W9-CFC-424

THE COMPLETE BOOK OF THE OLYMPICS

2012 EDITION

THE COMPLETE BOOK OF THE OLYMPICS

2012 EDITION

DAVID WALLECHINSKY
AND JAIME LOUCKY

Aurum sport

Tulare County Library

First published in Great Britain
2012 by Aurum Press Ltd
7 Greenland Street
London NW1 0ND
www.aurumpress.co.uk

Copyright © David Wallechinsky and Jaime Loucky 2012

David Wallechinsky and Jaime Loucky have asserted their moral right
to be identified as the authors of this work in accordance
with the Copyright Designs and Patents Act 1988.

All rights reserved. No part of this book may be reproduced or utilised
in any form or by any means, electronic or mechanical, including photocopying,
recording or by any information storage and retrieval system, without
permission in writing from Aurum Press Ltd.

A catalogue record for this book is available from the British Library.

ISBN 978 1 84513 695 6

1 3 5 7 9 10 8 6 4 2
2012 2014 2016 2015 2013

Designed and typeset by M Rules, London

Printed and bound in Finland by Bookwell

To Elijah, Aaron and Vanessa

Cheers for The Complete Book of the Olympics

"The newest edition of Wallechinsky's masterpiece, which he compiled with his nephew Jaime Loucky, may be the most entertaining book ever written."
—Anthony Lane, The New Yorker

"An indispensable addition to the shelves of both sportswriters and serious fans . . . an extremely meticulous—one may even say Olympian—piece of scholarship. . . . This is a volume that will be of service for many Olympiads to come."
—Erich Segal, New York Times Book Review

"If ever a book was properly titled, this is the one. . . . The ultimate Olympic source book . . . humanity in all its pride and wonder."
—Los Angeles Times

"A staggering compendium of results, highlights, and oddments dating from the first modern Games in 1896. . . . You'll have a hard time putting down the book to watch the Games on TV."
—Frederick C. Klein, Wall Street Journal

"The perfect source for someone who wants to know everything about the Summer Games. . . . Open it to virtually any page and a good story is waiting."
—USA Today

"Invaluable."
—The New Republic

"Wallechinsky has done a Herculean job of research on the Olympics and we are all the richer."
—Los Angeles Daily News

"The most-plundered of all the books available to the nation's sporting scribblers. . . . A guy can look real smart after reading Wallechinsky's treasure trove of Olympic good stuff."
—Houston Post

"Well-worn copies of this reference classic can be seen on the desks of sportswriters and editors."
—Atlanta Journal and Constitution

"Author David Wallechinsky has amassed mind-boggling information. He stirs an aura of excitement into his superb writing. . . . Not a dull passage mars this book."
—Wichita Falls (Texas) Times

"The writing manages to convey the breathless excitement of a radio announcer's staccato commentary, leaving you cheering the finale of events held long in the past."
—New Orleans Times-Picayune

"A mass of superbly informative and entertaining anecdotes about the winners and losers, the characters and crises, and the fascinating behind-the-scenes dramas behind the medals."
—Oldham Evening Chronicle

"Quickly outdistances any mere reference manual with the inclusion of hundreds of dramatic moments—in photos and essays—of the last century of competition."
—Detroit News

"A monster compendium."
—The Guardian

"An enormous plum pudding of a book. . . . The book is a gem and the deadpan delivery priceless."
—London Daily Telegraph

"David Wallechinsky deserves a gold medal for compiling The Complete Book of the Olympics.*"*
—Glasgow Sunday Post

"Everything you've ever wanted to know about the Olympics. Richly informative, amusing, and colorful, this is by far the most complete and accurate book of its kind."
—Athletics Weekly

"Told at a cracking pace . . . infinitely more interesting than watching the box."
—Ideal Home

"Comprehensive . . . concise . . . meticulous . . . well-presented, easily followed, and above all, clean of errors."
—Dublin Sunday Tribune

"Incredible narratives . . . mind-boggling tidbits . . . I am proud to have this book in my collection, not only as a reference book but as an entertaining read."
—Birmingham Post

"The supreme guide . . . guaranteed to make you an expert."
—New York Daily News

"It would not be blasphemous to call Wallechinsky's book the Bible of the Olympics."
—Gannett News Service

Contents

Acknowledgments

First of all I would like to thank my father, Irving Wallace, who introduced me to the world of the Olympics. In the course of my research I have encountered numerous people who have graciously helped me on my way, starting with C. Robert Paul, who made available to me the archives of the United States Olympic Committee. Mr. Paul was also kind enough to review my original manuscript in light of his long experience with the Olympic movement. I would also like to acknowledge the aid of David Kelly at the Library of Congress, Jan Foulstich and other members of the staff of Representative Anthony Beilenson, the staff of the library of Notre Dame University, Maynard Brichford and others at the University of Illinois, Champaign-Urbana, which houses the Avery Brundage Collection, Wayne Wilson and the staff of the Amateur Athletic Foundation library in Los Angeles, and Sandy Duncan of the British Olympic Association.

I would like to pay special thanks to the staff of the Lexis-Nexis database, who helped me immensely without knowing it, and I would like to thank the talented members of the Olympics research department of NBC television.

I am also indebted to Bill Mallon, Peter Diamond, John Lucas, and Harvey Abrams, who allowed me to enjoy and make use of their personal libraries. Special acknowledgments are due to my agent, Ed Victor, for his support and encouragement; and to the memory of Irv Goodman, who believed in this project from the start.

DW

I would first like to give special thanks to my uncle, David Wallechinsky, for his constant guidance and encouragement during the writing of this edition. Without his expertise and continued support this book would not exist, and I am honored to be a part of it. I would also like to thank my family, James Loucky, Maria Chavez and Vanessa Loucky, for their love and support during the writing of this book.

JL

The authors would also like to thank the following people for their help in the research process: Tony Bijkerk, Ove Karlsson, Wolf Lyberg and Gulu Ezekiel. Thanks also to Chris Freddi, Jess Cully, David Miller, Chris Wigginton, John Paul Leavey, Paul Jenes, Jim Constandt, Pierce O'Callahan, Malcom Fare . . . and Steve Futterman. And, for their help with accent marks and names, Ernesto Rodríguez, Andrew Dettre, Radoslav Simic, Migdalia Dominguez and Gabriel Stanescu.

Final thanks go to John Wheelwright for his excellent copy-editing and proofreading.

The authors of this book may be reached by email at: Maussane@aol.com and CompleteOlympics@gmail.com.

The Olympic Games

				Total Competitors	Women	Nations Represented	Events
I	1896	ATHENS, GREECE	April 6-15	c245	0 (0%)	14	43
II	1900	PARIS, FRANCE	May 14-October 28	c1118	21 (1.9%)	28	75[1]
III	1904	ST. LOUIS, U.S.A.	July 1-November 23	627	6 (1.0%)	12	84[2]
—	1906	ATHENS, GREECE	April 22-May 2	847	6 (0.7%)	20	74
IV	1908	LONDON, GREAT BRITAIN	April 27-October 31	2023	44 (2.2%)	22	109
V	1912	STOCKHOLM, SWEDEN	May 5-July 22	2490	55 (2.2%)	28	102
VI	1916	BERLIN, GERMANY	Not held because of war	—	—	—	—
VII	1920	ANTWERP, BELGIUM	April 20-September 12	2668	77 (2.9%)	29	154
VIII	1924	PARIS, FRANCE	May 4-July 27	3070	125 (4.0%)	44	126
IX	1928	AMSTERDAM, HOLLAND	May 17-August 12	3014	290 (9.6%)	46	109
X	1932	LOS ANGELES, U.S.A.	July 30-August 14	1328	127 (9.6%)	37	116
XI	1936	BERLIN, GERMANY	August 1-16	3956	328 (8.3%)	49	129
XII	1940	TOKYO, JAPAN; HELSINKI, FINLAND	Not held because of war	—	—	—	—
XIII	1944	LONDON, GREAT BRITAIN	Not held because of war	—	—	—	—
XIV	1948	LONDON, GREAT BRITAIN	July 29-August 14	4064	355 (8.7%)	59	136
XV	1952	HELSINKI, FINLAND	July 19-August 3	4879	518 (10.6%)	69	149
XVI	1956	MELBOURNE, AUSTRALIA[3]	November 22-December 8	3258	384 (11.8%)	72	151
XVII	1960	ROME, ITALY	August 25-September 11	5348	610 (11.4%)	83	150
XVIII	1964	TOKYO, JAPAN	October 10-24	5081	683 (13.4%)	93	163
XIX	1968	MEXICO CITY, MEXICO	October 12-27	5423	768 (14.2%)	112	172
XX	1972	MUNICH, GERMANY	August 26-September 10	7173	1058 (14.8%)	121	195
XXI	1976	MONTREAL, CANADA	July 17-August 1	6024	1246 (20.7%)	92[4]	198
XXII	1980	MOSCOW, U.S.S.R.	July 19-August 3	5217	1124 (21.5%)	80[5]	203
XXIII	1984	LOS ANGELES, U.S.A.	July 28-August 12	6797	1567 (23.1%)	140	221
XXIV	1988	SEOUL, SOUTH KOREA	September 17-October 2	8465	2189 (25.9%)	159[6]	237
XXV	1992	BARCELONA, SPAIN	July 24[7]-August 9	9370	2708 (28.9%)	169	257
XXVI	1996	ATLANTA, U.S.A.	July 19-August 4	10,310	3513 (34.1%)	197	271
XXVII	2000	SYDNEY, AUSTRALIA	September 13[8]-October 1	10,649	4069 (38.5%)	200	300
XXVIII	2004	ATHENS, GREECE	August 11[9]-29	10,560	4305 (40.8%)	201[10]	301
XXIX	2008	BEIJING, CHINA	August 8[11]-24	10,900	4608 (42.3%)	204	302
XXX	2012	LONDON, ENGLAND	July 25[12]-August 12				302

1 Figures for 1900 do not include shooting events for which cash prizes were awarded.
2 Figures for 1904 do not include boxing.
3 The equestrian events were held in Stockholm, Sweden, June 10-17, 1956.
4 Some sources list this figure as 88. Cameroon, Egypt, Morocco, and Tunisia all boycotted the 1976 Olympics; however, athletes from each of these countries had already competed before the boycott was officially announced.
5 Some sources list this figure as 81. Liberia entered seven athletes, but none of them competed.
6 Some sources list this figure as 160. However, the delegation from Brunei, which marched in the Opening Ceremony, included one official, but no athletes.
7 One soccer match, between Italy and the United States, took place on July 24, the day before the Opening Ceremony.
8 Six soccer matches took place in the two days preceding the Opening Ceremony on September 15.
9 Eight soccer matches took place during the two days preceding the Opening Ceremony on August 13.
10 Djibouti marched in the Opening Ceremony, but none of its athletes competed.
11 Fourteen soccer matches took place during the two days preceding the Opening Ceremony on August 8.
12 Fourteen soccer matches will take place during the two days preceding the Opening Ceremony on July 27.

National Medal Totals in Each Olympics

The International Olympic Committee does not officially recognize national medal totals. However, these totals are frequently included in Official Reports, and during the Olympic Games, they are often displayed on huge screens in the Main Press Center and are updated on a continuous basis for the benefit of the press and the public.

The awarding of gold medals for first place, silver medals for second place, and bronze medals for third place began in 1904. In the charts for 1896 and 1900, *G, S,* and *B* are used to indicate first, second, and third. Precise totals by nation for 1896-1906 are difficult to determine because until 1908 athletes entered the Olympics as individuals rather than as selected members of a national team. In addition, athletes from different nations sometimes joined forces in team sports, including tennis doubles. In the following charts, combined teams are listed as "COM." However, the combined East and West German teams of 1956-1964 are presented in these charts as a single team, although in the rest of the book individuals from each nation are identified as East or West Germans. Koreans who in 1936 were forced to compete for Japan, Irish who competed for Great Britain, and so forth are listed in the following charts under the team for which they were officially entered. The list for 1900 does not include those shooting or yachting events for which winners received cash prizes. For a full explanation, see page 933. The list for 1904 does not include the 18 boxing medals (7 gold, 7 silver and 4 bronze) that went to the US, because the competition was poorly organized and included only American boxers. For an explanation, please see the note on page 452.

G = gold, **S** = silver, **B** = bronze.

1896 Athens

	G	S	B
USA	11	7	2
GRE	10	16	19
GER	6	5	2
FRA	5	4	2
GBR	2	3	3
HUN	2	1	3
AUT	2	1	2
AUS	2	0	0
DEN	1	2	3
SWI	1	2	0
EGY	0	1	0
COM	1	1	1

1900 Paris

	G	S	B
USA	21	14	15
FRA	18	27	21
GBR	12	9	7
BEL	3	3	1
GER	3	2	2
ITA	3	2	0
AUS	2	0	3
CUB	1	1	0
CAN	1	0	1
LUX	1	0	0
SPA	1	0	0
AUT	0	3	3
HUN	0	2	2
HOL	0	1	2
BOH	0	1	1
NOR	0	1	1
DEN	0	0	2
MEX	0	0	1
SWE	0	0	1
COM	4	3	5

1904 St. Louis

	G	S	B
USA	62	66	69
GER	4	4	4
CAN	4	1	1
CUB	3	0	0
HUN	2	1	1
AUT	1	1	1
GBR	1	1	0
GRE	1	0	1
SWI	1	0	1*
FRA	0	1	0
COM	1	1	0

1906 Athens

	G	S	B
FRA	15	9	16
USA	12	6	6
GRE	8	13	12
GBR	8	11	5
ITA	7	6	3
GER	4	6	5
SWI	4	3	1
AUT	3	3	3
DEN	3	2	1
SWE	2	5	7
HUN	2	5	3
BEL	2	1	3
FIN	2	1	1
CAN	1	1	0
NOR	1	1	0
HOL	0	1	2
TUR	0	1	1
AUS	0	0	3
BOH	0	0	2
COM	0	1	0

1908 London

	G	S	B
GBR	56	51	39
USA	23	12	12
SWE	8	6	11
FRA	5	5	9
GER	3	5	5
HUN	3	4	2
CAN	3	3	10

*For more than a century, 1904 Olympic swimmer Frank Gailey was mistakenly listed in official records as an American. Born in Brisbane, Gailey competed for the Olympic Club of San Francisco at the St. Louis Olympics—winning three silver medals and one bronze—and returned to Australia soon afterwards. His four medals have been reallocated to Australia.

NOR	2	3	3
ITA	2	2	0
BEL	1	5	2
AUS	1	2	1
RUS	1	2	0
FIN	1	1	3
SAF	1	1	0
GRE	0	3	1
DEN	0	2	3
BOH	0	0	2
HOL	0	0	2
AUT	0	0	1
NZL	0	0	1

1912 Stockholm

	G	S	B
USA	25	18	20
SWE	23	24	17
GBR	10	15	16
FIN	9	8	9
FRA	7	4	3
GER	5	13	7
SAF	4	2	0
NOR	3	2	5
HUN	3	2	3
CAN	3	2	2
ITA	3	1	2
BEL	2	1	3
DEN	1	6	5
AUS	1	2	2
GRE	1	0	1
RUS	0	2	3
AUT	0	2	2
HOL	0	0	3
NZL	0	0	1
COM	1	0	0

1920 Antwerp

	G	S	B
USA	41	27	27
SWE	19	20	25
FIN	15	10	9
GBR	14	15	13
BEL	13	11	11
NOR	13	9	9
ITA	13	5	5
FRA	9	19	13
HOL	4	2	5
DEN	3	9	1
SAF	3	4	3
CAN	3	3	3
SWI	2	2	7
EST	1	2	0
BRA	1	1	1
AUS	0	2	1
JPN	0	2	0
SPA	0	2	0
GRE	0	1	0
LUX	0	1	0
CZE	0	0	2
NZL	0	0	1

1924 Paris

	G	S	B
USA	45	27	27
FIN	14	13	10
FRA	13	15	10
GBR	9	13	12
ITA	8	3	5
SWI	7	8	10
NOR	5	2	3
SWE	4	13	12
HOL	4	1	5
BEL	3	7	3
AUS	3	1	2
DEN	2	5	2
HUN	2	3	4
YUG	2	0	0
CZE	1	4	5
ARG	1	3	2
EST	1	1	4
SAF	1	1	1
URU	1	0	0
AUT	0	3	1
CAN	0	3	1
POL	0	1	1
HAI	0	0	1
JPN	0	0	1
NZL	0	0	1
POR	0	0	1
ROM	0	0	1

1928 Amsterdam

	G	S	B
USA	22	18	16
GER	10	7	14
FIN	8	8	9
SWE	7	6	12
ITA	7	5	7
SWI	7	4	4
FRA	6	10	5
HOL	6	9	4
HUN	4	5	0
CAN	4	4	7
GBR	3	10	7
ARG	3	3	1
DEN	3	1	2
CZE	2	5	2
JPN	2	2	1
EST	2	1	2
EGY	2	1	1
AUT	2	0	1
AUS	1	2	1
NOR	1	2	1
POL	1	1	3
YUG	1	1	3
SAF	1	0	2
IND	1	0	0
IRL	1	0	0
NZL	1	0	0
SPA	1	0	0
URU	1	0	0
BEL	0	1	2
CHI	0	1	0
HAI	0	1	0
PHI	0	0	1
POR	0	0	1

1932 Los Angeles

	G	S	B
USA	41	32	30
ITA	12	12	12
FRA	10	5	4
SWE	9	5	9
JPN	7	7	4
HUN	6	4	5
FIN	5	8	12
GBR	4	7	5
GER	3	12	5
AUS	3	1	1
ARG	3	1	0
CAN	2	5	8
HOL	2	5	0
POL	2	1	4
SAF	2	0	3
IRL	2	0	0
CZE	1	2	1
AUT	1	1	3
IND	1	0	0
DEN	0	3	3
MEX	0	2	0
LAT	0	1	0
NZL	0	1	0
SWI	0	1	0
PHI	0	0	3
SPA	0	0	1
URU	0	0	1

1936 Berlin

	G	S	B
GER	33	26	30
USA	24	20	12
HUN	10	1	5
ITA	8	9	5
FIN	7	6	6
FRA	7	6	6
SWE	6	5	9
JPN	6	4	8
HOL	6	4	7
GBR	4	7	3
AUT	4	6	3
CZE	3	5	0
ARG	2	2	3
EST	2	2	3
EGY	2	1	2
SWI	1	9	5
CAN	1	3	5
NOR	1	3	2
TUR	1	0	1
IND	1	0	0
NZL	1	0	0
POL	0	3	3
DEN	0	2	3
LAT	0	1	1
ROM	0	1	0
SAF	0	1	0
YUG	0	1	0
MEX	0	0	3
BEL	0	0	2
AUS	0	0	1
PHI	0	0	1
POR	0	0	1

1948 London

	G	S	B
USA	38	27	19
SWE	16	11	17
FRA	10	6	13
HUN	10	5	12
ITA	8	12	9
FIN	8	7	5
TUR	6	4	2
CZE	6	2	3
SWI	5	10	5
DEN	5	7	8
HOL	5	2	9
GBR	3	14	6
ARG	3	3	1
AUS	2	6	5
BEL	2	2	3
EGY	2	2	1
MEX	2	1	2
SAF	2	1	1
NOR	1	3	3
JAM	1	2	0
AUT	1	0	3
IND	1	0	0
PER	1	0	0
YUG	0	2	0
CAN	0	1	2
POR	0	1	1
URU	0	1	1
CUB	0	1	0
SPA	0	1	0
TRI	0	1	0
SRL	0	1	0
KOR	0	0	2
PAN	0	0	2
BRA	0	0	1
IRN	0	0	1
POL	0	0	1
PUR	0	0	1

1952 Helsinki

	G	S	B
USA	40	19	17
SOV	22	30	19
HUN	16	10	16
SWE	12	13	10
ITA	8	9	4
CZE	7	3	3
FRA	6	6	6
FIN	6	3	13
AUS	6	2	3
NOR	3	2	0
SWI	2	6	6
SAF	2	4	4
JAM	2	3	0
BEL	2	2	0
DEN	2	1	3
TUR	2	0	1
JPN	1	6	2
GBR	1	2	8
ARG	1	2	2
POL	1	2	1
CAN	1	2	0
YUG	1	2	0
ROM	1	1	2
BRA	1	0	2
NZL	1	0	2
IND	1	0	1
LUX	1	0	0
GER	0	7	17
HOL	0	5	0
IRN	0	3	4
CHI	0	2	0
AUT	0	1	1
LEB	0	1	1
IRL	0	1	0
MEX	0	1	0
SPA	0	1	0
KOR	0	0	2
URU	0	0	2
TRI	0	0	2
BUL	0	0	1
EGY	0	0	1
POR	0	0	1
VEN	0	0	1

1956 Melbourne

	G	S	B
SOV	37	29	32
USA	32	25	17
AUS	13	8	14
HUN	9	10	7
ITA	8	8	9
SWE	8	5	6
GER	7	13	7
GBR	6	7	11
ROM	5	3	5
JPN	4	10	5
FRA	4	4	6
TUR	3	2	2
FIN	3	1	11
IRN	2	2	1
CAN	2	1	3
NZL	2	0	0
POL	1	4	4
CZE	1	4	1
BUL	1	3	1
DEN	1	2	1
IRL	1	1	3
NOR	1	0	2
MEX	1	0	1
BRA	1	0	0
IND	1	0	0
YUG	0	3	0
CHI	0	2	2
BEL	0	2	0
ARG	0	1	1
KOR	0	1	1
ICE	0	1	0
PAK	0	1	0
SAF	0	0	4
AUT	0	0	2
BAH	0	0	1
GRE	0	0	1

SWI	0	0	1
URU	0	0	1

1960 Rome

	G	S	B
SOV	43	29	31
USA	34	21	16
ITA	13	10	13
GER	12	19	11
AUS	8	8	6
TUR	7	2	0
HUN	6	8	7
JPN	4	7	7
POL	4	6	11
CZE	3	2	3
ROM	3	1	6
GBR	2	6	12
DEN	2	3	1
NZL	2	0	1
BUL	1	3	3
SWE	1	2	3
FIN	1	1	3
AUT	1	1	0
YUG	1	1	0
PAK	1	0	1
ETH	1	0	0
GRE	1	0	0
NOR	1	0	0
SWI	0	3	3
FRA	0	2	3
BEL	0	2	2
IRN	0	1	3
HOL	0	1	2
SAF	0	1	2
ARG	0	1	1
EGY	0	1	1
CAN	0	1	0
GHA	0	1	0
IND	0	1	0
MOR	0	1	0
POR	0	1	0
SIN	0	1	0
TAI	0	1	0
BRA	0	0	2
BWI	0	0	2
IRQ	0	0	1
MEX	0	0	1
SPA	0	0	1
VEN	0	0	1

1964 Tokyo

	G	S	B
USA	36	26	28
SOV	30	31	35
JPN	16	5	8
GER	10	22	8
ITA	10	10	7
HUN	10	7	5
POL	7	6	10
AUS	6	2	10
CZE	5	6	3
GBR	4	12	2
BUL	3	5	2
FIN	3	0	2
NZL	3	0	2
ROM	2	4	6
HOL	2	4	4
TUR	2	3	1
SWE	2	2	4
DEN	2	1	3
YUG	2	1	2
BEL	2	0	1
FRA	1	8	6
CAN	1	2	1
SWI	1	2	1
BAH	1	0	0
ETH	1	0	0
IND	1	0	0
KOR	0	2	1
TRI	0	1	2
TUN	0	1	1
ARG	0	1	0
CUB	0	1	0
PAK	0	1	0
PHI	0	1	0
IRN	0	0	2
BRA	0	0	1
GHA	0	0	1
IRL	0	0	1
KEN	0	0	1
MEX	0	0	1
NGR	0	0	1
URU	0	0	1

1968 Mexico City

	G	S	B
USA	45	28	34
SOV	29	32	30
JPN	11	7	7
HUN	10	10	12
GDR	9	9	7
FRA	7	3	5
CZE	7	2	4
GER	5	11	10
AUS	5	7	5
GBR	5	5	3
POL	5	2	11
ROM	4	6	5
ITA	3	4	9
KEN	3	4	2
MEX	3	3	3
YUG	3	3	2
HOL	3	3	1
BUL	2	4	3
IRN	2	1	2
SWE	2	1	1
TUR	2	0	0
DEN	1	4	3
CAN	1	3	1
FIN	1	2	1
ETH	1	1	0
NOR	1	1	0
NZL	1	0	2
TUN	1	0	1
PAK	1	0	0
VEN	1	0	0
CUB	0	4	0
AUT	0	2	2
SWI	0	1	4
MGL	0	1	3
BRA	0	1	2
BEL	0	1	1
KOR	0	1	1
UGA	0	1	1
CAM	0	1	0
JAM	0	1	0
ARG	0	0	2
GRE	0	0	1
IND	0	0	1
TAI	0	0	1

1972 Munich

	G	S	B
SOV	50	27	22
USA	33	31	30
GDR	20	23	23
GER	13	11	16
JPN	13	8	8
AUS	8	7	2
POL	7	5	9
HUN	6	13	16
BUL	6	10	5
ITA	5	3	10
SWE	4	6	6
GBR	4	5	9
ROM	3	6	7
CUB	3	1	4
FIN	3	1	4
HOL	3	1	1

FRA	2	4	7
CZE	2	4	2
KEN	2	3	4
YUG	2	1	2
NOR	2	1	1
PRK	1	1	3
NZL	1	1	1
UGA	1	1	0
DEN	1	0	0
SWI	0	3	0
CAN	0	2	3
IRN	0	2	1
BEL	0	2	0
GRE	0	2	0
AUT	0	1	2
COL	0	1	2
ARG	0	1	0
KOR	0	1	0
LEB	0	1	0
MEX	0	1	0
MGL	0	1	0
PAK	0	1	0
TUN	0	1	0
TUR	0	1	0
BRA	0	0	2
ETH	0	0	2
GHA	0	0	1
IND	0	0	1
JAM	0	0	1
NIG	0	0	1
NGR	0	0	1
SPA	0	0	1

1976 Montreal

	G	S	B
SOV	49	41	35
GDR	40	25	25
USA	34	35	25
GER	10	12	17
JPN	9	6	10
POL	7	6	13
BUL	6	9	7
CUB	6	4	3
ROM	4	9	14
HUN	4	5	13
FIN	4	2	0
SWE	4	1	0
GBR	3	5	5
ITA	2	7	4
FRA	2	3	4
YUG	2	3	3
CZE	2	2	4
NZL	2	1	1
KOR	1	1	4
SWI	1	1	2
JAM	1	1	0
NOR	1	1	0
PRK	1	1	0
DEN	1	0	2
MEX	1	0	1
TRI	1	0	0
CAN	0	5	6
BEL	0	3	3
HOL	0	2	3
POR	0	2	0
SPA	0	2	0
AUS	0	1	4
IRN	0	1	1
MGL	0	1	0
VEN	0	1	0
BRA	0	0	2
AUT	0	0	1
BER	0	0	1
PAK	0	0	1
PUR	0	0	1
THA	0	0	1

1980 Moscow

	G	S	B
SOV	80	69	46
GDR	47	37	42
BUL	8	16	17
CUB	8	7	5
ITA	8	3	4
HUN	7	10	15
ROM	6	6	13
FRA	6	5	3
GBR	5	7	9
POL	3	14	15
SWE	3	3	6
FIN	3	1	4
CZE	2	3	9
YUG	2	3	4
AUS	2	2	5
DEN	2	1	2
BRA	2	0	2
ETH	2	0	2
SWI	2	0	0
SPA	1	3	2
AUT	1	2	1
GRE	1	0	2
BEL	1	0	0
IND	1	0	0
ZIM	1	0	0
PRK	0	3	2
MGL	0	2	2
TAN	0	2	0
MEX	0	1	3
HOL	0	1	2
IRL	0	1	1
UGA	0	1	0
VEN	0	1	0
JAM	0	0	3
GUY	0	0	1
LEB	0	0	1

1984 Los Angeles

	G	S	B
USA	83	61	30
ROM	20	16	17
GER	17	19	23
CHN	15	8	9
ITA	14	6	12
CAN	10	18	16
JPN	10	8	14
NZL	8	1	2
YUG	7	4	7
KOR	6	6	7
GBR	5	10	22
FRA	5	7	16
HOL	5	2	6
AUS	4	8	12
FIN	4	2	6
SWE	2	11	6
MEX	2	3	1
MOR	2	0	0
BRA	1	5	2
SPA	1	2	2
BEL	1	1	2
AUT	1	1	1
KEN	1	0	2
POR	1	0	2
PAK	1	0	0
SWI	0	4	4
DEN	0	3	3
JAM	0	1	2
NOR	0	1	2
GRE	0	1	1
NGR	0	1	1
PUR	0	1	1
COL	0	1	0
EGY	0	1	0
IRL	0	1	0
IVC	0	1	0
PER	0	1	0
SYR	0	1	0
THA	0	1	0
TUR	0	0	3
VEN	0	0	3

ALG	0	0	2
CAM	0	0	1
DOM	0	0	1
ICE	0	0	1
TAI	0	0	1
ZAM	0	0	1

1988 Seoul

	G	S	B
SOV	55	31	46
GDR	37	35	30
USA	36	31	27
KOR	12	10	11
GER	11	14	15
HUN	11	6	6
BUL	10	12	13
ROM	7	11	6
FRA	6	4	6
ITA	6	4	4
CHN	5	11	12
GBR	5	10	9
KEN	5	2	2
JPN	4	3	7
AUS	3	6	5
YUG	3	4	5
CZE	3	3	2
NZL	3	2	8
CAN	3	2	5
POL	2	5	9
NOR	2	3	0
HOL	2	2	5
DEN	2	1	1
BRA	1	2	3
FIN	1	1	2
SPA	1	1	2
TUR	1	1	0
MOR	1	0	2
AUT	1	0	0
POR	1	0	0
SUR	1	0	0
SWE	0	4	7
SWI	0	2	2
JAM	0	2	0
ARG	0	1	1
CHI	0	1	0
CRC	0	1	0
INA	0	1	0
IRN	0	1	0
NLA	0	1	0
PER	0	1	0
SEN	0	1	0
VIR	0	1	0
BEL	0	0	2
MEX	0	0	2
COL	0	0	1
DJI	0	0	1
GRE	0	0	1
MGL	0	0	1
PAK	0	0	1
PHI	0	0	1
THA	0	0	1

1992 Barcelona

	G	S	B
SOV	45	38	28
USA	37	34	37
GER	33	21	28
CHN	16	22	16
CUB	14	6	11
SPA	13	7	2
KOR	12	5	12
HUN	11	12	7
FRA	8	5	16
AUS	7	9	11
ITA	6	5	8
CAN	6	5	7
GBR	5	3	12
ROM	4	6	8
CZE	4	2	1
PRK	4	0	5
JPN	3	8	11
BUL	3	7	6
POL	3	6	10
HOL	2	6	7
KEN	2	4	2
NOR	2	4	1
TUR	2	2	2
INA	2	2	1
BRA	2	1	0
GRE	2	0	0
SWE	1	7	4
NZL	1	4	5
FIN	1	2	2
DEN	1	1	4
MOR	1	1	2
IRL	1	1	0
ETH	1	0	2
ALG	1	0	1
EST	1	0	1
LIT	1	0	1
SWI	1	0	0
JAM	0	3	1
NGR	0	3	1
LAT	0	2	1
AUT	0	2	0
NAM	0	2	0
SAF	0	2	0
BEL	0	1	2
CRO	0	1	2
IRN	0	1	2
YUG	0	1	2
ISR	0	1	1
MEX	0	1	0
PER	0	1	0
TAI	0	1	0
MGL	0	0	2
SLO	0	0	2
ARG	0	0	1
BAH	0	0	1
COL	0	0	1
GHA	0	0	1
MAL	0	0	1
PAK	0	0	1
PHI	0	0	1
PUR	0	0	1
QAT	0	0	1
SUR	0	0	1
THA	0	0	1

1996 Atlanta

	G	S	B
USA	44	32	25
RUS	26	21	16
GER	20	18	27
CHN	16	22	12
FRA	15	7	15
ITA	13	10	12
AUS	9	9	23
CUB	9	8	8
UKR	9	2	12
KOR	7	15	5
POL	7	5	5
HUN	7	4	10
SPA	5	6	6
ROM	4	7	9
HOL	4	5	10
GRE	4	4	0
CZE	4	3	4
SWI	4	3	0
DEN	4	1	1
TUR	4	1	1
CAN	3	11	8
BUL	3	7	5
JPN	3	6	5
KAZ	3	4	4
BRA	3	3	9
NZL	3	2	1
SAF	3	1	1
IRL	3	0	1

SWE	2	4	2
NOR	2	2	3
BEL	2	2	2
NGR	2	1	3
PRK	2	1	2
ALG	2	0	1
ETH	2	0	1
GBR	1	8	6
BLR	1	6	8
KEN	1	4	3
JAM	1	3	2
FIN	1	2	1
INA	1	1	2
YUG	1	1	2
IRN	1	1	1
SLV	1	1	1
ARM	1	1	0
CRO	1	1	0
POR	1	0	1
THA	1	0	1
BRD	1	0	0
CRC	1	0	0
ECU	1	0	0
HKG	1	0	0
SYR	1	0	0
ARG	0	2	1
NAM	0	2	0
SLO	0	2	0
AUT	0	1	2
MAL	0	1	1
MOL	0	1	1
UZB	0	1	1
AZR	0	1	0
BAH	0	1	0
LAT	0	1	0
PHI	0	1	0
TAI	0	1	0
TON	0	1	0
ZAM	0	1	0
GEO	0	0	2
MOR	0	0	2
TRI	0	0	2
IND	0	0	1
ISR	0	0	1
LIT	0	0	1
MEX	0	0	1
MGL	0	0	1
MOZ	0	0	1
PUR	0	0	1
TUN	0	0	1
UGA	0	0	1

2000 Sydney

	G	S	B
USA	38	24	33
RUS	32	28	29
CHN	28	16	14
AUS	16	25	17
GER	13	17	26
FRA	13	14	11
ITA	13	8	13
HOL	12	9	4
CUB	11	11	7
GBR	11	10	7
ROM	11	6	8
KOR	8	10	10
HUN	8	6	3
POL	6	5	3
JPN	5	8	5
BUL	5	6	2
GRE	4	6	3
SWE	4	5	3
NOR	4	3	3
ETH	4	1	3
UKR	3	10	10
KAZ	3	4	0
BLR	3	3	11
CAN	3	3	8
SPA	3	3	5
TUR	3	0	2
IRN	3	0	1
CZE	2	3	3
KEN	2	3	2
DEN	2	3	1
FIN	2	1	1
AUT	2	1	0
LIT	2	0	3
AZR	2	0	1
BAH	2	0	1
SLO	2	0	0
SWI	1	6	2
INA	1	3	2
SLV	1	3	1
MEX	1	2	3
ALG	1	1	3
UZB	1	1	2
LAT	1	1	1
YUG	1	1	1
NZL	1	0	3
EST	1	0	2
THA	1	0	2
CRO	1	0	1
CAM	1	0	0
COL	1	0	0
MOZ	1	0	0
BRA	0	6	6
JAM	0	6	3
NGR	1	2	0
BEL	0	2	3
SAF	0	2	3
ARG	0	2	2
MOR	0	1	4
TAI	0	1	4
PRK	0	1	3
MOL	0	1	1
SAU	0	1	1
TRI	0	1	1
IRL	0	1	0
URU	0	1	0
VIE	0	1	0
GEO	0	0	6
CRC	0	0	2
POR	0	0	2
ARM	0	0	1
BAR	0	0	1
CHI	0	0	1
ICE	0	0	1
IND	0	0	1
ISR	0	0	1
KUW	0	0	1
KYR	0	0	1
MAC	0	0	1
QAT	0	0	1
SRL	0	0	1

2004 Athens

	G	S	B
USA	36	39	27
CHN	32	17	14
RUS	27	27	38
AUS	17	16	16
JPN	16	9	12
GER	13	16	20
FRA	11	9	13
ITA	10	11	11
KOR	9	12	9
GBR	9	9	12
CUB	9	7	11
UKR	9	5	9
HUN	8	6	3
ROM	8	5	6
GRE	6	6	4
BRA	5	2	3
NOR	5	0	1
HOL	5	9	9
SWE	4	2	1
SPA	3	11	5
CAN	3	6	3

TUR	3	3	4
POL	3	2	5
NZL	3	2	0
THA	3	1	4
BLR	2	6	7
AUT	2	4	1
ETH	2	3	2
IRN	2	2	2
SLV	2	2	2
TAI	2	2	1
GEO	2	2	0
BUL	2	1	9
JAM	2	1	2
UZB	2	1	2
MOR	2	1	0
DEN	2	0	6
ARG	2	0	4
CHI	2	0	1
KAZ	1	4	3
KEN	1	4	2
CZE	1	3	4
SAF	1	3	2
CRO	1	2	2
LIT	1	2	0
EGY	1	1	3
SWI	1	1	3
INA	1	1	2
ZIM	1	1	1
AZR	1	0	4
BEL	1	0	2
BAH	1	0	1
ISR	1	0	1
CAM	1	0	0
DOM	1	0	0
UAE	1	0	0
PRK	0	4	1
LAT	0	4	0
MEX	0	3	1
POR	0	2	1
FIN	0	2	0
SER	0	2	0
SLO	0	1	3
EST	0	1	2
HKG	0	1	0
IND	0	1	0
PAR	0	1	0
COL	0	0	2
NGR	0	0	2
VEN	0	0	2
ERI	0	0	1
MGL	0	0	1
SYR	0	0	1
TRI	0	0	1

2008 Beijing

	G	S	B
CHN	51	21	28
USA	36	38	36
RUS	23	21	29
GBR	19	13	15
GER	16	10	15
AUS	14	15	17
KOR	13	10	8
JPN	9	6	10
ITA	8	9	10
FRA	7	16	18
UKR	7	5	15
NED	7	5	4
KEN	6	4	4
JAM	6	3	2
SPA	5	10	3
BLR	4	5	10
ROM	4	1	3
ETH	4	1	2
CAN	3	9	6
POL	3	6	1
HUN	3	5	2
NOR	3	5	1
BRA	3	4	8
CZE	3	3	0
NZL	3	2	4
SLV	3	2	1
GEO	3	0	3
CUB	2	11	11
KAZ	2	4	7
DEN	2	2	3
MGL	2	2	0
THA	2	2	0
SWI	2	1	4
PRK	2	1	3
ARG	2	0	4
MEX	2	0	1
TUR	1	4	3
ZIM	1	3	0
AZE	1	2	4
UZB	1	2	3

SLO	1	2	2
BUL	1	1	3
INA	1	1	3
FIN	1	1	2
LAT	1	1	1
BEL	1	1	0
DOM	1	1	0
EST	1	1	0
POR	1	1	0
IND	1	0	2
IRN	1	0	1
CMR	1	0	0
PAN	1	0	0
TUN	1	0	0
SWE	0	4	1
CRO	0	2	3
LTU	0	2	3
GRE	0	2	2
TRI	0	2	0
NGR	0	1	3
AUT	0	1	2
IRL	0	1	2
SRB	0	1	2
ALG	0	1	1
BAH	0	1	1
COL	0	1	1
KGZ	0	1	1
MOR	0	1	1
TJK	0	1	1
CHI	0	1	0
ECU	0	1	0
ICE	0	1	0
MAL	0	1	0
SAF	0	1	0
SIN	0	1	0
SUD	0	1	0
VIE	0	1	0
ARM	0	0	6
TAI	0	0	4
AFG	0	0	1
EGY	0	0	1
ISR	0	0	1
MOL	0	0	1
MRI	0	0	1
TOG	0	0	1
VEN	0	0	1

A Short History of the Modern Olympics

THE ANCIENT OLYMPIC GAMES

Beginning in about 776 BC, the ancient Olympic Games were held every four years in the valley of Olympia in southwestern Greece. The opening of the Games was marked by the lighting of a flame at the altar of Zeus. When the Games were completed, the flame was extinguished. In the early years, up to 40,000 people would crowd into the main stadium to join in religious ceremonies and to watch the single athletic contest: the *stadion*, a sprint of almost 200 meters.

The first recorded Olympic champion was Koroibos, a cook from Elis. The first repeat winner was Pantakles of Athens in 696 BC and 692 BC. Originally the runners wore loincloths, but when Orsippus of Megara ran naked and won the *stadion*, nudity became the standard.

As time went on, more events were added. Among the most popular were boxing, wrestling and the *pankration*, a no-holds-barred combination of boxing and wrestling. Other popular events were the *tethrippon*, a four-horse chariot race of about 14,000 meters, and the five-event pentathlon, which included a *stadion* race, the long jump, discus throw, javelin throw and wrestling. There were also some unusual contests such as the race in armor, the competition for trumpeters and the *apene* race, in which a chariot was pulled not by horses but by two mules.

The scope of the Olympic Games also grew, drawing contestants not only from Greece, but from throughout the Macedonian empire and the Roman empire. A month-long truce, the *hieromenia*, suspended warfare to allow the athletes safe passage to and from the Olympic Games.

The ancient Olympics had more in common with the modern Games than is commonly realized. Although the only prize for winners in the early Games was an olive wreath, athletes were fully supported in their training and amply rewarded when they returned to their home towns. As time went on, there were cases of cheating and bribery and even boycotts.

Athletes came from all social classes including slaves. Among the more famous competitors were Philip II of Macedon and his son, Alexander the Great. Pythagoras, the philosopher and mathematician, served as team doctor for Kroton, a city of Greek settlers on the Italian coast.

The most decorated champion was the runner Leonidas of Rhodes, who won twelve championships between 164 BC and 152 BC. The most famous of the ancient athletes was the wrestler Milon of Kroton. After winning the boys' wrestling contest in 540 BC, Milon took the senior title five straight times between 532 BC and 516 BC. In 512 BC he was finally defeated in the final match by Timasitheos of Kroton.

Originally the Olympics were for men only, but eventually women were allowed to compete. The first female champion was Kyniska of Sparta, who won the *tethrippon* in 396 BC and again in 392 BC.

The last recorded champion of the ancient Olympic Games was Varasdates, Prince of Armenia, who won the boxing competition in 369 AD. In 393 AD, the Games were abolished by Emperor Theodosius of Rome, who considered them pagan.

After lasting for more than 1100 years, it would be another 1500 years before they were revived.

1896

Although there had been previous attempts to create a modern revival of the ancient Olympic Games, Baron Pierre de Coubertin of France was the first person to possess the perseverance and organizational skills necessary to make it happen. Inspired by a model of ancient Olympia that he saw on display while touring the 1889 Paris Exposition, de Coubertin, at a sports conference in 1892, proposed a renewal of the Olympic Games. His proposal was rejected, but in 1894 he called a conference of his own and the project was launched. Initially, de Coubertin suggested that the first Games be staged in his hometown of Paris in 1900. However, Greek support for the idea was so enthusiastic that the date was moved up to 1896 and the site shifted to Greece. Because Olympia itself was remote and undeveloped, the Games were awarded to Athens.

Lacking any financial support from the Greek government, the Greek Organizing Committee, led by Crown Prince Constantine, raised money by selling souvenir stamps and medals. A wealthy businessman, Georgios Averoff, donated one million drachma. This donation facilitated the reconstruction of Athens' Pananthenaic Stadium, which had been originally built in 330 BC.

Although it was the Greeks who ran the show, it was Baron de Coubertin who created the form of the Games, including the Olympic Charter (in 1908) and the Opening and Closing Ceremonies. De Coubertin served as president of the International Olympic Committee from 1896 until 1925.

In the afternoon of April 6, 1896, King George I of Greece declared open the first modern Olympic Games. There were 245 athletes, all of them men, from 14 nations. The largest delegations were from Greece, Germany and France.

The first race of the modern Olympics was the opening heat of the 100-meter dash. It was won by Francis Lane of the United States, who went on to finish fourth in the final.

The triple jump (then two hops and a jump) was won by the US champion, James Connolly. The 27-year-old Connolly, who dropped out of Harvard University to travel to Athens and compete, thus became the first Olympic champion in 1527 years. First place winners in 1896 were awarded a silver medal, a crown of olive branches and a diploma. Those in second place were given a bronze medal, a crown of laurel and a diploma.

Forty-three separate events were contested, although some of them, such as the one-handed weightlifting contest and the 100-meter freestyle swimming race for members of the Greek navy, attracted only limited participation. Rowing and yachting were canceled because of bad weather, but the swimming events were contested—in open water in and around the Bay of Zea near Piraeus. The water temperature was 13°C (55°F). The winner of the 1200-meter race, Alfred Hajos of Hungary, later recalled, "My will to live completely overcame my desire to win."

In the military revolver shooting event, American brothers John and Sumner Paine became the first siblings to finish first and second in an event.

Germany's Carl Schuhmann earned medals in gymnastics and wrestling, as well as placing third in weightlifting and fifth in the triple jump. George Robertson of Great Britain greatly pleased the crowd at the Closing Ceremony by reading an ode which he had written in ancient Greek to honor the Olympic Games.

But the real hero of the 1896 Games was Spiridon Louis, a 24-year-old Greek shepherd from the village of Amarousion. There was no event that the Greek hosts wanted more to win than the 40,000-meter marathon race, which was created to honor the legend of Pheidippides, who allegedly carried the news of the Greek victory at the Battle of Marathon in 490 BC by running from Marathon to Athens.

On April 10, 1896, Louis set off from Marathon with sixteen other runners, took the lead four kilometers from the Panathenaic Stadium and, to the great joy of the 100,000 spectators in and around the stadium, won the race by more than seven minutes.

1900

After the success of the 1896 Games, many people supported the proposal that Athens should become the permanent host of the Olympics. Baron Pierre de Coubertin, the founder of the modern Olympic movement and the president of the International Olympic Committee, rejected this idea and insisted that the Games of 1900 be held in Paris as part of the Exposition Universelle Internationale—the Paris World's Fair. De Coubertin reasoned that the fair would increase awareness of the Olympics, but his plan backfired. The exposition organizers took control of the contests and relegated de Coubertin to a minor role. They spread the events over five months and de-emphasized their Olympic status to such an extent that many athletes died without ever knowing that they had participated in the Olympics.

Women made their first appearance in the modern Games. The first to compete were Mme. Brohy and Mlle. Ohnier of France in croquet. The first female champion was in tennis: Charlotte Cooper of Great Britain. Britain's Doherty brothers, Reginald and Laurie, were scheduled to face each other in the semifinals of the tennis singles competition, but Reginald stepped aside and allowed his younger brother to advance to the final, which Laurie won. That same day, the brothers combined to win the doubles final. Tennis was one of five sports in which athletes from different nations competed on the same team. The others were football, polo, rowing and tug of war.

The track and field competitions were thrown into confusion when several of the favorites from the United States refused to compete on Sunday. Nonetheless, the Americans still dominated. Alvin Kraenzlein, who is credited with introducing the leg-extended style of hurdling, won four events in three days and, on July 16, Ray Ewry, who had overcome childhood polio, won three championships in one day—all in the standing jump events.

The swimming events produced unusually fast times because they were held in the River Seine and swum *with* the current.

The 1900 Games included some unusual one-time events, most notably the equestrian high jump and long jump and the swimming obstacle race, which required the twelve entrants to climb a pole, scramble over a row of boats and swim *under* another row of boats.

Most of the winners in 1900 did not receive medals, but rather cups and trophies. Professionals were allowed to compete in fencing and when Albert Ayat of France won the épée for amateurs and masters, he was awarded a prize of 3000 francs.

The 1900 Games came to an ignominious end on October 28 without a Closing Ceremony. One great mystery remains. In the coxed pairs rowing event, the Dutch team chose a small French boy for their coxswain for the final on August 26. The team won. The boy joined in the victory ceremony, had his photograph taken and then disappeared. He is probably the youngest champion in Olympic history, but years of research by numerous historians have failed to turn up his name or his date of birth.

1904

To reward the United States for its enthusiastic support of the 1896 and 1900 Olympics, the International Olympic Committee awarded the 1904 Games to Chicago. However, the American city of St. Louis had scheduled a world's fair for 1904—the Louisiana Purchase Exhibition—and the fair organizers threatened to stage a competing international sports tournament. US president Theodore Roosevelt sided with St. Louis and the IOC voted to move the Games. It was an unfortunate decision. The St. Louis organizers repeated all of the worst mistakes of 1900. The Olympic competitions, spread out over four and a half months, were lost in the chaos of the world's fair. Baron de Coubertin did not bother to attend. Nor did very many athletes from outside North America. Less than half as many nations were represented as in 1900. Of the 84 events generally considered to have been part of the Olympic program, only 42 included athletes who were not from the United States.

The 1904 Olympics did have a few highlights. They were the first at which gold, silver and bronze medals were awarded for first, second and third place. Boxing and freestyle wrestling made their debuts, although only athletes from the United States took part. Len Tau and Jan Mashiani, Tswana tribesmen who were in St. Louis as part of the Boer War exhibit at the world's fair, became the first Africans to compete in the Olympics when they entered the marathon race. On August 31, Americans George Poage and Joseph Stadler became the first African-American athletes to win medals. Poage finished third in the 400-meter hurdles, while Stadler placed second in the standing high jump.

One of the most remarkable athletes of the St. Louis Games was the American gymnast George Eyser, who won three gold medals, two silvers and one bronze. What made his feats particularly impressive was that his left leg was made of wood. His leg had been amputated after he was run over by a train.

Chicago runner James Lightbody won the steeplechase and the 800 meters and then set a world record in the 1500 meters. The marathon was run in intense heat on dusty roads made dustier by the automobiles of the officials and journalists who often drove in front of the runners. The first person to cross the finish line was Fred Lorz of New York. He was about to be awarded the gold medal when it was discovered that he had stopped running after nine miles, ridden eleven miles in a car, and then resumed running. The real winner of the race was Thomas Hicks, an English-born brass worker from Massachusetts, who managed to survive the difficult conditions by drinking strychnine and brandy.The most unusual event of the 1904 Olympics was the plunge for distance. Contestants dived into the swimming pool and then remained motionless for 60 seconds or until their heads broke the surface of the water, whichever came first. William Dickey of the United States won with a plunge of 19.05 meters (62 feet 6 inches).

1906

After the debacles of 1900 and 1904, the Greeks held the Intercalated or "Intermediary" Games of 1906. Initially Baron de Coubertin opposed the idea, but, swayed by the enthusiasm of the Athens organizers, he eventually endorsed them. These Games, although not considered official by the International Olympic Committee, carried through the Olympic spirit until the next official Games in 1908. The question as to whether the 1906 Games should be considered official is a difficult one. Most of the participants thought they were competing in the Olympics, which is more than can be said of the "official" Games of 1900. In April 1906, the "Olympic Review," the official publication of the International Olympic Committee, published a special issue "on the occasion of the Olympic Games of Athens." However, in 1949, a three-man commission headed by Avery Brundage concluded that the 1906 Athens Games were not official and the International Olympic Committee has refused to reopen the issue since then. Despite the position of the IOC, the 1906 Olympics were the first to limit entries to athletes sent by national Olympics committees and the first at which there was a Parade of Nations.

1908

The 1908 Olympics were awarded to Rome. But when Mt. Vesuvius erupted in 1906, the Italian government decided that their limited financial resources were needed to rebuild Naples. The Olympics were reassigned to London. Within ten months, the English built a new stadium at Shepherd's Bush that included a running track, a cycling track, a football field, a swimming pool and a platform for gymnastics and wrestling. The competitions were well-organized and the British Olympic Association produced the first comprehensive Official Report.

For the first time (other than 1906), at the Opening Ceremony the athletes marched into the stadium by nation, as most countries sent selected national teams. The level of competition was high. In swimming, world records were established in five of the six events.

Archers Willy and Lottie Dod of Great Britain became the first brother and sister medalists, winning gold and silver respectively. Willy won on his 41st birthday. In fact, the 1908 Olympics were noteworthy for the number of older champions. Featherweight boxing winner Richard Gunn was 37 years old; Henry Blackstaffe triumphed in single sculls rowing at age 40; Josiah Ritchie won the men's singles tennis tournament at 37 and George Hillyard, who earned gold in men's doubles, was 44. But all of these British athletes were mere youngsters compared to Oscar Swahn of Sweden who became the oldest person ever to win an individual event when, at the age of 60, he defeated fourteen rivals to win the single shot running deer shooting event.

1908 marked the first appearance of diving and field hockey, as well as figure skating, which was transferred to the Olympic Winter Games when they were inaugurated in 1924.

In the football (soccer) tournament, Sophus Nielsen of Denmark scored ten goals in a match against France.

In the spirit of sportsmanship, the final in middleweight Greco-Roman wrestling between Sweden's Frithiof Martensson and Mauritz Andersson was postponed one day to allow Martensson to recover from a minor injury. Martensson won.

Ray Ewry of the United States won the standing high jump and the standing long jump for the third time and became the only person in Olympic history to win a career total of eight gold medals in individual events.

The biggest highlight of the 1908 Olympics—the event that caught the public imagination around the world—was the dramatic ending of the marathon. After 26 miles of running, the first man to enter the stadium was Dorando Pietri of Italy. But Dorando, as he came to be known, collapsed on the track five times and was finally carried across the finish line by well-meaning officials. He was disqualified for receiving outside aid, but he did become an international celebrity. The real winner of the race was Johnny Hayes, New York City.

1912

Held in Stockholm, the 1912 Olympics were a model of efficiency and set the standard for organization for decades to come. The Swedish hosts introduced the use of unofficial electronic timing devices for the track events, as well as the first use of a public address system.

Following a campaign by Baron de Coubertin, the modern pentathlon was added to the Olympic program. Women's events in swimming and diving were also introduced. Sweden would not allow boxing contests to be held in their country. After the Games, the International Olympic Committee decided to limit the power of host nations in deciding the Olympic program.

If there was an unofficial theme of the 1912 Games, it was endurance. The course for the cycling road race was 320 kilometers (199 miles), the longest race of any kind in Olympic history. The winner was Okey Lewis of South Africa in a time of 10 hours 42 minutes and 39 seconds. The Greco-Roman wrestling tournament saw two epic battles. The light-heavyweight final was declared a draw after Anders Ahlgren of Sweden and Ivar Böhling of Finland grappled for nine hours. The middleweight semifinal match between Estonian Martin Klein and Finland's Alfred Asikainen lasted even longer. Klein finally pinned his opponent after eleven hours, but he was so exhausted that he was unable to take part in the final. Hannes Kolehmainen of Finland won three gold medals in long-distance running. On July 8, he won the 10,000 meters. Two days later he set a world record in the 5000 meters. Three days after that he broke the world record at 3000 meters in a heat of the team race and, on July 15, he won the 12,000-meter cross-country race.

Despite these exploits, the most popular hero of the 1912 Games, and probably the greatest athlete of the 20th century, was Jim Thorpe of the United States. Thorpe began his Stockholm campaign by winning the five-event pentathlon. Then he placed fourth in the high jump and seventh in the long jump. Finally, over a period of three days, he earned a second gold medal by shattering the world record in the ten-event decathlon. Thorpe was so far ahead of his time that his performance would have earned him a silver medal at the *1948* Olympics.

Another athletics highlight was the final of the 800-meter run. In a tight and exciting finish, the first four runners, all from the United States, broke the world record. Winner Ted Meredith's time of 1:51.9 would last as a world record for the next fourteen years.

In a consolation match of the football tournament, Gottfried Fuchs of Germany scored ten goals against Russia to match Sophus Nielsen's 1908 feat.

One member of the Austrian team that finished

second in the team sabre fencing event was Otto Herschmann, who was, at that time, president of the Austrian Olympic Committee. Herschmann is the only sitting national Olympic committee president to win an Olympic medal. He died in a Nazi concentration camp on June 14, 1942.

1920

The 1916 Olympics were scheduled to be held in Berlin, but were canceled because of what came to be known as World War I. The 1920 Games were awarded to Antwerp to honor the suffering that had been inflicted on the Belgian people during the war. Although their presentation was spartan, the hosts were admired for their noble effort.

As aggressor nations in World War I, Germany, Austria, Hungary, Bulgaria and Turkey (over the objections of Baron de Coubertin) were not allowed to participate.

The Opening Ceremony was notable for the introduction of the Olympic flag and the presentation of the Athletes' Oath, which was spoken by Belgium's Victor Boin. Boin had previously earned two medals in water polo, silver in 1908 and bronze in 1912. In 1920 he would win another silver medal—in team épée fencing.

The 1920 Olympics featured numerous outstanding athletes. In a performance unequaled in Olympic history, Nedo Nadi of Italy earned gold medals in five of the six fencing events. His brother Aldo won three golds and one silver. Ethelda Bleibtrey of the United States won gold medals in all three women's swimming contests. Including preliminary heats, she swam in five races and broke the world record in every one. France's Suzanne Lenglen dominated women's tennis singles so completely that she lost only four games in the ten sets she played. She won a second gold medal in mixed doubles and a bronze in women's doubles. One of the members of the gold medal-winning US rugby team was Daniel Carroll, who had also been a member of Australia's winning team in 1908. Carroll remains one of only three people to earn gold medals for two distinctly different countries.

American boxer Eddie Eagan triumphed in the light-heavyweight division. Twelve years later he won another Olympic championship in bobsledding. He remains the only athlete to win gold medals in both the Summer and Winter Games.

Swedish shooter Oscar Swahn also made Olympic history. At age 72 he earned a silver medal in the team double-shot running deer event to become the oldest medalist ever. At the other end of the scale was American diver Aileen Riggin who won the springboard diving competition at age 14. She was also the smallest athlete at the Antwerp Games, measuring 4 feet 7 inches (1.40 meters) and weighing 65 pounds (29.5 kilograms).

1920 also produced several oddities. Ice hockey was included in the Summer Games for the first and only time. Tug of war appeared for the last time. Swimmer Duke Kahanamoku of the United States won the 100-meter freestyle not once but twice, when the final was ordered reswum after a protest. The 1920 12-foot dinghy yachting event was the only event in Olympic history to be held in two countries. The first race was staged in Belgium, but the last two races took place in the Netherlands because both entrants were Dutch. On July 9, Norway won seven yachting events. Their achievement was less impressive than it appears—in five of the events there were no other entrants.

1924

To the great relief of Baron de Coubertin, who was due to retire in 1925, the 1924 Olympics were awarded to Paris, giving the French a chance to redeem themselves for the disastrous 1900 Paris Games. But first, between January 25 and February 4, the inaugural Olympic Winter Games were held in Chamonix, France. In 1924 the Olympic motto, "*Citius, Altius, Fortius,*" (Swifter, Higher, Stronger) was introduced, as was the Closing Ceremony ritual of raising three flags: the flag of the International Olympic Committee, the flag of the host nation and the flag of the next host nation.

Raucous demonstrations broke out during the boxing and rugby competitions, and disputes during the fencing tournament led to two real duels. The French were particularly irritated by the Americans because the US government had only recently criticized the French occupation on the Ruhr. During a rugby match between France and the United States, an American art student was severely caned by an incensed French spectator who had become annoyed by the loud American "rooting." On the whole, however, the Games were well-organized and went smoothly. The number of participating nations jumped from 29 to 44, signaling widespread acceptance of the Olympics as a major event, as did the presence of 1000 journalists.

Women's fencing made its debut as Ellen Osiier of Denmark earned the gold medal without losing a single bout.

William DeHart Hubbard of the United States became the first black athlete to win an individual event. However, his victory in the long jump was overshadowed by the performance of Robert Legendre, who had failed to qualify for the US team in the long jump, but set a world record in the event while competing in the pentathlon the day before the long jump final.

The 1924 Olympics featured several athletes who went on to achieve greater fame in other fields. Johnny Weissmuller of the United States won two gold medals in swimming on July 20 alone. That same day he earned a bronze medal in water polo. He later went to Hollywood and starred as Tarzan in twelve movies.

A member of the Yale University crew that won the coxed eights rowing event was Ben Spock. Twenty years later he wrote *The Common Sense Book of Baby and Child Care,* which eventually sold more than 35 million copies. American swimmer Gertrude Ederle won a bronze medal in the 100-meter freestyle. Two years later she caused a sensation by becoming the first woman to swim across the English Channel (la Manche)—and in a time almost two hours faster than any man had ever achieved.

Arthur Porritt of New Zealand earned a bronze medal in the 100-meter dash. He later served as Governor-General of New Zealand and, for more than 30 years, as surgeon to the British royal family.

The greatest hero of the 1924 Games was the Finnish runner Paavo Nurmi, who won five gold medals to add to the three he had won in 1920. His most spectacular performance occurred on July 10. First he easily won the 1500 meters. Then, a mere 55 minutes later, he returned to the track and won the 5000 meters. Nurmi's teammate, Ville Ritola, didn't do badly either in 1924: he won four gold medals and two silver.

One gold medalist who retained his modesty was Pierre Coquelin de Lisle of France, who won the small-bore rifle, prone shooting event. After his victory he sent the following cable to his mother: "Am Olympic champion. World record beaten. Will arrive Tuesday morning."

1928

The Amsterdam Olympics of 1928 were (with the exception of the boxing tournament) held in an atmosphere of peace and harmony that preceded twenty years of economic uncertainty and war. Perhaps the Games were best exemplified by the experience of Australian rower Henry Pearce. Midway through his quarterfinal race, he stopped rowing to allow a family of ducks to pass single file in front of his boat. Pearce won the race anyway and, later, the gold medal as well.

At the Opening Ceremony, the team from Greece led the Parade of Nations and the host Dutch team marched in last. Greece first, hosts last would become a permanent part of the Olympic protocol.

Athletes from 28 different nations won gold medals in Amsterdam, a record that would last for 40 years.

The number of female athletes more than doubled as women were finally allowed to compete in gymnastics and track and field. It was with great reluctance that the male-dominated IAAF and IOC agreed to running races for women. When several finalists in the 800 meters (won by Lina Radke of Germany) collapsed in exhaustion after the race, antifeminists attacked such "feats of endurance" as dangerous. The new president of the International Olympic Committee, Henri de Baillet-Latour of Belgium, suggested that all women's sports be eliminated from the Olympic program. The uproar would have been humorous except that the IAAF actually did ban all races longer than 200 meters, and no women's race longer than half a lap was run at the Olympics for another 32 years.

For the first time, Asian athletes won gold medals. Mikio Oda of Japan won the triple jump, while his teammate, Yoshiyuki Tsuruta, won the 200-meter breaststroke. Meanwhile the team from India swept to victory in field hockey. Between 1928 and 1960, Indian teams won six straight gold medals.

Another winning streak began in 1928. Hungary earned the first of seven consecutive gold medals in team sabre fencing. Between 1924 and 1964, Hungarian sabre teams won 46 straight matches.

Two notable members of royalty earned gold medals in 1928. Crown Prince Olav of Norway was part of the crew that won the 6-meter yachting event. He later became a symbol of Norwegian resistance to the Nazis during World War II and was a popular king for 34 years until his death in 1991. Lord Burghley, heir to the Marquess of Exeter in Great Britain, won the 400-meter hurdles. Later he was elected to parliament, served as president of the International Amateur Athletic Federation for 30 years and as a member of the International Olympic Committee for 45 years. He was also chairman of the Organizing Committee of the 1948 Olympics.

1932

Because the 1932 Olympics were held in the middle of the Great Depression and in the comparatively remote city of Los Angeles, half as many athletes took part as had in 1928. The turnout was the lowest since the 1904 Games. Several events attracted only a handful of entrants and the football (soccer) tournament had to be canceled completely. Nevertheless, the level of competition was extremely high and 18 world records were either broken or tied. The crowds set records too, starting with the 100,000 people who attended the Opening Ceremony. The 1932 Games were also the first to turn a substantial profit—about $1 million.

The 1932 Olympics were the first to last 16 days. The duration of the Olympics has remained between 15 and 18 days ever since. Between 1900 and 1928, no Summer Olympics was shorter than 79 days.

For the first time, the male athletes were housed in a single Olympic Village, while the women stayed in a luxury hotel. At the victory ceremonies the medal winners stood on a victory stand and the flag of the winner was raised. Official automatic timing was introduced for the track events, as was the photo-finish camera. In fact, for the first time, the results of a final were changed after the film of the race was reviewed. Originally Jack Keller of the United States was awarded the bronze medal in the 110-meter hurdles. When the revised results gave third place to Donald Finley of Great Britain, Keller found Finley in the Olympic Village and gave him the medal.

In the interests of international goodwill, the US government suspended its prohibition against alcoholic beverages to allow French, Italian and other athletes to import and drink wine.

The United States won all twelve medals in diving, while the Japanese men swept nine of twelve gold and silver medals in swimming. Fourteen-year-old Kuzuo Kitamura won the 1500-meter freestyle to become the youngest male in any sport ever to earn a gold medal in an individual event.

Sprinter Liu Changchun excited interest as the first and only representative of the 400 million people of China.

Twenty-one-year-old American Babe Didrikson qualified for all five women's track and field events, but was only allowed to compete in three. She won the javelin throw and set world records in the high jump and the 80-meter hurdles.

Ivar Johansson, a Swedish policeman, won gold medals in both freestyle and Greco-Roman wrestling. Another Swedish wrestler, Carl Westergren, won his third Greco-Roman title, each in a different division. His previous victories had come in 1920 and 1924.

In the spirit of fair play, British fencer Judy Guinness gave up her hopes for a gold medal when she pointed out to officials that they had not noticed two touches scored against her by her final opponent, Ellen Preis of Austria.

One of the most bizarre controversies in Olympic history occurred in the equestrian dressage competition. Bertil Sandström of Sweden placed second, but was relegated to last place for encouraging his horse by making clicking noises. Sandström claimed the noises were made by a creaking saddle, but the Jury of Appeal was not convinced.

1936

In 1931, when Berlin was chosen as the site for the 1936 Olympics, few people suspected that a mere two years would see the rise to power of Adolf Hitler and the Nazi Party. Jewish groups in various countries asked for a boycott of the Berlin Olympics and in the United States a boycott proposal was only narrowly defeated. An alternative People's Olympics was scheduled to take place in Barcelona, Spain, but it was cancelled at the last moment when the Spanish Civil War broke out the day before competition was set to begin. The 1936 Olympics are best remembered for Hitler's failed attempt to use them to prove his theories of Aryan racial superiority. As it turned out, the most popular hero of the Games, even among the German people, was the African-American sprinter and long jumper Jesse Owens, who won four gold medals. During the long jump competition, Owens' German "rival," Luz Long, publicly befriended him in front of the Nazis.

1936 saw the introduction of the torch relay, in which a lighted torch is carried from Olympia to the site of the current Games. The 1936 Olympics were also the first to be broadcast on a form of television. Twenty-five large screens were set up throughout Berlin, allowing the local people to see the Games for free. The Berlin Games also produced the first noteworthy official film: *Olympia*, directed by Leni Riefenstahl. Although intended as a piece of Nazi propaganda, the film ended up as a celebration of the human spirit as well.

Basketball, canoeing and team handball made their first appearances, while polo was included in the Olympic program for the last time.

Thirteen-year-old Marjorie Gestring of the United States won the gold medal in springboard diving. She remains the youngest female gold medalist in the history of the Summer Olympics. Inge Sørensen of Denmark earned a bronze medal in the 200-meter breaststroke at the age of 12, making her the youngest medalist ever in an individual event.

Hungarian water polo player Olivier Halassy won his third medal (two golds and a silver) despite the fact that one of his legs had been amputated below the knee following a streetcar accident.

Rower Jack Beresford of Great Britain won a gold

medal in the double sculls event, marking the fifth Olympics at which he earned a medal.

Kristjan Palusalu of Estonia won the heavyweight division in both freestyle and Greco-Roman wrestling.

Norway's Jacob Tullin Thams took a silver medal in the 8-meter yachting event. Twelve years earlier he had won the ski jump at the inaugural Olympic Winter Games.

One of the many German heroes of the Berlin Games was Konrad von Wangenheim, who fell and broke his collarbone during the steeplechase portion of the equestrian three-day event. Knowing that the German team would be disqualified if he failed to finish, he remounted and completed the course without a fault. The next day, during the jumping competition, he fell again and his horse landed on him. Both of them recovered and finished, and the German team placed first.

One of the oddest hometown decisions took place in the cycling match sprint final when Germany's Toni Merkens fouled Arie van Vliet of the Netherlands. Instead of being disqualified, Merken was fined 100 marks.

1948

The 1940 Olympics were awarded to Japan—the Winter games to Sapporo and the Summer Games to Tokyo—but when Japan invaded China and became involved in a major war, the Games were reassigned to Helsinki. When Soviet troops invaded Finland, the Olympics were canceled all together. The same fate befell the 1944 Games, which had been scheduled for London.

The British Olympic Association took up the task of organizing the first Summer Olympics in twelve years. Because London was still rebuilding after World War II, financing was limited and the athletes had to be housed in Army camps and remodeled schoolrooms. As aggressor nations, Germany and Japan were banned from the Games, but a record-setting 59 nations did take part. The first political defection took place as Marie Provaznikova, the president of the technical commission of women's gymnastics, refused to return to Communist-ruled Czechoslovakia.

The 1948 Games were the first to be shown on home television, although very few people in Great Britain actually owned sets. A women's canoeing event was held for the first time—and won by Karen Hoff of Denmark. Audrey Patterson finished third in the 200-meter dash to become the first black woman to earn an Olympic medal. The next day, fellow American Alice Coachman won the high jump to become the first black female gold medalist.

17-year-old American Bob Mathias won the decathlon only four months after taking up the sport. He is the youngest athlete in Olympic history to win a men's track and field event.

Two athletes who were Olympic champions in 1936 managed to defend their titles twelve years later. They were Ilona Elek of Hungary in women's foil fencing and Jan Brzák of Czechoslovakia in the canoeing Canadian pairs 1000 meters.

As an 18-year-old, Fanny Blankers-Koen of the Netherlands had competed in the Berlin Games, but it was in 1948 that she became a star. She was the world record holder in six events, but, according to the rules of the day, was only allowed to enter four. She won all four: the 100-meter dash, the 80-meter hurdles, the 200 meters and the 4 × 100-meter relay. Concert pianist Micheline Ostermeyer of France won both the shot put and the discus throw.

Two father and son teams won the gold and silver medals in Star class yachting: Hilary Smart and Paul Smart of the United States and Carlos de Cárdenas and Carlos de Cárdenas, junior of Cuba.

Károly Takács was a member of the Hungarian world champion pistol shooting team in 1938 when a grenade shattered his right hand—his pistol hand. Takács taught himself to shoot with his left hand and, ten years later, he won an Olympic gold medal in the rapid-fire pistol event.

Another unusual disqualification took place in equestrian dressage. The Swedish team earned gold medals, but eight months later they were forced to return their medals because one of their members, Gehnall Persson, was only a noncommissioned officer and thus ineligible to compete.

1952

The 1952 Helsinki Games began dramatically as Paavo Nurmi, now 55 years old, carried the torch into the stadium and handed it to Hannes Kolehmainen, now 62, who lit the cauldron. The athletes of 69 nations, gathered on the infield, broke ranks to catch a glimpse of these living legends. It seemed appropriate that the most impressive achievements in Helsinki should be those of another long-distance runner, Emil Zátopek of Czechoslovakia. Zátopek had already won gold at 10,000 meters and silver at 5000 in 1948. In 1952 he defended his 10,000-meter title and then, four days later, he won the 5000. Later that day, Zátopek's wife, Dana, earned a gold medal in the javelin throw. Three days after that, Zátopek competed in the marathon for the first time in his life—and won by 2½ minutes, to become the only person in Olympic history to win the 5000, 10,000 and marathon at the same Olympics.

The Soviet Union entered the Olympics for the first time. Although their athletes were housed in a separate "village," warnings that Cold War rivalries would lead to clashes proved unfounded. Particularly impressive were the Soviet women gymnasts who won the team competition easily, beginning a streak that would continue for forty years until the Soviet Union broke up into separate republics.

One of the most versatile athletes of 1952 was the Russian Aleksandra Chudina, who achieved a unique triple when she took silver medals in the long jump and javelin throw and a bronze in the high jump.

One of the first women allowed to compete against men in the equestrian dressage was Lis Hartel of Denmark. Despite being paralyzed below the knees after an attack of polio, Hartel, who had to be helped on and off her horse, won a silver medal.

Lars Hall, a carpenter from Sweden, became the first nonmilitary winner of the modern pentathlon. France's Madeleine Moreau earned a silver medal in women's springboard diving. She was the first non-American to medal in the event since its inclusion in the Olympic program in 1920.

Back in 1924, Bill Havens had been chosen to represent the United States in coxed eights rowing, but declined in order to stay home with his wife, who was expecting their first child. Twenty-eight years later, that child, Frank Havens, won a gold medal in the Canadian singles 10,000 meters canoeing event.

Another case of delayed gratification concerned the Jamaican 4 × 400-meter relay squad. In 1948 the team of Arthur Wint, Leslie Laing, Herb McKenley and George Rhoden had hoped to defeat the US, but Wint, running the third leg, pulled a muscle and was unable to finish. The foursome stayed together and, four years later in Helsinki, they broke the world record by 4.3 seconds and defeated the US team by one yard to win the Olympic championship.

In the end, the Helsinki Games were so well-organized, and the fans were so enthusiastic and knowledgeable, that some observers suggested that the Olympics be held permanently in Scandinavia.

1956

Melbourne won the right to host the 1956 Olympics by one vote over Buenos Aires. Australian quarantine laws were too severe to allow the entry of foreign horses, so the equestrian events were held separately in Stockholm in June. The Melbourne Games were the first to be held in the southern hemisphere, so they were staged between November 22 and December 8—the latest in Olympic history. The 1956 Olympics were stung by two boycotts. Egypt, Iraq and Lebanon withdrew to protest the Israeli-led invasion of the Suez Canal, and the Netherlands, Spain and Switzerland boycotted to protest the Soviet invasion of Hungary. On the other hand, West and East Germany entered a combined team. This arrangement continued for the next two Olympics.

László Papp of Hungary became the first boxer to win three gold medals. American Pat McCormick won both diving events, just as she had in 1952. Two athletes dominated the gymnastics competition. On the men's side, Ukrainian Viktor Chukarin earned five medals, including three gold, to bring his career total to eleven medals, seven of them gold. Ágnes Keleti of Hungary brought her career total to ten medals by winning four gold medals and two silver.

The US basketball team, led by Bill Russell and K.C. Jones, put on the most dominant performance in Olympic history, scoring more than twice as much as their opponents and winning each of their games by at least 30 points.

In the swimming competition, the butterfly stroke was separated from the breaststroke. Georgios Roubanis of Greece introduced the fiberglass pole to the pole vault competition (although Bob Mathias used one in the 1952 decathlon).

The Melbourne Olympics also saw some unusual oddities, including a false start in the marathon. In the team pursuit cycling race, the team from Great Britain finished in third place—for the sixth straight Olympics.

American bantamweight weightlifter Charles Vinci found himself seven ounces (200 grams) over the weight limit only fifteen minutes before the weigh-in. A severe last minute haircut allowed him to qualify. He went on to win the gold medal and set a world record. On the other end of the weight spectrum was another US weightlifter—Paul Anderson, who weighed 137.9 kilograms (303¼ pounds). In weightlifting, ties are broken by awarding the higher place to the athlete with the lower body weight. Incredibly, this worked to Anderson's *advantage* when he tied for first with Humberto Selvetti of Argentina. Selvetti weighed 143.5 kilograms (316½ pounds) so Anderson was awarded the gold medal and Selvetti the silver.

The water polo final matched Hungary and the Soviet Union—one month after the Soviet invasion of Hungary. The game degenerated into a brawl before being halted with Hungary leading 4-0. Forty-five members of the Hungarian Olympic delegation refused to return to their occupied country.

Counteracting this tension was an innovation in the protocol of the Closing Ceremony. Prior to 1956, the athletes marched by nation, as they did in the Opening Ceremony. In Melbourne, following a suggestion by a young Australian named John Ian Wang, the athletes entered the stadium together, as a symbol of global unity. At the time, Wang refused public acknowledgment, and gladly went on to lead a normal life. When the Olympics returned to Australia 44 years later, a search went out for Wang, who was discovered running a Chinese restaurant in Bucharest, Romania. He was flown to Sydney and honored at the Closing Ceremony of the 2000 Olympics.

1960

Fifty-four years after Italy had to give up hosting the Olympics following the eruption of Mt. Vesuvius, Rome finally got its chance. It made the most of its dramatic history, holding the wrestling competition in the Basilica of Maxentius, site of wrestling contests 2000 years earlier. Among the other antique sites that were used were the Caracalla Baths (gymnastics) and the Arch of Constantine (finish of the marathon). Even the Pope became a spectator, catching the canoeing semifinals from a window of his summer residence.

The 1960 Olympics saw a changing of the guard as numerous national winning streaks were broken. Coxed eights crews from the United States had won eight straight gold medals since 1920, but it was Germany who finished first in Rome. The same thing happened in the men's 4 × 100-meter relay, where a late pass led to the disqualification of the US team and a victory for Germany. East German Ingrid Kramer won both springboard and platform diving, stopping American streaks in those events at eight and seven respectively. Another German, Armin Hary, became the first-ever sprinter from a non-English-speaking country to win the men's 100-meter dash, while Livio Berruti of Italy became the first non-North American to win the 200 meters. Since the beginning of the modern Olympics, the men's high jump had been dominated by athletes from English-speaking countries, but in Rome Robert Shavlakadze of Soviet Georgia earned the gold medal.

India had won six straight Olympic field hockey tournaments since first entering in 1928, but in Rome, after 30 consecutive victories, India was beaten in the final 1-0 by Pakistan. In the men's team foil event, a Russian foursome broke the French-Italian stranglehold that had covered the last eight Olympics.

Not all favorites fell by the wayside. Paul Elvstrøm of Denmark won the gold medal in Finn class yachting—for the fourth straight time. Hungarian fencer Aladár Gerevich earned his sixth consecutive gold medal in the team sabre event. In canoeing, Sweden's Gert Fredricksson won his sixth gold medal.

Yugoslavia, which qualified for the semifinal by winning a coin toss, won the football tournament after losing in the final three straight times.

Sante Gaiardoni of Italy became the only cyclist in Olympic history to win both the time trial and the match sprint events.

By winning the silver medal in light-welterweight boxing, Ike Quartey of Ghana became the first black African Olympic medalist. Five days later in the marathon, Abebe Bikila, running barefoot, outlasted Rhadi Ben Abdesselem of Morocco to become the first black African Olympic champion.

Rafer Johnson and C.K. Yang were decathlon training partners at UCLA, but in Rome Johnson represented the United States and Yang represented Taiwan. In a dramatic finish, they took first and second places and then, exhausted, fell against each other for support.

British race walker Don Thompson prepared for the Roman summer heat by exercising in a bathroom filled with heaters and boiling kettles. His strategy paid off when he won the 50,000-meter race.

Suffering from a concussion and a broken collarbone after a fall in the three-day equestrian event, Bill Roycroft left his hospital bed to compete in the jumping test and ensure the gold medal for Australia.

1964

The 1964 Tokyo Games were the first to be held in Asia. The Japanese expressed their successful reconstruction after World War II by choosing as the final torchbearer Yoshinori Sakai, who was born in Hiroshima the day that that city was destroyed by an atomic bomb.

South Africa was banned from competition because of its government's racist policies. In 1962 Indonesia hosted the Asian Games in Jakarta. When the Indonesian government refused to allow athletes from Israel and Taiwan to participate, the IOC suspended the Indonesian Olympic Committee until it agreed to abide by the rules of the IOC. Indonesia withdrew its team from the 1964 Olympics, as did North Korea.

Judo and volleyball were introduced to the Olympic program. The 1964 Games also saw the first Olympic wedding, as two Bulgarian athletes, long jumper Diana Yorgova and gymnast Nikolai Prodanov, exchanged vows at a ceremony in the Olympic Village.

In men's swimming, world records were set in eight of the ten events, while American swimmer Don Schollander won four gold medals. In the men's springboard contest, US divers earned the gold *and* silver medals for the tenth consecutive Olympics.

Abebe Bikila of Ethiopia became the first repeat winner of the marathon—less than six weeks after having his appendix removed. Russian rower Vyascheslav Ivanov won the single sculls for the third time, and Australian swimmer Dawn Fraser won the 100-meter freestyle for the third time. Al Oerter of the United States did the same in the discus throw despite cervical disc injury that forced him to wear a neck harness and torn rib cartilage incurred a week before the competition.

Hungarian water polo player Dezsö Gyarmati won his fifth medal in a row. Another Hungarian, Greco-Roman wrestler Imre Polyák, finally won a gold medal after finishing second in the same division at the last three Olympics.

By winning two medals of each kind, Larysa Latynina of the Ukraine brought her career medal total to an incredible 18. She is also one of only four athletes in any sport to win nine gold medals.

Helen "Lana" Dupont of the United States became the first woman to compete in the equestrian three-day event.

Hungarian fencers suffered their first loss in 40 years in the team sabre event. On the other hand, they won the team épée after 52 years of victories by Italy and France.

Two unusual events occurred in the cycling competitions. The finish of the 195-kilometer long road race was so close that even though Sture Pettersson of Sweden finished only sixteen-hundredths of a second behind the winner, Mario Zanin of Italy, he ended up in only 51st place. In a semifinal race of the match sprint, Giovanni Pettenella of Italy and Pierre Trentin of France set a dubious Olympic record by standing still for 21 minutes 57 seconds.

The most dramatic race of the Tokyo Games was the 10,000 meters, in which Billy Mills of the United States came from behind to beat Mohamed Gammoudi of Tunisia. Both Mills and Gammoudi were unknown runners who improved their personal best times by more than 45 seconds.

1968

The choice of Mexico City to host the 1968 Olympics was a controversial one because of the city's high altitude—2300 meters (7546 feet)—which meant that the air contained 30% less oxygen than at sea level. Sure enough, the rarefied air proved disastrous to many athletes competing in endurance events. The winning time in the 5000 meters was the slowest in 16 years and in the 3000-meter steeplechase and the 10,000 meters it was the slowest in 20 years. The world record holder in the 10,000, Ron Clarke of Australia, collapsed after finishing sixth and was unconscious for ten minutes.

On the other hand, the high altitude led to world records in all of the men's races that were 400 meters or shorter, including both relays, and in the long jump as well. In the triple jump, five different athletes broke the world record. Lee Evans' record of 43.86 seconds in the 400 meters would last for 19 years; Bob Beamon's spectacular long jump of 8.90 meters (29 feet 2½ inches) would last for 22 years; and the US 4 × 400-meter relay team's record of 2:56.16 would not be broken for 24 years. At the same time, many observers were dubious of the wind readings, which, for four world records, were exactly the maximum allowable: 2.0 meters per second.

The Mexico City Olympics, the first Summer Games to include sex testing for women, were blessed with many outstanding heroines. Mexican hurdler Enriqueta Basilio became the first woman to light the cauldron at the Opening Ceremony. Eulalia Rolinska of Poland and Gladys de Seminario of Peru were the first women to compete in shooting. Wyomia Tyus of the United States became the first repeat winner of the 100-meter dash, and fellow American Debbie Meyer was the first swimmer to win three gold medals in individual events at the same Olympics. Discus thrower Lia Manoliu of Romania competed in her fifth Olympics—and finally won a gold medal at age 36.

But the most popular female athlete of the 1968 Games was Vera Čáslavská, the Czech gymnast. After the Soviet invasion of Czechoslovakia two months before the Olympics, Čáslavská went into hiding for three weeks. She emerged to win four gold medals and two silvers and then, to the delight of a crowd of 10,000 well-wishers, was married in Mexico City during the Olympics.

On the male side, Al Oerter of the United States won the discus throw for the fourth time, and American high jumper Dick Fosbury revolutionized his event by clearing the bar head first with his back to the bar.

The Swedish team demonstrated sibling harmony. The four Pettersson brothers combined to win the silver medal in cycling's team time trial, and the three Sundelin brothers won the gold medal in the 5.5-meter yachting event.

Ten days before the Opening Ceremony, Mexican government troops opened fire on a crowd of unarmed demonstrators, killing at least 250 people. The IOC refused to take a stand, declaring the incident "an internal affair." Yet two weeks later, when African-American sprinters Tommie Smith and John Carlos staged a silent, non-violent protest during the award ceremony for the 200 meters, the IOC pressured the US Olympic Committee into ordering Smith and Carlos to leave the Olympic Village and the country.

The 1968 Games also saw the first drug disqualification, as a Swedish entrant in the modern pentathlon, Hans-Gunnar Liljenwall, tested positive for excessive alcohol.

1972

The 1972 Munich Games were the largest yet, setting records in all categories, with 195 events and 7173 athletes from 121 nations. They were supposed to celebrate peace and, for the first ten days, all did indeed go well. But then, in the early morning of September 5, eight Palestinian terrorists broke into the Olympic Village and made their way to the rooms of the Israeli team. Two Israelis were killed immediately and nine more were taken hostage. The terrorists demanded the release of 200 prisoners held in Israeli jails and safe passage for themselves out of Germany. They got as far as a military airport, where West German sharpshooters opened fire. In the ensuing battle, all nine Israeli hostages were killed, as were five of the terrorists and one policeman. The Olympics were suspended and a memorial service was held in the main stadium. In defiance of the terrorists, the International Olympic Committee ordered the competitions to resume after a pause of 34 hours.

Of course, all other details about the Munich Games paled in significance, but it did have its highlights. Archery was reintroduced to the Olympic program after a 52-year absence and team handball after a 36-year absence. Whitewater (or slalom) canoeing was included for the first time and all four events were won by the East Germans, who had built an exact replica of the Olympic course for their training. The 1972 Games were also the first to have a named mascot: Waldi the dachshund.

US swimmer Mark Spitz won an incredible seven gold medals to go with the two he had earned in 1968. Lasse Viren of Finland fell midway through the 10,000-meter final, but rose and set a world record to win the first of his four career gold medals

Freestyle wrestler Ivan Yarygin of Russia pinned all seven of his opponents en route to his first Olympic championship in the heavyweight division. But the real "big man" was super-heavyweight Chris Taylor of the United States, who weighed 186.88 kilograms (412 pounds). Taylor, who won the bronze medal, remained the heaviest athlete in Olympic history until 2008 when his record was broken by judoka Ricardo Blas Jr. Wrestling imposed a maximum weight limit of 130 kilograms in 1988.

Ulrike Meyfarth of West Germany won the women's high jump at age 16. She is the youngest winner of an individual athletics event in Olympic history. Another West German, Liselott Linsenhoff, competing in the dressage event, became the first female equestrian to win a gold medal in an individual event.

The media star of the Munich Games was the tiny gymnast, Olga Korbut, whose dramatic cycle of success in the team competition, failure in the individual competition and renewed success in the apparatus finals, captured the attention of fans worldwide. Back in her hometown of Grodno, Belarus, Korbut received so much fan mail that a special clerk had to be assigned to sort out her mail.

Many Olympic gold medal winners have exploited their success by pursuing movie careers. All but one of these athletes have been humans. The exception was Cornishman V, the British horse who helped two different riders win gold medals in the three-day event in 1968 and 1972. Cornishman V appeared in *Dead Cert* (1974) and *International Velvet* (1978).

1972 saw the end of three long US winning streaks. Vladimir Vasin of Russia won the men's springboard diving event after eleven consecutive US victories. In the pole vault, US athletes had gained victory in every Olympics since the modern Games began in 1896—16 times in a row. But in Munich, after a dispute regarding the banning of a new type of pole, the win streak was finally halted by Wolfgang Nordwig of East Germany. Even more controversial was the end of US domination of men's basketball. Since 1936, US teams had won 62 straight games and seven straight gold medals before losing the 1972 final to the USSR in a game in which the Soviets were given a reprieve after the final buzzer sounded.

1976

As a result of poor planning and corruption, the 1976 Montreal Olympics went almost unbelievably over budget, saddling the people of Montreal and Canada with a debt that it would take them decades to pay off. Despite this financial disaster, the Games themselves were well-organized and the competitions went smoothly.

The 1976 games did face a major political obstacle when the dictator of Tanzania, Julius Nyerere, called for a boycott of the Olympics because the national rugby team of New Zealand had toured South Africa, and New Zealand was scheduled to compete in the Olympics. The fact that South Africa had been banned from the Olympics for twelve years because of its racial policies did not seem to faze Nyerere. Nor did the fact that rugby was not affiliated with the Olympic movement. Still, 22 African governments ended up boycotting the Montreal Games, as did the South American nation of Guyana. The Guyanese sprinter, James Gilkes, asked to be allowed to compete as an independent participant, but the International Olympic Committee rejected his appeal.

Women's events were included for the first time in basketball, rowing and team handball.

Fourteen-year-old gymnast Nadia Comăneci of Romania caused a sensation when, for her performance on the uneven bars, she was awarded the first-ever perfect score of 10.0. She eventually earned seven 10.0s, as well as three gold medals, one silver and one bronze. On the men's side, Japan's Shun Fujimoto broke his leg while completing his floor exercises routine. The Japanese team was engaged in a close contest with the Soviet Union, so Fujimoto kept his injury secret. But when he dismounted from the rings, he dislocated his knee and was forced to withdraw.

World records were broken in 21 of the 26 swimming events and tied in one other. US swimmers won twelve of the thirteen men's events, finishing one-two in nine of the eleven individual events and winning both relays. The East German women were almost as dominant as the American men, winning eleven of thirteen events. However, unlike the American men, who had a long history of Olympic success, the East German women emerged from nowhere. In 1972, they had failed to win a single gold medal. This led to suspicions that they were taking steroids and other prohibited drugs, suspicions that later proved to be true.

Soviet wrestlers also put on an impressive show. Of the twenty who competed, eighteen won medals, including twelve gold.

The Japanese women's volleyball team won all their matches in straight sets, and in only one of fifteen games did an opponent score in double figures. On the other hand, the men's field hockey team from New Zealand won the gold medal despite winning only half their matches and giving up as many goals as they scored.

Individual stars included Klaus Dibiasi of Italy, who won his third straight gold medal in platform diving; Viktor Saneyev of Soviet Georgia, who won his third triple jump gold; and Irena Szewińska of Poland, winner of the 400-meter run, who brought her career total to seven medals—in five different events.

Alberto Juantorena of Cuba put together the first 400 meters/800 meters double victory. Miklos Németh of Hungary won the javelin throw to become the first son of a track and field gold medalist to win a gold of his own. His father, Imre, had won the hammer throw in 1948.

Clarence Hill of Bermuda earned a bronze medal in boxing's super-heavyweight division to give Bermuda the honor of being the least populous nation (53,500) ever to win a medal in the Summer Olympics.

1980

The 1980 Moscow Olympics were disrupted by another, even larger boycott, this one led by US president Jimmy Carter, part of a package of actions to protest the December 1979 Soviet invasion of Afghanistan. With his eyes on the upcoming presidential election, Carter engaged in extensive arm-twisting to gain support from other nations. Some governments, like those of Great Britain and Australia, supported the boycott but allowed the athletes to decide for themselves whether to go to Moscow. No such freedom of choice was allowed US athletes, as Carter threatened to revoke the passport of any athlete who tried to travel to the USSR. In the end, 65 nations turned down their invitations to the Olympics; probably 45 to 50 did so because of the US-led boycott. Eighty nations did participate—the lowest number since 1956.

Certain sports, such as yachting, equestrian events, field hockey and men's swimming, were particularly hard hit by the boycott. Yet the Games proceeded with much pomp, and more world records were set than in 1976. With traditional powers West Germany, Japan and the United States missing, some Soviet fans took out their aggressions by booing and heckling the Poles and East Germans.

Russian gymnast Nikolai Andrianov took the Athletes' Oath and then won five medals to bring his career total to fifteen: seven gold, five silver and three bronze. Fellow Russian Aleksandr Dityatin earned a medal in every men's gymnastics event (three gold, four silver and one bronze) to become the only athlete in history to win eight medals at one Olympics.

Cuban super-heavyweight Teófilo Stevenson became the first boxer to win the same weight division three times. Waldemar Cierpinski of East Germany matched Abebe Bikila's feat of winning the marathon twice. East German Gerd Wessig became the first male high jumper to set a world record at the Olympics. Valentyn Mankin of the Ukraine earned a gold medal in the Star class to become the first yachtsman to win gold medals in three different classes. Meanwhile, another yachtsman, Esko Rechardt, became the first Finn to win the Finn class.

The chemically-augmented East German women swimmers again won eleven of thirteen events while every one of the 54 East German rowers who competed in Moscow went home with a medal.

Russian swimmer Vladimir Salnikov won three gold medals, but his greatest achievement was in the 1500 meters, where he broke the 15-minute barrier for the first time (14:58.27).

The most dramatic confrontation matched Great Britain's Steve Ovett and Sebastian Coe at 800 meters and 1500 meters. Coe was favored in the 800 meters race and Ovett in the 1500. They did both win gold medals—but each in the other's specialty.

Károly Varga of Hungary broke his shooting hand two days before the small-bore rifle prone event, but earned the gold medal anyway.

The boycott deprived the inaugural women's field hockey tournament of all of its entrants except the host Soviet Union. Five weeks before the Opening Ceremony, a late invitation went out to Zimbabwe to send a team. Members were selected less than a week before the Games and rushed to Moscow, where they surprised everyone by finishing first.

Finally, observers of the medal ceremony for the men's coxless pairs rowing event might have been excused for rubbing their eyes. Both the gold- and silver-medal winning teams were identical twins. Bernd and Jorg Landvoigt of East Germany took first place, while Yuri and Nikolai Pimenov of Russia finished second.

1984

After the terrorist attack in 1972 and the financial disaster of 1976, only Los Angeles bid for the right to host the 1984 Olympics. Because the Los Angeles Games were the first since 1896 to be staged without government financing, the organizers depended heavily on existing facilities and corporate sponsors. Although criticized at the time, the 1984 Los Angeles Olympics became the model for future Games, particularly after it was revealed that they had produced a profit of $223 million.

With the Olympics being held in the United States only four years after the US-led boycott of the Moscow Games, it was not surprising that the Soviet Union organized a revenge boycott in 1984. This time only fourteen nations stayed away—but those nations accounted for 58% of the gold medals at the 1976 Olympics. Weightlifting lost 29 of the 30 medalists at the last world championships including all the gold medal winners. Freestyle wrestling lost 23 of 30 medalists and nine of ten world champions. Other sports that were hard hit were gymnastics, team handball, modern pentathlon and women's track and field.

Despite the boycott, a record 140 nations took part. Good feelings prevailed to such an extent that at the Opening Ceremony the athletes broke ranks to join in spontaneous dancing, such celebration usually being reserved for the Closing Ceremony.

Fifty-six years after doctors declared that women who ran 800 meters would "become old too soon," a women's marathon was added to the Olympic program. The inaugural race was won by Joan Benoit of the United States. Among the other events for women that were introduced in 1984 were the cycling road race (won by Connie Carpenter-Phinney of the United States), rhythmic gymnastics (won in an upset by Lori Fong of Canada), and synchronized swimming, which was added after the Soviet-led boycott was announced.

Carl Lewis of the United States matched Jesse Owens' 1936 feat by winning the 100 meters, the 200 meters, the long jump and the 4 × 100-meter relay. Nawal El Moutawakel of Morocco won the 400-meter hurdles to become the first female Olympic champion from an Islamic nation. Twelve years after setting a record as the youngest winner of an individual track and field event, Ulrike Meyfarth of West Germany won the high jump again to become the *oldest*-ever winner of that event. Sebastian Coe of Great Britain became the first repeat winner of the men's 1500 meters, while Edwin Moses of the United States won his second gold medal in the 400-meter hurdles despite having missed the last Olympics because of the US boycott.

In men's rowing, each of the eight events was won by a different country, with Pertti Karpinnen of Finland earning his third gold medal in single sculls.

Hans Marius Fogh of Canada won a bronze medal in Soling class yachting—24 years after he earned his first medal while competing for Denmark.

For the first time, professionals were allowed in the football tournament—as long as they had not yet taken part in the World Cup. This led to a spirited final—viewed by 101,799 spectators—in which France defeated Brazil 2-0.

Naroli Fairhall, an archer from New Zealand, competed in a wheelchair. She was the first paraplegic athlete to take part in a medal event at the Olympics.

An oddity occurred in men's 400-meter freestyle

swimming. Beginning in 1984, the eight fastest qualifiers took part in the "A" final and the ninth through sixteenth fastest swam in a consolation "B" final. For the only time in Olympic history, the winner of the "B" final, Thomas Fahrner of West Germany, recorded a faster time than the winner of the "A" final.

1988

The 1988 Olympics were held in Seoul, South Korea, a nation that turned democratic in order to welcome the world to the Summer Games. North Korea boycotted, and was joined by Cuba, Ethiopia and Nicaragua. Still, records were set with 159 nations participating, 52 winning medals and 31 taking home gold medals.

The Games got off to a dramatic start at the Opening Ceremony when the torch was run into the stadium by 76-year-old Sohn Kee-chung, the winner of the 1936 marathon. In 1936 Sohn had been forced to enter using a Japanese name because Korea was occupied by Japan.

Table tennis was admitted to the Olympic program and South Korea and China won all four gold medals, as well as nine of twelve total medals. Tennis was reintroduced after a gap of 62 years as Steffi Graf of West Germany capped off a Grand Slam season by winning Olympic gold.

In February 1988, Christa Luding-Rothenburger of East Germany won gold and silver in speed skating at the Calgary Winter Olympics. In Seoul she finished second in the inaugural women's cycling match sprint event to become the only person in history to earn medals in the Summer and Winter Games in the same year.

Several athletes whose nations boycotted the 1984 Olympics came back to successfully defend the titles they had won in 1980. Among them were Vladimir Salnikov of Russia in the 1500-meter freesyle, Lutz Hesslich of East Germany in the men's match sprint, and Serhei Bilohlazov of the Ukraine in freestyle wrestling. The three Soviet medalists in the 1980 hammer throw, Yuri Sedykh, Sergei Litvinov and Juri Tamm, all won medals again in 1988.

Peter Seisenbacher of Austria and Hitoshi Saito of Japan became the first repeat winners in judo. For the first time, all three medalists in equestrian dressage were women. Fencer Kerstin Palm of Sweden became the first woman to take part in seven Olympics.

In swimming, Kristin Otto of East Germany won six gold medals, but her achievements were tarnished when documents revealed that she had been fed a steady diet of prohibited drugs. On the men's side, Matt Biondi of the United States earned seven medals including five gold. For the seventh straight Olympics in which they competed, US men won all the relays. Between 1960 and 1988, they set world records in eighteen of nineteen swimming relays.

Greg Louganis of the United States became the first man to win both diving events twice—despite the fact that he hit his head on the board during the preliminary round of the springboard competition.

Ben Johnson of Canada set a world record in the 100-meter dash, but tested positive for steroids. Although Johnson was the 43rd Olympic athlete to be disqualified for drugs, he was the first "big fish" to be caught and the scandal rocked the sports world. Carl Lewis of the US was promoted to the official winner of the event. He was the first man to win the 100 meters twice and the first long jumper of either sex to win two gold medals.

US sprinter Florence Griffith Joyner won three gold medals and one silver, while her sister-in-law, Jackie Joyner-Kersee, won both the heptathlon and the long jump.

In an overwhelming performance in the shot put, all six puts by Natalya Lisovskaya of Russia were good enough for the gold medal.

1992

In the years following the 1988 Olympics, the world went through massive political changes. Apartheid was repealed in South Africa, allowing that nation to return to the Olympics for the first time since 1960. The Berlin Wall fell and West and East Germany were reunited, as were North and South Yemen. Communism collapsed in the Soviet Union, and the USSR split into fifteen separate countries. At the 1992 Barcelona Olympics, independent teams from Estonia and Latvia made their first appearance since 1936, and Lithuania fielded its first team since 1928. The remaining ex-Soviet republics competed as the "Unified Team," although individual winners were honored by the raising of the flag of their own republic. For the first time in twenty years, all nations were represented. The only controversy concerned Yugoslavia, which was the subject of United Nations sanctions because of its military aggression against Croatia and Bosnia-Herzegovina. In the end, Yugoslavia was banned from taking part in any team sports, but individual Yugoslav athletes were allowed to compete as "independent Olympic participants."

Baseball, which had appeared as an exhibition or demonstration sport at six Olympics, finally achieved medal status. Badminton and women's judo were also added to the Olympic program.

Men's basketball was opened to all professionals for the first time, leading to the creation of the US "Dream Team" that included Magic Johnson, Michael Jordan, Larry Bird and Charles Barkley. In eight games, they averaged 117 points and never called a time-out.

Gymnast Vitaly Scherbo of Belarus won six gold medals including a record four in one day.

Zhang Shan of China won the skeet contest to become the first woman to win a mixed-sex shooting event. She could also be the last, as men's and women's events were separated after the 1992 Games.

Hungarian swimmer Tamás Darnyi won both individual medley races, just as he had four years earlier.

Some of the team sports in Barcelona saw dramatic results. Italy needed six overtime periods to defeat Spain in the water polo final. Spain beat Poland in the football final on a goal with only 72 seconds to play. Spain scored a major upset by winning the men's team archery event even though none of their three team members had placed higher than 29th in the individual event. In the men's coxed eights rowing final, Canada beat Romania by less than 30 centimeters (one foot), in the closest rowing final in Olympic history. Spain's coxswain in the eights, 11-year-old Carlos Front, was the youngest competitor in the Summer Games since 1900.

Another close contest was the women's 100-meter dash. Merlene Ottey of Jamaica finished only six-hundredths of a second behind the winner, Gail Devers of the United States—and yet she ended up in only fifth place. The men's 100 was won by Great Britain's Linford Christie who, at the age of 32, was the event's oldest winner by four years.

Andreas Keller of the gold medal-winning German field hockey team was the third generation of his family to medal in the event. His grandfather Erwin earned a silver medal in 1936 and his father, Carsten, a gold in 1972.

The women's 10,000-meter run was won by Derartu Tulu of Ethiopia, the first black African female gold medalist in Olympic history. In second place was Elana Meyer, a white South African. Their shared victory lap symbolized hope for a new Africa—and for the Olympic movement, which had survived twenty years of terrorism and boycotts.

1996

Many observers had assumed that the 1996 Centennial Games would be awarded to Athens, host of the 1896 Olympics. However, the International Olympic Committee voted in favor of Atlanta 51-35. The Opening Ceremony was highlighted by an innovation in the Parade of Nations: instead of marching through a tunnel, the athletes entered from the top of the stadium and descended onto the field so that each of the 10,310 athletes from 197 nations was honored as a hero. Then the cauldron was lit by Muhammad Ali who, as Cassius Clay, had won a gold medal in light-heavyweight boxing in 1960.

Unfortunately, as soon as the Games began, it became clear that there were major organizational problems. The transportation system was overcrowded and chaotic, the computerized results system was primitive and failed repeatedly, and the volunteers who staffed many of the sites, although well-meaning, were poorly trained. In addition, many people were appalled by the commercial exploitation that surrounded the competition venues, particularly around Centennial Olympic Park. The park, which appeared to be part of the Olympics, was actually not included in the Olympic security system. In the early morning of July 27, a bomb exploded in the park, killing one person and injuring 111. A Turkish cameraman also died of a heart attack suffered while running to cover the scene. The crime remained unsolved until 1998, when the FBI connected the bombing with three others in Georgia and Alabama. In May 2003 anti-abortion extremist Eric Robert Rudolph was arrested for the bombings. He pleaded guilty and was sentenced to four consecutive life sentences.

Several new sports and events were added to the Olympic program including beach volleyball, mountain biking, lightweight rowing, women's football and softball.

Carl Lewis of the United States won the long jump to become only the third person in Olympic history to win the same individual event four times. This also made him only the fourth person to earn nine career gold medals.

Steve Redgrave of Great Britain won the coxless pairs to become the first rower to earn a gold medal in four different Olympics. Turkey's Naim Süleymanoğlu became the first weightlifter to win a third gold medal. Considering that Süleymanoğlu was the reigning world record holder in 1984, he might have won a fourth had not his nation at the time, Bulgaria, boycotted the Los Angeles Games.

Aleksandr Karelin of Russia became the first wrestler to win the same division three times with another victory in the Greco-Roman super-heavyweight category. Krisztina Egerszegi of Hungary won the 200-meter backstroke for the third time.

Birgit Schmidt of Germany won her fifth gold medal in kayak canoeing, sixteen years after her first victory, the first woman to earn gold medals so far apart.

Table tennis was dominated by the Chinese, who

won all four events, as well as collecting three silver medals and one bronze.

On the track, Marie-José Pérec of France and Michael Johnson of the United States both recorded wins in the 200 meters and the 400 meters, a feat never before achieved by either sex in an unboycotted Olympics.

Yachtsman Hubert Raudaschl of Austria became the first person ever to compete in nine Olympics. Before he began his streak in 1964, he was an alternate in 1960.

In the freestyle wrestling middleweight division, two brothers, Elmadi Jabrailov of Kazakhstan and Tucuman Jabrailov of Moldova, faced each other in the second round. Elmadi won the high-scoring but unusually friendly encounter 10-8.

For the first time, each team that qualified for the football tournament was allowed to include three professionals regardless of their age or of their World Cup experience. In an exciting final, Nigeria defeated Argentina 3-2. Cycling also opened its doors to professionals—and five-time Tour de France winner Miguel Indurain of Spain won the road time trial.

Athletes from a record-setting 79 nations won medals and 53 nations won gold.

2000

The Sydney 2000 Olympics were the largest yet, with 10,649 athletes taking part in 300 events, including, for the first time, triathlon, taekwondo and synchronized diving. Women's events were added in weightlifting, water polo and modern pentathlon. A record 80 nations won medals.

At the Sydney Olympics the International Olympic Committee finally cracked down against doping. Gymnast Andreea Raducan of Romania was stripped of her gold medal in the all-around competition because her team doctor gave her pills containing a prohibited substance. It was a harsh call, but a correct one.

In the end, the Sydney Games will be best remembered for the achievements of its athletes. Birgit Fischer of Germany won two gold medals in canoeing to become the first woman in Olympic history to win medals 20 years apart. She also became only the third woman in any sport to earn the seven gold medals and first female non-gymnast to win ten career medals. Steve Redgrave was a member of the victorious British coxless fours crew, making him the first rower to win gold medals in five straight Olympics. Chinese diver Fu Mingxia won her fourth and fifth gold medals. Michael Johnson of the United States became the first repeat winner in the men's 400 meters.

The most memorable race on the track was the thrilling duel at 10,000 meters, in which defending champion Haile Gebrselassie of Ethiopia just caught Paul Tergat of Kenya at the finish line. For the first time, the United States was left off the medal stand in the men's long jump. In swimming, Australia put an end to the Americans' undefeated record in the men's 4 × 100-meter freestyle relay. On the other hand, it was the United States that stopped Cuban domination in baseball. The Cubans had won every world and Olympic championship in which they had competed since 1969.

The US softball team won in stirring fashion, losing three straight games and then coming back to defeat each of the teams who had beaten them. In women's water polo, Australia defeated the United States in the final with a goal in the final second. In women's team handball, Denmark trailed by six points in the second half, but came from behind to beat Hungary 31-27.

The Lithuanian men's basketball team almost pulled off the upset of the century against a team of US all-stars when a final shot in their semifinal encounter fell short at the buzzer. Instead, the honor of upset winner of the Sydney Games went to unknown American Greco-Roman wrestler Rulan Gardner, who handed super-heavyweight legend Aleksandr Karelin of Russia his first defeat in 13 years.

By winning the women's 4 × 100-meter relay, the sprint quartet from the Bahamas (population 270,000) earned for their nation the honor of becoming the smallest country to win a team event in any sport.

Dutch cyclist Leontien Zijlaard gained three gold medals and one silver, competing both on the track and on the road. One of the most rewarding stories of perseverance was that of Japanese judoka Ryoko Tamura, who had lost in the final in both Barcelona and Atlanta, but came back to win the gold medal in Sydney.

2004

In 2004 the Olympic Games returned to Greece, the home of both the ancient Olympics and the first modern Olympics. The men's and women's shot put events were held in the ancient stadium in Olympia. The marathon races followed the same route as the 1896 race, beginning in Marathon and ending in Athens' Panathenaic Stadium. The archery events were also held in the Panathenaic Stadium. Women's wrestling was included in the program for the first time. Irini Merlini of Ukraine had the honour of being the first Olympic champion, and she earned it with the most dominating performance of any of the winners.

Canoeist Birgit Fischer earned a gold medal in the K-4 500 metres and a silver medal in the K-2 500 metres. In so doing, she became the first woman in any sport to win gold medals in six different Olympics, the first woman to win gold 24 years apart and the first person in Olympic history to win two or more medals in five different Games. At the age of 34, cyclist Leontien Zijlaard-van Moorsel crashed in the road race, but, despite bruises to her neck, hip and shoulder, she won the road time trial three days later to become the first female cyclist to earn four career gold medals and six total medals.

Hicham El Guerrouj of Morocco became the first runner since Paavo Nurmi in 1924 to win both the 1500 metres and the 5000 metres. In the 1500, he was passed by Bernard Lagat in the homestretch, but came back to win. In the 5000, he came from behind to defeat 10,000 metres champion Kenenisa Bekele. In Athens, El Guerrouj was also voted a member of the IOC. In women's athletics, Kelly Holmes won both the 800 metres and the 1500 metres. At 34, she was the oldest woman to win either event, much less both.

The US women's 4 × 200-meter swimming team of Natalie Coughlin, Carly Piper, Dana Vollmer and Kaitlin Sandeno finished the final 2½ seconds ahead of China. Their time of 7:53.32 broke the 17-year-old world mark, erasing the last record of the drug-tainted East German women of the 1980s. South African men had never even qualified for a final in swimming's relay events. Yet in Athens their 4 × 100-meter freestyle relay team of Roland Schoeman, Lyndon Ferns, Darian Townsend and Ryk Neethling finished first in world record time. Eighteen-year-old Michael Phelps of the United States earned six gold medals and two bronze medals to match gymnast Aleksandr Dityatin's feat of winning eight medals at one Olympics.

Synchronized swimmers Olga Brusnikina and Maria Kisseleva were part of the winning Russian team and both earned their third career gold medals, the first in their sport to do so. Although rhythmic gymnastics has been in the Olympics since 1984, in Athens, Natalia Lavrova became the first athlete to earn two gold medals in the sport. Catalina Ponor earned three gold medals in artistic gymnastics. In the floor exercise final her margin of victory was the largest in Olympic history.

Argentina's men's basketball team put an end to the domination of the US professionals, defeating them 89-81 in the semifinals. The Argentinians, led by Manu Ginobli, lost two preliminary matches, but beat Greece 69-64 in the quarterfinals and Italy 84-69 in the final. Before 2004, Argentina had not won gold medals in a team sport since polo was in the Olympics. Argentina also won the men's football title, winning all six of their matches, while scoring 17 goals and conceding none. The US softball team won the Olympic tournament by outscoring their nine opponents 51-1.

The mostly unlikely winners of the 2004 Olympics were Greek synchronized divers Nikolaos Siranidis and Thomas Bimas. The two were only allowed to compete because Greece, as the host nation, received an automatic qualification. Placed only fourth with one dive to go, they hit their final dives with near-perfection and won the host nation's first championship of the Athens Games.

2008

In its attempt to bring the Olympics to the world's most populous nation, China, the International Olympic Committee (IOC) ran into the problem that the Chinese government was also one of the most repressive in the world. Although only 5% of Chinese citizens were members of the Chinese Communist Party (CCP), the Party controlled all media and punished dissenters who spoke in favor of democracy and freedom of expression. The CCP's leaders promised the IOC that they would be more open, but as soon as their contract to host the Games was signed they ignored the IOC and cracked down even more harshly than before.

Although the IOC was seemingly helpless to react, the international human rights community used the Torch Relay to protest Chinese government policies, including suppression of Tibetans and Chinese support for the murderous regime in Sudan. Dogged by demonstrations around the world, the Chinese fought back . . . literally. Chinese paramilitary forces accompanying the torch assaulted French, British and US citizens, including torchbearers, in their own countries. They even punched Sebastian Coe, chair of the London 2012 Organising Committee.

Many foreign commentators mistakenly spread the idea that China was using the Olympics as a "coming out to the world" to show that it was an important member of the international community. In reality, the CCP's primary goal was to impress China's own citizens: to show that the party could provide a great spectacle and lots of gold medals, while at the same time demonstrating that the most important world nations recognized the CCP as the legitimate rulers of China. Many foreign leaders were happy to play along. Among those attending the Beijing Games were Vladimir Putin of Russia, Gordon Brown of the United Kingdom, Nicolas Sarkozy of France, Yasuo Fukuda of Japan and George W. Bush of the United States. In fact, Bush was the first US president to attend a foreign Olympics.

Unknown to many foreigners, the CCP reacted to the Torch Relay-related protests by blanketing domestic media with virulent anti-Western diatribes. This toxic atmosphere may have contributed to a tragic incident that took place the day after the Opening Ceremony. A deranged man went to the Drum Tower (a.k.a. Realizing Humiliation Tower), a symbol of foreign imperialism, and attacked two tourists and their Chinese guard, killing one of the tourists. The murder victim turned out to be Todd Bachman, father of 2004 US volleyball Olympian Elisabeth "Wiz" Bachman and father-in-law of Hugh McCutcheon, coach of the 2008 US men's volleyball team.

Once the competitions began, attention focused on the athletes, and there were numerous outstanding performances. US swimmer Michael Phelps became the first person in Olympic history to earn eight gold medals in one Olympics. Jamaican sprinter Usain Bolt won the 100 meters, the 200 meters and the 4 × 100-meter relay, breaking the world record in each event.

Also on the track, Ethiopian distance runners Kenenisa Bekele and Tirunesh Dibaba swept the men's and women's 5,000 meters and 10,000 meters. Brimin Kipruto gave Kenya its seventh consecutive victory in the 3,000-meter steeplechase, while US runners matched that streak in the men's 4 × 400-meter relay. American swimmers continued their own streak of winning the men's medley relay every time they entered—12 in a row.

Chris Hoy of the United Kingdom won three gold medals in cycling, as did Zou Kai of China in men's gymnastics and Stephanie Rice of Australia in swimming. American basketball player Lisa Leslie earned her fourth straight gold medal, while Buvaisa Saytiev of Russia won his third Olympic championship in freestyle wrestling and Briton Ben Ainslie did the same in sailing. In judo, Ryoko Tani (Tamura) earned a bronze medal in the extra-lightweight division to go with the two golds and two silvers she had won in the last four Olympics.

The US women's basketball team swept through the tournament, winning their eight games with an average victory margin of 37.6 points. China swept every possible medal in table tennis (six individual and two team), and in the women's singles event, all the top eight places were taken by players born in China, even though they represented five different countries.

The 2008 Olympic competitions were not without controversy, particularly in women's gymnastics. The Chinese team was caught using underage girls. However, the International Gymnastics Federation (FIG) chose to accept at face value whatever documentation the Chinese submitted, and the IOC declined to investigate.

China and the United States dominated the national medals table, the Chinese earning the most golds (51) and the Americans the most medals in total (110). Thirty-six of China's gold medals came in five sports—gymnastics (11), weightlifting (8), diving (7), shooting (5) and table tennis (4)—while the US gained more than half of its 36 golds in just two—swimming (12) and track and field (7).

Shelia Taormina of the United States competed in the modern pentathlon, becoming the first woman in Olympic history to participate in three sports. She had previously won a gold medal in swimming and twice took part in the triathlon. Competing in the open water swimming event, South Africa's Natalie du Toit was the first amputee to take part in the Olympics since gymnast George Eyser in 1904.

Florian Keller of Germany became the fifth member of his family to earn a medal in field hockey, following in the footsteps of his grandfather, father, brother and sister. Japanese equestrian Hiroshi Hokotsu became the first person to compete in Olympic Games 44 years apart: he had last participated in 1964. Another athlete to make the record books was Ricardo Blas Jr., a judoka from Guam. At 463 pounds (210 kilograms), he became the heaviest person ever to compete in the Olympics. And then there was the winner of the 53-kilogram category of women's weightlifting, who earned the title of the non-royal Olympic champion with the longest name in history . . . Prapawadee Jaroenrattanatarakoon. Born with a different name, she adopted her tongue-twister on the advice of a fortune teller who told her that if she did so she would win a gold medal. The fortune teller was right.

Issues

POLITICS IN THE OLYMPICS

There are only two places today where people from all parts of the world gather: the United Nations and the Olympics. The trouble with the United Nations is that many of the governments represented are ruled by dictators, royal families, and single parties that permit no opposition. Consequently, the people who represent these countries at the United Nations, far from being typical citizens, are generally the worst the country has to offer. Even those nations that aspire to democracy are represented by a most unrepresentative group: wealthy men and women, mostly men, who have gone to the right schools and know the right people.

Unlike UN delegates, Olympic athletes represent an almost complete economic cross-section of the world's population. In this book you will meet carpenters, farmers, housewives, teachers, psychiatrists, accountants, nurses, secretaries, and cartoonists, as well as the usual hordes of students, soldiers, and professional athletes. Some Olympians have been unemployed. Others came from families of sharecroppers or from no families at all. Even lawyers, businessmen, and royalty have taken part in the Olympics.

This is not to say that the Olympics are any less political than the United Nations. However, contrary to popular belief, the politicization of the Olympics is not a recent phenomenon. From the very beginning the Olympics were exploited by the ruling classes of the nations in which they were held. In 1896 and 1906 the Greek royal family was highly visible at the Games, placing its box at the finish line and inserting itself into the festivities at the most exciting parts—the moment of victory and the award ceremonies. The British royal family did the same thing in 1908. In 1912 awards were handed out not only by King Gustav of Sweden, but by Czar Nicholas of Russia as well.

Staging the Olympics also helped the ruling classes by providing a distraction from serious political and economic problems. During the 1906 Intercalated Games in Athens, British and American tourists were shocked when a riot broke out in front of their hotel. Government troops attacked a political demonstration, killing three people and injuring 57. Meanwhile the Greek royal family was busy entertaining the English royal family at Olympic-related functions, including the competitions themselves.

Several days after Adolf Hitler and the Nazi Party seized control of Germany in March 1933, a delegation of German Olympic leaders met with Hitler and received his enthusiastic support for organizing the 1936 Olympics, which had been awarded to Berlin two years earlier. Hitler was so enthusiastic that he began to see the Games as a showcase for Nazi power and ideology. The president of the German Organizing Committee, Dr. Theodore Lewald, was a Christian, but, because one of his grandparents was Jewish, he was threatened with removal from his position. The international community was quick to show concern but slow to act. Only three months after the Nazi ascension to power, the International Olympic Committee met to consider moving the Games from Germany. Pressure was brought to bear on the Nazis to keep Dr. Lewald and to allow a couple of token Jewish athletes on the German team. But although the debate raged for over two years, the Nazis were allowed to stage the Olympics. In several countries, most notably in the United States, the debate shifted to whether the Games should be boycotted. In the end, nothing was done, and the Nazis were allowed their showcase, although the message of Aryan superiority fell flat when Jesse Owens and other African-American athletes were hailed as the stars of the Olympics by the German people themselves.

Despite this history, it is often stated that the "intrusion" of politics into the Olympics began in a serious manner with the black-gloved, clenched-fist salutes of US sprinters Tommie Smith and John Carlos in Mexico City in 1968. Smith and Carlos staged their Black Power protest while "The Star-Spangled Banner" was being played during the medal ceremony for the 200-meter dash. They were immediately suspended by the IOC and ordered to leave the Olympic Village by the USOC. Yet they were hardly the first to make political gestures on the victory platform. During the 1936 Berlin Games, all German winners and several foreigners as well raised their right arms in the Nazi salute. Countless American athletes have placed their right hands over their hearts during the playing of their national anthem. Needless to say, none of these athletes was punished the way Smith and Carlos were.

The question then arises: If it was acceptable in 1936 to raise your right arm in the air with the open palm face down, and today it is acceptable to put your right hand over your heart, why was it *not* acceptable in 1968 to bow your head and raise your arm into the air with your gloved fist closed?

From the point of view of the IOC, the "crime" committed by Smith and Carlos was not that they had made a political statement, but that they had made the *wrong* political statement. Although Olympic *athletes* may be a representative group, IOC members and other Olympic leaders are not. They are, in fact, very much like UN delegates. They have definite political beliefs. They support nationalism, and, more often than not, they support the ruling elites of the various nations of the world, no matter if they are Communist or capitalist. Thus it was perfectly all right in 1936 for German athletes to give the Nazi salute, because that salute was approved by the German government. And it is quite within the rules for US athletes to put their hands over their hearts because this is a patriotic gesture which shows support for nationalism and the status quo.

It was *not* acceptable to the IOC to have Smith and Carlos raise clenched fists because their gesture, rather than showing support for a recognized nation-state, showed support for an unrecognized political entity—African-Americans.

By 1972 it had become clear that because the Olympics commanded such massive international interest, they could be used to attract attention to a political cause. On September 5, the pro-Palestinian Black September group infiltrated the Olympic Village and eventually murdered eleven members of the Israeli team. The incident did not do much to advance the Palestinian cause, but it did force future Olympic organizers to turn the athletes' village and the competition venues into heavily secured armed camps.

Although the first boycotts of the modern Olympics took place in 1956, boycotting became a fad in 1976 when black African governments, led by Julius Nyerere of Tanzania, refused to allow their athletes to compete in the Montreal Games as a protest against apartheid in South Africa. Although their cause was a righteous one, it is difficult to view the African boycott with anything but cynicism considering that the boycotting governments were mostly dictatorships that did not tolerate dissent from their own citizens, much less support the concept of self-determination. In addition, the issue that triggered the boycott was tenuous at best. The Organization of African Unity demanded that the IOC expel the team from New Zealand because a rugby team from that nation had toured South Africa. Rugby was not an Olympic sport and there was no connection between the New Zealand rugby team and any branch or twig of the Olympic movement.

Unfortunately, the success of the African boycott impressed at least one person: United States President Jimmy Carter. With the 1980 Olympics to be held in Moscow, Carter seized on a boycott as a way to punish the Soviet government for invading Afghanistan. Again the cause was a righteous one, but wouldn't it have been a more effective tactic to allow United States athletes to compete in Moscow and then ask them to display Afghan flags during the Parade of Nations? It went without saying that the Soviet Union would boycott the 1984 Los Angeles Olympics.

If ever there was an example of how the Olympics can have a *positive* effect on the political development of a country, it happened in 1988, when the Games were scheduled for Seoul. South Korea was ruled by a dictatorship that actually abdicated in favor of democratic elections in order to satisfy international opinion prior to the Olympics.

Perhaps it was this success that led almost half the members of the IOC to vote to award the 2000 Olympics to China, which, in an age of spreading democracy, continues to forbid free speech and free elections, imprisons dissenters, and kills political demonstrators. Cooler heads prevailed and Sydney defeated Beijing by two votes. However, eight years later, the IOC voted overwhelmingly to award the 2008 Olympics to Beijing.

The Olympics will always reflect the politics of the world, from which they provide a temporary respite, and, because they are followed by a larger audience than any event in the world, they will always be a tempting forum for individuals and groups with a political agenda to promote.

CORRUPTION AND EXPULSIONS

On November 24, 1998, Chris Vanocur, a reporter for KTVX-TV in Salt Lake City, broke a story about a letter he had received anonymously in which the Salt Lake Organizing Committee for the Olympic Winter Games 2002 informed the daughter of an IOC member from Cameroon that the Committee would no longer be able to pay her university tuition. Two weeks later, senior IOC member Marc Hodler publicly referred to the payment as a bribe. The story quickly exploded into the biggest scandal in the history of the International Olympic Committee. Over the next three months, a series of revelations made it clear that many IOC members supplemented their incomes by selling their votes to cities bidding to host future Olympics. Bid committees in turn kept dossiers on each IOC member and targeted them with gifts, free medical care and scholarships. By March 1999, four IOC members had resigned and six were expelled.

At the time, it was widely reported that these expulsions were the first in the history of the IOC. In fact, thirteen members had already been expelled. The first, on May 23, 1907, was José Zubiaur of Argentina, one of the IOC's founding members, who was drummed out because he had failed to attend a single meeting in thirteen years. It is worth noting that the unfortunate Zubiaur was a teacher who, at a time when IOC members were expected to pay their own way to meetings, was not wealthy enough to do so.

In 1913 the IOC ruled that absence from three consecutive meetings was grounds for expulsion. However this rule was only selectively enforced. Although, over the years, 53 IOC members never attended an official session, only six were actually expelled. Indeed the Olympic absence record belongs to a member who was never expelled: Arnaldo Guinle of Brazil, who missed 36 sessions in a row.

The second victim of expulsion was another Argentinian, Manuel Quintana Jr. who was punished in 1910 because he "used his position as an IOC member for personal publicity." More to the point, he staged an international sports meeting in Argentina and used the word "Olympic" without the permission of the IOC.

It would be another 25 years before another member was expelled from the IOC, but the case of Ernest Lee Jahncke of the United States is the most interesting on the list. At the time that Adolf Hitler took power in Germany, Jahncke, a New Orleans businessman, was one of three American IOC members. Although Jahncke was the son of a German immigrant, he called for the Olympics to be taken away from Berlin and urged American athletes to boycott the Games if they were held in Nazi Germany. The president of the United States Olympic Committee, Avery Brundage, viciously attacked boycott supporters and supported the Berlin Games. On July 30, 1936, the IOC expelled Jahncke and replaced him with Brundage. Ironically, after World War II, another IOC member, Giorgio Vaccaro of Italy, was expelled because he did support the Fascists during the war.

The first case that even remotely resembles the financial scandals of 1998-1999 was that of Saul Ferreira Pires of Portugal. He brought his family to the 1960 Rome Olympics and, after the Games were over, left without paying his hotel bill. A year-long IOC investigation led to his expulsion. One final odd case was the 1987 expulsion of General Zein El Abdin Mohamed Ahmed Abdel Gadir of Sudan. Gadir's transgression was that he missed three meetings without providing an excuse beforehand. His absence and silence were not surprising considering that he was in prison at the time, having been on the wrong side of a coup d'état. After he was released from prison, Gadir was reelected to the IOC. He was expelled again in 1999 because of corrupt practices. Among Gadir's scams was convincing the Salt Lake City organizing committee to send $1000 a month to his daughter in London. As it turned out, not only did Gadir not have a daughter in London, he did not have a daughter at all. The name of his fictional daughter, Zema, was actually an acronym for his own name. General Gadir is the only IOC member to be expelled twice.

The culture of corruption that was exposed in 1998-1999 had its roots in changes that occurred in the 1980s. Before the ascension of Juan Antonio Samaranch as president of the International Olympic Committee, the IOC was very much the domain of a wealthy elite. It was not until 1981, for example, that the IOC began paying travel expenses for members attending meetings. Two major developments set the stage for the corruption scandals. The first was the huge amounts of money that began to pour into the IOC coffers as a result of increased fees for television rights. The second development, which happened concurrently, was the democratization (relatively speaking) of the IOC membership, which grew and became more international. At the same time that the Olympics began producing real money, there appeared, for the first time, a large number of members who were not already rich.

By the late 1980s it was already apparent that certain IOC members were using their positions for personal profit. On December 3, 1991, Robert Helmick of the United States resigned rather than face a possible expulsion vote after it was revealed that, at the same time that he was serving as president of the United States Olympic Committee, he was also accepting consultancy fees from companies that did business with the USOC.

The 1984 Los Angeles Olympics proved that it was possible to organize the Olympics and make a profit. All over the world, business groups began looking at the Olympics as a money-making enterprise and the number of cities bidding for the Games multiplied. As the competiton to win the right to host the Olympics became more intensive, many IOC members seized the chance to play the warring bid committees against each other. Although it was Salt Lake City that was the first to be caught, there is no question that similar payoffs and favors were paid by Atlanta, Nagano and Sydney, not to mention cities that lost. The practice of IOC member-wooing became so overheated that it reached ludicrous levels. The story of Anani Matthia of Togo is a case in point. The Salt Lake organizing committee flew Matthia and his wife to Salt Lake City in February 1993 and threw in a $3,925 stopover in Paris. In 1995, the Salt Lake City folks wanted Matthia to visit their city again (even though this was against IOC regulations). Mr. Matthia, who lived in a country that had no snow or ice and had never entered the Winter Olympics, was understandably reluctant to return to Utah. But when the US ambassador to Togo, Jimmy Young, intervened, Matthia felt obligated to accept the invitation. Under the circumstances, the IOC decided not to expel Matthia, but rather to issue him a "serious warning."

In an attempt to clean shop, the IOC issued new regulations regarding the bidding process. These included prohibiting members from visiting bid cities. Although one can appreciate the IOC's sincere attempt to rid itself of corrupt practices, it is hard to imagine how IOC members can make informed choices if they are not allowed to study the venues and facilities first-hand. Another example of the IOC going overboard in its reforms was the passing of a rule forcing IOC members to resign at the age of 70. Again, one can appreciate the IOC's desire to keep its membership fresh, but by dumping all older members, the IOC is losing their wisdom and experience.

AMATEURISM

Contrary to popular belief, the Ancient Greek athletes were not amateurs. Not only were they fully supported throughout their training, but even though a winner received only an olive wreath at the Games, back home he was amply rewarded and could become quite rich.

The concept of amateurism actually developed in nineteenth-century England as a means of preventing the working classes from competing against the aristocracy. The wealthy could take part in sports without worrying about having to make a living, and thus could pursue the ideal of amateurism. Everyone else had to give up training time in order to earn a living, or else take money for sports performances and become a professional, ineligible for competitions such as the Olympics.

Baron de Coubertin, although a member of the French aristocracy, was well aware of the inequities of the amateur system. His solution was to have wealthy people come forward as "patrons" to support worthy working-class athletes.

The qualifications for being an amateur have varied from decade to decade and from sport to sport. In the 1920s British sportsmen accused the Americans of circumventing the rules of amateurism by the awarding of athletic scholarships to universities (although even the ancient Greek medical colleges recruited athletes). As late as the 1930s physical education teachers and recreation directors were considered professional athletes and thus ineligible for the Olympics.

After the 1988 Games, the IOC voted to declare all professionals eligible for the Olympics, subject to the approval of the international federations in charge of each sport. All but two federations eventually went along with the lifting of restrictions promoted by the IOC. Boxing continues to forbid professionals, while football (soccer) has agreed to allow each nation to include three professionals on their roster in addition to the professionals under the age of 23, against whom there is no prohibition. We believe the IOC has made the right decision in opening the doors to professionals because Olympic events should be competitions among the best athletes in the world.

DRUGS

The use of performance-enhancing drugs and concoctions by Olympic athletes is nothing new. The winner of the 1904 marathon, Thomas Hicks, was administered multiple doses of strychnine and brandy *during* the race. Just before the running of the 1920 men's 100 meters, the US sprint coach gave his soon-to-be-victorious team members a mixture of sherry and raw egg. In 1960, Danish cyclist Knut Enemark died during the Olympic road race as a result of ingesting amphetamines and nicotinyl tartrate.

It was not until 1967 that the Medical Commission of the International Olympic Committee began outlawing drugs. The following year, Hans-Gunnar Liljenwall, of the Swedish modern pentathlon team, was disqualified for using alcohol. Full-scale drug testing began in 1972. By this time the use of stimulants, sedatives, hormones, and steroids was so common that doctors and coaches were already coming up with masking agents to beat the tests and studying how close to competition an athlete could continue his or her drug program without risking a positive test result.

Although fewer athletes tested positive for drugs in 1988 than in 1984, it was in Seoul that the issue came to a head because one of those caught was sprinter Ben Johnson, the most visible hero of the Games. The subsequent investigation by the Canadian government into the use of banned substances by its athletes, as well as the revelations by athletes from East Germany and Czechoslovakia following the collapse of Communism in Eastern Europe, revealed that the use of steroids was widespread and extremely sophisticated.

Although doping is definitely an international problem, the details of the East German doping programs of 1968-1989 are especially hair-raising. In the late 1960s the East German government became convinced that athletic success, particularly at the Olympics, was an effective form of political propaganda. Doctors, researchers and coaches were ordered to use whatever means necessary to achieve this success. Some of the scientific studies that were undertaken and some of the training methods that were developed were legitimate advances and were adopted by other nations. However the experiments with steroids and testosterone were not only morally reprehensible, but criminal.

Apparently, the first East German athlete to be administered drugs was the shot putter Margitte Gummel, who began taking the steroid Oral-Turinabol on July 28, 1968. Although she was already 27 years old, Gummel improved her performance by two meters in eleven weeks. By 1978, East German athletes in every sport except sailing were being given anabolic steroids. The IOC banned steroids in 1974 and began testing for them at the 1976 Olympics. The East Germans had little trouble beating these tests. A key figure in overcoming the obstacle of drug testing was Manfred Höppner, the deputy director of the East German Sports Medical Service. Höppner also served on international drug commissions, monitored the new tests and passed on the details to his nation's sports authorities. By the time an effective test for testosterone was introduced, the East Germans had already discovered how to beat it. If a mistake occurred, Höppner simply switched urine samples or falsified test results. It was Höppner himself who helped reveal the truth about East German cheating by selling secret documents to *Stern* in 1990.

The East Germans achieved their greatest doping success with women, particularly with young swimmers, and therein lies the tragic side of the story. Many girls were given steroids without their knowledge before they reached puberty. They were ordered not to tell their parents about the "little blue pills." Dozens of these human guinea pigs suffered major health problems in later life. The first trial of East German coaches and doctors took place in 1998. In January 2000, Lothar Kipke, the chief doctor of the East German Swimming Federation from 1975 to 1985, was convicted of causing bodily harm to 58 swimmers. Swimmers and other athletes who competed against—and were beaten by—the chemically augmented East Germans, were cheated out of medals they should have earned. However many of the East German athletes were victims as well because they will never know if they could have won medals without the drugs.

The Burlingame Bay Area Laboratory Co-Operative (BALCO) was founded in 1984 by Victor Conte, a former athlete and bass player for the band Tower of Power. Originally a lab for blood and urine analysis, the company began to supply a number of athletes and sport stars with illegal steroids and growth hormones, including a new strain of steroid called Tetrahydrogestrinone (THG), which was undetectable by normal steroid tests. In June 2003, US sprint coach Trevor Graham, a former Olympic medalist from Jamaica, sent an anonymous tip to the US Anti-Doping Agency (USADA), naming Victor Conte as the head of a widespread doping ring. As proof, he provided a syringe filled with THG, nicknamed "the clear." Using the sample, the head of the Olympic drug-testing lab at UCLA, Dr. Don Catlin, developed a test for THG and retested hundreds of samples from athletes inside and outside track and field. Of the 550 tests, 20 came up positive. On Sept 3, 2003, the BALCO laboratory was raided by FBI, FDA and narcotics officers, who confiscated thousands of documents and emails including detailed drug schedules and regimens.

The ensuing scandal implicated dozens of athletes, including Olympic track stars Justin Gatlin, Kelli White, Marion Jones and Tim Montgomery, baseball star Barry Bonds and NFL player Bill Romanowski. In track alone, fifteen track athletes either tested positive or were banned because of links to Conte. Conte was indicted on 42 counts of money laundering, possession of human growth hormone, and conspiracy to distribute steroids. In July 2005 he pleaded guilty and agreed to share his knowledge with federal investigators. For his cooperation, Conte was sentenced to only four months in a federal work camp.

In addition to Conte, a number of other people pled guilty to various charges in the BALCO scandal, including James Valente, the former vice president of BALCO; Greg Anderson, former personal trainer of baseball star Barry Bonds; Patrick Arnold, a chemist; Remi Korchemny, a track coach; and Troy Ellerman, a defense lawyer.

In October, 2007, Marion Jones admitted in court to having taken THG for two years beginning in 1999, and said that she got it from her coach, Trevor Graham, who told her it was flaxseed oil. Jones was stripped of her five Olympic medals and given a two-year ban.

Ironically, before his involvement with BALCO, Conte's musical career included playing guitar in a number of short-lived bands, including one named The Pure Food and Drug Act.

According to current regulations there are nine

classes of banned substances and three banned methods. The doping classes are:

1. Stimulants, including amphetamines, bromantan, cocaine, ephedrine, fencamfamine, mesocarbe, pemoline, phenylpropanolamine and strychnine
2. Narcotics, including heroin, methadone, and morphine
3. Cannabinoids (hashish and marijuana), which are the only prohibited substances that are not performance-enhancing
4. Anabolic androgenic steroids and other anabolic (tissue building) agents, including clenbuterol, methandienone, nandrolone, stanozolol, excessive levels of testosterone and dehydrochloromethyltestosterone, which has the distinction of having the longest name of any prohibited substance
5. Peptide hormones, growth factors and related substances, mimetics and analogues, including corticotrophins (ACTH), growth hormone (GH), erythropoietin (EPO) and insulin
6. Beta 2 agonists, except certain asthma-related medicines that are permitted by inhalation only
7. Hormone and metabolic modulators, such as aromatase inhibitors and certain estrogen receptor modulators (SERMs)
8. Masking agents, including plasma expanders and diuretics such as furosemide
9. Glucocorticosteroids.

The prohibited methods are:

1. Enhancement of oxygen transfer, including blood doping, in which athletes remove some of their blood, freeze it, and then, once their blood level has returned to normal, reinject it, and products such as erythropoietin and modified haemoglobin products
2. The catch-all "chemical, and physical manipulation," which includes catheterization, urine substitution and/or tampering and alteration of testosterone and epitestosterone concentrations
3. Gene doping, which is defined as the non-therapeutic use of genes, genetic elements, or of the modulation of gene expression, having the capacity to enhance athletic performance.

Individual sports federations set their own standards for alcohol and beta-blockers. Alcohol is monitored in archery; beta-blockers in archery and shooting. Most sports administer doping tests to at least the three medalists in each event. When an athlete is chosen for doping control, he or she must produce a urine sample of at least 100 milliliters—not always an easy task after events that are seriously dehydrating. The urine sample is divided into two bottles. From this point on, the samples are labeled only by number. No one who tests the samples is aware of which athlete has produced which sample. If the "A" sample is positive, the athlete and his team are notified and are allowed to be present during the testing of the "B" sample. If the "B" sample also proves positive, the athlete is disqualified.

Drug testing at the Olympics is extremely reliable. The equipment is state of the art, and the technicians are highly competent. However, not all drug testing that affects the Olympics actually takes place *at* the Olympics. Testing is also conducted at international, regional, and national competitions around the world. In addition, many sports now conduct random, out-of-competition tests. The laboratories that analyze these various tests are not always up to Olympic standards. Most athletes who test positive for banned substances dispute the results even if they are guilty. However, in some cases the results really are wrong. One case, from the Winter Games, suggests that testing procedures are not infallible. In 1991, Soviet ice dancer Marina Klimova tested positive for a diuretic commonly used as a masking agent. The test was produced at an unaccredited laboratory in Bulgaria. Klimova seemed a highly unlikely suspect for drug use. Sure enough, when her "B" sample was analyzed at an accredited lab in Germany, the result was negative and she was cleared. Although the first result was probably due to incompetence, it is possible that Klimova's urine sample had been tampered with by supporters of her rivals, who hoped to destabilize her psychologically just before the world championships. When a female ice dancer tests positive for drugs, it automatically raises suspicions about the competency of the testing procedures. But what if the incorrectly analyzed positive test had been that of a muscular shot putter or weightlifter? One wonders if he would have been treated as sympathetically as Klimova was before and after the testing of her "B" sample. The Butch Reynolds case (see page 87) illustrates some of the problems and complications in the field of drug testing.

Drug testing is now administered by the World Anti-Doping Agency (WADA). In Beijing in 2008, 4,770 tests were performed including 817 blood tests. Fifteen competitors were disqualified, including six horses.

85 Positive Drug Tests at the Summer Games (in competition)

1968			
Hans-Gunnar Liljenwall	SWE	modern pentathlon	alcohol
1972			
Bakhaava Buidaa	MGL	judo—63 kg	caffeine
Miguel Coll	PUR	basketball	ephedrine
Rick DeMont	USA	swimming—400 free	ephedrine
Jaime Huelamo	SPA	cycling—road race	coramine
Walter Legel	AUT	weightlifting—67.5 kg	ephedrine
Mohamad Nasehi Ar Jomand	IRN	weightlifting—52 kg	ephedrine
Aad van den Hoek	HOL	cycling—team time trial	coramine
1976			
Blagoi Blagoev	BUL	weightlifting—82.5 kg	anabolic steroids
Mark Cameron	USA	weightlifting—110 kg	anabolic steroids
Paul Cerutti	MON	shooting—trap	amphetamines
Valentin Hristov	BUL	weightlifting—110 kg	anabolic steroids
Dragomir Cioroslan	ROM	weightlifting—75 kg	fencanfamine
Phillip Grippaldi	USA	weightlifting—90 kg	anabolic steroids
Zbigniew Kaczmarek	POL	weightlifting—67.5 kg	anabolic steroids
Lorne Leibel	CAN	sailing—tempest	phenylpropanolamine
Arne Norback	SWE	weightlifting—60 kg	anabolic steroids
Petř Pavlašek	CZE	weightlifting—110 kg	anabolic steroids
*Danuta Rosani	POL	track and field—shot put	anabolic steroids
1984			
Serafin Grammatikopoulos	GRE	weightlifting—110+ kg	nandrolone
Vesteinn Hafsteinsson	ICE	track and field—discus	nandrolone
Tomas Johansson	SWE	Greco-Roman wrestling—super heavy	methenolone
Stefan Laggner	AUT	weightlifting—110+ kg	nandrolone
Göran Pettersson	SWE	weightlifting—110 kg	nandrolone
Eiji Shimomura	JPN	volleyball	testosterone
Mikiyasu Tanaka	JPN	volleyball	ephedrine
Ahmed Tarbi	ALG	weightlifting—56 kg	nandrolone
Mahmoud Tarha	LEB	weightlifting—52 kg	nandrolone
Gianpaolo Urlando	ITA	track and field—hammer	testosterone
Martti Vainio	FIN	track and field—10,000 meters	methenolone
*Anna Verouli	GRE	track and field—javelin	nandrolone
1988			
Alidad	AFG	freestyle wrestling—62 kg	furosemide
Kerrith Brown	GBR	judo—71 kg	furosemide
Mitko Grablev	BUL	weightlifting—56 kg	furosemide
Angel Genchev	BUL	weightlifting—67.5 kg	furosemide
Ben Johnson	CAN	track and field—100 meters	stanozolol
Fernando Mariaca	SPA	weightlifting—67.5 kg	pemoline
Jorge Quesada	SPA	modern pentathlon	propranolol
Kalman Scengeri	HUN	weightlifting—75 kg	stanozolol
Andor Szanyi	HUN	weightlifting—100 kg	stanozolol
Alexander Watson	AUS	modern pentathion	caffeine
1992			
*Madina Biktagirova	BLR	track and field—marathon	norephedrine
*Bonnie Dasse	USA	track and field—shot put	clenbuterol

Jud Logan	USA	track and field—hammer	clenbuterol
*Nijole Medvedieva	LIT	track and field—long jump	mesocarde
*Wu Dan	CHN	volleyball	strychnine
1996			
*Natalya Shekhodanova	RUS	track and field—100 meter hurdles	stanozolol
*Iva Prandzheva	BUL	track and field—triple jump	metadienone
2000			
Ivan Ivanov	BUL	weightlifting—56 kg	furosemide
Sevdalin Minchev	BUL	weightlifting—62 kg	furosemide
*Izabela Dragneva	BUL	weightlifting—48 kg	furosemide
Andris Reinholds	LAT	rowing—single sculls	nandrolone
*Andreea Raducan	ROM	gymnastics	pseudoephedrine
Fritz Aanes	NOR	Greco-Roman wrestling—85 kg	norandrosterone and norethiocholanolone
Ashot Danielyan	ARM	weightlifting—super heavyweight	stanozolol
Alexander Leipold	GER	freestyle wrestling—76 kg	nandrolone
Oyunbileg Purevbaatar	MGL	freestyle wrestling—58 kg	furosemide
2004			
Adrian Annus	HUN	track and field—hammer	failure to appear for test
Robert Fazekas	HUN	track and field—discus	failure to provide adequate sample
*Irina Korzhanenko	RUS	track and field—shot put	stanozolol
**Waterford Crystal (Cian O'Connor)	IRL	equestrian—individual jumping	fluphenazine and zuclophenthixol
**Goldfever (Ludger Beerbaum)	GER	equestrian—team jumping	betamethasone
*Olena Olefirenko	UKR	rowing—quadruple sculls	ethamivan
*Aye Khine Nan	BUR	weightlifting—48 kg	anabolic steroid
Leonidas Sampanis	GRE	weightlifting—62 kg	testosterone
Ferenc Gyurkovics	HUN	weightlifting—102 kg	oxanfrolone
*Thingbaijam Sanamacha Chanu	IND	weightlifting—53 kg	furosemide
*Mabel Fonseca	PUR	wrestling—55 kg	stanozolol
2008			
Rashid Ramzi	BRN	athletics – 1500 meters	CERA
*Vanja Perišić	CRO	athletics – 800 meters	CERA
*Athanasia Tsoumeleka	GRE	athletics – 20 kilometer walk	CERA
Adam Seroczyński	POL	canoeing – kayak doubles	clenbuterol
Davide Rebellin	ITA	cycling – road race	CERA
Stefan Schumacher	GER	cycling – road race	CERA
**Cöster (Christian Ahlmann)	GER	equestrian	capsaicin
**Camiro (Tony André Hansen)	NOR	equestrian	capsaicin
**Cornet Obolensky (Marco Kutscher)	GER	equestrian	capsaicin
**Rufus (Rodrigo Pesssoa)	BRA	equestrian	capsaicin
**Chupca Chup (Bernardo Resende)	BRA	equestrian	capsaicin
**Lantinus (Denis Lynch)	IRL	equestrian	capsaicin
Đỗ Thị Ngân Thương	VIE	gymnastics	furosemide
Kim Jong-su	PRK	shooting	propranolol
Ihor Razoronov	UKR	weightlifting—heavyweight	nandrolone

*Women
**Horses

GIGANTISM

One problem that is currently of great concern to the International Olympic Committee is what the IOC calls "gigantism": in other words, that the Olympic Games have become too big. Specifically, according to the IOC, there are too many athletes and team officials who show up for the Games, putting an unnecessary burden on the organizing committee to provide them with housing, food, and transportation. Let us assume, for the sake of discussion, that the IOC's concerns are justified, that despite being given seven years to prepare, the organizing committees cannot handle more than 15,000 participants. The question is: How can the numbers be kept down? There are two basic solutions:

1. limit the number of entries in different sports and events by setting qualifying standards and/or hold regional qualifying tournaments;
2. eliminate certain events or entire sports.

The IOC has already placed a limit to entries, while attempting to maintain international diversity by allowing every nation to enter a combined total of up to four athletes in selected sports regardless of their ability to meet qualifying standards. This system seems to be working well, which is a good thing, because the second solution—eliminating events and sports—is much easier said than done.

For the public record, the IOC has taken the position that sports will be added or axed according to their international popularity. If a sport is widely practiced on every continent, it stays; if it is only practiced in a small number of nations or its popularity is geographically limited, it goes. In reality there are other factors that are more important, namely, whether the sport looks good on television (especially US television), and whether its proponents have power within the IOC. If international popularity was all that counted, canoeing would be eliminated, as would synchronized diving, women's rowing, dressage, synchronized swimming, all sailing events except windsurfing, and the entire Winter Olympics. They would be replaced by karate, squash, bowling and billiards. Of course, that won't happen. Canoeing, like modern pentathlon, fencing, and equestrian events, is a well-established Olympic sport whose elimination would outrage certain countries. All of these threatened sports have made successful attempts to enliven their presentation in order to keep their place on the Olympic program.

And while the IOC is complaining about gigantism, it has also added to the program such sports as beach volleyball and, in the Winter Games, snowboarding and curling, none of which has a great deal of appeal in Africa or Asia. For the record, by the way, the only sports that have produced gold-medal winners from every inhabited continent are track and field (athletics), boxing, swimming, weightlifting and tennis.

Frankly, the issue of gigantism is somewhat overstated. There are several sports and events that we could do without, but we recognize that large numbers of people like what we don't. If the IOC and the organizing committees are concerned that the Olympic Village is too crowded, why not cut down the number of team officials and non-athletes? Athletes need coaches, but the roster of Olympic participants is bloated with bureaucrats and hangers-on.

Another reform that the IOC refuses to seriously consider is lengthening the Summer Olympics by a week. They argue that host cities would not be able to handle the Olympics for that long and that television viewers would lose interest. In fact, as soon as the Olympics end, each host city hosts the Paralympic Games, so that they end up entertaining the world's athletes for an extra 12 days anyway. As for television, the second biggest sports event in the world, the World Cup, lasts for one month and, except in the United States, maintains high ratings throughout. Adding one week to the Olympics, with one or two rest days, would avoid the current situation in which, during the last few days of the Games, there are so many finals that some sports and events are not shown on television.

The Charts

SOURCES

It might seem to the casual reader that compiling the charts in this book was a simple task—just copy them from the Official Reports and fill in the blanks by consulting the International Olympic Committee. First of all, the Official Reports, particularly for 1896-1906 and 1920, are often terribly incomplete. Even as recently as 1956, the Official Report lists only the initial of each athlete's given name, not the name itself. As for the IOC, it has a beautiful library and a brilliantly staffed Olympic Studies Center. Unfortunately, it is only recently that the archives of the IOC have expanded from the study of the history of the IOC and its members to the history of the Olympic Games themselves.

There does exist a network of academics who study "Olympism" and the history of the Olympic movement. But the study of the competitions themselves is a less favored subject. When I began researching the first edition of this book in 1982, the archives of the United States Olympic Committee were housed in a converted meat locker. The USOC archives were at least well organized. At that time, the archives of the British Olympic Association were stored in a shed with ivy growing through cracks in the wall. The archives of the International Olympic Committee were kept in an unused bomb shelter.

It has been left to individual, independent historians, most of them working in their spare time, to compile the records of the Olympic competitions and Olympic athletes. On December 5, 1991, seven of us gathered in the Duke of Clarence, a London pub, and founded the International Society of Olympic Historians. We now have more than four hundred members. I am indebted to the intrepid researchers of the ISOH from around the world for the full names of athletes from the early Olympics and for the correct spelling and accent marks in languages with which I was unfamiliar. The charts in this book are really the distillation of the work of dozens of Olympic enthusiasts. Those readers who are interested in joining the ISOH should write to:

International Society of Olympic Historians
Vogelrijd 16
8428 HJ Fochteloo
Netherlands
E-mail: tony.bijkerk@planet.nl
www.isoh.org

The primary sources for the information included in the charts are the Official Reports of the various Olympics. The man who did the most to correct their inadequacies was the late Erich Kamper of Austria, author of *Enzyklopädie der Olympischen Spiele.* My search for correct spellings and accent marks has also led me to *Olympische Sommerspiele* by Volker Kluge of Germany; *Starozytme i Nowozytne Igrazyska Olimpyskie* by Zbigniew Porada of Poland; *Meet the Bulgarian Olympians* by Kostadinov, Georgiev, and Kambourov; *Az Olimpia-játékokon Indult Magyar Versenyzök Névsora 1896-1980*; *Die Deutschen Sportler der Olympischen Spiele 1896 bis 1968*; and *Sveriges Deltagare i de Olympiska Spelen 1896-1952.*

For the years 1896 through 1920, the most reliable sources are the *Results of the Early Modern Olympics* series by Bill Mallon and co-authored by Ture Widlund (1896 and 1912), Ian Buchanan (1908) and Anthony Th. Bijkerk (1920). These books are available from McFarland & Company, Box 611, Jefferson, North Carolina 28640, USA.

On the Internet there are two sites that are especially useful to readers who want to learn more about the Olympic Movement and the history of the Olympics. The first is www.olympic.org. This is the official site of the International Olympic Committee and, along with other valuable information, it provides links to the web sites of the international sports federations in charge of each sport and to many national Olympic committees. The second is http://www.la84foundation.org/5va/reports_frmst.htm. This site, operated by the LA84 Foundation of Los Angeles, includes the complete text of the Official Reports of all Olympic Games from 1896 through 2010, as well as a searchable archive of articles from scholarly journals including the Journal of Olympic History, which is published by the International Society of Olympic Historians.

HOW TO READ THEM

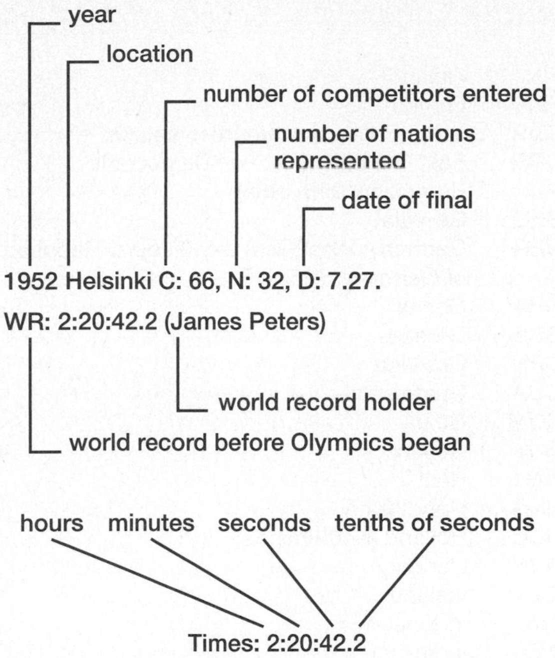

Numbers in the charts indicate times unless otherwise noted. A dash symbol in the numbers column means that the information was not taken or is otherwise unavailable.

Whenever possible we have included an athlete's first and last names. If the first name was unavailable, we have included the first initial. If that was unavailable we have just included the surname. In cases where an athlete was commonly known by his middle name, we have included the initial of his first name as well as the middle name in full. If a female athlete competed under her maiden name, then married and took part in a second Olympics using her married name, we have included her maiden name in parentheses.

The 1906 Intercalated Games are considered unofficial by the IOC, but we have included them because of their historical importance.

In 1956, 1960, and 1964, West Germany (GER) and East Germany (GDR) entered combined teams. Nevertheless we have indicated which athletes were actually from each country. We have also added to the nation an athlete represented the nation he or she would represent today. For example, "SOV/UKR" means the athlete competed for the Soviet Union but his homeland is now part of an independent Ukraine. "GBR/IRL" is a reminder that athletes from Ireland competed for Great Britain. Other examples are "YUG/CRO" (formerly Yugoslavia, now Croatia), colonies that are now independent (such as "FRA/ALG" for Algerians competing for France), and in the 1936 marathon, "JPN/KOR," Koreans competing for Japan. In team sports, "SOV" without a second national designation means the team combined athletes from more than one republic. In individual events, "SOV" without a second national designation means that the actual origin of the athlete is unclear, although in most of these cases they were probably from Russia. In 1992, 12 of the ex-Soviet republics competed as the Unified Team. But because winners were honored with the raising of the flag of their own republic, in the charts for 1992 we have indicated the specific republic for each athlete. In cases where athletes from more than one country competed for the same team, such as East and West Germany in 1956-1964 or in the early Olympics, we have used an ampersand rather than a slash. "GER&GDR" means a combined East and West German team. The designation "GBR[IRL]&GER," used in 1896 tennis doubles, indicates an Irish athlete representing Great Britain joining with a German athlete.

Key to Abbreviations

NATIONS

AFG	Afghanistan
ALG	Algeria
ANG	Angola
ARG	Argentina
ARM	Armenia
ASA	American Samoa
AUS	Australia
AUT	Austria
AZR	Azerbaijan
BAH	Bahamas
BAR	Barbados
BEL	Belgium
BER	Bermuda
BLR	Belarus
BOH	Bohemia
BOT	Botswana
BRA	Brazil
BRD	Burundi
BRN	Bahrein
BSH	Bosnia-Herzegovina
BUL	Bulgaria
BUR	Burma (Myanmar)
BWI	British West Indies (Jamaica and Trinidad)
CAM	Cameroon
CAN	Canada
CHI	Chile
CHN	China
CMR	Cameroon
COL	Colombia
CON	Congo
CRC	Costa Rica
CRO	Croatia
CUB	Cuba
CYP	Cyprus
CZE	Czech Republic (Czechoslovakia, 1920-1992)
DEN	Denmark
DJI	Djibouti
DOM	Dominican Republic
ECU	Ecuador
EGY	Egypt
ENG	England
ERI	Eritrea
ESA	El Salvador
EST	Estonia
ETH	Ethiopia
FIN	Finland
FRA	France
GBR	Great Britain and Northern Ireland
GDR	East Germany (German Democratic Republic, 1956-1988)
GEO	Georgia
GER	Germany; West Germany (Federal Republic of Germany, 1952-1988)
GHA	Ghana
GRE	Greece
GRN	Granada
GUA	Guatemala
GUM	Guam
GUY	Guyana
HAI	Haiti
HKG	Hong Kong
HOL	Holland (Netherlands)
HUN	Hungary
ICE	Iceland
INA	Indonesia
IND	India
INT	International team
IRL	Ireland (Eire)
IRN	Iran
IRQ	Iraq
ISR	Israel
ITA	Italy
IVC	Ivory Coast
JAM	Jamaica
JOR	Jordan
JPN	Japan
KAZ	Kazakhstan
KEN	Kenya
KGZ	Kyrgyzstan
KOR	South Korea
KOS	Kosovo
KUW	Kuwait
KYR	Kyrgyzstan
LAT	Latvia
LEB	Lebanon
LES	Lesotho
LIE	Liechtenstein
LIT	Lithuania
LUX	Luxembourg
MAC	Macedonia
MAD	Madagascar
MAL	Malaysia
MEX	Mexico

MGL	Mongolia
MLI	Mali
MLT	Malta
MLW	Malawi
MNE	Montenegro
MOL	Moldova
MON	Monaco
MOR	Morocco
MOZ	Mozambique
MRI	Mauritius
NAM	Namibia
NEP	Nepal
NGR	Nigeria
NIC	Nicaragua
NIG	Niger
NLA	Netherland Antilles
NOR	Norway
NRU	Nauru
NZL	New Zealand
OMA	Oman
PAK	Pakistan
PAN	Panama
PAR	Paraguay
PER	Peru
PHI	Philippines
PNG	Papua New Guinea
POL	Poland
POR	Portugal
PRK	North Korea (People's Republic of Korea)
PUR	Puerto Rico
QAT	Qatar
ROM	Romania
RUS	Russia
RWA	Rwanda
SAA	Saar
SAF	South Africa
SAM	Samoa
SAU	Saudi Arabia
SCO	Scotland
SEN	Senegal
SER	Serbia
SEY	Seychelles
SIN	Singapore
SKN	St. Kitts and Nevis
SLE	Sierra Leone
SLO	Slovenia
SLV	Slovakia
SMR	San Marino
SOM	Somalia
SOV	Soviet Union (Unified Team, 1992)
SPA	Spain
SRL	Sri Lanka (Ceylon)
SUD	Sudan
SUR	Suriname
SWE	Sweden
SWI	Switzerland
SYR	Syria
TAI	Taiwan
TAN	Tanzania
THA	Thailand
TJK	Tajikistan
TOG	Togo
TON	Tonga
TRI	Trinidad and Tobago
TRM	Turkmenistan
TUN	Tunisia
TUR	Turkey
UAE	United Arab Emirates
UGA	Uganda
UKR	Ukraine
URU	Uruguay
USA	United States of America
UZB	Uzbekistan
VEN	Venezuela
VIE	Vietnam
VIR	US Virgin Islands
YUG	Yugoslavia
ZAM	Zambia
ZIM	Zimbabwe

Please note that some of the national abbreviations used in this book are different than those used by the International Olympic Committee. These official abbreviations can be found on page 1333.

TERMS

AAA	Amateur Athletic Association
AAU	Amateur Athletic Union
AC	Also competed
AIBA	International Amateur Boxing Association
c	Approximately
C:	Number of competitors entered
D:	Date of final
Dec.	Won by judges' decision
DISC	Discus throw
DISQ	Disqualified
DNC	Did not compete in final
DNF	Did not finish
DNS	Did not start in final
e	Estimated
elim	Eliminated
EOR	Equaled Olympic record

EWR	Equaled world record
FINA	International Amateur Swimming Federation
FITA	International Archery Federation
FT.	Feet
GA	Goals against
GF	Goals for
GRW	Greco-Roman wrestling
H	Hurdles
HAM	Hammer throw
HJ	High jump
IAAF	International Amateur Athletic Federation
IN.	Inches
IOC	International Olympic Committee
JAV	Javelin throw
kg	Kilograms
km	Kilometers
KO	Knockout
L	Lost
lbs	Pounds
LJ	Long jump (broad jump)
M	Meters
m.p.h.	Miles per hour
m.p.s.	Meters per second
N:	Number of nations represented
NCAA	National Collegiate Athletic Association
OR	Olympic record
PA	Points against
Pen.	Penalty
PF	Points for
PTS.	Points
PV	Pole vault
RA	Runs against
Ret	Retired
RF	Runs for
RSC	Referee stopped contest
SLJ	Standing long jump
SP	Shot put
T:	Number of teams entered
T	Tied
TG	Touches given
TR	Touches received
USOC	United States Olympic Committee
W	Won
w	Wind-aided
with	Withdrawn
WB	World best
WADA	World Anti-Doping Agency
WO	Walkover
WR	World record
YDS.	Yards

Chapter 1 **Track & Field (Men)**

100 Meters
200 Meters
400 Meters
800 Meters
1500 Meters
5000 Meters
10,000 Meters
Marathon
110-Meter Hurdles
400-Meter Hurdles
3000-Meter Steeplechase
4 × 100-Meter Relay
4 × 400-Meter Relay
20,000-Meter Walk
50,000-Meter Walk
High Jump
Pole Vault
Long Jump
Triple Jump
Shot Put
Discus Throw
Hammer Throw
Javelin Throw
Decathlon
Discontinued Events

Paavo Nurmi, 1924

Breasting the tape to win the 1500 meters, just two hours before he'd capture another gold in the 5000 by a scant ²⁄₁₀ths of a second.

100 METERS

The 100-meter dash is run in lanes on a straightaway. Each lane is between 1.22 and 1.25 meters (4 feet and 4 feet 1¼ inches) wide. According to current rules, each runner is allowed one false start; a second false start results in disqualification. False starts are determined with the aid of pressure plates built into each runner's starting blocks. Although every finalist in the last five Olympics has been black, historically, the major division in this event has been not racial but linguistic. Since the modern Olympics were first held in 1896, 24 of 29 winners at 100 meters have been from English-speaking countries, as have 66 of the 87 medalists. In the following charts, the unofficial automatic times for 1936-1964, as compiled by Bob Sparks, have been included in parentheses. When a tailwind is measured at more than 2.0 meters per second (4.473 m.p.h.), times are not counted for record purposes. A runner is considered to have finished a race when his or her torso—from shoulder to waist—reaches the finish line. Heads, arms, legs, and feet do not count.

1896 Athens C: 15, N: 8, D: 4.10.
WR: 10.8 (Luther Cary)

1. Thomas Burke	USA	12.0
2. Fritz Hofmann	GER	12.2e
3. Francis Lane	USA	12.6e
3. Alajos Szokoli	HUN/SLV	12.6e
5. Alexandros Chalkokondilis	GRE	12.6e

DNS: Thomas Curtis (USA)

The very first race of the modern Olympics was the opening heat of the 100-meter dash. It was won by Frank Lane of Princeton in the time of 12⅕ seconds. The European crowd was fascinated by the "crouch" start of the Americans, as Thomas Curtis and quarter-mile specialist Thomas Burke, both of Boston, won the other two qualifying heats. Their teammates celebrated by chanting, "B.A.! Rah! Rah! Rah!" The Greek spectators had never heard organized cheering before. They liked it so much that the Boston men were called on to repeat it frequently throughout the remainder of their stay in Athens. The first two finishers in each of the heats qualified for the final four days later, but Curtis chose not to start, preferring to save himself for the 110-meter hurdles, which was the next race. Burke, who had registered the fastest time (12.0) in the heats, equaled his time in the final and defeated Hofmann by two meters. The other runners were bunched four meters farther back. Although

Hofmann was a champion sprinter, his athletic specialty was actually rope climbing. Thomas Burke also won the Olympic 400 meters final. The following year he served as the official starter for the inaugural Boston Marathon. He later became a lawyer and also wrote part-time for the *Boston Journal* and the *Boston Post.* Burke died on Valentine's Day, 1929, at the age of 53.

1900 Paris C: 20, N: 9, D: 7.14. WR: 10.8 (Luther Cary)

1. Frank Jarvis	USA	11.0
2. J. Walter Tewksbury	USA	11.1e
3. Stanley Rowley	AUS	11.2e

DNF: Arthur Duffey (USA)

The American runners had never competed before on a grass track, but this didn't prevent Jarvis of Princeton and Tewksbury of Pennsylvania from equaling the world record of 10.8 in the heats and semifinals, respectively. Despite these performances, the clear favorite was 5-foot 7-inch tall (1.70 meter) Arthur Duffey of Georgetown University, who had defeated both Jarvis and Tewksbury in London the previous week. As expected, Duffey burst into the lead and seemed well on his way to victory, when he suddenly began to wobble and fell to the ground at the 50-meter mark, the victim of a strained tendon in his left leg. Jarvis went on to win by about two feet. Duffey later told the press, "I do not know why my leg gave way. I felt a peculiar twitching after going twenty yards. I then seemed to lose control of it, and suddenly it gave out, throwing me on my face. But that is one of the fortunes of sport, and I cannot complain." In 1902 Duffey ran 100 yards in 9.6 seconds, setting a world record which stayed in the books for 24 years. Later he became a columnist for the *Boston Post.*

1904 St. Louis C: 13, N: 3, D: 9.3. WR: 10.8 (Luther Cary, Frank Jarvis, John Walter Tewksbury)

1. Charles "Archie" Hahn	USA	11.0
2. Nathaniel Cartmell	USA	11.2
3. William Hogenson	USA	11.2
4. Fay Moulton	USA	11.4e
5. Frederick Heckwolf	USA	—
6. Lawson Robertson	USA	—

Archie Hahn, "The Milwaukee Meteor," had already won the 60-meter and 200-meter dashes when he settled down for the final of the 100. Running into a heavy wind, he shot out to a fast start, had a one-yard lead by the 20-meter mark, and held off the fast-finishing Louisville sprinter Nate Cartmell to win by almost two yards. Hahn was only 5-feet 5-inches tall (1.65 meter) and weighed about 130 pounds. He did not take up track until he was 19 years old. The following year, 1900, he was recruited by representatives of the University of Michigan, who saw him win a race at a county fair.

1906 Athens C: 42, N: 14, D: 4.27. WR: 10.8 (Luther Cary, Frank Jarvis, John Walter Tewksbury)

1. C. "Archie" Hahn	USA	11.2
2. Fay Moulton	USA	11.3e
3. Nigel Barker	AUS	11.3e
4. William Eaton	USA	—
5. Lawson Robertson	USA	—
6. Knut Lindberg	SWE	—

William Eaton of Boston recorded the fastest time in the semifinals (11.2), but in the final Hahn, with a quick start, led the whole way and won by a yard. Back in the United States, Hahn studied law at Michigan, but never practiced his profession. Instead he devoted his life to coaching younger runners. His book *How to Sprint* is still considered a classic text.

1908 London C: 60, N: 16, D: 7.22. WR: 10.6 (Knut Lindberg)

1. Reginald Walker	SAF	10.8 EOR
2. James Rector	USA	11.0e
3. Robert Kerr	CAN	11.0e
4. Nathaniel Cartmell	USA	11.2e

In 1908 the excitement surrounding the 100-meter race rivaled that of the marathon. The tension was heightened by the fact that only the winner of each heat advanced to the next round. The favorites, James Rector, a University of Virginia student from Hot Springs, Arkansas, and Bobby Kerr, the Irish-born Canadian champion, did not disappoint their supporters in the opening heats. Rector was particularly impressive, tying the Olympic record of 10.8 seconds. He equaled this time in the semifinals, but so did Reggie Walker, a 19-year-old clerk from Durban. Arriving three weeks before the Olympics, Walker lost to Kerr in the final of the British AAA championship. Nevertheless he caught the eye of the famous coach Sam Mussabini, who took the young man under his wing and spent the next couple of weeks working with him on his start. Indeed, according to Rector, Mussabini asked Rector himself to help Walker, which he did. This last-minute training worked wonders. Running on the inside lane, Walker stormed into an early lead, gave way to Rector at the halfway point, and then was able to pull ahead once again to win by a "long yard," with Rector holding on to second by mere inches. The 5-foot 7-inch, 130-pound Walker, who had been previously unknown to the general public, became an instant hero, as the crowd of 49,000 cheered wildly and threw their hats and programs into the air, while friends and officials competed for the right to carry the embarrassed South African on their shoulders. James Rector later described the scene: "The bands were furiously playing national airs, while the bookmakers were calling their bets and the whole stadium seemed to be disordered." In the words of one US newspaper, "The Englishmen were gratified to see the monotonous succession of American victories broken by a Britisher, even if he was a colonist."

1912 Stockholm C: 70, N: 22, D: 7.7. WR: 10.5 (Richard Rau, Erwin Kern, Emil Ketterer)

1. Ralph Craig	USA	10.8
2. Alvah Meyer	USA	10.9
3. Donald Lippincott	USA	10.9
4. George Patching	SAF	11.0
5. Frank Belote	USA	11.0
DNS: Howard Drew (USA)		

Ralph Craig of the University of Michigan was considered the pre-Olympic favorite until he was beaten in the U.S trials by Howard Drew, a strong black student from Springfield, Massachusetts. Drew had honed his sprinting skill while working as a baggage handler at a railway station, earning extra tips by using his speed to reach arriving passengers and their bags before the other handlers. In the first round in Stockholm, Donald Lippincott, the star of the University of Pennsylvania track team, set an Olympic record by winning his heat in 10.6 seconds. The semifinals were run with only the winner of each race advancing to the final. The Americans showed their strength by winning all five of the heats in which they were entered. Unfortunately, Drew strained a tendon just before the finish of his heat and, despite qualifying, was unable to start in the final.

The final was marred by seven false starts, the first three by Craig. After one false start, Craig and Lippincott raced all the way to the finish line. At the eighth try a clean break was made, with Patching taking the early lead. Craig caught him at the 60-meter mark and went on to win by two feet. Thirty-six years later, Craig, by then a wealthy 59-year-old industrial engineer, reappeared at the London Olympics as an alternate on the US yachting team and was chosen to carry the United States' flag at the Opening Ceremony.

As for Drew, he went on to set an indoor record at 100 meters and an outdoor record at 200 meters. However, his success did not protect him from racial prejudice. While representing the University of Southern California at a college meet in San Francisco in 1915, Drew was denied entry to a public bus and had to walk to the stadium. Then the gatekeepers at the stadium refused to believe he was a college athlete and made him pay to enter. By the time Drew made it into the stadium, he had missed his race.

1920 Antwerp C: 61, N: 23, D: 8.16. WR: 10.5 (Richard Rau, Erwin Kern, Emil Ketterer)

1. Charles Paddock	USA	10.8
2. Morris Kirksey	USA	10.9e
3. Harry Edward	GBR	10.9e
4. Jackson Scholz	USA	10.9e
5. Émile Ali-Khan	FRA	11.0e
6. Loren Murchison	USA	11.1e

Charley Paddock was born in Gainesville, Texas, on August 11, 1900. A sickly child, he weighed only 7½ pounds at the age of 7 months. His parents moved to Southern California for his health, eventually settling in Pasadena. The change of climate must have done the trick, because by age 15, Charley was a barrel-chested 170-pounder with big strong legs and a sprinter's body. He loved to run long distances, but his father convinced him to concentrate on the 100 yards and the 220 yards. Paddock came to international

Charley Paddock, 1920

Spent anxious hours with his fellow 100-meter finalists (top, with Jackson Scholz, Loren Murchison and Morris Kirksey) before besting Kirksey at the wire (above).

attention in 1919 when he won both metric sprints at the Inter-Allied Games in Paris, with times of 10.8 and 21.6. Charley was a great crowd-pleaser, who delighted photographers with a flying finish in which he would leap at the tape from about 12 feet out, with his arms flung wide.

The semifinals of the Olympic championship were held in the early morning on Monday, August 16. The first heat was won by Guyanese-born Harry Edward and the second by Charley Paddock, both in 10.8. Scholz and Murchison had also run 10.8 in the earlier rounds. All four Americans qualified for the final and spent the next few hours together, waiting anxiously for their late afternoon race. The blond-haired Murchison kept muttering, half to himself, "I'm going to win. I've known it all along. . . . I can trim any sprinter who ever lived." The others tried to ignore him. Just before it was time to take the field, the four runners were approached by coach Lawson Robertson, who said, "What you fellows need to warm up is a glass of sherry and a raw egg." Murchison, Scholz, and Paddock were horrified by the suggestion, but when Stanford's Morris Kirksey agreed to try the drink, the others feared it would give him a psychological advantage to be the only one to follow the coach's advice, so they guzzled down the strange concoction as well.

Like many athletes, Charley Paddock followed a set of good-luck rituals. On the way to the starting line he would knock on "a friendly piece of wood." When called to his mark, he would put his hands far across the starting line and then draw them slowly back before the second call of "get set." Paddock was the last to stoop to his mark at the starting line of the 1920 100-meter final. The assistant starter, unaware of Charley's ritual, ordered him in French to pull back his hands, which he was actually already in the process of doing. The starter then called out *"prêt,"* the French equivalent of "get set." Murchison misinterpreted the exchange and thought the runners had been ordered to stand up, so he was just beginning to relax and rise when the gun went off. He was left 10 yards behind. Kirksey took the early lead, but at the halfway mark Scholz had a two-foot advantage, with Edward in second. Then Kirksey surged ahead again, with Paddock at his shoulder. In the words of Charley Paddock: "Then I saw the thin white string stretched to the breaking point in front of me. I drove my spikes into the soft cinders and felt my foot give way as I sprang forward in a final jump for the tape. . . . There was nothing more I could do. My eyes closed as my chest hit the string and when I opened them, my feet were on the ground again and I was yards ahead of the field. I did not know if I had been in front when the string was broken. I dared not ask." In fact, Charley Paddock had won the race by 12 inches. "My dream had come true," he later wrote, "and I thrilled to the greatest moment I felt that I should ever know . . . The real pleasure had been in the anticipation and in that single moment of glorious realization."

1924 Paris C: 82, N: 34, D: 7.7. WR: 10.2 (Charles Paddock)

1. Harold Abrahams	GBR	10.6 EOR
2. Jackson Scholz	USA	10.8
3. Arthur Porritt	NZL	10.9
4. Chester Bowman	USA	10.9
5. Charles Paddock	USA	10.9
6. Loren Murchison	USA	11.0

The story of Harold Abrahams' victory in Paris in 1924 is well told in the beautiful film *Chariots of Fire.* Unfortunately, despite its claim of being "a true story," the film contains several factual distortions. Abrahams did not race around the great courtyard of Trinity College at Cambridge. (It was Lord Burghley who did that.) He

Harold Abrahams, 1924

The real Harold Abrahams. Despite the film *Chariots of Fire*, Abrahams did not run around the courtyard at Trinity College, Cambridge. He did, however, win the 100-meter dash at the 1924 Olympics in Paris.

did not look at the 100-meter contest as a chance to redeem himself after his failure in the 200, since the running of the 100 actually preceded the 200 in real life. Although Abrahams did feel himself an outsider because he was Jewish, a much more important motivating factor in his quest for victory was a desire to do better than his two older brothers, both of whom were well-known athletes and one of whom had represented Great Britain in the long jump at the 1906 and 1912 Olympics. Abrahams himself had competed in the 100 and 200 meters in Antwerp in 1920, but had been eliminated in the quarter-finals. In the year preceding the Paris Olympics, Abrahams came under the direction of Sam Mussabini, who had successfully coached Reggie Walker to victory in 1908. Among other things, Mussabini stressed to Abrahams the importance of the length and number of his strides. During practice sessions Abrahams would place pieces of paper on the track, to indicate where each stride should end. Then he would try to pick them up on his spikes as he ran. He always carried with him a piece of string the length of his first stride. Before a race he would pull out the string, measure forward from the starting line, and make a mark on the track where his first step should land.

Abrahams was also a proficient long-jumper. One month before the Olympics he leaped 24 feet 2½ inches (7.38 meters) to set an English record that lasted until 1956. For this reason he was chosen to represent Great Britain in the long jump as well as the 100, 200, and 4 × 100 relay. When an anonymous letter appeared in the *Daily Express,* criticizing the decision to enter Abrahams in the long jump, few people knew that the letter had been written by Harold Abrahams himself. He made his point and was excused from that event.

Despite his great feats, the 6-foot ½-inch (1.84 meter), 175-pound Abrahams was considered a long shot in comparison to the US team, which included defending champion Charley Paddock as well as Antwerp finalists Jackson Scholz and Loren Murchison. On June 18, 1921, Paddock had stunned the track world by running 110 yards (which is actually longer than 100 meters) in the unheard-of time of 10.2 seconds, a record that remained unbeaten for 29 years. Although the Americans were the favorites, it was Harold Abrahams, running faster than he had ever run before, who registered the fastest times in the early heats, tying the Olympic record (10.6) twice, in the quarterfinals and the semifinals, where he overcame an awful start. For the first time Abrahams realized that he had a chance to win the Olympic gold, and for the first time he began to feel the pressure. For the next 3¾ hours, as he waited for the final, he "felt like a condemned man feels just before going to the scaffold." As he went to his mark at 7:05 p.m. on July 7, Abrahams recalled Sam Mussabini's final words of advice: "Only think of two things—the report of the pistol and the tape. When you hear the one, just run like hell till you break the other." After a perfect start, the runners ran almost even for the first 40 or 50 meters, but then Abrahams began to move ahead, gaining with each stride until he crossed the tape with a two-foot victory.

Harold Abrahams is a perfect example of an athlete who peaks at exactly the right moment. After that day at the Stade Colombes in Paris, he never raced well again. The following year he injured his thigh while long-jumping and retired from competition forever. He once wrote, "I wonder if, in a sense, that was not another piece of good bad-luck. How many people find it almost impossible to retire at the right time. Would I have gone downhill, and tried to go on? That was the decision I never had to make; it was made for me. Rather painfully, but it was made." Abrahams went on to great success as a radio commentator, lawyer, writer, statistician, and president of the British Amateur Athletic Association. Arthur Porritt, who took the bronze medal even though he failed to win a single heat, had an even more distinguished career, culminating in a five-year term as Governor-General of New Zealand and more than 30 years as Surgeon to the British royal family. Among his many legacies, Porrit was a vigorous proponent of the doctor's role as a personal friend to each of his patients. Until Abrahams' death in 1978, he and Porritt and their wives had dinner every year at 7:00 p.m. on July 7—the day and the hour of the 1924 100-meter final. As for Charley Paddock, he acted in a couple of Hollywood films, went into the newspaper business, and became active in local politics in Pasadena. During World War II he enlisted in the US Marine Corps and died in a plane crash in Alaska on July 21, 1943.

Harold Abrahams mounted his gold medal on a plinth with a plaque engraved with the signatures of the other five finalists of the 1924 100 meters. The gold medal was stolen before Abrahams' death and never recovered. In 1989 the rest of his major medals and awards were auctioned at Christie's and purchased by Mohamed al Fayed, who put them on display at his London department store, Harrod's. Al Fayed's son, Dodi, who later died in a car crash with Diana, Princess of Wales, had served as executive producer for the film *Chariots of Fire.*

1928 Amsterdam C: 81, N: 33, D: 7.30. WR: 10.2 (Charles Paddock)

1. Percy Williams	CAN	10.8
2. John "Jack" London	GBR	10.9
3. Georg Lammers	GER	10.9
4. Frank Wykoff	USA	11.0
5. Wilfred Legg	SAF	11.0
6. Robert McAllister	USA	11.0

Percy Williams was one of the most popular winners of the Amsterdam Games. Not considered a serious threat by the experts, the slim, almost frail-looking 20-year-old from Vancouver, British Columbia, caught the fancy of the crowd in the second round, when he tied the Olympic record of 10.6. This time was matched in both semifinals, first by Bob McAllister, "The Flying Cop" of New York City, who barely held off a slow-starting Williams, and then by Jack London, a Guyanese-born university student who was the first Briton to use starting blocks. In Amsterdam, Williams was joined by his coach, Bob Granger, a janitor who managed the trip by washing dishes on the train to Toronto and working on a freighter to Europe. He helped Williams practice his starts in his hotel room by racing into a mattress set against the wall. As the six finalists lined up for the deciding race, the 5-foot 6-inch (1.67 meter), 126-pound Williams seemed an unlikely bet to become Olympic champion, particularly as he was standing beside the muscular 6-foot 2-inch (1.87 meter), 200-pound London. After two false starts, by Legg and Wykoff (who had gained ten pounds on the boat ride from the United States), the runners were off. Williams took the lead immediately and kept it the entire way, holding off late rushes by London and Lammers to win by two feet. McAllister pulled a tendon 20 meters from the tape and finished last.

In the days before television, an unexpected winner like Williams could be famous and unrecognized at the same time. Only a few hours after his Olympic victory, Williams and a friend noticed a large crowd gathered in front of his hotel. "We joined the mob," Williams later recalled, "looking over their shoulders. I asked a person in front of me why they were there and he said, 'We're waiting for the Canadian runner Williams to come out of the hotel.' I didn't tell him who I was. I stood around waiting for him, too, and talking to some of the people—it was much more fun." Later that night, Williams wrote in his diary, "So I'm supposed to be the world's 100 meters champion. Crushed apples. No more fun in running now."

Upon his return to Canada, Williams, who also won the 200 meters, was greeted with an enthusiasm reminiscent of the ancient Greek Olympics. Crossing the continent by train with his mother, he stopped in Montreal, where he was presented with a gold watch. In Hamilton he received a silver tea service and in Winnipeg a bronze statue, a silver cup, and a golden retriever. When he finally reached Vancouver, a school holiday was declared, and he was met by tens of thousands of cheering fans. He was given a blue Graham-Paige sports car as well as $14,500 for his education.

1932 Los Angeles C: 32, N: 17, D: 8.1. WR: 10.2 (Charles Paddock, Ralph Metcalfe)

1. T. "Eddie" Tolan	USA	10.3 OR	(10.38)
2. Ralph Metcalfe	USA	10.3 OR	(10.38)
3. Arthur Jonath	GER	10.4	(10.50)
4. George Simpson	USA	10.5	(10.53)
5. Daniel Joubert	SAF	10.6	(10.60)
6. Takayoshi Yoshioka	JPN	10.7	(10.79)

Eddie Tolan was the third University of Michigan athlete to win the Olympic 100 meters gold medal, following in the tradition of Archie Hahn and Ralph Craig. The 5-foot 7-inch Tolan dominated US sprinting from 1929 to 1931, but he was dethroned by Ralph Metcalfe of Marquette University in Milwaukee, who breezed undefeated through the 1932 season. At the US Olympic trials Metcalfe beat Tolan in both sprints and went to Los Angeles as the favorite. But in the second round it was Tolan who set an Olympic record of 10.4. In the final, Yoshioka, an excellent starter, took the lead from the first step and held it for 40 meters, when he was caught by Tolan. Yoshioka faded at 60 meters, while Metcalfe began his famous finishing spurt. He pulled even with Tolan at 80 meters and the two ran neck and neck for the rest of the race, crossing the finish line in a near dead heat. Most of the spectators felt that there had been a tie or that Metcalfe had won. Several hours later, seven judges viewed a film of the race and determined that Tolan had *crossed* the line two inches ahead of Metcalfe. Current rules state that the first runner to *reach* the finish line is the winner. So close was the race that if the current rules had been in effect in 1932, Metcalfe would have been the winner.

There were also two also-rans who provoked interest in 1932. The first was Daniel Joubert, a white South African who spoke seven African dialects. Joubert arrived in Los Angeles in a somewhat weakened condition, having traveled 38 days to get there. Considering his ordeal, it was quite an achievement that he even made the final. The other was Liu Changchun, who marched in the opening day ceremony as the one and only representative of the 400,000,000 people of China. No Chinese athlete had ever competed at the Olympics. When the Japanese invaded northeastern China and set up the puppet Manchukuo government, they announced that they would send Liu to compete at the 1932 Olympics. Liu, a student at Northeastern University, refused. The head of the university, General Zhang Xueliang, then personally financed Liu's trip to Los Angeles. Liu finished last in his first round heat in both the 100 and 200. He also competed in both events at the Berlin Olympics four years later.

1936 Berlin C: 63, N: 30, D: 8.3. WR: 10.2 (Charles Paddock, Ralph Metcalfe, James "Jesse" Owens)

1. James "Jesse" Owens	USA	10.3
2. Ralph Metcalfe	USA	10.4
3. Martinus Osendarp	HOL	10.5
4. Frank Wykoff	USA	10.6
5. Erich Borchmeyer	GER	10.7
6. Lennart Strandberg	SWE	10.9

Jesse Owens assured himself a permanent place in sports history on May 25, 1935, when, while competing at the Big Ten championships at Ann Arbor, Michigan, he broke five world records and equaled a sixth in the space of 45 minutes. At 3:15 p.m. he won the 100-yard dash by five yards in 9.4 seconds to tie the world record. At 3:25 he long-jumped 26 feet 8¼ inches (8.13 meters), breaking the existing world record by six inches. It was his only jump of the day, but it wasn't beaten for 25 years. At 3:45 he scored a ten-yard victory in the 220-yard dash, clocking 20.3 seconds and bettering the listed record by three-tenths of a second. He was also given credit for lowering the world record in the shorter 200-meter dash. At 4:00 p.m. he flew over the 220-yard low hurdles in 22.6, the first man to beat 23 seconds. En route he also established a record for the 200-meter hurdles. Despite these and other sensational performances, in the following year Owens lost three times to the great Alabama-born sprinter Eulace

Jesse Owens, 1936
Owens' celebrity failed to earn him a living, and he was forced to make ends meet by racing against horses, dogs, and motorcycles. He eventually found his place as a "professional good example."

Peacock. And it wasn't until one week before the Olympic trials that Jesse was able to defeat Ralph Metcalfe.

But he peaked when he needed to, winning the 100, 200, and long jump at the trials, and he went to Berlin as the favorite in all three events.

Owens had little trouble living up to expectations. In the first round of the 100 meters he tied the Olympic record of 10.3. In the second round he ran a wind-aided 10.2. Jesse took it easy in the semifinals, winning his heat in 10.4 while Metcalfe won the other in 10.5. The final saw Owens take the lead from the first stride and pull out to a five-foot lead by the halfway mark. As usual Metcalfe started slowly and came on strong in the last 25 meters. He closed the gap, but was still a yard back when Owens broke the tape. Metcalfe, who was elected to the US Congress 34 years later, picked up his second straight 100 meters silver medal, while Osendarp became the first Dutchman to win an individual track and field medal. Osendarp later joined the German SS and was imprisoned for seven years after the Nazis were defeated. Strandberg appeared to be a sure medalist, but he strained a tendon at the 80-meter mark and limped home in last place. Before the week was out, Jesse Owens had earned three more gold medals.

Nazi propaganda had portrayed Negroes as inferior,

Jesse Owens, 1936
The son of sharecroppers won four gold medals and returned home to a hero's welcome and a ticker-tape parade down Broadway.

taunting the United States for relying on "black auxiliaries." Evidently, though, the message had little effect on the German masses, who considered Owens the hero of Berlin. Everywhere he went around town he was mobbed by fans seeking his autograph or photograph. They even shoved autograph books through his bedroom window in the Olympic Village while he tried to sleep.

Jesse Owens was born September 12, 1913, in Danville, Alabama, the son of sharecroppers and the grandson of slaves. By the age of 7 he was expected to pick 100 pounds of cotton a day. When he was 9 his family moved north to Cleveland, where Jesse pumped gas and delivered groceries. After he set national high school records in the long jump, the 100-yard dash, and the 220, he was recruited by 28 colleges. It was at this point in his life that the 19-year-old Owens first confronted the responsibilities of being a public figure and the need to maintain a positive public image. Local black newspapers and political leaders took a keen interest in his choice of universities and were critical when he chose Ohio State, a university that had earned a racist reputation. In 1935, while competing in California, Owens was photographed socializing with a wealthy white woman named Quincella Nickerson. On July 4, a Cleveland journalist confronted Owens with the fact that he was the father of a 2½-year-old daughter and that his newspaper would publish a photograph of the little girl if Jesse did not marry the girl's mother, Ruth Bolomon. Owens married Ruth the very next day.

The following month, Jesse faced another public relations crisis. While at Ohio State, he had worked as a freight elevator operator and then as a page in the state legislature. As Owens' fame grew, it came out that his page "job" had been one at which he had not had to work. Jesse settled the matter by paying back the salary he had received: $159.

There is an enduring myth that after Jesse won the 100 meters in Berlin he was snubbed by Adolf Hitler, who refused to meet Owens after he had personally congratulated three earlier gold medal winners. Actually, if such a snub did occur, the recipient was not Jesse Owens, but Cornelius Johnson and David Albritton, black Americans who had finished one-two in the high jump the previous day. Owens *was* snubbed by a different world leader—Franklin Delano Roosevelt. Although Jesse received tickertape parades in New York City and Cleveland, the President not only failed to invite him to the White House, he never even sent a letter of congratulations. Owens was also snubbed by the Amateur Athletic Union, which suspended him for refusing to run in a Swedish meet, which he had never agreed to enter. The AAU also bypassed him for the Sullivan award, which was presented to the best US amateur athlete of the year. In 1935, the year that Jesse Owens set six world records, the award was given to a golfer named Lawson Little. In 1936, the year of Owens' four gold medals, the award went to Glenn Morris, the Olympic decathlon champion.

After the Olympics, Jesse worked as a paid campaigner for presidential candidate Alf Landon. When Landon lost to Roosevelt in a landslide, and after a series of unsuccessful business and work ventures, Owens took a $130-a-month job as a playground instructor in Cleveland. In an attempt to make ends meet, the hero of Berlin, "The Ebony Antelope," allowed promoters to stage exhibitions in which he raced against horses, dogs, and motorcycles. Tiring of this, he returned to his job as a playground instructor. Then he lent his name to a chain of cleaning stores which went bankrupt, leaving Owens $114,000 in debt. In the 1950s he finally achieved financial security when he opened a public relations firm and became a public speaker on behalf of various corporate sponsors. He developed a repertoire of five basic speeches including ones on religion, patriotism, and marketing for salesmen. In the words of writer William Oscar Johnson, Jesse Owens had become "a professional good example."

In 1968 Owens took the side of the US Olympic Committee in its struggle with militant black athletes and two years later he wrote a book called *Blackthink,* which criticized racial militancy. However in 1972 he published another book, *I Have Changed,* retracting his earlier criticisms. After 35 years of pack-a-day cigarette smoking, Jesse Owens died of lung cancer in Tucson, Arizona, on March 31, 1980. Four years later a street in Berlin was renamed in his honor.

In the end, Jesse Owens filled an important need in American society, first among African-Americans and then among whites: the need for an honest clean-cut hero. Facts that might have tarnished his image, such as keeping a separate apartment for rendezvous with mistresses, or his 1966 conviction for non-payment of taxes, were ignored. Jesse eventually gave America what it wanted, inventing the sort of details about his life that the public wanted to hear. A typical example concerns the apocryphal Hitler snub. At first, Owens denied that it had happened and insisted that he had been treated well by all Germans. But the persistence of the Hitler snub story was so great that Jesse finally stopped denying it and actually incorporated it into his speeches.

Would-be Olympic sprint champions might be

interested to know the secret of Owens' success. In 1936 he told one London reporter, "I let my feet spend as little time on the ground as possible. From the air, fast down, and from the ground, fast up. My foot is only a fraction of the time on the track."

1948 London C: 66, N: 34, D: 7.31. WR: 10.2 (Charles Paddock, Ralph Metcalfe, James "Jesse" Owens, Harold Davis, Lloyd LaBeach, H. Norwood "Barney" Ewell)

1. W. Harrison Dillard	USA	10.3 EOR
2. H. Norwood "Barney" Ewell	USA	10.4
3. Lloyd LaBeach	PAN	10.4
4. Alastair McCorquodale	GBR	10.4
5. Melvin Patton	USA	10.5
6. E. McDonald Bailey	GBR/TRI	10.6

Harrison Dillard was a 13-year-old schoolboy in Cleveland when he attended the huge parade in 1936 in honor of Jesse Owens. Later he met Owens, who took a liking to the young man and presented him with his first pair of running shoes. Dillard put those shoes to good use. By 1952 he had matched his hero's total of four Olympic victories. From May 31, 1947, through June 26, 1948, "Bones" Dillard, running mostly the hurdles, ran up an unprecedented string of 82 consecutive victories. The streak finally came to an end at the AAU meet in Milwaukee when he tried to run four races in 67 minutes. First he lost the 100 meters to Barney Ewell and then he lost the 110-meter hurdles to Bill Porter. Nevertheless, when the Olympic trials were held the following week in Evanston, Illinois, there seemed no surer gold medal bet than Harrison Dillard, the world record holder in the 110-meters hurdles. However, in the final he uncharacteristically hit the first hurdle, lost his stride, hit two more hurdles, and stopped at the seventh hurdle as the others raced ahead. Dillard's Olympic hopes seemed over. Fortunately he had qualified the day before as third man in the 100 meters. But Dillard would face stiff competition in London. First there was the prerace favorite, USC's Mel Patton, who held the world record of 9.3 in the 100 yards. Then there was 30-year-old Barney Ewell, who had beaten Patton at the US trials in the world record time of 10.2. And there was Patton's arch rival, Lloyd LaBeach of UCLA, who had also run 100 meters in 10.2 and who went to London as the sole representative of his native country, Panama.

The three favorites and Dillard were joined in the Olympic final by two representatives of Great Britain, Mac Bailey of Trinidad, who, like Dillard, had been inspired by the feats of Jesse Owens, and Alastair McCorquodale, a burly Scot who had taken up running only a year earlier and who actually preferred rugby and cricket to track. After one false start, Dillard flashed into the lead and held it the entire way. Ewell caught him at the tape and, thinking he had won, danced around the field joyfully and embraced his opponents. But LaBeach told him, "Man, you no win; Bones win." LaBeach was right. When the photo-finish had been studied, it was announced that Dillard had won. Ewell graciously congratulated him on his good fortune, greatly impressing the crowd of 82,000 with his sportsmanship. LaBeach, whose parents were Jamaican, is the only Panamanian ever to have won an Olympic medal.

Harrison Dillard and Barney Ewell, 1948

1952 Helsinki C: 72, N: 33, D: 7.21. WR: 10.1 (Lloyd LaBeach)

1. Lindy Remigino	USA	10.4	(10.79)
2. Herbert McKenley	JAM	10.4	(10.80)
3. E. McDonald Bailey	GBR/TRI	10.4	(10.83)
4. F. Dean Smith	USA	10.4	(10.84)
5. Vladimir Sukharyev	SOV	10.5	(10.88)
6. John Treloar	AUS	10.5	(10.91)

The 1952 100-meter final produced one of the closest finishes in Olympic history and also one of the biggest sprint upsets. The title seemed pretty much up for grabs, particularly after the US college champion, Jim Golliday, was injured and unable to participate in the Olympics. The position of favorite shifted to 31-year-old Mac Bailey and Art Bragg of Morgan State College.

Tale of the Tape, 1952

Lindy Remigino (Lane 3 from top) edges Herb McKenley (Lane 2) by the slimmest of margins.

But Bragg pulled a muscle in the semifinals, which were won by Bailey and 30-year-old Herb McKenley, the 400-meter world record holder who had also entered the 100 as a means of practicing his start. With this race McKenley became the first—and only—man to qualify for a final in the 100 meters, 200 meters, and 400 meters. One of the surviving US representatives was Texan Dean Smith, who also competed in rodeos and who later became a stuntman in hundreds of television shows and films, including *Stagecoach* and *True Grit,* and doubled for Robert Redford three times in the early 1970s. The other was Lindy Remigino, a modest Manhattan College student from Hartford, Connecticut, who had barely qualified for the US Olympic tryouts by finishing fifth in the NCAA championship. Smith showed in front first, but Remigino had a clear lead at the halfway mark. He held on gamely for 90 meters, but was passed by McKenley just as they reached the tape.

"I was sure I had lost the race," said Remigino afterward. "I started my lean too early . . . and I saw Herb McKenley shoot past me. I was heartsick. I figured I had blown it." Lindy walked over to the delighted Jamaican and offered his congratulations. But a photo-finish showed that Remigino's right shoulder had reached the finish line an inch ahead of McKenley's chest, and the judges ruled him the winner. When someone told Remigino the results before they had been flashed on the scoreboard, he was incredulous and was sure there had been a mistake. Finally he turned to McKenley and is reputed to have said, "Gosh, Herb, it looks as though I won the darn thing." The closeness of the finish is shown by the fact that Dean Smith was only 14 inches (36 centimeters) behind the winner, yet placed only fourth.

1956 Melbourne C: 65, N: 31, D: 11.24. WR: 10.1 (Lloyd LaBeach, Willie Williams, Ira Murchison, Leamon King)

1. Bobby Joe Morrow	USA	10.5	(10.62)
2. W. Thane Baker	USA	10.5	(10.77)
3. Hector Hogan	AUS	10.6	(10.77)
4. Ira Murchison	USA	10.6	(10.79)
5. Manfred Germar	GER	10.7	(10.86)
6. Michael Agostini	TRI	10.7	(10.88)

The Olympic record was tied in the second round by the favorites, 6-foot 1½-inch (1.87 meter) Bobby Morrow and 5-foot 4½-inch (1.64 meter) Ira Murchison. The same pair won the two semifinal heats, with Morrow again running 10.3. The final was run into a nine-m.p.h. wind, which accounts for the slow times. Hec Hogan, the five-time Australian 100-yard champion from Queensland, took the early lead, but Morrow passed him after 50 meters and stormed to a decisive victory. Baker and Murchison caught Hogan with 25 yards to go, but Hogan churned out a final burst, and only a desperate lunge by Baker kept the Aussie from a silver medal. Morrow, a devout Christian from San Benito, Texas, never tried to anticipate the starters' gun with a rolling start because he considered it unsportsmanlike. A cotton and grain farmer, he relied on getting 11 hours' sleep a night to keep up his strength. "Whatever success I have had," he said, "is due to being so perfectly relaxed that I can feel my jaw muscles wiggle." Bronze medalist Hogan died of leukemia at the age of 29 on September 2, 1960, the day after the 100-meter final at Rome.

1960 Rome C: 61, N: 45, D: 9.1. WR: 10.0 (Armin Hary, Harry Jerome)

1. Armin Hary	GER	10.2 OR	(10.32)
2. David Sime	USA	10.2	(10.35)
3. Peter Radford	GBR	10.3	(10.42)
4. Enrique Figuerola Camue	CUB	10.3	(10.44)
5. Francis "Frank" Budd	USA	10.3	(10.46)
6. O. Ray Norton	USA	10.4	(10.50)

On June 21, 1960, controversial Armin Hary, an office worker from Frankfurt, became the first man to be credited with 10.0 in the 100 meters. Running in Zurich, this fast-starting son of a coal miner in Quierschied, Saarland, actually achieved the time twice in one day. On the first occasion he was accused of "taking a flyer," or beating the gun, a tactic for which he was notorious. When the starter ordered the race rerun, Hary protested, but went ahead and ran another 10.0. Three and a half weeks later, on July 15, the son of a Pullman coach attendant, 19-year-old Harry Jerome of Vancouver, recorded the second official 10.0 at the Canadian Olympic trials at Saskatoon.

Despite the achievements of Hary and Jerome, most track aficionados were predicting victory for Ray Norton, who had swept both sprints at the USA–USSR meet, the 1959 Pan American Games, and the 1960 US Olympic trials. Another contender was Dave Sime, a medical student from Fair Lawn, New Jersey. Sime set a rather unusual world record when he ran 100 yards in 9.8 seconds while dressed in a baseball uniform. The previous record had been set by Jesse Owens in 1936.

In the second round in Rome, Armin Hary beat Dave Sime by a yard and set an Olympic record of 10.2. The first semifinal was won by Peter Radford, a Walsall schoolteacher who had spent three childhood years in a wheelchair because of a kidney disease. Harry Jerome had been in the lead when he pulled a muscle and couldn't finish. The second semi saw Armin Hary beat both Sime and Norton, who was running unusually tightly.

The start of the final was a tense affair. First Hary and Sime broke without a gun, but neither was penalized. The next try for a start was halted when Figuerola needed his starting block repaired. Then Hary beat the gun and was penalized. One more false start and he would be disqualified. But the usually volatile Hary kept his poise and at the next attempt got off to a fair and perfect start. By the end of the first stride he was already in the lead, and at the five-meter mark he led by a full meter. In the second half of the race, Sime stormed back from last place to make up over three meters, but Hary held on to win by a "long foot." Not only was Armin Hary the first winner of the Olympic 100 meters to come from a non-English-speaking country, he was also the first German male to win an Olympic gold medal in a track event.

In the end Hary proved that his amazing "blitz start" was legitimate. He contended, however, that there was more to it than quick reflexes. "More important to me," he said, "is the fact that I have learned, through relaxation, how to achieve full stride and smooth forward action very early in the race." He did, however, employ one "trick." Whenever the starter called "set," Hary would stay down until all the other runners were hanging heavily in the set position. Only then would he rise. Unsuspecting starters would invariably wait for him and then pull the trigger for the start, allowing Hary, in effect, to control the beginning of the race. Knowing that the anxious starter would pull the trigger as soon as he was set, Hary would rise, pause a moment, and then take off just as the gun was sounding. Hary's competitive career came to an abrupt halt shortly after the Olympics, when his knee was severely injured in an auto accident. In 1981 his name reappeared in the news when he was convicted of diverting Roman Catholic Church funds for use in a personal investment.

1964 Tokyo C: 73, N: 49, D: 10.15. WR: 10.0 (Armin Hary, Harry Jerome, Horacio Estevez)

1. Robert Hayes	USA	10.0 EWR	(10.05)
2. Enrique Figuerola Camue	CUB	10.2	(10.25)
3. Harry Jerome	CAN	10.2	(10.27)
4. Wieslaw Maniak	POL	10.4	(10.42)
5. Heinz Schumann	GER	10.4	(10.46)
6. Gaoussou Kone	IVC	10.4	(10.47)
6. Melvin Pender	USA	10.4	(10.47)
8. Thomas Robinson	BAH	10.5	(10.57)

This was one 100-meter final that was run exactly to form. Any doubts that Hayes had not recovered from a June leg injury were quickly dispelled when the burly, pigeon-toed Florida speedster demolished the field in the first semifinal in a wind-aided 9.9. Harry Jerome won the second semi, ahead of Kone, Figuerola, and Pender. Pender led most of the way but tore a rib muscle and had to be carried off the field on a stretcher. Advised by doctors to withdraw from the final, he ran anyway and spent the next three days in the hospital as a result. Hayes, who was the first person to run 100 yards in 9.1 and the first person to break 6.0 for 60 yards, entered the Olympics with a record of 48 straight finals victories at 100 yards and 100 meters. The start was delayed 10 minutes while the curb lane, Hayes' lane, was raked after having been chewed up by the start of the 20-kilometer walk. The big three, Hayes,

Bob Hayes, 1964
An Olympic title and a world record (right), over Figuerola (80) and Jerome (56) en route to a nine-year career with the Dallas Cowboys (below).

Figuerola, and Jerome, had pulled away from the others by the 10-meter mark. Then Hayes unleashed his power, took a one-meter lead halfway, and pulled away to an awesome seven-foot victory. Both Figuerola, who became the first Cuban to win an Olympic track and field medal, and Jerome called it the best race they had run all year and had nothing but praise for the winner.

After the Olympics, Bob Hayes became the first Olympic champion to make a successful transition to professional football. He played nine years for the Dallas Cowboys and was twice chosen All-Pro as a wide receiver. He is the only athlete to earn both an individual Olympic gold medal and a Super Bowl victory ring. Hayes was so fast that opposing teams had to abandon their traditional man-to-man pass defenses and create the double zone defenses that are the standard today. When he retired from football, Hayes plunged into alcoholism and drug use. In 1978 he was arrested by undercover narcotics agents and the following year he pleaded guilty to selling cocaine and methaqualone. In 15 years he went from the top of the Olympic podium to a cell in a Texas prison. He served ten months, drifted back to alcohol and drugs, and then underwent successful rehabilitation. In 1994, at the age of 51, Bob Hayes earned a degree in elementary education from Florida A&M University. Hayes died of kidney failure on September 19, 2002. Two months later, a seven-foot (2.13-meter) bronze statue of him was unveiled at A. Philip Randolph Park in Jacksonville, Florida.

1968 Mexico City C: 64, N: 42, D: 10.14. WR: 9.9 (James Hines, Ronnie Ray Smith, Charles Greene)

1. James Hines	USA	9.95 WR
2. Lennox Miller	JAM	10.04
3. Charles Greene	USA	10.07
4. Pablo Montes	CUB	10.14
5. Roger Bambuck	FRA	10.16
6. Melvin Pender	USA	10.17
7. Harry Jerome	CAN	10.20
8. Jean-Louis Ravelomanatsoa	MAD	10.28

The first accredited time of 9.9 seconds for 100 meters was registered at the AAU championships in Sacramento, California, on June 20, 1968, by Jim Hines, the son of an Oakland construction worker. Hines had run a wind-aided 9.8 in a heat, and then followed with his history-making run in the semifinal. However, in the final he was beaten by Charlie Greene, a graduate of the University of Nebraska. Previous to the Olympics, Hines and Greene had met in 12 finals, with Greene winning eight of them. However two of Hines' four victories had been the last two times they met, at the US Olympic trials.

Competition was stiff in Mexico City. In the second round Heinz Erbstösser of East Germany had the distinction of being the first person to run 10.2 and not qualify for the semifinals. Greene clocked 10.0 in his first two heats, while Hines matched the time in the semis. Hermes Ramirez of Cuba also ran 10.0 in the second round, but was eliminated in the semis. The 1968 100 meters saw the first all-black final in Olympic history. Hines got off to what he later said was the best start of his career. However it was US Army captain Mel Pender, now 30, who took the early lead. By 50 meters Hines and Greene had pulled even, and at 70 meters Hines shifted gears and pulled away to win by a meter. Greene, discouraged and suffering a cramp, was nipped at the tape by Lennox Miller, who represented U.S.C. in US collegiate competition. Hines' electronically timed 9.95 was considered faster than the hand-timed world record of 9.9. Four days after his Olympic victory, Hines signed a contract with the Miami Dolphins football team. Another man who went into professional sports was Japan's Hideo Iijima, who made it to the semifinals in 1964 and 1968. As the fastest sprinter in Japanese history, Iijima attracted the attention of the Lotte Orions baseball team, who hired him to become a pinch-runner and base-stealer. The club insured Iijima's legs for 50 million yen. Unfortunately Iijima, though fast, hadn't played baseball since he was 12 and had no aptitude for getting a jump on a pitch or for sliding. After two years, during which he was caught stealing 17 of 40 times, he was finally dropped from the team.

Jim Hines, 1968
Lunging to a gold medal and a world record 9.95 seconds.

One night after his return from Mexico City, Jim Hines came home to his Houston apartment to discover that burglars had stolen his television and stereo, his wife's jewelry and his gold medals. Hines placed an ad in his local newspaper asking the thieves to return the gold medals. Eventually they arrived by mail in a plain brown envelope.

1972 Munich C: 84, N: 55, D: 9.1. WR: 9.95 (James Hines)

1. Valery Borzov	SOV/UKR	10.14
2. Robert Taylor	USA	10.24
3. Lennox Miller	JAM	10.33
4. Aleksandr Kornelyuk	SOV/AZR	10.36
5. Michael Fray	JAM	10.40
6. Jobst Hirscht	GER	10.40
7. Zenon Nowosz	POL	10.46

DNF: Hasely Crawford (TRI)

Valery Borzov was the clear favorite in 1972. The blond, blue-eyed Ukrainian from Sambir was extremely consistent and had not been beaten in almost two years. However, Eddie Hart of Pittsburg, California, and Rey Robinson of Lakeland, Florida, had both been timed at 9.9 in the US Olympic trials. Hart was considered the number-one threat to Borzov. The first round of 12 heats began at 11:09 a.m. on August 31. Borzov, Hart, and Robinson each won their heats. Vassilios Papageorgopoulous of Greece recorded the fastest time of the round, 10.24, a time that might have earned him a silver medal had he not suffered a groin injury that forced him to withdraw from the semifinals. The second round, the quarter-finals, was scheduled to commence at 4:15 p.m. As that time drew nearer, 1968 400-meter gold medalist Lee Evans noticed that Hart, Robinson, and the third US sprinter, Robert Taylor, had not yet arrived at the stadium. When he couldn't find them at the warm-up track, Evans began to worry. Scheduled to run in the 4 × 400-meter relay later in the week, he raced at top speed from the stadium to the Olympic Village three quarters of a mile away in search of the missing Americans. But it was too late.

Two minutes earlier, Hart, Robinson, and Taylor, thinking the quarterfinals didn't begin until 7 p.m., had casually left their quarters to return to the stadium. Accompanied by their coach, Stan Wright, who had been working from an outdated 18-month-old preliminary schedule, the trio made their way to the bus stop at the Village gate. While waiting for the track stadium bus, they wandered into the doorway of the ABC-TV headquarters and began watching the television monitor. What they saw on the screen was several 100-meter runners lining up at the starting line. Robinson asked if this was a rerun of the first round. Told that it was a live transmission, Robinson realized with horror that he was watching the very heat in which he had been scheduled to run. Hart was entered in the second heat and Taylor in the third. The three athletes and their coach were pushed into a car and driven at breakneck speed to the stadium by ABC employee Bill Norris. It was too late for Robinson and Hart, but Taylor, who, like Jim Hines, had studied at Texas Southern, arrived just in time to slip off his sweats, put on his shoes, do a couple knee bends, and settle into the starting blocks. He finished second in the heat, a yard behind Borzov, which is exactly where he ended up 25 hours later, in the final. In that race, Borzov took the lead after 30 meters and was never headed. He even eased up at the end, throwing his arms wide in exultation five meters from the finish. A last-chance dive gained dental student Lennox Miller third place over Aleksandr Kornelyuk, the 5-foot 5-inch (1.65-meter) surprise from Azerbaijan.

Oddly enough, Borzov almost missed the same quarterfinal heat that Hart and Robinson missed. First he was misinformed about the starting time of his heat. His coach convinced him to stay in the stadium. Borzov dozed off, and when he awoke his heat was being called. He raced to the track, but was stopped by a German official. Pushing aside the official, Borzov got to the line just in time to prepare his starting blocks.

Following the final, Borzov told reporters (in English) that he owed his success, "First and foremost to my country, secondly to my coach, Valentin Petrovsky, thirdly to all the people who helped me develop, and fourthly to myself." Borzov wasn't just toeing the party line. Listen to Petrovsky explain what went on at the Kiev Institute of Physical Culture, where Borzov was a graduate student: "We began with a search for the most up-to-date model of sprinting. We studied slow-motion films of leading world sprinters of past and present, figured out the push-off angle and the body incline at the breakaway and went deeply into a whole number of minor details. For Borzov to be able to clock ten seconds flat over 100 meters, a whole team of scientists conducted research resembling the work of, say, car or aircraft designers . . . When the mathematical equivalent of a runner was worked out and given a scientific basis, we began testing our

Valery Borzov, 1972

calculations in practice. It was subtle work, which could be compared to the training of a ballerina." Such statements give the impression that Borzov was just a machine, but he was quite human. He once said, "I very often have the following urge: I suddenly feel on the street that I have to run. I absolutely have to run, dressed in a suit, wearing my hat and tie, not paying any attention to the passers-by . . . Then convention gets the upper hand and I restrain myself." Borzov eventually married the famous gymnast Lyudmila Turischeva, who won even more gold medals than he did. He later served as the first President of the Ukranian Olympic Committee and as a member of the International Olympic Committee.

1976 Montreal C: 63, N: 40, D: 7.24. WR: 9.95 (James Hines)

1. Hasely Crawford	TRI	10.06
2. Donald Quarrie	JAM	10.07
3. Valery Borzov	SOV/UKR	10.14
4. Harvey Glance	USA	10.19
5. Guy Abrahams	PAN	10.25
6. John Jones	USA	10.27
7. Klaus-Dieter Kurrat	GDR	10.31
8. Peter Petrov	BUL	10.35

Several runners were given a strong chance to win, but the leading choices of track experts were Donald Quarrie, Silvio Leonard of Cienfuegos, Cuba, and Valery Borzov, who was aiming to become the first man to win two 100-meters gold medals (not counting Archie Hahn, whose second victory was in the Intercalated Games of 1906). In fact, Borzov was the first gold medalist even to attempt the feat since Percy Williams had been eliminated in the semifinals in 1932. The first of the leading contenders to fall by the wayside was the accident-prone Cuban Silvio Leonard. Leonard had won the 100 meters at the 1975 Pan

American Games in Mexico City, but had pulled a muscle as he crossed the finish line. Hobbling forward in pain, he was unable to stop himself and fell into the ten-foot moat that surrounded the track. Seriously injured, Leonard nonetheless regained his form in time for the Olympics. Ten days before the Games, however, he stepped on a cologne bottle during a bit of horseplay and cut his foot. He was eliminated in the quarterfinals.

Meanwhile, 6-foot 2¾-inch (1.90-meter) Hasely Crawford, a gear machinist from San Fernando, Trinidad, was breezing through his heats. In the quarterfinals he beat Borzov, and in the semis he defeated Quarrie. Crawford had been a finalist in Munich four years earlier but had stopped running after four or five strides, the victim of a hamstring pull and nervousness. He was still fighting his nerves in Montreal, but he was not the only one. In the staging room before the final Crawford ranted and raved and tried to intimidate his opponents. When he stared at Glance and Jones, who were only 19 and 18, respectively, their "eyes showed they were already defeated." Crawford later told reporters, "At the line I knew I could beat Borzov. I feared Don Quarrie." At the starting line, Crawford "shook a little bit," but got a good start anyway. Glance took the early lead. Quarrie caught him after 60 meters and passed him at 75 meters. Then Crawford flew past on the curb lane. He stumbled just before the finish, but held off the lunging Quarrie to win. Crawford kept running for another 150 meters, then stopped suddenly, as if the realization of his accomplishment had just hit him.

As Trinidad's first Olympic champion, Crawford received more than his share of honors. He was awarded the Trinity Cross, his picture appeared on two postage stamps, an airplane was named after him, and six different Calypso songs were written in his honor.

1980 Moscow C: 65, N: 40, D: 7.25. WR: 9.95 (James Hines)

1. Allan Wells	GBR	10.25
2. Silvio Leonard Tartabull	CUB	10.25
3. Petar Petrov	BUL	10.39
4. Aleksandr Aksinin	SOV/RUS	10.42
5. Osvaldo Lara Cañizares	CUB	10.43
6. Vladimir Muravyov	SOV/KAZ	10.44
7. Marian Woronin	POL	10.46
8. Hermann Panzo	FRA	10.49

Stanley Floyd of Albany, Georgia, won the US Olympic trials and also recorded the best time of the year (10.07). But with US athletes boycotted out of the Olympics the mantle of favorite fell to Silvio Leonard, who had successfully managed to steer clear of moats and cologne bottles. His most serious challengers were considered to be Marian Woronin, who predicted that he would win the gold medal in a time of 10.10, and Eugen Ray of East Germany. Aleksandr Aksinin recorded the fastest time of the first round—10.26. When the draw was announced for the second round, many eyebrows were raised. Of the nine first-round winners, four were thrown into the first heat, as was defending champion Hasely Crawford. On the other hand, heat number three saw Aksinin unburdened by competition from other first-round winners. Aksinin won that heat in 10.29, a time that would have placed him seventh in the first heat. Heat number one was won by Allan Wells, a marine engineer from Edinburgh who didn't start training fulltime until six months before the Olympics. His time of 10.11 pushed him to cofavorite with Leonard.

The final took place during the last round of the triple jump, an event of great interest to the Soviet crowd. Just as the starter called "set," a great roar went up for a jump made by local favorite Viktor Saneyev. The starter held the runners in their crouch, then shot the gun. Aksinin and Lara were off the fastest, with Leonard and Wells close behind. By 60 meters Lara had faded, and by 80 meters the race was between Leonard on the inside and Wells on the outside. Wells edged ahead, but Leonard drew even again. With seven meters to go the stocky Scot began an extreme lean which allowed his shoulder to cross the finish line two or three inches before Leonard's chest. Allan Wells had become Great Britain's first 100-meters winner since Harold Abrahams and Scotland's first track gold medalist since Eric Liddell. At 28 he was also the oldest winner of the 100 meters at that time. As a youngster Wells had enrolled in a Charles Atlas correspondence course in bodybuilding. His father was a blacksmith and his mother sewed nets for fishermen and worked as a hospital cleaner. Wells didn't turn from long-jumping to sprinting until 1976, at which time his personal best was only 10.9. Coached by his wife, Wells did not use starting blocks until 1980, when the International Amateur Athletic Federation (IAAF) required their use in international competitions. In the run-up to the Olympics, the British government of Margaret Thatcher attempted to persuade Wells to support their boycott of the Moscow Games by flooding his postbox with letters that contained photographs of dead Afghan children. He was awarded the Trinity Cross, his picture appeared on two postage stamps, an airplane was named after him, six different Calypso songs were written in his honor, and a stadium was named after him in Port of Spain.

1984 Los Angeles C: 82, N: 59, D: 8.4. WR: 9.93 (Calvin Smith)

1. F. Carlton Lewis	USA	9.99
2. Sam Graddy	USA	10.19
3. Benjamin Johnson	CAN	10.22
4. Ron Brown	USA	10.26
5. Michael McFarlane	GBR	10.27
6. Raymond Stewart	JAM	10.29
7. Donovan Reid	GBR	10.33
8. Tony Sharpe	CAN	10.35

The third son of two track coaches, Carl Lewis was born in Birmingham, Alabama, and raised in Willingboro, New Jersey. Small for his age and shy, Lewis began to grow so rapidly at the age of 15 (two and a half inches in one month) that he had to walk with crutches for three weeks while his body adjusted. Previously thought to be the least athletic member of his talented family, Lewis' achievements began to outstrip all around him. By 1981 he was ranked number one in the world in the 100-meter dash and in the long jump. In June of 1983, he won the 100, the 200, and the long jump at the US national championships, the first person to do so since Malcolm Ford in 1886. Two months later, he earned three gold medals at the Helsinki world championships. The following year he qualified for four events at the Los Angeles Olympics, giving him the opportunity to match Jesse Owens four-gold-medal feat of 1936.

Lewis' first stop was the 100 meters, the event at which he was considered most vulnerable. As it turned out, he dominated the field. His second-round time of 10.04 was the best ever at a low-altitude Olympics. In the final, Graddy and Johnson were out fastest. Graddy still led at the 80-meter mark. "I thought, 'Hey, I'm going to win a gold medal,'" Graddy would later say. "Then I saw him out of the corner of my eye." Lewis, who was clocked at 28 m.p.h. at the finish, pulled away so strongly that his winning margin was a remarkable eight feet—the widest in Olympic history. Carl Lewis had won the first of his four gold medals.

1988 Seoul C: 102, N: 69, D: 9.24. WR: 9.83 (Benjamin Johnson)

1. F. Carlton Lewis	USA	9.92 OR
2. Linford Christie	GBR	9.97
3. Calvin Smith	USA	9.99
4. Dennis Mitchell	USA	10.04
5. Robson Caetano da Silva	BRA	10.11
6. Desai Williams	CAN	10.11
7. Raymond Stewart	JAM	12.26

DISQ (Drugs): Benjamin Johnson (CAN) 9.79

Ben Johnson was born in Falmouth, Jamaica, on December 30, 1961. Small and shy, he began to stutter at the age of 12 as a result of constantly mimicking his older brother's stammer. When he was 14 he moved to Toronto with his mother and three of his five siblings. Like his future rival, Carl Lewis, Johnson experienced a rapid growth spurt when he was 15 years old. It was also at this time that Johnson came under the tutelage of sprint coach Charlie Francis, the man who would guide his running career for the next 11 years.

On August 29, 1980, Johnson took part in the Pan American Junior Championships in Sudbury, Ontario, finishing sixth with a time of 10.86. This seemingly unimportant race would, in retrospect, earn significance as the first encounter between Johnson and Lewis, who won the contest in 10.43. Johnson scored his first major international success two years later when he finished second at the 1982 Commonwealth Games. Two years after that he qualified for the 100-meter final at the Los Angeles Olympics. After purposely false-starting in an unsuccessful attempt to rattle Lewis, Johnson surprised track fans by earning the bronze medal behind Lewis and Sam Graddy.

In 1985, after seven consecutive losses, Johnson finally defeated Lewis. By 1986 there was no question that "Big Ben" had wrested the title of Fastest Man on Earth from "King Carl." By the time of their classic confrontation at the 1987 world championships in Rome, it was Johnson who had won their last four encounters.

Carl Lewis, 1984

Mike McFarlane's attention is diverted from the finish line as Carl Lewis breezes past to win the opening heat of the 1984 100 meters. Lewis went on to match Jesse Owens' four gold medals of 1936. Four years later he became the first man to win the 100 meters twice.

100-meter dash, 1988
The finish of the 1988 100-meter dash – without Ben Johnson

By that time, also, Johnson had developed a reputation as an incredibly fast starter who appeared to leap out of the blocks like a panther going after a kill or a guard dog attacking an intruder. In the Rome final he burst off the line with so much power that he almost fell over. After ten meters he was already in front by a full meter, a lead he would hold all the way to the finish line, which he reached in a mere 9.83 seconds, breaking the world record by a full tenth of a second. In less than ten seconds Ben Johnson had become an international celebrity. He would soon sign commercial endorsement contracts worth millions of dollars.

Meanwhile, Carl Lewis, who had equaled the world record of 9.93 only to finish second, was livid. Although he refused to name names, he made it clear that he thought Johnson was taking illegal, performance-enhancing drugs. Although many dismissed Lewis' charges as sour grapes, he was not alone in his suspicions. On the track circuit, Johnson's highly sculptured muscles and yellow-tinged eyes, two indications of steroid use, had earned Johnson the nickname "Benoid." However, as his coach, Charlie Francis, was quick to point out, Johnson had passed innumerable drug tests. In 1985 Johnson himself told Canada's *Athletics* magazine, "Drugs are both demeaning and despicable and when people are caught they should be thrown out of the sport for good . . . I want to be the best on my own natural ability and no drugs will pass into my body."

As 1988 began, Johnson seemed to have a lock on the Olympic gold medal. But then disaster struck. In February, he pulled a hamstring muscle. In May, he reinjured his leg. In June, he broke away from Charlie Francis for the first time. However, a few weeks later they reconciled and Johnson returned to competition in time to win the Canadian Olympic trials. On August 17 in Zurich, the site of Johnson's first victory over Lewis three years earlier, the two met again for the first time since the Rome world championships. As usual, Johnson broke in front, but this time Lewis mowed him down to win with a time of 9.93 seconds. Calvin Smith was second at 9.97 and Johnson third at 10.00. Five days later in Cologne, Johnson was again beaten into third place, this time by Smith and Dennis Mitchell.

While Johnson retreated to Canada for a final month of training, Lewis was installed as the overwhelming favorite to become the first male sprinter to retain his Olympic title. Johnson dismissed this growing consensus. "When the gun go off," he said, "the race be over."

In Seoul, Lewis appeared to be in perfect form. He registered the fastest time in each of the first two rounds: 10.14 and 9.99. Johnson, meanwhile, caused a minor sensation in the second round. The rules stated that the top two finishers in each of the six heats would advance to the semifinals, as would the four fastest of the remaining runners. Johnson, misjudging the size of his lead, eased up long before the end, and dropped to third behind Linford Christie and Dennis Mitchell. Fortunately, Johnson's 10.17 allowed him to advance anyway.

The semifinals were held the following day, Saturday, at noon. Lewis won the first heat in 9.97. In the second, Johnson was called for a false start, a ruling that infuriated him. Still, he managed to control his anger and win the race in 10.03 despite running into a 1.2-meters-per-second head wind.

Less than an hour and a half later, the eight finalists met at the starting line. Carl Lewis was in lane 3, Ben Johnson in lane 6. They were separated by Linford Christie and Calvin Smith. By now Johnson's muscles were so highly developed that, as he waited for the sound of the starter's pistol, they seemed to be separate beings on the verge of exploding out of his skin. As expected, Johnson charged into the lead immediately.

On May 5, 1987, Carl Lewis' father had died of cancer. At the funeral, Carl had reached into his pocket and pulled out the gold medal he had earned for winning the 100 meters in 1984. He placed the medal in his father's hand and said, "I want you to have this because it was your favorite event." Noting his mother's surprise, he added, "Don't worry, I'll get another one."

Now, halfway through the 1988 final, he glanced to

his right, saw Ben Johnson five feet ahead of him, and was convinced that he could catch him. At the 80-meter mark Lewis looked over again and discovered that he was still five feet behind. This time he knew the race was lost. "Damn," he thought. "Ben did it again. The bastard got away with it again. It's over, Dad." Just before the finish line, Johnson stared back at Lewis and thrust his right arm into the air, his index finger pointed to the sky. His time was an amazing 9.79.

Lewis, convinced that Johnson was on steroids, wanted to protest, but held his tongue. As he later wrote in his autobiography, *Inside Track*, "I didn't have the medal to replace the one I had given [my father], and that hurt. But I could still give something to my father by acting the way he had always wanted me to act, with class and dignity." He shook Johnson's hand and walked away, ignoring the taunts of a group of Canadian fans who chanted, "When the gun go off, the race be over."

Johnson accepted the accolades of the crowd, appeared live on Canadian television, and then went off to doping control where he required one and a half hours and several beers to produce a urine sample. Afterward he spent over an hour in a sauna, then celebrated by eating half of a cream cake given to him by his mother, dining with friends at an Italian restaurant, and visiting a disco.

Back in Canada, the population was in ecstasy. In the 12 Olympics prior to the boycotted Games of 1980 and 1984, Canada had averaged one gold medal per Olympics. Its last track-and-field gold had come in 1932. The headline in the *Toronto Star* summed up the mood of the nation: "Ben Johnson—a national treasure."

Meanwhile, Johnson's urine sample was delivered to the Olympic Doping Control Center, numbered, and divided into two parts labeled "A" and "B." On Sunday, the testing center, not knowing whose urine they were examining, discovered that the "A" sample contained steroids. This information was passed on to Prince Alexandre de Merode of Belgium, the chairman of the IOC's medical commission. He matched the sample to a list of athletes' numbers and became the first person to learn that the guilty party was Ben Johnson. De Merode wrote a letter to the Canadian team, which was delivered at 1:45 a.m., Monday. At 7:00 a.m., Carol Anne Letheren, the Canadian *chef de mission*, informed Johnson of the positive test. Three hours later, with Canadian representatives in attendance, the "B" sample was tested and it too registered positive.

At 3:30 Tuesday morning, Letheren revisited Johnson to collect his gold medal. "We love you," she told him, "but you're guilty."

At 10:00 a.m., the IOC called a press conference and issued the following statement: "The urine sample of Ben Johnson (Canada—Athletics—100 meters) collected on Saturday, 24th September 1988 was found to contain the metabolites of a banned substance namely stanozolol (anabolic steroid). . . . The IOC Medical Commission recommends the following sanction: disqualification of this competitor from the Games of the XXIV Olympiad in Seoul. Of course, the gold medal has been withdrawn by the IOC."

Although Johnson was the 43rd Olympic athlete to be disqualified because of drugs since testing began in 1968, he was the first "big fish" to be caught. His disgrace was front-page news all over the world. Initially, Johnson denied having taken steroids. Charlie Francis claimed that Johnson was a victim of sabotage, that he had been given a spiked drink. Francis even hinted that agents of Carl Lewis had been responsible.

The Canadian government, to its great credit, wasted no time in ordering an investigation into the use of banned substances by Canadian athletes, including several of Johnson's sprinting teammates and a number of weightlifters who tested positive before the Games and were not allowed to travel to Seoul. The investigation, much of which was televised live, became known as the Dubin Inquiry in honor of the man in charge of the hearings, Charles Dubin, an associate chief justice of the Ontario Supreme Court.

Testifying before the Dubin Commission, Charlie Francis and Johnson's doctor, George (Jamie) Astaphan, revealed that the sprinter began taking steroids in November 1981 because Francis convinced him that everyone else was taking them and that if he didn't, he would be left behind. Over the next seven years, Johnson took the anabolic steroids Dianabol, stanozolol, and furazabol, as well as testosterone, diuretics, which he used as masking agents, and human growth hormone, which was made from human cadavers. Although Astaphan had once labeled a bottle of steroids "Do Not Take Within 28 Days of Competition," he apparently gave Johnson an injection only 26 days before the Olympic final. The Dubin Commission concluded that this injection contained Winstrol-V, a stanozolol compound used to fatten cattle before they are sent to market.

On June 12, 1989, Johnson himself appeared before the Dubin Commission. He admitted taking steroids and lying to the public when he said he hadn't. The following day, he was asked if he had any message for young athletes who had considered him their idol. With tears in his eyes, he replied, "I want to tell them to be honest and don't take drugs. It happened to me. I've been there. I know what it's like to cheat."

Three months later, the IAAF, in a controversial decision, retroactively rescinded Johnson's 1987 world record even though he had passed the drug test in Rome. Johnson served out his standard two-year suspension and returned to competition in 1991. However, his times were not what they had been in his drug-augmented heyday. Johnson qualified for the 1992 Canadian Olympic team but was eliminated in the semifinals at the Olympics. Following a meet in Montreal on January 17, 1993, Johnson again tested positive for drugs—this time excessive levels of the male hormone testosterone—and he was banned for life. Although he had passed similar tests two days before and four days after the Montreal meet, Johnson chose not to appeal the ban.

The 1988 gold medal that Johnson lost did go to Carl Lewis after all, raising Lewis' career total to six golds and one silver.

In April 2003, it was revealed that at the 1988 US Olympic trials, Lewis had tested positive for the banned stimulants ephedrine, pseudoephedrine and phenylpropanaline. However, the United States Olympic Committee ruled that his use of the drugs had been inadvertent and Lewis was cleared to compete in Seoul. It is worth noting that the highest level Lewis recorded was six parts per million of the stimulants. Although this qualified as a positive result back in 1988, by 2000 research had shown that such a level was not performance-enhancing and the acceptable level was raised to ten parts per million for ephedrine and twenty-five parts per million for the other substances.

1992 Barcelona C: 81, N: 66, D: 8.1. WR: 9.86 (F. Carlton Lewis)

1. Linford Christie	GBR	9.96
2. Frank Fredericks	NAM	10.02
3. Dennis Mitchell	USA	10.04
4. Bruny Surin	CAN	10.09
5. Leroy Burrell	USA	10.10
6. Olapade Adeniken	NGR	10.12
7. Raymond Stewart	JAM	10.22
8. Davidson Ezinwa	NGR	10.26

Ben Johnson was not the only Jamaican-born sprinter who tested positive for prohibited drugs at the 1988 Olympics. Linford Christie's doping test revealed traces of the banned stimulant pseudoephedrine. But because the amount was so small, Christie was not disqualified or otherwise punished. The vote of the IOC medical commission was 11-10. On August 25, 1991, Christie was one of the entrants in one of the greatest 100-meter races of all time—the world championship final in Tokyo. Carl Lewis won that race, setting a world record of 9.86. He was followed by Leroy Burrell at 9.88, Dennis Mitchell at 9.91, Christie at 9.92, Frank Fredericks at 9.95, and Raymond Stewart at 9.96—the first and only time that six runners have beaten ten seconds in one race. Christie was so discouraged by the result that he considered retiring.

Christie had a mixed reputation. On the one hand, he was reasonably popular with the public and was voted Britain's sexiest athlete in 1991. On the other hand, his defensive and hypersensitive demeanor earned him less respect with the press and with fellow athletes. As quartermiler Derek Redmond put it, Christie was "Britain's best-balanced athlete, because he has a chip on both shoulders."

Christie's Barcelona chances were improved when Lewis, winner of every major championship race since 1983, was weakened by a virus and placed only sixth at the US Olympic trials, qualifying only for the 4 × 100-meter relay and the long jump.

Meanwhile, Christie, at age 32, was having his best season ever. His only loss was by 1/100 of a second to Olapade Adeniken. However, Christie still had to overcome former world record holder Leroy Burrell, who had beaten him ten straight times over the past three years. In the Olympic quarterfinals, Christie finally broke that streak, edging Burrell 10.07 to 10.08 in the last heat. The following day, running into a 1.2-meters-per-second headwind, Burrell beat Christie 9.97 to 10.00 in the first semifinal. The second semi was won by Fredericks in 10.17.

In the final, Burrell was charged with a false start even though he never left his blocks. Distressed, he was never a factor in the race. After a second delay, when Mitchell signaled that he was not ready, the runners finally took off. Haitian-born Bruny Surin grabbed the early lead and held it for 40 meters. Over the next 20 meters Christie caught first Fredericks and then Surin. By the 60-meter mark he was in first place and pulling away. Linford Christie is, by four years, the oldest man to win the Olympic 100 meters. Fredericks became the first black African to medal in the event, and, far from the hoopla and medal attention, Ray Stewart became the first man to run in three 100-meters finals.

1996 Atlanta C: 106, N: 75, D: 7.27. WR: 9.85 (Leroy Burrell)

1. Donovan Bailey	CAN	9.84 WR
2. Frank Fredericks	NAM	9.89
3. Ato Boldon	TRI	9.90
4. Dennis Mitchell	USA	9.99
5. Michael Marsh	USA	10.00
6. Davidson Ezinwa	NGR	10.14
7. Michael Green	JAM	10.16

DISQ: Linford Christie (GBR)

Donovan Bailey was born in Manchester, Jamaica, December 16, 1967, and moved to Canada when he was thirteen years old. In high school and college his favorite sport was basketball, but he ran track as well because it was a good way to meet girls. He graduated from Sheridan College in Toronto with a degree in economics and went to work as a marketing consultant for a brokerage firm. Later he created a successful business importing and exporting clothes. He did no competitive running for six years, but returned to the sport in 1991 because he knew he was naturally gifted. Still, prior to 1994, his best time was 10.36.

Under the direction of coach Dan Pfaff, Bailey progressed quickly and in 1995 he won the world championship with a time of 9.97. However the 1996 season saw others capturing the headlines. On June 1, Ato Boldon ran a 9.92; two weeks later, Dennis Mitchell matched that time. Both of them beat Bailey in Stockholm on July 8. On July 3, Frank Fredericks clocked a 9.86 into the wind for the fastest wind-adjusted time in history. Fredricks completed the pre-Olympic season undefeated.

In Atlanta, Boldon won his quarterfinal heats in 9.95. Two heats later, Fredericks ran a 9.93: the fastest non-final time ever recorded. The following evening, Fredericks won the first semifinal in 9.94, with Bailey, after a false start, placing second in 10.00. The second semifinal was won by Boldon in 9.93. Mitchell was second at 10.00 and third place was taken by defending champion Linford Christie who, at age 36, was already a grandfather.

The final was scheduled to start at 9 p.m., but it would be several minutes before the 10-second race was finally concluded. First Christie false started. Then Boldon false started. Then Linford Christie was charged with a second false start and was disqualified. It was the first time in his long career that he had suffered such a fate. Christie did not go quietly, arguing with the officials and, while the seven remaining finalists waited, refusing to leave the track. Finally, the track referee, John Chaplin, showed him the red marker indicating disqualification and Christie retreated into the tunnel, throwing his shoes into a trashcan.

On the fourth try, the runners broke cleanly. Bailey, as usual, was the slowest out of the blocks. Mitchell showed in front first, then Boldon. At 60 meters, Frank Fredericks took over the lead, but by this time Bailey, who had been fifth at 40 meters, was running an incredible 27 miles per hour (12.1 meters per second). He shot past the others and crossed the finish line in world record time. The race was so fast that Dennis Mitchell had the unfortunate and unprecedented experience of breaking ten seconds and not winning a medal. Immediately after his win Bailey dedicated the race to his uncle Keith, who was succumbing to pancreatic cancer. Unknown to Bailey, his uncle had passed away the night before the final, but his family did not tell him until after the race.

While Donovan Bailey set off on a victory lap, Linford Christie rather crudely ran past the stands himself, waving to the spectators who were giving Bailey a standing ovation. Even then, Christie's career of controversy was not over. In July 1998 he won a libel suit against a journalist who accused him of taking steroids. After the judgment, Christie told the press, "I am living proof that success achieved after hard, natural, drug-free work lasts so much longer and is so much sweeter." Seven months later, at a meet in Germany, he tested positive for the steroid nandrolone.

2000 Sydney C: 97, N: 71, D: 9.23. WR: 9.79 (Maurice Greene)

1. Maurice Greene	USA	9.87
2. Ato Boldon	TRI	9.99
3. Obadele Thompson	BAR	10.04
4. Dwain Chambers	GBR	10.08
5. Jonathan Drummond	USA	10.09
6. Darren Campbell	GBR	10.13
7. Kim Collins	SKN	10.17

DNF: Aziz Zakari (GHA)

Maurice Greene watched the 100 meters final at the 1996 Olympics from the stands. Tears came to his eyes as Donovan Bailey won in world record time. Greene told his father, "They will never have an Olympic 100-meter final without me again as long as I'm running." Two months later, Greene and his father drove from their home in Kansas City to Los Angeles so that Maurice could train with respected coach John Smith and his HIS training group. By the spring of 1997, Greene was discouraged, borrowing money and scanning the classified ads for a job. But then John Smith's instruction started to work for Greene. He won the US national title in 9.90 and edged Bailey to win the world championship in Athens in 9.86. On June 16, 1999, Greene returned to Athens and set a world record of 9.79. This was the same time that Ben Johnson, augmented by steroids, had run at the 1988 Olympics. Two months later, Greene successfully defended his world championship. By the end of the year, he had earned $3 million.

Although he lost four of eleven races in the 2000 pre-Olympic season, Greene went to Sydney as the overwhelming favorite. In his semifinal heat he was matched with two of his HIS training partners, Jon Drummond and Ato Boldon. They all qualified for the final by finishing 1-2-3. In the final, Greene showed ahead midway through the race and pulled away to a clear victory. By finishing third, Oba Thompson became the first athlete to earn an Olympic medal while representing Barbados. (In 1960, quarter-miler Jim Wedderburn had won a bronze medal as a member of the relay team of the British West Indies.)

2004 Athens C: 74, N: 57, D: 8.22. WR: 9.78 (Tim Montgomery)

1. Justin Gatlin	USA	9.85
2. Francis Obikwelu	POR	9.86
3. Maurice Greene	USA	9.87
4. Shawn Crawford	USA	9.89
5. Asafa Powell	JAM	9.94
6. Kim Collins	SKN	10.00
7. Obadele Thompson	BAR	10.10

DNF: Abdul Aziz Zakari (GHA)

The favorite in the 100-meter competition was defending Olympic champion Maurice Greene, who had returned to training after suffering a broken leg in a motorcycle accident on a Los Angeles freeway in 2002. In the first round in Athens, 25-year-old Shawn Crawford ran the fastest-ever first-round Olympic time: 10.02 seconds. Greene (10.18), Asafa Powell (10.06), Justin Gatlin (10.07) and Nigerian-born Francis Obikwelu (10.09) all won their heats as well. Crawford recorded the fastest time in the second round as well, in 9.89 seconds. In the first semifinal heat, Crawford edged out Gatlin 10.07-10.09, while in the second Asafa Powell finished in 9.95 seconds, ahead of both Obikwelu and Greene, tied at 9.97. The final seemed wide open. Gatlin and Collins got off to the fastest start, with Collins slightly ahead after 50 meters, Crawford in third just ahead of Obikwelu, and Greene in fifth. As Collins began to fade, Obikwelu moved up to second, but could not close the gap on Gatlin, who ran a personal best of 9.85 seconds to win gold. Obikwelu, also registering a personal best, held off Greene for silver. It was the first time in Olympic history that five runners broke the 10-second mark.

Gatlin attributed part of his speed to a pre-race confrontation in the locker room, when he was approached by a man seeking to take pictures of Gatlin's tattoos. The man, Alex Kolenko, was from the IAAF and was checking for advertising transfers, which some athletes use to covertly advertise their sponsors. Kolenko's request to see Gatlin's tattoo so fired up the athlete that he credited it for some of his speed, "He hyped me up . . . He made me so angry, I should thank him."

One hour after Gatlin crossed the finish line, his coach, Trevor Graham, admitted to his role in tipping off the Bay Area Laboratory Co-Operative (BALCO) investigation by anonymously sending a syringe of the previously unknown steroid THG to the US Anti-Doping Agency (USADA). The resulting doping scandal implicated eight of Graham's athletes and later led to Graham's own indictment for lying to federal investigators. The revelation was only the latest in a series of controversies in Gatlin's career. In 2001, at the US Junior World Championships, Gatlin tested positive for amphetimines and was subsequently given a two-year ban by the IAAF, which later reduced his sentence to one year after determining that the amphetamines came from a prescribed medicine for attention deficit disorder. Gatlin was reinstated in 2002 with the warning that another violation might trigger a lifetime ban.

Almost two years after winning the gold medal, in May 2006, Gatlin appeared to set a new world record in the 100 meters. He celebrated for two days before the IAAF announced that Gatlin's time of 9.766 had been incorrectly rounded down to 9.76 when it should have been rounded up to 9.77, and that rather than breaking the previous world record set by Asafa Powell, Gatlin had simply tied it.

In April 2006 Gatlin tested positive for testosterone after participating in the Kansas Relays. Although he maintained his innocence, Gatlin did not dispute the test result. Because of his prior positive test, Gatlin was given an eight-year ban by the US Anti-Doping Agency that was later reduced to four years. Trevor Graham claimed that Gatlin had been doped without his knowledge by Chris Whetstine, Gatlin's massage therapist, whom he accused of sabotaging Gatlin by rubbing steroid-laced ointment onto Gatlin's legs just before the race. In 2003 Whetstine had been disciplined by the Oregon Board of Massage Therapists for "unprofessional conduct," and he had been fired earlier in 2006, but rehired shortly before the Kansas race. Cedric Walker, the former manager of USA Track and Field's relay program, was quoted by the *Washington Post* as having witnessed the potential incident. "All I saw was the massage therapist go into a bag and bring out something else," Walker said. "He rubbed something else on Justin . . . It was right there in front of me." Graham also testified to having seen Whetstine rub Gatlin with cream from a white tube with a pink squiggle on it. Graham said he later searched the Internet for such a tube, and found a Deep Hydrating Essential Aloe Cream marketed by Sarati Laboratories (with a large pink S on the tube), which contained the hormone Dehydroepiandrosterone (DHEA).

The *Washington Post* later claimed to uncover evidence that Gatlin's positive test would have been consistent with the use of steroid cream, but noted that it would be impossible to tell conclusively. However, the

Post also concluded that it would have been foolish for Gatlin to have allowed himself to be rubbed with the cream, or for Graham to have knowingly allowed its use, as the active ingredient is not known to enhance athletic performance, but is easily detectible in doping tests.

2008 Beijing C: 80, N: 64, D: 8.16. WR: 9.72 (Usain Bolt)

1. Usain Bolt	JAM	9.69	WR
2. Richard Thompson	TRI	9.89	
3. Walter Dix	USA	9.91	
4. Churandy Martina	NLA	9.93	
5. Asafa Powell	JAM	9.95	
6. Michael Frater	JAM	9.97	
7. Marc Burns	TRI	10.01	
8. Darvis Patton	USA	10.03	

Four months before the start of the Beijing Olympics, at an international meet in Kingston, Jamaica, a little-known sprinter named Usain Bolt surprised himself by running the second-fastest 100 meters ever recorded: 9.76 seconds. The time was just two-hundredths of a second off the world record held by Asafa Powell. More impressive was the fact that Bolt was only running the distance, on the advice of his coach, as a speed workout for the 200 meters event, which Bolt considered his specialty.

Usain St. Leo Bolt was born in Sherwood Content, a small village in the farming community of Trelawny, Jamaica, known mainly for its yams. His father, Wellesley, owned a grocery store, and his mother, Jennifer, was a dressmaker. They raised Usain and his sisters, Sadiki and Sherine, in modest circumstances.

As a child, Bolt's primary interest was cricket, although he was never very good at it. By the age of ten, he had switched to track and began running for his primary school team, representing Trelawny at the national primary schools meet. By high school he was focusing seriously on the 200 meters and 400 meters, winning both events at the Jamaican high school championships during his senior year. Abnormally tall for a sprinter—a full 6ft 4in (1.93 meters) by the time he turned 15—Bolt made up for his slow start times with a long, powerful stride.

In 2002, one month shy of his 16th birthday, Bolt won the 2002 World Junior Championship 200 meters title, becoming the youngest junior world champion in history. The following year he defended his title, equaling the junior world record of 20.13 seconds. In 2004, at the CARIFTA Games in Bermuda, Bolt became the first junior athlete to break the 20-second barrier, setting a junior world record of 19.93 seconds.

Bolt was offered several track scholarships in the United States, but chose to stay and train in Jamaica.

After turning professional in 2004, he struggled with injuries, including scoliosis, which affected his hamstrings. In a terrible performance at the Athens Olympics he went out in the first round of the 200 meters. Despite his natural talents, Bolt had a reputation for being lazy and prone to partying. In late 2004 he switched coaches to Glen Mills, a veteran sprinting coach, and the following year he finished eighth at the 2005 world championships in Helsinki.

Over the next two years Bolt's performances slowly began to improve. He was interested in running the 100 meters event and made a deal with his coach: if he could break the 200 meters national record, Mills would let him compete in the 100 meters. At the 2007 Jamaican championships Bolt did just that, breaking the 36-year-old national record set by Don Quarrie with a run of 19.75. Then, less than a month after his near-world record in Kingston, he did break the world record at a meet in New York, finishing more than a yard ahead of reigning world champion Tyson Gay—whose own time was only one-hundredth of a second off his personal best (9.85). It was only the fourth time Bolt had run the 100 meters as a professional.

Bolt's main competition at the Olympics was expected to come from Gay, who was recovering from a difficult 2007 season (his long-time coach Lance Brauman had spent 366 days in prison after being found guilty of mail fraud and embezzlement). Two days before Brauman was released, Gay managed to sweep both the 100-meter and 200-meter titles at the 2007 world championships in Osaka, Japan, becoming the third man in history to do so.

Gay's pre-Olympic season was more problematic. He failed to qualify for the 200 meters event after suffering a severe cramp during the US qualifying trials, and then nearly missed out on the 100 meters when he eased up too early during a qualifying run. Gay managed to get across the line in time to advance, and then responded by setting a US record (9.77) in his quarterfinal heat: the fourth-fastest 100 meters ever run. One month before the Opening Ceremony, Gay recorded the fastest 100 meters ever recorded, 9.68 seconds, but it was not eligible for a world record due to a strong tailwind (+4.1m/s).

Rounding out the medal favorites was Asafa Powell, who had held the world record for nearly three years before losing it to Bolt. The youngest of six brothers, Powell had lost two of them in 2002 and 2003: one shot and killed in a New York taxi cab and another struck down by a heart attack while playing American football. Powell edged Bolt by one-hundredth of a second at a meet in Stockholm one month before the Games.

The preliminary round in Beijing went according to form, with Bolt, Powell and Gay finishing first in their heats. Bolt and Powell led their quarterfinal heats, while Gay was pipped by Richard Thompson. The biggest surprise came during the semifinal round, when a struggling Gay finished fifth in his heat and failed to advance. With Gay out of the final, the question was not whether Usain Bolt would win gold, but by how much—he had won each of his heats easily and recorded the fastest times in both the quarterfinal and semifinal rounds.

Racing with his left shoe unlaced, Bolt got off to the second-slowest start of the eight men in the final. At the 30-meter mark he was still in fourth place, but was already using his long stride to make up the deficit. By the halfway point he had moved into the lead and was pulling away with breathtaking ease. Fifteen meters short of the line he began to ease up and celebrate, spreading his arms and beating his chest as he crossed the finish line. Despite this, he managed to better his own world record by three-hundredths of a second.

This was the first 100-meter race in Olympic history in which six men finished in under 10 seconds. Bolt also earned Jamaica's first gold medal in the event. Several sprinters of Jamaican origin had won it previously, but always for other countries.

What would have happened had Bolt not eased up at the end? One month after the Olympics, a team of scientists at the University of Oslo attempted to answer the question, analyzing footage of the race from NBC, the BBC and the Norwegian Broadcasting Company. The team calculated that he could have recorded a time of 9.55 seconds had he not slowed down. Their findings were published in the *American Journal of Physics.*

As for Bolt, at the 2009 world championships in Berlin he shattered his world record with a time of 9.58 seconds, finishing 0.13 seconds ahead of Tyson Gay in second place. His world record-breaking margin (0.11) was the largest since the start of official digital time measurements in 1977.

The overwhelming favorite to repeat at the 2011 world championship, Bolt was disqualified when he false-started in the final.

200 METERS

The 200-meter race is one half lap—a sprint around a curve. Because the runners must stay in their lanes, there is a staggered start so that all runners end up covering the same distance. Like the 100 meters, the 200 meters has been dominated by runners from English-speaking countries. Anglophones have won 20 of 24 gold medals and a startling 62 of 72 total medals.

1896 not held

1900 Paris C: 8, N: 7, D: 7.22. WR (220 yards): 21.2 (Bernie Wefers)

1. J. Walter Tewksbury	USA	22.2
2. Norman Pritchard	GBR/IND	22.8
3. Stanley Rowley	AUS	22.9
4. William Holland	USA	—

With this victory, Walter Tewksbury earned his fifth medal of the games. He had already won the 400-meter hurdles, finished second in the 60-meter and 100-meter sprints, and third in the 200-meter hurdles. Second-place finisher Norman Pritchard has been the subject of much research by Olympic historians. His parents were English, but he was born in a suburb of Calcutta, India, on June 23, 1875. Pritchard visited England in 1900 and in competitions that he entered, he was listed as representing both the Bengal Presidency Athletic Club of India and the London Athletic Club, which has led to disputes as to his true nationality when he took part in the 1900 Olympics. Pritchard returned to India and served as secretary of the Indian Football Association. After being involved in the jute business, Pritchard turned to acting. He moved to the United States in 1913 and, as Norman Trevor, achieved success on the stage. He is known to have appeared in at least 28 plays on Broadway between 1914 and 1926. He also acted in 27 movies, most notably *Dancing Mothers* (1926) with Clara Bow, *Beau Geste* (1926) with Ronald Colman, and *The Love Trap* (1929), which was directed by William Wyler.

1904 St. Louis C: 7, N: 2, D: 8.31. WR (220 yards): 21.2 (Bernie Wefers)

1. C. "Archie" Hahn	USA	21.6 OR
2. Nathaniel Cartmell	USA	21.9
3. William Hogenson	USA	—
4. Fay Moulton	USA	—

Cartmell, Hogenson, and Moulton each false started once, which, according to the rules at that time, resulted in their being penalized two yards. In point of fact, however, they were only set back one yard because there was not enough room. Hahn took good advantage of his head start and led the entire way. Cartmell closed within one yard, but Hahn pulled away again and won by three yards. Commented Cartmell, "He's little, but he certainly can run."

1906 not held

1908 London C: 43, N 14, D: 7.23. WR: (220 yards): 21.2 (Bernie Wefers, Dan Kelly)

1. Robert Kerr	CAN	22.6
2. Robert Cloughen	USA	22.6e
3. Nathaniel Cartmell	USA	22.7e
4. George Hawkins	GBR	22.9e

Bobby Kerr was born in Enniskillen, Ireland. When he was seven years old his family moved to Canada, settling in Hamilton, Ontario. As a teenager Kerr joined the International Harvester Fire Brigade, which prided itself on the speed of its members. In 1904 Kerr represented Canada at the St. Louis Olympics sleeping on the floor of a friend's house to save money. He had hoped to compete at Athens in 1906, but not enough money could be raised to pay his passage. He did make it to London, where, ten days before the Olympics, he swept both sprints at the British AAA championships. At the 1908 Olympics he rebounded from the disappointment of finishing third in the 100 meters to win the 200 meters by less than a foot. The following year Kerr returned to Ireland and fulfilled his dream of representing the nation of his birth in an international meet. In 1928 he was the captain of the Canadian Olympic team, and in 1932 he was manager of the track and field division. Cloughen, the silver medalist, did not qualify for the US team and was only able to compete because his parents paid his way.

1912 Stockholm C: 61, N: 19, D: 7.11. WR (220 yards): 21.2 (Bernie Wefers, Dan Kelly, Ralph Craig)

1. Ralph Craig	USA	21.7
2. Donald Lippincott	USA	21.8
3. William Applegarth	GBR	21.9
4. Richard Rau	GER	22.2
5. Charles Reidpath	USA	22.3
6. Donnell Young	USA	22.3

1920 Antwerp C: 48, N: 22, D: 8.20. WR (220 yards): 21.2 (Bernie Wefers, Dan Kelly, Ralph Craig, Howard Drew, William Applegarth)

1. Allen Woodring	USA	22.0
2. Charles Paddock	USA	22.0e
3. Harry Edward	GBR	22.1e
4. Loren Murchison	USA	22.2e
5. George Davidson	NZL	22.3e
6. Jack Oosterlaak	SAF	22.4e

Allen Woodring of Syracuse University had qualified for the US team only as an alternate, but when George Massengale of Missouri was stiffened by an attack of rheumatism, Woodring was allowed to compete. In the final Paddock led from the start, but Woodring caught him at the 180-meter mark. Just as Paddock began the takeoff of his flying finish, Woodring flashed by him to steal the victory. The young New Yorker couldn't believe he had won and was sure that Paddock had graciously allowed him to finish first. Paddock finally convinced him that he had given his all and that the victory was legitimate.

1924 Paris C: 62, N: 32, D: 7.9. WR: 21.0 (Charles Paddock)

1. Jackson Scholz	USA	21.6	EOR
2. Charles Paddock	USA	21.7	
3. Eric Liddell	GBR	21.9	
4. George Hill	USA	22.0	
5. Bayes Norton	USA	22.0	
6. Harold Abrahams	GBR	22.3	

The day before the semifinals and final, Charley Paddock was convinced that he was over the hill and could never succeed the following day. His friend Douglas Fairbanks took him home, and together they dined and joked with Mary Pickford and Maurice Chevalier, who entertained them with imitations of Paavo Nurmi and Harold Abrahams, who had already won the 100 meters and who had beaten Charley in the first round of the 200 earlier that day. After dinner Fairbanks and Chevalier went for a walk while Mary Pickford gave Paddock an inspirational pep talk. She told him that his fate rested in his own hands. "If you believe in yourself," she said, "you will win tomorrow."

Paddock took her advice to heart, slept well, and awoke the next day refreshed and relaxed. He won his semifinal heat with ease, with Scholz winning the other semi. In the final Abrahams fell behind quickly while the others ran almost evenly. By the 120-meter mark Paddock had opened up a two-foot lead, but Scholz came on strong, reaching Paddock's shoulder with ten yards to go. In the final stride he moved ahead and won by less than a foot. Paddock pulled a ligament in his thigh in his final leap and collapsed to the ground beyond the finish line.

Scholz, who was born in Buchanan, Michigan, later made his living as an author of "pulp" fiction, publishing 31 sports novels. Interest in Scholz was renewed with the release of the film *Chariots of Fire,* which took great liberties in its portrayal of him. There is one scene in the film in which Scholz, just before the start of the 400 meters, approaches Eric Liddell and hands him a piece of paper inscribed with a religious message. Scholz actually did no such thing—he wasn't even religious. This put him in a difficult situation. When *Chariots of Fire* became a hit, the 84-year-old Scholz, now living in Delray Beach, Florida, was inundated with mail from people requesting spiritual inspiration. "I'm afraid," he told reporters, "that my religious background was rather casual." Indeed, when asked what he best remembered about Harold Abrahams, who had finished in front of him in the 1924 100 meters final, Scholz replied, "I remember his ass."

1928 Amsterdam C: 62, N: 30, D: 8.1. WR (track with curve): 20.6 (Roland Locke)

1. Percy Williams	CAN	21.8
2. Walter Rangeley	GBR	21.9
3. Helmuth Körnig	GER	21.9
4. Jackson Scholz	USA	21.9
5. John Fitzpatrick	CAN	22.1
6. Jakob Schüller	GER	22.2

The early rounds saw unusually stiff competition. In the quarterfinals Helmuth Körnig, pressed by Walter Rangeley of Salford, Lancashire, and Charlie Borah, the US champion, equaled the Olympic record of 21.6. Since only two from each heat advanced to the semifinals, Borah was eliminated. The first semi saw the fall of Charley Paddock, who finished fifth behind Williams and Rangeley. The second semi was won by Körnig, with defending champion Scholz second. In the final Körnig led coming out of the turn, but with 50 meters to go he was passed by Williams and Rangeley. Williams, running his eighth race in four days, pulled away and won by almost a yard. A dead heat was declared for third place between Körnig and Scholz, and a rerun between the two was ordered. However, by the time this decision had been reached, Scholz had already broken training, so he forfeited the runoff. Subsequent examination of the photo-finish revealed that Körnig had actually won third place anyway. That night Williams wrote in his diary: "Telegrams galore. The girls' team sent flowers to me. Hot dog!"

1932 Los Angeles C: 25, N: 13, D: 8.3. WR: 20.6 (Roland Locke, James Carlton)

1. T. "Eddie" Tolan	USA	21.2 OR (21.12)
2. George Simpson	USA	21.4
3. Ralph Metcalfe	USA	21.5
4. Arthur Jonath	GER	21.5
5. Carlos Bianchi Luti	ARG	21.6
6. William Walters	SAF	21.9

One man who did not compete in the 1932 Olympics was James Carlton of Lismore, New South Wales, who had beaten George Simpson twice. On January 16, 1932, Carlton shocked the world by winning the Australian 220-yard championship in 20.6, around the curve of an oval track. Speculation on Carlton's chance for an Olympic gold medal was cut short when the 24-year-old became a monk and retired to a monastery. In the quarterfinals at Los Angeles the Olympic record of 21.6, which had first been set by Archie Hahn back in 1904, was broken in each of the four heats. In the first two heats it was lowered to 21.5 by Metcalfe, who had won the US trials, and by Tolan, who had edged Metcalfe to win the 100 meters gold medal the day before. In the third heat Bianchi broke the record again, at 21.4, and in the fourth heat his time was matched by sportswriter Arthur Jonath. The following day the first heat of the semifinals was won by Metcalfe, with Simpson beside him. In the second semi, won by Jonath, Tolan was almost eliminated. Content to qualify for the final with a third-place finish, Tolan almost failed to notice the closing rush of Canadian Harold Wright, who closed within a foot but fell short.

Bianchi had the quickest start in the final, but as they came out of the turn Simpson of Ohio State was leading by almost a yard. Tolan, who chewed gum while he ran, surged ahead with 50 meters to go, stumbled just before the finish, and held on to win by five or six feet. When films of the race were viewed, it was discovered that Metcalfe had inadvertently been forced to dig his starting holes three or four feet behind the spot where they should have been, which deprived him of a silver medal. Metcalfe was offered a rerun by race officials, but he didn't want to jeopardize the US medal sweep and so declined.

1936 Berlin C: 44, N: 22, D: 8.5. WR: 20.6 (Roland Locke, James Carlton)

1. James "Jesse" Owens	USA	20.7 OR
2. M. "Mack" Robinson	USA	21.1
3. Martinus Osendarp	HOL	21.3
4. Paul Hänni	SWI	21.6
5. Lee Orr	CAN	21.6
6. Wijnand van Beveren	HOL	21.9

In the first round Jesse Owens set an Olympic record of 21.1 seconds, a time that he repeated in the second round and which was matched by Mack Robinson of Pasadena, California, in the semifinals. The final was run in a light rain, but this didn't prevent Owens from sprinting away from the field in record time. He led by almost two yards entering the straightaway and won by four yards to gain his third gold medal of the Berlin games. Silver medalist Robinson was something of a surprise. His high school coaches did not consider him athletic material and made his mother sign a statement absolving them of blame if his heart was damaged. Local businessmen paid his way to the US Olympic trials. His younger brother, Jackie Robinson, gained fame with the Brooklyn Dodgers as the first black major league player in modern baseball history.

Mel Patton, 1948
Redemption at 200 meters following a disappointing fifth-place finish in the 100.

1948 London C: 50, N: 26, D: 8.3. WR: 20.6 (Roland Locke, James Carlton)

1. Melvin Patton	USA	21.1
2. H. Norwood "Barney" Ewell	USA	21.1
3. Lloyd LaBeach	PAN	21.2
4. Herbert McKenley	JAM	21.2
5. Clifford Bourland	USA	21.3
6. Leslie Laing	JAM	21.6

McKenley and Bourland looked strongest in the preliminaries, both of them clocking 21.3 in each of the first two rounds. They also won their respective semifinal heats. In the final, however, it was the favorites who came through fastest. Patton, intent on making up for his disappointing fifth place finish in the 100, pulled away coming out of the turn and led by almost two meters. Ewell closed fast, but Patton held him off with a final spurt to win by two feet.

1952 Helsinki C: 71, N: 35, D: 7.23. WR: 20.6 (Roland Locke, James Carlton, Andrew Stanfield)

1. Andrew Stanfield	USA	20.7	EOR	(20.81)
2. W. Thane Baker	USA	20.8		(20.97)
3. James Gathers	USA	20.8		(21.08)
4. Emmanuel McDonald Bailey	GBR/TRI	21.0		(21.14)
5. Leslie Laing	JAM	21.2		(21.45)
6. Gerardo Bönnhoff	ARG	21.3		(21.59)

Andy Stanfield, a 6-foot 1-inch (1.85 meter), 24-year-old from Jersey City, New Jersey, was the unanimous favorite. As expected, he and Mac Bailey won the semifinals. Bailey ran well on the turn in the final, and as they hit the straightaway he was almost even with Stanfield, but Stanfield pulled away with ease and won by a yard and a half. The official times appear to be incorrect, since Bailey actually finished quite close to Gathers.

1956 Melbourne C: 67, N: 32, D: 11.27. WR: 20.6 (Roland Locke, James Carlton, Andrew Stanfield, Bobby Joe Morrow, W. Thane Baker)

1. Bobby Joe Morrow	USA	20.6	OR	(20.75)
2. Andrew Stanfield	USA	20.7		(20.97)
3. W. Thane Baker	USA	20.9		(21.05)
4. Michael Agostini	TRI	21.1		(21.35)
5. Boris Tokaryev	SOV/RUS	21.2		(21.42)
6. José Telles da Conceição	BRA	21.3		(21.56)

Bobby Morrow, the winner of the 100, was the favorite to win the 200 and become the first man since Jesse Owens to achieve a double in the Olympic sprints. He appeared for the first round with his left thigh bandaged, having suffered a slight groin pull in the final of the 100. Fortunately he was able to breeze through the early heats with little competition while allowing his muscle to heal. Abdul Khaliq of Pakistan ran 21.1 in both of the first two rounds, but wore himself out and was eliminated in the semifinals, which were won by Baker (21.1) and Stanfield (21.2). One unexpected finalist was Telles da Conceição, who had won the bronze medal in the high jump at Helsinki four years earlier. Baker was so upset at receiving the outside lane in the final, just as he had at Helsinki, that he put his starting blocks in backwards, necessitating a delay while he readjusted them. At the halfway mark Stanfield led Morrow by a foot, but 20 meters later Morrow swept past the defending champion and won going away, with Stanfield and Baker completing the second straight sweep of the 200 for the United States. Of the 15 medals awarded between 1932 and 1956, 13 were won by the United States, which took the first two places in five straight Olympics.

1960 Rome C: 62, N: 47, D: 9.3. WR: 20.5 (Peter Radford, Stonewall Johnson, O. Ray Norton)

1. Livio Berruti	ITA	20.5	EWR	(20.62)
2. Lester Carney	USA	20.6		(20.69)
3. Abdoulaye Seye	FRA/SEN	20.7		(20.83)
4. Marian Foik	POL	20.8		(20.90)
5. Stonewall Johnson	USA	20.8		(20.93)
6. O. Ray Norton	USA	20.9		(21.09)

On May 28, 1960, Peter Radford set a world record of 20.5. His record was matched five weeks later at the US Olympic trials by Stone Johnson of Dallas, Texas, and Ray Norton. In Rome, the first semifinal was won by Seye in 20.8. The second semi saw some bad seeding as the three world record holders were thrown together with local favorite Livio Berruti, with only three to qualify for the final. It was Radford who was left out, with Berruti, a chemistry student at the University of Padua, finishing first in the world record time of 20.5. The second semi was so hotly contested that last-place finisher, Paul Genevay of France, ran 21.0, good enough to take second place in the first semi.

"One hour before the final," Livio Berruti would later recall, "all the other athletes went down to the field to warm up. Me, I didn't go. They thought I was snubbing them; they didn't know that I was afraid. But this fear was my drug. I didn't join them until it was time to prepare my starting blocks fifteen minutes before the competition."

The final saw one false start by Berruti and Johnson, although neither was charged. Berruti, always strong on the curve, hit the straight with a one-yard lead, which he held until the finish. Norton was placed second with 80 meters to go, but he faded. After crossing the line, both Berruti, who ran with dark glasses, and Carney (of Akron, Ohio) fell to the ground. Berruti's victory was met with enthusiastic cheering that went on for five minutes, and after the medal ceremony he was led to the VIP box, where each Italian dignitary kissed him on both cheeks. Berruti was the first non-North American to win the 200 meters.

Thirty-six years later, Berruti would look back on his fellow athletes of 1960: "We were truly all friends, with an equality of souls and races and a desire to exchange ideas and compare our experiences. There was no nationality; we were citizens of the world. We were happy because we took part in sport for pleasure, with enthusiasm, with the primary idea of having a good time. The coach was still our friend and his scientific and physiological knowledge left a lot to be desired. Now athletes are research laboratories."

1964 Tokyo C: 57, N: 42, D: 10.17. WR: 20.2 (Henry Carr)

1. Henry Carr	USA	20.3	OR	(20.36)
2. O. Paul Drayton	USA	20.5		(20.58)
3. Edwin Roberts	TRI	20.6		(20.63)
4. Harry Jerome	CAN	20.8		(20.79)
5. Livio Berruti	ITA	20.8		(20.83)
6. Marian Foik	POL	20.8		(20.83)
7. Richard Stebbins	USA	20.8		(20.89)
8. Sergio Ottolina	ITA	20.9		(20.94)

This event went according to form. Drayton, a 25-year-old Army private, recorded the best series in the preliminaries (20.7, 20.9, and 20.5), but Carr, the world record holder, had paced himself well and turned it on in the final. Carr overtook Drayton quickly, led by a yard entering the stretch, and was able to extend his lead to win by over four feet. Carr had finished only fourth at the US Olympic trials, but was given the nod by US coaches over the third-place finisher, Bob Hayes.

After the Olympics, Carr became a professional football player for the New York Giants. Then he turned to gambling before straightening out his life. He worked with inner-city children, operated a

Henry Carr, 1964
From fourth at the US Olympic trials to a gold medal in Tokyo.

delicatessen, worked as a janitor and renovated houses. In 1998 he told the *Detroit News* how he and his running teammates circumvented the strict rules of amateurism that were enforced back in 1964: "I remember—like in the James Bond or mystery movies—in Tokyo . . . a shoe agent . . . goes into the bathroom and leaves an envelope under the stall, and I go into the stall after him . . . You get an envelope that had six, seven hundred or a couple of thousand dollars in fives and tens. You thought you were rich."

1968 Mexico City C: 49, N: 36, D: 10.16. WR: 19.92 (John Carlos)

1. Tommie Smith	USA	19.83	WR
2. Peter Norman	AUS	20.06	
3. John Carlos	USA	20.10	
4. Edwin Roberts	TRI	20.34	
5. Roger Bambuck	FRA	20.51	
6. Larry Questad	USA	20.62	
7. Michael Fray	JAM	20.63	
8. Joachim Eigenherr	GER	20.66	

There seemed little question that the battle for the gold medal would be between Tommie Smith and John Carlos, both students at San Jose State College in California and both members of the Olympic Project for Human Rights, a group of athletes organized to protest the treatment of blacks in the United States. The 6-foot 3-inch (1.90 meter), 180-pound Smith was an extraordinary runner who held 11 world records indoors and outdoors at distances up to 440 yards. He had also long-jumped 25 feet 11 inches (7.90 meters). Carlos, who grew up in Harlem, beat Smith for the first time (by three yards) at the US Olympic trials and clocked a world record time of 19.7 seconds. His record was never officially recognized because he was wearing multipronged "brush spike" shoes which, at the time, were considered illegal. At 6 feet 4 inches (1.93 meter) and 198 pounds, Carlos was the largest competitor in the 1968 200 meters, 90 pounds heavier than José Astacio, who represented El Salvador.

Tommie Smith, 1968

The joy – and the calm – of a world record run, before the storm that would rock the Olympics and, in a way, America.

In Mexico City Smith set the stage in the first round by tying the Olympic record of 20.3. But four heats later a surprise occurred when Peter Norman ran 20.2 to break the Olympic record. Norman, a 26-year-old physical education teacher and Salvation Army officer, had never beaten 20.5 until he arrived in Mexico. In the first heat of the second round Carlos slipped on the bend, but he regained his balance and won in 20.6. In the third heat Smith equaled Norman's earlier mark of 20.2. The semis were won by Carlos and Smith in 20.1, but Smith pulled an adductor muscle in his groin and limped off the field.

"I was 80 percent certain I was out," he said, but he made it to the starting line of the final anyway. Coming out of the turn Carlos led by one and one-half yards, but then Smith turned on his "Tommie-jets," in a stunning display of speed reminiscent of Bob Hayes' 4 × 100-meter relay anchor leg in Tokyo. He passed his teammate with 60 meters to go and won so decisively that he was able to raise his arms in victory ten yards from the tape and smile and wave as he crossed the finish line. Carlos turned his head to watch Smith go by, allowing Norman, who had been in only sixth place entering the straight, to slip by on the other side and take the silver medal with a final lunge.

Smith's victory caused a sensation, but it was nothing compared to the sensation that he and Carlos caused at the victory ceremony. Mounting the dais barefooted, they wore civil rights badges, as did Norman, who asked to join Smith and Carlos in their protest. Smith wore a black scarf around his neck and Carlos a string of beads as a memorial to those blacks who had been lynched. When "The Star-Spangled Banner" was played, Smith and Carlos bowed their heads and each raised one black-gloved hand in the Black Power salute. They later explained that their clenched fists symbolized black strength and unity and that their bare feet were a reminder of black poverty in the United States. They bowed their heads to express their belief that the words of freedom in the US national anthem only applied to Americans with white skin. Carlos told reporters, "White America will only give us credit for an Olympic victory. They'll say I'm an American, but if I did something bad, they'd say I was a Negro." Olympic officials were outraged. The International Olympic Committee demanded that the US Olympic Committee ban Smith and Carlos from further Olympic competition (i.e. the relays) and expel them from the Olympic Village. The USOC refused. The next morning the IOC told the USOC that if Smith and Carlos were not banned and expelled, the entire USA track and field team would be barred from competition. This time the US Olympic Committee complied.

The international response to the demonstration by Smith and Carlos was generally sympathetic, but back in the United States they were not so well received. Chicago sports columnist Brent Musburger spoke for the Establishment when he called them "black-skinned storm troopers." The two Olympic medalists found it difficult to make a living, and both their marriages broke up. Carlos' wife committed suicide. In 1972 Smith finally got a position as track coach at Oberlin College in Ohio. Six years later he moved to Santa Monica College in California. Carlos had an even tougher time—hustling, gambling, taking menial jobs. In 1977 he founded the John Carlos Youth Development Program in Los Angeles, which encouraged ghetto youth to become well educated. In February 1982, Carlos' Olympic experiences came full circle when he was hired by the Los Angeles Olympic Organizing Committee to promote the 1984 games and act as liaison with the black ghetto.

In retrospect, Smith and Carlos' gestures on the victory platform in Mexico City appear as eloquent expressions of nonviolent protest, while the reactions of the IOC and the USOC come off as knee-jerk traditionalism. Smith and Carlos made their point without interfering with anyone's free will. The same cannot be said of government-inspired boycotts or of the Black September guerrillas, whose attempt to stop the games was accompanied by murder. When Norman was asked why he had backed the Americans, he said that he supported human rights and opposed the "White Australia" immigration policy in his own country. John Carlos responded to criticisms that his political protest had tainted the games by pointing out that the Olympic movement was already highly political. "Why do you have to wear the uniform of your country?" he asked. "Why do they play national anthems? Why do we have to beat the Russians? Why do the East Germans want to beat the West Germans? Why can't everyone wear the same colors but wear numbers to tell them apart? What happened to the Olympic ideal of man against man?"

Thirty-two years after the Mexico City protest, John Carlos reflected on Peter Norman's role. Carlos told Mike Wise of the *New York Times*, "To wear the badge as a white individual, it made the statement even more powerful. During a crucial time in our lives, he was compassionate, understanding and he showed his manhood. I'll always respect and love him for that. Pete became my brother at that moment." And Carlos added: "A lot happened back then. But the most amazing thing was . . . I didn't know there was a white guy who could run that fast." On October 3, 2006, Norman died of a heart attack while mowing his front lawn. Smith and Carlos both served as pallbearers at his funeral.

1972 Munich C: 57, N: 42, D: 9.4. WR: 19.83 (Tommie Smith)

1. Valery Borzov	SOV/UKR	20.00
2. Larry Black	USA	20.19
3. Pietro Mennea	ITA	20.30
4. Lawrence Burton	USA	20.37
5. Charles Smith	USA	20.55
6. Siegfried Schenke	GDR	20.56
7. Martin Jellinghaus	GER	20.65
8. Hans-Joachim Zenk	GDR	21.05

Borzov completely dominated the opposition to become the first non-North American to win the Olympic sprint double. He won his first two heats in 20.64 and 20.30 despite the fact that he turned around several times to check the position of the other runners. In the first heat of the semifinals he turned and spoke to Larry Burton as he passed him with 50 meters to go. Burton was a 6-foot 2-inch (1.88 meter) Purdue football player who had run in his first track meet only eight months earlier, and had competed in his first 220-yard race a mere four and a half months before the Olympics. The winner of the second semi was Larry Black, a Florida-born student of North Carolina Central. In the final, Black came out of the turn with a slight lead, but with 70 meters to go Borzov appeared to shift into overdrive, rocketing ahead to a clear two-meter lead. With five meters left, Borzov turned back for a final look at Black and the others, then crossed the line with arms flung high. Mennea edged past Burton at the 175-meter mark to take third. During the second round Mennea had entertained the crowd by stripping down to his jock strap while changing into his running shorts. Borzov refused to participate in the postrace interview, stating, with some justification, that he had been treated in an insulting manner by US journalists after his victory in the 100.

Some people consider the athletes who finish fourth to be the big losers of the Olympics—so close to a medal, so far from glory. Not so Larry Burton. Burton returned to Purdue and earned All-American honors as a pass receiver. Prior to the Purdue–Notre Dame football game in 1974, a reporter suggested to Notre Dame coach Ara Parseghian that Burton would have a tough time against Notre Dame's pass defenders. "I don't know about that," replied Parseghian. "There are only three people in the world who are faster than Larry Burton, and they are not in the Notre Dame defensive backfield." Burton played five years in the NFL and then devoted his life to helping troubled young people at Boys' Town, Nebraska, and in California.

1976 Montreal C: 45, N: 33, D: 7.26. WR: 19.83 (Tommie Smith)

1. Donald Quarrie	JAM	20.22
2. Millard Hampton	USA	20.29
3. Dwayne Evans	USA	20.43
4. Pietro Mennea	ITA	20.54
5. Ruy da Silva	BRA	20.84
6. Bogdan Grzejszczak	POL	20.91
7. Colin Bradford	JAM	21.17
8. Hasely Crawford	TRI	1:19.60

Donald Quarrie's Olympic career began back in 1968 when he was 17 years old. He made it to Mexico City but injured himself during training and was unable to compete. In 1971 he won the Pan American Games in 19.86, the second-fastest electronically timed 200 on record, but at the Olympics in Munich he pulled a hamstring muscle in the semifinals and had to be carried off the field on a stretcher. At Montreal he had already finished second to Hasely Crawford in the 100 and was now the odds-on favorite to take the gold in the 200.

His challengers included one man who wanted to run but wasn't allowed to and another who didn't want to run but was forced to. James Gilkes of Guyana was the victor in the 1975 Pan American Games, but his government decided to boycott the Olympics. Gilkes appealed to the IOC to let him compete under the Olympic flag, but his request was denied. Pietro Mennea, on the other hand, was so disappointed with his performance at the Italian championships in July that he decided not to compete in Montreal. Public reaction to his decision was so strong that he changed his mind. Also in the running were Millard Hampton of San Jose and 17-year-old high school student Dwayne Evans of Phoenix.

Quarrie had the lead coming out of the turn. Hampton made a run at him, but Quarrie held on to win by two feet. His long quest for an Olympic gold medal finally fulfilled, Don Quarrie is now honored by a statue in his hometown of Kingston, Jamaica.

The three medalists took one of the slowest victory laps on record. Forced to stop when they encountered the victory ceremony for the javelin, it was ten minutes before they completed their circuit of the track.

Hasely Crawford, whom the official report lists as not finishing, suffered a cramp after 50 meters and ended up on the ground, but a California track fan named Pitch Johnson noted that Crawford never actually left his lane until after he had jogged past the finish line, so he did finish the race, albeit in a rather unusual time.

1980 Moscow C: 57, N: 37, D: 7.28. WR: 19.72 (Pietro Mennea)

1. Pietro Mennea	ITA	20.19
2. Allan Wells	GBR	20.21
3. Donald Quarrie	JAM	20.29
4. Silvio Leonard Tartabull	CUB	20.30
5. Bernhard Hoff	GDR	20.50
6. Leszek Dunecki	POL	20.68
7. Marian Woronin	POL	20.81
8. Osvaldo Lara Cañizares	CUB	21.19

Like Donald Quarrie before him, Pietro Mennea of Barletta, Italy, had to wait until his third try to gain an Olympic gold medal. In 1979 at the World Student Games in Mexico City, Mennea had run 19.72 to break Tommie Smith's 11-year-old world record. But that same year, before a hometown crowd at the European Cup in Torino, Mennea had lost to Allan Wells. For this insult, the otherwise blameless Wells had become known as "The Beast" in Mennea's household. For the final of the 1980 Olympics, Mennea drew the outside lane, with "The Beast" just behind him in Lane 7. At the sound of the gun Wells tore out of the blocks at full speed and had made up the stagger after only 50 meters. Coming out of the turn he had a two-meter lead over Leonard, with Quarrie and Mennea close behind. But Mennea, as usual, shifted gears in the straight, closing the gap with each stride until he moved ahead of Wells with less than ten meters to go.

Pietro Mennea, 1980
Besting the beast by 2/100ths of a second

At the last moment Wells attempted the same final dip which had brought him victory in the 100, but this time he fell short. Quarrie's third-place finish, impressive as it was, was all the more remarkable considering he had been injured in an auto accident the previous year. Mennea, employed by the public relations department of Fiat, had received his doctorate in political science two weeks before the Olympics. He had been a candidate for local office for the Social Democratic Party, which supported the Moscow boycott, but 15 years of training and his belief in the Olympic ideal proved more important than the party line, and he decided to enter anyway. Mennea did serve as a member of the European Parliament from 1999 to 2004.

1984 Los Angeles C: 76, N: 58, D: 8.8. WR: 19.72 (Pietro Mennea)

1. F. Carlton Lewis	USA	19.80 OR
2. Kirk Baptiste	USA	19.96
3. Thomas Jefferson	USA	20.26
4. João Batista da Silva	BRA	20.30
5. Ralf Lübke	GER	20.51
6. Jean-Jacques Boussemart	FRA	20.55
7. Pietro Mennea	ITA	20.55
8. Adeoye Mafe	GBR	20.85

Carl Lewis, holder of the low-altitude world record with a 1983 time of 19.75, won his third gold medal by getting off to an unusually fast start. He came out of the curve with a two meter lead and then held off the fast-finishing Kirk Baptiste to win by one and one-half meters. Considering that the race was run into the wind, Lewis' time was more impressive than Mennea's high-altitude world record of 19.72 or his own 19.75. Pietro Mennea, in seventh place, became the first runner to qualify for the final of the same event in four straight Olympics. He later revealed that in 1984 he had taken human growth hormone, which was not banned at the time.

1988 Seoul C: 72, N: 59, D: 9.28. WR: 19.72 (Pietro Mennea)

1. Joseph DeLoach	USA	19.75 OR
2. F. Carlton Lewis	USA	19.79
3. Robson Caetano da Silva	BRA	20.04
4. Linford Christie	GBR	20.09
5. Atlee Mahorn	CAN	20.39
6. Gilles Quénéhervé	FRA	20.40
7. Michael Rosswess	GBR	20.51
8. Bruno Marie-Rose	FRA	20.58

Carl Lewis suffered his first 200-meter defeat in two years when he was beaten 19.96-20.01 at the US Olympic trials by his training partner, 21-year-old Joe DeLoach of Bay City, Texas. The two had first met when DeLoach, the youngest of 13 children, had asked Lewis for his autograph. In Seoul, Lewis led coming out of the turn. DeLoach drew even after 150 meters, then surged ahead 30 meters from the finish. In 2003, it was revealed that both DeLoach and Lewis had tested positive for stimulants at the US Olympic Trials. They were both let off with a warning. By current standards, neither of them would have registered a positive result.

1992 Barcelona C: 79, N: 65, D: 8.6. WR: 19.72 (Pietro Mennea)

1. Michael Marsh	USA	20.01
2. Frank Fredericks	NAM	20.13
3. Michael Bates	USA	20.38
4. Robson Caetano da Silva	BRA	20.45
5. Olapade Adeniken	NGR	20.50
6. John Regis	GBR	20.55
7. Oluyemi Kayode	NGR	20.67
8. Marcus Adam	GBR	20.80

The overwhelming favorite in this event was world champion Michael Johnson of Texas. The first man to be ranked number one in both the 200 meters and 400 meters, since May 19, 1990, Johnson had won 29 straight finals at the shorter distance until he was beaten by Frank Fredericks in Rome on June 9. Nineteen days later he came roaring back to win the US Olympic trials in 19.79. But on July 13, Johnson contracted food poisoning after eating at a restaurant in Salamanca, Spain. He did not recover fully in time for the Olympics and was eliminated in the semifinals. Meanwhile, Mike Marsh was tearing up the track. In 1984 he had worked as a parking attendant at the Olympic fencing and volleyball venues. Eight years later he registered the fastest times in each of the first two rounds. In the semifinals he created a sensation when he was clocked in 19.73—a mere $\frac{1}{100}$ of a second shy of Pietro Mennea's 13-year-old world record. Because he didn't realize how fast he was running, Marsh, following the instructions of his coach, Tom Tellez, actually eased up over the last 15 meters in order to save his energy for the final.

By the time of the final the following evening, Marsh was feeling the pressure of being expected to break the world record. Determined to remain relaxed in the final, he overdid it and got off to an awful start. Marsh immediately took the situation in hand and streaked to a clear victory. Marsh was the third straight 200-meter champion to be coached by Tom Tellez.

Bronze medalist Michael Bates was actually a football player who ran track to stay in shape. He went on to a successful professional football career, earning places in the Pro Bowl as both a kickoff returner and as a defensive kick coverage specialist.

1996 Atlanta C: 78, N: 57, D: 8.1. WR: 19.66 (Michael Johnson)

1. Michael Johnson	USA	19.32 WR
2. Frank Fredericks	NAM	19.68
3. Ato Boldon	TRI	19.80
4. Obadele Thompson	BAR	20.14
5. Jeff Williams	USA	20.17
6. Jan Garcia	CUB	20.21
7. Patrick Stevens	BEL	20.27
8. Michael Marsh	USA	20.48

Michael Johnson's early elimination in Barcelona had been a bitter disapointment. He continued to dominate the 400 meters in 1993, but it wasn't until 1994 that he fully regained control at 200 meters. On July 28, 1994, he began another winning streak that included the 1995 world championship and climaxed on June 23, 1996, when, at the US Olympic Trials, he ran a 19.66 to break Pietro Mennea's seventeen-year-old world record.

Originally, the IAAF arranged the Olympic schedule so that the semifinals of the 200 meters were to be run the same day as the final of the 400 meters. Michael Johnson had won both events at the 1995 world championships and felt that he could do so again at the Olympics. He petitioned the IAAF to change the schedule. Initially the IAAF refused, but then relented and changed the schedule to allow completion of the entire 400 meters event, as well as a day of rest, before the opening round of the 200 meters.

On July 5, two weeks before the Olympics, Johnson's latest 200 meters win streak was stopped at 21, when Frank Fredericks beat him in Oslo 19.82 to 19.85. Still, Johnson held a 15-8 career advantage over Fredericks, who appeared to be his only serious challenger.

A university graduate with a degree in marketing, Johnson saw the Atlanta Games as an opportunity to elevate himself into the pantheon of running legends by becoming the first man to achieve a 200-400 double. He won the 400 in overwhelming fashion, but was irritated when his great moment was eclipsed by Carl Lewis who, on the same night, tied two venerable Olympic records by winning the same event (the long jump) for the fourth time and earning his ninth gold medal.

In addition, fifteen minutes before the men's 200 meters final, Marie-José Pérec won the women's 200 to match the same double that Johnson was attempting. Clearly, if Johnson wanted to reach the superstar status that he was aiming for, he would have to accomplish something special in the 200. And that is exactly what he did.

Johnson stumbled slightly coming out of the blocks, but recovered immediately. At 80 meters he accelerated dramatically and then, at 110 meters, he shifted into overdrive and pulled away to win by more than four meters. His time, an incredible 19.32, lowered the world record (and his own world record at that) by a phenomenal .34 seconds. Although Fredericks' 19.68 bettered Pietro Mennea's old world record, he seemed to be in a different race than Johnson, who ran the last 100 meters in 9.20 seconds.

Ato Boldon, who took the bronze medal, went straight up to Michael Johnson and bowed down in homage. Before taking his victory lap, Johnson, who had felt a twinge just before the finish line, wrapped his right hamstring with an ice bag. US decathlete Chris Huffins, who was on the infield at the time, commented, "The only thing that hurt his hamstring was the reentry burn," while Ato Boldon marveled, "19.32. That's not a time. It sounds like my dad's birthday."

When asked what it was like to run so fast, Johnson replied, "It was like the first time I went down the hill at the end of our street in the go-cart my father made for me."

Michael Johnson, 1996
A run for the ages, burying his own world record by an incredible .34 seconds.

2000 Sydney C: 97, N: 71, D: 9.23. WR: 19.32 (Michael Johnson)

1. Konstantinos Kenteris	GRE	20.09
2. Darren Campbell	GBR	20.14
3. Ato Boldon	TRI	20.20
4. Obadele Thompson	BAR	20.20
5. Christian Malcolm	GBR	20.23
6. Claudino da Silva	BRA	20.28
7. Coby Miller	USA	20.35
8. John Capel	USA	20.49

This race was supposed to be one of the highlights of the Sydney Olympics, the event where two superstars, 100 meters favorite Maurice Greene and 400 meters favorite Michael Johnson came together in a head-to-head duel. And both men had great credentials at 200 meters. Johnson was the world record holder and defending Olympic champion; Greene was the defending world champion. Their first clash, at the US Olympic trials on July 23, 2000, would also prove to be their last. Seventy meters into the trials final, Johnson grabbed his left thigh and fell to the ground. Barely twenty-five meters later, Greene also strained a hamstring muscle. Neither finished the race, which was then won by John Capel in 19.85.

By virtue of his trials victory, Capel became one of the new favorites, along with 100 meters medalists Ato Boldon and Oba Thompson. But there were more surprises to come. An early clue came in the first heat of the quarterfinals, when outsiders Darren Campbell and Kostas Kenteris recorded personal bests of 20.13 and 20.14. Capel also won his quarterfinal heat in 20.13. The following evening, Capel took the first semifinal, running 20.10 into the wind. In the second semi, Kenteris beat Campbell 20.20 to 20.23.

Capel looked to have the edge going into the final, but before the starter pulled the trigger, he jumped forward. The starter did not call a false start, so Capel reset himself. However, as he was doing so, the gun went off and Capel was left behind. Kenteris came out of the turn a meter behind Campbell, Boldon and Thompson, but sprinted past them all to gain a huge upset. Kenteris was the first Greek male runner to win an Olympic championship since Spiridon Louis won the marathon in 1896. Because the 27-year-old Kenteris had never won a major race, some were suspicious that his performance might have been chemically augmented. However, Kenteris, who had lost four years of his career to injuries, went on to win the world championship in 2001. As a point of information, all three medalists in the 2000 200 meters were born in the second half of 1973.

2004 Athens C: 54, N: 41, D: 8.26. WR: 19.32 (Michael Johnson)

1. Shawn Crawford	USA	19.79
2. Bernard Williams	USA	20.01
3. Justin Gatlin	USA	20.03
4. Frank Fredericks	NAM	20.14
5. Francis Obikwelu	POR	20.14
6. Stéphane Buckland	MRI	20.24
7. Tobias Unger	GER	20.64
DNS: Asafa Powell (JAM)		

On August 12, the day before the Athens Opening Ceremony, defending 200-meter Olympic champion Kostas Kenteris and defending 100-meter silver medalist Ekaterina Thanou failed to appear for a mandatory pre-competition drug test. The Greek duo, favorites in their respective events and revered by Greek fans, had been spotted in the Olympic village just hours earlier, but vanished before they could be reached by IOC officials for the test. Under Olympic rules, failing to show up for a drug test carries the same penalty as failing the test. What followed would turn out to be one of the strangest stories of the 2004 Olympics.

The pair turned up hours later in a nearby hospital, claiming that they had been involved in a motorcycle accident on the outskirts of Athens while rushing back to the Olympic Village for the drug test. Annoucing that they were too badly injured to travel, the pair spent five days in the hospital and failed to appear at an IOC disciplinary tribunal.

Police launched an investigation into the accident, describing it as "not natural." Despite the sprinters' claim that their motorcycle had skidded and crashed after hitting an oil slick on the outskirts of Athens, no accident had been reported and no ambulance was called for. For several days there were no known witnesses to the crash, nor any trace of the motorcycle involved. The pair said they had been picked up by a stranger who drove them to a hospital fifteen miles from the crash site, rather than one ten miles closer. The hospital issued a statement listing Kenteris and Thanou's injuries, including cranial trauma, whiplash, open leg wounds, abdominal bruises and muscle injuries.

As the police investigation continued, the story of the motorcycle accident unravelled. One man who claimed he had witnessed the accident was discovered to have an outstanding warrant for fraud after falsely posing as a lawyer. The man was sentenced to 14 months in prison. Twelve other people were charged with making false statements, including seven doctors at the hospital where the pair stayed. On August 17, Kenteris and Thanou left the hospital with no visible injuries, and appeared the next day before an IOC tribunal. After less than an hour of questioning, both athletes withdrew from the Olympic competition. On August 20, the police probe concluded that the pair had faked the motorcycle crash to avoid the drug test.

The same day, Greek investigators searched the office and warehouse owned by Christos Teskos, a former nutritional supplement salesman who coached both Kenteris and Thanou. Police found 30 boxes of steroids and 1,400 boxes of food supplements containing the banned stimulant ephedrine. An earlier raid in 2003 had uncovered 641 boxes of the banned supplement, leading to a $19,000 fine for Teskos. Emails soon surfaced linking Teskos to Victor Conte, founder of the Bay Area Laboratory Co-op (BALCO), the center of one of the largest doping scandals in Olympic history. Despite the fact that neither sprinter had actually failed a drug test, Kenteris and Thanou had been under suspicion after missing two other out-of-competition tests earlier that summer. After an IAAF investigation, the pair were handed two-year bans.

Shawn Crawford showed his speed in the quarterfinals, winning his heat easily in 19.95 seconds. The 100-meter champion, Justin Gatlin, Bernard Williams and 100-meter silver medalist Francis Obikwelu also won their heats. The next day, the semifinals were delayed when the largely Greek crowd began to whistle and chant "Kenteris, Kenteris!" Crawford and Williams faced each other in the first semi. They were even at the halfway-point, but Crawford pulled away to win 20.05 to 20.18. The second semi saw Gatlin edge Obikwelu by one hundredth of a second.

For the first time since 1912, the final was held the day after the semifinals, rather than the same day. The start of the final was delayed nearly ten minutes by a boisterous and rude Greek crowd, who whistled, chanted and hurled insults, ignoring pleas for quiet from Greek officials. When the final eventually did commence, Crawford trailed early, but surged past Gatlin and Williams off the turn and powered to victory in 19.79 seconds. Williams, third off the turn in front of Obikwelu, edged past Gatlin at the end to take silver. Crawford was known not only for his speed, but for his antics on the track. In addition to having appeared on a television show in a race against a zebra and a giraffe (the zebra and giraffe won), Crawford once tried to run the 200 meters while wearing a Phantom of the Opera mask. During the race, the mask slipped and Crawford veered off the course.

Both Crawford and Gatlin trained under controversial coach Trevor Graham, who was linked to eight positive drug tests by his athletes. As for Kenteris and Thanou, in June 2006, nearly two years after failing to show up for their pre-race drug tests, they admitted to violating doping rules and accepted their two-year bans from competition. They became re-eligible for competition in December of 2006.

2008 Beijing C: 63, N: 53, D: 8.20.
WR: 19.32 (Michael Johnson)

1. Usain Bolt	JAM	19.30	WR
2. Shawn Crawford	USA	19.96	
3. Walter Dix	USA	19.98	
4. Brian Dzingai	ZIM	20.22	
5. Christian Malcolm	GBR	20.40	
6. Kim Collins	SKN	20.59	

DISQ: Churandy Martina (NLA); Wallace Spearmon (USA)

In 2002, one month shy of his sixteenth birthday, Usain Bolt had won the 2002 World Junior Championship 200 meters title, becoming the youngest IAAF junior world champion in history. The following year he defended his title, equaling the junior world record of 20.13 seconds. In 2004, at the CARIFTA Games in Bermuda, he set a junior world record of 19.93 seconds, becoming the first junior athlete to break the 20-second barrier.

He was eliminated in the first round at the 2004 Athens Olympics, and the following year he finished eighth at the 2005 world championships in Helsinki. At the 2007 Jamaican championships, he broke the 36-year-old national record set by Don Quarrie with a run of 19.75. Two months later, at the 2007 world championships in Osaka, Japan, he earned the silver medal behind Tyson Gay.

By the time the 2008 Olympics rolled around, Bolt was the clear favorite in the 200 meters. His position was strengthened when Gay failed to qualify for the event after suffering a severe cramp in his left hamstring during the US Olympic trials. With Gay absent, the other top medal contenders included defending Olympic champion Shawn Crawford, 2003 world champion Kim Collins and double world championship medalist Wallace Spearmon.

Usain Bolt, 2008
Usain Bolt wins the 200 meters in world record time.

The 200 meters final was held four days after Bolt's victory in the 100 meters event and the day before his twenty-second birthday. As in the 100 meters, the gold medal was never seriously in doubt; this time, however, he did not ease up at the end. Clear of the field by the halfway mark, Bolt continued accelerating, dipping slightly at the line to finish eight meters ahead of Shawn Crawford in second place. It was the largest margin of victory since the event was first contested in 1900.

Bolt's time broke the world record set by Michael Johnson at the 1996 Olympics in Atlanta, and made him the first man since Carl Lewis in 1984 to win both Olympic sprints in the same Games, as well as the first ever to break the world records in both events at the same Olympics. Collins said later, "It's ridiculous. How fast can you go before the world record can't be broke? How fast can the human being go before there's no more going fast?"

While Bolt's victory was clear, second and third places were a bit more contentious. Third-place finisher Spearmon was disqualified for running outside his lane, prompting an immediate appeal by the US team. After reviewing the tape, US officials dropped the appeal, but then filed a successful protest against second-place finisher Churandy Martina for also running outside his lane. The subsequent disqualifications raised Crawford and Walter Dix into the silver and bronze medal spots. In a touching act of selflessness, Crawford gave his silver medal to Martina after the race along with a note saying, "I know this can't replace the moment, but I want you to have this because I believe it's rightfully yours."

In 2009 Bolt smashed the 200 meters world record yet again, recording a stunning 19.19 at the world championships in Berlin, and becoming the first man to hold both the Olympic and world championship titles in both sprints simultaneously. As a reward for his feat, the mayor of Berlin presented Bolt with a 12-foot (3.66 meters) high section of the Berlin Wall weighing nearly 3 tons (2,722 kilograms). It was transported to Jamaica and installed at Bolt's training center.

Bolt successfully defended his world title in Daegu in 2011, this time with a relatively modest time of 19.40.

400 METERS

The 400 meters is a one-lap race run in lanes with a staggered start. Athletes from the United States have finished first 18 of the 24 times they have entered and have captured more than half of the total medals.

1896 Athens C: 7, N: 4, D: 4.7. WR (440 yards): 48.5 (Henry Tindall, Edgar Bredin)

1. Thomas Burke	USA	54.2
2. Herbert Jamison	USA	55.2
3. Charles Gmelin	GBR	—
4. Fritz Hofmann	GER	—

The slow time was a result of the quality of the track rather than the quality of the contestants. The turns were so sharp that the runners had to slow down drastically to keep from falling. Burke, who won by more than 13 meters, had previously beaten the world record holder, Edgar Bredin. In 1896 Bredin, in the words of former 440-champion Montague Shearman, "voluntarily joined the professional ranks, a step which was received with great surprise, as he was a gentleman by birth and education."

1900 Paris C: 16, N: 6, D: 7.15. WR (440 yards): 48.5 (Henry Tindall, Edgar Bredin)

1. Maxwell "Maxey" Long	USA	49.4 OR
2. William Holland	USA	49.6e
3. Ernst Schultz	DEN	53.0e

DNS: Dixon Boardman (USA), Harry Lee (USA), William Moloney (USA)

Long was cheered heartily by the French spectators, who mistook his light-blue-and-white Columbia University uniform for that of the Racing Club of Paris. Boardman, Lee, and Moloney refused to compete in the final for religious reasons, since the race was run on a Sunday.

1904 St. Louis C: 13, N: 3, D: 8.29. WR (440 yards): 47.8 (Maxwell "Maxey" Long)

1. Harry Hillman	USA	49.2 OR
2. Frank Waller	USA	49.9
3. Herman Groman	USA	50.0
4. Joseph Fleming	USA	50.3e
5. Meyer Prinstein	USA	50.3e
6. George Poage	USA	—

One can only imagine the chaos of this race, which the 13 entrants ran without lanes even though the course was only 1¼ laps long. Poage of Milwaukee was one of the first two black athletes to compete in the Olympics.

1906 Athens C: 25, N: 8, D: 4.30. WR (440 yards): 47.8 (Maxwell "Maxey" Long)

1. Paul Pilgrim	USA	53.2
2. Wyndham Halswelle	GBR	53.8e
3. Nigel Barker	AUS	54.1e
4. Harry Hiliman	USA	—
5. Charles Bacon	USA	—
6. Fay Moulton	USA	—
7. William Anderson	GBR	—
8. M. Bellin du Coteau	FRA	—

Paul Pilgrim, 1906
Coming out of nowhere to win the 400 meters, he took the 800 the next day – and never won another major race.

The victory of Pilgrim came as a complete surprise. This was the first time that the United States sent an official team. Pilgrim, who had represented the New York Athletic Club in the 1904 4-mile team race, didn't make the team in 1906, but he paid his own way to Athens and was allowed to compete.

1908 London C: 37, N: 11, D: 7.25. WR (440 yards): 47.8 (Maxwell "Maxey" Long)

1. Wyndham Halswelle	GBR	50.0

DNS: William Robbins (USA), John Baxter Taylor (USA)
DISQ: John Carpenter (USA)

Few events in Olympic history have caused as much controversy as the final of the 1908 400 meters in London. The favorite was Lieutenant Wyndham Halswelle, a 26-year-old London-born Scot who had served in the Boer War. In 1906, Halswelle won the Scottish championship at 100, 200, 440 and 880 yards—on the same day. In London he set an Olympic record of 48.4 in the semifinals. Halswelle was joined in the final by three Americans—John Baxter Taylor, William Robbins, and John Carpenter of Cornell. The British, afraid that the Americans would use team tactics, stationed officials every 20 yards around the track. Robbins charged to the front and built up a 12-yard lead by the halfway mark. Coming into the homestretch he was passed by Carpenter and Halswelle. Halswelle then attempted to go by Carpenter on the outside, but the American ran wide and kept Halswelle from taking the lead. British officials yelled "foul" and "no race" and broke the tape before Carpenter reached it. Taylor was physically pulled off the track by officials. British and American partisans argued and yelled at each other for a half hour before the track could be cleared. Carpenter was disqualified and the race was ordered rerun without him two days later, this time with strings laid out to divide the lanes. Robbins and Taylor refused to participate, however, and Halswelle was left to run the race alone. Halswelle was so disgusted by the incident that he quit sports and returned to his regiment. Although later sources variously credit Gmelin and Hofmann as finishing third, 1896 sources credit Gmelin with the third-place finish. He was killed in World War I while fighting in France on March 31, 1915.

1912 Stockholm C: 49, N: 16, D: 7.13. WR (440 yards): 47.8 (Maxwell "Maxey" Long)

1. Charles Reidpath	USA	48.2 OR
2. Hanns Braun	GER	48.3
3. Edward Lindberg	USA	48.4
4. J. Edwin Meredith	USA	49.2
5. Carroll Haff	USA	49.5

The 400 meters was again the subject of controversy, this time occasioned by an incident at the beginning of the last heat of the semifinal round. Donnell Young of the United States jumped into the lead, but before the first curve the German champion, Hanns Braun, tried to cut in front of him. Young refused to allow this and rammed into Braun, throwing him to the outside. Young went on to win, but was disqualified. Young deserved to be disqualified; however, Braun's move was uncalled for and might have resulted in *his* disqualification had not Young responded so violently. The Swedish officials wisely decided that the final should be run in lanes. Braun took the lead at the halfway mark, but Charlie Reidpath of Buffalo, New York, and Syracuse University, passed him with 15 meters to go and won by two feet (61 centimeters). Braun, who was killed in World War I, was much honored in Germany. A street in Berlin was named after him, as was an annual sportsfest in Munich.

1920 Antwerp C: 37, N: 16, D: 8.20. WR (440 yards): 47.4 (J. Edwin Meredith, H. Binga Dismond)

1. Bevil Rudd	SAF	49.6
2. Guy Butler	GBR	49.9e
3. Nils Engdahl	SWE	49.9e
4. Frank Shea	USA	49.9e
5. John Ainsworth-Davis	GBR	50.0e
6. Harry Davel	SAF	50.1e

Born in Devonshire, raised in South Africa and educated at Oxford, Bevil Gordon D'Urban Rudd was an extremely popular winner who looked at running as a joyful experience. He was often seen smoking a pipe and drinking beer while watching the other athletes go through their strenuous exercises. Rudd served as athletic correspondent for the London *Daily Telegraph* from 1931 until his death in 1948.

1924 Paris C: 60, N: 27, D: 7.11. WR (440 yards): 47.4 (J. Edwin Meredith, H. Binga Dismond)

1. Eric Liddell	GBR	47.6	OR
2. Horatio Fitch	USA	48.4	
3. Guy Butler	GBR	48.6	
4. David Johnson	CAN	48.8	
5. John Coard Taylor	USA	56.0	

DNF: Josef Imbach (SWI)

Eric Liddell was born on January 16, 1902, in Tientsin, China, where his father was a missionary. He grew up in Scotland from the age of five. His favorite sport was rugby, but he gave up a promising career in it in order to concentrate on running. He gained national attention in 1923 when he won both sprints at the AAA championships. The following week his reputation was enhanced when he was knocked to the ground during a 440-yard race against England and Ireland. By the time he had regained his feet, Liddell was 20 yards behind the field. Yet he was able to overtake every runner and win the race. Afterward he repeated his oft-spoken dictum, "I do not like to be beaten."

In the film *Chariots of Fire* Eric Liddell is portrayed as a devout Christian who learns, as he is boarding a ship en route to the Paris Olympics, that the heats of the 100-meter dash, his specialty, will be run on a Sunday. Because of his respect for the Sabbath, he refuses to run. Finally another member of the British team, a cinematic version of Lord Burghley, offers Liddell his spot in the 400 meters. This highly dramatized rendition of Liddell's Olympic experience bears only a slight resemblance to reality.

Liddell was in fact a devout Christian, and it is true that he withdrew from the 100 because he wouldn't run on a Sunday. He dropped out of the relays for the same reason. However, he did *not* find out the Olympic schedule at the last minute. In real life Liddell learned the schedule over six months in advance, and once he had made his decision not to enter the 100, he was able to concentrate his training on the 200 and 400. As for Lord Burghley, he wasn't even entered in the 400 meters. Liddell did spend the Sunday of the 100-meter heats giving a sermon at a Scottish church in Paris, but he had doubts about his decision right up to the end, particularly as a result of criticism he received from certain quarters that he was being unpatriotic, since Scotland had few opportunities to win Olympic championships.

On July 9, Liddell finished third in the 200 meters, behind Jackson Scholz and Charley Paddock. The first two rounds of the 400 were held the next day, and Liddell qualified in respectable, but unspectacular times. The fastest race of the day was won by Imbach in 48.0. The first semifinal, held the morning of July 11, was won by Fitch in 47.8 and the second by Liddell in 48.2, an impressive performance by the "Flying Scot" considering that he had never before beaten the 49-second mark. The final, contested later in the day, was won by Liddell in an unorthodox and electrifying manner. Racing in the outside lane, Liddell took off as if he were running a short dash and passed the halfway mark in an extraordinary 22.2 seconds, only 0.3 seconds slower than he had run in the 200-meter final. Track experts considered this to be tactical foolishness, but Liddell was a man inspired. He actually increased his lead during the second half of the race and won by more than five meters. His pace was so fast that two of his opponents, Imbach and Taylor, fell while trying to keep up. Taylor crawled and scrambled the last few yards to the finish line. Liddell celebrated his victory by attending a Tango Tea Dance on the Champs Elysées.

Eric Liddell returned to Scotland a hero of heroes and was paraded through the streets of Edinburgh. A year after his Olympic triumph, he returned to China to join his father in missionary work. Liddell made two more trips to Scotland, but he was back in China during World War II. He died of a brain tumor in a Japanese internment camp in Weifang, on February 21, 1945. Forty-five years later, his unmarked grave was located by Charles Walker, a civil engineer based in Hong Kong. On June 9, 1991, a monument of Scottish granite was erected in Liddell's honor in Weifang. On it is a quotation from the book of Isaiah: "They shall mount up with wings as eagles; they shall run and not be weary."

Eric Liddell, 1932
The real life story of the "Flying Scot" didn't happen exactly as depicted in the film *Chariots of Fire*, but it's a pretty good one anyway.

1928 Amsterdam C: 51, N: 20, D: 8.3. WR: 47.0 (Emerson Spencer)

1. Raymond Barbuti	USA	47.8
2. James Ball	CAN	48.0
3. Joachim Büchner	GER	48.2
4. John Rinkel	GBR	48.4
5. Werner "Harry" Storz	GER	48.8
6. Herman Phillips	USA	49.0

On May 12, 1928, Emerson Spencer set a world record of 47.0. But he failed to qualify for the Olympics except as a member of the relay team, because of a major misunderstanding at the US final Olympic tryouts. Thinking he was running in a heat, he finished only fast enough to qualify for what he thought was the next round. Actually the race had been to decide the final places on the US team and Spencer lost out.

The semifinals in Amsterdam were won by Ball and Büchner in 48.6. In the final Barbuti, a former captain of the Syracuse football team, started his finishing kick at the 300-meter mark even though he had been instructed to wait an extra 30 meters. Fortunately for Barbuti, James Ball of Winnipeg made the opposite mistake. Unaccustomed to running in lanes, Ball misjudged his position until the final straightaway and then unleashed a great finishing kick. As they approached the finish line, Ball had closed within a foot of Barbuti, but he turned to see where his opponent was just as Barbuti lunged for the tape. The plucky New Yorker fell to the ground, scraping his arm, leg, and side, but he had gained the victory. Afterward he told reporters, "I never noticed the other runners after the start. I heard them, but all I kept thinking was 'run, kid, run.' I don't remember anything of the last 100 meters except a mad desire to get to that tape."

1932 Los Angeles C: 27, N: 15, D: 8.5. WR (440 yards): 46.4 (Benjamin Eastman)

1. William Carr	USA	46.2	WR	(46.28)
2. Benjamin Eastman	USA	46.4		(46.50)
3. Alexander Wilson	CAN	47.4		
4. William Walters	SAF	48.2		
5. James Gordon	USA	48.2		
6. George Golding	AUS	48.8		

Ben Eastman of Stanford University was considered king of the world at 400 and 800 meters, particularly after March 26, 1932, when he lowered his own world record at 440 yards (402.3 meters) by a full second in running the extraordinary time of 46.4. He ran 46.5 two months later and appeared to be a sure bet to win either the 400 or 800 at the Los Angeles Olympics. Then, seemingly from out of nowhere, came a new contender, University of Pennsylvania junior Bill Carr of Pine Bluff, Arkansas. At the US intercollegiate championships at Berkeley on July 2, Carr came from behind to gain a shocking 440 victory over Eastman, 47.0 to 47.2. Two weeks later at the US Olympic tryouts on Eastman's home track in Palo Alto, California, Carr again came from behind to defeat Eastman, 46.9 to 47.1.

Unfortunately, Eastman got caught up in a rivalry

Losing by a (turn of the) Head, 1928

James Ball (left) commits the classic error in the 400 meters, checking his position while Ray Barbuti surges past.

between his own coach, Dink Templeton of Stanford, and Carr's coach, Lawson Robertson of Pennsylvania, who had been chosen to coach the US Olympic team. Obsessed with beating Robertson, Templeton convinced Eastman to skip the Olympic 800 meters, which was actually his best event, and concentrate on beating Carr at 400 meters.

At the 1932 Olympics Carr posted the fastest time in each of the first two rounds. Then he won the first semifinal in 47.2. Eastman won the second in 47.6. In the final Eastman held a slight edge through most of the race. Carr drew even with 80 meters to go and gradually pulled away to win by two yards. Whatever Dink Templeton thought of the race, Ben Eastman himself was an amiable loser. "Bill's just too fast for me," he said. "You don't need to sympathize. I know when I'm licked by a better runner." Unfortunately, Bill Carr's running career came to an abrupt halt on March 17, 1933, when he broke both ankles and fractured his pelvis in an automobile accident.

1936 Berlin C: 42, N: 25, D: 8.7. WR: 46.1 (Archie Williams)

1. Archie Williams	USA	46.5	(46.66)
2. A. Godfrey Brown	GBR	46.7	(46.68)
3. James LuValle	USA	46.8	(46.84)
4. William Roberts	GBR	46.8	(46.87)
5. William Fritz	CAN	47.8	
6. John Loaring	CAN	48.2	

Prior to the 1936 season, Archie Williams of Oakland, California, had never run a quarter mile faster than 49 seconds. However, in April 1936, he ran 47.4, in May 46.8, and on June 19, at the NCAA championships in Chicago, he clocked 46.5 for 440 yards around one turn, passing the 400-meter mark in 46.1 to break Bill Carr's world record. In the Olympic final Williams and fellow Californian James LuValle led the field entering the homestretch. But Godfrey Brown, three yards behind with 100 meters to go, staged a thrilling stretch drive, passed LuValle 40 meters from the tape, and closed in on the exhausted Williams. Brown had pulled within seven inches and was still coming strong when Williams breasted the tape before Brown could get any closer. The official times appear to have been inaccurate; the photofinish camera yielded the following, more reliable results: Williams 46.66, Brown 46.68, LuValle 46.84, and Roberts 46.87. The day after Godfrey Brown won the 400 meters silver medal, his sister Audrey earned a silver medal of her own in the women's 4 × 100-meter relay. Godfrey added a gold medal to the family haul in the men's 4 × 400-meter relay. In 1939 Archie Williams earned a degree in mechanical engineering from the University of California, Berkeley, but, because he was black, he had to settle for a job digging ditches. Eventually he joined the Army Air Corps and trained pilots. When he retired from the military, he taught high school. James LuValle earned a doctorate in chemistry at Caltech and became director of the undergraduate chemistry labs at Stanford University. Since Godfrey Brown also taught school and became a headmaster, the 1936 400-meter medalists qualify as among the most academically accomplished in Olympic history.

1948 London C: 53, N: 28, D: 8.5. WR: 45.9 (Herbert McKenley) WR (440 yards): 46.0 (Rudolf Harbig, Grover Klemmer, Herbert McKenley)

1. Arthur Wint	JAM	46.2	EOR
2. Herbert McKenley	JAM	46.4	
3. Malvin Whitfield	USA	46.9	
4. David Bolen	USA	47.2	
5. Morris Curotta	AUS	47.9	
6. George Guida	USA	50.2	

Jesse Abramson of the *New York Herald Tribune* had called Herb McKenley "the surest sure thing of the Games," but whenever anyone asked McKenley about it, he told them that his older teammate, 6-foot 4½-inch (1.94 meter) Arthur Wint, was really the man to beat. McKenley may not have actually believed that himself at the time, but it turned out that he was absolutely correct. Wint, a minister's son whose mother was a Scot, had joined the Royal Air Force during World War II. Staying on in England after the war, Wint was a 28-year-old medical student at the University of London at the time of the 1948 Olympics. Consequently, he was quite a local favorite among London sports fans.

Disappointed at having lost to Mal Whitfield at 800 meters, Wint was determined to finish ahead of the American at 400 meters. Although Wint had never lost to McKenley at 400 meters, he was prepared to settle for a silver medal behind his friend and rival, who seemed to be in prime condition. McKenley's usual tactics, or lack of them, consisted of running as fast as he could as soon as the starter's gun went off. Normally he could keep up his all-out pace for 350 meters and then coast through the final 50 meters.

True to form, McKenley went away at breakneck speed in the London final. Coming out of the final curve he was four yards ahead of Whitfield. But, McKenley, uncharacteristically, broke stride about 25 meters early and began to fade. Noticing the plight of his fellow Jamaican, Wint took off after him, closed the gap, caught McKenley with about 20 yards to go, and went on to win by two and a half yards.

Dave Bolen, who finished fourth, was later appointed US ambassador to Botswana, Lesotho, and Swaziland, as well as East Germany. Arthur Wint became a diplomat as well, interrupting his medical career to serve as Jamaica's High Commisioner to Great Britain from 1974 to 1978.

1952 Helsinki C: 71, N: 35, D: 7.25. WR: 45.8 (V. George Rhoden)

1. V. George Rhoden	JAM	45.9 OR	(46.09)
2. Herbert McKenley	JAM	45.9 OR	(46.20)
3. Oliver "Ollie" Matson	USA	46.8	(46.94)
4. Karl-Friedrich Haas	GER	47.0	(47.22)
5. Arthur Wint	JAM	47.0	(47.24)
6. Malvin Whitfield	USA	47.1	(47.30)

In 1952 the track world had different expectations of Herb McKenley. The 30-year-old McKenley was considered a sure finalist but an unlikely medal winner. The favorite was George Rhoden, a 25-year-old from Kingston who had just graduated from Morgan State College in Baltimore. In the 1948 Olympics he had been eliminated in the semifinals, but by August of 1950 he had broken the 400-meter world record in 45.8.

Rhoden and McKenley were joined in the 1952 final by fellow Olympic veterans Arthur Wint and Mal Whitfield, who had already won the 800 meters, but was now fighting off a cold with Benzedrine. The other starters were University of San Francisco football star Ollie Matson, who later achieved success as a five-time All-Pro back in the National Football League, and Kaaro Haas, the only white finalist. McKenley had the sympathy of much of the crowd as a result of his photo-finish loss in the 100-meter final four days earlier.

The amazing thing about the 1952 400-meter final was that Wint and McKenley completely reversed the tactic that they had used in the 1948 final. McKenley, having learned from his experience four years earlier, began cautiously and saved his strength for the finish. Wint, on the other hand, for some reason unknown even to himself, took off at full speed and led by three yards at the 200-meter mark in 21.7—0.2 second faster than he had ever run the distance. Not surprisingly, Wint ran out of steam early and was passed by Rhoden, who entered the long final straightaway with a four-yard lead over McKenley. But then McKenley began to close the gap, pulling closer with every stride until he almost drew even. Rhoden recalled the moment after the race: "About 20 meters from home I heard the roar of the crowd and with split vision saw someone coming up. From someplace I summoned the necessary strength and held him off. I surely was glad to see that tape." Rhoden's margin of victory was about 18 inches (46 centimeters).

1956 Melbourne C: 42, N: 23, D: 11.29. WR: 45.2 (Louis Jones)

1. Charles Jenkins	USA	46.7	(46.85)
2. Karl-Friedrich Haas	GER	46.8	(47.12)
3. Voitto Hellsten	FIN	47.0	(47.15)
3. Ardalion Ignatyev	SOV/RUS	47.0	(47.15)
5. Louis Jones	USA	48.1	(48.35)
6. Malcolm Spence	SAF	48.3	(48.40)

Lou Jones set a world record of 45.2 at the US Olympic tryouts and went to Melbourne as the clear favorite. Ignatyev won the first semifinal in 46.8, with Jones coasting in third place to qualify for the final. The second semi was a hard-fought affair, won by the third-string US runner, Charley Jenkins of Cambridge, Massachusetts. Jenkins had barely made the semifinal round by finishing third in his first- and second-round heats. The second semifinal was so fast that Kevan Gosper of Australia was eliminated even though he finished in 46.2 seconds.

Jones led the final for the first 300 meters. Coming out of the final turn he had expected to have a three- or four-meter lead and was psychologically unprepared when he realized that Ignatyev was right behind him. The Soviet runner took the lead with 60 yards to go, but then Jenkins launched a finishing kick, passed Ignatyev 25 yards from the finish, and broke the tape just ahead of Haas, who came from last place to second in the final 100 meters. The photo-finish was unable to separate Hellsten and Ignatyev, so they were both awarded third place. After the race Jenkins modestly told reporters, "Jones is still the champ. That 45.2 is it."

1960 Rome C: 54, N: 41, D: 9.6. WR: 45.2 (Louis Jones)

1. Otis Davis	USA	44.9 WR	(45.07)
2. Carl Kaufmann	GER	44.9 WR	(45.08)
3. Malcolm Spence	SAF	45.5	(45.60)
4. Milkha Singh	IND	45.6	(45.73)
5. Manfred Kinder	GER	45.9	(46.04)
6. Earl Young	USA	45.9	(46.07)

This was the first time since 1912 that the final was held on a different day than the semifinals. The improvement in times spoke well for the new procedure. Spence, who required nine painkilling injections before the final, took the early lead and was still in front at 200 meters, followed by Kaufmann, Milkha Singh, and Davis. Then Davis accelerated dramatically, covering the next 100 meters in 10.8 seconds and entering the final straight with a four-yard lead over Brooklyn-born Carl Kaufmann. Next it was Kaufmann's turn to stage a sensational sprint. He almost caught Davis, but the American leaned forward just in time, crossing the finish line ahead of the flying Kaufmann, who ended up sprawled on the track from exhaustion.

The electronic timer gave Davis a victory of .01 second, both men being credited with a new world record.

Otis Davis was born in Tuscaloosa, Alabama. A basketball player at the University of Oregon, he didn't start running until he was 26 years old, two years before the Olympics. Like Charley Jenkins before him, Davis finished only third at the US Olympic tryouts. Carl Kaufmann went on to become an opera tenor, actor and theater director.

In 1994 Otis Davis' two gold medals (he won a second in the 4 × 400-meter relay) were stolen from his home. After an intensive "medal hunt," the Jersey City, New Jersey, police received an anonymous call and found Davis' prizes in a paper bag on the front steps of the police station.

There is an unusual story relating to the performance of fourth-place finisher Milkha Singh: "The Flying Sikh." Milkha Singh grew up in the Pakistani village of Gobindpura. In 1947, when he was 16 years old, fighting broke out between India and Pakistan and Milkha Singh's parents were shot to death while he watched. Three of his brothers were also killed. He escaped death himself by hiding among corpses and then fled to a refugee camp in Kashmir by hiding in the ladies' section of a train. The Indian 400 meters record that he set in the 1960 Rome final lasted so long that Milkha Singh became frustrated by the sad state of running in his country and offered a reward of 200,000 rupees ($4770) to any Indian who could break his record.

In November 1998, a Sikh police officer named Paramjeet Singh ran 45.70 in a local meet and claimed the prize since his time was faster than the electronic version of Milkha Singh's Rome time: 45.73. But Milkha refused to pay because his electronic time was unofficial while his official hand-timed 45.6 was still below Paramjeet's time. In addition, dubious of Indian officialdom, Milkha added a new caveat: that the record had to be set on foreign soil. Although some criticized Milkha Singh for being a poor sport, neither Paramjeet Singh nor any other Indian has been able to meet Milkha's conditions.

1964 Tokyo C: 50, N: 33, D: 10.19. WR: 44.9 (Otis Davis, Carl Kaufmann, Adolph Plummer, Michael Larrabee)

1. Michael Larrabee	USA	45.1	(45.15)
2. Wendell Mottley	TRI	45.2	(45.24)
3. Andrzej Badeński	POL	45.6	(45.64)
4. Robbie Brightwell	GBR	45.7	(45.75)
5. Ulis Williams	USA	46.0	(46.01)
6. Timothy Graham	GBR	46.0	(46.08)
7. Peter Vassella	AUS	46.3	
8. Edwin Skinner	TRI	46.8	

His students laughed when Los Angeles high school mathematics teacher Mike Larrabee told them he was going to try out for the Olympics, but their laughter turned to excitement when they saw the times he was producing on the school track and at local meets. Larrabee had been a major contender in 1960, until he injured a tendon. Most observers thought Larrabee's track career was finished, but he returned in 1964 and qualified for the US team at the age of 30. Sixth at the halfway mark of the final and fifth coming out of the final curve, Larrabee unleashed his patented finishing kick and churned past one runner after another. At last he caught Wendell Mottley of Yale ten meters from the finish and won by two feet. During a record-setting two-hour press conference following his victory, Larrabee told reporters, "I kept a copy of one story written about me that said I was too old. It's still on my wall. I think I'll take it down now." Larrabee was the first white winner of the 400 meters in 32 years.

1968 Mexico City C: 54, N: 35, D: 10.18. WR: 44.0 (Lee Evans)

1. Lee Evans	USA	43.86	WR
2. G. Lawrence James	USA	43.97	
3. Ronald Freeman	USA	44.41	
4. Amadou Gakou	SEN	45.01	
5. Martin Jellinghaus	GER	45.33	
6. Tegegne Bezabeh	ETH	45.42	
7. Andrzej Badeński	POL	45.42	
8. Amos Omolo	UGA	47.61	

A US sweep seemed inevitable, considering that the top 12 400-meter runners in the world were all Americans. With each nation limited to only three entrants per event, several first-class US runners had to be left behind. The big surprise was the success of the Africans, particularly Amadou Gakou of Senegal, who lowered his personal best from 46.7 to 45.0 and became the first black to hold the African 400-meter record.

Initially Lee Evans announced his intention to withdraw from the final after his friends John Carlos and Tommie Smith were expelled from the Olympic Village after their Black Power protest at the 200-meter victory ceremony. But Carlos personally convinced him to run and to win. Evans expected to have a five-yard lead when he reached the final straightaway. Instead he realized that Larry James was right behind him. "I felt faint . . . Three steps from the finish, Larry dropped his head. I knew I had it then . . . Larry ran three hundred ninety-five meters. I ran four hundred and one. That was the difference." The first seven finishers all bettered their pre-Olympic best times. Evans later served as coach to the national teams of Nigeria, Cameroon,

Qatar and Saudi Arabia and conducted clinics in more than twenty African nations.

At the medal ceremony, the three Americans wore black socks and berets and raised their fists, but removed their berets and lowered their fists during the US national anthem.

1972 Munich C: 64, N: 49. D: 9.7. WR: 43.86 (Lee Evans)

1. Vincent Matthews	USA	44.66
2. Wayne Collett	USA	44.80
3. Julius Sang	KEN	44.92
4. Charles Asati	KEN	45.13
5. Horst-Rüdiger Schlöske	GER	45.31
6. Markku Kukkoaho	FIN	45.59
7. Karl Honz	GER	45.68
DNF: John Smith (USA)		

Another US sweep seemed to be a distinct possibility even though defending champion Lee Evans, hampered by a hamstring pull, had finished fourth at the US Olympic trials and only qualified as a member of the 4 × 400 relay team. In his place was Vince Matthews, a New York City social worker who had just missed making the US entry in 1968. US officials and coaches were clearly disappointed that Evans hadn't qualified for the 400, and made Matthews feel extremely unwanted. The pre-Olympics favorites were Californians John Smith and Wayne Collett. In the final, Smith, running with an injured leg, pulled up lame after only 80 meters, but Collett and Matthews drove on. Matthews was somewhat shocked to find himself in the lead entering the final straight and still feeling strong. He held off Collett the rest of the way and won by four feet.

At the medal ceremony, Matthews and Collett showed little respect for the proceedings, talking and fidgeting during the playing of "The Star-Spangled Banner" rather than standing quietly at attention. The West German crowd booed them, and the International Olympic Committee, ignoring the US Olympic Committee, banned the two runners from further competition. Matthews and Collett denied that their actions had constituted an organized protest. "If we did have any ideas about a demonstration," Matthews said, "we could have done a better job than that." Collett added, "I couldn't stand there and sing the words [to the national anthem] because I don't believe they're true. I wish they were. I think we have the potential to have a beautiful country, but I don't think we do."

Stepping down from the victory platform, Matthews had taken off his gold medal and twirled it around his finger, leading some people to believe that the medal meant little to him. In an article in the *New York Times,* Matthews responded to this criticism: "I took it off to tell them this was my medal. A lot of people had forgotten about me and given up on me. . . . Twenty years from now, I can look at this medal and say, 'I was the best quarter-miler in the world that day.' If you don't think that's important, you don't know what's inside an athlete's soul."

John Smith, the frustrated favorite, finally achieved Olympic satisfaction when he coached Steve Lewis and Danny Everett to gold and bronze in 1988. Lewis, who wasn't certain he had won until he and Smith watched a replay of the race on the stadium scoreboard, then turned to Smith and said, "That one is for you, Coach." In 1992 Smith coached two more gold-medal winners—Quincy Watts and Kevin Young, in 1996 another: Marie-José Pérec, and in 2000 yet another: Maurice Greene.

1976 Montreal C: 44, N: 29, D: 7.29. WR: 43.86 (Lee Evans)

1. Alberto Juantorena Danger	CUB	44.26
2. Frederick Newhouse	USA	44.40
3. Herman Frazier	USA	44.95
4. Alfons Brijdenbach	BEL	45.04
5. Maxie Parks	USA	45.24
6. Richard Mitchell	AUS	45.40
7. David Jenkins	GBR	45.57
8. Jan Werner	POL	45.63

In 1972 Alberto Juantorena had been narrowly eliminated in the Olympic semifinals. He was unbeaten in 1973 and 1974, but before the 1975 season he

Alberto Juantorena, 1976
A gazelle's stride to eclipse Fred Newhouse in the 400 meters and complete the Games' first 400/800 double (not including Paul Pilgrim in the 1906 Intercalated Games).

underwent two operations on his foot. By the time of the Montreal Olympics he had emerged as the clear favorite at 400 meters. When he scored a surprising victory at 800 meters, it appeared that he had an excellent chance to become the first runner to score a 400/800 double since Paul Pilgrim in the Intercalated Games of 1906. Juantorena waltzed through the first two rounds, content to qualify without extending himself. After finishing his second-round heat, he kept on running, continuing through the tunnel and into the locker room without stopping. In the semifinals, Juantorena started poorly, then accelerated into first place and jogged home in 45.10, looking back at the other runners seven times on his way to the tape. Fred Newhouse, winner of the second semifinal in 44.89, sprinted into the lead in the final and was sure he was about to win the gold medal when Juantorena, the man with the nine-foot stride, appeared at his shoulder with 20 meters to go and moved right by him. Juantorena's winning time was a half-second faster than he had ever run before. The 6-foot 2-inch Cuban hero became the first man from a non-English-speaking country to win the 400 meters, although Juantorena himself actually spoke English quite well. Before the 1976 Olympics were over, Alberto Juantorena had run nine races and lost 11 pounds.

1980 Moscow C: 50, N: 32, D: 7.30. WR: 43.86 (Lee Evans)

1. Viktor Markin	SOV/RUS	44.60
2. Richard Mitchell	AUS	44.84
3. Frank Schaffer	GDR	44.87
4. Alberto Juantorena Danger	CUB	45.09
5. Alfons Brijdenbach	BEL	45.10
6. Michael Solomon	TRI	45.55
7. David Jenkins	GBR	45.56
8. Joseph Coombs	TRI	46.33

For the third straight time the 400 meters was won by the runner in lane 2. This time, though, the man in lane 2 was a complete outsider: a 23-year-old Siberian-born medical student named Viktor Markin. Markin gained the lead from Schaffer with 80 meters to go. Rick Mitchell also finished strongly, moving from last to second in the final 100 meters. Although Juantorena was only a shadow of his former self, his fourth-place finish was actually quite an achievement considering that he was still recovering from an Achilles tendon operation. Markin's time, 0.73 second faster than his previous best, was the fastest 400 meters to be run in over two years. "I don't know my own limits," he said afterward. "Everything came to me so quickly in the final . . . I finished like I was in a dream."

1984 Los Angeles C: 80, N: 57, D: 8.8. WR: 43.86 (Lee Evans)

1. Alonzo Babers	USA	44.27
2. Gabriel Tiacoh	IVC	44.54
3. Antonio McKay	USA	44.71
4. Darren Clark	AUS	44.75
5. Sunder Nix	USA	44.75
6. Sunday Uti	NGR	44.93
7. Innocent Egbunike	NGR	45.35

DNS: Bertland Cameron (JAM)

The battle on the track for the 400-meters title was preceded by a war of words between world champion Bert Cameron and US Olympic trials winner Antonio McKay. Cameron had stated that the gold medal already had his name written on it. McKay responded by vowing, "I'm going to destroy Cameron." Cameron seemed unconcerned about McKay, for whom the Olympics would be his first international meet. But he was worried about Air Force second lieutenant Alonzo Babers, who had handed Cameron his only two defeats of the past two years. "He is so relaxed when he's running," Cameron would say of Babers on the eve of the Games. "Maybe McKay should be watching him instead of me."

The first round included one bizarre occurrence. Innocent Egbunike, one of the secondary favorites, thought he had prepared for any eventuality. But shortly after the start of the third heat, Egbunike, running in the inside lane, found himself cut off by Secundino Borabota of the small, impoverished West African nation of Equatorial Guinea. After yelling at Borabota for 100 meters, Egbunike finally squeezed by on the inside and went on to win the heat. After the race, Borabota, evidently unaware that 400-meter runners are supposed to stay in the same lane from start to finish, explained rather cryptically that an injury led him to switch lanes temporarily. "Lane one is a good lane," he added.

The quarterfinals saw some surprisingly fast times. McKay led 18-year-old Darren Clark 44.72 to 44.77 in the first heat, and Babers recorded 44.75 in the third. The following day, the first semifinal was won by Egbunike over Babers 45.16 to 45.17. But the real drama began in the second semi which pitted Cameron against McKay for the first time. After 100 meters Cameron was charging down the backstretch when he suddenly leaped into the air and grabbed his left thigh, the victim of a pulled hamstring muscle. Cameron's Olympics seemed over, but, remarkably, he took off again, having lost a good eight to ten meters to the field. Last at the halfway point and seventh with 100 meters to go, Cameron caught up in the homestretch, finishing fourth and earning a place in the final. Cameron's phenomenal performance overshadowed a great race by Gabriel Tiacoh, who set an African record of 44.64, with Sunday Uti placing second in 44.83 and McKay third at 44.92.

Of the eight finalists, all but Clark were US collegians. Unfortunately, two days' rest did not heal Cameron's leg and he was forced to scratch from the final. Clark went out strongly and led the race all the way into the final straightaway. He thought the victory was his, but about 50 meters from the finish line, Tiacoh and Babers blew by him with Babers pulling away to win by 2½ meters. McKay just nipped Clark at the end for the bronze in what turned out to be the first 400-meter race in which six runners finished under 45 seconds. Babers' time of 44.27 was only one-hundredth of a second off Alberto Juantorena's sea-level best and was the fastest 400 meters in the world since Juantorena set that record at the 1976 Olympics. It was also .71 second better than Babers' pre-Olympic personal record. Tiacoh, who improved his own pre-Olympic best by .70 second, became the first representative of the Ivory Coast to win an Olympic medal. He died of viral meningitis eight years later, at the age of 28.

1988 Seoul C: 75, N: 55, D: 9.26. WR: 43.29 (Harry "Butch" Reynolds)

1. Steven Lewis	USA	43.87
2. Harry "Butch" Reynolds	USA	43.93
3. Danny Everett	USA	44.09
4. Darren Clark	AUS	44.55
5. Innocent Egbunike	NGR	44.72
6. Bertland Cameron	JAM	44.94
7. Ian Morris	TRI	44.95
8. Mohamed Al Malky	OMA	45.03

The US Olympic trials were won by 24-year-old Butch Reynolds in a time of 43.93, with Danny Everett close behind in 43.98. It was the first time that the 44-second barrier had been broken since the 1968 Olympics. The third US qualifier was Everett's UCLA teammate, 19-year-old Steve Lewis. As recently as May 1988, Lewis' personal record had been only 45.68, but in the semifinals of the trials he dropped it to 44.11. Four weeks later, on August 17, at the Weltklasse meet in Zurich, Reynolds shattered Lee Evans' 19-year-old world record, stopping the clock at 43.29 seconds.

Reynolds entered the Olympics as the overwhelming favorite, but Lewis recorded the fastest times in both of the first two rounds: 45.31 and 44.41. Lewis won the first semifinal in 44.35 and Reynolds the second in 44.33. The latter race saw the elimination of world champion Thomas Schönlebe of East Germany.

Everett led at the halfway point in the final, followed closely by Lewis. Reynolds, renowned for his powerful finishing kick, was sixth. With 100 meters to go, Lewis took the lead. Reynolds was still in only fifth place, a good 6 meters back. Then the world record holder made his move. But it was too late. He passed Everett 20 meters from the finish and had just caught Lewis when Lewis executed a perfect lean to snatch the victory. Lewis was the youngest male runner to win an individual gold medal since Reggie Walker took the 100 meters in 1908. Lewis was four days older than Walker had been. The Seoul final was the first race in history in which seven runners were clocked in less than 45 seconds.

1992 Barcelona C: 68, N: 52, D: 8.5. WR: 43.29 (Harry "Butch" Reynolds)

1. Quincy Watts	USA	43.50 OR
2. Steven Lewis	USA	44.21
3. Samson Kitur	KEN	44.24
4. Ian Morris	TRI	44.25
5. Robert Hernández Prendes	CUB	44.52
6. David Grindley	GBR	44.75
7. Ibrahim Ismail	OAT	45.10
8. Susumu Takano	JPN	45.18

Because runners from the United States have dominated the 400 meters, the US Olympic trials are often more nerve-wracking than the Olympics themselves. The procedure is simple. The best American quarter-milers face each other in head-to-head competition. The three fastest go to the Olympics. The next three qualify for the 4 × 400-meter relay team. The rest stay home. Clear and simple—except in 1992. The 1992 trials were held in New Orleans in late June. The

Derek Redmond, 1992

Comforted by his father as he walks to the finish line in the semifinals of the 1992 400 meters.

defending Olympic champion, Steve Lewis, was there. The defending world champion, Antonio Pettigrew, was there. And the world record holder, Butch Reynolds? That's where things got complicated.

On August 12, 1990, Reynolds competed in Monte Carlo and tested positive for the steroid nandrolone. He was given an automatic two-year suspension. Like many athletes who fail doping tests, Butch Reynolds denied taking prohibited drugs and challenged the test results. But Reynolds' case appeared to have more merit than the average drug denial. Reynolds' lawyers contended that the urine samples from Monte Carlo had not been kept safe from tampering and that a circle around the number of a different sample on the paperwork from the drug-testing laboratory in Paris suggested that the positive result actually belonged to a German woman. On December 3, 1991, the executive board of The Athletic Congress (TAC), the governing body of track and field in the United States, recommended that Reynolds' suspension be lifted. Five months later, after five postponements, an IAAF arbitration panel curtly denied Reynolds' appeal and reminded the Americans that if Reynolds was allowed to race, anyone who ran against him would also be banned from international competition.

On May 28, a federal judge in Columbus, Ohio, ruled that Reynolds should be allowed to run in order to pick up a qualifying time for the Olympic trials. Reynolds ran twice and qualified—and the IAAF promptly banned the athletes who ran against him. Because of the IAAF's "contamination" rule, the favorites in the 400 meters, Steve Lewis, Antonio Pettigrew, and veteran Danny Everett, joined the argument against Reynolds, stating that Reynolds' participation in the Olympic trials would cause them to be banned from the Olympics. On June 19, the day before the opening round of the 400 meters, an appellate judge in Ohio ruled against Reynolds and the issue appeared to be settled. But Reynolds' lawyers took the case to the US Supreme Court and, on June 20, Justice John Paul Stevens ordered TAC to allow Reynolds to compete in the Olympic trials. Chaos reigned in New Orleans. The 400-meter heats were postponed two hours, then overnight, and then two more days. On June 23 the IAAF agreed to lift its contamination rule for the US Olympic trials only. Reynolds responded by running 44.58, the fastest preliminary time ever. In the semifinals he ran 44.14, his best time since 1988. But in the final he faded to fifth place. Although he missed qualifying for the 400 meters, he did earn a spot as an alternate on the 4 × 400-meter relay team. On July 17, the US Olympic Committee dropped Reynolds from its list of entrants. (Reynolds did make it to the Olympics in 1996, but suffered a severe cramp and failed to finish his semifinal heat.) When the dust settled, the US Olympic entry turned out to be Danny Everett, who won the final in 43.81, the second-fastest time in history, Steve Lewis, and 6-foot 3-inch (1.90 meter) Quincy Watts, who ran a powerful 43.97 in the semifinals only 16 months after switching from the sprints to the 400. In 1991 Watts had qualified for the world championships, but a throat infection led him to give up his spot at the last minute to Danny Everett.

In Barcelona the first two rounds went as expected, but the first semifinal saw one of the most moving moments in Olympic history, a reminder that behind the hype and the money and the controversies, the Olympics is really about human beings.

Starting in lane 5 was Derek Redmond of Great Britain, a talented runner whose 45.03 was the fastest time of the opening round and whose quarterfinal time of 45.02 was good enough to win his heat. But Redmond's running career had been frustrated by a constant battle against injury. He had already undergone five operations, one on his toe and four on his Achilles tendon, the latest in April. In 1988 Redmond had been forced to withdraw less than two minutes before his opening heat in Seoul and for four years he had agonized that he wasn't really an "Olympic athlete." Now, four years later, he was running well and felt confident that he could lower his personal record.

Like many athletes, Redmond sometimes forgot how much his parents had sacrificed to allow him to fulfill his athletic potential. But as Derek Redmond settled into his blocks in the Olympic semifinals, his thoughts went to his father and all the "time and money and care" he had devoted to see Redmond through all his injuries and to get him where he was. Silently, Derek Redmond dedicated the race to his father. "This one's for you, Dad," he told himself.

Redmond got off to a clean start and was running smoothly when suddenly, about 150 meters into the race, he heard a pop—his right hamstring had torn—and he fell to the ground. When he looked up he saw the other runners racing down the homestretch and across the finish line. When Redmond noticed the stretcher-bearers rushing toward him, he realized how important it was to him to finish the race and not end his Olympic experience on a stretcher. He jumped up and, despite the pain, he continued down lane 5. He couldn't run, he could only hop, so he hobbled forward.

Meanwhile up in the stands, Derek Redmond's father, Jim, watched heartbroken as his son fell, his dreams shattered. When the medics failed to arrive immediately, Jim Redmond, a father seeing his boy in pain, instinctively ran through the stands, past the security guards, and onto the field. By this time Derek had risen and started his slow journey to the finish line. When Jim reached him, he was in the far turn.

"You don't have to do this," said the father to the son.

"I've got to finish," replied the son.

"Okay," said the father. "We started your career together, so we're going to finish this race together."

Jim Redmond put one arm around Derek's shoulder, held his hand, and together they headed toward the homestretch. After a few steps Derek leaned against his father and began sobbing. A few steps from the finish line, Jim Redmond let go of his son and allowed him to finish the course on his own, while the crowd of 65,000 gave the young runner a standing ovation.

Prior to the Olympics, Derek Redmond had had a hostile relationship with team captain (and 100-meter gold medalist) Linford Christie, and the two had criticized each other publicly. But as Derek Redmond was walking to the bus after his race, he was approached by Christie. The two men embraced and cried together.

Almost overlooked in the drama of Redmond's ordeal was the result of the race itself, which was won by Steve Lewis. The second semi was won by Quincy Watts, with an Olympic record of 43.71. Watts did even better in the final, entering the homestretch with a huge lead and holding on to win by over five meters. His margin of victory was the largest since Eric Liddell's in 1924. Watts was the fifth African-American since 1956 to win the Olympic 400-meter championship after finishing only third at the US Olympic trials.

There is a curious footnote about what happened to Quincy Watts after his sensational victory in Barcelona. As soon as the Olympics were over, he was forgotten by the American public. In Europe it was a different story. Nike chose Watts to star in a television commercial, shown in several countries, in which a Viking king offers to trade his "super-cushioned wife" for Watts' "supercushioned Air Max shoes." Watts takes one look at the massive Viking woman and sprints away at full speed while the super-cushioned wife bellows, "Quin-cy!"

"Quin-cy!" became the European equivalent of such immortal US advertising slogans as "Where's the beef?" and "Tastes great, less filling," transforming Watts into a continental celebrity.

1996 Atlanta C: 62, N: 42, D: 7.29. WR: 43.29 (Harry "Butch" Reynolds)

1. Michael Johnson	USA	43.49 OR
2. Roger Black	GBR	44.41
3. Davis Kamoga	UGA	44.53
4. Alvin Harrison	USA	44.62
5. Iwan Thomas	GBR	44.70
6. Roxbert Martin	JAM	44.83
7. Davian Clarke	JAM	44.99

DNF: Ibrahim Ismail (QAT)

For the past seven years Michael Johnson had completely dominated the 400 meters, winning 54 straight finals since April 1, 1989, including the 1993 and 1995 world championships. And yet, because of his food poisoning disaster in 1992, he still had not won an Olympic gold medal in an individual event.

Johnson cruised effortlessly through the opening rounds, recording the fastest times in both the quarterfinals and the semifinals. After the semifinal, he threw his shoes into the stands—forgetting that they had spikes. He appeared for the final wearing gold shoes. Running from lane four, he took control of the race at the halfway point, came out of the final curve with a five-meter lead and continued to pull away until he crossed the finish line, defeating Roger Black in second place by ten meters. It was the largest margin of victory in the event in 100 years.

Davis Kamoga, the surprise bronze medallist, had not run on a synthetic track until less than 14 months before the Olympics.

2000 Sydney C: 68, N: 44, D: 9.25. WR: 43.18 (Michael Johnson)

1. Michael Johnson	USA	43.84
2. Alvin Harrison	USA	44.40
3. Gregory Haughton	JAM	44.70
4. Sanderlei Parrela	BRA	45.01
5. Robert Mackowiak	POL	45.14
6. Hendrik Mokganyetsi	SAF	45.26
7. Antonio Pettigrew	USA	45.42
8. Danny McFarlane	JAM	45.55

Michael Johnson once said that he did not have a prerace ritual, but that he did have a post-race ritual: "I stand on the podium and have them put a gold medal around my neck."

Johnson arrived in Sydney as the overwhelming favorite at 400 meters. Over the past decade he had raced in sixty 400 meters finals and won fifty-seven of them. He was the defending Olympic champion and he had won the last four world championships. At the 1999 world championships in Seville, he ran 43.18 seconds to break Butch Reynolds' 11-year-old world record. He had run faster than 44 seconds twenty-one times. No one else had done it more than four times.

Alvin Harrison recorded the fastest time in each of the three pre-final rounds, 44.96 in the first round, 44.25 in the quarterfinals and 44.53 in the semifinals. The two semis were badly balanced. Avard Moncur of the Bahamas finished six hundreds of a second faster than the winner of the second semifinal (Antonio Pettigrew), but was eliminated because his time was only good enough for fifth place in the first semifinal.

In the final, Michael Johnson was last out of the blocks. Johnson's training partner, Greg Haughton, running in lane 8, burst into the lead. Johnson caught him after 300 meters and pulled away to win by four meters. Johnson became the first man to win the 400 meters twice. At 33 years, he was also the oldest athlete ever to win an Olympic championship at a distance shorter than 5000 meters.

2004 Athens C: 62, N: 48, D: 8.23. WR: 43.18 (Michael Johnson)

1. Jeremy Wariner	USA	44.00
2. Otis Harris	USA	44.16
3. Derrick Brew	USA	44.42
4. Alleyne Francique	GRN	44.66
5. Brandon Simpson	JAM	44.76
6. Davian Clarke	JAM	44.83
7. Leslie Djhone	FRA	44.94
8. Michael Blackwood	JAM	45.55

For the first time since 1912, the 400 meters was held with three rounds instead of four. Twenty-year-old Jeremy Wariner, from Irving, Texas, led the world rankings coming to Athens, having broken 45-seconds in every meet in which he competed in the four months before the Games. Wariner advanced easily to the semifinals, where he recorded the fastest time of the round, 44.87 seconds. In the final, the three Americans drew adjacent lanes, with Wariner in lane four, flanked by Derrick Brew on his left and Otis Harris on his right. Harris held a small lead until the 300-meter mark, when Wariner drew alongside him and then calmly began to pull away, covering the last 100 meters in 11.8 seconds. Harris held on for silver, recording a personal best, while Brew completed the American sweep ahead of Grenadan Alleyne Francique, a graduate of Louisiana State University. It was the sixth consecutive US victory in the event and the eleventh out of the last twelve in which Americans competed.

Known for his habit of wearing sunglasses during every race, Wariner was the first white male to win a sprint event since Viktor Markin won the 400 meters in the boycotted Games of 1980. Wariner, who had been recruited by Baylor University in 2002 as a wide receiver for their football team, switched to track when he discovered that he was not being awarded a football scholarship.

2008 Beijing C: 55, N: 40, D: 8.21. WR: 43.18 (Michael Johnson)

1. LaShawn Merritt	USA	43.75
2. Jeremy Wariner	USA	44.74
3. David Neville	USA	44.80
4. Chris Brown	BAH	44.84
5. Leslie Djhone	FRA	45.11
6. Martyn Rooney	GBR	45.12
7. Renny "Chicken" Quow	TRI	45.22
8. Johan Wissman	SWE	45.39

Since winning the gold medal in Athens, Jeremy Wariner had continued to dominate the 400 meters event, easily winning both the 2005 and 2007 world championship titles while also earning consecutive golds in the 4 × 400-meter relay events. Despite this success, in January 2008 Wariner parted ways with long-time coach Clyde Hart, who had coached him through the Olympic and world championship wins. The split was believed to have resulted from a disagreement over Hart's salary.

Wariner's dominance was also threatened by a rising star, 22-year-old LaShawn Merritt. Born in Portsmouth, Virginia, Merritt took up running as a junior in high school to help cope with the death of his older brother Antwan, who jumped to his death from an eighth-floor dormitory window to escape a fight at Shaw University in Raleigh, North Carolina. LaShawn was 13 at the time. In 2004 Merritt won three gold medals at the junior world championships. In 2005 he recorded what was then the second-fastest indoor 400 meters time ever, 44.93, at the Tyson Invitational in Arkansas. The time stood for five years as the fastest-ever junior indoor time, until bettered in 2011.

Although Wariner had beaten Merritt the first eleven times they had raced, the balance had begun to shift in the lead-up to the Olympics. At the 2007 world championships in Osaka, Japan, Merritt recorded his first sub-44-second time, 43.96 seconds, and won his first major international medal, beating 2000 Olympic champion Angelo Taylor for silver. Merritt finished the season ranked second behind Wariner. In June 2008, two months before the Olympics, Merritt finally managed to end Wariner's nine-race winning streak at a meet in Berlin. Merritt repeated the feat in July, beating Wariner by 0.20 seconds at the US Olympic trials in Eugene, Oregon. A little-known 24-year-old named David Neville finished third to qualify for the team. An accomplished drummer, Neville had played in the Indiana University marching band for a year because he was ineligible to run track as a freshman. He trained with his father and won a 200-meter silver behind sixteen-year-old Usain Bolt at the 2003 Junior Pan Am Games. He graduated with a music degree in 2007.

The preliminary rounds in Beijing held no major surprises; both Wariner and Merritt advanced easily through the quarter- and semi-final rounds, each winning both of their heats. Neville also managed to reach the final, despite finishing second behind French sprinter Leslie Djhone in both early rounds.

Merritt recorded the slowest response time in the final and was in third place behind Wariner and Neville coming out of the final turn. Thinking of Bolt's performance in the final stretch of the 200-meter final the previous day, Merritt surged into the lead down the final straight, pulling away with every stride and opening nearly a full second's lead over Wariner in second place. Merritt's time was a personal best and the largest margin of victory ever in the event. Neville secured the US sweep by taking a headlong tumble across the finish line to edge out Chris Brown of the Bahamas. "I did it because it was the only thing I could think to do in the [final] second," Neville said later. "God might have pushed me over."

A year later, Merritt again beat Wariner to win the 2009 world championship title in Berlin. In April 2010 the US Anti-Doping Agency revealed that three times between October 2009 and January 2010 Merritt had tested positive for a banned substance, DHEA. The cause? An over-the-counter "sexual enhancement" product called Expense. Merritt accepted a provisional suspension and then was handed a two-year suspension.

However, a US arbitration panel reduced his suspension by three months and he was able to compete in the 2011 world championships in Daegu, where he finished second behind teenager Kirani James of Grenada.

800 METERS

The 800 meters is a two-lap race with a staggered start. The runners stay in lanes until the end of the first curve, at which point they are allowed to break to the inside.

1896 Athens C: 9, N: 5, D: 4.9. WR (880 yards): 1:53.4 (Charles Kirkpatrick)

1. Edwin Flack	AUS	2:11.0
2. Nándor Dáni	HUN	2:11.8
3. Demitrios Golemis	GRE	2:28.0e

DNS: Albin Lermusiaux (FRA)

Teddy Flack was a 22-year-old accountant who took a month's holiday from his job with Price, Waterhouse and Company in London to travel to Athens and take part in the Olympics. Flack had a busy week. He also won the 1500 meters, took part in the marathon, and, on the very morning of the 800-meter final, played in the tennis tournament.

1900 Paris C: 18, N: 7, D: 7.16. WR (880 yards): 1:53.4 (Charles Kirkpatrick)

1. Alfred Tysoe	GBR	2:01.2
2. John Cregan	USA	2:01.8
3. David Hall	USA	2:03.0
4. Henri Deloge	FRA	—
5. Zoltán Speidl	HUN	—
6. John Bray	USA	—

David Hall won the first qualifying heat in 1:59.0, but was unable to repeat his time in the final, which was won by Alf Tysoe, who ran the last lap in 56.2 seconds. Tysoe was a farmhand from Skerton in Lancashire. He died of pleurisy at age 27, only one and a half years after his Olympic triumph.

1904 St. Louis C: 13, N: 3, D: 9.1. WR (880 yards): 1:53.4 (Charles Kirkpatrick)

1. James Lightbody	USA	1:56.0 OR
2. Howard Valentine	USA	1:56.3
3. Emil Breitkreutz	USA	1:56.4
4. George Underwood	USA	—
5. Johannes Runge	GER	—
6. William Frank Verner	USA	—

Lightbody ran most of the race in fifth place, then moved to the outside and passed the leaders to win by one and a half yards. Runge, who had led at the halfway mark, tired badly in the second half of the race. This may have been because, three days earlier, he had won the 880 yards handicap event, thinking it was the Olympic final.

1906 Athens C: 23, N: 8, D: 4.30. WR (880 yards) 1:53.4 (Charles Kirkpatrick)

1. Paul Pilgrim	USA	2:01.5
2. James Lightbody	USA	2:01.6e
3. Wyndham Halswelle	GBR	2:03.0e
4. Reginald Percy Crabbe	GBR	—
5. Kristian Hellström	SWE	—
6. Charles Bacon	USA	—
7. Eli Parsons	USA	—

DNF: Johannes Runge (GER)

Coming down the homestretch, Lightbody looked over his left shoulder to check the position of the other runners. Just then, Paul Pilgrim, the upset winner of the 400 meters the previous day, sped past him on the right to win by about two feet. Pilgrim never won a major race before or after the 1906 Games.

1908 London C: 38, N: 10, D: 7.21. WR (880 yards): 1:53.4 (Charles Kirkpatrick)

1. Melvin Sheppard	USA	1:52.8 WR
2. Emilio Lunghi	ITA	1:54.2e
3. Hanns Braun	GER	1:55.2e
4. Ödön Bodor	HUN	1:55.4e
5. Theodore Just	GBR	1:56.4e
6. John Halstead	USA	—

DNF: Clarke Beard (USA), Ivo Fairbairn-Crawford (GBR)

A minor controversy developed regarding the drawing of runners into heats. Because only the winners of each heat would advance to the final, the US and Swedish teams protested when some of their entrants were drawn into the same heats. The British officials agreed to a certain amound of reshuffling and, indeed, Mel Sheppard and John Halstead, who had originally been assigned the same heat, were separated, and both qualified for the final.

In the final, Fairbairn-Crawford raced into the lead and set a blistering pace, in the hope of wearing out 1500-meter winner Mel Sheppard for the benefit of Britain's number-one runner, Theodore Just. Fairbairn-Crawford opened a 15-yard gap after 200 meters and finished the first lap in 53 seconds. The British strategy failed, as Sheppard kept to his own pace, moved into the lead after 500 meters, and won by ten yards over the surprising Emilio Lunghi, who once won a long-distance road race in Genoa while carrying an open umbrella because it was raining. A second tape had been set up five yards four inches (4.68 meters) after the finish so that the winner's time could be measured at 880 yards. Sheppard slowed down so much that he needed 1.2 seconds to cover the extra distance, and thus missed breaking Kirkpatrick's 13-year-old half-mile world record.

1912 Stockholm C: 48, N: 15, D: 7.8. WR: 1:52.8 (Melvin Sheppard)

1. J. Edwin Meredith	USA	1:51.9 WR
2. Melvin Sheppard	USA	1:52.0
3. Ira Davenport	USA	1:52.0
4. Daniel Caldwell	USA	1:52.8e
5. Melville Brook	CAN	1:53.0e
6. Hanns Braun	GER	1:53.0e
7. Clarence Edmundson	USA	—
8. Herbert Putnam	USA	—

Sheppard led from the start, passing the halfway mark in 52.4. Ted Meredith edged ahead in the final straightaway and won by about 18 inches (46 centimeters), with the first four runners all breaking the world record. Meredith continued on to set a new 880-yard record of 1:52.5. According to the *New York Times,* "The excitement during the race was terrific, and was made more so by the terrible noise caused by thousands of throats yelling injunctions in every language to those in front to 'sit down.'"

1920 Antwerp C: 40, N: 17, D: 8.17. WR: 1:51.9 (James "Ted" Meredith)

1. Albert Hill	GBR	1:53.4
2. Earl Eby	USA	1:53.6
3. Bevil Rudd	SAF	1:54.0
4. Edgar Mountain	GBR	1:54.6
5. Donald Scott	USA	1:56.0
6. Albert Sprott	USA	1:56.4
7. Adriaan Paulen	HOL	1:56.4
8. Jean Esparbès	FRA	1:58.0

Albert Hill, a 31-year-old World War I veteran, won by about two meters an exciting race in which the lead changed hands numerous times. The final was run only a half hour after the semifinals. Hill was coached by Sam Mussabini, who had coached Reggie Walker to victory in the 1908 100 meters and would coach Harold Abrahams in 1924. A notable instance of gentlemanly good sportsmanship was related by bronze medalist Bevil Rudd. When Earl Eby accidentally bumped into Rudd 300 meters from the finish, he turned to the South African and said, "Sorry, Bevil." Adriaan Paulen, who placed seventh, became a hero of the Dutch resistance during World War II and later served as president of the IAAF.

1924 Paris C: 41, N: 21, D: 7.8. WR: 1:51.9 (J. Edwin Meredith)

1. Douglas Lowe	GBR	1:52.4
2. Paul Martin	SWI	1:52.5
3. Schuyler Enck	USA	1:52.9
4. Hyla "Henry" Stallard	GBR	1:53.0
5. William Richardson	USA	1:53.7
6. Ray Dodge	USA	1:54.2
7. John Watters	USA	1:54.8
8. Charles Hoff	NOR	1:56.7

The favorite, Henry Stallard, was suffering from an injured foot, but this didn't stop him from giving his all in the final and leading for the first 700 meters. Finally he was passed by Lowe and Martin, who engaged in a frantic battle, which Lowe won by about a yard. The final took place on Lowe's 22nd birthday. Charles Hoff, who finished in eighth place, was the reigning world record holder in the pole vault, an event in which he could not compete in Paris because of a foot injury. Ultimately, Hoff would become better known in Norway for his political actions than for his athletic feats. During the 1940-1945 occupation of Norway by Germany, Hoff collaborated with the Nazis. After World War II, he was convicted of treason and spent five years in prison. Paul Martin competed in every Olympic 800 meters contest from 1920 through 1936, one of only two male runners (Pietro Mennea is the other) to take part in five Olympics.

1928 Amsterdam C: 54, N: 26, D: 7.31. WR: 1:50.6 (Séraphin Martin)

1. Douglas Lowe	GBR	1:51.8 OR
2. Erik Byléhn	SWE	1:52.8
3. Hermann Engelhard	GER	1:53.2
4. Philip Edwards	CAN	1:54.0
5. Lloyd Hahn	USA	1:54.2
6. Séraphin Martin	FRA	1:54.6
7. Earl Fuller	USA	1:55.0
8. Jean Keller	FRA	1:57.0

The 1928 800 meters was an anxiously awaited contest among Germany's Dr. Otto Peltzer, who had broken Ted Meredith's 14-year-old world record in a classic showdown with Douglas Lowe in 1926, Lloyd Hahn, who had broken Peltzer's record, and Séra Martin, who had broken Hahn's record. Unfortunately, Peltzer became ill and was eliminated in the semifinals. As it turned out, the big confrontation was actually a rout, as defending champion Douglas Lowe swept past Hahn in the final curve and won by about eight yards. Following the Amsterdam Olympics, Peltzer received the following letter: "Dear Dr. Peltzer, The British halfmilers who have competed with you in the past feel duty bound to send you their deepest sympathy for the injury that prevented you from showing your best form in the Olympic Games. We realize what sadness this must have caused you, but we have to tell you that your sense of bitterness is fully shared not only by your compatriots, but also by all British sportsmen." The letter was signed, "Douglas Lowe." Peltzer endured hard times during the reign of the Nazis. First he was imprisoned for homosexuality. He was away from Germany when World War II broke out, but he was extradited by the Swedish government. The Nazis put him in the Mauthausen internment camp and kept him there for four years. After the war, Peltzer served as a popular coach in India.

1932 Los Angeles C: 19, N: 10, D: 8.2. WR: 1:50.0 (Benjamin Eastman)

1. Thomas Hampson	GBR	1:49.7 WR	(1:49:70)
2. Alexander Wilson	CAN	1:49.9	
3. Philip Edwards	CAN	1:51.5	
4. Edwin Genung	USA	1:51.7	
5. Edwin Turner	USA	1:52.5	
6. Charles Hornbostel	USA	1:52.7	
7. John Powell	GBR	1:53.1	
8. Séraphin Martin	FRA	1:53.6	

Missing from the competition was Ben Eastman, who had recorded 1:50.0 for 800 meters earlier in the year on his way to a time of 1:50.9 for 880 yards. Eastman had decided to concentrate on the 400 meters. Guyanese-born medical student Phil Edwards sprinted into the lead, covering the first lap in 52.3 seconds. Inevitably, he faded and was passed, first by Alex Wilson and then by 24-year-old schoolteacher Tommy Hampson, who had never before run faster than 1:52.4. Wilson and Hampson dueled stride for stride over the last 50 yards with Hampson just edging ahead to win by a foot.

Two days after his victory, Hampson recorded in his diary his impressions during the last half lap of the race: "Oh God help me—I'm tired. Oh Winnie [his fiancée], my darling, I cannot manage it. Yes I can, though, I beat Wilson two years ago. I beat Edwards twice two years ago. Oh damn this run—round the bend I can't see what's happening.

"We're in the straight. Oh God, let me get there—mustn't disappoint Winnie. Ah, goodbye Phil; now for Wilson. Wonder how far from the tape. I can't see. Caught him now for it. Harder, harder, harder—shall I do it? Yes, I will. Help me now, darling. I can't drop him; damn the man. At last, just in front—my shadow just ahead. Oh where is that tape? My legs won't take me there. What a row the crowd are making too! Ah, thank God, I felt it break, it must have been. Yes, here's Wilson, patting me: 'Well run, Tommy.'"

Hampson credited his victory to his love for his future wife. "I can truly say that but for her I would never have got where I am. A runner perhaps, for they can be made by diligence and hard work; a racer possibly, for they are born of experience in running; but a world beater must, like a great artist, be inspired—and what greater inspiration can anyone have than the love of such a beautiful, kind, gentle, sweet, good creature."

1936 Berlin C: 43, N: 24, D: 8.4. WR: 1:49.7 (Thomas Hampson)

1. John Woodruff	USA	1:52.9
2. Mario Lanzi	ITA	1:53.3
3. Philip Edwards	CAN	1:53.6
4. Kazimierz Kucharski	POL	1:53.8
5. Charles Hornbostel	USA	1:54.6
6. Harry Williamson	USA	1:55.8
7. Juan Carlos Anderson	ARG	—
8. Gerald Backhouse	AUS	—

John Woodruff was a 21-year-old University of Pittsburgh freshman—one of twelve African-Americans in a student body of more than 12,000—who came from a poor family in South Connellsville, Pennsylvania. His time of 1:52.7 was the fastest of the qualifying rounds. As usual, Phil Edwards, now a doctor, stormed into the lead and led the field around the first lap. Meanwhile Woodruff was executing one of the most unusual tactics ever seen in the Olympics. Finding himself boxed in after

300 meters, Woodruff came to a complete stop and let all the other runners pass him. Then he moved way to the outside and sprinted past his opponents one by one until he found himself in the lead with one lap to go. Edwards regained the lead on the backstretch, but Woodruff took over again in the last curve. Mario Lanzi staged a great finishing drive, but Woodruff used his loping ten-foot stride to stave off the challenge and win by two yards. Phil Edwards won his fifth Olympic bronze medal.

1948 London C: 41, N: 24, D: 8.2. WR: 1:46.6 (Rudolf Harbig)

1. Malvin Whitfield	USA	1:49.2 OR
2. Arthur Wint	JAM	1:49.5
3. Marcel Hansenne	FRA	1:49.8
4. Herbert Barten	USA	1:50.1
5. Ingvar Bengtsson	SWE	1:50.5
6. Robert Chambers	USA	1:52.1
7. Robert Chef d'Hôtel	FRA	1:53.0
8. Niels Hoist-Sörensen	DEN	1:53.4

Chef d'Hôtel held the early lead, but at the end of the first lap 23-year-old Air Force sergeant Mal Whitfield jumped the field and pulled away. Arthur Wint made a late charge, but Whitfield held on to win by three yards. Between 1948 and 1954 Whitfield won 66 of 69 half-mile races. He was inspired to be an Olympic runner when he sneaked into the Los Angeles Coliseum during the 1932 Olympics.

1952 Helsinki C: 50, N: 32, D: 7.22. WR: 1:46.6 (Rudolf Harbig)

1. Malvin Whitfield	USA	1:49.2 EOR	(1:49.34)
2. Arthur Wint	JAM	1:49.4	(1:49.63)
3. Heinz Ulzheimer	GER	1:49.7	(1:49.78)
4. Gunnar Nielsen	DEN	1:49.7	(1:49.84)
5. Albert Webster	GBR	1:50.2	(1:50.47)
6. Günter Steines	GER	1:50.6	(1:50.81)
7. Reginald Pearman	USA	1:52.1	(1:52.31)
8. Lars-Eric Wolfbrandt	SWE	1:52.1	(1:52.38)

Between Olympics Mal Whitfield had worked as a tail-gunner during the Korean War, flying 27 bomber missions. But on July 22, 1952, he was back in the final of the Olympic 800 meters run, once again facing the challenge of Arthur Wint. The 32-year-old Wint led the field around the first lap, reaching 400 meters with Ulzheimer second and Whitfield third. On the backstretch, with 250 meters to go, Whitfield made his move and entered the final curve in first place. Coming into the homestretch, Wint made a move of his own and gradually drew up to Whitfield's shoulder. But Whitfield had kept some extra strength in reserve and was able to pull away to a two-yard victory. Whitfield's time was exactly what it had been four years earlier, but Wint finished one yard closer.

Mal Whitfield spent 35 years setting up sports programs around the world under the auspices of the United States Information Agency.

1956 Melbourne C: 38, N: 24, D: 11.26. WR: 1:45.7 (Roger Moens)

1. Thomas Courtney	USA	1:47.7 OR	(1:47.75)
2. Derek Johnson	GBR	1:47.8	(1:47.88)
3. Audun Boysen	NOR	1:48.1	(1:48.25)
4. Arnold Sowell	USA	1:48.3	(1:48.41)
5. Michael Farrell	GBR	1:49.2	(1:49.29)
6. Lonnie Spurrier	USA	1:49.3	(1:49.38)
7. Emile Leva	BEL	1:51.8	(1:51.75)
8. Bill Butchart	AUS	1:52.5	

On August 3, 1955, Roger Moens of Belgium ran 1:45.7 to finally break Rudolf Harbig's 1939 world record. Unfortunately, Moens sustained a leg injury late in the 1956 season and was unable to compete in the Olympics. Nevertheless, the 800 meters final turned out to be the most dramatic race of the Melbourne Olympics. With Moens gone, the race shaped up to be the climactic chapter in the ongoing rivalry between Arnie Sowell of Pittsburgh and Tom Courtney of Livingston, New Jersey.

Sure enough, Courtney took the early lead, but Sowell quickly passed him and led the pack through the first lap and into the second. Toward the end of the backstretch, Courtney tried to pass Sowell, and the two ran shoulder to shoulder around the final curve. Emerging into the homestretch, the runners

800 meters, 1956

Tom Courtney (153) edges Derek Johnson (137) in the 800 meters final of 1956, the most dramatic race of the Melbourne Olympics. Courtney exhausted himself so thoroughly that the award ceremony had to be delayed an extra hour until he recovered.

found themselves confronted by a stiff wind. Courtney moved ahead and then shifted to the third lane in order to avoid the chewed up inner lane. Noticing the sudden opening between the two Americans, Derek Johnson dashed between them and, with 60 yards to go, pushed into first place. It looked like a major upset in the making, but Courtney was not about to give up. Courtney later recalled, "I looked at the tape just 40 yards away and realized this was the only chance I would ever have to win the Olympics." Ignoring the pain throughout his body, Courtney fashioned one last sprint out of nothing but determination. Step by step he gained on Johnson and lunged across the finish line. In a delirium, he turned to Johnson and asked who had won. "Why you did, Tom," came the reply.

"It was a new kind of agony for me," Courtney recalled. "I had never run myself into such a state. My head was exploding, my stomach ripping and even the tips of my fingers ached. The only thing I could think was, 'If I live, I will never run again!'" The victory ceremony had to be delayed for an hour until he recovered. Twenty years later, Tom Courtney wrote about his years of competitive running: "It is a world that is gone now, but I still enjoy going out to a local track and taking a run and, with a half lap to go, I kind of savor the idea that I am re-running the last half lap of the best part of my life."

1960 Rome C: 51, N: 35, D: 9.2. WR: 1:45.7 (Roger Moens)

1. Peter Snell	NZL	1:46.3 OR	(1:46.48)
2. Roger Moens	BEL	1:46.5	(1:46.55)
3. George Kerr	BWI/JAM	1:47.1	(1:47.25)
4. Paul Schmidt	GER	1:47.6	(1:47.82)
5. Christian Wägli	SWI	1:48.1	(1:48.19)
6. Manfred Matuschewski	GDR	1:52.0	(1:52.21)

The 1960 800 meters was expected to be a great duel between 30-year-old world record holder Roger Moens and George Kerr of Jamaica. Kerr won the first semifinal, but the second semi produced a surprise when Moens was beaten by a little-known New Zealander from Opunake named Peter Snell, whose pre-Olympic best had been 1:49.2 for 880 yards. However, Moens had not really extended himself, so Snell was still not taken seriously. Snell was unusually stocky for a middle-distance runner. Sports writer Leslie Hobbs would describe him as "a Sherman tank with overdrive."

As expected, Christian Wägli took the lead in the final and held on for 700 meters, at which point Moens moved ahead. In the homestretch he looked back three times to check the position of the other runners, particularly George Kerr. Moens was still ahead 25 yards from the tape when Snell, realizing for the first time that he actually had a chance to win, charged ahead on the inside. "All I remember from that point is hurling every ounce of effort into the finish, and flinging myself forward," Snell wrote in his autobiography, *No Bugles, No Drums.* Like Tom Courtney four years earlier, Peter Snell had no idea in which place he had finished. Then a dejected Roger Moens approached him with congratulations. "Who won?" asked Snell. "You did," replied Moens.

"It was a strange moment," Snell recalled. "What should I do now? Flashingly, I recalled films of past Olympics, and of champions who cavorted round the track, presumably letting their happy emotions run riot. But I felt in a semi-daze, partly from fatigue, partly from disbelief that this had actually happened to me." Snell did not take a victory lap. Instead he channeled his emotions into rooting for fellow New Zealander Murray Halberg, who won the next race on the schedule, the 5000 meters.

A word about one runner who never even made it to the starting line: Wym Essajas was the first person to represent the South American nation of Suriname at the Olympics. Unfortunately he was mistakenly told that the 800-meter heats would be held in the afternoon, so he spent the morning resting. When Essajas arrived at the stadium the heats were over, and he was forced to return to Suriname without having competed. It was eight years before Suriname sent another athlete to the Olympics.

Peter Snell, 1960

A surprise winner over world-record holder Roger Moens (237).

1964 Tokyo C: 47, N: 32, D: 10.16. WR: 1:44.3 (Peter Snell)

1. Peter Snell	NZL	1:45.1 OR
2. William Crothers	CAN	1:45.6
3. Wilson Kiprugut Chuma	KEN	1:45.9
4. George Kerr	JAM	1:45.9
5. Thomas Farrell	USA	1:46.6
6. Jerome Siebert	USA	1:47.0
7. Dieter Bogatzki	GER	1:47.2
8. Jacques Pennewaert	BEL	1:50.5

When Peter Snell arrived in Rome in 1960, no one had paid any attention, but four years later in Tokyo it was a completely different story. In one week in 1962 Snell had set world records of 3:54.4 for the mile and 1:44.3 for 800 meters. Now he was the favorite in both the 800 and 1500, although he didn't make his final decision to enter the 800 until the last minute. In the first round, Francis Chatelet of France had the unfortunate experience of recording the fifth-fastest time of the round, and yet being eliminated because he finished fifth in his heat, with only the top four from each heat advancing to the semifinals. The final saw stocky Wilson Kiprugut lead the field for 550 meters. Then Snell swung outside, stormed around the leaders into first place, and pulled away to win by four yards. Kiprugut tripped on George Kerr's heel 50 yards from the finish, but still managed to gain a bronze medal, the first Olympic medal ever won by a Kenyan. Snell's winning time was the best on record since his own world record performance.

After he retired from competition, Snell worked in the public relations department of a tobacco company. After several years he moved to the United States and, using money he earned in a Superstars competition, he put himself through graduate school and, at the age of 38, emerged with a doctorate in exercise physiology. In 1993, Snell became a US citizen and in 1998 he was US national age group champion (60-64) in the sport of orienteering.

1968 Mexico City C: 41, N: 31, D: 10.15. WR: 1:44.3 (Peter Snell)

1. Ralph Doubell	AUS	1:44.3 EWR	(1:44.40)
2. Wilson Kiprugut Chuma	KEN	1:44.5	(1:44.57)
3. Thomas Farrell	USA	1:45.4	(1:45.46)
4. Walter Adams	GER	1:45.8	(1:45.83)
5. Josef Plachý	CZE	1:45.9	(1:45.99)
6. Dieter Fromm	GDR	1:46.2	(1:46.30)
7. Thomas Saisi	KEN	1:47.5	(1:47.59)
8. Benedict Cayenne	TRI	1:54.3	(1:54.40)

Following the usual Kenyan tactics, Kiprugut led the field from the start and still had a six-yard lead after 600 meters. Unheralded Ralph Doubell, who had nipped Kiprugut in the second semifinal, repeated his come-from-behind performance in the final. He passed Kiprugut 50 yards from the finish and won by a long yard. As soon as the race was over, Doubell asked Farrell what the world record was. Farrell pointed to the scoreboard and said, "That's it." The top four finishers all set personal records while Plachý equaled his.

1972 Munich C: 61, N: 46, D: 9.2. WR: 1:44.3 (Peter Snell, Ralph Doubell, David Wottle)

1. David Wottle	USA	1:45.9	(1:45.86)
2. Yevhen Arzhanov	SOV/UKR	1:45.9	(1:45.89)
3. Michael Boit	KEN	1:46.0	(1:46.01)
4. Franz-Josef Kemper	GER	1:46.5	(1:46.50)
5. Robert Ouko	KEN	1:46.5	(1:46.53)
6. Andrew Carter	GBR	1:46.6	(1:46.55)
7. Andrzej Kupczyk	POL	1:47.1	(1:47.10)
8. Dieter Fromm	GDR	1:48.0	(1:47.96)

At the US Olympic tryouts, Dave Wottle of Canton, Ohio, had equaled the world record of 1:44.3, three seconds faster than he had ever run before. However, because of his lack of international experience and because he had suffered a recent attack of tendinitis, Wottle was not the favorite in Munich. This role fell rather naturally to Yevhen Arzhanov, who had not lost an 800-meter final in four years. As expected, the two Kenyans, Ouko and Boit, rushed into the early lead in the Olympic final, while Wottle ran in sixth place. Coming into the homestretch it looked like Arzhanov's race, and even Wottle, who had now begun his finishing kick, was only hoping for a medal. As the Kenyans faded, Wottle, who always wore an old golf cap while he ran, saw his chance for second place. Then, 20 yards from the finish, he realized that Arzhanov had run out of steam and that the gold medal was still a possibility. Drawing on his last reserve of energy, Wottle caught and passed Arzhanov, who stumbled two meters short of the tape and fell onto the synthetic track. "It is very disappointing," Arzhanov later told the press, "to lose in the very last stride by the length of your nose."

Wottle was so shocked by his victory that he forgot to take off his cap during the playing of "The Star-Spangled Banner" at the medal ceremony. He didn't realize what he had done until a reporter asked him if he had been staging a protest. Although nobody back in the United States actually held it against him, Wottle, a member of the Air Force ROTC at Bowling Green University, was embarrassed to the point of tears and felt obliged to make a formal apology to the American people.

1976 Montreal C: 42, N: 31, D: 7.25. WR: 1:43.7 (Marcello Fiasconaro)

1. Alberto Juantorena Danger	CUB	1:43.50 WR
2. Ivo van Damme	BEL	1:43.86
3. Richard Wohlhuter	USA	1:44.12
4. Willi Wülbeck	GER	1:45.26
5. Stephen Ovett	GBR	1:45.44
6. Luciano Susanj	YUG/CRO	1:45.75
7. Sriram Singh	IND	1:45.77
8. Carlo Grippo	ITA	1:48.39

Alberto Juantorena went to the Montreal Olympics as the favorite at 400 meters, but somewhat of an unknown quantity at 800 meters. Although he had recorded 1:44.9 in April, the second fastest time of the year (to Rick Wohlhuter's 1:44.8), Juantorena had very little experience at the distance. In fact, his coach had tricked him into entering 800-meter races by telling him they would build his endurance for the 400. Wohlhuter himself dismissed the Cuban as a non-contender, assuming that he would not have the stamina to make it through three rounds of metric half-mile races. Wohlhuter could not have been more wrong. In the final, Juantorena moved ahead as the runners broke to the inside after running the first 300 meters in lanes. He passed the halfway mark in 50.9 seconds. Sriram Singh took the lead briefly, but Juantorena fought him off, easily beat back a challenge from Wohlhuter, and won decisively, to become the first 800 meters gold medalist from a non-English-speaking country. Conspicuously missing from the competition was Mike Boit of Kenya, who was forced to watch the meet from the stands after his nation's government joined the African boycott. Four weeks later Boit ran 1:43.90 and 1:43.57, leaving track fans to wonder what might have been. Silver medalist Ivo van Damme died in a car crash on December 29, 1976. He was only 22 years old.

Olympic history, of course, is not just made up of medalists, and some mention should be made of Wilnor Joseph of the notorious Haitian track and field team. Joseph finished the second heat of the first round in 2:15.26, a time so slow that it would not have qualified him for the 800 meters final in 1900, much less 1976.

1980 Moscow C: 41, N: 28, D: 7.26. WR: 1:42.33 (Sebastian Coe)

1. Stephen Ovett	GBR	1:45.40
2. Sebastian Coe	GBR	1:45.85
3. Nikolai Kirov	SOV/BLR	1:45.94
4. Agberto Guimaraes	BRA	1:46.20
5. Andreas Busse	GDR	1:46.81
6. Detlef Wagenknecht	GDR	1:46.91
7. Jose Marajo	FRA	1:47.26
8. David Warren	GBR	1:49.25

Steve Ovett, 1980

Holding off the desperate charge of Sebastian Coe (254) in the stretch to best his arch-rival.

The final of the 1980 800 meters race was one of the most eagerly anticipated confrontations in Olympic history. Although there were six other runners in the race, the entire focus of sports fans around the world was on the two English world record holders, Sebastian Coe and Steve Ovett. The last time the two had met was at the 1978 European championships, where Ovett had beaten Coe at 800 meters, but both had lost to Olaf Beyer of East Germany. Since then Ovett and Coe had avoided each other like the plague, preferring to heat up their rivalry with increasingly faster times.

In 1979 Coe set the track world on its heels by breaking three world records in 41 days. On July 5 he ran 800 meters in 1:42.33 to lower Alberto Juantorena's world record by a full second. On July 17 Coe became the first person since Peter Snell to hold the records for both the 800 and the mile, when he ran the classic distance in 3:48.95. Then, on August 15, he covered 1500 meters in 3:32.03, to break Filbert Bayi's five-year-old mark.

The following year it was Steve Ovett's turn to enter the record books. On July 1, 1980, less than an hour after Coe set a new record for 1000 meters, Ovett gained great satisfaction by running a 3:48.8 mile to snatch the world record away from his rival. On July 15, nine days before the heats of the Olympic 800, Ovett beat a distinguished field of Olympic boycotters to win a 1500-meter race in 3:32.09, a time that rounded up to 3:32.1, the same as Coe's 3:32.03. The stage was definitely set for fireworks in the Olympics.

When Coe arrived in Moscow with the rest of the

British team, he was met by an army of no less than 400 journalists, who assaulted him with a barrage of inane questions, such as, "Do you think you will win?" "How do you feel as a human being?" (this one from the representative of Tass, the Soviet news agency), and "How do you like Moscow?" (he had been there only a few hours). Ovett, on the other hand, slipped in two days before he was due to run and, following his usual procedure, refused to talk to the press, a wise decision considering Coe's experience.

The consensus of track experts was that Coe was the favorite at 800 meters, but that the 1500 was a toss-up. Ovett, on the other hand, had issued a public statement that the 800 was a toss-up, but that he was 90 percent sure he would win the 1500. The two did not meet in the heats and semifinals of the 800 meters, the first middle-distance race to be contested.

The first round was run without incident, but the semifinals saw the surprise elimination of Olaf Beyer. The three semifinal heats were won by Ovett, Nikolai Kirov, and Coe.

The final, run at 7:25 p.m. on July 26, turned out to be a strange, almost sluggish race. The first lap was covered in the unusually slow time of 54.3 with Guimaraes in the lead, Ovett badly boxed in, in sixth place, and Coe running last. Dave Warren jumped into the lead, but in the backstretch Kirov moved in front by three meters, while Ovett pushed his way into second place, throwing so many elbows that he verged on disqualification. Meanwhile Coe was floundering, wasting his time in outside lanes and evidently unsure of what tactics to follow. By the time he finally made his move, it was too late. Ovett shot past Kirov 70 meters from the finish and won by more than three meters. Ironically, Ovett's winning time was the same as his fifth-place time in Montreal four years earlier. Coe outsprinted Kirov for the silver medal, a prize that would earn a place of honor in most homes, but which for Sebastian Coe was a symbol of failure.

As usual, Ovett declined to attend the postrace press conference. However Coe did not. Sorrowfully, he told the world, "I chose this day of all days to run the worst race of my life. I cannot explain why. I suppose I must have compounded more cardinal sins of middle-distance running in 1½ minutes than I've done in a lifetime. What a race to choose." Fortunately for Coe, he still had a chance to redeem himself six days later. "I've got to come back and climb the mountain again," he said. "The 1500 was going to be a hard event anyway, but now it's going to be the big race of my life. I must win it."

1984 Los Angeles C: 69, N: 55, D: 8.6. WR: 1:41.73 (Sebastian Coe)

1. Joaquim Carvalho Cruz	BRA	1:43.00 OR
2. Sebastian Coe	GBR	1:43.64
3. Earl Jones	USA	1:43.83
4. Billy Konchellah	KEN	1:44:03
5. Donato Sabia	ITA	1:44.53
6. Edwin Koech	KEN	1:44.86
7. Johnny Gray	USA	1:47.89
8. Stephen Ovett	GBR	1:52.28

Joaquim Cruz grew up in a poor neighborhood in Taguatinga, Brazil. Although his father worked from morning until night to support his wife and five children, it took a month's pay to produce enough extra to buy a pair of shoes for his only son. A few months after his father died in 1981, the 18-year-old Cruz, a reluctantly converted basketball player, set a world junior record of 1:44.3. His coach, Luiz de Oliveira, decided that if Cruz's potential was to be fulfilled, he would have to move north to the United States. So Cruz, de Oliveira, and de Oliveira's family went to live in Utah and then in Eugene, Oregon. By 1983 Cruz was ranked second in the world. The following year he entered the Olympics as a slight favorite over the veteran Sebastian Coe.

The young Brazilian was clearly in top form in Los Angeles. He won his first-round heat in 1:45.66, his quarterfinal heat in 1:44.84 and his semifinal in a personal best of 1:43.82. The other semi was won by Coe. In the final, Cruz positioned himself in second place and let Edwin Koech do the front-running, while Coe stayed right behind them. Coming out of the final turn, Cruz did a double-take at Coe behind him and then burst away from the other runners. Coe and Jones took off after him, but they never had a chance. Cruz's winning margin of five meters was the event's largest since 1928.

Sebastian Coe's silver medal was ample reward for a remarkable comeback. Only twelve months earlier, worn out by a prolonged debilitating illness, Coe had declared, "As far as the 800 meters goes, the game is up . . . I have been obliged to walk away from an event which I did not believe I had fully explored." As for defending Olympic champion Steve Ovett, he had struggled to qualify for the final, lunging across the line to gain the last spot ahead of Omar Khalifa of Sudan. Ovett's semifinal time of 1:44.81 was his fastest 800 in six years. After the final, Ovett, who had been battling bronchitis, collapsed twice in the tunnel leading away from the track. Taken away on a stretcher, he spent the next two nights in a hospital, suffering from broncho-spasms, which he attributed to the legendary Los Angeles smog. Courageously, or, as he would later say, foolishly, Ovett returned to the track to compete in the 1500 meters.

1988 Seoul C: 70, N: 53, D: 9.26. WR: 1:41.73 (Sebastian Coe)

1. Paul Ereng	KEN	1:43.45
2. Joaquim Carvalho Cruz	BRA	1:43.90
3. Saïd Aouita	MOR	1:44.06
4. Peter Elliott	GBR	1:44.12
5. Johnny Gray	USA	1:44.80
6. José Luiz Barbosa	BRA	1:46.39
7. Donato Sabia	ITA	1:48.03
8. Nixon Kiprotich	KEN	1:49.55

In 1988 the 800 meters was blessed with a talent-rich field led by Saïd Aouita, who hadn't lost a flat race at any distance between 800 and 10,000 meters in over three years. Challenging the multitalented Moroccan were Commonwealth champion Steve Cram, the man who had beaten Aouita at 1500 meters more than 50 races ago on July 16, 1985, and Joaquim Cruz, the defending Olympic champion. The big three were expected to be pressed by the world championship silver and bronze medalists, Peter Elliott, a carpenter at a steelworks in Rotherham, South Yorkshire, and José Luiz Barbosa, who grew up in Três Lagoas in the jungles of western Brazil, and by Johnny Gray, who had recorded the fastest time of the year, 1:42.65, just one month before the Olympics. No one paid any attention to Paul Ereng. And why should they?

A converted quarter-miler, the 21-year-old Ereng did not begin competing at 800 meters until 1988. Running for the University of Virginia, he won the NCAA title, then ran ten races in Europe, finishing first in only one. He was invited to the Kenyan Olympic trials only after someone sent Kenyan officials a newspaper article about Ereng's NCAA victory. In the absence of world champion Billy Konchellah, who was suffering a relapse of tuberculosis, the Kenyan trials were won by Nixon Kiprotich. Ereng, who led for most of the race, died at the end and barely held on for third place. He was the first member of the Turkana tribe to qualify for the Olympics.

Ereng still was not given serious consideration, even when he ran the fastest time of the opening round in Seoul (1:46.14). The quarterfinals saw the surprising elimination of Steve Cram. The semifinals were won by Ereng, in a personal record of 1:44.55, and Kiprotich in 1:44.71.

With two men in the final, the Brazilians planned a team race. Their strategy was to have Barbosa take out the first lap with a fast pace of between 49 and 50 seconds and try to disrupt Aouita by surging between 300 and 400 meters and 500 and 600, which was when they expected the Moroccan to accelerate. Then Cruz would take over in the backstretch and race to the tape.

The Kenyans had a similar plan, but with a twist. Kiprotich suggested that he set the early pace. Because he was better known, he reasoned, the others would not be expecting such a tactic and would be caught by surprise when Ereng made his move. Kiprotich did set a fast early pace (23.0 for 200 meters), so fast in fact that Ereng was horrified and almost yelled at him to stop. Barbosa moved ahead and led at the bell in 49.54, with Kiprotich second and Cruz third. Aouita was holding back in sixth place and Ereng in seventh.

The real scramble began in the backstraight. First Kiprotich regained the lead from Barbosa. Then Cruz shot by both of them with Elliott and Aouita close behind. Elliott tried to take the lead entering the final turn, but Cruz fought him off and reached the final straight looking like a winner. Meanwhile, though, Ereng was weaving his way between runners. While Elliott and Aouita engaged in a tough battle for second behind Cruz, Ereng slipped by both of them on the inside, then passed a shocked Cruz to win by 2 meters.

1992 Barcelona C: 59, N: 49, D: 8.5. WR: 1:41.73 (Sebastian Coe)

1. William Tanui	KEN	1.43.66
2. Nixon Kiprotich	KEN	1:43.70
3. Johnny Gray	USA	1:43.97
4. José Luiz Barbosa	BRA	1:45.06
5. Andrea Benvenuti	ITA	1:45.23
6. Curtis Robb	GBR	1:45.57
7. Reda Abdenouz	ALG	1:48.34
DNF: Mark Everett (USA)		

In the Olympic Village, Nixon Kiprotich dreamed that his teammate and friend, Air Force clerk William Tanui, would win the 800 meters final, and told him so. When the race was actually run, Johnny Gray burst into the lead and held it all the way into the homestretch. About 50 meters from the finish he was passed by Kiprotich and then, just at the end, both of them were passed by Tanui.

1996 Atlanta C: 55, N: 40, D: 7.31. WR: 1:41.73 (Sebastian Coe)

1. Vebjørn Rodal	NOR	1:42.58	OR
2. Hezekiél Sepeng	SAF	1:42.74	
3.Fred Onyancha	KEN	1:42.79	
4. Norberto Téllez	CUB	1:42.85	
5. Nico Motchebon	GER	1:43.91	
6. David Kiptoo	KEN	1:44.19	
7. Johnny Gray	USA	1:44.21	
8. Benyounés Lahlou	MOR	1:45.52	

Vebjørn Rodal found it difficult to train in the snow and ice of his hometown of Berkak, Norway, so the local power station allowed him to run in the 350-meter tunnel they had driven through a mountain. It wasn't until 1994 that he began training in modern facilities in nearby Trondheim. By 1995, he had earned a bronze medal at the world championship.

Meanwhile, in Potchefstroom, South Africa, Hezekiél Sepeng, the son of a poultry truck driver and a domestic servant, grew up running to school to avoid being late and running home to fight his brothers for food. He was discovered running barefoot and put into a high school with white students who pushed and elbowed him so much during races that he took to running in front to avoid them. Prior to the Olympics, Sepeng read an article in which Rodal listed his ten most dangerous challengers. Sepeng was not among them.

Both Rodal and Sepeng won their first round heats. There would be three semifinals, with the top two finishers in each advancing to the final along with the two fastest losers. Sepeng won his semi, but Rodal only placed third in his, behind Norberto Téllez and David Kiptoo. He squeezed into the final as the fastest loser.

As expected, Johnny Gray, competing in his fourth Olympic 800 meters final, broke into the lead, covering the first lap in 49.55 seconds. At the 500-meter mark, Rodal and Sepeng trailed the field. Over the next 100 meters, Rodal swept into second place and then passed Gray in the final turn. He opened a three-meter lead with Fred Onyancha and Téllez in hot pursuit. Sepeng, in sixth place with only 50 meters to go, moved past Onyancha into second place five meters from the line, but he couldn't catch Rodal. Vebjørn Rodal was the first Norwegian runner to win a gold medal, while Sepeng was the first-ever black South African medalist in any sport. The race was the first in which three runners bettered 1:43, much less four runners.

As fast and as exciting as the Olympic final was, it was difficult to forget that the overwhelming favorite, Wilson Kipketer, was not present in Atlanta. Ranked number one since 1994 and the defending world champion, Kipketer was undefeated in the pre-Olympic season, and had beaten Rodal twice. On July 10, three weeks before the Olympic final, Kipketer ran 1:42.51 in Nice—the fastest 800 meters in eleven years.

Kipketer was born in Kenya but moved to Denmark in 1990 to study electrical engineering. He applied for Danish citizenship, but Denmark refused to reduce their seven-year residence requirement. Kipketer could only compete for Denmark if Kenya signed a release allowing him to do so. The Kenyans suggested he represent his native country instead of Denmark. Kipketer refused to run for Kenya, the Kenyans refused to sign the release and the Danes refused to accelerate the citizenship process. Kipketer watched the Olympics on television. He completed the 1996 season undefeated, beating Rodal three more times. In 1997, in addition to defending his world championship, Kipketer equaled Sebastian Coe's 16-year-old world record and then, on August 13 and 24, beat it twice, running 1:41.24 and 1:41.11. After a severe bout with malaria, Kipketer earned a third world championship in 1999.

2000 Sydney C: 68, N: 46, D: 9.27. WR: 1:41.11 (Wilson Kipketer)

1. Nils Schumann	GER	1:45.08
2. Wilson Kipketer	DEN	1:45.14
3. Djabir Saïd-Guerni	ALG	1:45.16
4. Hezekiel Sepeng	SAF	1:45.29
5. André Bucher	SWI	1:45.40
6. Yury Borzakovsky	RUS	1:45.83
7. Glody Dube	BOT	1:46.24
DNF: Andrea Longo (ITA)		

As the world record holder and winner of the last three world championships, Wilson Kipketer was the clear favorite in Sydney. André Bucher had recorded the fastest time of the year, 1:43:12, and was also considered a serious contender. But the fast times of Kipketer and Bucher proved meaningless because the Olympic final was a slow, tactical race, the slowest in twenty years. It was so slow that, for the first time since 1936, the final was slower than the semifinals. European champion Nils Schumann, who had set a personal best of 1:44:22 in the semifinals, took an early lead in the final. Andrea Longo led the pack past the halfway mark in 53.43. Running even with Bucher as they approached the final turn, Longo inadvertently bumped Bucher onto the infield (the two were friends and training partners), leading to Longo's subsequent disqualification. Coming out of the turn, Longo was still in front, with Bucher, Schumann and 19-year-old Yury Borzakovsky close behind. Atlanta silver medalist Hezekiél Sepeng made a move on the inside, while Kipketer and Djabir Saïd-Guerni swung wide. Schumann, who had hoped for a silver or bronze medal, took the lead with 50 meters to go and held off the closing sprints of Kipketer and Saïd-Guerni to win the closest 800-meter group finish in Olympic history. As a sign of his seriousness, Schumann had gone without beer for three months before the Olympics.

2004 Athens C: 72, N: 58, D: 8.28. WR: 1:41.11 (Wilson Kipketer)

1. Yuri Borzakovsky	RUS	1:44.45
2. Mbulaeni Mulaudzi	SAF	1:44.61
3. Wilson Kipketer	DEN	1:44.65
4. Moussin Chéhibi	MOR	1:45.16
5. Wilfred Bungei	KEN	1:45.31
6. Hezekiél Sepeng	SAF	1:45.53
7. Djabir Saïd-Guerni	ALG	1:45.61
8. Ahmed Ismail	SUD	1:52.49

The competition was staged with only three rounds, despite attracting a record-setting 72 entrants. This led to highly-competitive heats and semifinals, with only the first two finishers in each race automatically qualifying for the next round.

Named after the Russian cosmonaut Yuri Gagarin, 2003 world champion silver medalist Yuri Borzakovsky qualified easily for the semis, as did world record holder Wilson Kipketer. In the first semifinal, world champion Djabir Saïd-Guerni edged out Mbulaeni Mulaudzi for first place. The second semifinal heat saw top-ranked Wilfred Bungei hold off Borzakovsky at the finish, while Kipketer led the third semi.

In the final, after 200 meters, Borzakovsky trailed the field by eight meters. At the second turn, the race slowed somewhat, allowing him to catch up, and by the end of the first lap the field was closely bunched, with Saïd-Guerni leading and Bungei in second place. Kipketer was in third, just ahead of Mulaudzi, with Ahmed Ismail and Borzakovsky close behind. Bungei took the lead in the backstretch, with Kipketer drawing even off the bend. With 80 meters to go, Borzakovsky, still in only fifth place, made his move, pulling past Saïd-Guerni, while Kipketer took the lead, followed by Mulaudzi on the inside. Kipketer, Mulaudzi and Borzakovsky were even with 25 meters to go, but then Borzakovsky pulled ahead and Mulaudzi edged out a fading Kipketer for silver. The first Russian to win the 800-meter event, Borzakovsky dedicated his medal to the victims of two Russian airplane crashes in Southern Russia linked to Chechen separatists.

2008 Beijing C: 58, N: 40, D: 8.23. WR: 1:41.11 (Wilson Kipketer)

1. Wilfred Bungei	KEN	1:44.65
2. Ismail Ahmed Ismail	SUD	1:44.70
3. Alfred Kirwa Yego	KEN	1:44.82
4. Gary Reed	CAN	1:44.94
5. Yusuf Saad Kamel	BRN	1:44.95
6. Yeimer López García	CUB	1:45.88
7. Nabil Madi	ALG	1:45.96
8. Nadjim Manseur	ALG	1:47.19

Defending Olympic champion Yuri Borzakovsky had continued to be a top international contender, winning the silver medal at the 2005 world championships and bronze at the 2007 championships. His main threats were from reigning world champion Alfred Kirwa Yego, silver medalist Gary Reed and 2006 world indoor champion Wilfred Bungei, who had finished in the top five at the 2004 Olympics and the past two world championships.

Another intriguing competitor was 19-year-old Abubaker Kaki of Sudan. In March 2008 Kaki became the youngest 800 meters indoor world champion in history at the age of 18 years 262 days. Then, two months before the Olympics, Kaki registered a 1:42.69 at a meet in Oslo, the fastest time in the world since Bungei had recorded a 1:42.52 in 2003. A product of the bare-bones Sudanese national sports program in Khartoum, Kaki and his teammate Ismail Ahmed Ismail represented both sides of the ongoing war in Darfur. Kaki was a member of the Misseriya tribe, connected with the government-supported mounted Arab militias that were ravaging the Darfur region of western Sudan, while Ismail was from the Fur tribe, the target of much of the violence. The team trained in an unfinished stadium with no lights, using paint cans filled with cement for weight training. The facilities were so poor that a runner for Somalia called it "the worst track I ever witnessed." The team was so poorly funded that Kaki and Ismail only made it to Beijing after a donation from the British Embassy helped pay for the trip.

The semi-final round of the Olympic competition eliminated several of the favorites, including Borzakovsky, Kaki and defending silver medalist Mbulaeni Mulaudzi. In the final, Bungei took the early lead, with a 53.35-second first lap ahead of Yego and Kenyan-born Yousef Saad Kamel. Bungei upped the pace in the final lap, but Ismail gradually moved up the field to challenge him over the final stretch. Bungei held on to win the gold medal by 0.05 seconds. Trapped in the pack with 100 meters remaining, Yego worked his way up from fifth to take bronze. Ismail's silver was Sudan's first-ever Olympic medal. It was also the first-ever African sweep of the event.

Bungei was born in the small village of Kabirirsang in Kenya's Rift Valley, the same area that produced world record holder Wilson Kipketer, double Olympic champion Kipchoge Keino and multiple world record setter Henry Rono. Bungei himself was Kipketer's second cousin and related to Rono through his mother.

1500 METERS

The "metric mile," the 1500 meters race, is 1640 yards 1 foot 3 inches long and covers three and three-quarter laps. Twelve runners take part in the final. On the fortieth anniversary of the day he broke the four-minute mile, Roger Bannister, speaking to an audience that included thirteen other mile record setters, had this to say about the life of world-class milers: "Old men, they say, forget. It's true we forget the pain and the fatigue and lashing yourself to try harder next time and next, illness and injury, real and perhaps sometimes imagined, the castigations of the press and coaches—all these fade away, because memory is kind. We remember the good times, the sun on our backs, running through the beauty of the countryside, running thousands and thousands of miles. We remember laughter and friends. For us, no matter what life may bring, whatever subsequent shadows there may be, no one can strip us of these memories."

1896 Athens C: 8, N: 5, D: 4.7. WR (1 mile): 4:12.8 (Walter George)

1. Edwin Flack	AUS	4:33.2
2. Arthur Blake	USA	4:34.0e
3. Albin Lermusiaux	FRA	4.37.0e
4. Karl Galle	GER	—

Flack outsprinted Blake in the final straightaway to win by about five meters. Two days later Flack also won the 800 meters race.

1900 Paris C: 9, N: 6, D: 7.15. WR: 4:10.4 (Albin Lermusiaux)

1. Charles Bennett	GBR	4:06.2 WR
2. Henri Deloge	FRA	4:07.0e
3. John Bray	USA	4:10.2e
4. David Hall	USA	—
5. Christian Christensen	DEN	—
6. Hermann Wraschtil	AUT	—

Two of the leading contenders, John Cregan and Alex Grant of the United States, withdrew because the race was held on a Sunday. Bennett, a railway engine driver from Shapwick, Dorset, ran the final lap in 70.2 seconds. He celebrated his victory by going to the Folies Bergère.

1904 St. Louis C: 9, N: 3, D: 9.3. WR: 4:06.2 (Charles Bennett)

1. James Lightbody	USA	4:05.4 WR
2. William Frank Verner	USA	4:06.8
3. Lacey Hearn	USA	—
4. David Munson	USA	—
5. Johannes Runge	GER	—
6. Peter Deer	CAN	—
7. Howard Valentine	USA	—
8. Harvey Cohn	USA	—

Lightbody moved into the lead at the end of the backstretch and won by six yards. The first three finishers were all members of the Chicago Athletic Association.

1906 Athens C: 20, N: 9, D: 4.30. WR: 4:05.4 (James Lightbody)

1. James Lightbody	USA	4.12.0
2. John McGough	GBR/IRL	4;12.6
3. Kristian Hellström	SWE	4:13.4
4. A. Gregory Wheatley	AUS	—
5. James Sullivan	USA	—
6. George Bonhag	USA	—
7. Reginald Percy Crabbe	GBR	—
8. Harvey Cohn	USA	—

Lightbody and McGough were fourth and seventh entering the final lap. Lightbody took the lead 200 meters from the finish.

1908 London C: 43, N: 15, D: 7.14. WR: 3:59.8 (Harold Wilson

1. Melvin Sheppard	USA	4:03.4 OR
2. Harold Wilson	GBR	4:03.6e
3. Norman Hallows	GBR	4:04.0e
4. John Tait	CAN	4:06.8e
5. Ivo Fairbairn-Crawford	GBR	4:07.6e
6. Joseph Deakin	GBR	4:07.9e

DNF: James Sullivan (USA), E. Vincent Loney (GBR)

Unfortunately, British officials decided to divide the 43 entrants into eight heats and allow only the winner of each heat to advance to the final. Because the runners were not seeded, this caused the elimination of several major contenders, most notably Emilio Lunghi, who ran the second fastest time (4:03.8), but lost his heat to Norman Hallows, who ran 4:03.4. The final looked like a victory for the 5-foot 4-inch (1.63 meter), 115-pound world record holder, Harold Wilson, until Mel Sheppard launched a sprint 100 yards from the tape, passed Wilson with 15 yards to go, and won by a yard and a half. For Sheppard, it was the first of his four Olympic gold medals. Ironically, Sheppard had applied to become a New York City policeman, but was rejected because he had a "weak heart."

1912 Stockholm C: 45, N: 14, D: 7.10. WR: 3:55.8 (Abel Kiviat)

1. Arnold Jackson	GBR	3:56.8 OR
2. Abel Kiviat	USA	3:56.9
3. Norman Taber	USA	3:56.9
4. John Paul Jones	USA	3:57.2
5. Ernst Wide	SWE	3:57.6
6. Philip Baker	GBR	3:59.6
7. John Zander	SWE	4:02.0e
8. Henri Arnaud	FRA	4:02.2e

The United States entered a powerful team, including defending champion Mel Sheppard, 1500-meter world record holder Abel Kiviat, and mile world record holder John Paul Jones. Kiviat took the lead entering the final lap, followed by Taber and Jones, with Jackson and Sheppard close behind. Sheppard faded first. Entering the final straight it still looked like an American sweep, as Kiviat, Taber, and Jones raced almost shoulder to shoulder. Thirty meters from the finish Kiviat seemed assured of victory, when suddenly Arnold Jackson of Great Britain burst by on the outside and won by almost two yards. A finish camera was used to sort out second and third place. This was the first time a photo finish was employed at the Olympics. Jackson later gained greater fame as Arnold Nugent Strode-Jackson following his participation in World War I, during which he was wounded three times. In 1918, at the age of 27, he became the youngest acting brigadier general in the British army. As an athlete, Jackson was rather casual in his training, prefering golf, walking, and massages to the more vigorous and acceptable techniques of keeping in shape. As for Kiviat, 72 years later, at the age of 91, he participated in the 1984 torch relay, carrying the flame for one kilometer in New York City.

1920 Antwerp C: 29, N: 12, D: 8.19. WR: 3:54.7 (John Zander)

1. Albert Hill	GBR	4:01.8
2. Philip Baker	GBR	4:02.3e
3. Lawrence Shields	USA	4:03.0e
4. Vaclàv Vohralík	CZE	4:04.6e
5. Sven Lundgren	SWE	4:06.3e
6. André Audinet	FRA	4:06.4e
7. Arturo Porro	ITA	4:06.6e
8. Joie Ray	USA	4:10.0e

The 31-year-old Hill completed his 800/1500 double with the help of Baker, who ran beside him for most of the final lap in order to "protect him from attacks." Baker later adopted his wife's maiden name and changed his name to Philip Noel-Baker. He served as a Member of Parliament for 36 years, but was considered so boring that he earned the nickname, "the chambermaid," because he always cleaned out the chamber whenever he spoke. A Quaker pacifist, Noel-Baker served in the Ambulance Corps during World War I. After the war, he worked on the draft of the Covenant of the League of Nations and after World War II he served on the sub-committee that created the preliminary agenda for the United Nations General Assembly. In 1959 Noel-Baker was awarded the Nobel Peace Prize in honor of his work in the pursuit of peace and disarmament and for his work on behalf of war refugees. In 1991, a different side of Philip Noel-Baker was revealed with the public disclosure of 554 love letters that he wrote to fellow MP Megan Lloyd George, during a 20-year adulterous affair, which Noel-Baker finally broke off when his wife died in 1956.

1924 Paris C: 40, N: 22, D: 7.10. WR: 3:52.6 (Paavo Nurmi)

1. Paavo Nurmi	FIN	3:53.6 OR
2. Wilhelm Schärer	SWI	3:55.0
3. Hyla "Henry" Stallard	GBR	3:55.6
4. Douglas Lowe	GBR	3:57.0
5. Raymond Buker	USA	3:58.5
6. Lloyd Hahn	USA	3:59.0
7. Raymond Watson	USA	3:59.9
8. Frej Liewendahl	FIN	4:00.3

The crowd at the Stade Colombes Stadium rose to their feet to watch the thrilling race to the finish line, as Willy Schärer moved ahead in the last few strides to defeat the desperately struggling Henry Stallard, who collapsed to the ground and remained unconscious for a half hour. It had been an exciting battle—for second place. The race for first place had been no race at all, due to the presence of "The Phantom Finn," Paavo Nurmi. Finnish Olympic officials had been extremely upset when the track and field schedule was announced and they learned that the final of the 1500 meters and the final of the 5000 meters would be separated by only a half hour, giving negligible time for recuperation to Nurmi, their star entrant in both events. A protest was filed, and the French organizers grudgingly agreed to expand the interval to two hours. It still seemed an impossible feat to attempt, particularly after Nurmi injured both legs in training. But the challenge simply made Nurmi more determined to succeed. On June 19, three weeks before the day of the two Olympic finals, Nurmi decided to simulate the task ahead of him. First he ran a 1500-meter race, setting a world record of 3:52.6. After a one-hour rest he returned to the track and ran 5000 meters, setting another world record of 14:28.2.

Needless to say, when the other runners lined up for the start of the Olympic 1500 final in Paris, they had little hope for the gold medal. Nurmi took off, stopwatch in hand, as usual, covering the first 400 meters in a blistering 58.0 designed to kill off the opposition. Ray Watson made the mistake of trying to keep up with the Finnish running machine, and paid for his folly by fading to a disappointing seventh place. As soon as Watson had dropped away, Nurmi consulted his stopwatch one last time, tossed it onto the infield, and sprinted away to a 40-meter lead. In order to save his strength for the 5000, he coasted the final 300 meters, picking up speed briefly just before the end to make sure the others did not catch up. After he crossed the finish line, he ignored the cheers of the crowd, picked up his stopwatch and his sweater, and disappeared into the dressing room to rest up for his next race.

1928 Amsterdam C: 54, N: 26, D: 8.2. WR: 3:51.0 (Otto Peltzer)

1. Harry Larva	FIN	3:53.2 OR
2. Jules Ladoumègue	FRA	3:53.8
3. Eino Purje-Borg	FIN	3:56.4
4. Hans-Georg Wichmann	GER	3:56.8
5. Cyril Ellis	GBR	3:57.6
6. Paul Martin	SWI	3:58.4
7. Helmut Krause	GER	3:59.0
8. William Whyte	AUS	4:00.0

Two hundred meters from the finish, Ladoumègue took the lead from Purje and appeared to be headed for victory. However he was passed 20 meters from the tape by "Harri" Larva, a goldsmith's engraver, who won by four yards. Larva was born to Swedish parents who lived in Turku, the hometown of Paavo Nurmi. He began training as a runner in 1924 after attending a post-Olympic race between Nurmi and Ritola. Ladoumègue, too, idolized Nurmi and kept a newspaper photo of the master underneath his bed. On the victory podium both Larva and Ladoumègue cried—the Finn from joy, the Frenchman from disappointment.

1932 Los Angeles C: 27, N: 15, D: 8.4. WR: 3:49.2 (Jules Ladoumègue)

1. Luigi Beccali	ITA	3:51.2 OR (3:51:20)
2. John "Jerry" Cornes	GBR	3:52.6
3. Philip Edwards	CAN	3:52.8
4. Glenn Cunningham	USA	3:53.4
5. Eric Ny	SWE	3:54.6
6. Norwood Hallowell	USA	3:55.0
7. John Lovelock	NZL	3:55.6
8. Frank Crowley	USA	3:56.6

Five months before the Los Angeles Games, world record holder Jules Ladoumègue was banned from competition by the French Athletics Federation after being charged with accepting payment for running in certain meets. The heated protests of French sports fans were to no avail. Still, the 1932 Olympic final was packed with splendid runners. The lead changed hands several times in the early going. Then, as the second lap came to a close, Glenn Cunningham, who was suffering a bad case of tonsilitis, burst ahead, followed by Phil Edwards. By the time the bell had rung to signal the final lap, Cunningham and Edwards had opened a 15-meter gap over the rest of the field. With 300 meters to go, John "Jerry" Cornes and 5-foot 6½-inch (1.69 meter) Luigi Beccali gave chase. In the backstretch Edwards passed Cunningham and took a five-yard lead. Beccali caught Cunningham at the head of the homestretch and then passed Edwards 100 yards from the finish. The young man from Milan won by six yards (5½ meters), breaking the tape by grabbing it in his hands and tearing it apart. At the medal ceremony Beccali gave the Fascist salute and became a national hero overnight. As a matter of fact, when he emerged from his cottage in the Olympic Village the next morning, he discovered that his Italian teammates had covered the walk from his bungalow with rugs from their own rooms and lined the path with wicker chairs adorned with flowers. Standing behind the chairs were his teammates, chanting, "Luigi, Luigi, Luigi." Beccali, choked with emotion, was speechless. He later emigrated to New York and went into the wine business. Meanwhile, Jerry Cornes joined the Colonial Service and spent many years in Palestine until he was almost killed when anti-British Jewish terrorists blew up the King David Hotel in Jeruselem in 1946.

1936 Berlin C: 44, N: 27, D: 8.6. WR: 3:48.8 (William Bonthron)

1. John Lovelock	NZL	3:47.8 WR
2. Glenn Cunningham	USA	3:48.4
3. Luigi Beccali	ITA	3:49.2
4. Archie San Romani	USA	3:50.0
5. Philip Edwards	CAN	3:50.4
6. John "Jerry" Cornes	GBR	3:51.4
7. Miklós Szabó	HUN	3:53.0
8. Robert Goix	FRA	3:53.8

The 1936 1500-meter final promised to be one of the great races of all time and, unlike many athletic contests with great expectations, it lived up to its advance billing. Among the starters were six of the top seven finishers from the 1932 Olympics. The favorites were defending champion Luigi Beccali, one-mile world record holder Glenn Cunningham of Elkhart, Kansas, whose leg had been severely burned in a schoolhouse fire when he was eight years old, and Jack Lovelock of New Zealand, who had beaten Cunningham in "The Mile of the Century" at Princeton in 1935. Lovelock, a former Rhodes scholar at Oxford, was now a medical student who ran numerous tests on himself in order to determine the conditions necessary to achieve an optimum performance. He was particularly interested in learning how long he could sustain a final sprint, and this led to his development of a secret strategy to win at the Berlin Olympics.

When the great race finally began at 4:18 p.m., there was a good deal of jockeying for position. Cunningham took the lead at 400 meters, followed by Lovelock, who later dropped back to fourth place. Just before the bell, Eric Ny passed Cunningham. Then, 300 yards from the tape, Lovelock passed Cunningham and reached Ny's shoulder. Cunningham followed him. Then Lovelock paused and so did Cunningham, thinking the move had been a false alarm. But one second later Lovelock was off again, beginning the unusually long sprint that he had planned so carefully. Cunningham raced after him, but Lovelock was able to open up a lead of six yards. Cunningham tried to close the gap, but he could get no closer than four yards. Lovelock ran the final 400 meters in 56.8 seconds and the last 200 meters in 27.2, even though he slowed up in the last 20 yards, realizing that his victory was assured. Lovelock didn't believe in setting records, only in winning, but he broke the world record by a full second because that was what was required to defeat Cunningham.

In 1940 Jack Lovelock was thrown from a horse during a hunt and lay unconscious for an hour before he was discovered. He recovered, but suffered double vision and occasional dizziness for the rest of his life. He and his wife moved to New York, where Lovelock obtained a position as assistant director of physical medicine at the Hospital for Special Surgery. On December 28, 1949, eight days before his 40th birthday, Lovelock began having dizzy spells and telephoned his wife that he would be coming home early. He was standing on the southbound platform of the Church Street subway station in Brooklyn when he suddenly pitched forward onto the tracks. He was struck by an oncoming train and died instantly.

1948 London C: 37, N: 22, D: 8.6. WR: 3:43.0 (Gunder Hägg, Lennart Strand)

1. Henry Eriksson	SWE	3:49.8
2. Lennart Strand	SWE	3:50.4
3. Willem Slijkhuis	HOL	3:50.4
4. Václav Čevona	CZE	3:51.2
5. Gösta Bergkvist	SWE	3:52.2
6. G. William Nankeville	GBR	3:52.6
7. Sándor Garay	HUN	3:52.8
8. Erik Jörgensen	DEN	3:52.8

The 1948 final was run on a rain-soaked track in the middle of a downpour. The two great Swedish runners Gunder Hägg and Arne Andersson had been banned as professionals, but the Swedes still fielded the strongest team in Lennart Strand, Henry Eriksson, and Gösta Bergkvist. Marcel Hansenne of France led for 1000 meters, at which point the three Swedes, led by Eriksson, made their move. Coming out of the final turn, Eriksson, who had never beaten Strand, held a three-yard lead. Strand closed up to his shoulder and ran even for another 20 yards, but with 50 yards to go he realized that he couldn't pass his teammate. Looking behind him he saw Slijkhuis coming with a great rush on the inside. Determined to preserve second place, Strand veered to his left and bumped the Dutch runner off the track long enough to prevent him from passing. It was the first time that Eriksson had beaten Strand. Eriksson was a fireman, Strand a linotype operator and pianist.

1952 Helsinki C: 52, N: 26, D: 7.26. WR: 3:43.0 (Gunder Hägg, Lennart Strand, Werner Lueg)

1. Josef Barthel	LUX	3:45.1 OR	(3:45.28)
2. Robert McMillen	USA	3:45.2	(3:45.39)
3. Werner Lueg	GER	3:45.4	(3:45.67)
4. Roger Bannister	GBR	3:46.0	(3:46.30)
5. Patrick El Mabrouk	FRA	3:46.0	(3:46.35)
6. Rolf Lamers	GER	3:46.8	(3:47.18)
7. Olle Åberg	SWE	3:47.0	(3:47.20)
8. Ingvar Ericsson	SWE	3:47.6	(3:47.70)

The 1952 1500 meters was up for grabs. If there were favorites they were probably Werner Lueg, who had tied the world record at the German championships on June 29, and Roger Bannister, whose greatest fame was yet to come. Bannister, a medical intern, had prepared himself very carefully for a competition that would include a heat and then a final two days later. Unfortunately, IAAF officials decided to add a semifinal round, which meant that the finalists would run three races in three days. This change of schedule greatly upset Bannister's plans. The semifinals were won by local favorite Denis Johansson in 3:49.8 and lightly regarded Josy Barthel, a small man from the small nation of Luxembourg, who finished in 3:50.4.

Audun Boysen of Norway was the first in front in the final, but he was soon passed by Rolf Lamers, who held the lead until the third lap, when he surrendered it to his teammate Werner Lueg. Coming into the backstretch, the action became frantic. Lueg fought off challenges from Olle Åberg, Patrick El Mabrouk, and Bannister. Lueg opened up a three-yard lead and held it around the final turn. However, almost unnoticed, two outsiders, Josy Barthel and Bob McMillen, had sprinted up from the very back of the field to within striking distance.

Fifty yards from the finish, Lueg began to tie up. With the crowd screaming wildly, first Barthel and then McMillen passed the German. Barthel could feel McMillen literally breathing down his back as the American inched closer with every stride until he

Josy Barthel, 1952
The pride of tiny Luxembourg, realizing a dream and besting, among others, a soon-to-be-famous Roger Bannister (177).

was only one and a half feet behind. Let Josy Barthel tell the rest of the story: "Five meters to run, the victory is mine, and, just as I had always dreamed in secret, I raised my arms, I smiled and I crossed the finish line.

"Afterward, I didn't appreciate right away that I had won. For me, as for the public, it was a surprise. I sat down, without being excited, on a bench in the middle of the infield. Then, no longer able to contain my joy, I cried. My friend Audun Boysen asked me, '*Eh bien,* Josy, why are you crying? Are you ill?' It was only then that I truly understood. 'No,' I replied, 'I am crying because I won.'"

Six of the 12 finalists had run their best time ever, including Barthel, whose previous best had been 3:48.4, and McMillen, who had never bettered 3:49.3. On the victory platform, as he listened to the national anthem of Luxembourg being played for the first and only time in Olympic history, Josy Barthel cried again. Roger Bannister recalled, "He raised his hand to wipe away a tear. His great strength was overcome by the tide of joy. Then he turned the movement into a wave of gratitude to the crowd . . . In the great joy of that single moment the agony of the previous week was quite forgotten. I had found new meaning in the Olympic words that the important thing was not the winning but the taking part—not the conquering but the fighting well."

1956 Melbourne C: 37, N: 22, D: 12.1. WR: 3:40.6 (István Rózsavölgyi)

1. Ron Delany	IRL	3:41.2 OR	(3:41.49)
2. Klaus Richtzenhain	GDR	3:42.0	(3:42.02)
3. John Landy	AUS	3:42.0	(3:42.03)
4. László Tábori	HUN	3:42.4	(3:42.55)
5. Brian Hewson	GBR	3:42.6	(3:42.69)
6. Stanislav Jungwirth	CZE	3:42.6	(3:42.80)
7. Neville Scott	NZL	3:42.8	(3:42.87)
8. Ian Boyd	GBR	3:43.0	(3:42.94)

May 6, 1954, stands as probably the greatest day in track and field history. Running in Oxford with the help of pace-setters Chris Brasher and Chris Chataway, Roger Bannister attempted to break the barrier of barriers—the four-minute mile. In his autobiography, appropriately entitled *The Four-Minute Mile,* Bannister recalled the final lap of that race: "I felt that the moment of a lifetime had come . . . The world seemed to stand still, or did not exist. The only reality was the next two hundred yards of track under my feet . . .

"I felt at that moment that it was my chance to do one thing supremely well. I drove on, impelled by a combination of fear and pride. The air I breathed filled me with the spirit of the track where I had run my first race. The noise in my ears was that of the faithful Oxford crowd. Their hope and encouragement gave me greater strength. I had now turned the last bend and there were only fifty yards more . . .

Ron Delany, 1956
A late surge and the classic race went to the youngest man in the field.

John Landy, 1956
After the race, John Landy goes to the aid of Delany, whom he assumes to be doubled over in pain. Instead he discovers that Delany is deep in prayer.

"Those last few seconds seemed never-ending. The faint line of the finishing tape stood ahead as a haven of peace, after the struggle. The arms of the world were waiting to receive me if only I reached the tape without slackening my speed. If I faltered, there would be no arms to hold me and the world would be a cold, forbidding place, because I had been so close. I leapt at the tape like a man taking his last spring to save himself from the chasm that threatens to engulf him."

The track announcer that day was none other than Norris McWhirter, who later became world famous as the compiler, along with his brother Ross, of *The Guinness Book of World Records*. McWhirter milked the dramatic moment for all it was worth. "Ladies and gentlemen," he began, "here is the result of event number nine, the one mile. First, number forty-one, R. G. Bannister of the Amateur Athletic Association and formerly of Exeter and Merton Colleges, with a time which is a new meeting and track record and which, subject to ratification, will be a new English Native, British National, British All-Corners', European, British Empire and World's record. The time is THREE . . ." The rest of the announcement was lost in the roar of the crowd. In fact, Bannister's time was 3:59.4.

In the two and a half years between that day in Oxford and the Melbourne Olympics, Bannister had retired from competition, but nine other runners had broken the four-minute barrier. All ten were present in Melbourne for the running of the 1500 meters—six on the track (John Landy, Brian Hewson, László Tábori, Ron Delany, Gunnar Nielsen, and István Rózsavölgyi) and four in the stands (Bannister, Jim Bailey, Chris Chataway, and Derek Ibbotson). Bannister presented to each of his successors a black silk tie with a monogram of a silver "4" and two gold "M"s within a gold laurel wreath.

The very first heat saw the elimination of several great runners, including Josy Barthel, István Rózsavölgyi, who had broken training during the Hungarian uprising against the USSR, Michel Jazy, who was to win a silver medal four years later in Rome, and an obscure Ethiopian named Mamo Wolde, who would gain fame 12 years later when he won the 1968 Olympic marathon.

The final turned out to be just as great a contest as had been expected. Before the race, the great sportsman John Landy, who once stopped in the middle of a race to help a fallen runner by the name of Ron Clarke, gave a pep talk to Ron Delany, the youngest of the four-minute milers, and told him, "I think you can win this one, Ron." The twelve finalists were so well matched that when they began the final lap, less than eight yards separated the leader from the man in last place. The official in charge of signaling the beginning of the final lap was so excited that he forgot to ring the bell. Hewson and Merv Lincoln of Australia were in the lead, but Lincoln, feeling a pain in his leg, began to fall back quickly. Meanwhile, Ron Delany was boxed in at tenth place. His coach at Villanova University, Jumbo Elliott, had always told him that if he was ever in a box just to relax. So Delany relaxed, even though there were only 300 yards left in the race.

Just then the runner in front of Delany, Gunnar Nielsen, realizing that he himself couldn't win the race, turned around and motioned Delany to pass him on the inside. Gradually Delany moved up; then, 120 meters from the finish, he burst out with all he had. The power of his sprint demoralized the other runners, and he was home free. He ran the last lap in 53.8, the last 200 meters in 25.6, and the final 100 meters in 12.9. He flew past the tiring Hewson and won by three yards. During his final training session in Berekeley, California, before leaving for Australia, the famous American coach, Brutus Hamilton, strung a piece of twine across the track and told Delany to run through it, spreading his arms wide in mock jubilation. In the real Olympic final, Delany breasted the tape with his arms spread wide and a huge grin on his face. After crossing the finish line, Delany fell to his knees. John Landy, thinking Delany was ill or injured, rushed up to help him, only to discover that the new Olympic champion was actually deep in prayer.

For the record, 43 years after Roger Bannister's four-minute mile breakthrough, Daniel Komen of Kenya ran back to back four-minute miles (3:59.2 and 3:59.4) winning a two-mile race in Brussels on July 19, 1997, in 7:58.61.

1960 Rome C: 39, N: 25, D: 9.6. WR: 3:36.0 (Herbert Elliot)

1. Herbert Elliott	AUS	3:35.6 WR
2. Michel Jazy	FRA	3:38.4
3. István Rózsavölgyi	HUN	3:39.2
4. Dan Waern	SWE	3:40.0
5. Zoltan Vamos	ROM	3:40.8
6. Dyrol Burleson	USA	3:40.9
7. Michel Bernard	FRA	3:41.5
8. James Grelle	USA	3:45.0

World record holder Herb Elliott of Perth was the clear favorite in 1960. After 950 meters he passed Michel Bernard and took off like a "scared bunny." To his opponents and to the 90,000 people in the stadium, Elliott appeared to be a sure winner, but Elliott himself refused to look behind him. Unaware that he had opened up an insurmountable 15-meter lead, he was sure that someone was close on his heels. When he reached the backstretch he saw his coach, Percy Cerutty, standing by the side of the track waving a white towel, which meant that a world record was achievable and that Elliott should give it all he had. The 66-year-old Cerutty had raced out of the stands and dashed across the protective moat that surrounded the track in order to signal his pupil. He was quickly grabbed by the police and hauled away. Actually, in the heat of the moment, Elliott couldn't remember if the white towel signal meant that a world record was possible or that there was another runner close behind him. Even that didn't make a difference because throughout his training, Elliott always imiagined a competitor on his shoulder. "The competitor had no face, no name." The competitor was extraordinary because he could "see into my brain and into my heart and [he] knew exactly what I was thinking and feeling at that moment. [He] would sense the weaknesses in me. I would have this competitor on my shoulder and I would think, 'You're not getting past me you bastard. . . . I had practiced a million times being challenged and winning that challenge, so when it came to the race, I had done it a million times. It became instinctive." Elliott strained to the finish line and won by the amazing margin of 20 yards (18 meters). His time of 3:35.6 was a new world record. Silver medalist Michel Jazy would later claim that he was the first man to cross the finish line. "Elliott," explained Jazy, "was a being from another planet."

Herb Elliott, whose diet consisted mostly of raw, natural foods, celebrated by going out drinking. His most difficult concern for the remainder of the Olympics was protecting his kangaroo-hide track shoes, which were almost stolen on three separate occasions. Between 1954 and 1960, Herb Elliott won 44 consecutive races at 1500 meters or one mile before retiring from competition at the age of 22. Many years later Elliott paid tribute to Cerutty. "He challenged my totality. I came to realize that spirit, as much as or more than physical conditioning, had to be stored up before a race. I would avoid running on tracks because tracks were spiritually depleting. I never studied my opponents—they were an irrelevancy to me. Poetry, music, forests, ocean, solitude—they were what developed enormous spiritual strength." Of his early retirement he said, "Once I had satisfied myself . . . that my spirit *could* dominate my body, there was no reason to continue."

1964 Tokyo C: 43, N: 34, D: 10.21. WR: 3:35.6 (Herbert Elliott)

1. Peter Snell	NZL	3:38.1
2. Josef Odložil	CZE	3:39.6
3. John Davies	NZL	3:39.6
4. Alan Simpson	GBR	3:39.7
5. Dyrol Burleson	USA	3:40.0
6. Witold Baran	POL	3:40.3
7. Michel Bernard	FRA	3:41.2
8. John Whetton	GBR	3:42.4

Before the Tokyo Olympics, Peter Snell had never run a race at 1500 meters, although he had competed in many one-mile contests. Running his sixth race in eight days, Snell was boxed in at the bell when John Whetton stepped aside and let him through. Snell ran away from the field in the backstretch and won by 12 yards, to gain his third Olympic gold medal.

Silver medalist Josef Odlozil married the famous Czech gymnast Věra Čáslavská at the 1968 Olympics (see page 706). In 1993, Odlozil was killed by their 19-year-old son during a fight.

1968 Mexico City C: 54, N: 37, D: 10.20. WR: 3:33.1 (James Ryun)

1. H. Kipchoge Keino	KEN	3:34.9 OR	(3:34.91)
2. James Ryun	USA	3:37.8	(3:37.89)
3. Bodo Tümmler	GER	3:39.0	(3:39.08)
4. Harald Norpoth	GER	3:42.5	(3:42.57)
5. John Whetton	GBR	3:43.8	(3:43.90)
6. Jacques Boxberger	FRA	3:46.6	(3:46.65)
7. Henryk Szordykowski	POL	3:46.6	(3:46.69)
8. Josef Odložil	CZE	3:48.6	(3:48.69)

Jim Ryun of Wichita, Kansas, went to the 1968 Olympics as the world record holder at 880 yards, 1500 meters, and the mile. He had not been beaten at 1500 or the mile in over three years. Yet his status as favorite was threatened by an attack of mononucleosis in June and by the fact that the Olympics were being held in the high altitude of Mexico City. For this reason, 28-year-old Kip Keino, an uncoached Nandi tribesman who had never defeated Ryun, was considered a serious contender. However Keino was having problems of his own. Recently he had been suffering violent stomach pains, which later turned out to be the result of a severe gall bladder infection. Ignoring the advice of doctors, Keino went ahead and entered not only the 1500, but also the 5000 and the 10,000. The 10,000 came first and Keino was running with the leaders with only two laps to go, when he suddenly doubled up in pain and fell onto the infield. When the stretcher-bearers came to get him, he jumped back onto the track and, even though he had been disqualified, he finished the race. Four days later he took second place in the 5000 meters.

As if he hadn't run enough already, the day of the 1500 meters final he got caught in a traffic jam and jogged the last mile to the stadium. Keino was well aware that Jim Ryun possessed a devastating finishing kick, so he decided to try a dangerous gamble, hoping to neutralize Ryun's sprint by building up a huge lead. "I was thinking, 'This is the race of my life,'" he would later recall. "'If I die, I die here.'"

After fellow Kenyan Ben Jipcho set a torrid pace of 56.0 for the first 400 meters, Keino took over and pulled away from the pack, passing the 800-meter mark in a seemingly suicidal 1:55.3. Everyone waited for Keino to run out of steam but, remarkably, he never did. Ryun's famous kick was impressive, but he was unable to close within 12 yards of Keino and finally eased up in pain, as the Kenyan went on to win by 20 meters, the largest margin of victory in Olympic 1500 meters history. Keino improved his personal best by 1.8 seconds and lowered his own high-altitude world record by a phenomenal five seconds. That same day, back in Kenya, Kip Keino's wife gave birth to their third daughter, who was named Milka Olympia Chelagat in honor of her father's achievement. Keino and his wife, Phyllis, eventually established a children's home and raised more than 200 orphaned and abandoned children.

Jacky Boxberger, who placed sixth in the 1968 1500 meters, eventually represented France in four Olympics at distances ranging up to the marathon. In 2001, when he was 52 years old, Boxberger died an unusual death. While on vacation with his family in Kenya, Boxberger was filming an elephant when the elephant suddenly turned around, picked Boxberger up with his trunk, slammed him against a tree, threw him to the ground and stomped him to death.

Mexico City, 1968
Kip Keino of Kenya scores the most decisive 1500 meters victory in Olympic history.

1972 Munich C: 66, N: 46, D: 9.10. WR: 3:33.1 (James Ryun)

1. Pekka Vasala	FIN	3:36.3	(3:36.33)
2. H. Kipchoge Keino	KEN	3:36.8	(3:36.81)
3. Rodney Dixon	NZL	3:37.5	(3:37.46)
4. Michael Boit	KEN	3:38.4	(3:38.41)
5. Brendan Foster	GBR	3:39.0	(3:39.02)
6. Herman Mignon	BEL	3:39.1	(3:39.05)
7. Paul-Heinz Wellmann	GER	3:40.1	(3:40.08)
8. Vladimir Pantelei	SOV/UKR	3:40.2	(3:40.24)

Track aficionados awaited another showdown between defending champion Kip Keino and Jim Ryun, who had retired, returned to competition, had his ups and downs, and was now in top form once again. What no one expected was that their last confrontation as amateurs would come not in the Olympic final, but in the opening round. Entrants in the Olympics are seeded according to their previous times, so that leading contenders are separated in the opening heats. US officials had submitted Ryun's superb time of 3:52.8 for the mile. However, somewhere along the line, this time was interpreted as being for 1500 meters, so the computer in charge of seeding treated Ryun as just another mediocre runner. Consequently, Ryun was thrown into the same first-round heat as top-seeded Kip Keino.

The fateful fourth heat, won easily by Keino, was to prove the end of Jim Ryun's amateur career. Caught in a box 550 meters from the finish, Ryun tried to squeeze his way between runners rather than pass on the outside. As early leader Mohamed Younis of Pakistan faded on the inside lane, Vitus Ashaba of Uganda stepped to the outside to avoid him, and moved right into the space that Ryun was trying to fill. Ryun tripped on Ashaba's heel and fell back on Billy Fordjour of Ghana, sending both of them crashing to the ground. Ryun landed on the curb and Fordjour landed on Ryun, who came away with a bruised hip, a scraped knee, a sprained left ankle, and a contusion of his Adam's apple. Stunned, Ryun lay on the track for eight seconds before he got up and began chasing after the field. The sympathetic German crowd rooted him on, but he had lost at least 75 meters and it proved impossible for him to catch up. Ryun was in shock. "All I know is everything was going well," he said, "and I felt good, and the next thing I knew I was trying to figure out what happened."

Two days later, in the final, Kip Keino faced the challenge of Pekka Vasala, by no means an outsider, even though he was known in Finland as "Mr. Unpredictable." Vasala had competed in the Mexico City Games, but, struck down by "Montezuma's Revenge," he had finished last in his heat. Nevertheless, he had been quite moved by the opening ceremonies and vowed to himself that "someday, somewhere, I would accomplish something great."

In Munich, Keino made his move after 600 meters and Vasala followed close behind, dogging the former goat-herder all the way until the homestretch, when he moved ahead to win by about three meters. Vasala had run the last 800 meters in the amazing time of 1:49.0.

The surprise bronze medalist was Rod Dixon of New Zealand, who began sobbing when he realized that his dream of an Olympic medal had come true. Still weeping, he was ushered backstage for the urine test. After producing a meager sample, Dixon sheepishly asked the German official if it was enough. "For the gold medal, no," was the reply, "but for the bronze medal, it will do."

Dixon was not the only one to be moved to tears. Pekka Vasala recalled, "When I walked into the dressing room after the race . . . I realized in a second I had won. Somehow I had not fully understood it on the track. All became misty and I was crying uncontrollably. I had completely lost control of myself. I was still confused on the victory stand. It was not until I put the gold medal into my pocket and grabbed it in my fingers that I finally woke up."

1976 Montreal C: 42, N: 28, D: 7.31. WR: 3:32.2 (Filbert Bayi)

1. John Walker	NZL	3:39.17
2. Ivo van Damme	BEL	3:39.27
3. Paul-Heinz Wellmann	GER	3:39.33
4. Eamonn Coghlan	IRL	3:39.51
5. Frank Clement	GBR	3:39.65
6. Richard Wohlhuter	USA	3:40.64
7. David Moorcroft	GBR	3:40.94
8. Graham Crouch	AUS	3:41.80

In 1976, black African nations boycotted the Olympics because a rugby team from New Zealand had played a team from South Africa. Ironically, this prevented Tanzanian world record holder Filbert Bayi from competing, and handed over an almost sure gold medal to New Zealand, which was represented by John Walker, who held the world record for the mile. It was Walker who had pushed Bayi to his 1500 meters record at the 1974 Commonwealth Games, and the two friends had been looking forward to their Olympics showdown ever since. Without Bayi and Kenyan Mike Boit to set the pace, the Olympic final was a slow, almost dull race that came down to the final sprint. Walker passed Eamonn Coghlan in the backstretch and won by a meter. His winning time was the slowest in 20 years. When asked why he hadn't tried for a record even with Bayi missing, Walker replied, "Every record set in Montreal will eventually be broken and forgotten. The gold medal is the thing they can never take away from you." On February 17, 1985, running on his home track at Mount Smart Stadium in Auckland, John Walker became the first person to run 100 sub-four-minute miles, beating out Steve Scott of the United States by barely three months. Walker had first broken the four-minute barrier 11½ years earlier. On February 20, 1994, Eamonn Coghlan set a record of his own when, at age 41, he became the first person over the age of 40 to break the four-minute mile.

1980 Moscow C: 40, N: 29, D: 8.1. WR: 3:32.1 (Sebastian Coe, Stephen Ovett)

1. Sebastian Coe	GBR	3:38.40
2. Jürgen Straub	GDR	3:38.80
3. Stephen Ovett	GBR	3:38.99
4. Andreas Busse	GDR	3:40.17
5. Vittorio Fontanella	ITA	3:40.37
6. Josef Plachý	CZE	3:40.66
7. José Marajo	FRA	3:41.48
8. Stephen Cram	GBR	3:41.98

It certainly seemed to most observers that Steve Ovett entered the 1500 meters final with a tremendous advantage. Not only had he defeated Sebastian Coe at Coe's best distance, the 800, but Ovett had won 42 consecutive races at 1500 meters and one mile, going back to May 1977. In the semifinals Ovett had been so relaxed and in control that he actually gave a victory wave to the crowd before he had even taken the lead. Coe, on the other hand, had struggled through his first-round heat and had been hounded and mercilessly criticized by the British press during the six days since the 800 meters final. As it turned out, however, Ovett's gold medal had taken away his competitive edge ever so slightly, while Coe had conquered his disappointment and depression, and couldn't wait to get out on the track to prove that he was a winner and not just a record-setter.

The withdrawal of Filbert Bayi, who had decided to concentrate on the 3000 meters steeplechase, left the race without a pace-setter, but before the first lap had ended it became clear that this was not going to be just a two-man race. Jürgen Straub took the lead at 400 meters, followed by Coe, who was determined to stay near the front and avoid the tactical errors he had committed in the 800. With 780 meters to go, Straub stepped up the pace, with Coe and Ovett close behind. It was just what Coe had hoped for: a long, open run to the finish.

With 200 meters to go, Straub was four meters ahead of Coe and six meters ahead of Ovett. Coming into the final curve, Coe unleashed his finishing kick, unaware that Ovett had chosen the exact same moment to make *his* move. Straub was not about to give in, but by the time they had hit the homestretch, Coe had taken the lead. A quick glance to each side to check the position of his opponents, and then, 80 meters from the finish line, Coe increased his speed again, crossing the finish line with a look of ecstatic relief that spoke far more than a thousand words. Straub, four meters back, held off Ovett for second place. Coe dropped to his knees and touched his forehead to the ground, seemingly unaware of the hearty congratulations being offered by Straub and Ovett. Coe had run the last lap in 52.2 seconds and the final 100 meters in 12.1.

Afterward, Coe and Ovett, who had been constantly portrayed by the press as bitter rivals, discussed the relief that they both felt and agreed to have a couple drinks together. On the victory stand, Coe looked up to the sky. When asked why he had done this, Coe replied, "Perhaps somebody, somewhere, loves me after all."

1984 Los Angeles C: 59, N: 40, D: 8.11. WR: 3:30.77 (Stephen Ovett)

1. Sebastian Coe	GBR	3:32.53 OR
2. Stephen Cram	GBR	3:33.40
3. José Manuel Abascal Gómez	SPA	3:34.30
4. Joseph Chesire	KEN	3:34.52
5. Jim Spivey	USA	3:36.07
6. Peter Wirz	SWI	3:36.97
7. Andres Vera	SPA	3:37.02
8. Omar Khalifa	SUD	3:37.11

Following his Olympic victory in 1980, Sebastian Coe had been forced to call it quits for the rest of the season because of a back injury. He came back with a vengeance in 1981 and set four world records—in the 800, the 1000, and twice in the mile. However his 1982 season was a disappointing one, due apparently to an attack of glandular fever. Early in 1983 he seemed to have recovered, but as the season progressed, he found himself losing race after race. Finally, after withdrawing from the world championships, he checked into a hospital, where he underwent surgery for removal of a lymph node. It was discovered that Coe had been suffering from toxoplasmosis, a rare, sometimes fatal, protozoan infection. It looked like his championship days were over. As noted track writer Bob Hersh put it in an early Olympic preview article for *The Runner* magazine: "Based on 1983, I'd write Coe off completely."

It was to prove a premature obituary. After months of treatments and much time spent lying in hospital beds, Coe was released to resume training in December 1983. In the meantime his throne had been usurped by Steve Cram who had gone undefeated at 1500 meters in 1983 and had beaten Steve Scott, Saïd Aouita, and Steve Ovett in a tactical race at the world championships. Coe's comeback was treated with scorn by much of the British press, particularly after he was selected for the 1500 meters Olympic event even though he lost to Peter Elliott at the British Amateur Athletic Association championships in June in what had been billed as a showdown for the final spot on the team.

The Olympic 1500 developed into a battle of survivors. Saïd Aouita withdrew to concentrate on the less competitive 5000 meters. Former world record holder Sydney Maree withdrew due to a hamstring tear that failed to heal. World championship finalist Dragan Zdravković was sent home by Yugoslav officials for refusing to wear Adidas shoes. World record holder Steve Ovett had collapsed after the 800-meter final and spent two nights in the hospital. Yet there he was the next day on the starting line of heat 3 of the opening round. Ovett won the heat, but right behind him yet another contender fell by the wayside. Ten meters from the finish line, world championship finalist Pierre Délèze of Switzerland tripped on Ovett's heel and sprawled on the ground just short of his goal. The fourth heat was won by 800-meter gold medalist Joaquim Cruz, but the next day he pulled out of the semifinals because of a head cold.

Still, when the twelve finalists gathered barely 24 hours after the semifinals, the four leading favorites, Cram, Scott, Ovett, and Coe, were right there on the starting line. Ovett did seem doubtful, having required medical attention following the semifinals, and, although Coe had looked strong in winning the 800 silver, he, like Ovett, was about to run his seventh race in nine days.

Coe broke to the front, but quickly relinquished the lead to Omar Khalifa. Less than 600 meters from the start came the big surprise. For many years 1500-meter races in major championships had been run as kickers' races: three slow laps, followed by a final sprint. Steve Scott had decided to turn the 1984 Olympic final into "a true miler's race." In the backstretch of the second lap, he tore into the lead and forced the pace, testing the strength of the other runners. He passed the 800-meter mark in 1:56.81, followed more closely than he had hoped by Coe, Abascal, Khalifa, Cram, and Ovett.

The next runner to make a move was José Abascal. Knowing that he too would lose a kicker's finish, Abascal took the lead with about a lap and a quarter to go. Coe and Cram chased after him while Scott began to fade to an eventual tenth-place finish. Three hundred and fifty yards from the finish, Steve Ovett, running in fourth place, was overcome by the same chest pains he had experienced four days earlier. He stepped off the track and was taken away on a stretcher. Abascal sprinted down the backstretch, but he couldn't shake Coe and Cram. Coming into the final curve, Cram made his move, pulling up to Coe's shoulder. Coe glanced up quickly to see who was there, then began his own kick. They both sped by Abascal, racing hard around the turn. Coe entered the final straight with a four-foot lead which he extended to a six-meter winning margin.

Coe crossed the finish line with a smile on his face. Then he turned in the direction of the British press, made a defiant gesture, and shouted, "Who says I'm finished?!" He had run the final 200 meters in 26.1 seconds and the last 100 meters in 13.04. At the age of 27, Sebastian Coe had become the first male repeat winner of the Olympic 1500 meters (excepting James Lightbody's victory in the 1906 Intercalated Games).

After retiring from athletics, Coe threw his energies into politics. In 1980 Coe had defied the Conservative government of Margaret Thatcher and competed in the Moscow Olympics. Twelve years later, running as a Conservative, he was elected to parliament. Driven from office at the next election, he became chief of staff for Conservative Party leader, William Hague. Later, Coe became chairman of the organizing committee for the 2012 Olympics.

1988 Seoul C: 59, N: 46, D: 10.1. WR: 3:29.46 (Saïd Aouita)

1. Peter Rono	KEN	3:35.96
2. Peter Elliott	GBR	3:36.15
3. Jens-Peter Herold	GDR	3:36.21
4. Stephen Cram	GBR	3:36.24
5. Steve Scott	USA	3:36.99
6. Han Kulker	HOL	3:37.08
7. S. Kipkoech Cheruiyot	KEN	3:37.94
8. Marcus O'Sullivan	IRL	3:38.39

On the eve of the Olympics, the favorites were world record holder Saïd Aouita; Steve Cram, who had recorded the fastest time of the year, 3:30.95, on August 19; and world champion Abdi Bile of Somalia. But Bile was forced to withdraw after sustaining a tibial stress fracture, and Aouita, also the victim of a leg injury, dropped out before the semifinals. Joaquim Cruz, the 800-meter silver medalist, also failed to appear for his semifinal heat. The finalists set out at a sluggish pace. With two laps to go, 5-foot 5¾-inch (1.67 meter), 117-pound Peter Rono decided he had had enough. "The other guys were holding me up," he would later explain. He rushed into the lead. "I thought some of the fellows behind would follow me, but they didn't."

Most likely, the other fellows didn't take Rono seriously. After all, the undersized economics student at Mount St. Mary's College in Emmitsburg, Maryland, had no major victories to his credit. Besides, they were too busy watching Steve Cram. With half a lap to go, Rono led by two meters over Elliott, with Cram and Herold close behind. Elliott tried desperately to close the gap but could make little headway. Rono, who looked back 13 times in the final 200 meters, ran the last 800 meters in 1 minute 50 seconds. Afterward, Rono seemed as surprised as anyone by the result. "It was tougher to win the Kenyan trials," he said. At 21 years of age, he was the youngest 1500-meter medalist in Olympic history.

1992 Barcelona C: 50, N: 39, D: 8.8. WR: 3:29.46 (Saïd Aouita)

1. Fermín Cacho Ruiz	SPA	3:40.12
2. Rachid El Basir	MOR	3:40.62
3. Mohamed Ahmed Suleiman	QAT	3:40.69
4. Joseph Chesire	KEN	3:41.12
5. Jonah Birir	KEN	3:41.27
6. Jens-Peter Herold	GER	3:41.53
7. Noureddine Morceli	ALG	3:41.70
8. Jim Spivey	USA	3:41.74

Few runners have dominated an event as thoroughly as Noureddine Morceli did the 1500 meters between 1990 and 1996. In 1991 he was undefeated at 1500 meters and one mile, crowning the season by winning the world championship by 15 meters. It seemed that nothing could stop him from winning Olympic gold except an injury. But early in 1992 Morceli did in fact injure his hip, reducing him to sudden, albeit temporary, vulnerability. He lost over six weeks' training, and on June 9 his 21-race winning streak was broken. On July 4, he lost again.

Nonetheless, Morceli did win the first semifinal in Barcelona. The second semi was won by Mohamed Suleiman from the small Persian Gulf emirate of Qatar in 3:34.77—the fastest preliminary time in Olympic history. The most notable development was the complete shutout of British runners. The 1992 final would be only the second 1500-meter final since 1904 without a runner from Great Britain. (The first was in 1960.)

The final was run at a shockingly slow pace. Led by 34-year-old Joseph Chesire, the field completed the first 800 meters in 2:06.83, more than one and three-quarters seconds slower than the women in their 1500-meter final. In the final backstretch Morceli was trapped in the pack, his every move marked by David Kibet of Kenya at his shoulder. When the real running started, he was unable to respond. Meanwhile local favorite Fermín Cacho of Agreda, Soria, had positioned himself behind Chesire, but found himself boxed in by Jens-Peter Herold on his right. Cacho's race plan was to begin his sprint with 150 meters to go, but about 50 meters before that suddenly, inexplicably, as they approached the final turn, Chesire drifted wide. Cacho reacted immediately, passed Chesire on the inside and, with a delirious crowd screaming his name, burst into a ten-meter lead. El Basir, moving from eighth to second in the final straightaway, closed the gap to four meters while Cacho, incredulous at the wonderful turn of events, looked back eight times in seeming disbelief before crossing the finish line. Although he ran the last lap in about 50.4 seconds, Cacho's winning time was the slowest since 1956. Cacho was the first Spanish runner to win a gold medal.

As for Morceli, he was so sickened by what had happened that he "could not eat or sleep for a week." However, he recovered his form immediately. Four weeks later he ran 3:28.86 to break Saïd Aouita's seven-year-old world record. A year later he set a world record for the mile and he defended his world championship in both 1993 and 1995.

1996 Atlanta C: 57, N: 37, D: 8.3. WR: 3:27.37 (Noureddine Morceli)

1. Noureddine Morceli	ALG	3:35.78
2. Fermín Cacho Ruiz	SPA	3:36.40
3. Stephen Kiprorir	KEN	3:36.72
4. Laban Rotich	KEN	3:37.39
5. William Tanui	KEN	3:37.42
6. Abdi Bile	SOM	3:38.03
7. Marko Koers	HOL	3:38.18
8. Ali Hakimi	TUN	3:38.19

The son of a factory worker in the coastal town of Ténès, Noureddine Morceli was coached by his older brother Abderahmane, who had represented Algeria himself at 1500 meters in 1980 and 1984. Morceli entered the Olympics as the overwhelming favorite. Since two weeks after the last Olympics, he had won 52 straight races at 1000 meters, 1500 meters or one mile. He had also won the last three world championships and was the reigning world record holder at 1500 meters and the mile (not to mention the 3000 meters).

Still, Morceli had gone into the 1992 Games in much the same position of dominance and had placed only seventh. In Atlanta he was expected to face a stiff challenge from the rising Moroccan star, 21-year-old Hicham El Guerrouj, who had placed second at the 1995 world championships.

In the first semifinal, Morceli ran the fastest non-final in history, edging defending Olympic champion Fermín Cacho 3:32.88 to 3:33.12. Indeed, the first semi was such a fast race that Abdelkader Chékhemani of France finished eighth and failed to qualify for the final even though his time of 3:34.84 would have been good enough to win any Olympic final (including 1996) other than that of 1984. El Guerrouj won the second semifinal ahead of Stephen Kiprorir.

Early in the final, Morceli found himself boxed in by Kenyans, just as he had been in the Barcelona final. This time he slipped out, swung wide and moved to the front of the pack at about the 900-meter mark. Pressing the pace, he strung out the field, with only El Guerrouj and Cacho able to maintain contact. Just before the bell, with about 430 meters to go, El Guerrouj tried to position himself at Morceli's shoulder. His knee hit Morceli's heel. Morceli stumbled and El Guerrouj stepped on Morceli's right heel, drawing blood. Morceli regained his balance, but El Guerrouj crashed to the ground, ultimately finishing in last place.

While the rest of the runners jumped over El Guerrouj or weaved around him, Morceli took off, quickly opening a five-meter lead over Cacho that he stretched to ten meters before relaxing when the race was clearly won. Noureddine Morceli had finally won the Olympic gold medal that he so richly deserved. A deeply spiritual man, Morceli knelt on the track with his hands and forehead down and thanked God.

He later told the press, "God teaches you to be dignified in defeat and modest in victory. The records and medals are wonderful, but they are mere trinkets in reality. They cannot feed all the people in the world who are hungry, clothe all those who are cold, comfort all those who are troubled or bring peace to all those who are at war. That is a race we must all run together."

One non-finalist particularly worthy of note was Dieudonné Kwizera of Burundi. Kwizera had tried to enter the Olympics in 1988 and 1992, but was unable to because Burundi did not have a national Olympic committee. Using money he had earned running, Kwizera and several of his fellow athletes formed a

Noureddine Morceli, 1996
With one lap to go in the final of the 1996 1500 meters, Hicham El Guerrouj trips on Noureddine Morceli's heel and falls. Morceli stumbles, but goes on to win the race.

committee and were recognized by the IOC in 1993. Kwizera did not qualify to run in the 1996 Olympics, but he was chosen to carry the flag of Burundi at the Opening Ceremony.

Then, two days before the opening round of the 1500 meters, Burundi's entrant in the event, world championship bronze medalist Vénuste Niyongabo, came to Kwizera and told him that he intended to drop out of the 1500 in order to take his chances instead at 5000 meters—a distance he had raced at only twice. Niyangabo suggested that Kwizera take his place in the 1500. Kwizera was not credentialed as an athlete in Altanta, only as a coach. He was allowed to compete anyway, but just to be on the safe side, he covered the "C" on his credential badge with his finger when he entered the changing room before the round one heats. Kwizera placed sixth in his heat and did not advance to the semifinals. But his smile as he crossed the finish line was as big as any gold-medal winner. The man who had almost singlehandedly brought his wartorn nation to the Olympics kissed the track, later explaining, "I was proud of myself. I was finally an Olympian."

2000 Sydney C: 41, N: 26, D: 9.29. WR: 3:26.00 (Hicham El Guerrouj)

1. Noah Ngeny	KEN	3:32.07
2. Hicham El Guerrouj	MOR	3:32.32
3. Bernard Lagat	KEN	3:32.44
4. Medhi Baala	FRA	3:34.14
5. Kevin Sullivan	CAN	3:35.50
6. Daniel Zegeye	ETH	3:36.78
7. Andrés Díaz	SPA	3:37.27
8. Juan Carlos Higuero	SPA	3:38.91

After the 1996 final, in which he had fallen and finished last, Hicham El Guerrouj retreated into a tunnel inside the stadium and sobbed uncontrollably. After ten minutes, someone handed him a cell phone. On the line was King Hassan II of Morocco. The king told El Guerrouj, "You are a champion in the eyes of the Moroccan people. Don't feel under pressure. Forget about this. You must persevere."

"After the call from His Majesty," El Guerrouj later recalled, "it was another El Guerrouj who was born. There is no similarity to the El Guerrouj before that call and El Guerrouj after."

A photographer snapped a picture of El Guerrouj while he was crying and El Guerrouj put a framed copy in his room at the national training center for inspiration. Over the next four years, he would lose only one race, a loss that he followed with 28 straight finals victories in the course of the three years leading to the Sydney Games. Among these victories were the world championships of 1997 and 1999. Running in Rome on July 14, 1998, he broke Noureddine Morceli's 1500 meters world record by an astonishing 1.37 seconds. A year later, on the same track, El Guerrouj ran the mile in 3:43.13 to set another world record. He accomplished this later feat because he was pushed to the limit by a 20-year-old Kenyan named Noah Ngeny.

Born on his parents' maize farm in Eldoret, home of running champions Kip Keino, Moses Kiptanui and Daniel Komen, Ngeny set world junior records for the 1500 meters and the mile and, in 1998, he served as pacesetter for El Guerrouj on the European circuit. His experience as pacesetter taught Ngeny that he was within reach of El Guerrouj and he returned in 1999 as a serious contender. In that mile world record on July 7, Ngeny had chased down El Guerrouj over the last 180 meters, drawing within a foot of him before the Moroccan fought him off. Even though he finished second, Ngeny also broke Morceli's world record. It was the first time since 1958 that two men had broken the mile record in the same race. Seven weeks later, El Guerrouj and Ngeny finished one-two at the world championships in Seville. By the time of the 2000 Olympics, El Guerrouj had defeated Ngeny four times, but Ngeny was confident that he would catch El Guerrouj eventually.

In Sydney, Ngeny recorded the fastest time of the first round, with defending champion Morceli second-fastest. Ngeny and El Guerrouj won the two semifinals, while Morceli stumbled in traffic in Ngeny's semi and did not qualify for the final.

Moroccan Youssef Baba set the pace in the final, but ran out of steam early, so El Guerrouj took the lead after 900 meters. Ngeny, fellow Kenyan Bernard Lagat and Medhi Baala of France went with him, while the rest of the field fell behind. Baala lost touch in the final turn, but El Guerrouj was unable to drop the Kenyans. Ngeny inched closer, caught El Guerrouj 50 meters from the finish and pulled ahead with 25 meters to go. A stunned El Guerrouj was left in tears again.

When Ngeny returned to Nairobi, he was met by a large crowd that included his wife and his newborn daughter—Marion Sydney. In 2001 Ngeny fractured his pelvis in a car crash in Kenya. The injury hampered his ability to compete and kept him out of the 2004 Olympics, eventually forcing him to retire in 2006.

Although El Guerrouj's disappointment was great, he resumed his undefeated ways and won the next two world championships, in 2001 and 2003. At the 2003 championships, he also picked up a silver medal in the 5000 meters.

2004 Athens C: 38, N: 26, D: 8.24. WR: 3:26.00 (Hicham El Guerrouj)

1. Hicham El Guerrouj	MOR	3:34.18
2. Bernard Lagat	KEN	3:34.30
3. Rui da Silva	POR	3:34.68
4. Timothy Kiptanui	KEN	3:35.61
5. Ivan Heshko	UKR	3:35.82
6. Michael East	GBR	3:36.33
7. Reyes Estévez López	SPA	3:36.63
8. Gert-Jan Liefers	HOL	3:37.17

Known as the "King of Middle Distance Running," Hicham El Guerrouj won the 1500-meter world championship four consecutive times between 1997 and 2003 and set world records in the 1500 meters and the mile. El Guerrouj began running at the age of 15, the same year he went to work as an assistant mechanic in a shop in Berkane, Morocco. Prior to the 2004 season, he had lost only three of 87 race finals in eight years, but two of those losses had been in the Olympics. Plagued by allergy-induced asthma, he was beaten twice in the pre-Olympic season, including a tough sub-3:28 loss to Bernard Lagat in Zurich, just a week before the Athens Opening Ceremony.

The qualifying round saw the elimination of world champion silver medalist Medhi Baala of France, who had sprained his ankle nine days earlier. In the final, Kenyan Isaac Songok set a slow pace of 60.42 seconds, with El Guerrouj making his move at 600 meters, easing past Reyes Estévez with a lap and a half to go. Lagat stayed with him, even as El Guerrouj began to increase his speed, with 25-year-old Ivan Heshko trailing in third ahead of Mulugeta Wendimu of Ethiopia and Estévez. El Guerrouj continued to press the pace, dropping everyone but Lagat. Lagat challenged in the last half lap and managed to move ahead by half a stride with only 50 meters to go. El Guerrouj drew even again and then surged ahead of Lagat at the finish, collapsing onto the track and bursting into tears. In ninth place coming into the final lap, Rui da Silva passed Ivan Heshko in the final 100 meters to take the bronze. After the victory, El Guerrouj leapt into the stands to kiss his 19-year-old wife and three-month old daughter, Hiba, whose name means "gift from God." El Guerrouj later described his emotional win: "It's amazing to think that in Sydney I was crying tears of sadness and here I am crying tears of joy. I'm like a five year-old with a toy, living something wonderful with the people I love and people who love me."

Hicham El Guerrouj, 2004

El Guerrouj edges past Bernard Legat to earn the first half of his 1500/5000 double in Athens.

2008 Beijing C: 48, N: 30, D: 8.19. WR: 3:26.00 (Hicham El Guerrouj)

1. Asbel Kiprop	KEN	3:33.11
2. Nick Willis	NZL	3:34.16
3. Mehdi Baala	FRA	3:34.21
4. Juan Carlos Higuero Mate	SPA	3:34.44
5. Abdalaati Iguider	MOR	3:34.66
6. Juan van Deventer	SAF	3:34.77
7. Belal Mansoor Ali	BRN	3:35.23
8. Andy Baddeley	GBR	3:35.37

DISQ (Drugs): Rashid Ramzi (BRN) 3:32.94

A year after winning double Olympic golds, Hicham El Guerrouj missed the 2005 world championships due to a persistent back injury. In his absence, another Moroccan-born runner took the title: Rashid Ramzi, who used to train with El Guerrouj. Born Rashid Khoula, Ramzi represented Morocco at the 1999 African junior championships, but moved to Bahrain at the end of 2001 as a laborer, later joining the military and gaining citizenship. He represented Bahrain at the 2004 Olympics, but fell during his semi-final heat and finished 11th. In Helsinki in 2005, Ramzi became the first athlete to complete the 1500-meter/800-meter double at a world championship.

Two years later, Ramzi lost his title to another foreign-born racer, who also completed an historic world championship double. Bernard Lagat, a double Olympic medalist for Kenya, had moved to the US in 1996 to attend college in Washington State, becoming a US citizen in 2004. Although he represented Kenya at the 2004 Olympics, winning the 1500 meters silver medal, Lagat missed out on the 2005 world championships because of his citizenship switch. In 2007 he became the first athlete in world championship history to record the 1500 meters/5000 meters double.

With El Guerrouj in retirement, the final looked to be a battle between the two double world champions. But Lagat, hampered by an Achilles injury, was eliminated in the semi-finals, leaving the final open for Ramzi. Bahrain's Kenyan-born Belal Mansoor Ali shot into the lead at the start of the final, but was soon joined by Asbel Kipruto Kiprop, who set a first-lap pace of 56.48. Augustine Choge moved to the front and led through the 1200 meters mark, but couldn't open a gap and was quickly overtaken when Ramzi began his kick with 300 meters to go. Ramzi maintained a punishing sprint down the final stretch, holding off a charging Kiprop by half a stride. Nick Willis moved up from 8th place over the final 300 meters to finish third.

In February 2009 the IOC retested urine samples from the Beijing Olympics after a new lab test became available. Five athletes subsequently tested positive for a new form of the banned blood-booster EPO-CERA, including Ramzi, who was subsequently stripped of his medal. Kiprop and Willis were moved up to gold and silver. Kiprop's previous international best was a fourth place finish at the 2007 world championships, which he led with only 100 meters to go. In January 2010, nearly a year-and-a-half after the competition, Mehdi Baala finally received his bronze medal in a special ceremony in Paris. Kiprop placed fourth at the 2009 world championships as well, but in 2011 he won the world title.

Few athletes had as difficult a road to the Olympics as semi-finalist Lopez Lomong. One of the Sudanese "Lost Boys", Lomong had been kidnapped from his family at the age of six and held captive for three weeks by an armed militia. He escaped with the help of three older boys from his village and made his way to a refugee camp in Kenya, where he spent ten years before being adopted by a foster family in New York. In 2003 Lomong was finally reunited with his family, who had assumed he had been killed and had buried him in absentia years before. Lomong qualified for the Olympics on July 6, 2008, exactly a year to the day after he became a US citizen. He was selected as the US flag-bearer for the Opening Ceremony, in a move that was perceived as a dig against the Chinese government for its support of the Sudanese dictatorship.

Along with Lomong, the US's other 1500 meters contestants were Lagat and Mexican-born teammate Leonel Manzano, so all three members of the squad were foreign-born.

5000 METERS

A race of 12½ laps, the 5000 meters is 3 miles 188 yards 2 inches. Fifteen runners take part in the final.

1896–1906 not held

1912 Stockholm C: 31, N: 11, D: 7.10. WR: 15:01.2 (Arthur Robinson)

1. Johan Kolehmainen	FIN	14:36.6	WR
2. Jean Bouin	FRA	14:36.7	
3. George Hutson	GBR	15:07.6	
4. George Bonhag	USA	15:09.8	
5. Tell Berna	USA	15:10.0	
6. Alex Decoteau	CAN	—	
7. Mauritz Karlsson	SWE	15:18.6	

Hannes Kolehmainen, a vegetarian bricklayer from a running family, had already won the 10,000 meters two days earlier, and was taking part in his fourth long-distance race in four days. He and Jean Bouin pulled away from the other eight finalists after a couple of laps and ran the rest of the race with Bouin in front and Kolehmainen right behind him. Every time Kolehmainen tried to pass, Bouin would resist his challenge. On the final curve of the final lap, Kolehmainen tried again. Bouin swung wide, forcing the Finn back in line. When they reached the homestretch, Kolehmainen tried once more, finally reaching Bouin's shoulder 20 meters from the tape. Bouin veered into Kolehmainen, but his legs began to buckle, and "Hannes the Mighty," as he became known, was able to win by less than a meter. Silver medalist Bouin and bronze medalist George Hutson were both killed in action in September 1914. Kolehmainen, on the other hand, moved to the United States and reappeared in Antwerp to win the 1920 marathon.

Hannes Kolehmainen, 1912

Passes Jean Bouin just before the finish of the 1912 5000 meters.

1920 Antwerp C: 38, N: 16, D: 8.17. WR: 14:36.6 (Johan Kolehmainen)

1. Joseph Guillemot	FRA	14:55.6
2. Paavo Nurmi	FIN	15:00.0
3. Eric Backman	SWE	15:13.0
4. Teodor Koskenniemi	FIN	15:17.0
5. Charles Blewitt	GBR	15:19.0
6. William Seagrove	GBR	15:21.0
7. Carlo Speroni	ITA	—
8. Alfred Nichols	GBR	—

This race, the first Olympic appearance by Paavo Nurmi, proved to be sweet, though temporary, revenge by the French for Kolehmainen's defeat of Bouin eight years earlier. Joseph Guillemot, whose heart was on the right side of his chest, smoked a pack of cigarettes a day. Before the final, his trainer gave the 5-foot 3-inch (1.61 meters) Guillemot a mysterious liquid concoction and said, "Swallow this and you will be unbeatable." Nurmi took the lead at the end of the third lap. Guillemot followed him closely until the final backstretch. Then, 200 meters from the finish, Guillemot sprinted away to win by 20 meters. And the mysterious concoction? It turned out to be water, sugar and rum.

1924 Paris C: 39, N: 22, D: 7.10. WR: 14:28.2 (Paavo Nurmi)

1. Paavo Nurmi	FIN	14:31.2 OR
2. Viljo "Ville" Ritola	FIN	14:31.4
3. Edvin Wide	SWE	15:01.8
4. John Romig	USA	15:12.4
5. Eino Seppälä	FIN	15:18.4
6. Charles Clibbon	GBR	15:29.0
7. Lucien Dolques	FRA	15:33.0
8. Axel Eriksson	SWE	15:38.0

Paavo Nurmi, 1924

Checks his watch during the running of the 1924 5000 meters. He is followed by fellow Finn Ville Ritola.

Paavo Nurmi

A rare photo of Paavo Nurmi smiling. Between 1920 and 1928 he won nine gold medals and three silver.

Paavo Nurmi had hoped to defend his 10,000 meters championship in Paris and was very resentful when Ville Ritola returned from four years in the United States to break Nurmi's world record and bump him from the Finnish 10,000 meters entry. On July 6, Ritola had proved his worth by winning the 10,000 in world record time. Nurmi got his chance to face Ritola four days later in the 5000, a race that began less than two hours after Nurmi had won the 1500 meters. Taking advantage of Paavo's lack of rest, his opponents set a torrid pace, passing the 1000-meter mark in 2:46.4, the same pace as the 1972 Olympic final 48 years later. Unruffled, Nurmi stayed close and then took the lead at the halfway mark, followed by Ritola. For the last eight laps, Nurmi, refusing to look behind him, stayed two yards ahead of his rival. With 500 meters to go he checked his watch for the last time, threw it to the grass, and picked up the pace. Twenty yards from the tape Ritola tried to pass, but Nurmi increased his speed and won—by two yards.

1928 Amsterdam C: 38, N: 18, D: 8.3. WR: 14:28.2 (Paavo Nurmi)

1. Vilho Ritola	FIN	14:38.0
2. Paavo Nurmi	FIN	14:40.0
3. Edvin Wide	SWE	14:41.2
4. Leo Lermond	USA	14:50.0
5. Ragnar Magnusson	SWE	14:59.6
6. Armas Kinnunen	FIN	15:02.0
7. Stepans Petkevics	LAT	—
8. Herbert "Johnny" Johnston	GBR	—

By 1928 it was a familiar sight to see Nurmi and Ritola pull away from the field, with only Edvin Wide able to keep close. This time Ritola drew clear of Nurmi in the final curve and won by over 12 yards. Wide picked up his fourth bronze medal to go with his one silver. Ritola finished his Olympic career with five gold medals and three silver medals.

1932 Los Angeles C: 19, N: 12, D: 8.5. WR: 14:17.0 (Lauri Lehtinen)

1. Lauri Lehtinen	FIN	14:30.0 OR	(14:29.91)
2. Ralph Hill	USA	14:30.0	
3. Lauri Virtanen	FIN	14:44.0	
4. John Savidan	NZL	14:49.6	
5. Jean-Gunnar Lindgren	SWE	14:54.8	
6. Max Syring	GER	14:59.0	
7. J. Alexander "Alec" Burns	GBR	15:04.0	
8. Daniel Dean	USA	15:08.5	

This race produced the ugliest incident of the 1932 Olympics. Running in last place for the first mile, Ralph Hill of Oregon gradually moved his way up to third place behind the Finnish favorites, Lehtinen and Virtanen. Then, with the surprised American crowd wild with excitement, Hill passed Virtanen, who faded back. Over the last two laps Lehtinen tried desperately to shake the pesky Hill, but couldn't. Fifty yards from the finish, Hill moved to pass Lebtinen on the outside, but the world record holder swerved out to the third lane and blocked his path. Hill broke stride, dropped back, and attempted to pass on the inside. Lehtinen swerved back into lane one, again impeding Hill's progress. Forced to break stride again, Hill made one more move, but Lehtinen was able to beat him to the tape by about three inches. After a moment of stunned silence, the audience broke into a loud chorus of boos, which didn't end until announcer Bill Henry got on the public address system and said, "Please remember, folks, that these people are our guests." Although films of the race clearly showed that Lehtinen had interfered with Hill, US officials declined to lodge a protest. At the victory ceremony, a chagrined Lehtinen attempted to lift Hill onto the first-place platform, but Hill refused. He did allow Lehtinen to pin an enameled Finnish flag to his sweater as the crowd applauded with approval.

Lauri Lehtinen, 1932

Lehtinen interfered with Ralph Hill during the home stretch of the 5000-meter run. However, Hill declined to file a protest.

1936 Berlin C: 41, N: 23, D: 8.7. WR: 14:17.0 (Lauri Lehtinen)

1. Gunnar Höckert	FIN	14:22.2 OR
2. Lauri Lehtinen	FIN	14:25.8
3. Henry Jonsson	SWE	14:29.0
4. Kohei Murakoso	JPN	14:30.0
5. Józef Noji	POL	14:33.4
6. Ilmari Salminen	FIN	14:39.8
7. Umberto Cerati	ITA	14:44.4
8. Louis Zamperini	USA	14:46.8

The 10,000 meters champion, Ilmari Salminen, lost his chance for a second medal when he tripped on Lehtinen with two laps to go and fell. At the same moment, Höckert made his move into the lead. Ahead by two yards at the bell, he sprinted away and won by 20 yards. Höckert died fighting on the Karelian Isthmus on February 11, 1940. In his honor, Lauri Lehtinen donated his gold medal from 1932 to be awarded to a Finnish soldier who fought with distinction on the Isthmus. Louis Zamperini, who placed eighth in the 1936 5000 meters, also served in World War II and was declared dead in 1944. However, he was actually still alive. A bombardier, he was flying a rescue mission when he crashed in the Pacific Ocean. He and his co-pilot spent 47 days adrift in a life raft (their tail gunner died after 33 days). Picked up by a Japanese patrol boat, Zamperini spent two years in brutal prison camps until the war ended.

1948 London C: 33, N: 20, D: 8.2. WR: 13:58.2 (Günder Hägg)

1. Gaston Reiff	BEL	14:17.6	OR
2. Emil Zátopek	CZE	14:17.8	
3. Willem Slijkhuis	HOL	14:26.8	
4. Erik Ahldén	SWE	14:28.6	
5. Bertil Albertsson	SWE	14:39.0	
6. Curtis Stone	USA	14:39.4	
7. Vaino Koskela	FIN	14:41.0	
8. Vaino Makela	FIN	14:43.0	

Zátopek was perhaps a bit too tired from winning the 10,000 meters three days earlier, particularly after he had unnecessarily sprinted at the end of his 5000 heat. Trailing Reiff by 50 meters at the bell in the final, Zátopek thrilled the crowd by sprinting around the rain-soaked track and pulling closer and closer. Reiff thought that the applause he heard was for him, until someone on the infield called his attention to Zátopek's unexpected spurt. Reiff was able to pick up his own speed just enough to reach the finish one and a half meters ahead of the charging Czech. Reiff was the first Belgian to win a track and field gold medal.

1952 Helsinki C: 45, N: 24, D: 7.24. WR: 13:58.2 (Günder Hägg)

1. Emil Zátopek	CZE	14:06.6	OR	(14:06.72)
2. Alain Mimoun	FRA	14:07.4		(14:07.58)
3. Herbert Schade	GER	14:08.6		(14:08.80)
4. D. Gordon Pirie	GBR	14:18.0		(14:18.31)
5. Christopher Chataway	GBR	14:18.0		(14:18.38)
6. Leslie Perry	AUS	14:23.6		(14:23.16)
7. Ernö Béres	HUN	14:24.8		
8. Åke Andersson	SWE	14:26.0		

After he had won the 10,000 meters for the second time, Emil Zátopek was asked if it was true that he would also contest the 5000. "The marathon contest won't be for a long time yet, so I simply must do something until then," he replied. With five runners in each of the three heats qualifying for the final, Zátopek decided to enjoy himself during his heat. As the laps piled up, the multilingual Czech chatted amiably with the other runners, particularly after it had become clear who the five qualifiers would be. As they approached the bell lap, Zátopek, in the lead, slowed down, waited for Aleksandr Anoufriev of the USSR, and motioned for him to pass, acting like a traffic cop clearing an intersection. As he rounded the final turn, Zátopek noticed Bertil Albertsson of Sweden sprinting for the finish. Slowing down again, he hailed Albertsson as if he were hitching a ride and engaged him in conversation. The two ran the last straight together, with Zátopek giving way just before the finish. He also took a liking to fourth-place finisher Les Perry of Australia and later presented him with a gift of his training suit.

The final was, of course, a more serious affair. Yet Zátopek still took the time to speak to Herbert Schade before the start, advising him to hold back for the first 2000 meters and not waste his energy setting the pace. Schade ignored this advice and paid the price. The race itself was full of action, with the lead changing hands numerous times. As the laps wound down, it appeared that any of five runners could win: Zátopek, Schade, Mimoun, Chataway, or Pirie. At the bell, Zátopek was in first place, hard-pressed by Schade. In the backstretch, Chris Chataway, who later paced Roger Bannister and John Landy to the first two sub-four-minute miles, dashed into the lead, followed by Mimoun and Schade, leaving Zátopek in fourth place. Entering the final curve, Zátopek made his move, swinging wide into lane 3. Halfway through the bend, he was already in front again and pulling away. Entering the home straightaway, Chataway, exhausted, stepped on the curb and fell. He was able to regain his feet and stagger home, but by that time Zátopek had already gained a five-yard victory over Mimoun, who finished second to Zátopek for the third time in an Olympic final and improved his personal best by over 14 seconds.

Later in the afternoon, Emil Zátopek learned that his wife, Dana, had won a gold medal in the javelin throw. When asked if it was true that he was going to try for another win in the marathon, Zátopek replied, "At present, the score of the contest in the Zátopek family is 2—1. This result is too close. To restore some prestige I will try to improve on it—in the marathon race."

Emil Zátopek, 1952
Making his move on the final turn as a fatigued Chris Chataway falls by the wayside.

1956 Melbourne C: 23, N: 13, D: 11.28. WR: 13:36.8 (Gordon Pirie)

1. Volodymyr Kuts	SOV/UKR	13:39.6 OR	(13:39.86)
2. D. Gordon Pirie	GBR	13:50.6	(13:50.78)
3. G. Derek Ibbotson	GBR	13:54.4	(13:54.60)
4. Miklos Szabó II	HUN	14:03.4	(14:03.38)
5. Albert Thomas	AUS	14:04.6	(14:05.03)
6. László Tábori	HUN	14:09.8	(14:09.99)
7. Maiyoro Nyandika	KEN	14:19.0	(14:18.99)
8. Thyge Thögersen	DEN	14:21.0	(14:21.81)

One athlete who was conspicuously missing from the 1956 Olympics was the great Hungarian runner, Sandor Iharos. Between May 14, 1955 and July 15, 1956, Iharos set world records at 1500 meters, 3000 meters, 3 miles, 5000 meters (twice), 6 miles and 10,000 meters. He was on his way to the Melbourne Games when the Soviet Union made preparations to invade Hungary. Iharos, who was in Austria, returned to Budapest and devoted himself to the unsuccessful defense of the telephone exchange.

After Volodymyr Kuts' decisive victory in the 10,000 five days earlier, it seemed a long shot that anyone would beat him in the 5000, although Gordon Pirie had defeated Kuts at this distance in world record time on June 19. In the Olympic final, Kuts went to the front immediately and was never headed, finishing 75 yards in front of Pirie and Ibbotson. Unfortunately for Kuts, the experimental training program which the Soviet coaches had imposed on him apparently took its toll. By 1960 he had suffered his first heart attack. His fourth heart attack killed him, on August 17, 1975, at the age of 48.

1960 Rome C: 48, N: 31, D: 9.2. WR: 13.35.0 (Volodymyr Kuts)

1. Murray Halberg	NZL	13:43.4	(13:43.76)
2. Hans Grodotzki	GDR	13:44.6	(13:45.01)
3. Kazimierz Zimny	POL	13:44.8	(13:45.09)
4. Friedrich Janke	GDR	13:46.8	(13:47.14)
5. David Power	AUS	13:51.8	(13:52.38)
6. Maiyoro Nyandika	KEN	13:52.8	(13:53.25)
7. Michel Bernard	FRA	14:04.2	(14:04.68)
8. Horst Flossbach	GER	14:06.6	(14:07.03)

When he was 17 years old, Murray Halberg was hit from behind in a crash tackle during a rugby match. He was left with a dislocated shoulder, ruptured veins and arteries, blood clots, and a paralyzed left arm. After two months in the hospital and two operations, he was released with a withered arm and shoulder. He had to relearn how to walk, run, dress himself, and feed himself. Prevented from competing in contact sports, Halberg concentrated on running. Six years after his accident, he represented New Zealand at the Melbourne Olympics and two years after that he broke the four-minute mile.

Murray Halberg, 1960
Collapsing to the infield grass, with the tape still in hand, after a strategic win.

Back in the Olympics in 1960, Halberg and his coach, Arthur Lydiard, devised a radical strategy to win the 5000 meters, a strategy they had tried successfully at the 1958 Commonwealth Games. With three laps to go, at the stage in the race when runners usually gather their strength for the last lap sprint, Halberg suddenly pushed to the front of the pack and then darted away as if the finish line was just around the next curve. The tactic worked perfectly. His startled opponents were confused, and before Grodotzki was able to respond, Halberg had covered the tenth lap in 61.1 seconds and opened up a lead of 25 yards. He also ran the next lap as fast as he could, preventing Grodotzki from closing any ground. Then Halberg faced the grim task of completing the final lap even though he was totally exhausted. Checking behind himself frequently, he watched as Grodotzki gradually whittled his lead down to 15 yards, 12 yards, 10 yards. But then Halberg reached the finish line with eight yards to spare. He collapsed on his back on the infield, still holding the tape between his fingers. In his autobiography, *A Clean Pair of Heels,* Halberg recalled, "I had always imagined an Olympic champion was something more than a mere mortal, in fact, a god. Now I knew he was just a human being."

1964 Tokyo C: 48, N: 29, D: 10.18. WR: 13:35.0 (Volodymyr Kuts)

1. Robert Schul	USA	13.48.8
2. Harald Norpoth	GER	13:49.6
3. William Dellinger	USA	13:49.8
4. Michel Jazy	FRA	13:49.8
5. H. Kipchoge Keino	KEN	13:50.4
6. William Baillie	NZL	13:51.0
7. Nikolai Dutov	SOV/RUS	13:53.8
8. Thor Helland	NOR	13:57.0

Bob Schul, 1964
His joy of victory (center) juxtaposed the agony of defeat of Michel Jazy (third from left), who dropped from first to fourth in the final 50 meters.

Ron Clarke of Australia led the way for most of the race, but gave up the lead to Michel Jazy shortly before the 4000-meter mark. With one and a half laps to go, Bill Dellinger moved ahead, but just after the bell Jazy regained the lead and pulled ahead by ten yards, with Norpoth second and the favorite, Bob Schul, third. Two hundred meters from the finish, Jazy was sure that he would win. "I was beside myself with joy." Suddenly, in the course of only three strides, his legs turned to lead and "weighed a ton each." Meanwhile, Schul, known for his finishing kick, had begun sprinting in the backstretch. By the final curve he had cut Jazy's lead to five yards. Coming out of the turn, Schul saw Jazy look back and noticed his shoulders tighten. "I smiled inwardly," said Schul. "I knew I had him." Jazy's thoughts turned to Volodymyr Kuts' defeat of Gordon Pirie in 1956. "You are Pirie," he told himself. "You are dead." Desperately he tried to draw an extra reserve of strength from his body, but there was nothing there. Schul passed the discouraged Frenchman 50 meters from the tape. Schul had run the last 300 meters in 38.7 seconds. Jazy was so drained that he wasn't even able to hold on to third place.

1968 Mexico City C: 37, N: 25, D: 10.17. WR: 13:16.6 (Ronald Clarke)

1. Mohamed Gammoudi	TUN	14:05.0	(14:05.01)
2. H. Kipchoge Keino	KEN	14:05.2	(14.05.16)
3. Naftali Temu	KEN	14:06.4	(14:06.41)
4. Juan Martínez	MEX	14:10.8	(14:10.76)
5. Ronald Clarke	AUS	14:12.4	(14:12.45)
6. Wohib Masresha	ETH	14:17.6	(14:17.70)
7. Nikolai Sviridov	SOV/RUS	14:18.4	(14:18.40)
8. Fikru Deguefu	ETH	14:19.0	(14:18.98)

Mohamed Gammoudi, a 29-year-old soldier, moved in front with two laps to go and, with great grit and determination, held off alternating challenges from Keino and Temu, finally winning by about four feet after running the last lap in 54.8 seconds. A Tunisian biography of Gammoudi claimed that a typical day's diet for the Olympic champion consisted of five yogurts, ten pieces of fruit, four cups of tea, two coffees, two pastries, large quantities of meat, fish, milk, and cheese, and as much parsley as he could eat. Gammoudi weighed 135 pounds.

1972 Munich C: 61, N: 35, D: 9.10. WR: 13:16.6 (Ronald Clarke)

1. Lasse Virén	FIN	13:26.4 OR	(13:26.42)
2. Mohamed Gammoudi	TUN	13:27.4	(13:27.33)
3. Ian Stewart	GBR	13:27.6	(13:27.61)
4. Steve Prefontaine	USA	13:28.4	(13:28.25)
5. Emiel Puttemans	BEL	13:30.8	(13:30.82)
6. Harald Norpoth	GER	13:32.6	(13:32.58)
7. Per Halle	NOR	13:34.4	(13:34.38)
8. Nikolai Sviridov	SOV/RUS	13:39.4	(13:39.31)

Before the competition, Steve Prefontaine had boldly warned that he would run the final mile in less than four minutes. Right on cue, Prefontaine took the lead with four laps to go and picked up the pace. Most of the field fell behind, but Virén and Gammoudi would not be shaken and were still shooting for the gold medal when the bell rang to signal the final lap. Virén led the way into the backstretch, was headed briefly by Gammoudi, but was back in the lead before the homestretch and couldn't be caught. Prefontaine faded and lost the bronze medal to the fast-finishing Ian Stewart. The last mile had been run in 4:01.2. Lasse Virén became the fourth runner to achieve a 5000/10,000 double, joining the ranks of Hannes Kolehmainen, Emil Zátopek, and Volodymyr Kuts. On May 30, 1975, Steve Prefontaine lost control of his sports car and was killed in a crash, at the age of 24. More than twenty years later, two different fictional films about his life were released: *Prefontaine* (1997) and *Without Limits* (1998).

1976 Montreal C: 36, N: 23, D: 7.30. WR: 13:13.0 (Emiel Puttemans)

1. Lasse Virén	FIN	13:24.76
2. Dick Quax	NZL	13:25.16
3. Klaus-Peter Hildenbrand	GER	13:25.38
4. Rodney Dixon	NZL	13:25.50
5. Brendan Foster	GBR	13:26.19
6. Willy Polleunis	BEL	13:26.99
7. Ian Stewart	GBR	13:27.65
8. Aniceto Silva Simoes	POR	13:29.38

Following his victory in the 10,000 meters, Lasse Virén was subjected to a double inquisition. First, members of the press grilled him about the practice of blood boosting. This unnatural, but, at that time, not illegal, procedure involves the extraction of a quart or more of blood from a runner before a major competition. This blood is frozen, while the runner's body rebuilds its blood to a normal level. Then, just before the race, the extracted blood is unfrozen and reinjected into the runner, increasing the body's hemoglobin level and oxygen-carrying capability, and thus providing the runner with greater endurance. Virén was accused of blood boosting because the procedure was first experimented with in Scandinavia, and because Virén only recorded his best performances in major competitions, particularly the Olympics. Virén always denied that he engaged in blood boosting and claimed that his training schedule was organized to peak at the Olympics, because only the Olympics really mattered to him.

The day before the 5000 meters final, Virén was called before the Technical Committee of the International Olympic Committee and asked to explain why he had carried his running shoes aloft while taking his victory lap following the 10,000 meters final. Accused of commercialism, the soft-spoken policeman said that he had removed his shoes because he had a blister. This seemed to satisfy the committee, which allowed him to continue competing.

The most notable performers in the 5000 heats were Brendan Foster, who set an Olympic record of 13:20.34 and Dieudonne Lamothe of Haiti, who led after the first lap, but finished five minutes after the other runners in his heat. His time, 18:50.07, was the slowest ever recorded in the Olympics.

In the final, most of the pace-setting was done by Virén and Foster, although the fourth kilometer saw Quax and Hildenbrand take their turns in front. With three laps to go, Virén picked up the pace, but at the start of the final lap there were still only five meters separating the first six runners. "At the bell," said Virén later, "I gave just one quick glance behind me and took in the situation in all its ghastliness. The wall at my heels was thick. . . . I had put in a couple of sixty-second laps and almost everybody was still chasing me, damn it! I was the fugitive now, and I realized I had to flee as if my life depended on it . . . In the far turn I had the most frightening experience of my career. Some guy in black was forcing himself past me. It was Quax, whom I really hadn't reckoned very seriously . . . I found my last gear, and it was just enough. The black shadow glided away from my eyes. The holy sanctuary of the finish line engulfed me—I had won!" Lasse Virén had earned his fourth gold medal and had become the first repeat winner of the 5000.

Virén was a strong believer in training in the woods. He explained it this way: "The tranquility of nature creates mental strength. When you run in the woods, you will have to change rhythm to avoid roots just in the same way as you have to be constantly alert in competitions. The humus layer developed through the years gives elasticity to the natural path and I never had, even during my active career, any foot injuries." In 1999, Virén was elected to Finland's parliament.

1980 Moscow C: 35, N: 22, D: 8.1. WR: 13:08.4 (Henry Rono)

1. Miruts Yifter	ETH	13:20.91
2. Suleiman Nyambui	TAN	13:21.60
3. Kaarlo Maaninka	FIN	13:22.00
4. Eamonn Coghlan	IRL	13:22.74
5. Markus Ryffel	SWI	13:23.03
6. Dietmar Millonig	AUT	13:23.25
7. John Treacy	IRL	13:23.62
8. Aleksandr Fedotkin	SOV/RUS	13:24.10

Miruts Yifter, 1980
Savoring the moment after an eight-year wait.

Miruts Yifter's quest for a gold medal at 5000 meters is a frustrating eight-year saga with a happy ending. Yifter first gained international attention in 1971 at a US–Africa meet in North Carolina, when he sprinted to an apparent victory over Steve Prefontaine in the 5000 meters race, only to discover that he had miscounted the laps and quit running one lap too soon. The next day he made up for his mistake by defeating Frank Shorter at 10,000 meters. At the Munich Olympics in 1972, Yifter gained a bronze medal at 10,000 meters, but missed the start of his heat in the 5000 meters race. Typical of the mystery surrounding Yifter is the fact that there were three explanations for his failure to appear at the starting line. The first is that he was directed to the wrong check-in gate at the stadium and was refused admittance by German guards. The second is that he spent too long in the toilet before the race, and the third is that he left the bathroom in time but got lost on the way to the track. In interviews twelve years later, Yifter added a fourth, characteristically vague, explanation. He implied that he ran into problems with team officials and with the Ethiopian government because he came from Tigre Province, a region involved in a civil war against the ruling dictatorship. Whether the team trainer purposely misinformed him about the starting time of his heat or whether he feared the consequences of what would happen if he did race is still unclear. In 1976 Yifter was prevented from competing when Ethiopia boycotted the Olympics.

In Moscow, the 5-foot 4-inch (1.63 meter), 117-pound father of six faced no such problems. For some strange reason, a semifinal round was added to the 5000 meters competition, despite the fact that the field of 35 was the smallest in 24 years. This didn't bother Yifter, who won his opening heat and finished second to teammate Yohannes Mohammed in the semifinals.

After 4000 meters of the final, the 12 finalists were still bunched within 12 meters. Ninety-nine-pound Mohammed Kedir led at the bell, as everyone waited for the infamous Yifter kick that had already brought victory in the 10,000 meters. However, in the backstretch Yifter was completely caught in a box, with Kedir in front of him, Eamonn Coghlan beside Kedir, and the pack behind him. Then, with less than 300 meters to go, Kedir turned around and asked Yifter if he was ready. A wave of the hand from the master and the selfless Kedir stepped aside. Yifter shot through on the inside as Coghlan watched in amazement. The rest was academic. Yifter ran the last 200 meters in 27.2 seconds to gain his long-awaited 5000 meters gold medal. Kedir got tripped up by the pack, lost his shoe, and finished last. Coghlan lost the bronze medal to Kaarlo Maaninka, who came from a family of 23 children in Lapland.

Part of the mystery of Miruts Yifter is the question of his age, which was variously reported as 33, 35, 36, 37, or 42. When asked for a definitive answer, Yifter would only reply, "I don't count the years. Men may steal my chickens, men may steal my sheep. But no man can steal my age."

1984 Los Angeles C: 56, N: 40, D: 8.11. WR: 13:00.41 (David Moorcroft)

1. Saïd Aouita	MOR	13:05.59 OR
2. Markus Ryffel	SWI	13:07.54
3. Antonio Leitão	POR	13:09.20
4. Timothy Hutchings	GBR	13:11.50
5. Paul Kipkoech	KEN	13:14.40
6. Charles Cheruiyot	KEN	13:18.41
7. Doug Padilla	USA	13:23.56
8. John Walker	NZL	13:24.46

Despite the fact that the 5000 meters field was decimated by injuries, illness, boycott, and drug disqualification, the 1984 Olympic final was the fastest mass race ever at that distance. The favorite was Saïd Aouita by virtue of his June 13 performance of 13:04.78, second only to Dave Moorcroft's world record. Aouita did not disappoint, although it was the Portuguese runners Ezequiel Canario and Antonio Leitão who created the pace. Canario led for the first 1000 meters. When he couldn't push any harder, Leitão took over. One by one he burned away the other runners with successive 64-second laps until, with 500 meters to go, only Aouita and Markus Ryffel remained. With one half lap left, Aouita sprinted ahead. Ryffel tried to keep up, but gave up in the final turn and concentrated on protecting second place. Aouita ran the final lap in 55.08 despite taking time to wave to the crowd during the last 50 yards. Ryffel, Hutchings, Kipkoech, and Cheruiyot all bettered their personal records by at least five seconds. To celebrate the victory, King Hassan II of Morocco gave Aouita a villa in Casablanca. The Rabat-to-Casablanca express train was also renamed in his honor. Aouita was undefeated at 5000 meters from 1979 until June 20, 1989. He withdrew from the 1988 Olympic competition because of injury.

1988 Seoul C: 56, N: 39, D: 10.1. WR: 12:58.39 (Saïd Aouita)

1. John Ngugi	KEN	13:11.70
2. Dieter Baumann	GER	13:15.52
3. Hansjörg Kunze	GDR	13:15.73
4. Domingos Castro	POR	13:16.09
5. Sydney Maree	USA	13:23.69
6. Jack Buckner	GBR	13:23.85
7. Stefano Mei	ITA	13:26.17
8. Yevgeny Ignatov	BUL	13:26.41

Before the race, Domingos Castro, who had consistently lost to John Ngugi in cross-country races, turned to Ngugi and said "You only know how to run in the bush. I am going to beat you on this track." In fact, Ngugi was a three-time cross country champion. Just before the 1000-meter mark of the Olympic final, Ngugi, aware that he could not match the finishing kicks of the other runners, suddenly burst into the lead and ran away from the pack. Covering the next 800 meters in a startling 2:00.25, he opened up a huge gap of almost 50 meters. With four laps to go it became clear that Ngugi was not going to fall apart, so Domingos Castro reluctantly gave chase. He managed to close within about 25 meters, 1000 meters from the finish, but Ngugi, constantly looking back to check for challengers, loped steadily onward to win by 30 meters. Ngugi would later say, "I owe it to Castro for his taunts which inspired me to win." Castro, for his part was passed . . . by 50 meters. Left without a medal, he spent the next half hour sobbing inconsolably. Ngugi went on to win two more cross-country world championships, but in 1993 he refused to take an out-of-competition drug test and was suspended from competition for two years, effectively ending his career.

1992 Barcelona C: 56, N: 41, D: 8.8. WR: 12:58.39 (Saïd Aouita)

1. Dieter Baumann	GER	13:12.52
2. Paul Bitok	KEN	13:12.71
3. Fita Bayisa	ETH	13:13.03
4. Moulay Brahim Boutaïb	MOR	13:13.27
5. Yobes Ondieki	KEN	13:17.50
6. Worku Bikila	ETH	13:23.52
7. Rob Denmark	GBR	13:27.76
8. Abel Antón Rodrigo	SPA	13:27.80

Dieter Baumann's pre-race strategy was simple: "Wait and see what the Kenyans will do." What the Kenyans did was very much to Baumann's liking. They set a decent pace without speeding up too early—perfect for a strong kicker like Baumann. Unfortunately for the 27-year-old from the small town of Blaustein, on the backstretch he found himself completely boxed in, surrounded by Bitok, Bayisa, Boutaïb, and Ondieki. On the final curve, as the Africans began sprinting, Baumann slipped out of the back of the box, swung wide and started picking off the leaders. He zipped right by Ondieki, then caught Boutaïb, wormed by Bayisa on the inside, cut back to the outside, passed Bitok 12 meters from the finish line, and won by one and a half meters. His time for the last 200 meters was 24.9 seconds. In October and November 1999, Baumann, a harsh critic of doping in sports, himself twice tested positive for the anabolic steroid nandrolone, which, in addition to being found in his urine, was discovered in his toothpaste. Baumann served out a two-year suspension, while never ceasing to insist that he had been framed.

Leo Garnes, who represented Barbados in the 1992 5000 meters, qualified for the Olympic dishonor role when, during a domestic dispute on August 31, 1999, he murdered his girlfriend and her sister.

1996 Atlanta C: 37, N: 22, D: 8.3. WR: 12:44.39 (Haile Gebrselassie)

1. Vénuste Niyongabo	BRD	13:07.96
2. Paul Bitok	KEN	13:08.16
3. Khalid Boulami	MOR	13:08.37
4. Dieter Baumann	GER	13:08.81
5. Tom Nyariki	KEN	13:12.29
6. Robert Kennedy	USA	13:12.35
7. Enrique Molina Vargas	SPA	13:12.91
8.Brahim Lahlafi	MOR	13:13.26

Vénuste Niyongabo was a Tutsi from the village of Vuglio in southern Burundi near the border with Tanzania. His father was a veterinarian and his mother a schoolteacher. A medal favorite at 1500 meters, he withdrew from that race to make way for a friend (see page 109) and entered the 5000 meters instead, even though he had competed at that distance only twice before. While Niyongabo was making his decision to join the 5000, the favorite, world record holder Haile Gebrselassie, was deciding to withdraw after hurting his foot while winning the 10,000 meters.

The early part of the 5000-meter final was run at a sluggish pace. Kenyans Tom Nyariki and Shem Kororia carried the field forward as Nyariki made periodic surges. With two laps to go, Bob Kennedy burst into the lead with Niyongabo at his shoulder and the race was on. Just before the bell, Niyongabo passed Kennedy and pulled away to a ten-meter lead. In the final curve, he began to tire, but he retained enough strength to barely hold off closing rushes by Paul Bitok and Khalid Boulami. Niyongabo ran the last lap in 54.9 seconds.

2000 Sydney C: 36, N: 23, D: 9.27. WR: 12:39.36 (Haile Gebrselassie)

1. Millon Wolde	ETH	13:35.49
2. Ali Saidi-Sief	ALG	13:36.20
3. Brahim Lahlafi	MOR	13:36.47
4. Fita Bayissa	ETH	13:37.03
5. David Chelule	KEN	13:37.13
6. Dagne Alemu	ETH	13:37.17
7. Serhiy Lebid	UKR	13:37.80
8. Jirka Arndt	GER	13:38.57

The Sydney 5000 meters contest was notable for who *wasn't* in the race. World record holder Haile Gebrselassie of Ethiopia chose to enter only the 10,000 meters, as did his Kenyan rival, Paul Tergat. World champion Salah Hissou of Morocco was injured, as was medal favorite Mohammed Mourhit of Belgium. This put Ali Saidi-Sief into the role of favorite. Saidi-Sief had won the African championship and had withdrawn from the 1500 meters to concentrate on the 5000. The pace in the Olympic final was unusually slow, which appeared to play into the hands of the fast-finishing Saidi-Sief. For most of the race the pack was tightly bunched. Brahim Lahlafi, who had the season's fastest time, 12:49:28, led the field at 3000 meters and once again at 4000 meters, with Millon Wolde, who had served as the pacesetter for Gebrselassie's 1996 world record, throwing in occasional surges. Saidi-Sief moved ahead with four laps to go and, based on his 1500 speed, he should have won easily. He was able to fight off Lahlafi and Fita Bayissa, but he was unable to shake Wolde, who drew alongside the Algerian with 100 meters to go and then pulled away to win by five meters. Although Wolde's winning time was the slowest since the high-altitude Olympics of 1968, he ran the last 800 meters in 1:54.1 and his 53.83-second last lap was the fastest in Olympic 5000 meters history. Wolde was an oddity among East African runners in that he was born and raised in the city. Lahlafi dedicated his bronze medal to fellow Moroccan Hicham El Guerrouj, who had been upset the day before in the final of the 1500 meters. At the 2001 world championships, Saidi-Sief tested positive for the steroid nandrolone and was banned from competition for two years.

2004 Athens C: 36, N: 22, D: 8.28. WR: 12:37.35 (Kenenisa Bekele)

1. Hicham El Guerrouj	MOR	13:14.39
2. Kenenisa Bekele	ETH	13:14.59
3. Eliud Kipchoge	KEN	13:15.10
4. Gebre-egziabher Gebremariam	ETH	13:15.35
5. Dejene Berhanu	ETH	13:16.92
6. John Kibowen	KEN	13:18.24
7. Zersenay Tadesse	ERI	13:24.31
8. Craig Mottram	AUS	13:25.70

The 5000 meters final matched Kenenisa Bekele, who won the 10,000 meters gold medal eight days earlier, and Hicham El Guerrouj, who won the 1500 meters four days earlier. After a sluggish start, Bekele and Eliud Kipchoge took charge of the pace, while El Guerrouj held his position in the middle of the front pack. Kipchoge had barely edged out El Guerrouj for the world championship in 2005. With 300 meters left in the Olympic final, Kipchoge led, with Bekele by his side. El Guerrouj was right behind Kipchoge, but he was boxed in by Bekele's Ethiopian teammate, Dejene Berhanu. As the pace increased, Berhanu could not keep up, and, with half a lap to go, El Guerrouj jumped to the outside, while Bekele moved ahead of Kipchoge and into the lead. "When I saw Bekele go out, I told myself I was going to win," El Guerrouj later explained. "They made a big mistake. Their strength is rhythm; my strength is the finish." El Guerrouj pulled even with Bekele with 60 meters left, and then pulled away before the finish. With his victory, El Guerrouj earned his second Olympic gold medal and became the first runner since Paavo Nurmi in 1924 to win both the 1500 meters and the 5000 meters in the same Olympics. After the race, El Guerrouj told the press, "When I arrived at the stadium I was talking to myself, and I was thinking of Paavo Nurmi. I was telling myself, 'This is a great day for you.'"

2008 Beijing C: 39, N: 24, D: 8.23. WR: 12:37.35 (Kenenisa Bekele)

1. Kenenisa Bekele	ETH	12:57.82	OR
2. Eliud Kipchoge	KEN	13:02.80	
3. Edwin Soi	KEN	13:06.22	
4. Moses Kipsiro	UGA	13:10.56	
5. Abreham Cherkos	ETH	13:16.46	
6. Tariku Bekele	ETH	13:19.06	
7. Juan Luis Barrios	MEX	13:19.79	
8. James Kwalia	QAT	13:23.48	

In 2004 Kenenisa Bekele was denied a 5000/10,000 meters Olympic double by Morocco's Hicham El Guerrouj, who completed the first 1500/5000 meters Olympic double since 1924. Four years later Bekele returned as the reigning 10,000 meters Olympic champion, the defending 5000 meters silver medalist, the three-time reigning 10,000 meters world champion, and widely regarded as the best long-distance runner in the world.

Born in Bekoji, a sleepy town outside Addis Ababa, Bekele's specialty was the 10,000 meters, a distance over which he had never been beaten. Although he had chosen not to compete in the 5000 meters at the past two world championships, he held the world records in both the 5000 and 10,000. Bekele's main challengers were expected to be reigning 5000 meters world champion Bernard Lagat, a Kenyan-born runner now competing for the United States, and defending Olympic bronze medalist and 2003 world champion Eliud Kipchoge.

Competing six days after winning gold in the 10,000 meters event, Bekele controlled the pace during the final, taking the lead after the first lap and alternating with his younger brother, Tariku, an outside medal contender, and fellow Ethiopian Abreham Cherkos. Kipchoge and Lagat remained in the chasing pack. With five laps to go, Bekele upped the pace, dropping most of the pack. Kipchoge and Edwin Cheruiyot Soi managed to stay within striking distance until the last lap, when Bekele began his final kick and calmly pulled away, opening a 25-meter lead over Kipchoge over the final stretch. Bekele recorded the first sub-13-minute time in Olympic history and was the first male athlete to complete the 5000/10,000 meters double since Miruts Yifter at the boycotted 1980 Moscow Games.

One year after his triumph in Beijing, Bekele faced Lagat once again in the 5000 meters final of the 2009 world championships in Berlin. Lagat, racing with four stitches in his leg after being spiked during the qualifying round, surged into the lead around the final turn, but Bekele managed to pass him in the final 20 meters to take gold. Bekele's earlier win in the 10,000 meters made him the first man in history to complete a 5000/10,000 meters double at a world championships.

10,000 METERS

A 25-lap race, the 10,000 meters is 6 miles 376 yards and 4 inches. Twenty runners take part in the final.

1896–1908 not held

1912 Stockholm C: 30, N: 13, D: 7.8, WR: 30:58.8 (Jean Bouin)

1. Johan Kolehmainen	FIN	31:20.8
2. Louis Tewanima	USA	32:06.6
3. Albin Stenroos	FIN	32:21.8
4. Joseph Keeper	CAN	32:36.2
5. Alfonso Orlando	ITA	33:31.2

Fifteen men qualified for the final but only 11 started. The hot sun and hard pace cut the field down further and only five finished. Twenty-two-year-old Hannes Kolehmainen took the lead in the first lap and won the first of his four Olympic gold medals without being challenged. Silver medalist Louis Tewanima was a Hopi Indian.

1920 Antwerp C: 34, N: 17, D: 8.20. WR: 30:58.8 (Jean Bouin)

1. Paavo Nurmi	FIN	31:45.8
2. Joseph Guillemot	FRA	31:47.2
3. James Wilson	GBR	31:50.8
4. Augusto Maccario	ITA	32:02.0
5. James Hatton	GBR	32:14.0
6. Jean-Baptiste Manhès	FRA	32:26.0
7. Heikki Liimatainen	FIN	32:28.0
8. Frederick Faller	USA	32:38.0

Paavo Nurmi was born in Turku, Finland, on June 13, 1897, the son of a carpenter who died when Paavo was 12. He gained early success in Finland at 3000 meters, but caused his first sensation while serving in the army in the early summer of 1919. He entered a 20-kilometer march with full equipment. Running was allowed, so Nurmi ran the entire distance. Carrying a rifle, a cartridge belt, and an 11-pound sack of sand, he finished the course so quickly that some officials thought he must have discovered a shortcut.

In Antwerp Nurmi lost his first final, the 5000 meters, to Joseph Guillemot, but sought revenge three days later in the 10,000. This time he let James Wilson of Scotland do most of the pace-setting. Nurmi took the lead with two laps to go. Guillemot passed him in the backstretch of the final lap, but Nurmi sprinted back into the lead almost immediately and won by eight yards.

Although Paavo Nurmi's first Olympic victory was not his most difficult, it *was* his most unpleasant, since Guillemot vomited on his shoes as soon as he crossed the finish line. The source of Guillemot's distress was a last-minute change in the starting time of the race. Guillemot had just finished a large lunch when he was informed that the race had been moved up from 5:30 p.m. to 2:15 p.m. at the request of the king of Belgium, who wished to appear at an art opening, leaving the Frenchman no time to digest his food.

1924 Paris C: 43, N: 17, D: 7.6. WR: 30:35.4 (Vilho "Ville" Ritola)

1. Vilho "Ville" Ritola	FIN	30:23.2 WR
2. Edvin Wide	SWE	30:55.2
3. Eero Berg	FIN	31:43.0
4. Väinö Sipilä	FIN	31:50.2
5. Ernest Harper	GBR	31:58.0
6. Halland Britton	GBR	32:06.0
7. Guillaume Tell	FRA	32:12.0
8. Earl Johnson	USA	32:17.0

For the first time, the 10,000 meters was run without heats. Ritola and Wide pulled away from the other 41 contestants after only two laps, but even Wide couldn't keep up with Ritola, who won by a half lap and broke his own world record by more than 12 seconds. He continued on for another quarter lap before the officials were able to convince him that the race was over. Paavo Nurmi had been prevented from entering this race by Finnish officials, who felt he was entering too many events. Back in Finland after the Games, Nurmi made his point by setting a world record of 30:06.2 that was to last for almost 13 years.

Competing between 1920 and 1928, Edvin Wide earned four bronze medals and one silver. He was born in Finland, but was granted Swedish citizenship in time for the 1920 Olympics. One of the many runners who collapsed during the 1924 cross-country race, he is reported to have said that he could die in peace, having run his last Olympic race. In fact, he lived another 72 years until the age of 100 before dying June 19, 1996.

1928 Amsterdam C: 24, N: 12, D: 7.29. WR: 30:06.2 (Paavo Nurmi)

1. Paavo Nurmi	FIN	30:18.8 OR
2. Vilho "Ville" Ritola	FIN	30:19.4
3. Edvin Wide	SWE	31:00.8
4. Jean-Gunnar Lindgren	SWE	31:26.0
5. Arthur Muggridge	GBR	31:31.8
6. Ragnar Magnusson	SWE	31:37.2
7. Toivo Loukola	FIN	31:39.0
8. Kalle Matılainen	FIN	31:45.0

Paavo Nurmi earned his ninth and last gold medal in the 10,000 meters flat race, the same event in which he had won his first gold medal. After nine laps only Ritola, Nurmi, and Wide were still in contention. During the 18th lap the Swede dropped back. Nurmi dogged Ritola for the remainder of the race, then passed him about 50 yards from the tape and won by two or three meters. Nurmi refused to be congratulated or photographed, and simply picked up his sweatsuit and walked off the track without a smile. The following week he gained two silver medals in the 5000 and the steeplechase.

Nurmi had planned to enter the 10,000 and the marathon in the 1932 Olympics, but was declared a professional by the International Amateur Athletic Federation after a 13-12 vote, and banned from competition. For a time Nurmi ran a construction business and then a men's clothing store, eventually gaining considerable financial security as a result of wise real estate investments. His last appearance on a track was a dramatic one. When the 1952 Olympics were held in Helsinki, Finland, the Opening Ceremony was staged in the Olympic Stadium, which was graced with a bronze statue of Nurmi in the front. After the athletes had paraded around the track and onto the infield, the audience awaited the arrival of the Olympic torch. When the final runner, whose name had not been announced, appeared from out of the tunnel bearing the torch aloft, the Finnish spectators broke into thunderous applause as they recognized the runner as none other than Paavo Nurmi, whose stride was unmistakable even though he was 55 years old. The athletes of the world broke rank and dashed to the side of the track to catch a glimpse of the legendary "flying Finn," who bounded up the steps and passed the torch to 62-year-old Hannes Kolehmainen, who lit the Olympic flame.

Paavo Nurmi, who set 29 world records at distances ranging from 1500 meters to 20,000 meters, died on October 2, 1973. Six Finnish gold medal winners served as pallbearers at his funeral. Nurmi left the bulk of his estate to help the cause of heart research. In 1987, Finland issued a ten-mark note with Nurmi on one side and the Olympic Stadium on the other.

1932 Los Angeles C: 16, N: 11, D: 7.31. WR: 30:06.2 (Paavo Nurmi)

1. Janusz Kusociński	POL	30:11.4 OR	(30:11.42)
2. Volmari Iso-Hollo	FIN	30:12.6	
3. Lauri Virtanen	FIN	30:35.0	
4. John Savidan	NZL	31:09.0	
5. Max Syring	GER	31:35.0	
6. Jean-Gunnar Lindgren	SWE	31:37.0	
7. Juan Morales Rodriguez	MEX	32:03.0	
8. Calvin Bricker	CAN	—	

Kusociński and Iso-Hollo dueled at close quarters for 24 of 25 laps. Iso-Hollo led by one yard entering the final lap, but then Kusociński sprinted away to a big lead, before slowing to a jog and finishing with ten yards to spare. Seventh-place finisher Juan Morales Rodriguez was a Yaqui Indian who ran barefoot. Among the unplaced entrants was Adalberto Cardoso of Brazil, who got stranded in San Francisco and didn't arrive in Los Angeles until the day of the race.

At the time of his Olympic triumph, Janusz Kusociński was a gardener in a Warsaw park. Following the German occupation of Poland in 1939, Kusociński, while employed as a waiter, worked secretly for the anti-Nazi resistance. Arrested by the Gestapo March 26, 1940 he was imprisoned, beaten and tortured. When it became clear that he would not reveal the names of his compatriots, he was executed on June 21, 1940.

1936 Berlin C: 30, N: 18, D: 8.2. WR: 30:06.2 (Paavo Nurmi)

1. Ilmari Salminen	FIN	30:15.4
2. Arvo Askola	FIN	30:15.6
3. Volmari Iso-Hollo	FIN	30:20.2
4. Kohei Murakoso	JPN	30:25.0
5. James "Alec" Burns	GBR	30:58.2
6. Juan Carlos Zabala	ARG	31:22.0
7. Max Gebhardt	GER	31:29.6
8. Donald Lash	USA	31:39.4

Murakoso fought valiantly against the three Finns, who ran a team race that included a good deal of jostling every time one of them passed him. However Murakoso finally had to give in with one lap to go. Salminen, a 33-year-old army sergeant, jumped the others at the start of the last lap, but Askola regained the lead in the backstretch. Salminen caught him again coming out of the final turn and gradually inched ahead for a narrow victory.

1948 London C: 27, N: 15, D: 7.30. WR: 29:35.8 (Viljo Heino)

1. Emil Zátopek	CZE	29:59.6	OR
2. Alain Mimoun	FRA	30:47.4	
3. Bertil Albertsson	SWE	30:53.6	
4. Martin Stokken	NOR	30:58.6	
5. Severt Dennolf	SWE	31:05.0	
6. Abdallah ben Said	FRA	31:07.8	
7. Stanley Cox	GBR	31:08.0	
8. James Peters	GBR	31:16.0	

World record holder Viljo Heino was expected to receive a stiff challenge from Czech army lieutenant Emil Zátopek. As it turned out, it was the challenger who controlled the race. Moving in front during the tenth lap, Zátopek ground out the laps at a steady 71-second pace until both Heino and his teammate, Heinstrom, were forced to drop out from exhaustion. Eventually Zátopek lapped all but two runners and won by more than 300 meters. The incompetent officials in charge of the race became confused by Zátopek's performance and announced the start of the final circuit one lap too soon. Fortunately Zátopek knew better, although others didn't. When the race was over, it was announced that Dennolf of Sweden had finished fourth and Stokken of Norway fifth. The Norwegians protested, but the matter was settled quickly when Dennolf himself supported their case. Sixth place was awarded to Robert Everaert of Belgium, who had actually dropped out of the race over five laps before the finish. Everaert pointed out the mistake, but the judges refused to change their decision until a Belgian official intervened. Martin Stokken, who finished fourth, won a silver medal at the 1952 Winter Olympics in the 4 × 10-kilometer cross-country relay.

At the time that Emil Zátopek won the 1948 10,000 meters, he was courting a Czech javelin thrower named Dana Ingrová. (They later married.) In London, Zátopek paid a forbidden visit to the lodgings of the Czech women. He stood under Dana's window and, as she looked down, he waved his gold medal at her. Unfortunately, it slipped out of his hand and dropped into a swimming pool. Zátopek stripped down to his underwear, dived into the pool and recovered his gold medal.

1952 Helsinki C: 33, N: 21, D: 7.20. WR: 29:02.6 (Emil Zátopek)

1. Emil Zátopek	CZE	29:17.0	OR
2. Alain Mimoun	FRA	29.32.8	
3. Aleksandr Anufriev	SOV/RUS	29:48.2	
4. Hannu Posti	FIN	29:51.4	
5. Frank Sando	GBR	29:51.8	
6. Valter Noström	SWE	29:52.8	
7. D. Gordon Pirie	GBR	30:09.5	
8. Fred Norris	GBR	30:09.8	

Looking back on the 1952 Olympics, Emil Zátopek once recalled, "I have to smile as I remember the respect I got from the other runners. When I went to the start of the 10,000 meters, the others stood back and asked where Zátopek would like to stand, and when the gun went off they all fell into place behind me like schoolboys in a procession." The result was never in doubt, as Zátopek wore out his opponents one by one, with Mimoun the last to go, four and a half laps from the finish. Zátopek won by about 100 yards to gain the first part of his unprecedented long-distance triple. Between 1948 and 1954 Emil Zátopek won 38 consecutive races at 10,000 meters.

In 1968, the Australian distance runner, Ron Clarke, visited Zátopek after failing in his last attempt to win an Olympic championship. Writing in *Athletics Weekly* in 1987, Clarke recalled, "As he marched me through customs and on to the plane on my way out of Prague, he shook hands and, in so doing, secretly transferred a small package into my grip. I thought I was smuggling some message to the outside world for him so did not dare open the little parcel until the plane was well outside Czechoslovakian territory.

"When I opened it up it, was his 1952 Olympic 10,000 meters gold medal. I thought back to the words he said as he passed it across to me, which at the time I did not understand: 'Because you deserved it,' he said. I wish I had.

"I do know no one cherishes any gift more than I do, my only Olympic gold medal and not because of what it is . . . but because of the man whose spirit it represents."

1956 Melbourne C: 25, N: 15, D: 11.23. WR: 28:30.4 (Volodymyr Kuts)

1. Volodymyr Kuts	SOV/UKR	28:45.6	OR	(28:45.59)
2. József Kovács	HUN	28:52.4		(28:52.36)
3. Allan Lawrence	AUS	28:53.6		(28:53.59)
4. Zdzislaw Kryszkowiak	POL	29:05.0		(29:05.41)
5. Kenneth Norris	GBR	29:21.6		
6. Ivan Chernyavsky	SOV/UKR	29:31.6		
7. David Power	AUS	29:49.2		
8. D. Gordon Pirie	GBR	29:49.6		

Volodymyr Kuts was a teenager when the Germans invaded his Ukrainian village in 1943. After the war, he joined the Soviet navy, and it was only then that he attracted the attention of Soviet coaches, who introduced him to competitive running at the age of 23.

Two months before the Melbourne Olympics, while running in Moscow, Kuts broke the world 10,000 meters record by over 12 seconds. By virtue of this performance, he was considered the favorite. But there were those who remembered that two months before that, Kuts had been beaten in England by Gordon Pirie

Pirie and Kuts, 1956

Gordon Pirie and Volodymyr Kuts, still friendly despite their intense rivalry. In 1956 Kuts defeated Pirie in both the 10,000 meters and the 5000 meters.

at 5000 meters, and although he had never run the 10,000 faster than 29:17.2, Pirie was also given a good shot at the gold medal.

Kuts took off like a flash and completed the first of 25 laps in only 61.2 seconds. Slowing down only slightly, he had outdistanced everyone but Pirie by the seventh lap. Kuts ran the first half of the race so quickly that he passed the 5000-meter mark at 14:07.0, which almost equaled Emil Zátopek's Olympic record for that distance. And he still had another 5000 meters to run. Between laps 8 and 20, Kuts tried a variety of tactics to rid himself of the stubborn Pirie. Several times he sprinted out at a seemingly insane pace, only to have Pirie catch up each time. Alternatively, Kuts would slow down, move to the outside, and wave Pirie past him. But Pirie refused to bite, preferring to remain at Kuts' shoulder.

Suddenly, at the end of the 20th lap, Kuts stopped so abruptly that Pirie was forced to take the lead. Relieved of the pressure of having Pirie on his heels, Kuts rested for a half lap while he studied his adversary in front of him. Then, just as suddenly as he had slowed, Kuts burst past Pirie to take the lead for good. Pirie struggled to keep pace, but with four laps to go, he gave up, eventually dropping back to eighth place. Kovács and Lawrence finished strongly, but Kuts' victory was never in doubt.

1960 Rome C: 32, N: 20, D: 9.8. WR: 28:30.4 (Volodymyr Kuts)

1. Pyotr Bolotnikov	SOV/RUS	28:32.2 OR	(28:32.18)
2. Hans Grodotzki	GDR	28:37.0	(28:37.22)
3. David Power	AUS	28:38.2	(28:37.65)
4. Aleksei Desyachikov	SOV/RUS	28:39.6	(28:39.72)
5. Murray Halberg	NZL	28:48.6	(28:49.11)
6. Max Truex	USA	28:50.2	(28:50.34)
7. Zdzislaw Krzyszkowiak	POL	28:52.4	(28:52.75)
8. John Merriman	GBR	28:52.6	(28:52.89)

Dave Power tried to pull away with seven laps to go, but Bolotnikov, Grodotzki, and Desyachikov were able to stay with him. Seven hundred meters from the finish, Bolotnikov, a 30-year-old pupil of Volodymyr Kuts, left the others behind, running the last lap in 57.4 seconds and winning by 30 yards. Nine of the first ten finishers achieved personal records, including Power, who bettered his previous best time by 53.8 seconds.

1964 Tokyo C: 29, N: 17, D: 10.14. WR: 28:15.6 (Ronald Clarke)

1. William Mills	USA	28:24.4 OR
2. Mohamed Gammoudi	TUN	28:24.8
3. Ronald Clarke	AUS	28:25.8
4. Degaga "Mamo" Wolde	ETH	28:31.8
5. Leonid Ivanov	SOV/KYR	28:53.2
6. Kokichi Tsuburaya	JPN	28:59.4
7. Murray Halberg	NZL	29:10.8
8. Anthony Cook	AUS	29:15.8

The 1964 10,000 meters produced one of the most electrifying upsets in Olympic history. Pregame predictions had the race as a tough battle among defending 5000-meter champion Murray Halberg, defending 10,000 meters champion Pyotr Bolotnikov, and the main favorite, world record holder Ron Clarke. By the halfway mark, Clarke, following a strategy of surging every other lap, had managed to eliminate from contention all but four runners: Mohamed Gammoudi and Mamo Wolde, who would both win gold medals four years later in Mexico City, local favorite Kokichi Tsuburaya, and Billy Mills, who had finished second at the US Olympic trials. Tsuburaya was the first to lose contact; then, with two and a half laps to go, Wolde dropped away.

At this point, Ron Clarke appeared assured of victory, since neither Gammoudi nor Mills had ever broken 29 minutes. It was surely just a matter of time before Clarke would break away. They reached the final lap with Clarke and Mills running abreast and Gammoudi right behind. The track was cluttered with stragglers, and the three leaders were forced to thread their way through the congestion. It was "like a dash for a train in a peak-hour crowd," Clarke would later recall. In the backstretch Clarke found himself faced with a problem. In front of him was a straggler who wouldn't move aside to be passed. To his right was Mills. Clarke tapped Mills a couple times, but he wouldn't step aside either. So Clarke gave him a shove that sent the American unknown careening to the outside. Seeing his chance, Gammoudi, putting one hand on Clarke and the other on Mills, pushed his way to the front and opened a sudden ten-yard lead. Clarke took off after the Tunisian, while Mills appeared to be out of the running. By this time, the audience was already going wild with excitement.

Clarke gradually closed the gap, finally passing Gammoudi at the beginning of the homestretch. But Gammoudi wasn't finished. With a major upset within his grasp, he pulled up to Clarke's shoulder once again. Then came one of those rare moments that sports fans never forget. Billy Mills, fighting his way through still more stragglers, let loose a final sprint that sent Clarke and Gammoudi into shock and carried him across the finish line with a three-yard victory that left the crowd of 75,000 as exhausted as the runners. Mills was immediately surrounded by Japanese officials, one of whom asked him, "Who are you?"

During the two weeks that he had spent in the Olympic Village prior to the opening of the games, not one reporter had asked Billy Mills a single question. Now he was besieged by journalists from all over the world, all asking the same question: "Who is Billy Mills?" Humble and calm (after crying on the victory platform), Mills explained that he was seven sixteenths Sioux Indian, and had been born in Pine Ridge, South Dakota, one of 12 siblings. Orphaned at 12, he had been sent to Haskell Institute, a school for Native Americans in Lawrence, Kansas. He had taken up running as training to become a boxer, but after losing a couple of fights, he had decided to stick to running. After attending the University of Kansas, he had joined the Marines and was now a motor pool officer at Camp Pendleton in California. His winning time in Tokyo was 46 seconds faster than his previous best (Gammoudi had improved

1964
Mohamed Gammoudi (second from left) pushes his way past Billy Mills (left) and Ron Clarke (right) during the spectacular last lap of the 1964 10,000 meters.

Billy Mills, 1964
Mills crosses the finish line in the 1964 10,000 meters.

his own personal record by 47 seconds). "I'm flabbergasted," said Mills. "I can't believe it. I suppose I was the only person who thought I had a chance."

In 1965 Billy Mills proved that his Olympic victory was no fluke by bettering Ron Clarke's six-mile world record by six seconds. That same year, he received an award that was to prove more meaningful to him than his gold medal—a ring made from Black Hills gold that was presented to him by the elders of the Oglala Sioux tribe. They also gave him warrior status, which he did not have because he was a half-breed, and an Indian name Makoce Teh'la: Loves His Country.

But there was one thing missing from Billy Mills' Olympic experience: because there were so many runners still finishing the race, he was not allowed to take a victory lap. Twenty years later, on a rainy day in 1984, Mills returned to the National Stadium in Tokyo along with his wife, Pat, US filmmaker Bud Greenspan, and a film crew. Mills described what followed in the book *Tales of Gold,* by Lewis Carlson and John Fogarty: "I knew what I wanted, and Pat knew what I was going to do. I went down onto the track and . . . went on around, taking that victory lap I so desperately needed. At the same time, in my mind, I was reliving the race. I could feel Clarke push me, and I could sense people in the stadium. Toward the end of my lap, I heard one person clapping; it was Pat, clapping for me. I started to cry. I needed that victory lap so badly, I started crying, and rather than let the group see me cry, I lifted my face up to the rain, walked up the track a way to get my composure, then finished my lap." The 1983 film, *Running Brave,* was based on Mills' life.

1968 Mexico City C: 37, N: 23, D: 10.13. WR: 27:39.4 (Ronald Clarke)

1. Naftali Temu	KEN	29:27.4	(29:27.40)
2. Degaga "Mamo" Wolde	ETH	29:28.0	(29:27.75)
3. Mohamed Gammoudi	TUN	29:34.2	
4. Juan Martinez	MEX	29:35.0	
5. Nikolai Sviridov	SOV/RUS	29:43.2	
6. Ronald Clarke	AUS	29:44.8	
7. Ronald Hill	GBR	29:53.2	
8. Wohib Masresha	ETH	29:57.0	

When the International Olympic Committee first announced that the 1968 Olympics would be held in Mexico City, there was much criticism that the competitions would be adversely affected by the high altitude. The IOC denied that the altitude would make a difference, but they couldn't have been more wrong.

The 10,000 meters was the first track and field event to be decided. With six laps to go, two runners were carried away on stretchers. The first surprise came after 8900 meters, when Kip Keino dropped out, suffering stomach cramps as a result of a gall bladder infection. Although 11 different men had led over the first 8000 meters, with 800 meters left, the only runners still in contention were Wolde, Clarke, Temu, and Gammoudi. One and a half laps from the finish, Clarke finally lost contact. A 64.4-second 24th lap by Temu got rid of Gammoudi, but just after the bell Wolde shot past Temu and opened up a five-yard gap. However, Temu had the most strength left. He caught Wolde 50 meters from the finish line and won by four yards. The first five finishers were all from high-altitude countries or had lived in high-altitude areas of their nations. The first non-high-altitude runner to finish was Ron Clarke, who collapsed and was unconscious for ten minutes. Clarke, by the way, had previously endured physical suffering because of the Olympics. In 1956, when he was 19 years old, Clarke was chosen to be the final runner in the torch relay and to light the Olympic cauldron. Sparks from the flame singed the hair on his arm and destroyed his t-shirt, but he escaped without serious injury.

Temu, a 23-year-old Kisii tribesman, was resentful, as well he should have been, when he learned that his victory was being belittled because of the altitude. In 1966 he had attracted attention by finishing first at the Commonwealth Games in Jamaica. "Now tell me," he said after his win in Mexico City, "I beat that Clarke they were talking about in Jamaica, and tell me . . . were there mountains in Kingston?" Temu was the first Kenyan to earn an Olympic gold medal. The 1968 10,000 meters marked the first time that Africans won all three medals in an Olympic event.

In January 2003 Temu was admitted into a state-run hospital in Nairobi, Kenya, for treatment for prostate cancer. He had been diagnosed many months earlier but had been unable to afford the $630 medical bill. The government eventually waived the fee after the story was picked up by the press, but Temu passed away soon after.

1972 Munich C: 50, N: 34, D: 8.31. WR: 27:39.4 (Ronald Clarke)

1. Lasse Virén	FIN	27:38.4 WR	(27:38.35)
2. Emiel Puttemans	BEL	27:39.6	(27:39.58)
3. Miruts Yifter	ETH	27:41.0	(27:40.96)
4. Mariano Haro Cisneros	SPA	27:48.2	(27:48.14)
5. Frank Shorter	USA	27:51.4	(27:51.32)
6. David Bedford	GBR	28:05.4	(28:05.44)
7. Daniel Korica	YUG/SER	28:15.2	(28:15.18)
8. Abdelkader Zaddem	TUN	28:18.2	(28:18.17)

With 50 runners entered, qualifying heats were reinstituted for the first time since 1920. In the first heat, Dave Bedford and Emiel Puttemans pulled away from the field. After reaching 8000 meters in 22:16.2, Bedford turned to Puttemans and asked him if they

Lasse Virén, 1972
A stumble, followed by a quick recovery – and, soon, the first of four gold medals.

should go for the world record. Puttemans declined. "But we're so close to the mark," said Bedford. Finally Puttemans convinced him that they should save themselves for the final, not to mention the 5000. The second heat saw the Olympic debut of Lasse Virén, a 23-year-old Finnish policeman from the small village of Myrskyla. Two and a half weeks earlier Virén had defeated Puttemans and Bedford in Stockholm, setting a two-mile world record of 8:14.0.

The third and last heat was highlighted by the appearance of Anilus Joseph of Haiti, who had evidently never taken part in a 10,000 meters race before. Joseph took off as if he was two laps from the finish line. He covered the first lap in 59.6 seconds, opening up a lead of 50 meters. He was still in first place after 800 meters, but then he ran out of steam, and by the 1000-meter mark he was in last place. By the eighth lap he had been lapped by all the other runners and by the twelfth he had been lapped again. When the bell rang to signal the final lap for the leaders, Joseph thought that it meant that he too only had one more lap to go, so he began sprinting again. Informed by an official that even though all the other runners had finished, he still had another mile to run, Joseph finally dropped out. He wasn't seen again in the Olympics, but his performance was only a prelude to the unusual feats that would be accomplished by the Haitian track team four years later in Montreal.

The final, two days later, was a more serious race. Although Bedford set a pace not unlike that of Joseph, he was able to sustain it for much longer. He was still in the lead after 4600 meters, when a surprising incident occurred behind him.

Running in fifth place, Lasse Virén, without being interfered with, stumbled and fell. Mohamed Gammoudi tripped on Virén and crashed to the ground. Gammoudi, stunned, was forced to give up a couple laps later, but Virén rose quickly and moved up to second place after only 230 meters.

Virén passed Bedford at the 6000-meter mark and Bedford began to fade soon after. Only Yifter, Haro, Puttemans, and Shorter were still in the hunt. The lead changed hands several times during the next few laps. Six hundred meters from the finish, Virén poured it on. Shorter fell back immediately, and Haro lost contact 100 meters later. Yifter fell away in the final backstretch. Puttemans tried desperately to keep up, but Virén had too much strength left and was able to pull away in the final straight to win by about six or seven yards. Virén's times for the last two laps were a remarkable 60.0 and 56.4. Lasse Virén had broken Ron Clarke's seven-year-old world record and won the first of his four gold medals.

1976 Montreal C: 41, N: 26, D: 7.26. WR: 27:30.8 (David Bedford)

1. Lasse Virén	FIN	27:40.38
2. Carlos Lopes	POR	27:45.17
3. Brendan Foster	GBR	27:54.92
4. Anthony Simmons	GBR	27:56.26
5. Ilie Floroiu	ROM	27:59.93
6. Mariano Haro Cisneros	SPA	28:00.28
7. Marc Smet	BEL	28:02.80
8. Bernard Ford	GBR	28:17.78

The final was a relatively simple race. Lopes took the lead after 3200 meters and eventually drew away from everyone but Virén, who passed him 450 meters from the finish and won easily by 30 meters.

However, the 1976 10,000 meters competition should not be left without making mention of Olmeus Charles of Haiti, whose performance in the opening heat was the ultimate expression of the Olympic ideal that what counts is not the winning, but the taking part. Charles completed the course in 42:00.11, the slowest time ever recorded in the Olympics, almost 14 minutes slower than Carlos Lopes, who won the heat, and over eight and one-half minutes slower than Chris McCubbins of Canada, who placed next to last. The entire schedule had to be held up while Charles plodded the final six laps alone. In 1972 and 1976 Haitian runners consistently finished in last place. At first reflection, one might feel sympathy for the Haitians. After all, Haiti is the poorest country in the Western Hemisphere, and malnutrition is widespread. However, there is no evidence that tryouts were actually held to determine the nation's best runners. Instead, "Baby Doc" Duvalier, the dictator of Haiti, simply chose his friends and other trusted soldiers, and rewarded them with a free trip to Canada. Unfortunately, none of them were athletes.

1980 Moscow C: 40, N: 26, D: 7.27. WR: 27:22.5 (Henry Rono)

1. Miruts Yifter	ETH	27:42.69
2. Kaarlo Maaninka	FIN	27:44.28
3. Mohammed Kedir	ETH	27:44.64
4. Tolossa Kotu	ETH	27:46.47
5. Lasse Virén	FIN	27:50.46
6. Jörg Peter	GDR	28:05.53
7. Werner Schildhauer	GDR	28:10.91
8. Enn Sellik	SOV/EST	28:13.72

The final resembled a dual meet between Ethiopia and Finland more than an international contest. The Ethiopians dominated the proceedings, changing the pace and the lead every few hundred meters. After lulling the pack into confusion for the first 5000 meters, they set off at a torrid clip until only Virén and Maaninka were left to challenge. In the 22nd lap Maaninka broke ahead, only to be passed by Kedir and Yifter. Then Virén took the lead, but Kedir moved ahead again just before the bell. Finally, the inevitable took place. With 300 meters left in the race, Miruts Yifter sprinted into the lead, covered the last 200 meters in 26.8 seconds, and won by ten meters. Virén faded to fifth, but Maaninka, who later admitted to blood boosting before the Olympics, finished strongly to prevent an Ethiopian sweep.

1984 Los Angeles C: 45, N: 33, D: 8.6. WR: 27:13.81 (Fernando Mamede)

1. Alberto Cova	ITA	27:47.54
2. Michael McLeod	GBR	28:06.22
3. Michael Musyoki	KEN	28:06.46
4. Salvatore Antibo	ITA	28:06.50
5. Christoph Herle	GER	28:08.21
6. Sosthenes Bitok	KEN	28:09.01
7. Yutaka Kanai	JPN	28:27.06
8. Stephen Jones	GBR	28:28.08

DISQ (Drugs): Martti Vainio (FIN) 27:51.10

In 1982, Alberto Cova won the European championships by outsprinting Werner Schildhauer of East Germany. In 1983, Cova won the world championships by outsprinting Schildhauer. In 1984, with Schildhauer missing because of the Soviet-bloc boycott, Cova's only competition was thought to be world record holder Fernando Mamede. But even Mamede was considered a doubtful challenger because of his long record of becoming overcome by nerves at important meets. True to form, Mamede, after winning his qualifying heat, raced off the track halfway through the final.

While Mamede was disappearing into the tunnel, Nick Rose of Great Britain was making the first significant move of an otherwise slow race. He opened a ten-meter lead, but was quickly hauled in by Martti Vainio and Cova. Vainio then ran away from the field—except for Cova, who tracked him relentlessly for two and one-half miles. The result seemed inevitable. With 200 meters to go, Cova shot past the tall Finn and pulled away to a 25-meter victory. The second 5000 meters of the race had been run in 13:27.71. Vainio was subsequently disqualified when his drug test turned up traces of an anabolic steroid, apparently contained in a batch of black market testosterone that Vainio injected 27 days before the final. Indeed, Vainio had tested positive for excess testosterone in May, but the Finnish Athletic Association had destroyed the results. As for Cova, he admitted to blood doping during this period, a dubious practice which was not yet forbidden.

One admirable characteristic of the audience at the 1984 track events was their tendency to vigorously applaud last-place finishers. One such also-ran was Basil Kilani of Jordan, who finished the first preliminary heat in 30 minutes and 43.54 seconds, almost two and one-half minutes behind Fernando Mamede. The crowd probably would have given Kilani an even bigger ovation had they realized that their support had helped Kilani improve his personal record by a surprising 2 minutes and 50 seconds.

1988 Seoul C: 52, N: 35, D: 9.26. WR: 27:13.81 (Fernando Mamede)

1. Moulay Brahim Boutaïb	MOR	27:21.46	OR
2. Salvatore Antibo	ITA	27:23.55	
3. Kipkemboi Kimeli	KEN	27:25.16	
4. Jean-Louis Prianon	FRA	27:36.43	
5. Arturo Barrios Flores	MEX	27:39.32	
6. Hansjörg Kunze	GDR	27:39.35	
7. Paul Arpin	FRA	27:39.36	
8. Moses Tanui	KEN	27:47.23	

Sicilian Salvatore Antibo rattled the field by running the first 800 meters in 2:07.4. Moses Tanui surged into the lead at the 2000-meter mark, carrying Kipkemboi Kimeli and Antibo with him. They were joined, three laps later, by Brahim Boutaïb, a former protege of Saïd Aouita, who had broken away from his mentor only a month before the Olympics. The rest of the runners were already out of the race, 40 meters back. Kimeli reached the halfway point in world record pace: 13:35.32. Boutaïb was on his heels. Tanui trailed by 10 meters with Antibo another 10 meters behind. One lap later Boutaïb made his move. By the end of the next lap he had opened up a 10-meter lead, which he gradually expanded to 40 meters by the bell. He slowed to a walk before the end, stopping completely just after the finish line in order to embrace Antibo, who passed Kimeli in the final straight to take the silver. At 21 years of age, Boutaïb was the youngest winner in the event's history. When asked "Where do you go from here?" he replied, "What can you ask a flower that is just blooming?"

1992 Barcelona C: 56, N: 38, D: 8.3. WR: 27:08.23 (Arturo Barrios Flores)

1. Khalid Skah	MOR	27:46.70
2. Richard Chelimo	KEN	27:47.72
3. Addis Abebe	ETH	28:00.07
4. Salvatore Antibo	ITA	28:11.39
5. Arturo Barrios Flores	MEX	28:17.79
6. Germán Silva Martínez	MEX	28:20.19
7. William Koech	KEN	28:25.18
8. Moses Tanui	KEN	28:27.11

Running is the purest of Olympic sports. There are no judges rating performances, crushing an athlete's dream with their personal prejudices. There is no sophisticated equipment, providing wealthy nations with an insurmountable advantage. Track champions come from rich families and poor families, warm regions and cold regions, superpower nations and tiny nations. In running races, each athlete covers the same distance and whoever crosses the finish line first is the winner. The results are simple and clear cut—usually. The 1992 men's 10,000-meter final was one of those rare races that was an exception to the rule.

By the 1990s the world of the 10,000 meters was dominated by East Africans and Moroccans with an occasional Italian or Mexican thrown in. In 1991, for example, eight of the eleven fastest runners in the world were from Kenya alone. But the Kenyans had a problem: a cocky Moroccan from Fez by the name of Khalid Skah. Skah, whose name in Arabic means "runaway," was a complete unknown when he shocked the Kenyans by winning the 1990 World Cross-Country Championship. He defended his title in 1991. By the time of the 1991 World Championships in Athletics, the Kenyans knew they had to take special measures to defeat Skah. The night before the 10,000 meters final Kenya's national coach, Mike Kosgei, devised a race plan that would send Moses Tanui and Richard Chelimo out front with a blistering pace, while Thomas Osano stayed behind to badger Skah, covering his spurts, passing him, slowing his pace and generally keeping the Moroccan occupied. The plan worked perfectly as Tanui and Chelimo finished first and second while Skah had to settle for third. At the post-race press conference, an angry Skah brashly predicted that the 5000-meter final would be different because in that race Skah would have other Moroccan runners to support him. But Kenya won that one too. The pattern was repeated at the 1992 World Cross-Country Championship as Skah was beaten back into fourth place. Morocco simply did not have enough talent to execute a team strategy against the Kenyans.

10,000 meters, 1992

An Olympic official tries to stop Hammou Boutayeb during the controversial final laps of the 1992 10,000 meters.

The Olympic final did not begin until after 10 p.m., but the temperature was still 85 degrees Fahrenheit (29 degrees centigrade). After a suitably slow start considering the hot and humid conditions, Chelimo and fellow Kenyan William Koech began to force the pace. By the 3000-meter mark only eight runners were still in contention. By 5000 meters Barrios and Antibo had lost contact; by 6000 meters so had Tanui and Fita Bayisa of Ethiopia. On the sixteenth lap, Addis Abebe and Koech fell back, leaving only Chelimo and Skah to fight it out for the last 3600 meters. During the 20th lap Skah took the lead for the first time and slowed the pace. He continued to lead for about 800 meters. Then, with about 1400 meters to go, things got a bit strange.

Skah and Chelimo had already lapped one runner, Jon Halvorsen of Norway. On the backstretch of the 22nd lap they encountered a second runner ready to be lapped: 36-year-old Hammou Boutayeb of Morocco. Unlike Halvorsen, Boutayeb was a surprising person to find in next to last place. In 1990 he had recorded the third-fastest time of the year and in 1991 he had placed eighth at the world championships. As they drew closer to Boutayeb, Skah drifted wide, allowing Chelimo to retake the lead. As Boutayeb did not move out to let the leaders pass, they went around him. Boutayeb kept pace with Chelimo and Skah, then, on the next backstretch, he accelerated and cut in front of Chelimo, forcing the Kenyan to alter his stride. Chelimo was now sandwiched between the two Moroccans, with Skah so close behind him that he was clipping his heels. What had been a two-man race turned into a three-man race.

Chelimo regained the "lead," but with 700 meters to go, Boutayeb cut in front of him again. By now the crowd of 63,525 had become enraged, and whistles and boos rained down on the Moroccan pair. Fifty meters before the bell, with Chelimo back in front and Boutayeb running beside him, Carl Gustaf Tollemar, chairman of the IAAF technical committee, stepped onto the track and tried to grab Boutayeb, who evaded his grasp.

Two hundred meters from the finish line, Boutayeb dropped out, while Skah passed Chelimo and sprinted for home, running the last half lap in 26.0 seconds. Chelimo stuck with him for 140 meters, but then gave way as Skah went on to win by about seven meters. Skah's victory lap was greeted by loud choruses of derision, not to mention soiled paper cups and other debris. Almost instantly the IAAF disqualified Skah and announced that Chelimo was the gold medal winner.

Skah was livid. He accused the Spanish race officials of being racists and thieves and even implied that unnamed US officials had instigated his disqualification. He also had harsh words for Boutayeb, whom he accused of being "an animal, an imbecile" who didn't even know how to read or write. (Skah himself was the son of a professor of classical literature.) Skah's supporters maintained that he was an intellectual, a decent man who would never cheat or lie. "Why, he's a law student," said one US television commentator, evidently unaware that most people consider lawyers and would-be lawyers *less* honest than most humans.

Perhaps it was Skah's lawyerly ambitions that helped him deal with some of the stickier aspects of the case. Chelimo claimed that Skah and Boutayeb had talked back and forth during the last three laps. At first Skah denied this. When video replays showed the two Moroccans exchanging words, Skah explained that he had been urging Boutayeb to go away and stop interfering. Skah also suggested that Boutayeb's actions were motivated by his fear of being humiliated as a result of being lapped by Skah, who was a member of a rival camp of runners in Morocco. He also postulated that Boutayeb might actually have been trying to help Chelimo. If Boutayeb was so proud, asked reporters, why did he fail to finish the race? The Moroccan team answer: because Skah had managed to convince him that he had been disqualified. In fact, Boutayeb was never disqualified. Boutayeb, for his part, had nothing to say to the press.

The Moroccan team immediately filed an appeal. Fourteen hours later an IAAF jury of appeal met to decide the case. Rule 143.2 of the IAAF handbook stated that "no competitor shall receive assistance during the progress of an event." Assistance was defined as including pacing by runners lapped or about to be lapped. The rulebook was specific about athletes who received assistance in field events—they should be cautioned after a first offense and debarred after a second—but no provision was made for penalties in running events. The jury of appeal, after viewing a videotape of the race, ruled that Chelimo's progress had not been physically impaired and voted unanimously to rescind the disqualification and reinstate Skah as the Olympic champion. Rule 143.2 was subsequently amended to include penalties for track athletes and for competitors who *give* assistance as well as those who receive it.

The Spanish crowd was not as forgiving as the IAAF. They whistled and booed throughout the medal ceremony. It remains a mystery whether Boutayeb acted on his own on the spur of the moment or whether his actions were the result of a pre-race strategy concocted by the Moroccan team to gain revenge on the Kenyans. There seems little doubt though that Khalid Skah was simply the fastest man on the track that night. If Hammou Boutayeb had not been in the race, Skah still would have won.

Richard Chelimo died of a brain tumor on August 15, 2001. He was thought to be 29 years old.

1996 Atlanta C: 46, N: 29, D: 7.29. WR: 26:43.53 (Haile Gebrselassie)

1. Haile Gebrselassie	ETH	27:07.34	OR
2. Paul Tergat	KEN	27.08.17	
3. Saleh Hissou	MOR	27:24.67	
4. Aloys Nizigama	BRD	27:33.79	
5. Josephat Machuka	KEN	27:35.08	
6. Paul Koech	KEN	27:35.19	
7. Khalid Skah	MOR	27:46.98	
8. Mathias Ntawulikura	RWA	27:50.73	

Haile Gebrselassie grew up on a farm outside the village of Assela, south of the Ethiopian capital of Addis Ababa. One of ten children, his mother died when he was ten. He ran ten kilometers to school and ten kilometers back. As an adult he ran with his left arm crooked, the effect of years spent running with books under his arm.

By 1996, the 5-foot 4-inch (1.64 meters), 23-year-old Gebrselassie was the clear favorite at 10,000 meters. He was the reigning world record holder and two-time defending world champion. However, it was expected that he would recieve a stiff challenge from Paul Tergat, the two-time defending world cross-country champion. Tergat finished only fourth at the Kenyan Trials, but he was entered at the Olympics because his record was consistent and he had been ill at the trials.

By no means would it be the first time that Gebrselassie clashed with the Kenyans. At the 1992 junior world championships, for example, the young Ethiopian stalked Kenya's Josephat Machuka for 24½ laps, refusing to share the pacemaking. When Gebrselassie finally sprinted by Machuka with 200 meters to go, Machuka was so angered by Gebrselassie's tactics that he hit him on the head as he went by and was disqualified. During the final of the 1993 world championships, Gebrselassie pursued the same tactics, running at the heels of Kenya's Moses Tanui. With one lap to go, Gebrselassie stepped on Tanui's heel, pulling loose his shoe. Tanui was forced to kick off the shoe and run the last lap with one shoe. After crossing the finish line after Gebrselassie, Tanui pulled off his remaining shoe and shoved it in Gebrselassie's face.

Burundi's Aloys Nizigama reluctantly led the field through the first half of the race in a careful 13:55.22. Then the Kenyans took over the pace, with Paul Koech and Machuka pushing hard enough to drop all but four runners: teammate Paul Tergat, Gebrselassie, Nizigama and Saleh Hissou.

At 8000 meters, Tergat threw in a 2:02.3 800 meters, leaving behind everyone but Gebrselassie, who tracked his Kenyan rival in his usual manner. Just before the bell, Gebrselassie pulled alongside Tergat, gave him a quick, hard study, and sprinted ahead. By the final turn, Gebrselassie was leading by twelve meters. Tergat cut the gap in half, but they hit the finish line before he could get closer. Gebrselassie had run the second 5000 meters in an amazing 13:11.4, a time that would have been good enough to win 19 of history's 21 Olympic 5000 meters finals.

Gebrselassie had intended to run the 5000 meters in Atlanta as well as the 10,000. He was the world record holder in that event as well. But the hard track, made for sprinters, forced him to finish the 10,000 in pain with bleeding feet, so he withdrew from the 5000.

In 1999, a film, *Endurance*, was released, telling the story of Gebrselassie in docudrama style.

2000 Sydney C: 34, N: 19, D: 9.25. WR: 26:22.75 (Haile Gebrselassie)

1. Haile Gebrselassie	ETH	27:18.20
2. Paul Tergat	KEN	27:18.29
3. Assefa Mezegebu	ETH	27:19.75
4. Patrick Ivuti	KEN	27:20.44
5. John Korir	KEN	27:24.75
6. Said Berioui	MOR	27:37.83
7. Toshinari Takaoka	JPN	27:40.44
8. Karl Keska	GBR	27:44.09

Haile Gebrselassie and Paul Tergat, 2000
For the second straight Olympics, Gebrselassie nips Tergat at the line in the 10,000 meters.

September 25, 2000, was one of the greatest nights in track and field history. Nine Olympic finals were contested. The inaugural women's pole vault turned into a tense and dramatic duel. In the women's 400 meters, Cathy Freeman brought joy to the Australian crowd with an electrifying victory. In the next race, Michael Johnson became the first man to win the 400 meters twice. Jonathan Edwards won the triple jump to lift the cloud of his 1996 disappointment. Maria Mutola, competing in her fourth Olympics, earned her first gold in the women's 800 meters. But for track aficionados, the best was the final final of the night: the men's 10,000 meters.

Haile Gebrselassie had not lost a 10,000 meters final in more than seven years. During that time, he had won the world championships four times, in 1993, 1995, 1997 and 1999. He had also earned the Olympic gold medal in 1996 and, on June 1, 1998, he had set the current world record, 26:22:75, averaging 63.3 seconds per lap for 25 laps. But for all his success, Gebrselassie was questionable for the 2000 Olympics because an Achilles tendon injury had forced him to lose three months training earlier in the year.

When it became clear that Gebrselassie *would* enter the 10,000, his great rival (and friend), Paul Tergat, who had qualified for the 5000 meters in the Kenyan Trials, petitioned the Kenyan federation to let him switch to the 10,000 meters so that he could face Gebrselassie. Tergat had finished second to Gebrselassie at the 1996 Olympics, the 1997 world championships and the 1999 world championships. But losing to Gebrselassie again in Sydney was not a foregone conclusion. Tergat won the world cross-country championship five times in a row (1995-9). He also set a 10,000 meters world record in August 1997, and recorded the fastest time of the pre-Olympic season in 2000, 27:03:87.

Tergat trained three times a day. "Often I will be on the track," he told Jason Henderson of *Athletics Weekly* in 1999, "running hard, collapsing, getting up and running hard again for up to three hours. And then, when I am done, I cannot eat. I feel sick. I have no energy to do anything other than take a drink of water and lie down. Then I think of Haile. I admire him very much and when I train hard, I know that he will be training even harder."

There was a crowd of 112,524 in the Sydney Olympic Stadium the night of the final. Among the twenty starters were three Ethiopians and three Kenyans. Aloys Nizigama of Burundi set the pace for the first 3000 meters. Then Patrick Ivuti of Kenya took over for 1400 meters and then slowed to let the lead pack catch up. Somali-born American Abdi Abdirahman surged ahead, but Ivuti was back in the lead at 6000 meters. Meanwhile Gebrselassie was pursuing a strategy of staying behind the leader, while occasionally showing in front and slowing the pace. Nizigama was back in front when, with less than seven laps left, Kenya's John Korir accelerated and cut the contenders to seven, running in single file. Gebrselassie took the lead with four laps to go and slowed the pace again, but Korir would have none of it. For the next three laps, Korir was in front, followed by Gebrselassie, Tergat, medal favorite Assefa Mezgebu of Ethiopia and Ivuti. It was three Kenyans against two Ethiopians.

As they approached the bell signaling the final lap, Mezgebu moved up beside Tergat, so that Tergat was boxed in with Gebrselassie in front of him and Mezgebu to his right. In the backstretch, with 250 meters to go, Tergat jumped back, swung to the outside and sprinted into the lead, gaining the rail before they entered the last turn. Gebrselassie went after him and began inching closer as they entered the final straight. Fifty meters from the finish line, Gebrselassie finally pulled alongside Tergat, but Tergat would not give in. Gebrselassie was unable to pass Tergat—until the very last strides, when he dipped ahead just as they reached the finish.

It was as exciting a distance race as one could hope for and the crowd rewarded the runners with a standing ovation. Tergat showed absolutely no bitterness at coming so close, and for a simple reason. As he explained to reporters, "I did my best. I can do no better than that. I had nothing left at the end." On September 28, 2003, Tergat became the first person to run a marathon in less than 2 hours and 5 minutes when he won the Berlin Marathon in 2:04:55.

2004 Athens C: 24, N: 14, D: 8.20. WR: 26:20.31 (Kenenisa Bekele)

1. Kenenisa Bekele	ETH	27:05.10	OR
2. Sileshi Sihine	ETH	27:09.39	
3. Zersenay Tadesse	ERI	27:22.57	
4. Boniface Kiprop	UGA	27:25.48	
5. Haile Gebrselassie	ETH	27:27.70	
6. John Korir	KEN	27:41.91	
7. Moses Mosop	KEN	27:46.61	
8. Ismaïl "Smail" Sghyr	FRA	27:57.09	

Two-time Olympic champion and four-time world champion Haile Gebrselassie was no longer the dominating force he had been over the past dozen years. Having been beaten at the 2003 world championships by compatriot Kenenisa Bekele, Gebrselassie arrived in Athens hampered by a Achilles tendon injury that had caused him to lose three weeks of training.

After seven laps, the three Ethiopians began to pick up the pace. Trading the lead, they set a fast enough pace that by the tenth lap more than half the runners had ceased to be serious threats. By the halfway point, the three Ethiopians were followed closely only by Boniface Kiprop, and two Kenyans, John Korir and Moses Mosop. When Gebrselassie began to have difficulty maintaining his pace, Bekele slowed down. "We wanted him with us," he would later explain. While Kiprop took the lead, Gebrselassie did catch up, but so did Zersenay Tadesse of Eritrea. With three laps remaining and Gebrselassie slowly fading again, Bekele and Sihine broke away, opening a 25-meter gap ahead of Tadesse and Kiprop. Bekele produced a 53-second final lap to defeat Sihine by 30 meters. Tadesse pulled ahead of Kiprop to earn the first Olympic medal for Eritrea since the country's independence in 1993. After finishing, Bekele and Sihine waited for Gebrselassie to cross the line. Then the trio ran a victory lap together.

On January 5, 2005, Bekele's fiancée, Alem Techale, died of a heart attack while the pair were on a training run. Two months later, the still-grieving Bekele successfully defended his IAAF World Cross Country Championship titles for the fourth consecutive time. The following year he repeated the feat and became the first person to win both the short and long races at the championships five years in a row.

2008 Beijing C: 38, N: 20, D: 8.17. WR: 26:17.53 (Kenenisa Bekele)

1. Kenenisa Bekele	ETH	27:01.17	OR
2. Sileshi Sihine	ETH	27:02.77	
3. Micah Kogo	KEN	27:04.11	
4. Moses Masai	KEN	27:04.11	
5. Zersenay Tadesse	ERI	27:05.11	
6. Haile Gebrselassie	ETH	27:06.68	
7. Martin Mathathi	KEN	27:08.25	
8. Ahmad Abdullah	QAT	27:23.75	

Kenenisa Bekele and Sileshi Sihine, 2008
Kenenisa Bekele satirizes Usain Bolt's signature celebration after winning the 10,000 meters in 2008.

In 2004, when 22-year-old reigning world champion and world record-holder Kenenisa Bekele won his first Olympic gold medal, fellow Ethiopian Sileshi Sihine took the silver. Bekele and Sihine repeated their 1–2 finishes at both the 2005 and 2007 world championships and looked to be a lock for the top of the podium at the Beijing Olympics. Adding to the Ethiopian excitement was the return of legendary marathoner and long-distance champion Haile Gebrselassie, the 1996 and 2000 Olympic champion. The 35-year-old Gebrselassie had originally planned to compete in the marathon, but pulled out over concerns about the air quality in Beijing. Together with Bekele and Sihine, the Ethiopians hoped to pull off a podium sweep. Their main challengers included defending bronze medalist Zersenay Tadesse of Eritrea and 22-year-old Boniface Kiprop of Kenya, who had finished just off the podium at both the 2004 Olympics and the 2005 world championships.

Tadesse led the group through the first half, with Gebrselassie taking the lead briefly to cheers from the large Ethiopian contingent in the crowd. With three laps remaining the pack was down to seven, but as the bell for the final lap rang Bekele quickly moved to the front and began to open a decisive lead. Gebrselassie followed, but was unable to keep up the pace and was soon passed by Sihine. He ultimately drifted back to sixth. As in the past three major championships, Bekele and Sihine finished 1–2. Close behind them, Micah Kogo edged out teammate Moses Masai for the bronze. Bekele's time, 27:01.17, was an Olympic record and set the stage for his successful attempt at a 5000/10,000 double six days later.

In 2009 Bekele extended his streak in the 10,000 meters event by winning gold at the Berlin world championships. It was Bekele's fourth straight world championship title, equaling Gebrselassie's record, and it maintained his remarkable 100% career record in the event over 12 races.

MARATHON
(42,195 Meters—26 Miles 385 Yards)

"If you want to win something, run the 100 meters.
If you want to experience something, run the marathon."
Emil Zátopek

The start and finish of the marathon may or may not take place within a stadium. The course should follow standard roads, although bicycle or footpaths are allowed. Refreshment stations must be provided every five kilometers. Competitors must not take refreshments between refreshment stations. However, water stations, to be used for drinking and sponging, must be provided between the refreshment stations. Any runner who receives outside assistance is automatically disqualified. An exception, added to the rules after 1984, allows a hands-on medical examination by designated medical personnel. If the official medical staff determines that an athlete is not fit to continue, the athlete must retire at once.

1896 Athens C: 17, N: 5, D: 4.10.
(40,000 Meters)

1. Spiridon Louis	GRE	2:58:50
2. Charilaos Vasilakos	GRE	3:06:03
3. Gyula Kellner	HUN	3:06:35
4. Ioannis Vrettos	GRE	—
5. Eleveitherios Papasimeon	GRE	—
6. Demetrios Deligannis	GRE	—
7. Evangelos Gerakakis	GRE	—
8. Stamatios Masouris	GRE	—

Spiridon Louis, 1896

The idea for a marathon race was inspired by the legend of Pheidippides, a professional runner who allegedly carried the news of the Greek victory over the Persians at the Battle of Marathon in 490 BC. Upon his arrival in Athens, he called out, "Be joyful, we win!" and then dropped dead of exhaustion. Actually there is no evidence that this dramatic incident ever took place. The fifth century BC historian Herodotus wrote about the Battle of Marathon, and made mention of a professional runner named Pheidippides. However, Herodotus, who thrived on such juicy tidbits, said nothing about a run from Marathon to Athens. The story didn't appear in print until the second century AD—more than 600 years after it was alleged to have occurred. However, Herodotus did write about an earlier incident in which a runner was sent from Athens to Sparta—a distance of about 230 kilometers—to ask that soldiers from Sparta be sent to help in the battle of Marathon. The longest race to be included in the ancient Greek Olympics was only 4614 meters.

However, when meetings began to be held in 1894 to organize an international revival of the Olympics, Michel Bréal, a French-Jewish linguist and historian, proposed that a long-distance race be included. He even offered to present a silver cup to the winner. Invoking the legend of Pheidippides, Bréal and Baron Pierre de Coubertin presented the idea to the Organizing Committee of the Athens Olympics. The Greeks, moved by the presumed historical importance associated with such a race, agreed immediately. Georgios Averoff, designer of the refurbished Panathinaikos Stadium and the primary financial supporter of the Games, added an antique vase to the offer of Bréal's silver cup.

Before long, the marathon race had come to be considered the most important event of the upcoming games, and two preliminary races for Greeks were held along the proposed route from the Marathon Bridge to the stadium in Athens. The first race, on March 10, was won by Charilaos Vasilakos in 3:17:00. He was followed by Spiridon Belokas and Demetrios Deligannis. The second race was, held on March 24, officially designated an Olympic trial and was contested by 38 runners. The winner was Georgios Lavrentis, in 3:11:27. In fifth place was a young man of 24 years, from the village of Amarousion, named Spiridon Louis.

On the afternoon of Friday, April 10, 17 runners were transported from Athens to an inn near the starting point of the race in Marathon. Among them were four foreigners, including the first three finishers in the 1500 meters: Edwin Flack, the London-based Australian accountant, who had won the 800 meters only a couple of hours earlier, Arthur Blake, and Albin Lermusiaux.

The next afternoon, the 17 entrants gathered on the Marathon Bridge and endured a preliminary speech by the starter, Major Papadiamantopoulos, who finally fired a gun to begin the race. Before they departed, one of the Greek entrants, Sokratis Lagoudakis, a medical student who spoke French, turned to the foreign athletes and said, "If you win, we will still think of you as brothers." There was much excitement among the Greek populace, and all along the route the runners were cheered by curious and enthusiastic peasants. Of the foreigners, only the Hungarian, Gyula Kellner, had ever run a race of such length, having qualified for the trip to Athens by running a 40-kilometer trial in Budapest. The other three set off relatively quickly and eventually paid for their inexperience. Lermusiaux set the early pace and soon built up a huge lead, which he carried past the halfway mark. He was followed midway by Flack, with Blake three minutes farther back. After another three-minute gap came Vasilakos and Louis in fourth and fifth. At the village of Palini (Charvati), the local people had built a triumphal arch. When Lermusiaux approached in first place, the villagers crowned him with a floral victor's wreath. By the 25-kilometer mark, which was reached in 94 minutes, Blake and four of the Greeks had already dropped out.

Shortly after Palini, there was an incline, and Lermusiaux began to stagger from exhaustion. A French companion, riding beside him on a bicycle, revived his countryman with an alcohol rubdown, but this delay allowed Flack to pass him at 30 kilometers and take the lead. Lermusiaux continued for some distance, but finally collapsed after 32 kilometers. Flack, who had never before run more than ten miles, had over-extended himself in his attempt to catch Lermusiaux. Louis caught him at 34 kilometers. The two men ran together for a few minutes and then Louis pulled away. With four kilometers to go, the race was his. After 37 kilometers, Flack began to weave and sway. Flack's companion, V.W. Delves-Broughton, asked a nearby Greek to keep the Australian from falling over while he rushed off to get a wrap. The delirious Rack, thinking that he was being attacked, smashed the helpful Greek with his fist and knocked him to the ground. Flack was loaded into a carriage and driven to the dressing room at the stadium, where he was tended to by Prince Nicholas himself, and revived with a drink of egg and brandy.

As the race progressed, messengers were sent to the stadium on horseback and bicycle to convey the identity of the leaders. The last news that the 100,000 spectators in and around the stadium heard was that Flack was in front, and their disappointment was great. Then Major Papadiamantopoulos entered the stadium on horseback and rushed to the royal box, where the king and queen and the rest of the royal family were anxiously awaiting the latest news. The word spread "with the rapidity of lightning," according to the Official Report of the Games. Shouts of *"Hellene! Hellene!"* ("A Greek! A Greek!") announced the joyous news that a Greek was in the lead. Then the Commissioner of Police appeared and formally announced what the growing roar of the crowd in the streets had already implied: the winner had arrived. At last, a small, dusty runner, Spiridon Louis, appeared at the marble entrance to the stadium. Prince George and Crown Prince Constantine rushed down to greet him and, one on each side, ran with him the rest of the way to the finish line, where Louis summoned enough energy to bow to the delighted King George. Louis was kissed and hugged and hauled off to the dressing room upon the shoulders of his admirers, while a collective ecstasy spread from the stadium throughout the city.

Seven minutes later, a second Greek, Charilaos Vasilakos, crossed the finish to be followed shortly by a third Greek, Spiridon Belokas. However, the fourth-place finisher, Gyula Kellner, raised a protest that Belokas had ridden part of the way in a carriage. Belokas admitted his deception, and was stripped of his awards, as well as his shirt, and thoroughly ostracized. Belokas was the only participant in the 1896 marathon to run the marathon again when the Olympics returned to Athens in 1906.

The story of Spiridon Louis is one of which legends are made. In fact, so many legends developed about Louis that it is difficult to sort out the truth. Was he a poor shepherd, a well-to-do farmer, a soldier, a post office messenger? In fact, he and his family were small farmers who owned a house and some fields. A modest man, Louis appeared in the stadium the day after the race to accept his prize, but then returned quickly to his village, allowing journalists to invent whatever details they saw fit. Typical of the rumors that quickly spread was that he had entered the race in hopes of convincing the king to grant clemency to his imprisoned brother—a romantic story that was deflated when it was learned that Louis didn't even have a brother. It is true that merchants throughout Athens tried to shower him with gifts, including watches, jewelry, wine, free haircuts, free clothing for life, free meals, free coffee for a year, monthly stipends, a shotgun, and a Singer sewing machine.

Amazingly, Spiridon Louis managed to return to a relatively normal life. In 1936, however, he was rediscovered by the German Olympic Organizing Committee, which brought him to Berlin. There he presented a laurel wreath from the sacred grove at Olympia to Adolf Hitler. Prior to and during his visit to Berlin, Louis was interviewed by numerous German journalists. Of particular interest is one article discovered by Olympic historian Karl Lennartz in the archive of the German Sports University in Cologne. In its June 13, 1936, issue, the Magdeburg *Sport Telegramm* presented a first-person account of the 1896 Marathon by Spiridon Louis, himself.

According to Louis, in 1895 he was finishing his military service in Athens as a groom for the horses belonging to General Mavromichalis. One day the two men rode by the spot where the Olympic stadium was being constructed. Mavromichalis pointed to the finish line and Louis became inspired.

The day before the Olympic Marathon, Louis and other runners from Amarousion traveled by horse-drawn cart in the rain for five hours until they reached the village of Marathon. There they were fed by the mayor who also provided them with wine. "What did we know about the rules of training and proper diet," Louis recalled. "We sang and ate and laughed until late in the evening."

The next morning, at eleven, milk was served and each runner was given two beers. Three hours later, after shivering in the cold, the runners took off. Louis was wearing shoes donated by his village. At Pikermi (kilometer 14), Louis' second stepfather handed him some red wine and an Easter egg. At Levkas he drank orange juice.

After Flack dropped out, Major Papadiamantopoulous rode alongside Louis most of the way to the stadium. When Louis asked for water, Papdiamantopoulous instead gave him cognac, which Louis promptly spat out. He did however accept some more wine from a fellow villager waiting along the route.

In 1936 Louis recalled the moments after his victory: "That hour was something unimaginable and it still appears to me in my memory like a dream. People were calling my name. Twigs and flowers were raining down on me. Everybody was calling out my name and throwing their hats in the air . . . Afterwards it was printed in the papers that I asked for horses and a wagon as a reward and also received them . . . It is untrue." Louis claimed that besides the formal prizes, the only gift he received was "a golden watch sent to the crown prince by a lady." However his father did buy three barrels of wine and spread their contents freely at an open celebration.

Spiridon Louis died on March 26, 1940, but his name entered the Greek language in the expression *"egine Louis"*: "became Louis," or, ran quickly. More than any other single event, the victory of Spiridon Louis served as an inspiration to keep the Olympics going through the hard times that the movement faced over the next 12 years.

1900 Paris C: 13, N: 5, D: 7.19.
(40,260 Meters)

1. Michel Théato	FRA/LUX	2:59:45
2. Emile Champion	FRA	3:04:17
3. Ernst Fast	SWE	3:37:14
4. Eugène Besse	FRA	4:00:43
5. Arthur Newton	USA	4:04:12
6. Ronald MacDonald	CAN	—
7. Richard Grant	USA	4:24:00e

This unfortunate event was held in 102-degree Fahrenheit (39 degrees centigrade) heat. The course began in the Bois de Boulogne, followed the old city wall, and ended up back in the Bois. The course was poorly marked and the runners sometimes took a wrong turn and had to double back. In addition, in

Michel Théato, 1900
Théato (right) on his way to victory in the 1900 marathon.

certain places, the roads were filled with pedestrians, bicyclists, runners joining in for the fun of it, automobiles and animals. The local favorite was Georges Touquet-Daunis. However, twelve kilometers into the race, he stopped at a café, drank a couple beers and decided it was too hot to continue. Indeed, only seven of the thirteen starters completed the course. Michel Théato, a 22-year-old salaried cabinetmaker from Saint-Mandé, took the lead around the halfway point and held it to the finish line, where he was met by 1500 spectators and a military band that launched into *La Marseillaise.* In the locker room, Théato told reporters, "I could not have dreamt of a sweeter victory for my pride as a runner and a Frenchman." In fact, Théato was born in Luxembourg and maintained Luxembourgian citizenship for his entire life. Théato did not know that the race he won was the Olympic marathon until twelve years later, when a list of Olympic records was first compiled and published.

Ernst Fast, who finished third, was an electrician working in the Swedish section of the Paris World's Fair and had already won a marathon in Copenhagen.

1904 St. Louis C: 32, N: 5, D: 8.30.
(c. 40,000 Meters)

1. Thomas Hicks	USA	3:28:53
2. Albert Corey	FRA	3:34:52
3. Arthur Newton	USA	3:47:33
4. Félix Carvajal de Soto	CUB	—
5. Demetrios Velouis	GRE	—
6. David Kneeland	USA	—
7. Henry Brawley	USA	—
8. Sidney Hatch	USA	—

The 1904 marathon ranks very high on the list of bizarre events in Olympic history. Among the more unusual entrants in the race was 5-foot-tall (1.52 meter) Félix Carvajal, a Cuban mail carrier, who raised the money for his trip to St. Louis by staging exhibitions in Havana. He took a boat to the United States and got as far as New Orleans, where he lost the rest of his savings in a crap game. After hitchhiking to St. Louis, he arrived on the starting line wearing heavy street shoes, long trousers, a long-sleeved shirt, and a beret. The start of the race was delayed while Martin Sheridan, the discus thrower, cut off Carvajal's pants at the knees. Also entered were the first Africans to participate in the Olympics: Tswana tribesmen Len Tau and Jan Mashiani, and Bob Harris, who was white. The three were members of a South African contingent who traveled to St. Louis to act out two famous battles from the recently concluded Anglo-Boer War, as part of the Boer War exhibit at the Louisiana Purchase Exposition. Another foreign contestant was Albert Corey, a professional strikebreaker, who had arrived in Chicago in 1903 during a butchers' strike and stayed around, since there was never a shortage of business for him in the Windy City.

Thomas Hicks (left) and Jan Mashiani (36) and Len Tau (35), 1904

The effects of the winner's strychnine and brandy concoction are evident, while the uniforms of the 12th- and ninth-place finishers testify to their late entry.

Among the American entrants were Sam Mellor, winner of the 1902 Boston Marathon; John Lordon, winner of the 1903 Boston Marathon; Michael Spring, winner of the 1904 Boston Marathon; Thomas Hicks, who had finished second at Boston in 1904; and

Félix Carvajal, 1904 marathon

Financing his own trip from Cuba, he lost all his money in a crap game in New Orleans. He hitchhiked to St. Louis and arrived at the starting line wearing long pants and heavy shoes. The start of the race was delayed while a sympathetic US athlete cut off Carvajal's pants at the knees.

Arthur Newton, who had finished fifth in Paris in 1900.

Unfortunately, the organizers of the race knew almost nothing about staging such an event. The course included seven hills and was run on dusty roads, made dustier by the many automobiles, which the judges, doctors, and journalists used to follow—and lead—the runners. The brutal nature of the contest was made worse by the fact that it was scheduled for the middle of the afternoon in 90-degree Fahrenheit (32 degrees centigrade) heat. In addition, the only water available to the runners was from a well located 12 miles from the stadium, where the race began and ended.

With all these obstacles in their path, it is not surprising that only 14 of the 32 starters made it back to the finish line. John Lordon, for example, began vomiting after ten miles and had to withdraw. William Garcia of San Francisco was discovered lying unconscious by the side of the road. Sam Mellor, the leader at the halfway mark, finally gave up after 16 miles. Meanwhile, one of the Africans, probably Mashiani, lost a great deal of valuable time when he was chased off the course and through a cornfield by two large dogs. The only runner who didn't seem bothered by all these catastrophes was Félix Carvajal, who stopped a number of times to chat with bystanders, discuss the progress of the race, and practice his English. He also quenched his thirst by snatching a couple of peaches from an official in one of the cars, and by raiding a farmer's orchard of some green apples. The latter detour caused him an attack of stomach cramps.

Back in the stadium, the spectators were unaware of all that had transpired, although the more knowledgeable sports fans may have wondered why three hours had passed without any of the runners showing up. Finally, after 3 hours and 13 minutes, Fred Lorz of New York appeared, and was immediately hailed as the winner. He had already been photographed with Alice Roosevelt, the daughter of the President of the United States, and was about to be awarded the gold medal, when it was discovered that he had actually stopped running after 9 miles, hitched a ride in a car for 11 miles, and then started running again. Lorz readily admitted his practical joke, but AAU officials were not amused, and he was slapped with a lifetime ban. However, he was reinstated well before the ban ran out and managed to win the Boston Marathon of 1905.

The real winner of the 1904 Olympic marathon was Thomas Hicks, an English-born brass worker from Cambridge, Massachusetts. If present-day rules had been enforced, however, he would have been disqualified. Second at the halfway point, Hicks found himself in front after Sam Mellor collapsed. Ten miles from the finish Hicks begged to be allowed to lie down, but his handlers wouldn't allow it, even though he had a lead of one and a half miles. Instead they administered to him an oral dose of strychnine sulfate mixed with raw egg white. A few miles later he was given more strychnine, as well as some brandy. He was also bathed with water made warm by being kept next to the boiler of the steam-powered automobile that accompanied him.

Hicks was forced to slow to a walk when faced with a final, steep hill two miles from the stadium, but a couple more doses of strychnine and brandy revived him enough to win the race by six minutes. Needless to say, Hicks was in something of a stupor afterward. He had lost ten pounds during the afternoon, and gladly announced his retirement. When he had finally recovered, he told reporters, "I would rather have won this race than be President of the United States." Everett Brown of the Chicago Athletic Association filed a protest, charging that Hicks had received unfair assistance during the race, but the protest was denied.

The athletes who suffered through the 1904 marathon may have received some satisfaction when they learned that two of the officials in charge of patrolling the course were badly injured as well, when their brand-new car swerved to avoid one of the runners and careened down an embankment.

1906 Athens C: 53, N: 15, D: 5.1.
(41,860 Meters)

1. William Sherring	CAN	2:51:23.6
2. Johan "John" Svanberg	SWE	2:58:20.8
3. William Frank	USA	3:00:46.8
4. Gustaf Törnros	SWE	3:01:00.0
5. John Alepous	GRE	3:09:25.4
6. George Blake	AUS	3:09:35.0
7. Constantinos Karvelas	GRE	3:15:54.0
8. Joseph Roffi Farrade	FRA	3:17:49.8

There was great excitement in Athens when it was learned that another Olympic-style marathon would be held. Local merchants offered the winner a statue of Hermes, a loaf of bread every day for a year, three coffees a day for a year, free shaves for life, and a free lunch for six every Sunday for a year—but only if the winner was a Greek.

Billy Sherring of Hamilton, Ontario, had other ideas. Convinced he could win, he gathered his savings from his job as a railway brakeman, but they weren't enough to pay his way to Greece. A local athletic club raised an extra $75, but it still wasn't enough. In desperation, Sherring turned over the $75 to a friendly bartender named Butch Collier, who bet the money on a horse named Cicely, who won and paid 6-1 odds. At last Billy Sherring was able to travel to Athens. He arrived two months early and took a job as a railway station porter, training every other day. On March 17, the Greeks staged a trial run that was won in 3:04:29.6. Sherring watched with pleasure, knowing that he had covered the same course, in secret, 20 minutes faster.

When the big day finally came, George Blake of Australia took the early lead. After four miles he was passed by William Frank of New York, who led for three miles before Blake regained the lead. Blake faded, however, and after 15 miles he was passed by Sherring and Frank. The two ran together for three more miles, at which point Sherring turned to Frank and said, "Well, goodbye, Billy." Then he took off and built up such a large lead that he was able to walk part of the way to the finish.

There was great disappointment in the Olympic Stadium when the news spread that the leader was not a Greek. However, when Sherring passed through the marble entrance, he was met by Prince George, who applauded him and ran with him around the track to the finish line, where Sherring bowed to the king, just as Spiridon Louis had done ten years earlier. Billy Sherring had weighed 135 pounds when he left Canada. By the morning of the race he was down to 112, and by the end of the race he had evaporated to 98 pounds. Sherring was no stranger to pain. According to news reports, while in the lead during the 1900 Boston Marathon, Sherring collapsed, "in a semi-conscious condition on the roadside" and was passed by five racers, before getting up to finish second. Sherring didn't receive all the goodies that had been offered a Greek winner, but he was presented with a three-foot statue of Athena and a young lamb. Back in Canada he did much better. The city of Hamilton gave him a purse of $5,000, while the city of Toronto chipped in $400.

One runner who was overlooked in 1906 was a 20-year-old Italian who developed stomach problems and dropped out after 24 kilometers. His name was Dorando Pietri. Before the decade was out, he would become a living legend.

1908 London C: 55, N: 16, D: 7.24.

1. Johnny Hayes	USA	2:55:18.4	OR
2. Charles Hefferon	SAF	2:56:06.0	
3. Joseph Forshaw	USA	2:57:10.4	
4. Alton Welton	USA	2:59:44.4	
5. William Wood	CAN	3:01:44.0	
6. Frederick Simpson	CAN	3:04:28.2	
7. Harry Lawson	CAN	3:06:47.2	
8. Johan "John" Svanberg	SWE	3:07:50.8	

DISQ: Dorando Pietri (ITA) 2:54:46.4

Marathon, 1908

Dorando Pietri collapses within sight of the finish of the 1908 marathon. This photo puts to rest Dorando's contention that he could have completed the course unaided if meddlesome British officials had not interfered with him.

Johnny Hayes, 1908
Winner of the 1908 marathon.

July 24, 1908, dawned hot (by English standards: 78° F, 25.6°C) and muggy. The talk of the town was the bitter hostilities that had erupted between the British and the Americans following the controversial running of the 400 meters final the previous day. People had been looking forward to the marathon race with great anticipation, and a large crowd lined the 26-mile route from Windsor Castle to the Olympic Stadium in Shepherd's Bush. The race was scheduled to conclude with 385 yards around the stadium track, so that the finish line would be directly in front of the royal box of Queen Alexandra. As it happened, this random distance of 26 miles and 385 yards would later become the standardized length for marathon races.

The first 26 miles of the 1908 marathon were actually quite exciting, although they were quickly forgotten as a result of the extraordinary incidents that occurred during the final 385 yards. The British runners, under great pressure to perform well, started off at far too fast a clip and later paid the price of their folly. Thomas Jack of Scotland led for the first five miles, but quickly exhausted himself. Fred Lord and Jack Price took his place in front. Lord began to fade after ten miles. At the halfway mark at Ruislip, Price led by 200 yards. Charles Hefferon had moved into second place, followed by Lord and Dorando Pietri. The American entrants, at this point, were calmly running their own race, unruffled by the fast pace of the leaders.

Shortly after the 14-mile mark, Hefferon passed Price, who dropped out not long after. Lord also began to fade, eventually finishing 15th. The well-known Onondaga Indian Tom Longboat, of Toronto, who had been one of the favorites, came up to challenge, but he too fell back, slowing to a walk and then retiring completely.

By the 18-mile mark, it appeared that only Hefferon and Pietri (or Dorando, as he became better known) had a chance for the gold medal. Hefferon led by 3 minutes 18 seconds. By 20 miles he had built up a lead of 3 minutes 52 seconds, but then Dorando began to close the gap. Two miles from the stadium, the exhausted Hefferon made a crucial mistake. He accepted a drink of champagne and, within a mile, he had developed stomach cramps and become dizzy. Dorando also committed a major tactical blunder. Urged on by the well-meaning but overzealous crowd, he picked up his pace too early. Meanwhile, Americans Johnny Hayes, Joseph Forshaw, and Alton Welton were drawing closer.

The spectators lining the route, having inadvertently damaged Dorando's chances for victory, now did the same to Hefferon. Hoping to boost his spirits, they slapped him on the back so many times that they sapped him of what little energy he had left. A mile from the entrance to the stadium, he was passed by Dorando.

The last report that had been received inside the stadium was that South Africa and Italy were in the lead. All eyes were on the entrance as Dorando Pietri, a small man from the small town of Carpi, near Modena, made his appearance. However, it immediately became obvious that something was wrong. Dorando appeared dazed and headed off in the wrong direction. Track officials rushed to his aid and pointed him the right way. But after going only a few yards, he collapsed on the track. The audience, which had never before seen or heard of Dorando, immediately became sympathetic. While many people screamed for the officials to help him, others, knowing that such aid would automatically disqualify the plucky Italian, called out to leave him alone. However, in the words of the official report, "It was impossible to leave him there, for it looked as if he might die in the very presence of the Queen." Doctors and officials rushed to help him, and Dorando managed to struggle to his feet and plod on, only to fall again. And again and again. By this time, a second runner had arrived on the track. However, much to the horror of the spectators, he was not Charles Hefferon, a good man of the Empire, but an American, 5-foot 4-inch (1.63 meter) Johnny Hayes, who had breezed past Hefferon 20 yards before the stadium grounds.

This was too much for the British officials. When Dorando started to collapse a fifth time, just short of the finish, Jack Andrew, the head organizer of the race, caught him and carried him across the line. The Italian flag was immediately run up the victory pole, even as Hayes, still in good shape, crossed the finish himself. The Americans wasted no time in lodging a protest, and while Dorando, who had been carried away on a stretcher, lay seemingly on the verge of death, the protest was allowed and Hayes was declared the winner.

Remarkably, Dorando was back on his feet the next day, complaining that the British officials should have left him alone and that he could have finished without their assistance. However, photos of the incident make it quite clear that this was highly unlikely, and that the stretcher probably should have been called for the first time he fell. At any rate, Dorando showed up at the stadium the day after the race and was presented with a special gold cup by the Queen. Overnight he became an international celebrity. Even in the United States, songs were written about him, including one by Irving Berlin. Unfortunately, Berlin completely missed the point of what had happened, entitling his song "Dorando He'sa Gooda for Not" and portraying the courageous Italian as a "bigga de flop."

Somewhat lost in the excitement was the actual winner, John Hayes, a 22-year-old who was paid to train by Bloomingdale's department store in New York City. Hayes, who had prepared for the big race by resting in bed for two days, had finished fifth in the 1906 Boston Marathon and third in 1907, before winning the 1907 Yonkers Marathon on Thanksgiving Day.

Dorando's sensational effort in London set off a marathon craze that swept around the world. He and Hayes were offered very good money to turn professional. Both of them did, and they each built up a good deal of capital running scores of races over the next couple of years, far more than Hayes could have earned at Bloomingdale's or than Dorando could have earned back in Carpi. The most notable contests were two match races between Hayes and Dorando held in New York City on November 25, 1908, and March 15, 1909, both of which were won by the Italian. Between these two races, Pietri was twice defeated by Tom Longboat. Between 1904 and 1911 Dorando competed in 128 long-distance races and won 88 of them. Dorando, whose opportunistic brother ran off with his fortune, lived out his life driving a taxi in Italy. He also received a stipend from the Italian government for scouting promising marathon runners.

1912 Stockholm C: 68, N: 19, D: 7.14. WB: 2:42:31.0 (Frederick "Harry" Barrett)

(40,200 Meters)

1. Kennedy McArthur	SAF	2:36:54.8
2. Christopher Gitsham	SAF	2:37:52.0
3. Gaston Strobino	USA	2:38:42.4
4. Andrew Sockalexis	USA	2:42:07.9
5. James Duffy	CAN	2:42:18.8
6. Sigfrid "Sigge" Jacobsson	SWE	2:43:24 9
7. John Gallagher	USA	2:44:19.4
8. Joseph Erxleben	USA	2:45:47.2

Once again, the Olympic marathon was held on an oppressively hot day that caused half of the runners to retire before the finish. Tatu Kolehmainen, the older brother of Hannes, took the lead before three miles had been covered, and held it until just before the turnaround point, when he was passed by Gitsham. McArthur was third, followed by Fred Lord. After 17 miles, Gitsham and Kolehmainen were running together, with McArthur only a meter or two behind. Two or three miles later, Kolehmainen was forced to retire, and the two South Africans went on alone. Two miles from the stadium they reached a refreshment stand, and Gitsham stopped to take a drink of water. McArthur had said he would wait for his teammate, but instead he kept on going, opening up a lead that Gitsham was unable to close. McArthur was born at Dervock in County Antrim, Ireland, on February 10, 1880. The son of a farmer, he worked as a postman, often running his entire 15-mile daily round. He emigrated to South Africa in 1905 and became a policeman. After his Olympic victory, McArthur went back to Dervock, where thousands of people traveled from all over the countryside to honor him. Upon his return to South Africa, the town council of Potchefstroom presented him with a piece of land, and it was there that he died 48 years later.

The 1912 marathon was marred by a sad note. The 21-year-old Portuguese runner Francisco Lazaro collapsed from sunstroke and heart trouble toward the end of the race and was taken to a hospital, where he died the following day. The cause of his death was described as "possibly meningitis, brought on by heat exhaustion." Lazaro was the first of only two athletes to die as a result of their participation in the Olympics. Jimmy Duffy, who placed fifth, went on to win the 1914 Boston Marathon, but when World War I broke out, Duffy volunteered and was killed during a suicidal charge against the Germans on April 23, 1915.

One unusual story concerns Shizo Kaniguri of Japan. Kaniguri dropped out of the marathon after 20 kilometers. A local family, seeing his distress, invited him in for some fruit juice. As one of Japan's two participants in the 1912 Olympics, and the nation's first Olympic entrants at that, Kaniguri was ashamed at failing to finish. Instead of contacting Japanese or Olympic authorities, he returned to Japan on his own. He did compete in the Olympics again, in 1920 and 1924. On the 50th anniversary of the Stockholm Games, Swedish journalist Oscar Söderland tracked down Kaniguri and invited him to go back to Sweden where Kaniguri, now 71 years old, symbolically completed the marathon course.

1920 Antwerp C: 48, N: 17, D: 8.22. WB: 2:36:06.6 (Alexis Ahlgren)
(42,750 Meters)

1. Johan Kolehmainen	FIN	2:32:35.8	WB
2. Jüri Lossmann	EST	2:32:48.6	
3. Valerio Arri	ITA	2:36:32.8	
4. Auguste Broos	BEL	2:39:25.8	
5. Juho Tuomikoski	FIN	2:40:18.8	
6. Sofus Rose	DEN	2:41:18.0	
7. Joseph Organ	USA	2:41:30.0	
8. Rudolf Hansen	DEN	2:41:39.4	

At last the Olympic marathon was contested on a cool day, and the runners responded with excellent times, particularly considering that the course was longer than ever before. Chris Gitsham took the early lead, but after 15 kilometers he was joined by Hannes Kolehmainen, who had returned from Brooklyn to compete for Finland. They reached the turnaround together, but after 27 kilometers, Kolehmainen moved ahead and began to draw away. Gitsham, suffering from foot trouble after one of his shoes tore open, retired after 37 kilometers. Meanwhile, Jüri Lossmann of Estonia closed the gap that separated him from the famous Finn, but Kolehmainen managed to hold on to his lead and win by 70 yards—until 1996 the closest marathon finish in Olympic history.

In direct contrast to previous marathons, the runners finished in good health. Valerio Arri, the Italian champion, even celebrated his bronze medal by performing three cartwheels as soon as he crossed the finish line.

1924 Paris C: 58, N: 20, D: 7.13. WB: 2:32:35.8 (Johan "Hannes" Kolehmainen)

1. Albin Stenroos	FIN	2:41:22.6
2. Romeo Bertini	ITA	2:47:19.6
3. Clarence DeMar	USA	2:48:14.0
4. Lauri Halonen	FIN	2:49:47.4
5. Samuel Ferris	GBR	2:52:26.0
6. Miguel Plaza Reyes	CHI	2:52:54.0
7. M. Boughèra El Ouafi	FRA/ALG	2:54:19.6
8. Gustav Kinn	SWE	2:54:33.4

The start of the race was delayed 2½ hours until 5:30 p.m. to lessen the impact of an oppressive heatwave. Albin Stenroos, a 35-year-old woodworker, had won a bronze medal in the 1912 10,000 meters race. However he did not run a single marathon between 1909 and May 18, 1924, when he placed second in the Finnish Olympic trial. In Paris, he passed Georges Verger of France after 19½ kilometers, and steadily drew away to a huge lead, winning by almost six minutes. Silver medalist Romeo Bertini was 31 years old, while bronze medalist Clarence DeMar was 36. In 1930 DeMar won his seventh Boston Marathon at the age of 41. In the 1924 Olympics, 28 of the 58 starters failed to finish the course.

1928 Amsterdam C: 68, N: 23, D: 8.5. WB: 2:29:01.8 (Albert Michelsen)

1. M. Boughèra El Ouafi	FRA/ALG	2:32:57
2. Miguel Plaza Reyes	CHI	2:33:23
3. Martti Marttelin	FIN	2:35:02
4. Kanematsu Yamada	JPN	2:35:29
5. Joie Ray	USA	2:36:04
6. Seiichiro Tsuda	JPN	2:36:20
7. Yrjo Korholin-Koski	FIN	2:36:40
8. Samuel Ferris	GBR	2:37:41

The lead changed several times during the first half of the race, with Joie Ray in first place at the turnaround.

M. Boughèra El Ouafi, 1928
A fine finish to the 1928 marathon, but a tragic ending 31 years later.

Shortly thereafter he was passed by Yamada and Tsuda. These three remained in front past 30 kilometers. By this time two outsiders, Algerian-born Boughèra El Ouafi and Miguel Plaza of Chile, had moved up to challenge. Plaza had evidently decided to run the race on El Ouafi's shoulder, just as he had four years earlier. Three kilometers short of the finish they had taken over second and third place, finally wearing down Yamada during the approach to the stadium. Both El Ouafi and Plaza finished strongly, with El Ouafi winning by about 150 meters. The victor was a former member of the French Colonial Army, who had settled in Paris and was employed as an automobile mechanic. Twenty-eight years later, when another Algerian-born Frenchman, Alain Mimoun, won the Olympic marathon, journalists sought out El Ouafi and discovered him unemployed and living in poverty in Paris. French sportsmen got together a fund to help the forgotten hero of Amsterdam. However, three years later, on October 18, 1959, El Ouafi was shot to death while sitting in a café on his 61st birthday.

1932 Los Angeles C: 29, N: 15, D: 8.7. WB: 2:29:01.8 (Albert Michelsen)

1. Juan Carlos Zabala	ARG	2:31.36 OR
2. Samuel Ferris	GBR	2:31.55
3. Armas Toivonen	FIN	2:32.12
4. Duncan McLeod Wright	GBR	2:32.41
5. Seiichiro Tsuda	JPN	2:35.42
6. Kim Eun-bae	JPN/KOR	2:37.28
7. Albert Michelsen	USA	2:39.38
8. Oskar Heks	CZE	2:41.35

Paavo Nurmi had been considered the favorite to win the 1932 marathon, until he was suspended by the IAAF one week before the race for accepting payments in excess of his expenses during an exhibition tour. Juan Carlos Zabala, a 20-year-old Argentinian, had set a world record at 30,000 meters in 1931. On June 25, 1932, the *Los Angeles Times* sponsored a marathon race. Zabala built up an eight-and-a-half-minute lead in that race, but developed foot problems and was ordered to withdraw by his trainer. Albert Michelsen went on to win.

Zabala took the early lead in the Olympics. He was passed briefly by Margarito Baños of Mexico, but regained the lead and held it for over 30 kilometers. At the 31-kilometer mark, Lauri Virtanen, who had already finished third in the 10,000 and 5000, sprinted ahead suddenly and opened up a 300-meter gap. This shook up the field, and there was much jockeying for position. Duncan Wright, following a well-laid-out British plan, forged to the front after 20 miles (35.5 kilometers), and as Virtanen faded, he moved a full minute ahead of Zabala, with Toivonen another half-minute further back. By 37 kilometers, Virtanen had dropped out and Wright had begun to fade. Zabala moved back into the lead, and Sam Ferris, taking over second place, took off after him. But he had waited too long. Zabala entered the Coliseum with a one-minute lead and was almost three quarters of the way around the track when Ferris appeared, followed closely by Toivonen and Wright. Thus, the crowd was treated to the rare spectacle of the first four finishers of the marathon being on the track at the same time. Zabala struggled across the finish line and then collapsed, whereas Ferris was still full of strength and probably would have won had the race continued for an extra half lap.

1936 Berlin C: 56, N: 27, D: 8.9. WB: 2:26:42.0 (Sohn Kee-chung)

1. Sohn Kee-chung	JPN/PRK	2:29:19.2 OR
2. Ernest Harper	GBR	2:31:23.2
3. Nam Seung-yong	JPN/KOR	2:31:42.0
4. Erkki Tamila	FIN	2:32:45.0
5. Väinö Muinonen	FIN	2:33:46.0
6. Johannes Coleman	SAF	2:36:17.0
7. Donald Robertson	GBR	2:37:06.2
8. Henry Gibson	SAF	2:38:04.0

On November 3, 1935, Sohn Kee-chung of Korea set a world marathon record of 2:26:42.0. Because Korea was, at the time, occupied by Japanese forces, Sohn's hopes for competing in the Olympics depended on his ability to qualify for the Japanese team. This he accomplished, as did fellow Korean Nam Seung-yong. Both young men were forced to endure the further insult of adopting Japanese names. Sohn, a fervent nationalist, always signed his Korean name in Berlin, and whenever he was asked where he was from, made it a point to explain that Korea was a separate nation which was currently a victim of Japanese imperialism.

Defending champion Juan Carlos Zabala had arrived in Berlin months in advance, and during his period of extended training had become a local favorite, particularly in the absence of a serious German threat in the marathon. As usual, Zabala tore into the lead and was 30 seconds in front at the four-kilometer mark. After 15 kilometers he was ahead by 1 minute and 40 seconds. He let the margin slip to 50 seconds at the turnaround, but pumped it back up to 90 seconds after 25 kilometers. For quite some time, Zabala had been followed by Sohn and 34-year-old coal miner Ernie Harper, who had been running together since the beginning. However, it came as a shock to Zabala when, after 28 kilometers, he was suddenly passed, first by Sohn and, ten meters later, by Harper. Zabala fell, got up, struggled on for four more kilometers, and then retired. Meanwhile, Sohn pulled away and won by over two minutes. Harper finished heroically, holding off the fast-closing Nam despite a bad blister that had filled one of his shoes with blood.

At the medal ceremony Sohn was forced to endure the humiliation of having his victory celebrated by the raising of the Japanese flag and by the playing of the Japanese national anthem. Both Sohn and Nam registered a silent protest by bowing their heads. Interviewed by the press afterwards, Sohn used the opportunity to educate the world about the plight of his nation. Few reporters were interested, and most seemed relieved when he turned to the race itself. "The human body can do so much," he said. "Then the heart and spirit must take over."

Back in Korea, however, Sohn was a national hero. One newspaper, *Dong-a-Ilbo,* published a wire-service photograph of Sohn on the victory platform—but with one alteration: they painted over the Japanese flag on his sweatshirt. The Japanese colonial government responded by jailing eight people connected with the paper and suspending its publication for nine months.

In 1948 Sohn was given the honor of carrying the South Korean flag in the Opening Ceremony of the London Olympics, the first to be attended by an independent Korea. Forty years later, in a moment that brought tears to an entire nation, Sohn Kee-chung entered the Seoul Olympic Stadium bearing the Olympic torch. The 76-year-old Sohn bounded around the track, leaping for joy and bursting with pride for himself and for his country.

1948 London C: 41, N: 21, D: 8.7. WB: 2:25:39.0 (Suh Yun-bok)

1. Delfo Cabrera	ARG	2:34:51.6
2. Thomas Richards	GBR	2:35:07.6
3. Etienne Gailly	BEL	2:35:33.6
4. Johannes Coleman	SAF	2:36:06.0
5. Eusebio Guiñez	ARG	2:36:36.0
6. Thomas Sidney Luyt	SAF	2:38:11.0
7. Gustav Ostling	SWE	2:38:40.6
8. John Systad	NOR	2:38:41.0

Twenty-five-year-old Etienne Gailly, running his first race longer than 32.5 kilometers, was in the lead by the ten-kilometer post and had opened up a 41-second gap by 25 kilometers, at which point he was followed by Guiñez, Ostling, and Cabrera. The field then began to close in on him, and after 32.5 kilometers he was passed by Choi Yoon-chil of Korea. At 35 kilometers, Choi led by 28 seconds, with Delfo Cabrera, a 29-year-old fireman also running his first marathon, in second place. Gailly was third and Guiñez fourth.

Delfo Cabrera, 1948
A rookie marathoner's finest 2½ hours.

But Choi had used up all his energy and soon retired. Five thousand meters from Wembley Stadium, Cabrera led Gailly by five seconds. Tom Richards, a 38-year-old Welsh nurse, had moved into third place. Gailly gathered his strength and regained the lead. A half mile from the stadium, he led Cabrera by 50 yards and Richards by 100. The exhausted Belgian was the first to enter the stadium, but by now he was barely running. Spectators were immediately reminded of the ordeal endured by Dorando Pietri the last time the Olympics had been held in London. Gailly managed to stay on his feet, but before he had covered 100 yards of the track, he was passed by Cabrera and then by Richards. Gailly staggered on, almost collapsing 60 yards short of his goal. But he did finally cross the finish line and gain a well-earned bronze medal, much to the relief of the sympathetic crowd. In fourth place was 38-year-old Johannes Coleman, who had finished sixth in the last Olympics 12 years earlier.

1952 Helsinki C: 66, N: 32, D: 7.27. WB: 2:20:42.2 (James Peters)

1. Emil Zátopek	CZE	2:23:03.2	OR
2. Reinaldo Gorno	ARG	2:25:35.0	
3. Gustaf Jansson	SWE	2:26:07.0	
4. Choi Yoon-chil	KOR	2:26:36.0	
5. Veikko Karvonen	FIN	2:26:41.8	
6. Delfo Cabrera	ARG	2:26:42.4	
7. József Dobronyi	HUN	2:28:04.8	
8. Erkki Puolakka	FIN	2:29:35.0	

Emil Zátopek, the son of a carpenter, was born in Koprivnice, Northern Moravia, on September 19, 1922, the exact same day that his wife, Dana, was born. He made his first appearance in the Olympics in 1948, finishing first in the 10,000 meters and second at 5000. Whenever he ran, his face was always contorted by a grimace, and his shoulders and body looked hunched with pain. Observers, on first viewing Zátopek, were sure that he was on the verge of collapse, but it turned out that that was just his style. Years later Zátopek was asked about this idiosyncrasy. He replied, "I was not talented enough to run and smile at the same time."

In 1952 Zátopek became the first runner since Hannes Kolehmainen to win both the 5000- and 10,000-meter races. But that wasn't enough for Zátopek. He decided to attempt an unprecedented triple by also competing in the marathon. The fact that he had never run a marathon before bothered him only slightly. He wasn't concerned about coming up with the necessary endurance, but it did worry him a bit that there might be pacing strategies with which he was not familiar. With this in mind, Zátopek decided to run along with the man whom he considered to be the favorite in the race—Jim Peters of Great Britain, who had run the fastest marathon in history only six weeks earlier. Zátopek took note of Peters' running number in the newspaper, and the next day he located Peters on the starting line and introduced himself.

Peters took off at what seemed to be an outlandish pace, but Zátopek, as well as Gustaf Jansson, kept contact with him. After 15 kilometers Zátopek and Jansson caught up with Peters, and the three ran together for a couple of miles. Then Zátopek turned to Peters and said, in English, "The pace? Is it good enough?" Peters, who had exhausted himself with his early running, pretended that he was still fresh, and replied, "Pace too slow." Zátopek mulled this over for a few moments and then said, "You say, 'too slow.' Are you sure the pace is too slow?" "Yes," came the reply. They continued on in silence for a short while, and then Zátopek zipped by Peters, taking Jansson with him.

They passed the turnaround together, with Peters ten seconds behind. Now Zátopek had to deal with Jansson. "He stopped at one feeding station," Zátopek later recalled, "and picked up a slice of lemon to suck. I was not so sure. I had never taken anything before in racing or training. But I thought, 'If he runs well, at the next feeding station I will take *two* lemons.'" Instead, Jansson began to fade. After 20 miles Peters developed a leg cramp and dropped out. By this time Zátopek had shaken off Jansson completely, and he was able to continue alone, chatting amiably with policemen, spectators, and cyclists along the route. He entered the stadium far ahead of the other runners. The huge crowd greeted him as the hero of the 1952 Games, chanting "Zá-to-pek, Zá-to-pek," as he completed the final lap. The Jamaican 4 × 400-meter relay team hoisted him on their shoulders and carried him around the field. Zátopek was already signing autographs by the time the next runner, the surprising Reinaldo Gorno, arrived. Zátopek greeted him at the finish line with a slice of orange. The top fifteen finishers all set personal bests.

Despite his convincing victory, Zátopek later said, "I was unable to walk for a whole week after that, so much did the race take out of me. But it was the most pleasant exhaustion I have ever known."

On May 30, 1954, Zátopek, running in Paris without pacesetters or even serous challengers, broke the 5000 meters world record with a time of 13:57.2. Two days later, he moved on to Brussels and ran a 28:54.2 to set a world record at 10,000 meters. Not since Hannes Kolehmainen at the 1912 Olympics had a runner broken world records at 5000 and 10,000 meters over a three-day period. However, by the time of the 1956 Olympics, Zátopek's times had been bettered by Volodymyr Kuts and Gordon Pirie. In Melbourne, Zátopek chose to stick to the marathon. But six weeks before the Games he had developed a hernia while trying to train with his wife on his shoulders. His doctors told him not to run for two months after his operation, but instead he resumed training the day after he left the hospital. Under the circumstances, his sixth-place finish could hardly be considered a failure.

Zátopek had been a member of the Czech army since 1944. His athletic successes gained him promotion to the rank of lieutenant-colonel, as well as a prominent position in the Communist Party. However, Emil Zátopek was not really a party man. In 1968 he signed the *2000 Words Manifesto*, which supported the establishment of freedom in Czechoslovakia. When Soviet tanks moved in and crushed the growing democratic movement in Czechoslovakia, Zátopek was expelled from both the army and the Communist Party. He was sent to work doing manual labor at a uranium mine and digging ditches and hauling sacks of cement for a geological survey team. He also drove a sprinkler truck for the Prague sanitation department. Seven years later, the Ministry of Sport, taking advantage of his facility with languages, hired him as a "sports spy," translating sports periodicals in a search for tips from foreign coaches. He served in this capacity until his retirement in 1982.

Emil Zátopek died on November 22, 2000, at the age of 78. He left an indelible impression on the world of sports that goes beyond his four gold medals and 18 world records. Unlike his predecessor Paavo Nurmi, Zátopek was greatly loved by his fellow competitors, as well as by all those who had the good fortune to meet him personally.

1956 Melbourne C: 46, N: 23, D: 12.1. WB: 2:17:39.4 (James Peters)

1. Alain Mimoun	FRA	2:25:00
2. Franjo Mihalić	YUG/CRO	2:26:32
3. Veikko Karvonen	FIN	2:27:47
4. Lee Chang-hoon	KOR	2:28:45
5. Yoshiaki Kawashima	JPN	2:29:19
6. Emil Zátopek	CZE	2:29:34
7. Ivan Filin	SOV/RUS	2:30:27
8. Evert Nyberg	SWE	2:31:12

Thirty-five-year-old Algerian-born Alain Mimoun had made a habit of finishing second to Emil Zátopek—three times in the Olympics and twice in the European championships. But he was sure that December 1, 1956, would be his lucky day. Frenchmen had won the Olympic marathon in 1900, and then 28 years later in 1928. Now, 28 more years had passed. In addition, Mimoun was wearing what he considered to be the lucky number 13. As if these weren't enough good omens, he had just learned that he had become a father.

For the first time in Olympic history, there was a false start in the marathon. It was also the first time that the runners followed a line painted on the ground. Mimoun stayed with the leading group for the first half of the race. Then he surged forward during an uphill segment before the turnaround. By the 25-kilometer mark he had opened a 50-second gap, and no one came close to him again. After 30 kilometers, however, Mimoun began to feel drained of energy. He thought of all he had gone through to get this far, including his six years fighting in World War II. In 1944 his left leg had been badly injured by a mine during the battle of Monte Cassino. He summoned all his strength and spirit, but he was still struggling. He was running with a moist handkerchief on his head, but it now felt so heavy that at 35 kilometers he pulled it off and threw it to the ground. Then he watched as "a pretty blonde girl" picked it up and blew him a kiss. Suddenly reenergized, Mimoun ran the rest of the race without fear. He knew he had an insurmountable lead when two police officers on motor bikes appeared at his side to escort him. When he entered the stadium, the roar from the crowd of 110,000 was so loud that it was, in the words of Mimoun, "like an atomic explosion." For the third time in a row, the Olympic marathon had been won by a converted track star competing in his first marathon.

At the finish line Mimoun waited for his old friend Emil Zátopek, who trotted home in a trance four and a half minutes later. "Emil," he asked, "why don't you congratulate me? I am an Olympic champion. It was I who won." Zátopek snapped out of his trance, took off his cap, saluted Mimoun, and then embraced him. "For me," Mimoun recalled, "that was better than the medal."

After his return to France, Mimoun was introduced to the president of France, General Charles de Gaulle, who had led the French troops during the war. After congratulating Mimoun, de Gaulle added, "You and I have something in common: we last." As a matter of fact, Mimoun's marathon career had only just begun. He proceeded to win the French championship six times, the last in 1966, when he was 45 years old. At the age of 51, Mimoun completed the 26-mile, 385-yard race in a time of 2:34:36.2. In the 38 years after his Olympic triumph, 38 French sports centers were named in his honor.

Looking back on his Olympic races, Mimoun observed, "I look at my career as a castle: my London silver medal is the foundation; my two Helsinki silver medals are the walls; my gold medal at Melbourne, the roof."

1960 Rome C: 69, N: 35, D: 9.10. WB: 2:15:17.0 (Sergei Popov)

1. Abebe Bikila	ETH	2:15:16.2 WB
2. Rhadi Ben Abdesselem	MOR	2:15:41.6
3. Arthur "Barry" Magee	NZL	2:17:18.2
4. Konstantin Vorobyev	SOV/RUS	2:19:09.6
5. Sergei Popov	SOV/RUS	2:19:18.8
6. Thyge Tögersen	DEN	2:21:03.4
7. Abebe Wakgira	ETH	2:21:10.0
8. Bakir Benaissa	MOR	2:21:22.0

Abebe Bikila, 1960
Making his move on Rhadi Ben Abdesselem en route to his first of back-to-back marathon triumphs.

The 1960 Olympic marathon was the first to be run at night, the first to start and end outside the stadium, and, as it turned out, the first to be won by a black African. After 18 kilometers, two men pulled away from the field: Rhadi Ben Abdesselem, who was one of the favorites, and barefooted Abebe Bikila, who was not. Rhadi was an international cross-country champion who had placed 14th in the Olympic 10,000 meters two days before the marathon. Abebe was born August 7, 1932—the day of the Los Angeles Olympic marathon. A member of the Ethiopian Imperial Bodyguard, he was running in his third marathon. Abebe and Rhadi ran side by side, mile after mile, never looking at each other, along a course lit by torches held by Italian soldiers, and lined by thousands of spectators who had to be restrained from interfering with the runners.

Reconnoitering the route some days earlier, Abebe and his Finnish coach, Onni Niskanen, had noticed that less than a mile from the finish line at the Arch of Constantine was the obelisk of Axum, which had been plundered from Ethiopia by Italian troops and hauled off to Rome. It seemed appropriate that the slight incline that followed the obelisk would be the proper place for Abebe to make his final move. Although none of the experts had even considered that the Ethiopian would still be in contention by that point, Abebe was sure that he would be. Right on schedule he pulled away from Rhadi, and his lead had increased to almost 200 yards by the time he breasted the tape. His final obstacle was a typical Roman driver, who had lurched his motor scooter onto the course 60 yards from the end.

1964 Tokyo C: 68, N: 35, D: 10.21. WB: 2:13:55.0 (B. Basil Heatley)

1. Abebe Bikila	ETH	2:12:11.2	WB
2. B. Basil Heatley	GBR	2:16:19.2	
3. Kokichi Tsuburaya	JPN	2:16:22.8	
4. Brian Kilby	GBR	2:17:02.4	
5. József Sütö	HUN	2:17:55.8	
6. Leonard "Buddy" Edelen	USA	2:18:12.4	
7. Aurele Vandendriessche	BEL	2:18:42.6	
8. Kenji Kimihara	JPN	2:19:49.0	

There was no clear-cut favorite in the 1964 marathon, with at least 15 runners in serious contention for the gold medal. Defending champion Abebe Bikila had undergone an appendectomy only 40 days before the race. The Australian Ron Clarke, running his fourth race in a week, rushed to an early lead, followed closely by Jim Hogan of Ireland. Abebe, running this time with shoes and socks, joined them before the seven-kilometer mark, and the three ran together for about half an hour. After 15 kilometers, Abebe, attempting to become the first person in history to win two Olympic marathons, began to apply pressure. By the turning point—Tobitakyu-machi, in Chofu city—Clarke had fallen behind and Abebe was five seconds ahead of Hogan. From 25 kilometers on, Abebe moved ahead steadily until, ten kilometers later, he led Hogan by two and a half minutes. Hogan slowed to a walk and then dropped out, leaving Kokichi Tsuburaya, who was running only the fourth marathon of his career, in second place.

When Abebe Bikila entered the stadium, he was greeted by 75,000 waving and cheering spectators. After crossing the finish line in the fastest marathon time ever recorded, Abebe entertained the crowd by doing stretching and bicycling exercises and generally looking like he was sorry the race had been so short. He told the press that he could have kept up the pace for another ten kilometers. At the medal ceremony later in the day, none of the Japanese officials knew the Ethiopian national anthem, so the band took the opportunity to play the Japanese anthem instead.

Tsuburaya was the second man to enter the stadium, followed ten yards later by Heatley. Despite the encouragement of the hometown crowd, Tsuburaya was exhausted, and when Heatley moved past him before the final curve, he was unable to respond. However, Tsuburaya's third-place finish brought him Japan's first track and field medal in 28 years, and he became a national hero.

Unfortunately, Kokichi Tsuburaya met a tragic end. A member of the Training School of the Japanese Ground Self-Defense Force, after the 1964 race he was ordered to stop seeing his fiancee and to begin training immediately for the 1968 Olympics. But in 1967 he suffered two injuries and was forced to spend three months in the hospital. The doctors declared him completely recovered, but when Tsuburaya started running again, he realized that his body had been irreversibly weakened and that he could not possibly win the next Olympic marathon. On January 9, 1968, two months after his release from the hospital and nine months before the Mexico City Olympics, Kokichi Tsuburaya ended his own life by cutting his right carotid artery with a razor blade. Beside him was a piece of paper on which he had written a single phrase: "Cannot run anymore."

Abebe Bikila also came up against tragedy. He entered the 1968 marathon, but had to withdraw after 17 kilometers because of a bone fracture in his leg. The following year he was driving his Volkswagen, a gift from the government following his second gold medal, when he crashed. He suffered a broken neck and a spinal cord injury that left him paralyzed below the waist. Confined to a wheelchair for the rest of his life, he died of a brain hemorrhage on October 25, 1973, at the age of 41.

1968 Mexico City C: 74, N: 41, D: 10.20. WB: 2:09:36.4 (Derek Clayton)

1. Degaga "Mamo" Wolde	ETH	2:20:26.4
2. Kenji Kimihara	JPN	2:23:31.0
3. Michael Ryan	NZL	2:23:45.0
4. Ismail Akcay	TUR	2:25:18.8
5. William Adcocks	GBR	2:25:33.0
6. Merawi Gebru	ETH	2:27:16.8
7. Derek Clayton	AUS	2:27:23.8
8. Timothy Johnston	GBR	2:28:04.4

Like Abebe Bikila, Mamo Wolde was a member of the Oromo tribe. Wolde had a long and unusual involvement in the Olympics. His first appearance was in Melbourne in 1956, where he had entered the 800 and 1500, and finished last in his heat in both events. He also ran the third leg for the Ethiopian 4 × 400 relay team, which finished last in its heat. He did not compete in 1960, but he was back in 1964. He failed to complete the marathon, but placed fourth in the 10,000. In 1968 he finished a close second to Naftali Temu in the 10,000, a week before the marathon. In the later race, Wolde and Temu let others set the pace without allowing the leaders to get too far ahead. Then, about the halfway mark, they picked up the pace considerably and left the others behind. Shortly after 30 kilometers Temu ran out of steam and began to drift back, eventually finishing 19th. This left Wolde with almost a two-minute lead at 35 kilometers. He went on to win as easily as Abebe Bikila had four years earlier. At the age of 36, he had finally come out from the shadow of his famous teammate and won an Olympic gold medal.

More than one hour after Mamo Wolde, the final runner, John Akhwari of Tanzania, entered the stadium. He had injured his knee in a fall. Bloodied and bandaged, he struggled to the finish line. When asked by filmmaker Bud Greenspan why he had not quit despite the obvious pain he was feeling, Akhwari replied, "My country did not send me 7000 miles away to start the race. They sent me 7000 miles to finish it."

In September 1992, Mamo Wolde was arrested for unspecified crimes committed by a previous government known as the Dergue. Twice he was released and then rearrested, definitively in April 1993. For years Wolde languished in prison without being charged. Meanwhile, the IOC sent financial assistance to his wife and children and hired a lawyer on his behalf. In March 1999, after more than six years in prison, Wolde finally went on trial. He was accused of shooting to death, on March 22, 1978, a teenager who belonged to an anti-government organization. On January 18, 2002, Wolde was finally convicted of murder and sentenced to six years. Since he had already spent nine years in prison, he was immediately released. However Wolde enjoyed only four months of freedom. He died, aged 69, on May 26, 2002. He was buried at St. Joseph's Cemetary in Addis Ababa next to his idol, Abebe Bikila.

1972 Munich C: 69, N: 35, D: 9.10. WB: 2:08:33.6 (Derek Clayton)

1. Frank Shorter	USA	2:12:19.8
2. Karel Lismont	BEL	2:14:31.8
3. Degaga "Mamo" Wolde	ETH	2:15:08.4
4. Kenneth Moore	USA	2:15:39.8
5. Kenji Kimihara	JPN	2:16:27.0
6. Ronald Hill	GBR	2:16:30.6
7. Donald Macgregor	GBR	2:16:34.4
8. Jack Foster	NZL	2:16:56.2

Munich-born Yale graduate Frank Shorter, annoyed by the slow pace, took the lead before the 15-kilometer mark and pulled away steadily as the race progressed. He was never challenged. Quite naturally, he entered the stadium expecting to be greeted by cheers and applause. Instead, all he heard was whistling and booing, and he wondered what he had done wrong. Unbeknownst to Shorter, a hoaxer had appeared on the track a couple of minutes before him and run a full lap before being hustled away by security guards. The sounds of derision had been aimed at the hoaxer, not

Frank Shorter, 1972
Reacting with puzzlement to the boos of the crowd, he soon discovered they weren't intended for him.

at Shorter. The silver medal went to previously undefeated Karel Lismont, and the bronze to Mamo Wolde, who ran his fastest marathon ever at the age of 40. Eighth-place finisher Jack Foster was also 40 years old. After the race, Shorter went back to his room and celebrated his victory by drinking three gins in the bathtub. It is a curious oddity of Olympic history that none of the three American men who have won the marathon were first to enter the stadium. In 1904, Thomas Hicks, like Shorter, was preceded by a hoaxer and in 1908 Johnny Hayes was beaten to the finish line by Dorando Pietri, who was subsequently disqualified.

1976 Montreal C: 67, N: 35, D: 7.31. WB: 2:08:33.6 (Derek Clayton)

1. Waldemar Cierpinski	GDR	2:09:55.0 OR
2. Frank Shorter	USA	2:10:45.8
3. Karel Lismont	BEL	2:11:12.6
4. Donald Kardong	USA	2:11:15.8
5. Lasse Virén	FIN	2:13:10.8
6. Jerome Drayton	CAN	2:13:30.0
7. Leonid Moseyev	SOV/RUS	2:13:33.4
8. Franco Fava	ITA	2:14:24.8

Defending champion Frank Shorter looked like the man to beat in 1976, although Lasse Virén was an unknown quantity. Virén had already run 30,000 meters during the last seven days, including victories in the 10,000 and, 24 hours before the marathon, in the 5000. This was his first marathon race. Bill Rodgers of the United States, who eventually finished 40th, guided the leading pack through the first ten kilometers, but the real action didn't begin until just before the 25-kilometer mark, when Shorter surged through the rain, leaving the others behind. Virén tried to keep up for 200 meters, but fell back. About four minutes later, Waldemar Cierpinski, a relatively unknown converted steeplechaser from East Germany, who had entered his first marathon on a whim in 1974, decided that Shorter wasn't really running so fast after all, and caught up with him.

"It was a wonderful feeling when I came alongside," Cierpinski later recalled. "I glanced at Shorter as I did so, and looked right into the eyes of the man who was my idol as a marathon runner. I knew all about him. And yet I could tell by the return glance that he didn't know much, if anything, about me. The psychological advantage was mine." In fact, for the entire race, Shorter thought Cierpinski was actually Carlos Lopes of Portugal. Cierpinski's coaches had told him to annoy Shorter by getting as close to his body as possible. This he did, until a couple shoves separated them. Shorter made periodic surges, but each time Cierpinski caught him. Then, after 34 kilometers, they disappeared from the sight of the crowds and the cameras during a short stretch through the campus of McGill University. When they emerged again, Cierpinski had taken the lead and begun to draw away. Shorter tried to close the gap, but couldn't.

Cierpinski entered the stadium just as the band had finished playing the East German national anthem to celebrate the victory of the women's 4 × 400-meter relay team. When he reached the finish line, Cierpinski noticed that the lap indicator read "1." Confused, he continued running for another lap and was surprised, when he crossed the finish again, to find Frank Shorter waiting to congratulate him. Cierpinski had bettered his personal best by two and one-half minutes.

Cierpinski's victory came as a shock even to his fellow countrymen. Back in the Olympic Village, the East German soccer team watched the race on television while waiting for their final match against Poland. Goalie Jürgen Croy later recalled, "We just sat there staring at each other, thinking that if this living example of mediocrity can lift himself up and win the marathon, and we don't beat Poland, we are never going to hear the end of it." They won.

After the fall of the Iron Curtain, documents began to surface proving widespread drug use among East German athletes. In 1997, Shorter, convinced that Cierpinski had taken prohibited drugs, wrote to Dr. Werner Franke, the German scientist who helped uncover the files. Franke provided Shorter with evidence that Cierpinski had indeed been taking steroids. Shorter, a lawyer, began to push to have the East German results, including Cierpinski's, overturned. Although unsuccessful, Shorter continued the fight against performance-enhancing drugs, serving as the chairman of the US Anti-Doping Agency from 2000 to 2003.

1980 Moscow C: 74, N: 40, D: 8.1. WB: 2:08:33.6 (Derek Clayton)

1. Waldemar Cierpinski	GDR	2:11:03
2. Gerhardus "Gerard" Nijboer	HOL	2:11:20
3. Satymkul Dzhumanazarov	SOV/KYR	2:11:35
4. Vladimir Kotov	SOV/BLR	2:12:05
5. Leonid Moseyev	SOV/RUS	2:12:14
6. Rodolfo Gómez	MEX	2:12:39
7. Dereje Nedi	ETH	2:12:44
8. Massimo Magnani	ITA	2:13:12

Vladimir Kotov led for the first half of the race. After 24 kilometers, Lasse Virén, who had been running with the leaders, suddenly rushed off into the bushes with diarrhea. He dropped out three kilometers later. Rodolfo Gómez took advantage of Virén's indisposition to jump into the lead, quickly opening a 100-meter gap. At the 30-kilometer mark, he led by 23 seconds. However, five and a half kilometers later he was passed by Gerard Nijboer. Six hundred meters further along, Cierpinski passed them both, and was never headed. He ran the last 200 meters in 33.4 seconds and won by about 80 meters. As he crossed the finish line, there were five runners on the track, an Olympic record. Although he was only two days shy of his 30th birthday, Waldemar Cierpinski was still described by East German sources as a "sports student." After becoming the only person besides Abebe Bikila to win two Olympic marathons, he was elevated to "sports teacher."

1984 Los Angeles C: 107, N: 60, D: 8.12. WB: 2:08.18 (F. Robert de Castella)

1. Carlos Lopes	POR	2:09:21	OR
2. John Treacy	IRL	2:09:56	
3. Charles Spedding	GBR	2:09:58	
4. Takeshi Soh	JPN	2:10:55	
5. F. Robert de Castella	AUS	2:11:09	
6. Juma Ikangaa	TAN	2:11:10	
7. Joseph Nzau	KEN	2:11:28	
8. Djama Robleh	DJI	2:11:39	

The 1984 men's marathon was an eagerly awaited race with a talent-packed field that included seven different runners who had clocked times under 2 hours and 9 minutes. The leading favorites were world champion Rob de Castella, who had won all four marathons he had run in the last three and one-half years, and the reclusive Japanese star, Toshihiko Seko, whose last loss in 1979 had been followed by five victories. Among the other highly regarded entrants was Carlos Lopes, the 1976 Olympic silver medalist at 10,000 meters. Lopes had completed only one of three marathons he had attempted, but that was a two-second loss to de Castella in 1983.

Not surprisingly, the Olympic marathon was closely fought for the first half of the race. By the 25-kilometer mark, Juma Ikangaa, one of the sub-2:09 men, was heading a lead pack that still contained twelve runners. At the 20-mile mark, de Castella slowed down to grab a cup of water and looked up to discover himself 50 meters behind the pack. He was never able to close the gap. The lead pack was down to seven. A mile later, Seko lost contact. Then Charlie Spedding, a dark horse despite having won the Houston and London Marathons earlier in the year, forced the pace. The only ones who were able to stay with him were the 37-year-old Lopes and John Treacy, who was running his first marathon. Treacy had placed ninth in the 10,000-meter run six days earlier.

Then Lopes turned on the pressure, running the next five kilometers in 14 minutes 33 seconds, a remarkable achievement, considering he had just run 21½ hot and humid miles against the best marathon field ever assembled. Spedding and Treacy had no choice but to let him go. Lopes breezed ahead to win the gold medal. Treacy ran a 67-second last lap to earn the silver, while Spedding, whose dedication was so great that he had foresworn alc for an entire week before the race, happily settled for the bronze. De Castella finished fifth and Seko fourteenth.

World-class athletes often face unexpected obstacles on their way to the Olympics. Lopes, for example, was hit by a Mercedes-Benz while training only fifteen days before the Olympic marathon. "There goes the Olympics," Lopes thought, as he rolled over the hood and watched his elbow crash through the windshield. As luck would have it, his injuries were minor. The same could not be said of the unfortunate Richard Mbewa, the Tanzanian marathon alternate, who was shot to death while jogging on a golf course by a policeman who mistook him for a thief. And then there is the story of the 78th and last man to cross the finish line in the 1984 Olympic marathon: Dieudonné Lamothe of Haiti. When last heard from, Lamothe had competed in the 1976 5000-meter race, recording the slowest time in Olympic history, but insisting on finishing. While in Los Angeles in 1984, Lamothe did not speak to the press. However, after the fall of Haitian dictator Baby Doc Duvalier, Lamothe revealed that Haitian Olympic officials had threatened to kill him if he failed to finish. He did make it across the finish line—in 2 hours 52 minutes and 18 seconds, a much more respectable time than his 1976 performance. In 1988, under considerably less pressure, Lamothe placed 20th in 2:16:15.

1988 Seoul C: 118, N: 66, D: 10.2. WB: 2:06:50 (Belayneh Densimo)

1. Gelindo Bordin	ITA	2:10:32
2. Douglas Wakiihuri	KEN	2:10:47
3. Houssein Ahmed Saleh	DJI	2:10:59
4. Takeyuki Nakayama	JPN	2:11:05
5. Stephen Moneghetti	AUS	2:11:49
6. Charles Spedding	GBR	2:12:19
7. Juma Ikangaa	TAN	2:13:06
8. F. Robert de Castella	AUS	2:13:07

The 1988 men's marathon was run in humid weather along a route lined with 36,000 policemen. By the 25-kilometer mark Juma Ikangaa was leading a pack of 13. Four kilometers later the pace was forced by the 1986 European champion, Gelindo Bordin, who, back in April 1981, had been presumed dead after being hit from behind by a car while training in Verona.

By 30 kilometers the lead pack was down to Bordin; Nakayama, who had won two marathons on the Seoul course in 1985 and 1986; world champion Douglas Wakiihuri; the favorite, Ahmed Saleh, who had also triumphed on the Seoul course at the 1987 World Cup; Ikangaa; Charlie Spedding; and Toshihiko Seko, whose disappointing performance at the 1984 Olympics remained his only loss in nine years. After 31 kilometers Nakayama surged, causing Spedding and Seko to fall behind, the latter eventually finishing ninth. Spedding fought his way back over the next few kilometers, but 400 meters past the 35-kilometer mark, Saleh and Nakayama increased the pace, and Spedding and Ikangaa lost contact for good. Just short of 37 kilometers, Nakayama fell back as well.

With three miles left, the medals were to be decided among Saleh, Wakiihuri, and Bordin, the same three who had medaled at the 1987 world championships in Rome. In that race the then unknown Wakiihuri had run away from Saleh just before the 38-kilometer mark, while Bordin had come from behind to snatch the bronze from Steve Moneghetti.

Now, 13 months later, it was Saleh who broke away at 38 kilometers, gradually opening a lead of about 25 meters over Wakiihuri. Bordin, exhausted and suffering leg cramps, resigned himself to third place. In order to distract himself from worrying about Nakayama behind him, Bordin focused his attention on Wakiihuri's back. One and a half miles from the finish, Bordin suddenly realized, to his great surprise, that he was gaining on the Kenyan. At 40 kilometers he passed him and set his sights on Saleh, who was now in pain and looking back frequently. At 40.5 kilometers Saleh glanced over his left shoulder and didn't see Bordin. He looked over his right shoulder and there he was, with a smile on his face, only three meters behind.

Fifty meters later Bordin drove past Saleh and, another 250 meters on, so did Wakiihuri. Bordin went on to win the closest Olympic marathon in 68 years. As soon as he crossed the finish line he crossed himself, then knelt down and kissed the track. Approached by reporters, he described the last two kilometers as "a war" and commented that he was "too tired even to be happy."

Six months after his Olympic triumph, Gelindo Bordin shocked Italian sports fans by announcing his retirement on national television. The next day, he returned to remind the public that the day before had been April Fool's Day.

1992 Barcelona C: 110, N: 72, D: 8.9. WB: 2:06:50 (Belayneh Densimo)

1. Hwang Young-cho	KOR	2:13:23
2. Koichi Morishita	JPN	2:13:45
3. Stephan Freigang	GER	2:14:00
4. Takeyuki Nakayama	JPN	2:14:02
5. Salvatore Bettiol	ITA	2:14:15
6. Salah Kokaich	MOR	2:14:25
7. Jan Huruk	POL	2:14:32
8. Hiromi Taniguchi	JPN	2:14:42

Although the race began at 6:30 p.m., for the third straight time the marathon was run in uncomfortably hot conditions. This time the demands on the runners were even more severe because, after 37½ kilometers, the course concluded with a brutal three-mile climb up Montjuïc to the Olympic Stadium. The field got off to a cautious start. After ten kilometers the first 50 runners were still bunched within 50 meters of each other, sharing water-soaked sponges, their rivalries forgotten before the common enemy: the course. At the halfway mark the lead pack still contained 30 men. It was Salvatore Bettiol who forced the pace after 23 kilometers, breaking up the pack at last. He was quickly

Marathon, 1992
Koichi Morishita (right) looks over his shoulder in the final mile and does not like what he sees.

hauled in, but by the 27-kilometer mark, three runners had pulled away: 24-year-old Koichi Morishita, who had recorded the fastest time of 1991, 22-year-old Hwang Young-cho, and Hwang's Korean teammate, Kim Wan-ki. Kim fell back seven kilometers later, eventually ending up in 28th place.

In 1936, Korean Sohn Kee-chung had won the Olympic marathon, but had been forced to endure the humiliation of competing for Japan, using a Japanese name. Now, 56 years later to the day, Hwang of Korea and Morishita of Japan were locked in a grim and dramatic struggle. Waiting in the stadium was Sohn himself, now 80 years old. For four kilometers, Hwang and Morishita ran side by side. Whenever one sped up, the other matched him. Then they reached the bottom of the awful Montjuïc hill. Still they pressed on, one surging, the other catching up. Finally, two kilometers from the stadium, Hwang accelerated, and Morishita, despite a noble effort, was unable to respond.

Hwang entered the stadium with a lead of more than 100 meters. Although he was able to smile and wave to the crowd, as soon as he crossed the finish line, he collapsed. Hwang wanted to take a victory lap carrying the South Korean flag, but his legs could go no farther. He was carried away on a stretcher. Fortunately a quick massage revived him and he was able to return for the medal ceremony, the raising of the Korean flag and the playing of the South Korean national anthem. Hwang tried to telephone his mother back in Korea, but was unable to reach her because she spent the whole day in a temple, praying for him. When he returned to Seoul, Hwang met Sohn Kee-chung and placed his gold medal around the older man's neck. Sohn told Hwang, "Now I can die without any regrets." Hwang himself dismissed the political significance of his triumph over a Japanese runner and reminded his fellow Koreans that he had worn Japanese-made running shoes during his Olympic victory.

For the first time in Olympic history marathon runners were told that they would not be allowed to finish in the stadium unless they completed the course within a time limit, 2 hours 45 minutes, so as not to interfere with preparations for the Closing Ceremony 45 minutes later. Twenty-three runners failed to complete the course, including defending champion Gelindo Bordin. Eighty-four runners met the time limit, which was extended by two minutes, but three did not, and they were redirected to a nearby warm-up track. The next-to-last finisher was Hussain Haleen of the Maldive Islands. Although his time of 3:04:16 was not impressive, Haleen did gain the distinction of being the first Maldivian athlete in any sport to finish ahead of an athlete from another country. The last finisher was Pyambuu Tuul of Mongolia, whose time of 4:00:44 was the slowest in 84 years. But Tuul's achievement had a touch of drama of its own. A construction worker, he was blinded by an explosion in 1978. Twelve years later he was discovered by Richard Traum, founder of the Achilles Club, a New York based organization that helped disabled athletes. Tuul, with the help of a guide, competed in the 1990 New York Marathon. Then, in January 1991, a cornea transplant restored sight in his right eye. One and a half years later he took part in—and finished—the Olympic Marathon, not to win but "to show that a man has many possibilities."

Far less inspirational is the story of the man who finished last at the 1988 Olympics (in a time of 3:14:02), Polin Belisle, who represented Belize. Although Belisle apparently did spend a few childhood years in Belize, he grew up and lived in Burbank, California. He convinced Belizean Olympic officials to let him compete in Seoul by sending them newspaper clippings that showed he had recorded an impressive time in the Long Beach Marathon. In fact there was no evidence that he had run any of the race except the beginning and the end. After 1988 he used his Olympic appearance to con people into donating money to support his "training." In 1992 he badgered the Belize Olympic Committee to send him to the Olympics again, but by this time the Belizeans were wise to him. So, armed with a Honduran birth certificate and more fake marathon results, he changed his name to Apolineria Belisle Gomez and won a place on the Olympic team of Honduras. But on the fifth day of the 1992 Olympics some Belizean athletes recognized Belisle's name on the entry list and told the president of the Belize Olympic Committee, who informed the president of the Honduras Olympic Committee, who kicked Belisle off the team. Not so easily discouraged, Belisle showed up on race day anyway, slipped into the first line of runners on the starting line and raced with the leaders for a mile before fading into the pack and disappearing. He was the first unauthorized athlete to compete in the Olympics since Madeline de Jesus of Puerto Rico took the place of her twin sister in the 1984 4 × 400-meter relay. Before that, the 1972 cycling road race was crashed by four members of the Irish Republican Army.

Finally, there is the story of Salvador Garcia, a sergeant in Mexico's presidential guard. After winning the 1991 New York Marathon, Garcia was promoted to lieutenant. In 1992 he placed ninth at the Olympics—and was demoted back to sergeant.

1996 Atlanta C: 124, N: 79, D: 8.4. WB: 2:06.50 (Belayneh Densimo)

1. Josia Thugwane	SAF	2:12:36
2. Lee Bong-ju	KOR	2:12:39
3. Eric Wainaina	KEN	2:12:44
4. Martín Fiz Martín	SPA	2:13:20
5. Richard Nerurkar	GBR	2:13:39
6. Germán Silva Martínez	MEX	2:14:29
7. Steve Moneghetti	AUS	2:14:35
8. Benjamín Paredes Martínez	MEX	2:14:55

Josia Thugwane was not one of the favorites in the Atlanta Olympic marathon. A member of the Ndebele tribe, Thugwane was abandoned by his parents and began working at the age of nine, tending cattle. When he was seventeen he switched from playing soccer to running when he learned that it was possible to earn money racing. His first success was in a local half-marathon that brought him 50 rand ($14). He attracted the attention of a nearby coal mine who wanted him for contests against other mines. He was given a job as a kitchen worker and he built a shack for his wife and children in Mzinoni Township in the highlands east of Johannesburg.

Thugwane was chosen to compete abroad, placing 14th in a 1994 race in Seoul. In 1995 he dropped out of the New York Marathon and then won the Honolulu Marathon. In the meantime, the coal mine had given him a better job: janitor in a workers' hostel. He also opened a beer bar in the shack next to his home.

When the 1996 South African Olympic team was chosen, Thugwane was not included. The regulations left him one last chance. Anyone who won the South African championship would automatically qualify. Thugwane won the race in a time of 2:11:46.

Two weeks later, Thugwane was driving his pickup truck, on his way to buy some cows, when he stopped to pick up a hitchhiker he knew. Two men jumped into his truck and threatened him with a gun. Thugwane leaped out of the car, but not before being shot in the chin. He ran home, but the encounter left him with a deep scar from the gunshot and a sore back from the jump. The Olympics were less than five months away.

In June, Thugwane and the other South African marathoners settled in Albuquerque, New Mexico for two months of high-altitude training. Thugwane arrived, with his long hair in dreadlocks, preoccupied with fear that his family would be attacked during his long absence from Mzinoni. Sometimes the South Africans would go on training runs with runners from other nations who were also preparing for the Olympics. Thugwane would always make sure he was ahead of the foreign runners. It was in Albuquerque that he first became aware that the Olympics was a big event, that "it was for runners what the World Cup is for football players."

Thugwane arrived in Atlanta ranked 41st in the world by time. At 1.58 meters (5 feet 2 inches) and 47 kilograms (99 pounds), he was the smallest of the 123 runners who started the race. Twenty-five years old, he could not read or write.

To avoid the terrible heat of mid-summer Atlanta, the race began at 7:05 a.m. It was foggy, but humid. The runners began so carefully that when they reached the halfway mark, there were still 48 runners in the lead pack. Luis dos Santos of Brazil pushed the pace, whittling the pack to twenty-one by the 30-kilometer mark. One kilometer later, Thugwane made his first move. He was joined by Lee Bong-ju, and the two opened a 50-meter lead. Eric Wainaina gradually closed the gap, moving into the lead at 35 kilometers. The trio of Thugwane, Lee and Wainaina had run the last 5000 meters in 15 minutes 11 seconds.

Thugwane threw in a series of short spurts that opened daylight between him and the other two, but each time Lee and Wainaina came back. One kilometer from the finish, Thugwane sprinted to a 30-meter lead over Wainaina, with Lee close behind Wainaina. Lee passed the Kenyan on the ramp leading into the stadium. For the first time since 1948, the first three runners were on the track at the same time. Despite a determined attempt by Lee to catch up, Thugwane won by three seconds, with Wainaina five seconds behind Lee. It was the closest marathon in Olympic history. Thugwane ran the second half of the race in 1 hour 5 minutes.

In an age of television coverage and shoe contracts, Josia Thugwane was still so unaware of the significance of the Olympics that he was preparing to leave the stadium when officials informed him that there would be a medal ceremony on the field. When his name was announced as the gold medal winner, he remained standing on the ground until another official motioned him to climb the platform. Thugwane celebrated his victory by buying a CD player and thirty CDs. But, as the first black South African gold medal winner, Thugwane's days of innocence were numbered.

Before he had time to prepare himself, Thugwane was inundated by journalists, sponsors, agents, politicians, beggars and criminals.

Among the also-rans were three men with particularly noteworthy stories. Turbo Tumo of Ethiopia, running in 60th place late in the race, entered the stadium, but was so disoriented by the heat that he lost his way and walked off the track without finishing. Of the 112 runners who did finish, Islam Djugum of Bosnia-Herzogovina was 107th. Djugum was the only member of the 10-person Bosnian Olympic team who remained in the country during his nation's bloody war with Yugoslavia. In fact, Djugum continued running on the streets two hours a day, changing his course each day to discourage snipers. Three different times he stopped in the middle of training runs when he encountered massacres and helped load the survivors into cars to be taken to hospitals. The 36-year-old Djugum carried his national flag at the Opening Ceremony.

Abdul Baser Wasigi was a 21-year-old from Kabul, Afghanistan with a personal best of 2 hours 33 minutes. At the 1992 Olympics, Afghanistan had been so disrupted by war that its athletes never arrived in Barcelona. Four years later, Wasigi injured his hamstring muscle shortly after his arrival in Atlanta and he was forced to give up training for the two weeks preceding the race. Wasigi was determined to compete and finish despite his injury. Two miles into the race, Wasigi was already three-quarters of a mile behind the other runners. When Josia Thugwane crossed the finish line, Baser Wasigi had just passed the 25-kilometer mark. Along the route, Wasigi caught the fancy of many spectators. After watching dozens of elite runners zip by, here, an hour or more later, was a runner they could relate to: an everyman stubbornly limping forward. Some ran alongside him and offered him water bottles.

In the stadium, grounds crews were already covering the track in preparation for the Closing Ceremony. Officials were going to wave Wasigi aside to finish at an alternative track, but let him proceed to the main stadium after all. Preparations for the Closing Ceremony were halted. Volunteers cut a piece of white plastic tape, wrote "ATLANTA 96" on it, and stretched it across the finish line. When Wasigi finally arrived inside the stadium, hundreds of volunteers lined the track and applauded while the band struck up a welcoming fanfare. Wasigi's time of 4:24:17 was the slowest in Olympic history, breaking the previous record of 4:22:45, set by George Lister of Canada in 1908. Wasigi finished 1 hour 24 minutes and 22 seconds behind the runner in next to last place.

2000 Sydney C: 100, N: 66, D: 10.1. WB: 2:05:42 (Khalid Khannouchi)

1. Gezahgne Abera	ETH	2:10:11
2. Eric Wainaina	KEN	2:10:31
3. Tesfaye Tola	ETH	2:11:10
4. Jon Brown	GBR	2:11:17
5. Giacomo Leone	ITA	2:12:14
6. Martín Fiz Martín	SPA	2:13:06
7. Abdel Kader El-Mouaziz	MOR	2:13:49
8. Mohamed Ouaadi	FRA	2:14:04

Gezahgne Abera of Ethiopia first attracted attention in 1999 when, after placing 11th at the world championships, he raced in the Fukuoka marathon. In Fukuoka, he misjudged the finish line and allowed Mohamed Ouaadi of France to pass him. When he realized his error, Abera sped up and repassed Ouaadi just in time to win the race. On April 17, 2000, Abera entered the Boston Marathon. Running on his 22nd birthday, he finished second between two Kenyans, Elijah Lagat and Moses Tanui. Abera claimed that Lagat and Tanui had kicked him, jostled him and stepped on him.

Five and a half months later, in the Olympic marathon, the race came down to two Ethiopians, Abera and Tesfaye Tola, and only one Kenyan, defending Olympic bronze medal-winner Eric Wainaina. Wainaina was only added to the Kenyan squad two months before the Sydney Games after a dispute led to the dismissal of both Lagat and Tanui. Wainaina, who began his athletic career by running away from bullies, had been living in Japan since 1993.

Venezuela's José Semprun was the first to show in front. Then Tiyapo Mosa of Botswana attempted to run away from the field. He built up a lead of more than a minute and still led by 35 seconds at the halfway mark. Mosa was finally reeled in after 24 kilometers and ended up finishing in 77th place. After 30 kilometers, the runners confronted a strong headwind that blew against them for the remainder of the race. By 31 kilometers, the lead group was down to four: Abera, Tola, Wainaina and Jon Brown, who was born in Wales, grew up in England, went to university in the United States, trained in Germany and then moved to Canada. Brown fell back after 34 kilometers and the medalists were decided. At the 37-kilometer mark, the Ethiopians slowed to pick up water-soaked sponges and Wainaina seized the opportunity to make a break. Earlier the Ethiopians had discussed how to deal with Wainaina because, in Abera's words, "the Kenyan chap was very tough and kept looking like he could get away." Now that Wainaina was doing just that, Tola found that he couldn't respond, so he told Abera, "I'm tired. You go. You win." Two kilometers later, Abera surged into the lead and held it for the rest of the race, winning by six seconds. At 22 years old, Abera was the youngest marathon champion in Olympic history. In 2001, Abera won the world championship to become the first person to achieve an Olympics/world championships marathon double. Abera became so popular that when he married fellow marathoner Elfenesh Alemu in 2003, the ceremony was held in the Ethiopian national football stadium and was attended by 25,000 people. Alemu's wedding dress measured 300 meters and was carried by 600 students.

2004 Athens C: 101, N: 59, D: 8.29. WB: 2:04:55 (Paul Tergat)

1. Stefano Baldini	ITA	2:10:55
2. Mebrahtom Keflezighi	USA	2:11:29
3. Vanderlei de Lima	BRA	2:12:11
4. Jon Brown	GBR	2:12:26
5. Shigeru Aburaya	JPN	2:13:11
6. Toshinari Suwa	JPN	2:13:24
7. Eric Wainaina	KEN	2:13:30
8. Alberto Chaíça	POR	2:14:17

Stretching from the town of Marathon to the newly rebuilt Panathinaikos Stadium, the 2004 marathon course followed the route used for the 1896 Olympic marathon The race was held in better weather than the women's marathon one week earlier, with 86° Farenheit (30° C) temperatures and clear skies. After a slow start on the challenging course, the first major break came after the 15-kilometer mark, when South African Hendrick Ramaala opened up a 50-meter gap ahead of the pack. Ramaala was unable to maintain his lead, and as the group caught up, Brazilian Vanderlei de Lima moved ahead, breaking away at the 20-kilometer point and opening a 25-second lead over the next five kilometers. De Lima continued to widen his lead, to nearly 47 seconds at the 30-kilometer mark, ahead of Eritrean-born Mebrahtom Keflezighi, European Champion Stefano Baldini and world record holder Paul Tergat. With five kilometers left, Tergat began to fade, and Baldini launched his attack. In fact, Baldini was not the only one who had planned to attack. Just before Baldini surged past Keflezighi to try for the lead, a religious fanatic dressed in a red kilt jumped onto the course and tackled de Lima. The attacker, a defrocked Irish priest, Neil Horan, who had previously been arrested for walking onto the track during the 2003 British Formula One Grand Prix race, knocked de Lima off the course and was promptly arrested. De Lima continued the race after a few stunned seconds, but was overtaken by Baldini at the two-hour mark and, a minute later, by Keflezighi. The three held their places through the final four kilometers.

Immediately after the race, Brazil filed a formal protest. Although the appeal for a second gold medal was denied, de Lima was awarded the Pierre de Coubertin medal for "exceptional demonstration of fair play and Olympic values." His attacker, who had a history of mental illness, was given a 12-month suspended jail sentence, a 3,000 euro fine and was barred from all future sports events. Silver medalist Mebrahtom Keflezighi emigrated from Eritrea to Italy after his father, Russom Keflezighi, fled persecution by walking 150 miles into Sudan. The family eventually settled in San Diego, California, where Keflezighi's father drove a taxi and cleaned the floors of various banks to pay for college for Mebrahtom and his ten siblings.

2008 Beijing C: 95, N: 56, D: 8.24. WB: 2:04:26 (Haile Gebrselassie)

1. Samuel Wanjiru	KEN	2:06:32 OR
2. Jaouad Gharib	MOR	2:07:16
3. Tsegaye Kebede	ETH	2:10:00
4. Deriba Merga	ETH	2:10:21
5. Martin Lel	KEN	2:10:24
6. Viktor Röthlin	SWI	2:10:35
7. Gashaw Asfaw	ETH	2:10:52
8. Yared Asmerom	ERI	2:11:11

After dominating the 10,000 meters event for nearly a decade, winning two Olympic gold medals and four consecutive world championships, long-distance legend Haile Gebrselassie turned his attention to the marathon. By 2007 he had broken the world record, and he entered the 2008 Olympic year as the favorite. A few months before the Olympics, however, Gebrselassie withdrew, citing concerns about air quality in Beijing and its impact on his asthma. As it turned out, he needn't have worried. Despite nearly three weeks of smog and oppressive heat during the Games, an overnight rain shower cleared the air the night before the marathon and the race was held on a clear, though humid, day.

With Gebrselassie out of the running, Kenya hoped to earn its first gold medal in the event. The team, however, had been hit by some bad luck. Robert Cheruiyot, a four-time Boston Marathon winner and the inaugural World Marathon Majors champion (a new series which includes the Boston, London, Berlin, Chicago and New York Marathons, as well as the Olympic and world championship Marathons), had aggravated a thigh injury and pulled out a week before the competition. He was replaced by reigning world champion Luke Kibet. Meanwhile three-time London Marathon winner and double New York Marathon winner Martin Lel was recovering from a recent bout of malaria and was still not at his peak.

Kenya's greatest hopes were pinned on 21-year-old rising star Samuel Wanjiru. Raised by his mother, whose maiden name he used, Wanjiru moved to Japan in 2002 on an athletic scholarship, where he attended high school and learned fluent Japanese. After graduating in 2005, he began training with 1992 silver medalist Koichi Morishita. At the age of 18, Wanjiru set a 10,000 meters junior world record. Two weeks later, he broke the world half-marathon record, held by Paul Tergat since 1998. He celebrated by buying his mother a five-acre farm.

Although his world record was broken by Gebrselassie in early 2006, Wanjiru reclaimed it the following year at a meet in the United Arab Emirates, and then lowered it still further, to 58:33, at a half-marathon in Holland. This time he celebrated by buying his mother a truck. Wanjiru ran his first full marathon in 2007 at Fukuoka in Japan, setting a course record of 2:06:39. His second competition at the distance was the London Marathon, which he lost narrowly to Lel in a sprint to the finish. Lel went on to become the first man to win both the London and New York marathons in the same year. Wanjiru missed the 2007 world championships after finishing fourth at the Kenyan national trials.

The Kenyans faced stiff opposition for the gold, including double world champion Jaouad Gharib of Morocco and reigning world champion silver medalist Mubarak Hassan Shami of Qatar.

Racing in his warm-up shoes, having forgotten to pack his race shoes, Wanjiru controlled the race from the start, setting a blistering pace and covering the first ten kilometers in less than 30 minutes. At that point only eight racers remained in the lead pack. By the 20-kilometer mark the lead pack had been reduced to five, including Wanjiru, Lel, Gharib, Eritrea's Yonas Kifle and Ethiopia's Deriba Merga. Merga's teammate Tsegaye Kebede trailed another 18 seconds back. Ten kilometers later, Wanjiru upped the pace again, dropping Gharib, Lel and Kifle. Gharib managed to work his way back up to join the leaders over the next few kilometers.

Shortly after the 35-kilometer mark, as an exhausted Merga began to fade, Wanjiru and Gharib found a yellow water bottle on the course. The two passed it back and forth to drink before Wanjiru pulled away from Gharib, opening a clear gap over the next five kilometers. Wanjiru finished strongly, breaking the previous Olympic record, set by Carlos Lopes in 1984, by nearly three minutes. Gharib took silver, also breaking the previous Olympic record, while Kebede overtook Merga on the final lap inside the stadium to take bronze. It was Wanjiru's third-ever marathon, and Kenya's first Olympic gold medal in the event's history.

The fast pace and intense heat proved too much for many racers. Nineteen of the 95 runners failed to finish, including Kibet, who dropped out shortly after the halfway point, due to stomach cramps.

The year after winning the Olympic gold, Wanjiru continued to dominate, beating the course records in both the London Marathon (by five seconds) and the Chicago Marathon (by one second). Not realizing how close he was to the Chicago record, he slowed at the end and began to wave to fans, but still managed to cross the line in time. For his performance Wanjiru earned an estimated $250,000 appearance fee, $100,000 in prize money and an additional $75,000 prize fee. He was also crowned the World Marathon Majors champion, which carried an additional $500,000 prize.

Despite his Olympic success, Wanjiru's life soon began to unravel. In December 2010 he was arrested after threatening his wife, a maid and a security guard with an AK-47 assault rifle. Five months later he died in a bizarre home accident after being caught in bed with another woman by his wife, who locked the pair inside the bedroom. Wanjiru apparently fell from the first-floor balcony of his home while attempting to stop his wife from leaving the house, and later died of his injuries. However, two of the three pathologists who studied his body reportedly said that the injuries were not consistent with an accident.

110-METER HURDLES

Contestants must clear ten hurdles, each of which is three feet six inches (1.07 meters) high. It is 45 feet (13.7 meters) to the first hurdle; the distance between hurdles is 30 feet (9.1 meters); and it is 46 feet (14 meters) from the last hurdle to the finish. The United States has dominated this event. Competing in 25 Olympics (including 1906), US hurdlers have won nineteen gold medals, eighteen silver, and sixteen bronze. No other nation has won more than five medals.

1896 Athens C: 8, N: 6, D: 4.10. WR (120 yards): 15.4 (Stephen Chase)

1. Thomas Curtis	USA	17.6
2. Grantley Goulding	GBR	17.6e

DNS: William Welles Hoyt (USA), Frantz Reichel (FRA)

Goulding led at the final hurdle, but Curtis passed him in the run-in to win by about two inches (five centimeters). Reichel gave up his spot in the final to serve as assistant to countryman Albin Lermusiaux who was running in the marathon at the same time. Welles Hoyt also declined to start, presumably to save himself for the pole vault later in the day, which he won. Curtis, who had studied at MIT, later wrote that when the Boston team arrived in Athens the day before the opening ceremony, they were marched directly to a banquet at City Hall where "great surprise was shown at our hesitation in drinking great bumpers of white wine which were forced upon us."

Alvin Kraenzlein, 1900
Won four gold medals in three days at the 1900 Paris Olympics. His wins came in the 60-meter dash, the long jump, and the 110- and 200-meter hurdles.

1900 Paris C: 9, N: 3, D: 7.14. WR (120 yards): 15.2 (Alvin Kraenzlein)

1. Alvin Kraenzlein	USA	15.4 OR
2. John McLean	USA	15.6e
3. Frederick Moloney	USA	15.6e
4. Jean Lécuyer	FRA	—

DNF: Norman Pritchard (GBR/IND)

Alvin Kraenzlein won the first of his four gold medals at the 1900 Games. Kraenzlein was responsible for introducing the leg-extended style to hurdling. He subsequently earned a dental degree from the University of Pennsylvania, but gave up dentistry to become a track coach at the University of Michigan. He also coached the national teams of Germany and Cuba.

1904 St. Louis C: 8, N: 2, D: 9.3. WR (120 yards): 15.2 (Alvin Kraenzlein)

1. Frederick Schule	USA	16.0
2. Thaddeus Shideler	USA	16.3
3. Lesley Ashburner	USA	16.4
4. Frank Castleman	USA	—

1906 Athens C: 15, N: 8, D: 5.1. WR (120 yards): 15.2 (Alvin Kraenzlein)

1. Robert Leavitt	USA	16.2
2. Alfred Healey	AUS	16.2e
3. Vincent Duncker	GER	16.3e
4. Hugo Friend	USA	16.3e
5. Henri Molinié	FRA	—

1908 London C: 25, N: 10, D: 7.25. WR (120 yards): 15.2 (Alvin Kraenzlein)

1. Forrest Smithson	USA	15.0 WR
2. John Garrels	USA	15.7e
3. Arthur Shaw	USA	15.8e
4. William Rand	USA	16.0e

Smithson, of Portland, Oregon, shot into the lead before the first hurdle and won by five yards. There is an enduring anecdote that Smithson, while running the final, carried a Bible in one hand as a protest against Sunday competition. There is no evidence to support this otherwise admirable story. It is not mentioned in any contemporary newspaper accounts and none of Smithson's races were held on a Sunday. A much-reprinted photograph of Smithson clearing a hurdle while holding a Bible is clearly a posed shot not taken during competition.

1912 Stockholm C: 22, N: 10, D: 7.12. WR: 15.0 (Forrest Smithson)

1. Frederick Kelly	USA	15.1
2. James Wendell	USA	15.2
3. Martin Hawkins	USA	15.3
4. John Case	USA	15.3
5. Kenneth Powell	GBR	15.5

DNF: John Nicholson (USA)

1920 Antwerp C: 24, N: 15, D: 8.18. WR (120 yards): 14.4 (Earl Thomson)

1. Earl Thomson	CAN	14.8 WR
2. Harold Barron	USA	15.1e
3. Frederick Murray	USA	15.1e
4. Harry Wilson	NZL	15.2e
5. Walker Smith	USA	15.3e
6. Carl-Axel Christiernsson	SWE	15.3e

Earl Thomson was born in Birch Hills, Saskatchewan, but grew up in Southern California from the age of eight. He represented Dartmouth in intercollegiate competition, but because he was still a Canadian citizen, he competed for Canada in the Olympics. Thomson, who survived a near-fatal rifle accident in 1914, took his hurdling very seriously, going so far as to tie his legs to the foot of his bed so that he wouldn't curl up and risk cramping. Thomson spent most of his life as a track coach, including 37 years as head coach of the Navy team at Annapolis. His Olympic time of 14.8 seconds was accepted as a world record even though his 14.4 for the slightly shorter distance of 120 yards was much more impressive.

1924 Paris C: 27, N: 15, D: 7.9. WR (120 yards): 14.4 (Earl Thomson)

1. Daniel Kinsey	USA	15.0
2. Sydney Atkinson	SAF	15.0
3. Sten Pettersson	SWE	15.4
4. Carl-Axel Christiernsson	SWE	15.5
5. Karl Anderson	USA	15.8

DISQ: George Guthrie (USA)

Atkinson was in the lead as he and Kinsey rose to clear the last hurdle. However, the South African clipped the barrier with his rear foot and stumbled. He recovered well, but lost by inches. Guthrie finished third, but was disqualified for knocking over three hurdles.

1928 Amsterdam C: 41, N: 24, D: 8.1. WR (120 yards): 14.4 (Earl Thomson)

1. Sydney Atkinson	SAF	14.8
2. Stephen Anderson	USA	14.8
3. John Collier	USA	14.9
4. Leighton Dye	USA	14.9
5. George Weightman-Smith	SAF	15.0
6. Frederick Gaby	GBR	15.2

In the semifinals, Weightman-Smith set a metric world record of 14.6 seconds.

1932 Los Angeles C: 17, N: 10, D: 8.3. WR (120 yards): 14.2 (Percy Beard)

1. George Saling	USA	14.6	(14.57)
2. Percy Beard	USA	14.7	(14.72)
3. Donald Finlay	GBR	14.8	(14.79)
4. Jack Keller	USA	14.8	(14.83)
5. David Burghley	GBR	14.8	(14.84)
DISQ: Willi Welscher (GER)			

Jack Keller won the first semifinal in 14.5 and George Saling the second in 14.4. In the final, Keller showed in front first, but hit the fifth hurdle, allowing Beard to move ahead. However, Beard hit the sixth hurdle. Saling then caught up and took the lead. He tripped on the ninth hurdle, but held on to win by a yard. Welscher finished fourth, but was disqualified for knocking over four hurdles, a prohibition that is no longer in the rules. For the first time in Olympic history, the results of a final were changed after a film of the race had been viewed. Originally Keller had been placed third and awarded the bronze medal. When the revised results were announced, Keller sought out Finlay in the Olympic Village and handed over the medal.

1936 Berlin C: 31, N: 20. D: 8.6. WR: 14.1 (Forrest Towns)

1. Forrest Towns	USA	14.2
2. Donald Finlay	GBR	14.4
3. Frederick "Fritz" Pollard	USA	14.4
4. Håkan Lidman	SWE	14.4
5. John Thornton	GBR	14.7
6. Lawrence O'Connor	CAN	15.0

The son of a railroad blacksmith, Forrest "Spec" Towns of Georgia equaled his own world record of 14.1 in the semifinals and then skimmed to a two-yard victory in the final. Towns became a hurdler by an unusual route. He had not competed in high school because his family was too poor to buy him track shoes. A couple years later a neighbor saw Towns high-jumping over a broomstick held by his father and brother. The neighbor told a local sportswriter, who wrote about the scene. Weems Baskin, the track coach at the University of Georgia, read the article, gave Towns a tryout and then a scholarship and then switched him to hurdling, an event Towns had never heard of. Three years later he was an Olympic champion.

1948 London C: 28, N: 18, D: 8.4. WR (120 yards): 13.6 (W. Harrison Dillard)

1. William Porter	USA	13.9 OR
2. Clyde Scott	USA	14.1
3. Craig Dixon	USA	14.1
4. Alberto Triulzi	ARG	14.6
5. Peter Gardner	AUS	14.7
6. Håkan Lidman	SWE	14.9

The absence of world record holder Harrison Dillard, who was eliminated at the US trials, did not prevent the US from sweeping the medals so decisively that the final appeared to be two separate races. At the starting line, the stadium was silent and the starter had already called out "on your mark" and "get set," when suddenly the wife of one of Bill Porter's former coaches yelled, "Come on, Bill!" Porter was so unnerved that he false started. In the re-start, to avoid disqualification, he had to come out of the blocks more carefully.

1952 Helsinki C: 30, N: 20, D: 7.24. WR: 13.5 (Richard Attlesey)

1. W. Harrison Dillard	USA	13.7 OR	(13.91)
2. Jack Davis	USA	13.7	(14.00)
3. Arthur Barnard	USA	14.1	(14.40)
4. Yevhen Bulanchyk	SOV/UKR	14.5	(14.73)
5. Kenneth Doubleday	AUS	14.7	(14.82)
6. Raymond Weinberg	AUS	14.8	(15.15)

Harrison Dillard began hurdling at the age of eight, running in an alley and using the springs from abandoned car seats as barriers. By 1948 Dillard was the unquestioned world champion of the high hurdles. However, he lost his stride in the US Olympic trials and failed to finish. He did qualify in the 100-meter dash and went on to win the gold medal. Despite this unexpected triumph, he still wanted to earn an Olympic victory in the hurdles. Four years later, at the age of 29, Dillard got his chance. He was hard-pressed by Jack Davis, who knocked down the ninth hurdle, allowing Dillard to achieve the victory "on which I had set my heart." The usually calm Dillard jumped for joy and exclaimed, "Good things come to those who wait."

While most observers thought Jack Davis missed a gold medal because he hit the ninth hurdle, Davis himself wondered if there wasn't another reason. In the Olympic Village in Helsinki, Davis shared a room with shot putter Parry O'Brien, discus thrower Sam Iness and javelin thrower Cy Young. Because the weather was cool, O'Brien wore his USC sweatshirt under his jersey the day of the shot put final. O'Brien won the gold

Harrison Dillard, 1952

The king of the high hurdles failed to qualify in that event for the 1948 Olympics, but won the 100-meter dash instead. Four years later, in Helsinki, he finally earned his high hurdles gold medal.

medal. The next day, O'Brien loaned the sweatshirt to discus thrower Sim Iness, who then won the gold medal. Young decided that the sweatshirt brought good luck, so the following day, he wore O'Brien's shirt when he competed in the javelin final. Young won the gold medal. The next day, it was Davis' turn to take part in the final of his event. But Davis balked at wearing the now sacred sweatshirt. "By the time the shirt got to me," he later recalled, "it was kind of ripe and stretched out with wear. I decided not to wear it, and I only got a silver medal. In the back of my mind, I can't help but think that if I'd worn the shirt, I'd have won the gold."

1956 Melbourne C: 24, N: 15, D: 11.26. WR: 13.4 (Jack Davis)

1. Lee Calhoun	USA	13.5 OR	(13.70)
2. Jack Davis	USA	13.5	(13.73)
3. Joel Shankle	USA	14.1	(14.25)
4. Martin Lauer	GER	14.5	(14.67)
5. Stanko Lorger	YUG/SLO	14.5	(14.68)
6. Boris Stolyarov	SOV/RUS	14.6	(14.71)

Once again, if each nation had not been limited to three entrants, the final would probably have been an all-American affair. Running into a 1.9-meters-per-second wind, Calhoun and Davis were even by the eighth hurdle. Using a lunge that he had learned from Davis, Calhoun got his shoulder across the finish line inches ahead. For the second straight time, Jack Davis had recorded the same time as the winner yet had been forced to settle for a silver medal.

1960 Rome C: 36, N: 21, D: 9.5. WR: 13.2 (Martin Lauer, Lee Calhoun)

1. Lee Calhoun	USA	13.8	(13.98)
2. Willie May	USA	13.8	(13.99)
3. Hayes Jones	USA	14.0	(14.17)
4. Martin Lauer	GER	14.0	(14.20)
5. Keith Gardner	JAM	14.4	(14.55)
6. Valentin Chistyakov	SOV/RUS	14.6	(14.71)

Lee Calhoun had to sit out the 1958 season after being suspended for receiving gifts on the television game show *Bride and Groom.* He was back in uniform in 1960, winning his second gold medal with the same lunge that he had used to win four years earlier, and United States hurdlers achieved their fourth consecutive sweep.

1964 Tokyo C: 37, N: 23, D: 10.18. WR: 13.2 (Martin Lauer, Lee Calhoun)

1. Hayes Jones	USA	13.6	(13.67)
2. H. Blaine Lindgren	USA	13.7	(13.74)
3. Anatoly Mikhailov	SOV/RUS	13.7	(13.78)
4. Eddy Ottoz	ITA	13.8	(13.84)
5. Gurbachan Singh Randhawa	IND	14.0	(14.09)
6. Marcel Duriez	FRA	14.0	(14.09)
7. Giovanni Cornacchia	ITA	14.1	(14.12)
8. Giorgio Mazza	ITA	14.1	(14.17)

A US sweep was prevented when Willie Davenport, the surprise winner of the US Olympic trials, succumbed to a thigh injury and was eliminated in the semifinals. Jones and Lindgren ran evenly for almost the entire race, but Lindgren started his lean too early and was nipped at the tape.

1968 Mexico City C: 33, N: 23, D: 10.17. WR: 13.2 (Martin Lauer, Lee Calhoun, Earl McCullouch)

1. Willie Davenport	USA	13.33 EOR
2. Ervin Hall	USA	13.42
3. Eddy Ottoz	ITA	13.46
4. Leon Coleman	USA	13.67
5. Werner Trzmiel	GER	13.68
6. Bo Forssander	SWE	13.73
7. Marcel Duriez	FRA	13.77
8. Pierre Schoebel	FRA	14.02

In 1968, 19 of the world's top 25 high hurdlers were from the United States. Since 1964, Willie Davenport had struggled through four years of injuries to gain another chance at an Olympic gold medal. He was so nervous before the start of the final that he almost fell while taking off his sweat pants, and he never even heard the starter say, "set." Yet "from the first step, the gun," he said, "I knew I had won the race. It was perhaps the only race I ever ran that way, but that first step was so perfect—right on the money. I coasted over the last three hurdles thinking, 'It's over, it's over.'" His official time of 13.3 equaled the Olympic record set by Erv Hall in the semifinals.

1972 Munich C: 39, N: 27, D: 9.7. WR: 13.2 (Martin Lauer, Lee Calhoun, Earl McCullouch, Willie Davenport); WR (120 yards): 13.0 (Rodney Milburn)

1. Rodney Milburn	USA	13.24 EWR
2. Guy Drut	FRA	13.34
3. Thomas Hill	USA	13.48
4. Willie Davenport	USA	13.50
5. Frank Siebeck	GDR	13.71
6. Leszek Wodzyński	POL	13.72
7. Lubomir Nadenicek	CZE	13.76
8. Petr Cech	CZE	13.86

Rod Milburn of Opelousas, Louisiana, almost pulled a Harrison Dillard in 1972. After going undefeated in 1971 and winning 27 consecutive finals, he hit two hurdles in the US Olympic trials and barely qualified in third place. However, in Munich his superiority was absolute. He was first over the first hurdle and almost two meters in front by the sixth hurdle, winning by one meter over fast-closing Guy Drut.

On November 11, 1997, Rod Milburn was unloading a hopper car filled with hot water and crystallized sodium chlorate at a paper plant in Port Hudson, Louisiana, when he fell in and died from burns caused by the scalding liquid. He was 47 years old.

1976 Montreal C: 23, N: 17, D: 7.28. WR: 13.0 (Guy Drut)

1. Guy Drut	FRA	13.30
2. Alejandro Casañas Ramírez	CUB	13.33
3. Willie Davenport	USA	13.38
4. Charles Foster	USA	13.41
5. Thomas Munkelt	GDR	13.44
6. James Owens	USA	13.73
7. Vyacheslav Kulebyakin	SOV/RUS	13.93
8. Victor Myasnikov	SOV/RUS	13.94

Early in 1975 Guy Drut predicted that he would win the Olympics in a time of 13.28. By 1976 he was under so much pressure from French sports fans that he was forced to train in secret. The son of a French father and an English mother, he was born in Oignies, on the same street as France's last male track and field medalist, Michel Jazy. Drut got off to a good start, took a slight lead after the third hurdle and held it the rest of the way. He was the first person from a non-English-speaking country to win the high hurdles. Drut was an excellent all-around athlete, whose other feats included pole-vaulting 17 feet ¾ inch, long-jumping 24 feet ½ inch, and high-jumping 6 feet 7 inches. Drut later entered politics. He was elected to the national assembly and appointed Minister of Youth and Sport. However, in 2005 Drut was convicted of corruption and receiving misused funds, after it was discovered that in the early 1990s he had held a fictitious job at a construction company, for which he was paid 3,000 Euro per month. Drut was given a 15-month suspended sentence and a 50,000 Euro fine, but was pardoned by French president Jacques Chirac in 2006.

Thirty-three-year-old bronze medalist Willie Davenport was competing in his fourth Olympics. In 1980 he also took part in the Winter Olympics, placing twelfth in the four-man bobsled event.

1980 Moscow C: 22, N: 16, D: 7.27. WR: 13.00 (Renaldo Nehemiah)

1. Thomas Munkelt	GDR	13.39
2. Alejandro Casañas Ramírez	CUB	13.40
3. Aleksandr Puchkov	SOV/RUS	13.44
4. Andrei Prokofyev	SOV/RUS	13.49
5. Jan Pusty	POL	13.68
6. Arto Bryggare	FIN	13.76
7. Javier Moracho	SPA	13.78
8. Yuri Chervanyov	SOV/BLR	15.80

Renaldo Nehemiah, Dedy Cooper, and Greg Foster of the United States would have been favorites to finish at least first and second. Without them, the winning time was the slowest since 1964. Thomas Munkelt, a good-humored 27-year-old dental student, commented before the final, "I will drill through my opposition." He ended up winning by the skin of his teeth. Alejandro Casañas, having lost in 1976 by 0.03 second, experienced the frustration of coming even closer in 1980—0.01 second.

After the disintegration of East Germany, documents surfaced showing that Munkelt, while a member of the University Club of Leipzig, had taken anabolic steroids.

1984 Los Angeles C: 26, N: 17, D: 8.6. WR: 12.93 (Renaldo Nehemiah)

1. Roger Kingdom	USA	13.20 OR
2. Gregory Foster	USA	13.23
3. Arto Bryggare	FIN	13.40
4. Mark McKoy	CAN	13.45
5. Anthony Campbell	USA	13.55
6. Stephane Caristan	FRA	13.71
7. Carlos Sala	SPA	13.80
8. Jeff Glass	CAN	14.15

When world record holder Renaldo Nehemiah gave up his eligibility to become a professional football player, the title of World's Best High Hurdler passed to Greg Foster. In the opening round, Foster equaled Rod Milburn's 12-year-old Olympic record of 13.24. In the first semifinal, the record was tied again, this time by fast-improving newcomer Roger Kingdom. Ten minutes later, Foster, running into the wind, clocked yet another 13.24.

In the final, Foster hesitated slightly after the gun, thinking he had false-started. But he recovered quickly and moved into the lead by the second hurdle. About four meters from the finish, Foster, in lane 1, glanced to his right as Kingdom, in lane 8, pulled even and lunged for the tape. Kingdom thought he had finished second and didn't believe he had won until he watched a slow-motion replay of the finish on the huge video screen at the end of the stadium. Only then did he begin leaping up and down with joy.

Nigel Walker, who made it to the semi-finals while representing Great Britain, later played rugby for the national team of Wales.

1988 Seoul C: 41, N: 31, D: 9.28. WR: 12.93 (Renaldo Nehemiah)

1. Roger Kingdom	USA	12.98 OR
2. Colin Jackson	GBR	13.28
3. Anthony Campbell	USA	13.38
4. Vladimir Shishkin	SOV/RUS	13.51
5. Jonathan Ridgeon	GBR	13.52
6. Anthony Jarrett	GBR	13.54
7. Mark McKoy	CAN	13.61
8. Arthur Blake	USA	13.96

On July 16, 1985, Roger Kingdom pulled his left hamstring muscle. As it was his first major injury, he did not take it seriously enough, and it failed to heal properly. The following year he injured it again. By 1987 he was no longer competing. When Greg Foster won the Rome world championships, Kingdom watched the race on television. He even had to listen to one of the TV commentators refer to him as "the forgotten man of the hurdles." However, when the 1988 season began, Kingdom was fully healed. He entered the Olympics undefeated with victories in 16 straight meets. Arthur Blake caught a flyer in the final. Kingdom started in third place, took the lead after the fourth hurdle, and powered to an impressive three-meter victory.

1992 Barcelona C: 39, N: 27, D: 8.3. WR: 12.92 (Roger Kingdom)

1. Mark McKoy	CAN	13.12
2. Michael "Tony" Dees	USA	13.24
3. Jack Pierce	USA	13.26
4. Anthony Jarrett	GBR	13.26
5. Florian Schwarthoff	GER	13.29
6. Emilio Valle	CUB	13.41
7. Colin Jackson	GBR	13.46
8. Hughie Teape	GBR	14.00

In 1988 Mark McKoy finished seventh in the high hurdles and then fled Seoul in the wake of the Ben Johnson scandal. Because Canadian team officials had expected him to make himself available for the 4 × 100-meter relay, he was suspended for two years. McKoy also admitted that he had taken steroids. In 1991 Welsh hurdler Colin Jackson invited McKoy and his family to move into his home in Rhoose, South Wales. Jackson and his coach, Malcolm Arnold, rekindled McKoy's enthusiasm for hurdling. The two friends agreed not to compete against each other until the Olympics. In the meantime Jackson established himself as the Barcelona favorite by defeating the US champions Pierce and Dees.

In the opening round, Jackson ran a 13.10, the fastest heat time in history. The final, however, belonged to McKoy, who led from start to finish. At age 30, he was the oldest winner in the event's history. He was also Canada's first gold medalist in track since 1928. Born in Guyana, McKoy lived in England, attended university in the United States, married a German, and, after the Olympics, became an Austrian citizen. But on the day he became an Olympic champion, Mark McKoy literally wrapped himself in the Canadian flag.

1996 Atlanta C: 62, N: 40, D: 7.29. WR: 12.91 (Colin Jackson)

1. Allen Johnson	USA	12.95 OR
2. Mark Crear	USA	13.09
3. Florian Schwarthoff	GER	13.17
4. Colin Jackson	GBR	13.19
5. Emiio Valle Álvarez	CUB	13.20
6. Eugene Swift	USA	13.23
7. Kyle Vander-Kuyp	AUS	13.40
8. Erick Batte Herrera	CUB	13.43

Defending world champion Allen Johnson knocked down eight of the ten hurdles on his way to victory. He took the lead between the third and fourth hurdles and expanded it to more than two meters before stepping hard on the final hurdle. Mark Crear, who had broken his arm two weeks before the Olympics, cut Johnson's lead in half on the run-in.

2000 Sydney C: 37, N: 31, D: 9.25. WR: 12.91 (Colin Jackson)

1. Anier García Ortiz	CUB	13.00
2. Terrence Trammell	USA	13.16
3. Mark Crear	USA	13.22
4. Allen Johnson	USA	13.23
5. Colin Jackson	GBR	13.28
6. Florian Schwarthoff	GER	13.42
7. Dudley Dorival	HAI	13.49
8. Robert Kronberg	SWE	13.61

Despite having to overcome a series of injuries, defending champion Allen Johnson was considered a slight favorite over Anier García. García won the first semi-final, while the second went to Terrence Trammell, who had finished third at the US Olympic Trials. The final was held two hours later. Johnson knocked down all ten hurdles and was left without a medal, as was Colin Jackson, who was competing in his fourth straight Olympic final. Meanwhile, García was having no such problems. Halfway through the race, he was sure he would win, which he did by almost two meters. Both García and Trammell recorded personal bests. Johnson's setback was to prove only temporary, as he went on to win the world championship in both 2001 and 2003.

2004 Athens C: 47, N: 34, D: 8.27. WR: 12.91 (Colin Jackson)

1. Liu Xiang	CHN	12.91 EWR
2. Terrence Trammell	USA	13.18
3. Anier García Ortiz	CUB	13.20
4. Maurice Wignall	JAM	13.21
5. Staņislavs Olijars	LAT	13.21
6. Charles Allen	CAN	13.48
7. Matheus Inocêncio	BRA	13.49
8. Ladji Doucouré	FRA	13.76

The son of a Shanghai truck driver, Liu Xiang initially trained in the high jump after being selected for a Junior Sports School in Shanghai in the fourth grade. Despite winning a national championship, Liu was asked to leave after bone tests revealed that he would not grow tall enough for a high jumper. Liu eventually switched to the hurdles and became one of the first Chinese athletes to take part in a massive scientific study to improve their techniques. Starting in 2001, the China Institute of Sport Science (CISS) recorded nearly every race Liu ran, often with three simultaneous cameras. In Athens, all three of his qualifying races were recorded and immediately analyzed by a team of scientists, with reports sent via email to Liu and his coach.

The first major surprise of the competition came in the quarterfinals, when Allen Johnson, the 1996 Olympic champion and the reigning world champion, hit two barriers, and then fell on the ninth and was disqualified. Maurice Wignall edged out Liu in the first semifinal, while Ladji Doucouré set a personal best of 13.06 seconds to win the second semi. In the final, Liu and 2000 silver medalist Terrence Trammell got out of the blocks the fastest, and ran evenly for four hurdles. By the midpoint, Liu's clean technique allowed him to pull ahead of Trammell, who made contact with several hurdles. Meanwhile, Doucouré moved up into second place, but hit the ninth hurdle and crashed against the tenth, finishing last. Liu recorded a time of 12.91 seconds, unexpectedly matching Colin Jackson's 11-year-old world record.

Liu was the first Chinese man ever to win an Olympic track gold medal. Asked how he planned to celebrate his victory, Liu responded, "Karaoke! I love karaoke. That is how I celebrate after all my medals at big championships."

On July 11, 2006, Liu gained undisputed control of the world record, setting a time of 12.88 seconds at a Super Grand Prix meet in Lausanne, Switzerland.

2008 Beijing C: 42, N: 32, D: 8.21. WR: 12.87 (Dayron Robles)

1. Dayron Robles Planes	CUB	12.93
2. David Payne	USA	13.17
3. David Oliver	USA	13.18
4. Ladji Doucouré	FRA	13.24
5. Artur Noga	POL	13.36
6. Maurice Wignall	JAM	13.46
7. Richard Phillips	JAM	13.60
8. Jackson Quiñónez Vernaza	SPA	13.69

Of all the events at the 2008 Olympics, none was more important to the host country China than the 110-meter hurdles. Four years earlier in Athens, Liu Xiang became the second-biggest superstar in China (behind only NBA basketball player Yao Ming) after winning China's first-ever track and field gold medal. Now, with the eyes of the world watching, the expectations of 1.3 billion Chinese rested on Liu's shoulders.

Liu's record over the previous four years gave reason for optimism about his medal chances. In August 2005 he finished second behind Ladji Doucouré at the world championships in Helsinki. One year later he set a world record, and the year after that he won the world championship title in Osaka, Japan, beating Terrence Trammell and David Payne of the United States. In the lead-up to the Beijing Olympics, however, Liu scaled back his competition schedule, preferring to train in isolation. His enormous popularity in China, however, meant that he had to use decoy cars to get to and from his training sessions, simply to avoid being mobbed by fans.

Liu's main challenge was expected to come from 21-year-old Dayron Robles of Cuba. Born in the province of Guantánamo, Robles had come to international attention in 2007 when he finished fourth in the world championships (behind Liu, Trammell and Payne) before going on to win the World Athletics Final and the Shanghai Grand Prix in China, beating Liu in the process. On June 12, two months before the Olympics, at a meet in Ostrava, Czech Republic, Robles broke Liu's world record, dropping it to 12.87 seconds. Although competitors, Robles and Liu were also friends, and the two would often offer each other congratulations after races.

The first round of competition held two big surprises. In the fifth heat, double Olympic silver medalist

Terrence Trammell cleared the first hurdle before veering off the track with a hamstring injury. In the following heat, Liu made his appearance in front of a stadium full of cheering Chinese fans. Grimacing and rubbing his right hamstring before getting into his crouch, Liu pulled up lame just steps into the first round heat. After a false start was called on Dutch hurdler Marcel van der Westen, the stunned crowd watched as Liu pulled off his lane numbers and limped off the track, the victim of a long-standing Achilles tendon injury that had resurfaced two days before the heat.

With Liu absent, the path was clear for Robles. He advanced easily through his quarter-final and semi-final heats, and dominated the final, taking the lead out of the starting blocks and recording the second-fastest time in Olympic history, behind Liu's 2004 time. The 26-year-old Payne edged out David Oliver at the line by one-hundredth of a second.

Some of the leading hurdlers in the 2008 Olympic competition would return at the 2011 world championships in a final that was marked by controversy. Robles was leading, but Liu was closing fast in the lane to his right. Robles knocked over the eighth hurdle. As he struggled on, his right arm hit the oncoming Liu, who was running at the edge of his own lane. Liu lost his momentum. Robles went on to cross the finish line first, with Liu in third. Robles was disqualified and the championship went to a surprised Jason Richardson of the united States.

400-METER HURDLES

Contestants in this event must clear ten three-foot-high hurdles. The distance from the starting line to the first hurdle is 45 meters; the distance between hurdles is 35 meters; and the distance from the last hurdle to the finish line is 40 meters. Athletes from the United States have won this event 17 of the 22 times they have entered. The only times the winner came from a non-English-speaking country were in 1980 when the United States boycotted the Olympics and in 2004.

1896 not held

1900 Paris C: 5, N: 4, D: 7.15. WR (440 yards): 57.2 (Godfrey Shaw)

1. J. Walter Tewksbury	USA	57.6
2. Henri Tauzin	FRA	58.3e
3. George Orton	CAN	58.8e

DNS: William Lewis (USA)

The results were a great disappointment to the French, since the Americans were unfamiliar with this event. This didn't prevent Tewksbury from easily defeating the previously unbeaten Tauzin. The "hurdles" were actually 30-foot-long telephone poles. A water jump was added just before the finish.

1904 St. Louis C: 4, N: 1, D: 8.31. WR (440 yards): 57.2 (Godfrey Shaw)

1. Harry Hillman	USA	53.0
2. Frank Waller	USA	53.2
3. George Poage	USA	56.8e
4. George Varnell	USA	—

An oddity in the world of US athletics, Harry Hillman was a 22-year-old bank teller who had never attended college. Writing in the September 1905 issue of *Physical Culture* magazine, Hillman advised aspiring hurdlers to avoid candy, pastries, tobacco, and meat, although he did recommend swallowing whole raw eggs, which he claimed were "excellent for the wind and stomach." He concluded by advising young men in the business world to take up athletics because it "gives one the needed virility demanded by modern business life." Hillman's time was not allowed as a world record because he tipped over one hurdle, and because the hurdles were only two feet six inches high anyway. George Poage was the first black runner to win an Olympic medal. On April 24, 1909, Harry Hillman and Lawson Robertson set a world record of 11.0 seconds in the 100-yard three-legged race.

1906 not held

1908 London C: 15, N: 6, D: 7.22. WR (440 yards): 57.2 (Godfrey Shaw)

1. Charles Bacon	USA	55.0	WR
2. Harry Hillman	USA	55.3	
3. Leonard "Jimmy" Tremeer	GBR	57.0	
4. Leslie Burton	GBR	58.0	

Bacon won a close and exciting contest despite the fact that he went over a hurdle in the wrong lane midway through the race. When the judges measured the course he had taken, they discovered that he had actually run farther than if he had stayed in his own lane, so he was saved from disqualification.

1912 not held

1920 Antwerp C: 19, N: 9, D: 8.16. WR (440 yards): 54.2 (John Norton)

1. Frank Loomis	USA	54.0	WR
2. John Norton	USA	54.6e	
3. August Desch	USA	54.7e	
4. Georges "Géo" André	FRA	54.8e	
5. Carl-Axel Christiernsson	SWE	55.4e	
6. Charles Daggs	USA	55.7e	

After the final, three American flags were raised and the European spectators watched with fascination as the US team celebrated by chanting, "Rah rah rah, U-S-A. A-M-E-R-I-C-A. Loomis! Loomis! Loomis!" Fourth-place finisher Géo André had won a silver medal in the high jump in 1908.

1924 Paris C: 23, N: 13, D: 7.7. WR: 54.0 (Frank Loomis)

1. F. Morgan Taylor	USA	52.6
2. Erik Vilén	FIN	53.8 OR
3. Ivan Riley	USA	54.1
4. Georges "Géo" André	FRA	56.1

DISQ: Charles Brookins (USA), Frederick Blackett (GBR)

Taylor's world record time was not allowed because he knocked down one hurdle, thus violating the rules of the time. Brookins finished second, but was disqualified for running out of his lane and clearing a hurdle improperly. Consequently, it was Erik Vilén who was credited with an Olympic record, even though he finished only third. "Géo" André again made the final, this time at age 34—sixteen years after his first Olympic appearance. Even after his retirement from competition he continued to be a late achiever. Having served as a pilot during World War I, he was anxious to do his part again in World War II. Too old to be a fighter pilot, he joined the infantry and was killed by the Germans near Tunis on May 4, 1943. He was 53 years old.

F. Morgan Taylor, 1924
Winner of the 1924 400-meter hurdles.

1928 Amsterdam C: 27, N: 16, D: 7.30. WR: 52.0 (F. Morgan Taylor)

1. David Burghley	GBR	53.4 OR
2. Frank Cuhel	USA	53.6
3. F. Morgan Taylor	USA	53.6
4. Sten Pettersson	SWE	53.8
5. Thomas Livingston-Learmonth	GBR	54.2
6. Luigi Facelli	ITA	55.8

David George Brownlow Cecil, Lord Burghley was one of the most popular winners of the 1928 Games. Heir to the Marquess of Exeter, he first appeared in the Olympics in 1924, when he was eliminated in the first round of the 110-meter hurdles. In 1927, during his last year at Cambridge, he caused a sensation by running around the Great Court at Trinity College in the time it took the Trinity Clock to toll 12 o'clock. A completely distorted version of this event was presented in the film *Chariots of Fire,* in which the feat is credited to Harold Abrahams. For this reason, Lord Burghley, who was then 76 years old, reportedly refused to view the film. Actually, Lord Burghley was not the first person to accomplish the Great Court run. It had been done in the 1890s by Sir Walter Borley Fletcher, but in Sir Walter's time the clock took five more seconds to complete its toll.

Lord Burghley, 1928
Lord Burghley, winner of the 1928 400-meter hurdles, clears a barrier in classic style during a preliminary heat.

Burghley was an extremely colorful character, who once set another unusual record by racing around the upper promenade deck of the ocean liner *Queen Mary* in 57 seconds, dressed in street clothes. Once he showed up for a meet in Antwerp but was denied admission at the main gate and told to circle the stadium and enter by the competitors' gate. Burghley took a few steps back, tightened his bowler hat on his head, got a firm grip on his attaché case, hurdled the four-foot fence, and dashed off before the astonished guards could react. Burghley is believed to be the first hurdler to place matchboxes on hurdles and practice knocking over the matchboxes with his lead foot without touching the hurdle. It is not true, despite his portrayal in *Chariots of Fire,* that he put glasses of champagne on the hurdles as well. In the words of his daughter, Lady Victoria Leatham, "He was never one to waste champagne." Burghley was elected to Parliament in 1931, but was granted a leave of absence to compete in the 1932 Olympics in Los Angeles. He later served as governor of Bermuda for three years, as well as president of the British Amateur Athletic Association for 40 years, president of the International Amateur Athletic Federation for 30 years, and as a member of the International Olympic Committee for 48 years. He was also chairman of the Organizing Committee of the 1948 Olympics.

1932 Los Angeles C: 18, N: 13, D: 8.1. WR: 52.0 (F. Morgan Taylor)

1. Robert Tisdall	IRL	51.7		(51.67)
2. Glenn Hardin	USA	51.9	WR	(51.85)
3. F. Morgan Taylor	USA	52.0		(51.96)
4. David Burghley	GBR	52.2		(52.01)
5. Luigi Facelli	ITA	53.0		
6. Johan Kjell Areskoug	SWE	54.6		

Bob Tisdall, a well-known athlete while a student at Cambridge, had run the 400-meter hurdles only once when, in March 1932, he decided to try out for the Irish Olympic team. He quit his job in London and, with his wife, moved into a converted railway carriage in an orchard in Sussex, where he spent the next three months training, although he had no hurdles to practice with. He won a match race in early June and then, on June 18, finished first in the All-Ireland Championships in a time of 54.2 seconds. Less than a month later he was on his way to Los Angeles with the rest of the Irish team. Weakened by the two-week journey, he stayed in bed for 15 hours a day until the morning of his first-round heat. Full of energy, he qualified easily. In the semifinals, he surprised even himself by winning in 52.8, equaling the Olympic record that had been set by Glenn Hardin in the first semi. The final was only Tisdall's seventh race at the distance, and he faced not only Hardin, but former champions Morgan Taylor and Lord Burghley as well. Completely relaxed, Tisdall took the lead early and approached the last hurdle five yards ahead of the others.

"At that moment," Tisdall recalled, "I experienced a strange feeling of loneliness. . . . Everything was strangely quiet. . . . I began to wonder if the rest of the field had fallen over." He mistimed his leap, knocked over the barrier, and stumbled for five or six yards before regaining his balance. Hardin and Taylor closed fast, but Tisdall beat them to the tape in world record time. According to the rules of the day, which were not changed until 1938, his record was disallowed because he had failed to clear the final barrier. So Glenn Hardin entered the record books as world record holder even though he only finished second.

Four days after his hurdles triumph, Bob Tisdall competed in the decathlon. Although he had never before contested the discus, the javelin or the pole vault, he still managed to finish in eighth place.

1936 Berlin C: 32, N: 20, D: 8.4. WR: 50.6 (Glenn Hardin)

1. Glenn Hardin	USA	52.4
2. John Loaring	CAN	52.7
3. Miguel White	PHI	52.8
4. Joseph Patterson	USA	53.0
5. Sylvio de Magalhães Padilha	BRA	54.0
6. Christos Mantikas	GRE	54.2

On July 26, 1934, while running in Stockholm, Glenn Hardin of Louisiana took a full second off the existing world record. His time of 50.6 was not beaten for more than 19 years. Following his second-place finish in the 1932 Olympics, Hardin never lost another race. In Berlin, he caught the fading Joe Patterson in the stretch and won by four yards. Patterson died in a submarine accident on May 23, 1939.

1948 London C: 25, N: 17, D: 7.31. WR: 50.6 (Glenn Hardin)

1. Leroy Cochran	USA	51.1	OR
2. Duncan White	SRL	51.8	
3. Rune Larsson	SWE	52.2	
4. Richard Ault	USA	52.4	
5. Yves Cros	FRA	53.3	
6. Ottavio Missoni	ITA	54.0	

The ninth of ten children from Richton, Mississippi, Roy Cochran won a second gold medal in the 4 × 400-meter relay.

1952 Helsinki C: 40, N: 24, D: 7.21. WR: 50.6 (Glenn Hardin)

1. Charles Moore	USA	50.8	OR	(51.06)
2. Yuri Lituyev	SOV/RUS	51.3		(51.57)
3. John Holland	NZL	52.2		(52.26)

4. Anatoly Yulin	SOV/BLR	52.8	(52.81)
5. Harold Whittle	GBR	53.1	(53.36)
6. Armando Filiput	ITA	54.4	(54.49)

Remarkably, the six finalists cleared the first five hurdles in unison. Then Moore, whose father had been an alternate on the 1924 US Olympic team, pulled ahead. Lituyev drew even by the eighth hurdle, but Moore moved ahead again and won by four yards. Moore's near-world record time was quite extraordinary considering that the track had been soaked by rain. He also ran 50.8 in the second round.

1956 Melbourne C: 28, N: 13, D: 11.24. WR: 49.5 (Glenn Davis)

1. Glenn Davis	USA	50.1 EOR	(50.29)
2. S. Edward Southern	USA	50.8	(50.94)
3. Joshua Culbreath	USA	51.6	(51.74)
4. Yuri Lituyev	SOV/RUS	51.7	(51.91)
5. David Lean	AUS	51.8	(51.93)
6. Gerhardus Potgieter	SAF	56.0	

On June 29, at the US Olympic trials, Glenn Davis set a world record of 49.5, pressed by Eddie Southern, who ran 49.7. In Melbourne Southern set an Olympic record of 50.1 in the semifinals, then set the pace in the final. Davis caught him midway and surged ahead at the seventh hurdle to win decisively. Potgieter was in third place when he hit the final hurdle and fell.

1960 Rome C: 34, N: 23, D: 9.2. WR: 49.2 (Glenn Davis)

1. Glenn Davis	USA	49.3 OR	(49.51)
2. Clifton Cushman	USA	49.6	(49.77)
3. Richard Howard	USA	49.7	(49.90)
4. Helmut Janz	GER	49.9	(50.05)
5. Jussi Rintamäki	FIN	50.8	(50.98)
6. Bruno Galliker	SWI	51.0	(51.11)

"Running scared," Glenn Davis ran off-stride until the seventh hurdle, when he regained his poise, passed Janz at the ninth hurdle and Howard at the tenth, to win by two meters. Silver medalist Cliff Cushman was lost in action in Vietnam in 1966. Bronze medalist Dick Howard died of a heroin overdose in 1967. They were 28 and 32 years old, respectively.

1964 Tokyo C: 39, N: 25, D: 10.16. WR: 49.1 (Warren "Rex" Cawley)

1. Warren "Rex" Cawley	USA	49.6
2. John Cooper	GBR	50.1
3. Salvatore Morale	ITA	50.1
4. Gary Knoke	AUS	50.4
5. James Luck	USA	50.5
6. Roberto Frinolli	ITA	50.7
7. Vasily Anisimov	SOV/UKR	51.1
8. Wilfried Geeroms	BEL	51.4

Rex Cawley ran off-stride until the sixth hurdle and was still three yards behind Frinolli at the eighth hurdle. Then the world record holder turned on his speed and pulled away to a clear victory. Silver medalist John Cooper was one of the 346 people who died in the famous Turkish Air Lines plane crash over France on March 3, 1974. He was 33 years old.

1968 Mexico City C: 30, N: 24, D: 10.15. WR: 48.8 (Geoffrey Vanderstock)

1. David Hemery	GBR	48.12 WR
2. Gerhard Hennige	GER	49.02
3. John Sherwood	GBR	49.12
4. Geoffrey Vanderstock	USA	49.07
5. Vyacheslav Skomorokhov	SOV/UKR	49.12
6. Ronald Whitney	USA	49.27
7. Rainer Schubert	GER	49.30
8. Roberto Frinolli	ITA	50.13

The 1968 final had all the makings of a spectacular race. The favorites were world record holder Geoff Vanderstock, fellow American Ron Whitney, and David Hemery, who had beaten Vanderstock at the NCAA championships. Hemery, although born in England, had spent 10 of his 24 years in the United States. Other finalists included John Sherwood, whose wife, Sheila, had won a silver medal in the long jump the day before, Vyacheslav Skomorokhov, who was deaf, and 1964 finalist Roberto Frinolli, who had stripped down to his bikini-style black jock strap before the race, unaware that he was being shown live on US television. Hemery was in lane 6, just inside Ron Whitney, the man he most feared because of his strong finishing kick.

Frinolli and Vanderstock were off quickest, but Hemery had taken the lead by the third hurdle. He passed the halfway mark in 23.3 and demoralized the rest of the field with an awesome display of speed in which he gained at least a yard between and over each of the next five hurdles. He crossed the finish line with an eight-yard lead, the largest winning margin since 1924. While millions of people around the world marveled at his extraordinary performance, Hemery himself wasn't even sure he had won. He had looked to his right at the end to check for Ron Whitney, but had failed to look to his left. It wasn't until he was approached by a BBC camera crew that his uncertainty was erased. At the victory ceremony, Hemery received his gold medal from David Burghley, who had won the same event 40 years earlier.

John Sherwood earned his bronze medal the day after his wife Sheila took a silver in the long jump.

Final mention should be made of US hurdler Boyd Gittins, who was eliminated at the US Olympic semi-trials when a pigeon dropping hit him in the eye and dislodged his contact lens just before the first hurdle. Fortunately, he won a runoff to qualify for the final Olympic trials, and then made the team. Unfortunately, a leg injury forced him to withdraw from his first-round heat.

1972 Munich C: 37, N: 25, D: 9.2. WR: 48.12 (David Hemery)

1. John Akii-Bua	UGA	47.82 WR
2. Ralph Mann	USA	48.51
3. David Hemery	GBR	48.52
4. James Seymour	USA	48.64
5. Rainer Schubert	GER	49.65
6. Yevgeny Gavrilenko	SOV/BLR	49.66
7. Stavros Tziortzis	GRE/CYP	49.66
8. Yuri Zorin	SOV/RUS	50.25

The second semifinal was filled with misfortune. James Seymour and Australia's Gary Knoke, running in the two outside lanes, mistook the echo of the starter's gun for a second shot and thought a false start had been declared. Seymour, in lane 7, realized his mistake quickly enough to avoid disaster and win the heat anyway, but Knoke, in lane 8, was unable to recover, and finished last. As the runners cleared the tenth hurdle, East Germany's Christian Rudolph, in lane 1, stumbled and fell heavily into lane 2, right into the path of Dieter-Wolfgang Büttner of West Germany, who also fell. Neither man was able to finish. The judges decided not to order a rerun, since Büttner was only in fifth place at the time of the mishap.

In the final David Hemery actually set an even faster pace than he had in Mexico City, covering the first 200 meters in 22.8 seconds. Thus it came as quite a shock when he discovered that John Akii-Bua, running in lane 1, was right beside him with 100 meters to go. Akii-Bua surged ahead between the eighth and ninth hurdles and won by six meters. Despite the fact that he had just set a world record, Uganda's first gold medalist kept right on going over the next two flights of hurdles. Akii-Bua, who was also Uganda's decathlon champion, said that he was "scared to death" when he learned that he had drawn lane 1. "When you are in lane 1," he said, "you are always the loser. I couldn't sleep that night." Akii-Bua's father had eight wives and 43 children, 29 of whom were still alive in 1972. A police instructor, John Akii-Bua fled Uganda in 1979, following the overthrow of Idi Amin, and spent a month in a Kenyan jail before he was recognized and released. He eventually returned and in 1987 was arrested again for illegal possession of a submachine gun. At the time of his death in 1997, at the age of 47, Akii-Bua was working again as a senior police superintendent.

1976 Montreal C: 22, N: 16, D: 7.25. WR: 47.82 (John Akii-Bua)

1. Edwin Moses	USA	47.63 WR
2. Michael Shine	USA	48.69
3. Yevgeny Gavrilenko	SOV/BLR	49.45
4. Quentin Wheeler	USA	49.86
5. José Carvalho	POR	49.94
6. Yanko Bratanov	BUL	50.03
7. Damaso Alfonso	CUB	50.19
8. Alan Pascoe	GBR	51.29

The African boycott prevented a potentially historic showdown. No matter how sympathetic one is to the movement to bring self-determination for blacks in South Africa, it is difficult to not be cynical when you realize that John Akii-Bua was not allowed to compete in Montreal because the leader of his nation's government, the notorious Idi Amin, was offended by human rights violations in another country.

With Akii-Bua gone and Alan Pascoe still recovering from a leg injury, the competition turned into a one-man show. Edwin Moses was a 20-year-old engineering and physics major at Atlanta's Morehouse College, a school without a track and which he had entered with an academic rather than an athletic scholarship. Basically self-coached, Moses had entered only one 400-meter hurdles race before March 27, 1976. The Olympics was

Edwin Moses, 1976

his first international meet. Moses wore down his last challenger, Yevgeny Gavrilenko, by the seventh hurdle and won by eight meters, the largest winning margin in the history of the event. Afterward, Moses said that his major regret was that training for the Olympics had interfered with his studies, allowing his grade-point average to dip to 3.57.

1980 Moscow C: 22, N: 19, D: 7.26. WR: 47.13 (Edwin Moses)

1. Volker Beck	GDR	48.70
2. Vasyl Arkhypenko	SOV/UKR	48.86
3. Gary Oakes	GBR	49.11
4. Mykola Vasilyev	SOV/UKR	49.34
5. Rok Kopitar	YUG/SLO	49.67
6. Horia Toboc	ROM	49.84
7. Franz Meier	SWI	50.00
8. Yanko Bratanov	BUL	56.35

The year 1980 saw a severely devalued competition as a result of the Jimmy Carter boycott. The preboycott favorite, Edwin Moses, set a world record of 47.13 on July 3, three weeks before the Olympics. The silver medal had been expected to be a toss-up among Harald Schmid of West Germany and James Walker and David Lee of the United States. In their absence, Volker Beck passed Arkhypenko on the run-in. His winning time was the slowest since 1964.

1984 Los Angeles C: 45, N: 30, D: 8.5. WR: 47.02 (Edwin Moses)

1. Edwin Moses	USA	47.75
2. Danny Harris	USA	48.13
3. Harald Schmid	GER	48.19
4. Sven Nylander	SWE	48.97
5. El Hadji Amadou Bâ	SEN	49.28
6. Tranel Hawkins	USA	49.42
7. Michel Zimmerman	BEL	50.69
8. Henry Amike	NGR	53.78

On August 26, 1977, Edwin Moses lost a race to Harald Schmid in Berlin. One week later in Düsseldorf he beat Schmid by 15 yards to begin an incredible winning streak that took him through 22 countries and extended, by the time of the 1984 Olympics, to 102 races including 89 finals. By this time the 48-second barrier had been broken 32 times: once by John Akii-Bua, once by Andre Phillips, three times by Harald Schmid, and 27 times by Edwin Moses, who also owned the nine fastest times ever recorded. Needless to say, Moses was a prohibitive favorite to win what should have been his third gold medal.

After being distracted at the starting line by the hundreds of cameras clicking away at him, Moses got off to a quick start and was never headed. Second place went to 18-year-old Danny Harris, who had not run his first 400-meter hurdle race until March 17, 1984. On June 4, 1987, it was Harris who finally ended Moses' finals winning streak at 107 by defeating him 47.56 to 47.69 in a race in Madrid. The streak had lasted nine years, nine months, and nine days.

1988 Seoul C: 37, N: 28, D: 9.25. WR: 47.02 (Edwin Moses)

1. Andre Phillips	USA	47.19 OR
2. Amadou Dia Bâ	SEN	47.23
3. Edwin Moses	USA	47.56
4. Kevin Young	USA	47.94
5. Winthrop Graham	JAM	48.04
6. Kriss Akabusi	GBR	48.69
7. Harald Schmid	GER	48.76
8. Edgar Itt	GER	48.78

Following Danny Harris' defeat of Edwin Moses in Madrid, the next big 400-meter hurdles race came at the world championships in Rome on September 1, 1987. Moses won that contest, leaning across the finish line in 47.46 to beat Harris and Harald Schmid by a mere six inches.

At the 1988 US Olympic trials, Moses won again, clocking 47.37 in the first race in which five runners went under 48 seconds. Andre Phillips was second in 47.58, with Danny Harris beaten back into fifth.

In Seoul the 29-year-old Phillips, who had lost more than 20 times to the 33-year-old Moses without a single victory, chose a strategy that mirrored Moses' usual tactic—racing as hard as possible through three hurdles, then surging again at the seventh hurdle. Phillips reacted quickly to the gun and led by almost two meters after the third hurdle. Moses gradually closed the gap, then inched ahead as they reached the seventh barrier. Between the seventh and ninth hurdles, Phillips, following his plan perfectly, regained a clear lead. Moses faded, while Amadou Bâ came on with a rush, passing Moses and almost catching Phillips. Phillips' first thought after he realized he had won was not that he was the Olympic champion, but that he had beaten Moses. Both Phillips and Bâ ran the race of their lives, the former improving his personal record by .32, the latter by .80. Phillips' margin of victory was provided by the seven hundredths of a second he gained over Bâ between the gun and his first stride. Bâ earned Senegal's first Olympic medal, although in 1960, Abdoulaye Seye, another Senegalese, had won a bronze in the 200 meters while competing for France.

Phillips went on to become a high school special education teacher.

1992 Barcelona C: 47, N: 35, D: 8.6. WR: 47.02 (Edwin Moses)

1. Kevin Young	USA	46.78	WR
2. Winthrop Graham	JAM	47.66	
3. Kriss Akabusi	GBR	47.82	
4. Stéphane Diagana	FRA	48.13	
5. Niklas Wallenlind	SWE	48.63	
6. Oleg Tverdokhleb	UKR	48.63	
7. Stéphane Caristan	FRA	48.86	
8. David Patrick	USA	49.26	

When Kevin Young arrived at the Olympic Village he taped to the walls of his room pieces of paper with the time "46.89" written on them. It was true that he was one of the favorites, having defeated world champion Samuel Matete of Zambia three times at the beginning of July. But breaking Edwin Moses' nine-year-old world record seemed a bit overly optimistic considering that Young's personal best was only 47.72—and that was set at the Olympic trials not of 1992, but of 1988. However, in the second semifinal (the first was won by Kriss Akabusi in 48.01), Young ran a 47.63. But he also suffered his first loss of the season because Winthrop Graham hit the finish line in 47.62. The big news of the second semi was that Matete, who placed third, was disqualified for knocking over the last hurdle—in the lane next to his.

In the final Young simply ran the race of his life. This is how his opponents described it:

Kriss Akabusi: "I thought I was running fast, but when Kevin came flying past me—and I mean flying—I thought, 'This guy means business.'"

Winthrop Graham: "It shocked me to come off the turn and see how far ahead Kevin was. I'd never had anybody be that far ahead of me going into the last stretch. It exhausted me right there."

David Patrick: "When I hit the line, I looked at the clock and thought, 'No wonder I'm so far behind.'"

Young smashed the last hurdle, but he was so far ahead that he was able to thrust his right arm into the air in triumph eight meters from the finish. "I always wanted to put my hand up at the end of a race," he said, "and I finally got my chance today."

1996 Atlanta C: 55, N: 35, D: 8.1. WR: 46.78 (Kevin Young)

1. Derrick Adkins	USA	47.54
2. Samuel Matete	ZAM	47.78
3. Calvin Davis	USA	47.96
4. Sven Nylander	SWE	47.98
5. Rohan Robinson	AUS	48.30
6. Fabrizio Mori	ITA	48.41
7. Everson Teixeira	BRA	48.57
8. Eronilde de Araújo	BRA	48.78

At the 1992 United States Olympic Trials, Derrick Adkins, hampered by an ankle injury, finished fourth, one place away from a trip to the Barcelona Olympics. When the Olympic final came on television, Adkins couldn't bring himself to watch it and went to the local mall instead.

In 1995, Adkins won the world championship, beating friendly rival Samuel Matete 47.98 to 48.03. A member of the Bemba tribe and the son of a truck driver, Matete began hurdling using five hurdles he built from kindling he found in his backyard. Later he discovered three rusty hurdles in storage at Lusaka Stadium and he used these for the next three years until he finished fifth at the world junior championships. By 1991, he was champion of the world.

Adkins' father was a former hurdler who coached him through high school. Although he was born in Lakeview, New York, Derrick lived in Atlanta for several years and earned a degree in mechanical engineering from Georgia Tech. At the 1996 Olympics, Adkins would experience both the pressure and the excitement of competing in front of a hometown crowd. In fact, Adkins was feeling suicidal and, in April 1996, he was diagnosed as being chronically clinically depressed as a result of a chemical imbalance in his brain. He began taking anti-depressants and his mood improved. However his athletic performance declined, so, on the eve of the US Olympic Trials, he stopped taking the medication.

While many elite-level rivals avoid each other outside of major competitions, Adkins and Matete had faced each other 37 times in the past five years, with Matete leading the series 22-15, including a 4-1 advantage in the 1996 pre-Olympic season.

In the opening heats, he recorded a 48.21: the fastest heat time in history. If he had matched that time in the semifinals, the final might have been a different race. Adkins won the first semi in 47.76. In the second semi, every runner but Matete beat or tied his personal best. The race was won in 47.91 by Calvin Davis, a converted 400-meter flat runner who began competing in hurdles races only 3½ months before the Olympics. Davis trained with and was mentored by none other than Samuel Matete. Matete eased up at the end of the semifinal heat and was nipped for second by Everson Teixeira. This put Matete in the bottom four draw for lanes for the final and he ended up in the sharp lane one.

Davis smashed the first hurdle, but recovered quickly and led in the early going. Sven Nylander moved in front at the midway point. Adkins caught Nylander in the last turn and entered the home straight with a lead that he wouldn't relinquish. Matete closed fast and Davis came from behind to outlean Nylander for the bronze.

In the category of Overcoming Adversity, credit

goes to Poland's Paweł Januszewski. At the Atlanta Olympics, Januszewski finished third in his first-round heat but didn't advance to the semifinal. In November 1997, Januszewski was severely injured in an automobile accident. He went into a coma, last rites were performed and his obituary appeared abroad. In fact, Januszewski did not die. Nine months later he won the European championship and in 2000 he placed sixth at the Sydney Olympics.

2000 Sydney C: 62, N: 45, D: 9.27. WR: 46.78 (Kevin Young)

1. Angelo Taylor	USA	47.50
2. Hadi Somayli	SAU	47.53
3. Llewellyn Herbert	SAF	47.81
4. James Carter	USA	48.04
5. Eronilde de Araújo	BRA	48.34
6. Paweł Januszewski	POL	48.44
7. Fabrizio Mori	ITA	48.78
8. Hennadiy Horbenko	UKR	49.01

Samuel Matete, at 31 the second-oldest of the 62 competitors, recorded the fastest time of the opening round, 48.98. He clocked the same time in the semifinals, but was eliminated: The first semi was won by Hadi Somayli, who had spent the previous five months training with John Smith in Los Angeles. The second semi matched the two favorites, Llewellyn Herbert and 21-year-old Angelo Taylor, with Herbert gaining the edge. The third semi went to James Carter, who alienated the crowd by taunting his rivals in the final strides.

Taylor was upset when he learned that he would run the final from lane one, but he received a slew of encouragement from family, friends and coaches culminating in a call on his cell phone while he was receiving a massage an hour before the race. The caller was his old high school teammate from Atlanta, Terrence Trammell, who had earned the silver medal in the 110-meter hurdles two days earlier. Trammell concluded by urging Taylor to think of lane one as a good sign beause it represented first place. Somayli led for most of the final and was still ahead as the runners entered the final straight, while Taylor did not start moving up from fourth place until after the eighth hurdle. Somayli was the first to clear the tenth and last hurdle, but Taylor caught him six meters from the finish line and managed to win by less than a foot. The first four finishers all set personal records.

Taylor gained notoriety following the 2004 Olympics, when he was arrested twice within three months for child molestation, after being caught having sex in his car with two different 15-year-old girls. In 2006 he pleaded guilty to all charges and was sentenced to three years probation and a $2,500 fine.

2004 Athens C: 35, N: 24, D: 8.26. WR: 46.78 (Kevin Young)

1. Félix Sánchez	DOM	47.63
2. Danny McFarlane	JAM	48.11
3. Naman Keita	FRA	48.26
4. James Carter	USA	48.58
5. Bayano Kamani	PAN	48.74
6. Marek Plawgo	POL	49.00
7. Alwyn Myburgh	SAF	49.07
8. Bennie Brazell	USA	49.51

Félix Sánchez was born to Dominican parents in New York City and grew up in Southern California. When a broken wrist forced him to take a break from his high school baseball team, he turned to track at the age of fifteen. After failing to make the finals at the 2000 Olympics, Sánchez began to wear a red plastic souvenir bracelet with blinking white lights at every race to remind himself of what happened in Sydney. Apparently the reminder helped, as Sánchez went on to win the 2001 and 2003 world championships, and he entered the 2004 Olympics as an overwhelming favorite, having won 35 straight finals. In the semifinals in Athens, Sánchez recorded the fastest time, 47.93, while Danny McFarlane, in only his second year of competitive hurdling, won the second semi in 48.00. After a false start by Sánchez and James Carter, the final got underway, and the two led through the first six hurdles. Carter opened a slight lead between the seventh and eighth hurdles, but Sánchez surged past him before the ninth barrier and never relinquished the lead. Carter faded in the final stretch, and McFarlane moved up to second, while Naman Keita came up from seventh place to nip Carter for the bronze. It was Carter's second fourth-place Olympic finish and the first US shutout in the event since 1968. Sánchez was the first Domincan to earn a gold medal in any sport.

2008 Beijing C: 26, N: 19, D: 8.18. WR: 46.78 (Kevin Young)

1. Angelo Taylor	USA	47.25
2. Kerron Clement	USA	47.98
3. Bershawn Jackson	USA	48.06
4. Danny McFarlane	JAM	48.30
5. Louis "L.J." van Zyl	SAF	48.42
6. Marek Plawgo	POL	48.52
7. Markino Buckley	JAM	48.60
8. Periklis Iakovakis	GRE	49.96

The US fielded an unusually strong team, including reigning world champion Kerron Clement, 2005 world champion Bershawn Jackson, and 2000 Olympic champion Angelo Taylor.

Twenty-five-year-old Bershawn Jackson was raised in Liberty City, an impoverished inner-city neighborhood of Miami. Nicknamed "Batman" for his large ears, Jackson rose to prominence after winning the US nationals in 2003, and then the world championship title in 2005. Jackson had had difficulty clearing the 10th hurdle in competition, however; in 2004 he missed a berth at the Olympics after clipping the final hurdle during the US Olympics trials, finishing fourth, and in 2007 he missed the chance to defend his world championships title after again clipping the final hurdle during the semi-finals and being eliminated.

At the age of 22, Kerron Clement was the youngest of the three Americans. Born in Trinidad, he moved to the US during high school, before running track at the University of Florida. In 2004 he became a US citizen and won the 400-meter hurdles and the 4 × 400-meter relay at the world junior championships. In 2006 he won the US national title in the 400-meter hurdles, and the following year he won the world championship title in Osaka, Japan, ahead of defending Olympic champion Félix Sánchez. By the end of 2007 Clement had moved to California and begun working with Bob Kersee, husband and former coach of six-time Olympic medalist Jackie Joyner-Kersee.

The third American athlete, Angelo Taylor, had returned to competition after several years of difficulty. In 2004 he failed to defend his Olympic title after being eliminated in the semi-finals, and he missed the 2005 season due to hip and shin injuries. In 2006 he narrowly avoided jail after being caught naked in a car with an underage girl; he pleaded guilty to contributing to the delinquency of two minors and was sentenced to three years probation. Taylor lost his Nike endorsement and was forced to work full-time as an electrician's apprentice.

In the winter of 2006 Taylor began to train with former Nigerian sprinter and coach Innocent Egbunike. Taylor's main strength was his speed at 400 meters. When he returned to competition in 2007 he won the flat 400 meters event at the US outdoor championships, and then went on to win bronze in the event at the world championships, as well as gold as part of the 4 × 400-meter relay team.

Taylor also faced complications surrounding his Athens 4 × 400 relay gold medal. In 2004 the medal was withdrawn after teammate Jerome Young was disqualified for doping; however in 2005 the Court of Arbitration for Sport reversed the decision and restored the medals. In August 2008, a week before the start of the Beijing Games, the medal was again taken away after another teammate, Antonio Pettigrew, also admitted to doping. Taylor was never implicated in the doping scandals.

Taylor was in impressive form in the first two rounds, although none of the Americans had difficulty reaching the final. All three won their first-round heats and then recorded the top three semi-final times, with Taylor the only racer to break 48 seconds. Defending Olympic champion Sánchez was injured and failed to advance out of the heats.

Racing in lane six, Taylor dominated the final, making up most of the stagger over the first 150 meters and taking the lead on the backstretch. Taylor recorded a career-best 47.25 seconds to lead the US sweep. Clement made up for a slow start, closing the gap behind Jackson and moving into second place over the final 50 meters to take silver. Once again, Jackson clipped the 10th hurdle, but managed to stay ahead of Jamaica's Danny McFarlane to win bronze. It was the fifth US sweep of the event in Olympic history, but the first since 1960.

3000-METER STEEPLECHASE

In the steeplechase, runners must negotiate a course of 28 hurdles and seven water jumps. The hurdles are three feet high and are solid, so that they cannot be knocked over. The tops of the hurdles are five inches wide, allowing the contestants to step on them. The water jump, which is preceded by a hedge, is 12 feet long, with a maximum depth of two feet three and one-half inches. Twelve runners take part in the final. The steeplechase event appears to have been introduced in Edinburgh in 1828, although the distance was not standardized at 3000 meters until 1920. It got its name from the fact that it was first run from the church steeple in one village to the church steeple in the next village.

1896 not held

1900 Paris C: 6, N: 6, D: 7.15.
(2500 Meters)

1. George Orton	CAN	7:34.4
2. Sidney Robinson	GBR	7:35.2e
3. Jacques Chastanié	FRA	7:44.0e
4. Arthur Newton	USA	—
5. Hermann Wraschtil	AUT	—
6. Franz Dühne	GER	—

Paralyzed as a child after falling out of a tree, George Orton regained his motor skills when he was twelve years old and ran everywhere, earning the nickname "The Boy Who Never Walked." Canada's first Olympic medalist, Orton competed in Paris wearing the colors of the University of Pennsylvania. Robinson and Chastanié led through most of the race. Orton made his move on the final straight and won going away. He ran the steeplechase only 45 minutes after finishing third in the 400-meter hurdles.

1904 St. Louis C: 7, N: 2, D: 8.29.
(2590 Meters)

1. James Lightbody	USA	7:39.6
2. John Daly	GBR/IRL	7:40.6
3. Arthur Newton	USA	7:46.0e
4. W. Frank Verner	USA	—

Lightbody, who had never before run a steeplechase, came from behind to win the first of his three gold medals at St. Louis.

1906 not held

1908 London C: 24, N: 6, D: 7.18.
(3200 Meters)

1. Arthur Russell	GBR	10:47.8
2. Archie Robertson	GBR	10:48.4
3. John Eisele	USA	11:00.8
4. C. Guy Holdaway	GBR	11:26.0e
5. Harold Sewell	GBR	—
6. William Galbraith	CAN	—

A rather unusual controversy developed during the heats, when some of the American runners showed up wearing white shorts, which were prohibited by AAA rules. They were finally allowed to compete after they had been provided with dark shorts. Russell and Robertson cleared the last hurdle together in the final, but Russell won by two yards in the run-in.

1912 not held

1920 Antwerp C: 16, N: 6, D: 8.20. WR: 9.49.8 (Josef Ternström)

1. Percy Hodge	GBR	10:00.4 OR
2. Patrick Flynn	USA	10:21.1e
3. Ernesto Ambrosini	ITA	10:32.0e
4. Gustaf Mattsson	SWE	10:32.1e
5. Michael Devaney	USA	10:34.3e
6. Albert Hulsebosch	USA	10:37.7e
7. Lars Hedvall	SWE	10:42.2e
8. Raymond Watson	USA	10:50.3e

The 29-year-old Hodge won easily by 100 yards. Earlier in the year he had entered the AAA steeplechase championship. In the second lap of that race, he was spiked and lost the heel of his shoe. Hodge stopped running, took off his shoe, readjusted and relaced it, and then took off again. He won by 60 yards. Hodge was a superb hurdler who gave exhibitions in which he cleared hurdles while carrying a tray, a bottle, and filled glasses without spilling a drop.

1924 Paris C: 21, N: 9, D: 7.9. WR: 9:33.4 (Paul Bontemps)

1. Vilho "Ville" Ritola	FIN	9:33.6 OR
2. Elias Katz	FIN	9:44.0
3. Paul Bontemps	FRA	9:45.2
4. B. Marvin Rick	USA	9:56.4
5. Karl Ebb	FIN	9:57.6
6. Evelyn Montague	GBR	9:58.0
7. Michael Devaney	USA	10:01.0
8. Albert Isola	FRA	10:14.8

Paul Bontemps had run a 9:33.4 on June 9, 1924, but was unable to repeat his performance one month later at the Olympics, as Ville Ritola won by 75 meters. Silver medalist Elias Katz was murdered by Arab terrorists on December 26, 1947, while working as a film projectionist at a British army base near Gaza. Sixth-place finisher Evelyn Aubrey Montague is introduced in the film *Chariots of Fire* as a good friend of Harold Abrahams, whose acquaintance he makes when they both arrive at Cambridge as freshmen. In reality, Abrahams and Montague were rivals, since Montague attended not Cambridge, but Oxford.

1928 Amsterdam C: 22, N: 10, D: 8.4. WR: 9.33.4 (Paul Bontemps)

1. Toivo Loukola	FIN	9:21.8 WR
2. Paavo Nurmi	FIN	9:31.2
3. Ove Andersen	FIN	9:35.6
4. Nils Eklöf	SWE	9:38.0
5. Henri Dartigues	FRA	9:40.0
6. Lucien Duquesne	FRA	9:40.6
7. Melvin Dalton	USA	—
8. William Spencer	USA	—

In the second heat of the qualifying round, Paavo Nurmi fell head over heels into the first water jump and had to be fished out by Lucien Duquesne. Nurmi repaid Duquesne's kindness by pacing him for the rest of the race, the two finishing together. The final marked the last Olympic appearances of Nurmi and Ville Ritola, both of whom were exhausted from their duel in the 5000 meters final the previous day. Ritola dropped out 600 yards short of the finish, but Nurmi held on grimly and placed second, 60 yards behind Toivo Loukola. Five years earlier Loukola had been declared unfit for military service because he had tuberculosis. He had then returned home and taken up running to restore his health.

1932 Los Angeles C: 15, N: 8, D: 8.6. WR: 9:08.4 (George Lermond)
(3460 Meters)

1. Volmari Iso-Hollo	FIN	10:33.4
2. Thomas Evenson	GBR	10:46.0
3. Joseph McCluskey	USA	10:46.2
4. Mart Matilainen	FIN	10:52.4
5. George Bailey	GBR	10:53.2
6. Glen Dawson	USA	10:58.0
7. Giuseppe Lippi	ITA	11:04.0
8. Walter Pritchard	USA	11:04.4

Volmari Iso-Hollo, a 25-year-old typesetter, crossed the finish line with a 40-yard lead, only to discover that there was no tape awaiting him and that the lap counter still read "1." He continued on for an extra lap and won by 75 yards. It was later determined that the lap checker, a substitute for the regular man, who was ill, had forgotten to change the lap count the first time the runners passed by. It didn't make any difference to Iso-Hollo, but the blunder had a profound effect on who won the silver medal. At the end of the regulation distance, McCluskey was in second place and Evenson in third. But during the extra lap Evenson passed McCluskey and beat him to the finish by two yards. When McCluskey pointed out to track officials what had happened, he was offered the opportunity of having the race re-run the next day. Quite exhausted, McCluskey declined, stating that anyway "a race has only one finish line."

1936 Berlin C: 28, N: 13, D: 8.8. WR: 9:08.2 (Harold Manning)

1. Volmari Iso-Hollo	FIN	9:03.8	WR
2. Kaarlo Tuominen	FIN	9:06.8	
3. Alfred Dompert	GER	9:07.2	
4. Martii Matilainen	FIN	9:09.0	
5. Harold Manning	USA	9:11.2	
6. Lars Larsson	SWE	9:16.6	
7. Woldemars Wihtols	LAT	9:18.8	
8. Glen Dawson	USA	9:21.2	

1948 London C: 26, N: 12, D: 8.5. WR: 8:59.6 (Erik Elmsäter)

1. Thore Sjöstrand	SWE	9:04.6
2. Erik Elmsäter	SWE	9:08.2
3. Göte Hagström	SWE	9:11.3
4. Alex Guyodo	FRA	9:13.6
5. Pentti Siltaloppi	FIN	9:19.6
6. Petar Šegedin	YUG/CRO	9:20.4
7. H. Browning Ross	USA	9:23.2
8. Constantino Miranda Justo	SPA	9.25.0

The only runner given a chance of defeating the Swedes was the European champion, Raphael Pujazon of France. However, Pujazon developed a stomach cramp midway through the final and was forced to retire.

1952 Helsinki C: 35, N: 12, D: 7.25. WR: 8:48.6 (Vladimir Kazantsey)

1. Horace Ashenfelter	USA	8:45.4 WR	(8:45.68)
2. Vladimir Kazantsev	SOV/RUS	8:51.6	(8:51.52)
3. John Disley	GBR	8:51.8	(8:51.94)
4. Olavi Rinteenpää	FIN	8:55.2	(8:55.60)
5. Curt Söderberg	SWE	8:55.6	(8:55.87)
6. Günther Hesselmann	GER	8:55.8	(8:55.98)
7. Mikhail Saltykov	SOV/BLR	8:56.2	(8:56.47)
8. Helmut Gude	GER	9:01.4	(9:01.36)

Twenty-nine-year-old FBI agent Horace Ashenfelter of Glen Ridge, New Jersey, caused something of a stir when he won his preliminary heat in 8:51.0. Not only was it the fastest time of the round, but Ashenfelter's previous best had been an undistinguished 9:06.4. Still, it seemed unlikely that Ashenfelter, who had trained at night, using park benches and a homemade bench as hurdles, could seriously challenge world record holder Vladimir Kazantsev. Mikhail Saltykov was the early leader in the final, but before the third lap had ended, Ashenfelter had moved ahead, followed closely by Kazantsev. They continued running together until the final lap. With half a lap to go, Kazantsev forged ahead, and it looked like the race was his. But Kazantsev stumbled slightly at the final water jump, while Ashenfelter moved to the outside, where the grass was drier and firmer, and breezed through without even breaking stride. Kazantsev had run out of energy, and Ashenfelter pulled away dramatically over the last 150 meters to win by almost 30 yards. Gleeful American sportswriters had a field day—it was the first time that an FBI man had allowed himself to be followed by a Russian. Ashenfelter delighted the Finnish crowd by interrupting his victory lap to run 30 rows into the stands to kiss his wife.

Horace Ashenfelter, 1952
FBI agent Ashenfelter leads favourite Vladimir Kazantsev during the 1952 steeplechase.

1956 Melbourne C: 23, N: 13, D: 11.29. WR: 8:35.6 (Sándor Rozsnyói)

1. Christopher Brasher	GBR	8:41.2	OR	(8:41.35)
2. Sándor Rozsnyói	HUN	8:43.6		(8:43.68)
3. Ernst Larsen	NOR	8:44.0		(8:44.05)

4. Heinz Laufer	GER	8:44.4	(8:44.53)
5. Semyon Rzhischin	SOV/RUS	8:44.6	(8:44.58)
6. John Disley	GBR	8:44.6	(8:44.79)
7. Neil Robbins	AUS	8:50.0	(8:50.36)
8. Eric Shirley	GBR	8:57.0	

Larsen led until two laps from the finish, after which Rzhischin surged ahead. Entering the final curve, Rozsnyói made his move, with Larsen at his shoulder. As they approached the fourth-to-last hurdle, Rozsnyói swung wide to give himself room to clear. Chris Brasher, a 28-year-old oil company executive, saw his chance, elbowed his way between the two leaders, and sprinted away to an unexpected 15-yard victory.

Twelve minutes later it was announced that Brasher had been disqualified for interfering with Larsen. However, Larsen made it clear that although he had been bumped, he considered the incident insignificant, and not worthy of disqualification. Rozsnyói, who was considerably more concerned about the fact that he hadn't heard from his wife or children since Soviet troops had invaded Hungary, also supported Brasher, as did Laufer, the potential bronze medalist. Three hours later, the Jury of Appeal voted unanimously to rescind the disqualification, giving Great Britain its first track and field gold medal since 1936.

Brasher, whose previous claim to fame had been pacing Roger Bannister when he broke the four-minute mile, spent the next 19 hours celebrating. This included sharing a "liquid lunch" with thirteen members of the British press. He arrived, in his own words, "blind drunk, totally blotto, on the Olympic podium. I have an asinine grin on my face and nearly fall flat on my face as I lean forward, breathing gin fumes all over an IOC Frenchman as he attempts to hang a medal around my neck." Brasher later worked as a journalist himself and later still founded the London Marathon, which was first contested in 1981.

1960 Rome C: 32, N: 20, D: 9.3. WR: 8:31.4 (Zdzislaw Krzyszkowiak)

1. Zdzislaw Krzyszkowiak	POL	8:34.2 OR	(8:34.30)
2. Nikolai Sokolov	SOV/RUS	8:36.4	(8:36.55)
3. Semyon Rzhischin	SOV/RUS	8:42.2	(8:42.34)
4. Gaston Roelants	BEL	8:47.6	(8:47.85)
5. Gunnar Tjörnebo	SWE	8:58.6	(8:58.87)
6. Ludwig Müller	GER	9:01.6	(9:01.57)
7. Charles "Deacon" Jones	USA	9:18.2	(9:18.22)
8. Aleksei Konov	SOV/RUS	9:18.2	(9:18.23)

The three Soviet runners ran a team race, hoping to wear down Krzyszkowiak. It didn't work. The 31-year-old Polish world record holder glided past Sokolov on the final backstretch and won by 15 yards.

1964 Tokyo C: 29, N: 19, D:10.17. WR: 8:29.6 (Gaston Roelants)

1. Gaston Roelants	BEL	8:30.8 OR
2. Maurice Herriott	GBR	8:32.4
3. Ivan Bylyayev	SOV/UKR	8:33.8
4. Manuel de Oliveira	POR	8:36.2
5. George Young	USA	8:38.2
6. Guy Texereau	FRA	8:38.6
7. Adolfas Alekseunas	SOV/LIT	8:39.0
8. Lars-Erik Gustafsson	SWE	8:41.8

Ahead by five yards after the first lap, Gaston Roelants broke away from the field and led by 50 yards at the start of the bell lap. Maurice Herriott closed the gap rapidly, but fell ten yards short. Between 1961 and 1966 Roelants won 45 straight steeplechase finals. In 1977, at the age of 40, he was clocked in 8:41.5. Roelants also competed in the 1968 Olympic marathon, placing eleventh.

1968 Mexico City C: 37, N: 26, D: 10.16. WR: 8:24.2 (Jouko Kuha)

1. Amos Biwott	KEN	8:51.0	(8:51.02)
2. Benjamin Kogo	KEN	8:51.6	(8:51.56)
3. George Young	USA	8:51.8	(8:51.86)
4. Kerry O'Brien	AUS	8:52.0	(8:52.08)
5. Aleksandr Morozov	SOV/RUS	8:55.8	(8:55.61)
6. Mikhail Chelev	BUL	8:58.4	(8:58.41)
7. Gaston Roelants	BEL	8:59.4	(8:59.50)
8. Arne Risa	NOR	9:09.0	(9:08.98)

Amos Biwott's rise to Olympic glory was sudden and unexpected. Early in 1968 he had just finished fourth in the 10,000 meters in a provincial championship, when he noticed that the steeplechase was scheduled for two hours later and decided to "just have a go." He

Amos Biwott, 1968

Biwott, defying accepted techniques, soars over the water barrier in the 1968 steeplechase.

finished second and was selected to take part in the national championship. He won that, placed second to Ben Kogo in the East Africa Championships, and found himself on the Kenyan Olympic team.

The 20-year-old Biwott literally leaped to international prominence in the third and final elimination heat. Either unaware of or disdainful of accepted racing tactics and steeplechase techniques, Biwott sprinted to a 30-yard lead in the first half lap and led by 70 yards before the first lap had been completed. But what really made the crowd go wild was Biwott's bizarre method of clearing the water jump. Contradicting the teachings of every coach in the world, he would jump onto the hedge and then hop over the water, triple-jump-style, landing on dry ground with the same foot he used to take off. His hurdle style was also unique: he jumped over the barriers with his feet together. In the words of Joe Henderson of *Track and Field News*, "He cleared the hurdles like he feared they had spikes imbedded on the top and leaped the water hazard as if he thought crocodiles were swimming in it." Despite his unorthodox approach, Biwott won his heat by 11.6 seconds.

Naturally, there was a great deal of curiosity as to how well Biwott would stand up in the final two days later against favorites Ben Kogo, Victor Kudinsky, and George Young. Surprisingly, Biwott started slowly, letting Kogo do most of the pace-setting. Unfortunately, Kudinsky withdrew with a hip injury during the second lap. With two laps to go, Gaston Roelants took the lead, while Biwott lingered in ninth place. By the start of the last lap, Kogo was back in the lead. Then, with 300 meters left, Young made his move, passing Kogo on the backstretch. Kogo fought him off, but out of nowhere came Amos Biwott. Kogo was still in front as they cleared the last hurdle, 60 meters from the finish, but Biwott loped right by him and won by three yards.

Four days after earning a bronze medal in the steeplechase, George Young competed in the marathon and finished sixteenth.

1972 Munich C: 49, N: 29, D: 9.4. WR: 8:21.98 (Kerry O'Brien)

1. H. Kipchoge Keino	KEN	8:23.6 OR	(8:23.64)
2. Benjamin Jipcho	KEN	8:24.6	(8:24.62)
3. Tapio Kantanen	FIN	8:24.8	(8:24.66)
4. Bronislaw Malinowski	POL	8:28.0	(8:27.92)
5. Dušan Moravčik	CZE	8:29.2	(8:29.06)
6. Amos Biwott	KEN	8:33.6	(8:33.48)
7. Romualdas Bite	SOV/LIT	8:34.6	(8:34.64)
8. Pekka Päivärinta	FIN	8:37.2	(8:37.17)

The second preliminary heat seemed to be cursed. Sergei Skrypka of the Soviet Union lost a shoe with six laps to go, but managed to stay with the leaders until the final water jump, when he slipped and fell headlong into the pond. World record holder Kerry O'Brien had similar bad luck, losing a shoe 200 meters from the finish and smashing into the water jump barrier. In the fourth heat, Amos Biwott set an Olympic record of 8:23.8.

The final was won by Kip Keino, who outkicked his teammate Ben Jipcho. Keino had little steeplechase experience, having entered the race as a challenge. "I had a lot of fun jumping the hurdles," he said, although his lack of experience caused him to jump "like an animal. My style is not good." Anders Gärderud, who was eliminated in the heats, set a world record ten days after the Olympic final.

1976 Montreal C: 24, N: 16, D: 7.28. WR: 8:09.70 (Anders Gärderud)

1. Anders Gärderud	SWE	8:08.2 WR	(8:08.02)
2. Bronislaw Malinowski	POL	8:09.2	(8:09.11)
3. Frank Baumgartl	GDR	8:10.4	(8:10.36)
4. Tapio Kantanen	FIN	8:12.6	(8:12.60)
5. Michael Karst	GER	8:20.1	(8:20.14)
6. Euan Robertson	NZL	8:21.1	(8:21.08)
7. Dan Glans	SWE	8:21.5	(8:21.53)
8. Antonio Campos	SPA	8:22.7	(8:22.65)

The 1976 final was one of the greatest steeplechase races of all time. Antonio Campos led for almost half the race. Then Bronislaw Malinowski, who had issued a warning that he planned to run away from the field in order to make it difficult for "followers" like Anders Gärderud, took over and tried to pull away. But Gärderud and Frank Baumgartl stayed with him. With 300 meters to go, Gärderud, who previously had had trouble living up to expectations in major competitions, flew by Malinowski, with Baumgartl right behind him. Gärderud cleared the final water jump beautifully and opened a five-yard lead. However, the surprising Baumgartl closed the gap as they approached the final hurdle. Gärderud cleared perfectly again, but Baumgartl clipped the barrier with his trail knee and sprawled to the ground. Malinowski jumped over the human hurdle and beat the world record, but he couldn't catch Gärderud. Baumgartl, recalling Lasse Viren's fall in the 1972 10,000 meters, leaped to his feet and salvaged the bronze medal, improving his personal best by 7.2 seconds, despite his mishap.

1980 Moscow C: 31, N: 18, D: 7.31. WR: 8:05.4 (Henry Rono)

1. Bronislaw Malinowski	POL	8:09.7	(8:09.70)
2. Filbert Bayi	TAN	8:12.5	(8:12.48)
3. Eshetu Tura	ETH	8:13.6	(8:13.57)
4. Domingo Ramón	SPA	8:15.8	(8:15.74)
5. Francisco Sanchez	SPA	8:18.0	(8:17.93)

Steeplechase, 1976
Coming off the final hurdle of the 1976 steeplechase, Bronislaw Malinowski (724) is forced to add a human hurdle to the obstacles in his path as Anders Gärderud streaks to vistory.

6. Giuseppe Gerbi	ITA	8:18.5	(8:18.47)
7. Boguslaw Mamiński	POL	8:19.5	(8:19.43)
8. Anatoly Dimov	SOV/RUS	8:19.8	(8:19.75)

No longer contemptuous of those who only follow during the early going, Bronislaw Malinowski was quite content to let Filbert Bayi set the pace in Moscow. Bayi, an air force mechanic from the Mbulu tribe, had little steeplechase experience, whereas Malinowski had been concentrating on the event for 13 years. The offspring of a Polish father and a Scottish mother, Malinowski had finished fourth in 1972 and second in 1976.

Bayi drove into the lead immediately and led by 35 meters with two laps to go, but about a half lap later he suddenly began to tire. Malinowski caught him on the backstretch and won easily, finally achieving his goal of an Olympic gold medal. When asked why he had followed such a suicidal race plan, Bayi replied, "Because it's fun. . . . It is fun to run as fast as one can until you are dead-tired." He was the first Tanzanian ever to win an Olympic medal. Unfortunately, Bronislaw Malinowski was killed in a car crash on September 26, 1981, near his hometown of Grudziadz. He was 30 years old.

1984 Los Angeles C: 35, N: 25, D: 8.10. WR: 8:05.4 (Henry Rono)

1. Julius Korir	KEN	8:11.80
2. Joseph Mahmoud	FRA	8:13.31
3. Brian Diemer	USA	8:14.06
4. Henry Marsh	USA	8:14.25
5. Colin Reitz	GBR	8:15.48
6. Domingo Ramón	SPA	8:17.27
7. Julius Kariuki	KEN	8:17.47
8. Pascal Debacker	FRA	8:21.51

After a slow first lap, Peter Renner of New Zealand moved to the front and set a hard pace for the first 2000 meters. With 500 meters to go, Washington State student Julius Korir took the lead. The pre-race favorite, Henry Marsh, moved into second shortly after the bell, positioning himself well for his famous finishing kick. But 220 meters from the finish line, Korir pulled away and scored a decisive victory. Mahmoud and Diemer passed Marsh in the stretch to gain the other medals. Marsh, suffering from a lingering virus, collapsed after the race and was taken away on a stretcher. Of the eight top finishers, all but Marsh and Ramón bettered their pre-Olympic personal records.

1988 Seoul C: 32, N: 24, D: 9.30. WR: 8:05.4 (Henry Rono)

1. Julius Kariuki	KEN	8:05.51 OR
2. Peter Koech	KEN	8:06.79
3. Mark Rowland	GBR	8:07.96
4. Alessandro Lambruschini	ITA	8:12.17
5. William Van Dijck	BEL	8:13.99
6. Henry Marsh	USA	8:14.39
7. Patrick Sang	KEN	8:15.22
8. Boguslaw Mamiński	POL	8:15.97

Francesco Panetta of Italy won the 1987 world championship with an inspired piece of frontrunning. He tried the same strategy at the Olympics, but with considerably less success. Panetta held a slight lead for the first 2000 meters, but then began to struggle. Kariuki, finding himself in front, turned back toward Koech and asked him to take over. Koech whipped into the lead, taking his teammate with him. Panetta faded to a ninth-place finish. With 600 meters to go, Kariuki moved past Koech and opened a ten-meter lead. He eased up at the finish, unaware that he was so close to breaking Henry Rono's ten-year-old world record. Kariuki seemed unconcerned. At the post-race press conference he asked, "What did you say the time was? 8:05.51? Ah, truly not bad." On July 3, 1989, Rono's record finally was beaten: by Peter Koech in 8:05.35.

1992 Barcelona C: 32, N: 23, D: 8.7. WR: 8:05.35 (Peter Koech)

1. Matthew Birir	KEN	8:08.84
2. Patrick Sang	KEN	8:09.55
3. William Mutwol	KEN	8:10.74
4. Alessandro Lambruschini	ITA	8:15.52
5. Steffen Brand	GER	8:16.60
6. Tom Hanlon	GBR	8:18.14
7. Brian Diemer	USA	8:18.77
8. Azzeddine Brahmi	ALG	8:20.71

Since 1968 Kenyans have won every Olympic steeplechase they have entered (Kenya boycotted in 1976 and 1980). By 1992 their dominance was overwhelming: seven of the eight fastest runners of the year were Kenyan. They approached the Olympics in a matter-of-fact fashion. As Patrick Sang explained: "Before the race started, we discussed the way each of us runs, our strengths and weaknesses. As Mutwol is a cross-country and 5000-meter runner we decided that he should set a fast pace and lead the group. Birir is a 1500-meter runner and it was decided he should move to the front with four laps to go. That's all there was to it. Our aim was to run most of the race together and leave it to the one who was strongest at the end to come home first for Kenya." The only glitch in the Kenyan plan came after 1000 meters when Birir was clipped by Azzeddine Brahmi, tore his shoe, and fell to one knee. Although the mishap dropped him to ninth place, he was back to fourth within 100 meters and went on to win.

World champion Moses Kiptanui of Kenya missed the Olympics because of a knee injury and a strained tendon. 'When the rest of the team went off to Barcelona I was injured," he explained later. "There was nothing I could do and I knew there were going to be no gold medals this year, so I decided to break some world records." Nine days after the Olympic final he broke the world record for the unimpeded 3000 meters, and then, three days after that, he set a steeplechase world record of 8:02.08.

1996 Atlanta C: 35, N: 22, D: 8.2. WR: 7:59.18 (Moses Kiptanui)

1. Joseph Keter	KEN	8:07.12
2. Moses Kiptanui	KEN	8:08.33
3. Alessandro Lambruschini	ITA	8:11.28
4. Matthew Birir	KEN	8:17.18
5. Mark Croghan	USA	8:17.84
6. Steffen Brand	GER	8:18.52
7. Brahim Boulami	MOR	8:23.13
8. Jim Svenøy	NOR	8:23.39

The favorite was three-time defending world champion Moses Kiptanui, who was also the world record holder. In 1992 he had been offered a place in the Olympics even though he finished fourth at the Kenyan trials. Kiptanui declined because it would have meant bumping from the team his friend William Mutwol. Mutwol went on to win a bronze medal.

Kiptanui, whose cousin, Richard Chelimo, had won the silver medal in the 1992 10,000 meters, took the lead after only 200 meters and eventually the three Kenyans opened a gap on the pack. But defending champion Matthew Birir faded with two laps to go and Lambruschini prevented a Kenyan sweep, just as he had done at the 1993 world championships.

Lambruschini caught up with Kiptanui and Keter at the bell, but they soon left him behind again. The unheralded Keter passed Kiptanui at the final water jump and sprinted to victory.

2000 Sydney C: 40, N: 29, D: 9.29. WR: 7:55.72 (Bernard Barmasai)

1. Reuben Kosgei	KEN	8:21.43
2. Wilson Boit Kipketer	KEN	8:21.77
3. Ali Ezzine	MOR	8:22.15
4. Bernard Barmasai	KEN	8:22.23
5. Luis Miguel Martín	SPA	8:22.75
6. Eliseo Martin	SPA	8:23.00
7. Brahim Boulami	MOR	8:24.32
8. Günther Weidlinger	AUT	8:26.70

The Kenyans were the favorites, as usual. Their team included 1997 world champion and 1999 runner-up Wilson Boit Kipketer and Bernard Barmasai, whose 1997 world record was still on the books. Yet it was the third Kenyan, 21-year-old Reuben Kosgei from Kapsabet, who won the gold medal. The final was run at such a slow pace that it seemed possible that a non-Kenyan might be able to pull off an upset. Luís Miguel Martín led after 1000 meters, but then Barmasai accelerated. At 2000 meters, Kosgei was in the lead, but the pace was still sluggish and when the bell rang for the final lap, there were still ten runners seemingly in contention. The Kenyans were running one-two-three. Martín tried to challenge on the backstretch, but to no avail. Kipketer caught Kosgei coming off the last hurdle. But Kosgei, who had been running on the rail, swung wide. The two bumped arms, causing Kipketer to lose stride and allowing Kosgei to reach the finish line first, while Ali Ezzine just pipped Barmasai to secure the bronze. Kosgei, who stood 1.73 meters (5 feet 8 inches) and weighed 55 kg. (121 lbs.), predicted that he would be remembered as "the little Olympic champion in Sydney 2000." The following year he became the first Olympic steeplechase champion to also win the world championship. At his Sydney press conference, Kosgei provided an insight into the relaxed Kenyan attitude. During the trials to make the Olympic team, Kosgei and Barmasai were staying in comfortable hotel rooms, when they were visited by friends of Barmasai who could not afford to stay in the hotel. So the two runners, with Olympics berths on the line, left the hotel and joined their friends at an inexpensive youth hostel. "We had a good time," explained Kosgei . . . and they both qualified for Sydney.

2004 Athens C: 39, N: 25, D: 8.24. WR: 7:55.28 (Brahim Boulami)

1. Ezekiel Kemboi	KEN	8:05.81
2. Brimin Kipruto	KEN	8:06.11
3. Paul Koech	KEN	8:06.64
4. Musa Amer Obaid	QAT	8:07.18
5. Luis Miguel Martín	SPA	8:11.64
6. Simon Vroemen	HOL	8:13.25
7. Bouabdellah Tahri	FRA	8:14.26
8. Ali Ezzine	MOR	8:15.58

In 2003, Stephen Cherono of Kenya, changed his name to Saif Saaeed Shaheen and switched his Kenyan citizenship to that of the oil-rich nation of Qatar. When, in August 2003, he defeated his former teammate, Ezekiel Kemboi, to win the world championship, Shaheen did not speak Arabic and he was unfamiliar with the Qatari national anthem that was played to celebrate his victory. Kemboi and Shaheen were expected to battle it out for gold in Athens, but Shaheen was declared ineligible to compete when the Kenyan Olympic Committee refused to waive the three-year restiction for athletes who switch nationalities. With Shaheen out of the running, the three Kenyans dominated the Olympic final, establishing their lead after the first lap. For the rest of the race, the only runner able to keep close to them was another Kenyan-turned-Qatari, Musa Amer Obaid (Moses Kipkirui). Koech, who held the fastest personal record of the trio, set a fast pace and surged ahead before the halfway point, followed by Kemboi and Kipruto, with Obaid in fourth. Just before the final water jump, Kemboi moved into the lead, with Kipruto a close second and Obaid moving up to challenge Koech. Kemboi pulled away in the final stretch, turning around to urge on his compatriots to complete the sweep and not let Obaid "spoil our party." Kipruto finshed second, while Koech sprinted to hold off Obaid at the finish. One week after the Kenyan sweep, Shaheen set a world record of 7:53.63.

2008 Beijing C: 39, N: 26, D: 8.18. WR: 7:53.63 (Saif Saaeed Shaheen)

1. Brimin Kipruto	KEN	8:10.34
2. Mahiedine Mekhissi-Benabbad	FRA	8:10.49
3. Richard Mateelong	KEN	8:11.01
4. Yacob Jarso	ETH	8:13.47
5. Bouabdellah "Bob" Tahri	FRA	8:14.79
6. Youcef Abdi	AUS	8:16.36
7. Ezekiel Kemboi	KEN	8:16.38
8. Abubaker Ali Kamal	QAT	8:16.59

One year after being declared ineligible to compete at the Athens Olympics, Kenyan-born Saif Saaeed Shaheen, competing for Qatar, led a *de facto* Kenyan sweep of the 2005 world championships, ahead of reigning Olympic champion Ezekiel Kemboi and Olympic silver medalist Brimin Kipruto. Shaheen was unable to defend his title two years later, after missing most of the season due to an unspecified injury. In his absence the 2007 world championships saw yet another Kenyan sweep, this time led by Brimin Kipruto, with Kemboi taking silver for the third straight time and Richard Mateelong capturing the bronze.

The third of nine children raised on a farm in Kenya's Rift Valley, Kipruto was the only one of his brothers or sisters to take up running. Kipruto's first name is actually Firmin, but a clerk mistakenly transcribed it as "Brimin" when he applied for a birth certificate in 2001, in order to get a passport. He later told the IAAF, "I thought I had to stay with what they wrote . . ." Kipruto won his first Olympic medal at the age of 19.

All three Kenyans managed to qualify for the final, although none bothered to win their first-round heats. The pace in the final was relatively slow, and by the final lap most of the main pack was still together. Kipruto moved up from seventh place to trail Mateelong and relative unknown Mahiedine Mekhissi-Benabbad of France before moving into the lead in the final stretch. Kemboi developed stomach cramps after clearing a barrier on the last lap of the final and faded to seventh. Mekhissi-Benabbad prevented a Kenyan 1–2 by outsprinting Mateelong to the line to take silver.

Born in Reims, France, of Algerian heritage, Mekhissi-Benabbad had only appeared in international competition once before, when he failed to reach the final of the 2007 world championships in Osaka, Japan. He was so little known before winning the silver that neither of the two Kenyan medalists had heard of him.

Kipruto's win extended Kenya's unbroken sequence of wins in the event to nine Olympics, stretching back to the 1968 Mexico City Games. The only two exceptions were the 1976 and 1980 Olympics, which Kenya boycotted. Of the nine Olympics, Kenya swept the medals twice (1992 and 2004) and went 1–2 six times.

4 × 100-METER RELAY

The 4 × 100-meter relay is a one-lap race run in lanes with a staggered start. The first runner for each team begins in starting blocks; the second, third, and fourth runners use a running start. The baton, made of wood or metal, is between 11 inches (28 centimeters) and 11¾ inches (30 centimeters) long and between 4¾ inches (12 centimeters) and 5 inches (13 centimeters) in circumference. It must weigh at least 50 grams (1.76 ounces). The baton must be carried by hand. If the baton is dropped, the runner may go out of his or her lane to retrieve it as long as that does not lessen the distance covered. Baton exchanges must take place within a 20-meter (21.87-yard) passing zone. It is the position of the baton, not the position of the runners' hands or bodies, that determines whether a pass is successful. A pass out of zone results in immediate disqualification. In the following charts and for all relay charts, runners who took part in preliminary heats but not in the final are included in brackets.

This event has been dominated by the United States, which has won it 15 of 21 times. Apart from 1996 and 2004, the only US losses had been the result of disqualification (1912, 1960, and 1988) and boycott (1980). The United States retained this edge by using raw speed to overcome mediocre passing.

1896–1908 not held

1912 Stockholm T: 8, N: 8, D: 7.9.

1. GBR	David Jacobs, Henry Macintosh, Victor D'Arcy, William Applegarth	42.4
2. SWE	Ivan Möller, Karl August "Charles" Luther, Ture Persson, Knut Lindberg	42.6

DISQ: GER: Otto Röhr, Max Herrmann, Erwin Kern, Richard Rau

The US team of Courtney, Belote, Wilson, and Cooke won the first semifinal in a time of 42.2, but was disqualified for passing out of the zone. The third semifinal was won by the German team, in 42.3; however they too were disqualified for passing out of the zone in the final, in which they finished second.

1920 Antwerp T: 13, N: 13, D: 8.22. WR: 42.3 (GER—Röhr, Herrmann, Kern, Rau)

1. USA	Charles Paddock, Jackson Scholz, Loren Murchison, Morris Kirksey	42.2 WR
2. FRA	René Tirard, René Lorain, René Mourlon, Émile Ali-Khan	42.5e
3. SWE	Agne Holmström, William Petersson [Björneman], Sven Malm, Nils Sandström	42.8e
4. GBR	William Hill, Harold Abrahams, Victor D'Arcy, Denis Black	43.0e
5. DEN	Henri Thorsen, Fritiof Andersen, August Sørensen, Marinus Sørensen	43.3e
6. LUX	Jean Colbach, Paul Hammer, Jean Proess, Alex Servais	43.6e

1924 Paris T: 15, N: 15, D: 7.13. WR: 42.2 (USA—Paddock, Scholz, Murchison, Kirksey)

1. USA	Francis Hussey, Louis Clarke, Loren Murchison, Alfred Leconey	41.0 EWR
2. GBR	Harold Abrahams, Walter Rangeley, Lancelot Royle, William Nichol	41.2
3. HOL	Jacob Boot, Henricus Broos, Jan de Vries, Marinus van den Berge	41.8
4. HUN	Ferenc Gerö, Lajos Kurunczy, László Muskát, Gusztáv Rózsahegyi	42.0
5. FRA	Maurice Degrelle, Albert Heise, René Mourlon, André Mourlon	42.2

DISQ: SWI: Karl Borner, Heinz Hemmi, Joseph Imbach, David Moriaud)

A wholesale assault on the world record began in the first heat of the first round, when Great Britain clocked 42.0. The Dutch team equaled this time in the next heat, but in the sixth heat the Americans ran away in 41.2. In the semifinal, the United States recorded a time of 41.0, and repeated this performance in the final. The most surprising aspect of the final was that the US leadoff runner, Francis Hussey of Stuyvesant High School in New York City, beat 100-meter gold medalist Harold Abrahams by two yards.

1928 Amsterdam T: 13, N: 13, D: 8.5. WR: 41.0 (USA—Hussey, Clarke, Murchison, Leconey; Newark Athletic Club, USA—Bowman, Currie, Pappas, Cumming; Sports Club Eintracht, GER—Geerling, Wichmann, Metzner, Salz)

1. USA	Frank Wykoff, James Quinn, Charles Borah, Henry Russell	41.0 EWR
2. GER	Georg Lammers, Richard Corts, Hubert Houben, Helmut Körnig	41.2
3. GBR	Cyril Gill, Edward Smouha, Walter Rangeley, Jack London	41.8
4. FRA	André Cerbonney, Gilbert Auvergne, Pierre Dufau, André Mourlon	42.0
5. SWI	Emmanuel Goldsmith, Willy Weibel, Willy Tschopp, Hans Niggl	42.6

DISQ: CAN: Ralph Adams, John Fitzpatrick, George Hester, Percy Williams

1932 Los Angeles T: 8, N: 8, D: 8.7. WR: 40.8 (GER—Jonath, Corts, Houben, Körnig; Sports Club Charlottenburg, GER—Körnig, Grosser, Natan, Schloske; University of Southern California, USA—Delby, Mauer, Guyer, Wykoff)

1. USA	Robert Kiesel, Emmett Toppino, Hector Dyer, Frank Wykoff	40.0 WR (40.10)
2. GER	Helmut Körnig, Friedrich Hendrix, Erich Borchmeyer, Arthur Jonath	40.9
3. ITA	Giuseppe Castelli, Ruggero Maregatti, Gabriele Salviati, Edgardo Toetti	41.2
4. CAN	Percy Williams, James Brown, Harold Wright, Birchall Pearson	41.3

5. JPN	Takayoshi Yoshioka, Chuhei Nambu, Izuo Anno, Itaro Nakajima	41.3	
6. GBR	Donald Finlay, Stanley Fuller, Stanley Engelhart, Ernest Page	41.4	

The US team set world records of 40.6 in the preliminaries and 40.0 in the final without having to use their leading sprinters, Eddie Tolan, Ralph Metcalfe, and George Simpson.

1936 Berlin T: 15, N: 15, D: 8.9. WR: 40.0 (USA—Kiesel, Toppino, Dyer, Wykoff)

1. USA	James "Jesse" Owens, Ralph Metcalfe, Foy Draper, Frank Wykoff	39.8	WR
2. ITA	Orazio Mariani, Gianni Caldana, Elio Ragni, Tuillo Gonnelli	41.1	(41.13)
3. GER	Wilhelm Leichum, Erich Borchmeyer, Erwin Gillmeister, Gerd Hornberger	41.2	(41.30)
4. ARG	Juan Lavenas, Antonio Sande, Carlos Hofmeister, Tomás Clifford Beswick	42.2	
5. CAN	Samuel Richardson, Arthur Bruce Humber, Lee Orr, Howard McPhee	42.7	

DISQ: HOL: Tjeerd Boersma, Wijnand van Beveren, Christiaan Berger, Martinus Osendarp

The 4 × 100-meter relay was the focus of one of the uglier incidents of the 1936 Games, one that caused great embarrassment to the United States. For weeks it had been assumed that the US team would consist of Sam Stoller, Marty Glickman, Frank Wykoff, and Foy Draper, and the foursome spent a good deal of time practicing their baton passing. On August 5, three days before the qualifying heats, Jesse Owens won the 200-meter dash, gaining his third gold medal. When asked if Owens would be added to the relay quartet, coach Lawson Robertson replied, "Owens has had enough glory and collected enough gold medals and oak trees to last him a while. We want to give the other boys a chance to enjoy the *'cérémonie protocolaire.'* Marty Glickman, Sam Stoller, and Frank Wykoff are assured places on the relay team. The fourth choice rests between Foy Draper and Ralph Metcalfe."

Two days later, however, Robertson announced that Owens would probably replace Glickman. Then, on the morning of the heats, the US coaches informed both Glickman and Stoller that they were being dropped from the team and replaced by Owens and Metcalfe. What made the situation ugly was that Stoller and Glickman were the only Jews on the US track team, and they returned to the United States as the only members of the squad who didn't compete. Robertson's excuse was that he feared the speed of the Dutch and German teams, and wanted to field the fastest foursome possible. Robertson's alleged fears turned out to be unfounded. If he had really been concerned about fielding the best teams possible, he should have paid more attention to the 4 × 400-meter relay team. In that event, Robertson bypassed medal winners Archie Williams, James LuValle, and Glenn Hardin, and stuck with the original foursome, who promptly lost to the British by over 12 yards.

At any rate, the US 4 × 100 team won easily by 15 yards, setting a world record that would last for 20 years. Frank Wykoff, running the anchor leg, won his third straight relay gold medal, setting a world record each time.

Fifty years after the Berlin Games, 68-year-old Marty Glickman visited the Olympic Stadium for the first time since he had been prevented from competing. Glickman blamed US Olympic Committee president Avery Brundage for making the decision against him so as not to humiliate Adolf Hitler. Glickman described his visit in the *New York Times:* "I went down into the well of the stadium and walked along the backstretch of the track, the portion I should have run so many years before. I stopped and looked across to the far side where Hitler and his entourage had watched the Games. Fifty feet to the right was the section reserved for the athletes where I had watched the races. Suddenly a wave of rage overwhelmed me. I thought I was going to pass out. I began to scream every dirty curse word, every obscenity I knew. How could you no-good, dirty so-and-sos do this to an 18-year-old kid, to any young man who worked so hard to get there, you rotten S.O.B.s. . . . For 49 years that anger and frustration, that rage, had been inside me. . . . But being there, visualizing and reliving those moments, caused the eruption which had been gnawing at me for so long and which I thought I had expunged years ago."

1948 London T: 15, N: 15, D: 8.7. WR: 39.8 (USA—Owens, Metcalfe, Draper, Wykoff)

1. USA	H. Norwood "Barney" Ewell, Lorenzo Wright, W. Harrison Dillard, Melvin Patton	40.6
2. GBR	John Archer, John Gregory, Alastair McCorquodale, Kenneth Jones	41.3
3. ITA	Michele Tito, Enrico Perucconi, Antonio Siddi, Carlo Monti	41.5
4. HUN	Ferenc Tima, László Bartha, György Csányi, Béla Goldoványi	41.6
5. CAN	Don McFarlane, James O'Brien, Donald Pettie, Edward Haggis	41.9
6. HOL	Jan Lammers, Johannes Meyer, Gabe Scholten, Jan Zwaan	41.9

The US team crossed the finish line six yards ahead of the British, but was disqualified when a judge claimed that the first pass, between Barney Ewell and Lorenzo

Wright, had taken place beyond the legal zone. The Americans were dumbfounded and immediately lodged a formal protest. The medal ceremony was held anyway, but three days later a Jury of Appeal viewed films of the race and discovered that the pass had been perfectly legal, and that the track official had been in error. The disqualification was therefore rescinded.

1952 Helsinki T: 22, N: 22, D: 7.27. WR: 39.8 (USA—Owens, Metcalfe, Draper, Wykoff)

1. USA	F. Dean Smith, W. Harrison Dillard, Lindy Remigino, Andrew Stanfield	40.1	(40.26)
2. SOV	Boris Tokaryev, Levan Kalyayev, Levan Sanadze, Vladimir Sukharyev	40.3	(40.58)
3. HUN	László Zarándi, Géza Varasdi, György Csányi, Béla Goldoványi	40.5	(40.83)
4. GBR	Emmanuel McDonald Bailey, William Jack, John Gregory, Brian Shenton	40.6	(40.85)
5. FRA	Alain Porthault, Etienne Bally, Yves Camus, René Bonino	40.9	(41.10)
6. CZE	František Brož, Jiři David, Miroslav Horčic, Zdenek Pospišil	41.2	(41.41)

The United States and the USSR were almost even after three legs, but Stanfield drew away from Sukharyev to win by two yards.

1956 Melbourne T: 18, N: 18, D: 12.1. WR: 39.8 (USA—Owens, Metcalfe, Draper, Wykoff)

1. USA	Ira Murchison, Leamon King, W. Thane Baker, Bobby Joe Morrow	39.5 WR	(39.60)
2. SOV	Boris Tokaryev, Vladimir Sukharyev, Leonid Bartenyev, Yuri Konovalov	39.8	(39.93)
3. GER	Lothar Knörzer, Leonhard Pohl, Heinz Fütterer, Manfred Germar	40.3	(40.34)
4. ITA	Franco Galbiati, Giovanni Ghiselli, Luigi Gnocchi, Vincenzo Lombardo	40.3	(40.43)
5. GBR	Kenneth Box, E. Roy Sandstrom, Brian Shenton, David Segal	40.6	(40.74)
6. POL	Marian Foik, Janusz Jarzembowski, Edward Schmidt, Zenon Baranowski	40.6	(40.75)

1960 Rome T: 19, N: 19, D: 9.8. WR: 39.5 (USA—Murchison, King, Baker, Morrow, GER—Steinbach, Lauer, Fütterer, Germar)

1. GER	Bernd Cullmann, Armin Hary, Walter Mahlendorf, Martin Lauer	39.5 EWR	(39.66)
2. SOV	Gusman Kosanov, Leonid Bartenyev, Yuri Konovalov, Edvins Ozoliņs	40.1	(40.24)
3. GBR	Peter Radford, David Jones, David Segal, J. Neville "Nick" Whitehead	40.2	(40.32)
4. ITA	Armando Sardi, Pier Giorgio Cazzola, Salvatore Giannone, Livio Berruti	40.2	(40.33)
5. VEN	S. Clive Bonas, Lloyd Murad, Emilio Romero, Rafael Romero	40.7	(40.83)

DISQ: USA: Frank Budd, O. Ray Norton, Stonewall Johnson, David Sime

The United States had won eight straight 4 × 100-meter relays, but in the opening round the West Germans served notice that they would be serious contenders when they equaled the world record of 39.5. Disaster struck the Americans in the final. Ray Norton, anxious to make up for his disappointing sixth-place finishes in the 100 and 200, took off too quickly on his second leg. Leadoff runner Frank Budd yelled at Norton, who came to almost a complete halt. But it was too late. He was already three yards beyond the twenty-meter passing zone. Norton didn't realize it at the time, and ran a strong leg anyway, moving the United States from fourth to second. Dave Sime's come-from-behind anchor leg brought the United States through the tape in first place, in world record time, but the disqualification gave the victory to the Germans, who equaled the world record again in the final.

1964 Tokyo T: 21, N: 21, D: 10.21. WR: 39.1 (USA—Jones, Budd, Frazier, Drayton)

1. USA	O. Paul Drayton, Gerald Ashworth, Richard Stebbins, Robert Hayes	39.0 WR	(39.06)
2. POL	Andrzej Zieliński, Wieslaw Maniak, Marian Foik, Marian Dudziak	39.3	(39.36)
3. FRA	Paul Genevay, Bernard Laidebeur, Claude Piquemal, Jocelyn Delecour	39.3	(39.36)
4. JAM	Pablo McNeil, Patrick Robinson, Lynworth Headley, Dennis Johnson	39.4	(39.49)
5. SOV	Edvins Ozoliņs, Boris Zubov, Gusman Kosanov, Boris Savchuk	39.4	(39.50)
6. VEN	Arquímedes Herrera, Lloyd Murad, Rafael Romero, Hortensio Herrera Fucil	39.5	(39.53)
7. ITA	Livio Berruti, Ennio Preatoni, Sergio Ottolina, Pasquale Giannattasio	39.5	(39.54)
8. GBR	Peter Radford, Ronald Jones, Walter Campbell, Lynn Davies	39.6	(39.69)

Poor baton passing put the United States in fifth place, three meters behind France, when Bob Hayes took over for the anchor leg. Hayes then unleashed one of the most awesome and breathtaking displays of sprinting ever seen. He swept into the lead after only 30 yards and crossed the finish line with a three-meter margin of victory. Observers disagreed as to Hayes' time for his flying-start 100-meter leg, but the slowest estimate was 8.9 seconds.

1968 Mexico City T: 19, N: 19, D: 10.20. WR: 38.6 (University of Southern California, USA/JAM—McCulloch, Kuller, Simpson, Miller)

1. USA	Charles Greene, Melvin Pender, Ronnie Ray Smith, James Hines	38.24 WR
2. CUB	Hermes Ramírez Limonta, Juan Morales Hechevarria, Pablo Montes Casanova, Enrique Figuerola Camue	38.40
3. FRA	Gérard Fénouil, Jocelyn Delecour, Claude Piquemal, Roger Bambuck	38.43
4. JAM	Errol Stewart, Michael Fray, Clifton Forbes, Lennox Miller	38.47
5. GDR	Heinz Erbstösser, Hartmut Schelter, Peter Hasse, Harald Eggers	38.66
6. GER	Karl-Peter Schmidtke, Gerhard Wucherer, Gert Metz, Joachim Eigenherr	38.76

7. ITA	Sergio Ottolina, Ennio Preatoni, Angelo Sguazzero, Livio Berruti	39.22
8. POL	Wieslaw Maniak, Edward Romanowski, Zenon Nowosz, Marian Dudziak	39.22

With Charlie Greene running with heavily bandaged legs, the United States was beaten to the tape by Cuba in both the opening round and the semifinals. Although Greene ran the final as if uninjured, mediocre baton passing left the United States in only third place when Jim Hines took over for the anchor leg. Five feet behind Enrique Figuerola at the exchange, Hines ripped into the lead after 30 yards and won by a yard. The Cubans mailed their silver medals to activist Stokely Carmichael as a symbol of support for US blacks.

1972 Munich T: 27, N: 27, D: 9.10. WR: 38.24 (USA—Greene, Pender, R. R. Smith, Hines)

1. USA	Larry Black, Robert Taylor, Gerald Tinker, Edward Hart	38.19 WR
2. SOV	Aleksandr Kornelyuk, Vladimir Lovetski, Juris Silovs, Valery Borzov	38.50
3. GER	Jobst Hirscht, Karlheinz Klotz, Gerhard Wucherer, Klaus Ehl	38.79
4. CZE	Jaroslav Matoušek, Juraj Demeč, Jiři Kynos, Ludvik Bohman	38.82
5. GDR	Manfred Kokot, Bernd Borth, Hans-Jürgen Bombach, Siegfried Schenke	38.90
6. POL	Stanislaw Wagner, Tadeusz Cuch, Jerzy Czerbniak, Zenon Nowosz	39.03
7. FRA	Patrick Bourbeillon, Jean-Pierre Grès, Gérard Fénouil, Bruno Cherrier	39.14
8. ITA	Vincenzo Guerini, Ennio Preatoni, Luigi Benedetti, Pietro Mennea	39.14

For the first time since 1932, the 4 × 100-meter relay was won by a team that did not include the 100-meter gold medalist. Eddie Hart, running the anchor leg for the United States, gained some degree of satisfaction after missing the start of his 100-meter quarterfinal heat.

1976 Montreal T: 20, N: 20, D: 7.31. WR: 38.19 (USA—Black, Taylor, Tinker, Hart)

1. USA	Harvey Glance, John Wesley Jones, Millard Hampton, Steven Riddick	38.33
2. GDR	Manfred Kokot, Jörg Pfeifer, Klaus-Dieter Kurrat, Alexander Thieme	38.66
3. SOV	Alexander Aksinin, Nikolai Kolesnikov, Juris Silovs, Valery Borzov	38.78
4. POL	Andrzej Świerczyrński, Marian Woronin, Bogdan Grzejszczak, Zenon Licznerski	38.83
5. CUB	Francisco Gómez, Alejandro Casañas Ramírez, Hermes Ramírez Limonta, Silvio Leonard Tartabull	39.01
6. ITA	Vincenzo Guerini, Luciano Caravani, Luigi Benedetti, Pietro Mennea	39.08
7. FRA	Claude Amoureux, Joseph Arame, Lucien Sainte-Rose, Dominique Chauvelot	39.16
8. CAN	Hugh Spooner, Marvin Nash, Albin Dukowski, Hugh Fraser	39.47

1980 Moscow T: 16, N: 16, D: 9.1. WR: 38.03 (USA—Collins, Riddick, Wiley, Williams)

1. SOV	Vladimir Muravyov, Nikolai Sidorov, Aleksandr Askinin, Andrei Prokotyev	38.26
2. POL	Krzysztof Zwolinski, Zenon Licznerski, Leszek Dunecki, Marian Woronin	38.33
3. FRA	Antoine Richard, Pascal Barré, Patrick Barré, Hermann Panzo	38.53
4. GBR	Michael McFarlane, Allan Wells, R. Cameron Sharp, Andrew McMaster	38.62
5. GDR	Sören Schiegel, Eugen Ray, Bernhard Hoff, Thomas Munkelt	38.73
6. BUL	Pavel Pavlov, Vladimir Ivanov, Ivailo Karaniotov, Peter Petrov	38.99
7. NGR	Hammed Adio, Kayode Elegbede, Samson Oyeledun, Peter Okodogbe	39.12
8. BRA	Milton Costa de Castro, Nelson Rocha Dos Santos, Katsuiko Nakaia, Altevir Araujo Filho	39.54

The French team included 21-year-old twins, Pascal and Patrick Barré.

1984 Los Angeles T: 20, N: 20, D: 8.11. WR: 37.86 (USA—King, Gault, C. Smith, Lewis)

1. USA	Sam Graddy, Ron Brown, Calvin Smith, F. Carlton Lewis	37.83 WR
2. JAM	Albert Lawrence, Gregory Meghoo, Donald Quarrie, Raymond Stewart, [Norman Edwards]	38.62
3. CAN	Benjamin Johnson, Tony Sharpe, Desai Williams, Sterling Hinds	38.70
4. ITA	Antonio Ullo, Giovanni Bongiorni, Stefano Tilli, Pietro Mennea	38.87
5. GER	Jürgen Koffler, Peter Klein, Jürgen Evers, Ralf Lübke, [Christian Zirkelbach]	38.99
6. FRA	Antoine Richard, Jean-Jacques Boussemart, Marc Gasparoni, Bruno Marie-Rose	39.10
7. GBR	Francis "Daley" Thompson, Donovan Reid, Michael McFarlane, Allan Wells	39.13
8. BRA	Arnaldo da Silva, Nelson Rocha Dos Santos, Katsuiko Nakaia, Paulo Correia, [Robson da Silva]	39.40

Running an 8.94 anchor leg, Carl Lewis won his fourth gold medal, as the US team set the only track and field world record of the Los Angeles Games. The second-place Jamaican squad included 33-year-old Donald Quarrie, who brought his three-Olympic medal total to one gold, two silver and one bronze.

1988 Seoul T: 30, N: 30, D:10.1. WR: 37.83 (USA—Graddy, Brown, Smith, Lewis)

1. SOV	Viktor Bryzhin, Vladimir Krylov, Vladimir Muravyov, Vitaly Savin	38.19
2. GBR	Elliott Bunney, John Regis, Michael McFarlane, Linford Christie, [Clarence Callender]	38.28
3. FRA	Bruno Marie-Rose, Daniel Sangouma, Gilles Quénéhervé, Max Morinière	38.40
4. JAM	Christopher Faulknor, Gregory Meghoo, Clive Wright, John Mair	38.47
5. ITA	Ezio Madonia, Sandro Floris, Pierfrancesco Pavoni, Stefano Tilli	38.54
6. GER	Fritz Heer, Christian Haas, Peter Klein, Dirk Schweisfurth	38.55
7. CAN	Desai Williams, Atlee Mahorn, Cyprian Enweani, Brian Morrison, [Andrew Mowatt]	38.93
8. HUN	György Bakos, László Karaffa, István Tatár, Attila Kovács	39.19

The favored US team was disqualified in the opening round when Lee McNeill, who had finished eighth at the US Olympic trials, failed to receive the pass from Calvin Smith until he was more than five meters beyond the passing zone.

1992 Barcelona T: 26, N: 26, D: 8.8. WR: 37.50 (USA—Cason, Burrell, Mitchell, Lewis)

1. USA	Michael Marsh, Leroy Burrell, Dennis Mitchell, F. Carlton Lewis, [James Jett]	37.40 WR
2. NGR	Oluyemi Kayode, Chidi Imoh, Olapade Adeniken, Davidson Ezinwa, [Osmond Ezinwa]	37.98
3. CUB	Andrés Simón Gómez, Joel Lamela Loaces, Joel Isasi González, Jorge Luis Aguilera Ruiz	38.00
4. GBR	Marcus Adam, Tony Jarrett, John Regis, Linford Christie, [Jason John]	38.08
5. SOV	Pavel Galkin, Edvin Ivanov, Andrei Fedoriv, Vitaly Savin	38.17
6. JPN	Shinji Aoto, Hisatsugu Suzuki, Satoru Inoue, Tatsuo Sugimoto	38.77
7. AUT	Christoph Postinger, Thomas Renner, Andreas Berger, Franz Ratzenberger	39.30
8. IVC	Franck Waotta, Jean Olivier Zirignon, Glues Bogui, Ouattara Lagazane	39.31

When Carl Lewis finished only sixth in the 100 meters at the US Olympic trials, his detractors claimed he was over the hill. Lewis said he had been suffering from a sinus infection that spread. Lewis was right. His sixth-place finish qualified him as only an alternate on the relay team, but when Mark Witherspoon ruptured an Achilles tendon in the semifinals of the 100 meters, Lewis was back where he wanted to be, anchoring the US squad in the Olympic final. Unusually fine passing earned the United States its 15th world record in an Olympic 4 × 100-meter race and brought Carl Lewis his eighth gold medal.

1996 Atlanta T: 39, N: 39, D: 8.3. WR: 37.40 (USA—Marsh, Burrell, Mitchell, Lewis)

1. CAN	Robert Esmie, Glenroy Gilbert, Bruny Surin, Donovan Bailey, [Carlton Chambers]	37.69
2. USA	Jon Drummond, Tim Harden, Michael Marsh, Dennis Mitchell, [Tim Montgomery]	38.05
3. BRA	Arnaldo de Oliviera Silva, Robson Caetano da Silva, Edson Luciano Ribeiro, André Domingos Silva	38.41
4. UKR	Kostya Rurak, Slava Dologodin, Serhiy Osovych, Oleh Kramarenko	38.55
5. SWE	Lars Hedner, Peter Karlsson, Patrik Strenius, Torbjörn Mårtensson, [Torbjörn Eriksson]	38.67
6. CUB	Joel Isassi González, Luis Alberto Pérez Rionda, Andrés Simón Gómez, Joel Lamelas Luaces, [Ivan García Sánchez]	39.39

DNF: FRA: Regis Groisard, Pascal Théophile, Needy Guims, Hermann Lomba, GHA: Aziz Zakar, Eric Nkansah, Albert Agyemang, Emmanuel Tuffour, [Christian Nsiah]

Since the 4 × 100-meter relay was first included in the program in 1912, no one had ever beaten the United States to the finish line in an Olympic final. The US had lost three times as a result of passing out of zone, but American teams had always finished first in finals they had started. At the 1995 world championships, the US bungled a pass in the first round and were disqualified. Canada, fielding the team of Robert Esmie, Glenroy Gilbert, Bruny Surin and Donovan Bailey, won with a time of 38.31.

At the Olympics, Esmie was replaced by Carlton Chambers. The Canadian team came within an inch of being disqualified in the opening round for passing outside of the zone. Replays showed that anchor Donovan Bailey had in fact left the zone before he received the baton from Bruny Surin, but the baton itself was still inside.

Canada won the first semifinal in 38.36, the United States the second in 37.96. On July 29, five days before the relay final, Carl Lewis won the long jump to earn his ninth career gold medal. If he could win one more, he would become the first Olympic athlete in any sport to win ten gold medals. Lewis started lobbying to be included in the relay final even though he had skipped the relay practice camp. This led to a media-inflamed debate within the American team. The Canadians watched these developments with rising fury. "There was absolutely no mention that *we* were the world champions last year," said Donovan Bailey. "All we heard about was Carl Lewis' 10th gold medal, as if it was automatic. That disrespect made us gel. We were on a mission."

The Americans did not choose Carl Lewis for the final. The Canadians, on the other hand, did make a change, bringing back Robert Esmie to replace an injured Carlton Chambers. Esmie, running the leadoff leg, celebrated this honor by shaving his head to read "RELAY BLAST OFF."

4 × 100-meter relay, 1992
Davidson Ezinwa and Jorge Luis Aguilera are just as thrilled with their finishes as Carl Lewis is with his victory.

The second leg would be run by Glenroy Gilbert who, like Bruny Surin, had competed in the long jump at the 1988 Olympics. At the 1992 Barcelona Games, Gilbert had been a part of the bungled pass that eliminated Canada in the 4 × 100 semifinals. In 1994, Gilbert represented Canada at the Olympic Winter Games in Lillehammer, placing 15th in the two-man bobsled and 11th in the four-man.

The Atlanta final was delayed for six minutes because of an incident regarding the team from Ghana. Ghana had used Christian Nsiah in the opening round, replaced him in the semifinal and then tried to bring him back for the final, a practice that was against the rules. They were disqualified, but refused to leave the track until the disqualification was confirmed.

Jon Drummond took a slight lead over Esmie on the opening leg. But the first US pass was cautious while the Canadian pass was perfectly smooth. Gilbert ran away from Tim Harden on the second leg and the race was effectively over by the halfway mark. By the time Surin handed the baton to anchor Donovan Bailey, Canada was so far ahead that Bailey was able to let up and raise his arm in celebration ten meters from the finish line. Bailey later apologized to his teammates for his action because it kept them from a possible world record.

None of the four Canadian finalists was born in Canada, Bailey and Esmie were born in Jamaica, Gilbert in Trinidad and Surin in Haiti.

2000 Sydney T: 40, N: 40, D: 9.30. WR: 37.40 (USA—Marsh, Burrell, Mitchell, Lewis)

1. USA	Jon Drummond, Bernard Williams III, Brian Lewis, Maurice Greene, [Kenneth Brokenburr, Tim Montgomery]	37.61
2. BRA	Vicente de Lima, Edson Ribeiro, André da Silva, Cláudio da Silva	37.90
3. CUB	José Angel Cesar, Luis Alberto Pérez, Ivan García, Freddy Mayola	38.04
4. JAM	Lindel Frater, Dwight Thomas, Christopher Williams, Llewelyn Bredwood, [Donovan Powell]	38.20
5. FRA	Frédéric Krantz, David Patros, Christophe Cheval, Needy Guims, [Jerome Eyana]	38.49

6. JPN	Shigeyuki Kojima, Koji Ito, Shingo Suetsugu, Nobuharu Asahara, [Shingo Kawabata]	38.66
7. ITA	Francesco Scuderi, Alessandro Cavallaro Maurizio Checcucci, Andrea Colombo	38.67
8. POL	Marian Nowak, Marian Urbas, Piotr Balcerzak, Ryszard Pilarczyk	38.96

The US victory was never in doubt. Anchor Maurice Greene, who had already won a gold medal in the 100 meters, took over with a two-meter lead and ran away from the rest of the field. In Greene's words: "I didn't really do anything. These three guys baked a cake. Jon Drummond whipped it up, Bernard baked it, Brian Lewis pulled it out of the oven and I just put the icing on it." The four Americans offended many people with their celebration, which included posing and clowning not only on their victory lap, but during the medal ceremony and during the playing of the "Star-Spangled Banner."

In 2002, two years after winning the gold medal with the US squad, Tim Montgomery set a 100 meters world record of 9.78 seconds at the Grand Prix final in Paris.

In 2005, in the aftermath of the BALCO scandal, Montgomery was found guilty of doping by the Court of Arbitration for Sport. He was handed a two-year ban and stripped of all results since 2001, including his 2002 100 meters world record.

In April 2006, Montgomery was arrested for his involvement in a New York-based multi-million dollar money laundering and check fraud scheme. He pled guilty in April 2007 to depositing bogus checks totaling $775,000. In May 2008, two weeks before being sentenced in the fraud case, a Virginia court indicted Montgomery for dealing 111 grams of heroin while out on bond. Montgomery was sentenced to nearly nine years in prison for the crimes.

He later admitted to having taken testosterone and human growth hormone before the Sydney Games.

2004 Athens T: 16, N: 16, D: 8.28. WR: 37.40 (USA—Drummond, Cason, Mitchell, Burrell)

1. GBR	Jason Gardener, Darren Campbell, Marlon Devonish, Mark Lewis-Francis	38.07
2. USA	Shawn Crawford, Justin Gatlin, Coby Miller, Maurice Greene [Darvis Patton]	38.08
3. NGR	Olusoji Fasuba, Uchenna Emedolu, Aaron Egbele, Deji Aliu	38.23
4. JPN	Hiroyasu Tsuchie, Shingo Suetsugu, Shinji Takahira, Nobuharu Asahara	38.49
5. POL	Zbigniew Tulin, Łukasz Chyła, Marcin Jedrusiński, Marcin Urba	38.54
6. AUS	Adam Basil, Paul di Bella, Patrick Johnson, Joshua Ross	38.56
7. TRI	Niconnor Alexander, Marc Burns, Ato Boldon, Darrel Brown	38.60
8. BRA	Cláudio Roberto de Souza, Edson Luciano Ribeiro, André Domingos da Silva, Vicente de Lima	38.67

The United States team included 100-meter gold medalist Justin Gatlin, 200-meter gold medalist Shawn Crawford and two-time gold medalist and five-time world champion Maurice Greene. Clearly, the Americans were the favorites. In the first semifinal, the US, despite resting Gatlin, ran a 38.02 to beat the British team by a half-second. Nigeria won the other semi in 38.27 seconds. In the final, the US was haunted by its traditional relay problem: poor passing. During the first exchange, Crawford was forced to slow down on his handoff to Gatlin, while Great Britain and Nigeria completed smooth handoffs. The second exchange was even worse. Coby Miller was forced to slow down to avoid running out of the passing zone, and Gatlin stepped on his foot, ripping a hole in his shoe and giving him a slow start on the third leg. Miller made up some time on his leg, pulling even with Nigeria's Aaron Egbele at the handoff to Greene, but the Americans were still about two meters behind Great Britain's handoff between Marlon Devonish and Mark Lewis-Francis. Greene closed the gap, but Lewis-Francis managed to hold him off at the line by one-hundredth of a second, the closest relay finish in Olympic history.

The gold medal was especially meaningful for two members of the British team, Darren Campbell and Marlon Devonish, who had been stripped of their silver medals at the 2003 world championships after anchor Dwain Chambers tested positive for steroids.

2008 Beijing T: 16, N: 16, D: 8.22. WR: 37.40 (USA–Drummond, Cason, Mitchell, Burrell)

1. JAM	Nesta Carter, Michael Frater, Usain Bolt, Asafa Powell, [Dwight Thomas]	37.10	WR
2. TRI	Keston Bledman, Marc Burns, Emmanuel Callander, Richard Thompson, [Aaron Armstrong]	38.06	
3. JPN	Naoki Tsukahara, Shingo Suetsugu, Shinji Takahira, Nobuharu Asahara	38.15	
4. BRA	Vicente Lima, Sandro Viana, Bruno de Barros, José Carlos Moreira	38.24	
5. GER	Tobias Unger, Till Helmke, Alexander Kosenkow, Martin Keller	38.58	
6. CAN	Hank Palmer, Anson Henry, Jared Connaughton, Pierre Browne	38.66	

DISQ: CHN (Wen Yongyi, Zhang Peimeng, Lu Bin, Hu Kai), HOL (Maarten Heisen, Guus Hoogmoed, Patrick van Luijk, Caimin Douglas)

One year before the Beijing Games, at the 2007 world championships, the United States edged out Jamaica by a mere 0.11 seconds in the final to win the title. However, by the time the Beijing Olympics rolled around the Jamaicans had overtaken the Americans as the gold-medal favorites. Their squad included Usain Bolt, who had already won two gold medals in the 100 and 200 meters events, both in world record times, and anchor Asafa Powell, who was the former 100-meter world record holder.

The anticipated US–Jamaica final never materialized, as the Americans once again struggled with their passing. In the lead in the first heat of round one, Darvis Patton reached anchor Tyson Gay for the handoff, but the two dropped the baton, and the team was disqualified. "It probably was my fault," Gay would say later. "If it hits your hand, you should have it. I'm a veteran. I've never dropped a stick in my life." Defending Olympic champion Great Britain was eliminated in the second heat for passing outside the designated zone.

With the US and the British out of the running, the only question remaining for the Jamaicans was their margin of victory. The final was close until the third leg, when Bolt built up a dominant lead. Powell increased the advantage on the anchor leg, finishing nearly a full second ahead of second-place Trinidad and Tobago. It was the largest winning margin since Jesse Owens led the US team in 1936. The Jamaicans also slashed three-tenths of a second off the world record, which had been held by the United States for 16 years. The victory earned Bolt a place as the fourth man in Olympic history to win all three sprint events at the same Games, and the first person to do so in all world record times.

4 × 400-METER RELAY

The 4 × 400-meter relay is begun in lanes from a staggered start with each runner covering one lap. The first runner remains in his or her lane. The second runner may cut to the inside after the first curve. The third and fourth runners, under the direction of an official, place themselves from lane 1 out, according to the order of their teams when the incoming runners are half a lap away. Even if the team order changes in the next 200 meters, the waiting runners must remain in their lanes. Incoming runners must stay in their lanes after passing the baton in order to avoid obstructing other teams. The construction of the baton and the length of the passing zones are the same as in the 4 × 100-meter relay. The United States has won this event 17 of the 22 times it has been contested.

1896–1906 not held

1908 London T: 7, N: 7, D: 7.25.
(Medley Relay: 200, 200, 400, 800)

1. USA	William Hamilton, Nathaniel Cartmell, John Baxter Taylor, Melvin Sheppard	3:29.4
2. GER	Arthur Hoffmann, Hans Eicke, Otto Trieloff, Hanns Braun	3:32.4
3. HUN	Pál Simon, Frigyes Mesei-Wiesner, József Nagy, Ödön Bodor	3:32.5

In this, the first-ever Olympic relay race, the runners did not pass a baton, but touched hands instead. The US team clocked 3:27.2 in the first round, but eased up in the final, winning by 25 yards. John Baxter Taylor, who ran the third leg, was the first black athlete to win an Olympic gold medal. He was just about to open up practice as a veterinarian, when he died of typhoid on December 2, 1908, at the age of 26.

1912 Stockholm T: 7, N: 7, D: 7.15. WR: 3:18.2 (USA—Schaaf, Sheppard, Gissing, Rosenberger)

1. USA	Melvin Sheppard, Edward Lindberg, J. Edwin Meredith, Charles Reidpath	3:16.6 WR
2. FRA	Charles Lelong, Robert Schurrer, Pierre Failliot, Charles Poulenard	3:20.7
3. GBR	George Nicol, Ernest Henley, James Soutter, Cyril Seedhouse	3:23.2

Sheppard, running in his ninth race in ten days, also competed in the 800 meters, 1500 meters, and 400 meters. Meredith, running his eighth race, took part in the 800 and the 400.

1920 Antwerp T: 6, N: 6, D: 8.23. WR: 3:16.6 (USA—Sheppard, Lindberg, Meredith, Reidpath)

1. GBR	Cecil Griffiths, Robert Lindsay, John Ainsworth-Davis, Guy Butler	3:22.2
2. SAF	Harry Davel, Clarence Oldfield, Jack Oosterlaak, Bevil Rudd	3:23.0e
3. FRA	Georges "Géo" André, Gaston Féry, Maurice Delvart, André Devaux	3:23.5e
4. USA	George Schiller, George Bretnall, J. Edwin Meredith, Frank Shea	3:23.6e
5. SWE	Sven Krokström, Sven Malm, Erik Sundblad, Nils Engdahl	3:24.3e
6. BEL	Jules Migeot, Auguste Corteyn, Omer Smet, François Morren	3:24.9e

Although only six teams entered the competition, the officials in charge insisted that a semi-final round be run with the top three in each semi qualifying for the final. Needless to say, all six teams qualified.

1924 Paris T: 7, N: 7, D: 7.13. WR: 3:16.4 (American Legion, Pennsylvania, USA—Rodgers, Eby, Brown, Maxam)

1. USA	Commodore Cochran, Alan Helffrich, J. Oliver MacDonald, William Stevenson	3:16.0	WR
2. SWE	Artur Svensson, Erik Byléhn, Gustaf Wejnarth, Nils Engdahl	3:17.0	
3. GBR	Edward Toms, George Renwick, Richard Ripley, Guy Butler	3:17.4	
4. CAN	Horace Aylwin, Allan Christie, David Johnson, William Maynes	3:22.8	
5. FRA	Raymond Fritz, Gaston Féry, Francis Galtier, Barthélemy Favaudon	3:23.4	
6. ITA	Guido Cominotto, Alfredo Gargiullo, Ennio Mattiolini, Luigi Facelli	3:28.0	

The British team was hampered by the absence of Eric Lidell, who was off preaching a sermon, it being a Sunday.

1928 Amsterdam T: 16, N: 16, D: 8.5. WR: 3:16.0 (USA—Cochrane, Helffrich, MacDonald, Stevenson)

1. USA	George Baird, Emerson "Bud" Spencer, Frederick Alderman, Raymond Barbuti	3:14.2	WR
2. GER	Otto Neumann, Richard Krebs, Werner "Harry" Storz, Hermann Engelhard	3:14.8	
3. CAN	Alexander Wilson, Philip Edwards, Stanley Glover, James Ball	3:15.4	
4. SWE	Björn Kugelberg, Bertil von Wachenfeldt, Erik Byléhn, Sten Pettersson	3:15.8	
5. GBR	Roger Leigh-Wood, W. William Craner, John Rinkel, Douglas Lowe	3:16.4	
6. FRA	Georges Krotoff, Joseph Jackson, Georges Dupont, René Féger	3:19.4	

1932 Los Angeles T: 7, N: 7, D: 8.7. WR: 3:12.6 (Stanford University, USA—Shore, A. Hables, L. Hables, Eastman)

1. USA	Ivan Fuqua, Edgar Ablowich, Karl Warner, William Carr	3:08.2	WR (3:08:14)
2. GBR	Crew Stoneley, Thomas Hampson, David Burghley, Godfrey Rampling	3:11.2	
3. CAN	Raymond Lewis, James Ball, Philip Edwards, Alexander Wilson	3:12.8	
4. GER	Joachim Büchner, Walter Nehb, Adolf Metzner, Otto Peltzer	3:14.4	
5. JPN	Itaro Nakajima, Iwao Masuda, Seikan Oki, Teiichi Nishi	3:14.6	
6. ITA	Giacomo Carlini, Giovanni Turba, Mario De Negri, Luigi Facelli	3:17.8	

The US team set a world record of 3:11.8 in the opening heat. In the final Bill Carr took off with a 12-yard lead. Godfrey Rampling closed the gap to six yards, at which point Carr pulled away and won by over 20 yards.

1936 Berlin T: 12, N: 12, D: 8.9. WR: 3:08.2 (USA—Fuqua, Ablowich, Warner, Carr)

1. GBR	Frederick Wolff, Godfrey Rampling, William Roberts, A. Godfrey Brown	3:09.0
2. USA	Harold Cagle, Robert Young, Edward O'Brien, Alfred Fitch	3:11.0
3. GER	Helmut Hamann, Friedrich von Stülpnagel, Harry Voigt, Rudolf Harbig	3:11.8
4. CAN	Marshall Limon, Philip Edwards, William Fritz, John Loaring	3:11.8
5. SWE	Sven Strömberg, Per Edfeldt, Olle Danielsson, Bertil von Wachenfeldt	3:13.0
6. HUN	Tibor Ribényi, Zoltán Zsitavi, József Vadas, József Kovacs	3:14.8

Compared to the Americans, the British team had an extremely casual view of training. As Godfrey Rampling once recalled, "I remember saying one day: 'Look here, chaps, we really ought to practice some baton-changing.' But we soon got bored and packed it in." But when Brown and Roberts finished second and fourth in the 400 meters, and the United States dropped Archie Williams and Jim LuValle, the gold and bronze medalists, from their relay squad, Rampling and his teammates suddenly realized, "We can beat these blighters."

Freddie Wolff was left over eight meters behind by the end of the first leg, but Rampling ran a spectacular lap to make up the deficit and take a two-meter lead. Roberts expanded the lead to four meters and Brown pulled away to win by about 11 meters.

This race marked the only medal-winning performance by the great German runner Rudolf Harbig, who competed in the 800 meters, but was eliminated in the first round. Between August 1938 and September 1940, Harbig won 55 consecutive races at distances ranging from 50 meters to 1000 meters. On July 15, 1939, he ran 800 meters in 1:46.6, setting a world record that would last for 16 years. On August 12, he set a 400-meter world record of 46.0 that wasn't bettered until 1948. Harbig was killed fighting the Russians in World War II, on March 5, 1944.

1948 London T: 15, N: 15, D: 8.7. WR: 3:08.2 (USA—Fuqua, Ablowich, Warner, Carr)

1. USA	Arthur Harnden, Clifford Bourland, Leroy Cochran, Malvin Whitfield	3:10.4
2. FRA	Jean Kerebel, François Schewetta, Robert Chef d'Hôtel, Jacques Lunis	3:14.8
3. SWE	Kurt Lundkvist, Lars Wolfbrandt, Folke Alnevik, Rune Larsson	3:16.0
4. FIN	Tauno Suvanto, Olli Talja, Runar Holmberg, Berth Storskrubb	3:24.8

DNF: JAM: V. George Rhoden, Leslie Laing, Arthur Wint, Herbert McKenley, ITA: Giovanni Rocca, Ottavio Missoni, Luigi Paterlini, Antonio Siddi

Roy Cochran's older brother Commodore won a gold medal in the same event 24 years earlier.

1952 Helsinki T: 18, N: 18, D: 7.27. WR: 3:08.2 (USA—Fuqua, Ablowich, Warner, Carr)

1. JAM	Arthur Wint, Leslie Laing, Herbert McKenley, V. George Rhoden	3:03.9 WR	(3:04.04)
2. USA	Ollie Matson, Gerald "Gene" Cole, Charles Moore, Malvin Whitfield	3:04.0	(3:04.21)
3. GER	Hans Geister, Günther Steines, Heinz Ulzheimer, Karl-Friedrich Haas	3:06.6	(3:06.78)
4. CAN	Douglas Clement, John Hutchins, John Carroll, James Lavery	3:09.3	(3:09.37)
5. GBR	Leslie Lewis, Alan Dick, Terence Higgins, Nicholas Stacey	3:10.0	(3:10.23)
6. FRA	Jean-Pierre Goudeau, Robert Bart, Jacques Degats, Jean-Paul Martin du Gard	3:10.1	(3:10.33)

In 1948, the Jamaican relay team had wanted more than anything to defeat the United States and win the gold medal. But Arthur Wint, running the third leg, had pulled a muscle and hobbled off the track in pain and anguish. Four years later the same four Jamaicans were back on the track, ready for another shot at their goal. Before the final began, Wint, Laing, McKenley, and Rhoden locked arms in a circle and said a prayer.

George Rhoden, Leslie Laing, Arthur Wint, Herb McKenley, 1948

Anguish in London, followed by euphoria four years later.

Wint ran the first leg and gave up a slight lead to Ollie Matson. Gerald Cole ran a tremendous second lap for the United States. When Herb McKenley took over for Jamaica, he was 12 yards behind 400-meter hurdles' champion Charley Moore. McKenley, competing in his fifth Olympic final without ever having won a gold medal, ran like a man inspired. Incredibly, he closed the gap and passed Moore in the last second, running a phenomenal 44.6 to Moore's far from shabby 46.3, and allowing 400-meter gold medalist George Rhoden to take off with a one-yard lead. Victory now seemed assured for the Jamaicans, since Mal Whitfield, the US anchor man, had run a disappointing sixth in the 400-meter final. But Whitfield didn't give in, refusing to yield an inch the entire way. However, Rhoden, wearing the same vest that Wint had worn to run the first leg, also refused to let up, and managed to break the tape exactly one yard ahead of Whitfield. The 20-year-old world record, set at the Los Angeles Games, had been demolished by 4.3 seconds. That night, the Jamaican foursome celebrated in their quarters by drinking whisky with the Duke of Edinburgh, out of the only available vessel—a toothbrush tumbler. The next day, the Governor of Jamaica declared a national holiday, which led to many arrests for drunkenness. When brought to court and asked their plea, most replied, "Helsinki," and received unusually mild sentences.

1956 Melbourne T: 15, N: 15, D: 12.1. WR: 3:03.9 (JAM—Wint, Laing, McKenley, Rhoden)

1. USA	Louis Jones, Jesse Mashburn, Charles Jenkins, Thomas Courtney	3:04.8	(3:04.81)
2. AUS	Leon Gregory, David Lean, Graham Gipson, Kevan Gosper	3:06.2	(3:06.19)
3. GBR	John Salisbury, Michael Wheeler, F. Peter Higgins, Derek Johnson	3:07.2	(3:07.19)
4. GER	Jürgen Kühl, Walter Oberste, Manfred Pörschke, Karl-Friedrich Haas	3:08.2	(3:08.27)
5. CAN	Laird Sloan, Murray Cockburn, Douglas Clement, Terry Tobacco	3:10.2	(3:10.33)

DISQ: JAM: Keith Gardner, George Kerr, Malcolm Spence, Melville Spence

1960 Rome T: 19, N: 19, D: 9.8. WR: 3:03.9 (JAM—Wint, Laing, McKenley, Rhoden)

1. USA	Jack Yerman, Earl Young, Glenn Davis, Otis Davis	3:02.2 WR	(3:02.37)
2. GER	Hans-Joachim Reske, Manfred Kinder, Johannes Kaiser, Carl Kaufmann	3:02.7	(3:02.84)
3. BWI/JAM& BAR	Malcolm Spence, James Wedderburn, Keith Gardner, George Kerr	3:04.0	(3:04.13)
4. SAF	Edward Jefferys, Edgar Davis, Gordon Day, Malcolm Spencer	3:05.0	(3:05.18)

5. GBR	H. Malcolm Yardley, Barry Jackson, John Wrighton, Robbie Brightwell	3:08.3	(3:08.47)
6. SWI	René Weber, Ernst Zaugg, Hansrüdi Bruder, Christian Wägli	3:09.4	(3:09.55)

Otis Davis began the anchor leg six yards ahead of Carl Kaufmann. Kaufmann closed the gap to one yard, but in the middle of the final curve, Davis accelerated and pulled away to win by four yards. In 1960, Jamaica, Trinidad, and Barbados competed as the British West Indies, also known as the West Indies Federation. Wedderburn was from Barbados; the rest of the relay team was from Jamaica.

1964 Tokyo T: 17, N: 17, D: 10.21. WR: 3:02.2 (USA—Yerman, Young, G. Davis, O. Davis)

1. USA	Ollan Cassell, Michael Larrabee, Ulis Williams, Henry Carr	3:00.7 WR
2. GBR	Timothy Graham, Adrian Metcalfe, John Cooper, Robbie Brightwell	3:01.6
3. TRI	Edwin Skinner, Kent Bernard, Edwin Roberts, Wendell Mottley	3:01.7
4. JAM	Lawrence Kahn, Malcolm Spence, Melville Spence, George Kerr	3:02.3
5. GER& GDR	Jörg Jüttner, Hans-Ulirich Schulz, Johannes Schmitt, Manfred Kinder	3:04.3
6. POL	Marian Filipiuk, Ireneusz Kluczek, Stanislaw Swatowski, Andrzej Badeński	3:05.3
7. SOV	Grigory Sverbetov, Victor Bychkov, Vasily Anisimov, Vadim Arkhipchuk	3:05.9
8. FRA	Michel Hiblot, Bernard Martin, Germain Nelzy, Jean Pierre Boccardo	3:07.4

1968 Mexico City T: 16, N: 16, D: 10.20. WR: 2:59.6 (USA—Frey, Evans, Smith, Lewis)

1. USA	Vincent Matthews, Ronald Freeman, G. Lawrence James, Lee Evans	2:56.2 WR	(2:56.16)
2. KEN	Daniel Rudisha, Matesi Munyoro Nyamau, Naftali Bon, Charles Asati	2:59.6	(2:59.64)
3. GER	Helmar Müller, Manfred Kinder, Gerhard Hennige, Martin Jellinghaus	3:00.5	(3:00.54)
4. POL	Jan Balachowski, Stanislaw Grędziński, Jan Werner, Andrzej Badeński	3:00.5	(3:00.58)
5. GBR	Martin Winbolt-Lewis, Colin Campbell, David Hemery, John Sherwood	3:01.2	(3:01.21)
6. TRI	George Simon, Euric Bobb, Benedict Cayenne, Edwin Roberts	3:04.5	(3:04.52)
7. ITA	Sergio Ottolina, Giacomo Puosi, Furio Fusi, Sergio Bello	3:04.6	(3:04.64)
8. FRA	Jean Nallet, Jacques Carette, Glues Bertould, Jean Pierre Boccardo	3:07.5	(3:07.51)

The final was really two separate races: the United States fighting for a world record and the other teams battling it out for second through eighth places. It was Ron Freeman's remarkable second leg that really did the trick for the Americans. His unofficial time of 43.2 was the fastest leg ever recorded in a 4 × 400-meter relay. Anchor man Lee Evans crossed the finish line 30 yards ahead of Charles Asati in second place. Kenya's leadoff man, Daniel Rudisha, is the only member of the Masai tribe to compete in the Olympics.

1972 Munich T: 21, N: 21, D: 9.10. WR: 2:56.16 (USA—Matthews, Freeman, Fames, Evans)

1. KEN	Charles Asati, Hezakiah Nyamau, Robert Ouko, Julius Sang	2:59.8	(2:59.83)
2. GBR	Martin Reynolds, Alan Pascoe, David Hemery, David Jenkins	3:00.5	(3:00.46)
3. FRA	Gilles Bertould, Daniel Velasques, Francis Kerbiriou, Jacques Carette	3:00.7	(3:00.65)
4. GER	Bernd Herrmann, Horst-Rüdiger Schlöske, Herrmann Köhler, Karl Honz	3:00.9	(3:00.88)
5. POL	Jan Werner, Jan Balachowski, Zbigniew Jaremski, Andrzej Badeński	3:01.1	(3:01.05)
6. FIN	Stig Lönnqvist, Ari Salin, Ossi Karttunen, Markku Kukkoaho	3:01.1	(3:01.12)
7. SWE	Eric Carlgren, Anders Faager, Kent Öhman, Ulf Rönner	3:02.6	(3:02.57)
8. TRI	Arthur Cooper, Pat Marshall, Charles Joseph, Edwin Roberts	3:03.6	(3:03.58)

Ten days before the heats, each nation submitted a list of six names from which a team of four could be chosen. The names submitted by the United States were Vince Matthews, Wayne Collett, Lee Evans, John Smith, Maurice Peoples, and Tommie Turner. Unfortunately, Matthews and Collett were banned from further competition because of their behavior on the victory platform following the 400-meter final. Meanwhile, Smith had pulled a hamstring muscle and was unable to run. This left the United States without a full team, so they were forced to withdraw.

The final was an exciting race, with the hometown West Germans in first place most of the way. But Julius Sang, running a 43.5 anchor leg, passed the fading Karl Honz 75 meters from the finish and went on to give Kenya a three-meter victory.

The British anchor, David Jenkins, was sent to prison in 1987 after pleading guilty to charges related to the manufacture and smuggling of anabolic steroids.

1976 Montreal T: 16, N: 16, D: 7.31. WR: 2:56.16 (USA—Matthews, Freeman, James, Evans)

1. USA	Herman Frazier, Benjamin Brown, Frederick Newhouse, Maxie Parks	2:58.65
2. POL	Ryszard Podlas, Jan Werner, Zbigniew Jaremski, Jerzy Pietrzyk	3:01.43
3. GER	Franz-Peter Hofmeister, Lothar Krieg, Harald Schmid, Bernd Herrmann	3:01.98
4. CAN	Ian Seale, Don Domansky, Leighton Hope, Brian Saunders	3:02.64
5. JAM	Leighton Priestley, Donald Quarrie, Colin Bradford, Seymour Newman	3:02.84

6. TRI	Michael Solomon, Horace Tuitt, Joseph Coombs, Charles Joseph	3:03.46
7. CUB	Eddy Gutierrez, Damaso Alfonso, Carlos Alvarez, Alberto Juantorena Danger	3:03.81
8. FIN	Hannu Mäkelä, Ossi Karttunen, Stig Lönnqvist, Markku Kukkoaho	3:06.51

With the defending champions from Kenya boycotted out of the Olympics, the Americans were left unchallenged. The final was run during a hard rain. Also missing because of the African boycott was the team from Gambia, which included two runners with unusually colorful names: Bambo Fatty and Bannana Jarju.

1980 Moscow T: 24, N: 24, D: 8.1. WR: 2:56.16 (USA—Matthews, Freeman, James, Evans)

1. SOV	Remigijus Valiulis, Mikhail Linge, NIkolai Chernetsky, Viktor Markin, [Viktor Burakov]	3:01.1	(3:01.08)
2. GDR	Klaus Thiele, Andreas Knebel, Frank Schaffer, Volker Beck	3:01.3	(3:01.26)
3. ITA	Stefano Malinverni, Mauro Zuliani, Roberto Tozzi, Pietro Mennea	3:04.3	
4. FRA	Jacques Fellice, Robert Froissart, Didier Dubois, Francis Demarthon	3:04.8	
5. BRA	Paulo Roberto Correia, Antonio Dias Ferreira, Agberto Conceição Guimaraes, Geraldo José Pegado	3:05.9	
6. TRI	Joseph Coombs, Charles Joseph, Rafee Mohammed, Michael Solomon	3:06.6	
7. CZE	Josef Lomicky, Dusan Malovec, Frantisek Brecka, Karel Kolar	3:07.0	

DNF: GBR: Alan Bell, R. Terence Whitehead, Roderic Milne, Glendon Cohen

With the top three teams—the United States, West Germany, and Kenya—absent because of the anti-Soviet boycott, this was a severely devalued contest. The Soviets, desperate for a victory, rested 400-meter champion Viktor Markin in the opening heat, then claimed that his replacement, Victor Burakov, had been injured, and brought Markin back for the final. They used the same trick to circumvent the anti-replacement rules in the women's 4 × 400 relay. The rejuvenated Markin fought off a surprisingly strong challenge from 400-meter hurdle gold medalist Volker Beck to gain a victory-at-any-cost for the USSR. The winning time was the slowest in 20 years. The slowest losing time since 1956 (3:25.0) was recorded by Sierra Leone.

1984 Los Angeles T: 25, N: 25, D: 8.11. WR: 2:56.16 (USA—Matthews, Freeman, James, Evans)

1. USA	Sunder Nix, Ray Armstead, Alonzo Babers, Antonio McKay, [Willie Smith, Walter McCoy]	2:57.91
2. GBR	Kriss Akabusi, Gary Cook, Todd Bennett, Philip Brown	2:59.13
3. NGR	Sunday Uti, Moses Ugbisie, Ulo Rotimi Peters, Innocent Egbunike	2:59.32
4. AUS	Bruce Frayne, Darren Clark, Gary Minihan, Rick Mitchell, [Peter Van Mittenberg]	2:59.70
5. ITA	Roberto Tozzi, Ernesto Nocco, Roberto Ribaud, Pietro Mennea, [Donato Sabia, Mauro Zuliani]	3:01.44
6. BAR	Richard Louis, David Peltier, Clyde Edwards, Elvis Forde	3:01.60
7. UGA	John Govile, Moses Kyeswa, Peter Rwamuhanda, Mike Okot	3:02.09
8. CAN	Michael Sokolowski, Doug Hinds, Bryan Saunders, Saunders, Tim Bethune	3:02.82

The United States almost lost this one in the semifinals, when Walter McCoy took five steps in the wrong lane. A formal protest was rejected because his violation was unintentional and had not impeded the progress of any other runners. McCoy squeezed a lot of mileage out of his good fortune. In 1988 he received a neck injury in an elevator accident at a Holiday Inn in Tampa, Florida. He sued the hotel owners and the elevator manufacturer, claiming that the injury deprived him of a good shot at a second gold medal at the Seoul Olympics. In July 1994 a jury sided with McCoy and awarded him $900,000.

The final was hotly contested and marked the first time that four teams broke three minutes in a single race. Sunday Uti gave Nigeria the first lap lead, while Darren Clark's 43.86 leg put Australia ahead at the midway point. Then Alonzo Babers ran a 43.75 lap to put the US in first place to stay.

1988 Seoul T: 22, N: 22, D: 10.1. WR: 2:56.16 (USA—Matthews, Freeman, James, Evans)

1. USA	Danny Everett, Steven Lewis, Kevin Robinzine, Harry "Butch" Reynolds, [Andrew Valmon, Antonio McKay]	2:56.16	EWR
2. JAM	Howard Davis, Devon Morris, Winthrop Graham, Bertland Cameron, [Trevor Graham, Howard Burnett]	3:00.30	
3. GER	Norbert Dobeleit, Edgar Itt, Jörg Vaihinger, Ralf Lübke, [Mark Heinrich, Bodo Kühn]	3:00.56	
4. GDR	Jens Carlowitz, Mathias Schersing, Frank Möller, Thomas Schönlebe, [Michael Schemer]	3:01.13	
5. GBR	Brian Whittle, Kriss Akabusi, Todd Bennett, Philip Brown, [Paul Harmsworth]	3:02.00	
6. AUS	Robert Ballard, Mark Garner, Miles Murphy, Darren Clark, [Leigh Miller]	3:02.49	
7. NGR	Sunday Uti, Moses Ugbisie, Henry Amok, Innocent Egbunike	3:02.50	
8. KEN	Tito Sawe, Lucas Sang, Paul Ereng, Simon Kipkemboi	3:04.69	

The US team found that their real race was not against the other teams, but against the world record set in the 1968 Olympics. When Butch Reynolds crossed the finish line 40 meters clear of the rest of the field, the scoreboard clock stopped at 2:56.17, a frustrating one

one-hundredth of a second short of the record. However, the official time turned out to be 2:56.16.

1992 Barcelona T: 24, N: 24, D: 8.8. WR: 2:56.16 (USA—Matthews, Freeman, James, Evans; USA—Everett, Lewis, Robinzine, Reynolds)

1. USA	Andrew Valmon, Quincy Watts, Michael Johnson, Steve Lewis, [Darnell Hall, Charles Jenkins]	2:55.74	WR
2. CUB	Lázaro Martínez Despaigne, Héctor Herrera Ortiz, Norberto Téllez, Roberto Hernández Prendes	2:59.51	
3. GBR	Roger Black, David Grindley, Kriss Akabusi, John Regis, [Mark Richardson, Duaine Ladejo]	2:59.73	
4. BRA	Robson Caetano Da Silva, Edielson Rocha Tenório, Sergio Matias De Menezes, Sidney Telles De Souza, [Eronilde Nunes de Araújo]	3:01.61	
5. NGR	Udeme Ekpeyong, Emmanuel Okoli, Hassan Bosso, Sunday Bada	3:01.71	
6. ITA	Alessandro Aimar, Marco Vaccari, Fabio Grossi, Andrea Nuti	3:02.18	
7. TRI	Alvin Daniel, Patrick Delice, Neil De Silva, Ian Morris	3:03.31	

DNF: KEN: Samson Kitur, Abednego Matilu, Simeon Kipkemboi, Simon Kemboi, [David Kitur]

At the 1991 world championships Great Britain upset the United States 2:57.53 to 2:57.57. Although there was much bickering in the United States camp as to who would run in the Olympic final, there was never any doubt that the Americans would exact revenge. As in 1988, there were two races: the United States versus the now 23-year-old world record and the battle for the other medals. This time the Americans, with a 43.1 leg from Quincy Watts and a 43.4 from Steve Lewis, won their race. Thirty meters behind Lewis, the other race was won by a gutsy Cuban squad when Roberto Hernández held off John Regis by two meters.

1996 Atlanta T: 35, N: 35, D: 8.3. WR: 2:54.29 (USA—Valmon, Watts, Reynolds, Johnson)

1. USA	LaMont Smith, Alvin Harrison, Derek Mills, Anthuan Maybank, [Jason Rouser]	2:55.99
2. GBR	Iwan Thomas, Jamie Baulch, Mark Richardson, Roger Black, [Du'aine Ladejo, Mark Hylton]	2:56.60
3. JAM	Michael McDonald, Robert Martin, Greg Haughton, Davian Clarke, [Dennis Blake, Garth Robinson]	2:59.42
4. SEN	Moustapha Diarra, Aboubakry Dia, Hachim Ndiaye, Ibou Faye	3:00.64
5. JPN	Shunji Karube, Koji Ito, Jun Osakada, Shigekazu Omori, [Kenji Tabata]	3:00.76
6. POL	Piotr Rysiukiewicz, Tomasz Jędrusik, Piotr Haczek, Robert Maćkowiak, [Paweł Januszewski]	3:00.96
7. BAH	Carl Oliver, Troy McIntosh, Dennis Darling, Timothy Munnings, [Theron Cooper]	3:02.71

DNS: KEN: Samson Kitur, Samson Yego, Simon Kemboi, Julius Chepkwony, Kennedy Ochieng; USA (Drummond, Cason, Mitchell, Burrell)

The US ran without Olympic 400-meter champion Michael Johnson and world record holder Butch Reynolds, both of whom were injured in Atlanta. The Americans led from the start to finish, but were hard-pressed throughout by the British team. The Jamaicans were in second place midway, but their third runner, Greg Haughton, was tripped by incoming runner Robert Martin and fell. Remarkably, Haughton did a shoulder roll and bounced back onto his feet, allowing Jamaica to hold onto third place.

2000 Sydney T: 34, N: 34, D: 9.30. WR: 2:54.20 (USA—Young, Pettigrew, Washington, Johnson)

1. USA	Alvin Harrison, Antonio Pettigrew, Calvin Harrison, Michael Johnson, [Jerome Young, Angelo Taylor]	2:56.35
2. NGR	Clement Chukwu, Jude Monye, Sunday Bada, Enefiok Udo-Obong	2:58.68
3. JAM	Michael Blackwood, Greg Haughton, Christopher Williams,Danny McFarlane, [Sanjay Ayre, Michael McDonald]	2:58.78
4. BAH	Avard Moncur, Troy McIntosh, Carl Oliver, Christopher Brown,	2:59.23
5. FRA	Emmanuel Front, Marc Foucan, Ibrahima Wade, Marc Raquil, [Pierre-Marie Hilaire, Bruno Wavelet]	3:01.02
6. GBR	Jared Deacon, Daniel Caines, Iwan Thomas, Jamie Baulch	3:01.22
7. POL	Piotr Rysiukiewicz, Robert Maćkowiak, Piotr Długosielski, Piotr Haczek, [Filip Walotka, Jacek Bocian]	3:03.22
8. AUS	Brad Jamieson, Blair Young, Patrick Dwyer, Michael Hazel, [Casey Vincent]; USA (Drummond, Cason, Mitchell, Burrell)	3:03.91

It was an exciting and hard-fought race down the final stretch. Christoper Brown of the Bahamas came out of the turn in the lead, but with fifty meters to go, he was passed by Jamaican Danny McFarlane. However Enefiok Udo-Obong passed them both and won the race—the race for second place, that is. More than 20 meters ahead of this trio, Michael Johnson was winning his fifth career gold medal for the United States. Two other members of the US team were 26-year-old twins Alvin and Calvin Harrison. The Harrisons were champions of perseverance. They both dropped out of high school in Salinas, California, and tried to run track at a local college. In 1995 they were forced to quit and make a living. They both landed jobs, Alvin handling hazardous materials and Calvin at a sporting goods store, but for a while they had to live in their 1987 Ford Mustang, Calvin in the front seat, Alvin in the back. In 1996, Alvin made the US Olympic team, placing fourth in the 400 meters and winning a gold medal in the relay. Six weeks later, the twins' younger sister was murdered. In 1998-1999, Calvin missed eight months of training because his left foot was partially paralyzed. In

Sydney, Alvin earned the silver medal in the 400 meters and the twins finally came together to share gold in the relay. Calvin's 43.55 third leg was the fastest leg of the race.

This event was hit by a series of delayed controversies. Three years after the race, in August 2003, it was revealed that Jerome Young, who ran in the preliminaries for the United States, had previously tested positive for the steroid nandrolone in 1999. He was initially suspended by USA Track & Field in a secret hearing, but another secret meeting held by a three-member "doping appeals board" on July 10, 2000—two months before the Olympics—cleared Young to compete in the Sydney Olympics.

On June 29, 2004, the Court of Arbitration for Sport ruled that Young should have been ineligible to take part in the Olympics because of the 1999 test. Three weeks later the IAAF moved to strip Young and the rest of the US team of their medals, lifting Nigeria, Jamaica and the Bahamas into first, second and third places.

The USOC appealed the decision, and on July 22, 2005, the CAS overturned the IAAF ruling and reinstated the US medals, although Young was still considered disqualified.

Ironically, during the year-long appeals process, three of the five members of the relay team were hit with additional doping violations. Young was banned for life after testing positive for the banned blood booster EPO, while twin brothers Alvin and Calvin Harrison received four- and two-year suspensions, Alvin for multiple doping violations related to the BALCO doping scandal (see pg XXX) and Calvin for a 2003 positive test for the stimulant modafinil.

In August 2008, the US relay team was disqualified for a second, and final time, after Antonio Pettigrew, who had never failed a doping test, admitted in court to having used EPO and human growth hormone from 1997 to 2001. Pettigrew and Young were both forced to testify during the trial of their former coach Trevor Graham.

In August 2010 Pettigrew was found dead in the back seat of his car, having committed suicide by ingesting sleeping pills.

2004 Athens T: 16, N: 16, D: 8.28. WR: 2:54.20 (USA–Young, Pettigrew, Washington, Johnson)

1. USA	Otis Harris, Derrick Brew, Jeremy Wariner, Darold Williamson [Kelly Willie, Andrew Rock]	2:55.91
2. AUS	John Steffensen, Mark Ormrod, Pat Dwyer, Clinton Hill	3:00.60
3. NGR	James Godday, Musa Audu, Saul Weigopwa, Enefiok Udo-Obong	3:00.90
4. JPN	Yuki Yamaguchi, Jun Osakada, Tomohiro Ito, Mitsuhiro Sato	3:00.99
5. GBR	Timothey Benjamin, Sean Baldock, Malachi Davis, Matt Elias	3:01.07
6. BAH	Nathaniel McKinney, Aaron Cleare, Andrae Williams, Chris Brown [Dennis Darling]	3:01.88
7. GER	Ingo Schultz, Kamghe Gaba, Ruwen Faller, Bastian Swillims	3:02.22
8. BOT	Johnson Kubisa, Calfornia Molefe, Gaolesiela Salang, Kagiso Kilego [Oganeditse Moseki]; USA (Drummond, Cason, Mitchell, Burrell)	3:02.49

The US team included all three 2004 400-meter medalists, as well as Darold Williamson, who had missed qualifying for a spot in the 400-meter competition by only one-hundredth of a second. In the qualifying round, the US was the only team to record a sub-three-minute time. Jamaica, which had won the bronze medals at the last two Olympics, was disqualified for an exchange violation on the first pass of the qualifying round. The result of the final was never in doubt, as Otis Harris took the lead and each US runner increased it. Their eventual margin of victory, 4.67 seconds, was the largest in Olympic history, and their time was the fastest in the event in six years. Australian anchor Clinton Hill took over in fifth place, but ran a 44.61 split to secure the silver. After the race, he lamented, "I thought if the US dropped the baton, we still wouldn't have caught them."

2008 Beijing T: 16, N: 16, D: 8.23. WR: 2:54.20 (USA–Young, Pettigrew, Washington, Johnson)

1. USA	LaShawn Merritt, Angelo Taylor, David Neville, Jeremy Wariner, [Kerron Clement, Regi Witherspoon]	2:55.39 OR
2. BAH	Dretti Bain, Michael Mathieu, Andrae Williams, Chris Brown, [Avard Moncur, Ramon Miller]	2:58.03
3. RUS	Maksim Dyldin, Vladislav Frolov, Anton Kokorin, Denis Alekseyev	2:58.06
4. GBR	Andrew Steele, Rob Tobin, Michael Bingham, Martyn Rooney	2:58.81
5. BEL	Kévin Borlée, Jonathan Borlée, Cédric Van Branteghem, Arnaud Ghislain	2:59.37
6. AUS	Sean Wroe, John Steffensen, Clinton Hill, Joel Milburn, [Mark Ormrod]	3:00.02
7. POL	Rafał Wieruszewski, Piotr Klimczak, Piotr Kędzia, Marek Plawgo	3:00.32
8. JAM	Michael Blackwood, Ricardo Chambers, Sanjay Ayre, Lansford Spence, [Allodin Fothergill]	3:01.45

After its overwhelming performance in Athens, the US continued to dominate the 4 × 400 relay event, winning both the 2005 and 2007 world championships. The 2008 US team featured all three medalists from the 400 meters sweep two days earlier: 2004 gold medalist Jeremy Wariner of Waco, Texas, who had anchored the team to both world championship titles, current 400 meters gold medalist LaShawn Merritt, and bronze medalist David Neville. The team was rounded out by Angelo Taylor, who had won the 400-meter hurdles five days earlier.

With such a strong team, the US seemed a lock for gold. The main favorite for silver was the Bahamas, led by 29-year-old anchor Chris Brown, who had helped them to silver behind the US at each of the past two championships.

The US was true to form in the final. Running the first leg, Merritt put the US ahead by a second over Belgium before the handover. Taylor and Neville maintained the advantage, while Wariner posted a 43.18 anchor leg. The US won the race in 2:55.39, breaking the Olympic record set by the 1992 US team. Still in second place going into the anchor leg, Belgium was passed by three teams in the final leg, ultimately finishing fifth. Brown held off Russian anchor Alekseyev by 0.03 seconds to win silver for the Bahamas.

It was the seventh straight Olympic gold medal in this event for the US, although the 2000 Sydney squad was stripped of their medals after multiple doping violations.

20,000-METER WALK

In walking races, the contestants must keep at least one foot in contact with the ground at all times. If a walker loses contact with the ground, he or she receives a warning for "lifting." Another rule requires walkers to straighten the leg at each step at the point of first contact with the ground. If three judges give a walker warnings, the third warning results in disqualification. The equivalent distance for 20,000 meters is 12.147 miles.

Official world records (WR)—as opposed to world bests (WB)—can be set only in walking races contested on a track. Since Olympic walking events are held on the road, winning times are not eligible for world record consideration, but are included in lists of world bests.

1896–1952 not held

1956 Melbourne C: 21, N: 10, D: 11.28. WR: 1:27:58.2 (Mikhail Lavrov)

1. Leonid Spirin	SOV/RUS	1:31:27.4
2. Antanas Mikėnas	SOV/LIT	1:32:03.0
3. Bruno Junk	SOV/EST	1:32:12.0
4. John Ljunggren	SWE	1:32:24.0
5. Stanley Vickers	GBR	1:32:34.2
6. Donald Keane	AUS	1:33:52.0
7. George Coleman	GBR	1:34:01.8
8. Roland Hardy	GBR	1:34:40.4

So many disputes had developed over the judging of the comparatively fast-paced 10,000-meter walk that it was replaced by the less controversial 20,000-meter event. Mikėnas, leading after 15 kilometers, received a warning, and resigned himself to second place, urging on Spirin, who had been placed only tenth at the halfway mark.

1960 Rome C: 36, N: 18, D: 9.2. WR: 1:27:05.0 (Volodymyr Holubnychy)

1. Volodymyr Holubnychy	SOV/UKR	1:34:07.2
2. Noel Freeman	AUS	1:34:16.4
3. Stanley Vickers	GBR	1:34:56.4
4. Dieter Lindner	GDR	1:35:33.8
5. Norman Read	NZL	1:36:59.0
6. Lennart Back	SWE	1:37:17.0
7. John Ljunggren	SWE	1:37:59.0
8. Ladislav Moc	CZE	1:38:32.4

Holubnychy, a 24-year-old Ukrainian who eventually competed in five Olympics, won the first of his four medals. Freeman, who apparently had not gone over the course beforehand, misjudged his closing surge and fell 50 yards short of victory. In 1968 Freeman became something of a *cause célèbre* in Australia when he was omitted from the national Olympic team despite the submission of a 41,000-signature petition to the Australian Olympic Federation.

1964 Tokyo C: 30, N: 15, D: 10.15. WR: 1:27:05.0 (Volodymyr Holubnychy)

1. Kenneth Matthews	GBR	1:29:34.0 OR
2. Dieter Lindner	GDR	1:31:13.2
3. Volodymyr Holubnychy	SOV/UKR	1:31:59.4
4. Noel Freeman	AUS	1:32:06.8
5. Gennady Solodov	SOV/RUS	1:32:33.0
6. Ronald Zinn	USA	1:32:43.0
7. Boris Khrolovich	SOV	1:32:45.4
8. John Edgington	GBR	1:32:46.0

Ken Matthews, an electrician at a power station near his hometown of Sutton Coldfield, had collapsed and failed to finish in 1960 after leading for eight kilometers. In 1964 he knew he would have a better chance of winning if his wife, Sheila, could join him in Tokyo. His mates agreed and collected £742 to send her along. Sure enough, Matthews crossed the finish line far ahead of the others. Sheila broke through stadium security, rushed onto the track, and gave her hubby what was probably the longest victory kiss in Olympic history. At the post-race interview, Matthews said, "My legs hurt me at the end of the race. They still do. But I wouldn't mind going dancing now."

Sixth-place finisher Ron Zinn died in the Vietnam War less than nine months later. He was 26 years old.

Ken Matthews, 1964
Celebrates his victory in the 1964 20,000-meter walk with his wife, Sheila.

1968 Mexico City C: 33, N: 20, D: 10.14. WR: 1:27:05.0 (Volodymyr Holubnychy)

1. Volodymyr Holubnychy	SOV/UKR	1:33:58.4
2. José Pedraza Zúñiga	MEX	1:34:00.0
3. Mykola Smaha	SOV/UKR	1:34:03.4
4. Rudolph Haluza	USA	1:35:00.2
5. Gerhard Sperling	GDR	1:35:27.2
6. Otto Barch	SOV/UKR	1:36:16.8
7. Hans Reimann	GDR	1:36:31.4
8. Stefan Ingvarsson	SWE	1:36:43.4

After 85 minutes of hard walking, Volodymyr Holubnychy entered the stadium in first place, followed closely by teammate Nikolai Smaga. Then the 60,000-plus spectators went wild as a third walker appeared—José Pedraza, a 31-year-old Mexican soldier. Two hundred meters from the finish, Pedraza passed Smaga and set his sights on Holubnychy. Pedraza's style seemed far from legal, but it would have taken a suicidal judge to disqualify the determined Pedraza while the stadium echoed with chants of "May-hee-co" and "Pay-drah-zah." An international incident was avoided when Holubnychy drew away slightly in the homestretch to win by a mere three yards.

1972 Munich C: 24, N: 12, D: 8.31. WR: 1:25:19.4 (Peter Frenkel, Hans Reimann)

1. Peter Frenkel	GDR	1:26:42.4 OR
2. Volodymyr Holubnychy	SOV/UKR	1:26:55.2
3. Hans-Georg Reimann	GDR	1:27:16.6
4. Gerhard Sperling	GDR	1:27:55.0
5. Mykola Smaha	SOV/UKR	1:28:16.6
6. V. Paul Nihill	GBR	1:28:44.4
7. Jan Ornoch	POL	1:32:01.6
8. Vittorio Visino	ITA	1:32:30.0

Frenkel, Reimann, and Holubnychy were even after 15 kilometers, with the deaf walker, Gerhard Sperling, six seconds behind. Approaching the stadium, Holubnychy moved ahead, but Frenkel had the strongest finishing kick and was able to enter the stadium with a small but growing lead. Part of Frenkel's success was due to an amazing invention of East German sports scientists: an underground room with artificially thin air that simulated altitude training. Frenkel was described in East German press handouts as a "color designer and decorator."

1976 Montreal C: 38, N: 21, D: 7.23. WR: 1:24:45.0 (Bernd Kannenberg)

1. Daniel Bautista Rocha	MEX	1:24:40.6 OR
2. Hans-Georg Reimann	GDR	1:25:13.8
3. Peter Frenkel	GDR	1:25:29.4
4. Karl-Heinz Stadtmüller	GDR	1:26:50.6
5. Raúl González Rodríguez	MEX	1:28:18.2
6. Armando Zambaldo	ITA	1:28.25.2
7. Volodymyr Holubnychy	SOV/UKR	1:29:24.6
8. Vittorio Visini	ITA	1:29:31.6

Volodymyr Holubnychy, 1968
Volodymyr Holubnychy holds off a frantic finish of dubious legality by local favorite José Pedraza to win the 20,000-meter walk in Mexico City in 1968.

The contestants in the 1976 20-kilometer walk covered one of the widest age ranges in the Olympics. Eighteen-year-old Bengt Simonsen of Sweden finished 26th, while 48-year-old Alex Oakley of Canada placed 35th. The winner, Daniel Bautista, brought Mexico its first-ever track and field gold medal. He was so dehydrated at the end that he had to drink ten cans of soft drinks before he could produce enough urine for the drug test. Bautista's time was not accepted as a world record because it was set on the road rather than on a track.

1980 Moscow C: 34, N: 20, D: 7.24. WR: 1:20:06.8 (Daniel Bautista)

1. Maurizio Damilano	ITA	1:23:35.5 OR
2. Pyotr Pochinchuk	SOV/BLR	1:24:45.4
3. Roland Wieser	GDR	1:25:58.2
4. Yevgeny Yevsyukov	SOV/RUS	1:26:28.3
5. José Marín	SPA	1:26:45.6
6. Raúl González Rodríguez	MEX	1:27:48.6
7. Bohdan Bulakowski	POL	1:28:36.3
8. Karl-Heinz Stadtmüller	GDR	1:29:21.7

In 1976 walk officials had been embarrassed by the publication of photographs which clearly showed gold medal winner Daniel Bautista with both feet off the ground during his final lap. In 1980 the officials decided to get tough. With less than 2500 meters to go, Bautista was in first place when he was suddenly disqualified and ordered off the course. This left Anatoly Solomin of the USSR in front, but a few hundred meters later he too was disqualified. By the end of the race seven walkers had been ordered off by the judges, including three of the six leaders at the 15-kilometer mark. These crackdowns allowed Maurizio Damilano to win a surprise gold medal. His twin brother, Giorgio, finished 11th. Thipsamay Chanthaphone of Laos, celebrating his 19th birthday, crossed the finish line in 2:20:22.0—over a half hour after the other walkers, and 21½ minutes slower than any contestant since the event began in 1952. But, unlike Bautista and Solomin, he *did* finish.

1984 Los Angeles C: 38, N: 22, D: 8.3. WR: 1:18:39.9 (Ernesto Canto)

1. Ernesto Canto	MEX	1:23:13 OR
2. Raúl González Rodríguez	MEX	1:23:20
3. Maurizio Damilano	ITA	1:23:26
4. Guillaume Leblanc	CAN	1:24:29
5. Carlo Mattioli	ITA	1:25:07
6. José Marín	SPA	1:25:32
7. Marco Evoniuk	USA	1:25:42
8. Erling Andersen	NOR	1:25:54

The Mexican population of Los Angeles is second only to that of Mexico City and it was out in force for the 20-kilometer walk, most of which was held on the streets surrounding the stadium. Guillaume Leblanc opened up an early lead, but by the halfway point, he had been passed by defending Olympic champion Maurizio Damilano and by world champion and world record holder Ernesto Canto. Damilano moved ahead by almost 40 meters in the next five kilometers, but was overhauled by Canto and González, who were enthusiastically rooted on by the home away from hometown crowd. The two Mexicans entered the stadium to tumultuous applause with Canto prevailing by 40 meters. For the first time in Olympic history, not one walker was disqualified for improper technique.

1988 Seoul C: 53, N: 28, D: 9.23. WR: 1:18:39.9 (Ernesto Canto)

1. Jozef Pribilinec	CZE/SLV	1:19:57 OR
2. Ronald Weigel	GDR	1:20:00
3. Maurizio Damilano	ITA	1:20:14
4. José Marín	SPA	1:20:34
5. Roman Mrázek	CZE	1:20:43
6. Mikhail Shchennikov	SOV/RUS	1:20:47
7. Carlos Mercenario	MEX	1:20:53
8. Axel Noack	GDR	1:21:14

After 15 kilometers, Pribilinec, 50-kilometer world champion Weigel, and defending Olympic champion Ernesto Canto were eight seconds clear of the rest of the field. But then Canto was disqualified, just as he had been at the 1987 world championships. Pribilinec entered the stadium less than ten meters ahead of Weigel but managed to extend his lead slightly on the track. After the finish, Pribilinec collapsed on his back.

Jozef Pribilinec (bottom) and Ronald Weigel, 1988

Pribilinec defeated Weigel by three seconds in the 1988 20,000-meter walk. When Pribilinec proved too exhausted to respond to Weigel's congratulations, Weigel kissed his conqueror and silently walked away.

Weigel knelt over him and tried to extend his congratulations. But the Slovak winner was so exhausted that he was unable to respond. Silently, Weigel kissed Pribilinec and walked away.

1992 Barcelona C: 42, N: 23, D: 7.31. WR: 1:18:35.2 (Stefan Johansson)

1. Daniel Plaza Montero	SPA	1:21.45
2. Guillaume Leblanc	CAN	1:22.25
3. Giovanni De Benedictis	ITA	1:23.11
4. Maurizio Damilano	ITA	1:23.39
5. Chen Shaoguo	CHN	1:24.06
6. James McDonald	IRL	1:25.16
7. Daniel García Córdova	MEX	1:25.35
8. Sándor Urbanik	HUN	1:26.08

Daniel Plaza made his home in El Prat de Llobregat, ten kilometers from the Olympic Stadium. For the 26-year-old Plaza that was just a short walk away. At the 1991 world championships in Tokyo, Plaza had crossed the finish line in third place only to learn ten minutes later that he had been disqualified. This time, too, he received warnings from the judges but, spurred on by the enthusiasm of the hometown fans, he held his technique. Veteran Maurizio Damilano led the pack for the first half of the race and more, but shortly before the 15-kilometer checkpoint, Plaza, Leblanc, and Plaza's Catalan teammate, Valentí Massana, shifted gears and pulled away. By the time they reached the steep hill leading to the stadium, Plaza had broken free from the others. Only 800 meters from the stadium Massana was disqualified while in second place.

Daniel Plaza gets credit for one of the most creative excuses for a positive drug test. In June 1996, Plaza tested positive for the steroid nandrolone. Because nandrolone is produced naturally by pregnant women, Plaza claimed that his positive result occured because he engaged in oral sex with his wife the night before his race. He was suspended anyway. However, ten years later, in 2006, Plaza was finally exonerated, when the Spanish Supreme Court ruled in his favor and overturned the two-year ban that had been imposed by the Spanish Committee for Sporting Discipline.

1996 Atlanta C: 60, N: 33, D: 7.26. WB: 1:17.25 (Bernardo Segura Rivera)

1. Jefferson Pérez Quezada	ECU	1:20:07
2. Ilya Markov	RUS	1:20:16
3. Bernardo Segura Rivera	MEX	1:20:23
4. Nick A'Hern	AUS	1:20:31
5. Rishat Shafikov	RUS	1:20:41
6. Aigars Fadejevs	LAT	1:20:47
7. Mikhail Shchennikov	RUS	1:21:09
8. Robert Korzeniowski	POL	1:21:13

Rishat Shafikov took the lead after five kilometers and still led by five seconds at the 16-kilometer mark. He was soon joined by teammate Ilya Markov. With two kilometers to go, Markov was in front and Shafikov right behind him. Four seconds farther back were Miguel Rodríguez of Mexico and unheralded Jefferson Pérez of Ecuador, a nation that had never won an Olympic medal in any sport. They were followed closely by world record holder Bernard Segura and hairdresser Nick A'hern. Pérez suggested to his friend Rodríguez that they pick up the pace, but Rodríguez was soon disqualified and Pérez was forced to go it alone. As Shafikov faded, Pérez passed Markov with 1000 meters to go. Markov tried to respond, but was unable to. Pérez pulled away to a 30-meter lead and held form for the victory.

Pérez, who had placed only 33rd at the 1995 world championships, prepared for all weather possibilities by training three days a week at the beach, once a week in the cool mountains and three days a week in the moderate climate of his hometown of Cuenca. As Ecuador's first Olympic champion, he was instantly transformed into a national hero and was flooded with gifts including cash, a car, free vacations, and a lifetime supply of yogurt. To celebrate his victory, Pérez spent 17 days walking 460 kilometers (285 miles) from Quito to Cuenca as the public came out to applaud him and join him.

2000 Sydney C: 47, N: 28, D: 9.22. WB: 1:17:46 (Julio Rene Martínez)

1. Robert Korzeniowski	POL	1:18:59
2. Noé Hernández	MEX	1:19:03
3. Vladimir Andreyev	RUS	1:19:27
4. Jefferson Pérez Quezada	ECU	1:20:18
5. Andreas Erm	GER	1:20:25
6. Roman Rasskazov	RUS	1:20:57
7. Francisco Fernández	SPA	1:21:01
8. Nathan Deakes	AUS	1:21:03

By the 16-kilometer mark, there were four walkers still in contention for a medal: defending 50-kilometer champion Robert Korzeniowski, Vladimir Andreyev, 1996 bronze medalist Bernardo Segura and his young (22 years old) Mexican teammate Noé Hernández. During the one kilometer transition from the circuit to the stadium, Andreyev lost contact and Korzeniowski, Hernández and Segura entered the stadium side by side. With 100 meters to go, Segura began to gradually move ahead and he crossed the finish line just two seconds before Korzeniowski. It was the closest walking finish in Olympic history. Meanwhile, though, there was trouble afoot. About 18 minutes from the finish, Segura had been given a red card for lifting. Eight minutes later, he earned a second red card for lifting.

Then, on the way back from the loop circuit to the stadium, the judges gave him a third card, thus disqualifying him. Walking rules state that the chief judge, in this case Lamberto Vacchi of Italy, must personally inform an athlete of his disqualification. Vacchi learned of Segura's disqualification while he was standing on the field after the race breaking the news of *his* disqualification to Maris Putenis of Latvia. Vacchi found Segura near the finish line, doing a live television interview. Segura, who had served in the Mexican national congress and was currently a mayoral candidate, was wearing sunglasses and a sombrero and he had a Mexican flag draped over his shoulders. He was also wearing earphones because he was conversing on air with the president of Mexico, Ernesto Zedilla. Vacchi was hesitant to interrupt this scene, but as the conversation drew to a close, he informed Segura that he was disqualified. In disgust, Segura threw down his sunglasses, the sombrero and the flag.

Meanwhile, Korzeniowski was speaking by cell phone to his wife in Krakow, when Polish officials rushed up and told him about Segura's disqualification. Korzeniowski screamed with joy and, as tears formed in his eyes, he told his wife, "Darling, darling, I'm getting crazy now. I am the winner."

2004 Athens C: 48, N: 28, D: 8.20. WB: 1:17:21 (Jefferson Pérez Quezada)

1. Ivano Brugnetti	ITA	1:19:40
2. Francisco Javier Fernández	SPA	1:19:45
3. Nathan Deakes	AUS	1:20:02
4. Jefferson Pérez Quezada	ECU	1:20:38
5. Juan Manuel Molina	SPA	1:20:55
6. Zhu Hongjun	CHN	1:21:40
7. Vladimir Andreyev	RUS	1:21:53
8. André Höhne	GER	1:21:56

After setting a world record in the world championships in 2003, Jefferson Pérez Quezada of Ecuador was the pre-race favorite for Olympic gold. But after a breakaway around the 12-kilometer mark, only three racers remained in contention for gold: 1999 world champion Ivano Brugnetti, 2003 10-kilometer world champion Francisco Fernández and Australian Nathan Deakes. The three remained close as they entered the stadium, with Brugnetti in the lead, Fernández close behind and Deakes trailing slightly. Brugnetti held off Fernández in the final meters to take gold, setting a personal best in the process. Deakes' bronze medal came three months after his parents had won AU$1,000,000 ($857,000) on a five-cent poker machine.

2008 Beijing C: 51, N: 30, D: 8.16. WB: 1:16:43 (Sergei Morozov)

1. Valeriy Borchin	RUS	1:19:01
2. Jefferson Pérez Quezada	ECU	1:19:15
3. Jared Tallent	AUS	1:19:42
4. Wang Hao	CHN	1:19:47
5. Ivano Brugnetti	ITA	1:19:51
6. Luke Adams	AUS	1:19:57
7. Francisco Javier Fernández Peláez	SPA	1:20:32
8. Robbie Heffernan	IRL	1:20:36

Long recognized as the greatest athlete in Ecuador's history, Jefferson Pérez was once again the favorite for gold. Four years after his first Olympic triumph in Atlanta, he had been disappointed by a fourth-place finish in Sydney and announced his retirement at the age of 26. He went back to Ecuador and completed his studies in business administration, but returned to competition the following year and went on to win the 2003 world championship and break the world best. He then suffered another disappointing fourth-place finish at the Athens Olympics, but a year later he was back on top, and successfully defended his world championship title in both 2005 and 2007. Now 34 and competing in his fifth Olympics, Pérez arrived in Beijing seeking his second Olympic gold medal, 12 years after winning his first.

Pérez' main adversary was long-time rival Francisco Fernández of Spain. Beginning in 2003 the two had faced each other at three consecutive world championships, with Pérez beating Fernández for the title each time. At the 2004 Olympics, however, Fernández won silver ahead of the fourth-place Pérez. Fernández's coach was four-time Olympic champion Robert Korzeniowski of Poland.

Pérez and Fernández expected to face stiff competition from the Russian contingent. Two months before the Olympics, at the Russian National Championships in Saransk, 20-year-old Sergei Morozov became the first man to break the 1:17 minute barrier in the event, setting a world best of 1:16.43; it was Morozov's first-ever 20-kilometer race. Second-place finisher Vladimir Kanaykin also broke the 1:17 barrier. Neither ended up competing, after reports surfaced that they and other Russian race walkers had tested positive for EPO.

Defending Olympic champion Ivano Brugnetti, Fernández and Pérez led the field over the opening three laps inside the Olympic stadium, followed closely by the rest of the field. Brugnetti maintained the lead throughout much of the first 15 kilometers, trailed closely by Fernández. Shortly after the 15th kilometer, Pérez upped the pace, stretching out the lead pack. Exactly one hour into the race, Pérez broke away, pursued by Australia's Jared Tallent, with Brugnetti a few meters adrift and Russia's Valeriy Borchin close behind.

Borchin began to surge at 16 kilometers, catching up with Pérez and Tallent before moving into the lead before the 18-kilometer mark. Borchin was never seriously threatened after that, with Pérez managing to hang on for silver and Tallent taking bronze despite vomiting on the finishing stretch.

Just 21 years old, Borchin had already served a one-year ban after testing positive for ephedrine in 2005. He returned to win silver at the 2006 European Championships two months after the ban ended. Borchin was one of the few Russian race walkers to actually compete in Beijing—Vladimir Kanaykin, Athens bronze medalist Alexei Voyevodin and Viktor Vurayev having tested positive for EPO in the run-up to the games. The three athletes were coached by Viktor Chegin, who also coached Borchin and Morozov. Morozov, still listed in the pre-race lineup, failed to appear for the start of the race.

One year after winning the gold medal in Beijing, Borchin won the world championship title in Berlin. He successfully defended his world title in Daegu in 2011.

50,000-METER WALK

The rules for this punishing race are the same as those for the 20,000-meter walk. The equivalent distance of 50,000 meters is 31.068 miles.

1896–1928 not held

1932 Los Angeles C: 15, N: 10, D: 8.3. WR: 4:34:03.0 (Paul Sievert)

1. Thomas Green	GBR	4:50:10
2. Jānis Daliņš	LAT	4:57:20
3. Ugo Frigerio	ITA	4:59:06
4. Karl Hähnel	GER	5:06:06
5. Ettore Rivolta	ITA	5:07:39
6. Paul Sievert	GER	5:16:41
7. Henri Quintric	FRA	5:27:25
8. Ernest Crosbie	USA	5:28:02

Tommy Green, a 38-year-old railway worker, took the lead seven miles from the finish and won easily. Ugo Frigerio added a bronze medal to the three golds he had won in 1920 and 1924. Green had to overcome considerable adversity to make it to the Olympics. Because he had rickets as a child, he was unable to walk until he was five years old. At 12, he lied about his age and joined the army. A couple of years later he was invalided out when a horse fell on him. Recalled to service in 1914, he was wounded three times in World War I and finally sent home again in 1917 after having been badly gassed while fighting in France. He did not enter his first walking contest until 1926, when he was 32 years old.

1936 Berlin C: 33, N: 16, D: 8.5. WR: 4:34:03.0 (Paul Sievert)

1. H. Harold Whitlock	GBR	4:30:41.4 OR
2. Arthur Schwab	SWI	4:32:09.2
3. Adalberts Bubenko	LAT	4:32:42.2
4. Jaroslav Štork	CZE	4:34:00.2
5. Edgar Bruun	NOR	4:34:53.2
6. Fritz Bleiweiss	GER	4:36:48.4
7. Karl Reiniger	SWI	4:40:45.0
8. Etienne Laisne	FRA	4:41:40.0

Harry Whitlock, a 32-year-old auto mechanic, moved into first place after 33 kilometers. However, at the 38-kilometer mark, he began to vomit. His sickness continued for five kilometers, but he kept walking, recovered, and won by a wide margin. In 1952 Whitlock came out of retirement to compete in the Helsinki Olympics, where he finished 11th at the age of 48.

1948 London C: 23, N: 11, D: 7.31. WR: 4:34:03.0 (Paul Sievert)

1. John Ljunggren	SWE	4:41:52
2. Godel Gaston	SWI	4:48:17
3. Terence "Tebbs" Lloyd-Johnson	GBR	4:48:31
4. Edgar Bruun	NOR	4:53:18
5. Harold Martineau	GBR	4:53:58
6. Rune Bjurström	SWE	4:56:43
7. Pierre Mazille	FRA	5:01:40
8. Claude Hubert	FRA	5:03:12

Ljunggren led from start to finish and won easily. Bronze medalist Tebbs Lloyd-Johnson was 48 years old, the oldest person ever to win an Olympic track and field medal.

1952 Helsinki C: 31, N: 16, D: 7.21. WR: 4:31:21.6 (Antal Róka)

1. Giuseppe "Pino" Dordoni	ITA	4:28:07.8 OR
2. Josef Doležal	CZE	4:30:17.8
3. Antal Róka	HUN	4:31:27.2
4. George Whitlock	GBR	4:32:21.0
5. Sergei Lobastov	SOV/RUS	4:32:34.2
6. Vladimir Ukhov	SOV/RUS	4:32:51.6
7. Dumitru Paraschivescu	ROM	4:41:05.2
8. Ionescu Baboie	ROM	4:41:52.8

1956 Melbourne C: 21, N: 10, D: 11.24. WR: 4:21:07.0 (Ladislav Moc)

1. Norman Read	NZL	4:30:42.8
2. Yevgeny Maskinskov	SOV/RUS	4:32:57.0
3. John Ljunggren	SWE	4:35:02.0
4. Abdon Pamich	ITA	4:39:00.0
5. Antal Róka	HUN	4:50:09.0
6. Raymond Smith	AUS	4:56:08.0
7. Adolf Weinacker	USA	5:00:16.0
8. Albert Johnson	GBR	5:02:19.0

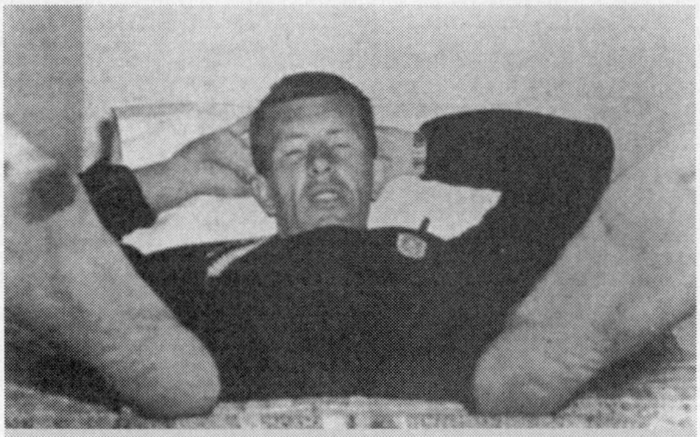

Norman Read, 1956
Celebrating his victory in the 1956 50,000-meter walk by resting his feet.

Norman Read moved from England to New Zealand in 1954. As the Melbourne Olympics approached, he wrote to the British AAA asking for permission to represent Great Britain as a walker. He was rejected. At first he was rejected in New Zealand as well, but a strong showing in races in Australia and New Zealand paved his way. After receiving his naturalization papers he was ready to fulfill his dream. On the day of the 50,000-meter race Read got lost in the corridors of the stadium and didn't find his way to the track until the other runners were already standing on the starting line. Maskinskov led over most of the course, with Read two and a half minutes back after 30 kilometers. At 42 kilometers, however, Read caught the tiring Soviet walker and pulled away to a decisive victory. His unexpected win caused wild cheering in the stadium, and a whole section of the New Zealand contingent had to be restrained from streaming onto the track.

1960 Rome C: 39, N: 20, D: 9.7. WR: 4:16:08.6 (Sergei Lobastov)

1. Donald Thompson	GBR	4:25:30.0 OR
2. John Ljunggren	SWE	4:25:47.0
3. Abdon Pamich	ITA	4:27:55.4
4. Aleksandr Stcherbina	SOV/UKR	4:31:44.0
5. Thomas Misson	GBR	4:33:03.0
6. Alexander Oakley	CAN	4:33:08.6
7. Giuseppe "Pino" Dordoni	ITA	4:33:28.8
8. Zora Singh	IND	4:37:45.0

In 1956, Don Thompson had been in fifth place with only 5000 meters to go, when he collapsed and failed to finish. With this bad memory in mind, he decided to acclimatize himself well in advance. But it is not easy to simulate a hot and humid September day in Rome when you live in Cranford, Middlesex. Fortunately, Don Thompson was quite a resourceful person. Several times each week, the 5-foot 5½-inch fire insurance clerk hauled paraffin heaters, hot water, and boiling kettles into his bathroom, sealed the doors and windows, and did his exercises in steaming 100-degree Fahrenheit (38-degree centigrade) heat. As he would later recall, "Half an hour was more than enough; I was feeling dizzy by then. It wasn't until several years later that I realised I wasn't feeling dizzy because of the heat; it was carbon monoxide from the stove."

Sure enough, the race began in 87-degree Fahrenheit (30.5-degree centigrade) weather, but Don Thompson, wearing a cap to which his mother had stitched a handkerchief in back, was ready. At the halfway point, he found himself in first place, following the disqualification of two of the leaders and the early overexertions of several others. Surprisingly, his only challenger was 1948 gold medalist John Ljunggren, who was two days shy of his 41st birthday. With 5000 meters to go, the two men were only one second apart. But then Thompson managed to pull away by 18 seconds over the next two kilometers, a lead that he was able to maintain the rest of the way. In Thompson's words, "Over the previous 25 kilometers, I'd been in a private race with Ljunggren and all I knew was I had to beat him. But once out there on the track with the spectators going crazy, I suddenly realized, 'gosh, this is for the Olympic gold medal.' It suddenly came to me that I was going to win the gold medal. It made me crack a bit. I froze up and was stiff and awkward coming down the finishing stretch. When I crossed the line, I wasn't so much excited—I was too tired for that—as smugly happy."

1964 Tokyo C: 34, N: 19, D: 10.18. WR: 4:14:02.4 (Abdon Pamich)

1. Abdon Pamich	ITA	4:11:12.4 OR
2. V. Paul Nihill	GBR	4:11:31.2
3. Ingvar Pettersson	SWE	4:14:17.4
4. Burkhard Leuschke	GDR	4:15:26.8
5. Robert Gardiner	AUS	4:17:06.8
6. Christoph Höhne	GDR	4:17:41.6
7. Anatoly Vedyakov	SOV/RUS	4:19:56.0
8. Kurt Sakowski	GDR	4:20:31.0

The race resolved into a two-man battle between Yugoslav-born Pamich and railwayman Nihill. At the 38-kilometer mark, Pamich was overcome by nausea and forced to take a 15-second vomit break. He regained the lead quickly, however, and fought off Nihill's challenges for the remainder of the race.

1968 Mexico City C: 36, N: 18, D: 10.17. WR: 4:10:41.8 (Christoph Höhne)

1. Christoph Höhne	GDR	4:20:13.6
2. Antal Kiss	HUN	4:30:17.0
3. Larry Young	USA	4:31:55.4
4. Peter Selzer	GDR	4:33:09.8
5. Stig-Erik Lindberg	SWE	4:34:05.0
6. Vittorio Visini	ITA	4:36:33.2
7. Bryan Eley	GBR	4:37:33.0
8. José Pedraza Zúñiga	MEX	4:37:52.0

Favorite Christoph Höhne drew away after passing the halfway mark, and won by an incredible ten-minute margin. Paul Nihill, who collapsed after 44 kilometers, suffered his only defeat in 86 races between December 1967 and June 1970. He finished ninth at the 1972 Olympics.

1972 Munich C: 36, N: 18, D: 9.3. WR: 3:52:44.6 (Bernd Kannenberg)

1. Bernd Kannenberg	GER	3:56:11.6 OR
2. Veniamin Soldatenko	SOV/KAZ	3:58:24.0
3. Larry Young	USA	4:00:46.0
4. Otto Barch	SOV/KYR	4:01:35.4
5. Peter Selzer	GDR	4:04:05.4
6. Gerhard Weidner	GER	4:06:26.0
7. Vittorio Visini	ITA	4:08:31.4
8. Gabriel Hernández	MEX	4:12:09.0

Kannenberg and Soldatenko walked together for 35 kilometers. Kannenberg, who had dropped out in the middle of the 20-kilometer race, noticed that Soldatenko was slow in taking his refreshments at the 35-kilometer food and drink stand, so he decided to pick up the pace. Soldatenko, worried because he had already received a warning, was unable to respond.

1976 not held

1980 Moscow C: 27, N: 14, D: 7.30. WR: 3:41:38.4 (Raúl González Rodríguez)

1. Hartwig Gauder	GDR	3:49:24 OR
2. Jorge Llopart Ribas	SPA	3:51:25
3. Yevgeny Ivchenko	SOV/UKR	3:56:32
4. Bengt Simonsen	SWE	3:57:08
5. Vyacheslav Fursov	SOV/RUS	3:58:32
6. José Marín	SPA	4:03:08
7. Stanislaw Rola	POL	4:07:07
8. Willi Sawall	AUS	4:08:25

Gold medalist Hartwig Gauder was born in West Germany, but his family moved to East Germany in 1960. Forty-two-year-old bronze medalist Yevgeny Ivchenko had been credited with a controversial time of 3:37:36.0 on the Olympic course on May 23, 1980.

In 1995 Gauder contracted a virus at a chicken farm that left his heart seriously weakened. After a near-disastrous experience using an artificial heart, Gauder underwent a second heart transplant in 1997. The following year he race walked the New York marathon and in 2003 he climbed Mt. Fuji.

1984 Los Angeles C: 31, N: 16, D: 8.11. WR: 3:41:38.4 (Raúl González Rodríguez)

1. Raúl González Rodríguez	MEX	3:47:26 OR
2. Bo Gustafsson	SWE	3:53:19
3. Alessandro Bellucci	ITA	3:53:45
4. Reima Salonen	FIN	3:58:30
5. Raffaello Ducceschi	ITA	3:59:26
6. Carl Schueler	USA	3:59:46
7. Jorge Llopart Ribas	SPA	4:03:09
8. José Pinto	POR	4:04:42

The popular 32-year-old veteran Raúl González, competing in his fourth Olympics, pushed the other walkers through a brutal early pace until the hot sun had worn out all of the leading challengers. Maurizio Damilano was the last to go, staying with González for 35 kilometers, before losing contact and then dropping out seven kilometers from the finish. Of the 31 starters, five were disqualified and nine more failed to complete the course.

1988 Seoul C: 42, N: 22, D: 9.30. WR: 3:41:38.4 (Raúl González Rodríguez)

1. Vyacheslav Ivanenko	SOV/RUS	3:38:29 OR
2. Ronald Weigel	GDR	3:38:56
3. Hartwig Gauder	GDR	3:39:45
4. Aleksandr Potashov	SOV/BLR	3:41:00
5. José Marín	SPA	3:43:03
6. Simon Baker	AUS	3:44:07
7. Bo Gustafsson	SWE	3:44:49
8. Raffaello Ducceschi	ITA	3:45:43

Vyacheslav Ivanenko was a 22-year-old machine repairman at a textile factory when he watched a television program that said that walking was good therapy for a bad back. The 5-foot 4½ -inch Ivanenko began walking the two and a half miles to work. Because he lived in Siberia, he walked fast. One day he was noticed by a coach, who began training him in earnest.

At the 20-kilometer mark in the Olympic contest, Hernán Andrade of Mexico led teammate Martín Bermúdez by 14 seconds; the rest of the walkers were at least 32 seconds farther back. Ten minutes later Andrade was disqualified. Bermúdez held a one-minute lead at the halfway point, but a group of five caught him in the 32nd kilometer and Bermúdez eventually faded to fifteenth. The favorites, Gauder, Weigel, and Ivanenko, pulled away from Martín and Potashov, with Ivanenko holding a three-second lead after 40 kilometers. Ivanenko then pressed the pace, dropping first Gauder and then Weigel, who resigned himself to protecting second place after receiving his second warning for lifting.

1992 Barcelona C: 42, N: 20, D: 8.7. WR: 3:41:38.4 (Raúl González Rodríguez)

1. Andrei Perlov	RUS	3:50.13
2. Carlos Mercenario Carbajal	MEX	3:52.09
3. Ronald Weigel	GER	3:53.45
4. Valery Spitsyn	RUS	3:54.39
5. Roman Mrázek	CZE	3:55.21
6. Hartwig Gauder	GER	3:56.47
7. Valentin Kononen	FIN	3:57.21
8. Miguel Rodríguez López	MEX	3:58.26

In 1991 Andrei Perlov, a construction engineer from Novosibirsk, Siberia, had a frustrating year. First he was disqualified after finishing first at the World Walking Cup, then, at the World Championships in Athletics, he and teammate Aleksandr Potashov tried to dead-heat by finishing arm in arm, but the judges ruled that Potashov had crossed the finish line first.

In Barcelona Potashov took the early lead, but was disqualified after 20 kilometers. Valentin Kononen took over and opened a 42-second gap at the 30-kilometer mark. By 35 kilometers he had been reeled in by Mercenario, Perlov, and Robert Korzeniowski of Poland and was soon left behind. At the 40-kilometer refreshment stand, without warning, Perlov shot ahead. Mercenario and Korzeniowski were unable to keep up with his pace. At the entrance to the stadium, Korzeniowski, in second place, was informed that he had been disqualified. In fact, he had received a record five warning cards, but it took a while for the recording system to catch up with him.

1996 Atlanta C: 51, N: 27, D: 8.2. WB: 3:37.41 (Andrei Perlov)

1. Robert Korzeniowski	POL	3:43:30
2. Mikhail Shchennikov	RUS	3:43:46
3. Valentí Massana Gracia	SPA	3:44:19
4. Arturo Di Mezza	ITA	3:44:52
5. Viktor Ginko	BLR	3:45:27
6. Ignacio Zamudio Cruz	MEX	3:46:07
7. Valentin Kononen	FIN	3:47:40
8. Sergei Korepanov	KAZ	3:48:42

Valentí Massana set the early pace and led by 39 seconds after 18 kilometers. The pack caught him at 27 kilometers. By 36 kilometers, the leading group consisted of Robert Korzeniowski, Massana, Daniel García of Mexico, Viktor Ginko and Ignacio Zamudio. Ginko lost contact at 40 kilometers as did García about a kilometer later. After 43 kilometers Korzeniowski began to gradually pull away. Four years earlier in Barcelona he had been disqualified at the stadium entrance while in second place. This time he completed the course without a single warning. Meanwhile, Mikhail Shchennikov was making his move. A 20-kilometer specialist, Shchennikov was so disappointed with his seventh place finish in that race that he entered the 50-kilometer even though he had competed only once before at that distance. He passed a fading Zamudio at 47 kilometers and caught Massana at 48 to earn a surprise silver medal.

Korzeniowski trained each day in two countries. He ate breakfast in France, walked across the border into Belgium and returned to France for lunch.

One unfortunate competitor was Duane Cousins of Australia. Track officials miscounted his laps and sent him to the finish line a lap early. He was officially recorded as "did not finish."

2000 Sydney C: 56, N: 28, D: 9.29. WB: 3:37:26 (Valery Spytsyn)

1. Robert Korzeniowski	POL	3:42:22
2. Aigars Fadejevs	LAT	3:43:40
3. Joel Sánchez	MEX	3:44:36
4. Valentí Massana Gracia	SPA	3:46:01
5. Nikolay Matyukhin	RUS	3:46:37
6. Nathan Deakes	AUS	3:47:29
7. Miguel Angel Rodríguez	MEX	3:48:12
8. Roman Magdziarczyk	POL	3:48:17

After winning the 20-kilometer walk, Robert Korzeniowski was asked if anything could stop him from defending his 50-kilometer title the following week. He replied, "Only the Tasmanian Devil". Korzeniowski was particularly confident because his bib number was 2711. For Korzeniowski the 27 stood for the 27th Olympiad and the 11 for two first place finishes. In fact, he pulled away after 42 kilometers and won by 78 seconds. In so doing, he entered the record books as the first walker to win both Olympic events and as the first person to win the 50 kilometers twice. The following year Korzeniowski became the first repeat winner at the world championships (he first won in 1997) and in 2003 he won the 50 kilometers world title for the third time.

2004 Athens C: 54, N: 29, D: 8.27. WB: 3:37:41 (Andrei Perlov)

1. Robert Korzeniowski	POL	3:38:46
2. Denis Nizhegorodov	RUS	3:42:50
3. Aleksei Voyevodin	RUS	3:43:34
4. Yu Chaohong	CHN	3:43:45
5. Jesús Ángel García	SPA	3:44:42
6. Roman Magdziarczyk	POL	3:48:11
7. Grzegorz Sudoł	POL	3:49:09
8. Santiago Pérez Alonso	SPA	3:49:48

With three world championship titles, a former world record and two consecutive 50-kilometer Olympic gold medals, including the first walking double in Olympic history, 36-year-old Robert Korzeniowski was en route to becoming the greatest racewalker ever. In

Athens, Korzeniowski, as expected, dominated the competition, setting a pace only three competitors could keep up with through the halfway point: Denis Nizhegorodov, Yu Chaohong, and Nathan Deakes, who had earned the bronze medal in the 20 kilometers one week earlier. At the 30-kilometer mark, Korzeniowski upped the pace even more, opening a 30-second lead ahead of Nizhegorodov in second place, and he was never seriously challenged thereafter. All three challengers paid a heavy price for trying to keep pace with Korzeniowski. Deakes lost his technique and was disqualified soon after the 30-kilometer mark. Yu faded at the end and lost the bronze when he was passed in the final 150 meters by Aleksei Voyevodin. Nizhegorodov staggered into the stadium four minutes after Korzeniowski, but managed to cross the finish line in second place before collapsing from exhaustion.

One week before the event, Korzeniowski's friend and training partner, Irish walker Jamie Costin, was involved in a head-on accident with a truck just after dropping Korzeniowski off after a practice session. Costin was driving Korzeniowski's car at the time, and incurred severe back and hand injuries.

Korzeniowski took up sports at the age of thirteen, after recovering from childhood rheumatism. Inspired by movie star Bruce Lee, he inititally took up martial arts, but the sport was unpopular with the Communist regime in power at the time. According to Korzeniowski, the authorities quickly closed the martial arts gym under the pretext of renovations, forcing him to take up the only other available option—athletics.

2008 Beijing C: 59, N: 32, D: 8.22. WB: 3:34:14 (Denis Nizhegorodov)

1. Alex Schwazer	ITA	3:37:09 OR
2. Jared Tallent	AUS	3:39:27
3. Denis Nizhegorodov	RUS	3:40:14
4. Jesús Ángel García Bragado	SPA	3:44:08
5. Erik Tysse	NOR	3:45:08
6. Horacio Nava Reza	MEX	3:45:21
7. Yuki Yamazaki	JPN	3:45:47
8. Rafał Fedaczyński	POL	3:46:51

After winning his third consecutive Olympic gold medal in the event, Robert Korzeniowski announced his retirement, opening the field to a new generation of race walkers. In the intervening four years, no overwhelming favorite had emerged, as each major event had had a different champion. In 2005 Russia's Sergei Kirdyapkin won the world championship title, ahead of 2004 bronze medalist Aleksei Voyevodin and Alex Schwazer. In 2006 France's Yohan Diniz, a former rave party organizer and wine expert, won the European championship ahead of Jesús García of Spain. And in 2007 Australia's Nathan Deakes won the world championship title, with Diniz in second, Schwazer again in third, and 2004 silver medalist Denis Nizhegorodov fourth.

Three months before the Olympics, Nizhegorodov set a world best at a race in Cherboksary, Russia, finishing three minutes ahead of Schwazer in second place. The two seemed well positioned to battle for gold, especially after reigning world champion Deakes withdrew from the competition a month before the Games due to a hamstring injury.

A lead group of four, including Tallent, Schwazer, China's Li Jianbo and Nizhegorodov, broke away early in Beijing. Nizhegorodov held the lead at the 15-kilometer mark, but was quickly reeled in by Li, Tallent and Schwazer. Twenty-four-year-old Schwazer and Tallent traded the lead over the next hour, with Nizhegorodov close behind, while Li slowly drifted out of medal contention. Diniz stayed close to the lead pack until the 30-kilometer mark, but slowed to a near standstill by the two-hour mark and ultimately dropped out with severe stomach pains.

Schwazer made his move after 42 kilometers, passing Tallent and surging over the next few kilometers to open a comfortable lead. His final time broke the Olympic record set by Vyacheslav Ivanenko in 1988. Tallent won silver with a personal best.

Two weeks after the Games, Tallent married his fiancée, Claire Woods, who competed in the women's 20-kilometer walk. The couple held their wedding in an appropriately named suburb of Adelaide . . . Walkerville.

HIGH JUMP

In high jump competitions, the crossbar is four meters (13 feet 1½ inches) long. The runway leading to the crossbar must be at least 20 meters (65 feet 7½ inches) long and preferably at least 25 meters (82 feet) long. Each contestant may place one or two markers along the runway to assist in the timing of his or her run-up and takeoff. There is a time limit of 1½ minutes for each jump, although when there are only two or three competitors remaining, three minutes are allowed before each jump. A contestant may begin at any height and may pass at any height. Three successive misses results in elimination, even if the misses are at different heights. Touching the crossbar is acceptable as long as the bar does not fall. Current rules decide ties in the following manner:

1. The competitor with the fewest misses at the last cleared height wins. If there is still a tie, then:
2. The competitor with the fewest total misses wins. If there is still a tie, it is recorded as such, unless the tie is for first place. In that case:
3. Each competitor is given one extra jump. If there is still a tie, then the bar is raised or lowered until the tie is broken.

High-jumpers must take off from one foot. In April 1954, US tumbler Dick Browning reportedly somersaulted over a bar set at 7 feet 6 inches (2.28 meters). In 1962 Gary Chamberlain did a back handspring with a back flip over a bar set at 7 feet 4 inches (2.23 meters). He landed on his feet.

1896 Athens C: 5, N: 3, D: 4.10. WR: 1.97, 6-5 (Michael Sweeney)

		M	FT.-IN.
1. Ellery Clark	USA	1.81	5-11¼
2. James Connolly	USA	1.65	5-5
2. Robert Garrett	USA	1.65	5-5
4. Henrik Sjöberg	SWE	1.60	5-3
5. Fritz Hofmann	GER	1.55	5-1

Ellery Clark was a 22-year-old Harvard undergraduate who was granted a leave of absence for the Olympics because of his high grade point average—but only on the condition that he not bring attention to the fact that he was associated with Harvard. Clark returned to the Olympics in 1904, placing fifth in the decathlon. He eventually authored nineteen books including a novel, *Loaded Dice,* that was made into a 1952 film entitled *Caribbean* that starred John Payne and Arlene Dahl.

1900 Paris C: 8, N: 7, D: 7.15. WR: 1.97, 6-5 (Michael Sweeney)

		M	FT.-IN.
1. Irving Baxter	USA	1.90	6-2¾ OR
2. Patrick Leahy	GBR/IRL	1.78	5-10
3. Lajos Gönczy	HUN	1.75	5-8¾
4. Carl-Albert Andersen	NOR	1.70	5-7
4. Eric Lemming	SWE	1.70	5-7
4. Waldemar Steffen	GER	1.70	5-7
7. Louis Monnier	FRA	1.60	5-3
8. Tore Blom	SWE	1.50	4-11

Two Americans, William Remington and Walter Carroll, refused to take part in the final because it was held on a Sunday. Silver medalist Pat Leahy had reportedly cleared 6 feet 4 inches at least six times back in Ireland, but in Paris he missed three times at 6 feet.

1904 St. Louis C: 6, N: 3, D: 8.29. WR: 1.97, 6-5 (Michael Sweeney)

		M	FT.-IN.
1. Samuel Jones	USA	1.80	5-11
2. Garrett Serviss	USA	1.77	5-9¾
3. Paul Weinstein	GER	1.77	5-9¾
4. Lajos Gönczy	HUN	1.75	5-9
5. Emil Freymark	USA	—	—
6. Ervin Barker	USA	1.70	5-7

Lajos Gönczy had brought with him to the United States several bottles of potent Hungarian wine, which were confiscated by Hungarian team officials prior to the competition. Unable to clear even 5 feet 9¾ inches, Gönczy finished a disappointing fourth. Several days later, Gönczy took part in an unofficial handicap event and successfully cleared 6 feet 2 inches. When the other Hungarians rushed up to congratulate him, they smelled his breath and discovered that he had found the hidden bottles of wine.

1906 Athens C: 24, N: 11, D: 5.1. WR: 1.97, 6-5 (Michael Sweeney)

		M	FT.-IN.
1. Cornelius "Con" Leahy	GBR/IRL	1.775	5-10
2. Lajos Gönczy	HUN	1.75	5-8¾
3. Themistoklis Diakidis	GRE	1.725	5-8
3. Herbert Kerrigan	USA	1.725	5-8
5. Gunnar Rönström	SWE	1.70	5-7
6. Halfdan Bjølgerud	NOR	1.675	5-5¾
6. Bruno Söderström	SWE	1.675	5-5¾
8. Paul Weinstein	GER	1.65	5-5

Herbert Kerrigan had been the favorite, but he was injured when a huge wave hit the ship that carried the US team to Athens. Con Leahy's brother Pat had placed second in the 1900 high jump.

1908 London C: 22, N: 10, D: 7.21. WR: 1.97, 6-5 (Michael Sweeney)

		M	FT.-IN.
1. Harry Porter	USA	1.905	6-3 OR
2. Georges "Géo" André	FRA	1.88	6-2
2. Cornelius "Con" Leahy	GBR/IRL	1.88	6-2
2. István Somodi	HUN	1.88	6-2
5. Herbert Gidney	USA	1.855	6-1
5. Thomas Moffitt	USA	1.855	6-1
7. Norman Patterson	USA	1.83	6-0
8. Axel Hedenlund	SWE	1.80	5-11

Silver medalist Géo André had never before jumped higher than 1.79 meters (5 feet 10 inches). At the 1912 Olympics he took part in the decathlon. During World War I he was badly injured and taken prisoner. After escaping at his sixth try, he rejoined the fight as an aviator. At the 1920 Olympics he competed in the 400-meter hurdles and the 4 × 400-meter relay. In 1924, again entered in the hurdles, he was chosen to take the

Athletes' Oath on behalf of all the athletes at the Paris Games.

In a 1922 interview, Géo André revealed an incident that occurred relating to the 1908 high jump. During the competition, André noticed that the US coaches periodically gave to their jumpers sips from blue bottles that they kept hidden underneath their warmup clothes. In the days before drug testing, there was nothing illegal about this, but André became convinced that this mysterious liquid allowed the Americans to jump with greater elasticity and he was determined to uncover their secret.

After the competition was over, André slipped over to the American side, stole one of the bottles and tried to hide it in his pocket. As he walked back to the locker room, he was stopped by the American coaches. Convinced he had been caught, André broke out in a cold sweat. But it turned out that the Americans only wanted to shake his hand and congratulate him.

Back in his room, André studied the bottle. On it was a label that read, "Sun Water." He brought the bottle back to Paris and tried drinking the liquid before jumping. But it didn't seem to help his performance.

Finally, his curiosity getting the better of him, André brought the bottle to a pharmacist. After analyzing the mysterious liquid, the pharmacist revealed to André its composition. The secret drink of the American jumpers was . . . water.

1912 Stockholm C: 37, N: 10, D: 7.8. WR: 2.005, 6-7 (George Horine)

		M	FT.-IN.
1. Alma Richards	USA	1.93	6-4 OR
2. Hans Liesche	GER	1.91	6-3¼
3. George Horine	USA	1.89	6-2¼
4. Egon Erickson	USA	1.87	6-1½
4. James Thorpe	USA	1.87	6-1½
6. Harry Grumpelt	USA	1.85	6-0¾
6. John Johnstone	USA	1.85	6-0¾
8. Karl-Axel Kullerstrand	SWE	1.83	6-0

Alma Richards was a tall, awkward-looking 22-year-old Mormon from Parowan, Utah who had never competed outside of Utah until he entered—and won—the US Trials. Despite his victory, he was initially left off the US team because he was so unknown. Finally he was added as a "supplemental" entry. On the ship from New York to Stockholm, he became the butt of countless "country boob" jokes made by the other members of the US team. In the final Olympic competition, Richards seemed to have quite a bit of trouble, missing as many jumps as he made. Yet when the bar was raised to 6 feet 3¼ inches, the only jumpers left were Richards, Hans Liesche of Germany, and the favorite, George Horine, inventor of what came to be known as the "western-roll" style of high-jumping. Liesche cleared smoothly on the first try, but Horine missed three times and was eliminated. Richards, however, cleared the bar on his third and final attempt.

The bar was then put up to 6 feet 4 inches. Alma Richards, scheduled to jump first, walked away from the high jump area to be by himself. He closed his eyes and bowed his head, and made a deal with God. "I told the Lord," he later wrote, "that if He would help me to win the high jump in the Olympic Games at Stockholm, I would do my best to be a good boy and set a good example." Without further hesitation, Richards, who had never before come close to jumping 6 feet 4 inches, dashed toward the bar and sailed over with almost two inches to spare. Liesche was completely unnerved. He failed twice. Then, just as he had composed himself for his final attempt, a gun went off to signal the start of a race. Liesche waited for the race to end and then composed himself once more. This time the band began to play. After nine minutes, a Swedish official approached him and asked him to hurry up. This was the final blow. Liesche ran at the bar, but missed completely. Alma Richards, transformed from a country bumpkin into a hero in the eyes of his teammates, went on to be a good boy for the rest of his life. He served in World War I and eventually spent 32 years as a science teacher at Venice High School in Los Angeles.

1920 Antwerp C: 22, N: 9, D: 8.17. WR: 2.01, 6-7¼ (Edward Beeson)

		M	FT.-IN.
1. Richmond Landon	USA	1.935	6-4 EOR
2. Harold Muller	USA	1.90	6-2¾
3. Bo Ekelund	SWE	1.90	6-2¾
4. Walter Whalen	USA	1.85	6-0¾
5. John Murphy	USA	1.85	6-0¾
6. B. Howard Baker	GBR	1.85	6-0¾
7. Pierre Lewden	FRA	1.80	5-10¾
7. Einar Thulin	SWE	1.80	5-10¾

In his book *Un Champion à la Hauteur,* Pierre Lewden, who placed seventh, describes how shocked he was by an incident that occurred during Bo Ekelund's final attempt at 6 feet 4 inches. While Ekelund was racing down the runway, an American official walked over and picked up the marker belonging to Dick Landon, which happened to be only a couple inches away from Ekelund's marker. His concentration broken, but unable to stop himself, Ekelund hit the bar head-on and the competition was decided in Landon's favor.

1924 Paris C: 21, N: 15, D: 7.7. WR: 2.03, 6-8¼ (Harold Osborn)

		M	FT.-IN.
1. Harold Osborn	USA	1.98	6-6 OR
2. Leroy Brown	USA	1.95	6-4¾
3. Pierre Lewden	FRA	1.92	6-3½
4. Thomas Poor	USA	1.88	6-2
5. Jenö Gáspár	HUN	1.88	6-2
6. Helge Jansson	SWE	1.85	6-0¾
7. Pierre Guilloux	FRA	1.85	6-0¾
8. Sverre Helgesen	NOR	1.83	6-0
8. Lawrence Roberts	SAF	1.83	6-0

Harold Osborn cleared every height on his first attempt. Five days later he earned a second gold medal in the decathlon.

1928 Amsterdam C: 35, N: 17, D: 7.29. WR: 2.03, 6-8¼ (Harold Osborn)

		M	FT.-IN.
1. Robert King	USA	1.94	6-4½
2. Benjamin Hedges	USA	1.91	6-3¼
3. Claude Ménard	FRA	1.91	6-3¼
4. Simeon Toribio	PHI	1.91	6-3¼
5. Harold Osborn	USA	1.91	6-3¼
6. Kazuo Kimura	JPN	1.88	6-2
7. André Cherrie	FRA	1.88	6-2
7. Pierre Lewden	FRA	1.88	6-2
7. Charles McGinnis	USA	1.88	6-2
7. Mikio Oda	JPN	1.88	6-2

Places two through five were decided by a jump-off.

1932 Los Angeles C: 14, N: 10, D: 7.31. WR: 2.03, 6-8¼ (Harold Osborn)

		M	FT.-IN.
1. Duncan McNaughton	CAN	1.97	6-5½
2. Robert Van Osdel	USA	1.97	6-5½
3. Simeon Toribio	PHI	1.97	6-5½
4. Cornelius Johnson	USA	1.97	6-5½
5. Ilmari Reinikka	FIN	1.94	6-4¼
6. Kazuo Kimura	JPN	1.94	6-4¼
7. Misao Ono	JPN	1.90	6-2¾
7. Jerzy Plawczyk	POL	1.90	6-2¾

Bob Van Osdel and Duncan McNaughton were good friends and fellow students at the University of Southern California in Los Angeles. Van Osdel had qualified for the US team, as expected, by clearing 6 feet 6⅝ inches at the US trials. McNaughton, on the other hand, had to wage a one-man campaign to convince the Canadian Olympic Association to let him compete. Undeterred by their constant refusals, McNaughton waited until the Canadian team arrived in Los Angeles, and then badgered them in person until they finally relented.

Van Osdel, McNaughton, Toribio, and 18-year-old Los Angeles High School student Cornelius Johnson

Duncan McNaughton, 1932

McNaughton pestered the Canadian Olympic Association into letting him complete in the 1932 Olympics, since he lived in Los Angeles anyway. He went on to win the gold medal in the high jump.

all cleared 6 feet 5½ inches, but they all missed at 6 feet 6¾ inches. Following the rules in force at the time, the bar was then raised, lowered, raised and lowered until the contest was decided. After Johnson and Toribio had been eliminated, Van Osdel, who had been informally coaching McNaughton ever since he had first arrived in Los Angeles from Vancouver two years earlier, approached his Canadian friend and advised him on improving his technique. He concluded, "Get your kick working and you will be over." That piece of advice and encouragement did the trick. McNaughton cleared the bar while Van Osdel missed.

If current tie-breaking rules had been used back in 1932, Van Osdel would have won the gold medal, Johnson the silver, and McNaughton the bronze.

In 1933, McNaughton's gold medal was stolen from his car. Van Osdel, now a dentist, made a mold from his own silver medal, poured gold into the mold, and sent this replica gold medal to McNaughton.

1936 Berlin C: 40, N: 24, D: 8.2. WR: 2.07, 6-9¾ (Cornelius Johnson, David Albritton)

		M	FT.-IN.
1. Cornelius Johnson	USA	2.03	6-8 OR
2. David Albritton	USA	2.00	6-6¾
3. Delos Thurber	USA	2.00	6-6¾
4. Kalevi Kotkas	FIN	2.00	6-6¾
5. Kimlo Yada	JPN	1.97	6-5½
6. Yoshiro Asakuma	JPN	1.94	6-4¼
6. Lauri Kalima	FIN	1.94	6-4¼
6. Hiroshi Tanaka	JPN	1.94	6-4¼
6. Gustav Weinkötz	GER	1.94	6-4¼

Johnson won the gold medal without a miss and didn't even take off his sweatsuit until the bar had reached 6 feet 6¾ inches. Places 2 through 4 were decided by a jump-off. Adolf Hitler had personally congratulated the winners of the first two events of the day, Germans and Finns, but he left the stadium before the ceremony honoring the three Americans. Both Johnson and Albritton were black. Fourth-place finisher Kotkas had finished seventh in the discus throw four years earlier.

David Albritton later became a high school teacher and coach and served six terms in the Ohio state legislature. When he died in 1994, his legacy was hundreds of people whom he motivated to pursue an education, respect themselves and respect others.

1948 London C: 26, N: 16, D: 7.30. WR: 2.11, 6-11 (Lester Steers)

		M	FT.-IN.
1. John Winter	AUS	1.98	6-6
2. Björn Paulson	NOR	1.95	6-4¾
3. George Stanich	USA	1.95	6-4¾
4. Dwight Eddleman	USA	1.95	6-4¾
5. Georges Damitio	FRA	1.95	6-4¾
6. Arthur Jackes	CAN	1.90	6-2¾
7. Alan Paterson	GBR	1.90	6-2¾
7. Hans Wähli	SWI	1.90	6-2¾

John Winter, a 23-year-old bank clerk from Perth, cleared 6 feet 6 inches on his first attempt. Then he watched in surprise as the remaining four jumpers, including two Americans who had had to clear 6 feet 7¼ inches just to make the team, failed three times each. For the first time in the Olympics, ties were decided according to fewer misses.

1952 Helsinki C: 36, N: 24, D: 7.20. WR: 2.11, 6-11 (Lester Steers)

		M	FT.-IN.
1. Walter "Buddy" Davis	USA	2.04	6-8½ OR
2. Kenneth Wiesner	USA	2.01	6-7
3. JoséTelles da Conceição	BRA	1.98	6-6
4. Gösta Svensson	SWE	1.98	6-6
5. Ronald Pavitt	GBR	1.95	6-4¾
6. Ion Söter	ROM	1.95	6-4¾
7. Arnold Betton	USA	1.95	6-4¾
8. Björn Gundersen	NOR	1.90	6-2¾

The 6-foot 8-inch, 206-pound Davis was an All-American basketball player from Texas A. & M. Stricken by polio at the age of eight, he had been unable to walk for three years. After the Olympics, Davis was drafted by the Philadelphia Warriors of the National Basketball Association (NBA). However, he refused to turn professional until he had set a world record in the high jump. On June 27, 1953, Davis jumped 6 feet 11⅝ inches (2.13 meters) to break Les Steers' 12-year-old world record. A few days later he signed a contract with Philadelphia and won NBA championships with both the Warriors and the St. Louis Hawks.

1956 Melbourne C: 28, N: 19, D: 11.23. WR: 2.15, 7-0½ (Charles Dumas)

		M	FT.-IN.
1. Charles Dumas	USA	2.12	6-11½ OR
2. Charles "Chilla" Porter	AUS	2.10	6-10¾
3. Igor Kashkarov	SOV/RUS	2.08	6-9¾
4. Stig Pettersson	SWE	2.06	6-9
5. Kenneth Money	CAN	2.03	6-8
6. Volodymyr Sytkin	SOV/UKR	2.00	6-6¾
7. Phil Reavis	USA	2.00	6-6¾
7. Colin Ridgeway	AUS	2.00	6-6¾

When Les Steers jumped 6 feet 11 inches on June 14, 1941, it seemed that the magic 7-foot barrier would be cleared at any time. But it was 12 years before Walt Davis bettered Steer's record with a leap of 6 feet 11½ inches, and even he was unable to go that extra half-inch. It was as if the 7-foot mark was guarded by a protective aura. It is true that 7-foot jumps had been claimed, most notably by Davis in an exhibition, but the first official, in-competition 7-foot jump wasn't achieved until June 29, 1956, when 19-year-old Charley Dumas glided over at the US Olympic trials. There was great interest in Dumas when he arrived in Melbourne, but some of that interest turned to hostility when it turned out that Dumas didn't believe in practicing or even training, other than a few stretching exercises each morning.

However, Dumas knew what he was up to. He won the gold medal with relative ease, despite the spirited challenge of local favorite Chilla Porter, who improved his personal best by two inches. Ken Money, who finished fifth, later became a space scientist and astronaut.

1960 Rome C: 32, N: 23, D: 9.1. WR: 2.23. 7-3¾ (John Thomas)

		M	FT.-IN.
1. Robert Shavlakadze	SOV/GEO	2.16	7-1 OR
2. Valery Brumel	SOV/UKR	2.16	7-1
3. John Thomas	USA	2.14	7-0¼
4. Viktor Bolshov	SOV/RUS	2.14	7-0¼
5. Stig Pettersson	SWE	2.09	6-10¼
6. Charles Dumas	USA	2.03	6-8
7. Jiři Lansky	CZE	2.03	6-8
7. Kjell-Åke Nilsson	SWE	2.03	6-8
7. Theo Püll	GER	2.03	6-8

American sportswriters boasted that the high jump was one gold medal that was "in the bag" for the United States. The US team consisted of 17-year-old Joe Faust, who had cleared 7 feet, defending champion Charley Dumas, and the 6-foot 5-inch world record holder John Thomas, who had jumped 7 feet over 30 times and hadn't been defeated in two years. But Faust, hampered by an ankle injury, was unable to clear 6 feet 6¾ inches. And Dumas, plagued by a knee injury that American officials had tried to convince him was imaginary, bowed out at 6 feet 10¼ inches. This left Thomas to battle it out with three jumpers from the USSR: Soviet champion Viktor Bolshov, 18-year-old Siberian-born Valery Brumel, who had suddenly improved three and a half inches in August to 7 feet 1½ inches, and Robert Shavlakadze, a mustachioed 27-year-old from Tbilisi, Georgia.

John Thomas (left) and Robert Shavlakadze, 1960
Thomas congratulates Shavlakadze after the latter's upset victory in the 1960 high jump.

At 6 feet 11½ inches Thomas passed. Bolshov and Shavlakadze went over the bar on their first attempts, while Brumel missed twice before clearing. This height also saw the departure of Stig Pettersson. The bar was raised to 7 feet ¼ inch. Brumel and Bolshov missed, but Shavlakadze cleared with his first try, the first time he had ever jumped over 7 feet in competition. Thomas missed, but the second time around, he and the other two Soviet jumpers all cleared the bar.

The next height was 7 feet 1 inch. The only one to clear on the first attempt was Shavlakadze, who had now made seven straight successful jumps since missing his first try of the afternoon at 6 feet 6¾ inches. Brumel cleared on his second try, but Bolshov and Thomas missed all three times. For Robert Shavlakadze, this was the greatest day of his career. For Valery Brumel, it was just the beginning. As for John Thomas, he was disappointed, but proud that he had earned an Olympic medal. Consequently, it came as a shock to the mild-mannered teenager when the very same sportswriters and fans who had been singing his praises only a few days earlier turned on him and accused him of getting carried away with all the publicity that they themselves had spread.

"That was the first time I learned people didn't like me," Thomas later recalled. "They only like winners. They don't give credit to a man for trying. I was called a quitter, a man with no heart. It left me sick." Thomas had nightmares for months until he finally came to accept that American sports fans were fickle. "American spectators are frustrated athletes," he concluded. "In the champion, they see what they'd like to be. In the loser, they see what they actually are, and they treat him with scorn."

1964 Tokyo C: 29, N: 20, D: 10.21. WR: 2.28, 7-5¾ (Valery Brumel)

		M	FT.-IN.
1. Valery Brumel	SOV/UKR	2.18	7-1¾ OR
2. John Thomas	USA	2.18	7-1¾ OR
3. John Rambo	USA	2.16	7-1
4. Stig Pettersson	SWE	2.14	7-0¼
5. Robert Shavlakadze	SOV/GEO	2.14	7-1¼
6. Ralf Drecoll	GER	2.09	6-10¼
6. Kjell-Åke Nilsson	SWE	2.09	6-10¼
8. Edward Caruthers	USA	2.09	6-10¼

By 1964 the pressure of great expectations had shifted from John Thomas to Valery Brumel, the current world record holder. And Brumel definitely felt that pressure. He lost to Shavlakadze at the 1964 USSR championships, and arrived in Tokyo in somewhat of a crisis. Well below form, he worked out in secret so that his image of invincibility wouldn't be tarnished. When he cleared 6 feet 9¾

Valery Brumel, 1964
The ecstasy – to be followed, within the year, by agony.

inches in practice, his coach lied to him and told him the bar had actually been two inches higher.

The Olympic qualifying round was held on October 20. Brumel missed twice at 6 feet 8 inches and was on the verge of not even making it to the final, when he got himself together and cleared the bar successfully, thus preventing a complete disaster.

The next day, for the final, Brumel was more composed. He made it through 6 feet 11½ inches without a miss, a feat matched only by Robert Shavlakadze. Pettersson, Rambo, and Thomas each cleared 6 feet 11½ inches with their second try. At 7 feet ¼ inch, only Rambo went over the first time, and only Pettersson made it the second time. The three medalists from 1960 were now each one miss from elimination. But all three literally rose to the challenge and sailed over without dislodging the bar. This seemed to be a turning point for Valery Brumel. With renewed confidence, he cleared 7 feet 1 inch on his first attempt. Thomas made it the second time around, and Rambo the third, while Pettersson and Shavlakadze failed at all three attempts. Rambo bowed out at 7 feet 1¾ inches, while Brumel and Thomas both succeeded

Valery Brumel and John Thomas, 1964
Brumel of the Soviet Union and John Thomas of the United States became friends despite their athletic rivalry and their nations' political differences.

with their first tries. However, neither man, by now good friends after four years of competition, was able to make it over 7 feet 2½ inches. Brumel and Thomas were both credited with the Olympic record, but Brumel was awarded first place because he had committed fewer misses.

On October 4, 1965, Valery Brumel was riding on the back of a motorcycle being driven by female motorcycle racing champion Tamara Golikova, when they skidded out of control. Although Golikova was unhurt, Brumel was smashed into a concrete pillar and suffered an open tibia fracture of his right leg. His right foot was hanging limply, barely connected to the rest of his body.

When Brumel had traveled to the United States to compete in a series of competitions against John Thomas, he had been shocked by the behavior of American crowds, which booed Thomas when he missed a jump or, worst of all, when he committed the sin of finishing second. But now that his own sporting career had come to a sudden end, Brumel learned that Soviet fans could be just as harsh. The newspapers lost interest in him, most of his friends drifted away, his wife, perhaps wondering what he had been doing whizzing around on the back of a motorcycle with Tamara Golikova in the first place, divorced him.

After his accident, Brumel received a telegram that

read, "Sometimes a twist of fate seems to have been put there to test a man's strength of character. Don't admit defeat. I sincerely hope you come back to jump again." It was signed "John Thomas." Remarkably, Valery Brumel, after more than twenty operations, did jump again. Although he never made it back to international competition, in 1970 he actually cleared 6 feet 11¾ inches. He was also able to channel his energy into other directions, earning a doctorate in sports psychology and publishing a novel, a play and an opera libretto.

1968 Mexico City C: 39, N: 25, D: 10.20. WR: 2.28, 7-5¾ (Valery Brumel)

		M	FT.-IN.
1. Richard Fosbury	USA	2.24	7-4¼ OR
2. Edward Caruthers	USA	2.22	7-3¼
3. Valentin Gavrilov	SOV/RUS	2.20	7-2½
4. Valery Skvortsov	SOV/RUS	2.16	7-1
5. Reynaldo Brown	USA	2.14	7-0¼
6. Giacomo Crosa	ITA	2.14	7-0¼
7. Günter Spielvogel	GER	2.14	7-0¼
8. Lawrie Peckham	AUS	2.12	6-11½

Dick Fosbury, 1968

Introduces the Fosbury Flop at the 1968 Olympics.

The 1968 Olympics marked the international debut of Dick Fosbury and his celebrated "Fosbury flop," which would soon revolutionize high-jumping. Fosbury's technique began by racing up to the bar at great speed and taking off with his left foot. But instead of swinging his right foot up and over the bar, as everyone else did, Fosbury would pivot his right leg back and approach head first with his back to the bar. While the coaches of the world, already exasperated by the steeplechase style of Amos Biwott, shook their heads in disbelief, the Mexico City audience was absolutely captivated by Fosbury. Fosbury cleared every height through 7 feet 3¼ inches without a miss and then achieved a personal record of 7 feet 4¼ inches to win the gold medal. By 1980, 13 of the 16 Olympic finalists were using the Fosbury flop. Actually Fosbury was not the first high jumper to jump with his back to the bar. In 1966 Debbie Brill of Canada was already practicing the "Brill Bend." In 2000, sportswriter Rial Cummings stumbled across a newspaper photo from May 24, 1963, that showed Bruce Quande flopping over the bar at the Montana state high school meet. The photo clearly shows Quande jumping head first with his back to the bar.

1972 Munich C: 40, N: 29, D: 9.10. WR: 2.29, 7-6 (Ni Zhiqin, Patrick Matzdorf)

		M	FT.-IN.
1. Jüri Tarmak	SOV/EST	2.23	7-3¾
2. Stefan Junge	GDR	2.21	7-3
3. Dwight Stones	USA	2.21	7-3
4. Hermann Magerl	GER	2.18	7-1¾
5. Ádám Szepesi	HUN	2.18	7-1¾
6. John Beers	CAN	2.15	7-0½
6. István Major	HUN	2.15	7-0½
8. Rustam Akhmyetov	SOV/UKR	2 15	7-0½

1976 Montreal C: 36, N: 23, D: 7.31. WR: 2.31, 7-7 (Dwight Stones)

		M	FT.-IN.
1. Jacek Wszola	POL	2.25	7-4½ OR
2. Gregory Joy	CAN	2.23	7-3¾
3. Dwight Stones	USA	2.21	7-3
4. Sergei Budalov	SOV/RUS	2.21	7-3
5. Serhei Senyukov	SOV/UKR	2.18	7-1¾
6. Rodolfo Bergamo	ITA	2.18	7-1¾
7. Rolf Beilschmidt	GDR	2.18	7-1¾
8. Jesper Torring	DEN	2.18	7-1¾

In 1972 Dwight Stones had been one of the darlings of the Munich Games. A mere 18 years old, he had delighted the crowd with his exuberance. Four years later in Montreal, it was a completely different story. Now he was the world record holder and heavy favorite. But several days before the competition began, Stones launched a verbal attack against the French-Canadian organizers of the Games for failing to complete the stadium as planned. Of particular concern to Stones was the nonappearance of a retractable roof, which would have kept out the rain. Fear of rain was an obsession with Stones because his approach to the bar was unusually fast and sharp. Stones called the Olympic organizers "rude" for forcing the athletes to compete in an unfinished stadium. But by the time that his remarks had been translated into the local papers, he was being accused of calling all French Canadians "rude."

When Stones appeared on the track for the qualifying round, he was loudly booed. Whenever his name was announced, he was booed; whenever he began a jump he was booed; whenever he missed or made a jump he was booed. The situation degenerated rather badly when US fans in the stadium retaliated by booing a French-Canadian high-jumper, Claude Ferragne.

The next day, Stones tried to make peace with the local crowd by wearing a shirt that bore on the back the slogan "I love French Canadians." Track officials made him take it off. Underneath he had on a 1972 Olympic shirt, which he was wearing because it had been made by a company with which he had a financial relationship. The officials made him take that one off too. By the time the bar had been raised to 7 feet 1¾ inches, a light rain had begun to fall. At 7 feet 3 inches, the rain had become heavy. Huge puddles formed in the high jump area. Stones, exasperated by the ineffectual attempts of the officials to clear the area, grabbed a squeegee and started mopping up the area himself. Other jumpers joined him, including surprise local favorite Greg Joy. For Stones it was a hopeless cause. Even the eventual winner, 19-year-old Jacek Wszola, when asked later at what point he knew he would win, replied, "When it started to rain." Four days later, in Philadelphia, Dwight Stones broke his own world record with a leap of 7 feet 7¼ inches.

In the years to come, Greg Joy's 1976 image would become embedded in the Canadian national consciousness because his final successful jump was included in CBC-TV's nightly sign-off montage.

1980 Moscow C: 30, N: 19, D: 8.1. WR: 2.35, 7-8½ (Jacek Wszola, Dietmar Mögenburg)

		M	FT.-IN.
1. Gerd Wessig	GDR	2.36	7-8¾ WR
2. Jacek Wszola	POL	2.31	7-7
3. Jörg Freimuth	GDR	2.31	7-7
4. Henry Lauterbach	GDR	2.29	7-6
5. Roland Dalhäuser	SWI	2.24	7-4¼
6. Vaso Komneni	YUG/SER	2.24	7-4¼
7. Adrian Proteasa	ROM	2.21	7-3
8. Aleksandr Grigoryev	SOV/RUS	2.21	7-3

The anticipated showdown between co-world record holders Jacek Wszola and Dietmar Mögenburg was spoiled when West Germany joined the anti-Soviet boycott. As it turned out, however, neither of them held the world record anymore once the competition was over. Gerd Wessig, a 6-foot 7-inch 21-year-old cook from Schwerin, was one of the big surprises of the 1980 Olympics. He had qualified for the East German team only two weeks earlier when he won the national championship with what was then his personal record of 7 feet 6½ inches. In Moscow he improved by over two inches to become the first man to set a world record in the high jump in the Olympics. Oddly enough, Wessig was also the first jumper since 1896 to make a successful jump beyond the height that had won him the gold medal.

1984 Los Angeles C: 30, N: 20, D: 8.11. WR: 2.39, 7-10 (Zhu Jianhua)

		M	FT.-IN.
1. Dietmar Mögenburg	GER	2.35	7-8½
2. Patrik Sjöberg	SWE	2.33	7-7¾
3. Zhu Jianhua	CHN	2.31	7-7
4. Dwight Stones	USA	2.31	7-7
5. Doug Nordquist	USA	2.29	7-6¼
6. Milton Ottey	CAN	2.29	7-6¼
7. Liu Yunpeng	CHN	2.29	7-6¼
8. Cai Shu	CHN	2.27	7-5¼

While the experts predicted the gold medal would go to world record holder Zhu Jianhua, with two-time bronze medalist Dwight Stones fighting it out for second place with Dietmar Mögenburg, *the* expert on the high jump knew better. That expert, loquacious Dwight Stones himself, picked the 6-foot 7-inch Mögenburg for the gold, Zhu for the silver and himself for the bronze. Had not 19-year-old Patrik Sjöberg equaled his personal record to take second, Stones' soothsaying would have been right on the mark. The most important factor, as Stones well knew, was that Mögenburg had a history of rising to the occasion at important meets, while Zhu seemed to falter when the going got rough.

Two months earlier Zhu had defeated Mögenburg in West Germany by setting a world record of 7 feet 10 inches, but in Los Angeles Zhu's concentration was broken by an unexpected occurrence. After recording his first miss at 7 feet 7¾ inches, Zhu was just about to try again when 1500-meter finalist Steve Ovett walked off the track and collapsed on the apron of the high jump area. Startled officials prevented Zhu from going ahead with his jump until Ovett had been tended to. By this time Zhu had changed his mind and decided to pass. His final two attempts were taken at 7 feet 8½ inches and he missed both. Meanwhile, Mögenburg cleared every height on the first try and gained the gold medal without a miss.

1988 Seoul C: 27, N: 18, D: 9.25. WR: 2.42, 7-11½ (Javier Sotomayor Sanabria)

		M	FT.-IN.
1. Hennady Avdeyenko	SOV/UKR	2.38	7-9¾ OR
2. Hollis Conway	USA	2.36	7-8¾
3. Rudolf Povarnytsyn	SOV/UKR	2.36	7-8¾
3. Patrik Sjöberg	SWE	2.36	7-8¾
5. Clarence Saunders	BER	2.34	7-8
6. Dietmar Mögenburg	GER	2.34	7-8
7. Dalton Grant	GBR	2.31	7-7
7. Igor Paklin	SOV/KYR	2.31	7-7
7. Carlo Thränhardt	GER	2.31	7-7

The 1988 high jump field included five former world record holders: Mögenburg, Zhu Jianhua (who failed to qualify for the final), Povarnytsyn, Paklin, and Sjöberg. None of them placed higher than third. Instead, the winner was 6-foot 7½-inch Hennady Avdeyenko, who made all five jumps he attempted through 7 feet 8¾ inches, and then cleared 7 feet 9¾ inches on his second try. Second place went to unheralded Hollis Conway, who, at 6 feet ¼ inch, was unusually short for a successful high jumper. Javier Sotomayor, kept out of the Olympics by the Cuban boycott, set a world record of 7 feet 11½ inches only 17 days before the Seoul final. On July 29, 1989, Sotomayor became the first person to clear 8 feet. In 1996 Igor Paklin was sent to prison for beating to death a business partner.

1992 Barcelona C: 43, N: 27, D: 8.2. WR: 2.44, 8-0 (Javier Sotomayor Sanabria)

		M	FT.-IN.
1. Javier Sotomayor Sanabria	CUB	2.34	7-8
2. Patrik Sjöberg	SWE	2.34	7-8
3. Hollis Conway	USA	2.34	7-8
3. Timothy Forsyth	AUS	2.34	7-8
3. Artur Partyka	POL	2.34	7-8
6. Ralf Sonn	GER	2.31	7-7
7. Troy Kemp	BAH	2.31	7-7
8. Charles Austin	USA	2.28	7-5¾
8. Marino Drake Rodríguez	CUB	2.28	7-5¾
8. Dragutin Topić	YUG/SER	2.28	7-5¾

It was a strange competition. Despite a high-quality field, the winning height was the lowest since 1976, and the last 20 attempts were all misses. Sotomayor earned the gold medal by being the only jumper to clear 7 feet 8 inches on his first try. The surprise medalist was 18-year-old Tim Forsyth from Thorpdale in Gippsland. Four years earlier Forsyth had been so uninterested in high jumping that when the Olympic final came on television he went outside and mowed the lawn.

In April 2011 Sjöberg released a memoir that

revealed that he had been sexually molested as a child by prominent coach Viljo Nousiainen. After the book was released, several other athletes, including Swedish track coach Yannick Tregaro, who had trained 2004 Olympic triple jump champion Christian Olsson, came forward with similar stories of abuse by Nousiainen. The reveleations came more than a decade after Nousiainen's death in 1999.

1996 Atlanta C: 37, N: 27, D: 7.28. WR: 2.45, 8-0½ (Javier Sotomayor Sanabria)

		M	FT.-IN.
1. Charles Austin	USA	2.39	7-10 OR
2. Artur Partyka	POL	2.37	7-9¼
3. Steve Smith	GBR	2.35	7-8½
4. Dragutin Topić	YUG/SER	2.32	7-7¼
5. Steinar Hoen	NOR	2.32	7-7¼
6. Lambros Papakostas	GRE	2.32	7-7¼
7. Timothy Forsyth	AUS	2.32	7-7¼
8. Lee Jin-taek	KOR	2.29	7-6¼

Charles Austin of Van Vleck, Texas, won the 1991 world championship, but, severely hampered by a knee injury, had not performed well in international competition since then. The youngest of ten children raised by his housekeeper mother, Austin had completely recovered his health in time for the 1996 Olympics. The same could not be said for favorite Javier Sotomayor. Sotomayor, competing with an inflamed knee, qualified for the final but cleared only one height and finished in a tie for 11th place.

At 6 feet ½ inch (1.84 meters), Austin was the shortest finalist. He advanced through 7 feet 8½ inches without a miss, as did Artur Partyka. Steve Smith cleared that height on his second attempt. The bar was raised to 7 feet 9¼ inches and Partyka, jumping first, cleared on his second try. Austin and Smith missed twice and then passed their third attempts. The bar went up to 7 feet 10 inches. Partyka missed. Austin had only one try left. If he and Smith missed, the gold went to Partyka. But Austin cleared, much to the delight of the partisan American crowd of more than 80,000. Smith missed his final attempt, Partyka missed twice at 7 feet 10¾ inches and the contest was over.

2000 Sydney C: 36, N: 24, D: 9.24. WR: 2.45, 8-0½ (Javier Sotomayor Sanabria)

		M	FT.-IN.
1. Sergei Klyugin	RUS	2.35	7-8½
2. Javier Sotomayor Sanabria	CUB	2.32	7-7¼
3. Abderrahmane Hammad	ALG	2.32	7-7¼
4. Stefan Holm	SWE	2.32	7-7¼
5. Konstantin Matusevich	ISR	2.32	7-7¼
6. Mark Boswell	CAN	2.32	7-7¼
6. Staffan Strand	SWE	2.32	7-7¼
8. Wolfgang Kressig	GER	2.29	7-6¼

In 1999, world record holder and 1992 Olympic champion Javier Sotomayor tested positive for cocaine at the 1999 Pan American Games. He was given a two year suspension, but on August 2, 2000, the IAAF, in a highly controversial decision, reinstated Sotomayor just in time to compete in the Sydney Olympics.

The final was held in windy conditions and was complicated when it started to rain an hour after the competition started. The favorite was world champion Vyacheslav Voronin, who had won 14 of 20 meets in the pre-Olympic season, during which he also recorded the best jump of the year: 2.40 meters (7 feet 10½ inches). However, Voronin was undone by the weather, went out at 2.32 meters and finished in only tenth place. Seven jumpers cleared that height. When the bar was raised to 2.35 meters, only Sergei Klyugin, jumping last, cleared on his first attempt. At this point, the rain, which had been light, turned heavy, and no one else was able to get over the bar, leaving Klyugin with the victory. Among Klyugin's pieces of advice for aspiring jumpers was one unusual one: drinking 50 grams of cognac before a competition. In eleventh place was an American with an appropriate name: Nathan Leeper. As for Sotomayor, in 2001 he failed another drug test, this time for the steroid nandrolone, and retired.

2004 Athens C: 38, N: 22, D: 8.22. WR: 2.45, 8-0½ (Javier Sotomayor Sanabria)

		M	FT.-IN.
1. Stefan Holm	SWE	2.36	7-8¾
2. Matt Hemingway	USA	2.34	7-8
3. Jaroslav Bába	CZE	2.34	7-8
4. Jamie Nieto	USA	2.34	7-8
5. Andriy Sokolovskiy	UKR	2.32	7-7¼
6. Yaroslav Rybakov	RUS	2.32	7-7¼
7. Mark Boswell	CAN	2.29	7-6¼
8. Svatoslav Ton	CZE	2.29	7-6¼

Stefan Holm arrived in Athens having won seventeen straight events in 2004, including the world indoor championship. In the final, when the bar reached 2.32 meters (7 feet 7¼ inches), 31-year-old Matt Hemingway cleared easily, while Holm missed his first attempt, but got over on his second. Eight competitors were still in the competition when the bar was raised to 2.34 meters (7 feet 8 inches). Hemingway matched his personal record on the first attempt, as did 19-year-old Jaroslav Bába. Holm missed his first two attempts, and would have dropped to fifth place had he not made the third, joining Hemingway, Nieto and Bába to attempt 2.36 meters (7 feet 8¾ inches), a height only Holm had cleared in competition. Holm cleared the bar on his first attempt, while Hemingway, who had no misses up to that point, failed three times. No other jumpers made it over, and the gold went to Holm.

Holm began high jumping at the age of eight, after watching three-time Olympic medalist Patrik Sjöberg on television. Within hours, Holm and his friends were practicing, using an old mattress for their landings. Standing 1.81 meters (5 feet 11¼ inches), Holm was one of the shortest jumpers in the competition.

2008 Beijing C: 40, N: 28, D: 8.19. WR: 2.45, 8-0½ (Javier Sotomayor Sanabria)

		M	FT.-IN.
1. Andrey Silnov	RUS	2.36	7-9
2. Germaine Mason	GBR	2.34	7-8
3. Yaroslav Rybakov	RUS	2.34	7-8
4. Stefan Holm	SWE	2.32	7-7¼
5. Raúl Spank	GER	2.32	7-7¼
6. Jaroslav Bába	CZE	2.29	7-6¼
7. Tomáš Jank	CZE	2.29	7-6¼
8. Tom Parsons	GBR	2.25	7-4½

In the four years since the Athens Olympics no dominant high jumper had emerged in international competition. The 2005 world championship was won by Yuri Krymarenko of Ukraine, the 2006 European championship by Andrey Silnov of Russia, and the 2007 world championship by Donald Thomas of the Bahamas, who was soon drafted by the Harlem Globetrotters basketball squad. Reigning indoor world champion Yaroslav Rybakov was also considered a top medal contender, having finished second at the 2001, 2005 and 2007 world championships.

The qualifying round proved difficult, eliminating Thomas, world champion bronze medalist Kyriakos Ioannou of Cyprus, and all three American competitors. In the final Silnov had a nearly perfect competition, clearing each height through 2.36 meters (7 ft. 9 in.) on his first jump. Defending Olympic champion Stefan Holm seemed on track for a medal as well until he missed an attempt at 2.34 (7 ft. 8 in.), passed, and failed his next two attempts to clear 2.36. Jamaican-born Germaine Mason and Rybakov were the only other two jumpers to clear 2.34, and both failed their three attempts at 2.36. Their medals were decided by fewest misses.

Silnov had originally failed to qualify for the Olympics after placing fourth at the Russian Olympic trials. He was granted a spot on the team a month before the Games after jumping a personal best of 2.38 meters (7 ft. 9¾ in.) at the London Grand Prix.

POLE VAULT

Contestants may use a pole of any length and made of any material or combination of materials. They are given two minutes to make a vault, although when the competition is reduced to two or three competitors, the time limit is extended to four minutes. The runway must be at least 40 meters (131 feet 3 inches) long and, preferably, at least 45 meters (147 feet 8 inches) long. Each vaulter may place one or two markers along the runway to assist in the timing of the approach and take-off. The vaulters plant their poles in a rigid box sunk level with the ground. The box is one meter long. It is 60 centimeters (1 foot 11½ inches) wide at the front and 15 centimeters (5¾ inches) wide at the stop board. The crossbar is 4.5 meters (14 feet 9¼ inches) long. As in the high jump, vaulters may touch the crossbar as long as they do not dislodge it. All other rules, including tie-breaking rules, are the same as those for the high jump.

Between 1896 and 1968 athletes from the United States won every Olympic pole vault competition (not including the unofficial games of 1906). At sixteen in a row, this remains the longest national winning streak in any event in any sport in Olympic history. The streak was finally broken, in controversial circumstances, in 1972.

1896 Athens C: 5, N: 2, D: 4.10. WR: 3.49, 11-5-⅜ (Walter Rodenbaugh)

		M	FT.-IN.
1. William Welles Hoyt	USA	3.30	10-10
2. Albert Tyler	USA	3.20	10-6
3. Evangelos Damaskos	GRE	2.60	8-6¼
3. Ioannis Theodoropoulos	GRE	2.60	8-6¼
5. Vasilios Xydas	GRE	2.40	7-10½

Hoyt and Tyler did not start vaulting until the bar was raised to 2.70 meters and the Greeks had already been eliminated. The Greek vaulters encouraged the two Americans by massaging their arms and legs and giving them warm drinks.

1900 Paris C: 8, N: 5, D: 7.15. WR: 3.62, 11-10½ (Raymond Clapp)

		M	FT.-IN.
1. Irving Baxter	USA	3.30	10-10 EOR
2. Meredith Colket	USA	3.25	10-8
3. Carl-Albert Andersen	NOR	3.20	10-6
4. Émile Gontier	FRA	3.10	10-2
4. Jakab Kauser	HUN	3.10	10-2
4. Eric Lemming	SWE	3.10	10-2
7. Karl Staaf	SWE	2.80	9-2¼
8. August Nilsson	SWE	2.60	8-6¼

This event was marred by indecision on the part of the officials in charge. Three of the leading American entrants, Bascom Johnson, Charles Dvorak, and

Daniel Horton, objected to the scheduling of the pole vault on a Sunday. Johnson and Dvorak showed up anyway, but were told that the event would be rescheduled, so they left. Then the officials changed their minds and went ahead with the contest without Johnson and Dvorak. In their absence, the pole vault was won by Irving Baxter, who was still on the field after winning the high jump. The next day Baxter finished second to Ray Ewry in the three standing jump events. In order "to appease the indignant visitors from across the seas," two more pole vault contests were staged. The first was won by Johnson at 11 feet 1¼ inches and the second by Horton at 11 feet 3¾ inches with Dvorak second at 11 feet.

1904 St. Louis C: 7, N: 2, D: 9.3. WR: 3.69, 12-1½ (Norman Dole)

		M	FT.-IN.
1. Charles Dvorak	USA	3.50	11-6 OR
2. Leroy Samse	USA	3.35	11-0
3. Louis Wilkins	USA	3.35	11-0
4. Ward McLanahan	USA	3.35	11-0
5. Claude Allen	USA	3.35	11-0
6. Walter Dray	USA	—	—
7. Paul Weinstein	GER	—	—

Places two through five were decided by jump-offs.

1906 Athens C: 11, N: 8, D: 4.25. WR: 3.74, 12-3¼ (Fernand Gonder)

		M	FT.-IN.
1. Fernand Gonder	FRA	3.50	11-6 EOR
2. Bruno Söderström	SWE	3.40	11-1¾
3. Edward Glover	USA	3.35	10-11¾
4. Theodoris Makris	GRE	3.25	10-8
5. Heikki Ahlmann (Pennola) (FIN), Georgios Banikas (GRE), Otto Haug (NOR), Imré Kiss (HUN), Stefanos Koudouriotis (GRE)		3.00	9-10

Gonder won first place by clearing 11 feet 6 inches with ease. When Glover attempted to clear the same height, an official crossed his path. Glover lost his balance and was injured. The Canadian vaulter, Ed Archibald, also had a tough time. His pole disappeared on a train ride through Italy. Olympic officials gave him some local models when he arrived in Athens, but when one of them broke and almost impaled him, he lost confidence and was unable to perform at his usual level.

1908 London C: 15, N: 7, D: 7.24. WR: 3.90, 12-9½ (Walter Dray)

		M	FT.-IN.
1. Edward Cooke	USA	3.71	12-2 OR
1. Alfred "A.C." Gilbert	USA	3.71	12-2 OR
3. Edward Archibald	CAN	3.58	11-9
3. Charles Jacobs	USA	3.58	11-9
3. Bruno Soderström	SWE	3.58	11-9
6. Georgios Banikas	GRE	3.50	11-6
6. Samuel Bellah	USA	3.50	11-6
8. Károly Szathmáry	HUN	3.35	11-0

Walter Dray set a world record of 12 feet 9½ inches only six weeks before the Olympic contest, but did not compete in London, apparently because his mother was worried he might injure himself. Competition in the pole vault was severely disrupted by the sensational incidents surrounding the finish of the marathon. The pole vault competition itself was the subject of controversy. The old method of vaulting was to use a pole with a nail or spike on the bottom and to plant the spike into the ground to start the launch. By 1908, a new technique was spreading in which the vaulters planted non-spiked poles into a hole dug at the end of the runway. The British officials refused to allow this technique, so the North Americans were forced to use spiked poles. In addition, the British did not provide a sand pit for landing or even bales of straw to soften the impact. Gold medalist A.C. Gilbert worked

A.C. Gilbert, 1908

Scaling the heights for a gold medal in the pole vault, a brief stop en route to inventing the Erector Set.

his way through Yale Medical School as a magician. He is best known today as the inventor of the Erector Set, one of the most popular toys of all time. In 1918, Gilbert was involved in an incident that caused quite a sensation. In the midst of World War I, the US government's Council of National Defense demanded that all segments of the American population make sacrifices for the war effort—including children. To this end, they proposed a ban on toy sales for Christmas. Gilbert led a group of toy makers to a meeting with the Council to argue in favor of toys. After giving a stirring speech in support of toys, Gilbert pulled out a toy submarine, a toy steam engine, tin soldiers, wire puzzles and other items. The secretary of the navy, the secretary of commerce and the other Council members tried out the toys and then withdrew their proposed ban. When word of the meeting made its way to journalists, A.C. Gilbert became known as "The Man Who Saved Christmas for Children."

1912 Stockholm C: 25, N: 11, D: 7.11. WR: 4.02, 13-2¼ (Marcus Wright)

		M	FT.-IN.
1. Harry Babcock	USA	3.95	12-11½ OR
2. Frank Nelson	USA	3.85	12-7½
2. Marcus Wright	USA	3.85	12-7¼
4. William Happeny	CAN	3.80	12-5½
4. Frank Murphy	USA	3.80	12-5½
4. Bertil Uggla	SWE	3.80	12-5½
7. Samuel Bellah	USA	3.75	12-3½
8. Frank Coyle	USA	3.65	11-11¾
8. Gordon Dukes	USA	3.65	11-11¾
8. William Fritz	USA	3.65	11-11¾

William Happeny was forced to withdraw after he broke two ribs while clearing 3.80 meters. Harold Babcock won the gold medal by completing seven vaults without a miss.

1920 Antwerp C: 16, N: 7, D: 8.20. WR: 4.02, 13-2¼ (Marcus Wright)

		M	FT.-IN.
1. Frank Foss	USA	4.09	13-5 WR
2. Henry Petersen	DEN	3.70	12-1½
3. Edwin Myers	USA	3.60	11-9¾
4. Edward Knourek	USA	3.60	11-9¾
5. Ernfrid Rydberg	SWE	3.60	11-9¾
6. Laurits Jørgensen	DEN	3.60	11-9¾
7. Eldon Jenne	USA	3.60	11-9¾
8. Georg Högström	SWE	3.50	11-6

Foss' world record vault, made in the midst of wind and rain, excited the crowd more than any other event in the 1920 Games. His 15½-inch margin of victory was by far the largest in Olympic history.

1924 Paris C: 20, N: 13, D: 7.10. WR: 4.21, 13-9¾ (Charles Hoff)

		M	FT.-IN.
1. Lee Barnes	USA	3.95	12-11½
2. Glenn Graham	USA	3.95	12-11½
3. James Brooker	USA	3.90	12-9½
4. Henry Petersen	DEN	3.90	12-9½
5. Victor Pickard	CAN	3.80	12-5½
6. Ralph Spearow	USA	3.70	12-1½
7. Maurice Henrijean	BEL	3.66	12-0

Charles Hoff, the Norwegian world record holder, withdrew because of an injury. He did, however, take part in the 400- and 800-meter runs, finishing eighth in the latter. In Hoff's absence, the pole vault was won by 17-year-old Lee Barnes, a student at Hollywood High School in Los Angeles. In 1927 Barnes appeared in the film *College,* as a stand-in for Buster Keaton in a scene that required him to pole vault into a second-story window.

1928 Amsterdam C: 20, N: 13, D: 8.1. WR: 4.31, 14-1¾ (Lee Barnes)

		M	FT.-IN.
1. Sabin Carr	USA	4.20	13-9¼ OR
2. William Droegemuller	USA	4.10	13-5¼
3. Charles McGinnis	USA	3.95	12-11½
4. Victor Pickard	CAN	3.95	12-11½
5. Lee Barnes	USA	3.95	12-11½
6. Yonataro Nakazawa	JPN	3.90	12-9½
7. Henry Lindblad	SWE	3.90	12-9½
8. János Karlovits	HUN	3.80	12-5½

On May 27, 1927, Sabin Carr of Yale had become the first vaulter to clear 14 feet. The Olympic final was held during a rainstorm.

1932 Los Angeles C: 8, N: 4, D: 8.3. WR: 4.37, 14-4¼ (William Graber)

		M	FT.-IN.
1. William Miller	USA	4.31	14-1¾ OR
2. Shuhei Nishida	JPN	4.30	14-1¼
3. George Jefferson	USA	4.20	13-9½
4. William Graber	USA	4.15	13-7½
5. Shizuo Mochizuki	JPN	4.00	13-1½
6. Lucio de Castro	BRA	3.90	12-9½
7. Peter Clentzos	GRE	3.75	12-3½

The 1932 competition was expected to provide a clean sweep for the United States, but no one had counted on the unexpected determination of Japan's Shuhei Nishida, who gained the support of the previously partisan crowd with his great performance and fine sportsmanship, sincerely congratulating Bill Miller when the latter broke the Olympic record. Nevertheless, most of the 80,000 American spectators breathed a sigh of relief when Miller avoided a vault-off by clearing 14 feet 1¾ inches on his third attempt.

1936 Berlin C: 30, N: 21, D: 8.5. WR: 4.43, 14-6½ (George Varoff)

		M	FT.-IN.
1. Earle Meadows	USA	4.35	14-3¼ OR
2. Shuhei Nishida	JPN	4.25	13-11¼
3. Sueo Oe	JPN	4.25	13-11¼
4. William Sefton	USA	4.25	13-11¼
5. William Graber	USA	4.15	13-7¼
6. Kiyoshi Adachi (JPN), Sylvanus Apps (CAN), Péter Bácsalmási (HUN), Josef Haunzwickel (AUT), Danilo Innocenti (ITA), Jan Korejs (CZE), Bo Ljungberg (SWE), Alfred Proksch (AUT), Wilhelm Sznajder (POL), Frederick Webster (GBR), Viktor Zsuffka (HUN)		4.00	13-1½

On July 4, 1936, George Varoff, a 22-year-old janitor from San Francisco, rose from obscurity to set a world record of 14 feet 6½ inches at the AAU championships in Princeton, New Jersey. Sportswriters rushed in to get his story. They learned that he came from a poor family of Ukrainian immigrants; that he was a music major at Oregon University who played the string fiddle; that he hoped to land a good job in order to help his family. VAROFF TYPIFIES SPIRIT OF AMERICA read a typical headline. But the following week at the US Olympic trials, Varoff bowed out at 14 feet 3 inches and failed to make the US team. The press moved on to other stories.

The 1936 Olympic final was another dramatic duel between the Americans and the Japanese. It lasted into the night and finished in the eerie glow of floodlights. After it had been determined that Meadows had finished first and Sefton fourth, Nishida and Oe refused to vault-off for second and third. Instead they decided by lot that Nishida would be placed second and Oe third. Back home in Japan, they brought their medals to a jeweler and had them cut in half lengthwise. Then they were fused back together so that each man had a medal that was half silver and half bronze.

1948 London C: 19, N: 10, D: 8.2. WR: 4.77, 15-7¾ (Cornelius Warmerdam)

		M	FT.-IN.
1. O. Guinn Smith	USA	4.30	14-1¼
2. Erkki Kataja	FIN	4.20	13-9¼
3. Robert Richards	USA	4.20	13-9¼
4. Erling Kaas	NOR	4.10	13-5¼
5. Ragnar Lundberg	SWE	4.10	13-5¼
6. Richmond Morcom	USA	3.95	12-11½
7. Hugo Göllors	SWE	3.95	12-11½
7. Valto Olenius	FIN	3.95	12-11½

The period between the 1936 and 1948 Olympics was dominated by Cornelius "Dutch" Warmerdam, the first person to vault 15 feet (on April 13, 1940.) Between 1940 and his retirement in 1944, Warmerdam, using a bamboo pole, cleared 15 feet 43 times. No one else accomplished the height until 1951. In fact, when he retired, Warmerdam's best vault was nine inches higher than anyone else's. His world record of 15 feet 7¾ inches, set on May 23, 1942, wasn't broken until April 1957.

The 1948 Olympic final was concluded during a downpour. With ties now decided on the basis of fewer misses, Erkki Kataja was poised for victory if no one could clear 14 feet 1¼ inches. But Guinn Smith made it on his final try, and the US pole vault winning streak was kept alive.

1952 Helsinki C: 25, N: 17, D: 7.22. WR: 4.77, 15-7¾ (Cornelius Warmerdam)

		M	FT.-IN.
1. Robert Richards	USA	4.55	14-11 OR
2. Donald Laz	USA	4.50	14-9
3. Ragnar Lundberg	SWE	4.40	14-5¼
4. Petro Denysenko	SOV/UKR	4.40	14-5¼
5. Valto Olenius	FIN	4.30	14-1¼
6. Bunkichi Sawada	JPN	4.20	13-9¼
7. Vladimir Brazhnik	SOV/UKR	4.20	13-9¼
8. Viktor Knyazev	SOV/RUS	4.20	13-9¼

The competition came down to a duel between Don Laz and "The Vaulting Vicar," Reverend Bob Richards, a theology professor in California. They both missed for the first time at 14 feet 9 inches and then cleared with their second attempts. When they both missed twice at 14 feet 11 inches, discussions began as to how a vault-off would be conducted. But Richards solved the problem quickly by clearing the bar on his third attempt. The year 1952 was the first time that the USSR competed in the Olympics, and many politicians, journalists, and athletes looked at the Olympics as a front-line battle in the Cold War. Bob Richards thought otherwise and was a major force in encouraging interaction and friendship between athletes from the United States and the USSR.

1956 Melbourne C: 19, N: 12, D: 11.26. WR: 4.77, 15-7¾ (Cornelius Warmerdam)

		M	FT.-IN.
1. Robert Richards	USA	4.56	14-11½ OR
2. Robert Gutowski	USA	4.53	14-10¼
3. Georgios Roubanis	GRE	4.50	14-9
4. George Mattos	USA	4.35	14-3¼
5. Ragnar Lundberg	SWE	4.25	13-11¼
6. Zenon Wazny	POL	4.25	13-11¼
7. Eeles Landström	FIN	4.25	13-11¼
8. Manfred Preussger	GDR	4.25	13-11¼

Bob Richards, 1956
"The Vaulting Vicar", the only double pole vault champion in Olympic history.

The qualifying round almost saw a major upset when Bob Richards missed twice at the shockingly low height of 13 feet 1½ inches. He cleared on his third attempt and was in control for the rest of the contest. Gusty winds and a patchy runway hampered the quality of performance in the final. As it happened though, the wind actually helped Richards on his winning vault. After missing once at 14 feet 11½ inches, he hit the bar on his second attempt. Richards lay on his back for 30 seconds watching the bar bounce and quiver. "I was scared to change my position in the pit in case the slightest vibration brought it down," he explained. But the wind kept the bar in place and Richards became the only person to win two gold medals and three total medals in the pole vault. Richards also made history by becoming the first athlete to appear on a box of Wheaties cereal.

It was silver medalist Bob Gutowski who finally broke Cornelius Warmerdam's world record with a vault of 15 feet 8¼ inches on April 27, 1957. Richards had predicted that Gutowski would someday be the first vaulter to break the 16-foot barrier. However, Bob Gutowski was killed in a car crash at the age of 25 on August 2, 1960.

The 1956 competition was also noteworthy because it saw the first appearance in the pole vault competition of the fiberglass pole, which would revolutionize pole vaulting. It was used by bronze medalist Georgios Roubanis, who improved his personal best by three and a half inches. The first Olympic athlete to use a fiberglass pole was Bob Mathias in the 1952 decathlon.

1960 Rome C: 30, N: 20, D: 9.7. WR: 4.80, 15-9¼ (Donald Bragg)

		M	FT.-IN.
1. Donald Bragg	USA	4.70	15-5 OR
2. Ronald Morris	USA	4.60	15-1
3. Eeles Landström	FIN	4.55	14-11
4. Rolando Cruz	PUR	4.55	14-11
5. Günter Malcher	GDR	4.50	14-9
6. Igor Petrenko	SOV/UKR	4.50	14-9
6. Matti Sutinen	FIN	4.50	14-9
8. Rudolf Tomášek	CZE	4.50	14-9

Don "Tarzan" Bragg began the final competition cautiously, but gained confidence with each leap and finished strongly. After he had won, Bragg, whose dream it was to play Tarzan in the movies, delighted the crowd by celebrating with a Tarzan yell.

Silver medalist Ron Morris had failed to clear the qualifying height of 14 feet 5¼ inches. However, Olympic rules state that at least 12 men must compete in the final. Since only 10 had made the required height, the three vaulters with the next best records were added to the final. One of them was Morris. Bragg, by the way, never did get to play Tarzan, although he did come close. Shooting had already begun for *Tarzan and the Jewels of Opar* in 1964, and Bragg was in front of the cameras, happily swinging from vines, when a court order halted the production because of copyright infringement. Forced to become a salesman of drug supplies, Bragg later opened a boys' camp in New Jersey.

1964 Tokyo C: 32, N: 20, D: 10.17. WR: 5.28, 17-4 (Frederick Hansen)

		M	FT.-IN.
1. Frederick Hansen	USA	5.10	16-8¾ OR
2. Wolfgang Reinhardt	GER	5.05	16-6¾
3. Klaus Lehnertz	GER	5.00	16-4¾
4. Manfred Preussger	GDR	5.00	16-4¾
5. Hennady Blyznetsov	SOV/UKR	4.95	16-2¾
6. Rudolf Tomášek	CZE	4.90	16-0¾
7. Pentti Nikula	FIN	4.90	16-0¾
8. Billy Pemelton	USA	4.80	15-9

The pole vault world record was broken 17 times between the Rome Olympics and the Tokyo Olympics, the last two times by Fred Hansen of Cuero, Texas. The 1964 final was a long, drawn-out competition that ended up lasting 8¾ hours. For the first eight hours, Hansen attempted only four vaults, all of them successful. When the bar was raised to 16 feet 6¾ inches, Hansen gambled by passing. Tomášek, Blyznetsov, Preussger, and Lehnertz all bowed out, but Wolfgang Reinhardt, who had beaten Hansen earlier in the year, cleared on his first try. The bar was moved up to 16 feet 8¾ inches and suddenly, after hours of boredom, the pole vault became a dramatic contest. Hansen and

Reinhardt both missed twice. If Hansen missed again, the gold medal would go to Reinhardt and the United States would lose the pole vault for the first time ever (not including the 1906 Intercalated Games). "Please don't think I'm corny," Hansen later said, "but I was thinking what I could do for my country, not for myself." Hansen had the uprights moved back eight inches. Then he prepared himself at great length, raced down the runway, and cleared the bar by half a foot. Reinhardt had one more attempt, but he missed, and the competition was finally over.

Back in 11th place was John Pennel, a Tennessee farm boy who set or tied the world record seven times in 1963 alone but injured his back three weeks before the Olympics. Although Pennel made history on August 24, 1963, by becoming the first vaulter to clear 17 feet (landing in a sawdust pit), his personal highlight came earlier in the year at a meet in Warsaw, Poland. After winning the event before a crowd of almost 100,000 people, Pennel asked for the bar to be moved above the existing world record (it was later remeasured at equal to the record). Because the stadium had no lights, meet officials illuminated the runway with car headlights and the plant box with a photographer's spotlight. Pennel still couldn't see the crossbar and missed his first attempt. Then the stadium became brighter as the audience improvised torches by lighting seat cushions and rolled-up programs. They also encouraged Pennel by singing a Polish folk song. Pennel successfully cleared the world record height. As the fans continued singing, Pennel asked a Polish man who spoke English to translate the phrase that they kept repeating. It was "May he live a thousand years." "These people," Pennel later told John Ortega of the *Los Angeles Times,* "who were beautiful people who loved life and wanted to go crazy, but couldn't because of the restrictions in Poland at the time, were all for me. It was like I had made their day. When he told me what they were singing, I just started crying. No amount of money or notoriety was worth that [experience]."

Fred Hansen, 1964

With his final attempt, Hansen clears 16 feet 8¾ inches to win the 1964 pole vault in Tokyo.

1968 Mexico City C: 23, N: 15, D: 10.16. WR: 5.41, 17-9 (Robert Seagren)

		M	FT.-IN.
1. Robert Seagren	USA	5.40	17-8½ OR
2. Claus Schiprowski	GER	5.40	17-8½ OR
3. Wolfgang Nordwig	GDR	5.40	17-8½ OR
4. Christos Papanicolaou	GRE	5.35	17-6½
5. John Pennel	USA	5.35	17-6½
6. Hennady Blyznetsov	SOV/UKR	5.30	17-4½
7. Herve d'Encausse	FRA	5.25	17-2¾
8. Heinfried Engel	GER	5.20	17-0¾

Bob Seagren had set a world record of 17 feet 9 inches at the US Olympic trials five weeks before the Olympics, but no one expected him to have an easy time of it in Mexico City, as the field was thick with great vaulters. Ignacio Sola of Spain cleared 17 feet ¾ inch and only placed ninth. Herve d'Encausse cleared 17 feet 2¾ inches. This put him in first place, so he elected to pass the next height of 17 feet 4½ inches. He then watched in horror as the remaining six vaulters all made the height, dropping d'Encausse to seventh, which is where he finished.

At 17 feet 6½ inches, Seagren passed. This was thought to be a dangerous but shrewd gamble, comparable to Fred Hansen's pass four years earlier. Actually it was an error due to Seagren's unfamiliarity with the metric system. "If I'd known the metric system better," he later revealed, "I wouldn't have passed that high—5.35 meters doesn't sound as high as 17 feet 6½ inches." Ironically, Seagren's mistake may have won him the gold medal. At any rate, it was now Seagren's turn to sit on the sidelines and watch as the remaining four competitors all cleared the bar, dropping Seagren from first to fifth.

Next the bar was raised to 17 feet 8½ inches, only one half-inch below Seagren's new world record. Papanicolaou, Nordwig, Seagren, Pennel, and Schiprowski all missed their first attempts. If they continued to miss, the victory would go to Nordwig, since he had only missed once at lower heights. The second time around, Papanicolaou and Nordwig missed again, but Seagren cleared, to move into the lead again. Then John Pennel made a successful clearance, but his pole passed under the bar. The IAAF had just voted a new rule making such an occurrence legal, but they had also decreed that the rule wouldn't take effect until the following May. Too late for Pennel, who lost out on at least a bronze medal. Schiprowski, whose pre-Olympic best was only 17 feet, then cleared 17 feet 8½ inches, bettering his previous record for the fifth time in one day. Papanicolaou, who would later become the first person to vault 18 feet, and Pennel failed one last time, but Nordwig made it.

The bar then went up to 17 feet 10½ inches, but before Nordwig, Seagren, and Schiprowski could start vaulting, the competition was delayed while the victory ceremony for the 200 meters took place. This turned out to be a sensational event, as Tommie Smith and John Carlos staged their now famous Black Power protest, which was greeted by booing and whistling. This may have disturbed the concentration of the vaulters, but it didn't prevent each of them from making superb efforts at the world record height. None of them succeeded, however, so the medals were decided on the basis of fewer misses. Personal records had been set by five of the top six vaulters and eight of the top 11.

1972 Munich C: 21, N: 12, D: 9.2. WR: 5.63, 18-5¾ (Robert Seagren)

		M	FT.-IN.	
1. Wolfgang Nordwig	GDR	5.50	18-0½	OR
2. Robert Seagren	USA	5.40	17-8½	
3. Jan Johnson	USA	5.35	17-6½	
4. Reinhard Kuretzky	GER	5.30	17-4½	
5. Bruce Simpson	CAN	5.20	17-0¾	
6. Volker Ohl	GER	5.20	17-0¾	
7. Hans Lagerqvist	SWE	5.20	17-0¾	
8. Francois Tracanelli	FRA	5.10	16-8¾	

The US monopoly of the pole vault was finally broken in 1972, but only after a series of disruptive and

Bob Seagren, 1972
Gracious with gold medalist Wolfgang Nordwig (left), but not quite so with IAAF official Adriaan Paulen (above).

disturbing events. On July 25, the Technical Committee of the International Amateur Athletic Federation announced that it was banning the new model of Cata-Poles, which was being used by most of the leading vaulters, including Olympic favorites Bob Seagren, Kjell Isaksson of Sweden, and Steve Smith of the United States. The original complaint, lodged by East Germany, was that the poles contained carbon fiber. Manufacturers of the poles pointed out that they didn't contain carbon fiber at all, while the vaulters referred to IAAF rules, which said that poles could be made of any material, anyway. The IAAF refused to withdraw the ban on the grounds that the new Cata-Poles "had not been available through normal supply channels" for at least 12 months prior to the Olympics. Once again it was pointed out that the IAAF rule book made no mention of such a requirement.

On August 27, four days before the competition was to begin, the IAAF reversed itself and lifted the ban. Relieved vaulters returned to practicing with their usual poles. Then, on August 30, the ban was reimposed. The night before the qualifying round, IAAF officials went to the athletes' rooms, confiscated all their poles, and took them off for inspection. Those vaulters who were found to be in possession of the now illegal poles were handed new ones, or rather, new old ones.

The qualifying round turned out to be a pretty sad affair. Only ten men were able to clear the qualifying height of 16 feet 8¾ inches, so four more who had only cleared 16 feet 4¾ inches were added for the final.

The vaulter who had benefited most by the ban on the new model Cata-Pole was Wolfgang Nordwig of East Germany, who had not adapted well to the new Cata-Pole and still used an old model. Nordwig, who kept out the noise of the stadium by stuffing his ears, missed once at 17 feet 4½ inches before clearing, which put him behind Seagren, who reached 17 feet 8½ inches without a miss. Nordwig made that height with his second attempt, while Seagren needed a third. This reversed their positions. At 17 feet 10½ inches, Nordwig went over the first time, but Seagren missed all three of his attempts. After his final miss, Seagren approached Adriaan Paulen, the IAAF official who had taken responsibility for the Cata-Pole ban, and thrust his pole into Paulen's lap. Seagren stated that Paulen had given him the unwanted pole and now he was returning it. Nordwig, a 29-year-old precision engineer, had the bar raised once more, and cleared 18 feet for the first time in his life.

1976 Montreal C: 27, N: 13, D: 7.26. WR: 5.70, 18-8¼ (David Roberts)

		M	FT.-IN.
1. Tadeusz Ślusarski	POL	5.50	18-0½ EOR
2. Antti Kalliomäki	FIN	5.50	18-0½ EOR
3. David Roberts	USA	5.50	18-0½ EOR
4. Patrick Abada	FRA	5.45	17-10½
5. Wojciech Buciarski	POL	5.45	17-10½
6. Earl Bell	USA	5.45	17-10½
7. Jean-Michel Bellot	FRA	5.45	17-10½
8. Itsuo Takanezawa	JPN	5.40	17-8½

Pre-Olympic prognostications had the battle for the gold medal among Earl Bell, who had set a world record of 18 feet 7¼ inches on May 29, Dave Roberts, who had broken Bell's record on June 22, and Wladyslaw Kozakiewicz, known for his strong performances in important meets. Surprisingly, Kozakiewicz, hampered by injury, was unable to clear 17 feet 10½ inches. Since he had passed the previous three heights, he ended up in 11th place. Roberts, too, was playing a passing game. He didn't even start jumping until 17 feet 6¾ inches. He missed his first attempt, a miss that would later prove crucial, but cleared the second time. Then he passed the next two heights before sailing over 18 feet ½ inch with his first try.

When the bar was raised to 18 feet 2½ inches, there were still six vaulters left in the competition. Roberts, following a strategy he had prepared a month earlier, passed. His reasoning was that the contest would go on for quite some time and that fewer misses and fewer attempts might become crucial. He was absolutely right about that. But then two things happened that were unexpected. All five of the other remaining vaulters missed every one of their attempts at 18 feet 2½ inches, leaving Roberts alone with the bar at 18 feet 4½ inches, and facing the other unexpected element—a strong and unpredictable headwind. He missed all three attempts and ended up in third place.

The silver medal went to surprising Antti Kalliomäki and the gold to Kozakiewicz's Polish teammate Tadeusz Ślusarski. Ślusarski had the same number of misses as Kalliomäki, but had made fewer attempts. As it turned out, if Dave Roberts hadn't missed his initial attempt at 17 feet 6¾ inches, he would have finished in first place.

On August 17, 1998, Ślusarski was killed, along with his friend 1972 shot put champion Wladyslaw Komar, when the car Ślusarski was driving was hit head-on by a driver who fell asleep at the wheel.

1980 Moscow C: 19, N: 10, D: 7.30. WR: 5.77, 18-11 (Philippe Houvion)

		M	FT.-IN.
1. Wladyslaw Kozakiewicz	POL	5.78	18-11½ WR
2. Tadeusz Ślusarski	POL	5.65	18-6½
2. Konstantin Volkov	SOV/RUS	5.65	18-6½
4. Philippe Houvion	FRA	5.65	18-6½
5. Jean-Michel Bellot	FRA	5.60	18-4½
6. Mariusz Klimczyk	POL	5.55	18-2½
7. Thierry Vigneron	FRA	5.45	17-10½
8. Sergei Kulibaba	SOV/KAZ	5.45	17-10½

The year 1980 was a banner one for pole vaulting. For the first time ever, three different men set world records in the same season. Wladyslaw Kozakiewicz began the onslaught on May 11 when his jump of 18 feet 9¼ inches broke Dave Roberts' 1976 record. Three weeks later, on June 1, Thierry Vigneron vaulted 18 feet 10¼ inches. On June 29, he repeated this feat. On July 17, less than two weeks before the Olympic competition, Philippe Houvion set a new

Wladyslaw Kozakiewicz, 1980
A world record, and a final word for the adoring Muscovite crowd.

record of 18 feet 11 inches. The stage was set for a classic showdown, particularly with the addition of defending champion Tadeusz Ślusarski and local favorite Konstantin Volkov.

Unfortunately, the competition was marred by the incredibly boorish behavior of many of the Soviet fans, who whistled and jeered at the foreign vaulters, particularly the Poles. The 3000 Poles in the audience responded in kind whenever Volkov vaulted. Through it all, Wladyslaw Kozakiewicz seemed unperturbed. Indeed, he seemed to gain strength from the hostility of the Russians. He won the gold medal without a miss and punctuated his winning leap with an obscene gesture to the crowd. Then he had the bar raised, and set a world record on his second attempt, the first pole vault world record to be set in the Olympics since Frank Foss' in 1920. Afterward, Kozakiewicz ran into the stands and shook hands with his compatriots, while the Poles, surrounded by Soviet soldiers, sang "Poland Is Not Beaten . . ." Subsequently, Kozakiewicz defected to West Germany.

1984 Los Angeles C: 19, N: 13, D: 8.8. WR: 5.90, 19-4¼ (Serhei Bubka)

		M	FT.-IN.
1. Pierre Quinon	FRA	5.75	18-10¼
2. Mike Tully	USA	5.65	18-6½
3. Earl Bell	USA	5.60	18-4½
3. Thierry Vigneron	FRA	5.60	18-4½
5. Kimmo Pallonen	FIN	5.45	17-10½
6. Doug Lytle	USA	5.40	17-8½
7. Felix Böhni	SWI	5.30	17-4½
8. Mauro Barella	ITA	5.30	17-4½

The pre-boycott favorite, Ukrainian Serhei Bubka, set a world record of 19 feet 4¼ inches two weeks before the Olympics began. Nine days after the Olympic final Bubka was beaten at the Friendship Games by Soviet teammate Konstantin Volkov, but two weeks after that he set another world record of 19 feet 5¾ inches.

In the absence of the Soviets, the Los Angeles competition became a French-American confrontation with both teams fielding two 19-foot vaulters. By the time the bar reached 18 feet 4½ inches, only the four favorites remained, although none of them had taken more than two vaults. At this point, Bell and Vigneron cleared on their first attempts, while Quinon and Tully passed. The bar was raised two inches, and, while Bell and Vigneron watched, Quinon and Tully each missed. Quinon then elected to pass again, while Tully, after one more miss, cleared 18 feet 6½ inches on his final attempt to take the lead. At the next height, 18 feet 8¾ inches, Tully passed, Quinon cleared immediately, and Bell and Vigneron missed all three attempts, finishing in a tie for third.

With Quinon vaulting first, the bar was raised to 18 feet 10¼ inches. The young Frenchman with a reputation for inconsistency cleared on his first try. Although a clearance at this height would have put Tully in a tie for first, he elected to pass. Neither man was successful at 19 feet ¼ inch, and the competition was over.

1988 Seoul C: 21, N: 13, D: 9.28. WR: 6.06, 19-10½ (Serhei Bubka)

		M	FT.-IN.
1. Serhei Bubka	SOV/UKR	5.90	19-4¼ OR
2. Rodion Gataullin	SOV/UZB	5.85	19-2¼
3. Grigory Yegorov	SOV/KAZ	5.80	19-0¼
4. Earl Bell	USA	5.70	18-8¼
5. Philippe Collet	FRA	5.70	18-8¼
5. Thierry Vigneron	FRA	5.70	18-8¼
7. István Bagyula	HUN	5.60	18-4½
8. Philippe d'Encausse	FRA	5.60	18-4½

Born in the coal-mining town of Lugansk (Voroshilovgrad) Serhei Bubka was the sort of child who makes parents grow old fast. When he was three years old he tried to run away from home. When he was four he almost drowned in a barrel of water used for salting cabbage. He also fell out of a tree and was saved from serious injury only when his suspenders caught on a branch. When he finally started flying through the air at the end of a pole, it was almost a relief. Bubka burst on the international scene when, as a 19-year-old, he won an upset victory at the 1983 world championships. He completely dominated the event for the next five years, setting nine outdoor world records and winning another world championship in 1987 with only two vaults.

A minor revolt developed during the Olympic qualifying round. The leading vaulters objected to the fact that the bar used by the contestants in Group A was being raised at a rate different from the bar in Group B. The vaulters refused to continue the competition and the officials were forced to advance 15 of the 21 competitors into the final.

Bubka and his main rival, medical student Rodion Gataullin, did not begin vaulting in the final until the bar reached 18 feet 8¼ inches. Gataullin cleared on his first attempt, but Bubka needed two tries, and even then he grazed the bar on the way down. Yegorov cleared 19 feet ¼ inch, while Bubka and Gataullin passed. Then Gataullin cleared 19 feet 2¼ inches on his third attempt to take the lead, dropping Yegorov to second and Bubka to fourth behind Bell, who had already missed three times at 18 feet 10¼ inches. Yegorov went out at 19 feet 4¼ inches. Meanwhile Bubka missed twice at the same height. Suddenly, one of the surest favorites of the 1988 Games was one miss away from finishing out of the medals. Desperately nervous, Bubka sprinted down the runway, hurled himself into the air and cleared the bar by a huge margin—perhaps 7 or 8 inches. Gataullin made three attempts at 19 feet 6¼ inches, but was never close.

1992 Barcelona C: 34, N: 25, D: 8.7. WR: 6.11, 20-0½ (Serhei Bubka)

		M	FT.-IN.
1. Maksim Tarasov	RUS	5.80	19-0¼
2. Igor Trandenkov	RUS	5.80	19-0¼
3. Javier García Chico	SPA	5.75	18-10¼
4. Kory Tarpenning	USA	5.75	18-10¼
5. David Volz	USA	5.65	18-6½
6. Asko Peltoniemi	FIN	5.60	18-4½
7. Philippe Collet	FRA	5.55	18-2½
8. Yevgeny Krasnov	ISR	5.40	17-8½

Once again, Serhei Bubka was a big, big favorite. Since May 26, 1984, he had set 30 world records, 16 indoors and 14 outdoors, the latest on June 13, just eight weeks before the Olympic final. In the days of communism, Bubka received 400 rubles for each world record; in the days of Nike, $100,000. Among his many feats: first person to clear 6 meters (Paris; July 13, 1988), first person to clear 20 feet indoors (San Sebastian; March 15, 1991), and first person to clear 20 feet outdoors (Malmö; August 5, 1991). Along the way he had also won all three world championships, in 1983, 1987, and 1991.

In Barcelona, as in Seoul four years earlier, Bubka did not start vaulting until 18 feet 8¼ inches. With time running out on the clock, he went under the bar on his first attempt. On his second try he cleared easily, but his momentum did not take him far enough and he dislodged the crossbar on his way down. Now he was down to one last vault. Unsettled, he passed to gain more time. The situation was critical, but not unprecedented. In both the 1988 Olympics and the 1991 world championships he had been one miss away from finishing out of the medals, but pulled it out and won. The bar was raised to 18 feet 10¼ inches. Bubka decided that the windy conditions he had faced during his first two attempts required a softer pole. He switched poles—and while he was on the runway the wind died. Bubka's final try was an awkward one: he hit the bar with his shins on the way up.

The spectators, delirious because Spaniard Javier García was still in the running, unkindly booed and whistled at Bubka. His fellow vaulters—there were six still left in the competition—were stunned by the unexpected turn of events. It was 21-year-old Maksim Tarasov of Yaroslavl who came out on top, clearing 19 feet ¼ inch on his first try, while teammate Igor Trandenkov needed three attempts. In fact, Tarasov won the gold medal even though he made a grand total of only two clearances.

Trandenkov explained his mood this way: "I've got one weeping eye and one smiling one. My very good friend and teacher Serhei Bubka didn't achieve what he wanted, but his pupil took the silver."

So what did go wrong for Bubka? The swirling winds were definitely disruptive, but they affected everyone, and Bubka himself had handled worse conditions before. On his way out of the stadium Bubka conceded that maybe he had just been too nervous. Later he presented a more unusual theory, that his biorhythms were "unbelievably bad, the sort of situation that might occur once in a year." Other observers suggested a more prosaic explanation. As the star of the pole vault, Bubka was used to having meet organizers, hungry for a world record, allow him more than the usual two minutes to prepare for a vault. Before the final, US vaulter Tim Bright approached the officials in charge of the competition and pointedly asked them not to show favoritism to Bubka. Forced to play by the same rules as everyone else, Bubka's first reaction had been, "To me it looked like the clock was running faster than usual."

Whatever the true cause of Bubka's Barcelona failure, it proved to be a mere glitch in his continued domination of the event. Twenty-three days after the Olympic final he set another world record and 13 days after that, yet another. In 1993, 1995 and 1997 he defended his world championship, becoming the only person to win the World Championship in Athletics every time it had been held.

1996 Atlanta C: 37, N: 24, D: 8.2. WR: 6.14, 20-1¾ (Serhei Bubka)

		M	FT.-IN.
1. Jean Galfione	FRA	5.92	19-5 OR
2. Igor Trandenkov	RUS	5.92	19-5 OR
3. Andrei Tivontchik	GER	5.92	19-5 OR
4. Igor Potapovich	KAZ	5.86	19-2¾
5. Pyotr Bochkaryov	RUS	5.86	19-2¾
6. Dmitri Markov	BLR	5.86	19-2¾
7. Tim Lobinger	GER	5.80	19-0¼
8. Lawrence Johnson	USA	5.70	18-8¼

The favorite, Serhei Bubka, was expected to receive a stiff challenge from the young South African, Okkert Brits. As it happened, neither of them made it to the final. While warming up for the qualifying round, Bubka discovered that because of an inflamed right Achilles' tendon, he was unable to run and he was forced to withdraw. Brits did compete, but missed all three attempts at his opening height of 5.60 meters.

Fourteen vaulters started the final and eleven were still in the contention when the bar was raised to 5.80 (19 feet ¾ inch). Trandenkov and Potapovich passed. Tim Lobinger was the only one to clear on his first attempt. Lobinger was so excited that he injured himself celebrating and failed to clear another height. Tivontchik, Bochkaryov and Jean Galfione went over on the second try, and Markov on the third. At 5.88 (19 feet 2¾ inches), Bochkaryov, Potapovich and Galfione cleared with their first vaults and Markov and Tivontchik with their second. Trandenkov missed twice and then saved his third attempt for the next height: 5.92 (19 feet 5 inches). He cleared this Olympic record height to briefly take the lead. Then Galfione went over 5.92 at his first attempt and this proved to be the gold medal vault. Tivontchik cleared with his second try to secure the bronze. Galfione was the nephew of Jean-Claude Magnan, who won four medals in foil fencing between 1964 and 1972.

2000 Sydney C: 13, N: 8, D: 9.29. WR: 6.14, 20-1¾ (Serhei Bubka)

		M	FT.-IN.
1. Nick Hysong	USA	5.90	19-4¼
2. Lawrence Johnson	USA	5.90	19-4¼
3. Maksim Tarasov	RUS	5.90	19-4¼
4. Michael Stolle	GER	5.90	19-4¼
5. Dmitri Markov	AUS	5.80	19-0¼
6. Viktor Khistyakov	AUS	5.80	19-0¼
7. Okkert Brits	SAF	5.80	19-0¼
8. Daniel Ecker	GER	5.80	19-0¼

Missing from the competition was Jeff Hartwig of the United States, who was the season leader with a vault of 6.03 meters. Hartwig failed to clear a height at the US Olympic trials and did not make the team. The Sydney field did include three Olympic champions. Serhei Bubka missed all three tries at 5.70 and Jean Galfione, who cleared 5.55, but missed at 5.65 and, like Bubka, did not qualify for the final. On the other hand, 1992 gold medalist Maksim Tarasov did make it to the final and was considered the favorite in 2000. Tarasov no-heighted at the 1996 Russian Olympic trials, but he came back to finish second at the World Championships in 1997 and first in 1999. In the final, two adopted Australians, Dmitri Markov and Viktor Khistyakov, cleared 5.80 meters on their first try, as did two Americans, Nick Hysong and Lawrence Johnson. Two Germans, Michael Stolle and Danny Ecker, went over on their second attempt, as did Okkert Brits of South Africa and Tarasov. It was the first time that eight vaulters had cleared 19 feet. When the bar was raised to 5.90 meters, Hysong set a personal best by going over on his first try. Johnson, who had dislocated his ankle and fractured his heel in a June 1999 motorcycle accident, cleared with his second attempt, while Tarasov and Stolle went over on their final try. That settled the medals, although no one knew it for quite a while, as there followed 15 missed attempts by seven different vaulters.

2004 Athens C: 39, N: 25, D: 8.27. WR: 6.14, 20-1¾ (Serhei Bubka)

		M	FT.-IN.
1. Timothy Mack	USA	5.95	19-6¼ OR
2. Toby Stevenson	USA	5.90	19-4¼
3. Giuseppe Gibilisco	ITA	5.85	19-2¼
4. Igor Pavlov	RUS	5.80	19-0¼
5. Danny Ecker	GER	5.75	18-10¼
6. Lars Börgeling	GER	5.75	18-10¼
7. Derek Miles	USA	5.75	18-10¼
8. Aleksandr Averbukh	ISR	5.65	18-6½

The qualification round was uneventful, except for the surprise eliminations of 2001 world champion Dmitri Markov and 2003 world champion silver medalist Okkert Brits. Nonetheless, sixteen vaulters made it into the final, the most since the 1976 Games. The field included world champion Guiseppe Gibilisco, and Germany's Tim Lobinger, who won the 2003 IAAF World Athletics Final and then caused a stir by mooning the crowd, for which he was penalized $5,000.

The first eliminations came at 5.65 meters (18 feet 6½ inches), and included Lobinger. Tim Mack, a 31-year-old from Cleveland, failed his first attempt at the height, but cleared with his second, while Gibilisco passed. Mack, Stevenson and Gibilisco all cleared 5.75 meters (18 feet 10¼ inches) on their first attempts, and all then passed the next height, 5.80 meters (19 feet ¼ inch). With six vaulters remaining at 5.85 meters (19 feet 2½ inches), both Mack and Stevenson missed their first vaults, but Gibilisco sailed over to take the lead. Lars Börgeling and Derek Miles were eliminated, while Igor Pavlov missed his first two attempts and passed. With the option to pass, Mack instead vaulted, clearing the height and moving ahead of Stevenson into second place. Stevenson responded by clearing on his second attempt and reclaiming second place. When the bar was raised to 5.90 meters (19 feet 4¼ inches), Mack cleared on his first attempt to take the lead, which Stevenson immediately regained after clearing on *his* first vault. Facing the same height that had won him the world championship, Gibilisco failed to clear the bar on his first attempt and passed his next two vaults. Pavlov missed his last attempt and finished in fourth place. The bar was then raised to 5.95 meters (19 feet 6¼ inches). Mack and Stevenson each came close on their first attempts, while Gibilisco aborted his jump. All three missed their second vaults, putting Gibilisco into third. With one final attempt, Mack cleared the height, bettering his personal best by two inches and setting an Olympic record. Stevenson almost made it over on his third try, but watched from the pit as the bar slipped off.

Stevenson was the only athlete in the competition, and practically the only one on the international circuit, to wear a helmet—a precaution he maintained after making a promise to his parents while in high school.

2008 Beijing C: 38, N: 25, D: 8.22. WR: 6.14, 20-1¾ (Serhei Bubka)

		M	FT.-IN.
1. Steve Hooker	AUS	5.96	19-6½ OR
2. Yevgeniy Lukyanenko	RUS	5.85	19-2¼
3. Denys Yurchenko	UKR	5.70	18-8¼
4. Derek Miles	USA	5.70	18-8¼
5. Dmitry Starodubtsev	RUS	5.70	18-8¼
6. Danny Ecker	GER	5.70	18-8¼
7. Jérôme Clavier	FRA	5.60	18-4¼
8. Raphael Holzdeppe	GER	5.60	18-4¼

Born in Melbourne, Steve Hooker took up pole vaulting full-time in 1999 after switching from Australian Rules Football. Both his parents were top-level athletes. His mother, Erica Nixon, was a long jumper who competed in the 1972 Olympics and won a silver medal at the 1978 Commonwealth Games, while his father Bill participated in the 1974 Commonwealth Games in the 800 meters and 4 × 400-meter relay.

Hooker represented Australia at the world junior championships in 2000, finishing fourth. The following year he began to suffer from a fear of heights, often losing his nerve at the take-off point and running straight under the bar. On the verge of giving up the sport, he finally overcame his fears after seeing a hypnotist and made a breakthrough in 2004, recording a personal best to make the Australian Olympic team. Despite failing to make the final, Hooker had regained his confidence, and by the end of 2006 he had risen to number one in the world.

The qualifying round in Beijing took more than three hours to narrow the field. Although the original qualifying height was 5.75 meters (18 ft. 10¼ in.), the event officials lowered it to 5.65 (18 ft. 6½ in.) and allowed all 13 athletes who had cleared the height to advance. Russia's Igor Pavlov and Yevgeniy Lukyanenko, who had come to Beijing with the second-best vault of the season, 6.01 meters (19 ft. 8½ in.), both cleared 5.65 meters on their first attempts, while Hooker only managed to clear the qualifying height on his third and final attempt. Reigning world champion Brad Walker of the United States arrived in Beijing with the best vault of the season, 6.04 meters, but failed to clear the bar on any of his Olympic qualifying jumps and was out of the competition.

Hooker got off to a good start in the final, clearing his opening height, 5.60 meters (18 ft. 4½ in.), on his first vault, while Lukyanenko needed three attempts to get over. At 5.80 meters (19 ft. ¼ in.), their situations were reversed, with Hooker requiring all three attempts to clear the bar and Lukyanenko clearing easily on his first try. By the time the bar was raised to 5.85 meters (19 ft. 2¼ in.), only Hooker and Lukyanenko remained in gold medal contention. Both cleared on their third and final attempts. Lukyanenko then failed three times at 5.90 (19 ft. 4¼ in.), while Hooker managed to clear the bar on his third attempt to secure the gold medal. He then went on to break the Olympic record by clearing 5.96 (19 ft. 6½ in.), again on his third and final try. In the end Hooker had survived a precarious competition, requiring twelve jumps to clear the final four heights, managing each on his third and final attempt.

In 2009 Hooker won the world championship title despite having suffered a hip injury less than two weeks before. Knowing that a local anesthetic would last only three hours, and the competition would probably take four hours, Hooker waited until midway through the final before receiving a shot.

LONG JUMP

The long jump runway must be at least 40 meters (131 feet 3 inches) long and, preferably, at least 45 meters (147 feet 8 inches) long. Each contestant may place one or two markers on the runway to assist with the timing of his or her run-up and takeoff. A valid jump must be made from behind the far edge of the takeoff board, which is eight inches (20 centimeters) wide and level to the ground. A plasticine indicator board abuts the takeoff board to help determine fouls. Somersaults are not allowed. There is a time limit of 1½ minutes per jump. Jumps are measured from the nearest impression made in the sand by any part of the jumper's body or limbs. Current competitions begin with a qualifying round, the results of which are not carried over to the final. In the final, each contestant is allowed three jumps. Then the first eight are allowed three more jumps. The long jump has been dominated by US athletes, who have won 22 of 26 times. Until 2000, the only US losses were by 2¼ inches, 1½ inches, and one boycott.

1896 Athens C: 9, N: 5, D: 4.7. WR: 7.21, 23-8 (J. J. Mooney)

		M	FT.-IN.
1. Ellery Clark	USA	6.35	20-10
2. Robert Garrett	USA	6.00	19-8¼
3. James Connolly	USA	5.84	19-2
4. Alexandros Chalkokondilis	GRE	5.74	18-10

Ellery Clark described his victory in a 1911 article : "My own win was about as close a thing as could well have been. In America the invariable custom is for the jumper to measure off his run, and to mark the spot where he begins to run his hardest with something that will readily catch the eye. I myself was very dependent upon this mark, and practically lost without it. . . . Thus my discomforture was great when Prince George of Greece, who was superintending the event, emphatically forbade any measurements or marks. Apparently this, to his mind, savored of professionalism. We made a faint attempt to argue, were promptly suppressed, and remembering the cautions we had received at home, lest possible international bad feeling should arise out of the games, we meekly bowed to the decision."

Each man was allowed three jumps. Clark fouled the first two times. "It was little short of agony," he wrote. "I shall never forget my feelings as I stood at the end of the path for my third—and last—try. Five thousand miles, I reflected, I had come; and was it to end in this? Three fouls, and then five thousand miles back again, with that for my memory of the games." Fortunately, his last jump was not only valid, but good enough to win. Clark was a popular figure in Athens, particularly after he sewed the arms of the Greek royal family on his jersey above the American flag.

1900 Paris C: 12, N: 6, D: 7.15. WR: 7.50, 24-7¼ (Meyer Prinstein)

		M	FT.-IN.
1. Alvin Kraenzlein	USA	7.185	23-7 OR
2. Meyer Prinstein	USA	7.175	23-6½
3. Patrick Leahy	GBR/IRL	6.95	22-9¾
4. William Remington	USA	6.825	22-4¾
5. Albert Delannoy	FRA	6.755	22-2
6. John McLean	USA	6.655	21-10
7. Thaddeus McClain	USA	6.435	21-1¼
8. Waldemar Steffen	GER	6.30	20-8

Prinstein achieved his 23-foot 6¼-inch jump in the qualifying round, which, according to the rules of the time, counted in the final placings. The final was held on the next day, which was a Sunday. The official in charge of the Syracuse University team prohibited Prinstein from competing on a Sunday even though Prinstein was Jewish. Kraenzlein, who was Christian, did take part in the Sunday final and bettered Prinstein's mark by one centimeter. Peter O'Connor of Ireland was entered but did not compete. The following month he broke Prinstein's world record with a leap of 24 feet 7¾ inches. On August 5, 1901, he jumped 24 feet 11¾ inches to set a record that would last 20 years. In fact, O'Connor's jump remained an Irish national record until Carlos O'Connell broke it on June 2, 1990!

1904 St. Louis C: 10, N: 3, D: 9.1. WR: 7.61, 24-11¾ (Peter O'Connor)

		M	FT.-IN.
1. Meyer Prinstein	USA	7.34	24-1 OR
2. Daniel Frank	USA	6.89	22-7¼
3. Robert Stangland	USA	6.88	22-7
4. Fred Englehardt	USA	6.63	21-9
5. George Van Cleaf	USA	—	—
6. John Hagerman	USA	—	—

Prinstein earned his well-deserved Olympic long jump championship after a four-year wait.

1906 Athens C: 27, N: 10, D: 4.27. WR: 7.61, 24-11¾ (Peter O'Connor)

		M	FT.-IN.
1. Meyer Prinstein	USA	7.20	23-7½
2. Peter O'Connor	GBR/IRL	7.025	23-0½
3. Hugo Friend	USA	6.96	22-10
4. Hjalmar Mellander	SWE	6.585	21-7¼
5. Sidney Abrahams	GBR	6.21	20-4½
6. Thomas Cronan	USA	6.185	20-3½
7. Gunnar Rönström	SWE	6.15	20-2¼
8. István Somodi	HUN	6.045	19-10

This event saw an early example of international politics spilling over into the Olympics. When Peter O'Connor and his Irish teammates Con Leahy and John Daly arrived in Athens, they were outraged to discover that they were described in the athletics program as "British" rather than Irish. O'Connor filed a protest with the Greek Olympic Organizing Committee. But the Committee voted to support the British claim that because Ireland was part of the United Kingdom, they should compete for the British team.

After Prinstein was declared the winner over O'Connor, O'Connor filed another protest claiming that Prinstein had been allowed to jump out of order to take advantage of a smoother runway, that Matthew Halpin of the United States was allowed to act as the sole official, judge and measurer for the long jump, and that Halpin had, without reason, declared foul a jump of O'Connor's that had surpassed Prinstein's winning mark. His protest was rejected.

When three flags were required to indicate the nationality of the medalists, the British Union Jack was flown to represent O'Connor. This was too much for the proud Irish nationalist. He climbed the flagpole, unfurled a green Irish flag and waved it vigorously while Con Leahy stood guard at the foot of the pole. O'Connor recalled that this flag incident took place after the long jump, however some newspaper accounts suggest it happened after the triple jump. Including the Intercalated Games of 1906, Meyer Prinstein won four gold medals and one silver in the long jump and triple jump.

Third-place finisher Hugo Friend became a judge in Chicago and presided at the famous 1921 Black Sox trial in which members of the Chicago White Sox baseball team were accused of throwing the 1919 World Series.

1908 London C: 32, N: 9, D: 7.22. WR: 7.61, 24-11¾ (Peter O'Connor)

		M	FT.-IN.
1. Francis "Frank" Irons	USA	7.48	24-6½ OR
2. Daniel Kelly	USA	7.09	23-3¼
3. Calvin Bricker	CAN	7.08	23-3
4. Edward Cook	USA	6.97	22-10½
5. John Brennan	USA	6.86	22-6¼
6. Frank Mount Pleasant	USA	6.82	22-4½
7. Albert Weinstein	GER	6.77	22-2¾
8. Timothy Ahearne	GBR/IRL	6.72	22-0¾

The victory of 5 foot 5½ inch Frank Irons came as quite a surprise since his pre-Olympic best was only 22 feet 7½ inches. Many British sports enthusiasts were disgusted by the exuberant displays of the Americans whenever a US athlete won an event. One London paper described the American response to Irons' victory: "They were entertained then from the American stand by the singing of 'There'll be a hot time in the old town tonight,' by the fluttering of United States flags, and by the blowing of a new squeaking instrument of torture such as is employed at country fairs [probably a kazoo]. The Americans made themselves a nuisance and behaved in a manner which is happily quite foreign to the athletic grounds of England."

1912 Stockholm C: 30, N: 13, D: 7.12. WR: 7.61, 24-11¾ (Peter O'Connor)

		M	FT.-IN.
1. Albert Gutterson	USA	7.60	24-11¼ OR
2. Calvin Bricker	CAN	7.21	23-8
3. Georg Åberg	SWE	7.18	23-6¾
4. Harry Worthington	USA	7.03	23-0¾
5. Eugene Leroy Mercer	USA	6.97	22-10½
6. Fred Allen	USA	6.94	22-9¼
7. James Thorpe	USA	6.89	22-7¼
8. Robert Pasemann	GER	6.82	22-4½

Gutterson, of Andover, Vermont, settled the competition with his first jump, which was the best in the world since Peter O'Connor's record of 1901.

Although he failed to qualify for the Olympic final, Greek competitor Grigorios Lambrakis went on to lead an unusually eventful life. An active member of the Greek resistance movement during the Axis occupation, Lambrakis graduated from medical school after WWII and opened a gynecology clinic to treat indigent patients. An avowed pacifist, he later joined the United Democratic Left party and was elected to the Greek

Parliament, continuing to march in anti-war protests. On May 22, 1963, Lambrakis was attacked by two right-wing extremists while giving a speech at a pacifist rally. He sustained a serious brain injury and died five days later. Lambrakis' funeral sparked a demonstration of half a million people against the right-wing government, and the annual Marathon Peace Rally continues to be held in his honor. Lambrakis' life was the basis of the political novel, and later movie, *Z.*

1920 Antwerp C: 29, N: 11, D: 8.18. WR: 7.61, 24-11¾ (Peter O'Connor)

		M	FT.-IN.
1. William Petersson (Björneman)	SWE	7.15	23-5½
2. Carl Johnson	USA	7.095	23-3¼
3. Erik Abrahamsson	SWE	7.08	23-2¾
4. Robert "Dink" Templeton	USA	6.95	22-9¾
5. Erling Aastad	NOR	6.885	22-7
6. Rolf Franksson	SWE	6.73	22-1
7. Solomon Butler	USA	6.60	21-8
8. Einar Raeder	NOR	6.585	21-7¼

William Petersson, who later changed his last name to Björneman, was preparing to take his first jump when he noticed a silver coin lying on the runway. He picked it up and discovered that it was an American quarter. He put it in his left shoe for good luck and went on to win the gold medal. The favorite, Sol Butler, pulled a tendon on his first jump and had to withdraw. Fourth-place finisher Dink Templeton later became a famous track coach at Stanford University.

1924 Paris C: 34, N: 21, D: 7.8. WR: 7.69, 25-3 (Edward Gourdin)

		M	FT.-IN.
1. William DeHart Hubbard	USA	7.44	24-5
2. Edward Gourdin	USA	7.27	23-10¼
3. Sverre Hansen	NOR	7.26	23-10
4. Vilho Tuulos	FIN	7.07	23-2½
5. Louis Wilhelme	FRA	6.99	22-11¼
6. C. Christopher Mackintosh	GBR	6.92	22-8½
7. Virgilio Tommasi	ITA	6.89	22-7¼
8. Jacob Boot	HOL	6.86	22-6¼

A student at the University of Michigan, DeHart Hubbard, the son of a chauffeur, was the first black athlete to win an individual Olympic gold medal. His performance, however, was overshadowed by that of Robert LeGendre the day before. LeGendre, who had failed to make the US long jump team, set a world record of 25 feet 5¾ inches while competing in the pentathlon. In 1958, silver medalist Edward Gourdin became the first African-American member of the Massachusetts Supreme Court. Christopher Mackintosh, who placed sixth, was an all-around athlete who represented Scotland in rugby, dominated British skiing from 1923 through 1933, and was a member of the British team that won the four-man event at the 1938 World Bobsleigh Championships.

William DeHart Hubbard, 1924
Hubbard became the first black athlete to win an Olympic gold medal in an individual event when he won the 1924 long jump in Paris.

1928 Amsterdam C: 41, N: 23, D: 7.31. WR: 7.90, 25-11 (Edward Hamm)

		M	FT.-IN.
1. Edward Hamm	USA	7.73	25-4½ OR
2. Silvio Cator	HAI	7.58	24-10½
3. Alfred Bates	USA	7.40	24-3½
4. Willi Meier	GER	7.39	24-3
5. Erich Köchermann	GER	7.35	24-1½
6. Hannes de Boer	HOL	7.32	24-0¼
7. Edward Gordon	USA	7.32	24-0¼
8. Erik Svensson	SWE	7.29	23-11

Six weeks after the Olympic competition, while competing in Paris, silver medalist Silvio Cator became the first man to break the 26-foot barrier with a jump of 26 feet ¼ inch. Cator was also the captain of the Haitian soccer team. As it turned out, five different past and future gold medal winners took part in the 1928 long jump. In addition to Hamm, 1924 winner DeHart Hubbard finished 11th, 1932 winner Ed Gordon placed seventh, 1928 triple jump winner Mikio Oda tied with Hubbard for 11th, and 1932 triple jump winner Chuhei Nambu finished ninth.

1932 Los Angeles C: 12, N: 9, D: 8.2. WR: 7.98, 26-2¼ (Chuhei Nambu)

		M	FT.-IN.
1. Edward Gordon	USA	7.64	25-0¾
2. C. Lambert Redd	USA	7.60	24-11¼
3. Chuhei Nambu	JPN	7.45	24-5½
4. Erik Svensson	SWE	7.41	24-3¾
5. Richard Barber	USA	7.39	24-3
6. Naoto Tajima	JPN	7.15	23-5½
7. Hector Berra	ARG	6.66	21-10¼
8. Clovis de Figueiredo Raposo	BRA	6.43	21-1¼

1936 Berlin C: 43, N: 27, D: 8.4. WR: 8.13, 26-8¼ (James "Jesse" Owens)

		M	FT.-IN.
1. James "Jesse" Owens	USA	8.06	26-5½ OR
2. Carl Ludwig "Luz" Long	GER	7.87	25-10
3. Naoto Tajima	JPN	7.74	25-4¾
4. Wilhelm Leichum	GER	7.73	25-4½
4. Arturo Maffei	ITA	7.73	25-4½
6. Robert Clark	USA	7.67	25-2
7. John Brooks	USA	7.41	24-3¾
8. Robert Paul	FRA	7.34	24-1

On May 25, 1935, Jesse Owens had jumped 26 feet 8¼ inches, setting a world record that would last for 25 years and 79 days. He seemed a sure bet to win the Olympic gold medal. But when he walked over to the long jump area, he was surprised to see a tall, blue-eyed, blond German taking practice jumps in the 26-foot range. Owens was fully aware of the Nazis' desire to prove their theory of "Aryan superiority" and he was also fully aware that Hitler and his followers had a particular distaste for Negroes. With this in mind, Jesse, still in his sweatsuit, took a practice run down the runway and into the pit. To his surprise, the officials in charge counted this as his first attempt of the qualifying round. Somewhat rattled, he fouled his second attempt. He was now one foul away from being eliminated from his best event.

Luz Long and Jesse Owens, 1936
Rivals and friends, Nazi ideology notwithstanding.

According to Owens, at this point he was approached by the tall, blue-eyed, blond German, who introduced himself, in English, as Luz Long.

"Glad to meet you," said Owens tentatively. "How are you?"

"I'm fine," replied Long. "The question is: How are *you?*"

"What do you mean?" asked Owens.

"Something must be *eating* you," said Long, proud to display his knowledge of American slang. "You should be able to qualify with your eyes closed." For the next few minutes the black son of sharecroppers and the white model of Nazi manhood chatted. It turned out that Luz Long didn't believe in the theory of Aryan superiority and the two joked about the fact that he looked the part anyway. Then Long made a suggestion. Since the qualifying distance was only 23 feet 5½ inches, why didn't Owens make a mark several inches before the takeoff board and jump from there to play it safe. Owens did just that. He took off one and a half feet before the board and qualified by just one centimeter.

The final was held that afternoon. Jesse Owens opened with an Olympic record of 25 feet 5½ inches and then followed with 25 feet 10 inches. In the fifth of six rounds, Luz Long brought the German crowd to life by matching Owens' jump exactly. Inspired by the challenge, Owens leaped 26 feet 3¾ inches. Then, with his final jump, he hit 26 feet 5½ inches, to clinch his second of four gold medals. The first person to congratulate Owens, in full view of Adolf Hitler, was Luz Long. "You can melt down all the medals and cups I have," Jesse Owens later wrote, "and they wouldn't be a plating on the 24-carat friendship I felt for Luz Long at that moment." Long was killed in the Battle of St. Pietro on July 14, 1943, but Owens continued to correspond with his family.

1948 London C: 21, N: 17, D: 7.31. WR: 8.13, 26-8¼ (James "Jesse" Owens)

		M	FT.-IN.
1. Willie Steele	USA	7.82	25-8
2. T. William (Bill) Bruce	AUS	7.55	24-9¼
3. Herbert Douglas	USA	7.54	24-9
4. Lorenzo Wright	USA	7.45	24-5½
5. Adegboyega Folaranmi Adedoyin	GBR/NGR	7.27	23-10¼
6. Georges Damitio	FRA	7.07	23-2½
7. Harold Whittle	GBR	7.03	23-0¾
8. Felix Wurth	AUT	7.00	22-11½

Fifth-place finisher Prince Adegboyega Folaranmi Adedoyin was a member of the royal family of the kingdom of Ijebu-Remo in Nigeria. A medical student at Queen's University in Belfast, he represented Great Britain, since Nigeria was not yet considered an independent nation.

1952 Helsinki C: 27, N: 19, D: 7.21. WR: 8.13, 26-8¼ (James "Jesse" Owens)

		M	FT.-IN.
1. Jerome Biffle	USA	7.57	24-10
2. Meredith Gourdine	USA	7.53	24-8½
3. Ödön Földessy	HUN	7.30	23-11½
4. Ary Façanha de Sá	BRA	7.23	23-8¾
5. Jorma Valtonen	FIN	7.16	23-6
6. Leonid Grigoryev	SOV/RUS	7.14	23-5¼
7. Karl-Erik Israelsson	SWE	7.10	23-3½
8. Paul Faucher	FRA	7.02	23-0½

George Brown of UCLA had won 41 straight competitions before placing third at the US Olympic trials. Yet he was still the heavy favorite to win in Helsinki. In the final, however, he fouled three times in a row and was eliminated. Gold medalist Jerome Biffle was an army private who came out of two years' retirement to compete. Neville Price of South Africa jumped 24 feet 1¾ inches in the qualifying round, but was unable to take part in the final because of an injury.

Silver medalist Meredith Gourdine, whose father was a painter and a janitor, became an engineer and physicist with twenty-seven patents to his credit. Chief executive of an energy firm, he helped develop a device to eliminate fog above airports and another to convert low-grade coal into high-voltage electrical energy.

1956 Melbourne C: 32, N: 21, D: 11.24. WR: 8.13, 26-8¼ (James "Jesse" Owens)

		M	FT.-IN.
1. Gregory Bell	USA	7.83	25-8¼
2. John Bennett	USA	7.68	25-2½
3. Jorma Valkama	FIN	7.48	24-6½
4. Dmitri Bondarenko	SOV/UKR	7.44	24-5
5. Karim Olowu	NGR	7.36	24-1¾
6. Kazimierz Kropidlowski	POL	7.30	23-11½
7. Neville Price	SAF	7.28	23-10¾
8. Oleg Fyedoseyev	SOV/RUS	7.27	23-10¼

A short, loose runway and a strong fluctuating wind caused all entrants to perform well below their normal standards.

1960 Rome C: 49, N: 34, D: 9.2. WR: 8.21, 26-11¼ (Ralph Boston)

		M	FT.-IN.
1. Ralph Boston	USA	8.12	26-7¾ OR
2. Irvin "Bo" Roberson	USA	8.11	26-7¼
3. Igor Ter-Ovanesyan	SOV/RUS	8.04	26-4½
4. Manfred Steinbach	GER	8.00	26-3
5. Jorma Valkama	FIN	7.69	25-2¾
6. Christian Collardot	FRA	7.68	25-2½
7. Henk Visser	HOL	7.66	25-1¾
8. Dmitri Bondarenko	SOV/UKR	7.58	24-10½

On August 12, 1960, two weeks before the opening of the Rome Olympics, Ralph Boston finally broke Jesse Owens' 25-year-old world record with a leap of 26 feet 11¼ inches. He was expected to receive his stiffest challenge from Armenian Igor Ter-Ovanesyan, who had fouled out of the 1956 final and who would eventually go on to take part in five Olympics. Ter-Ovanesyan led at 25 feet 11 inches after the first round of the final. Bo Roberson, whose pre-Olympic best had been 26 feet 0 inches, jumped 26 feet 4¼ inches in the second round to take the lead. However, the third round saw Boston's big jump of 26 feet 7¾ inches. There were no changes in position during the next two rounds, but the competition was far from over. With his last attempt, Ter-Ovanesyan leaped 26 feet 4½ inches to edge into second place. An exhausted Bo Roberson had considered passing, but now he had to give it one last try. He zoomed seven inches beyond his pre-Olympic record, but landed one centimeter short of a gold medal. This was the first meet in which four men jumped over 26 feet.

The last of ten children, the son of a farmer and handyman, Ralph Boston grew up in Laurel, Mississippi. As a teenager, he borrowed his father's tools and built a track on a nearby lot that included a high jump set made of bamboo and a sawdust landing pit. At that time, Laurel was a center for Ku Klux Klan violence. After he earned his gold medal in Rome, Boston returned to a town in which he could only use segregated restaurants, restrooms and water fountains. "I was a citizen of the world," said Boston, "but not a citizen of Mississippi." Thirty-six years later, Boston served as a grand marshal of the Laurel Christmas parade.

(left to right) Bo Robertson, Ralph Boston, and Igor Ter-Ovanesyan, 1960

The three medalists in the 1960 long jump.

1964 Tokyo C: 32, N: 23, D: 10.18. WR: 8.34, 27-4¼ (Ralph Boston)

		M	FT.-IN.
1. Lynn Davies	GBR	8.07	26-5¾
2. Ralph Boston	USA	8.03	26-4¼
3. Igor Ter-Ovanesyan	SOV/RUS	7.99	26-2¾
4. Wariboko West	NGR	7.60	24-11¼
5. Jean Cochard	FRA	7.44	24-5
6. Luis Felipe Areta	SPA	7.34	24-1
7. Mike Ahey	GHA	7.30	23-11½
8. Andrzej Stalmach	POL	7.26	23-10

Lynn Davies, a physical education teacher from Nantymoel, Glamorganshire, in Wales, wasn't on anyone's list of potential winners in 1964. In fact, he barely made it into the final, qualifying with his last attempt. But the weather, cold, windy, and raining, was much more familiar to Davies than it was to the favorites, Ralph Boston and Igor Ter-Ovanesyan. "The Welsh gods must have been looking down on Tokyo that day," Davies later explained. "I'm convinced that had it been a warm, sunny day in Tokyo, I wouldn't have won the gold." The American and Soviet champions tried to convince the officials to reverse the running of the event, so that they would be jumping with the wind behind them instead of against them, but to no avail.

Ter-Ovanesyan took the first-round lead at 25 feet 6¼ inches. Boston moved ahead in the second round with a jump of 25 feet 9¼ inches. In the fourth round, he improved to 25 feet 10¼ inches. Entering the fifth round, Lynn Davies was in third place. "I remember thinking, this is it," he recalled. "I glanced up at the flag at the top of the stadium. Boston told me about this in New York, four months previously. 'If the flag drops,' he had said, 'it's a good indication that the wind is about to fade inside the stadium.' And as I looked up at it, it dropped dead." Davies took off down the runway immediately and hit the best jump of his career—26 feet 5¾ inches.

Ter-Ovanesyan followed with 26 feet 2¾ inches to move back into second place. The competition came down to Ralph Boston's final leap. Davies covered his face and peeked through his fingers. Boston's jump was long and Davies prepared himself for disappointment. But the measurement showed Boston had missed by four centimeters, and Lynn Davies had become the first Welshman ever to win an Olympic gold medal in an individual event. Davies also competed in the 100 meters and the 4 × 100-meter relay.

In 1999, Lynn Davis' leap was voted the greatest moment in Welsh sporting history.

1968 Mexico City C: 35, N: 22, D: 10.18. WR: 8.35, 27-4¾ (Ralph Boston, Igor Ter-Ovanesyan)

		M	FT.-IN.
1. Robert Beamon	USA	8.90	29-2½ WR
2. Klaus Beer	GDR	8.19	26-10½
3. Ralph Boston	USA	8.16	26-9¼
4. Igor Ter-Ovanesyan	SOV/RUS	8.12	26-7¾
5. Tõnu Lepik	SOV/EST	8.09	26-6½
6. Allen Crawley	AUS	8.02	26-3¾
7. Jacques Pani	FRA	7.97	26-1¾
8. Andrzej Stelmach	POL	7.94	26-0¾

All three medalists from 1964, Lynn Davies, Ralph Boston, and Igor Ter-Ovanesyan, were back in 1968, and all three were in good enough shape to win the gold medal. However, none of them was the favorite. That distinction fell to Bob Beamon, a 6-foot 3-inch 22-year-old from South Jamaica in New York. In 1968 Beamon had won 22 of 23 meets, losing only once indoors. But Beamon was by no means a sure bet. Unlike the other leading contenders, he made no checkmarks on the side of the runway to help him with his stride, so he was

Bob Beamon, 1968

Beamon stunned the sports world when he bettered the world long jump record by 21¾ inches with a leap of 29 feet 2½ inches, in 1968.

Bob Beamon, 1968
When he finally realized what he had accomplished, Beamon suffered a cataplectic seizure and fell to the ground in shock.

unusually prone to fouling. In addition, he had been without the benefit of a regular coach since mid-April, when he had been suspended from the track team at the University of Texas at El Paso for refusing to compete against Brigham Young University, as a protest against the racial policies of the Mormon Church.

Beamon almost met disaster in the qualifying round. His first jump took off a full foot after the board and his second jump was also a foul. He was now one foul away from elimination. Remembering the Jesse Owens—Luz Long incident of 1936, Ralph Boston, who had been informally coaching Beamon, walked up to the nervous favorite and had a few words with him. He told Beamon to relax and to take off from a mark a few inches before the takeoff board. Like Jesse Owens 32 years earlier, Bob Beamon made a mark one foot up the runway, then raced down the path and qualified easily.

The night before the most important final of his career, Bob Beamon did something he had never done before: he engaged in sexual intercourse the night before a major competition. At the moment of orgasm, he was suddenly overcome with the horrible feeling that he had blown it, that his chances for a gold medal and for thc world record he had boldly predicted he would achieve had been thrown away right there in bed.

The following day was gloomy, with occasional rain, the kind of day that supposedly favored Lynn Davies. There were 17 finalists ready to begin the competition at 3:40 p.m. Beamon's jumping order was fourth, Davies'12th, Ter-Ovanesyan's 13th, and Ralph Boston's 17th. The first three jumpers fouled. Then it was Bob Beamon's turn. Boston called out to him, "Come on, make it a good one." For 20 seconds Beamon stood at the beginning of the runway, gathering his strength and telling himself, "Don't foul, don't foul." Then he tore down the runway (he was a 9.5 sprinter at 100 yards), hit the takeoff board perfectly, and sailed through the air at what seemed to be an uncommon elevation, estimated by observers to be between five and a half and six feet. He hit the sand so powerfully that he bounced back up and landed outside the pit.

"That's over 28 feet," Ralph Boston said to Lynn Davies. "With his first jump?" replied Davies. "No, it can't be." They trotted over to the pit to get a better look. Officials slid the marker of the sophisticated optical measuring device down its rail to the point where Beamon's feet had hit the sand. But before it got there, the marker fell off the end of the rail. An official turned to Beamon and murmured, "Fantastic. Fantastic." An old-fashioned steel tape was called for. A couple measurements were taken and then the result was flashed on the electronic scoreboard: 8.90 meters. Beamon knew he had set a record, but being unfamiliar with the metric system, he didn't really understand how far he had jumped. He ran up to Ralph Boston, the man who had helped him so much, and embraced him. Boston then told Beamon, "Bob, you jumped 29 feet."

Beamon was stunned. "What do I do now?" he asked. "Ralph, I know you're gonna kick my ass."

"No, no," said Boston. "It's over for me. I can't jump that far."

"What about the Great Britain dude?" asked Beamon. "And what about the Russian?"

"The Russian," Igor Ter-Ovanesyan, had turned to Lynn Davies and said, "Compared to this jump, we are as children." Davies told Boston, "I can't go on. What is the point? We'll all look silly." Then he turned to Beamon and said, "You have destroyed this event."

By this time, Beamon's jump had been officially converted to 29 feet 2½ inches. Suddenly, Beamon realized what he had done. In his autobiography, *The Man Who Could Fly,* Beamon described his feelings at that moment: "All that emotion, those years of rejection, disappointment and confusion that had been sublimated into push-ups and sprints up mountains and bounding drills and visualization, flooded my psyche and were transformed into tears and nausea. My legs collapsed and I slid to the ground. . . ." Beamon had experienced what doctors would later describe as a "cataplectic seizure," an "atonic state of the somatic muscles which develops suddenly on the heels of emotional excitement." He was helped to his feet by Boston and US teammate Charlie Mays, who supported him until he recovered from his dizziness.

The contest continued, but just as Ter-Ovanesyan began his first jump, the skies began pouring rain. Beamon took one more jump of 26 feet 4½ inches but then passed his last four opportunities. Boston, Ter-Ovanesyan, and Davies (who finished ninth), who had waited four years for another chance at Olympic victory, were dazed and unable to perform up to par. Klaus Beer of East Germany, on the other hand, had had no such grand expectations, and was able to take the silver medal by bettering his personal best by four inches. Lepik and Crawley also had their best jumps ever.

Beamon's 29-foot 2½-inch jump was hailed as the greatest athletic achievement of all time, although detractors criticized the suspicious Mexican wind readings which measured the exact legal maximum of 2.0 meters per second. In the 33 years since Jesse Owens' 1935 jump of 26 feet 8¼ inches, the world record had progressed eight and a half inches. In a matter of seconds, Beamon had added another 21¾ inches. Ironically—since Beamon completely bypassed the 28-foot barrier—the first 28-foot jump didn't take place until the 1980 Olympics. Beamon himself never again jumped farther than 26 feet 11½ inches.

1972 Munich C: 36, N: 25, D: 9.9. WR: 8.90, 29-2½ (Robert Beamon)

		M	FT.-IN.
1. Randy Williams	USA	8.24	27-0½
2. Hans Baumgartner	GER	8.18	26-10
3. Clarence "Arnie" Robinson	USA	8.03	26-4¼
4. Joshua Owusu	GHA	8.01	26-3½
5. Preston Carrington	USA	7.99	26-2¾
6. Max Klauss	GDR	7.96	26-1¾
7. Alan Lerwill	GBR	7.91	25-11½
8. Leonid Barkovsky	SOV/UKR	7.75	25-5¼

Nineteen-year-old Randy Williams, the youngest entrant, led the qualifying round with a jump of 27 feet 4¼ inches—over a foot farther than his pre-Olympic, non-wind-aided best. He was followed by Preston Carrington at 26 feet 11¾ inches, 7¾ inches better than *his* pre-Olympic record. Neither American was able to do as well in the final. Williams, who kept a good-luck teddy bear with him at all times, injured his leg warming up before the final, and wisely decided to put all his effort into his first leap, which turned out to be good enough for the gold medal.

1976 Montreal C: 33, N: 25, D: 7.29. WR: 8.90, 29-2½ (Robert Beamon)

		M	FT.-IN.
1. Clarence "Arnie" Robinson	USA	8.35	27-4¾
2. Randy Williams	USA	8.11	26-7¼
3. Frank Wartenberg	GDR	8.02	26-3¾
4. Jacques Rousseau	FRA	8.00	26-3
5. João Carlos de Oliveira	BRA	8.00	26-3
6. Nenad Stekić	YUG/SER	7.89	25-10¾
7. Valery Pidluzhny	SOV/UKR	7.88	25-10¼
8. Hans Baumgartner	GER	7.82	25-8

For the third straight time, the long jump was won with a first round leap, and for the tenth time in 12 Olympics, it was won by an African-American.

1980 Moscow C: 32, N: 24, D: 7.28. WR: 8.90, 29-2½ (Robert Beamon)

		M	FT.-IN.
1. Lutz Dombrowski	GDR	8.54	28-0¼
2. Frank Paschek	GDR	8.21	26-11¼
3. Valery Pidluzhny	SOV/UKR	8.18	26-10
4. László Szalma	HUN	8.13	26-8¼
5. Stanislaw Jaskulka	POL	8.13	26-8¼
6. Viktor Belsky	SOV/BLR	8.10	26-7
7. Antonio Corgos	SPA	8.09	26-6½
8. Yordan Yanev	BUL	8.02	26-3¾

Before the Moscow Olympics, the longest jump other than Bob Beamon's had been 27 feet 11½ inches, by Larry Myricks of the United States. Myricks had qualified for the 1976 final, but fractured a bone in his foot and had to withdraw. In 1980, he was kept out again, this time by the Jimmy Carter boycott. Without him, the long jump competition was dominated by Lutz Dombrowski, who put together a tremendous series that averaged 27 feet 3¼ inches. His fifth-round jump of 28 feet ¼ inch was the first ever in the 28-foot range. Something of a rebel, Dombrowski kept running away from the schools to which he had been assigned by the East German government in order to return home to his family, his girlfriend, and his soccer team. When he broke his left leg playing soccer in 1979, he finally gave in to the East German coaches, although he continued to insist that he preferred the triple jump to the long jump. In 1991 Dombrowski admitted that between 1979 and 1987 he had delivered secret reports on his teammates to the Stasi security police.

1984 Los Angeles C: 31, N: 25, D: 8.6. WR: 8.90, 29-2½ (Robert Beamon)

		M	FT.-IN.
1. F. Carlton Lewis	USA	8.54	28-0¼
2. Gary Honey	AUS	8.24	27-0½
3. Giovanni Evangelisti	ITA	8.24	27-0½
4. Larry Myricks	USA	8.16	26-9¼
5. Liu Yuhuang	CHN	7.99	26-2¾
6. Joey Wells	BAH	7.97	26-1¾
7. Junichi Usui	JPN	7.87	25-10
8. Kim Jong-il	KOR	7.81	25-7½

When Carl Lewis was seven years old his parents began a track club. Carl and his five-year-old sister, Carol, used the landing area in the long jump pit to build sand castles. As they grew older, Carl and Carol used the pit for more conventional purposes. By 1981, Carl Lewis was the world's leading long-jumper. After losing an indoor meet to Larry Myricks on February 28, 1981, Lewis won 36 straight competitions leading up to the Olympics, including 16 meets in which he leaped over 28 feet. Twice he reached 28 feet 10¼ inches, both times at low-altitude. Once, in 1982, he landed about thirty feet from the take-off board, but the jump was ruled a foul after a controversial judge's decision.

At the Los Angeles Olympics, Lewis secured the gold medal with a first-round leap into the wind that once again surpassed 28 feet. He took one more jump and then, with six races behind him and five more to go, he passed the last four rounds.

Meanwhile, the battle for second place continued hot and heavy. Giovanni Evangelisti took the first-round non-Lewis lead at 26 feet 6½ inches. In the third round he was passed by Gary Honey's personal record of 26 feet 10 inches. Evangelisti led off the final round with his first-ever jump over 27 feet. But Honey, next down the runway, matched him to the centimeter and won the silver medal by virtue of a better second jump.

Unfortunately, Carl Lewis' performance was met by boos by many in the crowd who resented his refusal to challenge Bob Beamon's record by taking four more jumps. These boorish "fans" seemed unappreciative of Lewis' exacting Olympic schedule, and unaware that he had never taken a full complement of jumps at a meet in which he also competed in the sprints. It is also worth noting that the legendary Jesse Owens, to whom Lewis was often compared, took only one jump on the day he set his 1935 world record that would last for 25 years and, during his entire career, only twice did Owens take a full set of jumps.

At the 1984 Olympics, Carl Lewis' sister, Carol, placed ninth in the women's long jump.

1988 Seoul C: 41, N: 31, D: 9.26. WR 8.90, 29-2½ (Robert Beamon)

		M	FT.-IN.
1. F. Carlton Lewis	USA	8.72	28-7¼
2. Michael Powell	USA	8.49	27-10¼
3. Larry Myricks	USA	8.27	27-1½
4. Giovanni Evangelisti	ITA	8.08w	26-6w
5. Antonio Corgos	SPA	8.03	26-4¼
6. László Szalma	HUN	8.00	26-3
7. Norbert Brige	FRA	7.97	26-1¾
8. Leonid Voloshin	SOV/RUS	7.89	25-10¾

Carl Lewis went to the Olympics with a winning streak of 55 meets over seven and a half years. His latest victory came in a dramatic seesaw battle with longtime rival Larry Myricks at the US Olympic trials. Lewis won that one 28 feet 9 inches (8.76 meters) to 28 feet 8¼ inches (8.74 meters). In Seoul, however, Lewis faced a tough assignment: the long jump final began only 55 minutes after he finished competing in the preliminaries of the 200-meter dash. Drawn to jump in the first position, Lewis appealed to the officials in charge of the event and was allowed to jump twelfth and last instead. He took the first-round lead with a leap of 27 feet 7 inches, then lengthened his lead with a wind-aided second jump of 28 feet.

After the third round, a new official arrived on the scene and ordered Lewis to begin jumping first instead of last. Lewis argued that if he had to comply, he should at least be allowed a 10-minute break. The Korean official refused, but then the long jump clock malfunctioned and Lewis got his break anyway. He responded with his winning leap of 28 feet 7¼ inches.

Lewis, who registered the four longest jumps of the competition, became the first repeat winner in the history of the event (not including Meyer Prinstein's victory at the 1906 Intercalated Games).

1992 Barcelona C: 50, N: 37, D: 8.6. WR: 8.95, 29-4½ (Michael Powell)

		M	FT.-IN.
1. F. Carlton Lewis	USA	8.67	28-5½
2. Michael Powell	USA	8.64	28-4¼
3. Joe Greene	USA	8.34	27-4
4. Iván Pedroso Soler	CUB	8.11	26-7¼
5. Jaime Jefferson Guilarte	CUB	8.08	26-6¼
6. Konstantinos Koukodimos	GRE	8.04	26-4½
7. Dmitri Bagryanov	RUS	7.98	26-2¼
8. Huang Geng	CHN	7.87	25-10

The greatest duel in long jump history took place in Tokyo on the evening of August 30, 1991. By that time, Bob Beamon's Mexico City world record had stood for 22 years 316 days. But there was definitely a feeling in the air that something special was going to happen, that this could be the night. Carl Lewis had won 65 straight meets over a period of the last 10 years 170 days. But the 65th win had been a close call. At the US National Championships on June 15, he had defeated 27-year-old Mike Powell by only one centimeter with his final jump. In the third round at the world championships in Tokyo, Lewis jumped a wind-aided 28 feet 11¾ inches. In the fourth round he stretched beyond Beamon's world record at 29 feet 2¾ inches, but that jump too was wind-aided. Then, in the fifth round, Powell, who had lost to Lewis 15 straight times over the past eight years, uncorked the jump everyone had been waiting for, a legal 29 feet 4½ inches. Lewis was stunned that the record he had sought for so long should fall to someone else, but he did not fold. Instead he responded with a jump of 29 feet 1¼ inches, his longest legal jump ever. In the final round he hit 29 feet exactly. Lewis had put together the greatest series in history, but it was Powell who had broken Beamon's record, ending Lewis' win streak.

The Olympic final a year later was not nearly so dramatic. Lewis, who had leaped 28 feet 5¾ inches to lead the qualifying round, went 28 feet 5½ inches with his first try in the final. Powell started poorly and then improved with each of his other four legal jumps. After hitting 28 feet in the fifth round, he prayed at the top of the runway and then took his final jump. It was his best of the evening, but he fell 1¼ inches short. Carl Lewis, who had become a vegetarian between Olympics, won his third straight long jump gold medal. He then offended many in the crowd by taking his victory lap in the outside lane while a 5000-meter semifinal was in progress.

1996 Atlanta C: 52, N: 40, D: 7.29. WR: 8.95, 29-4½ (Michael Powell)

		M	FT.-IN.
1. F. Carlton Lewis	USA	8.50	27-10¾
2. James Beckford	JAM	8.29	27-2½
3. Joe Greene	USA	8.24	27-0½
4. Emmanuel Bangue	FRA	8.19	26-10½
5. Michael Powell	USA	8.17	26-9¾
6. Gregor Cankar	SLO	8.11	26-7¼
7. Aleksandr Glovatsky	BLR	8.07	26-5¾
8. Mattias Sunneborn	SWE	8.06	26-5¼

After his loss to Carl Lewis at the Barcelona Olympics, Mike Powell won 34 straight long jump contests including the 1993 world championship. In 1995, however, it was Cuba's Iván Pedroso who dominated the event, surpassing 28 feet in thirteen different meets and winning the world championship. Pedroso was also involved in a controversial incident in the high-altitude venue of Sestriere, Italy, on July 29, 1995. Pedroso jumped beyond Mike Powell's world record mark, landing at 8.96 meters (29 feet 4¾ inches). It appeared to be a world record, but doubts were immediately raised about the wind reading, which had been within the acceptable range. Of the 60 jumps taken that day only

Carl Lewis, 1996

After winning the long jump for the fourth time, Carl Lewis takes home some sand from the landing pit.

four had been wind-legal and three of those had been by Pedroso. A few days later, a videotape was discovered that clearly showed an Italian coach, Luciano Gemello, standing in front of the wind gauge, thus preventing an accurate measurement. The jump was not submitted for world record verification. Unfortunately, Pedroso experienced a severe hamstring tear in March 1996. Although he qualified for the Olympic final, he was not a factor and finished twelfth.

While all this was going on, few observers considered Carl Lewis, the three-time defending Olympic champion, to be a serious contender. He barely qualified for the Atlanta Games, placing third at the US trials, a mere one inch (3 centimeters) ahead of Mike Conley. Powell won the trials with a leap of 27 feet 6½ inches (8.39 meters).

After two of the three qualifying rounds, Carl Lewis was lying in 15th place, with only the top twelve eligible for the final. But with his last jump he hit 27 feet 2½ inches (8.29 meters), not only qualifying, but doing so in first place.

Emmanuelle Bangue took the early lead in the final the following evening with a first round jump of 26 feet 10½ inches (8.19 meters). Lewis ran through his first try and then hit a cautious 26 feet 8½ inches (8.14 meters) with his second to guarantee the extra three attempts accorded the top eight jumpers after three rounds. This put Lewis in third place behind Bangue and Powell. Joe Greene took the lead with a leap of 27 feet ½ inch (8.24 meters). Then came Carl Lewis' third attempt. With the crowd of 82,000 rooting him on, he bounded to 27 feet 10¾ inches (8.50 meters). It was his best sea level jump since the 1992 Olympics. Although there was great tension over the final three rounds as Powell, Greene and James Beckford, in particular, tried to match Lewis' distance, the fact was that of the eight finalists, only Beckford was able to improve in the last three rounds, moving from fifth to second with his final leap. The most dramatic moment came when Mike Powell, having strained a groin muscle in the fifth round, tried to jump one last time, only to land face first in the sand.

Twelve years after his triumph in Los Angeles (or, as Lewis put it, "fourteen hairstyles" later), Carl Lewis was still the Olympic long jump champion. He became only the fourth athlete in any sport to win nine gold medals and only the third to win the same individual event four times. One of those other two, discus thrower Al Oerter, was there to embrace Lewis at his press conference. Before leaving the field, Lewis scooped some of the sand from the landing pit into a bag and took it home with him.

After retiring the following year, Lewis started a clothing company and designed numerous items including a leather tuxedo.

2000 Sydney C: 53, N: 38, D: 9.28. WR: 8.95, 29-4½ (Michael Powell)

		M	FT.-IN.
1. Iván Pedroso Solar	CUB	8.55	28-0¾
2. Jai Taurima	AUS	8.49	27-10¼
3. Roman Schurenko	UKR	8.31	27-3¼
4. Oleksiy Lukashevych	UKR	8.26	27-1¼
5. Kofi Amoah Prah	GER	8.19	26-10½
6. Peter Burge	AUS	8.15	26-9
7. Luis Meliz Linares	CUB	8.08	26-6¼
8. Dwight Phillips	USA	8.06	26-5¼

Iván Pedroso had been the dominating force in long jumping for the past five years, winning the world championships of 1995, 1997 and 1999, but he had yet to earn an Olympic medal. He placed fourth at the 1992 Barcelona Games, but in 1996 he was hampered by a hamstring injury and could do no better than twelfth. In addition, he had recorded the best jump of the pre-Olympic season: 8.65 meters. In Sydney, Pedroso found himself in a duel with Jai Taurima, a half-Maori Australian who admitted to smoking a pack of cigarettes a day and drinking a good deal of alcohol on a regular basis. Taurima's personal record was only 8.35 meters, but he was spurred on by a wildly appreciative Australian crowd of more than 100,000. Both Taurima and Pedroso fouled in the first round, but in the second round Taurima took the lead with a jump of 8.18, only to have Pedroso top him at 8.34. Taurima matched that jump in the third round and moved into first place on the basis of his superior second-best jump. It also gave him the opportunity to jump last in each of three final rounds. In round four, Pedroso retook the lead with a leap of 8.41, while Taurima set a personal best of 8.40. Taurima moved ahead again with a fifth round jump of 8.49—an improvement of 14 centimeters over his pre-Olympic personal best. The crowd was going wild, but Taurima was not ready to celebrate. "I knew on his last jump that Pedroso was going to get me," said Taurima. "He always gets people on his last jump." Sure enough, Pedroso came through with a leap of 8.55. Taurima had one last try, but fell short at 8.28. Meanwhile, Roman Schurenko, who was in sixth place after five rounds, snatched the bronze medal with a final jump of 8.31. This marked the first time in Olympic history that US long jumpers competed, but failed to win a medal.

For the record, Taurima's parents came up with the name Jai because that was the name of the child who Tarzan adopted in the 1962 film *Tarzan Goes to India*.

2004 Athens C: 40, N: 30, D: 8.26. WR: 8.95, 29-4½ (Michael Powell)

		M	FT.-IN.
1. Dwight Phillips	USA	8.59	28-2¼
2. John Moffitt	USA	8.47	27-9½
3. Joan Lino Martínez	SPA	8.32	27-3½
4. James Beckford	JAM	8.31	27-3
5. Chris Tomlinson	GBR	8.25	27-0¾
6. Ignisious Gaisah	GHA	8.24	27-0½
7. Iván Pedroso	CUB	8.23	27-0
8. Bogdan Tăru	ROM	8.21	26-11¼

Dwight Philips' athletic career nearly came to an end at the age of fourteen, when he broke both his legs after being struck by a motorcycle while playing street football. According to Philips, "The doctors thought I wouldn't walk again, but my parents and I always thought I would." In 2003, Phillips won both the IAAF indoor and outdoor world championships, and during the pre-Olympic season he recorded the world's six longest jumps. In Athens, Phillips led the qualifying round. In the final he hit what would be his winning distance of 8.59 meters (28 feet 2¼ inches) with his first jump. Trying to outdo this first attempt, Philip fouled his next two jumps, falling flat on his face on his third jump. The rest of the field struggled to catch up. In the second round, Joan Lino Martínez recorded a personal record of 8.35 meters (27 feet 3¾ inches), although the jump, which ultimately earned him the bronze medal, would prove controversial. Video replays showed that Martínez's foot clearly went over the board, however no mark was found in the plasticine and so no foul was called. A protest lodged by Great Britain was denied. John Moffit earned the silver medal in the fifth round with a personal record of 8.47 meters (27 feet 9½ inches).

Although Phillips did not qualify for the 2008 Olympics, he continued to flourish at the world championships, winning the world title in 2005, 2009 and 2011, and finishing third in 2007.

2008 Beijing C: 39, N: 32, D: 8.18. WR: 8.95, 29-4½ (Michael Powell)

		M	FT.-IN.
1. Irving Saladino Aranda	PAN	8.34	27-4¼
2. Godfrey Khotso Mokoena	SAF	8.24	27-0¼
3. Ibrahim Camejo Savas	CUB	8.20	26-10¾
4. Ngonidzashe Makusha	ZIM	8.19	26-10½
5. Wilfredo Martínez Caraba	CUB	8.19	26-10½
6. Ndiss Kaba Badji	SEN	8.16	26-9¼
7. Luis Felipe Méliz Linares	SPA	8.07	26-5¾
8. Roman Novotný	CZE	8.00	26-3

After finishing sixth at the 2005 world championships, Panama's Irving Saladino had a breakout season, winning 15 of 17 competitions in 2006 and seven straight competitions in the lead-up to the 2007 world championships in Osaka, Japan. There Saladino held the lead until the final round, when Italy's Andrew Howe recorded an 8.47-meter (27 ft 9½ in.) jump. Saladino responded with a personal best of 8.57 meters (28 ft. ½ in.) on his final attempt to earn his first major international title. In third place was reigning Olympic champion and 2005 world champion Dwight Phillips, and in fifth place was South Africa's Godfrey Mokoena, who had competed in Athens in 2004 but failed to move past the qualifying round, after arriving late at the competition due to a scheduling misunderstanding by his coach.

Both Saladino and Howe struggled with injuries in 2008. Saladino was hampered by a persistent knee injury, while Howe suffered a shoulder injury and a hamstring injury after competing in the 200 meters event at the European Cup in June. By May Saladino had regained form enough to record a spectacular 8.73-meter (28 ft. 7¾ in.) leap at a meet in Hengelo, Netherlands, making him the clear favorite in Beijing. Phillips ultimately missed the chance to defend his gold medal after suffering an abdominal strain at the US Olympic trials, finishing fourth and failing to qualify.

The first round of the Olympic competition proved difficult, taking out Howe and all three American competitors. Except for the boycotted 1980 Games, this would be the first Olympic long jump final to take place without a representative of the United States.

In the final, Zimbabwe's Ngoni Makusha took the early lead after a first-round jump of 8.19 (26 ft. 10½ in.) meters, but Saladino passed him in the third round. Mokoena briefly moved into first place early in the fourth round, but Saladino retook the lead with a jump of 8.34 meters (27 ft. 4¼ in.), which would end up being the gold-medal-winning jump. Twenty-six-year-old Ibrahim Camejo, second on the 2008 world season list going into Beijing, edged out Makusha for the bronze medal with his sixth and final jump.

Saladino's gold was Panama's first-ever Olympic gold medal, and its first medal of any color since Lloyd LaBeach had won bronze in the 100- and 200-meter sprints at the 1948 London Games.

In 2009 Phillips beat Mokoena to regain the world championship title, as Saladino fouled all three of his attempts in the final.

TRIPLE JUMP

This used to be known as the hop, step, and jump, which accurately describes the event. The contestants land on the same foot with which they take off, take one step onto the other foot, and then jump. Other rules are the same as those for the long jump.

1896 Athens C: 7, N: 5, D: 4.6. WR: 15.25, 50-0½ (Daniel Shanahan)

		M	FT.-IN.
1. James Connolly	USA	13.71	44-11¾
2. Alexandre Tuffère	FRA	12.70	41-8
3. Ioannis Persakis	GRE	12.52	41-0¾
4. Alajos Szokoly	HUN/SLV	11.26	36-11½
5. Carl Schumann	GER	—	—

James Brendan Connolly came from a poor Irish-American family in South Boston, Massachusetts. He was a 27-year-old, self-educated freshman at Harvard when he read about the revival of the Olympic Games. As the national triple jump champion, he decided to go to Athens and take part. He asked permission for a leave of absence. When his dean refused, he dropped out and went anyway. Connolly's travel expenses were paid for by the Suffolk Athletic Club and by the proceeds of a bake sale organized by his local parish church.

James Connolly

Connolly of Boston became the first Olympic champion in 1527 years when he won the triple jump in 1896. He later became a well-known writer.

Ten American athletes and one trainer spent 16½ days on a ship to Naples, where Connolly's wallet was stolen. Then they took the train to Athens, arriving at 9 p.m. on April 5. According to Connolly, at 4 a.m. the following morning, they were awakened by a brass band and discovered, to their shock, that the competition was to begin that day rather than twelve days hence as they had expected. Apparently the Americans had forgotten that the Greek calendar differed from the American one.

At 2 p.m., on April 6, the first modern Olympic Games were officially opened. Connolly was the last to jump in the triple jump competition. After his second try he turned to the Englishman raking the pit and said, "They ought to tell how far each man jumps. Then a fellow won't be breaking his back when there's no need of it." The pit raker replied, "As far as the measurements go, there's nobody within a yard of you." James Connolly had become the first Olympic champion since the boxer Prince Varasdates of Armenia in 369 AD. Actually, Connolly had performed two hops and a jump rather than a hop, step, and jump, which was acceptable according to the rules of the competition at the time. Later in the Games, he finished third in the long jump and second in the high jump. He returned to the Olympics in 1900 and placed second in the triple jump.

Connolly later became a noted journalist and war correspondent, and also authored 25 novels and 200 short stories. Connolly covered the 1908 London Olympics as a journalist and responded to the numerous judging controversies by producing an unpublished manuscript entitled "The English as Poor Loser." Connolly died on January 20, 1957, at the age of 88. His victor's medal is at the Colby College library in Waterville, Maine, and there is a statue of Connolly in Columbus Park in South Boston.

1900 Paris C: 13, N: 6, D: 7.16. WR: 15.25, 50-0½ (Daniel Shanahan)

		M	FT.-IN.	
1. Meyer Prinstein	USA	14.47	47-5¾	OR
2. James Connolly	USA	13.97	45-10	
3. Lewis Sheldon	USA	13.64	44-9	
4. Patrick Leahy	GBR/IRL	—	—	
5. Albert Delannoy	FRA	—	—	
6. Alexandre Tuffère	FRA	—	—	

Prinstein made up for his disappointment at not being allowed to take part in the previous day's long jump final.

1904 St. Louis C: 7, N: 1, D: 9.1. WR: 5.25, 50-0½ (Daniel Shanahan)

		M	FT.-IN.
1. Meyer Prinstein	USA	14.35	47-1
2. Fred Englehardt	USA	13.90	45-7¼
3. Robert Stangland	USA	13.36	43-10
4. John Fuhler	USA	12.91	42-4½
5. George Van Cleaf	USA	—	—
6. John Hagerman	USA	—	—
7. Samuel Jones	USA	—	—

Prinstein won with his sixth and final jump.

1906 Athens C: 21, N: 9, D: 4.30. WR: 15.25, 50-0½ (Daniel Shanahan)

		M	FT.-IN.
1. Peter O'Connor	GBR/IRL	14.075	46-2¼
2. Cornelius "Con" Leahy	GBR/IRL	13.98	45-10½
3. Thomas Cronan	USA	13.70	44-1½
4. Oscar Guttormsen	NOR	13.34	43-9¼
5. Dimitrios Müller	GRE	13.125	43-0¾
6. Francis Connolly	USA	12.75	41-10
7. Vasilios Stournaras	GRE	12.725	41-9
8. Carl Pedersen	NOR	12.68	41-7

Peter O'Connor began training for the triple jump while still a boy, although he was probably not aware of the existence of such an event at the time. "I became imbued with the ambition, when a small lad, to reach by doing a hop, step and jump from the doorstep of my home, a grass margin, over an intervening gravel space." He did this almost every morning for several years until he could not only reach the grass margin, but jump far beyond it.

1908 London C: 20, N: 8, D: 7.25. WR: 15.25, 50-0½ (Daniel Shanahan)

		M	FT.-IN.	
1. Timothy Ahearne	GBR/IRL	14.92	48-11¼	OR
2. J. Garfield MacDonald	CAN	14.76	48-5¼	
3. Edvard Larsen	NOR	14.39	47-2¾	
4. Calvin Bricker	CAN	14.10	46-3	
5. Platt Adams	USA	14.07	46-2	
6. Frank Mount Pleasant	USA	13.97	45-10	
7. Karl Fryksdal	SWE	13.65	44-9¼	
8. John Brennan	USA	13.59	44-7	

Ahearne won with his final jump.

Tim Ahearne was the older brother of Dan Ahearn, who dropped the last "e" in his name when he passed through Ellis Island on his way to the United States, and who represented the US in the triple jump at the 1920 Antwerp Games.

1912 Stockholm C: 20, N: 8, D: 7.15. WR: 15.52, 50-11 (Daniel Ahearn)

		M	FT.-IN.
1. Gustaf Lindblom	SWE	14.76	48-5¼
2. Georg Åberg	SWE	14.51	47-7¼
3. Erik Almlöf	SWE	14.17	46-6
4. Erling Vinne	NOR	14.14	46-4¾
5. Platt Adams	USA	14.09	46-2¾
6. Edvard Larsen	NOR	14.06	46-1½
7. Hjalmar Olsson	SWE	14.01	45-11¾
8. Nils Fixdal	NOR	13.96	45-9¾

1920 Antwerp C: 21, N: 8, D: 8.21. WR: 15.52, 50-11 (Daniel Ahearn)

		M	FT.-IN.
1. Vilho Tuulos	FIN	14.505	47-7
2. Folke Jansson	SWE	14.48	47-6
3. Erik Almlöf	SWE	14.27	46-9¾
4. Ivar Sahlin	SWE	14.17	46-6
5. Sherman Landers	USA	14.17	46-6
6. Daniel Ahearn	USA	14.08	46-2¼
7. Ossian Nylund	FIN	13.74	45-0½
8. B. Howard Baker	GBR	13.675	44-10

1924 Paris C: 20, N: 12, D: 7.12. WR: 15.52, 50-11 (Daniel Ahearn)

		M	FT.-IN.	
1. Anthony "Nick" Winter	AUS	15.525	50-11¼	WR
2. Luis Brunetto	ARG	15.425	50-7¼	
3. Vilho Tuulos	FIN	15.37	50-5	
4. Väinö Rainio	FIN	15.01	49-3	
5. Folke Jansson	SWE	14.97	49-1½	
6. Mikio Oda	JPN	14.35	47-1	
7. R. Earle Wilson	USA	14.235	46-8	
8. Ivar Sahlin	SWE	14.16	46-5½	

Nick Winter, a 29-year-old fireman, was the first Australian to compete in a field event. The triple jump was so little known in Australia that it was not included in the national championships until six years *after* Winter earned his gold medal. The son of the proprietor of a snooker salon, Winter specialized in odd events, such as backward cycling and the individual tug-of-war. In setting a world record with his final jump, Nick Winter improved on his pre-Olympic best by 14½ inches.

1928 Amsterdam C: 24, N: 13, D: 8.2. WR: 15.525, 50-11¼ (Anthony Winter)

		M	FT.-IN.
1. Mikio Oda	JPN	15.21	49-11
2. Levi Casey	USA	15.17	49-9¼
3. Vilho Tuulos	FIN	15.11	49-7
4. Chuhei Nambu	JPN	15.01	49-3
5. Toimi Tulikoura	FIN	14.70	48-2¾
6. Erkki Järvinen	FIN	14.65	48-0¾
7. Willem Peters	HOL	14.55	47-9
8. Väinö Rainio	FIN	14.41	47-3½

Mikio Oda of Hiroshima Prefecture was the first Asian to win an individual Olympic gold medal. The pole that bore the Olympic flag during the 1964 Tokyo

Olympics was 15.21 meters high in honor of Oda's winning jump 36 years earlier.

1932 Los Angeles C: 16, N: 12, D: 8.4. WR: 15.58, 51-1½ (Mikio Oda)

		M	FT.-IN.
1. Chuhei Nambu	JPN	15.72	51-7 WR
2. Eric Svensson	SWE	15.32	50-3¼
3. Kenkichi Oshima	JPN	15.12	49-7¼
4. Eamon Fitzgerald	IRL	15.01	49-3
5. Willem Peters	HOL	14.93	48-11¾
6. Sol Furth	USA	14.88	48-10
7. Sidney Bowman	USA	14.87	48-9½
8. Rolland Romero	USA	14.85	48-8¾

Chuhei Nambu was the world record holder in the long jump, but a leg injury prevented him from placing better than third in Los Angeles. Two days later he entered the triple jump and finished first, achieving the rare distinction of holding the world record in both horizontal jump events. A native of Sapporo in northern Japan, Nambu tried to practice indoors during the winter. In fact, he was banned from local department stores because he would do his workouts by weaving among the customers while running up and down the stairs. Nambu honed his technique by studying the world around him. To learn how to run, he watched horses. To learn how to leap, he watched frogs and monkeys. To learn how to move his arms, he watched the wheels of trains. After retiring from competition, Nambu worked as a sports editor for *Mainichi Shimbun*, served as head athletics coach for Japan at the 1964 Tokyo Olympics, and worked as a college professor and president. He died July 23, 1997, at the age of 93.

Chuhei Nambu, 1932
A world record triple jump, followed by a leap for joy.

1936 Berlin C: 31, N: 19, D: 8.6. WR: 15.78, 51-9¼ (Jim Metcalfe)

		M	FT.-IN.
1. Naoto Tajima	JPN	16.00	52-6 WR
2. Masao Harada	JPN	15.66	51-4½
3. Jack Metcalfe	AUS	15.50	50-10¼
4. Heinz Wöllner	GER	15.27	50-1¼
5. Rolland Romero	USA	15.08	49-5¾
6. Kenkichi Oshima	JPN	15.07	49-5½
7. Erich Joch	GER	14.88	48-10
8. Dudley Wilkins	USA	14.83	48-8

Tajima duplicated Nambu's feat of winning the triple jump gold medal two days after he had earned a bronze medal in the long jump. Long jump silver medalist Luz Long placed tenth in the triple jump.

1948 London C: 29, N: 18, D: 8.3. WR: 16.00, 52-6 (Naoto Tajima)

		M	FT.-IN.
1. Arne Åhman	SWE	15.40	50-6¼
2. George Avery	AUS	15.36	50-4¾
3. Ruhi Sarialp	TUR	15.02	49-3½
4. Preben Larsen	DEN	14.83	48-8
5. Geraldo de Oliveira	BRA	14.82	48-7½
6. Valdemar Rautio	FIN	14.70	48-2¾
7. Leslie McKnead	AUS	14.53	47-8
8. Helio Coutinho de Silva	BRA	14.49	47-6½

1952 Helsinki C: 35, N: 23, D: 7.23. WR: 16.01, 52-6½ (Adhemar Ferreira da Silva)

		M	FT.-IN.
1. Adhemar Ferreira da Silva	BRA	16.22	53-2¾ WR
2. Leonid Sherbakov	SOV/RUS	15.98	52-5¼
3. Arnoldo Devonish	VEN	15.52	50-11
4. Walter Ashbaugh	USA	15.39	50-6
5. Rune Nilsen	NOR	15.13	49-7¾
6. Yoshio Iimuro	JPN	14.99	49-2¼
7. Geraldo de Oliveira	BRA	14.95	49-0¾
8. Roger Norman	SWE	14.89	48-10¼

The son of a railroad worker and a domestic servant, Adhemar da Silva put on an incredible show, breaking his old world record four times in six attempts in the final. Arnoldo Devonish was the first Venezuelan to win an Olympic medal.

1956 Melbourne C: 32, N: 20, D: 11.27. WR: 16.56, 54-4 (Adhemar Ferreira da Silva)

		M	FT.-IN.	
1. Adhemar Ferreira da Silva	BRA	16.35	53-7¾	OR
2. Vilhjálmur Einarsson	ICE	16.26	53-4¼	
3. Vitold Kreyer	SOV/RUS	16.02	52-6¾	
4. William Sharpe	USA	15.88	52-1¼	
5. Martin Rehák	CZE	15.85	52-0	
6. Leonid Sherbakov	SOV/RUS	15.80	51-10	
7. Koji Sakurai	JPN	15.73	51-7¼	
8. Teruji Kogake	JPN	15.64	51-3¾	

The second round of the final produced a tremendous shock, when a completely unknown Icelander, 22-year-old Vilhjálmur Einarsson, took the lead with a jump of 53 feet 4¼ inches, improving his personal record by 17 inches. Nevertheless, defending champion da Silva regained the lead in the fourth round and won his second gold medal. Afterward, reporters searched frantically to find an Icelandic interpreter, only to have Einarsson save them the trouble by explaining that he spoke English quite well, since he had just graduated from Dartmouth College, in New Hampshire. Einarsson was Iceland's first Olympic medal winner.

In 1958 Adhemar Ferreira da Silva acted in the internationally acclaimed film *Black Orpheus.* He is the only South American athlete to win two Olympic gold medals.

1960 Rome C: 39, N: 24, D: 9.6. WR: 17.03, 55-10½ (Józef Schmidt)

		M	FT.-IN.	
1. Józef Schmidt	POL	16.81	55-2	OR
2. Vladimir Goryayev	SOV/BLR	16.63	54-6¾	
3. Vitold Kreyer	SOV/RUS	16.43	53-11	
4. Ira Davis	USA	16.41	53-10¼	
5. Vilhjálmur Einarsson	ICE	16.37	53-8 ½	
6. Ryszard Malcherczyk	POL	16.01	52-6½	
7. Manfred Hinze	GDR	15.93	52-3¼	
8. Karl Rahkamo	FIN	15.84	51-11¾	

On August 5, 1960, Józef Schmidt had jumped 55 feet 10½ inches to become the first person to break both the 55-foot barrier and the 17-meter barrier, bettering the world record by 13 inches (33 centimeters). In Rome, he won easily.

1964 Tokyo C: 34, N: 21, D: 10.16. WR: 17.03, 55-10½ (Józef Schmidt)

		M	FT.-IN.	
1. Józef Schmidt	POL	16.85	55-3½	OR
2. Oleg Fyedoseyev	SOV/RUS	16.58	54-4¾	
3. Viktor Kravchenko	SOV/RUS	16.57	54-4½	
4. Frederick Alsop	GBR	16.46	54-0	
5. Şerban Ciochină	ROM	16.23	53-3	
6. Manfred Hinze	GDR	16.15	53-0	
7. Georgi Stoikovski	BUL	16.10	52-10	
8. Hans-Jürgen Rückborn	GDR	16.09	52-9½	

Józef Schmidt had dominated the triple jump for six years. However, he underwent an operation to his knee less than two months before the Tokyo Games, and his condition was still in doubt. Competing in pain, needing an injection of Novocain, Schmidt jumped 54 feet 7½ inches in the second round of the final and then set an Olympic record of 55 feet 3½ inches with his last attempt.

1968 Mexico City C: 34, N: 24, D: 10.17. WR: 17.03, 55-10½ (Józef Schmidt)

		M	FT.-IN.	
1. Viktor Saneyev	SOV/GEO	17.39	57-0¾	WR
2. Nelson Prudêncio	BRA	17.27	56-8	
3. Giuseppe Gentile	ITA	17.22	56-6	
4. Arthur Walker	USA	17.12	56-2	
5. Nikolai Dudkin	SOV/BLR	17.09	56-1	
6. Philip May	AUS	17.02	55-10¼	
7. Józef Schmidt	POL	16.89	55-5	
8. Mamadou Mansour-Dia	SEN	16.73	54-10¾	

Giuseppe Gentile, a bearded 25-year-old law student who later played opposite Maria Callas in the film version of *Medea,* produced a stunning performance in the qualifying round when he leaped 56 feet 1¼ inches to break Józef Schmidt's eight-year-old world record. But this was just a prelude to the extraordinary events of the following day's final.

In the very first round, Gentile hit a whopping 56 feet 6 inches, 19 inches farther than his pre-Olympic best, and it seemed that he had surely put a lock on the gold medal. But in the second round, Nelson Prudêncio, who had never jumped beyond 53 feet 5¾ inches before Mexico City, leaped an ominous 55 feet 11¼ inches. In the third round it was the turn of Viktor Saneyev, a graduate of the Georgian Sub-Tropical Plant Cultivation Institute. The pre-Olympic favorite, Saneyev reached 56 feet 6½ inches to move ahead of Gentile by one centimeter.

In the fifth round, Nikolai Dudkin moved into third place with 56 feet 1 inch. Two jumps later, Prudêncio exploded with another world record of 56 feet 8 inches. With his last jump, Prudêncio again broke Schmidt's old record with a jump of 56 feet 3¼ inches. Saneyev, Art Walker, and Gentile each had one jump remaining. It was Saneyev who came up with the clutch performance, extending to 57 feet ¾ inch for yet another world record. Walker jumped 56 feet 2 inches, leaving Nikolai Dudkin in fifth place even though he had bettered the pre-Olympic world record. Gentile closed the amazing competition with his fourth foul in five jumps and had to settle for a bronze medal after twice setting a world record. The best jumps of Saneyev and Prudêncio were both accompanied by suspicious wind readings of exactly 2.0 m.p.s., which didn't affect the competition, but did affect their validity as world records, since 2.0 m.p.s. happened to be the maximum allowable wind speed.

1972 Munich C: 36, N: 28, D: 9.4. WR: 17.40, 57-1 (Pedro Pérez Dueñas)

		M	FT.-IN.
1. Viktor Saneyev	SOV/GEO	17.35	56-11¼
2. Jörg Drehmel	GDR	17.31	56-9½
3. Nelson Prudêncio	BRA	17.05	55-11¼
4. Carol Corbu	ROM	16.85	55-3½
5. John Craft	USA	16.83	55-2¾
6. Mamadou Mansour-Dia	SEN	16.83	55-2¾
7. Michal Joachimowski	POL	16.69	54-9¼
8. Kristen Flogstad	NOR	16.44	53-11¼

This was expected to be a dramatic showdown between defending champion Viktor Saneyev and his rival Jörg Drehmel, who had twice beaten Saneyev in important meets. But Saneyev belted out the third best jump of all time in the first round of the final, and Drehmel was unable to even come close until the fifth round. World record holder Pedro Pérez withdrew in the middle of the qualifying round because of injury. Nelson Prudêncio's final jump was his best since the 1968 Olympic final.

1976 Montreal C: 25, N: 18, D: 7.30. WR: 17.89, 58-8½ (João Carlos de Oliveira)

		M	FT.-IN.
1. Viktor Saneyev	SOV/GEO	17.29	56-8¾
2. James Butts	USA	17.18	56-4½
3. João Carlos de Oliveira	BRA	16.90	55-5½
4. Pedro Pérez Dueñas	CUB	16.81	55-2
5. Tommy Haynes	USA	16.78	55-0¾
6. Wolfgang Kolmsee	GER	16.68	54-8¾
7. Eugeniusz Biskupski	POL	16.49	54-1¼
8. Carol Corbu	ROM	16.43	53-11

On October 15, 1975, João Carlos de Oliveira, competing at the Pan American Games in Mexico City, triple-jumped 58 feet 8½ inches to better Viktor Saneyev's world record by an incredible 17¾ inches. At the Montreal Olympics, de Oliveira led the qualifying round with a reserved jump of 55 feet 2 inches, followed by Saneyev at 55 feet ¼ inch. In the final, Pérez took the first-round lead at 55 feet 2 inches, but Saneyev moved ahead in the third round with a jump of 55 feet 11¾ inches. In the fourth round, James Butts, aiming to become the first US triple jump medalist in 48 years, leaped into the lead at 56 feet 4½ inches. However, Saneyev, ever the clutch performer, rebounded in the fifth round with a jump of 56 feet 8¾ inches, and that settled the issue. He joined standing jumper Ray Ewry, hammer thrower John Flanagan, and discus champion Al Oerter as the track and field athletes to win three or more individual gold medals in the same event. They have since been joined by long jumper Carl Lewis and javelin thrower Jan Železný.

1980 Moscow C: 23, N: 19, D: 7.25. WR: 17.89, 58-8½ (João Carlos de Oliveira)

		M	FT.-IN.
1. Jaak Uudmäe	SOV/EST	17.35	56-11¼
2. Viktor Saneyev	SOV/GEO	17.24	56-6¾
3. João Carlos de Oliveira	BRA	17.22	56-6
4. Keith Connor	GBR	16.87	55-4¼
5. Ian Campbell	AUS	16.72	54-10¼
6. Atanas Chochev	BUL	16.56	54-4
7. Béla Bakosi	HUN	16.47	54-0½
8. Kenneth Lorraway	AUS	16.44	53-11¼

Unfortunately, this event was marred by ugly scenes: Soviet spectators whistling while de Oliveira jumped, and controversial officiating that caused leading non-Soviet contenders de Oliveira and Ian Campbell to be charged with nine fouls in 12 jumps. In the third round Campbell received a no-jump after allegedly dragging his trail leg during the step stage. He argued his case, but the pit was raked before impartial observers could arrive. The very next jump was the gold medal winner for 25-year-old Estonian Jaak Uudmäe. The final round was highlighted by a near world record by de Oliveira that was ruled a foul, and by 34-year-old Viktor Saneyev's noble attempt to match Al Oerter's feat of four consecutive gold medals. He landed four and a half inches short, but did manage to edge past de Oliveira for the silver medal. On December 22, 1981, João Carlos de Oliveira was badly injured in an auto accident in which he was struck head-on by a drunken driver being chased by the police. After a nine-and-a-half month battle to salvage his athletic career, his right leg was finally amputated below the knee. De Oliveira served two terms as a state legislator, but after being voted out of office his life turned downhill and he died of liver and lung diseases at the age of 45.

1984 Los Angeles C: 28, N: 21, D: 8.4. WR: 17.89, 58-8½ (João Carlos de Oliveira)

		M	FT.-IN.
1. Alfredrick Joyner	USA	17.26 w	56-7½ w
2. Michael Conley	USA	17.18	56-4½
3. Keith Connor	GBR	16.87	55-4¼
4. Zou Zhenxian	CHN	16.83	55-2¾
5. Peter Bouschen	GER	16.77	55-0¼
6, William Banks	USA	16.75	54-11½
7. Ajayi Agbebaku	NGR	16.67	54-8¼
8. Eric McCalla	GBR	16.66	54-8

Mike Conley solidified his role of favorite by leading the qualifying round with a near Olympic record jump of 56 feet 11½ inches. The next morning, Conley's teammate Al Joyner was watching a television preview of the day's events when he saw pictures of Conley and the third US triple-jumper, Willie Banks, come on the screen. "I thought they would show me too," Joyner would later recall, "but they didn't. So I wanted to go out and let everybody know who I was."

Joyner's first-round jump, aided by the only significant tailwind of the day, held up for the gold medal. He also recorded three of the four next best jumps as well. The first seven places were decided by the second round, although Conley almost pulled it out with a huge last-round leap that turned out to be a foul.

Joyner, of East St. Louis, Illinois, competed at the same time that his younger sister, Jackie, was taking part in the heptathlon. In fact, he passed his fourth-round turn in order to root her on during the last lap of the 800-meter run. On the way to the triple jump award ceremony he ran into Jackie coming off the platform after receiving her silver medal. Several days after the competition, while other athletes were nursing injured leg muscles, upset winner Al Joyner confided that he was suffering from sore cheek muscles—from smiling so much. In 1987 Joyner married sprinter Florence Griffith, who went on to win three gold medals at the 1988 Olympics.

1988 Seoul C: 43, N: 31, D: 9.24. WR: 17.97, 58-11½ (William Banks)

		M	FT.-IN.
1. Khristo Markov	BUL	17.61	57-9¼ OR
2. Igor Lapshin	SOV/BLR	17.52	57-5¾
3. Aleksandr Kovalenko	SOV/BLR	17.42	57-1¾
4. Oleg Protsenko	SOV/RUS	17.38	57-0¼
5. Charles Simpkins	USA	17.29	56-8¾
6. William Banks	USA	17.03	55-10½
7. Ivan Slanař	CZE	16.75	54-11½
8. Jacek Pastusiński	POL	16.72	54-10¼

Markov's first-round attempt held up for the gold medal, but Lapshin gained the silver with his final try.

1992 Barcelona C: 47, N: 32, D: 8.3. WR: 17.97, 58-11½ (William Banks)

		M	FT.-IN.
1. Michael Conley	USA	18.17 w	59-7¼ w
2. Charles Simpkins	USA	17.60	57-9
3. Frank Rutherford	BAH	17.36	56-11½
4. Leonid Voloshin	RUS	17.32	56-10
5. Brian Wellman	BER	17.24	56-6¾
6. Yoelbi Quesada Fernández	CUB	17.18	56-4½
7. Aleksandr Kovalenko	RUS	17.06	55-11¾
8. Zou Sixin	CHN	17.00	55-9¼

After earning a silver medal in 1984, Mike Conley missed out on making the United States team in 1988 when judges at the Olympic trials ruled that his shorts grazed the sand four and a quarter inches before his feet. By 1992 Conley was taking no chances: he wore a formfitting bodysuit instead of loose shorts. Conley took the lead in the second round with a jump of 56 feet 10¼ inches. In the final round he leaped almost eight inches beyond Willie Banks' world record. But the wind gauge flashed 2.1 meters per second—the smallest possible amount above the legal limit. Conley's jump was the only wind-assisted measurement of the competition. Eight years earlier Conley had lost the gold medal when Al Joyner won with the only wind-assisted measurement of that competition. In Barcelona, Charlie Simpkins moved from fourth to second with his final jump.

1996 Atlanta C: 43, N: 32, D: 7.27. WR: 18.29, 60-0¼ (Jonathan Edwards)

		M	FT.-IN.
1. Kenny Harrison	USA	18.09	59-4 OR
2. Jonathan Edwards	GBR	17.88	58-8
3. Yoelbi Quesada Fernández	CUB	17.44	57-2½
4. Michael Conley	USA	17.40	57-1
5. Armen Martirosyan	ARM	16.97	55-8
6. Brian Wellman	BER	16.95	55-7¼
7. Galin Georgiev	BUL	16.92	55-6¼
8. Robert Howard	USA	16.90	55-5½

The year 1995 belonged to Jonathan Edwards, a geneticist whose religious beliefs kept him from competing on Sundays until he had a change of heart in 1993. At a meet in Salamanca, Spain, on July 18, 1995, Edwards jumped 17.98 meters (59 feet) to break Willie Banks' ten-year-old world record. Three weeks later, in the finals of the world championship in Göteborg, Sweden, he became the first person to break the 18-meter barrier with a leap of 18.19 meters (59 feet 7 inches). That was his opening round attempt. In the next round he followed up with the first ever 60-foot jump (18.29 meters). By the time the Olympics rolled around, Edwards had won 22 straight meets.

Meanwhile, Kenny Harrison, who described the triple jump as "power ballet" because it combines speed, strength, and grace, was emerging as the mystery factor in the contest. Harrison won the world championship in 1991, but had been plagued by injuries ever since. He didn't qualify for the US Olympic team in 1992. The 1996 US Olympic Trials was his first competition in fifteen months. He took one jump and won with a wind-aided 18.01 meters (59 feet 1¼ inches). However he was removed from the US team because he had not met the qualifying standard of a non-wind-aided 16.85

meters (55 feet 3½ inches). At the last minute, the IAAF gave Harrison credit for an indoor performance and he was allowed to compete.

Harrison, again jumping only once, led the qualifying round at 17.58 meters (57 feet 8½ inches). The following evening, he entered the Olympic final having taken a grand total of three jumps in competition over the past 16 months.

With his first attempt in the final, Harrison rattled his opponents by recording a huge leap of 17.99 meters (59 feet ¼ inch). Between rounds he watched his girlfriend, Gail Devers, run in the 100-meter semifinals. Edwards fouled his first two tries, before moving into third place with his third jump and earning a place in the last three rounds. In the fourth round, Edwards stretched out to 17.88 meters (58 feet 8 inches). Put on alert, Harrison extended his lead with a jump of 18.09 meters (59 feet 4¼ inches) and the contest was over.

2000 Sydney C: 40, N: 27, D: 9.25. WR: 18.29, 60-0¼ (Jonathan Edwards)

		M	FT.-IN.
1. Jonathan Edwards	GBR	17.71	58-1¼
2. Yoel García Luis	CUB	17.47	57-3¾
3. Denis Kapustin	RUS	17.46	57-3½
4. Yoelbi Quesada Fernández	CUB	17.37	57-0
5. Onochie "Larry" Achike	GBR	17.29	56-8¾
6. Phillips Idowu	GBR	17.08	56-0½
7. Robert Howard	USA	17.05	55-11¼
8. Paolo Camossi	ITA	16.96	55-7¾

Jonathan Edwards was already 34 years old in 2000, but he was, in his own words, "a young 34 years." After being upset at the Atlanta Olympics, Edwards had finished second at the world championships in 1997 and third in 1999. Still, Edwards had registered the longest jump of the pre-Olympic season (17.62 meters; 57 feet 9¾ inches) and he arrived in Sydney as the favorite again. In the third round of the final, Edwards jumped 17.71 meters (58 feet 1¼ inches). Since no one but Edwards himself had jumped that far in three years, the battle for the gold medal was effectively over. Behind Edwards, the competition was intense. Denis Kapustin's second round leap of 17.46 kept him in the silver medal position until the final round, and Onochie Achike's first round 17.29 put him in line for bronze. But clutch performances by the Cubans, Yoelbi Quesada and Yoel García, shook up the standings. Quesada's final jump of 17.37 bumped Achike out of the medals. Then García hit 17.47 to leapfrog from fifth to second.

2004 Athens C: 45, N: 34, D: 8.22. WR: 18.29, 60-0¼ (Jonathan Edwards)

	M		FT.-IN.
1. Christian Olsson	SWE	17.79	58-4¼
2. Marian Oprea	ROM	17.55	57-7
3. Danil Burkenya	RUS	17.48	57-4
4. Yoandri Betanzos	CUB	17.47	57-3¾
5. Jadel Gregório	BRA	17.31	56-9½
6. Khristos Meletoglou	GRE	17.13	56-2¼
7. Viktor Gushchinskiy	RUS	17.11	56-1½
8. Yoelbi Quesada Fernández	CUB	16.96	55-7¾

Christian Olsson recorded the longest qualifying jump, 17.68 meters (58 feet ¼ inch). On his first attempt of the final, he lost his balance slightly, but still hit 17.69 meters (58 feet ½ inch), which would turn out to be good enough for gold. Marian Oprea, who had broken Olsson's 29-competition winning streak less than three weeks before the Olympics began, earned the silver medal with his first leap. In the second round, Olsson solidified his lead with a jump of 17.79 meters (58 feet 4¼ inches), his best result ever in an outdoor competition. With the Olympic gold, Olsson completed his collection of titles, having already won both the indoor and outdoor world championships.

2008 Beijing C: 39, N: 26, D: 8.21. WR: 18.29, 60-0¼ (Jonathan Edwards)

		M	FT.-IN.
1. Nelson Évora	POR	17.67	57-11½
2. Phillips Idowu	GBR	17.62	57-9¾
3. Leevan Sands	BAH	17.59	57-8½
4. David Giralt, Rivero	CUB	17.52	57-5¾
5. Marian Oprea	ROM	17.22	56-6
6. Jadel Gregório	BRA	17.20	56-5¼
7. O. Lawrence Achike	GBR	17.17	56-4
8. Viktor Kuznyetsov	UKR	16.87	55-4¼

Born in the Ivory Coast, Nelson Évora moved to Portugal with his family at the age of five. The family moved into an apartment building on the floor above triple-jump coach and former Portuguese national record holder João Ganço, who convinced Nelson to take up jumping. He first began to compete as a high jumper, but a knee injury at the age of 15 forced him to change events. Évora represented Cape Verde until 2002, when he formally took Portuguese citizenship. In 2005 he competed at the world championships in Helsinki, missing qualification for the final by six centimeters. The following year he finished sixth at the world indoor championships in Moscow. His real breakthrough came at the 2007 world championships, when he earned his first major championship medal by recording a personal best jump of 17.74 meters (58 ft. 2½ in.) to win the title ahead of Brazil's Jadel Gregório.

Another top medal contender was Britain's Phillips Idowu. Born in East London to Nigerian parents, he participated in the 2004 Olympics, but fouled out after three missed jumps, failing to make the final. In March 2008 he recorded a jump of 17.75 meters (58 ft. 2¾ in.) to earn the world indoor title in Valencia, Spain, and by the time he arrived in Beijing, he was on a 10-competition winning streak.

With defending Olympic champion Christian Olsson out due to injury, and 2005 world champion Walter Davis out after failing to qualify at the US Olympic trials, the gold medal looked to be a toss-up between Idowu and Évora. Unsurprisingly, the two recorded the top two jumps of the qualifying round, Idowu leading with 17.44 meters (57 ft. 2½ in.) and Évora second with 17.34 (56 ft. 10¾ in.).

Jumping fifth, Évora took the lead briefly in the first round of the final with a 17.31-meter (56 ft. 9½ in.) jump, but was surpassed by Idowu's first attempt of 17.51 meters (57 ft. 5¼ in.). Évora moved back into first place in the second round with a jump of 17.56 (57 ft. 5¼ in.). The lead changed again in the third round, when Idowu managed a 17.62 meters (57 ft. 9¾ in.) jump, his best of the year, while Évora fouled. Leevan Sands of the Bahamas took over third place with his third-round jump of 17.59 meters (57 ft. 8½ in.). The turning point came in the fourth round, when Évora recorded a 17.67 (57 ft. 11½ in.) jump to move back into first place. Neither Idowu nor Sands was able to improve their mark, finishing in second and third places respectively. This was the first gold medal for Portugal in any sport for twelve years, since Fernanda Ribeiro won gold in the women's 10,000 meters event in Atlanta.

One year after missing out on the gold medal, Idowu came back to win the 2009 world championships in Berlin, recording a personal best of 17.73 meters (58 ft. 2 in.) to beat Évora for the title.

SHOT PUT

A shot is a 16-pound ball made of iron or brass. It must be put rather than thrown and must not drop below the level of the contestant's shoulder. The shot circle is 2.135 meters (7 feet) in diameter. At the front of the circle is a wooden stop board 10 centimeters (4 inches) high. Contestants must not leave the circle until the shot lands. As with all throwing events, the twelve finalists are given three tries. The top eight are then given three more.

1896 Athens C: 7, N: 4, D: 4.7. WR: 14.32, 47-0 (George Gray)

		M	FT.-IN.
1. Robert Garrett	USA	11.22	36-9¾
2. Miltiades Gouskos	GRE	11.03	36-2¼
3. Georgios Papasideris	GRE	10.36	34-0
4. Viggo Jensen	DEN	—	—

Garrett, who had placed first in the discus the day before, won the shot put with his first attempt.

1900 Paris C: 11?, N: 6, D: 7.15. WR: 14.68, 48-2 (Denis Horgan)

		M	FT.-IN.
1. Richard Sheldon	USA	14.10	46-3¼ OR
2. Josiah McCracken	USA	12.85	42-2
3. Robert Garrett	USA	12.35	40-6½
4. Rezsö Crettier	HUN	12:07	39-7¼
5. Panagiotis Paraskevopoulos	GRE	11.52	37-9½
6. Gustaf Söderström	SWE	11.18	36-8¼
7. Artur Coray	HUN	11.13	36-6¼
8. Thomas Truxton Hare	USA	10.92	35-10

McCracken and Garrett made their throws in the qualifying round and then refused to compete in the final because it was held on a Sunday.

1904 St. Louis C: 8, N: 2, D: 8.31. WR: 14.68, 48-2 (Denis Horgan)

		M	FT.-IN.
1. Ralph Rose	USA	14.81	48-7 WR
2. W. Wesley Coe	USA	14.40	47-3
3. Lawrence Feuerbach	USA	13.37	43-10½
4. Martin Sheridan	USA	12.39	40-8
5. Charles Chadwick	USA	—	—
6. Albert Johnson	USA	—	—
7. John Guiney	USA	—	—

Ralph Rose was a 6-foot 6-inch, 265-pound giant from California. Before his Olympic career was over, he had won three gold medals, two silver and one bronze. He died of pneumonia on October 16, 1913, at the age of 28. Nicolaos Georgantas of Greece was also entered in this event, but after his first two attempts were disallowed for throwing, he withdrew in disgust.

1906 Athens C: 17, N: 8, D: 4.27. WR: 15.09, 49-6 (Wesley Coe)

		M	FT.-IN.
1. Martin Sheridan	USA	12.325	40-5¼
2. Mihály Dávid	HUN	11.83	38-9¾
3. Eric Lemming	SWE	11.26	36-11½
4. André Tison	FRA	11.02	36-2
5. Vasilios Papageorgiou	GRE	11.00	36-1

Martin Sheridan was the star of the Intercalated Games, winning two gold medals and three silver medals. In 1908 he added two gold and a silver.

(left to right) Patrick McDonald (gold), Lawrence Whitney (bronze), and Ralph Rose (silver)
The winners of the 1912 shot put. Rose also won gold medals in 1904 and 1908.

1908 London C: 25, N: 8, D: 7.16. WR: 15.12, 49-7½ (Ralph Rose)

		M	FT.-IN.
1. Ralph Rose	USA	14.21	46-7½
2. Denis Horgan	GBR/IRL	13.62	44-8¼
3. John Garrels	USA	13.18	43-3
4. W. Wesley Coe	USA	13.07	42-10½
5. Edward Barrett	GBR/IRL	12.89	42-3½
6. Marquis "Bill" Horr	USA	12.82	42-1
7. Jalmari Sauli	FIN	12.58	41-3½
8. Leander Talbott	USA	11.63	38-2

Denis Horgan was 37 years old and past his prime. His second-place performance was particularly noteworthy considering that he had almost been killed the year before. On duty as a New York City policeman, Horgan tried to break up a brawl and was severely attacked with sticks and shovels. After his surprising recovery, he was given a pension and allowed to return to Ireland.

One of the most enduring Olympic myths is that the US flagbearer at the 1908 Opening Ceremony infuriated the English spectators by refusing to dip the US flag to the King of England, stating that "this flag dips to no earthly king." This story became so inbedded in American culture that in 1942 the US Congress actually passed a law stipulating that "the flag of the United States of America . . . should not be dipped to any person or thing." The quotation, "this flag dips to no earthly king," is usually attributed to the discus thrower Martin Sheridan and so it has been assumed that is was also Sheridan who carried—and refused to dip—the flag. In fact it was shot putter Ralph Rose who carried the flag. Contemporaneous accounts, as compiled by historians Bill Mallon and Ian Buchanan, make it clear that Rose did in fact refuse to dip the flag, although the English spectators appear not to have cared or even noticed.

As for the famous "earthly king" quote, there is no evidence that Martin Sheridan or anyone else said this. Sheridan himself, in an article written in 1908, talked about Rose not dipping the flag, but made no mention of his own involvement in the incident. Indeed, the quotation did not appear in print until 1952—44 years after its alleged utterance.

1912 Stockholm C: 22, N: 14, D: 7.10. WR: 15.545, 51-0 (Ralph Rose)

		M	FT.-IN.
1. Patrick McDonald	USA	15.34	50-4 OR
2. Ralph Rose	USA	15.25	50-0½
3. Lawrence Whitney	USA	13.93	45-8½
4. Elmer Niklander	FIN	13.65	44-9½
5. George Philbrook	USA	13.13	43-1
6. Imre Mudin	HUN	12.81	42-0½
7. Einar Nilsson	SWE	12.62	41-5
8. Patrick Quinn	GBR	12.53	41-1½

McDonald, another enormous (6 feet 5 inches, 300 pounds) New York City policeman, surprised Rose in the fourth round of six by achieving the best put of his career. Eight years later, McDonald won another gold medal, this time in the 56-pound weight throw. He eventually served 41 years in the New York City Police Department (1905–1946) and was one of the city's best known and most visible officers because it was his job to direct traffic in Times Square.

1920 Antwerp C: 20, N: 10, D: 8:18. WR: 15.545, 51-0 (Ralph Rose)

		M	FT.-IN.
1. F. Wilhelm (Ville) Pörhölä	FIN	14.81	48-7¼
2. Elmer Niklander	FIN	14.155	46-5¼
3. Harry Liversedge	USA	14.15	46-5¼
4. Patrick McDonald	USA	14.08	46-2½
5. Einar Nilsson	SWE	13.87	45-6¼
6. Harald Tammer	EST	13.605	44-7½
7. George Bihlman	USA	13.575	44-6½
8. Howard Cann	USA	13.52	44-4¼

Bronze medalist Harry Liversedge later became a regimental commander in the US Marines during World War II and led the troops who raised the flag on Mount Suribachi on Iwo Jima. He eventually rose to the rank of brigadier general.

1924 Paris C: 28, N: 15, D: 7.8. WR: 15.545, 51-0 (Ralph Rose)

		M	FT.-IN.
1. L. Clarence "Bud" Houser	USA	14.99	49-2¼
2. Glenn Hartranft	USA	14.89	48-10¼
3. Ralph Hills	USA	14.64	48-0½

4. Hannes Torpo	FIN	14.45	47-5
5. Norman Anderson	USA	14.29	46-10¾
6. Elmer Niklander	FIN	14.26	49-9½
7. Frans "Ville" Pörhölä	FIN	14.10	46-3¼
8. Berth Jansson	SWE	13.76	45-1¾

1928 Amsterdam C: 22, N: 14, D: 7.29. WR: 15.79, 51-9¾ (Emil Hirschfeld)

		M	FT.-IN.
1. John Kuck	USA	15.87	52-0¾ WR
2. Herman Brix	USA	15.75	51-8¼
3. Emil Hirschfeld	GER	15.72	51-7
4. Eric Krenz	USA	14.99	49-2¼
5. Armas Wahlstedt	FIN	14.69	48-2½
6. Wilhelm Uebler	GER	14.69	48-2½
7. Harlow Rothert	USA	14.68	48-2
8. József Darányi	HUN	14.35	47-1

On May 6, 1928, Emil Hirschfeld finally broke Ralph Rose's 1909 world record. He was in good form in Amsterdam, but Kuck and Brix were superb. Kuck, a farmboy from Wilson, Kansas, started his road to shot put gold when, at the age of four, he discovered a three-pound agate sphere and began throwing it around his yard. His practice shot turned out to be a 20,000-year-old Native American relic. Brix later became a well-known movie actor, appearing in more than 100 films. Among his early roles was Tarzan in *The New Adventures of Tarzan* (1935). Unfortunately, Brix became so associated with the role of Tarzan that, in 1939, he had to change his name to Bruce Bennett in order to continue his career. Although he appeared in such critically acclaimed features as *Mildred Pierce* (1945) and *The Treasure of Sierra Madre* (1948), Bennett also acted in such clunkers as *The Alligator People* (1959) and *The Fiend of Dope Island* (1961).

1932 Los Angeles C: 15, N: 10, D: 7.31. WR: 16.05, 52-8 (Zygmunt Heljasz)

		M	FT.-IN.
1. Leo Sexton	USA	16.00	52-6 OR
2. Harlow Rothert	USA	15.67	51-5
3. František Douda	CZE	15.61	51-2¾
4. Emil Hirschfeld	GER	15.56	51-0¾
5. Nelson Gray	USA	15.47	50-9¼
6. Hans-Heinrich Sievert	GER	15.07	49-5½
7. Zygmunt Heljasz	POL	14.80	48-6¾
8. József Darányi	HUN	14.68	48-2

Leo Sexton was a 6-foot 4-inch insurance broker from New York. World record holder Zygmunt Heljasz of Poland was able to place only ninth.

1936 Berlin C: 22, N: 14, D: 8.2. WR: 17.40, 57-1 (Jack Torrance)

		M	FT.-IN.
1. Hans Woellke	GER	16.20	53-1¾ OR
2. Sulo Bärlund	FIN	16.12	52-10¾
3. Gerhard Stöck	GER	15.66	51-4½
4. Samuel Francis	USA	15.45	50-8¼
5. Jack Torrance	USA	15.38	50-5½
6. Dimitri Zaitz	USA	15.32	50-3¼
7. František Douda	CZE	15.28	50-1¾
8. Arnold Viiding	EST	15.23	49-11¾

Hans Woellke, a 25-year-old policeman, was the first German to win a track and field gold medal. Another policeman, 304-pound world record holder Jack Torrance of Baton Rouge, Louisiana, was out of shape and finished a disappointing fifth.

1948 London C: 24, N: 14, D: 8.3. WR: 17.68, 58-03⁄8 (Charles Fonville)

		M	FT.-IN.
1. Wilbur Thompson	USA	17.12	56-2 OR
2. F. James Delaney	USA	16.68	54-8¾
3. James Fuchs	USA	16.42	53-10½
4. Mieczyslaw Lomowski	POL	15.43	50-7½
5. Gösta Arvidsson	SWE	15.37	50-5¼
6. Yrjö Lehtilä	FIN	15.05	49-4½
7. Pentti Jouppila	FIN	14.59	47-10½
8. Čestmir Kalina	CZE	14.55	47-9

The American putters were so strong that world record holder Charles Fonville failed to make the US team. In London the Americans outdistanced the rest of the world by over three feet.

1952 Helsinki C: 20, N: 14, D: 7.21. WR: 17.95, 58-10½ (James Fuchs)

		M	FT.-IN.
1. W. Parry O'Brien	USA	17.41	57-1½ OR
2. C. Darrow Hooper	USA	17.39	57-0¾
3. James Fuchs	USA	17.06	55-11¾
4. Otto Grigalka	SOV/RUS	16.78	55-0¾
5. Roland Nilsson	SWE	16.55	53-3¾
6. John Savidge	GBR	16.19	53-1½
7. Georgi Fyodorov	SOV/RUS	16.06	52-8¼
8. Per Stavem	NOR	16.02	52-6¾

World record holder Jim Fuchs had won 88 consecutive meets when he was beaten at the 1951 AAU championships by Parry O'Brien. At the 1952 US Olympic trials, O'Brien was beaten by Darrow Hooper. It was his last loss for four years, during which time he won 116 straight meets. O'Brien and Hooper were almost the exact same size and weight. Their similarity also extended to their performances in the Olympics. O'Brien, who was two days older than Hooper, outputted him by only two centimeters. Parry O'Brien, a student at the University of Southern California, practiced at the Los Angeles Memorial Coliseum, site of the 1932 and 1984 Olympics, by sneaking over a fence late at night while no one was there. He revolutionized shot putting by

Parry O'Brien, 1952
Gold by a sliver, and by a country mile four years later in Melbourne.

introducing a new style in which he began with his back to the front of the throwing circle and then used every bit of momentum he could gather before he let go of the shot.

1956 Melbourne C: 14, N: 10, D: 11.28. WR: 19.25, 63-2 (W. Parry O'Brien)

		M	FT.-IN.
1. W. Parry O'Brien	USA	18.57	60-1¼ OR
2. William Nieder	USA	18.18	59-7¾
3. Jiři Skobla	CZE	17.65	57-11
4. Kenneth Bantum	USA	17.48	57-4¼
5. Boris Balyayev	SOV/RUS	16.96	55-7¾
6. Erik Uddebom	SWE	16.65	54-7½
7. Karlheinz Wegmann	GER	16.63	54-6¾
8. Georgios Tsakanikas	GRE	16.56	54-4

On May 8, 1954, two days after Roger Bannister broke the four-minute mile, Parry O'Brien became the first person to put the shot more than 60 feet, with a toss of 60 feet 5¼ inches. In Melbourne, at the 1956 Olympics, O'Brien overwhelmed the field, recording the five best puts of the competition. Even his worst put was beaten only by Bill Nieder's best. Parry O'Brien became the first reigning world record holder to win the shot put at the Olympics since 1908. Bronze medalist Jiři Skobla was the son of Jaroslav Skobla, who won the heavyweight weight-lifting gold medal in 1932. The younger Skobla died of kidney cancer in 1978 at the age of 48. The results of his autopsy were not released and it was widely believed that his premature death was associated with steroid use.

1960 Rome C: 24, N: 16, D: 8.31. WR: 20.06, 65-10 (William Nieder)

		M	FT.-IN.
1. William Nieder	USA	19.68	64-6¾ OR
2. W. Parry O'Brien	USA	19.11	62-8½
3. Dallas Long	USA	19.01	62-4½
4. Viktor Lipsnis	SOV/UKR	17.90	58-8¾
5. Michael Lindsay	GBR	17.80	58-4¾
6. Alfred Sosgórnik	POL	17.57	57-7¾
7. Dieter Urbach	GER	17.47	57-3¾
8. Martyn Lucking	GBR	17.43	57-2¼

Bill Nieder had failed to qualify for the US team after finishing fourth in the Olympic trials. But a wrist injury suffered by Dave Davis, and a world record put by Nieder, convinced US officials to make a rare replacement. In Rome, Nieder showed that they had made the right decision. Parry O'Brien led after four rounds, but in the fifth round, Nieder, recalling O'Brien's disparaging remark that he was a "cow pasture performer" who choked in important meets, let loose a monster toss that was almost two feet better than anything the defending champion was able to produce.

1964 Tokyo C: 22, N: 13, D: 10.17. WR: 20.68, 67-10 (Dallas Long)

		M	FT.-IN.
1. Dallas Long	USA	20.33	66-8½ OR
2. James Randel Matson	USA	20.20	66-3¼
3. Vilmos Varjú	HUN	19.39	63-7½
4. W. Parry O'Brien	USA	19.20	63-0
5. Zsigmond Nagy	HUN	18.88	61-11½
6. Nikolai Karassev	SOV/RUS	18.86	61-10½
7. Leslie Mills	NZE	18.52	60-9¼
8. Adolfas Varanauskas	SOV/LIT	18.41	60-4¾

Twenty-four-year-old Dallas Long, a 6-foot 4-inch, 260-pound dental student from Los Angeles, took the lead with a first-round toss of 64 feet 4 inches. In the third round, 19-year-old Randy Matson of Pampa, Texas, moved ahead at 65 feet 2¾ inches. With his next throw he improved to 66 feet 3¼ inches, a new Olympic record. However, his record was short-lived. Two minutes later, Long countered with a put of 66 feet 8½ inches that held up for first place.

1968 Mexico City C: 19, N: 14, D: 10.14. WR: 21.78, 71-5½ (James Randel Matson)

		M	FT.-IN.
1. J. Randel Matson	USA	20.54	67-4¾
2. George Woods	USA	20.12	66-0¼
3. Eduard Gushchin	SOV/RUS	20.09	65-11
4. Dieter Hoffmann	GDR	20.00	65-7½
5. David Maggard	USA	19.43	63-9
6. Wladyslaw Komar	POL	19.28	63-3¼
7. Uwe Grabe	GDR	19.03	62-5¼
8. Heinfried Birlenbach	GER	18.80	61-8¼

Although he only placed third at the US Olympic trials, 6-foot 6½-inch, 265-pound Randy Matson was still the overwhelming favorite by virtue of the fact that he had completely dominated the event over the previous four years. On May 8, 1965, he had demolished the world record with a put of 70 feet 7¼ inches, bettering the previous record by 2 feet 9¼ inches. By the time of the Mexico City Olympics, Matson had registered 23 of the 25 longest puts in history. He led the qualifying round with an Olympic record of 67 feet 10¼ inches. His first toss of the final w as 67 feet 4¾ inches. No one else came close to that for the rest of the competition. US shot putters finished first and second for the fifth straight time. Like many athletes during the Vietnam War period, Randy Matson was declared unfit for military service because of knee problems.

1972 Munich C: 29, N: 19, D: 9.9. WR: 21.78, 71-5½ (James Randel Matson)

		M	FT.-IN.
1. Wladyslaw Komar	POL	21.18	69-6 OR
2. George Woods	USA	21.17	69-5½
3. Hartmut Briesenick	GDR	21.14	69-4¼
4. Hans-Peter Gies	GDR	21.14	69-4¼
5. Allan Feuerbach	USA	21.01	68-11¼
6. Brian Oldfield	USA	20.91	68-7¼
7. Heinfried Birlenbach	GER	20.37	66-10
8. Vilmos Varjú	HUN	20.10	65-11½

The 6-foot 5¼-inch, 276-pound Wladyslaw Komar had twice been kicked off the Polish team for "misbehavior," including once when he received a "life ban." However, he was back again in Munich for his third Olympics. Ninth in 1964, sixth in 1968, the 32-year-old Komar connected with the greatest put of his career in the first round of the 1972 final, bettering his previous best by seven and a quarter inches. Woods, Briesenick, and Gies all came very, very close, but each fell short by inches. George Woods' last toss caused much controversy since it hit the marker that indicated Komar's best put. Many observers were quite surprised when it was measured at only 69 feet ¾ inch, and Woods himself believed that at the very least he deserved an extra put. But the officials in charge ruled it a valid toss and called an end to the competition. Films of the incident were inconclusive.

Wladyslaw Komar became an actor and appeared in Roman Polanski's *Pirates.* In 1993, after the fall of Communism, Komar ran for office as a candidate of the Polish Party of Beer Lovers. He was killed in an automobile accident on August 17, 1998, while a passeneger in a car driven by former pole vaulter Tadeusz Ślusarski. They were hit head-on by a driver who fell asleep at the wheel.

1976 Montreal C: 23, N: 18, D: 7.24. WR: 22.00, 72-2¼ (Aleksandr Baryshnikov)

		M	FT.-IN.
1. Udo Beyer	GDR	21.05	69-0¾
2. Yevgeny Mironov	SOV/RUS	21.03	69-0
3. Aleksandr Baryshnikov	SOV/RUS	21.00	68-10¾
4. Allan Feuerbach	USA	20.55	67-5¼
5. Hans-Peter Gies	GDR	20.47	67-2
6. Geoffrey Capes	GBR	20.36	66-9¾
7. George Woods	USA	20.26	66-5¾
8. Hans Hoglund	SWE	20.17	66-2¼

Missing from the Olympics was the number-one shot putter in the world, Brian Oldfield, who owned the four longest unofficial puts in history, including one of 75 feet. Oldfield was a professional and thus ineligible to compete. The amateur record of 72 feet 2¼ inches was set by Aleksandr Baryshnikov on July 10. Baryshnikov looked good as gold when his one put of the qualifying round sailed 69 feet 11½ inches to break the Olympic record. Baryshnikov also took the lead in the first round of the final with a toss of 67 feet 4¼ inches. In the second round he was passed by Al Feuerbach's 67 feet 5 inches. Baryshnikov boomed back in front with a third-round 68 feet 10¾ inches. Then, in the fifth round, 20-year-old Udo Beyer, the youngest man in the competition, unleashed a put of 69 feet ¾ inch. Beyer had only been added to the East German team one week before the Olympics began. Yevgeny Mironov, who had been mired inconspicuously in sixth place, followed a few minutes later with 69 feet 0 inches, and the medals were decided. Most of the leading contenders fell several feet short of their best performances. Although the pressure of the Olympics may have been a contributing factor, most observers felt that the institution of steroid testing played a more important role. Documents released after the fall of the Berlin Wall revealed that Udo Beyer, for example, took 3,955 milligrams of steroids a year.

1980 Moscow C: 16, N: 11, D: 7.30. WR: 22.15, 72-8 (Udo Beyer)

		M	FT.-IN.
1. Volodymyr Kyselyov	SOV/UKR	21.35	70-0½ OR
2. Aleksandr Baryshnikov	SOV/RUS	21.08	69-2
3. Udo Beyer	GDR	21.06	69-1¼
4. Reijo Ståhlberg	FIN	20.82	68-3¾
5. Geoffrey Capes	GBR	20.50	67-3¼
6. Hans-Jürgen Jacobi	GDR	20.32	66-8
7. Jaromir Vlk	CZE	20.24	66-5
8. Vladimir Milić	YUG/SLO	20.07	65-10¼

Volodymyr Kyselyov was the only shot putter to achieve a personal best, ending Udo Beyer's string of 34 consecutive victories. In 1985 Kyselyov lost 25 kilograms (56 pounds) and almost died as a result of past use of prohibited substances, specifically testosterone.

1984 Los Angeles C: 19, N: 13, D: 8.11. WR: 22.22, 72-10¾ (Udo Beyer)

		M	FT.-IN.
1. Alessandro Andrei	ITA	21.26	69-9
2. Michael Carter	USA	21.09	69-2½
3. Dave Laut	USA	20.97	68-9¾
4. Augie Wolf	USA	20.93	68-8
5. Werner Günthör	SWI	20.28	66-6½
6. Marco Montelatici	ITA	19.98	65-6¾
7. Sören Tallhem	SWE	19.81	65-0
8. Erik de Bruin	HOL	19.65	64-5¾

The quality of the 1984 shot put competition, already lessened by the Soviet-bloc boycott, was further diminished when the final was interrupted by no less than six medal award ceremonies. Michael Carter took the first-round lead with a put of 67 feet 8¼ inches. But 25-year-old Florence policeman Alessandro Andrei moved ahead with a second-round toss of 68 feet 9¾ inches. He improved by almost a foot with his next attempt. Carter improved as well, but still had to settle for the silver. Six days after the Olympic final, Carter was playing in his first professional football pre-season game, and six months later, he was taking part in the San Francisco 49ers' Super Bowl victory.

1988 Seoul C: 21, N: 17, D: 9.23. WR: 23.06, 75-8 (Ulf Timmermann)

		M	FT.-IN.	
1. Ulf Timmermann	GDR	22.47	73-8¾	OR
2. E. Randolph Barnes	USA	22.39	73-5½	
3. Werner Günthör	SWI	21.99	72-1¾	
4. Udo Beyer	GDR	21.40	70-2½	
5. Remigius Machura	CZE	20.57	67-5¾	
6. Gert Weil	CHI	20.38	66-10¼	
7. Alessandro Andrei	ITA	20.36	66-9½	
8. Sergei Smirnov	SOV	20.36	66-9½	

World champion Werner Günthör set an Olympic record with an opening put of 70 feet 4½ inches. Later in the first round, Ulf Timmermann, who had broken the world record on May 22, took the lead at 72 feet 3 inches. Timmermann improved to 72 feet 8½ inches in the third round and to 73 feet 1½ inches in the fifth round. People began congratulating the East German, but Timmermann wisely noted that it was too early for a victory celebration. He breathed a little easier after Günthör failed to improve on his fifth-round best of 72 feet 1¾ inches. Then 22-year-old Randy Barnes, who was languishing in fourth place, uncorked a toss of 73 feet 5½ inches and suddenly the shot put circle was the site of high drama. Two throwers later, Timmermann stepped up for the last put of the competition. Concentrating intensely, he shut out the outside world. "It was like I went into a tunnel" he later told *Track and Field News*. "Time became just a blur, a haze; throwing was just a reflex. . . . I knew inside that this was my big chance; I could make my place in Olympic history." Timmermann heaved with everything he had—and managed to outdistance Barnes by a mere 3¼ inches.

On May 20, 1990, Randy Barnes broke Timmermann's world record, but two and a half months later he tested positive for methyltestosterone, an anabolic steroid, and was subsequently slapped with a two-year suspension.

1992 Barcelona C: 26, N: 18, D: 7.31. WR: 23.12, 75-10¼ (E. Randolph Barnes)

		M	FT.-IN.
1. Michael Stulce	USA	21.70	71-2½
2. James Doehring	USA	20.96	68-9¼
3. Vyacheslav Lykho	RUS	20.94	68-8½
4. Werner Günthör	SWI	20.91	68-7¼
5. Ulf Timmermann	GER	20.49	67-2¾
6. Klaus Bodenmüller	AUT	20.48	67-2¼
7. Dragan Perić	YUG/SER	20.32	66-8
8. Aleksandr Klimenko	UKR	20.23	66-4½

The 1992 shot put competition may not have been the first in which all the medalists had taken prohibited drugs, but it was definitely the first in which all the medalists had actually served suspensions for taking prohibited drugs. Stulce tested positive for excessive testosterone on March 20, 1990, and was banned for two years. Doehring also tested positive for excessive testosterone in December 1990. He sat out 14 months until his ban was lifted because of procedural irregularities. However, Doehring had further drug problems. In December 1991, he pleaded guilty to possessing and conspiring to sell methamphetamine. Given a suspended sentence and probation, he left a halfway house a month before the US Olympic trials. Lykho tested positive for stimulants in 1990 and served a three-month suspension.

In Barcelona, Stulce set three personal records, starting with a first-round heave of 70 feet 6¼ inches. He improved to 70 feet 9¾ inches in the second round and 71 feet 2½ inches in the fifth. The only drama came just before Stulce's winning throw, when double world champion Werner Günthör reached 71 feet 6 inches but fouled by touching beyond the ring with his fingers while trying to keep his balance. Stulce's margin of victory was the largest since 1900. At the 1993 world championships, Stulce again tested positive for testosterone as well as for mestanolone, a steroid-like substance.

1996 Atlanta C: 36, N: 24, D: 7.26. WR: 23.12, 75-10¼ (E. Randolph Barnes)

		M	FT.-IN.
1. E. Randolph Barnes	USA	21.62	70-11¼
2. John Godina	USA	20.79	68-2½
3. Oleksandr Bagach	UKR	20.75	68-1

4. Paolo Dal Soglio	ITA	20.74	68-0½
5. Oliver-Sven Buder	GER	20.51	67-3½
6. Roman Virastyuk	UKR	20.45	67-1
7. Cottrell "C. J." Hunter	USA	20.39	66-10¾
8. Dragan Perić	YUG/SER	20.07	65-10¼

The United States entered a powerful team. C. J. Hunter was ranked number one in the world in 1994; John Godina was the reigning world champion and Randy Barnes, winner of the US trials, was the world record holder.

The warmup track was the scene of some unusual activity just before the final. Godina rattled his opponents by hoisting a couple throws in the 74-foot range. With one throw, Godina did more than rattle Randy Barnes—he hit him. Barnes was slow to leave the field after retrieving his shot. He heard yelling, looked up, and saw Godina's shot heading at his face. Barnes ducked and the 16-pound ball hit him on the back below his neck.

The final itself was safer, but no less exciting. The three Americans seemed overwhelmed at first by the huge, partisan crowd of 82,000. Oleksandr Bagach took the first round lead at 20.14 meters. He increased to 20.50 meters in the second round, but then Paolo Dal Soglio, throwing last, took the lead at 20.65 meters. Midway through the competition, the order stood: Dal Soglio, Bagach, Barnes, Hunter, Buder, Virastyuk and Godina. In the fourth round Godina hit 20.64 meters and moved into second place, only one centimeter behind Dal Soglio. Dal Soglio responded by closing out the round with a put of 20.74 meters. In the fifth round Godina moved ahead with a 20.79. He was the fourth person to lead the contest. With one round to go, the medal positions belonged to Godina, Dal Soglio and Buder (who threw 20.51 meters in the fifth round).

Godina misfired his final attempt. At this point, Randy Barnes was in sixth place. Eight years earlier he had been in first place when Ulf Timmermann beat him with his final throw. In Atlanta, Barnes reversed roles. A beautiful toss of 21.62 meters secured him the gold medal and dropped Godina to silver. Bagach then came up and hit 20.75 meters to squeeze past Dal Soglio into third place. It was the first time all night that Dal Soglio had been out of the medal positions. His was the final throw. His put reached 21 meters, but he foot-fouled.

Except for Barnes' winning throw, the quality of the results was poor. Godina's silver medal toss would not have earned a medal in any other Olympics since 1968.

Those people who enjoy coincidences should note the similarities between Randy Barnes and javelin thrower Jan Železný. Both men were born on June 16, 1966. Both of them were deprived of a gold medal in 1988 by an opponent's last round throw. Both of them came back to win a gold medal in 1996.

On April 1, 1998, Randy Barnes tested positive for androstenedione, an adrenal hormone that increases the body's ability to produce testosterone. As recently as the 1988 Olympics, all East German athletes took androstenedione one or more hours before competing. Three months after the test, Barnes was banned for life because this was his second positive test for steroids. The case was a curious one though. Androstenedione was considered an over-the-counter supplement in the United States. It had been added to the IOC's prohibited list less than four months before Barnes' positive test. Barnes readily admitted taking it, claiming he did not know it had been banned.

The great irony was that baseball star Mark McGuire was taking androstenedione at the same time Barnes was. But while McGuire was being hailed as a national hero and a baseball legend for hitting 70 home runs in one year, Randy Barnes was being banned for life, his reputation tarnished.

Bronze medalist Oleksandr Bagach also subsequently drew a lifetime ban. In 1989 he received a two-year suspension after testing positive for excess testosterone. In 1997 he won the world championship, but was disqualified when he tested positive for ephedrine. Finally, in 2000, he failed a test for steroids and his competitive career was over.

2000 Sydney C: 37, N: 27, D: 9.22. WR: 23.12, 75-10¼ (E. Randolph Barnes)

		M	FT.-IN.
1. Arsi Harju	FIN	21.29	69-10¼
2. Adam Nelson	USA	21.21	69-7
3. John Godina	USA	21.20	69-6¾
4. Andrew Bloom	USA	20.87	68-5¾
5. Yuri Bilonoh	UKR	20.84	68-4½
6. Manuel Martínez Gutiérrez	SPA	20.55	67-5¼
7. Janus Robberts	SAF	20.32	66-8
8. Oliver-Sven Buder	GER	20.18	66-2½

Arsi Harju was an unexpected winner. Ranked only eighth in the world, Harju suddenly attracted attention when he led the qualifying round with a throw of 21.39 meters (70 feet 2¼ inches), bettering his two-year-old personal best by a startling 35 centimeters (13¾ inches). With his red beard, pink-checkered bandana and pot belly, he looked like a biker. In fact, back home in the small town of Perho, he did drive around on a Harley-Davidson. The final began eight hours after the preliminaries. Harju took the first round lead with a toss of 21.20. Adam Nelson, an Atlanta native who had spent the 1996 Olympics serving coffee in the Olympic village, matched Harju's distance in the second round, but the Finn came right back with a throw of 21.29. Nelson added a centimeter in the third round to secure the silver medal. John Godina was added to the US team at the last minute when world champion C.J. Hunter withdrew in Sydney as news leaked that he had failed four doping tests over the summer. Godina took advantange of his good fortune by earning the bronze medal with a fifth round put of 21.20.

It is a Finnish tradition to reward Olympic champions by giving them a house or a plot of land. Unfortunately, the 3200 inhabitants of Perho were too poor to afford this luxury. However they did come up with a suitable alternative: they presented him with a brand new Harley-Davidson.

2004 Athens–Olympia C: 39, N: 26, D: 8.18. WR: 23.12, 75-10¼ (E. Randolph Barnes)

		M	FT.-IN.
1. Yuri Bilonoh	UKR	21.16	69-5
2. Adam Nelson	USA	21.16	69-5
3. Joachim Olsen	DEN	21.07	69-1½
4. Manuel Martínez Gutiérrez	SPA	20.84	68-4½
5. Andrei Mikhnevich	BLR	20.60	67-7
6. Yuri Belov	BLR	20.34	66-8¾
7. Justin Anlezark	AUS	20.31	66-7½
8. Ralf Bartels	GER	20.26	66-5½

With the Olympics returning to their roots in Greece, the organizers could not resist taking advantage of the opportunity to stage at least one event in Olympia, the site of the ancient Olympics from about 776 BC through 368 AD. They had hoped to use the sacred site for the discus throw, an event that was actually included in the ancient Games, but the setting was too vulnerable and it would have been dangerous for the spectators. So it was decided to use the ancient field for the shot put, an event that was never part of the original ancient Olympics.

Adam Nelson qualified for the final with his first put, 21.12 meters (69 feet 4¾ inches), the best of the qualifying round. In the final, he took the lead on his first throw, 21.16 meters (69 feet 5 inches). He then fouled each of his next four attempts, dropping the shot on one and falling down on another. Nelson's first throw held up until the final round, when Yuri Bilonoh matched the distance exactly. Nelson still had one more attempt. The rules stated that ties would be broken by comparing each athlete's second-best throw. Because Nelson had no legal throws other than his first one, he needed to better Belinoh's second-best, 21.15 meters, to win the competition. His throw went about 21.30 meters, but it was ruled a foul. Nelson staged a vigorous protest, but video replays confirmed the foul. This was the first time in the history of the Olympics that a gold medal in a field event was decided by a second-best mark.

In 2009 fourth-place finisher Manuel Martínez starred in a Spanish film, Estigmata, in which he played a gentle giant dealing with the consequences of stigmata.

2008 Beijing C: 44, N: 34, D: 8.15. WR: 23.12, 75-10-0¼ (E. Randolph Barnes)

		M	FT.-IN.
1. Tomasz Majewski	POL	21.51	70-6¾
2. Christian Cantwell	USA	21.09	69-2¼
3. Andrey Mikhnevich	BLR	21.05	69-0¾
4. Dylan Armstrong	CAN	21.04	69-0¼
5. Pavel Lyzhin	BLR	20.98	68-10
6. Yuriy Bilonoh	UKR	20.63	67-8¼
7. Reese Hoffa	USA	20.53	67-4¼
8. Pavel Sofin	RUS	20.42	66-11¾

The US team arrived in Beijing with high hopes for a shot put sweep. The team included double Olympic silver medalist Adam Nelson, who had gone on to win the 2005 world championships, as well as 2007 world champion Reese Hoffa, who won the title in Osaka, Japan, with a put of 22.04 meters (72 ft. 3¾ in.). Born in Georgia, Hoffa had been put up for adoption after accidentally burning down his family's home at the age of four. As a senior at the University of Georgia he found and re-established contact with his birth mother through a website, and the two subsequently built a strong relationship. Rounding out US hopes in the event was 27-year-old Christian Cantwell of Missouri, who beat Hoffa at the 2008 world indoor championships in Valencia, Spain.

The three Americans qualified easily, but the top qualifying throw was recorded by 26-year-old Tomasz Majewski, who recorded a personal best of 21.04 meters (69 ft. ¼ in.) to advance to the final. A relative unknown, Majewski's best international result had been a bronze at the 2008 world indoor championships, behind Cantwell and Hoffa. He represented Poland at the 2004 Olympics but failed to advance past the qualifying round.

Majewski took the lead in the final after a first-round throw of 20.80 meters (68 ft. 3 in.), but was passed in the second round by 2003 world champion Andrey Mikhnevich, with a 21.05 (69 ft. ¾ in.); Dylan Armstrong, whose 21.04-meter (69 ft. ½ in.) throw was a Canadian record; and Cantwell with a 20.98 (68 ft. 10 in.). Nelson was eliminated in the third round after fouling three times, while Majewski moved back into the lead with a throw of 21.21 meters (69 ft. 7 in.), another personal best. Majewski clinched the gold medal with his fourth throw, yet another personal record of 21.51 meters (70 ft. 6 ¾ in.), the only throw that surpassed 70 feet.

No other throws came close to challenging Majewski's lead, although Cantwell moved up from sixth to take silver on his final throw, dropping Armstrong out of the medals.

In 2009 Cantwell recorded a season's best throw of 22.03 meters (72 ft. 3½ in.) to win the world championship title ahead of Majewski.

DISCUS THROW

The men's discus weighs 2 kilograms (4 pounds 6.55 ounces) and has a diameter of 22 centimeters (inches). The discus circle has a diameter of 2.5 meters (8 feet 2½ inches). The discus throw is the only track and field event in which a world record has never been set in the Olympics.

1896 Athens C: 9, N: 6, D: 4.6. WR: 27.81, 91-2¾ (Panagiotis Paraskevopoulos)

		M	FT.-IN.
1. Robert Garrett	USA	29.15	95-7½
2. Panagiotis Paraskevopoulos	GRE	28.955	95-0
3. Sotirios Versis	GRE	27.78	91-1¾
4. George Robertson	GBR	25.20	82-8

Twenty-year-old Robert Garrett came from a wealthy Baltimore banking family. While a student at Princeton, he was shown a drawing of an ancient Greek discus by his history professor William Milligan Sloane, who had a facsimile made for Garrett. It weighed ten kilograms. Garrett practiced with it, but it proved too heavy and unwieldy and so he lost interest quickly. However, while strolling on the field in Athens, he chanced upon a similar object and was told that this was a real discus, which turned out to be much lighter (two kilograms) than his American version. Encouraged, yet risking what he feared would be great embarrassment; he entered the Olympic discus contest. To the disappointment of the Greeks, he won the event with his final throw. Before the games were over, Garrett had won two events, placed second in two more, and third in yet another two.

1900 Paris C: 15, N: 8. D: 7.15. WR: 36.20, 118-9 (Charles Henneman)

		M	FT.-IN.
1. Rudolf (Rezsö) Bauer	HUN	36.04	118-3 OR
2. František Janda-Suk	BOH/CZE	35.14	115-3
3. Richard Sheldon	USA	34.60	113-6
4. Panagiotis Paraskevopoulos	GRE	34.50	111-8
5. Rezsö Crettier	HUN	33.65	110-4½
6. Gustaf Söderström	SWE	33.07	108-5½
7. John Flanagan	USA	33.00	108-3
8. Eric Lemming	SWE	32.50	106-7
8. Carl Winckler	DEN	32.50	106-7

The challenge of this event was heightened by the fact that the landing area was a narrow lane between two rows of trees. Inaccurate throws hit the trees.

1904 St. Louis C: 6, N: 2, D: 9.3. WR: 40.71, 133-6½ (Martin Sheridan)

		M	FT.-IN.
1. Martin Sheridan	USA	39.28	128-10½ OR
2. Ralph Rose	USA	39.28	128-10½
3. Nicolaos Georgantas	GRE	37.68	123-7½
4. John Flanagan	USA	36.14	118-7
5. John Biller	USA	—	—
6. James Mitchel	USA	—	—

Sheridan and Rose finished in a tie, so, for the only time in Olympic history, a throw-off was held to determine first place. Each man was given three throws. Sheridan won 127-10¼ (38.97) to 120-6¾ (36.74).

1906 Athens C: 21, N: 9, D: 4.25. WR: 42.14, 138-3 (Martin Sheridan)

		M	FT.-IN.
1. Martin Sheridan	USA	41.46	136-0
2. Nicolaos Georgantas	GRE	38.06	124-10
3. Werner Järvinen	FIN	36.82	120-9
4. Eric Lemming	SWE	35.62	116-10
5. André Tison	FRA	34.81	114-2

In 1906, Martin Sheridan competed in seven events. He won the discus and the shot put; finished second in the stone throw, the standing high jump, and standing long jump; and fourth in the Greek-style discus throw. He tried to take part in the pentathlon, but had to withdraw after the first event because of a knee injury.

1908 London C: 42, N: 11, D: 7.16. WR: 42.63, 139-10½ (Martin Sheridan)

		M	FT.-IN.
1. Martin Sheridan	USA	40.89	134-2 OR
2. Merritt Giffin	USA	40.70	133-6½
3. Marquis "Bill" Horr	USA	39.4.4	129-5
4. Werner Järvinen	FIN	39.42	129-4½
5. Arthur Dearborn	USA	38.52	126-4½
6. Leander Talbott	USA	38.40	126-0
7. György Luntzer	HUN	38.34	125-9
8. André Tison	FRA	38.30	125-8

Competing in the 1904, 1906, and 1908 Games, Irish-born New York policeman Martin Sheridan won five gold medals, three silver and one bronze. He died of pneumonia on March 27, 1918, the day before his 37th birthday.

1912 Stockholm C: 41, N: 15, D: 7.12. WR: 47.58, 156-1 (James Duncan)

		M	FT.-IN.
1. Armas Taipale	FIN	45.21	148-3 OR
2. Richard Leslie Byrd	USA	42.32	138-10
3. James Duncan	USA	42.28	138-8
4. Elmer Niklander	FIN	42.09	138-1
5. Hans Tronner	AUT	41.24	135-4
6. Arlie Mucks	USA	40.93	134-3
7. George Philbrook	USA	40.92	134-2½
8. Emil Magnusson	SWE	39.91	130-11

1920 Antwerp C: 16, N: 8, D: 8.22. WR: 47.58, 156-1 (James Duncan)

		M	FT.-IN.
1. Elmer Niklander	FIN	44.685	146-7
2. Armas Taipale	FIN	44.19	145-0
3. Augustus Pope	USA	42.13	138-2
4. Edvin Zallhagen	SWE	41.07	134-9
5. Kenneth Bartlett	USA	40.875	134-1
6. Allan Eriksson	SWE	39.41	129-3
7. Valther Jensen	DEN	38.23	125-5
8. F. Wilhelm (Ville) Pörhölä	FIN	38.19	125-3

1924 Paris C: 32, N: 18, D: 7.13. WR: 47.58, 156-1 (James Duncan)

		M	FT.-IN.
1. L. Clarence "Bud" Houser	USA	46.15	151-4 OR
2. Vilho Niittymaa	FIN	44.95	147-5
3. Thomas Lieb	USA	44.83	147-0
4. Augustus Pope	USA	44.42	145-9
5. Ketil Askildt	NOR	43.40	142-5
6. Glenn Hartranft	USA	42.49	139-4
7. Elmer Niklander	FIN	42.09	138-1
8. Heikki Malmivirta	FIN	41.16	135-0

Bud Houser also won the shot put five days later. He was the last male athlete to achieve such a double in the Olympics.

1928 Amsterdam C: 34, N: 19, D: 8.1. WR: 48.20, 158-2 (L. Clarence "Bud" Houser)

		M	FT.-IN.
1. L. Clarence "Bud" Houser	USA	47.32	155-3 OR
2. L. Antero Kivi	FIN	47.23	154-11
3. James Corson	USA	47.10	154-6
4. Harald Stenerud	NOR	45.80	150-3
5. John Anderson	USA	44.87	147-2
6. Eino Kenttä	FIN	44.17	144-10
7. Ernst Paulus	GER	44.15	144-9
8. Johan Trandem	NOR	43.97	144-3

1932 Los Angeles C: 18, N: 11, D: 8.3. WR: 51.73, 169-9 (Paul Jessup)

		M	FT.-IN.
1. John Anderson	USA	49.49	162-4 OR
2. Henri Jean Laborde	USA	48.47	159-0
3. Paul Winter	FRA	47.85	156-11
4. Jules Noël	FRA	47.74	156-7
5. István Donogán	HUN	47.08	154-5
6. Endre Madarász	HUN	46.52	152-7
7. Kalevi Kotkas	FIN	45.87	150-5
8. Paul Jessup	USA	45.25	148-5

Two of the favorites, József Remecz of Hungary and Paul Jessup, the 6-foot 7-inch world record holder, failed to qualify for the final round of six. But the final competition was still hotly contested, as Anderson and Laborde traded the lead, with Anderson breaking the previous Olympic record four times in six throws. The Americans may have won the medals, but it was the fourth-place finisher, Jules Noël, who made the news. Because the 1932 Olympics were held in the United States during Prohibition, the French team had to receive special permission to import several thousand bottles of wine into the United States. The French successfully argued that although alcohol might be illegal in the United States, it was an essential part of the diet of many of the French athletes.

Evidently, Jules Noël was one of those athletes, as he caused the American track and field officials great consternation during the competition by making periodic visits to the dark tunnel that joined the field to the locker rooms. There he swigged champagne with his compatriots.

On his fourth attempt, Noël lofted a great throw that appeared to land just beyond the flag that marked Anderson's first-place effort. Unfortunately, every one of the officials in charge of the discus was, at that moment, distracted by the tense proceedings of the pole vault, taking place nearby, so none of them saw where Noël's discus had landed. Embarrassed by this blunder, they awarded Noël an extra throw in addition to the two that he still had coming. However, the Frenchman was unable to come up with another big throw and he was forced to return home without a medal.

1936 Berlin C: 31, N: 17, D: 8.5. WR: 53.10, 174-2 (Willy Schröder)

		M	FT.-IN.
1. W. Kenneth Carpenter	USA	50.48	165-7 OR
2. Gordon Dunn	USA	49.36	161-11
3. Giorgio Oberweger	ITA	49.23	161-6
4. Reidar Sörlie	NOR	48.77	160-0
5. Willy Schröder	GER	47.93	157-3
6. Nicolaos Syllas	GRE	47.75	156-7
7. Gunnar Bergh	SWE	47.22	154-11
8. Åke Hedvall	SWE	46.20	151-7

The two favorites, Harald Andersson of Sweden and Willy Schröder of Germany, were unable to rise to the occasion. Andersson, hampered by injury, failed to qualify for the semifinals, while Schröder only made it to the final group of six by winning a throw-off against Bergh. Carpenter overhauled Dunn and Oberweger with his next to last attempt.

Silver medalist Gordon Dunn served as mayor of

Fresno, California, from 1949 until 1957. During his terms of office, he led a vigorous campaign to rid the town of gambling halls, transient hotels and other manifestations of vice and corruption. For his efforts, he earned the sobriquet "No Fun Dunn."

1948 London C: 28, N: 18, D: 8.2. WR: 54.93, 180-3 (Robert Fitch)

		M	FT.-IN.
1. Adolfo Consolini	ITA	52.78	173-2 OR
2. Giuseppe Tosi	ITA	51.78	169-10
3. Fortune Gordien	USA	50.77	166-6
4. Ivar Ramstad	NOR	49.21	161-5
5. Ferenc Klics	HUN	48.21	158-2
6. Veikko Nyqvist	FIN	47.33	155-3
7. Nicolaos Syllas	GRE	47.25	155-0
8. Stein Johnson	NOR	46.54	152-8

Adolfo Consolini held the world record from October 1941 until June 1948. Two months after earning the Olympic gold medal, he regained the world record.

Tosi also finished second to Consolini in three consecutive European Championships; 1946, 1950 and 1954.

1952 Helsinki C: 32, N: 20, D: 7.22. WR: 56.97, 186-11 (Fortune Gordien)

		M	FT.-IN.
1. Simeon Iness	USA	55.03	180-6 OR
2. Adolfo Consolini	ITA	53.78	176-5
3. James Dillion	USA	53.28	174-10
4. Fortune Gordien	USA	52.66	172-9
5. Ferenc Klics	HUN	51.13	167-9
6. Otto Grigalka	SOV/RUS	50.71	166-4
7. Roland Nilsson	SWE	50.06	164-3
8. Giuseppe Tosi	ITA	49.03	160-10

When Sim Iness was born in Keota, Oklahoma, he weighed 13 pounds 8 ounces (6.12 kilograms). His father was a sharecropper. His family fled the Dust Bowl and ended up in Tulare, California, where he played on the Tulare High School football team with another future Olympic champion, Bob Mathias. In Helsinki, Iness bettered Consolini's Olympic record with all six of his throws in the final. Nicolaos Syllas of Greece, who had finished sixth in 1936, was still able to place ninth 16 years later.

1956 Melbourne C: 20, N: 15, D: 11.27. WR: 59.28, 194-6 (Fortune Gordien)

		M	FT.-IN.
1. Alfred Oerter	USA	56.36	184-11 OR
2. Fortune Gordien	USA	54.81	179-9
3. Desmond Koch	USA	54.40	178-6
4. Mark Pharaoh	GBR	54.27	178-0
5. Otto Grigalka	SOV/RUS	52.37	171-9
6. Adolfo Consolini	ITA	52.21	171-3
7. Ferenc Klics	HUN	51.82	170-0
8. Dako Radosević	YUG/SER	51.69	169-7

When Al Oerter of West Babylon, New York, was 15 years old, a discus bounced onto the track where he was practicing sprinting. He threw it back farther than the discus throwers had thrown it in his direction. A coach who was watching suggested that Oerter switch events and a legend was born. At the Melbourne Olympics, Oerter, now 20 years old, watched the favorites, Adolfo Consolini and Fortune Gordien, make their first-round throws. When his turn came, he felt "keyed up" and "inspired" and let loose the best throw of his career—184 feet 11 inches. No one else came within five feet as Oerter ended up with the three longest throws of the competition. On the victory rostrum he suddenly realized that he had actually won. His knees buckled and he almost fell. As it turned out, in the years to come Al Oerter would have plenty of opportunities to get used to standing on the gold medal platform at Olympic medal ceremonies.

Silver medalist Fortune Gordien later earned his living as an escape artist and illusionist.

1960 Rome C: 35, N: 22, D: 9.7. WR: 59.91, 196-6 (Edmund Pi tkowski, Richard "Rink" Babka)

		M	FT.-IN.
1. Alfred Oerter	USA	59.18	194-2 OR
2. Richard "Rink" Babka	USA	58.02	190-4
3. Richard Cochran	USA	57.16	187-6
4. József Szécsényi	HUN	55.79	183-0
5. Edmund Piątkowski	POL	55.12	180-10
6. Viktor Kompaniyets	SOV/UKR	55.06	180-8
7. Carmelo Rado	ITA	54.00	177-2
8. Kim Bukhantsev	SOV/RUS	53.61	175-10

In 1957 Al Oerter was involved in a near-fatal car crash, but he recovered fully and was back in shape before long. Then, at the US Olympic trials, he suffered his first defeat in over two years when he lost to giant Rink Babka. Oerter was still considered a slight favorite at the Olympics, but he was definitely under great pressure. While warming up for the qualifying round, he casually threw the discus beyond the world record marker and then qualified with an Olympic record of 191 feet 8 inches. But the day of the final he was "so tense I could barely throw." Babka led off with a toss of 190 feet 4 inches. Oerter followed with 189 feet 1 inch, but couldn't get closer over the next three rounds. As Oerter prepared for his fifth throw, Babka told him that he seemed to be carrying his left arm too low as he spun. Oerter made the necessary adjustment and threw his discus 194 feet 2 inches—a personal record. He thanked Babka and wished him luck on his last throw, but Babka fell short and settled for the silver medal.

1964 Tokyo C: 28, N: 21, D: 10.15. WR: 64.54, 211-9 (Ludvik Daněk)

		M	FT.-IN.
1. Alfred Oerter	USA	61.00	200-1 OR
2. Ludvik Daněk	CZE	60.52	198-7
3. David Weill	USA	59.49	195-2
4. L. Jay Silvester	USA	59.09	193-10
5. József Szécsényi	HUN	57.23	187-9
6. Zenon Begier	POL	57.06	187-2
7. Edmund Piątkowski	POL	55.81	183-1
8. Vladimir Trusenev	SOV/RUS	54.78	179-9

On May 18, 1962, Al Oerter became the first discus thrower to break officially the 200-foot barrier, with a throw of 200 feet 5 inches. Surprisingly, it was his first world record. It lasted only 17 days, when it was broken by Vladimir Trusenev. But 27 days later Oerter had the record back again.

In 1964, however, Oerter knew that he would be in for a real struggle if he wanted to win a third gold medal. Not only did he have to face current world record holder Ludvik Daněk, who had won 45 straight competitions, but he had also been suffering for quite some time from a chronic cervical disc injury, which caused him to wear a neck harness. As if that wasn't trouble enough, Oerter tore the cartilage in his lower ribs while practicing in Tokyo less than a week before the competition. Doctors advised him to rest for six weeks, but the day of the preliminary round, he showed up anyway, shot up with Novocain and wrapped with ice packs and tape. With his first throw Oerter set an Olympic record of 198 feet 8 inches.

Al Oerter, 1964

The first athlete to win the same Olympic track and field event four straight times, he earned four gold medals in the discus throw in 1956, 1960, 1964 and 1968.

Ludvik Daněk opened the final at 195 feet 11 inches. Before the competition, Al Oerter had told a fellow athlete, "If I don't do it on the first throw, I won't be able to do it at all." But his first attempt only went 189 feet 1 inch. After four rounds Oerter was in third place behind Daněk and David Weill. Then, with his fifth throw, Oerter gave it everything he had. While he doubled over in pain, his discus sailed 200 feet 1 inch to set another Olympic record and earn Oerter a third gold medal.

1968 Mexico City C: 27, N: 19, D: 10.15. WR: 68.40, 224-5 (L. Jay Silvester)

		M	FT.-IN.
1. Alfred Oerter	USA	64.78	212-6 OR
2. Lothar Milde	GDR	63.08	206-11
3. Ludvik Daněk	CZE	62.92	206-5
4. Hartmut Losch	GDR	62.12	203-10
5. L. Jay Silvester	USA	61.78	202-8
6. Gary Carlsen	USA	59.46	195-1
7. Edmund Piątkowski	POL	59.40	194-10
8. B. Richard Bruch	SWE	59.28	194-6

Jay Silvester, the 31-year-old world record holder, was the favorite in Mexico City. And yet, one couldn't help but wonder if Al Oerter might pull off one more miracle. Silvester dampened such speculations in the qualifying round by opening up with an Olympic record of 207 feet 10 inches, 16½ feet less than his own best, but several inches better than anything Oerter had ever done.

The final was delayed an hour because of rain, and this seemed to upset Silvester in particular. Lothar Milde took the first-round lead with a throw of 204 feet 10 inches and then improved to 206 feet 11 inches with his second attempt. The third round began with Oerter in fourth place, behind Milde, Losch, and Silvester. But, as if out of a fairy tale, the incomparable Oerter uncorked a throw of 212 feet 6 inches—five feet farther than he had ever thrown before. The rest of the finalists were demoralized, particularly Silvester, who fouled three times in a row. Oerter, meanwhile, added throws of 212 feet 5 inches and 210 feet 1 inch. Al Oerter had become the first track and field athlete to win four gold medals in the same event.

Oerter, after throwing the discus 33,000 times, didn't take part in the 1972 or 1976 Olympics, but then he came out of retirement to try out for the 1980 US team. At the age of 43, he finished fourth at the US Olympic trials, which were held after the anti-Soviet boycott had been declared. But who knows, if the top three had really been assured of going to Moscow instead of settling for symbolic honors, Al Oerter, the ultimate clutch performer, just might have qualified after all.

1972 Munich C: 29, N: 19, D: 9.2. WR: 68.40, 224-5 (L. Jay Silvester, Björn "Ricky" Bruch)

		M	FT.-IN.
1. Ludvik Daněk	CZE	64.40	211-3
2. L. Jay Silvester	USA	63.50	208-4
3. Björn "Ricky" Bruch	SWE	63.40	208-0
4. John Powell	USA	62.82	206-1
5. Géza Fejér	HUN	62.62	205-5
6. Detlef Thorith	GDR	62.42	204-9
8. Tim Vollmer	USA	60.24	197-8
7. Ferenc Tégla	HUN	60.60	198-10

With Al Oerter gone, Ludvik Daněk and Jay Silvester, both 35 years old, could finally relax and get down to the business of winning a gold medal. They had previously met 24 times, with Daněk finishing ahead 12 times and Silvester 12 times. In Munich they also had to contend with high-strung but increasingly consistent Ricky Bruch. Daněk led the qualifying round with an impressive throw of 211 feet. In the final, Géza Fejér took the first-round lead at 205 feet 1 inch. John Powell moved ahead in the second-round at 206 feet 1 inch, and then Silvester took over at the halfway mark with 208 feet 4 inches. With one round to go, the order was Silvester, Bruch, Powell, Fejér, and Daněk, who hadn't come within five feet of his qualifying toss. Since no Olympic discus contest had been won in the final round since 1896, it seemed a good bet that Jay Silvester was on the verge of victory. But Daněk, who had enlisted the aid of a psychologist to help him prepare for just such last-ditch situations, broke tradition and won with a final throw of 211 feet 3 inches.

1976 Montreal C: 30, N: 20, D: 7.25. WR: 70.86, 232-6 (M. Maurice "Mac" Wilkins)

		M	FT.-IN.
1. M. Maurice "Mac" Wilkins	USA	67.50	221-5
2. Wolfgang Schmidt	GDR	66.22	217-3
3. John Powell	USA	65.70	215-7
4. Norbert Thiede	GDR	64.30	210-11
5. Siegfried Pachale	GDR	64.24	210-9
6. Pentti Kahma	FIN	63.12	207-1
7. Knut Hjeltnes	NOR	63.06	206-11
8. L. Jay Silvester	USA	61.98	203-4

With his first and only throw of the preliminary round, Mac Wilkins, a 25-year-old schoolteacher from Oregon, set an Olympic record of 224 feet. The next day, his second-round throw of 221 feet 5 inches put a quick end to any doubt as to who would win the final. Wilkins was sharply criticized by the US press for congratulating East German silver medallist Wolfgang Schmidt, with whom he had become quite friendly, while ignoring American bronze medallist John Powell, with whom he did not get along. The criticism seemed ironic in view of the concern that was simultaneously being expressed about excessive nationalism in the Olympics.

Beginning in 1982, Schmidt was imprisoned for 15 months for "antisocial behavior" because of his opposition to Communism and his friendships with Western athletes. He was unable to return to competition until 1988, after he was given permission to emigrate to West Germany. He placed fourth at the 1991 world championships.

1980 Moscow C: 18, N: 12, D: 7.28. WR: 71.16, 233-5 (Wolfgang Schmidt)

		M	FT.-IN.
1. Viktor Rashchupkin	SOV/RUS	66.64	218-8
2. Imrich Bugár	CZE/SLV	66.38	217-9
3. Luis Delís Fournier	CUB	66.32	217-7
4. Wolfgang Schmidt	GDR	65.64	215-4
5. Yuri Dumchev	SOV/RUS	65.58	215-2
6. Ihor Dugynets	SOV/UKR	64.04	210-1
7. Emil Vladimirov	BUL	63.18	207-3
8. Velko Velev	BUL	63.04	206-10

Conspicuously missing because of the anti-Soviet boycott were Knut Hjeltnes of Norway and Mac Wilkins, John Powell, and Ben Plucknett, each of whom had to throw over 223 feet just to make the US team. With these leading contenders absent, Wolfgang Schmidt seemed a sure bet for the gold medal, but a foot injury upset his performance and he had to settle for fourth place. The first-round lead in the final went to Imrich Bugár at 213 feet 8 inches. The lead changed hands four more times before Rashchupkin moved from fourth place to first with his gold-medal-winning fourth-round throw. His pre-Olympic best had only been 216 feet 6 inches. The contest ended in controversy, as many observers felt that Luis Delís' final throw had been marked about a foot short, keeping him from a silver medal or maybe even a gold.

1984 Los Angeles C: 20, N: 14, D: 8.10. WR: 71.86, 235-9 (Yuri Dumchev)

		M	FT.-IN.
1. Rolf Danneberg	GER	66.60	218-6
2. M. Maurice "Mac"' Wilkins	USA	66.30	217-6
3. John Powell	USA	65.46	214-9
4. Knut Hjeltnes	NOR	65.28	214-2
5. Arthur Burns	USA	64.98	213-2
6. Alwin Wagner	GER	64.72	212-4
7. Luciano Zerbini	ITA	63.50	208-4
8. Stefan Fernholm	SWE	63.22	207-5

With pre-boycott favorites Luis Delís and Imrich Bugár among the missing, a US sweep seemed a distinct possibility. Olympic record holder Mac Wilkins took the early lead at 216 feet 5 inches, but in the fourth round, unheralded Rolf Danneberg, a bearded, 6-foot 6-inch unemployed schoolteacher, unleashed a toss of 218 feet 6 inches. Wilkins improved by a foot in the fifth round but could come no closer. The 31-year-old Danneberg, who wore dark glasses while competing, was the least-expected track and field winner of the 1984 Olympics.

1988 Seoul C: 29, N: 20, D: 10.1. WR: 74.08, 243-0 (Jürgen Schult)

		M	FT.-IN.
1. Jürgen Schult	GDR	68.82	225-9 OR
2. Romas Ubartas	SOV/LIT	67.48	221-5
3. Rolf Danneberg	GER	67.38	221-1
4. Yuri Dumchev	SOV/RUS	66.42	217-11
5. Maurice "Mac" Wilkins	USA	65.90	216-2
6. Gejza Valent	CZE	65.80	215-10
7. Knut Hjeltnes	NOR	64.94	213-1
8. Alois Hannecker	GER	63.28	207-7

World champion and world record holder Jürgen Schult earned the gold medal with his first throw. He also recorded the three next best throws of the competition. Dumchev held second place until the fifth round, when he was passed by Danneberg. But it was Lithuanian Ubartas who grabbed the silver medal with his final attempt.

1992 Barcelona C: 32, N: 24, D: 8.5. WR: 74.08, 243-0 (Jürgen Schult)

		M	FT.-IN.
1. Romas Ubartas	LIT	65.12	213-8
2. Jürgen Schult	GER	64.94	213-1
3. Roberto Moya Sandoval	CUB	64.12	210-4
4. Costel Grasu	ROM	62.86	206-3
5. Attila Horváth	HUN	62.82	206-1
6. Juan Martínez	CUB	62.64	205-7
7. Dmitri Kovtsun	UKR	62.04	203-6
8. Dmitri Shevchenko	RUS	61.78	202-8

Romas Ubartas led the qualifying round with a toss of 216 feet 9 inches. Jürgen Schult took the first-round lead in the final at 210 feet 10 inches. Ubartas moved ahead in round three with a throw of 211 feet 2 inches. The competition came to a head in the fifth round. First Schult hit 213 feet 1 inch, then Ubartas came right back with a throw of 213 feet 8 inches that held up for the win. The 6-foot 7½-inch, 270-pound Ubartas was Lithuania's first Olympic champion. He had refused to take part in the 1991 world championships rather than represent the Soviet Union, which then collapsed, allowing Lithuania to recapture its independence. Ubartas' stint as a national hero was short-lived—in 1993 he tested positive for anabolic steroids at the world championships in Stuttgart and was slapped with a four-year suspension.

1996 Atlanta C: 40, N: 30, D: 7.31. WR: 74.08, 243-0 (Jürgen Schult)

		M	FT.-IN.
1. Lars Riedel	GER	69.40	227-8 OR
2. Vladimir Dubrovshchik	BLR	66.60	218-6
3. Vasily Kaptyukh	BLR	65.80	215-10
4. Anthony Washington	USA	65.42	214-8
5. Virgilijus Alekna	LIT	65.30	214-3
6. Jürgen Schult	GER	64.62	212-0
7. Vitaliy Sidorov	UKR	63.78	209-3
8. Vaclovas Kidykas	LIT	62.78	206-0

Lars Riedel of Chemnitz in the former East Germany had been the dominant force in discus throwing for the past five years, having won the last three world championships. However, at the 1992 Olympics, he had failed to advance out of the qualifying round. In Atlanta he avoided the same fate. In fact, he led the qualifiers with a throw of 64.66 meters (218 feet 8 inches). But in the final it looked like Olympic disaster would strike Riedel again. His first two throws smashed into the wire mesh of the cage. He was one throw away from elimination. Riedel needed to find a refuge where he could meditate and gather his strength before his third attempt. He retreated to the men's toilet.

This oasis seemed to do the trick. His third throw was successful and he moved into fourth place behind Vladimir Dubrovshchik, Vasily Kaptyukh and Anthony Washington. In the fifth round, Riedel put the competition away with a toss of 69.40 meters (227 feet 8 inches) and then concluded with a 69.24 (227-2) for good measure. In 1997, Riedel won a fourth world championship.

2000 Sydney C: 45, N: 28, D: 9.25. WR: 74.08, 243-0 (Jürgen Schult)

		M	FT.-IN.
1. Virgilijus Alekna	LIT	69.30	227-4
2. Lars Riedel	GER	68.50	224-9
3. Frantz Kruger	SAF	68.19	223-8
4. Vasily Kaptyukh	BLR	67.59	221-9
5. Adam Setliff	USA	66.02	216-7
6. Jason Tunks	CAN	65.80	215-10
7. Vladimir Dubrovshchik	BLR	65.13	213-8
8. Jürgen Schult	GER	64.41	211-4

Virgilijus Alekna, who worked part-time as a security guard for an ex-president of Lithuania, had an extraordinary pre-Olympic season. In addition to winning 14 straight meets, he became the first person to surpass 70 meters three times in one series. At the Lithuanian Championships, he recorded the two longest throws since Jürgen Schults's 1986 world record, 73.88 meters and 72.55 meters. Yet Alekna's victory in Sydney was not seen as a sure thing because two weeks before the Olympics Lars Riedel beat him in Berlin—albeit by only two centimeters—and Alekna had never defeated Riedel at a major competition. In the Olympic final, Frantz Kruger took the first round lead with a throw of 67.89 meters (222 feet 9 inches). In the third round, Riedel moved ahead with a 68.50 throw (224 feet 9 inches) and Kruger improved to 68.19 (223 feet 8 inches). But then Alekna followed Kruger into the circle and hit 68.73 meters (225 feet 6 inches). That settled the medal places, although Alekna did improve to 69.30 (227 feet 4 inches) in the fifth round.

2004 Athens C: 39, N: 26, D: 8.23. WR: 74.08, 243-0 (Jürgen Schult)

		M	FT.-IN.
1. Virgilijus Alekna	LIT	69.89	229-3 OR
2. Zoltán Kővágó	HUN	67.04	219-11
3. Aleksander Tammert	EST	66.66	218-8
4. Vasily Kaptyukh	BLR	65.10	213-7
5. Frantz Kruger	SAF	64.34	211-1
6. Casey Malone	USA	64.33	211-0
7. Lars Riedel	GER	62.80	206-0
8. Hannes Hopley	SAF	62.58	205-0

DISQ (Drugs): Róbert Fazekas (HUN) 70.93 (232-8)

Róbert Fazekas of Hungary originally finished first, but was disqualified for failing to produce a sufficiently large urine sample for the post-competition drug test. He was later caught with a bag containing stored urine hidden on his body. The gold went instead to defending Olympic and world champion Virgilijus Alekna, who had recorded an Olympic-record-breaking distance of 69.89 meters (229 feet 3 inches) with his first throw. Fortunately, Fazekas' positive test came early enough that Alekna was able to receive his gold medal at the regularly scheduled victory ceremony. Fazekas' disqualification also negated what may have been another Olympic record: during his victory lap after his apparent win, he carried a flag so large that he needed help from teammate Zoltán Kővágó just to hold it.

2008 Beijing C: 37, N: 29, D: 8.19. WR: 74.08, 243-0 (Jürgen Schult)

		M	FT.-IN.
1. Gerd Kanter	EST	68.82	225-9
2. Piotr Małachowski	POL	67.82	222-6
3. Virgilijus Alekna	LIT	67.79	222-5
4. Robert Harting	GER	67.09	220-1
5. Frank Casañas Hernández	SPA	66.49	218-2
6. Bogdan Pishchalnikov	RUS	65.88	216-2
7. Rutger Smith	HOL	65.39	214-6
8. Róbert Fazekas	HUN	63.43	208-1

After winning his second consecutive Olympic gold medal in Athens, Lithuania's Virgilijus Alekna continued to dominate international competition. In 2005 he defended his world championship title by recording a championship record throw of 70.17 meters (230 ft. 2½ in.) on his final attempt to beat Estonia's Gerd Kanter for the title. It was the first time anyone had surpassed 70 meters in a world championship. The following year he won the European Championship, again ahead of Kanter.

Alekna's reign finally ended in 2007, when a short final throw left him in fourth place at the world championships, behind Kanter, Germany's Robert Harting and Holland's Rutger Smith. It was Alekna's first major championship loss since he finished second to Lars Reidel at the 2001 worlds, and it ended a two-year, 37-competition winning streak and a four-year reign as the first-ranked thrower in the world.

Alekna and Kanter were the clear favorites at the 2008 Olympics. The competition also saw the return of Hungary's Róbert Fazekas, who had come back after being stripped of his gold medal and given a two-year ban for a doping violation in 2004. The top throw of the qualifying round went to Poland's Piotr Małachowski. A former firefighter from the town of Biezhun, near Warsaw, Małachowski had become involved briefly in the criminal underworld in Poland before taking up discus with a military sports club.

Małachowski took the lead after the first round, with a throw of 66.45 meters (218 ft. ¼ in.), ahead of Harting and Smith, with Alekna fouling his first throw. He expanded his lead with a 67.82-meter (222 ft. 6 in.) throw in the second round, as Kanter moved up to second and Alekna into third. Małachowski stayed in the lead until the fourth round, when Kanter's 68.82-meter (225 ft. 9½ in.) throw dropped him to second place. Alekna, who had briefly fallen to fourth place in the third round, recorded a 67.79-meter (222 ft. 4¾ in.) fourth-round effort to move back into third. None of the top three were able to improve on their standings in the final two rounds, with Kanter taking gold by a full meter.

Kanter, a 29-year-old business major, celebrated his win by crouching down in the starting blocks of the 100 meters and sprinting down the track draped in an Estonian flag.

HAMMER THROW

The hammer is a 16-pound metal sphere attached to a grip by means of a spring steel wire not longer than 3 feet 11¾ inches (121.5 centimeters). It is thrown from a circle with a diameter of 2.135 meters (7 feet). Most throwers spin around three or four times before releasing the implement. This potentially dangerous sport appears to have had it origins in the practice of sledgehammer throwing in 15th- and 16th-century England and Scotland.

1896 not held

1900 Paris C: 5, N: 2, D: 7.16. WR: 51.105, 167-8 (John Flanagan)

		M	FT.-IN.
1. John Flanagan	USA	51.01	167-4½
2. T. Truxtun Hare	USA	46.26	151-9
3. Josiah McCracken	USA	43.58	143-0
4. Eric Lemming	SWE	—	—
5. Karl Gustaf Staaf	SWE	—	—

Irish-born John Flanagan emigrated to the United States in 1897 and became a policeman in New York City. Truxtun Hare was a four-time All-American football selection from the University of Pennsylvania.

1904 St. Louis C: 6. N: 1, D: 8.29. WR: 52.705, 172-11 (John Flanagan)

		M	FT.-IN.
1. John Flanagan	USA	51.23	168-1 OR
2. John DeWitt	USA	50.26	164-11
3. Ralph Rose	USA	45.73	150-0
4. Charles Chadwick	USA	42.78	140-4
5. James Mitchel	USA	—	—
6. Albert Johnson	USA	—	—

1906 not held

1908 London C: 19, N: 8, D: 7.14. WR: 53.35, 175-0 (Matthew McGrath)

		M	FT.-IN.
1. John Flanagan	USA	51.93	170-4¼ OR
2. Matthew McGrath	USA	51.18	167-11
3. Cornelius Walsh	CAN	48.51	159-1½
4. Thomas Nicolson	GBR	48.09	157-9¼
5. Leander Talbott	USA	47.87	157-0¼
6. Marquis "Bill" Horr	USA	46.95	154-0¼
7. Simon Gillis	USA	45.59	149-6½
8. Eric Lemming	SWE	43.06	141-3

With his last attempt, Flanagan won his third straight hammer throw gold medal. On July 24, 1909, Flanagan threw the hammer 184 feet 4 inches to become the oldest world record breaker in the history of track and field. He was 41 years, 196 days old. He returned to Ireland in 1911 and lived there until his death in 1938.

1912 Stockholm C: 14, N: 4, D: 7.14. WR: 57.10, 187-4 (Matthew McGrath)

		M	FT.-IN.
1. Matthew McGrath	USA	54.74	179-7 OR
2. Duncan Gillis	CAN	48.39	158-9
3. Clarence Childs	USA	48.17	158-0
4. Robert Olsson	SWE	46.50	152-7
5. Carl Johan "Masse" Lind	SWE	45.61	149-7
6. Denis Carey	GBR	43.78	143-8
7. Nils Linde	SWE	43.32	142-1
8. Carl Jahnzon	SWE	42.58	139-8
8. Ralph Rose	USA	42.58	139-8

Irish-American policeman Matt McGrath was truly in a class by himself in Stockholm. The *shortest* of his six throws—173 feet 4 inches—was almost 15 feet longer than anyone else's *longest* throw. McGrath's Olympic record held up for 24 years and would have earned a silver medal in the 1948 Olympics.

Matt McGrath, 1912
On the beat and on the job, where he won a gold and two silvers in four Olympics.

1920 Antwerp C: 12, N: 5. D: 8.18. WR: 57.77, 189-6 (Patrick Ryan)

		M	FT.-IN.
1. Patrick Ryan	USA	52.875	173-5
2. Carl Johan "Masse" Lind	SWE	48.43	158-10
3. Basil Bennet	USA	48.25	158-3
4. Malcom Svensson	SWE	47.29	155-1
5. Matthew McGrath	USA	46.67	153-1
6. Thomas Nicolson	GBR	45.70	149-11
7. Nils Linde	SWE	44.885	147-3
8. James McEachern	USA	44.70	146-8

Pat Ryan emigrated from Ireland to New York in 1910. On August 17, 1913, he set a world record of 189 feet 6 inches that would last for 25 years. It remained as a US record until 1953. In Antwerp, Ryan was unchallenged, particularly after Matt McGrath injured his knee and was forced to withdraw after only two throws.

1924 Paris C: 15, N: 10, D: 7.10. WR: 57.77, 189-6 (Patrick Ryan)

		M	FT.-IN.
1. Frederick Tootell	USA	53.295	174-10
2. Matthew McGrath	USA	50.84	166-9
3. Malcolm Nokes	GBR	48.875	160-4
4. Erik Eriksson	FIN	48.74	159-11
5. Ossian Skiöld	SWE	45.285	148-7
6. James McEachern	USA	45.225	148-4
7. Carl Johan "Masse" Lind	SWE	44.785	146-11
8. John Murdock	CAN	42.48	139-4

In 1920, Johnny Magee, the coach of the track team at Bowdoin College in Maine, asked Fred Tootell if he had ever thrown a hammer. Confused, Tootell answered that his father was a contractor, so he had used a hammer while helping him do some roofing, but, no, he had never actually thrown a hammer. Magee explained that that was not the kind of hammer he meant. Tootell learned quickly. Although he qualified for the US Olympic team in 1924, Tootell injured a tendon in his ankle at the US trials and was forced to wear a cast during his voyage to Paris. He did not remove the cast until the day before the Olympic competition. Tootell was the first American-born winner of the hammer throw. Silver medalist Matt McGrath was 45 years old.

1928 Amsterdam C: 16, N: 11, D: 7.30. WR: 57.77, 189-6 (Patrick Ryan)

		M	FT.-IN.
1. Patrick O'Callaghan	IRL	51.39	168-7
2. Ossian Skiöld	SWE	51.29	168-3
3. Edmund Black	USA	49.03	160-10
4. Armando Poggioli	ITA	48.37	158.8
5. Donald Gwinn	USA	47.15	154-8
6. Frank Connor	USA	46.75	153-4
7. Federico Kleger	ARG	46.60	152-11
8. Ricardo Bayer	CHI	46.34	152-0

Pat O'Callaghan, of Derrygallon in North Cork, was a rugby player who had only been competing with the hammer for 13 months when he won an Olympic gold medal with his next-to-last throw, improving his personal best by 20 inches.

1932 Los Angeles C: 14, N: 9, D: 8.1. WR: 57.77, 189-6 (Patrick Ryan)

		M	FT.-IN.
1. Patrick O'Callaghan	IRL	53.92	176-11
2. F. Wilhelm (Ville) Pörhölä	FIN	52.27	171-6
3. Peter Zaremba	USA	50.33	165-1
4. Ossian Skiöld	SWE	49.24	161-6
5. Grant McDougall	USA	49.12	161-2
6. Federico Kleger	ARG	48.33	158-7
7. Gunnar Jansson	SWE	47.79	156-9
8. Armando Poggioli	ITA	46.90	153-10

Ville Pörhölä, who had won the shot put gold medal 12 years earlier in Antwerp, led after five rounds. However, defending champion Dr. Pat O'Callaghan, who spent every free moment between throws filing down the spikes on his shoes, came through with a dramatic victory in his final attempt.

1936 Berlin C: 27, N: 16, D: 8.3. WR: 57.77, 189-6 (Patrick Ryan)

		M	FT.-IN.
1. Karl Hein	GER	56.49	185-4 OR
2. Erwin Blask	GER	55.04	180-7
3. O. Fred Warngård	SWE	54.83	179-10
4. Gustaf Alfons Koutonen	FIN	51.90	170-3
5. William Rowe	USA	51.66	169-6
6. Donald Favor	USA	51.01	167-4
7. Bernhard Greulich	GER	50.61	166-0
8. Koit Annamaa	EST	50.46	165-7

Hein, a 28-year-old Hamburg carpenter, scored an upset victory with his final throw. All three medalists achieved personal records.

1948 London C: 24, N: 16, D: 7.31. WR: 59.02, 193-8 (Imre Németh)

		M	FT.-IN.
1. Imre Németh	HUN	56.07	183-11
2. Ivan Gubijan	YUG/CRO	54.27	178-0
3. Robert Bennett	USA	53.73	176-3
4. Samuel Felton	USA	53.66	176-0
5. Lauri Tamminen	FIN	53.08	174-2
6. Bo Ericson	SWE	52.98	173-10
7. Teseo Taddia	ITA	51.74	169-9
8. Einar Söderqvist	SWE	51.48	168-11

Imre Németh, who broke Erwin Blask's ten-year-old world record two weeks before the Olympics began, weighed a mere 85 kilograms (184 pounds).

1952 Helsinki C: 33, N: 18, D: 7.24. WR: 59.88, 196-5 (Imre Németh)

		M	FT.-IN.	
1. József Csérmák	HUN	60.34	197-11	WR
2. Karl Storch	GER	58.86	193-l	
3. Imre Németh	HUN	57.74	189-5	
4. Jiři Dadák	CZE	56.80	186-4	
5. Mykola Redkin	SOV/UKR	56.55	185-6	
6. Karl Wolf	GER	56.49	185-4	
7. Sverre Strandli	NOR	56.36	184-11	
8. Georgi Dybenko	SOV/UKR	55.03	180-6	

Twenty-year-old József Csérmák, a pupil of defending champion Imre Németh, broke the 60-meter barrier for the first time with his third throw. Silver medalist Karl Storch, who had first cleared 190 feet in 1939, was 38 years old.

1956 Melbourne C: 22, N: 14, D: 11.24. WR: 68.54, 224-10 (Harold Connolly)

		M	FT.-IN.	
1. Harold Connolly	USA	63.19	207-3	OR
2. Mikhail Krivonosov	SOV/BLR	63.03	206-9	
3. Anatoly Samotsvetov	SOV/RUS	62.56	205-3	
4. Albert Hall	USA	61.96	203-3	
5. Jósef Csérmák	HUN	60.70	199-2	
6. Krešimir Račić	YUG/SER	60.36	198-0	
7. Dmitri Yegorov	SOV/UKR	60.22	197-7	
8. Sverre Strandli	NOR	59.21	194-3	

For several months, Harold Connolly and Mikhail Krivonosov had been carrying on a long-distance duel between Boston and Minsk, breaking each other's most recent records. Krivonosov was a Belarussian who attracted the attention of athletic coaches during a hand-grenade throwing contest. In 1952 he had hoped to go to the Helsinki Olympics as a discus thrower, but finished only fourth in the USSR trials and failed to make the team. Two days later he qualified in the hammer throw instead. In Helsinki he fouled twice, fell once, and failed to register a valid throw. Concentrating on the hammer from then on, Krivonosov set his first world record in 1954. His sixth record, 220 feet 10 inches, was made on October 22, 1956. Eleven days later, Harold Connolly, whose left arm was withered as a result of an accident at birth, broke Krivonosov's record by four feet. Three weeks later the two rivals met at the Melbourne Olympics.

The first-round lead went to Siberia's Anatoly Samotsvetov at 203 feet 9 inches. Krivonosov moved ahead in the second round with a throw of 206 feet 8 inches. His last three attempts were all fouls. Hal Connolly, wearing ballet shoes to improve his footing, finally won the contest with a fifth-round heave of 207 feet 3 inches.

What gained Connolly international attention was not his gold medal but his Olympic Village romance with Czechoslovakian discus champion Olga Fikotová. After a great deal of pressure, the Iron Curtain was drawn open long enough for Olga and Harold to wed. Forty thousand well-wishers attended their civil ceremony in Prague, which was followed by two more services, one Catholic and one Protestant. The couple then settled in the United States. Harold eventually took part in four Olympics and Olga in five. After they divorced in 1973, Harold married three-time Olympian Pat Daniels. What few people knew about Connolly, because he tried to keep it hidden, was that his left arm was four inches shorter than his right and was dysfunctional.

1960 Rome C: 28, N: 18, D: 9.3. WR: 70.33, 230-9 (Harold Connolly)

		M	FT.-IN.	
1. Vasily Rudenkov	SOV/BLR	67.10	220-2	OR
2. Gyula Zsivótzky	HUN	65.79	215-10	
3. Tadeusz Rut	POL	65.64	215-4	
4. John Lawlor	IRL	64.95	213-1	
5. Olgierd Cieply	POL	64.57	211-10	
6. Zvonko Bezjak	YUG/SER	64.21	210-7	
7. Anatoly Samotsvetov	SOV/RUS	63.60	208-8	
8. Harold Connolly	USA	63.58	208-7	

Harold Connolly broke his own world record only two weeks before the Olympics began but was troubled by injury and finished a disappointing eighth in Rome. Meanwhile, metal worker Vasily Rudenkov set an Olympic record of 219 feet 10 inches in the qualifying round and then led the final from start to finish.

1964 Tokyo C: 24, N: 13, D: 10.18. WR: 70.66, 231-10 (Harold Connolly)

		M	FT.-IN.	
1. Romuald Klim	SOV/BLR	69.74	228-10	OR
2. Gyula Zsivótzky	HUN	69.09	226-8	
3. Uwe Beyer	GER	68.09	223-4	
4. Yuri Nikulin	SOV/RUS	67.69	222-1	
5. Yuri Bakarinov	SOV/RUS	66.72	218-11	
6. Harold Connolly	USA	66.65	218-8	
7. Edward Burke	USA	65.66	215-5	
8. Olgierd Cieply	POL	64.82	212-8	

Romuald Klim, a 31-year-old from Belarus, won with his fourth throw.

1968 Mexico City C: 22, N: 12, D: 10.17. WR: 73.76, 242-0 (Gyula Zsivótsky)

		M	FT.-IN.	
1. Gyula Zsivótzky	HUN	73.36	240-8	OR
2. Romuald Klim	SOV/BLR	73.28	240-5	
3. Lázár Lovász	HUN	69.78	228-11	
4. Takeo Sugawara	JPN	69.78	228-11	
5. Sándor Eckschmidt	HUN	69.46	227-11	
6. Gennady Kondrashov	SOV/RUS	69.08	226-8	
7. Reinhard Theimer	GDR	68.84	225-10	
8. Helmut Baumann	GDR	68.26	223-11	

On September 4, 1965, Gyula Zsivótzky threw the hammer 241 feet 11 inches to better the world record by a shocking 8 feet 2 inches. Three years later he bumped the record up an extra inch, but at the Olympics he was not the favorite. Romuald Klim, unbeaten in three years, had defeated Zsivótzky nine straight times. Zsivótzky seemed to be held back by a psychological barrier whenever he faced Klim, but he received a big boost when he threw 247 feet 1 inch in practice one week before the competition began.

Klim's first throw of the final was 237 feet, but Zsivótzky, throwing immediately after Klim, gained further confidence by recording 237 feet 9 inches with his second throw. However, the third round saw Klim take the lead at 238 feet 11 inches, while Zsivótzky could only respond with 238 feet, two inches less than the Olympic record he had set in the qualifying round the previous day. In the fourth round of the final, Klim reached 240 feet 5 inches, while Zsivótzky fouled. However, the Hungarian put it together with his next-to-last throw and won with 240 feet 8 inches.

Takeo Sugawara, the smallest man in the competition at 5 feet 8½ inches and 185 pounds, tied with Lázár Lovász, but Lovász was awarded the bronze medal because his second-best throw was one foot longer than Sugawara's.

1972 Munich C: 31, N: 18, D: 9.7. WR: 76.40, 250-8 (Walter Schmidt)

		M	FT.-IN.	
1. Anatoly Bondarchuk	SOV/UKR	75.50	247-8	OR
2. Jochen Sachse	GDR	74.96	245-11	
3. Vasily Khmelevski	SOV/RUS	74.04	242.11	
4. Uwe Beyer	GER	71.52	234-8	
5. Gyula Zsivótzky	HUN	71.38	234-2	
6. Sándor Eckschmidt	HUN	71.20	233-7	
7. Edwin Klein	GER	71.14	233-5	
8. Shigenobu Murofushi	JPN	70.88	232-6	

The favorite, 32-year-old Anatoly Bondarchuk, settled matters early in the final with an opening throw of 247 feet 8 inches. He claimed to have thrown the hammer 100,000 times in the previous 13 years.

1976 Montreal C: 20, N: 13, D: 7.28. WR: 79.30, 260-2 (Walter Schmidt)

		M	FT.-IN.	
1. Yuri Sedykh	SOV/RUS	77.52	254-4	OR
2. Aleksei Spiridonov	SOV/RUS	76.08	249-7	
3. Anatoly Bondarchuk	SOV/UKR	75.48	247-8	
4. Karl-Hans Riehm	GER	75.46	247-7	
5. Walter Schmidt	GER	74.72	245-2	
6. Jochen Sachse	GDR	74.30	243-9	
7. Christopher Black	GBR	73.18	240-1	
8. Edwin Klein	GER	71.34	234-1	

On May 19, 1975, Karl-Hans Riehm had a truly remarkable day. Competing at Rehlingen, he bettered the previous world record with all six of his throws, his best of the day being 257 feet 6 inches. Three months later, he lost the record to Walter Schmidt, who was famous for achieving his best performances at minor meets. In Montreal, Riehm led the qualifying round at 244 feet 3 inches, but in the final, he and Schmidt had to take a backseat to the Soviet trio. Yuri Sedykh, a 21-year-old student of Anatoly Bondarchuk, won the competition with his second throw. Sedykh was introduced to the sport that would become his specialty in an unusual way. When he was 12 years old he chased a soccer ball onto a field, not realizing that hammer throwers were practicing nearby. He came very close to being decapitated by a flying hammer. He lingered—at a respectful distance—long enough to become fascinated, then returned every day until he was allowed to join in.

1980 Moscow C: 17, N: 12, D: 7.31. WR: 81.68, 267-11 (Sergei Litvinov)

		M	FT.-IN.	
1. Yuri Sedykh	SOV/RUS	81.80	268-4	WR
2. Sergei Litvinov	SOV/RUS	80.64	264-7	
3. Jüri Tamm	SOV/EST	78.96	259-1	
4. Roland Steuk	GDR	77.54	254-5	
5. Detlef Gerstenberg	GDR	74.60	244-9	
6. Emannouil Dulgherov	BUL	74.04	242-11	
7. Gianpaulo Urlando	ITA	73.90	242-5	
8. Ireneusz Golda	POL	73.74	241-11	

Unfortunately missing because of the anti-Soviet boycott was Karl-Hans Riehm, who threw 265 feet 1 inch the day before the Olympic final. Riehm was the only man capable of threatening the Soviets, who dominated hammer throwing so thoroughly that three of their team members set world records during one nine-day period. On May 16, 1980, Sedykh took the record away from Riehm with a throw of 263 feet 8 inches. Then Jüri Tamm entered the circle and threw 263 feet 9 inches. Not to be outdone, Sedykh countered with 264 feet 7 inches. Eight days later, Sergei Litvinov beat them both with a new record of 267 feet 11 inches.

In Moscow, Sedykh opened the Olympic final with a world record of 268 feet 4 inches. Litvinov's first throw gained him the silver medal. He followed with five straight fouls. Two of Yuri Sedykh's three wives were Olympic champions: Lyudmila Kondratyeva (1980 100 meters) and Natalya Lisovskaya (1988 shot put).

1984 Los Angeles C: 23, N: 13, D: 8.6. WR: 86.34, 283-3 (Yuri Sedykh)

		M	FT.-IN.
1. Juha Tiainen	FIN	78.08	256-2
2. Karl-Hans Riehm	GER	77.98	255-10
3. Klaus Ploghaus	GER	76.68	251-7
4. Orlando Bianchini	ITA	75.94	249-2
5. William Green	USA	75.60	248-0
6. Harri Huhtala	FIN	75.28	247-0
7. Walter Ciofani	FRA	73.46	241-0
8. Robert Weir	GBR	72.62	238-3

DISQ (Drugs): Gianpaolo Urlando (ITA) 75.96 249-3

On July 3, 1984, Yuri Sedykh added 7 feet 3 inches to Sergei Litvinov's world record. Sadly, the Soviet boycott prevented these two great champions from battling it out at the Olympics. Juha Tiainen, the only one of the top twelve ranked hammer throwers present in Los Angeles, won with his third-round throw. Fourth-place finisher Urlando was disqualified when his doping test registered positive for excessive testosterone.

1988 Seoul C: 30, N: 16, D: 9.26. WR: 86.74, 284-7 (Yuri Sedykh)

		M	FT.-IN.
1. Sergei Litvinov	SOV/RUS	84.80	278-2 OR
2. Yuri Sedykh	SOV/RUS	83.76	274-10
3. Jüri Tamm	SOV/EST	81.16	266-3
4. Ralf Haber	GDR	80.44	263-11
5. Heinz Weis	GER	79.16	259-8
6. Tibor Gécsek	HUN	78.36	257-1
7. Imre Szitás	HUN	77.04	252-9
8. Ivan Tanev	BUL	76.08	249-7

The three medalists from 1980 returned to the victory platform in 1988. Two-time world champion Sergei Litvinov settled the competition with a first-round heave of 278 feet 1 inch, then added a slightly longer throw in the fifth round.

1992 Barcelona C: 27, N: 19, D: 8.2. WR: 86.74, 284-7 (Yuri Sedykh)

		M	FT.-IN.
1. Andrei Abduvaliyev	TJK	82.54	270-9
2. Igor Astapkovich	BLR	81.96	268-11
3. Igor Nikulin	RUS	81.38	267-0
4. Tibor Gécsek	HUN	77.78	255-2
5. Jüri Tamm	EST	77.52	254-4
6. Heinz Weis	GER	76.90	252-3
7. Lance Deal	USA	76.84	252-1
8. Sean Carlin	AUS	76.16	249-10

DISQ (Drugs): Jud Logan (USA) 79.00 259-2

Astapkovich and Abduvaliyev faced each other nine times in 1992. Astapkovich won eight of those encounters, but the ninth happened to be the Olympics. Astapkovich was leading when Abduvaliyev let fly his winner in the fourth round. Bronze medalist Igor Nikulin was the son of Yuri Nikulin, who placed fourth in 1964. The fourth-place finisher in 1992, Jud Logan, tested positive for the recently banned steroid substitute Clenbuterol and was disqualified.

1996 Atlanta C: 37, N: 22, D: 7.28. WR: 86.74, 284-7 (Yuri Sedykh)

		M	FT.-IN.
1. Balázs Kiss	HUN	81.24	266-6
2. Lance Deal	USA	81.12	266-2
3. Oleksiy Krykun	UKR	80.02	262-6
4. Andriy Skvaruk	UKR	79.92	262-2
5. Heinz Weis	GER	79.78	261-9
6. Ilya Konovalov	RUS	78.72	258-3
7. Igor Astapkovich	BLR	78.20	256-7
8. Sergei Alay	BLR	77.38	253-10

Born in Veszprén, Hungary, Balázs Kiss was a four-time US university champion representing the University of Southern California. Except for a few minutes in the second round, he led the final from start to finish. The fight for second place was more dramatic. After the third round, Lance Deal was tied for eighth place with Enrico Sgrulletti of Italy at 76.94 meters. Because Sgrulletti had a better second throw, Deal assumed that he was eliminated from the last three rounds of the competition. In fact, the rules did not provide for a tiebreaker and both men advanced. At that point, Andriy Skvaruk was in second place at 79.92 meters. The situation remained the same until the final round: Kiss leading, followed by Skvaruk and Oleksiy Krykun.

When Deal came up for his last throw, he was still in eighth place. But he uncorked a beauty that scared Kiss until it was measured at 81.12 meters, twelve centimeters short of Kiss' mark. Oleksiy Krykun threw an 80.02 to move ahead of Skvaruk, who dropped from silver to no medal in the final round.

2000 Sydney C: 44, N: 24, D: 9.24. WR: 86.74, 284-7 (Yuri Sedykh)

		M	FT.-IN.
1. Szymon Ziółkowski	POL	80.02	262-6
2. Nicola Vizzoni	ITA	79.64	261-3
3. Igor Astapkovich	BLR	79.17	259-9
4. Ivan Tikhon	BLR	79.17	259-9
5. Ilya Konovalov	RUS	78.56	257-9
6. Loris Paoluzzi	ITA	78.18	256-6
7. Tibor Gécsek	HUN	77.70	254-11
8. Vladimir Maska	CZE	77.32	253-8

The qualifying round saw the mass elimination of most of the favorites. Among the throwers who fell by the wayside were all of the medalists from the 1999 world championships—Karsten Kobs of Germany, Zsolt Németh of Hungary and Vladyslav Piskunov of Ukraine—1997 world champion Heinz Weis of Germany, defending Olympic silver medalist, Lance Deal of the United States, and Gilles Dupray of France, who had recorded a throw of 82.38 meters, the longest of the pre-Olympic season.

When the survivors gathered the next day for the final, they found themselves forced to compete in a rainstorm. Their first throws were all sluggish, but in the second round, lightly-regarded Szymon Ziółkowski, who had placed tenth at the 1996 Olympics, scored with a throw of 79.87 meters (262 feet). In the next round, another outsider, Nicola Vizzoni, hit a personal best of 79.64 meters (261 feet 3 inches) to take over second place. Ziólkowski added 15 centimeters in the fourth round, but from a competitive point of view, the only interest left was the battle for third place between two Belarussians, 37-year-old Igor Astapkovich and 24-year-old Ivan Tikhon. Tikhon reached 79.17 in the third round and Astapkovich matched him in the fifth round. However, Tikhon was still ahead on the basis of his superior second best throw: 78.11 meters. Then, with his final attempt, Astapkovich landed a throw of 79.06 to win the bronze medal.

2004 Athens C: 35, N: 24, D: 8.22. WR: 86.74, 284-7 (Yuri Sedykh)

		M	FT.-IN.
1. Koji Murofushi	JPN	82.91	272-0
2. Ivan Tikhon	BLR	79.81	261-10
3. Eşref Apak	TUR	79.51	260-10
4. Vadim Devyatovskiy	BLR	78.82	258-7
5. Krisztián Pars	HUN	78.73	258-3
6. Primož Kozmus	SLO	78.56	257-8
7. Libor Charfreitag	SLV	77.54	254-4
8. Karsten Kobs	GER	76.30	250-3

DISQ (Drugs): Adrian Annus (HUN) 83.19 (272-11)

Adrian Annus of Hungary was originally awarded the gold medal, but came under suspicion after his teammate, discus thrower Róbert Fazekas, was disqualified after being caught with a bag of urine hidden on his body. Fazekas and Annus trained together under the same coach. Annus, who passed his post-competition drug test, left the Olympic Village before he could be reached by officials for a second test, and he immediately announced his retirement. After Annus failed to show up for a second drug test, he was disqualified and stripped of his gold medal. He was the third Hungarian athlete to be stripped of a medal for doping violations during the Athens Games.

The gold medal passed to Koji Murofushi, who had placed second and third in the previous two world championships, and whose winning distance came on his final throw. His margin of victory was the largest in the event since 1920. When Eşref Apak moved up to bronze after Annus' disqualification, it meant that both Japan and Turkey earned a throwing medal for the first time. Murofushi came from a family of hammer throwers: his father Shigenobu was a three-time Olympian who finished eighth in 1972, and his sister Yuka placed 27th in the Athens Games. Murofushi won a bronze medal at the 2008 Olympics. Three years later, at the 2011 world championships in Daegu, he earned a surprise world title at the age of 37.

2008 Beijing C: 33, N: 26, D: 8.17. WR: 86.74, 284-7 (Yuri Sedykh)

		M	FT.-IN.
1. Primož Kozmus	SLO	82.02	269-1
2. Krisztián Pars	HUN	80.96	265-7
3. Koji Murofushi	JPN	80.71	264-10
4. Olli-Pekka Karjalainen	FIN	79.59	261-1
5. Szymon Ziółkowski	POL	79.22	259-11
6. Libor Charfreitag	SVK	78.65	258-0
7. Markus Esser	GER	77.10	253-0
8. András Haklits	CRO	76.58	251-3

DISQ (doping): Vadim Devyatovsky (BLR) 81.61m/267ft. 9in., Ivan Tikhon (BLR) 81.51/267ft. 5in.

Except for his second place finish at the 2004 Olympics, Ivan Tikhon had dominated international competition since 2003, winning back-to-back world championship titles and the 2006 European championship. At the 2007 world championships in Osaka, Japan, Slovenia's Primož Kozmus held the lead until the final round, when Tikhon recorded the longest throw of the year, 83.63 meters, to win his third straight world championship title. Defending Olympic champion Koji Murofushi finished a disappointing sixth at these championships after an exceptional 2006 season, going undefeated in eight competitions and winning the World Cup in Athens and World Athletics Final in Stuttgart.

As the Olympics approached, Tikhon was the clear favorite for gold, having recorded the longest throw of the year, 84.51 meters (277 ft. 3¼ in.). Meanwhile, Murofushi, in addition to training for the Olympics, pursued and obtained a doctoral degree in biomechanics, researching the mechanics of hammer throwing while also studying the history of Japanese sword fighting.

Tikhon, Murofushi and Kozmus made it through the qualifying round easily, with Hungary's Krisztián Pars recording the longest throw of the round, 80.07 meters (262 ft. 8¼ in.). In the final, Kozmus took the lead after the first round, with a throw of 80.75 (264 ft. 11¼ in.). He solidified this lead with a 82.02-meter (269 ft. 1 in.) throw in the second round, while Bulgaria's Vadim Devyatovsky moved into second place followed by Pars, Murofushi and Tikhon. None of the leaders were able to improve their results until the fifth round, when Tikhon moved into third place with a throw of 81.51 meters (267 ft. 5 in.). Kozmus became the first Olympic gold medalist to represent Slovenia. One year later, he won the world championship title in Berlin, and two months later he announced his surprise retirement from the sport.

The silver and bronze medals were more complicated. In a post-competition doping test, both Devyatovsky and Tikhon tested positive for elevated levels of testosterone. Four months after the competition, the IOC reached a decision to strip the two of their medals, moving Pars and Murofushi up to silver and bronze. Devyatovsky, who had already served a two-year drug suspension in 2000–2002, was hit with a lifetime ban, while Tikhon was given a two-year suspension.

In June 2010, however, the Court of Arbitration for Sport reinstated Devyatovsky and Tikhon, ruling that their doping results were invalid because the Beijing National Laboratory, which had carried out the tests, had violated "documentation and reporting requirements" by having the same analyst test both the A and B samples for each athlete. The CAS panel also noted, however, that the decision "should not be interpreted as an exoneration of the athletes" and that they did not say that the athletes were free of any doping suspicion.

The IOC has not yet responded to the CAS ruling.

JAVELIN THROW

A javelin must weigh a minimum of 800 grams (1 pound 12¼ ounces) and measure between 2.60 meters (8 feet 6¼ inches) and 2.70 meters (8 feet 10¼ inches). The shaft may be either wood or metal. In 1986, the balance point and grip of the men's javelin was moved up 10cm. and the tail was made narrower. These modifications were instituted in response to the increased frequency of dangerously long throws. For a throw to be considered valid the pointed metal head must break the turf. The javelin is thrown on the run and must be released above the shoulder. The runway is between 30 meters (98 feet 5 inches) and 36.5 meters (119 feet 9 inches) long. Each competitor may place one or two markers along the runway to assist in his or her run-up. Spinning around before throwing is illegal, since this technique could seriously discourage spectators from coming anywhere near the part of the stadium where the javelin competition is taking place.

1896–1906 not held

1908 London C: 16, N: 6, D: 7.17. WR: 54.40, 178-6 (Eric Lemming)

		M	FT.-IN.
1. Eric Lemming	SWE	54.825	179-10 WR
2. Arne Halse	NOR	50.57	165-11
3. Otto Nilsson	SWE	47.105	154-6
4. Aarne Salovaara	FIN	45.89	150-6
5. Armas Pesonen	FIN	45.18	148-3
6. Juho Halme	FIN	44.96	147-6
7. Jalmari Sauli	FIN	—	—

Eric Lemming, a 6-foot 3-inch, 26-year-old Stockholm policeman, had dominated javelin throwing since 1899.

1912 Stockholm C: 25, N: 7, D: 7.6. WR: 58.27, 191-2 (Eric Lemming)

		M	FT.-IN.
1. Eric Lemming	SWE	60.64	198-11 WR
2. Juho Saaristo	FIN	58.66	192-5
3. Móric Kovács-Kóczán	HUN/SLV	55.50	182-1
4. Juho Halme	FIN	54.65	179-3
5. Väinö Siikaniemi	FIN	52.43	172-0
6. Richard Åbrink	SWE	52.20	171-3
7. Arne Halse	NOR	51.98	170-6
8. Jonnas "Jonni" Myrrä	FIN	51.33	168-4

Lemming received a standing ovation from the hometown crowd after he made the world's first 60-meter throw. Three days later, while competing in the now discontinued combined left- and right-hand event, Juho Saaristo set a world record of 200 feet 1 inch using his right hand.

Eric Lemming, 1912
Perfect form and a pair of gold medals.

1920 Antwerp C: 25, N: 12, D: 8.15. WR: 66.10, 216-10 (Jonnas "Jonni" Myrrä)

		M	FT.-IN.
1. Jonnas "Jonni" Myrrä	FIN	65.78	215-10 OR
2. Urho Peltonen	FIN	63.605	208-8
3. Paavo "Pekka" Johansson-Jaale	FIN	63.095	207-0
4. Juho Saaristo	FIN	62.395	204-9
5. Aleksander Klumberg-Kolmpere	EST	62.39	204-8
6. Gunnar Lindström	SWE	60.52	198-7
7. Milton Angier	USA	59.275	194-5
8. Erik Blomqvist	SWE	58.18	190-10

1924 Paris C: 30, N: 13, D: 8.15. WR: 66.10, 216-10 (Jonnas "Jonni" Myrrä)

		M	FT.-IN.
1. Jonnas "Jonni" Myrrä	FIN	62.96	206-7
2. Gunnar Lindström	SWE	60.92	199-10
3. Eugene Oberst	USA	58.35	191-5
4. Yrjö Ekqvist	FIN	57.56	188-10
5. William Neufeld	USA	56.96	186-10
6. Erik Blomqvist	SWE	56.85	186-6
7. Urho Peltonen	FIN	55.66	182-7
8. Paavo "Pekka" Johansson-Jaale	FIN	55.10	180-9

The 32-year-old Myrrä successfully defended his title. However, he lost his world record two months later, when Lindström threw 66.62 meters (218 feet 7 inches).

1928 Amsterdam C: 28, N: 18, D: 8.2. WR: 69.88, 229-3 (Eino Penttilä)

		M	FT.-IN.
1. Erik Lundkvist	SWE	66.60	218-6 OR
2. Béla Szepes	HUN	65.26	214-1
3. Olav Sunde	NOR	63.97	209-10
4. Paavo Liettu	FIN	63.86	209-6
5. W. Bruno Schlokat	GER	63.40	208-0
6. Eino Penttilä	FIN	63.20	207-4
7. Stanley Lay	NZL	62.89	206-3
8. Johannes Meimer	EST	61.46	201-8

On October 8, 1927, Eino Penttilä recorded a throw of 69.88 meters (229 feet 3 inches) to improve the world record by an impressive 3.45 meters (10 feet 8 inches). In Amsterdam, however, Penttilä suffered from overtraining, the pressure of high expectations, and a sore foot, and was only able to finish sixth. The winner, sign painter Erik Lundkvist, went on to set a world record of 71.00 meters (232 feet 11 inches) two weeks later.

1932 Los Angeles C: 13, N: 7, D: 8.4. WR: 74.02, 242-10 (Matti Järvinen)

		M	FT.-IN.
1. Matti Järvinen	FIN	72.71	238-6 OR
2. Matti Sippala	FIN	69.80	229-0
3. Eino Penttilä	FIN	68.70	225-5
4. Gottfried Weimann	GER	68.18	223-8
5. Lee Bartlett	USA	64.46	211-6
6. Kenneth Churchill	USA	63.24	207-6
7. Malcolm Metcalf	USA	61.89	203-0
8. Kohsaku Sumiyoshi	JPN	61.14	200-7

Three sons of Finland's first gold medal winner, Verner Järvinen, took part in the 1932 Olympics, but only the youngest, Matti, won a gold medal. Matti's first five throws were the best of the competition, and all of them bettered the previous Olympic record. Matti didn't bother to take off the trousers of his track suit until the contest was over and it was time for photographs to be taken. Between 1930 and 1936 Matti Järvinen broke the javelin world record ten times and became known as "Mr. Javelin."

Matti Järvinen, 1932
Throwing for photographers after his gold medal performance, achieved while still wearing his sweat pants.

1936 Berlin C: 28, N: 19, D: 8.6. WR: 77.23, 253-4 (Matti Järvinen)

		M	FT.-IN.
1. Gerhard Stöck	GER	71.84	235-8
2. Yrjö Nikkanen	FIN	70.77	232-2
3. Kaarlo Kalervo Toivonen	FIN	70.72	232-0
4. Lennart Attervall	SWE	69.20	227-0
5. Matti Järvinen	FIN	69.18	227-0
6. Alton Terry	USA	67.15	220-4
7. Eugeniusz Lokajski	POL	66.39	217-9
8. József Várszegi	HUN	65.30	214-3

Gerhard Stöck, who had finished third in the shot put four days earlier, was in fifth place after four rounds. It was then that Adolf Hitler arrived in the stadium. With the crowd chanting, "Stöck, Stöck, don't be a wet blanket,' go ahead and finally throw 70 meters," Stöck unleashed a throw of almost 72 meters that turned out to be sufficient for the gold medal. Matti Järvinen, suffering from a back injury, was only able to place fifth.

1948 London C: 22, N: 15, D: 8.4. WR: 78.70, 258-2 (Yrjö Nikkanen)

		M	FT.-IN.
1. Kai Tapio Rautavaara	FIN	69.77	228-10
2. Steve Seymour	USA	67.56	221-8
3. József Várszegi	HUN	67.03	219-11
4. Pauli Vesterinen	FIN	65.89	216-2
5. Odd Maehlum	NOR	65.32	214-3
6. Martin Biles	USA	65.17	213-9
7. Mirko Vujačić	YUG/MNE	64.89	212-10
8. Robert Likens	USA	64.51	211-7

Marty Biles led the qualifying round with a throw of 222 feet, which would have been good enough for a silver medal if he had been able to repeat it in the final. Two years after his Olympic triumph, Tapio Rautavaara won a world championship gold medal—in team archery. He later became a successful folksinger and film actor. While posing for a photograph, he fell and hit his head on a concrete floor; he died on September 25, 1979, at the age of 64. The 1999 fictional film *Kulkuri ja joutsen* was based on that period of Rautavaara's life when he was a travelling singer.

1952 Helsinki C: 26, N: 16, D: 7.23. WR: 78.70, 258-2 (Yrjö Nikkanen)

		M	FT.-IN.
1. Cyrus Young	USA	73.78	242-1 OR
2. William Miller	USA	72.46	237-9
3. Toivo Hyytiäinen	FIN	71.89	235-10
4. Viktor Tsybulenko	SOV/UKR	71.72	234-4
5. Branko Dangubić	YUG/SER	70.55	231-5
6. Vladimir Kuznetsov	SOV/RUS	70.37	230-10
7. Ragnar Ericzon	SWE	69.04	226-6
8. Soini Nikkinen	FIN	68.80	225-9

The two American medalists presented an unusual contrast. Cy Young, who celebrated his 24th birthday by winning the gold medal, was 6 feet 5 inches (1.96 meters) tall, while Bill Miller was only 5 feet 9 inches (1.75 meters). When a third American, ninth-place finisher Bud Held, broke Yrjö Nikkanen's 15-year-old world record in 1953, it looked like the United States had found itself another specialty. However, the expected US dominance did not materialize.

1956 Melbourne C: 21, N: 12, D: 11.26. WR: 83.66, 274-6 (Janusz Sidlo)

		M	FT.-IN.
1. Egil Danielsen	NOR	85.71	281-2 WR
2. Janusz Sidlo	POL	79.98	262-5
3. Viktor Tsybulenko	SOV/UKR	79.50	260-10
4. Herbert Koschel	GER	74.68	245-0
5. Jan Kopyto	POL	74.28	243-8
6. Giovanni Lievore	ITA	72.88	239-1
7. Michel Macquet	FRA	71.84	235-8
8. Aleksandr Gorshkov	SOV/RUS	70.32	230-8

Cy Young led the qualifying round with a throw of 245 feet 3 inches. After three rounds of the final, Sidlo was in first place, followed by Tsybulenko and Koschel. Egil Danielsen, who had won 36 consecutive meets, was only in sixth place. At this time, all throwers were using wooden javelins—except Janusz Sidlo, who was using a new Swedish one made of steel. Sidlo suggested that Danielsen try the steel implement. Danielsen accepted the offer and began preparing for his next throw. At that moment, Michel Macquet approached Danielsen and offered him a cup of strong coffee. "I never drink coffee," Danielsen later recalled. "After this cup, I almost had a shock. My heart began to beat fast and I was sweating. I took the steel javelin, made a good run and a powerful stroke." Danielsen's enormous throw broke the world record and almost landed on the runway of the pole vault. "Such a fantastic result I never suspected—85.71 meters! I was crazy with joy. Sidlo was the first to congratulate me." It would prove to be the longest throw of Danielsen's career.

1960 Rome C: 28, N: 18, D: 9.8. WR: 86.04, 282-3 (Albert Cantello)

		M	FT.-IN.
1. Viktor Tsybulenko	SOV/UKR	84.64	277-8
2. Walter Krüger	GDR	79.36	260-4
3. Gergely Kulcsár	HUN	78.57	257-9
4. Väinö Kuisma	FIN	78.40	257-3
5. Willy Rasmussen	NOR	78.36	257-1
6. Knut Fredriksson	SWE	78.33	256-11
7. Zbigniew Radziwonowicz	POL	77.30	253-7
8. Janusz Sidlo	POL	76.46	250-10

In 1960 the javelin throw turned out to be a strange contest. The preliminary round was led by Janusz Sidlo at 279 feet 4 inches and Al Cantello at 261 feet 6 inches. If Sidlo and Cantello had been able to reproduce their form in the final, they would have finished first and third. Instead, they ended up eighth and tenth. The preliminary round also saw the elimination of defending champion Egil Danielsen and Bill Alley of the United States, who had a pending (and subsequently never ratified) world record of 283 feet 8 inches. The final was settled early with Viktor Tsybulenko's first-round throw of 277 feet 8 inches. Gusty winds and rain disrupted the competition from the second round on, and no one, Tsybulenko included, was able to do better than 257 feet 1 inch after that.

1964 Tokyo C: 25, L: 15, D: 10.14. WR: 91.72, 300-11 (Terje Pedersen)

		M	FT.-IN.
1. Pauli Nevala	FIN	82.66	271-2
2. Gergely Kulcsár	HUN	82.32	270-1
3. Jānis Lūsis	SOV/LAT	80.57	264-4
4. Janusz Sidlo	POL	80.17	263-0
5. Urs von Wartburg	SWI	78.72	258-3
6. Jorma Kinnunen	FIN	76.94	252-5
7. Rolf Herings	GER	74.72	245-2
8. Vladimir Kuznetsov	SOV/RUS	74.26	243-8

On September 2, 1964, Terje Pedersen shocked the track and field world with a monster throw of 300 feet 11 inches that bettered his own world record by 15 feet 1 inch. Yet six weeks later in Tokyo, he could do no better than 236 feet 6 inches, and failed to qualify for the final. The 1964 Olympic competition, like the one in 1960, was marred by wind and rain. Janusz Sidlo had the best throw of the first round of the final at 263 feet. Jānis Lūsis took the lead in the second round with a throw of 264 feet 4 inches. But the real action took place in the fourth round. Ever-consistent Gergely Kulcsár reached 270 feet 1 inch, only to be topped by unheralded Pauli Nevala at 271 feet 2 inches. Von Wartburg's final throw appeared good enough for a silver medal, but was declared invalid on the grounds that it landed incorrectly, a ruling that raised many eyebrows.

Finnish Olympic officials had been criticized for wasting their money sending Nevala to Tokyo, particularly after he had failed to win the national championship. "Even if I'm not the Finnish champion," Nevala commented, "at least I've won the Olympics."

1968 Mexico City C: 27, N: 18, D: 10.16. WR: 91.98, 301-9 (Jānis Lūsis)

		M	FT.-IN.	
1. Jānis Lūsis	SOV/LAT	90.10	295-7	OR
2. Jorma Kinnunen	FIN	88.58	290-7	
3. Gergely Kulcsár	HUN	87.06	285-7	
4. Wladislaw Nikiciuk	POL	85.70	281-2	
5. Manfred Stolle	GDR	84.42	277-0	
6. Åke Nilsson	SWE	83.48	273-11	
7. Janusz Sidlo	POL	80.58	264-4	
8. Urs von Wartburg	SWI	80.56	264-4	

A surprising thing happened in the 1968 javelin competition: for the first time since 1932, it was won by the favorite. The first-round lead went to 5-foot 9-inch, 165-pound Jorma Kinnunen. Popular Jānis Lūsis of Latvia, who was married to Elvira Ozolina, winner of the 1960 women's javelin, edged ahead by four centimeters in the second round. In the fourth round, Gergely Kulcsár moved in front with a personal and Olympic record of 285 feet 7 inches. And so the situation stood with one round remaining: Kulcsár in first, followed by Lūsis and Kinnunen. Lūsis calmly took his spear in hand and made his last attempt his best—295 feet 7 inches. He had one more moment of concern when Kinnunen also came up with a clutch performance, 290 feet 7 inches, but the Finn had to be content with second place. Janusz Sidlo, competing in his fifth Olympics, finished a creditable seventh. Kinnunen's son, Kimmo, placed fourth in 1992 after winning the 1991 world championship.

1972 Munich C: 23, N: 15, D: 9.3. WR: 93.80, 307-9 (Jānis Lūsis)

		M	FT.-IN.	
1. Klaus Wolfermann	GER	90.48	296-10	OR
2. Jānis Lūsis	SOV/LAT	90.46	296-9	
3. William Schmidt	USA	84.42	277-0	
4. Hannu Siitonen	FIN	84.32	276-8	
5. Björn Grimnes	NOR	83.08	272-7	
6. Jorma Kinnunen	FIN	82.08	269-3	
7. Miklos Németh	HUN	81.98	268-11	
8. Frederick Luke	USA	80.06	262-8	

Jānis Lūsis dominated javelin throwing between Olympics. In 1972 no one came within 17 feet of his performance of the year until one week before the Munich Games, when Klaus Wolfermann hit 296 feet 7 inches. In the Olympic final, Lūsis had the first big throw—291 feet 7 inches in the first round. He improved to 293 feet 9 inches with his third attempt. Wolfermann, cheered on by the German crowd, picked up steam in the fourth round with a throw of 290 feet. Then, in the fifth round, he caused the spectators to roar with excitement when he exploded for a personal best of 296 feet 10 inches. However, Jānis Lūsis still had one attempt left, and many remembered his dramatic last-round victory four years earlier. Sure enough, Lūsis let loose a big one. Wolfermann and his supporters waited anxiously for the measurement. And then it came—296 feet 9 inches. The two-centimeter difference is the smallest unit of measurement used in javelin competitions. One more inch and Lūsis would have won on the basis of a longer second throw.

When Jānis Lūsis was six years old, he had been forced to watch the execution of his father by Russian soldiers.

Tuita Lolesio, who had finished in eleventh place, was the first Olympian to hail from the small French colony of Wallis and Futuna in the South Pacific.

1976 Montreal C: 23, N: 15, D: 7.25. WR: 94.08, 308-8 (Klaus Wolfermann)

		M	FT.-IN.
1. Miklos Németh	HUN	94.58	310-4 WR
2. Hannu Siitonen	FIN	87.92	288-5
3. Gheorghe Megelea	ROM	87.16	285-11
4. Pyotr Bielczyk	POL	86.50	283-9
5. Sam Colson	USA	86.16	282-8
6. Vasyl Yershov	SOV/UKR	85.26	279-9
7. Seppo Hovinen	FIN	84.26	276-5
8. Jānis Lūsis	SOV/LAT	80.26	263-4

Miklos Németh was less than two years old when his father, Imre, won the gold medal for the hammer throw at the 1948 Olympics in London. His father pressed him to take up the hammer, but Miklos preferred the javelin, and by 1967 he was ranked second in the world. But he never performed well in major championships. In the 1968 Olympics an elbow injury kept Miklos from qualifying for the final. In 1972 he was one of the favorites, but finished a disappointing seventh. His father said he was too gentle. His critics said he was a choker. Miklos himself said, "It is not an easy thing in my country to be the son of an Olympic champion."

Then came Montreal. Now 29 years old and no longer a favorite, Miklos Németh was almost ignored as interest centered on the leading contenders, Hovinen, Siitonen, and Bielczyk. Németh was the tenth man up in the final, and with his first attempt he uncorked a beauty. He tried not to watch it, but kept looking back as the spear sailed on and on until it finally landed 310 feet 4 inches away from the throwing area. It was ten and a half feet farther than Németh had ever thrown before. It was also a new world record.

While Németh jumped for joy, the rest of the javelin throwers were absolutely demoralized. The remaining medals, it turned out, were also decided by first-round throws. Hovinen, who had led the qualifiers at 294 feet 6 inches, could do no better than 276 feet 5 inches. Nineteen-year-old Phil Olson of Canada, who had qualified with a throw of 287 feet 11 inches, finished 11th at 254 feet 11 inches. Németh was so excited that he had to pass the next two rounds. His winning margin was the widest in any field event in Olympic history (excluding the Intercalated Games of 1906). Imre and Miklos Németh are the only father-and-son combination ever to win track and field gold medals at the Olympics.

1980 Moscow C: 18, N: 11, D: 7.27. WR: 96.72, 317-4 (Ferenc Paragi)

		M	FT.-IN.
1. Dainis Kūla	SOV/LAT	91.20	299-2
2. Aleksandr Makarov	SOV/RUS	89.64	294-1
3. Wolfgang Hanisch	GDR	86.72	284-6
4. Heino Puuste	SOV/EST	86.10	282-6
5. Antero Puranen	FIN	85.12	279-3
6. Pentti Sinersaari	FIN	84.34	276-8
7. Detlef Fuhrrnann	GDR	83.50	273-11
8. Miklos Németh	HUN	82.40	270-4

Only twice since World War II has the leader of the qualifying round in the javelin gone on to victory, the exceptions being Klaus Wolfermann in 1972 and Jan Železny in 1992. Unfortunately for world record holder Ferenc Paragi, the jinx continued. After a preliminary throw of 291 feet 2 inches, his best in the final was only 260 feet 11 inches and he placed tenth. After two rounds, the leader was Wolfgang Hanisch, followed by Heino Puuste. The decisive moment came at the end of the third round. The last man to throw was Dainis Kūla, a 21-year-old Latvian. Having fouled on his first two attempts, Kūla needed not only a valid throw, but a big one, just to qualify for the extra three attempts accorded the top eight. To most observers, Kūla's third try appeared to land tail first and then bounce, which should have led to his immediate elimination. Instead, Soviet officials rushed out to measure it and announced a valid throw of 291 feet 7 inches. Taking advantage of his questionable reprieve, Kūla followed with an excellent, and perfectly legal, throw of 299 feet 2 inches that held up for the gold medal.

The US team trials had been won by Rod Ewaliko at 291 feet, but Bruce Kennedy, who finished second, set what must be an Olympic record—and a most unfortunate one. A citizen of Zimbabwe, then known as Rhodesia, Kennedy had gone to Munich in 1972 as part of his nation's Olympic team. However, pressure from black African nations opposed to Rhodesia's white minority government prevented the Rhodesians from competing. In 1976 Kennedy was again selected to compete in the Olympics, but again Rhodesia was excluded. Meanwhile, Kennedy had moved to the United States and married an American. In 1977 he became a US citizen. In 1980 he qualified for the US team, but, for the third time, he was prevented from competing in the Olympics because of politics. Ironically, Zimbabwe, now ruled by its black majority, was readmitted into the Olympic movement and allowed to take part in the Moscow Games. In 1984 Bruce Kennedy, who by this time had earned a master's degree from Stanford University, finally made it inside an Olympic Stadium—as an usher.

1984 Los Angeles C: 28, N: 19, D: 8.5. WR: 104.80, 343-10 (Uwe Hohn)

		M	FT.-IN.
1. Arto Härkönen	FIN	86.76	284-8
2. David Ottley	GBR	85.74	281-3

3. Kenth Eldebrink	SWE	83.72	274-8
4. Wolfram Gambke	GER	82.46	270-6
5. Masami Yoshida	JPN	81.98	268-11
6. Einar Vilhjalmsson	ICE	81.58	267-8
7. A. Roald Bradstock	GBR	81.22	266-6
8. Laslo Babits	CAN	80.68	264-8

On May 15, 1983, Tom Petranoff of the United States broke Ferenc Paragi's three-year-old world record by almost ten feet with a throw of 327 feet 2 inches (99.72 meters). At the world championships three months later, Petranoff was beaten by East Germany's Detlef Michel, with 1980 Olympic champion Dainis Kūla in third place. It seemed just a matter of time before Petranoff or Michel broke through the 100-meter barrier. However, on July 20, 1984, it was another East German, 22-year-old Uwe Hohn, who accomplished the feat. And Hohn, who also held the East German national record for throwing a 21-ounce grenade (328 feet 2 inches), did it in grand style with a massive throw of 343 feet 10 inches (104.80 meters)—the greatest world record improvement in javelin history.

With Hohn, Michel, and Kūla among the boycott missing, Petranoff found himself in the unusual and uncomfortable position of being the favorite in the most important meet of his career, the 1984 Olympics. Petranoff led the qualifying round with a throw of 282 feet, but like Ferenc Paragi four years earlier, he could do no better than tenth place in the final. David Ottley took the surprise early lead with a near-personal best of 281 feet 3 inches. But in the fourth round, Arto Härkönen, whose father was the coach of women's silver medallist Tuna Lillak, launched a throw of 284 feet 8 inches, to bring Finland its first javelin gold medal in twenty years.

1988 Seoul C: 38, N: 22, D: 9.25. WR: 87.66, 287-7 (Jan Železný)

		M	FT.-IN.
1. Tapio Korjus	FIN	84.28	276-6
2. Jan Železný	CZE	84.12	276-0
3. Seppo Räty	FIN	83.26	273-2
4. Klaus Tafelmeier	GER	82.72	271-5
5. Viktor Yevsyukov	SOV/UKR	82.32	270-1
6. Gerald Weiss	GDR	81.30	266-9
7. Vladimir Ovchinnikov	SOV/RUS	79.12	259-7
8. Dag Wennlund	SWE	78.30	256-11

World record holder Jan Železný recorded the longest throw of the qualifying round at 281 feet 10 inches. In the final, Tapio Korjus took the first-round lead with a throw of 271 feet 5 inches. The second round was highlighted by throws of 270 feet 1 inch by both Železný and Viktor Yevsyukov. Seppo Räty, practically unknown when he won the 1987 world championship, moved ahead in the third round with a throw of 273 feet 2 inches. Meanwhile, Korjus passed his next two opportunities because of a cramp in his left leg. In his absence, Železný regained the lead by 8 inches. Korjus returned for the fifth round, but fouled. In the sixth and final round, Železný reached 276 feet to lengthen his lead. Korjus, in third place, was the final thrower of the competition. "This is all or nothing," he thought. "It was a good throw," he said of his last attempt. "You know it when you see only a dot against the sky." It landed 6 inches beyond Železný's mark to give Finland its seventh javelin gold.

1992 Barcelona C: 32, N: 21, D: 8.8. WR: 91.46, 300-1 (Stephen Backley)

		M	FT.-IN.
1. Jan Železný	CZE	89.66	294-2 OR
2. Seppo Räty	FIN	86.60	284-1
3. Stephen Backley	GBR	83.38	273-7
4. Kimmo Kinnunen	FIN	82.62	271-1
5. Sigurdur Einarsson	ICE	80.34	263-7
6. Juha Laukkanen	FIN	79.20	259-10
7. Michael Barnett	USA	78.64	258-0
8. Andrei Shevchuk	RUS	77.74	255-1

On July 4, Jan Železný obliterated the world record with a throw of 310 feet 10 inches. However, controversy immediately developed over whether Železný's Németh 2000 javelin, which had already been disallowed for the Olympics itself, was a legal implement. The issue was considered of such great significance in Finland that Finnish track officials took apart the Németh 2000 on live television to show that it contained graphite fiber and did not meet IAAF specifications. When the javelin area was laid out on the morning of the Olympic final, a marker was set at 310 feet 10 inches to indicate the world record. But less than an hour before the beginning of the competition, the marker was moved back to 300 feet 1 inch, the record set by Steve Backley on January 25. Far from being discouraged by this setback, Železný was inspired. Since his silver medal at the 1988 Olympics, he had not done well in major meets, failing to qualify for the final in the 1990 European Championships and the 1991 World Championships in Athletics. Now he had the added incentive of losing his world record. In fact, Železný settled the matter with his first throw, breaking his own Olympic record by 12 feet 4 inches.

1996 Atlanta C: 34, N: 21, D: 8.3. WR: 98.48, 323-1 (Jan Železný)

		M	FT.-IN.
1. Jan Železný	CZE	88.16	289-3
2. Stephen Backley	GBR	87.44	286-11
3. Seppo Raty	FIN	86.98	285-4
4. Raymond Hecht	GER	86.88	285-0
5. Boris Henry	GER	85.68	281-1
6. Sergei Makarov	RUS	85.30	279-10
7. Kimmo Kinnunen	FIN	84.02	275-8
8. Tom Pukstys	USA	83.58	274-3

At 77 kilograms (173 pounds), Jan Železný was the lightest of the 34 competitors. Nonetheless, he was very much the favorite. He was the defending Olympic champion, the two-time defending world champion and the reigning world record holder since 1993 (including a new record on May 25, 1996).

Jan Železný, 1996
Spearing a second of three gold medals, to go with the silver he won in his first Olympics at Seoul.

Železný's rival—and sometimes training partner—Steve Backley opened the final with a toss of 87.44 meters. In the second round, Železný threw 88.16 meters and the race for gold and silver was over. Seppo Raty edged past Raymond Hecht in the final round to secure the bronze so that all three medalists from 1992 were back on the podium in 1996.

2000 Sydney C: 36, N: 26, D: 9.23. WR: 98.48, 323-1 (Jan Železný)

		M	FT.-IN.
1. Jan Železný	CZE	90.17	295-10
2. Steve Backley	GBR	89.85	294-9
3. Sergei Makarov	RUS	88.67	290-11
4. Raymond Hecht	GBR	87.76	287-11
5. Aki Parvianen	FIN	86.62	284-2
6. Konstantinos Gatsioudis	GRE	86.53	283-10
7. Boris Henry	GER	85.78	281-5
8. Emeterio González Silva	CUB	83.33	273-4

Jan Železný's illustrious career appeared to come to an abrupt end one day in April 1998. He was doing sprint training with a weighted elastic band when the ten-kilogram weight hit him on the ankle. He fell and landed badly, separating his right shoulder. He resumed training seven months later and, at the age of 34, he was ready to continue his rivalry with Steve Backley, who also happened to be a friend and training partner. By this time, Železný had set five world records and won two Olympic gold medals and two world championships. Backley had earned bronze and silver at the Olympics and two silver medals at world championships, but he had also won the European championship three times in a row.

Železný led the qualifying round with a throw of 89.39 meters (293 feet 3 inches). In the opening round of the final, he threw down the gauntlet with a toss of 89.41 meters (293 feet 4 inches). Sergei Makarov, whose father had won a silver medal in the 1980 javelin competition, followed with an 88.67 opener that would ultimately hold up for the bronze medal. Backley rose to the occasion with a second round throw of 89.85 meters (294 feet 9 inches), his longest throw in eight years and an Olympic record. Zelezný felt ready to respond in the third round, but he was forced to wait while the runway was blocked for the medal presentation of the women's 100 meters. Železný paced impatiently. When he was finally allowed to resume the competition, he threw 90.17 meters (295 feet 10 inches) to regain first place. The top five positions remained unchanged for the remainder of the contest, although Železný did add a final throw of 88.97 (291 feet 10 inches) for good measure. Železný became the first javelin thrower to earn three gold medals and the first to win four total medals. Neither Železný nor Backley was finished with their careers: Železný won another world championship in 2001, while Backley won a fourth European title in 2002.

2004 Athens C: 33, N: 23, D: 8.28. WR: 98.48, 323-1 (Jan Železný)

		M	FT.-IN.
1. Andreas Thorkildsen	NOR	86.50	283-9
2. Vadims Vasilevskis	LAT	84.95	278-8
3. Sergei Makarov	RUS	84.84	278-4
4. Steve Backley	GBR	84.13	276-0
5. Aleksandr Ivanov	RUS	83.31	273-3
6. Andrus Värnik	EST	83.25	273-1
7. Ēriks Rags	LAT	83.14	272-9
8. Tero Pitkämäki	FIN	83.01	272-4

Twenty-two-year-old Andreas Thorkildsen was a surprise gold medalist, having placed only eleventh at the 2003 world championships. He entered the final in Athens with only the ninth-best qualifying throw. American Breaux Greer, who was suffering from a torn anterior cruciate ligament (ACL) in his left knee, recorded a huge first throw of 87.25 meters (286 feet 3 inches) to lead the qualifying round, a distance that would have earned him the gold medal had he been able to reproduce it in the final. However, he reinjured his knee in the process, and instead placed last in the final. Meanwhile, 22-year-old Vadims Vasilevskis recorded a personal best of 84.95 meters (278 feet 8 inches) with his first throw to take the lead in the final, while 2003 world champion Sergei Makarov, the favorite in the event, held second place with a throw of 84.84 meters (278 feet 4 inches). Thorkildsen opened in third place with a throw of 84.83 meters (278 feet 3 inches), the second-best throw of his career. In round two, Thorkildsen shocked the field by moving into first place with a personal record of 86.50 meters (283 feet 9 inches), that held up for the gold medal. After the competition, Thorkildsen remarked, "If you had said the words 'Olympic champion' to me yesterday, I wouldn't have believed you. But now it sounds great."

2008 Beijing C: 38, N: 29, D: 8.23. WR: 98.48, 323-1 (Jan Železný)

		M	FT.-IN.
1. Andreas Thorkildsen	NOR	90.57	297-2 OR
2. Ainārs Kovals	LAT	86.64	284-3
3. Tero Pitkämäki	FIN	86.16	282-8
4. Tero Järvenpää	FIN	83.95	275-5
5. Teemu Wirkkala	FIN	83.46	273-10
6. Jarrod Bannister	AUS	83.45	273-9
7. Ilya Korotkov	RUS	83.15	272-10
8. Uladzimir Kazlou	BLR	82.06	269-3

After his surprising win at the 2004 Olympics, where he improved his personal best by nearly a meter, Thorkildsen had developed a friendly rivalry with Finland's Tero Pitkämäki.

Thorkildsen finished second in the 2005 world championships, behind Estonia's Andrus Värnik, and then won the 2006 European championship ahead of Pitkämäki. In July 2007, at an IAAF Golden League event in Rome, a throw by Pitkämäki veered off course and struck French long-jumper Salim Sdiri in the back, puncturing his liver and kidney—Sdiri was rushed to hospital, but made a full recovery—while understandably distracted Pitkämäki finished second behind Thorkildsen. The competition was held on Friday the 13th. A month and a half later, Pitkämäki beat Thorkildsen at the world championships in Osaka, Japan. The two had also topped the IAAF world rankings each year since 2004, with Thorkildsen number one in 2004 and 2006 and Pitkämäki number one in 2005 and 2007.

Thorkildsen was never seriously challenged in Beijing, recording the longest throws in each of the first three rounds and breaking Jan Železný's Olympic record with a fifth-round throw of 90.57 meters (297 ft. 1¾ in.). In third place after the first three rounds, Pitkämäki moved into second place in the fourth round, but was passed in the final round by Ainārs Kovals, who recorded a personal best on his final throw to take the silver.

One year after defending his Olympic gold medal, Thorkildsen won his first world championship title and became the first javelin thrower to simultaneously hold the world, Olympic and European titles.

DECATHLON

The decathlon consists of ten events held over a two-day period. On the first day, the athletes take part in the 100-meter dash, long jump, shot put, high jump, and 400-meter run. On the second day they compete in the 110-meter hurdles, discus throw, pole vault, javelin throw, and 1500-meter run. Rules for these events are generally the same as for the equivalent individual events. Notable exceptions are that in the running events each contestant is allowed two false starts instead of one, and in the long jump and the three throwing events, each contestant is allowed only three attempts. Points are scored according to a set of tables approved by the International Amateur Athletic Federation. The tables currently in use were devised in 1962 and revised in 1971 and 1977 to take into account the advent of automatic electronic timing, with accuracy to ⅟₁₀₀ second. They were further adjusted in 1985. The 1985 equivalent of each athlete's performance is included here for the purpose of historical comparison. If two contestants finish with the same point total, the tie is won by whichever competitor had a higher point total in the most separate events. If a tie still exists, the winner is the competitor who earned the most points for any single event.

Decathletes tend to show up later as movie actors. Jim Thorpe was an extra in several Westerns, Glenn Morris played Tarzan, Floyd Simmons was in *South Pacific,* Bob Mathias acted with Jayne Mansfield in *It Happened in Athens.* Rafer Johnson and C.K. Yang also appeared in movies. The 1976 gold medalist Bruce Jenner made his screen debut in *Can't Stop the Music,* one of the worst films ever made. Dennis Weaver, who became famous for his roles in the television series *Gunsmoke* and *McCloud,* placed sixth in the 1948 US Olympic trials.

1896–1900 not held

1904 St. Louis C: 7, N: 2, D: 7.4.

		100 YDS	SP	HJ	800-YD WALK	HAM	PV	120-YD. H	56-LB. THROW	LJ	MILE	TOTAL POINTS
1. Thomas Kiely	IRL	11.2e	10.82	1.52	3:59.0	36.76	2.74	17.8	8.91	5.94	5:51.0	6036
2. Adam Gunn	USA	11.2e	12.21	1.65	4:13.0	31.40	2.97	17.9e	7.22	5.53	5:45.0	5907
3. T. Truxtun Hare	USA	10.8	12.09	1.52	4:20.0	36.28	2.44	18.27e	7.59	6.07	5:40.0	5813
4. John Holloway	IRL	10.9e	10.01	1.68	3:59.0	27.51	2.89	18.33e	5.98	5.53	5:40.0	5273
5. Ellery Clark	USA	11.0	10.26	1.62	4:11.0	29.11	DNF	—	—	—	—	2778
6. John Grieb	USA	11.2e	10.54	1.62	4:49.0	DNF	—	—	—	—	—	2199

This competition was known as the "All-Around Championship" and was noteworthy because all ten events were held on the same day. Offered a free trip if he would compete for Great Britain, 34-year-old Tom Kiely, of Ballyneale in County Tipperary, refused, paid his own way, and competed for Ireland. In 1899 Kiely had held the world record in the hammer throw for a period of 46 days.

1906–1908 not held

1912 Stockholm C: 29, N: 12, D: 7.13-15. WR: 7414 (James Austin Menaul)

		100 M	LJ	SP	HJ	400 M	DISC	110 H	PV	JAV	1500 M	TOTAL POINTS	1985 TABLES
1. James Thorpe	USA	11.2	6.79	12.89	1.87	52.2	36.98	15.6	3.25	45.70	4:40.1	8413 WR	6564
2. Hugo Wieslander	SWE	11.8	6.42	12.14	1.75	53.6	36.29	17.2	3.10	50.40	4:45.0	7724	5965
3. Charles Lomberg	SWE	11.8	6.87	11.67	1.80	55.0	35.35	17.6	3.25	41.83	5:12.2	7414	5721
4. Gustaf "Gösta" Holmér	SWE	11.4	5.98	10.98	1.70	53.2	31.78	17.0	3.20	46.28	4:41.9	7348	5768
5. James Donahue	USA	11.8	6.48	9.67	1.65	51.6	29.95	16.2	3.40	37.09	4:44.0	7083	5701
6. Eugene Leroy Mercer	USA	11.0	6.84	9.76	1.65	49.9	21.95	16.4	3.60	32.32	4:46.3	7075	5825
7. J. Valdemar Wickholm	FIN	11.5	5.95	11.09	1.60	52.3	29.78	17.0	3.25	42.58	4:43.9	7059	5676
8. Erik Kugelberg	SWE	12.3	6.20	9.98	1.65	55.8	31.48	17.2	3.00	45.67	4:43.5	6759	5346

James Francis Thorpe was born on May 28, 1887, on a farm near the town of Bellemont in what was then known as the Oklahoma Territory. His father was part Irish, part Sac and Fox Indian. His mother, who was part Potawatomie and Kickapoo Indian and part French, gave him the Indian name Wa-Tho-Huck, or "Bright Path." Jim's twin brother, Charles, died of pneumonia at the age of 8. His mother died when he was 12 and his father when he was 15. Educated at the government-run Indian schools of Haskell and Carlisle, Jim Thorpe did not become a noteworthy athlete until 1907. In the spring of that year he walked past the track area where the high jumpers were trying—and failing—to clear 5 feet 9 inches. Thorpe, dressed in work clothes, went over the bar on his first attempt, setting a school record.

He first came to national prominence as a football player. In 1911, tiny Carlisle upset Harvard 18-15, with Thorpe scoring all of Carlisle's points on four field goals and a touchdown. The following year against Army, he ran 92 yards for a touchdown, only to have the score nullified because of a penalty. On the next play, he ran 97 yards for a touchdown. Thorpe was chosen as an All-American halfback in both 1911 and 1912. An all-around athlete, he earned varsity letters in 11 different sports, and even won the 1912 intercollegiate ballroom

Jim Thorpe, 1912
Thorpe led a ticker-tape parade in New York City following his victories in the decathlon and pentathlon in 1912. "I heard people yelling my name," he recalled, "and I couldn't realize how one fellow could have so many friends."

dancing championship. He so excelled at track and field that he was chosen to represent the United States at the 1912 Olympics.

In Stockholm, Thorpe began by winning the pentathlon. The next day, while the other pentathletes were recuperating, Thorpe was back on the field taking fourth place in the high jump. He also finished seventh in the long jump. Finally, he took part in the decathlon, which was spread over three days because of the large number of entrants. Although he had never before competed in a decathlon, and had never thrown a javelin until two months earlier, he won easily. His performance was so impressive that it would have earned him a silver medal in the *1948* Olympics.

Besides his gold medals, Thorpe was awarded a jewel-encrusted chalice by Czar Nicholas of Russia, in honor of his victory in the decathlon, and a bronze bust of King Gustav V of Sweden for winning the pentathlon. When Gustav handed Jim the bust, he said, "Sir, you are the greatest athlete in the world." To which Thorpe allegedly replied shyly, "Thanks, King."

Back in the United States, Jim Thorpe had become a national hero. Honored with a ticker-tape parade down Broadway in New York City, Jim marveled at the experience. "I heard people yelling my name—and I couldn't realize how one fellow could have so many friends," he recalled.

But in January 1913, Thorpe received a hard blow. It was revealed that in 1909 and 1910 he had earned $25 a week playing minor league baseball in North Carolina. Thus, by the strictest definition of the word, he had been a professional athlete and therefore ineligible to compete in the Olympics. Thorpe wrote a letter to James E. Sullivan, chairman of the Amateur Athletic Union, admitting what he had done but asking for leniency.

"I hope I will be partly excused by the fact that I was simply an Indian schoolboy and did not know all about such things," he wrote. "In fact, I did not know that I was doing wrong because I was doing what I knew several other college men had done except that they did not use their own names.

"I have received offers amounting to thousands of dollars since my victories last summer, but I have turned them all down because I did not care to make money from my athletic skill. . . . I hope the Amateur Athletic Union and the people will not be too hard in judging me."

The "people" were not hard in judging Jim Thorpe, and generally rallied to his side. The AAU, on the other hand, was very hard in judging him. He was publicly vilified and his name was stricken from all record books. The American Olympic Committee issued a formal apology to the International Olympic Committee,

Jim Thorpe
A man for all seasons.

which asked for the return of Thorpe's medals and trophies.

As soon as he was declared a professional, Thorpe received offers to play major-league baseball. He signed with the New York Giants first, and played as well for the Cincinnati Reds and the Boston Braves until 1919. He also played professional football between 1915 and 1928. During the Depression, Jim Thorpe drifted from job to job. He was discovered wielding a pick and shovel at a construction site in Los Angeles, and when the 1932 Olympics came to town he was invited to sit with US Vice-President Charles Curtis, who was also part Indian. Such high spots were few, however. He worked as an extra in Hollywood, mostly playing Indian chiefs (although he did appear as a dancer in *King Kong*), gave lectures, joined the Merchant Marine in 1945, and took a job as a bouncer in 1949.

In February 1950, a poll of sportswriters taken by the Associated Press voted Thorpe the greatest athlete of the first half of the century. The following year *Jim Thorpe—All-American,* a film based on his life and starring Burt Lancaster, was released. Yet two months later, when Jim was hospitalized with cancer of the lip, he was admitted as a charity case because he had no money. He had sold the film rights to his life to MGM in 1931 for $1500. When MGM sold the rights to Warner Bros., Thorpe thought he would be paid again, but he had failed to read the fine print. He died of a heart attack in Lomita, California, on March 28, 1953. Thorpe was buried in Mauch Chunk, Pennsylvania, a small town which agreed to change its name to Jim Thorpe in return for the right to have his body.

The movement to reinstate Jim Thorpe's records and trophies began in 1914, but met with no success during his lifetime. "Rules are like steam rollers," he once wrote. "There is nothing they won't do to flatten the man who stands in their way." It is interesting to note that Avery Brundage, who was President of the International Olympic Committee from 1952 to 1972, and who did nothing to help Jim Thorpe's cause, also took part in the 1912 pentathlon and decathlon, placing sixth in the former and failing to finish the latter. Not until October 13, 1982, did the IOC finally lift the ban against Thorpe and allow his name to be returned to the record books. On January 18, 1983, his gold medals were presented to his children. It is worth noting that even according to the rules of 1912, Thorpe's medals never should have been taken from him in the first place. The official rules clearly stated that any challenge to the qualification of a competitior had to be submitted to the Swedish Olympic Committee within 30 days of the distribution of prizes. The objection of the AAU did not come until six months after the end of the Olympics. In fact, the Swedes immediately cited this passing of the statute of limitations, but the American officials ignored the point and appealed directly to the IOC for Thorpe to be punished.

There is an unusual story relating to the pre-Olympic world record. The official world record was the 7244 points recorded by Hugo Wieslander of Sweden. Back in 1912 the US Olympic team was chosen by committee. In the decathlon, for example, Jim Thorpe was selected based on his well-deserved reputation, while Eugene Mercer, who would place sixth in Stockholm, was chosen because he was a favorite of Olympic coach Lawson Robertson. There were three regional Olympic trials. One of them was won by Chicago's J. Austin Menaul. Because the order of finish was based on placement points, no one bothered to check Menaul's results against the point charts that would be used at the Olympics—no one in his lifetime, that is. In 1987, decathlon historian Frank Zarnowski finally did the calculations and discovered that Menaul had topped Wieslander's record by 170 points.

Menual traveled to the Olympics with the US team, but after their arrival in Europe he injured his shoulder while practicing the javelin throw. He managed to place fifth in the pentathlon, but was forced by his injury to withdraw from the decathlon.

1920 Antwerp C: 23, N: 11, D: 8.20-21. WR: 7751 (James Thorpe)

		100 M	LJ	SP	HJ	400 M	110 H	DISC	PV	JAV	1500 M	TOTAL POINTS	1985 TABLES
1. Helge Løvland	NOR	12.0	6.28	11.19	1.65	54.8	16.2	37.34	3.20	48.01	4:48.4	6803	5803
2. Brutus Hamilton	USA	11.4	6.325	11.61	1.60	55.0	17.3	36.14	3.30	48.08	4:57.8	6771	5739
3. Bertil Ohlson	SWE	12.0	6.435	11.07	1.65	55.0	17.0	37.78	3.30	39.89	4:50.6	6580	5639
4. Gustaf "Gosta" Holmér	SWE	11.8	5.92	11.06	1.70	56.5	16.6	34.82	3.20	47.62	5:01.6	6532	5551
5. Evert Nilsson	SWE	12.2	5.67	11.39	1.75	55.7	20.0	34.77	3.40	49.28	4:45.6	6434	5371
6. J. Valdemar Wickholm	FIN	11.6	6.12	11.44	1.60	52.8	16.8	32.30	3.00	42.76	4:45.6	6405	5630
7. Eugene Vidal	USA	12.0	6.13	1116	1.65	55.7	17.1	37.30	3.30	35.32	4:46.6	6359	5489
8. Axel-Erik Gyllenstolpe	SWE	12.0	6.35	10.69	1.65	55.8	16.8	33.65	2.90	49.31	5:01.4	6331	5482

Løvland passed Hamilton in the last event. His margin of victory was the equivalent of six seconds in the 1500 meters. In 1952 Brutus Hamilton served as coach of the US Olympic track team. Following the Nazi occupation of Norway in 1940, Helge Løvland organized a "Sports Strike" in which Norwegian athletes refused to take part in official competitions. Løvland's letter to the various sports federations calling for the strike was intercepted by his pro-Nazi fellow Olympian Charles Hoff (see page 91) and Løvland was forced to go underground.

1924 Paris C: 36, N: 22, D: 7.11-12. WR: 7482 (Aleksander Klumberg-Kolmpere)

		100 M	LJ	SP	HJ	400M	110H	DISC	PV	JAV	1500M	TOTAL POINTS	1985 TABLES
1. Harold Osborn	USA	11.2	6.92	11.435	1.97	53.2	16.0	34.51	3.50	46.69	4:50.0	7711 WR	6476
2. Emerson Norton	USA	11.6	6.92	13.04	1.92	53.0	16.6	33.11	3.80	42.09	5:38.0	7351	6117
3. Aleksander Klumberg-Kolmpere	EST	11.6	6.96	12.27	1.75	54.4	17.6	36.795	3.30	57.70	5:16.0	7329	6056
4. Anton Huusari	FIN	12.0	6.16	12.025	1.70	53.4	16.6	33.15	3.20	53.65	4:37.2	7005	5952
5. Edward Sutherland	SAF	11.6	6.67	10.865	1.80	56.0	16.6	30.83	3.30	51.015	5:19.0	6794	5928
6. Ernst Gerspach	SWI	11.4	6.46	10.355	1.70	53.4	16.8	33.91	3.40	44.82	5:08.2	6744	5765
7. Helge Jansson	SWE	11.6	6.32	12.22	1.83	54.2	17.8	32.08	3.10	47.20	5:22.0	6656	5633
8. Harry Frieda	USA	11.6	5.94	11.01	1.60	54.0	19.0	35.095	3.40	54.90	5:02.6	6618	5541

Norton led after eight events, but fell off badly in the javelin, and barely finished the 1500 meters. Osborn, having already won a gold medal in the high jump on July 7, achieved a unique double.

1928 Amsterdam C: 38, N: 19, D: 8.3-4. WR: 7995 (Paavo Yrjölä)

		100M	LJ	SP	HJ	400M	110 H	DISC	PV	JAV	1500 M	TOTAL POINTS	1985 TABLES
1. Paavo Yrjölä	FIN	11.8	6.72	14.11	1.87	53.2	16.6	42.09	3.30	55.70	4:44.0	8053 WR	6607
2. Akilles Järvinen	FIN	11.2	6.87	13.64	1.75	51.4	15.6	36.95	3.30	55.58	4:52.4	7932	6645
3. John Kenneth Doherty	USA	11.6	6.61	11.85	1.80	52.0	15.8	38.72	3.30	56.56	4:54.0	7707	6428
4. James Stewart	USA	11.2	6.61	13.04	1.87	52.8	16.6	40.90	3.30	48.07	5:17.0	7624	6310
5. Thomas Churchill	USA	11.6	6.32	12.28	1.70	52.2	16.8	38.19	3.60	50.93	4:55.0	7417	6165
6. Helge Jansson	SWE	11.4	6.85	13.59	1.87	53.2	16.6	36.83	3.30	41.73	5:27.0	7286	6111
7. Ludwig Vesely	AUT	11.6	6.73	12.58	1.70	52.2	15.8	35.46	3.20	47.44	4:47.0	7274	6224
8. Albert Andersson	SWE	12.0	6.30	12.19	1.75	54.0	15.8	36.64	3.30	45.81	4:44.2	7109	6031

Yrjölä lived on a farm and trained with his brother, using equipment he fashioned himself out of local lumber.

1932 Los Angeles C: 14, N: 9, D: 8.5-6. WR: 8255 (Akilles Järvinen)

		100M	LJ	SP	HJ	400M	110 H	DISC	PV	JAV	1500 M	TOTAL POINTS	1985 TABLES
1. James Bausch	USA	11.7	6.95	15.32	1.70	54.2	16.2	44.58	4.00	61.91	5:17.0	8462 WR	6735
2. Akilles Järvinen	FIN	11.1	7.00	13.11	1.75	50.6	15.7	36.80	3.60	61.00	4:47.0	8292	6879
3. Wolrad Eberle	GER	11.4	6.77	13.22	1.65	50.8	16.7	41.34	3.50	57.49	4:34.4	8031	6661
4. Wilson "Buster" Charles	USA	11.2	7.24	12.56	1.85	51.2	16.2	38.71	3.40	47.72	4:39.8	7985	6716
5. Hans-Heinrich Sievert	GER	11.4	6.97	14.50	1.78	53.6	16.1	44.54	3.20	53.91	5:18.0	7941	6515
6. Paavo Yrjölä	FIN	11.8	6.59	13.68	1.75	52.6	17.0	40.77	3.10	56.12	4:37.4	7688	6385
7. Clyde Clifford Coffman	USA	11.3	6.77	11.86	1.70	51.8	17.8	34.40	4.00	48.88	4:48.0	7534	6265
8. Robert Tisdall	IRL	11.3	6.60	12.58	1.65	49.0	15.5	33.31	3.20	45.26	4:34.4	7327	6398

Akilles Järvinen, older brother of javelin gold medallist Matti Järvinen, was the heavy favorite to win the decathlon. He did in fact break his own world record, but he was only able to place second. The upset winner was ex-University of Kansas football star Jim Bausch, whose entire decathlon career lasted less than 16 months. Fifth after the first day's events, Bausch took advantage of splendid performances in the discus and pole vault to build an insurmountable lead. Although Järvinen did win his second silver medal, had the 1985 tables been in use at the time he would have finished first in both 1928 and 1932.

1936 Berlin C: 28, N: 17, D: 8.7-8. WR: 7880 (Glenn Morris)

		100 M	LJ	SP	HJ	400 M	110 H	DISC	PV	JAV	1500M	TOTAL POINTS	1985 TABLES
1. Glenn Morris	USA	11.1	6.97	14.10	1.85	49.4	14.9	43.02	3.50	54.52	4:33.2	7900 WR	7254
2. Robert Clark	USA	10.9	7.62	12.68	1.80	50.0	15.7	39.39	3.70	51.12	4:44.4	7601	7063
3. Jack Parker	USA	11.4	7.35	13.52	1.80	53.3	15.0	39.11	3.50	56.46	5:07.8	7275	6760
4. Erwin Huber	GER	11.5	6.89	12.70	1.70	52.3	15.8	35.46	3.80	56.45	4:35,2	7087	6588
5. Reindert Brasser	HOL	11.6	6.69	13.49	1.90	51.5	16.2	39.45	3.40	55.75	5:06.0	7046	6570
6. Armin Guhl	SWI	11.3	7.04	12.30	1.80	52.3	15.6	40.97	3.30	51.20	4:49.2	7033	6818
7. Olle Bexell	SWE	11.6	6.68	13.54	1.75	54.9	16.0	38.83	3.70	57.07	4:40.4	7024	6558
8. Helmut Bonnet	GER	11.6	6.66	13.45	1.75	53.7	16.2	39.16	3.60	58.15	4:54.0	6939	6489

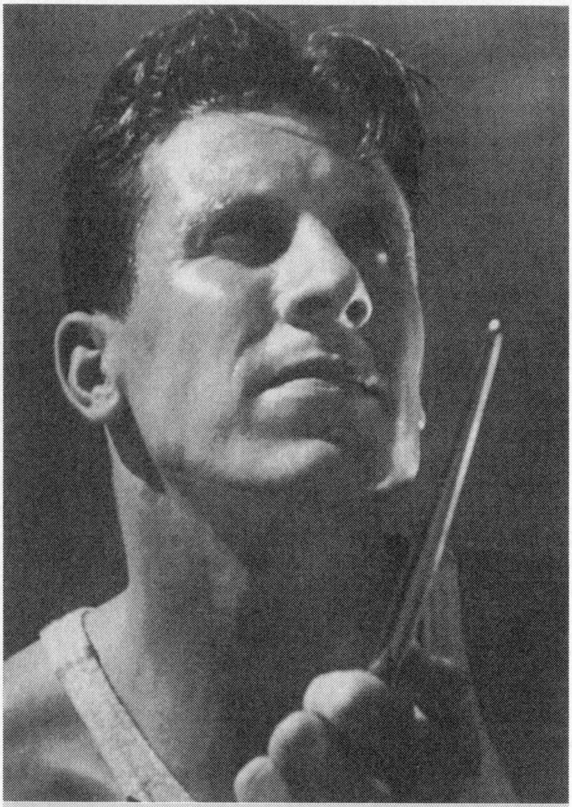

Glenn Morris, 1936
Photographed by Leni Riefenstahl, was an automobile salesman when he won the Olympic decathlon in Berlin in 1936.

A new set of tables was instituted in 1934, which accounts for the lower scores. Just before the running of the 1500 meters, it was announced that Glenn Morris, a 24-year-old automobile salesman from the small town of Simla (population 500) in Colorado, needed to run 4:32.0 in order to set a new world record. This was 16 seconds faster than Morris, who was only competing in his third decathlon, had ever run. When he crossed the finish line in 4:33.2, there was much disappointment. But then it was discovered that an error had been made in computing his score, and that he had in fact broken the record after all. Morris's victory earned him an invitation to Hollywood, where he appeared in two bad films, *Tarzan's Revenge* and *Hold That Co-Ed*. He also joined the Detroit Lions football team, but sustained a career-ending injury in his first game. During World War II he commanded an amphibious-assault landing craft that transported troops and equipment and he took part in the Battle of Leyte Gulf.

In her 1987 autobiography, Leni Riefenstahl, who directed the official film of the 1936 Olympics, describes her brief but passionate love affair with Glenn Morris. Of particular interest is her version of the medal ceremony for the decathlon. "The dim light prevented any filming of the ceremony, and when Glenn Morris came down the steps he headed straight towards me. I held out my hand and congratulated him, but he grabbed me in his arms, tore off my blouse and kissed my breasts, right in the middle of the stadium, in front of a hundred thousand spectators. A lunatic, I thought. I wrenched myself out of his grasp and dashed away. But I could not forget the wild look in his eyes . . ."

Bob Mathias, 1948
Seventeen-year-old Bob Mathias was the youngest winner of a men's track and field gold medal in Olympic history.

1948 London C: 35, N: 20, D: 8.5-6. WR: 7900 (Glenn Morris)

		100 M	LJ	SP	HJ	400M	110 H	DISC	PV	JAV	1500 M	TOTAL POINTS	1985 TABLES
1. Robert Mathias	USA	11.2	6.615	13.04	1.86	51.7	15.7	44.00	3.50	50.32	5:11.0	7139	6628
2. Ignace Heinrich	FRA	11.3	6.895	12.85	1.86	51.6	15.6	40.94	3.20	40.98	4:43.8	6974	6559
3. Floyd Simmons	USA	11.2	6.725	12.80	1.86	51.9	15.2	32.73	3.40	51.99	4:58.0	6950	6531
4. C. Enrique Kistenmacher	ARG	10.9	7.08	12.67	1.70	50.5	16.3	41.11	3.20	45.06	4:49.6	6929	6542
5. Erik Peter Andersson	SWE	11.6	6.595	12.66	1.75	52.0	15.9	36.07	3.60	51.04	4:34.0	6877	6486
6. Peter Mullins	AUS	11.2	6.645	12.75	1.83	53.2	15.2	33.94	3.40	51.32	5:17.6	6739	6334
7. Per Axel Eriksson	SWE	11.9	6.80	11.96	1.80	52.5	16.2	34.91	3.30	56.70	4:35.8	6731	6391
8. Irving Mondschein	USA	11.3	6.810	12.74	1.83	51.6	16.6	38.74	3.50	36.81	4:49.8	6715	6331

Bob Mathias was only 17 years old when Virgil Jackson, his track coach at Tulare High School in Central California, suggested that he take up the decathlon. Mathias learned quickly and less than three months later he had qualified for the US Olympic team and was on his way to London. His inexperience led to one setback in the shot put. After lofting the 16-pound ball over 45 feet, he was surprised when an official raised the red flag that indicated a foul. The perplexed teenager was informed that he had left the throwing circle from the front, which was against the rules. Nobody had ever told Mathias about this particular rule, but there was nothing he could do about it. His best throw after that was only 42 feet 9¼ inches.

The next event was the high jump, and here Mathias almost met disaster, as he missed twice at the mediocre height of 5 feet 9 inches. Faced with virtual elimination, he ignored formal technique and threw himself over the bar with a jump that was clumsy, but successful. He went on to clear 6 feet 1¼ inches. After the first day's events, Mathias was in third place behind Enrique Kistenmacher and Ignace Heinrich.

The second day's competition began at 10 a.m., but bad weather and general confusion caused it to drag on into the night. The discus was Bob Mathias' specialty, and he connected with a good throw of about 145 feet. Unfortunately, the marker for his throw got knocked over. After a half hour search in the rain and gloom for the hole left by his discus, officials gave him credit for 144 feet 4 inches. Mathias' older brother, Gene, who had gained access to the field by flashing a bogus press pass, raced up to Bob and urged him to press the search. But Bob felt guilty about the delay he was causing, and so accepted his fate. The throw was good enough, however, to put him into first place. Because there were no infield lights, before the javelin throw began, cars were driven into the stadium and their headlights were turned on to illuminate the foul line. By the time he staggered across the finish line at the end of the 1500 meters, it was 10:35 p.m. and Bob Mathias had become the youngest winner of a men's track and field event in the history of the Olympics. His father and a team trainer rushed onto the track, grabbed him and walked him up and down for ten minutes because he was nauseated and his feet were cramping. In the dressing room afterward, the exhausted teenager was asked how he intended to celebrate his victory. He replied, "I'll start shaving, I guess." In fact, he was so drained that he went right to sleep and had to be awakened to take part in the victory ceremony the next day.

Bob Mathias, 1948

After his victory in the 1948 decathlon, Mathias returned to Tulare, California, for the small-town equivalent of a ticker-tape parade.

Back home in Tulare, a small farming town of 12,000, the entire population had been on pins and needles waiting for the results from London. When the news came over the radio that Mathias had won, the town went wild. Factory whistles and fire sirens blared for 45 minutes, businesses closed down, and a spontaneous three-hour parade of cars clogged the downtown area and the nearby interstate highway. The local telegraph office had to stay open into the night as friends stood in line to send their congratulations to the hometown boy who had made good. When Mathias finally returned three weeks later, the excitement was so great that the airplane he was on had to delay its landing until the crowd could be cleared from around the runway.

Four days after Mathias' Olympic victory, 26-year-old Heino Lipp scored 7584 points in a meet in Tartu, Estonia. Between 1920 and 1936 Estonia had competed as an independent nation. However, Estonia lost its independence during World War II and was annexed by the Soviet Union. The USSR chose not to compete in the 1948 Olympics and Lipp was left without a country. The USSR did take part in the 1952 Olympics, but Lipp was considered a security risk and was forced to stay home again. After the fall of Communism in the Soviet Union, Estonia regained its independence and Estonia entered a separate team at the 1992 Olympics. When the Estonian team marched into the stadium at the Opening Ceremony for the first time in 56 years, the Estonian flag was proudly carried by 70-year-old Heino Lipp.

1952 Helsinki C: 28, N: 16, D: 7.25-26. WR: 7825 (Robert Mathias)

		100M	LJ	SP	HJ	400M	100 M	DISC	PV	JAV	1500 M	TOTAL POINTS	1985 TABLES
1. Robert Mathias	USA	10.9	6.98	15.30	1.90	50.2	14.7	46.89	4.00	59.21	4:50.8	7887 WR	7580
2. Milton Campbell	USA	10.7	6.74	13.89	1.85	50.9	14.5	40.50	3.30	54.54	5:07.2	6975	6948
3. Floyd Simmons	USA	11.5	7.06	13.18	1.92	51.1	15.0	37.77	3.60	54.69	4:53.4	6788	6903
4. Vladimir Volkov	SOV/RUS	11.4	7.09	12.62	1.75	51.2	15.8	38.04	3.80	56.68	4:33.2	6674	6868
5. Josef Hipp	GER	11.4	6.85	13.26	1.75	51.3	16.1	45.84	3.50	54.14	4:57.2	6449	6705
6. Göran Widenfeldt	SWE	11.4	6.76	11.61	1.94	51.3	16.1	39.53	3.50	49.36	4:38.6	6388	6661
7. Kjell Tännander	SWE	11.4	6.90	12.97	1.85	52.6	15.8	39.30	3.50	52.79	4:57.2	6308	6607
8. Friedel Schirmer	GER	11.7	6.37	12.69	1.80	50.5	16.0	37.01	3.50	54.00	4:47.6	6118	6464

World records for this period get very confusing, since yet another new set of tables was devised in 1950 and revised a few days before the Olympics. It made little difference to Bob Mathias, who won by the largest margin in Olympic history. His only problem developed in the javelin, when his first two throws fell far short of his capabilities. Up in the stands, Jack Weiershauser, Mathias' track coach at Stanford, convinced a bunch of American rooters to chant, "Oh Bob, hey you, don't forget to follow through." Bob got the message, and followed through with a throw of 194 feet 3 inches.

Although he made no attempt to exploit his Olympic success, Mathias was one of the first gold medal winners to benefit financially from his victories. In the first year after Helsinki, Mathias earned $50,000 for advertising appearances. He also acted in four films (including *The Bob Mathias Story*) and was elected to the US Congress, where he served for eight years.

1956 Melbourne C: 15, N: 8, D: 11.29-30. WR: 7985 (Rafer Johnson)

		100 M	LJ	SP	HJ	400 M	110 H	DISC	PV	JAV	1500 M	TOTAL POINTS	1985 TABLES
1. Milton Campbell	USA	10.8	7.33	14.76	1.89	48.8	14.0	44.98	3.40	57.08	4:50.6	7937 OR	7565
2. Rafer Johnson	USA	10.9	7.34	14.48	1.83	49.3	15.1	42.17	3.90	60.27	4:54.2	7587	7422
3. Vassily Kuznetsov	SOV/RUS	11.2	7.04	14.49	1.75	50.2	14.9	44.33	3.95	65.13	4:53.8	7465	7330
4. Uno Palu	SOV/EST	11.5	6.65	13.39	1.89	50.8	15.4	40.38	3.60	61.59	4:35.6	6930	7028
5. Martin Lauer	GER	11.1	6.83	12.86	1.83	48.2	14.7	39.38	3.10	50.66	4:43.8	6853	6910
6. Walter Meier	GDR	11.3	6.80	12.99	1.86	49.3	16.1	37.59	3.70	47.97	4:20.6	6773	6910
7. Torbjörn Lassenius	FIN	11.8	6.62	13.45	1.70	50.8	15.9	41.36	3.80	59.33	4:36.2	6565	6782
8. Yang Chuan-kwang	TAI	11.2	6.90	11.56	1.95	51.3	15.0	33.92	3.30	57.88	5:00.8	6521	6697

World record holder Rafer Johnson was hampered by injury, but even in full health he probably couldn't have beaten Milt Campbell in Melbourne. Campbell, a 22-year-old sailor from Plainfield, New Jersey, had hoped to qualify for the US Olympic team as a hurdler, but only finished fourth in the final tryouts. "I was stunned," he said. '"But then God seemed to reach into my heart and tell me he didn't want me to compete in the hurdles, but in the decathlon."

In the Olympics he led from start to finish. A time of 14.0 in the hurdles earned him 1124 points and assured him the victory. He lost his shot at a world record when he could do no better than 11 feet 1¾ inches in the pole vault, almost 20 inches below his best performance. But, paced and urged on by 11th-place finisher Ian Bruce of Australia, he ran the 1500 meters in 4:50.6 to gain the Olympic record.

Milt Campbell, 1956
Paced to a gold medal and Olympic record by Aussie Ian Bruce.

1960 Rome C: 30, N: 20, D: 9.5-6. WR: 8683 (Rafer Johnson)

		100 M	LJ	SP	HJ	400 M	110 H	DISC	PV	JAV	1500 M	TOTAL POINTS	1985 TABLES
1. Rafer Johnson	USA	10.9	7.35	15.82	1.85	48.3	15.3	48.49	4.10	69.76	4:49.7	8392 OR	7901
2. Yang Chuan-kwang	TAI	10.7	7.46	13.33	1.90	48.1	14.6	39.83	4.30	68.22	4:48.5	8334	7820
3. Vassily Kuznetsov	SOV/RUS	11.1	6.96	14.46	1.75	50.2	15.0	50.52	3.90	71.20	4:53.8	7809	7527
4. Yuri Kutenko	SOV/UKR	11.4	6.93	13.97	1.80	51.1	15.6	45.63	4.20	71.44	4:44.2	7567	7401
5. Evert Kamerbeek	HOL	11.3	7.21	13.76	1.80	51.1	14.9	44.31	3.80	57.49	4:43.6	7236	7212
6. Franco Sar	ITA	11.4	6.69	13.89	1.80	51.3	14.7	49.58	3.80	55.74	4:49.2	7195	7140
7. Markus Kahma	FIN	11.5	6.93	14.55	1.75	50.5	15.9	44.93	3.60	60.50	4:22.8	7112	7161
8. Klaus Grogorenz	GDR	10.8	6.93	12.42	1.73	48.0	16.9	40.12	3.70	60.81	4:27.0	7032	7078

Rafer Johnson and Yang Chuan-kwang grew up in very different circumstances, yet they came together as fellow students at UCLA, and then as friendly rivals at the Rome Olympics. Johnson was born in Hillsboro, Texas. In 1945, when Rafer was nine, his family moved to the small mostly Swedish town of Kingsburg, California, less than 25 miles from Bob Mathias' hometown of Tulare.

Yang, the son of a rice farmer, was a member of the Takasago ethnic group, which inhabited the island of Formosa long before the Chinese arrived. He visited the United States for a couple of months and decided to stay. At UCLA Johnson and Yang, now known as C.K. Yang, trained together, but in Rome Johnson represented the United States and Yang, Taiwan.

The first day of competition, interrupted by an 80-minute thunder shower, didn't end until 11 p.m. After five events, Johnson led Yang by only 55 points. They were back on the track again at 9 a.m. for the sixth event, the 110-meter hurdles, which was one of Johnson's specialties. But the poorly rested American hit the first hurdle badly and took 15.3 seconds to reach the finish line, far slower than his best of 13.9. He made

Rafer Johnson and Yang Chuan-kwang, 1960
The UCLA teammates collapse against each other after completing the final event of the 1960 decathlon.

up the lost points in the pole vault by achieving a personal record of 13 feet 5½ inches.

With only the 1500 meters left to run, Johnson led Yang by 67 points. This meant that if Yang, whose best time for the distance was 4:36.0, could beat Johnson by ten seconds, he would become Taiwan's first-ever gold medalist. Johnson's 1500 best was the 4:54.2 that he had recorded at the 1956 Olympics. Before the race, Johnson walked over to the stands to speak to his coach, Ducky Drake. Drake advised Johnson to stay on Yang's heels, not let him pull away and be prepared for "a hellish sprint" at the end. Then Yang approached his coach, the same Ducky Drake. Drake told Yang to build up as big a lead as possible over Johnson and then go all out on the final lap.

The two very tired rivals took off at 9:15 p.m., with Yang in front and Johnson dogging him the entire way. Yang tried desperately to pull away in the final lap, but Johnson stuck close and earned the gold medal by finishing only six yards behind, in a career best of 4:49.7. Johnson and Yang wobbled on for a few yards and then fell against each other for support, while Italian fans chanted, "Give them both the gold medal." Yang was the first Taiwanese athlete to gain an Olympic medal.

Rafer Johnson later became a film actor and television sportscaster before becoming involved in politics. On June 5, 1968, Johnson was walking through the kitchen in the Ambassador Hotel in Los Angeles with Robert Kennedy, when the Presidential candidate was shot and killed. In 1984, it was Johnson who was chosen to light the torch at the Opening Ceremony of the Los Angeles Olympics.

Rafer Johnson's daughter, Jenny, represented the United States in beach volleyball at the 2000 Sydney Olympics.

1964 Tokyo C: 22, N: 14, D: 10.19-20. WR: 8089 (Yang Chuan-kwang)

		100 M	LJ	SP	HJ	400 M	110 H	DISC	PV	JAV	1500 M	TOTAL POINTS	1985 TABLES
1. Willi Holdorf	GER	10.7	7.00	14.95	1.84	48.2	15.0	46.05	4.20	57.37	4:34.3	7887	7726
2. Rein Aun	SOV/EST	10.9	7.22	13.82	1.93	48.8	15.9	44.19	4.20	59.06	4:22.3	7842	7677
3. Hans-Joachim Walde	GER	11.0	7.21	14.45	1.96	49.5	15.3	43.15	4.10	62.90	4:37.0	7809	7668
4. Paul Herman	USA	11.2	6.97	13.89	1.87	49.2	15.2	44.15	4.35	63.35	4:25.4	7787	7651
5. Yang Chuan-kwang	TAI	11.0	6.80	13.23	1.81	49.0	14.7	39.59	4.60	68.15	4:48.4	7650	7539
6. Horst Beyer	GER	11.2	7.02	14.32	1.90	49.8	15.2	45.17	3.80	58.17	4:23.6	7647	7488
7. Vassily Kuznetsov	SOV/RUS	10.9	6.98	14.06	1.70	49.5	14.9	43.81	4.40	67.87	5:02.5	7569	7454
8. Mikhail Storozhenko	SOV/RUS	11.0	7.22	16.37	1.84	53.6	15.0	43.20	4.00	59.10	5:00.7	7464	7307

On April 28, 1963, Yang Chuan-kwang had severely disrupted the scoring of the decathlon by pole-vaulting 15 feet 10½ inches, which put him above the maximum height accounted for by the charts then in use. The new charts, known as the 1962 tables, were not released until August 1964. They tended to equalize the ten events, and were particularly damaging to Yang, whose pole-vault best was suddenly worth 501 points less than it had been.

Using the old tables, Yang's best total of 1964 had been 485 points higher than anyone else's. With the new tables, he trailed both Holdorf and Beyer.

At the end of the first day in Tokyo, Holdorf led with 4090 points. He was followed by Walde with 4074 and Aun with 4067. After nine events, Holdorf led Walde by 60 points and Aun by 137. The 1500, however, was one of Aun's strong points. To win, Holdorf had to finish within 17 seconds of Aun, but his best time of the year was more than 30 seconds slower than Aun's. Holdorf's coach, Friedel Schirmer, purposely misled him, telling Holdorf that he had only 12 seconds to spare.

Aun finished in 4:22.3, while Holdorf pushed himself as hard as he could. Forty yards from the finish, he began to weave and appeared on the verge of collapse. But he struggled on until the end, crossing the finish with a time of 4:34.3—exactly 12 seconds slower than Aun. Then he collapsed. Aun tried to congratulate his fallen conqueror, but Holdorf was too dazed to comprehend. Eventually he was revived and shown the scoreboard that displayed his winning score.

1968 Mexico City C: 33, N: 20, D: 10.18-19. WR: 8319 (Kurt Bendlin)

		100 M	LJ	SP	HJ	400M	110 H	DISC	PV	JAV	1500 M	TOTAL POINTS	1985 TABLES
1. William Toomey	USA	10.4	7.87	13.75	1.95	45.6	14.9	43.68	4.20	62.80	4:57.1	8193 OR	8158
2. Hans-Joachim Walde	GER	10.9	7.64	15.13	2.01	49.0	14.8	43.54	4.30	71.62	4:58.5	8111	8120
3. Kurt Bendlin	GER	10.7	7.56	14.74	1.80	48.3	15.0	46.78	4.60	75.42	5:09.8	8064	8096
4. Mykola Avilov	SOV/UKR	10.9	7.64	13.41	2.07	49.9	14.5	46.64	4.10	60.12	5:00.8	7909	7884
5. Joachim Kirst	GDR	10.5	7.61	16.43	1.98	50.2	15.6	46.89	4.15	57.02	5:20.1	7861	7791
6. Thomas Waddell	USA	11.3	7.47	14.45	2.01	51.2	15.3	43.73	4.50	63.70	5:04.5	7719	7694
7. Rick Sloan	USA	11.2	6.72	14.07	2.10	51.0	15.5	45.58	4.85	49.90	4:44.0	7692	7553
8. Steen Smidt-Jensen	DEN	10.9	7.17	13.03	1.95	50.2	14.9	41.07	4.85	46.80	4:41.3	7648	7507

"Behind every good decathlon man, there's a good doctor," Bill Toomey once declared, and he was an expert on the subject. When he was 12 years old, an accident left him with 75 percent paralysis in his right hand. Aside from the usual array of illnesses and pulled muscles, Toomey also suffered through hepatitis, mononucleosis, and a shattered kneecap on his way to an Olympic gold medal. A 29-year-old English teacher from California, Toomey faced his moment of truth in the pole vault. Leading after seven events, he suddenly found himself one miss away from elimination at the opening height of 11 feet 9¼ inches.

"I had done so many things wrong on my first two jumps," he later recalled, "I couldn't figure out how to correct anything. . . . Everything was closing in on me—the people in that huge arena, the people watching on television back home, my whole life, all those years of working and waiting for this moment. If I missed, it would be like dying." Fortunately, Toomey didn't miss. "All the technique I had learned and practiced . . . had been forgotten in the fear and frustration I felt. I was like a beginner, clumsy and uncertain. But I had made that jump on sheer determination. I'm not even sure I needed my pole."

Toomey went on to clear 13 feet 9½ inches, his best ever in competition, and then managed to stave off the competition through the final two events.

Army physician Tom Waddell, who placed sixth, became a gay activist who organized the Gay Games to highlight the accomplishments of homosexual athletes. He died of AIDS on July 11, 1987, at the age of 49.

1972 Munich C: 33, N: 19, D: 9.7-8. WR: 8417 (William Toomey)

		100 M	LJ	SP	HJ	400M	110 H	DISC	PV	JAV	1500 M	TOTAL POINTS	1985 TABLES
1. Mykola Avilov	SOV/UKR	11.00	7.68	14.36	2.12	48.45	14.31	46.98	4.55	61.66	4:22.8	8454 WR	8466
2. Leonid Lytvynenko	SOV/UKR	11.13	6.81	14.18	1.89	48.40	15.03	47.84	4.40	58.94	4:05.9	8035	7970
3. Ryszard Katus	POL	10.89	7.09	14.39	1.92	49.11	14.41	43.00	4.50	59.96	4:31.9	7984	7936
4. Jefferson Bennett	USA	10.73	7.26	12.82	1.86	46.25	15.58	36.58	4.80	57.48	4:12.2	7974	7920
5. Stetan Schreyer	GDR	10.82	7.44	15.02	1.92	49.5	15.00	45.08	4.40	50.42	4:48.2	7950	7907
6. Freddy Herbrand	BEL	11.00	7.30	13.91	2.04	49.78	14.87	47.12	4.40	50.42	4:27.1	7947	7897
7. Steen Smidt-Jensen	DEN	11.07	6.95	13.35	2.01	50.10	14.65	44.80	4.80	55.24	4:24.7	7947	7908
8. Tadeusz Janczenko	POL	10.64	7.28	14.45	2.04	49.10	16.89	45.26	4.50	63.80	5:01.5	7861	7791

The 1972 decathlon looked to be a wide-open affair, with at least four men considered leading contenders: two-time European champion Joachim Kirst of East Germany, Jeff Bannister of the United States, veteran Lennart Hedmark of Sweden, and the fast-improving Ukrainian, Mykola Avilov of the USSR. Unfortunately, Hedmark, troubled by an injured foot, was forced to withdraw after three events. After five events, Kirst was in first place with 4364 points, followed by Avilov with 4345, and Tadeusz Janczenko and Ryszard Skowronek of Poland with 4266 and 4240, respectively. The turning point came shortly after 9 a.m. the following morning, in the second heat of the high hurdles. Kirst hit the first hurdle, fell heavily at the next and pulled a muscle. Bannister, in the next lane, was thrown off stride, fell after the fourth hurdle, pushed over the next one, and was disqualified. Janczenko, forced to add the fallen Bannister to the obstacles in his path, was slowed down so much that it may have cost him a medal. Meanwhile, Avilov, unaware of the chaos behind him, finished first with a time of 14.31. In addition to all this, Skowronek had pulled a muscle in his heat and had to retire in the middle of the next event.

Avilov, who suddenly found himself with a huge lead, finished the day brilliantly, eventually recording personal records in seven of the ten decathlon events, and equaling his best in an eighth. A strong finish in the 1500 earned him a world record. Fellow Ukrainian Leonid Lytvynenko ran an even better 1500-meter race, enabling him to move from eighth place after nine events to second after ten.

The first to congratulate Avilov was the man whose record he had broken, Bill Toomey, on hand as a television commentator. Both Toomey and Avilov married Olympic medallists. Toomey wed 1964 long jump champion Mary Rand, and Avilov married Valentina Kozyr, winner of the bronze medal in the 1968 high jump.

Mykola Avilov, 1972
With personal bests in eight of the 10 events, both Olympic gold and a world record were his.

1976 Montreal C: 28, N: 17, D: 7.29-30. WR: 8538 (Bruce Jenner)

		100 M	LJ	SP	HJ	400M	110 H	DISC	PV	JAV	1500 M	TOTAL POINTS	1985 TABLES
1. Bruce Jenner	USA	10.94	7.22	15.35	2.03	47.51	14.84	50.04	4.80	68.52	4:12.6	8618 WR	8634
2. Guido Kratschmer	GER	10.66	7.39	14.74	2.03	48.19	14.58	45.70	4.60	66.32	4:29.1	8411	8416
3. Mykola Avilov	SOV/UKR	11.23	7.52	14.81	2.14	48.16	14.20	45.60	4.45	62.28	4:26.3	8369	8403
4. Raimo Pihl	SWE	10.93	6.99	15.55	2.00	47.97	15.81	44.30	4.40	77.34	4:28.8	8218	8216
5. Ryszard Skowronek	POL	11.02	7.26	13.74	1.91	47.91	14.75	45.34	4.80	62.22	4:29.9	8113	8099
6. Siegfried Stark	GDR	11.35	6.98	15.08	1.91	49.14	15.65	45.48	4.65	74.18	4:24.9	8048	8051
7. Leonid Lytvynenko	SOV/UKR	11.12	6.92	14.20	1.91	48.44	14.71	46.26	4.60	53.66	4:11.4	8025	7963
8. Lennart Hedmark	SWE	11.36	7.09	15.00	1.91	49.80	14.79	46.42	4.30	78.58	4:44.2	7974	8002

The 1976 decathlon was looked forward to as a classic duel between Mykola Avilov, the defending champion and holder of the automatically timed world record, and Bruce Jenner, tenth in Munich, but now the holder of the official, albeit hand-timed, world record. From the very first event, however, it was Jenner who was in control. Hoping to be within 200 points of the leaders, Kratschmer and Avilov, at the end of the first day, Jenner found himself only 35 points behind Kratschmer and 17 points behind Avilov. He went to bed completely confident of victory since the second day's events were his best.

By the time eight events had been completed, Jenner's victory was assured, and he began to cry as he realized that his goal was about to be achieved, and that his athletic career was about to come to an end. Encouraged by his wife, Chrystie, who had supported the young couple with her job as an air hostess, Jenner had totally immersed himself in the world of the decathlon. At night, he dreamed about the different events so often that Chrystie could tell which one he was unconsciously practicing. As Jenner rested on the infield in Montreal, his reverie was broken by Leonid Lytvynenko, who patted him on the shoulder and said, "Bruce, you going to be Olympic champion."

"Thanks," said Jenner.

Lytvynenko stared at Jenner for a few seconds, and then asked, "Bruce, you going to be a millionaire?"

Jenner just laughed.

Unlike most decathletes, who dread the 1500 meters, Jenner actually looked forward to it, and ran his final race full of strength, leaning forward as he crossed the finish line. The North American crowd roared with delight, but eventually Bruce made his way through the adulation, found Chrystie, and told her, "Congratulations. We did it together." When he left the stadium, he didn't even bother to take his vaulting poles with him, because he knew he wouldn't need them where he was going.

Bruce Jenner did become rich and famous, just as Lytvynenko had wondered, but his marriage didn't last. Since the media had constantly portrayed Bruce and Chrystie as the All-American couple, their divorce was a difficult one. Jenner later married Linda Thompson, former girlfriend of Elvis Presley, before settling into a third, more successful marriage.

1980 Moscow C: 21, N: 12, D: 7.25-26. WR: 8649 (Guido Kratschmer)

		100 M	LJ	SP	HJ	400M	110 H	DISC	PV	JAV	1500 M	TOTAL POINTS	1985 TABLES
1. Francis "Daley" Thompson	GBR	10.62	8.00	15.18	2.08	48.01	14.47	42.24	4.70	64.16	4:39.9	8495	8522
2. Yuri Kutsenko	SOV/RUS	11.19	7.74	14.50	2.08	48.67	15.04	39.86	4.90	68.08	4:22.6	8331	8369
3. Sergei Zhelanov	SOV/RUS	11.40	7.60	14.17	2.18	49.27	14.83	42.80	4.60	57.30	4:27.5	8315	8135
4. Georg Werthner	AUT	11.44	7.27	13.45	2.03	49.26	15.08	38.14	4.85	73.66	4:23.4	8050	8084
5. Josef "Sepp" Zeilbauer	AUT	11.29	7.14	15.31	2.03	50.91	14.80	44.00	4.50	64.86	4:30.6	8007	7989
6. Dariusz Ludwig	POL	11.35	7.51	13.32	2.08	50.55	15.38	45.82	4.80	58.38	4:29.7	7978	7972
7. Atanas Andonov	BUL	11.38	6.86	15.59	2.00	50.36	14.83	47.62	4.70	53.54	4:29.2	7927	7887
8. Steffen Grummt	GDR	11.35	6.86	16.15	1.94	49.39	14.82	48.56	4.30	55.24	4:30.2	7892	7840

In Montreal Daley Thompson had been the youngest entrant in the decathlon, finishing 18th at the age of 18. Four years later this gregarious offspring of a Nigerian father and a Scottish mother was expected to face a tough battle for the gold medal against Guido Kratschmer of West Germany. When West Germany joined the Jimmy Carter boycott, Thompson broke training, so that he could compete against Kratschmer. He beat his rival in May, and set a world record of 8622 in the process. Kratschmer responded with another world record of 8649 in June, but he would have been hard-pressed to beat Thompson in Moscow.

At the Olympics, Thompson was not seriously challenged. His nearest rival, Valery Kachanov of the USSR, pulled a calf muscle during the pole vault and had to withdraw while in second place. Thompson's world record pace was thwarted by rain on the second day, but the Soviet fans, who had been none too friendly to foreign athletes, gave Thompson a standing ovation anyway when he finished the 1500 meters.

Bruce Jenner, 1976

Jenner completes his world record performance in the 1976 decathlon.

Daley Thompson, 1980

Clicking up his heels after the first of his two decathlon gold medals.

1984 Los Angeles C: 26, N: 18, D: 8.8-9. WR: 8798 (Jürgen Hingsen)

		100 M	LJ	SP	HJ	400M	110 H	DISC	PV	JAV	1500 M	TOTAL POINTS	1985 TABLES
1. Francis "Daley" Thompson	GBR	10.44	8.01	15.72	2.03	46.97	14.33	46.56	5.00	65.24	4:35.00	8798 EWR	8847
2. Jürgen Hingsen	GER	10.91	7.80	15.87	2.12	47.69	14.29	50.82	4.50	60.44	4:22.60	8673	8695
3. Siegfried Wentz	GER	10.99	7.11	15.87	2.09	47.78	14.35	46.60	4.50	67.68	4:33.96	8412	8416
4. Guido Kratschmer	GER	10.80	7.40	15.93	1.94	49.25	14.66	47.28	4.90	69.40	4:47.99	8326	8357
5. William Motti	FRA	11.28	7.45	14.42	2.06	48.13	14.71	50.92	4.50	63.76	4:35.15	8266	8278
6. John Crist	USA	11.33	6.98	14.05	2.06	48.45	15.01	46.18	4.80	61.88	4:23.78	8130	8115
7. Jim Wooding	USA	11.04	7.01	13.90	1.97	47.62	14.57	47.38	4.60	57.20	4:28.31	8091	8054
8. David Steen	CAN	11.20	7.41	12.57	2.03	48.09	15.39	44.04	4.80	56.92	4:17.70	8047	8034

In 1982, Jürgen Hingsen entered the European Championships as the world record holder. Daley Thompson beat him. In 1983, Jürgen Hingsen entered the world championships as the world record holder. Daley Thompson beat him. In 1984, Jürgen Hingsen entered the Olympics as the world record holder. Guess what?

This time the crucial moment in the meet came in the seventh event, the discus throw. While Thompson was flubbing his first two attempts, Hingsen hit a strong 166 feet 9 inches. If the defending Olympic champion couldn't improve with his final attempt, Hingsen would take the lead for the first time. Thompson, who relished moments such as these, threw 152 feet 9 inches to pick up 100 points and put himself back in front. During the next event, the pole vault, Hingsen became ill, performed well below standard, and the rest of the contest was a mere formality. Except that Daley Thompson still had a shot at Hingsen's world record. He needed to run the 1500 meters in 4:34.98, much slower than his personal best. However, the irreverent champion exasperated the crowd by easing off at the tape and finishing in 4:35.00. He then took a victory lap wearing a sweat shirt which read on the front: "THANKS AMERICA FOR A GOOD GAMES AND A GREAT TIME." On the back was another message: "BUT WHAT ABOUT THE TV COVERAGE," a reference to the myopic nationalism displayed by the US television network that covered the Games.

In 1986, the IAAF announced that close examination of the electric phototimer revealed that Thompson had actually completed the 110-meter hurdles in 14.33 seconds rather than 14.34 seconds. One more point was added to his Olympic total, and he was given a belated share of the world record despite himself.

1988 Seoul C: 39, N: 26, D: 9.28-29. WR: 8847 (Francis "Daley" Thompson)

		100 M	LJ	SP	HJ	400M	110 H	DISC	PV	JAV	1500 M	TOTAL POINTS
1. Christian Schenk	GDR	11.25	7.43	15.48	2.27	48.90	15.13	49.28	4.70	61.32	4:28.95	8488
2. Torsten Voss	GDR	10.87	7.45	14.97	1.97	47.71	14.46	44.36	5.10	61.76	4:33.02	8399
3. David Steen	CAN	11.18	7.44	14.20	1.97	48.29	14.81	43.66	5.20	64.16	4:23.20	8328
4. Francis "Daley" Thompson	GBR	10.62	7.38	15.02	2.03	49.06	14.72	44.80	4.90	64.04	4:45.11	8306
5. Christian Plaziat	FRA	10.83	7.62	13.58	2.12	48.34	14.18	43.06	4.90	52.18	4:34.07	8272
6. Alain Blondel	FRA	11.02	7.43	12.92	1.97	47.44	14.40	41.20	5.20	57.46	4:16.64	8268
7. Timothy Bright	USA	11.18	7.05	14.12	2.06	49.34	14.39	41.68	5.70	61.60	4:51.20	8216
8. Robert de Wit	HOL	11.05	6.95	15.34	2.00	48.21	14.36	41.32	4.80	63.00	4:25.86	8189

The competition began on a startling note when, in the first heat of the 100 meters, Jürgen Hingsen was disqualified for committing three false starts. Christian Schenk, a 6-foot 7-inch medical student from Rostock, moved into the lead when he high jumped 7 feet 5¼ inches, using the archaic straddle technique. At the end of the first day, Schenk was in first place with 4470 points, Plaziat was second at 4375, Thompson third at 4332, and Voss fourth at 4299. Schenk's lead shrank to 25 points after the pole vault, but when Plaziat blew his javelin throw, Schenk found himself a solid 62 points ahead of Voss and 78 ahead of Thompson. The 23-year-old Schenk, who had won only one previous decathlon, had no trouble maintaining his lead in the final event. Dave Steen, in only eighth place after nine events, ran a strong 1500 meters to snatch the bronze medal from Thompson.

Silver medalist Torsten Voss competed in the 1998 Winter Olympics as a pusher for the German four-man bobsleigh team that placed eighth.

1992 Barcelona C 36, N: 24, D: 8.5-6. WR: 8847 (Francis "Daley" Thompson)

		100 M	LJ	SP	HJ	400 M	110 H	DISC	PV	JAV	1500 M	TOTAL POINTS
1. Robert Změlík	CZE	10.78	7.87	14.53	2.06	48.64	13.95	45.00	5.10	59.06	4:27.21	8611
2. Antonio Peñalver	SPA	11.09	7.54	16.50	2.06	49.66	14.58	49.68	4.90	58.64	4:38.02	8412
3. David Johnson	USA	11.16	7.33	15.28	2.00	49.76	14.76	49.12	5.10	62.86	4:36.62	8309
4. Dezsó Szabó	HUN	11.09	7.42	13.73	1.97	48.24	14.86	39.22	5.30	59.14	4:19.96	8199
5. Robert Muzzio	USA	11.36	6.94	16.02	2.00	50.00	14.75	50.74	4.90	61.64	4:31.52	8195
6. Paul Meier	GER	10.75	7.54	15.34	2.15	48.33	15.22	42.14	4.60	55.44	4:38.21	8192
7. William Mottl	FRA	11.42	7.13	16.44	2.12	50.44	15.02	50.58	4.70	67.50	4:48.89	8164
8. Ramil Ganiyev	UZB	10.97	7.49	14.35	2.12	49.30	14.78	45.08	4.90	54.70	4:42.20	8160

It was supposed to be the Dan and Dave show—at least according to the Reebok shoe company's $25 million advertising campaign. "Dan" was Dan O'Brien, the reigning world champion. "Dave" was Dave Johnson, who held the record for the highest second-day score. Dan was the favorite; Dave was the worthy contender. But at the United States Olympic trials, something went wrong. Dan O'Brien was on world record pace when he failed to clear his opening height of 15 feet 9 inches in the pole vault. Dave Johnson was left to carry the United States and Reebok flags in the decathlon. But he too almost ran aground in Barcelona. His first two shot put attempts were fouls. The red flag went up again on his final try when an official ruled that his foot had touched the top of the toe board. The head judge overruled the decision, but after that the Spanish crowd, rooting for Antonio Peñalver, jeered Johnson's every move. At the end of the first day, Paul Meier, a weak second-day decathlete, led with 4510 points, followed by Robert Změlík with 4435, and Peñalver with 4357. Johnson was back in ninth place with 4154 and it was clear that something more than the heckling crowd was hurting him. It turned out that he was trying to keep secret the fact that he was suffering from the effects of a stress fracture in his right ankle.

Změlík took the lead after the first event of the second day, survived the discus, and then pulled away over the last three events. The good news for Reebok was that Změlík too was a Reebok man.

Decathlon, 1992

Competitors in the 1992 decathlon reach out to help each other after the tenth and final event.

1996 Atlanta C: 40, N: 24, D: 7.29–8.1. WR: 8891 (Dan O'Brien)

		100 M	LJ	SP	HJ	400 M	110 H	DISC	PV	JAV	1500 M	TOTAL POINTS
1. Dan O'Brien	USA	10.50	7.57	15.66	2.07	46.82	13.87	48.78	5.00	66.90	4:45.89	8824
2. Frank Busemann	GER	10.60	8.07	13.60	2.04	48.34	13.47	45.04	4.80	66.86	4:31.41	8706
3. Tomáš Dvořák	CZE	10.64	7.60	15.82	1.98	48.29	13.79	46.28	4.70	70.16	4:31.25	8664
4. Steve Fritz	USA	10.90	7.77	15.31	2.04	50.13	13.97	49.84	5.10	65.70	4:38.26	8644
5. Eduard Hämäläinen	BLR	10.85	7.48	16.32	1.98	46.91	13.95	49.62	5.00	57.66	4:34.68	8613
6. Erki Nool	EST	10.65	7.88	14.01	2.01	47.26	15.03	42.98	5.40	65.48	4:43.36	8543
7. Robert Změlík	CZE	10.83	7.64	13.53	1.95	49.55	14.17	43.44	5.40	67.20	4:38.45	8422
8. Ramil Ganiyev	UZB	10.84	7.61	14.71	2.13	49.14	14.88	44.86	5.20	53.70	4:42.72	8318

Like Daley Thompson, Dan O'Brien was born to a white mother and a black father. But O'Brien's parents gave him up at birth. He lived in foster homes and was named first Wesley and then Dion before being adopted at the age of two by Jim and Virginia O'Brien, a white couple from Klamath Falls, Oregon. The O'Briens adopted five other children of various races to join two from Virginia's previous marriage.

Dan recieved an athletic scholarship to the University of Idaho, but his grades were so bad that he was not allowed to compete. For 33 months he did not even train. He did find time to develop a serious alcohol problem. He was arrested for driving under the influence and also for cashing bad checks. On Christmas Day 1987 he woke up hungover and alone and realized he had to take control of his life. He returned to training. When VISA funded a program to support the best decathletes in the United States, O'Brien was able to concentrate on his sport. In 1991 he won the world championship. He was the clear favorite to win the 1992 Olympics, but his pole vault no-height at the US trials left him out in the cold. But O'Brien was not to be deterred. On September 5, one month after the Barcelona Olympic final, he scored 8891 points at a meet in Talence, France, to break Daley Thompson's eight-year-old world record. He went on to win the world championship of 1993 and 1995. By the time of the 1996 Olympics, he had won ten straight decathlons and was once again the favorite for gold.

This time, he qualified easily. O'Brien took the lead in Atlanta after the shot put and never relinquished it. The only surprise was the strong performance of 21-year-old Frank Busemann, who beat his personal best by 184 points to take the silver medal. In order to avoid jinxing himself, Dan O'Brien did not bring with him to the stadium the sweatsuit he was supposed to wear at the medal ceremony. When he did win, he wore sweats borrowed from sprinter Michael Johnson.

2000 Sydney C: 38, N: 23, D: 9.28. WR: 8994 (Tomáš Dvořák)

		100 M	LJ	SP	HJ	400 M	110 H	DISC	PV	JAV	1500 M	TOTAL POINTS
1. Erki Nool	EST	10.68	7.76	15.11	2.00	46.71	14.48	43.66	5.00	65.82	4:29.48	8641
2. Roman Šebrle	CZE	10.92	7.62	15.22	2.12	48.20	13.87	44.39	4.80	64.04	4:28.79	8606
3. Chris Huffins	USA	10.48	7.71	15.27	2.09	48.31	13.91	49.55	4.70	56.62	4:38.71	8595
4. Dean Macey	GBR	10.81	7.77	14.62	2.09	46.41	14.53	43.37	4.80	60.38	4:23.45	8567
5. Tom Pappas	USA	10.82	7.41	14.87	2.21	48.64	14.15	41.42	4.90	62.26	4:45.10	8425
6. Tomáš Dvořák	CZE	10.91	7.50	15.91	1.97	49.11	14.34	47.15	4.40	69.94	4:32.23	8385
7. Frank Busemann	GER	10.91	7.64	14.52	2.09	48.97	14.16	33.71	5.00	64.91	4:25.32	8351
8. Attila Zsivoczky	HUN	11.10	7.00	14.96	2.06	48.61	15.27	47.43	4.80	65.87	4:23.37	8277

The pre-Olympic favorite was Tomáš Dvořák who, since his bronze medal at the 1996 Olympics, had won the1997 and 1998 world championships and, on July 4, 1999, set a world record that came within six points of hitting the 9000-point barrier. Unfortunately, in Sydney, Dvořák was hampered by injuries and, although he gave it his best shot, he could do no better then sixth place.

Chris Huffins took the lead after the first event and was still ahead at the end of the first day, albeit by only 8 points over Dean Macey and 49 points over Erki Nool. The next day, Huffins expanded his lead to 196 over Šebrle after the seventh event: the discus. It was this event that was to prove the turning point in the competition. Nool fouled his first two attempts and needed a valid throw on his last try to avoid a zero and thus remain in contention. He appeared to touch the edge of the circle and the official in charge of the discis immediately raised the red flag to indicate a foul. The Estonians filed a protest and the competition officials overruled the discus judge and validated Nool's throw. A counter-protest was filed by the British, American and Czech teams, but it was rejected.

Meanwhile, with only the 1500 meters to be run, Huffins led Nool by 14 points, Šebrle by 54 and Macey and Tom Pappas by 128 and 131 points. However, Huffins was a notoriously poor 1500 meters runner and needed a personal best to retain a shot at any medal at all. In fact, in a courageous performance, Huffins bettered his personal record by an amazing 12½ seconds and edged Macey for the bronze. In fact, Nool, Šebrle and Macey also recorded personal bests for the 1500, leading to the closest decathlon in Olympic history, with only 74 points separating the top four finishers.

Back in Estonia, Erki Nool became so popular that he had to trademark his name to protect it from being used on a wide range of products. Meanwhile, though, the controversy about Nool's discus foul/non-foul did not go away. The Czech Athletic Federation hired a Czech firm called Euro G.V. to perform a computer analysis of Nool's throw. In February 2001, Euro G.V issued a 30-page report that concluded that Nool had avoided overstepping the edge of the rink by 9 millimeters and that the validation of his throw was correct after all. In 2007 Nool was elected to the Estonian Parliament.

In the end it was not Tomás Dvořák, but Roman Šebrle who finally broke the 9000-point barrier, scoring 9026 point at Götzis, Austria, on May 26-27, 2001.

2004 Athens C: 39, N: 26, D: 8.24. WR: 9026 (Roman Šerble)

		100 M	LJ	SP	HJ	400 M	110 H	DISC	PV	JAV	1500 M	TOTAL POINTS
1. Roman Šebrle	CZE	10.85	7.84	16.36	2.12	48.36	14.05	48.72	5.00	70.52	4:40.01	8893 OR
2. Bryan Clay	USA	10.44	7.96	15.23	2.06	49.19	14.13	50.11	4.90	69.71	4:41.65	8820
3. Dmitry Karpov	KAZ	10.50	7.81	15.93	2.09	46.81	13.97	51.65	4.60	55.54	4:38.11	8725
4. Dean Macey	GBR	10.89	7.47	15.73	2.15	48.97	14.56	48.34	4.40	58.46	4:25.42	8414
5. Chiel Warners	HOL	10.62	7.74	14.48	1.97	47.97	14.01	43.73	4.90	55.39	4:38.05	8343
6. Attila Zsivoczky	HUN	10.91	7.14	15.31	2.12	49.40	14.95	45.62	4.70	63.45	4:29.54	8287
7. Laurent Hernu	FRA	10.97	7.19	14.65	2.03	48.73	14.25	44.72	4.80	57.76	4:24.35	8237
8. Erki Nool	EST	10.80	7.53	14.26	1.88	48.81	14.80	42.05	5.40	61.33	4:36.33	8235

Bryan Clay took an early lead in the 100-meter event, finishing just ahead of 23-year-old Dmitry Karpov. He then set a personal best in the long jump, again finishing first, this time ahead of world record holder Roman Šebrle. Clay hung on to the lead despite finishing eighth in the shot put, which Karpov led with a personal record throw. Karpov took over the lead after the high jump, while Šebrle cleared 2.12 meters (6 feet 11½ inches) to move even with Clay. Karpov strengthened his lead with another personal record in the 400 meters, and Šebrle moved ahead of Clay. At the end of the first day, the scoreboard read: Karpov 4689, Šebrle 4594, Clay 4554.

On the second day of competition, Karpov placed first in the 100-meter hurdles, recording the only subfourteen-second time, while Šebrle and Clay held on to second and third places. Karpov expanded his lead to 166 points after the discus throw, and Clay moved within 21 points of Šebrle. Karpov finally began to falter after a disappointing nineteenth-place finish in the pole vault, as Šebrle began to make his move, vaulting five meters and closing within 46 points of Karpov. Šebrle then exploited his strength in the javelin throw to finally take over first place, and Clay moved past Karpov as well with a personal best of 69.71 meters (228 feet 8 inches), even though Karpov himself equalled his own personal best. Šebrle entered the 1500 meters in first place, with a 63-point lead over Clay, who needed to finish within 18 seconds of Karpov to retain the silver. All three athletes recorded personal bests in the event and none of the three moved up or down in the rankings. Clay's second-place score of 8820 was the highest non-winning total ever. Karpov dedicated his medal to the memory of his mother, Vera, a former pentathlete who had died of stomach cancer in March.

Another notable competitor in Athens was Iceland's Jón Arnar Magnússon, who dropped out of the competition before the high jump. It was the second consecutive Olympics that Magnússon had been unable to finish, along with all five World Championships he had contested since 1995.

2008 Beijing C: 40, N: 28, D: 8.22. WR: 9026 (Roman Šebrle)

		100 M	LJ	SP	HJ	400 M	110 H	DISC	PV	JAV	1500 M	TOTAL POINTS
1. Bryan Clay	USA	10.44	7.78	16.27	1.99	48.92	13.93	53.79	5.0	70.97	5:06.59	8791
2. Andrei Krauchanka	BLR	10.96	7.61	14.39	2.11	47.30	14.21	44.58	5.0	60.23	4:27.47	8551
3. Leonel Suárez Fajardo	CUB	10.90	7.33	14.49	2.05	47.91	14.15	44.45	4.7	73.98	4:29.17	8527
4. Aleksandr Pogorelov	RUS	11.07	7.37	16.53	2.08	50.91	14.47	50.04	5.0	64.01	5:01.56	8328
5. Romain Barras	FRA	11.26	7.08	15.42	1.96	49.51	14.21	45.17	5.0	65.40	4:29.29	8253
6. Roman Šebrle	CZE	11.21	7.68	14.78	2.11	49.54	14.71	45.50	4.8	63.93	4:49.63	8241
7. Oleksiy Kasianov	UKR	10.53	7.56	15.15	1.96	47.70	14.37	48.39	4.3	51.59	4:28.94	8238
8. André Niklaus	GER	11.12	7.29	13.23	2.05	49.65	14.37	45.39	5.2	60.21	4:32.90	8220

Bryan Clay and Roman Šebrle had been rivals and friends over the years. After finishing second to Šebrle at the 2004 Olympics, Clay defeated his rival to win the 2005 world championship, his first major international title. The following year Šebrle won the 2006 European championship. Both Clay and Šebrle had a challenging 2007 season. During a training session in South Africa in early 2007 Šebrle was hit in the shoulder by a javelin that came within 10 centimeters of puncturing his lung and 20 centimeters from hitting his throat. He recovered in time to compete in the world championships, whereas Clay, hampered by a lingering quad injury, dropped out after the high jump event. With Clay out of the running, Šebrle managed to come back from a late deficit to win the title in the last two events. It was the narrowest margin in world championship history: a mere 32 points. Šebrle's victory made him the second man in history—after Britain's Daley Thompson—to simultaneously hold the Olympic, European and world championship decathlon titles, as well as the world record. The next year Clay regained his momentum after recording a personal best score of 8832 to win the

US Olympic Trials, while Šebrle battled his own injury, this time with his hamstring.

Born in Texas to an African-American father and a Japanese-American mother, Bryan Clay spent most of his childhood in Hawaii. At the age of 10 he was so affected by his parents' divorce that his mother didn't let him play team sports because she was worried about his interactions with others. "I told him he would have to play an individual sport . . . swimming, tennis or track and field."

Competing in intermittent rains, Clay took the lead after the first event in Beijing, the 100 meters, and never relinquished his advantage. In round two Clay recorded a season-best long jump (7.78 meters/25 ft. 6¼ in.) and then finished second in the shot put behind Aleksandr Pogorelov of Russia. Despite struggling in the high jump and 400-meter events, placing 11th and 10th overall, Clay carried an 88-point lead over second-place Andrei Krauchanka into the second day of competition, with Šebrle back in fifth place.

Clay expanded his lead on the second day of competition, finishing second in the 110-meter hurdles and winning the discus event. By the final event, the 1500 meters, Clay had built a huge 479-point lead over Krauchanka, needing only to finish to take the gold medal. Krauchanka held on for silver, while 20-year-old Leonel Suárez edged past Pogorelov in the final event to take bronze.

An exhausted Šebrle finished sixth, but pulled himself up from the track to raise Clay's hand in victory. Asked how he was planning on celebrating, Clay responded, "I am going home and going straight to bed."

DISCONTINUED EVENTS

60 METERS

1900 Paris C: 10, N: 6, D: 7.15.

1. Alvin Kraenzlein	USA	7.0 WR
2. J. Walter Tewksbury	USA	7.1e
3. Stanley Rowley	AUS	7.2e
4. Edmund Minahan	USA	7.2e

1904 St. Louis C: 15, N: 3, D: 8.29. WR: 7.0 (Alvin Kraenzlein)

1. C. "Archie" Hahn	USA	7.0	EWR
2. William Hogenson		USA	7.2
3. Fay Moulton		USA	7.2
4. Clyde Blair		USA	7.2
5. Meyer Prinstein		USA	—
6. Frank Castleman		USA	—

Hahn won the first of his three gold medals at the St. Louis Games. One of the runners eliminated in the first heat of the first round was George Poage who, with this race, became the first African-American to compete in the Olympics.

5 MILES (8047 METERS)

1906 Athens C: 28, N: 12, D: 4.25. WR: 24:33.4 (Alfred Shrubb)

1. Henry Hawtrey	GBR	26:11.8
2. Johan "John" Svanberg	SWE	26:19.4
3. Edward Dahl	SWE	26:26.2
4. George Bonhag	USA	—
5. Pericle Pagliani	ITA	—
6. George Blake	AUS	—

DISQ: John Daly (IRL) 26:26.0e

Hawtrey took the lead after two miles and pulled away to win by 50 yards. John Daly of Ireland finished third, but was disqualified for staggering in front of Dahl and impeding his progress.

1908 London C: 36, N: 14, D: 7.18. WR: 24:33.4 (Alfred Shrubb)

1. Emil Voigt	GBR	25:11.2
2. Edward Owen	GBR	25:24.0
3. Johan "John" Svanberg	SWE	25:37.2
4. Charles Hefferon	SAF	25:44.0
5. Arthur "Archie" Robertson	GBR	26:13.0
6. Frederick Meadows	CAN	26:16.2
7. John Fitzgerald	CAN	—
8. Frederick Bellars	USA	—

The heats of the five-mile run were held the same day as the final of the three-mile team race. Archie Robertson finished second individually in the three-mile team race. Three hours later he won his heat in the five-mile competition. Voigt, a 5-foot 5-inch vegetarian from Manchester, sprinted away in the final lap and won by 70 yards. He later emigrated to Australia, where he set up a radiio station and became President of the Australian Federation of Broadcasting Stations. Voigt retired to New Zealand and died October 16, 1973, at the age of ninety.

CROSS-COUNTRY, INDIVIDUAL

1912 Stockholm C: 45, N: 10, D: 7.15. (ca. 12,000 Meters)

1. Johan "Hannes" Kolehmainen	FIN	45:11.6
2. Hjalmar Andersson	SWE	45:44.8
3. John Eke	SWE	46:37.6
4. Jalmari "Lauri" Eskola	FIN	46:54.8
5. Josef Ternström	SWE	47:07.7
6. Albin Stenroos	FIN	47:23.4
7. Wilhelm "Ville" Kyrönen	FIN	47:32.0
8. Leonard Richardson	SAF	47:33.5

Hannes Kolehmainen won his third gold medal of the Stockholm Games, having already triumphed in the 5000 meters and 10,000 meters.

1920 Antwerp C: 47, N: 11, D: 8.23.
(ca. 8000 Meters)

1. Paavo Nurmi	FIN	27:15.0
2. Erik Backman	SWE	27:17.6
3. Heikki Liimatainen	FIN	27:37.0
4. James Wilson	GBR	27:45,2
5. A. Frank Hegarty	GBR	27:57.0
6. Teodor Koskenniemi	FIN	27:57.2
7. Julien van Campenhout	BEL	28:00.0
8. Gaston Heuet	FRA	28:10.0

Nurmi and Joseph Guillemot had split the 5000 and 10,000. The cross-country was to be the tie-breaker, but three kilometers from the finish Guillemot stepped in a hole, injured his ankle, and had to withdraw. Approaching the stadium, Nurmi held a lead of 50 meters. He slowed down and let Backman enter the stadium first. Then, 200 meters from the finish line, he sprinted away to an easy victory.

1924 Paris C: 38, N: 10, D: 7.12. (ca. 10,000 Meters)

1. Paavo Nurmi	FIN	32:54.8
2. Vilho "Ville" Ritola	FIN	34:19.4
3. Earl Johnson	USA	35:21.0
4. Ernest Harper	GBR	35:45.4
5. Henri Lauvaux	FRA	36:44.8
6. Arthur Studenroth	USA	36:45.4
7. Carlo Martinenghi	ITA	37:01.0
8. August Fager	USA	37:40.2

This event proved to be an almost total disaster, which put an end to cross-country races in the Olympics. Thirty-eight runners started off in the afternoon of one of the hottest days in Parisian history. Only fifteen finished. The course was unusually difficult, including stone paths that were covered in knee-high thistles and weeds. The race was also run too close to an energy plant that was belching out poisonous fumes. The first man to enter the stadium and cross the finish line was Paavo Nurmi. He appeared so fresh and untroubled that the spectators had no reason to suspect that anything was wrong. But as soon as the other runners started to arrive, the horrible situation began to unfold. One after another, strong athletes staggered onto the track. Aguilar of Spain collapsed, hit his head on a marker, and began bleeding. Sewell of Great Britain headed the wrong way. Pointed in the right direction, he collided with another runner. Both of them fell and failed to finish. Out on the roads

Paavo Nurmi, 1924
Nurmi leads the field during the running of the murderous 1924 cross-country race that put an end to cross-country as an Olympic event.

there had been worse scenes of carnage, as various contestants were overcome by sunstroke and vomiting. Hours later, the Red Cross and Olympic officials were still searching the sides of the road for missing runners.

When the full extent of the tragedy became known, the remarkable performance of Paavo Nurmi was seen as even more impressive. Not only had the race taken place only two days after Nurmi had won the 1500 meters and the 5000 meters on the same day, but the very next day after the catastrophe, while most of the other cross-country runners were recuperating in bed or in the hospital, Nurmi was back again, winning another gold medal in the 3000 meters team race.

3000-METER TEAM RACE

1912 Stockholm T: 5, N: 5, D: 7.13.

	TEAM TOTALS	
1. USA	9	1—Tel Berna 8:44.6, 3—Norman Taber 8:45.2. 5—George Bonhag 8:46.6
2. SWE	13	2—Thorild Ohlsson 8:44.6, 4—Ernst Wide 8:46.2, 7—Bror Fock 8:47.1
3. GBR	23	6—William Cottrill 8:46.8, 8—George Hutson 8:47.2. 9—Cyril Porter 8:48.0

Finland was eliminated in the first-round heat by the well-balanced US team, despite the fact that Hannes Kolehmainen set a world record of 8:36.9.

1920 Antwerp T: 6, N: 6, D: 8.22.

	TEAM TOTALS	
1. USA	10	1—H. Hallock Brown 8:45.4, 3—Arlie Schardt 8:46.3e, 6—Ivan Dresser 8:51.4e
2. GBR	20	5—Charles Blewitt 8:49.3e, 7—Albert Hill, 8—William Seagrove
3. SWE	24	2—Erik Backman 8:45.6e, 10—Sven Lundgren, 12—Edvin Wide
4. FRA	30	4—Armand Burtin, 11—Gaston Heuet, 15—Edmond Brossard
5. ITA	36	9—Ernesto Ambrosini, 13—Augusto Maccario, 14—Carlo Speroni

For the team race, only the placings for the first three finishers from each country were counted.

1924 Paris T: 9, N: 9, D: 7.13.

	TEAM TOTALS	
1. FIN	8	1—Paavo Nurmi 8:32.0, 2—Vilho "Ville" Ritola 8:40.6, 5—Elias Katz 8:45.4
2. GBR	14	3—Bertram Macdonald 8:44.0, 4—Herbert "Johnny" Johnston, 7—George Webber
3. USA	25	6—Edward Kirby 8:53.0, 8—William Cox, 11—Willard Tibbets
4. FRA	31	9—Paul Bontemps, 10—Armand Burtin, 12—Leonard Mascaux

Paavo Nurmi, running his seventh race in six days, won his fifth gold medal.

3-MILE TEAM RACE (4828 METERS)

1908 London T: 6, N: 6, D: 7.15.

	TEAM TOTALS	
1. GBR	6	1—Joseph Deakin 14:35.6e, 2—Arthur Robertson, 14:41.0, 3—Wilfred Coales 14:41.6
2. USA	19	4—John Eisele 14:41.8,6—George Bonhag 15:05.0e, 9—Herbert Trube 15:11.0e
3. FRA	32	8—Louis de Fleurac 15:08.4e, 11—Joseph Dreher 15:40.0e, 13—Paul Lizandier 16:03.0e

On July 14, Jean Bouin of France recorded the fastest time in the preliminary round, 14:53. As it happened to be the French national holiday, Bouin celebrated his victory by getting drunk on beer in the bars of Soho. He got into a fight and was arrested and thrown into jail. He was bailed out the next morning by team officials and put onto the starting line for the afternoon final. He started the race but was forced to withdraw. The incident failed to diminish Bouin's popularity back in France, and four years later he returned to the Olympics to win a silver medal in the 5000 meters.

5000-METER TEAM RACE

1900 Paris T: 2, N: 3, D: 7.22.

	TEAM TOTALS	
1. GBR/AUS	26	1—Charles Bennett 15:29.2 WR, 2— John Rimmer, 6—Sidney Robinson, 7—Alfred Tysoe, 10—Stanley Rowley [AUS] DNF
2. FRA	29	3—Henri Deloge, 4—Gaston Ragueneau, 5—Jacques Chastanié, 8—André Castanet, 9—Michel Chainpoudry

The United States team refused to take part because the race was held on a Sunday. Although only the first four finishers on each team counted for the team score, French officials insisted that each team start five runners, all of whom must finish. The British team was one man short, so they recruited Australian sprinter Stanley Rowley, who had already finished third in the 60-, 100-, and 200-meter races. Not accustomed to long distances, Rowley ran one lap and then slowed to a leisurely walk. After several more very slow laps, the French officials conceded the absurdity of the situation and allowed Rowley to retire. Bennett pulled away from Rimmer on the final lap and won by about 25 yards.

4-MILE TEAM RACE (6437 METERS)

1904 St. Louis T: 2, N: 2, D: 9.3.

	TEAM TOTALS	
1.USA (New York A.C.)	27	1—Arthur Newton 21:17.8, 5—George Underwood, 6—Paul Pilgrim, 7—Howard Valentine, 8—David Munson
2. USA & FRA (Chicago A.A.)	28	2—James Lightbody, 3—William Frank Verner, 4—Lacey Hearn, 9—Albert Corey [FRA], 10—Sidney Hatch

CROSS-COUNTRY TEAM RACE

1912 Stockholm T: 6, N: 6, D: 7.15. (ca. 12,000 Meters)

	TEAM TOTALS	
1. SWE	10	2—Hjalmar Andersson 45:44.8, 3—John Eke 46:37.6, 5—Jósef Ternström 47:07.1
2. FIN	11	1—Johan "Hannes" Kolehmainen 45:11.6, 4—Jalmari "Lauri" Eskola 46:54.8, 6—Albin Stenroos 47:23.4
3. GBR	49	15—Frederick Hibbins 49:18, 2, 16—Ernest Glover 49:53.7, 18—Thomas Humphreys 50:28.0
4. NOR	61	19—Olav Hovdenak 50:40.8, 20—Parelius Finnerud 51:16.2, 22—Johannes Andersen 51:47.4
5. DEN	63	14—Lauritz Christiansen, 49:06.4, 23—Viggo Pedersen 53:00.8, 26—Gerhard Topp 54:24.9

1920 Antwerp T: 7, N: 7, D: 8.23. (ca. 8000 Meters)

	TEAM TOTALS	
1. FIN	10	1—Paavo Nurmi 27:15.0, 3—Heikki Liimatainen 27:37.00, 6—Teodor Koskenniemi 27:57.2
2. GBR	21	4—James Wilson 27:45.2, 5—Frank Hegarty 27:57.0, 12—Arthur Nichols 28:20.0
3. SWE	23	2—Erik Backman 27:17.6, 10—Gustaf Mattsson 28:16.0, 11—Hilding Ekman 28:17.0
4. USA	36	9—Patrick Flynn 28:12.0, 13—Frederick Faller, 14—Max Bohland
5. FRA	40	8—Gaston Heuet 28:10.0, 15—Gustave Lauvaux, 17—Joseph Servella
6. BEL	48	7—Julien van Campenhout 28:00.0, 20—Henri Smets, 21—Aimé Proot
7. DEN	53	16—Albert Andersen, 18—Henrik Sorensen, 19—Jón Jónsson

1924 Paris T: 7, N: 7, D: 7.12. (ca. 10,000 Meters)

	TEAM TOTALS	
1. FIN	11	(1—Paavo Nurmi 32:54.8, 2—Vilho "Ville" Ritola 34:19.4, 8—Heikki Liimatainen 38:12.0)
2. USA	14	(3—Earl Johnson 35:21.0, 5—Arthur Studenroth 36:45.4, 6—August Fager 37:40.2)
3. FRA	20	(4—Henri Lauvaux 36:44.8. 7—Gaston Heuet 37:52.0, 9—Maurice Norland 41:38.6)

The same horrible race that was the individual cross-country also counted as the team race. In order for Finland to win, at least three men had to cross the finish line. Nurmi and Ritola finished easily, but Liimatainen, staggering along in the oppressive heat, halted 30 meters short of his goal. Thinking he had already crossed the finish line, he turned and headed off the track. The crowd shouted at him and he stopped. After standing for a while with his back to the finish line, he finally regained control of his senses, turned around, and walked across the finish. It took him two minutes to cover the last 30 meters. The British, Italian, Spanish, and Swedish teams failed to complete the course.

200-METER HURDLES

1900 Paris C: 11, N: 5, D: 7:16. WR: 23.6 (Alvin Kraenzlein)

1. Alvin Kraenzlein	USA	25.4
2. Norman Pritchard	GBR/IND	26.0e
3. J. Walter Tewksbury	USA	26.1e
4. Eugène Choisel	FRA	—

Kraenzlein won his fourth gold medal of the Paris Games.

1904 St. Louis C: 5, N: 1, D: 9.1. WR: 23.6 (Alvin Kraenzlein)

1. Harry Hillman	USA	24.6 OR
2. Frank Castleman	USA	24.9
3. George Poage	USA	25.2e
4. George Varnell	USA	—
5. Frederick Schule	USA	

4000-METER STEEPLECHASE

1900 Paris C: 8. N: 5, D: 7.16.

1. John Rimmer	GBR	12:58.4
2. Charles Bennett	GBR	12:58.6e
3. Sidney Robinson	GBR	12:58.8e
4. Jacques Chastanié	FRA	—
5. George Orton	CAN	—
6. Franz Duhne	GER	—

AC: Alexander Grant (CAN), Thaddeus McClain (USA)

Rimmer led from start to finish, pulling away at the beginning of the final lap and then holding off the closing rushes of Bennett and Robinson to win by one and a half yards over Bennett and two over Robinson.

1500-METER WALK

1906 Athens C: 9, N: 6, D: 4:30.

1. George Bonhag	USA	7:12.6
2. Donald Linden	CAN	7:19.8
3. Konstantin Spetsiotis	GRE	7:22.0
4. Georgios Saridakis	GRE	—
5. Charilaos Vasilakos	GRE	—
6. Alexandros Kouris	GRE	—
7. György Sztantics	HUN	—

DISQ: Richard Wilkinson (GBR), Eugen Spiegler (AUT)

Wilkinson and Spiegler finished first and second, but were disqualified for illegal technique. This left Bonhag with first place, although he too was disqualified by two of the four judges. The deciding vote in favor of Bonhag was cast by the president of the jury, Prince George. Bonhag had actually never entered a walking race before. Disappointed by his showings in the 5-mile run and the 1500-meter run in which he had finished fourth and sixth, Bonhag entered the 1500-meter walk hoping to make up for his previous failures. He approached Donald Linden asking for advice and Linden obliged by teaching Bonhag rules and technique. Linden was one of many who thought that Bonhag should have been disqualified. It was widely thought, even among some Americans, that the chief judge, James Sullivan of the United States, had been blinded by patriotic fever. Vasilakos, who placed fifth, had finished second in the 1896 marathon.

Bonhag is the only athlete to have won Olympic gold in both running and walking events.

3000-METER WALK

1906 Athens C: 8, N: 5, D: 5.2.

1. György Sztantics	HUN	15:13.2
2. Hermann Müller	GER	15:20.0
3. Georgios Saridakis	GRE	15:33.0
4. Pandelis Ektoros	GRE	—
5. Ioannis Panagoulopoulos	GRE	—

DISQ: Richard Wilkinson (GBR), Eugen Spiegler (AUT), Konstantin Spetsiotis (GRE)

The day after the controversial 1500-meter walk, a second contest was hastily scheduled at 3000 meters with Crown Prince Konstantinos as head judge. Once again Wilkinson and Spiegler moved to the front. Fifty meters from the finish, they both began to run and were again disqualified. In honor of Sztantics' victory, the mayor of his hometown in Hungary sent him money to buy two barrels of wine, which were then shared in a large hall with the athletes of many nations.

1908–1912 not held

1920 Antwerp C: 22, N: 12, D: 8.21. WR: 12:53.8 (Gunnar Rasmussen)

1. Ugo Frigerio	ITA	13:14.2 OR
2. George Parker	AUS	13:19.6e
3. Richard Remer	USA	13:22.2e
4. Cecil McMaster	SAF	13:23.6e
5. Thomas Maroney	USA	13:25.0e
6. Charles Dowson	GBR	13:28.0e
7. William Hehir	GBR/IRL	13:29.8e
8. William Roelker	USA	13:30.4e

Ugo Frigerio was such a colorful character that his flamboyance often obscured the fact that he was a superb athlete who combined great speed with perfect style. While other walkers became nervous or annoyed when a judge got down on his hands and knees to scrutinize their style Frigerio seemed to enjoy the attention, and always made it a point to thank the judge when he was finished. Frigerio also enjoyed the attentions of the crowd, sometimes taking the time to exchange remarks with spectators, and even leading cheers for himself.

Just before the beginning of the 3000-meter walk, Frigerio approached the conductor of the band in the middle of the field and handed him several pages of sheet music which he requested to be played during the course of the race. Accompanied by the proper background music, Frigerio moved quickly to the front and led the entire race, pausing only once toward the end to admonish the band for not playing at the correct tempo. He won easily by 20 meters.

Ugo Frigerio, 1920
Musically minded crowd-pleaser Frigerio won a total of three walking gold medals in 1920 and 1924.

3500-METER WALK

1908 London C: 23, N: 8, D: 7.14.

1. George Larner	GBR	14:55.0
2. Ernest Webb	GBR	15:07.4
3. Harry Kerr	AUS/NZL	15:43.4
4. George Goulding	CAN	15:49.8
5. Arthur Rowland	AUS/NZL	16:07.0
6. Charles Westergaard	DEN	17:21.8
7. Einar Rothman	SWE	17:50.0

DNF: William Palmer (GBR)

George Larner, a 33-year-old Brighton policeman, came out of retirement to take part in the Olympics. He won by 45 yards. Bronze medalist Harry Kerr had been a professional, but, according to Australian rules in effect at the time, he was able to regain his amateur status by avoiding competition for two years. During that break (1905–1906), Kerr worked on his family's farm at Tariki, near Stratford. Kerr almost missed the start of the final because he was chatting with some officials underneath the stands.

10,000-METER WALK

1912 Stockholm C: 22, N: 11, D: 7.11. WR: 45:15.6 (Ernest Webb)

1. George Goulding	CAN	46:28.4
2. Ernest Webb	GBR	46:50.4
3. Fernando Altimani	ITA	47:37.6
4. Aage Rasmussen	DEN	48:00.0

George Goulding, an English-born Canadian, had competed in the 1908 Olympics as both a walker and a runner, placing fourth in the 3500-meter walk and 22nd in the marathon. In 1912 he kept up such a rapid pace in the 10,000-meter walk that three of the ten finalists dropped out and another three were disqualified for lifting. After his victory, the laconic Canadian sent a telegram to his wife which read simply, "Won—George." Ten days later, his wife gave birth to a baby boy, whom his parents named George Beverly Olympic Goulding. Ernest Webb, who earned his third Olympic silver medal, was 40 years old.

1920 Antwerp C: 23, N: 13, D: 8.18. WR: 45:26.4 (Gunnar Rasmussen)

1. Ugo Frigerio	ITA	48:06.2
2. Joseph Pearman	USA	49:40.2e
3. Charles Gunn	GBR	49:43.9e
4. Cecil McMaster	SAF	50:04.0e
5. William Hehir	GBR/IRL	50:11.8e
6. Thomas Maroney	USA	50:24.4e
7. Jean Seghers	BEL	50:32.4e
8. Antoine Doyen	BEL	56:30.0e

Frigerio, as boisterous as ever, won by 250 meters to gain the first of his three gold medals.

1924 Paris C: 23, N: 13, D: 7:13. WR: 45:26.4 (Gunnar Rasmussen)

1. Ugo Frigerio	ITA	47:49.0
2. Gordon Goodwin	GBR	48:37.9
3. Cecil McMaster	SAF	49:08.0
4. Donato Pavesi	ITA	49:17.0
5. Arthur Tell Schwab	SWI	49:50.0
6. F. Ernest Clarke	GBR	49:59.2e
7. Armando Valente	ITA	—
8. Luigi Besatra	ITA	—

Frigerio's final gold medal was won by 200 meters.

1928–1936 not held

1948 London C: 19, N: 10, D: 8.7. WR: 42:39.6 (Verner Hardmo)

1. John Mikaelsson	SWE	45:13.2
2. Ingemar Johansson	SWE	45:43.8
3. Fritz Schwab	SWI	46:00.2
4. Charles Morris	GBR	46:04.0
5. Harold Churcher	GBR	46:28.0
6. Emile Maggi	FRA	47:02.8
7. Richard West	GBR	—
8. Gianni Corsano	ITA	—

Mikaelsson set an Olympic record of 45:03.0 in the first round. The final saw the disqualification of the great Verner Hardmo, who set 29 ratified and unratified world records between 1943 and 1945, at distances ranging from 3000 meters to 10 miles.

1952 Helsinki C: 23, N: 12, D: 7.27. WR: 42:39.6 (Verner Hardmo)

1. John Mikaelsson	SWE	45:02.8 OR	(45:02.85)
2. Fritz Schwab	SWI	45:41.0	(45:41.03)
3. Bruno Junk	SOV/EST	45:41.0	(45:41.05)
4. Louis Chevalier	FRA	45:50.4	(45:50.28)
5. George Coleman	GBR	46:06.8	(46:06.69)
6. Ivan Yarmysh	SOV/UKR	46:07.0	(46:07.07)
7. Emile Maggi	FRA	46:08.0	(46:08.16)
8. Bruno Fait	ITA	46:25.6	

Mikaelsson was 38 years old when he won his second gold medal. Silver medallist Fritz Schwab was the son of Arthur Schwab, who won the 50-kilometer silver medal in 1936. Both Schwab and Junk began running 30 yards from the finish, making the judges, who had disqualified seven men in the heats and final, look foolish. The controversies that resulted from this race led Olympic officials to drop the 10,000 meters event and replace it with a 20,000 meters contest in 1956.

10-MILE WALK (16,093 METERS)

1908 London C: 25, N: 8, D: 7.17. WR: 1:14:45.0 (J. W. Raby)

1. George Larner	GBR	1:15:57.4
2. Ernest Webb	GBR	1:17:31.0
3. Edward Spencer	GBR	1:21:20.2
4. Frank Carter	GBR	1:21:20.2
5. Ernest Larner	GBR	1:24:26.2

DNF: William Palmer (GBR), Richard Harrison (GBR)

Larner broke the 11-year-old world's amateur record of 1:17:38.4 in winning his second gold medal in four days. Larner practiced unusual training techniques. "When circumstances permit," he advised, "all clothing should be removed for a run round a secluded garden, especially if it is raining at the time."

STANDING HIGH JUMP

1900 Paris C: 3, N: 1, D: 7.16. WR: 1.63, 5-4¼ (Raymond Ewry)

		M	FT.-IN.
1. Raymond Ewry	USA	1.655	5-5 WR
2. Irving Baxter	USA	1.525	5-0
3. Lewis Sheldon	USA	1.50	4-11

Ray Ewry won eight Olympic gold medals in 1900, 1904, and 1908, and added two more in the Intercalated Games of 1906. Yet he is almost unknown today because his unprecedented feats were performed in events that are no longer held. Born on October 18, 1873, in Lafayette, Indiana, Ewry contracted polio as a small boy. Confined to a wheelchair, it was thought that he might be paralyzed for life. However he began exercising on his own, and not only regained the use of his legs, but eventually grew up to be a superb athlete who specialized in the standing jumps. On July 16, 1900, Ewry won three gold medals in Paris, sweeping the standing high jump, the standing long jump, and the standing triple jump. He made a great impression in France and was dubbed "The Human Frog." His final clearance of 5 feet 5 inches would have been good enough for a silver medal in 1896 – in the running high jump. Ewry repeated his sweep in 1904. With the triple jump eliminated from the Games, he had to settle for double victories in 1906 and 1908. The standing jumps were dropped from the Olympics after 1912. Ewry also held the amateur record for the backward standing long jump—9 feet 3 inches. He died on September 27, 1937, at the age of 63.

1904 St. Louis C: 5, N: 2, D: 8.31. WR: 1.65, 5-5 (Raymond Ewry)

		M	FT.-IN.
1. Raymond Ewry	USA	1.60	5-3
2. Joseph Stadler	USA	1.45	4-9
3. Lawson Robertson	USA	1.45	4-9
4. John Biller	USA	1.42	4-8
5. Lajos Gönczy	HUN	1.35	4-5

Joseph Stadler was the first black athlete to win an Olympic medal in a field event. He was awarded second place after a jump-off.

1906 Athens C: 11, N: 6, D: 5.1. WR: 1.65, 5-5 (Raymond Ewry)

		M	FT.-IN.
1. Raymond Ewry	USA	1.56	5-1¼
2. Léon Dupont	BEL	1.40	4-7
2. Lawson Robertson	USA	1.40	4-7
2. Martin Sheridan	USA	1.40	4-7
5. Lajos Gönczy	HUN	1.35	4-5
6. Konstantinos Tsiklitiras	GRE	1.30	4-3¼
7. Themistoklis Diakidis	GRE	1.25	4-1¼
7. Paul Weinstein	GER	1.25	4-1¼

Martin Sheridan took part in the standing high jump at the same time that he was competing in the discus throw, Greek style.

1908 London C: 23, N: 11, D: 7.23. WR: 1.65, 5-5 (Raymond Ewry)

		M	FT.-IN.
1. Raymond Ewry	USA	1.575	5-2
2. John Biller	USA	1.55	5-1
2. Konstantinos Tsiklitiras	GRE	1.55	5-1
4. F. Leroy Holmes	USA	1.525	5-0
5. Platt Adams	USA	1.47	4-10
5. Georges "Géo" André	FRA	1.47	4-10
5. Alfred Motté	FRA	1.47	4-10
8. William Blystad (NOR), Léon Dupont (BEL), Walter Henderson (GBR), Francis Irons (USA), Svend Langkjær (DEN), Arthur Mallwitz (GER)		1.42	4-8

1912 Stockholm C: 18, N: 9, D: 7.13. WR: 1.65, 5-5 (Raymond Ewry)

		M	FT.-IN.
1. Platt Adams	USA	1.63	5-4¼
2. Benjamin Adams	USA	1.60	5-3
3. Konstantinos Tsiklitiras	GRE	1.55	5-1
4. Richard Byrd	USA	1.50	4-11
4. Leo Goehring	USA	1.50	4-11
4. Evald Möller	SWE	1.50	4-11

Platt Adams was 27 years old. His brother Ben was 22. In 1980, Rune Almen of Sweden cleared 1.90 meters (6 feet 2¾ inches) in the standing high jump to set the current record in the event.

STANDING LONG JUMP

1900 Paris C: 4, N: 2, D: 7.16.

		M	FT.-IN.
1. Raymond Ewry	USA	3.30	10-10
2. Irving Baxter	USA	3.135	10-3¼
3. Emile Torcheboeuf	FRA	3.03	9-11¼
4. Lewis Sheldon	USA	3.02	9-10¾

1904 St. Louis C: 4, N: 1, D: 8.29.

		M	FT.-IN.
1. Raymond Ewry	USA	3.476	11-4 WR
2. Conant King	USA	3.28	10-9
3. John Biller	USA	3.26	10-8¼
4. Henry Field	USA	3.19	10-5½

1906 Athens C: 30, N: 11, D: 4.25.

		M	FT.-IN.
1. Raymond Ewry	USA	3.30	10-10
2. Martin Sheridan	USA	3.095	10-1¾
3. Lawson Robertson	USA	3.05	10-0
4. Léon Dupont	BEL	2.975	9-9
5. Axel Ljung	SWE	2.955	9-8¼
6. Istzán Somodi	HUN	2.86	9-4½
7. Alexandre Tuffère	FRA	2.855	9-4
8. Konstantinos Tsiklitiras	GRE	2.84	9-3¾

1908 London C: 24, N: 11, D: 7.20.

		M	FT.-IN.
1. Raymond Ewry	USA	3.335	10-11¼
2. Konstantinos Tsiklitiras	GRE	3.235	10-7¼
3. Martin Sheridan	USA	3.23	10-7
4. John Biller	USA	3.215	10-6½
5. Ragnar Ekberg	SWE	3.195	10-5¾
6. Platt Adams	USA	3.11	10-2½
6. F. LeRoy Holmes	USA	3.11	10-2½

1912 Stockholm C: 19, N: 8, D: 7.8.

		M	FT.-IN.
1. Konstantinos Tsiklitiras	GRE	3.37	11-0¾
2. Platt Adams	USA	3.36	11-0¼
3. Benjamin Adams	USA	3.28	10-9
4. Gustaf Malmsten	SWE	3.20	10-6
5. Leo Goehring	USA	3.14	10-3½
5. Evald Möller	SWE	3.14	10-3½
7. András Baronyi	HUN	3.13	10-3¼
8. R. Leslie Byrd	USA	3.12	10-2¾

Tsiklitiras died of meningitis the year after his Olympic triumph while fighting in the Balkan War. He was 25 years old.

In 1962 Johann Evandt of Norway performed a standing long jump of 11 feet 11¾ inches. The claims of professional jumpers are difficult to substantiate. Joe Darby of Great Britain was said to have jumped 12 feet 1½ inches on May 28, 1890, and W. Barker was reputed to have leaped 12 feet 6½ inches in May 1904.

STANDING TRIPLE JUMP

1900 Paris C: 10, N: 4, D: 7.16.

		M	FT.-IN.
1. Raymond Ewry	USA	10.58	34-8½
2. Irving Baxter	USA	9.95	32-7¾
3. Robert Garrett	USA	9.50	31-2
4. Lewis Sheldon	USA	9.45	31-0

1904 St. Louis C: 4, N: 1, D: 9.3.

		M	FT.-IN.
1. Raymond Ewry	USA	10.54	34-7¼
2. Conant King	USA	10.16	33-4
3. Joseph Stadler	USA	9.60	31-6
4. Garrett Serviss	USA	9.53	31-3¼

STONE THROW (6.35 kg—14 lbs.)

1906 Athens C: 16, N: 8, D: 4.27.

		M	FT.-IN.
1. Nicolaos Georgantas	GRE	19.925	65-4½
2. Martin Sheridan	USA	19.035	62-5½
3. Michalis Dorizas	GRE	18.585	60-11¾
4. Eric Lemming	SWE	18.21	59-9

The American favorite, James Mitchel was unable to compete because he had suffered a dislocated shoulder when the ship carrying the US team to Europe was hit by a large wave.

SHOT PUT (BOTH HANDS)

1912 Stockholm C: 7, N: 4, D: 7.11.

		M	TWO HANDS	FT.-IN.
1. Ralph Rose	USA	27.70	(15.23 + 12.47)	90-10½
2. Patrick McDonald	USA	27.53	(15.08 + 12.45)	90-4
3. Elmer Niklander	FIN	27.14	(14.71 + 12.43)	89-0½
4. Lawrence Whitney	USA	24.09	(13.48 + 10.61)	79-0½
5. Einar Nilsson	SWE	23.37	(12.52 + 10.85)	76-8¼
6. Paavo Aho	FIN	23.30	(12.72 + 10.58)	76-5½
7. Migir Migiryan	TUR	19.78	(10.85 + 8.93)	64-10¾

The current world record for this event is 121 feet 6¼ inches, set by Al Feuerbach on August 24, 1974. He put 70 feet 1¾ inches with his right hand and 51 feet 5 inches with his left.

56-POUND WEIGHT THROW (25.4 KG)

1904 St. Louis C: 6, N: 2, D: 9.1.

		M	FT.-IN.
1. Étienne Desmarteau	CAN	10.465	34-4
2. John Flanagan	USA	10.16	33-4
3. James Mitchel	USA	10.135	33-3
4. Charles Henneman	USA	9.18	30-1½
5. Charles Chadwick	USA	—	—
6. Ralph Rose	USA	8.53	28-0e

Martin Sheridan, 1908
Falling short of a medal in the Greek-style discus depicted here, he won five gold and four silver medals over three games.

Refused a leave of absence from his job as a Montreal policeman to compete in the St. Louis Games, Étienne Desmarteau went anyway and was fired. When it was learned that he had won a gold medal, his dismissal notice was conveniently lost. Unfortunately, Desmarteau, who was the first individual Olympic champion to represent Canada, died of typhoid the following year at the age of 32. A park was named in his honor.

1906–1912 not held

1920 Antwerp C: 12, N: 4, D: 8.21. WR: 12.36, 40-6¾ (Matthew McGrath)

		M	FT.-IN.
1. Patrick McDonald	USA	11.265	36-11½ OR
2. Patrick Ryan	USA	10.965	35-11½
3. Carl Johan "Masse" Lind	SWE	10.255	33-7½
4. Archie McDiarmid	CAN	10.12	33-2½
5. Malcolm Svensson	SWE	9.455	31-0
6. Petter Pettersson	FIN	9.375	30-9
7. Edward Roberts	USA	9.36	30-8½
8. Elmer Niklander	FIN	8.865	29-1

McDonald is the oldest person ever to win an Olympic track and field gold medal. He was 42 years and 26 days old.

DISCUS (GREEK-STYLE)

1906 Athens C: 21, N: 9, D: 5.1.

		M	FT.-IN.
1. Verner Järvinen	FIN	35.17	115-4½
2. Nicolaos Georgantas	GRE	32.80	107-7
3. István Mudin	HUN	31.91	104-8½
4. Martin Sheridan	USA	31.50	103-4
5. György Luntzer	HUN	30.26	99-3¼
6. František Soucek	BOH/CZE	27.55	90-4½
7. Miroslav Sustera	BOH/CZE	27.08	88-10

Contestants threw the discus from a pedestal that sloped forward, and they were required to follow a restricted set of movements. The discus had to be released from a standing position, with no spinning allowed. Verner Järvinen had four sons, three of whom competed in the 1932 Olympics.

1908 London C: 23, N: 8, D: 7.18. WR: 35.17, 115-4½ (Verner Järvinen)

		M	FT.-IN.
1. Martin Sheridan	USA	38.00	124-8 OR
2. Marquis "Bill" Horr	USA	37.33	122-5½
3. Verner Järvinen	FIN	36.48	119-8¼
4. Arthur Dearborn	USA	35.65	116-11½
5. Michalis Dorizas	GRE	33.35	109-4½
6. Nicolaos Georgantas	GRE	33.20	108-11¼
7. István Mudin	HUN	33.11	108-7½
8. Wilbur Burroughs	USA	32.73	107-4¾

DISCUS (BOTH HANDS)

1912 Stockholm C: 20, N: 6, D: 7.13.

		M	TWO HANDS	FT.-IN.
1. Armas Taipale	FIN	82.86	(44.68 + 38.18)	271-10
2. Elmer Niklander	FIN	77.96	(40.28 + 37.68)	255-9
3. Emil Magnusson	SWE	77.37	(40.58 + 36.79)	253-10
4. Einar Nilsson	SWE	71.40	(40.99 + 30.41)	234-3
5. James Duncan	USA	71.13	(39.78 + 31.35)	233-4½
6. Emil Muller	USA	69.56	(39.83 + 29.73)	229-2
7. Folke Fleetwood	SWE	68.22	(34.20 + 33.82)	223-10
8. Carl Johan "Masse" Lind	SWE	68.02	(34.98 + 32.12)	223-2

The current record for this event, 324 feet 6 inches (178-0 + 146-6) was set by Hank Kraychir on March 24, 1984. This broke Fortune Gordien's 30-year-old record of 305 feet 10 inches.

JAVELIN (FREESTYLE)

1906 Athens C: 22, N: 7, D: 7.27. WR: 53.79, 176-5 (Eric Lemming)

		M	FT.-IN.
1. Eric Lemming	SWE	53.90	176-10 WR
2. Knut Lindberg	SWE	45.17	148-2
3. Bruno Söderström	SWE	44.92	147-4
4. Hjalmar Mellander	SWE	44.30	145-4
5. Verner Järvinen	FIN	44.25	145-2
6. Arne Halse	NOR	43.60	143-0
7. Conrad Carlsrud	NOR	—	—

1908 London C: 33, N: 9, D: 7.15. WR: 57.33, 188-1 (Eric Lemming)

		M	FT.-IN.
1. Eric Lemming	SWE	54.45	178-7½
2. Michalis Dorizas	GRE	51.36	168-6
3. Arne Halse	NOR	49.73	163-1¾
4. Charalambos Zouras	GRE	48.61	159-5¾
5. Hugo Wieslander	SWE	47.55	156-0
6. Armas Pesonen	FIN	46.04	151-0½
7. Imre Mudin	HUN	45.95	150-9
8. Jalmari Sauli	FIN	43.31	142-1

Since all of the successful throwers held the javelin in the middle, just as they did in the regular javelin event, the freestyle javelin was dropped from the Olympics.

JAVELIN (BOTH HANDS)

1912 Stockholm C: 14, N: 4, D: 7.9.

		M	TWO HANDS	FT.-IN.
1. Juho Saaristo	FIN	109.42	(61.00 WR + 48.42)	359-0
2. Väinö Siikaniemi	FIN	101.13	(54.09 + 47.04)	331-9½
3. Urho Peltonen	FIN	100.24	(53.58 + 46.66)	328-10
4. Eric Lemming	SWE	98.59	(58.33 + 40.26)	323-5½
5. Arne Halse	NOR	96.92	(55.05 + 41.87)	318-0
6. Richard Åbrink	SWE	93.12	(50.04 + 43.08)	305-6
7. Daniel Johansen	NOR	92.82	(48.78 + 44.04)	304-6
8. Otto Nilsson	SWE	88.90	(50.21 + 38.69)	291-8

When Finnish team officials realized that all three finalists were from Finland, they asked that the final round be canceled and that the preliminary results be allowed to stand. Swedish Olympic officials agreed with the request.

TRIATHLON

1904 St. Louis C: 118, N: 4, D: 7.2.

		LJ	SP	100 YARDS	PTS.
1. Max Emmerich	USA	21-7	32-2¼	10.6	35.7
2. John Grieb	USA	20-2¼	33-7	11.0	34.0
3. William Merz	USA	19-10¾	31-1	10.8	32.95
4. George Mayer	USA	18-1	36-7	11.4	32.4
5. John Bissinger	USA	18-4¾	32-9½	11.4	30.8
6. Phillip Kassel	USA	19-2¼	28-9½	11.2	30.1
7. Christian Busch	GER	18-10¾	31-3½	11.6	30.05
8. Fred Schmind	USA	19-4¾	30-2¼	11.6	30.0

This event was part of a combined gymnastics and track and field competition known as "'turning" or "turnverein gymnastics."

PENTATHLON

Unlike the decathlon, the pentathlon was decided according to placement points. After the first three events, all but the top 12 athletes were eliminated. After the fourth event, only the top six could continue. Oddly enough, despite these rules, seven men competed in the final event in 1912, 1920, and 1924. In 1912, this was the result of a tie; in 1920, it was due to a controversy concerning the eligibility of Hugo Lahtinen; and in 1924 it was because of a mistake in computing the point total of Göran Unger. Ties in the final places were decided according to the decathlon tables.

1906 Athens C: 26, N: 11, D: 4.28.
(Standing Long Jump, Greek-Style Discus, Javelin, 192-Meter Race, Greco-Roman Wrestling)

		SLJ	DISC	JAV	192 M	GRW	PTS.
1. Hjalmar Mellander	SWE	7	5	5	4	3	24
2. István Mudin	HUN	6	1	9	8	1	25
3. Erik Lemming	SWE	15	2	1	7	4	29
4. Uno Häggman (Tuomela)	FIN	18	9	2	3	2	34
5. Knut Lindberg	SWE	16	11	3	2	5	37
6. Lawson Robertson	USA	1	17	11	1	6	36
7. Edward Archibald	CAN	10	13	4	6	—	—
8. Julius Wagner	GER	8	6	18	5	—	—

The events of the 1906 pentathlon were the same as those of the ancient Greek pentathlon. Robertson withdrew during the wrestling competition and was placed behind Lindberg despite his lower score.

1908 not held

1912 Stockholm C: 26, N: 11, D: 7.7.

		LJ	JAV	200 M	DISC	1500 M	TOTAL PTS.
1. James Thorpe	USA	7.07 (1)	46.71 (3)	22.9 (1)	35.75 (1)	4.44.8 (1)	7
2. Ferdinand Bie	NOR	6.85 (2)	46.45 (4)	23.5 (5)	31.79 (4)	5:07.8 (6)	21
3. James Donahue	USA	6.83 (3)	38.28 (10)	23.0 (2)	29.64 (11)	4:51.0 (3)	29
4. Frank Lukeman	CAN	6.45 (6)	36.02 (11)	23.2 (4)	33.76 (3)	5:00.2 (5)	29
5. J. Austin Menaul	USA	6.40 (8)	35.85 (12)	23.0 (2)	31.38 (6)	4:49.6 (2)	30
6. Avery Brundage	USA	6.58 (4)	42.85 (7)	24.2 (11)	34.72 (2)	DNF (7)	31
7. Hugo Wieslander	SWE	6.27 (10)	49.56 (1)	24.1 (10)	30.74 (7)	4:51.1 (4)	32
8. Gustuf "Gosta" Holmér	SWE	6.02 (12)	45.46 (5)	24.0 (8)	31.78 (5)	—	—

Thorpe and Bie clinched the gold and silver medals respectively before the 1500 meters was even run.

1920 Antwerp C: 19, N: 8, D: 8.16.

		LJ	JAV	200 M	DISC	1500 M	TOTAL PTS.
1. Eero Lehtonen	FIN	6.635 (2)	54.67 (2)	23.0 (1)	34.64 (7)	4:40.2 (2)	14
2. Everett Bradley	USA	6.61 (3)	49.16 (8)	23.0 (1)	36.78 (6)	5:10.0 (6)	24
3. Hugo Lahtinen	FIN	6.59 (4)	54.25 (3)	23.6 (5)	31.12 (13)	4:36.0 (1)	26
4. Robert LeGendre	USA	6.505 (5)	44.60 (11)	23.0 (1)	37.39 (4)	4:46.0 (5)	26
5. Helge Løvland	NOR	6.32 (7)	53.13 (4)	24.0 (10)	39.51 (2)	4:45.8 (4)	27
6. Brutus Hamilton	USA	6.86 (1)	48.36 (10)	23.4 (4)	37.13 (5)	5:12.8 (7)	27
7. Bertil Ohlson	SWE	6.27 (9)	43.68 (12)	23.6 (5)	39.80 (1)	4:42.8 (3)	30
8. Aleksander Klumberg-Kolmpere	EST	6.25 (10)	60.76 (1)	25.3 (15)	38.62 (3)	—	—

1924 Paris C: 31, N: 17, D: 7.7.

		LJ	JAV	200 M	DISC	1500 M	TOTAL PTS.
1. Eero Lehtonen	FIN	6.68 (7)	50.93 (4)	23.0 (1)	40.44 (1)	4:47.1 (1)	14
2. Elemér Somfay	HUN	6.77 (5)	52.07 (2)	23.4 (5)	37.76 (2)	4:48.4 (2)	16
3. Robert LeGendre	USA	7.765 (1)	48.04 (9)	23.0 (1)	36.76 (4)	4:52.6 (3)	18
4. Leo Leino	FIN	6.72 (6)	54.12 (1)	23.2 (4)	33.62 (8)	4:55.4 (4)	23
5. Morton Kaer	USA	6.96 (2)	50.20 (5)	23.0 (1)	32.70 (10)	5:38.6 (6)	24
6. Hugo Lahtinen	FIN	6.895 (3)	48.66 (7)	23.6 (7)	36.08 (5)	4:55.6 (5)	27
7. Brutus Hamilton	USA	6.83 (4)	48.96 (6)	24.4 (11)	37.70 (3)	—	—
8. Göran Unger	SWE	6.55 (8)	48.45 (8)	23.8 (8)	35.11 (6)	—	—

The highlight of this competition was the surprising world record of 25 feet 5¾ inches (7.77 meters) set in the long jump by Robert LeGendre of Georgetown University. First place was not decided until Lehtonen edged Somfay in the 1500 meters.

Chapter 2 Track & Field (Women)

100 METERS

1896–1924 not held

1928 Amsterdam C: 31, N: 13, D: 7.31. WR: 12.2 (Elizabeth Robinson)

1. Elizabeth Robinson	USA	12.2	EWR
2. Fanny "Bobbie" Rosenfeld	CAN	12.3	
3. Ethel Smith	CAN	12.3	
4. Erna Steinberg	GER	12.4	

DISQ: Myrtle Cook (CAN), Helene "Leni" Schmidt (GER)

This was the first women's track event to be contested in the Olympics, so the entrants were unusually nervous, as was the primarily male audience. The men found it particularly unsettling when the three Canadian finalists hugged and kissed each other before the race. First Cook and then Schmidt were disqualified for false-starting twice. The winner—by 18 inches (46 centimeters), Betty Robinson was a 16-year-old high school student from Riverdale, Illinois. Robinson didn't know that she was a really fast runner until her biology teacher saw her running for a train and asked if he could time her running down the school corridor. Robinson competed in her first meet in March 1928. In her second meet—her first outdoors—she broke the world record. The Olympics was only her fourth track meet of any kind. Three years after her victory she was badly injured in a small plane crash, receiving a concussion, a cracked hip, a broken leg, a crushed arm, and a severe cut across her forehead and eyelid. The man who found Robinson and her cousin thought they were dead. He put them in his car trunk and drove them to a mortician, who discovered they were still alive. Robinson was unconscious for seven weeks and was unable to walk normally for two years. However, she regained the use of her leg and returned to competitive running. Because she could

Wyomia Tyus, 1968
After winning the 100-meter dash for a second time, Tyus (center), joined Barbara Ferrell (left) and Irena Szewinska on the podium.

not bend her leg fully at the knee, she could not assume the crouched starting position of a sprinter. She could, however, run in relays. In 1936, Betty Robinson won a second gold medal as a member of the US 4 × 100-meter relay team.

1932 Los Angeles C: 20, N: 10, D: 8.2. WR: 11.9 (Tollien Schuurman)

1. Stanisława Wałasiewicz	POL	11.9	EWR
2. Hilda Strike	CAN	11.9	
3. Wilhełmina Von Bremen	USA	12.0	
4. Marie Dollinger	GER	12.2	
5. Eileen Hiscock	GBR	12.3	
6. Elizabeth Wilde	USA	12.3	

Stanisława Wałasiewicz was born in Rypin, Poland, on April 3, 1911. When she was still an infant her family moved to the United States and settled in Cleveland, Ohio, where she grew up and became known as Stella Walsh. On May 30, 1930, she became the first woman to break the 11-second barrier for 100 yards. By 1932 US track enthusiasts were looking forward to a gold medal from her in the Olympics. But Stella Walsh had a problem: as a result of the worldwide depression, her job with the New York Central Railroad had been eliminated. She was offered a position with the Cleveland Recreation Department, but taking it would have made her ineligible for the Olympics, since Olympic regulations at the time disqualified athletes who made their living from physical education or recreation. With no

Stella Walsh, 1932
What deep, dark secret prevented Walsh from smiling even after she had won the gold medal in then 1932 100-meter dash?

help forthcoming from her adopted country, Stella Walsh made a major decision in her life. Twenty-four hours before she was scheduled to take out US naturalization papers, she accepted a job offer from the Polish consulate in New York and decided to compete for Poland.

Stella Walsh's performance in Los Angeles was no disappointment. Running with what the Canadian official report called "long man-like strides," Stella Walsh equaled Tollien Schuurman's two-month-old world record in every one of her three races. In the final she was hard-pressed by Hilda Strike, but managed to win by half a yard. While some US observers pointed to the loss of Walsh to Poland as an example of the consequences of the lack of support for women's athletics in the US, there were also those who held a grudge against Walsh herself, and she was not granted her naturalization papers until 1947.

1936 Berlin C: 30, N: 15, D: 8.4. WR: 11.6 (Helen Stephens)

1. Helen Stephens	USA	11.5w
2. Stanisława Wałasiewicz	POL	11.7
3. Käthe Krauss	GER	11.9
4. Marie Dollinger	GER	12.0
5. Annette Rogers	USA	12.2
6. Emmy Albus	GER	12.3

Helen Stephens was a 6-foot farm girl from Calloway County, Missouri, who loved to run. When she entered Fulton High School she was routinely timed in the 50-yard dash. Coach Burton Moore was astounded to discover that Stephens had run the race in 5.8 seconds, equaling the existing world record held by Betty Robinson. Moore taught Stephens the various events of track and field and then entered her in the 1935 national AAU meet, which was being held in St. Louis. Wearing a borrowed sweatshirt and shoes, she won the shot put, set a world record in the 200 meters, and set another world record in the standing long jump. But the real sensation came when she beat Stella Walsh in the 50-yard dash, this time officially tying the world record. Walsh was outraged by such impudence and referred to Stephens as a "greenie from

Helen Stephens, 1936
Adolf Hitler made advances to Stephens after her win in the 100 meters, but she turned him down.

the sticks." When Stephens and Walsh met again in the Olympics in Berlin there was never any question as to who would take the gold medal. In the opening round Helen Stephens ran a wind-aided 11.4 to win her heat by ten yards. She ran wind-aided 11.5 in the semifinals and final, finishing the latter two yards ahead of Stella Walsh. After the race, Stephens was taken to meet Adolf Hitler in his private glass-enclosed box. "Hitler comes in and gives me the Nazi salute," she later recalled. "I gave him a good old Missouri handshake. Immediately Hitler goes for the jugular vein. He gets ahold of my fanny, and he begins to squeeze and pinch and hug me up, and he said, 'You're a true Aryan type. You should be running for Germany.' So after he gave me the once-over and a full massage, he asked me if I'd like to spend the weekend in Berchtesgaden." She declined.

After only two and a half years of competition, Helen Stephens retired from amateur athletics with an undefeated record in running events. For a while she made a living playing basketball and softball and then served as a marine during World War II. Later she worked until retirement for the Defense Mapping Agency Aerospace Center in St. Louis.

The rivalry between Helen Stephens and Stella Walsh had an ironic and long-delayed ending. After Stephens' victory in Berlin, a Polish journalist accused her of actually being a man, and German officials were forced to issue a statement that they had given her a sex check and that she had passed. Forty-four years later, on December 4, 1980, Stella Walsh went to a discount store in Cleveland to buy ribbons for a reception for the Polish national basketball team. In the parking lot she was shot to death during a robbery attempt. When an autopsy was performed afterward, it turned out that although Helen Stephens may not have had male sexual organs, Stella Walsh did. The autopsy revealed that Walsh had a condition known as "mosaicism" in which she had both male and female chromosomes. She had a tiny penis and testes, but no female organs. All the while that Walsh had been setting 11 world records, winning 41 AAU titles and two Olympic medals, she was, by current rules, a man.

1948 London C: 38, N: 21, D: 8.2. WR: 11.5 (Helen Stephens)

1. Francina "Fanny" Blankers-Koen	HOL	11.9
2. Dorothy Manley	GBR	12.2
3. Shirley Strickland	AUS	12.2
4. Viola Myers	CAN	12.3e
5. Patricia Jones	CAN	12.3e
6. Cynthia Thompson	JAM	12.4e

A farmer's daughter, Fanny Koen was 18 years old when she was chosen to join the Dutch team for the 1936 Olympics in Berlin. She tied for sixth place in the high jump and was part of the 4 × 100-meter relay team that finished fifth. The highlight of the games for her was when she got Jesse Owens' autograph. When the Olympics resumed after a 12-year break, Fanny was the holder of six world records—in the 100 yards, the 80-meter hurdles, the high jump, the long jump, and in two relays. In the interim she had also married her coach, Jan Blankers, and given birth to two children. At 30 years of age she was thought by some to be too old to win the Olympic sprints, despite her string of records. She quieted her critics almost immediately by recording the best time of the opening round (12.0) in the 100-meter dash. She went on to win the final in the mud by three yards. Later in the week she also won gold medals in the 80-meter hurdles, the 200 meters, and the 4 × 100-meter relay. Of the nine women's track and field events included in the 1948 Olympics, Fanny Blankers-Koen won four of them. If she had entered the long jump she probably would have won that too, considering that the winning jump was 22 inches shorter than Fanny's world record. When she returned to Amsterdam she was driven through the crowded streets in an open carriage drawn by four gray horses. Her neighbors gave her a bicycle, "so she won't have to run so much."

1952 Helsinki C: 56, N: 27, D: 7.22. WR: 11.5 (Helen Stephens, Francina "Fanny" Blankers-Koen)

1. Marjorie Jackson	AUS	11.5 EWR	(11.67)
2. Daphne Häsenjager	SAF	11.8	(12.05)
3. Shirley de la Hunty Strickland	AUS	11.9	(12.12)
4. Winsome Cripps	AUS	11.9	(12.16)
5. Maria Sander	GER	12.0	(12.27)
6. Mae Faggs	USA	12.1	(12.27)

Marjorie Jackson first gained international attention when she twice defeated Fanny Blankers-Koen in Australia in 1949. Jackson was used to competing on grass and digging her starting holes before the race. In order to prepare her for the Olympics, the people of her hometown of Lithgow built a cinder track, and her father made her a set of starting blocks. Looking back on the 100 meters final, Jackson recalled, "Suddenly I am in the final. My heart was thumping, my legs were like jelly and I thought how could I race, I could hardly walk. When I won, my smile swallowed the world." British fans, who had been looking forward to the playing of "God Save the Queen" following the victory by Jackson, whom they considered a British subject, were stunned when what they heard instead was "Advance Australia Fair." Back home in Australia, the residents of Lithgow welcomed her with a 250-pound cake to help her break training.

Studies of the film of the race have shown that Sander and Faggs actually tied for fifth place. In 2001, Marjorie Jackson was chosen to be Governor of South Australia.

1956 Melbourne C: 34, N: 16, D: 11.26. WR: 11.3 (Shirley Strickland de la Hunty)

1. Elizabeth Cuthbert	AUS	11.5	(11.82)
2. Christa Stubnick	GDR	11.7	(11.92)
3. Marlene Matthews	AUS	11.7	(11.94)
4. Isabelle Daniels	USA	11.8	(11.98)
5. Giuseppina Leone	ITA	11.9	(12.07)
6. Heather Armitage	GBR	12.0	(12.10)

Eighteen-year-old Betty Cuthbert broke the Olympic record in the first round with an 11.4. In the semifinals she was beaten by Stubnick, but in the final she led from start to finish to win by five feet. Like Marjorie Jackson before her, Betty Cuthbert was as unassuming a heroine as one could hope for. In her autobiography, *Golden Girl*, Cuthbert wrote, "I broke the tape in 11.5s just like in any other race and there seemed nothing special about it. I couldn't realize then just what I had done and even later, when the telegrams, letters, honours, victory functions and the like started, I was too shy and self-conscious fully to appreciate it . . . However, at the time, Mum must have realized what I had done because I looked up in the crowd just after the race was over and saw her crying her eyes out." Four days later Cuthbert won the 200-meter dash and then earned another gold medal as part of the Australian 4 × 100-meter relay team.

1960 Rome C: 31, N: 18, D: 9.2. WR: 11.3 (Shirley Strickland de la Hunty, Vira Krepkina)

1. Wilma Rudolph	USA	11.0w	(11.18)
2. Dorothy Hyman	GBR	11.3	(11.43)
3. Giuseppina Leone	ITA	11.3	(11.48)
4. Maria Itkina	SOV/RUS	11.4	(11.54)
5. Catherine Capdeville	FRA	11.5	(11.64)
6. Jennifer Smart	GBR	12.0	(11.72)

Wilma Rudolph was born in St. Bethleham, Tennessee, on June 23, 1940, the 20th of her father's 22 children. She was born prematurely and weighed only 4½ pounds at birth. She suffered through polio, double pneumonia, and scarlet fever, which caused her to lose the use of her left leg. From the age of 6 she wore a brace. Her mother learned from doctors that rubbing her daughter's leg might help, so each day Wilma received four leg rubs from her brothers, sisters, and mother. Eventually she graduated from a brace to an orthopedic shoe and she joined her brothers playing basketball whenever she could. When Wilma was 11, her mother returned home one day to find her daughter playing basketball barefooted, having thrown away her corrective shoe. By the time she was 16, Rudolph had developed into a star runner and had qualified for the US Olympic team. In Melbourne in 1956 she was eliminated in the first round of the 200 meters, but earned a bronze medal running the third leg of the US 4 × 100-meter relay team. The same day that she returned from Australia to her hometown of Clarksville, Tennessee, she played for her high school's basketball team.

Wilma Rudolph, 1960

As a child in rural Tennessee, Rudolph suffered through polio, double pneumonia, and scarlet fever. Yet she grew up to win three gold medals in 1960, in the 100- and 200-meter dashes and the 4 × 100-meter relay

Four years later, the 5-foot 11-inch Rudolph, now a mother and a member of the Tennessee State University "Tigerbelles," went to the Rome Olympics as the favorite to succeed Betty Cuthbert as the world's fastest woman. She dominated the competition from the beginning. She actually fell asleep while waiting for her semifinal heat. Well-rested, she swept to a three-yard victory, equaling the world record of 11.3. She won the final by the same wide margin and was clocked in 11.0. However her time was not accepted as a world record because the wind was 2.752 meters per second—above the acceptable limit of 2 meters per second. She went on to match Betty Cuthbert's triple gold by winning the 200 meters and the 4 × 100-meter relay. Rudolph died of brain cancer on November 12, 1994.

1964 Tokyo C: 44, N: 27, D: 10.16. WR: 11.2 (Wilma Rudolph)

1. Wyomia Tyus	USA	11.4	(11.49)
2. Edith McGuire	USA	11.6	(11.62)
3. Ewa Klobukowska	POL	11.6	(11.64)
4. Marilyn White	USA	11.6	(11.67)
5. Miguelina Cobián	CUB	11.7	(11.72)
6. Marilyn Black	AUS	11.7	(11.73)
7. Halina Górecka	POL	11.8	(11.83)
8. Dorothy Hyman	GBR	11.9	(11.90)

Until the Olympics, 19-year-old Wyomia Tyus of Griffin, Georgia, had been overshadowed by her Tennessee State teammate Edith McGuire, whom she had never beaten. But in Tokyo, Tyus improved her personal best from 11.5 to 11.2 to equal Wilma Rudolph's world record in the second round. She won the final handily by two yards. Bronze medalist Klobukowska was later the subject of much controversy. On September 15, 1967, she was barred from international competition after she failed a sex chromosome test. Although she passed a visual examination she was subsequently stripped of all her records.

1968 Mexico City C: 41, N: 20, D: 10.15. WR: 11.1 (Irena Szewińska [Kirszenstein], Wyomia Tyus, Barbara Ferrell, Lyudmila Samotyosova, Margaret Bailes)

1. Wyomia Tyus	USA	11.08	WR
2. Barbara Ferrell	USA	11.15	
3. Irena Szewińska (Kirszenstein)	POL	11.19	
4. Raelene Boyle	AUS	11.20	
5. Margaret Bailes	USA	11.37	
6. Dianne Burg	AUS	11.44	
7. Chi Cheng	TAI	11.53	
8. Miguelina Cobián	CUB	11.61	

Competition was particularly stiff in 1968. In the first round, all three Americans, Tyus, Bailes, and Ferrell, equaled the Olympic record of 11.2. The second round saw Ferrell and Szewińska tie the world record of 11.1, while Wyomia Tyus ran a wind-aided 11.0. The semifinals, run in the rain, were won by Szewińska and Tyus, as co-world record holder Lyudmila Samotyosova was eliminated. The final matched four of the five world record holders. After false-starting, Tyus won a clear victory to become the first runner, male or female, to win an Olympic sprint title twice in a row.

1972 Munich C: 47, N: 33, D: 9.2. WR: 11.08 (Wyomia Tyus)

1. Renate Stecher	GDR	11.07	WR
2. Raelene Boyle	AUS	11.23	
3. Silvia Chivás	CUB	11.24	
4. Iris Davis	USA	11.32	
5. Annegret Richter	GER	11.38	
6. Alice Annum	GHA	11.41	
7. Barbara Ferrell	USA	11.45	
8. Eva Gleskova	CZE	12.48	

Wyomia Tyus, 1968

In 1968 Tyus became the first sprinter to win the 100-meter dash twice.

Although 17-year-old Silvia Chivás recorded the fastest times of the first two rounds (11.18 and 11.22), there was never any doubt that Stecher would win the gold. In 1997 Raelene Boyle auctioned her silver medal to raise money to rebuild her life after surviving treatment for breast cancer. That same year, documents were released showing that Renate Stecher had been given the anabolic steroid Oral-Turinabol for the two years leading up to the Munich Olympics.

1976 Montreal C: 39, N: 22, D: 7.25. WR: 10.8 (Renate Stecher, Annegret Richter); 11.04 (Inge Helten)

1. Annegret Richter	GER	11.08
2. Renate Stecher	GDR	11.13
3. Inge Helten	GER	11.17
4. Raelene Boyle	AUS	11.23
5. Evelyn Ashford	USA	11.24
6. Chandra Cheeseborough	USA	11.31
7. Andrea Lynch	GBR	11.32
8. Marlies Oelsner	GDR	11.34

Richter defeated Stecher 11.19 to 11.21 in heat number 6 of the first round. In the second round she ran an impressive 11.05. The next day she set a world record of 11.01 in the semifinals, before leading a German sweep in the final. Less than a yard separated the three medalists at the finish.

1980 Moscow C: 40, N: 25, D: 7.26. WR: 10.88 (Marlies Göhr [Oelsner])

1. Lyudmila Kondratyeva	SOV/RUS	11.06
2. Marlies Göhr (Oelsner)	GDR	11.07
3. Ingrid Auerswald	GDR	11.14
4. Linda Haglund	SWE	11.16
5. Romy Müller	GDR	11.16
6. Kathryn Smallwood	GBR	11.28
7. Chantal Rega	FRA	11.32
8. Heather Hunte	GBR	11.34

Haglund led at the halfway mark, but Kondratyeva and Göhr stormed by her after 60 meters. Göhr edged ahead with a few meters to go, but Kondratyeva came back and, despite pulling a hamstring muscle at the finish, won by the smallest margin imaginable.

Kondratyeva went on to marry two-time Olympic hammer throw champion Yuri Sedykh, although they would later divorce.

1984 Los Angeles C: 46, N: 33, D: 8.5. WR: 10.79 (Evelyn Ashford)

1. Evelyn Ashford	USA	10.97 OR
2. Alice Brown	USA	11.13
3. Merlene Ottey-Page	JAM	11.16
4. Jeanette Bolden	USA	11.25
5. Grace Jackson	JAM	11.39
6. Angela Bailey	CAN	11.40
7. Heather Oakes (Hunte)	GBR	11.43
8. Angella Taylor	CAN	11.62

In 1976, 19-year-old Evelyn Ashford competed at the Montreal Olympics, finishing fifth in the 100 meters. Three years later, back in Montreal, she gained international acclaim at the World Cup meet by defeating East German world record holder Marita Koch in the 200, 21.83 to 22.02, and then beating the 100-meter world record holder, Marlies Göhr, 11.06 to 11.17. Ashford seemed right on track to fulfill her dreams of Olympic glory—until Jimmy Carter announced that US athletes would not be allowed to go to Moscow. When the boycott was made official, Ashford was competing in Canada. She and her coach and a teammate went to a bar, where Evelyn, completely out of character, "got sloppy drunk," stood up and fell on her face.

Ashford reset her goals for the 1983 inaugural world championships in Helsinki and for the 1984 Olympics. In June of 1983 she was beaten by Göhr in Los Angeles 11.39 to 11.53, but one week later, competing in Colorado, she set a world record of 10.79. Annoyed that her record was not properly respected because it was set at high altitude, Ashford vowed to prove herself by defeating Göhr in Helsinki. She recorded the fastest time in each of the three preliminary rounds, but in the final she pulled a hamstring muscle and fell to the ground while Göhr sped on to victory, followed closely by Marita Koch.

For all of her frustrations, Ashford still had the Los Angeles Olympics to look forward to. But as she warmed up for her semifinal heat at the US trials on June 18, 1984, Ashford felt a twinge in her right hamstring muscle. Running very carefully, she qualified for the Olympic team, but, although she had hoped to win three gold medals at the Olympics, she withdrew from the 200 meters to protect her leg.

With Göhr boycotted out of the Olympics, only the very real threat of injury stood between Evelyn Ashford and her long-awaited goal of an Olympic title. In Los Angeles, her leg held up as she again recorded the fastest time in each of the three preliminary rounds. In the final, she took command at the midway point and won going away.

Over the years Evelyn Ashford had earned a reputation as a shy, somewhat unfriendly loner, who shunned the media and rarely expressed her emotions. "They should be bottled up inside," she would say. "You want it to come out on the track." But after crossing the finish line and hearing the track announcer say that she had broken the Olympic record, the years of frustration and anguish gave way to tearful relief. After collapsing into the arms of teammate Jeannette Bolden, she cried her way through her victory lap while she received a standing ovation.

"When I caught my first glimpse of the gold medal while I waited on the victory stand," she would later recall, "I was emotionally overcome. I couldn't believe it was over. I couldn't stop crying."

Actually it wasn't all over. Not quite. Evelyn Ashford was now the world record holder and the Olympic champion, but one more challenge remained: she wanted to beat Marlies Göhr. In fact, on August 16, Göhr won the Friendship Games meet with a time of 10.95, faster than Ashford's Olympic record. But the next day, in Berlin, Ashford clocked 10.92 and 10.94. Then, on August 22, the two met head-to-head in Zurich. Ashford overcame Göhr's fast start and final surge to gain the victory—and set a new world record of 10.76 in the process. When the time was announced, Göhr and East German teammate Ingrid Auerswald, gracious in defeat, each took one of Ashford's hands and raised it in the air. Finally, ten years after she had begun competing for the *boys'* track team at Roseville High School in California, Evelyn Ashford had proved that she was the fastest woman in the world.

1988 Seoul C: 64, N: 42, D: 9.25. WR: 10.49 (D. Florence Griffith Joyner)

1. D. Florence Griffith Joyner	USA	10.54w
2. Evelyn Ashford	USA	10.83
3. Heike Drechsler (Daute)	GDR	10.85
4. Grace Jackson	JAM	10.97
5. Gwendolyn Torrence	USA	10.97
6. Natalya Pomoshchnikova	SOV/RUS	11.00
7. Juliet Cuthbert	JAM	11.26
8. Anelia Vechernikova	BUL	11.49

Delorez Florence Griffith was born December 21, 1959. The seventh of eleven children, she grew up in Watts, a neighborhood in Los Angeles best known as the site of a black uprising in 1965. Griffith was always a bit eccentric. Once she was asked to leave a local shopping mall because she was wearing her pet boa constrictor like a muffler. But what really set her apart from her peers was her speed. She began racing at age 7 and continued to compete until 1979 when she was forced to drop out of college in order to help support her family.

Sprint coach Bob Kersee found Griffith working as a bank teller and helped her get financial aid so that she could attend UCLA. Griffith first gained serious international attention when she placed fourth in the 200 meters at the 1983 world championships. The following year she earned a silver medal in the 200 at the Los Angeles Olympics, although her six-inch, wildly painted fingernails gained her more press than her running.

By 1986, Griffith, seemingly a perennial runner-up, was in semi-retirement, working in a bank again and also as a beautician. She returned to serious training in 1987 and finished second to Silke Gladisch of East Germany in that year's world championship 200. Her marriage to 1984 triple jump Olympic champion Al Joyner and her loss to Gladisch marked a turning point in her career. Now known as Florence Griffith Joyner, she became determined to end her string of second places. She obtained a videotape of Ben Johnson's explosive start in the world championship 100-meter final and watched it every day. After consulting with Johnson, she embarked on a vigorous weight-lifting program. She also incorporated endurance runs into her training and, along with her studies of Ben Johnson's start, she watched tapes of Carl Lewis to analyze his form and his ability to run in a relaxed manner.

Griffith Joyner was still considered a 200-meter specialist, but on June 25, 1988, she ran a 10.89 100 in San Diego. Then, at the US Olympic trials, exactly three weeks later, she achieved a stunning breakthrough. Running in a quarterfinal heat, she crossed the finish line in 10.49 seconds, obliterating Evelyn Ashford's 1984 world record of 10.76. In fact her time was faster than the automatically timed *men's* record in a wide range of nations, including Ireland, New Zealand, Norway, Iran, and Turkey. Griffith Joyner's shocking performance was not without controversy. Although the wind gauge next to the triple jump runway 30 feet away registered an unacceptable 4.3 meters per second, the gauge at the track registered exactly 0.0. Because gusty winds were sweeping through the stadium, it was assumed that the instrument had malfunctioned. But Omega Electronics defended their measuring device. In an official memo to the IAAF, the company explained that a wind of 2.80 meters per second had blown across the track, but in a direction of 91 degrees perpendicular to the track. Subsequent analysis by Australian physicist Nicholas Linthorne has shown that the true wind reading was probably *5.5* meters per second or more. Nonetheless, Griffith Joyner's record stood. The next day she won the final in 10.61 with a legal wind of 1.2 meters per second.

Her spectacular times, coupled with her outrageous running suits, which she changed for each race, brought Florence Griffith Joyner overnight celebrity. She acquired yet another name: Flojo. Because of the wind controversy and because her record had been set at a domestic meet, the European sports press was still skeptical of Griffith Joyner's abilities. In Seoul, she put their doubts to rest. In the opening round she set an Olympic record of 10.88. Evelyn Ashford matched that time in the second round, but one heat later, Flojo ran a 10.62. She followed that with a wind-aided 10.70 in the semifinals.

In the final Griffith Joyner showed that her obsessive study of Ben Johnson's start was not wasted. Her reaction time of 0.131 seconds was not only the best in the race, it was faster than that of Johnson himself. Halfway through the race a smile began to spread across her face, and by the time she flashed across the finish line in a wind-aided 10.54, she was positively beaming. Behind her, Ashford edged Heike Drechsler for second place to become, at age 31, the oldest female sprint medalist in Olympic history. Anelia Vechernikova was even with Ashford at 80 meters, but pulled a muscle and hobbled in in last place.

Florence Griffith Joyner went on to win two more gold medals and one silver. Unfortunately, the disqualification of Ben Johnson left a cloud of suspicion over Flojo's performances as well. Skeptics pointed to her sudden improvement and her bulging muscles as evidence that she might be using steroids or human growth hormone. Griffith Joyner fueled this speculation by announcing her retirement on February 25, 1989, on the eve of the institution of mandatory random drug testing. On September 21, 1998, Florence Griffith Joyner died in her sleep at the age of 38. An autopsy revealed that she had a congenital brain abnormality known as cavernous angioma. She had apparently experienced a form of epileptic seizure while lying prone and died of suffocation.

1992 Barcelona C: 54, N: 41, D: 8.1. WR: 10.49 (D. Florence Griffith Joyner)

1. Y. Gail Devers	USA	10.82
2. Juliet Cuthbert	JAM	10.83
3. Irina Privalova	RUS	10.84
4. Gwendolyn Torrence	USA	10.86
5. Merlene Ottey	JAM	10.88
6. Anelia Nuneva (Vechernikova)	BUL	11.10
7. Mary Onyali	NGR	11.15
8. Liliana Allen Doll	CUB	11.19

When the Berlin Wall fell in 1989, no East German athlete was as well placed to take advantage of German reunification as sprinter Katrin Krabbe. She won both the 100 meters and 200 meters at the 1990 European championships and repeated the double at the 1991 world championships. She was voted the most popular female athlete in Germany, more popular even than tennis player Steffi Graf. Tall, blond, and beautiful, Krabbe was the perfect poster girl for newly unified Germany and she quickly signed endorsement contracts that made her rich. All was not rosy, however, for Katrin Krabbe. The tabloids dogged her wherever she went and the details of her romantic life were revealed as front-page gossip. When she returned to her hometown of Neubrandenburg in East Germany, she was greeted with hostility by some bitter neighbors for whom reunification had been a financial disaster. In addition, there was hostility between the athletes of what had been East and West Germany. The easterners produced far superior results, leading the westerners to accuse them of using prohibited drugs.

In January 1992, Katrin Krabbe and some of her East German teammates went to train in South Africa. Detractors accused them of fleeing Germany to escape drug testing. On January 24, a team of German medical officials flew down to South Africa and tested Krabbe and the others. The results were revealed on February 9: none of the women had tested positive, but the urine samples submitted by Krabbe, Grit Breuer, and Silke Müller all came from the same person. Six days later the German Track Federation charged the three women with tampering with a drug test and suspended them for four years. Because Krabbe was expected to be *the* German heroine of the upcoming Barcelona Olympics, the scandal was enormous. There was a flurry of appeals and hearings, and on April 4, the German Track Federation, much to the disgust of the rest of the world, revoked the suspensions, claiming that the urine samples might have been subject to outside tampering while they had been transferred from South Africa to the testing laboratory in Germany. On June 28 the IAAF arbitration panel cleared Krabbe's path to the Olympics on a technicality: the constitution of the German Track Federation did not yet provide for random drug testing. Nevertheless, Krabbe did not take part in the Olympics. On July 2, she bowed out, claiming that the emotional ordeal of the past months had left her unable to perform at her usual standards. On July 21, Krabbe was given another test. This time the results showed traces of Clenbuterol, a steroid substitute. Krabbe never competed again.

With Katrin Krabbe out of the running, the role of favorite shifted to Gwen Torrence of Decatur, Georgia, who had finished second to Krabbe in both sprints at the 1991 world championships. Torrence's toughest challenge was expected to come from Merlene Ottey, who had been undefeated at 100 meters between the 1988 Olympics and the 1991 world championships, but who was known as "Ms. Bronze" because of a string of third-place finishes going back to the 200 meters at the 1980 Olympics and extending to both sprints at the 1984 Olympics, the 1987 world championships, and the 1991 world championships.

As it turned out, the most serious contenders were Juliet Cuthbert, who called herself a "Jamerican" because she grew up in Jamaica before moving to the United States with her mother when she was 16 years old, and Gail Devers, who had placed second behind Torrence at the United States Olympic trials. The story of Devers' travails the past four years almost defied belief. In June 1988 Devers began getting migraine headaches. She also experienced dizziness and temporary loss of sight in one eye. She managed to qualify for the Olympics in her speciality, the 100-meter hurdles, but in Seoul she was eliminated in the semifinals. At first it had been easy to assume that Devers' symptoms were the result of stress, but her condition continued to deteriorate. Unfortunately, it was two years before doctors finally came up with a correct diagnosis: Graves' disease. In order to control her hyperactive thyroid, Devers began radiation therapy on September 12, 1990. The therapy worked, but then she developed awful reactions to the radiation. She hemorrhaged blood clots, her weight fluctuated dramatically, and she experienced second-degree burns on her feet, which became infected and swollen. Incredibly, after missing 2½ years of training, Devers returned to competition and finished second in the 100-meter hurdles at the 1991 world championships.

The 100-meter final in Barcelona was the closest in Olympic history, even closer than the 1952 men's final. Devers and Privalova ran almost even most of the race, but Cuthbert, Torrence, and Ottey all came on at the end. It was impossible to tell who had won until slow-motion replays of the finish were shown in the stadium. Even then, one couldn't be sure. The official announcement finally gave the victory to Devers. Devers, Cuthbert, and Torrence had all set personal records, while Ottey ended up in fifth place even though she was less than one-tenth of a second behind the winner. Gail Devers was the third straight winner of the women's 100 meters to have attended UCLA.

Shut out of the medals, Gwen Torrence managed to spoil the event for the winners by publicly stating that two of the three medalists were drug users. At first she refused to name names. Then, under pressure from the media, she said she didn't mean Devers, which left Cuthbert and Privalova. The next day Cuthbert confronted Torrence, who told her she had meant Devers and Privalova. Finally, under threat of suspension by the IAAF, Torrence made a public apology, but the damage had been done and Torrence came away more tainted than those she had accused.

1996 Atlanta C: 56, N: 39, D: 7.27. WR: 10.49 (D. Florence Griffith Joyner)

1. Y. Gail Devers	USA	10.94
2. Merlene Ottey	JAM	10.94
3. Gwendolyn Torrence	USA	10.96
4. Chandra Sturrup	BAH	11.00
5. Marina Trandenkova	RUS	11.06
6. Natalya Voronova	RUS	11.10
7. Mary Onyali	NGR	11.13
8. Zhanna Pintusevych	UKR	11.14

Like the 1992 Olympic final, the final of the 1993 world championships was so close that a photo-finish was needed to determine the winner. Gail Devers and Merlene Ottey were both timed in 10.82 (Gwen Torrence was third in 10.89), but the officials gave first place to Devers by one centimeter. Ottey refused to believe she had been beaten and, indeed, many observers wondered why a dead-heat had not been declared. At the 1995 world championships, Torrence won a relatively clear (for the era) victory over Ottey 10.85 to 10.94, while Devers concentrated on what was theoretically her strongest event, the 100-meter hurdles.

After defeating Devers at the US Olympic trials 10.82 to 10.91, Torrence went to Atlanta as the slight favorite. Actually, she didn't *go* to Atlanta—she stayed there. Torrence was born 1½ miles from the Olympic stadium.

It was Devers who recorded the fastest time of the opening rounds: 10.92 and 10.94. The next evening, Ottey won the first semifinal, defeating Torrence 10.93 to 10.97, while Devers won the second semi in 11.00.

In the final, Devers burst into the lead almost immediately. After sixty meters, Ottey, on her right, began to close the gap, finally catching Devers just as they reached the finish line. In an eerie repeat of the 1993 world championship, Devers, Ottey and Torrence stood on the track and watched video replays of the finish on the giant stadium screen. It was impossible to tell who had won. Finally the standings were announced. Again Devers and Ottey were given the same time but Devers was declared the winner (by two centimeters) with Torrence third. And again Ottey protested, but her protest was rejected. Surprisingly, as in 1992, Devers lost her speciality and won a gold medal in her secondary event. In fact, although Devers won the world championship in the 110-meter hurdles three times and finished second twice, she never won a single hurdles medal of any kind in the Olympics. All three of her gold medals came in other races.

2000 Sydney C: 84, N: 63, D: 9.24. WR: 10.49 (D. Florence Griffith Joyner)

1. —		
2. Ekaterina Thanou	GRE	11.12
2. Tayna Lawrence	JAM	11.18
3. Merlene Ottey	JAM	11.19
4. Zhanna Pintusevych	UKR	11.20
6. Chandra Sturrup	BAH	11.21
6. Sevatheda Fynes	BAH	11.22
7. Debbie Ferguson	BAH	11.29

DISQ (Drugs): Marion Jones (USA) 10.75

Marion Jones was born in Los Angeles, but held dual citizenship because her mother was from Belize. When Jones began to compete internationally, she chose to represent the United States. She had to make the decision early because she was clearly an athletic prodigy. When she was still only 15 years old, Jones came within .04 seconds of qualifying for the 1991 US world championship team at 200 meters. When she was 16, she did qualify as an alternate for the Olympic 4 × 100 meter relay. However she declined the invitation and stayed home. Track was not Jones' only sport—she was also a star basketball player. As a freshman at the University of North Carolina, she was the starting point guard, averaging 16.8 points per game and helping lead her team to the 1994 NCAA championship. During the summer of 1995, Jones broke a bone in her left foot during basketball training for the World University Games and in 1996 another Olympics came and went without Jones taking part. In December of that year, she broke the same bone while trampolining.

At this point, Jones made the decision to concentrate on track and field. Her rewards came quickly. She won the 100 meters at the 1997 world championship and successfully defended her title in 1999. By the time of the Sydney Olympics, Jones had gone undefeated at 100 meters for three years, during which time she won 32 straight finals.

The runup to the Olympics saw a good deal of controversy regarding Merlene Ottey, who was the last person to beat Jones at 100 meters back in 1997. Ottey, who was now 40 years old, had failed a doping test for steroids in 1999, but had been reinstated early so that she could take part in the Jamaican Olympic trials. There she finished only fourth, but was put on the team anyway in place of one of the runners who had beaten her.

The second-best sprinter in the world was thought to be Ekaterina Thanou, which is to say that Thanou was the favorite to win the silver medal, since Jones was correctly perceived to be in a class of her own. Jones and Thanou faced each other in three of the four rounds in Sydney. Jones won their quarterfinal matchup 10.83 to 10.99 and their semifinal encounter 11.01 to 11.10. The other semifinal was won by Ottey in 11.22.

The final went exactly to form. Jones secured a clear lead by the halfway point and pulled away to win by about three and a half meters, a margin of victory matched only by Marjorie Jackson in 1952. Thanou took second place as expected, but the battle for bronze was decided by photofinish, as the next five runners finished within four hundredths of a second of one another. Eventually it was determined that Ottey had been edged out by Jamaican teammate Tayna Lawrence. Lawrence, whose family had moved from Jamaica to Miami eight years earlier, was so used to being incorrectly referred to as Tanya rather than Tayna, that she didn't bother to correct the mistake either in the official database of the Sydney Olympics or when reporters questioned her at the post-race press conference.

In 2007 Jones was stripped of her gold medal after admitting to taking steroids in 2000 and 2001. In December 2009, the IOC decided to reallocate Jones' medals in the 100 meters, 200 meters and long jump events. In the 100 meters event, Lawrence and Ottey were awarded the silver and bronze medals, but the IOC declined to award Thanou the 100 meters gold medal because of her behavior at the 2004 Athens Olympics, in which she and sprinter Kostas Kenteris were accused of faking a motorcycle accident to avoid a doping test. In May 2011, an Athens court found Thanou and Kenteris guilty of perjury. However, in September an appeals court acquitted them on grounds of reasonable doubt. Although it was the first time in Olympic history that no gold medal was awarded due to improper behavior by the silver medalist, there were at least two precedents for Olympic events having been held with no gold medals awarded. In 1908, the four finalists in the cycling match sprint jockeyed for position so long that the time allotted for the event was exceeded and no medals were awarded (see page 543). In 1912, the two finalists in the 82.5 kilogram (182 lb) Greco-Roman wrestling event fought for nine hours and finally became so exhausted that they ended the fight. The IOC did not award medals to either combatant because nobody had actually won (see page 1308).

When this book went to press, the IOC had not yet determined whether to upgrade Thanou to gold.

2004 Athens C: 63, N: 51, D: 8.21. WR: 10.49 (D. Florence Griffith Joyner)

1. Yuliya Nesterenko	BLR	10.93
2. Lauryn Williams	USA	10.96
3. Veronica Campbell	JAM	10.97
4. Ivet Lalova	BUL	11.00
5. Aleen Bailey	JAM	11.05
6. Sherone Simpson	JAM	11.07
7. Debbie Ferguson	BAH	11.16
8. LaTasha Colander-Richardson	USA	11.18

The 2004 100 meters saw a changing of the guard. Defending champion Marion Jones failed to qualify for the competition after finishing fifth at the US Olympic trials, while 1992 and 1996 gold medalist Gail Devers was eliminated in the Olympic semifinals, as was four-time 100 meters finalist Merlene Ottey, now 44 years old. Americans Kelli White and Torri Edwards, who finished one-two at the 2003 World Championships, were barred from competing because of doping violations.

In the absence of the more famous sprinters, relatively unheralded Yuliya Nesterenko swept through the first two qualifying heats with ease, recording the only sub-11 times in both rounds. In the semifinals, Nesterenko led the faster of the two heats, edging out Veronica Campbell by one-hundredth of a second. Twenty-year-old Lauryn Williams won the second semi. In the final, Williams was out of the blocks slowly, but soon moved to the front and was still in the lead after

70 meters. However, Nesterenko finished strongly and overtook Williams, who began her lean prematurely with ten meters still to go. Nesterenko was the first non-American to win the event since the boycotted Games of 1980. She was also the first woman ever to record wind-legal sub-eleven-second times in all four rounds of an Olympics, a feat made more impressive by the fact that she had never broken eleven seconds prior to the Athens Games. She credited her improvement to a new training regimen, a new masseur, and, most importantly, to the fact that she and her husband moved out of her parents' house into their own apartment. Williams dedicated her silver medal to her father, David, who had been diagnosed with leukemia in 1989 and who relied on regular kidney dialysis to stay alive. He was able to watch his daughter in Athens as a result of a $10,000 donation from a cancer survivor in his home state of Pennsylvania.

After the Games it emerged that Nesterenko had tested positive for clenbuterol at a Polish league meet in May 2002. Because the Warsaw lab conducting the test was not accredited by the IOC or WADA, no action was taken.

2008 Beijing C: 85, N: 69, D: 8.17. WR: 10.49 (D. Florence Griffith Joyner)

1. Shelly-Ann Fraser	JAM	10.78
2. Sherone Simpson	JAM	10.98
2. Kerron Stewart	JAM	10.98
4. Lauryn Williams	USA	11.03
5. Muna Lee	USA	11.07
6. Jeannette Kwakye	GBR	11.14
7. Debbie Ferguson-McKenzie	BAH	11.19
8. Torri Edwards	USA	11.20

The 100-meter final in Beijing was expected to be a showdown between defending silver and bronze medalists Lauryn Williams and Veronica Campbell-Brown. The two had battled each other for the intervening two world championship titles—Williams beating Campbell by two-hundredths of a second in 2005 and Campbell edging out Williams by less than one-hundredth of a second in 2007. (In November 2007 Campbell married fellow Jamaican sprinter Omar Brown.)

The expected showdown never materialized, as Campbell-Brown narrowly failed to qualify for the Jamaican 100-meter line-up, finishing fourth in an Olympic trial in which the top four all finished in under 10.90 seconds. So Jamaica was represented by Kerron Stewart, Sherone Simpson and 21-year-old Shelly-Ann Fraser, who ran a personal best of 10.85 to qualify. Fraser had never competed at a world championship or major international championship, and was so little-known that a Jamaican newspaper ran a story about her a few weeks before the Olympics under the headline "Who is Shelly-Ann Fraser?"

The event also saw the return of 2003 world champion Torri Edwards, who had been excluded from competing at the Athens Games after testing positive for the banned stimulant nikethamide in April 2004. Edwards returned to competition in 2005, winning the 2007 US Nationals.

The three Jamaican women advanced easily through the early rounds, topping their respective quarter-final heats. Stewart was the only one to record a time under 11 seconds in the preliminary rounds, finishing her quarter-final heat in 10.98 seconds to beat Williams. By the semi-finals it was clear that the US/Jamaica match-up was materializing, with the top six times all posted by sprinters from the two countries.

At the start of the final, several runners thought that Torri Edwards had false-started—including Edwards herself—causing them to pull back. The mistake cost them dearly, Edwards ended up finishing last while Muna Lee recovered to fifth place. The real show was put on by the Jamaicans, however, as Fraser pulled away to lead the first-ever sweep of the women's 100-meter event, in a personal-best time of 10.78 seconds. Stewart recovered from the second-slowest start-time to match Simpson at the line. A review of the photo-finish couldn't separate the two, so both Stewart and Simpson were given silver medals. Fraser's margin of victory, though, was the largest since 1988, when Florence Griffith Joyner set the world record. "I can't stop smiling," a beaming Fraser said after the race, "my braces are hurting me."

Raised in a violent inner-city ghetto near Kingston, Fraser went to the same track club as Asafa Powell, the former 100-meter world record holder. Her mother, a former athlete turned street vendor, supported three children by selling underwear, socks and rags.

Another competitor who faced significant hardships on her path to the Olympics was Robina Jalali of Afghanistan. Raised during the Taliban regime, Jalali and her seven sisters were secretly tutored at home. She took up running at the age of 16 after the Taliban's fall from power and competed in both the 2004 and 2008 Olympics, failing to advance out of her first-round heats both times.

One year after winning gold, Shelly-Ann Fraser went on to win the 100 meters world championship title in Berlin, recording the third-fastest 100-meter time ever, 10.73. In May 2010 at an IAAF Diamond League event in Shanghai, she tested positive for oxycodone, a non-performance-enhancing painkiller. She admitted having taken it before the race to treat a toothache and served a six-month suspension.

200 METERS

1896–1936 not held

1948 London C: 33, N: 17, D: 8.6. WR: 23.6 (Stanisława Wałasiewicz)

1. Francina "Fanny" Blankers-Koen	HOL	24.4
2. Audrey Williamson	GBR	25.1
3. Audrey "Mickey" Patterson	USA	25.2
4. Shirley Strickland	AUS	25.2e
5. Margaret Walker	GBR	25.4e
6. Daphne Robb	SAF	25.5e

Fanny Blankers-Koen had already won two gold medals in the 100-meter dash and the 80-meter hurdles. Far from being exuberant about these accomplishments, she felt tremendous pressure to win a third gold medal and was close to a mental breakdown. Prior to the semifinals of the 200 meters she told her husband, Jan, that she wanted to withdraw. Jan tried to calm her down and gave her words of encouragement, but to no avail. In desperation he evoked memories of her parents and her two children, and she burst into tears. When she finally came out of her cry, she had recovered and was once again eager to run. She went out and won her heat by six yards, establishing an Olympic record of 24.3 seconds. The next day, running on a muddy track, she won the final by seven yards, the largest margin ever recorded in the women's 200 meters.

Fanny Blankers-Koen, 1948
She won four of the nine women's track and field events.

Mickey Patterson was the first African-American woman to win an Olympic medal. She almost didn't survive the US trials. The morning of the qualifying heats, she burned her leg with an iron. Then, before the final, she was accidentally locked inside the dressing room and only made it to the starting line when her panicked coach found her. In 1975, the photo finish of the Olympic final was discovered. It revealed that Strickland had actually finished ahead of Patterson.

1952 Helsinki C: 38, N: 21, D: 7.26. WR: 23.6 (Stanisława Wałasiewicz)

1. Marjorie Jackson	AUS	23.7	(23.89)
2. Bertha Brouwer	HOL	24.2	(24.25)
3. Nadezhda Khnykina	SOV/GEO	24.2	(24.37)
4. Winsome Cripps	AUS	24.2	(24.40)
5. Helga Klein	GER	24.6	(24.72)
6. Daphne Hasenjager (Robb)	SAF	24.6	(24.72)

One of the longest-lasting women's track and field world records ever was set by Stanisława Wałasiewicz on August 15, 1935, when she/he ran the 200 meters in 23.6 seconds. Almost 17 years later, Marjorie Jackson tied that record in the first round of the 1952 Helsinki Olympics, and in the first semifinal she ran a 23.4 to finally break it. In the final she reached the tape four yards ahead of her nearest rival.

1956 Melbourne C: 27, N: 12, D: 11.30. WR: 23.2 (Elizabeth Cuthbert)

1. Elizabeth Cuthbert	AUS	23.4 EOR	(23.55)
2. Christa Stubnick	GDR	23.7	(23.89)
3. Marlene Matthews	AUS	23.8	(24.10)
4. Norma Croker	AUS	24.0	(24.22)
5. June Paul (Foulds)	GBR	24.3	(24.30)
6. Gisela Köhler	GDR	24.3	(24.68)

For the first and only time in Olympic history, the medalists in the two sprints (100 and 200 meters) finished in the exact same order.

1960 Rome C: 29, N: 17, D: 9.5. WR: 22.9 (Wilma Rudolph)

1. Wilma Rudolph	USA	24.0	(24.13)
2. Jutta Heine	GER	24.4	(24.58)
3. Dorothy Hyman	GBR	24.7	(24.82)
4. Maria Itkina	SOV/RUS	24.7	(24.85)
5. Barbara Janiszewska	POL	24.8	(24.96)
6. Giuseppina Leone	ITA	24.9	(25.01)

Wilma Rudolph dominated the event, setting an Olympic record of 23.2 in her opening heat. Silver medalist Jutta Heine was the daughter of a millionaire, while the father of bronze medalist Dorothy Hyman was a Yorkshire miner.

1964 Tokyo C: 29, N: 21, D: 10.19. WR: 22.9 (Wilma Rudolph, Margaret Burvill)

1. Edith McGuire	USA	23.0	OR	(23.05)
2. Irena Kirszenstein	POL	23.1		(23.13)
3. Marilyn Black	AUS	23.1		(23.18)
4. Una Morris	JAM	23.5		(23.58)
5. Lyudmila Samotyosova	SOV/RUS	23.5		(23.59)
6. Barbara Sobotta (Janiszewska)	POL	23.9		(23.97)
7. Janet Simpson	GBR	23.9		(23.98)
8. Daphne Arden	GBR	24.0		(24.01)

1968 Mexico City C: 36, N: 21, D: 10.18. WR: 22.7 (Irena Szewińska [Kirszenstein])

1. Irena Szewińska (Kirszenstein)	POL	22.58	WR
2. Raelene Boyle	AUS	22.74	
3. Jennifer Lamy	AUS	22.88	
4. Barbara Ferrell	USA	22.93	
5. Nicole Montandon	FRA	23.08	
6. Wyomia Tyus	USA	23.08	
7. Margaret Bailes	USA	23.18	
8. Jutta Stöck	GER	23.25	

Irena Kirszenstein was born in Leningrad to Jewish parents from Poland on May 24, 1946. Beginning in 1964 she competed in five Olympics, winning seven medals in five different events. As an 18-year-old at the 1964 Tokyo Olympics she finished second in the long jump and the 200 meters and ran the second leg on the Polish 4 × 100-meter relay team, which scored an upset victory. In 1967 she culminated a five-year courtship by marrying Janusz Szewińsk, and when she arrived in Mexico City for the 1968 Olympics she was running under the name Irena Szewińska. She was disappointed in her first two events, failing to qualify for the final of the long jump and finishing third in the 100 meters, but in the final of the 200 meters she overcame a slow start to win in world record time.

Most people attribute the plethora of world records which were set in Mexico City to the altitude, but another factor was the unusual method that the Mexicans used for determining wind conditions. With the acceptable limit for world records set at a wind speed of 2 meters per second, the measurement during the women's 200 meters was exactly 2.0 m.p.s. The same recording of exactly 2.0 m.p.s. was registered when Bob Beamon made his famous 29-foot 2½-inch leap and when Nelson Prudencio and Viktor Saneyev set world records in the triple jump.

Eighth-place finisher Jutta Stöck was the daughter of 1936 javelin gold-medalist Gerhard Stöck.

1972 Munich C: 37, N: 27, D: 9.7. WR: 22.4 (Chi Cheng)

1. Renate Stecher	GDR	22.40	EWR
2. Raelene Boyle	AUS	22.45	
3. Irena Szewińska (Kirszenstein)	POL	22.74	
4. Ellen Stropahl	GDR	22.75	
5. Christina Heinich	GDR	22.89	
5. Annegret Kroniger	GER	22.89	
7. Alice Annum	GHA	22.99	
8. Rosie Allwood	JAM	23.11	

Between August 1970 and June 1974, Renate Stecher won 90 straight outdoor races at 100 meters and 200 meters.

1976 Montreal C: 36, N: 21, D: 7.28. WR: 22.21 (Irena Szewińska [Kirszenstein])

1. Bärbel Eckert	GDR	22.37	OR
2. Annegret Richter	GER	22.39	
3. Renate Stecher	GDR	22.47	
4. Carla Bodendorf	GDR	22.64	
5. Inge Helten	GER	22.68	
6. Tetyana Prorochenko	SOV/UKR	23.03	
7. Denise Robertson	AUS	23.05	
8. Chantal Rega	FRA	23.09	

The first shock came in the semifinals, when five-time sprint finalist Raelene Boyle was disqualified for false-starting twice. Boyle was furious and protested unsuccessfully. The electronic starting device had registered a clean start the first time, but the recall judge claimed that Boyle's head and shoulders had been

Irena Szewinska, 1976
Between 1964 and 1976, she won seven medals in five different events, second only to Merlene Ottey's eight.

moving. Unaware that she had actually been charged with a false start rather than a mere warning, Boyle was stunned when she was disqualified after her next false start. The real surprise was 21-year-old Bärbel Eckert, East Germany's third-string sprinter. In the quarterfinals she equaled her personal best of 22.85. She won her semifinal heat in 22.71 and then set an Olympic record to win the final.

1980 Moscow C: 35, N: 25, D: 7.30. WR: 21.71 (Marita Koch)

1. Bärbel Wöckel (Eckert)	GDR	22.03	OR
2. Natalya Bochina	SOV/RUS	22.19	
3. Merlene Ottey	JAM	22.20	
4. Romy Müller	GDR	22.47	
5. Kathryn Smallwood	GBR	22.61	
6. Beverley Goddard	GBR	22.72	
7. Denise Boyd (Robertson)	AUS	22.76	
8. Sonia Lannaman	GBR	22.80	

Defending champion Bärbel Eckert of Leipzig, now married, a mother, and renamed Wöckel, made it through to the final without winning a single heat. She finished second each time, once to Lyudmila Maslakova of the USSR, and twice to Merlene Ottey. Meanwhile, 18-year-old Natalya Bochina ran a 22.26 in the second round to break Wöckel's Olympic record. In the final, however, it was Wöckel who took the lead coming out of the turn and won going away. Missing from the competition were the two women who had clocked the fastest times in the world: Marita Koch, who chose to concentrate on the 400 meters, and Evelyn Ashford, who suffered the double blow of injury and boycott.

In 1991, a letter was discovered by researcher Werner Frank in which Koch complained to the head of the state-owned pharmaceutical company that Wöckel was receiving larger doses of steroids because Wöckel had a relative who worked for the drug company.

1984 Los Angeles C: 37, N: 28, D: 8.9. WR: 21.71 (Marita Koch)

1. Valerie Brisco-Hooks	USA	21.81	OR
2. D. Florence Griffith	USA	22.04	
3. Merlene Ottey-Page	JAM	22.09	
4. Kathryn Cook (Smallwood)	GBR	22.10	
5. Grace Jackson	JAM	22.20	
6. Randy Givens	USA	22.36	
7. Rose-Aimée Bacoul	FRA	22.78	
8. Liliane Gaschet	FRA	22.86	

In 1982, Valerie Brisco-Hooks was a retired runner, forty pounds overweight after giving birth to a baby boy. Encouraged by her family and her coach, she returned to the track the following year and found that childbirth and motherhood had actually increased her strength. In 1984, she seemed to come out of nowhere to make the US team. Three days after winning the 400 meters, Brisco-Hooks overcame a mediocre start to become the first person to record a 200-400 double win in the Olympics. Coincidentally, her winning times in both races were exactly the same as the winning times in the 1992 Olympics.

1988 Seoul C: 59, N: 42, D: 9.29. WR: 21.71 (Marita Koch, Heike Drechsler)

1. D. Florence Griffith Joyner	USA	21.34	WR
2. Grace Jackson	JAM	21.72	
3. Heike Drechsler (Daute)	GDR	21.95	
4. Merlene Ottey	JAM	21.99	
5. Silke Möller (Gladisch)	GDR	22.09	
6. Gwendolyn Torrence	USA	22.17	
7. Maya Azarashvili	SOV/GEO	22.33	
8. Galina Malchugina	SOV/RUS	22.42	

Florence Griffith Joyner set an Olympic record of 21.76 in the quarterfinals. In the semifinals she ran a 21.56 to break the nine-year-old world record. The final, run 100 minutes later, was more of the same: Griffith Joyner pulled away in the second half of the race and leaped joyously across the finish line, stopping the clock in an almost unbelievable 21.34. Grace Jackson took almost a half second off her pre-Olympic best and came within one one-hundredth of a second of the pre-Olympic world record, yet found herself 4 meters behind Griffith Joyner at the finish.

1992 Barcelona C: 51, N: 40, D: 8.6. WR: 21.34 (D. Florence Griffith Joyner)

1. Gwendolyn Torrence	USA	21.81
2. Juliet Cuthbert	JAM	22.02
3. Merlene Ottey	JAM	22.09
4. Irma Privalova	RUS	22.19
5. Carlette Guidry	USA	22.30
6. Grace Jackson Small	JAM	22.58
7. Michelle Finn	USA	22.61
8. Galina Malchugina	RUS	22.63

Torrence ran 21.72 in the semifinals to better her personal best by .30 seconds. In the final she pulled away after hitting the final straight. Torrence also won medals in both relays, but her performance was tainted by the fact that her mouth ran even faster than her feet. After finishing out of the medals in the 100 meters, Torrence leveled unsupported accusations of drug use at her opponents (see page 295). At the press conference after the 200 meters, Juliet Cuthbert confronted Torrence, noting that when she spoke with her own mother after earning a silver medal in the 100, the elder Cuthbert immediately asked her daughter if it was true that she was taking drugs. Torrence appeared only mildly repentant and left the impression that she didn't understand the difference between being outspoken and being slanderous.

In 2002 Cuthbert was robbed at gunpoint in downtown Kingston. The robber took her cell phone and demanded money. "After I realized I had no money to give," Cuthbert recounted, "I told him who I was. He put his gun away, gave me back my cell phone and said, 'I'm sorry. I didn't know it was you, and times are hard.' That's the respect an athlete gets in Jamaica."

1996 Atlanta C: 47, N: 34, D: 8.1. WR: 21.34 (D. Florence Griffith Joyner)

1. Marie-José Pérec	FRA	22.12
2. Merlene Ottey	JAM	22.24
3. Mary Onyali	NGR	22.38
4. Inger Miller	USA	22.41
5. Galina Malchugina	RUS	22.45
6. Chandra Sturrup	BAH	22.54
7. Juliet Cuthbert	JAM	22.60
8. Carlette Guidry	USA	22.61

For four years the 200 meters had been dominated by the triumvirate of Gwen Torrence, Merlene Ottey and Irina Privalova. But Torrence finished fourth at the US trials, missing Olympic qualification by one hundredth of a second, and questions were raised about Privalova's health (in fact she dropped out before the semifinals). This left Ottey with the mantle of favorite.

Merlene Ottey was born May 10, 1960, in the community of Pondside in the rural parish of Hanover, Jamaica. When Ottey was fourteen years old she was chosen to represent Hanover at 200 meters in an All-Island meet in the Jamaican capital of Kingston. She carried with her a small purse containing spending money given to her by her mother as well as bus fare entrusted to her by teammates. Fearful that the purse would be stolen, she carried it with her to the starting line. Ottey burst into the lead, but dropped the purse. She hesitated, considered retrieving it, then ran on, regaining the lead and winning the race—all this in 200 meters. When she went back for the purse it had been stolen, but her running career, which would turn out to be one of the longest and most successful in track history, had been launched.

Ottey attended the University of Nebraska in the United States and first represented Jamaica at the Olympics in 1980, earning a bronze at 200 meters. At the 1984 Games in Los Angeles, she won two more bronzes, at 100 meters and 200 meters. Slowed by an unhealed hamstring injury, she placed out of the medals in 1988, but returned to the Olympics in 1992 to win yet another bronze at 200 meters. Although she had won the world championships in 1993 and 1995, she was still driven by the need to win a gold medal in the Olympics. In Atlanta she lost the 100 meters to Gail Devers in a photo-finish. At age 36, the 200 meters appeared to be her last chance for Olympic victory.

Since her 400 meters victory at the 1992 Olympics, Marie-José Pérec had become such a popular celebrity in France that she was unable to concentrate on her training and was forced to leave the country. She settled in Los Angeles and began training with UCLA coach John Smith. After the IAAF changed the Olympic schedule to allow Michael Johnson to try for a 200-400 double, word leaked that Pérec would enter the 200 as well. Pérec insisted she would only run the 400. However, with Torrence out and Privalova weakened, Pérec signed up for the double after all. She had run the distance at the 1988 Olympics, but was eliminated in the heats. Although her personal record was 21.99, her best result in competition was fourth place at the 1993 world championships.

In Atlanta, Pérec, having already earned gold in the 400 meters, won the first semifinal at 200 meters in 22.07. Ottey won the second semi in 22.08 to become the first runner to qualify for the final in the same event five times.

Michael Johnson's attempt to double had been accompanied by a huge media buildup. Many American spectators were confused when Pérec lined up to steal his thunder fifteen minutes before the men's final. Ottey took the early lead. After 100 meters, Pérec, a relatively slow starter, was still in fifth place. But in the straightaway, she made up ground quickly. She caught Ottey fifteen meters from the finish and won by about one meter. With the final contested only one hour and forty-five minutes after the semifinals, none of the finalists was able to better her semifinal time.

Merlene Ottey, after running in the 4 × 100-meter relay, brought her Olympic medal total to two silvers and five bronzes. There was speculation that she would continue until the 2000 Olympics, but on the eve of the 1999 world championships it was announced that, on July 5, she had tested positive for the steroid nandrolone. While Jamaica and the track world reeled in shock, Ottey was suspended for two years, although she was reinstated early and did compete in Sydney after all.

2000 Sydney C: 51, N: 35, D: 9.28. WR: 21.34 (D. Florence Griffith Joyner)

1. Pauline Davis-Thompson	BAH	22.27
2. Susanthika Jayasinghe	SRI	22.28
3. Beverly McDonald	JAM	22.35
4. Debbie Ferguson	BAH	22.37
5. Melinda Gainsford-Taylor	AUS	22.42
6. Cathy Freeman	AUS	22.53
7. Zhanna Pintusevych	UKR	22.66

DISQ (Drugs): Marion Jones (USA) 21.84

On September 23, Marion Jones won the 100 meters, the first step in her longshot quest for five gold medals at the Sydney 2000 Olympics. Her next stop was the 200 meters, but before the 200 heats began four days later, Jones had to deal with a bombshell revelation: her husband, world champion shot-putter C.J. Hunter, had tested positive for steroids four times during the summer. Although there was no evidence that Jones herself had taken prohibited substances, it was hard to imagine that she was unaware of her husband's activities. Jones continued to meet with the press, but refused to discuss Hunter's test results.

When the 200 meters competition began, Jones seemed unaffected by the turmoil. After easing through the opening rounds, she won her semifinal heat easily. Pauline Davis finished just ahead of Susanthika Jayasinghe in the second semi. Jones lived up to expectations in the final, coming out of the turn with a clear lead and winning by four meters, the event's largest margin of victory since Wilma Rudolph. Davis came from behind to pip Jayasinghe for the silver medal as both clocked personal bests.

What with Jones' second gold medal and her husband's drug scandal, the post-race press conference was jammed with reporters. But the world's sportswriters were soon to learn that Marion Jones wasn't the only women's sprinter with a compelling story. Pauline Davis had just won her first individual medal after competing in five Olympics and she was in a very good mood. Asked about the key events in her career, she told this story: "When I was fourteen, I went to a meet in Jamaica and a woman in the stands said, 'That girl's never going to make it because she's heavy busted and has a big butt.' So my coach's sister took me all over Nassau to find a sports bra and, back then, they were hideous. She got me a red one and told me I had to wear it day and night. I slept in it. I never took it off." Then Davis pointed to her "jugalugs," as she put it, and added, "Look, it worked, because here I am today." Davis also told about her first meeting with Aboriginal Australian Cathy Freeman, whom she asked, "Girl, just what color are you?" The two later became good friends.

If Davis' story was entertaining, Jayasinghe's was harrowing. The first Sri Lankan medalist since Duncan White in the 1948 400-meter hurdles, Jayasinghe grew up in the remote village of Atnawala, northwest of Colombo. At the time of her birth, her father was an unemployed driver and her mother worked as a rubber tree tapper. Discovered during a high school relay, she improved quickly and became a national hero when she earned a silver medal at the 1997 world championships. But then her troubles began. According to Jayasinghe, the Sri Lankan sports minister demanded that she have sex with him. Jayasinghe, who was married, refused. In April of 1998, athletics officials appeared at her home to collect a urine sample for doping tests. Jayasinghe complied, but when she demanded that the colleting jar be sealed in her presence, the officials refused. The resulting test was positive for steroids and Jayasinghe was publicly reviled. She claimed that the sample had been spiked and protested. The IAAF took her side and her two-year suspension was lifted. Under continued pressure at home, Jayasinghe sold some of her trophies to pay for a visa and flew to the United States to train. During the Sydney Olympics, she infuriated the Sri Lankan government by wearing on her wrist a yellow ribbon that symbolized the desire that upcoming elections in Sri Lanka be free and fair.

And Marion Jones? She did win three more medals, although only one of them was gold. And five months later, she and C.J. Hunter separated. In fact, after the 2000 Olympics, Jones' career went into a tailspin. Hunter, told reporters that he had seen Jones inject banned substances. In 2003, Jones' boyfriend, former world-record holder Tim Montgomery, was implicated in the BALCO doping scandal and received a two-year ban. Then, in June 2006, Jones tested positive for Erythropoietin (EPO) at the US track and field championships in Indianapolis. She was cleared after her B sample tested negative, however, the following month, Jones was implicated in a multimillion-dollar check-counterfeiting scheme, which resulted in criminal charges against Montgomery. In 2007, Jones married Obadele Thompson, the 100 meters bronze medalist in 2000. By then, legal fees and loss of corporate sponsorship had left Jones in severe financial troubles, with a bank balance that she claimed was only $2,000. One of the first women in track and field to become a millionaire, Jones was forced to sell her $2.5 million mansion in North Carolina, as well as two other houses in the state, including the one in which her mother was living. In October 2007, Jones admitted in federal court to having used steroids in the run-up to the Sydney Olympics. She was stripped of her five medals and sentenced to six months in prison for lying to federal prosecutors.

2004 Athens C: 43, N: 32, D: 8.25. WR: 21.34 (D. Florence Griffith Joyner)

1. Veronica Campbell	JAM	22.05
2. Allyson Felix	USA	22.18
3. Debbie Ferguson	BAH	22.30
4. Aleen Bailey	JAM	22.42
5. Ivet Lalova	BUL	22.57
6. Kim Gevaert	BEL	22.84
7. Muna Lee	USA	22.87
7. Abiodun Oyepitan	GBR	22.87

Twenty-two-year-old Veronica Campbell entered the final with a four-year winning streak at 200 meters and with a bronze medal in the 100 meters four days earlier. Her main challenge came from 18-year-old Allyson Felix, who recorded the fastest time in the first qualifying round, winning her heat in 22.39 seconds. Both Campbell and Felix won their heats in all three preliminary rounds, with Campbell setting a personal record of 22.13 in the semifinals. In the final, they faced each other for the first time ever. Campbell, one lane to the outside of Felix in lane four, accelerated in the curve and came out of the turn with a lead that she never relinquished. Debbie Ferguson earned the bronze medal despite running on her own in lane eight.

2008 Beijing C: 46, N: 36, D: 8.21. WR: 21.34 (D. Florence Griffith Joyner)

1. Veronica Campbell-Brown	JAM	21.74
2. Allyson Felix	USA	21.93
3. Kerron Stewart	JAM	22.00
4. Muna Lee	USA	22.01
5. Marshevet Hooker	USA	22.34
6. Sherone Simpson	JAM	22.36
7. Debbie Ferguson-McKenzie	BAH	22.61
8. Cydonie Mothersill	CAY	22.68

Four years after losing to Veronica Campbell in the 200-meter final in Athens, Allyson Felix had become the unquestioned favorite leading up to the Beijing Games. In 2005 Felix won her first major international title, beating Campbell at the world championships and ending her 42-race winning streak. Two years later the 22-year-old Felix defended her title in impressive style, beating Campbell for the second time, this time with a 0.53-second margin of victory, the largest in a world championship or Olympic final since the 1948 Olympics in London.

Campbell—who hailed from Trelawny, the same Jamaican parish as Usain Bolt—had also had a successful season, winning three medals at the 2007 world championships, including gold in the 100 meters, despite the fact that her coach, Lance Brauman, was serving a year-long prison term for embezzlement and fraud. After failing to qualify for the Jamaican team in the 100-meter event, Campbell was focused entirely on defending her 2004 Olympic title.

The 2008 Olympic competition was a near-exact repeat of 2004. Once again Campbell and Felix both won their semi-final heats easily and faced off in the final, drawing adjacent lanes with Campbell on the inside. And, just like in 2004, Campbell accelerated on the curve and pulled away over the final straight. Felix moved up from fourth over the final 70 meters to edge Kerron Stewart for silver, but finished well behind Campbell, whose time of 21.74 seconds was a personal best and matched the eighth-best 200 meters time ever. "Déjà vu," Felix said afterwards, "and not in a good way."

In 2009, Felix once again beat Campbell in the world championship final to win her third consecutive 200-meter title, becoming the first-ever woman to achieve a hat-trick in a sprint event at the world championships. At the post-race press conference Felix confessed to Campbell, "I would love to trade my three world championships for your gold."

Campbell-Brown finally won a 200 meters world championship in 2011, while Felix placed third behind Carmelita Jeter of the United States.

400 METERS

1896–1960 not held

1964 Tokyo C: 23, N: 17, D: 10.17. WR: 51.4 (Dan Shin-geum)

1. Elizabeth Cuthbert	AUS	52.0 OR	(52.01)
2. Ann Packer	GBR	52.2	(52.20)
3. Judith Amoore	AUS	53.4	
4. Antonia Munkácsi	HUN	54.4	
5. Maria Itkina	SOV/RUS	54.6	
6. Mathilda "Tilly" van der Zwaard	HOL	55.2	
7. Gertrud Schmidt	GDR	55.4	
8. Evelyne Lebret	FRA	55.5	

World record holder Dan Shin-geum of North Korea was barred from participating in the Olympics because of a dispute between the IOC and the North Korean government. In her absence, the inaugural Olympic 400 meters was won by Betty Cuthbert, the remarkable

Ann Packer, Betty Cuthbert and Judith Amoore, 1964
The medalists in the 1964 women's 400 metres.

Australian who had earned three gold medals eight years earlier in Melbourne. At the Rome Olympics in 1960 she was suffering from a hamstring pull and was forced to withdraw from competition after only one race. In Tokyo she coasted through the opening round and the semifinals, satisfied to qualify for the final. Then, on October 16, she ran what she later called "the only perfect race I have ever run" to finish a long yard ahead of Ann Packer. In 1969, Cuthbert developed multiple sclerosis and has spent the rest of her life in a wheelchair.

1968 Mexico City C: 29, N: 21, D: 10.16. WR: 51.2 (Dan Shin-geum)

1. Colette Besson	FRA	52.03	EOR
2. Lillian Board	GBR	52.12	
3. Natalya Pechenkina	SOV/RUS	52.25	
4. Janet Simpson	GBR	52.57	
5. Aurelia Penton	CUB	52.75	
6. Jarvis Scott	USA	52.79	
7. Helga Henning	GER	52.89	
8. Hermina Van Der Hoeven	HOL	53.02	

The victory of Colette Besson, a 22-year-old physical education teacher from Bordeaux, came as a complete surprise. Her best time previous to the Olympics was 53.8, but she was able to improve by 1.8 seconds when it counted. She passed the favorite, Lillian Board, just before the finish line and won by almost two feet. Although the harsher members of the British sports press were critical of Board for missing the gold medal, she was only 19 years old and seemed a good bet for the 1972 Olympics in Munich. She did make it to Munich, but the circumstances were tragic. In 1970 she developed cancer, complicated by peritonitis. She died in a Munich clinic 13 days after her 22nd birthday.

1972 Munich C: 49, N: 29, D: 9.7. WR: 51.0 (Marilyn Neufville, Monika Zehrt)

1. Monika Zehrt	GDR	51.08	OR
2. Rita Wilden (Jahn)	GER	51.21	
3. Kathy Hammond	USA	51.64	
4. Helga Seidler	GDR	51.86	
5. Mable Fergerson	USA	51.96	
6. Charlene Rendina	AUS	51.99	
7. Dagmar Käsling	GDR	52.19	
8. Györgyi Balogh	HUN	52.39	

Despite the absence of injured co-world record holder Marilyn Neufville of Jamaica, the competition was excellent. The Olympic record was broken by five different women before the final was run. However 19-year-old Monika Zehrt of Berlin seemed unaffected by the pressure of her opponents or by her role as favorite. She had taken the lead by the halfway mark and held off a late challenge by local favorite Rita Wilden to win by a meter.

1976 Montreal C: 38, N: 19, D: 7:29. WR: 49.75 (Irena Szewińska [Kirszenstein])

1. Irena Szewińska (Kirszenstein)	POL	49.28	WR
2. Christina Brehmer	GDR	50.51	
3. Ellen Streidt (Stropahl)	GDR	50.55	
4. Pirjo Häggman (Wilmi)	FIN	50.56	
5. Rosalyn Bryant	USA	50.65	
6. Sheila Ingram	USA	50.90	
7. Riita Salin	FIN	50.98	
8. Debra Sapenter	USA	51.66	

The amazing Irena Szewińska had already won Olympic medals in the 100 meters, 200 meters, long jump, and 4 × 100-meter relay when she switched to the 400 meters in 1973. The following year she became the first woman to break 50 seconds in what was only the second 400 meters race of her career. Early in 1976 her world record was broken by Christina Brehmer. But later in the year Szewińska regained the record, and an Olympic showdown between the 18-year-old Brehmer and the 30-year-old Szewińska was eagerly awaited. Irena coasted through the first two rounds and then set an Olympic record of 50.48 in the semifinals. For the first 300 meters, the final was a close race, but then Szewińska pulled away dramatically to win by almost ten meters. Her total of seven medals (three gold, two silver, and two bronze) ranks her along with Shirley Strickland as one of the most successful female track and field athletes in Olympic history. Between 1974 and 1978 she won 34 straight 400-meter finals, until she was finally beaten by Marita Koch at the European championships. In 1980 Szewińska took part in the Moscow Olympics, but was eliminated in the semifinals when she pulled a muscle.

Pirjo Häggman, who finished fourth in Montreal, later became the first woman to be elected to the IOC. She resigned in 1999, but not before being joined in the IOC by Szewínska.

1980 Moscow C: 38, N: 22, D: 7.28. WR: 48.60 (Marita Koch)

1. Marita Koch	GDR	48.88	OR
2. Jarmila Kratochvilová	CZE	49.46	
3. Christina Lathan (Brehmer)	GDR	49.66	
4. Irina Nazarova	SOV/RUS	50.07	
5. Nina Zyuskova	SOV/UKR	50.17	
6. Gabriele Löwe	GDR	51.33	
7. Pirjo Häggman	FIN	51.35	
8. Linsey MacDonald	GBR	52.40	

Marita Koch had been one of the favorites in 1976, but was forced to withdraw from her semifinal heat because of injury. In 1979 she became the first woman to break 22 seconds for 200 meters as well as the first woman to beat 49 seconds for 400 meters. In Moscow, using the same spikes she had used four years earlier in Montreal, Koch won a clear victory over Kratochvilová and

Lathan, both of whom recorded personal bests. The race was the first in history in which three women broke the 50-second barrier.

1984 Los Angeles C: 28, N: 18, D: 8.6. WR: 47.99 (Jarmila Kratochvilová)

1. Valerie Brisco-Hooks	USA	48.83 OR
2. Chandra Cheeseborough	USA	49.05
3. Kathryn Cook (Smallwood)	GBR	49.43
4. Marita Payne	CAN	49.91
5. Lillie Leatherwood	USA	50.25
6. Ute Thimm	GER	50.37
7. Charmaine Crooks	CAN	50.45
8. Ruth Waithera	KEN	51.56

At the US trials, Cheeseborough had come from behind to defeat Brisco-Hooks, but in the Olympic final, competing only three miles from where her older brother had been shot to death by a stray bullet ten years earlier while jogging on a high school track, Brisco-Hooks held off Cheeseborough's finishing kick to win the first of her three gold medals.

Of the 28 women who took part in the 400-meter competition in 1984, the slowest was Zeina Mina who finished last in her heat with a time of 59.56. However, it is worth bearing in mind the difficulties which Mina faced training in her hometown—Beirut. Lebanon's leading heptathlete, Mina was unable to train for her specialty because shelling prevented her from reaching the stadium. So she ran on the beach, in the subway, anywhere she could find. For a year she didn't run on a track, until two weeks before the Olympics. Her performance in Los Angeles did not bother her. "It is wonderful here," she said, "away from the bombs."

1988 Seoul C: 46, N: 33, D: 9.26. WR: 47.60 (Marita Koch)

1. Olha Bryzhina	SOV/UKR	48.65 OR
2. Petra Müller	GDR	49.45
3. Olga Nazarova	SOV/RUS	49.90
4. Valerie Brisco	USA	50.16
5. Diane Dixon	USA	50.72
6. Denean Howard-Hill	USA	51.12
7. Helga Arendt	GER	51.17
8. Maree Holland	AUS	51.25

Defending champion Valerie Brisco took the early lead. World champion Olha Bryzhina, fifth at the halfway mark, caught Brisco after 300 meters, opened up an 8-meter lead and won by 6 meters. Her husband, Viktor Bryzhin, also won a gold medal in the 4 × 100-meter relay. With the exception of Bryzhina and Müller, the times in the final were surprisingly slow. In the semis all three Americans had broken 50 seconds, while Olga Nazarova had clocked a 49.11. Unlike the men's 400-meter runners, the women were not allowed a day off between the semifinals and the final.

1992 Barcelona C: 41, N: 29, D: 8.5. WR: 47.60 (Marita Koch)

1. Marie-José Pérec	FRA	48.83
2. Olha Bryzhina	UKR	49.05
3. Ximena Restrepo Gaviria	COL	49.64
4. Olga Nazarova	RUS	49.69
5. Jillian Richardson-Briscoe	CAN	49.93
6. Rochelle Stevens	USA	50.11
7. Sandie Richards	JAM	50.19
8. Phylis Smith	GBR	50.87

Marie-Jose Pérec was born in Basse-Terre on the island of Guadeloupe in the Caribbean. She moved to Paris with her mother when she was 16 years old. Because of her natural ability, coaches practically forced her to become a sprinter. By 1988 she was representing France in the Olympics at 200 meters. She improved rapidly and in 1991 she won a clear victory in the 400 meters final at the world championships. Her athletic success, along with her model's body (5 feet 10¾ inches [1.80 meters], 132 pounds [60 kg.], and long, long legs), catapulted her into major stardom in France. In the months leading up to the 1992 Olympics, the French media followed her every move, scrutinizing her training regimen, photographing her visit to her grandmother in Guadeloupe, even analyzing her opponents in greater detail than the press in their own countries. Despite this pressure, Pérec did not disappoint her followers. She was hard-pressed by defending champion Olha Bryzhina, who took an early lead and was still in front as the finalists entered the final straightaway. But then Pérec used her long, graceful strides to pull away and win by almost two meters.

Pérec's time of 48.83 was the first sub-49-second 400 to be run since 1988. At the post-race press conference, Pérec was asked if she thought she could someday break Marita Koch's world record of 47.60. She startled the audience by bluntly replying, "I think the world record is the race I ran today. I don't think that anyone has run under 49 seconds until now. To run this race today I didn't need any 'biological preparation.' She thus accused of doping not only Marita Koch, but also five other runners, including Valerie Brisco and Olha Bryzhina, who was sitting beside her. Bryzhina did not respond. One of the five, Olga Nazarova, did in fact fail a doping test in 1996.

1996 Atlanta C: 49, N: 35, D: 7.29. WR: 47.60 (Marita Koch)

1. Marie-José Pérec	FRA	48.25 OR
2. Catherine Freeman	AUS	48.63
3. Falilat Ogunkoya	NGR	49.10
4. Pauline Davis	BAH	49.28
5. Jearl Miles	USA	49.55
6. Fatima Yusuf	NGR	49.77
7. Sandie Richards	JAM	50.45
8. Grit Breuer	GER	50.71

Between Olympics, Marie-José Pérec worked as a model, left her French coach, moved to Los Angeles, set a French record in the 400-meter hurdles and dabbled with the 200 meters. She arrived in Atlanta as the clear favorite at 400 meters and she did not disappoint. As expected, her most serious challenge came from Cathy Freeman. In 1993, while returning to Australia from the world championships, where she had been eliminated in the 200 meters semifinals, Freeman wrote the following goal on an air sickness bag: "48.60 ATLANTA." Three years later in Atlanta, Freeman ran 48.63 to become the first Aborigine to medal in an individual event. Pérec, meanwhile, passed Freeman coming off the final turn and pulled away to win by three meters. Her time of 48.25 was the fastest in ten years. Pérec, Freeman, Ogunkoya and Davis all beat their personal bests by more than half a second, while Pérec became the first athlete of either sex to win the 400 meters twice.

2000 Sydney C: 57, N: 42, D: 9.25. WR: 47.60 (Marita Koch)

1. Cathy Freeman	AUS	49.11
2. Lorraine Graham	JAM	49.58
3. Katharine Merry	GBR	49.72
4. Donna Fraser	GBR	49.79
5. Ana Guevara Espinoza	MEX	49.96
6. Heide Seyerling	SAF	50.05
7. Falilat Ogunkoya	NGR	50.12
8. Olga Kotlyarova	RUS	51.04

Catherine Astrid Salome Freeman was born in Mackay, North Queensland, on February 16, 1973. Her ethnic heritage mirrored the history of Australia. Her mother's father was a Syrian who came to Australia to deliver camels. One great-grandfather came from China in search of gold and somewhere in the family tree was probably a convict. But most of Freeman's ancestors were Aborigines, the native people of Australia, now reduced to 1% of the population. Freeman's grandmother was a member of the "Stolen Generation," light-skinned Aborigines who were taken away from their families to be raised by whites. Freeman's father's father was a rugby player who, in 1936, was invited to play in Great Britain. However, the Australian government refused to issue him a passport.

Cathy Freeman's own athletic abilities were noticed early. When she was only 16 years old, she was a member of Australia's victorious 4 × 100-meter relay team at the 1990 Commonwealth Games. At the 1992 Olympics, she ran in the 400 meters and the 4 × 400 meter relay. But it was at the 1994 Commonwealth Games that Freeman came into her own, not only as an athlete but as a national figure. She won the 400 meters and, before taking hold of the Australian flag, she wrapped herself in the red, yellow and black Aboriginal flag. The head of the Australian delegation, Arthur Tunstall, reprimanded her and announced that henceforth only the Australian flag could be displayed during victory laps. A few days later, Freeman gave her response: she won the 200 meters and, during her victory lap, she waved both the Aboriginal and Australian flags. Although her gesture stirred a great deal of controversy in the press, back home in Australia the public reaction was overwhelmingly positive. Gradually, Cathy Freeman became the symbol of the Australian desire to recognize its past racist excesses and to reconcile whites and Aborigines.

Meanwhile, on the track, Freeman kept getting better and better. She finished second behind Marie-José Pérec at the 1996 Atlanta Olympics, and then won the world championship at 400 meters in both 1997 and 1999. By the time of the Sydney Olympics, Freeman had won 37 of 38 finals, going back to the start of the 1997 season. Her only loss was the result of a foot injury that put her out of action for six months in 1998.

If anyone was considered capable of challenging Freeman in Sydney, it was thought to be Marie-José Pérec. In reality, though, Pérec, despite her impressive history, was considered a complete mystery. After losing to Freeman in a post-Atlanta match-up, she had not run a 400 meters race in four years. In March 1998, Pérec fell ill with Epstein-Barr virus, which left her with chronic fatigue. When she recovered sufficiently to recommence training, Pérec zigzagged around the world in search of coaches. At the beginning of 2000, she settled, in a bizarre twist of events, on Wolfgang Meier, the East German husband of Marita Koch, the woman she had openly accused of doping at her post-race press conference at the 1992 Olympics (see above). Pérec finally returned to competition in July, but she only raced twice, finishing second in a 200-meter race and third, behind Katharine Merry and Lorraine Graham, at 400 meters. Her time in the 400, 50.32 seconds, was not going to win any medals, but it wasn't bad after a four-year break, so the mystery of her condition remained. Pérec's behavior also seemed strange. In July she announced that an Australian had tried to buy her training secrets from Meier. When she arrived in Sydney on September 8, she fled from the press and secluded herself in her hotel suite.

For Freeman, there was no avoiding the public. The climax of the Opening Ceremony on September 15 came when Freeman lit the Olympic cauldron to mark the beginning of the Sydney Games. For Freeman, this responsibility was more nerve-wracking than the competition itself. Once it was over and she could concentrate on running, she was relieved. "Running is like breathing for me," she explained.

The heats for the 400 meters were scheduled for September 22, but two days earlier, a surprising event occurred: Marie-José Pérec, accompanied by her boyfriend, 1996 gold medalist Anthuan Maybank, fled Sydney. On the way to France, they changed planes in Singapore, but were detained by police when Maybank attacked a photographer. Pérec claimed she had been threatened with attack at her room in Sydney by someone posing as a delivery man.

With Pérec out of the picture, all attention centered on Freeman. She recorded the fastest time of the quarterfinals, 50.32 seconds, and then won her semifinal heat in 50.01. Graham won the other semi in 50.28. The night of the final, 112,524 people jammed into the Olympic stadium while almost half of Australia watched on television. Freeman's race was the third most watched event in the history of Australian television, topped only by the Sydney Opening Ceremony and by the funeral of Princess Diana. Freeman, wearing a hooded bodysuit, started cautiously. Coming out of the turn she was even with Graham, with Merry just behind. Eighty meters from the finish line, Freeman began to pull away. The roar of the crowd was so loud that, in Freeman's words, "it vibrated through my body." Freeman increased her lead and won by four meters. Behind her, Graham, Merry and Donna Fraser all recorded personal bests. After she crossed the finish line, Freeman pulled down her hood and sat down on the track. She remained there for a full two minutes, overwhelmed by relief. When her friend, Donna Fraser, tried to congratulate her, Freeman was unable to respond. "She was in her own world," said Fraser, "a special place I guess." Later, Freeman explained, "I could feel the crowd around me, all over me. I felt everybody's emotion. Happiness and joy absorbed into every pore of my body. I had to sit down to make myself feel normal and get comfortable. . . . All I know is that I've made a lot of people happy, with all kinds of backgrounds who call Australia home. And I'm happy." Freeman took her victory lap with both the Australian and Aboriginal flags.

2004 Athens C: 42, N: 31, D: 8.24. WR: 47.60 (Marita Koch)

1. Tonique Williams-Darling	BAH	49.41
2. Ana Guevara Espinoza	MEX	49.56
3. Natalya Antyukh	RUS	49.89
4. Monique Hennagan	USA	49.97
5. DeeDee Trotter	USA	50.00
6. Sanya Richards	USA	50.19
7. Christine Amertil	BAH	50.37
8. Natalya Nazarova	RUS	50.65

One month before the Olympics, at the IAAF Golden League meet in Rome, Tonique Williams-Darling beat world champion Ana Guevara, breaking Guevara's two-year, 23-meet winning streak. One month later the pair met again, in Zurich, and again Williams-Darling gained a narrow victory. Both Williams-Darling and Guevara made it to the final easily, each winning their heats in the first round and semifinals. In the final, Monique Hennagan burst out to a quick lead, but Williams-Darling caught up by 200 meters and led until the final 50 meters, when Guevara pulled even for first time, with Richards and Hennagan battling for bronze. Williams-Darling pulled away in the final stretch to finish a step ahead of Guevara. She was the first Bahamian to win a gold medal in an individual event in any sport.

2008 Beijing C: 50, N: 40, D: 8.19. WR: 47.60 (Marital Koch)

1. Christine Ohuruogu	GBR	49.62
2. Shericka Williams	JAM	49.69
3. Sanya Richards	USA	49.93
4. Yuliya Gushchina	RUS	50.01
5. Anastasiya Kapachinskaya	RUS	50.03
6. Tatyana Firova	RUS	50.11
7. Rosemarie Whyte	JAM	50.68
8. Amantle Montsho	BOT	51.18

Christine Ohuruogu had a controversial path to the 2008 Olympics. One of seven children born to Nigerian immigrants in East London, she first rose to prominence in England after winning the 400 meters title at the Commonwealth Games in 2006, beating reigning world and Olympic champion Tonique Williams-Darling. Less than six months later, the 22-year-old Ohuruogu received a one-year ban by the IAAF for missing three out-of-competition drug tests over a ten-month period. She blamed the misses on youthful forgetfulness, and the Court of Arbitration for sport, while upholding the ban, noted, "There is no suggestion that she is guilty of taking drugs in order to enhance her performance or otherwise and, indeed, this case can be viewed in all the circumstances as a busy young athlete being forgetful."

Despite having never returned a positive drug test, Ohuruogu faced significant criticism at home. She considered quitting the sport, but continued to train, returning to competition in time to win the 2007 world championship in Osaka, Japan, 24 days after her suspension expired. Under British Olympic Association (BOA) rules, any athlete banned for a doping offense is automatically ineligible for future Olympic Games. After winning the world championship title Ohuruogu challenged the BOA bylaw and had her Olympic ban overturned.

Her redemption nearly complete, Ohuruogu still faced stiff competition from two-time US National champion Sanya Richards. Born in Trelawny, Jamaica, Richards's parents moved to Florida when she was 12 to provide her better athletic training. Richards had dominated the 2005–2006 season, taking silver at the 2005 world championships and winning six out of six IAAF Golden League races in 2006. She finished the season ranked number one overall and was named the 2006 World Athlete of the Year by the IAAF, along with Asafa Powell.

That same year, Richards was also diagnosed with Behçet's syndrome, a rare and painful virus that causes chronic inflammation of blood vessels throughout the body. The virus flared up in 2007, causing ulcers and lesions on her legs so bad that Richards could barely talk, eat or stretch. She finished fourth at the world trials, her first loss of the season, and failed to qualify for the world championships. By 2008, though, she had returned to form, winning the US Trials easily. She beat Ohuruogu three separate times in the run-up to the Olympics and looked to be a favorite for gold.

Richards recorded the fastest times of the qualifying and semi-final rounds, and was the only athlete to break the 50-second barrier in the preliminary rounds.

In the final, Richards got off to a strong start, leading through the first 300 meters. In fourth with 100 meters remaining, Ohuruogu looked out of medal contention, but she maintained a controlled pace and gradually closed the gap, moving past Richards, who faded to third after suffering a cramped hamstring in the final 70 meters. Ohuruogu held off a hard-charging Shericka Williams at the line to win gold in 49.62 seconds, just one-hundredth of a second off her personal best. She was the first British woman to win the Olympic 400 meters gold, and one of only four British runners (including Steve Ovett, Sally Gunnell and Linford Christie) to hold both the world and Olympic titles in the same event.

In 2009 Richards finally won her first international title, at the world championships in Berlin, recording a time of 49 seconds flat, the fastest of the season, to finish 0.32 seconds ahead of second-place Williams. It was the 38th time in Richards' career that she had broken the 50-second barrier.

800 METERS

1896–1924 not held

1928 Amsterdam C: 25, N: 13, D: 8.2. WR: 2:19.6 (Karoline "Lina" Radke)

1. Karoline "Lina" Radke	GER	2:16.8 WR
2. Kinue Hitomi	JPN	2:17.6
3. Inga Gentzel	SWE	2:18.8
4. Jenny "Jean" Thompson	CAN	2:21.4
5. Fanny "Bobbie" Rosenfeld	CAN	2:22.4
6. Florence McDonald	USA	2:22.6
7. Marie Dollinger	GER	2:23.0
8. Gertruda Kilos	POL	2:28.0

The 1928 women's 800-meter race touched off a major controversy in the athletic world. The competition itself was exciting enough. Kinue Hitomi took the early lead. The three German finalists, Lina Radke, Marie Dollinger, and Elfriede Wever, ran a team race, with Dollinger and Wever wearing down the opposition and keeping a steady pace for Radke, who pulled away in the

Lina Radke, 1928
Male officials were so shocked to see women run the long distance of 800 meters in 1928 that all women's races longer than 200 meters were kept out of the Olympics for 32 years.

final 300 meters. Hitomi, meanwhile, had fallen back in the pack, but started a late charge in the final turn to capture the silver medal despite the fact that she had never competed at 800 meters before the Olympics. Radke's winning time was a world record that lasted for sixteen years.

After the race, several of the women dropped to the ground while they recuperated and had to be given aid. Antifeminists in the press and in the International Amateur Athletic Federation (IAAF) seized on their condition as evidence that women should be banned from running races of more than 200 meters. The London *Daily Mail* quoted doctors who said that women who took part in races of 800 meters and other such "feats of endurance" would "become old too soon." The president of the International Olympic Committee, Comte de Baillet-Latour, spoke out in favor of eliminating all women's sports from the Olympics and returning to the ancient Greek custom of an all-male competition. But there were those who supported women's athletics, and they pointed out that men frequently fainted after races just as women did. In fact, male rowers were *expected* to be nearly comatose at the finish of important races, such as those between Oxford and Cambridge or Harvard and Yale. In retrospect, of course, the arguments of the antiwomen forces seem foolish and ridiculous, particularly in light of the inclusion of a women's marathon in the 1984 Olympics. What makes the story more of a tragedy than a comedy, however, is that the executive committee of the IAAF actually *did* ban races longer than 200 meters, and no women's race longer than ½ lap was run at the Olympics for another 32 years.

Some of the early women athletes were extremely versatile. Fifth-place finisher Bobbie Rosenfeld, who worked in a Toronto chocolate factory, also took second in the 100 meters and first in the 4 × 100-meter relay. Silver medalist Kinue Hitomi of Okayama was the world record holder in the 200 meters and the long jump. Since neither event was included in the Olympics program, she took part instead in the 100 meters and the 800 meters. At the third Women's World Games, held in Prague in 1930, Hitomi delighted the crowd by winning four medals: a gold in the long jump, a silver in the triathlon, and bronzes in the 60-meter dash and the discus. The following year Kinue Hitomi died of tuberculosis at the age of 24.

1932–1956 not held

1960 Rome C: 27, N: 15, D: 9.7. WR: 2:04.3 (Lyudmyla Shevtsova)

1. Lyudmyla Shevtsova	SOV/UKR	2:04.3 EWR	(2:04.50)
2. Brenda Jones	AUS	2:04.4	(2:04.58)
3. Ursula Donath	GDR	2:05.6	(2:05.73)
4. Vera Kummerfeldt	GER	2:05.9	(2:06.07)
5. Antje Gleichfeld	GER	2:06.5	(2:06.63)
6. Joy Jordan	GBR	2:07.8	(2:07.95)
7. Gizella Csoka	HUN	2:08.0	(2:08.11)
8. Beata Zbikowska	POL	2:11.8	(2:11.91)

Dixie Willis of Australia led the field for most of the race, but, in the final straightaway, she tired, lost her balance and stepped onto the infield. She returned to the track and crossed the finish line in ninth place. Brenda Jones took the lead, but was passed by world record holder Lyudmyla Shevtsova just before the finish.

1964 Tokyo C: 23, N: 15, D: 10.20. WR: 1:58.0 (Dan Shin-geum)

1. Ann Packer	GBR	2:01.1 OR
2. Maryvonne Dupureur	FRA	2:01.9
3. M. Ann Marise Chamberlain	NZL	2:02.8
4. Zsuzsa Szabó	HUN	2:03.5
5. Antje Gleichfeld	GER	2:03.9
6. Laine Erik	SOV/EST	2:05.1
7. Gerarda Kraan	HOL	2:05.8
8. Anne Smith	GBR	2:05.8

With unofficial world record holder Dan Shin-geum out because of politics and official world record holder (2:01.2) Dixie Willis out because of illness, the 800 meters looked like an open race. In the semifinals, Maryvonne Dupureur, a housewife and physical education teacher from Lille, set an Olympic record of 2:04.1. In the final Dupureur had a five-yard lead entering the last straightaway, but Britain's Ann Packer, who had already won a silver medal in the 400 meters, turned on a fantastic finishing kick, passed Dupureur with 70 yards to go, and won by five yards. The 800 meters was not really Packer's race. She had finished fifth in her opening heat and third in her semifinal heat. She had considered skipping the final and going shopping instead, but when her fiancé, Robbie Brightwell, finished a disappointing fourth in the men's 400 meters, she decided to go all-out in his honor. "It was so easy, I could not believe I had won," she told reporters afterward. "I was thinking about him and not about myself, and so I wasn't nervous."

1968 Mexico City C: 24, N: 16, D: 10.19. WR: 1:58.0 (Dan Shin-geum)

1. Madeline Manning	USA	2:00.9 OR	(2:00.92)
2. Ileana Silai	ROM	2:02.5	(2:02.58)
3. Maria Gommers	HOL	2:02.6	(2:02.63)
4. Sheila Taylor	GBR	2:03.8	(2:03.81)
5. Doris Brown	USA	2:03.9	(2:03.98)
6. Patricia Lowe	GBR	2:04.2	(2:04.25)
7. Abigail Hoffman	CAN	2:06.8	(2:06.99)
8. Maryvonne Dupureur	FRA	2:08.2	(2:08.28)

The most shocking incident of the 1968 women's events occurred in the first semifinal heat, when the 20-year-old favorite, and official world record holder (2:00.5) Vera Nikolić of Yugoslavia, overcome by the pressure of being her nation's only hope for a track and field medal, dropped out after 300 meters and left the stadium. Rumors quickly spread that she had gone straight to a nearby bridge and was only prevented from committing suicide by her coach, who had followed her. That race was won by 20-year-old Madeline Manning, a Tennessee State "Tigerbelle" from Cleveland. Two days later, in the final, Manning took the early lead, then, spurred on by the garlicky perspiration of one of the other runners, she pulled away in the backstretch of the final lap and won by more than ten meters. Manning later became an ordained minister and served as chaplain to US Olympic athletes.

1972 Munich C: 38, N: 26, D: 9.3. WR: 1:58.0 (Dan Shin-geum)

1. Hildegard Falck	GER	1:58.6 OR	(1:58.55)
2. Nijolė Sabaitė	SOV/LIT	1:58.7	(1:58.65)
3. Gunhild Hoffmeister	GDR	1:59.2	(1:59.19)
4. Svetla Zlateva	BUL	1:59.7	(1:59.72)
5. Vera Nikolić	YUG/SER	2:00.0	(1:59.98)
6. Ileana Silai	ROM	2:00.0	(2:00.04)
7. Rosemary Stirling	GBR	2:00.2	(2.00.15)
8. Abigail Hoffman	CAN	2:00.2	(2.00.17)

The fireworks started in the second heat of the first round, when Svetla Zlateva slashed three seconds off her personal best to set an Olympic record of 1:58.9. Vera Nikolić finished close behind her in 1:59.6. Previous to this race, the only women to better two minutes had been Dan Shin-geum, Hildegard Falck, and Vasilena Amzina of Bulgaria, who had run a 1:59.9 a week before the Olympics began. In the fourth heat of the first round Amzina collided with Raisa Ruus of the USSR and fell to the ground. She got up and finished the race with blood on her face, but she failed to qualify for the next round. The first semifinal was won by Lithuanian Nijolė Sabaitė and the second by local favorite Hildegard Falck, a 23-year-old schoolteacher. In the second semi, defending champion Madeline Manning was eliminated when she misjudged the finish line and was passed just before the real line by Rosemary Stirling. The final was a thrilling race. Falck, urged on by the partisan crowd, pulled away coming out of the last curve and held off a final burst by Sabaitė.

1976 Montreal C: 35, N: 20, D: 7.26. WR: 1:56.0 (Valentina Gerassimova)

1. Tatyana Kazankina	SOV/RUS	1:54.94 WR
2. Nikolina Shtereva	BUL	1:55.42
3. Elfi Zinn	GDR	1:55.60
4. Anita Weiss	GDR	1:55.74
5. Svetlana Styrkina	SOV/BLR	1:56.44
6. Svetla Zlateva	BUL	1:57.21
7. Doris Gluth	GDR	1:58.99
8. Mariana Suman	ROM	2:02.21

The level of the competition was so high that world record holder Valentina Gerassimova, European champion Liliana Tomova of Bulgaria, Commonwealth champion Charlene Rendina of Australia, and 1968 Olympic champion Madeline Jackson (Manning) were all eliminated in the semifinals. Anita Weiss, who lowered the Olympic record by two seconds with a 1:56.53 in her semifinal heat, broke the world record in the final, but didn't even win a medal. Kazankina, a 1500-meter specialist who had been entered in the 800 meters as well on the final day for entries, moved from fifth place to first in the last 50 meters and slashed the world record by over a second.

Madeline Manning, 1976

The winner in 1968 in the 800 meters went on to become an ordained minister and (above) record a gospel music album.

1980 Moscow C: 28, N: 17, D: 7.27. WR: 1:54.85 (Nadiya Olizarenko)

1. Nadiya Olizarenko	SOV/UKR	1:53.43 WR
2. Olga Mineyeva	SOV/RUS	1:54.81
3. Tatyana Providokhina	SOV/RUS	1:55.46
4. Martina Kämpfert	GDR	1:56.21
5. Hildegard Ullrich	GDR	1:57.20
6. Jolanta Januchta	POL	1:58.25
7. Nikolina Shtereva	BUL	1:58.71
8. Gabriella Dorio	ITA	1:59.12

For the first time in Olympic history, all three medals in a women's track event were won by athletes from the same nation. Olizarenko, a 26-year-old military office worker from Odessa, ran a spectacular race, leading from start to finish (a rarity at 800 meters) and clipping almost one and a half seconds from her own world record, set only six weeks earlier.

1984 Los Angeles C: 25, N: 20, D: 8.6. WR: 1:53.28 (Jarmila Kratochvilová)

1. Doina Melinte	ROM	1:57.60
2. Kimberly Gallagher	USA	1:58.63
3. Rafira Fita Lovin	ROM	1:58.83
4. Gabriella Dorio	ITA	1:59.05
5. Lorraine Baker	GBR	2:00.03
6. Ruth Wysocki	USA	2:00.34
7. Margrit Klinger	GER	2:00.65
8. Caroline O'Shea	IRL	2:00.77

Melinte, known for her fast times, but disappointing performances in important meets, took the lead from Dorio with about 225 meters to go and won by over five meters. Conspicuously missing because of the Soviet-bloc boycott was Czech world record holder Jarmila Kratochvilová, who had caused a sensation at the 1983 world championships by winning the 400- and 800-meter races, a most unusual double.

1988 Seoul C: 29, N: 20, D: 9.26. WR: 1:53.28 (Jarmila Kratochvilová)

1. Sigrun Wodars	GDR	1:56.10
2. Christine Wachtel	GDR	1:56.64
3. Kimberly Gallagher	USA	1:56.91
4. Slobodanka Čolović	YUG/SER	1:57.50
5. Delisa Floyd	USA	1:57.80
6. Inna Yevseyeva	SOV/UKR	1:59.37
7. Teresa Zúñiga	SPA	1:59.82
8. Diane Edwards	GBR	2:00.77

The two Ws, Wodars and Wachtel, had a lot in common. They were both born in 1965, they were both 5 feet 5¼ inches tall, they ran for the same club and trained under the same coach, Walter Gladrow, and they both liked champagne, ice cream, and chocolate. Most important of all, they were both experts at running 800 meters. In 1987, Wachtel defeated Wodars four straight times, but in the biggest meet of the year, the world championships in Rome, Wodars came out on top.

In 1988, Wachtel was again dominant, finishing ahead of Wodars seven of eight times in the run-up to the Olympics. In Seoul, the two Ws took turns setting the pace. Wodars forged ahead in the final straightaway and went on to win by 5 meters. Unfortunately, the Cuban boycott prevented the participation of Ana Quirot, who had won all 13 of her 800-meter races in 1988, including victories over both Wodars and Wachtel. The entire Romanian squad also missed the Games; they were victims of blundering team officials who forgot to file their entry forms.

In 1990, Sigrun Wodars earned a footnote in sports history when she edged Wachtel again at 800 meters to win the final event of the final East German championships. In 1992, it was revealed that Wodars had been given steroids from 1983 until 1989 and Wachtel from 1985 until 1989.

1992 Barcelona C: 36, N: 26, D: 8.3. WR: 1:53.28 (Jarmila Kratochvilová)

1. Ellen van Langen	HOL	1:55.54
2. Lilia Nurutdinova	RUS	1:55.99
3. Ana Fidelia Quirot Moret	CUB	1:56.80
4. Inna Yevseyeva	UKR	1:57.20
5. Maria de Lurdes Mutola	MOZ	1:57.49
6. Ella Kovacs	ROM	1:57.95
7. Joetta Clark	USA	1:58.06
8. Lyubov Gurina	RUS	1:58.13

It was widely assumed that the medals would be divided among the first four finishers at the 1991 world championships: Nurutdinova, Quirot, Kovacs, and Mutola. Few people outside of the Netherlands took it seriously when three weeks before the opening of the Olympics Ellen van Langen ran the fastest time of the year (1:55.63) and beat Nurutdinova and Kovacs in the process. A good race, but the 26-year-old van Langen had never before won a medal in a major championship.

Nurutdinova set a blistering pace, covering the first 400 meters in 55.72 seconds. Mutola was right beside her with Quirot third and van Langen back in sixth place. With 150 meters to go, Quirot began moving away from the curb to prepare herself for an attempt to pass Nurutdinova. Kovacs, now running behind Quirot, followed her. Seeing a gap, van Langen moved up on the inside. Into the homestretch Nurutdinova grappled to stay ahead, with van Langen at her heels. In her desperate effort, Nurutdinova veered to the outside. Again van Langen was quick to slip through the gap. She drew even with Nurutdinova with 50 meters to go and then pulled away to win by about three meters. The following year, at the 1993 world championships, Nurutdinova was banned after she tested positive for the "Ben Johnson steroid," Stanozolol.

1996 Atlanta C: 36, N: 30, D: 7.27. WR: 1:53.28 (Jarmila Kratochvilová)

1. Svetlana Masterkova	RUS	1:57.73
2. Ana Fidelia Quirot Moret	CUB	1:58.11
3. Maria de Lurdes Mutola	MOZ	1:58.71
4. Kelly Holmes	GBR	1:58.81
5. Yelena Afanasyeva	RUS	1:59.57
6. Patricia Djaté-Taillard	FRA	1:59.61
7. Natalya Dukhnova	BLR	2:00.32
8. Toni Hodgkinson	NZL	2:00.54

On January 23, 1993, Ana Quirot, while seven months pregnant, was washing clothes in the kitchen of her Havana home using a kerosene cooker. The cooker exploded, sending out flames that left Quirot with third-degree burns on 38% of her body. Doctors induced labor, but the baby died after only a few days. Quirot spent three months in the hospital and eventually underwent 21 surgical operations including seven skin grafts. To protect her legs, which had been untouched by the fire, doctors used skin from her back for the grafts. Quirot, whose sister had competed at the 1980 Olympics as a basketball player, returned to competition in November. She completed a spectacular comeback by winning the world championship in 1995.

Maria Mutola was a football (soccer) player in Maputo, Mozambique, when a popular poet, José Craverinhas, turned her in the direction of athletics. At the 1988 Olympics, the 15-year-old Mutola was eliminated in the heats. The International Olympic Committee, as part of its Solidarity Program, gave Mutola a scholarship in 1991 to study and train in Eugene, Oregon. At the 1992 Barcelona Olympics, she finished fifth in the 800 meters and ninth in the 1500 meters. The following year she won the world championship at 800 meters.

By the time of the 1995 world championships, Mutola had won 42 straight races at 800 meters and had not been beaten in three years. But in the semifinals she was disqualified for stepping on the lane divider line during the first curve. She did not lose again in the lead up to the Atlanta Olympics. Quirot and Mutola were expected to engage in a tight duel, and they did—for second place.

Svetlana Masterkova was born and raised in the small town of Achinsk in southern Siberia. In 1991, Masterkova recorded the fastest time of the year, but at the world championships she only placed eighth. In 1993 she was second at the indoor world championships, but injury kept her out of the outdoor meet. A notorious overracer, she then took off two years to have a baby. When she entered a meet in France in late May of 1996, it was her first outdoor race in 32 months.

Masterkova was plagued by ongoing weight problems. At one point the 1.68-meter (5′ 6″) Masterkova weighed 85 kilograms (187 lbs.). While searching for a coach, she visited the office of Pavel Litovchenko, who assumed she was a javelin thrower. She trained down to middle-distance size, but during pregnancy she ballooned back to 80 kg. (176 lbs.). Back in excellent shape in 1996, she maintained her running weight by not eating after 2 p.m. Although she won the Russian Olympic trials at both 800 and 1500 meters, there was nothing in her international results to indicate that she could run with Quirot and Mutola.

However, in the Olympic final, Masterkova ran a brilliant tactical race. She led from the start and, occasionally aided by teammate Yelena Afanasyeva, she controlled the pace completely, surging, slowing and surging again. Only Quirot was close to her in the homestretch. But with 80 meters to go, Masterkova surged one last time and maintained a two-stride lead until the finish. One week later, Masterkova earned a second gold medal at 1500 meters. By finishing third, Maria Mutola became Mozambique's first Olympic medalist.

2000 Sydney C: 38, N: 30, D: 9.25. WR: 1:53.28 (Jarmila Kratochvilová)

1. Maria de Lurdes Mutola	MOZ	1:56.15
2. Stephanie Graf	AUT	1:56.64
3. Kelly Holmes	GBR	1:56.80
4. Brigita Langerholc	SLO	1:58.51
5. Helena Fuchsová	CZE	1:58.56
6. Zulia Calatayud	CUB	1:58.66
7. Hazel Clark	USA	1:58.75
8. Hasna Benhassi	MOR	1:59.27

The favorites were Maria Mutola, who was competing in her fourth Olympics, and world champion Ludmila Formanová of the Czech Republic. Mutola had been the dominant force in the 800 meters for the past seven years, yet her only major title had been the 1993 world championship. Since then she had been disqualified at the 1995 world championships, finished third at the 1996 Olympics, third at the 1997 world championships and second at the 1999 world championships. Formanová, hit by an untimely ankle injury, pulled out of her opening round heat after running one lap.

In the final, another Czech, Helena Fuchsová, burst into the lead and set a torrid pace, completing the first lap in 55.04 seconds. After 500 meters, Hazel Clark pulled up to Fuchsová's shoulder. Then Kelly Holmes made her move. As they came out of the final turn, Holmes, who was recovering from injury, was amazed to find herself with a two-meter lead. She pushed on, but in the last 50 meters, first Mutola and then Stephanie Graf drove past her. Graf, Langerholc, Fuchsová, Calatayud and Clark all achieved personal bests. For Mutola, the victory was particularly sweet because it was Mozambique's first Olympic gold medal and it came on a national holiday for her country, which had suffered through a bad year of flooding that displaced 450,000 people. Mutola definitely broke her big meet jinx, as she went on to win the world championship in 2001 and again in 2003.

The US entry was unusual in that it consisted of two sisters, Joetta and Hazel Clark, and their sister-in-law, Jearl Miles-Clark, who was married to their brother JJ, who coached all three women. The father of Joetta, Hazel and JJ was Joe Clark, the New Jersey high school principal whose efforts were portrayed in the 1989 film *Lean on Me*.

2004 Athens C: 43, N: 36, D: 8.23. WR: 1:53.28 (Jarmila Kratochvilová)

1. Kelly Holmes	GBR	1:56.38
2. Hasna Benhassi	MOR	1:56.43
3. Jolanda Čeplak	SLO	1:56.43
4. Maria Mutola	MOZ	1:56.51
5. Tatyana Andrianova	RUS	1:56.88
6. Jearl Miles-Clark	USA	1:57.27
7. Maria Cioncan	ROM	1:59.62
8. Zulia Calatayud	CUB	2:00.95

Kelly Holmes began running track at the age of 12, but quit at the age of 18 to enlist in the British Army with the goal of becoming a physical training instructor. In 1992, Holmes decided to return to athletics after watching Lisa York, a former school rival, compete for Great Britain at the Barcelona Olympics. For two years Holmes lived and trained with Maria Mutola, the three-time world champion and defending Olympic gold medalist. But in an indoor race in February 2004, Mutola tripped over Holmes and fell, and the two stopped training together.

The final got off to a fast start, with 37-year-old Jearl Miles-Clark forcing the pace. Holmes settled into last place, but began to move up the field after 300 meters. Miles-Clark was still in front with half a lap to go, but 100 meters from the finish, Mutola surged past her, followed closely by Holmes, who then took the lead. Meanwhile, Hasna Benhassi and Jolanda Čeplak both finished with a rush, Čeplak moving up from sixth place with only 100 meters left. Benhassi and Čeplak edged ahead of Mutola in the last two strides, but Holmes held on for the victory. It was the first time that Holmes had beaten Mutola in a major race. At the age of 34, she was the oldest woman to win the 800 meters.

In the run-up to the Olympics, Holmes had a minor scare after suffering a pain in her left leg. Worried it might be a muscle injury, she was relieved when she found a four-inch centipede in her bed that had bitten her during the night.

2008 Beijing C: 42, N: 33, D: 8.18. WR: 1:53.28 (Jarmila Kratochvilova)

1. Pamela Jelimo	KEN	1:54.87
2. Janeth Jepkosgei Busienei	KEN	1:56.07
3. Hasna Benhassi	MOR	1:56.73
4. Svetlana Klyuka	RUS	1:56.94
5. Maria Mutola	MOZ	1:57.68
6. Kenia Sinclair	JAM	1:58.24
7. Yuliya Krevsun	UKR	1:58.73
8. Tatyana Andrianova	RUS	2:02.63

After taking silver in Athens, Hasna Benhassi continued to be a top international performer, but kept missing out on the top slot. In 2005 she took silver at the world championships in Helsinki (behind Zulia Calatayud of Cuba), and two years later she earned silver again at the world championships in Osaka, this time behind Janeth Jepkosgei of Kenya.

In addition to Benhassi and Jepkosgei, two other runners looked to be in gold medal contention. The first was Yelena Soboleva of Russia, who had recorded a 1:54.85, the fastest time of the year, at a meet in Russia one month before the Games. Just before the start of the Olympics, however, Soboleva and six other Russian women were suspended by the IAAF for using substitute urine during drug tests.

The other major contender was 18-year-old breakout star Pamela Jelimo. The fourth of nine children raised by a single mother, Jelimo was completely unknown before 2007, when she became the African junior champion in the 400 meters. She hailed from Kabirisang, the same village in Kenya's Rift Valley as Jepkosgei, and the two became friends and training partners. In early 2008 Jepkosgei convinced Jelimo to switch to the 800 meters event. The change was immediately successful. In early May, Jelimo won the African championship, beating three-time world champion and 2000 Olympic gold medalist Maria Mutola. Twenty days later Jelimo broke the junior world record in her European debut in Hengelo, and eight days after that she recorded a 1:54.99 at her Golden League debut in Berlin, the fastest 800-meter time in nearly 11 years. By the time she reached Beijing, Jelimo had beaten Jepkosgei five times, each time by a large margin, and was the clear favorite for gold.

Jelimo and Jepkosgei both won their preliminary and semi-final heats easily and reached the final along with Benhassi and Mutola. In the final, Jepkosgei took the lead through the first 200 meters, but was soon passed by Jelimo, who opened a sizeable lead and was never seriously challenged. Jelimo cruised to victory in 1:54.87, recording a junior world record in the process.

Less than a month after winning the Olympic gold, Jelimo won a $1m jackpot after winning all six IAAF Golden League meets. On her return to Kenya her home village held a feast that included more than 100 chickens, ten sheep, four cows, 100 crates of soda and 1000 kilograms (2204 lbs) of rice. Her new-found success also brought a surge of attention, both in the form of swarms of marriage offers and of at least seven men claiming to be her father.

1500 METERS

1896–1968 not held

1972 Munich C: 36, N: 21, D: 9.9. WR: 4:06.9 (Lyudmila Bragina)

1. Lyudmila Bragina	SOV/RUS	4:01.4 WR	(4:01.38)
2. Gunhild Hoffmeister	GDR	4:02.8	(4:02.83)
3. Paola Cacchi	ITA	4:02.9	(4:02.85)
4. Karin Burneleit	GDR	4:04.1	(4:04.11)
5. Sheila Carey (Taylor)	GBR	4:04.8	(4:04.81)
6. Ilja Keizer	HOL	4:05.1	(4:05.13)
7. Tamara Pangelova	SOV/UKR	4:06.5	(4:06.45)
8. Jennifer Orr	AUS	4:12.2	

Twenty-nine-year-old Lyudmila Bragina exploded onto the international scene six weeks before the Olympics when she chopped 2.7 seconds off Karin Burneleit's world record by running a 4:06.9 in a *heat* of the Soviet championships. A few weeks later she ran 3000 meters in 8:53.0, to better the world record at that distance by over 16 seconds. In the first heat of the first round of the 1500 meters at Munich, Bragina led from start to finish and broke her own world record in 4:06.47, carrying 17-year-old Glenda Reiser of Canada with her in 4:06.71. Three days later Bragina again broke the world record with a 4:05.07 in her semifinal heat. The semifinals saw 13 women better the pre-Olympic world record. In the final, Bragina moved to the front after two laps and pulled away to a 12-meter lead, which she held for the entire last lap. In a postrace interview, Bragina told reporters, "We shall be running 3 minutes 56 seconds before the next Olympics." She hit it right on the button, as 3:56.0 was exactly the world record at the time of the 1976 Olympics.

1976 Montreal C: 36, N: 19, D: 7.30. WR: 3:56.0 (Tatyana Kazankina)

1. Tatyana Kazankina	SOV/RUS	4:05.48
2. Gunhild Hoffmeister	GDR	4:06.02
3. Ulrike Klapezynski	GDR	4:06.09
4. Nikolina Shtereva	BUL	4:06.57
5. Lyudmila Bragina	SOV/RUS	4:07.20
6. Gabriella Dorio	ITA	4:07.27
7. Ellen Wellmann	GER	4:07.91
8. Janice Merrill	USA	4:08.54

Bragina's Munich world record went unbeaten until one month before the next Olympics, when Kazankina lowered it by 5.4 seconds. Track fans who had hoped for a new record in the Olympic final were disappointed, as the race turned into a tactical contest. With one lap to go, Bragina took the lead, but 200 meters later, with elbows flying, she was passed by the two East German training mates, Hoffmeister on the inside and Klapezynski on the outside. Meanwhile, Kazankina, who had already won the 800 meters gold medal, steered clear of the elbowing and moved up on the outside to take the lead with 50 meters to go. She won by three meters. Defending champion Lyudmila Bragina had to settle for fifth place, but her career was hardly over. A few days later, at a USA vs. USSR meet, she ran the 3000 meters in 8:27.2, 18.3 seconds faster than the previous world record. This put her only 50 years behind the men's pace, something of a record in women's track events.

1980 Moscow C: 24, N: 14, D: 8.1. WR: 3:55.0 (Tatyana Kazankina)

1. Tatyana Kazankina	SOV/RUS	3:56.6 OR	(3:56.56)
2. Christiane Wartenberg	GDR	3:57.8	(3:57.71)
3. Nadiya Olizarenko	SOV/UKR	3:59.6	(3:59.52)
4. Gabriella Dorio	ITA	4:00.3	(4:00.30)
5. Ulrike Bruns (Klapezynski)	GDR	4:00.7	(4:00.62)
6. Lyubov Smolka	SOV/UKR	4:01.3	(4:01.25)
7. Maricica Puică	ROM	4:01.3	(4:01.26)
8. Ileana Silai	ROM	4:03.0	(4:02.98)

Covering the final 800 meters in 1:59.0, Kazankina took the lead with 600 meters to go and had left the other runners 20 meters behind by the time she reached the last curve. Twelve days later she lowered the world record to 3:52.47 and became the first woman to run 1500 meters faster than Paavo Nurmi. In September 1984, Kazankina received an 18-month suspension when the Soviet team manager refused to let her submit to a test for drugs following a 5000-meter race in Paris.

1984 Los Angeles C: 22, N: 15, D: 8.11. WR: 3:52.47 (Tatyana Kazankina)

1. Gabriella Dorio	ITA	4:03.25
2. Doina Melinte	ROM	4:03.76
3. Maricica Puică	ROM	4:04.15

4. Roswitha Gerdes	GER	4:04.41
5. Christine Benning	GBR	4:04.70
6. Christina Boxer	GBR	4:05.53
7. Brit McRoberts	CAN	4:05.98
8. Ruth Wysocki	USA	4:08.92

At the 1983 world championships, the first five places had gone to Mary Decker, three Soviet runners, and Wendy Sly of Great Britain. With all five absent, the roles of favorites went to the two Romanians, Maricica Puică, who had won the 3000-meter gold 24 hours earlier, and Doina Melinte, who had been victorious in the 800 meters five days before the final of the 1500. But Gabriella Dorio had other ideas. Having suffered from taking the early lead in the 800, she held back in the 1500, allowing Chris Boxer to set a slow pace. Then, with 1½ laps to go, Dorio moved to the front, followed closely by Melinte. Melinte took the lead on the final lap and it looked like a repeat of the 800. But this time Dorio had saved an extra charge of energy for the finish. She regained the lead coming into the homestretch and could not be caught. Puică, who waited too long to make her final sprint, finished strongly to take the bronze. Among the many rewards that came Dorio's way as a result of her victory was an unusual one: her husband had promised her that if she won a gold medal he would give her a bath—in wine.

1988 Seoul C: 28, N: 19, D: 10.1. WR: 3:52.47 (Tatyana Kazankina)

1. Paula Ivan	ROM	3:53.96 OR
2. Laimutė Baikauskaitė	SOV/LIT	4:00.24
3. Tetyana Samolenko	SOV/UKR	4:00.30
4. Christina Cahill (Boxer)	GBR	4:00.64
5. Lynn Williams	CAN	4:00.86
6. Andrea Hahmann	GDR	4:00.96
7. Shireen Bailey	GBR	4:02.32
8. Mary Slaney (Decker)	USA	4:02.49

Until 1988, the career of 25-year-old Paula Ivan had been decent but undistinguished. Beginning in July of the Olympic year, she suddenly showed rapid and spectacular improvement. On August 17, she ran 3:56.22 for her third personal best in 6 weeks. Only Mary Slaney's 3:58.92 at the US Olympic trials came within 4 seconds of Ivan's pre-Olympic time. In Seoul, 6 days before the 1500-meter final, Ivan thought she was about to win the gold medal at 3000 meters, when Tetyana Samolenko sprinted by her to steal the victory.

In order to neutralize Samolenko's kick, Ivan decided to try to run away from the field early in the 1500. Her strategy worked perfectly. She led by 3 meters after 400 meters, 10 meters after 800, and then seemed to increase her lead with each step for the remainder of the race, until she crossed the finish line with an unprecedented margin of victory of 40 meters. The battle for second was won by Lithuanian Laimutė Baikauskaitė, who came from last place at the halfway mark to nip Samolenko in a photo finish.

1992 Barcelona C: 43, N: 31, D: 8.8. WR: 3:52.47 (Tatyana Kazankina)

1. Hassiba Boulmerka	ALG	3:55.30
2. Lyudmila Rogacheva	RUS	3:56.91
3. Qu Yunxia	CHN	3:57.08
4. Tetyana Dorovskikh (Samolenko)	UKR	3:57.92
5. Liu Li	CHN	4:00.20
6. Maite Zúñiga Domínguez	SPA	4:00.59
7. Matgorzata Rydz	POL	4:01.91
8. Yekaterina Podkopayeva	RUS	4:02.03

Since World War II, women's middle-distance running had been dominated by runners from Communist nations, with an occasional interruption by the likes of Ann Packer, Madeline Manning, and Mary Decker. In 1991 a new quarter was heard from when, in the same week that the Soviet Union collapsed, 23-year-old Hassiba Boulmerka of Algeria scored a stunning victory over Tetyana Dorovskikh and Lyudmila Rogacheva at the World Championship in Athletics. The men's 1500 had also been won by an Algerian, Noureddine Morceli. When Boulmerka and Morceli returned to Algiers they were driven through the streets while women showered them with flowers, candles, and wheat seeds, as they would at a wedding celebration. Overnight, Boulmerka was transformed not only into a national heroine but into a symbol for Arab women who wanted to break away from traditional Islamic restrictions. Heroine though she was for most Algerians, she was singled out for condemnation by one group: Islamic fundamentalists. In mosques across the country Boulmerka was denounced for "running with naked legs in front of thousands of men." In fact, Boulmerka herself was a devout Muslim. But her father had worked for many years as a truck driver in France and both he and his wife supported their daughter's educational and athletic pursuits. Distracted by the political situation in Algeria, Boulmerka retreated to a training camp in Germany for the weeks preceding the Olympics, and then showed up refreshed in Barcelona.

Rogacheva set a torrid pace in the final, covering the first 400 meters in 60.66 seconds. Applying relentless pressure, she burned away most of the field but was unable to shake Boulmerka. With a little more than 200 meters to go, Boulmerka drove past Rogacheva and cruised to victory. When she crossed the finish line Boulmerka screamed out, "Algérie! Algérie!" and pointed to the name of the nation on her jersey. The race was the first in which four women dipped below four minutes. It was such a fast race that nine of the top ten finishers (except 40-year-old Podkopayeva) set personal bests. Five of the runners—Boulmerka, Rogacheva, Qu, Zúñiga, and Maria Mutola in ninth place—improved their personal records by more than four seconds.

If Hassiba Boulmerka was the star of 1992, it was the 19-year-old bronze medalist, Qu Yunxia, who would capture the headlines the following year. Trained by controversial coach Ma Junren, Qu, like the rest of "Ma's Detachment," ran 150 miles a week, ate soft-shell turtle soup, drank an elixir containing caterpillars, made frequent trips to the high altitude of the Qinghai-Tibet Plateau, and was forbidden to pursue romantic affairs until the age of 22. In 1993, Qu won the world championships 3000 meters and then, at the Chinese national championships, ran the 1500 meters in 3:50.46 to break Tatyana Kazankina's 13-year-old world record.

1996 Atlanta C: 32, N: 21, D: 8.3. WR: 3:50.46 (Qu Yunxia)

1. Svetlana Masterkova	RUS	4:00.83
2. Gabriela Szabo	ROM	4:01.54
3. Theresia Kiesl	AUT	4:03.02
4. Leah Pells	CAN	4:03.56
5. Margaret Crowley	AUS	4:03.79
6. Carla Sacramento	POR	4:03.91
7. Lyudmila Borisova	RUS	4:05.90
8. Małgorzata Rydz	POL	4:05.92

Before the Olympics, it was assumed that the medals would be divided by Hassiba Boulmerka, the defending champion; Sonia O'Sullivan, who won nine of ten races in 1995 and recorded the second fastest pre-Olympic time of 1996 (3:59.91); and army sergeant Kelly Holmes, the world championship runner-up. In the end, none of the three favorites won a medal.

Earlier in the Games, O'Sullivan, after picking up an intestinal disorder, had dropped out of the 5000 meters final. She tried to compete in the 1500 meters, but could do no better than tenth in her qualifying heat and was eliminated. At the beginning of the last lap of the first semifinal, Boulmerka stumbled in traffic, smashed her kneecap into Theresia Kiesl's heel and finished last.

The situation looked encouraging for Kelly Holmes, but she knew she had to deal with Svetlana Masterkova, who had won the Russian championships in 3:59.30. Although this was the fastest time of the year, it was also Masterkova's first race at 1500 meters in twelve years and her Olympic prospects were considered something of a mystery. Then she actually won the gold medal at 800 meters, pushing Holmes out of the medals at that distance. In the 800, Masterkova had led from the start and controlled the pace. In the 1500 she rushed into the lead again and tried the same tactic. This time Holmes would have none of it. She passed Masterkova immediately and held the lead herself through the first three laps. Masterkova moved up to her shoulder after 2½ laps. With 200 meters to go, Masterkova pulled away. Discouraged, Holmes drifted back to eleventh place. Masterkova fought off challenges from Kiesl and Szabo and went on to complete an unexpected and impressive double.

2000 Sydney C: 42, N: 27, D: 9.30. WR: 3:50.46 (Qu Yunxia)

1. Nouria Merah-Benida	ALG	4:05.10
2. Violeta Szekely	ROM	4:05.15
3. Gabriela Szabo	ROM	4:05.27
4. Kutre Dulecha	ETH	4:05.33
5. Lidia Chojecka	POL	4:06.42
6. Anna Jakubczak	POL	4:06.49
7. Kelly Holmes	GBR	4:08.02
8. Marla Runyan	USA	4:08.30

The Sydney women's 1500 meters was a hard race to call. Defending champion Svetlana Masterkova had also won the 1998 European championship and the 1999 world championship, but her 2000 pre-Olympic season had been uninspired. Atlanta silver medalist Gabriela Szabo had already won the 5000 meters at the Sydney Olympics. On July 28, two months before the start of the Olympic competition, American Suzy Favor Hamilton had defeated most of the top contenders at the Bislett Games in Oslo by running 3:57.40, the best time of the season. And after that, 35-year-old Violeta Szekely had looked impressive in winning the Monaco Grand Prix in 3:58.29. Nobody paid attention to Nouria Merah-Benida, including Algerian Olympic officials. Before leaving Algeria for Sydney, they divided their athletes into three classes: medal contenders, possible finalists and others. Merah-Benida was put into the last category. As such, she was not allowed to bring with her husband/trainer, Amar Benida. Nouria considered withdrawing, but the Algerian Minister of Sport intervened, pointing out that by finishing third in the Monaco race, Merah-Benida had recorded the fourth fastest time of the year. Amar Benida was allowed to go to Sydney.

The opening round saw the demise of Masterkova, who injured her calf in a collision and did not finish the race. The next day, Merah-Benida edged Favor Hamilton to win the first semifinal, while Szekely took the second semi.

The final itself was not a pleasant race. The first lap was so slow that Marla Runyan, who was unable to see out of the center of her eyes and was legally blind, felt compelled to abandon her race strategy and push the pace. The opening 400 meters was covered in only 70.56 seconds. Favor Hamilton took over after 600 meters and was tracked by 1997 world champion Carla Sacramento. About 300 meters later, Britain's Hayley Tullett fell. Szabo was forced to jump over her and almost came to a complete stop. Meanwhile, up front, Sacramento tried to pass Favor Hamilton, but the American fought her off. Sacramento did succeed in taking the lead just after the bell. She was followed by Favor Hamilton, Szekely and Merah-Benida. With 200 meters to go, Sacramento faded and Favor Hamilton regained the lead. At this point Szabo was still back in ninth place. As they came out of the final turn, the race turned hectic. With 120 meters to go, Merah-Benida moved into the lead as Favor Hamilton became dizzy. Eighty meters from the finish, the American collapsed. As the rest of the runners swept past her, she slowly rose and managed to walk across the line before she collapsed again. She was eventually taken away in a wheelchair, the victim of dehydration, apparently due to stress and the various legal drugs she had been taking (anti-inflammatories, Advil and sleeping pills).

Meanwhile, Merah-Benida began to run out of steam as she approached the finish, while the Romanians closed fast. Merah-Benida crossed the line just before Szekely caught her, while Szabo, running the last 100 meters in 14.5 seconds, ran out of room as well.

Szabo and Szekely were teammates only as an accident of birth. Szekely had served a three-year drug ban from 1995 until 1998 and Szabo felt she shouldn't be allowed to return. When both earned medals at the 1998 world indoor championship, they sat at opposite sides of the room at the post-race press conference and refused to even look at each other. After the Olympics, the Romanian edition of *Playboy* published an interview with Szabo that was to lead to all sorts of problems for the Olympic champion and national heroine. Szabo claimed that the reason Szekely was not invited to the major meets was that she was "ugly" and also had a poor running style. Szekely responded by suing Szabo for moral damages and calling her "short and hunched." Szabo countersued. Szabo apologized on live national television, but Szekely refused to accept the apology. Eventually Szabo was forced to pay Szekely about $5000. She was also fined $240 for slander. On the other side, Szekely was ordered to pay Szabo one lei. Considering that, at the time, there were about 31,500 lei to the dollar, this did not cause a great hardship for Szekely.

In the same *Playboy* interview, Szabo characterized a coach, Carmen Hodas, as an alcoholic who doped her athletes. Szabo accused Hodas of trying to slip prohibited substances into the track star's coffee. Hodas also sued Szabo. A Bucharest court awarded Hodas about $10,000, as Szabo was again found guilty of slander.

2004 Athens C: 45, N: 27, D: 8.28. WR: 3:50.46 (Qu Yunxia)

1. Kelly Holmes	GBR	3:57.90
2. Tatyana Tomashova	RUS	3:58.12
3. Maria Cioncan	ROM	3:58.39
4. Natalya Yevdokimova	RUS	3:59.05
5. Daniela Yordanova	BUL	3:59.10
6. Lidia Chojecka	POL	3:59.27
7. Anna Jakubczak	POL	4:00.15
8. Elvan Abeylegesse	TUR	4:00.67

Natalya Yevdokimova eliminated the possibility of a tactical final, by setting a hard pace and stringing out the field. Kelly Holmes, who had won the 800 meters five days earlier, employed the same strategy she had used in the 800, staying close for most of the race and then striking in the final lap. Still in only fifth place with half a lap to go, Holmes accelerated around the final curve and swept into the lead. World champion Tatyana Tomashova tried to catch her, but it was too late. Holmes bettered her seven-year-old personal record. In fact, seven of the twelve finalists set personal bests, including all of the first five finishers. Aged 34, Holmes was the oldest woman to win the Olympic 1500 meters.

2008 Beijing C: 33, N: 18, D: 8.23. WR: 3:50.46 (Qu Yunxia)

1. Nancy Langat	KEN	4:00.23
2. Iryna Lishchynska	UKR	4:01.63
3. Nataliya Sydorenko-Tobias	UKR	4:01.78
4. Lisa Dobriskey	GBR	4:02.10
5. Maryam Jamal	BRN	4:02.71
6. Natalia Rodríguez Martínez	SPA	4:03.19
7. Shannon Rowbury	USA	4:03.58
8. Iris Fuentes-Pila Ortiz	SPA	4:04.86

Three days before the Beijing Opening Ceremony, a doping controversy erupted among the Russian athletics team, when officials from the IOC and IAAF announced the suspension of seven athletes after a 16-month investigation. Although none of the athletes had returned positive drug tests, DNA analysis had shown that the athletes had been tampering with and switching urine samples. The suspended athletes included the reigning 1500-meter world indoor champion and 2007 world champion silver medalist Yelena Soboleva, defending Olympic silver medalist and 2005 world champion Tatyana Tomashova, and 2008 indoor silver medalist Yuliya Fomenko.

With the three top Russians out of the competition, the remaining medal contenders included reigning world champion Maryam Yusuf Jamal and world champion bronze medalist Iryna Lishchynska. The Ethiopian-born Jamal had claimed refugee status in Switzerland, later moving to Bahrain and gaining citizenship.

Both Jamal and Lishchynska won their first-round heats, as did 2004 African champion Nancy Langat of Kenya.

The first two laps of the final were led by the sole remaining Russian athlete, Anna Alminova, followed closely by Lishchynska. Jamal moved into the lead at the 500 meters mark and held it through the 1200 meters mark, followed closely by Langat. Langat maintained her position until the final turn, when she cranked up the pace to move past a tiring Jamal and pulled away to finish in 4:00.23, bettering her personal best by more than two seconds; Jamal faded to fifth. Langat's victory came one day after her 27th birthday.

5000 METERS

1896–1992 not held

1996 Atlanta C: 46, N: 25, D: 7.28. WR: 14:36.45 (Fernanda Ribeiro)

1. Wang Junxia	CHN	14:59.88 OR
2. Pauline Konga	KEN	15:03.49
3. Roberta Brunet	ITA	15:07.52
4. Michiko Shimizu	JPN	15:09.05
5. Paula Radcliffe	GBR	15:13.11
6. Yelena Romanova	RUS	15:14.09
7. Elena Fidatov	ROM	15:16.71
8. Rose Cheruiyot	KEN	15:17.33

In 1992 the world of women's distance running was turned upside down by the protégés of eccentric and tyrannical coach Ma Junren, rewriting the record book and dominating the world championships in Stuttgart. None of Ma's runners was more impressive than Wang Junxia, a fisherman's daughter, who won the 10,000-meters championship and set world records at 3000 meters and 10,000 meters, the latter by an incredible 41.96 seconds. In December 1994 Wang fled Ma's camp, claiming, among other things, that Ma had tried to force her to marry his son and that he had refused to hand over to her the Mercedes-Benz she had earned by winning the world championship. Wang and the rest of "Ma's Detachment" vanished from the high levels of competition. But, unlike the others, Wang reemerged in 1996 and qualified for the Chinese Olympic team at both 5000 meters and 10,000 meters. Because the two events overlapped, all non-Chinese runners chose to enter one or the other. Wang decided to go for both.

On July 26, Wang ran in the opening round of the 5000, cautiously placing fourth, which was the minimum required to qualify for the final. On July 27, she ran in a 10,000 meter heat, again qualifying carefully for the final. On July 28, in the final of the 5000 meters, she faced favorite Sonia O'Sullivan, the defending world champion. But O'Sullivan, apparently weakened by diarrhea, was clearly off form, fell off the pace, and dropped out after 4100 meters. With two laps to go, Wang made her move. By the bell she was ahead by 30 meters and the race for gold was over. Silver medalist Pauline Konga was the first Kenyan woman to win an Olympic medal.

And Wang Junxia's Mercedes? In 1998, the Chinese National Sports Commission finally released it to her, although by then it was five years old.

2000 Sydney C: 49, N: 32, D: 9.25. WR: 14:28.09 (Jiang Bo)

1. Gabriela Szabo	ROM	14:40.79
2. Sonia O'Sullivan	IRL	14:41.02
3. Gete Wami	ETH	14:42.23
4. Ayelech Worku	ETH	14:42.67
5. Irina Mikitenko	GER	14:43.59
6. Lydia Cheromei	KEN	14:47.35
7. Worknesh Kidane	ETH	14:47.40
8. Olga Yegorova	RUS	14:50.31

Arriving at the Sydney Olympics, Gaby Szabo had the credentials to be a legitimate favorite at 5000 meters: she won the 1997 world championships, she won the 1999 world championships, she had earned $500,000 by winning every 1999 Golden League race at 3000 and 5000 meters and she had become the first track and field athlete to earn more than $1 million in prize money in one year. In four years, Szabo had lost only one 5000-meter race, the 1998 European Championship, where she was beaten by Sonia O'Sullivan. Only one race, that is, until the Berlin Grand Prix on September 1, only two weeks before the Olympics, when Leah Malot of Kenya beat her with a time of 14:39.83. But Malot did not make the Kenyan Olympic team. That left O'Sullivan to lead the challenge to Szabo, along with season leader Gete Wami (14:30.88) and her Ethiopian teammate, Ayelech Worku.

The finalists got off to a cautious start. After 1000 meters, Wami and Worku took charge of the pace with Szabo sticking close to them. Over the next 1000 meters, O'Sullivan drifted back through the pack until she was 40 meters back in tenth place. Wami led throughout most of the middle of the race, with Worku doing her share as well. By the 3000-meter mark, O'Sullivan had climbed back in touch with the lead group. At 4000 meters, the third Ethiopian, 18-year-old Worknesh Kidane was in front, followed by Worku, then Szabo and Wami running side by side, with O'Sullivan fifth.

With a lap and a half to go, Szabo took the lead and Wami went with her. O'Sullivan pulled up to third at the bell signaling the final lap. Szabo began her much-feared sprint finish. Only O'Sullivan could go with her. In the backstretch she pulled up to Szabo's shoulder, but the Romanian would not let her pass. As they dueled around the curve and down the homestretch, they presented a distinctive sight. Szabo was 5′2″ (1.58 meters) and weighed 93 pounds (42 kg). O'Sullivan was 5′9″ (1.75 meters) and weighed 121 pounds (55kg). O'Sullivan made repeated attempts to pass Szabo, but each time Szabo responded by sprinting a little harder and she managed to reach the finish line two meters ahead of O'Sullivan. O'Sullivan was the first Irish woman to win a running medal. Szabo went on to add a bronze medal in the 1500 meters.

2004 Athens C: 41, N: 28, D: 8.23. WR: 14:24.68 (Elvan Abeylegesse)

1. Meseret Defar	ETH	14:45.65
2. Isabella Ochichi	KEN	14:48.19
3. Tirunesh Dibaba	ETH	14:51.83
4. Yelena Zadorozhnaya	RUS	14:55.52
5. Jo Pavey	GBR	14:57.87
6. Gulnara Samitova	RUS	15:02.30
7. Irina Mikitenko	GER	15:03.36
8. Sun Yingjie	CHN	15:07.23

In 2003, 18-year-old Tirunesh Dibaba became the youngest world 5000 meters champion when she moved up from sixth place in the last 200 meters. Another Ethiopian, 20-year-old Mereset Defar, was originally chosen as an alternate, but was promoted after positive results in training. The final got off to an exceptionally slow start, with a first lap of about 85 seconds. After the fifth lap, the world record holder, Ethiopian-born Elvan Abeylegesse, who was representing Turkey, began to pull away from the pack. Shortly after the midway point in the race, Isabella Ochichi, a sergeant with the Kenyan Airports Police Unit, took over, while Abeylegesse drifted back, eventually finishing in twelfth place. Only Defar was able to keep up with Ochichi. The Kenyan remained ahead into the final lap, but with 200 meters to go Defar struck, powering past Ochichi and winning by almost fifteen meters. Defar went on to break the 5000 meters world record in New York City on June 3, 2006, (14:24.53) and again in Oslo on June 15, 2007 (14:16.63).

2008 Beijing C: 31, N: 19, D: 8.22. WR: 14:11.15 (Tirunesh Dibaba)

1. Tirunesh Dibaba	ETH	15:41.40
2. Elvan Abeylegesse	TUR	15:42.74
3. Meseret Defar	ETH	15:44.12
4. Sylvia Kibet	KEN	15:44.96
5. Vivian Cheruiyot	KEN	15:46.32
6. Liliya Shobukhova	RUS	15:46.62
7. Alemitu Bekele Degfa	TUR	15:48.48
8. Meselech Melkamu	ETH	15:49.03

Competing one week after winning gold in the 10,000 meters event, Tirunesh Dibaba was aiming to achieve the first 5000 meters/10,000 meters double in women's

Kelly Holmes, 2004
Holmes won both the 800 meters and the 1500 meters, becoming the oldest woman to win either.

Tirunesh Dibaba and Elvan Abeylegesse, 2008
Tirunesh Dibaba and Elvan Abeylegesse celebrate their 1-2 finish in the 2008 5000 meters, one week after a similar result in the 10,000 meters.

Olympic history. The biggest obstacle standing in her way was long-time rival and reigning Olympic and world champion Meseret Defar.

The rivalry between Tirunesh Dibaba and Meseret Defar had spanned more than six years: most of their competitive careers. In 2002 Defar became the first person to complete a 3000 meters/5000 meters double at a junior championships, beating Dibaba in the 5000 meters event. The following year Dibaba won her first international title at the 2003 world championships in Paris after Defar fell in the heats and failed to advance. The two continued to face each other over the ensuing years. Defar won her first Olympic gold medal in Athens in 2004, with Dibaba finishing third. Dibaba was dominant in 2005, leading Defar in an Ethiopian sweep of the 5000 meters event and becoming the first woman to win the 5000- and 10,000-meter titles at the world championships in Helsinki.

By 2006 the rivalry had taken on both athletic and financial implications. Needing to win at a Golden League final in Berlin to get a $125,000 share of the $500,000 prize, Dibaba lost to Defar in a last-lap sprint. The pair did not exchange words after the race. The following year the two athletes each won a world championship title, Dibaba in the 10,000 meters and Defar in the 5000 meters. Two months before the Olympics, Dibaba broke Defar's world record by 5.48 seconds at a Golden League meet in Oslo.

Reigning world silver medalist Vivian Cheruiyot set the early pace in the Olympic final, followed by Dibaba, Defar and Meselech Melkamu. Ethiopian-born Elvan Abeylegesse, who had won the 10,000 meters silver medal behind Dibaba one week earlier, took the lead with nine laps remaining and upped the pace. She was followed by Defar and Russia's Gulnara Samitova-Galkina, who had won the 3000-meter steeplechase gold medal five days previously. Samitova-Galkina led the field through the three-kilometer mark, at a slow 9:58.13. Dibaba moved to the front with three laps to go, but waited until the final lap to begin her kick, clocking a 59.54-second final lap to clinch the gold medal and record the first 5000 meters/10,000 meters women's Olympic double in history. Abeylegesse held off Defar to earn her second Olympic silver medal in as many weeks.

The race was also notable for the slowest-ever finish in a 5000 meters Olympic or world championship final.

10,000 METERS

1896–1984 not held

1988 Seoul C: 34, N: 20, D: 9.30. WR: 30:13.74 (Ingrid Kristiansen)

1. Olga Bondarenko	SOV/RUS	31:05.21 OR
2. Elizabeth McColgan	GBR	31:08.44
3. Olena Zhupiyova	SOV/UKR	31:19.82
4. Kathrin Ullrich	GDR	31:29.27
5. Frances Larrieu Smith	USA	31:35.52
6. Lynn Jennings	USA	31:39.93
7. Wang Xiuting	CHN	31:40.23
8. Susan Lee	CAN	31:50.51

Ingrid Kristiansen of Norway had dominated this event since 1985 when she set her first world record at 10,000 meters at the Bislett Games in Oslo. The following year, at the next Bislett Games, she ran a 30:13.74 to take an amazing 45.72 seconds off her own record. She also won the 1986 European championship and the 1987 world championship. But at the 1988 Bislett Games on July 2, she suffered her first defeat at 10,000 meters. At the 9000-meter mark Kristiansen experienced such a severe stomach cramp that she stopped running. She still managed to finish second, behind Scotland's Liz McColgan. A few days later, Kristiansen, who did not know that she was pregnant, suffered a miscarriage.

In Seoul, Kristiansen won the first qualifying heat, McColgan the second. The final began uneventfully. The early pace was set by Lyudmila Matveyeva of the Soviet Union and Lynn Nelson of the United States. Kristiansen moved in front after six laps, but then, at the end of the seventh lap, she suddenly stepped off the track—she had badly bruised the sole of her right foot in the preliminary round.

While Kristiansen was carried away on a stretcher, Kathrin Ullrich unexpectedly found herself in first place with a lead of 10 meters. She eventually increased the gap to 30 meters. McColgan finally hauled her in after 4800 meters, with Zhupiyova and Bondarenko close behind. Ullrich lost contact with the leaders after 7600 meters and Zhupiyova fell back after 8800. That left only McColgan and Bondarenko in contention with three laps to go. The 5-foot ¾-inch, 91-pound Bondarenko patiently tracked McColgan until the middle of the last lap. Then she shot past her on the back straightaway, ran the final 200 meters in 31.2 seconds, and won by 20 meters. Bondarenko was one of the pioneers of the women's 10,000-meter run, having set world records at the distance in 1981 and 1984. After her Olympic triumph, Bondarenko told the press, "I'm too happy to say anything original."

1992 Barcelona C: 48, N: 28, D: 8.7. WR: 30:13.74 (Ingrid Kristiansen)

1. Derartu Tulu	ETH	31:06.02
2. Elana Meyer	SAF	31:11.75
3. Lynn Jennings	USA	31:19.89
4. Zhong Huandi	CHN	31:21.08
5. Elizabeth McColgan	GBR	31:26.11
6. Wang Xiuting	CHN	31:28.06
7. Uta Pippig	GER	31:36.45
8. Judi St. Hilaire	USA	31:38.04

Liz McColgan won the 1991 world championships by grinding out one 75-second lap after another until she had worn out all of the other runners. The last to lose contact was Derartu Tulu, who drifted back to eighth place while McColgan went on to win by over 20 seconds. McColgan tried the same tactic at the Olympics, but in one year the world had caught up with her. After 5000 meters a large pack was still right behind her. At the 6100-meter mark, Elana Meyer moved outside to grab a sponge and then suddenly darted into the lead. McColgan did not respond and Meyer soon opened a ten-meter gap. It was Tulu who went after Meyer, eventually settling in at her shoulder. Soon the two of them had pulled 50 meters ahead of the rest of the runners. Lap after lap they continued, Meyer in front, Tulu just behind her to the right. Twice Meyer moved to the outside and invited Tulu to take the lead and set the pace. Tulu refused. At last, with 420 meters to go, she was ready. Effortlessly, Tulu moved into the lead and, covering the last lap in 65.9 seconds, went on to win by 30 meters. Tulu waited for Meyer at the finish line and then Tulu, the first black African woman to earn an Olympic medal, and Meyer, South Africa's first medalist since it was banned after the 1960 Games, set off hand in hand on a shared victory lap that seemed to symbolize hope for a new Africa. Tulu bettered her pre-Olympics personal best by 19.23 seconds, Meyer improved hers by 21.71 seconds, and Lynn Jennings, in third place, beat her pre-Olympics record by 20.04 seconds.

A member of the Oromo ethnic group, Derartu

Derartu Tulu and Elana Meyer, 1992

The new Africa: Tulu and Meyer, gold and silver medalists in the 1992 10,000 meters.

Tulu was a shepherd who grazed cattle near the village of Bekoji in the Arsi highlands of Ethiopia. She did not realize that she was a fast runner until she was sixteen years old. She returned from her Olympic victory as a national heroine. In 1995, after winning the cross-country world championships, she led a successful protest march against corrupt and incompetent officials of the Ethiopan track federation.

1996 Atlanta C: 35, N: 19, D: 8.2. WR: 29:31.78 (Wang Junxia)

1. M. Fernanda Ribeiro	POR	31:01.63 OR
2. Wang Junxia	CHN	31:02.58
3. Gete Wami	ETH	31:06.65
4. Derartu Tulu	ETH	31:10.46
5. Masako Chiba	JPN	31:20.62
6. Tegla Leroupe	KEN	31:23.22
7. Yuko Kawakami	JPN	31:23.23
8. Iulia Negura	ROM	31:26.46

The favorites were Fernanda Ribeiro, the world record holder at 5000 meters, who had earned gold at 10,000 meters and silver at 5000 meters at the 1995 world championships, and Wang Junxia, the world record holder at 10,000 meters, who had won all 13 of her races at the distance since she first attempted it in 1992. Defending Olympic champion Derartu Tulu and her training partner, Gete Wami, were also considered serious contenders. Wang, who won the 5000 meters five days before the 10,000 meters final, was the only leading runner to attempt the 5000/10,000 double in Atlanta because of overlapping schedules.

Catherina McKiernan of Ireland pulled the finalists through the first 4000. Ribeiro, Sally Barsosio of Kenya and others took their turns in front. When the pace slowed, Julia Vaquero of Spain, working in tandem with Ribeiro, pushed the pace between 6000 and 8000 meters. Ribeiro returned to the lead, but with 600 meters to go, Wang moved ahead and opened a 15-meter lead. Three hundred meters from the finish, Ribeiro began closing the gap. With 50 meters to go, she sprinted by Wang and won the race.

During a dark period, while Fernanda Ribeiro was hobbled by injury, she vowed that if she won the gold medal at the 1996 Olympics, she would walk 175 kilometers (110 miles) from Oporto to the shrine of Fatima and give thanks to the Virgin Mary. She completed the walk in two days.

2000 Sydney C: 41, N: 25, D: 9.30. WR: 29:31.78 (Wang Junxia)

1. Derartu Tulu	ETH	30:17.49
2. Gete Wami	ETH	30:22.48
3. M. Fernanda Ribeiro	POR	30:22.88
4. Paula Radcliffe	GBR	30:26.97
5. Tegla Loroupe	KEN	30:37.26
6. Sonia O'Sullivan	IRL	30:53.37
7. Ji Li	CHN	31:06.94
8. Elana Meyer	SAF	31:14.70

There were four favorites for the 10,000 meters in 2000. Gete Wami was the reigning world champion and had already earned a bronze medal in Sydney in the 5000 meters. Wami's training partner, Derartu Tulu, had won the Olympic title in 1992 and placed fourth in 1996. She missed almost three years of competition because of injury and childbirth. But by early 2000, Tulu was back in form and won the world cross-country championship. Fernanda Ribeiro, the defending Olympic champion, had not won an outdoor title since Atlanta, but she was always in a medal position. Fifth in the 1996 Olympic 5000 meters, Paula Radcliffe switched to the 10,000 meters in 1998 and was rewarded with a silver medal at the 1999 world championships. Early in 2000, Radcliffe missed 13 weeks of training because of a bizarre injury: she spent too much time on her knees while writing thank-you notes for wedding gifts and had to undergo minor surgery.

Lacking a strong finishing kick, Radcliffe had led almost throughout the 1999 world championship final, only to be passed by Wami on the last lap. For the Olympic final, Radcliffe concluded that her only chance for victory was to press the pace even harder. So Radcliffe jumped into the lead on the very first lap and began to churn out a series of 72-second laps. By the 2000-meter mark, only 8 of the 20 starters were still in contention. By 3000 meters, the only runners able to keep up with Radcliffe were Tulu, Wami, Ribeiro and Kenya's Tegla Loroupe, who had run in the marathon only three days before the heats of the 10,000. Radcliffe reached the halfway point in 15:05.07. Then she moved to the outside and tried to get one of the other runners to take over the lead. There were no takers. It was not until the 20th of 25 laps that the others moved forward: first Wami and Ribeiro, then Tulu. Radcliffe regained the lead a half lap later. With two laps to go, the order was Radcliffe, Ribeiro, Wami, Tulu and Loroupe. Just before the bell announcing the last lap, Tulu and Wami shot past Radcliffe and took off, with Ribeiro following. Tulu won by covering the final lap in 60.25 seconds. Wami held off Ribeiro for second. Radcliffe, for all her courageous front-running, was left without a medal. Eight of the top eleven finishers set personal bests, including Tulu, Wami, Ribeiro and Radcliffe.

2004 Athens C: 31, N: 20, D: 8.27. WR: 29:31.78 (Wang Junxia)

1. Xing Huina	CHN	30:24.36
2. Ejegayehu Dibaba	ETH	30:24.98
3. Derartu Tulu	ETH	30:26.42
4. Werknesh Kidane	ETH	30:28.30
5. Lornah Kiplagat	HOL	30:31.92
6. Sun Yingjie	CHN	30:54.37
7. Jeļena Čelnova-Prokopčuka	LAT	31:04.10
8. Lidiya Grigoryeva	RUS	31:04.62

The Ethiopian team was so deep that reigning world champion Berhane Adere was unable to qualify. The Ethiopian Olympic entry did include two-time gold medalist Derartu Tulu and 2003 world championship silver medalist Werknesh Kidane. The Olympic final began slowly. After the eleventh lap, Kidane took the lead and picked up the pace, remaining in front for the next eight laps. With seven laps to go, the Ethiopians had dropped everyone but Kenyan-born Lornah Kiplagat and lightly-regarded Xing Huina, a 20-year-old from Shandong Province who had set a junior world record the previous year. Kiplagat took a brief lead, but was soon passed by the Ethiopian trio, while Xing moved up to third behind Ejegayehu Dibaba and Kidane with less than three laps to go. Coming into the final stretch, Dibaba held a narrow lead, with Xing on her shoulder and Tulu trying to move up from third. Xing managed to edge past Dibaba in the straightaway, bettering her personal best by more than seven seconds to win the gold medal by four meters. Dibaba, thinking Xing was a lapped runner, began to celebrate before realizing her error.

2008 Beijing C: 31, N: 17, D: 8.15. WR: 29:31.78 (Wang Junxia)

1. Tirunesh Dibaba	ETH	29:54.66	OR
2. Elvan Abeylegesse	TUR	29:56.34	
3. Shalane Flanagan	USA	30:22.22	
4. Linet Masai	KEN	30:26.50	
5. Mariya Konovalova	RUS	30:35.84	
6. Inga Abitova	RUS	30:37.33	
7. Lucy Wangui	KEN	30:39.96	
8. Lornah Kiplagat	HOL	30:40.27	

Tirunesh Dibaba grew up in Bekoji, the small farming village in Ethiopia that produced three-time Olympic gold medalist Kenenisa Bekele and long-distance giant Haile Gebrselassie. Inspired by her cousin, two-time Olympic gold medalist and 10,000 meters world champion Derartu Tulu, Dibaba took up running as a teenager and moved to Addis Ababa at the age of 14 to attend high school. Unfortunately, she arrived six days after the school registration deadline. Not wanting to return home, Dibaba entered a cross-country race held at a local horse track, finished fifth, and was promptly signed by the Prison Police Sports Club. Three years later she gained her first international title, winning the 5000 meters event at the Paris world championships and becoming the youngest individual winner in the history of the championships, at the age of 17 years 333 days. Both Tirunesh and her sister Ejegayehu earned medals at the 2004 Olympics, Tirunesh taking bronze in the 5000 meters and Ejegayehu claiming silver in the 10,000 meters.

Two years later in Helsinki, Tirunesh became the first woman to record a 5000-meter/10,000-meter world championship double, leading her sister in an Ethiopian sweep of the 10,000 meters and outsprinting her biggest rival, fellow Ethiopian Meseret Defar, at the head of a four-person Ethiopian sweep of the 5000 meters. Dibaba managed to defend her 10,000 meters title in Osaka in 2007 despite suffering abdominal pains midway through the race. She became the first woman to win back-to-back 10,000-meter titles.

In Beijing, Kenyan-born Lornah Kiplagat took the early lead, covering the first 5000 meters in 15:09.98 and dropping most of the field. By the 7000-meter mark, Ethiopian-born Elvan Abeylegesse had taken the lead, followed closely by Tirunesh. Ejegayehu faded, eventually finishing 14th. Tirunesh waited until the final bell before making her move, pulling away smoothly from Abeylegesse to record an Olympic record and becoming the second woman to break 30 minutes. Her pacing pulled Abeylegesse under the 30-minute barrier as well.

Meanwhile, in ninth place with four laps remaining, Shalane Flanagan surged over the final two laps to take bronze. She had suffered a severe bout of food poisoning less than a week before the event and had nearly withdrawn from competition. Because the leaders had begun lapping other racers, Flanagan was unsure where she had finished until she received confirmation from race officials.

MARATHON

1896–1980 not held

1984 Los Angeles C: 50, N: 28, D: 8.5. WB: 2:22:43 (Joan Benoit)

1. Joan Benoit	USA	2:24:52
2. Grete Waitz	NOR	2:26:18
3. Rosa Mota	POR	2:26:57
4. Ingrid Kristiansen	NOR	2:27:34
5. Lorraine Moller	NZL	2:28:34
6. Priscilla Welch	GBR	2:28:54
7. Lisa Martin	AUS	2:29:03
8. Sylvie Ruegger	CAN	2:29:09

Women were not allowed to compete in the original 1896 Olympic race on April 10. However, a woman

Joan Benoit, 1984
Benoit, first across the finish line in the inaugural women's marathon.

named Stamata Revithi attempted to sign up for the Olympic race, but was rejected by the commission in charge of entries. Revithi was an impoverished mother from Siro who lived in Piraeus. Three months earlier, one of her two children died. On April 11, the day after the Olympic race, she left Marathon in the morning and arrived at the outskirts of Athens about 5½ hours later, having stopped on the way to watch ships go by.

The first woman to be officially timed in a marathon run was Violet Piercy of Great Britain who, on October 3, 1926, completed the Chiswick course in three hours forty minutes and twenty-two seconds. Her "record" stood, completely unchallenged, for 37 years until Merry Lepper of the US ran a 3:37:07 on December 16, 1963. The three-hour barrier was first broken, and well broken at that, on September 10, 1971, when Australia's Adrienne Beames clocked a 2:46:30. On April 17, 1983, Grete Waitz, the popular Norwegian runner, brought her own record down to 2:25:29. The next day, Joan Benoit of Freeport, Maine, smashed Waitz's record, finishing the Boston Marathon in 2:22:43.

Although Benoit did not compete in another marathon until the US Olympic trials 13 months later, her Boston feat qualified her as co-favorite with Grete Waitz. Waitz, a two-time Olympian at 1500 meters, was undefeated in the seven marathons she had completed and had beaten Benoit at various distances 10 of the 11 times they had met. She was also the victor at the 1983 world championships, finishing a full 3 minutes ahead of Marianne Dickerson in second place.

Favorites though they were, both Benoit and Waitz considered themselves blessed to make it to the Olympic starting line at all. Benoit had undergone arthroscopic surgery on her right knee only seventeen days before the US Olympic trials, which she won anyway. Waitz woke up the morning before the Olympic marathon with a sore back that left her unable to run or even stand up straight. She spent the day crying with disappointment, but by racetime the next day the pain had disappeared.

As an event, the inaugural women's Olympic marathon was charged with emotion. The long struggle to achieve recognition for women's long-distance running had finally reached fruition and many spectators along the route were moved to tears as the women dashed by. As a race, however, there wasn't much to it. Benoit, wearing a white painter's cap with the flap in back, moved ahead after only 14 minutes and pulled away at will, amazed that no one went with her.

As Waitz watched her disappear in the distance, she was convinced that Benoit had taken a reckless gamble and would eventually fade back to the pack. She never did. At 15 km., Benoit's lead was 51 seconds, by 25 km. it was 1 minute and 51 seconds. Waitz began to reel her in after 30 km., but by then it was too late. Meanwhile, Benoit had simply ploughed ahead, smiling only once when she spotted a banner of Bowdoin College, her alma mater. When she reached the Marina Freeway, a three-mile stretch where no spectators were allowed, Benoit chuckled to herself at the irony that this hunk of concrete had provided her with the peace and quiet she was used to during her training runs back home in Maine. "The one thing I'll tell my grandchildren," she later mused, "is that one time I ran alone on an LA freeway." One half mile from the stadium, she passed an enormous wall mural depicting her crossing of the finish line at the Boston Marathon.

As she approached the tunnel leading to the Coliseum track, she heard the crowd erupt and sensed

Gabriele Andersen-Scheiss, 1984
Andersen-Scheiss gained unsought celebrity as a result of her staggering 5-minute 44-second final lap in the 1984 women's marathon.

the audience rise to its feet. In the tunnel, Benoit, a very private person, not comfortable with celebrity, told herself, "When you come out from underneath the tunnel, you're going to be a different person. Do you want to come out of the tunnel?" It was too late to turn back. "When I came into the stadium," she later recalled, "and saw all the colors and everything, I told myself, 'Listen, just look straight ahead, because if you don't you're probably going to faint.'" She ended up finishing 400 meters ahead of silver medalist Grete Waitz. During the long break between the end of the race and the awards ceremony, Benoit put on a hat and sunglasses, walked outside the Coliseum and mingled with the spectators and tourists in search of stamps for her collection.

The race for the medals may have lacked suspense, but there was still high drama ahead. Twenty minutes after Joan Benoit entered the stadium, a ghostly figure emerged from the tunnel. It was 39-year-old Gabriele Andersen-Scheiss, an Idaho ski instructor, who had taken advantage of her dual citizenship to represent Switzerland. Suffering from heat prostration (but fortunately not heatstroke), she staggered forward, her left arm hanging limply, her right leg stiffened. It was as if Dorando Pietri had reappeared after 76 years. The audience gasped in horror, but when medical officers approached her, Andersen-Scheiss waved them off. As with Pietri in 1908, the crowd alternately cheered her on and begged for her to be stopped. Doctors accompanying her around the track noted that she was sweating profusely, a good sign, and let her proceed. For 5 minutes and 44 seconds she lurched along, occasionally stopping, blacking out on her feet, holding her head. Finally she fell across the finish line into the waiting arms of three medics. The records will show that Gabriele Andersen-Scheiss placed 37th.

Remarkably, she recovered rapidly and was released by medical personnel only two hours later to return to the Olympic Village and grab a bite to eat. Ten hours after her ordeal, Andersen-Scheiss was being interviewed on television. Two weeks later she was finishing fifth in a Utah "ride and tie" competition in which she ran twenty miles and rode a horse for eighteen. As a result of the controversy surrounding her condition during that final lap, the IAAF passed the "Scheiss rule," which allows athletes to receive a hands-on medical examination without being subject to disqualification.

The travails of Gaby Andersen-Scheiss received a great deal of attention, but those of another runner received too little. Anne Audain of New Zealand, one of the secondary favorites, became ill after the 18th mile and began asking people the location of the nearest aid station. No one seemed to know, so she staggered on until she collapsed, as luck would have it, in front of two Los Angeles Fire Department paramedics who had stopped to watch the race. They carried her to their ambulance and drove her to a nearby hospital where she was treated for dehydration.

One more contestant worth noting was a late entrant, Leda Diaz de Cano of Honduras. De Cano fell behind immediately, trailing all of the other runners by 6½ minutes after only five kilometers. She was 27½ minutes behind at the 20-kilometer mark. Shortly thereafter, race officials, concerned less with the Olympic credo of taking part being more important than winning than they were with not interrupting the day's schedule at the track, convinced de Cano to leave the course and allow vehicular traffic to recapture the streets of Los Angeles.

1988 Seoul C: 69, N: 39, D: 9.23. WB: 2:21:06 (Ingrid Kristiansen)

1. Rosa Mota	POR	2:25:40
2. Lisa Martin	AUS	2:25:53
3. Katrin Dörre	GDR	2:26:21
4. Tetyana Polovynska	SOV/UKR	2:27:05
5. Zhao Youfeng	CHN	2:27:06
6. Laura Fogli	ITA	2:27:49
7. Danièle Kaber	LUX	2:29:23
8. Maria Curatolo	ITA	2:30:14

In 1982, Rosa Mota was a 24-year-old middle-distance runner who was enjoying her sport, but whose career was going nowhere. At the European championships in Athens that year she finished twelfth at 3000 meters and then decided to enter the marathon as an experiment. Previously, she had never run more than 20 kilometers, even in practice. To everyone's surprise, including her own, she won. Two years later, she placed third in Los Angeles to become the first Portuguese woman ever to earn an Olympic medal.

By 1986, the 5-foot 1¾-inch, 97-pound Mota was not only winning every marathon she entered, she was winning big. She took the European championship by 4 minutes 14 seconds and the Tokyo Marathon by 4 minutes 39 seconds. In 1987, she won the Boston Marathon by 4 minutes 29 seconds and the world championship by a stunning 7 minutes 11 seconds. She tuned up for the Olympics by repeating at Boston in 1988, this time by 4 minutes 54 seconds.

Mota arrived in Seoul as the overwhelming favorite. She did not disappoint her fans. By the 30-kilometer mark the lead group had dwindled to Mota in front, with Martin, Dörre, and Polovynska close behind. At 32 kilometers, Mota motioned for the others to take their turn in the lead, but found no takers. Four kilometers later, Polovynska faded and the medal winners were decided, although who got what was still in doubt. About 2½ miles from the finish, Mota's coach and lover, José Pedroza, appeared on his bicycle and asked how she was feeling. When she replied that she was feeling fine, he advised her to follow their original plan: to take off when she reached the next hill, one of only a few bumps in an unusually flat course.

Immediately, Mota made her move. Martin, mesmerized and feeling "inert," failed to respond until it was too late. She pulled away from Dörre, but was unable to catch Mota, who went on to win by about 75 meters. In 1995, Mota was elected to the Portuguese parliament.

1992 Barcelona C: 47, N: 31, D: 8.1. WB: 2:21:06 (Ingrid Kristiansen)

1. Valentina Yegorova	RUS	2:32:41
2. Yuko Arimori	JPN	2:32:49
3. Lorraine Moller	NZL	2:33:59
4. Sachiko Yamashita	JPN	2:36:26
5. Katrin Dörre	GER	2:36:48
6. Mun Gyong-ae	PRK	2:37:03
7. Manuela Machado	POR	2:38:22
8. Ramilia Burangulova	RUS	2:38:46

DISQ (Drugs): Madina Biktagirova (BLR) 2:35:39

When Valentina Yegorova qualified for the Olympics, all her neighbors in the small farming village of Iziderkino were thrilled. They couldn't wait to watch her on television . . . There was just one problem: no one in the village owned a television set. So all 1500 villagers chipped in and bought a single, 30-year-old black-and-white set that was placed at the entrance of the home of Yegorova's parents and faced out toward the street.

It was 84° Fahrenheit (29° centigrade) when Yegorova and 46 other marathoners set off at a cautious pace on a long, exposed course that culminated in a punishing climb of Montjuïc to the Olympic Stadium. Lisa Ondieki (Martin) led the field through the first 20 kilometers. Then Madina Biktagirova made a break and pulled away by about 200 meters. She was reeled in by Manuela Machado, who was soon passed by Yegorova. By the 30-kilometer mark Yegorova had opened a lead of 54 seconds, but five kilometers later she found herself joined by Yuko Arimori. Over the final kilometers Yegorova repeatedly surged and Arimori repeatedly caught up to her. They raced up the hill and then, less than 300 meters from the stadium, Yegorova burst ahead and Arimori could not keep pace. Yegorova's margin of victory was barely 40 meters. Back in Iziderkino the villagers stayed up past midnight to watch Yegorova receive her gold medal—even if it was in black and white.

Biktagirova was disqualified after she tested positive for the stimulant norephedrine.

1996 Atlanta C: 88, N: 51, D: 7.28. WB: 2:21:06 (Ingrid Kristiansen)

1. Fatuma Roba	ETH	2:26:05
2. Valentina Yegorova	RUS	2:28:05
3. Yuko Arimori	JPN	2:28:39
4. Katrin Dörre-Heinig	GER	2:28:45
5. María Ríos Pérez	SPA	2:30:50
6. Lidia Simon	ROM	2:31:04
7. Manuela Machado	POR	2:31:11
8. Sonja Krolik	GER	2:31:16

Among the favorites were defending world champion Manuela Machado; defending Olympic champion Valentina Yegorova; Barcelona runner-up Yuko Arimori, who was making a comeback after three years away from competition; and Uta Pippig, who had won the last three Boston Marathons as well as the last five marathons she had run. Not among the favorites was Fatuma Roba, a relative newcomer of indefinite age. Roba was born and raised in Bokeji, the same village as 1992 10,000 meters Olympic champion Derartu Tulu.

The start of the race was moved up to 7:05 a.m. to avoid the oppressive Atlanta heat. At it turned out, rain showers ended just before the race and although the humidity was high, the temperature remained relatively cool.

Pippig tried to steal the race by running away from the pack almost immediately. After 5 kilometers she already led by 13 seconds. By 8 kilometers she had increased her lead by 25 seconds. She still led by 20 seconds after 15 kilometers, but by 17 kilometers the lead pack reeled her in. Machado, Yegorova, Lidia Simion, Roba and Arimori swept by her. Pippig struggled on for another hour and then dropped out after 37 kilometers. Roba moved in front and pulled away steadily for the rest of the race, finally winning by two minutes. In so doing, Roba improved her personal best by three minutes. Behind her, Yegorova drew clear of Arimori, just as she did in 1992, but this time it was for second place. Fatuma Roba went on to continued success in the United States, winning the Boston Marathon in 1997, 1998, and 1999.

One official action of note was the vaporization of the records of two of the participants. Valentina Enaki of Moldova and Virginia Gloum of the Central African Federation were listed on the official entry list and ran the race, but as soon as it was over they were declared "unofficial competitors" because of bureaucratic blunders by their team officials and their results were stricken from the record.

After the Olympics, bronze medalist Arimori told the Asahi News Service what the Olympics meant to her: "I think the Olympics is a special stage where people of high ability can compete, delight and grieve. It is a field of battle, but I feel something peaceful there."

2000 Sydney C: 53, N: 36, D: 9.24. WB: 2:20:43 (Tegla Loroupe)

1. Naoko Takahashi	JPN	2:23:14
2. Lidia Simon	ROM	2:23:22
3. Joyce Chepchumba	KEN	2:24:45
4. Esther Wanjiru	KEN	2:26:17
5. Madina Biktagirova	RUS	2:26:33
6. Elfenesh Alemu	ETH	2:26:54
7. Eri Yamaguchi	JPN	2:27:03
8. Ham Bong-sil	PRK	2:27:07

Naoko Takahashi vaulted onto the international stage in December 1998 when she won the marathon at the Asian Games in Bangkok. It wasn't just that she won, but the way she won. Competing in 90° Fahrenheit (32°C) heat with 90% humidity, Takahashi won by more than 13 minutes, or more than two miles. Her time, 2:21:47, the best ever in a women's only race, was so fast that some suspected that the course was short. (It wasn't.) Takahashi was unable to take part in the 1999 world championships because of a late injury. In her absence, the race was won by Jong Song-ok of North Korea. Jong explained her surprising victory by describing her own version of sports psychology: "I imagined in my mind the image of our leader, Kim Jong-Il, and this inspired me. This was the source of my power." Jong promptly retired and was not heard from again. It was thought that Takahashi's chief rival at the Olympics would be world record holder Tegla Loroupe of Kenya. Unfortunately, Loroupe woke up the morning of the marathon with stomach problems that reappeared early in the race. She insisted on completing the course, but could do no better than 13th place.

Before the marathon could begin, Sydney workmen towed 137 cars that were parked along the course. Marleen Renders of Belgium sprinted to an early lead, but the pack caught up with her after 12 kilometers and she eventually dropped out. The first important break came at the 17-kilometer mark, as Takahashi, teammate Ari Ichihashi, who had finished second to Jong at the world championships, perennial big meet medalist Lidia Simon and North Korean Kim Chang-ok opened a 9-second gap over the others. By the halfway point, Joyce Chepchumba, double winner of both the London and Chicago marathons, had reestablished contact with the leaders. Then Takahashi and Simon began to pull away. At the 30-kilometer mark they had established a 43-second lead over Ichihashi, with Chepchumba in fourth.

Takahashi had been wearing sunglasses, but now she wanted to discard them. However they were so expensive that she hesitated. After 34 kilometers she heard her father call out to her. She spotted him and flung the glasses to him. Then she made her decisive move. Over the next six kilometers she opened a 28-second gap over Simon. Takahashi entered the stadium to the roar of the crowd, but she was aware that Simon had not given up. The Romanian sprinted on the track and closed the gap, but Takahashi managed to win by 8 seconds. Chepchumba headed the wrong way on the track, but turned around and took the bronze medal easily.

Naoko Takahashi's victory was watched on television by 59% of Japanese. She became a national heroine and the subject of a weekly comic strip based on her life. She did not run another marathon until a year later, but it was a good one. Competing in Berlin on September 30, 2001, Takahashi became the first woman to run a marathon in less than 2 hours 20 minutes when she won with a time of 2:19:46.

More than 45 minutes after Takahashi finished the Olympic marathon, Aguida Amaral of East Timor entered the stadium in 43rd place. She stopped and kneeled on the track with her hands in a position of prayer. An official explained to her that she still had a lap to go. She rose, completed the lap and then kneeled again and kissed the track. A marathon is a long way to run, but for Amaral the journey was much longer than 42 kilometers. Her nation had been wracked by more than 20 years of war as the Indonesian government tried to stop the Timorese movement for independence. In 1999, Amaral and her three children were forcibly separated from her husband and sent to live in a refugee camp where they slept on the ground next to a dirt road. An Australian-led international force entered East Timor and stopped the Indonesian killing of the Timorese. Amaral and her children were reunited with her husband. However her running shoes had been stolen, so she trained barefoot. East Timor did achieve independence, but not in time for the Sydney Olympics. However, the International Olympic Committee allowed four Timorese to compete anyway. When Aguida Amaral celebrated her completion of the Olympic marathon course, she was also honoring the perseverance of her people.

2004 Athens C: 82, N: 47, D: 8.22. WR: 2:15:25 (Paula Radcliffe)

1. Mizuki Noguchi	JPN	2:26:20
2. Catherine Ndereba	KEN	2:26:32
3. Deena Drossin-Kastor	USA	2:27:20
4. Elfenesh Alemu	ETH	2:28:15
5. Reiko Tosa	JPN	2:28:44
6. Olivera Jevtić	SER	2:31:15
7. Naoko Sakamoto	JPN	2:31:43
8. Lyudmila Petrova	RUS	2:31:56

The favorites in 2004 included world record holder Paula Radcliffe of Great Britain, who had battled a calf injury in the weeks before the Olympics, and Catherine Ndereba, the previous world record holder and the reigning world champion. Ndereba had gained her 2003 world championship by defeating Mizuki Noguchi by nineteen seconds, but had lost to Radcliffe both times they had met in competition.

The race was held in sweltering 95° Fahrenheit (35° C) heat. The course started in the town of Marathon, namesake of the event, and ended at the Panathinaikos Stadium, which had been used in the first modern Olympics in 1896. Along the way, the course included a series of grueling climbs and steep descents, including a 195-meter climb in the middle 12 kilometers and a 170-meter drop over the final 10 kilometers. Radcliffe dictated the pace for most of the first half of the race, with Noguchi and Elfenesh Alemu close behind. The first important break came at the 25-kilometer mark, when Noguchi accelerated on a series of inclines. Shadowed by Alemu, the pair gained about 50 meters on Radcliffe and Ndereba. Alemu soon faded, while Ndereba moved up from fifth place into second, still 30 seconds behind Noguchi. Struggling to maintain fourth place, Radcliffe faltered just before the 36-kilometer mark and then collapsed by the side of the road. Entering Panathinaikos Stadium, Ndereba continued to gain ground on Noguchi, whittling her lead down to 12 seconds, but Noguchi managed to maintain her pace and hold off Ndereba's charge. Meanwhile, Deena Drossin-Kastor ran a technically perfect race, moving up from 23rd early in the race to 12th at the halfway point. Kastor entered the stadium unsure whether she was in third or fourth place. After hearing her name announced over the loudspeaker as third, she finished her last lap while sobbing with emotion. At 1.50 meters (4 feet 11 inches) and weighing in at 41 kilograms (90 pounds), Noguchi was the smallest-ever Olympic track champion.

2008 Beijing C: 81, N: 45, D: 8.17. WB: 2:15:25 (Paula Radcliffe)

1. Constantina Diţă-Tomescu	ROM	2:26:44
2. Catherine Ndereba	KEN	2:27:06
3. Zhou Chunxiu	CHN	2:27:07
4. Zhu Xiaolin	CHN	2:27:16
5. Martha Komu	KEN	2:27:23
6. Mara Yamauchi	GBR	2:27:29
7. Irina Timofeyeva	RUS	2:27:31
8. Lidia Şimon	ROM	2:27:51

Born in Turburea, Romania, Constantina Diţă-Tomescu had built a reputation as an aggressive runner, who would build up an imposing lead over the first half of a race only to be reeled in and passed over the final kilometers. Her reckless pacing had left her in 10th place at the 2001 world championships, had caused her to drop out of the 2003 championships and had dropped her to 20th at the 2004 Olympics in Athens. Diţă came back to win her first major race at the 2004 Chicago Marathon and finished third at the 2005 world championships in Helsinki.

The real favorite in Beijing was reigning world

champion Catherine Ndereba, known as "Catherine the Great." Ndereba had won the 2003 world championship title, taken silver in 2005 and amassed a record that included victories in four Boston Marathons and two Chicago Marathons.

Despite concerns over Beijing's notorious heat, humidity and poor air quality, the women's marathon was held under hot but relatively bearable conditions, 22° C (72° F) and 88% humidity. Nonetheless, the race began incredibly slowly, with Diţă setting the pace in the lead pack over the first 20 kilometers (12.4 miles) before making a clear break from the rest of the field. "I was surprised nobody came with me," she said later. "Maybe everybody was thinking about the weather. Maybe they worried about the humidity. In the last kilometers, I was looking back, because I didn't want to lose the medal." By the 30-kilometer mark Diţă had built a 5-second lead, and the only question was whether or not she could maintain her pace. In fact, she had extended her lead to 70 seconds by the 35-kilometer mark, and she entered the stadium alone and in no danger of being passed. At the age of 38, Diţă became the oldest-ever Olympic marathon champion.

Meanwhile, in the chasing pack, Ndereba was battling it out with 2007 world champion silver medalist Zhou Chunxiu for second place. Ndereba was passed briefly in the final stretch, but made a final push to retake the lead and edge out Zhou by one second.

100-METER HURDLES

Women clear ten hurdles 2 feet 9 inches (.838 meters) high. It is 13 meters (14 yards 7¾ inches) from the start line to the first hurdle, 8½ meters (8 yards 2 feet 10 inches) between hurdles, and 10½ meters (11 yards 5 inches) from the last hurdle to the finish line.

1896–1928 not held

1932 Los Angeles C: 9, N: 6, D: 8.4. WR: 11.8 (Marjorie Clark)
(80 Meters)

1. Mildred "Babe" Didrikson	USA	11.7 WR
2. Evelyne Hall	USA	11.7
3. Marjorie Clark	SAF	11.8
4. Simone Schaller	USA	11.9
5. Violet Webb	GBR	11.9
6. Alda Wilson	CAN	12.0

Babe Didrikson had already won a gold medal in the javelin throw when she began competition in the 80-meter hurdles. In her opening heat she tied the world record of 11.8 seconds. In the final she committed one false start and then broke the record, apparently beating Evelyne Hall of Chicago, who cut her neck on the finish line, by about two inches. Many observers thought the race was actually a dead heat. Fourth-place finisher Simone Schaller of Pasadena, California, had taken up hurdling only three months earlier.

1936 Berlin C: 22, N: 11, D: 8.6. WR: 11.6 (Ruth Engelhard)
(80 Meters)

1. Trebisonda Valla	ITA	11.7
2. Anni Steuer	GER	11.7
3. Elizabeth Taylor	CAN	11.7
4. Claudia Testoni	ITA	11.7
5. Catharina ter Braake	HOL	11.8
6. Doris Eckert	GER	12.0

The finish was so close that the judges spent 30 minutes studying the photo-finish before they were able to sort out the places and announce the results. In the semifinals, Ondina Valla had run a wind-aided 11.6, which was recognized as an Olympic record but not a world record.

1948 London C: 21, N: 12, D: 8.4. WR: 11.0 (Francina "Fanny" Blankers-Koen)
(80 Meters)

1. Francina "Fanny" Blankers-Koen	HOL	11.2 OR
2. Maureen Gardner	GBR	11.2
3. Shirley Strickland	AUS	11.4
4. Yvette Monginou	FRA	11.8e
5. Maria Oberbreyer	AUT	11.9e
6. Libuše Lomská	CZE	11.9e

Fanny Blankers-Koen had already won the 100-meter dash, but she was quite nervous about 19-year-old Maureen Gardner in the hurdles. She didn't meet her rival until the day of the opening heats, when Gardner showed up at the warmup track with her own set of hurdles. In the semifinals Gardner hit a hurdle and stumbled, barely qualifying in third place. But in the final it was Blankers-Koen who had a tough race. Left behind at the start, she caught Gardner at the fifth barrier, but hit the hurdle and lurched clumsily to the finish line, leaning so low that the tape cut her neck, causing her to bleed. It was unclear who had won, and the first three finishers waited impatiently for the results. Suddenly the band struck up "God Save the King" and Fanny thought that meant she had lost. Actually the band was playing not because Maureen Gardner had won, but because the British royal family had just arrived at the stadium. Then the results appeared on the scoreboard, and Fanny Blankers-Koen had gained her second gold medal. The fact that she was a devoted mother and housewife and that Maureen

Babe Didrikson, 1932

Didrikson qualified for all five individual women's track and field events in 1932, but was allowed to compete in only three of them. She won the javelin throw and the 80-meter hurdles and set a world record in the high jump, despite being placed second. She was later voted the greatest female athlete of the first half of the twentieth century.

Gardner was a ballet instructor did much to counter the pre-World War II masculine image of women athletes that had been established by Stella Walsh, Babe Didriksen, and Helen Stephens. Bronze medalist Shirley Strickland also finished third in the 100 meters, fourth in the 200, and second in the relay. Her official time of 11.4 is undoubtedly a mistake, since she was less than a meter behind the winner.

1952 Helsinki C: 33, N: 21, D: 7.24. WR: 11.0 (Francina "Fanny" Blankers-Koen)
(80 Meters)

1. Shirley de la Hunty (Strickland)	AUS	10.9	WR	(11.01)
2. Maria Golubnichaya	SOV/RUS	11.1		(11.24)
3. Maria Sander	GER	11.1		(11.38)
4. Anneliese Seonbuchner	GER	11.2		(11.46)
5. Jean Desforges	GBR	11.6		(11.75)

DNF: Francina "Fanny" Blankers-Koen (HOL)

Shirley Strickland, a 27-year-old teacher from Western Australia with a degree in physics, equaled Fanny Blankers-Koen's world record in the first heat. The Dutch defending champion, suffering from a carbuncle on her leg, ran 11.2 and 11.3 to qualify for the final, while Strickland ran a wind-aided 10.8 in the semifinals. In the final, Blankers-Koen hit the first two hurdles and stopped running. Meanwhile, Shirley Strickland streaked to victory in world record time. Because there was a dispute as to which song to play for Australia's national anthem, the peacemaking Finnish hosts played *two* anthems: "God Save the Queen" and "Advance Australia Fair."

1956 Melbourne C: 22, N: 11, D: 11.28. WR: 10.6 (Kreszentia Gastl)
(80 Meters)

1. Shirley de la Hunty (Strickland)	AUS	10.7	OR	(10.96)
2. Gisela Köhler	GDR	10.9		(11.12)
3. Norma Thrower	AUS	11.0		(11.25)
4. Galina Bystrova	SOV/RUS	11.0		(11.25)
5. Maria Golubnichaya	SOV/RUS	11.3		(11.50)
6. Gloria Cooke	AUS	11.4		(11.60)

By 1956 Shirley Strickland had become a mother and was employed as an assistant lecturer in physics and mathematics at Perth Technical College. Her decisive two-yard victory in the 80-meter hurdles and her gold medal in the relay gave her a total of seven Olympic medals: three gold, one silver, three bronze.

One morning in February 1999, de la Hunty, then 73 years old, was watering her front garden in Perth, when a man set fire to her car by throwing a Molotov cocktail through the window. The attack was probably related to de la Hunty's leadership of a campaign to halt logging of old-growth forests. In 2001, de la Hunty sold a huge collection of her sporting memorabilia, including her Olympic medals, in order to raise money for her grandchildren's education and to support environmental causes.

1960 Rome C: 28, N: 17, D: 9.1. WR: 10.5 (Gisela Birkemeyer [Köhler])
(80 Meters)

1. Iryna Press	SOV/UKR	10.8	(10.93)
2. Carole Quinton	GBR	10.9	(10.99)
3. Gisela Birkemeyer (Köhler)	GDR	11.0	(11.13)
4. Mary Bignal	GBR	11.1	(11.22)
5. Galina Bystrova	SOV/RUS	11.2	(11.26)
6. Rimma Koschelyova	SOV/RUS	11.2	(11.28)

Iryna Press, the younger sister of shot put and discus champion Tamara Press, set an Olympic record of 10.6 in the semifinals before winning a clear start-to-finish victory in the final.

1964 Tokyo C: 27, N: 19, D: 10.19. WR: 10.5 (Gisela Birkemeyer [Köhler], Betty Moore, Karin Balzer, Iryna Press, Draga Stamejčić)
(80 Meters)

1. Karin Balzer	GDR	10.5w	(10.54w)
2. Teresa Ciepla-Wieczorek	POL	10.5	(10.55)

3. Pamela Kilborn	AUS	10.5	(10.56)
4. Iryna Press	SOV/UKR	10.6	(10.62)
5. Ikuko Yoda	JPN	10.7	(10.72)
6. Maria Piatkowska	POL	10.7	(10.76)
7. Draga Stamejčić	YUG/SLO	10.8	(10.86)
8. Rosie Bonds	USA	10.8	(10.88)

Hometown favorite Ikuko Yoda delighted the crowd with her unusual prerace routine, which included sweeping her lane up to the first hurdle, sucking a lemon, and dabbing cream behind her ears. She led until the third hurdle, but couldn't hold off the favorites. The three medalists finished within 12 inches of one another. Their world record time was disallowed because of a 2.23 meters per second wind. The competition was marred in the opening round when Canadian Marion Snider crashed into a hurdle and was carried away, unconscious, on a stretcher.

1968 Mexico City C: 32, N: 23, D: 10.18. WR: 10.2 (Vera Korsakova)
(80 Meters)

1. Maureen Caird	AUS	10.39 OR
2. Pamela Kilborn	AUS	10.46
3. Chi Cheng	TAI	10.51
4. Patricia Van Wolvelaere	USA	10.60
5. Karin Balzer	GDR	10.61
6. Danuta Straszyńska	POL	10.66
7. Elżbieta Zebrowska	POL	10.66
8. Tatyana Talysheva	SOV/RUS	10.72

When word spread from the USSR that unknown Vera Korsakova had broken Iryna Press's world record, many eyebrows were raised. Cynics doubted her time of 10.2 and said that it was just the Soviets' way of removing from the record books the names of the Press sisters, who had disappeared from competition following the institution of sex tests. Sure enough, Korsakova was eliminated in the semifinals after clocking only 10.6 and 10.8. Pam Kilborn had been undefeated since the Tokyo Olympics, but she suffered a slow start in the final and was unable to catch her 17-year-old teammate Maureen Caird. Caird competed in the 1972 Olympics but was eliminated in the first round. Back home she underwent surgery for stomach cancer and then retired from competition. She retired so completely that over the next 29 years she gave only one interview. Then, in 2001, to honor a request of her deceased mother, Caird came forward to display a certificate she had been given by the New South Wales Amateur Athletic Association stating that on January 17, 1967, Caird, then 15 years old, had won the 80-meter hurdles in 10.2 seconds, which would have made her the youngest runner to set a world record in an Olympic event. Chi Cheng, the first Asian woman in 40 years to win an Olympic track and field medal, was elected to the Taiwan parliament in 1981.

1972 Munich C: 25, N: 15, D: 9.8. WR: 12.5 (Anneliese Ehrhardt, Pamela Ryan [Kilborn])

1. Anneliese Ehrhardt	GDR	12.59 WR
2. Valeria Bufanu	ROM	12.84
3. Karin Balzer	GDR	12.90
4. Pamela Ryan (Kilborn)	AUS	12.98
5. Teresa Nowak	POL	13.17
6. Danuta Straszyńska	POL	13.18
7. Annerose Krumpholz	GDR	13.27
8. Grażyna Rabsztyn	POL	13.44

Esther Shakhamorov had the potential of becoming Israel's first Olympic finalist, but she withdrew following the terrorist murder of Israeli athletes, including her coach, Amitzur Shapira. Anneliese Ehrhardt was never seriously challenged. The final was noteworthy for the success of the "older women," including 34-year-old Karin Balzer and 33-year-old Pam Ryan.

1976 Montreal C: 27, N: 15, D: 7.29. WR: 12.59 (Anneliese Ehrhardt)

1. Johanna Schaller	GDR	12.77
2. Tatiana Anisimova	SOV/RUS	12.78
3. Natalya Lebedeva	SOV/RUS	12.80
4. Gudrun Behrend	GDR	12.82
5. Grażyna Rabsztyn	POL	12.96
6. Esther Rot (Shakhamorov)	ISR	13.04
7. Valeria Stefanescu	ROM	13.35
8. Ileana Ongar	ITA	13.51

The semifinals saw an unusual incident. In the second heat, Lyubov Kononova of the USSR stumbled and smashed into Valeria Stefanescu in the next lane. At first both women were disqualified, but fair play prevailed. Stefanescu was reinstated, and a rerun was ordered for the next day, 75 minutes before the final. This rerun allowed Stefanescu to replace injured defending champion Ehrhardt as the eighth finalist. The final was so close that only one and a half feet separated Schaller from fourth-place finisher Behrend. Esther Shakhamorov, now married and living then in Tarzana, California, at last succeeded in becoming Israel's first finalist.

1980 Moscow C: 20, N: 11, D: 7.28. WR: 12.36 (Grażyna Rabsztyn)

1. Vera Komisova	SOV/RUS	12.56 OR
2. Johanna Klier (Schaller)	GDR	12.63
3. Lucyna Langer	POL	12.65
4. Kerstin Claus	GDR	12.66
5. Grażyna Rabsztyn	POL	12.74
6. Irina Litovchenko	SOV/RUS	12.84
7. Bettine Gärtz	GDR	12.93
8. Zofia Bielczyk	POL	13.08

Twenty-seven-year-old Vera Komisova was one of the surprise winners of the Moscow Games, as she improved her pre-Olympic best by .28 seconds, even greater than Schaller's 1976 Olympic improvement of .22.

1984 Los Angeles C: 22, N: 14, D: 8.10. WR: 12.36 (Grażyna Rabsztyn)

1. Benita Fitzgerald-Brown	USA	12.84
2. Shirley Strong	GBR	12.88
3. Michele Chardonnet	FRA	13.06
3. Kim Turner	USA	13.06
5. Glynis Nunn	AUS	13.20
6. Marie Noèlle-Savigny	FRA	13.28
7. Ulrike Denk	GER	13.32
8. Pamela Page	USA	13.40

In 1984 all of the leading contenders in the 100-meter hurdles came from boycotting nations, including the twelve women who registered the fastest times of the year.

Originally a dead-heat was announced for third place, but after viewing films of the race for 50 minutes, a Jury of Appeal awarded sole possession to Turner. Unfortunately, Chardonnet was not informed of this decision until she was standing in the award ceremony area. When her name was not announced, she was led away in tears. Three and a half months later, the IAAF reversed the decision of the Jury of Appeal and Chardonnet was awarded her bronze medal.

Benita Fitzgerald later became president of the Women's Sports Foundation, director of the US Olympic training center and president of Women in Cable and Telecommunications.

1988 Seoul C: 36, N: 24, D: 9.30. WR: 12.21 (Yordanka Donkova)

1. Yordanka Donkova	BUL	12.38	OR
2. Gloria Siebert	GDR	12.61	
3. Claudia Zackiewicz	GER	12.75	
4. Natalya Hryhoryeva	SOV/UKR	12.79	
5. Florence Colle	FRA	12.98	
6. Julie Rocheleau	CAN	12.99	
7. Monique Ewanje-Épée	FRA	13.14	
8. Cornelia Oschkenat	GDR	13.73	

In 1986, Yordanka Donkova broke the world record four times in 27 days. The following year she lost the record to teammate Ginka Zagorcheva and finished a disappointing fourth at the world championship in Rome. However, in 1988 she continued her pattern of excelling in even-numbered years. She regained the world record on August 20th and won all 15 finals that she entered, including the Olympics, which she led from start to finish. Her chief rivals both bowed out to injuries in Seoul—Zagorcheva failed to complete her opening-round heat and Cornelia Oschkenat pulled a hamstring in the final while running in third place.

1992 Barcelona C: 37, N: 23, D: 8.6. WR: 12.21 (Yordanka Donkova)

1. Paraskevi "Voula" Patoulidou	GRE	12.64
2. LaVonna Martin	USA	12.69
3. Yordanka Donkova	BUL	12.70
4. Lynda Tolbert	USA	12.75
5. Y. Gail Devers	USA	12.75
6. Aliuska López	CUB	12.87
7. Natalya Kolovanova	UKR	13.01
8. Odalys Adams	CUB	13.57

This was expected to be a duel between world champion Lyudmila Narozhilenko of Russia, who had recorded the five fastest times of the year, and Gail Devers, who had finished second to Narozhilenko at the world championships and had already won the 100-meter dash in Barcelona. However, Narozhilenko pulled out of her semifinal heat after straining a hamstring. In the final, Devers moved in front by the fourth hurdle and seemed to be home free with only one hurdle left. But she came up to the final barrier too quickly, and just as she rose to clear it, she glanced briefly to her right. She hit the hurdle with her lead foot on the way up and lost her balance. As she scraped and scrambled toward the finish line, her lead vanished and she did well to place fifth despite her fall.

Meanwhile Tolbert, Martin, Patoulidou and Donkova finished almost in a line. The day before, Patoulidou, whose pre-Olympic personal best was only 12.96, had celebrated joyously because she had qualified for the final. Now she thought she had actually earned a bronze medal. When she saw the replay in the stadium she realized she had won the race. To say that Patoulidou's victory was a surprise would be a gross understatement. Previously her best performance had been a second-place in the Mediterranean Games. Patoulidou was the first Greek woman to qualify for a track final, the first Greek woman to win a medal in any sport (excluding the 1906 Intercalated Games), and the first Greek athlete of either sex to earn a gold medal in track and field since Konstantin Tsiklitiras won the standing long jump in 1912. At the 1996 Olympics, Patoulidou finished eleventh in the long jump.

LaVonna Martin, who took the silver medal, had been suspended after testing positive for a banned diuretic. However, she was reinstated three months before the United States Olympic trials because her coach claimed that he had given her the drug without her knowledge.

1996 Atlanta C: 44, N: 28, D: 7.31. WR: 12.21 (Yordanka Donkova)

1. Ludmila Engquist	SWE	12.58
2. Brigita Bukovec	SLO	12.59
3. Patricia Girard-Leno	FRA	12.65
4. Y. Gail Devers	USA	12.66
5. Dione Rose	JAM	12.74
6. Michelle Freeman	JAM	12.76
7. Lynda Goode	USA	13.11

DISQ (Drugs): Natalya Shekhodanova (RUS) 12.80

Few athletes have had as rocky a road to gold as Ludmila Engquist. A mother at age 18, she first competed in the Olympics in 1988 as a representative of the Soviet Union. At the time her name was Lyudmila Narozhilenko. In her semifinal heat she fell and did not finish. In 1992 she again qualified for the semifinals but had to withdraw because of a hamstring injury. On February 13, 1993, she tested positive for anabolic steroids. She was banned for four years, but then her husband, Nikolai, came forward in court and claimed that he had slipped steroids into her protein powder to punish her for initiating divorce proceedings against him after she fell in love with her manager, Johan Engquist.

She married Engquist, moved to Sweden and applied for citizenship. Her suspension was lifted because of "exceptional circumstances," but she had already lost two years of competition. While she was gone, Gail Devers won both world championships—in 1993 and 1995. Engquist hoped to compete in the 1996 Olympics, but found herself in nationality limbo. On June 20, she was granted Swedish citizenship and on July 5, only two weeks before the Opening Ceremony, the Russian Olympic Committee released her to compete for Sweden. Engquist led the qualifying round with a time of 12.66 and then clocked an impressive 12.47 in the quarterfinals. Two days later she won her semifinal in 12.51. In the final, Brigita Bukovec led at the halfway mark. Engquist edged ahead over the last hurdle and won in a photo-finish.

In March 1999, Engquist was diagnosed as having breast cancer. On April 21, her 35th birthday, she submitted to a masectomy and then began chemotherapy. Taking a break from the chemo, she participated in the world championships in Seville in August and, incredibly, won a bronze medal. After completing chemotherapy, Engquist switched sports—to bobsleigh, with the goal of winning a medal at the 2002 Winter Olympics. She and her partner, Karin Olsson, placed fourth at the 2001 world championships, but then, in November of 2001, the roller coaster ride of Engquist's career took a big plunge. She was picked for a random drug test. Before the results could be analyzed, she admitted that she had taken steroids, which she had purchased in Russia. Engquist was fined $1900 for drug smuggling, suspended from competition for two years, and the breakfast cereal that bore her name was taken off the shelves of supermarkets.

2000 Sydney C: 38, N: 26, D: 9.27. WR: 12.21 (Yordanka Donkova)

1. Olga Shishigina	KAZ	12.65
2. Glory Alozie	NGR	12.68
3. Melissa Morrison	USA	12.76
4. Delloreen Ennis-London	JAM	12.80
5. Aliuska López	CUB	12.83
6. Nicole Ramalalanirina	FRA	12.91
7. Linda Ferga	FRA	13.11
8. Brigitte Foster	JAM	13.49

Gail Devers' bizarre Olympics story continued in Sydney. Although she had won two gold medals in the 100-meter sprint, she had never won a medal in her strongest event, the 100-meter hurdles. 1988—out in the semifinals; 1992—hit the last hurdle while in the lead and placed fifth; 1996—missed a medal by one one-hundredth of a second. She arrived at the 2000 Olympics as the reigning world champion. She had also recorded the three fastest times of the pre-Olympic season, including a 12.33 at the US Olympic trials.

Devers' main rivals also had full stories. Olga Shishigina, a 31-year-old with a 12-year-old son, had missed the last Olympics because of a positive test for steroids. Melissa Morrison almost gave up sports after the deaths of four close family members between 1996 and 1998, including her sister and her father. Glory Alozie grew up on a farm in a remote corner of Nigeria, 18 hours from the nearest track. When she competed at the 1999 world championships, it was the first time she had participated in a meet with rounds. She won the silver medal. One week before the Opening Ceremony, Alozie's fiancé, Hyginus Anugo, was killed in Sydney while crossing a street at night. Alozie was so shocked and grief-stricken that her coach had to spoon-feed her and she lost 13 pounds (6kg) in two weeks. A popular figure, she received overwhelming support from her fellow athletes and others and decided to compete in honor of Anugo.

Devers recorded the fastest time of the opening round, 12.62 seconds. As it would turn out, this was the fastest time of the entire competition. Shishigina led the quarterfinals with a 12.66. Madagascar-born Nicole Ramalalanirina won the first semifinal in 12.77 seconds and Alozie the second in 12.68. The biggest news of the semis was that Devers, hampered by a hamstring injury, stopped running midway through the first semi, as her Olympic hurdles jinx continued.

In the final, Alozie led halfway through the race, followed by Morrison and Shishigina. Shishigina closed, drawing even with Alozie over the last hurdle and just pulling ahead on the run-in. She did not know she had won until she watched the replay on the stadium screen.

2004 Athens C: 37, N: 23, D: 8.24. WR: 12.21 (Jordanka Donkova)

1. Joanna Hayes	USA	12.37	OR
2. Olena Ovcharova-Krasovska	UKR	12.45	
3. Melissa Morrison	USA	12.56	
4. Mariya Koroteyeva	RUS	12.72	
5. Lacena Golding-Clarke	JAM	12.73	
6. Angela Whyte	CAN	12.81	

DNF: Perdita Felicien (CAN), Irina Shevchenko (RUS)

The favorite in Athens was reigning world champion Perdita Felicien, who had also won six straight meets in the run-up to the Olympics. Felicien easily won the first semifinal in 12.49, while 27-year-old Joanna Hayes took the second semi in 12.48. In the final, Felicien, running in the fifth lane, hit the first hurdle with her lead leg, stepped on top of it, stumbled into the lane to her right, plowing into Irina Shevchenko and knocking her to the ground. Hayes, on the other side of Felicien, was unaffected by the accident and continued the race. Despite brushing two hurdles, Hayes was unchallenged and set an Olympic record. Russian officials filed a protest on behalf of Shevchenko, requesting that the final be rerun without Felicien, but their petition was denied.

2008 Beijing C: 40, N: 31, D: 8.19. WR: 12.21 (Jordanka Donkova)

1. Dawn Harper	USA	12.54
2. Sally McLellan	AUS	12.64
3. Priscilla Lopes-Schliep	CAN	12.64
4. Damu Cherry	USA	12.65
5. Delloreen Ennis-London	JAM	12.65
6. Brigitte Foster	JAM	12.66
7. Lolo Jones	USA	12.72
8. Sarah Claxton	GBR	12.94

One month before the Beijing Games, two-time reigning world champion Michelle Perry failed to qualify for the US Olympic Team after a season-long struggle with an injured hamstring. With Perry out, the top US medal contender seemed to be 26-year-old Lolo Jones. Born in Des Moines, Iowa, Jones missed competing at the 2004 Olympics after clipping the ninth hurdle in the semi-finals of the US Olympic trials. She struggled for a year without a contract, living in a church basement and working as a waitress and at hardware retailer Home Depot to pay her bills. In March 2008 she won the 60-meter hurdles at the IAAF indoor world championships, and four months later she won the US Olympic trials in a wind-aided time of 12.29 seconds.

True to expectations, Jones was the only American to finish first in her first-round heat. In the semi-final round, however, all three of the top times were recorded by Americans. Jones won the first semi in 12.43 seconds, the fastest time of the year. The second semi was won by 30-year-old Damu Cherry in 12.62, with 24-year-old Dawn Harper right behind at 12.66.

Jones came out strong in the final, taking the early lead and building a clear gap over the first eight hurdles. In a repeat of her 2004 qualifying run, Jones hit the ninth hurdle and stumbled, managing to stay on her feet but losing all momentum. As Jones dropped to seventh place, Harper recorded a personal best to take the gold. Only two-hundredths of a second separated second and sixth places, and all were decided by photo finish, with Sally McLellan earning silver and Priscilla Lopes-Schliep bronze.

Born in East St Louis, Harper was inspired to take up hurdling by three-time Olympic gold medalist and fellow East St Louis native Jackie Joyner-Kersee. In middle school Harper set up a foam hurdle in her driveway to practice, and after graduating from UCLA she began training with Bob Kersee. She earned her spot on the 2008 Olympic team by a margin of 0.007 seconds.

400-METER HURDLES

Rules are the same as those for men except that the ten hurdles are 2 feet 6 inches (.762 meters) high.

1896–1980 not held

1984 Los Angeles C: 26, N: 20, D: 8.8. WR: 53.58 (Margarita Ponomaryova)

1. Nawal El Moutawakel	MOR	54.61	OR
2. Judi Brown	USA	55.20	
3. Cristina Cojocaru	ROM	55.41	
4. Pilavullakandi "P.T." Usha	IND	55.42	
5. Ann-Louise Skoglund	SWE	55.43	
6. Debra Flintoff	AUS	56.21	
7. Tuija Helander	FIN	56.55	
8. Sandra Farmer	JAM	57.15	

Nawal El Moutawakel, who led from start to finish and improved her personal best by .76 seconds, was the first woman from an Islamic nation to win an Olympic medal. She was also the first ever gold-medal winner from Morocco, a fact which did not go unnoticed in her hometown of Casablanca, where the 400-meter hurdle final was televised live at 2 a.m. After she crossed the finish line in first place and took her victory lap carrying a huge Moroccan flag, people poured into the streets of Casablanca to celebrate, and the king of Morocco decreed that all women born on the day of her victory be named Nawal. In 1998, El Moutawakel became the first Islamic woman to be named to the International Olympic Committee.

1988 Seoul C: 35, N: 25, D: 9.28. WR: 52.94 (Marina Stepanova)

1. Debra Flintoff-King	AUS	53.17	OR
2. Tatyana Ledovskaya	SOV/BLR	53.18	
3. Ellen Fiedler	GDR	53.63	
4. Sabine Busch	GDR	53.69	
5. Sally Gunnell	GBR	54.03	
6. Gudrun Abt	GER	54.04	
7. Tatyana Kurochkina	SOV/BLR	54.39	
8. LaTanya Sheffield	USA	55.32	

On the day that she and the rest of the Australian team left for Seoul, Debbie Flintoff-King attended the funeral of her sister, who had died of a heart attack three days earlier. In the semifinals, Flintoff-King edged Tatyana Ledovskaya 54.00 to 54.01. Halfway through the final she was in fifth place behind Ledovskaya, Fiedler, Kurochkina, and world champion Sabine Busch. By the eighth hurdle Fiedler was slightly in front of Ledovskaya, Busch had passed Kurochkina, and Flintoff-King was still fifth. Ledovskaya moved decisively into the lead over the ninth hurdle. As they cleared the tenth and final barrier, Flintoff-King caught Busch, but still trailed Fiedler and Ledovskaya, the latter by .24. She sprinted past the East German. Then, at the finish line, Ledovskaya failed to lean and Flintoff-King nipped her in the final stride.

1992 Barcelona C: 27, N: 18, D: 8.5. WR: 52.94 (Marina Stepanova)

1. Sally Gunnell	GBR	53.23
2. Sandra Farmer-Patrick	USA	53.69
3. Janeene Vickers	USA	54.31
4. Tatyana Ledovskaya	BLR	54.31
5. Vera Ordina	RUS	54.83
6. Margarita Ponomaryova	RUS	54.83
7. Deon Hemmings	JAM	55.58
DNF: Myrtle Bothma (SAF)		

Farmer-Patrick was leading when she had trouble with the seventh hurdle. Gunnell, a farmer's daughter from Chigwell, Essex, caught her at the beginning of the final straightaway, moved ahead at the ninth hurdle, and pulled away to win by three and a half meters.

1996 Atlanta C: 30, N: 21, D: 7.31. WR: 52.61 (J. Kimberly Batten)

1. Deon Hemmings	JAM	52.82	OR
2. J. Kimberly Batten	USA	53.08	
3. Tonja Buford-Bailey	USA	53.22	
4. Debbie-Ann Parris	JAM	53.97	
5. Heike Meissner	GER	54.03	
6. Rosey Edeh	CAN	54.39	
7. Ionela Târlea	ROM	54.40	
8. Silvia Rieger	GER	54.57	

Growing up in St. Ann, Jamaica, Deon Hemmings was a good student and an okay runner. When Central State University in Ohio recruited five Jamaican runners in 1989, they gave a sixth scholarship to Hemmings to give the deal academic credibility. She discovered the 400-meter hurdles in 1990 and improved so quickly that by 1992 she was an Olympic finalist.

At the 1993 world championships, Sally Gunnell broke the seven-year-old world record. Injured, she watched the 1995 world championships final from the stands while working as a commentator for the BBC. What she saw shocked her. Two Americans, Kim Batten and Tonja Buford, shattered her record, with Batten gaining the victory 52.61 to 52.62. Deon Hemmings finished third.

When Hemmings read the Olympic preview issue of *Track and Field News*, she saw that the editors predicted a US sweep: Batten, Buford-Bailey and Sandra Farmer-Patrick. Picked for fifth behind the Americans and Gunnell, Hemmings crossed out the names ahead of her and put herself first.

In Atlanta, Hemmings led the qualifying round with a time of 54.70. The next evening she stunned her opponents by winning the first semifinal in 52.99, bettering her personal best by half a second. The second semi, won by Batten, saw the elimination of Farmer-Patrick (by one hundredth of a second) and Gunnell, who succumbed to injury midway in the race.

In the final, Hemmings led by two meters at the halfway mark. Batten and Buford-Bailey pulled even at the eighth hurdle, but by the final hurdle, Hemming reestablished her two-meter lead. She won going away to become the first Jamaican gold medal winner in twenty years and the first Jamaican woman Olympic champion ever. Hemmings, Meissner, Edeh and Târlea all set personal records in both the semifinals and the final.

2000 Sydney C: 33, N: 21, D: 9.27. WR: 52.61 (J. Kimberly Batten)

1. Irina Privalova	RUS	53.02
2. Deon Hemmings	JAM	53.45
3. Nezha Bidiouane	MOR	53.57
4. Daimi Pernia	CUB	53.68
5. Tetyana Antipova-Tereshchuk	UKR	53.98
6. Ionela Târlea	ROM	54.35
7. Guðrún Arnardóttir	ISL	54.63
8. Natasha Danvers	GBR	55.00

Irina Privalova followed an unusually circuitous path to Olympic gold. After trying figure skating, she achieved childhood success as a speed skater. She switched to track and field and dabbled in various events before settling on the sprints. At the 1992 Olypmics, she picked up as silver medal in the 4 × 100-meter relay and a bronze in the 100 meters and finished fourth in the 200 meters. At the 1996 Olympics, she was eliminated in the semifinals of both sprints and placed fourth in the relay. Her sporting career was revived in 1999 when she was given a tissue transplant for her Achilles tendon using tissue from a deceased soldier. Privalova did not enter her first hurdles race until 2000. The opening round of the Sydney Olympics was only her sixth race in the event. In the semifinals she won her heat with a personal best of 54.02. In the final, Privalova and defending champion Deon Hemmings were even until the seventh hurdle. Between the seventh and eighth hurdles, Privalova surged and kept pulling away, eventually winning by almost four meters. All three medalists were 31 years old.

2004 Athens C: 33, N: 25, D: 8.25. WR: 52.34 (Yuliya Pechenkina)

1. Fani Halkia	GRE	52.82
2. Ionela Târlea-Monolache	ROM	53.38
3. Tetyana Antipova-Tereshchuk	UKR	53.44
4. Sheena Johnson	USA	53.83
5. Jana Pittman	AUS	53.92
6. Yekaterina Bikert	RUS	54.18
7. Brenda Taylor	USA	54.97
8. Yuliya Novosa-Pechenkina	RUS	55.79

World record holder Yuliya Pechenkina recorded the fastest time in the preliminary round and was considered the favorite until unheralded 25-year-old Fani Halkia set an Olympic record of 52.77 in the semifinals. Halkia was such an unknown that her name was not listed in the IAAF official track guide.

Nevertheless, she dominated the final, surging ahead of Jana Pittman, Ionela Târlea-Manolache and Tetyana Antipova-Tereshchuk between the 7th and 8th barriers, and increasing her lead to more than half a second before the finish. During her victory lap, Halkia bowed down before her coach, Yiorgos Panayiotopoulos. Originally a high jumper and 400-meter runner, Halkia had never won a major international competition, and had never recorded a sub-56-second time until three months before the Olympics.

At the press conference after her surprise win, Halkia was peppered with questions from suspicious journalists because of her sudden improvement at a relatively late age and because her coach had trained under Christos Tsekos, coach to the soon-to-be-disgraced Greek sprinters Kostantinos Kenteris and Ekaterina Thanou. A former student of broadcast journalism, Halkia attributed her improvement and her victory to patriotism and good coaching. "When I entered the stadium," she explained, "I was certain I would win. It may sound arrogant, but I felt it very intensely with all these people. I wanted to show the world that the Greeks are born for the top."

2008 Beijing C: 27, N: 21, D: 8.20. WR: 52.34 (Yuliya Pechonkina)

1. Melaine Walker	JAM	52.64	OR
2. Sheena Johnson-Tosta	USA	53.70	
3. Tasha Danvers	GBR	53.84	
4. Anastasiya Rabchenyuk	UKR	53.96	
5. Anna Olichwierczuk-Jesień	POL	54.29	
6. Yekaterina Bikert	RUS	54.96	
7. Zuzana Hejnová	CZE	54.97	
8. Tiffany Ross-Williams	USA	57.55	

The 2008 400-meter hurdles was notable for who wasn't there. At the end of June world ranked number one Lashinda Demus failed to qualify for Beijing after finishing fourth at the US Olympic trials. Then in July, reigning world champion Jana Rawlinson of Australia announced that she would be unable to compete due to complications from a toe injury suffered the previous year. The same week, 2005 world champion and world record holder Yuliya Pechonkina announced that she would also be unable to compete, after heart problems resulting from a sinus infection incurred during a training session in Portugal earlier in the season.

Finally, less than 24 hours before the start of the qualifying heats, the IOC announced that defending Olympic gold medalist Fania Halkia had tested positive for the banned substance methyltrienolone at a Greek training camp in Japan prior to arriving in Beijing. Halkia flew home just hours before the competition started and was later hit with a two-year ban.

With the competition wide open, 25-year-old Melaine Walker established herself as the surprise favorite for gold, recording the fastest time of the qualifying round (54.46) and winning her semi-final heat easily. Sheena Tosta barely made it to the semi-finals after finishing fifth in her qualifying heat, but won her semi-final heat to advance to the final.

In the final, Tosta took the early lead but was passed by Walker at the seventh hurdle. Walker pulled away in the final stretch, setting an Olympic record and recording the fourth-fastest time in history. Natasha Danvers took bronze despite having incurred an Achilles injury three months before the games, and after suffering a torn hamstring on her first day back in training.

One year after the Olympics Walker went on to win the 2009 400-meter hurdles world title in Berlin, setting a championship record in the process. At the 2011 world championships she finished second behind Lashinda Demus.

3000-METER STEEPLECHASE

1896–2004 not held

2008 Beijing C: 51, N: 30, D: 8.17. WR: 9:01.59 (Gulnara Samitova)

1. Gulnara Samitova-Galkina	RUS	8:58.81	WR
2. Eunice Jepkorir	KEN	9:07.41	
3. Yekaterina Volkova	RUS	9:07.64	
4. Tatyana Petrova	RUS	9:12.33	
5. Cristina Casandra	ROM	9:16.85	
6. Ruth Bisibori	KEN	9:17.35	
7. Zemzem Ahmed	ETH	9:17.85	
8. Wioletta Janowska-Frankiewicz	POL	9:21.76	

Making its Olympic debut, the women's steeplechase competition was expected to be dominated by Russia. Two Russians, Yekaterina Volkova and Tatyana Petrova, had gone 1-2 at the 2007 world championships, and another, Gulnara Samitova, had set two world records in the event in 2003 and 2004.

Because women's steeplechase was not an Olympic event at the time of the 2004 Athens Games, Samitova competed instead in the 5000 meters event, finishing a disappointing sixth. Immediately after the Games she married 400 meters runner Anton Galkin, who had tested positive for stanozolol in Athens and had been banned from competition for two years. Samitova also disappeared from international competition for the duration of her husband's suspension. The two then returned using double-surnames. Samitova-Galkina competed at the 2007 world championships, but finished seventh.

The only two athletes expected to challenge the Russians were Eunice Jepkorir and Ruth Bisibori of Kenya, who had finished third and fourth at the 2007 world championships.

In the final Samitova-Galkina led from the beginning and was never headed. She was followed in the early going by Petrova, Jepkorir, Bisibori and Zemzem Ahmed. By the 1000-meter mark, she had dropped all but Petrova and Jepkorir, and by the final lap she had built a nearly 40-meter gap. Samitova-Galkina beat her own world record and became the first woman to break the nine-minute barrier. Meanwhile, Volkova, who hadn't been in the lead pack during the first half of the race, caught up with the leaders and moved into second place in the final stretch. Jepkorir managed to outsprint Volkova to the line to take silver.

4 × 100-METER RELAY

1896-1924 not held

1928 Amsterdam T: 8, N: 8, D: 8.5. WR (440 yards): 49.8 (GBR—Scovler, Haynes, Edwards, Thompson)

1. CAN	Fanny "Bobbie" Rosenfeld, Ethel Smith, Florence Jane Bell, Myrtle Cook	48.4	WR
2. USA	Mary Washburn, Jessie Cross, Loretta McNeil, Elizabeth Robinson	48.8	
3. GER	Rosa Kellner, Helene "Leni" Schmidt, Anni Holdmann, Helene "Leni" Junker	49.0	
4. FRA	Georgette Gagneux, Yvonne Plancke, Marguerite Radideau, Lucienne Velu	49.6	
5. HOL	Mechelina Aengenendt, Maria Briejer, Jeannette Hendrika Grooss, Elisabeth ter Horst	49.8	
6. ITA	Luisa Bonfanti, Giannina Marchini, Derna Polazzo, Vittorina Vivenza	53.6	

After Bobbie Rosenfeld false-started once, the Americans led for the first half of the race. Then Jane Bell ran a strong turn to give the Candians a three-yard lead that anchor Myrtle Cook was able to extend. The relay victory was sweet revenge for the Canadian team, particularly for Rosenfeld, who had lost first place in the 100 meters on a disputed judges' decision, and for Cook, who had cried by the side of the track for a half hour after being disqualified in the 100 meters final. Training restrictions for the Canadian runners were so strict that they were not allowed to drink soda pop. Myrtle Cook and Bobbie Rosenfeld both became sports editors for Canadian newspapers.

1932 Los Angeles T: 6, N: 6, D: 8.7. WR: 48.4 (CAN—Rosenfeld, Smith, Bell, Cook)

1. USA	Mary Carew, Evelyn Furtsch, Annette Rogers, Wilhelmina "Billie" Von Bremen	46.9	WR (46.86)
2. CAN	Mildred Frizzel, Lilian Palmer, Mary Frizzel, Hilda Strike	47.0	
3. GBR	Eileen Hiscock, Gwendolina Porter, Violet Webb, Nellie Halstead	47.6	
4. HOL	Johanna Dalmolen, Cornelia Aalten, Elisabeth du Mee, Tollien Schurrman	48.0	
5. JPN	Mie Muraoka, Michi Nakanishi, Asa Dogura, Sumiko Watanabe	48.9	
6. GER	Grete Heublein, Ellen Braumüller, Ottilie "Tilly" Fleischer, Marie Dollinger	—	

1936 Berlin T: 8, N: 8, D: 8.9. WR: 46.5 (GER—Albus, Krauss, Dollinger, Dörffeldt)

1. USA	Harriet Bland, Annette Rogers, Elizabeth Robinson, Helen Stephens	46.9
2. GBR	Eileen Hiscock, Violet Olney, Audrey Brown, Barbara Burke	47.6
3. CAN	Dorothy Brookehaw, Mildred Dolson, Hilda Cameron, Aileen Meagher	47.8
4. ITA	Lydia Bongiovanni, Trebisonda Valla, Fernanda Bullano, Claudia Testoni	48.7
5. HOL	Catharina ter Braake, Francina "Fanny" Koen, Alida de Vries, Elisabeth Koning	48.8

DISQ: GER: Emmy Albus, Käthe Krauss, Marie Dollinger, Ilse Dörffeldt

In the opening round the German team set a world record of 46.4 that was to remain unbroken for sixteen years. In the final they led by eight meters as Marie Dollinger prepared to make the final pass to Ilse Dörffeldt. However, as Adolf Hitler, King Boris of Bulgaria, and 100,000 others watched, Ilse Dörffeldt dropped the baton. The US team, anchored by the heroic 1928 100 meters winner Betty Robinson and the 1936 100 meters winner Helen Stephens, took advantage of the German catastrophe and won by eight yards. Hitler was so moved by the sight of Dörffeldt sobbing after the race that he called the four German women to his booth and comforted them.

1948 London T: 10, N: 10, D: 8.7. WR: 46.4 (GER—Albus, Krauss, Dollinger, Dörffeldt)

1. HOL	Xenia Stad-de Jong, Jeanette Witziers-Timmer, Gerda van der Kade-Koudijs, Francina '"Fanny" Blankers-Koen	47.5
2. AUS	Shirley Strickland, June Maston, Elizabeth McKinnon, Joyce King	47.6
3. CAN	Viola Myers, Nancy MacKay, Diane Foster, Patricia Jones	47.8
4. GBR	Dorothy Manley, Muriel Pletts, Margaret Walker, Maureen Gardner	48.0
5. DEN	Grete Lövsöe [Nielsen], Bente Bergendorff, Birte Nielsen, Hildegard Nissen	48.2
6. AUT	Grete Jenny, Elfi Steurer, Grete Pavlousek, Maria Oberbreyer	49.2

Fanny Blankers-Koen took over in fourth place, but was able to race through the field and catch Joyce King just before the finish. She thus became the only woman to win four track and field gold medals in one Olympics.

1952 Helsinki T: 15, N: 15, D: 7.27. WR: 46.4 (GER—Albus, Krauss, Dollinger, Dörffeldt)

1. USA	H. Mae Faggs, Barbara Jones, Janet Moreau, Catherine Hard	45.9	WR	(46.14)
2. GER	Ursula Knab, Maria Sander, Helga Klein, Marga Petersen	45.9	WR	(46.18)
3. GBR	Sylvia Cheeseman, June Foulds, Jean Desforges, Heather Armitage	46.2		(46.41)
4. SOV	Irma Turova, Yevgenya Setshenova, Nadezhda Khnykina, Vyera Kalashnikova	46.3		(46.42)
5. AUS	Shirley Strickland de la Hunty, Verna Johnson, Winsome Cripps, Marjorie Jackson	46.6		(46.86)
6. HOL	Grietje de Jongh, Bertha Brouwer, Neeltje Büch, Wilhelmina Lust	47.8		(47.16)

Australian 4 × 100-meter Relay Team, 1952
They set a world record in their qualifying heat and were on the way to winning the final when Winsome Cripps and Marjorie Jackson dropped the baton in the last changeover.

The Australians set a world record of 46.1 in the very first heat. They led by one meter in the final at the last changeover. Winsome Cripps made a clean pass to Marjorie Jackson, winner of both sprints, but as Jackson took off, her hand hit Cripps's knee and the baton was jarred loose. Jackson caught it on a bounce and raced on, but the delay proved decisive. One of the four black women who made up the US team was 15-year-old Barbara Jones of Chicago, who is the youngest person in Olympic history to win a gold medal in track and field.

1956 Melbourne T: 9, N: 9, D: 12.1. WR: 45.2 (SOV—Krepkina, Itkina, Kocheleva, Bochkaryova)

1. AUS	Shirley Strickland de la Hunty, Norma Croker, Fleur Mellor, Elizabeth Cuthbert	44.5	WR	(44.65)
2. GBR	Anne Pashley, Jean Scrivens, June Paul [Foulds], Heather Armitage	44.7		(44.70)
3. USA	H. Mae Faggs, Margaret Matthews, Wilma Rudolph, Isabelle Daniels	44.9		(45.04)

4. SOV	Vira Krepkina, Galina Reschikova, Maria Itkina, Irina Botchkaryova	45.6	(45.81)
5. ITA	Maria Musso, Letizia Bertoni, Maria Greppi, Giuseppina Leone	45.7	(45.90)
6. GDR & GER	Maria Sander, Christa Stubnick, Gisela Köhler, Barbara Mayer	47.2	(47.29)

Pressed by the Germans, the Australian team set a world record of 44.9 in the opening heat. In the final, though, it was the British women who put on the pressure. Heather Armitage finished only half a yard behind Betty Cuthbert (a closer margin than indicated by Great Britain's time of 44.7). Anne Pashley, who ran the opening leg for the British team, later gained renown as a mezzo-soprano.

1960 Rome T: 10, N: 10, D: 9.8. WR: 44.5 (AUS—Strickland de la Hunty, Croker, Mellor, Cuthbert)

1. USA	Martha Hudson, Lucinda Williams, Barbara Jones, Wilma Rudolph	44.5	(44.72)
2. GER	Martha Langbein, Annie Biechl, Brunhilde Hendrix, Jutta Heine	44.8	(45.00)
3. POL	Teresa Wieczorek, Barbara Janiszewska, Celina Jesionowska, Halina Richter	45.0	(45.19)
4. SOV	Vira Krepkina, Valentina Maslovskaya, Maria Itkina, Iryna Press	45.2	(45.39)
5. ITA	Letizia Bertoni, Sandra Valenti, Piera Tizzoni, Giuseppina Leone	45.6	(45.80)

DNF: GBR: Carole Quinton, Dorothy Hyman, Jennifer Smart, Mary Bignal

Marie Dollinger was one of the two unfortunate German women who dropped their baton in 1936, during the changeover from the third runner to the fourth. Twenty-four years later she sat in the stands in Rome and watched tensely as her daughter, Brunhilde Hendrix, the third runner on the German team, prepared to pass the baton to Jutta Heine. Fortunately all went well, and the 1960 German team finished impressively in second place. The US team from Tennessee State had a two-yard lead that was lost in a sloppy final pass. However Wilma Rudolph was able to regain the lead and cross the tape in first place for the ninth time in the Rome Games. The US women had set a world record of 44.4 in the semifinals.

1964 Tokyo T: 15, N: 15, D: 10.21. WR: 44.3 (USA—White, Pollards, Brown, Rudolph)

1. POL	Teresa Ciepla [Wieczorek], Irena Kirszenstein, Halina Górecka [Richter], Ewa Klobukowska	43.6	(43.69)
2. USA	Willye White, Wyomia Tyus, Marilyn White, Edith McGuire	43.9	(43.92)
3. GBR	Janet Simpson, Mary Rand [Bignal], Daphne Arden, Dorothy Hyman	44.0	(44.09)
4. SOV	Galina Gaide, Renata Lace, Lyudmila Samotysova, Galina Popova	44.4	(44.44)
5. GER	Karin Frisch, Erika Pollmann, Martha Pensberger [Langbein], Jutta Heine	44.7	
6. AUS	Dianne Bowering, Marilyn Black, Margaret Burvill, Joyce Bennett	45.0	
7. HUN	Erzsébet Bartos Heldt, Margit Nemesházi Markó, Antónia Munkácsi, Ida Such	45.2	
8. FRA	Marlene Canguio, Danièle Gueneau, Michele Lurot, Denise Guénard	46.1	

The Polish team was originally credited with a world record, but their names were later struck from the record books when Ewa Klobukowska became the first

Ewa Klobukowska, 1964

In 1964 Klobukowska won a bronze medal in the 100-meter dash and a gold in the 4 × 100-meter relay. Three years later she became the first athlete to fail a sex test.

athlete to fail a sex test—even though she passed a "visual verification" exam. British runner Janet Simpson won a bronze medal, just as her mother, Violet Webb, had in the same event in 1932.

1968 Mexico City T: 14, N: 14, D: 10.20. WR: 43.6 (SOV—Zharkova, Bukharina, Popkova, Samotysova)

1. USA	Barbara Ferrell, Margaret Bailes, Mildrette Netter, Wyomia Tyus	42.88	WR
2. CUB	Marlene Elejarde, Fulgencia Romay, Violetta Quesada, Miguelina Cobián	43.36	
3. SOV/RUS	Lyudmila Zharkova, Galina Bukharina, Vyera Popkova, Lyudmila Samotysova	43.41	
4. HOL	Geertruida Hennipman, Mieke Sterk, Cornelia Bakker, Wilhelmina van den Berg	43.44	
5. AUS	Jennifer Lamy, Joyce Bennett, Raelene Boyle, Dianne Burge	43.50	
6. GER	Renate Meyer, Jutta Stöck, Rita Jahn, Ingrid Becker	43.70	
7. GBR	Anita Neil, Maureen Tranter, Janet Simpson, Lillian Board	43.78	
8. FRA	Michele Alayrangues, Gabrielle Meyer, Nicole Montandon, Silviane Telliez	44.30	

The American women set a world record of 43.4 in the first heat. This time was equaled, surprisingly, in the second heat by the unheralded Dutch team. In the final the US team overcame mediocre baton-passing with rare speed to win by five yards and establish a new world record.

1972 Munich T: 15, N: 15, D: 9.10. WR: 42.88 (USA—Ferrell, Bailes, Netter, Tyus)

1. GER	Christiane Krause, Ingrid Mickler [Becker], Annegret Richter, Heidemarie Rosendahl	42.81	WR
2. GDR	Evelyn Kaufer, Christina Heinich, Bärbel Struppert, Renate Stecher	42.95	
3. CUB	Marlene Elejarde, Carmen Valdes, Fulgencia Romay, Silvia Chivás	43.36	
4. USA	Martha Watson, Mattiline Render, Mildrette Netter, Iris Davis	43.39	
5. SOV/RUS	Marina Sidorova, Galina Bukharina, Lyudmila Zharkova, Nadezhda Besfamilnaya	43.59	
6. AUS	Maureen Caird, Raelene Boyle, Marion Hoffman, Penelope Gillies	43.61	
7. GBR	Andrea Lynch, Della Pascoe, Judith Vernon, Anita Neil	43.71	
8. POL	Helena Fliśnik, Barbara Bakulin, Urszula Jóźwik, Danuta Jędrejek	44.20	

The East Germans had edged the West Germans in the European championships. Rematched in a poorly seeded opening heat, the East Germans again finished ahead, 42.88 to 42.97. In the final, however, long jump gold medalist Heide Rosendahl began the anchor leg with a one-meter advantage and raced flat-out to hold off Renate Stecher, who had won both the 100 meters and 200 meters earlier in the games.

1976 Montreal T: 10, N: 10, D: 7.31. WR: 42.50 (GDR—Maletzki, Stecher, Heinich, Eckert)

1. GDR	Marlies Oelsner, Renate Stecher, Carla Bodendorf, Bärbel Eckert	42.55	OR
2. GER	Elvira Possekel, Inge Helten, Annegret Richter, Annegret Kroniger	42.59	
3. SOV	Tetyana Prorochenko, Lyudmila Maslakova [Zharkova], Nadezhda Besfamilnaya, Vera Anisimova	43.09	
4. CAN	Margaret Howe, Patty Loverock, Joanne McTaggart, Marjorie Bailey	43.17	
5. AUS	Barbara Wilson, Deborah Wells, Denise Robertson, Raelene Boyle	43.18	
6. JAM	Leleith Hodges, Rose Allwood, Carol Cummings, Jacqueline Pusey	43.24	
7. USA	Martha Watson, Evelyn Ashtord, Debra Armstrong, Chandra Cheeseborough	43.35	
8. GBR	Wendy Clarke, Denise Ramsden, Sharon Colyear, Andrea Lynch	43.79	

The 200 meters champion, Bärbel Eckert, made up a one-meter deficit on the anchor leg to win by a foot. The East German victory brought Renate Stecher's Olympic medal total to six: three gold, two silver, and one bronze.

1980 Moscow T: 8, N: 8, D: 8.1. WR: 41.85 (GDR—Müller, Wöckel [Eckert], Auerswald, Göhr [Oelsner])

1. GDR	Romy Müller, Bärbel Wöckel [Eckert], Ingrid Auerswald, Marlies Göhr [Oelsner]	41.60	WR
2. SOV/RUS	Vera Komisova, Lyudmila Maslakova [Zharkova], Vera Anisimova, Natalya Bochina	42.10	
3. GBR	Heather Hunte, Kathryn Smallwood, Beverley Goddard, Sonia Lannaman	42.43	
4. BUL	Sofka Popova, Liliana Panayotova, Maria Shishkova, Galina Encheva	42.67	
5. FRA	Veronique Grandrieux, Chantal Rega, Raymonde Naigre, Emma Sulter	42.84	
6. JAM	Leleith Hodges, Jacqueline Pusey, Rosie Allwood, Merlene Ottey	43.19	
7. POL	Lucyna Langer, Elzbieta Satchurska, Zofia Bielczyk, Grazyna Rabsztyn	43.59	

DNF: SWE: Linda Haglund, Lena Moller, Ann-Louise Skoglund, Helena Pihl

Unusually poor baton passing failed to prevent the East Germans from winning by five meters and breaking their own world record.

1984 Los Angeles T: 11, N: 11, D: 8.11. WR: 41.53 (GDR—Gladisch, Koch, Auerswald, Göhr [Oelsner])

1. USA	Alice Brown, Jeanette Bolden, Chandra Cheeseborough, Evelyn Ashford	41.65
2. CAN	Angela Bailey, Marita Payne, Angella Taylor, France Gareau	42.77
3. GBR	K. Simmone Jacobs, Kathryn Cook [Smallwood], Beverley Callender [Godard], Heather Oakes [Hunte]	43.11
4. FRA	Rose-Aimée Bacoul, Liliane Gaschet, Marie France Coval, Raymonde Naigre	43.15
5. GER	Edith Oker, Michaela Schabinger, Heide-Elke Gaugel, Ute Thimm	43.57
6. BAH	Eldece Clarke, Pauline Davis, Debbie Greene, Oralee Fowler	44.18
7. TRI	Janice Bernard, Gillian Forde, Ester Hope-Washington, Angela Williams	44.23

8. JAM	Juliette Cuthbert, Grace Jackson, Veronica Findlay, Merlene Ottey-Page, [Janet Burke]	53.54

1988 Seoul T: 19, N: 19, D: 10.1. WR: 41.37 (GDR—Gladisch, Reiger, Auerswald, Göhr [Oelsner])

1. USA	Alice Brown, Sheila Echols, D. Florence Griffith Joyner, Evelyn Ashford [Dannette Young]	41.98
2. GDR	Silke Möller [Gladisch], Kerstin Behrendt, Ingrid Lange [Auerswald], Marlies Göhr [Oelsner]	42.09
3. SOV/RUS	Lyudmila Kondratyeva, Galina Malchugina, Marina Zhirova, Natalya Pomoshchnikova	42.75
4. GER	Sabine Richter, Ulrike Sarvari, Andrea Thomas, Ute Thimm	42.76
5. BUL	Tzvetanka Ilieva, Valia Demireva, Nadezhda Georgieva, Yordanka Donkova	43.02
6. POL	Joanna Smolarek, Jolanta Janota, Ewa Pisiewicz, Agnieszka Siwek	43.93
7. FRA	Françoise Leroux, Muriel Leroy, Laurence Bily, Patricia Girard	44.02

DNS: JAM: Ethlyn Tate, Grace Jackson, Juliet Cuthbert, Merlene Ottey, [Viviene Spence, Laurel Johnson]

In the semifinals, Evelyn Ashford, running the anchor leg, almost took off too quickly to receive the baton from Florence Griffith Joyner. In the final, Ashford overcompensated. Although Griffith Joyner reached her in first place, by the time Ashford achieved a tenuous grip on the baton, she trailed her rival of 12 years, Marlies Göhr, as well as Natalya Pomoshchnikova. Pomoshchnikova passed Göhr but then pulled a hamstring muscle 40 meters from the finish. She still managed to hobble across the line in third place. Meanwhile, Ashford was tearing up the track. She passed Göhr 20 meters before the finish and won by 1 meter to gain her third Olympic gold medal.

The Jamaican team qualified for the final but was forced to withdraw because of an injury to Merlene Ottey.

1992 Barcelona T: 14, N: 14, D: 8.8. WR: 41.37 (GDR—Gladisch, Reiger, Auerswald, Göhr [Oelsner])

1. USA	Evelyn Ashford, Esther Jones, Carlette Guidry, Gwendolyn Torrence, [Michelle Finn]	42.11
2. RUS	Olga Bogoslovskaya, Galina Malchugina, Marina Trandenkova, Irma Privalova	42.16
3. NGR	Beatrice Utondu, Faith Idehen, Christy Opara Thompson, Mary Onyali	42.81
4. FRA	Patricia Girard, Odiah Sidibe, Laurence Bily, Marie-José Pérec	42.85
5. GER	Andrea Philipp, Silke Knoll, Andrea Thomas, Sabine Günther	43.12
6. AUS	Melissa Moore, Melinda Gainsford, Kathleen Sambell, Kerry Johnson	43.77

DNF: CUB: Eusebia Riquelme Terrazón, Aliuska López, Idalmis Bonne Rauseauk, Liliana Allen Doll; JAM: Michele Freeman, Juliet Cuthbert, Dahlia Duhaney, Merlene Ottey

Nigerian Team, 1992

The 4 × 100-meter relay team celebrate their bronze medal in 1992.

Torrence, the United States anchor, took the baton one meter behind Privalova, ran her down, and won by one-half meter. Ashford brought her career total to four gold medals and one silver. The Jamaican team, medal favorites, were thwarted again when Juliet Cuthbert pulled a hamstring mid-race.

1996 Atlanta T: 22, N: 22, D: 8.3. WR: 41.37 (GDR—Gladisch, Reiger, Auerswald, Göhr [Oelsner])

1. USA	Chryste Gaines, Y. Gail Devers, Inger Miller, Gwendolyn Torrence, [Carlette Guidry]	41.95
2. BAH	Eldece Clarke, Chandra Sturrup, Sevatheda Fynes, Pauline Davis, [Debbie Ferguson]	42.14
3. JAM	Michelle Freeman, Juliet Cuthbert, Nikole Mitchell, Merlene Ottey, [Gillian Russell, Andria Lloyd]	42.24
4. RUS	Yekaterina Leshchova, Galina Malchugina, Natlya Voronova, Irina Privalova	42.27
5. NGR	Chioma Ajunwa, Mary Tombiri-Shirey, Christy Opara-Thompson, Mary Onyali	42.56
6. FRA	Sandra Citte, Odiah Sidibe, Patricia Girard-Leno, Marie-José Pérec, [Delphine Combe]	42.76
7. AUS	Sharon Cripps, Kylie Hanigan, Lauren Hewitt, Jodi Lambert	43.70
8. GBR	Angie Thorp, Marcia Richardson, Simmone Jacobs, Katharine Merry	43.93

The Bahamian women actually held a slight lead over the US team after two runners, but third leg Inger Miller put the US in front and Gwen Torrence extended the margin. Miller's gold medal completed the set for her family: her father, Lennox Miller, won a silver in the 1968 100 meters and a bronze in 1972. The US victory was expected, but the performance by the women from the Bahamas was a surprise. Never before had such a small nation (population 275,000) earned a medal in a team event.

2000 Sydney T: 25, N: 25, D: 9.30. WR: 41.37 (GDR—Gladisch, Reiger, Auerswald, Göhr [Oelsner])

1. BAH	Sevatheda Fynes, Chandra Sturrup, Pauline Davis-Thompson, Debbie Ferguson [Eldece Clarke-Lewis]	41.95
2. JAM	Tanya Lawrence, Veronica Campbell, Beverly McDonald, Merlene Ottey [Merlene Frazer]	42.13
3. USA	Chryste Gaines, Torri Edwards, Nanceen Perry, Marion Jones* [Passion Richardson]	42.20
4. FRA	Linda Ferga, Muriel Hurtis, Fabe Dia, Christine Arron [Sandra Citté]	42.42
5. RUS	Natalya Ignatova, Marina Trandenkova, Irina Khabarova, Natalya Voronova [Marina Kislova]	43.02
6. GER	Gabi Rockmeier, Sabrina Mulrain, Andrea Philipp, Marion Wagner	43.11
7. NGR	Glory Alozie, Benedicta Ajudua, Mercy Nku, Mary Onyali-Omagbemi	44.05
8. CHN	Zeng Xiujun, Liu Xiaomei, Qin Wangping, Li Xuemei	44.87

*Marion Jones was stripped of her medal in 2007.

At the medalists' press conference following the women's 100 meters, Pauline Davis of the Bahamas turned to Marion Jones of the United States and said, "We are only a small country with 270,000 people, so small that you can hardly find us on the map. So what does it tell you about our nation that we had three women in the final of the 100 meters? We have never been given the credit we deserve collectively despite all the titles we have won [i.e. 1996 Olympics silver and 1999 world championships gold], but I am telling you Marion, that is just going to make our victory all the sweeter when it comes. We are going to give you one hell of a race."

Davis wasn't kidding. The Bahamians beat the United States in the semifinals 42.42 to 42.82. Jamaica won the second semi in 42.15. In the final, the poorly prepared Americans put themselves out with sloppy passing on two of the three exchanges. Meanwhile, the Bahamians led from the start, concluded three prefect passes and beat the Jamaicans by about two and a half meters. The anchor for Jamaica was 40-year-old Merlene Ottey, who became the first female runner to compete in six Olympics. Ottey was a controversial addition to the Jamaican team. In 1999 she was suspended for a doping violation, but a year later an IOC arbitration panel lifted the suspension a year early and she qualified for the Jamaican relay lineup. However other Jamaican runners protested when Ottey was selected as one of their nation's three entries in the 100 meters event even though she only placed fourth at the Jamaican Olympic trials. Ottey missed a medal in the 100 by only one one-hundredth of a second and then ran a strong leg in the relay to earn her eighth career medal (3 silver and 5 bronze), the most ever won by a woman in track and field.

In 2007, the IOC disqualified the US squad after Marion Jones admitted to having used steroids in the months leading up to the Sydney Olympics. However, in July 2010, the Court of Arbitration for sport modified the IOC's decision and reinstated Jones' relay teammates in the 4 × 100 meters and 4 × 400 meters events.

2004 Athens T: 16, N: 16, D: 8.27. WR: 41.37 (GDR—Gladisch, Reiger, Auerswald, Göhr [Oelsner])

1. JAM	Tanya Lawrence, Sherone Simpson, Aleen Bailey, Veronica Campbell, [Beverly McDonald]	41.73
2. RUS	Olga Fyodorova, Yuliya Tabakova, Irina Khabarova, Larisa Kruglova	42.27
3. FRA	Véronique Mang, Muriel Hurtis, Sylviane Felix, Felix Arron	42.54
4. BAH	Timicka Clarke, Chandra Sturrup, Shandria Brown, Debbie Ferguson	42.69
5. BLR	Yuliya Nesterenko, Natalya Safronnikova, Yelena Nevmerzhitskaya, Oksana Dragun	42.94
6. BEL	Katleen De Caluwé, Lien Huyghebaert, Elodie Ouédraogo, Kim Gevaert	43.11
7. NGR	Gloria Kemasoude, Mercy Nku, Oludamola Osayomi, Endurance Ojokolo	43.42

DNF: USA: Angela Williams, Marion Jones, Lauryn Williams, LaTasha Colander-Richardson

The US team underwent late changes after the Olympic Trials, when rising star Torri Edwards was given a two-year ban following a positive doping test and Gail Devers opted to focus on individual events. The revised team included three-time gold medalist Marion Jones, whose career had been rocked by scandal after her name was mentioned in the BALCO doping trial. Controversial and makeshift though it may have been, the US team was fast, recording a 41.67 in Munich three weeks before the Olympics, the fastest time in the world since 1997. Clear favorites for the gold, the US recorded another 41.67 in their qualifying heat, the fastest preliminary time in Olympic history. Russia led the other semifinal, finishing .08 seconds ahead of Jamaica. In the final, Jamaica's Tanya Lawrence led after the first leg, with the US a close second, followed by Russia. Jones, running the second leg an hour after competing in the long jump final, held her ground, but was unable to make up any distance on Jamaica's Sherone Simpson. Disaster struck for the Americans on their second handoff, when Lauryn Williams started a bit early and Jones struggled for breath too soon. Stretching herself as far as possible, Jones attempted two swipes before she could get the baton into Williams' flailing hand, but by that time Williams had left the passing zone. With the

US out of the running, the race for gold came down to Jamaica and Russia. Aleen Bailey gave Jamaica a one-meter lead after the third leg, and anchor Veronica Campbell, who had already won bronze in the 100 meters and gold in the 200 meters, pulled away for the victory.

2008 Beijing T: 16, N: 16, D: 8.22. WR: 41.37 (GDR–Gladisch, Reiger, Auerswald, Göhr [Oelsner])

1. RUS	Yevgeniya Polyakova, Aleksandra Fedoriva, Yuliya Gushchina, Yuliya Chermoshanskaya	42.31
2. BEL	Olivia Borlée, Hanna Mariën, Elodie Ouédraogo, Kim Gevaert	42.54
3. NGR	Franca Idoko, Gloria Kemasoude, Halimat Ismaila, Damola Osayomi, [Agnes Osazuwa]	43.04
4. BRA	Rosemar Coelho Neto, Lucimar de Moura, Thaissa Presti, Rosangela Santos	43.14
5. GER	Anne Möllinger, Verena Sailer, Cathleen Tschirch, Marion Wagner	43.28

DNF: GBR (Jeannette Kwakye, Montell Douglas, Emily Freeman, Emma Ania); JAM (Shelly-Ann Fraser, Sherone Simpson, Kerron Stewart, Veronica Campbell-Brown, [Sheri-Ann Brooks, Aleen Bailey])
DISQ: POL (Ewelina Klocek, Daria Korczy ska, Dorota J drusi ska, Joanna Kocielnik, [Marta Jeschke])

After a botched pass took them out of the 2004 Olympics, the United States had returned to the top in the 4 × 100-meter relay. US squads won both the 2005 and 2007 world championship titles.

Despite the US championship record, the gold medal seemed destined for the Jamaican squad, which included Veronica Campbell-Brown, who had won the 200 meters the day before the relay final and was the reigning 100 meters world champion, and Shelly-Ann Fraser, Sherone Simpson and Kerron Stewart, who had gone 1-2-3 in the 100 meters five days earlier.

The expected match-up never materialized, however. In the first heat of the first round, Americans Torri Edwards and Lauryn Williams botched the final exchange and the US team was disqualified. The dropped pass occurred just 30 minutes after the US men's team dropped the baton during their qualifying heat and were also eliminated.

With the US out of the running, Jamaica seemed the sure bet for gold. They won their first-round heat easily, finishing in 42.24 seconds to advance to the final.

In the final, 100 meters gold medalist Fraser gave Jamaica a clear lead after the first leg, with Simpson expanding the margin in the second leg. But disaster struck during the second handoff when Stewart started running early and failed to get a grip on the baton before leaving the passing zone. Suddenly, the overwhelming favorites were out of the race. With Jamaica gone, the Russian squad powered to a decisive win over Belgium, whose squad members became the first Belgian women to win Olympic track and field medals. Nigeria edged out Brazil for third, while Great Britain failed to finish after another botched pass, and Poland was also disqualified for passing out of the zone.

According to lead-off runner Yevgeniya Polyakova, the Russian coach gave them a traditional Russian-style encouragement before the race, telling them "You can't get anything." The team answered back, "God damn you."

4 × 400-METER RELAY

1896–1968 not held

1972 Munich T: 14, N: 14, D: 9.10. WR: 3:28.8 (GDR—Käsling, Seidler, Zehrt, Rohde)

1. GDR	Dagmar Käsling, Rita Kühne, Helga Seidler, Monika Zehrt	3:23.0	WR	(3:22.95)
2. USA	Mable Fergerson, Madeline Manning, Cheryl Toussaint, Kathy Hammond	3:25.2		(3:25.15)
3. GER	Anette Rückes, Inge Bödding, Hildegard Falck, Rita Wilden	3:26.5		(3:26.51)
4. FRA	Martine Duvivier, Colette Besson, Bernadette Martin, Nicole Duclos	3:27.5		(3:27.52)
5. GBR	Verona Bernard, Janet Simpson, Janette Roscoe, Rosemary Stirling	3:28.7		(3:28.74)
6. AUS	Alison Rose-Edwards, Raelene Boyle, Cheryl Peasley, Charlene Rendina	3:28.8		(3.28.84)
7. FIN	Marika Eklund, Pirjo Wilmi, Tuula Rautanen, Mona-Lisa Strandvall	3:29.4		(3:29.44)
8. SOV	Lyubov Runtso, Olga Syrovatskaya, Natalya Chistyakova, Nadezhda Kolesnikova	3:31.9		

1976 Montreal T: 11, D: 7.31. WR: 3:23.0 (GDR—Käsling, Kühne, Seidler, Zehrt)

1. GDR	Doris Maletzki, Brigitte Rohde, Ellen Streidt, Christina Brehmer	3:19.23	WR
2. USA	Debra Sapenter, Sheila Ingram, Pamela Jiles, Rosalyn Bryant	3:22.81	
3. SOV	Inta Klimoviča, Lyudmyla Aksenova, Natalya Sokolova, Nadezhda Ilyina	3:24.24	
4. AUS	Judith Canty, Verna Burnard, Charlene Rendina, Bethanie Nail	3:25.56	
5. GER	Claudia Steger, Dagmar Fuhrmann, Elke Barth, Rita Wilden	3:25.71	
6. FIN	Marika Lindholm, Pirjo Häggman [Wilmi], Mona-Lisa Pursiainen [Strandvall], Riita Salin	3:25.87	
7. GBR	Elizabeth Barnes, Gladys Taylor, Verona Elder [Bernard], Donna Murray	3:28.01	
8. CAN	Margaret Stride, Joyce Yakubowich, Rachelle Campbell, Yvonne Saunders	3:28.91	

The remarkable East German women won by almost 30 meters.

1980 Moscow T: 11, N: 11, D: 8.1. WR: 3:19.23 (GDR—Maletzki, Rohde, Streidt, Brehmer)

1. SOV	Tetyana Prorochenko, Tatyana Goistchik, Nina Zyuskova, Irma Nazarova, [Olga Mineyeva, Lyudmila Chernoval]	3:20.2	(3:20.12)
2. GDR	Gabriele Löwe, Barbara Krug, Christina Lathan [Brehmer], Marita Koch	3:20.4	(3:20.35)
3. GBR	Linsey MacDonald, Michelle Probert, Joslyn Hoyte-Smith, Donna Hartley [Murray], [Janine Macgregor]	3:27.5	
4. ROM	Iboia Korodi, Niculina Lazarciuc, Maria Samungi, Elena Tarita	3:27.7	
5. HUN	Irén Orosz, Judit Forgacs, Éva Toth, Ilona Pál, [Ibolya Petrika]	3:27,9	
6. POL	Grażyna Oliszewska, Elżbieta Katolik-Skowrońska, Jolanta Januchta, Malgorzata Dunecka	3:27.9	
7. BEL	Lea Alaerts, Regine Berg, Anne Michel, Rosine Wallez	3:31.6	

DNF: BUL: Svobodka Damianova, Rossitza Stamenova, Milena Andonova, Bonka Dimova

The defeat of the East German 4 × 400-meter relay team was a major upset, but it took an unusual set of circumstances to produce the result. Olympic rules at the time stated that the same athletes who ran in the heats had to run in the final, unless official certificates could be produced proving that they were medically unfit to run. The USSR came up with two such certificates to replace Olga Mineyeva and Lyudmila Chernova with two fresh runners—Nina Zyuskova and Irma Nazarova, who had finished fifth and fourth respectively in the individual 400 meters event. At the beginning of the third leg, East Germany's Christina Lathan shot ahead of Zyuskova, but the Soviet runner pushed back in front as Lathan stepped on the curb and lost her rhythm. Nazarova took over with a lead of about 10 meters, but 400 meters champion Marita Koch slowly but surely closed the gap. As they entered the final straight it looked as if Koch would move ahead. However Nazarova, inspired by the wildly cheering hometown crowd of 100,000, managed to hold off Koch's challenge and win by one meter.

1984 Los Angeles T: 10, N: 10, D: 8.11. WR: 3:15.92 (GDR—Walther, Busch, Rübsam, Koch)

1. USA	Lillie Leatherwood, Sherri Howard, Valerie Brisco-Hooks, Chandra Cheeseborough, [Diane Dixon, Denean Howard]	3:18.29	OR
2. CAN	Charmaine Crooks, Jillian Richardson, Molly Killingbeck, Marita Payne, [Dana Wright]	3:21.21	
3. GER	Heike Schulte-Mattler, Ute Thimm, Heide-Elke Gaugel, Gaby Bussmann, [Christina Sussiek, Nicole Leistenschneider]	3:22.98	
4. GBR	Michelle Scutt [Probert], Helen Barnett, Gladys Taylor, Joslyn Hoyte-Smith	3:25.51	
5. JAM	Ilrey Oliver, Cynthia Green, Cathy Rattray, Grace Jackson, [Andrea Thomas]	3:27.51	
6. ITA	Patrizia Lombardo, Cosetta Compana, Marisa Masullo, Erica Rossi, [Giuseppina Ciruli]	3:30.82	
7. IND	M.D. Valsamma, Vandana Rao, Kurisingal "Shiny" Abraham, Pilavullakandi "PT" Usha	3:32.49	

DNS: PUR: Evelyn Mathieu, Madeline de Jesus, Angelita Lind, Marie Lande Mathieu, [Margaret de Jesus]

Valerie Brisco-Hooks earned her third gold medal of the Los Angeles Games, while Chandra Cheeseborough won two gold medals in one hour, becoming the first athlete of either sex to win golds in both Olympic relays. The Puerto Rican coach refused to let his team take part in the final when he discovered that the woman who ran the second leg for the Puerto Ricans in their qualifying heat was not team member Madeline de Jesus, but her twin sister Margaret. After being injured in the long jump, Madeline had asked her sister, who was in Los Angeles as a spectator, to take her place in the relay.

1988 Seoul T: 13, N: 13, D: 10.1. WR: 3:15.92 (GDR—Walther, Busch, Rübsam, Koch)

1. SOV	Tatyana Ledovskaya, Olga Nazarova, Mariya Pinihina, Olha Bryzhina, [Lyudmila Dzhigalova]	3:15.17	WR
2. USA	Denean Howard-Hill, Diane Dixon, Valerie Brisco, D. Florence Griffith Joyner, [Lillie Leatherwood, Sherri Howard]	3:15.51	
3. GDR	Dagmar Neubauer [Rübsam], Kirsten Emmelmann, Sabine Busch, Petra Müller, [Grit Breuer]	3:18.29	
4. GER	Ute Thimm, Helga Arendt, Andrea Thomas, Gudrun Abt, [Michaela Schabinger, Gisela Kinzel]	3:22.49	
5. JAM	Sandi Richards, Andrea Thomas, Cathy Rattray-Williams, Sharon Powell, [Marcia Tate]	3:23.13	
6. GBR	Linda Keough, Jennifer Stoute, Angela Piggford, Sally Gunnell, [Janet Smith]	3:26.89	
7. FRA	Fabienne Ficher, Nathalie Simon, Nadine Debois, Evelyne Elien	3:29.37	

DNF: CAN: Charmaine Crooks, Molly Killingbeck, Marita Payne-Wiggins, Jillian Richardson, [Esmie Lawrence]

Running the third leg, Valerie Brisco of the United States cut a Soviet lead of about 8 meters down to 2. The anchor leg pitted 400-meter gold medalist Olha Bryzhina against Florence Griffith Joyner, who had won her third gold medal only 40 minutes earlier in the 4 × 100-meter relay. Griffith Joyner, who had never before run a 4 × 400-meter relay in an international meet, tucked in behind Bryzhina and chased the Soviet champion around the track. Although Griffith Joyner ran the fastest split of any of the US runners, Bryzhina maintained her 2-meter lead all the way to the finish line.

1992 Barcelona T: 14, N: 14, D: 8.8. WR: 3:15.17 (SOV—Ledovskaya, Nazarova, Pinigina, Bryzhina)

1. SOV	Yelena Ruzina, Lyudmila Dzhigalova, Olga Nazarova, Olha Bryzhina, [Marina Shmonina, Lilia Nurutdinova]	3:20.20
2. USA	Natasha Kaiser, Gwendolyn Torrence, Jearl Miles, Rochelle Stevens, [Denean Hill, Dannette Young]	3:20.92
3. GBR	Phylis Smith, Sandra Douglas, Jennifer Stoute, Sally Gunnell	3:24.23
4. CAN	Rosey Edeh, Charmaine Crooks, Camille Noel, Jillian Richardson, [Karen Clarke]	3:25.20
5. JAM	Catherine Scott, Cathy Rattray Williams, Juliet Campbell, Sandi Richards, [Claudine Williams]	3:25.68
6. GER	Uta Rohländer, Heike Meissner, Linda Kisabaka, Anja Rücker	3:26.37
7. AUS	Catherine Freeman, Susan Andrews, Renee Poetschka, Michelle Lock	3:26.42
8. POR	Marta Moreira, Lucrécia Jardim, Elsa Amaral, Eduarda Coelho	3:36.85

Gwen Torrence brought the United States from third to first place on the second leg, giving Jearl Miles a lead of three meters. Olga Nazarova pulled almost even at the final exchange. Bryzhina tucked in behind Stevens for the first 250 meters of the last lap. She tried to pass her entering the final curve, found it difficult, waited, then shot by 60 meters from the finish to win by five meters. The following year, three of the six members of the team of ex-Soviets, Shmonina, Dzhigalova, and Nurutdinova, tested positive for steroids and were given suspensions.

1996 Atlanta T: 14, N: 14, D: 8.3. WR: 3:15.17 (SOV—Ledovskaya, Nazarova, Pinigina, Bryzhina)

1. USA	Rochelle Stevens, Maicel Malone, Kim Graham, Jearl Miles, [Linetta Wilson]	3:20.91
2. NGR	Olabisi Afolabi, Fatima Yusuf, Charity Opara-Thompson, Falilat Ogunkoya	3:21.04
3. GER	Uta Rohländer, Linda Kisabaka, Anja Rücker, Grit Breuer	3:21.14
4. JAM	Merlene Frazer, Sandie Richards, Juliet Campbell, Deon Hemmings, [Tracy Barnes, Inez Turner]	3:21.69
5. RUS	Tatyana Chebykina, Svetlana Goncharenko, Yekaterina Kulikova, Olga Kotlyarova	3:22.22
6. CUB	Idalmis Bonne Rosseaux, Julia Duporty Torres, Surella Morales Rosillo, Ana Fidelia Quirot Moret	3:25.85
7. CZE	Nadžda Koštovalová, Ludmila Formanová, Helena Fuchsová, Hana Benešová	3:26.99
8. FRA	Francine Landre, Viviane Dorsile, Evelyne Elien, Elsa De Vassoigne	3:28.46

Olabisi Afolabi and Fatima Yusuf gave Nigeria the lead after 800 meters. When Kim Graham began the third leg for the United States, she was in third place, about seven meters off the pace. She passed Yekaterina Kulikova of Russia in the backstretch, but still trailed Charity Opara by six meters entering the final turn. She made up five meters in the turn and took a five-meter lead of her own before handing over to Jearl Miles. Falilat Ogunkoya, anchoring for Nigeria, ran the fastest leg of the race. Three meters behind at the beginning of the homestretch, she closed to Miles' shoulder, but could get no closer.

2000 Sydney T: 21, N: 21, D: 9.30. WR: 3:15.17 (SOV—Ledovskaya, Nazarova, Pinigina, Bryzhina)

1. USA	Jearl Miles-Clark, Monique Hennagan, Marion Jones*, LaTasha Colander-Richardson, [Andrea Anderson]	3:22.62
2. JAM	Sandie Richards, Catherine Scott-Pomales, Deon Hemmings, Lorraine Graham [Charmaine Howell, Michelle Burgher]	3:23.25
3. RUS	Yuliya Sotnikova, Svetlana Goncharenko, Olga Kotlyarova, Irina Privalova, [Olesya Zykina, Nataliya Nazarova]	3:23.46
4. NGR	Olabisi Afolabi, Charity Opara-Thompson, Rosemary Okafor, Falilat Ogunkoya, [Doris Jaob]	3:23.80
5. AUS	Nova Peris-Kneebone, Tamsyn Lewis, Melinda Gainsford-Taylor, Cathy Freeman, [Susan Andrews, Jana Pittman]	3:23.81
6. GBR	Natasha Danvers, Donna Fraser, Allison Curbishley, Katharine Merry, [Helen Frost]	3:25.67
7. CZE	Jitka Burianová, Hana Benesová, Lenka Ficková, Helena Fuchsová	3:29.17
8. CUB	Zulia Calatayud, Daysi Duporte, Idalmis Bonne, Daimi Pernia	3:29.47

*Marion Jones was stripped of her medal in 2007.

The final quickly evolved into a duel between Jamaica and the United States. Jamaica held a narrow lead at both the first and second handovers. Marion Jones ran the third leg for the Americans . . . less than two hours after running an unsatisfying anchor leg in the 4 × 100-meter relay. This time, Jones turned up the heat in the backstretch and turned over a 15-meter lead to LaTasha Colander-Richardson. Colander-Richardson had to hold off not only Lorraine Graham of Jamaica, but 400-meter champion Cathy Freeman of Australia and 400-meter hurdles champion Irina Privalova. Colander-Richardson tied up halfway down the homestretch, but held on to win by five meters. Freeman's 49.4 matched Jones for the fastest leg of the race, but it was not enough to catch Graham and Privalova. Jones brought her Sydney medal total to five—three gold and two bronze. Jones, Colander-Richardson and second-leg Monique Hennagan were all graduates of the University of North Carolina.

In 2007, the IOC disqualified the US squad after Marion Jones admitted to having used steroids in the months leading up to the Sydney Olympics. However, in July 2010, the Court of Arbitration for sport modified the IOC's decision and reinstated Jones' relay teammates in the 4 × 100 meters and 4 × 400 meters events.

2004 Athens T: 16, N: 16, D: 8.28. WR: 3:15.17 (SOV—Ledovskaya, Nazarova, Pinigina, Bryzhina)

1. USA	DeeDee Trotter, Monique Henderson, Sanya Richards, Monique Hennagan, [Crystal Cox, Moushaumi Robinson]	3:19.01
2. RUS	Olesya Krasnomvets, Nataliya Nazarova, Olesya Zykina, Natalya Antyukh, [Natalya Ivanova, Tatyana Firova]	3:20.16
3. JAM	Novlene Williams, Michelle Burgher, Nadia Davy, Sandie Richards, [Ronetta Smith]	3:22.00
4. GBR	Donna Fraser, Catherine Murphy, Christine Ohuruogu, Lee McConnell, [Helen Karagouris]	3:25.12
5. POL	Zuzanna Radecka, Monika Bejnar, Małgorzata Pskit, Grażyna Prokopek	3:25.22
6. ROM	Angela Moroşanu, Alina Râpanu, Maria Rus, Ionela Târlea-Monolache	3:26.81
7. IND	Geetha Satti, Kalayathum Matthew Beenamol, Chitra Soman, Rajwinder Kaur	3:28.51
8. GRE	Hariklia Bouda, Khrysoula Goudenoudi, Dimitra Dova, Fani Halkia	3:45.70

The United States, Jamaica and Russia continued their dominance of the long relay, battling amongst themselves for the medals. Twenty-one-year-old DeeDee Trotter gave the US the early lead with a 49.8 leg. At the handoff, Russia held second place, just ahead of Jamaica. Monique Henderson put the US a full second ahead of Russia at the halfway mark. The third leg saw Sanya Richards steadily increase the US advantage over Russia with a 49.81 split, while Jamaica began to lose ground. Russian anchor Natalya Antyukh attempted a late challenge, but was unable to overtake Monique Hennagan, who cruised to the third consecutive American 4 × 400 Olympic victory. The US time of 3:19.01 was the first sub-3:20 women's relay time since 1993.

The slow time registered by the Greek team was the result of Khrysoula Goudenoudi stepping on teammate Dimitra Dova's shoe during the second exchange. Dova stepped off the track and readjusted her shoe before continuing.

2008 Beijing T: 16, N: 16, D: 8.23. WR: 3:15.17 (SOV–Ledovskaya, Nazarova, Pinigina, Bryzhina)

1. USA	Mary Wineberg, Allyson Felix, Monique Henderson, Sanya Richards, [Natasha Hastings]	3:18.54
2. RUS	Yuliya Gushchina, Lyudmila Litvinova, Tatyana Firova, Anastasiya Kapachinskaya, [Yelena Migunova, Tatyana Veshkurova]	3:18.82
3. JAM	Shericka Williams, Shereefa Lloyd, Rosemarie Whyte, Novlene Williams, [Bobby-Gaye Wilkins]	3:20.40
4. BLR	Anna Kozak, Irina Khlyustova, Ilona Usovich, Svetlana Usovich, [Yuliyana Yushchenko]	3:21.85
5. GBR	Christine Ohuruogu, Kelly Sotherton, Marilyn Okoro, Nicola Sanders	3:22.68
6. CUB	Roxana Díaz Sánchez, Zulia Calatayud Torres, Susana Clement Quezada, Indira Terrero Letuce	3:23.21
7. NGR	Joy Amechi Eze, Folashade Abugan, Oluoma Nwoke, A.J. Odumosu	3:23.74
8. GER	Jonna Tilgner, Sorina Nwachukwu, Florence Ekpo-Umoh, Claudia Hoffman	3:28.45

The US was the clear favorite in the event, having won the last three 4 × 400-meter Olympic events and the 2007 world championships. The US squad included two members from the 2004 gold medal-winning team, Sanya Richards and Monique Henderson, and three members of the 2007 world championship squad: Richards, Allyson Felix and Mary Wineberg.

Their main competition was expected to come from defending Olympic silver medalists Russia, who had also won the 2005 world championships after the US team was disqualified for running outside its lane during the preliminary round. Defending bronze medalists, and two-time consecutive world silver medalists, the Jamaicans were also considered medal contenders.

The first rounds of the men's and women's 4 × 400-meter relay events were held two days after both US squads had been eliminated from the 4 × 100-meter relays in the first rounds for dropping their batons. This time, the US qualified easily, beating Jamaica in their preliminary heat, with Russia finishing first in the other heat.

In the final, the US trailed Russia and Jamaica after the first leg by Mary Wineberg. Taking over the second leg, Allyson Felix tore past Jamaica's Shereefa Lloyd and Russia's Lyudmila Litvinova to take the lead, recording a 48.55-second split, the fastest of any runner in the final, and giving a 0.25 second advantage to Monique Henderson. The lead changed again in the third leg, as Russia's Tatyana Firova moved past Henderson going into the anchor leg. Sill stinging from her disappointing performance in the 400-meter event, in which she dropped from first to third place in the final 80 meters, Richards took her time moving up on Russia's Anastasia Kapachinskaya. Richards waited until the final 120 meters to make her move and then surged into the lead with 30 meters to go to give the United States the victory.

The medalists finished in the same order as the 2004 Olympics.

20,000-METER WALK

1896–1996 not held

2000 Sydney C: 57, N: 31, D: 9.28. WB: 1:25.28 (Tatyana Gudkova)

1. Wang Liping	CHN	1:29:05
2. Kjersti Tysse Plätzer	NOR	1:29:33
3. Maria Vasco	SPA	1:30:23
4. Erica Alfridi	ITA	1:31:25
5. Guadalupe Sánchez	MEX	1:31:33
6. Norica Cimpean	ROM	1:31:50
7. Kerry Junna-Saxby	AUS	1:32:02
8. Tatyana Gudkova	RUS	1:32:35

With four kilometers to go, it looked like a three-woman race. Reigning world champion Liu Hongyu led local favorite Jane Saville and 1996 Olympic 10-kilometer walk silver medalist Elisabeth Perrone of Italy. Kjersti Plätzer and Wang Liping trailed the three leaders by seven and eleven seconds. But as Liu, Saville and Perrone battled, their technique loosened. First Liu was given the red paddle. At the 17-kilometer mark, Perrone was disqualified. She thought it was a mistake, so she kept walking with Saville until she saw a red marker next to her name on the warning board. Saville entered the stadium tunnel with a safe 30-meter lead over Wang. Saville could already hear the cheers of the Australian crowd when, only 150 meters from the finish line, chief judge Lamberto Bacchi blocked her way and held up the red paddle. Grabbing her head in horror, Saville turned around and ran back out the entrance of the tunnel. Expecting the arrival of Saville, the stunned Australian crowd applauded politely as 24-year-old Wang crossed the finish line in first place.

2004 Athens C: 57, N: 35, D: 8.23. WB: 1:26:52 (Olympiada Ivanova)

1. Athanasia Tsoumeleka	GRE	1:29:12
2. Olimpiada Ivanova	RUS	1:29:16
3. Jane Saville	AUS	1:29:25
4. Margarita "Ryta" Turava	BLR	1:29:39
5. Melanie Seeger	GER	1:29:52
6. Elisa Rigaudo	ITA	1:29:57
7. María del Monte Vascó	SPA	1:30:06
8. Wang Liping	CHN	1:30:16

Olimpiada Ivanova led throughout most of the race, until local favorite Athanasia Tsoumeleka, cheered on by the throngs of Greeks lining the course, surged ahead at the 17th kilometer. Tsoumeleka, whose previous best was a seventh-place finish at the 2003 world championships, led throughout the 2-kilometer loop leading to the Olympic Stadium, with Olimpiada Ivanova close behind. Ivanova tried to pass Tsoumeleka outside the stadium, and managed to pull even briefly, but was unable to overtake her and dropped back to a frustrated second place. Jane Saville, who had been disqualified from the 2000 event in the tunnel of the Olympic Stadium, earned an emotional bronze medal. Ivanova's silver came three days before her 34th birthday. One year later, she won the 2005 world championships, setting a world record of 1:25.41.

As for Tsoumeleka, she finished ninth at the 2008 Olympics. However, a retest for the following year of a urine sample she provided two days before the Beijing Olympics showed a positive result for the banned blood-booster erythropoietin. Her 2008 results were expunged and she announced her immediate retirement from the sport.

2008 Beijing C: 48, N: 30, D: 8.21. WB: 1:25.41 (Olimpiada Ivanova)

1. Olga Kaniskina	RUS	1:26:31	OB
2. Kjersti Tysse-Plätzer	NOR	1:27:07	
3. Elisa Rigaudo	ITA	1:27:12	
4. Liu Hong	CHN	1:27:17	
5. María Vasco Pes Gallardo	SPA	1:27:25	
6. Beatriz Pascual Rodríguez	SPA	1:27:44	
7. Olive Loughnane	IRL	1:27:45	
8. Ana Cabecinha	POR	1:27:46	

Olga Kaniskina took up race walking at the age of 14, making her debut at the 1999 Russian championships. Her first prize was a box of candy after finishing in last place. Four years later she was spotted by coach Victor Chegin while competing at the Russian Junior Championships and invited to train at the Mordovian Race Walking Center in Saransk, the center of the Russian race walking world. In 2007 Kaniskina qualified for her first world championship, in Osaka, Japan. She and training partner Tatyana Shemyakina set the pace throughout the race and finished 1-2, ahead of Spain's María Vasco and 2000 Olympic silver medalist Kjersti Plätzer of Norway.

In early 2008 Kaniskina set her sights on breaking the world best set by compatriot and reigning Olympic silver medalist Olimpiada Ivanova at the 2005 world championships in Helsinki. Kaniskina recorded the fastest-ever time, 1:25.11, at the Russian national championships in February, but the time could not be ratified as a world record as there were no international judges present at the race. In May, at a World Cup race in Cheboksary, Russia, Kaniskina missed breaking the record by a single second.

The Olympic race was held in pouring rain. Although Ivanova appeared on the start list for Beijing, pain from an old skiing accident prevented her from competing. In her absence, 23-year-old Kaniskina took the lead from the start of the race and was never seriously challenged, going on to win by 36 seconds. In second place with two kilometers remaining, Plätzer held on to take silver, while Italy's Elisa Rigaudo took bronze. The top twelve finishers all broke the previous Olympic record of 1:29:05.

Kaniskina went on to dominate the event, winning the world championship in 2007, 2009 and 2011.

HIGH JUMP

1896–1924 not held

1928 Amsterdam C: 20, N: 9, D: 8.5. WR: 1.61, 5-3¼ (Carolina Gisolf)

		M	FT.-IN.
1. Ethel Catherwood	CAN	1.59	5-2½
2. Carolina Gisolf	HOL	1.56	5-1¼
3. Mildred Wiley	USA	1.56	5-1¼
4. Jean Shiley	USA	1.51	4-11½
5. Marjorie Clark	SAF	1.48	4-10¼
6. Helma Notte	GER	1.48	4-10¼
7. Inge Braumüller	GER	1.48	4-10¼
8. Catherine Maguire	USA	1.48	4-10¼

Ethel Catherwood was born in Hannah, North Dakota, and raised in Scott, Saskatchewan. Her family moved to the growing city of Saskatoon when she was 17 years old and it was there that her athletic abilities became apparent. When she first competed in Toronto in 1927 she caused a sensation, not only by setting national records in the high jump and javelin throw, but, dressed in a pure white uniform and a purple cloak, with her exceptional beauty. One reporter dubbed her "The Saskatoon Lily" and it was by that sobriquet that she became known. In Amsterdam, Catherwood became a favorite of the spectators and the photographers. During the three-hour competition she kept herself wrapped up in a big red blanket and didn't even take off her sweatsuit until the five-foot mark had been reached. Before each jump she would face the bar, smile and then go over. Her return to Saskatoon caused the largest celebration since the signing of the 1918 Armistice. She was presented with a $3000 education trust fund to be used to continue her piano studies. When asked about rumors that she had received offers to go to Hollywood, Catherwood replied, "I'd rather gulp poison than try my hand at motion pictures." However, she did move to the United States, eventually settling in San Francisco and marrying fellow Olympic high jump champion Harold Osborn. She did maintain her distaste for public attention. For the rest of her life she refused to talk to reporters and would not respond when invited to reunions or even when she was inducted into the Canadian Hall of Fame. Although she died in California on September 18, 1987, her death was not discovered in Canada until seven months later.

1932 Los Angeles C: 10, N: 6, D: 8.7. WR: 1.62, 5-3¾ (Carolina Gisolf)

		M	FT.-IN.	
1. Jean Shiley	USA	1.657	5-5¼	WR
2. Mildred "Babe" Didrikson	USA	1.657	5-5¼	WR
3. Eva Dawes	CAN	1.60	5-3	
4. Carolina Gisolf	HOL	1.58	5-2¼	
5. Marjorie Clark	SAF	1.58	5-2¼	
6. Annette Rogers	USA	1.58	5-2¼	
7. Helma Notte	GER	1.55	5-1	
8. Yuriko Hirohashi	JPN	1.49	4-10½	

Ethel Catherwood, 1928
"The Saskatoon Lily" won the high jump and the crowd.

Jean Shiley and Babe Didrikson had tied for first place in the US Olympic trials and they tied again in Los Angeles. Both women cleared 5 feet 5¼ inches but failed at 5 feet 6 inches. A jump-off was ordered, and both cleared a world record height of 5 feet 5¾ inches. At this point the judges intervened and declared that Didrikson's western-roll style caused her head to clear the bar before her body. This was deemed "diving" and ruled illegal. Deprived of her third gold medal, Babe was nonetheless given a share of the world record. Her jumping style was legalized not long afterward. Shiley wanted to try out for the US team in 1936, but was declared ineligible because she had once worked as a swimming instructor.

1936 Berlin C: 17, N: 12, D: 8.7. WR: 1.67, 5-5¾ (Jean Shiley, Mildred "Babe" Didriksen)

		M	FT.-IN.
1. Ibolya Csák	HUN	1.60	5-3
2. Dorothy Odam	GBR	1.60	5-3
3. Elfriede Kaun	GER	1.60	5-3
4. Herman "Dora" Ratjen	GER	1.58	5-2¼
5. Marguerite Nicolas	FRA	1.58	5-2¼
6. Francina "Fanny" Blankers-Koen	HOL	1.55	5-1
6. Doris Carter	AUS	1.55	5-1
6. Annette Rogers	USA	1.55	5-1

Ibolya Csák was Hungary's national champion in 1935 when she married and settled in as a housewife. However she kept in shape by chopping wood, shoveling snow and practicing gymnastics exercises. She returned to competition in 1936. At the Olympics, Csák was awarded first place after clearing 1.62 meters in a jump-off. If the current tie-breaking rules had been in force, 16-year-old Dorothy Odam would have won the gold medal. The German high jump entry was riddled with controversy. Gretel Bergmann, a German Jew, won the Olympic trials with a jump of 1.64 meters, but two weeks before the opening of the Games, she was told by the German Olympic Committee that, because of her "mediocre performance," she would not be allowed to compete. Her place was not filled. Fourth-place finisher Dora Ratjen was barred from competition in 1938, when it was announced that she was a hermaphrodite, a rare sexual group for which international athletics has made no provisions. In 1957, Ratjen revealed that she was really *Herman* Ratjen and that he had been ordered to pose as a woman by officials of the Nazi Youth Movement.

1948 London C: 19, N: 10, D: 8.7. WR: 1.71, 5-7¼ (Francina "Fanny" Blankers-Koen)

		M	FT.-IN.
1. Alice Coachman	USA	1.68	5-6 OR
2. Dorothy Tyler (Odam)	GBR	1.68	5-6 OR
3. Micheline Ostermeyer	FRA	1.61	5-3¼
4. Vinton Beckett	CAN	1.58	5-2¼
4. Doreen Dredge	CAN	1.58	5-2¼
6. Bertha Crowther	GBR	1.58	5-2¼
7. Iso Steinegger	AUT	1.55	5-1
8. Dora Gardner	GBR	1.55	5-1

Once again, Dorothy Odam, now Dorothy Tyler, lost a tie despite having fewer misses than the winner. This time Alice Coachman of Albany, Georgia, was awarded first place because she cleared the final height on her first try, while Tyler required a second attempt. Coachman was the first black woman from any country to win an Olympic gold medal. When Coachman returned to Georgia, a 175-mile motorcade in her honor was cheered by blacks and whites alike, but when she arrived at the Albany Municipal Auditorium for an official welcome, the audience was segregated and she was not allowed to speak. Four years later Coachman was chosen by Coca-Cola to become the first black female athlete to endorse an international consumer product. Bronze medalist

Alice Coachman, 1948

Coachman, the first black woman from any country to earn an Olympic gold medal, shares the victory platform for the 1948 high jump with Dorothy Tyler and Micheline Ostermeyer.

Micheline Ostermeyer had already won the shot put and discus.

1952 Helsinki C: 17, N: 10, D: 7.27. WR: 1.72, 5-7¾ (Sheila Lerwill)

		M	FT.-IN.
1. Esther Brand	SAF	1.67	5-5¾
2. Sheila Lerwill	GBR	1.65	5-5
3. Aleksandra Chudina	SOV/RUS	1.63	5-4¼
4. Thelma Hopkins	GBR	1.58	5-2¼
5. Olga Modrachová	CZE	1.58	5-2¼
6. Theodora Schenk-Solms	AUT	1.58	5-2¼
7. Nina Kossova	SOV/RUS	1.58	5-2¼
7. Dorothy Tyler (Odam)	GBR	1.58	5-2¼

1956 Melbourne C: 19, N: 12, D: 12.1. WR: 1.75, 5-8¼ (Iolanda Balaş)

		M	FT.-IN.
1. Mildred McDaniel	USA	1.76	5-9¼ WR
2. Thelma Hopkins	GBR	1.67	5-5¾
2. Maria Pissaryeva	SOV/RUS	1.67	5-5¾
4. Gunhild Larking	SWE	1.67	5-5¾
5. Iolanda Balaş	ROM	1.67	5-5¾
6. Michele Mason	AUS	1.67	5-5¾
7. Mary Donaghy	NZL	1.67	5-5¾
8. Hermina Geyser	SAF	1.64	5-4¼
8. Jiřina Vobořilová	CZE	1.54	5-4½

1960 Rome C: 23, N: 15, D: 9.8. WR: 1.86, 6-1¼ (Iolanda Balaş)

		M	FT.-IN.
1. Iolanda Balaş	ROM	1.85	6-0¾ OR
2. Jaroslawa Jóźwiakowska	POL	1.71	5-7¼
2. Dorothy Shirley	GBR	1.71	5-7¼
4. Galina Dolya	SOV/RUS	1.71	5-7¼
5. Taisa Chenchyk	SOV/UKR	1.68	5-6
6. Helen Frith	AUS	1.65	5-5
6. Inga-Briff Lorentzon	SWE	1.65	5-5
6. Frances Slaap	GBR	1.65	5-5

Few people have dominated an event as completely as Iolanda Balaş dominated the women's high jump. Following her fifth-place finish at the Melbourne Olympics, she won an incredible 140 consecutive competitions over the next ten and a half years. She set 14 world records and was the first woman to high-jump 6 feet. By the time a second woman, Michele Brown of Australia, had cleared that barrier, Balaş had done it in 46 different meets. On July 16, 1961, the 6-foot Balaş jumped 6 feet 3¼ inches, a height that wasn't beaten until September 4, 1971.

1964 Tokyo C: 27, N: 18, D: 10.15. WR: 1.91, 6-3¼ (Iolanda Balaş)

		M	FT.-IN.
1. Iolanda Balaş	ROM	1.90	6-2¾ OR
2. Michele Brown (Mason)	AUS	1.80	5-11
3. Taisa Chenchyk	SOV/UKR	1.78	5-10
4. Aida Dos Santos	BRA	1.74	5-8½
5. Dianne Gerace	CAN	1.71	5-7¼
6. Frances Slaap	GBR	1.71	5-7¼
7. Olga Pluic	YUG/SER	1.71	5-7¼
8. Eleanor Montgomery	USA	1.71	5-7¼

Iolanda Balaş, 1964

Balaş completely dominated the high jump between 1957 and 1967, setting fourteen world records and winning two Olympic gold medals

1968 Mexico City C: 24, N: 14, D: 10.17. WR: 1.91, 6-3¼ (Iolanda Balaş)

		M	FT.-IN.
1. Miloslava Režková	CZE	1.82	5-11½
2. Antonina Okorokova	SOV/RUS	1.80	5-10¾
3. Valentyna Kozyr	SOV/UKR	1.80	5-10¾
4. Jaroslava Valentová	CZE	1.78	5-10
5. Rita Schmidt	GDR	1.78	5-10
6. Maria Faithová	CZE	1.78	5-10
7. Karin Schulze	GDR	1.76	5-9¼
8. Ilona Gusenbauer	AUT	1.76	5-9¼

Eighteen-year-old Milena Režková was a popular winner. Not only was she a complete outsider who had improved her personal best by 6 inches since the beginning of the year and who jumped 5 inches over her own height, but she was a Czech who won a dramatic showdown against two women from the USSR. Her victory was gained on her third and final try at 5 feet 11½ inches. Had Režková missed, Okorokova would have won on the basis of fewer misses.

1972 Munich C: 40, N: 22, D: 9.4. WR: 1.92, 6-3½ (Ilona Gusenbauer)

		M	FT.-IN.
1. Ulrike Meyfarth	GER	1.92	6-3½ EWR
2. Yordanka Blagoyeva	BUL	1.88	6-2

3. Ilona Gusenbauer	AUT	1.88	6-2
4. Barbara Inkpen	GBR	1.85	6-0¾
5. Rita Schmidt	GDR	1.85	6-0¾
6. Sara Simeoni	ITA	1.85	6-0¾
7. Rosemarie Witschas	GDR	1.85	6-0¾
8. Deborah Brill	CAN	1.82	5-11½

If Režková's win in Mexico City was considered an upset, then the victory of 16-year-old Ulrike Meyfarth in Munich was more like a fairy tale. The 6-foot ½-inch Köln-Rodenkirchen schoolgirl, who had only finished third in the West German trials, jumped 2¾ inches higher than her pre-Olympic best. Blagoyeva appeared to have cleared the bar on her last attempt at 6 feet 2¾ inches and was already starting to put her sweatsuit back on, when the bar fell and the judges ruled a miss. The admirably neutral German audience jeered the decision, which was, however, entirely in keeping with the rules of the competition. Gusenbauer looked the other way as Meyfarth equaled the world record that the Austrian had set exactly one year earlier to the day. Three weeks later, Blagoyeva raised the world record to 6 feet 4½ inches. Ulrike Meyfarth is the youngest person of either sex to win an individual track and field gold medal in the Olympics.

1976 Montreal C: 35, N: 23, D: 7.28. WR: 1.96, 6-5¼ (Rosemarie Ackermann [Witschas])

		M	FT.-IN.
1. Rosemarie Ackermann (Witschas)	GDR	1.93	6-4 OR
2. Sara Simeoni	ITA	1.91	6-3¼
3. Yordanka Blagoyeva	BUL	1.91	6-3¼
4. Mária Mrachnová	CZE	1.89	6-2½
5. Joni Huntley	USA	1.89	6-2½
6. Tatyana Shlyahto	SOV/BLR	1.87	6-1½
7. Annette Tannander	SWE	1.87	6-1½
8. Cornelia Popa	ROM	1.87	6-1½

The qualifying rounds saw the surprising early elimination of Ulrike Meyfarth, Rita Kirst (Schmidt), Debbie Brill of Canada, and Vera Bradacová of Czechoslovakia, all of whom had cleared 6 feet 3 inches previously. Although the competition was won by the favorite, Rosemarie Ackermann, the field had such depth that 18 women cleared 6 feet and 13 were still in the running after three hours. On August 26, 1977, Ackermann, a shop clerk from Cottbus, became the first woman to jump two meters—9½ inches over her own head.

1980 Moscow C: 20, N: 13, D: 7.26. WR: 2.01, 6-7 (Sara Simeoni)

		M	FT.-IN.
1. Sara Simeoni	ITA	1.97	6-5½ OR
2. Urszula Kielan	POL	1.94	6-4¼
3. Jutta Kirst	GDR	1.94	6-4¼
4. Rosemarie Ackermann (Witschas)	GDR	1.91	6-3¼
5. Marina Sysoyeva	SOV/KYR	1.91	6-3¼
6. Christine Stanton	AUS	1.91	6-3¼
7. Andrea Reichstein	GDR	1.91	6-3¼
8. Cornelia Popa	ROM	1.88	6-2

The ever-popular Sara Simeoni had switched to high-jumping at the age of 12 after being told that she couldn't be a ballet dancer because she was too tall and her feet were too big. She lost six out of seven meets to Rosemarie Ackermann between 1973 and 1977. Then she beat her in a dramatic showdown at the European championships in Prague in August 1978, and the tide turned. In Moscow Simeoni recorded her first miss at 1.94, but cleared on her second attempt to earn the gold medal. Fifth-place finisher Marina Sysoyeva jumped 6 feet 4 inches earlier in the year to set a women's world record for jumping higher than one's own height—10¼ inches.

1984 Los Angeles C: 29, N: 18, D: 8.10. WR: 2.07, 6-9½ (Lyudmila Andonova)

		M	FT.-IN.
1. Ulrike Meyfarth	GER	2.02	6-7½ OR
2. Sara Simeoni	ITA	2.00	6-6¾
3. Joni Huntley	USA	1.97	6-5½
4. Maryse Ewanje-Épée	FRA	1.94	6-4¼
5. Deborah Brill	CAN	1.94	6-4¼
6. Vanessa Browne	AUS	1.94	6-4¼
7. Zheng Dazhen	CHN	1.91	6-3¼
8. D. Louise Ritter	USA	1.91	6-3¼

Twelve years after becoming the youngest Olympic track and field champion ever, Ulrike Meyfarth earned her second gold medal to become the *oldest* person to win an Olympic high jump competition. The largest woman in the field, at 6 feet 2 inches and 154 pounds, Meyfarth also became the only female track and field athlete besides Irena Szewińska to win gold medals twelve years apart. Three of the top five places in 1984 belonged to women who had been finalists in Munich in 1972.

1988 Seoul C: 24, N: 15, D: 9.30. WR: 2.09, 6-10¼ (Stefka Kostadinova)

		M	FT.-IN.
1. D. Louise Ritter	USA	2.03	6-8 OR
2. Stefka Kostadinova	BUL	2.01	6-7¼
3. Tamara Bykova	SOV/RUS	1.99	6-6¼
4. Olga Turchak	SOV/KAZ	1.96	6-5¼
5. Lyudmila Andonova	BUL	1.93	6-4
5. Galina Astafei	ROM	1.93	6-4
7. Christine Stanton	AUS	1.93	6-4
8. Diana Davies	GBR	1.90	6-2¾
8. Kim Hee-sun	KOR	1.90	6-2¾

Between 1985 and 1987 Stefka Kostadinova of Plovdiv, Bulgaria, won 73 of 77 meets and set three world records, the last at the 1987 world championships. By the time of the Seoul Olympics, she had cleared 6 feet 8 inches at 29 different meets, compared to 10 times for all other jumpers combined. She also owned 11 of the top 12 jumps in history. Although she had lost twice in late June, she had also won 19 meets in 1988, so she entered the Olympic competition as the prohibitive favorite.

Favored for second place was 30-year-old Louise Ritter, who grew up in the tiny Texas town of Red Oak. Ritter's injury-riddled career had seen many disappointments, including eighth-place finishes at the 1984 Olympics and the 1987 world championships. However she had also earned a bronze medal at the 1983 world championships and handed Kostadinova two of her three defeats in 1987.

Kostadinova and Ritter both cleared seven heights without a miss to knock out the rest of their opponents. But then they both missed all three attempts at 6 feet 8 inches, forcing a sudden-death jump-off. Kostadinova missed a fourth time at 6 feet 8 inches and it was Ritter's turn. The lanky Texan realized that this was probably her last chance for victory. "My hamstrings were about to fall off my legs," she would later explain in her thick drawl. Besides, she knew that Kostadinova was too good a competitor to miss again.

Ritter moved the start of her run-up back 1 foot, raced down the runway and leapt for all she was worth. She grazed the bar with her right thigh, but not hard enough to dislodge it, and the victory was hers.

1992 Barcelona C: 41, N: 26, D: 8.8. WR: 2.09, 6-10¼ (Stefka Kostadinova)

		M	FT.-IN.
1. Heike Henkel	GER	2.02	6-7½
2. Galina Astafei	ROM	2.00	6-6¾
3. Ioamnet Quintero Alvarez	CUB	1.97	6-5½
4. Stefka Kostadinova	BUL	1.94	6-4¼
5. Sigrid Kirchmann	AUT	1.94	6-4¼
6. Silvia Costa Acosta	CUB	1.94	6-4¼
7. Megumi Sato	JPN	1.91	6-3¼
8. Alison Inverarity	AUS	1.91	6-3¼

Competing in her third Olympics, world champion Heike Henkel did not begin jumping until 6 feet 3¼ inches (1.91 meters). At 6 feet 5¾ (1.97 meters) she faced unexpected problems. After missing twice, she cleared on her final attempt and seemed to regain confidence. Meanwhile, Galina Astafei, returning from a pregnancy sabbatical, cleared seven straight heights without a miss through 6 feet 6¾ inches (2 meters). At 6 feet 7½ inches (2.02 meters), Henkel went over on her first try while Astafei missed three times.

Henkel was married to two olympians, swimmer Rainer Henkel and decathlete Paul Meier.

1996 Atlanta C: 32, N: 24, D: 8.3. WR: 2.09, 6-10¼ (Stefka Kostadinova)

		M	FT.-IN.
1. Stefka Kostadinova	BUL	2.05	6-8¾ OR
2. Niki Bakogianni	GRE	2.03	6-8
3. Inha Babakova	UKR	2.01	6-7¼
4. Antonella Bevilacqua	ITA	1.99	6-6¼
5. Yelena Gulyayeva	RUS	1.99	6-6¼
6. Alina (Galina) Astafei	GER	1.96	6-5¼
6. Tatyana Motkova	RUS	1.96	6-5¼
6. Nele Zilinskiene	LIT	1.96	6-5¼

There were two eligibility controversies during the buildup to the Olympics. In 1992, Alina (then Galina) Astafei had earned the silver medal while representing her native Romania. The following year Astafei, whose brother Petr was a well-known martyr of the 1989 revolution, moved to Germany and refused to continue competing for Romania. She gained German citizenship in February 1996, but, although she had represented Germany at the 1995 world indoor championships (and won), she could not do so at the Olympics without the permission of the Romanian Olympic Committee. Amid rumors of a "donation" paid by a German corporate sponsor, in April the committee voted 4-3 to allow Astafei to represent Germany in Atlanta.

In May, Italy's Antonella Bevilacqua twice tested positive for ephedrine. Bevilacqua readily admitted to taking a Chinese herbal preparation which contained the ingredient Ma Huong, but claimed that she did not know that "Ma Huong" is the Chinese word for ephedra. The IAAF referred the case to arbitration to be held after the Olympics.

For the past ten years the dominant force in the women's high jump had been Stefka Kostadinova. She set three world records and won two world championships (1987 and 1995). She cleared 2.05 meters twenty times. The rest of the world's high jumpers had done it a total of five times. But for all her success, her Olympic results had only been second in 1988 and fourth in 1992.

The qualifying round was held during a downpour. Despite the adverse weather conditions, 14 women cleared 1.93 meters (6 feet 4 inches). Every one of them cleared it again two days later in the final. At 1.99 (6 feet 6¼ inches), Bevilacqua, Kostadinova and Inha Babakova went over at the first try. Niki Bakogianni, whose pre-Olympic best had been 1.97 (6 feet 5½ inches) missed once and then cleared, as did Yelena Gulyayeva. At 2.01 (6 feet 7 inches), Kostadinova and

Babakova maintained their perfect records. Bakogianni went over on her second try and the medalists were decided.

Kostadinova cleared 2.03 (6 feet 8 inches) with her first jump. Babakova missed all three times, but Bakogianni went over on her final attempt to set her third personal best of the evening. Kostadinova finally won the competition by clearing 2.05 meters (6 feet 8¾ inches) with her second try.

Bakogianni, who was 1.71 meters tall (5 feet 7¼ inches), set a record by jumping 32 centimeters (12½ inches) over her head.

In 2005, Kostadinova was elected President of the Bulgarian Olympic Committee, after then-President Ivan Slavkov was expelled from the IOC for corruption.

2000 Sydney C: 38, N: 27, D: 9.30. WR: 2.09, 6-10¼ (Stefka Kostadinova)

		M	FT.-IN.
1. Yelena Yelesina	RUS	2.01	6-7¼
2. Hestrie Cloete	SAF	2.01	6-7¼
3. Kajsa Bergqvist	SWE	1.99	6-6¼
3. Oana Pantelimon-Muşunoi	ROM	1.99	6-6¼
5. Inha Babakova	UKR	1.96	6-5¼
6. Svetlana Zalevskaya	KAZ	1.96	6-5¼
7. Vita Palamar	UKR	1.96	6-5¼
8. Amewu Mensah	GER	1.93	6-4

Yelena Yelesina led the world with a jump of 2.02 meters (6 feet 7 inches) . . . back in 1990. The following year she earned a silver medal at the world championships. A series of injuries kept her away from the big-time for several years, but she rebounded to take another silver medal at the 1999 world championships. She moved to Melbourne in October 1999, but, at the age of 30, she represented Russia at the Olympics . . . her first.

Although it wouldn't be known until later, the critical point came when Hestrie Cloete missed once at 1.96 meters (6 feet 5 inches), while Yelesina (and four others) went over on her first try. At 1.99 meters (6 feet 6¼ inches), first Cloete and then Yelesina cleared immediately. Kajsa Bergqvist and little known Oana Pantelimon made it on their second tries and their identical records earned them both bronze medals. Both Cloete and Yelesina missed once at 2.01 meters (6 feet 7 inches) and then cleared the second time around. The competition concluded with ten missed jumps. Yelesina's winning height was the lowest in 20 years.

2004 Athens C: 34, N: 25, D: 8.28. WR: 2.09, 6-10¼ (Stefka Kostadinova)

		M	FT.-IN.	
1. Yelena Slesarenko	RUS	2.06	6-9	OR
2. Hestrie Storbeck-Cloete	SAF	2.02	6-7½	
3. Viktoria "Vita" Styopina	UKR	2.02	6-7½	
4. Amy Acuff	USA	1.99	6-6¼	
5. Iryna Mikhalchenko	UKR	1.96	6-5¼	
6. Anna Chicherova	RUS	1.96	6-5¼	
7. Oana Pantelimon-Muşunoi	ROM	1.93	6-4	
8. Monica Iagăr-Dinescu	ROM	1.93	6-4	

The 2004 competition saw an intense duel between two-time defending world champion Hestrie Storbeck-Cloete and Yelena Slesarenko, who had burst onto the scene early in 2004, winning the world indoor championship in Budapest, Hungary, with a jump of 2.04 meters (6 feet 8¼ inches). Cloete was nicknamed "The Flying Bird" for her habit of swinging her arms on the approach to the bar. In Athens, neither Slesarenko nor Cloete missed a single jump for the first six heights, beginning at 1.85 meters (6 feet ¾ inch) and continuing through 2.02 meters (6 feet 7½ inches). At 2.04 meters (6 feet 8¼ inches), Slesarenko again cleared on her first attempt, while Cloete missed twice and then a third time at 2.06. With the gold medal clinched, Slesarenko cleared 2.06 meters (6 feet 9 inches) on her first attempt, setting an Olympic record with a personal best. Cloete, who turned 26 on the day of the qualifying round, was an avid smoker, averaging nearly a pack of cigarettes a day.

2008 Beijing C: 32, N: 24, D: 8.23. WR: 2.09, 6-10¼ (Stefka Kostadinova)

		M	FT.-IN.
1. Tia Hellebaut	BEL	2.05	6-8¾
2. Blanka Vlašić	CRO	2.05	6-8¾
3. Anna Chicherova	RUS	2.03	6-8
4. Yelena Slesarenko	RUS	2.01	6-7¼
5. Vita Palamar	UKR	1.99	6-6¼
6. Chaunte Howard	USA	1.99	6-6¼
7. Ruth Beitía Vila	SPA	1.96	6-5¼
7. Ariane Friedrich	GER	1.96	6-5¼

Blanka Vlašić, the product of one of Croatia's top sporting couples, was named after the Moroccan city of Casablanca, where her father was competing when she was born. Her father Joško set a Croatian national record in the decathlon, while her mother, Venera, was a cross-country skier and basketball player. Blanka made her first Olympic appearance in Sydney at the age of 16, and won her first major title at the world junior championships less than a month later. In 2003 she won her first Golden League event with a jump of 1.99 meters (6 ft. 6¼ in.), and then broke the two-meter barrier in front of a hometown crowd in Zagreb at a Grand Prix event.

The following year Vlašić struggled with lethargy, which was diagnosed as a hyperthyroid condition. After surgery in 2005 she came back to clear 2.05 meters (6 ft. 8¾ in.) indoors and 2.06 meters (6 ft. 9¼ in.) outdoors in 2006, but failed to win a medal at the European championships. By 2007, however, Vlašić had emerged as the world's top female high jumper. She won 18 of 19 outdoor competitions, including the world championship title in Osaka, Japan. To commemorate the occasion, the Croatian postal service released a commemorative stamp on her 24th birthday. By the time she arrived in Beijing Vlašić was riding a 34-meet winning streak, the longest of any track and field athlete at the 2008 Games.

Despite her apparent dominance, Vlašić had serious competition in Beijing. Her biggest challenger was Belgium's Tia Hellebaut, a former pentathlete who had turned to the high jump because of a shoulder injury. Hellebaut made her Olympic debut in Athens in 2004, finishing 12th, but her breakthrough came in 2006, when she broke the two-meter barrier at a Golden League event in Paris before capturing the 2006 European high jump title, her first major international victory. After struggling with injuries in 2007, she came back to win the world indoor pentathlon title in Valencia. Despite the win, Hellebaut chose to concentrate on the high jump rather than the pentathlon, mainly because of concerns about a nagging Achilles' tendon injury in her left foot.

The final in Beijing was one of the finest high jump competitions in Olympic history. By the time the bar reached 2.01 meters (6 ft. 7¼ in.), six jumpers still remained in contention, including Vlašić and Hellebaut, defending Olympic champion Yelena Slesarenko, reigning world silver medalist Anna Chicherova and 2005 world silver medalist Chaunte Howard.

Howard was the first to go out, after missing three attempts at 2.01 meters. Ukraine's Vita Palamar and Slesarenko were next, both failing to clear 2.03 meters (6 ft. 8 in.). Vlašić and Chicherova made it over on their first attempts, while Hellebaut needed two tries.

Perfect up to this point in the competition, Vlašić had her first miss at 2.05 meters, while Hellebaut cleared on her first attempt. Vlašić cleared on her second try, but Slesarenko failed to get over the bar on three attempts and settled for bronze. Vlašić made three attempts at 2.07 meters (6 ft. 9½ in.), which would have been an Olympic record, but was unable to clear the height, and the gold medal went to Hellebaut on count-back. It was Belgium's first female Olympic track and field gold, coming a day after its first female track and field medals: the 4 × 100 meter relay squad's silvers.

Hellebaut's victory was one of the biggest upsets of the Beijing Olympics, but Vlašić kept the loss in perspective. "I won a silver medal and jumped 2.05," she said after the competition. "How can that be a disappointment?"

Two weeks after the Olympic final, Vlašić traveled to Brussels to compete in the IAAF Golden League series finale. In a near repeat of Beijing, Vlašić lost to new rival Ariane Friedrich on count-back after both cleared 2.01 meters. The loss cost Vlašić a share of the $1 million IAAF jackpot.

Four months after the Olympics, Hellebaut announced her retirement from the sport. The reason? She and her coach and partner Wim Vandeven were expecting a baby.

In 2009 Vlašić successfully defended her world championship title in Berlin, despite suffering a freak accident on the morning of the qualifying round (cutting her head on a door frame while warming up in the hallway of her hotel). She had six stitches and bounced back to win with a jump of 2.04 meters (6 ft. 8¼ in.). "If I can survive this, I can survive anything," she said afterwards.

POLE VAULT

1896–1996 not held

2000 Sydney C: 30, N: 20, D: 9.25. WR: 4.63, 15-2¼ (Stacy Dragila)

		M	FT.-IN.
1. Stacy Dragila	USA	4.60	15-1
2. Tatiana Grigorieva	AUS	4.55	14-11¼
3. Vala Flosadóttir	ICE	4.50	14-9¼
4. Daniela Bartová	CZE	4.50	14-9¼
5. Nicole Humbert	GER	4.45	14-7¼
6. Yvonne Buschbaum	GER	4.40	14-5¼
7. Monika Pyrek	POL	4.40	14-5¼
8. Marie Bagger-Rasmussen	DEN	4.35	14-3¼

Until the mid-1990s, women's pole vaulting was widely viewed as an oddity, an insurance risk or one of those sports at which women were so far behind men that it wasn't worth watching. In 1995, Daniela Bartová, who had represented Czechoslovakia in the 1992 Olympics—as a gymnast—set ten world records in the pole vault. The next big name in the event was Australian Emma George, who, until the age of thirteen, had performed as a circus acrobat. Between 1995 and 1999, the glamorous George broke the outdoor world record twelve times. On December 17, 1995, she became the first woman to clear 14 feet (4.28 meters) and on February 21, 1998, the first to clear 15 feet (4.57 meters). George was eclipsed by

Stacy Dragila, a former youth rodeo performer, who won the inaugural women's pole vault world championship in 1999 by equaling the world record of 4.60 meters (15 feet 1 inch). Dragila broke the record twice in the 2000 pre-Olympic season, including a vault of 4.63 meters (15 feet 2¼ inches) at the US Olympic trials.

The qualifying round at the Olympics saw the elimination of Emma George, but the final turned into a riveting contest that took place in the midst of the exciting atmosphere surrounding the 400-meter victories of Michael Johnson and Cathy Freeman. There were seven vaulters still in the running when the bar was raised to 4.45 meters (14 feet 7¼ inches). Dragila went over on her first try, as did Russian-born Australian Tatiana Grigorieva. Grigorieva had converted from hurdling to vaulting because her husband, Viktor Chistiakov, was a vaulter and she found herself with access to excellent coaching. Grigorieva had earned the bronze medal at the 1999 world championships. In Sydney, Vala Flosadóttir also cleared 4.45 the first time. Bartová and Nicole Humbert went over on their third and final attempts, while Humbert's German teammate, Yvonne Buschbaum, and Monika Pyrek were eliminated. The bar went up to 4.50 meters (14 feet 9¼ inches) and Bartová and Flosadóttir went over on the first attempt. For Flosadóttir, it was her seventh clearance without a miss and a personal best, and it put her in first place as she tried to become the first Icelandic woman to win an Olympic medal. Grigorieva cleared with her second try, while Dragila missed twice and found herself one vault away from finishing out of the medals. But her try was successful and the bar was raised to 4.55 meters (14 feet 11¼ inches). Of the remaining competitors, only Dragila and Humbert had cleared that height. Bartová, Humbert and Flosadóttir all missed three times. However, Grigorieva, with the home crowd loudly rooting her on, went over with her first attempt to set a personal best and vault into first place. Dragila stayed in contention by clearing with her second try. At 4.60 meters (15 feet 1 inch), Dragila went right over the first time, while Grigorieva missed. They both tried a world record height of 4.65 meters, but the contest was over.

Prior to the Olympics, both Dragila and Grigorieva had posed nude, Dragila for a calendar, Grigorieva for a magazine. After the competition was over, Dragila did a good job of summing up the status of women's pole vaulting: "We're dang exciting. Back when I started, meet directors didn't want us. They thought we were boring. Now that there's hot chicks out there clearing fifteen feet, they want us." In 2007, sixth place finisher Yvonne Buschbaum announced her decision to undergo hormone treatment to become a man.

"For many years I've felt a sense of being in the wrong body," Buschbaum explained. In 2008 Buschbaum announced that his new first name was Balian, after a character in the film *Kingdom of Heaven*.

2004 Athens C: 35, N: 22, D: 8.24. WR: 4.90, 16-0¾ (Yelena Isinbayeva)

		M	FT.-IN.
1. Yelena Isinbayeva	RUS	4.91	16-1¼ WR
2. Svetlana Feofanova	RUS	4.75	15-7
3. Anna Rogowska	POL	4.70	15-5
4. Monika Pyrek	POL	4.55	14-11¼
5. Þórey Edda Elísdóttir	ICE	4.55	14-11¼
6. Naroa Agirre Kamio	SPA	4.40	14-5¼
6. Anzhela Balakhonova	UKR	4.40	14-5¼
6. Vanessa Boslak	FRA	4.40	14-5¼
6. Dana Ellis	CAN	4.40	14-5¼

The competition in Athens matched the reigning world record holder, Yelena Isinbayeva, and the reigning world champion, Svetlana Feofanova. During the six

Yelena Isinbayeva, 2004
Isinbayeva broke her own world record in winning the 2004 pole vault.

months preceding the Olympics, Isinbayeva broke the world record five times and Feofanova twice.

In Athens, the serious action began when the bar reached 4.70 meters. Feofanova cleared on her first attempt, as did Anna Rogowska. Isinbayeva missed, dropping her to third place. With nothing to gain by trying the height again, she passed, and the bar was raised to 4.75 meters (15 feet 7 inches). All three remaining vaulters missed their first attempts, but Feofanova cleared on her second try. Rogowska went out with two more misses, but Isinbayeva passed again. This left her with one last attempt . . . at 4.80 meters (15 feet 9 inches), a height that only she and Feofanova had ever cleared. After a miss by Feofanova, Isabayeva, exhuding confidence, went over the bar and moved into first place. Now it was Feofanova who was forced to pass. As the clock passed midnight, the bar went up to 4.85 meters (15 feet 11 inches) Feofanova missed, but Isinbayeva had no problem going over the bar. Feofanova was forced to pass again and make her final try at 4.90 meters (16 feet ¾ inch), which was two centimeters higher than her personal best. She missed and the contest was over. With the gold medal secure, Isinbayeva had the bar raised to 4.91 meters (16 feet 1¼ inch), which she cleared to break her own world record.

A plumber's daughter from Volgograd, the 22-year-old Isinbayeva began her career as a gymnast, but was considered too tall for the sport and switched to the pole vault. In 2005, Isinbayeva became the first woman to clear 5 meters (16 feet 4¾ inches).

2008 Beijing C: 36, N: 24, D: 8.18.
WR: 5.03, 16-6 (Yelena Isinbayeva)

		M	FT.-IN.
1. Yelena Isinbayeva	RUS	5.05	16-6¾ WR
2. Jenn Stuczynski	USA	4.80	15-9
3. Svetlana Feofanova	RUS	4.75	15-7
4. Yuliya Golubchikova	RUS	4.75	15-7
5. Monika Pyrek	POL	4.70	15-5
6. Caroline Hingst	GER	4.65	15-3
7. Silke Spiegelburg	GER	4.65	15-3
8. April Steiner-Bennett	USA	4.55	14-11¼

Of all the athletes competing in Beijing, few seemed such overwhelming favorites as Yelena Isinbayeva. Four years after making her Olympic debut in Athens, winning the gold medal and setting a world record in the process, Isinbayeva had won every major international competition leading to the 2008 Olympics, including back-to-back world championships and the intervening European championship. Not content simply to dominate the sport, she had also undergone a complete overhaul of her technique in 2006, learning to use a stiffer pole, changing her grip and adopting a new swing technique developed by her coach Vitaly Petrov. After a few months of struggling, she improved enough to win the European championship.

Isinbayeva's biggest problem was the lack of a real challenger. "I love to win of course, but when you win every time you lose your appetite," she told the IAAF. "It's like someone who loves to eat chocolate and eats it every day and eventually you have so much you hate it." This finally changed in 2007, with the rise of Jennifer Stuczynski. A star basketball player at Roberts Wesleyan College in Rochester, New York, Stuczynski was a reluctant convert to pole vault. In 2005 she shocked the US track and field community by winning the US indoor nationals just ten months after being convinced by local coach Rick Suhr to take up the sport. The following year she won the US outdoor nationals, and in 2007 she became the first US woman to vault 16 feet (4.88 meters), tying former world record holder Svetlana Feofanova as the second-best performer of all time behind Isinbayeva. Then, one month before the Olympics, Stuczynski set a national record at the US Olympic trials, vaulting 4.92 meters (16 ft. 1¾ in.) to move ahead of Feofanova.

Isinbayeva responded by improving her own world record to 5.03 meters (16 ft. 6 in.) at an event in Rome five days later, and then improved it further to 5.04 meters (16 ft. 6½ in.) at a meet in Monaco in late July. By the time she arrived in Beijing, Isinbayeva had brought her career total of world records to 23, second only to pole vaulting great Sergei Bubka's career total of 35.

True to expectations, the competition in Beijing was fierce. Seven athletes still remained in contention at 4.70 meters (15 ft. 5 in.), at which point Isinbayeva deigned to make her first vault. She cleared on her first attempt, as did Stuczynski and Russia's Yuliya Golubchikova. The 2005 world silver medalist, Monika Pyrek, made it over on her second vault, and reigning Olympic silver medalist Svetlana Feofanova passed.

Pyrek missed all three attempts at 4.75 meters (15 ft. 7 in.), the silver-medal winning height in Athens, while Isinbayeva passed. The competition narrowed further after 4.80 meters (15 ft. 9 in.), as Feofanova and Golubchikova both missed all three attempts. Isinbayeva again passed, leaving only Stuczynski, who cleared on her first attempt. Isinbayeva cleared 4.85 meters (15 ft. 11 in.) on her first vault, while Stuczynski passed. At 4.90 meters (16 ft. 1 in.), Isinbayeva passed again, leaving Stuczynski to attempt a height she had cleared only once before. Stuczynski missed all three attempts, and the gold medal was Isinbayeva's.

But the event was far from over. With the gold medal secure, Isinbayeva missed her first two attempts at 4.95 meters (16 ft. 2¾ in.), but cleared on her third attempt. She then had the bar raised to 5.05 meters (16 ft. 6¾ in.), to attempt a world record. After two misses, She made it over on her third vault, to set her 24th world record.

For her performance, and a season in which she won 12 of 13 competitions, including all nine outdoor competitions, Isinbayeva was named the IAAF World Athlete of The Year, along with sprinter Usain Bolt.

LONG JUMP

1896–1936 not held

1948 London C: 26, N: 13, D: 8.4. WR: 6.25, 20-6¼ (Francina "Fanny" Blankers-Koen)

		M	FT.-IN.
1. Olga Gyarmati	HUN	5.695	18-8¼
2. Noémi Simonetta de Portela	ARG	5.60	18-4½
3. Ann-Britt Leyman	SWE	5.575	18-3¼
4. Gerda van der Kade-Koudijs	HOL	5.57	18-3¼
5. Neeltje Karelse	HOL	5.545	18-2¼
6. Kathleen Russell	JAM	5.495	18-0¼
7. Judy Canty	AUS	5.38	17-7¾
8. Yvonne Curtet-Chabot	FRA	5.35	17-6½

The importance of this competition was somewhat muted by the absence of world record holder Fanny Blankers-Koen, who was busy winning gold medals in four other events.

1952 Helsinki C: 34, N: 22, D: 7.23. WR: 6.25, 20-6¼ (Francina "Fanny" Blankers-Koen)

		M	FT.-IN.
1. Yvette Williams	NZL	6.24	20-5¾ OR
2. Aleksandra Chudina	SOV/RUS	6.14	20-1¾
3. Shirley Cawley	GBR	5.92	19-5¼
4. Irmgard Schmelzer	GER	5.90	19-4¼
5. Wilhelmina Lust	HOL	5.81	19-0¾
6. Nina Tyurkina	SOV/RUS	5.81	19-0¾
7. Mabel "Dolly" Landry	USA	5.75	18-10½
8. Verna Johnston	AUS	5.74	18-10

Twenty-three-year-old Yvette Williams led the qualifying rounds with a jump of 6.16 meters (20 feet 2½ inches). She faulted twice in the final and was one jump away from elimination. However, her third jump of 5.90 meters (19 feet 4½ inches) was good enough to put her in the top six who qualified for three more jumps. Her fourth attempt was the winning one, and none of the leaders was able to improve after that. Williams also finished sixth in the shot put and tenth in the discus. However, the real award for versatility in field events went to Chudina, who took second in the long jump, second in the javelin, and third in the high jump. Chudina was also a champion speed skater and volleyball player. She was also the object of much suspicion because she spoke with a deep voice, possessed "masculine" musculature, and refused to shower with her teammates.

1956 Melbourne C: 19, N: 11, D: 11.27. WR: 6.35, 20-10 (Elżbieta Krzesińska)

		M	FT.-IN.
1. Elżbieta Krzesińska	POL	6.35	20-10 EWR
2. Willye White	USA	6.09	19-11¾
3. Nadezhda Dvalischvili (Khnykina)	SOV/GEO	6.07	19-11
4. Erika Fisch	GER	5.89	19-4
5. Marthe Lambert	FRA	5.88	19-3½
6. Valentina Schaprunova	SOV/RUS	5.85	19-2¼
7. Beverly Weigel	NZL	5.85	19-2¼
8. Nancy Borwick	AUS	5.82	19-1¼

Krzesińska, a 21-year-old medical student, was in a class by herself. Seventeen-year-old Willye White, who was born in Money, Mississippi, was a surprise silver medalist. She was so new to high-level competition that she had spent the summer of 1956 picking cotton for two dollars a day. At the Olympics, she read the New Testament between jumps and won second place with her final leap. She also competed in the next four Olympics, earning another silver medal as a member of the 1964 US 4 × 100-meter relay team.

1960 Rome C: 30, N: 18, D: 8.31. WR: 6.40, 21-0 (Hildrun Claus)

		M	FT.-IN.
1. Vira Krepkina	SOV/UKR	6.37	20-10¾ OR
2. Elżbieta Krzesińska	POL	6.27	20-7
3. Hildrun Claus	GDR	6.21	20-4½
4. Renate Junker	GER	6.19	20-3¾
5. Lyudmyla Radchenko	SOV/UKR	6.16	20-2½
6. Helga Hoffmann	GER	6.11	20-0½
7. Johanna Bijleveld	HOL	6.11	20-0½
8. Valentina Schaprunova	SOV/RUS	6.01	19-8¾

Krepkina's victory came as a complete surprise, since she was better known as a sprinter. In fact, she was coholder of the world record for 100 meters.

1964 Tokyo C: 31, N: 20, D: 10.14. WR: 6.70, 21-11¾ (Tatyana Schelkanova)

		M	FT.-IN.
1. Mary Rand (Bignal)	GBR	6.76	22-2¼ WR
2. Irena Kirszenstein	POL	6.60	21-8
3. Tatyana Schelkanova	SOV/RUS	6.42	21-0¾
4. Ingrid Becker	GER	6.40	21-0
5. Viorica Viscopoleanu	ROM	6.35	20-10
6. Diana Yorgova	BUL	6.24	20-5¾
7. Hildrun Laufer (Claus)	GDR	6.24	20-5¾
8. Helga Hoffmann	GER	6.23	20-5¼

In 1960 Mary Rand (then Mary Bignal) had been considered the favorite in the long jump, particularly after she had led the qualifying round with a personal best of 20 feet 9¼ inches. That jump would have won her a silver medal if she had been able to repeat it in the final. Instead she ran through twice and had to settle for ninth place with her third jump. She also finished fourth in the 80-meter hurdles the following day. Four years later in Tokyo, Mary Rand again had the best jump of the qualifying round—21 feet 4¾ inches. This time, though, everything went right in the final. Four of her six jumps were her best ever, and her whole series was so consistent that her worst leap would have earned her a silver medal. Her fifth jump registered 6.76 meters. Unfamiliar with the metric system, she raced back to her bag, pulled out the program, and learned that she had broken the world record. And this despite the fact that she had jumped into a 1.69 meters per second wind. Mary Rand was the first British woman to win an Olympic gold medal in track and field. Later in the week she also won a silver medal in the pentathlon and a bronze in the 4 × 100-meter relay. In 1967 she went to Mexico City and met her future second husband, the US decathlon champion Bill Toomey.

The woman who finished sixth in 1964, Bulgarian Diana Yorgova, made the news several days later when she and Bulgarian gymnast Nikolai Prodanov held the first-ever Olympic wedding. The ceremony took place in the International Club of the Olympic Village in front of a huge Olympic flag and a photo of the Olympic flame. The couple honeymooned in Kyoto, but returned to Tokyo in time for the closing ceremonies.

1968 Mexico City C: 27, N: 19, D: 10.14. WR: 6.76, 22-2¼ (Mary Rand [Bignal])

		M	FT.-IN.
1. Viorica Viscopoleanu	ROM	6.82	22-4½ WR
2. Sheila Sherwood	GBR	6.68	21-11
3. Tatyana Talisheva	SOV/RUS	6.66	21-10¼
4. Burghild Wieczorek	GDR	6.48	21-3¼
5. Miroslawa Sarna	POL	6.47	21-2¾
6. Ingrid Becker	GER	6.43	21-1¼
7. Berit Berthelsen	NOR	6.40	21-0
8. Heidemarie Rosendahl	GER	6.40	21-0

Viscopoleanu recorded her winning jump on her first attempt of the final. The 29-year-old Romanian improved on her pre-Olympic personal best by no less than nine inches.

1972 Munich C: 33, N: 19, D: 8.31. WR: 6.84, 22-5¼ (Heidemarie Rosendahl)

		M	FT.-IN.
1. Heidemarie Rosendahl	GER	6.78	22-3
2. Diana Yorgova	BUL	6.77	22-2½
3. Eva Šuranová	CZE/SLV	6.67	21-10¾
4. Marcia Garbey	CUB	6.52	21-4¾
5. Heidi Schüller	GER	6.51	21-4¼
6. Meta Antenen	SWI	6.49	21-3½
7. Viorica Viscopoleanu	ROM	6.48	21-3¼
8. Margrit Olfert	GDR	6.46	21-2½

Heidemarie Rosendahl brought great joy to the crowd by becoming the first West German gold medal winner of the Munich Games. Her first leap of 6.78 meters appeared to be good enough for first place until the fourth round, when Diana Yorgova, the first Bulgarian to win a track and field medal, hit the best jump of her career. But it was one centimeter too short. Yorgova's last jump was also a long one, but was disallowed because her foot went over the board. Later in the Games Rosendahl picked up a silver medal in the pentathlon and another gold in the 4 × 100-meter relay.

1976 Montreal C: 30, N: 19, D: 7.23. WR: 6.99, 22-11¼ (Siegrun Siegl)

		M	FT.-IN.
1. Angela Voigt	GDR	6.72	22-0¾
2. Kathy McMillan	USA	6.66	21-10¼
3. Lidiya Alfeyeva	SOV/UKR	6.60	21-8
4. Siegrun Siegl	GDR	6.59	21-7½
5. Ildikó Szabó	HUN	6.59	21-7½
6. Jarmila Nygrýnová	CZE	6.54	21-5½
7. Heidemarie Wycisk	GDR	6.39	20-11¾
8. Elena Vintila	ROM	6.38	20-11¼

For the third straight time the women's long jump was won with a first-round jump. Angela Voigt had held the world record for ten days earlier in the year, but she had a reputation for doing poorly in important meets. The last jumper of the competition, 18-year-old Kathy McMillan of Raeford, North Carolina, finished with the longest leap of the day; however she had stepped an inch or so over the board, and a no-jump was declared.

1980 Moscow C: 19, N: 11, D: 7.31. WR: 7.09, 23-3¼ (Vilma Bardauskiene)

		M	FT.-IN.
1. Tatyana Kolpakova	SOV/KYR	7.06	23-2 OR
2. Brigitte Wujak	GDR	7.04	23-1¼
3. Tetyana Skachko	SOV/UKR	7.01	23-0
4. Anna Wlodarczyk	POL	6.95	22-9¾
5. Siegrun Siegl	GDR	6.87	22-6½
6. Jarmila Nygrýnová	CZE	6.83	22-5
7. Siegrid Heimann	GDR	6.71	22-0¼
8. Lidiya Alfeyeva	SOV/UKR	6.71	22-0¼

This was, without question, the most exciting women's Olympic long-jump contest ever. In 1978 Vilma Bardauskiene had become the first woman to break the 7-meter barrier, but two years later, hampered by injuries, she was unable to make the Soviet team. With one round to go Skachko was in first place as a result of her third round leap of 7.01 meters. She was followed by Wujak and Wlodarczyk, with 6.88 each, and Kolpakova with 6.87. Wlodarczyk's final jump of 6.95 put her into second place and had her crying for joy, but she and Skachko watched in horror as the situation changed dramatically in the next two minutes. First Kolpakova, third string on the USSR team, jumped into first place with a 7.06—nine inches further than her pre-Olympic best. Then Wujak improved her personal best by 5½ inches to take the silver medal. Skachko, who had been in front for two hours, was forced to settle for a bronze medal, and Wlodarczyk was left without any medal at all. At the postrace press conference, Kolpakova, a shy 20-year-old from Frunze in the Kirghiz Soviet Socialist Republic, summed up the competition by saying, "I think that one should always fight until the end, and my last attempt confirmed it."

1984 Los Angeles C: 23, N: 17, D: 8.9. WR: 7.43, 24-4½ (Anişoara Cuşmir-Stanciu)

		M	FT.-IN.
1. Anişoara Cuşmir-Stanciu	ROM	6.96	22-10
2. Valeria Ionescu	ROM	6.81	22-4¼
3. Susan Hearnshaw	GBR	6.80	22-3¾
4. Angela Thacker	USA	6.78	22-3
5. Jacqueline Joyner	USA	6.77	22-2½
6. Robyn Lorraway	AUS	6.67	21-10¾
7. Glynis Nunn	AUS	6.53	21-5¼
8. Shonel Ferguson	BAH	6.44	21-1½

The Soviet bloc boycott prevented the anticipated showdown between world record holder Anişoara Cuşmir-Stanciu and the rising East German star Heike Daute, who had upset Stanciu at the Helsinki world championships. At the Olympics Stanciu went ahead on her own, taking a first-round lead of 6.80 and sealing the victory in the fourth round.

1988 Seoul C: 30, N: 20, D: 9.29. WR: 7.52, 24-8¼ (R. Galina Čištjaková)

		M	FT.-IN.	
1. Jacqueline Joyner-Kersee	USA	7.40	24-3¼	OR
2. Heike Drechsler (Daute)	GDR	7.22	23-8¼	
3. R. Galina Čištjaková	SOV/UKR	7.11	23-4	
4. Olena Belevska	SOV/UKR	7.04	23-1¼	
5. Nicole Boegman	AUS	6.73	22-1	
6. Fiona May	GBR	6.62	21-8¾	
7. Agata Karczmarek	POL	6.60	21-7¾	
8. Sabine John	GDR	6.55	21-5¾	

This event pitted world record holder Galina Čištjaková against former world record holders Heike Drechsler and Jackie Joyner-Kersee. Drechsler, then known by her maiden name, Heike Daute, had won the 1983 world championship at the tender age of 18. She was ranked number one in the world four years in a row. Then her 27-meet winning streak was broken when she finished third at the 1987 world championships after injuring her knee on her fourth jump. The winner of that competition was Jackie Joyner-Kersee with a jump of 24 feet 1¾ inches (7.36 meters).

Five days before the Olympic final, Joyner-Kersee won a gold medal in the heptathlon, setting an Olympic long jump record of 23 feet 10½ inches (7.27 meters) in the process.

Čištjaková took the first-round lead with a leap of 7.11, but, hampered by injury, she was unable to improve after that. In the second round, Olena Belevska jumped 7.04 and Drechsler followed with a 7.06. She improved to 7.18 with her next jump, while Joyner-Kersee moved into second at 7.16. In the fourth round, Drechsler improved again, this time to 7.22, while Joyner-Kersee fouled. As she prepared for her fifth jump, Joyner-Kersee noticed that her opponents were tiring and decided to go for one big one. Her husband and coach, Bob Kersee, called out to her, "You have a 7.40 in you." Concentrating on keeping her knees high and staying in the air as long as possible, Joyner-Kersee then won the competition with a jump of exactly 7.40 meters.

1992 Barcelona C: 35, N: 24, D: 8.7. WR: 7.52, 24-8¼ (R. Galina Čištjaková)

		M	FT.-IN.
1. Heike Drechsler (Daute)	GER	7.14	23-5¼
2. Inessa Kravets	UKR	7.12	23-4½
3. Jacqueline Joyner-Kersee	USA	7.07	23-2½
4. Mirela Dulgheru	ROM	6.71	22-0¼
5. Irma Mushailova	RUS	6.68	21-11
6. Sharon Couch	USA	6.66	21-10¼
7. Sheila Echols	USA	6.62	21-8¾
8. Susen Tiedtke	GER	6.60	21-8

DISQ (Drugs): Nijole Medvedeva (LIT) 6.76 22-2¼

Jackie Joyner-Kersee defeated Heike Drechsler at the 1987 world championships, the 1988 Olympics, and the 1991 world championships. In Barcelona, Drechsler finally came out on top. Inessa Kravets, the world record holder in the triple jump, took the first-round lead with a leap of 7.12 meters. She and Joyner-Kersee never improved on their opening jumps. Drechsler moved into third place in the second round and then hit her winning jump in the fourth round.

As a major athletics star, Drechsler experienced the best and worst of the East German system. On the one hand, she served in parliament; on the other hand, she had to submit a written request to have a baby. After the collapse of communism, Brigette Berendonk and Werner Franke published a book that included details of Drechsler's annual dose of steroids. Drechsler accused Berendonk of lying. Berendonk sued for libel and, in 1995, won. Drechsler was convicted of perjury and was forced to issue a public apology. On the other hand, the records also showed that Drechsler's performances improved as her steroid use was decreased and, indeed, her greatest success was achieved after the fall of the Berlin Wall.

1996 Atlanta C: 48, N: 36, D: 8.2. WR: 7.52, 24-8¼ (R. Galina Čištjaková)

		M	FT.-IN.
1. Chioma Ajunwa	NGR	7.12	23-4½
2. Fiona May	ITA	7.02	23-0½
3. Jacqueline Joyner-Kersee	USA	7.00	22-11½
4. Niki Xanthou	GRE	6.97	22-10½
5. Iryna Chekhovtsova	UKR	6.97	22-10½
6. Agata Karczmarek	POL	6.90	22-7¾
7. Nicole Boegman	AUS	6.73	22-1
8. Tünde Vaszi	HUN	6.60	21-8

DISQ (Drugs): Iva Prandzheva (BUL) 6.82 22-4½

Chioma Ajunwa was among the most unexpected winners at the Atlanta Olympics. Born in the village of Umuihiokwu Ogbe in the state of Imo, she moved to Lagos and worked as a police inspector. She played midfield on the Nigerian football (soccer) team and competed in the 1991 Women's World Cup. In 1992, she was the national champion at 100 meters and the long jump. But on June 11, she tested positive for methylandenome and Codeine and was handed a four-year suspension. She did not return to competition—at 100 meters—until five weeks before the Olympics. Ajunwa had high hopes for the 100 meters. Upon arriving in Atlanta she was surprised to learn she had also been entered in the long jump. In the 100 meters, she was eliminated in the semifinals, missing the final in a photo-finish.

Four days later, Ajunwa qualified for the long jump final by leaping 6.81 meters, second only to Fiona May's 6.85. Is the final the following evening, she recorded a first-round jump of 7.12 meters, a personal best that held up for the victory. May, who had married an Italian and changed citizenship between Olympics, gained the silver with a second-round personal best of 7.02. The final round did see a piece of drama. Jackie Joyner-Kersee, at 34 years of age, was the pre-Olympic favorite. Hampered by a right hamstring injury, she was placed only seventh. But with her final attempt, she hit 7 meters and leapfrogged onto the medal platform.

Chioma Ajunwa was the first Nigerian to win an Olympic gold medal in any sport, and the first African to win a field event. At 1.60 meters (5 feet 3 inches) she was also the shortest athlete in the competition.

Shabaza Akhtar, who finished 34th, was the first woman to represent Pakistan, even though Pakistan, the seventh most populous nation in the world, had been entering the Olympics since 1948.

2000 Sydney C: 39, N: 25, D: 9.27. WR: 7.52, 24-8¼ (R. Galina Čištjaková)

		M	FT.-IN.
1. Heike Drechsler (Daute)	GER	6.99	22-11¼
2. Fiona May	ITA	6.92	22-8½
3. Tatyana Kotova	RUS	6.83	22-5
4. Olga Rublyeva	RUS	6.79	22-3¼
5. Susan Tiedtke	GER	6.74	22-1¼
6. Jackie Edwards	BAH	6.59	21-7½
7. Tünde Vaszi	HUN	6.59	21-7½
8. Lyndmila Galkina	RUS	6.56	21-6¼

DISQ (Drugs): Marion Jones (USA) 6.92 22-8½

Almost all media attention was focused on Marion Jones, who had already won gold medals in both sprints on her way to her goal of five gold medals. Yet the actual favorite was Tatyana Kotova, who had won ten of eleven meets in the pre-Olympic season. Jones had jumped 7.31 meters (23 feet 11 inches) in 1998, but she had managed only one 7 meter jump in 1999 and one in 2000. The Olympic field also included three former world champions: Ludmila Galkina (1997), who would ultimately end up in ninth place, Fiona May (1995) and Heike Drechsler, the winner of the first World Championships of Athletics, as an 18-year-old in 1983. After winning at the 1992 Olympics, Drechsler had missed both the 1996 Olympics and 1999 world championships because of injury. Drechsler had more than 400 7-meter jumps to her credit, but two years had passed since her last one.

Drechsler recorded the longest qualifying jump, 6.84 meters, followed by May and Jones. As it would turn out, that was the exact order of finish two days later in the final. May took the first round lead at 6.76 meters. When Olga Rublyeva hit 6.79 in the second round, May responded with 6.82. Kutova was in third place, Jones in fourth and Drechsler in eighth. The third round would prove decisive. Drechsler took advantage of a 1.9 mph tailwind to reach 6.99 meters. Jones jumped 6.92 meters. May matched Jones' distance, but took over second place as a result of her superior second jump. Jones fouled all three of her last attempts and none of the eight women who made it to the second half of the final improved in the last three rounds.

2004 Athens C: 39, N: 28, D: 8.27. WR: 7.52, 24-8¼ (R. Galina Čištjaková)

		M	FT.-IN.
1. Tatyana Lebedeva	RUS	7.07	23-2½
2. Irina Simagina	RUS	7.05	23-1½
3. Tatyana Kotova	RUS	7.05	23-1½
4. Bronwyn Thompson	AUS	6.96	22-10
5. Marion Jones	USA	6.85	22-5½
6. Anju Bobby George	IND	6.83	22-5
7. Jade Johnson	GBR	6.80	22-3¼
8. Tünde Vaszi	HUN	6.73	22-1

The two-time defending world champion in the triple jump, Tatyana Lebedeva finished a disappointing third at the Athens Olympics. Two days later she entered the long jump, in which she had the longest jump of the year, and led the qualifying round with a jump of 6.95 meters (22 feet 9¾ inches). In the final, teammates Irina Simagina and Tatyana Kotova both jumped 7.05 meters (23 feet 1½ inches) to take the first round lead. In the second round, Lebedeva moved ahead of her fellow Russians with a leap of 7.07 meters (23 feet 2½ inches). Simagina followed with a jump of 7.02 meters (23 feet ½ inch), which ultimately secured her the silver medal as a better backup mark than that of Kotova, and, as it turned out, all the medals were decided. The Russian sweep was the first in any women's athletics event since the Soviet sweeps of the 800 meters and the pentathlon in 1980.

2008 Beijing C: 42, N: 33, D: 8.22. WR: 7.52, 24-8¼ (R. Galina ištjaková)

		M	FT.-IN.
1. Maurren Maggi	BRA	7.04	23-1¼
2. Tatyana Lebedeva	RUS	7.03	23-0¼
3. Blessing Okagbare	NGR	6.91	22-8
4. Chelsea Hammond	JAM	6.79	22-3¼
5. Brittney Reese	USA	6.76	22-2¼
6. Oksana Udmurtova	RUS	6.70	21-11¾
7. Jade Johnson	GBR	6.64	21-9¼
8. Grace Upshaw	USA	6.58	21-7

Maurren Maggi's father was a big fan of The Beatles and named his daughter after drummer Ringo Starr's first wife, Maureen. A spelling error on her birth certificate, however, turned the name to Maurren. Raised in the city of São Carlos, Maggi moved to São Paolo in 1994 to pursue an athletics career, eventually winning the long jump event at the South American championships in Bogota, Colombia, in 1999. Her jump, 7.26 meters (23 ft. 9¾ in.), put her among the top 10 jumpers of all time.

Maggi made her first Olympic appearance in Sydney in 2000, but was injured in the qualifying round and withdrew. The following year she finished seventh at the world championships despite being a pre-race favorite. After winning bronze at the world indoor championships in 2003 Maggi tested positive for the anabolic steroid clostebol and received a two-year suspension; she blamed the positive test on hair removal cream. Although she was later cleared by the Brazilian Athletics Federation, the IAAF appealed the ruling to the Court of Arbitration for Sport, and Maggi chose to serve the two-year ban rather than attend the hearing. During her ban from competition she met and married Formula 1 racer Antonio Pizzonia and gave birth to a daughter. She returned to competition in 2006, winning the South American championships and finishing sixth at the 2007 world championships. In 2008 she finished second at the world indoor championships behind Portugal's Naide Gomes and was one of the favorites coming into Beijing.

In addition to Maggi and Gomes, the Russian contingent remained serious medal contenders. Three years after Tatyana Lebedeva led the first-ever sweep of the women's long jump at the 2004 Athens Olympics, she repeated the feat by leading a sweep of the 2007 world championships, with 2006 European champion Lyudmila Kolchanova taking silver and 2005 world champion and defending Olympic bronze medalist Tatyana Kotova in third.

The qualifying round saw the elimination of Gomes, who fouled her first two jumps and managed only 6.29 meters (20 ft. 7¾ in.) on her final attempt. In the final Lebedeva took the lead with her first jump, 6.97 meters (22 ft. 10½ in.), but was quickly passed by Maggi, who landed a first-round jump of 7.04 meters (23 ft. 1¼ in.). Lebedeva faulted on her next four attempts before coming just short of the gold medal with a final jump of 7.03 meters (24 ft. ¾ in.).

Maggi was the first Brazilian woman to win an Olympic athletics medal. Lebedeva, who had won silver in the triple jump event five days earlier, finished with silver. Bronze medalist Blessing Okagbare was a surprise addition to the final, after finishing 13th in the qualifying round and failing to make the qualifying distance of 6.75 meters (22 ft. 1¾ in.). Blessing managed to advance to the final when third-place qualifier Lyudmila Blonska tested positive for the steroid methyltestosterone after finishing second in the heptathlon. Blessing recorded her bronze-medal-winning jump on her first attempt.

TRIPLE JUMP

1896–1992 not held

1996 Atlanta C: 32, N: 24, D: 7.31. WR: 15.50, 50-10¼ (Inessa Kravets)

		M	FT.-IN.
1. Inessa Kravets	UKR	15.33	50-3½
2. Inna Lasovskaya	RUS	14.98	49-1¾
3. Sárka Kaspárková	CZE	14.98	49-1¾
4. Ashia Hansen	GBR	14.49	47-6½
5. Olga Vasdeki	GRE	14.44	47-4½
6. Ren Ruiping	CHN	14.30	46-11
7. Rodica Mateescu	ROM	14.21	46-7½
8. Jelena Blazevica	LAT	14.12	46-4

DISQ (Drugs): Iva Prandzheva (BUL) 14.92 48-11¼

The women's triple jump was accorded world record status by the IAAF in 1991. It was Inessa Kravets who established the standard at 14.95 meters. Ana Biryukova of Russia was the first to break the 15-meter barrier, jumping 15.09 meters to win the 1993 world championship. Kravets missed that meet while serving a three-month suspension for ephedrine. At the 1995 world championships, Kravets fouled twice, studied a photograph of British triple jump star Jonathan Edwards, and leaped 15.50 meters to break Biryukova's world record by 41 centimeters (16 inches).

At the inaugural Olympic competition in Atlanta, Biryukova could do no better than 14.19 meters and missed qualifying for the final. In the final, Lasovskaya and Kaspárková leaped 14.98 meters in the second and third rounds respectively. Kravets, in third place, connected with a fifth-round jump of 15.33 meters to gain the victory. Lasovskaya won the silver medal because her second-best leap, 14.70 meters, was one centimeter better than Kaspárková's.

The morning after the triple jump final, Kravets took part in the qualifying round of the long jump, but she fouled all three of her tries.

2000 Sydney C: 27, N: 22, D: 9.24. WR: 15.50, 50-10¼ (Inessa Kravets)

		M	FT.-IN.
1. Tereza Marinova	BUL	15.20	49-10½
2. Tatyana Lebedeva	RUS	15.00	49-2½
3. Olena Hovorova	UKR	14.96	49-1
4. Yamile Aldama	CUB	14.30	46-11
5. Baya Rahouli	ALG	14.17	46-5¾
6. Cristina Elena Nicolau	ROM	14.17	46-5¾
7. Olga Vasdeki	GRE	14.15	46-5
8. Oksana Rogova	RUS	13.97	45-10

Tatyana Lebedeva had won 13 of 14 pre-Olympic meets. Her only loss was to Tereza Marinova and then by only 7 centimeters (3 inches). After the loss, Lebedeva beat Marinova twice in the run-up to the Olympics. Lebedeva recorded the longest jump of the qualifying round, 14.91 meters (48 feet 11 inches). The final was accompanied by wind and hard rain, but when the competition began, it was only misty. Marinova quickly took advantage with a first-round jump of 15.20 meters (49 feet 10½ inches). Olena Hovorova was second at 14.96 meters (49 feet 1 inch) and Lebedeva third at 14.77 (48'5½"). Marinova fouled all five of her remaining jumps, while Lebedeva, after improving to 14.91 meters (48 feet 11 inches), took over the silver medal position with a fifth-round leap of 15 meters (49 feet 2½ inches).

2004 Athens C: 33, N: 24, D: 8.23. WR: 15.50, 50-10¼ (Inessa Kravets)

		M	FT.-IN.
1. Françoise Mbango Etone	CAM	15.30	50-2¼
2. Khrysopigi Devetzi	GRE	15.25	50-½
3. Tatyana Lebedeva	RUS	15.14	49-8¼
4. Trecia Smith	JAM	15.02	49-3½
5. Yamilé Aldama	SUD	14.99	49-2
6. Baya Rahouli	ALG	14.86	48-9
7. Magdelín Martínez	ITA	14.85	48-8½
8. Anna Pyatykh	RUS	14.79	48-6¼

Two-time world champion Tatyana Lebedeva travelled to Athens looking for double golds in the triple jump and long jump. Khrysopigi Devetzi, who had placed only eighth at the previous year's world championship, led the qualifying round by 43 centimeters (17 inches) with a startling jump of 15.32 meters (50 feet 3¼ inches). In the first round of the final, Devetzi took the lead at 14.96 meters (49 feet 1 inch). In the second round, Trecia Smith briefly led at 15.02 meters (49 feet 3½ inches), before two-time world championship silver medalist Françoise Mbango tore into first place with an African record of 15.30 meters (50 feet 2½ inches). Devetzi moved back into second place in the third round with a leap of 15.14 meters (49 feet 8¼ inches). In the fourth round, with the loud support of the Greek crowd, she improved to 15.25 meters (50 feet ½ inch). Lebedeva, finally moved into a medal position in the fifth round, jumping 15.04 meters (49 feet 4¼ inches). With her final attempt, Mbango duplicated her winning distance of 15.30 meters, earning Cameroon's first ever individual gold medal. Alhough she had only topped 15 meters twice before 2004 Olympics, she did so with five of her six jumps in Athens. The 28-year-old Mbango had trained without a coach since April 2003 because she could not afford the cost.

2008 Beijing C: 36, N: 26, D: 8.17. WR: 15.50, 50-10¼ (Inessa Kravets)

		M	FT.-IN.	
1. Françoise Mbango Etone	CMR	15.39	50-5¾	OR
2. Tatyana Lebedeva	RUS	15.32	50-3¼	
3. Khrysopigi "Pigi" Devetzi	GRE	15.23	49-11½	
4. Olga Rypakova	KAZ	15.11	49-6¾	
5. Yargelis Savigne Herrera	CUB	15.05	49-4½	
6. Marija Martinović-Šestak	SLO	15.03	49-3¾	
7. Viktoriya Gurova	RUS	14.77	48-5½	
8. Anna Pyatykh	RUS	14.73	48-4	

After the Athens Olympics, it finally looked as though Françoise Mbango's contentious relationship with the Cameroon Athletic Federation had improved. As Cameroon's first-ever female Olympic medalist and first-ever medalist in athletics, Mbango was promised a bonus of CFA 80,000,000 ($170,000) to support her training and preparation for the Beijing Olympics. Previously, lack of financial support had forced Mbango to train with her younger sister instead of a coach.

One year later however, the relationship had already begun to sour. In 2005 Mbango made a last-minute decision not to compete at the world championships in Helsinki. She pointed to the fact that her mother, who had been diagnosed with cancer, had been unable to get medical travel documents from government officials and that the situation had left her unable to face high-level competition. Taking a break from competition, Mbango moved to the United States and began to settle into family life, giving birth to a son. She reappeared only briefly in 2006 to complain about her treatment by the Cameroonian authorities, including their failure to pay her the promised financial support.

Françoise Mbango Etone, 2008

Françoise Mbango celebrates after successfully defending her triple jump championship in 2008.

Mbango eventually returned to training in January 2007, but failed to show up at the All-Africa Games in Algiers in July, despite having collected a stipend and airline ticket for the event. The no-show was the last straw, and Mbango was suspended indefinitely by the Cameroon Athletics Federation. Despite the suspension, Mbango qualified for and won the 2008 African Championships, earning a berth at the Beijing Olympics. It was all the more impressive because it was her first major competition since the 2004 Olympics. The Cameroon Ministry of Sports and Physical Education finally intervened, sponsoring her trip to Beijing.

After all the drama, the competition itself was rather straightforward. Reigning world champion Yargelis Savigne recorded the longest jump of the qualifying round (14.99 meters; 49 feet 2 inches). But in the final Mbango led after the first round with a 15.19-meter (49 ft. 10 in.) jump. Defending Olympic silver medalist Khrysopigi Devetzi moved into first place briefly in the second round with a 15.23-meter (49 ft. 11½ in.) leap, but Mbango responded by recording the second-longest jump in history, just 11 centimeters short of the world record. Reigning Olympic and world long jump champion Tatyana Lebedeva moved into second place in the third round, while Savigne could do no better than fifth place.

To celebrate her victory, Mbango was awarded the Cameroon National Order of Merit and hailed by the Prime Minister for "resisting the nomadic nationality syndrome of sports men and women." However, in 2010 Mbango officially changed her nationality to French.

SHOT PUT

The women's shot weighs 4 kilograms (8 pounds 14¾ ounces).

1896–1936 not held

1948 London C: 19, N: 12, D: 8.4. WR: 14.89, 48-10¼ (Tatyana Sevryukova)

		M	FT.-IN.
1. Micheline Ostermeyer	FRA	13.75	45-1½
2. Amelia Piccinini	ITA	13.09	42-11½
3. Ine Schäffer	AUT	13.08	42-11
4. Paulette Veste	FRA	12.985	42-7¼
5. Jaroslava Komárková	CZE	12.92	42-4¾
6. Anni Bruk	AUT	12.50	42-0¼
7. Maria Radosavjevic	YUG/SER	12.355	40-6½
8. Bevis Reid	GBR	12.17	39-11¼

Three months before the Olympics, pianist Micheline Ostermeyer had graduated with high honors from the Paris Conservatory of Music. In London she used the hands that so delicately played the piano to win gold medals in both the shot put and discus. She also placed third in the high jump. She celebrated her shot put victory by performing an impromptu Beethoven recital back at the French team headquarters. Ostermeyer's success in track and field actually hurt her reputation as a concert pianist, and for the next six years she was afraid to play Liszt because he was too *"sportif."* However, Ostermeyer continued to defend her "divided life." "Sport," she said, "taught me to relax; the piano gave me strong biceps and a sense of motion and rhythm."

1952 Helsinki C: 20, N: 13, D: 7.26. WR: 15.19, 49-10 (Galina Zybina)

		M	FT.-IN.
1. Galina Zybina	SOV/RUS	15.28	50-1¾ WR
2. Marianne Werner	GER	14.57	47-9¾
3. Klavdia Tochenova	SOV/RUS	14.50	47-7
4. Tamara Tyshkevich	SOV/RUS	14.42	47-3¾
5. Gertrud Kille	GER	13.84	45-5
6. Yvette Williams	NZL	13.35	43-9¾
7. Maria Radosavjevic	YUG/SER	13.30	43-7¾
8. Meeri Saari	FIN	13.02	42-8¾

As a ten-year-old child, Galina Zybina had watched her mother and brother die of cold and starvation during World War II. She barely survived herself and entered adolescence thin and sickly. However, ten years after her ordeal, she proved to be one of the strongest women in the world. In Helsinki Zybina had the three longest throws of the competition and had already secured first place when she broke the world record on her final attempt. Werner moved from fourth to second on her final throw to prevent a Soviet sweep.

1956 Melbourne C: 18, N: 9, D: 11.30. WR: 16.76, 55-0 (Galina Zybina)

		M	FT.-IN.
1. Tamara Tyshkevich	SOV/RUS	16.59	54-5 OR
2. Galina Zybina	SOV/RUS	16.53	54-2¾
3. Marianne Werner	GER	15.61	51-2¾
4. Zinaida Doynikova	SOV/RUS	15.54	51-0
5. Valerie Sloper	NZL	15.34	50-4
6. Earlene Brown	USA	15.12	49-7¼
7. Regina Branner	AUT	14.60	47-10¾
8. Nadya Kotlušek	YUG/SLO	14.56	47-9¼

Zybina took the lead in the first round and appeared to be headed for a second gold medal. However, in the final round her 231-pound teammate, Tamara Tyshkevich, scored a dramatic victory by heaving the shot 2¼ inches further than Zybina's best. Los Angeles housewife Earlene Brown made a great impression on the Australians and became a local favorite. Arriving in Melbourne early, she took part in a regional meet and won. When a fan informed her that she had just broken the Victoria state record, Brown replied, "I'm sorry, honey. If I'd known I was going to do that I wouldn't have thrown it so far."

Shot Put Medalists, 1956
Left to right, Marianne Werner, Tamara Tyshkevich, and Galina Zybina.

1960 Rome C: 18, N: 12, D: 9.2. WR: 17.78, 58-4 (Tamara Press)

		M	FT.-IN.
1. Tamara Press	SOV/UKR	17.32	56-10 OR
2. Johanna Lüttge	GDR	16.61	54-6
3. Earlene Brown	USA	16.42	53-10½
4. Valerie Sloper	NZL	16.39	53-9¼
5. Zinaida Doynikova	SOV/RUS	16.13	52-11
6. Renate Garisch	GDR	15.94	52-3¾
7. Galina Zybina	SOV/RUS	15.56	51-0¾
8. Wilfriede Hoffmann	GDR	15.14	49-8¼

Between them, Tamara Press and her younger sister Iryna set 26 world records and won five Olympic gold medals and one silver. Unfortunately, when sex tests were instituted at international competitions, the careers of both Press sisters came to a sudden halt.

1964 Tokyo C: 16, N: 11, D: 10.20. WR: 18.55, 60-10½ (Tamara Press)

		M	FT.-IN.
1. Tamara Press	SOV/UKR	18.14	59-6¼ OR
2. Renate Garisch-Culmberger	GDR	17.61	57-9½
3. Galina Zybina	SOV/RUS	17.45	57-3
4. Valerie Young-Sloper	NZL	17.26	56-7½
5. Margitta Helmboldt	GDR	16.91	55-5¾
6. Iryna Press	SOV/UKR	16.71	54-10
7. Nancy McCredie	CAN	15.89	52-1¾
8. Ana Salagean	ROM	15.83	51-11¼

Tamara Press won the discus gold the day before the shot put. Zybina's bronze gave her a complete set of Olympic medals.

1968 Mexico City C: 14, N: 10, D: 10.20. WR: 18.87, 61-11 (Margitta Gummel [Helmboldt])

		M	FT.-IN.
1. Margitta Gummel (Helmboldt)	GDR	19.61	64-4 WR
2. Marita Lange	GDR	18.78	61-7½
3. Nadezhda Chizhova	SOV/RUS	18.19	59-8¼
4. Judit Bognar	HUN	17.78	58-4
5. Renate Boy (Garisch-Culmberger)	GDR	17.72	58-1¾
6. Ivanka Hristova	BUL	17.25	56-7¼
7. Marlene Fuchs	GER	17.11	56-1¾
8. Els Van Noorduyn	HOL	16.23	53-3

In the very first round Marita Lange heaved the shot 61 feet 7½ inches to improve her personal best by over a yard. Gummel broke the world record in the third round and then unleashed an amazing fifth-round toss of 64 feet 4 inches to better her own pre-Olympic world record by 29 inches. It was later revealed that Gummel was one of the first East Germans to be administered steroids, although she was not given her first dose of Twinabol until July 28, 1968, less than three months before the Mexico City Olympics.

1972 Munich C: 18, N: 11, D: 9.7. WR: 20.63, 67-8¼ (Nadezhda Chizhova)

		M	FT.-IN.
1. Nadezhda Chizhova	SOV/RUS	21.03	69-0 WR
2. Margitta Gummel (Helmboldt)	GDR	20.22	66-4¼
3. Ivanka Hristova	BUL	19.35	63-6
4. Esfir Dolzhenko	SOV/MOL	19.24	63-1½
5. Marianne Adam	GDR	18.94	62-1¾
6. Marita Lange	GDR	18.85	61-10¼
7. Helena Fibingerová	CZE	18.81	61-8½
8. Yelena Stoyanova	BUL	18.34	60-2

Tamara Press, 1964
Press dominated the shot put, but disappeared from international competition when sex tests began.

Siberian-born Nadezhda Chizhova put the championship out of reach on her first attempt with a world record of 69 feet.

1976 Montreal C: 13, N: 8, D: 7.31. WR: 21.89, 71-10 (Ivanka Hristova)

		M	FT.-IN.
1. Ivanka Hristova	BUL	21.16	69-5¼ OR
2. Nadezhda Chizhova	SOV/RUS	20.96	68-9¼
3. Helena Fibingerová	CZE	20.67	67-9¾
4. Marianne Adam	GDR	20.55	67-5¼
5. Ilona Schoknecht	GDR	20.54	67-4¾
6. Margitta Droese	GDR	19.79	64-11¼
7. Eva Wilms	GER	19.29	63-3½
8. Yelena Stoyanova	BUL	18.89	61-11¾

The 1976 shot put competition matched the world record holder against three former world record holders. Defending champion Chizhova led after the first round with a throw of 68 feet 4½ inches. In the second round Hristova hit 68 feet 6 inches, but Chizhova responded with 68 feet 9¼ inches. However, Chizhova slipped and injured her leg and was unable to come up with another serious throw. Her lead held up until the fifth round, when Hristova secured the victory with a new Olympic record of 69 feet 5¼ inches. Hristova's win culminated a steady rise in her career. In the 1964 Olympics she finished tenth. In 1968 she was sixth, and in 1972 she was third. Finally, at the age of 34, she won a gold medal, the first ever by a Bulgarian track and field athlete. Chizhova matched Galina Zybina's feat of earning a complete set of medals.

1980 Moscow C: 14, N: 8, D: 7.24. WR: 22.45, 73-8 (Ilona Slupianek [Schoknecht])

		M	FT.-IN.
1. Ilona Slupianek (Schoknecht)	GDR	22.41	73-6¼ OR
2. Svetlana Krachevskaya (Esfir Dolzhenko)	SOV/RUS	21.42	70-3½
3. Margitta Pufe (Droese)	GDR	21.20	69-6¾
4. Nunu Abashidze	SOV/UKR	21.15	69-4¾
5. Verginia Vesselinova	BUL	20.72	67-11¾
6. Elena Stoyanova	BUL	20.22	66-4¼
7. Natalya Akhrimenko	SOV/RUS	19.74	64-9¼
8. Ines Reichenbach	GDR	19.66	64-6

Slupianek was forced to sit out the 1979 season when she was caught taking steroids. She was the first East German athlete to fail a doping test. In Moscow Slupianek put on an extraordinary performance, outclassing the opposition. The last to throw, she broke the Olympic record on her first attempt and then went over 70 feet on each of her five remaining throws. Her *worst* put, 70 feet 3½ inches, was equal to the *best* put of silver medalist Svetlana Krachevskaya.

1984 Los Angeles C: 13, N: 8, D: 8.3. WR: 22.53, 73-11 (Natalya Lisovskaya)

		M	FT.-IN.
1. Claudia Losch	GER	20.48	67-2¼
2. Mihaela Loghin	ROM	20.47	67-2
3. Gael Martin	AUS	19.19	62-11½
4. Judith Oakes	GBR	18.14	59-6¼
5. Li Meisu	CHN	17.96	58-11¼
6. Venissa Head	GBR	17.90	58-8¾
7. Carol Cady	USA	17.23	56-6½
8. Florenta Craciunescu	ROM	17.23	56-6½

Claudia Losch, a 24-year-old Bavarian optician, defeated a severely depleted field by edging Mihaela Loghin with her final throw. Bronze medalist Gael Martin had tested positive for steroids in 1981, but returned to competition in time for the Olympics. She failed another doping test in 1988, while taking part in the World Powerlifting Championships.

1988 Seoul C: 25. N: 14, D: 10.1. WR: 22.63, 74-3 (Natalya Lisovskaya)

		M	FT.-IN.
1. Natalya Lisovskaya	SOV/RUS	22.24	72-11¾
2. Kathrin Neimke	GDR	21.07	69-1½
3. Li Meisu	CHN	21.06	69-1¼
4. Ines Müller	GDR	20.37	66-10
5. Claudia Losch	GER	20.27	66-6
6. Heike Hartwig	GDR	20.20	66-3¼
7. Natalya Akhrimenko	SOV/RUS	20.13	66-0½
8. Huang Zhihong	CHN	19.82	65-0¼

The 6-foot 2-inch (1.88 meters), 218-pound (99 kilograms) Lisovskaya so dominated the competition that *any* of her six throws would have won the gold medal. The battle for the silver, on the other hand, was extremely close, as Neimke came from behind to edge Li by 1 centimeter with her final throw. In 1995, Lisovskaya married hammer throwing great Yuri Sedykh.

1992 Barcelona C: 18, N: 11, D: 8.7. WR: 22.63. 74-3 (Natalya Lisovskaya)

		M	FT.-IN.
1. Svetlana Krivelyova	RUS	21.06	69-1¼
2. Huang Zhihong	CHN	20.47	67-2
3. Kathrin Neimke	GER	19.78	65-2¾
4. Belsis Laza Muñoz	CUB	19.70	64-7¾
5. Zhou Tianhua	CHN	19.26	63-2¼
6. Svetlana Mitkova	BUL	19.23	63-1¼
7. Stephanie Storp	GER	19.10	62-8
8. Viktoriya Pavlysh	UKR	18.69	61-4

Krivelyova took the first round lead with a heave of 66 feet 8¾ inches (20.34 meters). In the third round Huang moved into first place at 67 feet 2 inches (20.47 meters). This was beyond Krivelyova's personal best and appeared to settle the question of who would win the gold medal. But in the fifth round Krivelyova, in a clutch performance, reached 68 feet 6½ inches (20.89 meters). She improved to 69 feet 1¼ inches in the final round to better her pre-Olympic best by 2 feet 3½ inches.

Huang was a welcome contrast to obsessed athletes. "I didn't like the shot at all," she once said. "How could anyone like those heavy metal lumps? If I knew the shot put would make me so fat, I wouldn't have taken it up." After she won the 1991 world championship, she was asked how it felt to be the first Asian to win a world athletics title. She replied, "What I have done is no more newsworthy than if I had swallowed 500 eels."

1996 Atlanta C: 25, N: 16, D: 8.2. WR: 22.63, 74-3 (Natalya Lisovskaya)

		M	FT.-IN.
1. Astrid Kumbernuss	GER	20.56	67-5½
2. Sui Xinmei	CHN	19.88	65-2¾
3. Irina Khudoroshkina	RUS	19.35	63-5¾
4. Viktoriya Pavlysh	UKR	19.30	63-3¾
5. Connie Price-Smith	USA	19.22	63-0¾
6. Stephanie Storp	GER	19.06	62-6½
7. Kathrin Neimke	GER	18.92	62-1
8. Irina Korzhanenko	RUS	18.68	61-3½

Astrid Kumbernuss entered the Olympics with a 37-meet winning streak including the 1995 world championships which she won by an unprecedented 1.18 meters (3 feet 10½ inches). In Atlanta she secured the gold medal with her first throw. She eventually ran her victory streak to 53, lost twice at the beginning of 1997 and then won 27 more meets. After skipping the 1998 season to have a baby, she returned in 1999 and won her third straight world championship.

2000 Sydney C: 25, N: 18, D: 9.28. WR: 22.63, 74-3 (Natlaya Lisovskaya)

		M	FT.-IN.
1. Yanina Korolchik	BLR	20.56	67-5½
2. Larisa Peleshenko	RUS	19.92	65-4¼
3. Astrid Kumbernuss	GER	19.62	64-4½
4. Svetlana Krivelyova	RUS	19.37	63-6½
5. Krystyna Danilczyk-Zabawska	POL	19.18	62-10
6. Yumileidi Cumbá	CUB	18.70	61-4¼
7. Kalliopi Ouzouni	GRE	18.63	61-1½
8. Nadine Kleinert-Schmitt	GER	18.49	60-8

Astrid Kumbernuss' winning streak was finally stopped at 53 when Vita Pavlysh of Ukraine beat her at the 1997 world indoor championships. Kumbernuss won the 1997 world championships, took a year off to have a baby and then, with Pavlysh out with a steroids ban, won the 1999 world championships. In 2000, Kumbernuss won 10 of 12 meets in the pre-Olympic outdoor season and arrived in Sydney as the favorite to defend her Olympic title.

Yanina Korolchik led the qualifying round with a put of 19.36 meters (63 feet 6¼ inches). She also took the first round lead in the final at 19.43 meters (63 feet 9 inches) with Kumbernuss in second place (19.38 meters). In the second round, Larisa Peleshenko, back after a four-year drug ban, hit 19.92 meters (65 feet 4¼ inches). She retained her lead all the way into the final round. Kumbernuss' last put, 19.62 meters (64 feet 4½ inches), moved her into the silver medal position, but then, out of the blue, Korolchik bettered her personal best by 24 centimeters and won a surprise gold medal with a put of 20.56 meters (67 feet 5½ inches).

Korolchik was unable to defend her title in 2004 because she was slapped with a two-year ban after testing positive for clenbuterol in 2003.

2004 Athens–Olympia C: 38, N: 28, D: 8.18. WR: 22.63, 74-3 (Natalya Lisovskaya)

		M	FT.-IN.
1. Yumileidi Cumbá	CUB	19.59	64-3¼
2. Nadine Kleinert	GER	19.55	64-1½
3. Svetlana Krivelyova	RUS	19.49	63-11¼
4. Nadezhda Ostapchuk	BLR	19.01	62-4¼
5. Natalya Khoronenko	BLR	18.96	62-2¼
6. Krystyna Danilczyk-Zabawska	POL	18.64	61-1¾
7. Misleydis González	CUB	18.59	60-11¾
8. Valerie Adams	NZL	18.56	60-10½

DISQ (Drugs): Irina Korzhanenko (RUS) 21.06 69-1

The shot put competition was held in the ancient stadium at Olympia, home to the original ancient Olympic Games, in which women were not allowed to compete. Kristin Heaston of the United States had the honor of being the first Olympic athlete to perform in the stadium in 1,635 years. Nadezhda Ostapchuk led the qualifying round with a put of 19.69 meters (64 feet 7¼ inches), a distance that would have earned her the gold medal had she repeated it in the final. The final appeared to be completely dominated by Irina Korzhanenko, who recorded the four longest puts, all beyond 20 meters (65 feet 7 inches). In the second round, Nadine Kleinert moved into second place with a 19.55-meter put, immediately followed by a toss of 19.49 meters by reigning world champion and 1992 Olympic champion Svetlana Krivelyova. In sixth place going into the final throw, Yumileidi Cumbá edged past Kleinert into second with a put of 19.59 meters (64 feet 3¼ inches).

Korzhanenko's victory was not long-lived. Immediately after the event, she tested positive for the steroid stanozolol. After a test on her backup sample confirmed the result, Korzhanenko was stripped of her gold medal. With the disqualification, Cumbá moved into first place, Kleinert into second, and Krivelyova into third. It was Korzhanenko's second doping

Kristin Heaston, 2004
Shot Put in Ancient Olympia Stadium. Heaston was the first Olympic athlete to perform in the stadium in 1,635 years.

violation. The first came at the 1999 world indoor championships, when she was stripped of her silver medal and given a two-year ban, preventing her from competing in the 2000 Olympics. Korzhanenko, who faced a lifetime ban because of the second positive test, refused to give back her medal. One year later she was named a coach for the Russian national athletics team.

2008 Beijing C: 35, N: 22, D: 8.16. WR: 22.63, 74-3 (Natalya Lisovskaya)

		M	FT.-IN.
1. Valerie Adams-Vili	NZL	20.56	67-5½
2. Nataliya Khoronenko-Mikhnevich	BLR	20.28	66-6½
3. Nadezhda Ostapchuk	BLR	19.86	65-1¾
4. Misleydis González Tamayo	CUB	19.50	63-11¾
5. Gong Lijao	CHN	19.20	62-11¾
6. Anna Omarova	RUS	19.08	62-7¼
7. Nadine Kleinert-Schmitt	GER	19.01	62-4¼
8. Li Meiju	CHN	19.00	62-4

Valerie Adams was a reluctant convert to shot putting. Picked on as a child for her height and size, Adams became shy and withdrawn. At the age of 14 she was pressured into participating in a regional schools competition by her Physical Education teacher and managed to break a school shot put record that had stood for twenty years. When her mother died of cancer in 2000, just after the Opening Ceremony of the Sydney Olympics, Adams vowed to honor her memory by winning a gold medal. The following year she won gold at the World Youth Championships in Hungary, and a year after that won gold at the World Junior Championships in Jamaica. By 2003 Adams had moved up to senior competition, finishing fifth at the world championships. She made her Olympic debut in Athens in 2004; she was stricken with appendicitis the week before she was due to leave New Zealand, but, after surgery, managed to recover sufficiently to finish eighth. On her return home she became engaged to, and later married, New Caledonian discus-thrower Bertrand Vili.

Four years later, Adams-Vili arrived in Beijing the reigning world champion and one of the top contenders for the gold medal. Her biggest challenge was expected to come from 2005 world champion Nadezhda Ostapchuk, whom she had beaten for the

2007 world title by a mere six centimeters. Also in the running for a spot on the podium were reigning European champion Natalya Mikhnevich and defending Olympic silver medalist and reigning world bronze medalist Nadine Kleinert.

In the end, the competition for gold was over almost before it began. In the morning Adams recorded the longest throw of the qualifying round, 19.73 meters (64 ft. 8¾ in.), and that evening, in the final, she unleashed a personal record 20.56-meter (67 ft. 5½ in.-) throw in the opening round. Mikhnevich managed to top 20 meters (65 ft. 7½ in.) in the second round, but could not beat Adams's first-round throw. Adams then broke the 20-meter barrier with each of her four subsequent throws, although without improving on her first distance. Ostapchuk moved into third place with her fifth-round throw.

Adams dedicated her gold medal to the memory of her parents, her father having passed away in 2007. In 2009 she successfully defended her world title in Berlin against the home favorite Kleinert, and then won again in 2011, defeating Ostapchuk.

DISCUS THROW

The women's discus weighs 1 kilogram (2 pounds 3.27 ounces).

1896–1924 not held

1928 Amsterdam C: 21, N: 12, D: 7.31. WR: 39.18, 128-6 (Halina Konopacka)

		M	FT.-IN.
1. Halina Konopacka	POL	39.62	129-11¾ WR
2. Lillian Copeland	USA	37.08	121-8
3. Ruth Svedberg	SWE	35.92	117-10
4. Emilie "Milly" Reuter	GER	35.86	117-8
5. Grete Heublein	GER	35.56	116-8
6. Liesl Perkaus	AUT	33.54	110-0½
7. MayBelle Reichardt	USA	33.52	110-0
8. Genowefa Kobielska	POL	32.72	107-4

This was the first women's track and field event to be decided in the history of the Olympics.

1932 Los Angeles C: 9, N: 4, D: 8.2. WR: 42.43, 139-2½ (Jadwiga Wajs)

		M	FT.-IN.
1. Lillian Copeland	USA	40.58	133-2 OR
2. Ruth Osburn	USA	40.12	131-7
3. Jadwiga Wajs	POL	38.74	127-1
4. Tilly Fleischer	GER	36.12	118-6
5. Grete Heublein	GER	34.66	113-8
6. Stanisława Wałasiewicz	POL	33.60	110-3
7. Mitsue Ishizu	JPN	33.52	110-0
8. Ellen Braumüller	GER	33.15	108-9

Twenty-seven-year-old Lillian Copeland, a law student at the nearby University of Southern California, won the contest on her final throw. She told reporters, "The only thing I could think of as I stood there waiting for my last throw of the day was Dr. O'Callaghan, who won the hammer throw [the previous day] on *his* last throw of the day." Copeland, who was Jewish, boycotted the 1936 Olympic to protest the Nazi refusal to allow Jewish athletes on the German team. After retiring from sport Copeland went on to serve 24 years as an officer for the LA County Sheriff's Department.

1936 Berlin C: 19, N: 11, D: 8.4. WR: 48.31, 158-6 (Gisela Mauermayer)

		M	FT.-IN.
1. Gisela Mauermayer	GER	47.63	156-3 OR
2. Jadwiga Wajs	POL	46.22	151-8
3. Paula Mollenhauer	GER	39.80	130-7
4. Ko Nakamura	JPN	38.24	125-5
5. Hide Mineshima	JPN	37.35	122-6
6. Birgit Lundström	SWE	35.92	117-10
7. Anna Niesink	HOL	35.21	115-6
8. Gertrude Wilhemsen	USA	34.43	112-11½

Three weeks before the games began, Gisela Mauermayer heaved the discus 158 feet 6 inches to set a world record that would last for twelve years. Mauermayer was a modest 22-year-old, a 6-foot blonde, who was hailed in Germany as the perfect example of Aryan womanhood. She gave the Nazi salute on the victory stand and became a top-ranking member of the Nazi women's organization. During World War II she was a teacher in Munich. After the war she lost her job because of her high-profile Nazi involvement. Starting over at the Zoological Institute of Munich University she gained a doctor's degree by studying the social behavior of ants. Like Helen Stephens, another star of the 1936 games, Mauermayer eventually settled down as a librarian.

1948 London C: 21, N: 11, D: 7.30. WR: 48.31, 158-6 (Gisela Mauermayer)

		M	FT.-IN.
1. Micheline Ostermeyer	FRA	41.92	137-6
2. Edera Cordiale-Gentile	ITA	41.17	135-0
3. Jacqueline Mazéas	FRA	40.47	132-9
4. Jadwiga Wajs-Marcinkiewicz	POL	39.30	128-11
5. Charlotte "Lotte" Haidegger	AUT	38.81	127-3
6. Anna Panhorst Niesink	HOL	38.74	127-1
7. Majken Aberg	SWE	38.48	126-3
8. Ingeborg Mello	ARG	38.44	126-1

Ostermeyer moved from third to first with her final throw to win the first of her three medals in 1948.

Discus Medalists, 1948

Left to right, Edera Cordiale Gentile (silver), Micheline Ostermeyer (gold), and Jacqueline Mazéas (bronze).

1952 Helsinki C: 20, N: 16, D: 7.20. WR: 53.37, 175-1 (Nina Dumbadze)

		M	FT.-IN.
1. Nina Romaschkova	SOV/RUS	51.42	168-8 OR
2. Yelisaveta Bagryantseva	SOV/RUS	47.08	154-5
3. Nina Dumbadze	SOV/GEO	46.29	151-10
4. Toyoko Yoshino	JPN	43.81	143-8
5. Charlotte "Lotte" Haidegger	AUT	43.49	142-8
6. Lia Manoliu	ROM	42.65	139-11
7. Ingeborg Pfuller	ARG	41.73	136-11
8. Ilona Jozsa	HUN	41.61	136-6

Romaschkova's margin of victory in Helsinki was extraordinary, particularly considering the presence of world record holder Nina Dumbadze. The following month Romaschkova broke Dumbadze's record, but on October 18, Dumbadze threw the discus 187 feet 1½ inches to set a world record that would last for almost eight years. Olympic silver medalist Yelisaveta Bagryantseva was the mother of Irma Bagryantseva, who, under her married name, Nazarova, won a gold medal in the 4 × 400-meter relay in 1980.

1956 Melbourne C: 22, N: 12, D: 11.23. WR: 57.04, 187-1½ (Nina Dumbadze)

		M	FT.-IN.
1. Olga Fikotová	CZE	53.69	176-1 OR
2. Irina Beglyakova	SOV/RUS	52.54	174-4
3. Nina Ponomaryeva (Romaschkova)	SOV/RUS	52.02	170-8
4. Earlene Brown	USA	51.35	168-5
5. Albina Yelkina	SOV/UKR	48.20	158-2
6. Isabel Ercilia Avellán	ARG	46.73	153-3
7. Jiřina Voborilova	CZE	45.84	150-5
8. Stepanka Mertová	CZE	45.78	150-2

A former member of the Czechoslovakian national basketball team, Fikotová was taught by her first discus coach to regard the event as a dance step and was allowed to practice to the sounds of "The Blue Danube." In 1956, she gained great fame as a result of her Cold War-thawing romance with and marriage to US hammer thrower Harold Connolly. The couple eventually settled in California, although they divorced in 1973. Olga took part in four more Olympics, finishing seventh in 1960, twelfth in 1964, sixth in 1968, and

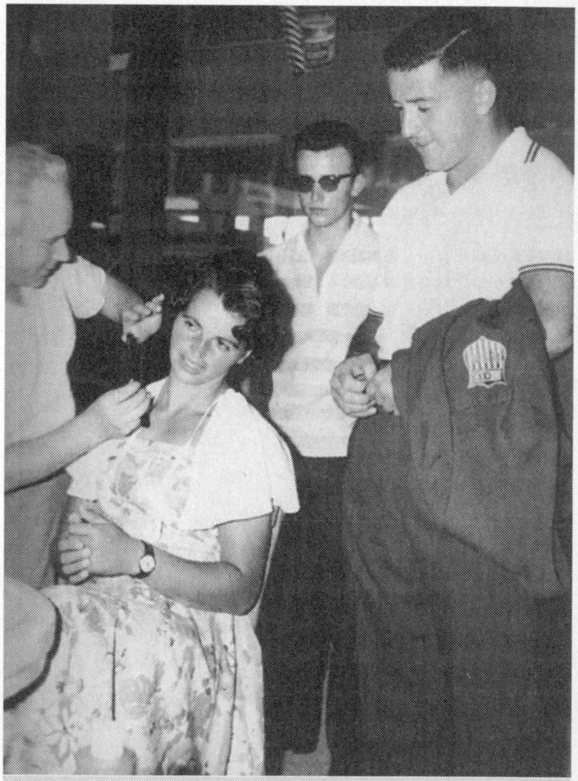

Olga Fikotová and Harold Connolly, 1956

The romance between the Czech discus thrower and American hammer thrower made worldwide headlines.

sixteenth in 1972. In 1972 Olga Connolly was elected by her teammates to carry the United States flag at the Opening Ceremony. The United States Olympic Committee, miffed by her outspoken opposition to United States involvement in the Vietnam War, tried to intervene, but Connolly was allowed to carry out the honor anyway.

1960 Rome C: 24, N: 15, D: 9.5, WR: 57.04, 187-1½ (Nina Dumbadze)

		M	FT.-IN.
1. Nina Ponomaryeva (Romaschkova)	SOV/RUS	55.10	180-9 OR
2. Tamara Press	SOV/UKR	52.59	172-4
3. Lia Manoliu	ROM	52.36	171-9
4. Krimhild Hausmann	GER	51.47	168-10
5. Yevgenya Kuznetsova	SOV/RUS	51.43	168-8
6. Earlene Brown	USA	51.29	168-3
7. Olga Connolly (Fikotová)	USA	50.95	167-2
8. Jiřina Nemcova (Voborilova)	CZE	50.12	164-5

The 1960 discus competition matched two former gold medal winners and two future gold medal winners. Ponomaryeva took the lead in the second round and won with the contest's three longest throws. A week later, Tamara Press set a world record of 57.15 meters (187 feet 6 inches). Back in 1956, Ponomaryeva had gained dubious notoriety when she was arrested in London for stealing five hats from a shop in Oxford Street.

1964 Tokyo C: 21, N: 15, D: 10.19. WR: 59.28, 194-5¾ (Tamara Press)

		M	FT.-IN.
1. Tamara Press	SOV/UKR	57.27	187-10 OR
2. Ingrid Lotz	GDR	57.21	187-8
3. Lia Manoliu	ROM	56.97	186-10
4. Virzhinia Mikhailova	BUL	56.70	186-0
5. Yevgenya Kuznetsova	SOV/RUS	55.17	181-0
6. Jolán Kleiber	HUN	54.87	180-0
7. Krimhild Limberg (Hausmann)	GER	53.81	176-6
8. Olimpia Catarama	ROM	53.08	173-11

After four rounds, world record holder Tamara Press was only in fourth place. Her fifth attempt, however, stretched two inches beyond Ingrid Lotz's first-round mark and gave Press the closest victory in Olympic discus history.

1968 Mexico City C: 15, N: 8, D: 10.18. WR: 62.54, 205-2¼ (Liesel Westermann)

		M	FT.-IN.
1. Lia Manoliu	ROM	58.28	191-2 OR
2. Liesel Westermann	GER	57.76	189-6
3. Jolán Kleiber	HUN	54.90	180-1
4. Anita Otto	GDR	54.40	178-6
5. Antonina Popova	SOV/RUS	53.42	175-3
6. Olga Connolly (Fikotová)	USA	52.96	173-9
7. Christine Spielberg	GDR	52.86	173-5
8. Brigitte Berendonk	GER	52.80	173-3

Lia Manoliu, 1968
Manoliu, the first track and field athlete to take part in six Olympics, finally won a gold medal on her fifth attempt, in the 1968 discus throw.

On November 5, 1967, while competing in Brazil, Liesel Westermann became the first woman to throw the discus over 200 feet, with a heave of 201 feet (61.26 meters). In Mexico City she was one of the three favorites, along with the East German Christine Spielberg and the Romanian Lia Manoliu, who was taking part in her fifth Olympics. In 1952 Manoliu had finished sixth, in 1956 ninth, in 1960 third, and in 1964 third again. Manoliu entered the competition in 1968 with a sore elbow, so she decided to put everything she had into her first throw. It went 191 feet 2 inches, good enough to take the lead after the first round. After that she fouled three times, passed once, and got off one poor throw. However, a rainstorm arrived during the second round, and the rest of the competition was severely impaired as the throwing circle became wetter and wetter. It turned out that Lia Manoliu's first toss held up to take first place, and the 36-year-old Manoliu became the oldest woman in Olympic history to win a track and field gold medal. She took part in one more Olympics in 1972, finishing ninth. Only one other female track and field athlete, Tessa Sanderson, has taken part in six different Olympic Games. In 1990 Manoliu was appointed president of the Romanian Olympic Committee. She died of a heart attack January 9, 1998, following surgery for a brain tumor.

1972 Munich C: 17, N: 10, D: 9.10. WR: 66.76, 219-0¼ (Faina Melnik)

		M	FT.-IN.
1. Faina Melnik	SOV/ARM	66.62	218-7 OR
2. Argentina Menis	ROM	65.06	213-5
3. Vassilka Stoyeva	BUL	64.34	211-1
4. Tamara Danilova	SOV/RUS	62.86	206.3
5. Liesel Westermann	GER	62.18	204-0
6. Gabriele Hinzmann	GDR	61.72	202-6
7. Carmen Ionescu	ROM	60.42	198-3
8. Lyudmila Muraviova	SOV/RUS	59.00	193-7

Argentina Menis, who wore makeup and false eyelashes while competing, led after three rounds, with world champion Faina Melnik struggling in fifth place. However, Melnik, who yelled at the top of her lungs with each throw, came within 5½ inches of her best ever on her fourth attempt. Menis gave one last mighty effort on her final try, nearly decapitating a marker judge with a throw of 212 feet 11 inches. Less than two weeks later Menis set a world record of 220 feet 10 inches.

1976 Montreal C: 15, N: 9, D: 7.29. WR: 70.50, 231-3½ (Faina Melnik)

		M	FT.-IN.
1. Evelin Schlaak	GDR	69.00	226-4 OR
2. Maria Vergova	BUL	67.30	220-9
3. Gabriele Hinzmann	GDR	66.84	219-3
4. Faina Melnik	SOV/ARM	66.40	217-10
5. Sabine Engel	GDR	65.88	216-2
6. Argentina Menis	ROM	65.38	214-6
7. Maria Betancourt	CUB	63.86	209-6
8. Natalya Gorbachova	SOV/RUS	63.46	208-2

Twenty-year-old Schlaak shocked the opposition with a 69-meter first throw that held up for the victory. It was originally announced that Faina Melnik had taken second place by virtue of her fifth-round toss of 225 feet 1 inch (68.60 meters). However, the throw was later ruled illegal because Melnik had balked, having started her throwing action and then stopped. Danuta Rosani of Poland qualified for the final, but was disqualified after failing the test for anabolic steroids. She was the first Olympic track and field athlete to be disqualified for taking drugs.

1980 Moscow C: 17, N: 10, D: 8.1. WR: 71.80, 235-7 (Maria Petkova [Vergova])

		M	FT.-IN.
1. Evelin Jahl (Schlaak)	GDR	69.96	229-6 OR
2. Maria Petkova (Vergova)	BUL	67.90	222-9
3. Tatyana Lesovaya	SOV/KAZ	67.40	221-1
4. Gisela Beyer	GDR	67.08	220-1
5. Margitta Pufe (Droese)	GDR	66.12	216-11
6. Florența Țacu	ROM	64.38	211-2
7. Galina Murashova	SOV/LIT	63.84	209-5
8. Svetla Gunleva	BUL	63.14	207-1

Now married and a first lieutenant in the army, Jahl had lost her world record to Petkova a few weeks before the games. However, in Moscow she posted the four longest throws of the competition after Petkova had taken the opening-round lead.

1984 Los Angeles C: 17, N: 14, D: 8.11. WR: 73.26, 240-4¼ (Galina Savinkova)

		M	FT.-IN.
1. Ria Stalman	HOL	65.36	214-5
2. Leslie Deniz	USA	64.86	212-9
3. Florența Craciunescu (Țacu)	ROM	63.64	208-9
4. Ulla Lundholm	FIN	62.84	206-2
5. Margaret Ritchie	GBR	62.58	205-4
6. Ingra Manecke	GER	58.56	192-1
7. Venissa Head	GBR	58.18	190-10
8. Gael Martin	AUS	55.88	183-4

In a competition severely depleted by the Soviet-bloc boycott, Ria Stalman won a dramatic victory over her former Arizona State U. roommate, Leslie Deniz. Stalman took the lead with her first throw of 64.50, but was passed in the fifth round by Deniz's 64.86. But the 32-year-old Stalman was able to secure the gold medal with a final toss of 65.36. Stalman was subsequently caught trying to smuggle steroid tablets into the United States from Mexico.

1988 Seoul C: 22, N: 13, D: 9.29. WR: 76.80, 252-0 (Gabriele Reinsch)

		M	FT.-IN.
1. Martina Hellmann	GDR	72.30	237-2½ OR
2. Diana Gansky	GDR	71.88	235-10
3. Tzvetanka Hristova	BUL	69.74	228-10
4. Svetla Mitkova	BUL	69.14	226-10
5. Ellina Zvereva	SOV/BLR	68.94	226-2
6. Zdeňka Šilhavá	CZE	67.84	222-7
7. Gabriele Reinsch	GDR	67.26	220-8
8. Hou Xuemei	CHN	65.94	216-4

Gabriele Reinsch, whose pre-1988 best was 220 feet 5 inches (67.18 meters), added more than seven feet to Zdeňka Šilhavá's 1984 world record with a throw of 252 feet on July 9, 1988. At the Olympics two and a half months later, she needed all three attempts to make it out of the preliminary round, then placed a disappointing seventh in the final. Meanwhile, her teammate, two-time world champion Martina Hellmann, hit a 71.84 in the first round and extended to 72.30 with her fourth throw, to outdistance the third East German, Diana Gansky, whose fifth-round throw earned her the silver.

1992 Barcelona C: 28, N: 16, D: 8.3. WR: 76.80, 252-0 (Gabriele Reinsch)

		M	FT.-IN.
1. Maritza Martén García	CUB	70.06	229-10
2. Tzvetanka Khristova	BUL	67.78	222-4
3. Daniela Costian	AUS	66.24	217-4
4. Larissa Korotkevich	BLR	65.52	214-11
5. Olga Burova	RUS	64.02	210-0
6. Hilda Ramos Manez	CUB	63.80	209-4
7. Irina Yatchenko	BLR	63.74	209-1
8. Stefania Simova	BUL	63.42	208-1

Korotkevich led the qualifying round at 222 feet 10 inches (67.92 meters), but the favorite remained Ilke Wyludda of Germany. Wyludda had won 41 consecutive meets between 1988 and 1991, when she was upset at the world championships on the last throw by Tzvetanka Khristova. In the final, the early lead was taken by unheralded 28-year-old Maritza Martén of Havana. Kristova took over in the second round with a throw of 222 feet 4 inches. Through the fourth round, Khristova still led by 2 feet 10½ inches, with Martén in second, Korotkevich third, and Costian fourth. Wyludda, in ninth place, did not qualify for the final three throws. The medals were decided in the fifth round. First Costian reached 217 feet 4 inches to move into third place and then Martén hit 229 feet 10 inches to secure a decisive victory. Born in Romania Daniela Costian had a colorful history. In 1986 she was suspended for a drug violation. Returning to competition in 1988, she defected during the Balkan Games in Turkey and settled in Australia. In 1993 Khristova tested positive for steroids and was banned from competition.

1996 Atlanta C: 39, N: 24, D: 7.29. WR: 76.80, 252-0 (Gabriele Reinsch)

		M	FT.-IN.
1. Ilke Wyludda	GER	69.66	228-7
2. Natalya Sadova	RUS	66.48	218-1
3. Ellina Zvereva	BLR	65.64	215-4
4. Franka Dietzsch	GER	65.48	214-10
5. Xio Yanling	CHN	64.72	212-4
6. Olga Chernyavskaya (Burova)	RUS	64.70	212-3
7. Nicoleta Grasu	ROM	63.28	207-7
8. Lisa-Marie Vizaniari	AUS	62.48	205-0

Ilke Wyludda had dominated the women's discus since 1988, but had faced nothing but frustration when it came to the big meets: the Olympics and the world championships. In 1988 she was passed over by the East German coaches; in Barcelona she didn't make it out of the qualifying round. Her world championship results were: 1987—fourth, 1991—second, 1992—eleventh and 1995—second. In Atlanta, Wyludda made up for all those disappointments by obliterating her opposition. Her first five throws were all better than anything anyone else could produce and her winning margin was the largest since 1952. After the competition, reporters were quick to ask her what changes she had made in her preparations that allowed her to overcome her big-meet curse. "I will tell you my secret," she replied. "For six weeks I have not eaten ice cream."

2000 Sydney C: 32, N: 20, D: 9.27. WR: 76.80, 252-0 (Gabriele Reinsch)

		M	FT.-IN.
1. Ellina Zvereva	BLR	68.40	224-5
2. Anastasia Kelesidou	GRE	65.71	215-7
3. Irina Yachenko	BLR	65.20	213-11
4. Nataliya Sadova	RUS	65.00	213-3
5. Styliani "Stella" Tsikouna	GRE	64.08	210-3
6. Franka Dietzsch	GER	63.18	207-3
7. Ilke Wyludda	GER	63.16	207-3
8. Lisa-Marie Vizaniari	AUS	62.57	205-3

World champion Franka Dietzsch won 14 of 16 meets in the pre-Olympic season. But in Sydney she struggled, qualifying for the final by only one centimeter and then placing sixth. Thirty-nine-year-old Ellina Zvereva, the 1996 bronze medal winner, led the qualifying round at 64.81 meters (212 feet 7 inches). In the final, her first four throws were all long enough to earn the gold medal. Anastasia Kelesidou's first round throw held up for second place, while 35-year-old Irina Yachenko took the bronze with her fifth round attempt. Ellina Zvereva is the oldest woman to win an Olympic track and field championship. In last place was Mariana Canillas of Paraguay. Her only legal throw, 32.31 meters (106 feet) was the shortest Olympic result in 36 years. Canillas was 15 years old.

2004 Athens C: 42, N: 27, D: 8.21. WR: 76.80, 252-0 (Gabriele Reinsch)

		M	FT.-IN.
1. Natalya Sadova	RUS	67.02	219-10
2. Anastasia Kelesidou	GRE	66.68	218-9
3. Irina Yachenko	BLR	66.17	217-1
4. Věra Pošpísilová-Cechlová	CZE	66.08	216-9
5. Olena Antonova	UKR	65.75	215-8
6. Nicoleta Grăsu-Gradinaru	ROM	64.92	212-11
7. Beatrice Faumuina	NZL	63.45	208-2
8. Aikaterini Vongoli	GRE	62.37	204-7

Despite earning a silver medal at the 2000 Olympics, as well as silvers at the 1999 and 2003 world championships, Anastasia Kelesidou had never won a gold medal in an international meet bigger than the Mediterranean Games. The hometown hero had serious competition in Athens, both from reigning world champion Irina Yachenko and from 1996 silver medalist Natalya Sadova. Sadova also won the 2001 world championship, but was stripped of her title and given a public warning after testing positive for excessive caffeine, which was later taken off the banned list.

During the closely-matched Olympic final, the crowd followed the women's discus competition with unusual interest because three of the twelve finalists were Greek. Sadova led the first round with a throw of 64.78 meters, but dropped to second in the next round when Věra Cechlová reached 66.08 meters. In round three, Yachenko briefly took the lead with a 66.17-meter throw, before being surpassed by Kelesidou, who thrilled the hometown crowd with a toss of 66.68 meters. Kelesidou's lead held up until the fifth round when Sadova, in fourth place, unleashed her winning throw of 67.02 meters.

In 2006, the World Anti-Doping Agency handed Sadova a two-year ban after she tested positive for the anabolic steroid methandienone at a meet in Hengelo, Netherlands.

2008 Beijing C: 38, N: 24, D: 8.18. WR: 76.80, 252-0 (Gabriele Reinsch)

		M	FT.-IN.
1. Stephanie Brown Trafton	USA	64.74	212-5
2. Yarelis Barrios	CUB	63.64	208-10
3. Olena Antonova	UKR	62.59	205-4
4. Song Aimin	CHN	62.20	204-1
5. Věra Pospíšilová-Cechlová	CZE	61.75	202-7
6. Ellina Zvereva	BLR	60.82	199-6
7. Li Yanfeng	CHN	60.68	199-1
8. Mélina Robert-Michon	FRA	60.66	199-0

Despite having competed in four Olympics, German discus thrower Franka Dietzsch had never managed to win an Olympic medal. After a disappointing finish in Athens, where she failed to advance past the qualifying round, Dietzsch showed she was still a dominant force in the sport, winning back-to-back world championship titles in 2005 and 2007 and taking silver at the 2006 European championships. Unfortunately, her Olympic bad luck continued in 2008 when a combination of high blood pressure, thyroid and knee problems forced her to withdraw a week and a half before the Beijing Games.

With Dietzsch out of the running, the favorite seemed to be reigning European champion and 2007 world silver medalist Darya Pishchalnikova. But Pishchalnikova was implicated in a Russian urine-tampering scandal and suspended just before the start of the Beijing Games.

With the event now wide open, relative unknown Stephanie Brown Trafton took the lead on her first attempt in the final, recording a 64.74-meter (212 ft. 4¾ in.) throw that bettered the field by more than a meter and a half. In second place after the first round, Yarelis Barrios improved to 63.64 meters (208 ft. 9½ in.), but could not beat Brown's opener. Brown fouled on her next three attempts, and managed only 61.30 meters (201 ft. 1½ in.) on her final throw, but was never threatened. It was the first US medal in the event in 76 years, since Lillian Copeland won at the 1932 Los Angeles Olympics. It was also the shortest Olympic winning distance since 1968.

Brown was an unlikely gold medalist, with almost no international experience. She made her first appearance at the Olympics in 2004, but failed to reach the final, and had never qualified for a world championship. In 2008 she was the last of the three US athletes to qualify for the event. At the age of 4, Brown had been inspired to become a gymnast after watching Mary Lou Retton perform during the 1984 Los Angeles Olympics, but switched to basketball after growing to be 6 ft. 4 in. (1.93m) tall. Maintaining her Olympic dreams Brown switched to the discus after suffering a tear in her anterior cruciate ligament (ACL) that ended her basketball career.

HAMMER THROW

1896–1996 not held

2000 Sydney C: 28, N: 20, D: 9.29. WR: 76.07, 249-7 (Mihaela Melinte)

		M	FT.-IN.
1. Kamila Skolimowska	POL	71.16	233-6
2. Olga Kuzenkova	RUS	69.77	228-11
3. Kirsten Münchow	GER	69.28	227-4
4. Yipsi Moreno	CUB	68.33	224-2
5. Debbie Sosimenko	AUS	67.95	222-11
6. Lyudmila Gubkina	BLR	67.08	220-1
7. Dawn Ellerbe	USA	66.80	219-2
8. Amy Palmer	USA	66.15	217-0

Since the women's hammer throw achieved a reasonable level of respectability in 1994, it had been dominated by Mihaela Melinte of Romania and Olga Kuzenkova of Russia. Between them they had 10 of the 12 best throws of all-time and all 17 of the longest throws of the pre-Olympic season. Melinte, the reigning world record holder, won the first two major international competitions, the 1998 European Championships and the 1999 world championships. Kuzenkova finished second both times.

The Olympic competition got off to a shocking start. As the throwers were warming up for the qualifying round, officials approached Melinte and escorted her off the field because two days earlier the IAAF had informed her that she had failed a doping test. This should have opened the door for Kuzenkova, who did in fact lead the qualifying round with a throw of 70.66 meters (231 feet 7 inches). Australian favorite, Debbie Sosimenko, another of the sport's pioneers, opened the final with a personal best of 67.95 meters (222 feet 11 inches). Her lead held up until the third round when 17-year-old Kamila Skolimowska connected with the best throw of her brief career, 71.16 meters (233 feet 6 inches). Skolimowska later said that she was inspired when, just before the competition began, she heard the Polish national anthem being played in honor of the victory of walker Robert Korzeniowski. Kuzenkova moved into second place with a throw of 69.64 (228 feet 6 inches) and improved in the fourth round to 69.77 (228 feet 11 inches). In the fifth round, Yipsi Moreno moved past Sosimenko into third place, but Kirsten Münchow immediately followed with a longer throw to secure the bronze medal. Skolimowska was the youngest track and field champion since the high jumper Ulrike Meyfarth in 1972. Less than three weeks later, Skolimowska competed in the world junior championships . . . and failed to make it out of the qualifying round.

2004 Athens C: 48, N: 27, D: 8.25. WR: 76.07, 249-7 (Mihaela Melinte)

		M	FT.-IN.	
1. Olga Kuzenkova	RUS	75.02	246-1½	OR
2. Yipsi Moreno	CUB	73.36	240-8	
3. Yunaika Crawford Rogert	CUB	73.16	240-0¼	
4. Betty Heldler	GER	72.73	238-7¼	
5. Kamila Skolimowska	POL	72.57	238-1	
6. Olga Tsander	BLR	72.27	237-1	
7. Zhang Wenxiu	CHN	72.03	236-3¾	
8. Iryna Sekachova	UKR	70.40	230-11½	

The two clear favorites in 2004 were reigning world champion Yipsi Moreno of Cuba and 33-year-old Olga Kuzenkova of Russia. The rivals had faced each other in the finals of both the 2001 and 2003 world championships, with Moreno edging out Kuzenkova both times. In fact, Kuzenkova had quite a history of placing second in major meets, having also done so in the 1998 European Championships, the 1999 world championships and the 2000 Olympics. In Athens, Kuzenkova took the lead with her first throw, an Olympic-record breaking distance of 73.18 meters. In the second round, Moreno moved up to second place with a 72.68-meter throw, while Kuzenkova improved to 74.27 meters. The third round saw a number of changes, as 21-year-old Yunaika Crawford moved past Moreno into the silver-medal position, with a personal record of 73.12 meters, before 20-year-old Betty Heidler dropped Moreno to fourth place with a throw of 72.73 meters. Kuzenkova then unleashed her biggest throw, 75.02 meters. In the fifth round, Moreno climbed back into the silver medal position with a heave of 73.36 meters. "I got used to the label of silver medalist," Kuzenkova told the press, "but that was a mistake." Kuzenkova went on the win the 2005 world championship as well.

2008 Beijing C: 50, N: 30, D: 8.20. WR: 77.80, 255-3 (Tatyana Lysenko)

		M	FT.-IN.	
1. Aksana Miankova	BLR	76.34	250-6	OR
2. Yipsi Moreno González	CUB	75.20	246-9	
3. Zhang Wenxiu	CHN	74.32	243-10	
4. Darya Pchelnik	BLR	73.65	241-8	
5. Manuela Montebrun	FRA	72.54	238-0	
6. Anita Włodarczyk	POL	71.56	234-9	
7. Clarissa Claretti	ITA	71.33	234-0	
8. Martina Danišová-Hrašnová	SVK	71.00	232-11	

By the time she arrived in Beijing, Yipsi Moreno had had a long streak of second-place finishes at major international tournaments. In 2004, after winning back-to-back world championship titles, she was beaten by Olga Kuzenkova for the Olympic gold. The following year she again finished second behind Kuzenkova at the world championships in Helsinki. Two years later, Moreno was once again second on the world championship podium, this time behind Germany's Betty Heidler, whose great-grandfather, Martin Riefstahl, had participated in the first Olympic torch relay in 1936.

It looked as if Moreno would finally get her shot at the top of the podium in 2008. Reigning Olympic champion Kuzenkova had failed to qualify for the Olympics, while reigning world champion Heidler only narrowly made it out of the qualification round and was eliminated after three rounds of the final. Moreno finished first in the qualifying round with a throw of 73.92 meters (242 ft. 6¼ in.), slightly ahead of 2007 world bronze medalist Zhang Wenxiu.

Twenty-six-year-old Aksana Miankova took the lead in the final with a first-round throw of 74.40 meters (244 ft. 1¼ in.) and held on to the lead through the next four rounds, followed by Zhang and Moreno. Moreno briefly took the lead in the fifth round with a throw of 74.70 meters (245 ft. 1 in.), but then Miankova managed to reach 76.34 meters (250 ft. 5½ in.), an Olympic record. That was enough for the gold medal, even though Moreno improved to 75.20 meters on her final attempt.

Miankova had taken up athletics at the age of 14 against the wishes of her mother, who wanted her to follow in her footsteps as a doctor, like all of her sisters. She briefly considered taking up rowing, but switched to the hammer throw after seeing ice in the local river.

Her 2008 Olympic victory was the only non-age group podium performance of her career.

JAVELIN THROW

The women's javelin must weigh a minimum of 600 grams (26.16 ounces) and measure between 2.20 meters (7 feet 2⅝ inches) and 2.30 meters (7 feet 6½ inches).

1896–1928 not held

1932 Los Angeles C: 8, N: 4, D: 7.31. WR: 46.75, 153-4½ (Nan Gindele)

		M	FT.-IN.
1. Mildred "Babe" Didrikson	USA	43.68	143-4 OR
2. Ellen Braumüller	GER	43.49	142-8
3. Ottilie "Tilly" Fleischer	GER	43.00	141-1
4. Masako Shimpo	JPN	39.07	128-2
5. Nan Gindele	USA	37.95	124-6
6. Gloria Russell	USA	36.73	120-6
7. Maria Uribe Jasso	MEX	33.66	110-5
8. Mitsue Ishizu	JPN	30.81	101-1

Mildred "Babe" Didriksen was born June 26, 1911, in Port Arthur, Texas and raised in nearby Beaumont. Her parents were immigrants from Norway. After her name was misspelled in school as "Didrikson," she decided to retain the misspelling. She first heard about the Olympics in 1928 and vowed to be an Olympic champion in 1932. She was so determined that she convinced homeowners on her block to trim their hedges to the same height so she could use them to practice hurdling. She was already an all American basketball player when she gained sudden and dramatic national attention as a track and field star. On July 4, 1932, the women's AAU championships, which also served as the Olympic trials, were held in Evanston, Illinois, on the campus of Northwestern University. Babe caused a sensation at the opening parade when she appeared as the entire team representing the Employers Casualty Insurance Company of Dallas, which had recruited her to play basketball for the company team. In the next three hours she took part in eight of the ten events and won six of them. She set world records in the 80-meter hurdles, the javelin, and the high jump, in which she tied with Jean Shiley. She also won the shot put, long jump, and baseball throw, and finished fourth in the discus. When the point totals were tallied, it was announced that Babe Didrikson had won the team title with 30 points. In second place with 22 points was the University of Illinois, which had sent a 22-woman contingent.

Olympic rules limited Babe to only three events, even though she had qualified for five, so she chose the three at which she had set world records. On the train across the country to the Los Angeles Olympics, the 21-year-old Babe irritated her fellow teammates by playing the harmonica, exercising in the aisles, and bragging about her numerous feats, which included earning a blue ribbon for sewing at the Texas State Fair (in reality it was a local fair). The same qualities that annoyed the athletes delighted reporters. Upon arrival in California, she told them, "I am out to beat everybody in sight, and that's just what I'm going to do." Her first event was the javelin, in which her first throw of 143 feet 4 inches was good enough for the gold medal even though the javelin slipped out of her hand. Before the Olympics were over she had recorded new world marks in the 80-meter hurdles and the high jump.

Overnight Babe Didrikson became a celebrity. But before the year was out she had been barred from amateur competition because she had allowed a photo of herself and an interview to be used in an automobile ad campaign. For a time she toured as the only female and only nonbearded member of the House of David baseball team. But making a living as an athlete was difficult for a woman in the 1930s. In addition, Babe soon discovered that the brash, tough, good ol' boy public image that she had cultivated on the road to fame, did not work so well once she reached the top. In her later life, Didrikson actually avoided talking about her years in track and field and she worked hard to make her image more feminine and respectable. Eventually she turned to golf, and it was there that she gained her greatest success. Encouraged by her 285-pound husband, wrestler George Zaharias, she became the greatest woman golfer in the world. During one 12-month period from 1946 to 1947, she won 14 straight tournaments and became the first American woman to win the British Amateur Open.

In 1953 Babe learned that she had cancer and was forced to undergo an emergency colostomy. Three and a half months after the surgery she was back on the circuit, finishing third in a minor tournament. The following year she won the US Open by 12 strokes. But the cancer returned, and on September 17, 1956, Babe Didrikson, who had been voted the greatest female athlete of the half-century in an Associated Press poll, died at the age of 45.

1936 Berlin C: 14, N: 10, D: 8.2. WR: 46.75, 153-4½ (Nan Gindele)

		M	FT.-IN.	
1. Ottilie "Tilly" Fleischer	GER	45.18	148-3	OR
2. Luise Krüger	GER	43.29	142-8	
3. Maria Kwaśniewska	POL	41.80	137-2	
4. Hermine "Herma" Bauma	AUT	41.66	136-8	
5. Sadako Yamamoto	JPN	41.45	135-11	
6. Lydia Eberhardt	GER	41.37	135-8	
7. Gertrude Wilhelmsen	USA	37.35	122-6	
8. Gerda de Kock	HOL	36.93	121-2	

1948 London C: 15, N: 10, D: 7.31. WR: 50.32, 165-1 (Klavdia Mayuchaya)

		M	FT.-IN.	
1. Hermine "Herma" Bauma	AUT	45.57	149-6	OR
2. Kaisa Parviainen	FIN	43.79	143-8	
3. Lily Carlstedt	DEN	42.08	138-1	
4. Dorothy Dodson	USA	41.96	137-8	
5. Johanna Tenunissen Waalboer	HOL	40.92	134-3	
6. Johanna Koning	HOL	40.33	132-3	
7. Dana Ingrová	CZE	39.64	130-0	
8. Elly Dammers	HOL	38.23	125-5	

1952 Helsinki C: 19, N: 13, D: 7.24. WR: 53.41, 175-2¾ (Nina Smirnitskaya)

		M	FT.-IN.	
1. Dana Zátopková (Ingrová)	CZE	50.47	165-7	OR
2. Aleksandra Chudina	SOV/RUS	50.01	164-0	
3. Yelena Gorchakova	SOV/RUS	49.76	163-3	
4. Galina Zybina	SOV/RUS	48.35	158-7	
5. Lily Kelsby-Carlstedt	DEN	46.23	151-8	
6. Marlies Müller	GER	44.37	145-6	
7. Maria Ciach	POL	44.31	145-4½	
8. Jutta Kruger	GER	44.30	145-4	

Shortly before the competition began, Dana Zátopková's husband, Emil Zátopek, was awarded a gold medal for winning the 5000 meters. After the ceremony, she rushed up to him and said, "You've won! Splendid! Show me that medal." After examining it, she added, "I'll take it with me for luck." She put it in her bag and left. On her first throw she set an Olympic record and earned a gold medal of her own. That evening Emil claimed that he deserved partial credit for his wife's gold medal because he had inspired her. Naturally, Dana was quite offended and replied, "What? All right, go and inspire some other girl and see if she throws a javelin fifty meters."

1956 Melbourne C: 19, N: 12, D: 11.28. WR: 55.48, 182-0 (Nadezhda Konyayeva)

		M	FT.-IN.	
1. Inese Jaunzeme	SOV/LAT	53.86	176-8	OR
2. Marlene Ahrens	CHI	50.38	165-3	
3. Nadiya Konyayeva	SOV/UKR	50.28	164-11½	
4. Dana Zátopková (Ingrová)	CZE	49.83	163-5½	
5. Ingrid Almqvist	SWE	49.74	163-2	
6. Urszula Figwer	POL	48.16	158-0	
7. Erszébeth Vig	HUN	48.07	157-8½	
8. Karen Anderson	USA	48.00	157-5½	

Dana Zátopková and Emil Zátopek, 1952
Keeping it all in the family in Helsinki.

1960 Rome C: 20, N: 14, D: 9.1. WR: 59.54, 195-4 (Elvira Ozoliņa)

		M	FT.-IN.	
1. Elvira Ozoliņa	SOV/RUS	55.98	183-8	OR
2. Dana Zátopková (Ingrová)	CZE	53.78	176-5	
3. Birutė Kalėdienė	SOV/LIT	53.45	175-4	
4. Vlasta Pesková	CZE	52.56	172-5	
5. Urszula Figwer	POL	52.33	171-8	
6. Anna Pazera	AUS	51.15	167-9	
7. Susan Platt	GBR	51.01	167-4	
8. Alevtina Shastitko	SOV/RUS	50.92	167-1	

Ozoliņa unleashed her winning throw at her first attempt. Zátopková was 18 days shy of her 38th birthday when she won her second Olympic medal. Not only was she the oldest woman in Olympic history to win a track and field medal, but two years earlier she had thrown the javelin 182 feet 10 inches to become the oldest female world record breaker.

In the third round, Susan Platt of Great Britain threw past the 177-foot mark. However she was so excited that she stepped over the line on her way to see where the spear had fallen. The judge immediately ruled a foul and Platt had to settle for seventh place.

1964 Tokyo C: 16, N: 10, D: 10.16. WR: 61.38, 201-4½ (Elvira Ozoliņa)

		M	FT.-IN.
1. Mihaela Peneş	ROM	60.54	198-7
2. Márta Rudas	HUN	58.27	191-2
3. Yelena Gorchakova	SOV/RUS	57.06	187-2
4. Birutė Kalėdienė	SOV/LIT	56.31	184-8
5. Elvira Ozoliņa	SOV/RUS	54.81	179-9
6. Maria Diaconescu	ROM	53.71	176-2
7. Hiroko Sato	JPN	52.48	172-2
8. Anneliese Gerhards	GER	52.37	171-10

The 1964 javelin competition was full of surprises. On the very first throw of the qualification round, 31-year-old Yelena Gorchakova set a world record of 62.40 meters (204 feet 9 inches). This boosted her up to co-favorite along with defending champion Elvira Ozoliņa. However, when the final began a few hours later, it was 17-year-old high school student Mihaela Peneş of Bucharest who stunned the crowd with a throw of 198 feet 7 inches—17 feet further than she had ever thrown before. No one came close to her for the rest of the competition. Ozoliņa fouled on her last four attempts and had to settle for fifth place. She was so distressed by her performance that she went straight to the hairdresser at the Olympic Village and asked to have her head shaved. When the Japanese hairdresser refused, Ozoliņa took the clippers herself and removed a chunk of her long tresses. The hairdresser finished the job and Ozoliņa left the parlor bald, refusing a scarf to hide her shame. Ozoliņa was not the first Olympic athlete to react to defeat by having her head shaved, although she was the first woman. Four years earlier, in Rome, the entire Japanese wrestling team had had their heads shaved after an all-around poor showing.

Elvira Ozoliņa, 1964

Ozoliņa, winner of the 1960 javelin throw, was so humiliated at finishing only fifth in 1964 that she shaved off all her hair and refused to wear a scarf to hide her shame.

1968 Mexico City C: 16, N: 11, D: 10.14. WR: 62.40, 204-8¾ (Yelena Gorchakova)

		M	FT.-IN.
1. Angéla Németh	HUN	60.36	198-0
2. Mihaela Peneş	ROM	59.92	196-7
3. Eva Janko	AUT	58.04	190-5
4. Márta Rudas	HUN	56.38	185-0
5. Daniela Jaworska	POL	56.06	183-11
6. Nataša Urbančić	YUG/SLO	55.42	181-10
7. Ameli Koloska	GER	55.20	181-1
8. Kaisa Launela	FIN	53.96	177-0

1972 Munich C: 19, N: 10, D: 9.1. WR: 65.06, 213-5½ (Ruth Fuchs)

		M	FT.-IN.
1. Ruth Fuchs	GDR	63.88	209-7 OR
2. Jacqueline Todten	GDR	62.54	205-2
3. Kathryn Schmidt	USA	59.94	196-8
4. Liutvian Mollova	BUL	59.36	194-9
5. Nataša Urbančić	YUG/SLO	59.06	193-9
6. Eva Janko	AUT	58.56	192-1
7. Ewa Gryziecka	POL	57.00	187-0
8. Svetlana Korolyova	SOV/RUS	56.36	184-11

Yelena Gorchakova's 1964 qualifying toss of 204 feet 8¾ inches had been in the books as a world record for over seven and a half years when it was suddenly beaten twice in one day. On June 11, 1972, Ewa Gryziecka, competing in Bucharest, threw the javelin 205 feet 8 inches (62.70 meters). One half-hour later, in Potsdam, East Germany, Ruth Fuchs began her domination of women's javelin with a throw of 213 feet 5½ inches (65.06 meters). Two and a half months later, at the Munich Olympics, Fuchs took the lead from Kate Schmidt in the second round, improved in the fourth round, and broke the Olympic record in the fifth round. The competition ended on an exciting note when Urbančić's final throw almost skewered a wandering photographer.

1976 Montreal C: 15, N: 10, D: 7.24. WR: 69.12, 226-9¼ (Ruth Fuchs)

		M	FT.-IN.
1. Ruth Fuchs	GDR	65.94	216-4 OR
2. Marion Becker	GER	64.70	212-3
3. Kathryn Schmidt	USA	63.96	209-10
4. Jacqueline Hein (Todten)	GDR	63.84	209-5
5. Sabine Sebrowski	GDR	63.08	206-11
6. Svetlana Babich (Korolyova)	SOV/RUS	59.42	194-11
7. Nadezhda Yakubovich	SOV/BLR	59.16	194-1
8. Karin Smith	USA	57.50	188-8

Marion Becker reached the victory platform in Montreal after an unusual odyssey. Born in Hamburg in West Germany in 1950, she was nonetheless raised in East Germany. After marrying, she moved to Romania and represented Romania at the 1972 Olympics in Munich, finishing seventeenth. After the games, she stayed behind in West Germany and four years later competed for the nation of her birth in the 1976 Olympics. In the qualifying round she broke the Olympic record with a throw of 213 feet 8 inches (65.14 meters). However, in the competition proper, Ruth Fuchs knocked out her opposition with an opening throw of 216 feet 4 inches (65.94 meters).

1980 Moscow C: 21, N: 14, D: 7.25. WR: 70.08, 229-10 (Tatyana Biryulina)

		M	FT.-IN.
1. María Colón Rueñes	CUB	68.40	224-5 OR
2. Saida Gunba	SOV/GEO	67.76	222-2
3. Ute Hommola	GDR	66.56	218-4
4. Ute Richter	GDR	66.54	218-4
5. Ivanka Vancheva	BUL	66.38	217-9
6. Tatyana Biryulina	SOV/UZB	65.08	213-6
7. Eva Raduly-Zorgo	ROM	64.08	210-3
8. Ruth Fuchs	GDR	63.94	209-9

Ruth Fuchs continued to be the queen of javelin throwing all the way into 1980. On April 29 she set a world record of 69.96 meters (229 feet 6 inches) and she looked poised to become the first woman to break the 70-meter barrier. However, on July 12 a complete unknown, Tatyana Biryulina, improved her personal best by 27½ feet with a throw of 70.08. Less than two weeks later, at the Olympics, Biryulina could do no better than 65.08 and sixth place. In fact, the women with the four best pre-Olympic records all had disappointing performances. Fuchs, competing with a back injury, finished eighth, Raduly was seventh, and Tessa Sanderson, who had thrown 69.70, failed to qualify for the final. It was left to María Colón to win the competition on her first throw. She was the first Cuban woman to win an Olympic gold medal and the first non-white athlete of either sex to win an Olympic throwing event. From 1970 through 1980 Ruth Fuchs took part in 129 meets

Ruth Fuchs, 1978
Winner of two gold medals in the 1970s, Fuchs, while a member of parliament, later admitted to taking steroids.

and won 113 of them, including 30 straight from 1972 to 1974. In April 1994, Fuchs admitted that she had taken steroid tablets during the winters between 1972 and 1980. At the time of her admission, one of the first by a former East German athlete, Fuchs was a member of parliament.

1984 Los Angeles C: 24, N: 16, D: 8.6. WR: 74.73, 245-3 (Ilse "Tiina" Lillak)

		M	FT.-IN.
1. Theresa "Tessa" Sanderson	GBR	69.56	228-2 OR
2. Ilse "Tiina" Lillak	FIN	69.00	226-4
3. Fatima Whitbread	GBR	67.14	220-3
4. Tuula Laaksalo	FIN	66.40	217-10
5. E. Katrine Hattestad (Solberg)	NOR	64.52	211-8
6. Ingrid Thyssen	GER	63.26	207-6
7. Beate Peters	GER	62.34	204-6
8. Karin Smith	USA	62.06	203-7

Jamaican-born Tessa Sanderson, competing in her third Olympics, broke the Olympic record with her first throw. World record holder Tiina Lillak had won the 1983 world championship with a dramatic last round throw in front of an adoring hometown crowd. In Los Angeles her second round effort came within two feet of Sanderson's best, but she was forced to pass her last four chances because of a stress fracture of her right foot. Sanderson's record held up for the gold medal, while Fatima Whitbread, who had beaten Sanderson three times in a row after losing 21 of their first 22 confrontations, overhauled Laaksalo in the fifth round to secure the bronze. Sanderson was the first British athlete to win an Olympic throwing event. She eventually competed in three more Olympics, culminating in a fourteenth place finish in 1996. Sanderson and discus thrower Lia Maniliu are the only women track and field athletes to take part in six Olympics.

1988 Seoul C: 29, N: 18, D: 9.26. WR: 80.00, 262-5 (Petra Felke)

		M	FT.-IN.
1. Petra Felke	GDR	74.68	245-0 OR
2. Fatima Whitbread	GBR	70.32	230-8½
3. Beate Koch	GDR	67.30	220-10
4. Iryna Kostyuchenkova	SOV/UKR	67.00	219-10
5. Silke Renk	GDR	66.38	217-9
6. Natalya Yermolovich	SOV/BLR	64.84	212-9
7. Donna Mayhew	USA	61.78	202-8
8. Ingrid Thyssen	GER	60.76	199-4

Between 1984 and the opening of the 1988 Olympics, Petra Felke won 69 of 76 meets. Her last three losses were all to Fatima Whitbread, who defeated her at the two most important meets—the 1986 European championships and the 1987 world championships. Eight days before the opening of the Seoul Games, Felke served notice that she was finally ready to win the big one when she became the first woman to throw a javelin 80 meters. In Seoul she delivered the three longest throws of the competition. Whitbread secured the silver medal despite the fact that in the 12 preceding months she had experienced a trapped nerve in her throwing shoulder, a foot injury, a mouth infection, an abscess in her back, hamstring problems, glandular fever, and a car crash.

1992 Barcelona C: 25, N: 17, D: 8.1. WR: 80.00, 262-5 (Petra Felke)

		M	FT.-IN.
1. Silke Renk	GER	68.34	224-2
2. Natalya Shikolenko	BLR	68.26	223-11
3. Karen Forkel	GER	66.86	219-4
4. Theresa "Tessa" Sanderson	GBR	63.58	208-7
5. E. Katrine Hattestad (Solberg)	NOR	63.54	208-5
6. Heli Rantanen	FIN	62.34	204-6
7. Petra Meier (Felke)	GER	59.02	193-8
8. Dulce García Gil	CUB	58.26	191-1

Shikolenko's first round throw of 223 feet 11 inches appeared to be good enough for the gold. But in the final round, Silke Renk, then in third place, extended the start of her run-up all the way back to lane 8 of the track and beat Shikolenko by 3 inches.

1996 Atlanta C: 32, N: 23, D: 7.27. WR: 80.00, 262-5 (Petra Felke)

		M	FT.-IN.
1. Heli Rantanen	FIN	67.94	222-11
2. Louise McPaul	AUS	65.54	215-0
3. E. Katrine Hattestad (Solberg)	NOR	64.98	213-2
4. Isel López Ramírez	CUB	64.68	212-2
5. Xiomara Rivero Azcuy	CUB	64.48	211-7
6. Karen Forkel	GER	64.18	210-7
7. Mikaela Ingberg	FIN	61.52	201-10
8. Li Lei	CHN	60.74	199-3

The pre-Olympic favorites were world champion Natalya Shikolenko and Trine Hattestad, the former world champion who was returning after maternity leave. Hattestad, competing in her fourth Olympics, holds a unique spot in athletics history. After a doping test in 1989, she became the first athlete to win a reversal of her suspension by the IAAF Doping Commission.

Felicia Tilea of Romania led the qualifying round with a throw of 66.94 meters while Heli Rantanen set a personal best of 66.54 meters. Rantanen went first in the final. Defying her coach's advice to take it easy at the beginning, she went all out and was rewarded with another personal record that held up for the gold medal. The battle for silver and bronze went down to the wire. With one round to go, the order stood: Rantanen, López, Rivero, McPaul, Forkel and Hattestad. But with their final attempts, McPaul moved from fourth to second and Hattestad jumped from sixth to third. Shikolenko was particularly unlucky. Her second throw hit an overhead camera cable. She was awarded an extra try, but she was unable to match the cable shot and she ended up in twelfth place. Tilea, too, bombed out in the final, placing tenth.

Heli Rantanen was the seventh Finnish javelin thrower to win a gold medal, but the first woman.

2000 Sydney C: 35, N: 27, D: 9.30. WR: 69.48, 227-11 (Trine Hattestad)

		M	FT.-IN.
1. E. Katrine Hattestad (Solberg)	NOR	68.91	226-1
2. Mirela Manjani-Tzelili	GRE	67.51	221-6
3. Osleidys Menéndez	CUB	66.18	217-2
4. Steffi Nerius	GER	64.84	212-9
5. Sonia Bisset	CUB	63.26	207-7
6. Xiomara Rivero	CUB	62.92	206-5
7. Tatyana Shikolenko	RUS	62.91	206-5
8. Nikola Tomecková	CZE	62.10	203-9

The javelin was redesigned and all records started fresh in 1998. Veteran Trine Hattestad established the world record for the new implement on July 28, 2000. Thirty four years old and competing in her fifth Olympics, Hattestad settled the gold medal with her first throw. Albanian-born Mirela Tzelili secured the silver medal with a third-round throw, while Osleidys Menéndez made three throws that were long enough for the bronze medal.

2004 Athens C: 45, N: 31, D: 8.27. WR: 71.54 (Osleidys Menéndez)

		M	FT.-IN.
1. Osleidys Menéndez	CUB	71.53	234-8
2. Steffi Nerius	GER	65.82	215-11
3. Mirela Manjani	GRE	64.29	210-11
4. Nikola Tomečková-Brejchová	CZE	64.23	210-8
5. Sonia Bisset	CUB	63.54	208-5
6. Laverne Eve	BAH	62.77	205-11
7. Noraida Bicet	CUB	62.51	205-1
8. Tetyana Liakhovych	UKR	61.75	202-7

World record holder and 2001 world champion Osleidys Menéndez arrived in Athens hoping to make up for a disappointing fifth place finish in the 2003 world championships, where her best throw fell more than four meters short of first-place Mirela Manjani. Manjani, who had also won the championship title in 1999 and the silver medal at the 2000 Olympics, had finished second behind Menéndez in 2001. On her first attempt of the 2004 Olympic final, Menéndez recorded a huge throw of 71.53 meters (234 feet 8 inches), just one centimeter short of her world record, effectively ending the competition for gold. Three rounds later, she sealed her lead with a throw of 68.60 meters (225 feet 1 inch), which also would have been good enough for gold. The battle for the remaining two medals culminated in the final round, when Steffi Nerius, the daughter of two volleyball coaches, moved into second place with a personal best of 65.82 meters (215 feet 11 inches). Manjani pleased the crowd with a final throw of 64.29 meters (210 feet 11 inches) that earned her the bronze medal.

In 2005, Menéndez won her second world championship with a world record throw of 71.70 meters (235 feet 3 inches).

2008 Beijing C: 54, N: 40, D: 8.21. WR: 71.70, 235-3 (Osleidys Menéndez)

		M	FT.-IN.
1. Barbora Špotáková	CZE	71.42	234-4
2. Mariya Abakumova	RUS	70.78	232-3
3. Christina Obergföll	GER	66.13	217-0
4. Goldie Sayers	GBR	65.75	215-9
5. Steffi Nerius	GER	65.29	214-2
6. Osleidys Menéndez	CUB	63.35	207-10
7. Barbara Madejczyk	POL	62.02	203-6
8. Katharina Molitor	GER	59.64	195-8

In a relatively wide-open competition, reigning world champion and world number one Barbora Špotáková seemed to be the gold medal favorite. True to expectations, she finished first in the qualifying round, ahead of two-time reigning world silver medalist Christina Obergföll and reigning Olympic silver medalist Steffi Nerius.

In the final, however, 22-year-old relative unknown Mariya Abakumova took the lead with her first throw, a Russian national record of 69.32 meters (227 ft. 5¼ in.). Špotáková responded with a Czech national record, 69.22 meters (227 ft. 1¼ in.). The two stayed in first and second place for the next five rounds, with Abakumova improving to 70.78 meters (232 ft. 2½ in.) on her fourth attempt to become the second-longest thrower in history. On her sixth and last throw, Špotáková unleashed a throw of 71.42-meters (234 ft. 3¾ in.) to move past Abakumova into the gold medal spot. Obergföll moved into third place on her first attempt and held on through the next five rounds, while defending Olympic champion and world record holder Osleidys Menéndez finished in sixth place after fouling five times.

Abakumova started her career as a rhythmic gymnast, but was expelled for being too tall and not skinny enough. She switched to heptathlon, but found she was terrible at the 800 meters. She then focused on the hurdles, but crashed so often that she kept getting injured. Abakumova finally decided to focus on the javelin, and placed second in her first competition, the 2002 Russian Championships.

At the 2009 world championships, Špotáková and Abakumova finished second and third behind 37-year-old Nerius. Two years later at the 2011 world championships in Daegu, the two engaged in another dramatic battle. Špotáková took the first round lead, but Abakumova moved ahead in the second round with a throw of 71.25 meters (223 feet 9 inches). This held up as the leading throw until the fifth round, when Špotáková reached 71.58 (234 feet 10 inches). But when Abakumova followed her to the line, she threw a 71.99 (236 feet 2 inches) to take the title.

HEPTATHLON/PENTATHLON

In 1984 the five-event pentathlon was replaced by the seven-event heptathlon. On the first day, athletes compete in the 100-meter hurdles, the high jump, the shot put, and the 200-meter dash. On the second day, they conclude with the long jump, the javelin and the 800-meter run. Points are scored according to a set of tables approved by the International Amateur Athletic Federation.

1896–1960 not held

1964 Tokyo C: 20, N: 15, D: 10.16-17. WR: 5194 (Iryna Press)

		80M H	SP	HJ	LJ	200M	TOTAL
1. Iryna Press	SOV/UKR	10.7	17.16	1.63	6.24	24.7	5246 WR
2. Mary Rand (Bignal)	GBR	10.9	11.05	1.72	6.55	24.2	5035
3. Galina Bystrova	SOV/RUS	10.7	14.47	1.60	6.11	25.2	4956
4. Mary Peters	GBR	11.0	14.48	1.60	5.60	25.4	4797
5. Draga Stamejčić	YUG/SLO	10.9	12.73	1.54	6.19	25.2	4790
6. Helga Hoffman	GER	11.2	10.67	1.60	6.44	25.0	4737
7. Patricia Winslow	USA	12.0	13.04	1.63	5.90	24.6	4724
8. Ingrid Becker	GER	11.6	11.62	1.60	6.17	24.6	4717

Press's margin of victory was provided in the shot put, where she outpointed Rand 1173 to 789 with a throw of 56 feet 2½ inches, which was 16½ inches farther than she was able to throw in the shot put competition three days later.

1968 Mexico City C: 33, N: 24, D: 10.15-16. WR: 5246 (Iryna Press)

		80M H	SP	HJ	LJ	200M	TOTAL
1. Ingrid Becker	GER	10.9	11.48	1.71	6.43	23.5	5098
2. Elisabeth Prokop	AUT	11.2	14.61	1.68	5.97	25.1	4966
3. Annamária Tóth	HUN	10.9	12.68	1.59	6.12	23.8	4959
4. Valentina Tikhomirova	SOV/RUS	11.2	14.12	1.65	5.99	24.9	4927
5. Manon Bornholdt	GER	11.0	12.37	1.59	6.42	24.8	4890
6. Patricia Winslow	USA	11.4	13.33	1.65	5.97	24.5	4877
7. Ingeborg Bauer	GDR	11.4	13.00	1.59	6.22	24.5	4849
8. Meta Antenen	SWI	10.7	11.06	1.62	6.30	24.9	4848

Heidemarie Rosendahl of West Germany was considered the pre-Games favorite, but she pulled a muscle while warming up and was unable to compete. Liese Prokop was the surprise leader after four events, but Ingrid Becker, competing in her third Olympics, ran the fastest 200 meters of the competition to take the gold medal.

1972 Munich C: 28, N: 18, D: 9.2-3. WR: 4775 (Burglinde Pollak)

		100M H	SP	HJ	LJ	200M	TOTAL
1. Mary Peters	GBR	13.29	16.29	1.82	5.98	24.08	4801 WR
2. Heidemarie Rosendahl	GER	13.34	13.86	1.65	6.83	22.96	4791
3. Burglinde Pollak	GDR	13.53	16.04	1.76	6.21	23.93	4768
4. Christine Bodner	GDR	13.25	12.51	1.76	6.40	23.66	4671
5. Valentina Tikhomirova	SOV/RUS	13.77	14.64	1.74	6.15	24.25	4597
6. Nedialka Angelova	BUL	13.84	13.96	1.68	6.32	24.58	4496
7. Karen Mack	GER	14.45	14.10	1.76	6.11	24.72	4449
8. Ilona Bruzsenyák	HUN	13.65	12.48	1.65	6.29	24.35	4419

In 1971, the 80-meter hurdles was replaced by the 100-meter hurdles, necessitating a change in the scoring tables and a reevaluation of the world record. Mary Peters, a 33-year-old English-born secretary from Belfast, Northern Ireland, finished fourth at Tokyo in 1964 and ninth in Mexico City in 1968. During the first day of competition in Munich she recorded personal bests in two of the three events—the 100-meter hurdles and the high jump. The high jump was a particularly magical moment for her, as the German crowd rooted her on and chanted her name despite the fact that she was competing against local favorite Heide Rosendahl, who had won the long jump two days earlier. At the end of the first day, Peters was 97 points ahead of Pollak and 301 points ahead of

Pentathlon Medalists, 1972

Heidemarie Rosendahl (silver), Mary Peters (gold) and Burglinde Pollak (bronze).

Rosendahl, who was in fifth place. But the two events of the second day, the long jump and the 200 meters, were Rosendahl's best and Peters' worst. Sure enough, Rosendahl jumped 22 feet 5 inches, 1 centimeter short of her world record. The 200 meters saw both women achieve personal bests. If Mary Peters had run one-tenth of a second slower she would have lost the gold medal. Afterward she told the press that she had become so exhausted in the last 50 meters of the 200 that her legs felt like jelly. In her autobiography, *Mary P.,* she revised her description and wrote that her legs felt like lead.

1976 Montreal C: 20, N: 13, D: 7.25-26. WR: 4932 (Burglinde Pollak)

		100M H	SP	HJ	LJ	200M	TOTAL
1. Siegrun Siegl	GDR	13.31	12.92	1.74	6.49	23.09	4745
2. Christine Laser (Bodner)	GDR	13.55	14.29	1.78	6.27	23.48	4745
3. Burglinde Pollak	GDR	13.30	16.25	1.64	6.30	23.64	4740
4. Lyudmila Popovskaya	SOV/RUS	13.33	15.02	1.74	6.19	24.10	4700
5. Nadezhda Tkachenko	SOV/UKR	13.41	14.90	1.80	6.08	24.61	4669
6. Diane Jones	CAN	13.79	14.58	1.80	6.29	25.33	4582
7. Jane Frederick	USA	13.54	14.55	1.76	5.99	24.70	4566
8. Margit Papp	HUN	14.14	14.80	1.78	6.35	25.43	4535

Anyone who enjoys close finishes need look no further than the 1976 pentathlon. With four events finished and only the 200 meters to be run, the standings were as follows:

1. Tkachenko	3788	5. Laser	3757
2. Popovskaya	3772	6. Papp	3726
3. Pollak	3768	7. Siegl	3718
4. Jones	3764	8. Frederick	3693

All the leaders were matched against one another in the final heat. When the dust cleared 26 seconds later, officials and fans hurriedly consulted their scoring tables. It was discovered that Siegl, the world record holder in the long jump, and Laser, who had achieved personal records in the high jump and 200, had finished with the exact same point total, while Pollak was only five points behind. Siegl was finally awarded first place on the basis of having beaten Laser in three of the five events. Had Pollak run six one-hundredths of a second faster she would have won the gold medal. Instead she had to settle for her second straight bronze. While Siegl jumped from seventh to first in one event, Tkachenko had the misfortune of dropping from first to fifth in less than 25 seconds.

1980 Moscow C: 19, N: 12, D: 7.23-24. WR (with 800m): 4856 (Olga Kuragina)

		100M H	SP	HJ	LJ	800M	TOTAL
1. Nadezhda Tkachenko	SOV/UKR	13.29	16.84	1.84	6.73	2:05.2	5083 WR
2. Olga Rukavishnikova	SOV/RUS	13.66	14.09	1.88	6.79	2:04.8	4937
3. Olga Kuragina	SOV/RUS	13.26	12.49	1.84	6.77	2:03.6	4875
4. Ramona Neubert	GDR	13.93	13.68	1.77	6.63	2:07.7	4698
5. Margit Papp	HUN	13.96	14.94	1.74	6.35	2:15.8	4562
6. Burglinde Pollak	GDR	13.74	16.67	1.68	5.93	2:14.4	4553
7. Valentina Dimitrova	BUL	14.39	15.65	1.74	5.91	2:15.5	4458
8. Emilia Kunova	BUL	13.73	11.98	1.74	6.10	2:11.1	4431

The 1980 pentathlon saw tremendous performances by all three Soviet athletes, each of whom broke the existing world record. Thirty-one-year-old Nadezhda Tkachenko followed a long road to her gold medal. Ninth in Munich, fifth in Montreal, she won the European title in 1978 only to lose it after failing a test for anabolic steroids. Handed an 18-month suspension by the IAAF, she was back in time for the 1980 Olympics. In Moscow she achieved personal bests in four of the five events and fell only three-quarters of an inch short of her lifetime record in the shot put. Rukavishnikova has the unusual distinction of setting the shortest-lived world record in history—two-fifths of a second. When she crossed the finish line of the 800 meters she became the world record holder in the pentathlon. But when Tkachenko finished right behind her, a new record was set.

1984 Los Angeles C: 23, N: 13, D: 8.3-4. WR: 6867 (Sabine Paetz)

		100M H	HJ	SP	200M	LJ	JT	800M	TOTAL
1. Glynis Nunn	AUS	13.02	1.80	12.82	24.06	6.66	35.58	2:10.57	6390 OR
2. Jacqueline Joyner	USA	13.63	1.80	14.39	24.05	6.11	44.52	2:13.03	6385
3. Sabine Everts	GER	13.54	1.89	12.49	24.05	6.71	32.62	2:09.05	6363
4. Cindy Greiner	USA	13.71	1.83	13.36	24.40	6.15	40.86	2:11.75	6281
5. Judith Simpson	GBR	13.07	1.86	13.86	24.95	6.33	33.64	2:13.01	6280
6. Sabine Braun	GER	13.61	1.80	12.09	24.22	6.10	44.14	2:12.48	6236
7. Tineke Hidding	HOL	13.70	1.74	13.48	24.12	6.35	33.94	2:12.84	6147
8. Kim Hagger	GBR	13.39	1.86	12.29	24.72	6.37	35.42	2:18.44	6127

With all of the leading medal contenders among the boycott missing, the first Olympic heptathlon became an open competition. After the four events of the first day, Simpson led with 3759 points. She was followed closely by Joyner at 3739, Nunn with 3731 and Everts with 3721. The first event of the second day; the long jump, turned out to be the turning point. This was Joyner's specialty. But after fouling her first two tries, she played it safe with her final jump, taking off over a foot before the takeoff board and registering only 20 feet ½ inch, 26 inches less than she would achieve in placing fifth in the long jump competition five days later. Meanwhile, Everts moved into first place, one point ahead of Nunn. However, Joyner took the lead for the first time following the javelin throw.

As Jackie Joyner struggled through the 800-meter run, she was rooted on by her brother Al, who was in the midst of winning the triple jump. When the race was over, coaches and officials rushed to their scoring tables booklets to compute the results. Initially, Glynis Nunn, a 24-year-old schoolteacher, thought she had lost by 3 points. In fact, she had improved her personal record by 108 points and won by 5 points. If Joyner had long-jumped 3 centimeters farther or finished the 800 0.33 seconds faster, the victory would have been hers. Later in the Olympics Nunn placed seventh in the long jump and fifth in the 100-meter hurdles.

1988 Seoul C: 29, N: 19, D: 9.23-24. WR: 7215 (Jacqueline Joyner-Kersee)

		100M H	HJ	SP	200M	LJ	JT	800M	TOTAL
1. Jacqueline Joyner-Kersee	USA	12.69	1.86	15.80	22.56	7.27	45.66	2:06.51	7291 WR
2. Sabine John (Paetz)	GDR	12.85	1.80	16.23	23.65	6.71	42.56	2:06.14	6897
3. Anke Behmer	GDR	13.20	1.83	14.20	23.10	6.68	44.54	2:04.20	6858
4. Natalya Shubenkova	SOV/RUS	13.51	1.74	14.76	23.93	6.32	47.46	2:07.90	6540
5. Remigia Sablovskaite	SOV/LIT	13.61	1.80	15.23	23.92	6.25	42.78	2:12.24	6456
6. Ines Schulz	GDR	13.75	1.83	13.50	24.65	6.33	42.82	2:05.79	6411
7. Jane Flemming	AUS	13.38	1.80	12.88	23.59	6.37	40.28	2:12.54	6351
8. Cindy Greiner	USA	13.55	1.80	14.13	24.48	6.47	38.00	2:13.65	6297

The baby girl born into the Joyner family on March 3, 1962, was named Jacqueline after the wife of US President John Kennedy because, in the words of her grandmother, "Someday this girl will be the First Lady of something." How right she was. But before that day could come, Joyner-Kersee endured a number of tragedies as a child. Growing up in a poor neighborhood in East St. Louis, Illinois, at the age of eleven she saw a man murdered across the street from her house. Three years later, her grandmother was shot and killed by her drug-addicted boyfriend. During Jackie's first year in college, she received a phone call from her aunt informing her that her mother had contracted a highly contagious form of meningitis and had slipped into a coma. It was Jackie who had to make the difficult choice to take her mother off life-support. After finishing second in the 1984 Olympics, Jackie Joyner won all nine heptathlons that she entered over the next four years. She also married her coach, Bob Kersee, who told her that she couldn't use his name until she broke a world record. She became Jackie Joyner-Kersee in Moscow on July 7, 1986, when she became the first woman to break the 7000-point mark with a score of 7148. She set another world record 26 days later and another one at the US Olympic trials in 1988.

By that time, Joyner-Kersee was so much better than all the other heptathletes that her husband had to create a new opponent for her: Wilhelmina World Record. In Seoul, Joyner-Kersee beat Wilhelmina again. Five days after the heptathlon, Joyner-Kersee earned a second gold medal in the long jump.

1992 Barcelona C: 32, N: 22, D: 8.1-2. WR: 7291 (Jacqueline Joyner-Kersee)

		100M H	HJ	SP	200M	LJ	JT	800M	TOTAL
1. Jacqueline Joyner-Kersee	USA	12.85	1.91	14.13	23.12	7.10	44.98	2:11.78	7044
2. Irina Belova	RUS	13.25	1.68	13.77	23.34	6.82	41.90	2:05.06	6845
3. Sabine Braun	GER	13.25	1.94	14.23	24.27	6.02	51.12	2:14.35	6649
4. Liliana Nastase	ROM	12.86	1.82	14.34	23.70	6.49	41.30	2:11.22	6619
5. Svetla Dimitrova	BUL	13.23	1.70	14.68	23.31	6.11	44.48	2:07.90	6464
6. Peggy Beer	GER	13.48	1.82	13.23	23.93	6.01	48.10	2:09.49	6434
7. Birgit Clarius	GER	14.10	1.82	15.33	24.86	6.13	45.14	2:08.83	6388
8. Urszula Włodarczyk	POL	13.57	1.82	13.91	24.81	6.20	43.46	2:14.96	6333

Although there was some pre-Olympic talk that Sabine Braun—who won the 1991 world championship when Jackie Joyner-Kersee injured a hamstring mid-contest—might challenge Joyner-Kersee at the Olympics, it was not to be. Joyner-Kersee took the lead after the first event and never looked back. Her 7044 points was the sixth-highest total ever—the top five scores were also hers. Belova set personal records in five of the seven events and bettered her pre-Olympic total by 320 points. In 1994 Belova was suspended for four years after she tested positive for testosterone.

1996 Atlanta C: 29, N: 21, D: 7.27-28. WR: 7291 (Jacqueline Joyner-Kersee)

		100M H	HJ	SP	200M	LJ	JT	800M	TOTAL
1. Ghada Shouaa	SYR	13.72	1.86	15.95	23.85	6.26	55.70	2:15.43	6780
2. Natasha Sazanovich	BLR	13.56	1.80	14.52	23.72	6.70	46.00	2:17.92	6563
3. Denise Lewis	GBR	13.45	1.77	13.92	24.44	6.32	54.82	2:17.41	6489
4. Urszula Włodarczyk	POL	13.48	1.86	14.36	24.27	6.30	43.28	2:12.35	6484
5. Eunice Barber	SLE	13.50	1.77	12.87	24.67	6.57	45.26	2:13.27	6342
6. Rita Ináncsi	HUN	13.95	1.83	14.69	24.92	6.32	46.46	2:17.37	6336
7. Sabine Braun	GER	13.55	1.83	14.48	24.89	6.21	48.72	2:22.87	6317
8. Kelly Blair	USA	13.62	1.80	12.29	24.49	6.32	50.32	2:16.87	6307

A former center for the Syrian national basketball team, Ghada Shouaa was her nation's first Olympic champion. Six-feet two and a half inches tall (1.89 meters), she was said to have an arm span of two meters. Shouaa, the 1995 world champion, was expected to be challenged by defending Olympic champion Jackie Joyner-Kersee. But Joyner-Kersee, trying to compete with a damaged hamstring, dropped out after the hurdles.

On the first day, Shouaa set personal bests in the 100-meter hurdles and the shot put. By day's end, she led Włodarczyk by 112 points and Sazanovich by 136. Sazanovich moved ahead by 6 points after the long jump. But Shouaa threw the javelin 182 feet 9 inches, a national record, to regain the lead by 182 points and the battle for gold was effectively over.

2000 Sydney C: 33, N: 23, D: 9.23-24. WR: 7291 (Jacqueline Joyner-Kersee)

		100M H	HJ	SP	200 M	LJ	JAV	800 M	TOTAL
1. Denise Lewis	GBR	13.23	1.75	15.55	24.34	6.48	50.19	2:16.83	6584
2. Yelena Prokhorova	RUS	13.63	1.81	13.21	23.72	6.59	45.05	2:10.32	6531
3. Nataliya Sazanovich	BLR	13.45	1.84	14.79	24.12	6.50	43.97	2:16.41	6527
4. Urszula Włodarczyk	POL	13.33	1.78	14.45	24.29	6.31	46.16	2:12.15	6470
5. Sabine Braun	GER	13.49	1.81	14.33	24.74	6.22	48.56	2:19.14	6355
6. Nataliya Roshchupkina	RUS	13.70	1.84	14.03	23.53	5.47	43.87	2:12.24	6237
7. Karin Ertl	GER	13.43	1.78	13.55	24.64	6.22	42.70	2:16.25	6209
8. Tiia Hautala	FIN	13.62	1.78	13.31	25.00	6.12	45.40	2:14.90	6173

The Sydney heptathlon was expected to be a duel between world champion Eunice Barber, originally from Sierra Leone, but now representing France, and Denise Lewis, who had placed second at the last two world championships after earning the bronze medal at the 1996 Olympics. Barber's condition was considered a mystery because she had skipped meets because of injury and broken with her coach just before the Olympics. Yet she started strongly and was in first place after two events, leading Atlanta runner-up Natalya Sazanovich by 71 points. Lewis, meanwhile, had performed poorly in the high jump and fallen to eighth place. The third event, the shot put, was a turning point. Barber could do no better than 11.27 meters (36 feet 11¾ inches) and plummeted to eighth place, while Lewis jumped to second place with a best put of 15.55 meters (51 feet ¼ inch). At the end of the first day, after four events, Sazanovich had 3903 points, Natalya Roshchupkina 3872 points and Lewis 3852. The next day, Barber took one attempt at the long jump and withdrew. Lewis pulled within 57 points of Sazanovich, while Yelena Prokhorova moved into third place, 103 points out of first. Lewis' strong performance in the javelin put her into the lead, with Sazanovich 62 points back and Prokhorova, an excellent 800 meters runner, 146 points behind. To win, Lewis needed to stay within 4.3 seconds of Sazanovich and about 8 seconds behind Prokhorova. With her calves and one ankle heavily bandaged, Lewis met the challenge and held on to win by 53 points.

2004 Athens C: 34, N: 24, D: 8.20-21. WR: 7291 (Jacqueline Joyner-Kersee)

		100M H	HJ	SP	200 M	LJ	JAV	800 M	TOTAL
1. Carolina Klüft	SWE	13.21	1.91	14.77	23.27	6.78	48.89	2:14.15	6952
2. Austra Skujytė	LIT	14.03	1.76	16.40	24.82	6.30	49.58	2:15.92	6435
3. Kelly Sotherton	GBR	13.44	1.85	13.29	23.57	6.51	37.19	2:12.27	6424
4. Shelia Burell	USA	13.17	1.70	13.14	24.06	6.25	47.69	2:15.32	6296
5. Yelena Prokhorova	RUS	13.84	1.79	13.67	24.71	6.21	45.58	2:11.31	6289
6. Sonja Kesselschläger	GER	13.38	1.76	14.53	25.23	6.42	42.99	2:15.21	6287
7. Marie Collonvillé	FRA	13.65	1.85	12.35	25.26	6.19	49.14	2:13.62	6279
8. Natalia Dobrynska	UKR	13.89	1.82	14.70	25.02	6.23	44.08	2:17.01	6255

From the time she won the 2002 European championship at the age of 19, Carolina Klüft dominated the heptathlon. She defeated Eunice Barber of France by 246 points to win the 2003 world championship. With Barber out with an injury, Klüft took the lead after the second event at the Olympics and was never seriously challenged. At the end of the first day, she led her friend Kelly Sotherton by 240 points.

On day two of the competition, Klüft expanded her lead with each event. Austra Skujytė, in fifth place after day one, passed Sotherton with a strong javelin throw to move into second place, and then held onto the silver medal by eleven points by keeping within four seconds of Sotheran in the 800 meters.

2008 Beijing C: 43, N: 28, D: 8.16. WR: 7291 (Jacqueline Joyner-Kersee)

		100M H	HJ	SP	200 M	LJ	JAV	800 M	TOTAL
1. Nataliya Dobrynska	UKR	13.44	1.80	17.29	24.39	6.63	48.60	2:17.72	6733
2. Hyleas Fountain	USA	12.78	1.89	13.36	23.21	6.38	41.93	2:15.45	6619
3. Tatyana Chernova	RUS	13.65	1.83	12.88	23.95	6.47	48.37	2:06.50	6591
4. Kelly Sotherton	GBR	13.18	1.83	13.87	23.39	6.33	37.66	2:07.34	6517
5. Jessica Zelinka	CAN	12.97	1.77	13.79	23.64	6.12	43.91	2:07.95	6490
6. Anna Bogdanova	RUS	13.09	1.86	14.08	24.24	6.45	35.41	2:09.45	6465
7. Karolina Tymi ska	POL	13.62	1.77	14.08	23.39	6.53	35.97	2:07.08	6428
8. Lilli Schwarzkopf	GER	13.73	1.80	14.61	25.25	5.96	51.88	2:10.91	6379

DISQ (Drugs): Lyudmila Blonska (UKR) 6700

Carolina Kluft, the reigning Olympic champion, twice European champion and three times world champion, was the overwhelming favorite for gold in Beijing. In March 2008, however, Kluft announced that she was withdrawing from the competition to focus on the long jump and triple jump, citing a lack of motivation. A week later, reigning world indoor champion Tia Hellebaut pulled out to focus on the long jump, and to rest a nagging ankle injury,

With the two favorites out of the competition, the competition was wide open. Twenty-seven-year-old Hyleas Fountain got off to a strong start, finishing first in both the 100-meter hurdles and high jump events, both in personal best times. Fountain had made a splash at the 2008 US Olympic trials, breaking Jackie Joyner-Kersee's 10-year US record in the 100-meter hurdles and recording a personal best of 6667 total points, the season's best score to date. Fountain's coach, Lynn Smith, had been one of the 111 people injured in the Centennial Park bombing at the 1996 Atlanta Olympics.

Fountain's main challenger was 26-year-old Natalia

Dobrynska, who moved into the lead after the third phase with a shot put of 17.29 meters (56 ft. 8 ¾ in.), a personal best, having also recorded a personal best in the hurdles. Fountain came back to retake the lead by recording the fastest time in the 200 meters, 23.21 seconds, ending the first day with a 64-point lead over Dobrynska, with 2004 Olympic bronze medalist Kelly Sotherton in third place, another 58 points back.

Dobrynska moved back into the lead by 16 points at the beginning of the second day, recording the best long jump of the competition, another personal best. Fountain slipped to second place after fouling her first two jumps and managing only 6.38 meters (20 ft. 11¼ in.) on her third attempt. Dobrynska cemented her lead in the javelin event, breaking her personal best twice to finish with 48.60 meters (159 ft. 5¼ in.) and a 145-point lead over Fountain. Dobrynska completed the 800 meters in the modest time of 2:17.72 to clinch the gold medal, having recorded six personal bests during the competition.

The 2007 world silver medalist, Lyudmila Blonska, originally finished in second place, but tested positive for the steroid methyltestosterone and was disqualified, moving Fountain and Tatyana Chernova into second and third place. Blonska had previously failed a doping test in 2003 and had served a two-year ban, so the second positive result earned her a lifetime ban.

DISCONTINUED EVENTS

3000 METERS

1984 Los Angeles C: 31, N: 21, D: 8.10. WR: 8:26.78 (Svetlana Ulmasova)

1. Maricica Puică	ROM	8:35.96	OR
2. Wendy Sly	GBR	8:39.47	
3. Lynn Williams	CAN	8:42.14	
4. Cindy Bremser	USA	8:42.78	
5. Cornelia Bürki	SWI	8:45.20	
6. Aurora Cunha	POR	8:46.37	
7. Zola Budd	GBR	8:48.80	
8. Joan Hansen	USA	8:51.53	

They called her "Little Mary Decker" when she first attracted international attention in 1973 by upsetting Olympic 800-meter silver medalist Nijolė Sabaitė at a USA–USSR dual meet in Minsk. And why not? Five feet tall and weighing 86 pounds, the fawn-like Decker was only 14 years old at the time. She had discovered running at age 11, during a period when her life was in turmoil. Her family had just moved from New Jersey to California and her parents were on the road to divorce. Mary Decker threw herself into her new pursuit. During one seven-day period when she was 12 years old, she competed in a marathon (finishing with a time of 3:09), a 440, an 880, a mile race and a two-mile. The next day she was hospitalized for an emergency appendectomy.

In 1974, Decker again caused a minor sensation at a USA–USSR dual meet, this time in Moscow. Running the anchor leg in a 4 × 800-meter relay, she was shoved off the indoor track by Latvian Sarmite Shtula. Decker responded by throwing her relay baton at Shtula. She retrieved the baton and continued the race, but at the finish line Decker again threw the baton at Shtula. Both teams were disqualified, and Decker was admonished for her unsportsmanlike behavior. However, no one in the United States had ever been condemned for responding violently to blatant Soviet aggression, so she was quickly forgiven. Besides, she was still only 15 years old.

At this point, Mary Decker's career took a drastic downward turn. Her intense, some would say obsessive, devotion to running began to take its toll on her still-growing body. Her legs, in particular, began to give in to the strain, and for the next three years she went from doctor to doctor and treatment to treatment desperately trying to relieve her pain. In tears she watched the 1976 Olympics on television, as runners she had beaten two years earlier collected medals that should have been hers.

Then in 1977, she chanced to meet 1976 10,000-meter silver medalist Dick Quax, who immediately recognized her physical problems as Compartment Syndrome in which the sheaths of tissues surrounding muscles fail to expand with the muscles' growth. An operation on her calf relieved the pain. After surviving two automobile accidents and then another operation, her times began improving again.

In 1980 she set her first world record, running the mile in 4:21.7. She qualified easily for the US Olympic team, but the anti-Soviet boycott prevented her from competing. Again she watched the Olympics on television. Then she flew to Europe where she was beaten at 1500 meters by Olympic champion Tatyana Kazankina and by Gabriella Dorio, who became the first Western woman to run the 1500 in less than four minutes. Despite increasing pain in her legs, Decker kept running until finally she had to be operated on to repair a partial tear of her Achilles' tendon. In 1981 she underwent a third operation on her shins and was forced to sit out the year.

The following year was her best yet. In June she set a 5000-meter world record of 15:08.26. On July 9, in Paris, she broke the mile record again with a time of 4:18.08. On the 14th, in Lausanne, she ran the 800 in 1:58.33. Two days later, after flying back to Eugene, Oregon, she

1. Disaster strikes the women's 3,000-meter run as gold-medal favorite Mary Decker steps on the barefooted heel of Zola Budd.

2. Decker falls to the ground as Budd tries to regain her balance, and the eventual winner, Maricica Puică (behind Budd), sidesteps Decker.

3. Zola Budd looks back to see her idol hit the infield in pain.

4. Mary Decker, too injured to continue, writhes in agony as the race goes on without her.

set a 10,000-meter world record with a time of 31:35.3. 1983 would see further improvements. Until this time Decker was still considered unproven, because she had not beaten the Eastern Europeans who dominated women's middle-distance running. But then came Mary Decker's masterpieces. At the inaugural world championships in Helsinki she scored a thrilling start to finish victory in the 3000 meters, stunning triple Olympic champion Tatyana Kazankina, as well as world record holder Svetlana Ulmasova. Four days later, in the 1500 meters, she again led from the beginning. Entering the final curve she was passed and cut off by Zamira Zaitseva. Decker lost her momentum, but in the homestretch she came roaring back. After a heart-stopping stretch run she nipped Zaitseva at the finish to complete a spectacular double victory. Immediately, Decker became the early favorite for the 1984 Olympics, which would take place in her former hometown, Los Angeles.

Mary Decker returned to the United States as a national hero. Beautiful and strong, she had defeated the Soviets. She seemed to symbolize all that was good about the American character. Of course, track aficionados were all too aware of the dark side of Decker's personality. For example, there was the ugly incident that took place at the 1983 Millrose Games in New York. When Angelita Lind, a Puerto Rican runner about to be lapped, failed to move to the outside to let Decker pass, America's sweetheart shoved her to the ground and forged ahead. Decker's belated sensitivity to this incident would have tragic consequences 18 months later at the Olympics. In the meantime, all over the nation, all over the world in fact, young girls dreamed of becoming like Mary Decker.

One such hero-worshiper, half a world away, was a slight, shy South African teenager named Zola Budd, who kept a poster of Decker on the wall beside her bed. Like Decker, Budd was a precocious talent. When she first told her father that she was winning races at school, he thought that was nice, but when he watched her win one such race by a lap—in a three-lap race—he realized that he should take the situation more seriously and find her a coach. As Budd's times improved, word of her accomplishments began to trickle out to the outside world. In 1983, at the age of 17, the 5-foot, 82-pound Budd was ranked number one in the world at 5000 meters by *Track and Field News*. On January 5, 1984, Budd, who always competed barefooted, ran the distance in 15:01.83 to break Mary Decker's world record by more than six seconds. Clearly Zola Budd was ready for international competition. However, South Africa had been banned by the IAAF in 1976 and had not been allowed in the Olympics since 1960. As long as Budd remained a South African citizen, her running career had no future.

But for Zola Budd, there was a loophole. Because her paternal grandfather was British, she could move to Great Britain and change her citizenship. On March 24, with all expenses paid by the *Daily Mail* newspaper, Zola and her parents arrived in England and set up residency in Guildford, Surrey. Less than two weeks later Zola Budd was granted British citizenship. The next four months would be enormously traumatic for the shy young girl. Accustomed to the quiet life on her farm in Bloemfontein in Orange Free State, she suddenly found herself the object of intense hostility—from other British runners, from the *Daily Mail's* rivals and from the many opponents of South Africa's racial policies. She ran her first race in England on April 14, then withdrew from another to avoid confrontations with the left-wing local government. On April 25, she won a 1500-meter race, but crossed the finish line in tears after being taunted throughout the race by blacks displaying signs that read, "WHITE TRASH GO HOME." Amidst all this turmoil, she also had to qualify for the British team. This she did, by winning every race that she was required to. After one race, teammate Jane Furniss, who had initially harshly criticized Budd, hugged her and gave her a kiss. At last, it seemed, Zola Budd would be allowed to get on with her running.

Back in the United States, Mary Decker had come up against another setback. In Helsinki she had been able to achieve her 1500/3000 double because the heats for the 1500 hadn't begun until after the final of the 3000. The Olympic schedule was different. The two events overlapped, making a double more difficult. The US trials were set up with the same schedule as the Olympics, giving Decker an opportunity to try it out. She won the 3000, but was upset by Ruth Wysocki in the 1500. On July 11, 2½ weeks before the Games would begin, Decker announced that she would withdraw from the 1500 and compete only in the 3000, the same race that Zola Budd would be entering.

The scheduled Decker-Budd confrontation encouraged the US media to indulge in an absolute orgy of pre-Olympic hype, much to the annoyance of both parties concerned. The problem was that all track fans knew that Budd was not really ready to compete at Decker's level, especially since Budd specialized at longer distances which were not yet a part of the Olympic program. Decker's real threat came not from Zola Budd, but from 34-year-old Maricica Puică. Although Puică had missed the Helsinki championships because of an injury sustained while playing basketball, her credentials were solid. Not only had she previously competed in the 1976 and 1980 Olympics, but she was the current world record holder in the mile and the reigning world cross-country champion. She had also recorded the fastest 3000-meter time of the pre-Olympic season: 8:33.57.

The qualifying heats of the Olympic 3000 were held on August 8. The first heat was won by Mary Decker, the second by Brigitte Kraus of West Germany, who had placed second behind Decker in the world championship 3000. In the third heat Budd led from the start but was passed in the run-in by Puică and Cindy Bremser. "It's unusual to run with a pack of people," commented Budd afterwards. "I'm happy to be running here, it's very nice."

The final was held two days later. The intense midday heat had cooled to a pleasant 75° Fahrenheit (24° centigrade) by race time. Decker took the early lead and set a fast pace, followed closely by Budd, Puică and Wendy Sly, although all of the runners were tightly packed. At the 1400-meter mark Joan Hansen tripped on Aurora Cunha's heel and fell. She recovered quickly and continued running. At 1600 meters, Sly moved up to challenge Decker along the backstretch, but Budd moved between them and took the lead entering the turn. As the pace accelerated, Budd, Decker, Sly and Puică began to pull away from the others.

Coming out of the turn Budd was in front, running on the outside edge of lane one. Decker, on the inside of the lane, maintained her position and pace. At about the 1700-meter mark, Decker hit one of Budd's legs, throwing Budd off balance just a bit. Five strides later, they bumped again. This time Budd landed awkwardly, her left leg shooting out in search of balance. Decker, running straight and hard, tripped on Budd's right leg, her spikes cutting deeply into Budd's heel. Decker lost her balance and pitched forward onto the infield. Puică, running directly behind Decker, hurdled over her leg. Budd looked back to see her idol falling to the ground. As the runners zipped by, Mary Decker attempted to rise. But her hard landing had caused her to suffer a pulled left hip stabilizer muscle. "It was like I was tied to the ground," she would later explain. As the race continued, Decker was left writhing in agony, weeping in frustration.

The partisan crowd of over 85,000 was stunned. At first the stadium went silent. Then the booing began. Fifty-two years earlier, in the same stadium, a similar incident had occurred between a US athlete and a foreign athlete during the running of the men's 5000-meter final at the 1932 Olympics. That time the track announcer, Bill Henry, had silenced the crowd by reminding them that "these people are our guests." In 1984 there was no Bill Henry to intervene. As the race continued, Zola Budd was met by booing at every turn. Bleeding, and in tears because of the crowd's reaction, she kept running, but her spirit was gone.

Five hundred meters from the finish, Sly and Puică passed Budd, entering the final lap with Sly in the lead. With 250 meters to go, Puică moved effortlessly ahead of Sly and went on to win by more than fifteen meters. Budd, still in third only 200 meters from the finish, slowed to a jog and finished seventh.

In the tunnel leading away from the track, Mary Decker was being comforted by her fiancé, discus thrower Richard Slaney. As the other runners filed by, they offered their condolences. Budd approached Decker and said, "I'm sorry. I'm sorry. I'm sorry."

"Don't bother," replied Decker, "I don't want to talk to you."

As Budd stood crying, fifth place finisher Cornelia Burki, a Swiss runner who was born in South Africa, came to Budd's defense. "It wasn't Zola's fault, Mary!" she said. "Not her fault."

"Yes, it was," Decker shot back. "I know it was. It was!"

Initially Budd was disqualified on the testimony of two track officials, both Americans. But upon reviewing videotapes of the incident from various angles, a jury of appeal voted unanimously to reinstate her. Decker, however, would not budge from her position that Zola Budd was at fault for cutting in before she had established a clear lead.

The controversy raged across the Atlantic Ocean. At first the US media supported Decker, while the British press took Budd's side. The issue was so emotional that the comments of Maricica Puică, who was the closest witness to the incident, were quoted completely differently in the U.S. and Great Britain. American newspapers, without exception, limited their coverage of Puică's remarks to "It was tough for me to decide [who was at fault]. I'm sorry for what happened to Mary. She is a fine competitor." In Great Britain, and the rest of the world, Puică was quoted as saying that Decker was at fault because Budd was in the lead and Decker tried to pass her on the inside, an assertion that Decker flatly denied.

As the public viewed repeated replays of the race, opinions on both sides of the Atlantic began to soften and almost everyone apologized. The truth is that neither Budd nor Decker was actually *at fault*, although both made mistakes. Budd should not have cut in so sharply. However such moves are not uncommon and are never cause for disqualification. Decker, for her part, should have known better than to bull forward like a tailgating commuter rushing home on a Friday evening. She could have given Budd a slight push, perhaps not quite as hard as the one she gave Angelita Lind at the Millrose Games. It is true that reaction to the Millrose incident might have haunted Decker. At her post-race press conference in Los Angeles, she said, "Looking back, I should have pushed her, but the headlines tomorrow would have read 'DECKER PUSHES ZOLA.'" Decker's other alternative was to do what she had done in Helsinki when she was cut off by Zaitseva in the last lap of the 1500: slow down and pass on the outside. In Los Angeles she even had the luxury of 1300 meters left in the race rather than 200.

Mary Decker did not run again in 1984. However, by 1985 she had recovered from her injuries and had a brilliant season, which she completed undefeated. Amongst her victories was a sensational mile race in Zurich in which she defeated both Puică and Budd, and stripped Puică of her world record to boot. Decker returned to the Olympics in 1988, placing tenth in the 3000 and eighth in the 1500. In 1996 she was eliminated in the opening round of the 5000 meters.

If Decker's performance in Seoul was disappointing, at least she was able to compete. Zola Budd was not so lucky. She won the world cross-country championship in 1985 and 1986, then was forced to take time off because of injury. She returned to competition, but in April 1988, the IAAF recommended that the British Amateur Athletic Board suspend her from international athletics for at least twelve months because she *attended* a cross-country event in Brakpan, South Africa, even though she didn't compete in it. On the verge of emotional collapse, Budd gave up her Olympic dreams and returned to her family in South Africa. During her tumultuous four years in Great Britain, Zola Budd had steadfastly refused to comment on South Africa's racial policies, even though a simple statement against apartheid would have helped her personal cause immensely. Instead, she waited until 1989, when her racing career appeared to be finished, to issue an unequivocal denouncement of apartheid. After apartheid was dismantled, she represented South Africa at the 1992 Olympics and was eliminated in the heats of the 3000 meters.

Maricica Puică's life also crossed into the world of politics. During the 1989 Romanian revolution against dictator Nicolae Ceauşescu, Puică spoke on national television praising the youthful revolutionaries and urging, "if we have to die, let us die together."

1988 Seoul C: 35, N: 24, D: 9.25. WR: 8:22.62 (Tatyana Kazankina)

1. Tetyana Samolenko	SOV/UKR	8:26.53 OR
2. Paula Ivan	ROM	8:27.15
3. Yvonne Murray	GBR	8:29.02
4. Yelena Romanova	SOV/RUS	8:30.45
5. Natalya Artemova	SOV/RUS	8:31.67
6. Vicki Huber	USA	8:37.25
7. Wendy Sly	GBR	8:37.70
8. Lynn Williams	CAN	8:38.43

Mary Slaney (Decker) rushed into the lead, taking the pack through a torrid world record pace for the first 1000 meters. She was still in front at the halfway mark, but, much to her disappointment, nine other runners were close behind her. Shortly before the 2000-meter mark, Vicki Huber swept by Slaney with Yvonne Murray, Paula Ivan, and the 27-year-old world champion, Tetyana Samolenko, right on her heels. With 450 meters to go, Murray made her move. Ivan and Samolenko followed easily. On the backstretch, about 200 meters from the finish, Ivan took the lead and tried to pull away. But Samolenko was not to be denied. Running a 59.4 last lap, she edged past a surprised Ivan 50 meters from the finish. Thanks in part to the pace-setting Americans, the final times were excellent. Samolenko, Ivan, Romanova, and Huber each improved their personal bests by over 9 seconds, Murray by over 8 seconds and Artemova by 7½.

On the darker side is the story of the South Korean record holder, Lim Chun-ae. A complete unknown from a poor rural family, Lim became a national hero in 1986 when, at the age of 17, she won three gold medals at the Asian Games. In June of 1987, word leaked out that Lim had been hospitalized for two weeks with a broken eardrum after her coach, Kim Pon-il, beat her as punishment for performing poorly in training. Kim was not punished, while Lim publicly accepted blame for her "accident." When the Olympics came to Seoul, Lim Chun-ae was chosen to be the final bearer of the Olympic torch. As the whole world watched, it was Lim who carried the torch around the track in the main stadium and handed it to the cauldron lighters. Six days later, Lim took part in her only individual event: the 3000 meters. Unfortunately, she finished fifteenth and last in her qualifying heat, crossing the finish line over fourteen seconds after the other runners were done. She immediately fell to the ground, buried her head between her legs, and wept. The following year, she retired from competition.

1992 Barcelona C: 33, N: 21, D: 8.2. WR: 8:22.62 (Tatyana Kazankina)

1. Yelena Romanova	RUS	8:46.04
2. Tetyana Dorovskikh (Samolenko)	UKR	8:46.85
3. Angela Chalmers	CAN	8:47.22
4. Sonia O'Sullivan	IRL	8:47.41
5. Patricia "PattiSue" Plumer	USA	8:48.29
6. Yelena Kopytova	RUS	8:49.55
7. Shelly Steely	USA	8:52.67
8. Yvonne Murray	GBR	8:55.85

Dorovskikh had won the 1987 world championships, the 1988 Olympics, and the 1991 world championships, but had done nothing outstanding in 1992. Still, the unusually slow pace of the final appeared to play right into the hands of Dorovskikh, who was known for her strong finishing kick. With 580 meters to go, Murray surged into the lead but was unable to shake the pack. At the beginning of the backstretch, O'Sullivan passed Murray, who was quickly left behind. Behind O'Sullivan came Romanova, Dorovskikh, Plumer, and Chambers. As the leaders entered the final straightaway, Romanova darted past O'Sullivan on the outside while Dorovskikh passed her on the inside. It was Romanova, rather than Dorovskikh, who had the most powerful kick, as she covered the last 200 meters in 28.6 seconds and pulled away to win by six meters.

One also-ran worth noting was Mirsada Burić of Bosnia-Herzegovina. Burić had trained in the rubble-strewn streets of Sarajevo in the midst of her nation's civil war. Twice she was shot at by snipers. At the beginning of June, she and other Muslim women and children were seized by Serb militiamen and held for 13 days during which her daily diet was one cup of tea and one slice of bread. When she was finally released in a prisoner exchange on June 13, all her sports equipment, including her track shoes, had been confiscated; the opening of the Olympics was only six weeks away. Burić and the rest of the Bosnian team managed to make it to Barcelona just six hours before the Opening Ceremony. Burić finished last in her heat, but for her merely making it to the starting line was a victory.

As for Dorovskikh, her career achievements were tainted when she tested positive for steroids in June 1993.

10,000-METER WALK

1992 Barcelona C: 44, N: 21, D: 8.3. WR: 41:30 (Kerry Junna-Saxby)

1. Chen Yueling	CHN	44:32
2. Yelena Nikolayeva	RUS	44:33
3. Li Chunxiu	CHN	44:41
4. Sari Essayah	FIN	45:08
5. Cui Yingzi	CHN	45:15
6. Madelein Svensson	SWE	45:17
7. Annarita Sidoti	ITA	45:23
8. Yelena Sayko	RUS	45:28

Chen entered the stadium with a 20-meter lead over Li. Twenty meters behind Li, Alma Ivanova of the Ukraine was beginning to make a move. Nikolayeva was thirty meters behind Ivanova. Ivanova raced past Li and Chen, provoking two quick red warning cards in the process. Chen tried to stay with her, but with 150 meters to go, Ivanova took off again. Her technique was so unacceptable that even the relatively uninitiated audience gasped as she skipped along the homestretch. Ivanova crossed the finish line first, but was disqualified. Chen, who held off a late surge by Nikolayeva, learned about her victory back in the locker room. Because the fourth walker across the line, Ileana Salvador of Italy, was also disqualified, Li had the strange experience of winning the bronze medal even though she was the fifth person to cross the finish line. Although a bronze statue was built in her honor in her hometown of Tieling, Chen Yueling emigrated to California and represented the United States at the 2000 Olympics, placing 38th in the 20-kilometer walk.

1996 Atlanta C: 44, N: 26, D: 7.29. WR: 41:04 (Yelena Nikolayeva)

1. Yelena Nikolayeva	RUS	41:49 OR
2. Elisabetta Perrone	ITA	42:12
3. Wang Yan	CHN	42:19
4. Gu Yan	CHN	42:34
5. Rossella Giordano	ITA	42:43
6. Olya Kardapoltseva	BLR	43:02
7. Katarzyna Radtke	POL	43:05
8. Valentina Tsybulskaya	BLR	43:21

The Russians entered 19-year-old world champion Irina Stankina, and Yelena Nikolayeva, who had set a world record at the Russian trials on April 20. The two shared the lead at the halfway mark, but Stankina was soon disqualified, leaving Nikolayeva with a 19-second lead that she increased to 27 seconds with 2000 meters to go.

Chapter 3 Archery

MEN	WOMEN
Individual	Individual
Team	Team
Discontinued Events	Discontinued Event

Archery targets are 122 centimeters (four feet) in diameter. The bulls-eye is 4.8 inches across (12.2 centimeters). This is the equivalent of shooting across three tennis courts laid end to end and hitting a grapefruit. Targets are divided into five colored rings: gold on the inside, then red, blue, black, and finally white on the outside. Each ring is divided in half. The inner gold zone is worth ten points, the outer gold nine points, on down to the outer white, which is worth one point. Modern bows are extremely complicated and are augmented by bowsights, bowmarks, foresights, and stabilizers.

Few Olympic sports have gone through as many rule changes in so short a time as archery did between 1984 and 1992. From 1972 to 1984, competitions consisted of two FITA rounds. A FITA round is 36 arrows shot at each of four distances: 90, 70, 50, and 30 meters for men and 70, 60, 50 and 30 meters for women. In 1988, all competitors took part in an opening FITA round. The top twenty-four then moved on to the eighth final, where they shot nine arrows at each distance. The top eighteen in that round advanced to the quarter-final. The top twelve in the quarter-final advanced to the semi-final. The top eight in the semi-final qualified for the final. The scores were not cumulative. In the semi-final and final rounds the distances were reversed: 30, 50, 70, and 90 meters. In 1992, following a preliminary FITA round, the top 32 archers moved on to single-elimination match play, with each match consisting of twelve arrows shot at 70 meters. Since 1996 the 64 entrants in each individual event begin with a 144-arrow qualification round. All 64 then advance to match play according to their placement in the qualifying round, with the highest qualifier playing the lowest, second playing 63rd, etc. Matches are played over the best of five sets, with each set consisting of three arrows per archer at 70 meters.

Thirty-two of the 64 entrants in each individual event qualify based on their performances at the most recent World Archery Championships: three each from eight highest-scoring teams and eight from nations whose teams did not place in the top eight, with a maximum of one per nation. Thirteen archers qualify for the Olympics from five regional tournaments, nine from a Final World Team Qualification Tournament, and four from a Final World Individual Team Qualification Tournament. Three places are reserved for the host nation, and the final three spots are wildcards selected by the International Archery Federation (FITA). No nation is allowed more than three entries per gender.

MEN

INDIVIDUAL

1896–1968 not held

1972 Munich C: 55, N: 24, D: 9.10. WR: 2445 (John Williams)

		1st ROUND	2nd ROUND	TOTAL POINTS
1. John Williams	USA	1268 WR	1260	2528 WR
2. Gunnar Jarvil	SWE	1229	1252	2481
3. Kyösti Laasonen	FIN	1213	1254	2467
4. Robert Cogniaux	BEL	1205	1240	2445
5. Edwin Eliason	USA	1193	1245	2438
6. Donald Jackson	CAN	1225	1212	2437
7. Viktor Sidorouk	SOV/UKR	1205	1222	2427
8. Arne Jacobsen	DEN	1188	1235	2423

The reigning world champion, John Williams, was an 18-year-old army private from Cranesville, Pennsylvania, who spent 42 hours a week in training. In the first FITA round he broke Arne Jacobsen's single round world record despite missing the target completely with one arrow.

1976 Montreal C: 37, N: 23, D: 7.30. WR: 2570 (Darrell Pace)

		1st ROUND	2nd ROUND	TOTAL POINTS
1. Darrell Pace	USA	1264	1307	2571 WR
2. Hiroshi Michinaga	JPN	1226	1276	2502
3. Giancarlo Ferrari	ITA	1220	1275	2495
4. Richard McKinney	USA	1230	1241	2471
5. Vladimir Chendarov	SOV/RUS	1217	1250	2467
6. Willi Gabriel	GER	1203	1232	2435
7. David Mann	CAN	1190	1241	2431
8. Takanobu Nishi	JPN	1191	1231	2422

1980 Moscow C: 38, N: 25, D: 8.2. WR (single round): 1341 (Darrell Pace)

		1st ROUND	2nd ROUND	TOTAL POINTS
1. Tomi Poikolainen	FIN	1220	1235	2455
2. Boris Isachenko	SOV/BLR	1217	1235	2452
3. Giancarlo Ferrari	ITA	1215	1234	2449
4. Mark Blenkarne	GBR	1224	1222	2446
5. Béla Nagy	HUN	1225	1221	2446
6. Vladimir Yesheyev	SOV/RUS	1222	1210	2432
7. Kyösti Laasonen	FIN	1212	1207	2419
8. Martinus Reniers	HOL	1205	1213	2418

1984 Los Angeles-Long Beach C: 62, N: 25, D: 8.11. WR: 1341 (Darrell Pace)

		1st ROUND	2nd ROUND	TOTAL POINTS
1. Darrell Pace	USA	1317	1299	2616 OR
2. Richard McKinney	USA	1295	1269	2564
3. Hiroshi Yamamoto	JPN	1276	1287	2563
4. Takayoshi Matsushita	JPN	1264	1288	2552
5. Tomi Poikolainen	FIN	1275	1263	2538
6. Göran Bjerendal	SWE	1275	1247	2522
7. Marnix Vervinck	BEL	1260	1259	2519
8. Koo Ja-chung	KOR	1226	1274	2500

Darrell Pace and Rick McKinney grew up 85 miles apart in Reading, Ohio, and Muncie, Indiana. Their rivalry began in 1973 when both were teenagers and Pace, at 16, won a place on the US world championship team by finishing one point ahead of McKinney at the trials. In 1975, Pace won the next world championship and the following year added an Olympic victory. A discouraged McKinney decided to give himself one more year before retiring from competition. Relaxed and unpressured, McKinney won the 1977 world championship, with Pace slipping to fourth. However, Pace regained the title in 1979.

Pace and McKinney's most dramatic confrontation came at the 1983 world championship held at the Olympic site in Long Beach. Pace needed to fire all tens with his final three arrows to clinch another world championship. His first two arrows were bull's-eyes. But his final shot was so perfect that the arrow struck the nock of one of the first two arrows and glanced off into the nine ring.

McKinney, firing two targets away, heard Pace's arrow hit the nock and knew that if *he* could hit the ten ring with his final shot *he* would be the world champion. After many moments of quiet tension, McKinney released his bow and achieved his ten.

Ten months later, at the Los Angeles Olympics, there was no such drama, at least not for the gold medal. Pace took a 13-point lead after the first of four days and steadily widened the gap to win easily. McKinney, however, needed to fire a ten with his final arrow to secure second place. He did and the silver medal was his.

1988 Seoul C: 84, N: 34, D: 9.30. WR: 1341 (Darrell Pace)

		OPEN ROUND	8th FINAL	QUART. FINAL	SEMI-FINAL	GRAND FINAL	GRAND TOTAL
1. Jay Barrs	USA	1294 (3)	313 (13)	326 (4)	334 (2)	338 (1)	2605
2. Park Sung-soo	KOR	1303 (2)	322 (4)	324 (5)	329 (4)	336 (2)	2614
3. Vladimir Yesheyev	SOV/RUS	1304 (1)	313 (14)	320 (9)	328 (5)	335 (3)	2600
4. Chun In-soo	KOR	1284 (6)	326 (2)	323 (6)	334 (1)	331 (4)	2598
5. Martinus Reniers	HOL	1286 (5)	328 (1)	328 (2)	324 (8)	327 (5)	2593
6. Richard McKinney	USA	1288 (4)	321 (6)	327 (3)	332 (3)	324 (6)	2592
7. Pentti Vikström	FIN	1273 (13)	312 (15)	320 (10)	324 (7)	323 (7)	2552
8. Hiroshi Yamamoto	JPN	1271 (14)	316 (7)	318 (12)	324 (6)	321 (8)	2550

Twenty-six-year-old Jay Barrs, who listened to heavy metal music between rounds, gained his victory by picking up 2 points on Park during the final 18 arrows. Defending champion Darrell Pace finished ninth. In last place was Derrick Tenai, a security guard from the Solomon Islands, who had never seen a modern bow until he arrived in Seoul. In the open round, Tenai hit the target 89 times and missed 55 times. None of the other 83 contestants missed the target more than 5 times and 65 of them had no misses at all.

1992 Barcelona C: 75, N: 34, D: 8.3. WR: 12 Arrow Match—111 (Chung Jae-hun)

1. Sébastien Flute	FRA
2. Chung Jae-hun	KOR
3. Simon Terry	GBR
4. Bertil Martinus Grov	NOR
5. Jari Lipponen	FIN
6. Hendra Setijawan	INA
7. Jay Barrs	USA
8. Vadim Shikarev	TJK

Final: Flute 110-107 Chung
3rd Place: Terry 109-103 Grov

The 20-year-old European champion, Sébastien Flute, defeated all three South Korean archers on his way to the Olympic title. He and Chung were tied after nine arrows in the final, but Flute coolly scored 10, 9, and 10 with his last shots to earn a mild upset. An unemployed roofer, Simon Terry was Britain's first medalist in archery in 80 years. Yet when he returned home to Sleaford, Lincolnshire, he discovered that his unemployment benefits had been cut off because, while he was in Barcelona, he was not available for work.

1996 Atlanta-Stone Mountain C: 64, N: 31, D: 8.2. WR: 12 Arrow Match—119 (Park Kyung-mo)

1. Justin Huish	USA
2. Magnus Petersson	SWE
3. Oh Kyo-moon	KOR
4. Paul Vermeiren	BEL
5. Kim Bo-ram	KOR
6. Michele Frangilli	ITA
7. Jang Yong-ho	KOR
8. Lionel Torres	FRA

Final: Huish 112-107 Petersson
3rd Place: Oh 115-110 Vermeiren

Michele Frangilli led the ranking round with a 72-arrow score of 684. In the quarterfinals Frangilli faced Justin Huish, who was ranked only 24th in the world. With his ponytail, backwards facing baseball cap, and his carefree personality, the crowd-pleasing Huish would soon be transformed into a media darling. Huish led by two points with one arrow to go, but scored only eight points with his final shot, and Frangilli was able to force a shoot-out by hitting a ten. Huish shot a ten and Frangilli matched it. Frangilli then shot a nine and Huish followed with a ten to secure the upset. Huish had an easier time in the semifinals and final, defeating Paul Vermeiren 112-103 and Magnus Petersson 111-108.

Justin Huish qualified for the 2000 US Olympic Team, but withdrew after he was arrested for selling marijuana.

2000 Sydney C: 64, N: 31, D: 9.20. WR: 12 Arrow Match—119 (Park Kyung-mo)

1. Simon Fairweather	AUS
2. Victor Wunderle	USA
3. Wietse van Alten	HOL
4. Magnus Petersson	SWE
5. Kim Chung-tae	KOR
6. Oh Kyo-moon	KOR
7. Balzhinima Tsyrempilov	RUS
8. Sébastien Flute	FRA

Final: Fairweather 113-106 Wunderle
3rd Place: van Alten 114-109 Petersson

Simon Fairweather placed 16th at the 1988 Olympics. But when he won the 1991 world championships, he went to the Barcelona Olympics as one of the favorites. He ended up in 25th place and then dropped to 52nd at the 1996 Olympics. Meanwhile, Korean archers had won every world championship since Fairweather's triumph. In Sydney, the Koreans took the top three places in the ranking round, with Jang Yong-ho first, Atlanta bronze medalist Oh Kyo-moon second and Kim Chung-tae third. Jang, who recorded the highest score of each of the first three rounds, was eliminated in the round of 16 by Balzhinima Tsyrempilov, who was in turn beaten 113-104 in the quarterfinals by Fairweather. In the other quarterfinals, Wietse van Alten defeated 1992 champion Sébastien Flute 106-102, 1996 silver medalist Magnus Petersson edged Kim 112-111 and Vic Wunderle, who had survived a one-point victory over Ukrainian Serhei Antonov in the round of 32, beat Oh 108-105. In the semifinals, Fairweather defeated van Alten 112-110 and Wunderle squeezed out a victory over Petersson 108-107. Before an enthusiastic crowd of 4500, Fairweather then led the final from the first arrow and gradually increased his lead to earn the gold medal by seven points.

2004 Athens C: 64, N: 35, D: 8.19. WR: 12 Arrow Match—119 (Park Kyung-mo)

1. Marco Galiazzo	ITA
2. Hiroshi Yamamoto	JPN
3. Tim Cuddihy	AUS
4. Laurence Godfrey	GBR
5. Park Kyung-mo	KOR
6. Im Dong-hyun	KOR
7. Chen Szu-yuan	TAI
8. Victor Wunderle	USA

Final: Galiazzo 111-109 Yamamoto
3rd Place: Cuddihy 113-112 Godfrey

In 2004, the archery events were held in the ancient Panathinaikos Stadium, built in 329 BC and the site of the first modern Olympic Games in 1896.

South Korea entered the competition with high hopes for their first gold in the men's individual event. Their three archers all placed in the top five during the ranking round, with 18-year-old Im Dong-hyun setting a 72-arrow world record of 687 points. However their dreams began to fade in the round of 16 when 17-year-old Tim Cuddihy edged Jang Yong-ho 166-165. In the quarterfinals, Cuddihy eliminated Park Kyung-mo 112-111, while Im was beaten 111-110 by Hiroshi Yamamoto, a 41-year-old high school teacher competing in his fifth Olympics. Yamamoto already owned one bronze medal . . . from 1984. After failing to qualify for the 2000 Games, Yamamoto lost his will to compete. However, his high school archery students reignited his spirit, and he even competed using a bowstring made for him by one of his students.

In the semifinals, Yamamoto tied Cuddihy, but beat him 10-9 in the one-arrow shootout. The other semi matched Laurence Godfrey, a helicopter repair engineer for Rolls-Royce, with 21-year-old Marco Galiazzo, who had finished only 49th in the previous world championships. Both Godfrey and Galiazzo barely escaped the round of 32 with one-point victories. In the quarterfinals, Galiazzo had to contend with defending silver medalist Vic Wunderle. Wunderle built a two-point lead at the halfway point, but Galiazzo came back with to win 109-108.

In the 12-arrow gold medal match, Yamamoto led by one point after three arrows, but Galiazzo came from behind to win 111-109. He was Italy's first Olympic archery champion.

Although the South Koreans did not get their gold medal, they were not completely shut out of the event. Both Galiazzo and Cuddihy were trained by South Korean coaches.

2008 Beijing C: 64, N: 37, D: 8.15. WR: 12 Arrow Match—120 (Choi Won-jong)

1. Viktor Ruban	UKR
2. Park Kyung-mo	KOR
3. Bair Badenov	RUS
4. Juan René Serrano	MEX
5. Juan Carlos Stevens	CUB
6. Vic Wunderle	USA
6. Ryuichi Moriya	JPN
8. Cheng Chu Sian	MAL

Final: Ruban 113-112 Park
3rd Place: Badenov 115-110 Serrano

The first major upset of the competition came during the round of sixteen, when reigning world champion Im Dong-hyun was knocked out of the tournament by 2000 Olympic silver medalist Vic Wunderle. Wunderle had finished twenty-fourth at the 2007 world championships and was 41st after the ranking round in Beijing.

With Im out of the running, the path to gold seemed open for Park Kyung-mo. Park had been tied with Im atop the World Cup standings going into the Olympics, and the two had won gold medals in the team events in both 2004 and 2008. Park faced 2007 Pan Am Games silver medalist Juan Carlos Stevens in the quarter-finals and trailed Stevens by two points before the last arrow. Park shot a perfect 10 to Stevens's 8 to take the match to sudden-death shoot-off, and then finished him off with another perfect 10 to advance. He had an easier time in the semis, advancing on a 115-112 win over Juan René Serrano, who had finished first in the ranking round with 679 points.

Park faced world number five Viktor Ruban in the gold-medal match. Ruban, who had won a bronze medal at the 2004 Athens Olympics in the team event, had advanced easily through the early rounds but had only narrowly reached the final, after a 112-112 tie against Bair Badenov that he won in a two-arrow 20-18 shoot-off.

In the final, Park looked to be on the verge of winning Korea's first-ever individual men's gold medal when he shot an eight on his second-to-last arrow, leaving both archers tied at 103 points. Ruban managed a perfect 10 on his final shot, while Park shot a nine to lose by one point.

Park's penultimate arrow mistake was a repeat of the women's individual final one day earlier, when gold medal favorite Park Sung-hyun shot an eight on her second-to-last arrow to give an opening to China's Zhang Juanjuan, who went on to win the gold medal by a single point.

The individual archery events were not a complete loss for South Korea. Two weeks after the Olympics, Park Kyung-mo and Park Sung-hyun announced that they had been dating since autumn 2007. They married in December 2008.

TEAM

In 1988, scores from the individual open round were used to determine the 16 teams that advanced to team play. The top 12 teams in a qualifying round then moved to the semi-finals, and the top eight in that round went on to the final. In each team round, each archer shot nine arrows at each of four distances. Since 2008, team competition begins with a ranking round. The top four teams advance directly into the quarter-finals. The next eight teams compete in single-elimination match play for the chance to enter the quarter-final round. Each match consists of 24 arrows, eight by each archer, at 70 meters. Team members take turns shooting two arrows in four ends, with all three archers required to finish shooting within two minutes per end. Ties are broken by the number of 10s shot in that round, and then by the number of Xs (inner 10s) shot in the round. In team events, unlike individual events, archers may be coached while on the shooting line.

1896–1984 not held

1988 Seoul T: 22, N: 22, D: 10.1. WR: 3948 (USA—McKinney, Barrs, Pace)

		OPEN ROUND	SEMI-FINAL	GRAND FINAL
1. KOR	Chun In-soo, Lee Han-sup, Park Sung-soo	3862 (1)	960 (6)	986 (1)
2. USA	Jay Barrs, Richard McKinney, Darrell Pace	3839 (2)	992 (1)	972 (2)
3. GBR	Steven Hallard, Richard Priestman, Leroy Watson	3733 (8)	965 (4)	968 (3)
4. FIN	Ismo Falck, Tomi Poikolainen, Pentti Vikström	3797 (4)	960 (7)	956 (4)
5. SOV	Konstyantin Shkolny, Vladimir Yesheyev, Yuri Leontyev	3799 (3)	976 (2)	949 (5)
6. JPN	Terushi Furuhashi, Takayoshi Matsushita, Hiroshi Yamamoto	3766 (5)	958 (8)	948 (6)
7. TAI	Chiu Ping-kun, Hu Pei-wen, Yen Man-sung	3693 (11)	968 (3)	937 (7)
8. SWE	Gent Bjerendal, Göran Bjerendal, Mats Nordlander	3759 (6)	964 (5)	925 (8)

The Koreans trailed the US team by two points before surging ahead at the final distance of 90 meters.

1992 Barcelona T: 20, N: 20, D: 8.4. WR: FITA Round—3963 (SOV—Zabrodsky, Shikarev, Yesheyev)

1. SPA Juan Carlos Holgado Romero, Alfonso Menéndez Vallín, Antonio Vázquez Megido
2. FIN Ismo Falck, Jari Lipponen, Tomi Poikolainen
3. GBR Steven Hallard, Richard Priestman, Simon Terry
4. FRA Bruno Felipe, Sébastien Flute, Michael Taupin
5. KOR Chung Jae-hun, Han Seung-hoon, Lim Hee-sik
6. USA Jay Barrs, Richard "Butch" Johnson, Richard McKinney
7. SOV Vadim Shikarev, Vladimir Yesheyev, Stanislav Zabrodsky
8. AUS Simon Fairweather, Grant Greenham, Scott Hunter-Russell

Final: SPA 238-236 FIN
3rd Place: GBR 233-231 FRA

The victory by the Spanish team was one of the biggest upsets of the Barcelona Games. In the individual competition, Vázquez had placed 29th, Menéndez 42nd, and Holgado 45th. Seeded tenth, they scored surprise victories over Denmark, the Unified Team, and Great Britain. In the final, Spain led by nine points after twenty arrows, and then held off a strong comeback by the Finns.

1996 Atlanta-Stone Mountain T: 15, C: 15, D: 8.2. WR: 27 Arrow Match—259 (KOR—Oh K.M, Chung J.H, Park K.M)

1. USA Justin Huish, Richard "Butch" Johnson, Rodney White
2. KOR Jang Yong-ho, Kim Bo-ram, Oh Kyo-moon
3. ITA Matteo Bisiani, Michele Frangilli, Andrea Parenti
4. AUS Simon Fairweather, Jackson Fear, Matthew Gray
5. SLO Peter Koprivnikar, Matevž Krumpestar, Samo Medved
6. SWE Göran Bjerendal, Mikael Larsson, Magnus Petersson
7. UKR Aleksandr Yatsenko, Valery Yevetsky, Stanislav Zabrodsky
8. FIN Jari Lipponen, Tomi Poikolainen, Tommi Tuovila

Final: USA 251-249 KOR
3rd Place: ITA 248-244 AUS

A model of consistency, the US team shot 251 in each of their four matches. The South Koreans set a world record in the ranking round, but faltered slightly in the final. Initially the scoreboard read 250-250, but when the judges examined the target, the Americans gained one point and the South Koreans lost one.

2000 Sydney T: 14, N: 14, D: 9.22. WR: 27 Arrow Match—260 (KOR—Hong S.C., Jang Y.H., Kim B.R.)

1. KOR Jang Yong-ho, Oh Kyo-moon, Kim Chung-tae
2. ITA Matteo Bisiani, Michele Frangilli, Ilario Di Buò
3. USA Rodney White, Victor Wunderle, Richard "Butch" Johnson
4. RUS Balzhinima Tsyrempilov, Bayr Badenov, Yuri Leontyev
5. TUR Serdar Şatir, Özdemir Akbal, Hasan Orbay
6. SWE Magnus Petersson, Niklas Eriksson, Mattias Eriksson
7. KAZ Stanislav Zabrodsky, Aleksandr Li, Vadim Shikaryev
8. UKR Igor Parkhomenko, Serhiy Antonov, Viktor Kurchenko

Final: KOR 255-247 ITA
3rd Place: USA 239/29-239/26 RUS

This marked the first time that the home team did not win the men's team title, as the Australians finished in twelfth place out of fourteen. Less than three weeks before the Olympics, the Korean team engaged in an unusual practice session. They gathered in Seoul's Chamsil Stadium before the start of a baseball game and, for forty minutes, they shot at bulls-eyes while the crowed booed and cheered in order to simulate the conditions the archers would face in Sydney. The Koreans surprisingly did not win a medal in the individual competition, but they made up for it in the team event. After leading the ranking round by 59 points, they set an Olympic 27-arrow record of 258 in their quarterfinal victory over Ukraine. They beat Russia 240-229 in the semifinals, while Italy defeated the United States 244-241 in the other semi. South Korea led the final 87-84 after the first nine arrows, but Italy drew even at 167 after eighteen arrows. Kim Chung-tae's three straight ten-pointers helped South Korea pull away to a 255-247 victory.

One unexpected medalist was Rod White of the United States. The US Olympic Trials were held in September 1999 with the top three finishers qualifying for the Olympic team. White, who had earned a gold medal in the team event in 1996, finished a disappointing fifth. White tossed his bow into his basement and tried to get on with his life. Then Shane Parker, who had placed third, was suspended for cheating (he shot two extra arrows at the Trials) and White was moved up to team alternate. In March 2000, Justin Huish, who had finished second at the Trials, withdrew after being arrested for selling marijuana. Suddenly White, who had not picked up his Olympic bow for six months, found himself on the US team after all. He began shooting 200-300 arrows a day to get back "in quiver." The Americans were defeated in the semifinals and then faced the Russian team in the bronze medal match. After 27 arrows, the two teams were tied 239-239. Each archer shot one arrow and the Americans won 29-26.

2004 Athens T: 13, N: 13, D: 8.21.

1. KOR Im Dong-hyun, Park Kyung-mo, Jang Yong-ho
2. TAI Wang Cheng-pang, Liu Ming-huang, Chen Szu-yuan
3. UKR Dmytro Hrachov, Viktor Ruban, Oleksandr Serdiuk
4. USA Richard "Butch" Johnson, John Magera, Victor Wunderle
5. HOL Pieter Custers, Wietse van Alten, Ron van der Hoff
6. AUS David Barnes, Tim Cuddihy, Simon Fairweather
7. ITA Ilario Di Buò, Michele Frangilli, Marco Galiazzo
8. JPN Takaharu Furukawa, Yuji Hamano, Hiroshi Yamamoto

Final: KOR 251-245 TAI
3rd Place: UKR 237-236 USA

The South Korean team entered the competition determined to make up for their disappointing performance in the individual event, when all three archers failed to advance past the quarterfinals. The Koreans eked out a 250-249 victory over the Netherlands in the quarterfinals and then advanced to the finals with another close win over Ukraine, 242-239.

In the final, the South Koreans led Taiwan 82-81 after the first nine arrows and never relinquished the lead. Needing only four points with his final shot to secure the gold, Park Kyung-mo calmly hit a bulls-eye, for a 251-245 victory.

2008 Beijing T: 12, N: 12, D: 8.11. WR: 24 Arrow Match—231 (KOR—Lee C.H., Kim Y.C., Im D.H.)

1. KOR	Im Dong-hyun, Lee Chang-hwan, Park Kyung-mo
2. ITA	Ilario Di Buò, Marco Galiazzo, Mauro Nespoli
3. CHN	Lin Jiang, Li Wenquan, Xue Haifeng
4. UKR	Markiyan Ivashko, Viktor Ruban, Oleksandr Serdiuk
5. POL	Rafał Dobrowolski, Piotr Piątek, Jacek Proć
6. MAL	Cheng Chu Sian, Wan Khalmizam, Muhammad Marbawi
7. TAI	Chen Szu-yuan, Kuo Cheng-wei, Wang Cheng-pang
8. RUS	Andrey Abramov, Bair Badenov, Balzhinima Tsyrempilov

Final: KOR 227-225 ITA
3rd Place: CHN 222-219 UKR

Despite having never won a men's individual gold medal, South Korea remained the world's dominant archery nation. Not only had they won the men's team gold medal at three of the past five Olympics, they had also won every major international tournament since the 2004 Athens Games, including both world championships, the 2006 Asian Games, and the 2007 Olympic test event.

Led at the Beijing Olympics by reigning world champion Im Dong-hyun and 2006 FITA world cup winner Park Kyung-mo, the team finished first in the ranking round to receive a bye into the quarterfinal round. They advanced past Poland 224–222 in the quarterfinals, and then beat China 221-218 to reach the final, where they faced Italy.

The Italians were led by defending individual gold medalist Marco Galiazzo. The two teams fought to a tie going into the final three arrows. Italy's Mauro Nespoli shot a seven. The Korean team answered with two nines and a ten on their final three arrows, clinching Korea's third straight gold medal and setting a 24-arrow Olympic record of 227 points. Part of South Korea's success may have been due to their detailed training regime. To prepare their athletes for the noise and distraction of an Olympic competition, Korean officials built a full replica of the Beijing archery venue at their practice grounds, complete with stands full of screaming spectators and loudspeakers blasting music.

Despite finishing last in the ranking round, the Chinese defeated Great Britain, Russia and the Ukraine to earn their first-ever Olympic archery medal. The Chinese squad was led by 28-year-old Xue Haifeng, a member of the Xibo ethnic minority group from northeast China, who traditionally give their children an archery bow on their first birthday.

DISCONTINUED EVENTS

In early editions of this book, I included results from the 1900 Paris Exposition and the 1904 St. Louis Louisiana Purchase Exposition. The truth is that these contests were really national championships and only by the most extreme definition of the term could they be considered "Olympic" competitions. Those readers wishing to pursue the results of the archery contests in Paris in 1900 and those in St. Louis in 1904 should read *The Unofficial Report of the 1900 Olympic Games* and *The Unofficial Report of the 1904 Olympic Games*, both by Bill Mallon. Both books are available from McFarland & Company, Inc.; Box 611; Jefferson, North Carolina 28640; USA. The archery competitions of 1908 and 1920 were only marginally more international, but in London and Antwerp designations of official Olympic events were more clearly defined than in 1900 and 1904.

1908 London C: 27, N: 3, D: 7.18.
York Round (100 Yards—80 Yards—60 Yards)

		PTS.
1. William Dod	GBR	815
2. Reginald Brooks-King	GBR	768
3. Henry Richardson	USA	760
4. John Penrose	GBR	709
5. John Bridges	GBR	687
6. Harold James	GBR	652
7. Theodore Robinson	GBR	647
8. Hugh Nesham	GBR	643

Willy Dod was born into a family so wealthy that during his 87-year life span he never attended school, never worked, and never even married. In fact, he never attempted anything difficult until, in a burst of patriotic enthusiasm four weeks after the outbreak of World War I, he enlisted—at age 47—in the Sportsman's Battalion of the Royal Fusiliers and found himself serving as a private on the front lines in France. His zeal cooled rapidly and he managed a transfer to the navy as an administrative officer. Dod did not take up archery until he was 39 years old, but apparently it was in his blood: one of his ancestors, Sir Anthony Dod of Edge, commanded the victorious English archers at the Battle of Agincourt against the French in 1415. The Olympic competition was held over two days. Dod took a ten-point lead after the first day, during which action was delayed because of heavy rain, and then pulled away on the second day to take the title on his 41st birthday. When Dod's sister, Lottie, finished in second place in the women's archery contest, they became the first brother-sister medalists in Olympic history.

1908 London C: 17, N: 2, D: 7.20.

Continental Style (50 Meters)

		PTS.
1. Eugène Grisot	FRA	263
2. Louis Vernet	FRA	256
3. Gustave Cabaret	FRA	255
4. Charles Aubras	FRA	231
5. Charles Querviel	FRA	223
6. Albert Dauchez	FRA	222
7. L.A. Salingre	FRA	215
8. H. Berton	FRA	212

In the continental style event, shots were fired one at a time rather than in flights of three. An unofficial entrant, R.O. Backhouse of Great Britain, finished second with a score of 260 and was awarded a certificate for special merit. Another unofficial entrant, Hugh Nesham of Great Britain, shot 221.

1920 Antwerp

Individual

The top finisher from each nation in the team events qualified for the individual events.

28 Meters: C: 24, N: 3, D: 8.5.

		PTS.
1. Hubert van Innis	BEL	144
2. Léonce Quentin	FRA	115

33 Meters: C: 16, N: 2, D: 8.5.

		PTS.
1. Hubert van Innis	BEL	139
2. Julien Brulé	FRA	94

50 Meters: C: 16, N: 2, D: 8.5.

		PTS.
1. Julien Brulé	FRA	134
2. Hubert van Innis	BEL	106

Van Innis outshot Brulé 404 to 380 in the qualifying round.

Teams

28 Meters: T: 3, N: 3, D: 8.4.

	PTS.
1. HOL Adrianus Theeuwes, Johannes van Gastel, Theodorus Willems, Petrus de Brouwer, Adrianus van Merrienboer, Joep Packbiers, Driekske van Bussel, Tiest van Gestel	3087
2. BEL Hubert van Innis, Alphonse Allaert, Edmond de Knibber, Louis Delcon, Jérôme de Maeyer, Louis van Beeck, Pierre van Thielt, Louis Fierens	2924
3. FRA Léonce Quentin, Julien Brulé, Pascal Fauvel, Eugène Grisot, Eugène Richez, Paul Leroy, Artun Mabellon, Léon Epin	2328

A Dutch newspaper of the time provided this evocative description of the Dutch victory in neighboring Belgium: "When the Dutch archery team had won the championship, they sang their national anthem at the top of their voices. Some people from the audience begrudged the Dutchmen the championship and called them cheeseheads ('kaaskoppen'). But our plucky archers were not at all disturbed about this abuse and sang even louder."

33 Meters: T: 2, N: 2, D: 8.5.

	PTS.
1. BEL Hubert van Innis, Alphonse Allaert, Edmond de Knibber, Louis Delcon, Jérôme de Maeyer, Louis van Beeck, Pierre van Thielt, Louis Fierens	2958
2. FRA Léonce Quentin, Julien Brulé, Pascal Fauvel, Eugène Grisot, Eugène Richez, Paul Leroy, Artur Mabellon, Léon Epin	2586

50 Meters: T: 2, N: 2, D: 8.5.

	PTS.
1. BEL Hubert van Innis, Pierre van Thielt, Edmond de Knibber, Louis van Beeck, Louis Fierens, Alphonse Allaert, Louis Delcon, Jérôme de Maeyer	2701
2. FRA Julien Brulé, Pascal Fauvel, Léonce Quentin, Eugène Grisot, Eugène Richez, Paul Leroy, Artur Mabellon, Léon Epin	2493

Pole Targets

Archers shot at bird-shaped targets on crossbeams attached to a 31-meter high pole.

Pole, Small Birds C: 6, N: 1, D: 8.3.

		PTS.
1. Edmond van Moer	BEL	11
2. Louis van de Perck	BEL	8
3. Joseph Hermans	BEL	6
4. Firmin Flamand	BEL	5
5. Edmond Cloetens	BEL	4
6. Auguste van de Verre	BEL	1

Pole, Large Birds C: 6, N: 1, D: 8.3.

		PTS.
1. Edmond Cloetens	BEL	13
2. Louis van de Perck	BEL	11
3. Firmin Flamand	BEL	7
4. Edmond van Moer	BEL	6
5. Joseph Hermans	BEL	5
6. Auguste van de Verre	BEL	3

Pole, Small Birds, Team T: 1, N: 1, D: 8.3.

	PTS.
1. BEL Edmond van Moer, Louis van de Perck, Joseph Hermans, Firmin Flamand, Edmond Cloetens, Auguste van de Verre	25

Pole, Large Birds, Team T: 1, N: 1, D: 8.3.

	PTS.
1. BEL Edmond Cloetens, Louis van de Perck, Firmin Flamand, Edmond van Moer, Joseph Hermans, Auguste van de Verre	31

WOMEN

Prior to 1992, women's Olympic archery rules differed from men's only in that the distances were 70, 60, 50, and 30 meters. Now the rules are exactly the same.

INDIVIDUAL

1896–1968 not held

1972 Munich C: 40, N: 21, D: 9.10. WR: 2380 (Emma Gapchenko)

		1st ROUND	2nd ROUND	TOTAL POINTS
1. Doreen Wilber	USA	1198	1226	2424 WR
2. Irena Szydlowska	POL	1224	1183	2407
3. Emma Gapchenko	SOV/RUS	1201	1202	2403
4. Keto Losaberidze	SOV/GEO	1195	1207	2402
5. Linda Myers	USA	1200	1185	2385
6. Maria Maczyńska	POL	1173	1198	2371
7. Kim Ho-gu	PRK	1195	1174	2369
8. Alla Peounova	SOV/UKR	1180	1184	2364

Wilber was a 42-year-old housewife from Jefferson, Iowa.

1976 Montreal C: 27, N: 16, D: 7.30. WR: 2465 (Zebiniso Rustamova)

		1st ROUND	2nd ROUND	TOTAL POINTS
1. Luann Ryon	USA	1217	1282	2499 WR
2. Valentyna Kovpan	SOV/UKR	1182	1278	2460
3. Zebiniso Rustamova	SOV/TJK	1202	1205	2407
4. Jang Sun-yong	PRK	1200	1205	2405
5. Lucille Lemay	CAN	1181	1220	2401
6. Jadwiga Wilejto	POL	1200	1195	2395
7. Linda Myers	USA	1180	1213	2393
8. Maria Urban	GER	1216	1160	2376

Ryon, a 23-year-old student from Riverside, California, had never before competed in an international tournament.

1980 Moscow C: 29, N: 19, D: 8.2. WR (Single Round): 1321 (Natalya Butuzova)

		1st ROUND	2nd ROUND	TOTAL POINTS
1. Keto Losaberidze	SOV/GEO	1257	1234	2491
2. Natalya Butuzova	SOV/UZB	1251	1226	2477
3. Päivi Meriluoto	FIN	1217	1232	2449
4. Ždenka Padevetova	CZE	1206	1199	2405
5. O Gwang-sun	PRK	1195	1206	2401
6. Catherina Floris	HOL	1186	1196	2382
7. Maria Szeliga	POL	1190	1175	2365
8. Lotti Tschanz	SWI	1184	1162	2346

1984 Los Angeles-Long Beach C: 47, N: 24, D: 8.11. WR: 1325 (Lyudmila Arzhanikova)

		1st ROUND	2nd ROUND	TOTAL POINTS
1. Seo Hyang-soon	KOR	1275	1293	2568 OR
2. Li Lingjuan	CHN	1279	1280	2559
3. Kim Jin-ho	KOR	1276	1279	2555
4. Hiroko Ishizu	JPN	1263	1261	2524
5. Päivi Meriluoto	FIN	1259	1250	2509
6. Manuela Dachner	GER	1260	1248	2508
6. Katrina King	USA	1265	1243	2508
8. Wu Yanan	CHN	1240	1253	2493

Two-time world champion Kim Jin-ho was upset by 18-year-old Li Lingjuan and 17-year-old Seo Hyang-soon, the latter coming from behind to win on the final day of competition.

Finishing in 35th place was New Zealand's Neroli Fairhall, the first paraplegic athlete to take part in the Olympics. Paralyzed from the waist down following a motorbike accident, she competed while seated in a wheelchair.

1988 Seoul C: 62, N: 30, D: 9.30. WR: 1338 (Kim Soo-nyung

		OPEN ROUND	8th FINAL	QUART. FINAL	SEMI-FINAL	GRAND FINAL	GRAND TOTAL
1. Kim Soo-nyung	KOR	1331 (1)	331 (2)	337 (1)	340 (1)	344 (1)	2683
2. Wang Hee-kyung	KOR	1298 (2)	320 (5)	330 (2)	332 (2)	332 (2)	2612
3. Yun Young-sook	KOR	1296 (3)	328 (3)	326 (5)	326 (7)	327 (3)	2593
4. Lyudmila Arzhanikova	SOV/RUS	1279 (6)	332 (1)	326 (6)	329 (5)	327 (4)	2593
5. Jenny Sjöwall	SWE	1294 (4)	306 (16)	327 (4)	330 (3)	325 (5)	2581
6. Claudia Kriz	GER	1250 (17)	311 (11)	322 (8)	326 (8)	318 (6)	2527
7. Joanne Franks	GBR	1281 (5)	301 (18)	327 (3)	330 (4)	318 (7)	2557
8. Tetyana Muntyan	SOV/UKR	1272 (7)	319 (6)	316 (12)	328 (6)	314 (8)	2549

The three Korean medalists were 17, 18, and 17 years old, respectively.

1992 Barcelona C: 61, N: 27, D: 8.2. WR: 12 Arrow Match—114 (Kim Soo-nyung)

1. Cho Youn-jeon	KOR
2. Kim Soo-nyung	KOR
3. Natalya Valeyeva	MOL
4. Wang Xiaozhu	CHN
5. Khatuna Kvrivichvili	GEO
6. Lai Fang-Mei	TAI
7. Alison Williamson	GBR
8. Denise Parker	USA

Final: Cho 112-105 Kim
3rd Place: Valeyeva 104-102 Wang

Cho set a world record of 1375 in the qualifying round. The previous record holder, Lee Eun-kyung, was defeated in the round of 16 by Wang of China. When asked how she calmed her nerves before competitions, Cho replied, "I take long walks at night through the cemetery."

1996 Atlanta-Stone Mountain C: 64, N: 29, D: 7.31. WR: 12 Arrow Match—117 (Kim Kyo-jeong, Wang Xiaozhu)

1. Kim Kyung-wook	KOR
2. He Ying	CHN
3. Olena Sadovnycha	UKR
4. Elif Altinkaynak	TUR
5. Olga Yakusheva	BLR
6. Kim Jo-sun	KOR
7. Wang Xiaozhu	CHN
8. Barbara Mensing	GER

Final: Kim 113-107 He
3rd Place: Sadovnycha 109-102 Altinkaynak

Lina Herasymenko of Ukraine led the ranking round, but was eliminated in the third match round by Wang Xiaozhu. Reigning world champion Natalya Valeyeva was beaten in the round of 16 by Barbara Mensing, whom she had beaten in the 1995 world championship final. Meanwhile, Kim Kyung-wook and He Ying, who were coincidentally tied in 31st place in the world rankings, were wending their ways to the final. Kim's most difficult match was a high-scoring (165-164) third round victory over teammate Youn Hye-young. In the final, Kim led from start to finish. Kim, along with other members of the South Korean archery team, had to endure an unusual training regimen. For Kim the low point came in 1994 when she had to pick up a live snake and lightly bite its body. She was so frightened that her trainer had to hold the snake while Kim bit it.

Paola Fantato of Verona, Italy, became the second archer to compete from a wheelchair. A victim of childhood polio and winner of the 1992 Paralympics, she placed 54th in Atlanta.

2000 Sydney T: 34, N: 34, D: 9.19. WR: 12 Arrow Match—117 (Kim Kyo-jeong, Wang Xiaozhu)

1. Yun Mi-jin	KOR
2. Kim Nam-soon	KOR
3. Kim Soo-nyung	KOR
4. Choe Ok-sil	PRK
5. Sayoko Kawauchi	JPN
6. Nataliya Bolotova	RUS
7. Natalya Valeyeva	ITA
8. Joanna Nowicka	POL

Final: Yun 107-106 Kim N.S.
3rd Place: Kim S.N. 103-101 Choe

The powerful South Koreans boasted Asian Games champion Kim Jo-sun, world champion Lee Eun-kyung and world record holders Choi Nam-ok and Kim Won-jeong. But the South Koreans were so strong and so deep that none of them qualified for the Olympic team. In the end, all three of the South Koreans who did qualify made it all the way to the semifinals . . . along with yet another Korean, North Korean Choe Ok-sil. One of three South Koreans was veteran Kim Soo-nyung. As a 17-year-old, Kim won the gold medal at the 1988 Olympics and then added the 1989 and 1991 world championships and the silver medal at the 1992 Olympics. Then, at the age of 21, Kim retired. After seven years, during which she married and raised two children, Kim returned to training in 1999. In the semifinals she was defeated 107-105 by 17-year-old Yun Mi-jin. In the other semi Kim Nam-soon easily beat Choe 114-107. In the bronze medal match, Kim Soo-nyung held off Choe to secure a South Korean sweep. Yun and Kim Nam-soon were tied after seven arrows in the final. Yun picked up a point each in the eighth and tenth rounds, while Kim gained back a point with her eleventh arrow. They both shot 9s in the last round and Yun came away with the victory.

2004 Athens C: 64, N: 31, D: 8.19. WR: 12 Arrow Match—118 (Song Mi-jing)

1. Park Sung-hyun	KOR	WR
2. Lee Sung-jin	KOR	
3. Alison Williamson	GBR	
4. Yuan Shu-chi	TAI	
5. Yun Mi-jin	KOR	
6. Wu Hui-ju	TAI	
7. Evangelia Psarra	GRE	
8. He Ying	CHN	

Final: Park 110-108 Lee
3rd Place: Williamson 105-104 Yuan

Competing in her first Olympics, 21-year-old Park Sung-hyun set a world record of 682 points during the ranking round. She won each of her first five matches by at least ten points and then faced compatriot Lee Sung-jin in the final. Trailing at one point by three points, Park came back to earn a tie with one shot left. With her final shot, Park managed a bulls-eye for the maximum 10 points. Lee scored 8 points to take silver.

2008 Beijing C: 64, N: 35, D: 8.14. WR: 12 Arrow Match—119 (Yun Ok-hee)

1. Zhang Juanjuan	CHN
2. Park Sung-hyun	KOR
3. Yun Ok-hee	KOR
4. Kwon Un-sil	PRK
5. Khatuna Kvrivishvili-Lorig	USA
6. Nami Hayakawa	JPN
7. Joo Hyun-jung	KOR
8. Mariana Avitia Martínez	MEX

Final: Zhang 110-109 Park
3rd Place: Yun 109-106 Kwon

South Korean archers had won six straight women's individual gold medals over 24 years, the longest active winning streak in the Olympics in any sport. Led by defending gold medalist Park Sung-hyun, the three South Koreans finished 1-2-3 in the ranking round, and all three advanced easily to the quarter-finals. The prospects for another gold medal, or even a possible sweep, seemed strong, especially after Joo knocked out reigning world champion Natalya Valeyeva 110-108 in the second round.

South Korea's biggest obstacle turned out to be China's Zhang Juanjuan, who finished just 27th in the ranking round, last of China's three archers. Zhang's previous best results included a 10th place at the 2004 Athens Olympics and a sixth place at the 2007 world championships. Zhang faced number three seed Joo in the quarter-finals, recording a 106-101 upset victory to move on to the semis. There she faced number two seed Yun, and pulled off another upset, 115-109, to make it to the gold medal match. In the final Zhang trailed Park 101-109 before her final arrow, with which she scored nine out of ten to win by a single point. Zhang was China's first-ever archery gold medalist and the first non-Korean to win an individual women's archery gold medal since Keto Losaberidze in 1980.

TEAM

1896-1984 not held

1988 Seoul T: 15, N: 15, D: 10.1. WR: 3981 (KOR—Lee H.Y., Kim K.W., Kim S.N.)

		OPEN ROUND	SEMI-FINAL	GRAND FINAL
1. KOR	Kim Soo-nyung, Wang Hee-kyung, Yun Young-sook	3925 (1)	1000(1)	982 (1)
2. INA	Lilies Handayani, Nurfitriyana Saiman, Kusuma Wardhani	3720 (5)	975 (4)	952 (2)
3. USA	Debra Ochs, Denise Parker, Melanie Skillman	3742 (4)	988 (2)	952 (3)
4. SOV	Lyudmila Arzhanikova, Natalya Butuzova, Tetyana Muntyan	3818 (2)	978 (3)	951 (4)
5. GBR	Pauline Edwards, Joanne Franks, Cheryl Sutton	3692 (7)	962 (5)	933 (5)
6. GER	Doris Haas, Claudia Kriz, Christa Öckl	3702 (6)	953 (6)	931 (6)
7. SWE	Liselotte Andersson, Carina Jonsson, Jenny Sjöwall	3662 (10)	949 (8)	930 (7)
8. FRA	Marie-Josée Bazin, Nathalie Hibon, Catherine Pellen	3653 (11)	950 (7)	898 (8)

The unheralded Indonesian team earned their nation's first-ever Olympic medals by defeating the US in a shoot-out, 72-67. Said the Indonesian coach, Donald Pandiangan, "It is a silver, but for us it is more than one hundred gold medals, it is more than even a gold mine."

1992 Barcelona T: 17, N: 17, D: 8.1. WR: FITA Round—4025 (KOR—Kim S.N., Wang H.K., Park M.K.)

1. KOR	Cho Youn-jeong, Kim Soo-nyung, Lee Eun-kyung
2. CHN	Ma Xiangjun, Wang Hong, Wang Xiaozhu
3. SOV	Lyudmila Arzhanikova, Khatuna Kvrivichvili, Natalya Valeyeva
4. FRA	Severine Bonal, Christine Gabillard, Nathalie Hibon
5. SWE	Liseiotte Djerf, Kristina Persson, Jenny Sjöwall
6. TUR	Elif Ekşi, Natalia Çakir, Zehra Öktem
7. PRK	Kim Jong-hwa, Li Myong-gum, Sin Song-hui
8. USA	Sherry Block, Jennifer O'Donnell, Denise Parker

Final: KOR 236-228 CHN
3rd Place: SOV 240-222 FRA

The South Korean women obliterated the world record in the qualifying round by scoring 4094 points. Still, they had to survive a tie-breaker against the Swedes in the quarterfinals before they recovered their composure to breeze though the semifinals and finals.

1996 Atlanta-Stone Mountain T: 15, C: 15, D: 8.1. WR: 27 Arrow Match—250 (CHN—Lin S., Wang X., Zhang F.)

1. KOR	Kim Jo-sun, Kim Kyung-wook, Youn Hye-young
2. GER	Barbara Mensing, Cornelia Pfohl, Sandra Wagner
3. POL	Iwona Dzięcioł, Katarzyna Klata, Joanna Nowicka
4. TUR	Elif Altinkaynak, Elif Ekşi, Natalia Nasaridze
5. UKR	Natalya Bilukha, Lina Herasymenko, Olena Sadovnycha
6. CHN	He Ying, Wang Xiaozhu, Yang Jianping
7. SWE	Christa Bäckman, Kristina Persson, Jenny Sjövall
8. KAZ	Irina Leonova, Anna Mozhar, Yana Tuniiantse

Final: KOR 245-235 GER
3rd Place: POL 244-239 TUR

Once again, the South Korean women set a world record in the ranking round and then won with relative ease. In the final they fell behind the Germans early and then gradually closed the gap to one point after 18 arrows. When Cornelia Pfohl scored only 1 point on the 19th arrow, the South Koreans pounced and went on to win by ten points.

2000 Sydney C: 12, N: 12, D: 9.21. WR: 27 Arrow Match—253 (KOR—Kang H.J., Yun H.Y., Hwang J. H.)

1. KOR	Kim Soo-nyung, Kim Nam-soon, Yun Mi-jin
2. UKR	Olena Sadovnycha, Kateryna Serdyuk, Nataliya Burdeyna
3. GER	Cornelia Pfohl, Barbara Mensing, Sandra Sachse-Wagner
4. TUR	Elif Altınkaynak, Natalia Nasaridze, Zekiye Şatir
5. USA	Janet Dykman, Karen Scavotto, Denise Parker
6. CHN	Yu Hui, He Ying, Yang Jianping
7. ITA	Natalia Valeyeva, Cristina Ioriatti, Irene Franchini
8. TAI	Liu Pi-yu Liu, Lin Yi-yin, Wen Chia-ling

Final: KOR 251-239 UKR
3rd Place: GER 240-234 TUR

Having swept the medals in the individual event, the South Koreans were the overwhelming favorites to win the team contest. They did not disappoint. After setting a world record of 1994 points in the ranking round, they defeated the United States 252-240, Germany 251-238 and Ukraine 251-239. Their 54-arrow total of 502 in the semis and the final was also a world record. Kim Soo-nyung brought her career medal total to six: 4 gold, 1 silver and 1 bronze.

2004 Athens T: 15, N: 15, D: 8.20. WR: 27 Arrow Match—258 (KOR—Park S.H., Yun M.J., Lee S.J.)

1. KOR	Lee Sung-jin, Park Sung-hyun, Yun Mi-jin
2. CHN	He Ying, Lin Sang, Zhang Juanjuan
3. TAI	Wu Hui-ju, Chen Li-ju, Yuan Shu-chi
4. FRA	Alexandra Fouace, Bérangère Schuh, Aurore Trayan
5. GRE	Evangelia Psarra, Elpida Romantzi, Fotini Vavatsi
6. UKR	Tetiana Berezhna, Natalia Burdeina, Kateryna Palekha
7. GER	Anja Hitzler, Wiebke Nulle, Cornelia Pfohl
8. IND	Dola Banerjee, Reena Kumari, Sumangala Sharma

Final: KOR 241-240 CHN
3rd Place: TAI 242-228 FRA

The South Korean team set a world record of 2,030 during the 216-arrow ranking round. After defeating Greece by 12 points and France by 15 points, the South Koreans faced China in the final. With three arrows left for their last shooter, Park Sung-hyun, South Korea needed 27 points to secure the victory. Park scored a nine and an eight on her next two arrows and one of the Chinese archers, Zhang Juanjuan, began to do a victory dance. But then Park hit a perfect 10 with her last arrow to give South Korea the gold. "Do you know," said Park, "if I aimed for a 10, I am sure I would not have got 10. I resigned myself to the divine will and then I calmed down."

To help their archers prepare for the competition in Athens, the South Korean archery federation had their archers train under simulated conditions of Panathinaikos Stadium–complete with thousands of cheering fans—by having the team practice in a full baseball stadium prior to a game.

2008 Beijing T: 10, N: 10, D: 8.10. WR: 24 Arrow Match—228 (KOR–Lee, Yun, Yun)

1. KOR	Joo Hyun-jung, Park Sung-hyun, Yun Ok-hee
2. CHN	Ling Chen, Dan Guo, Zhang Juanjuan
3. FRA	Virginie Arnold, Sophie Dodemont, Bérangère Schuh
4. GBR	Charlotte Burgess, Naomi Folkard, Alison Williamson
5. ITA	Pia Lionetti, Elena Tonetta, Natalia Valeeva
6. POL	Małgorzata Ćwienczek (Sobieraj), Iwona Marcinkiewicz (Dzi cioł), Justyna Mospinek
7. IND	Dola Banerjee, Bombayla Devi, Pranitha Vardhineni
8. JPN	Nami Hayakawa, Yuki Hayashi, Sayoko Kawauchi-Kitabatake

Final: KOR 224-215 CHN
3rd Place: FRA 203-201 GBR

South Korea had won every women's team gold medal since the event's debut as an Olympic sport in 1988. Since 2004 its teams had also won two world championships, the 2006 Asian Games and the 2007 Olympic test event. Led by double Olympic gold medalist Park Sung-hyun, the Korean squad was never seriously challenged. The team recorded a 216-arrow Olympic record of 2,004 points in the ranking round, as well as a 24-arrow world record of 231 points in their quarter-final match against Italy. They outshot France 213-184 in the semi-final before taking on China in the gold-medal match. Shooting last, Park needed just a 2 to clinch the gold medal, but she hit a perfect 10 to finish at 224-215.

The bronze medal match was more suspenseful. France's Sophie Dodemont needed seven points to win with one arrow remaining. She managed eight points, giving France its first-ever women's Olympic archery medal.

DISCONTINUED EVENT

1908 London C: 25, N: 1, D: 7.20.

National Round (60 Yards—50 Yards)

		PTS.
1. Sybil "Queenie" Newall	GBR	688
2. Charlotte "Lottie" Dod	GBR	642
3. Beatrice Hill-Lowe	GBR/IRL	618
4. Jessie Wadworth	GBR	605
5. G.W. H. Honnywill	GBR	587
6. S.H. Armitage	GBR	582
7. C. Priestley Foster	GBR	553
8. Lillian Wilson	GBR	534

Newall trailed Dod by ten points at the end of the first day but surged ahead on the second day. Fifty-three years old at the time of her victory, Newall remains the oldest female medalist in Olympic history.

Silver medalist "Lottie" Dod was an exceptional athlete. In 1887, at the age of 15, she won the first of five Wimbledon tennis championships. To this day, Dod remains the youngest person to win a singles championship at Wimbledon. (Martina Hingis was three days younger than Dod when she gained the doubles title in 1996.) She was also a champion golfer and field hockey player. In 1894 she became one of the first women to attempt the Cresta Run at St. Moritz. She was also a fine skater who once played a cricket match on ice skates. The greatest female archer of the time, Alice Legh, did not take part in the Olympics. A week later, however, she defeated Queenie Newall by 151 points.

Sybil "Queenie" Newall, 1908
Winner of the women's archery competition at age 53, Newall is the oldest female medalist in Olympic history.

Chapter 4 **Badminton**

MEN	WOMEN	MIXED
Singles	Singles	Doubles
Doubles	Doubles	

The sport of badminton appears to have been invented around 1860 when the daughters of the Duke of Beaufort ran a string across the great hall of Badminton House and hit a shuttle back and forth over the string. Modern badminton is played on a court 44 feet (13.4 meters) long and across a net 5 feet 1 inch (1.55 meters) high at the post, which sags 1 inch at the center. The playing area is 17 feet (5.18 meters) wide for singles and 20 feet (6.1 meters) wide for doubles. Players use a racket to hit a leather-covered cork-tipped shuttlecock that is topped by 16 goose feathers taken from the same goose, usually from the left wing, which is considered stronger. Shuttles travel at speeds in excess of 150 mph (240 k.p.h.)—much faster than the other Olympic net sports: tennis, table tennis, and volleyball.

Badminton uses a "rally points scoring system." If the serving side wins a rally, that side scores a point and serves again. If the receiving side wins a rally, that side scores a point and becomes the new serving side. Matches are played over the best of three games. Each game is won by the first player or team to reach 21 points, or, after 20, by a margin of two points. If the score reaches 29-29, the next point wins. Players are allowed a 90-second rest between the first and second games of a match and a rest of five minutes between the second and third games.

In 1992, pool play was followed by a direct elimination format. Between 1996 and 2008, the tournament was changed to direct elimination with the eight highest ranked players or teams seeded and the rest placed in a blind draw. In 2012 the format will revert to a two-stage format. All events will begin with a preliminary round, with competitors divided into groups, and each player and doubles pair playing everyone else in their group. The best players from this stage (16 for the singles events, eight pairs for doubles events) will qualify for the knockout stage of the competition.

Eighty-two players per gender qualify for the Olympics according to their world rankings, which are based on their performances in a series of international events. Three more entrants are selected by a Tripartite Commission. The host nation is allowed two entries and each of five regions must be represented by at least one player or pair. Each nation is limited to three entries per individual event and two pairs per doubles event.

In May 2011, in an attempt to revive interest in the sport in the lead-up to the 2012 London Olympics, the Badminton World Federation instituted a dress code requiring female players to wear skirts or dresses rather than shorts or pants. One month later, after widespread criticism of the rule as sexist and offensive, the proposed rule was shelved.

MEN

SINGLES

1896–1988 not held

1992 Barcelona C: 56, N: 32, D: 8.4.

		MATCHES		GAMES	
		W	L	W	L
1. Allan Budi Kusuma	INA	6	0	12	0
2. Ardy Wiranata	INA	4	1	8	3
3. Thomas Stuer-Launidsen	DEN	4	1	8	3
3. Hermawan Susanto	INA	3	1	7	3
5. Poul-Erik Høyer-Larsen	DEN	2	1	4	2
5. Kim Hak-kyun	KOR	2	1	4	3
5. Rashid Sidek	MAL	2	1	4	2
5. Zhao Jianhua	CHN	2	1	5	2

Final: Kusuma—Wiranata 15-12, 18-13

The critical match of the early rounds came in the quarter-finals when world champion Zhao Jianhua staved off six match points but was finally beaten, 15-2, 14-17, 17-14, by Hermawan Susanto.

The final was an 84-minute marathon, which Kusuma won by earning 11 of the last 13 points. His victory came two hours after his girlfriend, Susi Susanti, won the women's title. Prior to the victories by Susanti and Kusuma, Indonesia, the fourth most populous nation in the world, had never earned a gold medal, despite taking part in the Olympics since 1952. Not surprisingly, the pair became national heroes and their return to Jakarta was cause for an enormous celebration that included a two-hour parade led by a car carrying a gigantic shuttlecock. Susanti and Kusuma were also awarded $200,000 each.

1996 Atlanta C: 48, N: 29, D: 8.1.

1. Poul-Erik Høyer-Larsen	DEN
2. Dong Jiong	CHN
3. Rashid Sidek	MAL
4. Heryanto Arbi	INA

5. Allan Budi Kusuma (INA), Lee Kwang-jin (KOR), Park Sung-woo (KOR), Joko Suprianto (INA)
Final: Høyer-Larsen—Dong 15-12, 15-10
3rd Place: Sidek—Arbi 5-15, 15-11, 15-6

Høyer-Larsen was the only non-Asian badminton medalist of the Atlanta Games. In the first game of the final he trailed Dong 2-6 and 8-11 before prevailing 15-12. The second game was easier. Høyer-Larsen led 5-0 and 12-7. Dong closed to 12-10 before Høyer-Larsen finished him off 15-10. Bronze medalist Rashid Sidek was the younger brother of Razif and Jalani Sidek, who earned bronze medals of their own in the 1992 doubles.

2000 Sydney C: 35, N: 22, D: 9.23.

1. Ji Xinpeng	CHN
2. Hendrawan	INA
3. Xuanze Xia	CHN
4. Peter Gade	DEN

5. Marleve Mario Mainaky (INA), Jun Sun (CHN), Taufik Hidayat (INA), Wong Choong-Hann (MAL)
Final: Ji—Hendrawan 15-12, 15-4
3rd Place: Xia—Gade 15-13, 15-5

Seeded only seventh, Ji Xinpeng earned his gold medal the hard way by beating all three of the world's leading players. Ji got off to a tentative start, losing his first game against Wei Ng 7-15 before winning 15-4 and 15-11. After defeating Kevin Han of the United States, Ji faced number one seed Taufik Hidayat and scored a startling 15-12, 15-5 upset. In the semifinals Ji defeated world number one Peter Gade 15-9, 1-15, 15-9. Ji's final opponent was veteran Hendrawan, who had qualified for the gold medal match by winning all four of his matches without losing a game. Ji easily won the first game of the final 15-4. In the second game, Hendrawan led 9-4, but Ji roared back to win 15-13. Ji never won another major tournament.

2004 Athens C: 32, N: 21, D: 8.21.

1. Taufik Hidayat	INA
2. Shon Seung-mo	KOR
3. Soni Dwi Kuncoro	INA
4. Boonsak Ponsana	THA

5. Ronald Susilo (SIN), Peter Gade (DEN), Park Tae-sang (KOR), Chen Hong (CHN)
Final: Hidayat—Shon 15-8, 15-7
3rd Place: Kuncoro—Ponsana 15-11, 17-16

Hidayat had earned a reputation as the wild child of Indonesia. In 2000 the Indonesian Badminton Association suspended him from two international competitions after he publicly criticized officials. In 2001, at the Indonesian National Championships, he threw his water bottle at a shouting fan, and then climbed into the stands and hit the spectator with his racket. Hidayat later moved to Singapore and threatened to switch his national allegiance after his coach, Mulyo Handoyo, was fired. The pair returned to Indonesia to train in early 2004.

Anxious to erase the memory of his premature exit at the 2000 Olympics in Sydney, Hidayat ran into problems in the round of 16 when he dropped the opening game to Malaysia's Wong Choong-hann. However, Hidayat recovered and won the match. He breezed through his next three matches and then faced Shon Seung-mo in the final. Shon, the son of a taxi driver in the port city of Masan, underwent a cornea transplant after being hit by a shuttlecock during his freshman year of high school, leaving him partially blind in one eye. Shon quickly established a 6-0 lead over a nervous Hidayat in the first game. Hidayat came back to tie the score 7-7 and only allowed one more point to win the game 15-8. In the second game, a calm and collected Hidayat dominated the play, winning 15-7.

Earning Olympic gold did not improve Hidayat's reputation for trouble. In 2006, he was suspended from the world championships because he walked off the court in the middle of a match against Lin Dan after disputing a line call in the Hong Kong Open.

2008 Beijing C: 41, N: 35, D: 8.17.

1. Lin Dan	CHN
2. Lee Chong Wei	MAL
3. Chen Jin	CHN
4. Lee Hyun-il	KOR

5. Peter Gade (DEN), Hsien Yu-hsing (TAI), Bao Chunlai (CHN), Sony Dwi Kuncoro (INA)
Final: Lin—Lee 21-12, 21-8
3rd Place: Chen—Lee 21-16, 12-21, 21-14

Twice reigning world champion and three-time All-England champion Lin Dan arrived in Beijing as the top-ranked player in the world and one of the clearest favorites for gold. Along with his girlfriend Xie Xingfeng—also a double world and thrice All-England champion—Lin was one of the biggest stars of international badminton.

Despite his international success, Super Dan, as he was popularly known, faced several strong opponents in Beijing, including defending Olympic champion Taufik Hidayat and world second-ranked player Lee Chong Wei. Lin had suffered a painful 15-3, 15-7 defeat to Hidayat in the final of the 2005 world championships in Anaheim, California, and then lost to him again in straight sets in the final of the Asian Games the following year in Doha, Qatar. Two months before the Beijing Olympics, Lin suffered another defeat, this time to Lee Chong Wei in the semi-final of the Thomas Cup in Jakarta, Indonesia.

Lin, Lee and Hidayat all received byes to advance to the second round. Hidayat, who had been hospitalized a week before the Olympics due to fever, was the first to drop out of the tournament, after a surprising second-round loss to Malaysia's Wong Choong Hann. Lin and

Lee cruised through the early rounds, winning every match in straight sets through the quarter-finals.

Lin faced reigning All-England champion Chen Jin in the semi-finals. Chen had won the All-England title by beating Lin 22-20, 25-23 in a hard-fought final five months earlier. This time Lin had an easy time of it, dispatching Chen 21-12, 21-18. In the other semi-final, Lee Chong Wei defeated Lee Hyun-il 21-18, 13-21, 21-13.

Lin dominated the final against Lee from the beginning, winning the first set 21-12 and taking an 11-1 lead in the second set before cruising to a 21-8 victory.

DOUBLES

1896–1988 not held

1992 Barcelona T: 30, N: 21, D: 8.4.

		MATCHES		GAMES	
		W	L	W	L
1. KOR	Kim Moon-soo, Park Joo-bong	4	0	8	1
2. INA	Eddy Hartono, Rudy Gunawan	3	1	6	2
3. CHN	Li Yongbo, Tian Bingyi	3	1	6	5
3. MAL	Jalani Sidek, Razif Sidek	3	1	6	2
5. DEN	Jan Paulsen, Henrik Svarrer	2	1	5	2
5. INA	Rexy Mainaky, Ricky Subagja	2	1	4	2
5. JPN	Shuji Matsuno, Shinji Matsuura	2	1	4	2
5. KOR	Lee Sang-bok, Shon Jin-hwan	2	1	4	3

Final: Kim/Park—Hartono/Gunawan 15-11,15-7

This tournament went completely according to form, with the favorites winning in every instance. There was a bit of controversy in the first round when China's Li Yongbo was almost disqualified for delaying the match when he twice gained several minutes of much-needed rest by slowly rewrapping the bandage on his injured ankle.

1996 Atlanta T: 25, N: 14, D: 7.31.

1. INA Rexy Mainaky, Ricky Subagja
2. MAL Cheah Soon Kit, Yap Kim Hock
3. INA Antonius Irianto, Denny Kantono
4. MAL Soo Beng Kiang, Tan Kim Her
5. Huang Zhanzhong/Jiang Xin (CHN), Simon Archer/Chris Hunt (GBR), Ha Tae-kwon/Kang Kyung-jin (KOR), Andrei Antropov/ Nikolai Zuyev (RUS)

Final: Mainaky/Subagja—Cheah/Yap 5-15, 15-13,15-12
3rd Place: Antonius/Kantono—Soo/Tan 15-4, 12-15, 15-8

The final, between the two top seeded teams, was an exciting 89-minute tussle. Ricky and Rexy, as they were commonly known, were the favorites, having beaten Yap and Cheah several times and lost only once. But in the first game, the Malaysian pair overwhelmed Ricky and Rexy, jumping out to an 11-1 lead and winning 15-5. Ricky and Rexy took charge of the second game and led 9-2 before Yap and Cheah reeled off nine unanswered points. Three points from defeat at 11-12, Ricky and Rexy came from behind to win 15-13 and force a deciding game. This was a seesaw battle that was tied eight times until Yap and Cheah pulled ahead 12-10. Three points from defeat once again, Ricky and Rexy scored the next five points to gain an emotional victory.

2000 Sydney T: 22, N: 15, D: 9.21.

1. INA R. Candra Wijaya, Tony Gunawan
2. KOR Lee Dong-soo, Yoo Yong-sung
3. KOR Ha Tae-kwon, Kim Dong-moon
4. MAL Choong Tan-fook, Lee Wan-wah
5. Flandy Limpele/Hian Eng (INA), Rexy Ronald Mainaky/Ricky Achmad Subagja (INA), Jens Eriksen/Jesper Larsen (DEN), Nathan Robertson/Simon Archer (GBR)

Final: Gunawan/Wijaya—Lee/You 15-10, 9-15, 15-7
3rd Place: Ha/Kim—Choong/Lee 15-2, 15-8

Candra Wijaya and Sigit Budiarto won the 1997 world championship, but the following year Budiarto tested positive for the steroid nandrolone and was suspended for a year. Wijaya found a new partner, Tony Gunawan. Although Wijaya and Budiarto did compete together again in May 2000, Wijaya stuck with Gunawan for the Olympics, which they entered as the number one seeds. In the semifinals they faced South Koreans Ha Tae-kwon and Kim Dong-moon. Kim had won the mixed doubles gold medal at the 1996 Olympics. It took Wijaya and Gunawan six match points before they finally prevailed 15-13, 15-11. The final was an exciting 77-minute marathon, which the Indonesian pair won by jumping out to a quick lead in the deciding game and holding off the challenges of Lee and Yoo. At Candra Wijaya's wedding a few months after the Olympics, both Budiarto and Gunawan served as groomsmen, while the bride's gowns were designed with Olympic themes: the shoulders of her morning gown were covered with a replica of the Sydney Opera House and her evening gown included on the shoulders an imitation of Sydney's Harbour Bridge made of pleated fabric.

2004 Athens T: 22, N: 14, D: 8.20.

1. KOR Kim Dong-moon, Ha Tae-kwon
2. KOR Lee Dong-soo, Yoo Yong-sung
3. INA Hian Eng, Flandy Limpele
4. DEN Jens Eriksen, Martin Lundgaard Hansen
5. Yim Bang-eun/Kim Yong-hyun (KOR), Zheng Bo/Sang Yang (CHN), Tan Fook Choong/Wan Wah Lee (MAL), Fu Haifeng/Cai Yun (CHN)

Final: Kim/Ha—Lee/Yoo 15-11, 15-4
3rd Place: Eng/Limpele—Eriksen/Hansen 15-13, 15-7

Close friends since childhood, Kim Dong-moon and Ha Tae-kwon won the tournament without losing a single game. Kim had already earned a gold medal in mixed doubles in 1996 and a bronze medal, with Ha, in men's doubles in 2000.

2008 Beijing T: 16, N: 10, D: 8.15.

1. INA	Markis Kido, Hendra Setiawan
2. CHN	Cai Yun, Fu Haifeng
3. KOR	Lee Jae-jin, Hwang Ji-man
4. DEN	Lars Paaske, Jonas Rasmussen

5. Koo Kien Keat/Tan Boon Heong (MAL), Michał Łogosz/Robert Mateusiak (POL), Keita Masuda/Tadashi Ohtsuka (JPN), Howard Bach/Bob Malaythong (USA)
Final: Kido/Setiawan—Cai/Fu 12-21, 21-11, 21-16
3rd Place: Lee/Hwang—Paaske/Rasmussen 13-21, 21-18, 21-17

Although different doubles pairs had won every major international competition since 2004, the favorites in the men's doubles event seemed to be reigning world champions and twice Asian Games champions Markis Kido and Hendra Setiawan, the top-ranked pair in the world. Their main challengers, world number twos Cai Yun and Fu Haifeng, had been eliminated in the quarter-finals in Athens 2004, but had gone on to win the 2006 world championships.

Kido and Setiawan had a difficult first-round match against Guo Zhendong and Xie Zhongbo of China, narrowly winning the first set 22-20 and losing the second set 10-21 before pulling back to a 21-17 win in the third set. After that initial scare, Kido and Setiawan settled into a rhythm, beating 2006 Asian Games champions Koo Kien Keat and Tan Boon Heong in straight sets in the quarter-finals and dispatching Danish pair Lars Paaske and Jonas Rasmussen 21-19, 21-10 in the semi-finals.

The gold-medal match was much more exciting. Kido and Setiawan lost their first set against Cai and Fu 12-21, but stormed back to take a 10-5 lead early in the second set and held on for a 21-11 win. The Indonesians maintained their momentum in the final set, building a quick 11-4 lead and moving on a 21-16 victory to clinch the gold medal. It was Indonesia's only gold medal at the Beijing Olympics.

WOMEN

SINGLES

1896–1988 not held

1992 Barcelona C: 52, N: 27, D: 8.4.

		MATCHES		GAMES	
		W	L	W	L
1. Susi Susanti	INA	5	0	10	1
2. Bang Soo-hyun	KOR	4	1	9	3
3. Huang Hua	CHN	3	1	6	2
3. Tang Jiuhong	CHN	3	1	6	3
5. Somhasurthai Jaroensiri	THA	3	1	6	4
5. Sarwendah Kusumawardhani	INA	2	1	5	2
5. Anna Lao	AUS	2	1	6	3
5. Lee Heun-soon	KOR	2	1	5	2

Final: Susanti—Bang 5-11, 11-5, 11-3

Susanti crushed her first four opponents, outscoring them 88-22. In the final, the pressure of being Indonesia's first-ever gold-medal hope caused her to falter. However, she regained her composure midway through the second game and won with ease.

1996 Atlanta C: 47, N: 29, D: 8.1.

1. Bang Soo-hyun	KOR
2. Mia Audina	INA
3. Susi Susanti	INA
4. Kim Ji-hyun	KOR

5. Han Jingna (CHN), Camilla Martin (DEN), Yao Yan (CHN), Ye Zhaoying (CHN)
Final: Bang—Audina 11-6, 11-7
3rd Place: Susanti—Kim 11-4, 11-1

The big upset came in the quarterfinals when Kim Ji-hyun shocked world champion Ye Zhaoying 11-5, 12-11. Bang Soo-hyum, the daughter of a popular South Korean comedian, crushed her first three opponents by a combined score of 66 to 10. In the semifinals she faced Susi Susanti, who had defeated her in the 1992 Olympic final. This time Bang prevailed 11-9, 11-8. In the final Bang faced 16-year-old sensation Mia Audina, whom she had beaten all six times they had met. Bang fell behind 5-6 in the first game before rallying to win 11-6. The second game followed the same pattern as Audina led 7-5 before Bang scored the last six points. Audina later married a Dutch gospel singer and represented the Netherlands in the 2000 Olympics, where she was eliminated in the quarterfinals by Camilla Martin.

2000 Sydney C: 40, N: 23, D: 9.22.

1. Gong Zhichao	CHN
2. Camilla Martin	DEN
3. Zhaoying Ye	CHN
4. Dai Yun	CHN

5. Huang Chia-Chi (TAI), Kim Ji-hyun (KOR), Mia Audina (HOL), Yasuko Mizui (JPN)
Final: Gong—Martin 13-10, 11-3
3rd Place: Ye—Dai 8-11, 11-2, 11-6

This tournament went according to form, as seven of the eight seeds made it to the quarterfinals and the four top seeds made it to the semifinals. Both Camilla Martin and tiny Gong Zhichao cruised to the final. Martin outscored her four opponents 88-26 and Gong outscored her opponents 88-44. Martin stunned defending silver medalist Mia Audina 11-2, 11-1 in 19 minutes and number three seed Dai Yun 11-5, 11-0 in 20 minutes. Martin led Gong 9-5 and 10-7 in the first game of the final, but Gong scored 6 straight points to win 13-10. The second game was tied 3-3 when Gong took control and scored the last 8 points.

2004 Athens C: 32, N: 21, D: 8.19.

1. Zhang Ning	CHN
2. Mia Audina	HOL
3. Zhou Mi	CHN
4. Gong Ruina	CHN

5. Cheng Shao-chieh (TAI), Tracey Hallam (GBR), Petya Nedelcheva (BUL), Wang Chen (HKG)
Final: Zhang—Audina 8-11, 11-6, 11-7
3rd Place: Zhou—Gong 11-2, 8-11, 11-6

When Zhang Ning and Mia Audina met in the final, it was the culmination of a ten-year rivalry. The two had first faced one another in 1994 in the Uber Cup, the prestigious women's team competition. Zhang lost a key match to the then-14-year-old Audina, breaking China's ten-year win streak. Audina went on to win the silver medal in the 1996 Olympics while Zhang was not included in the Chinese Olympic team in 1996 or 2000.

Zhang, left her home in Liaonong Province at the age of twelve to train full-time. In a country where most athletes above the age of 25 are forcibly retired, Zhang defended her spot on the national team through determination and sacrifice. When she and her then-fiancée Yu Yang received their marriage license in 2001, they delayed having a ceremony for three years, until after the 2004 Games. Until the end of the Games the couple had never spent more than two months together at a stretch. By the time of the Athens Games, Zhang was 29 years old and the reigning world champion.

Audina won the first game of the final 11-8, but soon began to tire, allowing Zhang to rally to an 11-6 win in the second game and secure gold with an 11-7 victory in the third.

In March 2008, in an interview on CCTV, Chinese badminton coach Li Yongbo admitted to fixing the results of the semifinal match between Zhou Mi and Zhang Ning. Zhou, who lost her first set 11-6 to Zhang, was asked to give up the second set to allow Zhang to save her energy for the gold-medal match. Zhang advanced 11-6, 11-4. Li defended his actions as a way "to make sure the gold medal would end up in Chinese hands," adding that he felt "proud of our team spirit".

After the Olympics Zhou quit the Chinese team and moved to Hong Kong. In 2008 she represented Hong Kong at the BWF Super Series Masters Final, winning the women's singles title.

2008 Beijing C: 47, N: 43, D: 8.15.

1. Zhang Ning	CHN
2. Xie Xingfang	CHN
3. Maria Yulianti	INA
4. Lu Lan	CHN

5. Huaiwen Xu (GER), Wong Mew Choo (MAL), Saina Nehwal (IND), Pi Hongyan (FRA)
Final: Zhang—Xie 21-12, 10-21, 21-18
3rd Place: Yulianti—Lu 11-21, 21-13, 21-15

The depth of China's badminton lineup was evidenced by who was not selected for the team: 24-year-old reigning world champion Zhu Lin. Limited to three athletes, China instead sent the top three ranked players in the world, two-time world champion Xie Xingfang, reigning All-England silver medalist Lu Lan, and 33-year-old defending Olympic champion Zhang Ning.

Zhang got off to a shaky start in the tournament, losing her first set 21-23 to Thailand's Salakjit Ponsana before advancing by winning the next two sets 21-17 and 21-7. Xie won her first match 21-1, 21-9, while Lu prevailed 21-3, 7-1 when her opponent withdrew because of injury. All three advanced to the quarter-finals on straight sets. The first major upset of the tournament came during the third round, when reigning All-England champion Tine Rasmussen was knocked out in three sets by unseeded 23-year-old Maria Yulianti.

Yulianti made it to the semi-finals after a hard-fought 26-28, 21-14, 21-15 win over Saina Nehwal, in which she saved eight game points. Zhang also had a tough quarter-final against Chinese-born Pi Hongyan, advancing 21-8, 19-21, 21-19. Xie qualified for the gold-medal match with a 7-21, 21-10, 21-12 win over Lu, while Zhang dispatched Yulianti in straight sets 21-15, 21-15.

Zhang faced Xie in the gold-medal match. The two had previously met in the finals of both the 2005 and 2006 world championships, with Xie winning both times. This time, Zhang won the first set 21-12, but Xie took a 5-0 lead in the second set, and went on to win 21-10. Zhang built a 13-6 lead in the third set before Xie came back with six consecutive points. The score reached 16-16, but then Zhang pulled ahead with a first match point at 20-17, before winning 21-18 to clinch the gold medal. At the age of 33, Zhang was the oldest woman in Olympic history to win a badminton gold.

Yulianti, who had never reached the podium of a major international tournament, beat Lu for the bronze medal despite dropping the first set.

DOUBLES

1896–1988 not held

1992 Barcelona T: 29, N: 20, D: 8.4.

		MATCHES		GAMES	
		W	L	W	L
1. KOR	Hwang Hye-young, Chung So-young	4	0	8	1
2. CHN	Guan Weizhen, Nong Qunhua	3	1	7	3
3. CHN	Lin Yanfen, Yao Fen	2	1	4	2
3. KOR	Gil Young-ah, Shim Eun-jung	3	1	7	2
5. AUS	Rhonda Cator, Anna Lao	2	1	4	2
5. GBR	Julie Bradbury, Gillian Clark	2	1	4	3
5. IND	Aadijatmiko Finarsih, Lili Tampi	2	1	4	2
5. SWE	Catrine Bengtsson, Maria Bengtsson	2	1	4	3

Final: Hwang/Chung—Guan/Nong 18-16, 12-15, 15-13

The final, matching the two top-seeded pairs, lasted for almost two hours. With the score tied 10-10 in the deciding game, Guan scored a go-ahead point, only to have it disallowed because her racket crossed the net. Hwang and Chung then scored three straight points. Trailing 13-14, Guan served an ace, but was again penalized, this time for a foot fault. Finally, after fighting off four match points, Guan let one of Chung's serves fall—and it landed in, giving the Koreans the victory.

1996 Atlanta T: 27, N: 18, D: 7.31.
1. CHN Ge Fei, Gu Jun
2. KOR Gil Young-ah, Jang Hye-ock
3. CHN Qin Yiyuan, Tang Yongshu
4. DEN Helene Kirkegaard, Rikke Olsen
5. Chen Ying/Peng Xingyong (CHN), Ann Jorgensen/Lotte Olsen, (DEN), Lisbet Stuer-Lauridsen/Marlene Thomsen (DEN), Eliza Nathanael/Zelin Resiana (INA)
Final: Ge/Gu—Gil/Jang 15-5, 15-5
3rd Place: Qin/Tang—Kirkegaard/Olsen 7-15, 15-4, 15-8

Ge Fei and Gu Jun from Jiangsu Province had been playing together since they were nine years old. Twelve years later they ran roughshod through the Olympic field, outscoring the four teams they played 120 to 39. In the final, as expected, they faced Gil Young-ah and Jang Hye-ock, the reigning world champions. The two sides had met ten times with Ge and Gu holding a 6-4 advantage. In Atlanta the Chinese pair attacked relentlessly and Gil and Jang were unable to establish their own rhythm. The match was over in 36 minutes.

2000 Sydney T: 26, N: 17, D: 9.23.
1. CHN Ge Fei, Gu Jun
2. CHN Huang Nanyan, Yang Wei
3. CHN Gao Ling, Qin Yiyuan
4. KOR Chung Jae-hee, Ra Kyung-min
5. Helene Kirkegaard/Rikke Olsen (DEN), Donna Kellogg/Joanne Wright-Goode (GBR), Lotte Jonathans/Nicole van Hooren (HOL), Cynthia Tuwankotta/Eti Lesmina Tantra (INA)
Final: Ge/Gu—Huang/Yang 15-5, 15-5
3rd Place: Gao/Qin—Chung/Ra 15-10, 15-4

Ge Fei and Gu Jun continued their doubles dominance between Olympics, winning the 1997 world championships, the 1998 Asian Games and the 1999 world championships. In fact, they were unbeaten for four and a half years until compatriots Yang Wei and Huang Nanyan upset them at the Japan Open in April 2000. There would be no such surprises in Sydney. Ge and Gu outscored their four opponents 120-45. The only time they gave up more than seven points in a game was in the semifinals when Gao Ling and Qin Yiyuan managed 12 points in the second game before succumbing.

2004 Athens T: 23, N: 16, D: 8.21.
1. CHN Zhang Jiewen, Yang Wei
2. CHN Huang Sui, Gao Ling
3. KOR Ra Kyung-min, Lee Kyung-won
4. CHN Zhao Tingting, Wei Yili
5. Saralee Thungthongkam/Sathinee Chankrachangwong (THA), Lotte Bruil-Jonathans/Mia Audina (HOL), Lee Hyo-jung/Hwang Yu-mi (KOR), Ann-Lou Jørgensen/Rikke Olsen (DEN)
Final: Zhang/Yang—Huang/Gao 7-15, 15-4, 15-8
3rd Place: Ra/Lee—Zhao/Wei 10-15, 15-9, 15-7

The two Chinese pairs had been involved in a controversial match one year earlier, when they faced each other in the quarterfinals of the 2003 World Championships in Birmingham, England. After winning a hard-fought first set, Gao and Huang won the second set easily, raising suspicions that Zhang and Yang had handed their compatriots an easy win to conserve their energy for their semifinal match against a Dutch team. Zhang and Yang were reprimanded for failing to use their best efforts throughout the match, while Gao and Huang went on to win the championship. In the Olympic final, Gao and Huang, who held a 7-4 career match advantage over Zhang and Yang, took the first game 15-7. However, the top-seeded Zhang and Yang came back to win the second game 15-4. In the deciding game, Zhang and Yang scored the first seven points and held on to their advantage to win 15-8.

2008 Beijing T: 16, N: 12, D: 8.15.
1. CHN Du Jing, Yu Yang
2. KOR Lee Hyo-jung, Lee Kyung-won
3. CHN Wei Yili, Zhang Yawen
4. JPN Miyuki Maeda, Satoko Suetsuna
5. Yang Wei/Zhang Jiewen (CHN), Jiang Yanmei/Lee Yujia (SIN), Cheng Wen-hsing/Chien Yu-chin (TAI), Kumiko Ogura/Reiko Shiota (JPN)
Final: Du/Yu—Lee/Lee 21-15, 21-13
3rd Place: Wei/Zhang—Maeda/Suetsuna 21-17, 21-10

Seeded 1-2-3 in the tournament, the three Chinese pairs included defending Olympic champions and double world champions Yang Wei and Zhang Jiewen, 2006 world silver medalists and 2007 All-England champions Wei Yili and Zhang Yawen and 2008 All-England silver medalists Du Jing and Yu Yang. The only non-Chinese pair that seemed to have a shot at the medal podium were the South Korean pair Lee Hyo-jung and Lee Kyung-won, who had beaten Du and Yu in the final of the 2008 All-England Open five months before the Olympics.

As it turned out, number-one seeds Yang and Zhang were knocked out in the quarter-finals by Miyuki Maeda and Satoko Suetsuna 8-21, 23-21, 21-14. Maeda and Suetsuna were subsequently beaten 22-20, 21-15 by Lee and Lee, while Du and Yu defeated Wei and Zhang 21-19, 21-12. Played in front of a loud, flag-waving Chinese crowd, neither of the final matches was particularly close, with both the gold and bronze medals going to the home teams in straight sets.

MIXED

DOUBLES

1896–1992 not held

1996 Atlanta T: 32, N: 18, D: 8.1.
1. KOR Gil Young-ah, Kim Dong-moon
2. KOR Ra Kyung-min, Park Joo-bong
3. CHN Sun Man, Liu Jianjun
4. CHN Peng Xingyong, Chen Xingdong
5. Wang Xiaoyuan/Tao Xiaoqiang (CHN), Rikke Olsen/Michael Søgaard, (DEN), Rosalina Riseu/Nimpele Flandy (INA), Minarti Timur/Trikus Harjanto (INA)

Final: Kil/Kim—Ra/Park 13-15, 15-4, 15-12
3rd Place: Sun/Liu—Peng/Chen 13-15, 17-15, 15-4

Park Joo-bong won a gold medal in men's doubles at the 1992 Olympics, then extended his career to take part in the inaugural mixed doubles event. In the final, he and his young partner, Ra Kyung-min (he was 31, she was 19), faced Kim Dong-moon, who had been Park's student at Seoul University, and Gil Young-ah, who, the day before, had won a silver medal in women's doubles.

Park and Ra led the first game 9-5 and 14-9. Kim and Gil closed to 14-13 before succumbing 15-13. The second game was an easy win for Kim and Gil, but the tiebreaking game was full of drama. Park and Ra took a 10-5 lead, but Kim and Gil gradually fought back to an 11-11 tie. The two sides traded points before Kim and Gil moved ahead 14-12. Park and Ra fended off one match point before Kim and Gil prevailed.

2000 Sydney T: 27, N: 14, D: 9.21.
1. CHN Gao Ling, Zhang Jun
2. INA Minarti Timur, Tri Kusharyanto
3. GBR Joanne Wright-Goode, Simon Archer
4. DEN Rikke Olsen, Michael Søgaard
5. Zelin Resiana/Bambang Suprianto (INA), Erica van den Heuvel/Chris Bruil (HOL), Mette Schjoldager/Jens Eriksen (DEN), Ra Kyung-min/Kim Dong-moon (KOR)

Final: Gao/Zhang—Timur/Heryanto 1-15, 15-13, 15-11
3rd Place: Wright-Goode/Archer—Olsen/Søgaard 15-4, 12-15, 17-14

Zhang Jun and Gao Ling had only been playing together for a year when they entered the 2000 Olympics as the number seven seed. Their victory did not come easily. In their opening match, they lost the first game 10-15 to the German pair, Björn Siegemund and Karen Stechmann, before winning the next two. In their semifinal battle against Michael Søgaard and Rikke Olsen, they again lost the first game 10-15. After winning the second game 15-6, they ran into trouble again in the decider. The Danish pair led 14-7, but Zhang and Gao fended off match point, fought back and won 17-16. In the final they came up against the number one seeds, Tri Kusharyanto and Minarti Timur. The Indonesian pair breezed through the first game in nine minutes, crushing Zhang and Gao 15-1. In the second game, Zhang and Gao fell behind 1-3 and 5-8, before scoring seven points in a row to lead 12-8. But then Kusharyanto and Timur won five straight points to regain the lead, 13-12. Zhang and Gao finally pulled out the game 15-13. They jumped out to a 4-0 lead in the deciding game. The Indonesians pulled up to 4-3, Zhang and Gao scored seven in a row to lead 11-3 and Kusharyanto and Timur drew back to 13-11. Zhang and Gao managed two more points to earn a hard-fought victory.

2004 Athens T: 23, N: 17, D: 8.19.
1. CHN Zhang Jun, Gao Ling
2. GBR Nathan Robertson, Gail Emms
3. DEN Jens Eriksen, Mette Schjoldager
4. DEN Jonas Rasmussen, Rikke Olsen
5. Kim Dong-moon/Ra Kyung-min (KOR), Chen Qiqiu/Zhao Tingting (CHN), Nova Widianto/Vita Marissa (INA), Fredrik Bergström/Johanna Persson (SWE)

Final: Zhang/Gao—Robertson/Emms 15-1, 12-15, 15-12
3rd Place: Eriksen/Schjoldager—Rasmussen/Olsen 15-5, 15-5

Defending Olympic champions Zhang Jun and Gao Ling breezed into the finals, outscoring their three opponents 90-25. They continued their domination in the first game of the final, blitzing Nathan Robertson and Gail Emms 15-1. In the second game, the British pair built leads of 6-1 and 10-6 and held on to win 15-12. The deciding game was a see-saw battle. Robertson and Emms pulled ahead 11-8, but Zhang and Gao scored the next six points to gain match point at 14-11. They went on to win 15-12.

2008 Beijing T: 16, N: 12, D: 8.17.
1. KOR Lee Hyo-jung, Lee Yong-dae
2. INA Lilyana Natsir, Nova Widianto
3. CHN He Hanbin, Yu Yang
4. INA Flandy Limpele, Vita Marissa
5. Nadia Kostiuczyk/Robert Mateusiak (POL), Kamilla Rytter Juhl/Thomas Laybourn (DEN), Gail Emms/Nathan Robertson (GBR), Sudket Prapakamol/Saralee Thungthongkam (THA)

Final: Lee/Lee—Natsir/Widianto 21-11, 21-17
3rd Place: He/Yu—Limpele/Marissa 19-21, 21-17, 23-21

Arguably the most exciting match of the mixed doubles tournament came during the first round, when twice Olympic gold medalist Gao Ling and her new partner Zheng Bo, the reigning All-England champions, were drawn against 2004 silver medalists and 2006 world champions Gail Emms and Nathan Robertson. The two pairs went the full three sets, with Emms and Robertson pulling out a narrow 21-16, 16-21, 21-19 win to advance to the quarter-finals.

With Gao and Zheng out of the running, the path seemed clear for Lilyana Natsir and Nova Widianto, the top-ranked mixed doubles team in the world and the winners of both the 2005 and 2007 world championship titles. The pair advanced easily into the semi-finals where they beat fourth-seeded He Hanbin and Yu Yang 15-21, 21-11, 23-21 to make it to the gold-medal match.

Natsir and Widianto's opponents in the final were the unseeded pair of Lee Hyo-jung and Lee Yong-dae. Only 19 years old, Lee Yong-dae had already made a name for himself in South Korea as a badminton prodigy. He took up the sport in the second grade as a way to lose weight and by his freshman year in high school had earned a spot on South Korea's junior national team. By his senior year he had won three gold medals at the Asia Junior Championships and three more at the World Junior Championships.

The Lees made it to the gold-medal match after beating Emms and Robertson 21-19, 21-12 in the quarter-finals, and then achieving an exciting 21-9, 12-21, 21-17 victory over Flandy Limpele and Vita Marissa in the semi-finals.

In the final, the Lees won the first set easily. They took a 9-2 lead in the second set, but Natsir and Widianto gradually closed the gap to 19-17. Two straight points by the Lees finally gave South Korea their first mixed-doubles gold medal since the 1992 Barcelona Olympics. The win also brought Lee Hyo-jung her second gold medal at the Beijing Olympics, three days after her victory in the women's doubles event.

Gao Ling and Zhang Jun, 2004

Gao and Zhang won the mixed doubles championship in both 2000 and 2004.

Chapter 5 **Basketball**

Olympic basketball matches are played on a court 28 meters (91 feet 10 inches) long and 15 meters (49 feet 2½ inches) wide. The object of the game is to dribble and pass the ball downcourt and shoot it into a netted basket 3.05 meters (10 feet) above the ground. The open ring or hoop into which the ball is shot is 45 centimeters (1 foot 5¾ inches) in diameter. A successful shot is worth two points. Extending in an arc 6.25 meters (20 feet 6 inches) from the basket is the three-point line. Any successful shot launched from beyond that line is worth three points. Free throws, awarded as a result of fouls, are taken from behind a line 5.8 meters (19 feet ¼ inch) from the endline. A successful free throw is worth one point.

Each team consists of five players. Substitutions may be made at any break in the play of the game. Substituted players may return at any time.

Olympic basketball matches are made up of two 20-minute halves. If the score is tied at the end of 40 minutes of play, a five-minute overtime period is played. Further overtime periods are added until the tie is broken. Tie games are not tolerated in basketball.

According to Olympic rules, the offensive team must take a shot within 30 seconds of gaining possession of the ball.

Personal fouls involve bodily contact with an opposing player. Common fouls include blocking the progress of an opponent, charging into an opponent, holding, pushing, and hand-checking. If a foul is committed on a player who is not in the act of shooting, the game resumes with a throw-in from out of bounds. If the foul is committed on a player who is in the act of shooting, if the goal is made, it counts and the fouled player is awarded one free throw. If the shot is unsuccessful, the shooter is awarded two free throws. If the shot was from beyond the three-point line and was unsuccessful the shooter is awarded three free throws. If a foul is committed by a player whose team is in possession of the ball, the opposing team is given possession with a throw-in from out of bounds. A technical foul is assessed when a player or coach acts in a violent or disrespectful manner. The opposing team is awarded two free throws and possession of the ball.

A player who commits five fouls must leave the game and may not return. Each team is allowed seven fouls per half. Each team foul after the seventh one is penalized by the awarding of two free throws to the opposing team even if the foul was not committed during the act of shooting.

One rule that newcomers to basketball find confusing is the three-second restriction. The restricted area on each end of the court begins at the endline, extending three meters (9 feet 10 inches) to each side of the basket, and extends to the free throw line. A player whose team has possession of the ball may not spend more than three seconds in the opposing team's restricted area. A violation of this rule is penalized by loss of possession of the ball.

Spectators familiar with basketball as played in the National Basketball Association (NBA) should be aware of certain differences in Olympic rules. Most notably, in Olympic basketball each team is allowed only two time-outs per half; balls bouncing on the rim after a shot may be touched; only a team's coach may call a time-out.

The 12 teams in an Olympic tournament play in two round-robin pools. The top four teams from each pool advance to direct-elimination quarterfinals, semifinals, and finals.

MEN

1896–1932 not held

1936 Berlin T: 21, N: 21, D: 8.14.

	W	L	PF	PA
1. USA	4	0	152	69
2. CAN	5	1	176	104
3. MEX	4	2	160	115
4. POL	1	4	119	180
5. PHI	4	1	159	145
6. URU	2	3	125	136
7. ITA	3	2	160	129

Final: USA 19-8 CAN
3rd Place: MEX 26-12 POL
5th Place: PHI 33-23 URU

1. USA—Ralph Bishop, Joe Fortenberry, Carl Knowles, Jack Ragland, Carl Shy, William Wheatley, Francis Johnson, Samuel Balter, John "Tex" Gibbons, Frank Lubin, Arthur Mollner, Donald Piper, Duane Swanson, Willard Schmidt
2. CAN—Gordon Aitchison, Jan Allison, Arthur Chapman, Charles Chapman, Douglas Peden, James Stewart, Malcolm Wiseman, Edward John Dawson, Irving Meretsky
3. MEX—Carlos Borja Morca, Victor Hugo Borja Morca, Raúl Fernández Robert, Francisco Martínez Cordero, Jesús Olmos Moreni, Greer Skousen Spilsbury, Luis Ignacio de la Vega Leija, Rodolfo Choperno Irizarri, José Pamplona Lecuanda, Andrés Gómez Domínguez, Silvio Hernández del Valle
4. POL—Zdzislaw Filipkiewicz, Florian Grzechowiak, Jakub Kopowski, Edwaryst Lój, Andrzej Pluciński, Zenon Rózycki, Edward Szostak, Zdzislaw Kasprzak, Janusz Patrzykont, Pavel Stok

5. PHI—Charles Bork, Jacinto Cruz Ciria, Franco Marquicias, Primitivo Martinez, Jesús Marzan, Amador Obordo, Ambrosio Padilla, Bibiano Ouano, Fortunato Yamboa
6. URU—Gregorio Agos, Rodolfo Braseili, Leandro Gómez Harley, Alejo González Roig, Victor Lato Jaimeu, Prudencio de Pena, Tabaré Quintans, Humberto Bernasconi, Carlos Gabin
7. ITA—Enrico Castelli, Galeazzo Dondi, Livio Franeschini, Emilio Giasetti, Giancarlo Marinelli, Sergio Paganella, Egidio Premiani, Gino Basso

The first official Olympic basketball tournament was held outdoors in a tennis stadium on courts of clay and sand surrounded by a raised concrete border. Half the US squad was made up of members of the winner of the US trials—the team from Universal Pictures. Universal decided that they did not want their players involved in an Olympics that would be sponsored by the Nazis and studio executives threatened to fire any player who traveled to Berlin. The players, one of whom, Sam Balter, was Jewish, decided to go anyway and raised the money for the voyage by playing exhibitions. During the tournament, the International Basketball Federation passed a rule that banned all players who were taller than 6 feet 3 inches (1.90 meters). The United States, which would have lost three of its players, objected, and the rule was withdrawn. The day of the final saw heavy rain, which turned the courts into mud. The players found it quite difficult to dribble on wet sand, which undoubtedly contributed to the low score. The United States led 15-4 at the half. Six-foot 8-inch center Joe Fortenberry of McPherson, Kansas, scored eight points to match the score of the entire Canadian team. The medal was presented by Dr. James Naismith, the inventor of basketball.

1948 London T: 23, N: 23, D: 8.13.

	W	L	PF	PA
1. USA	8	0	524	256
2. FRA	5	2	331	281
3. BRA	7	1	374	263
4. MEX	5	2	314	264
5. URU	5	3	369	301
6. CHI	4	4	391	301
7. CZE	5	3	315	294
8. KOR	3	5	364	279

Final: USA 65-21 FRA
3rd Place: BRA 52-47 MEX

1. USA—Clifford Barker, Donald Barksdale, Ralph Beard, Lewis Beck, Vincent Boryla, Gordon Carpenter, Alexander Groza, Wallace Jones, Robert Kurland, Raymond Lumpp, Robert Pitts, Jesse Renick, Robert Robinson, Kenneth Rollins
2. FRA—André Barrais, Michel Bonnevie, André Buffière, René Chocat, René Dérency, Maurice Desaymonnet, André Even, Maurice Girardot, Fernand Guillou, Raymond Offner, Jacques Perrier, Yvan Quénin, Lucien Rebuffic, Pierre Thiolon
3. BRA—Zenny de Azevedo, João Francisco Bráz, Marcus Vinicius Dias, Alfonso Azevedo Évora, Ruy de Freitas, Alexandre Gemignani, Alberto Marson, Alfredo Rodrigues da Mota, Nilton Pacheco de Oliveira, Massinet Sorcinelli
4. MEX—Angel Acuna Lizaña, Isaac Alfaro Loza, Alberto Bienvenu Barajas, José de la Cruz Cabrera Gándara, Jorge Cardiel Gaitán, Rodolfo Diaz Mercado, Francisco Galindo Chávez, Jorge Gudiño Goya, Héctor Guerrero Delgado, Emilio López Enriquez, Ignacio Romo Porchas, José Rojas Herrera, Fernando Rojas Herrera, José Santos de León
5. URU—Martín Acosta y Lara, Néstor Anton, Victorio Cieslinskas, Nelson Demarco, Miguel Diab, Abraham Eidlin, Eduardo Folle, Héctor García Otero, Eduardo Gordon, Adesio Lombardo, Roberto Lovera, Gustavo Marganiños, Carlos Rosselló, Héctor Ruiz
6. CHI—Eduardo Cordero Fernández, Exequiel Figueroa Reyes, Juan Gallo Chinchilla, Roberto Hammer Casadio, Eduardo Kapstein Suckel, Manuel Ledesma Barraies, Victor Mahana Badrie, Luis Marmentini Gil, Andres Mitrovic Guic, Antonio Moreno Rodillo, Eduardo Parra Rojas, Hernán Raffo Abarca, Marcos Sanchez Carmona, Guillermo Verdugo Yáñez
7. CZE—Karel Belohradsky, Cyril Benacek, Jiři Chlup, Jiři Drvota, Josef Ezr, Jozef Kalina, Jan Kozak, Vaclav Krasa, Zdenek Krenicky, Jozef Krepela, Ivan Mrazek, Jiři Siegel, Josef Toms, Ladislav Trpkos
8. KOR—Ahn Byung-suk, Bang W., Chang Chin-ri, Chyo Joon-deuk, Kang Hyun-bong, Kim Shin-chung, Lee Yung-choon, Lee Hoon-sang, Oh Chul-soo

The 1948 tournament had some unusual highlights: A British referee was knocked unconscious during a preliminary game between Chile and Iraq. In the fiercely contested match for third place, da Motta of Brazil lost his pants and had to retire to the dressing room. Iraq lost by 100 points twice—to Korea and China (which finished eighteenth), and gave up an average of almost 104 points per game while scoring only 23.5. Ireland's offense was even less effective, averaging only 17 points a game. Meanwhile, the US team, which brought together the best players from the Phillips 66 Oilers and the University of Kentucky, survived an early 59-57 scare against Argentina and then breezed through the rest of its games. The halftime score in the final was 28-9. Don Barksdale was the first African-American to represent the United States in basketball. José Llanusa Gobel of the Cuban team went on to become Minister of Education under Fidel Castro.

Fereidoun M. Esfandiary of the Iranian team later became a well-known futurist, changing his name to FM-2030 and predicting that humans would become "post-biological organisms", possessed of limitless resources and eventual immortality; when he died in 2000, at the age of 69, his body was placed in cryogenic suspension.

1952 Helsinki T: 23, N: 23, D: 8.2.

	W	L	PF	PA
1. USA	8	0	562	406
2. SOV	6	2	468	431
3. URU	5	3	486	471
4. ARG	5	3	600	523
5. CHI	4	4	447	508
6. BRA	4	4	469	436
7. BUL	4	4	451	506
8. FRA	4	4	468	460

Final: USA 36-25 SOV
3rd Place: URU 68-59 ARG
5th Place: CHI 58-49 BRA
7th Place: BUL 58-44 FRA

1. USA—Charles Hoag, William Hougland, Melvin Dean Kelley, Robert Kenney, Clyde Lovellette, Marcus Freiberger, Victor Wayne Glasgow, Frank McCabe, Daniel Pippin, Howard Williams, Ronald Bontemps, Robert Kurland, William Lienhand, John Keller
2. SOV—Viktor Vlassov, Stepas Butautas, Joann Lössov, Kazys Petkevičius, Nodar Dshordshikiya, Anatoly Konyev, Otar Korkiya, Ilmar Kullam, Yuri Ozerov, Aleksandr Moiseyev, Heino Kruus, Justinas Lagunavičius, Maigonis Valdmanis, Stasys Stonkus
3. URU—Martín Acosta y Lara, Enrique Baliño, Victorio Cieslinskas, Héctor Costa, Nelson Demarco, Héctor Garcia Otero, Roberto Lovera, Adesio Lombardo, Tabaré Larre Borges, Sergio Matto, Wilfredo Peláez, Carlos Rosselló
4. ARG—Rubén Menini, Hugo Del Vecchio, Leopoldo Contarbio, Raúl Pérez Varela, Juan Gaszo, Roberto Viau, Ricardo González, Juan Urder, Omar Monza, Rubén Pagliari, Rafael Liedo, Oscar Furlong, Alberto López, Ignacio Poletti
5. CHI—Juan Gallo Chinchilla, Victor Mahana Badrie, Exequiel Figueroa Reyes, Eduardo Cordero Fernández, Rufino Bernedo Zorzano, Alvaro Salvadores Salvi, Eric Maehn Godoy, Hernán Ramos Muñoz, Hugo Fernández Diaz, Orlando Silva Infante, Hernán Raffo Abarca, Pedro Araya Zabala, Juan Ostoic
6. BRA—Zenny de Azevedo, Sebastião Gimenez, Ruy de Freitas, Mayr Facci, Raymundo Carvalho dos Santos, Angelo Bonfietti, João Francisco Bráz, Alfredo Rodrigues da Motta, Almir Nelson de Almeida, Mario Jorge da Fonseca Hermes, Thales Monteiro, José Luiz Santos Azevedo, Helio Marquez Pereira
7. BUL—Kiril Semov, Hristo Donchev, Vasil Manchenko, Peter Shishkov, Georgi Panov, Konstantin Totev, Anton Kuzov, Gencho Rashkov, Ivan Nikolov, Veselin Penkov, Kontantin Georgiev, Vladimir Slavov
8. FRA—Bernard Planque, Robert Monclar, René Chocat, Jean Perniceni, Louis Devoti, Robert Guillin, Robert Crost, Jacques Dessemme, André Buffière, André Vacheresse, André Chavet, Jean-Paul Beugnot, Roger Haudegand, Jean-Pierre Salignon

Having been crushed by the United States 86-58, in the semifinal round, the Soviet team decided to freeze the ball in the final match. After ten minutes, the United States led 4-2. At halftime the score was still only 17-15. With five minutes to play, Clyde Lovellette scored a basket to give the United States a lead of 31-25. The next time the Americans got the ball, it was their turn to stall. One Soviet player became so exasperated that he sat down on the floor until his coach ordered him to stand up.

The tournament was enlivened by the participation of Uruguay. In the semifinal round, France had a 66-64 lead over the team from South America, which had been reduced to three players due to excessive fouling. With one minute to play, Uruguay tied the score, whereupon the American referee, Vincent Farrell, whistled a foul against Uruguay. The Uruguayan team rushed off the bench and abused Farrell for five minutes until he was finally able to communicate that the foul had occurred after the basket and that the 2 points had not been disallowed. France took the ball out of bounds and worked the ball to Jacques Dessemme, who scored an easy layup to win the game. At this point Uruguayan players and spectators attacked Farrell again. This time he was kicked in the groin and had to be carried from the court. Two Uruguayan players, Wilfredo Peláez and Carlos Roselló, were banned from further competition. Three days later it was the USSR's turn to face the volatile Uruguayans. In the second half, three Soviet players had to receive first aid. The following day, the now exhausted Uruguayans faced their bitter rival, Argentina, in the match for third place. They mustered up enough energy for one more brawl with 25 people involved. So many fouls were called that Uruguay finished the game with only four players and Argentina with only three.

1956 Melbourne T: 15, N: 15, D: 12.1.

	W	L	PF	PA
1. USA	8	0	793	365
2. SOV	5	3	574	524
3. URU	6	2	568	559
4. FRA	5	3	542	497
5. BUL	5	3	568	545
6. BRA	3	4	500	535
7. PHI	4	4	534	599
8. CHI	2	5	490	518

Final: USA 89-55 SOV
3rd Place: URU 71-62 FRA
5th Place: BUL 64-52 BRA
7th Place: PHI 75-68 CHI

1. USA—Carl Cain, William Hougland, K.C. Jones, William Russell, James Walsh, William Evans, Burdette Haldorson, Ronald Tomsic, Richard Boushka, Gilbert Ford, Robert Jeangerard, Charles Darling
2. SOV—Valdis Muižnieks, Maigonis Valdmanis, Vladimir Torban, Stasys Stonkus, Kazys Petkevičius, Arkady Bochkaryov, Jānis Krūmiņš, Mikhail Semyonov, Algirdas Lauritenas,Yuri Ozerov, Viktor Zubkov, Mikhail Studenetsky
3. URU—Carlos Blixen, Ramiro Cortes, Héctor Costa, Nelson Chelle, Nelson Demarco, Héctor García Otero, Carlos González, Sergio Matto, Oscar Moglia, Raúl Mera, Ariel Olascoaga, Milton Scarón
4. FRA—Roger Haudegand, Christian Baltzer, Robert Monclar, Roger Veyron, Gérard Sturla, Henri Rey, Roger Antoine, Henri Grange, Yves Gominon, Maurice Buffière, Andrè Schlupp, Jean-Paul Beugnot
5. BUL—Atanas Atanasov, Vladimir Slavov, Ilia Mirchev, Victor Radev, Georgi Kunev, Vasil Manchenko, Georgi Panov, Konstantin Totev, Tsviatko Slavov, Lyubomir Panov, Nikola Ilov
6. BRA—Zenny de Azevedo, Noel Marques Lisboa, Wlamir Marques, Angelo Bonfietti, Jamil Gedeão, Wilson Bombarda, Jorge Dortas Oliviere, Mayr Facci, Edson Bispo dos Santos, José Luiz Santos Azevedo, Fausto Sucena Rasga Filho, Amaury Antônio Passos
7. PHI—Ramon Manulat, Ramon Campos, Carlos Badion, Loreto Carbonel, Martin Urra, Rafael Barretto, Leo-Leonardo Marquicias, Antonio Villamor, Mariano Tolentino, Carlos Loyzaga, Antonio Genato, Eduardo Lim
8. CHI—Luis Salvadores, Juan Ostoic, Maximiliano Garafulic, Pedro Araya Zabala, Rufino Bernedo Zorzano, Victor Mahana Badrie, Orlando Silva Infante, Raul Urra, Hernán Raffo Abarca, Orlando Etcheverre-Garay, Juan Arremdondo, Rolando Etchepare

Led by Bill Russell and K.C. Jones, who later became great professional stars with the Boston Celtics, the team from the United States won all eight of its games by at least 30 points and scored over 100 points four times. Their average score was 99-46.

1960 Rome T: 16, N: 16, D: 9.10.

	W	L	PF	PA
1. USA	8	0	815	476
2. SOV	6	2	596	497
3. BRA	6	2	568	573
4. ITA	4	4	603	653
5. CZE	5	3	632	594
6. YUG	4	4	582	603
7. POL	4	4	582	653
8. URU	2	6	548	678

Final: USA 81-57 SOV
BRA 78-75 ITA
USA 112-81 ITA
SOV 64-62 BRA
SOV 78-70 ITA
USA 90-63 BRA

1. USA—Jay Arnette, Walter Bellamy, Robert Boozer, Terry Dischinger, Jerry Lucas, Oscar Robertson, Adrian Smith, Burdette Haldorson, Darrall Imhoff, Allen Kelley, Lester Lane, Jerry West
2. SOV—Yuri Korneyev, Jānis Krūmiņš, Guram Minaschvili, Valdis Muižnieks, Cēzars Ozers, Aleksandr Petrov, Mikhail Semyonov, Vladimir Ugrekhelidze, Maigonis Valdmanis, Albert Valtin, Gennady Volnov, Viktor Zubkov
3. BRA—Edson Bispo dos Santos, Moyses Blas, Waldemar Blalkauskas, Zenny de Azevedo, Carmo de Souza, Carlos Domingos Massoni, Waldyr Geraldo Boccardo, Wlamir Marques, Amaury Antônio Passos, Fernando Pereira de Freitas, Antônio Salvador Sucar, Jatyr Eduardo Schall
4. ITA—Augusto Giomo, Gabriele Vianello, Alessandro Riminucci, Gianfranco Lombardi, Gianfranco Pieri, Alessandro Gamba, Mario Alesini, Achille Canna, Antonio Calebotta, Paolo Vittori, Giovanni Gavagnin, Gianfranco Sardagna
5. CZE—Jaroslav Tetiva, Josef Kinský, Zdeněk Bobrovský, Boris Lukašik, Franišek Konvička, Zdeněk Konečný, Dušan Lukašik, Bohuslav Rylich, Jiři Baumruk, Vladimir Pištělák, Jiři Štastný Bohumil Tomášek
6. YUG—Slobodan Gordić, Ivo Daneu, Sreten Dragojlović, Josip Djerdja, Nemanja Djurić, Marjan Kandus, Radivoje Korać, Boris Kristančić, Miha Lokar, Miodrag Nikolić, Zvonimir Petričević, Radovan Radović
7. POL—Jerzy Piskun, Janusz Wichowski, Andrzej Pstrokoński, Andrzej Nartowski, Jerzy Mlynarczyk, Ryszard Olszewski, Krzysztof Sitkowski, Mieczyslaw Lopatka, Zbigniew Dregien, Bogdan Przywarski, Tadeysz Pacula, Dariusz Świerczewski
8. URU—Sergio Matto, Raul Mera, Nelson Chelle, Waldemar Rial, Washington Poyet, Carlos Blixen, Milton Scaron, Aldofo Lubnicki, Hector Costa, Danilo Coito, Edison Ciavattone, Manuel Gadea

Ten members of the 1960 US squad went on to play professionally in the National Basketball Association. The team was so strong that future Boston Celtic star John Havlicek qualified only as an alternate. Led by Jerry Lucas and Oscar Robertson, both of whom averaged 17 points a game, the Americans won every game by at least 24 points despite a much improved international field. The US team averaged 102 points per game while giving up only 59.5. In the final match against Brazil, the United States built up a 41-14 lead after only 14 minutes and coasted for the rest of the game.

1964 Tokyo T: 16, N: 16, D: 10.23.

	W	L	PF	PA
1. USA	9	0	704	434
2. SOV	8	1	674	544
3. BRA	6	3	596	565
4. PUR	5	4	595	592
5. ITA	6	3	649	602
6. POL	5	4	608	596
7. YUG	6	3	670	583
8. URU	4	5	596	642

Final: USA 73-59 SOV
3rd Place: BRA 76-60 PUR
5th Place: ITA 79-59 POL
7th Place: YUG 78-55 URU

1. USA—James Barnes, William Bradley, Lawrence Brown, Joseph Caldwell, Mel Counts, Richard Davis, Walter Hazzard, Lucius Jackson, John McCaffrey, Jeffrey Mullins, Jerry Shipp, George Wilson
2. SOV—Valdis Muižnieks, Mykola Bahley, Armenak Alachachyan, Aleksandr Travin, Vyacheslay Khrynin, Jānis Krūmiņš, Levan Mosechvili, Yuri Korneyev, Aleksandr Petrov, Gennady Voinov, Jaak Lipso, Juris Kalniņš
3. BRA—Amaury Antônio Passos, Wlamir Marques, Ubiratan Pereira Maciel, Carlos Domingos Massoni, Friedrich Wilhelm Braun, Carmo de Souza, Jatyr Eduardo Schall, Edson Bispo dos Santos, Antônio Salvador Sucar, Victor Mirshawka, Sérgio de Toledo Machado, José Edvar Simões
4. PUR—William McCadney, Evelio Droz Ramos, Rubén Adorno Meléndez, Teófilo Cruz Downs, Juan Vicens Sastre, Alberto Zamot Bula, Martín Anza Ortiz, Jaime Frontera Colley, Juan Ramon Baez Marino, Angel García Lucas, Angel Cancel Acevedo, Thomas Gutierrez Ferrer
5. ITA—Augusto Giomo, Giusto Pellanera, Gianfranco Lombardi, Gianfranco Pieri, Gianfranco Bertini, Paolo Vittori, Gianfranco Sardagna, Ottorino Flaborea, Massimo Masini, Sauro Bufalini, Gabrielle Vianello, Giovanni Gavagnin
6. POL—Janusz Wichowski, Andrzej Pstrokonski, Tadeusz Blauth, Andrzej Perka, Stanislaw Olejniczak, Krystian Czernichowski, Zbigniew Dregier, Kazimierz Frelkiewicz, Bogdan Liszko, Mieczyslaw Lopatka, Jerzy Piskun, Krzysztof Sitkowski
7. YUG—Slobodan Gordić, Radivoje Korać, Trajko Rajković, Dragan Kovačić, Josip Djerdja, Dragoslav Ražnatović, Ivo Daneu, Zvonko Petričević, Vital Eiselt, Vladimir Cvetković, Nenamja Djurić, Miodrag Nikolic
8. URU—Washington Poyet, Walter Marquez, Julio Cesar Gómez, Luis Eduardo Koster, Edison Ciavattone, Alvaro Eduardo Roca, Sergio Pisano, Luis Agustín García, Manuel Roberto Gadea, Ramiro Eduardo de León, Waldemar José Rial, Jorge Maya

Once again the Americans went through the tournament undefeated. They were pressed only by the Yugoslavs, whom they beat 69–61. In the final, the USSR led 16–13 after the first ten minutes, but the United States went on an 18–4 spurt and was never headed again. The Peruvian team sported four brothers, Ricardo, Enrique, Raul, and Luis Duarte. Michale Ahmatt of the Australian team was the first Aborigine to compete in the Olympics.

1968 Mexico City T: 16, N: 16, D: 10.25.

	W	L	PF	PA
1. USA	9	0	739	505
2. YUG	7	2	705	638
3. SOV	8	1	774	524
4. BRA	6	3	677	563
5. MEX	7	2	641	580
6. POL	5	4	604	631
7. SPA	5	4	717	693
8. ITA	5	4	686	693

Final: USA 65-50 YUG
3rd Place: SOV 70-53 BRA
5th Place: MEX 76-65 POL
7th Place: SPA 88-72 ITA

1. USA—John Clawson, Kenneth Spain, Joseph "Jo-Jo" White, Michael Barrett, Spencer Haywood, Charles Scott, William Hosket, Calvin Fowler, Michael Silliman, Glynn Saulters, James King, Donald Dee
2. YUG—Aljoša Žorga, Radivoje Korać, Zoran Maroević, Trajko Rajković, Vladimir Cvetković, Dragoslav Ražnatović, Ivo Daneu, Krešimir Čosić, Damir Šolman, Nikola Plećaš, Dragutin Čermak, Petar Skansi
3. SOV—Anatoly Krikun, Modestas Paulauskas, Zurab Sakandelidze, Vadim Kapranov, Yuri Selikhov, Anatoly Polyvoda, Sergei Belov, Priit Tomson, Sergei Kovalenko, Gennady Volnov, Jaak Lipso, Vladimir Andreyev
4. BRA—Sérgio de Toledo Machado, Wlamir Marques, Ubiratan Pereira Maciel, Celso Luiz Scarpini, Helio Rubens Garcia, Carmo de Souza, José Aparecido dos Santos, Luiz Claudio Menon, Antônio Salvador Sucar, José Edvar Simões, José Geraldo de Castro, Carlos Domingos Massoni
5. MEX—Rafael Heredia Estrella, Arturo Guerrero, Fernando Tiscareño, Miguel Arellano, Antonio Ayala, Oscar Asiain, Luis Grajeda, Alejandro Guzmán, Carlos Quintanar, Ricardo Pontvianne, John Hatch, Mañuel Raga
6. POL—Grzegorz Korcz, Wlodzimierz Trams, Czeslaw Malec, Henryk Cegielski, Andrzej Kasprzak, Edward Jurkiewicz, Adam Niemiec, Bogdan Liszko, Mieczyslaw Lopatka, Kazimierz Frelkiewicz, Boleslaw Kwiatkowski, Andrzej Pasiorowski
7. SPA—Juan Martínez, Vicente Ramos, Luis Santiago, Jesús Codina, Enrique Margall, Antonio Nava, Emiliano Rodríguez, Clifford Luyk, José Vela Sagi, Francisco Buscato, Lorenzo Alocén, Alfonso Martínez
8. ITA—Carlo Recalcati, Giusto Pellanera, Gianfranco Lombardi, Enrico Bovone, Massimo Masini, Paolo Vittori, Gabriele Vianello, Guido Gatti, Ottorino Flaborea, Sauro Fufalini, Massimo Cosmelli, Gianluigi Jessi

The best of the US college players stayed away from the Olympic trials for various reasons. Notable absentees included Elvin Hayes, who had signed a professional contract, and Lew Alcindor (Kareem Abdul-Jabbar), who gave two reasons: not wanting to take time off from his studies and support for the threatened black boycott of the Olympics. But the US team, although held to a 5-point victory by Puerto Rico, made it to the final by beating Brazil 75-63. In the other semifinal, Yugoslavia's Vladimir Cvetković sank two free throws with four seconds to play to upset the USSR 63-62. At the end of the first half of the final, the Yugoslavs trailed the United States by only three points, 32-29. But at the beginning of the second half Spencer Haywood and Jo-Jo White went on a rampage, as the US outscored Yugoslavia 22-3 to put the game out of reach. The vocal Mexican crowd, which had been rooting for the underdog Yugoslavs, was so impressed by the display of Haywood and White that they switched allegiance. The only incident of the tournament occurred when some photographers attempted to shoot pictures of the weeping Cuban team, which had just lost to Mexico by one point. The Cubans took out their frustrations by chasing the photographers across the court. There were no injuries.

1972 Munich T: 16, N: 16, D: 9.10.

	W	L	PF	PA
1. SOV	9	0	757	590
2. USA	8	1	660	401
3. CUB	7	2	687	577
4. ITA	5	4	650	605
5. YUG	7	2	734	617
6. PUR	6	3	743	683
7. BRA	3	5	625	642
8. CZE	4	5	625	642

Final: SOV 51-50 USA
3rd Place: CUB 66-65 ITA
5th Place: YUG 86-70 PUR
7th Place: BRA 87-69 CZE

1. SOV—Anatoly Polyvoda, Modestas Paulauskas, Zurab Sakandelidze, Alshan Sharmukhamedov, Aleksandr Boloshev, Ivan Edeshko, Sergei Belov, Mishako Korkia, Ivan Dvorni, Gennady Volnoy, Aleksandr Belov, Serhei Kovalenko
2. USA—Kenneth Davis, Douglas Collins, Thomas Henderson, Michael Bantom, Robert Jones, Dwight Jones, James Forbes, James Brewer, Tommy Burleson, Thomas McMillen, Kevin Joyce, Ed Ratleff
3. CUB—Juan Domecq, Roberto Herrera Tabio, Juan Roca, Pedro Chappé García, Jose Alvarez Pozo, Rafael Cãnizares Poey, Conrado Pérez Armenteros, Miguel Calderón Gómez, Tomás Herrera Martínez, Oscar Varona, Alejandro Urgellés Guibot, Franklin Standard
4. ITA—Ottorino Flaborea, Giuseppe Brumatti, Giorgio Giomo, Mauro Cerioni, Massimo Masini, Renzo Bariviera, Marino Zanatta, Dino Meneghin, Pierluigi Marzorati, Luigi Serafini, Ivan Bisson, Giulio Jellini
5. YUG—Ratko Tvrdič, Ljubodrag Simonovič, Vinko Jelovać, Zarko Knezević, Miroljub Damnjanović, Dragan Kapidžić, Blagoje Georgievski, Krešimir Čošić, Damir Šolman, Nikola Plećaš, Dragutin Cermak, Milun Marovič
6. PUR—Joe Hatton, Neftali Rivera, James Thordsen, Rubén Rodríguez, Eric William Baum, Hector Blondet, Earl Brown, Mariano Ortiz, Teófilo Cruz Downs, Raymond Dalmau, Ricardo Calzada
7. BRA—Joseph Washington, Radvilas Gorauskas, Maciel Pereira Ubiratan, Sergio Francisco Garcia, Rubens Helio Garcia, Abdalla Marcos Leite, José Aparecido dos Santos, Luiz Claudio Menon, Adilson de Nascimento, José Edivar Simões, José Geraldo de Castro, Carlos Domingos Massoni
8. CZE—Petr Novický, Zdenek Douša, Jiři Konopašek, Jiři Pospisil, Zdeněk Kos, Jiři Balastik, Jiři Zidek, Jiři Zedniček, Jan Bobrovsky, Kamil Brabeneč, Jan Blazek, Jiři Ruzicka

Aleksandr Belov, 1972
Belov scoring the winning layup against the United States in the disputed final of 1972.

One of the greatest controversies in the history of international sports took place in Munich in the early morning hours of Sunday, September 10. The United States entered the final match with a record of 62 wins and no losses in Olympic basketball competition. The game began at 11:45 p.m., in order to accommodate US television. One of the American team's strengths was speed, but the United States coach, Hank Iba, chose not to exploit it, ordering his squad to play at a more cautious and deliberate pace instead.

The USSR scored first, led 26–21 at the half, and was ahead by eight points with 6:07 to play. But then the United States applied a full-court press and the Soviet team began to crumble. Nonetheless, with six seconds to play, the Soviets had the ball and clung to a one-point lead. Then Soviet star Sasha Belov inadvertently threw the ball toward Doug Collins of Illinois State. With three seconds left, Collins was fouled intentionally by Sako Sakandelidze. In fact, he was fouled so hard that he momentarily lost consciousness. Dazed, he mechanically followed his free throw routine—"three dribbles, a little spin, and then shoot"—and coolly sank two free throws to give the United States its first lead of the game, 50-49. The Soviet team in-bounded the ball, but two seconds later head referee Renato Righetto of Brazil noted a disturbance at the scorer's table and called an administrative time-out. The Soviet coach, Vladimir Kondrashkin, claimed that he had called for a time-out after Collins' first shot. Indeed, the time-out horn had gone off just as Collins released his second free throw attempt. According to the rules of the day, a coach calling for a time-out in a free throw situation could ask that the time-out begin before or after the first shot. Kondrashkin wanted his time-out *after* Collins' first shot. The German officials, in the excitement of the moment, apparently forgot about this option and, noting the Soviet players go to the line for Collins' first shot, thought that Kondrashkin had canceled his request, and so they failed to inform the referees of a time-out.

With one second on the clock, the USSR was awarded a time-out. When play resumed, they in-bounded the ball and time ran out. The United States players began a joyous celebration.

But at this point Great Britain's R. William Jones, the Secretary-General of the International Amateur Basketball Federation (FIBA), intervened and ordered the clock set back to three seconds, which was how much time remained on the clock when Kondrashkin originally tried to call time-out. Technically, Jones had no right to make any decisions, but he ruled FIBA with an iron hand, and hardly anyone dared to question his authority. Kondrashkin brought in Ivan Edeshko, who threw a long pass to Sasha Belov. Belov caught the pass perfectly, pushed past two defenders, and scored the winning basket. The United States filed a protest, which was heard by a five-man Jury of Appeal. Jones appointed Ferenc Hepp of Hungary to be chairman of the committee, and Hepp provided the deciding vote in favor of the USSR. He was joined by representatives of Poland and Cuba, while representatives of Italy and Puerto Rico voted to disallow Belov's basket. The US team voted unanimously to refuse their silver medals. Coach Hank Iba felt doubly robbed. At two a.m., while he was signing the official protest, his pocket was picked and he lost $370.

The loss haunted many of the United States players for years to come, but others were able to put it in perspective. In 1992, Kenny Davis told *Sports Illustrated,* "I went back to my room and cried alone that night. But every time I get to feeling sorry for myself, I think of the Israeli kids who were killed at those Games . . .

Think of being in a helicopter with your hands tied behind your back and a hand grenade rolling toward you and compare *that* to not getting a gold medal. If that final game is the worst injustice that ever happens to the guys on that team, we'll all come out of this life pretty good."

As for Sasha Belov, he died in mysterious circumstances on October 3, 1978. He was 26 years old.

UNITED STATES' BASKETBALL WINNING STREAK

1936

USA	52—28	EST
USA	56—23	PHI
USA	25—0	MEX
USA	19—8	CAN

1948

USA	86—21	SWI
USA	53—28	CZE
USA	59—57	ARG
USA	68—28	EGY
USA	61—33	PER
USA	63—28	URU
USA	71—40	MEX
USA	65—21	FRA

1952

USA	66—48	HUN
USA	72—47	CZE
USA	57—44	URU
USA	86—58	SOV
USA	103—55	CHI
USA	57—53	BRA
USA	85—76	ARG
USA	36—25	SOV

1956

USA	98—40	JPN
USA	101—29	THA
USA	121—53	PHI
USA	84—44	BUL
USA	113—51	BRA
USA	85—55	SOV
USA	101—38	URU
USA	89—55	SOV

1960

USA	88—54	ITA
USA	125—66	JPN
USA	107—63	HUN
USA	104—42	YUG
USA	108—50	URU
USA	81—57	SOV
USA	112—81	ITA
USA	90—63	BRA

1964

USA	78—45	AUS
USA	77—51	FIN
USA	60—45	PER
USA	83—28	URU
USA	69—61	YUG
USA	86—53	BRA
USA	116—50	KOR
USA	62—42	PUR
USA	73—59	SOV

1968

USA	81—46	SPA
USA	93—36	SEN
USA	96—75	PHI
USA	73—58	YUG
USA	95—50	PAN
USA	100—61	ITA
USA	61—56	PUR
USA	75—63	BRA
USA	65—50	YUG

1972

USA	65—35	CZE
USA	81—55	AUS
USA	67—48	CUB
USA	61—54	BRA
USA	96—31	EGY
USA	72—56	SPA
USA	99—33	JPN
USA	68—38	ITA

1976 Montreal T: 12, N: 12, D: 7.27.

	W	L	PF	PA
1. USA	7	0	584	500
2. YUG	5	2	527	522
3. SOV	6	1	732	535
4. CAN	4	3	595	611
5. ITA	5	2	526	491
6. CZE	3	4	584	580
7. CUB	4	3	616	574
8. AUS	2	5	625	652

Final: USA 95-74 YUG
3rd Place: SOV 100-72 CAN
5th Place: ITA 98-75 CZE
7th Place: CUB 92-81 AUS

1. USA—Phil Ford, Steve Sheppard, Adrian Dantley, Walter Davis, William "Quinn" Buckner, Ernie Grunfeld, Kenneth Carr, Scott May, Michel Armstrong, Thomas La Garde, Philip Hubbard, Mitchell Kupchak
2. YUG—Blagoje Georgievski, Dragan Kićanović, Vinko Jelovać, Rajko Žižić, Željko Jerkov, Andro Knego, Zoran Slavnić, Krešimir Ćosić Damir Šolman, Žarko Varajić, Dražen Dalipagić, Mirza Delibašić
3. SOV—Vladimir Arzamaskov, Aleksand Salnikov, Valery Miloserdov, Alshan Sharmukhamedov, Andrei Makeev, Ivan Edeshko, Sergei Belov, Vladimir Tkachenko, Anatoly Myshkin, Mikhail Korkiya, Aleksandr Belov, Vladimir Zhigily
4. CAN—Alexander Devlin, Martin Riley, Bill Robinson, John Cassidy, Derek Sankey, Robert Sharpe, Cameron Hall, James Russell, Robert Town, Romel Raffin, Lars Hansen, Phillip Tollestrup
5. ITA—Giulio Jellini, Carlo Recalcati, Luciano Vendemini, Fabrizio Della Fiori, Renzo Baniviera, Marino Zanatta, Dino Meneghin, Pierluigi Marzorati, Luigi Serafini, Ivan Bisson, Gianni Bertolotti
6. CZE—Vladimir Ptaček, Petr Vojtech, Jiři Konopašek, Justin Sedlak, Stanislav Kropilak, Jaroslav Kanturek, Zedenek Kos, Jiři Pospišil, Vladimir Padrta, Kamil Brabeneč Zdenek Douša, Gustav Hraška
7. CUB—Juan Domecq, Roberto Herrera Tabio, Juan Roca, Pedro Alejandro Ortiz Herrera, Rafael Cãnizares Poey, Daniel Scott Brice, Angel Padron, Tomás Herrera Martínez, Oscar Varona, Alejandro Urgellés Guibot, Felix Morales Alphonso
8. AUS—Andrew Campbell, Ian Watson, Robert Cadee, Anthony Barnett, Edward Palubinskas, Andris Blicavs, Michael Tucker, Perry Crosswhite, Russell Simon, Peter Walsh, John Maddock, Ray Tomlinson

For four years the United States waited to gain revenge for their loss to the USSR, but their train was almost derailed by a young man from New York who also had something to prove. Butch Lee of Marquette University had been prevented from trying out for the US team when his college coach, Al McGuire, sent another player to the tryouts instead. Lee returned to his birthplace of Puerto Rico and made the team there. Puerto Rico faced the United States in the second game of the Olympic tournament: Lee shot 15 of 18 from the field and scored 35 points, while his teammate Neftalí Rivera added 26. But the gutsy Puerto Ricans fell one point short and lost 95-94. However, the US—USSR showdown was not to be. In the semifinals, an inspired Yugoslav team upset the Soviets 89-84. The final was no contest, as the Americans took an 8-0 lead and never looked back. High scorer in the tournament for the United States was Adrian Dantley of Notre Dame, who averaged 19.3 points a game.

1980 Moscow T: 12, N: 12, D: 7.30.

	W	L	PF	PA
1. YUG	9	0	920	768
2. ITA	5	4	744	757
3. SOV	7	2	943	797
4. SPA	4	5	871	843
5. BRA	4	4	745	712
6. CUB	2	6	660	704
7. POL	5	3	709	656
8. AUS	6	2	641	596

Final: YUG 86-77 ITA
3rd Place: SOV 117-94 SPA

1. YUG—Andro Knego, Dragan Kićanović, Rajko Žižić, Mihovil Nakić Vojnović, Željko Jerkov, Branko Skroče, Zoran Slavnić, Krešimir Ćosić, Ratko Radovanović, Duje Krstulović, Dražen Dalipagić, Mirza Delibašić
2. ITA—Romeo Sacchetti, Roberto Brunamonti, Michael Sylvester, Enrico Gilardi, Fabrizio Della Fiori, Marco Solfrini, Marco Bonamico, Dino Meneghin, Renato Villalta, Renzo Vecchiato, Pierluigi, Marzorati, Pietro Generali
3. SOV—Stanislav Eremin, Valery Miloserdov, Sergei Tarakanov, Oleksander Salnikov, Andrei Lopatov, Nikolai Deruguin, Sergei Belov, Volodymyr Tkachenko, Anatoly Myshkin, Sergejus Jovaiša, Oleksander Bilostinny, Vladimir Zhigily
4. SPA—Wayne Brabender, José Luis Llorente Gento, Candido-Antonio Sibilio, José María Margall Tauler, Manuel Flores, Fernando Romay Pereiro, Luis-Miguel Santillana, Juan Antonio Corbalán Alfocea, Ignacio Solozábal Igartua, Juan Domingo De La Cruz Fermanelli, Juan López Iturriaga, Juan Antonio San Epifanio Ruiz
5. BRA—André Ernesto Stoffel, Luiz Gustavo de Lage, José Carlos Saiani, Milton Setrini, Wagner Machado da Silva, Marcos Abdalla Leite, Gilson Trindade de Jesus, Marcel Ramon de Souza, Adilson de Nascimento, Marcelo Vido, Oscar Daniel Schmidt, Ricardo Cardoso Guimarães
6. CUB—Jorge More Rojas, Ruperto Herrera Tabio, Pedro Alejandro Ortiz Herrera, Noangel Luaces Rodríguez, Generoso Márquez Saes,Raul Dubois Cumbath, Pedro Abreu Pascual, Miguel Calderón Gómez, Tomás Herrera Martinez, Daniel Scott Brice, Alejandro Urgellés Guibot, Félix Morales Alphonso
7. POL—Daniusz Zelig, Leszek Dolńiski, Wojciech Rosinski, Eugeńiusz Kijewski, Jerzy Bińkowski, Andrzej Michalski, Ireneusz Mulak, Justyn Weglorz, Mieczyslav Mylarnski, Zdzislaw Myrda, Ryszard Prostak, Kryzstof Fikiel
8. AUS—Melvyn Dalgleish, Gordon McLeod, Philip Smyth, Larry Sengstock, Peter Ali, Michael Tucker, Stephan Berheny, Les Riddle, Ian Davies, Peter Walsh, Danny Morseu, Perry Crosswhite

The Yugoslavs were led by Dalipagić and Kicanović, who averaged 24.4 and 23.6 points per game respectively. Although the United States boycotted the 1980 Olympics, there was one American who earned a medal in Moscow. Mike Sylvester, a guard on the Italian team, was born and raised in the United States, but gained dual citizenship in 1977 after living in Italy for three years. The team from India brought back memories of the 1948 Iraqi squad, losing their eight matches by an average score of 65.5 to 116.

1984 Los Angeles-Inglewood T: 12, N: 12, D: 8.10.

	W	L	PF	PA
1. USA	8	0	763	506
2. SPA	6	2	697	688
3. YUG	7	1	716	604
4. CAN	4	4	681	639
5. ITA	6	2	718	614
6. URU	3	5	688	776
7. AUS	4	4	654	683
8. GER	2	6	600	635

Final: USA 96-65 SPA
3rd Place: YUG 88-82 CAN
5th Place: ITA 111-102 URU
7th Place: AUS 83-78 GER

1. USA—Steve Alford, Leon Wood, Patrick Ewing, Vern Fleming, Alvin Robertson, Michael Jordan, Joseph Kleine, Jon Koncak, Wayman Tisdale, Christopher Mulllin, Samuel Perkins, Jeffrey Turner
2. SPA—Fernando Arecega Aperte, José Manuel Beirán Lozano, Juan Antonio Corbalán Alfocea, Juan Domingo De La Cruz Fermanelli, Andres Jiménez Fernández, José Luis Llorente Gento, José Manuel López Iturriaga, José María Margall Tauler, Fernando Martín Espina, Fernando Romay Pereiro, Juan Antonio San Epifanio Ruiz, Ignacio Solozábal Igartua
3. YUG—Dražen Petrović, Aleksandar Petrović, Nebojsa Zorkić, Rajko Žižić, Ivan Sunara, Emir Mutapcić, Saabit Hadžić, Andro Knego, Ratko Radovanović, Mihovil Nakić Vojnovic, Dražen Dalipagić, Branko Vukicević
4. CAN—Howard Kelsey, Tony Simms, I. Enrico Pasquale, Karl Tilleman, Gerald François Kazanowski, James Triano, John Hatch, Gord Herbert, Bill Wennington, Romel Raffin, Greg Wiltjer, Dan Meagher
5. ITA—Carlo Caglieris, Roberto Premier, Marco Bonamico, Enrico Gilardi, Walter Magnifico, Roberto Brunamonti, Renato Villata, Dino Meneghin, Antonello Riva, Renzo Vecchiato, Pierluigi Marzorati, Romeo Sacchetti
6. URU—Horacio López, Luis Larrosa, Luis Pierri Barros, Hebert Núñez González, Wilfredo Ruiz Bruno, Horacio Perdomo Shaban, Carlos Peinado Stagnero, Julio Pereyra Mele, Alvaro Tito Moreno, Juan Mignone Crisena, Victor Frattini Bonomi
7. AUS—Andrew Campbell, Damian Keogh, Philip Smyth, Larry Sengstock, Mark Dalton, Wayne Carroll, Melvyn Dalgleish, Andrew Gaze, Ian Davies, Daniel Morseu, Bradley Dalton, Raymond Borner
8. GER—Christoph Korner, Vladimir Kadlec, Uwe Brauer, Uwe Sauer, Ulrich Peters, Klaus Zander, Michael Pappert, Armin Sowa, Detlef Schrempf, Uwe Blab, Ingo Mendel, Christian Welp

The powerful US team breezed through the tournament, winning by an average of 32 points per game. Their only weak game was a 78-67 quarterfinal victory over West Germany. The well-balanced American squad included Michael Jordan, who averaged 17.1 points per game, Wayman Tisdale, who led the team in rebounding, Patrick Ewing, the tournament blocked-shot leader with 18, Leon Wood, the tournament assist leader with 63, and Alvin Robertson, who shot 65% from the field and registered 17 steals.

1988 Seoul T: 12, N: 12, D: 9.30.

	W	L	PF	PA
1. SOV	7	1	728	637
2. YUG	6	2	717	603
3. USA	7	1	733	490
4. AUS	4	4	625	651
5. BRA	5	3	905	808
6. CAN	3	5	738	747
7. PUR	4	4	618	677
8. SPA	4	4	741	701

Final: SOV 76-63 YUG
3rd Place: USA 78-49 AUS
5th Place: BRA 106-90 CAN
7th Place: PUR 93-92 SPA

1. SOV—Aleksandr Volkov, Tiit Sokk, Sergei Tarakanov, R. Šarūnas Marčiulionis, Igors Miglinieks, Vadim Tikhonenko, Rimas Kurtinaitis, Arvydas Sabonis, Victor Pankracskin,Valdemaras Chomičius, Oleksander Bilostinny, Valery Goborov
2. YUG—Dražen Petrović, Zdravko Radulović, Zoran Čutura, Toni Kukoč, Žarko Paspalj, Želimir Obradović, Jurij Zdovc, Stojan Vranković, Vlade Divac, Franjo Arapović, Dino Radja, Danko Cvjetičanin
3. USA—Mitchell Richmond, Charles D. Smith, Vernell Coles, Hersey Hawkins, Jeffrey Grayer, Charles E. Smith, Willie Anderson, Stacey Augmon, Daniel Majerle, Danny Manning, Herman Reid, David Robinson
4. AUS—Darryl Pearce, Philip Smyth, Larry Sengstock, Damian Keogh, Wayne Carroll, Lucien Longley, Andrew Gaze, Mark Bradtke, Bradley Dalton, Andrew Vlahov, Raymond Borner
5. BRA—Paulo Almeida, Jorge Guerra, Gerson Victalino, João “Pipoka” Vianna, Rolando Ferreira, Ricardo Cardoso Guimarães, Maury Ponikwar De Souza, Marcel Ponikwar De Souza, Luiz Azevedo, Paulo Silva, Oscar Schmidt Bezerra, Israel Andrade
6. CAN—Norman Clarke, David Turcotte, I. Enrico Pasquale, Karl Tilleman, Alan Kristmanson, James Triano, Dwight Walton, John Hatch, Barry Mungar, Romel Raffin, Wayne Yearrwood, Gerald François Kazanowski
7. PUR—José Ortiz Rijos, Federico López Camacho, Raymond Gause Santiago, Vicente Ithier, Jerome Mincy Clark, Roberto Rios, Angel Cruz, Ramon Rivas Contreras, Mario Morales Micheo, Edgar De León Cruz, Francisco León, Ramon Ramos
8. SPA—Jordi Villacampa, José Luis Llorente Gento, José Biryukov, José María Margall Tauler, Andrés Jiménez Fernández, Enrique Andreu, José António Montero, Fernando Arcega Aperte, Ignacio Solozábal Igartua, Ferrán Martínez, Antonio Martin, Juan Antonio San Epifanio Ruiz

The long-awaited Olympic rematch between the US and the USSR finally took place in the semifinal round at Seoul, 16 years after the controversial 1972 Munich final. This time the Soviets took a 10-point halftime lead, beat back every American challenge, and won 82-76. With this bit of history out of the way, the Soviets faced their arch rivals, the Yugoslavs, in the final, in what would be the sixth match between the two teams in six months.

Although the Yugoslavs had won four of the five previous encounters, including a 92-79 victory in the tournament's opening round, they had to have been haunted by memories of two earlier losses. In the semifinals of the 1986 world championships, Yugoslavia led by 9 points with 47 seconds left in the game. The Soviets then hit three straight three-point shots and went on to win by 1 point in overtime. In the 1988 European Olympic qualifying tournament, the Soviets overcame a 15-point second-half deficit to defeat the Yugoslavs 86-83.

Magic Johnson and Michael Jordan, 1992
Johnson and Jordan of the 1992 US “Dream Team.”

In the Olympic final, Yugoslavia took a 24-12 lead. However the Soviets, led by Lithuanians Marčiulionis, Sabonis, and Kurtinaitis, went on a 19-2 run and were never headed again.

In a preliminary-round loss to Spain, Brazil's Oscar Schmidt scored an Olympic record 55 points. Schmidt also *averaged* 42½ points per game for the entire tournament.

1992 Barcelona T: 12, N: 12, D: 8.8.

	W	L	PF	PA
1. USA	8	0	938	588
2. CRO	6	2	681	656
3. LIT	6	2	753	725
4. SOV	5	3	660	606
5. BRA	4	4	692	741
6. AUS	4	4	686	683
7. GER	3	5	620	710
8. PUR	3	5	692	737

Final: USA 117-85 CR0
3rd Place: LIT 82-78 SOV
5th Place: BRA 90-80 AUS
7th Place: GER 96-86 PUR

1. USA—Larry Bird, Earvin “Magic” Johnson, David Robinson, Patrick Ewing, Scottie Pippen, Michael Jordan, Clyde Drexler, Karl Malone, John Stockton, Christopher Mullin, Charles Barkley, Christian Laettner
2. CRO—Dražen Petrović, Velimir Perasović, Danko Cvjetićanin, Toni Kukoč, Vladan Alanović, Franio Arapović, Zan Tabak, Stoiko Vranković, Alan Gregov, Arijan Komazec, Dino Radja, Aramis Naglić
3. LIT—Valdemaras Chomičius, Aluydas Pazdrazdis, Arunas Visockas, Darius Dimavičius, Romanas Brazdauskis, Gintaras Krapikas, Rimas Kurtinaitis, Arvydas Sabonis, Artūras Karnišovas, R. Šarūnas Marčiulionis, Gintaras Einikis, Sergejus Jovaiša

4. SOV—Goundars Vetra, Sergei Bazarevich, Igor Miglinieks, Vladimir Gorin, Sergei Panov, Vadim Tikhonenko, Viktor Berezhnoi, Vitaly Nosov, Dmitri Sukharev, Elshad Gadashev, Aleksandr Volkov, Oleksandr Bilostinny
5. BRA—Paulo Villas Boas, Jorge Guerra, Gerson Victalino, João "Pipoka" Vianna, Ricardo Cardoso Guimarães, Maury Ponikwar De Souza, Marcel Ponikwar De Souza, Aristides Josuel Dos Santos, Wilson Fernando Minuci, Oscar Schmidt, Rolando Ferreira, Israel Machado
6. AUS—Kevin Dorge, Michael McKay, Philip Smyth, Larry Sengstock, Damian Keogh, Leroy Loggins, Andrew Gaze, Shane Heal, Mark Bradtke, Lucien Longley, Andrew Vlahov, Raymond Borner
7. GER—Gunther Behnke, Henrik Rödl, Armin Andres, Stephan Baeck, Arnd Neuhaus, Henning Harnisch, Uwe Blab, Detlef Schrempf, Hans Gnad, Kai Nurnbenger, Jens Kujawa, Michael Jackel
8. PUR—José Ortiz Rijos, Federico López Camacho, Raymond Gause Santiago, Edwin Pellot Rosa, Jerome Mincy Clark, James Carter, Javier Colón Rodríguez, Ramon Rivas Contreras, Mario Morales Micheo, Edgar De León Cruz, Eddie Casiano, Richard Soto

On April 17, 1989, the International Amateur Basketball Federation (FIBA) voted 56-13 to allow NBA players to participate in the Olympics. A myth soon developed that the United States, humiliated by the defeat of its college all-stars in 1988, had manipulated the vote to regain dominance in the Olympics. In fact, the United States was one of the 13 nations that voted *against* the proposal. USA Basketball, the organization in charge of international basketball in the United States, had two major objections to allowing American professionals in the Olympics: They feared that the presence of a dozen millionaires representing the United States would kill their fundraising efforts in support of women's and junior basketball, and they feared that the inevitable lopsided nature of the games would adversely effect television ratings. Other basketball powers, such as the Soviet Union and Yugoslavia, saw the situation differently. They were willing to concede the gold medal to the United States in exchange for allowing their own best players to play in the NBA and still remain eligible for the Olympics. Those nations that had little or no chance for a medal reasoned that as long as they were going to lose anyway, they would rather lose to the best.

And so was born the greatest basketball team ever assembled. Coached by Chuck Daly, the United States squad was captained by veterans Magic Johnson and Larry Bird, and included Michael Jordan, Charles Barkley, Patrick Ewing, and Karl Malone. It wasn't just hype when they gained their nickname the Dream Team. A lot of Americans whined that it was overkill to send the Dream Team to Barcelona, but in the rest of the world the decision was greeted with enormous enthusiasm, especially in Barcelona itself, home of one of Spain's leading professional teams.

Before they could play for the gold medal, the United States squad had to go through the formality of qualifying for the Olympics in the Tournament of the Americas. The Americans' first opponent was the team from Cuba. For over thirty years, the governments of the United States and Cuba had treated each other as the bitterest of enemies. It soon became apparent that this enmity did not extend to the basketball court. The start of the game had to be delayed briefly—the Cubans asked if they could have their photographs taken with the US players. The United States won 136-57, but the Cubans seemed content. This set the tone for the rest of the Tournament of the Americas as well as the Olympics. For opposing teams, playing against the NBA giants was a dream come true; it was something they would tell their grandchildren about.

The United States won the Olympic tournament as easily as expected. The Americans scored more than 100 points in every game and averaged a record-setting 117¼ points. Their closest victories were over Croatia, 103-70 and 117-85. Charles Barkley (18.0) and Michael Jordan (14.9) led the team in scoring, Malone and Ewing in rebounds, and Scottie Pippen and Magic Johnson in assists. Jordan had a tournament high 37 steals.

If the final lacked drama, the bronze-medal match made up for it. Lithuanians had traditionally played a significant role in Soviet basketball. However, for 52 years Lithuania had been a reluctant member of the Soviet Union, and support for independence ran high. In 1988, the Soviet players posed for a team photo after winning the gold medal. After the session was over, the four Lithuanian members of the team gathered for their own "team" photo. Four years later, in Barcelona, those four players were back in the Olympics representing an independent Lithuania. Another four members of the 1988 Soviet team were also in Barcelona—playing for the Unified Team of ex-Soviet republics. One of the four, Igor Miglinieks, was actually from Latvia, but competed for the Unified Team rather than miss the Olympics.

In pool play the ex-Soviets overcame a 19-point deficit to beat Lithuania 92-80. The Lithuanian players were heartbroken by the loss, but a week later they were given a chance for revenge when Croatia, trailing by six points with 65 seconds to play in the semifinals, upset the ex-Soviets 75-74. This meant that Croatia earned the silver medal while Lithuania and the ex-Soviets battled for the final platform at the medal ceremony. This time Lithuania, led by Šarunas Marčiulionis and Arvydas Sabonis with 29 and 27 points, led for most of the game, kept their poise, and won 82-78.

In the end, the inclusion of the Dream Team at the

Olympics was a big success. Although they were so much better than the rest of the teams that Coach Daly never called a single time-out, their average margin of victory—43¾ points—was not as great as the US team of 1956, nor did they double the scores of their opponents, as did the US teams of 1936 and 1948.

1996 Atlanta T: 12, N: 12, D: 8.3.

	W	L	PF	PA
1. USA	8	0	816	562
2. YUG	7	1	741	578
3. LIT	5	3	664	600
4. AUS	5	3	712	690
5. GRE	5	3	674	664
6. BRA	3	5	725	757
7. CRO	4	4	686	624
8. CHN	2	6	581	844

Final: USA 95-69 YUG
3rd Place: LIT 80-74 AUS
5th Place: GRE 91-72 BRA
7th Place: CRO 99-85 CHN

1. USA—Anfernee Hardaway, Charles Barkley, David Robinson, Gary Payton, Grant Hill, Hakeem Olajuwon, John Stockton, Karl Malone, Mitch Richmond, Reggie Miller, Scottie Pippen, Shaquille O'Neal
2. YUG—Aleksandar Djordjević, Dejan Bodiroga, Dejan Tomašević, Milenko Topić, Miroslav Berić, Nikola Lonččar, Predrag Danilović, Sasa Obradović, Vlade Divac, Zarko Paspalj, Zeljko Rebrača, Zoran Savić
3. LIT—Arturas Karnisovas, Arvydas Sabonis, Darius Lukminas, Eurelijus Zukauskas, Gintaras Einikis, Mindaugas Zukauskas, Rimas Kurtinaitis, Rytis Vaisvila, R. Šarūnas Marčiulionis, Saulius Stombergas, Tomas Pacesas
4. AUS—Andrew Gaze, Andrew Vlahov, Brett Maher, John Dorge, Mark Bradtke, Pat Reidy, Ray Borner, Sam MacKinnon, Scott Fisher, Shane Heal, Tonny Jensen, Tony Ronaldson
5. GRE—Costas Patavoukas, Dimitris Papanikolaou, Dinos Agelidis, Efthimios Bakatsias, Efthimis Rentzias, Eleftherios Kakiousis, Fragiskos Alvertis, Giorgios Sigalas, Nikos Economou, Panayotis Fassoulas, Panayotis Giannakis, Theofanis Christodoulou
6. BRA—Andre "Rato" Fonseca, Antonio José Santana, Aristides Josuel Dos Santos, Caio Cassiolato, Caio Silveira, Carlos "Olivia" Do Nascimento, Demétrius Ferraciu, João "Pipoka" Vianna, Joelcio Joerke, Oscar Schmidt, Rogério Klafke, Wilson Fernando Minuci
7. CRO—Arijan Komazec, Damir Mulaomerović, Davor Marcelic, Dino Radja, Josip Vranković, Slaven Rimac, Stojan Vranković, Toni Kukoč, Velimir Perasović, Veljko Mršić, Vladan Alanović, Zan Tabak
8. CHN—Ba Tere, Gong Xiaobin, Hu Weidong, Li Nan, Li Xiaoyong, Liu Yudong, Shan Tao, Sun Jun, Wang Zhizhi, Wu Naiqin, Wu Qinglong, Zheng Wu

The performance of the US was somewhat of a letdown after the excitement of 1992. For most of the tournament, the Americans, clearly superior to the rest of the teams, appeared sluggish and detached. In the final they faced Yugoslavia, which was anxious to perform well after being forbidden to take part in the Barcelona Games.

Yugoslavia led 23-16 midway through the first half. The US tied the score at 34 with four minutes to play and led at halftime 43-38. Six minutes into the second half, Yugoslavia had whittled the US lead to 51-50, but then the Americans took charge, outscoring the Yugoslavs 44 to 19 for the remainder of the game. David Robinson scored 28 points in the final and Reggie Miller 20.

2000 Sydney T: 12, N: 12, D: 10.1.

	W	L	PF	PA
1. USA	8	0	760	587
2. FRA	4	4	591	574
3. LIT	5	3	620	558
4. AUS	4	4	596	634
5. ITA	4	3	463	473
6. YUG	4	3	494	463
7. CAN	5	2	582	524
8. RUS	3	4	520	499

Final: USA 85-75 FRA
3rd Place: LIT 89-71 AUS
5th Place: ITA 69-59 YUG
7th Place: CAN 86-83 RUS

1. USA—Allan Houston, Alonzo Mourning, Antonio McDyess, Gary Payton, Jason Kidd, Kevin Garnett, Ray Allen, Shareff Abdur-Rahim, Steve Smith, Tim Hardaway, Vin Baker, Vince Carter
2. FRA—Antoine Rigaudeau, Cyril Julian, Frédéric Weis, Crawford Palmer, Jim Bilba, Laurent Foirest, Laurent Sciarra, Makan Dioumassi, Moustapha Sonko, Stéphane Risacher, Thierry Gadou, Tann Bonato
3. LIT—Audrius Giedraitis, Dainius Adomaitis, Darius Maskoliunas Eurelijus Zukauskas, Gintaras Einikis, Kestutis Marčiulionis, Mindaugas Timinskas, Darius Songaila, Ramunas Šiškauskas, Šarūnas Jasikevičius, Saulius Štombergas, Tomas Masiulis
4. AUS—Chris Anstey, Mark Bradtke, Martin Cattalini, Andrew Gaze, Ricky Grace, Shane Heal, Luc Longley, Sam MacKinnon, Brett Maher, Paul Rogers, Jason Smith, Andrew Vlahov
5. ITA—Alessandro Abbio, Gianluca Basile, Roberto Chiacig, Marcelo Dilglay Damio, Gregor Fucka, Giacomo Galanda, Denis Marconato, Andrea Meneghin, Michele Mian, Carlton Myers, German Claudio Scarone, Agostino Antonio Li Vecchi
6. YUG—Dejan Bodiroga, Predrag Danilović, Predrag Drobnjak, Nikola Jestratijević, Dragan Lukovski, Igor Rakočević, Željko Rebrača, Vlado Ščepanović, Predrag Stojaković, Dragan Tarlać, Dejan Tomašević, Saša Obradović
7. CAN—Rowan Barrett, David Daniels, Greg Francis, Pete Guarasci, Sherman Hamilton, Eric Hinrichsen, Todd MacCulloch, Andrew Mavis, Michael Meeks, Steve Nash, Greg Newton, Shawn Swords
8. RUS—Ruslan Avleyev, Aleksandr Bakhminov, Sergey Basarevich, Andrey Fetisov, Andrey Kirilenko, Yevgeny Kisurin, Valentin Kubrakov, Nikita Morgunov, Yevgeny Pashutin, Zakhar Pashutin, Sergey Panov, Sergey Chikalkin

Since American professional players began appearing in the Olympics, US teams had won all 16 of their games by at least 22 points. In 2000, they again began with two easy victories over China and Italy, but then the nature of the tournament changed. The Americans defeated Lithuania, but the score was only 85-76. After rolling over New Zealand, they beat France 106-94 in a game that was highlighted by a spectacular slam dunk by Vince Carter, who leaped over French center Frédéric Weis on his way to the basket. Jumping over any player is quite a feat but Weis, known to his teammates as "Big Fred," happened to be 7 feet 2 inches

(2.18 meters) tall. After a blowout of New Zealand, Team USA defeated Russia in the quarterfinals, 85-70.

In the semifinals, the Americans faced a rematch with the Lithuanians and came breathtakingly close to suffering the biggest upset in Olympic history. The US led 48-36 at halftime, but Lithuania opened the second half with a 20-6 run and took a lead of 56-54. The last 15½ minutes of the game were so close that at no time did either team lead by more than three points. With 1:36 to go, former University of Maryland guard Sarunas Jasikevičius made two free throws to put Lithuania ahead 80-79. Seventeen seconds later, Vince Carter made one of two free throws to tie the game at 80. With 43.4 seconds to play, Antonio McDyess fouled Ramunas Siskauskas while he was attempting a three-pointer. Siskauskas had been 16 for 16 at the free throw line since the start of the tournament, but this time he missed his first two tries before sinking the third to put Lithuania back in front 81-80. Carter answered with a floater from the side and the US led 82-81 with 31 seconds left. Kevin Garnett stole the ball and was fouled. He missed both free throws, but McDyers grabbed the offensive rebound and scored to make it 84-81. Jasikevičius made a short jumper with 9.4 seconds to play and it was 84-83. The Lithuanians quickly fouled Jason Kidd, who made the first free throw, but missed the second. After a scramble for the rebound, a jump ball was called, but McDyers was called for a violation on the jump and Lithuania was awarded the ball trailing by two, with 5.2 seconds left. Jasikevičius, closely and carefully guarded by Jason Kidd, dribbled down court and launched a 22-foot off-balance three-point shot as time ran out. If it had gone in, Lithuania would have defeated the NBA all-stars, but the ball fell a foot short and the Americans escaped disaster. Commenting on what would have happened if Jasikevičius had made the shot, Kidd said, "About twelve guys would have to change their identities. We'd all have to move as far away as possible. New Zealand would be my pick."

The Americans faced France again in the final. They led 46-32 at the half and were still ahead by 16 points when the French went on a 16-4 run and cut the US lead to 76-72 with 4:26 to play. This time the Americans took charge when they needed to and kept France from getting any closer, as Team USA finally won 85-75.

For the entire tournament, Vince Carter led the US with 14.8 points per game, while Kevin Garnett's 9.1 rebounds a game was tops for all teams at the Olympics.

2004 Athens T: 12, N: 12, D: 8.28.

	W	L	PF	PA
1. ARG	6	2	656	610
2. ITA	5	3	623	586
3. USA	5	3	705	668
4. LIT	6	2	750	693
5. GRE	4	3	538	487
6. PUR	3	4	555	579
7. SPA	6	1	591	527
8. CHN	2	5	454	569

Final: ARG 84-69 ITA
3rd Place: USA 104-96 LIT
5th Place: GRE 85-75 PUR
7th Place: SPA 92-76 CHN

1. ARG—Carlos Francisco Delfino, Gabriel Diego Fernández, Emanuel "Manu" David Ginobili, Leonardo Gutiérrez, Walter Herrmann, Alejandro Montecchia, Andrés Marcelo Nocioni, Fabricio Raúl Jesús Oberto, Juan Ignacio Sánchez, Luis Alberto Scola, Hugo Ariel Sconochini, Rubén Oscar Wolkowyski
2. ITA—Gianluca Basile, Massimo Bulleri, Roberto Chiacig, Giacomo Galanda, Luca Garri, Denis Marconato, Michele Mian, Gianmarco Pozzecco, Nikola Radulovic, Alex Righetti, Rodolfo Rombaldoni, Matteo Soragna
3. USA—Carmelo Anthony, Carlos Boozer, Tim Duncan, Allen Iverson, LeBron James, Richard Jefferson, Stephon Marbury, Shawn Marion, Lamar Odom, Emeka Okafor, Amare Stoudemire, Dwayne Wade, Jr.
4. LIT—Vidas Ginevičius, Šarūnas Jasikevičius, Kšištov Lavrinovič, Dainius Šalenga, Ramūnas Šiškauskas, Eurelijus Žukauskas, Mindaugas Žukauskas, Robertas Javtokas, Arvydas Macijauskas, Donatas Slanina, Darius Songaila, Saulius Štombergas
5. GRE—Frangiskos "Frankie" Alvertis, Dimitrios Diamantidis, Dimosthenis Dikoudis, Antonios Fotsis, Mikhail Kakiouzis, Nikolaos Khatzivrettas, Lazaros Papadopoulos, Theodoros Papaloukas, Dimitrios Papanikolaou, Vasileios Spanoulis, Konstantinos Tsartsaris, Nikolaos Zisis
6. PUR—Rick Apodaca, Carlos Arroyo, Elias "Larry" Ayuso, Eddie Casiano, Christian Dalmau, Sharif Karim Fajardo, Roberto Hatton, Rolando Hourruitiner, José Rafael "Piculin" Ortíz, Peter John Ramos, Jorge Rivera, Daniel Santiago
7. SPA—Oscar Yebra Fernández, José Manuel Calderón Borrallo, Jaume Comas Castro, Rodrigo de la Fuente Morgado, Roberto Dueñas Hernández, Rodolfo Fernández Farres, Jorge Joaquín Garbajosa Chaparro, Carlos Jiménez Sánchez, Iker Iturbe Martínez de Lecea, Juan Carlos Navarro Feijoo, Felipe Reyes Cabanas, Pau Gasol Sáez
8. CHN—Mengke Bateer, Chen Ke, Du Feng, Guo Shiqiang, Li Nan, Liu Wei, Mo Ke, Yao Ming, Yi Jianlian, Zhang Jinsong, Zhang Yunsong, Zhu Fangyu

The United States had difficulty assembling a team for the Athens Games, as seven of the nine original choices for the squad turned down the offer to compete in the Olympics, and the US basketball federation had to ask thirty players before they could fill the 12-man roster. Instead of the expected lineup of NBA all-stars, the US fielded its youngest team since 1988, with an average age of 23½ years. Led by coach Larry Brown of the Detroit Pistons, the team arrived in Athens with a 109-2 all-time record in Olympic competition, their only losses being to the Soviet Union in the 1972 final and the 1988 semifinals.

However, US dominance in the sport had long been in decline. In 1992 the average winning margin for the team was almost 44 points, but in 1996 it dropped to 32 points, and in 2000 to 22 points. The Americans had also received a major wake-up call at the 2002 World Championships in Indianapolis, in the US, losing three games (to Argentina, Spain and Yugoslavia) and finishing a disappointing sixth, breaking their ten-year, 58-game winning streak in the process. Twelve days before the start of the Olympics the US suffered yet another painful loss, a lopsided 78-95 exhibition match against Italy.

On the first day of the 2004 competition, the US faced Puerto Rico in Group B of the preliminaries. Puerto Rico had suffered three 20-point losses in the run up to the Olympics and had been given virtually no chance to medal. As expected, the game was a lopsided one—however it was the US that suffered. Led by point guard Carlos Arroyo, the Puerto Ricans effectively controlled the game, building up a 22-point lead by halftime and going on to win 92-73. It was the first Olympics loss for the United States since NBA players were allowed on the roster in 1992.

The US team next played Greece, which, as host nation, had been given an automatic berth. Again the US struggled, connecting on just three of 21 three-point shots, but managing to come from behind for a 77-71 win. The Americans committed 41 turnovers during their first two games. The US won its next game against Australia 89-79, but then faced Lithuania, the team that had come so close to knocking the US out in the semifinals in 2000. This time, Lithuanian point guard Šarūnas Jasikevičius made up for his 2000 missed shot, scoring 12 points in less than two minutes to give Lithuania a 93-87 lead with 56 seconds left. They held on to win 94-90 and give the US their second loss of the tournament—an Olympic first.

In a key match-up in Group A, Argentina faced Serbia and Montenegro, who (then playing as Yugoslavia) had beaten them in overtime in the 2002 world championship final. This time the Argentines won the match 83-82 on a last-second, off-balance three-point bank shot by Manu Ginobili. The reigning world champions, Serbia gave their worst Olympic performance ever, finishing last in their group.

Having survived the round robin, the US earned an important 102-94 quarterfinal win over previously undefeated Spain. In the semifinals, the Americans faced Argentina, which, at the 2002 World Championships, had handed the United States its first loss in ten years. Argentina led 43-38 at the half, then came out strong in the third quarter with Ginobili scoring nine points in the less than three minutes. The Argentines widened their lead to 70-57 by the end of the third quarter and the Americans were unable to close the gap, losing 89-81 and failing to make the final for the first time since 1988. The other semifinal match was also a major upset. Lithuania, which had not yet lost a game, faced an Italian team with no NBA players on the roster. Italy stayed in the game by capitalizing on its three-point shots, hitting 64 percent from outside the arc to make 18 three-pointers, and earning a place in the final with a 100-91 win.

Argentina played in the final without their starting forward, Fabricio Oberto, who broke his right arm during the semifinal victory over the United States. Argentina started with a solid lead, opening a 34-22 gap before Italy rallied back to a two-point deficit, 41-43, at halftime. Back-to-back three-pointers by Matteo Soragna and Gianmarco Pozzecco gave Italy a 54-51 advantage with 4:41 left in the third quarter, but Argentina came back with nine unanswered points, taking a 60-54 lead into the fourth quarter. With 9:09 left in the game, Italy's Massimo Bulleri scored five consecutive points to put Italy ahead 61-59 but Argentina's Alejandro Montecchio responded with two 3-pointers and Scola added four points during a 10-1 run, pushing Argentina ahead 71-60 with 5:25 to play. The Argentines expanded their lead to complete a 84-69 victory. It was Argentina's first medal of any kind in Olympic basketball.

For security reasons, the US men's and women's basketball teams were housed in suites on the *Queen Mary II*, anchored in the Port of Piraeus. Security measures for the port included 24-hour police and open-sea surveillance, continuous coast guard patrols, and permanent submarine control systems and seabed detectors.

2008 Beijing T: 12, N: 12, D: 8.24.

	W	L	PF	PA
1. USA	8	0	850	627
2. SPA	6	2	688	632
3. ARG	6	2	673	615
4. LIT	5	3	680	646
5. GRE	3	3	493	455
6. CRO	3	3	458	452
7. AUS	3	3	542	521
8. CHN	2	4	434	494

Final: USA 118-107 SPA
3rd Place: ARG 87-75 LTU

1. USA—Carmelo Anthony, Carlos Boozer, Chris Bosh, Kobe Bryant, Dwight Howard, LeBron James, Jason Kidd, Chris Paul, Tayshaun Prince, Michael Redd, Dwyane Wade Jr., Deron Williams
2. SPA—José Manuel Calderón Borallo, Rudy Fernández Farrés, Jorge Garbajosa Chaparro, Marc Gasol Sáez, Pau Gasol Sáez, Carlos Jiménez Sánchez, Raúl López Molist, Álex Mumbrú Murcia, Juan Carlos Navarro Feijoo, Felipe Reyes Cabanas, Berni Rodríguez Arias, Ricky Rubio Vives

3. ARG—Carlos Delfino, Manu Ginóbili, Román González, Juan Pedro Gutiérrez Lanas, Leonardo Gutiérrez, Federico Kammerichs, Andrés Nocioni, Fabricio Oberto, Antonio Porta Pernigotti, Pablo Prigioni, Paolo Quinteros, Luis Scola Balvoa
4. LIT— Simas Jasaitis, Šar nas Jasikevičius, Robertas Javtokas, Rimantas Kauk nas, Linas Kleiza, Darjuš Lavrinovič, Kšištof Lavrinovič, Mindaugas Lukauskis, Jonas Mačiulis, Marijonas Petravičius, Marius Prekevičius, Ram nas Šiškauskas
5. GRE— Ioannis Bourousis, Dimitrios Diamantidis, Antonios Fotsis, Andreas Glyniadakis, Theodoros Papaloukas, Michail Pelekanos, Georgios Printezis, Sofoklis Schortsanitis, Vasileios Spanoulis, Kostas Tsartsaris, Panagiotis Vasilopoulos, Nikos Zisis
6. CRO— Marko Banić, Stanko Barać, Davor Kus, Krešimir Lončar, Sandro Nicević, Zoran Planinić, Marko Popović, Nikola Prkačin, Marin Rozić, Damjan Rudež, Marko Tomas, Roko-Leni Ukić
7. AUS— David Andersen, Chris Anstey, David Barlow, Andrew Bogut, C. J. Bruton, Joe Ingles, Patrick Mills, Brad Newley, Matt Nielsen, Shawn Redhage, Glen Saville, Mark Worthington
8. CHN— Chen Jianghua, Du Feng, Li Nan, Liu Wei, Sun Yue, Wang Lei, Wang Shipeng, Wang Zhizhi, Yao Ming, Yi Jianlian, Zhang Qinpeng, Zhu Fangyu

After a disappointing bronze-medal finish in Athens, the United States overhauled its method of building an Olympic basketball team, hiring a new managing director, Jerry Colangelo, and bringing on Duke University Hall of Famer and West Point graduate Mike Krzyzewski as the head coach. In early 2006 the team approached some thirty players, asking for a three-year commitment to play on the US national team in order to build team chemistry.

The result was the so-called "The Redeem Team". With an average age of 26 years 1 month, the core of the team included three rookie members from the Athens 2004 squad: LeBron James, Dwyane Wade and Carmelo Anthony, all of whom had been drafted into the NBA in 2003. The team also included several more experienced players, including 10-time NBA All-Star and recent MVP (recipient of the NBA's Most Valuable Player award) Kobe Bryant and 35-year-old Jason Kidd, who had earned a gold medal as part of the 2000 US team.

The group played together regularly over the next three years. In 2006 they competed at the World Championships in Saitama, Japan, losing 101-95 to eventual silver medalists Greece in the semi-finals before beating Argentina 96-81 to finish third. The following year they qualified for the Olympics by sweeping through the Tournament of the Americas, winning all 10 of their games by an average margin of nearly 40 points.

Despite the new energy and dedication, the US faced a formidable field in Beijing, including reigning world champion Spain, whose squad included Kobe Bryant's Los Angeles Lakers' teammate, 7-foot (2.13-meter) center Pau Gasol, the leading scorer at the 2004 Olympics, and 17-year-old rising star Ricky Rubio. Defending Olympic champions Argentina, led by three-time NBA championship winner Manu Ginóbili, were also considered strong contenders, despite having finished fourth at the 2006 world championships.

The US opened preliminary play against China, who were led by 7-ft 6-in (2.29-meter) center Yao Ming, the tallest player in the tournament and one of the tallest men ever to play in the NBA. Yao was nearly two feet (60 centimeters) long at birth and was a full 6 feet (1.83 meters) tall by the time he was nine. It was Yao's first game after a stress fracture in his left foot had ended his season in February, and he opened the scoring with a perfect 3-point shot. The Chinese team fought to a 29-29 tie with six minutes left in the first half before the US responded with a 16-3 run capped by dunks from James, Bryant and Chris Bosh. By the second half the US was clearly dominant, powering to a 101-70 rout.

The Americans next faced Angola, the underdogs of the tournament. The two teams had met three times in the past four Olympics, with the US winning by an average margin of nearly 47 points. This time the scrappy Angolan team, cheered on by a handful of raucous fans, held their own, trailing by just 7 points at one point in the second quarter and outscoring the US 23-16 in the fourth quarter. Despite the 97-76 loss, Angola remained upbeat. As forward Joaquim Gomes put it, "losing by 20 points is not bad at all."

The first real challenge for the US was against Greece. At the 2006 world championships the Greeks had trounced the US in the semifinals, executing an efficient pick-and-roll offense to shoot 63%. This time the US played a strong defensive game, preventing the Greeks from making any 3-point shots in the first half and building a 19-point lead before the break. The Americans then maintained the advantage, eventually winning 92-69.

By the time they faced Spain for the first time, the US team was on fire. They hit seven of their first 10 attempts beyond the arc and led 61-45 by the half. An 11-3 surge to open the second half increased the advantage to 72-48, and it reached 119-82 by the end of the game. The US closed pool play with a 106-57 victory over Germany, for a clean record, an average margin of victory of 32.2 points and an average of 103 points per game. Spain were second in the group, having managed a 85-75 overtime win over China.

Lithuania led the other round-robin group, beating Argentina 79-75 and Croatia 86-73 before losing 106-75 to Australia. Argentina finished second in the group with just the single loss to Lithuania, while Croatia and Australia advanced with two losses apiece.

The most exciting quarter-final match by far was a tense nail-biter between Argentina and Greece that saw Greece pull within two points in the last 30 seconds, although Argentina held on for an 80-78 win. The US advanced to the semi-finals with a 116-85 rout of Australia. The Australians, led by Aboriginal point guard Patrick Mills, maintained a narrow 25-24 lead after the first quarter until the Americans came back with 14 unanswered points after the break. Bryant led US scoring with 25 points, his highest total of the tournament. Lithuania and Spain also advanced easily into the semis, beating China 94-68 and Croatia 72-59, respectively.

In the semi-finals, the US faced defending Olympic champions Argentina, who had beaten them 89-81 in the Athens semi-finals. This time, the US built a 21-4 lead in the first quarter. Six and a half minutes into play, Argentina's leading scorer, Ginóbili, re-injured his left ankle and was forced to withdraw. Despite the setback, Argentina put up a tough fight, cutting a 21-point deficit to just six points before the half, after which the US powered back to a 101-81 victory.

Spain reached the final after a close game against Lithuania in which neither team held more than an eight-point lead. A three-pointer by Kšištof Lavrinovič gave Lithuania a 74-73 lead with seven minutes remaining, but Spain's Rudy Fernández answered with another three-pointer to retake the lead, which his team never relinquished.

Argentina, playing without Ginóbili, faced Lithuania in the bronze-medal match. After an evenly matched first quarter, Argentina sank six three-pointers in the second quarter to pull ahead 46-34 and never trailed.

The final was even more exciting, with Spain making seven of their first nine shots and maintaining the lead for much of the first quarter. The US came back to build a 14-point lead at one point in the first half, but Spain narrowed it to only 69-61 at the break after shooting a 61% from the floor. With 2:22 minutes left in the final quarter, Spain closed the gap to four points on a 3-pointer from Carlos Jiménez, but late 3-pointers by Dwyane Wade and Kobe Bryant held off the Spanish assault and clinched the gold medal for the US.

WOMEN

1896–1972 not held

1976 Montreal T: 6, N: 6, D: 7.27.

	W	L	PF	PA
1. SOV	5	0	504	346
2. USA	3	2	415	417
3. BUL	3	2	365	377
4. CZE	2	3	351	359
5. JPN	2	3	405	400
6. CAN	0	5	336	477

1. SOV—Angelė Rupšienė, Tatyana Zakharova, Raisa Kurvyakova, Olga Barisheva, Tatyana Ovechkina, Nadezhda Shuvayeva, Uljana Semjonova, Nadezhda Zakharova, Nelly Feriabnikova, Olga Sukharnova, Tamara Dauinene, Natalya Klimova
2. USA—Cindy Brogdon, Susan Rojcewicz, Ann Meyers, Lusia Harris, Nancy Dunkle, Charlotte Lewis, Nancy Lieberman, Gail Marquis, Patricia Roberts, Mary Anne O'Connor, Patricia Head, Julienne Simpson
3. BUL—Nadka Golcheva, Penka Metodieva, Petkana Makaveyeva, Snezhana Mihailova, Krassima Gyurova, Krassimira Bogdanova, Todorka Yordanova, Diana Dilova, Margarita Shturkelova, Mania Stoyanova, Girgina Skerlatova, Penka Stoyanova
4. CZE—Ludmila Kraliková, Dana Ptáčková, Pavla Davidová, Ludmila Chmeliková, Martina Balaštiková, Ivana Kořínková, Marta Pechová, Hana Doušová, Božena Miklošovičová
5. JPN—Kazuko Kadoya, Kimi Wakitashiro, Mieko Fukui, Miyako Otsuka, Miho Matsuoka, Kazuyo Hayashida, Teruko Miyamoto, Keiko Namai, Reiko Aonuma, Sachiyo Yamamoto, Misako Satake
6. CAN—Joyce Douthwright, Joanne Sargent, Anne Hurley, Christine Critelli, Beverly Bland, Coleen Dufresne, Sheila Strike, Sylvia Sweeney, Carol Turney, Donna Hobin, Angela Johnson, Beverly Barnes

The Soviet women's basketball team had not lost a game for five years and was undefeated in international tournament competition since 1958. Not surprisingly, they won the Olympic gold medal with ease. When the Americans boasted that they would upset the Soviets, Soviet coach Lydia Alekseyeva pledged that their match would be "a punitive expedition." The USSR won 112-77. High scorer for the Soviets was 6-foot 10½-inch, 284-pound Uljana Semjonova of Riga, who suffered from a rare pituitary gland condition called gigantism. Semjonova averaged 19.4 points and 12.4 rebounds a game, despite the fact that she spent more than half the time on the bench. The United States was awarded second place by virtue of its 95-79 victory over Bulgaria.

Just how big was Semjonova? United States' player Nancy Lieberman recalled one non-Olympic game in which 6-foot 8-inch Anne Donovan was assigned to guard the Latvian giant. "I'd have the ball on the point," said Lieberman, "and Anne would get position on Uljana. But I couldn't see Anne. I'd dribble the ball and yell, 'Anne, where are you?' and I'd hear this voice, 'I'm back here.'"

Ten years after the Montreal Olympics, Nancy

Lieberman became the first woman to play in a men's professional league when she took the court for the Springfield, Mass., Fame of the United States Basketball League.

1980 Moscow T: 6, N: 6, D: 7.30.

	W	L	PF	PA
1. SOV	6	0	657	389
2. BUL	4	2	513	509
3. YUG	4	2	424	429
4. HUN	2	4	409	475
5. CUB	1	4	346	403
6. ITA	0	5	308	452

Final: SOV 104-73 BUL
3rd Place: YUG 68-65 HUN

1. SOV—Angelé Rupšien, Lyubov Sharmay, Vida Beselien, Olga Korosteleva, Tatyana Ovechkina, Nadezhda Olkhova [Shuvayeva], Uljana Semjonova, Lyudmila Rogozina, Nelly Feriabnikova, Olga Sukharnova, Tatyana Nadyrova [Zakharova], Tatyana Ivinskaya
2. BUL—Nadka Golcheva, Penka Metodieva, Petkana Makaveyeva, Snezhana Mihailova, Vania Denmandzhieva, Krassimira Bogdanova, Angelina Mihailova, Diana Brainova [Dilova], Eviadia Zakatanova, Kostadinka Radkova, Silvia Germanova, Penka Stoyanova
3. YUG—Vera Djurašković, Mersada Bećirspahić, Jelica Komnenović, Mira Bjedov, Vukica Mitić, Sanja Ožegović, Sofija Pekić, Marija Tonković, Zorica Djurković, Vesna Despotović, Biljana Majstorović, Jasmina Perazić
4. HUN—Éva Gulyás, Ágnes Németh, Ilona Kovács, Györgyi Vertetics, Zsuzsa Boksay, Ione Lörincz, Katalin Szuchy, Magda Gulyás, Ildikó Gulyás, Judit Medgyesi, Lenke Kiss, Erzsébet Szentesi
5. CUB—Leonor Borrell Hernández, Nancy Aties Sánchez, Barbara Becquer Rivero, Maria Moret Hernández, Inocenta Corbea Aguirre, Caridad Despaigne Savig, Matilde Charro Mendoza, Maria de Los Santos Iglesias, Sonia de La Paz Galan, Virginia Pérez Viart, Margarita Skeet Quiñones, Vicenta Salom Smith
6. ITA—Chiara Guzzonato, Nunziata Sernadimigni, Roberta Faccin, Lidia Gorlin, Emanuela Silimbani, Wanda Sandon, Bianca Rossi, Antoinetta Baistrocchi, Marinella Draghetti, Rosanna Vergnano, Mariangela Piancastelli, Orietta Grossi

The USSR had an even easier time than they had had in 1976, winning all their games by 31 points or more. Their average score was 109.5 to 65. Semjonova, now 27 years old, was high scorer in the tournament, with 21.8 points a game. She also averaged 12.5 rebounds. In fact, Semjonova and her 6-foot 3-inch teammate Olga Sukharnova pulled down more rebounds than the entire 12-woman Italian team.

1984 Los Angeles-Inglewood T: 6, N: 6, D: 8.7.

	W	L	PF	PA
1. USA	6	0	516	320
2. KOR	4	2	347	387
3. CHN	3	3	381	405
4. CAN	2	4	370	398
5. AUS	1	4	267	317
5. YUG	1	4	293	347

Final: USA 85-55 KOR
3rd Place: CHN 63-57 CAN

1. USA—Teresa Edwards, Lea Henry, Lynette Woodard, Anne Donovan, Cathy Boswell, Cheryl Miller, Janice Lawrence, Cindy Noble, Kim Mulkey, Denise Curry, Pamela McGee, Carol Menken-Schaudt
2. KOR—Choi Aei-young, Kim Eun-sook, Lee Hyung-sook, Choi Kyung-hee, Lee Mi-ja, Moon Kyung-ja, Kim Hwa-soon, Jeong Myung-hee, Kim Young-hee, Sung Jung-a, Park Chan-sook
3. CHN—Chen Yuefang, Li Xiaoqin, Ba Yan, Song Xiaobo, Qui Chen, Wang Jun, Xiu Lijuan, Zheng Haixia, Cong Xuedi, Zhang Hui, Liu Qing, Zhang Yueqin
4. CAN—Lynn Polson, Tracie McAra, Anna Pendergast, Debbie Huband, Carol Jane Sealey, Alison Lang, Bev Smith, Sylvia Sweeney, Candi Clarkson-Lohr, Toni Kordic, Andrea Blackwell, Misty Thomas
5. AUS—Robyn Maher, Bronwyn Marshall, Jennifer Cheesman, Patricia Cockrem, Donna Quinn, Patricia Mickan, Julie Nykiel, Kathryn Foster, Marina Moffa, Karen Dalton, Wendy Laidlaw, Susanna Geh
5. YUG—Sanja Ožegović, Slavica Suka, Jelica Komnenović, Zagorka Počeković, Stojna Vangeloyska, Slavica Pecikoza, Sladjana Golić, Polona Dornik, Biljana Majstorović, Jasmina Perazić, Gvetana Dekleva, Marija Uzelac

In 1982 the Soviet women's 24-year winning streak was finally broken by a US team that beat them 85–83 in Budapest. The following year the Soviets came back to score a two-point victory of their own in the final of the world championships. The eagerly anticipated Olympic showdown between the two squads was prevented by the Soviet boycott.

The US team cruised through the Olympic tournament, winning all of their games by 28 points or more. Cheryl Miller, averaging 16.5 points and 7 rebounds per game, led the team in scoring, rebounding, steals and assists. Another US star, Lynette Woodard, later became the first female member of the Harlem Globetrotters.

As for the big US–USSR showdown, it finally took place two years later in Moscow, when the American women crushed the Soviets 83-60 in the finals of the Goodwill Games. Five weeks later, again in Moscow, the two teams met in the title match of the world championships, and again the US won easily, 108-88.

1988 Seoul T: 8, N: 8, D: 9.29.

	W	L	PF	PA
1. USA	5	0	461	392
2. YUG	3	2	326	344
3. SOV	3	2	364	343
4. AUS	2	3	287	321
5. BUL	3	2	400	393
6. CHN	2	3	371	411
7. KOR	2	3	416	375
8. CZE	0	5	339	382

Final: USA 77-70 YUG
3rd Place: SOV 68-53 AUS
5th Place: BUL 102-74 CHN
7th Place: KOR 77-59 CZE

1. USA—Teresa Edwards, Mary Ethridge, Cynthia Brown, Anne Donovan, Teresa Weatherspoon, Bridgette Gordon, Victoria Bullett, Andrea Lloyd, Katrina McClain, Jennifer Gillom, Cynthia Cooper, Suzanne McConnell

2. YUG—Stojna Vangeloyska, Mara Lakić, Žana Lelas, Eleonora Vild, Kornelija Kvesić, Danira Nakić, Sladjana Golić, Polona Dornik, Razija Mujanović, Vesna Bajkuša, Andjelija Arbutina, Bojana Milošević
3. SOV—Olga Yevkova, Irina Gerlits, Olesya Barel, Irina Sumnikova, Olga Buryakina, Olga Yakovleva, Irina Minkh, Aleksandra Leonova, Yelena Khudashova, Vitalija Tuomaite, Galina Savitskaya, Natalya Zasulskaya
4. AUS—Robyn Maher, Jennifer Cheesman, Michele Timms, Donna Brown, Patricia Mickan, Julie Nykiel, Debra Slimmon, Marina Moffa, Karen Dalton, Shelley Gorman, Maree White
5. BUL—Nina Khadzhiyankova, Larissa Spasova, Mariana Naydenova, Tzonka Vaysilova, Vania Dermendzhieva, Sonia Dragomirova, Radmila Vasileva, Kostadinka Radkova, Yevladiya Stefanova, Madlen Staneva, Polina Tzekova, Mariana Chobanova
6. CHN—Han Qingling, Ling Guang, Li Xiaoqin, Zhao Wei, Peng Ping, Zheng Haixia, Cong Xuedi, Xue Cuilan, Liu Qing, Xu Chunmei
7. KOR—Lee Keum-jin, Kim Mal-lyun, Choi Kyung-hee, Lee Hyung-sook, Park Chan-mi, Woo Eun-kyung, Chung Mi-kyung, Kim Hwa-soon, Kim Hye-youn, Park Chan-sook, Sung Jung-a, Cho Mun-joo
8. CZE—Svatava Kysilková, Alena Kašová, Eva Kalužáková, Ivana Nováková, Zuzana Hájková, Anna Janoštinová, Zora Brziaková, Hana Zarevúcka, Erika Dobrovičová, Eva Křižová, Irma Valová, Eva Berková

The victorious US team was led by playmaker Teresa Edwards, who averaged 16.6 points a game, and her former University of Georgia teammate, Katrina McClain, who led the Americans in scoring (17.6 points a game) and rebounding (10.4 per game).

1992 Barcelona-Badalona T: 8, N: 8, D: 8.7.

	W	L	PF	PA
1. SOV	4	1	399	361
2. CHN	3	2	380	372
3. USA	4	1	479	334
4. CUB	3	2	390	427
5. SPA	3	2	332	376
6. CZE	1	4	315	363
7. BRA	2	3	385	398
8. ITA	0	5	353	402

Final: SOV 76-66 CHN
3rd Place: USA 88-74 CUB
5th Place: SPA 59-58 CZE
7th Place: BRA 86-83 ITA

1. SOV—Yelena Zhirko, Yelena Baranova, Irina Gerlits, Yelena Tornikidu, Yelena Shvaybovich, Marina Tkachenko, Irina Minkh, Yelena Khudashova, Irina Sumnikova, Elen Bunatiants, Natalya Zasulskaya, Svetlana Zaboluyeva
2. CHN—Cong Xuedi, Li Xin, Liu Jun, Wang Fang, Zheng Dongmei, He Jun, Peng Ping, Zhen Haixia, Zheng Xiulin, Li Dongmei, Liu Quing, Zhan Shuping
3. USA—Teresa Edwards, Daedra Charles, Clarissa Davis, Tammy Jackson, Teresa Weatherspoon, Vickie Orr, Victoria Bullett, Carolyn Jones, Katrina McClain, Medina Dixon, Cynthia Cooper, Suzanne McConnell
4. CUB—Leonor Borrel Hernández, Ana Hernández Álvárez, Olga Vigil Gómez, Grisel Herrera Méndez, Biosotis Lagnó Frómeta, Judith Aguila Hernández, María León Molinet, Yamilet Martínez Calderón, Dalia Henry Hernández, Lissett Castillo Iglesias, Regla Hernández Buides, Milayda Enrique Parrado
5. SPA—Patrica Hernández Arencibia, Carolina Mújica Vallejo, Blanca Ares Torres, Pilar Alonso López, Mónica Pulgar Machado, Margarita Geuer Draeger, Almudena Vara Rivera, Ana Álvaro Bascuñana, Mónica Messa López, Marina Ferragut Castillo, Elisabeth Cebrián Scheurer, Carlota Castrejana Fernández
6. CZE—Iveta Bieliková, Martina Liptáková, Anna Janoštinová, Eva Nemcová, Andrea Chupíková, Eva Antalecová, Renata Hiráková, Adriana Chamajová, Erika Buriánová, Kamila Vodicková, Milena Razgova, Eva Berková
7. BRA—Hortência Marcari Oliva, Helen Santos Luz, Nádia De Lima, Vania Souza, Maria Paula Silva, Janeth Arcain, Adriana Santos, Marta De Souza Sobral, Ruth Souza, Maria Bertolotti, Joycenara Batista, Simone Pontello
8. ITA—Elena Paparazzo, Monica Bastiani, Mara Fullin, Stefania Salvemini, Anna Costalunga, Francesca Rossi, Angela Arcangeli, Catarina Pollini, Stefania Stanzani, Silvia Todeschini, Giuseppina Tufano, Stefania Passaro

Between 1982 and 1991 the United States' women won 42 straight games at international tournaments. However, at the Pan American Games in Havana the Americans were beaten by both Brazil and Cuba. Still, at the Barcelona Olympics the United States team looked unbeatable, crushing their three opponents in the qualifying pool by an average of 45.7 points. Meanwhile, the team from the former Soviet Union looked sluggish, even losing their opening game against Cuba 91-89. But in the semifinals, the ex-Soviets stunned the Americans 79-73. The other semifinal was won by the dark-horse team from China, who, surprisingly, overwhelmed the Cubans 109-70. In the final, China led 16–14 after six minutes. Then the ex Soviets scored 16 points in a row and never relinquished the lead again. The victors were led by 6-foot 2½-inch power forward Natalya Zasulskaya, who averaged 17.4 points and 8.6 rebounds a game. She also led the tournament in fouls received with 7.2 per game. Zasulskaya was from Lithuania, but chose to continue playing with her teammates from the former Soviet republics so that she could take part in the Olympics.

1996 Atlanta T: 12, N: 12, D: 8.4.

	W	L	PF	PA
1. USA	8	0	820	590
2. BRA	7	1	693	600
3. AUS	5	3	580	538
4. UKR	4	4	529	555
5. RUS	6	2	619	559
6. CUB	3	5	586	639
7. JPN	3	5	608	653
8. ITA	3	5	519	527

Final: USA 111-87 BRA
3rd Place: AUS 66-56 UKR
5th Place: RUS 91-74 CUB
7th Place: JPN 81-69 ITA

1. USA—Teresa Edwards, Ruthie Bolton, Sheryl Swoopes, Lisa Leslie, Katrina McClain, Dawn Staley, Jennifer Azzi, Carla McGhee, Katy Steding, Rebecca Lobo, Venus Lacey, Nikki McCray

2. BRA—Hortência Marcari Oliva, Maria Paula Silva, Janeth Arcain, Marta De Souza Sobral, Alessandra Oliveira, Maria "Branca" Silva, Adriana Santos, Leila Sobral, Roseli Gustavo, Silvia "Silvinha" Luz, Cintia Santos, Claudia Maria Pastor
3. AUS—Carla Boyd, Michelle Brogan, Sandra Brondello, Michelle Chandler, Allison Cook, Trisha Fallon, Robyn Maher, Fiona Robinson, Shelley Sandie, Rachael Sporn, Michele Timms, Jenny Whittle
4. UKR—Ruslana Kyrytchenko, Viktoriya Burenok, Yelena Zhirko, Marina Tkachenko, Lyudmila Nazarenko, Yelena Oberemko, Viktorya Paradiz, Viktoya Leleka, Oksana Dovgalyuk, Diana Sadovnikova, Natalya Silyanova, Olga Shylakova
5. RUS—Yevgenia Nikonova, Lyudmila Konovalova, Irina Rutkovskaya, Mariya Stepanova, Yelena Baranova, Natalya Svinukhova, Svetlana Kuznetsova, Oksana Zakaulyuzhanaya, Irina Sumnikova, Elen Shakirova [Bunatiants], Yelena Pshikova, Svetlana Antipova
6. CUB—Tania Seino Borbón, Maria León Molinet, Yamilé Martínez García, Delia Henry Hernández, Milayda Enríquez Parrado, Lisdeivys Víctores Pompa, Olga Vigil Gómez, Grisel Herrera Méndez, Biosotis Lagnó Frómeta, Judith Águila Hernández, Cariola Hechevarría García, Gertrudis Gomez
7. JPN—Aki Ichijo, Chikako Murakami, Taeko Oyama, Mikiko Hagiwara, Kikuko Mikawa, Kagari Yamada, Takako Kato, Yuka Harada, Akemi Okazato, Mayumi Kawasaki, Mutsuko Nagata, Noriko Hamaguchi
8. ITA—Susann Bonfiglio, Mara Fullin, Nicoletta Caselin, Catarina Pollini, Giuseppina Tufano, Stefania Zanussi, Elena Paparazzo, Valentina Gardellin, Viviana Ballabio, Marta Rezoagli, Morenza Arnetoli, Novella Schiesaro

After losing to the Soviet Union in the semifinals of the 1992 Olympics and to Brazil in the final of the 1994 world championship, the US formed a permanent national squad in 1995. During the 8½ months preceding the 1996 Olympics, the US team played and won 52 games including 25 against other national teams. In Atlanta they were never seriously challenged, winning every game by at least 12 points. Lisa Leslie averaged 19.5 points and 7.2 rebounds per game, Katrina McClain 14.1 points and 8.2 rebounds. Teresa Edwards, playing in her fourth Olympics, averaged 8 assists per game.

2000 Sydney T: 12, N: 12, D: 9.30.

	W	L	PF	PA
1. USA	8	0	648	474
2. AUS	7	1	588	440
3. BRA	4	4	562	527
4. KOR	4	4	588	578
5. FRA	5	2	468	414
6. RUS	3	4	524	464
7. SLV	3	4	401	407
8. POL	3	4	432	479

Final: USA 76-54 AUS
3rd Place: BRA 84-73 KOR
5th Place: FRA 71-59 RUS
7th Place: SLV 64-57 POL

1. USA—Ruthie Bolton-Holifield, Teresa Edwards, Yolanda Griffith, Lisa Leslie, Nikki McCray, Delisha Milton, Katie Smith, Dawn Staley, Sheryl Swoopes, Natalie Williams, Kara Wolters
2. AUS—Carla Boyd, Sandra Brondello, Trisha Fallon, Michelle Griffiths, Kristi Harrower, Jo Hill, Lauren Jackson, Annie la Fleur, Shelly Sandie, Rachael Sporn, Michele Timms, Jenny Whittle
3. BRA—Janeth Arcain, Ilisaine David, Lilian Gonçalves, Helen Cristina Luz, Silvia Andrea Luz, Claudia Neves, Alessandra Oliveira, Adriana Pinto, Cintia Santos, Adriana Santos, Kelly Santos, Marta Sobral
4. KOR—Chun Joo-weon, Chung Eun-soon, Jang Sun-hyoung, Jung Sun-min, Kang Ji-sook, Kim Ji-yoon, Lee Eun-ju, Lee Jong-ae, Lee Mi-sun, Park Jung-eun, Wang Su-jin, Yang Jung-ok
5. FRA—Nicole Antibe, Isabelle Fijalkowski, Edwige Lawson, Sandra le Drean, Nathalie Lesdema, Catherine Melain, Laetitia Moussard, Audrey Sauret, Laure Savasta, Yannick Souvre, Dominique Tonnerre, Stephanie Vivenot
6. RUS—Svetlana Abrosimova, Anna Arkhipova, Yelena Shakirova, Yelena Khudashova, Yevgenia Nikonova, Irina Rutkkovskaya, Irina Sumnikova, Mariya Stepanova, Natalya Zasulskaya, Yelena Pshikova, Olga Artekhina
7. SLV—Slavka Frniaková, Martina Godalyová, Renata Hiraková, Dagmar Hutková, Marcela Kalistová, Anna Kotocová, Alena Kovacová, Livia Libicová, Jana Lichnerová, Martina Luptakková, Katařina Poláková, Zužana Zirková
8. POL—Dorota Bukowska, Joanna Cupryś, Patrycja Czepiec, Katarzyna Dydek, Malgorzata Dydek, Edyta Koryzna, Ilona Mądra, Beata Predehl, Krystyna Szymańska-Lara, Elżbieta Trześniewska, Anna Wielebnowska, Sylwia Wlaźlak

The United States won with relative ease, averaging 81 points per game and giving up 59.3 points. They received their stiffest challenge from Russia during pool play. The Russians led twice by eight points before the US pulled away to win 88-77. In the knockout stage, the Americans beat Slovakia 58-43 in the quarterfinals and South Korea 78-65 in the semifinals. The final was held before a raucous hometown crowd that also included the US men's basketball team, the Australian swimming team and the US women's soccer team. The game itself was anticlimatic, as the Americans, at the top of their game, led by 13 points at halftime and won by 22 points. The game did have an unusual highlight: in the closing minutes, the 6-foot 5-inch stars of the two teams, Lisa Leslie of the US and Lauren Jackson of Australia, clashed while scrambling for the ball and Jackson came away with a strange object in her hand . . . Leslie's ponytail hair extension. Jackson dropped it on the floor. Leslie picked it up and threw it into the crowd, where it hit a photographer in the face. For the entire tournament, Leslie averaged 15.8 points per game, as well as almost 8 rebounds, while Sheryl Swoopes scored 13.4 points per game and Yolanda Griffith averaged 11.5 points and 8.75 rebounds. After the final ended and both teams left the court, one American player stayed behind. Teresa Edwards, having completed the final game of her fifth Olympics, sat down in the center of the court and absorbed the moment.

The bronze game, held just before the gold medal contest, was an exciting one in which Brazil, after trailing the South Koreans throughout most of the game, tied them in regulation and then won in overtime.

2004 Athens T: 12, N: 12, D: 8.28.

	W	L	PF	PA
1. USA	8	0	672	482
2. AUS	7	1	663	517
3. RUS	6	2	592	510
4. BRA	4	4	634	583
5. CZE	4	3	536	513
6. SPA	4	3	499	480
7. GRE	3	4	512	577
8. NZL	2	5	459	595

Final: USA 74-63 AUS
3rd Place: RUS 71-62 BRA
5th Place: CZE 79-68 SPA
7th Place: GRE 87-83 NZL

1. USA—Sue Bird, Swintayla "Swin" Cash, Tamika Catchings, Yolanda Griffith, Shannon Johnson, Lisa Leslie, Ruth Riley, Katie Smith, Dawn Staley, Sheryl Swoopes, Diana Taurasi, Tina Thompson
2. AUS—Suzy Batkovic, Sandra Brondello, Trish Fallon, Kristi Harrower, Lauren Jackson, Natalie Porter, Alicia Poto, Belinda Snell, Rachael Sporn, Laura Summerton, Penny Taylor, Allison Tranquilli
3. RUS—Anna Arkhipova, Olga Arteshina, Yelena Baranova, Diyana Gustilina, Mariya Kalmykova, Yelena Karpova, Ilona Korstin, Irina Osipova, Oksana Rakhmatulina, Tatyana Shchyegoleva, Mariya Stepanova, Natalya Vodopyanova
4. BRA—Janeth Arcain, Karla Cristina da Costa, Kelly Santos, Vivian Lopes, Helen Cristina Luz, Iziane Marques, Alessandra de Oliveira, Adriana "Adrianinha" Pinto, Sílvia Cristina Rocha, Cíntia "Cíntia Tuiú" dos Santos, Leila Sobral, Érika de Souza
5. CZE—Irena Borecká, Romana Hamzová, Michala Hartigová, Zuzana Klimešová, Petra Kulichová, Hana Machová, Michaela Pavlíčková, Michaela Uhrová, Ivana Večeřová, Jana Veselá, Eva Vítečková, Ivana Vořačková
6. SPA—Elisabeth "Elisa" Aguilar Lopez, Sonia Blanco Bernal, Elisabeth Cebrián Scheurer, Marta Fernández Farres, Marina Ferragut Castillo, Begoña García Piñero, Nuria Martínez Prat, Laia Palau Altés, María Lucila Pascua Suárez, Ingrid Pons Molina, Rosa Sánchez Luján, Amaya Valdemoro Madariaga
7. GRE—Aikaterini Deli, Dimitra Kalentzou, Tatiana Kavvadia, Athena Khristoforaki, Sofia Klingopoulou, Anastasia Kostaki, Evanthia Maltsi, Maria Samoroukova, Polymnia Sarengou, Eirini Stakhtiari, Atalandi Tasouli, Eleni Vasileiou
8. NZL—Megan Compain, Rebecca Cotton, Gina Farmer, Sally Farmer, Aneka Kerr, Donna Loffhagen, Angela Marino, Julie Ofsoski, Jody Tini, Tania Brunton-Tupu, Leanne Walker, Kim Wielens

After breezing to the gold in 2000, the United States women's team went on to earn the 2002 world championship with a 79-74 win over Russia. Although they had only eleven days to prepare for the Athens Olympics, the US team included three starters, Dawn Staley (guard), Sheryl Swoopes (forward), and Lisa Leslie (center), who had played on the gold-medal teams in 1996 and 2000.

As expected, Australia and Russia dominated Group A, with the Australians cruising through the round robin with an 85-73 win over Nigeria, a 75-56 defeat of Russia, and solid wins over Japan (97-78), Greece (77-40) and Brazil (84-66). Meanwhile, Russia lost only the one game against Australia to finish second in the group. In Group B, the US steamrolled to a 99-47 win over New Zealand, and then beat the Czech Republic (80-61) and Korea (80-57) before shutting down China 100-62.

The quarterfinals saw few surprises, with the US, Australia and Russia all winning easily, the US 100-72 over Greece, Russia 70-49 over the Czech Republic, and Australia 94-55 over New Zealand. The US faced its first real challenge in its semifinal match against Russia. Early in the game, the Americans found their inside game neutralized by the 7-foot Russian center, Maria Stepanova. Forced to rely on outside shots, the American women shot poorly. Still, they led 37-33 at halftime and 51-44 after three quarters. Led by Oksana Pakhmatulina, the Russians closed the gap to 60-58 with 4:23 to play. Then Swoopes scored two baskets—her first of the game—in 37 seconds, and the Americans held on to win 66-62.

The final was a rematch of the 2000 final. As in Sydney, both the United States and Australia entered the game undefeated. The Americans led 29-26 after the first half. In the third quarter, the Australians quickly took the lead and were still ahead, 49-45 with 1:25 left in the quarter. Lauren Johnson scored at the buzzer to put the US ahead 52-50 going into the final quarter, and the Americans never trailed again. They opened the fourth quarter with a 9-1 run and went on to win 74-63.

2008 Beijing T: 12, N: 12, D: 8.23.

	W	L	PF	PA
1. USA	8	0	754	453
2. AUS	7	1	658	513
3. RUS	6	2	569	546
4. CHN	5	3	572	592
5. SPA	3	3	422	408
6. BLR	2	4	386	409
7. CZE	2	4	392	435
8. KOR	2	4	387	464

Final: USA 92-65 AUS
3rd Place: RUS 94-81 CHN

1. USA—Seimone Augustus, Sue Bird, Tamika Catchings, Sylvia Fowles, Kara Lawson, Lisa Leslie, DeLisha Milton-Jones, Candy Parker, Cappie Pondexter, Katie Smith, Diana Taurasi, Tina Thompson
2. AUS—Suzy Batkovic, Tully Bevilaqua, Rohanee Cox, Hollie Grima, Kristi Harrower, Lauren Jackson, Erin Phillips, Emma Randall, Jenni Screen, Belinda Snell, Laura Summerton, Penny Taylor
3. RUS—Svetlana Abrosimova, Becky Hammon, Marina Karpunina, Ilona Korstin, Marina Kuzina, Yekaterina Lisina, Irina Osipova, Oksana Rakhmatulina, Tatyana Shchyegoleva, Irina Sokolovskaya, Maria Stepanova, Nataliya Vodopyanova
4. CHN—Bian Lan, Chen Nan, Chen Xiaoli, Liu Dan, Miao Lijie, Shao Tingting, Song Xiaoyun, Sui Feifei, Zhang Hanlan, Zhang Wei, Zhang Xiaoni, Zhang Yu

5. SPA—Tamara Abalde Díaz, Elisa Aguilar López, Cindy Lima García, Nuria Martínez Prat, Anna Montañana Gimeno, Laura Nicholls González, Laia Palau Altés, Lucila Pascua Suárez, María Revuelto Sánchez Aguilera, Isabel Sánchez Fernández, Alba Torrens Salom, Amaya Valdemoro Madariaga
6. BLR—Nataliya Anufriyenko, Viktoriya Gasper, Marina Kress, Yelena Levchenko, Tatyana Likhtarovich, Nataliya Marchenko, Olga Masilenene, Olga Podobed, Yekaterina Snytina, Nataliya Trofimova, Tatyana Troina, Anastasiya Veremeyenko
7. CZE—Kate ina Elhotová, Michala Hartigová, Romana Hejdová, Petra Kulichová, Hana Horáková (Machová), Markéta Mokrošová, Edita Šujanová, Miloslava Svobodová, Michaela Uhrová, Ivana Veče ová, Jana Veselá, Eva Vítečková
8. KOR—Byeon Nyeon-ha, Choi Yun-a, Jin Mi-jeong, Sin Jeong-ja, Kim Jeong-eun, Kim Gye-ryeong, Kim Yeong-ok, Lee Jong-Ae, Lee Mi-seon, Park Jeong-eun, Jeong Seon-min

The US women's basketball team, led by three-time Olympic champion Lisa Leslie, was the overwhelming favorite in Beijing. In three Olympics and three world championships over a 12-year period, the Americans had a 50-1 record. Their only loss since 1994 was 75-68 to Russia in the semi-finals of the 2006 world championships in Brazil, in which they finished third.

The leading challenger for gold was expected to be the reigning world champions Australia, whose squad included arguably the best female basketball player in the world, Lauren Jackson. Jackson, a 6-ft 5-in (1.95-meter) center, was twice a WNBA MVP who had led scoring in two consecutive world championships. Just before the Olympics, the US had faced Australia in the final of the FIBA Diamond Ball, an Olympics warm-up tournament, managing a close 71-67 win.

Another potential contender was Russia, which had been extremely consistent over the previous six years, winning silver in the last three world championships and bronze at the 2004 Olympics. Led by 6ft 8-in (2.03-meter) Maria Stepanova, the squad also featured US-born Becky Hammon, a South Dakota native who caused some controversy by becoming a naturalized Russian citizen after being passed over for the US Olympic team.

There were no major surprises in pool play. Australia and Russia were drawn into the same pool and faced each other after three straight victories each. Australia won 75-55 and finished first in the group. The US cruised through Group B undefeated, winning by an average of 43 points; their closest match was a 96-60 rout of New Zealand.

Russia and the US met in the semi-finals. The US, looking to make up for their loss at the world championships, trailed 33-38 early in the third quarter, but then Tina Thompson kicked off a 12-point run. Hammon struggled with her shooting, scoring just three points, as the rest of the Russian team missed thirteen of fourteen 3-point attempts. The US pulled away to a 67-52 win and advanced to a gold-medal match meeting with Australia, who routed China 90-56 in the other semi-final.

In the bronze-medal match China kept pace with Russia through the first quarter, but then two 3-pointers from Shchyegoleva and a 21-7 run in the second quarter gave Russia a 22-point lead by the half. China shot 55 percent for the game, including 26 points from Chen Nan, but were unable to close the gap. Hammon led Russian scoring with 22 points, giving Russia a 94-81 victory and their second straight Olympic bronze.

The gold-medal match, like the 2000 and 2004 Olympic finals, pitted the United States against Australia. The Australians took the early lead, but a 24-4 run through the first and second quarters gave the Americans a 47-30 advantage at half time. Australia's Jackson contributed 20 points and 10 rebounds, but the team continued to struggle with their shooting, managing only 25% from the field throughout the game and giving the US an easy 92-65 victory.

The win brought the US Olympic streak to 33 games. Leslie joined former teammate Teresa Edwards as the second basketball player in Olympic history to earn four gold medals. The US won their eight games by an average margin of 37.6 points, the highest in women's Olympic history.

Chapter 6 **Boxing**

MEN

Light Flyweight—49 Kg
Flyweight—52 Kg
Bantamweight—56 Kg
Lightweight—60 Kg
Light Welterweight—64 Kg
Welterweight—69 Kg
Middleweight—75 Kg
Light Heavyweight—81 Kg
Heavyweight—91 Kg
Super Heavyweight—Unlimited Weight
Discontinued Event

WOMEN

Flyweight—48 Kg
Light Welterweight—57 Kg
Light Heavyweight—69 Kg

Richard Gunn, 1908

At 37, 1908 Featherweight champion Richard Gunn was the oldest boxing gold medalist in Olympic history.

Traditionally, amateur boxing matches have consisted of three three-minute rounds with one-minute breaks between rounds. In 2000 this format was changed to four two-minute rounds. In 2009 the IOC voted to reduce the number of men's events to ten and to introduce three women's events. Bouts take place in a square ring measuring 20 feet (6.1 meters) on each side. Olympic tournaments are single elimination and boxers are not seeded. For this reason it is possible—and indeed often happens—that the two best fighters in a division meet in their first match rather than in the final. Between 1904 and 1948, losing semifinalists faced off in a bronze medal fight; however, since 1952 both defeated semifinalists have been awarded bronze medals.

Several measures have been taken to protect the safety of the fighters, including the wearing of protective headgear. In addition, a boxer who has been knocked down or stunned may not resume fighting until the count of eight. Three eight counts in a round or four in a fight result in automatic defeat for the downed boxer. A single ten count is deemed a knockout, ending the fight. The referee is empowered to stop a contest if he believes a boxer is receiving excessive punishment or is otherwise in danger. Boxers must be as least 17 years old and no more than 34 years old. Although these age restrictions are a recent addition to the rules, in fact only one Olympic champion, Jackie Fields (1924 featherweight), has been younger than 17, and only one, Richard Gunn (1908 featherweight), has been older than 34. Boxers are not allowed to wear beards.

Since 1960, Olympic bouts have been judged by five ringside judges. Like any judged sport, boxing is open to controversy. However no other sport has had anything approaching the tumultuous history of boxing, complete with attacks on referees and judges, sit-down strikes by boxers, and full-scale riots. These incidents peaked in the 1920s and returned in the 1980s. In the wake of several absurd decisions and outrageous scenes at the 1988 Seoul Games, the International Amateur Boxing Association (AIBA) instituted numerous reforms that were put in force in Barcelona in 1992. These included daily alcohol tests for all referees and judges, an attempt to keep referees and judges "out of reach" of national associations and their officials, and a requirement that referees and judges not attend cocktail parties without the permission of the AIBA executive committee.

The most visible reform related to the method of scoring. Prior to 1992 each judge voted for a winner based on his scoring of each round. The boxer who gained the vote of a majority of judges won the fight. (In 1984, whenever the judges split 3–2, the decision was referred to a five-member Jury of Appeals.) In 1992, however, AIBA introduced computerized scoring. Each judge was given a console. Whenever a boxer connected with a punch, the judge pushed a button corresponding to that boxer. If three of the five judges pushed their buttons within one second, the boxer automatically received a point. Whichever boxer registered the most points at the end of three rounds was declared the winner. Unfortunately, this system was not without its flaws. For example, in the words of a post-Olympic report issued by AIBA vice-president Emil Jetchev, it was discovered that "in some judges the eyesight was found to be poor," "judges have different motor reactions," "a certain degree of uncertainty and even fear is noticeable among judges in regard of electronics," and—imagine this—"there exist different criteria among the judges in assessing a bout." Because of these problems, there were several notable cases in Barcelona in which one boxer would batter his opponent throughout a round and yet receive no points, or in which all five judges would give the nod to one boxer, yet his opponent would win the fight. In fact, the AIBA was so embarrassed by the results of the Griffin-Lozano light-flyweight bout that they ceased to allow the public access to individual judge's scores and, to this day, the complete Barcelona results remain under lock and key. After the 2004 Olympics growing concerns about lack of transparency and the potential for manipulation in judging scores led the IOC to withhold a total of $1.1 million in Olympic television revenues from the AIBA. In response AIBA instituted a randomized system for assigning judges and revamped its computer scoring system, which now requires three of the five judges to register a punch within a second of each other for a point to count. Video monitors were also installed at the Beijing venue so that fans and media could monitor judging as a bout progressed.

If one boxer builds an advantage of 20 points, the bout is stopped and he is awarded the victory. In the event of a tie, the scorecards of the five judges are examined. For each fighter, the high and low scores are dropped and the three remaining scores are added.

Boxing is the only Olympic sport in which professionals are not allowed to compete, although dozens of Olympic boxers have gone on to become professional champions. This is probably a wise restriction, considering the dangers involved in potential mismatches. However, in practice this gives an unfair advantage to nations with Communist governments that don't allow professional boxing, and especially to Cuba, the only remaining Communist nation with a boxing tradition.

In the charts that follow, defeated quarterfinalists are listed as tied for fifth place, but defeated quarterfinalists who did not win a match are not included. Beginning in 2000, defeated finalists have been awarded specific places based on their quarterfinal results.

NOTE: It has been commmon practice in Olympic circles to include the boxing events of 1904 as official events. They were in fact open to amateurs of all nations, although only US boxers actually took part. However, in one case a fighter was allowed to compete even though he failed to make weight and in another case, one boxer fought in two divisions. On the whole, the 1904 tournament does not deserve to be accorded Olympic status. The results are included here for historical interest.

LIGHT FLYWEIGHT
(49 kg—108 lbs)

1896–1964 not held

1968 Mexico City C: 24, N: 24, D: 10.26.

		FINAL MATCH
1. Francisco "Morochito" Rodríguez	VEN	Dec 3–2
2. Jee Yong-ju	KOR	
3. Harlan Marbley	USA	
3. Hubert Skrzypczak	POL	

5. Joseph Donovan (AUS), Hatha Karunaratne (SRL), Alberto Morales (MEX), Gabriel Ogun (NGR)

Morochito Rodríguez broke his thumb in the last round of the final. After his victory was announced, few in the crowd could fail to be moved by the sight of the 23-year-old Venezuelan joyfully weeping into the national flag that his seconds had draped over his shoulders. Rodríguez is the only Venezuelan gold medalist in Olympic history. Eventually he signed a professional contract, but before he actually fought he took his mother to see a pro fight. At one point, one of the boxers was hit in the mouth and his bloody mouthpiece landed in Rodríguez's mother's lap. She begged Rodríguez to give up fighting and he cancelled his contract.

Aboriginal boxer Joe Donovan lost a disputed decision in the quarterfinals to to Hubert Skrzypczak. Donovan wanted to file a protest but was told that he would have to pay the $50 appeal fee himself. He was unable to afford it, so the decision went unchallenged.

1972 Munich C: 31, N: 31, D: 9.10.

		FINAL MATCH
1. György Gedó	HUN	Dec 5–0
2. Kim U-Gil	PRK	
3. Ralph Evans	GBR	
3. Enrique Rodríguez	SPA	

5. Rafael Carbonell (CUB), Chanyalew Haile (ETH), Vladimir Ivanov (SOV/RUS), James Odwori (UGA)

1976 Montreal C: 27, N: 27, D: 7.31.

		FINAL MATCH
1. Jorge Hernández	CUB	Dec 4–1
2. Li Byong-uk	PRK	
3. Orlando Maldonado	PUR	
3. Payao Pooltarat	THA	

5. György Gedó (HUN), Armando Guevara (VEN), Park Chan-lee (KOR), Hector Patri (ARG)

Hernández was the reigning world amateur and Pan American champion. Eighteen-year-old bronze medalist Payao Pooltarat from Prachub Khiri Khan was the first Thai athlete to win an Olympic medal. He accomplished this by outpointing defending champion Gedó in the quarterfinals. Pooltrat went on to be a professional champion and a member of parliament.

1980 Moscow C: 22, N: 22, D: 8.2.

		FINAL MATCH
1. Shamil Sabirov	SOV/RUS	Dec 3–2
2. Hipólito Ramos	CUB	
3. Ismail Hjuseinov	BUL	
3. Li Byong-uk	PRK	

5. György Gedó (HUN), Dietmar Geilich (GDR), Dumitru Şchiopu (ROM), Ahmed Siad (ALG)

Gedó became the only boxer to compete in four Olympics.

1984 Los Angeles C: 24, N: 24, D: 8.11.

		FINAL MATCH
1. Paul Gonzales	USA	Default
2. Salvatore Todisco	ITA	
3. José Marcelino Bolívar	VEN	
3. Keith Mwila	ZAM	

5. Mamoru Kunoiwa (JPN), John Lyon (GBR), Carlos Motta-Taracena (GUA), Rafael Ramos (PUR)

It was less than four miles from Paul Gonzales' home in the Aliso Village housing project to the gold medal platform at the 1984 Olympics, but so rocky was the road he traveled to get there that they might as well have been a continent apart.

Growing up in what he called "a ghetto's ghetto," Gonzales saw his father walk out when he was 7, leaving his mother to raise 8 children on her own. By the time he was nine years old, Paul Gonzales had joined Primera Flats, one of 13 "major" gangs operating in his area. When he was 12 years old, he and his buddies were out cruising one night, when their '64 Chevy Impala stalled in an area controlled by a rival gang. Shots were fired through the car window and Gonzales was hit in the side of the head. Following a well-known local procedure, he washed his head in a lake at a nearby park and then had his cousin remove the remaining pieces of shot and glass with a pair of tweezers.

When he was 15, Gonzales was arrested on a murder charge. Fortunately he had a perfect alibi—he was boxing at the time—and his coach was a policeman. That policeman, Al Stankie, had convinced Gonzales to try his hands at boxing after seeing the 10-year-old in a street fight. At first Gonzales climbed into the gym through a back window, since it was located in the basement of the police station and he didn't want his fellow gang members to think he was a snitch.

As he began to take boxing more seriously, his friends would mock him because he stopped drinking, went home each night at 9 o'clock, and was up at 5 in the morning, running. But as he achieved more and more success, his friends became protective, making sure that he didn't stay out late or break training.

When he was 17, Gonzales missed 11 months of competition because of surgery to remove a bone spur from the back of his right hand. His first bout after the layoff was an upset victory over defending Olympic champion Shamil Sabirov.

At the Los Angeles Olympics, Gonzales blocked out the pressure and expectations of the wildly enthusiastic local crowd by imagining, as he entered the ring for each bout, that he was fighting in his opponent's hometown. His performances were impressive enough to earn him the Val Barker award for the best boxer at the Olympics.

He won his final match in a walkover, when his opponent, Salvatore Todisco, showed up with his hand in a cast, having broken his thumb in his semifinal bout. Gonzales himself had sustained a hairline stress fracture above his right wrist during his first round fight, requiring post-Olympic surgery and a cast of his own.

When he mounted the gold-medal platform, Paul Gonzales carried with him a United States flag in one hand and a Mexican flag in the other. He also carried with him the hopes and dreams of many disadvantaged youths, to whom he sent a message: "I won this gold medal, not just for myself or my mom or my coach, but for the kids like me who are always told, 'You're nothing.' The only way you're going to make it come true is by dreaming it, and when you dream something, you've got to turn it into reality. Because if you don't, you just die with your dreams."

Gonzales turned his Olympic dream into reality, but his dream of becoming a professional champion never materialized. In 1986 he broke a knuckle in a street fight and in 1987 he broke his ankle and injured his knee when he accidentally engaged the gear shift in his

Corvette convertible and ran over his own leg. In 1988 he fractured his hip in a bicycle accident. Although he did not personally fulfill his potential as a professional, Gonzales paved the way for other low-weight boxers to earn the kind of money that had previously been reserved for heavier fighters.

1988 Seoul C: 34, N: 34, D: 10.1.

		FINAL MATCH
1. Ivailo Hristov [Ismail Hjuseinov]	BUL	Dec 5–0
2. Michael Carbajal	USA	
3. Róbert Isaszegi	HUN	
3. Leopoldo Serantes	PHI	

5. Aleksandr Makhmutov (SOV/RUS), Mahjoub M'Jirih (MOR), R. Scott Olson (CAN), Chatchai Sasakul (THA)

Ivailo Hristov, a 28-year-old sailor, used a quick left jab and clever counterpunching to earn his gold medal. However, he was aided by a secret weapon: his frequent changes of name. Few ringside observers in Seoul were aware that Hristov was the same fighter who won an Olympic bronze medal in 1980 using the name Ismail Hjuseinov, a world championship in 1982 as Ismail Mustafov, and a silver medal at the 1985 European championship as Ivajlo Marinov. The name changes were not meant to cause confusion or to put his opponents off their guard—Hristov, a member of Bulgaria's Turkish minority, was forced to change his name because of the Bulgarian government's attempt to crush all remnants of Turkish ethnic identity.

Michael Carbajal went on to a successful professional career and was the first junior flyweight to be paid $1 million for a fight.

1992 Barcelona-Badalona C: 30, N: 30, D: 8.8.

		FINAL MATCH
1. Rogelio Marcelo García	CUB	Pts 24–10
2. Daniel Petrov Bojilov	BUL	
3. Jan Quast	GER	
3. Roel Velasco	PHI	

5. Valentin Barbu (ROM), Pál Lakatos (HUN), Rafael Lozano Muñoz (SPA), Rowan Williams (GBR)

No boxer in the 1992 Olympic tournament except Félix Savón was considered more of a gold medal shoo-in than two-time world champion Eric Griffin of the United States. Griffin's only serious challenge was expected to come from Rogelio Marcelo, and Griffin had beaten him easily each of the five times they had met. But in his second fight in Barcelona, Griffin ran up against an opponent he couldn't beat—the new computerized scoring system. All five judges had Griffin outpointing hometown favorite Rafael Lozano (19-9, 18-9, 26-17, 8-5 and 10-9) but he lost the bout 5-6 because the judges didn't push the buttons of their consoles at the same time. In the closing seconds of the second round, Griffin landed a flurry of five hard blows to Lozano's head, leading the referee to step in and call a standing eight-count. Yet Griffin earned not a single point for the barrage. With Griffin out, Marcelo breezed to the gold medal. His closest match was an 11-3 quarterfinal victory over Lozano. Lozano was also involved in a bit of history in his opening match. His opponent, Fana Twala, was the first black athlete to officially represent South Africa. (The two Tswana runners who competed in the 1904 marathon were independent entries.)

1996 Atlanta C: 30, N: 30, D: 8.3.

		FINAL MATCH
1. Daniel Petrov Bojilov	BUL	Pts 19–6
2. Mansueto "Onyok" Velasco	PHI	
3. Oleh Kiryukhin	UKR	
3. Rafael Lozano Muñoz	SPA	

5. Hamid Berhili (MOR), Albert Guardado (USA), Somrot Kamsing (THA), Lamasara Lapaini (INA)

The winners of the last two world championships, Nshan Munchyan of Armenia and Daniel Bojilov, faced each other in their opening bouts. Bojilov won 11-5. Bojilov, a computer hacker in his free time, won his four fights by a combined total of 65 to 25. Onyok Velasco, a sailor, was the younger brother of Roel Velasco, who won a bronze medal in the same division in 1992. Onyok went on to act in movies and television.

An unexpected incident enlivened the preliminary round. Afred Tetteh of Ghana was fighting Hamid Berhili when his protective cup fell out of his trunks and bounced along the canvas. The bout was halted while Tetteh's cornermen reinserted the cup. Tetteh lost the fight, but gained the support of the fans by good-naturedly waving to the crowd.

2000 Sydney C: 27, N: 27, D: 9.30.

		FINAL MATCH
1. Brahim Asloum	FRA	Pts 23–10
2. Rafael Lozano	SPA	
3. Kim Un-chol	PRK	
3. Maikro Romero Esquirol	CUB	
5. Kim Ki-suk	KOR	
6. Suleiman Wanjau Bilali	KEN	
7. Valeri Sidorenko	UKR	
8. Ivan Stapovic	LIT	

The luck of the draw brought together two of the favorites in the first round as world champion Brian Viloria defeated 1998 European champion Sergei Kazarov of Russia 8-6. Viloria's next opponent was Brahim Asloum, whom Viloria had beaten in a controversial match at the 1999 world championships in Houston, Texas. Asloum had been ahead 3-1 when Vilora scored two points in the last fifteen seconds and then was awarded the victory based on the total punches tiebreaker. At the Olympics, it was Asloum who won a controversial decision. The final score was 6-4, but neither boxer was awarded a single point for a body blow, of which there were many, particularly by Viloria. In the quarterfinals Asloum defeated Kim Ki-suk 12-8 to earn a semifinal duel with 1996 Olympic flyweight champion Maikro Romero. Asloum built an 8-3 lead in the third round. Romero fought back in an exciting toe-to-toe battle, but Asloum held on to win 13-12. The final was something of an anticlimax. Asloum was 15 centimeters (6 inches) taller than Atlanta bronze medalist Rafael Lozano. Asloum outpointed Lozano in each round and won 23-10. Asloum was France's first Olympic boxing champion in 64 years.

2004 Athens C: 29, N: 29, D: 8.29.

		FINAL MATCH
1. Yan Barthelemy Varela	CUB	Pts 21–16
2. Atagün Yalçınkaya	TUR	
3. Sergei Kazakov	RUS	
3. Zou Shiming	CHN	

5. Joseph Jermia (NAM), Alfonso Pinto (ITA), Aleksan Nalbandyan (ARM), Hong Moo-won (KOR)

Of the four medalists in the flyweight category, three had met previously in international competition, with varied results. Yan Barthelemy defeated Sergei Kazakov 20-17 in the quarterfinals of the 2001 world championships, before going on to win the title in a walkover against Romania's Marian Velicu, who was hospitalized for back pains, reportedly due to kidney infection and dehydration from trying to make weight. Two years later, Kazakov won the 2003 world championship, with a 23-19 win over Zou Shiming in the final. Earlier in the competition Zou had gained a surprise victory over Barthelemy in the round of 16, and his silver was the first medal by a Chinese boxer in world championship boxing.

In Athens, Barthelemy and Zou both advanced easily through the preliminary rounds, and faced off in the semifinals. Zou led 11-7 after the second round, but Barthelemy came back in the third round, pulling ahead 20-14 before going on to a 29-17 win.

The surprise semifinalist was Atagün Yalçınkaya, a 17-year-old Turkish boxer. Yalçınkaya advanced to the semis, where he defeated Sergei Kazakov 26-20. In the gold medal match, Yalçınkaya took an early 4-2 lead in the first round before Barthelemy managed to find his rhythm, coming back to move ahead 11-8 after two rounds and then win 21-16. Yalçınkaya became the youngest Turk to earn an Olympic medal in any sport.

2008 Beijing C: 29, N: 29, D: 8.24.

		FINAL MATCH	
1. Zou Shiming	CHN	Ret 2	0:19
2. Pürevdorjin Serdamba	MGL		
3. Yampier Hernández Gonzales	CUB		
3. Paddy Barnes	IRL		

5. Łukasz Maszczyk (POL), Birzhan Zhakypov (KAZ), Amnat Ruenroeng (THA), Paulo Carvalho (BRA)

Four years after winning China's first-ever Olympic boxing medal, Zou Shiming had developed into the world's foremost light flyweight boxer. In 2005 he gained his first major international title, winning the world championship final in front of a hometown crowd in Mianyang. The following year he won the Asian Games title, and in 2007 he successfully defended his world title.

Zou advanced easily through the first round in Beijing, defeating Venezuela's Eduard Bermúdez 11-2, but faced a fierce challenge in the second round from French national champion Nordine Oubaali. With less than 40 seconds remaining in the final round, Oubaali pulled ahead on a quick head shot. Zou connected with a punch in the final fifteen seconds to tie the bout, and then advanced after winning the tie-breaking decision.

He had less trouble in the quarter-final, defeating Birzhan Zhakypov 9-4. His semi-final bout against Paddy Barnes raised some controversy after Barnes was shocked not to be awarded a single point against Zou in his 15-0 victory. "The only way I could win here is if the judges got knocked out," he complained.

Zou's opponent in the final was 23-year-old Pürevdorjin Serdamba. Serdamba had suffered a shoulder injury during qualifications in March and had aggravated the injury during his semi-final bout against Yampier Hernández. By the time he reached the final, he was barely able to lift his arms. Zou scored a single point in the first round before Serdamba retired due to injury.

Originally from Guizhou Province in the southwest, one of the poorest provinces in China, Zou had dreamed of becoming a French chef, hairdresser or DJ before settling on boxing.

FLYWEIGHT
(52 kg—115 lbs)

1896–1900 not held

1904 St. Louis C: 2, N: 1, D: 9.22.
(47.63 kg—105 lbs)

		FINAL MATCH
1. George Finnegan	USA	RSC 1
2. Miles Burke	USA	

For some unknown reason Burke was allowed to compete even though he was almost four pounds over the weight limit.

1906–1912 not held

1920 Antwerp C: 16, N: 9, D: 8.24.
(50.80 kg—112 lbs)

		FINAL MATCH
1. Frank DiGennara	USA	Dec
2. Anders Petersen	DEN	
3. William Cuthbertson	GBR	
4. Charles Albert	FRA	

5. Joseph Charpentier (BEL), Jean-Baptiste Rampignon (FRA), Nicolas Zegwaard (HOL), Peter Zivic (USA)

Seven and a half years later, DiGennara, fighting under the name Frankie Genaro, won the World Flyweight title by defeating Albert "Frenchy" Belanger in Toronto.

1924 Paris C: 19, N: 13, D: 7.20.
(50.80 kg—112 lbs)

		FINAL MATCH
1. Fidel LaBarba	USA	Dec
2. James McKenzie	GBR	
3. Raymond Fee	USA	
4. Rinaldo Castellenghi	ITA	

5. Oscar Bergström (SWE), R. Biete-Berdes (SPA), John MacGregor (CAN), Stephen Rennie (CAN)

LaBarba, an 18-year-old Los Angeles high school student, went on to a successful professional career. In 1925 he defeated Frankie Genaro for the American Flyweight title, and in 1927 he won the vacant World Flyweight title. LaBarba later graduated from Stanford University with a degree in journalism and spent most of his life as a sportswriter and working in Hollywood.

1928 Amsterdam C: 19, N: 19, D: 8.11.
(50.80 kg—112 lbs)

		FINAL MATCH
1. Antal Kocsis	HUN	Dec
2. Armand Appell	FRA	
3. Carlo Cavagnoli	ITA	
4. B. "Buddy" Lebanon	SAF	

5. Hubert Ausböck (GER), Barend "Ben" Bril (HOL), Alfredo Gaona (MEX), Cuthbert Taylor (GBR)

In the first contest of the tournament, 16-year-old Hyman Miller of California appeared to have easily defeated Marcel Santos of Belgium. When the decision was announced in Santos' favor, Miller's confident smile turned to convulsive sobbing. The US boxing team was so outraged that they requested permission to withdraw all their boxers from the Olympics. However the president of the US Olympic Committee, Major-General Douglas MacArthur, refused permission, stating, "Americans never quit." The eventual winner, Antal Kocsis, was Hungary's first Olympic gold medalist in boxing. The following year he turned professional and emigrated to the United States.

1932 Los Angeles C: 12, N: 12, D: 8.13.
(50.80 kg—112 lbs)

		FINAL MATCH
1. István Énekes	HUN	Dec
2. Francisco Cabañas	MEX	
3. Louis Salica	USA	
4. Thomas Pardoe	GBR	

5. Edelweis Rodriguez (ITA), Werner Spannagel (GER)

Francisco Cabañas paid his own way to the Olympics by borrowing money from his mother and his friends.

1936 Berlin C: 25, N: 25, D: 8.15.
(50.80 kg—112 lbs)

		FINAL MATCH
1. Willi Kaiser	GER	Dec
2. Gavino Matta	ITA	
3. Louis Daniel Laurie	USA	
4. Alfredo Carlomagno	ARG	

5. Raoul Degryse (BEL), William Passmore (SAF), Edmund Sobkowiak (POL), Fidel Tricánico (URU)

1948 London C: 26, N: 26, D: 8.13.

		FINAL MATCH
1. Pascual Pérez	ARG	Dec
2. Spartaco Bandinelli	ITA	
3. Han Soo-ann	KOR	
4. František Majdloch	CZE	

5. Alex Bollaert (BEL), Hermanus Corman (HOL), Luis Martínez Zapata (SPA), Frank Sodano (USA)

Pascual Pérez, a 22-year-old clerk in the Chamber of Deputies in Buenos Aires, faced his most difficult challenge *before* the fighting began. Pérez was unexpectedly disqualified for being overweight. However, it was later discovered that officials had confused him with his bantamweight teammate Arnoldo *Pares*. Pérez, who was only 1.50 meters (4 feet 11 inches) tall, went on to a successful professional career, gaining the World Flyweight Title by defeating Yoshio Shirai on November 26, 1954, and defending it nine times before losing to Pone Kingpeter April 16, 1960. An unusually hard hitter for a flyweight, Pérez knocked out 62 percent of his opponents as a professional.

1952 Helsinki C: 28, N: 28, D: 8.2.

		FINAL MATCH
1. Nathan Brooks	USA	Dec 3–0
2. Edgar Basel	GER	
3. Anatoly Bulakov	SOV/RUS	
3. William Toweel	SAF	

5. Thorbjorn Clausen (NOR), David Dower (GBR), Mircea Dobrescu (ROM), Han Soo-ann (KOR)

1956 Melbourne C: 19, N: 19, D: 12.1.

		FINAL MATCH
1. Terence Spinks	GBR	Dec
2. Mircea Dobrescu	ROM	
3. John Caldwell	IRL	
3. René Libeer	FRA	

5. Warner Batchelor (AUS), Ray Perez (USA), Vladimir Stolnikov (SOV/RUS), Kenji Yonekura (JPN)

About two hours before the weigh-in for the final, it was discovered that Terry Spinks was one and a half pounds overweight. His coach, Jack Roy, shut all the doors and windows in the lounge of the British team house and lit a fire to raise the temperature. Spinks skipped rope for more than a half hour without stopping and successfully sweated off enough weight to qualify for the final against veteran Mircea Dobrescu. Spinks was a great crowd favorite because he was baby-faced and small, even for a flyweight.

1960 Rome C: 33, N: 33, D: 9.5.

		FINAL MATCH
1. Gyula Török	HUN	Dec 3–2
2. Sergei Sivko	SOV/RUS	
3. Abdelmoneim Elguindi	EGY	
3. Kiyoshi Tanabe	JPN	

5. Humberto Barrera (USA), Miguel Botta (ARG), Mircea Dobrescu (ROM), Manfred Homberg (GER)

1964 Tokyo C: 28, N: 28, D: 10.23.

		FINAL MATCH
1. Fernando Atzori	ITA	Dec 4–1
2. Artur Olech	POL	
3. Robert Carmody	USA	
3. Stanislav Sorokin	SOV/RUS	

5. Otto Babiasch (GER), Choh Dong-kih (KOR), Constantin Ciucă (ROM), John McCafferty (IRL)

After one minute and six seconds of the first round of his quarterfinal bout against Stanislav Sorokin, Korean boxer Choh Dong-kih was disqualified for holding his head too low. Unable to accept this verdict, Choh sat down in the middle of the ring and refused to leave. His sitdown strike continued for 51 minutes, until officials persuaded him to abandon his protest. Ironically, Sorokin was forced to withdraw before his next fight because of a cut that wasn't healing. The winner, Sardinian house-painter Fernando Atzori, fought the final with a black eye.

1968 Mexico City C: 26, N: 26, D: 10.26.

		FINAL MATCH
1. Ricardo Delgado	MEX	Dec 5–0
2. Artur Olech	POL	
3. Servilio Oliveira	BRA	
3. Leo Rwabwogo	UGA	

5. Tibor Badari (HUN), Joseph Destimo (GHA), Tetsuaki Nakamura (JPN), Nicolai Novikov (SOV/RUS)

Heriberto Cintrón of Puerto Rico was standing in the ring waiting for his first-round bout with Polish policeman Artur Olech when he was suddenly disqualified for being younger than the minimum age of 17 years. He was, in fact, 16 years and one month old.

1972 Munich C: 37, N: 37, D: 9.10.

		FINAL MATCH
1. Georgi Kostadinov	BUL	Dec 5–0
2. Leo Rwabwogo	UGA	
3. Leszek Blazyński	POL	
3. Douglas Rodríguez	CUB	

5. Neil McLaughlin (IRL), Calixto Pérez (COL), You Chong-man (KOR), Boris Zoniktuev (SOV/RUS)

Most Olympic boxers who went on to become world champions were also Olympic champions, or at least medalists. But there is one boxing star who made little impression in his Olympic debut. As an underage 15-year-old representative of Puerto Rico, Wilfredo Gómez lost a 4-1 decision in the first round to Mohamed Selin of Egypt, who was in turn knocked out in his next fight. Less than five years later, on May 21, 1977, Gómez won the WBC Junior Featherweight championship and defended it 17 times. On March 9, 1979, he won the Junior Featherweight title. He added the WBC Featherweight title on May 31, 1984.

1976 Montreal C: 26, N: 26, D: 7.31.

		FINAL MATCH
1. Leo Randolph	USA	Dec 3–2
2. Ramón Duvalon	CUB	
3. Leszek Blazyński	POL	
3. David Torosyan	SOV/ARM	

5. Ian Clyde (CAN), Jong Jo-ung (PRK), David Larmour (IRL), Alfredo Pérez (VEN)

Leo Randolph, an 18-year-old high school student from Tacoma, Washington, called his surprise victory "the best thing that happened to me since I became a Christian in 1969."

1980 Moscow C: 20, N: 20, D: 8.2.

		FINAL MATCH
1. Peter Lessov	BUL	RSC 2 2:08
2. Viktor Mynoshnychenko	SOV/UKR	
3. Hugh Russell	IRL	
3. János Váradi	HUN	

5. Gilberto Román Saldaña (MEX), Daniel Radu (ROM), Henryk Średnicki (POL), Yo Ryon-sik (PRK)

1984 Los Angeles C: 31, N: 31, D: 8.11.

		FINAL MATCH
1. Steven McCrory	USA	Dec 4–1
2. Redžep Redžepovski	YUG/MAC	
3. Ibrahim Bilali	KEN	
3. Eyup Can	TUR	

5. Peter Ayesu (MLW), Jeffrey Fenech (AUS), Heo Yong-mo (KOR), Laureano Ramírez (DOM)

Detroit's Steve McCrory, the younger brother of World Welterweight champion Milton McCrory, won a close decision over veteran Redžep Redžepovski, who complained, "As long as an American is standing on his feet for three rounds it is hard to get a decision over him." Steven McCrory, who pawned his gold medal and abused illegal drugs, was only 37 years old when, in 2000, he died in poverty of an undisclosed illness.

1988 Seoul C: 44, N: 44, D: 10.2.

		FINAL MATCH
1. Kim Kwang-sun	KOR	Dec 4–1
2. Andreas Tews	GDR	
3. Mario González	MEX	
3. Timofei Skriabin	SOV/MOL	

5. Benaissa Abed (ALG), Meluin Deleon (DOM), Alfred Amon Kotey (GHA), Serafim Todorov (BUL)

In 1984, Kim Kwang-sun was favored to win the light flyweight division in Los Angeles. However, he was upset in his first-round bout by eventual gold-medal winner Paul Gonzales. Deeply depressed, Kim vowed that he would return to the Olympics and win a gold medal himself. For four years his mother went to a Buddhist temple every day and prayed for her son. In 1988, Kim, by then a flyweight, blasted his way through four opponents and into the final. There he faced European champion Andreas Tews, who had beaten him 3-2 at the 1987 World Cup. This time Kim dominated the last two rounds, bringing great joy to the highly partisan crowd.

1992 Barcelona-Badalona C: 31, N: 31, D: 8.9.

		FINAL MATCH
1. Choi Chol-su	PRK	Pts 12–2
2. Raúl González Sánchez	CUB	
3. Timothy Austin	USA	
3. István Kovács	HUN	

5. Héctor Ávila (DOM), Benjamin Mwangata (TAN), Robert Peden (AUS), David Sernadas Suárez (VEN)

The critical bout took place in the semifinals when world champion István Kovács faced Choi Chol-su, the man he had beaten 25-15 to win the 1991 title. This time it was Choi who came out on top, 10-5. In the round of 16 Choi had barely survived a late rush by Paul Ingle of Great Britain, winning 13-12. The North Korean had no such problems in the final, easily outgunning González.

1996 Atlanta C: 32, N: 32, D: 8.4.

		FINAL MATCH
1. Maikro Romero Esquirol	CUB	Pts 12–11
2. Bulat Jumadilov	KAZ	
3. Zoltan Lunka	GER	
3. Albert Pakeyev	RUS	

5. Mahdi Assous (ALG), Damaen Kelly (IRL), Elias Recaido (PHI), Daniel Reyes (COL)

The gold medal bout was one of the most exciting of the Atlanta tournament. Using superior speed and a quick left hook, Jumadilov took a 5-2 lead in the first round and an 8-5 lead after two rounds. But in the final round, Jumadilov ran out of steam and Romero was able to force the action. He squeezed ahead 11-10 with less than one minute to go and managed to hold his slim advantage to the end.

2000 Sydney C: 28, N: 28, D: 9.29.

		FINAL MATCH
1. Wijan Ponlid	THA	Pts 19–12
2. Bulat Jumadilov	KAZ	
3. Jérôme Thomas	FRA	
3. Vladimir Sidorenko	UKR	
5. Manuel Mantilla Rodríguez	CUB	
6. Vakhtang Darchinian	ARM	
7. Andrzej Rzany	POL	
8. José Navarro	USA	

The final matched Bulat Jumadilov, who was expected to be there, and Wijan Ponlid, who wasn't. In addition to winning the silver medal at the Atlanta Olympics, Jumadilov had earned a silver medal at the 1995 world championships and a bronze at the 1997 world championships before becoming world champion in 1999. In Sydney, Jumadilov overcame Kennedy Kanyata of Kenya 12-9 and Vakhtang Darchinian of Armenia 15-8 to qualify for a semifinal bout against Jérôme Thomas. Thomas was born with Paulan's syndrome, which left him with one hand that would not close, one pectoral muscle too few and a left arm that was 7 centimeters shorter than his right arm. Thomas, who underwent 15 surgeries as a child—including seven on his left hand alone—claimed that his mismatched arms were actually an advantage because after a few jabs with his left hand, an opponent would be unprepared when Thomas followed with a hard blow from his surprisingly long right arm. After a hard-fought four rounds, Jumadilov won 22-16.

Meanwhile, Ponlid, a southpaw police officer, was picking up one unexpected victory after another. After stopping Vardan Zakarjan of Germany in the fourth round and outpointing Canada's Andrew Kooner 11-7, Ponlid faced 1997 world champion Manuel Mantilla of Cuba in the quarterfinals. When Ponlid scored a clear victory, 19-8, Thai fans began to pay attention. Back in Bangkok, the senate delayed a vote on an election reform bill so that the senators could watch Ponlid's semifinal contest against two-time European champion Vladimir Sidorenko. Ponlid trailed 4-6 after two rounds, but outscored Sidorenko 7-1 in the third round and held on to win 14-11.

In Thailand, Ponlid's father joined the provincial governer on top of an elephant that led a procession of villagers to seek blessings from the statue of Chao Muang Dong, founder of the village where Ponlid was born in Sukohthai province. Against Jumadilov, Ponlid took a 4-1 lead after the first round. Jumadilov closed to 9-7 in the second round, but Ponlid increased his lead to 13-9 and stayed at least four points ahead for the rest of the match. After his victory was announced, the 24-year-old Ponlid held aloft a photograph of the King of Thailand. When Ponlid left Thailand for the Olympics, he was unknown. When he returned, he was a national hero and was presented with rewards and gifts worth $700,000.

2004 Athens C: 27, N: 27, D: 8.28.

		FINAL MATCH
1. Yuriorkis Gamboa Toledano	CUB	Pts 38–23
2. Jérôme Thomas	FRA	
3. Rustamhodza Rahimov	GER	
3. Fuad Aslanov	AZR	

5. Paulus Ambunda (NAM), Georgy Balakshin (RUS), Andrzej Rżany (POL), Tulashboy Doniyorov (UZB)

At the 2003 World Championships, Yuriorkis Gamboa was narrowly beaten 22-23 by Somjit Jongjohor, who went on to win the title. Jongjohor and Gamboa faced each other again in Athens in the round of 16. Jongjohor, using a hit and run strategy, had built up a 19-16 lead when Gamboa launched a comeback in the final round to earn a 26-21 victory. It would be Gamboa's closest match of the competition. Meanwhile, 2000 silver medalist Jérôme Thomas made his way to the finals with two lopsided victories in the preliminary rounds and two closer wins, both 23-18, against US boxer Ron Siler in the quarterfinals and Fuad Aslanov in the semis. Since the last Olympics, Thomas had won the 2001 world championship title and earned silver at the 2003 Worlds. Gamboa dominated the Athens final, using a combination of superior footwork and quick left-right combinations to manage a comfortable 38-23 victory.

2008 Beijing C: 27, N: 27, D: 8.23.

		FINAL MATCH
1. Somjit Jongjohor	THA	Pts 8–2
2. Andry Laffita Hernández	CUB	
3. Georgiy Balakshin	RUS	
3. Vincenzo Picardi	ITA	

5. McWilliams Arroyo (PUR), Jitender Kumar (IND), Walid Cherif (TUN), Anvar Yunusov (TJK)

Twenty-one-year-old reigning world champion and three times US national champion, Rau'shee Warren was eliminated in the first round when he lost 9-8 to 2005 world champion Lee Ok-sung. With Warren out, the gold-medal favorite seemed to be 33-year-old veteran and world silver medalist Somjit Jongjohor.

Jongohor advanced easily through the competition, giving up only five points in his first four bouts. He faced 30-year-old Andry Laffita in the final. The two had faced each other previously in the first round of the 2005 world championships, when Laffita beat Jongjohor on his way to winning the silver medal. This time Jongohor scored the first six points and held steady for an 8-2 win.

BANTAMWEIGHT

(56 kg—123 lbs)

1896–1900 not held

1904 St. Louis C: 2, N: 1, D: 9.22.
(52.16 kg—115 lb.)

		FINAL MATCH
1. Oliver Kirk	USA	RSC 3
2. George Finnegan	USA	

1906 not held

1908 London C: 6, N: 2, D: 10.27.
(52.62 kg—116 lbs)

		FINAL MATCH
1. A. Henry Thomas	GBR	Dec
2. John Condon	GBR	
3. William Webb	GBR	

1912 not held

1920 Antwerp C: 12, N: 7, D: 8.24.
(53.52 kg—118 lbs)

		FINAL MATCH
1. Clarence Walker	SAF	Dec
2. Chris Graham	CAN	
3. George McKenzie	GBR	
4. Henri Hébrants	BEL	

5. Edward Hartman (USA), Henri Ricard (FRA), Sam Vogel (USA)

1924 Paris C: 21, N: 15, D: 7.20.
(53.52 kg—118 lbs)

		FINAL MATCH
1. William Smith	SAF	Dec
2. Salvatore Tripoli	USA	
3. Jean Ces	FRA	
4. Oscar Andrén	SWE	

5. Albert Barber (GBR), Antonio Sánchez Dietz (SPA), Jacques Lemouton (FRA), Benjamín Pertuzzo (ARG)

Joe Lazarus of Cornell University had the unusual misfortune of knocking out his opponent, Oscar Andrén of Sweden, and yet being declared the loser. As Andrén was being revived, the referee, Maurice Siegel of France, announced that Lazarus was disqualified for striking the knockout punch while breaking from a clinch. Siegel later apologized to US officials for his mistaken call and Andrén and the Swedish team manager urged Lazarus to file a protest. Moved by the Swedes' good sportsmanship, Lazarus declined, as did the US officials.

In 1943, Lazarus, then an insurance broker, intervened in a street brawl between one of his clients and two British merchant seamen. Lazarus managed to bring peace to the group and everyone had shaken hands, when suddenly one of the sailors punched Lazarus, sending him through a drugstore window. The fall severed an artery in his thigh and he bled to death.

1928 Amsterdam C: 18, N: 18, D: 8.11.
(53.52 kg—118 lbs)

		FINAL MATCH
1. Vittorio Tamagnini	ITA	Dec
2. John Daley	USA	
3. Harry Isaacs	SAF	
4. Edward Traynor	IRL	

5. John Garland (GBR), Vincent Glionna (CAN), Carmelo Robledo (ARG), János Széles (HUN)

Controversy developed when Harry Isaacs was announced the winner of his semifinal bout with John Daley. In what the US Official Report would refer to as "a demonstration never equalled in Olympic history," American supporters stormed the judges' table demanding that the decision be reversed. After several minutes, it was announced that one of the judges had transposed his figures for the two fighters. Daley was declared the victor. He moved on to the final while Isaacs went home certain that he had been robbed. It was, in the words of the London *Daily Express*, "an example of vacillation unprecedented in the history of a meeting of such worldwide scope."

In the final, Daley, perhaps rattled by his earlier experience, fought below his usual standard and Tamagnini was given a narrow victory. Again the Americans howled their disapproval. Complained one British reporter, "For more than two hours, there was little else save din and clatter, screeching and raving, and several skirmishes with the police. . . ." This time it was to no avail: the decision stood.

1932 Los Angeles C: 10, N: 10, D: 8.13.

		FINAL MATCH
1. Horace Gwynne	CAN	Dec
2. Hans Ziglarski	GER	
3. José Villanueva	PHI	
4. Joseph Lang	USA	
5. Carlos Alberto Pereyra	ARG	

Although he made his living as a jockey, Toronto's Lefty Gwynne started boxing when he was 4 years old. He and his 6-year-old brother put on exhibitions for British army troops in Wales. In Los Angeles Gwynne made no attempt to study the other fighters and didn't even bother to learn who his next opponent would be until he arrived at the arena. When Gwynne, now 19, returned to Toronto after winning the Olympic gold medal, the city honored him with a small reception and a gold watch. Gwynne, well aware of the realities of the Depression, immediately asked the mayor for a job. The mayor just laughed. Although Gwynne did fight professionally until 1939, there was little money for bantamweights and he was forced to supplement his income by working as a security guard at a Ford Motors auto plant. In an era before corporate sponsorship, Gwynne offered to endorse his favorite chocolate drink: Vi-Tone. He was turned down. Gwynne spent most of his working life as a jockey's agent.

1936 Berlin C: 24, N: 24, D: 8.15.
(53.52 kg—118 lbs)

		FINAL MATCH
1. Ulderico Sergo	ITA	Dec
2. Jack Wilson	USA	
3. Fidel Ortiz	MEX	
4. Stig Cederberg	SWE	

5. Joseph Cornelis (BEL), Oscar Larrazabal (PHI), Alexander Hannan (SAF), Shunpei Haskioka (JPN)

1948 London C: 30, N: 30, D: 8.13.

		FINAL MATCH
1. Tibor Csík	HUN	Dec
2. Giovanni Battista Zuddas	ITA	
3. Juan Venegas	PUR	
4. Alvaro Vicente Domenech	SPA	

5. James Carruthers (AUS), Celestino González Henríquez (CHI), Willie Lenihan (IRL), Albert Perera (SRL)

Argentina's Arnoldo Pares, although innocent of any wrongdoing, was the center of much confusion and controversy. At the weigh-in he was found to be overweight. In a panic, his supporters cut off his hair, rubbed him down with a towel, scrubbed the soles of his feet, and blew the dust off the scales. He even wept for a few minutes which further reduced his weight. It was no use: he still couldn't make the limit. The Argentinians filed a protest, and weights and measures experts were sent for. Sure enough, it turned out that the scales were inaccurate, and Pares was allowed to compete. In his first match the nearly bald Pares won a disputed decision over Vic Toweel of South Africa. Toweel didn't let this setback hurt his career. He turned professional and, less than two years later, won the World Bantamweight title, which he held for two and a half years before losing to Jimmy Carruthers of Australia, who happened to have been Arnoldo Pares' second opponent at the 1948 Olympics. Carruthers won that fight but sustained an eye injury that forced him to withdraw from his quarterfinal bout with Tibor Csík. The unusually lucky Csík was thus able to move on to the semifinals even though he had fought only one regular fight. (His first-round opponent had been disqualified.) Csík fought in the 1956 anti-Communist revolution. When Soviet troops put down the uprising, Csík was forced to leave Hungary and he spent the rest of his life in Australia.

1952 Helsinki C: 23, N: 23, D: 8.2.

		FINAL MATCH
1. Pentti Hämäläinen	FIN	Dec 2–1
2. John McNally	IRL	
3. Gennady Garbuzov	SOV/RUS	
3. Kang Joon-ho	KOR	

5. Vincenzo Dall'Osso (ITA), František Majdloch (CZE), David Moore (USA), Helmuth Von Gravenitz (SAF)

The victory of Hämäläinen, a 23-year-old typewriter mechanic from Kotka, was greeted with great enthusiasm by the local Finnish crowd, although the Irish felt they had gotten a raw deal. Nevertheless, Belfast's John McNally was the first Irishman to win an Olympic boxing medal.

1956 Melbourne C: 18, N: 18, D: 12.1.

		FINAL MATCH
1. Wolfgang Behrendt	GDR	Dec
2. Song Soon-chun	KOR	
3. Claudio Barrientos	CHI	
3. Frederick Gilroy	IRL	

5. Eder Jofre (BRA), Owen Reilly (GBR), Mario Sitri (ITA), Carmelo Tomaselli (ARG)

Twenty-year-old Berlin machine-fitter Wolfgang Behrendt was the first Olympic champion from the German Democratic Republic (East Germany). Behrendt went on to a career as a sports photographer for the German newspaper *Neues Deutschland*, winning international acclaim for his black and white photos.

1960 Rome C: 33, N: 33, D: 9.5.

		FINAL MATCH
1. Oleg Grigoryev	SOV/RUS	Dec
2. Primo Zamparini	ITA	
3. Brunon Bendig	POL	
3. Oliver "Frankie" Taylor	AUS	

5. Jerry Armstrong (USA), Fernández Alfred Carbajo (SPA), Horst Rascher (GER), Myint Thein (BUR)

In the third round of competition, Oleg Grigoryev won a much-disputed split decision over 17-year-old Frankie Taylor of Great Britain. Although a British protest was rejected, all three judges who voted for Grigoryev were fired, as were no less than half of the 30 referees and judges involved in the Olympic tournament.

1964 Tokyo C: 32, N: 32, D: 10.23.

		FINAL MATCH	
1. Takao Sakurai	JPN	RSC 2	1:18
2. Chung Shin-cho	KOR		
3. Juan Fabila Mendoza	MEX		
3. Washington Rodríguez	URU		

5. Fermin Espinosa (CUB), Oleg Grigoryev (SOV/RUS), Nicolae Puiu (ROM), Karimu Young (NGR)

The final contest was stopped after Sakurai had knocked down Chung four times in less than four and a half minutes. After a brief career as a professional, Sakurai opened a coffee shop in Tokyo called "The Medalist."

1968 Mexico City C: 39, N: 39, D: 10.26.

		FINAL MATCH
1. Valery Sokolov	SOV/RUS	RSC 2 2:15
2. Eridari Mukwanga	UGA	
3. Chang Kyou-chull	KOR	
3. Eiji Morioka	JPN	

5. Robert Cervantes (MEX), Michael Dowling (IRL), Samuel Mbugua (KEN), Horst Rascher (GER)

1972 Munich C: 38, N: 38, D: 9.10.

		FINAL MATCH
1. Orlando Martínez	CUB	Dec 5–0
2. Alfonso Zamora	MEX	
3. Ricardo Carreras	USA	
3. George Turpin	GBR	

5. Ferry Egberty Moniaga (INA), John Mwaura Nderu (KEN), Juan Francisco Rodríguez (SPA), Vassily Solomin (SOV/RUS)

Martínez was the first Cuban to win an Olympic gold medal since Ramón Fonst, the fencer, in 1904.

1976 Montreal C: 24, N: 24, D: 7.31.

		FINAL MATCH
1. Gu Yong-ju	PRK	Dec 5–0
2. Charles Mooney	USA	
3. Patrick Cowdell	GBR	
3. Victor Rybakov	SOV/RUS	

5. Stefan Förster (GDR), Reynaldo Fortaleza (PHI), Hwang Chul-soon (KOR), Veerachat Saturngrum (THA)

1980 Moscow C: 33, N: 33, D: 8.2.

		FINAL MATCH
1. Juan Hernández	CUB	Dec 5–0
2. Bernardo José Piñango	VEN	
3. Michael Anthony	GUY	
3. Dumitru Cipere	ROM	

5. Geral Issaick (TAN), Samson Khachatrian (SOV/ARM), John Sirakibbe (UGA), Daniel Zaragoza (MEX)

Seventeen-year-old Hernández was the second youngest boxer at the Moscow Olympics. He stopped two African boxers before the fights had gone the distance, and he defeated his other three opponents with clear-cut decisions.

1984 Los Angeles C: 35, N: 35, D: 8.11.

		FINAL MATCH
1. Maurizio Stecca	ITA	Dec 4–1
2. Hector López	MEX	
3. Pedro Nolasco	DOM	
3. Dale Walters	CAN	

5. Pedro Rubén Décima (ARG), Ndaba Dube (ZIM), Moon Sung-kil (KOR), Robinson Pitalúa Tamara (COL)

Stecca immediately turned professional, compiling a career record of 49-4-0 and twice winning the WBO featherweight title.

1988 Seoul C: 48, N: 48, D: 10.1.

		FINAL MATCH
1. Kennedy McKinney	USA	Dec 5–0
2. Alexander Hristov	BUL	
3. Phajol Moolsan	THA	
3. Jorge Julio Rocha	COL	

5. Nyamaa Altankhuyag (MGL), Aleksandr Artemyev (SOV/RUS), Katsuyuki Matsushima (JPN), Stephen Mwema (KEN)

Since 1924, Olympic boxing tournaments have been plagued by riots and demonstrations of varying magnitude. In 1988, however, a new twist was added to the ringside ugliness when a referee was attacked, not by spectators, but by Korean boxing officials and security guards.

The incident was rooted in the 1984 Los Angeles Olympics, when the Korean team became upset by what they perceived as biased judging against their boxers. They were particularly incensed by the dubious victory of light welterweight Jerry Page of the US over Kim Dong-kil. Four years later the wound was reopened when Korean light flyweight favorite Oh Kwang-soo was narrowly upset by Michael Carbajal of the US.

The day after the Carbajal-Oh fight, Korean bantamweight Byun Jong-il faced one of the division favorites, Alexander Hristov of Bulgaria. The fight was not a pretty one. There was much pushing, shoving, grabbing, and general brawling. Referee Keith Walker of New Zealand tried to control the bout, cautioning both boxers, but he focused his reprimands on Byun. After warning Byun three times to stop using his head as a battering ram, Walker ordered the judges to deduct a point from the Korean's score. Another head butt in the final round led to the deduction of a second point. As it turned out, those two points decided the outcome of the fight. Without the penalties Byun would have won the decision; instead, he lost 4-1.

As soon as the verdict was announced, Korean boxing trainer Lee Heung-soo charged into the ring and struck Keith Walker on the back. Other Koreans, apparently under the mistaken assumption that Walker had also refereed the Carbajal-Oh fight, followed suit. Within seconds the ring was filled with angry Koreans pummeling Walker. Walker's fellow referees came to his aid and held off his attackers until security personnel could escort him out of the arena. Unfortunately, some of the security guards also took part in the riot, one of them aiming a kick at Walker's head as he fled. Another guard, Yoon S. L., who took off his uniform jacket before going after Walker, was quoted as saying, "I acted instinctively for the love of my fatherland."

Walker went straight from the arena to his hotel, checked out and took the next flight to New Zealand. Earlier in the tournament, Walker had been criticized

Choh Dong-kih, 1964
In 1964 South Korean flyweight Choh Dong-kih staged a 51-minute sitdown strike after being disqualified for holding his head too low.

Byun Jong-il, 1988
In 1988 bantamweight Byun Jong-il beat his countryman's sit-down record by 16 minutes.

by Irish officials for *not* penalizing Korean welterweight Song Kyung-sup when he engaged in head butting.

Another victim of the Koreans' fury was Emil Jetchev, the Bulgarian president of the Referees' Committee of the International Amateur Boxing Association. When a Korean coach attempted to smash Jetchev on the head with a plastic box, a US judge, Stan Hamilton, reached out and blunted the blow. Hamilton had to be treated for a badly cut hand.

After the ring was cleared of unauthorized personnel and miscellaneous debris, Byun sat down in the middle of the ring and staged a silent protest. After 35 minutes he was given a chair. He finally left after 67 minutes, breaking the Olympic sit-in record of 51 minutes set in 1964 by his countryman, flyweight Choh Dong-kih. Before leaving the arena, Byun returned to the ring and bowed to the remaining spectators.

Eventually, five Korean boxing officials were suspended, the president of the Korean Olympic Committee resigned, and the Korean government apologized to the government of New Zealand. Three days after the incident, Lee Heung-soo, the supposedly suspended trainer who had led the charge on Walker, was back in the arena shouting orders to his boxers from a ringside seat.

Hristov, who had slipped out of the stadium without harm, squeaked into the final by winning agonizingly close 3-2 decisions over Aleksandr Artemyev and Jorge Julio Rocha. The latter verdict led to bitter protests from the Colombian corner.

In the final, Hristov ran out of luck. Kennedy McKinney of Killeen, Texas, floored him with a right and left hook combination only 11 seconds into the fight. Although Hristov rose and completed the bout without going down again, McKinney was the clear winner. McKinney went on to a troubled professional career, testing positive for cocaine after his third professional bout and ultimately making a living selling the soil from his 5.8-acre plot of land in Oliver Branch, Mississippi.

One final note about a boxer who never made it to the starting gate: Eduard Paululum was scheduled to be the first-ever Olympic competitor from the small Pacific island nation of Vanuatu. Unfortunately, Paululum ate a large breakfast *before* the weigh-in and was disqualified for being one pound overweight.

1992 Barcelona-Badalona C: 31, N: 31, D: 8.8.

		FINAL MATCH
1. Joel Casamayor Johnson	CUB	Pts 14–8
2. Wayne McCullough	IRL	
3. Mohamed Achik	MOR	
3. Li Gwang-sik	PRK	

5. Roberto Jalnaiz (PHI), Remigio Molina Ferreyra (ARG), Sabo Mohammed (NGR), Serafim Todorov (BUL)

Between 1989 and 1991 the bantamweight division was dominated by Cuba's Enrique Carrión and Bulgaria's Serafim Todorov, and it was assumed that these two would be the favorites in Barcelona. However, when Carrión lost to Todorov at the 1991 world championships and was beaten twice by American Sergio Reyes, the Cubans replaced him with 21-year-old ex-featherweight Joel Casamayor, the son of a hog farmer from Guantánamo. Todorov almost didn't make it to the Olympics either when the AIBA threatened to punish him for skipping the 1992 World Championships Challenge in order to fight in a pseudo-professional German club match. Another contender was Li Gwang-sik of North Korea, who had earned bronze medals at the 1989 and 1991 world championships. At the Barcelona Olympics, Li eliminated Reyes 15-8 and Todorov 16-15 before losing in the semifinals 21-16 to Wayne McCullough in what many observers considered the best fight of the Games. In the final, Casamayor took a 10-2 lead into the last round and then withstood an increasingly vigorous onslaught by the slow-starting McCullough. McCullough, a Protestant from Belfast, carried the Irish flag at the 1988 Seoul Games.

In 1996, Casamayor, scheduled to defend his Olympic title, was training with the Cuban team in Guadalajara, Mexico. On the night of June 27, he fled the camp and headed north, defecting to the United States only three weeks before he was supposed to compete.

1996 Atlanta C: 31, N: 31, D: 8.3.

		FINAL MATCH
1. István Kovács	HUN	Pts 14–7
2. Arnaldo Mesa Bonell	CUB	
3. Vichai Rachanond Khadpo	THA	
3. Raimkoul Malakhbekov	RUS	

5. Rachid Bouaita (FRA), Hicham Nafil (MOR), G. Crinu Olteanu Raicu (ROM), Davaatseren Tseyen-Oidov (MGL)

A flyweight bronze medalist in 1992, István Kovács was not seriously challenged on his way to the bantamweight final in 1996, outpointing his four opponents 68 to 15. In the gold medal bout he faced Arnaldo Mesa, a fighter with a tempestuous history. At the 1991 World Championships Mesa lost his semifinal fight because of a penalty call and had to be restrained after threatening the referee and judges. Mesa was supposed to represent Cuba at the 1992 Barcelona Olympics, but his name was withdrawn after he engaged in a fist fight with a teammate. In Atlanta, Mesa was originally entered in the featherweight division, but was asked to drop down to bantamweight when Joel Casamayor defected three weeks before the Games. Mesa squeezed into the final with the narrowest of wins over Tajik-born Raimkoul Malakhbekov. The two tied 14-14 in their semifinal contest, but Mesa won the total punch tiebreak 75-73. In the final, however, he was no match for the stylish Kovács, who was so thrilled by his victory that he began running around the ring in celebration even before the final bell sounded. An award for perseverance goes to Vichai Rachanond, who was competing in his third Olympics. In both Seoul and Barcelona he lost his first bout, but in Atlanta he put together a string of three wins and earned a bronze medal.

2000 Sydney C: 28, N: 28, D: 9.30.

		FINAL MATCH
1. Guillermo Rigondeaux Ortiz	CUB	Pts 18–12
2. Raimkul Malakhbekov	RUS	
3. Clarence Vinson	USA	
3. Sergey Danilchenko	UKR	
5. Agasi Ağagüloğlu	TUR	
6. Alisher Rahimov	UZB	
7. G. Crinu Olteanu Raicu	ROM	
8. Justin Kane	AUS	

Guillermo Rigondeaux began his Olympic career in impressive fashion, knocking out Moez Zemzemi in only 23 seconds. He then shut out Japan's Kazumasa Tsujimoto 15-0 and defeated reigning European champion Agasi Ağagüloğlu 14-5. In the semifinals he outclassed Clarence Vinson 18-6. On his twentieth birthday, Rigondeaux fought the final against two-time world champion Raimkoul Malakhbekov. Rigondeaux led 4-3 after the first round; Malakhbekov moved ahead 7-6 in the second round. In the second half of the fight, the young Cuban took charge, outscoring Malakhbekov 5-2 in round three and 7-3 in round four.

2004 Athens C: 27, N: 27, D: 8.29.

		FINAL MATCH
1. Guillermo Rigondeaux Ortiz	CUB	Pts 22–13
2. Worapoj Petchkoom	THA	
3. Bahodirjon Sultonov	UZB	
3. Ağasi Mammadov (Agasi Ağagüloğlu)	AZR	

5. Andrew Kooner (CAN), Gennady Kovalyev (RUS), Nestor Bolum (NGR), Maksym Tretiak (UKR)

One year after defeating Agasi Ağagüloğlu in the quarterfinals of the 2000 Olympic competition, Guillermo Rigondeaux beat him again in the final of the 2001 world championship, this time by a score of 30-24. Two years later, Ağagüloğlu gained his revenge by beating Rigondeaux 16-13 win in the second round of the 2003 world championships. It was Guillermo Rigondeaux's first loss in international competition. Ağagüloğlu went on the win the world title. Both Rigondeaux and Ağagüloğlu—now competing for Azerbaijan under the name Ağasi Mammadov—advanced easily into the semi-finals, and fans expected the gold medal bout to be a rematch between the two rivals. However, Thai boxer Worapoj Petchkoom upset Mammadov in the semifinals, using long-range shots to advance 27-19. Ultimately Worapoj proved no match for Rigondeaux, who earned his second gold medal by taking a 6-2 lead after the first round of the final and never relinquishing control.

2008 Beijing C: 27, N: 27, D: 8.24.

		FINAL MATCH
1. Enkhbatyn Badar-Uugan	MGL	Pts 16–5
2. Yankiel León Alarcón	CUB	
3. Bruno Julie	MRI	
3. Veaceslav Gojan	MOL	

5. Worapoj Petchkoom (THA), Héctor Manzanilla (VEN), Akhil Kumar (IND), Khumiso Ikgopoleng (BOT)

After the 2004 Athens Olympics, Cuba was hit by a string of high-profile defections. In December 2006 three Olympic gold medalists—light flyweight Yan Barthelemy, flyweight Yuriokis Gamboa and super heavyweight Odlanier Solis—defected while training in Venezuela. They eventually reappeared in Germany and turned professional.

The following year, at the Pan American Games in Rio de Janeiro, two-time reigning bantamweight gold medalist Guillermo Rigondeaux attempted to defect, along with 2005 world welterweight champion Erislandy Lara. The two were later taken into police custody and returned to Cuba, where they were subsequently removed from the national team. The situation got so bad that Cuba declined to send any boxers to the 2007 world championships in Chicago.

With Rigondeaux out of the running, the contest was wide open. The current world champion, Sergei Vodopyanov, was eliminated in the second round of the competition when his opponent, 2006 Commonwealth champion Akhil Kumar, fought back from a second-round 2-6 deficit to tie the bout 9-9 after four rounds, eventually winning on decision.

Meanwhile, Rigondeaux's replacement on the Cuban team, 26-year-old Yankiel León, received a bye into the second round and advanced easily into the semi-finals, beating 2004 Olympic silver medalist Worapoj Petchkoom 10-2 in the quarter-final round. He then made it to the final after a close 7-5 win over Bruno Julie, who became Mauritius' first-ever Olympic medalist.

In the final León faced reigning world silver medalist Enkhbatyn Badar-Uugan, who had cruised through the tournament, winning his four bouts with a total combined score of 54-10.Cheered on by a group of countrymen chanting "Mon-go-li-a", Badar-Uugan led 4-2 after the first round, stretching this to 8-5 after the second round. He clinched the gold with eight straight points to win 16-5. It was Mongolia's first ever Olympic boxing gold medal.

LIGHTWEIGHT
(60 kg—132 lbs)

1896–1900 not held

1904 St. Louis C: 8, N: 1, D: 9.22.
(61.24 kg—135½ lbs)

		FINAL MATCH
1. Harry Spanger	USA	Dec
2. Jack Eagan	USA	
3. Russell Van Horn	USA	
4. Peter Sturholdt	USA	

A well-known local boxer, Carroll Burton, entered the tournament and won his first match. However, it was then discovered that the victor was not Burton at all, but a man named Bollinger posing as Burton. Bollinger was disqualified and his opponent, Sturholdt, was advanced to the next round.

1906 not held

1908 London C 12, N: 3, D: 10.27.
(63.50 kg—140 lbs)

		FINAL MATCH
1. Frederick Grace	GBR	Dec
2. M. Frederick Spiller	GBR	
3. Harry Johnson	GBR	

4. Harold Holmes (GBR), George Jessup (GBR), Matthew Wells (GBR)

Early in the second round, the two finalists swung hard at each other. Both missed and fell on their faces.

1912 not held

1920 Antwerp C: 16, N: 10, D: 8.24.
(61.24 kg—135½ lbs)

		FINAL MATCH
1. Samuel Mosberg	USA	Dec
2. Gotfred Johansen	DEN	
3. Clarence "Chris" Newton	CAN	
4. Richard Beland	SAF	

5. Frank Cassidy (USA), Frederick Grace (GBR), Julian van Muyzen (BEL), Johan Sæterhaug (NOR)

Grace tried to defend his 12-year-old Olympic title at age 36, but lost a close quarterfinal decision to Mosberg. In the semifinals, Mosberg knocked out Beland in only 15 seconds.

1924 Paris C: 30, N: 22, D: 7.20.
(61.24 kg—135½ lbs)

		FINAL MATCH
1. Hans Nielsen	DEN	Dec
2. Alfredo Copello	ARG	
3. Frederick Boylstein	USA	
4. Jean Tholey	FRA	

5. Richard Breland (SAF), Alfred Genon (BEL), Haakon Hansen (NOR), Benjamin Rothwell (USA)

1928 Amsterdam C: 24, N: 24, D: 8.11.
(61.24 kg—135½ lbs)

		FINAL MATCH
1. Carlo Orlandi	ITA	Dec
2. Stephen Michael Halaiko	USA	
3. Gunnar Berggren	SWE	
4. Hans Nielsen	DEN	

5. Dirk Baan (HOL), Cecil Bissett (ZIM), Pascual Bonfiglio (ARG), Jorge Díaz Hernández (CHI)

1932 Los Angeles C: 13, N: 13, D: 8.13.
(61.24 kg—135½ lbs)

		FINAL MATCH
1. Lawrence Stevens	SAF	Dec
2. Thure Ahlqvist	SWE	
3. Nathan Bor	USA	
4. Mario Bianchini	ITA	

5. Frank Genovese (CAN), Franz Kartz (GER), Gaston Mayor (FRA)

1936 Berlin C: 26, N: 26, D: 8.15.
(61.24 kg—135½ lbs)

		FINAL MATCH
1. Imre Harangi	HUN	Dec
2. Nikolai Stepulov	EST	
3. Erik Ågren	SWE	
4. Poul Kops	DEN	

5. Carlos Lillo (CHI), Lidoro Oliver (ARG), José "Pepe" Padilla, Jr. (PHI), Andrew Scrivani (USA)

Prior to the Olympics, Harangi was urged by doctors to retire from boxing and undergo an operation on his nose, which had been badly injured in previous fights. Harangi refused and went on to win the gold medal in Berlin. One unfortunate competitor was Thomas Hamilton-Brown of South Africa. In his opening-round match, he lost a split decision to Carlos Lillo of Chile. However, it was later discovered that one of the judges had mistakenly reversed his scores for the two boxers and that Hamilton-Brown was in fact the winner and thus eligible to move on to the next round. Unfortunately, Hamilton-Brown, who had had trouble making the weight limit, had softened the disappointment of his loss by going on an eating binge. By the time the South African manager found him it was after midnight and the boxer had already put on nearly five pounds. In desperation, his trainer tried to boil him down, but it was no use. The next day Hamilton-Brown, still over the weight limit, was disqualified and Lillo was allowed to advance in his place. Quarterfinalist Jose "Pempe" Padilla became a well-known movie actor after World War II.

1948 London C: 28, N: 28, D: 8.13.
(62 kg—135½ lbs)

		FINAL MATCH
1. Gerald Dreyer	SAF	Dec
2. Joseph Vissers	BEL	
3. Svend Wad	DEN	
4. Wallace Smith	USA	

5. Øivind Breiby (NOR), Edward Haddad (CAN), Michael "Maxie" McCullagh (IRL), Ralf Benedito Zumbano (BRA)

1952 Helsinki C: 27, N: 27, D: 8.2.

		FINAL MATCH
1. Aureliano Bolognesi	ITA	Dec 2–1
2. Aleksy Antkiewicz	POL	
3. Gheorghe Fiat	ROM	
3. Erkki Pakkanen	FIN	

5. Américo Bonetti (ARG), István Juhász (HUN), Vicente Matute (VEN), Frederick Reardon (GBR)

1956 Melbourne C: 18, N: 18, D: 12.1.

		FINAL MATCH
1. Dick McTaggart	GBR	Dec
2. Harry Kurschat	GER	
3. Anthony Byrne	IRL	
3. Anatoly Lagetko	SOV/RUS	

5. Edward Beattie (CAN), Zygmunt Milewski (POL), Louis Molina (USA), André Vairolatto (FRA)

McTaggart came from a family of 18 children (8 of whom died before he was born) in Dundee, Scotland. His return to Dundee was almost as dangerous as his fights in Melbourne. He was met at the railway station by members of his boxing club, who lifted him onto their shoulders, carried him up the stairs . . . and banged his head on the ceiling. McTaggart competed in two more Olympics, losing both times to Polish boxers who went on to win the gold medal.

1960 Rome C: 34, N: 34, D: 9.5.

		FINAL MATCH
1. Kazimierz Paździor	POL	Dec 4–1
2. Sandro Lopopolo	ITA	
3. Abel Laudonio	ARG	
3. Richard McTaggart	GBR	

5. Velikton Barannikov (SOV/RUS), Harry Campbell (USA), Ferenc Kellner (HUN), Salah Shokweir (UAR/EGY)

Paździor, a 25-year-old blacksmith from Radom, used his experience of 175 fights to outpoint five straight opponents, although he had a tough time with McTaggart in the semifinals.

1964 Tokyo C: 34, N: 34, D: 10.23.

		FINAL MATCH
1. Józef Grudzień	POL	Dec
2. Velikton Barannikov	SOV/RUS	
3. Ronald Allan Harris	USA	
3. James McCourt	IRL	

5. Rodolfo Arpon (PHI), Domingo Barrera Corpas (SPA), János Kajdi (HUN), Stoyan Pilichev (BUL)

1968 Mexico City C: 37, N: 37, D: 10.26.

		FINAL MATCH
1. Ronald W. Harris	USA	Dec 5–0
2. Józef Grudzień	POL	
3. Calistrat Cutov	ROM	
3. Zvonimir Vujin	YUG/SER	

5. Luis Minami (PER), Mohamed Muruli (UGA), Enzo Petriglia (ITA), Stoyan Pilichey (BUL)

1972 Munich C: 37, N: 37, D: 9.10.

		FINAL MATCH
1. Jan Szczepański	POL	Dec 5–0
2. László Orbán	HUN	
3. Samuel Mbugua	KEN	
3. Alfonso Pérez	COL	

5. Eraslan Doruk (TUR), Kim Tai-ho (KOR), Charles Nash (IRL), Sven Erik Paulsen (NOR)

The 32-year-old European champion, Szczepański, was almost upset in the round of 16 when he won the closest of split decisions over Chaidau Altankhuiag of Mongolia. He won his next two fights on a disqualification and a walkover. Then he took a close but unanimous decision from Orbán, the 1969 European champion.

1976 Montreal C: 23, N: 23, D: 7.31.

		FINAL MATCH
1. Howard Davis	USA	Dec 5–0
2. Simion Cutov	ROM	
3. Ace Rusevski	YUG/MAC	
3. Vassily Solomin	SOV/RUS	

5. András Botos (HUN), Yves Jeudy (HAI), Ove Lundby (SWE), Tsvetan Tsvetkov (BUL)

The year 1976 was a full one for Howard "John John" Davis. The father of a 2-year-old boy, Davis played guitar in a rock and soul group, having previously played drums for James Brown. In January he graduated from Glen Cove High School on Long Island. In February he turned 20. In July he went to Montreal with the intention of beating the favorite, European champion Simion Cutov. Two days before the start of the Olympics, Davis' mother, Catherine, died of a heart attack. Davis, deciding to honor his mother by winning the gold medal, was voted the Val Barker award for most outstanding boxer of the Olympics. Two of his five fights were stopped in the first round and the other three were won by unanimous decision.

Howard Davis's gold medal took as strange a journey as any ever awarded. In 1981 the gold medal was stolen from Davis's home on Long Island, New York. Apparently the robber threw it out the window of his car while being chased by police. Ten years later, a landscaper named Jake Fiesel was trimming the long grass beside the Long Island Freeway when he came upon a heavy piece of round metal. Fiesel took it home, cleaned it up and, for the next four years, used it as a paperweight. In 1995 a visitor studying the paperweight realized that it was actually an Olympic gold medal, and Howard Davis's gold medal at that. Fourteen years after his Olympic medal was stolen, Davis received a phone call from Jake Fiesel, who then presented him with the medal.

1980 Moscow C: 29, N: 29, D: 8.2.

		FINAL MATCH	
1. Angel Herrera	CUB	RSC 3	0:13
2. Viktor Demyanenko	SOV/KAZ		
3. Kazimierz Adach	POL		
3. Richard Nowakowski	GDR		

5. Galsandorj Batbileg (MGL), George Gilbody (GBR), Yordan Lessov (BUL), Florin Livadaru (ROM)

Herrera, who had won the 1976 Olympic Featherweight title, moved up successfully to Lightweight four years later, winning four unanimous decisions on his way to the final.

1984 Los Angeles C: 40, N: 40, D: 8.11.

		FINAL MATCH	
1. Pernell Whitaker	USA	Ret 2	2:57
2. Luis Ortiz	PUR		
3. Chun Chil-sung	KOR		
3. Martin Ndongo Ebanga	CAM		

5. Leopoldo Cantancio (PHI), Reiner Gies (GER), José Antonio Hernando (SPA), Fahri Sumer (TUR)

Whitaker, of Norfolk, Va., like Herrera four years earlier, won four unanimous decisions on his way to the final. Ortiz's semifinal split decision victory over Ndongo Ebanga was roundly booed. In the final, Ortiz's handlers stopped the fight following a standing eight-count three seconds before the end of the second round. Whitaker went on to win the lightweight title of all three international professional federations, unifying the division in 1990 for the first time in 8 years. Later he won junior welterweight, welterweight, and junior middleweight titles as well. He defended his welterweight title eight times between 1993 and 1997. However, Whitaker said that winning these championships did not compare to winning an Olympic gold medal. "They placed that medal around my neck and played the national anthem. Nothing else I do in life will top that feeling. I came out of the ring and put that medal on my mother. After winning the gold medal, everything else is icing on the cake."

After he stopped fighting, Whitaker built up a record of alcohol- and drug-related arrests. The most colorful of these occurred on August 10, 2001, when Whitaker was sentenced to four days in jail after pleading guilty to speeding and driving without a license. While sheriff's deputies were taking an inventory of his possessions before taking him away to jail, a packet of cocaine fell out of his money roll. This indiscretion led to a new sentence of one year probation. Whitaker violated this probation by driving drunk and, in 2003, he was sentenced to 27 months in prison. After his release, he was inducted into the International Boxing Hall of Fame.

1988 Seoul C: 39, N: 39, D: 10.1.

		FINAL MATCH
1. Andreas Zuelow	GDR	Dec 5–0
2. George Cramne	SWE	
3. Romallis Ellis	USA	
3. Nerguy Enkhbat	MGL	

5. Mohamed Hegazy (EGY), Charles Kane (GBR), Kamal Marjonane (MOR), Emil Chuprenski (BUL)

The key matchup of the tournament took place in the round of 16 when Andreas Zuelow, a technically pure boxer, faced Kostya Tsyzu of the Soviet Union, who had knocked out his first two opponents in the first round. Two judges gave Zuelow the nod, two more gave the edge to Tsyzu, while the fifth judge, Abdul Hani of Iraq, scored the bout a draw. Olympic rules require each judge to designate a winner. Hani leaned toward Zuelow, who went on to win the gold medal with three straight unanimous decisions. George Cramne, who fought for Sweden, was born in Liberia. Tsyzu moved to Australia and won the professional Super-Lightweight championship in 1997.

1992 Barcelona-Badalona C: 29, N: 29, D: 8.8.

		FINAL MATCH
1. Oscar De La Hoya	USA	Pts 7–2
2. Marco Rudolph	GER	
3. Namjil Bayarsaikhan	MGL	
3. Hong Sung-sik	KOR	

5. Donald Chávez (PHI), Julien Lorcy (FRA), Haji Matumla (TAN), Tontcho Tonchev (BUL)

Like 1984 light flyweight gold medalist Paul Gonzales, Oscar De La Hoya hailed from the East Los Angeles barrio. Both his father and his grandfather were boxers, and Oscar began his own career when he was seven years old. By the age of 17 he had conquered the world at the Goodwill Games. Two months later De La Hoya's good life was shattered when his 38-year-old mother, Cecelia, died of breast cancer. Just before her death, he promised her that he would win an Olympic gold medal. It seemed like a reasonable goal until De La Hoya lost his first bout at the 1991 world championships. His conqueror, by a score of 17-13, was Marco Rudolph, a hotel restaurant charcutier from Cottbus in eastern Germany, who went on to win the world title. Despite this setback, De La Hoya continued to be regarded as a hero in East Los Angeles. One night he was surrounded on the street by five hoodlums with guns. They stole his wallet, which contained $150 in cash. Two hours later De La Hoya found the wallet on his front porch. When the thieves had opened it and discovered who they had robbed, they returned it. The $150 was still inside.

At the Barcelona Olympics De La Hoya breezed through his first two fights, celebrating each victory by kneeling and pointing skyward in honor of his mother. In the quarterfinals, De La Hoya led Tontcho Tonchev 7-6 after two rounds and then won the third round 9-1. Then, in the semifinals, he ran into Hong Sung-sik, a brawler whose style seemed more suited to a wrestling mat than a boxing ring. Both boxers were penalized three points for repeated infractions. The referee was so flustered that he forgot to disqualify Hong after his fourth warning and actually issued him a fifth warning. In the end De La Hoya escaped with an 11-10 win. In the final he faced a rematch with Marco Rudolph. Leading only 3-2 after two rounds, De La Hoya finally put the fight away when he floored Rudolph with 1:09 left in the third round. A gracious loser, Rudolph embraced De La Hoya as soon as the bout was over. At the victory ceremony De La Hoya carried the United States' flag in one hand and a Mexican flag in the other—the latter in honor of his Mexican-born mother. Back in Los Angeles De La Hoya fulfilled his vow to his mother by visiting her grave with the Olympic gold medal.

De La Hoya went on to a highly successful professional career, winning world titles at weights ranging from junior lightweight to light middleweight. Most notably, he defeated Pernell Whitaker for the World Welterweight title April 12, 1997, and then defended the title seven times before losing to Felix Trinidad September 18, 1999.

1996 Atlanta C: 31, N: 31, D: 8.3.

		FINAL MATCH
1. Hocine Soltani	ALG	Pts 3–3 (20–16)
2. Tontcho Tontchev	BUL	
3. Terrance Cauthen	USA	
3. Leonard Doroftei	ROM	

5. Shin Eun-chui (KOR), Koba Gogoladze (GEO), Phongsit Wiangviset (THA), Michael Strange (CAN)

The final was a breathtakingly dull affair that had fans of all races booing and whistling. Soltani led 2-1 in the third round when he was penalized two points for slapping. Suddenly behind, he maintained his composure and scored with a left cross with 30 seconds to go. This tied the score 3-3 and Soltani won the tiebreaker 20-16. He was Algeria's first boxing gold medal winner.

2000 Sydney C: 28, N: 28, D: 9.30.

		FINAL MATCH
1. Mario César Kindelán Mesa	CUB	Pts 14–4
2. Andriy Kotelnyk	UKR	
3. Aleksandr Maletin	RUS	
3. Cristian Bejarano Benítez	MEX	
5. Tingran Ouzlian	GRE	
6. Nurzhan Karimzhanov	KAZ	
7. Selim Palyani	TUR	
8. Almazbek Raymkulov	KYR	

Mario Kindelán had dominated the division for more than two years, winning the Goodwill Games and the World Cup in 1998 and the Pan-American Games and the World Championships in 1999. At the Olympics he outpointed his four opponents 79-36. His closest fight was his first, a 14-8 victory over Thailand's Phongsit Wiangviset. Kindelán was the cousin of Orestes Kindelán, a two-time gold medal winner in baseball and Cuba's greatest home run hitter.

2004 Athens C: 28, N: 28, D: 8.29.

		FINAL MATCH
1. Mario César Kindelán Mesa	CUB	Pts 30–22
2. Amir Khan	GBR	
3. Serik Yeleyev	KAZ	
3. Murat Khrachev	RUS	

5. Domenico Valentino (ITA), Baik Jong-sub (KOR), Rövşen Hüseynov (AZR), Sam Rukundo (UGA)

After earning the gold medal in 2000, Mario Kindelán continued to dominate the lightweight division. He won the 2001 world championship and defended his title in 2003, despite suffering a hairline fracture in his left arm during his second bout.

If Kindelán was the overwhelming favorite for gold, the favored underdog was Amir Khan, a 17-year-old from Bolton, England, and the sole British boxer at the Olympics. Khan had been introduced to boxing at the age of eight by his father, a car mechanic, as a way to channel his energy and keep him out of trouble at school. England's Amateur Boxing Association refused to allow Khan to compete in Athens because of his age. However, Khan discovered he was eligible on the website of the International Amateur Boxing Association despite being too young to compete as a senior in England. Khan was soon courted by Pakistan, the birthplace of both of his parents, and the United States, convincing Britain to support the young boxer.

Kindelán and Khan faced each other in a test event before the start of the Games. The 33-year-old Kindelán dominated the fight, winning 33-13. In the Olympic competition, both boxers breezed through the field. When they met in the final, Kindelán had been undefeated for five years, and had fought more than 330 amateur fights in his career, losing only 22. It was Kahn's 14th senior bout. In the final, Khan scored the first point and estabished a 4-3 lead in the first round, but was outmatched 11-5 in the second round and trailed 14-22 by the end of the third. Khan tried to launch several counterattacks in the final round, but Kindelán stayed out of reach and continued to calmly pick off shots, winning the match 30-22. After the fight, Kindelán announced his intention to retire. However, the two would meet in the ring once more one year later, in a rematch that was to be the final amateur fight for both boxers. Khan won 19-13. After the match, Khan turned pro, while Kindelán retired permanently. In 2006 Kindelán was chosen as a coach for the British Olympic boxing team.

2008 Beijing C: 27, N: 27, D: 8.24.

		FINAL MATCH
1. Aleksei Tishchenko	RUS	Pts 11–9
2. Daouda Sow	FRA	
3. Hrachik Javakhyan	ARM	
3. Yordenis Ugás Hernández	CUB	

5. Baek Jong-seop (KOR), Darley Pérez (COL), Georgian Popescu (ROM), Hu Qing (CHN)

After competing in the lightweight division since 2006, reigning Olympic featherweight champion and 2005 world champion Aleksei Tishchenko was expected to be a major gold-medal contender. He had won the 2006 European title, defeating Armenia's Hrachik Javakhyan 39-15 in the final, and had finished third at the 2007 world championships.

The 2008 Olympic competition also featured 2005 world champion Yordenis Ugás, the only one of the four Cubans to win world titles in 2005 who had not defected or tried to defect before the 2008 Olympics. Ugás, who was also the 2007 Pan Am champion, missed the opportunity to defend his world title when Cuba skipped the world championship due to fears of further defections, but had won the 2008 Americas Olympic qualifying tournament to secure a berth at the Beijing Olympics.

The first big surprise of the tournament came before the competition started, when 22-year-old reigning world champion Frankie Gavin of Great Britain dropped out because he didn't think he could make the 60-kilogram weight limit. With Gavin out, Tishchenko and Ugás both advanced easily to the semi-finals, where Tishchenko beat Javakhyan 15-8 to reach the gold-medal match. In the other semi Ugás led Daouda Sow 7-5 after two rounds before the 25-year-old came back with 10 points to win 15-8.

The final was fairly evenly matched, with Tishchenko building a slim 10-8 lead over the first three rounds. Sow cut the lead to a single point in the last round, but Tishchenko held on and connected with a short punch in the final with 12 seconds to go to secure the gold medal.

LIGHT WELTERWEIGHT

(64 kg—141 lbs [1952-2000: 63.5 kg—140 lbs])

1896–1948 not held

1952 Helsinki C: 28, N: 28, D: 8.2.

		FINAL MATCH
1 Charles Adkins	USA	Dec 2–1
2. Viktor Mednov	SOV/RUS	
3. Erkki Mallenius	FIN	
3. Bruno Visintin	ITA	

5. Terence Milligan (IRL), Jean Paternotte (BEL), Alexander Webster (SAF), René Weismann (FRA)

The final saw the first-ever boxing match between fighters from the United States and the USSR. Adkins, a 20-year-old police administration student from Gary, Indiana, had had no trouble with his preliminary fights.

Mednov, on the other hand, entered the ring with stitches over both eyes, the result of a brutal second-round fight with Francisco Ambrus of Romania, which was finally stopped by a doctor due to injuries to both men. Fortunately for Mednov, his semifinal opponent, Erkki Mallenius, injured his hand and had to withdraw, allowing the Soviet boxer an extra day to heal. In the final bout Mednov fought gallantly, but was no match for Adkins' powerful two-handed hooking.

1956 Melbourne C: 22, N: 22, D: 12.1.

		FINAL MATCH
1. Vladimir Yengibaryan	SOV/ARM	Dec
2. Franco Nenci	ITA	
3. Constantin Dumitrescu	ROM	
3. Henry Loubscher	SAF	

5. Hwang Ei-kyung (KOR), Antonio Marcilla (ARG), Claude Saluden (FRA), Joseph Shaw (USA)

1960 Rome C: 34, N: 34, D: 9.5.

		FINAL MATCH
1. Bohumil Nemeček	CZE	Dec 5–0
2. Clement "Ike" Quartey	GHA	
3. Quincey Daniels	USA	
3. Marian Kasprzyk	POL	

5. Piero Brandi (ITA), Sayed Elnahas (EGY), Kim Duck-bong (KOR), Vladimir Yengibaryan (SOV/ARM)

The final matched two underdogs and was won by Bohumil Nemeček, a 22-year-old railway worker from Decin. Ike Quartey, however, gained distinction by becoming the first black African to win an Olympic medal. Quartey's father had 27 children with five wives. The youngest of the 27 was also named Ike. He competed in the 1988 Olympics and later, as a professional, won the WBA Welterweight title in 1994.

1964 Tokyo C: 35, N: 35, D: 10.23.

		FINAL MATCH
1. Jerzy Kulej	POL	Dec 5–0
2. Yevgeny Frolov	SOV/RUS	
3. Eddie Blay	GHA	
3. Habib Galhia	TUN	

5. Felix Betancourt (CUB), Joao Henrique da Silva (BRA), Vladimír Kućera (CZE), Iosif Mihalic (ROM)

1968 Mexico City C: 35, N: 35, D: 10.26.

		FINAL MATCH
1. Jerzy Kulej	POL	Dec 3–2
2. Enrique Regueiferos	CUB	
3. Arto Nilsson	FIN	
3. James Wallington	USA	

5. Yevgeny Frolov (SOV/RUS), Kim Sa-yong (KOR), Peter Stoichev (BUL), Peter Tiepold (GDR)

Policeman Jerry Kulej beat Enrique Regueiferos, a strong puncher eight years his junior, to win a rare repeat Olympic boxing title.

1972 Munich C: 32, N: 32, D: 9.10.

		FINAL MATCH
1. Ray Seales	USA	Dec 3–2
2. Angel Angelov	BUL	
3. Issaka Daborg	NIG	
3. Zvonimir Vujin	YUG/SER	

5. Srisook Bantow (THA), Andrés Molina Casañola (CUB), Graham Moughton (GBR), Kyoji Shinohara (JPN)

The final between Angel Angelov and "Sugar Ray" Seales of Tacoma, Washington, was a surprisingly dull affair. Many observers felt that Sugar Ray's mother, who rooted him on enthusiastically from ringside, had shadow boxed a better fight than her son's. Born in the US Virgin Islands, Seales turned professional and was reasonably successful until his career was ended by encroaching blindness.

1976 Montreal C: 32, N: 32, D: 7.31.

		FINAL MATCH
1. Ray Leonard	USA	Dec 5–0
2. Andrés Aldama	CUB	
3. Vladimir Kolev	BUL	
3. Kazimierz Szczerba	POL	

5. Ulrich Beyer (GDR), Calistrat Cutov (ROM), József Nagy (HUN), Luis Portillo (ARG)

Ray Leonard, of Palmer Park, Maryland, made it two in a row for light welterweights nicknamed "Sugar Ray." He faced a tough customer in Andrés Aldama, who had stopped his first three opponents in the second round and knocked out Kolev in the semifinals. But Sugar Ray, wearing photos of his girlfriend and their 2-year-old son pinned to his socks, won a clear victory. He turned professional a few months later and won the World Welter-weight championship on November 30, 1979. He lost the title to Robert Duran on June 20, 1980, but regained it five months later. In 1982 he retired as a result of an eye injury. However, he returned to the ring in 1987 and scored a controversial victory over Marvin Hagler in a fight for the World Middleweight championship.

1980 Moscow C: 30, N: 30, D: 8.2.

		FINAL MATCH
1. Patrizio Oliva	ITA	Dec 4–1
2. Serik Konakbayev	SOV/KAZ	
3. José Aguilar	CUB	
3. Anthony Willis	GBR	

5. Farouk Chanchoun Jawad (IRQ), William Lyimo (TAN), José Angel Molina (PUR), Ace Rusevski (YUG/MAC)

Bronze medalist Tony Willis followed in the great British tradition of middleweight Chris Finnegan and hurdler David Hemery when he required three hours, an orangeade, and a glass of water to produce enough urine to be used for a drug test. He passed.

1984 Los Angeles C: 32, N: 32, D: 8.11.

		FINAL MATCH
1. Jerry Page	USA	Dec 5–0
2. Dhawee Umponmaha	THA	
3. Mircea Fulger	ROM	
3. Mirko Puzović	YUG/SER	

5. Lotti Belkhir (TUN), Kim Dong-kil (KOR), Jorge Maisonet (PUR), Jean Pierre Mbereke (CAM)

The light welterweight division was disrupted by controversy in 1984. In a preliminary bout, Jorge Maisonet of Puerto Rico was declared a split decision winner over Nigeria's Charles Nwokolo. While the crowd chanted references to animal excrement, Colonel J. Whyte Ukor, the president of the Nigerian Boxing Association, rushed towards the jury waving his walking stick. After striking at least one boxing official, he was restrained by his coaches and removed from the arena.

Two days later, eventual gold medal winner Jerry Page was awarded a 4–1 quarterfinal victory over South Korean medal favorite Kim Dong-kil, in a match that most ringside observers thought Page had lost. The Korean delegation was so enraged that they threatened to withdraw from the tournament, but they later admitted that the threat was primarily an attempt to call attention to a string of controversial pro-US jury decisions.

1988 Seoul C: 45, N: 45, D: 10.2.

		FINAL MATCH
1. Vyacheslav Yanovsky	SOV/BLR	Dec 5–0
2. Grahame Cheney	AUS	
3. Reiner Gies	GER	
3. Lars Myrberg	SWE	

5. Sodnomdar Jaa Altansukh (MGL), Todd Foster (USA), Antony Mwamba (ZAM), Humberto Rodríguez (MEX)

Because there were so many entrants in the 1988 boxing tournament, two rings were used simultaneously until the quarterfinals. To avoid confusion, the end of a round was announced by a bell in ring A and a buzzer in ring B. The system did not work perfectly, leading to a bizarre incident in the round of 16 during the bout between Todd Foster of Great Falls, Montana, and Chun Jin-chul of South Korea.

The match was held in ring B. Just before the fight began, Foster's coaches reminded him to ignore the bell and listen only for "the horn." With 17 seconds left in round one, the bell sounded in ring A. In ring B Foster, Chun, and the Hungarian referee, Sandor Pajar, hesitated for a moment. Chun dropped his hands and took a step toward his corner. The referee called "Stop."

Foster, realizing that Chun and the referee had made a mistake, blasted Chun with a left hook that caught the Korean in his eye. Chun looked to his corner, then collapsed to the canvas, pretending to be knocked down in an attempt to have Foster disqualified for a late blow. Pajar began to count Chun out, but stopped at four and walked over to the judges for a consultation. Jury president Emil Jetchev called the bout a no-contest and ordered a rematch for the following day. An hour and a half later, Foster was sitting in the stands waiting to watch another American fight when he was told that, as a result of a US protest, the rematch would take place in 45 minutes. Foster opened the second bout by charging after Chun and knocking him to the canvas only 6 seconds into the fight. In the final minute of the first round Chun pounded Foster's nose, splattering blood on both boxers. Round two began with the spilling of more Foster blood, but the American took charge, knocking out Chun with a left hook to the chin.

In his next bout, Foster lost a split decision to Grahame Cheney, who later became Australia's first Olympic boxing finalist in eighty years. In the final, Cheney fought gamely, but was no match for the experienced 31-year-old Yanovsky.

1992 Barcelona-Badalona C: 30, N: 30, D: 8.9.

		FINAL MATCH
1. Héctor Vinent Charón	CUB	Pts 11–1
2. Mark Leduc	CAN	
3. Leonard Doroftei	ROM	
3. Jyri Kjäll	FIN	

5. Laid Bouneb (ALG), Oleg Nikolayev (RUS), Peter Richardson (GBR), László Szücs (HUN)

Vinent, a 20-year-old from Santiago de Cuba, was one of the most impressive fighters at the Barcelona Olympics, outpointing his five opponents by a combined score of 91 to 12. Leduc, a 30-year-old homosexual boxer from Toronto who once served three years in prison for armed robbery, had beaten Vinent two years earlier in Canada but was no match for him in Barcelona.

1996 Atlanta C: 32, N: 32, D: 8.4.

		FINAL MATCH
1. Héctor Vinent Charón	CUB	Pts 20–13
2. Oktay Urkal	GER	
3. Fethi Missaoui	TUN	
3. Bolat Niyazymbetov	KAZ	

5. Mohamed Allalou (ALG), Babak Moghimi (IRN), Nordine Mouchi (FRA), Edward Zaharov (RUS)

Between Olympics, Vinent won both world championships, in 1993 and 1995. He had little trouble defending his Olympic title in Atlanta. In the final he led 7-3 after one round and 14-7 after two.

2000 Sydney C: 27, N: 27, D: 9.29.

		FINAL MATCH
1. Mahamatkadir Abdullayev	UZB	Pts 27–20
2. Ricardo Williams	USA	
3. Diógenes Luna Martínez	CUB	
3. Mohamed Allalou	ALG	
5. Sergey Bukovsky	BLR	
6. Aleksandr Leonov	RUS	
7. Sven Paris	ITA	
8. Saleh Abdelbary Abdel Maksoud	EGY	

The tournament was enlivened by two particularly good fights. In the second elimination round, Sergey Bukovsky of Belarus trailed Nurhan Süleymanoğlu of Turkey 1-6 after three rounds, but outscored him 7-2 in the final round to achieve an 8-8 tie. Bukovsky won the tiebreaker 40-38. In the semifinals Ricardo Williams and Diógenes Luna clashed in what would turn out to be the best bout of the Sydney Olympics. The two fought toe-to-toe for almost the entire 8 minutes. Luna led 13-10 after the first round and 29-15 after the second. Olympics rules state that a fight is stopped if one boxer builds a 15-point lead. Williams went into the third round one point away from elimination. He then outscored Luna 20-2 to take a 35-31 lead. Luna won back two points in the closing seconds of the round. Exhausted, Williams switched tactics and ran and jabbed in the fourth round. He expanded his lead to 38-33, but Luna fought back and moved ahead 40-39. Williams scored three times and then Luna scored once to make it 42-41 Williams with 20 seconds left. Williams avoided Luna until the round ended and advanced to the final.

Mahamatkadir Abdullayev forged an easier path to the final. The reigning world champion, he was seriously challenged only once, in the quarterfinals against Bukovsky. Abdullayev won that one 9-6. The son of a truck driver, Abdullayev had defeated Williams 11-4 in an early round of the world championships. At the Olympics, he led 10-5 after two rounds. Williams closed the gap to 16-13 early in the final round. Abdullayev scored three straight points and held on to win 27-20.

2004 Athens C: 27, N: 27, D: 8.28.

		FINAL MATCH
1. Manus Boonjumnong	THA	Pts 17–11
2. Yudel Johnson Cedeno	CUB	
3. Boris Georgiev	BUL	
3. Ionut Gheorghe	ROM	

5. Dilshod Mahmudov (UZB), Nurzhan Karimzhanov (KAZ), Willy Blain (FRA), Michele Di Rocco (ITA)

Manus Boonjumnong used an ultracautious approach to frustrate his opponents, punching in flurries and then dancing away to safety. In the quarterfinals he scored a surprise 20-18 upset against reigning world champion Willy Blain. who found himself unable to reach the backpedaling Boonjumnong. In the final against Yudel Johnson, Boonjumnong continued to use the fighting style taught him by his Cuban coach, Juan Fontanilis, darting in to land a punch and then skipping out of range. He opened up a 6-2 lead after the first round, then held off Johnson's counterattacks to finish 17-11.

After Boonjumnong's victory, he received a phone call from Thailand's King Bhumibol Adulyadej, and was rewarded with more than 20 million baht (US $480,000) in prizes, not to mention the chance to see, for the first time, his six-week old son, named Athens.

Within two years, Boonjumnong had spent his prize money and earned a reputation as a big-spending playboy. In an attempt to straighten him out for the 2008 Olympics, the Thai amateur boxing association sent Boonjumnong to train in Cuba—without any money. The lesson appeared to have worked: when Boonjumnong won a gold medal at the Asian Games in 2006, he celebrated by shaving his head and spending two weeks in a Buddhist monastery.

2008 Beijing C: 28, N: 28, D: 8.23.

		FINAL MATCH
1. Félix Díaz Guzman	DOM	Pts 12–4
2. Manus Boonjumnong	THA	
3. Rosniel Iglesias Sotolongo	CUB	
3. Alexis Vastine	FRA	

5. Serik Sapiyev (KAZ), Gennady Kovalyov (RUS), Morteza Sepahvandi (IRN), Uranchimegiin Mönkh-Erdene (MGL)

Despite a two-year descent into partying and gambling, defending Olympic champion Manus Boonjumnong had worked himself back into fighting shape in time for the 2006 Asian Games. He faced 2005 world champion Serik Sapiyev in the final, and pulled off a narrow 22-18 victory. The following year, Boonjumnong had less success, losing his first bout against eventual bronze medalist Masatsugu Kawachi of Japan.

Boonjumnong's return to form notwithstanding, the real favorite in the light welterweight division was double world champion Serik Sapiyev. In eleven bouts over the two world championships no opponent had got closer than eleven points, and only two of his six 2007 bouts went the full four rounds.

The much anticipated meeting of Sapiyev and Boonjumnong materialized in the quarter-finals, after both received first-round byes and advanced easily through the next round. Boonjumnong led 3-1 after the first two rounds before Sapiyev found his range and leveled the score to 5-5 at the end of the third. Boonjumnong came back with two points in the fourth round to advance 7-5 over the world champion.

With Sapiyev out, Boonjumnong had little difficulty reaching the final, beating Rosniel Iglesias 10-5 after Iglesias was penalized in the third round for a head butt. Boonjumnong spent the fourth round avoiding Iglesias to hold on to his lead.

Boonjumnong's opponent in the final was 24-year-old relative unknown Félix Díaz. Díaz had had a difficult path to the final, advancing to the quarter-finals on a hard-fought 11-11 decision over Ireland's Johnny Joyce. His semi-final bout against Alexis Vastine was even more controversial, as Vastine, who towered a full seven inches over Díaz, was harshly penalized not once but twice for holding. Vastine screamed and wept after a second two-point penalty in the final seconds of the bout gave Díaz the victory.

The judging controversy erupted into a full-scale scandal when AIBA technical delegate Rudel Obreja held an impromptu press conference immediately after the semi-finals, in which he made sweeping allegations of bias in the referee selection process . Obreja was quickly suspended, although AIBA admitted that it had been tracking "possible attempts at manipulation" for more than two months. Nothing ever came of its investigation.

After all that, the gold medal match was relatively straightforward. Díaz came out strong and fast, scoring with a series of rights to the head and body blows, and pulled away by the third round to an eventual 12-4 victory. Díaz turned professional in 2009 and maintained an unbeaten professional record of ten bouts over two years.

WELTERWEIGHT

(69 kg—152 lbs [1948-2000: 67 kg—148 lbs])

1896–1900 not held

1904 St. Louis C: 4, N: 1, D: 9.22.

(65.77 kg—145 lbs)

		FINAL MATCH
1. Albert Young	USA	Dec
2. Harry Spanger	USA	
3. Jack Eagan	USA	
3. Joseph Lydon	USA	

1906–1912 not held

1920 Antwerp C: 18, N: 11, D: 24.

(66.68 kg—147 lbs)

		FINAL MATCH
1. Albert Schneider	CAN/USA	Dec
2. Alexander Ireland	GBR	
3. Frederick Colberg	USA	
4. William Clark	USA	

5. Léon Gillet (FRA), Aage Steen (NOR), Trygve Stokstad (NOR), August Suhr (DEN)

Bert Schneider of Canada was actually a US citizen. Born in Cleveland, his family moved to Montreal when he was 9 years old. Unaware that boxing was an Olympic sport, Schneider learned that he had been chosen for the Canadian team when he read it in a newspaper. His final bout with Ireland ended in a draw, so the referee ordered the two exhausted fighters to square off for an extra round. Schneider had the most energy left and earned the gold medal.

1924 Paris C: 29, N: 18, D: 7.20.
(68.68 kg—147 lbs)

		FINAL MATCH
1. Jean Delarge	BEL	Dec
2. Héctor Méndez	ARG	
3. Douglas Lewis	CAN	
4. Patrick Dwyer	IRL	

5. Hugh Haggerty (USA), Roy Ingram (SAF), Alfons Mello (USA), Teodor Stauffer (SWI)

The first two rounds of the final match were all Delarge's, as Méndez tried unsuccessfully to land his notorious knockout right. He finally caught the Belgian in the third round and pummeled him around the ring. But it was too late. Delarge wouldn't go down, and he had already built up a big enough lead to secure the victory. When the verdict was announced, pandemonium broke loose as thousands of Argentinians began chanting, "Méndez! Méndez! Méndez!" A furious Belgian rushed in among them and unfurled a Belgian flag, which led to further chaos. The demonstration went on for more than fifteen minutes before order was restored. This incident was actually a mere anticlimax after what had occurred following a preliminary match three days earlier. On that day an English referee, T.H. Walker, disqualified an Italian boxer named Giuseppi Oldani for persistent holding of his opponent. Oldani fell to the floor, sobbing, while his supporters pelted Walker with sticks, coins, and walking stick knobs. This went on for almost an hour, until Walker was finally escorted from the arena by a contingent of British, American, and South African boxers, headed by the 265-pound wrestler Con O'Kelly.

1928 Amsterdam C: 22, N: 22, D: 8.11.
(66.68 kg—147 lbs)

		FINAL MATCH
1. Edward Morgan	NZL	Dec
2. Raúl Landini	ARG	
3. Raymond Smillie	CAN	
4. Robert Galataud	FRA	

5. Cornelis Blommers (HOL), Romano Caneva (ITA), Johan Hellstrom (FIN), Kintaro Usuda (JPN)

When 22-year-old Ted Morgan left New Zealand by ship, he was a lightweight. When he arrived in Amsterdam six weeks later he was a welterweight. Despite fighting with a dislocated knuckle, he became the first gold medalist to represent New Zealand.

1932 Los Angeles C: 16, N: 16, D: 8.13.
(66.68 kg—147 lbs)

		FINAL MATCH
1. Edward Flynn	USA	Dec
2. Erich Campe	GER	
3. Bruno Ahlberg	FIN	
4. David McCleave	GBR	

5. Robert Barton (SAF), Luciano Fabbroni (ITA), Lucien Laplace (FRA), Carl Jensen (DEN)

After the Olympics Flynn turned professional and fought just long enough to finance his way through dental school, eventually setting up practice in Tampa, Florida. Flynn once explained, "Oh, boxing's all right. But I'm getting kind of sick of putting on gloves and hitting some fellow in the face when I've got nothing against him."

1936 Berlin C: 25, N: 25, D: 8.15.
(66.68 kg—147 lbs)

		FINAL MATCH
1. Sten Suvio	FIN	Dec
2. Michael Murach	GER	
3. Gerhard Petersen	DEN	
4. Roger Tritz	FRA	

5. Simplicio de Castro (PHI), Heinrich Dekkers (HOL), Imre Mándi (HUN), Raúl Rodríguez (ARG)

1948 London C: 26, N: 26, D: 8.13.

		FINAL MATCH
1. Július Torma	CZE/SLV	Dec
2. Horace Herring	USA	
3. Alessandro D'Ottavio	ITA	
4. Douglas Du Preez	SAF	

5. William Boyce (AUS), Zygmunt Chychla (POL), Aurelio Díaz Cadaveda (SPA), Eladio Herrera (ARG)

Before his second-round bout with Gerald Blackburn of Canada, Július Torma of Czechoslovakia attempted to shake hands with his opponent in the dressing room. When Blackburn refused, Torma became angry and decided to give the Canadian a lesson in the ring. This he did, with the referee stopping the fight in the second round. However, Torma's final left hook fractured a bone in his hand and it looked as if he might have to withdraw. Instead the 26-year-old Hungarian-born store clerk was able to hide his injury from his next three opponents, winning with careful defense and judicious use of his right hand.

1952 Helsinki C: 29, N: 29, D: 8.2.

		FINAL MATCH
1. Zygmunt Chychla	POL	Dec 3–0
2. Sergei Scherbakov	SOV/RUS	
3. Günther Heidemann	GER	
3. Victor Jörgensen	DEN	

5. Nicholaas Linneman (HOL), Ronald Norris (IND), Július Torma (CZE), Franco Vescovi (ITA)

1956 Melbourne C: 16, N: 16, D: 12.1.

		FINAL MATCH
1. Nicolae Linca	ROM	Dec 3–2
2. Frederick Tiedt	IRL	
3. Nicholas Gargano	GBR	
3. Kevin Hogarth	AUS	

5. Nicholas André (SAF), András Döri (HUN), Francisco Gelaberti (ARG), Pearce Allen Lane (USA)

Tiedt actually received more total points than Linca, but the Romanian was given the nod by three of the five judges. Romania has a strange history in Olympic boxing. Although twenty-one different Romanian boxers have earned medals, Linca is the only one to have won a gold.

1960 Rome C: 33, N: 33, D: 9.5.

		FINAL MATCH
1. Giovanni Benvenuti	ITA	Dec 4–1
2. Yuri Radonyak	SOV/RUS	
3. Leszek Drogosz	POL	
3. James Lloyd	GBR	

5. A. Phillip Baldwin (USA), Henry Loubscher (SAF), Shishman Mitsev (BUL), Andrés Moreno Navarro (SPA)

The European Light Middleweight champion Nino Benvenuti dropped down in weight class for the Olympics. He floored Radonyak toward the end of the first round, but the Soviet boxer came back strongly and was the aggressor in the final round. Benvenuti turned professional in 1961 and won the World Junior Middleweight title in 1965. On April 17, 1967, he defeated Emile Griffith for the World Middleweight championship, a title which he held for three of the next three and a half years.

1964 Tokyo C: 30, N: 30, D: 10.23.

		FINAL MATCH
1. Marian Kasprzyk	POL	Dec 4–1
2. Ričardas Tamulis	SOV/LIT	
3. Silvano Bertini	ITA	
3. Pertti Purhonen	FIN	

5. Issaka Daborg (NIG), Kichijiro Hamada (JPN), Ernest Powell Mabwa (UGA), Michael Varley (GBR)

1968 Mexico City C: 33, N: 33, D: 10.26.

		FINAL MATCH
1. Manfred Wolke	GDR	Dec 4–1
2. Joseph Bessala	CAM	
3. Mario Guilloti	ARG	
3. Volodymyr Musalimov	SOV/UKR	

5. Armando Muñiz Hurtado (USA), Alfonso Ramírez Gutiérrez (MEX), Celal Sandal (TUR), Victor Zilberman (ROM)

Joseph Bessala was the first Cameroonian athlete to earn a medal at the Olympics, and he returned home a hero, receiving a car and a house from his nation's President. Unfortunately, after spending four years in France pursuing an unsuccessful professional career, Bessala returned to find his house occupied by a stranger—and realized that he had forgotten to ask for official papers for the house. Bessala was given a second house by the state, but was evicted without explanation several years later. He used the last of his savings to build a small house where he safely settled.

1972 Munich C: 37, N: 37, D: 9.10.

		FINAL MATCH
1. Emilio Correa	CUB	Dec 5–0
2. János Kajdi	HUN	
3. Dick "Tiger" Murunga	KEN	
3. Jesse Valdez	USA	

5. Maurice Hope (GBR), Anatoly Khohlov (SOV/RUS), Sergio Lozano (MEX), Günter Meier (GER)

The final matched the 19-year-old Pan American champion, Emilio Correa, and the 32-year-old European titleholder, János Kajdi. The Cuban won a close but unanimous decision.

1976 Montreal C: 31, N: 31, D: 7.31.

		FINAL MATCH
1. Jochen Bachfeld	GDR	Dec 3–2
2. Pedro Gamarro	VEN	
3. Reinhard Skricek	GER	
3. Victor Zilberman	ROM	

5. Clinton Jackson (USA), Michael McCallum (JAM), Carmen Rinke (CAN), Carlos Santos (PUR)

Silver medalist Pedro Gamarro was the surprise of the tournament. In his third bout he stopped defending Olympic and world amateur champion Emilio Correa, and in the quarterfinals he defeated favorite Clinton Jackson on a split decision. The 21-year-old Venezuelan almost went all the way, but he lost a close split decision in the title match to 24-year-old Jochen Bachfeld.

1980 Moscow C: 29, N: 29, D: 8.2.

		FINAL MATCH
1. Andrés Aldama	CUB	Dec 4–1
2. John Mugabi	UGA	
3. Karl-Heinz Krüger	GDR	
3. Kazimierz Szczerba	POL	

5. Mehmet Bogujevi (YUG/Kosovo), Ionel Budușan (ROM), Joseph Frost (GBR), Plamen Yankov (BUL)

John Mugabi needed a total of only nine minutes to knock out his first three opponents. He got by Kazimierz Szczerba on a split decision but was defeated by Andrés Aldama, who had won the Light Welterweight silver medal four years earlier.

1984 Los Angeles C: 36, N: 36, D: 8.11.

		FINAL MATCH
1. Mark Breland	USA	Dec 5–0
2. An Young-su	KOR	
3. Luciano Bruno	ITA	
3. Joni Nyman	FIN	

5. Dwight Frazer (JAM), Vesa Koskela (SWE), Alexander Künzler (GER), Genaro León (MEX)

At 6 feet 2 inches, Brooklyn's Mark Breland, the most ballyhooed boxer at the Los Angeles Olympics, towered over his fellow welterweights. He also sported a 78-inch reach. Entering the tournament, Breland was the overwhelming favorite, having won the 1982 world amateur championship and having beaten everyone in his division including those from boycotting nations. His pre-Olympic record was 104 wins and 1 loss. As if all this wasn't intimidating enough to his opponents, Breland, who sparred with Tommy Hearns and with a professional karate champion, also received pre-fight advice from Muhammad Ali, Sugar Ray Robinson and Sugar Ray Leonard. A well-composed student of yoga, the 20-year-old Breland had already gained fame outside the world of boxing by starring in the 1983 film *The Lords of Discipline.*

1988 Seoul C: 44, N: 44, D: 10.1.

		FINAL MATCH	
1. Robert Wangila	KEN	KO 2	0:44
2. Laurent Boudouani	FRA		
3. Jan Dydak	POL		
3. Kenneth Gould	USA		

5. Adewale Adegbusi (NGR), Hristo Furnigov (BUL), Joni Nyman (FIN), Song Kyung-sup (KOR)

Wangila, a Nairobi brewery worker, was the first black African boxer to win an Olympic championship. This was also the first welterweight final to be decided by a knockout after 16 consecutive decisions. On July 22, 1994, Wangila lost a professional fight in Las Vegas to David Gonzales, walked back to the dressing room, and suddenly lapsed into a coma. He died 36 hours later. When his body was returned to Nairobi, fighting broke out between the police and local Moslems over what form of burial he should receive. Born a Christian, Wangila converted to Islam while in the United States. His will stated that he should be buried according to the wishes of his wife, who was Moslem. Wangila's mother challenged the will, as did the relatives of a man they claimed was Wangila's father. Finally a Kenyan judge ruled in favor of an Islamic burial.

1992 Barcelona-Badalona C: 30, N: 30, D: 8.8.

		FINAL MATCH
1. Michael Carruth	IRL	Pts 13–10
2. Juan Hernández Sierra	CUB	
3. Aníbal Acevedo Santiago	PUR	
3. Arkhom Chenglai	THA	

5. Sören Antman (SWE), Vitalijus Karpačiauskas (LIT), Andreas Otto (GER), Francisc Vaştag (ROM)

The stereotypical Irishman loves a good fight, but until 1992 no boxer representing Ireland had ever won a gold medal. So it was a great day for the Irish on August 8, when not one but two Irish fighters made it to the finals in Barcelona—such a thing had never happened before. Despite the fact that it was the Cubans who had dominated the tournament, qualifying for five of the six finals being held that day, it was the Irish fans who filled the Joventut Pavilion with drum-beating, singing, and raucous celebration. The first Irish finalist, bantamweight Wayne McCullough, was thought to have the best chance of becoming Ireland's first Olympic champion in any sport since Ron Delany won the 1500 meters back in 1956. McCullough fought gamely, but was outpointed by Cuban Joel Casamayor. If McCullough couldn't defeat a Cuban opponent, what possible chance could Michael Carruth have? After all, Juan Hernández was the reigning world champion; Carruth wasn't even ranked in the top fifteen. Even the bookmakers in Ireland were giving 7-2 odds in favor of Hernández.

Carruth, an army corporal, came from a family of ten children in Greenhills, south Dublin, and was the last-born of triplets. At the Seoul Olympics, fighting as a light welterweight, Carruth won one bout then lost his second. At the 1989 world championships he earned a bronze medal, losing 18-1 in the semifinals to Andreas Otto of Germany. At the Barcelona Olympics, three years later, Carruth faced Otto again, this time in the quarterfinals. When the fight was over the scoreboard read 6-6. In the event of a tie, the officials turn to the total punches registered by the five judges combined. This time Carruth came out on top, 35-22. By defeating Arkhom Chenglai 11-4 in the semis, he unexpectedly fought himself into the final against Hernández, who had overwhelmed his four opponents, stopping two of them in the second round and outpointing the other two 6-0 and 11-2.

Despite his long-shot status, Carruth had a couple things going for him. Because of a gymnastics injury, his right arm was more than two inches shorter than his left. Although he was right-handed, he was forced to fight as a southpaw, making him strong with both hands. Most important, in his corner he had something few other boxers had—a Cuban coach, Nicolas Cruz, not to mention a special trainer: his own father, Austin Carruth.

Sitting in the dressing room just before the final, Michael Carruth began to lose heart. It was hard for him to imagine defeating Hernández. Austin Carruth walked over and guessed what was going on. He pointed to his son's legs and said, "There's your ticket to the gold medal. That's the way you're going to win this fight—by using them." Michael closed his eyes, concentrated, and, as he later recalled, "miraculously, the self-doubt began to recede. I grabbed hold of Dad and the man nearly passed out on the spot with fright. 'Dad,' I told him, 'I'm going to win this fight. I'm going to bring the gold medal back with me to Dublin. Ronnie Delany's time is up.'"

In the first round Carruth successfully crowded the taller Hernández and came away with a 4-3 lead. In the second round, he was penalized three points for holding, but gained back a couple points as the round closed. The score was 8-8. Back in his corner Carruth suggested that he should "have a real go" at Hernández and try to back him into a corner. His father and Cruz bawled him out and told him to stick to his game plan of forcing Hernández to come to him and sneaking inside. They pointed across to the Cuban corner, where tempers were flaring and frustration and panic were starting to show. Sure enough, in the final three minutes, Hernández's impatience led to errors and Carruth was able to take the round, 5-2, and with it the fight and the Olympic championship. When the verdict was announced, the arena reverberated with the cheers of the Irish supporters. But the celebration in Barcelona was nothing compared to what went on back in Dublin. Carruth was instantly promoted to sergeant. Army helicopters flew over Carruth's house to salute his victory. And, most incredible of all, on the day of his return to Ireland, local pubs dropped the price of beer to that of 1956. For one day in 1992 a pint of Guinness could be bought for four pence.

1996 Atlanta C: 32, N: 32, D: 8.3.

		FINAL MATCH
1. Oleg Saitov	RUS	Pts 14–9
2. Juan Hernández Sierra	CUB	
3. Daniel Santos	PUR	
3. Marian Simion	ROM	

5. Hasan Al (DEN), Nariman Atayev (UZB), Kamel Chater (TUN), Nurzhan Smanov (KAZ)

Juan Hernández had dominated the welterweight division for the past five years, winning the world championship in 1991, 1993 and 1995. Other than a questionable disqualification for a low blow at the 1995 Pan-American Games, his only loss had been in the 1992 Olympic final. In Atlanta, Hernández breezed through four preliminary bouts. In the gold medal match he faced Oleg Saitov, the boxer he had beaten 4-2 in the 1995 world championship final. Hernández jumped out to a quick 2-0 lead, but Saitov took charge in the second round and led 8-4. In the third round Saitov surprised Hernández by continuing to attack rather than defending his lead. Nonetheless, when the verdict was announced, it was met by booing and jeering from the usually anti-Cuban crowd. In reality, Saitov probably did deserve the victory, although not by as wide a margin as the final score implied.

2000 Sydney C: 27, N: 27, D: 9.30.

		FINAL MATCH
1. Oleg Saitov	RUS	Pts 24–16
2. Sergei Dotsenko	UKR	
3. Dorel Simion	ROM	
3. Vitaly Grusak	MOL	
5. Ruslan Khairov	AZE	
6. Danijar Muneitbasov	KAZ	
7. Steven Kuchler	GER	
8. Bulent Ulusoy	TUR	

Hostility towards Oleg Saitov seemed to carry over from the 1996 final to the 2000 tournament. Even his opening 15-1 victory over Francisco Calderon of Colombia was booed, as his punch and run style turned off the spectators. In the quarterfinals, Ruslan Khairov staged a stirring comeback against Saitov. The bout ended 10-10, but Saitov won the total points tiebreaker 55-47, much to the disgust of the crowd. Saitov's 19-10 semifinal win against Dorel Simion was also met by loud booing, while his final victory over Sergei Dotsenko was greeted by more grumbling. The lack of respect that Saitov received despite his success was epitomized by an earlier incident in which he went straight from the ring into the stands in order to watch another fight. Although he was still wearing his uniform and his hands were still wrapped, he was stopped by a security official who demanded to see Saitov's accreditation.

2004 Athens C: 27, N: 27, D: 8.29.

		FINAL MATCH
1. Bakhtiyar Artayev	KAZ	Pts 36–26
2. Lorenzo Aragón Armenteros	CUB	
3. Kim Jung-joo	KOR	
3. Oleg Saytov	RUS	

5. Juan Camilo Novoa (COL), Ruslan Xeyirov (AZR), Sherzod Husanov (UZB), Viktor Poliakov (UKR)

Fans expected to see a gold medal match-up between two-time world champion Lorenzo Aragón and two-time gold medalist Oleg Saitov, but in the semifinals Bakhtiyar Artayev ended Saitov's hopes for a third consecutive gold by defeating him 20-18. Trailing Aragón one point after the first round of the final, Artayev staged a strong comeback, establishing a 10-point lead by the end of the third round, and maintaining it to win 36-26. Artayev also earned the Val Barker trophy for the best boxer in the Athens Olympics.

2008 Beijing C: 29, N: 29, D: 8.24.

		FINAL MATCH
1. Bakhyt Sarsekbayev	KAZ	Pts 18–9
2. Carlos Banteux Suárez	CUB	
3. Hanati Silamu	CHN	
3. Kim Jeong-ju	KOR	

5. Hosam Abdin (EGY), Toureano Johnson (BAH), Dilshod Makhmudov (UZB), Demetrius Andrade (USA)

Twenty-year-old Demetrius Andrade seemed to be the United States' best chance at a boxing gold medal in Beijing. Known by his long-time family nickname "Boo Boo", Andrade had dominated the 2007 world championships in Chicago, winning each of his six bouts by at least eleven points.

Beyond Andrade, the medal competition seemed wide open. Defending Olympic champion Bakhtiyar Artayev of Kazakhstan had moved up to the middleweight division, while 2005 world champion Erislandy Lara, having attempted to defect after the 2007 Pan American Games, had been removed from the Cuban national team. Lara's replacement, Carlos Banteux, won the American Olympic qualification tournament and seemed to be a medal contender. So did Non Boonjumnong, the 2006 Asian Games champion and brother of 2004 light welterweight Olympic champion Manus Boonjumnong.

Andrade had a tough first-round bout against Georgia's Kakhaber Zhvania, winning 11-9, but easily dispatched 2006 European champion Andrei Balanov of Russia 14-3 in the second round. He then faced 2004 Athens silver medalist Kim Jung-joo in the quarterfinals, with both boxers starting out cautiously and having to be ordered twice by the referee to throw more punches. Kim established a slim lead and pulled off an 11-9 upset to advance to the semis.

Meanwhile Bakhyt Sarsekbayev rolled through the tournament, beating 2005 world light welterweight silver medalist Dilshod Makhmudov 12-7 in the quarterfinals to face Kim in the semis. He won 10-6 to progress to the gold-medal match, in which he won a decisive 18-9 victory over Banteux, leaving Cuba with no gold medals for the first time since the 1968 Olympics in Mexico City.

MIDDLEWEIGHT

(75 kg—165½ lbs)

1896–1900 not held

1904 St. Louis C: 2, N: 1, D: 9.22.

(71.67 kg—158 lbs)

		FINAL MATCH	
1. Charles Mayer	USA	RSC 3	1:40
2. Benjamin Spradley	USA		

1906 not held

1908 London C: 10, N: 3, D: 10.27.

(71.67 kg—158 lbs)

		FINAL MATCH
1. John Douglas	GBR	Dec
2. Reginald "Snowy" Baker	AUS	
3. William Philo	GBR	
4. Ruben Warnes	GBR	
5. William Childs	GBR	

John William Henry Tyler (JWHT) Douglas was a well-known cricketer, known in Australia as "Johnny Won't Hit Today" Douglas because of his defensive batting. Silver medalist Reginald "Snowy" Baker also took part in the springboard diving competition and the 4 × 200-meter freestyle relay at the 1908 Olympics. In fact, Baker was probably the greatest all-around athlete ever produced by Australia. He competed in twenty-nine different sports and represented Australia in international competition in five of them. He also knocked out Douglas in a rematch a few days after the Olympics. In later years, Baker starred in several silent films, most notably *The Fighting Breed* (1921), moved to Hollywood, and taught fencing, riding, and swimming to stars such as Greta Garbo and Douglas Fairbanks.

1912 not held

1920 Antwerp C: 17, N: 10, D: 8.24.

(72.57 kg—160 lbs)

		FINAL MATCH
1. Henry Mallin	GBR	Dec
2. Georges Prud'homme	CAN	
3. Montgomery "Moe" Herscovitch	CAN	
4. Hjalmar Strømme	NOR	

5. William Bradley (SAF), Samuel Lagonia (USA), Martin Olsen (DEN), Marcel Rey-Golliet (FRA)

1924 Paris C: 23, N: 14, D: 7.20.
(72.57 kg—160 lbs)

		FINAL MATCH
1. Henry Mallin	GBR	Dec
2. John Elliott	GBR	
3. Joseph Beecken	BEL	
4. Leslie Black	CAN	

5. Roger Brousse (FRA), Daniel Daney (FRA), T. Harry Henning (CAN), James Murphy (IRL)

Olympic boxing has a long and glorious history of protests, demonstrations, and general outrages. But of all the incidents and controversies, the real gold medal winner was the Brousse-Mallin Affair, which occurred in Paris in 1924. Harry Mallin, the defending champion, was a 32-year-old London policeman. In the quarterfinals he faced 23-year-old Roger Brousse of France. As soon as the fight ended, Mallin approached the Belgian referee and displayed several well-defined teeth marks on his chest. The referee ignored him and proceeded to read out the verdict. Although most ringside observers gave the fight to Mallin, it was Brousse who won the decision, 2-1. The Italian judge and the Belgian referee voted for Brousse, while the South African judge sided with Mallin. Mallin, who had never lost a fight, left the ring without further comment. However, a protest was lodged by Mr. Söderland, a Swedish member of the International Boxing Association, and an inquiry was held. Examination of Mallin's chest revealed that he had most definitely been bitten, and quite robustly at that. In fact, in his previous bout Brousse had also been accused of biting his opponent, Manolo Gallardo of Argentina. Brousse's supporters claimed that he had an odd habit of snapping his jaw whenever he threw a punch. What had happened, they said, was that Mallin had ducked one of Brousse's punches and, coming back up, bumped his chest against Brousse's snapping mouth. The Jury of Appeal ruled that Brousse's bite had been unintentional, but disqualified him anyway. When this decision was announced at the Vélodrome d'Hiver the following evening, Brousse leapt to his feet and burst into tears. Immediately the hall became a scene of turmoil. Brousse was hoisted upon the shoulders of his loyal fans and paraded about the arena. Hundreds of demonstrators hooted and hollered and attempted to enter the ring. They were repulsed by the police. After about a half hour the commotion died down, but Brousse's supporters continued to launch attacks against the judges and referees for the rest of the evening.

The boxing finals were held the following night. The evening began with the announcement that two Italian boxers, flyweight Rinaldo Castellenghi and light heavyweight Carlo Saraudi, had withdrawn from their bronze-medal matches to protest the poor officiating. After the Méndez-Delarge welterweight final the arena was in an uproar, with hundreds of Argentinians expressing their outrage and anger vociferously. The confusion was added to when Mallin and Jack Elliot entered the ring, for the mere sight of Mallin set off the French spectators in their own chorus of catcalls. Not surprisingly, the two English middleweights had a hard time concentrating on their contest, which Mallin won in an uncharacteristically uninspired manner. The official report of the British Olympic Association included this account of the bout: "Mallin eventually won a close fight, but we are unable to give a more detailed description, owing to the fact that we were seated in the centre of a group of excited and gesticulating Frenchmen,

Harry Mallin, 1924
"Unroasted human beef of Old England": Mallin, the 1920 and 1924 Middleweight gold medalist.

who, not content with making themselves ridiculous . . . also refused to allow anyone in their proximity to get a view of the fight." The British press had a field day with the affair. "It was found necessary," said the *Daily Sketch,* "to substitute for a mere boxer a man-eating expert named Brousse, whose passion for raw meat led him to attempt to bite off portions of his opponents' anatomies." Another reporter wrote, "Having got his teeth into a piece of Argentine meat during one of the earlier contests, M. Brousse decided to vary the menu by sampling some of the unroasted human beef of Old England." Less light-hearted observers called for an end to boxing, an end to the Olympics, and, at the very least, an end to the French. However, life did go on, and so did boxing; so did the Olympics and so did the French.

1928 Amsterdam C: 17, N: 17, D: 8.11.
(72.57 kg—160 lbs)

		FINAL MATCH
1. Piero Toscani	ITA	Dec
2. Jan Heřmánek	CZE	
3. Leonard Steyaert	BEL	
4. Frederick Mallin	GBR	

5. John Chase (IRL), Humberto Curi (ARG), Harry Henderson (USA), Oscar Kjällander (SWE)

Wild scenes and alleged injustice hit the Middleweight division again in Amsterdam. In the final Heřmánek appeared to be the winner, but Toscani was awarded the gold medal. Heřmánek was hoisted on the shoulders of his countrymen and dumped at the feet of the judges, where he argued his case while the demonstration spread, erupting into violence in the back of the hall. While the light heavyweight finalists, Avendaño and Pistulla, prepared for their bout, Heřmánek's seconds tried to push him back into the ring. Finally the police intervened, and action *inside* the ring resumed.

1932 Los Angeles C: 10, N: 10, D: 8.13.
(72.57 kg—160 lbs)

		FINAL MATCH
1. Carmen Barth	USA	Dec
2. Amado Azar	ARG	
3. Ernest Pierce	SAF	
4. Roger Michelot	FRA	

5. Hans Bernlöhr (GER), Manuel Cruz (MEX), Aldo Longinotti (ITA), Lajos Szigeti (HUN)

1936 Berlin C: 19, N: 19, D: 8.15.
(72.57 kg—160 lbs)

		FINAL MATCH
1. Jean Despeaux	FRA	Dec
2. Henry Tiller	NOR	
3. Raúl Villarreal	ARG	
4. Henryk Chmielewski	POL	

5. Adolf Baumgarten (GER), James Atkinson (USA), Gerardus Dekkers (HOL), Josef Hrubes (CZE)

1948 London C: 25, N: 25, D: 8.13.
(73 kg—161 lbs)

		FINAL MATCH
1. László Papp	HUN	Dec
2. John Wright	GBR	
3. Ivano Fontana	ITA	
4. Michael McKeon	IRL	

5. August Cavignac (BEL), Aime-Joseph Escudie (FRA), Dogomar Martínez (URU), Jan Schubart (HOL)

This was the first milestone in László Papp's illustrious career. In 1952 he would go on to win the Light Middleweight gold medal and in 1956 he would successfully defend his title. The following year, at the age of 31, Papp gained permission from the Hungarian government to become the first boxer from a Communist country to fight professionally. He won the European Middleweight championship, but the Hungarian government refused to let him challenge for the world championship. He retired undefeated in 1965 and became a coach for the Hungarian Olympic team.

1952 Helsinki C: 23, N: 23, D: 8.2.

		FINAL MATCH	
1. Floyd Patterson	USA	KO 1	1:14
2. Vasile Tiţă	ROM		
3. Boris Nikolov	BUL		
3. Stig Sjölin	SWE		

5. Leonardus Jansen (HOL), Anthony Madigan (AUS), Walter Sentimenti (ITA), Dieter Wemhöner (GER)

Seventeen-year-old Floyd Patterson, who came from a family of 11 children in Brooklyn, breezed through his four bouts in the easiest manner imaginable. When the bell sounded at the start of the final, Patterson spun around in a circle, which earned him a warning from the Polish referee. A tremendous uppercut to Tiţă's chin ended the contest after 74 seconds. Four years later Patterson knocked out Archie Moore to win the vacant World Heavyweight title and became the youngest heavyweight champion until Mike Tyson. In 1959 he lost the title to Ingemar Johansson; then, in 1960, he defeated Johansson to become the first boxer to regain the heavyweight championship.

1956 Melbourne C: 14, N: 14, D: 12.1.

		FINAL MATCH
1. Gennady Shatkov	SOV/RUS	KO 1
2. Ramón Tapia Zapata	CHI	
3. Gilbert Chapron	FRA	
3. Víctor Zalazar	ARG	

5. Giulio Rinaldi (ITA), Július Torma (CZE/SLV), Dieter Wemhöner (GER)

László Papp, 1956

The first boxer to win three Olympic gold medals, Papp was Middleweight champion in 1948 and Light Middleweight champion in 1952 and 1956. Behind him are John McCormack and José Torres.

1960 Rome C: 25, N: 25, 9.5.

		FINAL MATCH
1. Edward Crook	USA	Dec 3–2
2. Tadeusz Walasek	POL	
3. Vevgeny Feofanov	SOV/RUS	
3. Ion Monea	ROM	

5. Hans Buechi (SWI), Chang Lo-Pu (TAI), Luigi Napoleoni (ITA) Frederik Van Rooyen (SAF)

The announcement of Crook's victory over Walasek was greeted by prolonged booing and whistling, which caused a delay in the awards ceremony. Crook went on to serve two tours in Vietnam as a command sergeant major, earning two purple hearts, one silver star and a bronze.

1964 Tokyo C: 20, N: 20, D: 10.23.

		FINAL MATCH	
1. Valery Popenchenko	SOV/RUS	RSC 1	2:05
2. Emil Schulz	GER		
3. Franco Valle	ITA		
3. Tadeusz Walasek	POL		

5. Joe Darkey (GHA), Ahmed Hassan (EGY), Ion Monea (ROM), Guillermo Salinas (CHI)

1968 Mexico City C: 22, N: 22, D: 10.26.

		FINAL MATCH
1. Christopher Finnegan	GBR	Dec 3–2
2. Aleksei Kiselyov	SOV/RUS	
3. Alfred Jones	USA	
3. Agustín Zaragoza Reyna	MEX	

5. Simeon Georgiev (BUL), Jan Hejdik (CZE), Mate Parlov (YUG/CRO), Wieslaw Rudkowski (POL)

Chris Finnegan, 1968

Outspoken Finnegan, on his way to victory in the 1968 Middleweight division. His biggest challenge was producing a urine sample for the post-fight drug test.

Chris Finnegan, a 24-year-old bricklayer from Iver, Buckinghamshire, almost didn't make it to the Olympics when an eye injury prevented him from taking part in the Amateur Boxing Association (ABA) championships that supposedly determined the Olympic team. He drowned his disappointment in a two-week drinking binge but was rescued by his trainer Dick Gunn, when Gunn helped secure a box-off for Finnegan based on Finnegan's excellent record. At the Mexico City Olympics, he survived two standing eight-counts in his semifinal bout against Al Jones of Detroit and was awarded an unpopular 4-1 decision. In the final Finnegan faced Aleksei Kiselyov, who had won the Light Heavyweight silver medal four years earlier. Kiselyov started strong, but was already tiring by the second round. The fight was close, but Finnegan thought he had won. "Then we were called to the centre of the ring for the announcement," he recalled in his autobiography *Finnegan: Self-Portrait of a Fighting Man.* "At first I couldn't cotton on to the jabber, but all of a sudden I heard the magic word which sounds the same in any language—FINNEGAN!" Three judges had voted 59-58 for Finnegan and two had voted 59-58 for Kiselyov. "I shall never be able to properly describe my feelings as I climbed up on that rostrum for the medal presentation," he went on. "The nearest I've felt to it was when walking down the aisle with my old woman after our wedding. . . . Only there was no gold medal at the end of that—only the golden rivet."

But Finnegan's most difficult challenge was still ahead: the urine test for drugs. As Finnegan put it: "Now if there's one thing I've never been able to do, it's have a piss while someone's watching me. I can never stand at those long urinals you get in gents' bogs, with all the other blokes having a quick squint." Sure enough, he was unable to produce. People turned on water faucets, whistled, whispered encouragement. He drank several glasses of water. Still nothing. Then he downed three or four pints of beer, but still without the desired result. After giving a television interview, Finnegan was hauled off to a local restaurant for a victory meal. Two Olympic officials tagged along with the necessary collection equipment. Finally, at 1:40 a.m., Finnegan jumped up and shouted, "Who wants some piss?" The officials followed him to the men's room, secured their sample, and returned to the lab. The test, of course, proved negative.

1972 Munich C: 22, N: 22, D: 9.10.

		FINAL MATCH
1. Vyacheslav Lemechev	SOV/RUS KO 1	2:17
2. Reima Virtanen	FIN	
3. Prince Amartey	GHA	
3. Marvin Johnson	USA	

5. Poul Knudsen (DEN), Nazif Kuran (TUR), Alejandro Montoya (CUB), Witold Stachurski (POL)

Lemechev's performance was so impressive that only one of his five opponents lasted the full three rounds. In the semifinals he stopped Marvin Johnson in the second round to avenge an earlier loss in the Soviet Union. In the final, Lemechev, a great counterpuncher, scored a sharp right cross over Virtanen's left lead that put the Finnish boxer out cold for a minute.

1976 Montreal C: 19, N: 19, D: 7.31.

		FINAL MATCH	
1. Michael Spinks	USA	RSC 3	1:54
2. Rufat Riskiyev	SOV/UZB		
3. Luis Martínez	CUB		
3. Alec Năstac	ROM		

5. Siraj Din (PAK), Fernando Martins (BRA), Ryszard Pasiewicz (POL), Dragomir Vujkovic (YUG/SER)

Twenty-year-old Michael Spinks of St. Louis won the gold medal even though he fought only two fights—his path to the title included one bye and two forfeits. Six months earlier Spinks had been beaten by Riskiyev in Tashkent, but in the third round of the final in Montreal, Spinks landed a tremendous blow to the Soviet boxer's stomach, causing Riskiyev to double up in pain and the referee to stop the contest. Spinks went on to great success as a professional boxer, gaining the WBA Light Heavyweight championship in 1981 and adding the WBC title in 1983. In 1985, he defeated Larry Holmes for the World Heavyweight championship.

1980 Moscow C: 19, N: 19, D: 8.2.

		FINAL MATCH
1. José Gómez	CUB	Dec 4–1
2. Viktor Savchenko	SOV/UKR	
3. Jerzy Rybicki	POL	
3. Valentin Silaghi	ROM	

5. Jang Bong-mun (PRK), Mark Kaylor (GBR), Peter Odhiambo (UGA), Manfred Trauten (GDR)

Savchenko won his first four fights by technical knockouts, but Gómez, the favorite, was too much for him in the final.

1984 Los Angeles C: 27, N: 27, D: 8.11.

		FINAL MATCH
1. Shin Joon-sup	KOR	Dec 3–2
2. Virgil Hill	USA	
3. Arístides González Ortíz	PUR	
3. Mohamed Zaoui	ALG	

5. Moses Mwaba (ZAM), Jeremiah Okorodudu (NGR), Damir Škaro (YUG/CRO), Pedro van Raamsdonk (HOL)

Of the 38 fights involving US boxers at the Los Angeles Olympics that went the full three rounds, 37 of them were decided in favor of the Americans. The only exception was the middleweight final in which Virgil Hill of North Dakota lost a very close decision to 23-year-old Shin Joon-sup, providing a cathartic happy ending for an otherwise frustrated and embittered Korean boxing squad. Four of Shin's five victories were by split decision.

1988 Seoul C: 33, N: 33, D: 10.1.

		FINAL MATCH
1. Henry Maske	GDR	Dec 5–0
2. Egerton Marcus	CAN	
3. Chris Sande	KEN	
3. Hussain Shah Syed	PAK	

5. Zoltán Füzesy (HUN), Michele Mastrodonato (ITA), Sven Ottke (GER), Franco Wanyama (UGA)

The most respected boxer in the middleweight division, Angel Espinoza of Cuba, was unable to compete because his government boycotted the Seoul Games. This put 6-foot 3½-inch Henry Maske into the role of favorite. Maske did not disappoint, registering unanimous decisions in each of his four fights. Maske's last victim, Guyana-born Egerton Marcus, fought the final with an injured right hand. Marcus' uncle, Charlie Amos, represented Guyana in the 1968 Olympics. His mother was a boxer as well.

In a repeat of the 1972 men's 100-meter sprint snafu, the US entrant, Anthony Hembrick, failed to show up on time for his opening bout when his coaches misread the day's schedule.

1992 Barcelona-Badalona C: 28, N: 28, D: 8.8.

		FINAL MATCH
1. Ariel Hernández Ascuy	CUB	Pts 12–7
2. Chris Byrd	USA	
3. Chris Johnson	CAN	
3. Lee Seung-bae	KOR	

5. Ahmed Dine (ALG), Sven Ottke (GER), Albert Papilaya (INA), Stefan Trendafilov (BUL)

Hernández and Byrd, whose father, Joe, was the United States' head coach, were far and away the class of the division. Hernández qualified for the final by outpointing his four opponents 47-9; Byrd outscored his four opponents 75-15. Both fighters were specialists in counterpunching. Unfortunately, this did not make for a thrilling final. The score was tied 4-4 after two rounds, but Hernández used his speed to pull out the victory in the final two minutes.

1996 Atlanta C: 31, N: 31, D: 8.3.

		FINAL MATCH
1. Ariel Hernández Azcuy	CUB	Pts 11–3
2. Malik Beyleroğlu	TUR	
3. Mohamed Bahari	ALG	
3. Rhoshii Wells	USA	

5. Tomasz Borowski (POL), Aleksandr Lebziak (RUS), Brian Magee (IRL), Dilshood Yarbekov (UZB)

Ariel Hernández was the overwhelming favorite to defend his Olympic title and he did not disappoint. His closest fight was a 5-0 victory over Sven Ottke of Germany, who spent almost the entire bout protecting himself and who threw almost no punches. Silver medalist Malik Beyleroğlu was born in Azerbaijan and changed his surname from Agayev to Beyleroğlu when he assumed Turkish citizenship. The oldest fighter in the competition was 32-year-old Randall Thompson of Canada. In 1984, 1988 and 1992, Thompson placed second at the Canadian Olympic trials and missed making the team. Finally, with his fourth try, he qualified. Alas, Thompson went out after only one bout, losing his opening match to Brian Magee 13-5. The Czech Republic was represented by Ludovit Plachetka, a Romany (Gypsy). He won one fight and lost one. Less than a year later, Plachetka, who worked as a bouncer at a disco, was arrested for shooting to death the mother of his former girlfriend following a dispute over child visitation rights. He would have shot his girlfriend too, but his pistol jammed. Plachetka was sentenced to thirteen years in prison.

2000 Sydney C: 27, N: 27, D: 9.30.

		FINAL MATCH
1. Jorge Gutiérrez Espinosa	CUB	Pts 17–15
2. Gaydarbek Gaydarbekov	RUS	
3. Vugar Alekperov	AZE	
3. Zsolt Erdei	HUN	
5. Adrian Diaconu	ROM	
6. Jeff Lacy	USA	
7. Akaki Kakauridze	TUR	
8. Aleksandr Zubrihin	UKR	

Jorge Gutiérrez won the middleweight division in the 1998 World Cup and the light middleweight division at the 1999 Pan-American Games. He was one bout away from winning the 1999 World Championships as a light middleweight when Cuba withdrew from the competition to protest the judging. Back as a middleweight in the Sydney Olympics, Gutiérrez faced Gaydarbek Gaydarbekov in the gold medal match. At no point did either boxer lead by more than two points. Gaydarbekov led 15-14 with one minute left in the fight. Gutiérrez scored a tying blow and then won by picking up two more points in the last 35 seconds.

2004 Athens C: 28, N: 28, D: 8.28.

		FINAL MATCH
1. Gaydarbek Gaydarbekov	RUS	Pts 28–18
2. Gennady Golovkin	KAZ	
3. Andre Dirrell	USA	
3. Suriya Prasathinphimai	THA	

5. Ramadan Yasser Abdel Ghaffar (EGY), Yordani Despaigne Herrera (CUB), Hassan Ndam Njikam (CAM), Oleh Mashkin (UKR)

Coming off a win at the 2004 European Championships, Gaydarbekov arrived in Athens hoping to improve on his silver-medal finish in Sydney. At the 2004 Olympics, he faced reigning world champion Gennady Golovkin in the final, and overcame a 2-6 deficit after the first round, staging a comeback in the third and fourth rounds to win 28-18.

2008 Beijing C: 28, N: 28, D: 8.23.

		FINAL MATCH
1. James DeGale	GBR	Pts 16–14
2. Emilio Correa Bayeux	CUB	
3. Darren Sutherland	IRL	
3. Vijender Singh	IND	

5. Alfonso Blanco Parra (VEN), Bakhtiyar Artayev (KAZ), Elshod Rasulov (UZB), Carlos Góngora (ECU)

The most hotly anticipated bout of the middleweight competition occurred in the second round, when twice (and reigning) world champion and 2006 European champion Matvey Korobov of Russia faced 2004 Olympic welterweight champion Bakhtiyar Artayev, a trained lawyer and captain of the Kazakh boxing team. Artayev had moved up to the middleweight division in 2007, just in time to win bronze at the world championships.

The two boxers were fairly evenly matched in Beijing, with Korobov holding a 7-6 lead in the third round before Artayev scored four consecutive points to advance 10-7. Artayev next faced 22-year-old James "Chunky" DeGale, the silver medalist at the 2006 European championships. DeGale came out strong, opening a three-point lead in the second round and holding off Artayev for an 8-3 win.

DeGale faced a serious challenge from Darren Sutherland in the semi-finals. The two boxers had faced each other five times before, with Sutherland winning all but one bout. This time DeGale built a two-point lead at the end of the second round and racked up a 10-3 victory with accurate counter-punches in the third and fourth rounds.

DeGale's final opponent was 2005 world bronze medalist and 2007 Pan American champion Emilio Correa. DeGale held a 6-1 lead by the end of the first round after Correa had two points deducted for biting was still ahead by DeGale's shoulder. DeGale was also penalized two points for holding in the third round, but was still ahead by two points going into the final round. The bout deteriorated quickly as both boxers began to tire, falling over each other no less than five times as DeGale held on to his lead.

DeGale turned professional in 2009 and won his first ten bouts, eight by knockout, before losing to Commonwealth super middleweight title-holder George Graves in May 2011.

LIGHT HEAVYWEIGHT
(81 kg—179 lbs)

1896–1912 not held

1920 Antwerp C: 11, N: 6, D: 8.24.
(79.38 kg—175 lbs)

		FINAL MATCH
1. Edward Eagan	USA	Dec
2. Sverre Sørsdal	NOR	
3. Harold Franks	GBR	
4. Hugh Brown	GBR	

5. Thomas Holdstock (SAF), Edwin Schell (USA)

Eddie Eagan is the only person to have won a gold medal in both Summer and Winter Olympics sports. Eagan grew up in a poor family in Denver, but made his way through Yale, Harvard Law School, and Oxford, became a successful lawyer, and married an automobile heiress. He lived his life according to the precepts of Frank Merriwell, the fictional hero of dime novels. In 1932, he wrote, "To this day I have never used tobacco, because Frank didn't. My first glass of wine, which I do not care for, was taken under social compulsion in Europe. Frank never drank." Twelve years after his boxing victory at the Antwerp Olympics, he reappeared as a member of the four-man bobsled team led by Billy Fiske that finished first at the Lake Placid Games.

Eagan's opponent in the gold-medal bout was 20-year-old Sverre Sørsdal, who had been a boxer for less than a year. Sørsdal went on to win a bronze medal at the 1924 Paris Olympics. He subsequently became the chief physician of a small Norwegian hospital near the Russian border. During World War II, when the hospital was bombed, Sørsdal went back into the burning building to rescue several injured patients. He was later awarded a Royal Medal for his bravery.

1924 Paris C: 21, N: 15, D: 7.20.
(79.38 kg—175 lbs)

		FINAL MATCH
1. Harry Mitchell	GBR	Dec
2. Thyge Petersen	DEN	
3. Sverre Sørsdal	NOR	
4. Carlo Saraudi	ITA	

5. John Courtis (GBR), Thomas Kirby (USA), George Mulholland (USA), G. Rossignon (FRA).

1928 Amsterdam C: 16, N: 16, D: 8.11.
(79.38 kg—175 lbs)

		FINAL MATCH
1. Víctor Angel Avendaño	ARG	Dec
2. Ernst Pistulla	GER	
3. Karl Leendert Miljon	HOL	
4. Donald McCorkindale	SAF	

5. Donald Carrick (CAN), Alfred Jackson (GBR), Juozas Vinca (LIT), William Murphy (IRL)

1932 Los Angeles C: 8, N: 8, D: 8.13.
(79.38 kg—175 lbs)

		FINAL MATCH
1. David Carstens	SAF	Dec
2. Gino Rossi	ITA	
3. Peter Jörgensen	DEN	
4. James Murphy	IRL	

Eddie Eagan, 1920
Eagan won the Light Heavyweight gold medal in 1920. Twelve years later, as a member of the winning four-man bob-sled team, he became the only person to earn gold medals in both the Summer and Winter Olympics.

1936 Berlin C: 22, N: 22, D: 8.15.
(79.38 kg—175 lbs)

		FINAL MATCH
1. Roger Michelot	FRA	Dec
2. Richard Vogt	GER	
3. Francisco Risiglione	ARG	
4. Sidney Leibbrandt	SAF	

5. Thomas Griffin (GBR), František Havelka (CZE), Borge Holm (DEN), Johannes Koivunen (FIN)

Michelot's most satisfying moment of the Berlin Games came when Adolf Hitler arrived during the medal ceremony and was obliged to remain standing during the playing of the "Marseillaise." Sidney Leibbrandt, who placed fourth, became enamoured of the Nazis during his stay in Berlin. He later agreed to work as a pro-Nazi agent in South Africa. However he was arrested, convicted of treason and spent seven years in prison.

1948 London C: 24, N: 24, D: 8.13.
(80 kg—177 lbs)

		FINAL MATCH
1. George Hunter	SAF	Dec
2. Donald Scott	GBR	
3. Gualberto Mauro Cía	ARG	
4. Adrian Holmes	AUS	

5. Giacomo Di Segni (ITA), Hugh O'Hagan (IRL), Harri Siljander (FIN), Franciszek Szymura (POL)

Before the match for third place, Maurio Cia had his broken right hand shot up with cocaine, then used it to knock down Adrian Holmes, who broke his ankle when he fell. Gold medalist George Hunter, a 21-year-old boilermaker, was awarded the Val Barker trophy for the best boxer of the Olympics.

1952 Helsinki C: 18, N: 18, D: 8.2.

		FINAL MATCH
1. Norvel Lee	USA	Dec 3–0
2. Antonio Pacenza	ARG	
3. Anatoly Perov	SOV/RUS	
3. Harri Siljander	FIN	

5. Giovanni Battista Alfonsetti (ITA), Lucio Grotone (BRA), Tadeusz Grzelak (POL), Karl Kistner (GER)

Norvel Lee went to Helsinki as a reserve heavyweight. Informed that he could compete as a light heavyweight if he made the weight limit, he lost twelve pounds and won the gold medal. In the semifinals, Lee faced local favorite Harri Siljander and made a great impression on the Finnish observers. The local news service, Unsisuomi, wrote, "Siljander had trouble with the pleasant half-Negro who controlled the situation with his calm and smooth way of fighting." An exception among boxers, Lee already had a master's degree in adult education. In 1948 Lee had been arrested in his hometown of Covington, Kentucky, for being one of the first blacks to sit in the all-white front section of a local bus.

1956 Melbourne C: 11, N: 11, D: 12.1.

			FINAL MATCH
1.	James Boyd	USA	Dec
2.	Gheorghe Negrea	ROM	
3.	Carlos Lucas	CHI	
3.	Romualdas Murauskas	SOV/LIT	

5. Rodolfo Díaz (ARG), Anthony Madigan (AUS), Ottavio Panunzi (ITA), Andrzej Wojciechowski (POL)

1960 Rome C: 19, N: 19, D: 9.5.

			FINAL MATCH
1.	Cassius Clay	USA	Dec 5–0
2.	Zbigniew Pietrzykowski	POL	
3.	Anthony Madigan	AUS	
3.	Giulio Saraudi	ITA	

5. Gennady Shatkov (SOV/RUS), Rafael Gargiulo (ARG), Gheorghe Negrea (ROM), Petar Stankov (BUL)

Long before Muhammad Ali became one of the most famous people in the world, he was Cassius Marcellus Clay, a brash and friendly 18-year-old who traveled to Rome from his hometown of Louisville, Kentucky, with hopes of winning a gold medal. Clay thrived in the atmosphere of the Olympic Village, garrulously introducing himself to people of all countries, joking with them, having his picture taken with them.

In the ring he was equally in his element. After stopping Yan Becaus of Belgium in the second round, he defeated the 1956 Olympic Middleweight champion, Gennady Shatkov, and the Australian Tony Madigan, by unanimous decisions. In the final he met the three-time European champion, Zbigniew Pietrzykowski, who was a veteran of 231 fights. Clay spent the first two rounds nimbly avoiding everything Pietrzykowski threw at him. Then in the last round he overwhelmed the Pole to earn a clear, unanimous decision.

At a press conference after the fight, a Soviet journalist asked Clay how he, as a Negro, felt about the fact that he wasn't allowed to eat at certain restaurants back home. Sensing an attempt to exploit him, Clay shot back, "Russian, we got qualified men working on that problem. We got the biggest and the prettiest cars. We get all the food we can eat. America is the greatest country in the world, and as far as places I can't eat goes, I got lots of places I can eat—more places I can than I can't."

And so Cassius Marcellus Clay achieved his goal of winning a gold medal. But the story of what happened to that medal tells volumes about the state of race relations in America at the beginning of the 1960s. Clay loved his medal. He slept with it, he ate with it, he wore it all the time. He wore it so much in fact that the gold began to wear off, revealing a common lead base. He returned to a hero's welcome in Louisville. The porch of his house was decorated with American flags, and his father had painted the steps red, white and blue. Cassius posed for photographers with his father—and his medal—while his father sang "The Star-Spangled Banner."

It wasn't long before Cassius turned professional and signed a contract with ten white Louisville millionaires, who agreed to sponsor his career. The millionaires gave him a slip of paper with all their phone numbers on it in case he ever needed help.

One day the mayor of Louisville asked Clay to come to his office so he could show off the gold medal to some visiting dignitaries. The mayor boasted to his visitors about the response Cassius had given to the Soviet reporter about the status of Negroes in the United States. The mayor told them, "Why, Cassius stood up tall, 'Look here, Commie . . . I'd rather live here in Louisville than in Africa cause at least I ain't fightin' off no snakes and alligators and livin' in mud huts.' He sho' told 'em! He's our own boy, Cassius, our next world champion."

Cassius Clay, 1960
Cassius Clay (later known as Muhammad Ali) with Bing Crosby.

By now Clay was sorry he had responded to the Soviet journalist the way he had. On the way home, he and a friend, Ronnie King, stopped at a whites-only restaurant and attempted to order two hamburgers and two vanilla milk shakes. They were refused service. "Miss," Clay told the waitress, "I'm Cassius Clay, the Olympic champion," and he showed off his gold medal with its red, white, and blue ribbons. The waitress turned to the owner of the restaurant, who boomed out, "I don't give a damn who he is! I done told you, we don't serve no niggers!" Several members of a white motorcycle gang happened to be in the restaurant and they rose and joined the owner by the counter. Ronnie King pulled out the paper with the names and numbers of Clay's millionaire sponsors and urged his friend to call them up for help. But Cassius just couldn't ask. In his book, *The Greatest,* Ali wrote, "I had earned my Gold Medal without their permission. It should mean something without their permission. I wanted that medallion to mean that I owned myself. And to call seemed to me to be exchanging one Owner for the Other."

According to Ali, he and Ronnie King left the restaurant. "Whatever illusions I'd built up in Rome as the All-American Boy were gone. My Olympic honeymoon was over." In the parking lot Clay was approached by one of the gang members, who ordered him to hand over his gold medal. Instead, he and Ronnie King raced off on their motor bikes, well aware that this gang had already seriously beaten several blacks who had been caught in white neighborhoods. Two of the gang leaders caught up with Clay and King at the Jefferson County Bridge on the Indiana border. A violent confrontation followed, which left the gang members bleeding and badly injured. When they left, Clay and King walked down to the river to wash the blood off their bodies and clothes. Ronnie King took the gold medal, cleaned it carefully, and hung it over his neck. It was the first time the medal had been away from Clay's chest. "For the first time," he wrote, "I saw it as it was. Ordinary, just an object." King put the gold medal back around Clay's neck, and the two friends walked back to the bridge. When they got to the middle of the bridge, Cassius Clay walked over to the side, pulled the gold medal off his chest, and threw it into the Ohio River. Later Ali wrote, "The medal was gone, but . . . I felt calmly relaxed, confident. My holiday as a White Hope was over. I felt a new, secret strength."

There are those who say that Muhammad Ali invented the story about throwing his gold medal in the Ohio River and that in reality, he merely lost it. If he did lose the medal, he did a good job of it, because it was never seen in public again. On August 3, 1996, at the Atlanta Olympics, the IOC presented Ali with a replacement medal. In order to satisfy the needs of US television, the presentation was made not at the boxing venue, but during halftime of the men's basketball final.

On February 25, 1964, Cassius Clay won the World Heavyweight championship by defeating Sonny Liston. He defended his title nine times over the next three years. Then he converted to Islam, announced that Cassius Clay was a slave name, and changed his name to Muhammad Ali. When he refused to be drafted during the Vietnam War, he was stripped of his title and didn't fight again for 3½ years. He won back the title on October 30, 1974, by knocking out George Foreman in Zaire. He defended his championship ten more times before losing to Leon Spinks on February 15, 1978. He regained the title from Spinks seven months later.

In 1996 Ali was chosen to light the cauldron during the Opening Ceremony of the Atlanta Olympics.

1964 Tokyo C: 19, N: 19, D: 10.23.

		FINAL MATCH
1. Cosimo Pinto	ITA	Dec 3–2
2. Aleksei Kiselyov	SOV/RUS	
3. Alexander Nikolov	BUL	
3. Zbigniew Pietrzykowski	POL	

5. Rafael Luis Gargiulo (ARG), Sayed Mersal (EGY), František Poláček (CZE), Jürgen Schlegel (GDR)

1968 Mexico City C: 18, N: 18, D: 10.26.

		FINAL MATCH
1. Danas Pozniakas	SOV/LIT	Default
2. Ion Monea	ROM	
3. Stanistaw Dragan	POL	
3. Georgi Stankov	BUL	

5. Fatai Ayinia (NGR), Walter Facchinetti (ITA), Bernard Malherbe (FRA), Jürgen Schlegel (GDR)

Monea suffered a broken nose in his semifinal victory over Dragan and was unable to compete in the final.

1972 Munich C: 28, N: 28, D: 9.10.

		FINAL MATCH
1. Mate Parlov	YUG/CRO	RSC 2 2:39
2. Gilberto Carrillo	CUB	
3. Janusz Gortat	POL	
3. Isaac Ikhouria	NGR	

5. Nikolai Anfimov (SOV/RUS), Miguel Ángel Cuello (ARG), Rudi Hornig (GER), Harald Skog (NOR)

Parlov blasted his way through the tournament, winning one walkover and stopping three of his other four opponents in the second round. Parlov turned professional in 1975 and three years later won the World Light Heavyweight title.

1976 Montreal C: 18, N: 18, D: 7.31.

		FINAL MATCH	
1. Leon Spinks	USA	RSC 3	1:09
2. Sixto Soria	CUB		
3. Costică Dafinoiu	ROM		
3. Janusz Gortat	POL		

5. Robert Burgess (BER), Wolfgang Gruber (GER), Ottomar Sachse (GDR), Juan Domingo Suárez (ARG)

Marine Corps Lance Corporal Leon Spinks stepped into the ring for his Olympic final immediately after his younger brother, Michael, had won the Middleweight championship. He faced knockout artist Sixto Soria, who had required only 9 minutes and 5 seconds to dispose of his first three opponents. However, the Cuban met his match in Spinks, who knocked him down in the first round and continued to batter him until the referee stopped the fight.

A year and a half later, in his eighth professional bout, Spinks defeated Muhammad Ali to win the World Heavyweight championship. Over the next seven months Spinks was arrested four times on charges ranging from driving the wrong way down a one-way street to possession of marijuana and cocaine. When Spinks faced Ali in a rematch eight months after their first fight, he had only trained a total of ten days, and Ali made history as the first man to win the world heavyweight title three times. One of Spinks' sons, Cory, was undisputed welterweight champion for more than a year, beginning in December 2003.

1980 Moscow C: 15, N: 15, D: 8.2.

		FINAL MATCH
1. Slobodan Kačar	YUG/SER	Dec 4–1
2. Pawel Skrzeck	POL	
3. Herbert Bauch	GDR	
3. Ricardo Rojas	CUB	

5. Georgică Donici (ROM), David Kvachadze (SOV/GEO), Michael Madsen (DEN), Geoffrey Pike (AUS)

1984 Los Angeles C: 24, N: 24, D: 8.11.

		FINAL MATCH
1. Anton Josipović	YUG/BSH	Default
2. Kevin Barry	NZL	
3. Evander Holyfield	USA	
3. Mustapha Moussa	ALG	

5. Georgică Donici (ROM), Jean Paul Nanga (CAM), Syivaus Okello (KEN), Anthony Wilson (GBR)

Despite all of the uproar about pro-American judging at the Los Angeles Olympics, it was a US boxer who was the victim of the most controversial decision of all. Evander Holyfield, who had defeated world amateur champion Ricky Womack to qualify for the US team, had stopped his first three opponents and was on the verge of knocking out a fourth, when an unusual incident occurred. A few seconds before the end of the second round of his semifinal bout with Kevin Barry, Holyfield lashed out a right to the ribs and followed with a left hook that floored Barry for good. The referee, Gligorije Novicić of Yugoslavia, motioned Holyfield to a neutral corner, counted out Barry, then turned to Holyfield and disqualified him for throwing the left hook after Novicić had yelled, "Stop." Subsequent viewing of the videotapes of the fight confirmed the late hit, but also showed that Barry and Holyfield had previously thrown four late blows each.

When the decision was announced, Barry turned to Holyfield and said, "You won the fight fair and square." Then he took the American's hand and raised it in the air. The crowd went berserk, raining abuse and refuse on the Yugoslavian referee. The police had to be brought in to escort Novicić from the arena. Novicić had been scheduled to work one of the final bouts three days later, but was relieved of his obligation for security reasons.

What made the incident all the more shocking was the subsequent ruling that because Barry had been declared a knockout victim, amateur boxing regulations prevented him from fighting again for 28 days. This meant that the gold medal was awarded by default to the other semifinal winner, Anton Josipović, who, like referee Novicić, happened to hail from Yugoslavia.

At the medal ceremony, Josipović, a handsome 22-year-old literature student from Bosnia, endured loud booing. But after the playing of the Yugoslav national anthem, he reached down and pulled up a surprised Holyfield to join him on the gold-medal platform. Afterwards, he told reporters, "It is a great honor to win the gold medal in this city of light and sun. I would have liked to fight Holyfield, to show what I am capable of doing and to win the medal that way. I am a bit disappointed that the audience doesn't realize that this is not the way I wanted it. I took the opportunity to have Holyfield join me on the top step because I believe the Olympics are the spirit of friendliness and goodwill."

Holyfield went on to an extremely successful professional career, winning the World Heavyweight championship three times. Josipović became a sports journalist and established a friendship with Holyfield when he covered his fights. In November 1997, Josipović, a Bosnian Croat, visited his hometown of Banja Luka for the first time in six years after being invited to attend a boxing tournament. Within 48 hours he was shot and wounded by a masked gunman.

1988 Seoul C: 26, N: 26, D: 10.2.

		FINAL MATCH
1. Andrew Maynard	USA	Dec 5–0
2. Nurmagomed Shanavazov	SOV/RUS	
3. Henryk Petrich	POL	
3. Damir Škaro	YUG/CRO	

5. Joseph Akhasamba (KEN), Ahmed Elnagar (EGY), Lajos Erös (HUN), Andrea Magi (ITA)

The 12th of 14 children, Andrew Maynard grew up on the streets of Cheverly, Maryland. His mother died when he was 3 years old; his father, a truck driver, was frequently on the road. Maynard, who was once a marijuana dealer, was in and out of juvenile court for such charges as assault and breaking and entering. Finally, a judge told him that he would have to go to college, join the Army or go to jail. Maynard chose the Army. In the armed service, he became a cook and a boxer. He also married, became a father, and generally turned his life around. The Olympic final, a turgid affair that resembled two bears dancing, was not a fair representation of either boxer's talents. Maynard gave his gold medal to his father. "By winning the medal," he explained, "I was saying 'Forgive me for being a bad kid.' . . . Giving him that medal was the proudest moment of my life." Bronze medalist Damir Škaro set a curious record by losing to the eventual silver-medal winner for the third straight Olympics. In 1980 and 1984 he had competed as a middleweight.

1992 Barcelona-Badalona C: 26, N: 26, D: 8.9.

		FINAL MATCH
1. Torsten May	GER	Pts 8–3
2. Rostislav Zaulichnyi	UKR	
3. Wojciech Bartnik	POL	
3. Zoltán Béres	HUN	

5. Ángel Espinosa Capo (CUB), Montell Griffin (USA), Roland Raform (SEY), Stephen Wilson (GBR)

Southpaw Torsten May was the surprise winner of the 1991 world championships but entered the Olympic tournament as the clear favorite. He won his first two matches easily but ran into major trouble in the quarterfinals. His opponent, Montell Griffin, was only 5 feet 7 inches tall—six inches shorter than May. The score was 1-1 after two rounds. However, less than a minute into the final round, Griffin opened a big cut over May's right eye, causing the taller German to bleed profusely. The referee, Osvaldo Bisbal of Argentina, stopped the fight, but the ring doctor, Oscar Ramírez of Cuba, allowed the bout to continue. A minute later Bisbal issued a third warning to Griffin for "ducking"—leading with his head instead of his fists—which automatically added three points to May's score. The penalty proved decisive, as May eventually won 6-4.

The Americans were furious, but the rest of the world had little sympathy for Griffin, who had alienated boxing fans by showboating in the closing seconds of his previous fight. May's 8-6 semifinal victory over Wojciech Bartnik was roundly booed and jeered because May spent much of the match clinching in order to protect his cut eye.

The official records show that 26 light heavyweights competed in the 1992 Olympic tournament. In fact, 27 showed up in the arena. Ali Kazemi of Iran made it to the ring in time for his opening bout with Ashghar Muhammad of Pakistan. Unfortunately, he wasn't wearing any gloves. His handlers frantically searched for a pair, but he was disqualified after five minutes for not being ready on time.

1996 Atlanta C: 31, N: 31, D: 8.4.

		FINAL MATCH
1. Vassily Zhirov	KAZ	Pts 17–4
2. Lee Seung-bae	KOR	
3. Antonio Tarver	USA	
3. Thomas Ulrich	GER	

5. Daniel Bispo (BRA), Stipe Drvis (CRO), Enrique Flores (PUR), Troy Amos Ross (CAN)

For 22-year-old Vassily Zhirov, the gold medal match was the easy part. In the round of 16, he faced Pietro Aurino of Italy, a tough customer with a reputation for giving it everything he had for an entire bout. Sure enough, Zhirov and Aurino fought at full speed for all nine minutes. At the end, the audience gave the two boxers a standing ovation. Zhirov won 18-13. After defeating Troy Amos Ross 14-8 in the quarterfinals, Zhirov met Antonio Tarver in the semifinals. The 27-year-old Tarver was the reigning world champion. Only one of Tarver's three preliminary opponents had survived three rounds. Tarver led Zhirov 9-8 after two rounds, but had exhausted all his energy in the process. Zhirov outscored him 7-0 in the last round to win 15-9. A bronze medalist as a middleweight in Barcelona, Lee was too slow for Zhirov who won the final easily, 17-4.

2000 Sydney C: 28, N: 28, D: 10.1.

		FINAL MATCH
1. Aleksandr Lebziak	RUS	Pts 20–6
2. Rudolf Kraj	CZE	
3. Andrey Fedshuk	UKR	
3. Sergey Mikhaylov	UZB	
5. John Dovi	FRA	
6. Jegbefumere Albert	NGR	
7. Olzhas Orazaliyev	KAZ	
8. Gurcharan Singh	IND	

Aleksandr Lebziak first attracted major attention when, as a middleweight, he earned the silver medal at the 1991 World Championships. After competing in the 1992 and 1996 Olympics, Lebziak moved up to light heavyweight and won every major tournament he entered. At the Sydney Olympics, Lebziak's only serious challenge came in the quarterfinals against John Dovi. However Lebziak eventually prevailed 13-11.

2004 Athens C: 28, N: 28, D: 8.29.

		FINAL MATCH
1. Andre Ward	USA	Pts 20–13
2. Mahomed Aripgadzhiev	BLR	
3. Utkirbek Khaydarov	UZB	
3. Ahmed Ismail	EGY	

5. Yevgeny Makarenko (RUS), İhsan Yıldırım Tarhan (TUR), Elias Pavlidis (GRE), Lei Yuping (CHN)

Andre Ward's training for the Olympics included pushing his trainer's 1999 Cadillac across a parking lot and asking his family to move temporarily to Washington State to allow him to focus. The 20-year-old father of two from Oakland, California, arrived in Athens without having lost a match in six years, although he had never competed in a major international tournament. In the quarterfinals, Ward faced Yevgeny Makarenko, a two-time world champion with a five-year winning streak and a six-inch height advantage. Ward managed a 23-16 upset by sneaking inside Makarenko's reach, landing straight punches to his head, and quickly retreating out of range. In the final against Mahomed Aripgadzhiev, Ward trailed 9-7 after the two rounds. He came back in the third round with quick inside punches to take a 14-11 lead, and followed with a comfortably aggressive fourth round to win 20-13. Ward competed with a photo of his father, Frank, who died of a heart attack in 2002, taped to his shoe. He also carried two tattoos on his forearms, one saying "Frank" and the other "Ward."

2008 Beijing C: 28, N: 28, D: 8.24.

		FINAL MATCH
1. Zhang Xiaoping	CHN	Pts 11–7
2. Kenny Egan	IRL	
3. Tony Jeffries	GBR	
3. Yerkebulan Shynaliyev	KAZ	

5. Imre Szellő (HUN), Washington Silva (BRA), Abdelhafid Benchabla (ALG), Dzhakhon Kurbanov (TJK)

The two favorites in the event, reigning world champion Abbos Atayev of Uzbekistan and reigning world silver medalist and 2006 European champion Artur Beterbiyev of Russia, were both eliminated in the early rounds. Atayev fell to world bronze medalist Yerkebulan Shynaliyev 11-3 in the first round, while Beterbiyev was upset in the second round by hometown favorite Zhang Xiaoping, who came from behind to score eight unanswered points in the final three rounds.

Originally from China's Inner Mongolia Autonomous Region, Zhang had never reached the podium in a major international tournament. He assured himself of a medal by beating Algeria's Abdelhafid Benchabla 12-7 to advance to the semifinals, where he faced Yerkebulan Shynaliyev. Shynaliyev had had an unpleasant experience in his quarter-final bout: he was leading 12-6 in the third round when his opponent, Dzhakhon Kurbanov, bit him on the shoulder and was disqualified. Zhang and Shynaliyev fought to a 4-4 tie after four rounds, and Zhang was declared the winner.

The gold-medal match pitted Zhang against 2006 European bronze medalist Kenny Egan, who had outscored his first four opponents 50-7. Zhang opened a 2-0 lead in the first round and held the lead throughout the next three rounds, as several blows by Egan, particularly in the third round, failed to be recorded, leading to booing from the non-Chinese portion of the audience.

HEAVYWEIGHT
(91 kg—200½ lbs)

1896–1980 not held

1984 Los Angeles C: 15, N: 15, D: 8.11.

		FINAL MATCH
1. Henry Tillman	USA	Dec 5–0
2. William de Wit	CAN	
3. Angelo Musone	ITA	
3. Arnold Vanderlijde	HOL	

5. Håkan Brock (SWE), Dodovic Owiny (UGA), George Stefanopoulos (GRE), Tevita Taufoou (TON)

Henry Tillman, who learned to box while serving time for armed robbery, qualified for the US team by twice defeating future World Heavyweight champion Mike Tyson. The Olympic tournament was held at the Sports Arena, just five miles from where Tillman grew up in South Central Los Angeles. Tillman's semifinal victory was a controversial jury reversal decision over Angelo Musone, a decision that the Italian newspapers referred to as "hallucinatory" and "scandalous." In the final, Tillman upset Willie de Wit, who had beaten the American in their two previous encounters.

Henry Tillman's post-Olympic ride was an unusual one. At the Opening Ceremony of the Los Angeles Games, Tillman fell in love with the young woman who ran the torch into the stadium: Gina Hemphill, the granddaughter of Jesse Owens. The couple eventually met and married. Tillman's professional career was satisfactory but not outstanding. When he retired in 1992, his record was 25 wins and 6 losses. Meanwhile, Tillman devoted himself to helping young people who were prone to trouble, giving not only money, but time, serving as a counselor and trainer at the Community Youth, Sports and Arts Foundation. Tillman appeared to be a perfect role model. He had pulled himself out of a world of drugs, theft and violence, achieved international acclaim through hard work, and gave back to the community he could have left behind.

But there was a dark side to Henry Tillman's life. Despite being a role model and well-spoken, he had difficulty finding a job. In 1994 he pleaded no contest to a charge of using a credit card not in his name. The judge gave him probation and community service. Then he was videotaped at a casino in Inglewood trying to use a counterfeit credit card with a fake name even though he was wearing a jacket with "TILLMAN" stenciled across the back. He pleaded guilty and in 1996 was sentenced to at least two years in prison. But even before the sentencing, he had gotten into worse trouble. This time he was charged with murdering one man outside a nightclub and shooting another. Eventually, Tillman pleaded no contest to charges of attempted murder and voluntary manslaughter. Released from prison in 2002, he returned in 2004 after pleading guilty in another case involving counterfeit checks and credit cards. As it happens, the man Tillman defeated in the 1984 Olympic final, Willie de Wit, also ended up spending a lot of time in courtrooms . . . as a lawyer.

1988 Seoul C: 18, N: 18, D: 10.1.

		FINAL MATCH
1. Raymond Mercer	USA	KO 1 2:16
2. Baik Hyan-man	KOR	
3. Andrzej Golota	POL	
3. Arnold Vanderlijde	HOL	

5. Gyula Alvics (HUN), Luigi Gaudiano (ITA), Maik Heydeck (GDR), Harold Obunga (KEN)

World champion Félix Savón was conspicuously missing from the tournament because of Cuba's boycott of the Seoul Games. In Savón's absence, 27-year-old infantryman Ray Mercer blasted his way through the tournament. His four opponents, none of whom survived the full three rounds, lasted a total of 17 minutes 6 seconds. An oddity among boxers, Mercer did not take up the sport until he was 22, and only then because being a sparring partner for the camp champion meant that he wouldn't have to take part in a 30-day winter survival field exercise. In 1993 Mercer was involved in a bizarre incident. He was charged with offering an opponent, Jesse Ferguson, a $100,000 bribe *during* a fight on February 6 at Madison Square Garden. He was eventually acquitted of the charge. Bronze medal winner Andrzej Golota turned professional in 1992 and fought successfully for several years. However he is best known for twice losing by disqualification to Riddick Bowe in 1996 after repeated low blows while clearly winning. He was also twice arrested for assault during bar brawls in Poland.

1992 Barcelona-Badalona C: 23, N: 23, D: 8.8.

		FINAL MATCH
1. Félix Savón Fabré	CUB	Pts 14–1
2. David Izonritei	NGR	
3. David Tua	NZL	
3. Arnold Vanderlijde	HOL	

5. Paul Douglas (IRL), Kirk Johnson (CAN), Danell Nicholson (USA). Vojtěch Rückschloss (CZE)

Three-time world champion Félix Savón had dominated the Heavyweight division since 1986. It was expected that his march to Olympic gold would be practically uncontested. However, in the quarterfinals he ran into an unexpected and unlikely obstacle: Chicago's Danell Nicholson, whose pre-Olympic international boxing experience consisted of one fight. Nicholson, who had spent over 3½ years in prison for armed robbery, had only been back in the outside world for 14 months. Instead of cowering in terror like most of Savón's opponents, Nicholson stood his ground and slugged it out. He shocked most observers by leading Savón 4-1 after the first round and 8-6 after the second. In the third round Savón finally took charge and pulled out a well-deserved 13-11 victory. In the semifinals Savón defeated 6 foot 6 inch Arnold Vanderlijde 23-3. It was the eighth time in eight tries that Vanderlijde had lost to Savón. The Dutchman did gain some consolation, however: he became the only boxer in Olympic history to earn three bronze medals.

1996 Atlanta C: 24, N: 24, D: 8.3.

		FINAL MATCH
1. Félix Savón Fabré	CUB	Pts 20–2
2. David Defiagbon	CAN	
3. Nate Jones	USA	
3. Luan Krasniqi	GER	

5. Sergei Dychkov (BLR), Giorgi Kandelaki (GEO), Christophe Mendy (FRA), Jiang Tao (CHN)

Félix Savón was expected to win his second gold medal without being seriously challenged and that was exactly what happened. He was sluggish in his first fight, a 9-3 victory over Andrei Kumyavka of Kyrgystan. Back in form for his second bout, he knocked out Kioamena

Turkson of Sweden in the first round and then helped the referee carry a groggy Turkson to his corner. In the quarterfinals, Giorgi Kandelaki was only trailing 4-3 midway through the second round, when Savon took charge and went on to win 20-4. Savón was scheduled to meet Kosovo-born Luan Krasniqi in the semifinals, but Krasniqi, perhaps recalling the 1995 world championship final, in which Savón had pummeled him until the fight was stopped in the second round, did not appear at the weigh-in and Savón won in a walkover.

Savón's opponent in the final was David Defiagbon, who had represented Nigeria as a light middleweight at the 1992 Olympics. After moving to Canada, Defiagbon gleefully put on 45 pounds and became a heavyweight. In Atlanta, Defiagbon began by beating highly-touted Ahmed Omar of Kenya 15-4. In the quarterfinals he faced Christophe Mendy, who had twice given Savón a close fight before losing. Mendy was leading 10-9 with two minutes to go, when he was accused of hitting Defiagbon below the belt and was disqualified in a controversial decision. Defiagbon recovered to surprise Nate Jones in the semifinals 16-10 and advance to the gold medal bout against Savón. But just as Krasniqi had been satisfied with a bronze medal, Defiagbon was content with a silver. He spent the entire fight protecting his head and trying to stay on his feet. He succeded, but meanwhile Savón used him for target practice and won 20-2.

2000 Sydney C: 16, N: 16, D: 9.30.

			FINAL MATCH
1.	Félix Savón Fabré	CUB	Pts 21–13
2.	Sultan Ahmed Ibragimov	RUS	
3.	Sebasten Kober	GER	
3.	Vladimir Chanturia	GEO	
5.	Michael Bennett	USA	
6.	Jackson Chanet	FRA	
7.	Mark Simmons	CAN	
8.	Ruslan Chagayev	UZB	

By the time of the Sydney Olympics, Félix Savón had dominated the heavyweight division for 14 years. However, at the last two world championships, he had experienced glitches in his career. In the 1997 final, Savón was actually defeated 14-4 by Ruslan Chagayev of Uzbekistan. It was later learned that Chagayev had fought professional bouts in the United States, so the AIBA took away his world title and gave it to Savón, who thus won his sixth straight world championship, with two Olympic titles thrown in. At the 1999 World Championships, which were held in Houston, Texas, Savón was scheduled to fight American Michael Bennett in the final. However, following a series of controversial decisions, the Cubans withdrew their team and Bennett was awarded the championship in a walkover. Savón did meet Bennett in the quarterfinals of the Olympics, easily outpointing him 23-8 after less than six minutes of fighting. Savón's closest fight was a 14-8 semifinal victory over Sebastien Kober. In his four bouts, Savón scored 76 points while his opponents scored only 32.

2004 Athens C: 15, N: 15, D: 8.28.

			FINAL MATCH
1.	Odlanier Solís Fonte	CUB	Pts 22–13
2.	Viktar Zuyev	BLR	
3.	Naser El-Shami	SYR	
3.	Mohamed El-Sayed	EGY	
5.	Wilmer José Vásquez Torres (VEN), Vuhar Mursal Alakbarov (AZR), Devin Vargas (USA), Adam Forsyth (AUS)		

With Félix Savón finally out of the competition due to age restrictions, the favorites in the field were two-time world champion Odlanier Solis and reigning European champion Alexandr Alekseyev of Russia. The two had met in the final of the 2003 world championships, with Solis narrowly defeating Alekseyev 18-15 for the title. As it happened, their Olympic encounter came in the first round of competition. Alekseyev put up a strong fight until the final round, when Solis used his greater speed and accuracy to pull ahead, winning 24-21. Solis breezed through the remaining matches, advancing to the semifinals with a 24-4 rout over Vásquez Torres of Venezuela and then stopping Naser El-Shami in the third round, before earning gold with a 22-13 win over Viktar Zuyev.

2008 Beijing C: 16, N: 16, D: 8.23.

			FINAL MATCH
1.	Rakhim Chakhkiev	RUS	Pts 4–2
2.	Clemente Russo	ITA	
3.	Osmay Acosta Duarte	CUB	
3.	Deontay Wilder	USA	
5.	Ilias Pavlidis (GRE), John M'Bumba (FRA), Mohamed Arjaoui (MOR), Oleksandr Usik (UKR)		

The final bout of the Olympic heavyweight division in Beijing was a repeat of the 2007 world championship final in Chicago ten months earlier. There Clemente Russo won a narrow 7-6 victory over Rakhim Chakhkiev in a fight that could have gone either way. Both Russo and Chakhkiev had dominated their earlier bouts, with Chakhkiev winning each by at least 11 points and Russo with margins of eight or more.

Both boxers swept through the Olympic tournament. Chakhkiev started with a 7-3 win over 2007 Asian champion Ali Mazaheri of Iran and made it to the final after beating 2007 Pan American champion Osmay Acosta 7-4 in the semis. Acosta came from one of the toughest neighborhoods of Havana and practiced judo until the age of 13, when he switched to boxing.

Meanwhile Russo began with a 7-1 win over Athens 2004 silver medalist Viktar Zuyev and then won his next two bouts easily, beating Oleksandr Usik 7-4 and 22-year-old Deontay Wilder 7-1, to reach the final. Wilder, who had worked previously as a truck driver and cook, had only taken up boxing in late 2005 to make money for the care of his daughter, who was born with congenital spinal disorder.

The final was the lowest-scoring bout of the heavyweight tournament, with the two boxers recording just two points each in the first three rounds. Chakhkiev scored the only two points in the fourth round to clinch the gold medal.

Russo was a huge fan of the movie *Dances with Wolves*, starring Kevin Costner. He named his beloved horse, Sisko, after Costner's horse, and, inspired by the movie, had a tattoo of a bison applied to his right ribcage. After turning professional in 2009 Chakhkiev went on to win 11 straight bouts, nine of them by knockout.

SUPER HEAVYWEIGHT

(Over 91 kg—200½ lbs)

This division, which is the unlimited weight class, was known as Heavyweight from 1904 to 1980.

1896–1900 not held

1904 St. Louis C: 3, N: 1, D: 9.22.

(Over 71.67 kg—158 lbs)

		FINAL MATCH
1. Samuel Berger	USA	Dec
2. Charles Mayer	USA	
3. William Michaels	USA	

The first Olympic heavyweight champion, Sam Berger was a Jewish boxer from San Francisco. Berger fought briefly as a professional. Then, in 1910, he served as a sparring partner for Jim Jefferies in his comeback attempt against Jack Johnson.

1906 not held

1908 London C: 6, N: 1, D: 10.27.

(Over 71.67 kg—158 lbs)

		FINAL MATCH
1. Albert Oldman	GBR	KO 1 2:00
2. Sydney Evans	GBR	
3. Frederick Parks	GBR	

Policeman Albert Oldman knocked out Ian Myrams of Manchester in less than a minute, received a bye in the semifinals and needed only two minutes to dispose of Evans.

1912 not held

1920 Antwerp C: 9, N: 7, D: 8.24.

(Over 79.38 kg—175 lbs)

		FINAL MATCH
1. Ronald Rawson	GBR	KO 2
2. Søren Petersen	DEN	
3. Xavier Eluère	FRA	
4. William Spengler	USA	

Rawson won all three of his fights by knockout or technical knockout.

1924 Paris C: 16, N: 11, D: 7.20.

(Over 79.38 kg—175 lbs)

		FINAL MATCH
1. Otto von Porat	NOR	Dec
2. Søren Petersen	DEN	
3. Alfredo Porzio	ARG	
4. Henk de Best	HOL	

5. Ricardo Bertazzolo (ITA), Arthur Clifton (GBR), Edward Greathouse (USA), Robert Larsen (DEN)

The final was a popular battle that saw Petersen almost knocked out in the first round and von Porat almost put away in the second. The Norwegian rebounded in the final round to earn the victory.

1928 Amsterdam C: 10, N: 10, D: 8.11.

(Over 79.38 kg—175 lbs)

		FINAL MATCH
1. Arturo Rodríguez Jurado	ARG	RSC 1
2. Nils Ramm	SWE	
3. M. Jacob Michaelsen	DEN	
4. Sverre Sørsdal	NOR	

5. Georges Gardebois (FRA), Alexander Kaletchetz (USA), Sam Oliji (HOL), Hans Schönrath (GER)

1932 Los Angeles C: 6, N: 6, D: 8.13.

(Over 79.38 kg—175 lbs)

		FINAL MATCH
1. Santiago Alberto Lovell	ARG	Dec
2. Luigi Rovati	ITA	
3. Frederick Feary	USA	
4. George Maughan	CAN	

5. Gunnar Bärlund (FIN), Heinz Kohlhaas (GER)

1936 Berlin C: 17, N: 17, D: 8.15.

(Over 79.38 kg—175 lbs)

		FINAL MATCH
1. Herbert Runge	GER	Dec
2. Guillermo Lovell	ARG	
3. Erling Nilsen	NOR	
4. Ferenc Nagy	HUN	

5. Jose Feans (URU), Vincent Stuart (GBR), Olle Tandberg (SWE), Ernest Toussaint (LUX)

Runge was a slaughterhouse worker from Wuppertal in the Rhineland.

1948 London C: 17, N: 17, D: 8.13.
(Over 80 kg—176½ lbs)

		FINAL MATCH
1. Argentino Rafael Iglesias	ARG	KO 2
2. Gunnar Nilsson	SWE	
3. John Arthur	SAF	
4. Hans Müller	SWI	

5. Uber Baccilieri (ITA), Adam Faul (CAN), Jack Gardner (GBR), E. Jay Lambert (USA)

1952 Helsinki C: 22, N: 22, D: 8.2.
(Over 81 kg—179 lbs)

		FINAL MATCH
1. H. Edward Sanders	USA	DISQ 2
2. Ingemar Johansson	SWE	
3. Ilkka Koski	FIN	
3. Andries Nieman	SAF	

5. Giacomo Di Segni (ITA), Edgar Hearn (GBR), Tomislav Krizmanić (YUG/SER), Algirdas Schocikas (SOV/LIT)

Evidently the punishment that Ed Sanders inflicted on his first three opponents made a great impression on Ingemar Johansson, because the Swede spent all his time in the ring back-pedaling, without throwing a single punch. After receiving several warnings from the referee, he was finally disqualified for not "giving of his best." Because of the disqualification, he was not awarded his silver medal and he returned to Sweden in shame. Johansson's version of the fight was that he had seen that Sanders' strength was as a counter-puncher. Consequently he refused to attack and tried to lure Sanders into attacking so that he himself could counter-punch. As it happened, it was not Sanders but Johansson who went on to a successful professional career, knocking out Floyd Patterson on June 29, 1959, to win the World Heavyweight championship. Johansson later recalled, "At the moment of victory, at the summit of glory for a boxer, I could think of only one thing: 'It's over. Now I am able to go home with my head held high.'" Johansson was finally awarded his silver medal in 1981. Sanders died of a brain hemorrhage on December 12, 1954, after being knocked out in his ninth professional bout.

1956 Melbourne C: 11, N: 11, D: 12.1.
(Over 81 kg—179 lbs)

		FINAL MATCH	
1. T. Peter Rademacher	USA	RSC 1	2:27
2. Lev Mukhin	SOV/RUS		
3. Daniel Bekker	SAF		
3. Giacomo Bozzano	ITA		

5. Thorner Åhsman (SWE), José Giorgetti (ARG), Josef Němec (CZE), Ulrich Nitzschke (GER)

The final looked as if it would be a classic. Mukhin had beaten all three of his opponents by knockout or technical knockout, coming off the floor himself in two of the fights. Rademacher, a soldier from Yakima, Washington, never gave Mukhin a chance to make a third comeback. He knocked down the Soviet boxer in the first 50 seconds. Mukhin got up, but Rademacher flattened him twice more in the next 80 seconds, and the referee finally stopped the fight. Four weeks earlier, Soviet troops had invaded Hungary. As soon as the fight ended, several Hungarian athletes rushed into the ring and hoisted Rademacher onto their shoulders. Eight and a half months later, Rademacher became the first boxer to fight for the Heavyweight title in his first professional contest. Rademacher, who had never gone more than three rounds, sent champion Floyd Patterson to the canvas in the second round, but Patterson came back to win in round 6.

1960 Rome C: 17, N: 17, D: 9.5.
(Over 81 kg—179 lbs)

		FINAL MATCH
1. Franco De Piccoli	ITA	KO 1 1:30
2. Daniel Bekker	SAF	
3. Josef Nemec	CZE	
3. Günter Siegmund	GDR	

5. Andrei Abramov (SOV/RUS), Vasile Mariutan (ROM), Percy Price (USA), Obrad Sretenović (YUG/SER)

1964 Tokyo C: 14, N: 14, D: 10.23.
(Over 81 kg—179 lbs)

		FINAL MATCH
1. Joseph Frazier	USA	Dec 3–2
2. Hans Huber	GER	
3. Giuseppe Ros	ITA	
3. Vadim Yemelyanov	SOV/RUS	

5. Santiago Alberto Lovell, Jr. (ARG), Vasile Mariutan (ROM), Athol McQueen (AUS)

In 1964 Joe Frazier worked at a Kosher slaughterhouse in Philadelphia. He made it to the Olympics as a late substitute for 293-pound Buster Mathis, who had broken his knuckle. Frazier demolished his first three opponents and then won a much tamer split decision over Regensburg bus mechanic Hans Huber in the final, which Frazier fought with a broken left thumb. In 1970 Frazier won the World Heavyweight championship. He held it for almost three years until he was beaten by George Foreman. Frazier also engaged in three memorable fights with Muhammad Ali, the first of which was Ali's first professional defeat. Frazier had the honor of being involved in four bouts that were chosen as *Ring Magazine*'s Fight of the Year: his 1969 seventh round TKO of Jerry Quarry, the 1971 defeat of Ali, his 1973 second round loss to

George Foreman and the 1975 "Thrilla in Manila" with Ali.

1968 Mexico City C: 16, N: 16, D: 10.23.
(Over 81 kg—179 lbs)

		FINAL MATCH
1. George Foreman	USA	RSC 2
2. Jonas Čepulis	SOV/LIT	
3. Giorgio Bambini	ITA	
3. Joaquín Rocha Herrera	MEX	

5. Ion Alexe (ROM), Bernd Anders (GDR), Rudolfus Lubbers (HOL), Kiril Pandov (BUL)

The relatively inexperienced Foreman, who had fought only 18 times before the Olympics, had little trouble winning the gold medal. After his final victory he paraded around the ring holding aloft a small US flag. On January 22, 1973, Foreman knocked out Joe Frazier to win the World Heavyweight title. Foreman retired in 1977, became an active Christian, and opened a youth center in Humble, Texas. Then, in 1987, at the age of 38, Foreman began a comeback. Longtime ring observers scoffed or shook their heads sadly. It was the old story of the boxer who is addicted to the ring and to glory and who doesn't know when to quit. But Foreman's comeback was different. He took his time, and on November 5, 1994, he shocked the world by knocking out undefeated Michael Moorer in the 10th round and winning the WBA Heavyweight championship—at age 45. Like Joe Frazier, Foreman was involved in four matches that were selected *Ring Magazine*'s Fight of the Year. The first was his 1973 second round stoppage of Joe Frazier. The second was his 1974 loss to Muhammad Ali in Zaire. The third was in 1976 when Foreman was knocked down twice in the fourth round by Ron Lyle, but came back to knock out Lyle in the fifth round. Foreman's fourth Fight of the Year was his 1977 loss by decision to Jimmy Young. It was following this fight that Foreman had a religious vision and quit boxing for ten years.

1972 Munich C: 14, N: 14, D: 9.10.
(Over 81 kg—179 lbs)

		FINAL MATCH
1. Teófilo Stevenson Lorenzo	CUB	Default
2. Ion Alexe	ROM	
3. Peter Hussing	GER	
3. Hasse Thomsén	SWE	

5. Duane Bobick (USA), Jürgen Fanghänel (GDR), Carroll Morgan (CAN)

Teófilo Stevenson, a handsome Jamaican-born 6-foot 3½-inch Cuban from Las Tunas, Oriente, was the most impressive Olympic boxer since Cassius Clay. After disposing of Poland's Ludwik Denderys in one round, he faced Duane Bobick of the US Navy. In 1971 Bobick had beaten Stevenson in the semifinals of the Pan American Games. Now, at the Munich Olympics, Bobick wasn't too worried about Stevenson. "I know he's tall and strong," he told reporters, "but the last time all he had was a good jab—no right hand." Unbeknownst to Bobick, the Cuban had spent twelve months working on just that problem. Using a stinging left jab and a now powerful right hand, Stevenson plastered Bobick until the fight was stopped in the third round.

Stevenson's semifinal opponent was Peter Hussing of Germany. He lasted 4 minutes and 3 seconds. "I have never been hit so hard in all my 212 bouts," said the good-natured Hussing. "You just don't see his right hand. All of a sudden it is there—on your chin." The other semifinal matched Alexe of Romania and Thomsén of Sweden, both of whom had been knocked out by Stevenson in previous tournaments. Some observers suggested that the *loser* should be forced to face Stevenson in the final.

In fact, neither of them did. Alexe won a unanimous decision over Thomsén, but showed up for the final with his hand in plaster, the result of a broken thumb. Although capitalist fight promoters drooled at the prospect, Stevenson refused to turn professional, stating that he was more interested in his studies and in revolution than he was in making a million dollars. In fact, he turned down an offer of $2,000,000. "Professional boxing treats a fighter like a commodity to be bought and sold and discarded when he is no longer of use," he said. "I wouldn't exchange my piece of Cuba for all the money they could give me."

1976 Montreal C: 15, N: 15, D: 7.31.
(Over 81 kg—179 lbs)

		FINAL MATCH
1. Teófilo Stevenson Lorenzo	CUB	KO 3 2:35
2. Mircea Simion	ROM	
3. Clarence Hill	BER	
3. Johnny Tate	USA	

5. Peter Hussing (GER), Atanas Suvandzhiev (BUL)

In the four years since the Munich Olympics, Stevenson had lost two fights—both to Igor Vysotsky of the USSR, who had knocked out the Cuban in Minsk three months before the 1976 Olympics. However, Vysotsky was unable to compete in Montreal because of eye injuries, and the road seemed clear for Stevenson to defend his title. He demolished his first three opponents in a record 7 minutes and 22 seconds. His last victim was Mircea Simion, who avoided Stevenson completely for the first two rounds. Although this same tactic had earned Ingemar Johansson a disqualification 24 years earlier, it seemed quite understandable in Simion's case. When Stevenson finally hit Simion in the third round, the Romanian's seconds immediately threw in the towel. Simion later defected to the United States. Clarence Hill's bronze made Bermuda (pop. 53,500) the smallest country ever to win a Summer Olympics medal.

1980 Moscow C: 14, N: 14, D: 8.2.
(Over 81 kg—179 lbs)

		FINAL MATCH
1. Teófilo Stevenson Lorenzo	CUB	Dec 4–1
2. Pyotr Zayev	SOV/RUS	
3. Jürgen Fanghänel	GDR	
3. István Levai	HUN	

5. Francesco Damiani (ITA), Grzegorz Skrzecz (POL), Peter Stoimenov (BUL)

In the semifinals, Levai ran around the ring for three rounds, becoming the first Olympic boxer to go the distance against Stevenson. Stevenson, in turn, became the first boxer to win three Olympic gold medals in the same division. As late as 1986, he proved that he was still the best amateur boxer in the world by winning the world championship at age 34.

1984 Los Angeles C: 11, N: 11, D: 8.11.

		FINAL MATCH
1. Tyrell Biggs	USA	Dec 4–1
2. Francesco Damiani	ITA	
3. Azis Salihu	YUG/KOS	
3. Robert Wells	GBR	

5. Peter Hussing (GER), Willie Isangura (TAN), Lennox Lewis (CAN), Viliami Pulu (TON)

1988 Seoul C: 17, N: 17, D: 10.2.

		FINAL MATCH
1. Lennox Lewis	CAN	RSC 2 0:43
2. Riddick Bowe	USA	
3. Aleksandr Miroshnichenko	SOV/KAZ	
3. Janusz Zarenkiewicz	POL	

5. Petr Hrivňák (CZE), Ulli Kaden (GDR), Kim Yoo-hyun (KOR), Andreas Schneiders (GER)

Lennox Lewis of Kitchener, Ontario, needed only 10 minutes 16 seconds to dispatch his three opponents. Most startling was his 34-second knockout of World Cup champion Ulli Kaden in the quarterfinals. Both Lewis and Bowe graduated to successful professional careers, each of them claiming at least a share of the heavyweight championship. Bowe's career was highlighted by his three fights with Evander Holyfield. The first—and best—took place on November 13, 1992, when Bowe won a unanimous decision over the previously unbeaten Holyfield. A year later, Holyfield gained a split decision in a fight that was interrupted for 21 minutes when a parachutist crashed onto the ring apron. Finally, in a 1995 bout, Bowe came back from being knocked down for the first time in his career and stopped Holyfield in the eighth round. Lewis gained his first Heavyweight title by default in 1992 when Bowe refused to fight him. Lewis also had two memorable fights with Holyfield, both in 1999. The first was judged a draw, even though it appeared to be a victory for Lewis, while the second was a unanimous decision in favor of Lewis. A rarity among professional boxers, Lewis retired in 2004 while he was still the reigning Heavyweight champion.

One unfortunate boxer in Seoul was Mohamed Hammad of Sudan. When the bell rang to begin his opening round bouth with South Korean Kim Yoo-hyun, Hammad took three steps forward and discovered that the fight was over and he was the loser. His coach, Abdellatif Mohamed Abbas, had literally thrown in the towel as a protest against an earlier decision in which South Korean light middleweight Park Si-hun had been declared the winner over Sudan's Abdallah Ramadan. Park had incapacitated Ramadan with an illegal kidney punch.

Another unusual highlight was the appearance of 5-foot 11-inch, 260-pound Ali Albaluchi of Kuwait. Clearly out-classed by the more athletically shaped Aleksandr Miroshnichenko, the good-natured Albaluchi took advantage of his moment in the spotlight to imitate Muhammad Ali. While Kuwaiti supporters chanted, "Ali, Ali," Albaluchi performed the rope-a-dope and the Ali Shuffle. He dropped his gloves, stuck out his chin and dared Miroshnichenko to hit him. Miroshnichenko won the fight easily, but it was Albaluchi who received the only standing ovation of the entire 429-match Seoul tournament.

1992 Barcelona–Badalona C: 17, N: 17, D: 8.9.

		FINAL MATCH
1. Roberto Balado Méndez	CUB	Pts 13–2
2. Igbeneghu Richard	NGR	
3. Brian Nielsen	DEN	
3. Svilen Russinov	BUL	

5. Larry Donald (USA), Wilhelm Fischer (GER), Peter Hrivňák (CZE), Gitas Juškevičius (LIT)

Two time world champion Roberto Balado outpointed his four opponents 54-9. In March he lost to American Larry Donald 16-14 in a fight held in Tampa, Florida, but in Barcelona, Balado outclassed Donald in the quarterfinals, 10-4. On July 2, 1994, Balado was killed when the car he was driving was struck by a train. He was 25 years old and had won his last 56 fights.

1996 Atlanta C: 19, N: 19, D: 8.4.

		FINAL MATCH
1. Wladimir Klitschko	UKR	Pts 7–3
2. Paea Wolfgramm	TON	
3. Duncan Dokiwari	NGR	
3. Aleksei Lezin	RUS	

5. Attila Levin (SWE), Adaliat Mamedov (AZR), René Monse (GER), Alexis Rubalcaba Polledo (CUB)

It would be hard to imagine a more unexpected medalist at the 1996 Olympics than Paea Wolfgramm. A 309-pound (140 kg) former rugby player, his pre-Olympic highlight was a third-place finish at the 1994 Commonwealth Games. He accomplished this feat by winning one fight. Before each match, Wolfgramm chanted a traditional mantra from his nation, Tonga (population 106,000): "Tonga mounga kihe loto"—"Your mountains are your hearts." According to Wolfgramm, "Tonga was always easy to invade. We had no mountains to hide behind, so we had to rely on our hearts and our souls."

In Atlanta Wolfgramm began by eking out a 10-9 victory over Sergei Dahovich of Belarus. In the quarterfinals, he faced hard-hitting 6-foot 7-inch (2-meter) Alexis Rubalcaba. The chances of a Tongan boxer beating a Cuban boxer were so minute that few observers paid attention to the fight. But Wolfgramm stood his ground and scored a shocking upset, 17-12. Suddenly, the sports world became interested in Wolfgramm and sought information about him. It wasn't easy to find. Tonga did not have a press information officer or even a team book. Reporters were reduced to checking the entry form questionnaire that all Olympic athletes were required to answer. Wolfgramm, who was 26 years old, had listed his occupation as "househusband" and the person who was most influential in his career as "my wife." In fact, he worked as a clerk in Auckland or, as Wolfgramm himself put it, he was "a mild-mannered clerk."

Wolfgramm's semifinal opponent was Duncan Dokiwari, who was something of a mystery man himself, although he had won the All Africa Games in 1995. In Atlanta Dokiwari had stopped all three fighters he had faced, and used up only 11 minutes 27 seconds in doing it. The bout was tied 6-6 when Wolfgramm connected with a last-second shot that gave him the victory. Back in Tonga, the nation went wild. Unfortunately, Tonga's only television station was a Christian one that didn't broadcast sports. Meanwhile, though, King Taufa'ahou Topou IV ordered a national day of fasting and prayer. Later Wolfgramm was asked if he himself ever fasted. Wolfgramm pointed to his 309-pound frame and replied, "Do I look like I've fasted a lot?"

Wolfgramm's opponent in the final was Wladimir Klitschko. Klitschko's older brother, Vitali, had won a silver medal at the 1995 world championships, losing in the final to Aleksei Lezin. A few months later Vitali was suspended for drug use and Wladimir took his place as the Ukrainian super heavyweight. At the 1996 European championships, in April, Wladimir made it to the final, but he too lost to Lezin. At the Olympics, Klitschko met up with Lezin again, this time in the semifinals. Klitschko ground out a 4-1 win to earn the right to meet Wolfgramm in the final. Unfortunately, the Tongan had broken his wrist against Dokiwari and would have withdrawn had it not been the Olympic gold medal match. Klitschko led 3-2 after two rounds and then wore down Wolfgramm in the last round to win 7-3.

Still, Wolfgramm's silver meant that Tonga was the smallest nation ever to win a medal in the Summer Olympics. When Wolfgramm returned home, the king declared a national holiday and a local rugby team carried him on a chair through his home village of Utungako (population 500). Wolfgramm let anyone who asked wear his medal. "I felt like it was national property," he explained.

In retrospect, the 1996 super heavyweight tournament turned out to be an unusually violent one. Of the 14 bouts in which Wolfgramm did not take part, only four lasted the full three rounds.

As for Klitschko, he and his brother Vitali were oddities in the world of boxing in that both spoke four languages and graduated university with Ph.D.s in sports science. In 2006 they were honored as UNESCO Champions For Sport, for their work to bring sport and education to poor children in Namibia, Brazil and Romania.

2000 Sydney C: 16, N: 16, D: 10.1.

		FINAL MATCH
1. Audley Harrison	GBR	Pts 30–16
2. Mukhtarkhan Dildabekov	KAZ	
3. Paolo Vidoz	ITA	
3. Rustam Saydov	UZB	
5. Art Binkowski	CAN	
6. Oleksiy Mazikin	UKR	
7. Alexis Rubalcaba Polledo	CUB	
8. Samuel Peter	NGR	

In the first round of the tournament, European champion Aleksei Lezin was leading Audley Harrison 8-6 in the fourth round when Harrison stunned him with a powerful left cross. Although Lezin stayed on his feet, the referee stopped the fight with only 70 seconds to go. Earlier in the day, Alexis Rubalcaba had knocked Cengiz Koc of Germany unconscious with one blow 84 seconds into the fight. It was an impressive performance by the big Cuban, but in his next bout he met his match in 1999 world championship runner-up Mukhtarkhan Dildabekov. Rubalcaba led 7-4 after the first round, but the smaller Dildabekov (1.90 meters to 2.40 meters) floored Rubalcaba in the second round and eventually pulled away to win 25-12. Harrison defeated Oleksiy Mazikin 19-9 in the quarterfinals and Paolo Vidoz 32-16 in the semifinals. Harrison fought the final with a badly swollen knuckle. He led Dildabekov 9-4 after two rounds. The Kazakh scored four straight points to pull within one point, but Harrison outscored him 21-8 the rest of the way. At the post-fight press conference, Harrison sang a rap song taunting those who had dismissed his chances before the Olympics. He also quoted the French playwright, Pierre Corneille: "Triumph without risk is triumph without glory."

2004 Athens C: 16, N: 16, D: 8.29.

		FINAL MATCH
1. Aleksandr Povetkin	RUS	Walkover
2. Mohamed Aly	EGY	
3. Roberto Cammarelle	ITA	
3. Michel López Núñez	CUB	

5. Mukhtarkhan Dildabekov (KAZ), Oleksiy Mazikin (UKR), Jaroslavas Jakšto (LIT), Jason Estrada (USA)

Reigning world champion and two-time European champion Aleksandr Povetkin won his first Olympic gold in a walkover when Mohamed Aly failed his pre-match medical test due to sprained shoulder sustained during his 18-16 semifinal upset of Cuba's Michel López.

2008 Beijing C: 16, N: 16, D: 8.24.

		FINAL MATCH
1. Roberto Cammarelle	ITA	RSC 4 0:19
2. Zhang Zhilei	CHN	
3. Vyacheslav Glazkov	UKR	
3. David Price	GBR	

5. Newfel Ouatah (ALG), Ruslan Myrsatayev (KAZ), Óscar Rivas Torres (COL), Jaroslavas Jakšto (LIT)

Although he had won the 2007 world championship title, Roberto Cammarelle was hardly an overwhelming favorite for the gold medal. For one thing, although he had won silver at the 2002 and 2004 European championships, bronze at the 2004 Athens Games and bronze at the 2005 world championships, the first time he had topped the podium in a major international tournament was in 2007. Second, two of his world championship bouts were won on walkover, after opponents failed to show up.

Cammarelle's shot at the gold medal was made easier by the absence of 2004 Athens heavyweight gold medalist and three-times world champion Odlanier Solís. Solís was one of three Athens gold medalists who defected from Cuba in 2006 while training in Venezuela, eventually turning up in Germany and signing professional contracts.

Cammarelle started with a 13-1 rout of Croatian kick boxer Marko Tomasović, and then beat 2007 Pan American silver medalist Óscar Rivas 9-5 in the quarterfinals. He cruised past David Price in the semi-finals, scoring nine unanswered points before connecting with a powerful right halfway through the second round that ended the match.

The final pitted Cammarelle against 2007 bronze medalist Zhang Zhilei, who had reached the gold-medal match on a walkover after reigning world silver medalist Vyacheslav Glazkov withdrew with an elbow injury. Cammarelle had already built an overwhelming 14-4 lead by the start of the fourth round when a staggering blow to Zhang's head caused the referee to stop the bout.

One year later, Cammarelle defended his world title by beating Ukraine's Roman Kapitonenko 10-5.

DISCONTINUED EVENTS

FEATHERWEIGHT
(57 kg—126 lbs)

1896–1900 not held

1904 St. Louis C: 3, N: 1, D: 9.22.
(56.70 kg—125 lbs)

		FINAL MATCH
1. Oliver Kirk	USA	Dec
2. Frank Haller	USA	
3. Fred Gilmore	USA	

Kirk is the only person to win two boxing titles at a single Olympics. The importance of his achievement is certainly muted by the fact that he fought only one bout in each division (Bantamweight and Featherweight).

1906 not held

1908 London C: 8, N: 2, D: 10.27.
(57.15 kg—126 lbs)

		FINAL MATCH
1. Richard Gunn	GBR	Dec
2. Charles Morris	GBR	
3. Hugh Roddin	GBR	
4. Thomas Ringer	GBR	

At 37, Gunn was the oldest fighter ever to win an Olympic championship. He had been British amateur champion from 1894 to 1896. Unfortunately, his superiority over other British featherweights was so pronounced that his entry in a tournament caused others to drop out. Consequently, amateur boxing authorities asked him to retire from competition and Gunn, ever the sportsman, agreed. He came out of retirement for the London Olympics and defeated one Frenchman and two Englishmen to win the gold medal. Then he retired again, having lost only one fight in 15 years.

1912 not held

1920 Antwerp C: 17, N: 9, D: 8.24.
(57.15 kg—126 lbs)

		FINAL MATCH
1. Paul Fritsch	FRA	Dec
2. Jean Gachet	FRA	
3. Edoardo Garzena	ITA	
4. Jack Zivic	USA	

5. Philippe Bovy (BEL), James Cater (GBR), Nicolaj Clausen (DEN), Paul Erdahl (NOR)

1924 Paris C: 24, N: 17, D: 7.20.
(57.15 kg—126 lbs)

		FINAL MATCH
1. John Fields	USA	Dec
2. Joseph Salas	USA	
3. Pedro Quartucci	ARG	
4. Jean Devergnies	BEL	

5. Carlos Abarca González (CHI), Marcel Depont (FRA), Harry Dingley (GBR), Bruno Petrarca (ITA)

Jackie Fields and Joe Salas were best friends back home in Los Angeles. At 16, Fields, whose real name was Yonkel—or Jacob—Finkelstein was the youngest boxer at the Paris Olympics. Salas later recalled, "We had to dress in the same room. When they knocked on the door to call us to the fight, we looked up at each other and started to cry and hugged. Ten minutes later we were beating the hell out of each other." After his victory over Salas in the final, Fields was so upset at having defeated his buddy that he went back to the dressing room and cried again. In 1929 Fields won the World Welterweight title. Fields and Salas died eight days apart in June 1987.

1928 Amsterdam C: 18, N: 18, D: 8.11.
(57.15 kg—126 lbs)

		FINAL MATCH
1. Lambertus van Klaveren	HOL	Dec
2. Víctor Peralta	ARG	
3. Harold Devine	USA	
4. Lucien Biquet	BEL	

5. George Boireau (FRA), Jan Górny (POL), Frederick Perry (GBR), Olavi Vakeva (FIN)

There seemed little question in anyone's mind that Peralta had outclassed van Klaveren. Anyone, that is, except the judges who awarded the decision to the Dutch fighter. "It was as plain as a pike-staff which was the master," wrote the reporter for the London *Daily Telegraph*. A battle ensued between Argentinian spectators and Dutch police, and the commotion was still bubbling when the decision of the next match, the Lightweight championship, set off outrage among the Americans in the crowd. Bep van Klaveren, known as "The Dutch Windmill," is the only Dutch boxer ever to win an Olympic title.

1932 Los Angeles C: 10, N: 10, D: 8.13.
(57.15 kg—126 lbs)

		FINAL MATCH
1. Carmelo Robledo	ARG	Dec
2. Josef Schleinkofer	GER	
3. Carl Carlsson	SWE	
4. Gaspare Alessandri	ITA	

5. John Keller (CAN), Henri Walter (FRA)

1936 Berlin C: 25, N: 25, D: 8.15.
(57.15 kg—126 lbs)

		FINAL MATCH
1. Oscar Casanovas	ARG	Dec
2. Charles Catterall	SAF	
3. Josef Miner	GER	
4. Dezsö Frigyes	HUN	

5. Theodore Ernst Kara (USA), William Marquart (CAN), Aleksander Polus (POL), John Treadway (GBR)

Casanovas described his emotions after receiving his gold medal and hearing the Argentine national anthem: "My greatest ambition had been achieved. I had succeeded for my country, my parents, and my friends. I was overjoyed. Unable to contain myself, I shed a few tears thinking of my dear parents, thanking them in my heart for having brought me into this world. I am sure that if at that moment Death had come to claim me, I would have welcomed him with a smile."

1948 London C: 30, N: 30, D: 8.13.
(58 kg—128 lbs)

		FINAL MATCH
1. Ernesto Formenti	ITA	Dec
2. Dennis Shephard	SAF	
3. Aleksy Antkiewicz	POL	
4. Francisco Núñez	ARG	

5. Edward Johnson (USA), Edward Kerschbaumer (AUT), Armand Savoie (CAN), Su Bung-nan (KOR)

A new style in Olympic boxing protests was created following the announcement that American Eddie Johnson had been declared the winner over 33-year-old

Jury of Appeal, 1948
Supporters of Uruguayan featherweight Basilio Alves storm the table of the Jury of Appeal following Alves' 1948 loss to American Eddie Johnson

Basilio Alves of Uruguay in their second-round match. While the crowd booed for more than fifteen minutes, Alves' supporters hoisted him on their shoulders and stormed the table of the Jury of Appeal. In the semifinals, it was the turn of the Argentinians to protest. Upset over the loss of Núñez to Shephard, they grabbed Núñez, who had refused to leave the ring, lifted him to their shoulders, and attempted a Uruguayan charge toward the Jurors table. Repulsed by a phalanx of twelve attendants, the Argentinians listened to speeches by two of their officials and were finally convinced to end their protest by an Argentinian member of the Jury of Appeal, Señor Oriani. The final saw Shephard enter the ring with six stitches over his right eye, the result of a cut that had been opened in four of his five preliminary bouts. He fought gamely but was finally worn down by Formenti in the final minute and a half.

1952 Helsinki C: 30, N: 30, D: 8.2.

		FINAL MATCH
1. Ján Zachara	CZE/SLV	Dec 2–1
2. Sergio Caprari	ITA	
3. Leonard Leisching	SAF	
3. Joseph Ventaja	FRA	

5. Edson Brown (USA), Leszek Drogosz (POL), János Erdei (HUN), Leonard Walters (CAN)

1956 Melbourne C: 18, N: 18, D: 12.1.

		FINAL MATCH
1. Vladimir Safronov	SOV/RUS	Dec
2. Thomas Nicholls	GBR	
3. Pentti Hämäläinen	FIN	
3. Henryk NiedźwiedzkiPOL		

5. Andre De Sousa (FRA), Tristán Falfán (ARG), Shinetsu Suzuki (JPN), Ján Zachara (CZE)

Safronov, an artist from Siberia, gained the USSR's first Olympic boxing title. He was added to the team at the last minute when Soviet champion Aleksandr Zasukhin injured his hand in training.

1960 Rome C: 31, N: 31, D: 9.5.

		FINAL MATCH
1. Francesco Musso	ITA	Dec 4–1
2. Jerzy Adamski	POL	
3. Jorma Limmonen	FIN	
3. William Meyers	SAF	

5. Abel Bekker (ZIM), Ernest Chervet (SWI), Constantin Gheorghiu (ROM), Boris Nikanorov (SOV/RUS)

In the first round of the tournament, Boris Nikanorov outpointed Nick Spanakos to become the first Soviet boxer to defeat an American.

1964 Tokyo C: 32, N: 32, D: 10.23.

		FINAL MATCH
1. Stanislav Stepashkin	SOV/RUS	Dec 3–2
2. Anthony Villanueva	PHI	
3. Charles Brown	USA	
3. Heinz Schulz	GDR	

5. Constantin Crudu (ROM), José Durán Aguirre (MEX), Piotr Gutman (POL), Tun Tin (BUR)

After all the hoopla and uproar that had gone on as a result of unpopular decisions in Olympic boxing, it was left to Spanish featherweight Valentín Lorén to register the ultimate protest. Disqualified for repeated holding and open-glove hitting in the second round of his first fight, Loren turned on the Hungarian referee, György Sermer, and punched him in the face. This unfortunate indiscretion caused the Zaragoza southpaw to receive a lifetime ban from international boxing. Silver medalist

Valentín Lorén, 1964
Disqualified in his fight in the 1964 Olympics, Spanish featherweight Lorén takes out his frustration on the Hungarian referee.

Anthony Villanueva was the son of José "Cely" Villanueva, who had won the Bantamweight bronze medal at the 1932 Olympics in Los Angeles. Anthony tried a brief career as a movie actor and then turned professional boxer. Stepashkin won his first four fights by knockout and technical knockout before gaining a split decision over Villanueva.

1968 Mexico City C: 28, N: 28, D: 10.26.

		FINAL MATCH
1. Antonio Roldán	MEX	DISQ 2
2. Albert Robinson	USA	
3. Ivan Mihailov	BUL	
3. Philip Waruinge	KEN	

5. Miguel García (ARG), Abdel Khallaf (EGY), Valery Plotnikov (SOV/RUS), Seyfi Tatar (TUR)

The final match came to a sudden end when Robinson was disqualified for butting. Although the Mexican crowd was delighted with the dubious victory, Roldán himself seemed apologetic. As the first disqualified finalist since Ingemar Johansson in 1952, Robinson was prevented from receiving his silver medal. After a protest by American officials, Robinson was finally awarded the medal after his return to the United States. In 1971 Robinson was injured while training and lapsed into a coma in which he remained until his death three years later.

1972 Munich C: 45, N: 45, D: 9.10.

		FINAL MATCH
1. Boris Kuznetsov	SOV/RUS	Dec 3–2
2. Philip Waruinge	KEN	
3. András Botos	HUN	
3. Clemente Rojas	COL	

5. Kazuo Kobayashi (JPN), Jouko Lindberg (FIN), Gabriel Pometcu (ROM), Antonio Rubio (SPA)

1976 Montreal C: 26, N: 26, D: 7.31.

		FINAL MATCH	
1. Angel Herrera	CUB	KO 2	2:18
2. Richard Nowakowski	GDR		
3. Leszek Kosedowski	POL		
3. Juan Paredes	MEX		

5. Davey Armstrong (USA), Choi Choon-gil (KOR), Gheorghe Ciochină (ROM), Bratislav Ristić (YUG/SER)

1980 Moscow C: 35, N: 35, D: 8.2.

		FINAL MATCH
1. Rudi Fink	GDR	Dec 4–1
2. Adolfo Horta	CUB	
3. Krzysztof Kosedowski	POL	
3. Viktor Rybakov	SOV/RUS	

5. Tzacho Andreikovski (BUL), Sidnei Dalrovere (BRA), Winfred Kabunda (ZAM), Luis Pizarro (PUR)

1984 Los Angeles C: 36, N: 36, D: 8.11.

		FINAL MATCH
1. Meldrick Taylor	USA	Dec 5–0
2. Peter Konyegwachie	NGR	
3. Turgut Aykaç	TUR	
3. Omar Catari Peraza	VEN	

5. Mohamed Hegazy (EGY), Charles Lubulwa (UGA), Park Hyeong-oc (KOR), John Wanjau (KEN)

As a professional, Meldrick Taylor was involved in one of boxing's most memorable fights. On March 17, 1990, Taylor challenged Julio César Chávez for the WBC Super Lightweight championship. Both fighters were undefeated. After 11 rounds Taylor appeared to be ahead on points and needed only to survive the final round to win the title. Instead of sticking to his fight plan by staying close to Chávez, with one minute to go Taylor stepped back and stood up. Chávez quickly took advantage of Taylor's mistake, battering Taylor with all the strength he had left. With less than 15 seconds left in the fight, Taylor finally went down. He picked himself up at the count of six, but referee Richard Steele noted Taylor's lack of responsiveness, decided that Taylor had had enough, and stopped the fight—with two seconds remaining on the clock. A check of the judges' scorecards confirmed that if Taylor had been able to last two more seconds, he would have won the championship.

1988 Seoul C: 48, N: 48, D: 10.2.

		FINAL MATCH	
1. Giovanni Parisi	ITA	RSC 1	1:41
2. Daniel Dumitrescu	ROM		
3. Abdelhak Achik	MOR		
3. Lee Jae-hyuk	KOR		

5. Liu Dong (CHN), Tomasz Nowak (POL), Jacov Shmuel (ISR), Regilio Tuur (HOL)

An unusual incident occurred during the first-round match between Jamie Pagendam of Canada and Tserendorj Awarjargal of Mongolia. Pagendam, a 22-year-old crane operator from St. Catharines, Ontario, registered three knockdowns in the second round (including one standing eight-count). According to amateur rules, Pagendam should automatically have been declared the winner after the third knockdown. However, the referee, Marius Guiramo Lougbo of the Ivory Coast, lost count of the knockdowns and allowed the bout to continue. When Pagendam was himself floored in the third round, Lougbo stopped the fight and gave the victory to Awarjargal. A protest was filed and the decision was in fact overturned. However, because Pagendam's final knockdown was the result of a blow to his head, he received a 30-day medical suspension and was not allowed to advance in the tournament. Neither was Lougbo—he was suspended for the remainder of the Olympics.

1992 Barcelona-Badalona C: 31, N: 31, D: 8.9.

		FINAL MATCH
1. Andreas Tews	GER	Pts 16–7
2. Faustino Reyes López	SPA	
3. Ramazi Palyani	GEO	
3. Hocine Soltani	ALG	

5. Victoriano Damián Sosa (DOM), Daniel Dumitrescu (ROM), Park Duk-kyu (KOR), Eddy Suárez Edua (CUB)

At the 1988 Olympics Andreas Tews represented East Germany and won a silver medal in the flyweight division. In 1992 he represented a united Germany, moved up two divisions to featherweight, and earned a gold medal. And earn it he did, defeating world champion Kirkor Kirkorov of Bulgaria 9-5, world champion runner-up Park Duk-kyu 17-7, and, in the final, the hero of the local fans, 17-year-old Faustino Reyes. One loser who did not go quietly was the European champion, Paul Griffin. Griffin, Ireland's first European champion in 42 years, was eliminated in his first bout. After Zambia's Steven Chungu knocked him down twice in the second round, the ring doctor stopped the fight. Griffin was so outraged that he kicked his gumshield into the fourth row, engaged in abusive language, and had to be restrained from attacking the doctor. This outburst earned him a six-month suspension.

1996 Atlanta C: 31, N: 31, D: 8.4.

		FINAL MATCH
1. Somluck Kamsing	THA	Pts 8–5
2. Serafim Todorov	BUL	
3. Julio Pablo Chacón	ARG	
3. Floyd Mayweather	USA	

5. Lorenzo Aragón Armenteros (CUB), Falk Huste (GER), Janos Nagy (HUN), Ramazi Palyani (RUS)

Once again, the featherweight division saw a disgruntled athlete suspended for protesting a decision. This time it was John Kelman of Barbados. When referee Najah Moussa of Morocco stopped his preliminary round fight against Janos Nagy, Kelman left the ring and then threw his glove back inside. Suspension: one year.

The final matched Serafim Todorov, who had won the last three world championships, and sailor Somluck Kamsing, whose brother Somrot was competing in the light flyweight class. Todorov, taking part in his third Olympics, each in a different weight class, barely survived the semifinals. He defeated Floyd Mayweather 10-9, but the fight was so close that when Todorov was declared the winner, referee Hamadi Hafez Shouman of Egypt instinctively raised Mayweather's hand by mistake.

Kamsing took a 5-2 lead into the final round and surprised Todorov with effective counterpunching to stay ahead. As Thailand's first Olympic champion in any sport, Kamsing, who hailed from the poor northeastern town of Khon Kaen, was celebrated as a national hero and given more than $1 million by the government and corporate admirers. Todorov, a member of Bulgaria's Turkish minority, defected to Turkey in 1997.

2000 Sydney C: 28, N: 28, D: 9.29.

		FINAL MATCH
1. Bekzat Sattarkhanov	KAZ	Pts 22–14
2. Ricardo Juarez	USA	
3. Kamil Dzhamalutdinov	RUS	
3. Tahar Tamsamani	MOR	
5. Ramazan Palyani (Ramazi Palyani)	TUR	
6. Kamsing Somluck	THA	
7. Israel Héctor Pérez	ARG	
8. Yosvany Aguilera Zamora	CUB	

Both Rocky Juarez and Bekzat Sattarkhanov had one tough fight on their way to the final. For world champion Juarez, it was a 17-15 win over Falk Huste of Germany. For Sattarkhanov, it was a 12-11 quarterfinal squeaker over Ramazan Palyani, who was competing in his third Olympics and for his third country. When he won a bronze medal in 1992, the Georgian flag was raised in his honor. In 1996 he represented Russia. Then he moved to Turkey, changed his name from Ramazi to Ramazan and won the 1998 and 2000 European championships as a Turk. Juarez, a native of Houston, Texas, entered the final with a 68-match winning streak. He had trouble adjusting to Sattarkhanov, who surged to a 15-4 lead after two rounds. Juarez fought back to 18-13, but trailed by seven points going into the final round. Sattarkhanov, by this time, had clearly run out of steam and spent the fourth round holding and escaping. After Sattarkhanov was given a 22-14 victory, US officials filed a protest. They used video footage to prove that the Russian referee, Stanislav Kirsanov, had cautioned Sattarkhanov for holding nine times without issuing a "warning" which would have resulted in a penalty. Further warnings would have led to disqualification. The International Amateur Boxing Federation refused to overturn the verdict, but, in a bizarre twist, they did suspend Kirsanov for four years.

On New Year's Eve 2000, only three months after he became an Olympic champion, Bekzat Sattarkhanov was killed in a car crash in heavy fog. He was 20 years old.

2004 Athens C: 28, N: 28, D: 8.28.

		FINAL MATCH
1. Aleksei Tishchenko	RUS	Pts 39–17
2. Kim Song-guk	PRK	
3. Vitali Tajbert	GER	
3. Jo Seok-hwan	KOR	

5. Muideen Ganiyu (NGR), Viorel Simion (ROM), Galib Dzhafarov (KAZ), Luis Franco Vásquez (CUB)

Competing in his first Olympics, 20-year-old Aleksei Tishchenko had never won a major international title. This did not stop him from rolling over the competition, defeating world champion Galib Dzhafarov 40-22 on his way to the final. Meanwhile, fellow Olympic newcomer Kim Song-guk edged out German favorite Vitali Tajbert 29-24 in the semifinal round The final was a lopsided match, with Tishchenko leaping to a 13-2 lead over Kim in the first round and expanding his lead to 21-3 by the end of the second round. Kim attempted to come back in the final rounds, but Tishchenko powered to a 39-17 win.

2008 Beijing C: 28, N: 28, D: 8.23.

		FINAL MATCH
1. Vasyl Lomachenko	UKR	RSC 1 1:51
2. Khédafi Djelkhir	FRA	
3. Yakup Kiliç	TUR	
3. Şahin İmranov	AZR	

5. Abdelkader Chali (ALG), Li Yang (CHN), Arturo Santos Reyes (MEX), Idel Torriente Leal (CUB)

Due to an unfortunate draw, the most anticipated bout of the featherweight tournament occurred during the first round, when reigning world champion Albert Selimov faced world silver medalist Vasyl Lomachenko. The match was a repeat of the 2007 world championship final, which Selimov had won 16-11. This time Selimov built a 5-2 lead early in the second round before Lomachenko came roaring back with 11 consecutive points, leading to a 14-7 victory.

The 20-year-old Lomachenko powered through the rest of the tournament easily. In the second round he dispatched 2004 Olympic bronze medalist Bahodirjon Sultonov 13-1. He then demolished both 2007 world bronze medalists, Li Yang and Yakup Kiliç, 12-3 and 10-1 in the quarter- and semi-finals. Lomachenko was so dominant in the final bout that the referee stopped the fight with nine seconds left in the first round, with Lomachenko up 9-1 and Khédafi Djelkhir having already endured three standing eight counts.

By the end of the tournament Lomachenko had outpointed his five opponents 58-13. He was subsequently awarded the Val Barker trophy for the best boxer of the Olympics. One year later, Lomachenko beat Sergey Vodopyanov to win the 2009 featherweight world title.

Although he failed to advance beyond the first round, Ghana's entry in the featherweight competition attracted attention for his unusual name: Prince Octopus Dzanie.

LIGHT MIDDLEWEIGHT
(71 kg—156 lbs)

1952 Helsinki C: 23, N: 23, D: 8.2.

		FINAL MATCH
1. László Papp	HUN	Dec 3–0
2. Theunis van Schalkwyk	SAF	
3. Eladio Herrera	ARG	
3. Boris Tishin	SOV/RUS	

5. Paulo de Jesus Cavalheiro (BRA), Guido Mazzinghi (ITA), Erich Schöppner (GER), Peter Stankov (BUL)

Papp had a tough time with van Schalkwyk until the final round of their bout, when a right hook dropped the South African to his knees for an eight-count.

1956 Melbourne C: 14, N: 14, D: 12.1.

		FINAL MATCH
1. László Papp	HUN	Dec
2. José Torres	USA	
3. John McCormack	GBR	
3. Zbigniew Pietrzykowski	POL	

5. Ulrich Kienast (GER), Boris Nikolov (BUL), Franco Scisciani (ITA)

In defeating Torres, the 30-year-old Papp became the first boxer to win three Olympic gold medals (he had won the Middleweight title in 1948). In 1965 Torres won the World Light Heavyweight professional title by knocking out Willie Pastrano. He later became commissioner of boxing for the State of New York.

1960 Rome C: 23, N: 23, D: 9.5.

		FINAL MATCH
1. Wilbert McClure	USA	Dec 4–1
2. Carmelo Bossi	ITA	
3. William Fisher	GBR	
3. Boris Lagutin	SOV/RUS	

5. John Bukowski (AUS), Henryk Dempc (POL), Souleymane Diallo (FRA), Celedonio Lima (ARG)

"Skeeter" McClure of Toledo, Ohio, a quick and intelligent boxer, survived two very close split decisions over Lima and Lagutin to qualify for the final. Against Bossi, he used his strong in-fighting abilities to wear down the aggressive Italian. McClure later became a professor at Northeastern University in Boston, president of his own counseling firm and chairman of the Massachusetts State Boxing Commission.

1964 Tokyo C: 25, N: 25, D: 10.23.

		FINAL MATCH
1. Boris Lagutin	SOV/RUS	Dec 4–1
2. Joseph Gonzales	FRA	
3. Józef Grzesiak	POL	
3. Nojim Maiyegun	NGR	

5. Anthony Barber (AUS), Tom Bogs (DEN), Eddie Davies (GHA), Vasile Mirza (ROM)

Boris Lagutin's path to the final included a victory by disqualification over José Chirino of Argentina, who was penalized for punching the referee, and a walkover in the quarterfinals. After two rounds with Gonzales, Lagutin had matters well in hand. But in the third round he decided to mix it up and received for his efforts a cut eye and a warning for pulling Gonzales. Maiyegun was the first Nigerian to win an Olympic medal.

1968 Mexico City C: 27, N: 27, D: 10.26.

		FINAL MATCH
1. Boris Lagutin	SOV/RUS	Dec 5–0
2. Rolando Garbey	CUB	
3. John Baldwin	USA	
3. Günther Meier	GER	

5. Mario Benítez (URU), Eric Blake (GBR), David Jackson (UGA), Ianos Kovacs (ROM)

The 30-year-old Lagutin outclassed all of his opponents to win his third straight medal. His final match with Garbey was an ugly, brawling contest, which led the crowd to boo and throw coins and burning newspapers at the Korean referee for failing to take action.

1972 Munich C: 33, N: 33, D: 9.10.

		FINAL MATCH
1. Dieter Kottysch	GER	Dec 3–2
2. Wieslaw Rudkowski	POL	
3. Alan Minter	GBR	
3. Peter Tiepold	GDR	

5. Rolando Garbey (CUB), Loucif Hamani (ALG), Mohamed Majeri (TUN), Emeterio Villanueva (MEX)

Kottysch eked out controversial split decisions over Minter and Rudkowski to take the gold medal. However, the most disputed verdict came in the opening round of the tournament when a battered and bleeding Valery Tregubov of the USSR was declared the winner against Reggie Jones of the United States. The announcement was met by a quarter-hour of international catcalls, which continued throughout the next bout.

1976 Montreal C: 23, N: 23, D: 7.31.

		FINAL MATCH
1. Jerzy Rybicki	POL	Dec 5–0
2. Tadija Kačar	YUG/BSH	
3. Rolando Garbey	CUB	
3. Viktor Savchenko	SOV/UKR	

5. Vasile Didea (ROM), Wilfredo Guzman (PUR), Kalevi Kosunen (FIN), Alfredo Lemus (VEN)

1980 Moscow C: 23, N: 23, D: 8.2.

		FINAL MATCH
1. Armando Martínez	CUB	Dec 4–1
2. Aleksandr Koshkin	SOV/RUS	
3. Ján Franek	CZE/SLV	
3. Detlef Kästner	GDR	

5. Francisco Carlos Jesus (BRA), Wilson Kaoma (ZAM), Leonidas Njunwa (TAN), Nicholas Colin Wilshire (GBR)

1984 Los Angeles C: 34, N: 34, D: 8.11.

		FINAL MATCH
1. Frank Tate	USA	Dec 5–0
2. Shawn O'Sullivan	CAN	
3. Christophe Tiozzo	FRA	
3. Manfred Zielonka	GER	

5. Israel Cole (SLE), Roderick Douglas (GBR), Christopher Kapopo (ZAM), Gnohere Sery (IVC)

As expected, the final matched Frank Tate and Shawn O'Sullivan, who had split two previous fights with each other. What was not expected was that both boxers would reach the final as a result of unpopular decisions. Tate's came in his first bout against Lotfi Ayed, a Tunisian-born Swede. Despite being staggered and outpunched, Tate won a unanimous verdict.

Even more controversial was O'Sullivan's semifinal victory over Christophe Tiozzo. The judges voted 3-2 in Tiozzo's favor. However, new rules instituted before the 1984 Games required that all 3-2 decisions be submitted to a 5-man jury. If the jury voted 4-1 or 5-0 for the loser of the split decision, then the decision was reversed. The jury gave the nod to O'Sullivan, 4-1.

In the second round of the championship bout, Tate was twice given a standing eight-count. Nevertheless, four of the five judges awarded him the round. The announcement of Tate's victory by unanimous decision was met by a chorus of boos, but O'Sullivan, who was raised with the teachings of Henry David Thoreau, was philosophical. "It was an unfortunate decision," he told reporters. "I dearly wish things had gone different, but they didn't, and there's no gain in crying over spilled milk."

As the years went by, however, O'Sullivan watched as Frank Tate became wealthy, while he made ends meet by working as a janitor. He thought about the decision daily and hid his silver medal in a desk drawer.

Roy Jones, Aldo Leoni and Park Si-hun, 1988
Shock accompanies the announcement of the decision in the final of the 1988 Light Middleweight division.

1988 Seoul C: 36, N: 36, D: 10.2.

		FINAL MATCH
1. Park Si-hun	KOR	Dec 3–2
2. Roy Jones	USA	
3. Raymond Downey	CAN	
3. Richard Woodhall	GBR	

5. Martin Kitel (SWE), Vincenzo Nardiello (ITA), Rey Rivera (PUR), Yevgeny Zaitsev (SOV/KAZ)

Probably no gold medalist in Olympic history has been less deserving of his prize than Park Si-hun, who benefited from five "hometown" decisions. Park's first bout, against Abdalla Ramadan of Sudan, was halted in the second round with Ramadan doubled over in pain and unable to continue following two illegal blows to the hip and kidney. The Australian referee, Ronald Mark Gregor, undoubtedly haunted by the attack on referee Keith Walker five days earlier, was hesitant to disqualify Park. Instead, he consulted the five judges, one of whom, Elmo Adolph of the US, told him that because Gregor had failed to caution Park after the low blows and because the fouls were not "flagrant," disqualification was inappropriate. Gregor ruled that the injured Ramadan had "retired" and declared Park the winner.

Park's second opponent was one of the favorites, Torsten Schmitz of East Germany. Most observers thought Schmitz had won the fight; however, Park was judged the victor in a narrow but unanimous decision. While the East Germans vented their fury, Park moved on to the quarterfinals and a bout with Vincenzo Nardiello of Acilia, Italy. Once again, it appeared to most observers that Park had been defeated. In fact, Nardiello was ahead on the cards of all five judges after the first two rounds. Two of the judges gave Nardiello the final round as well. However, the other three judges decided that Park had won the round by such a wide margin that they gave him the fight. When the verdict was announced, Nardiello fell to his knees and pounded the canvas. Then he charged out of the ring and began screaming at the jury. Italian team officials dragged him off to the dressing room. He raced back into the arena crying and screaming, only to be hauled back to his room.

In the semifinals, Park won another narrow but unanimous victory, defeating Ray Downey by the same margin by which he had beaten Schmitz. He was becoming known as the "unbeatable Park Si-hun." Now all that stood between Park and a gold medal was 19-year-old Roy Jones, Jr., of Pensacola, Florida. Jones had already alienated local fight fans and many others as well with his arrogant demeanor and showboating style. In the ring he emulated the theatrical ways of Muhammad Ali and Sugar Ray Leonard, dropping his guard and taunting his opponents, doing the Ali shuffle. Outside the ring, he gracelessly referred to one defeated opponent as "a bum." Nevertheless, Jones had also shown that he was a skillful boxer with unusually quick hands. He made it to the final without being seriously challenged. Three days before the gold-medal bout, Jones told reporters, "I know how tough it is to get a decision against a South Korean, but it doesn't matter. If they cheat me, that's OK. I'll know if I really won it." Still, to be on the safe side, Jones announced that he would be going for a knockout.

He didn't get the knockout, but he did pummel Park, dominating all three rounds. Compubox, a private company that kept track of punches thrown and connected for NBC, the US television network, registered 86 hits for Jones and only 32 for Park. Incredibly, three of the five judges gave the victory to the Korean. Veteran ring observers of all nationalities, reporters, referees and fans agreed that it was the worst decision they had ever seen. The French sports newspaper *L'Equipe* summed up the consensus in blunt terms: "Scandalous. To vomit." The decision was so bad that Korean fans were embarrassed, telephoning local newspapers and television stations to complain. Even Park himself apologized to Jones, telling him, through an interpreter, "I am sorry. I lost the fight. I feel very bad." On the victory stand, Park raised Jones' arm in triumph.

So how could such an unjust decision have been made? There were accusations that officials of the Korea Amateur Boxing Federation had bribed or otherwise persuaded some of the judges as a payback for pro-US decisions at the 1984 Olympics. *Sports Illustrated* reported that one judge, Hiouad Larbi of Morocco, told angry journalists, "The American won easily; so easily, in fact, that I was positive my four fellow judges would score the fight for the American by a wide margin. So I voted for the Korean to make the score only 4-1 for the American and not embarrass the host country." Unfortunately, the judges from Uruguay and Uganda did the same thing.

The Park-Jones affair, as well as numerous other dubious decisions, forced the International Boxing Federation to institute radical changes in scoring in 1989. Ringside computers are now used to allow the judges to push a button whenever a scoring punch is made. If a majority of the judges push the button simultaneously, a point is recorded on a scoreboard visible to all in the arena. The winner is known the instant a bout is over.

In 1997 the International Olympic Committee reopened the Park-Jones case and concluded that there was no evidence that someone had bribed the judges.

As a professional, Roy Jones won world titles in four weight divisions and, between 1989 and 2003, he compiled a record of 48 wins and one loss, the loss coming by disqualification after a late blow.

1992 Barcelona-Badalona C: 30, N: 30, D: 8.9.

		FINAL MATCH
1. Juan Carlos Lemus García	CUB	Pts 6–1
2. Orhan Delibas	HOL	
3. György Mizsei	HUN	
3. Robin Reid	GBR	

5. Ole Klemetsen (NOR), Raul Marquez (USA), Fao Maselino (ASA), Igors Shaplavskis (LAT)

World champion Lemus was never seriously challenged. He stopped one opponent in the first round and outpointed the other four by a combined score of 39 to 4. Runner-up Orhan Delibas was born in Turkey.

1996 Atlanta C: 31, N: 31, D: 8.4.

		FINAL MATCH
1. David Reid	USA	KO 3
2. Alfredo Duvergel Adams	CUB	
3. Ezmouhan Ibzaimov	KAZ	
3. Karim Tulaganov	UZB	

5. Markus Beyer (GER), Rival Cadeau (SEY), Mohamed Salah Marmouri (TUN), Antonio Perugino (ITA)

The situation looked very bleak for US boxing head coach Al Mitchell. The US was one bout away from being shut out of gold for the first time in 48 years. In fact, only one American had even made it as far as the final. That American was 22-year-old David Reid of North Philadelphia. As it happened, Reid had been coached since the age of ten by Al Mitchell himself. In fact, the two were so close that they called each other "father" and "son." They had seen each other through rough times. Only one month before the Olympics, Reid was arrested for domestic violence and battery following an altercation with his girlfriend. Charges were dropped before the Games began.

The favorite in the light-welterweight division, Francisc Vaştag, who had moved up from welterweight after the 1992 Olympics and won the world championship in 1993 and 1995. Both times he won lopsided decisions over Alfredo Duvergel. In Atlanta, Vaştag was upset in his first fight, losing to Markus Beyer 17-12. But Duvergel was still there—waiting for David Reid in the final.

Duvergel took a 7-5 lead in the first round. In the second round he attacked Reid with one hard straight left after another to score eight unanswered points. With one round to go, Reid was behind by ten points, an almost impossible gap to make up in only three minutes. Between rounds, Al Mitchell told Reid, "We cannot win this boxing. You've got to meet him with the right hand." He urged Reid to stay inside, watch for Duvergel's straight left and then counter with an overhead right.

Duvergel made no attempt to protect his lead, but instead went after Reid as aggressively as he had in the first two rounds. Twenty-five seconds into the third round, Duvergel tried a straight left. Reid slipped away and buried a short right into Duvergel's face. Duvergel collapsed onto the canvas. It was hard to tell who was more shocked, Duvergel or Reid, who fell to his knees in the neutral corner. Duvergel struggled to his feet, but was counted out. Of the 343 fights at the 1996 Olympics, this was the only one in which a boxer who was behind on points knocked out his opponent. It was also the first light middleweight final to not go the distance.

After the medal ceremony, Muhammed Ali, who was sitting ringside, motioned to Reid. Ali whispered something to Reid and Reid laughed. Later, reporters asked Reid what Ali had said. Reid replied, "He said, 'You're a baaaaad boy.' "

2000 Sydney C: 28, N: 28, D: 10.1.

		FINAL MATCH
1. Yermakhan Ibraimov	KAZ	Pts 25–23
2. Marian Simion	ROM	
3. Jermain Taylor	USA	
3. Pornchai Thongburan	THA	
5. Juan Hernández Sierra	CUB	
6. Frédéric Esther	FRA	
7. Adnan Catic	GER	
8. Hekal Mohamed Abdel Mawgod	EGY	

Yermakhan Ibraimov entered the Sydney Olympics with a solid and consistent record. He had earned a bronze medal at the 1998 Olympics, a silver medal at the 1997 world championships and another bronze medal at the 1999 world championships. Each time, he was beaten by a Cuban. Thus, Ibraimov's moment of truth came in the quarterfinals, when he faced Juan Hernández. A two-time Olympic silver medalist in the welterweight division, Ibraimov won 16-9. After outpointing Jermain Taylor 29-14 in the early seconds of the fourth round, Ibraimov moved on to the gold medal match, where he faced Marian Simion. Simion came from a boxing family. His father, Gheorghe, competed in the 1984 Olympics and Marian's younger brother, Dorel, earned a bronze medal in 2000. Marian himself had won a bronze medal as a welterweight at the 1996 Olympics and a gold medal at the 1999 world championships. Ibraimov jumped out to a 7-3 lead after the first round. Simion fought his way back and managed to move ahead 19-18 in the third round. However Ibraimov dominated the final round and held on for a narrow, two-point victory.

THE VAL BARKER CUP

The Val Barker Cup, named in honor of the first General-Secretary of the International Amateur Boxing Association, is awarded to the boxer who displays the best style and technique.

1936	Louis Laurie	USA	flyweight	bronze
1948	George Hunter	SAF	light heavyweight	gold
1952	Norvel Lee	USA	light heavyweight	gold
1956	Richard McTaggart	GBR	lightweight	gold
1960	Giovanni Benvenuti	ITA	welterweight	gold
1964	Valery Popenchenko	SOV/RUS	middleweight	gold
1968	Philip Waruinge	KEN	featherweight	bronze
1972	Teófilo Stevenson	CUB	super heavyweight	gold
1976	Howard Davis	USA	lightweight	gold
1980	Patrizio Oliva	ITA	light welterweight	gold
1984	Paul Gonzales	USA	light flyweight	gold
1988	Roy Jones	USA	light middleweight	silver
1992	Roberto Balado	CUB	super heavyweight	gold
1996	Vassily Zhirov	KAZ	light heavyweight	gold
2000	Oleg Saitov	RUS	welterweight	gold
2004	Bakhtiyar Artayev	KAZ	welterweight	gold
2008	Vasyl Lomachenko	UKR	featherweight	gold

WOMEN

FLYWEIGHT
(51 kg–112½ lbs)

This event will be held for the first time in 2012.

LIGHTWEIGHT
(57 kg–126 lbs)

This event will be held for the first time in 2012.

MIDDLEWEIGHT
(75 kg–165½ lbs)

This event will be held for the first time in 2012.

Chapter 7 **Canoeing**

MEN
Kayak Singles 200 Meters
Kayak Singles 1000 Meters
Kayak Pairs 200 Meters
Kayak Pairs 1000 Meters
Kayak Fours 1000 Meters
Canadian Singles 200 Meters
Canadian Singles 1000 Meters
Canadian Pairs 200 Meters
Canadian Pairs 1000 Meters
White-water (Slalom)
Kayak Slalom Singles
Canadian Slalom Singles
Canadian Slalom Pairs
Discontinued Events

WOMEN
Kayak Singles 200 Meters
Kayak Singles 500 Meters
Kayak Pairs 500 Meters
Kayak Fours 500 Meters
Kayak Slalom Singles

Olympic canoeing events are divided into two types, depending on the kind of paddle that is used. In *kayak* events, a paddle with a blade on each end is used. The canoeist alternately paddles one blade on the left side and the other on the right side. The paddle in *Canadian* canoeing has only one blade. The canoeist sits in a half-kneeling position, switching the blade from side to side.

One-person canoes and kayaks are about 5.18 meters (17 feet) long, two-person boats are about 6.4 meters (21 feet) long, and four-person kayaks are about 11 meters (36 feet) long. The lanes are nine meters (29 feet 6 inches) wide. The boats must stay in the middle of their lanes and are not allowed to come within five meters (16 feet 6 inches) of another boat, which keeps competitors from gaining an advantage by riding in the wake of the other boat. Each boat is allowed one false start. A second false start results in disqualification.

Canoeing contests begin with qualifying heats. The two or three winners of each heat advance directly to the semifinals, while the rest take part in a *repêchage*, or second-chance round (*repêchage* being the French word for "fishing again"). The three or four fastest participants in each *repêchage* race join the semifinals. Until 1984 the top six semifinalists took part in the final, while the other six took part in a *petit final* to determine seventh through twelfth places. In 1984 the final was expanded to nine participants and the *petit final* was eliminated.

MEN

KAYAK SINGLES 200 METERS

This event will be held for the first time in 2012.

KAYAK SINGLES 1000 METERS

1896–1932 not held

1936 Berlin-Grunau C: 15, N: 15, D: 8.8.

1. Gregor Hradetzky	AUT	4:22.9
2. Helmut Cämmerer	GER	4:25.6
3. Jacobus Kraaier	HOL	4:35.1
4. Ernest Riedel	USA	4:38.1
5. Joel Rahmqvist	SWE	4:39.5
6. Henri Eberhardt	FRA	4:41.2
7. Max Birger Johansson	FIN	4:42.2
8. Ivar Iversen	NOR	4:44.2

The final took place during a heavy downpour with thunder and lightning. Cämmerer took the early lead, but Hradetzky passed him after 700 meters. Gregor Hradetzky later achieved great success as a master organ builder.

1948 London-Henley-on-Thames C: 15, N: 15, D: 8.12.

1. Gert Fredriksson	SWE	4:33.2
2. Johan Frederik Kobberup	DEN	4:39.9
3. Henri Eberhardt	FRA	4:41.4
4. Hans Martin Gulbrandsen	NOR	4:41.7
5. Willem Frederik van der Kroft	HOL	4:43.5
6. Harry Åkerfelt	FIN	4:44.2
7. Lubomir Vambera	CZE	4:44.3
8. Walter Piemann	AUT	4:50.3

In the first heat Fredriksson showed his superiority by casually lying in fourth place for the first 950 meters and then sprinting at the end to take first. The final was no contest, as Fredriksson attained the longest winning margin in any Olympic kayak final other than 10,000 meters.

1952 Helsinki C: 20, N: 20, D: 7.28.

1. Gert Fredriksson	SWE	4:07.9
2. Thorvald Strömberg	FIN	4:09.7
3. Louis Gantois	FRA	4:20.1
4. Willem Frederik van der Kroft	HOL	4:20.8
5. Meinrad Miltenberger	GER	4:21.6
6. Lubomir Vambera	CZE	4:24.0
7. Hendrik Verbrugghe	BEL	4:25.0
8. Lev Nikitin	SOV/RUS	4:26.2

Fredriksson started a long, sustained sprint from the halfway mark, which wore down his opponents and allowed him to turn the tables on Strömberg, who had beaten him the previous evening in the 10,000 meters.

1956 Melbourne-Ballarat C: 13, N: 13, D: 12.1.

1. Gert Fredriksson	SWE	4:12.8
2. Igor Pissarev	SOV/RUS	4:15.3
3. Lajos Kiss	HUN	4:16.2
4. Stefan Kaplaniak	POL	4:19.8
5. Louis Gantois	FRA	4:22.1
6. Ladislav Čepčianský	CZE	4:23.2
7. Villy Christiansen	DEN	4:25.2
8. Ernst Steinhauer	GER	4:25.5

Fredriksson earned his fifth individual Olympic gold medal.

1960 Rome-Lake Albano C: 22, N: 22, D: 8.29.

1. Erik Hansen	DEN	3:53.00
2. Imre Szöllösi	HUN	3:54.02
3. Gert Fredriksson	SWE	3:55.89
4. Ibragim Khasanov	SOV/TJK	3:56.38
5. Ronald Rhodes	GBR	4:01.15
6. Rolf Olsen	NOR	4:02.31
7. Wolfgang Lange	GDR	4:03.05
8. Simo Kusimanen	FIN	4:03.66

1964 Tokyo-Lake Sagami C: 15, N: 15, D: 10.22.

1. Rolf Peterson	SWE	3:57.13
2. Mihály Hesz	HUN	3:57.28
3. Aurel Vernescu	ROM	4:00.77
4. Erich Suhrbier	GER	4:01.62
5. Günther Pfaff	AUT	4:03.56
6. Antonius Geurts	HOL	4:04.48
7. Erik Hansen	DEN	4:04.72
8. Alastair Wilson	GBR	4:05.80

Mihály Hesz and Aurel Vernescu, the reigning world champion, were the favorites, but were upset by Rolf Peterson, a 22-year-old student from Halmstad.

1968 Mexico City-Xochimilco C: 20, N: 20, D: 10.25.

1. Mihály Hesz	HUN	4:02.63
2. Oleksander Shaparenko	SOV/UKR	4:03.58
3. Erik Hansen	DEN	4:04.39
4. Wladyslaw Szuszkiewicz	POL	4:06.36
5. Rolf Peterson	SWE	4:07.86
6. Václav Mára	CZE	4:09.35
7. Andrei Contolenco	ROM	4:09.96
8. Wolfgang Lange	GDR	4:10.03

Lying fifth at the halfway mark, Hesz waited to make his move until there were only 200 meters to go. In the last 100 meters he passed Hansen, the 1960 Olympic champion, and Shaparenko, the reigning world champion.

1972 Munich C: 24, N: 24, D: 9.9.

1. Oleksander Shaparenko	SOV/UKR	3:48.06
2. Rolf Peterson	SWE	3:49.38
3. Géza Csapó	HUN	3:49.38
4. Jean-Pierre Burny	BEL	3:50.29
5. Ladislav Souček	CZE	3:51.05
6. Joachim Mattern	GDR	3:51.94
7. Erik Hansen	DEN	3:52.15
8. Grzegorz Śledziewski	POL	3:53.22

Gert Fredriksson, 1956
Fredriksson won six canoeing gold medals between 1948 and 1960.

1976 Montreal C: 19, N: 19, D: 7.31.

1. Rüdiger Helm	GDR	3:48.20
2. Géza Csapó	HUN	3:48.84
3. Vasile Dîba	ROM	3:49.65
4. Oreste Perri	ITA	3:51.13
5. Oleksander Shaparenko	SOV/UKR	3:51.45
6. Berndt Andersson	SWE	3:52.46
7. Douglas Parnham	GBR	3:52.64
8. Grzegorz Śledziewski	POL	3:54.29

In the opening heats Oreste Perri, the world champion, and Vasile Dîba were disqualified for using underweight boats. However, the decision was reversed when the judges announced that the super sensitive electronic scales had responded to a change in atmospheric pressure. Helm made his move in the last quarter of the race, passed Csapó, and shouted with joy as he stormed across the finish line. At 19, he was the youngest competitor in the event.

1980 Moscow C. 20, N: 20, D: 8.2.

1. Rüdiger Helm	GDR	3:48.77
2. Alain Lebas	FRA	3:50.20
3. Ion Bîrlădeanu	ROM	3:50.49
4. John Sumegi	AUS	3:50.63
5. Oreste Perri	ITA	3:51.95
6. Felix Masár	CZE	3:52.19
7. Milan Janić	YUG/CRO	3:53.50
8. Ian Ferguson	NZL	3:53.78

Two hours after this race, Helm joined his teammates in winning the Kayak Fours, to bring his Olympic medal total to five: three gold and two bronze.

1984 Los Angeles-Lake Casitas C: 19, N: 19, D: 8.11.

1. Alan Thompson	NZL	3:45.73
2. Milan Janić	YUG/CRO	3:46.88
3. Gregory Barton	USA	3:47.38
4. Kalle Sundqvist	SWE	3:48.09
5. Peter Genders	AUS	3:49.11
6. Philippe Boccara	FRA	3:49.38
7. Vasile Dîba	ROM	3:51.61
8. Stephen Jackson	GBR	3:52.25

1988 Seoul C: 19, N: 19, D: 10.1.

1. Gregory Barton	USA	3:55.27
2. Grant Davies	AUS	3:55.28
3. André Wohllebe	GDR	3:55.55
4. Dmitri Bankovsky	SOV/RUS	3:56.49
5. Gunnar Olsson	SWE	3:56.84
6. Alan Thompson	NZL	3:56.91
7. Attila Szabó	CZE	3:57.52
8. Morten Ivarsen	NOR	3:59.18

Greg Barton was a mechanical engineer who grew up in Homer, Michigan, a small town with more pigs than human beings. He was born with two club feet, a condition that was only aggravated by four operations. In Seoul, Barton and Davies crossed the finish line in a near dead heat. Barton was told by Korean officials that he had won. Then the scoreboard flashed the news that Davies was the victor. While the Australians celebrated and Barton prepared for the final of the 1000-meter pairs, the jury of the International Canoe Federation examined the finish line photo. A few minutes later they announced that Barton had won by .005 seconds—less than 1 centimeter. Greg Barton had become the first US kayaker to win an Olympic gold medal. Davies was stoic. "If that's the biggest disappointment in my life," he said, "I can handle it."

1992 Barcelona-Castelldefels C: 26, N: 26, D: 8.8.

1. Clint Robinson	AUS	3:37.26
2. Knut Holmann	NOR	3:37.50
3. Gregory Barton	USA	3:37.93
4. Marin Popescu	ROM	3:38.37
5. Beniamino Bonomi	ITA	3:41.12
6. José Garcia	POR	3:41.60
7. Thor Nielsen	DEN	3:41.70
8. Renn Crichlow	CAN	3:43.46

Robinson, a 20-year-old from Maroochydore, Queensland, upset two-time world champion Knut Holmann by staying close to the Norwegian throughout the race and then surging ahead at the end. He pushed himself so hard that, for the first time in his life, his whole body went numb. He was also so dehydrated that it would be six hours before he could produce a urine sample for doping control. Robinson was also a specialist in the sport of surf lifesaving, in particular the single ski event, in which he won the Australian national championship for the eleventh time in 2003.

1996 Atlanta-Lake Lanier C: 24, N: 24, D: 8.3.

1. Knut Holmann	NOR	3:25.785
2. Beniamino Bonomi	ITA	3:27.073
3. Clint Robinson	AUS	3:29.713
4. Lutz Liwowski	GER	3:30.025
5. Agustín Calderón Díez	SPA	3:31.397
6. Andrzej Gajewski	POL	3:32.521
7. Marin Popescu	ROM	3:34.549
8. Sebastian Cuattrin	BRA	3:34.669

Robinson went out hard and led at 250 meters, but knew already that it wasn't his day. Holmann, using a wooden boat, led at the halfway mark. Bonomi, who wore one long sideburn for good luck, moved ahead briefly at 750 meters, but Holmann quickly regained the lead and pulled away to win by more than a boat length.

2000 Sydney-Penrith C: 31, N: 31, D: 9.30.

1. Knut Holmann	NOR	3:33.269
2. Petar Merkov	BUL	3:34.649
3. Tim Brabants	GBR	3:35.057
4. Michael Kolganov	ISR	3:35.099
5. Javier Correa	ARG	3:35.687
6. Torsten Tranum	DEN	3:37.811
7. Pierre Lubac	FRA	3:37.931
8. Jacopo Majocchi	ITA	3:38.105

Knut Holman made his move after 350 meters and then held off a late challenge from Petar Merkov who refused to attend the post-race press conference after media reports that he had failed a doping test in Bulgaria.

2004 Athens-Schinias C: 25, N: 25, D: 8.27.

1. Eirik Verås Larsen	NOR	3:25.897
2. Ben Fouhy	NZL	3:27.413
3. Adam van Koeverden	CAN	3:28.218
4. Nathan Baggaley	AUS	3:28.310
5. Tim Brabants	GBR	3:30.553
6. Roland Kökény	HUN	3:31.121
7. Emanuel da Silva	POR	3:33.862
8. Björn Goldschmidt	GER	3:34.381

The 2002 world champion, 28-year-old Eirik Larsen maintained close ties to his leading adversary, Adam van Koeverden. In 2002, Larsen invited Koeverden to stay with him and his girlfriend in their tiny one-room apartment in Oslo. The pair lived and trained together until the young van Koeverden began to surpass his host, beating him at the 2003 world championships to take silver. Realizing he was helping to train a potential rival, Larsen told van Koeverden they could no longer train together.

In the Olympic final, van Koeverden jumped out to a 1.2-second lead after the first 250 meters, but began to slow by the halfway point. Larsen gained a .29 second lead by the 750-meter mark and never relinquished the lead, while Van Koeverden fell to third behind Ben Fouhy in the final 100 meters. An hour after his victory, Larsen added a bronze in the K-2 1000.

2008 Beijing-Shunyi C: 26, N: 26, D: 8.22.

1. Tim Brabants	GBR	3:26.323
2. Eirik Verås Larsen	NOR	3:27.342
3. Kenneth Wallace	AUS	3:27.485
4. Ben Fouhy	NZL	3:29.193
5. Max Hoff	GER	3:29.391
6. Markus Oscarsson	SWE	3:30.198
7. Stjepan Jani	CRO	3:30.495
8. Adam van Koeverden	CAN	3:31.793

A medical doctor by training, Sydney Olympics bronze medalist Tim Brabants took an 18-month break from competition to concentrate on medicine after a disappointing fifth-place finish at the 2004 Athens Olympics. Brabants finished his studies and practised as a doctor in New Jersey before returning to action in 2006, when he won the European championship and finished second at the world championships, a mere 0.06 seconds behind Markus Oscarsson. The next year, he showed he was in top form, finishing ahead of all three Athens medalists to win the 2007 world championship title by more than half a second.

Brabants won his first-round heat to advance straight to the final, along with defending Olympic champion and 2005 world champion Eirik Verås Larsen and double Olympic medalist and reigning world silver medalist Adam van Koeverden, who had won five of six pre-Olympic World Cup races in 2008.

In the final, Brabants led from the start, pulling ahead by six-tenths of a second by the halfway point. Second-place Van Koeverden began to close the gap, but in the final 400 meters Brabants upped the pace, and van Koeverden faded fast, dropping all the way to eighth place. Larsen finished strongly to take silver, while Australia's Ken Wallace moved up from last at the halfway point to capture bronze.

In 2010 friendly rivals van Koeverden, Anders Gustafsson of Sweden and Ken Wallace spent two months training together in Hungary. The training paid off for van Koeverden, who won the 2011 K-1 1000-meter world championship title more than three seconds ahead of Gustafsson.

KAYAK PAIRS 200 METERS

This event will be held for the first time in 2012.

KAYAK PAIRS 1000 METERS

1896–1932 not held

1936 Berlin-Grünau T: 12, N: 12, D: 8.8.

1. Adolf Kainz, Alfons Dorfner	AUT	4:03.8
2. Ewald Tilker, Fritz Bondroit	GER	4:08.9
3. Nicolaas Tates, Willem Frederik van der Kroft	HOL	4:12.2
4. František Brzák-Felix, Josef Dusil	CZE	4:15.2
5. Rudolf Vilim, Werner Klingelfuss	SWI	4:22.8
6. Edward Deir, Francis Willis	CAN	4:24.5
7. Werner Lövgreen, Axel Svendsen	DEN	4:26.6
DISQ: Sixten Jansson, Gunner Lundqvist (SWE)		

Jansson and Lundqvist finished second, but were disqualified for bumping into Tilker and Bondroit.

1948 London-Henley-on-Thames T: 16, T: 16, D: 8.12.

1. Hans Berglund, Lennart Klingström	SWE	4:07.3
2. Ejvind Hansen, Bernhard Jensen	DEN	4:07.5
3. Thor Axelsson, Nils Björklof	FIN	4:08.7
4. Ivar Mathisen, Knut Östbye	NOR	4:09.1
5. Otto Kroutil, Miloš Pech	CZE	4:09.8
6. Cornelis Gravesteyn, Willem Pool	HOL	4:15.8
7. Gerald Covey, Henry Harper	CAN	4:56.8
DISQ: János Toldi, Gyula Andrási (HUN)		

Toldi and Andrási were disqualified for "hanging" in the wake of another canoe. It was thought by many that the ruling was a harsh one.

1952 Helsinki T: 19, N: 19, D: 7.28.

1. Kurt Wires, Yrjö Hietanen	FIN	3:51.1
2. Lars Glassér, Ingemar Hedberg	SWE	3:51.1
3. Max Raub, Herbert Wiedermann	AUT	3:51.4
4. Gustav Schmidt, Helmut Noller	GER	3:51.8
5. Ivar Mathisen, Knut Östbye	NOR	3:54.7
6. Maurice Graffen, Marcel Renaud	FRA	3:55.1
7. István Granek, János Kulcsár	HUN	3:55.1
8. Cornelis Koch, Abraham Klingers	HOL	3:55.8

Wires and Hietanen, who had already won the 10,000 meter pairs, were awarded a second set of gold medals only after a photo-finish had been studied.

1956 Melbourne-Ballarat T: 15, N: 15, D: 7.28.

1. Michael Scheuer, Meinrad Miltenberger	GER	3:49.6
2. Mikhail Kaaleste, Anatoly Demitkov	SOV/RUS	3:51.4
3. Max Raub, Herbert Wiedermann	AUT	3:55.8
4. Mircea Anastasescu, Stavru Teodorov	ROM	3:56.1
5. Maurice Graffen, Michel Meyer	FRA	3:58.3
6. Henri Verbrugghe, Germain van de Moere	BEL	3:58.7
7. Walter Brown, Dennis Green	AUS	3:59.1
8 Miroslav Jemelka, Rudolph Klabouch	CZE	4:01.4

1960 Rome-Lake Albano T: 23, N: 23, D: 8.29.

1. Gert Fredriksson, Sven-Olov Sjödelius	SWE	3:34.73
2. György Mészáros, András Szente	HUN	3:34.91
3. Stefan Kaplaniak, Wladislaw Zielinski	POL	3:37.34
4. Nikolas Rudzinskas, Ivan Holovachov	SOV	3:37.48
5. Kaj Schmidt, Vagn Schmidt	DEN	3:39.06

6. František Riha, František Vršovsky	CZE	3:40.78
7. Rudolf Knuppe, Antonius Geurts	HOL	3:41.01
8. Wolfgang Lange, Dieter Krause	GDR	3:41.46

Fredriksson completed his Olympic career with six gold medals, one silver medal, and one bronze medal. Four years later in Tokyo he was the coach of the Swedish team.

1964 Tokyo-Lake Sagami T: 14, N: 14, D: 10.22.

1. Sven-Olov Sjödelius, Nils Gunnar Utterberg	SWE	3:38.54
2. Antonius Geurts, Paul Hoekstra	HOL	3:39.30
3. Heinz Büker, Holger Zander	GER	3:40.69
4. Haralambie Ivanov, Vasile Nicoară	ROM	3:41.12
5. György Mészáros, Imre Szöllösi	HUN	3:41.39
6. Cesare Beltrami, Cesare Zilioli	ITA	3:43.55
7. Erik Kalugin, Ibragim Khasanov	SOV	3:44.19
8. Gordan Jeffery, Adrian Powell	AUS	3:44.52

1968 Mexico City-Xochimilco T: 20, N: 20, D: 10.25.

1. Oleksander Shaparenko, Volodymyr Morozov	SOV/UKR	3:37.54
2. Csaba Giczi, István Timár	HUN	3:38.44
3. Gerhard Seibold, Günther Pfaff	AUT	3:40.71
4. Paul Hoekstra, Antonius Geurts	HOL	3:41.36
5. Lars Andersson, Nils Gunnar Utterberg	SWE	3:41.99
6. Atanase Sciotnic, Aurel Vernescu	ROM	3:45.18
7. Jean-Pierre Burny, Herman Naegels	BEL	3:45.21
8. Cesare Beltrami, Cesare Zilioli	ITA	3:46.08

1972 Munich T: 25, N: 25, D: 9.9.

1. Nikolai Gorbachev, Viktor Kratasyuk	SOV	3:31.23
2. József Deme, János Rátkai	HUN	3:32.00
3. Wladyslaw Szuszkiewicz, Rafal Piszcz	POL	3:33.83
4. Reiner Kurth, Alexander Slatnow	GDR	3:34.16
5. Costel Coşnită, Vasile Simiocenco	ROM	3:35.66
6. Jean-Pierre Cordebois, Didier Niquet	FRA	3:36.51
7. Günther Pfaff, Helmut Hediger	AUT	3:36.61
8. Hans-Jürgen Riemenschneider, Horst Mattern	GER	3:38.67

1976 Montreal T: 24, N: 24, D: 7.31.

1. Serhei Nahorny, Vladimir Romanovsky	SOV	3:29.01
2. Joachim Mattern, Bernd Olbricht	GDR	3:29.33
3. Zoltán Bakó, István Szabó	HUN	3:30.36
4. Jean-Paul Hanquier, Alain Lebas	FRA	3:33.05
5. Guillermo del Riego Gordón, José Seguín	SPA	3:33.16
6. Jean-Pierre Burny, Paul Hoekstra	BEL	3:33.86
7. Policarp Malihin, Larion Serghei	ROM	3:34.27
8. Steve King, Denis Barre	CAN	3:34.46

1980 Moscow T: 16, N: 16, D: 8.2.

1. Vladimir Parfenovich, Serhei Chukhray	SOV	3:26.72
2. István Szabó, István Joós	HUN	3:28.49
3. Luis Gregorio Ramos Misioné, Herminio Menéndez Rodriguez	SPA	3:28.66
4. Alexandru Giura, Nicolae Ticu	ROM	3:28.94
5. Peter Hempel, Harry Nolte	GDR	3:31.02
6. José Marrero Rodriguez, Reynaldo Cunill Infante	CUB	3:31.12
7. Ron Stevens, Gert-Jan Lebbink	HOL	3:33.18
8. Alan Thompson, Geoffrey Walker	NZL	3:33.83

1984 Los Angeles-Lake Casitas T: 17, N: 17, D: 8.11.

1. Hugh Fisher, Alwyn Morris	CAN	3:24.22
2. Bernard Bregeon, Patrick Lefoulon	FRA	3:25.97
3. Barry Kelly, Grant Kenny	AUS	3:26.80
4. Olney Kent, Terry White	USA	3:27.01
5. Matthias Seack, Oliver Seack	GER	3:27.28
6. Daniele Scarpa, Francesco Uberti	ITA	3:27.46
7. Herminio Menéndez Rodríguez, Guillermo Del Riego Gordón	SPA	3:27.53
8. Bengt Andersson, Kalle Sundqvist	SWE	3:29.39

Alwyn Morris, a Mohawk Indian from the Caughawaga Reserve in Quebec, carried with him to the medal ceremony a decorated eagle feather to honor his late grandfather and to symbolize the sharing of his victory with the native people of North America. The feather had been presented to him by a California Indian group.

1988 Seoul T: 20, N: 20, D: 10.1.

1. Gregory Barton, Norman Bellingham	USA	3:32.42
2. Ian Ferguson, Paul MacDonald	NZL	3:32.71
3. Peter Foster, Kelvin Graham	AUS	3:33.76
4. Niels Ellwanger, Carsten Lömker	GER	3:34.63
5. Guido Behling, Torsten Krentz	GDR	3:35.44
6. Daniel Stoian, Angelin Velea	ROM	3:35.75
7. Anders Ohlsén, Hans Olsson	SWE	3:36.13
8. Svein Egil Solvang, Harald Amundsen	NOR	3:38.16

Pre-Olympic favorites Philippe Boccara and Pascal Boucherit of France were disqualified in the semifinals when they failed to make it to the starting line on time. Barton, the son of a pig farmer, and Bellingham, the son of a CIA agent, came from behind in the last 250 meters to nip Ferguson and MacDonald, who happened to have been Bellingham's mentors.

1992 Barcelona-Castelldefels T: 27, N: 27, D: 8.8.

1. Kay Bluhm, Torsten Gutsche	GER	3:16.10
2. Gunnar Olsson, Karl Sundqvist	SWE	3:17.70
3. Grzegorz Kotowicz, Dariusz Białkowski	POL	3:18.86
4. Gregory Barton, Norman Bellingham	USA	3:19.26
5. Paolo Luschi, Daniele Scarpa	ITA	3:20.34
6. Krisztián Bártfai, András Rajna	HUN	3:20.71
7. René Kučera, Petr Hruška	CZE	3:23.12
8. Ian Ferguson, Paul MacDonald	NZL	3:26.84

Bluhm and Gutsche had won the event at the last three world championships. In the Olympic final they pulled out to a lead of almost three seconds at the halfway mark, continued to apply pressure over the next 250 meters, and held on for the victory.

1996 Atlanta-Lake Lanier T: 24, N: 24, D: 8.3.

1. Antonio Rossi, Daniele Scarpa	ITA	3:09.190
2. Kay Bluhm, Torsten Gutsche	GER	3:10.518
3. Andrian Dushev, Milko Kazanov	BUL	3:11.206
4. Grzegroz Kotowicz, Dariusz Białkowski	POL	3:11.262
5. Pierre Lubac, Patrick Lancereau	FRA	3:11.402
6. Thor Nielsen, Jesper Stahl	DEN	3:12.054
7. Peter Scott, Grant Leury	AUS	3:13.054
8. Staffan Malmsten, Markus Oscarsson	SWE	3:14.182

Competing in his fourth Olympics, each time with a different partner, Daniele Scarpa of Venice finally broke through to the medal platform. Bluhm and Gutsche led throughout the first half of the race, but could not match the finishing power of Rossi and Scarpa. The next day, Scarpa switched partners and earned a silver medal in the K-2 500 meters. Back in Venice, Scarpa was elected to the local government as a representative of the Greens Party.

2000 Sydney-Penrith T: 18, N: 18, D: 9.30.

1. Antonio Rossi, Beniamino Bonomi	ITA	3:14.461
2. Henrik Nilsson, Markus Oscarsson	SWE	3:16.075
3. Krisztián Bártfai, Krisztián Veréb	HUN	3:16.357
4. Andreas Ihle, Olaf Winter	GER	3:16.627
5. Babak Amir-Tahmasseb, Philippe Aubertin	FRA	3:17.635
6. Juraj Baca, Michal Riszdorfer	SLV	3:18.325
7. Yevgeny Salakhov, Oleg Goroby	RUS	3:18.937
8. Marek Twardowski, Adam Wysocki	POL	3:19.939

The year after the 1996 Olympics, Daniele Scarpa quit the Italian national team because of what he claimed was widespread drug abuse. Antonio Rossi teamed with Luca Negri and won the 1997 and 1998 world championships. In 1999 Rossi replaced Negri with Beniamino Bonomi even though Bonomi, like Rossi, was a bow paddler. By the time of the 2000 Olympics, they had adjusted and were able to win the gold medal. Bonomi was so excited that, after saluting the Italian team, he lost his balance and fell overboard.

2004 Athens-Schinias T: 16, N: 16, D: 8.27.

1. Markus Oscarsson, Henrik Nilsson	SWE	3:18.420
2. Antonio Rossi, Beniamino Bonomi	ITA	3:19.484
3. Eirik Verås Larsen, Nils Olav Fjeldheim	NOR	3:19.528
4. Daniel Collins, David Rhodes	AUS	3:19.956
5. Wouter D'Haene, Bob Maesen	BEL	3:20.196
6. Jan Schäfer, Marco Herszel	GER	3:20.548
7. Ian Wynne, Paul Darby-Dowman	GBR	3:20.848
8. Ben Fouhy, Steven Ferguson	NZL	3:21.336

Defending Olympic champions Antonio Rossi and Beniamino Bonomi had a difficult time qualifying for the Athens Games. They competed at the 2003 world championships two months after Rossi was involved in a severe bicycle accident, breaking his nose, cheekbone and a bone in his right hand. The pair earned their place at the Olympics with a fifth-place finish, but the clear favorites in Greece were the 2000 silver medalists, two-time world champions Markus Oscarsson and Henrik Nilsson. Despite finishing sixth in their heat, Rossi and Bonomi did make it to the final. However, Oscarsson and Nilsson dominated the race, winning by more than a second, while Rossi and Bonomi edged out Eirik Larsen and Nils Fjeldheim for silver.

2008 Beijing-Shunyi T: 14, N: 14, D: 8.22.

1. Martin Hollstein, Andreas Ihle	GER	3:11.809
2. Kim Knudsen, René Poulsen	DEN	3:13.580
3. Andrea Facchin, Antonio Scaduto	ITA	3:14.750
4. Zoltán Kammerer, Gábor Kucsera	HUN	3:15.049
5. Mike Walker, Steven Ferguson	NZL	3:15.329
6. Philippe Colin, Cyrille Carre	FRA	3:16.532
7. Krists Straume, Kristaps Za upe	LAT	3:19.387
8. Shen Jie, Huang Zhipeng	CHN	3:22.058

DISQ (drugs): Adam Seroczy ski, Marius Kujawski (POL) 3:14.828

Double world champion Gábor Kucsera and three-time Olympic champion Zoltán Kammerer were the clear favorites in Beijing (despite a disappointing third-place finish at the 2007 world championships behind surprise winners Philippe Colin and Cyrille Carre). They first paired up in 2006, winning the world championship title by more than a second ahead of defending world silver medalist Andreas Ihle and his new partner Rupert Wagner.

In Beijing, Ihle was partnered by 21-year-old newcomer, Martin Hollstein, who had never reached the podium in a major international event. The pair showed promise from the start, winning their first-round heat a full 2.722 seconds ahead of Kim Knudsen and René Poulsen. Kammerer and Kucsera also won their first-round heat, automatically advancing to the final.

In the final Kammerer and Kucsera jumped out to an early lead, drawing a full boat length ahead in the first 250 meters and maintaining a strong pace until the final 200 meters, when they began to fade. Hollstein and Ihle surged ahead, holding off Knudsen and Poulsen to take the gold medals, while Kammerer and Kucsera dropped to fifth.

After the Games it emerged that fourth-place finisher Adam Seroczy ski had tested positive for the steroid clenbuterol; he was banned from competition for two years and his results were expunged. His partner and fellow 2007 world silver medalist Marius Kujawski was not implicated.

KAYAK FOURS 1000 METERS

1896–1960 not held

1964 Tokyo-Lake Sagami T: 14, N: 14, D: 10.22.

1. SOV	Mykola Chuzhykov, Anatoly Grishin, Vyacheslav Ionov, Volodymyr Morozov	3:14.67
2. GER	Günther Perleberg, Bernhard Schulze, Friedhelm Wentzke, Holger Zander	3:15.39
3. ROM	Simion Cuciuc, Atanase Sciotnic, Mihai Turcaş, Aurel Vernescu	3:15.51
4. HUN	Imre Kemecsey, György Mészáros, András Szente, Imre Szöllösi	3:16.24
5. SWE	Rolf Peterson, Sven-Olov Sjödelius, Nils Gunnar Utterberg, Carl von Gerber	3:17.47

6. ITA	Claudio Agnisetta, Cesare Beltrami, Angelo Pedroni, Cesare Zilioli	3:19.32
7. HOL	Paul Hoekstra, Theodorus van Halteren, Gulllaume Weijzen, Jan Wittenberg	3:19.36
8. YUG	Dragan Desancić, Vladimir Ignjatijević, Aleksandar Kercov, Stanisa Radmanović	3:19.79

1968 Mexico City-Xochimilco T: 19, N: 19, D: 10.25.

1. NOR	Steinar Admundsen, Egil Söby, Tore Berger, Jan Johansen	3:14.38
2. ROM	Anton Calenic, Dimitrie Ivanov, Haralambie Ivanov, Mihai Turcaş	3:14.81
3. HUN	Csaba Giczi, István Timár, Imre Szöllösi, István Csizmadia	3:15.10
4. SWE	Per Larsson, Hans Nilsson, Tord Sahlén, Åke Sandin	3:16.68
5. FIN	Karl-Gustav von Alfthan, Heikki Mäkelä, Jorma Lehtosalo, Ilkka Nummisto	3:17.28
6. GDR	Joachim Wenzke, Klaus-Uwe Will, Erhard Riedrich, Klaus-Peter Ebeling	3:18.03
7. AUT	Helmut Hediger, Kurt Lindlgruber, Günther Pfaff, Gerhard Seibold	3:18.95
8. POL	Ewald Janusz, Ryszard Marchlik, Rafał Piszcz, Wladyslaw Zieliński	3:22.10

Much credit for the Norwegians' upset victory went to their trainer, Stein Johnson, who had successfully coached track and field, skiing, and speed skating before trying his hand at canoeing. Johnson himself placed eighth in the 1948 discus throw.

1972 Munich T: 20, N: 20, D: 9.9.

1. SOV	Yuri Filatov, Yuri Stetsenko, Volodymyr Morozov, Valery Didenko	3:14.02
2. ROM	Aurel Vernescu, Mihal Zafiu, Roman Vartolomeu, Atanase Sciotnic	3:15.07
3. NOR	Egil Söby, Steinar Amundsen, Tore Berger, Jan Johansen	3:15.27
4. ITA	Alberto Ughi, Pier Angelo Congiu, Mario Pedretti, Oreste Perri	3:15.60
5. GER	Rudolf Blass, Eberhard Fischer, Rainer Hennes, Hans-Erich Pasch	3:16.63
6. HUN	István Szabó, Peter Várhelyi, Zoltán Bakó, Csongor Vargha	3:16.88
7. FIN	Kari Markkanen, Heikki Mäkelä, Ilkka Nummisto, Jorma Lehtosalo	3:16.92
8. SWE	Lars Andersson, Nils Gunnar Utterberg, Per Larsson, Hans Nilsson	3:17.39

1976 Montreal T: 20, N: 20, D: 7.31.

1. SOV	Serhei Chukhray, Aleksandr Degtyarev, Yuri Filatov, Volodymyr Morozov	3:08.69
2. SPA	José María Esteban Celorrio, José Ramón López Díaz-Flor, Herminio Menéndez Rodríguez, Luis Gregorio Ramos Misioné	3:08.95
3. GDR	Peter Bischof, Bernd Duvigneau, Rüdiger Helm, Jürgen Lehnert	3:10.76
4. ROM	Nicuşor Eşanu, Vasile Simioncenco, Nicolae Simioncenco, Mihai Zafiu	3:11.35
5. POL	Henryk Budzicz, Kazimierz Górecki, Grzegorz Koltan, Ryszard Oborski	3:12.17
6. NOR	Morten Mörland, Einar Rasmussen, Olaf Söyland, Jostein Stige	3:12.28
7. BUL	Ivan Manev, Bojidar Milenkov, Nikolai Nachev, Vasil Chilingirov	3:12.94
8. HUN	József Deme, Csaba Giczi, János Rátkai, Zoltán Romhányi	3:14.67

The Soviet team came from third place in the last 250 meters to nose out Spain, which had been the surprise winner of the 1975 world championship.

1980 Moscow T: 12, N; 12, D: 8.2.

1. GDR	Rüdiger Helm, Bernd Olbricht, Harald Marg, Bernd Duvigneau	3:13.76
2. ROM	Mihai Zafiu, Vasile Dîba, Ion Geanta, Nicuşor Eşanu	3:15.35
3. BUL	Borislav Borissov, Bozhidar Milenkov, Lazar Hristov, Ivan Manev	3:15.46
4. POL	Ryszard Oborski, Grzegorz Koltan, Daniel Welna, Grzegorz Śledziewski	3:16.33
5. HUN	József Deme, János Rátkai, József Kosztyán, Zoltán Sztaniti	3:17.27
6. FRA	François Barouh, Patrick Berard, Philippe Boccara, Patrick Lefoulon	3:17.60
7. SOV	Gennady Makhnev, Serhei Nahorny, Aleksandrs Avdejevs, Vladimir Tainikov	3:19.83
8. AUS	Barry Kelly, Robert Lee, Ken Vidler, Crosbie Baulch	3:19.87

1984 Los Angeles-Lake Casitas T: 15, N: 15, D: 8.11.

1. NZL	Grant Bramwell, Ian Ferguson, Paul MacDonald, Alan Thompson	3:02.28
2. SWE	Per-Inge Bengtsson, Tommy Karls, Lars-Erik Moberg, Thomas Ohlsson	3:02.81
3. FRA	François Barouh, Philippe Boccara, Pascal Boucherit, Didier Vavasseur	3:03.94
4. ROM	Ionel Constantin, Nicolae Fedosei, Ionel Letcaie, Angelin Velea	3:04.39
5. GBR	Grayson Bourne, Andrew Sherriff, Kevin Smith, Jeremy West	3:04.59
6. SPA	Iván González Santos, Luis Gregorio Ramos Misioné, Juan José Román Mangas, Juan Manuel Sánchez de Castro	3:04.71
7. AUS	John Doak, Robert Doak, Raymond Martin, Scott Wooden	3:06.02
8. GER	Bernd Hessel, Oliver Kegel, Dieter Schmidt, Reiner Scholl	3:06.47

1988 Seoul T: 18, N: 18, D: 10.1.

1. HUN	Zsolt Gyulay, Ferenc Csipes, Sándor Hódosi, Attila Ábrahám	3:00.20
2. SOV	Aleksandr Motuzenko, Serhei Kyrsanov, Ihor Nahayev, Viktor Denisov	3:01.40
3. GDR	Kay Bluhm, André Wohllebe, Andreas Stähle, Hans-Jörg Bliesener	3:02.37
4. AUS	Bryan Thomas, Steven Wood, Grant Kenny, Paul Gilmour	3:03.70
5. POL	Maciej Freimut, Wojciech Kurpiewski, Grzegorz Krawców, Kazimierz Krzyżański	3:04.73
6. GER	Gilbert Schneider, Reiner Scholl, Dirk Joestel, Thomas Reineck	3:05.43
7. ITA	Beniamino Bonomi, Daniele Scarpa, Alessandro Pieri, Francesco Mandragona	3:05.97
8. SWE	Per-Inge Bengtsson, Lars-Erik Moberg, Karl Axel Sundkvist, Bengt Andersson	3:06.03

The Hungarians, seventh at the halfway point, blew away the field in the third quarter.

1992 Barcelona-Castelldefels T: 19, N: 19, D: 8.8.

1. GER	Oliver Kegel, Thomas Reineck, Mario Von Appen, André Wohllebe	2:54.18
2. HUN	Attila Ábrahám, Ferenc Csipes, László Fidel, Zsolt Gyulay	2:54.82
3. AUS	Ramon Andersson, Kelvin Graham, Ian Rowling, Steven Wood	2:56.97
4. CZE	Róbert Erban, Juraj Kadnár, Attila Szabó, Jozef Turza	2:57.06
5. ROM	Geza Magyar, Sorin Petcu, Romica Serban, Daniel Stoian	3:00.11
6. POL	Maciej Freimut, Grzegorz Kaleta, Grzegorz Krawców, Wojciech Kurpiewski	3:01.43
7. SWE	Jonas Fager, Pablo Grate, Anders Ohlsén, Hans Olsson	3:01.46
8. BUL	Petar Godev, Nikolay Georgiev, Milko Kazanov, Evlogiev Yordanov	3:02.08

The Hungarians had won every world and Olympic championship since 1986. They were expected to repeat in Barcelona, especially since their main rivals, the Germans, had lost one of their key members, Detlef Hofmann, to a positive drug test (testosterone) two months before the Games began. However, the German team took the lead in the second quarter and never relinquished it.

1996 Atlanta-Lake Lanier T: 16, N: 16, D: 8.3.

1. GER	Detlef Hofmann, Olaf Winter, Thomas Reineck, Mark Zabel	2:51.528
2. HUN	Attila Adrovicz, Ferenc Csipes, Gabor Horvath, Andras Rajna	2:53.184
3. RUS	Sergei Verlin, Oleg Gorobi, Anatoly Tishenko, Georgy Tsybulnikov	2:53.996
4. POL	Grzegorz Kaleta, Piotr Markiewicz, Marek Witkowski, Adam Wysocki	2:54.772
5. SPA	Miguel García Fernández, Jovino González, Comesaña Emilio Merchan, Gregorio Vicente	2:55.884
6. SWE	Paw Madsen, Mattias Oscarsson, Henrik Nilsson, Jonas Fager	2:55.908
7. CAN	Mihai Apostol, Peter Giles, Liam Jewell, Renn Crichlow	2:56.664
8. BUL	Petar Karadzhov, Petar Merkov, Nikolay Yordanov, Georgi Choykov	2:56.696

The German team stayed close to the leading Hungarians for 750 meters and then pulled away to win decisively.

2000 Sydney-Penrith T: 13, N: 13, D: 9.30.

1. HUN	Gábor Horváth, Zoltán Kammerer, Botond Storcz, Ákos Vereckei	2:55.188
2. GER	Björn Bach, Jan Schäfer, Stefan Ulm, Mark Zabel	2:55.704
3. POL	Dariusz Białkowski, Grzegorz Kotowicz, Adam Seroczyński, Marek Witkowski	2:57.192
4. SLV	Róbert Erban, Richard Riszdorfer, Juraj Tarr, Erik Vlček	2:57.696
5. BUL	Milcho Kazanov, Petar Merkov, Yordan Yordan, Petar Sibinkić	2:59.112
6. USA	Stein Jorgensen, John Mooney, Peter Newton, Angel Pérez	2:59.472
7. RUS	Oleg Goroby, Yevgeny Salakhov, Anatoly Tishchenko, Roman Zarubin	2:59.778
8. SWE	Jonas Fager, Anders Gustafsson, Erik Lindeberg, Niklaes Persson	3:01.326

The German-Hungarian rivalry continued throughout the 1990s. After the Atlanta Olympics, the Germans won close victories at the 1997 and 1998 world championships. The Hungarians finally finished first at the 1999 world championships, but two months before the Olympics, the Germans scored a comparatively easy victory at the European championships. In the final of the Sydney Games, the Hungarians won by about 2½ meters (8 feet).

2004 Athens-Schinias T: 9, N: 9, D: 8.27.

1. HUN	Zoltán Kammerer, Botond Storcz, Ákos Vereckei, Gábor Horváth	2:56.919
2. GER	Andreas Ihle, Mark Zabel, Björn Bach, Stefan Ulm	2:58.659
3. SLV	Richard Riszdorfer, Michal Riszdorfer, Erik Vlček, Juraj Bača	2:59.314
4. BUL	Milcho Kazanov, Ivan Khristov, Petar Merkov, Yordan Yordanov	2:59.622
5. NOR	Jacob Lorentz Norenberg, Alexander Wefald, Andreas Gjersøe, Mattis Næss	3:01.698
6. BLR	Raman Piatrushenka, Aleksey Abalmasau, Dziamyan Turchyn, Vadzim Makhneu	3:02.419
7. ROM	Marian Baban, Alexandru Ceauşu, Corneli Vasile Curuzan, Ştefan Vasile	3:03.107
8. POL	Tomasz Mendelski, Rafał Głażewski, Adam Seroczyński, Dariusz Białkowski	3:03.562

The Slovak four had won the previous two world championships, but the Olympic final was a near repeat of the 2000 final, with the same Hungarian foursome facing a German team that had made only one change. The Hungarians led the Germans by less than half a second at the halfway point, and then pulled away for gold.

2008 Beijing-Shunyi T: 10, N: 10, D: 8.22.

1. BLR	Roman Petrushenko, Aleksey Abalmasov, Artur Litvinchuk, Vadim Makhnev	2:55.714
2. SVK	Richard Riszdorfer, Michal Riszdorfer, Erik Vlček, Juraj Tarr	2:56.593
3. GER	Lutz Altepost, Norman Bröckl, Torsten Eckbrett, Björn Goldschmidt	2:56.676
4. ITA	Franco Benedini, Antonio Rossi, Alberto Ricchetti, Luca Piemonte	2:57.626
5. HUN	Márton Sík, István Beé, Ákos Vereckei, Gábor Bozsik	2:59.009
6. POL	Marek Twardowski, Tomasz Mendelski, Paweł Baumann, Adam Wysocki	2:59.505
7. CHN	Li Zhen, Liu Haitao, Zhou Peng, Lin Miao	3:00.078
8. RUS	Ilya Medvedev, Yevgeny Salakhov, Anton Vasilyev, Konstantin Vishnyakov	3:00.654

Despite significant turnover in both teams, Germany and Hungary had continued to dominate the men's kayak fours 1000 meters event in the years leading up to the Beijing Olympics, winning all three intervening world championship titles. Germany's squad in Beijing included three members of the reigning world championship team—Lutz Altepost, Norman Bröckl and Björn Goldschmidt—two of whom, Altepost and Bröckl, had also been members of the 2005 world championship team.

Defending Olympic champions Hungary had been more inconsistent. After being eliminated in the semifinals of the 2005 world championships, the team came back to win the 2006 world championship title, beating Poland and Belarus, with Germany in fourth place. In 2007 the team found less success, finishing just off the podium in fourth place.

Besides the two perennial favorites, two-time reigning silver medalists Poland and Athens bronze medalists Slovakia were also in contention. Slovakia had retained three of its paddlers from Athens and had won world silver in 2005 and bronze in 2007.

Germany and Hungary were in the same first-round heat, with Germany edging out their rivals by less than a tenth of a second as both teams qualified for the final, along with 2006 world bronze medalists Belarus, a second-and-a-half behind the leaders.

As expected, the final was a close battle between two teams … however the teams turned out to be Slovakia and Belarus. They led the field from the beginning, with Slovakia ahead at the halfway point before Belarus moved into the lead with 250 meters remaining and held on for the gold. Slovakia edged out Germany for silver, while Hungary was never a threat, finishing fifth. For the first time in 24 years, a country other than Germany or Hungary had won the K-4 1000 meters Olympic gold.

CANADIAN SINGLES 200 METERS

This event will be held for the first time in 2012.

CANADIAN SINGLES 1000 METERS

1896–1932 not held

1936 Berlin-Grünau C: 6, N: 6, D: 8.8.

1. Francis Amyot	CAN	5:32.1
2. Bohuslav Karlik	CZE	5:36.9
3. Erich Koschik	GER	5:39.0
4. Otto Neumüller	AUT	5:47.0
5. Joseph Hasenfus	USA	6:02.6
6. Joseph Treinen	LUX	7:39.5

Amyot, who once saved three Ottawa Rough Riders football players from drowning, took an early lead but was passed by Karlik at the 750-meter mark. A 31-year-old veteran, Amyot refused to be rattled and continued stroking smoothly, until he had burst past Karlik with 50 meters to go. Amyot was Canada's only gold medal winner at the Berlin Olympics, thus embarrassing the Canadian Olympic Committee, which had refused to pay his way.

1948 London-Henley-on-Thames C: 6, N: 6, D: 8.12.

1. Josef Holeček	CZE	5:42.0
2. Douglas Bennett	CAN	5:53.3
3. Robert Boutigny	FRA	5:55.9
4. Ingemar Andersson	SWE	6:06.0
5. Frank Havens	USA	6:14.3
6. Henry Maidment	GBR	6:37.0

1952 Helsinki C: 10, N: 10, D: 7.28.

1. Josef Holeček	CZE	4:56.3
2. János Parti	HUN	5:03.6
3. Olavi Ojanperä	FIN	5:08.5
4. Frank Havens	USA	5:13:7
5. Ingemar Andersson	SWE	5:15.0
6. Ralf Berckhan	GER	5:22.8
7. Jean Molle	FRA	5:24.1
8. Vladimir Kotyrev	SOV/RUS	5:24.5

1956 Melbourne-Ballarat C: 9, N:9, D: 12.1.

1. Leon Rotman	ROM	5:05.3
2. István Hernek	HUN	5:06.2
3. Gennady Bukharin	SOV/RUS	5:12.7
4. Karel Hradil	CZE	5:15.9
5. Franz Johannsen	GER	5:18.6
6. Verner Wettersten	SWE	5:28.0
7. Bryan Harper	AUS	5:37.6
8. George Bossy	CAN	5:39.4

1960 Rome-Lake Albano C: 13, N: 13, D: 8.29.

1. János Parti	HUN	4:33.93
2. Aleksandr Silayev	SOV/RUS	4:34.41
3. Leon Rotman	ROM	4:35.87
4. Ove Emanuelsson	SWE	4:36.46
5. Tibor Polakovič	CZE	4:39.28
6. Detlef Lewe	GER	4:39.72
7. Don Stringer	CAN	4:40.65
8. Bogdan Ivanov	BUL	4:42.52

János Parti won silver medals in 1952 and 1956 (in the 10,000-meter event) before striking gold in 1960 using a canoe of his own design.

1964 Tokyo-Lake Sagami C: 11, N: 11, D: 10.22.

1. Jürgen Eschert	GDR	4:35.14
2. Andrei Igorov	ROM	4:37.89
3. Yevgeny Penyayev	SOV/RUS	4:38.31
4. András Törö	HUN	4:39.95
5. Ove Emanuelsson	SWE	4:42.70
6. Bogdan Ivanov	BUL	4:44.76
7. Paul Stahl	CAN	5:04.79
8. Dennis Van Valkenburgh	USA	5:12.55

1968 Mexico City-Xochimilco C: 12, N: 12, D: 10.25.

1. Tibor Tatai	HUN	4:36.14
2. Detlef Lewe	GER	4:38.31
3. Vitaly Galkov	SOV/RUS	4:40.42
4. Jiři Čtvrtečka	CZE	4:40.74
5. Boris Lyubenov	BUL	4:43.43
6. Ove Emanuelsson	SWE	4:45.80
7. Ivan Patzaichin	ROM	4:49.32
8. Andreas Weigand	USA	4:50.42

Tibor Tatai made the Hungarian team only as a reserve, but he drove the other finalists to exhaustion and won decisively.

1972 Munich C: 13, N: 13, D: 9.9.

1. Ivan Patzaichin	ROM	4:08.94
2. Tamás Wichmann	HUN	4:12.42
3. Detlef Lewe	GER	4:13.63
4. Dirk Weise	GDR	4:14.38
5. Vasyl Yurchenko	SOV/UKR	4:14.43
6. Boris Lyubenov	BUL	4:14.65
7. Jiři Čtvrtečka	CZE	4:14.98
8. Roberto Altamirano	MEX	4:20.39

1976 Montreal C: 15, N: 15, D: 7.31.

1. Matija Ljubek	YUG/CRO	4:09.51
2. Vasyl Yurchenko	SOV/UKR	4:12.57
3. Tamás Wichmann	HUN	4:14.11
4. Borislav Ananiev	BUL	4:14.41
5. Ivan Patzaichin	ROM	4:15.08
6. Roland Iche	FRA	4:18.23
7. Wilfried Stephan	GDR	4:22.43
8. Ulrich Eicke	GER	4:22.77

Matija Ljubek, a carpenter from Belisce, was the only finalist to paddle the second half of the race faster than the first. He was fourth at the halfway mark but won going away. Ljubek also earned a bronze medal in the C-1 500 and added two more medals in 1984. He went on to become vice-president of the Croatian Olympic Committee and *chef de mission* of the Croatian Olympic team. Six days after returning to Zagreb from the 2000 Olympics, Ljubek was shot to death while trying to defend his mother from an estranged brother-in-law.

1980 Moscow C: 12, N: 12, D: 8.2.

1. Lyubomir Lyubenov	BUL	4:12.38
2. Serhei Postryekhin	SOV/UKR	4:13.53
3. Eckhard Leue	GDR	4:15.02
4. Libor Dvořák	CZE	4:15.25
5. Lipat Varabiev	ROM	4:16.68
6. Timo Grönlund	FIN	4:17.37
7. Thomas Falk	SWE	4:20.66
8. Matija Ljubek	YUG/CRO	4:22.40

1984 Los Angeles-Lake Casitas C. 11, N: 11, D: 8.11.

1. Ulrich Eicke	GER	4:06.32
2. Larry Cain	CAN	4:08.67
3. Henning Jakobsen	DEN	4:09.51
4. Timo Grönlund	FIN	4:15.58
5. Costică Olaru	ROM	4:16.39
6. Stephen Train	GBR	4:16.64
7. Bruce Merritt	USA	4:18.17
8. Kiyoto Inoue	JPN	4:18.72

1988 Seoul C: 15, N: 15, D: 10.1.

1. Ivans Klemenjevs	SOV/LAT	4:12.78
2. Jörg Schmidt	GDR	4:15.83
3. Nikolay Bukhalov	BUL	4:18.94
4. Larry Cain	CAN	4:20.70
5. Aurel Macarencu	ROM	4:21.72
6. Imre Pulai	HUN	4:21.86
7. Petr Pales	CZE	4:22.14
8. Ivan Šabjan	YUG/CRO	4:24.67

1992 Barcelona-Castelldefels C: 19, N: 19, D: 8.8.

1. Nikolay Bukhalov	BUL	4:05.92
2. Ivans Klementjevs	LAT	4:06.60
3. György Zala	HUN	4:07.35
4. Matthias Röder	GER	4:08.96
5. Pascal Sylvoz	FRA	4:09.82
6. Andrew Train	GBR	4:12.58
7. Victor Partnoi	ROM	4:14.27
8. Jan Bartůněk	CZE	4:15.25

Having defeated three-time world champion Mykhaylo Slyvynsky in the 500-meter event the day before, Bukhalov did the same to the 1000-meter three-time world champion, Ivans Klementjevs. As with the 500, Bukhalov had bested Klementjevs at 1000 on the Olympic course in 1991. In the Olympic final Bukhalov led from start to finish, while Klementjevs moved up from fifth to second in the last 250 meters.

1996 Atlanta-Lake Lanier C: 18, N: 18, D: 8.3.

1. Martin Doktor	CZE	3:54.418
2. Ivans Klementjevs	LAT	3:54.954
3. György Zala	HUN	3:56.366
4. Patrick Schulze	GER	3:57.778
5. Pascal Sylvoz	FRA	3:59.014
6. Victor Partnoi	ROM	3:59.858
7. Roman Bundz	UKR	4:02.078
8. Ivan Sabjan	CRO	4:04.066

Doktor led from start to finish. Klementjevs and Zala repeated their silver and bronze medals from 1992.

2000 Sydney-Penrith C: 18, N: 18, D: 9.30.

1. Andreas Dittmer	GER	3:54.379
2. Ledys Frank Balceiro Pajón	CUB	3:56.071
3. Steve Giles	CAN	3:56.437
4. Eric Le Leuch	FRA	3:57.217
5. Christian Frederiksen	NOR	3:58.159
6. Maksim Opalev	RUS	3:58.813
7. Efims Klementjevs	LAT	4:00.931
8. Martin Doktor	CZE	4:02.335

A 28-year-old bank teller, Andreas Dittmer converted to singles paddling after winning a gold medal in the C-2 1000 at the 1996 Olympics.

2004 Athens-Schinias C: 19, N: 19, D: 8.27.

1. David Cal Figueroa	SPA	3:46.201
2. Andreas Dittmer	GER	3:46.721
3. Attila Vajda	HUN	3:49.025
4. Martin Doktor	CZE	3:50.405
5. Steve Giles	CAN	3:51.457
6. Dagnis Vinogradovs	LAT	3:53.537
7. Marián Ostrčil	SLV	3:54.629
8. Karel Aguilar Chacón	CUB	3:54.957

Defending C-1 1000 gold medalist and three-time world champion, Andreas Dittmer got off to an quick lead in the final, but was surprised by an early surge from David Cal, who opened nearly a one-second gap by the 500-meter mark. Dittmer tried to close the distance but Cal held on to capture the gold. One year later Dittmer got his revenge, beating Cal by more than a second to win the 2005 C-1 500 meter world championship title.

2008 Beijing-Shunyi C: 22, N: 22, D: 8.22.

1. Attila Vajda	HUN	3:50.467
2. David Cal Figueroa	SPA	3:52.751
3. Thomas Hall	CAN	3:53.653
4. Vadim Menkov	UZB	3:54.237
5. Aleksandr Zhukovsky	BLR	3:55.645
6. Florin Mironcic	ROM	3:57.876
7. Mathieu Goubel	FRA	3:57.889
8. Andreas Dittmer	GER	3:57.894

Athens rivals Andreas Dittmer and David Cal were no longer the overwhelming favorites they had once been. A year after he beat Cal at the 2005 world championships, Dittmer suffered a surprise loss, finishing second to Mexico's José Cristobal at the 2006 world championships, while Cal could do no better than fifth. It was Athens bronze medalist and reigning world champion Attila Vajda who arrived in Beijing as the strongest contender for the gold medal. He had finished more than two seconds ahead of Slovakia's Marián Ostrčil to win the 2007 world title, with Cal and Dittmer in third and fourth place.

Vajda won his first-round heat easily, advancing straight to the final, as did Cal, who beat Dittmer by nearly two seconds. Dittmer made it to the final after finishing second in his semi-final heat, while Ostrčil finished fifth in the other semi-final and was eliminated.

Vadim Menkov held the lead through the first half of the final, but Vajda, who moved up from sixth place, passed him with 250 meters remaining and proceeded to hold off Cal to win the gold medal. Canada's Thomas Hall passed Menkov in the final 100 meters to take bronze.

Vajda wore a black armband during the competition and dedicated his medal to teammate and twice Olympic champion György Kolonics, who, one month before the Beijing Olympics, had died at the age of 26 after collapsing with a heart attack in his canoe while training.

CANADIAN PAIRS 200 METERS

This event will be held for the first time in 2012.

CANADIAN PAIRS 1000 METERS

1896–1932 not held

1936 Berlin-Grünau T: 5, N: 5, D: 8.8.

1. Vladimir Syrovátka, Jan Brzák-Felix	CZE	4:50.1
2. Rupert Weinstabl, Karl Proisl	AUT	4:53.8
3. Frank Saker, Harvey Charters	CAN	4:56.7
4. Hans Wedemann, Heinrich Sack	GER	5:00.2
5. Clarence McNutt, Robert Graf	USA	5:14.0

1948 London-Henley-on-Thames T: 8, N: 8, D: 8.12.

1. Jan Brzák-Felix, Bohumil Kudrna	CZE	5:07.1
2. Stephen Lysak, Stephan Macknowski	USA	5:08.2
3. Georges Dransart, Georges Gandil	FRA	5:15.2
4. Douglas Bennett, Harry Poulton	CAN	5:20.7
5. Karl Molnar, Viktor Salmhofer	AUT	5:37.3
6. Gunnar Johansson, Verner Wettersten	SWE	5:44.9
7. John Symons, Henry Van Zwananberg	GBR	5:50.8

DNF: Hubert Coomans, Jean Dubois (BEL), man overboard

Jan Brzák was one of the few gold medal winners at the Berlin Olympics who was able to retain his championship 12 years later in London. In 1955, when he was 43 years old, Brzák teamed with 46-year-old Bohuslav Karlik to paddle the 118 miles from Ceské Budějovice to Prague in 20 hours.

1952 Helsinki T: 11, N: 11, D: 7.28.

1. Bent Peder Rasch, Finn Haunstoft	DEN	4:38.3
2. Jan Brzák-Felix, Bohumil Kudrna	CZE	4:42.9
3. Egon Drews, Wilfried Soltau	GER	4:48.3
4. Georges Dransart, Armand Loreau	FRA	4:48.6
5. István Bodor, József Tuza	HUN	4:51.9
6. Kurt Liebhart, Englebert Lulla	AUT	4:55.8
7. John Haas, Frank Krick	USA	4:59.0
8. Arthur Johnson, Thomas Hodgson	CAN	5:01.4

1956 Melbourne-Ballarat T: 10, N: 10, D: 12.1.

1. Alexe Dumitru, Simion Ismailciuc	ROM	4:47.4
2. Pavel Kharine, Gratsian Botev	SOV/RUS	4:48.6
3. Károly Wieland, Ferenc Mohácsi	HUN	4:54.3
4. Georges Dransart, Marcel Renaud	FRA	4:57.7
5. William Jones, Thomas Ohman	AUS	5:03.0
6. Otto Schindler, Walter Waldner	AUT	5:04.4
7. William Collins, Bert Oldershaw	CAN	5:11.0

DISQ: Kai Sylvan, Gerner Christiansen (DEN)

1960 Rome-Lake Albano T: 11, N: 11, D: 8.29.

1. Leonid Geishtor, Serhei Makarenko	SOV	4:17.94
2. Aldo Dezi, Francesco La Macchia	ITA	4:20.77
3. Imre Farkas, András Törö	HUN	4:20.89
4. Igor Lipalit, Alexe Dumitru	ROM	4:22.36
5. Jiři Kodeš, Václav Vokal	CZE	4:27.66
6. Marin Gopov, Toma Sokolov	BUL	4:31.52
7. Willi Mehlberg, Werner Ulrich	GDR	4:31.68
8. Georges Turlier, Michel Picard	FRA	4:35.48

1964 Tokyo-Lake Sagami T: 12, N: 12, D: 10.22.

1. Andriy Khymych, Stepan Oschepkov	SOV	4:04.64
2. Jean Boudehen, Michel Chapuis	FRA	4:06.52
3. Peer Norrbohm Nielsen, John Sörensen	DEN	4:07.48
4. Antal Hajba, Árpád Soltesz	HUN	4:08.97
5. Igor Lipalit, Achim Sidorov	ROM	4:09.88
6. Klaus Böhle, Detlef Lewe	GER	4:13.18
7. Andor Ebert, Fred Heese	CAN	4:21.99
8. Miloslav Houzim, Rudolf Penkava	CZE	4:22.89

1968 Mexico City-Xochimilco T: 12, N: 12, D: 10.25.

1. Ivan Patzaichin, Serghei Covaliov	ROM	4:07.18
2. Tamás Wichmann, Gyula Petrikovics	HUN	4:08.77
3. Naum Prokupets, Mikhail Zamotin	SOV/RUS	4:11.30
4. Juan Martínez, Félix Altamirano	MEX	4:15.24
5. Berndt Lindelöf, Erik Zeidlitz	SWE	4:16.60
6. Jürgen Harpke, Helmut Wagner	GDR	4:22.53
7. Roland Kapf, Klaus Lewandowsky	GER	4:26.36
8. Ivan Vulov, Alexander Damianov	BUL	4:26.74

Ivan Patzaichin and Serghei Covaliov were fishermen from the village of Crisan-Mila, in the Danube delta. Silver medalist Tamás Wichmann was a chef.

1972 Munich T: 16, N: 16, D: 9.9.

1. Vladislavas Česiunas, Yuri Lobanov	SOV	3:52.60
2. Ivan Patzaichin, Serghei Covaliov	ROM	3:52.63
3. Fedia Damianov, Ivan Burchin	BUL	3:58.10
4. Hans-Peter Hoffmann, Hermann Glaser	GER	3:59.24
5. Miklós Darvas, Péter Povázsay	HUN	4:00.42
6. Roland Muhlen, Andreas Weigand	USA	4:01.28
7. Dirk Weise, Dieter Lichtenberg	GDR	4:01.50
8. Berndt Lindelöf, Eric Zeidlitz	SWE	4:01.60

Česiunas and Lobanov took an early lead, but at the 700-meter mark Patzaichin and Covaliov mounted a furious challenge that brought them to the finish line only three one-hundredths of a second too late.

One does not imagine the world of canoeing as fertile ground for secret agents and international intrigue, but the two did come together at least once in what came to be known as The Česiunas Affair.

Seven years after his Olympic triumph in Munich, Vladislavas Česiunas traveled to Duisburg, West Germany to attend, as a spectator, the 1979 kayak and canoe world championships. At some point, Česiunas vanished. The West German government subsequently said that he defected. Several weeks later, he reappeared in Vilnius, Lithuania, and read a statement that he had returned voluntarily. The West Germans claimed he was kidnapped. The Soviets said that Česiunas had met a young woman named Ursula Vorkehrt who invited him to spend the night and then drugged him. Soon he was meeting with anti-Communist Lithuanians and being asked to speak out in favor of a boycott of the 1980 Moscow Olympics. This was more that two months before the Soviet Union invaded Afghanistan and US president Jimmy Carter called for an Olympic boycott. Česiunas then made his way—"not without incident"—to the Soviet Embassy in Bonn and thence to the motherland. Later the Soviets would tone down their rhetoric and simply state that Česiunas had "got into dubious company," stayed in the West and then changed his mind. West Germans would continue to maintain that Česiunas had been kidnapped.

1976 Montreal T: 15, N: 15, D: 7.31.

1. Serhei Petrenko, Aleksandr Vinogradov	SOV	3:52.76
2. Gheorghe Danielov, Gheorghe Simionov	ROM	3:54.28
3. Tamás Buday, Oszkár Frey	HUN	3:55.66
4. Jerzy Opara, Andrzej Gronowicz	POL	3:59.56
5. Detlef Bothe, Hans-Jürgen Tode	GDR	4:00.37
6. Jiři Čtvrtečka, Tomáš Sach	CZE	4:01.48
7. Ivan Burchin, Krasimir Hristov	BUL	4:02.44
8. Hermann Glaser, Heinz Lucke	GER	4:03.86

1980 Moscow T: 11, N: 11, D: 8.2.

1. Ivan Patzaichin, Toma Simionov	ROM	3:47.65
2. Olaf Heukrodt, Uwe Madeja	GDR	3:49.93
3. Vasyl Yurchenko, Yuri Lobanov	SOV	3:51.28
4. Matija Ljubek, Mirko Nišović	YUG/CRO	3:51.30
5. Jiři Vrdlovec, Petr Kubiček	CZE	3:52.50
6. Marek Dopiérala, Jan Pinczura	POL	3:53.01
7. Raiko Kurmadzhiev, Kamen Kutzev	BUL	3:53.89
8. Tamás Buday, Oszkár Frey	HUN	3:54.31

1984 Los Angeles-Lake Casitas T: 10, N: 10, D: 8.11.

1. Ivan Patzaichin, Toma Simionov	ROM	3:40.60
2. Matija Ljubek, Mirko Nišović	YUG/CRO	3:41.56
3. Didier Hoyer, Eric Renaud	FRA	3:48.01
4. Wolfram Faust, Ralf Wienand	GER	3:52.69
5. John Plankenhorn, Rodney McClain	USA	3:52.72
6. Enrique Miguez Gómez, Narciso Suárez Amador	SPA	3:56.92
7. Steve Botting, Eric Smith	CAN	3:56.99
8. Arturo Ferrer, Victor Velasco	MEX	3:57.49

Thirty-four-year-old Ivan Patzaichin closed out his Olympic career with four gold medals and three silvers.

1988 Seoul T: 17, N: 17, D: 10.1.

1. Victor Reneisky, Nikolai Zhuravsky	SOV	3:48.36
2. Olaf Heukrodt, Ingo Spelly	GDR	3:51.44
3. Marek Dopierala, Marek Lbik	POL	3:54.33
4. Christian Frederiksen, Arne Nielsson	DEN	3:54.94
5. Hartmut Faust, Wolfram Faust	GER	3:55.62
6. Grigore Obreja, Gheorghe Andriev	ROM	3:56.56
7. Gábor Takács, Gusztáv Leikep	HUN	4:04.18
8. Pascal Sylvoz, Didier Hoyer	FRA	4:04.75

1992 Barcelona-Castelldefels T: 14, N: 14, D: 8.8.

1. Ulrich Papke, Ingo Spelly	GER	3:37.42
2. Arne Nielsson, Christian Frederiksen	DEN	3:39.26
3. Didier Hoyer, Olivier Boivin	FRA	3:39.51
4. Gheorghe Andriev, Nicolae Juravschi (Nicolai Zhuravsky)	ROM	3:39.88
5. Attila Pálizs, György Kolonics	HUN	3:42.86
6. Martin Marinov, Blagovest Stoyanov	BUL	3:43.97
7. Larry Cain, David Frost	CAN	3:46.21
8. Aleksei Igrayev, Aleksandr Gromovich	SOV	3:53.90

Papke and Spelly, defending two-time world champions, fought off a mid-race challenge from Nielsson and Frederiksen and won going away.

1996 Atlanta-Lake Lanier T: 17, N: 17, D: 8.3.

1. Andreas Dittmer, Gunar Kirchbach	GER	3:31.870
2. Antonel Borsan, Marcel Glavan	ROM	3:32.294
3. Csaba Horváth, György Kolonics	HUN	3:32.514
4. Martin Marinov, Blagovest Stoyanov	BUL	3:34.382
5. Nikolae Juravschi (Nikolai Zhuravsky), Viktor Reneisky	MOL	3:35.198
6. Andrew Train, Stephen Train	GBR	3:36.694
7. Csaba Orosz, Peter Pales	SLV	3:36.938
8. José Alfredo Bea García, Oleg Shelestenko Sánchez	SPA	3:37.154

Borsan and Glavan established an early lead and expanded it gradually through 750 meters. Dittmer and Kirchbach, meanwhile, were in ninth and last place after 250 meters. A second quarter surge brought them up to fourth at the halfway mark. They gathered strength during the third quarter and then launched a sustained sprint that allowed them to make up 2.15 seconds in the final 250 meters and catch the Romanians just before the line.

2000 Sydney-Penrith T: 14, N: 14, D: 9.30.

1. Florin Popescu, Mitica Pricop	ROM	3:37.355
2. Leobaldo Pereira, Ibrahim Rojas Blanco	CUB	3:38.753
3. Lars Kober, Stefan Utess	GER	3:41.129
4. Aleksandr Kostoglod, Aleksandr Kovalev	RUS	3:41.267
5. Ferenc Novák, Imre Pulai	HUN	3:43.103
6. Ramón Ferrer, Antonio Romero	MEX	3:46.457
7. Attila Buday, Tamás Buday, Jr.	CAN	3:48.017
8. Paweł Baraszkiewicz, Michał Gajownik	POL	3:52.229

Two-time defending world champions Aleksandr Kovalev and Aleksandr Kostoglod recorded the fastest qualifying time, but finished out of the medals in the final.

2004 Athens-Schinias T: 14, N: 14, D: 8.27.

1. Christian Gille, Tomasz Wylenzek	GER	3:41.802
2. Aleksandr Kostoglod, Aleksandr Kovalyov	RUS	3:42.990
3. György Kozmann, György Kolonics	HUN	3:43.106
4. Silviu Simioncencu, Florin Popescu	ROM	3:43.858
5. Michał Śliwiński, Łukasz Woszczyński	POL	3:44.338
6. Richard Dalton, Michael Scarola	CAN	3:45.638
7. José Alfredo Bea García, David Mascato García	SPA	3:45.766
8. Ibrahim Rojas Blanco, Ledis Frank Balceiro Pajon	CUB	3:50.346

Christian Gille raced with a black armband in honor of his former partner, Tomas Zereska, who had died of leukemia earlier that year.

2008 Beijing-Shunyi T: 13, N: 13, D: 8.22.

1. Andrei Bogdanovich, Aleksandr Bogdanovich	BLR	3:36.365
2. Christian Gille, Tomasz Wylenzek	GER	3:36.588
3. György Kozmann, Tamás Kiss	HUN	3:40.258
4. Constantin Popa, Niculae Flocea	ROU	3:40.342
5. Chen Zhongyun, Zhang Zhiwu	CHN	3:40.593
6. Andrew Russell, Gabriel Beauchesne-Sévigny	CAN	3:41.165
7. Wojciech Tyszy ski, Paweł Baraszkiewicz	POL	3:42.845
8. Sergey Ulegin, Aleksandr Kostoglod	RUS	3:44.669

Defending Olympic gold medalists and reigning world champions Christian Gille and Tomasz Wylenzek jumped out to a solid lead at the start, leading by a second-and-a-half after the first 250 meters. Brothers Andrei and Aleksandr Bogdanovich were nearly one second behind when they began their final push, but overtook Gille and Wylenzek in the final 100 meters to win the gold. Wylenzek pushed himself so hard at the end that he lost consciousness and had to be taken to a nearby hospital to be treated for dehydration.

Bronze medalists György Kozmann and 21-year-old Olympic newcomer Tamás Kiss dedicated their medal to Kozmann's former partner, four-time Olympic medalist György Kolonics, who had collapsed during a training session and died of heart failure only a month earlier. Shocked, Kozmann had initially refused to compete, only changing his mind after conferring with his teammates, coaches and Kolonic's friends.

WHITE-WATER (SLALOM)

This unusual sport requires the canoeist to paddle down an obstacle course in much the same manner as the slalom races in skiing. Courses include 18-25 gates, of which at least six must be negotiated upstream. The last gate is 25 meters from the finish line. In 1972 the course was 600 meters long and included 30 gates. In 1992 the course was 340 meters long and in 1996 415 meters. A 2-point penalty is assessed if the canoeist negotiates the gate but touches one of the two gate poles. A 50-point penalty is assessed if the canoeist (1) pushes the gate intentionally, (2) crosses the gate line upside down, (3) negotiates a gate in the wrong direction, (4) misses a gate, (5) touches a gate during a failed negotiation, (6) crosses a gate underwater. Each penalty point equals one second. Each competitor runs the course twice, with only the better run, as defined by both time and penalty points, counting.

KAYAK SLALOM SINGLES

1896–1968 not held

1972 Munich-Augsburg C: 37, N: 15, D: 8.28.

		TIME	PENALTIES	PTS
1. Siegbert Horn	GDR	4:18.56	10	268.56
2. Norbert Sattler	AUT	4:20.76	10	270.76
3. Harald Gimpel	GDR	4:17.95	20	277.95
4. Ulrich Peters	GER	4:12.82	30	282.82
5. Alfred Baum	GER	4:18:01	30	288.01
6. Marian Havliček	CZE	4:09.56	40	289.56
7. Eric Evans	USA	4:25.34	30	296.34
8. Jürgen Bremer	GDR	4:23.15	40	303.15

The West Germans spent 17 million marks ($4 million) constructing an artificial river at Augsburg for the competition, and they hoped to gain several medals at the Olympics. However, a year before the Munich games, the East Germans came over, studied the facilities at Augsburg, and built an exact replica back home in Zwickau. In 1972 East Germany won all four canoe slalom events. Their first winner was world champion Siegbert Horn, a 22-year-old army sergeant from Leipzig. Horn keeled over in the first run and finished 17th. But the second time he paddled a smooth race and, although his time was only the eighth best, he picked up so few penalty points that he won anyway.

1976–1988 not held

1992 Barcelona-Seu d'Urgell C: 44, N: 21, D: 8.2.

		TIME	PENALTIES	PTS
1. Pierpaolo Ferrazzi	ITA	1:46.89	0	106.89
2. Sylvain Curinier	FRA	1:47.06	0	107.06
3. Jochen Lettmann	GER	1:48.52	0	108.52
4. Richard Fox	GBR	1:48.85	0	108.85
5. Laurent Brissaud	FRA	1:49.37	0	109.37
6. Marjan Štrukelj	SLO	1:50.11	0	110.11
7. Melvyn Jones	GBR	1:50.40	0	110.40
8. Ian Wiley	IRL	1:50.45	0	110.45

Ferrazzi, who trained full-time as a member of a government-sponsored canoe club, placed only 17th in the first run, which was won by Jochen Lettmann.

1996 Atlanta-Ocoee River C: 44, N: 28, D: 7.28.

		TIME	PENALTIES	PTS
1. Oliver Fix	GER	2:21.22	0	141.22
2. Andraz Vehovar	SLO	2:21.65	0	141.65
3. Thomas Becker	GER	2:22.79	0	142.79
4. Laurent Burtz	FRA	2:24.33	0	144.33
5. Ian Wiley	IRL	2:25.21	0	145.21
6. Rich Weiss	USA	2:25.78	0	145.78
7. Jernej Abramic	SLO	2:25.81	0	145.81
8. Jochen Lettmann	GER	2:25.99	0	145.99

The 1996 slalom events were staged in the Ocoee River in the state of Tennessee. The site of the 415-meter course had been dry since 1950. Water was redirected into the dry riverbed in 1994, but usually it was diverted through a tunnel to a power plant. In 1996, water was released into the course for 77 days to allow for training, a pre-Olympic event and the Olympics.

Oliver Fix was born in Augsburg, site of the 1972 Olympic slalom events. He first paddled the Olympic course when he was nine years old. He was the youngest person ever to negotiate the course. After winning the 1995 world championship, he paid five visits to the Ocoee River, not only to familiarize himself with the course, but to feel psychologically comfortable with the area as "home ground." At the Olympics, Fix had trouble with gate 24 on the first run, but his time held up for the victory.

2000 Sydney-Penrith C: 23, N: 18, D: 9.20.

		TIME	PENALTIES	PTS
1. Thomas Schmidt	GER	3:37.25	0	217.25
2. Paul Ratcliffe	GBR	3:39.71	4	223.71
3. Pierpaolo Ferrazzi	ITA	3:45.03	0	225.03
4. Helmut Oblinger	AUT	3:44.45	2	226.45
5. Scott Shipley	USA	3:44.67	2	226.67
6. Manuel Köhler	AUT	3:44.80	2	226.80
7. Tomaš Kobes	CZE	3:44.99	2	226.99
8. Laurent Burtz	FRA	3:43.63	4	227.63

Thomas Schmidt was not expected to qualify for the Olympics, much less win the gold medal. The top-ranked German was Thomas Becker, who had earned a bronze medal at the 1996 Olympics and won the 1997 world championship. But Schmidt beat Becker at each of three selection races. At the Olympics the favorite was Paul Ratcliffe, who had won the 1998 and 1999 World Cups, as well as the 1999 Pre-Olympic Regatta on the Penrith Olympic course. Schmidt built a 3.15-point lead in the first round of the final by paddling a flawless run and recording the fastest time of the 15 finalists. In second place was Pierpaolo Ferrazzi, whose 1992 Olympic victory was a lone peak in the plains of his career as he never placed higher than 11th in any of the world championships in which he competed, and finished 17th at the 1996 Olympics. Radcliffe was in third. Both Ratcliffe and Ferrazzi rolled over just before the finish line of the second run, losing valuable time. Yet it would have made no difference as Schmidt again paddled a perfect run and again recorded the fastest time.

2004 Athens C: 25, N: 21, D: 8.20.

		TIME	PENALTIES	PTS
1. Benoît Peschier	FRA	3:07.96	0	187.96
2. Campbell Walsh	GBR	3:10.17	0	190.17
3. Fabien Lefèvre	FRA	3:06.99	4	190.99
4. David Ford	CAN	3:10.58	2	192.58

5. Thomas Schmidt	GER	3:10.93	2	192.93
6. Scott Parsons	USA	3:14.76	0	194.76
7. Grzegorz Polaczyk	POL	3:14.57	2	196.57
8. Sam Oud	HOL	3:11.28	6	197.28

The slalom course in Athens was the first to use saltwater, pumped directly from the Aegean Sea. Campbell Walsh held a quarter-second lead after the first run, but Benoît Peschier came from behind with an agressive and penalty-free second run. Two-time defending world champion Fabien Lefèvre was hit with two two-second penalties, one in each run, and had to settle for bronze despite his leading times. Just before Walsh started his second run, a spume of whitewater triggered the start timer, initially causing him to be shown to have finished out of the medals. After an official review, his time was corrected and he was awarded the silver medal.

2008 Beijing-Shunyi C: 21, N: 21, D: 8.12.

		TIME	PENALTIES	PTS
1. Alexander Grimm	GER	2:51.70	0	171.70
2. Fabien Lefèvre	FRA	2:53.30	0	173.30
3. Benjamin Boukpeti	TOG	2:53.45	0	173.45
4. Eoin Rheinisch	IRL	2:56.91	0	176.91
5. Warwick Draper	AUS	2:57.85	0	177.85
6. David Ford	CAN	2:56.35	2	178.35
7. Helmut Oblinger	AUT	2:56.83	2	178.83
8. Dariusz Popiela	POL	2:59.68	0	179.68

Only 21 years old, Alexander Grimm had already been ranked number three in the world two years in a row. In fourth place after the first run, Grimm executed a flawless second run to take the gold medal. Athens bronze medalist Fabien Lefèvre earned silver with two strong runs.

The real crowd favorite, however, was world-ranked number 56, Benjamin Boukpeti of Togo, who led after the first run and managed to hold on to bronze with his second run. He was so excited after the race that he snapped his paddle in half in celebration. Born in France to a French mother and a Togolese father, Boukpeti retained dual citizenship. He was Togo's first-ever Olympic medalist, as well as the first non-European man to win an Olympic canoeing slalom medal.

CANADIAN SLALOM SINGLES

1896–1968 not held

1972 Munich-Augsburg C: 22, N: 9, D: 7.28.

		TIME	PENALTIES	PTS
1. Reinhard Eiben	GDR	4:45.84	30	315.84
2. Reinhold Kauder	GER	5:07.89	20	327.89
3. James McEwan	USA	4:55.95	40	335.95
4. Jochen Förster	GDR	4:44.42	70	354.42
5. Wolfgang Peters	GER	4:46.25	70	356.25
6. Jürgen Köhler	GDR	5:12.88	60	372.88
7. Karel Tresnak	CZE	5:15.07	70	385.07
8. Petr Sodomka	CZE	5:01.11	90	391.11

The victory of Reinhard Eiben, a 20-year-old industrial blacksmith from Zwickau, came as a complete surprise. He had placed 13th at the 1971 world championships and only sixth in the East German championships. However, at the Olympics he recorded the best score in both rounds to finish well ahead of the favorite, Reinhold Kauder.

1976–1988 not held

1992 Barcelona-Seu d'Urgell C: 31, N: 15, D: 8.1.

		TIME	PENALTIES	PTS
1. Lukáš Pollert	CZE	1:53.69	0	113.69
2. Gareth Marriott	GBR	1:51.48	5	116.48
3. Jacky Avril	FRA	1:57.18	0	117.18
4. Jon Lugbill	USA	1:53.62	5	118.62
5. Renato De Monti	ITA	1:59.02	0	119.02
6. Martin Lang	GER	1:59.19	0	119.19
7. Emmanuel Brugvin	FRA	1:54.19	5	119.19
8. Juraj Ontko	CZE	2:00.23	0	120.23

Jon Lugbill competed in his first world championship at the age of 15 and dominated the sport of Canadian white-water canoeing for over a decade. He won his first world championship in 1979 and his fifth in 1989. Unfortunately, during his entire reign, white-water canoeing was not an Olympic sport. When it was finally reintroduced in 1992, Lugbill was already 31 years old. Still, he came within inches of winning a gold medal, brushing gate 23 with his shoulder on his first run. The five-second penalty turned out to be the difference between first and fourth place.

Winner Lukáš Pollert earned a silver medal four years later at the Atlanta Games. He then sold his medals to a Czech brokerage firm. To some journalists he said he did so to protest the commercialization and politicalization of the Olympics, but to others he said he needed the money to buy an apartment. A qualified pediatrician, on April 9, 1999, he helped save a fellow canoeist from drowning. The son of a chemist and a microbiologist, Pollert took part in the demonstrations that led to the overthrow of Communism in Czechoslovakia in 1989. He later said that taking part in the "Velvet Revolution," as it came to be known, was more important to him than winning the Olympic gold medal.

1996 Atlanta-Ocoee River C: 30, N: 18, D: 7.27.

		TIME	PENALTIES	PTS
1. Michal Martikán	SLV	2:31.03	0	151.03
2. Lukáš Pollert	CZE	2:31.17	0	151.17
3. Patrice Estanguet	FRA	2:32.84	0	152.84
4. Gareth Marriot	GBR	2:35.83	0	155.83
5. Hervé Delamarre	FRA	2:35.98	0	155.98
6. Emmanuel Brugvin	FRA	2:31.71	5	156.71
7. Martin Lang	GER	2:34.91	5	159.91
8. Ryszard Mordarski	POL	2:36.00	5	161.00

At the age of 16, Michal Martikán became the youngest winner of a World Cup event when he placed first in a race on the Ocoee Olympic course. Three months later, Martikán, now 17 years old, was in sixth place after the first run at the Olympics. With nothing to lose, he went all out on the second run and just barely bettered Lukáš Pollert's first run time. Martikán was the first Olympic champion to represent independent Slovakia.

One unfortunate competitor was Nenad Trpovski of Macedonia. During his second run, Trpovski flipped over and was hurled past three gates, the finish line and a pedestrian bridge before being fished from the water.

2000 Sydney-Penrith C: 16, N: 13, D: 9.18.

		TIME	PENALTIES	PTS
1. Tony Estanguet	FRA	3:49.87	2	231.87
2. Michal Martikán	SLV	3:51.76	2	233.76
3. Juraj Minčik	SLV	3:54.22	0	234.22
4. Emmanuel Brugvin	FRA	3:56.42	2	238.42
5. Stefan Pfannmöller	GER	3:55.72	4	239.72
6. Sören Kaufmann	GER	3:58.18	2	240.18
7. Simon Hočevar	SLO	4:00.64	0	240.64
8. Stuart McIntosh	GBR	3:59.61	4	243.61

In November 1997, while driving faster than the speed limit, Michal Martikán hit and killed a pedestrian. He was sentenced to seven months probation and ordered not to drive. He broke this probation by driving to the police station to turn in his driver's license. Martikán entered the 2000 Olympics as the favorite, having consistently finished near the top in every major competition and in each World Cup series. He registered the best score in the qualifying round, followed closely by Tony Estanguet, whose older brother Patrice had earned a bronze medal in 1996. Tony Estanguet negotiated a perfect run in the first round of the final and also recorded the fastest time. This gave him a lead of 2.30 points over Juraj Minčik, while Martikán was in fifth place 3.92 points back. In the second run, it was Martikán who was fastest and flawless, but Estanguet, although he touched a pole in the second half of the course, had built up too large a lead to be caught. Back in Slovakia, Martikán was scheduled to serve a prison term, but after his return from Sydney, the president of Slovakia, Rudolf Schuster, granted him a pardon, much to the disgust of the Justice Ministry.

2004 Athens C: 16, N: 14, D: 8.18.

		TIME	PENALTIES	PTS
1. Tony Estanguet	FRA	3:09.16	0	189.16
2. Michal Martikán	SLV	3:07.28	2	189.28
3. Stefan Pfannmöller	GER	3:12.56	0	191.56
4. Robin Bell	AUS	3:10.83	2	192.83
5. Tomáš Indruch	CZE	3:13.28	2	195.28
6. Simeon Hočevar	SLO	3:17.78	2	199.78
7. Jordi Sangrá Gibert	SPA	3:18.41	2	200.41
8. Stuart McIntosh	GBR	3:27.19	4	211.19

In a rematch of the 2000 competition, Tony Estanguet and Michal Martikán were neck and neck throughout the competition, with Martikán beating Estanguet by a .09 margin in the preliminary races and taking a .12-second lead into the final. Martikán appeared to have won the gold with an error-free final run, but a post-race review showed he had hit the fifth gate, and the resulting two-point penalty dropped him to second place. Estanguet was the first person to successfully defend an individual whitewater title.

2008 Beijing-Shunyi C: 16, N: 16, D: 8.12.

		SEMI-FINAL RUN		FINAL RUN		TOTAL POINTS
1. Michal Martikán	SVK	1:26.92	2	1:25.73	2	176.65
2. David Florence	GBR	1:28.46	2	1:28.15	0	178.61
3. Robin Bell	AUS	1:29.16	2	1:29.43	0	180.59
4. Ander Elosegui Alcain	SPA	1:30.19	2	1:27.93	2	182.12
5. Stanislav Ježek	CZE	1:29.85	0	1:28.44	4	182.29
6. Benn Fraker	USA	1:32.27	0	1:30.87	0	183.14
7. Khristos Tsakmakis	GRE	1:30.18	2	1:30.49	4	186.67
8. Krzysztof Bieryt	POL	1:30.08	0	1:48.13	2	200.21

Since winning the gold medal in 1996, Michal Martikán had lost to only one man in an Olympic final: two-time gold medalist Tony Estanguet. Estanguet had beaten Martikán not only at the last two Olympics but also at the 2006 world championships in Prague, and had edged him out for the silver medal at the 2005 world championships in Penrith, Australia—won by hometown favorite Robin Bell. Martikán turned the tables in 2007, beating both Estanguet and Bell to win the world title in Brazil.

In Beijing Martikán recorded the fastest times in both the qualifying and semi-final rounds, while Estanguet struggled to get a feel for the course, finishing ninth in the semi-final and failing to qualify for the final.

Martikán recorded the fastest two runs of the final and clinched the gold medal despite incurring a two-second penalty in each run.

The silver medalist, 26-year-old David Florence, had applied to be an astronaut at the European Space

Agency, but was rejected shortly before the start of the Olympics. Three days after the competition Florence learned that his family had been struck by lightning after being caught in a thunderstorm while sightseeing on the Great Wall of China. Nobody in the family was seriously injured.

CANADIAN SLALOM PAIRS

1896–1968 not held

1972 Munich-Augsburg T: 20, N: 9, D: 8.30.

		TIME	PENALTIES	PTS
1. Walter Hofmann, Rolf-Dieter Amend	GDR	4:30.68	40	310.68
2. Hans Otto Schumacher, Wilhelm Baues	GER	4:51.90	20	311.90
3. Jean-Louis Olry, Jean-Claude Olry	FRA	5:05.10	10	315.10
4. Jürgen Kretschmer, Klaus Trummer	GDR	4:59.57	30	329.57
5. Jan Frączek, Ryszard Seruga	POL	5:26.21	40	366.21
6. Janez Andrijašič, Peter Guzelj	YUG/SLO	5:18.01	50	368.01
7. Michael Reimann, Olaf Fricke	GER	5:01.86	70	371.86
8. Heimo Müllneritsch, Helmar Steindl	AUT	5:05.14	70	375.14

Canoe Slalom, 1972
The exotic sport of slalom, or white-water, canoeing was included in the 1972 Olympics and dominated by the East Germans, who had constructed an exact copy of the West German course that was used for the Olympics.

1976–1988 not held

1992 Barcelona-Seu d'Urgell T: 17, N: 8, D: 8.2.

		TIME	PENALTIES	PTS
1. Scott Strausbaugh, Joe Jacobi	USA	2:02.41	0	122.41
2. Miroslav Šimek, Jiří Rohan	CZE	1:59.25	5	124.25
3. Franck Adisson, Wilfrid Forgues	FRA	2:04.38	0	124.38
4. James McEwan, Jacob "Lecky"Haller	USA	2:08.05	0	128.05
5. Ueli Matti, Peter Matti	SWI	2:03.55	5	128.55
6. Pavel Štercl, Petr Štercl	CZE	2:10.42	0	130.42
7. Jan Petříček, Tomáš Petříček	CZE	2:06.86	5	131.86
8. Thierry Saïdi, Emmanuel del Rey	FRA	2:07.29	5	132.29

Strausbaugh and Jacobi were the only pair to paddle penalty-free on both runs. They led after the first run but needed to improve their time on the second run to stay ahead of Šimek and Rohan. Jamie McEwan of the fourth-place United States team had earned a bronze medal the last time canoe slalom races were included in the Olympics—20 years earlier. McEwan was the only Munich slalom veteran to compete at the Barcelona Games.

1996 Atlanta-Ocoee River T: 15, N: 10, D: 7.28.

		TIME	PENALTIES	PTS
1. Franck Adisson, Wilfrid Forgues	FRA	2:38.82	0	158.82
2. Miroslav Šimek, Jiři Rohan	CZE	2:40.16	0	160.16
3. Andre Ehrenberg, Michael Senft	GER	2:38.72	5	163.72
4. Manfred Berro, Michael Trummer	GER	2:43.72	0	163.72
5. Emmanuel Del Rey, Thierry Saïdi	FRA	2:40.47	5	165.47
6. Petr Stercl, Pavel Stercl	CZE	2:43.45	5	168.45
7. Krzysztof Kolomanski, Michal Staniszewski	POL	2:44.95	5	169.95
8. Benoit Gauthier, François Letourneau	CAN	2:47.67	5	172.67

Both of the favorites, Adisson and Forgues and Šimek and Rohan, had poor first runs and found themselves in 10th and 14th places respectively. None of the thirteen pairs completed a clean run the first time down and, as it would turn out, thirteen of the fifteen pairs would record a better score on the second run. Ehrenberg and Senft were awarded the bronze medals over Berro and Trummer based on their superior non-counting score.

2000 Sydney-Penrith T: 12, N: 10, D: 9.20.

		TIME	PENALTIES	PTS
1. Pavol Hochschorner, Peter Hochschorner	SLV	3:55.74	2	237.74
2. Krzysztof Kołomański, Michał Staniszewski	POL	4:03.81	0	243.81
3. Marek Jiřas, Tomáš Mader	CZE	4:03.45	6	249.45
4. Stuart Bowman, Nick Smith	GBR	4:07.93	2	249.93
5. Jaroslav Volf, Ondřej Štěpánek	CZE	4:09.36	4	253.36
6. Andrzej Wójs, Sławomir Mordarski	POL	4:07.51	8	255.51

7. Franck Adisson, Wilfrid Forgues	FRA	3:58.91	52	290.91
8. Andre Ehrenberg, Michael Senft	GER	4:07.78	54	301.78

Twins Pavol and Peter Hochschorner won two pre-Olympic competitions on the Olympic course, as well as the 1999 World Cup. Defending champions Franck Adisson and Wilfrid Forgues led the Hochschorners by 1.73 points after the first run, but they ran into trouble late in the second run, touching the 18th gate and missing the 21st. The missed gate left them in seventh place rather than second as the Hochschorners completed the run almost three seconds faster than the other finalists and did so without a penalty.

2004 Athens T: 12, N: 12, D: 8.20.

		TIME	PENALTIES	PTS
1. Pavol Hochschorner, Peter Hochschorner	SLV	3:25.16	2	207.16
2. Marcus Becker, Stefan Henze	GER	3:26.98	4	210.98
3. Jaroslav Volf, Ondřej Štěpánek	CZE	3:26.86	6	212.86
4. Christian Bahmann, Michael Senft	GER	3:31.45	2	213.45
5. Philippe Quemerais, Yann le Pennec	FRA	3:32.79	4	216.79
6. Andrea Benetti, Erik Masoero	ITA	3:36.06	4	220.06
7. Marek Jiras, Tomáš Máder [First round only]	CZE	1:44.35	6	110.35
8. Matt Taylor, Joe Jacobi [First round only]	USA	1:49.14	2	111.14

The Hochschorner twins easily defended their Olympic gold, despite touching the third-to-last gate in their final run. The Hochhschorners even celebrated in unison, pumping their right fists into the air.

2008 Beijing-Shunyi T: 12, N: 12, D: 8.15.

		SEMI-FINAL RUN		FINAL RUN		TOTAL POINTS
1. Pavol Hochschorner, Peter Hochschorner	SVK	1:32.88	2	1:33.94	2	190.82
2. Jaroslav Volf, Ondřej Štřpánek	CZE	1:35.33	0	1:37.56	0	192.89
3. Mikhail Kuznetsov, Dmitry Larionov	RUS	1:38.57	0	1:36.80	2	197.37
4. Cédric Forgit, Martin Braud	FRA	1:38.76	4	1:35.43	0	198.19
5. Andrea Benetti, Erik Masoero	ITA	1:41.64	2	1:38.48	2	204.12
6. Felix Michel, Sebastian Piersig	GER	1:34.38	0	1:48.05	2	204.43
7. Mark Bellofiore, Lachie Milne	AUS	1:38.17	6			
8. Paweł Sarna, Marcin Pochwała	POL	1:45.32	0			

The Hochschorner brothers, gold medalists at the previous two Olympics and reigning world champions, were once again the clear favorites in the Canadian pairs slalom event. Their main rivals were 2004 Olympic bronze medalists and 2006 world champions Jaroslav Volf and Ondřej Štřpánek, who had finished behind them in the 2007 world cup standings.

The Hochschorners completed the qualifying round in first place, but incurred a two-second penalty during their semi-final run, slipping to second behind Felix Michel and Sebastian Piersig, with Volf and Štřpánek in third.

Volf and Štřpánek had a slow final run, 1:37.56, but avoided any penalties and were in first place with just the Hochschorner brothers and Michel and Piersig still to go. The Hochschorners managed a 1:33.94 run, which put them back in first place despite incurring another two-second penalty. Michel and Piersig had a chance to take gold with their final run until their boat capsized, dropping them to sixth place.

DISCONTINUED EVENTS

KAYAK SINGLES 500 METERS

1896–1972 not held

1976 Montreal C: 18, N: 18, D: 7.30

1. Vasile Dîba	ROM	1:46.41
2. Zoltán Sztanity	HUN	1:46.95
3. Rüdiger Helm	GDR	1:48.30
4. Herminio Menéndez Rodríguez	SPA	1:48.40
5. Grzegorz Śledziewski	POL	1:48.49
6. Sergei Lizunov	SOV/RUS	1:49.21
7. Oreste Perri	ITA	1:50.27
8. Douglas Parnham	GBR	1:50.33

1980 Moscow C: 17, N: 17, D: 8.1.

1. Vladimir Parfenovich	SOV/BLR	1:43.43
2. John Sumegi	AUS	1:44.12
3. Vasile Dîba	ROM	1:44.90
4. Milan Janić	YUG/CRO	1:45.63
5. Frank-Peter Bischof	GDR	1:45.97
6. Anders Andersson	SWE	1:46.32
7. Ian Ferguson	NZL	1:47.36
8. Felix Masár	CZE	1:48.18

Parfenovich, a 21-year-old physical education instructor from Minsk, won three gold medals at the Moscow Olympics. He was later elected to the national legislature of Belarus and became a spokesman for the movement to bring true democracy to his nation.

1984 Los Angeles-Lake Casitas C: 19, N: 19, D: 8.10.

1. Ian Ferguson	NZL	1:47.84
2. Lars-Erik Moberg	SWE	1:48.18
3. Bernard Bregeon	FRA	1:48.41
4. Vasile Dîba	ROM	1:48.77
5. David Upson	GBR	1:49.32
6. Daniele Scarpa	ITA	1:49.60
7. Guillermo del Riego Gordón	SPA	1:49.71
8. Reiner Scholl	GER	1:49.89

A trained accountant, Ian Ferguson retired from kayaking after the Moscow Olympics and opened a business in Auckland repairing and distributing video-game machines. But when the New Zealand Sports Federation offered increased financial support to kayakers, Ferguson returned to the sport and won a silver medal at the 1983 world championships. The following year, at age 32, he won three gold medals at the Los Angeles Olympics.

1988 Seoul C: 18, N: 18, D: 9.30.

1. Zsolt Gyulay	HUN	1:44.82
2. Andreas Stähle	GDR	1:46.38
3. Paul MacDonald	NZL	1:46.46
4. Michael Herbert	USA	1:46.73
5. Karl Axel Sundqvist	SWE	1:46.76
6. Attila Szabó	CZE	1:47.38
7. Martin Hunter	AUS	1:47.66
8. Dirk Joestel	GER	1:47.91

1992 Barcelona-Castelldefels C: 28, N: 28, D: 8.7.

1. Mikko Kolehmainen	FIN	1:40.43
2. Zsolt Gyulay	HUN	1:40.64
3. Knut Holmann	NOR	1:40.71
4. Norman Bellingham	USA	1:40.84
5. Sergei Kalesnik	BLR	1:40.90
6. Roberto Liberato	SWI	1:41.98
7. Daniele Scarpa	ITA	1:42.00
8. Marin Popescu	ROM	1:42.24

The 27-year-old Kolehmainen won from behind after being placed only seventh at the halfway mark.

1996 Atlanta-Lake Lanier C: 26, N: 26, D: 8.4.

1. Antonio Rossi	ITA	1:37.423
2. Knut Holmann	NOR	1:38.339
3. Piotr Markiewicz	POL	1:38.615
4. Geza Magyar	ROM	1:38.975
5. Lutz Liwowski	GER	1:39.307
6. Miguel García	SPA	1:40.047
7. Mikko Kolehmainen	FIN	1:40.331
8. Robert Erban	SLV	1:40.407

The previous day, Knut Holmann had won the K-1 1000 meters and Antonio Rossi had won the K-2 1000 meters. When they met in the K-1 500 meters, Rossi started fast and led wire to wire.

2000 Sydney-Penrith C: 31, N: 31, D: 10.1.

1. Knut Holmann	NOR	1:57.847
2. Petar Merkov	BUL	1:58.393
3. Michael Kolganov	ISR	1:59.563
4. Ákos Vereckei	HUN	2:00.145
5. Lutz Liwowski	GER	2:00.259
6. Jovino González	SPA	2:03.889
7. Alvydas Duonela	LIT	2:04.591
8. Alan van Coller	SAF	2:04.981

The canoeing regatta got underway under a shroud of controversy after Bulgarian newspapers reported that two Bulgarian canoeists, one of whom was world champion silver medalist Petar Merkov, had tested positive in July for a diuretic used for masking steroids. More than a dozen canoeing nations submitted a petition to the International Canoeing Federation asking for an investigation, but the Bulgarians stonewalled the issue, Merkov refused to speak to the press and he was allowed to compete and to eventually win two silver medals.

Despite strong winds gusting up to 50 miles (80 kilometers) per hour, regatta officials attempted to start the race on time. However, as the competitors prepared themselves, one race official sank in his aluminum dinghy and then it was discovered that the starting gates for lanes seven and eight were broken. The start of the race was delayed while equipment was repaired, officials held meetings and the wind died down—somewhat. After five hours, both the participants and the spectators were getting edgy. Suddenly about 30 spectators stripped down to their underwear, dived into the water and raced to the medal podium on the opposite bank. The first three climbed onto the pontoon holding the platform and mounted the gold, silver and bronze places, at which point police and security personnel sent them all back.

The K-1 500 was finally run about an hour later. Knut Holmann added a third gold medal to his collection and brought his career medal total to six. Pre-Olympic favorite Ákos Vereckei was beaten for the bronze medal by Uzbeki-born Israeli Michael Kolganov, who trained on the Sea of Galilee where, according to the New Testament, Jesus walked on water. The United States was represented by 34-year-old Cliff Meidl, who, fourteen years earlier, was electrocuted while working for a construction company in southern California. He received 30,000 volts of electricity (electric chair executions use 1500 volts) and experienced three cardiac arrests. Meidl was unable to walk unaided for three years. He competed in the K-4 1000 meters in 1996. In Sydney he was eliminated in the semifinals of the K-1 500.

2004 Athens-Schinias C: 28, N: 28, D: 8.28.

1. Adam van Koeverden	CAN	1:37.919
2. Nathan Baggaley	AUS	1:38.467
3. Ian Wynne	GBR	1:38.547
4. Eirik Verås Larsen	NOR	1:38.667
5. Ákos Vereckei	HUN	1:39.315
6. Lutz Altepost	GER	1:39.647
7. Bâbak Amir-Tahmasseb	FRA	1:40.187
8. Javier Correa	ARG	1:40.639

After almost quitting the sport following a disappointing performance at the Sydney Games, Nathan Baggaley came back to win two world championship titles and entered the 2004 Olympics as the strong favorite for gold. He shot to a full-second lead in the first 250 meters of the final, but began to flag, allowing Adam van Koeverden to pull ahead for a half-second victory. The grandson of Hungarian immigrants, van Koeverden was born in Canada after his mother's family fled the 1956 Hungarian revolution. According to his mother, Beata Bokrossy, the family could as easily have ended up in Australia, "but the Canadian ship came first." A 2003 world championship silver medalist in the K-1 1000, the 22-year-old van Koeverden had never trained for the K-1 500. Van Koeverden lived and trained with 1984 gold and silver medalist Larry Cain, the last Canadian man to have won a canoeing or kayaking medal. In September 2005, shortly after winning the world championship title in the K-1 500 meters event, Baggaley tested positive for the steroids stanozolol and methindione. He blamed the positive test on having accidentally drunk from a container of juice that his brother, who was recovering from a shoulder injury, had mixed with steroids. The International Canoe Federation was unconvinced and banned Baggaley from competition for two years. Just before the ban was lifted, Baggaley faced a second drug charge after police found 762 ecstasy tablets in a car he was driving. He was sentenced to nine years in prison.

2008 Beijing-Shunyi C: 29, N: 29, D: 8.23.

1. Ken Wallace	AUS	1:37.252
2. Adam van Koeverden	CAN	1:37.630
3. Tim Brabants	GBR	1:37.671
4. Eirik Verås Larsen	NOR	1:37.949
5. Anton Ryakhov	RUS	1:38.187
6. Ákos Vereckei	HUN	1:38.318
7. Anders Gustafsson	SWE	1:38.447
8. Steven Ferguson	NZL	1:38.512

Defending Olympic champion and reigning world champion Adam van Koeverden seemed unbeatable in the early rounds, setting a world best of 1:35.554 in his first-round heat and winning his semi-final heat more than half a second ahead of 2006 world silver medalist Anton Ryakhov. Still smarting from a disappointing eighth-place finish in the K-1 1000 meters final the previous day, he came out strong in the final, building a half-boat-length lead by the midway point. With 150 meters left, Olympic newcomer Ken Wallace stormed into the lead from the middle of the pack, passing van Koeverden and holding on for the gold medal. Van Koeverden was also very nearly passed by 2007 world silver medalist Tim Brabants, but managed to hold on to silver. The two finished so close that the scoreboard initially listed Brabants in second place before it was determined that van Koeverden had actually beaten him.

The 25-year-old Wallace had originally competed in the Australian Ironman, a combination of four different disciplines of surf life-saving—swimming, board paddling, ski paddling and running—before switching to kayak sprint events at the age of 16.

KAYAK SINGLES 10,000 METERS

1936 Berlin-Grünau C: 15, N: 15, D: 8.7.

1. Ernst Krebs	GER	46:01.6
2. Fritz Landertinger	AUT	46:14.7
3. Ernest Riedel	USA	47.23.9
4. Jacobus van Tongeren	HOL	47:31.0
5. Evert Johansson	FIN	47:35.5
6. František Brzák-Felix	CZE	47:36.8
7. Bruno Lips	SWI	48:01.2
8. Elio Sasso Sant	ITA	49:20.0

1948 London-Henley-on-Thames C: 13, N: 13, D: 8.11.

1. Gert Fredriksson	SWE	50:47.7
2. Kurt Wires	FIN	51:18.2
3. Elvind Skabo	NOR	51:35.4
4. Knud Ditlevsen	DEN	51:54.2
5. Henri Eberhardt	FRA	52:09.0
6. Jochem Bobeldijk	HOL	52:13.2
7. Czesław Sobieraj	POL	52:51.0
8. Alfred Corbiaux	BEL	53:23.5

1952 Helsinki C: 17, N: 17, D: 7.27.

1. Thorvald Strömberg	FIN	47:22.8
2. Gert Fredriksson	SWE	47:34.1
3. Michael Scheuer	GER	47:54.4
4. Ejvind Hansen	DEN	47:58.8
5. Hans Martin Gulbrandsen	NOR	48:12.9
6. Miloš Pech	CZE	48:25.8
7. Ivan Sotnikov	SOV/UKR	48:36.8
8. Jochem Bobeldijk	HOL	49:36.2

Fredriksson spent most of the race hanging in the wake of Strömberg's bow, but when he finally made his move, the 21-year-old Finnish fisherman had saved enough for a spurt of his own and pulled away to victory.

1956 Melbourne-Ballarat C: 11, N: 11, D: 11.30.

1. Gert Fredriksson	SWE	47:43.4
2. Ferenc Hatlaczky	HUN	47:53.3
3. Michael Scheuer	GER	48:00.3
4. Thorvald Strömberg	FIN	48:15.8
5. Igor Pissaryev	SOV/RUS	49:58.2
6. Ladislav Čepcianský	CZE	50:08.2
7. Svend Fromming	DEN	50:10.0
8. Knut Östbye	NOR	51:28.2

FOLDING KAYAK SINGLES 10,000 METERS

1936 Berlin-Grünau C: 13, N: 13, D: 87

1. Gregor Hradetzky	AUT	50:01.2
2. Henri Eberhardt	FRA	50:04.2
3. Xaver Hörmann	GER	50:06.5

4. Lennart Dozzi	SWE	51:23.8
5. František Svoboda	CZE	51:52.5
6. Hans Mooser	SWE	52:43.8
7. Frans Nordberg	FIN	52:45.8
8 George Lawton	GBR	52:50.0

Hradetzky and Eberhardt passed Hörmann after 3000 meters, but all three battled closely for the rest of the race.

KAYAK PAIRS 500 METERS

1896–1972 not held

1976 Montreal T: 21, N: 21, D: 7.28.

1. Joachim Mattern, Bernd Olbricht	GDR	1:35.87
2. Serhei Nahorny, Vladimir Romanovsky	SOV	1:36.81
3. Larion Serghei, Policarp Malihin	ROM	1:37.43
4. José Seguín, Guillermo del Riego Gordón	SPA	1:38.50
5. József Deme, János Rátkai	HUN	1:38.81
6. Hannu Kojo, Kari Markkanen	FIN	1:39.59
7. Anders Andersson, Lars Andersson	SWE	1:39.63
8. John Southwood, John Sumegi	AUS	1:39.77

1980 Moscow T: 18, N: 18, D: 8.1.

1. Vladimir Parfenovich, Serhei Chukhray	SOV	1:32.38
2. Herminio Menéndez Rodríguez, Guillermo del Riego Gordón	SPA	1:33.65
3. Rüdiger Helm, Bernd Olbricht	GDR	1:34.00
4. Francis Hervieu, Alain Lebas	FRA	1:36.22
5. Barry Kelly, Robert Lee	AUS	1:36.45
6. Alexandru Giura, Ion Bîrlădeanu	ROM	1:36.96
7. Waldemar Merk, Zdzislaw Szubski	POL	1:37.20
8. László Szabó, Zoltán Romhányi	HUN	1:37.66

1984 Los Angeles-Lake Casitas T: 21, N: 21, D: 8.10.

1. Ian Ferguson, Paul MacDonald	NZL	1:34.21
2. Per-Inge Bengtsson, Lars-Erik Moberg	SWE	1:35.26
3. Hugh Fisher, Alwyn Morris	CAN	1:35.41
4. Daniele Scarpa, Francesco Uberti	ITA	1:35.50
5. Nicolae Feodosei, Angelin Velea	ROM	1:35.60
6. Francis Hervieu, Daniel Legras	FRA	1:36.40
7. Matthias Seack, Oliver Seack	GER	1:36.51
8. Andrew Sherriff, Jeremy West	GBR	1:36.73

1988 Seoul T: 22, N: 22, D: 9.30.

1. Ian Ferguson, Paul MacDonald	NZL	1:33.98
2. Ihor Nahayev, Viktor Denisov	SOV	1:34.15
3. Attila Ábrahám, Ferenc Csipes	HUN	1:34.32
4. Reiner Scholl, Thomas Pfrang	GER	1:34.40
5. Daniel Stoian, Angelin Velea	ROM	1:35.96
6. Maciej Frejmut, Wojciech Kurpiewski	POL	1:36.22
7. Kay Bluhm, André Wohllebe	GDR	1:36.49
8. Olney Kent, Terry White	USA	1:36.62

Ferguson and MacDonald opened a big lead and managed to lunge across the finish line before the field could catch them.

1992 Barcelona-Castelldefels T: 30, N: 30, D: 8.7.

1. Kay Bluhm, Torsten Gutsche	GER	1:28.27
2. Maciej Freimut, Wojciech Kurpiewski	POL	1:29.84
3. Antonio Rossi, Bruno Dreossi	ITA	1:30.00
4. Juan José Román Mangas, Juan Manuel Sánchez de Castro	SPA	1:30.93
5. Karl Sundqvist, Gunnar Olsson	SWE	1:31.48
6. Jesper Staal, Thor Nielsen	DEN	1:31.84
7. Ferenc Csipes, Zsolt Gyulay	HUN	1:32.34
8. Michael Harbold, Peter Newton	USA	1:33.02

Bluhm and Gutsche won the first of their two 1992 gold medals by recording the largest winning margin ever in a men's kayak 500 event. In 1988, Bluhm had earned a bronze medal as a member of East Germany's four-man team.

1996 Atlanta-Lake Lanier T: 25, N: 25, D: 8.4.

1. Kay Bluhm, Torsten Gutsche	GER	1:28.697
2. Beniamino Bonomi, Daniele Scarpa	ITA	1:28.729
3. Daniel Collins, Andrew Trim	AUS	1:29.409
4. Oleg Goroby, Anatoly Tishchenko	RUS	1:29.677
5. Maciej Freimut, Adam Wysocki	POL	1:29.937
6. Krisztián Bártfai, Zsolt Gyulay	HUN	1:30.001
7. Daniel Stoian, Romica Serban	ROM	1:30.053
8. Milko Kazanov, Andrian Dushev	BUL	1:30.513

Gyulay and Bártfai led after 250 meters but faded, leaving Bluhm and Gutsche in first. Bonomi and Scarpa moved ahead fifty meters from the finish, but Bluhm and Gutsche pulled even again with ten meters to go and edged ahead to successfully defend their title.

2000 Sydney-Penrith T: 19, N: 19, D: 10.1.

1. Zoltán Kammerer, Botond Storcz	HUN	1:47.055
2. Andrew Trim, Daniel Collins	AUS	1:47.895
3. Ronald Rauhe, Tim Wieskötter	GER	1:48.771
4. Babak Amir-Tahmasseb, Philippe Aubertin	FRA	1:48.921
5. Marek Twardowski, Adam Wysocki	POL	1:48.963
6. Peter Newton, Angel Pérez	USA	1:52.617
7. Antonio Rossi, Beniamino Bonomi	ITA	1:52.635
8. Petar Sibinkić, Milcho Kazanov	BUL	1:52.725

Six hundred enthusiastic Hungarian fans concluded their trip to the Sydney Olympics by attending the final day of canoeing. Unfortunately, bad weather conditions delayed the program and the Hungarians were forced to leave for the airport before the races began. They missed a battle between their heroes, Botond Storcz and Zoltán Kammerer, and local favorites Daniel Collins and Andrew Trim. Three times, the compeititors were told to prepare for the start and three times the race was delayed. When it did finally get under way—five hours late—the canoeists faced 40 mile-an-hour (64-kilometer) headwinds and choppy water that resembled that used in whitewater canoeing. The Australian pair moved up from third to first with only 50 meters to go, but Storcz and Kammerer were able to surge ahead to win by about a boat-length. Because of the adverse weather conditions, their winning time was almost 16 seconds slower than the time they recorded in their qualifying heat four days earlier.

2004 Athens-Schinias T: 19, N: 19, D: 8.28.

1. Ronald Rauhe, Tim Wieskötter	GER	1:27.040
2. Clint Robinson, Nathan Baggaley	AUS	1:27.920
3. Raman Piatrushenka, Vadzim Makhneu	BLR	1:27.996
4. Marek Twardowski, Adam Wysocki	POL	1:28.048
5. Zoltán Kammerer, Botond Storcz	HUN	1:29.096
6. Damián Vindel Marín, Francisco Llera Blanco	SPA	1:29.532
7. Alvydas Duonėla, Egidijus Balčiūnas	LIT	1:29.868
8. Antonio Rossi, Beniamino Bonomi	ITA	1:30.804

After earning bronze at the 2000 Olympics, Ronald Rauhe and Timö Wieskötter won every major K-2 500 title until the 2004 Olympics. At the Athens Games, they were never seriously challenged. After winning the gold they continued their dominance, earning their fifth straight world championships in 2006.

2008 Beijing-Shunyi T: 16, N: 16, D: 8.23.

1. Saúl Craviotto Rivero, Carlos Pérez Rial	SPA	1:28.736
2. Ronald Rauhe, Tim Wieskötter	GER	1:28.827
3. Roman Petrushenko, Vadim Makhnev	BLR	1:30.005
4. Zoltán Kammerer, Gábor Kucsera	HUN	1:30.285
5. Kim Knudsen, René Poulsen	DEN	1:30.569
6. Richard Dober, Jr., Andrew Willows	CAN	1:30.857
7. Vincent Lecrubier, Sébastien Jouve	FRA	1:31.312
8. Marek Twardowski, Adam Wysocki	POL	1:31.869

The clear gold medal favorites in the K-2 500 meters event were defending Olympic champions Ronald Rauhe and Tim Wieskötter. Besides gaining six consecutive world championship titles, the pair had also won seven straight European championships over 500 meters.

Their main challengers were expected to be 2004 Olympic bronze medalists Roman Petrushenko and Vadim Makhnev, who had finished just 0.164 seconds behind them to take silver at the 2007 world championships. World bronze medalists twice running, Zoltán Kammerer and Gábor Kucsera, were also to be reckoned with.

True to form, Rauhe and Wieskötter won their first-round heat, more than a second ahead of France's Vincent Lecrubier and Sébastien Jouve. Petrushenko and Makhnev also won their heat, ahead of Spanish policemen Saúl Craviotto and Carlos Pérez.

In the final Craviotto and Pérez got off to the fastest start, building up enough of a lead to hold off a late charge by Rauhe and Wieskötter. This was Rauhe and Wieskötter's first loss in eight years. Petrushenko and Makhnev finished third to earn their second consecutive Olympic bronze medal.

Craviotto and Pérez had earned their right to represent Spain by placing second at the European championships three months before the Olympics.

KAYAK PAIRS 10,000 METERS

1936 Berlin-Grünau T: 12, N: 12, D: 8.7.

1. Paul Wevers, Ludwig Landen	GER	41:45.0
2. Viktor Kalisch, Karl Steinhuber	AUT	42:05.4
3. Tage Falhborg, Helge Larsson	SWE	43:06.1
4. Werner Lövgreen, Axel Svendsen	DEN	44:39.8
5. Hendrik Starreveld, Gerardus Siderius	HOL	45:12.5
6. Werner Zimmermann, Othmar Bach	SWI	45:14.6
7. William Gaehler, William Lofgren	USA	45:15.4
8. Zdenek Cernicky, Jaroslav Humpal	CZE	46:05.4

1948 London-Henley-on-Thames T: 15, N: 15, D: 8.11.

1. Gunnar Åkerlund, Hans Wetterström	SWE	46:09.4
2. Ivar Mathisen, Knut Östbye	NOR	46:44.8
3. Thor Axelsson, Nils Björklof	FIN	46:46.2
4. Alfred Christensen, Finn Rasmussen	DEN	47:17.5
5. Gyula Andrási, János Urányi	HUN	47:33.1
6. Cornelius Koch, Hendrik Stroo	HOL	47:35.6
7. Ludvik Klima, Oldřich Lomecky	CZE	48:14.9
8. Hilaire Deprez, Jozef Massy	BEL	48.23.1

1952 Helsinki T: 18, N: 18, D: 7.27.

1. Kurt Wires, Yrjö Hietanen	FIN	44:21.3
2. Gunnar Åkerlund, Hans Wetterström	SWE	44:21.7
3. Ferenc Varga, József Gurovits	HUN	44:26.6
4. Max Raub, Herbert Wiedermann	AUT	44:29.1
5. Ivar Mathiesen, Knut Östbye	NOR	45:04.7
6. Karl-Heinz Schäfer, Meinrad Miltenberger	GER	45:15.2
7. Rudolf Klabouch, Bedřich Dvořák	CZE	45:39.6
8. Ingvard Norregaard, Svend Fromming	DEN	45:59.6

Although Wires and Hietanen led from start to finish, they won by only half a meter.

1956 Melbourne-Ballarat T: 12, N: 12, D: 11.30.

1. János Urányi, László Fábián	HUN	43:37.0
2. Fritz Briel, Theo Kleine	GER	43:40.6
3. Dennis Green, Walter Brown	AUS	43:43.2
4. Hans Wetterström, Carl-Axel Sundin	SWE	44:06.7
5. Yevhen Yatsynenko, Sergei Klimov	SOV	45:49.3
6. Miloslav Jemelka, Rudolf Klabouch	CZE	46:13.1
7. Yrjö Hietanen, Simo Kuismanen	FIN	46:40.4
8. Brian Bullivant, Raymond Blick	GBR	47:03.7

FOLDING KAYAK PAIRS 10,000 METERS

1936 Berlin-Grünau T: 13, N: 13, D: 8.7.

1. Sven Johansson, Eric Bladström	SWE	45:48.9
2. Willi Horn, Erich Hanisch	GER	45:49.2
3. Cornelis Wijdekop, Pieter Wijdekop	HOL	46:12.4
4. Adolf Kainz, Alfons Dorfner	AUT	46:26.1
5. Otokar Kouba, Ludvik Klima	CZE	47:46.2
6. Eugen Knoblauch, Emil Bottlang	SWI	47:54.4
7. John Lysak, James O'Rourke	USA	49:46.0
8. Charles Pasquier, Armand Pagnoulle	BEL	49:57.1

This race proved to skeptics that canoeing could be an exciting sport. Horn and Hanisch were neck and neck with Johansson and Bladström for most of the second half of the contest. The Swedes edged ahead in the final

200 meters to win by only a few centimeters after 10,000 meters of paddling.

KAYAK SINGLES RELAY 4 x 500 METERS

1960 Rome-Lake Albano T: 18, N : 18, D : 8.29.

1. GDR/GER	Paul Lange,Günter Perleberg, Friedhelm Wentzke, Dieter Krause	7:39.43
2. HUN	Imre Szöllösi, Imre Kemecsey, András Szente, György Mészáros	7:44.02
3. DEN	Helmuth Sörensen, Arne Höyer, Erling Jessen, Erik Hansen	7:46.09
4. POL	Stefan Kaplaniak, Wladislaw Zieliński, Ryszard Skwarski, Ryszard Marchlik	7:49.93
5. SOV	Igor Pissaryev, Anatoly Kononyenko, Fedir Lyakhovsky, Volodymyr Natalukha	7:50.72
6. ROM	Mircea Anastasescu, Aurel Vernescu, Ion Sideri, Stavru Teodorov	7:53.00

CANADIAN SINGLES 500 METERS

1896–1972 not held

1976 Montreal C: 15, N: 15, D: 7.30.

1. Aleksandr Rogov	SOV/RUS	1:59.23
2. John Wood	CAN	1:59.58
3. Matija Ljubek	YUG/CRO	1:59.60
4. Borislav Ananiev	BUL	1:59.92
5. Wilfried Stephan	GDR	2:00.54
6. Károly Szegedi	HUN	2:01.12
7. Ivan Patzaichin	ROM	2:01.40
8. Ulrich Eicke	GER	2:02.30

John Wood thrilled the Canadian crowd of 5000 by leading from the start until the last few strokes, when he was overtaken by the favorite, Aleksandr Rogov.

1980 Moscow C: 11, N: 11, D: 8.1.

1. Serhei Postryekhin	SOV/UKR	1:53.37
2. Lyubomir Lyubenov	BUL	1:53.49
3. Olaf Heukrodt	GDR	1:54.38
4. Tamás Wichmann	HUN	1:54.58
5. Marek Lbik	POL	1:55.90
6. Timo Grönlund	FIN	1:55.94
7. Lipat Varabiev	ROM	1:56.80
8. Radomir Blazik	CZE	1:56 83

1984 Los Angeles-Lake Casitas C: 13, N: 13, D: 8.10.

1. Larry Cain	CAN	1:57.01
2. Henning Jakobsen	DEN	1:58.45
3. Costică Olaru	ROM	1:59.86
4. Philippe Renaud	FRA	1:59.95
5. Timo Grönlund	FIN	2:01.00
6. Kiyoto Inoue	JPN	2:01.79
7. Hartmut Faust	GER	2:01.86
8. Robert Rozanski	NOR	2:02.12

In 1988, Larry Cain finished fourth in the C-1 1000. He was bitterly disappointed at having missed out on earning another medal. That night his friends boosted his spirits by presenting him with an "aluminum medal" made from the top of a beer can.

1988 Seoul C: 18, N: 18, D: 9.30.

1. Olaf Heukrodt	GDR	1:56.42
2. Mikhailyo Slyvynsky	SOV/UKR	1:57.26
3. Martin Marinov	BUL	1:57.27
4. Attila Szabó	HUN	1:59.87
5. Jan Pinozura	POL	1:59.90
6. Aurel Macarencu	ROM	2:00.98
7. Narciso Suárez Amador	SPA	2:01.33
8. Petr Procházka	CZE	2:01.36

Five-time world champion Olaf Heukrodt of Magdeburg moved up from last place at the halfway mark. Heukrodt, who was married to world champion swimmer Birgit Meineke, would have been the clear favorite four years earlier in Los Angeles had not East Germany boycotted the 1984 Games.

1992 Barcelona-Castelldefels C: 19, N: 19, D: 8.7.

1. Nikolay Bukhalov	BUL	1:51.15
2. Mikhailyo Slyvynsky	UKR	1:51.40
3. Olaf Heukrodt	GER	1:53.00
4. Slavomir Kňazovický	CZE	1:54.51
5. Imre Pulai	HUN	1:54.86
6. Stephen Giles	CAN	1:55.80
7. Pascal Sylvoz	FRA	1:55.96
8. Victor Partnoi	ROM	1:57.34

Slyvynsky had won the previous three world championships, but Bukhalov had bested him on the Olympic course in 1991.

1996 Atlanta-Lake Lanier C: 17, N: 17, D: 8.4.

1. Martin Doktor	CZE	1:49.934
2. Slavomir Kňazovický	SLV	1:50.510
3. Imre Pulai	HUN	1:50.758
4. Mikhaylo Slyvynsky	UKR	1:51.714
5. Thomas Zereske	GER	1:52.358
6. Christian Frederiksen	DEN	1:52.846
7. Konstantin Negodyayev	KAZ	1:53.158
8. Stephen Giles	CAN	1:53.326

Martin Doktor won his second gold medal by making his move at 350 meters. In order to ensure that he was comfortable in Atlanta, Doktor's mother cooked *knedliky* (dumplings) for him, using dozens of kilos of flour that she brought with her to the United States from the Czech Republic.

2000 Sydney-Penrith C: 18, N: 18, D: 10.1.

1. György Kolonics	HUN	2:24.813
2. Maksim Opalev	RUS	2:25.809
3. Andreas Dittmer	GER	2:27.591
4. Maxime Boilard	CAN	2:29.259
5. Slavomír Kňazovický	SLV	2:29.613
6. Ledys Frank Balceiro Pajón	CUB	2:32.229
7. Mykhaylo Slivinsky	UKR	2:33.129
8. Martin Doktor	CZE	2:37.467

György Kolonics, a C-2 specialist, had won gold and bronze medals at the last Olympics. After he and his partner, Csaba Horváth failed to place well at the first of two Hungarian Olympic trials, they split up and Kolonics managed to qualify in the C-1 500 at the second trial in August. Kolonics' last significant performance as a singles canoeist had been back in 1993 when he finished second in the world championships. Nonetheless, at the 2000 Olympics he was able to upset two-time defending world champion Maksim Opalev.

2004 Athens-Schinias C: 19, N: 19, D: 8.28.

1. Andreas Dittmer	GER	1:46.383
2. David Cal Figueroa	SPA	1:46.723
3. Maksim Opalev	RUS	1:47.767
4. Aleksandr Zhukusky	BLR	1:47.903
5. Martin Doktor	CZE	1:47.999
6. Richard Dalton	CAN	1:48.103
7. Márton Joób	HUN	1:48.195
8. Stanimir Atanasov	BUL	1:49.759

One day after finishing second behind David Cal in the C-1 1000 event after allowing the Spaniard to build too large a lead, Andreas Dittmer learned his lesson, staying close to his rival the entire race before pulling ahead at the end to earn his third Olympic gold medal. Dittmer went on to win both the C-1 500 and 1000 meter titles at the 2005 world championships in Zagreb, Croatia.

2008 Beijing-Shunyi C: 22, N: 22, D: 8.23.

1. Maksim Opalev	RUS	1:47.140
2. David Cal Figueroa	SPA	1:48.397
3. Yuriy Cheban	UKR	1:48.766
4. Mathieu Goubel	FRA	1:49.056
5. Aleksandr Zhukovsky	BLR	1:49.092
6. Li Qiang	CHN	1:49.287
7. Florin Mironcic	ROM	1:49.861
8. Paweł Baraszkiewicz	POL	1:50.048

Although he had medals from the past two Olympics and had earned eleven world championship titles, 29-year-old Maksim Opalev had never won an Olympic gold. His biggest obstacles in the C-1 500 meters event appeared to be defending Olympic champion Andreas Dittmer and reigning world champion and defending Olympic silver medalist David Cal.

Opalev and Cal both won their first-round heats to advance directly to the final. Dittmer finished fourth in his heat to move into the semi-final, where he again finished fourth and was eliminated.

Opalev stayed in the pack through most of the final, and was in fifth place at the halfway point. He made his move in the final 100 meters, pulling past leader Aleksandr Zhukovsky, who faded to fifth. Cal won his second successive Olympic silver medal in the 500-meter event, one day after also gaining silver in the C-1 1000 meters.

CANADIAN SINGLES 10,000 METERS

1948 London-Henley-on-Thames C: 5, N: 5, D: 8.11.

1. František Čapek	CZE	1:02:05.2
2. Frank Havens	USA	1:02:40.4
3. Norman Lane	CAN	1:04:35.3
4. Raymond Argentin	FRA	1:06:44.2
5. Ingemar Andersson	SWE	1:07:27.1

Čapek, a 33-year-old bank clerk from Prague, used a "crooked" canoe which curved at the keel, allowing him to paddle on one side and not waste energy maintaining a straight course.

1952 Helsinki C: 10, N: 10, D: 7.27.

1. Frank Havens	USA	57:41.1
2. Gábor Novák	HUN	57:49.2
3. Alfréd Jindra	CZE	57:53.1
4. Bengt Backlund	SWE	59:02.8
5. Norman Lane	CAN	59:26.4
6. Jan Fagerström	FIN	59:45.9
7. Franz Johannsen	GER	1:00.26.5
8. Robert Boutigny	FRA	1:01.15.2

The long-distance canoeing events were held in a bay and the Finnish hosts lined up merchant boats across the mouth to hold back the choppy water. Jindra led most of the way, but Havens, a 28-year-old auto insurance adjuster from Arlington, Virginia, overtook him on the home stretch of the last lap and won by about 18 yards. In 1924, Havens' father, Bill, had skipped the Olympics and missed out on a gold medal in the rowing eights in order to be with his wife when she gave birth to Frank. Twenty-eight years later, Frank sent a telegram from Helsinki to his father that ended, "I'm coming home with the gold medal you should've won."

1956 Melbourne-Ballarat C: 9, N: 9, D: 11.30.

1. Leon Rotman	ROM	56:41.0
2. János Parti	HUN	57:11.0
3. Gennady Bukharin	SOV/RUS	57:14.5
4. Jiři Vokněr	CZE	57:44.5
5. Franz Johannsen	GER	58:50.1
6. Verner Wettersten	SWE	59:24.7
7. Donald Stringer	CAN	59:57.5
8. Frank Havens	USA	1:01:23 6

CANADIAN PAIRS 500 METERS

1896–1972 not held

1976 Montreal T: 15, N: 15, D: 7.30.

1. Serhei Petrenko, Aleksandr Vinogradov	SOV	1:45.81
2. Andrzej Gronowicz, Jerzy Opara	POL	1:47.77
3. Tamás Buday, Oszkár Frey	HUN	1:48.35
4. Gheorghe Danielov, Gheorghe Simionov	ROM	1:48.84
5. Gerald Delacroix, Jean-François Millot	FRA	1:49.74

6. Ivan Burchin, Krasimir Hristov	BUL	1:50.43
7. Gregory Smith, John Wood	CAN	1:50.74
8. Jiři Čtvrtečka, Tomáš Sach	CZE	1:50.85

1980 Moscow T: 10, N: 10, D: 8.1.

1. László Foltán, István Vaskuti	HUN	1:43.39
2. Petre Capusta, Ivan Patzaichin	ROM	1:44.12
3. Borislav Ananiev, Nikolai Ilkov	BUL	1:44.63
4. Jerzy Dunajski, Marek Wisla	POL	1:45,10
5. Petr Kubiček, Jiři Vrdlovec	CZE	1:46.48
6. Serhei Petrenko, Aleksandr Vinogradov	SOV	1:46.95
7. Santos Magaz, Narciso Suárez Amador	SPA	1:48.18
8. Bernt Lindelof, Erik Zeidlitz	SWE	1:48.69

1984 Los Angeles-Lake Casitas T: 11, N: 11, D: 8.10.

1. Matija Ljubek, Mirko Nišović	YUG/CRO	1:43.67
2. Ivan Patzaichin, Toma Simionov	ROM	1:45.68
3. Enrique Miguez Gómez, Narciso Suárez Amador	SPA	1:47.71
4. Didier Hoyer, Eric Renaud	FRA	1:47.72
5. Steve Botting, Eric Smith	CAN	1:48.81
6. Wolfram Faust, Ralf Wienand	GER	1:48.97
7. Eric Jamieson, Andrew Train	GBR	1:49.59
8. Shusei Fukuzato, Hiroyuki Izumi	JPN	1:50.22

Ljubek and Nišović won the gold with a devastating closing spurt that pushed them past the Romanians after 400 meters.

1988 Seoul T: 17, N: 17, D: 9.30.

1. Viktor Reneisky, Nikolai Zhuravsky	SOV	1:41.77
2. Marek Dopierala, Marek Lbik	POL	1:43.61
3. Philippe Renaud, Joël Bettin	FRA	1:43.81
4. Deyan Bonev, Petar Bozhilov	BUL	1:44.32
5. Alexander Schuck, Thomas Zereske	GDR	1:44.36
6. János Kis Sarusi, István Vaskuti	HUN	1:44.85
7. Grigore Obreja, Gheorghe Andriev	ROM	1:45.84
8. Christian Frederiksen, Arne Nielsson	DEN	1:45.90

Third-place finisher Philippe Renaud was the third member of his family to win a canoeing medal. His father, Marcel, earned a silver in the 10,000-meter Canadian pairs in 1956. In 1984, Philippe's brother, Eric, took a bronze in the 1000-meter Canadian pairs. In addition, his uncle, also named Marcel, placed fourth in the 1924 team pursuit cycling race.

1992 Barcelona-Castelldefels T: 15, N: 15, D: 8.7.

1. Aleksandr Maseikov, Dmitri Dovgalenok	BLR	1:41.54
2. Ulrich Papke, Ingo Spelly	GER	1:41.68
3. Martin Marinov, Blagovest Stoyanov	BUL	1:41.94
4. Gheorghe Andriev, Nicolae Juravschi (Nikolai Zhuravsky)	ROM	1:42.84
5. Arne Nielsson, Christian Frederiksen	DEN	1:42.92
6. Didier Hoyer, Olivier Boivin	FRA	1:43.04
7. Attila Pálizs, György Kolonics	HUN	1:43.27
8. Jan Bartůněk, Waldemar Fibigr	CZE	1:44.70

The people of Romania and the people of Moldova are actually members of the same ethnic group and speak the same language. In 1988, Moldavan Nikolai Zhuravsky won two gold medals for the USSR while teamed with Viktor Reneisky of Belarus. When the Soviet Union collapsed in 1991, Zhuravsky crossed the border, changed his name to Nicolae Juravschi, and obtained Romanian citizenship six weeks before the opening of the Barcelona Olympics. Teamed with Gheorghe Andriev, he managed to place fourth in both the C-2 500 and the C-2 1000—an impressive achievement, considering the pair had begun competing together only two weeks before the Olympics.

1996 Atlanta-Lake Lanier T: 19, N: 19, D: 8.4.

1. Csaba Horváth, György Kolonics	HUN	1:40.42
2. Nikolae Juravschi (Nikolai Zhuravsky), Viktor Reneisky	MOL	1:40.45
3. Gheorghe Andriev, Grigore Obreja	ROM	1:41.33
4. Andreas Dittmer, Gunar Kirchbach	GER	1:41.76
5. Martin Marinov, Blagovest Stoyanov	BUL	1:42.20
6. Andrei Kabanov, Pavel Konovalov	RUS	1:42.49
7. José Alfredo Bea García, Oleg Shelestenko Sánchez	SPA	1:43.57
8. Csaba Orosz, Peter Pales	SLV	1:44.11

After the Barcelona Olympics, Nikolae Juravschi moved back to Moldova. In 1994 he convinced his old partner, Viktor Reneisky, to join him in Kishinev and have another go at the Olympics. Reneisky had been working as a coach in Belarus. So, in Atlanta, Juravschi participated in his third Olympics—each time for a different country. In a photo-finish they lost to Kolonics and Horváth by less than two centimeters (¾ inch).

2000 Sydney-Penrith T: 15, N: 15, D: 10.1.

1. Ferenc Novák, Imre Pulai	HUN	1:51.284
2. Paweł Baraszkiewicz, Daniel Jedraszko	POL	1:51.536
3. Florin Popescu, Mitiča Pricop	ROM	1:54.260
4. David Mascato, José Alfredo Bea García	SPA	1:56.600
5. Christian Gille, Thomas Zereske	GER	1:59.294
6. Aleksandr Kovalev, Aleksandr Kostoglod	RUS	2:00.134
7. Zhomart Zatubaldin, Konstantin Negodyayev	KAZ	2:01.436
8. Serhiy Klymnyuk, Dmytro Sablin	UKR	2:02.612

Imre Pulai had already competed in three Olympics as a singles paddler before he switched to pairs and teamed with Ferenc Novák in 1999. The two were known as "The Monster and the Little Guy" because Pulai was 1.99 meters (6 feet 6¼ inches) tall and weighed 97 kilograms (214 pounds), while Novák was 1.72 meters (5 feet 8 inches) tall and weighed 77 kilograms (170 pounds). Because of the powerful winds on the day of the final, Pulai decided to take no chances and taped his smaller partner's leg to the boat so that he wouldn't fall out.

2004 Athens T: 14, N: 14, D: 8.28.

1. Meng Guanliang, Yang Wenjun	CHN	1:40.278
2. Ibrahim Rojas Blanco, Ledis Frank Balceiro Pajón	CUB	1:40.350
3. Aleksandr Kostoglod, Aleksandr Kovalyov	RUS	1:40.442
4. Silviu Simioncencu, Florin Popescu	ROM	1:40.618
5. Christian Gille, Tomasz Wylenzek	GER	1:40.802
6. Aleksandr Kurliandchyk, Aleksandr Bahdanovich	BLR	1:40.858
7. György Kozmann, György Kolonics	HUN	1:41.138
8. Attila Buday, Tamás Buday	CAN	1:41.210

Prior to the Athens Games, no Chinese canoeist had ever qualified for an Olympic final, much less earned a medal, and the Chinese looked at the 2004 Olympics as a chance to gain experience before the 2008 Beijing Games. Just weeks after winning their first world cup race, the Meng Guanliang and Yang Wenjun drew a qualifying heat with all three of the top medal favorites. They finished almost a second ahead of the second-place Cubans, with the Russians and Romanians close behind. The final was a photo finish with less than a second separating all eight pairs. The results were so close that race officials were unable to determine the results until most competitors were out of their canoes and on the dock.

2008 Beijing-Shunyi T: 15, N: 15, D: 8.23.

1. Meng Guanliang, Yang Wenjun	CHN	1:41.025
2. Sergei Ulegin, Aleksandr Kostoglod	RUS	1:41.282
3. Christian Gille, Tomasz Wylenzek	GER	1:41.964
4. Andrei Bogdanovich, Aleksandr Bogdanovich	BLR	1:41.996
5. Andrew Russell, Gabriel Beauchesne-Sévigny	CAN	1:42.450
6. Iosif Chirilă, Andrej Cuculici	ROM	1:43.195
7. Deyan Georgiev, Adnan Aliev	BUL	1:43.971
8. Sergiy Bezugliy Maksym Prokopenko	UKR	1:44.157

Cheered on by a raucous Chinese crowd, defending Olympic champions Meng Guanliang and Yang Wenjun led the final from start to finish, establishing a half-second lead over 2006 world champions Sergei Ulegin and Aleksandr Kostoglod in the first 250 meters. They held off a late charge by the Russians, lunging across the finish line so hard that their boat capsized. Christian Gille and Tomasz Wylenzek, the 2005 world champions, edged Andrei and Aleksandr Bogdanovich—who had won gold in the C-2 1000 meters event the day before—to take silver.

Two months before the Olympics, Yang was featured in a *New York Times* article exposing the enormous pressure Chinese athletes were under to prepare for the Beijing Games. He disclosed that he had been given the deed to a three-bedroom apartment as a reward for his 2004 gold medal but had never had the chance to actually live in it, spending all his time at a training center 250 miles away, and that he had not seen his parents in three years due to the intense training regimen. Yang also described how he had tried to retire after the 2004 Olympics . . . until sports officials threatened to withhold his retirement payments if he did not compete in Beijing. "I do not want to work as an athlete," he said, "but as an athlete here I have no freedom to choose my future."

CANADIAN PAIRS 10,000 METERS

1936 Berlin-Grünau T: 5, N: 5, D: 8.7.

1. Václav Mottl, Ždenek Škrdlant	CZE	50:35.5
2. Frank Saker, Harvey Charters	CAN	51:15.8
3. Rupert Weinstabl, Karl Proisl	AUT	51:28.0
4. Walter Schuur, Christian Holzenberg	GER	52:35.6
5. Joseph Hasenfus, Walter Hasenfus	USA	57:06.2

1948 London-Henley-on-Thames T: 6, N: 6, D: 8.11.

1. Stephen Lysak, Stephen Macknowski	USA	55:55.4
2. Václav Havel, Jiři Pecka	CZE	57:38.5
3. Georges Dransart, Georges Gandil	FRA	58:00.8
4. Karl Molnar, Viktor Salmhofer	AUT	58:59.3
5. Bert Oldershaw, William Stevenson	CAN	59:48.4
6. Gunnar Johansson, Verner Wettersten	SWE	1:03:34.4

Stephen Lysak, age 26, and Stephen Macknowski, age 33, of Yonkers, New York, using a homemade mahogany canoe, took the lead after only five strokes and went on to win by an enormous margin.

1952 Helsinki T: 9, N: 9, D: 7.27.

1. Georges Turlier, Jean Laudet	FRA	54:08.3
2. Kenneth Lane, Donald Hawgood	CAN	54:09.9
3. Egon Drews, Wilfried Soltau	GER	54:28.1
4. Valentin Orischenko, Nikolai Perevozchikov	SOV/RUS	54:36.6
5. John Haas, Frank Krick	USA	54:42.5
6. Bohuslav Karlík, Oldřich Lomecký	CZE	55:10.9
7. Ernö Söptei, Róbert Söptei	HUN	55:35.3
8. Rune Blomqvist, Harry Lindbeck	SWE	55:41.3

With only 200 meters to go, Turlier and Laudet trailed Lane and Hawgood by half a boatlength. Turlier, exhausted, called out to his partner, "That's enough, we've already got the silver. That's not bad, let it go, I can't go on!" Laudet responded, "Shut up! We can beat them; the line is right there!" The French pair increased their speed and swept past the surprised Canadians just before the finish.

1956 Melbourne-Ballarat T: 10, N: 10, D: 11.30.

1. Pavel Kharin, Gratsian Botev	SOV/RUS	54:02.4
2. Georges Dransart, Marcel Renaud	FRA	54:48.3
3. Imre Farkas, József Hunics	HUN	55:15.6
4. Egon Drews, Wilfried Soltau	GER	55:21.1
5. Alexe Dumitru, Simion Ismailciuc	ROM	55:51.1
6. Aksel Dunn, Finn Haunstoft	DEN	55:54.3
7. William Jones, Thomas Ohman	AUS	56:18.6
8. Otto Schindler, Walter Waldner	AUT	56:48.7

WOMEN

KAYAK SINGLES 200 METERS

This event will be held for the first time in 2012.

KAYAK SINGLES 500 METERS

1896-1936 not held

1948 London-Henley-on-Thames C: 10, N: 10, D: 8.12.

1. Karen Hoff	DEN	2:31.9
2. Alida van der Anker-Doedens	HOL	2:32.8
3. Fritzi Schwingl	AUT	2:32.9
4. Klára Bánfalvi	HUN	2:33.8
5. Ružena Koštalová	CZE	2:38.2
6. Sylvi Saimo	FIN	2:38.4
7. Anna van Marcke	BEL	2:43.4
8. Catherine Vautrin	FRA	2:44.4

1952 Helsinki C: 13, N: 13, D: 7.28.

1. Sylvi Saimo	FIN	2:18.4
2. Gertrude Liebhart	AUT	2:18.8
3. Nina Savina	SOV/RUS	2:21.6
4. Alida van der Anker-Doedens	HOL	2:22.3
5. Bodil Svendsen	DEN	2:22.7
6. Cecília Hartmann	HUN	2:23.0
7. Marta Kroutilová	CZE	2:23.8
8. Josefa Köster	GER	2:25.9

1956 Melbourne-Ballarat C: 10, N: 10, D: 12.1.

1. Yelizaveta Dementyeva	SOV/RUS	2:18.9
2. Therese Zenz	GER	2.19.6
3. Tove Soby	DEN	2.22 3
4. Cecília Berkes (Hartmann)	HUN	2:23.5
5. Edith Cochrane	AUS	2.23.8
6. Daniela Walkowiak	POL	2:24.1
7. Patricia Moody	GBR	2:25.3
8. Eva Marion	FRA	2:27.9

Dementyeva false-started once, then spurted into the lead and held on to win by six feet (two meters). Zenz had competed at the 1952 Helsinki Olympics as a representative of Saar, which was recognised by the IOC while it sought independence, but which joined West Germany before the next Olympics. Edith Cochrane had never trained with or competed against women before the Olympics.

1960 Rome-Lake Albano C: 13, N: 13, D: 8.29.

1. Antonina Seredina	SOV/RUS	2:08.08
2. Therese Zenz	GER	2:08.22
3. Daniela Walkowiak	POL	2:10.46
4. Annemarie Werner-Hansen	DEN	2:13.88
5. Klára Fried-Bánfalvi	HUN	2:14.02
6. Else Marie Lindmark	SWE	2:14.17
7. Alberta Zanardi	ITA	2:14.31
8. Eva Kutova	CZE	2:15.30

1964 Tokyo-Lake Sagami C: 13, N: 13, D: 10.22.

1. Lyudmila Khvedosyuk	SOV/RUS	2:12.87
2. Hilde Lauer	ROM	2:15.35
3. Marcia Jones	USA	2:15.68
4. Elke Felten	GER	2:15.94
5. Else Marie Ljungdahl (Lindmark)	SWE	2:16.00
6. Hanneliese Spitz	AUT	2:16.11
7. Daniela Pilecka	POL	2:17.52
8. Mária Roka	HUN	2:17.85

1968 Mexico City-Xochimilco C: 13, N: 13, D: 10.25.

1. Lyudmila Pinayeva (Khvedosyuk)	SOV/RUS	2:11.09
2. Renate Breuer	GER	2:12.71
3. Viorica Dumitru	ROM	2:13.22
4. Marcia Smoke (Jones)	USA	2:14.68
5. Ivona Vávrová	CZE	2:14.78
6. Anita Nüssner	GDR	2:16.02
7. Ingmårie Svensson	SWE	2:16.04
8. Mieke Jaapies	HOL	2:18.38

In the middle of the race the ninth finalist, Anna Pfeffer of Hungary, spun over in the water and was rescued by a special emergency craft following the kayakists. One and a half hours later she was back in action, winning a silver medal in the kayak pairs.

1972 Munich C: 15, N: 15, D: 9.5.

1. Yulia Ryabchynska	SOV/UKR	2:03.17
2. Mieke Jaapies	HOL	2:04.03
3. Anna Pfeffer	HUN	2:05.50
4. Irene Pepinghege	GER	2:06.55
5. Bettina Müller	GDR	2:06.85
6. Maria Nichiforov	ROM	2:07.13
7. Kate Olsen	DEN	2:07.16
8. Ingmårie Svensson	SWE	2:07.61

Four months after winning her gold medal, Ryabchynska, exhausted and flushed after a winter training session, fell into the cold water of Lake Paleostomi in Soviet Georgia and died as a result of abrupt cooling. Every spring, in Moscow, an international competition is held in her honor.

1976 Montreal C: 15, N: 15, D: 7.30.

1. Carola Zirzow	GDR	2:01.05
2. Tatiana Korshunova	SOV/RUS	2:03.07
3. Klára Rajnai	HUN	2:05.01
4. Ewa Kamińska	POL	2:05.16
5. Maria Mihoreanu	ROM	2:05.40
6. Anastazie Hajná	CZE	2:06.72
7. Julie Leach	USA	2:06.92
8. Irene Peppinghege	GER	2:07.80

East German boat designers spent a month in Montreal studying the layout of the Olympic course. Then they went home and constructed special fiberglass canoes and kayaks that curved inward when placed in the water, becoming longer and faster. Using one of these kayaks, Carola Zirzow, a 5-foot 10-inch, 21-year-old student of physiotherapy, overcame a poor start to take first place.

1980 Moscow C: 11, N: 11, D: 8.1.

1. Birgit Fischer	GDR	1:57.96
2. Vania Gesheva	BUL	1:59.48
3. Antonina Melnikova	SOV/BLR	1:59.66
4. Maria Ştefan (Mihoreanu)	ROM	2:00.90
5. Ewa Eichler	POL	2:01.23
6. Agneta Andersson	SWE	2:01.33
7. Katalin Povázsán	HUN	2:01.52
8. Beatrice Knopf	FRA	2:02.91

1984 Los Angeles-Lake Casitas C: 11, N: 11, D: 8.10.

1. Agneta Andersson	SWE	1:58.72
2. Barbara Schüttpelz	GER	1:59.93
3. Annemiek Derckx	HOL	2:00.11
4. Tecla Marinescu	ROM	2:00.12
5. Beatrice Basson	FRA	2:01.21
6. Sheila Conover	USA	2:02.38
7. Lucie Guay	CAN	2:02.49
8. Elizabeth Blencowe	AUS	2:02.63

Agneta Andersson earned medals in all three women's canoeing events in 1984: two gold and one silver. She claimed that she did not start winning medals until she switched to eating organic foods, although the Soviet-led boycott was at least as important a factor.

1988 Seoul C: 15, N: 15, D: 9.30.

1. Vania Gesheva	BUL	1:55.19
2. Birgit Schmidt (Fischer)	GDR	1:55.31
3. Izabela Dylewska	POL	1:57.36
4. Rita Köbán	HUN	1:57.58
5. Yvonne Brandstrup Knudsen	DEN	1:58.80
6. Traci Phillips	USA	2:00.81
7. Galina Savenko	SOV/RUS	2:00.88
8. Agneta Andersson	SWE	2:01.00

In 1980, Birgit Schmidt, then 18 years old, defeated Vania Gesheva to become the youngest-ever winner of an Olympic canoeing event. If East Germany had not boycotted the 1984 Games, she would have been favored to win all three women's kayak events, just as she did in the world championships of 1981, 1982, 1983, 1985, and 1987. She took off 1986 to have a baby. Schmidt was the overwhelming favorite again in Seoul but was upset in the final by the fast-finishing Gesheva.

1992 Barcelona-Castelldefels C: 16, N: 16, D: 8.7.

1. Birgit Schmidt (Fischer)	GER	1:51.60
2. Rita Köbán	HUN	1:51.96
3. Izabela Dylewska	POL	1:52.36
4. Josefa Idem	ITA	1:52.78
5. Ursula Profanter	AUT	1:53.17
6. Sabine Goetschy	FRA	1:53.53
7. Caroline Brunet	CAN	1:54.82
8. Sanda Toma	ROM	1:54.84

1996 Atlanta-Lake Lanier C: 23, N: 23, D: 8.4.

1. Rita Köbán	HUN	1:47.655
2. Caroline Brunet	CAN	1:47.891
3. Josefa Idem	ITA	1:48.731
4. Birgit Fischer	GER	1:49.383
5. Susanne Gunnarsson (Wiberg)	SWE	1:49.591
6. Ursula Profanter	AUT	1:50.271
7. Katrin Borchert	AUS	1:50.811
8. Ingrid Haralamow	SWI	1:50.875

Although each nation is limited to one entry in canoeing events, the K-1 500 meters finals included three women who were born in Germany. In addition to the official German representative, Birgit Fischer, there was Josefa Idem who competed for West Germany in 1984 and 1988 before moving to Italy, and Katrin Borchert, who switched from Germany to Australia after the 1992 Olympics. Of the nine finalists, only one, Aneta Pastuszka of Poland, was less than 27 years old. Pastuszka finished last. Caroline Brunet of Lac Beauport, Quebec, led from the start, but was overtaken in the last 50 meters of Rita Köbán. Köbán, a strict vegetarian, brought her career Olympic medal total to 2 golds, 2 silvers and 1 bronze—eight years after winning her first. Heidi Lehrer of Antigua recorded an unusually slow time—3:00.672—in her heat. She was 52.86 seconds slower than the second slowest canoeist. Lehrer did not take part in the *repêchage*.

2000 Sydney-Penrith C: 17, N: 17, D: 10.1.

1. Josefa Idem Guerrini	ITA	2:13.848
2. Caroline Brunet	CAN	2:14.646
3. Katrin Borchert	AUS	2:15.138
4. Nataša Janić	YUG/SER	2:16.506
5. Elżbieta Urbańczyk	POL	2:18.018
6. Rita Kőbán	HUN	2:19.668
7. Ruth Nortje	SAF	2:20.274
8. Ursula Profanter	AUT	2:20.598

Competing in her fourth Olympics at the age of 31, Caroline Brunet had won all three world championships since the last Olympics and had not lost a race in more than two years. In the 2000 final, which was delayed five hours because of wind, Brunet led at the halfway mark, but was passed by 36-year-old Josefa Idem Guerrini, who was competing in her fifth Olympics and who won by half a boat length. Less than two weeks after the closing of the Sydney Games, the Italian newspaper *Corriere della Sera* revealed that Idem was one of 61 Italian athletes who tested positive for unnatural levels of human growth hormone (HGH), which was on the IOC's banned list, but for which there was no approved test. An investigation into the HGH scandal was halted by the Italian Olypmic Committee on the basis that it violated confidentiality laws.

2004 Athens-Schinias C: 23, N: 23, D: 8.28.

1. Nataša Janić	HUN	1:47.741
2. Josefa Idem	ITA	1:49.729
3. Caroline Brunet	CAN	1:50.601

4. Katrin Wagner	GER	1:52.557
5. Marcela Erbanová	SLV	1:52.685
6. Larisa Kosorukova-Pesyakhovich	ISR	1:53.089
7. Lucy Hardy	GBR	1:53.717
8. Jenni Honkanen	FIN	1:53.937

The daughter of 1984 K-1 1000 silver medalist Milan Janić, Nataša Janić was allowed to switch nationality from Serbia to Hungary barely three months before the Olympics. In the final, she powered to an early lead and held off a late challenge by defending Olympic champion Josefa Idem.

2008 Beijing-Shunyi C: 25, N: 25, D: 8.23.

1. Inna Osypenko-Radomska	UKR	1:50.673
2. Josefa Idem-Guerrini	ITA	1:50.677
3. Katrin Wagner-Augustin	GER	1:51.022
4. Katalin Kovács	HUN	1:51.139
5. Zhong Hongyan	CHN	1:52.220
6. Špela Ponomarenko	SLO	1:52.363
7. Lucy Hardy	GBR	1:53.102
8. Jennifer Hodson	SAF	1:53.353

Reigning world champion Katalin Kovács finished first in her heat to advance directly to the final, as did Athens 2004 silver medalist Josefa Idem and Athens fourth-place finisher Katrin Wagner. Kovács took the lead in the final, but couldn't maintain her pace in the final sprint, slipping to fourth as Idem and Athens K-4 500 meters bronze medalist Inna Osypenko battled for the gold. The finish was too close to call, and the two paddlers waited in their kayaks until Osypenko's name flashed on the scoreboard—the winner by 0.004 seconds. Idem's silver medal came 24 years after her first Olympic medal, a bronze in the K-2 500 meters at the 1984 Los Angeles Olympics.

KAYAK PAIRS 500 METERS

1896–1956 not held

1960 Rome-Lake Albano T: 11, N: 11, D: 8.29.

1. Maria Chubina, Antonina Seredina	SOV/RUS	1:54.76
2. Therese Zenz, Ingrid Hartmann	GER	1:56.66
3. Klára Fried-Bánfalvi, Vilma Egresi	HUN	1:58.22
4. Daniela Walkowiak, Janina Mendalska	POL	1:59.03
5. Annemarie Werner-Hansen, Birgit Jensen	DEN	2:01.36
6. Maria Szekeli, Elena Lipalit	ROM	2:01.68
7. Gabriella Cotta Ramusino, Luciana Guindani	ITA	2:02.47
8. Eva Kutova, Eva Kolinska	CZE	2:02.76

1964 Tokyo-Lake Sagami T: 10, N: 10, D: 10.22.

1. Roswitha Esser, Annemarie Zimmermann	GER	1:56.95
2. Francine Fox, Glorianne Perrier	USA	1:59.16
3. Hilde Lauer, Cornelia Sideri	ROM	2:00.25
4. Nina Gruzintseva, Antonina Seredina	SOV/RUS	2:00.69
5. Birthe Hansen, Annemarie Werner-Hansen	DEN	2:00.88
6. Else-Marie Ljungdahl (Lindmark), Eva-Britt Sisth	SWE	2:02.24
7. Katalin Benkö, Mária Roka	HUN	2:03.67
8. Izabella Antonowicz, Daniela Pilecka	POL	2:04.31

Silver medalist Francine Fox was only 15 years old, while her partner, Glorianne Perrier, was 20 years older.

1968 Mexico City-Xochimilco T: 11, N: 11, D: 10.25.

1. Roswitha Esser, Annemarie Zimmermann	GER	1:56.44
2. Anna Pfeffer, Katalin Rozsnyói	HUN	1:58.60
3. Lyudmila Pinayeva (Khvedosyuk), Antonina Seredina	SOV/RUS	1:58.61
4. Valentina Serghei, Viorica Dumitru	ROM	1:59.17
5. Anita Kobuss, Karin Haftenberger	GDR	2:00.18
6. Mieke Jaapies, Tjeentje Bergers-Duif	HOL	2:02.02
7. Sperry Rademaker, Marcia Smoke (Jones)	USA	2:02.97
8. Lesley Oliver, Barbara Mean	GBR	2:03.70

1972 Munich T: 12, N: 12, D: 9.9.

1. Lyudmila Pinayeva (Khvedosyuk), Kateryna Nahirna-Kuryshko	SOV	1:53.50
2. Ilse Kaschube, Petra Grabowski	GDR	1:54.30
3. Maria Nichiforov, Viorica Dumitru	ROM	1:55.01
4. Anna Pfeffer, Katalin Hollósy	HUN	1:55.12
5. Roswitha Esser, Renate Breuer	GER	1:55.64
6. Izabella Antonowicz-Szuszkiewicz, Ewa Grajkowska	POL	1:57.45
7. Mieke Jaapies, Maria van der Holst	HOL	1:58.11
8. Natasha Petrova, Petrana Koleva	BUL	1:59.40

1976 Montreal T: 14, N: 14, D: 7.30.

1. Nina Gopova, Galina Kreft	SOV/RUS	1:51.15
2. Anna Pfeffer, Klára Rajnai	HUN	1:51.69
3. Bärbel Köster, Carola Zirzow	GDR	1:51.81
4. Nastasia Nichitov, Agafia Orlov	ROM	1:53.77
5. Barbara Lewe-Pohlmann, Heiderose Wallbaum	GER	1:53.86
6. Maria Kazanecka, Katarzyna Kulczak	POL	1:55.05
7. Maria Mincheva, Natasha Yanakieva	BUL	1:55.95
8. Anne Dodge, Susan Holloway	CAN	1:56.75

1980 Moscow T: 12, N: 12, D: 8.1.

1. Carsta Genäuss, Martina Bischof	GDR	1:43.88
2. Galina Alexeyeva (Kreft), Nina Trofimova (Gopova)	SOV/RUS	1:46.91
3. Éva Rakusz, Mária Zakariás	HUN	1:47.95
4. Elisabeta Băbeanu, Agafia Buhaev	ROM	1:48.04
5. Agneta Andersson, Karin Olsson	SWE	1:49.27
6. Anne-Marie Loriot, Valerie Leclerc	FRA	1:49.48
7. Ewa Eichler, Ewa Wojtaszek	POL	1:51.31
8. Frances Wetherall, Lesley Smither	GBR	1:52.76

Genäuss and Bischof achieved the most decisive victory ever in women's Olympic canoeing.

1984 Los Angeles-Lake Casitas T: 10, N: 10, D: 8.10.

1. Agneta Andersson, Anna Olsson	SWE	1:45.25
2. Alexandra Barre, Susan Holloway	CAN	1:47.13
3. Josefa Idem, Barbara Schüttpelz	GER	1:47.32
4. Agafia Constantin (Buhaev), Nastasia Ionescu	ROM	1:47.56
5. Shirley Dery, Leslie Klein	USA	1:49.51
6. Bernadette Hettich, Cathérine Mathevon	FRA	1:51.40
7. Kari Ofstad, Anne Wahl	NOR	1:51.61
8. A. Lucy Perrett, Lesley Smither	GBR	1:51.73

Silver medalist Sue Holloway had represented Canada in Nordic skiing in 1976.

1988 Seoul T: 15, N: 15, D: 9.30.

1. Birgit Schmidt (Fischer), Anke Nothnagel	GDR	1:43.46
2. Vania Gesheva, Diana Paliiska	BUL	1:44.06
3. Annemiek Derckx, Annemarie Cox	HOL	1:46.00
4. Erika Mészáros, Éva Rakusz	HUN	1:46.58
5. Irma Salomykova, Irma Khmelevskaya	SOV/RUS	1:47.68
6. Anna Olsson, Agneta Andersson	SWE	1:48.39
7. Sheila Conover, Cathy Marino-Geers	USA	1:50.33
8. Barbara Olmsted, Sheila Taylor	CAN	1:51.03

One and a half hours after being upset in the singles final, Birgit Schmidt teamed with Anke Nothnagel to win a gold medal in the pairs.

1992 Barcelona-Castelldefels T: 18, N: 18, D: 8.7.

1. Ramona Portwich, Anke von Seck (Nothnagel)	GER	1:40.29
2. Agneta Andersson, Susanne Gunnarsson (Wiberg)	SWE	1:40.41
3. Rita Köbán, Éva Dónusz	HUN	1:40.81
4. Sanda Toma, Carmen Simion	ROM	1:42.12
5. Alison Herst, Klari MacAskill	CAN	1:42.14
6. Izabela Dylewska, Elżbieta Urbanczyk	POL	1:42.44
7. Zhao Xiaoli, Ning Menghua	CHN	1:42.46
8. Jeanette Brandstrup Knudsen, Yvonne Brandstrup Knudsen	DEN	1:43.98

1996 Atlanta-Lake Lanier T: 20, N: 20, D: 8.4.

1. Agneta Andersson, Susanne Gunnarsson (Wiberg)	SWE	1:39.329
2. Ramona Portwich, Birgit Fischer	GER	1:39.589
3. Katrin Borchert, Anna Wood (Annemarie Cox)	AUS	1:40.641
4. Rita Köbán, Szilvia Mednyanszki	HUN	1:40.893
5. Marie-Josee Gibeau, Corrina Kennedy	CAN	1:41.313
6. Izaskun Aramburu Balda, Beatriz Manchón Portillo	SPA	1:42.621
7. Izabela Dylewska-Swiatowiak, Elżbieta Urbanczyk	POL	1:42.753
8. Larissa Kosorukova, Natalya Guliy	RUS	1:43.237

Agneta Andersson was 35 years old and Susanne Gunnarsson 32. Both of them won their first medals back in 1984. Andersson brought her Olympic career medal total to seven: 3 gold, 2 silver and 2 bronze. By finishing second, Birgit Fischer raised her medal total to eight (5 gold and 3 silver) despite missing the 1984 Games because of the East German boycott. She matched the Olympic canoeing record set by Swedish great Gert Fredriksson in 1960. Fischer's partner Ramona Portwich, won her fifth medal (3 gold, 2 silver). The bronze medals went to two foreign-born Australians. Anna Wood won a bronze medal for the Netherlands in 1988 and moved to Australia the following year. Katrin Borchert earned a silver medal for Germany in 1992 and emigrated to Australia in February 1994. Although both Wood and Borchert were solidly Australian, they had only nine years residency in the country between them.

2000 Sydney-Penrith T: 13, N: 13, D: 10.1.

1. Birgit Schmidt (Fischer), Katrin Wagner	GER	1:56.996
2. Katalin Kovács, Szilvia Szabó	HUN	1:58.580
3. Beata Sokolowska, Aneta Pastuszka	POL	1:58.784
4. Raluca Ioniță, Mariana Limbau	ROM	1:59.264
5. Caroline Brunet, Karen Furneaux	CAN	2:01.046
6. Katrin Borchert, Anna Wood	AUS	2:01.472
7. María Isabel García Suarez, Belén Sánchez Jiménez	SPA	2:04.208
8. Anna Olsson, Ingela Ericsson	SWE	2:04.574

With this race, 38-year-old Birgit Fischer became the first woman to win two or more medals at four Summer Olympics. She also became only the fourth woman to earn seven career gold medals and, along with swimmer Jenny Thompson, the only woman to win ten medals in a summer sport other than gymnastics.

2004 Athens-Schinias T: 15, N: 15, D: 8.28.

1. Katalin Kovács, Nataša Janić	HUN	1:38.101
2. Birgit Fischer-Schmidt, Carolin Leonhardt	GER	1:39.533
3. Aneta Pastuszka, Beata Sokołowska-Kulesza	POL	1:40.077
4. Xu Linbei, Zhong Hongyan	CHN	1:40.913
5. Beatriz Manchón Portillo, María Teresa Portela Rivas	SPA	1:42.409
6. Delyana Dacheva, Bonka Pindzheva	BUL	1:42.553
7. Caroline Brunet, Mylanie Barré	CAN	1:42.833
8. Sofia Paldanius, Anna Karlsson	SWE	1:43.077

Birgit Fischer, 2004

Fischer was the 'first' woman in any sport to win medals 24 years apart. Between 1980 and 2004 she earned eight gold medals and four silver.

Seventy minutes after winning the K-1 500 event, Nataša Janić joined Katalin Kovács in the K-2 500 final. The Hungarian pair used a late-race charge to edge past eight-time Olympic gold medalist Birgit Fischer and Carolin Leonhardt, preventing Fischer from winning a ninth career gold medal, which would have equaled the record of Soviet gymnast Larysa Latynina as the most successful female Olympian of all time. It was Fischer's fourth silver, and her twelfth overall medal.

2008 Beijing-Shunyi T: 17, N: 17, D: 8.23.

1. Katalin Kovács, Natasa Janics	HUN	1:41.308
2. Beata Mikołajczyk, Aneta Konieczna [Pastuszka]	POL	1:42.092
3. Marie Delattre, Anne-Laure Viard	FRA	1:42.128
4. Fanny Fischer, Nicole Reinhardt	GER	1:42.899
5. Shinobu Kitamoto, Mikiko Takeya	JPN	1:43.291
6. Hannah Davis, Lyndsie Fogarty	AUS	1:43.969
7. Anne Rikala, Jenni Honkanen-Mikkonen	FIN	1:44.176
8. Michala Strnadová, Jana Blahová	CZE	1:44.870

Defending Olympic gold medalists and twice world champions Katalin Kovács and Natasa Janics recorded the fastest first-round time and had little difficulty in the final, finishing with a comfortable margin over the bronze medalists of the two previous Olympics, Beata Mikołajczyk and Aneta Konieczna. Twice world champion bronze medalists Marie Delattre and Anne-Laure Viard edged out the reigning world champions Fanny Fischer and Nicole Reinhardt to finish third.

KAYAK FOURS 500 METERS

1896–1980 not held

1984 Los Angeles-Lake Casitas T: 7, N: 7, D: 8.11.

1. ROM	Agafia Constantin [Buhaev], Nastasia Ionescu, Tecla Maninescu, Maria Ştefan [Mihoroanu]	1:38.34
2. SWE	Agneta Andersson, Anna Olsson, Eva Karlsson, Susanne Wiberg	1:38.87
3. CAN	Alexandra Barre, Lucie Guay, Susan Holloway, Barbara Olmsted	1:39.40
4. USA	Sheila Conover, Shirley Dery, Leslie Klein, Ann Turner	1:40.49
5. GER	Josefa Idem, Regina Schmidt, Barbara Schüttpelz, Judith Skolnik	1:42.68
6. NOR	Wenche Legraid, Kari Ofstad, Ingeborg Rasmussen, Anne Wahl	1:42.97
7. GBR	Janine Lawler, A. Lucy Perrett, Lesley Smither, Deborah Watson	1:46.30

1988 Seoul T: 13, N: 13, D: 10.1.

1. GDR	Birgit Schmidt (Fischer), Anke Nothnagel, Ramona Portwich, Heike Singer	1:40.78
2. HUN	Erika Géczi, Erika Mészáros, Éva Rakusz, Rita Kőbán	1:41.88
3. BUL	Vania Gesheva, Diana Paliiska, Ogniana Petkova, Borislava Ivanova	1:42.63
4. SOV	Irma Salomykova, Irina Khmelevskaya, Aleksandra Apanovich, Nadezhda Kovalevich	1:44.26
5. GER	Josefa Idem, Claudia Österheld, Andrea Martin, Ruth Domgörgen	1:45.62
6. SWE	Anna Olsson, Agneta Andersson, Susanne Wiberg, Liselotte Olsson	1:45.67
7. DEN	Yvonne Brandstrup Knudsen, Susanne Sanggaard Petersen, Jeanette Brandstrup Knudsen, Birgitte Lynning Froberg	1:47.10
8. POL	Bozena Ksiazek, Jolanta Lukaszewicz, Elżbieta Urbanczyk, Katarzyna Weiss	1:47.40

1992 Barcelona-Castelldefels T: 16, N: 16, D: 8.8.

1. HUN	Éva Dónusz, Kinga Czigány, Rita Kőbán, Erika Mészáros	1:38.32
2. GER	Katrin Borchert, Ramona Portwich, Birgit Schmidt (Fischer), Anke von Seck (Nothnagel)	1:38.47
3. SWE	Agneta Andersson, Maria Haglund, Anna Olsson, Susanne Rosenqvist	1:39.79
4. ROM	Viorica Iordache, Claudia Nicula, Carmen Simion, Sanda Toma	1:41.02
5. CHN	Ning Menghua, Wang Jing, Wen Yanfang, Zhao Xiaoli	1:41.12
6. CAN	Caroline Brunet, Alison Herst, Klari MacAskill, Kevyn Stafford	1:42.28
7. USA	Sheila Conover, Alexandra Harbold, Cathy Marino, Traci Phillips	1:43.00
8. AUS	Denise Cooper, Lynda Lehmann, Gayle Mayes, Anna Wood	1:43.88

The Hungarians finally defeated the Germans after four years of finishing second behind them in every major competition. Gold medal winner Erika Mészáros was the daughter of György Mészáros, who had won a silver in the 1960 kayak pairs 1000 meters. With this race Birgit Fischer raised her Olympic medal total to six—four gold and two silver—while Anke von Seck won her first silver to go with her three golds.

1996 Atlanta-Lake Lanier T: 16; N: 16; D: 8.3.

1. GER	Ramona Portwich, Manuela Mucke, Birgit Schmidt (Fischer), Anett Schuck	1:31.077
2. SWI	Daniela Baumer, Sabine Eichenberger, Ingrid Haralamow, Gabi Mueller	1:32.701
3. SWE	Agneta Andersson, Ingela Ericsson, Anna Olsson, Susanne Rosenqvist	1:32.917
4. CHN	Xian Bangdi, Gao Beibei, Dong Ying, Zhang Qin	1:33.089
5. CAN	Marie-Josee Gibeau, Alison Herst, Klari Macaskill, Corrina Kennedy	1:33.093
6. SPA	Izaskun Aramburu Balda, Beatriz Manchón Portillo, Ana María Penas Balchada, Belén Sánchez Jiménez	1:33.577
7. RUS	Olga Tishchenko, Tatyana Tishchenko, Larissa Kosorukova, Natalya Guliy	1:34.345
8. AUS	Natalie Hunter, Lynda Lehmann, Yanda Nossiter, Shelley Oates	1:34.673

Birgit Fischer became the first woman in any sport to win gold medals 16 years apart. Her first Olympic victory came in the 1980 Moscow Games in the K-1 event.

2000 Sydney-Penrith T: 10, N: 10, D: 9.30.

1. GER	Birgit Schmidt (Fischer), Manuela Mucke, Anett Schuck, Katrin Wagner	1:34.532
2. HUN	Rita Kőbán, Katalin Kovács, Szilvia Szabó, Erzsébet Viski	1:34.946
3. ROM	Raluca Ioniţă, Mariana Limbau, Elena Radu, Sanda Toma	1:37.010
4. POL	Aneta Michalak, Aneta Pastuszka, Joanna Skowron, Beata Sokolowska	1:37.076
5. UKR	Hanna Balbunova, Olena Cherevatova, Natalia Fiklisova, Mariya Ralcheva	1:37.544
6. BLR	Alesya Bakunova, Yelena Bet, Nataliya Bondarenko, Svetlana Vakula	1:37.748
7. RUS	Nataliya Guly, Yelena Tissina, Olga Tishchenko, Galina Poryvayeva	1:38.624
8. SPA	Izaskun Aramburu Balda, Beatriz Manchón Portillo, Ana María Penas Balchada, Belén Sánchez Jiménez	1:33.577

In 2000, three women, swimmer Dara Torres, rower Elisabeta Lipă and basketball player Teresa Edwards, matched Birgit Fischer's record of winning gold medals 16 years apart. But with this race, Fischer moved ahead again by becoming the first woman in any sport to earn gold medals 20 years apart. She also became the first woman to win a gold medal in five different Olympic Games. For her part, Rita Kőbán's silver medal brought her career medal total to six: 2 gold, 3 silver and 1 bronze.

2004 Athens-Schinias T: 10, N: 10, D: 8.27.

1. GER	Birgit Fischer-Schmidt, Maike Nollen, Katrin Wagner, Carolin Leonhardt	1:34.340
2. HUN	Katalin Kovács, Szilvia Szabó, Erzsébet Viski, Kinga Bóta	1:34.536
3. UKR	Inna Osipenko, Tetiana Teklyan-Semykina, Hanna Balabanova, Olena Cherevatova	1:36.192
4. POL	Karolina Sadalska, Joanna Skowroń, Małgorzata Czajczyńska, Aneta Michalak-Białkowska	1:36.376
5. SPA	María Isabel García Suárez, Beatriz Manchón Portillo, Jana Smidaková Krompolcova, María Teresa Portela Rivas	1:37.908
6. AUS	Chantal Meek, Amanda Rankin, Kate Barclay, Lisa Oldenhof	1:38.116
7. CHN	Xu Linbei, Zhong Hongyan, He Jing, Gao Yi	1:38.144
8. CAN	Karen Furneaux, Carrie Lightbound, Kamini Jain, Jillian D'Alessio	1:39.952

Seven-time gold medalist Birgit Fischer came out of retirement at the age of 42 to compete in the Athens Games. In the final, the Hungarians held a slight lead at the halfway marker, but the Germans edged past them for the win. With this victory, Fischer became the first woman in any sport to earn medals 24 years apart.

2008 Beijing-Shunyi T: 10, N: 10, D: 8.22.

1. GER	Fanny Fischer, Nicole Reinhardt, Katrin Wagner-Augustin, Conny Wassmuth	1:32.231
2. HUN	Katalin Kovács, Gabriella Szabó, Danuta Kozák, Natasa Janics	1:32.971
3. AUS	Lisa Oldenhof, Hannah Davis, Chantal Meek, Lyndsie Fogarty	1:34.704
4. POL	Beata Mikołajczyk, Aneta Konieczna [Pastuszka], Edyta Dzieniszewska, Dorota Kuczkowska	1:34.752
5. SPA	Beatriz Manchón Portillo, Jana Smidaková, Sonia Molanes Costa, María Teresa Portela Rivas	1:35.366
6. JPN	Shinobu Kitamoto, Ayaka Kuno, Mikiko Takeya, Yumiko Suzuki	1:36.465
7. SAF	Michele Eray, Carol Joyce, Nicola Mocke, Jennifer Hodson	1:36.724
8. ITA	Stefania Cicali, Alessandra Galiotto, Fabiana Sgroi, Alice Fagioli	1:36.770

Germany and Hungary had finished in the top two at three of the last four Olympics and the last two world championships (with Hungary beating Germany for the 2006 world title, and Germany beating Hungary in 2007). In Beijing both teams won their first-round heats easily to advance to the final. There Germany took the lead early in the race and maintained the advantage through the finish, winning their fourth straight Olympic gold medal in the event.

KAYAK SLALOM SINGLES

1896–1968 not held

1972 Munich-Augsburg C: 22, N: 10, D: 8.30.

		TIME	PENALTIES	PTS
1. Angelika Bahmann	GDR	5:04.50	60	364.50
2. Gisela Grothaus	GER	5:38.15	60	398.15
3. Magdalena Wunderlich	GER	5:40.50	60	400.50
4. Maria Ćwiertniewicz	POL	5:42.30	90	432.30
5. Kunegunda Godawska	POL	6:21.05	60	441.05
6. Victoria Brown	GBR	5:53.71	90	443.71
7. Ulrike Deppe	GER	6:06.44	90	456.44
8. Bohumila Kapplova	CZE	6:00.16	100	460.16

1976–1988 not held

1992 Barcelona-Seu d'Urgell C: 36, N: 13, D: 8.1.

		TIME	PENALTIES	PTS
1. Elisabeth Micheler	GER	2:06.41	0	126.41
2. Danielle Woodward	AUS	2:08.27	0	128.27
3. Dana Chladek	USA	2:06.75	5	131.75
4. Eva Roth	GER	2:07.29	5	132.29
5. Marianne Agulhon	FRA	2:12.89	0	132.89
6. Kordula Striepecke	GER	2:09.49	5	134.49
7. Zdenka Grossmannová	CZE	2:10.79	5	135.79
8. Joanne Woods	CAN	2:08.06	10	138.06

The defending world champion, Micheler, was born and raised in Augsburg, site of the 1972 Olympic whitewater competition. Silver medalist Woodward was a detective with Australia's federal police.

Gilda Montenegro of Costa Rica accumulated 470 penalty points on her first run, then spent most of the second run upside-down before giving up with 11 gates to go. At one point, Montenegro hit her head on the bottom of the course with such force that her helmet cracked. Some observers wondered how Montenegro could have qualified for the Olympics. In fact, she didn't. She was working as a raft guide for Rafael Gallo, who happened to be the manager of the Costa Rican canoe team. One month before the Barcelona Games, Gallo learned that Costa Rica had been awarded an extra entry. Gallo offered the place to Montenegro even though she had never trained for slalom. Montenegro was so shaken by her Olympic experience that she didn't get into a slalom boat again for a year and a half. Then she decided to try to return to the Olympics in 1996 and complete a run without missing a gate. She succeded on her second run and placed 28th of 30, ahead of paddlers from Macedonia and Latvia. She also married men's gold medalist Oliver Fix.

1996 Atlanta-Ocoee River C: 30, N: 18, D: 7.27.

		TIME	PENALTIES	PTS
1. Štěpánka Hilgertová	CZE	2:44.49	5	169.49
2. Dana Chladek	USA	2:44.49	5	169.49
3. Myriam Fox-Jérusalmi	FRA	2:46.00	5	171.00
4. Cristina Giai Pron	ITA	2:46.84	5	171.84
5. Gabriela Broskova	SLV	2:47.57	5	172.57
6. Anne Boixel	FRA	2:42.79	10	172.79
7. Cathy Hearn	USA	2:53.03	0	173.03
8. Margaret Langford	CAN	2:48.59	5	173.59

Both the gold and silver medals went to athletes born in Czechoslovakia. Dana Chladek moved with her family to the United States when she was five years old. Chladek and Štěpánka Hilgertová finished in a tie, but Hilgertová's non-counting second run was far better than Chladek's non-counting first run, during which she capsized, missed four gates and placed last. Lynn Simpson of Great Britain, the world champion and pre-Olympic favorite, flipped during her first run. Her second run would have won the gold medal, but she just missed the eleventh gate and ended up in 23rd place. Although the course was not unusually difficult, the water was strong and turbulent and only six of the sixty runs were clear.

2000 Sydney-Penrith C: 20, N: 16, D: 9.18.

		TIME	PENALTIES	PTS
1. Štěpánka Hilgertová	CZE	4:07.04	0	247.04
2. Brigitte Guibal	FRA	4:07.88	4	251.88
3. Anne-Lise Bardet	FRA	4:14.77	0	254.77
4. Elena Kaliska	SLV	4:11.95	4	255.95
5. Irene Pavelková	CZE	4:14.11	2	256.11
6. Mandy Planert	GER	4:13.85	4	257.85
7. Rebecca Giddens	USA	4:14.69	4	258.69
8. Danielle Woodward	AUS	4:17.89	4	261.89

Defending champion Štěpánka Hilgertová paddled two flawless runs in both the qualifying round and the final. She trailed Brigitte Guibal by .23 points after the first run of the final, but her second run was more than three seconds faster than the other finalists and she scored a clear victory. When asked if she had been motivated by the $24,000 bonus she earned for winning, Hilgertová replied, "I would compete even if there were no bonus. First, I like winning, and second, as any woman, I am vain, and I like to be the center of attention." Back in Prague, Hilgertová celebrated by taking a bath in a tub filled with 160 bottles of champagne.

2004 Athens C: 19, N: 16, D: 8.18.

		TIME	PENALTIES	PTS
1. Elena Kaliská	SVK	3:30.03	0	210.03
2. Rebecca Giddens	USA	3:34.62	0	214.62
3. Helen Reeves	GBR	3:32.77	6	218.77
4. Peggy Dickens	FRA	3:32.80	6	218.80
5. Štěpánka Hilgertová	CZE	3:36.75	4	220.75
6. Nagwa El Desouki	SWI	3:43.04	2	225.04
7. Louise Natoli	AUS	3:47.44	0	227.44
8. Maria Cristina Giai Pron	ITA	3:45.36	4	229.36

Elena Kaliská finished at the top of the 2000, 2001 and 2003 world cup standings, despite never having won a world championship title. In Athens she produced two near-perfect runs, finishing more than four and a half seconds ahead of 2002 world champion Rebecca Giddens.

2008 Beijing-Shunyi C: 21, N: 21, D: 8.15.

		SEMI-FINAL RUN		FINAL RUN		TOTAL POINTS
1. Elena Kaliská	SVK	1:37.13	0	1:35.51	0	192.64
2. Jacqueline Lawrence	AUS	1:39.40	4	1:43.54	0	206.94
3. Violetta Oblinger-Peters	AUT	1:48.65	2	1:40.12	4	214.77
4. Yurika Takeshita	JPN	1:47.86	0	1:47.44	4	219.30
5. Agnieszka Stanuch	POL	1:54.46	2	1:42.62	2	221.08
6. Ariane Herde	HOL	1:53.60	4	1:48.39	6	231.99
7. Emilie Fer	FRA	1:36.50	2	1:39.46	54	251.96
8. Heather Corrie	USA	1:52.51	2	1:44.37	52	270.88

Defending Olympic champion Elena Kaliská remained the person to beat in the kayak slalom singles event, having won the 2005 world championship and heading the 2005 and 2006 world cup standings. Her path to the gold medal was made easier when her main challenger, 25-year-old reigning world champion Jennifer Bongardt of Germany, missed two gates on her semi-final run and failed to qualify for the final.

Kaliská led coming into the final and produced two flawless runs, finishing with a lead of more than 14 points ahead. In second place after her first run, the relatively unknown Jacqui Lawrence captured the silver medal after world number one Štřpánka Hilgertová capsized and finished ninth. Lawrence, who grew up on a cattle farm in New South Wales, had earned a place in Beijing by beating her sister Kate in the Australian Olympic trials.

Chapter 8 **Cycling**

MEN	WOMEN
Match Sprint	Match Sprint
4000-Meter Team Pursuit	Omnium
Team Sprint	Road Time Trial
Keirin	Road Race
Omnium	Mountain Bike Cross-Country
Road Time Trial	BMX Race
Road Race	Discontinued Events
Mountain Bike Cross-Country	
BMX Race	
Discontinued Events	

Traditionally there have been two types of Olympic cycling contests: those held on a track, and those held on the road. In 1996 a third type of cycling was added to the program: mountain bike racing. Another major change that occurred in 1996 was the inclusion of professional cyclists for the first time. In 2008 BMX racing was included for the first time.

For 2012, the lineup of Olympic track cycling events has undergone another significant overhaul, with men's and women's Individual Pursuit and Points Races and men's Madison events dropped to make room for women's Team Pursuit, Team Sprint and Keirin, and the addition of a new Omnium event consisting of six competitions, including an individual pursuit and points race. In addition, nations will now be limited to a single rider in the Sprint, Keirin and Omnium events.

MEN

MATCH SPRINT

The individual match sprint, or scratch, is a tactical, and sometimes violent, race. Between 1906 and 2000 this event was held over 1000 meters, however since 2004 the match races were have been 750 meters. For the first 550 meters the cyclists circle the track, carefully maneuvering for position, usually trying to avoid taking the lead so that they can take advantage of the slipstream created by the leader. Then they sprint for the finish line. Times are usually taken only for the final 200 meters.

Current rules provide for a qualifying round to be held over 875 meters with a flying start. The racers are then seeded based on their times, and a tournament begins. Winners of the opening races advance to a round of 16; losers compete in a *repêechage* round. There is also a *repêechage* round for the losers in the round of 16.

Since 1928 separate races have been held to determine first place and third place. Since 1976 all four defeated quarterfinalists have raced off for places 5 through 8.

1896 Athens C: 4, N: 3, D: 4.11.
(2000 Meters)

1. Paul Masson	FRA	4:58.2
2. Stamatios Nikolopoulos	GRE	5:00.2
3. Léon Flameng	FRA	—
4. Joseph Rosemeyer	GER	—

1900 Paris C: 69, N: 5, D: 9.13.
(2000 Meters)

1. Georges Taillandier	FRA	2:52.0	(last 200 meters 13.0)
2. Fernand Sanz	FRA	—	
3. John Henry Lake	USA	—	

Taillandier defeated Sanz by one half length, with Lake another half length behind.

1904 not held

1906 Athens C: 28, N: 10, D: 4.23.
(1000 Meters)

1. Francesco Verri	ITA	1:42.2
2. Herbert Bouffler	GBR	—
3. Eugene Debougnie	BEL	—

1908 London C: 40, N: 9, D: 7.16.
(1000 Meters)

The final was declared void because the time limit was exceeded. The finalists were: 1. Maurice Schilles (FRA), 2. Benjamin Jones (GBR). DNF: Victor Johnson (GBR) and Clarence Kingsbury (GBR).

Johnson suffered a punctured tire shortly after the start. The other three crawled around the track, carefully jockeying for position. At the beginning of the last bank, Kingsbury also punctured. Then the remaining two raced to the finish line, with Schilles winning by inches. However, the time limit of 1 minute 45 seconds had been exceeded, so the race was declared void. Much to the surprise of most of those present, the judges of the National Cyclists' Union refused to allow the race to be rerun.

1912 not held

1920 Antwerp C: 37, N: 11, D: 8.9.
(1000 Meters)

1. Mouritius "Maurice" Peeters	HOL	13.0	(last 200 meters)
2. Thomas Johnson	GBR	—	
3. Harry Ryan	GBR	—	

Peeters defeated Johnson by inches with Ryan three lengths behind. At age 38, Peeters was the oldest cycling gold medalist in Olympic history. Four years later he won a bronze in the tandem event to become the sport's oldest medalist.

1924 Paris C: 31, N: 17, D: 7.27.
(1000 Meters)

1. Lucien Michard	FRA	12.8	(last 200 meters)
2. Jacob Meijer	HOL	—	
3. Jean Cugnot	FRA	—	

1928 Amsterdam C: 18, N: 18, D: 8.7.

1. Roger Beaufrand	FRA	13.2	(last 200 meters)
2. Antoine Mazairac	HOL	—	
3. Willy Falck-Hansen	DEN		
4. Hans Bernhardt	GER		

5. Jerzy Koszutski (POL), Antonio Malvassi (ARG), Jack Standen (AUS), Yves van Massenhove (BEL)

1932 Los Angeles C: 9, N: 9, D: 8.3.
(1000 Meters)

		1ST RACE	2ND RACE	3RD RACE
1. Jacobus van Egmond	HOL	—	12.6	12.6
2. Louis Chaillot	FRA	12.5	—	—
3. Bruno Pellizzari	ITA			
4. Edgar "Dunc" Gray	AUS			

5. Ernest Chambers (GBR), Willy Gervin (DEN), Leo Marchiori (CAN), Robert Thomas (USA)

Beginning in 1932, it was necessary to win two out of three races. Louis Chaillot won the first race of the final by inches. But Jacobus van Egmond set the pace in the second, leading all the way to the finish. He then won the tie-breaker by a foot. Dunc Gray withdrew from the bronze-medal race in order to save himself for the time trial the same evening.

1936 Berlin C: 20, N: 20, D: 8.7.
(1000 Meters)

		1ST RACE	2ND RACE
1. Toni Merkens	GER	11.8	11.8
2. Arie van Vliet	HOL	—	—
3. Louis Chaillot	FRA		
4. Benedetto Pola	ITA		

5. Henri Collard (BEL), Edgar "Dunc'" Gray (AUS), Carl Magnussen (DEN), Werner Wagelin (SWI)

As Arie van Vliet began to overtake Toni Merkens in the first race of the final, the German swerved to his right and blatantly interfered with his rival. No foul was called, and a disconcerted van Vliet lost the second race as well. The Dutch team protested. In a bizarre twist, cycling officials decided not to disqualify Merkens, but to fine him 100 marks instead. The next day, van Vliet returned to win the 1000-meter time trial. Merkens died toward the end of World War II after being wounded while fighting the Russians.

1948 London C: 23, N: 23, D: 8.9.
(1000 Meters)

		1ST RACE	2ND RACE
1. Mario Ghella	ITA	12.2	12.0
2. Reginald Harris	GBR	—	—
3. Axel Schandorff	DEN		
4. Charles Bazzano	AUS		

5. John Heid (USA), Hernán Masanés Gimeno (CHI), Luis Rocca (URU), Emile Van de Velde (BEL)

In 1940 Reg Harris was serving as a tank driver with the 10th Hussars in North Africa when his tank was destroyed by German fire. Harris was the only survivor and spent the next year in military hospitals and convalescent homes before being discharged as medically unfit. Fortunately he was fit enough to return to his main passion: cycling. By the time of the London Olympics, Harris was the reigning world sprint champion. However he was struck from the British team a few days before the Olympics because he insisted on staying in his hometown of Manchester instead of training with the rest of the team in London. After a public outcry, Harris was reinstated, but not until he had won a ride-off against his tandem partner, Alan Bannister. In the final he faced 20-year-old Mario Ghella, a student from Turin. In the first race, Ghella caught Harris in a moment of inattention with 350 meters to go, slipped inside of him, and won easily. In the second race, Ghella fought off three challenges from Harris to earn a dramatic and emotional victory.

Harris immediately turned professional and won the professional world sprint title four times. He retired from competition in 1957, but returned 14 years later and, incredibly, in 1974 he won the British sprint championships at the age of 54. Harris was remarkably well-known considering that he excelled at a sport which was not terribly popular in Great Britain. His name became synonymous with cycling speed and any youngster who rode his bicycle fast would be good-naturedly nicknamed, "Reg." One day when Harris was in his mid-sixties he was cycling on the streets when, as aggressive as ever, he jumped a red light and was pulled over by a police officer. The officer approached Harris and said, "Who do you think you are, Reg Harris?"

Harris suffered a stroke while riding the country lanes of Cheshire and died June 22, 1992. He was 72 years old. A bronze statue of Harris can be seen in Manchester, overlooking the south curve of Britain's first indoor velodrome.

1952 Helsinki C: 27, N: 27, D: 7.31.
(1000 Meters)

1. Enzo Sacchi	ITA	12.0
2. Lionel Cox	AUS	—
3. Werner Potzernheim	GER	

4. Cyril Peacock (GBR), Raymond Robinson (SAF), Béla Szekeres (HUN)

1956 Melbourne C: 19, N: 19, D: 12.6. WR: 11.0 (Arie van Vliet)
(1000 Meters)

		1ST RACE	2ND RACE
1. Michel Rousseau	FRA	11.4	11.4
2. Guglielmo Presenti	ITA	—	—
3. Richard Ploog	AUS		
4. Warren Johnston	NZL		

5. Jack Disney (USA), Ladislav Fouček (CZE), Boris Romanov (SOV/RUS), Thomas Shardelow (SAF)

1960 Rome C: 30, N: 18, D: 8.29. WR: 10.8 (Antonio Maspes)
(1000 Meters)

		1ST RACE	2ND RACE
1. Sante Gaiardoni	ITA	11.1	11.5
2. Leo Sterckx	BEL	—	—
3. Valentino Gasparella	ITA		
4. Ronald Baensch	AUS		

5. Anesio Argenton (BRA), Lloyd Binch (GBR), Antoine Pellegrina (FRA), August Rieke (GER)

For the third straight time, the Olympic sprint championship was won by the reigning world champion. The 5-foot 6-inch, 174-pound Gaiardoni had already won the 1000-meter time trial when he swept through the sprint competition without being seriously challenged. Gaiardoni is the only cyclist to win both the sprint and the time trial.

1964 Tokyo C: 39, N: 22, D: 10.19. WR: 10.8 (Antonio Maspes)
(1000 Meters)

		1ST RACE	2ND RACE
1. Giovanni Pettenella	ITA	13.85	13.69
2. Sergio Bianchetto	ITA	—	—
3. Daniel Morelon	FRA		
4. Pierre Trentin	FRA		

5. Willi Fuggerer GER), Patrick Sercú (BEL), Mario Vanegas Jiménez (COL), Zbyslaw Zajaç (POL)

In the semifinals Pettenella and Trentin set an Olympic record by standing still for 21 minutes 57 seconds.

1968 Mexico City C: 46, N: 27, D: 10.19. WR: 10.61 (Omar Pkhakadze)
(1000 Meters)

		1ST RACE	2ND RACE
1. Daniel Morelon	FRA	11.27	10.68
2. Giordano Turrini	ITA	—	—
3. Pierre Trentin	FRA		
4. Omar Pkhakadze	SOV/GEO		

5. Jürgen Barth (GER), Johannes Jansen (HOL), Leijn Loevesijn (HOL), Dino Verzini (ITA)

The tactical highlight of the competition came in the first race of the quarterfinal contest between Dino Verzini and Omar Pkhakadze. The first time out they stood and watched each other until a restart was ordered. The second attempt saw them both stop again, with Pkhakadze slipping off the banking and causing both of them to slide into the infield. The next restart, the two cyclists stopped for 4 minutes 47 seconds before continuing. This time they made it all the way to the finish with Verzini in the lead. However, Pkhakadze won the next two races and advanced to the semifinals, where he lost two out of three to Daniel Morelon, the eventual gold medalist. Morelon was a police officer from Bourg-en-Bresse, northeast of Lyon.

1972 Munich C: 51, N: 29, D: 9.2. WR: 10.61 (Omar Pkhakadze)
(1000 Meters)

		1ST RACE	2ND RACE
1. Daniel Morelon	FRA	11.69	11.25
2. John Nicholson	AUS	—	—
3. Omar Pkhakadze	SOV/GEO		
4. Klaas Balk	HOL		

5. Niels Fredborg (DEN), Hans-Jürgen Geschke (GDR), Massimo Marino (ITA), Peter van Doorn (HOL)

1976 Montreal C: 25, N: 25, D: 7.24. WR: 10.61 (Omar Pkhakadze)
(1000 Meters)

		1ST RACE	2ND RACE	3RD RACE
1. Anton Tkáč	CZE/SLV	10.78	—	11.17
2. Daniel Morelon	FRA	—	11.58	—
3. Hans-Jürgen Geschke	GDR			
4. Dieter Berkmann	GER			
5. Serhei Kravtsov	SOV/UKR			
6. Yoshika Cho	JPN			
7. Niels Fredborg	DEN			
8. Giorgio Rossi	ITA			

This was the first time that Olympic cycling events were held indoors. The Czechoslovakian team got off to a bad start at the Montreal Olympics when all of their wheels and spare tires were inadvertently picked up by garbage collectors and fed into a trash compactor. The final was held the day before the 32nd birthday of Daniel Morelon, the sentimental as well as the betting favorite. But Anton Tkáč, a pipe fitter from Bratislava, jumped early in the tie-breaker, took a five-length lead, and was too strong to be caught. In the first race Tkáč had crossed the finish line at almost 42 miles per hour. Morelon's second-place finish earned him his fifth Olympic medal: two golds, one silver, and one bronze in the sprint, and one more gold in the tandem.

1980 Moscow C: 15, N: 15, D: 7.26. WR: 10.61 (Omar Pkhakadze)
(1000 Meters)

		1ST RACE	2ND RACE	3RD RACE
1. Lutz Hesslich	GDR	11.40	—	12.01
2. Yave Cahard	FRA	—	10.86	—
3. Sergei Kopylov	SOV/RUS			
4. Anton Tkáč	CZE/SLV			
5. Henrik Salee	DEN			
6. Heinz Isler	SWI			
7. Kenrick Tucker	AUS			
8. Octavio Dazzan	ITA			

1984 Los Angeles-Carson C: 33, N: 25, D: 8.3. WR: 10.249 (Sergei Kopylov)
(1000 Meters)

		1ST RACE	2ND RACE
1. Mark Gorski	USA	10.49	10.95
2. Nelson Vails	USA	—	—
3. Tsutomu Sakamoto	JPN		
4. Philippe Vernet	FRA		
5. Gerhard Scheller	GER		
6. Marcelo Alexandre	ARG		
7. Kenrick Tucker	AUS		
8. Fredy Schmidtke	GER		

With the winners of the last four world championships, Lutz Hesslich and Sergei Kopylov, boycotted out of the Olympics, the final became an all-American contest.

In 1981, Nelson Vails, the youngest of ten children and a father himself since age 15, was living in Harlem, working eight hours a day as a bicycle messenger in Manhattan and training two hours a night in New York City's Central Park. In 1981, Mark Gorski had given up on cycling following a bad spill that left him with a broken collarbone and a severe concussion. Gorski returned to racing and, in 1983, defeated Kopylov three times. He had also defeated the fast-improving Vails three times before their Olympic encounter. After making it four in a row for the gold medal, Gorski took his 13-month-old son, Alexander, along with him on his victory lap.

1988 Seoul C: 25, N: 25, D: 9.24. WR: 10.118 (Michael Hübner)
(1000 Meters)

		1ST RACE	2ND RACE
1. Lutz Hesslich	GDR	13.98	11.82
2. Nikolai Kovsh	SOV/RUS	—	—
3. Gary Neiwand	AUS		
4. Edward Alexander	GBR		
5. Vratislav Šuster	CZE		
6. Erik Schoefs	BEL		
7. Frank Weber	GER		
8. Maxwell Cheesman	TRI		

In the last three world championships, all three medals had gone to East Germans. In the Olympics, however, each nation is allowed only one entrant. Thus it came as no surprise that Hesslich, having defeated his friend and rival Michael Hübner to qualify for the East German team, was not seriously challenged in Seoul.

1992 Barcelona C: 23, N: 23, D: 7.31. WR: 10.118 (Michael Hübner)
(1000 Meters)

		1ST RACE	2ND RACE
1. Jens Fiedler	GER	10.995	10.778
2. Gary Neiwand	AUS	—	—
3. Curt Harnett	CAN	10.930	11.120
4. Roberto Chiappa	ITA	—	—
5. Ken Carpenter	USA	11.648	
6. José Lovito Morales	ARG	—	
7. Nikolai Kovsh	RUS	—	
8. José Moreno Periñán	SPA	—	

Once again the Olympic competition suffered from the fact that the two leading sprinters, 1989 and 1990 world champion Bill Huck and 1991 world champion Jens Fiedler, were both from Germany and each nation was only allowed one entrant. It was the 22-year-old Fiedler

Gary Neiwand and Jens Fiedler, 1992
Battling for the lead in the match sprint.

who won the right to compete. Everything went according to form in Barcelona. The four cyclists who recorded the fastest times in the qualifying time trial placed in the same order in the end; of the eight match-ups to be decided by the best two out of three races, none required a third race. However, the final itself was full of drama. It took a photo-finish camera to decide the winner of the first race. The photo showed that Fiedler had held off Neiwand's come-from-behind effort by about two inches. In the second race, when Fiedler tried to move ahead in the middle of the race, Neiwand moved up the banking, forcing Fiedler to the outside of the track. With one 250-meter lap to go, Fiedler cut in front, forcing Neiwand to backpedal and drop back four lengths. Neiwand fought back furiously and crossed the line first. After a five-minute delay it was announced that Neiwand had been "declassed for dangerous riding" and that Fiedler was the winner. Despite their bitter struggle, Fiedler immediately consoled the distraught Neiwand and the two embraced on the infield.

1996 Atlanta-Stone Mountain C: 24, N: 16, D: 7.28. WR: 9.865 (Curtis Harnett)
(1000 Meters)

		1ST RACE	2ND RACE
1. Jens Fiedler	GER	10.664	11.074
2. Marty Nothstein	USA	—	—
3. Curtis Harnett	CAN	10.947	10.949
4. Gary Neiwand	AUS	—	—
5. Darryn Hill	AUS	11.027	
6. Frédéric Magne	FRA	—	
7. Eyk Pokorny	GER	—	
8. Florian Rousseau	FRA	—	

Three or four different cyclists were given a good chance to win the gold medal. Defending champion Jens Fiedler was not one of them. Since the 1992 Olympics, he had not placed higher than fourth at a world championship. In the meantime, Gary Neiwand won the world title in 1993, Marty Nothstein in 1994 (the first American to do so since 1912) and Darryn Hill in 1995. In Atlanta Nothstein eliminated Hill in the quarterfinals. In the first semifinal, Fiedler took two straight from Neiwand, just as he did in the 1992 final. In the second semi, Nothstein won two in a row against Harnett. Before the final, Fiedler communicated by telephone with his old East German coach, Carsten Schmarkus. Together they constructed a plan to take advantage of the short track (250 meters) and negate Notrhstein's power by racing from the front. In the first race, Fiedler led and stayed in front the entire way. Nothstein caught him at the line and it was impossible to tell who had won. The photo gave Fiedler the victory by one centimeter. Nothstein led the second race. Fiedler jumped him early, diving into the lead with 1½ laps to go. He fought off Nothstein's challenge and won by about 15 inches (38 centimeters).

2000 Sydney C: 19, N: 14, D: 9.20. WR: 9.865 (Curtis Harnett)
(1000 Meters)

		1ST RACE	2ND RACE
1. Marty Nothstein	USA	10.874	11.066
2. Florian Rousseau	FRA	—	—
3. Jens Fiedler	GER	10.732	10.918
4. Laurent Gané	FRA	—	—
5. Jan van Eijden	GER	11.040	
6. José Villanueva	SPA	—	
7. Sean Eadie	AUS	—	
8. Craig MacLean	GBR	—	

The semifinals brought together four match sprint world champions: Jens Fiedler (1991), Marty Nothstein (1994), Florian Rousseau (1997 and 1998) and Laurent Gané (1999). The first semi matched Fiedler, who had placed second at the last three world championships, and Nothstein, who had been waiting for this day for four years. "Jens beat me in '96," explained Nothstein, "and it's been haunting me every day. Every sit-up I did, every pound I lifted, I've been thinking of this race. There's been a lot of sacrifices . . . a lot of tears, a lot of skin lost." In the end, Nothstein defeated Fiedler rather handily, coming from behind on the final turn in both heats. In the other semifinal, Gané won the first race, but Rousseau won the next two to advance to the final. Against Rousseau, Nothstein followed the same strategy he used against Fiedler, moving to the outside on the last turn and powering to victory. Nothstein was the first American cyclist to win a gold medal in an Olympics held outside the United States.

2004 Athens C: 19, N: 13, D: 8.24. WR: 9.865 (Curtis Harnett)
(750 Meters)

		1st Race	2nd Race	3rd Race
1. Ryan Bayley	AUS	—	10.661	10.743
2. Theo Bos	HOL	10.710	—	—
3. René Wolff	GER	10.677	10.612	
4. Laurent Gané	FRA	—	—	
5. Ross Edgar	GBR	11.214		
6. Barry Forde	BAR	—		
7. Damian Zieliński	POL	—		
8. Mickael Bourgain	FRA	—		

Less than three months before the 2004 Olympics, Ryan Bayley and Theo Bos faced each other in the semifinals of the world championships. They split the first two races. In the final heat, Bos rode aggressively, pushing Bayley into the duckboards and causing him to lose momentum in the final turn. Awarded the victory, Bos went on to win his first international title. Facing each other in the Olympic final, two days after Bos' 21st birthday, the two riders again split the first two heats. Bos won the first, edging past Bayley by two centimeters at the finish line, but Bayley responded in the second, surging ahead at the line and lifting his front wheel to win by five centimeters. In the deciding race, Bayley managed a decisive win to become the first Australian rider to win a gold medal in the sprint event.

Despite dating a nutritionist, Bayley was nicknamed "The KFC Kid" in honor of his diet of junk food, fried chicken and fried potatoes. Bayley had a difficult childhood. His father fell into a pit of boiling lime when Bayley was a child, leaving him almost blind and forcing his mother to take multiple jobs to keep the family afloat. Bayley quit school in the 10th grade to concentrate on cycling.

2008 Beijing C: 21, N: 15, D: 8.19. WR: 9.772 (Theo Bos)
(750 Meters)

		1st Race	2nd Race	3rd Race
1. Chris Hoy	GBR	10.228	10.216	
2. Jason Kenny	GBR	—	—	
3. Mickaël Bourgain	FRA	11.047	—	10.560
4. Maximilian Levy	GER	—	10.666	—
5. Kévin Sireau	FRA	10.719		
6. Teun Mulder	HOL	—		
7. Theo Bos	HOL	—		
8. Mohd Azizulhasni Awang	MAL	—		

Athens silver medalist Theo Bos had won the last two world championships, in 2006 and 2007, and looked to be the overwhelming favorite in Beijing. However, in the quarter-finals of the 2008 world championships, five months before the Olympics, he was eliminated by Athens 1-kilometer Time Trial gold medalist Chris Hoy, who went on to win the championship. It was Bos's first world championship or world cup loss since 2005.

By the time they faced each other in the match sprint in Beijing, Hoy had already won gold medals in the Keirin and team sprint events. He set an Olympic record, 9.815, in the qualifying round and had no difficulty reaching the final. Bos made it to the quarter-finals, but was eliminated by double world bronze medalist Mickaël Bourgain, whom Hoy then beat in the semi-final round.

Hoy's opponent in the final was his 20-year-old teammate and fellow team sprint gold medalist Jason Kenny, who had reached the final by beating Germany's Maximilian Levy. Hoy had no difficulty beating his less experienced compatriot to complete a hat trick of all three sprint gold medals in Beijing.

Hoy had been inspired to take up cycling at the age of six after watching the BMX scene in Steven Spielberg's *ET*.

Chris Hoy, 2008
Chris Hoy shows off the three gold medals he earned at the Beijing Olympics.

4000-METER TEAM PURSUIT

In pursuit races, two cyclists or teams of cyclists start off on opposite sides of the track. If one team catches the other, the race is over. Otherwise the winner is the first one to cross the finish line. Two teams take part in the race for first place. Since 1996 the bronze medal has been awarded to the fastest semi-final loser. Places five through eight are determined by times recorded in the quarter-finals or distance covered before being overtaken. For this reason, the times for third through eighth places are often faster than those for first and second. Before the 1992 Olympics official world records could not be set unless there were no other competitors on the track.

The official time is that of the third rider on each team. Riders who took part in preliminary rounds but not in the finals are included in brackets.

1896–1906 not held

1908 London T: 5, N: 5, D: 7.17.
(1810.5 Meters)

1. GBR	Leonard Meredith, Benjamin Jones, Ernest Payne, Clarence Kingsbury	2:18.6
2. GER	Hermann Martens, Bruno Götze, Karl Neumer, Richard Katzer	2:28.6
3. CAN	William Morton, Walter Andrews, Frederick McCarthy, William Anderson	2:29.6
4. HOL	Johannes van Spengen, Antonie Gerrits, Dorotheus Nijland, Gerard Bosch van Drakestein	2:44.0

A few months after winning two gold medals at the Olympics, Ernie Payne signed a contract with the Manchester United soccer team. He played two league games and scored one goal before returning to cycling.

1912 not held

1920 Antwerp T: 8, N: 8, D: 8.10.

1. ITA	Franco Giorgetti, Ruggero Ferrario, Arnaldo Carli, Primo Magnani	5:14.2
2. GBR	Albert White, Thomas Johnson, William Stewart, Cyril Alden	—
3. SAF	James Walker, William Smith, Henry Kaltenbrun, Harry "Sammy" Goosen	—
4. BEL	Albert de Bunne, Charles van Doorselaer, Gustave de Schryver, Jean Janssens	—

The British team was leading when the Italians caught their trail rider, Albert White. White tried to pull wide so that they could pass, but he waited too long. Two Italians passed him on each side, shouting at him as they went by. Great Britain finished first, but Italy filed a protest. One member of the three-man protest jury was British and a second was Italian. Both judges recused themselves and the remaining judge, who was French, voted in favor of the Italians.

1924 Paris T: 10, N: 10, D: 7.27.

1. ITA	Angelo De Martino, Alfredo Dinale, Aleardo Menegazzi, Francesco Zucchetti	5:15.0
2. POL	Józef Lange, Jan Lazarski, Tomasz Stankiewicz, Franciszek Szymczyk	—
3. BEL	Léonard Daghelinckx, Henri Hoeveneers, Fernand Saive, Jean van den Bosch	—
4. FRA	Lucien Choury, Joseph Vuillemin, René Hournon, Marcel Renaud	—

The French team set an Olympic record of 5:11.4 in the heats.

1928 Amsterdam T: 12, N: 12, D: 8.7.

1. ITA	Luigi Tasselli, Giacomo Gaioni, Cesare Facciani, Mario Lusiani	5:01.8OR
2. HOL	Adriaan Braspenninx, Jacobus Maas, Johannes Pijnenburg, Piet van der Horst	5:06.2
3. GBR	Frederick Wyld, Leonard Wyld, Percy Wyld, M. George Southall	—
4. FRA	André Aumerle, Octave Dayen, René Brossy, André Trantoul	—

5. BEL: August Meuleman, Yves van Massenhove, Albert Muylle, Jean van Buggenhout; CAN: L.R. Elder, James Davies, A. Houting, William Peden; GER: Josef Steger, Anton Joksch, Kurt Einsiedel, Hans Dornebach; POL: Józef Lange, Artur Reul, Jan Zybert, Józef Oksiutycz

The British team set an Olympic record of 5:11.2 in the quarter finals. Three of the four British riders were the Wyld brothers from Derby: Frank, Leonard, and Percy.

1932 Los Angeles T: 5, N: 5, D: 8.3.

1. ITA	Marco Cimatti, Paolo Pedretti, Alberto Ghilardi, Nino Bosari	4:53.0
2. FRA	Amédée Fournier, René Legrèves, Henri Mouillefarine, Paul Chocque	4:55.7
3. GBR	Ernest Johnson, William Harvell, Frank Southall, Charles Holland	4:56.0
4. CAN	Lewis Rush, Glen Robbins, Russell Hunt, Francis Elliott	6:04.0

The Italian team set an Olympic record of 4:52.9 in the heats.

1936 Berlin T: 13, N: 13, D: 8.8.

1. FRA	Robert Charpentier, Jean Goujan, Guy Lapébie, Roger Le Nizerhy	4:45.0
2. ITA	Bianco Bianchi, Mario Gentili, Armando Latini, Severino Rigoni	4:51.0
3. GBR	Harold Hill, Ernest Johnson, Charles King, Ernest Mills	4:53.6
4. GER	Erich Arndt, Heinz Hasselberg, Heiner Hoffman, Karl Klöckner	4:55.0

The French team set an Olympic record of 4:41.8 in the heats.

1948 London T: 15, N: 15, D: 8.9.

1. FRA	Charles Coste, Serge Blusson, Ferdinand Decanali, Pierre Adam	4:57.8
2. ITA	Arnaldo Benfenati, Guido Bernardi, Anselmo Citterio, Rino Pucci	5:36.7
3. GBR	R. Alan Geldard, Thomas Godwin, David Ricketts, Wilfred Waters	4:55.8
4. URU	Atilio François, Juan De Armas, Luis De Los Santos, Walter Bernatsky	5:04.4

5. AUS: Sidney Patterson, Jim Nestor, Jack Hoobin, Russell Mockridge; BEL: Joseph DeBeukelaere, Maurice Blomme, Lionel van Brabant, Raphael Glorieux; DEN: Max Jorgensen, Borge Gissel, Borge Mortensen, Benny Schnoor; SWI: Walter Bucher, Gaston Gerosa, Eugen Kamber, Hans Pfenninger

1952 Helsinki T: 22, N: 22, D: 7.29.

1. ITA Marino Morettini, Guido Messina, Mino De Rossi, Loris Campana 4:46.1
2. SAF Thomas Shardelow, Alfred Swift, Robert Fowler, George Estman 4:53.6
3. GBR Ronald Stratton, Alan Newton, George Newberry, Donald Burgess 4:51.5
4. FRA Henri Andrieux, Pierre Michel, Jean-Marie Joubert, Claude Brugerolles 4:51.9
5. BEL: Gabriel Glorieux, José Pauwels, Robert Raymond, Paul de Paepe; DEN: Knud Andersen, Edvard Preben Lundgren-Kristensen, Jean Hansen, Bent Jorgensen; HOL: Johannes Plantaz, Adrianus Voorting, Daniel de Groot, Jules Maenen; SWI: Hans Pfenninger, Heini Müller, Max Wirth, Oscar von Büren

1956 Melbourne T: 16, N: 16, D: 12.4.

1. ITA Leandro Faggin, Valentino Gasparella, Antonio Domenicali, Franco Gandini, [Valentino Pizzali] 4:37.4 OR
2. FRA Michel Vermeulin, Jean-Claude Lecante, René Bianchi, Jean Graczyk 4:39.4
3. GBR Donald Burgess, Michael Gambrill, John Geddes, Thomas Simpson 4:42.4
4. SAF Alfred Swift, Robert Fowler, Charles Jonker, Anne-Jan Hettema 4:43.8
5. BEL: André Bar, Gustave de Smet, François de Wagheneire, Guillaume Van Tongerloo; CZE: Jaroslav Cihlar, Jiři Opavsky, Jiři Nouza, František Jursa; NZL: Warwick Dalton, Donald Eagle, Leonard Kent, Neil Ritchie; SOV: Victor Illine, Vladimir Mitine, Rostislav Tchijikov, Eduard Gusev

Great Britain won its sixth straight bronze medal in the team pursuit. One member of the British team, Thomas Simpson, later became the only cyclist to die during the Tour de France.

1960 Rome T: 19, N: 19, D: 8.29.

1. ITA Luigi Arienti, Franco Testa, Mario Vallotto, Marino Vigna 4:30.90
2. GDR Siegfried Köhler, Peter Gröning, Manfred Klieme, Bernd Barleben 4:35.78
3. SOV Stanislav Moskvin, Viktor Romanov, Leonid Kolumbet, Arnold Belgardt 4:34.05
4. FRA Marcel Delattre, Jacques Suire, Guy Claud, Michel Nedelec 4:35.72
5. ARG: Alberto Trillo, Ernesto Contreras, Héctor Acosta, Juan Brotto; CZE: Slavoy Cerny, Ferdinand Duchon, Jan Chlistovsky, Josef Volt; DEN: John Lundgren, Leif Larsen, Jens Sorensen, Kurt Stein; HOL: Jacob Oudkerk, Theodorus Nikkessen, Hendrix Nijdam, Petrus van der Lans

The Italian team set an Olympic record of 4:28.88 in the semifinals.

1964 Tokyo T: 18, N: 18, D: 10.21. WR: 4:26.60 (West Germany)

1. GER Lothar Claesges, Karlheinz Henrichs, Karl Link, Ernst Streng 4:35.67
2. ITA Luigi Roncaglia, Vincenzo Mantovani, Carlo Rancati, Franco Testa 4:35.74
3. HOL Gerard Koel, Hendrik Cornalissen, Jacob Oudkerk, Cornelis Schuuring 4:38.99
4. AUS Kevin Brislin, Robert Baird, Victor Browne, Hendrikus Vogels 4:39.42
5. ARG: Carlos Alvarez, Ernesto Contreras, Juan Alberto Merlos, Alberto Trillo; CZE: Jiři Daler, Antonin Kritz, Jiři Pecka, František Rezac; DEN: Bent Kurt Hansen, Preben Isaksson, Alf Johansen, Kurt Vid Stein; SOV: Dzintars Lacis, Leonid Kolumbet, Stanislav Moskvin, Sergei Terechenkov

The world champion German team broke the Italian pursuit monopoly in dramatic fashion. The two teams raced evenly for the last quarter of the contest. The finish was so close that it took ten minutes to determine the winner, despite the use of electronic timing devices.

1968 Mexico City T: 20, N: 20, D: 10.21. WR: 4:20.64 (Italy)

1. DEN Gunnar Asmussen, Per Pedersen Lyngemark, Reno Olsen, Mogens Frey Jensen 4:22.44
2. GER Udo Hempel, Karl Link, Karlheinz Henrichs, Jürgen Kissner 4:18.94
3. ITA Lorenzo Bosisio, Cipriano Chemello, Luigi Roncaglia, Giorgio Morbiato 4:18.35
4. SOV Dzintars Lacis, Stanislav Moskvin, Vladimir Kuznyetsov, Mikhail Kolyuschev 4:33.39
5. BEL: Ernest Bens, Ronny Vanmarcke, Willy Debosscher, Paul Crapez; CZE: Jiři Daler, Pavel Kondr, Milan Puzrla, František Rezac; FRA: Bernard Darmet, Daniel Rebillard, Jack Mourioux, Alain Van Lancker; POL: Wojciech Matusiak, Janusz Kierzkowski, Wacław Latocha, Rajmund Zieliński

In the qualifying round the West Germans set a world record of 4:19.90, which was broken quickly by the Italians at 4:16.10. In the first semifinal the Germans took back the record by beating the Italians 4:15.76 to 4:16.21. The final saw the exhausted West Germans hold on to finish first. But with one lap to go, Jürgen Kissner touched his teammate Karlheinz Henrichs on the back. East German officials, bitter because West German team member Kissner was a defector from the east, protested that the "touch" had been an illegal shove. Their protest was upheld, and West Germany was disqualified. At first it was announced that Italy would receive the silver medal and the USSR the bronze, but a post-Olympic decision allowed the West Germans to retain second place.

1972 Munich T: 22, N: 22, D: 9.4.

1. GER Jürgen Colombo, Günter Haritz, Udo Hempel, Günther Schumacher 4:22.14
2. GDR Thomas Huschke, Heinz Richter, Herbert Richter, Uwe Unterwalder 4:25.25
3. GBR Michael Bennett, Ian Hallam, Ronald Keeble, William Moore 4:23.78
4. POL Bernard Kręczyński, Pawel Kaczorowski, Janusz Kierzkowski, Mieczyslaw Nowicki 4:26.06
5. BUL: Nikifor Petrov, Plamen Timchev, Dimo Angelov, Ivan Stanoyev; HOL: Ad Dekkers, Gerard Kamper, Herman Ponsteen, Roy Schuiten; SOV: Viktor Bykov, Vladimir Kuznetsov, Anatoly Stapanenko, Aleksandr Yudin; SWI: Martin Steger, Xaver Kurmann, René Savary, Christian Brunner

The dramatic confrontation between the two German teams turned out to be a one-sided affair, as the West Germans took an early lead and were up by 3.82 seconds with 1000 meters to go.

1976 Montreal T: 16, N: 16, D: 7.24.

1. GER	Gregor Braun, Hans Lutz, Günther Schumacher, Peter Vonhof	4:21.06
2. SOV/RUS	Vladimir Osokin, Aleksandr Perov, Vitaly Petrakov, Viktor Sokolov	4:27.15
3. GBR	Ian Banbury, Michael Bennett, Robin Croker, Ian Hallam	4:22.41
4. GDR	Norbert Dürpisch, Thomas Huschke, Uwe Unterwalder, Matthias Wiegand	4:22.75

5. CZE: Ždenek Dohnal, Michal Klasa, Petr Koček, Jiři Pokorny; HOL: Gerrit Mohlmann, Peter Nieuwenhuis, Herman Ponsteen, Gerrit Slot; ITA: Sandro Callari, Cesare Cipollini, Rino de Candido, Giuseppe Saronni; POL: Jan Jankiewicz, Czesław Lang, Krzysztof Sujka, Zbigniew Szczepkowski

The world champion West German team filled their tires with helium instead of air because it was lighter. They also arrived in Montreal with one-piece silk racing suits, which they were not allowed to use because of the unfair aerodynamic advantage it would have given them.

1980 Moscow C: 13, N: 13, D: 7.26.

1. SOV	Viktor Manakov, Valery Movchan, Vladimir Osokin, Vitaly Petrakov, [Aleksandr Krasnov]	4:15.70
2. GDR	Gerald Mortag, Uwe Unterwalder, Matthias Wiegand, Volker Winkler	4:19.67
3. CZE	Teodor Černý, Martin Penc, Jiři Pokorný, Igor Sláma	
4. ITA	Pierangelo Bincoletto, Guido Bontempi, Ivano Maffei, Silvestro Milani	Overtaken

5. AUS: Colin Fitzgerald, Kevin Nichols, Kelvin Poole, Garry Sutton; FRA: Alain Bondue, Philippe Chevalier, Pascal Poisson, Jean-Marc Rebière; GBR: Anthony Doyle, Malcolm Elliott, Glen Mitchell, Sean Yates; SWI: Robert Dill-Bundi, Urs Freuler, Hans Kaenel, Hans Ledermann

The Soviet team set a world best of 4:14.64 in the quarterfinals, achieving a speed of 56.55 kilometers per hour.

1984 Los Angeles-Carson C: 14, N: 14, D: 8.3.

1. AUS	Michael Grenda, Kevin Nichols, Michael Turtur, Dean Woods	4:25.99
2. USA	David Grylls, Steve Hegg, R. Patrick McDonough, Leonard Harvey Nitz, [Brent Emery]	4:29.85
3. GER	Reinhard Alber, Rolf Gölz, Roland Günther, Michael Marx	4:25.60
4. ITA	Roberto Amadio, Massimo Brunelli, Maurizio Colombo, Silvio Martinello	4:26.90
5. DEN	Dan Frost, Michael Marcussen, Jörgen Pedersen, Brian Holm Sörensen	4:25.16
6. FRA	Didier Garcia, Eric Louvel, Pascal Potie, Robert Pascal	4:30.28
7. SWI	Daniel Huwyler, Hans Ledermann, Hansrüdi Märki, Jörg Müller	4:30.47
8. BEL	Rudi Ceyssens, Roger Ilegems, Peter Roes, Joseph Smeets	4:31.53

In the final, the toe strap of US team member Dave Grylls came loose almost immediately, forcing the Americans to complete the race with only three riders. The Australians took an early lead, allowed the Americans to pull close by the halfway mark, and then drew away for a clear victory.

1988 Seoul T: 19, N: 19, D: 9.24. WR: 4:17.710 (CZE—Soukup, Buchta, Cerny, Trčka)

1. SOV	Vyacheslav Ekimov, Artūras Kasputis, Dmitri Nelyubin, Gintautas Umaras	4:13.31 OR
2. GDR	Steffen Blochwitz, Roland Hennig, Dirk Meier, Carsten Wolf, [Uwe Preissler]	4:14.09
3. AUS	Brett Dutton, Wayne McCarney, Stephen McGlede, Dean Woods, [Scott McGrory]	4:16.02
4. FRA	Hervé Dagorne, Pascal Lino, Didier Pasgrimaud, Pascal Potie	4:22.23
5. CZE	Svatopluk Buchta, Zbynek Fiala, Pavel Soukup, Aleš Trčka, [Pavel Tesař]	4:19.05
6. ITA	Ivan Beltrami, Gianpaolo Grisandi, David Solari, Fabrizio Trezzi, [Fabio Baldato]	4:20.90
7. POL	Ryszard Dawidowicz, Joachim Halupczok, Andrzej Sikorski, Marian Turowski	4:22.50
8. DEN	Peter Clausen, Dan Frost, Jimmi Madsen, Lars Olsen, [Ken Frost]	4:25.30

Four different teams beat the world record in the qualifying round, with the Soviets leading the way in 4:16.10. In the quarterfinals they lowered their time to 4:14.22, then set a third record in the final. The East Germans almost edged the Soviets for the gold. They trailed by only three tenths of a second with half a lap to go and were closing fast when two of their riders, Wolf and Hennig, misjudged the finish line and sat up in their seats.

1992 Barcelona T: 20, N: 20, D: 7.31. WR: 4:16.100 (SOV—Ekimov, Kasputis, Nelyubin, Umaras)

1. GER	Guido Fulst, Michael Glöckner, Jens Lehmann, Stefan Steinweg, [Andreas Walzer]	4:08.791 OR
2. AUS	Brett Aitken, Stephen McGlede, Shaun O'Brien, Stuart O'Grady	4:10.218
3. DEN	Ken Frost, Klaus Kynde Nielsen, Jimmi Madsen, Jan Petersen, [Ivan Frost, Michael Sandstod]	4:15.860
4. ITA	Ivan Beltrami, Rossano Brasi, Ivan Cerioli, Fabrizio Trezzi, [Giovanni Lombardi]	4:18.291
5. GBR	Christopher Boardman, Paul Jennings, Bryan Steel, Glen Sword	4:14.350
6. SOV	Valery Baturo, Aleksandr Gonchenkov, Dmitri Nelyubin, Roman Saprykin, [Nikolai Kuznetzov]	4:16.685
7. NZL	Gary Anderson, Nigel Donnelly, Carlos Marryatt, Stuart Williams, [Glenn McLeay]	Overtaken
8. CZE	Svatopluk Buchta, Rudolf Juřický, Jan Panáček, Pavel Tesař	Overtaken

The Australians set a world best of 4:11.245 in the qualifying round, but the Germans twice lowered that time with a 4:10.980 in overtaking New Zealand in the quarterfinals, and a 4:10.446 while defeating Denmark in the semis. They broke quickly in the final and the Australian team was unable to reel them in. In last place, the team from Guam finished 37.621 seconds behind the next-to-last team, Iran. By contrast, Iran was only 34.5 seconds behind Australia, the top qualifier. Because there are no velodromes on the island of Guam, the Guamanian cyclists trained in a parking lot.

1996 Atlanta-Stone Mountain T: 17, N: 17, D: 7.27. WR: 4:03.840 (AUS—Aitken, O'Grady, O'Shannessey, Shearsby)

1. FRA	Christophe Capelle, Philippe Ermenault, Jean-Michel Monin, Francis Moreau	4:05.930
2. RUS	Anton Chantyr, Eduard Gritsun, Nikolai Kuznetsov, Aleksei Markov	4:07.730
3. AUS	Brett Aitken, Bradley McGee, Stuart O'Grady, Dean Woods, [Timothy O'Shannessey]	4:07.570
4. ITA	Adler Capelli, Mauro Trentini, Andrea Collinelli, Cristiano Citton	4:08.460
5. SPA	Juan Martínez, Juan Llaneras, Santos González, Adolfo Alperi	4:11.310
6. USA	Dirk Copeland, Mariano Friedick, Adam Laurent, Michael McCarthy	4:12.470
7. UKR	Oleksandr Fedenko, Andriy Yatsenko, Serhiy Matveyev, Alexander Simonenko, [Bohdan Bondaryev]	4:12.794
8. NZL	Gregory Henderson, Brendon Cameron, Timothy Carswell, Julian Dean	4:15.610

This was expected to be a duel between the world champion Australians and the hosts from the United States. The two teams did meet—in the quarterfinals. The Australians won easily by 2.82 seconds, but they were beaten in the semifinals by the surprising team from Russia, which rallied to win in the final kilometer. In the other semifinal, the lead changed hands four times before France prevailed over Italy. The final matched the seasoned French (average age 29½) and a team of Russian amateurs from Lokomotiv Sports Club in St. Petersburg (average age 20½). Although the Russians occasionally narrowed the gap, the French led from start to finish.

2000 Sydney T: 12, N: 12, D: 9.19. WR: 4:00.958 (ITA—Capelli, Citton, Collinelli, Trentini)

1. GER	Guido Fulst, Robert Bartko, Daniel Becke, Jens Lehmann, [Olaf Pollack]	3:59.710
2. UKR	Oleksandr Fedenko, Oleksandr Symonenko, Serhiy Matveyev, Sergiy Chernyavsky	4:00.830
3. GBR	Bryan Steel, Paul Manning, Bradley Wiggins, Chris Newton, [Jonny Clay]	4:01.979
4. FRA	Cyril Bos, Philippe Ermenault, Francis Moreau, Jerome Neuville	4:05.991
5. AUS	Brett Aitken, Graeme Brown, Bradley McGee, Michael Rogers, [Brett Lancaster]	4:06.361
6. NZL	Tim Carswell, Lee Vertongen, Gary Anderson, Greg Henderson	4:06.495
7. HOL	Peter Schep, Robert Slippens, Jens Mouris, Wilco Zuijderwijk, [John den Braber]	4:09.590
8. RUS	Vladimir Karpets, Aleksey Markov, Sergey Klimov, Denis Smyslov, [Vladislav Borisov]	4:09.910

The Ukrainian team set a world record of 4:00.830 in the semifinals against Great Britain, but in the final, a half hour later, the Germans led all the way and made history by breaking the four-minute barrier. They dedicated their victory to their coach, Robert Lange, who had been killed six months earlier by a drunken driver while riding his bike on the Spanish island of Majorca. The four German riders paid for Lange's widow and daughter to fly to Sydney and attend the final.

2004 Athens T: 10, N: 10, D: 8.23. WR: 3:57.280 (Brown, Dawson, Lancaster, Roberts)

1. AUS	Graeme Brown, Brett Lancaster, Bradley McGee, Luke Roberts, [Peter Dawson, Stephen Wooldridge]	3:58.233
2. GBR	Steve Cummings, Rob Hayles, Paul Manning, Bradley Wiggins, [Chris Newton, Bryan Steel]	4:01.760
3. SPA	Carlos Castaño Panadero, Sergi Escobar Roure, Asier Maeztu Villalabeitia, Carlos Torrent Tarres	4:05.523
4. GER	Robert Bartko, Guido Fulst, Christian Lademann, Leif Lampater	4:07.193
5. HOL	Levi Heimans, Jens Mouris, Peter Schep, Jeroen Straathof	4:04.605
6. UKR	Volodymyr Diudia, Roman Kononenko, Serhiy Matvieiev, Vitaliy Popkov	4:05.266
7. FRA	Matthieu Ladagnous, Anthony Langella, Jérôme Neuville, Fabien Sanchez	Overtaken
8. LIT	Linas Balčiūnas, Ignatas Konovalovas, Tomas Vaitkus, Raimondas Vilčinskas, [Aivaras Baranauskas]	Overtaken

The Australian team broke their own world record in their first round race against Lithuania with a time of 3:57.280. In the final, they trailed the British foursome in the first half, before pulling away to win by three and a half seconds.

2008 Beijing T: 10, N: 10, D: 8.18. WR: 3:56.322 (GBR – Clancy, Manning, Thomas, Wiggins)

1. GBR	Ed Clancy, Paul Manning, Geraint Thomas, Bradley Wiggins	3:53.314	WR
2. DEN	Michael Mørkøv, Casper Jørgensen, Jens-Erik Madsen, Alex Rasmussen, [Michael Færk Christensen]	4:00.040	
3. NZL	Sam Bewley, Hayden Roulston, Marc Ryan, Jesse Sergent, [Westley Gough]	3:57.776	
4. AUS	Jack Bobridge, Graeme Brown, Mark Jamieson, Luke Roberts, [Brad McGee]	3:59.006	
5. HOL	Levi Heimans, Jens Mouris, Robert Slippens, Wim Stroetinga	Overtaken	
6. RUS	Yevgeny Kovalyov, Aleksey Markov, Aleksandr Petrovsky, Aleksandr Serov, Nikolay Trusov	Overtaken	
7. SPA	Sergi Escobar Roure, Asier Maeztu Villabeitia, David Muntaner Juaneda, Antonio Miguel Parra	Overtaken	
8. FRA	Damien Gaudin, Matthieu Ladagnous, Christophe Riblon, Nicolas Rousseau	DISQ	

Led by two-time individual pursuit gold medalist Bradley Wiggins, Great Britain had won the past two world championships by wide margins. The team recorded the fastest time in the qualifying round in Beijing and set a world record, 3:55.202, in the semifinals, breaking the record they had set in March 2008 at the world championships in Manchester. The final was a repeat of those 2008 world championships; once again the British squad had no trouble, leading from start to finish and setting yet another world record in their win over Denmark.

TEAM SPRINT

Similar to the team pursuit, the three-lap team sprint is contested by three-man teams with each team member leading for one lap. Teams start on opposite sides of the track. As in the team pursuit, the eight fastest teams in the opening round proceed to the quarterfinals. Times are based on the performance of the third rider on each team.

1896–1996 not held.

2000 Sydney T: 12 , N: 12, D: 9.17.

1. FRA	Laurent Gané, Florian Rousseau, Arnaud Tournant	44.233
2. GBR	Chris Hoy, Craig MacLean, Jason Queally	44.680
3. AUS	Sean Eadie, Darryn Hill, Gary Neiwand	45.161
4. GRE	Lambros Vasilopoulos, Dimitrios Georgalis, Kleanthis Barngas	45.332
5. JPN	Narihiro Inamura, Yuichiro Kamiyama, Tomohiro Nagatsuka	45.079
6. SLV	Peter Bazálik, Jan Lepka, Jaroslav Jeřábek	45.523
7. GER	Jens Fiedler, Sören Lausberg, Stefan Nimke	45.537
8. LAT	Viesturs Berzins, Ainars Kiksis, Ivo Lakucs	45.589

France had won the last three world championships. In the final against Great Britain, Laurent Gané put the French into the lead, Florian Rousseau lengthened the gap in the second lap and Arnaud Tournant, twenty-four hours after his disappointing performance in the kilometer time trial, guaranteed the victory.

2004 Athens T: 12, N: 12, D: 8.21.

1. GER	Jens Fiedler, Stefan Nimke, René Wolff	43.980
2. JPN	Toshiaki Fushimi, Masaki Inoue, Tomohiro Nagatsuka	44.246
3. FRA	Mickael Bourgain, Laurent Gané, Arnaud Tournant	44.359
4. AUS	Ryan Bayley, Sean Eadie, Shane Kelly	44.404
5. GBR	Chris Hoy, Jamie Staff, Jason Queally, [Craig MacLean]	44.075
6. HOL	Jan Bos, Theo Bos, Teun Mulder	44.370
7. SPA	José Antonio Escuredo Raimóndez, Salvador Meliá Mangriñán, José Antonio Villanueva Trinidad	44.687
8. GRE	Georgios Khimonetos, Dimitrios Georgalis, Lambros Vasilopoulos	45.708

Jens Fiedler, the 2004 world champion in the sprint, keirin and the Olympic sprint, gave the German team an early edge with a blazing start, and Nimke and Wolff finished strongly to secure the gold. After the win, Fiedler placed his four-year-old son on his handlebars for the victory lap.

2008 Beijing T: 13, N: 13, D: 8.15.

1. GBR	Chris Hoy, Jason Kenny, Jamie Staff	43.128
2. FRA	Grégory Baugé, Kévin Sireau, Arnaud Tournant	43.651
3. GER	René Enders, Maximilian Levy, Stefan Nimke	44.014
4. AUS	Ryan Bayley, Daniel Ellis, Mark French, [Shane Kelly]	44.022
5. HOL	Theo Bos, Teun Mulder, Tim Veldt	44.212
6. JPN	Kiyofumi Nagai, Tomohiro Nagatsuka, Kazunari Watanabe	44.437
7. MAL	Mohd Azizulhasni Awang, Josiah Ng, Mohd Rizal Tisin	44.822
8. USA	Michael Blatchford, Adam Duvendeck, Giddeon Massie	45.423

France and Great Britain had faced each other in the final at each of the past three world championships. Led by Grégory Baugé and anchored by Sydney gold medalist Arnaud Tournant, France had won all three times.

Britain led the qualifying round, setting a world record of 42.950. As expected, both teams reached the final easily. Britain's Jamie Staff, a former BMXer who had trained specifically for the opening lap of the team sprint, recorded the fastest first lap in the event's history, 17.1 seconds, to pull ahead of Baugé. Twenty-year-old Olympic newcomer Jason Kenny then expanded the lead slightly over Kévin Sireau. Athens time trial gold medalist Chris Hoy proved unstoppable in the final lap, increasing the lead further over Tournant and giving Britain a margin of 0.523 for the victory. Hoy would go on to win two more sprint gold medals in Beijing.

In contrast, the bronze medal match between Germany and Australia was incredibly close, coming down to a margin of 0.008 seconds . . . about 12 centimeters (4½ inches).

KEIRIN

The Keirin (pronounced "kay-rin") is an eight-lap race. For the first 5½ laps, the riders are paced by a motorbike. The motorbike begins at a speed of 25 kilometers per hour and gradually increases to 45 kilometers per hour before leaving the track with 2½ laps to go. The riders then sprint to the finish. The keirin originated as a betting race in Japan in the 1940s.

1896–1996 not held

2000 Sydney C: 20, N: 15, D: 9.21.

1. Florian Rousseau	FRA	11.020
2. Gary Neiwand	AUS	
3. Jens Fiedler	GER	
4. Jan van Eijden	GER	
5. Marty Nothstein	USA	
6. Frédéric Magne	FRA	

When the motorbike pulled away in the final, 34-year-old Gary Neiwand was in front. Jens Fiedler, the two-time defending world champion, immediately passed him. In the last lap, Neiwand retook the lead, but just before the finish line Florian Rousseau edged ahead to earn his second gold medal and third total medal in five days.

2004 Athens C: 22, N: 15, D: 8.25.

1. Ryan Bayley	AUS	10.601
2. José Antonio Escuredo Raimondez	SPA	
3. Shane Kelly	AUS	
4. Mickael Bourgain	FRA	
5. René Wolff	GER	
6. Onn Lam "Josiah" Ng	MAL	
7. Łukasz Kwiatkowski	POL	
8. Jens Fiedler	GER	

The day after his victory in the sprint competition, Ryan Bayley added the Keirin title. Bayley started the day with breakfast at McDonald's, then won all three rounds of the Keirin, surging past a group of five riders a lap and a half out from the finish and opening a solid gap to secure the win. Shane Kelly, a four-time world champion, earned his third Olympic medal when third-place finisher René Wolff was disqualified for interference.

2008 Beijing C: 25, N: 16, D: 8.16.

1. Chris Hoy	GBR
2. Ross Edgar	GBR
3. Kiyofumi Nagai	JPN
4. Shane Kelly	AUS
5. Carsten Bergemann	GER
6. Arnaud Tournant	FRA
7. Grégory Baugé	FRA
8. Ryan Bayley	AUS

When the 1-kilometer time trial event was discontinued from the Olympics, 2004 gold medalist Chris Hoy was forced to branch out into the other track sprinting events—sprint, team sprint and Keirin. He turned out to be good at them too, winning world championship gold medals in each, including back-to-back victories. In Beijing he competed in the Keirin event one day after anchoring the British team to the gold medal in the team sprint.

Hoy had no difficulty reaching the final, winning each round easily. Other medal favorites were not so lucky. The 2005 world champion, Teun Mulder, was eliminated in the first round, while 2006 world champion Theo Bos and 2004 Olympic gold medalist Ryan Bayley fell in the semi-finals—in Bos's case literally, when he crashed alongside Polish racer Kamil Kuczynski and was not allowed to restart.

Hoy was never seriously threatened in the final, taking a commanding lead before the final lap and finishing unchallenged. Fellow Scot Ross Edgar took silver with a late burst ahead of Kiyofumi Nagai. Fourteen-times world champion Arnaud Tournant finished sixth.

Nagai had taken a significant pay cut to train for and compete in the Beijing Olympics, earning approximately $26,000 during the year, less than 10% of what he normally earned competing on the Japanese Keirin circuit.

OMNIUM

The two-day men's Olympic omnium event will consist of six disciplines: 1) flying start 250-meter time trial, 2) 30-kilometer points race, 3) 4,000-meter pursuit, 4) 15-kilometer scratch race, 5) 1,000-meter time trial and 6) elimination race. In the elimination race, the racers will start in a bunch and every two laps the cyclist in last place will be eliminated. Scoring is based on placements in each discipline with one point for first place. The athlete with the lowest total places for all six events is the winner.

ROAD TIME TRIAL

This is a race on the road against the clock. Riders start at one-and-a-half-minute intervals. The men's course may vary from 45 to 55 kilometers. The 2000 course will be 45.8 kilometers. The riders begin on a launching ramp, where they are held by a race official and then released. The same official holds and releases all entrants.

1896–1908 not held

1912 Stockholm C: 123, N: 16, D: 7.7.
315.4 KM

1. Rudolph "Okey" Lewis	SAF	10:42:39.0
2. Frederick Grubb	GBR	10:51:24.2
3. Carl Schutte	USA	10:52:38.8
4. Leon Meredith	GBR	11:00:02.6
5. Frank Brown	CAN	11:01:00.0
6. Antti Raita	FIN	11:02:20.3
7. Eric Friborg	SWE	11:04:17.0
8. Ragnar Malm	SWE	11:08:14.5

This grueling 196-mile race around Lake Mälar began at 2:00 a.m. The competitors were sent out on the course at two-minute intervals over the next four hours. "Okey"

Lewis of South Africa began at an unusually fast pace and held an 11½-minute lead at the 120 km control station. He increased this lead to 17 minutes at 200 km and held on for the last 4¼ hours to win by 8¾ minutes. While racing in Germany, Lewis got caught up in World War I. He was wounded several times and incarcerated in prison camps. He returned to Johannesburg after the war in very poor health, but survived until 1933.

There was one terrible accident at the beginning of the race. A few hundred meters after the start, Karl Landsberg of Sweden was hit by a motor-wagon and dragged along for some distance before the wagon stopped. Another competitor, Fyodor Borisov of Russia, fell into a swamped ditch and lay there unconscious until he was discovered by a farmer.

1920 Antwerp C: 46, N: 12, D: 8.12.
175 KM

1. Harry Stenqvist	SWE	4:40:01.8
2. Henry Kaltenbrun	SAF	4:41:26.6
3. Fernand Canteloube	FRA	4:42:54.4
4. Jean Janssens	BEL	4:44:20.6
5. Albert de Bunne	BEL	4:45:23.4
6. Georges Detreille	FRA	4:46:13.4
7. Ragnar Malm	SWE	4:46:22.0
8. Piet Ikelaar	HOL	4:46:54.0

The course was intersected by six railway crossings which might be closed at any time. Timekeepers were posted at each crossing to record any delays. At first it appeared that Kaltenbrun had won, and his victory was acknowledged by triumphant music in the stadium. However, it was later learned that Stenqvist had been held up for four minutes at a railway crossing, and the subtraction from his time put him into first place.

1924 Paris C: 72, N: 22, D: 7.23.
188 KM

1. Armand Blanchonnet	FRA	6:20:48.0
2. Henri Hoevenaers	BEL	6:30:27.0
3. René Hamel	FRA	6:30:51.6
4. Gunnar Sköld	SWE	6:33:36.2
5. Albert Blattmann	SWE	6:34:09.0
6. Alphonse Pardondry	BEL	6:35:57.0
7. Eric Bohlin	SWE	6:36:12.4
8. Georges Wambst	FRA	6:38:34.4

1928 Amsterdam C: 63, N: 21, D: 8.7.
168 KM

1. Henry Hansen	DEN	4:47:18
2. Frank Southall	GBR	4:55:06
3. Gösta Carlsson	SWE	5:00:17
4. Allegro Grandi	ITA	5:02:05
5. John Lauterwasser	GBR	5:02:57
6. Gottlieb Amstein	SWI	5:04:48
7. Leo Nielsen	DEN	5:05:37
8. André Aumerle	FRA	5:07:12

1932 Los Angeles C: 33, N: 11, D: 8.4.
100 KM

1. Attilio Pavesi	ITA	2:28:05.6
2. Guglielmo Segato	ITA	2:29:21.4
3. Bernhard Britz	SWE	2:29:45.2
4. Giuseppe Olmo	ITA	2:29:48.2
5. Frode Sörensen	DEN	2:30:11.2
6. Frank Southall	GBR	2:30:16.2
7. Giovanni Cazzulani	ITA	2:31:07.2
8. Sven Hoglund	SWE	2:31:29.4

1936–1992 not held

1996 Atlanta C: 38, N: 23, D: 8.3.
52.2 KM

1. Miguel Indurain Larraya	SPA	1:04:05
2. Abraham Olano Manzano	SPA	1:04:17
3. Christopher Boardman	GBR	1:04:36
4. Maurizio Fondriest	ITA	1:04:51
5. Tony Rominger	SWI	1:06:05
6. Lance Armstrong	USA	1:06.28
7. Alex Zülle	SWI	1:06:33
8. Patrick Jonker	AUS	1:06:54

Miguel Indurain was barely 20 years old when he first competed in the Olympics: in Los Angeles in 1984. He entered the road race but did not finish. The opening of the Olympics to cycling professionals allowed Indurain to return in 1996. In the interim, the taciturn Spaniard had become a living legend, the first person in history to win the Tour de France five straight times (1991-1995). Indurain had a lung capacity of 8 liters, heart circulation of 50 liters per minute and a resting heart rate of 30 beats per minute. His powerful legs were able to generate 550 watts of power. In 1996, Indurain's Tour de France streak was finally broken and he finished only 11th. Exhausted, he wanted to drop out of the Olympics, which had already started. A personal appeal by fellow Spaniard Juan Antonio Samaranch, the president of the International Olympic Committee, convinced him to travel to Atlanta. On July 31, ten days after the end of the Tour de France, he placed only 26th in the road race. Three days later he raced in the time trial, an event in which he was the defending world champion.

The race was held in intermittent rain that reached deluge proportions while the middle starters were on the course, flooding the streets up to six inches at one point. By the time the last group of ten started, the sun had returned. Indurain was the last to start, right after Abraham Olano. He moved ahead of Chris Boardman's pace after 20 kilometers and gained a clear victory.

2000 Sydney C: 38, N: 26, D: 9.30.
46.8 KM

1. Vyacheslav Ekimov	RUS	57:40.420
2. Jan Ullrich	GER	57:48.333
3. Lance Armstrong	USA	58:14.267

4. Abraham Olano Manzano	SPA	58:31.647
5. Laurent Jalabert	FRA	58:44.455
6. Andrei Teteryuk	KAZ	58:52.342
7. Thor Hushovd	NOR	59:00.015
8. Santos González Capilla	SPA	59:03.202

Two months after the 1996 Olympics, Lance Armstrong discovered that his body was riddled with dozens of cancerous tumors. After surgery and chemotherapy, he was declared cancer-free a year later. In 1999, Armstrong won the Tour de France and, two months before the 2000 Olympics, he won it again. Then, one month before the Olympic road time trial, Armstrong was training when he crashed into a car and fractured a neck vertebrae. Still, he was considered a co-favorite with 1999 world champion Jan Ullrich. Ullrich and Armstrong did both make it to the medal podium, but, in an upset, the gold was won by Armstrong's US Postal Service teammate, 34-year-old Vyacheslav Ekimov. Ekimov had previously earned a gold medal in the team pursuit event in 1988.

2004 Athens-Vouliagmeni C: 38, N: 26, D: 8.18.
48 KM

1. Tyler Hamilton	USA	57:31.74
2. Vyacheslav Ekimov	RUS	57:50.58
3. Bobby Julich	USA	57:58.19
4. Michael Rogers	AUS	58:01.67
5. Michael Rich	GER	58:09.46
6. Aleksandr Vinokurov	KAZ	58:58.14
7. Jan Ullrich	GER	59:02.04
8. Santiago Botero	COL	59:04.76

Four weeks before the opening of the Olympics, Tyler Hamilton was forced to withdraw during the 13th stage of the Tour de France after sustaining back injuries in a fall a week earlier while racing at 65 mph. To make matters worse, his beloved golden retriever, Tugboat, died the day after his fall. Hamilton's bad luck seemed to follow him to Athens—shortly after starting the time trial his radio broke, and he rode most of the race without communication. Hamilton lagged in third place for the first three splits, but he managed to pull ahead and build up a strong lead to gain a clear victory. Hamilton raced in the final with Tugboat's red dog tags tucked in his helmet.

Hamilton's gold medal came into question when a post-race doping test showed evidence of a blood transfusion. The test, which used a relatively new procedure, initially came out negative, but with a note stating that the sample was "suspicious". When the medical director of the IOC, Patrick Schamasch, was informed, he declined to take further action, and the B sample of Hamilton's blood was subsequently frozen. However, the science director of the World Anti-Doping Agency (WADA), Dr. Olivier Rabin, called for a review of the case by a panel of experts, who changed the result to a positive. Because Hamilton's B sample had already been frozen, the backup test proved inconclusive, and on September 21 the IOC ended its inquiry without taking action. The IOC report noted the "honest endeavour and honourable intent of all the key players involved," but cited a "lack of confidence in the laboratory's general ability to meet the criteria . . . necessary to make a valid report."

Meanwhile, a similar test performed during the Vuelta de España returned both A and B positive results for Hamilton, indicating evidence of a blood transfusion. As a result, Hamilton lost his contract with Phonak and was handed a two-year ban from competitive cycling. A subsequent appeal to the Court of Arbitration for Sport (CAS) was rejected and the ban was upheld.

In the summer of 2006, Hamilton was connected to the "Operación Puero" scandal, which implicated 58 cyclists, mostly Spanish, in an extensive doping program led by Dr. Eufemiano Fuentes. A seized fax sent to Hamilton's wife showed payments for a battery of banned drugs and practices. Despite the implication, the United States Anti-Doping Agency did not file charges against Hamilton, and in November 2006 he returned to professional cycling with the Tinkoff Credit Systems team. However, in 2009 Hamilton failed another doping test and was hit with an eight-year ban.

Bronze medalist Bobby Julich competed with an undiagnosed broken wrist, also sustained in the ill-fated 13th stage of the Tour de France.

2008 Beijing C: 39, N: 29, D: 8.13.
47.3 KM

1. Fabian Cancellara	SWI	1:02:11.43
2. Gustav Larsson	SWE	1:02:44.79
3. Levi Leipheimer	USA	1:03:21.11
4. Alberto Contador Velasco	SPA	1:03:29.51
5. Cadel Evans	AUS	1:03:34.97
6. Samuel Sánchez González	SPA	1:04:37.24
7. Svein Tuft	CAN	1:04:39.44
8. Michael Rogers	AUS	1:04:46.85

Starting 32nd of 39 riders, unheralded Gustav Larsson, who had finished in 72nd place in the 2004 Olympic road race, rode the race of his life. He was followed by Levi Leipheimer, who had finished third overall in the 2007 Tour de France. Leipheimer moved into second place, and nobody bettered their times until the final racer, double world champion Fabian Cancellara. Cancellara got off to a slow start and was placed third at the first checkpoint. By halfway, however, he had already overtaken his biggest rival, Stefan Schumacher, who had beaten him in both Tour de France time trials earlier in the year and who had started a minute and a half ahead of him. Cancellara finished 33 seconds ahead of Larsson, his professional teammate, to win the gold medal.

ROAD RACE

The traditional road race, also known as the in-line road race, begins with a mass start. The first rider across the finish line is the winner. Current rules require repeated circuits of a course 12 to 18 kilometers long. The total distance of the men's race must be between 210 and 240 kilometers. In 1996 any rider who fell 15 minutes behind the lead pack was ordered to leave the course. In 2000 lapped riders were eliminated, except on the final lap.

1896 Athens C: 7, N: 3, D: 4.12.

87 KM

1. Aristidis Konstantinidis	GRE	3:21:10
2. August Goedrich	GER	3:31:14
3. Edward Battell	GBR	

The cyclists raced from Athens to Marathon, where they signed their names, and then rode back again on the same road. Konstantinidis fell three times and had to change bikes twice. Battell was a servant at the British Embassy in Athens. Some British residents tried to prevent him from entering the race because, according to them, as he was not a "gentleman" he could not be an amateur.

1900–1904 not held

1906 Athens C: 24, N: 9, D: 5.1.

84 KM

1. Fernand Vast	FRA	2:41:28.0
2. Maurice Bardonneau	FRA	2:41:28.4
3. Edmond Luguet	FRA	2:41:28.6
4. Prospère Verschelden-Romeo	BEL	2:41:45.0
5. Adolf Böhm	GER	2:41:46.6
6. Ioannis Petritsas	GRE	2:41:47.0
7. Carl Andresen	DEN	—
8. Hans Holly	AUT	—

1908–1932 not held

1936 Berlin C: 100, N: 29, D: 8.10.

100 KM

1. Robert Charpentier	FRA	2:33:05.0
2. Guy Lapébie	FRA	2:33:05.2
3. Ernst Nievergelt	SWI	2:33.05.8
4. Fritz Scheller	GER	2:33:06.0
4. Charles Holland	GBR	2:33:06.0
4. Robert Dorgebray	FRA	2:33:06.0
7. Pierino Favalli	ITA	2:33:06.2
8. Auguste Garrebeek	BEL	2:33:06.6
8. Armand Putzeys	BEL	2:33:06.6
8. Talat Tuncalp	TUR	2:33:06.6

For the first time since 1906, all the road competitors started together rather than at intervals. This, coupled with the narrow road, led to numerous accidents and injuries during the last five kilometers. Charpentier had already won a gold medal in the team pursuit two days earlier.

1948 London C: 101, N: 29, D: 8.13.

194.63 KM

1. José Beyaert	FRA	5:18:12.6
2. Gerardus Petrus Voorting	HOL	5:18:16.2
3. Lode Wouters	BEL	5:18:16.2
4. Léon Delathouwer	BEL	5:18:16.2
5. Nils Johansson	SWE	5:18:16.2
6. Robert Maitland	GBR	5:18:16.2
7. Jack Hoobin	AUS	5:18:18.2
8. Gordon Thomas	GBR	5:18:18.2

During World War II, José Beyaert worked with the French resistance, moving weapons on his bike. With a reputation as a street thug in his hometown of Pantin, Beyaert's arrival at the 1948 Olympics was delayed when the mayor of Pantin refused to sign his good conduct certificate. At the London Games, Beyaert sprinted ahead with half a mile to go and won by eight lengths. In 1952 Beyaert moved to Colombia, where he entered the emerald and timber trade. In 2001 Beyaert escaped a kidnapping attempt and moved back to France, where he died in 2005.

1952 Helsinki C: 112, N: 30, D: 8.2.

190.4 KM

1. André Noyelle	BEL	5:06:03.4
2. Robert Grondelaers	BEL	5:06:51.2
3. Edi Ziegler	GER	5:07:47.5
4. Lucien Victor	BEL	5:07:52.0
5. Dino Bruni	ITA	5:10:54.0
6. Vincenzo Zucconelli	ITA	5:11:16.5
7. Gianni Ghidini	ITA	5:11:16.8
8. Oscar Zeissner	GER	5:11:18.5

1956 Melbourne C: 88, N: 28, D: 12.7.

187.73 KM

1. Ercole Baldini	ITA	5:21:17
2. Arnaud Geyre	FRA	5:23:16
3. Alan Jackson	GBR	5:23:16
4. Horst Tüller	GDR	5:23:10
5. Gustav-Adolf Schur	GDR	5:23:16
6. Arthur Stanley Brittain	GBR	5:23:40
7. Arnaldo Pambianco	ITA	5:23:40
8. Maurice Moucheraud	FRA	5:23:40

The year 1956 was known as "Baldini's Year," because the 23-year-old Italian won the world championship in the 4000-meter pursuit, set a world record for the one-hour time trial, and won the Olympic road race by a full mile. His victory was protested by the French and British, who charged that in the later stages of the race he had been protected from the hot sun by the Olympic film unit van that rode alongside him. As Baldini received his gold medal he felt disappointed

Ercole Baldini, 1956
Baldini won the road race by a full mile.

Viktor Kapitonov (left) and Livio Trapé, 1960
Kapitonov edges Trapé at the finish line in the road race, only to discover that he still has one more lap to go. Twenty-four minutes later, Kapitonov defeated Trapé again.

because his national anthem was not played. He was preparing to leave the podium when an anonymous spectator began singing the Italian anthem. In an emotionally charged moment, the lone singer was soon joined by all the other Italians in the crowd. The identity of the singer remained unknown for forty-one years, until a radio program, Pronto Australia, Qui Italia, received a phone call from an Italian-born Australian named Gualberto Gennai, who identified himself as the man who sang at the 1956 medal ceremony. In 1997, in Sydney, Baldini and Gennai met for the first time. After photos were taken, Gennai burst into song once again.

The protest was rejected. The start of the race was delayed fifteen minutes when it was discovered that two "unauthorized" Irish bicyclists, butcher Tom Gerrard and carpenter Paul Fitzgerald, were in the middle of the 88 starters. After they were removed, they joined 200 supporters in passing out Irish nationalist literature.

1960 Rome C: 148, N: 42, D: 8.30.
175.38 KM

1. Viktor Kapitonov	SOV/RUS	4:20:37
2. Livio Trapé	ITA	4:20:37
3. Willy van den Berghen	BEL	4:20:57
4. Yuri Melikhov	SOV/RUS	4:20:57
5. Ion Cosma	ROM	4:20:57
6. Stanislaw Gazda	POL	4:20:57
7. Benoni Beheyt	BEL	4:20:57
8. Janez Žirovnik	YUG/SLO	4:20:57

Kapitonov sprinted to the finish line to defeat Trapé by inches, only to discover that he still had one more 14½-km lap to go. Twenty-four-minutes later, the scene was repeated but this time Kapitonov's victory was official. Kapitonov later joined the editorial board of *Theory and Practice of Physical Culture* magazine and became the manager and head coach of the USSR cycling team.

1964 Tokyo C: 132, N: 35, D: 10.22.
194.83 KM

1. Mario Zanin	ITA	4:39:51.63
2. Kjell Åkerström Rodian	DEN	4:39:51.65
3. Walter Godefroot	BEL	4:39:51.74
4. Raymond Bilney	AUS	4:39:51.74
5. José López Rodríguez	SPA	4:39:51.74
6. Wilfried Peffgen	GER	4:39:51.74
7. Gösta Pettersson	SWE	4:39:51.74
8. Delmo Delmastro	ARG	4:39:51.74

A spectacular finish saw Zanin, a mechanic from Treviso, emerge from the pack with 20 meters to go and win by a wheel. Sture Pettersson of Sweden finished only sixteen-hundredths of a second behind Zanin, yet he ended up in 51st place.

1968 Mexico City C: 144, N: 44, D: 10.23.
196.2 KM

1. Pierfranco Vianelli	ITA	4:41:25.24
2. Leif Mortensen	DEN	4:42:49.71
3. Gösta Pettersson	SWE	4:43:15.24
4. Stephan Abrahamian	FRA	4:43:36.54
5. Marinus Pijnen	HOL	4:43:36.81
6. Jean-Pierre Monsère	BEL	4:43:51.77
7. Tomas Pettersson	SWE	4:43:58.11
8. Giovanni Bramucci	ITA	4:43:58.19

Iraq was represented by George Tajirian who, thirty years later, was convicted in one of the largest immigrant smuggling cases in United States history. He admitted to smuggling more than 1000 people and was sentenced to thirteen years in prison.

1972 Munich C: 163, N: 48, D: 9.7.
182.4 KM

1. Hennie Kuiper	HOL	4:14.37
2. Keven Clyde Sefton	AUS	4:15:04
3. Bruce Biddle	NZE	4:15:04
4. Philip Bayton	GBR	4:15:07
5. Philip Edwards	GBR	4:15.13
6. Wilfried Trott	GER	4:15:13
7. Francesco Moser	ITA	4:15:13
8. Miguel Samaca	COL	4:15:21

DISQ (Drugs): Jaime Huélamo (SPA) 4:15:04

The four Dutch contestants rode a team race with Cees Priem and Fedor den Hertog protecting Kuiper and fighting off challengers. Freddy Maertens was so frustrated by Priem's dogged persistence in sticking to his wheel that he tried to hit Priem in the face. Said Priem, "We worked for Hennie because he is one of the nicest blokes around." Four Irish Republican Army cyclists joined the race to protest the fact that the Irish Cycling Federation competed against cyclists from Northern Ireland. One of them tried to run Irish Olympian Noel Taggart into a ditch. The four IRA cyclists were arrested but later released without charge.

Third-place finisher Jaime Huelamo was disqualified after he tested positive for Coramine.

1976 Montreal C: 134, N: 40, D: 7.26.
175 KM

1. Bernt Johansson	SWE	4:46:52
2. Giuseppe Martinelli	ITA	4:47:23
3. Mieczyslaw Nowicki	POL	4:47:23
4. Alfons de Wolf	BEL	4:47:23
5. Nikolai Gorelov	SOV/RUS	4:47:23
6. George Mount	USA	4:47:23
7. Jean René Bernaudeau	FRA	4:47:23
8. Vittorio Algeri	ITA	4:47:23

Peter Thaler of Germany crossed the finish line in second place, but was demoted to ninth because he had interfered with Martinelli in the final sprint.

1980 Moscow C: 112, N: 32, D: 7.28.
189 KM

1. Sergei Sukhoruchenkov	SOV/RUS	4:48:28.9
2. Czesław Lang	POL	4:51:26.9
3. Yuri Barinov	SOV	4:51:29.9
4. Thomas Barth	GDR	4:56:12.9
5. Tadeusz Wojtas	POL	4:56:12.9
6. Anatoly Yarkin	SOV	4:56:54.9
7. Adri van der Poel	HOL	4:56:54.9
8. Christian Faure	ERA	4:56:54.9

Sukhoruchenkov pulled away with 20 miles to go and won by the largest Olympics margin since 1928.

1984 Los Angeles-Mission Viejo C: 135, N: 43, D: 7.29.
190.2 KM

1. Alexi Grewal	USA	4:59:57
2. Steve Bauer	CAN	4:59:57
3. Dag Otto Lauritzen	NOR	5:00:18
4. Morten Saether	NOR	5:00:18
5. Davis Phinney	USA	5:01:16
6. Thurlow Rogers	USA	5:01:16
7. Bojan Ropret	YUG/SLO	5:01:16
8. Nestor Mora	COL	5:01:16

The son of a Sikh father from India and a British mother of German descent, Alexi Grewal was considered too temperamental and too much of a loner to be an effective member of the US team. Two places on the team were to be decided by the combined results of three trials; the other two were to be filled by the team coaches. Since US head coach Eddie Borysewicz was definitely *not* a fan of Grewal's, the 23-year-old naturalized US citizen had no choice but to make it as one of the two automatic qualifiers. He succeeded, but his troubles were not yet over. Ten days before the Olympic road race, Grewal won a 92-mile contest in Colorado, but his post-race doping test turned up positive for phenyethylamine, apparently caused by a Chinese herbal tablet which he had casually popped before the race. The US Cycling Federation immediately slapped him with a 30-day suspension and dropped him from the Olympic team.

Grewal appealed the ruling by pointing out that he regularly took albuterol, a legal drug, for asthma, and that the doping test had not been sophisticated enough to distinguish between the asthma drug and the herbal pill. On the Monday before the Sunday Olympic race, Grewal was reinstated.

In Los Angeles, with a crowd of 300,000 lining the route, Grewal broke away from the pack 20 kilometers from the finish and opened up a 24-second lead after 11 of 12 laps. With 10 kilometers to go he appeared exhausted and began to wobble and weave. Steve Bauer of Fenwick, Ontario, passed him. Grewal faced a moment of panic and confusion. Then someone threw a bucket of water in his face. He regained his self-control and caught Bauer. The two raced the final lap together. After almost 5 hours of riding, the gold medal was to be decided by a sprint, which was Bauer's specialty. Bauer made his jump 100 meters from the finish, but Grewal zipped by with less than 50 meters to go and won by little more than a bike length.

Bronze medalist Dag Otto Lauritzen took up cycling in 1981 to rehabilitate his knee after suffering an injury while parachute jumping.

1988 Seoul C: 136, N: 54, D: 9.27.
196.8 KM

1. Olaf Ludwig	GDR	4:32:22
2. Bernd Gröne	GER	4:32:25
3. Christian Henn	GER	4:32:46
4. Robert Mionske	USA	4:32:46
5. Djamolidin Abdoujaparov	SOV/UZB	4:32:46
6. Edward Salas	AUS	4:32:46
7. Roberto Pelliconi	ITA	4:32:46
8. Graeme Miller	NZE	4:32:46

The unusually flat course laid out by the Seoul organizers was good news for talented sprinter Olaf Ludwig of Gera-Thiesehity. Eight years earlier, in Moscow, Ludwig had taken a silver in the team time trial and finished thirty-second in the road race. In Seoul he placed fourteenth in the points race three days before winning the road race.

A sidelight of note: by finishing ninth, 21-year-old Emili Perez became the highest placed athlete in Olympic history in any sport from the minuscule European nation of Andorra (pop. 50,000).

1992 Barcelona-Sant Sadurní d'Anoia C: 154, N: 59, D: 8.2.
194 KM

1. Fabio Casartelli	ITA	4:35.21
2. Hendrik Dekker	HOL	4:35.22
3. Dainis Ozols	LAT	4:35.24
4. Erik Zabel	GER	4:35.56
5. Lauri Aus	EST	4:35.56
6. Andrzej Sypykowski	POL	4:35.56
7. Sylvain Bolay	FRA	4:35.56
8. Arvis Piziks	LAT	4:35.56

Casartelli, the third man on the three-man Italian team, led the decisive break at the end of the penultimate lap. Only Dekker came with him, although Ozols joined them as the bell rang for the final lap. Two hundred and fifty meters from the finish, the 21-year-old from Como sprinted away to a clear victory. On July 18, 1995, Casartelli was competing in his first Tour de France when he lost control on a fast, steep, descending curve in the Pyrénées Mountains. Helmetless, he flew headfirst into a concrete pylon. Although doctors were on the scene within ten seconds, Casartelli's life could not be saved.

1996 Atlanta C: 183, N: 57, D: 7.31.
221.85 KM

1. Pascal Richard	SWI	4:53:56
2. Rolf Sørensen	DEN	4:53:56
3. Maximilian Sciandri	GBR	4:53:58
4. Francisco Andreu	USA	4:55:10
5. Richard Virenque	FRA	4:55:10
6. Melchior Mauri	SPA	4:55:11
7. Fabio Baldato	ITA	4:55:24
8. Michele Bartoli	ITA	4:55:24

Pascal Richard and Max Sciandri, recuperating from the Tour de France and recently arrived in Atlanta, went out for a training ride. They chanced upon Rolf Sørensen, who took them to see the Olympic course. Five days later the three would ride together again, but this time it was over the last 33 kilometers of the Olympic final. With 700 meters to go, Sciandri, an Anglo-Italian, launched a sprint that gave him a brief 15-meter lead. But it didn't last. With 200 meters to go, it was Sørensen's turn. Sciandri could not respond, but Richard did. Less than 50 meters from the finish line, Richard swung left and bolted past Sørensen to win by less than a wheel. Sørensen slammed his handlebars in frustration. By early next morning, however, he had recovered his spirits sufficiently to be found in a local nightclub dancing on a table while wearing his silver medal and little else.

2000 Sydney C: 154, N: 41, D: 9.27.
239.4 KM

1. Jan Ullrich	GER	5:29:08
2. Aleksandr Vinokurov	KAZ	5:29:17
3. Andreas Klöden	GER	5:29:20
4. Michele Bartoli	ITA	5:31:34
5. Laurent Jalabert	FRA	5:31:34
6. Frank Høj	DEN	5:31:34
7. Piotr Wadecki	POL	5:31:34
8. George Hincapie	USA	5:31:34

With 25 kilometers to go in the 239-kilometer race, Jan Ullrich broke away from the peloton. Only Aleksandr Vinokurov and Andreas Klöden were able to go with him. Three kilometers from the finish, Ullrich said goodbye to the other two and rode away to victory. In their professional lives, Ullrich, Vinokurov and Klöden all raced for the same team, Deutsche Telekom and, since Vinokourov and Klöden served as domestiques for Ullrich in major races, it was not surprising that Ullrich won. Ullrich went through a particularly bad patch in his life in 2002. On April 30, while drunk, he backed his Porsche into, of all things, a bike rack, destroying several bikes. Six weeks later, Ullrich tested positive for amphetamines and was suspended for nine months.

On June 30, 2006, one day before the start of the Tour de France, Ullrich was suspended after being linked to a large Spanish doping scandal, nicknamed

Operación Puerto, and was subsequently fired from his team, T-Mobile. In September, police raided Ullrich's home in Switzerland while he was on his honeymoon and collected DNA samples, which were matched to blood samples seized during Operación Puerto, but no charges were filed against him. However, six months later, after winning two stages of the 2007 Tour de France, Vinokurov tested positive for the presence of foreign blood cells, evidence that he had participated in a banned blood transfusion. Vinokurov was suspended and his entire team, Astana, withdrew from the race. When his B sample came back positive, Vinokurov was fired from the team and faced a two-year suspension.

2004 Athens C: 144, N: 43, D: 8.14.

224.4 KM

1. Paolo Bettini	ITA	5:41:44
2. Sérgio Paulinho	POR	5:41:45
3. Axel Merckx	BEL	5:41:52
4. Erik Zabel	GER	5:41:56
5. Andrej Hauptman	SLO	5:41:56
6. Kim Kirchen	LUX	5:41:56
7. Roger Hammond	GBR	5:41:56
8. Frank Høj	DEN	5:41:56

With two laps to go, Paolo Bettini and Sérgio Paulinho opened a wide gap over the peloton. They kept together until the end when Bettini, a 30-year-old from Cecina, Italy, edged out Paulinho in a sprint to the finish. Only 75 of the 144 racers finished the 224-kilometer race, which was held in 100° Fahrenheit heat (37.8° C) through the streets of old Athens.

2008 Beijing C: 143, N: 55, D: 8.9.

245.4 KM

1. Samuel Sánchez González	SPA	6:23:49
2. Fabian Cancellara	SWI	6:23:49
3. Aleksandr Kolobnev	RUS	6:23:49
4. Andy Schleck	LUX	6:23:49
5. Michael Rogers	AUS	6:23:49
6. Santiago Botero Echeverry	COL	6:24:01
7. Mario Aerts	BEL	6:24:01
8. Michael Barry	CAN	6:24:05

DISQ (Drugs): Davide Rebellin (ITA) 6:23:49

The Beijing road race was conducted over a 245.4 kilometer (152.5 mile) course, the longest in Olympic history. Held under hot and humid conditions, more than a third of the 143 participants did not finish, including 2007 Tour de France winner Alberto Contador. The first major breakaway came after 60 kilometers as 26 riders moved ahead and stayed in front for nearly 125 kilometers (77 miles) before being caught by the peloton. Six riders broke into the lead on the last lap, with all six finishing within a bike length. Sánchez finished a wheel ahead of Davide Rebellin, who was competing on his 37th birthday. None of the pre-race favorites were in serious medal contention. Three-time world champion Alejandro Valverde finished 13th, 22 seconds behind, while defending Olympic champion and two-time reigning world champion Paolo Bettini finished 18th, 1:10 behind.

In April 2009 the IOC announced that Rebellin had tested positive for CERA, an advanced version of the blood-booster EPO. He was stripped of his silver medal and banned from competition for two years. Cancellara and Kolobnev were moved up to silver and bronze.

MOUNTAIN BIKE CROSS-COUNTRY

The cross-country race is run on forest roads, fields, earth, and gravel paths. Paved and tarred roads cannot exceed 15% of the total route. The men's course is between 40 and 50 kilometers. There is a mass start and the first rider across the finish line is the winner. All dangerous obstacles are preceded by warning signs 30 meters in advance.

1896–1992 not held

1996 Atlanta-Conyers C: 43, N: 26, D: 7.30.

48.7 KM

1. Bart Brentjens	HOL	2:17:38
2. Thomas Frischknecht	SWI	2:20:14
3. Miguel Martinez	FRA	2:20:36
4. Christophe Dupouey	FRA	2:25:03
5. Daniele Pontoni	ITA	2:25:08
6. José Andres Brenes Mata	CRC	2:25:51
7. Lennie Kristensen	DEN	2:26:02
8. Luca Bramati	ITA	2:26:05

Mountain biking was added to the Olympic program in 1993, less than twenty years after it was created as a sport and only six years after the staging of the first world championships.

World champion Bart Brentjens prepared for the expected heat and humidity of Atlanta by training on an indoor bike in a hot, steamy room. He also drew a complete map of the course and memorized it. When the day of the Olympic championship dawned hot and muggy, Brentjens was ready. He and Luca Bramati broke ahead of the field almost immediately. Steadily they pulled away from the others. Midway through the race, Bramati cracked and Brentjens rode the second half alone. At 1.88 meters (6 feet 2 inches), Brentjens was the tallest racer in the field. On the other hand, Miguel Martinez, the bronze medalist was, at 1.64 meters (5 feet 4¼ inches), the smallest entrant. Thomas Frishnecht, who won the silver medal, was fined 5000 Swiss francs for competing in a sleeveless jersey. The day after the mountain biking event,

Frischknecht, using a cyclo-cross bike, took part in the road race. He placed 110th.

2000 Sydney-Fairfield C: 49, N: 30, D: 9.24.
49.4 KM

1. Miguel Martinez	FRA	2:09:02.50
2. Filip Meirhaeghe	BEL	2:10:05.51
3. Christoph Sauser	SWI	2:11:21.40
4. José Antonio Hermida Ramos	SPA	2:11:43.31
5. Lado Fumic	GER	2:11:58.28
6. Thomas Frischknecht	SWI	2:12:42.49
7. Cadel Evans	AUS	2:13:32.05
8. Carsten Bresser	GER	2:13:37.23

Atlanta bronze medal winner Miguel Martinez established himself as the favorite when, three months before the 2000 Olympics, he won the world championship by 2 minutes and 53 seconds. At the Sydney Games, it was another 1996 medalist, Thomas Frischknecht who surged to the early lead and tried to run away with the race. He opened a 50-second lead after the first of seven laps. He was still ahead by almost 55 seconds after four laps. But then Frischknecht began to drift back. Filip Meirhaeghe passed him with 17 kilometers to go, as did Martinez, who then stormed away as if he had no competitors. Martinez's last two laps were the fastest of the race and he won by more than a minute.

2004 Athens-Parnitha C: 50, N: 32, D: 8.27.
43.3 KM

1. Julien Absalon	FRA	2:15:02
2. José Antonio Hermida Ramos	SPA	2:16:02
3. Bart Brentjens	HOL	2:17:05
4. Roel Paulissen	BEL	2:18:10
5. Liam Killeen	GBR	2:18:32
6. Ralph Näf	SWI	2:19:15
7. Thomas Frischknecht	SWI	2:19:39
8. Manuel Fumic	GER	2:20:29

After winning the test event prior to the Olympics, Julien Absalon was among the favorites for gold. The 24-year-old from the Alsace-Lorraine region of France led throughout the 43.3 km race, pulling away in the second half to finish exactly one minute ahead of second-place José Antonio Hermida. Absalon was cheered on by a group of seventy fans from his hometown of Raon-aux-Bois, population 1,032. Watching from the sidelines, Absalon's wife, Emilie, fainted from the intense summer heat just as he made his final push for the finish.

2008 Beijing C: 50, N: 33, D: 8.23.
35.6 KM

1. Julien Absalon	FRA	1:55:59
2. Jean-Christophe Peraud	FRA	1:57:06
3. Nino Schurter	SWI	1:57:52
4. Christoph Sauser	SWI	1:57:54
5. Marco Fontana	ITA	1:59:59
6. Christoph Soukup	AUT	2:00:11
7. Liam Killeen	GBR	2:00:14
8. Iñaki Lejarreta Errasti	SPA	2:00:21

After earning the gold medal in Athens, Julien Absalon won four consecutive world championships. His only loss was at the 2008 world championships in Val di Sole, Italy, two months before the Beijing Olympics, when he dropped out of the race due to heatstroke. Double world silver medalist Christoph Sauser went on to win.

Despite the oppressive heat (32°C/90°F) and 90% humidity in Beijing, any doubts about Absalon's performance quickly vanished as he moved into the lead on the second lap and was never challenged. His teammate, Jean-Christophe Peraud, took silver, with 22-year-old Nino Schurter edging out his Swiss teammate Sauser for bronze.

BMX RACE

BMX, or Bicycle Motocross, uses specially-designed bikes with 20-inch (51-cm) wheels. Each competition includes 32 athletes, with two qualifying rounds. The best round for each cyclist determines seeding into the quarter-finals. Each race, or moto, includes up to eight riders. In elimination rounds the top four riders advance to the next round. National slots are determined based on International Cycling Union national rankings and the 2008 UCI World Championships. In the Men's event 24 places will be determined by UCI ranking, six by the World Championship and two by host country invitation, with a maximum of three men per nation.

1896–2004 not held

2008 Beijing C: 32, N: 20, D: 8.22.

1. Māris Štrombergs	LAT	36.190
2. Mike Day	USA	36.606
3. Donny Robinson	USA	36.972
4. Andrés Jiménez	COL	39.137
5. Rob van den Wildenberg	HOL	39.772
6. Jared Graves	AUS	2:19.233

DNF: Sifiso Nhlapo (SAF), Damien Godet (FRA)

Making its Olympic debut, the BMX competition featured cheerleaders, blaring rock music and plenty of crashes, including one in the quarter-finals that eliminated three-time world champion Kyle Bennett with a dislocated shoulder. Double world champion medalist Mike Day finished first in the qualifying round and won both his quarter- and semi-final heats. Reigning world champion Māris Štrombergs did the same and started the final in the No. 1 gate slot. Štrombergs, Day and Robinson all finished within one second of each other. Štrombergs had been riding BMX for 16 years and was already considered a veteran at only 21 years old.

DISCONTINUED EVENTS

ONE-LAP RACE

1896 Athens C: 8, N: 5, D: 4.11.
(333.33 Meters)

1. Paul Masson	FRA	24.0
2. Stamatios Nikolopoulos	GRE	26.0
3. Adolf Schmal	AUT	26.0
4. Edward Battel	GBR	26.2
5. Theodor Flameng	GER	27.0
5. Frank Keeping	GBR	27.0
5. Theodor Leupold	GER	27.0
8. Joseph Rosemeyer	GER	27.2

Nikolopoulos was awarded second place after defeating Schmal in a race-off 25.4 to 26.6.

1900–1904 not held

1906 Athens C: 24, N: 9, D: 4.24.
(333.33 Meters)

1. Francesco Verri	ITA	22.8
2. Herbert Crowther	GBR	23.2
3. Henri Menjou	FRA	23.2
4. Émile Demangel	FRA	23.2
5. Eugène Debougnie	BEL	23.6
6. Federico Della Ferrera	ITA	23.8
6. Alexandros Verdesopoulos	GRE	23.8

8. Herbert Bouffler (GBR), Bruno Götze (GER), Max Götze (GER), T. John Matthews (GBR) 24.2

Crowther was awarded second place after winning a race-off. His time was 22.8, while Menjou clocked 23.2 and Demangel 23.6.

1908 London C: 46, N: 9, D: 7.15.
(603.49 Meters)

1. Victor Johnson	GBR	51.2
2. Émile Demangel	FRA	—
3. Karl Neumer	GER	—
4. Daniel Flynn	GBR	—

Johnson defeated Demangel by only a few inches. In 1909 Johnson recorded a time of 28.0 seconds for a quarter mile from a standing start. This was recognized as a world record for 21 years until stricter standards for records were enforced.

¼ MILE TRACK RACE (402.34 METERS)

1904 St. Louis C: 11, N: 1, D: 8.3.

1. Marcus Hurley	USA	31.8
2. Burton Downing	USA	—
3. Edwin Billington	USA	—
4. Oscar Goerke	USA	—

Hurley won by one and a half lengths.

⅓ MILE TRACK RACE (536.45 METERS)

1904 St. Louis C: 10, N: 1, D: 8.5.

1. Marcus Hurley	USA	43.8
2. Burton Downing	USA	—
3. Edwin Billington	USA	—
4. Charles Schlee	USA	—

Hurley won by one length.

½ MILE TRACK RACE (804.67 METERS)

1904 St. Louis C: 16, N: 1, D: 8.2.

1. Marcus Hurley	USA	1:09.0
2. Edwin Billington	USA	—
3. Burton Downing	USA	—
4. George Wiley	USA	—

Hurley won by one and a half lengths

1000-METER TIME TRIAL

In the time trial, the competitors take turns racing against the clock from a standing start.

1928 Amsterdam C: 14, N: 14, D: 8.7.

1. Villy Falck Hansen	DEN	1:14.4
2. Gerard Bosch van Drakestein	HOL	1:15.2
3. Edgar "Dunc" Gray	AUS	1:15.6
4. Octave Dayen	FRA	1:16.0
5. Kurt Einsiedel	GER	1:17.2
6. Edward Kerridge	GBR	1:18.0
6. Józef Lange	POL	1:18.0
8. Jean Aerts	BEL	1:18.6

The bronze medalist, Dunc Gray, had never ridden in a time trial before the Olympics. Four years later he was the Olympic champion. The Sydney Olympic velodrome was named in his honor.

1932 Los Angeles C: 9, N: 9, D: 8.1.

1. Edgar "Dunc" Gray	AUS	1:13.0 OR
2. Jacobus van Egmond	HOL	1:13.3
3. Charles Rampelberg	FRA	1:13.4
4. Luigi Consonni	ITA	1:14.7
4. William Harvell	GBR	1:14.7
6. Lewis Rush	CAN	1:15.6
7. Harald Christensen	DEN	1:16.0
8. Bernard Mammes	USA	1:18.0

1936 Berlin C: 19, N: 19, D: 8.8.

1. Arie van Vliet	HOL	1:12.0 OR
2. Pierre Georget	FRA	1:12.8
3. Rudolf Karsch	GER	1:13.2
4. Benedetto Pola	ITA	1:13.6
5. László Orczán	HUN	1:14.0
5. Arne Pedersen	DEN	1:14.0
7. Raymond Hicks	GBR	1:14.8
8. George Giles	NZL	1:15.0

1948 London C: 21, N: 21, D: 8.11. WR: 1:10.0 (Fabio Battesini)

1. Jacques Dupont	FRA	1:13.5
2. Pierre Nihant	BEL	1:14.5
3. Thomas Godwin	GBR	1:15.0
4. Hans Fluckiger	SWI	1:15.3
5. Axel Schandorff	DEN	1:15.5
6. Sidney Patterson	AUS	1:15.7
7. John Heid	USA	1:16.2
8. Walter Freitag	AUT	1:16.8

1952 Helsinki C: 27, N: 27, D: 7.31. WR: 1:09.8 (Reginald Harris)

1. Russell Mockridge	AUS	1:11.1 OR
2. Marino Morettini	ITA	1:12.7
3. Raymond Robinson	SAF	1:13.0
4. Clodomiro Cortoni	ARG	1:13.2
5. Donald McKellow	GBR	1:13.3
6. Ib Vagn Hansen	DEN	1:14.4
6. Ion Ionită	ROM	1:14.4
8. Johannes Hijzelendoorn	HOL	1:14.5

Russell Mockridge believed that cycling was somewhat boring, but he felt compelled to keep returning to it because it was clearly something that he was very good at. Mockridge worked as a journalist but quit his job. He studied art but dropped out. After competing in the road race at the 1948 London Olympics and winning two gold medals at the 1950 British Empire Games, Mockridge told the press, "I feel there is a lot more to this life than riding a bicycle," and announced that he was giving up cycling to become a minister in the Church of England. A few months later he changed his mind again and returned to competitive cycling.

Mockridge seemed assured a place on the 1952 Australian Olympic team until he refused to sign a statement that he would refrain from turning professional for two years. While the controversy over his participation was reaching the floor of Parliament, Mockridge was racing in Europe. A month before the Olympics he became the first amateur to win the Paris Open Grand Prix. Back in Australia, Mockridge's hometown of Geelong worked out a face-saving compromise with the Australian Olympic Federation by which the agreement was limited to one year.

Mockridge arrived in Helsinki four days before he was scheduled to compete. On July 31 he won the gold medal for the time trial and then teamed with Lionel Cox to win a second gold medal in the tandem. Six years later Mockridge was in Melbourne, competing in the 140-mile Tour of Gippsland. Three miles after the start, Mockridge and five other cyclists, followed in a car by Mockridge's wife and 3-year-old daughter, were crossing an intersection when a bus came up on the right and struck Mockridge, killing him instantly. He was 30 years old.

1956 Melbourne C: 22, N: 22, D: 12.6. WR: 1:08.6 (Reginald Harris)

1. Leandro Faggin	ITA	1:09.8 OR
2. Ladislav Fouček	CZE	1:11.4
3. Alfred Swift	SAF	1:11.6
4. Warren Scarfe	AUS	1:12.1
5. Alan Danson	GBR	1:12.3
5. Boris Savostin	SOV/RUS	1:12.3
5. Louis Serra	URU	1:12.3
8. Warwick Dalton	NZL	1:12.6

1960 Rome C: 25, N: 25, D: 8.26. WR: 1:07.5 (Sante Gaiardoni)

1. Sante Gaiardoni	ITA	1:07.27 WR
2. Dieter Gieseler	GER	1:08.75
3. Rostislav Vargashkin	SOV/RUS	1:08.86
4. Pieter van der Touw	HOL	1:09.20
5. Ian Chapman	AUS	1:09.55
6. Anesio Argenton	BRA	1:09.96
7. Jean Govaerts	BEL	1:10.23
8. Josef Helbling	SWI	1:10.42

1964 Tokyo C: 27, N: 27, D: 10.16. WR: 1:07.27 (Sante Gaiardoni)

1. Patrick Sercu	BEL	1:09.59
2. Giovanni Pettenella	ITA	1:10.09
3. Pierre Trentin	FRA	1:10.42
4. Pieter van der Touw	HOL	1:10.68
5. Jiři Pecka	CZE	1:10.70
6. Lothar Claesges	GER	1:10.86
7. Wacław Latocha	POL	1:11.12
8. Roger Gibbon	TRI	1:11.19

Known as "The Flemish Arrow," Patrick Sercu turned professional in 1965 and, over the next eighteen years, set a record by winning 88 six-day races.

1968 Mexico City C: 32, N: 32, D: 10.17. WR: 1:04.61 (Gianni Sartori)

1. Pierre Trentin	FRA	1:03.91 WR
2. Niels Fredborg	DEN	1:04.61
3. Janusz Kierzkowski	POL	1:04.63
4. Gianni Sartori	ITA	1:04.65
5. Roger Gibbon	TRI	1:04.66
6. Leijn Loevesijn	HOL	1:04.84
7. Jocelyn Lovell	CAN	1:05.18
8. Serhei Kravtsov	SOV/UKR	1:05.21

Trentin won three medals in Mexico City: a gold in the time trial, a gold in the tandem, and a bronze in the sprint.

1972 Munich C: 32, N: 32, D: 8.31. WR: 1:03.91 (Pierre Trentin)

1. Niels Fredborg	DEN	1:06.44
2. Daniel Clark	AUS	1:06.87
3. Jürgen Schütze	GDR	1:07.02
4. Karl Köther	GER	1:07.21
5. Janusz Kierzkowski	POL	1:07.22
6. Dimo Angelov	BUL	1:07.55
7. Christian Brunner	SWI	1:07.71
8. Eduard Rapp	SOV/RUS	1:07.73

1976 Montreal C: 30, N: 30, D: 7.20. WR: 1:03.91 (Pierre Trentin)

1. Klaus-Jürgen Grünke	GDR	1:05.927
2. Michel Vaarten	BEL	1:07.516
3. Niels Fredborg	DEN	1:07.617
4. Janusz Kierzkowski	POL	1:07.660
5. Eric Vermeulen	FRA	1:07.846
6. Hans Michalsky	GER	1:07.878
7. Harald Bundli	NOR	1:08.093
8. Walter Baeni	SWE	1:08.12

One of the favorites, Eduard Rapp of the USSR was eliminated due to an unfortunate incident. He started before the gun and, assuming he would be ordered to restart, he stopped racing. But the officials ruled his start to be legal, and he was disqualified for stopping.

1980 Moscow C: 18, N: 18, D: 7.22. WR: 1:04.225 (José Ruchansky)

1. Lothar Thoms	GDR	1:02.955 OR
2. Aleksandr Panfilov	SOV/UZB	1:04.845
3. David Weller	JAM	1:05.241
4. Guido Bontempi	ITA	1:05.478
5. Yave Cahard	FRA	1:05.584
6. Heinz Isler	SWI	1:06.273
7. Petr Kocek	CZE	1:06.368
8. Bjarne Carl Sorensen	DEN	1:07.422

Thom's time was recognized as a world indoor record. David Weller is the only Jamaican to win a medal in a sport other than track and field.

1984 Los Angeles-Carson C: 25, N: 25, D: 7.30. WR: 1:02.547 (Maic Malchow)

1. Fredy Schmidtke	GER	1:06.10
2. Curtis Harnett	CAN	1:06.44
3. Fabrice Colas	FRA	1:06.65
4. Gene Samuel	TRI	1:06.69
5. Craig Adair	NZE	1:06.96
6. David Weller	JAM	1:07.24
7. Marcelo Alexandre	ARG	1:07.29
8. Rory O'Reilly	USA	1:07.39

1988 Seoul C: 30, N: 30, D: 9.20. WR: 1:02.091 (Maic Malchow)

1. Oleksandr Kyrychenko	SOV/UKR	1:04.499
2. Martin Vinnicombe	AUS	1:04.784
3. Robert Lechner	GER	1:05.114
4. Kurt Kenneth Ropke	DEN	1:05.168
5. Bernardo González	SPA	1:05.281
6. Maic Malchow	GDR	1:05.393
7. Anthony Graham	NZL	1:05.744
8. Frédéric Magné	FRA	1:06.142

Kyrychenko's rear tire began to deflate with one lap to go. By the time he crossed the finish line, half the air was gone. According to the rules of the competition, Kyrychenko could have demanded a restart, but his coach, Boris Vasilyev (a bronze medalist in the 1960 tandem), refused, reasoning that Kyrychenko would be too exhausted to improve his time. Soviet team officials were furious and let it be known that Vasilyev could begin looking for a new job. When the last rider, the favorite, Martin Vinnicombe, crossed the finish line without bettering Kyrychenko's time, Vasilyev tearfully embraced Kyrychenko and thanked him for saving his job.

1992 Barcelona C: 32, N: 32, D: 7.27. WR: 1:02.091 (Maic Malchow)

1. José Manuel Moreno Periñán	SPA	1:03.342
2. Shane Kelly	AUS	1:04.288
3. Erin Hartwell	USA	1:04.753
4. Jens Glücklich	GER	1:04.798
5. Adler Capelli	ITA	1:05.065
6. Frédéric Lancien	FRA	1:05.157
7. Jon Andrews	NZL	1:05.240
8. Gene Samuel	TRI	1:05.485

José Manuel Moreno was the defending world champion and very familiar with the Olympic Velodrome. But the Spanish team decided to take no chances in securing their nation's first gold medal of the Barcelona Games. Moreno warmed up at a track a few kilometers away and was then airlifted by helicopter to the Velodrome just in time for his ride. After breaking his left collarbone in 1991, Moreno prayed at his local church in Chiclana de la Frontera and vowed that if he won the world championship he would donate his medal to the church. His gold medals from the world championships and the Olympics are on display at the church, as are the jerseys he wore.

1996 Atlanta-Stone Mountain C: 20, N: 20, D: 7.24. WR: 1:00.613 (Shane Kelly)

1. Florian Rousseau	FRA	1:02.712 OR
2. Erin Hartwell	USA	1:02.940
3. Takanobu Jumonji	JPN	1:03.261
4. Soren Lausberg	GER	1:03.514
5. Jean-Pierre van Zyl	SAF	1:04.214
6. Grzegorz Krejner	POL	1:04.697
7. Dimitrios Georgalis	GRE	1:04.995
8. Ainars Kiksis	LAT	1:05.457

Florian Rousseau of Orléans won the world championship in 1993 and 1994. But in 1995 he was beaten by Australia's Shane Kelly, who set a world record in the process. Rousseau and Kelly were the last two to ride at the Olympics. Rousseau broke the 16-year-old Olympic record to secure at least a silver medal. Kelly took off—and immediately his left foot slipped out of the pedal clasp. He never finished the course. Dirk van Hameren of the Netherlands, who placed twelfth, was fined 500 Swiss francs for wearing an unorthodox jersey. The surprise bronze medal winner, Takanobu Jumonji, thanks to the generosity of various cycling associations, was awarded 41 million yen, far more than any other Japanese medal winner in any sport.

2000 Sydney C: 16, N: 15, D: 9.16. WR: 1:00.148 (Arnaud Tournant)

1. Jason Queally	GBR	1:01.609
2. Stefan Nimke	GER	1:02.487
3. Shane Kelly	AUS	1:02.818
4. Sören Lausberg	GER	1:02.937
5. Arnaud Tournant	FRA	1:03.023
6. Dimitrios Georgalis	GRE	1:04.018
7. Grzegorz Krejner	POL	1:04.156
8. Garen Bloch	SAF	1:04.478

In May 1995, Jason Queally was a 25-year-old research technician at Lancaster University. While training to try the triathlon, he joined a local bike club and did a time trial in 1 minute 9 seconds, only two seconds slower than the British national record. Pleased to find something he was good at, he concentrated on cycling. The following year, however, he fell during a track race in Edinburgh and two thick 18-inch splinters of the track border jammed into his back. He came away from the near-fatal accident with 70 stitches and a year-long recovery. In Sydney he thought he might have a shot at the bronze medal since the gold and silver were conceded to two-time defending world champion and world record holder Arnaud Tournant and local favorite Shane Kelly. Queally later explained that after completing the course, "it felt the same as usual when I raced. So when I saw the board showing 1:01:6, I thought, 'What's this?' But it was my time." He had just improved his personal best by 1.4 seconds and his sea level best by more than 1.8 seconds. Before the Olympics, Queally had bemoaned his late start in the sport, noting, "Sometimes . . . I think, 'Crikey, what if I'd started at the age of 12 or 13. I could've been Olympic champion.'" As it turned out, his timing was perfect.

2004 Athens C: 17, N: 13, D: 8.20. WR: 58.875 (Arnaud Tournant)

1. Christopher Hoy	GBR	1:00.711 OR
2. Arnaud Tournant	FRA	1:00.896
3. Stefan Nimke	GER	1:01.186
4. Shane Kelly	AUS	1:01.224
5. Theo Bos	HOL	1:01.986
6. François Pervis	FRA	1:02.328
7. Craig MacLean	GBR	1:02.369
8. Carsten Bergemann	GER	1:02.551

An Edinburgh native, Chris Hoy began his career competing in BMX. Starting last, Hoy watched nervously as the Olympic record was beaten three times, by Shane Kelly, Stefan Nimke and, finally, by four-time world champion Arnaud Tournant. On his turn Hoy got off to a fast start and never slipped behind Tournant's mark. Only six days before the competition Hoy was riding in the Olympic village when he ran over melting tar and fell, landing on his knee, thigh and elbow. Fortunately, the accident occurred in front of the Village first aid headquarters. Hoy had a history of sustaining injures prior to major competitions: in 1997, while competing in the junior World Championships, he broke his wrist before earning silver in the team sprint; in 2002 he severed a tendon in his foot shortly before winning the Commonwealth title; and in March 2004 he was knocked off his bike by a police van while training for the world championship (which he won).

ONE MILE TRACK RACE (1609.34 METERS)

1904 St. Louis C: 13, N: 1, D: 8.3.

1. Marcus Hurley	USA	2:41.6
2. Burton Downing	USA	—
3. Edwin Billington	USA	—
4. Oscar Goerke	USA	—

Marcus Hurley won four of the seven amateur cycling events in 1904 and placed third in another. He later became an All-American basketball player for Columbia University.

TWO MILE TRACK RACE (3218.69 METERS)

1904 St. Louis C: 13, N: 1, D: 8.3.

1. Burton Downing	USA	4:57.8
2. Oscar Goerke	USA	—
3. Marcus Hurley	USA	—
4. Edwin Billington	USA	—

Downing defeated Goerke by about one wheel.

5000 METER TRACK RACE

1906 Athens C: 26, N: 9, D: 4.25.

1. Francesco Verri	ITA	7:28.6
2. Herbert Crowther	GBR	—
3. Fernand Vast	FRA	—
4. Emile Demangel	FRA	—
5. Max Götze	GER	—

1908 London C: 42, N: 8, D: 7.18.

1. Benjamin Jones	GBR	8:36.2
2. Maurice Schilles	FRA	—
3. André Auffray	FRA	—
4. Emile Maréchal	FRA	—
5. Clarence Kingsbury	GBR	—
6. Johannes van Spengen	HOL	—
7. Gerard Bosch van Drakestein	HOL	—

In the final of the 1000-meter sprint, Schilles beat Jones by inches. However, the race was declared void because the time limit was exceeded. Two days later in the 5000 meters it was Jones who held off Schilles' finishing sprint to win by 6 inches. Jones was a coal miner from Wigan.

5 MILE TRACK RACE (8046.72 METERS)

1904 St. Louis C: ?, N: 1, D: 8.5.

1. Charles Schlee	USA	13:08.2
2. George Wiley	USA	—
3. Arthur Andrews	USA	—
4. Julius Schaefer	USA	—

Most of the riders fell in a crash precipitated by the aptly nicknamed J. Nash "Crash" McCrea. Schlee defeated Wiley by five lengths.

10 KM TRACK RACE

1896 Athens C: 6, N: 4, D: 4.11.

1. Paul Masson	FRA	17:54.2
2. Léon Flameng	FRA	17:54.8
3. Adolf Schmal	AUT	—
4. Joseph Rosemeyer	GER	—

AC: Aristidis Konstantinidis (GRE)
DNF: Georgios Kolettis (GRE)

20 KM TRACK RACE

1906 Athens C: 24, N: 9, D: 4.25.

1. William Pett	GBR	29:00.0
2. Maurice Bardonneau	FRA	29:30.0
3. Fernand Vast	FRA	29:32.0
4. Hans Holly	AUT	—
5. Erich Dannenberg	GER	—
6. Edmond Luguet	FRA	—

DNF: Adolf Böhm (GER)

Billy Pett did not begin cycling until he was 20 years old. His training was hampered by the fact that he worked 11 hours a day in the wine cellars at Harrods. He was 32 when he earned his gold medal in Athens.

1908 London C: 43, N: 10, D: 7.14.

1. Clarence Kingsbury	GBR	34:13.6
2. Benjamin Jones	GBR	—
3. Joseph Werbrouck	BEL	—
4. Louis Weintz	USA	—

Kingsbury, of Portsmouth, won by 3 inches. From the Olympics, Kingsbury went to the world championships in Leipzig, Germany. After triumphing there he returned home to a hero's welcome attended by tens of thousands of people.

25 KM TRACK RACE

1900 Paris C: 7, N: 2, D: 9.15.

1. Louis Bastien	FRA	25:36.2
2. Louis Hildebrand	FRA	28:09.4
3. Daumain	FRA	29:36.2
4. Bertrand	FRA	—

25 MILE TRACK RACE (40,233.61 METERS)

1904 St. Louis C: 10, N: 1, D: 8.5.

1. Burton Downing	USA	1:10:55.4
2. Arthur Andrews	USA	—
3. George Wiley	USA	—
4. Samuel LaVoice	USA	—

Downing passed Andrews on the backstretch of the last lap and won by one and a half lengths.

50 KM TRACK RACE

1920 Antwerp C: 31, N: 10, D: 8.10.

1. Henry George	BEL	1:16:43.2
2. Cyril Alden	GBR	—
3. Piet Ikelaar	HOL	—
4. Ruggero Ferrario	ITA	—
5. Herbert MacDonald	CAN	—
6. Franco Giorgetti	ITA	—
7. William Smith	SAF	—

8. Gaston Alancourt (FRA), Charles Cadron (BEL), Gustave de Schryver (BEL), Thomas Harvey (GBR), Primo Magnani (ITA), William Steward (GBR), James Walker (SAF).

Eyewitnesses said that Ikelaar actually finished second. The Jury of Appeal eventually agreed, but refused to reverse the judges' verdict, since it had already been announced.

1924 Paris C: 36, N: 16, D: 7.27.

1. Jacobus Willems	HOL	1:18:24.0
2. Cyril Alden	GBR	—
3. Frederick Wyld	GBR	—
4. Angelo De Martino	ITA	—
5. Józef Lange	POL	—
6. Alfredo Dinale	ITA	—

100 KM TRACK RACE

1896 Athens C: 9, N: 5, D: 4.8.

1. Léon Flameng	FRA	3:08:19.2
2. Georgios Kolettis	GRE	—

The race required 300 circuits of the track. Once, when Kolettis' bike needed repair, Flameng stopped and waited for him. Flameng fell towards the end of the race, but still won by eleven laps. He raced with a French flag tied around his leg.

1900–1906 not held

1908 London C: 43, N: 11, D: 7.16.

1. Charles Bartlett	GBR	2:41:48.6
2. Charles Denny	GBR	—
3. Octave Lapize	FRA	—
4. William Pett	GBR	—
5. Pierre Teixier	FRA	—
6. Walter Andrews	CAN	—
7. D.C. Robertson	GBR	—
8. Sydney Bailey	GBR	—

This was considered the most important cycling contest of the 1908 Olympics, and there were so many entrants that qualifying heats had to be run to cut down the field. In the second of these heats, a bad accident occurred when Harry Venn, a walking official, walked right onto the track and collided with Coeckelberg of Belgium. Coeckelberg fell to the ground and was cut on the thigh and head, but he managed to finish the race, qualifying for the final as a consequence of his having led much of the way. The final was contested on a wet track with rain still falling when the race began. After 70 kilometers Bartlett fell and was forced to mount a new bike. He lost a lap but caught up with one lap to go. By this time the race had come down to Octave Lapize of France and three representatives of Great Britain, Bartlett, Charles Denny, and Billy Pett. The four were moving around at a crawl when Bartlett suddenly darted to the inside, took the lead, and sprinted home to win by almost a length.

Octave Lapize won the Tour de France in 1910. A fighter pilot during World War I, he was shot down over Vouziers in July 1917 and died at the age of 27.

C.H. Bartlett, 1908

Bartlett won the 100-kilometer track race in 1908 despite falling and being forced to mount a new bicycle.

12-HOUR RACE

1896 Athens C: 7, N: 4, D: 4.13.

		KM
1. Adolf Schmal	AUT	295.3
2. Frank Keeping	GBR	294.654

DNF: Georgios Paraskevopoulos (GRE), Konstantinos Kenstantinou (GRE), Loverdos (GRE), A. Tryfiatis-Tripiaris (GRE), Josef Welzenbacher (GER)

Frank Keeping was apparently the butler of the British ambassador in Athens.

2000-METER TANDEM

1906 Athens T: 6, N: 4, D: 4.24.

1. GBR	T. John Matthews, Arthur Rushen	2:15.0
2. GER	Max Götze, Bruno Götze	—
3. GER	Karl Arnold, Otto Küpferling	—

Matthews and Rushen upset the Götze brothers, winning by 20 yards.

1908 London T: 17, N: 7, D: 7.15.

1. FRA	Maurice Schilles, André Auffray	3:07.6
2. GBR	Frederick Hamlin, Horace "Tiny" Johnson	—
3. GBR	Colin Brooks, Walter Isaacs	—

Schilles and Auffray had never ridden together before the first round of this contest.

1912 not held

1920 Antwerp T: 11, N: 6, D: 8.10.

1. GBR	Harry Ryan, Thomas Lance	2:49.2
2. SAF	James Walker, William Smith	—
3. HOL	Frans de Vreng, Piet Ikelaar	—
4. GBR	William Stewart, Cyril Alden	—

Ryan and Lance covered the last 200 meters in 11.2 seconds to win by a length.

1924 Paris T: 5, N: 5, D: 7.27.

1. FRA	Lucien Choury, Jean Cugnot	12.6 (last 200 meters)
2. DEN	Willy Falck Hansen, Edmund Hansen	—
3. HOL	Gerard Bosch van Drakestein, Mouritius "Maurice" Peeters	—

1928 Amsterdam T: 7, N: 7, D: 8.7.

1. HOL	Bernhard Leene, Daniel van Dijk	11.8
2. GBR	John Sibbitt, Ernest Chambers	—
3. GER	Karl Köther, Hans Bernhardt	—
4. ITA	Francesco Malatesta, Adolf Corsi	—

1932 Los Angeles T: 5, N: 5, D: 8.3.

		1ST RACE	2ND RACE
1. FRA	Maurice Perrin, Louis Chaillot	12.3	12.0
2. GBR	Ernest Chambers, Stanley Chambers	—	—
3. DEN	Willy Gervin, Harald Christensen		
4. HOL	Bernhard Leene, Jacobus van Egmond		

1936 Berlin T: 11, N: 11, D: 8.8.

		1ST RACE	2ND RACE
1. GER	Ernst Ihbe, Carl Lorenz	11.0	11.0
2. HOL	Bernhard Leene, Hendrik Ooms	—	—
3. FRA	Pierre Georget, Georges Maton		
4. ITA	Carlo Legutti, Bruno Loatti		

5. François Cools, Roger Pirotte (BEL), Heino Dissing, Bjorn Stièler (DEN), Ernest Chambers, John Sibbitt (GBR), William Logan, Albert Sellinger (USA)

1948 London T: 10, N: 10, D: 8.11.

		1ST RACE	2ND RACE	3RD RACE
1. ITA	Ferdinando Teruzzi, Renato Perona	—	11.3	11.6
2. GBR	Reginald Harris, Alan Bannister	11.1	—	—
3. FRA	René Faye, Georges Dron			
4. SWI	Jean Roth, Max Aeberli			

5. Louis van Schill, Roger de Pauw (BEL), Hans Andersen, Evan Klamer (DEN), Nicolaas Buchly, Martinus van Gelder (HOL), Marvin Thompson, Alfred Stiller (USA)

In a thrilling finish, held in the dark, Teruzzi and Perona won the tie-breaker by a mere six inches.

1952 Helsinki T: 14, N: 14, D: 7.31.

1. AUS	Lionel Cox, Russell Mockridge	11.0
2. SAF	Raymond Robinson, Thomas Shardelow	—
3. ITA	Antonio Maspes, Cesare Pinarello	
4. FRA	Franck Le Normand, Robert Vidal	

5. Jens Eriksen, Olaf Holmstrup (DEN), Leslie Wilson, Alan Bannister (GBR), Istán Schillerwein, Imre Furmen (HUN), Colin Dickinson, Clarence Simpson (NZL)

1956 Melbourne T: 10, N: 10, D: 6.12.

1. AUS	Ian Browne, Anthony Marchant	10.8
2. CZE	Ladislav Fouček, Václav Machek	—
3. ITA	Giuseppe Ogna, Cesare Pinarello	
4. GBR	Peter Brotherton, Eric Thompson	

5. Robert Vidal, André Gruchet (FRA), Richard Johnston, Warren Johnston (NZL), Thomas Shardelow, Raymond Robinson (SAF), James Rossi, Donald Ferguson (USA)

Browne and Marchant were surprise winners. They finished last in their first-round heat and lost the *repêchage* to Czechoslovakia. However, in another *repêchage*, the Germans and Soviets crashed, leaving the Soviet riders unable to restart. In need of opponents for the German pair, the officials turned to the already-eliminated Australians and Americans. Browne and Marchant won the race, scored two more unexpected victories in the quarterfinals and semifinals, and then upset Fouček and Machek in the final.

1960 Rome T: 12, N: 12, D: 8.27.

		1ST RACE	2ND RACE
1. ITA	Giuseppe Beghetto, Sergio Bianchetto	10.7	10.8
2. GDR	Jürgen Simon, Lothar Stäber	—	—
3. SOV/RUS	Boris Vasilyev, Vladimir Leonov	walkover	
4. HOL	Marinus Paul, Melis Gerritsen		

5. Juraj Miklusica, Dusan Skvarenin (CZE), Roland Surrugue, Michael Scob (FRA), David Handley, Eric Thompson (GBR), Jack Hartman, David Sharp (USA)

1964 Tokyo T: 13, N: 13, D: 10.20.

		1ST RACE	2ND RACE	3RD RACE
1. ITA	Angelo Damiano, Sergio Bianchetto	—	10.85	10.75
2. SOV	Imant Bodnieks, Viktor Logunov	10.80	—	—
3. GER	Willi Fuggerer, Klaus Kobusch			
4. HOL	Arie de Graaf, Pieter van der Touw			

5. Ian Browne, Daryl Perkins (AUS), Karel Paar, Karel Stark (CZE), Niels Fredborg, Per Jorgensen (DEN), Richárd Bicskey, Ferenc Habony (HUN)

1968 Mexico City T: 14, N: 14, D: 10.21.

		1ST RACE	2ND RACE
1. FRA	Daniel Morelon, Pierre Trentin	10.03	9.83
2. HOL	Johannes Jansen, Leijn Loevesijn	—	—
3. BEL	Daniel Goens, Robert van Lancker		
4. ITA	Walter Gorini, Luigi Borghetti		

5. Ivan Kucirek, Milos Jelinek (CZE), Werner Otto, Jürgen Geschke (GDR), Klaus Kobusch, Martin Stenzel (GER), Igor Tselovalnikov, Imant Bodnieks (SOV)

1972 Munich T: 14, N: 14, D: 9.3.

		1ST RACE	2ND RACE	3RD RACE
1. SOV/UKR	Volodymyr Semenets, Ihor Tselovalnykov	—	10.52	10.60
2. GDR	Jürgen Geschke, Werner Otto	10.68	—	—
3. POL	Andrzej Bek, Benedykt Kocot			
4. FRA	Daniel Morelon, Pierre Trentin			

5. Manu Snellinx, Noel Scetaert (BEL), Ivan Kucirek, Vladimir Popelka (CZE), Jürgen Barth, Rainer Müller (GER), Klaas Balk, Peter van Doorn (HOL)

TEAM TIME TRIAL

Until 1960 the results of the individual road race were used to determine the team winner. However, starting with the 1960 Rome Olympics a separate team event was held in which four cyclists from each team raced against the clock, riding together in a line and periodically changing positions as in the team pursuit. The official time was that of the third rider for each team.

1912 Stockholm T: 15, N: 14, D: 7.7.
315.4 KM

		COMBINED TIME
1. SWE	Eric Friborg, Ragnar Malm, Axel Persson, Algot Lönn	44:35:33.6
2. GBR/ENG	Frederick Grubb, Leon Meredith Charles Moss, William Hammond	44:44:39.4
3. USA	Carl Schutte, Alvin Loftes, Albert Krushel, Walter Martin	44:47:55.5
4. GBR/SCO	John Wilson, Robert Thompson John Miller, David Stevensen	46:29:55.6
5. FIN	Antti Raita, Vilho Tilkanen, Johan Kankonnen, Hjalmar Väre	46:34:03.5
6. GER	Franz Lemnitz, Rudolf Baier, Oswald Rathmann, Georg Warsow	46:35:16.1
7. AUT	Robert Rammer, Adolf Kofler, Rudolf Kramer, Josef Hellensteiner	46:57:26.4
8. DEN	Olaf Meyland-Smith, Charles Hansen, Johannes Reinwaldt, Godtfred Olsen	47:16:07.0

1920 Antwerp T: 11, N: 11, D: 8.12.
175 KM

		COMBINED TIME
1. FRA	Fernand Canteloube, Georges Detreille, Achille Souchard, Marcel Gobillot	19:16:43.4
2. SWE	Harry Stenqvist, Ragnar Malm, Axel Person, Sigfrid Lundberg	19:23:10.0
3. BEL	Jean Janssens, Albert de Bunne, André Vercruysse, Albert Wyckmans	19:28:44.4
4. DEN	Christian Johansen, Arnold Lundgren, Kristian Frisch, Ahrensborg Claussen	19:52:32.2
5. ITA	Federico Gay, Pietro Bestetti, Camillo Arduino, Dante Ghindani	20:26:44.0
6. HOL	Piet Ikelaar, Nico de Jong, Arie van der Stel, Pieter Kloppenburg	20:28:39.2
7. USA	Ernest Kockler, August Nogara, James Freeman, John Otto	21:32:36.6
8. NOR	Helge Flatby, Paul Henrichsen, Olaf Nygaard, Thorstein Stryken	21:35:11.8

1924 Paris T: 16, N: 16, D: 7.23.
168 KM

		COMBINED TIME
1. FRA	Armand Blanchonnet, René Hamel, Georges Wambst	19:30:14.0
2. BEL	Henri Hoevenaers, Alphonse Parfondry, Jean van den Bosch	19:46:55.4
3. SWE	Gunnar Sköld, Erik Bohlin, Ragnar Malm	19:59:41.6
4. SWI	Albert Blattmann, Otto Lehner, Georg Antenen	20:11:15.0
5. ITA	Ardito Bresciani, Antonio Negrini, Nello Ciaccheri	20:19:59.2
6. HOL	Cornelis Heeren, Jan Maas, Phillippus Hendrik Innemee	20:37:27.8

1928 Amsterdam T: 15, N: 15, D: 8.7.
168 KM

		COMBINED TIME
1. DEN	Henry Hansen, Leo Nielsen, Orla Jörgensen	15:09:14.0
2. GBR	Frank Southall, John Lauterwasser, John Middleton	15:14:49.0
3. SWE	Gösta Carlsson, Erik Jansson, E. Georg Johnsson	15:27:49.0
4. ITA	Allegro Grandi, Michele Orecchia, Ambrogio Beretta	15:33:12.0
5. BEL	Jean Aerts, Pierre Houdé, Joseph Lowagie	15:33:50.0
6. SWI	Gottlieb Amstein, Jakob Caironi, Tütel Wanzenried	15:35:21.0
7. FRA	André Aumerle, Louis Bessière, Octave Dayen	15:38:20.0
8. ARG	Cosine Saavedra, Francisco Bonvehi, José López	15:42:55.0

1932 Los Angeles T: 8, N: 8, D: 8.4.
100 KM

		COMBINED TIME
1. ITA	Attilo Pavesi, Guglielmo Segato, Giuseppe Olmo	7:27:15.2
2. DEN	Frode Sörensen, Leo Nielsen, Henry Hansen	7:38:50.2
3. SWE	Bernhard Britz, Sven Höglund, A. Arne Berg	7:39:12.6
4. GBR	Frank Southall, Charles Holland, Stanley Butler	7:44:53.0
5. FRA	Paul Chocque, Amédée Fournier, Henri Mouillefarine	7:46:31.8
6. USA	Henry O'Brien, Frank Connell, Otto Luedeke	7:51:55.6
7. CAN	Francis Elliott, James Jackson, Glen Robbins	8:01:38.0
8. GER	Hubert Ebner, Werner Lange-Wittich, Julius Maus	8:21:21.2

1936 Berlin T: 22, N: 22, D: 8.10.
100 KM

		COMBINED TIME
1. FRA	Robert Charpentier, Guy Lapébie, Robert Dorgebray	7:39:16.2
2. SWI	Ernst Nievergelt, Edgar Buchwalder, Kurt Ott	7:39:20.4
3. BEL	Auguste Garrebeek, Armand Putzeys, Francois Vandermette	7:39:21.0
4. ITA	Pierino Favalli, Glauco Servadei, Corrado Ardizzoni	7:39:22.0
5. AUT	Virgilius Altmann, Hans Höfner, Hans Schnalek	7:39:24.0

1948 London T: 25, N: 25, D: 8.13.
194.63 KM

		COMBINED TIME
1. BEL	Lode Wouters, Léon Delathouwer, Eugène van Roosbroeck	15:58:17.4
2. GBR	Robert Maitland, Gordon Thomas, C.S. Ian Scott	16:03:31.6
3. FRA	José Beyaert, Alain Moineau, Jacques Dupont	16:08:19.4
4. ITA	Alfo Ferrari, Silvio Pedroni, Franco Fanti	16:13:05.2
5. SWE	Nils Johansson, Harry Snell, Åke Olivestedt	16:20:26.6
6. SWI	Jakob Schenk, Jean Brun, Walter Reiser	16:23:04.2

7. ARG	Ceferino Perone, Dante Benvenuti, Miguel Sevillano	16:39:46.2

1952 Helsinki T: 27, N: 27, D: 8.2.
190.4 KM

		COMBINED TIME
1. BEL	André Noyelle, Robert Grondelaers, Lucien Victor	15:20:46.6
2. ITA	Dino Bruni, Vincenzo Zucconelli, Gianni Ghidini	15:33:27.3
3. FRA	Jacques Anquetil, Alfred Tonello, Claude Rover	15:38:58.1
4. SWE	Yngve Lundh, Stig Mårtensson, Allan Carlsson	15:41:34.3
5. GER	Edi Ziegler, Oskar Zeissner, Paul Maue	15:43:50.5
6. DEN	Hans Andersen, Jörgen Rasmussen, Poul Östergaard	15:48:02.0
7. LUX	André Moes, Roger Ludwig, Nicolas Morn	15:49:04.0
8. HOL	Arend Van't Hof, Johannes Planatz, Adrianus Voorting	15:52:22.7

Jacques Anquetil of the French team went on to win the Tour de France five times.

1956 Melbourne T: 20, N: 20, D: 12.7.
187.73 KM

		PTS.
1. FRA	2—Arnaud Geyre, 8—Maurice Moucheraud, 12—Michel Vermeulin	22
2. GBR	3—Alan Jackson, 6—Arthur Stanley Brittain, 14—William Holmes	23
3. GDR& GER	4—Horst Tüller, 5—Gustav-Adolf Schur, 18—Reinhold Pommer	27
4. ITA	1—Ercole Baldini, 7—Arnaldo Pambianco, 28—Dino Bruni	36
5. SWE	10—Lars Nordwall, 17—Karl-Ivan Andersson, 20—Roland Ströhm	47
6. SOV	15—Anatoly Cherepovich, 16—Mykola Kolumbet, 32—Viktor Kapitonov	63
7. BEL	23—Norbert Verougstraete, 24—Gustave De Smet, 42—François van den Bosch	89
8. COL	13—Ramon Hoyos Vallejo, 39—Pablo Hurtado Castañeda 40—Jaime Villegas	92

In 1956 the placings in the team road race were determined not by combined times, but by adding together the individual placings of the team members. Great Britain lost its chances for a gold medal when Billy Holmes crashed into a photographer who had stepped onto the course. Holmes was injured, but worse still, was delayed two and a half minutes while he changed a wheel. Holmes caught up with the leaders eleven miles later, but had he finished one second earlier, Britain would have taken first place.

1960 Rome T: 32, N: 32, D: 8.26.
100 KM

1. ITA	Antonio Bailetti, Ottavio Cogliati, Giacomo Fornoni, Livio Trapé	2:14:33.53
2. GDR	Gustav-Adolf Schur, Egon Adler, Erich Hagen, Günter Lörke	2:16:56.31
3. SOV/ RUS	Viktor Kapitonov, Yevgeny Klevzov, Yuri Melikhov, Aleksei Petrov	2:18:41:67
4. HOL	Johannes Hugens, Cornelis Lotz, Albert Sluis, Pieter van Kreuningen	2:19:15.71
5. SWE	Owe Adamson, Gunnar Göransson, Oswald Johansson, Gösta Pettersson	2:19:36.37
6. ROM	Ion Cosma, Gabriel Moiceanu, Aurel Şelaru, Ludovic Zanoni	2:20:18.91
7. FRA	Henri Duez, François Hamon, Roland Lacombe, Jacques Simon	2:20:36.38
8. SPA	Ignacio Astigarraga Uriarte, Juan Sanchez Camero, José Momene Campo, Ramon Saez Marzo	2:21:34:59

This race, which was run in 93-degree (34°C) heat, was marred by the death of Danish cyclist Knut Enemark, who collapsed from sunstroke and suffered a fractured skull. It was later determined that before the race Enemark had taken Ronicol, a blood circulation stimulant. Enemark was the first person to die in Olympic competition since the 1912 marathon.

1964 Tokyo T: 33, N: 33, D: 10.14.
109.89 KM

1. HOL	Evert Dolman, Gerben Karstens, Johannes "Jan" Pieterse, Hubertus "Bar" Zoet	2:26:31.19
2. ITA	Severino Andreoli, Luciano Dalla Bona, Pietro Guerra, Ferrucio Manza	2:26:55.39
3. SWE	Sven Hamrin, Erik Pettersson, Gösta Pettersson, Sture Pettersson	2:27:11.52
4. ARG	Héctor Acosta, Roberto Breppe, Delmo Delmastro, Rubén Placanica	2:27:58.55
5. SOV/ RUS	Yuri Melikhov, Anatoly Olizarenko, Aleksei Petrov, Gaynan Saidkhuschin	2:28:26.48
6. FRA	Marcel-Ernest Bidault, Georges Chappe, André Desvages, Jean-Claude Wuillemin	2:28:52.74
7. DEN	Flemming Hansen, Henning Petersen, Ole Pedersen, Ole Ritter	2:29:10.33
8. SPA	José Goyeneche, José López, Mariano Díaz, Luis Santamarina	2:30:55.26

This event took a special place in Olympic history because it was the first in which experimental drug testing was carried out. A series of tests were imposed before and after the race.

1968 Mexico City T: 30, N: 30, D: 10.15.
104 KM

1. HOL	Fedor den Hertog, Jan Krekels, Marinus Pijnen, Gerardes Zoetemelk	2:07:49.06
2. SWE	Erik Pettersson, Gösta Pettersson, Sture Pettersson, Tomas Pettersson	2:09:26.60
3. ITA	Giovanni Bramucci, Vittorio Marcelli, Mauro Simonetti, Pierfranco Vianelli	2:10:18.74
4. DEN	Verner Blaudzun, Jörgen Emil Hansen, Ole Hojlund Pederson, Leif Martensen	2:12:41.41
5. NOR	Thorleif Andresen, Ornulf Andresen, Tore Milsett, Leif Yli	2:14:32.85
6. POL	Jan Magiera, Zenon Czechowski, Marian Kegel, Andrzej Blawdzin	2:14:40.98
7. ARG	Juan Merlos, Carlos Alvarez, Roberto Breppe, Ernesto Contreras	2:15:34.24
8. GER	Burkhard Ebert, Jürgen Tschan, Ortwin Czarnowski, Dieter Koslar	2:15:37.25

The Pettersson Brothers, 1968
The Swedish brothers joined forces to win silver medals in the cycling team time trial.

The four Swedish silver medalists were all brothers. They won the world championship in 1967, 1968, and 1969. Three of them subsequently changed their last names from Pettersson to that of their home village, Fåglum.

1972 Munich T: 35, N: 35, D: 8.29.

100 KM

1. SOV/ RUS	Boris Shukhov, Valery Yardy, Gennady Komnatov, Valery Likhachov	2:11:17.8
2. POL	Lucjan Lis, Edward Barcik, Stanisław Szozda, Ryszard Szurkowski	2:11:47.5
3. BEL	Ludo Delcroix, Gustaaf Hermans, Gustaaf Van Cauter, Louis Verreydt	2:12:36.7
4. NOR	Thorleif Andresen, Arve Haugen, Knut Knudsen, Magne Orre	2:13:20.7
5. SWE	Lennart Fagerlund, Tord Filipsson, Leif Hansson, Sven-Åke Nilsson	2:13:36.9
6. HUN	Tibor Decreceni, Imre Géra, József Peterman, András Takács	2:14:18.8
7. SWI	Gilbert Bischoff, Bruno Hubschmid, Roland Schaer, Ulrich Sutter	2:14:33.6
8. ITA	Osvaldo Castellan, Pasqualino Moretti, Francesco Moser, Giovanni Tonoli	2:14:36.2

DISQ (Drugs): HOL: Fedor den Hertog, Hennie Kuiper, Cees Priem, Aad van den Hoek 2:12:27.1

The Dutch team was disqualified after it was determined that one of their members, Aad van den Hoek, had taken Coramine, a drug which was permitted by the International Cyclists' Union but forbidden by the International Olympic Committee. It was decided that the Belgian team would not be awarded bronze medals because its members had not been tested for drugs.

1976 Montreal T: 28, N: 28, D: 7.18.

100 KM

1. SOV	Anatoly Chukanov, Valery Chaplygin, Vladimir Kaminsky, Aavo Pikkuus	2:08:53
2. POL	Tadeusz Mytnik, Mieczyslaw Nowicki, Stanisław Szozda, Ryszard Szurkowski	2:09:13
3. DEN	Verner Blaudzun, Gert Frank, Jörgen Hansen, Törgen Lund	2:12:20
4. GER	Hans-Peter Jakst, Olaf Paltian, Friedrich von Löffelholz, Peter Weibel	2:12:35
5. CZE	Petr Buchaček, Petr Matoušek, Milan Puzrla, Vladimir Vondraček	2:12:56
6. GBR	Paul Carbutt, Philip Griffiths, M. Dudley Hayton, F. William Nickson	2:13:10
7. SWE	Tord Filipsson, Bernt Johansson, Sven-Åke Nilsson, Tommy Prim	2:13:13
8. NOR	Stein Bråthen, Geir Digerud, Arne Klavenes, Magne Orre	2:13:17

1980 Moscow T: 23, N: 23, D: 7.20.

101 KM

1. SOV	Yuri Kashirin, Oleg Logvin, Sergei Shelpakov, Anatoly Yarkin	2:01:21.7
2. GDR	Falk Boden, Bernd Drogan, Olaf Ludwig, Hans-Joachim Hartnick	2:02:53.2
3. CZE	Michal Klasa, Vlastibor Konečný, Alipi Kostadinov, Jiří Škoda	2:02:53.9
4. POL	Stefan Ciekanski, Jan Jankiewicz, Czesław Lang, Witold Plutecki	2:04:13.8
5. ITA	Mauro De Pellegrin, Gianni Giacomini, Ivano Maffei, Alberto Minetti	2:04:36.2
6. BUL	Borislav Assenov, Venelin Houbenov, Yordan Penchev, Nencho Staikov	2:05:55.2
7. FIN	Harry Hannus, Kari Puisto, Patrick Wackstrom, Sixten Wackstrom	2:05:58.2
8. YUG	Bruno Bilic, Vinko Poloncic, Bojan Ropret, Bojan Udović	2:07:12.0

1984 Los Angeles T: 26, N: 26, D: 8.5.
100 KM

1. ITA	Marcello Bartalini, Marco Giovannetti, Eros Poli, Claudio Vandelli	1:58.28
2. SWI	Alfred Achermann, Richard Trinkler, Laurent Vial, Benno Wiss	2:02:38
3. USA	Ronald Kiefel, Roy Knickman, Davis Phinney, Andrew Weaver	2:02:46
4. HOL	Johan Alberts, Erik Breukink, Martinus Ducrot, Gert Jakobs	2:02:57
5. SWE	Bengt Asplund, Per Christiansson, Magnus Knutsson, Håkan Larsson	2:04:46
6. FRA	Jean François Bernard, Philippe Bouvatier, Thierry Marie, Denis Pelizzari	2:05:07
7. DEN	John Carlsen, Kim John Eriksen, Lars Erik Jensen, Sören Liholt	2:05:31
8. GBR	Steven Poulter, Keith Reynolds, Peter Sanders, Darryl Webster	2:06:51

The Soviet Union surely would have been the gold medal favorite had their team not been prevented by their government from competing. The USSR had won the last three Olympic team time trials as well as the 1983 world championship. However, as it turned out, they would have been hard-pressed to defeat the amazing Italians who, equipped with revolutionary spokeless carbon fiber disc wheels, completed the course in the fastest time ever recorded, despite losing 20 seconds while changing a wheel. Their winning margin of 4 minutes 10 seconds was unheard of at international-level competition.

The site of the race was one of the dullest venues in Olympic history—a 15½ mile concrete stretch of the Artesia Freeway between the Harbor Freeway and the Santa Ana Freeway. During the medal ceremony, the winning teams enjoyed the rare privilege of seeing their national flags raised in front of the Regal Plastic Company and a freeway exit sign for Avalon Blvd.

1988 Seoul T: 31, N: 31, D: 9.18.
100 KM

1. GDR	Uwe Ampler, Mario Kummer, Maik Landsmann, Jan Schur	1:57:47.7
2. POL	Joachim Halupczok, Zenon Jaskula, Marek Leśniewski, Andrzej Sypytkowski	1:57:54.2
3. SWE	Björn Johansson, Jan Karlsson, Michel Lafis, Anders Jarl	1:59:47.3
4. FRA	Laurent Bezault, Eric Heulot, Pascal Lance, Thierry Laurent	1:59:49.8
5. ITA	Roberto Maggioni, Eros Poli, Mario Scirea, Flavio Vanzella	1:59:58.3
6. GER	Ernst Christl, Bernd Gröne, Rajmund Lehnert, Remig Stumpf	2:00:06.3
7. SOV	Vassily Zhdanov, Viktor Klimov, Asyat Saitov, Igor Sumnikov	2:00:27.0
8. CZE	Vladimír Hruza, Vladimír Kinst, Milan Křen, Jozef Regec	2:00:57.1

1992 Barcelona T: 30, N: 30, D: 7.26.
102.8 KM

1. GER	Bernd Dittert, Christian Meyer, Uwe Peschel, Michael Rich	2:01:39
2. ITA	Flavio Anastasia, Luca Colombo,2:02:39 Gianfranco Contri, Andrea Peron	
3. FRA	Hervé Boussard, Didier Faivre-Pierret, Philippe Gaumont, Jean-Louis Harel	2:05:25
4. SOV	Igor Dzyuba, Oleg Galkin, Igor Pastukhovich, Igor Patenko	2:05:34
5. SPA	Miguel Fernández Fernández, Álvaro González Gladeano, Eleuterio Mancebo Herrero, David Plaza Romero	2:06:11
6. POL	Grzegorz Piwowarski, Andrzej Sypytkowski, Dariusz Baranowski, Marek Leśniewski	2:06:34
7. SWI	Thomas Boutellier, Roland Meier, Beat Meister, Theodor Rinderknecht	2:06:35
8. CZE	Jaroslav Bílek, Miroslav Lipták, Pavel Padrnos, František Trkal	2:06:44

4000-METER INDIVIDUAL PURSUIT

In pursuit races, two cyclists or teams of cyclists start off on opposite sides of the track. If one cyclist, or team, catches the other, the race is over. Otherwise, the winner is the first one to cross the finish line. Two cyclists or teams take part in the race for first place. In 1996 the bronze medal was awarded to the fastest semifinal loser. Places five through eight are determined by times recorded in the quarterfinals or distance covered before being overtaken. For this reason, the times for third through eighth place are often faster than those for first and second. Prior to the 1992 Olympics, official world records could not be set unless there were no other competitors on the track.

1964 Tokyo C: 24, N: 24, D: 10.17. WR: 4:51.20 (Van Looy)

1. Jiři Daler	CZE	5:04.75
2. Giorgio Ursi	ITA	5:05.96
3. Preben Isaksson	DEN	5:01.90
4. Tiemen Groen	HOL	5:04.21

5. Lucjan Józefowicz (POL), Stanislav Moskvin (SOV/RUS), Hugh Porter (GBR), Lothar Spiegelberg (GER)

1968 Mexico City C: 28, N: 28, D: 10.18. WR: 4:45.94 (Jiři Daler)

1. Daniel Rebillard	FRA	4:41.71
2. Mogens Frey Jensen	DEN	4:42.43
3. Xaver Kurmann	SWI	4:39.42
4. John Bylsma	AUS	4:41.60

5. Cipriano Chamello (ITA), Paul Crapez (BEL), Rupert Kratzer (GER), Radamés Treviño (MEX)

Jensen set a world record of 4:37.54 in the quarterfinals to defeat the favorite, Chamello. Rebillard went to Mexico City as the fourth man in the team pursuit, but he performed so well in practice that he was given the French place in the individual pursuit.

1972 Munich C: 28, N: 28, D: 9.1. WR: 4:37.54 (Mogens Frey Jensen)

1. Knut Knudsen	NOR	4:45.74
2. Xaver Kurmann	SWI	4:51.96
3. Hans Lutz	GER	4:50.80
4. John Christopher Bylsma	AUS	4:54.93

5. Carlos Miguel Alvarez (ARG), Luciano Borgognoi (ITA), Luis Diaz (COL), Roy Schuiten (HOL)

Knut Knudsen was such an outsider that he didn't even get nervous until the final. Using wheels lent to him by the Danish team, the 21-year-old welder from Levanger took the lead from Kurmann after the fourth of 14 laps and pulled away to win comfortably.

1976 Montreal C: 28, N: 28, D: 7.22. WR: 4:37.54 (Mogens Frey Jensen)

1. Gregor Braun	GER	4:47.61
2. Herman Ponsteen	HOL	4:49.72
3. Thomas Huschke	GDR	4:52.71
4. Vladimir Osokin	SOV/RUS	4:57.34

5. Jan Georg Iversen (NOR), Michal Klasa (CZE), Orfeo Pizzoferrato (ITA), Garry Sutton (AUS)

The crucial match-up occurred in the semifinals, when the 20-year-old Braun upset Osokin by 0.17 seconds, as both men recorded personal bests.

1980 Moscow C: 14, N: 14, D: 7.24. WR: 4:34.66 (Uwe Unterwalder)

1. Robert Dill-Bundi	SWI	4:35.66
2. Alain Bondue	FRA	4:42.96
3. Hans-Henrik Örsted	DEN	4:36.54
4. Harald Wolf	GDR	4:37.58

5. Pierangelo Bincoletto (ITA), Vladimir Osokin (SOV/RUS), Martin Penc (CZE), Sean Yates (GBR)

In the semifinals Robert Dill-Bundi set a world record of 4:32.29. After his victory in the final he got off his bike and kissed the track. When US president Jimmy Carter called for a boycott of the Moscow Games, some nations chose a middle ground of protest: competing but refusing to display their flags. The medal ceremony for the individual pursuit was the first at which all three national flags were replaced by the Olympic flag.

1984 Los Angeles-Carson C: 33, N: 21, D: 8.1. WR: 4:32.29 (Robert Dill-Bundi)

1. Steve Hegg	USA	4:39.35
2. Rolf Gölz	GER	4:43.82
3. Leonard Harvey Nitz	USA	4:44.03
4. Dean Woods	AUS	4:44.08
5. Jörgen Pedersen	DEN	
6. Jelle Nijdam	HOL	
7. Robert Pascal	FRA	
8. Michael Grenda	AUS	

Former US downhill ski champion Steve Hegg stunned his fellow cyclists by posting an opening round qualifying time that was almost 11 seconds faster than that of any of the other 32 riders. Considered a dark horse for a medal, the 20-year-old Hegg powered his way into the final against the more experienced Gölz. The night before the gold medal race, Hegg, who began cycling after reading that his hero, Jean-Claude Killy, cycled, dreamt that he had skied the greatest run of his life. The next day he scored a decisive victory when Gölz, unnerved by the enthusiastic pro-US crowd and by the bizarre space-age bicycles being used by the US team, pushed the pace too quickly and was unable to withstand Hegg's finishing rush. After the race, Gölz bitterly told Hegg, "You wouldn't have beaten me in Germany." To which Hegg replied, "I really don't care—this is Los Angeles."

As it turned out, it wasn't just the hometown crowd and the advanced technology that gave Hegg an extra edge. Less than a week before the competition, Hegg, bronze medalist Leonard Harvey Nitz, and six other members of the US cycling team, encouraged by their coach, Eddie Borysewicz, had taken advantage of the dubious practice called blood boosting.

Blood boosting, which first became an Olympic issue as a result of long-distance runner Lasse Viren's successes in 1976 (see p. 117), is a procedure whereby blood is extracted from an athlete's body and frozen while the athlete's blood returns to a normal level. Then, before an important competition, it is reinjected, increasing the athlete's hemoglobin level and endurance. Borysewicz, who had also experimented with giving his cyclists caffeine suppositories, seemed to approach the issue with the same nonchalance that allowed US track coach Lawson Robertson to suggest to his sprinters that they drink warm sherry and a raw egg before the 1920 100-meter final (see p. 46).

Ethically questionable to begin with, blood boosting was given an uglier twist by the US cyclists. Because it was too late to remove and freeze their own blood, the eight US team members went to a nearby motel and injected other people's blood, some of them relatives, some of them not. The two US points racers, Mark Whitehead and Danny Van Haute, both became ill. Match sprinter Nelson Vails seemed to think the procedure was required of team members and was standing in line waiting for his transfusion when team doctor Thomas Dickson informed him that it was optional and discouraged him from going ahead with it. A relieved Vails left immediately. Blood boosting was finally banned in 1985.

In 1988, Steve Hegg was chosen to represent the US in the team pursuit. However, one week before the Games began, he was kicked off the team when he tested positive for excessive caffeine. Hegg returned to the Olympics in 1996. Racing in a support role, he placed 93rd in the road race and then finished 16th in the time trial.

1988 Seoul C: 22, N: 22, D: 9.22. WR: 4:31.160 (Gintautas Umaras)

1. Gintautas Umaras	SOV/LIT	4:32.00 OR
2. Dean Woods	AUS	4:35.00
3. Bernd Dittert	GDR	4:34.17
4. Colin Sturgess	GBR	4:34.90
5. Ryszard Dawidowicz	POL	4:39.44
6. Peter Clausen	DEN	4:42.62
7. Gary Anderson	NZL	4:42.82
8. Ivan Beltrami	ITA	Overtaken

In the final, Woods rushed out to an early lead. However, Umaras, the 25-year-old world champion from Klaipeda, Lithuania, caught him just after the halfway point and went on to an easy victory.

1992 Barcelona C: 29, N: 29, D: 7.29. WR: 4:31.16 (Gintautas Umaras)

1. Christopher Boardman	GBR	
2. Jens Lehmann	GER	Overtaken
3. Gary Anderson	NZL	4:31.061
4. Mark Kingsland	AUS	4:32.716
5. Philippe Ermenault	FRA	4:28.838
6. Cedric Mathy	BEL	4:33.942
7. Adolfo Alperi Plaza	SPA	4:34.760
8. Ivan Beltrami	ITA	4:36.541

Boardman caused a sensation when he appeared with his revolutionary bike, described as an "advanced composite monocoque with minimum-drag aerodynamic cross-sections, formed with unidirectional and stitched high-strength carbon fibre in an epoxy resin matrix." Designed by Mike Burrows and built by Lotus, the bike weighed less than 20 pounds. In the preliminary rounds Boardman recorded world records of 4:27.357 and 4:24.496, demoralizing the rest of the field even before the semifinals. In the final he lapped world champion Jens Lehmann, an unprecedented achievement in an Olympic final. Lehmann, with the graciousness typical of athletes from East Germany, dismissed talk about Boardman's bike, insisting that he had been beaten by the rider not the bike. Boardman earned Britain's first cycling gold medal since 1920. Six and a half weeks later, Boardman rode 55.291 kilometers in one hour to add a phenomenal 1.084 kilometers to the hour world record. Boardman competed in the road time trial at the next two Olympics, earning a bronze medal in 1996 and placing 11th in 2000. In 2000, the International Cycling Union (UCI) changed the rules by decreeing that hour world records had to be set using an old-style bike with a steel triangular frame, unbladed spoked wheels and drop handlebars and no aerohelmet. The hour record reverted to Eddy Merckx's 1972 mark of 49.431 kilometers. On October 27, 2000, Chris Boardman, after struggling with osteoporosis for two years, beat Merckx's record by ten meters.

1996 Atlanta-Stone Mountain C: 18, N: 18, D: 7.25. WR: 4:20.894 (Graeme Obree)

1. Andrea Collinelli	ITA	4:20.893
2. Philippe Ermenault	FRA	4:22.794
3. Bradley McGee	AUS	4:26.121
4. Aleksei Markov	RUS	4:26.828
5. Juan Martínez	SPA	4:28.310
6. Heiko Szonn	GER	4:31.583
7. Andriy Yatsenko	UKR	Overtaken (lap 15)
8. Walter Fernando Pérez	ARG	Overtaken (lap 12)

Andrea Collinelli set a world record of 4:19.699 in the qualifying round and then broke his own record three hours later with a 4:19.153 in the quarterfinals. Ermenault raced into the lead in the final, but Collinelli caught him after one kilometer, pulled away to a 2.3 second lead at the three kilometer mark and won easily. One month later, at the World Track Championship in Manchester, Chris Boardman, who did not compete in the Olympic pursuit, brought the world record down to 4:13.353 and then, in the final against Collinelli, to 4:11.114. Collinelli was prevented from defending his Olympic title in 2000 when he tested positive for a banned stimulant and a banned painkiller only two months before the Sydney Olympics.

2000 Sydney C: 17, N: 12, D: 9.17. WR: 4:11.114 (Christopher Boardman)

1. Robert Bartko	GER	4:18.515
2. Jens Lehmann	GER	4:19.613
3. Bradley McGee	AUS	4:19.250
4. Rob Hayles	GBR	4:21.350
5. Philippe Gaumont	FRA	4:22.142
6. Oleksandr Symonenko	UKR	4:23.983
7. Serhiy Matveyev	UKR	4:25.380
8. Walter Fernando Pérez	ARG	4:30.757

The final was a rematch of the 1999 world championship where Robert Bartko had overtaken fellow East German Jens Lehmann. The Germans endured unusual difficulties to get there. In May, Bartko was hit by a car and had to have shoulder surgery. Then, only eleven days before the qualifying round for the individual pursuit, Lehmann was hit by a car while training in Royal National Park south of Sydney. Lehmann hit the windshield and rolled off the car. Fortunately, Lehmann came away with only minor cuts and bruises. In the Olympic final, Lehmann led at the halfway point, but Bartko, who had set an Olympic record in the semifinals, moved ahead and scored a decisive victory. The bronze medal race was a dramatic confrontation between Rob

Hayles and local hero Brad McGee. Just five days before Lehmann's accident, McGee had crashed while training and broken his collarbone, necessitating surgery to insert a plate in his shoulder. Urged on by the enthusiastic Australian crowd, McGee trailed the entire race until he pulled ahead just before the finish line.

2004 Athens C: 15, N: 11, D: 8.21. WR: 4:11.114 (Christopher Boardman)

1. Bradley Wiggins	GBR	4:17.947
2. Bradley McGee	AUS	4:22.291
3. Sergi Escobar Roure	SPA	4:16.304
4. Rob Hayles	GBR	4:20.346
5. Luke Roberts	AUS	4:20.336
6. Fabien Sanchez	FRA	4:21.235
7. Volodymyr Diudia	UKR	4:22.720
8. Robert Bartko	GER	4:26.184

Bradley Wiggins, who won an Olympic bronze in the team pursuit in 2000 and silver medals in the 2001 and 2002 world championships, gained his first international title at the 2003 world championships. Born in Ghent, Belgium, of Australian and British parents, Wiggins set an Olympic record in the qualifying round. In the final, he built nearly a one-second lead after the first lap, and finished more than four seconds ahead of his friend and former teammate Bradley McGee. Wiggins was trained and mentored by 1992 gold medal winner Chris Boardman.

2008 Beijing C: 18, N: 12, D: 8.16. WR: 4:11.114 (Christopher Boardman)

1. Bradley Wiggins	GBR	4:16.977
2. Hayden Roulston	NZL	4:19.611
3. Steven Burke	GBR	4:20.947
4. Aleksey Markov	RUS	4:24.149
5. Volodymyr Diudia	UKR	4:22.471
6. Antonio Tauler Llull	SPA	4:24.974
7. Taylor Phinney	USA	4:26.644
8. Aleksandr Serov	RUS	4:25.391

After winning the gold medal in Athens, Bradley Wiggins switched his focus to road racing, finishing fourth in the London prologue of the 2007 Tour de France. He returned to track cycling in 2007 in time to win the world pursuit title ahead of double world champion Robert Bartko of Germany; the following year he defended his title, beating Jenning Huizenga of the Netherlands and earning gold medals in the team pursuit and Madison events.

Wiggins set an Olympic record of 4:15.031 in his Beijing qualifying run, almost four seconds ahead of second-place qualifier Hayden Roulston. In the final, Wiggins and Roulston were practically tied after the first 2500 meters, but Wiggins began to pull away, eventually finishing more than two seconds ahead. He was the first cyclist in Olympic history to successfully defend an individual pursuit gold medal.

Roulston had been a rider on Lance Armstrong's Discovery team, but had resigned after being convicted of assault following a bar fight. A year later he was diagnosed with potentially fatal heart arrythmia, forcing him to give up professional cycling. However, he was able to return to competition after discovering reiki, a Japanese hands-on healing practice.

Seventh-place finisher Taylor Phinney came from a prominent cycling family. His father, Davis Phinney, was the first American to win a stage of the Tour de France and his mother, Connie Carpenter-Phinney, won the gold medal in the inaugural women's road race in 1984. She also competed in speed skating at the 1972 Sapporo Olympics.

POINTS RACE

The points race was full of action but difficult to follow. The race ended when one rider completed the course. The winner was chosen from among those cyclists who were on the same lap as the first finisher. Points were awarded for sprints that took place every two kilometers—basically 20 races within the race. The winner of a sprint earned five points, second place three points, third place two points, and fourth place one point. Double points were awarded for the final sprint. A rider who had been lapped was not eligible to gain points; a rider who had been lapped twice was eliminated.

1900 Paris C: 28, N: 3, D: 9.15.
5 KM

		POINTS
1. Enrico Brusoni	ITA	21
2. Karl Duill	GER	9
3. Louis Trousellier	FRA	9
4. Chaput	FRA	8
5. Bérard	FRA	5
6. Cayron	FRA	4
7. Coisy	FRA	4
7. Ferdinand Vasserot	FRA	4

1904–1980 not held

1984 Los Angeles-Carson C: 43, N: 25, D: 8.3.
50 KM

		LAPS DOWN	POINTS
1. Roger Ilegems	BEL	0	37
2. Uwe Messerschmidt	GER	0	15
3. José Manuel Youshimatz	MEX	1	29
4. Jörg Müller	SWI	1	23
5. Juan Esteban Curuchet	ARG	1	20
6. Glenn Clarke	AUS	1	13
7. Brian Fowler	NZL	1	12
8. Derk van Egmond	HOL	2	56

Roger Ilegems, Belgium's only gold-medal winner of the Los Angeles Games, moved into the lead after 110 laps. World champion and heavy favorite Michael Marcussen of Denmark was relegated to ninth place.

1988 Seoul C: 34, N: 34, D: 9.24.
50 KM

		LAPS DOWN	POINTS
1. Dan Frost	DEN	0	38
2. Leo Peelen	HOL	0	26
3. Marat Ganeyev	SOV/RUS	1	46
4. Robert Burns	AUS	1	20
5. Juan Esteban Curuchet	ARG	1	18
6. Uwe Messerschmidt	GER	2	28
7. Pascal Lino	FRA	2	21
8. Frankie Andreu	USA	2	21

1992 Barcelona C: 38, N: 38, D: 7.31.
50 KM

		LAPS DOWN	POINTS
1. Giovanni Lombardi	ITA	0	44
2. Leon van Bon	HOL	0	43
3. Cedric Mathy	BEL	0	41
4. Glenn McLeay	NZL	0	30
5. Lubor Tesař	CZE	0	30
6. Eric Magnin	FRA	0	24
7. Guido Fulst	GER	0	24
8. Andreas Aeschbach	SWI	0	23

The final was an excellent race, averaging more than 49 kilometers per hour. The pace was so fast that no one could break away and gain a lap on the field. With only the last double-point sprint left, van Bon led with 41 points, followed by Lombardi with 38, and Mathy with 31. The crowd was on its feet and cheering as the riders began the final lap. Mathy, in the middle, appeared well-placed to win the sprint, van Bon was prepared to protect second place on the outside, while Lombardi was caught in a box. Suddenly, McLeay challenged van Bon on the outside, a gap opened, and in a split second Lombardi zipped through. Van Bon raised his arms in victory and the Dutch fans celebrated. But the videotape showed that the order of finish was Mathy (10 points), Lombardi (6 points), McLeay (4 points), and van Bon (2 points). Lombardi had won the gold medal by one point.

1996 Atlanta-Stone Mountain C: 28, N: 28, D: 7.28.
40KM

		LAPS DOWN	POINTS
1. Silvio Martinello	ITA	0	37
2. Brian Walton	CAN	0	29
3. Stuart O'Grady	AUS	0	27
4. Vasyl Yakovlev	UKR	0	24
5. Francis Moreau	FRA	0	21
6. Juan Llaneras Roselló	SPA	0	17
7. Cho Ho-sung	KOR	1	15
8. Glenn McLeay	NZL	1	8

Silvio Martinello was the defending world champion. He had last competed in the Olympics in 1984, placing fourth in the team pursuit and 16th in the points race. In Atlanta, he took the lead on the sixth of the twenty sprints and won with relative ease. Unheralded Brian Walton moved from fourth to second by winning the final sprint. Stuart O'Grady suffered from a heart condition called superventricular tachycardia and experienced a seizure the day before the points race. He earned a bronze medal anyway in both the team pursuit and the points race.

2000 Sydney C: 23, N: 23, D: 9.20.
40KM

		LAPS DOWN	POINTS
1. Juan Llaneras Roselló	SPA	0	14
2. Milton Wynants	URU	1	18
3. Aleksei Markov	RUS	1	16
4. Cho Ho-sung	KOR	1	15
5. Jame Carney	USA	1	10
6. Franz Stocher	AUT	1	8
7. Glen Thomson	NZL	1	6
8. Silvio Martinello	ITA	1	5

Stuart O'Grady of Australia scored the most points, 26, but finished two laps back and only placed tenth. Meanwhile, two-time points world champion Juan Llaneras scored on only four of the sixteen sprints but went with both breaks and ended up a lap ahead of everyone else.

2004 Athens C: 23, N: 23, D: 8.24.
40 KM

		LAPS DOWN	POINTS
1. Mikhail Ignatyev	RUS	0	93
2. Juan Llaneras Roselló	SPA	1	82
3. Guido Fulst	GER	1	79
4. Greg Henderson	NZL	1	68
5. Milan Kadlec	CZE	1	65
6. Mark Renshaw	AUS	2	60
7. Peter Schep	HOL	2	58
8. Angelo Ciccone	ITA	2	49

Nineteen-year-old Mikhail Ignatyev's strategy was to stick with every attack and build up points by lapping the field. He took the lead after the fifth sprint, lapping the peloton to earn 20 points. Although Ignatyev won only one of the sixteen sprints, he eventually lapped the field four times, to gain a total of 80 lap points. Juan Llaneras won three consecutive sprints late in the race to finish second.

2008 Beijing C: 23, N: 23, D: 8.16.
40 KM

		LAPS DOWN	POINTS
1. Joan Llaneras Roselló	SPA	0	60
2. Roger Kluge	GER	0	58
3. Chris Newton	GBR	0	56
4. Cameron Meyer	AUS	1	36
5. Vasily Kiriyenko	BLR	1	34
6. Daniel Kreutzfeldt	DEN	1	29
7. Zachary Bell	CAN	1	27
8. Makoto Iijima	JPN	1	23

Joan Llaneras had won medals in the points race at each of the two previous Olympics and had taken the 2007 world championship title, making him the pre-race favorite. He was part of a five-man breakaway that lapped the rest of the field after the sixth sprint. Llaneras, Roger Kluge and Chris Newton all lapped the field a second time. Llaneras beat Kluge in the 100th and 120th laps to clinch the gold medal at the age of 39, while Kluge beat Newton in the final sprint to take silver.

MADISON

Similar to the points race, the 60-kilometer Madison was contested by two-man teams who took turns riding and sprinting for points every five kilometers. The riders traded off by gripping hands. The outgoing lead rider gave the oncoming rider a "handsling," propelling him forward. Scoring was the same as that used for the points race. The event derived it's name from the fact that it was first contested in New York City's Madison Square Garden.

2000 Sydney T: 14, N: 14, D: 9.21.
60 KM

		LAPS DOWN	POINTS
1. AUS	Scott McGrory, Brett Aitken	0	26
2. BEL	Étienne De Wilde, Matthew Gilmore	0	22
3. ITA	Marco Villa, Silvio Martinello	0	15
4. GBR	Bradley Wiggins, Rob Hayles	0	13
5. AUT	Werner Riebenbauer, Roland Garber	0	10
6. GER	Thorsten Rund, Guido Fulst	0	9
7. ARG	Juan Esteban Curuchet, Gabriel Ovidio	0	9
8. HOL	Danny Stam, Robert Slippens	0	8

At the 1999 world championships, Brett Aitken and Scott McGrory were fighting for a medal when Aitken clashed with a French cyclist, crashed and was knocked unconscious for five minutes. In the months leading up to the Sydney Olympics, the two Australians each faced family tragedies. McGrory's 11-week-old son died of a heart condition and Aitken's two-year-old daughter was diagnosed with Rett's syndrome, a developmental disorder. At the Olympics, the British team of Bradley Wiggins and Rob Hayles led McGrory and Aitken 12-8 after the fourth of twelve sprints. The Australians moved ahead after the seventh sprint, scoring seven straight times. With only the final double sprint to go, McGrory and Aitken had built an insurmountable 14-point lead. All they had to do was avoid being lapped or falling. The Swiss team of Bruno Risi and Kurt Betschart pulled away to a half lap lead but could get no farther and ended up in 11th place. With two laps to go, three riders did go down and McGrory barely avoided the mess. As he approached the finish line, he let go of his handlebars and raised his arms in triumph. This slowed him down just enough over the last ten meters to allow Italy to squeak by and pick up the two points they needed to snatch the bronze medals from the British pair, as Rob Hayles was one of the riders involved in the late crash. The Belgians who won the silver medals were an odd pair: Matthew Gilmore had competed for Australia, but after a series of non-selections switched his citizenship, while Étienne de Wilde made the Olympic podium at the age of 42.

2004 Athens T: 18, N: 18, D: 8.25
60 KM

		LAPS DOWN	POINTS
1. AUS	Graeme Brown, Stuart O'Grady	0	22
2. SWI	Franco Marvulli, Bruno Risi	0	15
3. GBR	Rob Hayles, Bradley Wiggins	0	12
4. GER	Robert Bartko, Guido Fulst	0	9
5. UKR	Volodymyr Rybin, Vasyl Yakovlev	0	9
6. SPA	Miguel Alzamora Riera, Juan Llaneras Roselló	0	7
7. NZL	Greg Henderson, Hayden Roulston	0	2
8. AUT	Roland Garber, Franz Stocher	1	8

Graeme Brown and Stuart O'Grady established a strong lead by the halfway point and won points on most of the sprints. The British pair, Rob Hayles and Bradley Wiggins, managed bronze despite Hayles crashing half-way through the race.

2008 Beijing T: 16, N: 16, D: 8.19.
50 KM

		LAPS DOWN	POINTS
1. ARG	Juan Esteban Curuchet, Walter Pérez	0	8
2. SPA	Joan Llaneras Roselló, Antonio Tauler Llull	0	7
3. RUS	Mikhail Ignatyev, Aleksey Markov	0	6
4. BEL	Iljo Keisse, Kenny De Ketele 1	17	
5. GER	Roger Kluge, Olaf Pollack	1	15
6. DEN	Michael Mørkøv, Nicki Rasmussen	1	14
7. FRA	Matthieu Ladagnous, Jérôme Neuville	1	12
8. HOL	Jens Mouris, Peter Schep	1	6

Reigning world champions Mark Cavendish and Bradley Wiggins were the pair to beat in Beijing. Cavendish had won the world championship in 2005 and had won four stages of the Tour de France—the first British rider ever to do so—before dropping out to focus on training for Beijing. By the time the Madison final was held, Wiggins had already successfully defended his 2004 individual pursuit gold medal and had led Britain to gold in the team pursuit.

As it turned out, Cavendish and Wiggins were never a major threat, as the Argentine, Spanish and Russian pairs gained an early lap on the other thirteen teams. Competing in his sixth Olympics, 43-year-old Juan Esteban Curuchet and partner Walter Pérez won the gold medal after scoring five points in the third sprint. (Curuchet had won silver with his brother Gabriel at the inaugural Madison event at the 1995 world championships.)

Seven-time world champion Joan Llaneras earned silver with new partner Toni Tauler (he had won two world titles with partner Isaac Gálvez, who died in 2006 after a fall during the Six Days of Gent race). His only Madison competition after Gálvez's death was at the Beijing Olympics, and he announced his retirement immediately afterwards.

WOMEN

MATCH SPRINT

1896–1984 not held

1988 Seoul C: 12, N: 12, D: 9.24. WR: 11.383 (Isabelle Gautheron)

		1ST RACE	2ND RACE	3RD RACE
1. Erika Salumäe	SOV/EST	—	12.00	12.58
2. Christa Luding-Rothenburger	GDR	11.68	—	—
3. Connie Young	USA			
4. Isabelle Gautheron	FRA			
5. Julie Speight	AUS			
6. Zhou Suying	CHN			
7. Louise Jones	GBR			
8. Yang Hsiu-chen	TAI			

In 1984 Christa Rothenburger of Dresden won a gold medal in the 500-meter speed skating event in Sarajevo. In 1988, in Calgary, she missed another gold in the 500 by two one-hundredths of a second, but came back three days later to win the 1000-meter event. Eight years earlier, her coach, Ernst Luding, had persuaded her to take up cycling in the off-season. When she saw her first match sprint race she was terrified. "I was convinced that as soon as I tried to ride I would undoubtedly topple right over." Rothenburger learned quickly. But when asked to be allowed to enter competitions, East German sports officials turned her down and told her to stick to skating. She went over their heads and petitioned the president of East Germany's sports federation, Manfred Ewald, who gave her permission. At the 1986 world championships, her first international competition, she upset Estonian Erika Salumäe for the gold medal. Although Salumäe turned the tables in 1987, Rothenburger, who married Luding after Calgary, was on target to become the first person to win medals in the Winter and Summer Olympics in the same year.

In Seoul Luding-Rothenburger ensured her place in sports history by defeating Gautheron in the semifinals. She won the first race of the final and it looked like she might match Eddie Eagan's feat of winning Olympic championships in both winter and summer sports. But Salumäe outmaneuvered her twice in a row and Luding-Rothenburger ended up instead like Jacob Tullin: gold in winter, silver in summer.

1992 Barcelona C: 12, N: 12, D: 7.31. WR: 11.101 (Galina Yenyukhina)

		1ST RACE	2ND RACE	3RD RACE
1. Erika Salumäe	EST	—	12.667	12.244
2. Annett Neumann	GER	12.776	—	—
3. Ingrid Haringa	HOL	12.402	12.410	
4. Félicia Ballanger	FRA	—	—	
5. Galina Yenyukhina	RUS	12.575		
6. Tanya Dubnicoff	CAN	—		
7. Mika Kuroki	JPN	—		
8. Wang Yang	CHN	—		

As a member of the Soviet team, Erika Salumäe won the inaugural women's sprint in Seoul. When she returned to the Estonian capital of Tallinn, where she had been raised in an orphanage, she was welcomed as a hero. At the victory parade in her honor, one sign read OUR OWN TEAM IN BARCELONA IN 1992. Once upon a time, Estonia did have its own Olympic team, competing as an independent nation between 1920 and 1936 and winning 23 medals, 7 gold, 6 silver, and 10 bronze, most of them in wrestling and weightlifting. Then, in 1940, the Soviet Union annexed Estonia and those Estonian athletes who took part in the Olympics did so under the banner of the USSR. In 1988, at the time of Salumäe's victory parade, the idea of a separate Estonian Olympic team seemed a fantasy. But miracles do happen. Between Olympics, the Soviet Union disintegrated, Estonia declared its independence, and on July 25, 1992, Erika Salumäe and 36 other Estonian athletes marched behind the Estonian flag at the Opening Ceremony in Barcelona.

Salumäe faced stiff competition on the track. Although she had won the 1989 world championship, the political and economic chaos in her country made it difficult for her to train properly. One of her "rivals," Connie Paraskevin-Young, who had won the world championship in 1990 (not to mention 1982, 1983, and 1984), arranged for Salumäe to train once a year in the United States, but in the run-up to the Olympics, Salumäe was further handicapped by a back injury. Besides Paraskevin-Young, another favorite was Ingrid Haringa, a policewoman and ex-speed skater who switched to cycling and surprised everyone by winning the 1991 world championship only five months after taking up the sport. It was Haringa who set the standard in the qualification round with a time of 11.419. Salumäe and Paraskevin-Young recorded only the sixth and seventh best times in a field of twelve. The next round consisted of four heats with the winner of each heat advancing to the quarterfinals and the rest fighting it out in a *repêchage* round. Haringa and Salumäe went through, but Paraskevin-Young, although she finished first in her heat, was disqualified for interfering with Félicia Ballanger. The American was then eliminated by Annett Neumann after her own protest against the German rider was denied.

In the quarterfinals, Salumäe needed a tie-breaker to defeat world record holder Galina Yenyukhina. She had less trouble with Ballanger in the semifinals. The other semifinal, between Haringa and Neumann, turned out to be a dramatic struggle. Haringa won the first race but was disqualified in the second for passing too low on the inside. The winner of the next race would go on to the final. With a little over a lap to go, Haringa fell and a rerace was ordered. This time Neumann crashed. She almost fell again in the third try, but came from behind to win at last. Neumann also won the first race in the final, but Salumäe then took two in a row for the gold medal. It was an emotional moment at the award ceremony when the Estonian flag was raised at the Olympics for the first time in 56 years. Unfortunately, it was raised upside down. This blunder on the part of the Spanish officials failed to dampen Salumäe's enthusiasm. "The next time," she noted with a smile, "they will get it right."

1996 Atlanta-Stone Mountain C: 14, N: 14, D: 7.27. WR: 10.831 (Olga Slyusaryeva)

		1ST RACE	2ND RACE	3RD RACE
1. Félicia Ballanger	FRA	11.903	12.096	
2. Michelle Ferris	AUS	—	—	
3. Ingrid Haringa	HOL	—	12.074	11.782
4. Annett Neumann	GER	12.620	—	—
5. Oksana Grishina	RUS	12.416		
6. Erika Salumaë	EST	—		
7. Wang Yan	CHN	—		
8. Tanya Dubnicoff	CAN	—		

On May 27, 1996, Félicia Ballanger made history by earning second place in the French championship in the non-Olympic team sprint event—for men. The reigning world champion in the match sprint—for women—Ballanger won the gold medal in Atlanta without losing a race. In her second quarterfinal ride against defending champion Erika Salumaë, Ballanger matched a three-minute standstill by the Estonian (the maximum allowable according to current rules) and Salumaë was forced to stay in the lead until Ballanger shot by her to win.

2000 Sydney C: 12, N: 12, D: 9.20. WR: 10.831 (Olga Slyusaryeva)

		1ST RACE	2ND RACE	3RD RACE
1. Félicia Ballanger	FRA	11.810	—	12.533
2. Oksana Grishina	RUS	—	13.112	—
3. Iryna Yanovych	UKR	12.156	12.310	
4. Michelle Ferris	AUS	—	—	
5. Szilvia Noémi Szabolcsi	HUN	12.426		
6. Tanya Lindenmuth	USA	—		
7. Tanya Dubnicoff	CAN	—		
8. Daniela Larreal	VEN	—		

Since finishing second at the 1994 world championships, Félicia Ballanager had won every major sprint contest. She had beaten Michelle Ferris in the final of four of those events, the 1996 Olympics and the last three world championships. The two met again in Sydney, but this time it was in the semifinals. Ballanger won both heats easily. In the final, Ballanger defeated Oksana Grishina in the first heat, but in the second heat, she succumbed to a moment of tactical indecision, Grishina shot ahead and Ballanger responded too late. For the first time in three years, Ballanger was forced to a third heat. On the second lap, Ballanger ground to a halt in an attempt to make Grishina pass her, but Grishina stopped as well. Suddenly Ballanger exploded into a full sprint and opened up such a huge lead that Grishina was out of draft range. The race seemed over, but with half a lap to go she slowed, allowing Grishina to cut the gap in half before Ballanger awoke from her daze and reaccelerated to win comfortably to earn her second gold medal of the week and her third career gold medal.

Iryna Yanovych's bronze medal was a satisfying reward in the face of adversity. The day before the Opening Ceremony she was hit by a car and spent six hours in a hospital with a shoulder injury.

2004 Athens C: 12, N: 11, D: 8.24. WR: 10.831 (Olga Slyusaryeva)

		1ST RACE	2ND RACE
1. Lori-Ann Muenzer	CAN	12.042	11.822
2. Tamilla Abasova	RUS	—	—
3. Anna Meares	AUS	12.126	12.140
4. Svetlana Grankovskaya	RUS	—	—
5. Natalia Tsylinskaya	BLR	12.457	

6. Katrin Meinke	GER	—
7. Simona Krupeckait	LIT	—
8. Daniela Larreal	VEN	—

Lori-Ann Muenzer did not begin cycling until the age of 23. At 38, she was the oldest female cyclist in the competition. Muenzer's most difficult challenges on the way to gold came well before the final, which she won convincingly. Prior to the quarterfinals, Muenzer blew two disc wheels and, in order to compete she had to borrow wheels and a tire from the Australian and French teams. In the semifinal, Muenzer faced her most serious challenger, the 20-year-old 2004 world champion, Anna Meares. Muenzer lost the first heat but came back to win the second and third heats, and move on to the final, which she won in straight heats.

2008 Beijing C: 12, N: 11, D: 8.19.
750M

		1ST RACE	2ND RACE
1. Victoria Pendleton	GBR	11.363	11.118
2. Anna Meares	AUS	—	—
3. Guo Shuang	CHN	11.420	11.617
4. Willy Kanis	HOL	—	—
5. Clara Sánchez	FRA	12.264	
6. Nataliya Tsilinskaya	BLR		
7. Jennie Reed	USA		
8. Simona Krupeckaitė	LIT		

Vicki Pendleton had won three of the past four world championships. She set an Olympic record, 10.863, to lead in the qualifying round, followed by 2007 world silver medalist Guo Shuang and Athens 500-meter time trial gold medalist Anna Meares. Meares took out Guo in three races in the semi-final to meet Pendleton in the final, but Pendleton was unbeatable, winning easily in two races. Guo defeated double BMX world champion Kanis to win bronze.

Silver medalist Meares had come back from a horrific crash in January 2008 in which she suffered heavy skin grazing, torn tendons and a fractured vertebra near the base of her skull, nearly resulting in paralysis.

OMNIUM

The two-day women's Olympic omnium event will consist of six disciplines: 1) flying start 250-meter time trial, 2) 20-kilometer points race, 3) 3,000-meter pursuit, 4) 10-kilometer scratch race, 5) 500-meter time trial and 6) elimination race. In the elimination race, the racers will start in a bunch and every two laps the cyclist in last place will be eliminated. Scoring is based on placements in each discipline with one point for first place. The athlete with the lowest total places for all six events is the winner.

ROAD TIME TRIAL

The rules for the women's road time trial are the same as those for the men's except that the course is between 25 and 35 kilometers long.

1896–1992 not held

1996 Atlanta C: 24, N: 16, D: 8.3.
26.1 KM

1. Zulfia Zabirova	RUS	36:40
2. Jeannie Longo-Ciprelli	FRA	37:00
3. Clara Hughes	CAN	37:13
4. Kathryn Watt	AUS	37:53
5. Marion Clignet	FRA	38:14
6. Tea Vikstedt-Nyman	FIN	38:24
7. Jolanta Polikeviciute	LIT	38:27
8. Imelda Chiappa	ITA	38:47

The favorites were Jeannie Longo, Clara Hughes and Kathy Watt, who had finished 1-2-3 at the 1995 world championships. They finished in the same order in Atlanta, but this time 1-2-3 turned out to be 2-3-4. The race was won by Zulfia Zabirova, about whom almost nothing was known. She was not even included in the organizing committee's official database of athletes. Curious reporters learned that Zabirova, although competing for Russia, was born in Uzbekistan, and obtained one useful quick quote: "I have never ridden so calmly in my life." Zabirova, who had placed sixth in the road race, did not show up for the medalists' press conference because, according to Russian officials, she had a flight to catch. Zabirova later finished second at the world championships of 1997 and 1998. After recovering from head injuries following a crash two months before the 2000 Olympics, she placed 12th in the time trial in Sydney and 7th in the road race. In 2002 she came back to earn the world championship in the time trial.

2000 Sydney C: 23, N: 13, D: 9.30.
31.2 KM

1. Leontien Zijlaard (van Moorsel)	HOL	42:00
2. Mari Holden	USA	42:37
3. Jeannie Longo-Ciprelli	FRA	42:52
4. Anna Wilson	AUS	42:58
5. Joane Somarriba Arrola	SPA	43:06
6. Clara Hughes	CAN	43:12
7. Judith Arndt	GER	43:31
8. Hanka Kupfernagel	GER	43:37

Leontien Zijlaard had already won two gold medals and one silver medal in 2000, when she started the time trial, an event in which she was the two-time defending world champion. Not surprisingly, she won easily, by 37 seconds. Mari Holden's surprise silver medal was redemption for her 1996 disappointment when she won the time trial at the US Olympic Trials, but was passed over when the leaders of USA Cycling chose their team members based upon who would do well in the road race rather than the time trial. Jeannie Longo, at age 41, brought her Olympic career medal total to four.

2004 Athens-Vouliagmeni C: 25, N: 16, D: 8.18.

1. Leontien Zijlaard-van Moorsel	HOL	31:11.53
2. Dede Demet-Barry	USA	31:35.62
3. Karin Thürig	SWI	31:54.89
4. Christine Thorburn	USA	32:14.82
5. Lada Kozlíková	CZE	32:15.41
6. Oenone Wood	AUS	32:16.00
7. Joane Somarriba Arrola	SPA	32:25.93
8. Zulfiya Zabirova	RUS	32:30.08

Three days after crashing in the penultimate lap of the road race, three-time gold medalist Leontien van Moorsel defended her gold medal in the time trial, building up a massive lead by the halfway point and maintaining it for the rest of the race. The win made van Moorsel the most successful female cyclist in Olympic history.

2008 Beijing C: 25, N: 17, D: 8.13.
23.5 KM

1. Kristin Armstrong	USA	34:51.72
2. Emma Pooley	GBR	35:16.01
3. Karin Thürig	SWI	35:50.99
4. Jeannie Longo-Ciprelli	FRA	35:52.62
5. Christine Thorburn	USA	35:54.16
6. Judith Arndt	GER	35:59.77
7. Christiane Soeder	AUT	36:20.75
8. Priska Doppmann	SWI	36:27.79

Starting fifth, Emma Pooley posted a time that held up until 2006 world champion Kristin Armstrong took to the course. Armstrong trailed Pooley's pace through the first half of the race, but gradually moved up to finish just over 24 seconds ahead. Switzerland's Karin Thürig successfully defended her bronze medal.

Kristin Armstrong started as a triathlete, but arthritis in both her hips forced her to focus exclusively on cycling. She is often confused with Lance Armstrong's ex-wife, also named Kristin Armstrong, but the two are not related.

Competing in her seventh Olympics, 49-year-old Jeannie Longo-Ciprelli missed earning a fifth career Olympic medal by less than two seconds.

ROAD RACE

1896–1980 not held

1984 Los Angeles-Mission Viejo C: 45, N: 16, D: 7.29.
79.2 KM

1. Connie Carpenter-Phinney	USA	2:11:14
2. Rebecca Twigg	USA	2:11:14
3. Sandra Schumacher	GER	2:11:14
4. Unni Larsen	NOR	2:11:14
5. Maria Canins	ITA	2:11:14
6. Jeannie Longo	FRA	2:12:35
7. Helle Sörensen	DEN	2:13:28
8. Ute Enzenauer	GER	2:13:28

At the age of 14, Connie Carpenter had competed at the 1972 Winter Olympics in Sapporo, finishing seventh in the 1500-meter speed skating event. An ankle injury forced her to switch to cycling four years later. She gave up the sport for rowing, but returned to the track in 1981, dominating US women's cycling until the arrival of another early achiever, Rebecca Twigg of Seattle. Twigg's early achievements were not athletic, but academic. After completing 8th grade, the 14-year-old Twigg skipped four years of secondary schooling and went straight to the University of Washington, where she studied biology.

In 1982, when she was 19, Twigg beat Carpenter to become the world pursuit champion. She did not defend her championship, preferring to concentrate on road racing, since that would be the only women's cycling event contested at the Los Angeles Olympics. In her absence, Carpenter took the world pursuit title despite competing less than two months after breaking her arm.

In the Olympic road race, six women broke away at the mid-point. With 800 meters to go, Jeannie Longo clashed wheels with Maria Canins, causing Longo's rear

Connie Carpenter-Phinney and Rebecca Twigg, 1984
Carpenter-Phinney (foreground) edges ahead of Twigg in the last second of the women's road race.

derailleur to break and her chain to come off. The remaining five prepared for the final sprint. Canins took off first, 500 meters from the finish. Schumacher, a 17-year-old surprise, was the next to make her move. With 200 meters to go it was the turn of Carpenter and Twigg. Twigg seemed to have a decisive lead at the 100-meter mark and Carpenter thought she had lost the gold as late as the 50-meter mark. But she sped on, caught Twigg a mere three meters from the finish line and, using a technique which she had practiced every day for a month, she threw her bike forward and won by less than half a wheel.

Carpenter's husband, Davis Phinney, who had taught her the bike-throw move, also competed at the 1984 Olympics, finishing fifth in the men's road race and earning a bronze medal in the team time trial.

1988 Seoul C: 53, N: 23, D: 9.26.

82 KM

1. Monique Knol	HOL	2:00:52
2. Jutta Niehaus	GER	2:00:52
3. Laima Zilporite	SOV/LIT	2:00:52
4. Genevieve Brunet	CAN	2:00:52
5. Valentyna Yevpak	SOV/UKR	2:00:52
6. Maria Blower	GBR	2:00:52
7. Marie Höljer	SWE	2:00:52
8. Inga Benedict	USA	2:00:52

Until the very end, this was a dull race inspired by a dull course. The only attempt at a break came from Inga Benedict with about 5 kilometers to go. But she was hauled in by the heavy favorite, Jeannie Longo, who took the pack with her. Longo, still recovering from a hip fracture and bruise, eventually finished twenty-first. As they neared the finish line, 45 of the 53 starters were still in a pack. With 400 meters to go, 24-year-old substitute teacher Monique Knol, as she put it, "saw a little hole—*schwoook*—I went away and that was it. I sprinted by myself."

1992 Barcelona-Sant Sadurní d'Anoia C: 57, N: 26, D: 7.26.

81 KM

1. Kathryn Watt	AUS	2:04.42
2. Jeannie Longo-Ciprelli	FRA	2:05.02
3. Monique Knol	HOL	2:05.03
4. Natalya Kyschuk	UKR	2:05.03
5. Monica Valvik	NOR	2:05:03
6. Jeanne Golay	USA	2:05.03
7. Kathleen Shannon	AUS	2:05.03
8. Luzia Zberg	SWI	2:05.03

Three kilometers from the finish line Jeannie Longo, four-time world champion, three-time winner of the women's Tour de France, pulled away from the pack, took a lead of 100 meters, and never looked behind her. Attacking for the rest of the race, she crossed the finish line one second ahead of defending champion Monique Knol and 29 other riders. It was a classic, gutsy performance by Longo, who had finally earned the one prize that was missing from her trophy collection: an Olympic gold medal. The French team raised their arms in triumph. There was only one problem: the real winner, 5-foot ½-inch (1.54 meters) Kathy Watt, had already crossed the finish line 20 seconds earlier. With one ten-mile circuit to go, Watt slipped away from the main pack while another rider was coming back, and many riders didn't see her go. Watt took off after the two leaders, Maria Turcotto of Italy and Marie Purvis of Great Britain, and rode right past them without hesitating. She opened a 38-second lead and won handily. Like Longo, Watt, a 27-year-old from the small town of Warragul, did not know what place she was in. She was so dizzy when she crossed the finish that when she looked up and saw two riders nearby, she thought she had finished third. (The other two had failed to finish and were waiting for teammates.)

1996 Atlanta C: 58, N: 30, D: 7.21.

104.4 KM

1. Jeannie Longo-Ciprelli	FRA	2:36:13
2. Imelda Chiappa	ITA	2:36:38
3. Clara Hughes	CAN	2:36:44
4. Vera Hohfeld	GER	2:37:06
5. Jolanta Polikeviciute	LIT	2:37:06
6. Zulfiya Zabirova	RUS	2:37:06
7. Alessandra Cappellotto	ITA	2:37:06
8. Barbara Heeb	SWI	2:37:06

By the time of the 1996 Olympics, 37-year-old Jeannie Longo had won ten world championships: five in the road race, one in the road time trial, three in the individual pursuit and one in the points race. Longo was so much the dominant woman's cyclist of the past eleven years that she had even won a world championship silver medal in mountain biking. But Olympic success had escaped her. In the 1984 road race, a last-minute collision left her in sixth place. In 1988, a month after breaking her hip, she could do no better than 21st. In 1992, she was second to Kathy Watt. In Barcelona she also entered the pursuit, but was beaten in the quarterfinals (barely) by Rebecca Twigg.

Ever the individualist, Longo followed her own training strategy for the 1996 Olympics. While others were arriving in Atlanta early to acclimatize to the heat and humidity, Longo rented a home in the mountains of Colorado, trained in the cool fresh air, and arrived in Atlanta two days before the road race.

The contest began in the late morning and was disrupted by a midrace downpour that had the racers skidding and falling. The course consisted of eight 13-kilometer laps. Alessandra Cappellotto of Italy made a solo break during the third lap. Imelda Chiappa counterattacked during the fifth lap. Longo went with her, as did Anna Wilson of Australia and Clara Hughes. Wilson fell back quickly, but the other three gradually pulled away from the peloton. Eleven kilometers from the finish, Longo made her move and Chiappa and Hughes were left behind.

2000 Sydney C: 57, N: 23, D: 9.26.
119.7 KM

1. Leontien Zijlaard (van Moorsel)	HOL	3:06:31
2. Hanka Kupfernagel	GER	3:06:31
3. Diana Ziliute	LIT	3:06:31
4. Anna Wilson	AUS	3:06:31
5. Svetlana Bubnenkova	RUS	3:06:31
6. Magali le Floc'h	FRA	3:06:31
7. Zulfia Zabirova	RUS	3:06:31
8. Heidi Van de Vijver	BEL	3:06:31

The Dutch team executed an efficient game plan as Chantal Beltman helped control the pace in the first half of the race, while Mirjam Melchers, in the second half, hauled in mini-breaks, controlled the peloton and wore down some of the leading sprinters. Two hundred and fifty meters from the finish line, Melchers sat up and Leontien Zijlaard, with a two bike-length lead over Hanka Kupfernagel, pulled out of Melchers' draft and sprinted into the lead. With 50 meters to go, Zijlaard raised her arms in triumph, celebrating the second of her three Sydney gold medals.

2004 Athens C: 67, N: 30, D: 8.15.

1. Sara Carrigan	AUS	3:24:24
2. Judith Arndt	GER	3:24:31
3. Olga Slyusaryeva	RUS	3:25:03
4. Oenone Wood	AUS	3:25:03
5. Nicole Cooke	GBR	3:25:03
6. Mirjam Melchers	HOL	3:25:06
7. Joane Somarriba Arrola	SPA	3:25:06
8. Kristin Armstrong	USA	3:25:06

Leontien Zijlaard-Van Moorsel, 2004
The most successful female cyclist in Olympic history, van Moorsel won her fourth gold medal three days after crashing in the road race.

The pack stayed together throughout most of the first half of the race. Defending gold medalist Leontien van Moorsel fell with two laps to go, incurring a mild concussion and putting her out of the competition. In the final lap, 23-year-old Sara Carrigan broke from the group, but was quickly caught by Judith Arndt. The two opened a 20-second gap over the peloton, with Arndt doing most of the work. Carrigan drafted behind Arndt for most of the final lap, and with 100 meters to go faked to the left before slingshotting around Arndt and sprinting to gold. As Arndt crossed the finish line she shocked spectators with an obscene gesture. In the post-race interview she insisted that the gesture was not directed at Carrigan. Rather it was a protest against the German cycling federation's treatment of her teammate and lover, the 1992 pursuit gold medalist Petra Rossner, who was not selected for the 2004 team. The International Cycling Union fined Arndt 200 Swiss Francs for her "one-fingered salute."

2008 Beijing C: 66, N: 33, D: 8.10.
126.4 KM

1. Nicole Cooke	GBR	3:32:24
2. Emma Johansson	SWE	3:32:24
3. Tania Guderzo	ITA	3:32:24
4. Christiane Soeder	AUT	3:32:28

5. Linda Villumsen	DEN	3:32:33
6. Marianne Vos	HOL	3:32:45
7. Priska Doppmann	SWI	3:32:45
8. Paulina Brzeźna	POL	3:32:45

Nicole Cooke, 2008
Nicole Cooke outsprints Emma Johansson to win the 2008 Road Race.

A month before the Beijing Games, 2007 world champion Marta Bastianelli tested positive for the illegal stimulant flenfluramine and was barred from competing. That left 2006 world champion and 2007 world silver medalist Marianne Vos seemingly the favorite in the event.

Much of the race was held in pouring rain and wind, and several crashes occurred. The 2004 world silver medalist, Tania Guderzo, broke away with 13 kilometers remaining in the final lap, but was caught by a group of four riders, including twice Tour de France winner Nicole Cooke. Cooke was at the back of the quintet in the final 350 meters but moved to the front over the final hill and won the sprint to the finish.

MOUNTAIN BIKE CROSS-COUNTRY

The women's course must be between 30 and 40 kilometers.

1896–1992 not held

1996 Atlanta-Conyers C: 29, N: 19, D: 7.30.
31.9 KM

1. Paola Pezzo	ITA	1:50:51
2. Alison Sydor	CAN	1:51:58
3. Susan DeMattei	USA	1:52:36
4. Gunn-Rita Dahle	NOR	1:53:50
5. Elsbeth Vink	HOL	1:54:38
6. Annabella Stropparo	ITA	1:55:56
7. Regina Marunde	GER	1:57:21
8. Kathy Lynch	NZL	1:57:40

Alison Sydor won six of the seven pre-Olympic World Cup races, but the Italian team did not take part, spending the two months before the Olympics in a closed training camp. It was an Italian, Paola Pezzo, who would stand out on a day of sweltering heat. The glamour girl of mountain biking, Pezzo caused a sensation in Italy by posing provocatively as various fairy tale characters in a series of advertisements for her shoe sponsor. *Cycling Weekly* described her arrival in Atlanta by saying that "The Olympic camp [was] buzzing with talk of Pezzo's evident physical form." This statement would prove to have multiple meanings. Pezzo raced the Olympic course with her jersey unzipped almost to her navel. After the Olympics, her cleavage would earn almost as much space in the Italian press as her performance.

Early in the race, Pezzo fell in a hairpin turn and scraped her knees. She remounted quickly and gradually caught up with the leaders. Shortly after the 11-kilometer mark, during an uphill stretch, she powered into the lead so fast that the other racers knew they were in trouble. Sure enough, Pezzo kept pulling away until her lead reached 1 minute 42 seconds. Sydor closed the gap by 35 seconds, but by that time Pezzo was safely across the finish line. The bronze medal was won by surprising Susan DeMattei, a registered nurse who was undoubtably aided by the fact that her fiancé was one of the designers of the course. In 25th place was Gao Hongying of China who gained dubious notoriety after the race when she was fined 300 Swiss francs for using "foul language" and showing disrespect for officials.

In 1997, Paola Pezzo dominated the World Cup season, but then news leaked that she had tested positive for the steroid nandrolone. Threatened with a six-month suspension (and damage to her million-dollar image), Pezzo was able to show that similar tests taken a few days earlier and later had been negative.

Paola Pezzo, 1996

Pezzo on the way to victory in the inaugural women's mountain bike race.

The International Cycling Union, faced with the possibility of an expensive and high-profile lawsuit, dropped the case against Pezzo.

2000 Sydney C: 30, N: 20, D: 9.23.

35.7 KM

1. Paola Pezzo	ITA	1:49:24.38
2. Barbara Blatter	SWI	1:49:51.42
3. Margarita Fullana Riera	SPA	1:49:57.39
4. Alla Yepifanova	RUS	1:50:45.43
5. Alison Sydor	CAN	1:52:19.32
6. Mary Grigson	AUS	1:53:22.57
7. Alison Dunlap	USA	1:53:53.05
8. Chrissy Redden	CAN	1:54:07.38

Barbara Blatter led after the first of five laps, Alla Yepifanova after the second, and two-time defending world champion Margarita Fullana after the third. The critical moment of the race came late in the fourth lap. Defending Olympic champion Paolo Pezzo passed Blatter to move into second place. Then she pulled alongside Fullana. On a downhill section, Pezzo and Fullana collided. Fullana went down. Pezzo came out of her pedals, but stayed upright, moved into the lead and drove to the finish line, never to be caught, while Blatter passed Fullana in the final lap to take the silver medal.

2004 Athens-Parnitha C: 30, N: 24, D: 8.27.

1. Gunn Rita Dahle	NOR	1:56:51
2. Marie-Hélène Prémont	CAN	1:57:50
3. Sabine Spitz	GER	1:59:21
4. Alison Sydor	CAN	1:59:47
5. Elsbeth van Rooy-Vink	HOL	2:01:41
6. Maja Włoszczowska	POL	2:02:08
7. Ivonne Kraft	GER	2:05:18
8. Laurence Leboucher	FRA	2:05:34

In 2003, one year after winning the world championship title, Gunn Rita Dahle became the first mountain biker in history to sweep the World Cup, winning all five of the season's races and extending her World Cup streak to eight consecutive wins. Most impressive was her average margin of victory in the World Cup races, two minutes and seven seconds, which included one narrow eight-second victory and seven dominating wins.

Marie-Hélène Prémont and Alison Sydor managed to keep pace with Dahle for the first lap at the Olympics, but she soon left them far behind, opening a 67-second gap over Prémont by the end of the second lap, with Sydor another 48 seconds behind. Despite having difficulties with her gears, Dahle maintained nearly a full minute lead for the rest of the race, finishing 59 seconds ahead of Prémont. Sydor faded at the end and was overtaken for the bronze by the reigning world champion, Sabine Spitz.

2008 Beijing C: 30, N: 22, D: 8.23.

26.7 KM

1. Sabine Spitz	GER	1:45:11
2. Maja Włoszczowska	POL	1:45:52
3. Irina Kalentyeva	RUS	1:46:28
4. Catharine Pendrel	CAN	1:46:37
5. Ren Chengyuan	CHN	1:47:40
6. Petra Henzi	SWI	1:48:41
7. Mary McConneloug	USA	1:50:34
8. Georgia Gould	USA	1:50:51

The 2008 women's mountain bike race was postponed a day due to heavy rain. The defending Olympic bronze medalist, 36-year-old Sabine Spitz, led almost from start to finish, moving ahead of reigning world champion Maja Włoszczowska on the first lap. Spitz opened up such a large lead that she stopped five meters from the finish, hopped off her bike and carried it across the finish line. Defending gold medalist Gunn-Rita Dahle only completed three laps before dropping out due to mechanical problems.

BMX RACE

The women's event includes 16 athletes, 12 based on International Cycling Union (UCI) national rankings, three by the 2008 UCI World Championship, and one by host country invitation, with a maximum of two women per nation. The women's course is approximately 350 meters long.

1896–2004 not held

2008 Beijing C: 16, N: 13, D: 8.22.

1. Anne-Caroline Chausson	FRA	35.976
2. Laetitia le Corguille	FRA	38.042
3. Jill Kintner	USA	38.674
4. Sarah Walker	NZL	38.805
5. Gabriela Díaz	ARG	39.747
6. Nicole Callisto	AUS	1:19.609

DNF: Samantha Cools (CAN), Shanaze Reade (GBR)

Originally a BMX racer, Anne-Caroline Chausson had achieved major success after shifting to mountain biking, winning nine downhill world titles, four dual slalom and four-cross titles. She switched back to BMX in 2007 after learning the event was being added to the Olympic lineup.

Chausson reached the final along with two-time reigning world champion Shanaze Reade and four-time four-cross world champion Jill Kintner of Seattle. Trailing Chausson in the final turn Reade attempted to move into the lead, but crashed on the last corner and didn't finish.

DISCONTINUED EVENTS

500-METER TIME TRIAL

2000 Sydney C: 17, N: 12, D: 9.16. WR: 34.010 (Félicia Ballanger)

1. Félicia Ballanger	FRA	34.140
2. Michelle Ferris	AUS	34.696
3. Cuihua Jiang	CHN	34.768
4. Yan Wang	CHN	35.013
5. Chris Witty	USA	35.230
6. Ulrike Weichelt	GER	35.315
7. Kathrin Freitag	GER	35.473
8. Tanya Dubnicoff	CAN	35.486

Spurred on by a loud and supportive Australian crowd, Michelle Ferris broke her five-year-old personal record. However, there was little doubt that Félicia Ballanger would win the gold medal. She held the world record and she had won the world championship all five times it had been held since 1995 and always by decisive margins. Sure enough, Ballanger bettered Ferris' best time by more than half a second, an impressive gap in an event that lasts less than 35 seconds. Chris Witty, who placed fifth with a personal best, had earned two medals in speed skating at the 1998 Winter Olympics and then won a gold medal at the 2002 Winter Games in Salt Lake City.

2004 Athens C: 12, N: 11, D: 8.20. WR: 34.000 (Jiang Yonghua)

1. Anna Meares	AUS	33.952 WR
2. Jiang Yonghua	CHN	34.112
3. Natalya Tsylinskaya	BLR	34.167
4. Simona Krupeckait	LIT	34.317
5. Yvonne Hijgenaar	HOL	34.532
6. Vicki Pendleton	GBR	34.626
7. Lori-Ann Muenzer	CAN	34.628
8. Nancy Contreras Reyes	MEX	34.783

Riding last, 20-year-old part-time bank teller Anna Meares posted the fastest times over both 250-meter splits, becoming the first woman to break the 34-second mark. Meares' sister, Kerrie, had been the favorite to represent Australia, but a back injury kept her out of the competition. Silver medalist Jiang Yonghua had also finished second to Meares at the 2004 world championships. Three-time world champion Natalya Tsylinskaya took the bronze.

3000-METER INDIVIDUAL PURSUIT

1992 Barcelona C: 17, N: 17, D: 7.31. WR: 3:38.190 (Jeannie Longo)

1. Petra Rossner	GER	3:41.753
2. Kathryn Watt	AUS	3:43.438
3. Rebecca Twigg	USA	3:52.429
4. Hanne Malmberg	DEN	3:53.516
5. Jeannie Longo-Ciprelli	FRA	3:46.547
6. Svetlana Samokhvalova	RUS	3:47.444
7. Tea Vikstedt-Nyman	FIN	3:48.918
8. Leontien van Moorsel	HOL	3:49.795

During the 1980s, before the women's pursuit was included in the Olympics, the event was dominated by two riders: Rebecca Twigg of the United States and Jeannie Longo of France. Twigg won the world championship in 1982, 1984, 1985, and 1987; Longo in 1986, 1988, and 1989. Then they both retired. But when the news came that the pursuit was being added to the Olympic program in Barcelona, both Twigg and Longo returned to the track. They faced each other prematurely—in the quarterfinals. Twigg led by 0.306 seconds with 750 meters to go. Gradually, Longo closed the gap, moving ahead by 0.110 with only one lap remaining. With a half lap to go Longo's lead was down to 0.009. Twigg barely edged ahead to win 3:46.508 to 3:46.549—a difference of four one-hundredths of a second. Twigg was no match for Kathy Watt in the semifinals, but she did earn a bronze medal as the faster semifinal loser. In the final, Watt tried to shake the defending world champion, Petra Rossner, by rocketing off the mark and building a lead of 2.323 seconds. But Rossner ignored her, kept to her own pace, took the lead with 2½ laps to go, and won going away.

1996 Atlanta-Stone Mountain C: 12, N: 12, D: 7.26. WR: 3:31.924 (Antonella Bellutti)

1. Antonella Bellutti	ITA	3:33.595
2. Marion Clignet	FRA	3:38.571
3. Judith Arndt	GER	3:38.744
4. Yvonne McGregor	GBR	3:40.885
5. Rebecca Twigg	USA	3:41.611
6. Rasa Mazeikyte	LIT	3:42.129
7. Sarah Ulmer	NZL	3:45.761
8. Kathryn Watt	AUS	Overtaken

Antonella Bellutti of Bolzano had hoped to compete in the 1992 Olympics—as a hurdler—but knee injuries ruined her chances. She emerged as a world-class cyclist in 1994 and set the world record 3½ months before the Olympics. In the Atlanta final she defeated Marion Clignet, who was born in the United States to French parents. When she was 22 years old Clignet had an epileptic seizure while driving a car. Her license was suspended and she took up bike riding to get to work. She fell in love with cycling and was soon competing. She moved to France in November 1990 after a dispute with US coaches.

2000 Sydney C: 12, N: 12, D: 9.18. WR: 3:30.974 (Marion Clignet)

1. Leontien Zijlaard (van Moorsel)	HOL	3:33.360
2. Marion Clignet	FRA	3:38.751
3. Yvonne McGregor	GBR	3:38.850
4. Sarah Ulmer	NZL	3:38.930
5. Antonella Bellutti	ITA	3:36.967
6. Judith Arndt	GER	3:37.609
7. Alayna Burns	AUS	3:38.223
8. Erin Mirabella	USA	3:38.431

The medalists in this event represented the virtues of perseverance. Leontien van Moorsel, the youngest of the three at age 30, had been considered a glamorous prodigy who flourished both on the road and on the track. She won the individual pursuit world championship in 1990 and the road race world championship in 1991 and 1993. However she missed most of the next three seasons while she dealt with anorexia and bulimia as her weight fluctuated between 43 and 85 kilograms (105 and 190 pounds). She married her coach, Michael Zijlaard, conquered her eating disorders and returned to international competition in 1998. At that year's world championships she won the road time trial and placed second in the individual pursuit.

Marion Clignet, who was 36 years old at the time of the Sydney Olympics, had followed up her 1996 Olympic pursuit silver medal by winning the world championship the same year. But then she too had to withdraw from competition. Already struggling with bulimia and exercise-induced asthma, Clignet began to suffer the effects of genetic arthritis. The medication she took to combat the pain led to epileptic seizures, one of which occurred in 1998 while she was swimming in a pool in Sydney. Clignet returned to competition in May 1999 and regained her world championship in the pursuit. Clignet went to the 2000 Olympics as the reigning world champion and world record holder. However, in the semifinals, van Moorsel, now competing as Leontien Zijlaard, broke Clignet's four-year-old world record with a time of 3:30.816. The final was an anti-climax, as Zijlaard won easily.

What the final lacked in drama, was found instead in the bronze medal race. Yvonne McGregor of Yorkshire was an extreme example of a late bloomer. A converted triathlete, she did not take up competitive cycling until she was 30 years old. By the time of the Sydney Olympics, she was 39. In the race for third place, she fell behind Sarah Ulmer early and still trailed by 1¾ seconds with 1000 meters to go. McGregor finally caught up with Ulmer about 125 meters from the finish and won by less than a tenth of a second.

2004 Athens C: 12, N: 10, D: 8.22. WR: 3:30.604 (Sarah Ulmer)

1. Sarah Ulmer	NZL	3:24.537	WR
2. Katie Mactier	AUS	3:27.650	
3. Leontien Zijlaard-van Moorsel	HOL	3:27.037	
4. Katherine Bates	AUS	3:31.715	
5. Karin Thürig	SWI	3:34.831	
6. Olga Slyusaryeva	RUS	3:36.263	
7. Yelena Chalykh	RUS	3:36.442	
8. Emma Davies	GBR	3:35.069	

After earning the gold medal in Sydney, Leontien van Moorsel won three consecutive World Championships, the first woman to do so in 29 years. In 2004, however, she lost the world championship title to Sarah Ulmer, who had broken the world record with her qualifying time. In the Olympic final, Katie Mactier took a slight advantage in the first kilometer, but Ulmer surged ahead to a full second lead by the two-kilometer mark and finished with a stunning time of 3:24.537 seconds, six seconds faster than her pre-Olympic world record. Conditions at the velodrome were so fast that all three medalists rode under the world record not once but twice during the competition.

2008 Beijing C: 13, N: 11, D: 8.17.

4KM

1. Rebecca Romero	GBR	3:28.321
2. Wendy Houvenaghel	GBR	3:30.395
3. Lesya Kalitovska	UKR	3:31.413
4. Alison Shanks	NZL	3:34.156
5. Sarah Hammer	USA	3:34.237
6. Vilija Sereikaitė	LIT	3:36.808
7. Katie Mactier	AUS	3:37.296
8. Lada Kozlíková	CZE	DNF

Rebecca Romero had won a silver medal as a member of Britain's quadruple sculls rowing team in Athens, but was forced to retire in 2006 because of a persistent back injury. She took up cycling instead, winning a silver medal in the pursuit in her international debut at a UCI World Cup event in Moscow. In 2007 she won her first world championship medal, finishing second to defending world champion Sarah Hammer, and the following year she beat Hammer to win her first international title.

Hammer struggled in Beijing, finishing fifth in the qualifying round and losing her first-round match to Alison Shanks. With Hammer out, Romero's opponent in the final turned out to be team-mate Wendy Houvenaghel, a dental surgeon who had only taken up cycling at the age of 27 to keep her husband company on his training rides. The final was not close, with Romero leading Houvenaghel at each kilometer split and winning by more than two seconds.

POINTS RACE

The rules for the women's points race were the same as those for the men's except that the distance was 25 kilometers.

1996 Atlanta-Stone Mountain C: 21, N: 21, D: 7.28.

		LAPS DOWN	POINTS
1. Nathalie Even-Lancien	FRA	0	24
2. Ingrid Haringa	HOL	0	23
3. Lucy Tyler-Sharman	AUS	0	17
4. Svetlana Samokhvalova	RUS	0	14
5. Maureen Kaila Vergara	ESA	0	11
6. Lyudmila Gorozhanskaya	BLR	0	11
7. Tea Vikstedt-Nyman	FIN	0	9
8. Jacqueline Nelson	NZL	0	8

With only the last double-point sprint to go, there were four cyclists still in contention : three favorites and one surprise. Nathalie Lancien was in first place with 18 points. Reigning world champion Svetlana Samokhvalova was second with 14 points. Tied for third with 13 points were two-time world champion Ingrid Haringa and the outsider: Lucy Tyler-Sharman. Tyler-Sharman was born and raised in Louisville, Kentucky. Her road to the Olympis was a rocky one. In 1989 she was hit by a car going 50 miles per hour. In 1993, exasperated by her inability to gain selection for international competitions, she gave up on the US system and became an Australian citizen. Tyler-Sharman, who wore ten earrings in each ear, thought she had qualified for the individual pursuit, when a court of appeals in Sydney gave Australia's spot in that event to Kathy Watt on the day of the Opening Ceremony. Tyler-Sharman was still entered in the points race, but she hadn't practiced sprints for a year.

On the penultimate lap, Tyler-Sharman attacked. Samokhvalova was caught in the pack, but Lancien and Haringa gave chase. They caught her just before the finish line with Haringa barely nipping Lancien. Haringa's ten points raised her to 23, while Lancien's six points for second place gave her 24 and the gold medal. Tyler-Sharman, like Marion Clignet in the pursuit, was born in the United States, gave up on the US national team, settled in another country and returned to the US to win an Olympic medal.

By finishing fifth, Maureen Kaila became the highest placed athlete from El Salvador in any sport. In ninth place was Seiko Hashimoto of Japan, who, at the age of 31, was competing in her seventh Olympics: four as a speedskater in the Winter Games and three as a cyclist. Her training was no doubt disrupted by the demands of her profession: in 1995 she was elected to Japan's parliament, the House of Councillors.

2000 Sydney C: 17, N: 17, D: 9.21.

		LAPS DOWN	POINTS
1. Antonella Bellutti	ITA	0	19
2. Leontien Zijlaard (van Moorsel)	HOL	0	16
3. Olga Slyusaryeva	RUS	0	15
4. Judith Arndt	GER	0	12
5. Belem Guerrero Méndez	MEX	0	12
6. Marion Clignet	FRA	0	11
7. Teodora Ruano Sanchón	SPA	0	10
8. Sarah Ulmer	NZL	0	9

Antonella Bellutti, who had won a gold medal in the pursuit in 1996, had announced that she would retire after the Sydney Olympics. Three days before the points race, she placed fifth in the pursuit. After the third of ten sprints, Olga Slyusaryeva led with 10 points, followed by Bellutti with 9. Leontien Zijlaard won the next two sprints and at the halfway mark the score stood Slyusaryeva-11, Zijlaard-10, Judith Arndt-10 and Bellutti-9. Marion Clignet won sprints six and seven, while Bellutti picked up three more points by finishing second in the seventh sprint. After the eighth sprint, Bellutti, Slyusaryeva and Arndt were tied at 12. Bellutti and Slyusaryeva finished one-two in the penultimate sprint to make it 17-15. Zijlaard, in fifth place with 10 points, used the double points from her second place in the final sprint to jump up to the silver medal spot while Bellutti secured her gold medal by adding two more points. Bellutti did retire after the Olympics—but only from cycling. She switched to bobsleigh and, as brakewoman for Gerda Weissensteiner, placed seventh at the 2002 Winter Olympics.

2004 Athens C: 19, N: 19, D: 8.25.

		POINTS
1. Olga Slyusaryeva	RUS	20
2. Bélem Guerrero	MEX	14
3. Maria Luisa Calle Williams	COL	12
4. Erin Mirabella	USA	9
5. Vera Carrara	ITA	8
6. Sarah Ulmer	NZL	8
7. Gema Pascual Torrecilla	SPA	7
8. Katherine Bates	AUS	7

Four-time defending world champion Olga Slyusaryeva was expected to dominate the competition—and dominate she did, winning three of the ten sprints and placing in four others. She gained her gold medal on her mother's birthday and dedicated the medal to her. Third-place finisher Maria Luisa Calle Williams tested positive for the banned stimulant heptaminol and was disqualified, promoting Erin Mirabella to bronze. Calle Williams appealed the decision, and after a long deliberation, the Court of Arbitration for Sport reversed the ruling, finding that Calle Williams had taken a headache medicine containing a substance that "transforms to heptaminol during laboratory analyses." Fourteen months after the competition, Calle Williams was reinstated to third place and Mirabella was asked to return her bronze medal.

2008 Beijing C: 22, N: 22, D: 8.18.

		POINTS
1. Marianne Vos	HOL	30
2. Yoanka González Pérez	CUB	18
3. Leire Olaberria Dorronsoro	SPA	13
4. María Luisa Calle Williams	COL	13
5. Lesia Kalytovska	UKR	10
6. Kate Bates	AUS	10
7. Pascale Jeuland	FRA	8
8. Olga Slyusareva	RUS	8

Twenty-one-year-old Marianne Vos had been the world champion in the cyclo-cross and road race in 2006 and arrived in Beijing the reigning points world champion. She won the first field sprint and led by 10 points after the first five sprints. Immediately after the sixth sprint she broke from the peloton and lapped the entire field, earning 20 points and securing the gold medal. Yoanka González, in fifth place after seven sprints, won the eighth and tenth to move into second place. Leire Olaberria and María Luisa Calle both finished with 13 points, but Olaberria took bronze by finishing second in the final sprint.

González's husband, Cuban cyclist Pedro Pablo Pérez, was involved in a car crash one month before the Olympics and spent several days in a coma.

Chapter 9 **Diving**

MEN	WOMEN
Springboard	Springboard
Platform	Platform
Synchronized Springboard	Synchronized Springboard
Synchronized Platform	Synchronized Platform
Discontinued Event	

DIVING TERMS

Positions

Straight—body remains straight
Pike—body bent at the waist with legs straight
Tuck—body bent at the knees and hips with the knees held together against the chest
Free—a combination of positions used in twisting dives

Categories

Forward—body facing forward and dive made forward
Backward—back to the water, rotating away from the board
Reverse—facing forward, rotating back toward the board
Inward—back to the water, rotating toward the board
Forward with a twist—body facing forward and twisting in the air
Armstand—the diver begins with a steady handstand on the edge of the board (used in the platform event only)

MEN

SPRINGBOARD

This event is performed from a springboard three meters (9 feet 10 inches) above the water. The board must be at least 4.8 meters long and a half-meter wide. The scores of the seven judges are multiplied by a coefficient that is determined by the degree of difficulty of the attempted dive. The easiest dive, with a coefficient of 1.2, is a simple forward dive in the tuck position. The most difficult, with a coefficient of 3.7, is the reverse 1½ somersault with 4½ twists free. Olympic competitions begin with a preliminary round. Between 1968 and 1992 the top twelve divers then advanced to the final, which in 1992 consisted of 11 dives—five required and six voluntary. In 1996 a new system was introduced: the top 18 divers in the preliminary advance to a semifinal. The top 12 semifinalists go on to the final. Scores in the semifinal are added to scores in the final to determine the winners. The semifinal in the men's springboard comprises five dives with a total degree of difficulty not to exceed 9.5. The final comprises six dives with unlimited degree of difficulty.

1896–1906 not held

Pat McCormick, 1956
Displaying the spoils of her second straight Olympic diving double, achieved just eight months after giving birth to a bouncing baby boy.

1908 London C: 23, N: 8, D: 7.18.

		PTS.
1. Albert Zürner	GER	85.5
2. Kurt Behrens	GER	85.3
3. George Gaidzik	USA	80.8
3. Gottlob Walz	GER	80.8

1912 Stockholm C: 18, N: 7, D: 7.9.

		ORDINALS	PTS.
1. Paul Günther	GER	6	79.23
2. Hans Luber	GER	9	76.78
3. Kurt Behrens	GER	22	73.73
4. Albert Zürner	GER	23	73.33
5. Robert Zimmerman	CAN	24	72.54
6. Herbert Pott	GBR	28	71.45
7. Johan Jansson	SWE	32	69.64
8. George Gaidzik	USA	36	68.01

The competition consisted of two dives from a one-meter board and five from a three-meter board.

1920 Antwerp C: 14, N: 9, D: 8.27.

		ORDINALS	PTS.
1. Louis Kuehn	USA	6	675.4
2. Clarence "Bud" Pinkston	USA	11	655.3
3. Louis Balbach	USA	15	649.5
4. Gustaf Blomgren	SWE	19	587.05
5. Gunnar Ekstrand	SWE	27	559.25
6. Johan Jansson	SWE	27	544.75

The 1920 diving events were held outdoors in a moat. The water was so dark that some of the divers became disoriented. They performed from both one meter and three meters.

1924 Paris C: 17, N: 9, D: 7.17.

		ORDINALS	PTS.
1. Albert White	USA	7	696.4
2. Ulise "Pete" Desjardins	USA	8	693.2
3. Clarence "Bud" Pinkston	USA	15	653.0
4. Edmund Lindmark	SWE	22	599.1
5. Richmond Eve	AUS	26	564 3
6. Adolf Hellqvist	SWE	30	544 9
7. Kurt Sjöberg	SWE	34	538.3
8. Hendrik Hemsing	HOL	39	490.8

A recent graduate of Stanford University, 29-year-old Albert White was the first diver in Olympic history to win both the springboard and platform events.

1928 Amsterdam C: 24, N: 15, D: 8.8.

		ORDINALS	PTS.
1. Ulise "Pete" Desjardins	USA	5	185.04
2. Michael Galitzen (Mickey Riley)	USA	14	174.06
3. Farid Simaika	EGY	13	172.46
4. Harold "Dutch" Smith	USA	18	168.96
5. Arthur Mund	GER	29.5	154.72
6. Ewald Riebschläger	GER	31	153.86
7. Heinz Plumanns	GER	32.5	150.18
8. Alfred Phillips	CAN	37	149.48

Born in Canada, and raised from the age of 10 in Miami Beach, 5-foot 3-inch Pete Desjardins was a graduate of Stanford University. In Amsterdam, Desjardins received tens for two of his dives, a half gainer and a gainer 1½. He later turned professional and was billed as "The Little Bronze Statue from the Land of Real Estate, Grapefruits and Alligators."

Galitzen was awarded the silver medal over Simaika, even though he had more ordinals, because three of the five judges ranked him higher than Simaika.

1932 Los Angeles C: 13, N: 7, D: 8.8.

		PTS.
1. Michael Galitzen (Mickey Riley)	USA	161.38
2. Harold "Dutch" Smith	USA	158.54
3. Richard Degener	USA	151.82
4. Alfred Phillips	CAN	134.64
5. Leo Esser	GER	134.30
6. Kazuo Kobayashi	JPN	133.76
7. Emile Poussard	FRA	128.66
8. Tetsutaro Namae	JPN	125.18

Pete Desjardins, 1928

Desjardins (center), who won both diving events in 1928, with Al White and Johnny Weissmuller.

1936 Berlin C: 24, N: 15, D: 8.11.

		PTS.
1. Richard Degener	USA	163.57
2. Marshall Wayne	USA	159.56
3. Albert Greene	USA	146.29
4. Tsuneo Shibahara	JPN	144.92
5. Erhard Weiss	GER	141.24
6. Leo Esser	GER	137.99
7. Winfried Marauhn	GER	134.61
8. Tomio Koyanagi	JPN	133.07

Dick Degener's margin of victory was provided by an almost perfect full twist with a one and a half somersault. He was awarded a score of 19.55. Wayne attempted the same dive but earned only 15.54 points.

1948 London C: 26, N: 15, D: 8.3.

		PTS.
1. Bruce Harlan	USA	163.64
2. Miller Anderson	USA	157.29
3. Samuel Lee	USA	145.52

4. Joaquin Capilla Pérez	MEX	141.79
5. Raymond Mulinghausen	FRA	126.55
6. Svante Johansson	SWE	120.20
7. Kamal Hassan	EGY	119.90
8. Thomas Christiansen	DEN	114.59

Miller Anderson culminated a long comeback in London by earning the first of two silver medals. A highly decorated pilot in the army air corps during World War II, Anderson was shot down over Italy. His leg was almost torn off by the plane's tail. He spent a month in a German hospital until it was captured by United States troops. An operation at a United States Army hospital left him with silver plates attached to his left thigh bone. After a four-year absence, Anderson returned to competition in 1946. In 1966 he died of a heart attack, at the age of 42. Gold medalist Bruce Harlan also died young. On June 21, 1959, when he was 33 years old, Harlan took part in an exhibition in Fairfield, Connecticut. Following the performance, Harlan was helping dismantle the scaffolding of the diving tower when he fell 27 feet to his death.

1952 Helsinki C: 36, N: 20, D: 7.28.

		PTS.
1. David "Skippy" Browning	USA	205.29
2. Miller Anderson	USA	199.84
3. Robert Clotworthy	USA	184.92
4. Joaquin Capilla Pérez	MEX	178.33
5. Roman Brener	SOV/RUS	165.63
6. Milton Busin	BRA	155.91
7. Anthony Turner	GBR	151.90
8. Aleksei Zigalov	SOV/RUS	151.31

The divers were somewhat distracted by the presence of too many people near the board, including a photographer in a frogman outfit who actually stationed himself in the pool. After his victory, Skippy Browning was arrested for shinnying up a flag pole in Helsinki and trying to steal an Olympic flag. A navy jet pilot, Browning was killed in a crash in Kansas on March 14, 1956. He was 24 years old.

1956 Melbourne C: 24, N: 19, D: 8.29.

		PTS.
1. Robert Clotworthy	USA	159.56
2. Donald Harper	USA	156.23
3. Joaquin Capilla Pérez	MEX	150.69
4. Glen Whitten	USA	148.55
5. Gennady Udalov	SOV/RUS	140.64
6. Roman Brener	SOV/RUS	139.14
7. Gunther Mund	CHI	137.53
8. József Gerlach	HUN	136.08

1960 Rome C: 32, N: 19, D: 8.29.

		PTS.
1. Gary Tobian	USA	170.00
2. Samuel Hall	USA	167.08
3. Juan Botella	MEX	162.30
4. Alvaro Gaxiola	MEX	150.42
5. Ernest Meissner	CAN	144.07
6. Lamberto Mari	ITA	143.97
7. Toshio Yamano	JPN	140.46
8. Hans-Dieter Pophal	GDR	133.95

After the preliminary round, one judge, a Soviet woman, was replaced for being overly nationalistic in her scoring. Silver medalist Sam Hall gained dubious international fame in December 1986, when he was arrested as a freelance spy in Nicaragua. Hall, who once served in the Ohio House of Representatives, described himself as a "self-employed military advisor and counterterrorist." He was subsequently released by the Nicaraguan government, who declared him a victim of mental illness.

1964 Tokyo C: 27, N: 16, D: 10.14.

		PTS.
1. Kenneth Sitzberger	USA	159.90
2. Francis Gorman	USA	157.63
3. Larry Andreasen	USA	143.77
4. Hans-Dieter Pophal	GDR	142.58
5. Göran Lundqvist	SWE	138.65
6. Boris Polulyakh	SOV/GEO	138.64
7. Mikhail Safonov	SOV/RUS	134.00
8. Vladimir Vasin	SOV/RUS	133.48

Navy Lieutenant Frank Gorman actually outscored Ken Sitzberger on nine of his ten dives. But he missed badly with his ninth round back, two-and-a-half somersault tuck, and lost 11.20 points.

Both Sitzberger and bronze medalist Larry Andreasen met unusual deaths. Sitzberger died January 2, 1984 from a traumatic head injury. He had been involved in the murky world of cocaine trafficking. Because he was due to testify in six weeks as a Federal witness in a drug trial, there was speculation that his death might have been related to the case. However, his wife, fellow 1964 diving medalist Jeanne Collier, told authorities that Sitzberger had hit his head on a table during a New Year's party.

In 1988, toward the end of the Seoul Olympics, Larry Andreasen, then 42 years old, dived 160 feet from the center of the Gerald Desmond Bridge in Long Beach, California. Andreasen was under the mistaken impression that he was breaking the record for the highest dive. In fact, the record was 174 feet 8 inches. He survived the dive uninjured, but was arrested. Andreasen than became obsessed with another, higher bridge: the Vincent Thomas Bridge in Los Angeles Harbor, in particular its 385-foot west tower. Three times police removed him from the bridge tower. Finally, on October 26, 1990, he took the plunge and died of multiple injuries. His death was not ruled a suicide, but an accident.

1968 Mexico City C: 28, N: 16, D: 10.20.

		PTS.
1. Bernard Wrightson	USA	170.15
2. Klaus Dibiasi	ITA	159.74
3. James Henry	USA	158.09
4. Luis Niño de Rivera	MEX	155.71
5. Franco Giorgio Cagnotto	ITA	155.70
6. Keith Russell	USA	151.75
7. Tord Anderson	SWE	151.50
8. Donald Wagstaff	AUS	150.18

Bernie Wrightson moved up from third place to first with his last three dives.

1972 Munich C: 32, N: 16, D: 8.30.

		PTS.
1. Vladimir Vasin	SOV/RUS	594.09
2. Franco Giorgio Cagnotto	ITA	591.63
3. Craig Lincoln	USA	577.29
4. Klaus Dibiasi	ITA	559.05
5. Michael Finneran	USA	557.34
6. Vyacheslav Strahov	SOV/RUS	556.20
7. Falk Hoffmann	GDR	544.95
8. Norbert Huda	GER	524.16

The US string of eleven straight springboard victories was finally broken. The next to last dive was the decisive one. Cagnotto missed and was awarded only 48.72 points, while Vasin recorded 75.60 points, the highest score of the competition. Vasin finished eighth in 1964 and eleventh in 1968.

1976 Montreal C: 30, N: 16, D: 7.22.

		PTS.
1. Philip Boggs	USA	619.05
2. Franco Giorgio Cagnotto	ITA	570.48
3. Aleksandr Kosenkov	SOV/BLR	567.24
4. Falk Hoffmann	GDR	553.53
5. Robert Cragg	USA	548.19
6. Gregory Louganis	USA	528.96
7. Carlos Giron	MEX	523.59
8. Klaus Dibiasi	ITA	516.18

At the time of his Olympic triumph, Phil Boggs was a captain in the United States Air Force. As the reigning world champion, he expected to defend his Olympic title in 1980, but the US boycott of the Moscow Games kept him at home. Boggs died of lymphoma on July 2, 1990, at the age of 40.

1980 Moscow C 24, N: 16, D: 7.23.

		PTS.
1. Aleksandr Portnov	SOV/BLR	905.025
2. Carlos Girón	MEX	892.140
3. Franco Giorgio Cagnotto	ITA	871.500
4. Falk Hoffmann	GDR	858.510
5. Aleksandr Kosenkov	SOV/BLR	855.120
6. Christopher Snode	GBR	844.470
7. Vyacheslav Troshin	SOV/RUS	820.050
8. Ricardo Camacho	SPA	749.340

Aleksandr Portnov's victory was clouded by controversy. Distracted by the noise of the crowd watching the final of the men's 100-meter butterfly, Portnov turned a two-and-a-half backward somersault into a belly flop. He immediately protested and was awarded a re-dive, which he hit beautifully. Giron, Cagnotto, and Hoffman objected, claiming that they had been subjected to similar distractions. Hoffman was particularly annoyed, since his later claim that one of his dives had been disrupted by a photographer's flash was denied. The medal ceremony was delayed for two days until a final decision was announced by the International Amateur Swimming Federation (FINA). In Mexico City demonstrations were held outside the Soviet embassy to protest the ruling.

1984 Los Angeles C: 30, N: 19, D: 8.8.

		PTS.
1. Gregory Louganis	USA	754.41
2. Tan Liangde	CHN	662.31
3. Ronald Merriott	USA	661.32
4. Li Hongping	CHN	646.35
5. Christopher Snode	GBR	609.51
6. Piero Italiani	ITA	578.94
7. Albin Killat	GER	569.52
8. Stephen Foley	AUS	561.93

Of Samoan and northern European ancestry, Greg Louganis was given up for adoption by his 15-year-old parents. Like so many future Olympic champions, Louganis suffered through a difficult childhood. Taunted by his classmates in El Cajon, California, he was called "retarded" because he was dyslexic, and "nigger" because he had dark skin. He began smoking tobacco when he was 9 years old and marijuana when he was 12. When he turned 13, he kicked his adoptive mother in the chest, injuring her. His parents turned him over to the police. As a teenager Louganis depended so heavily on alcohol that he considered himself an alcoholic. But Louganis survived these hard times by escaping into the world of diving. He was so good that he qualified for the Montreal Olympics at the age of 16. He finished sixth in the springboard event and second in the platform. Favored to win two gold medals at the 1980 Olympics, he was shut out by the US boycott, but accomplished the feat instead at the 1982 world championships. In 1984 he performed brilliantly despite the heavy pressure of being the overwhelming favorite. His winning margin of over 92 points was unprecedented in Olympic history.

1988 Seoul C: 35, N: 23, D: 9.20.

		PTS.
1. Gregory Louganis	USA	730.80
2. Tan Liangde	CHN	704.88
3. Li Deliang	CHN	665.28
4. Albin Killat	GER	661.47
5. Mark Bradshaw	USA	642.99
6. Jorge Mondragón Vázquez	MEX	616.02
7. Jesús Mena	MEX	598.77
8. Edwin Jongejans	HOL	588.33

Greg Louganis won 19 consecutive international springboard competitions between 1982 and 1987. Then, in 1988, he was beaten twice by Tan Liangde, who had been studying videotapes of Louganis for 6 years. In Seoul, Louganis was leading the preliminary round when he stepped onto the board for his ninth dive, a reverse two and a half somersault in the pike position. The defending Olympic champion leapt into the air, but failed to push out far enough. When he came down, he hit his head on the board and fell clumsily into the water. It was not Louganis' first confrontation with diving danger. Once, in 1976, he hit the bottom of the platform and ended up with two black eyes and a bloody nose. In 1979 in Tbilisi in Soviet Georgia he hit the top of the platform and was knocked unconscious. He had to be rescued from the pool. He woke up 20 minutes later surrounded by doctors. In 1981 he broke his collarbone when he hit the bottom of a pool. In 1984 he became disoriented during a platform dive in New Zealand and landed on his back. In 1987, at the US Indoor Championship, in an incident eerily similar to the one in Seoul, he came within an inch or two of hitting the springboard on a reverse one and a half in the layout position.

In Seoul, Louganis climbed out of the pool unassisted. Four temporary sutures were applied to his head and, incredibly, 35 minutes later he was back on the board ready for his next dive: another reverse somersault. He scored 87.12 points, the highest score by any diver in the preliminaries. After qualifying for the final with his last dive, he was taken to the hospital where the sutures were replaced by five mattress stitches and a waterproof patch.

The next day, despite great pressure from Tan, Louganis hit all 11 of his dives—including the one he had botched in the preliminaries—and earned his third gold medal.

One week later Louganis won another gold medal in the platform event. As he came out of the water, an international television audience watched as he sobbed in the arms of his coach, Ron O'Brien, who whispered to him words unheard. Most people assumed that Louganis was crying because he had won a close contest with the final dive of his career. Although this was a contributing factor to the release of Louganis' emotion, there was much more to the story.

What O'Brien had said to Louganis in those touching moments was, "Nobody will ever know what we've been through." For more than six years this was true. But in 1995 Louganis went public with the full story. Six months before the Olympics Louganis learned that he had tested HIV-positive and that he might already have AIDS. By the time he got to Seoul, he was taking the drug AZT every four hours and was frightened that teammates might hear the alarm that woke him in the middle of each night so that he wouldn't miss a dose. When a fellow diver asked about the pills he popped all day long, Louganis told him they were aspirins for a sore shoulder. Only Ron O'Brien and a handful of others knew that Louganis was HIV-positive. When Louganis hit his head on his ninth dive of the springboard prelims, he felt blood on his head and was horrified that he might have bled in the pool, possibly

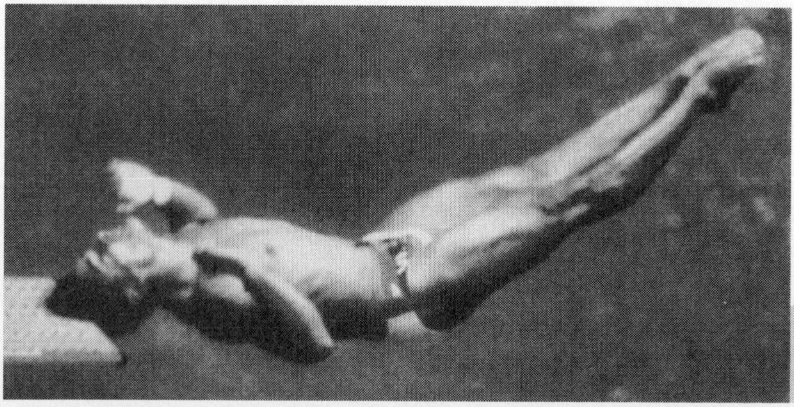

Greg Louganis, 1988
Louganis hits his head on the board during the 1988 springboad diving competiton

infecting other divers. He later learned that the water would have diluted his blood enough to keep it from being dangerous. But he did risk contaminating two other people. Ron O'Brien, who was aware that Louganis was HIV-positive, wiped away a trickle of blood on Louganis' neck so that his Chinese rivals wouldn't see it and gain confidence. Dr. Jim Puffer, who treated Louganis' wound and sewed the sutures, did not know about Louganis' condition. Both O'Brien and Puffer later took AIDS tests that proved negative.

1992 Barcelona C: 32, N: 22, D : 7.29.

		PTS.
1. Mark Lenzi	USA	676.53
2. Tan Liangde	CHN	645.57
3. Dmitri Sautin	RUS	627.78
4. Michael Murphy	AUS	611.97
5. Kent Ferguson	USA	609.12
6. Jorge Mondragón Vázquez	MEX	604.14
7. Edwin Jongejans	HOL	581.40
8. Valery Statsenko	UKR	577.92

Mark Lenzi of Federicksburg, Virginia, didn't begin diving until, at the age of 16, he watched Greg Louganis performing on television at the 1984 Olympics. Until that time Lenzi had been a wrestler. Seven years later he became the first person to score over 100 points on a single dive when he earned 101.85 points for a reverse 3½ somersault tuck at the 1991 United States Indoor Championship.

In the Barcelona final, Albin Killat of Germany held a slight lead over Tan Liangde and Lenzi. But then Killat slipped as he began his seventh dive, belly-flopping a forward 3½ somersault pike. Instantly, he dropped from first place to last (he ended up tenth), and Lenzi sprang into the lead. By day's end Lenzi had earned the three highest scores of the competition, leaving Tan with his third consecutive silver medal.

1996 Atlanta C: 39, N: 27, D: 7.29.

		PTS.
1. Xiong Ni	CHN	701.46
2. Yu Zhuocheng	CHN	690.93
3. Mark Lenzi	USA	686.49
4. Scott Donie	USA	666.93
5. Dmitri Sautin	RUS	644.67
6. Michael Murphy	AUS	640.95
7. Jan Hempel	GER	622.32
8. Fernando Platas Alvarez	MEX	619.98

As a teenager, Xiong Ni of Changsha had earned two medals in platform diving: a silver in 1988 and a bronze in 1992. After 1994, plagued by injuries, he switched to springboard. In Atlanta his most serious challenge came from teammate Yu Zhuocheng, the reigning world champion. Xiong entered the final in first place, with defending Olympic champion Mark Lenzi and favorite Dmitri Sautin 1.71 points behind. Yu jumped in front in the third round, but Xiong recaptured the lead with his fourth dive and expanded it with each of his last two dives.

2000 Sydney C: 49, N: 35, D: 9.26.

		PTS.
1. Xiong Ni	CHN	708.72
2. Fernando Platas Alvarez	MEX	708.42
3. Dmitri Sautin	RUS	703.20
4. Xiao Hailiang	CHN	671.04
5. Dean Pullar	AUS	647.40
6. Troy Dumais	USA	642.72
7. Mark Ruiz	USA	638.22
8. Ken Terauchi	JPN	634.47

After the semifinals, world champion Dmitri Sautin was in first place, followed by Xiao Hailiang, Fernando Platas and defending Olympic champion Xiong Ni. Sautin held onto his lead throughout most of the final. Going into the last round of dives, Sautin was 10.98 points ahead of Xiong and 13.33 points ahead of Platas. With his final dive, a forward 2½ somersault with 2 twists, Platas earned 83.64 points. Sautin attempted a reverse 2½ somersault with 1½ twists, but missed it. His scores ranged from 5.5 to 6.5 and he ended up with only 65.10, which dropped him below Platas. Xiong Ni, attempting an inward 3½ somersault, needed 81.31 points to win the gold medal. The judges awarded him a 9.0, an 8.5, three 8.0s and two 7.5s for a total of 81.60 points. Two days later, Xiong added another gold medal in the synchronized springboard event.

2004 Athens C: 32, N: 19, D: 8.24.

		PTS.
1. Peng Bo	CHN	787.38
2. Alexandre Despatie	CAN	755.97
3. Dmitri Sautin	RUS	753.27
4. Wang Feng	CHN	750.72
5. Fernando Platas Alvarez	MEX	704.25
6. Troy Dumais	USA	701.46
7. Aleksandr Dobroskok	RUS	697.29
8. Ken Terauchi	JPN	690.00

Placed second behind Dmitri Sautin going into the final, Peng Bo proved untouchable, giving a near-perfect performance, including a forward 3½ somersault in the second round that earned him five scores of 10.0. In second place after the first two dives of the final, 2004 world cup winner Alexandre Despatie mistimed his third dive, a reverse 3½ somersault, and dropped to third place behind Sautin. Despatie came back with three more strong dives, edging past Dmitri Sautin with his final attempt, a forward 2½ somersault with two twists, to earn silver. Despite a shoulder injury that kept him out of competition for the beginning of the season, the 30-year-old Sautin managed to earn a place on the podium, bringing his total medal count to seven over four Olympics, including two gold, one silver and four bronze.

2008 Beijing C: 29, N: 20, D: 8.19.

		PTS.
1. He Chong	CHN	572.90
2. Alexandre Despatie	CAN	536.65
3. Qin Kai	CHN	530.10
4. Dmitri Sautin	RUS	512.65
5. Pavlo Rozenberg	GER	485.60
6. Troy Dumais	USA	472.50
7. Yahel Castillo Huerta	MEX	462.10
8. Patrick Hausding	GER	462.05

China had won the past three springboard gold medals and was well-positioned to extend the streak in Beijing, where they were represented by reigning world champion Qin Kai and reigning world cup champion He Chong. He and Qin led the qualifying round, followed by world number two Yahel Castillo and thrice Olympic bronze medalist Dmitri Sautin, who was competing in his fifth Olympics.

The 21-year-old He dominated the semi-finals, recording the toughest dive of the round, a forward 2½ somersault with three twists that earned 102.60 points, to finish nearly 30 points ahead of Alexandre Despatie in second place. The 2005 world champion, Despatie had had a difficult 2008, fighting a back injury and fracturing his right foot while playing soccer during a training session in April. Despatie finished the qualifying round in ninth place, but moved up to second after the semifinals.

He Chong led after the first dive of the final, scoring four perfect 10s from the judges and cheers from the mostly Chinese crowd, and never relinquished the lead, going on to win by more than 36 points. Despatie moved into second place with his second dive and held off third-place Qin for silver. Sautin recorded a nearly-perfect final dive—a reverse 2½ somersault 1½ twist in pike position which scored 99.75 points—but was unable to overtake Qin and finished fourth.

PLATFORM

This event is staged from a rigid platform ten meters (32 feet 9¾ inches) above the water. The platform must be at least six meters long and two meters wide. Since 1996 the semifinalists perform four dives with a total degree of difficulty not to exceed 7.6. The finalists perform six dives with unlimited degree of difficulty.

1896–1900 not held

1904 St. Louis C: 5, N: 2, D: 9.7.

		PTS.
1. George Sheldon	USA	12.66
2. Georg Hoffmann	GER	11.66
3. Frank Kehoe	USA	11.33
4. Alfred Braunschweiger	GER	11.33
5. Otto Hooff	GER	—

George Sheldon, the first Olympic diving champion, was a 30-year-old eye doctor from St. Louis. The German team protested Sheldon's victory, but their protest was rejected by James Sullivan, the US official in charge. Kehoe and Braunschweiger tied, and a dive-off was ordered. Braunschweiger refused to take part, so Kehoe was awarded third place. Many Olympic historians credit Braunschweiger with a share of third anyway. The Americans and Germans disagreed as to what constituted a proper dive. The Americans felt that the manner in which a diver hit the water was important, while the Germans, who attempted more difficult dives but tended to land on their stomachs and chests, contended that landings didn't matter. George Sheldon died November 25, 1907, as a result of an organic heart lesion.

1906 Athens C: 24, N: 8, D: 4.28.

		PTS.
1. Gottlob Walz	GER	156.0
2. Georg Hoffmann	GER	150.2
3. Otto Satzinger	AUT	147.4
4, Albert Zürner	GER	144.6
5. Gordon Melville Clarke	GBR	144.0
6. Hjalmar Johansson	SWE	143.4
7. Robert Andersson	SWE	142.2
8. Fritz Nicolai	GER	138.0

1908 London C: 23, N: 6, D: 7.24.

		PTS.
1. Hjalmar Johansson	SWE	83.75
2. Karl Malmström	SWE	78.73
3. Arvid Spångberg	SWE	74.00
4. Robert Andersson	SWE	68.30
5. George Gaidzik	USA	56.30

In the preliminary round, George Cane of Great Britain landed awkwardly and was knocked unconscious. He was fished out of the water and saved by Hjalmar Johansson, the ultimate winner. George Gaidzik achieved the highest score in the preliminary round, but in the semifinals he was disqualified because one of the three judges accused him of receiving coaching signals from a teammate on the ground. The US protested and Gaidzik was advanced to the final as an extra qualifier. However he was apparently shaken by the turmoil and performed far below his usual standards in the final.

1912 Stockholm C: 23, N: 7, D: 7.15.

		ORDINALS	PTS.
1. Erik Adlerz	SWE	7	73.94
2. Albert Zürner	GER	10	72.60
3. Gustaf Blomgren	SWE	16	69.56
4. Hjalmar Johansson	SWE	22	67.80
5. George Yvon	GBR	22	67.66
6. Harald Arbin	SWE	31	62.62
7. Albin Carlsson	SWE	32	63.16
8. Toivo Aro	FIN	40	57.05

The divers performed two dives from five meters and five dives from ten meters.

1920 Antwerp C: 15, N: 7, D: 8.29.

		ORDINALS	PTS.
1. Clarence "Bud" Pinkston	USA	7	503.3
2. Erik Adlerz	SWE	10	495.4
3. Haig "Harry" Prieste	USA	16	468.65
4. Gustaf Blomgren	SWE	23	453.8
5. Yngve Johnson	SWE	27	441.8
6. Louis Balbach	USA	28	424.0
7. Adolfo Wellisch	BRA	29	423.8

The competition included dives from both five and ten meters. Hal Haig Prieste, the winner of the bronze medal, was apparently the first of a long line of Olympic athletes to steal official Olympic flags, climbing a 15-foot flagpole to snatch his souvenir. After keeping the flag in a suitcase for 80 years, Prieste returned it to the IOC's president, Juan Antonio Samaranch, at a ceremony at the Sydney Olympics. In return, Samaranch presented the 103-year-old Olympian with a box containing a commemorative Olympic medal. The hard-of-hearing Prieste responded, "What is it? Kleenex?" Prieste was born in Fresno, California, in 1896, the same year the modern Olympics began. He died on April 19, 2001, at the age of 104.

After the Olympics Prieste acted in Mack Sennett's Keystone Kops series. He also worked vaudeville and performed in the Ice Follies and with the Ringling Brothers and Barnum & Bailey Circus.

1924 Paris C: 20, N: 10, D: 7.20.

		ORDINALS	PTS.
1. Albert White	USA	9	97.46
2. David Fall	USA	11.5	97.30
3. Clarence "Bud" Pinkston	USA	6.5	94.60
4. Erik Adlerz	SWE	19	93.78
5. Eugène Lenormand	FRA	24	87.54
6. Helge Öberg	SWE	31	85.80
7. Svend Palle Sørensen	DEN	36	80.92
8. Adolf Hellqvist	SWE	37.5	80.64

1928 Amsterdam C: 24, N: 12, D: 8.11.

		ORDINALS	PTS.
1. Ulise "Pete" Desjardins	USA	6	98.74
2. Farid Simaika	EGY	9	99.58
3. Michael Galitzen (Mickey Riley)	USA	15	92.34
4. Walter Colbath	USA	21	87.78
5. Ewald Riebschläger	GER	27	82.44
6. Karl Schumm	GER	28	80.54
7. Alfred Phillips	CAN	35	77.26
8. Albert Reginald Knight	GBR	41	72.22

Simaika was originally announced as the winner, and the Egyptian national anthem was played. Then it was declared that a mistake had been made, that ordinals (place-figures), not total points, determined the winner. Consequently, Desjardins was given his second gold medal. In fact, only one of the five judges ranked Simaika ahead of Desjardins. Simaika and Desjardins later gave diving exhibitions together in Europe. In March 1942, Simaika became a United States citizen. He joined the United States Army Air Corps as a pilot and was shot down over New Guinea.

1932 Los Angeles C: 8, N: 5, D: 8.13.

		PTS.
1. Harold "Dutch" Smith	USA	124.80
2. Michael Galitzen (Mickey Riley)	USA	124.28
3. Frank Kurtz	USA	121.98
4. Josef Staudinger	AUT	103.44
5. Carlos Curiel	MEX	83.82
6. Jesús Flores Albo	MEX	77.94
7. Alfred Phillips	CAN	77.10
8. Hidekatsu Ishida	JPN	75.92

Frank Kurtz began supporting himself when he was 12 years old. At 14 he was selling newspapers in Kansas City, Missouri, and diving at local meets when Johnny Weissmuller saw him and advised him to find a good coach in California. Kurtz hitchhiked to Los Angeles and was taken in by coach Clyde Swendsen. Seven years later, Kurtz won a bronze medal at the 1932 Olympics. During World War II he became one of the US's most famous fighter pilots, flying a plane called the Swoose. When his wife gave birth to a daughter in 1944, they named her Swoosie after the plane. Swoosie Kurtz grew up to be a well known actress.

1936 Berlin C: 26, N: 15, D: 8.15.

		PTS.
1. Marshall Wayne	USA	113.58
2. Elbert Root	USA	110.60
3. Hermann Stork	GER	110.31
4. Erhard Weiss	GER	110.15
5. Frank Kurtz	USA	108.61
6. Tsuneo Shibahara	JPN	107.40
7. Siegfried Viebahn	GER	105.00
8. Tomio Koyanagi	JPN	94.54

While serving in World War II as an Air Force colonel, Marshall Wayne was shot down on a flight over Italy. He suffered a torn ligament in the crash, but managed to make his way to a British Aid Station and eventually to England. After the war Wayne became a Pan Am pilot.

1948 London C: 25, N: 15, D: 8.5.

		PTS.
1. Samuel Lee	USA	130.05
2. Bruce Harlan	USA	122.30
3. Joaquín Capilla Pérez	MEX	113.52
4. Lennart Brunnhage	SWE	108.62
5. Peter Heatly	GBR	105.29
6. Thomas Christiansen	DEN	105.22
7. Raymond Mulinghausen	FRA	103.01
8. George Athans	CAN	100.91

Sammy Lee was a 28-year-old Korean-American army doctor. For his last dive he chose a forward three and a half somersault. Once, when performing a similar dive, he had mistaken the sky for the water and pulled out too soon. Now with the Olympic title on the line, he was afraid he would repeat the mistake. "I dove, hit the water, felt numb and tingling and decided: 'I did a belly flop.'" When he popped out of the water he discovered that, far from belly-flopping, his dive had been rated almost perfect. "I just walked on water out of that pool," he later recalled. Lee was the first male Asian-American Olympic medalist.

1952 Helsinki C: 31, N: 17, D: 8.1.

		PTS.
1. Samuel Lee	USA	156.28
2. Joaquín Capilla Pérez	MEX	145.21
3. Günther Haase	GER	141.31
4. John McCormack	USA	138.74
5. Alberto Capilla Pérez	MEX	136.44
6. Rodolfo Perea	MEX	128.28
7. Aleksandr Bakatin	SOV/RUS	126.86
8. Roman Brener	SOV/RUS	126.31

Sammy Lee celebrated his 32nd birthday by winning his second gold medal. He later coached double gold medalist Bob Webster and quadruple gold medalist Greg Louganis.

1956 Melbourne C: 22, N: 10, D: 12.6.

		PTS.
1. Joaquín Capilla Pérez	MEX	152.44
2. Gary Tobian	USA	152.41
3. Richard Connor	USA	149.79
4. József Gerlach	HUN	149.25
5. Roman Brener	SOV/RUS	142.95
6. William Farrell	USA	139.12
7. Ferenc Siák	HUN	138.83
8. Mikhail Chachba	SOV/RUS	134.51

Third in 1948 and second in 1952, Capilla, a 27-year-old architect, completed his set of platform diving medals by executing a superb forward one and a half somersault with a double twist on his final dive. The highest-scored dive of the competition, it gave Capilla a 0.03 point edge over Tobian. The US team lodged a protest against the Soviet and Hungarian judges, but FINA Secretary Bertil Sallfors rejected the complaint, explaining, "There can be no protests against the judges." Soviet judge Eva Bozd-Morskaya had given Gary Tobian an average score of 6.35, while his average overall score had been 7.3. On the other hand, she had scored Mikhail Chachba 7.38, while his overall average had been 6.37. This incident led to a change in the rules which allowed individual judges to be eliminated because of incompetence.

1960 Rome C: 28, N: 18, D: 9.2.

		PTS.
1. Robert Webster	USA	165.56
2. Gary Tobian	USA	165.25
3. Brian Phelps	GBR	157.13
4. Roberto Madrigal García	MEX	152.86
5. Rolf Sperling	GDR	151.83
6. Gennady Galkin	SOV/RUS	141.69
7. Fritz Enskat	GER	138.86
8. Anatoly Sysoyev	SOV/RUS	135.59

Webster moved from third place to first with his last three dives. Bronze medalist Brian Phelps went on to found a gymnastics and trampoline club in the south of England. In 2008 he was arrested and charged with sexually abusing three young girls whom he trained in the 1970s and 1980s. Phelps pleaded guilty and was sent to prison for nine years.

1964 Tokyo C: 30, N: 16, D: 10.18.

		PTS.
1. Robert Webster	USA	148.58
2. Klaus Dibiasi	ITA	147.54
3. Thomas Gompf	USA	146.57
4. Roberto Madrigal García	MEX	144.27
5. Viktor Palagin	SOV/RUS	143.77
6. Brian Phelps	GBR	143.18
7. Rolf Sperling	GDR	142.24
8. Toshio Otsubo	JPN	142.05

This time Webster was only in sixth place with three dives to go, but still managed to withstand the pressure and successfully defend his championship.

1968 Mexico City C: 35, N: 17, D: 10.26.

		PTS.
1. Klaus Dibiasi	ITA	164.18
2. Alvaro Gaxiola	MEX	154.49
3. Edwin Young	USA	153.93
4. Keith Russell	USA	152.34
5. José Robinson	MEX	143.62
6. Lothar Matthes	GDR	141.75
7. Luis Niño de Rivera	MEX	141.16
8. Franco Giorgio Cagnotto	ITA	138.89

Coached by his father, Carlo, who had finished tenth in the 1936 Olympics, Klaus Dibiasi of Bolzano practiced between 130 and 150 dives a day, six days a week. In Mexico City, Dibiasi began his amazing Olympic winning streak by becoming the first Italian ever to win a gold medal in a swimming or diving event.

1972 Munich C: 35, N: 18, D: 9.4.

		PTS.
1. Klaus Dibiasi	ITA	504.12
2. Richard Rydze	USA	480.75
3. Franco Giorgio Cagnotto	ITA	475.83
4. Lothar Matthes	GDR	465.75
5. David Ambartsumyan	SOV/ARM	463.56
6. Richard Early	USA	462.45
7. Vladimir Kapirulin	SOV/RUS	459.21
8. Carlos Girón	MEX	442.41

Klaus Dibiasi, 1972

The first Italian to earn swimming or diving gold, not to mention three Olympic titles in platform diving.

1976 Montreal C: 25, N: 14, D: 7.27.

		PTS.
1. Klaus Dibiasi	ITA	600.51
2. Gregory Louganis	USA	576.99
3. Vladimir Aleynik	SOV/BLR	548.61
4. Kent Vosler	USA	544.14
5. Patrick Moore	USA	538.17
6. Falk Hoffmann	GDR	531.60
7. David Ambartsumyan	SOV/ARM	516.21
8. Carlos Girón	MEX	513.93

Seventeen-year-old Soviet diver Sergei Nemtsanov finished a disappointing ninth, and then caused something of a sensation when he disappeared mysteriously from the Olympic Village. Soviet officials charged that he had been abducted. When he showed up again, the Western press claimed that Nemtsanov had left the Village voluntarily, but that the Soviets had tracked him down and hauled him back against his will.

1980 Moscow C: 23, N: 14, D: 7.28.

		PTS.
1. Falk Hoffmann	GDR	835.650
2. Vladimir Aleynik	SOV/BLR	819.705
3. David Ambartsumyan	SOV/ARM	817.440
4. Carlos Girón	MEX	809.805
5. Dieter Waskow	GDR	802.800
6. Thomas Knuths	GDR	783.975
7. Sergei Nemtsanov	SOV/RUS	775.860
8. Niki Sajkovic	AUT	725.145

1984 Los Angeles C: 26, N: 18, D: 8.12.

		PTS.
1. Gregory Louganis	USA	710.91
2. Bruce Kimball	USA	643.50
3. Li Kongzheng	CHN	638.28
4. Tong Hui	CHN	604.77
5. Albin Killat	GER	551.97
6. Dieter Dörr	GER	536.07
7. Christopher Snode	GBR	524.40
8. David Bedard	CAN	518.13

As Greg Louganis stood 33 feet above the water, preparing for his final dive, he told himself, "No matter what I do, my mother is still going to love me." He then executed a near-perfect reverse tuck to become the first platform diver to score over 700 points and the first male since 1928 to win both the springboard and platform competitions. Bruce Kimball overtook Li Kongzheng with his final dive to win the silver medal. In 1981 Kimball was struck head-on by a drunken driver. Every bone in his face was broken, his skull was fractured, his left leg broken, the ligaments in his knee torn, his liver was lacerated, and his spleen had to be removed. When he returned to diving nine months later, he earned the nickname "The Comeback Kid." On August 1, 1988, two weeks before the US Olympic diving trials, Kimball, himself drunk, plowed into a crowd of teenagers while driving 75 miles per hour, killing two boys and injuring six others. Despite the tragedy, Kimball took part in the trials but failed to make the team. He subsequently pleaded guilty to vehicular manslaughter and was sentenced to 17 years in prison. He was released on November 24, 1993, after serving less than five.

1988 Seoul C: 26, N: 15, D: 9.27.

		PTS.
1. Gregory Louganis	USA	638.61
2. Xiong Ni	CHN	637.47
3. Jesús Mena	MEX	594.39
4. Georgy Chogovadze	SOV/GEO	585.96
5. Jan Hempel	GDR	583.77
6. Li Kongzheng	CHN	543.81
7. Steffen Haage	GDR	541.02
8. Vladimir Timoshinin	SOV/RUS	534.66

Greg Louganis, hoping to become the first male diver to win both the springboard and platform events twice in a row, found himself in an unusually close battle with 14-year-old Xiong Ni. The difference in their scores was never more than 10 points. With one dive remaining, Xiong led by exactly three points. His final dive was a brilliantly executed inward three and a half somersault in the tuck position. With a degree of difficulty of 3.2, it earned him 82.56 points. This meant that Louganis needed to score 85.56 points on *his* last dive, a reverse three and a half somersault in the tuck position, also known as the "Dive of Death" because it had proved fatal to two divers. Louganis performed it beautifully, although his entry was less than perfect. However, the high degree of difficulty, 3.4, allowed him to score 86.70 points and squeeze out a narrow, highly emotional victory. And just how young was Xiong Ni? After one dive he came out of the water with blood on his face. At first it was thought that he had injured himself. But it turned out that all he had suffered was a broken pimple.

1992 Barcelona C: 23, N: 14, D: 8.4.

		PTS.
1. Sun Shuwei	CHN	677.31
2. Scott Donie	USA	633.63
3. Xiong Ni	CHN	600.15
4. Jan Hempel	GER	574.17
5. Robert Morgan	GBR	568.59
6. Dmitri Sautin	RUS	565.95
7. Michael Kühne	GER	558.54
8. Keita Kaneto	JPN	529.14

Tiny Sun Shuwei of Jeyang in Guangdong Province burst onto the international scene when he won the 1990 Asian Games at the age of 14. The following year he won the world championships. Less than three months before the Olympics, at the Dive Canada meet, Sun set a world record for the most points earned on a single dive: he was awarded perfect tens on a reverse 3½ somersault tuck for a total score of 102.00 points. Standing 5 feet 1 inch (1.55 m) and weighing 99 pounds (45 kg), Sun took the lead in the fourth round of the Olympic final and won easily.

1996 Atlanta C: 37, N: 26, D: 8.2.

		PTS.
1. Dmitri Sautin	RUS	692.34
2. Jan Hempel	GER	663.27
3. Xiao Hailiang	CHN	658.20
4. Tian Liang	CHN	648.18
5. Vladimir Timoshinin	RUS	628.59
6. David Pichler	USA	607.11
7. Fernando Platas Alvarez	MEX	603.03
8. Michael Kühne	GER	583.98

In December 1991 Dmitri Sautin was stabbed several times during a street argument in his hometown of Voroneig. He spent almost two months in the hospital, but recovered in time to compete in the Barcelona Olympics. He won a bronze medal in the springboard competition and placed sixth in the platform. Sautin arrived in Atlanta as a favorite in both events, but finished a dissapointing fifth in the springboard. The platform event went more to form. Jan Hempel entered the final with a lead over Sautin of 2.58 points. Sautin moved ahead with his first dive and extended his lead to 41.28 points after four dives. Hempel's last two dives were the highest scoring of the competition, but Sautin still won a clear victory.

2000 Sydney C: 42, N: 28, D: 9.30.

		PTS.
1. Tian Liang	CHN	724.53
2. Hu Jia	CHN	713.55
3. Dmitri Sautin	RUS	679.26
4. Alexandre Despatie	CAN	652.35
5. Ken Terauchi	JPN	636.90
6. Mark Ruiz	USA	625.92
7. Igor Lukashin	RUS	624.51
8. Mathew Helm	AUS	618.24

The two Chinese entrants, Tian Liang, the 21-year-old son of a truck driver, and Hu Jia, a late replacement for an injured teammate, put on a spectacular duel. Hu took a 5.16-point lead into the final, but Tian moved ahead with his first dive of the final, a back 1½ somersault with 3½ twists that earned him perfect 10.0s from three of the seven judges. Hu regained the lead in the second round and then gave himself a 30-point cushion with a back 3½ somersault dive that brought him 99 points when all but one of the judges awarded him a 10.0. However, Hu blew his next dive, while Tian, attempting the extremely difficult back 3½ somersault pike, earned 101.52 points—the highest scoring dive in Olympic history at that time. This gave Tian a lead of 19.2 points and he held on in the last two rounds to win by 10.98 points. By winning the bronze medal, Dmitri Sautin brought his career medal total to six: two gold, one silver and three bronze. Alexandre Despatie, who placed fourth, was only fifteen years old.

2004 Athens C: 33, N: 19, D: 8.28.

		PTS.
1. Hu Jia	CHN	748.08
2. Mathew Helm	AUS	730.56
3. Tian Liang	CHN	729.66
4. Alexandre Despatie	CAN	707.46
5. Peter Waterfield	GBR	669.24
6. Leon Taylor	GBR	663.12
7. Heiko Meyer	GER	646.56
8. Robert Newbery	AUS	640.65

Tian Liang led for the first four dives of the final but was passed by the 21-year-old 2000 silver medalist Hu Jia in the last two dives, including a back 2½ somersault 1½ twist pike which earned Hu five perfect 10s and 100.98 points. Hu had entered the final in only fourth place. With his final dive, Mathew Helm edged past Tian Liang with a back 2½ somersault with 1½ pike twists that earned him four perfect 10s and the silver medal.

2008 Beijing C: 30, N: 18, D: 8.23

		PTS.
1. Matt Mitcham	AUS	537.95
2. Zhou Luxin	CHN	533.15
3. Gleb Galperin	RUS	525.80
4. Huo Liang	CHN	508.40
5. José Antonio Guerra Oliva	CUB	507.15
6. Mathew Helm	AUS	467.70
7. Tom Daley	GBR	463.55
8. Rommel Pacheco Manrufo	MEX	460.20

Chinese divers had already swept all seven of the other diving events in Beijing, with only the men's platform left on the program. However, it was the only event in which they were not the heavy favorite. China's top medal candidate, Zhou Luxin, had been beaten at both the 2007 world championships and at the 2008 world cup, losing to Gleb Galperin and Germany's Sascha Klein respectively.

Zhou started strongly, finishing first in the qualifying round, but dropped to third after the semi-finals, behind teammate Huo Liang and 20-year-old Australian Matt Mitcham, who had finished fifth at the 2008 world cup in February.

Zhou led the final from the start, but scored only 74.80 points on his final dive, his lowest score in the competition. Mitcham trailed Zhou by 32.5 points going into the final dive, but his ultimate attempt produced the highest-scoring dive in the history of the Olympics: a back 2½ somersault with 2½ twists that earned him 112.10 points and gave him the gold medal. Mitcham, who described his victory as "absolutely surreal", was Australia's first male Olympic diving gold medalist since Dick Eve in 1924. Originally a trampoline gymnast, Mitcham was one of only ten openly gay athletes to compete at the Beijing Olympics and the only openly gay male. One day after his victory, the Australia Post issued a 50-cent stamp in his honor.

SYNCHRONIZED SPRINGBOARD

Thanks to the television ratings success of diving, the International Olympic Committee agreed to double the number of Olympic diving events by introducing synchronized diving. There are nine judges: five for synchronization and four for execution (two for each diver). The highest and lowest scores for both synchronization and execution are discarded. The remaining scores are added and then multiplied by the degree of difficulty. Eight pairs of divers compete in each synchronized event.

1896–1996 not held

2000 Sydney T: 8, N: 8, D: 9.28.

		PTS.
1. Xiao Hailiang, Xiong Ni	CHN	365.58
2. Aleksandr Dobroskok, Dmitri Sautin	RUS	329.97
3. Robert Newbery, Dean Pullar	AUS	322.86
4. Troy Dumais, David Pichler	USA	320.91
5. Fernando Platas Alvarez, Eduardo Rueda Pedroza	MEX	317.70
6. Gilles Emptoz-Lacote, Frédéric Pierre	FRA	310.08
7. Antonio Ali, Mark Shipman	GBR	296.64
8. Nicola Marconi, Donald Miranda	ITA	286.38

Xiao Hailiang and Xiong Ni recorded the highest score in each of the five rounds of diving.

2004 Athens T: 8, N: 8, D: 8.16.

		PTS.
1. Nikolaos Siranidis, Thomas Bimis	GRE	353.34
2. Andreas Wels, Tobias Schellenberg	GER	350.01
3. Robert Newbery, Steven Barnett	AUS	349.59
4. Jorge Betancourt García, Erick Fornaris Alvarez	CUB	338.46
5. Tony Ally, Mark Shipman	GBR	334.98
6. Justin Dumais, Troy Dumais	USA	327.06
7. Dmitri Sautin, Aleksandr Dobroskok	RUS	312.24
8. Peng Bo, Wang Kenan	CHN	283.89

Nikolaos Siranidis was an experienced Olympian, having taken part in the 1996 and 2000 Games, but he was far from being a favorite when he competed before a hometown crowd at the 2004 Athens Olympics. In 1996, Siranidis had placed 26th in the springboard event and in 2000 he had placed 36th. As the host nation, Greece was automatically allowed to enter a pair in the synchronized springboard diving event without participating in a qualifying tournament. The Greeks were represented by Siranidis and fellow Athenian Thomas Bimis, who had placed 32nd in the 2000 springboard event. There were eight teams and a straight final with no preliminary round. Each pair performed five dives. The contest took place late at night on the third day of Olympic competition and Greece had yet to win a gold medal in any sport. Siranidis and Bimis got off to a good start, taking the lead after the first dive. However they soon drifted back into the pack. They were in fifth place after three dives and fourth after four.

Leading by twelve points with one dive remaining, Peng Bo and Wang Kenan seemed a sure shot for the gold, particularly as they had never lost a major international competition together. However, Wang lost control on his final dive, earning zero points from the judges and dropping the pair to last place. Next, the reigning world champions, Dmitri Sautin and Aleksandr Dobroskok, botched their final dive when Sautin hit his head on the board, dropping them to seventh place. With a chance for gold, the US team of Justin and Troy Dumais were stymied by a poor takeoff by Troy, leaving them in fifth place. Siranidis and Bimis, encouraged by the wild support of the crowd, performed a spectacular last dive—an inward 3½ somersault tuck—and unexpectedly won the event by 2.40 points. The upset nature of the Siranidis and Bimis' gold medals was underscored a week later when Siranidis took part in the individual springboard event. With 32 divers in the competition, he ended up in 28th place.

2008 Beijing T: 8, N: 8, D: 8.13.

		PTS.
1. Wang Feng, Qin Kai	CHN	469.08
2. Dmitri Sautin, Yuri Kunakov	RUS	421.98
3. Illya Kvasha, Oleksiy Pryhorov	UKR	415.05
4. Chris Colwill, Jevon Tarantino	USA	410.73
5. Alexandre Despatie, Arturo Miranda	CAN	409.29
6. Pavlo Rozenberg, Sascha Klein	GER	402.84
7. Nick Robinson-Baker, Ben Swain	GBR	402.36
8. Scott Robertson, Robert Newbery	AUS	393.60

Twenty-nine-year-old Wang Feng had won all four synchronized world championship and world cup gold medals since the Athens Olympics, the last two with partner Qin Kai. The pair dominated the competition in Beijing, recording the highest-scoring dive in each of the six rounds of the final. European champions and 2008 world cup silver medalists Dmitri Sautin and Yuri Kunakov had a scare in the fifth round, dropping from second to fourth place after a poor dive that earned only 67.32 points, but the pair moved back into second place with their final dive. World platform champion Alexandre Despatie and partner Arturo Miranda dropped from third to fifth place after their fourth dive and were never able to recover.

It was the eighth Olympic medal for the 34-year-old Sautin, the most by any diver in Olympic history. Sautin won his first Olympic medal at the age of 18 when he took bronze in the springboard event at the 1992 Barcelona Olympics.

SYNCHRONIZED PLATFORM

1896–1996 not held

2000 Sydney T: 8, N: 8, D: 9.23.

		PTS.
1. Dmitri Sautin, Igor Lukashin	RUS	365.04
2. Liang Tian, Jia Hu	CHN	358.74
3. Jan Hempel, Heiko Meyer	GER	338.88
4. Leon Taylor, Peter Waterfield	GBR	335.34
5. Robert Newbery, Mathew Helm	AUS	333.24
6. Roman Volod'kov, Oleksandr Skrypnik	UKR	332.22
7. David Pichler, Mark Ruiz	USA	321.69
8. Gilles Emptoz-Lacote, Frédéric Pierre	FRA	314.94

This was a tight competition between the Russians and the Chinese. Lukashin and Sautin led by 3 points after the first dive and 2.4 points after the second. Hu and Tian moved ahead by 3.12 points in the third round, but Lukashin and Sautin quickly regained the lead and then won by 6.3 points.

2004 Athens T: 8, N: 8, D: 8.14.

		PTS.
1. Tian Liang, Yang Jinghui	CHN	383.88
2. Peter Waterfield, Leon Taylor	GBR	371.52
3. Mathew Helm, Robert Newbery	AUS	366.84
4. Roman Volod'kov, Anton Zakharov	UKR	357.66
5. Philippe Comtois, Alexandre Despatie	CAN	351.90
6. Dmitry Dobroskok, Gleb Galperin	RUS	348.60
7. Sotirios Trakas, Ioannis Gavriliis	GRE	331.44
8. Mark Ruiz, Kyle Prandi	USA	325.44

Tian Liang and Yang Jinghui earned seven perfect 10s on their way to the gold medal. Tian was rumored to be dating springboard gold medalist and fellow Olympic champion Guo Jingjing. The couple were dubbed the Romeo and Juliet of Chinese sport after performing the roles for a TV commercial, but they never publicly admitted to being a couple. In 2005 Tian was kicked off the Chinese national team for pursuing too many commercial endorsements and for insisting that he be allowed a six-month break from training.

In 2005 Tian was kicked off the Chinese national team for pursuing too many commercial endorsements, including contact-lens solution, wooden flooring and bathroom fixtures, and for insisting that he be allowed a six-month break from training.

2008 Beijing T: 8, N: 8, D: 8.11.

		PTS.
1. Lin Yue, Huo Liang	CHN	468.18
2. Patrick Hausding, Sascha Klein	GER	450.42
3. Gleb Galperin, Dmitri Dobroskok	RUS	445.26
4. Mathew Helm, Robert Newbery	AUS	444.84
5. David Boudia, Thomas Finchum	USA	440.64
6. Víctor Ortega Serna, Juan Guillermo Urán Salazar	COL	423.66
7. José Antonio Guerra Oliva, Erick Fornaris Álvarez	CUB	409.38
8. Blake Aldridge, Tom Daley	GBR	408.48

Aged 17 and 18 respectively, Lin Yue and Huo Liang had won the last three major international titles, including the 2007 world championships and 2006 and 2008 world cups, and were the clear gold-medal favorites in Beijing. Their main competitors were Patrick Hausding and Sascha Klein, who won silver at the 2008 world cup, and Gleb Galperin and Dmitri Dobroskok, the 2005 world champions and 2007 world silver medalists.

True to form, Lin and Huo led from the start and were never headed. Their second dives were nearly flawless, earning seven perfect 10s from the judges. Galperin and Dobroskok looked to be on track for the silver medal until Dobroskok made a mistake on the fifth dive, opening the door for Hausding and Klein, who produced the best dives of the final round to move up to second place.

DISCONTINUED EVENT

PLAIN HIGH DIVING

The plain high dive was just that—nothing fancy, no twists or somersaults.

1912 Stockholm C: 31, N: 9, D: 7.11.

		ORDINALS	PTS.
1. Erik Adlerz	SWE	7	40.0
2. Hjalmar Johansson	SWE	12	39.3
3. Johan Jansson	SWE	12	39.1
4. Victor Crondahl	SWE	22	37.1
5. Tovio Aro	FIN	26	36.5
6. Axel Runström	SWE	26	36.0
7. Ernst Brandsten	SWE	28	36.2

DNF: Paul Günther (GER)

1920 Antwerp C: 22, N: 11, D: 8.25.

		ORDINALS	PTS.
1. Arvid Wallman	SWE	7	183.5
2. Nils Skoglund	SWE	8	183.0
3. John Jansson	SWE	16	175.0
4. Erik Adlerz	SWE	19	173.0
5. Yrjö Valkama	FIN	23	167.5
6. Herold Jansson	DEN	27	159.0
7. Fernand Sauvage	BEL	34	148.5
8. Adolfo Wellish	BRA	37	153.0

Silver medalist Nils Skoglund was 14 years 11 days old. He is the youngest male ever to win a medal in an individual event in the history of the Olympics.

1924 Paris C: 25, N: 10, D: 7.15.

		ORDINALS	PTS.
1. Richmond Eve	AUS	13.5	160.0
2. Johan Jansson	SWE	14.5	157.0
3. Harold Clarke	GBR	15.5	158.0
4. Ben Trash	USA	23.5	145.0
5. Raymond Vincent	FRA	26.5	144.0
6. Ulise "Pete" Desjardins	USA	28	141.0
7. Albert Reginald Knight	GBR	31	137.0
8. Arvid Wallman	SWE	31	136.0

Dick Eve came from one of Australia's most famous swimming families, with various members specializing in racing and stunts. Two of Eve's uncles died in the water: one while trying to stay underwater for three minutes and the other while attempting to swim across Seattle Harbor. Eve had hoped to continue competing after the Paris Olympics, but in 1925 he was declared a professional because he received travel expenses for a diving exhibition. His older brother Jim was secretary of the New South Wales amateur swimming association that banned him.

WOMEN

SPRINGBOARD

This event is performed from a springboard three meters above the water. Prior to 1996 each finalist made five compulsory dives and five voluntary dives. Now there are five preliminary dives. The semifinal comprises four dives with a total degree of difficulty not to exceed 9.5. The 12 finalists take five more dives with no limit on the degree of difficulty.

1896–1912 not held

1920 Antwerp C: 4, N: 1, D: 8.29.

		ORDINALS	PTS.
1. Aileen Riggin	USA	9	539.9
2. Helen Wainwright	USA	9	534.8
3. Thelma Payne	USA	12	534.1
4. Aileen Allen	USA	20	489.9

Tiny Aileen Riggin of Newport, Rhode Island, was only 14 years old when she won her Olympic gold medal. At 4 feet 7 inches (1.40 meters) and 65 pounds (29.48 kilograms), she was the smallest athlete at the 1920 Olympics. Silver medalist Helen Wainwright was also 14 years old. Both Riggin and Wainwright were members of the Women's Swimming Association of New York. In Antwerp, they had a chaperone, but no coach

Aileen Riggin and Helen Wainwright, 1920

Riggin and Wainwright were both 14 years old when they earned the gold and silver medals in the 1920 springboard diving contest.

and there were no hot showers. The competition was held outdoors in a moat filled with cold, muddy water. The stress of competing was the least of Riggin's worries. As she later explained, "I had another mental block. It was about sticking in the mud at the bottom . . . I kept thinking, the water is black and nobody could find me if I really got stuck down there. And if I were coming down with force, I might go up to my elbows and I'd be stuck permanently, and nobody would miss me and I'd die a horrible drowning death."

In 1922 Riggin was the subject of the first underwater and slow-motion swimming films. She returned to the Olympics in 1924 and won a silver medal for springboard diving and a bronze in the 100-meter backstroke. Later she turned professional, played the part of a slave dancer in the 1933 film *Roman Scandals*, and starred in Billy Rose's first Aquacade. She also became one of America's first women sportswriters and, at the age of 82, she set nine national age-group swim records. At the age of 86 she won six age-group titles at the World Masters Swimming Championships.

1924 Paris C: 17, N: 7, D: 7.18.

		ORDINALS	PTS.
1. Elizabeth Becker	USA	8	474.5
2. Aileen Riggin	USA	12	460.4
3. Caroline Fletcher	USA	16	436.4
4. Eva Olliwier	SWE	20	412.6
5. Signe Johanson	SWE	21	412.6
6. Klara Bornett	AUT	28	370.2

Fifth-place finisher Signe Johansson passed away on 9 May 2010, aged 104 years, 11 months and 12 days. She holds the record as the longest-lived female Olympian.

1928 Amsterdam C: 10, N: 4, D: 8.9.

		ORDINALS	PTS.
1. Helen Meany	USA	6	78.62
2. Dorothy Poynton	USA	13	75.62
3. Georgia Coleman	USA	14	73.38
4. Ilse Meudtner	GER	22	67.42
5. Margret Borgs	GER	26	65.16
6. Lini Söhnchen	GER	34	63.28
7. Aida van Leeuwen	HOL	35	59.82
8. Geertruida Klapwijk	HOL	35	60.98

Competing in her third Olympics, Helen Meany won her first medal at age 23.

1932 Los Angeles C: 8, N: 6, D: 8.10.

		PTS.
1. Georgia Coleman	USA	87.52
2. Katherine Rawls	USA	82.56
3. Jane Fauntz	USA	82.12
4. Olga Jordan	GER	77.60
5. Doris Ogilvie	CAN	77.00
6. Magdalene Epply	AUT	63.70
7. Etsuko Kamakura	JPN	60.78
8. Ingrid Larsen	DEN	57.26

Georgia Coleman, the first woman to do a two and a half forward somersault, completed her Olympic career with four medals: one gold, two silver, and one bronze. She died in 1941 at the age of 29. In 1932 the system of ordinals (place-figures) was dropped and total points became the determining factor in deciding places.

1936 Berlin C: 16, N: 9, D: 8.12.

		PTS.
1. Marjorie Gestring	USA	89.27
2. Katherine Rawls	USA	88.35
3. Dorothy Poynton Hill	USA	82.36
4. Gerda Daumerlang	GER	78.27
5. Olga Jentsch-Jordan	GER	77.98
6. Masayo Osawa	JPN	73.94
7. Suse Heinze	GER	71.49
8. Fusako Kono	JPN	70.27

Gold medalist Marjorie Gestring of Los Angeles was only 13 years and 9 months old. She remains the youngest person in Summer Olympic history to win an individual gold medal in any sport. Katy Rawls repeated her silver medal and, two days later, added a bronze medal as a member of the US freestyle relay team.

1948 London C: 16, N: 8, D: 8.3.

		PTS.
1. Victoria Draves	USA	108.74
2. Zoe Ann Olsen	USA	108.23
3. Patricia Elsener	USA	101.30
4. Nicole Pellissard	FRA	100.38
5. Gudrun Grömer	AUT	93.30
6. Edna Child	GBR	91.63
7. Madeleine Moreau	FRA	89.43
8. Jacoba Heck	HOL	87.61

Vicki Draves had a Filipino father and an English mother, but she was born and raised in San Francisco. She did not begin diving until she was 16 years old. The first ever Asian-American Olympic medalist, Draves faced racial discrimination early in her career. Her first swim club required that she drop her father's name and use her mother's maiden name, Taylor, instead. Silver medalist Zoe Ann Olsen married baseball star Jackie Jensen before the next Olympics.

1952 Helsinki C: 15, N: 7, D: 7.30.

		PTS.
1. Patricia McCormick	USA	147.30
2. Madeleine Moreau	FRA	139.34
3. Zoe Ann Jensen-Olsen	USA	127.57
4. Ninel Krutova	SOV/RUS	116.86
5. Charmain Welsh	GBR	116.38
6. Lyubov Shigalova	SOV/RUS	113.83
7. Nicole Pellissard	FRA	111.98
8. Phyllis Long	GBR	108.82

Pat McCormick of Long Beach, California, won the first of her four gold medals. Mady Moreau became the first non-American woman to win a springboard medal after six straight US sweeps. The Olympics were still low-profile enough in 1952 that when McCormick returned home, some of her neighbors asked if the reason she had been gone was that she was on vacation.

1956 Melbourne C: 17, N: 8, D: 12.4.

		PTS.
1. Patricia McCormick	USA	142.36
2. Jeanne Stunyo	USA	125.89
3. Irene MacDonald	CAN	121.40
4. Barbara Gilders	USA	120.76
5. Valentina Chumicheva	SOV/RUS	118.50
6. Phyllis Long	GBR	107.61
7. Nicole Darrigrand (Pellissard)	FRA	106.32
8. Kanoko Tsutani	JPN	103.12

Pat McCormick, 1956
In 1952 and 1956 McCormick swept both the springboard and platform diving competitions.

Eight months before the Melbourne Olympics, Pat McCormick gave birth to a baby boy. She had continued training throughout her pregnancy and swam a half-mile a day up until two days before childbirth. In 1956 she repeated her double gold medal performance of 1952.

1960 Rome C: 16, N: 10, D: 8.27.

		PTS.
1. Ingrid Krämer	GDR	155.81
2. Paula Jean Pope (Myers)	USA	141.24
3. Elizabeth Ferris	GBR	139.09
4. Mary "Patsy" Willard	USA	137.82
5. Ninel Krutova	SOV/RUS	136.11
6. Irene MacDonald	CAN	134.69
7. Phyllis Long	GBR	129.63
8. Dorothea DuPon	HOL	123.35

The US string of eight consecutive springboard victories was finally broken by 17-year-old Ingrid Krämer of Dresden. The Rome Games were the fourth straight Olympics at which both diving events were won by the same woman.

1964 Tokyo C: 21, N: 9, D: 10.12.

		PTS.
1. Ingrid Engel-Krämer	GDR	145.00
2. Jeanne Collier	USA	138.36
3. Mary "Patsy" Willard	USA	138.18
4. Sue Gossick	USA	129.70
5. Tamara Fyedosova	SOV/RUS	126.33
6. Yelena Anokhina	SOV/RUS	125.60
7. Kanoko Mabuchi	JPN	125.28
8. Angelika Hilbert	GER	123.27

Ingrid Engel-Krämer took over the lead from Patsy Willard on her seventh dive and went on to win her third gold medal.

1968 Mexico City C: 22, N: 15, D: 10.18

		PTS.
1. Sue Gossick	USA	150.77
2. Tamara Pogosheva (Fyedosova)	SOV/RUS	145.30
3. Keala O'Sullivan	USA	145.23
4. Maxine "Micki" King	USA	137.38
5. Ingrid Gulbin (Engel-Krämer)	GDR	135.82
6. Vyera Baklanova	SOV/RUS	132.31
7. Beverly Boys	CAN	130.31
8. Yelena Anokhina	SOV/RUS	129.17

Twenty-year-old Sue Gossick of Tarzana, California, didn't move into the lead until the ninth round. Pogosheva, leading after seven dives, missed her eighth dive badly, but earned the highest score of the competition with her final attempt, to jump back from fourth place to second. In fifth place was the one and only Ingrid Krämer, competing in her third Olympics, each under a different name.

1972 Munich C: 30, N: 18, D: 8.28

		PTS.
1. Maxine "Micki" King	USA	450.03
2. Ulrika Knape	SWE	434.19
3. Marina Janicke	GDR	430.92
4. Janet Ely	USA	420.99
5. Beverly Boys	CAN	418.89
6. Agneta Henriksson	SWE	417.48
7. Cynthia Potter	USA	413.58
8. Elzbieta Wierniuk	POL	408.36

In Mexico City Micki King of Pontiac, Michigan, had been in first place after eight dives. But during her ninth dive, a reverse one and a half layout, she hit the board and broke her left forearm. She completed her final dive, but dropped to fourth place. Four years later in Munich, King, now a 28-year-old air force captain, took the lead from Ulrika Knape with her eighth dive and this time steered clear of the diving board to win the gold medal. Her final dive, a reverse one and a half somersault with one and a half twists, was the same dive she had attempted four years earlier with a broken arm. After her victory she had to submit to a drug test. However it took King two hours to produce a urine sample. By that time everyone but the doctors had gone home, so she returned alone to the Olympic Village and had a chocolate drink. Three Australian weightlifters told her "a gold medalist shouldn't be drinking chocolate" and shared with her a bottle of wine.

1976 Montreal C: 27, N: 15, D: 7.20.

		PTS.
1. Jennifer Chandler	USA	506.19
2. Christa Köhler	GDR	469.41
3. Cynthia Potter	USA	466.83
4. Heidi Ramlow	GDR	462.15
5. Karin Guthke	GDR	459.81
6. Olga Dmitrieva	SOV/RUS	432.24
7. Irina Kalinina	SOV/RUS	417.99
8. Barbara Nejman	USA	365.07

Jennifer Chandler was a 17-year-old high school junior from the Birmingham, Alabama, area.

1980 Moscow C: 24, N: 13, D: 7.21.

		PTS.
1. Irina Kalinina	SOV/RUS	725.910
2. Martina Proeber	GDR	698.895
3. Karin Guthke	GDR	685.245
4. Zhanna Tsyrulnikova	SOV/UKR	673.665
5. Martina Jäschke	GDR	668.115
6. Valerie McFarlane	AUS	651.045
7. Irina Sidorova	SOV/BLR	650.265
8. Lourdes Gonzalez	CUB	640.005

1984 Los Angeles C: 24, N: 18, D: 8.6.

		PTS.
1. Sylvie Bernier	CAN	530.70
2. Kelly McCormick	USA	527.46
3. Christina Seufert	USA	517.62
4. Li Yihua	CHN	506.52
5. Li Qiaoxian	CHN	487.68
6. Elsa Tenorio	MEX	463.56
7. Lesley Smith	ZIM	451.89
8. Debbie Fuller	CAN	450.99

The women's springboard event had been billed as a showdown between the Americans and the Chinese, but a consistent performance by 20-year-old Sylvie Bernier of Ste. Foy, Quebec, gave her the victory. Bernier, who had a history of caving in in pressure situations, solved her problem by completely ignoring the standings throughout the competition. She even drowned out the public-address announcer by listening to the soundtrack from the movie "Flashdance" between dives. It wasn't until she had completed her final dive that her coach informed her the gold medal would be hers unless Kelly McCormick, daughter of four-time Olympic champion Pat McCormick, scored over 70 points on her last dive. McCormick's dive was an excellent one, but earned her only 67.20 points.

1988 Seoul C: 27, N: 19, D: 9.25.

		PTS.
1. Gao Min	CHN	580.23
2. Li Qing	CHN	534.33
3. Kelly McCormick	USA	533.19
4. Irina Lashko	SOV/RUS	526.65
5. Marina Babkova	SOV/RUS	506.43
6. Wendy Lucero	USA	498.81
7. Brita Baldus	GDR	479.19
8. Daphne Jongejans	HOL	465.45

In 1988, world champion Gao Min of Zigong in Sichuan Province became the first female diver to score over 600 points in a springboard competition. In Seoul, the 18-year-old Gao took the lead with her sixth dive, finished with the three highest scores of the day, and achieved the most decisive women's diving victory since Pat McCormick's in 1956. When she first began diving, as a child, Gao was troubled by stiff arches that made it difficult to point her toes in the manner preferred by diving judges. Her teammates said she had "hoe feet." In desperation she supplemented her toe stretching exercises by tying the tips of her feet to the end of her bed whenever she went to sleep.

1992 Barcelona C: 29, N: 20, D: 8.3.

		PTS.
1. Gao Min	CHN	572.40
2. Irina Lashko	RUS	514.14
3. Brita Baldus	GER	503.07
4. Heidemarie Bártová	CZE	491.49
5. Julie Ovenhouse	USA	477.84
6. Vera Ilyina	RUS	470.67
7. Simona Koch	GER	468.96
8. Mary DePiero	CAN	449.49

Competing in pain because of shoulder injuries, Gao moved ahead in the sixth round and pulled away to win by an even larger margin than she had four years earlier. This was the first time in the history of the event that divers from the United States had competed but failed to win a medal.

1996 Atlanta C: 30, N: 21, D: 7.30.

		PTS.
1. Fu Mingxia	CHN	547.68
2. Irina Lashko	RUS	512.19
3. Annie Pelletier	CAN	509.64
4. Melisa Moses	USA	507.99
5. Olena Zhupyna	UKR	507.27
6. Yuki Motobuchi	JPN	506.04
7. Vera Ilyina	RUS	493.56
8. Anna Lindberg	SWE	489.81

The preliminary round saw the spectacular elimination of one of the favorites: 1994 world champion Tan Shuping. During her third dive, a 3½ somersault pike, her hand slipped off her knee and she landed face first. Her score was 4.65 points. Her fourth dive was the highest scoring of the round and moved her back into a position to qualify for the semifinal. But then she blew her final dive and was gone. Fu Mingxia, who had already won the platform event, entered the final in third place behind Lashko and Ilyina, but performed with great consistency to win her third Olympic gold medal. Second place went—as usual—to Irina Lashko. Lashko had previously finished second at the 1990 Goodwill Games, the 1991 world championships, the 1992 Olympics and the World Cups of 1987, 1989, and 1993. Annie Pelletier, who was in only 17th place after the preliminaries, jumped from fifth to third with her last dive of the final, while Yuki Motobuchi dropped from second to sixth on the final dive.

2000 Sydney C: 43, N: 28, D: 9.28.

		PTS.
1. Fu Mingxia	CHN	609.42
2. Guo Jingjing	CHN	597.81
3. Dörte Lindner	GER	574.35
4. Yuliya Pakhalina	RUS	570.42
5. Anna Lindberg	SWE	559.17
6. Vera Ilyina	RUS	555.15
7. Chantelle Michell	AUS	550.68
8. Jenny Keim	USA	534.18

After the 1996 Olympics, Fu Mingxia retired from diving and began studying economics at Qinghua University. After two years, she unretired and began preparations to defend her Olympic springboard title. However, during the pre-Olympic season, she was beaten five times by Guo Jingjing. Yet Guo knew that, given Fu's reputation, she would have to perform far better than her celebrated teammate. Before competing against each other, Fu and Guo teamed up to earn silver medals in the synchronized springboard event. In the individual event, Guo led by 8.4 points after the semifinals. Guo built her lead up to 10.83 points following the second of the five dives of the final. But then Fu took charge, earning the highest score in each of the last three rounds. She edged ahead of Guo in the penultimate round and then won by 11.61 points. After the Olympics, Fu was chosen as the Chinese spokeswoman for the soft drink Sprite. Unfortunately her commercial career got off to a rocky start when Fu, who didn't speak English, appeared at a Sprite press conference in Guangzhou wearning pants emblazoned with English-language swear words. In 2002, she married the financial secretary of Hong Kong, Antony Leung.

2004 Athens C: 33, N: 20, D: 8.26.

		PTS.
1. Guo Jingjing	CHN	633.15
2. Wu Minxia	CHN	612.00
3. Yuliya Pakhalina	RUS	610.62

4. Vera Ilyina	RUS	589.11
5. Blythe Hartley	CAN	573.00
6. Loudy Tourky	AUS	566.94
7. Irina Lashko	AUS	551.97
8. Tania Cagnotto	ITA	550.38

Guo Jingjing led after her first dive, scoring the only two perfect 10s of the competition, on her second and fourth dives, to take a commanding lead that survived a weak final dive. Guo's win extended the Chinese women's springboard streak to five. After her win, Guo Jingjing was given a villa worth an estimated one million yuan ($120,000) by an anonymous businessman from her hometown of Shijiazhuang. She also earned so many commercial contracts, including ones with Coca-Cola, McDonalds and Budweiser, that she was forced to make a public apology for her selfishness to avoid being booted off the Chinese national team.

2008 Beijing C: 30, N: 19, D: 8.17.

		PTS.
1. Guo Jingjing	CHN	415.35
2. Yuliya Pakhalina	RUS	398.60
3. Wu Minxia	CHN	389.85
4. Blythe Hartley	CAN	374.60
5. Tania Cagnotto	ITA	349.20
6. Anna Lindberg	SWE	342.15
7. Sharleen Stratton	AUS	331.00
8. Nancilea Foster	USA	316.70

Nicknamed the "diving queen," 26-year-old defending Olympic champion Guo Jingjing was the face of China's powerful diving team, appearing on billboards and advertisements throughout the country during the lead-up to the Olympics. Guo was also the overwhelming favorite in the springboard event, having won both the individual and synchronized events in four consecutive world championships.

Competing a week after winning the gold medal in the synchronized springboard event along with partner Wu Minxia, Guo led after the qualifying and semi-final rounds. In the final round, she tied with defending Olympic bronze medalist and five-time European champion Yulia Pakhalina for first, after both received 81.00 points for their first dives. Guo pulled into the lead with her second dive and thereafter was never headed.

It was Guo's sixth Olympic medal, including four gold medals, making her the most decorated female diver in Olympic history and the first to win back-to-back individual and synchronized Olympic diving titles.

Guo Jingjing, 2008
Guo Jingjing on her way to one of her 4 gold medals.

PLATFORM

This event is performed from a static board ten meters above the water. Prior to 1996 each finalist attempted four compulsory dives and four voluntary dives. Since 1996, semifinalists perform four dives, with a total degree of difficulty not to exceed 7.6. The 12 finalists perform five more dives with no limit on degree of difficulty.

1896–1908 not held

1912 Stockholm C: 14, N: 3, D: 7.13.

		ORDINALS	PTS.
1. Margareta Johanson	SWE	5	39.9
2. Lisa Regnell	SWE	11	36.0
3. Isabel "Belle" White	GBR	17	34.0
4. Elsa Regnell	SWE	20	33.2
5. Ellen Eklund	SWE	22	31.9
6. Elsa Andersson	SWE	25	31.3
7. Selma Andersson	SWE	36	28.3
8. A. Viktoria Larsson	SWE	39	26.8

Seventeen-year-old Greta Johanson was the unanimous choice of the five judges.

1920 Antwerp C: 15, N: 6, D: 8.28.

		ORDINALS	PTS.
1. Stefanie Clausen	DEN	6	173.0
2. B. Eileen Armstrong	GBR	10	166.0
3. Eva Olliwer	SWE	11	166.0
4. Isabel "Belle" White	GBR	18	158.5
5. Aileen Riggin	USA	20	157.0
6. Betty Grimes	USA	30	133.5

1924 Paris C: 11, N: 6, D: 7.20.

		ORDINALS	PTS.
1. Caroline Smith	USA	10.5	33.2
2. Elizabeth Becker	USA	11	33.4
3. Hjördis Töpel	SWE	15.5	32.8
4. Edith Bechmann-Nielsen	DEN	17.5	31.6
5. Helen Meany	USA	22	29.6
6. Isabel "Belle" White	GBR	28.5	28.0

National prejudice reared its ugly head in the judging of the women's high dive. The Danish judge gave first place to Bechmann-Nielsen of Denmark. The Swedish judge voted for Töpel of Sweden, and the American judge registered a three-way tie for first among the three Americans. The British judge voted for Smith and the French judge for Becker.

1928 Amsterdam C: 17, N: 8, D: 8.11.

		ORDINALS	PTS.
1. Elizabeth Becker Pinkston	USA	9	31.6
2. Georgia Coleman	USA	10.5	30.6
3. Lama Sjöquist	SWE	13.5	29.2
4. Mietje Baron	HOL	21	27.2
5. Greta Onnela	FIN	25	26.0
6. Hanni Rehborn	GER	26	25.6

Elizabeth Becker Pinkston balanced her 1924 springboard gold with first place in the platform diving four years later. Between Olympics she had married Clarence Pinkston, whom she had met when both were members of the 1924 US diving team in Paris. Husband and wife eventually won seven Olympic medals between them.

1932 Los Angeles C: 7, N: 5, D: 8.12.

		PTS.
1. Dorothy Poynton	USA	40.26
2. Georgia Coleman	USA	35.56
3. Marion Roper	USA	35.22
4. Lala Sjöquist	SWE	34.52
5. Ingrid Larsen	DEN	31.96
6. Etsuko Kamakura	JPN	31.36
7. Magdalene Epply	AUT	26.76

1936 Berlin C: 22, N: 10, D: 8.13.

		PTS.
1. Dorothy Poynton Hill	USA	33.93
2. Velma Dunn	USA	33.63
3. Käthe Köhler	GER	33.43
4. Reiko Osawa	JPN	32.53
5. Cornelia Gilissen	USA	30.47
6. Fusako Kono	JPN	30.24
7. Jean Gilbert	GBR	30.16
8. Anne Ehseheidt	GER	29.90

Stylish Dorothy Poynton Hill, competing in her third Olympics at the age of 21, gained her fourth medal. She won two gold medals in the platform and a silver and bronze in the springboard.

1948 London C: 15, N: 9, D: 8.6.

		PTS.
1. Victoria Draves	USA	68.87
2. Patricia Elsener	USA	66.28
3. Birte Christoffersen	DEN	66.04
4. Ali Staudinger	AUT	64.59
5. Juno Stover	USA	62.63
6. Nicole Pellissard	FRA	61.07
7. Eva Petersen	SWE	59.86
8. Inge Beeken-Gregersen	DEN	59.54

Vicki Draves became the first female diver to win two gold medals in one Olympics.

1952 Helsinki C: 15, N: 8, D: 8.2

		PTS.
1. Patricia McCormick	USA	79.37
2. Paula Jean Myers	USA	71.63
3. Juno Irwin (Stover)	USA	70.49
4. Nicole Pellissard	FRA	66.89
5. Phyllis Long	GBR	63.19
6. Tatyana Vereina	SOV/RUS	61.09
7. Diana Spencer	GBR	60.76
8. Eugenia Bogdanovskaya	SOV/RUS	57.50

This was the second of Pat McCormick's four gold medals. Bronze medalist Juno Irwin was three and a half months' pregnant with her second child.

1956 Melbourne C: 18, N: 10, D: 12.7.

		PTS.
1. Patricia McCormick	USA	84.85
2. Juno Irwin (Stover)	USA	81.64
3. Paula Jean Myers	USA	81.58
4. Nicole Darrigrand (Pellissard)	FRA	78.80
5. Tatyana Karakashyants-Vereina	SOV/RUS	76.95
6. Lyubov Shigalova	SOV/RUS	76.40
7. Phyllis Long	GBR	76.15
8. Birte Hansson	SWE	75.21

Pat McCormick moved ahead of Juno Irwin after the sixth of seven dives to win her fourth gold medal. McCormick was a 26-year-old mother of one, Irwin a 28-year-old mother of three.

1960 Rome C: 18, N: 12, D: 8.30.

		PTS.
1. Ingrid Krämer	GDR	91.28
2. Paula Jean Pope (Myers)	USA	88.94

3. Ninel Krutova	SOV/RUS	86.99
4. Juno Irwin (Stover)	USA	83.59
5. Raisa Gorokhovskaya	SOV/UKR	83.03
6. Norma Thomas	GBR	82.21
7. Nicole Darrigrand (Pellissard)	FRA	81.18
8. Phyllis Long	GBR	80.98

Krämer clinched her diving double with a final one and a half forward somersault with a double twist that turned out to be the highest-scoring dive of the competition. Paula Jean Pope, a 25-year-old mother of two, won her third straight platform medal.

1964 Tokyo C: 24, N: 11, D: 10.15.

		PTS.
1. Lesley Bush	USA	99.80
2. Ingrid Engel-Krämer	GDR	98.45
3. Galina Alekseyeva	SOV/RUS	97.60
4. Linda Cooper	USA	96.30
5. Christine Lanzke	GDR	92.92
6. Ingeborg Pertmayr	AUT	92.70
7. Natalya Kuznetsova	SOV/RUS	90.91
8. Barbara Talmage	USA	89.60

Seventeen-year-old Lesley Bush of Princeton, New Jersey, finished only third at the US trials. In Tokyo she took the lead after the first dive and was never headed. Asked afterward how she felt when she realized she was in first place and might upset Ingrid Krämer's attempt to match Pat McCormick's four gold medals, Bush replied, "It was sort of scary, but gee, gosh, it was great."

1968 Mexico City C: 24, N: 15, D: 10.23.

		PTS.
1. Milena Duchková	CZE	109.59
2. Natalya Lobanova (Kuznetsova)	SOV/RUS	105.14
3. Ann Peterson	USA	101.11
4. Beverly Boys	CAN	97.97
5. Boguslawa Pietkiewicz	POL	95.28
6. Regina Krause	GER	93.08
6. Keiko Ohsaki	JPN	93.08
8. Nancy Robertson	CAN	90.66

Duchková overcame Lobanova with her last two dives, much to the delight of the crowd, which favored the 16-year-old Czechoslovakian because she was small and because her nation was occupied by Soviet troops.

1972 Munich C: 27, N: 17, D: 9.2.

		PTS.
1. Ulrika Knape	SWE	390.00
2. Milena Duchková	CZE	370.92
3. Marina Janicke	GDR	360.54
4. Janet Ely	USA	352.68
5. Maxine "Micki" King	USA	346.38
6. Sylvia Fiedler	GDR	341.67
7. Nancy Robertson	CAN	334.02
8. Ingeborg Pertmayr	AUT	321.03

Knape took the lead from Duchková after the sixth of eight dives and then earned the gold medal with a final dive that received the highest score of the competition. Knape's daughter, Anna Lindberg, represented Sweden at the 1996 Olympics, at the age of 14, and again in 2000.

1976 Montreal C: 25, N: 12, D: 7.25.

		PTS.
1. Elena Vaitsekovskaia	SOV/RUS	406.59
2. Ulrika Knape	SWE	402.60
3. Deborah Wilson	USA	401.00
4. Irina Kalinina	SOV/RUS	398.67
5. Cindy Shatto	CAN	389.50
6. Teri York	CAN	378.39
7. Melissa Briley	USA	376.86
8. Heidi Ramlow	GDR	365.64

Eighteen-year-old Elena Vaitsekovskaya jumped from fifth place to first with her fifth dive, a superbly executed backward two and a half somersault, piked. Vaitsekovskaia later became a sportswriter specializing in figure skating.

1980 Moscow C: 17, N: 11, D: 7.26.

		PTS.
1. Martina Jäschke	GDR	596.250
2. Servard Emirzyan	SOV/ARM	576.465
3. Liana Tsotadze	SOV/GEO	575.925
4. Ramona Wenzel	GDR	542.070
5. Yelena Matyushenko	SOV/RUS	540.180
6. Elsa Tenorio	MEX	539.445
7. Valerie McFarlane	AUS	499.785
8. Ildikó Kelemen	HUN	476.535

In fourth place after the preliminaries, Jäschke swept into first place on the fifth dive of the final round.

1984 Los Angeles C: 21, N: 14, D: 8.10.

		PTS.
1. Zhou Jihong	CHN	435.51
2. Michele Mitchell	USA	431.19
3. Wendy Wyland	USA	422.07
4. Chen Xiaoxia	CHN	419.76
5. Valerie Beddoe	AUS	388.56
6. Debbie Fuller	CAN	371.49
7. Elsa Tenorio	MEX	360.45
8. Guadalupe Canseco	MEX	352.89

At five-feet, one-inch and weighing 92 pounds, 19-year-old Zhou Jihong of Hubei Province was unusually small for a diver. She also differed from her competitors in the choice of music she listened to on her headphones between dives. While the others received inspiration from upbeat popular songs, Zhou relaxed with piano concertos. This tactic seemed to help her avoid the last-minute choking for which Chinese divers had become famous.

1988 Seoul C: 20, N: 14, D: 9.18.

		PTS.
1. Xu Yanmei	CHN	445.20
2. Michele Mitchell	USA	438.95
3. Wendy Lian Williams	USA	400.44
4. Angela Stasiulevich	SOV/BLR	386.22
5. Chen Xiaodan	CHN	384.15
6. Yelena Miroshina	SOV/RUS	381.93
7. Kamilla Gamme	NOR	366.45
8. Silke Abicht	GDR	350.61

After seven dives, the 17-year-old favorite, Xu Yanmei, led Michele Mitchell by only .27 of a point. For her final dive, Xu earned mostly 8s for a back 2½ pike for a total of 68.73 points. Mitchell, next to dive, missed slightly on the entry of her forward 3½ tuck and was awarded 7.5s for 60.75 points. The last diver was 14-year-old Chen Xiaodan, who had led the preliminary round, but who now stood firmly in third place, a formidable 83.82 points away from a gold medal. But Chen had scored 81.18 on her last dive and decided to forego caution and instead try "to win the whole meet." However, she went way too far over on a back 3½ tuck and almost landed on her stomach. Scores ranging from 1.5 to 3.0 left her with 22.77 points and fifth place. The ecstatic beneficiary of Chen's mistake was Wendy Lian Williams. Williams had been in last place after three dives and only fifth place after seven.

1992 Barcelona C: 28, N: 17, D: 7.27.

		PTS.
1. Fu Mingxia	CHN	461.43
2. Yelena Miroshina	RUS	411.63
3. Mary Ellen Clark	USA	401.91
4. Zhu Jinhong	CHN	400.56
5. Inga Afonina	UKR	398.43
6. María Alcalá Izguerra	MEX	394.35
7. Ellen Owen	USA	392.10
8. Verónica Ribot De Canales	ARG	384.03

When Fu Mingxia was 9 years old she was plucked from her home in Wuhan and taken 600 miles away to a diving school in Beijing. There she practiced seven days a week. To correct her posture and her bulging knees she was made to sit upright on a chair with her legs stretched out on a bench in front of her. Then an adult would sit on her knees and urge her to endure the excruciating pain. She was allowed to see her parents twice a year. When asked at the Barcelona Olympics what kind of work her parents did, she didn't know. She won the 1990 Goodwill Games title 12 days before her twelfth birthday, and the 1991 world championship at the age of 12½. The International Amateur Swimming Federation responded to Fu's success by passing a rule that required Olympic divers to be at least 14 years old in the Olympic year. Fu was able to compete because she turned 14 twenty days after the Olympic platform final. In that competition she moved ahead of her rivals with her third dive and then pulled away to the most decisive women's platform victory in sixty years.

On December 18, 1995, silver medalist Yelena Miroshina committed suicide by jumping out of a ninth-floor window in Moscow. She was 21 years old.

1996 Atlanta C: 33, N: 21, D: 7.27.

		PTS.
1. Fu Mingxia	CHN	521.58
2. Annika Walter	GER	479.22
3. Mary Ellen Clark	USA	472.95
4. Rebecca Ruehl	USA	455.19
5. Guo Jingjing	CHN	447.21
6. Olena Zhupyna	UKR	437.01
7. Irina Vyguzova	KAZ	432.60
8. Olga Kristoforova	RUS	426.12

Fu Mingxia, now 17 years old and 30 pounds (13.6 kilograms) heavier, took the lead on the fifth of fourteen dives and held it to the end. The final began at 10 p.m. in order to qualify for live television coverage in the United States. Repeating bronze medalist Mary Ellen Clark, who had stopped diving for nine months because of vertigo, was 33 years old.

2000 Sydney C: 40, N: 24, D: 9.24.

		PTS.
1. Laura Wilkinson	USA	543.75
2. Li Na	CHN	542.01
3. Anne Montminy	CAN	540.15
4. Sang Xue	CHN	513.03
5. Emilie Heymans	CAN	511.92
6. Olena Zhupyna	UKR	489.09
7. Anja Richter-Libiseller	AUT	482.16
8. Svetlana Timoshinina	RUS	478.89

On March 8, 2000, three and a half months before the US Olympic trials, Laura Wilkinson broke three bones in her right foot while doing dry-land training. After spending ten weeks with casts on her foot, she qualified for the Olympics anyway. The two Chinese divers, 16-year-old Li Na and 15-year-old Sang Xue, led going into the final, while Wilkinson languished in eighth place, 23.19 points off the pace. After the first two dives of the final, Li was still in first place, while lawyer Anne Montminy, competing in her third Olympics, had edged ahead of Sang into the second and Wilkinson had moved up to fifth place. The third round would change everything. Both Li and Sang botched their dives while Wilkinson hit hers and suddenly found herself in first place, albeit only 0.72 points ahead of Montminy and 1.17 points ahead of Li. Wilkinson's fourth dive was a inward 2½ somersault pike, which she had blown in the preliminary round, earning only 6.5s and 7.0s from the judges. This time she did it right and the judges rewarded her with scores ranging from 8.5 to 9.5. Still, with only one dive to go, she led Montminy by only a quarter of a point and Li by 5.34 points. All three made successful final dives, but because Montminy's had a lower degree of difficulty she slipped down to third place, while Wilkinson managed to stay 1¾ points ahead of Li.

2004 Athens C: 34, N: 21, D: 8.22.

		PTS.
1. Chantelle Michell-Newbery	AUS	590.31
2. Lao Lishi	CHN	576.30
3. Loudy Tourky	AUS	561.66
4. Emilie Heymans	CAN	555.03
5. Laura Wilkinson	USA	549.72
6. Li Ting	CHN	546.48
7. Myriam Boileau	CAN	530.25
8. Tania Cagnotto	ITA	518.67

The mother of a 2½-year-old son, Chantelle Newbery trailed Chinese favorites Lao Lishi and Li Ting going into the final, but scored the highest points on her last three dives to secure the gold. Chantelle's victory broke Australia's 80-year gold medal drought in diving.

2008 Beijing C: 29, N: 19, D: 8.21.

		PTS.
1. Chen Ruolin	CHN	447.70
2. Émilie Heymans	CAN	437.05
3. Wang Xin	CHN	429.90
4. Paola Espinosa Sánchez	MEX	380.95
5. Tatiana Ortíz Galicia	MEX	343.60
6. Melissa Wu	AUS	338.15
7. Marie-Éve Marleau	CAN	332.10
8. Tonia Couch	GBR	328.70

Aged 15 and 16 respectively, Chen Ruolin and Wang Xin had finished in the top two at the last two major international tournaments, with Chen winning the 2008 world cup and Wang winning the 2007 world championships. Performing exactly the same dive list, the two finished first and second in the qualifying round, Chen leading with 428.80 points to Wang's 420.30. Chen also led the semi-final round, earning 444.60 points, as Wang slipped to third behind 2008 world cup bronze medalist Paola Espinosa, who was trained by two Chinese diving coaches.

Chen took the lead with her first dive, followed closely by 2003 world champion Émilie Heymans. She maintained it until the fourth dive, when Heymans earned 95.20 points on a reverse 3½ somersault, the best dive of the final to that point. Chen responded with a near-perfect backward 2½ somersault with 1½ twist on her fifth and final dive, receiving four perfect 10s from the judges and earning 100.30 points to move back into first place. Chen's gold medal came one week after she and Wang teamed up to win the synchronized platform championship.

Born in Brussels to Belgian parents, the 26-year-old Heymans moved to Quebec at the age of one, five years after her mother, Marie-Paule Van Eyck, represented Belgium in the foil fencing event at the Montreal Olympics. Standing 5 feet 7 inches (1.70 meters) and weighing 137 pounds (62.14 kg), Heyman weighed more than the two Chinese medalists combined. After the Olympics it emerged that Chen, who weighed 66 pounds (30 kilograms) at the time of the Olympics, had been ordered to skip dinner for a year to keep her body weight down. "Sometimes I would get really hungry, but I was only allowed to drink water." Chen said, "I would tell myself to hold on until after the Olympics."

SYNCHRONIZED SPRINGBOARD

1896–1996 not held

2000 Sydney T: 8, N: 8, D: 9.23.

		PTS.
1. Vera Ilyina, Yulia Pakhalina	RUS	332.64
2. Jingjing Guo, Mingxia Fu	CHN	321.60
3. Ganna Sorokina, Olena Zhupyna	UKR	290.34
4. Loudy Tourky, Chantelle Michell	AUS	283.05
5. Eryn Bulmer, Blythe Hartley	CAN	279.00
6. Jashia Luna Alfaro, María Alcalá Izguerra	MEX	273.84
7. Conny Schmalfuss, Dörte Lindner	GER	263.76
8. Jacqueline Schneider, Catherine Maliev-Aviolat	SWI	256.20

Vera Ilyina, a graduate of the University of Texas, was competing in her third Olympics. She and Yulia Pakhalina earned the highest scores in four of the five rounds.

2004 Athens T: 8, N: 8, D: 8.14.

		PTS.
1. Wu Minxia, Guo Jingjing	CHN	336.90
2. Vera Ilyina, Yuliya Pakhalina	RUS	330.84
3. Irina Lashko, Chantelle Michell-Newbery	AUS	309.30
4. Tandi Gerrard, Jane Smith	GBR	302.25
5. Laura Sánchez, Paola Milagros Espinosa Sánchez	MEX	286.92
6. Ditte Kotzian, Conny Schmalfuss	GER	279.69
7. Blythe Hartley, Emilie Heymans	CAN	276.90
8. Diamantina Georgatou, Sotiria Koutsopetrou	GRE	270.33

After losing to Vera Ilyina and Yuliya Pakhalina in 2000, Guo Jingjing and Wu Minxia beat them at the 2003 world championships. In Athens, the Chinese pair dove consistently to build up a solid lead. The Russian pair ended on a high note, with a forward 2½ somersault with one twist that earned the highest score of the competition, but it wasn't enough to put them in first place.

2008 Beijing T: 8, N: 8, D: 8.10.

		PTS.
1. Guo Jingjing, Wu Minxia	CHN	343.50
2. Yuliya Pakhalina, Anastasia Pozdnyakova	RUS	323.61
3. Ditte Kotzian, Heike Fischer	GER	318.90
4. Kelci Bryant, Ariel Rittenhouse	USA	314.40
5. Briony Cole, Sharleen Stratton	AUS	311.34
6. Noemi Batki, Francesca Dallapè	ITA	296.70
7. Mariya Voloshchenko, Hanna Pysmenska	UKR	293.10
8. Tandi Gerrard-Indergaard, Hayley Sage	GBR	278.25

The clear favorites for the gold medals were defending Olympic champions and three times world champions Guo Jingjing and Wu Minxia. True to expectations, they took the lead after the second dive and were never seriously challenged, producing the best scores in all but the final round and bowing to the judges after each dive.

Reigning European champions Yuliya Pakhalina and Anastasia Pozdnyakova were tied with Kelci Bryant and Ariel Rittenhouse for second place until the fourth round, when Bryant and Rittenhouse slipped to third on a weak dive that earned only 69.30 points. The 2007 world silver medalists, Ditte Kotzian and Heike Fischer, subsequently edged Bryant and Rittenhouse out of bronze-medal position on their final dive, a reverse 2½ somersault that earned them 76.50 points, the third highest score of the competition.

SYNCHRONIZED PLATFORM

1896–1908 not held

2000 Sydney T: 8, N: 8, D: 9.28.

		PTS.
1. Na Li, Xue Sang	CHN	345.12
2. Emilie Heymans, Anne Montminy	CAN	312.03
3. Rebecca Gilmore, Loudy Tourky	AUS	301.50
4. Marion Reiff, Anja Richter-Libiseller	AUT	294.00
5. Jenny Keim, Laura Wilkinson	USA	291.42
6. Yevgeniya Olshevskaya, Svetlana Timoshinina	RUS	288.30
7. Odile Arboles-Souchon, Julie Danaux	FRA	277.14
8. María Alcalá Izguerra, Azul Almazán López	MEX	264.30

Li and Sang had dominated the event for the past two years. Overwhelming favorites, they won easily.

2004 Athens T: 8, N: 8, D: 8.14.

		PTS.
1. Lao Lishi, Li Ting	CHN	352.14
2. Nataliya Goncharova, Yuliya Koltunova	RUS	340.92
3. Blythe Hartley, Emilie Heymans	CAN	327.78
4. Loudy Tourky, Lynda Folauhola	AUS	313.92
5. Paola Milagros Espinosa Sánchez, Jashia Luña Alfaro	MEX	307.74
6. Annett Gamm, Nora Subschinski	GER	303.30
7. Cassandra Cardinell, Sara Reiling-Hildebrand	USA	302.22
8. Evtykhia Pappa-Papavasilopoulou, Florentia Sfakianou	GRE	272.40

The reigning world champions, 16-year-old Lao Lishi and 17-year-old Li Ting, earned the highest scores in four of the five rounds to gain a clear victory.

2008 Beijing T: 8, N: 8, D: 8.12.

1. Wang Xin, Chen Ruolin	CHN	363.54
2. Briony Cole, Melissa Wu	AUS	335.16
3. Paola Espinosa Sánchez, Tatiana Ortíz	MEX	330.06
4. Annett Gamm, Nora Subschinski	GER	310.29
5. Mary Beth Dunnichay, Haley Ishimatsu	USA	309.12
6. Choe Kum-hui, Kim Un-hyang	PRK	308.10
7. Meaghan Benfeito, Roseline Filion	CAN	305.91
8. Tonia Couch, Stacie Powell	GBR	303.48

After winning the 2006 world cup and 2007 world championship synchronized titles with Jia Tong, Chen Ruolin was paired with reigning individual world champion Wang Xin to win the 2008 world cup title. The pair led throughout the Olympic final, producing the best dive in each of the five rounds to finish more than 28 points ahead of 2007 world silver medalists Bree Cole and Melissa Wu.

Wang initially trained as a gymnast before being transferred to diving. Originally named Wang Ruoxue, her name was changed to Wang Xin after a suggestion by her coach, who thought the original name sounded too weak and delicate. Wang and Chen won the Olympic competition one day after Wang's sixteenth birthday.

Chapter 10 **Equestrian**

Three-Day Event, Individual
Three-Day Event, Team
Jumping, Individual
Jumping (Prix des Nations), Team
Dressage, Individual
Dressage, Team
Discontinued Events

As with many Olympic sports, equestrian regulations require a minimum age limit for participants: 18 years old. A lesser known fact is that the horses, too, must be of a certain age: at least seven years old. They must also have an official passport approved by the International Equestrian Federation and they are subject to drug testing. Riders in jumping and dressage must wear formal dress unless they belong to a military or police force; if so, they may wear their uniforms.

THREE-DAY EVENT, INDIVIDUAL

The three-day event consists of three parts: dressage, cross-country and show jumping. The dressage and jumping portions follow the same basic rules and scoring as the regular dressage and jumping events. According to rules in place since 2004, a first disobedience at a jump will incur a 20-point penalty; a second disobedience at the same jump will incur an 40-point penalty; a third disobedience at the same obstacle results in elimination. A fall will be penalized by 65 points; a second fall by elimination. Penalty points are also assessed for exceeding the optimum time limit. It used to be possible to score bonus points by beating the time limit, but this rule was changed before the 1976 Olympics. Since 2008 the individual and team events have been run concurrently.

1896–1908 not held

1912 Stockholm C: 27, N: 7, D: 7.17.

		HORSE	PTS.
1. Axel Nordlander	SWE	Lady Artist	46.59
2. Friedrich von Rochow	GER	Idealist	46.42
3. Jean Cariou	FRA	Cocotte	46.32
4. Nils Adlercreutz	SWE	Atout	46.31
5. Ernst Casparsson	SWE	Irmelin	46.16
5. Richard, Graf von Schaesberg-Tannheim	GER	Grundsee	46.16
7. Benjamin Lear	USA	Poppy	45.91
8. Eduard von Lütcken	GER	Blue Boy	45.90

The competition, spread over four days, was limited to commissioned officers on active duty.

1920 Antwerp C: 25, N: 8, D: 9.10.

		HORSE	PTS.
1. Helmer Mörner	SWE	Germania	1775.00
2. Åge Lundström	SWE	Ysra	1738.75
3. Ettore Caffaratti	ITA	Caniche	1733.75
4. Roger Moeremans d'Emaüs	BEL	Sweet Girl	1652.50
5. Garibaldi Spighi	ITA	Otello	1647.50
6. Harry Chamberlin	USA	Nigra	1568.75
7. William West	USA	Black Boy	1558.75
8. Georg von Braun	SWE	Diana	1543.75

The competition consisted of jumping, a 20-kilometer course, and a 50-kilometer course, but no dressage.

1924 Paris C: 44, N: 13, D: 7.26.

		HORSE	DRESSAGE	ENDURANCE	JUMPING	TOTAL PTS.
1. Adolph van der Voort van Zijp	HOL	Silver Piece	174.0	1402.0	400.0	1976.0
2. Frode Kirkebjerg	DEN	Meteor	164.0	1409.5	280.0	1853.5
3. Sloan Doak	USA	Pathfinder	156.0	1369.5	320.0	1845.5
4. Charles Pahud de Mortanges	HOL	Johnny Walker	174.0	1334.0	320.0	1828.0
5. Claës König	SWE	Bojar	166.0	1284.0	280.0	1730.0
6. Baudoin de Brabandère	BEL	Modestie	138.0	1190.5	400.0	1728.5
6. Edward de Fonblanque	GBR	Copper	133.0	1275.5	320.0	1728.5
8. Frank Carr	USA	Proctor	154.0	1333.0	240.0	1727.0

1928 Amsterdam C: 46, N: 17, D: 8.11.

		HORSE	DRESSAGE	ENDURANCE	JUMPING	TOTAL PTS.
1. Charles Pahud de Mortanges	HOL	Marcroix	237.82	1432.0	300.0	1969.82
2. Gerard de Kruyff	HOL	Va-tt-en	251.26	1416.0	300.0	1967.26
3. Bruno Neumann	GER	Ilja	208.42	1438.0	300.0	1944.42
4. Adolph van der Voort van Zijp	HOL	Silver Piece	224.60	1404.0	300.0	1928.60
5. Hans Olof von Essen	FIN	El Kaid	180.64	1444.0	300.0	1924.64
6. Bjart Ording	NOR	And Over	200.98	1412.0	300.0	1912.98
7. Nils Kettner	SWE	Caesar	197.66	1404.0	300.0	1901.66
8. Arthur Quist	NOR	Hidalgo	221.14	1404.0	270.0	1895.14

1932 Los Angeles C: 14, N: 5, D: 8.13.

		HORSE	DRESSAGE	ENDURANCE	JUMPING	TOTAL PTS.
1. Charles Pahud de Mortanges	HOL	Marcroix	311.833	1242.0	260.00	1813.833
2. Earl Thomson	USA	Jenny Camp	300.000	1271.0	240.00	1811.000
3. Clarence von Rosen	SWE	Sunnyside Maid	310.666	1241.5	257.25	1809.416
4. Harry Chamberlin	USA	Pleasant Smiles	340.333	1107.5	240.00	1687.833
5. Ernst Hallberg	SWE	Marokan	290.333	1129.0	260.00	1679.333
6. Karel Johan Schummelketel	HOL	Duiveltje	267.500	1105.0	242.00	1614.500
7. Morishige Yamamoto	JPN	Kingo	257.333	1092.5	259.75	1609.583
8. Edwin Argo	USA	Honolulu Tomboy	333.000	907.5	299.25	1539.750

Lieutenant Pahud de Mortanges raised his Olympic medal total to four gold medals and one silver. Captured by the Nazis in 1942, he escaped and became second in command of the free Dutch fighting the Germans. After World War II, Pahud served as president of The Netherlands Olympic Committee and as a member of the International Olympic Committee.

1936 Berlin C: 50, N: 19, D: 8.16.

		HORSE	DRESSAGE	ENDURANCE	JUMPING	TOTAL PTS.
1. Ludwig Stubbendorff	GER	Nurmi	-96.7	+69	-10	-37.7
2. Earl Thomson	USA	Jenny Camp	-127.9	+38	-10	-99.9
3. Hans Mathiesen-Lunding	DEN	Jason	-134.2	+42	-10	-102.2
4. Vincens Grandjean	DEN	Grey Friar	-115.9	+11	0	-104.9
5. Agoston Endrödy	HUN	Pandur	-134.7	+39	-10	-105.7
6. Rudolf Lippert	GER	Fasan	-118.6	+27	-20	-111.6
7. Alec Scott	GBR	Bob Clive	-152.3	+45	-10	-117.3
8. Mario Mylius	SWI	Saphir	-122.0	-3	-20	-145.0

The course was so difficult that three horses met their deaths and only 27 of the 50 entrants finished the competition.

1948 London C: 45, N: 16, D: 8.10.

		HORSE	DRESSAGE	ENDURANCE	JUMPING	TOTAL PTS.
1. Bernard Chevallier	FRA	Aiglonne	-104	+108	0	+4
2. Frank Henry	USA	Swing Low	-117	+96	0	-21
3. Robert Selfelt	SWE	Claque	-109	+84	0	-25
4. Charles Anderson	USA	Reno Palisade	-111	+96	-11.5	-26.5
5. Joaquín Nogueras Márquez	SPA	Epsom	-128	+87	0	-41
6. Erik Carlsen	DEN	Ezja	-113	+69	0	-44
7. Aecio Morrot Coelho	BRA	Guapo	-114	+72	-10	-52
8. Fernando Marques Cavaleiro	POR	Satari	-135	+90	-10	-55
8. Fabio Mangilli	ITA	Guerriero da Capestrano	-85	+72	-42	-55

1952 Helsinki C: 59, N: 21, D: 8.2.

		HORSE	DRESSAGE	ENDURANCE	JUMPING	TOTAL PTS.
1. Hans von Blixen-Finecke, Jr.	SWE	Jubal	-123.33	+105	-10	-28.33
2. Guy Lefrant	FRA	Verdun	-119.50	+75	-10	-54.50
3. Wilhelm Büsing	GER	Hubertus	-103.50	+48	0	-55.50
4. Pedro Mercado	ARG	Mandinga	-130.80	+78	-10	-62.80
5. Klaus Wagner	GER	Dachs	-109.66	+54	-10	-65.66
6. Piero D'Inzeo	ITA	Pagoro	-118.80	+52	0	-66.80
7. Albert Hill	GBR	Stella	-126.33	+69	-10	-67.33
8. Olof Stahre	SWE	Komet	-108.66	+81	-41.75	-69.41

Blixen-Finecke's father won a bronze medal in the 1912 dressage. His aunt was Karen Blixen, who, writing under the name Isak Dinesen, was an acclaimed author. Her works "Babette's Feast" and *Out of Africa* were adapted into successful films.

1956 Stockholm C: 57, N: 19, D: 6.14.

		HORSE	DRESSAGE	ENDURANCE	JUMPING	TOTAL PTS.
1. Petrus Kastenman	SWE	Iluster	-116.40	+69.87	-20	-66.53
2. August Lütke-Westhues	GER	Trux von Kamax	-129.60	+64.73	-20	-84.87
3. Francis Weldon	GBR	Kilbarry	-103.20	+37.72	-20	-85.48
4. Lev Baklychkine	SOV/RUS	Guimnast	-119.20	+42.55	-20	-96.65
5. Genko Rashkov	BUL	Euphoria	-146.00	+44.77	-10	-111.23
6. A. Laurence Rook	GBR	Wild Venture	-101.60	-44.29	-13.75	-119.64
7. Giancarlo Gutierrez	ITA	Wiston	-138.80	+12.37	-10	-136.43
8. Juan Martín Merbilháa	ARG	Gitana I	-150.00	+23.54	-10	-136.46

1960 Rome C: 73, N: 19, D: 9.10.

		HORSE	DRESSAGE	ENDURANCE	JUMPING	TOTAL PTS.
1. Lawrence Morgan	AUS	Salad Days	-106.00	+128.4	-15.25	+7.15
2. Neale Lavis	AUS	Mirrabooka	-124.50	+108.0	0	-16.50
3. Anton Bühler	SWI	Gay Spark	-89.01	+50.8	-13	-51.21
4. Michael Bullen	GBR	Cottage Romance	-129.00	+66.4	0	-62.60
5. Saibattal Mursalimov	SOV/KYR	Satrap	-79.00	+46.0	-30.75	-63.75
6. Jack Le Goff	FRA	Image	-108.51	+55.6	-20	-72.91
7. Lev Baklychkine	SOV/RUS	Bazis	-103.50	+58.4	-20.25	-85.35
8. Marian Babirecki	POL	Volt	-127.00	+61.6	-20	-85.40

The endurance course was unnecessarily dangerous, and two horses were killed. The Italian organizers seemed unprepared for such disasters. The Danish horse Rolf II had to wait two and a half hours for the arrival of a veterinarian, and the Romanian horse Mures II, driven across the finish line despite a fatal injury, lay dead for hours before he was finally removed. Only 35 of the 73 entrants completed the competition.

1964 Tokyo C: 48, N: 12, D: 10.19

		HORSE	DRESSAGE	ENDURANCE	JUMPING	TOTAL PTS.
1. Mauro Checcoli	ITA	Surbean	-54.00	+118.4	0	+64.40
2. Carlos Moratorio	ARG	Chalán	-42.00	+98.4	0	+56.40
3. Fritz Ligges	GER	Donkosak	-32.00	+91.2	-10	+49.20
4. Michael Page	USA	Grasshopper	-43.00	+90.4		+47.40
5. Anthony Cameron	IRL	Black Salmon	-70.67	+117.2	0	+46.53
6. Horst Karsten	GER	Condora	-49.00	+95.6	-10	+36.60
7. J. William Roycroft	AUS	Eldorado	-65.00	+97.2	0	+32.20
8. Richard Meade	GBR	Barberry	-52.67	+118.4	-36	+29.73

Mauro Checcoli, a 21-year-old student from Bologna, won the gold medal, but it was the 33rd-place finisher who made equestrian history. Lana duPont of the United States became the first woman to compete in the Olympic three-day event.

1968 Mexico City C: 49, N: 13, D: 10.21.

		HORSE	DRESSAGE	ENDURANCE	JUMPING	TOTAL PTS.
1. Jean-Jacques Guyon	FRA	Pitou	-73.01	+44.4	-10.25	-38.86
2. Derek Allhusen	GBR	Lochinvar	-85.01	+44.4	0	-41.61
3. Michael Page	USA	Foster	-107.51	+59.2	-4	-52.31
4. Richard Meade	GBR	Cornishman V	-97.01	+54.8	-22.25	-64.46
5. Reuben Jones	GBR	The Poacher	-68.51	+4.4	-5.75	-69.86
6. James Wofford	USA	Kilkenny	-101.51	+71.2	-43.75	-74.06
7. Juliet Jobling-Purser	IRL	Jenny	-72.51	+5.6	-1	-79.11
8. Wayne Roycroft	AUS	Zhivago	-103.50	+21.2	-12.75	-95.05

Two more horses were killed during the endurance competition. This time they died of exhaustion. Silver medalist Derek Allhusen was a 54-year-old grandfather. He also won a gold medal in the team event. Offered an MBE for his achievements, he declined because his teammates were not given the same honor.

1972 Munich C: 73, N: 19, D: 9.1.

		HORSE	DRESSAGE	ENDURANCE	JUMPING	TOTAL PTS.
1. Richard Meade	GBR	Laurieston	-50.67	+108.4	0	+57.73
2. Alessandro Argenton	ITA	Woodland	-48.67	+92.0	0	+43.33
3. Jan Jönsson	SWE	Sarajevo	-50.33	+90.0	0	+39.67
4. Mary Gordon-Watson	GBR	Cornishman V	-51.33	+81.6	0	+30.27
5. Kevin Freeman	USA	Good Mixture	-51.33	+91.2	-10	+29.87
6. J. William Roycroft	AUS	Warrathoola	-36.00	+65.6	0	+29.60
7. Richard Sands	AUS	Depeche	-64.33	+99.2	-10	+24.87
8. Bruce Davidson	USA	Plain Sailing	-40.33	+74.8	-10	+24.47

In 2001, Richard Meade made the news when he was expelled from the Royal Society for the Prevention of Cruelty to Animals (RSPCA) on the grounds that he was encouraging hunters to join the RSPCA and thus disrupt the organization's anti-hunting policies.

1976 Montreal C: 49, N: 13, D: 7.25.

		HORSE	DRESSAGE	ENDURANCE	JUMPING	TOTAL PTS.
1. Edmund "Tad" Coffin	USA	Bally-Cor	-64.59	-50.4	0	-114.99
2. J. Michael Plumb	USA	Better & Better	-66.25	-49.6	-10	-125.85
3. Karl Schultz	GER	Madrigal	-46.25	-63.2	-20	-129.45
4. Richard Meade	GBR	Jacob Jones	-73.75	-57.6	-10	-141.35
5. Wayne Roycroft	AUS	Laurenson	-80.84	-97.2	0	-178.04
6. Gerard Sinnott	IRL	Croghan	-101.25	-77.6	0	-178.85
7. Jean Valat	FRA	Vampire	-92.50	-95.2	0	-187.70
8. Yuri Salnikov	SOV/RUS	Rumpel	-86.66	-102.8	0	-189.46

1980 Moscow C: 28, N: 7, D: 7.27.

		HORSE	DRESSAGE	ENDURANCE	JUMPING	TOTAL PTS.
1. Euro Federico Roman	ITA	Rossinan	-54.4	-49.2	-5	-108.6
2. Aleksandr Blinov	SOV/KYR	Galzun	-64.4	-56.4	0	-120.8
3. Yuri Salnikov	SOV/RUS	Pintset	-53.0	-93.6	-5	-151.6
4. Valery Volkov	SOV/RUS	Tskheti	-54.0	-125.6	-5	-184.6
5. Tzvetan Donchev	BUL	Medisson	-66.4	-114.4	-5	-185.8
6. Miroslaw Sziapka	POL	Erywan	-52.4	-184.4	-5	-241.8
7. Anna Casagrande	ITA	Daleye	-61.2	-190.0	-15	-266.2
8. Mauro Roman	ITA	Dourakine 4	-63.4	-218.0	0	-281.4

The equestrian events were badly hit by the anti-Soviet boycott, and an alternative competition was held in August at Fontainebleau, France, with 42 riders representing 14 nations. The winner was Nils Haagensen of Denmark, with Americans James Wofford and Torrance Watkins finishing second and third.

1984 Los Angeles-Arcadia C: 48, N: 15, D: 8.3.

		HORSE	DRESSAGE	ENDURANCE	JUMPING	TOTAL PTS.
1. Mark Todd	NZL	Charisma	-51.6	0	0	-51.6
2. Karen Stives	USA	Ben Arthur	-49.2	0	-5	-54.2
3. Virginia Holgate	GBR	Priceless	-56.4	-0.4	0	-56.8
4. Torrance Watkins Fleischmann	USA	Finvarra	-57.6	-2.8	0	-60.4
5. Pascal Morvillers	FRA	Gulliver "B"	-52.6	-10.4	0	-63.0
6. Lucinda Green	GBR	Regal Realm	-63.8	0	0	-63.8
7. Marina Sciocchetti	ITA	Master Hunt	-67.0	0	0	-67.0
8. Mauro Checcoli	ITA	Spey Cast Boy	-60.4	-1.6	-5	-67.0

Thirty-three-year-old Karen Stives, the final rider of the competition, entered the arena knowing that her ride would decide both the individual and team gold medals. If she cleared all 12 obstacles without a fault, she would come away with both golds. If she dislodged the rail of one fence, she would lose the individual gold to Mark Todd, but she would still secure first place for the US team. If she knocked down two fences the team gold would be won by Great Britain. As the capacity crowd watched nervously, Stives successfully guided Ben Arthur over the first ten obstacles. But then, at the next to last obstacle—a triple jump—the horse nicked the top of the middle fence, sending the pole to the ground. Stives and Ben Arthur recovered to complete the course without incident. Mark Todd was a 28-year-old dairy farmer who sold most of his herd to finance his Olympic quest.

1988 Seoul C: 50, N: 16, D: 9.22.

		HORSE	DRESSAGE	ENDURANCE	JUMPING	TOTAL PTS.
1. Mark Todd	NZL	Charisma	-37.6	0	-5	-42.6
2. Ian Stark	GBR	Sir Wattie	-50.0	-2.8	0	-52.8
3. Virginia Leng (Holgate)	GBR	Master Craftsman	-43.2	-8.8	-10	-62.0
4. Claus Erhorn	GER	Justyn Tyme	-39.6	-16.0	-6.75	-62.35
5. Judith "Tinks" Pottinger	NZL	Volunteer	-65.8	0	0	-65.8
6. Matthias Baumann	GER	Shamrock	-50.6	-13.2	-5	-68.8
7. Jean Teulère	FRA	Mohican V	-57.6	-6.4	-5	-69.0
8. Andrew Hoy	AUS	Kiwi	-57.0	-32.0	0	-89.0

Todd and Charisma led the field in both the dressage and endurance stages, then knocked over just one fence to become only the second repeat winners of the three-day event. Todd later wrote a 112-page biography of Charisma.

1992 Barcelona C: 82, N: 25, D: 7.30.

		HORSE	DRESSAGE	ENDURANCE	JUMPING	TOTAL PTS.
1. Matthew Ryan	AUS	Kibah Tic Toc	-57.8	-7.2	-5	-70.0
2. Herbert Blöcker	GER	Feine Dame	-52.2	-27.6	-1.5	-81.3
3. Blyth Tait	NZL	Messiah	-78.8	-8.8	0	-87.6
4. Vicky Latta	NZL	Chief	-58.0	-24.8	-5	-87.8
5. Andrew Hoy	AUS	Kiwi	-58.8	-25.6	-5	-89.4
6. Karen Dixon (Straker)	GBR	Get Smart	-44.6	-42.8	-5	-92.4
7. Luis Álvarez Cervera	SPA	Mr. Chrisalis	-65.0	-37.2	0	-102.2
8. Karin Donckers	BEL	Britt	-75.4	-24.0	-5	-104.4

Unheralded Matt Ryan held a lead of 5.4 points over Andrew Nicholson of New Zealand after the endurance test but was considered suspect at show jumping after knocking over five fences while qualifying for the Olympics at the prestigious Badminton event. He had no such problems in Barcelona and came away with the gold medal. The same could not be said of Nicholson, who dislodged nine fences, incurred 45 penalty points—the most of any competitor—and finished in 16th place. Blyth Tait staged a remarkable comeback: placed only 69th after the dressage test, he performed so well the rest of the way that he was able to salvage the bronze medal.

1996 Atlanta-Conyers C: 35, N: 18, D: 7.26.

		HORSE	DRESSAGE	ENDURANCE	JUMPING	TOTAL PTS.
1. Blyth Tait	NZL	Ready Teddy	-51.60	-5.20	0.00	-56.80
2. Sally Clark	NZL	Squirrel Hill	-51.20	-9.20	0.00	-60.40
3. Kerry Millikin	USA	Out and About	-47.60	-19.60	-6.50	-73.70
4. Jean Teulere	FRA	Rodosto	-41.20	-26.00	-10.00	-77.20
5. David O'Connor	USA	Custom Made	-37.60	-30.80	-11.75	-80.15
6. Mara Depuy	USA	Hopper	-40.20	-44.80	0.00	-85.00
7. Hendrik von Paepcke	GER	Amadeus 18	-56.20	-26.00	-5.00	-87.20
8. Constant van Rijckevorsel	BEL	Ootis	-55.80	-21.60	-10.00	-87.40

To combat the effects of Georgia's torrid summer heat, the endurance phase began at 7 a.m. and the course was shortened. Unshaded portions of the course were protected by mesh that filtered out ultraviolet light and huge misting fans were employed to cool the horses. In addition, 80 veterinarians were on site (for 64 horses) and three equine ambulances were at the ready.

Blythe Tait wasn't entered in the individual event until Mark Todd's horse pulled a muscle four days before the competition began. Riding the inexperienced Ready Teddy, Tait entered the jumping phase with a 3.6-point lead over Sally Clark. When Clark rode a clear round, Tait was forced to do the same. At the twelfth of fifteen jumps, one of Ready Teddy's rear hooves hit the top rail. "The jump went 'klunk,'" said Tait, "and so did my heart." But the rail stayed up and Tait went on to match Clark's clear round.

Like Tait, bronze medalist Kerry Millikin was a late entry, added to the competition twelve days before it began. Unlike almost all equestrian stars, Millikan actually had a non-horse-related job: she worked at a hospital as a respiratory neuro-surgical nurse.

2000 Sydney C: 38, N: 21, D: 9.22.

		HORSE	DRESSAGE	ENDURANCE	JUMPING	TOTAL PTS.
1. David O'Connor	USA	Custom Made	-29.00	-0.00	-5.00	-34.00
2. Andrew Hoy	AUS	Swizzle in	-39.80	-0.00	0.00	-39.80
3. Mark Todd	NZL	Eyespy II	-39.00	-0.00	-3.00	-42.00
4. Rodolphe Scherer	FRA	Bambi de Brier	-41.40	-0.00	-5.00	-46.40
5. Fabio Magni	ITA	Cool 'n Breezy	-44.00	-0.00	-5.00	-49.00
6. Heidi Antikatzidis	GRE	Michaelmas	-37.40	-0.00	-13.00	-50.40
7. Mary King	GBR	Star Appeal	-47.00	-0.00	-5.00	-52.00
8. Robert Costello	USA	Chevalier	-42.40	-0.00	-10.00	-52.40

David O'Connor of Plains, Virginia, placed first in the dressage stage and completed the cross-country course without losing a point, thus earning the right to ride last on the jumping course. With a lead of 10.80 points, O'Connor knew that he could knock down two rails if he completed the course within 90 seconds. He and Custom Made hit the sixth fence. At this point, O'Connor made a potentially critical error: he turned his head to see if the rail had fallen. When he turned back, he became disoriented and was not sure which way to go. As the crowd called out, "The wall, the wall," he located the next obstacle and completed the course with only one penalty. His time was 89.82 seconds. The course turned out to be quite dangerous. Two riders had to be hospitalized and four horses were injured, including one that was subsequently put to death.

2004 Athens-Markopoulo C: 75, N: 23, D: 8.18.

		HORSE	DRESSAGE	ENDURANCE	JUMPING	TOTAL PTS.
1. Leslie Law	GBR	Shear L'Eau	-43.2	-44.4	-0	-44.4
2. Kim Severson	USA	Winsome Adante	-36.2	-36.2	-9	-45.2
3. Philippa "Pippa" Funnell	GBR	Primmore's Pride	-31.4	-42.6	-4	-46.6
4. Jean Teulère	FRA	Espoir de la Mare	-38.4	-38.4	-12	-50.4
5. Hinrich Romeike	GER	Marius	-44.4	-45.2	-6	-51.2
6. Amy Tryon	USA	Poggio II	-50.6	-51.8	-0	-51.8
7. Heelan Tompkins	NZL	Glengarrick	-44.0	-44.0	-8	-52.0
8. Nicolas Touzaint	FRA	Galan de Sauvagere	-29.4	-29.4	-23	-52.4

German rider Bettina Hoy, wife of three-time Australian gold medalist Andrew Hoy, rode a flawless first show jumping round, but was penalized fourteen points for crossing the starting line twice, dropping her to eighth place going into the final round. Just before the final show jumping round, a successful appeal by the German Olympic committee led to Hoy's penalty points being rescinded. This reinstated her gold medal in the team event and moved her up to second place, and within reach of the gold, in the individual competition. Hoy performed a perfect final ride to earn her second gold medal of the night . . . or so it seemed. Three days later, the Court of Arbitration for Sport overturned the previously successful German appeal and ordered that the fourteen penalty points be reapplied. Hoy was dropped to ninth place and the gold medal passed to Britain's Leslie Law.

2008 Beijing-Hong Kong C: 69, N: 24, D: 8.12.

		HORSE	DRESSAGE	ENDURANCE	JUMPING	TOTAL PTS.
1. Hinrich Romeike	GER	Marius	-37.4	-12.8	-4.0	-54.2
2. Gina Miles	USA	McKinlaigh	-39.3	-16.8	-0.0	-56.1
3. Tina Cook	GBR	Miners Frolic	-40.2	-17.2	-0.0	-57.4
4. Megan Jones	AUS	Irish Jester	-35.4	-15.6	-8.0	-59.0
5. Ingrid Klimke	GER	Abraxxas	-33.5	-17.2	-9.0	-59.7
6. Didier Dhennin	FRA	Ismène du Temple	-42.8	-14.0	-3.0	-59.8
7. Clayton Fredericks	AUS	Ben Along Time	-37.0	-16.4	-8.0	-61.4
8. Andreas Dibowski	GER	Butts Leon	-39.6	-17.6	-8.0	-65.2

Two months before the Olympics reigning world champion and gold-medal favorite Zara Phillips was forced to withdraw after her horse Toytown was injured in training. Phillips – the granddaughter of Queen Elizabeth II and daughter of 1972 equestrian gold medalist Mark Phillips and Princess Anne, who competed at the 1976 Montreal Olympics – had also missed the Athens Olympics when Toytown suffered a similar injury.

Germany's Hinrich Romeike, a full-time dentist, led after the dressage and cross-country stages, followed closely by teammate Ingrid Klimke, the daughter of dressage legend Reiner Klimke. Less than four points separated the top eight competitors going into the final round of jumping, the equivalent of one dropped rail.

Sixth-place Tina Cook moved into the lead with a clear final run, but was overhauled shortly afterwards by 34-year-old Gina Miles, who also managed to get round the course cleanly. Australia's Megan Jones entered the final round in second place but dropped to fourth after her gelding, Irish Jester, dislodged a rail with his hind legs on the final jump. Jumping last, Romeike made it through the course cleanly to clinch the gold medal: his second of the night, after helping Germany to gold in the team event.

THREE-DAY EVENT, TEAM

According to current rules, each team has four members, but the scores of only the top three finishers are counted.

1896–1908 not held

1912 Stockholm T: 7, N: 7, D: 7.17.

	HORSE		TOTAL PTS.
1. SWE			139.06
Axel Nordlander	Lady Artist	46.59	
Nils Adlercreutz	Atout	46.31	
Ernst Casparsson	Irmelin	46.16	
2. GER			138.48
Friedrich von Rochow	Idealist	46.42	
Rudolf, Graf von Schaesberg-Tannheim	Grundsee	46.16	
Eduard von Lütcken	Blue Boy	45.90	
3. USA			137.33
Benjamin Lear	Poppy	45.91	
John Montgomery	Deceive	45.88	
Guy Henry	Chiswell	45.54	
4. FRA			136.77
Jean Cariou	Cocotte	46.32	
Bernard Meyer	Allons-y	45.30	
Albert Seigner	Dignité	45.15	

Benjamin Lear of the US team rose to the rank of lieutenant general in time for World War II. In July 1941 Lear was playing golf in Memphis, Tennessee, when he witnessed a motorized regiment whistle and shout, "Yoo-hoo," at a group of young women in shorts. Outraged by this lack of discipline, Lear immediately ordered the 325 soldiers to drive 150 miles in the opposite direction, turn around and come back. Then he made them cover the final fifteen miles on foot. The incident was debated in Congress where Lear was criticized for "mass punishment of guilty and innocent alike." For the rest of his life he was known as "Yoo-Hoo" Lear.

1920 Antwerp T: 6, N: 6, D: 9.10.

	HORSE		TOTAL PTS.
1. SWE			5057.50
Helmer Mörner	Germania	1775.00	
Åge Lundström	Yrsa	1738.75	
Georg von Braun	Diana	1543.75	
2. ITA			4735.00
Ettore Caffaratti	Caniche	1733.75	
Garibaldi Spighi	Otello	1647.50	
Giulio Cacciandra	Facetto	1353.75	
3. BEL			4560.00
Roger Moeremans d'Emaüs	Sweet Girl	1652.50	
Oswald Lints	Martha	1515.00	
Jules Bonvalet	Weppelghem	1392.50	
4. USA			4477.50
Harry Chamberlin	Nigra	1568.75	
William West	Black Boy	1558.75	
John Barry	Raven	1350.00	

1924 Paris T: 10, N: 10, D: 7.26.

	HORSE		TOTAL PTS.
1. HOL			5297.5
Adolph van der Voort van Zijp	Silver Piece	1976.0	
Charles Pahud de Mortanges	Johnny Walker	1828.0	
Gerard de Kruyff	Addio	1493.5	
2. SWE			4743.5
Claès König	Bojar	1730.0	
Carl Torsten Sylvan	Amita	1678.0	
Gustaf Hagelin	Varius	1335.5	
3. ITA			4512.5
Alberto Lombardi	Pimplo	1572.0	
Alessandro Alvisi	Capiliglo	1536.0	
Emanuele di Pralormo	Mount Felix	1404.5	
4. SWI			4338.5
Hans Bühler	Mikosch	1477.5	
Charles Stoffel	Kreuzritter	1466.0	
Werner Fehr	Prahihans	1395.0	
5. BEL			4233.5
Baudoin de Brabandère	Modestie	1728.5	
Jules Bonvalet	Weppelghem	1428.0	
Joseph Fallon	Le Divorce	1077.0	
6. GBR			4064.5
Edward de Fonblanque	Copper	1728.5	
Keith Hervey	Wild Gal	1354.0	
Alec Tod	White Surrey	982.0	
7. POL			3571.5
Karol Rómmel	Krechowiak	1648.5	
Kazimierz Szosland	Helusia	961.5	
Kazimierz Rostowo-Suski	Lady	958.5	

1928 Amsterdam T: 14, N: 14, D: 8.11.

	HORSE		TOTAL PTS.
1. HOL			5865.68
Charles Pahud de Mortanges	Marcroix	1969.82	
Gerard de Kruyff	Va-t'en	1967.26	
Adolph van der Voort van Zijp	Silver Piece	1928.60	
2. NOR			5395.68
Bjart Ording	And Over	1912.98	
Arthur Quist	Hidalgo	1895.14	
Eugen Johansen	Baby	1587.56	
3. POL			5067.92
Michal Antoniewicz	Moja Mita	1822.50	
Józef Trenkwald	Lwi Pazur	1645.20	
Karol Rómmel	Doneuse	1600.22	

1932 Los Angeles T: 4, N: 4, D: 8.13.

	HORSE		TOTAL PTS.
1. USA			5038.083
Earl Thomson	Jenny Camp	1811.000	
Harry Chamberlin	Plesant Smiles	1687.833	
Edwin Argo	Honolulu Tomboy	1539.250	
2. HOL			4689.083
Charles Pahud de Mortanges	Marcroix	1813.833	
Karel Johan Schummelketel	Duiveltje	1614.500	
Aernout van Lennep	Henk	1260.750	

1936 Berlin T: 14, N: 14, D: 8.16.

	HORSE		TOTAL PTS.
1. GER			-676.65
Ludwig Stubbendorff	Nurmi	-37.70	
Rudolf Lippert	Fasan	-111.60	
Konrad von Wangenheim	Kurfürst	-527.35	
2. POL			-991.70
Henryk Rojcewicz	Arlekin III	-253.00	
Zdzislaw Kawecki	Bambino	-300.70	
Seweryn Kulesza	Tosca	-438.00	

Konrad von Wangenheim, 1936

A hero in Berlin, he broke his collarbone during the steeplechase portion of the equestrian three-day event. The next day he was thrown from his horse a second time, but completed the competition, enabling the German team to win the gold medal.

3. GBR			-9195.50
Alec Scott	Bob Clive	-117.30	
Edward Howard-Vyse	Blue Steel	-324.00	
Richard Fanshawe	Bowie Knife	-8754.20	
4. CZE			-18952.70
Václav Procházka	Harlekyn	-324.30	
Josef Dobes	Leskov	-497.70	
Otomar Bureš	Mirko	-18130.70	

Lieutenant Konrad, Freiherr von Wangenheim was one of the German heroes of the Berlin Games. During the steeplechase portion of the endurance run, his horse, Kurfürst, stumbled at the fourth obstacle, a hurdle and pond, throwing the 26-year-old von Wangenheim to the ground and breaking his collarbone. Knowing that the German team would be disqualified if he failed to finish, von Wangenheim remounted and negotiated the remaining 32 obstacles without a fault. But the jumping competition still remained. The next day von Wangenheim appeared in the stadium with his arm in a sling. Just before he mounted Kurfürst, the sling was removed and his arm was tightly bound. However, at one of the early obstacles, a double jump, Kurfürst rushed ahead and von Wangenheim was forced to pull the reins with both hands. The horse reared up, fell backward, and landed on von Wangenheim, who managed to crawl out from underneath. Kurfürst lay still and was thought to be dead, but suddenly jumped back up. Von Wangenheim remounted and again completed the course without another fault. The stadium crowd of 100,000 gave von Wangenheim a prolonged standing ovation, as Germany won the gold medal. The German team had spent 18 months practicing full-time on a replica of the Olympic course that had been built on a private estate.

The unusually enormous number of penalty points accumulated by Lieutenant Bureš of Czechoslovakia was a result of his taking 2 hours 46 minutes and 36 seconds to complete the eight-kilometer cross-country course, for which the time limit was 17 minutes 46 seconds.

As for Konrad von Wangenheim, he fought on the Eastern Front during World War II and was captured by the Soviet army in July 1944. He remained in custody long after the war ended and finally committed suicide January 28, 1953.

1948 London T: 14, N: 14, D: 8.12.

	HORSE		TOTAL PTS.
1. USA			-161.50
Frank Henry	Swing Low	-21.00	
Charles Anderson Rano	Palisade	-26.50	
Earl Thomson	Reno Rhythm	-114.00	
2. SWE			-165.00
Robert Selfelt	Claque	-25.00	
Olof Stahre	Komet	-70.00	
Sigurd Svensson	Dust	-70.00	
3. MEX			-305.25
Humberto Mariles Cortés	Parral	-61.75	
Raúl Campero	Tarahumara	-120.50	
Joaquín Solano Chagoya	Malinche	-123.00	
4. SWI			-404.50
Alfred Blaser	Mahmud	-59.25	
Anton Bühler	Amour Amour	-95.00	
Pierre Musy	Französin	-250.25	
5. SPA			-422.50
Joaquín Nogueras Márquez	Epsom	-41.00	
Fernando Gazapo de Sarraga	Vlvlan	-179.25	
Santiago Martínez Larraz	Fogoso	-202.25	

1952 Helsinki T: 19, N: 19, D: 8.2.

	HORSE		TOTAL PTS.
1. SWE			-221.94
Hans von Blixen-Finecke, Jr.	Jubal	-28.33	
Olof Stahre	Komet	-69.41	
Karl Folke Frölén	Fair	-124.20	
2. GER			-235.49
Wilhelm Büsing	Hubertus	-55.50	
Klaus Wagner	Dachs	-65.66	
Otto Rothe	Trux von Kamax	-114.33	
3. USA			-587.16
Charles Hough	Cassivellannus	-70.66	
Walter Staley	Craigwood Park	-168.50	
John Wofford	Benny Grimes	-348.00	
4. POR			-618.00
Fernando Marques Cavaleiro	Caudel	-183.00	
António Pereira de Almeida	Florentina	-216.20	
Joaquim Miguel Duarte Silva	Faial	-218.80	
5. DEN			-828.86
Hans Anderson	Tom	-222.20	
Otto Acthon	Sirdar	-267.66	
Aage Rybaeck-Nielsen	Sahara	-339.00	
6. IRL			-953.52
Henry Freeman-Jackson	Cuchulain	-268.66	
Ian Dudgeon	Hope	-269.20	
Mark Darley	Emily Little	-415.66	

1956 Stockholm T: 19, N: 19, D: 6.14.

	HORSE		TOTAL PTS.
1. GBR			-355.48
Francis Weldon	Kilbarry	-85.48	
A. Laurence Rook	Wild Venture	-119.64	
Albert Hill	Countryman III	-150.38	
2. GER			-475.91
August Lütke-Westhues	Trux von Kamax	-84.87	
Otto Rothe	Sissi	-158.04	
Klaus Wagner	Prinzeß	-233.00	
3. CAN			-572.72
John Rumble	Cilroy	-162.53	
James Elder	Colleen	-193.69	
Brian Herbinson	Tara	-216.50	
4. AUS			-619.98
Brian Crago	Radar	-147.42	
Wyatt Thompson	Brown Sugar	-155.06	
Ernest Barker	Dandy	-317.50	
5. ITA			-691.14
Giancarlo Gutierrez	Wiston	-136.43	
Adriano Capuzzo	Tuft of Heather	-139.41	
Giuseppe Molinari	Uccello	-415.30	
6. ARG			-724.18
Juan Martín Merbilháa	Gitana I	-136.46	
Eduardo Cano	Why	-242.01	
Carlos de la Serna Bustamante	Fanion	-345.71	

7. SOV/RUS			-1112.33
Lev Baklychkine	Guimnast	-96.65	
Nikolai Chelenkov	Satrap	-297.68	
Valerian Kouibychev	Perekop	-718.00	
8. SWI			-1360.90
Emil-Otto Gmür	Romeo	-378.51	
Roland Perret	Erlfried	-405.18	
Samuel Koechlin	Goya	-577.21	

1960 Rome T: 18, N: 18, D: 9.10.

	HORSE		TOTAL PTS.
1. AUS			-128.18
Lawrence Morgan	Salad Days	+7.15	
Neale Lavis	Mirrabooka	-16.50	
J. William Roycroft	Our Solo	-118.83	
2. SWI			-386.02
Anton Bühler	Gay Spark	-51.21	
Hans Schwarzenbach	Burn Trout	-131.45	
Rudolf Günthardt	Atbara	-203.36	
3. FRA			-515.71
Jack Le Goff	Image	-72.91	
Guy Lefrant	Nicias	-208.50	
Jean Raymond Le Roy	Gardem	-234.30	
4. GBR			-516.21
Michael Bullen	Cottage Romance	-62.60	
Albert Hill	Wild Venture	-215.60	
Francis Weldon	Samuel Johnson	-238.01	
5. ITA			-528.21
Lucio Tasca	Rahin	-125.80	
Ludovico Nava	Arcidosso	-161.91	
Giovanni Grignolo	Court Hill	-240.50	
6. IRL			-674.00
Edward Harty	Harlequin	-112.30	
Anthony Cameron	Sonnet	-251.55	
Ian Dudgeon	Corrigneagh	-310.15	

Suffering from a concussion and a broken collarbone as a result of a fall during the endurance test, 45-year-old Bill Roycroft insisted on leaving his hospital bed to compete in the jumping test, thus ensuring that the gold medal would go to Australia. Over the next 16 years, three of Roycroft's sons represented Australia in the Olympics. He himself competed four more times.

1964 Tokyo T: 12, N: 12, D: 10.19.

	HORSE		TOTAL PTS.
1. ITA			+85.80
Mauro Checcoli	Surbean	+64.40	
Paolo Angioni	King	+17.87	
Giuseppe Ravano	Royal Love	+3.53	
2. USA			+65.86
Michael Page	Grasshopper	+47.40	
Kevin Freeman	Gallopade	+17.13	
J. Michael Plumb	Bold Minstrel	+1.33	
3. GER&GDR			+56.73
Fritz Ligges	Donkosak	+49.20	
Horst Karsten	Condora	+36.60	
Gerhard Schulz	Balza X	-29.07	
4. IRL			+42.86
Anthony Cameron	Black Salmon	+46.53	
Thomas Brennan	Kilkenny	+1.13	
John Harty	San Michele	-4.80	
5. SOV/RUS			+19.63
German Gazyumov	Gran	+23.47	
Boris Konkov	Rumb	-10.97	
Pavel Deyev	Satrap	-32.13	
6. ARG			-34.80
Carlos Moratorio	Chalán	+56.40	
Elvio Flores	Legitima	-2.73	
Juan Gesualdi	Morrina	-88.47	
7. AUS			-67.27
J. William Roycroft	Eldorado	+32.20	
Brian Cobcroft	Stony Crossing	+8.40	
John Kelly	Brigalow	-107.87	
8. FRA			-133.87
Jack Le Goff	Leopard	-37.87	
Jean de Crouttede St. Martin	Mon Clos	-38.47	
Hughes Landon	Laurier	-57.53	

1968 Mexico City T: 12, N: 12, D: 10.21.

	HORSE		TOTAL PTS.
1. GBR			-175.93
Derek Allhusen	Lochinvar	-41.61	
Richard Meade	Cornishman V	-64.46	
Reuben Jones	The Poacher	-69.86	
2. USA			-245.87
Michael Page	Foster	-52.31	
James Wofford	Kilkenny	-74.06	
J. Michael Plumb	Plain Sailing	-119.50	
3. AUS			-331.26
Wayne Roycroft	Zhivago	-95.05	
Brian Cobcroft	Depeche	-108.76	
J. William Roycroft	Warrathoola	-127.55	
4. FRA			-505.83
Jean-Jacques Guyon	Pitou	-38.86	
André Le Goupil	Olivette B	-107.26	
Jean Sarrazin	Joburg	-359.71	
5. GER			-518.22
Horst Karsten	Adagio	-102.96	
Jochen Mehrdorf	Lapiz Lazuli	-199.41	
Klaus Wagner	Abdulla	-215.85	
6. MEX			-631.56
Ernesto del Castillo	Coficioso	-170.60	
Ramón Mejía	Centinela	-182.90	
Evaristo Avalos	Ludmilla II	-278.06	
7. GDR			-690.72
Karl-Heinz Fuhrmann	Saturn	-218.25	
Uwe Plank	Kranich	-231.01	
Helmut Hartmann	Ingwer	-241.46	
8. CAN			-787.68
Robin Hahn	Taffy	-95.41	
Norman Elder	Questionnaire	-332.46	
Barry Sonshine	Durlas Elie	-359.81	

Australia's bronze medalist team included the father-son combination of Bill and Wayne Roycroft. The Roycrofts repeated their performance in 1976, when father Bill was 61 years old. Two more of Bill Roycroft's sons competed in the Olympics: Clarke in 1972 and Barry in 1976 and 1988. Wayne's wife, Vicki, took part in 1984, 1988 and 1996.

1972 Munich T: 18, N: 18, D: 9.1.

	HORSE		TOTAL PTS.
1. GBR			+95.53
Richard Meade	Laurieston	+57.73	
Mary Gordon-Watson	Cornishman V	+30.27	
Bridget Parker	Cornish Gold	+7.53	
2. USA			+10.81
Kevin Freeman	Good Mixture	+29.87	
Bruce Davidson	Plain Sailing	+24.47	
J. Michael Plumb	Free and Easy	-43.53	
3. GER			-18.00
Harry Klugmann	Christopher Rob	+8.00	
Ludwig Goessing	Chikago	-0.40	
Karl Schultz	Pisco	-25.60	
4. AUS			-27.86
J. William Roycroft	Warrathoola	+29.60	
Richard Sands	Depeche	+24.87	
Brian Schrapel	Wakool	-82.33	
5. GDR			-127.93
Rudolf Beerbohm	Ingolf	+3.80	
Jens Niehls	Big-Ben	-60.00	
Joachim Brohmann	Uranio	-71.73	
6. SWI			-156.43
Paul Hürlimann	Grand Times	-11.03	
Anton Bühler	Wukari	-19.87	
Alfred Schwarzen-bach	Big Boy	-125.53	
7. SOV			-190.06
Sergei Mukhin	Reisfeder	-0.13	
Valentin Gorelkin	Rok	-34.93	
Vladimir Lanugin	Zimar	-155.00	
8. ITA			-203.58
Alessandro Argenton	Woodland	+43.33	
Dino Costantini	Lord Jim	-98.18	
Mario Turner	Forgotten Fred	-148.73	

Many Olympic gold-medal winners have exploited their success by pursuing movie careers. Almost all of these athletes-turned-actors have been human. One exception is Cornishman V, who helped two different riders to Olympic victory, in 1968 and 1972. He later appeared in *Dead Cert* (1974), based on a Dick Francis novel, and *International Velvet* (1978).

1976 Montreal T: 12, N: 12, D: 7.25.

	HORSE		TOTAL PTS.
1. USA			-441.00
Edmund "Tad" Coffin	Bally-Cor	-114.99	
J. Michael Plumb	Better & Better	-125.85	
Bruce Davidson	Irish-Cap	-200.16	
2. GER			-584.80
Karl Schultz	Madrigal	-129.45	
Herbert Blöcker	Albrant	-213.15	
Helmut Rethemeier	Pauline	-242.00	
3. AUS			-599.54
Wayne Roycroft	Laurenson	-178.04	
Mervyn Bennett	Regal Reign	-206.04	
J. William Roycroft	Version	-215.46	
4. ITA			-682.24
Euro Federico Roman	Shamrock	-194.14	
Mario Turner	Tempest Blisland	-213.19	
Alessandro Argenton	Woodland	-274.91	
5. SOV			-721.55
Yuri Salnikov	Rumpel	-189.46	
Valery Dvorianinov	Zeila	-218.25	
Viktor Kalinin	Araks	-313.84	
6. CAN			-808.81
Juliet Graham	Sumatra	-202.69	
Cathy Wedge	City Fella	-286.76	
Robin Hahn	L'Esprit	-319.36	

1980 Moscow T: 7, N: 7, D: 7.27.

	HORSE		TOTAL PTS.
1. SOV			-457.00
Aleksandr Blinov	Galzun	-120.80	
Yuri Salnikov	Pintset	-151.60	
Valery Volkov	Tskheti	-184.60	
2. ITA			-656.20
Euro Federico Roman	Rossinan	-108.80	
Anna Casagrande	Daleye	-266.20	
Mauro Roman	Dourakine 4	-281.40	
3. MEX			-1172.85
Manuel Mendivil Yocupicio	Remember	-319.75	
David Barcena Ríos	Bombon	-362.50	
José Luis Pérez Soto	Quelite	-490.80	
4. HUN			-1603.40
László Cseresnyes	Fapipa	-436.20	
István Grozner	Biboros	-498.60	
Zoltán Horvath	Lamour	-668.60	

The substitute three-day event, held in August at Fountainbleau, was won by France, with West Germany second and Australia third.

1984 Los Angeles-Arcadia T: 11, N: 11, D: 8.3.

	HORSE		TOTAL PTS.
1. USA			-186.00
Karen Stives	Ben Arthur	-54.20	
Torrance Watkins Fleischman	Finvarra	-60.40	
J. Michael Plumb	Blue Stone	-71.40	
2. GBR			-189.20
Virginia Holgate	Priceless	-56.80	
Lucinda Green	Regal Realm	-63.80	
Ian Stark	Oxford Blue	-68.60	
3. GER			-234.00
Dietmar Hogrefe	Foliant	-74.40	
Bettina Overesch	Peacetime	-79.60	
Claus Erhorn	Fair Lady	-80.00	
4. FRA			-236.00
Pascal Morvillers	Gulliver "B"	-63.00	
Marie Christine Duroy	Harley	-85.40	
Armand Bigot	Jacquou du Bois	-87.60	
5. AUS			-258.40
Andrew Hoy	Davey	-80.00	
Mervyn Bennett	Regal Reign	-87.40	
Vicki Roycroft	Looking Ahead	-91.00	
6. NZL			-280.00
Mark Todd	Charisma	-51.60	
Mary Hamilton	Whist	-98.00	
Andrew Nicholson	Kahlua	-130.40	

7. ITA			-280.70
Mauro Checcoli	Spey Cast Boy	-67.00	
Marina Sciocchetti	Master Hunt	-67.00	
Bartolo Ambrosione	Brick	-146.70	
8. SWE			-339.85
Jan Jonsson	Isolde	-86.40	
Göran Breisner	Bobalong	-99.65	
Christian Persson	Joel	-153.80	

1988 Seoul T: 10, N: 10, D: 9.22.

	HORSE		TOTAL PTS.
1. GER			-225.95
Claus Erhorn	Justyn Thyme	-62.35	
Matthias Baumann	Shamrock	-68.80	
Thies Kaspareit	Sherry	-94.80	
2. GBR			-256.80
Ian Stark	Sir Wattle	-52.80	
Virginia Leng (Holgate)	Master Craftsman	-62.00	
Karen Straker	Get Smart	-142.00	
3. NZL			-271.20
Mark Todd	Charisma	-42.60	
Judith "Tinks" Pottinger	Volunteer	-65.80	
Andrew Bennie	Grayshott	-162.80	
4. POL			-389.60
Bogusław Jarecki	Niewiaza	-111.40	
Krzystof Rogowski	Alkierz	-114.80	
Jerzy Rafalak	Dzwinograd	-163.40	
5. AUS			-457.60
Andrew Hoy	Kiwi	-89.00	
Scott Keach	Trade Commissioner	-176.60	
David Green	Shannagh	-192.00	
6. FRA			-498.80
Jean Teulère	Mohican V	-69.00	
Vincent Berthet	Jet Crub	-202.20	
Pascal Morvillers	Frangin III	-227.60	
7. KOR			-740.15
Choi Myung-jin	Snuffler	-130.55	
Park Dong-joo	Aqaba Legend	-227.00	
Park So-woon	Moisson d'Avril	-382.60	

1992 Barcelona T: 18, N: 18, D: 7.30.

	HORSE		TOTAL PTS.
1. AUS			-288.6
Matthew Ryan	Kibah Tic Toc	-70.0	
Andrew Hoy	Kiwi	-89.4	
Gillian Rolton	Peppermint Grove	-129.2	
2. NZL			-290.8
Blyth Tait	Messiah	-87.6	
Vicky Latta	Chief	-87.8	
Andrew Nicholson	Spinning Rhombus	-115.4	
3. GER			-300.3
Herbert Blöcker	Feine Dame	-81.3	
Ralf Ehrenbrink	Kildare	-108.4	
Cord Mysegaes	Ricardo	-110.4	
4. BEL			-333.05
Karin Donckers	Britt	-104.4	
Jet Desmedt	Dolleman	-108.4	
Willy Sneyers	Drum	-120.25	
5. SPA			-388.8
Luis Álvarez Cervera	Mr. Chrisalis	-102.2	
Santiago de la Rocha Mille	Kinvarra B'92	-122.4	
Fernando Villalón Gómez	Clever Night	-164.2	
6. GBR			-406.6
Karen Dixon (Straker)	Get Smart	-92.4	
Mary Thomson	King William	-105.4	
Richard Walker	Jacana	-208.8	
7. JPN			-434.8
Yoshihiko Kowata	Hell at Dawn	-135.8	
Eiki Miyazaki	Mystery Cargo	-137.8	
Kojiro Goto	Retalic	-161.2	
8. IRL			-445.8
Eric Smiley	Enterprise	-140.4	
Mairead Curran	Watercolour	-149.4	
Melanie Duff	Rathlin Roe	-156.0	

New Zealand led Australia by 32.8 points after the endurance test and seemed a lock for the gold medals. Indeed, with Andrew Nicholson on Spinning Rhombus left to jump for New Zealand and Matt Ryan on Kibah Tic Toc left for Australia, the Kiwis had actually lengthened their lead to 37.8 points. But Nicholson had a disastrous round, knocking over nine obstacles worth 45 points. This meant that if Ryan could clear all but one jump, Australia would earn an unexpected victory. Despite the pressure, Ryan and Kibah Tic Toc cleared all but the last obstacle.

1996 Atlanta-Conyers T: 16; N: 16; D: 7.24.

	HORSE		TOTAL PTS.
1. AUS			-203.85
Wendy Schaeffer	Sunburst	-61.00	
Phillip Dutton	True Blue Girdwood	-69.40	
Andrew Hoy	Darien Powers	-73.45	
2. USA			-261.10
David O'Connor	Giltedge	-76.00	
Bruce Davidson	Heyday	-79.50	
Karen O'Connor	Biko	-105.60	
3. NZL			-268.55
Blyth Tait	Chesterfield	-70.10	
Vaughn Jefferis	Bounce	-97.80	
Andrew Nicholson	Jagermeister II	-100.65	
4. FRA			-307.65
Jacques Dulcy	Upont	-78.90	
Rodolphe Scherer	Urane des Pins	-109.15	
Koris Vieules	Tandresse de Canta	-119.60	
5. GBR			-312.90
Karen Dixon (Straker)	Too Smart	-88.55	
Gary Parsonage	Magic Rogue	-106.80	
William Fox-Pitt	Cosmopolitan II	-117.55	
6. JPN			-326.15
Kazuhiro Iwatani	Sejane de Vozerier	-101.00	
Takeaki Tsuchiya	Right on Time	-102.65	
Yoshihiko Kowata	Hell at Dawn	-122.50	
7. SWE			-345.25
Linda Algotsson	Lafayette	-78.45	
Paula Tornqvist	Monaghan	-99.00	
Therese Olavssion	Hector T	-167.80	
8. SPA			-621.65
Santiago Centenera	Just Dixon	-161.00	
Javier Revuelta	Toby	-187.25	
Luis Álvarez de Cervera	Pico's Nippur	-273.40	

Sixth after the dressage test, the Australian team built an insurmountable 61-point lead on the endurance course.

Team member Wendy Schaeffer had broken her leg only two months before the Olympics.

2000 Sydney T: 12; N: 12; D: 9.19.

	HORSE		TOTAL PTS.
1. AUS			-146.80
Stuart Tinney	Jeepster	-41.00	
Andrew Hoy	Darien Powers	-45.60	
Matt Ryan Kibah	Sandstone	-60.20	
2. GBR			-161.00
Philippa "Pippa" Funnell	Supreme Rock	-45.40	
Leslie Law	Shear H2O	-54.00	
Jeanette Brakewell	Over To You	-61.60	
3. USA			-175.80
Karen O'Conner	Prince Panache	-43.00	
David O'Connor	Giltedge	-46.80	
Nina Fout	3 Magic Beans	-86.00	
4. GER			-241.80
Ingrid Klimke	Sleep Late	41.20	
Marina Koehncke	Sir Toby 4	-70.40	
Andreas Dibowski	Leonas Dancer	-130.20	
5. IRL			-270.00
Patricia Donegan	Don't Step Back	-65.80	
Susan Shortt	Joy of My Heart	-80.00	
Nicola Cassidy	Mr Mullins	-124.20	
6. BRA			-333.00
Augusto Luiz Faria	Hunefer	-79.40	
Vicente Neto Araujo	Teveri	-124.80	
Eder Pagoto	Amazonian	-128.80	
7. SPA			-1341.20
Enrique Sarasola	Super Djarvis	-164.80	
Ramón Beca	Pereus	-176.40	
Jaime Matossian	New Venture	ret	
8. NZL			-2065.60
Mark Todd	Diamond Hall Re	-65.60	
Vaughn Jefferis	Bounce	with	
Blyth Tait	Ready Teddy	elim	

New Zealand was in third place after the cross-country portion of the competition, but when Blyth Tait's horse, Reddy Teddy, failed the veterinary inspection, the Kiwis were left with only two entries for the show jumping course. The Australians led the competition from beginning to end, as Andrew Hoy became the first rider to win the three-day team event three times. Ian Stark of the British team earned his fourth Olympic silver medal twelve years after he won his last one. David and Karen O'Connor, who earned their second medals in the event, were husband and wife.

2004 Athens-Markopoulo T: 14, N: 14, D: 8.18.

	HORSE		TOTAL PTS.
1. FRA			-140.4
Nicolas Touzaint	Galan de Sauvagere	-33.4	
Jean Teulère	Espoir de la Mare	-46.4	
Didier Courreges	Debat d'Estruval	-60.6	
2. GBR			-143.0
Philippa "Pippa" Funnell	Primmore's Pride	-42.6	
Leslie Law	Shear L'Eau	-44.4	
Mary Elizabeth Thomson-King	King Solomon III	-56.0	
3. USA			-145.6
Kim Severson	Winsome Adante	-41.2	
Amy Tryon	Poggio II	-51.8	
Darren Chiacchia	Windfall 2	-52.6	
4. GER			-147.8
Hinrich Romeike	Marius	-45.2	
Bettina Overesch-Böker-Hoy	Ringwood Cockatoo	-49.6	
Andreas Dibowski	Little Lemon	-53.0	
5. NZL			-176.2
Heelan Tompkins	Glengarrick	-48.0	
Matthew Grayling	Revo	-59.2	
Blyth Tait	Ready Teddy	-69.0	
6. AUS			-185.8
Rebel Morrow	Oaklea Groover	-50.2	
Phillip Dutton	Nova Top	-50.8	
Stuart Tinney	Jeepster	-84.8	
7. BEL			-193.0
Constantin Van Rijckevorsel	Withcote Nellie	-54.4	
Karin Donckers	Gormley	-56.4	
Hendrik Degros	Mr. Noppus	-82.2	
8. IRL			-217.0
Mark Kyle	Drunken Disorderly	-67.0	
Niall Griffin	Lorgaine	-73.2	
Susan Shortt	Just Beauty Queen	-76.8	

Bettina Hoy first competed in the Olympics in 1984, earning a bronze medal in the team event. The daughter of riding instructor and national-level show jumper Edi Overesch, in 2001 Hoy married Australian rider and three-time gold medalist Andrew Hoy. The pair lived on the estate of Great Britain's Princess Anne, and made their living training the princess' second daughter, Zara Phillips, in eventing.

Hoy rode a clear show jumping round, giving Germany a score of 133.8 points and earning her team the Olympic title. Less than twenty minutes later, however, the ground jury panel decided to review the results, expressing concerns that Hoy may have crossed the start line twice and that the 90-second event clock should have started the first time she crossed it. Using a video replay of Hoy's round and a printed back-up timing record as evidence, the panel decided that an infraction had occurred and docked Hoy fourteen points, dropping Germany to fourth place and out of the medals.

Germany responded by lodging an appeal, stating that the event clock did not start running when Hoy crossed the line the first time and that she had been led to believe that the clock had been reset. "The rules say I have 45 seconds to cross the start line after the bell rings," Hoy explained. "When I was close to the start line I saw 35 seconds left on the clock so I decided to do another circle. After I finished my round, I had a clear round inside the time." Hugh Thomas, a British member of the appeal committee, agreed. "There were two mistakes made at the start," he said. "First, the clock was restarted when it shouldn't have been, and then there was no sign for Bettina when she looked at the clock that her round had started, so she circled again. When a mistake is made by the management, we have to be sure that the athlete does not suffer." The appeals committee reversed the penalty, citing technical failure and a "clear injustice" done to Hoy, and reinstated the original score, putting Germany back in the gold medal position.

However, the story did not end there. France, Britain and the United States quickly filed a joint complaint with the Court of Arbitration for Sport, arguing that a clear violation of the rules had occurred and that all riders know that once they cross the start line their round has begun.

Three days after the event, the CAS reversed the pro-German appeal decision, ruling that the appeals panel did not have the authority to overturn the initial ground jury decision. The fourteen penalty points were reinstated, dropping Germany back to fourth place and stripping Hoy of the gold medal for the second time in three days.

In March 2008, while preparing for the 2008 Olympics, Darren Chiacchia of the US team nearly died after his horse fell on him during a competition in Tallahassee, Florida. He sustained broken bones, a punctured lung and was in a coma for 42 days. He recovered and returned to competition less than a year later. In early 2010 he made headlines again, this time after being arrested when a former lover accused Chiacchia of exposing him to HIV. The charges were later dropped because, under Florida state law, homosexual sex does not qualify as sexual intercourse.

2008 Beijing-Hong Kong T: 11, N: 11, D: 8.12.

	HORSE		TOTAL PTS.
1. GER			-166.1
Hinrich Romeike	Marius	-54.2	
Ingrid Klimke	Abraxxas	-54.7	
Andreas Dibowski	Butts Leon	-57.2	
2. AUS			-171.2
Megan Jones	Irish Jester	-55.0	
Clayton Fredericks	Ben Along Time	-57.4	
Sonja Johnson	Ringwould Jaguar	-58.8	
3. GBR			-185.7
Tina Cook	Miners Frolic	-57.4	
Mary Thomson-King	Call Again Cavalier	-64.1	
William Fox-Pitt	Parkmore Ed	-64.2	
4. SWE			-230.5
Linda Algotsson	Stand By Me	-64.3	
Katrin Norling	Pandora	-73.0	
Dag Albert	Tubber Rebel	-93.2	
5. NZL			-240.9
Caroline Powell	Lenamore	-73.2	
Mark Todd	Gandalf	-77.6	
Joe Meyer	Snip	-90.1	
6. ITA			-246.4
Vittoria Panizzon	Rock Model	-69.0	
Susanna Bordone	Ava	-86.6	
Roberto Rotatori	Irham De Viages	-90.8	
7. USA			-250.0
Gina Miles	McKinlaigh	-56.1	
Phillip Dutton	Connaught	-68.2	
Becky Holder	Courageous Comet	-125.7	
8. IRL			-276.1
Austin O'Connor	Hobby Du Mee	-87.2	
Geoffrey Curran	Kilkishen	-94.1	
Louise Lyons	Watership Down	-94.8	

Four years after being stripped of the team gold medal in Athens, the members of the German squad were back and aiming for the top spot on the podium. The Germans had beaten Great Britain and Australia at the 2006 world championships and were in first place after the dressage and cross-country rounds at the Olympics. Australia trailed by only 3.9 points going into the final jumping stage, the equivalent of less than one dropped rail.

The final went down to the last rider on each team. As both Hinrich Romeike and Megan Jones knocked down a fence, Germany came away with the victory. All five members of Australia's team were making their Olympic debuts. Australia had been struck by an outbreak of equine influenza in the summer of 2007, which stopped all major equestrian tournaments until just four months before the Beijing Olympics.

JUMPING, INDIVIDUAL

Each horse and rider jumps three qualifying rounds. Competitors who finish in the top 45 of the qualifying rounds advance to final course A. The top 20 (and those tied for 20th) in that round qualify for final course B. The results are determined by adding the scores from both rounds. Ties for the medal places are decided by a jump-off. If a tie still exists, the competitor with the fastest time in the jump-off is declared the winner. Course A must be between 600 and 700 meters long and include 10 to 12 obstacles and a water jump. The obstacles may vary from 1.4 meters (4 feet 7 inches) to 1.6 meters (5 feet 3 inches) in height. Course B must be between 500 and 600 meters long. It must be different from course A and must include ten obstacles varying in height from 1.4 meters to 1.6 meters (5 feet 3 inches). Course A must include three double jumps or one double and one triple; course B must include one double or one triple, with a water jump being optional.

Faults are assessed for disobedience at an obstacle and backtracking. First disobedience at an obstacle is penalized by 4 penalties and a second disobedience by disqualification. If an obstacle is knocked down or the horse's hoof touches the white border of a water jump, 4 penalties are assessed. A fall by either horse or rider is penalized by 8 penalties; a second fall results in elimination. Riders exceeding the time limit in the qualifying rounds are penalized 1 point for each 4 seconds. In the final, the penalty is 1 point per second.

1896 not held

1900 Paris C: 37, N: 5, D: 5.29.

		HORSE	
1. Aimé Haageman	BEL	Benton II	2:16.0
2. Georges Van de Poële	BEL	Windsor Squire	2:17.6
3. Louis de Champsavin	FRA	Terpsichore	2:26.0

1904–1908 not held

1912 Stockholm C: 31, N: 8, D: 7.16.

		HORSE	POINTS	JUMP-OFF
1. Jean Cariou	FRA	Mignon	186	55
2. Rabod Wilhelm von Kröcher	GER	Dohna	186	53
3. Emanuel de Blommaert de Soye	BEL	Clonmore	185	
4. Herbert Scott	GBR	Shamrock	184	
5. Sigismund Freyer	GER	Ultimus	183	
6. Nils Adlercreutz	SWE	Ilex	181	
6. Ernst Casparsson	SWE	Kiriki	181	
6. Wilhelm, Graf von Hohenau	GER	Pretty Girl	181	

1920 Antwerp C: 25, N: 6, D: 9.12.

		HORSE	FAULTS
1. Tommaso Lequio di Assaba	ITA	Trebecco	2
2. Alessandro Valerio	ITA	Cento	3
3. Carl-Gustaf Lewenhaupt	SWE	Mon Coeur	4
4. Paul Michelet	NOR	Ravn	5
5. Ferdinand de la Serna	BEL	Arsinoe	6
5. Lars von Stockenström	SWE	Reward	6
7. Henry Allen	USA	Don	7
7. Santorre de Rossi di Santa Rosa	ITA	Neruccio	7
7. Roger Moeremans d'Emaüs	BEL	Sweet Girl	7

1924 Paris C: 43, N: 11, D: 7.27.

		HORSE	FAULTS	
1. Alphonse Gemuseus	SWI	Lucette	6	
2. Tommaso Lequio di Assaba	ITA	Trebecco	8.75	
3. Adam Królikiewicz	POL	Picador	10	
4. Philip Bowden-Smith	GBR	Billy Boy	10.5	
5. António Borges de Almeida	POR	Reginald	12	2:28.8
6. Åke Thelning	SWE	Loke	12	2:30.4
7. Axel Ståhle	SWE	Cecil	12.25	
8. Nicolas Leroy	BEL	Vif Argent	14.75	

1928 Amsterdam C: 46, N: 16, D: 8.12.

		HORSE	FAULTS	1ST JUMP-OFF	2ND JUMP-OFF
1. František Ventura	CZE/SLV	Eliot	0	0	0
2. Pierre Bertran de Balanda	FRA	Papillon	0	0	2
3. Charley Kuhn	SWI	Pepita	0	0	4
4. Kazimierz Gzowski	POL	Mylord	0	2	1:33.0
5. José Navarro Morenés	SPA	Zapatazo	0	2	1:36.0
6. Karl Hansen	SWE	Gerold	0	2	1:39.0
7. Francisco Fourquet	ITA	Joe Aleshire	0	DISQ	
8. Alphonse Gemuseus	SWI	Lucette	2		

1932 Los Angeles C: 11, N: 4, D: 8.14.

		HORSE	FAULTS
1. Takeichi Nishi	JPN	Uranus	8
2. Harry Chamberlin	USA	Show Girl	12
3. Clarence von Rosen, Jr.	SWE	Empire	16
4. William Bradford	USA	Joe Aleshire	24
5. Ernst Hallberg	SWE	Kornett	50.5

An extremely wealthy man, Takeichi Nishi was a lieutenant in the Japanese army when he won his gold medal. Promoted to colonel toward the end of World War II, he was made commander of a tank regiment on Iwo Jima. During the fierce fighting on that island, some of the US officers learned that Nishi was on the island and hoped to meet him. They never got a chance. Nishi, who had many American friends, including Will Rogers, Mary Pickford, and Douglas Fairbanks, refused to surrender and instead joined a mass Japanese suicide.

Silver medal winner Harry Chamberlin was an all-around athlete who, 23 years before his Olympic success, scored the winning touchdown in the 1909 Army-Navy football game.

1936 Berlin C: 54, N: 18, D: 8.16.

		HORSE	FAULTS	JUMP-OFF	
1. Kurt Hasse	GER	Tora	4	4	59.2
2. Henri Rang	ROM	Delfis	4	4	1:12.8
3. József Platthy	HUN	Sello	8	0	1:02.6
4. Georges van der Meersch	BEL	Ibrahim	8	0	1:09.0
5. Carl Raguse	USA	Dakota	8	4	
6. José Beltrão	POR	Biscuit	12		
6. Xavier Bizard	FRA	Bagatelle	12		
6. Johan Jacob Greter	HOL	Ernica	12		
6. Maurice Gudin de Vallerin	FRA	Ecuyère	12		
6. Cevat Koula	TUR	Sapkin	12		

1948 London C: 44, N: 15, D: 8.14.

		HORSE	FAULTS	JUMP-OFF	
1. Humberto Mariles Cortés	MEX	Arete	6.25		
2. Rubén Uriza	MEX	Harvey	8	0	
3. Jean d'Orgeix	FRA	Sucre de Pomme	8	4	38.9
4. Franklin Wing	USA	Democrat	8	4	40.1
5. Jaime García Cruz	SPA	Bizarro	12		
5. Eric Sörensen	SWE	Blatunga	12		
7. Max Fresson	FRA	Decametre	16		
7. Henry Llewellyn	GBR	Foxhunter	16		
7. Henry Nicoll	GBR	Kilgeddin	16		

General Mariles won the title in dramatic fashion. The last rider to enter the arena, he needed to incur fewer than eight faults to win the gold medal. This he did, clearing every obstacle but the water jump and losing 2¼ points for being eight seconds overtime. On the night of August 14, 1964, the 51-year-old Mariles was driving home from a party in his honor in Mexico City when another motorist attempted to force him off the road. At the next traffic light Mariles pulled out a gun and shot the man. He was sent to prison, but later released by presidential pardon. In 1972 Mariles was arrested in Paris during a raid in which 132 pounds of pure heroin were seized. He died in prison before coming to trial.

1952 Helsinki C: 51, N: 20, D: 8.3.

		HORSE	FAULTS	JUMP-OFF	
1. Pierre Jonquères d'Oriola	FRA	Ali Baba	8	0	
2. Óscar Cristi Gallo	CHI	Bambi	8	4	
3. Fritz Thiedemann	GER	Meteor	8	8	38.5
4. Eloi Massey Oliveira de Menezes	BRA	Bigua	8	8	45.0
5. Wilfred White	GBR	Nizefella	8	12	
6. Humberto Mariles Cortés	MEX	Petrolero	8.75		
7. César Mendoza Durán	CHI	Pillán	12		3:08.8
8. Argentino Molinuevo	ARG	Discutido	12		3:13.0

On July 24 d'Oriola watched as his young cousin, Christian d'Oriola, was awarded the gold medal in foil fencing. Throughout the tournament Christian had worn a white cap for good luck. Pierre asked if he could wear the cap now that Christian no longer needed it. Christian handed it over and ten days later Pierre too earned a gold medal.

Fritz Thiedemann commanded a German cavalry unit during World War II. He was captured and the end of the war found him in a Russian prison camp. At the Helsinki Olympics he earned bronze medals in both individual show jumping and team dressage to become the only rider in Olympic history to win medals in two equestrian disciplines at the same Games.

1956 Stockholm C: 66, N: 24, D: 6.16.

		HORSE	FAULTS
1. Hans-Günter Winkler	GER	Halla	4
2. Raimondo D'Inzeo	ITA	Merano	8
3. Piero D'Inzeo	ITA	Uruguay	11
4. Fritz Thiedemann	GER	Meteor	12
4. Wilfred White	GBR	Nizefella	12
6. Pierre Jonquères d'Oriola	FRA	Voulette	15
7. Henrique Callado	POR	Martingil	16
8. Carlos D'Elía	ARG	Discutido	19

Hans-Günther Winkler and his horse, Halla, had already won back-to-back world championships in show jumping when they competed at the 1956 Olympics. During the first round, Halla took off early for the penultimate fence. Winkler was thrown into the air, landed heavily back in the saddle and pulled a groin muscle. He knew that if he withdrew from the final round, the German team would be eliminated. Dizzy and in pain, he rode anyway. Halla, sensing that Winkler was not well, took charge and completed the course without a fault, as Winkler just hung on. They earned gold in both the individual and team events. Winkler eventually competed in six Olympics and won five gold medals, one silver medal and one bronze medal. His 1956 show jumping gold was the only one he earned in an individual event. Halla was the first horse to win three gold medals. Gigolo, ridden by Isabell Werth of Germany, became the second, ultimately winning four gold medals between 1992 and 2000.

1960 Rome C: 60, N: 23, D: 9.7.

		HORSE	FAULTS
1. Raimondo D'Inzeo	ITA	Posillipo	12
2. Piero D'Inzeo	ITA	The Rock	16
3. David Broome	GBR	Sunsalve	23
4. George Morris	USA	Simjon	24
5. Hans-Günter Winkler	GER	Halla	25
6. Fritz Thiedemann	GER	Meteor	25.5
7. Naldo Dasso	ARG	Final	28
7. Bernard de Fombelle	FRA	Buffalo	28
7. Hugh Wiley	USA	Master William	28

1964 Tokyo C: 46, N: 17, D: 10.24.

		HORSE	FAULTS	JUMP-OFF
1. Pierre Jonquères d'Oriola	FRA	Lutteur	9	
2. Hermann Schridde	GER	Dozent	13.75	
3. Peter Robeson	GBR	Firecrest	16	0
4. Thomas Fahey	AUS	Bonvale	16	8
5. Joaquim Miguel Duarte Silva	POR	Jeune France	20	
5. Nelson Pessoa Filho	BRA	Huipil	20	
7. Frank Chapot	USA	San Lucas	20.5	
8. Kurt Jarasinski	GER	Torro	22.25	

1968 Mexico City C: 41, N: 15, D: 10.23.

		HORSE	FAULTS	JUMP-OFF	
1. William Steinkraus	USA	Snowbound	4		
2. Marion Coakes	GBR	Stroller	8		
3. David Broome	GBR	Mister Softee	12	0	35.3
4. Frank Chapot	USA	San Lucas	12	0	36.8
5. Hans-Günter Winkler	GER	Enigk	12	0	37.5
6. James Elder	CAN	The Immigrant	12	0	39.2
7. Monika Bachmann	SWI	Erbach	16		
7. Piero D'Inzeo	ITA	Fidux	16		
7. Argentino Molinuevo	ARG	Don Gustavo	16		
7. Alwin Schockemöhle	GER	Donal Rex	16		

1972 Munich C: 56, N: 22, D: 9.3.

		HORSE	FAULTS	JUMP-OFF
1. Graziano Mancinelli	ITA	Ambassador	8	0
2. Ann Moore	GBR	Psalm	8	3
3. Neal Shapiro	USA	Sloopy	8	8
4. James Day	CAN	Steelmaster	8.75	
4. Hugo Simon	AUT	Lavendel	8.75	
4. Hartwig Steenken	GER	Simona	8.75	
7. Jean-Marcel Rozier	FRA	Sans Souci	12	
8. Alfonso Segovia	SPA	Tic Tac	16	
8. Fritz Ligges	GER	Robin	16	

For a long time Mancinelli was a rider for the Milan horse-dealing company of Fratelli Rivolta. Consequently he was considered a professional, and many observers were surprised when he was included as a member of the Italian team in Tokyo in 1964. Banned from the team the day before the competition was to begin, he was reinstated at the last minute. The ruling turned in his favor when it was revealed that he was the adopted son of one of the Rivolta brothers—part of the family and therefore not a professional. Eight years later in Munich, Mancinelli rode a perfect round in the jump-off to earn the individual gold medal.

1976 Montreal C: 48, N: 20, D: 7.27.

		HORSE	FAULTS	JUMP-OFF
1. Alwin Schockemöhle	GER	Warwick Rex	0	
2. Michel Vaillancourt	CAN	Branch County	12	4
3. François Mathy	BEL	Gai Luron	12	8
4. Deborah Johnsey	GBR	Moxy	12	15.25
5. Frank Chapot	USA	Viscount	16	
5. Guy Creighton	AUS	Mr. Dennis	16	
5. Marcel Rozier	FRA	Bayard de Maupas	16	
5. Hugo Simon	AUT	Lavendel	16	

A 39-year-old factory owner, Alwin Schockemöhle was the first rider to complete the Olympic competition without a fault since František Ventura in 1928.

1980 Moscow C: 14, N: 7, D: 8.3.

		HORSE	FAULTS	JUMP-OFF	
1. Jan Kowalczyk	POL	Artemor	8		
2. Nikolai Korolkov	SOV/RUS	Espadron	9.5		
3. Joaquín Pérez Heras	MEX	Alymony	12	4	43.23
4. Oswaldo Méndez Herbruger	GUA	Pampa	12	4	43.59
5. Viktor Pohanovsky	SOV/UKR	Topky	15.5		
6. Wieslaw Hartman	POL	Norton	16		
7. Barnabas Hevesi	HUN	Bohem	24		
8. Marian Kozicki	POL	Bremen	24.5		

The Rotterdam Show Jumping Festival for Olympic boycotters was won by Hugo Simon of Austria, with John Whitaker of Great Britain second and Melanie Smith of the United States third.

1984 Los Angeles-Arcadia C: 51, N: 21, D: 8.12.

		HORSE	FAULTS	JUMP-OFF
1. Joe Fargis	USA	Touch of Class	4	0
2. Conrad Homfeld	USA	Abdullah	4	8
3. Heidi Robbiani	SWI	Jessica V	8	0
4. Mario Deslauriers	CAN	Aramis	8	4
5. Bruno Candrian	SWI	Slygof	8	8
6. Luis Álvarez Cervera	SPA	Jexico De Park	8.5	
7. Frédéric Cottier	FRA	Flambeau C	12	
7. Paul Schockemöhle	GER	Deister	12	
7. Melanie Smith	USA	Calypso	12	

Joe Fargis and Conrad Homfeld were companions and business partners who owned a breeding stable in Petersburg, Virginia. Fargis would have won the gold medal without a jump-off had not he and Touch of Class knocked down the final rail in the second round. This was their only fault in six rounds of Olympic competition.

1988 Seoul C: 74, N: 24, D: 10.2.

		HORSE	FAULTS	JUMP-OFF	
1. Pierre Durand	FRA	Jappeloup	1.25		
2. Greg Best	USA	Gem Twist	4	4	45.70
3. Karsten Huck	GER	Nepomuk	4	4	54.75
4. David Broome	GBR	Countryman	8		
4. Anne Kursinski	USA	Starman	8		
6. Jaime Azcarraga	MEX	Chin Chin	8		
7. Joe Fargis	USA	Mill Pearl	12		
7. Marcus Fuchs	SWI	Shandor II	12		
7. Thomas Fuchs	SWI	Diners Dollar Girl	12		
7. Jos Lansink	HOL	Felix	12		
7. Nicholas Skelton	GBR	Apollo	12		
7. Franke Sloothaak	GER	Walzerkönig	12		
7. Johannes "Jan" Tops	HOL	Doreen	12		

In 1984, France lost its chance for bronze in the team jumping competition when Pierre Durand fell. Four years later in Seoul, Durand, a 33-year-old bankruptcy administrator from Libourne, near Bordeaux, was given a chance to redeem himself. If he could ride a clear round, the bronze would go to the French. If he made even one mistake, the Canadians would take part in the medal ceremony. This time the team of Durand and Jappeloup was faultless. Four days later, in the individual final, it was Karsten Huck who needed a perfect round to win. But he and Nepomuk knocked down the next-to-last fence and the victory went to Durand.

1992 Barcelona C: 87, N: 30, D: 8.9.

		HORSE	FAULTS
1. Ludger Beerbaum	GER	Classic Touch	0
2. Piet Raymakers	HOL	Ratina Z	0.25
3. Norman Dello Joio	USA	Irish	4.75
4. Hervé Godignon	FRA	Quidam De Revel	6.25
5. Johannes "Jan" Tops	HOL	Top Gun	8.25
6. Maria Gretzer	SWE	Marcoville	10.25
7. Ludo Philippaerts	BEL	Darco	12.25
8. Merethe Jensen	DEN	Maxime	12.75

Piet Raymakers rode clear on both final courses, but incurred a quarter-point penalty when he exceeded the time limit on course B by 0.66 seconds. This fraction of a second kept Raymakers from a jump-off for the gold medal when the final rider, Ludger Beerbaum, also jumped clear, but beat the limit by more than six seconds. When Beerbaum was 15 years old, he and his horse fell at a cross-country obstacle. The horse landed on him, knocking him unconscious, breaking five of his ribs and severely damaging his right lung. Doctors removed one-third of his lung and he spent six weeks in the hospital.

1996 Atlanta-Conyers C: 82, N: 24, D: 8.4.

		HORSE	FAULTS	JUMP-OFF	
1. Ulrich Kirchhoff	GER	Jus de Pommes	1		
2. Willi Melliger	SWI	Calvaro	4	0	38.07
3. Alexandra Ledermann	FRA	Rochet M	4	0	41.46
4. Hugo Simon	AUT	Et	4	4	
5. Urs Fah	SWI	Jeremia	4	4	
6. Geoff Billington	GBR	It's Otto	4	4	
7. Johannes "Jan" Tops	HOL	Top Gun	4	8	
8. Alvaro Miranda Neto	BRA	Aspen	4	16	

Ulrich Kirchhoff was the only rider to compete two clear rounds. Nineteen days later, his horse, Jus de Pommes, died of a circulatory collapse following treatment for intestinal congestion.

2000 Sydney C:74, N: 28, D:10.1.

		HORSE	FAULTS	JUMP-OFF	
1. Jeroen Dubbeldam	HOL	Sjiem	4	0	
2. Albert Voorn	HOL	Lando	4	4	44.72
3. Khaled Al-Eid	SAU	Khashm Al-Aan	4	4	44.86
4. Lars Nieberg	GER	Esprit Frh	8		
5. Ludo Philippaerts	BEL	Otterongo	8		
6. André Johannpeter	BRA	Calei	8		
7. Marcus Ehning	GER	For Pleasure	8		
8. Otto Becker	GER	Cento	8		

Ranked number one in the world, Rodrigo Pessoa of Brazil had dominated show jumping since the last Olympics. In April 2000, he became the first rider in the 22-year history of the World Cup Final to win three titles in a row. In Sydney he recorded the best score of the qualifying round and then was one of four contestants to ride a perfect course in the first round of the final. But in the second half of the final, Pessoa's horse, Baloubet du Rouet, unexpectedly refused three times at the seventh of ten obstacles and was eliminated. This left two Dutchmen, Jeroen Dubbeldam and Albert Voorn, tied for first place with Khaled Al-Eid of Saudi Arabia. Dubbeldam won the jump-off by riding clear, while the other two each knocked down a rail. The final was held in the midst of disruptive high winds that forced volunteers to hold down some of the top rails until a rider approached.

2004 Athens-Markopoulo C: 77, N: 27, D: 8.27.

		HORSE	FAULTS	JUMP-OFF
1. Rodrigo Pessoa	BRA	Baloubet du Rouet	8	4 49.42
2. Chris Kappler	USA	Royal Kaliber	8	ret
3. Marco Kutscher	GER	Montender	9	
4. Kevin Babington	IRL	Carling King	12	
4. Rolf-Göran Bengtsson	SWE	Mac Kinley	12	
4. Dirk Demeersmann	BEL	Clinton	12	
4. Peder Fredricsson	SWE	Magic Bengtsson	12	
4. Ludo Philippaerts	BEL	Parco	12	
4. Robert Smith	GBR	Mr Springfield	12	

DISQ (Drugs): Cian O'Connor (IRL)/Waterford Crystal 0

After 24-year-old Cian O'Connor was awarded the gold medal, an unusual scandal developed when his horse, Waterford Crystal, tested positive for banned sedatives in his urine. O'Connor and his veterinary surgeon, James Sheeran, claimed that the positive test came from medicine given to Waterford Crystal during treatment of a minor fetlock injury sustained in July, five weeks before the Olympic event, and that the substance should have passed out of the horse's system by then. According to FEI rules, even banned substances are allowed outside of competition.

O'Connor requested that a test of Waterford Crystal's backup urine sample be conducted at the Horseracing Forensic Laboratory in England, where his technician could witness the test. On October 21 the B sample was sent by courier from the International Equestrian Federation lab in Paris. It never arrived. A police investigation learned later that the sample had been stolen by someone posing as a lab staff member, who convinced the courier to let him sign for the package in the driveway rather than inside the office. The lab only realized the theft several days later.

On November 1, burglars ransacked the Irish Equestrian Federation headquarters, stealing documents relating to another of O'Connor's horses, ABC Landliebe, who had tested positive six months previously in Rome for the same banned substances as Waterford Crystal. Police reports suggested that the break-in was staged to protect someone in the office who was leaking the information to news media, but nobody was ever linked to the break-in.

Cian O'Connor on Waterford Crystal, 2004
Waterford Crystal was the first horse to fail a doping test.

As it turned out, both blood and urine samples had been taken from Waterford Crystal, and the backup blood sample had stayed in Paris. It was subsequently sent to a lab in New York and tested under armed guard. The test showed minute amounts of Fluphenazine and Zuclopenthixol, drugs used to treat humans suffering schizophrenia and known doping substances used to calm down nervous horses. Because of the second positive test, O'Connor was stripped of his gold medal. Though he faced a ban of up to two years for the doping violation, the FEI ruled that the drugs had not been administered to improve performance and gave O'Connor a light three-month ban.

The gold medal passed to 34-year-old Rodrigo Pessoa, son of Brazilian equestrian legend Nelson Pessoa, who earned eight faults in the first round of the final and followed with a perfect second round. Pessoa faced Kappler in a jump-off, during which Kappler's horse, Royal Kaliber, injured a front leg tendon, forcing Kappler to stop. The horse was eventually put to death, one of three horses who incurred tendon injuries at the Markopoulo Olympic Equestrian Centre during the Athens Games.

2008 Beijing-Hong Kong C: 77, N: 29, D: 8.21.

		HORSE	FAULTS	JUMP-OFF	
1. Eric Lamaze	CAN	Hickstead	0	0	38.39
2. Rolf-Göran Bengtsson	SWE	Ninja	0	4	38.39
3. Beezie Madden	USA	Alpapillon-Armanie	4	0	35.25
4. Meredith Michaels-Beerbaum	GER	Shutterfly	4	0	35.37
6. McLain Ward	USA	Sapphire	4	4	35.39
7. Ludger Beerbaum	GER	All Inclusive	4	4	36.16
8. Marc Houtzager	HOL	Opium	4	8	36.77

DISQ (Drugs): Rodrigo Pessoa/Rufus (BRA) 4/4 37.04

Eric Lamaze and 2004 team silver medalist Rolf-Göran Bengtsson both completed their two final runs without a penalty, so the gold medal was decided by a jump-off. Lamaze delivered another clean run, while Bengtsson knocked down the final rail, incurring four penalty points and dropping to second place.

Beezie Madden, who had won a team gold medal in 2004, earned bronze in a jump-off against six other riders, jumping clean in 35.25 seconds and beating 2007 European champion Meredith Michaels-Beerbaum by a tenth of a second. Madden saved time by taking a tight turn and jumping over a decorative island of shrubbery that was not part of the actual course.

Lamaze overcame a difficult background to reach the Beijing Games. Raised in Montreal by an alcoholic grandmother after his mother was jailed for drug trafficking, he developed a serious substance abuse problem himself as a teenager and dropped out of school in the seventh grade. His life began to turn round after he got a job in a stable, and he gradually worked his way up to riding. Lamaze missed both the 1996 and 2000 Olympics, each time for testing positive for cocaine. His lawyers managed to successfully appeal two separate lifetime bans and Lamaze was deemed eligible for the Canadian team for the Beijing Olympics.

Rodrigo Pessoa was disqualified and banned for 4½ months after his horse tested positive for nonivamide, a prohibited pain-reliever.

JUMPING (PRIX DES NATIONS), TEAM

The team jumping final consists of two rounds contested on the same course. The course must be between 600 and 800 meters long and include 12 to 15 obstacles and a water jump. Ties for medal placings are decided by a jump-off over a course of 350 to 450 meters with six obstacles. If a tie still exists, the faster team is declared the winner. Each team consists of three or four riders and horses, but only the best three scores in each round are used to determine the team score. Thus, a rider's score may count in one round but not in the other. Beginning in 1992, only those team members whose scores counted in at least one round were awarded medals.

1896–1908 not held

1912 Stockholm T: 6, N: 6, D: 7.17.

	HORSE	POINTS	TOTAL PTS.
1. SWE			545
Gustaf Kilman	Gatan	180	
Hans von Rosen	Lord Iron	177	
Fredrik Rosencrantz	Drabant	171	
2. FRA			538
Michel d'Astafort	Amazone	185	
Jean Cariou	Mignon	182	
Bernard Meyer	Allons-y	171	
3. GER			530
Sigismund Freyer	Ultimus	181	
Wilhelm, Graf von Hohenau	Pretty Girl	177	
Ernst Hubertus Deloch	Hubertus	172	
4. USA			527
John Montgomery	Deceive	180	
Guy Henry	Chisel	174	
Benjamin Lear	Poppy	173	
5. RUS			520
Aleksandr Rodzianko	Eros	176	
Aleksei Selikhov	Tugela	172	
Michail Plechkov	Yvette	172	
6. BEL			510
Emanuel de Blommaert de Soye	Clonmore	188	
Gaston de Trannoy	Capricieux	162	
Paul Covert	La Sioute	160	

1920 Antwerp T: 5, N: 5, D: 9.12.

	HORSE	FAULTS	TOTAL PTS.
1. SWE			14.00
Claës König	Tresor	2	
Daniel Norling	Eros II	6	
Hans von Rosen	Poor Boy	6	
2. BEL			16.25
Henri Laame	Biscuit	2.75	
André Coumans	Lisette	5.25	
Herman de Gaiffier d'Hestroy	Miss	8.25	
3. ITA			18.75
Ettore Caffaratti	Traditore	1.50	
Alessandro Alvisi	Raggio di Sole	6.25	
Giulio Cacciandra	Fortunello	11	
4. FRA			34.75
Auguste de Laissardière	Othello	7.50	
Henri Horment	Dignité	13.25	
Théophile Carbon	Incas	14	
5. USA			42.00
Harry Chamberlin	Nigra	9	
Karl Greenwald	Moses	12	
Vincent Erwin	Joffre	21	

1924 Paris T: 11, N: 11, D: 7.27.

	HORSE	FAULTS	TOTAL PTS.
1. SWE			42.25
Åke Thelning	Loke	12.00	
Axel Ståhle	Cecil	12.25	
Åge Lundström	Anvers	18.00	
2. SWI			50.00
Alphonse Gemuseus	Lucette	6.00	
Werner Stüber	Girandole	20.00	
Hans Bühler	Sailor Boy	24.00	

3. POR			53.00
António Borges de Almeida	Reginald	12.00	
Hélder de Souza Martins	Avro	19.00	
José Mousinho do Albuquerque	Hetrugo	22.00	
4. BEL			57.00
Nicolas Leroy	Vif Argent	14.75	
Jacques Misonne	Torino	19.50	
Gaston Mesmaekors	As de Pique	22.75	
5. ITA			57.50
Tommaso Lequio di Assaba	Trebecco	8.75	
Leone Valle	Struffo	20.00	
Alessandro Alvisi	Grey Fo	28.75	
6. POL			58.50
Adam Królikiewicz	Picador	10.00	
Karol Rómmel	Faworyt	18.00	
Zdzislaw Dziadulski	Zefer	30.50	
7. GBR			65.75
Philip Bowden-Smith	Billy Boy	10.50	
Capel Brunker	Peter	25.50	
Geoffrey Brooke	Daddy Long Legs	29.75	
8. SPA			73.75
José Álvarez de las Asturias Bohórquez y Goyeneche (Marqués de los Trujillos)	Acabado	18.00	
Nemesio Martínez Hombre	Zapatillero	22.00	
José Navarro Morenés	Grande Couronne	33.75	

1928 Amsterdam T: 15, N: 15, D: 8.12.

	HORSE	FAULTS	TOTAL PTS.
1. SPA			4
José Navarro Morenés	Zapatazo	0	
José Álvarez de las Asturias Bohórquez y Goyeneche (Marqués de los Trujillos)	Zalamero	2	
Julio García Fernández	Revistada	2	
2. POL			8
Kazimierz Gzowski	Mylord	0	
Kazimierz Szosland	Ali	2	
Michal Antoniewicz	Readgleadt	6	
3. SWE			10
Karl Hansen	Gerold	0	
Carl Björnstjerna	Kornett	2	
Ernst Hallberg	Loke	8	
4. FRA			12
Pierre Bertran de Balanda	Papillon	0	
Jacques Couderc de Fonlongue	Vangerville	4	
Pierre Clavé	Le Trouvère	8	
4. ITA			12
Francesco Forquet	Capineca	0	
Alessandro Bettoni-Cazzago	Aladino	6	
Tommaso Lequio di Assaba	Trebecco	6	
4. POR			12
Luiz Ivens Ferraz	Marco Visconti	4	
Henrique de Sousa Martins	Avro	4	
José Mousinho de Albuquerque	Hebraico	4	
7. GER			14
Eduard Krüger	Donauwelle	2	
Richard Sahla	Correggio	4	
Carl Friedrich, Freiherr von Langen-Parow	Falkner	8	
8. SWI			18
Charles Kuhn	Pepita	0	
Alphonse Gemuseus	Lucette	2	
Pierre do Muralt	Notas	16	

1932 Los Angeles T: 3, N: 3, D: 8.14.

No nation completed the course with three riders.

1936 Berlin T: 18, N: 18, D: 8.16.

	HORSE	FAULTS	TOTAL PTS.
1. GER			44.00
Kurt Hasse	Tora	4.00	
Marten von Barnekow	Nordland	20.00	
Heinz Brandt	Alchimist	20.00	
2. HOL			51.50
Johan Jacob Greter	Ernica	12.00	
Jan Adrianus de Bruine	Trixie	15.00	
Henri Louis van Schaik	Santa Bell	24.50	
3. POR			56.00
José Beltrão	Biscuit	12.00	
Domingos António de Sousa Coutinho (Marqués do Funchal)	Merle Blanc	20.00	
Luiz Mena e Silva	Faussette	24.00	
4. USA			72.50
Carl Raguse	Dakota	8.00	
William Bradford	Don	27.00	
Cornelius Jadwin	Ugly	37.50	
5. SWI			74.50
Arnold Mettler	Durmitor	15.00	
Jürg Fehr	Corona	29.00	
Max Iklé	Exile	30.50	
6. JPN			75.00
Manabu Iwahashi	Falaise	15.25	
Takeichi Nishi	Uranus	20.75	
Hirotsugu Inanami	Asafuji	39.00	
7. FRA			75.25
Xavier Bizard	Bagatelle	12.00	
Maurice Gudin de Vallerin	Ecuyère	12.00	
Jean de Tilière	Adriano	51.25	

1948 London T: 14, N: 14, D: 8.14.

	HORSE	FAULTS	TOTAL PTS.
1. MEX			34.25
Humberto Mariles Cortés	Arete	6.25	
Rubén Uriza Castro	Harvey	8.00	
Alberto Valdés Ramos	Chihuchoc	20.00	
2. SPA			56.50
Jaime García Cruz	Bizarro	12.00	
José Navarro Morenés	Quorum	20.00	
Marcelino Gavilán y Ponce de León	Forajido	24.50	
3. GBR			67.00
Henry Llewellyn	Foxhunter	16.00	
Henry Nicoll	Kilgeddin	16.00	
Arthur Carr	Monty	35.00	

The course was so difficult that only three of the 14 teams managed to finish intact.

1952 Helsinki T: 15, N: 15, D: 8.3.

	HORSE	FAULTS	TOTAL PTS.
1. GBR			40.75
Wilfred White	Nizefella	8.00	
Douglas Stewart	Aherlow	16.00	
Henry Llewellyn	Foxhunter	16.75	
2. CHI			45.75
Oscar Cristi	Bambi	8.00	
César Mendoza	Pillán	12.00	
Ricardo Echeverría	Lindo Peal	25.75	
3. USA			52.25
William Steinkraus	Hollandia	13.25	
Arthur John McCashin	Miss Budweiser	16.00	
John Russell	Democrat	23.00	
4. BRA			56.50
Eloi Massey Oliveira de Menezes	Bigua	8.00	
Renyldo Guimaraes Ferreira	Bibelot	20.50	
Alvaro Dias de Toledo	Eldorado	28.00	
5. FRA			59.00
Pierre Jonquères d'Oriola	Ali Baba	8.00	
Bertran Pernot du Breuil	Tourbillon	20.00	
Jean-François d'Orgeix	Arlequin D.	31.00	
6. GER			60.00
Fritz Thiedemann	Meteor	8.00	
Georg Höltig	Fink	20.00	
Hans-Hermann Evers	Baden	32.00	
7. ARG			60.75
Sergio Dellacha Chiaron	Santa Fe	12.00	
Argentino Molinuevo	Discutido	12.00	
Julio Sagasta	Don Juan	36.75	
8. POR			64.00
João Craveiro Lopes	Raso	20.00	
Henrique Alves Calado	Caramulo	20.00	
José Alves Carvalhosa	Mondina	24.00	

It was the last event of the last day of the Helsinki Olympics. The British team had failed to win a single event in any sport and were on the verge of being shut out of the gold for the first time since 1904—before the days of official national teams. In the first round of the team jumping final, the British trio of Wilf White, Duggie Stewart, and Harry Llewellyn had picked up 28.75 faults, including 16.75 by Llewellyn alone, and they were buried back in fifth place. But both White and Stewart knocked over only one fence each and Britain was back in the game. If Llewellyn and his horse, Foxhunter, could complete the course with no more than one mistake, they would save the day for their nation. In fact, they rode a completely clear round and Great Britain had its gold medal. The dramatic nature of the final ride created a national hero: Foxhunter. White and Stewart received a little bit of credit and Llewellyn a bit more, but it was the horse who became a media star. He was inundated with fan letters and gifts, and when a rumor spread that Foxhunter had learned to sign his own name, Llewellyn was flooded with requests for Foxhunter's autograph. After Foxhunter died, his skeleton was preserved by the Royal College of Veterinary Surgeons.

1956 Stockholm T: 20, N: 20, D: 6.16.

	HORSE	FAULTS	TOTAL PTS.
1. GER			40.00
Hans-Günter Winkler	Halla	4.00	
Fritz Thiedemann	Meteor	12.00	
Alfons Lütke-Westhues	Ala	24.00	
2. ITA			66.00
Raimondo D'Inzeo	Merano	8.00	
Piero D'Inzeo	Uruguay	11.00	
Salvatore Oppes	Pagoro	47.00	
3. GBR			69.00
Wilfred White	Nizefella	12.00	
Patricia Smythe	Flanagan	21.00	
Peter Robeson	Scorchin	36.00	
4. ARG			99.50
Carlos César D'Elia	Discutido	19.00	
Pedro Mayorga	Coriolano	32.00	
Naldo Dasso	Ramito	48.50	
5. USA			104.50
Hugh Wiley	Trail Guide	24.00	
William Steinkraus	Night Owl	28.00	
Frank Chapot	Belair	52.25	
6. SPA			117.25
Carlos López Quesada	Tapatio	27.75	
Francisco Goyoaga	Fahnenkönig	28.00	
Carlos Figueroa Castillejo	Gracieux	61.50	
7. IRL			131.25
Kevin Barry	Ballyneety	35.00	
William Ringrose	Liffey Vale	44.00	
Patrick Kiernan	Ballynonty	52.25	
8. FRA			154.50
Pierre Jonquères d'Oriola	Voulotte	15.00	
Bernard Jevardat de Fombelle	Doria	52.75	
Georges Calmon	Virtuoso	86.75	

Pat Smythe of Great Britain and Brigitte Schockaert of Belgium were the first women to compete in Olympic jumping.

1960 Rome T: 18, N: 18, 9.11.

	HORSE	FAULTS	TOTAL PTS.
1. GER			46.50
Hans-Günter Winkler	Halla	13.25	
Fritz Thiedemann	Meteor	16.00	
Alwin Schockemöhle	Ferdl	17.25	
2. USA			66.00
Frank Chapot	Trail Guide	20.00	
William Steinkraus	Ksar d'Esprit	21.50	
George Morris	Sinjon	24.50	
3. ITA			80.50
Raimondo D'Inzeo	Posillipo	8.00	
Piero D'Inzeo	The Rock	32.00	
Antonio Oppes	The Scholar	40.50	
4. EGY			135.50
Gamal Harres	Nefertiti	24.00	
Mohammed Zaki	Artos	48.00	
Alwi Gazi	Mabrouk	63.50	
5. FRA			168.75
Bernard Jevardat de Fombelle	Buffalo	32.50	
Max Fresson	Grand Veneur	50.25	
Pierre Jonquères d'Oriola	Eclair au Chocolat	86.00	

6. ROM			175.00
Vasile Pinciu	Barsan	41.50	
Virgil Bărbuceanu	Robot	57.75	
Gheorghe Langa	Rubin	75.75	

1964 Tokyo T: 14, N: 14, D: 10.24.

	HORSE	FAULTS	TOTAL PTS.
1. GER			68.50
Hermann Schridde	Dozent	13.75	
Kurt Jarasinski	Torro	22.25	
Hans-Günter Winkler	Fidelitas	32.50	
2. FRA			77.75
Pierre Jonquères d'Oriola	Lutteur	9.00	
Janou Lefebvre	Kenavo D	32.00	
Guy Lefrant	Monsieur de Littry	36.75	
3. ITA			88.50
Piero D'Inzeo	Sunbeam	24.50	
Raimondo D'Inzeo	Posillipo	28.00	
Graziano Mancinelli	Rockette	36.00	
4. GBR			97.25
Peter Robeson	Firecrest	16.00	
David Broome	Jacopo	37.00	
David Barker	North Flight	44.25	
5. ARG			101.00
Jorge Antonio Cánaves	Confinado	29.50	
Hugo Arrambide	Chimbote	34.25	
Carlos César D'Elia	Popin	37.25	
6. USA			107.00
Frank Chapot	San Lucas	20.50	
Kathyrn Kusner	Untouchable	29.75	
Mary Mairs	Tomboy	56.75	
7. AUS			109.00
Thomas Fahey	Bonvale	16.00	
Bridget Macintyre	Coronation	39.50	
Kevin Bacon	Ocean Foam	53.50	
8. SPA			118.75
Francis Goyoaga Caamaño	Kif-Kif B.	35.00	
Enrique Martínez de Vallejo	Eolo IV	40.00	
Manglano Antonio Queipo de Llano y Acuña	Infernal	43.75	

1968 Mexico City T: 15, N: 15, D: 10.27.

	HORSE	FAULTS	TOTAL PTS.
1. CAN			102.75
James Elder	The Immigrant	27.25	
James Day	Canadian Club	36.00	
Thomas Gayford	Big Dee	39.50	
2. FRA			110.50
Janou Lefebvre	Rocket	29.75	
Marcel Rozier	Quo vadis	33.50	
Pierre Jonquères d'Oriola	Nagir	47.25	
3. GER			117.25
Alwin Schockemöhle	Donald Rex	18.75	
Hans-Günter Winkler	Enigk	28.25	
Hermann Schridde	Dozent	70.25	
4. USA			117.50
Frank Chapot	San Lucas	25.00	
Kathryn Kusner	Untouchable	44.50	
Mary Chapot	White Lightning	48.00	
5. ITA			129.25
Raimondo D'Inzeo	Bellevue	24.25	
Piero D'Inzeo	Fidux	47.50	
Graziano Mancinelli	Donerailo	57.50	
6. SWI			136.75
Paul Weier	Satan	36.75	
Monica Bachmann	Erbach	49.50	
Arthur Blickenstorfer	Marianka	50.50	
7. BRA			138.00
Nelson Pessoa	Pass-Op	38.75	
Lucia Faria	Rush du Camp	44.75	
José Reynoso	Cantal	54.50	
8. GBR			159.50
David Broome	Mr. Softee	20.00	
R. Harvey Smith	Madison Time	45.00	
Marion Coakes	Stroller	94.50	

1972 Munich T: 17, N: 17, D: 9.11.

	HORSE	FAULTS	TOTAL PTS.
1. GER			32.00
Fritz Ligges	Robin	8.00	
Gerhard Wiltfang	Askan	12.00	
Hartwig Steenken	Simona	12.00	
Hans-Günter Winkler	Torphy	16.00	
2. USA			32.25
William Steinkraus	Main Spring	4.00	
Neal Shapiro	Sloopy	8.25	
Kathryn Kusner	Fleet Apple	32.00	
Frank Chapot	White Lightning	36.00	
3. ITA			48.00
Vittorio Orlandi	Fulmer Feather	8.00	
Raimondo D'Inzeo	Fiorello II	12.00	
Graziano Mancinelli	Ambassador	28.00	
Piero D'Inzeo	Easter Light	135.25	
4. GBR			51.00
Michael Saywell	Hideaway	16.00	
R. Harvey Smith	Summertime	20.00	
David Broome	Manhaton VI	20.00	
Ann Moore	Psalm	32.00	
5. SWI			61.25
Monica Weier	Erbach	17.75	
Paul Weier	Wulf	20.00	
Max Hauri	Haiti	23.50	
Hermann von Siebenthal	Royal Havana	135.25	
6. CAN			64.00
James Elder	Houdini	8.00	
James Day	Happy Fellow	24.00	
Terrance Miller	Le Dauphin	35.00	
Ian Millar	Shoeman	44.00	
7. SPA			66.00
Alfonso Segovia	Tic Tac	19.00	
Enrique Martínez Vallejo	Val de Loire	19.00	
Luis Álvarez Cervera	Acorn	28.00	
Luis Jaime Carvajal Salas (Duque do Aveyro)	Sunday Beau	115.25	
8. ARG			121.00
Hugo Arrambide	Camalote	27.00	
Roberto Tagle	Simple	46.00	
Jorge Llambi	Okey Amigo	48.00	
Argentino Molinuevo	Abracadabra	135.25	

Beginning in 1972, team totals were determined by adding the three best scores for each round rather than the three best scores for both rounds combined.

1976 Montreal T: 14, N: 14, D: 8.1.

	HORSE	FAULTS	TOTAL PTS.
1. FRA			40.00
Hubert Parot	Rivage	12.00	
Marcel Rozier	Bayard de Maupas	12.00	
Marc Roguet	Belle de Mars	24.00	
Michel Rocho	Un Espoir	32.00	
2. GER			44.00
Alwin Schockemöhle	Warwick Rex	12.00	
Hans-Günter Winkler	Torphy	16.00	
Sönke Sönksen	Keep	20.00	
Paul Schockemöhle	Agent	24.00	
3. BEL			63.00
Eric Wauters	Gute Sitte	15.00	
François Mathy	Gal Luron	20.00	
Edgar Gupper	Le Champion	28.00	
Stanny van Paeschen	Porsche	36.00	
4. USA			64.00
Frank Chapot	Viscount	16.00	
Robert Ridland	South Side	20.00	
William Brown	Sandsablaze	28.00	
Michael Matz	Grande	40.00	
5. CAN			64.50
James Day	Sympatico	20.00	
Michel Vaillancourt	Branch County	20.50	
Ian Millar	Countdown	27.50	
James Elder	Raffles II	36.00	
6. SPA			71.00
Luis Álvarez Cervera	Acorne	16.00	
Alfonso Segovia	Val de Loire	23.00	
José Rosillo	Agamenon	36.00	
Eduardo Amorós Lluch	Limited Edition	39.00	
7. GBR			76.00
Deborah Johnsey	Moxy	24.00	
Rowland Fernyhough	Bouncer	31.00	
Peter Robeson	Law Court	32.00	
Graham Fletcher	Hideaway	36.00	
8. MEX			76.25
Fernando Hernández	Fascination	24.00	
Fernando Senderos	Jet Run	24.00	
Luis Razo	Pueblo	28.50	
Carlos Aguirre	Consejero	38.25	

1980 Moscow T: 6, N: 6, D: 7.29.

	HORSE	FAULTS	TOTAL PTS.
1. SOV			20.25
Vyacheslav Chukanov	Gepatit	4.00	
Viktor Pohanovsky	Topky	8.25	
Viktor Asmayev	Reis	11.25	
Nikolai Korolkov	Espadron	12.00	
2. POL			56.00
Jan Kowalczyk	Artemor	12.00	
Wiesław Hartman	Norton	24.00	
Marian Kozicki	Bremen	37.50	
Janusz Bobik	Szampan	40.00	
3. MEX			59.75
Joaquín Pérez Heras	Alymony	12.00	
Alberto Valdés Lacarra	Lady Mirka	20.75	
Gerardo Tazzer Valencia	Caribe	31.75	
Jesús Gómez Portugal	Massacre	35.25	
4. HUN			124.00
Barnabás Hevesy	Bohem	28.00	
Ferenc Krucsó	Vadrozsa	32.00	
József Varró	Gambrinusz	97.75	
András Balogi	Artemis	101.75	
5. ROM			150.50
Alexandru Bozan	Prejmer	43.75	
Dania Popescu	Sonor	53.00	
Dumitru Velicu	Fudul	73.75	
Ioan Popa	Licurici	95.50	
6. BUL			159.50
Nikola Dimitrov	Vals	46.75	
Dimitar Ghenov	Makbet	56.00	
Boris Pavlov	Monblan	60.75	
Hristo Katchov	Povdo	73.00	

The surprise winners of the Rotterdam Show Jumping Festival were the Canadians. Great Britain was second and Austria was third.

1984 Los Angeles-Arcadia T: 15, N: 15, D: 8.7.

	HORSE	FAULTS	TOTAL PTS.
1. USA			12.00
Joe Fargis	Touch of Class	0	
Conrad Homfeld	Abdullah	8.00	
Leslie Burr	Albany	12.00	
Melanie Smith	Calypso	with	
2. GBR			36.75
Michael Whitaker	Overton Amanda	8.00	
John Whitaker	Ryan's Son	20.75	
Steven Smith	Shining Example	27.00	
Timothy Grubb	Linky	28.25	
3. GER			39.25
Paul Schockemöhle	Deister	8.00	
Peter Luther	Livius	12.00	
Franke Sloothaak	Farmer	19.25	
Fritz Ligges	Ramzes	29.00	
4. CAN			40.00
Ian Millar	Big Ben	12.00	
Hugh Graham	Elrond	16.00	
James Elder	Shawline	20.00	
Mario Deslauriers	Aramis	24.50	
5. SWI			41.00
Heidi Robbiani	Jessica V	5.00	
Bruno Candrian	Slygof	12.00	
Philippe Guerdat	Pybalia	32.00	
Willi Melliger	Van Gogh	32.00	
6. FRA			49.75
Philippe Rozier	Jiva	20.00	
Frédéric Cottier	Flambeau C	20.00	
Eric Navet	J't'Adore	21.75	
Pierre Durand	Jappeloup	elim	
7. SPA			52.00
Alberto Honrubia	Kaoua	8.00	
Luis Álvarez Cervera	Jexico De Park	11.00	
Rutherford Latham	Idaho E	33.00	
Luis Astolfi	Feinschnitt "Z"	56.50	
8. ITA			75.25
Giorgio Nuti	Impedoumi	16.00	
Filippo Moyersoen	Adam II	16.00	
Graziano Mancinelli	Ideal de la Haye	20.00	
Bruno Scolari	Joyau d'Or	39.25	

1988 Seoul T: 16, N: 16, D: 9.28.

	HORSE	FAULTS	TOTAL PTS.
1. GER			17.25
Ludger Beerbaum	The Freak	4.25	
Wolfgang Brinkmann	Pedro	10.00	
Dirk Hafemeister	Orchidee	12.00	
Franke Sloothaak	Walzerkönig	with	

2. USA			20.50
Joe Fargis	Mill Pearl	4.25	
Greg Best	Gem Twist	8.00	
Lisa Jacquin	For the Moment	8.25	
Anne Kursinski	Starman	16.00	
3. FRA			27.50
Pierre Durand	Jappeloup	5.00	
Michel Robert	Pequignet La Fayette	10.00	
Frédéric Cottier	Flambeau	16.00	
Hubert Bourdy	Morgat	16.50	
4. CAN			28.75
Ian Millar	Big Ben	8.00	
Mario Deslauriers	Box Car Willie	12.00	
Lisa Carlsen	Kahlua	16.00	
Laura Tidball-Balisky	Lavendel	22.75	
5. HOL			32.25
Wout-Jan van der Schans	Treffer	8.25	
Robbertus Ehrens	Sunrise	12.00	
Johannes "Jan" Tops	Doreen	16.00	
Jos Lansink	Felix	20.00	
6. GBR			40.00
Nicholas Skelton	Apollo	12.00	
David Broome	Countryman	16.00	
Malcolm Pyrah	Anglezarke	16.00	
Joseph Turi	Vital	20.00	
7. SWI			44.25
Markus Fuchs	Shandor II	12.00	
Thomas Fuchs	Diners Dollar Girl	12.25	
Philippe Guerdat	Lanciano II	20.00	
Walter Gabathuler	Jogger	36.25	
8. BRA			75.00
Christina Johannpeter	Société	25.50	
André Johannpeter	Heartbreaker	27.50	
Vitor Teixeira	Going	30.50	
Paulo Stewart	Platon	42.00	
8. SPA			75.00
Alfredo Fernández Durán	Kaoua	21.00	
Pedro Sanchez Aleman	Nuit de Tourelles	28.25	
Juan García Trevijano	Tirol	32.75	
Luis Álvarez Cervera	Mirage Mexicain	45.00	

1992 Barcelona T: 19, N: 19, D: 8.4.

	HORSE	FAULTS	TOTAL PTS.
1. HOL			12.00
Jos Lansink	Egano	0	
Piet Raymakers	Ratina Z	4.00	
Johannes "Jan" Tops	Top Gun	8.00	
2. AUT			16.75
Thomas Frühmann	Genius	0	
Hugo Simon	Apricot D	4.00	
Jörg Münzner	Graf Grande	12.75	
3. FRA			24.75
Hervé Godignon	Quidam de Revel	4.75	
Hubert Bourdy	Razzia du Poncel	12.00	
Eric Navet	Quito de Baussy	16.00	
Michel Robert	Nonix	20.25	
4. SPA			25.50
Luis Astolfi	Fino	4.00	
Luis Álvarez Cervero	Let's Go B'92	5.50	
Enrique Sarasola Marulanda	Minstrel	16.00	
5. SWI			28.00
Lesley McNaught-Mändli	Pirol B	8.00	
Thomas Fuchs	Dylano	8.00	
Markus Fuchs	Shandor II	12.00	
5. USA			28.00
Michael Matz	Heisman	4.00	
Lisa Jacquin	For the Moment	8.00	
Norman Dello Joio	Irish	20.00	
Anne Kursinski	Cannonball	elim	
7. GBR			28.75
John Whitaker	Milton	4.00	
Michael Whitaker	Monsanta	8.00	
Timothy Grubb	Denizen	17.00	
Nick Skelton	Dollar Girl	elim	
8. SWE			37.00
Peter Eriksson	Moritz	0	
Maria Gretzer	Marcoville	13.00	
Ulrika Hedin	Lipton	24.00	

The one-two finish by the Dutch and Austrian teams came as a shock. Neither country had ever earned medals in this event before and Austria's best Olympic performance prior to Barcelona was 11th, in 1976.

1996 Atlanta-Conyers T: 19, N: 19, D: 8.1.

	HORSE	FAULTS	TOTAL PTS.
1. GER			1.75
Ludger Beerbaum	Ratina	0.25	
Ulrich Kirchhoff	Jus de Pommes	1.50	
Lars Nieberg	For Pleasure	12.00	
Franke Sloothaak	Joly	60.25	
2. USA			12.00
Peter Leone	Legato	4.00	
Anne Kursinski	Eros	8.00	
Michael Matz	Rhum	8.00	
Leslie Burr Howard	Extreme	14.00	
3. BRA			17.25
Rodrigo Pessoa	Tomboy	0.75	
Alvaro Miranda Neto	Aspen	8.25	
Luiz Felipe Azevedo	Cassiana	12.00	
André Johannpeter	Calei	12.25	
4. FRA			20.25
Hervé Godignon	Viking du Tillard	4.25	
Alexandra Ledermann	Rochet M	8.00	
Roger-Yves Bost	Souviens Toi	8.00	
Patrice Delaveau	Roxane de Gruchy	16.00	
5. SPA			-29.75
Fernando Sarasola	Ennio	0.25	
Alejandro Jordá	Hernando du Sablon	13.50	
Rutherford Latham	Sourire d'Aze	16.00	
Pedro Sánchez Alemán	Riccardo	20.00	
6. SWI			32.00
Willi Melliger	Calvaro	12.00	
Beat Mandli	City Banking	12.00	
Urs Fäh	Jeremia	12.00	
Markus Fuchs	Adelfos	24.00	
7. HOL			32.25
Johannes "Jan" Tops	Top Gun	4.25	
Jozef Lansink	Carthago	16.00	
Emile Hendrix	Finesse	16.00	
Bert Romp	Samantha	20.00	
8. IRL			34.50
Peter Charles	Beneton	4.00	
Jessica Chesney	Diamond Exchange	12.50	
Eddie Macken	Schalkhaar	18.00	

The German team got off to a rough start when their first rider, world champion Franke Sloothaak, fell and cut his wrist so badly that he needed stiches. Unfazed, the three other Germans were almost flawless. In fact, Sloothaak himself came back for the second round and rode clear. The team from Argentina, which placed 17th, was later disqualified when it was learned that, prior to coming to Atlanta, they had been forcing their horses to practice by jumping over obstacles topped with wire and nails.

Michael Matz of the US team had gained fame seven years earlier when, on July 19,1989, he and his wife, D.D., survived a plane crash in Sioux City, Iowa, that killed 112 people. After escaping the wreckage, Matz went back and saved two children.

2000 Sydney T: 14, N: 14, D: 9.28

	HORSE	FAULTS	TOTAL PTS.
1. GER			15.00
Marcus Ehning	For Pleasure	7.00	
Lars Nieberg	Esprit Frh	8.00	
Ludger Beerbaum	Goldfever 3	36.25	
2. SWI			16.00
Markus Fuchs	Tinka's Boy	8.00	
Beat Mändli	Pozitano	8.00	
Lesley McNaught-Mändli	Dulf	23.50	
3. BRA			24.00
Luis Felipe De Azevedo	Ralph	8.00	
Alvero Neto Miranda	Aspen	16.00	
Andre Johannpeter	Calei	24.00	
4. FRA			24.00
Thierry Pomel	Thor des Chaînes	8.00	
Philippe Rozier	Barbarian	16.00	
Patrice Delaveau	Caucalis	72.50	
5. HOL			32.00
Jeroen Dubbeldam	Sjiem	12.00	
Jes Lansink	Carthago Z	12.00	
Johannes "Jan" Tops	Roofs	25.25	
6. USA			36.00
Laura Kraut	Liberty	12.00	
Lauren Hough	Clasiko	16.00	
Nona Garson	Rhythmical	36.00	
7. SWE			36.75
Lisen Bratt	Casanova	16.00	
Maria Gretzer	Feliciano	20.25	
Malin Birgitta Baryard	Butterfly Flip	20.75	
8. GBR			40.50
Michael Whitaker	Prince of Wales	16.00	
Geoff Billington	It's Otto	20.75	
Carl Edwards	Bit More Candy	32.50	

The Germans had won every major competition since the last Olympics and, although it could hardly have been closer, they continued their victory streak in Sydney. Although his score was dropped in both rounds, Ludger Beerbaum took home a gold medal for the fourth straight Olympics.

2004 Athens-Markopoulo T: 27, N: 27, D: 8.24.

		HORSE	FAULTS	TOTAL PTS.	JUMP-OFF
1. USA				20	131.09
	Beezie Madden	Authentic	0		
	Chris Kappler	Royal Kaliber	4		
	McLain Ward	Sapphire	16		
2. SWE				20	138.48
	Malin Birgitta Baryard	Butterfly Flip	4		
	Rolf-Göran Bengtsson	Mac Kinley	0		
	Peter Eriksson	Cardento	4		
	Peder Fredricsson	Magic Bengtsson	12		
3. GER				21	
	Christian Ahlmann	Coster	12		
	Otto Becker	Cento	9		
	Marco Kutscher	Montender	0		
4. HOL				24	
	Gert-Jan Bruggink	Joel	4		
	Gerco Bernardus Schröder	Monaco	4		
	Wim Schröder	Montreal	4		
	Leopold van Asten	Fleche Rouge	12		
5. SWI				26	
	Fabio Crotta	Mme Pompadour M	12		
	Markus Fuchs	Tinka's Boy	4		
	Steve Guerdat	Olympic	2		
	Christina Liebherr	No Mercy	8		
6. BEL				28	
	Dirk Demeersmann	Clinton	8		
	Jos Lansink	Cumano	0		
	Ludo Philippaerts	Parco	4		
	Stanny van Paesschen	O De Pomme	16		

7. ITA				44
	Roberto Arioldi	Dime De La Cour	10	
	Bruno Chimirri	Landknecht	13	
	Vincenzo Chimirri	Delfi Platiere	12	
	Juan Carlos García	Albin III	9	
8. KOR				51
	Sohn Bong-gak	Cim Christo	5	
	Woo Jung-ho	Seven Up	8	
	Joo Jung-hyun	Epsom Gesmeray	23	
	Hwang Soon-won	C. Chap	15	

DISQ (Drugs): Ludger Beerbaum (GER)/Goldfever
DISQ (Drugs): IRL
Cian O'Connor/Waterford Crystal (Drugs), 36
Marion Hughes/Fortunus, Jessica Chesney-Kuerten/Castle Forbes Maike, Kevin Babington/Carling King

In addition to Cian O'Connor's disqualification, which eliminated the Irish team, Ludger Beerbaum's horse, Goldfever, tested positive for the banned steroid betamethasone, eliminating his score and giving the gold medal to the United States. Even without Beerbaum, Germany's score was enough to earn them the bronze medals.

2008 Beijing-Hong Kong T: 16, N: 16, D: 8.18.

		HORSE	FAULTS	TOTAL PTS.	JUMP-OFF
1. USA			20	0	115.41
	McLain Ward	Sapphire	4		
	Laura Kraut Cedric		4		
	Beezie Madden	Alpapillon-Armanie	15		
	Will Simpson	Carlsson vom Dach	16		
2. CAN			20	4	76.67
	Ian Millar In Style		4		
	Mac Cone Ole		4		
	Eric Lamaze	Hickstead	18		
	Jill Henselwood	Special Ed	DNF		
3. SWI				30	
	Steve Guerdat	Jalisca Solier	9		
	Pius Schwizer	Nobless M	9		
	Niklaus Schurtenberger	Cantus	12		
	Christina Liebherr	No Mercy	27		
4. HOL				34	
	Marc Houtzager	Opium	6		
	Angelique Hoorn	O'Brien	12		
	Gerco Schröder	Monaco	16		
5. GBR				37	
	Ben Maher Rolette		4		
	Tim Stockdale	Corlato	12		
	Nick Skelton	Russel	21		
5. SWE				38	
	Rolf-Göran Bengtsson	Ninja	4		
	Peter Eriksson	Jaguar Mail	12		
	Lotta Schultz	Calibra II	25		
	Helena Lundbäck	Erbblume		39	
7. AUS			41		
	Edwina Alexander	Itot Du Chateau	0		
	Laurie Lever	Drossel Dan	20		
	Matt Williams	Leconte	21		
	Peter McMahon	Genoa	DNF		
8. NOR				49	
	Morten Djupvik	Casino	16		
	Stein Endresen	Le Beau	16		
	Geir Gulliksen	Cattani	17		

DISQ (Drugs): GER 34

Switzerland was tied with the US in the lead after the first round, but dropped to third in the final round. In fourth place after the first round, Canada moved up to tie the US with 20 penalties apiece, leading to a jump-off. The first three US riders, McLain Ward, Laura Kraut and Will Simpson all went clean in the jump-off; Canada, competing with just three riders after Marc Cone's horse Ole suffered an injury, were forced to settle for silver after Jill Henselwood dropped a pole.

The Canadian team featured 61-year-old Ian Millar, competing in his ninth Olympics (and equaling Austrian sailor Hubert Raudashchl's record for the most Olympic appearances). This was his first Olympic medal.

Norway originally placed third, however after the competition, Tony André Hansen of Norway was disqualified because his horse, Camino, tested positive for the banned pain reliever capsaicin, derived from chili peppers. Without his score, Norway dropped to eighth place, with Switzerland moving into third. Christian Ahlman of Germany was also disqualified when his horse, Cöster, tested positive for the same drug. Almost two years after the Olympics, in June 2010, a second German rider, Marco Kutscher, was disqualified for allowing his horse, Cornet Obolensky, to be treated with a banned substance, Lactanase, used to delay muscle fatigue. The Germans, who had originally tied for fourth place, were dropped from the standings.

DRESSAGE, INDIVIDUAL

Until knitting is added to the Olympic program, dressage will remain the least action-packed of Olympic events. The object of dressage is to demonstrate the horse's responsiveness to the rider's commands by taking the horse through a series of prearranged movements. The closest human-only equivalent is the compulsory figures in figure skating—which were eliminated after 1988 because they were too boring. Five judges grade each movement in dressage on a scale of 0 to 10. The horses canter, trot, and perform four varieties of walking. In addition to the movements, the judges award four "collective" marks, worth up to 10 points each, for freedom and regularity of the paces, the "impulsion" of the horse, the submission of the horse, and the form and position of the rider. Bizarre as it may seem to non-afficianados, horses are actually judged by their "attitude." A horse that appears happy and alert is rewarded, while a horse that exhibits signs of tension and stress, such as swishing its tail, tossing its head or pinning back its ears, is marked down. The scores of the five judges are added to determine the final score for each rider. The team event is used as the qualifying competition for the individual event. In 2008 the top 25 competitors in the team event will participate in the individual final, although only three riders per nation will be allowed to advance. The top 15 in the initial phase of the individual final then advance to a final of freestyle dressage, which is performed to music. The 1996 games saw the first appearance of freestyle dressage in the Olympic Games.

1896–1908 not held

1912 Stockholm C: 21, N: 8, D: 7.15.

		HORSE	PTS.
1. Carl Bonde	SWE	Emperor	15
2. Gustaf-Adolf Boltenstern, Sr.	SWE	Neptun	21
3. Hans von Blixen-Finecke, Sr.	SWE	Maggie	32
4. Friedrich von Osterley	GER	Condor	36
5. Carl Rosenblad	SWE	Miss Hastings	43
6. Oskar af Ström	SWE	Irish Lass	47
7. Felix Burkner	GER	King	51
8. Carl Kruckenberg	SWE	Kartusch	51

1920 Antwerp C: 17, N: 5, D: 9.9.

		HORSE	PTS.
1. Janne Lundblad	SWE	Uno	27.9375
2. Bertil Sandström	SWE	Sabel	26,3125
3. Hans von Rosen	SWE	Running Sister	25.125
4. Wilhelm von Essen	SWE	Nomeg	24.875
5. Hédoin de Maillé de la Tour Landry	FRA	Chéri Biribi	23.9375
6. Michel Artola	FRA	Plumard	23.4375
7. Gaston de Trannoy	BEL	Bouton d'Or	23.125
8. Jens Falkenberg	NOR	Hjørdis	22.375
DISQ: Gustaf-Adolf Boltenstern, Sr.	SWE	Iron	26.1875

Colonel Boltenstern, on Iron, finished in third place, but was disqualified for practicing in the ring before the competition began.

1924 Paris C: 24, N: 9, D: 7.25.

		HORSE	PTS.
1. Ernst Linder	SWE	Piccolomini	276.4
2. Bertil Sandström	SWE	Sabel	275.8
3. Xavier Lesage	FRA	Plumard	265.8
4. Wilhelm von Essen	SWE	Zobel	260.0
5. Victor Ankarcrona	SWE	Corona	256.5
6. Emanuel Thiel	CZE	Ex	256.2
7. Robert Wallon	FRA	Magister	243.2
7. Hans von der Weid	SWI	Uhlard	243.2

1928 Amsterdam C: 29, N: 12, D: 8.11.

		HORSE	PTS.
1. Carl Friedrich von Langen-Parow	GER	Draufgänger	237.42
2. Charles Marion	FRA	Linon	231.00
3. Ragnar Ohlson	SWE	Gunstling	229.78
4. Janne Lundblad	SWE	Blackmar	226.70
5. Emanuel Thiel	CZE	Loki	225.96
6. Hermann Linkenbach	GER	Gimpel	224.26
7. Robert Wallon	FRA	Clough-banck	224.08
8. Jan van Reede	HOL	Hans	220.70

1932 Los Angeles C: 10, N: 4, D: 8.10.

		HORSE	PTS.	ORDINALS
1. Xavier Lesage	FRA	Tame	343.75	6
2. Charles Marion	FRA	Linon	305.42	14
3. Hiram Tuttle	USA	Olympic	300.50	14
4. Thomas Byström	SWE	Gulliver	293.50	16
5. André Jousseaume	FRA	Sorelta	290.42	17
6. Isaac Kitts	USA	American Lady	282.08	17
7. Alvin Moore	USA	Water Pat	276.33	20
8. Gustaf-Adolf Boltenstern, Jr.	SWE	Ingo	277.83	21

Bertil Sandström of Sweden came in second but was relegated to last place for encouraging his horse, Kreta, by making clicking noises. He claimed that the noises were actually made by a creaking saddle, but the Jury of Appeal was not convinced. Moore was awarded seventh place, ahead of Boltenstern, because places were determined not by total points but by the rankings of the judges, using a system of ordinals such as is used in figure skating.

1936 Berlin C: 29, N: 11, D: 8.13.

		HORSE	PTS.
1. Heinz Pollay	GER	Kronos	1760.0
2. Friedrich Gerhard	GER	Absinth	1745.5
3. Alois Podhajsky	AUT	Nero	1721.5
4. Gregor Adlercreutz	SWE	Teresina	1675.0
5. André Jousseaume	FRA	Favorite	1642.5
6. Gérard de Ballore	FRA	Debaucheur	1634.0
7. Peder Jensen	DEN	His Ex	1596.0
8. Pierre Versteegh	HOL	Ad Astra	1579.0

1948 London C: 19, N: 9, D: 8.9.

		HORSE	PTS.
1. Hans Moser	SWI	Hummer	492.5
2. André Jousseaume	FRA	Harpagon	480.0
3. Gustaf-Adolf Boltenstern, Jr.	SWE	Trumf	477.5
4. Robert Borg	USA	Klingson	473.5
5. Henri Saint Cyr	SWE	Djimm	444.5
6. Jean Saint Fort Paillard	FRA	Sous les Ceps	439.5
7. Alois Podhajsky	AUT	Teja	437.5
8. Earl Thomson	USA	Pancraft	421.0
DISQ: Gehnäll Persson	SWE	Knaust	444.0

The absurdity of the rules governing Olympic dressage reached its pinnacle in 1948, when sixth-place finisher Gehnäll Persson was disqualified when it was discovered that he was only a noncommissioned officer and thus ineligible to compete.

1952 Helsinki C: 27, N: 10, D: 7.29.

		HORSE	PTS.
1. Henri Saint Cyr	SWE	Master Rufus	561.0
2. Lis Hartel	DEN	Jubilee	541.5
3. André Jousseaume	FRA	Harpagon	541.0
4. Gustaf-Adolf Boltenstern, Jr.	SWE	Krest	531.0
5. Gottfried Trachsel	SWI	Kursus	531.0
6. Henri Chammartin	SWI	Wohler	529.5
7. Gustav Fischer	SWI	Soliman	518.5
7. Heinz Pollay	GER	Adular	518.5

Between 1948 and 1952 dressage competition underwent a radical change. Not only were noncommissioned officers allowed to enter in 1952, so were other enlisted men. And not only were enlisted men allowed to enter, so were men who were civilians. And not only were men who were civilians allowed to enter, but for the first time in Olympic equestrian history, four women were allowed to compete against men. One of those women was Lis Hartel of Denmark. In 1944 Hartel, a 23-year-old pregnant mother, was one of Denmark's leading riders. Then, one morning in September, she awoke with a headache and a strange stiffness in her neck. A few days later paralysis began spreading throughout her body—she had become a victim of polio. But Lis Hartel was determined to regain her health. First she learned to lift her arm, then she regained the use of her thigh muscles. Then she gave birth to a healthy daughter. Soon she was

Lis Hartel, 1952

Paralyzed below the knee from polio, Denmark's Hartel had to be helped on and off her horse on her way to a silver medal in the individual dressage event.

crawling, and eight months after the attack, she was able to walk a bit by using crutches. Her friends hailed her recovery, but she was not finished. She insisted on mounting a horse. Reactivating the muscles necessary to keep from falling was so exhausting that she had to rest for two weeks before she tried a second time. Slowly but surely, Lis Hartel improved until, three years after her polio attack, she was able to compete in the Scandinavian riding championship, finishing second in the women's dressage. She remained paralyzed below the knees, but learned to do without those muscles. In 1952 she was chosen to represent Denmark in the Olympics, and she responded by earning the silver medal, even though she had to be helped on and off her horse. When gold medalist Henri Saint Cyr helped her up onto the victory platform for the medal presentation, it was one of the most emotional moments in Olympic history. Four years later, in Stockholm, she won another silver medal.

1956 Stockholm C: 36, N: 17, D: 6.16.

		HORSE	PTS.
1. Henri Saint Cyr	SWE	Juli	860
2. Lis Hartel	DEN	Jubilee	850
3. Liselott Linsenhoff	GER	Adular	832
4. Gehnäll Persson	SWE	Knaust	821
5. André Jousseaume	FRA	Harpagon	814
6. Gottfried Trachsel	SWI	Kursus	807
7. Gustaf-Adolf Bolterstern, Jr.	SWE	Krest	794
8. Henri Chammartin	SWI	Woehler	789

The judging caused something of a scandal. The German judge, General Berger, ranked the three German riders first, second, and third and the Swedish judge, General Colliander, ranked the three Swedish riders first, second, and third. First-place finisher Henri Saint Cyr completed his harvest of four gold medals. The fifth-place finisher, 61-year-old André Jousseaume, was competing in his fifth Olympics. Between 1932 and 1952 he won two gold medals, two silver, and one bronze.

1960 Rome C: 17, N: 10, D: 9.6.

		HORSE	PTS.
1. Sergei Filatov	SOV/RUS	Absent	2144
2. Gustav Fischer	SWI	Wald	2087
3. Josef Neckermann	GER	Asbach	2082
4. Henri Saint Cyr	SWE	L'Etoile	2064
5. Ivan Kalita	SOV/RUS	Korbey	2007
6. Patricia Galvin	USA	Rath Patrick	995
7. Rosemarie Springer	GER	Doublette	985
8. Henri Chammartin	SWI	Wolfdietrich	978

Finishing in 16th place was Kroum Lekarski of Bulgaria, whose first Olympic appearance had been in the three-day event in 1924.

1964 Tokyo C: 22, N: 9, D: 10.23.

		HORSE	PTS.
1. Henri Chammartin	SWI	Woermann	1504
2. Harry Boldt	GER	Remus	1503
3. Sergei Filatov	SOV/RUS	Absent	1486
4. Gustav Fischer	SWI	Wald	1485
5. Josef Neckermann	GER	Antoinette	1429
6. Reiner Klimke	GER	Dux	1404
7. Marianne Gossweiler	SWI	Stephan	802
8. Patricia Galvin de la Tour d'Auvergne	USA	Rath Patrick	783

1968 Mexico City C: 26, N: 9, D: 10.25.

		HORSE	PTS.
1. Ivan Kizimov	SOV/RUS	Ikhor	1572
2. Josef Neckermann	GER	Mariano	1546
3. Reiner Klimke	GER	Dux	1537
4. Ivan Kalita	SOV/RUS	Absent	1519
5. Horst Köhler	GDR	Neuschnee	1475
6. Yelena Petushkova	SOV/RUS	Pepei	1471
7. Gustav Fischer	SWI	Wald	1465
8. Liselott Linsenhoff	GER	Piaff	855

Toward the end of the long flight from Europe to Mexico, the Russian equestrian team members heard loud noises coming from the cargo area where the horses were being held. It turned out to be Ivan Kizimov's horse, Ikhor, banging against the walls. The Russian vetenarian, Anatoly Doilnev, was able to calm Ikhor, who, nonetheless, emerged from the plane with his legs covered in blood. Fortunately, they arrived two weeks before the Opening Ceremony and by the time the dressage competition began, Ikhor was fully recovered.

1972 Munich C: 33, N: 13, D: 9.7.

		HORSE	PTS.
1. Liselott Linsenhoff	GER	Piaff	1229
2. Yelena Petushkova	SOV/RUS	Pepel	1185
3. Josef Neckermann	GER	Venetia	1177
4. Ivan Kizimov	SOV/RUS	Ikhor	1159
5. Ulla Håkansson	SWE	Ajax	1126
6. Ivan Kalita	SOV/RUS	Tarif	1130
7. Karin Schlüter	GER	Liostro	1113
8. Maud Von Rosen	SWE	Lucky Boy	1088

Twenty-one of the 33 riders were women, including Liselott Linsenhoff, the first female individual gold medalist. Second-place finisher Petushkova was a professor of biology at the University of Moscow and was, for some time, married to high-jumper Valery Brumel.

1976 Montreal C: 27, N: 11, D: 7.30.

		HORSE	PTS.
1. Christine Stückelberger	SWI	Granat	1486
2. Harry Boldt	GER	Woycek	1435
3. Reiner Klimke	GER	Mehmed	1395
4. Gabriela Grillo	GER	Ultimo	1257
5. Dorothy Morkis	USA	Monaco	1249
6. Viktor Ugryumov	SOV/BLR	Said	1247
7. Christilot Boylen (Hansen)	CAN	Gaspano	1217
8. Ulla Petersen	DEN	Chigwell	1192

1980 Moscow C: 14, N: 6, D: 8.1.

		HORSE	PTS.
1. Elisabeth Theurer	AUT	Mon Cherie	1370
2. Yuri Kovshov	SOV/UZB	Igrok	1300
3. Viktor Ugryumov	SOV/BLR	Shkval	1234
4. Vira Misevych	SOV/UKR	Plot	1231
5. Kyra Kyrklund	FIN	Piccolo	1121
6. Anghelache Donescu	ROM	Dor	960
7. Georgi Gadzhev	BUL	Vnimatelen	881
8. Svetoslav Ivanov	BUL	Aleko	850

Theurer was the only leading dressage rider to enter the Olympics. All the rest took part in the Dressage Festival the following week, which was won by Christine Stückelberger.

1984 Los Angeles-Arcadia C: 43, N: 18, D: 8.10.

		HORSE	PTS.
1. Reiner Klimke	GER	Ahlerich	1504
2. Anne Grethe Jensen	DEN	Marzog	1442
3. Otto Hofer	SWI	Limandus	1364
4. Ingamay Bylund	SWE	Aleks	1332
5. Herbert Krug	GER	Muscadeur	1323
6. Christopher Bartle	GBR	Wily Trout	1279
6. Uwe Sauer	GER	Montevideo	1279
8. Annemarie Sanders-Keyzer	HOL	Amon	1271

Dr. Reiner Klimke, a 48-year-old lawyer from Münster, won his first individual gold medal to bring his Olympic total to 5 golds and 2 bronzes. In 1988, he was awarded another gold in the team competition.

1988 Seoul C: 55, N: 18, D: 9.27.

		HORSE	PTS.
1. Nicole Uphoff	GER	Rembrandt	1521
2. Margit Otto-Crépin	FRA	Corlandus	1462
3. Christine Stückelberger	SWI	Gauguin De Lully	1417
4. Cynthia Ishoy	CAN	Dynasty	1401
5. Kyra Kyrklund	FIN	Matador	1393
6. Monica Theodorescu	GER	Ganimedes	1385
7. Otto Hofer	SWI	Andiamo	1383
8. Ann-Kathrin Linsenhoff	GER	Courage	1374

This was the first time all three dressage medals were won by women.

1992 Barcelona C: 48, N: 18, D: 8.5.

		HORSE	PTS.
1. Nicole Uphoff	GER	Rembrandt	1626
2. Isabell Werth	GER	Gigolo	1551
3. Nikolaus "Klaus" Balkenhol	GER	Goldstern	1515
4. Anky van Grunsven	HOL	Bonfire	1447
5. Kyra Kyrklund	FIN	Edinburgh	1428
6. Carol Lavell	USA	Gifted	1408
7. Pia Laus	ITA	Adrett	1389
8. Elisabeth Max-Theurer	AUT	Liechtenstein	1380

Monica Theodorescu of Germany placed fourth in the qualifying round on Grunox but was left out of the individual final because the three riders ahead of her were also from Germany. Rembrandt became the first horse to win the dressage title twice. Bronze medalist Klaus Balkenhol was a 52-year-old policeman from Düsseldorf.

1996 Atlanta-Conyers C: 50, N: 17, D: 8.3.

		HORSE	PTS.
1. Isabell Werth	GER	Gigolo	235.09
2. Anky van Grunsven	HOL	Bonfire	233.02
3. Sven Rothenberger	HOL	Weyden	224.94
4. Monica Theodorescu	GER	Grunox	224.56
5. Michelle Gibson	USA	Peron	222.83
6. Nikolaus "Klaus" Balkenhol	GER	Goldstern	221.81
7. Margit Otto-Crepin	FRA	Lucky Lord	219.80
8. Guenter Seidel	USA	Graf George	215.02

For the first time, kür, or freestyle dressage to music, was added to the competition. Besides pleasing the spectators, this inclusion also changed the results. Going into the freestyle, Isabell Werth trailed Anky van Grunsven by 1.35 points. But, performing to a medley that included "Just a Gigolo" and Monty Python's "Bright Side of Life," Werth came from behind for the victory.

2000 Sydney C: 48, N: 18, D: 9.29.

		HORSE	PTS.
1. Anky van Grunsven	HOL	Bonfire	239.18
2. Isabell Werth	GER	Gigolo	234.19
3. Ulla Salzgeber	GER	Rusty	230.57
4. Nadine Capellmann	GER	Farbenfroh	225.88
5. Coby van Baalen	HOL	Ferro	221.36
6. Ellen Bontje	HOL	Silvano	217.59
7. Lone Jorgensen	DEN	Kennedy	216.90
8. Susan Blinks	USA	Flim Flam	214.65

Beginning with the 1995 European Championships, Anky van Grunsven had finished second to Isabell Werth in every major competition until the 1999 European Championship, when Werth's favorite horse, Gigolo, was unable to compete because of injury and van Grunsven finally won. Gigolo was back for the 2000 Olympics, but the tide had turned. Werth led by 1.32 points after the Grand Prix, but van Grunsven was clearly superior over the final two stages and won by almost 5 points. In 2000, van Grunsven raised her career medal total to 1 gold and 4 silver, while Werth brought hers to 4 gold and 2 silver.

2004 Athens-Markopoulo C: 52, N: 18, D: 8.25.

		HORSE	PTS.
1. Anky van Grunsven	HOL	Salinero	79.278
2. Ulla Salzgeber	GER	Rusty	78.833
3. Beatriz Ferrer-Salat	SPA	Beauvalais	76.667
4. Deborah McDonald	USA	Brentina	75.653
5. Hubertus Schmidt	GER	Wansuela Suerte	74.883
6. Robert Dover	USA	Kennedy	74.713
7. Jan Brink	SWE	Briar	73.727
8. Rafael Soto Andrade	SPA	Invasor	73.606

After the first round, defending Olympic champion Anky van Grunsven was in third place behind Ulla Salzgeber and Beatriz Ferrer-Salat, trailing by a full four points. She narrowed the gap to half a point behind Salzgeber with a strong performance in the special, and then secured gold with the top scores in the freestyle.

2008 Beijing-Hong Kong C: 46, N: 22, D: 8.19.

		HORSE	PTS.
1. Anky van Grunsven	HOL	Salinero	78.680
2. Isabell Werth	GER	Satchmo	76.650
3. Heike Kemmer	GER	Bonaparte 67	74.455
4. Steffen Peters	USA	Ravel	74.150
5. Hans Peter Minderhoud	HOL	Nadine	73.035
6. Aleksandra Korelova	RUS	Balagur	72.625
7. Emma Hindle	GBR	Lancet	72.345
8. Kyra Kyrklund	FIN	Max	71.985

Long-time rivals Anky van Grunsven and Isabell Werth had been swapping places on the podium for the past decade, and the pattern continued in the lead-up to Beijing. At the 2006 world championships Werth beat van Grunsven for gold in the Grand Prix Special, with van Grunsven winning the Grand Prix Freestyle. The opposite happened the following year at the European championships in La Madrina, Italy, van Grunsven topping the Special event and Werth the freestyle.

At the Beijing Olympics Werth led after both the Grand Prix and Grand Prix Special, despite losing points when her horse, Satchmo, shied violently during a piaff (step in place). In the final freestyle round van Grunsven and her black gelding Salinero shone, earning both the highest technical and artistic points, 38.9 and 43.5, for a combined freestyle total of 82.4 points and a final average of 78.680. Werth earned the second-highest technical and artistic scores, despite losing control of Satchmo again during the piaff. Her combined freestyle score of 78.1 left her in second place overall, with two-time team dressage gold medalist Heike Kemmer in third. It was van Grunsven's third consecutive individual gold medal.

The dressage event featured the oldest athlete at the Beijing Olympics, 67-year-old Hiroshi Hoketsu, who tied for 34th place. Hoketsu had also competed at the 1964 Tokyo Olympics, and the gap of 44 years between Olympic appearances is a record, by far eclipsing the previous record of 28 years held by six athletes.

In June 2009, Werth's horse, Whisper, tested positive for the banned stimulant fluphenazine. Werth was suspended for six months.

DRESSAGE, TEAM

Each team may enter four riders and horses, but only the scores of the top three finishers for each team are counted. In case of a tie, the team whose third rider had the highest score is declared the winner. Every time Germany has entered this event, their team has won a medal: 12 gold, 2 silver, 1 bronze.

1896–1924 not held

1928 Amsterdam T: 8, N: 8, D: 8.11.

	HORSE		TOTAL PTS.
1. GER			669.72
Carl Friedrich von Langen-Parow	Draufgänger	237.42	
Hermann Linkenbach	Gimpel	224.26	
Eugen, Freiherr von Lotzbeck	Caracalla	208.04	
2. SWE			650.86
Ragnar Ohlson	Gunstling	229.78	
Janne Lundblad	Blackmar	226.70	
Carl Bonde	Ingo	194.38	
3. HOL			642.96
Jan van Reede	Hans	220.70	
Pierre Versteegh	His Excellence	216.44	
Gerard Le Heux	Valerine	205.82	
4. FRA			642.18
Charles Marion	Linon	231.00	
Robert Wallon	Clough-banck	224.08	
Pierre Danloux	Rempart	187.10	
5. CZE			637.94
Emanuel Thiel	Loki	225.96	
Otto Schöniger	Ex	210.28	
Jaroslav Hauf	Elegant	201.70	
6. AUT			600.40
Arthur von Pongracz	Turridu	204.28	
Wilhelm Jaich	Graf	204.16	
Gustav Grachegg	Daniel	191.96	
7. SWI			569.08
Adolphe Mercier	Queen-Mary	203.34	
Otto Frank	Solon	190.62	
Werner Stuber	Ulhard	175.12	
8. BEL			499.70
Oscar Lints	Rira-t-elle	185.86	
Henri Laame	Belga	167.70	
René Delrue	Dreypuss	146.14	

1932 Los Angeles T: 3, N: 3, D: 8.10.

	HORSE		TOTAL PTS.
1. FRA			2818.75
Xavier Lesage	Tame	1031.25	
Charles Marion	Linon	916.25	
André Jousseaume	Sorelta	871.25	
2. SWE			2678.00
Bertil Sandström	Kreta	964.00	
Thomas Byström	Gulliver	880.50	
Gustaf-Adolf Boltenstern, Jr.	Ingo	833.50	
3. USA			2576.75
Hiram Tuttle	Olympic	901.50	
Isaac Kitts	American Lady	846.25	
Alvin Moore	Water Pat	829.00	

1936 Berlin T: 9, N: 9, D: 8.13.

	HORSE		TOTAL PTS.
1. GER			5074.0
Heinz Pollay	Kronos	1760.0	
Friedrich Gerhard	Absinth	1745.5	
Hermann von Oppeln-Bronikowski	Gimpel	1568.5	
2. FRA			4846.0
André Jousseaume	Favorite	1642.5	
Gerard de Ballore	Debaucheur	1634.0	
Daniel Gillois	Nicolas	1569.5	
3. SWE			4660.5
Gregor Adlercreutz	Teresina	1675.0	
Sven Colliander	Kal	1530.5	
Folke Sandström	Pergoia	1455.0	
4. AUT			627.5
Alois Podhajsky	Nero	1721.5	
Albert Dolleschall	Infant	1476.0	
Arthur von Pongracz	Georgine	1430.0	
5. HOL			4382.0
Pierre Versteegh	Ad Astra	1579.0	
Gérard Le Heux	Zonnetje	1422.0	
Daniel Camerling-Helmolt	Wodan	1381.0	
6. HUN			4090.0
Gusztáv von Pados	Ficsur	1424.0	
Lászlo von Magasházy	Tucsok	1415.5	
Pál Kerméry	Csintaian	1250.5	
7. NOR			4050.5
Arthur Quist	Jaspis	1438.0	
Eugene Johansen	Sorte Mand	1388.0	
Bjorn Bjornseth	Invictus	1224.5	
8. CZE			4026.0
Frantisek Jandl	Nestor	1453.0	
Matej Pechmann	Ideal	1319.0	
Otto Schöniger	Helios	1254.0	

The oldest competitor at the Berlin Olympics was 72-year-old General Arthur von Pongracz, of Austria's fourth-place team. Von Pongracz made his Olympic debut in Paris in 1924, when he was a mere youngster of 60.

1948 London T: 5, N: 5, D: 8.9.

	HORSE		TOTAL PTS.
1. FRA			1269.0
André Jousseaume	Harpagon	480.0	
Jean Saint Fort Paillard	Sous les Ceps	439.5	
Maurice Buret	Saint Ouen	349.5	
2. USA			1256.0
Robert Borg	Klingson	473.5	
Earl Thomson	Pancraft	421.0	
Frank Henry	Reno Overdo	361.5	
3. POR			1182.0
Fernando Pais da Silva	Matamas	411.0	
Franciso Valadas	Feitico	405.0	
Luiz Mena e Silva	Fascinante	366.0	
4. ARG			1005.5
Justo Iturralde	Pajarito	397.0	
Humberto Terzano	Bienvenido	327.0	
Oscar Goulú	Grillo	281.5	
DISQ: SWE			1366.0
Gustav-Adolf Boltenstern, Jr.	Trumf	477.5	
Henri Saint Cyr	Djimm	444.5	
Gehnäll Persson	Knaust	444.0	

In the middle of the competition, Commandant Hector of France, the Secretary General of the International Equestrian Federation, suddenly pointed to Gehnäll Persson, who had been entered as an officer, and said, "This man is not an officer. He is riding in the cap of a sergeant." Initially the Swedish team was allowed to keep their gold medals, but eight months later they were formally disqualified and forced to turn over the medals to the French team.

1952 Helsinki T: 8, N: 8, D: 7.29.

	HORSE		TOTAL PTS.
1. SWE			1597.5
Henri Saint Cyr	Master Rufus	561.0	
Gustaf-Adolf Boltenstern, Jr.	Krest	531.0	
Gehnäll Persson	Knaust	505.5	
2. SWI			1579.0
Gottfried Trachsel	Krusus	531.0	
Henri Chammartin	Wohler	529.5	
Gustav Fischer	Solimon	518.5	
3. GER			1501.0
Heinz Pollay	Adular	518.5	
Ida von Nagel	Afrika	503.0	
Fritz Thiedemann	Chronist	479.5	
4. FRA			1423.5
André Jousseaume	Harpagon	541.0	
Jean Peitevin de Saint André	Vol au vent	479.0	
Jean Saint-Ford Paillard	Tapir	403.5	
5. CHI			1340.5
José Larrain	Rey de Oros	473.5	
Hector Clavel	Frontalera	452.0	
Ernesto Silva	Viareggio	415.0	
6. USA			1253.5
Robert Borg	Bill Biddle	492.0	
Marjorie Haines	The Flying Dutchman	446.0	
Hartmann Pauly	Reno Overdue	315.5	
7 SOV/RUS			1205.5
Vladimir Raspopov	Imeninnik	433.5	
Vassily Tihonov	Pevec	395.0	
Nikolai Sitko	Cesar	377.0	
8. POR			1196.5
Antonio Reymão Nogueira	Napeiro	428.4	
Francisco Valadas Júnior	Feitico	422.0	
Fernando Paisda Silva	Matamas	346.0	

1956 Stockholm T: 8, N: 8, D: 6.16.

	HORSE		TOTAL PTS.
1. SWE			2475.0
Henri Saint Cyr	Juli	860.0	
Gehnäll Persson	Knaust	821.0	
Gustaf-Adolf Boltenstern, Jr.	Krest	794.0	
2. GER			2346.0
Liselott Linsenhoff	Adular	832.0	
Hannelore Weygand	Perkunos	785.0	
Anneliese Küppers	Afrika	729.0	
3. SWI			2346.0
Gottfried Trachsel	Kursus	807.0	
Henri Chammartin	Wohler	789.0	
Gustav Fischer	Vasello	750.0	

4. SOV/RUS			2170.0
Sergei Filatov	Ingas	744.0	
Aleksandr Vtorov	Repertoir	726.0	
Nikolai Sitko	Skatschek	700.0	
5. DEN			2167.0
Lis Hartel	Jubilee	850.0	
Hermann Zobel	Monty	673.0	
Inger Lemvigh-Müller	Bel Ami	644.0	
6. FRA			2016.0
André Jousseaume	Harpagon	814.0	
Jean-Albert Brau	Vol d'Amour	648.0	
Jean Salmon	Kipling	554.0	
7. NOR			1912.5
Else Christophersen	Diva	739.0	
Anne Lise Kielland	Clary	601.5	
Bodil Russ	Corona	572.0	
8. ROM			1862.0
Gheorghe Teodorescu	Palatin	721.0	
Nicolae Mihalcea	Mihnea	625.0	
Niculae Marcoci	Corvin	516.0	

1960 not held

1964 Tokyo T: 6, N: 6, D: 10.23.

	HORSE		TOTAL PTS.
1. GER			2558.0
Harry Boldt	Remus	889.0	
Reiner Klimke	Dux	837.0	
Josef Neckermann	Antoinette	832.0	
2. SWI			2526.0
Henri Chammartin	Wormann	870.0	
Gustav Fischer	Wald	854.0	
Marianne Gossweiler	Stephan	802.0	
3. SOV/RUS			2311.0
Sergei Filatov	Absent	847.0	
Ivan Kizimov	Ikhor	758.0	
Ivan Kalita	Moar	706.0	
4. USA			2130.0
Patricia Galvin de la Tour d'Auvergne	Rath Patrick	783.0	
Anne Newberry	Forstrat	707.0	
Karen McIntosh	Malteser	640.0	
5. SWE			2068.0
William Hamilton	Delicado	777.0	
Hans Wikne	Gaspari	753.0	
Bengt Ljungquist	Karat	538.0	
6. JPN			1779.5
Kikuko Inoue	Katsunobori	648.0	
Nagahira Okabe	Seiha	589.5	
Yoritsune Matsudaira	Hamachidori	542.0	

1968 Mexico City T: 8, N: 8, D: 10.24.

	HORSE		TOTAL PTS.
1. GER			2699
Josef Neckermann	Mariano	948	
Reiner Klimke	Dux	896	
Liselott Linsenhoff	Piaff	855	
2. SOV/RUS			2657
Ivan Kizimov	Ikhor	908	
Ivan Kalita	Absent	879	
Yelena Petushkova	Pepel	870	
3. SWI			2547
Gustav Fischer	Wald	866	
Henri Chammartin	Wolfdietrich	845	
Marianne Gossweiler	Stephan	836	
4. GDR			2357
Horst Köhler	Neuschnee	875	
Gerhard Brockmüller	Tristan	789	
Wolfgang Müller	Marios	693	
5. GBR			2332
Domini Lawrence	San Fernando	793	
H. Lorna Johnstone	El Guapo	777	
Johanna Hall	Conversano Caprice	762	
6. CHI			2015
Guillermo Squella	Colchaguino	693	
Antonio Piraíno	Ciclón	672	
Patricio Escudero	Prete	650	
7. CAN			2012
Inez Fischer-Credo	Marius	732	
Christilot Hanson	Bonheur	677	
Zoltan Sztehlo	Virtuose	603	
8. USA			1919
Kyra Downton	Cadet	657	
Edith Master	Helios	646	
Donnan Plumb	Attache	616	

1972 Munich T: 10, N: 10, D: 9.7.

	HORSE		TOTAL PTS.
1. SOV/RUS			5095
Yelena Petushkova	Pepel	1747	
Ivan Kizimov	Ikhor	1701	
Ivan Kalita	Tarif	1647	
2. GER			5083
Liselott Linsenhoff	Piaff	1763	
Josef Neckermann	Venetia	1706	
Karin Schlüter	Liostro	1614	
3. SWE			4849
Ulla Håkansson	Ajax	1649	
Ninna Swaab	Casanova	1622	
Maud Von Rosen	Lucky Boy	1578	
4. DEN			4606
Aksel Mikkelsen	Talisman	1597	
Ulla Petersen	Chigwell	1534	
Charlotte Ingemann	Souliman	1475	
5. GDR			4552
Gerhard Brockmüller	Marios	1545	
Wolfgang Müller	Semafor	1521	
Horst Köhler	Imanuel	1486	
6. CAN			4418
Christilot Hanson	Armagnac III	1615	
Cynthia Neal	Bonne Annee	1424	
Lorraine Stubbs	Venezuela	1379	
7. SWI			4383
Christine Stückelberger	Granat	1528	
Hermann Duer	Sod	1466	
Marita Aeschbacher	Charlamp	1389	
8. HOL			4309
Johanna van Doorne	Pericles	1480	
Kees Benedictus-Lieftinck	Turista	1420	
John Swaab	Maharadscha	1409	

1976 Montreal T: 8, N: 8, D: 7.29.

	HORSE		TOTAL PTS.
1. GER			5155
Harry Boldt	Woycek	1863	
Reiner Klimke	Mehmed	1751	
Gabriela Grillo	Ultimo	1541	
2. SWI			4684
Christine Stückelberger	Granat	1869	
Ulrich Lehmann	Widin	1425	
Doris Ramseier	Roch	1390	
3. USA			4647
Hilda Gurney	Keen	1607	
Dorothy Morkis	Monaco	1559	
Edith Master	Dahlwitz	1481	
4. SOV			4542
Viktor Ugryumov	Said	1597	
Ivan Kalita	Tarif	1520	
Ivan Kizimov	Rebus	1425	
5. CAN			4538
Christilot Boylen (Hanson)	Gaspano	1590	
Lorraine Stubbs	True North	1549	
Barbara Stracey	Jungherr II	1399	
6. DEN			4448
Ulla Petersen	Chigwell	1552	
Tonny Jensen	Fox	1521	
Niels Haagensen	Lowenstern	1375	
7. HOL			4380
Jo Rutten	Banjo	1533	
Louky Van Olphen	Aleric	1449	
Marjolyn Greeve	Lucky Boy	1398	
8. GBR			4076
Sarah Whitmore	Junker	1375	
A. Jennifer Loriston-Clarke	Kadett	1375	
Diana Mason	Special Ed	1326	

1980 Moscow T: 4, N: 4, D: 7.31.

	HORSE		TOTAL PTS.
1. SOV			4383
Yuri Kovshov	Igrok	1588	
Viktor Ugryumov	Shkval	1541	
Vira Misevych	Plot	1254	
2. BUL			3580
Peter Mandazhiev	Stchibor	1244	
Svetoslav Ivanov	Aleko	1190	
Georgi Gadjev	Vnimatelen	1146	
3. ROM			3346
Anghelache Donescu	Dor	1255	
Dumitru Veliku	Decebal	1076	
Petre Roşca	Derbist	1015	
4. POL			2945
Józef Zagor	Hellios	1061	
Elżbieta Morciniec	Sum	954	
Wanda Wąsowska	Damask	930	

The Goodwood Dressage Festival, held as an alternative to the Olympics, was won by West Germany, with Switzerland second and Denmark third.

1984 Los Angeles-Arcadia T: 12, N: 12, D: 8.9.

	HORSE		TOTAL PTS.
1. GER			4955
Reiner Klimke	Ahlerich	1797	
Uwe Sauer	Montevideo	1582	
Herbert Krug	Muscadeur	1576	
2. SWI			4673
Otto Hofer	Limandus	1609	
Christine Stückelberger	Tansanit	1606	
Amy-Cathérine de Bary	Aintree	1458	
3. SWE			4630
Ulla Håkansson	Flamingo	1589	
Ingamay Bylund	Aleks	1582	
Louise Nathhorst	Inferno	1459	
4. HOL			4586
Annemarie Sanders-Keyzer	Amon	1591	
Tineke Bartels de Vries	Duco	1539	
Jo Rutten	Ampere	1456	
5. DEN			4574
Anne Grethe Jensen	Marzog	1701	
Torben Ulsö Olsen	Patricia	1496	
Marie-Louise Castenskiöld	Stradivarius	1377	
6. USA			4559
Hilda Gurney	Keen	1530	
Sandy Pflueger-Clarke	Marco Polo	1516	
Robert Dover	Romantico	1513	
7. CAN			4503
Christilot Boylen (Hanson)	Anklang	1540	
Bonny Chesson	Satchmo	1496	
Eva-Maria Pracht	Little Joe	1467	
8. GBR			4463
Christopher Bartle	Wily Trout	1547	
Jane Bartle-Wilson	Pinocchio	1489	
Jennie Loriston-Clarke	Prince Consort	1427	

1988 Seoul T: 12, N: 12, D: 9.25.

	HORSE		TOTAL PTS.
1. GER			4302
Nicole Uphoff	Rembrandt	1458	
Monica Theodorescu	Ganimedes	1433	
Ann-Kathrin Linsenhoff	Courage	1411	
2. SWI			4164
Christine Stückelberger	Gauguin De Lully	1430	
Otto Hofer	Andiamo	1392	
Daniel Ramseier	Random	1342	
3. CAN			3969
Cynthia Ishoy	Dynasty	1363	
Ashley Nicoll	Reipo	1308	
Gina Smith	Malte	1298	
4. SOV			3926
Nina Menkova	Dixon	1395	
Olha Klymko	Buket	1272	
Yuri Kovshov	Barin	1259	
5. HOL			3903
Ellen Bontje	Petit Prince	1312	
Annemarie Sanders-Keyzer	Amon	1303	
Tineke Bartels de Vries	Olympic	1288	
6. FIN			3883
Kyra Kyrklund	Matador	1416	
Tuulikki Sohlberg	Pakistan	1242	
Jennifer Eriksson	My Way	1225	

6. USA			3883
Robert Dover	Federleicht	1327	
Jessica Ransehousen	Orpheus	1308	
Belinda Baudin	Christopher	1248	
8. FRA			3832
Margit Otto-Crépin	Corlandus	1455	
Dominique d'Esmé	Hopal Fleury Hn	1219	
Philippe Limousin	Iris de la Fosse	1158	

Eva-Maria Pracht was a non-scoring member of the Canadian dressage team that placed third. As she bent down to have the bronze medal placed around her neck at the award ceremony, she suddenly remembered an incident that had occurred a year earlier. A Gypsy palm-reader in Toronto told her that the following summer she would go on a long trip and that she would receive "a huge honor" and wear something shiny around her neck. "I was immediately covered with goosebumps," Pracht later recalled. "I wished I could have shared my happiness with her, but I never saw her again."

1992 Barcelona T: 11, N: 11, D: 8.2.

	HORSE		TOTAL PTS.
1. GER			5224
Nicole Uphoff	Rembrandt	1768	
Isabell Werth	Gigolo	1762	
Nikolaus "Klaus" Balkenhol	Goldstern	1694	
2. HOL			4742
Anky Van Grunsven	Bonfire	1631	
Ellen Bontje	Olympic Larius	1577	
Tineke Bartels de Vries	Olympic Courage	1534	
3. USA			4643
Carol Lavell	Gifted	1629	
Charlotte Bredahl	Monsieur	1507	
Robert Dover	Lectron	1507	
4. SWE			4537
Tinne Wilhelmsson	Caprice	1522	
Ann Behrenfors	Leroy	1514	
Annica Westerberg	Taktik	1501	
5. DEN			4533
Anne van Olst	Chevalier	1542	
Anne Grethe Törnblad (Jensen)	Ravel	1540	
Lene Hoberg	Bayar	1451	
6. SWI			4524
Otto Hofer	Renzo	1548	
Ruth Hunkeler	Afghadi	1498	
Doris Ramseier	Renatus	1478	
7. GBR			4522
Carl Hester	Giorgione	1523	
Emile Faurie	Virtu	1513	
Laura Fry	Quarryman	1486	
8. ITA			4491
Pia Laus	Adrett	1571	
Paolo Margi	Destino Di Acci	1481	
Daria Fantoni Camilla	Sonny Boy	1439	

1996 Atlanta-Conyers T: 10, N: 10, D: 7.27.

	HORSE		TOTAL PTS.
1. GER			5553
Isabell Werth	Gigolo	1915	
Monica Theodorescu	Grunox	1845	
Nikolaus "Klaus" Balkenhol	Goldstern	1793	
2. HOL			5437
Anky van Grunsven	Bonfire	1893	
Sven Rothenberger	Weyden	1854	
Tineke Bartels-de Vries	Olympic Barbria	1690	
3. USA			5309
Michelle Gibson	Peron	1880	
Guenter Seidel	Graf George	1734	
Steffen Peters	Udon	1695	
4. FRA			5045
Margit Otto-Crepin	Lucky Lord	1783	
Dominique Brieussel	Akazie	1650	
Dominique d'Esmé	Arnoldo	1612	
5. SWE			4996
Annette Solmell	Strauss	1673	
Ulla Håkansson	Bobby	1666	
Louise Nathhorst	Walk on Top	1657	
6. SWI			4893
Christine Stückelberger	Aquamarin	1662	
Hans Staub	Dukaat	1628	
Eva Senn	Renzo	1603	
7. SPA			4875
Ignacio Rambla Algarín	Evento	1744	
Beatriz Ferrer Salat	Brillant	1604	
Rafael Soto Andrade	Invasor	1527	
8. GBR			4761
Richard Davison	Askari	1668	
Joanna Jackson	Mester Mouse	1577	
Vicky Thompson	Enfant	1516	

Germany is such a hotbed of dressage excellence that in 1996 not only did Germany win the gold medal, but three German-born riders earned medals for other countries. Sven Rothenberger represented the Netherlands, while Guenter Seidel and Steffen Peters rode for the United States.

2000 Sydney T: 9, N: 9, D: 9.27.

	HORSE		TOTAL PTS.
1. GER			5632
Isabell Werth	Gigolo	1908	
Nadine Capellmann	Farbenfroh	1867	
Alexandra Simons de Ridder	Chacomo	1857	
2. HOL			5579
Anky van Grunsven	Bonfire	1875	
Coby van Baalen	Ferro	1873	
Arjen Teeuwissen	Goliath	1831	
3. USA			5166
Christine Traurig	Etienne	1746	
Susan Blinks	Flim Flam	1725	
Guenter Seidel	Foltaire	1695	
4. DEN			5149
Lone Jorgensen	Kennedy	1796	
Jon Pedersen	Esprit de Valde	1728	
Anne van Olst	Any How	1625	

5. SPA			5011
Beatiz Ferrer-Salat	Beauvalais	1710	
Rafael Soto	Invasor	1663	
Juan Antonio Jiménez	Guizo	1638	
6. AUS			4925
Kristy Oatley-Nist	Wall Street	1704	
Rachael Downs	Aphrodite	1613	
Mary Hanna	Limbo	1608	
7. SWI			4924
Daniel Ramseier	Rali Baba	1664	
Christine Stueckelberger	Aquamarin	1637	
Francoise Cantamessa	Sir S	1623	
8. GBR			4898
Emile Faurie	Rascher Hopes	1674	
Carl Hester	Argentile Gulli	1622	
Richard Davison	Askari	1602	

Competing in the rain, the Germans, Dutch and Americans finished first, second and third for the third consecutive Olympics.

2004 Athens-Markopoulo T: 18, N: 18, D: 8.27.

	HORSE		TOTAL PTS.
1. GER			74.653
Ulla Salzgeber	Rusty	78.208	
Martin Schaudt	Weltall	73.417	
Hubertus Schmidt	Wansuela Suerte	72.333	
2. SPA			72.917
Beatriz Ferrer-Salat	Beauvalais	74.667	
Rafael Soto Andrade	Invasor	72.792	
Juan Antonio Jiménez	Guizo	71.292	
3. USA			71.500
Deborah McDonald	Brentina	73.375	
Robert Dover	Kennedy	71.625	
Guenter Seidel	Aragon	69.500	
4. HOL			71.264
Anky van Grunsven	Salinero	74.208	
Sven Rothenberger	Barclay II	69.833	
Imke Schellekens-Bartels	Lancet	69.750	
5. DEN			69.333
Per Sandgaard	Zancor	70.667	
Jon Pedersen	Esprit De Valdemar	69.000	
Andreas Helgstrand	Cavan	68.333	
6. SWE			68.917
Jan Brink	Briar	73.250	
Tinne Eva Wilhelmsson	Just Mickey	66.917	
Louise "Lussan" Nathhorst	Guinness	66.583	
7. GBR			68.903
Carl Hester	Escapado	70.667	
Richard Davison	Ballaseyr Royale	68.542	
Emma Hindle	Wie Weltmeyer	67.500	
8. AUT			66.570
Victoria Max-Theurer	Falcao	68.667	
Nina Stadlinger	Egalité	67.375	
Friedrich "Fritz" Gaulhofer	Wels	63.667	

Trailing Spain with just one rider to go, Germany pulled out their sixth straight gold medal in the team dressage event when Ulla Salzgeber earned the highest score of the competition by more than three and a half points.

2008 Beijing-Hong Kong T: 11, N: 11, D: 8.14.

	HORSE		TOTAL PTS.
1. GER		72.917	
Isabell Werth	Satchmo	76.417	
Heike Kemmer	Bonaparte 67	72.250	
Nadine Capellmann	Elvis Va	70.083	
2. HOL			71.750
Anky van Grunsven	Salinero	74.750	
Imke Schellekens-Bartels	Sunrise	70.875	
Hans Peter Minderhoud	Nadine	69.625	
3. DEN			68.875
Nathalie zu Sayn-Wittgenstein	Digby	70.417	
Andreas Helgstrand	Don Schufro	68.833	
Anne van Olst	Clearwater	67.375	
4. SWE			67.347
Jan Brink	Briar	68.875	
Patrik Kittel	Floresco	67.125	
Tinne Silfvén	Solos Carex	66.042	
5. GBR			66.806
Emma Hindle	Lancet	71.125	
Laura Bechtolsheimer	Mistral Hojris	65.917	
Jane Gregory	Lucky Star	63.375	
6. FRA			65.403
Hubert Perring	Diabolo St Maurice	66.833	
Marc Boblet	Whitini Star	66.125	
Julia Chevanne-Gimel	Calimucho	63.250	
7. AUS			64.625
Kristy Oatley-Nist	Quando Quando	65.750	
Hayley Beresford	Relampago	65.583	
Heath Ryan	Greenoaks Dundee	62.542	
8. CAN		63.514	
Ashley Nicoll-Holzer	Pop Art	67.042	
Jacqueline Brooks	Gran Gesto	63.750	
Leslie Reid	Orion	59.750	
DISQ (Drugs): USA 67.81			

Led by four-time Olympic gold medalist and six-time world champion Isabell Werth, the Germans looked well-placed to extend their run of six Olympic wins in this event. All three members of the team were previous gold medalists and all had been on the reigning 2006 world championship team. The only other team with a credible shot at gold at the Beijing Games was the Netherlands, led by twice individual dressage gold medalist Anky van Grunsven. A year before the Olympics the Dutch had edged out Germany to win the European championship.

As expected, Werth and van Grunsven recorded the highest scores of the competition, 76.417 and 74.750 points respectively, with Heike Kemmer recording the third-highest score, 72.250 points, to help Germany to the victory. Denmark finished third, pipping the United States (defending bronze medalists for the fourth time in a row) after Debbie McDonald scored 63 points on a shaky performance. The US was later disqualified when Courtney King-Dye's horse Mythilus tested positive for the banned anti-inflammatory felbinac. On March 3 2010 King-Dye incurred a traumatic brain injury falling from her horse while riding without a helmet. The campaign Riders4Helmet was created as a result of her injury.

DISCONTINUED EVENTS

HIGH JUMP

1900 Paris C: 18?, N: 5, D: 6.2.

		HORSE	M	FT.-IN.
1. Dominique Maximien Gardères	FRA	Canela	1.85	6-0¾
1. Giovanni Giorgio Trissino	ITA	Oreste	1.85	6-0¾
3. Georges van de Poële	BEL	Ludlow	1.70	5-6¾
4. Giovanni Giorgio Trissino	ITA	Melopo	1.70	5-6¾

The current record for the equestrian high jump is 2.47 meters (8 feet 1¼ inches), set on February 5, 1949 by Alberto Larraguibel of Chile on Huaso.

LONG JUMP

1900 Paris C: 17?, N: 5, D: 5.31.

		HORSE	M	FT.-IN.
1. Constant van Langhendonck	BEL	Extra Dry	6.10	20-0¼
2. Giovanni Giorgio Trissino	ITA	Oreste	5.70	18-9½
3. de Bellegarde	FRA	Tolla	5.30	17-4¾
4. Napoléon Murat	FRA	Bayard	4.90	16-1

The current record for the equestrian long jump is 8.40 meters (27 feet 6¾), set in 1975 by André Ferreira of South Africa on Something.

MAIL COACH (FOUR-IN-HAND)

1900 Paris C: 31?, N: 6, D: 6.2.

1. Georges Nagelmackers	BEL
2. Léon Thome	FRA
3. de Neuflize	FRA
4. Philippe Vernes	FRA

HACK AND HUNTER COMBINED (CHEVAUX DE SELLE)

1900 Paris C: 51?, N: 4, D: 5.31.

		HORSE
1. Napoléon Murat	FRA	The General
2. Archenoul	FRA	Retournelle
3. de Montesquiou-Fezensac	FRA	Grey Leg
4. Marcel Haëntjens	BEL	Mavourneen

One of the participants in this event was Elvira Guerra of France, who appears to have been the first woman to compete in the Olympics. Some historians have assigned this honor to yachtswoman Helen de Pourtales, but, for several reasons, the yachting events of 1900 do not qualify as Olympic contests (see page 838). One contemporary source mentions a Mlle. Moulin as also competing in the *chevaux de selle* event.

FIGURE RIDING, INDIVIDUAL

1920 Antwerp C: 18, N: 3, D: 9.11.

		PTS.
1. Daniel Bouckaert	BEL	30.5
2. Field	FRA	29.5
3. Louis Finet	BEL	29.0
4. van Ranst	BEL	28.0
5. van Schauwbroeck	BEL	27.25
6. van Cauwenberg	BEL	26.666
7. Salins	FRA	26.333
8. Victor Claes	BEL	26.163

This event was open only to army officers. It included several acrobatic moves such as jumping on and off a horse and standing on a horse, as well as jumping *over* horses.

FIGURE RIDING, TEAMS

1920 Antwerp T: 3, N: 3, D: 9.11.

		PTS.
1. BEL	Daniel Bouckaert, Louis Finet, van Ranst	87.5
2. FRA	Field, Salins, Cauchy	81.083
3. SWE	Carl Green, Anders Mårtensson, Oskar Nilsson	59.416

Chapter 11 **Fencing**

MEN	WOMEN
Foil, Individual	Foil, Individual
Foil, Team	Foil, Team
Épée, Individual	Épée, Individual
Sabre, Individual	Épée, Team
Sabre, Team	Sabre, Individual
Discontinued Events	Discontinued Event

SOME COMMON FENCING TERMS

Balestra—A short jump forward immediately followed by a lunge
Barrage—A fence-off, used to decide ties
En garde—The position taken before combat begins. Standing sideways, with the rear arm curled up for balance, the fencer tries to present the smallest possible target area to the opponent.
Flêche—A running attack toward the opponent
Lunge—An attack in which the front leg is extended to a point where the knee is over the ankle and the back leg is straight
Parry—A blocking of an opponent's thrust
Piste—The dueling surface. For foil events it is two meters (6 ft. 7 in.) wide and 14 meters (46 feet) long. For épée and sabre events it is the same width but the length is 18 meters (59 feet). The *en garde* lines are two meters (6 ft. 7 in.) from the center line.
Reprise—An attack that follows a recovery from an opponent's lunge
Riposte—An offensive action that follows a parry
Thrust—An attack with a quick extension of the blade but no foot movement

Three weapons are used in fencing: foil, épée and sabre.

The *foil* has a flexible rectangular blade, and hits are scored with the point, but are valid only if they contact a conductive metallic jacket covering just the torso.

The *épée*, the traditional sword of duels, has a rigid triangular blade, and hits are scored with the point on any part of the body.

The *sabre* has a flexible triangular blade and hits are scored both with the point and the cutting edges, being valid on the mask and a metallic jacket covering the body above the waist.

All weapons are linked to an electrical scoring system. In the case of foil and épée, wires run from the tip of the weapon along a groove in the blade to a socket inside the guard and then via the fencer's body wire to a reel that is connected to the scoring apparatus. When a hit is made a light comes on and a buzzer sounds. The sabre blade has no wires, but the sudden contact of blade against metallic jacket or mask triggers an electric circuit in the guard that is conveyed to the scoring machine in the same way as the other weapons. Sabre was the last weapon to be electrified, but the first to use a wireless scoring system, introduced at the 2004 Athens Olympics before being adapted for épée and foil at the 2008 Olympics. Competitors wear special conductive T-shirts next to their skin. A hit activates a transmitter attached to the fencer's waist, which triggers a light on the mask and transmits a signal to the scoreboard in the arena.

Christian d'Oriola
The Frenchman won four gold medals and two silver medals in foil fencing between 1948 and 1956.

Over the years Olympic fencing tournaments have used a variety of formats. These days a single elimination format is used, each match in the individual tournaments being fenced up to 15 hits or whoever is leading after nine minutes. If the scores are level, one minute of sudden-death overtime is contested, a random electronic indicator showing which fencer will be declared the winner if no hit is scored at the end of that final minute.

Team events are contested by teams of three. The first pair fence for three minutes or until one fencer has scored five hits. The next pair takes over for another three minutes or until one team reaches 10 points. This continues until all members of a team have fenced their opposite numbers and one side has reached 45 points or time has expired. If the teams are tied at the end of regulation time, an additional minute of fencing is allowed and, as in individual events, a random indicator shows which team will win if there is no further score.

Since 2004 women's sabre has been added to the individual events and in theory to the team events also, but the IOC awards medals in only 10 of the 12 fencing disciplines. Therefore the International Fencing Federation (FIE) has to drop two events for each Olympics. In 2012 these will be the men's team épée and women's team sabre.

MEN

FOIL, INDIVIDUAL

1896 Athens C: 8, N: 2, D: 4.7.

		W	L	TG	TR
1. Eugène-Henri Gravelotte	FRA	4	0	12	7
2. Henri Callot	FRA	3	1	11	7
3. Perikles Pierrakos-Mavromichalis	GRE	2	1	7	4
3. Athanasios Vouros	GRE	2	1	5	4
5. Henri de Laborde	FRA	1	2	5	7
5. Konstantinos Komnios-Milliotis	GRE	1	2	5	4
7. Georgios Balakakis	GRE	0	3	3	9
7. Ioannis Poulos	GRE	0	3	4	9

Final: Gravelotte 3-2 Callot

Gravelotte, France's first Olympic champion, was a medical student. He defeated his friend Callot 3-2 in the final. That evening he celebrated his triumph by drinking a glass of retzina at the Acropolis.

1900 Paris C: 54, N: 8, D: 5.21.

		W	L
1. Emile Costé	FRA	6	1
2. Henri Masson	FRA	5	2
3. Marcel Jacques Boulenger	FRA	4	3
4. Debax	FRA	4	3
5. Pierre d'Hugues	FRA	3	4
6. Prospère Sénat	FRA	3	4
7. Georges Dillon-Kavanagh	FRA	2	5
8. Rudolf Brosch	AUT	1	6

1904 St. Louis C: 9, N: 3, D: 9.7.

		W	L
1. Ramón Fonst Segundo	CUB	3	0
2. Albertson Van Zo Post	USA	2	1
3. Charles Tatham	USA	1	2
4. Gustav Casmir	GER	0	3

1906 Athens C: 37, N: 12, D: 4.25.

1. Georges Dillon-Kavanagh	FRA
2. Gustav Casmir	GER
3. Pierre d'Hugues	FRA
4. Martin Harden	AUT
5. Simon Okker	HOL

DNF: Federico Cesarano ITA

1908 not held

The committee in charge of fencing at the London Games considered foil fencing an art form rather than a sport and allowed its inclusion in the program only as an exhibition.

1912 Stockholm C: 94, N: 15, D: 7.8.

		W	L	TG	TR
1. Nedo Nadi	ITA	7	0	35	8
2. Pietro Speciale	ITA	5	2	29	24
3. Richard Verderber	AUT	4	3	27	25
4. László Bertl	HUN	4	3	23	25
5. Edoardo Alaimo	ITA	4	3	27	26
6. Edgar Seligman	GBR	3	4	23	29
7. Béla Békessy	HUN	1	6	20	34
8. Robert Montgomerie	GBR	0	7	22	35

Nadi was a mere 18 years old when he won his first Olympic gold medal. The French team boycotted the competition after their proposal to include the upper arm as an attackable surface was rejected.

1920 Antwerp C: 56, N: 10, D: 8.18.

		W	L	TR
1. Nedo Nadi	ITA	10	1	
2. Philippe Cattiau	FRA	9	2	14
3. Roger Ducret	FRA	9	2	19
4. André Labatut	FRA	7	4	
5. Aldo Nadi	ITA	6	5	19
6. Fernand de Montigny	BEL	6	5	27
7. Oreste Puliti	ITA	5	6	
8. Ivan Osiier	DEN	4	7	

Nadi's performance at Antwerp was nothing short of spectacular, as he won an unprecedented and unequaled five gold medals. Not only did he win both the individual foil and sabre, but he was also the leader of the winning Italian teams in the foil, épée, and sabre. His record in the individual foil tournament was 22-2. However, he almost didn't win because his second loss was to Ducret in the final round. Ducret, in his memoirs, described what happened next: "I was the Olympic champion: I struggled to contain the joy that was overflowing in my heart. I thanked destiny for having given me this marvelous form and, in the Olympic period, this day of invincibility, the kind that fencers rarely encounter in their lives. Meanwhile, Nedo Nadi was crying in his corner. All that remained for me was one match against the last place of the pool [Pietro Speciale of Italy, who was 0-10 in the final]. A final formality that didn't worry me in the least. Crossing swords with this adversary was like stretching my legs. I had, without effort, touched him a dozen times in a row. I could beat him with my eyes closed. I attacked immediately (too hastily perhaps, because I missed). I was touched. Bah! Not

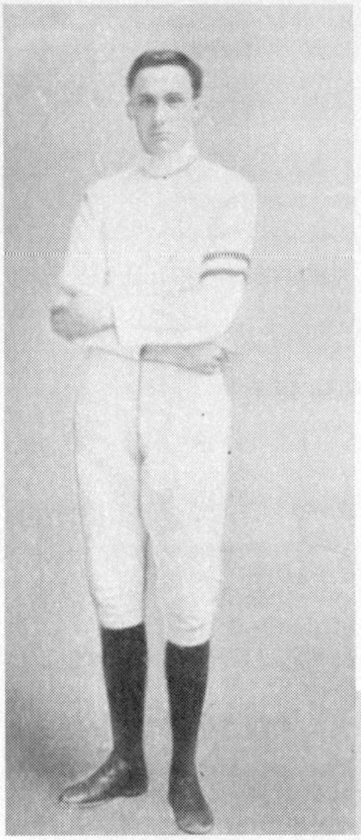

Nedo Nadi, 1920
Nedo Nadi won gold medals in five of the six fencing events of 1920.

important. I aimed again, with a casual assurance. This thrust was well parried; I received the riposte without making a counter riposte: 2-0. It was starting to go badly. Alas! Having believed the contest won, I had relaxed my pace to such a degree that I was unable to regain my rhythm. I no longer understood anything. I lost completely the flow and the match and the title, all at the same time." But Ducret had learned his lesson. Four years later in Paris he would win his gold medal at last by keeping his concentration when he needed it most.

1924 Paris C: 49, N: 17, D: 7.4.

		W	L	TG	TR
1. Roger Ducret	FRA	6	0	30	14
2. Philippe Cattiau	FRA	5	1	29	11
3. Maurice van Damme	BEL	4	2	23	16
4. Jacques Coutrot	FRA	3	3	18	25
5. Roberto Larraz	ARG	2	4	21	25
6. Ivan Osiier	DEN	1	5	14	27
7. Balthazar de Beuckelaer	BEL	0	6	13	30

DNS: Edgar Seligman GBR

In the absence of the Italians, who had withdrawn following an incident during the team foil, the individual competition was dominated by the French. Particularly formidable was Philippe Cattiau, who whipped through the tournament with an outstanding record of 23 wins and one loss and 119 touches given, as opposed to only 54 received. Unfortunately, his only loss was in the final pool to 26-year-old Roger Ducret, who beat Cattiau five touches to four to win the gold medal. Ducret had suffered six defeats (against 13 wins) on his way to the final.

1928 Amsterdam C: 54, N: 23, D: 8.1.

						BARRAGE			
		W	L	TG	TR	W	L	TG	TR
1. Lucien Gaudin	FRA	9	2	49	24	2	0	10	5
2. Erwin Casmir	GER	9	2	49	33	1	1	6	8
3. Giulio Gaudini	ITA	9	2	53	34	0	2	7	10
4. Oreste Puliti	ITA	8	3	51	27				
5. Philippe Cattiau	FRA	7	4	43	32				
6. Raymond Bru	BEL	7	4	42	41				
7. Ugo Pignotti	ITA	4	7	40	48				
8. Fritz August Gazzera	GER	4	7	37	49				

Lucien Gaudin and Oreste Puliti entered the finals undefeated, but Puliti lost to Gaudin, Erwin Casmir, and Raymond Bru. In the final Casmir beat Gaudin 5-4, but in the barrage Gaudin was the victor, 5-1. However Gaudin still needed to face Gaudini. With the score tied 2-2, Gaudini grazed Gaudin's fencing jacket. The referee called out, "No touch." The Italians were furious and began protesting vehemently. Gaudin removed his mask, walked over to the jury, and calmly announced, "I was touched." Gaudini was awarded the point and then earned another. However, Gaudin then scored three times in a row to win 5-4. Gaudin was 41 years old.

1932 Los Angeles C: 26, N: 12, D: 8.5.

		W	L	TG	TR
1. Gustavo Marzi	ITA	9	0	45	17
2. Joseph Levis	USA	6	3	38	35
3. Giulio Gaudini	ITA	5	4	34	27
4. Gioacchino Guaragna	ITA	5	4	37	33
5. Erwin Casmir	GER	5	4	36	34
6. John Emrys Lloyd	GBR	5	4	36	34
7. Roberto Larraz	ARG	3	6	33	31
8. René Bougnol	FRA	3	6	28	41

Twenty-three-year-old Gustavo Marzi completed the tournament with a record of 21-2.

1936 Berlin C: 62, N: 22, D: 8.6.

		W	L	TG	TR
1. Giulio Gaudini	ITA	7	0	35	20
2. Edward Gardère	FRA	6	1	33	25
3. Giorgio Bocchino	ITA	4	3	28	22
4. Erwin Casmir	GER	4	3	31	29
5. Gioacchino Guaragna	ITA	3	4	30	28
6. Raymond Bru	BEL	3	4	25	31
7. André Gardère	FRA	1	6	23	32
8. Georges de Bourguignon	BEL	0	7	17	35

Between 1928 and 1936 the 6-foot 3½-inch Gaudini won three gold medals, four silver, and two bronze. The 1936 foil was his only individual gold.

Giulio Gaudini, 1936
Between 1928 and 1936, Gaudini earned nine medals in foil and sabre fencing.

1948 London C: 63, N: 25, D: 8.4.

		W	L	TG	TR
1. Jehan Buhan	FRA	7	0	35	14
2. Christian d'Oriola	FRA	5	2	29	18
3. Lajos Maszlay	HUN	4	3	25	22
4. John Emrys Lloyd	GBR	4	3	23	29
5. René Bougnol	FRA	3	4	28	26
6. Manlio Di Rosa	ITA	3	4	22	27
7. Paul Valcke	BEL	1	6	23	31
8. Ivan Ruben	DEN	1	6	15	33

Buhan, a 36-year-old wine merchant, had gone to London to compete in the épée and was only entered in the foil at the last minute. Runner-up d'Oriola had surprised the fencing world in 1947 by winning the world championship in Lisbon at the tender age of 18. Buhan finished the tournament with a record of 24-1.

After competing in the Olympics, Cuban fencer Jorge Agostini joined Castro's Revolutionary forces in the fight against the country's president Fulgencio Batista. In June 1955 Agostini was found by Batista's forces and brutally killed; an autopsy revealed 21 bullet holes scattered throughout his body.

1952 Helsinki C: 61, N: 25, D: 7.24.

		W	L	TG	TR
1. Christian d'Oriola	FRA	8	0	40	12
2. Edoardo Mangiarotti	ITA	6	2	21	
3. Manlio Di Rosa	ITA	5	3	22	
4. Jacques Lataste	FRA	4	4	31	
5. Jehan Buhan	FRA	4	4	29	33
6. Mahmoud Younes	EGY	4	4	27	33
7. Salah Dessouki	EGY	2	6	35	
8. Giancarlo Bergamini	ITA	2	6	36	

All three medalists were left-handed.

1956 Melbourne C: 32, N: 14, D: 11.26.

						BARRAGE			
		W	L	TG	TR	W	L	TG	TR
1. Christian d'Oriola	FRA	6	1	33	17				
2. Giancarlo Bergamini	ITA	5	2	33	26	1	0	5	4
3. Antonio Spallino	ITA	5	2	30	21	0	1	4	5
4. Allan Jay	GBR	4	3	29	26				
5. József Gyuricza	HUN	3	4	21	25				
6. Claude Netter	FRA	3	4	19	30				
7. Mark Midler	SOV/RUS	2	5	19	30				
8. Raymond Paul	GBR	0	7	15	35				

D'Oriola was a 27-year-old law student when he became the first man since Nedo Nadi to win two individual foil gold medals. D'Oriola, a native of Perpignan, had some trouble adapting to the new electric foil, but he solved it quite well in time for the Melbourne Olympics.

1960 Rome C: 78, N: 31, D: 8.30.

						BARRAGE			
		W	L	TG	TR	W	L	TG	TR
1. Viktor Zhdanovich	SOV/RUS	7	0	35	20				
2. Yuri Sissikin	SOV/RUS	4	2	27	21				
3. Albert Axelrod	USA	3	3	23	24	2	0	10	7
4. Witold Woyda	POL	3	3	24	23	1	1	9	7
5. Mark Midler	SOV/RUS	3	4	28	25	0	2	5	10
6. Roger Closset	FRA	2	2	14	16				
7. Henry Hoskyns	GBR	2	5	21	33				
8. Christian d'Oriola	FRA	1	6	22	32				

A 22-year-old student teacher from Leningrad, Zhdanovich was the first Soviet fencer to win a gold medal. As such, he became a hero and was known in the newspapers as "Viktor the Victor."

1964 Tokyo C: 55, N: 21, D: 10.14.

		W	L	TG	TR
1. Egon Franke	POL	3	0	15	9
2. Jean-Claude Magnan	FRA	2	2	14	10
3. Daniel Revenu	FRA	1	3	12	11
4. Roland Losert	AUT	0	3	4	15
5. Jenő Kamuti	HUN				
6. Tim Gerresheim	GER				
7. Henry Hoskyns	GBR				
7. Sándor Szabó	HUN				

Egon Franke, a 29-year-old technical administrator from the small town of Gliwice, was an unexpected and popular winner.

1968 Mexico City C: 64, N: 25, D: 10.16.

						BARRAGE			
		W	L	TG	TR	W	L	TG	TR
1. Ionel Drimbă	ROM	4	1	22	15				
2. Jenő Kamuti	HUN	3	2	19	14	1	0	5	4
3. Daniel Revenu	FRA	3	2	22	17	0	1	4	5
4. Christian Noël	FRA	2	3	14	18				
5. Jean-Claude Magnan	FRA	2	3	18	22				
6. Mihai Tiu	ROM	1	4	14	23				
7. Tănase Mureşan	ROM								
7. German Sveshnikov	SOV/RUS								

Ion Drimbă, a 26-year-old physical training instructor, went through the tournament with a record of 19-2. Two years later he defected to the West and retired from competition.

1972 Munich C: 58, N: 26, D: 8.30.

		W	L	TG	TR
1. Witold Woyda	POL	5	0	25	7
2. Jenő Kamuti	HUN	4	1	23	19
3. Christian Noël	FRA	2	3	17	18
4. Mihai Tiu	ROM	2	3	17	20
5. Vladimir Denissov	SOV/RUS	2	3	17	21
6. Marek Dąbrowski	POL	0	5	10	25

Thirty-three-year-old Witold Woyda qualified for the final with a modest record of 14-6, but then he completely dominated his last five opponents to take the gold medal.

1976 Montreal C: 56, N: 23, D: 7.21.

						BARRAGE			
		W	L	TG	TR	W	L	TG	TR
1. Fabio Dal Zotto	ITA	4	1	24	15	1	0	5	1
2. Aleksandr Romankov	SOV/BLR	4	1	21	13	0	1	1	5
3. Bernard Talvard	FRA	3	2	19	21				
4. Vasyl Stankovych	SOV/UKR	2	3	19	18				
5. Frédéric Pietruszka	FRA	2	3	13	19				
6. Gregory Benkö	AUS	0	5	15	25				
7. Vladimir Denissov	SOV								
7. Christian Noèl	FRA								

Dal Zotto, a student from Venice, celebrated his 19th birthday three days before the competition began.

1980 Moscow C: 37, N: 16, D: 7.23.

						BARRAGE			
		W	L	TG	TR	W	L	TG	TR
1. Volodymyr Smirnov	SOV/UKR	4	1	24	16	1	1	9	5
2. Pascal Jolyot	FRA	4	1	24	17	1	1	5	5
3. Aleksandr Romankov	SOV/BLR	4	1	22	15	1	1	5	9
4. Sabirzhan Ruziyev	SOV/UZB	2	3	20	19				
5. Lech Koziejowski	POL	1	4	15	21				
6. Petru Kuki	ROM	0	5	8	25				
7. Frédéric Pietruszka	FRA								
7. István Szelei	HUN								

Two years after winning the Olympic gold medal, Smirnov was defending his world championship in Rome when the foil of his opponent, Matthias Behr of West Germany, snapped, pierced Smirnov's mask, penetrated his eyeball and entered his brain. The 28-year-old Soviet fencer died nine days later.

1984 Los Angeles-Long Beach C: 58, N: 26, D: 8.2.

1. Mauro Numa	ITA
2. Matthias Behr	GER
3. Stefano Cerioni	ITA
4. Frédéric Pietruszka	FRA
5. Andrea Borella	ITA
6. Mathias Gey	GER
7. Philippe Omnès	FRA
8. Thierry Soumagne	BEL

Final: Numa 10-9 Behr
3rd Place: Cerioni 10-5 Pietruszka

Mauro Numa may have won the gold medal, but his victory did not come easily. In his quarterfinal bout with Philippe Omnès, Numa trailed 6-8 with one minute left and then scored four straight touches in 49 seconds to win 10-8. In his semifinal match, he trailed Stefano Cerioni 1-6 before coming from behind to win 11-9. In the final against Matthias Behr, Numa was behind 3-7 with one minute to go. Again he scored four straight touches. Then Behr moved ahead 8-7. Numa was back with two quick scores. However, with two seconds remaining, Behr evened the count, sending the contest into sudden-death overtime. Within seconds Numa finally secured the win. Among the boycott missing was five-time world champion Aleksandr Romankov, who had won the last two world championships.

1988 Seoul C: 68, N: 29, D: 9.21.

1. Stefano Cerioni	ITA
2. Udo Wagner	GDR
3. Aleksandr Romankov	SOV/BLR
4. Ulnich Schreck	GER
5. Zsolt Érsek	HUN
6. Mauro Numa	ITA
7. Jens Howe	GDR
8. Mathias Gey	GER

Final: Cerioni 10-7 Wagner
3rd Place: Romankov 10-8 Schreck

Cerioni's victory capped a successful comeback following a 15-month suspension. During the 1986 world championships, the volatile Spanish-born fencer had offended tournament officials by screaming wildly and making obscene gestures.

1992 Barcelona C: 59, N: 25, D: 7.31.

1. Philippe Omnès	FRA
2. Sergiy Golubytsky	UKR
3. Elvis Gregory Gil	CUB
4. Udo Wagner	GER
5. Andrea Borella	ITA
6. Marian Sypniewski	POL
7. Guillermo Betancourt Scull	CUB
8. Joachim Wendt	AUT

Final: Omnès—Golubytsky 6-5, 3-5, 5-2
3rd Place: Gregory—Wagner 5-3, 2-5, 5-3

The 31-year-old Omnès had won the world championship in 1990 but was considered past his prime by the time of the Barcelona Olympics. He lost to Borella, but qualified for the final eight through *repêchage.* In the semifinals Omnès defeated Wagner 5-3, 5-6, 5-3, and Golubitsky, who had also come through the *repêchage* round, beat Gregory 3-5, 5-2, 5-1.

1996 Atlanta C: 45, N: 19, D: 7.22.

1. Alessandro Puccini	ITA
2. Lionel Plumenail	FRA
3. Franck Boidin	FRA
4. Wolfgang Wienand	GER
5. Rolando Tucker León	CUB
6. Sergiy Golubytsky	UKR
7. Philippe Omnès	FRA
8. Kim Young-ho	KOR

Final: Puccini 15-12 Plumenail
3rd Place: Boidin 15-11 Wienand

Reigning world champion, Dmitri Shevchenko of Russia had a reputation for beating the best fencers, but losing to weaker opponents. Sure enough, he was defeated 15-13 in his very first match by Kim Young-ho, who was ranked 50th in the world. None of the four top seeds made it to the semifinal. 1994 world champion Rolando Tucker was beaten 15-12 in the quarterfinals by Wolfgang Wienand. Sergiy Golubytsky also went out in the quarterfinals, losing to Lionel Plumenail 15-13. The real sensation of the tournament occurred in the round of 16 when Cuba's Elvis Gregory faced defending Olympic champion Philippe Omnès. The score was 14-14 when, according to Cuban officials, Omnès told Gregory, "You are nothing." Omnès then took the final point and the match. Gregory initially refused to shake hands with Omnès. As they left the floor, the French team began taunting Gregory. The Cubans supported Gregory and the two sides came to blows. They were separated by security personnel, and reporters were barred from the arena. Meanwhile, Alessandro Puccini, a successful team fencer who had never won a major individual event, survived a close quarterfinal bout against Kim Young-ho and finally prevailed 15-14. In the semifinals, Plumenail defeated Wienand 15-9 and Puccini beat Franck Boidin 15-13.

2000 Sydney C: 40, N: 23, D: 9.20.

1. Kim Young-ho	KOR
2. Ralf Bissdorf	GER
3. Dmitry Shevchenko	RUS
4. Jean-Noël Ferrari	FRA
5. Salvatore Sanzo	ITA
6. Sergiy Golubytsky	UKR
7. Richard Breutner	GER
8. Márk Marsi	HUN

Final: Kim 15-14 Bissdorf
3rd Place: Shevchenko 15-14 Ferrari

Sergiy Golubytsky had been the most successful foil fencer of the 1990s, yet he had met frustration at the Olympics, losing to France's Philippe Omnès in the 1992 final and to another Frenchman, Lionel Plumenail, in the 1996 quarterfinals. Between the Atlanta and Sydney Olympics, Golubytsky won all three world championships. Golubytsky's self-assessment? "I am a genius. There's no other explanation for my results." In the 2000 quarterfinals, Golubytsky met Kim Young-ho, the man he had beaten in the final of the 1997 world championship. This time Kim scored a surprisingly easy 15-5 victory. It was particularly surprising in that it was the only one of Kim's five Sydney matches that wasn't nervewrackingly close. Before meeting Golubytsky, Kim came from behind to defeat Brice Guyart of France 15-13 and then trailed Cliff Bayer of the United States 7-11, 10-13 and 13-14, before winning 15-14. In a wild semifinal match that took only 2 minutes 40 seconds, Kim came from behind yet again, beating Dmitri Shevchenko 15-14. In the final, Kim trailed Ralf Bissdorf 6-9 and then scored five straight points to lead 11-9. At 14-11, Kim needed only one more point, but Bissdorf fought back to a 14-14 tie. Finally Kim touched Bissdorf's shoulder to gain his third 15-14 victory and, with it, the gold medal. When Kim discovered fencing at the age of 14, his mother tried to stop him from pursuing the sport because she thought it would lead him to a life of crime.

2004 Athens C: 36, N: 20, D: 8.16.

1. Brice Guyart	FRA
2. Salvatore Sanzo	ITA
3. Andrea Cassara	ITA
4. Renal Ganeyev	RUS
5. Simone Vanni	ITA
6. Peter Joppich	GER
7. Wu Hanxiong	CHN
8. Richard Kruse	GBR

Final: Guyart 15-13 Sanzo
3rd Place: Cassara 15-12 Ganeyev

A gold-medal winner in the team event in 2000, at the age of nineteen, Brice Guyart defeated number-one-ranked Andrea Cassara in the semifinals, 15-14. In the rough and physical final, former world champion Salvatore Sanzo took an early 4-0 lead, but Guyart evened the score at 5-5. The two traded the lead, evening the score seven times until it stood at 12 all. Two quick strikes brought Guyart within reach of the gold, 14-12, but he bent his sword while giving up a point on next touch. Guyart changed swords and scored the final point to earn gold.

2008 Beijing C: 26, N: 21, D: 8.13.

1. Benjamin Kleibrink	GER
2. Yuki Ota	JPN
3. Salvatore Sanzo	ITA
4. Zhu Jun	CHN
5. Peter Joppich	GER
6. Andrea Cassarà	ITA
7. Erwann Le Péchoux	FRA
8. Lei Sheng	CHN

Final: Kleibrink 15-9 Ota
3rd Place: Sanzo 15-14 Zhu

The clear favorite in the men's individual foil event was two-time reigning world champion Peter Joppich. One month before the Olympics, his chances of a gold medal improved significantly when his most serious rival, Andrea Baldini, tested positive for the banned diuretic furosemide at the European championships in Kiev and was dropped from the Italian Olympic team. Baldini, the top-ranked fencer in the world, had won the two previous world championship silver medals behind Joppich.

The competition saw several early upsets. Defending Olympic champion Brice Guyart was eliminated in the second round after losing 10-15 to teammate Erwann Le Péchoux. Meanwhile, Joppich advanced to the quarterfinals with a narrow 10-9 win over 2006 European silver medalist Richard Kruse, but fell in the quarterfinals to 22-year-old Yuki Ota.

Ota faced 2005 world champion Salvatore Sanzo in the semifinals and managed a close 15-14 win. In the final his opponent was 2007 world bronze medalist Benjamin Kleibrink. Kleibrink built up a 9-3 lead in the first six minutes, eventually scoring the winning touch with sixteen seconds remaining in the match and becoming the first German in Olympic history to win an individual foil gold medal.

Ota started fencing at the age of 8 at the urging of his father, a former fencer himself, who promised the youngster a video game if he took up the sport.

FOIL, TEAM

1896–1900 not held

1904 St. Louis T: 2, N: 2, D: 9.8.

		WON
1. CUB&USA	Ramón Fonst Segundo—CUB, Manuel Diaz Martínez—CUB, Albertson Van Zo Post—USA	7
2. USA	Charles Tatham, Fitzhugh Townsend, Arthur Fox	2

1906–1912 not held

1920 Antwerp T: 8, N: 8, D: 8.17.

			MATCHES	
	WON	**LOST**	**W**	**L**
1. ITA	4	0	50	14
2. FRA	3	1	45	19
3. USA	2	2	22	42
4. DEN	1	3	26	38
5. GBR	0	4	17	47
6. BEL				
6. CZE				
6. HOL				

1. ITA—Baldo Baldi, Tommaso Constantino, Aldo Nadi, Nedo Nadi, Abelardo Olivier, Oreste Puliti, Pietro Speciale, Rodolfo Terlizzi
2. FRA—Lionel de Castellane, Gaston Amson, Phillippe Cattiau, Roger Ducret, André Labatut, Georges Trombert, Marcel Perrot, Lucien Gaudin
3. USA—Henry Breckinridge, Francis Honeycutt, Arthur Lyon, Harold Rayner, Robert Sears
4. DEN—Ivan Osiier, Georg Hegner, Ejnar Levison, Poul Rasmussen, Kay Schrøder
5. GBR—Edgar Seligman, Richard Willoughby, Philip Doyne, Robert Montgomerie, H. Evan James, Cecil Kershaw
6. BEL—Marcel Berré, Charles Crahay, Marcel Cuypers, Fernand de Montigny, Emile de Schepper, Robert Hennet, Léon Tom, Charles Pape
6. CZE—Josef Javůrek, Antony Mikala, Vilém Tvrzský, František Dvořák
6. HOL—Wouter Brouwer, Raphaël "Felix" Vigeveno, Salomon Zeldenrust, Andrianus de Jong, Jan van der Wiel

Italy defeated France 9-7 in the decisive match-up of the final pool.

1924 Paris T: 12, N: 12, D: 6.30.

			MATCHES	
	WON	**LOST**	**W**	**L**
1. FRA	3	0	31	6
2. BEL	2	1	12	20
3. HUN	1	2	9	23
4. ITA	0	3	1	4
5. ARG				

1. FRA—Lucien Gaudin, Philippe Cattiau, Jacques Coutrot, Roger Ducret, Henri Jobier, André Labatut, Guy de Luget, Joseph Peroteaux
2. BEL—Désiré Beaurain, Charles Crahay, Fernand de Montigny, Maurice van Damme, Marcel Bérré, Albert de Roocker
3. HUN—László Berti, Sándor Posta, Zoltán Schenker, Ödön Tersztyánszky, István Lichteneckert
4. ITA—Oreste Puliti, Giorgio Pessina, Valentine Argento, Giorgio Chiavacci, Giullo Gaudini, Aldo Boni, Luigi Cuomo, Dante Carniel
5. ARG—Francisco Bollini, Horacio Casco, Carlos Guerrico, Roberto Larraz, Luis Lucchetti, Carmelo Merlo, Ángel Santamarina, José Sosa

When the French and Italian teams met in the final pool at the Vélodrome d'Hiver, it was assumed that the winner would go on to take the gold medal. France took a 3-1 lead. In the fifth assault, Lucien Gaudin and Aldo Boni were tied at four touches each when the jury awarded a decisive, and questionable, fifth touch to Gaudin. Boni was incensed and launched a verbal attack against György Kovács, the Hungarian judge. Kovács approached the Jury of Appeal and demanded an apology, whereupon

Boni denied everything. Kovács then produced a witness, the Italian-born Hungarian fencing master Italo Santelli, who reluctantly supported Kovács' allegations of abusive language. The Italian team withdrew in protest, singing the Fascist hymn as they left, and their remaining matches were declared forfeited. Lost in the excitement was a brilliant performance by Gaudin, who scored 22 victories without a defeat and recorded 110 touches while receiving only 21.

However, the affair was not over. Back in Italy, the Italian foil team issued a statement which accused Santelli of testifying against them because he feared the Italians would defeat the Hungarian team, which he had coached. When he heard about this insult, Santelli, who was over 60 years old, challenged Adolfo Contronei, the Italian captain, to a real duel. Government permission was obtained to fight the duel, but before the two men could meet, Santelli's 27-year-old son, Giorgio, invoked the *code duello* and demanded that he fight in his father's place. In the small town of Abazzia near the Hungarian border, Giorgio and Contronei met and fought with heavy sabres. After two minutes the younger Santelli slashed Contronei deeply on the side of the head, drawing blood. Doctors rushed in and halted the duel. Giorgio Santelli later moved to the United States, where he became the coach of the US team. He taught fencing to 8,000 people and spent more than 100,000 hours with a sword in his hand, but he never again engaged in a real duel.

1928 Amsterdam T: 16, N: 16, D: 7.30.

	WON	LOST	MATCHES W	MATCHES L
1. ITA	3	0	34	14
2. FRA	2	1	23	25
3. ARG	1	2	23	25
4. BEL	0	3	16	32
5. HUN				
5. USA				

1. ITA—Ugo Pignotti, Oreste Puliti, Giullo Gaudini, Giorgio Pessina, Giorgio Chiavacci, Gioacchino Guaragna
2. FRA—Lucien Gaudin, Philippe Cattiau, Roger Ducret, André Labatut, Raymond Flacher, André Gaboriaud
3. ARG—Roberto Larraz, Raúl Anganuzzi, Luis Lucchetti, Héctor Lucchetti, Carmelo Camet
4. BEL—Max Janlet, Pierre Pecher, Raymond Bru, Albert de Roocker, Jean Verbrugghe, Charles Crahay
5. HUN—Ödön Tersztyánszky, György Rozgonyi, György Jekelfalussy-Piller, József Rády, Gusztáv Kálniczky, Péter Toth
5. USA—George Calnan, René Peroy, Joseph Levis, Harold Rayner, Henry Breckinridge, Dernell Every

In Amsterdam the Italians gained their revenge against the French with a 10-6 victory. The Italian team was led by Chiavacci, who finished the tournament with 22 wins and two losses, and Gaudini, who was 30-2, including four straight victories against the French.

1932 Los Angeles T: 6, N: 6, D: 8.1.

	WON	LOST	MATCHES W	MATCHES L	BARRAGE WON	BARRAGE LOST	BARRAGE MATCHES W	BARRAGE MATCHES L
1. FRA—Philippe Cattiau, Edward Gardère, René Lemoine, René Bondoux, Jean Piot, René Bougnol	2	1	26	22	2	0	19	13
2. ITA—Giulio Gaudini, Gustavo Marzi, Ugo Pignotti, Giorgio Pessina, Gioacchino Guaranga, Rodolfo Terlizzi	2	1	31	17	1	1	17	9
3. USA—George Calnan, Joseph Levis, Hugh Allesandroni, Dernell Every, Richard Steere, Frank Righeimer	2	1	22	26	0	2	6	20
4. DEN—Axel Bloch, Erik Kofoed-Hansen, Aage Leidersdorff, Ivan Osiier	0	3	17	31				

Italy and France tied in the barrage, 8-8, but France was awarded the victory on fewer touches received, 58-62.

1936 Berlin T: 18, N: 18, D: 8.4.

	WON	LOST	MATCHES W	MATCHES L
1. ITA	3	0	38	7
2. FRA	2	1	27	18
3. GER	1	2	13	33
4. AUT	0	3	13	33
5. BEL				
5. USA				
7. ARG				
7. HUN				

1. ITA—Giulio Gaudini, Gioacchino Guaranga, Gustavo Marzi, Giorgio Bocchino, Manlio Di Rosa, Ciro Verratti
2. FRA—Jacques Coutrot, André Gardère, René Lemoine, René Bougnol, Edward Gardère, René Bondoux
3. GER—Siegfried Lerdon, August Heim, Julius Eisenecker, Erwin Casmir, Stefan Rosenbauer, Otto Adam
4. AUT—Hans Lion, Roman Fischer, Hans Schönbaumsfeld, Ernst Baylon, Josef Losert, Karl Sudrich
5. BEL—Georges de Bourguignon, André van de Werve de Vorsselaer, Henri Paternoster, Raymond Bru, Heeremans, Paul Valcke
5. USA—Joseph Levis, Hugh Alessandroni, John Potter, John Hurd, Warren Dow, William Pecora
7. ARG—Roberto Larraz, Héctor Luchetti, Àngel Gorordo Palacios, Luis Luccheti, Rodolfo Valenzuela, Manuel Torrente
7. HUN—József Hátszeghy, Lajos Maszlay, Aladár Gerevich, Béla Bay, Ottó Hatszeghy Hatz, Antal Zirczy

France was the slight favorite, but the Italians breezed through the tournament with 104 wins and 19 losses.

Verratti was 23-1 and Marzi 18-1. The deciding match with France was halted when Italy achieved an unbeatable 9-4 advantage.

1948 London T: 16, N: 16, D: 7.31.

	WON	LOST	MATCHES W	MATCHES L
1. FRA	3	0	28	18
2. ITA	2	1	28	15
3. BEL	1	2	19	27
4. USA	0	3	14	29
5. ARG				
5. EGY				
5. GBR				
5. HUN				

1. FRA—André Bonin, René Bougnol, Jehan Buhan, Jacques Lataste, Christian d'Oriola, Adrian Rommel
2. ITA—Renzo Nostini, Manlio Di Rosa, Edoardo Mangiarotti, Giuliano Nostini, Giorgio Pellini, Saverio Ragno
3. BEL—Georges de Bourguignon, Henri Paternoster, Edouard Yves, Raymond Bru, André van de Werwe de Vorsselaer, Paul Valcke
4. USA—Daniel Bukantz, Dean Cetrulo, Dernell Every, Silvio Giolito, Nathaniel Lubell, Austin Prokop
5. ARG—José Rodriguez, Fulvio Galimi, Manuel Torrente, Félix Galimi
5. EGY—Osman Abdelhafiz, Salah Dessouki, Mahmoud Younes, Mohamed Zulficar, Hassan Hosni Tawfik, Mahmoud Abdin
5. GBR—R. René Paul, Albert Smith, Harold Cooke, John Emrys Lloyd, Pierre Turquet, Ulrich Wendon
5. HUN—Béla Bay, Aladár Gerevich, József Hátszeghy, Lajos Maszlay, Pál Dunay, Endre Palócz

An incident marred the semifinal round. Dissatisfied with a call by the president of the judges, the Argentine team gave three cheers for their opponents, the Belgians, and withdrew in protest. A more pleasant kind of event took place in the semifinal match between Great Britain and the United States. Harry Cooke of Britain was trailing Dean Cetrulo 3-4, when the two men collided. Cooke's mask smashed into his face, cutting his nose. The American team immediately administered first aid to their opponent. After a rest Cooke returned to action and rallied to win 5-4. Prior to their deciding match against the Italians, the French team found themselves in a difficult situation. They were exhausted and unable to find proper French nourishment. English cuisine was making them ill—in fact, an hour before the match, Bougnol was so sick he had to be replaced by Lataste. Fifteen minutes before they were due to enter the piste, French team member Jehan Buhan, who happened to be a wine merchant, managed to obtain a case of good French vintage. Revived, the French jumped out to a 6-3 lead. But the Italians came from behind to win five of the last seven fights. However, France won anyway on fewer touches received, 60-62.

1952 Helsinki T: 15, N: 15, D: 7.22.

	WON	LOST	MATCHES W	MATCHES L
1. FRA	3	0	35	11
2. ITA	2	1	34	12
3. HUN	1	2	16	31
4. EGY	0	3	8	39
5. ARG				
5. BEL				

1. FRA—Jehan Buhan, Christian d'Oriola, Adrian Rommel, Claude Netter, Jacques Noël, Jacques Lataste
2. ITA—Giancarlo Bergamini, Antonio Spallino, Manlio Di Rosa, Giorgio Pellini, Renzo Nostini, Edoardo Mangiarotti
3. HUN—Endre Tilli, Aladár Gerevich, Endre Palócz, Lajos Maszlay, Tibor Berczelly, József Sákovics
4. EGY—Salah Dessouki, Mohamed Ali Riad, Osman Abdelhafiz, Mahmoud Younes, Mohamed Zulficar, Hassan Hosni Tawfik
5. ARG—Fulvio Galimi, José Rodríguez, Eduardo Sastre, Félix Galimi, Santiago Massini
5. BEL—Pierre van Houdt, André Verhalle, Alex Bourgeois, Paul Valcke, Edouard Yves, Gustave Balister

As usual, France and Italy dominated all other countries, entering their final showdown with match records of 54-9 and 55-6, respectively. Christian d'Oriola was the star of the tournament, winning ten matches without a loss. In the deciding confrontation he swept all four Italians by the scores of 5-0, 5-0, 5-1, and 5-2, leading the French team to an 8-6 victory.

1956 Melbourne T: 9, N: 9, D: 11.23.

	WON	LOST	MATCHES W	MATCHES L
1. ITA	3	0	26	22
2. FRA	2	1	28	20
3. HUN	1	2	22	24
4. USA	0	3	18	28
5. GBR				
5. SOV				

1. ITA—Edoardo Mangiarotti, Giancarlo Bergamini, Antonio Spallino, Luigi Carpaneda, Manlio Di Rosa, Vittorio Lucarelli
2. FRA—Christian d'Oriola, Bernard Baudoux, Claude Netter, Jacques Lataste, Roger Closset, René Coicaud
3. HUN—József Gyuricza, József Sákovics, Mihály Fülöp, Endre Tilli, Lajos Somodi, Sr., József Marosi
4. USA—Albert Axelrod, Daniel Bukantz, Harold Goldsmith, Byron Kreiger, Nathaniel Lubell, Sewall Shurtz
5. GBR—R. René Paul, Henry Hoskyns, Raymond Paul, Allan Jay, Arnold Ralph Cooperman
5. SOV—Yuri Rudov, Yuri Ossipov, Mark Midler, Aleksandr Ovsyankin, Viktor Zhdanovich, Yuri Ivanov

Once again the championship was between France and Italy, and once again d'Oriola swept the Italians, receiving only seven hits in four assaults. This time, though, Italy's team was better balanced. Going into the last bout, Italy led 8-7, but because the touches were even at 57, whoever won the last bout, which matched Spallino and Netter, would win the gold medal. Netter took an early lead, but Spallino came from behind to tie 4-4 and then win the championship for Italy on the final touch.

1960 Rome T: 16, N: 16, D: 9.2.
1. SOV/RUS—Viktor Zhdanovich, Mark Midler, Yuri Sissikin, German Sveshnikov, Yuri Rudov
2. ITA—Alberto Pellegrino, Luigi Carpaneda, Mario Curletto, Aldo Aureggio, Edoardo Mangiarotti
3. GER—Jürgen Brecht, Tim Gerresheim, Eberhard Mehl, Jürgen Theuerkauff
4. HUN—Ferenc Czvikovsky, Jenő Kamuti, Mihály Fülöp, László Kamuti, József Gyuricza, József Sákovics
5. FRA—Jacky Courtillat, Jean-Claude Magnan, Guy Barrabino, Claude Netter, Christian d'Oriola
5. GBR—Henry Hoskyns, Allan Jay, Arnold Ralph Cooperman, R. Angus McKenzie, Raymond Paul
5. POL—Egon Franke, Ryszard Parulski, Janusz Rózycki, Ryszard Kunze, Witold Woyda
5. USA—Eugene Glazer, Harold Goldsmith, Joseph Paletta, Albert Axelrod, Daniel Bukantz

Final: SOV 9-4 ITA
3rd Place: GER 9-5 HUN

The Soviet Union became the first team since 1904 to break the Franco-Italian monopoly of the team foil event. In the final, Zhdanovich and Midler provided seven of the nine Soviet wins.

1964 Tokyo T: 16, N: 16, D: 10.16.
1. SOV/RUS—German Sveshnikov, Yuri Sissikin, Mark Midler, Viktor Zhdanovich, Yuri Sharov
2. POL—Zbigniew Skrudlik, Witold Woyda, Egon Franke, Ryszard Parulski, Janusz Rózycki
3. FRA—Daniel Revenu, Jacky Courtillat, Pierre Rodocanachi, Christian Noël, Jean-Claude Magnan
4. JPN—Kazuhiko Tabuchi, Fujio Shimizu, Kazuo Mano, Heizaburo Okawa, Sosuke Toda
5. GER—Jürgen Brecht, Dieter Wellmann, Eberhard Mehl, Tim Gerresheim, Jürgen Theuerkauff
6. ROM—Tănase Mureşan, Ionel Drimbă, Iuliu Falb, Ştefan Haukler, Atilla Csipler
7. HUN—Jenő Kamuti, László Kamuti, Jósef Gyuricza, Sándor Szabó, Béla Gyarmati
7. ITA—Gianguido Milanesi, Pasquale La Ragione, Arcangelo Pinelli, Nicola Granieri

Final: SOV 9-7 POL
3rd Place: FRA 9-4 JPN
5th Place: GER 860-857 ROM

1968 Mexico City T: 17, N: 17, D: 10.19.
1. FRA—Daniel Revenu, Gilles Berolatti, Christian Noël, Jean-Claude Magnan, Jacques Dimont
2. SOV—German Sveshnikov, Yuri Sharov, Vasyl Stankovych, Viktor Putyatin, Yuri Sissikin
3. POL—Witold Woyda, Ryszard Parulski, Egon Franke, Zbigniew Skrudlik, Adam Lisewski
4. ROM—Ionel Drimbă, Mihai Tiu, Ştefan Haukier, Tănase Mureşan, Iuliu Falb
5. HUN—Sándor Szabó, Jenő Kamuti, László Kamuti, Gábor Füredi, Attila May
6. GER—Jürgen Theuerkauff, Friedrich Wessel, Tim Gerresheim, Jürgen Brecht, Dieter Wellmann
7. ITA—Pasquale La Ragione, Alfredo Del Francia, Nicola Granieri, Arcangelo Pinelli, Michelle Maffei
7. JPN—Masaya Fukuda, Heizaburo Ohkawa, Fujio Shimizu, Kazuhiko Wakasugi, Kazuo Mano

Final: FRA 9-6 SOV
3rd Place: POL 9-3 ROM
5th Place: HUN 9-4 GER

1972 Munich T: 13, N: 13, D: 9.2.
1. POL—Lech Koziejowski, Witold Woyda, Marek Dąbrowski, Jerzy Kaczmarek, Arkadiusz Godel
2. SOV—Vasyl Stankovych, Viktor Putyatin, Leonid Romanov, Anatoly Koteshev, Vladimir Denisov
3. FRA—Daniel Revenu, Bernard Talvard, Gilles Berolatti, Jean-Claude Magnan, Christian Noël
4. HUN—Sándor Szabó, Csaba Fenyvesi, László Kamuti, István Marton, Jenő Kamuti
5. GER—Klaus Reichert, Friedrich Wessel, Harald Hein, Dieter Wellmann, Erk Sens-Gorius
6. JPN—Shiro Maruyama, Masaya Fukuda, Hiroshi Nakajima, Kiyoshi Uehara, Ichiro Serizawa
7. CUB—Evelio González, Eduardo Jhons, Jesus Gil, Enrique Salvat, Jorge Garbey
7. ROM—Iuliu Falb, Ştefan Haukler, Mihai Tiu, Tănase Mureşan, Aurel Ştefan

Final: POL 9-5 SOV
3rd Place: FRA 9-7 HUN
5th Place: GER 9-7 JPN

Poland secured the gold medal despite an early loss to Germany. In the same round, the USSR was defeated by Japan. The match for first place was highlighted by Woyda's sweep of the four Soviet fencers. The French had been the favorites, but they lost in the semifinals, 9-6, to the Soviet Union.

1976 Montreal T: 14, N: 14, D: 7.24.
1. GER—Harald Hein, Thomas Bach, Erk Sens-Gorius, Klaus Reichert, Matthias Behr
2. ITA—Fabio Dal Zotto, Attilio Calatroni, Carlo Montano, Stefano Simoncelli, Giovan Battista Coletti
3. FRA—Daniel Revenu, Christian Noël, Didier Flament, Bernard Talvard, Frédéric Pietruszka
4. SOV—Sabirzhan Ruziyev, Aleksandr Romankov, Vladimir Denisov, Vasyl Stankovych
5. POL—Leszek Martewicz, Lech Koziejowski, Ziemowit Wojciechowski, Arkadiusz Godel, Marek Dąbrowski
6. GBR—Geoffrey Grimmett, Barry Paul, Robert Bruniges, Graham Paul, Nicholas Bell
7. HUN—József Komatits, Csaba Fenyvesi, Lajos Somodi, Jr., Jenő Kamuti, Sándor Erdős
7. USA—Martin Lang, Edward Ballinger, Edward Wright, Edward Donofrio, Brooke Mackler

Final: GER 9-6 ITA
3rd Place: FRA 9-4 SOV
5th Place: POL 9-1 GBR

1980 Moscow T: 9, N: 9, D: 7.26.
1. FRA—Didier Flament, Pascal Jolyot, Frédéric Pietruszka, Philippe Bonnin, Bruno Boscherie

2. SOV—Aleksandr Romankov, Volodymyr Smirnov, Ashot Karagyan, Vladimir Lapitsky, Sabirzhan Ruziyev
3. POL—Bogusław Zych, Adam Robak, Marian Sypniewski, Lech Koziejowski
4. GDR—Siegmar Gutzeit, Hartmuth Behrens, Adrian Germanus, Klaus Kotzmann, Klaus Haertter
5. ROM—Petru Kuki, Mihai Tiu, Sorin Roca, Tudor Petruş
6. HUN—István Szelei, Ernő Kolczonay, András Papp, László Demény, Jenő Pap
7. CUB—Efigenio Favier, Guillermo Betancourt Scull, Heriberto González, Pedro Hernández
8. GBR—John Llewellyn, Steven Paul, Robert Bruniges, Pierre Harper, Neal Mallett

Final: FRA 868-860 SOV
3rd Place: POL 9-5 GDR
5th Place: ROM 9-7 HUN

In the semifinals, Soviet world champion Vladimir Lapitsky was accidentally run through the chest when his Polish opponent's foil broke his leather protective clothing. The sword severed a blood vessel but missed his heart. France's victory marked their 13th team foil medal in 14 Olympics.

1984 Los Angeles-Long Beach T: 14, N: 14, D: 8.7.

1. ITA—Mauro Numa, Andrea Borella, Stefano Cerioni, Angelo Scuri, Andrea Cipressa
2. GER—Matthias Behr, Mathias Gey, Harald Hein, Frank Beck, Klaus Reichert
3. FRA—Philippe Omnès, Patrick Groc, Frédéric Pietruszka, Pascal Jolyot, Marc Cerboni
4. AUT—Joachim Wendt, Dieter Kotlowski, Georg Somloi, Robert Blaschka, Georg Loisel
5. USA—Michael Marx, Gregory Massialas, Peter Lewison, Mark Smith, Michael McCahey
6. GBR—William Gosbee, Pierre Harper, Nicholas Bell, Robert Bruniges, Graham Paul
7. CHN—Chu Shisheng, Cui Yining, Yu Yifeng, Wang Wei, Zhang Jian
8. BEL—Thierry Soumagne, Peter Joos, Stefan Joos, Stephane Ganeff

Final: ITA 8-7 GER
3rd Place: FRA 9-3 AUT
5th Place: USA 9-6 GBR
7th Place: CHN 9-0 BEL forfeit

1988 Seoul T: 16, N: 16, D: 9.27.

1. SOV—Vladimir Aptsiauri, Anvar Ibragimov, Boris Koretsky, Ilgar Mamedov, Aleksandr Romankov
2. GER—Matthias Behr, Thomas Endres, Mathias Gey, Ulrich Schreck, Thorsten Weidner
3. HUN—István Busa, Zsolt Érsek, Róbert Gátai, Pál Szekeres, István Szelei
4. GDR—Aris Enkelmann, Adrian Germanus, Jens Gusek, Jens Howe, Udo Wagner
5. POL—Leszek Bandach, Waldemar Ciesielczyk, Piotr Kiełpikowski, Marian Sypniewski, Bogusław Zych
6. FRA—Laurent Bel, Patrick Groc, Youssef Hocine, Patrice Lhotellier, Philippe Omnès
7. ITA—Andrea Borella, Stefano Cerioni, Federico Cervi, Andrea Cipressa, Mauro Numa
8. CHN—Lao Shaopei, Liu Yunhong, Ye Chong, Zhang Zhicheng

Final: SOV 9-5 GER
3rd Place: HUN 9-5 GDR
5th Place: POL 860-853 FRA
7th Place: ITA 9-4 CHN

The underdog Soviet team received its stiffest challenge from the Hungarians in the semifinals. Both sides won eight matches, but the USSR won on touches, 57-51.

1992 Barcelona T: 12, N: 12, D: 8.5.

1. GER—Alexander Koch, Ulrich Schreck, Thorsten Weidner, Udo Wagner, Ingo Weissenborn
2. CUB—Guillermo Betancourt Scull, Tullo Díaz Babier, Hermenegildo García Marturell, Óscar García Pérez, Elvis Gregory Gil
3. POL—Piotr Kielpikowski, Adam Krzesiński, Marian Sypniewski, Cezary Siess, Ryszard Sobczak
4. HUN—István Busa, Zsolt Érsek, Róbert Gátai, Róbert Kiss, Zsolt Németh
5. SOV—Dmitri Shevchenko, Serhiy Golubytsky, Vyacheslav Grigoryev, Anvar Ibragimov, Ilgar Mamedov
6. ITA—Marco Arpino, Andrea Borella, Stefano Cerioni, Mauro Numa, Alessandro Puccini
7. FRA—Patrick Groc, Youssef Hocine, Olivier Lambert, Patrice Lhotellier, Philippe Omnès
8. KOR—Kim Young-ho, Kim Seung-pyo, Lee Ho-sung, Lee Seung-yong, You Bong-hyung

Final: GER 865-853 CUB
3rd Place: POL 9-4 HUN
5th Place: SOV 9-5 ITA
7th Place: FRA 9-2 KOR

At the 1991 world championships, the Cuban team shocked the fencing world by defeating Germany 9-6 in the final. In the quarterfinals at the Olympics they survived a close 8(59)-8(53) victory over South Korea. In the final the Cubans took a 7-3 lead, but the Germans fought back and won on touches.

1996 Atlanta T: 11, N: 11, D: 7.25.

1. RUS—Dmitri Shevchenko, Ilgar Mamedov, Vladislav Pavlovich
2. POL—Adam Krzesiński, Piotr Kielpikowski, Ryszard Sobczak
3. CUB—Elvis Gregory Gil, Oscar García Pérez, Rolando Tucker León
4. AUT—Jochim Wendt, Marco Falchetto, Michael Ludwig
5. HUN—Mark Marsi, Robert Kiss, Zsolt Ersek
6. GER—Alexander Koch, Uwe Römer, Wolfgang Wienand
7. KOR—Chung Soo-ki, Kim Yong-kook, Kim Young-ho
8. ITA—Alessandro Puccini, Marco Arpino, Stefano Cerioni

Final: RUS 45-40 POL
3rd Place: CUB 45-28 AUT
5th Place: HUN 45-44 GER
7th Place: KOR 45-34 ITA

The Russian team's road to victory was far from easy. Opening against Hungary they trailed 22-25 before pulling off a 45-43 victory. In the semifinals, the Russians faced the self-proclaimed "black musketeers" of Cuba. With the score 44-44 the match came down to the final touch between Dmitri Shevchenko and Rolando Tucker. Shevchenko scored and the Russians moved on to the final against Poland, which had earlier survived a 45-44 cliffhanger against Germany. In the final, Russia led 20-15 and 25-23 before Adam Krzesiński outscored Vladislav Pavlovich 7-3 to give Poland a 30-28 lead. Ilgar Mamedov put the Russians back in front 35-33 and Poland never caught up again.

2000 Sydney T: 8, N: 8, D: 9.22.
1. FRA—Jean-Noël Ferrari, Lionel Plumenail, Brice Guyart, Patrice Lhotellier
2. CHN—Dong Zhaozhi, Wang Haibin, Ye Chong
3. ITA—Salvatore Sanzo, Matteo Zennaro, Daniele Crosta, Gabriele Magni
4. POL—Sławomir Mocek, Ryszard Sobczak, Adam Krzesiński
5. UKR—Oleksiy Kruglyak, Sergiy Golubytsky, Oleksiy Bryzgalov
6. GER—Wolfgang Wienand, Ralf Bissdorf, Richard Breutner, David Hausmann
7. CUB—Elvis Grégory Gil, Oscar García Pérez, Rolando Tucker León
8. RUS—Dmitri Shevchenko, Ilgar Mamedov, Andrei Deyev, Aleksandr Lakatosh

Final: FRA 45-44 CHN
3rd Place: ITA 45-38 POL
5th Place: UKR 45-43 GER
7th Place: CUB 45-39 RUS

The French team opened with a contest against Cuba. Trailing 30-35, Jean-Noël Ferrari outscored Rolando Tucker 10-3 to give France a 40-38 lead. Lionel Plumenail, who was only 2-10 until then, took over and held Elvis Grégory even to give France a 45-43 victory. In the semifinals, France led throughout and held off a late challenge from Poland to win 45-38. In the other half of the table, China advanced to the final with two clear victories, 45-30 over Russia and 45-32 against Italy. For the final, France replaced Plumenail with Patrice Lhotellier. The French built a 20-13 lead, but then Ye Chong scored six unanswered points against Ferrari to make the score 20-19. Wang Haibin outscored Lhotellier 11-8 to give China a 30-28 lead. Ye expanded the lead to 35-31 against Brice Guyart. Lhotellier gained back a point from Dong Zhaozhi and it was left to Ferrari to try to battle back from a 34-37 deficit against Wang. The two went at it at a furious pace, scoring 18 touches between them in 2 minutes 8 seconds. At one point, Wang went flying off the piste. Then Wang was penalized one point for talking back to Polish referee Marian Sypniewski. Wang's lack of self-control would prove critical, as the score went to 44-44. At the 1999 world championships, France and China had also gone to a last decisive point in the final. That time, the French were awarded a controversial winning touch. This time, at the Olympics, Ferrari scored a clear touch to give France its first Olympic team foil championship in 20 years.

2004 Athens T: 8, N: 8, D: 8.21.
1. ITA—Andrea Cassara, Salvatore Sanzo, Simone Vanni
2. CHN—Dong Zhaozhi, Wang Haibin, Wu Hanxiong, Ye Chong
3. RUS—Renal Ganeyev, Yuri Molchan, Ruslan Nasibulin, Vyacheslav Pozdnyakov
4. USA—Jedediah Dupree, Dan Kellner, Jonathan Tiomkin
5. FRA—Loïc Attely, Jean-Noël Ferrari, Brice Guyart, Erwan le Pechoux
6. GER—Ralf Bissdorf, Peter Joppich, Simon Senft, André Wessels
7. KOR—Choi Byung-chul, Ha Chang-duk, Kim Woon-sung, Park Hee-kyung
8. EGY—Mostafa Anwar, Mostafa Nagaty, Tamer Mohamed Tahoun, Ali Tarek Madgy

Final: ITA 45-42 CHN
3rd Place: RUS 45-38 USA
5th Place: FRA 45-38 GER
7th Place: KOR 45-35 EGY

The Italian team swept into the final, easily defeating Egypt 45-20 and Russia 45-27. There the Italians faced China, the team they had beaten to win the 2003 world championships. The Chinese had advanced with victories of 45-36 over South Korea and 45-35 over the United States. Led by Simone Vanni, the Italians were leading the final 42-35, when Dong Zhaozhi scored seven straight points to even the score 42-42. Salvatore Sanzo earned the last three touches to secure the gold. The next day an official review of the final showed six clear scoring mistakes by Hungarian referee Joszef Hidasi, all in favor of Italy. In each case Hidasi awarded points to the wrong fencer. The mistakes took place in the second and fifth bouts, which Italy won 8-2 and 5-2, respectively. Although Chinese officials wrote a letter of appeal, there was no mechanism for filing a formal protest, and the president of the International Fencing Federation (FIE), René Roch, declared that the results would not be changed. Hidasi was subsequently banned for two years.

2008 not held

ÉPÉE, INDIVIDUAL

1896 not held

1900 Paris C: 104, N: 9, D: 6.14.

1. Ramón Fonst Segundo	CUB
2. Louis Perrée	FRA
3. Léon Sée	FRA
4. Georges de la Falaise	FRA
5. Eduardo Camet	ARG
6. Edmond Wallace	FRA
7. Gaston Alibert	FRA
8. Léon Thiébaut	FRA

Ramón Fonst was only 16 years old when he won the Olympic championship. His teacher, Albert Ayot, won the competition for masters.

1904 St. Louis C: 5, N: 3, D: 9.7.

1. Ramón Fonst Segundo	CUB
2. Charles Tatham	USA
3. Albertson Van Zo Post	USA
4. Gustav Casmir	GER
5. Fitzhugh Townsend	USA

Not only did Fonst achieve a rare double victory in winning both the foil and épée but he is also the only repeat winner in the individual épée.

1906 Athens C: 29, N: 10, D: 4.25.

1. Georges de la Falaise	FRA
2. Georges Dillon-Kavanagh	FRA
3. Hendrik van Blijenburgh	HOL
4. Raphael Vigeveno	HOL
5. Emil Schön	GER
6. Maurits Jacob van Löben Sels	HOL

1908 London C: 85, N: 14, D: 7.24

					BARRAGE	
	W	L	TG	TR	W	L
1. Gaston Alibert	FRA	5	0	2		
2. Alexandre Lippmann	FRA	4	2	1	2	0
3. Eugène Olivier	FRA	4	3	0		
4. Robert Montgomerie	GBR	4	1	2	0	2
5. Paul Anspach	BEL	2	5	0		
5. Cecil Haig	GBR	2	5	0		
5. Alfred Labouchère	HOL	2	3	2		
8. Martin Holt	GBR	1	5	1		

Gaston Alibert completed the tournament with 20 wins, no losses, and five double hits, or ties. Two other contestants worth noting were Alfred Labouchère, who attracted quite a bit of attention because he was 6 feet 9 inches (2.06 meters) tall and Ivan Osiier, a 19-year-old from Denmark. Osiier ultimately competed in seven Olympics, making his first and final appearances in London—40 years apart. Along the way he qualified for nine finals, achieving his greatest success in 1912, when he won the individual épée silver medal. His wife, Ellen, was the first female Olympic fencing champion.

Gaston Alibert, 1908
The Frenchman was triumphant in the épéé discipline.

1912 Stockholm C: 93, N: 15, D: 7.13.

		W	L	T
1. Paul Anspach	BEL	6	1	0
2. Ivan Osiier	DEN	5	2	0
3. Philippe Le Hardy de Beaulieu	BEL	4	2	1
4. Victor Boin	BEL	4	2	1
5. Einar Sörensen	SWE	3	4	0
6. Edgar Seligman	GBR	2	4	1
7. Léon Tom	BEL	1	6	0
8. Martin Holt	GBR	0	4	3

The Italian Fencing Federation proposed that the length of the épée blade be extended to 94 cm. When this was rejected, the Italians refused to participate, thus joining the French, who boycotted the entire fencing competition. Between 1908 and 1924 Paul Anspach won a total of five medals: two gold, two silver and one bronze.

1920 Antwerp C: 80, N: 13, D: 8.23.

		WON
1. Armand Massard	FRA	9
2. Alexandre Lippmann	FRA	7
3. Gustave Buchard	FRA	6
4. Ernest Gevers	BEL	6
5. Georges Casanova	FRA	5
6. Antonio Mascarenhas de Menezes	POR	5
6. Emile Moreau	FRA	5
6. Abelardo Olivier	ITA	5

Massard later served as president of the French Olympic Committee and vice-president of the International Olympic Committee.

1924 Paris C: 67, N: 18, D: 7.11.

				1st BARRAGE		2nd BARRAGE	
		WON	LOST	W	L	W	L
1. Charles Delporte	BEL	8	3				
2. Roger Ducret	FRA	7	4	2	1	1	0
3. Nils Hellsten	SWE	7	4	2	1	0	1
4. Emile Cornereau	FRA	7	4	1	2	1	0
5. Armand Massard	FRA	7	4	1	2	0	1
6. Virgilio Mantegazza	ITA	6	5				
7. Gustave Buchard	FRA	5	6				
7. Léon Tom	BEL	5	6				

1928 Amsterdam C: 59, N: 22, D: 8.7.

							EXTRA	FINAL		
		W	L	T	TG	TR	W	L	TG	TR
1. Lucien Gaudin	FRA	8	0	1	18	5	2	0	20	12
2. Georges Buchard	FRA	7	2	0	15	8	1	1	19	21
3. George Calnan	USA	6	3	0	14	9	1	1	21	19
4. Léon Tom	BEL	6	2	1	15	9	0	2	12	20
5. Nils Hellsten	SWE	5	4	0	12	13				

6. Charles Delporte	BEL	4	5	0	11	13
7. Charles Debeur	BEL	3	6	0	10	15
8. S. Cicurel	EGY	3	6	0	10	15

Gaudin's record for the tournament was an impressive 34 wins and five losses, as he became the only fencer besides Ramón Fonst to win both the foil and épée. Buchard later claimed that Gaudin had begged and pleaded with him to allow Gaudin to win their match and that Buchard had agreed to do so.

1932 Los Angeles C: 28, N: 12, D: 8.9.

		W	L	T	TG	TR
1. Giancarlo Cornaggia-Medici	ITA	8	1	2	31	18
2. Georges Buchard	FRA	8	3	0	27	17
3. Carlo Agostoni	ITA	7	3	1	30	17
4. Saverio Ragno	ITA	7	4	0	27	20
5. Bernard Schmetz	FRA	7	4	0	26	22
6. Philippe Cattiau	FRA	6	5	0	23	22
7. George Calnan	USA	6	5	0	22	22
8. Balthazar de Beuckelaer	BEL	4	7	0	19	25

1936 Berlin C: 68, N: 26, D: 8.11.

		W	L	T	TG	TR
1. Franco Riccardi	ITA	5	1	3	25	18
2. Saverio Ragno	ITA	6	3	0	24	15
3. Giancarlo Cornaggia-Medici	ITA	6	3	0	22	16
4. Hans Drakenberg	SWE	4	3	2	20	20
5. Charles Debeur	BEL	4	4	1	21	21
6. Henrique da Silveira	POR	4	5	0	18	19
7. Raymond Stasse	BEL	3	4	2	21	21
8. Ian Campbell-Gray	GBR	3	4	2	18	24

Riccardi's total record was 24 wins, three losses, and four ties. In the quarterfinal pool, defending champion Cornaggia-Medici demonstrated his acute awareness of distance. Perplexed by the call of two straight double hits, he insisted that his opponent's blade was the wrong length. Measurements showed that it was in fact a half-inch too long.

1948 London C: 66, N: 25, D: 8.9.

						BARRAGE	
		W	L	TG	TR	TG	TR
1. Luigi Cantone	ITA	7	2	24	15		
2. Oswald Zappelli	SWI	5	4	20	17	3	0
3. Edoardo Mangiarotti	ITA	5	4	20	17	0	3
4. Henri Guérin	FRA	5	4	20	19		
5. Jean Radoux	BEL	5	4	19	20		
6. Henri Lepage	FRA	4	5	19	20		
7. Carlo Agostoni	ITA	4	5	22	21		
8. Emile Gretsch	LUX	3	6	16	22		

Thirty-one-year-old Luigi Cantone was allowed to compete at the last minute after Dario Mangiarotti injured his foot and had to withdraw. In the final pool, which took five and a half hours, Cantone lost his first two bouts to Carlo Agostoni and Edoardo Mangiarotti. Then he won seven straight to take first place without a barrage.

1952 Helsinki C: 76, N: 29, D: 7.28.

		W	L	TR
1. Edoardo Mangiarotti	ITA	7	2	12
2. Dario Mangiarotti	ITA	6	3	16
3. Oswald Zappelli	SWI	6	3	18
4. Léon Buck	LUX	6	3	19
5. József Sákovics	HUN	5	4	17
6. Carlo Pavesi	ITA	4	5	21
7. Per Carleson	SWE	3	6	20
8. Carl Forsell	SWE	3	6	23

Milanese fencing master Giuseppe Mangiarotti began giving his sons lessons when they turned eight years old. Although both were right-handed, Giuseppe converted the younger boy, Edoardo, into a left-hander because he considered it an advantage in competition. When he was 11, Edoardo won the Italian junior foil title. But Giuseppe had been Italian professional épée champion 17 times, so when Edoardo turned 15 his father started training him with that weapon. At age 17, Edoardo was a member of the Italian épée team that won the gold medal at Berlin. By 1960 Edoardo had won 13 Olympic medals: four gold and one silver in team épée, one gold and two bronze in individual épée, one gold and three silver in team foil, and one silver in individual foil. His older brother, Dario, gained one gold and two silver.

1956 Melbourne C: 40, N: 17, D: 11.30.

						1st BARRAGE				2nd BARRAGE			
		W	L	TG	TR	W	L	TG	TR	W	L	TG	TR
1. Carlo Pavesi	ITA	5	2	29	20	1	1	9	7	2	0	10	5
2. Giuseppe Delfino	ITA	5	2	30	27	1	1	7	7	1	1	10	8
3. Edoardo Mangiarotti	ITA	5	2	30	17	1	1	7	9	0	2	3	10
4. Richard Pew	USA	4	3	25	28								
5. Lajos Balthazár	HUN	4	3	30	29								
6. René Queyroux	FRA	3	4	29	25								
7. Per Carleson	SWE	2	5	22	29								
8. Rolf Wiik	FIN	0	7	15	35								

Giuseppe Delfino came within one touch of winning the gold, but lost 5-4 to Richard Pew and was forced into the barrage.

1960 Rome C: 79, N: 32, D: 9.6.

						BARRAGE	
		W	L	TG	TR	TG	TR
1. Giuseppe Delfino	ITA	5	2	39	32	5	2
2. Allan Jay	GBR	5	2	39	23	2	5
3. Bruno Habārovs	SOV/LAT	4	3	32	23	8	7
4. József Sákovics	HUN	4	3	30	31	7	8
5. Roger Achten	BEL	3	4	31	30		
6. Yves Dreyfus	FRA	3	4	30	30		
7. Armand Mouyal	FRA	3	4	25	30		
8. Giovanni Breda	ITA	1	6	19	34		

The 38-year-old Delfino utilized a rather unusual style to achieve his long-awaited gold medal. Rather than waste his energy going for a five-touch victory, he would content himself with a tie until time ran out. Then he would concentrate on, and usually win, the single sudden-death over-time hit. This tactic defeated Allan Jay in the final pool to force the barrage.

1964 Tokyo C: 65, N: 25, D: 10.19.

						BARRAGE			
		W	L	TG	TR	W	L	TG	TR
1. Hryhory Kryss	SOV/UKR	2	1	12	11	1	0	5	2
2. Henry Hoskyns	GBR	2	1	15	12	0	1	2	5
3. Guram Kostava	SOV/GEO	1	2	12	12	1	0	5	0
4. Gianluigi Saccaro	ITA	1	2	10	14	0	1	0	5
5. Bogdan Gonsior	POL								
6. Claude Bourquard	FRA								
7. Orvar Lindwall	SWE								
8. Franz Rompza	GER								

In the final pool Kryss, a 23-year-old soldier from Kiev, defeated Hoskyns in a bout that saw four straight double (or simultaneous) hits. Hoskyns was a 33-year-old Somerset fruit farmer.

1968 Mexico City C: 73, N: 28, D: 10.22.

						BARRAGE				
		W	L	TG	TR	W	L	T	TG	TR
1. Győző Kulcsár	HUN	4	1	24	14	2	0	0	10	5
2. Hryhory Kryss	SOV/UKR	4	1	25	19	0	1	1	8	10
3. Gianluigi Saccaro	ITA	4	1	21	19	0	1	1	7	10
4. Viktor Modzalevsky	SOV/RUS	2	3	20	23					
5. Herbert Polzhuber	AUT	1	4	17	24					
6. Jean-Pierre Allemand	FRA	0	5	17	25					
7. Peter Loetscher	SWI									
7. Henryk Nielaba	POL									

The hero of Hungary's team épée victory four years earlier in Tokyo, Kulcsár completed the 1968 individual tournament with 17 wins and only one loss.

1972 Munich C: 72, N: 28, D: 9.6.

		W	L	TG	TR
1. Csaba Fenyvesi	HUN	4	1	25	10
2. Jacques la Degaillerie	FRA	3	2	23	19
3. Győző Kulcsár	HUN	3	2	20	19
4. Anton Pongratz	ROM	3	2	19	20
5. Rolf Edling	SWE	1	4	15	22
6. Jacques Brodin	FRA	0	5	13	25

Two of the three medals went to fencers from Budapest. Csaba Fenyvesi was a 29-year-old physician, Győző Kulcsár a 31-year-old engineer.

1976 Montreal C: 64, N: 25, D: 7.23.

						BARRAGE			
		W	L	TG	TR	W	L	TG	TR
1. Alexander Pusch	GER	3	2	22	18	2	0	10	7
2. Jürgen Hehn	GER	3	2	18	20	1	1	9	7
3. Győző Kulcsár	HUN	3	2	22	19	0	2	5	10
4. István Osztrics	HUN	2	3	18	19				
5. Jerzy Janikowski	POL	2	3	20	21				
6. Rolf Edling	SWE	2	3	18	21				
7. Csaba Fenyvesi	HUN								
7. Göran Floodström	SWE								

In the barrage Pusch defeated Hehn, 5-4, in a seesaw battle, and then scored the last two touches to beat Kulcsár 5-3. Pusch was only 21 years old.

1980 Moscow C: 42, N: 16, D: 7.28.

		W	L	TG	TR
1. Johan Harmenberg	SWE	4	1	22	21
2. Ernő Kolczonay	HUN	3	2	23	19
3. Philippe Riboud	FRA	3	2	20	17
4. Rolf Edling	SWE	3	2	18	16
5. Aleksandr Mozhayev	SOV/RUS	1	4	18	22
6. Ioan Popa	ROM	1	4	18	24
7. Jaroslav Jurka	CZE				
7. Boris Lukomsky	SOV/RUS				

1984 Los Angeles-Long Beach C: 63, N: 26, D: 8.8.

1. Philippe Boisse	FRA
2. Björne Väggö	SWE
3. Philippe Riboud	FRA
4. Stefano Bellone	ITA
5. Michael Poffet	SWI
6. Elmar Borrmann	GER
7. Alexander Pusch	GER
8. Volker Fischer	GER

Final: Boisse 10-5 Väggö
3rd Place: Riboud 10-7 Bellone

Björne Väggö, ranked only 44th in the world, registered four straight upsets to qualify for the gold medal match, defeating World Cup champion Olivier Lenglet, World Cup runner-up Angelo Mazzoni, world champion Elmar Borrmann and World University Games champion Stefano Bellone. In the final, however, he was no match for 29-year-old Paris radiologist Philippe Boisse, who had survived a tight 12-11 semifinal bout against teammate Philippe Riboud, with whom he fenced twice a week.

1988 Seoul C: 79, N: 32, D: 9.24.

1. Arnd Schmitt	GER
2. Philippe Riboud	FRA
3. Andrei Shuvalov	SOV/RUS
4. Sandro Cuomo	ITA
5. Torsten Kühnemund	GDR
6. Jerri Bergström	SWE
7. Martin Brill	NZE

8. Vladimir Reznitšenko SOV/EST
Final: Schmitt 10-9 Riboud
3rd Place: Shuvalov 10-8 Cuomo

Andrei Shuvalov compiled a record of 16 wins and only one loss before being tipped 10-9 in the semifinals by 23-year-old dental student Arnd Schmitt. In the final, Schmitt defeated two-time world champion Philippe Riboud by the same score.

1992 Barcelona C: 70, N: 30, D: 8.1.
1. Éric Srecki FRA
2. Pavel Kolobkov RUS
3. Jean-Michel Henry FRA
4. Kaido Kaaberma EST
5. Elmar Borrmann GER
6. Angelo Mazzoni ITA
7. Mauricio Rivas Nieto COL
8. Iván Kovács HUN
Final: Srecki-Kolobkov 6-5, 5-2
3rd Place: Henry-Kaaberma 2-5, 5-2, 5-3

Éric Srecki, a 28-year-old bank employee, had a reputation as a consistently high-level performer who could never quite make it to the medal podium. At the last three world championships he had finished fourth, seventh, and fifth. In Barcelona he survived the *repêchage* by beating defending world champion Andrei Shuvalov of Russia 5-3, 5-2. In the semifinals he encountered Kaido Kaaberma, who had earlier defeated him 5-3, 3-5, 6-5. This time Srecki came out on top 5-2, 5-3. In the final he spotted Kolobkov a 1-3 lead and then outscored him 10-4 to take the gold medal.

1996 Atlanta C: 45, N: 21, D: 7.20.
1. Aleksandr Beketov RUS
2. Iván Trevejo Pérez CUB
3. Géza Imre HUN
4. Iván Kovács HUN
5. Sandro Cuomo ITA
6. Jean-Michel Henry FRA
7. Kaido Kaaberma EST
8. Mariusz Strzalka GER
Final: Beketov 15-14 Trevejo
3rd Place: Imre 15-9 Kovács

In the round of 16, 18th seed Aleksandr Beketov upset defending Olympic and world champion Eric Srecki 15-10. In the quarterfinals, Beketov upset another Frenchman, 1992 bronze medalist Jean-Michel Henry, 15-13. After defeating medal favorite Iván Kovács 15-8 in the semifinals, Beketov faced fellow outsider Iván Trevejo in the final. Trevejo took a 10-6 lead, but Beketov never gave up. After the match was tied nine times, including 14-14, Beketov won with a final lunge to Trevejo's right side. The bronze medal went to the youngest fencer in the competition, 21-year-old Geza Imre, who won his first three bouts 15-14 before succumbing to Trevejo 15-10 in the semifinals. Seven of the eight quarterfinalists were left-handed.

2000 Sydney C: 42, N: 22, D: 9.16.
1. Pavel Kolobkov RUS
2. Hugues Obry FRA
3. Lee Sang-ki KOR
4. Marcel Fischer SWI
5. Peter Vanky SWE
6. Iván Trevejo Pérez CUB
7. Éric Srecki FRA
8. Gang Zhao CHN
Final: Kolobkov 15-12 Obry
3rd Place: Lee 15-14 Fischer

Pavel Kolobkov had won at least one medal in each of the last three Olympics, but he had yet to win a gold medal. Seeded number one, Kolobkov's only serious obstacle on the road to the final was Iván Trevejo, whom Kolobkov defeated in the quarterfinals 15-14. His opponent in the gold medal match was Hugues Obry, who had gained a controversial semifinal victory. In that match Obry beat Marcel Fischer 15-13 after being awarded two penalty points in the last minute when Fischer was accused of running into Obry. Fischer in turn charged Obry with acting. The final saw nine double hits as Kolobkov took a 7-6 lead and held off Obry for the rest of the bout.

2004 Athens C: 37, N: 21, D: 8.17.
1. Marcel Fischer SWI
2. Wang Lei CHN
3. Pavel Kolobkov RUS
4. Eric Boisse FRA
5. Fabrice Jeannet FRA
6. Silvio Fernández VEN
7. Soren Thompson USA
8. Daniel Strigel GER
Final: Fischer 15-9 Wang
3rd Place: Kolobkov 15-8 Boisse

Marcel Fischer earned a decisive victory over 23-year-old Wang Lei, gaining an early 8-2 lead and never relinquishing control. Fisher became the first Swiss fencer to win gold, while Wang was the first Chinese male fencer to earn a medal in an individual event. Fischer's closest match of the tournament was a 15-13 defeat of Silvio Fernández in the quarterfinals.

2008 Beijing C: 41, N: 23, D: 8.10.
1. Matteo Tagliariol ITA
2. Fabrice Jeannet FRA
3. José Luis Abajo Gómez SPA
4. Gábor Boczkó HUN
5. Jung Jin-sun KOR
6. Radosław Zawrotniak POL
7. Diego Confalonieri ITA
8. Bas Verwijlen HOL
Final: Tagliariol 15-9 Jeannet
3rd Place: Abajo 8-7 Boczkó

The men's épée competition included a number of early-round upsets. Athens Olympic silver medalist and 2006 world champion Wang Lei was eliminated in the second round, beaten 15-10 by Holland's Bas Verwijle, as was reigning world champion Krisztián Kulcsár of Hungary, who lost 15-9 to China's Yin Lianchi. In the third round, medal favorite Jérôme Jeannet lost 15-9 to José Luis Abajo.

Jérôme's younger brother, Fabrice Jeannet, made it to the final with a 15-12 victory over Boczkó and faced world number three Matteo Tagliariol. Tagliariol took control early in the final match, scoring six unanswered points to build an 8-3 lead and then went on to win 15-9.

Tagliariol was Italy's first individual épée gold medalist since Giuseppe Delfino won at the 1960 Rome Olympics. Tagliariol was inspired to take up fencing by Alexandre Dumas' novel *The Three Musketeers.* "Others dream of being footballers," he said, "I dreamed of being d'Artagnan, and I kept on dreaming for 25 years."

SABRE, INDIVIDUAL

1896 Athens C: 5, N: 3, D: 4.9.

		W	L	TG	TR
1. Ioannis Georgiadis	GRE	4	0	12	6
2. Telemachos Karakalos	GRE	3	1	11	5
3. Holger Nielsen	DEN	2	2	10	9
4. Adolf Schmal	AUT	1	3	7	11
5. Georgios Iatridis	GRE	0	4	3	12

The competition was almost finished when King George I and his entourage arrived. The jury decided to restart the tournament from the beginning so that the king would be better entertained. This decision drastically changed the outcome as Adolf Schmal had already beaten Georgiadis and Nielsen, but lost to both the second time around.

1900 Paris C: 33, N: 7, D: 6.25.

		W	L
1. Georges de la Falaise	FRA	6	1
2. Léon Thiébaut	FRA	5	2
3. Siegfried Flesch	AUT	4	3
4. Ámon, Ritter von Gregurich	HUN	4	3
5. Gyula von Iványi	HUN	3	4
6. de Boissière	FRA	3	4
7. Heinrich von Tenner	AUT	2	5
8. Camillo Müller	AUT	1	6

1904 St. Louis C: 5, N: 2, D: 9.8.

					BARRAGE	
		W	L	TG	W	L
1. Manuel Díaz Martínez	CUB	3	0	21		
2. William Grebe	USA	2	1	20	1	0
3. Albertson Van Zo Post	USA	2	1	18	0	1
4. Theodore Carstens	USA	1	2			
5. Arthur Fox	USA	0	4			

Díaz defeated Grebe 7-6 and Van Zo Post 7-4.

1906 Athens C: 29, N: 8, D: 4.28.

1. Ioannis Georgiadis	GRE
2. Gustav Casmir	GER
3. Federico Cesarano	ITA
4. Georges de la Falaise	FRA
5. Ervin Mészáros	HUN
6. Jenö Apáthy	HUN

1908 London C: 76, N: 11, D: 7.24.

					BARRAGE	
		W	L	T	W	L
1. Jenő Fuchs	HUN	6	0	1	1	0
2. Béla Zulavszky	HUN	6	1	0	0	1
3. Vilém Goppold z Lobsdorfu, Sr.	BOH/CZE	4	2	1		
4. Jenö Szántay	HUN	3	3	1		
5. Péter Tóth	HUN	3	4	0		
6. Lajos Werkner	HUN	2	5	0		
7. Jetze Doorman	HOL	1	5	1		
7. Georges de la Falaise	FRA	1	6	0		

Dr. Jenő Fuchs, the winner of four sabre gold medals in 1908 and 1912, recorded 22 wins, two losses, and one draw in the individual competition. Fuchs was also active in rowing and bobsledding.

Richard Schoemaker of the Netherlands, who was eliminated in the second round, was an Underground commander during the German occupation of his country in World War II. Arrested by the Nazis, he was executed on May 3, 1942.

1912 Stockholm C: 64, N: 12, D: 8.18.

		W	L	TG	TR
1. Jenő Fuchs	HUN	6	1	18	10
2. Béla Békéssy	HUN	5	2	17	11
3. Ervin Mészáros	HUN	5	2	17	12
4. Zoltán Schenker	HUN	4	3	17	13
5. Nedo Nadi	ITA	4	3	16	17
6. PéterTóth	HUN	2	5	12	17
7. Lajos Werkner	HUN	1	6	13	19
8. Dezső Földes	HUN	1	6	9	20

1920 Antwerp C: 42, N: 9, D: 8.26.

		W	L	TR
1. Nedo Nadi	ITA	11	0	
2. Aldo Nadi	ITA	9	2	
3. Adrianus de Jong	HOL	6	5	19
4. Oreste Puliti	ITA	6	5	19
5. Jan van der Wiel	HOL	6	5	22
6. Léon Tom	BEL	5	6	24
7. Robert Hennet	BEL	5	6	24
8. Robin Dalglish	GBR	5	6	27

The only break in Hungary's incredible 56-year domination of individual sabre occurred in 1920. Having been on the losing side of World War I, Hungary was not invited to the Antwerp Olympics.

1924 Paris C: 47, N: 15, D: 7.18.

						BARRAGE			
		W	L	TG	TR	W	L	TG	TR
1. Sándor Posta	HUN	5	2	26	20	2	0	8	1
2. Roger Ducret	FRA	5	2	22	18	1	1	4	7
3. János Garay	HUN	5	2	23	20	0	2	4	8
4. Zóltan Schenker	HUN	4	3	24	21	1	0	4	3
5. Adrianus de Jong	HOL	4	3	24	21	0	1	3	4
6. Ivan Osiier	DEN	2	5	15	24	1	0	4	2
7. Georges Conraux	FRA	2	5	23	22	0	1	2	4
8. Héctor Casco	ARG	1	6	16	27				

The Italians, led by Oreste Puliti, had already defeated the Hungarians to win the team sabre title, and another showdown seemed certain in the individual championship as four Italians and three Hungarians were among the twelve who qualified for the final round. The final matches began with the Official Jury of Appeal ordering the four Italians—Puliti, Bertinetti, Bini, and Sarrocchi—to fight off against each other. As expected, Puliti beat the other three with ease. But the judges were not satisfied. Led by Kovács, the Hungarian judge, they maintained that the other three had thrown their matches against Puliti in order to increase his chances for a gold medal.

Outraged by these accusations, Puliti threatened to cane Judge Kovács. Puliti was disqualified, and Bertinetti, Bini, and Sarrocchi walked out in protest. Two days later Puliti and Kovács ran into each other at a music hall and renewed their argument. When Kovács haughtily told Puliti that he couldn't understand the furious fencer because he didn't speak Italian, Puliti hit the Hungarian in the face and said that Kovács surely couldn't fail to understand that. The two men were pulled apart, but further words were exchanged and a formal duel was proposed.

Four months later Puliti and Kovács met again, at Nagykanizsa on the Yugoslav-Hungarian border. This time they were accompanied by seconds, swords, and spectators. After slashing away at each other for an hour, the two were finally separated by spectators, who had become concerned about the wounds which both men had received. Their honor restored, Puliti and Kovács shook hands and made up.

As for the Olympic competition, it was won by Sándor Posta in a three-way fence-off against fellow Hungarian János Garay and the French champion Roger Ducret, who left the 1924 Olympics with three gold medals and two silver.

1928 Amsterdam C: 44, N: 17, D: 8.11.

						BARRAGE	
		W	L	TG	TR	TG	TR
1. Ödön Tersztyánszky	HUN	9	2	51	33	5	2
2. Attila Petschauer	HUN	9	2	52	28	2	5
3. Bino Bini	ITA	8	3	49	32		
4. Gustavo Marzi	ITA	8	3	49	34		
5. Sándor Gombos	HUN	8	3	49	38		
6. Erwin Casmir	GER	6	5	44	32		
7. Arturo De Vecchi	ITA	5	6	44	36		
8. Roger Ducret	FRA	5	6	42	47		

Lieutenant Colonel Tersztyánszky died in an auto accident outside Budapest ten months after winning his gold medal. He was 40 years old.

1932 Los Angeles C: 25, N: 12, D: 8.13.

		W	L	TG	TR
1. György Jekelfalussy-Piller	HUN	8	1	42	19
2. Giulio Gaudini	ITA	7	2	39	28
3. Endre Kabos	HUN	5	4	36	29
4. Erwin Casmir	GER	5	4	32	30
5. Attila Petschauer	HUN	5	4	37	32
6. John Huffman	USA	5	4	38	35
7. Ivan Osiier	DEN	4	5	32	35
8. Arturo De Vecchi	ITA	3	6	27	36

Colonel Piller completed the tournament with a record of 19-2.

1936 Berlin C: 71, N: 26, D: 8.15.

		W	L	TG	TR
1. Endre Kabos	HUN	7	1	37	20
2. Gustavo Marzi	ITA	6	2	35	22
3. Aladár Gerevich	HUN	6	2	37	26
4. László Rajcsányi	HUN	5	3	34	25
5. Vincenzo Pinton	ITA	5	3	32	28
6. Giulio Gaudini	ITA	3	5	27	28
7. Antoni Sobik	POL	2	6	22	34
8. Josef Losert	AUT	2	6	20	36

As a student, Kabos received a fencing outfit as a birthday gift from his godfather. He hid it in his wardrobe, but his friends came across it and teased him. The next day he enrolled in a fencing club to spite them. At the Berlin Olympics Kabos compiled a record of 24-1 to win the gold medal. Kabos was killed during World War II when the Budapest Margaret Bridge blew up, the day before his 38th birthday.

1948 London C: 60, N: 24, D: 8.13.

		W	L	TG	TR
1. Aladár Gerevich	HUN	7	0	35	18
2. Vincenzo Pinton	ITA	5	2	32	23
3. Pál Kovács	HUN	5	2	33	24
4. Jacques Lefèvre	FRA	4	3	27	26
5. George Worth	USA	2	5	26	27
6. Gastone Darè	ITA	2	5	25	30
7. Tibor Nyilas	USA	2	5	20	31
8. Antonio Oliva Haro	MEX	1	6	15	34

Aladár Gerevich competed in six Olympics between 1932 and 1960 (when he was 50 years old). He won seven gold medals, one silver, and two bronze. In

Aladár Gerevich
Gerevich won seven gold medals, one silver and two bronze between 1932 and 1960 (when he was 50 years old).

winning his only individual gold medal Gerevich scored 19 victories against only one defeat.

1952 Helsinki C: 66, N: 26, D: 8.1.

		W	L	TR
1. Pál Kovács	HUN	8	0	19
2. Aladár Gerevich	HUN	7	1	16
3. Tibor Berczelly	HUN	5	3	22
4. Gastone Darè	ITA	5	3	27
5. Werner Plattner	AUT	4	4	34
6. Jacques Lefèvre	FRA	3	5	25
7. Vincenzo Pinton	ITA	2	6	32
8. Heinz Lechner	AUT	2	6	35

Kovács was the third straight Hungarian to win the sabre gold after winning the bronze in the previous Olympics. Kovács was 40 years old and had first won the world sabre championship fifteen years earlier. In the final pool he needed one last victory to clinch the gold medal. Trailing Pinton 4-2, he scored three hits in the final minute to secure the championship with an undefeated record of 19-0. A mechanic, Kovács ultimately earned six Olympic gold medals.

1956 Melbourne C: 35, N: 17, D: 12.5.

						BARRAGE	
		W	L	TG	TR	TG	TR
1. Rudolf Kárpáti	HUN	6	1	32	19		
2. Jerzy Pawłowski	POL	5	2	30	22		
3. Lev Kuznetsov	SOV/RUS	4	3	29	24	5	2
4. Jacques Lefèvre	FRA	4	3	27	25	2	5
5. Aladár Gerevich	HUN	3	4	30	31		
6. Wojciech Zabłocki	POL	2	5	17	29		
7. Pál Kovács	HUN	2	5	25	30		
8. Luigi Narduzzi	ITA	2	5	21	31		

The 36-year-old Kárpáti, eventual winner of six Olympic gold medals, earned his first individual championship by putting together 18 victories against only one loss (to Pawłowski). Kárpáti believed that his love of music contributed to his skills as a fencer, since both are based on rhythm and timing.

1960 Rome C: 70, N: 29, D: 9.8.

						BARRAGE			
		W	L	TG	TR	W	L	TG	TR
1. Rudolf Kárpáti	HUN	5	2	31	25				
2. Zoltán Horváth	HUN	4	3	29	26	2	1	14	8
3. Wladimiro Calarese	ITA	4	3	31	29	2	1	13	2
4. Claude Arabo	FRA	4	3	31	29	2	1	11	12
5. Wojciech Zabłocki	POL	4	3	27	26	0	3	9	15
6. Jerzy Pawłowski	POL	3	4	28	28				
7. David Tyshler	SOV/RUS	2	5	24	29				
8. Yakov Rylsky	SOV/RUS	2	5	21	32				

Following the quarterfinal round, the French team lodged a protest against Rudolf Kárpáti, claiming the defending champion had purposely lost to Ladislau Rohonyi of Romania in order to ensure that he, instead of Jacques Lefèvre of France, would advance to the next round. The protest was overruled. In the semifinals Kárpáti's loss to Arabo allowed the Frenchman to qualify for the final without a barrage. This time no protest was filed.

1964 Tokyo C: 52, N: 21, D: 10.20.

						BARRAGE	
		W	L	TG	TR	TG	TR
1. Tibor Pézsa	HUN	2	1	13	13	5	2
2. Claude Arabo	FRA	2	1	14	9	2	5
3. Umyar Mavlikhanov	SOV/RUS	1	2	9	13	5	3
4. Yakov Rylsky	SOV/RUS	1	2	11	12	3	5
5. Emil Ochyra	POL						
6. Marcel Parent	FRA						
7. Walter Köstner	GER						
8. Dieter Wellmann	GER						

Pézsa won despite a relatively unimpressive overall record of 12 wins and seven losses.

1968 Mexico City C: 40, N: 16, D: 10.17.

						BARRAGE	
		W	L	TG	TR	TG	TR
1. Jerzy Pawłowski	POL	4	1	22	18	5	4

2. Mark Rakita	SOV/RUS	4	1	24	16	4	5
3. Tibor Pézsa	HUN	3	2	20	16		
4. Vladimir Nazlymov	SOV/RUS	3	2	21	17		
5. Rolando Rigoli	ITA	1	4	11	21		
6. Józef Nowara	POL	0	5	15	25		
7. Umyar Mavlikhanov	SOV/RUS						
8. Serge Panizza	FRA						

In June, Pawłowski, a 35-year-old major in the Polish army, received his master's degree in law, having written his dissertation on "A Critique of Hayek's Neo-Liberal Conception of Liberty and Law." In the final pool Pawłowski defeated world champion Mark Rakita 5-4. Then he beat him again by the same score in the barrage, to achieve a final win-loss total of 16-2. Pawłowski became interested in fencing at age 16 when he saw films of the 1948 London Olympics. He was world sabre champion three times (in 1957, 1965 and 1966) and runner-up four times. In his military pursuits, Pawłowski was considered a protégé of General Wojciech Jaruzelski, who later became premier of Poland. However, Pawłowski was also working as a spy for the CIA, although it is unclear whether he was motivated by ideology or money. Arrested in 1975, he was sentenced to twenty-five years in prison. Ten years later, he was exchanged for three Communist spies, but he chose to remain in Poland.

1972 Munich C: 54, N: 23, D: 8.31.

		W	L	TG	TR
1. Viktor Sidyak	SOV/RUS	4	1	23	15
2. Péter Marót	HUN	3	2	21	20
3. Vladimir Nazlymov	SOV/RUS	3	2	21	21
4. Michele Maffei	ITA	3	2	20	21
5. Regis Bonissent	FRA	1	4	19	22
6. Tamás Kovács	HUN	1	4	17	22

Maffei, Kovács, and Sidyak each entered the final pool with records of 17-3, but Sidyak, emitting a growl each time he scored a hit, prevailed.

1976 Montreal C: 46, N: 18, D: 7.22.

		W	L	TG	TR
1. Viktor Krovopuskov	SOV/RUS	5	0	25	14
2. Vladimir Nazlymov	SOV/RUS	4	1	23	18
3. Viktor Sidyak	SOV/RUS	3	2	22	20
4. Ioan Popa	ROM	2	3	22	20
5. Mario Montano	ITA	1	4	16	21
6. Michele Maffei	ITA	0	5	13	25
7. Francisco de La Torre	CUB				
7. Imre Gedővári	HUN				

1980 Moscow C: 30, N: 12, D: 7.25.

						BARRAGE	
		W	L	TG	TR	TG	TR
1. Viktor Krovopuskov	SOV/RUS	4	1	24	17	5	3
2. Mikhail Burtsev	SOV/RUS	4	1	23	18	3	5
3. Imre Gedővári	HUN	3	2	23	21		
4. Vassil Etropolski	BUL	2	3	17	23		
5. Hristo Etropoiski	BUL	1	4	19	21		
6. Michele Maffei	ITA	1	4	15	21		
7. Ferdinando Meglio	ITA						
7. Vladimir Nazlymov	SOV/RUS						

Burtsev beat Krovopuskov in the final pool, 5-4, but Krovopuskov turned the tables in the barrage to become the third repeat winner in individual sabre.

1984 Los Angeles-Long Beach C: 33, N: 14, D: 8.4.

1. Jean-François Lamour	FRA
2. Marco Marin	ITA
3. Peter Westbrook	USA
4. Hervé Granger-Veyron	FRA
5. Pierre Guichot	FRA
6. Marin Mustață	ROM
7. Giovanni Scalzo	ITA
8. Ioan Popa	ROM

Final: Lamour 12-11 Marin
3rd Place: Westbrook 10-5 Granger-Veyron

The sabre competition was severely depleted by the Soviet-bloc boycott. However, Lamour's performance was nonetheless impressive, as he won all 19 of his bouts.

1988 Seoul C: 40, N: 18, D: 9.23.

1. Jean-François Lamour	FRA
2. Janusz Olech	POL
3. Giovanni Scalzo	ITA
4. Philippe Delrieu	FRA
5. György Nébald	HUN
6. Heorgy Pohosov	SOV/UKR
7. Felix Becker	GER
8. Jürgen Nolte	GER

Final: Lamour 10-4 Olech
3rd Place: Scalzo 10-2 Delrieu

When Lamour first competed in the Olympics in 1980, he was the only member of the 16-man French squad to go home without a medal. He finished twenty-first. When he was crowned Olympic champion in 1984, many French fencing aficionados scorned his victory over a boycott-depleted field and spoke of him winning a medal not of gold, but of chocolate. Lamour silenced his critics by winning the 1987 world championships and then repeating his Olympic triumph in Seoul. He later served as France's minister of sports.

1992 Barcelona C: 44, N: 19, D: 8.2.

1. Bence Szabó	HUN
2. Marco Marin	ITA
3. Jean-François Lamour	FRA
4. Giovanni Scalzo	ITA
5. Antonio García Hernández	SPA
6. Ferdinando Meglio	ITA
7. Robert Kocielniakowski	POL
8. Jürgen Nolte	GER

Final: Szabó–Marin 5-1, 5-1
3rd Place: Lamour–Scalzo 3-5, 6-5, 5-1

Both Szabó and Marin reached the final with semifinal victories over opponents who had beaten them earlier in the tournament. Szabó had lost to Scalzo 6-4, 6-5, but came back in the semis to win 5-3, 3-5, 6-4. Marin's defeat of Lamour was even sweeter. They had faced each other in the 1984 final with Marin coming back from a 9-5 deficit, only to lose 12-11. In Barcelona, Lamour, at age 36, was trying for a third gold medal. In the elimination round he beat Marin 6-4, 5-2, but in the semifinals Marin prevailed, 6-4, 5-3. The final was never close. Szabó was the first fencer from Hungary to win the individual sabre since the Hungarian dynasty of 1908 to 1964.

1996 Atlanta C: 43, N: 20, D: 7.21.

1. Stanislav Pozdnyakov	RUS
2. Sergei Sharikov	RUS
3. Damien Touya	FRA
4. József Navarette	HUN
5. Felix Becker	GER
6. Vadym Guttsayt	UKR
7. Rafal Sznajder	POL
8. Steffen Wiesinger	GER

Final: Pozdnyakov 15-12 Sharikov
3rd Place: Touya 15-7 Navarette

Pozdnyakov led 11-6 in the final. Sharikov closed to 13-12, but Pozdnyakov scored the last two hits.

2000 Sydney C: 39, N: 20, D: 9.21.

1. Mihai Covaliu	ROM
2. Mathieu Gourdain	FRA
3. Wiradech Kothny	GER
4. Domonkos Ferjancsik	HUN
5. Damien Touya	FRA
6. Aleksey Frosin	RUS
7. Tonhi Terenzi	ITA
8. Victor Gaureanu	ROM

Final: Covaliu 15-12 Gourdain
3rd Place: Kothny 15-11 Ferjancsik

Mihai Covaliu and Mathieu Gourdain qualified for the final by knocking out the favorites. In Gourdain's case it was a round of 16 upset of defending champion Stanislav Pozdnyakov by a score of 15-11. Covaliu gained a 15-14 quarterfinal victory over 1996 bronze medalist Damien Touya. Gourdain beat another favorite, Domonkos Ferjancsik, 15-12 in the semifinals, while Covaliu defeated Thai-born Wiradech Kothny 15-12. The final was fast-paced, as Covaliu, who had never placed higher than third in a Grand Prix event, took an 11-7 lead and won 15-12 in only 1 minute 41 seconds.

2004 Athens C: 39, N: 21, D: 8.14.

1. Aldo Montano	ITA
2. Zsolt Nemcsik	HUN
3. Vladislav Tretiak	UKR
4. Dmitri Lapkes	BLR
5. Volodymyr Lukashenko	UKR
6. Stanislav Pozdnyakov	RUS
7. Mihai Covaliu	ROM
8. Sergei Sharikov	RUS

Final: Montano 15-14 Nemcsik
3rd Place: Tretiak 15-11 Lapkes

In the final, Zsolt Nemcsik took a 5-1 lead. Aldo Montano closed the gap to 9-11, after which he was issued a warning for arguing with the referee. Montano scored the next three touches to take the lead. Then he called timeout to change a glove. Unperturbed by Montano's psychological tactics, Nemcsik regained the lead at 14-13, but Montano won the last two touches and the match. The 25-year-old Montano, from Livorno, was the third generation in his family to win an Olympic medal in the sabre competition. His grandfather, also named Aldo, earned silver medals in the team event in 1936 and 1948, and his father, Mario, won a team gold and two silvers between 1972 and 1980.

2008 Beijing C: 40, N: 21, D: 8.12.

1. Zhong Man	CHN
2. Nicolas Lopez	FRA
3. Mihai Covaliu	ROM
4. Julien Pillet	FRA
5. Luigi Tarantino	ITA
6. Keeth Smart	USA
7. Jorge Pina Pérez	SPA
8. Aleksandr Buykevich	BLR

Final: Zhong 15-9 Lopez
3rd Place: Covaliu 15-11 Pillet

Several favorites fell in the early rounds, including two-time defending world champion Stanislav Pozdnyakov of Russia, who lost to France's Nicolas Lopez 15-8 in the second round. Athens gold medalist and 2007 world silver medalist Aldo Montano was eliminated in the third round on a narrow 15-14 loss to 2007 European champion Jorge Pina, who was then beaten 15-10 by Lopez in the quarter-finals.

By the semi-final round, the field had shrunk to Lopez, Julien Pillet, Sydney Olympic champion Mihai Covaliu, and 2008 Asian champion Zhong Man. Zhong defeated Pillet 15-9 to reach the final, while Lopez beat Covaliu 15-13.

The final bout was a tense back-and-forth affair, as Lopez scored the first touch but was quickly overtaken. The score was tied three times, at 4-4, 6-6 and 9-9. But then Zhong recorded six unanswered touches to clinch the gold medal.

Zhong started his athletics career as a runner, but switched to fencing after being spotted by a coach who thought that his tall frame would give him an edge in the sport.

SABRE, TEAM

1896–1904 not held

1906 Athens T: 4, N: 4, D: 4.28.

1. GER—Gustav Casmir, Jacob Erckrath de Bary, August Petri, Emil Schön
2. GRE—Ioannis Georgiadis, Menelaos Sakorraphos, Khristos Zorbas, Triantafilos Kordogiannis
3. HOL—James van Carnbée, Johannes Osten, George van Rossem, Maurits van Löben Sels
4. HUN—Péter Tóth, Jenő Apáthy, Ervin Mészáros, Béla Nagy

1908 London T: 8, N: 8, D: 7.23.

1. HUN—Jenő Fuchs, Oszkár Gerde, Péter Tóth, Lajos Werkner, Dezső Földes
2. ITA—Riccardo Nowak, Alessandro Pirzio-Biroli, Abelardo Olivier, Marcello Bertinetti, Sante Ceccherini
3. BOH/CZE—Vilém Goppold z Lobsdorfu, Sr., Jaroslav "Tuček" Šourek, Vlastimil Lada-Sázavský, Otakar Lada, Bedřich Schejbal
4. FRA—Georges de la Falaise, Bernard de Lesseps, Marc Perrodon, Jean-Joseph Renaud

Final: HUN 9-7 BOH

Péter Tóth of the Hungarian team became involved in a fight with a fellow student at age 15 and was challenged to a duel. After consultation with their classmates, the boys decided to postpone the duel until after final examinations. In the meantime Tóth enrolled in a fencing school and became so proficient that when final exams were over his opponent decided to drop the matter. Eleven years later Tóth won the first of his team sabre gold medals. Dr. Dezső Földes, another member of the Hungarian team, emigrated to the United States in 1912 and set up a clinic for the poor in Cleveland.

Jean-Joseph Renaud of the French team wrote more than sixty novels and several plays. However, he was best known as the organizer and director of several hundred illegal private duels. He justified his role in these clandestine encounters by explaining that "generally both parties are so nervous that nobody gets hurt, the offended hero soothes his honor, and everyone goes away happy."

In 1908, second place was contested by a pool of those teams which had lost to Hungary. Bohemia refused to take part, so Italy defeated Germany for second place.

1912 Stockholm T: 11, N: 11, D: 7.15.

			MATCHES	
	WON	LOST	W	L
1. HUN	3	0	24	8
2. AUT	2	1	24	20
3. HOL	1	2	14	30
4. BOH/CZE	0	3	14	18
5. BEL				
5. ITA				
7. GBR				

1. HUN—Jenő Fuchs, László Berti, Ervin Mészáros, Dezső Földes, Oszkár Gerde, Zoltán Schenker, Péter Tóth, Lajos Werkner
2. AUT—Richard Verderber, Otto Herschmann, Rudolf Cvetko SLO, Friedrich Golling, Albert Bogen, Andreas Suttner, Reinhold Trampler
3. HOL—Willem Hubert van Blijenburgh, George van Rossem, Adrianus de Jong, Jetze Doorman, Dirk Scalongne, Hendrik de Iongh
4. BOH/CZE—Vilém Goppold z Lobsdorfu, Sr., Josef Pfeiffer, Bedřich Schejbal, Josef Čipera, Otakar Švorčik
5. BEL—Léon Tom, Robert Hennet, Marcel Berré, Philippe Le Hardy de Beaulieu, Henri Anspach, Paul Anspach
5. ITA—Nedo Nadi, Ugo Di Nola, Giovanni Benfratello, Fernando Cavallini, Edoardo Alaimo, Gino Belloni
7. GBR—Edward Brookfield, Harry Butterworth, Archibald Corble, Richard Crawshay, William Marsh, A. Ridley Martin

Otto Herschmann of the second-place Austrian team had previously won a bronze medal in the 1896 100-meter freestyle swimming event. At the time of the 1912 Games, Herschmann was president of the Austrian Olympic Committee, making him the only sitting national Olympic committee president to win an Olympic medal. Herschmann died at the Nazi concentration camp of Izbica in Poland on June 14, 1942.

1920 Antwerp T: 8, N: 8, D: 8.26.

			MATCHES	
	WON	LOST	W	L
1. ITA	7	0	76	20
2. FRA	6	1	53	42
3. HOL	5	2	51	45
4. BEL	4	3	47	47
5. USA	3	4	37	58
6. DEN	2	5	39	55
7. GBR	1	6	30	50
8. CZE	0	7	16	32

1. ITA—Nedo Nadi, Aldo Nadi, Oreste Puliti, Baldo Baldi, Francesco Gargano, Giorgio Santelli, Dino Urbani
2. FRA—Georges Trombert, Jean Margraff, Marc Perrodon, Henri de Saint Germain
3. HOL—Jan van der Wiel, Adrianus de Jong, Jetze Doorman, Willem Hubert van Blijenburgh, Albert Delaunoij, Salomon Zeldenrust, Henri Wijnoldij-Daniëls
4. BEL—Robert Hennet, Pierre Calle, Alexis Simonson, Léon Tom, Robert Feyerick, Charles Delporte, Harry Dombeeck
5. USA—Edwin Fulinwidder, Arthur Lyon, Joseph Brooks Parker, John Dimond, Frederick Cunningham, Claiborne Walker, C. Bradford Fraley, Roscoe Bowman
6. DEN—Ivan Osiier, Poul Rasmussen, Ejnar Levison, Aage Berntsen, Verner Bonde
7. GBR—A. Ridley Martin, William Marsh, William Hammond, Cecil Kershaw, Ronald Campbell, Robin Dalglish, Herbert Huntingdon
8. CZE—Josef Javůrek, Otakar Švorčik, František Dvořák, Antony Mikala, Josef Jungmann

1924 Paris T: 14, N: 14, D: 7.15.

	WON	LOST	MATCHES W	L
1. ITA	3	0	28	20
2. HUN	2	1	33	15
3. HOL	1	2	18	30
4. CZE	0	3	17	31
5. ARG				
5. FRA				

1. ITA—Renato Anselmi, Guido Balzarini, Marcello Bertinetti, Bino Bini, Vincenzo Cuccia, Oreste Moricca, Oreste Puliti, Giulio Sarrocchi
2. HUN—László Berti, János Garay, Sándor Pósta, Jozsef Rády, Zoltán Schenker, László Széchy, Ödön Tersztyánszky, Jenő Uhlyárik
3. HOL—Adrianus de Jong, Jetze Doorman, Hendrik Scherpenhuizen, Jan van der Wiel, Maarten van Dulm, Henri Wijnoldij-Daniëls
4. CZE—František Dvořák, Alexander Bárta, Josef Jungmann, Luděk Oppl, Otakar Švorčík
5. ARG—Carmelo Camet, Horacio Casco, Carlos Guerrico, Carmelo Merlo, Pedro Nazar Anchorena, Antonio Ponce Costa, Roberto Sola, Santiago Torres Blanco
5. FRA—Georges Conraux, Henri de Saint-Germain, Jean Jannekeyn, Louis Lifschitz, Jean Margraff, Marc Perrodon, Maurice Taillandier, Georges Trombert

The crucial match between Italy and Hungary ended in an 8-8 tie, but Italy won by four touches, 46 to 50. Puliti was the star of the tournament, winning 26 of 28 bouts and scoring 110 touches while receiving only 39.

1928 Amsterdam T: 12, N: 12, D: 8.9.

	WON	LOST	MATCHES W	L
1. HUN	2	0	23	9
2. ITA	1	1	21	11
3. POL	1	1	11	21
4. GER	0	2	9	23
5. FRA				
5. HOL				
7. BEL				
7. TUR				

1. HUN—Ödön Tersztyánszky, Sándor Gombos, Attila Petschauer, János Garay, József Rády, Gyula Glykais
2. ITA—Bino Bini, Renato Anselmi, Gustavo Marzi, Oreste Puliti, Emilio Salafia, Giullo Sarrocchi
3. POL—Adam Papée, Tadeusz Friedrich, Kazimierz Laskowski, Władysław Segda, Aleksander Małecki, Jerzy Zabielski
4. GER—Erwin Casmir, Heinrich Moos, Hans Halberstadt, Hans Thomson
5. FRA—René Fristeau, Roger Ducret, Jean Lacroix, Maurice Taillandier, Jean Piot, Paul Oziol de Pignol
5. HOL—Cornelis Ekkart, Hendrik Hagens, Maarten van Dulm, Jan van der Wiel, Adrianus de Jong, Henri Wijnoldij-Daniëls
7. BEL—Joseph Stordeur, Marcel Cuypers, Jacques Keste-Loot, Edouard Yves, Gaston Kaanen
7. TUR—Muhiddin Turhan Okyayyüz, Ergun Fouad, Nami Demir Yayak, Enver Balkan

Hungary defeated Italy 9-7 in the decisive match. The Hungarian team was led by the high-strung 23-year-old Attila Petschauèr of Budapest, who won all 20 of his bouts. While fighting in the Ukraine in 1943, Petschauer was tortured to death by anti-Semitic Hungarian army officers. Another Jewish member of the Hungarian team, János Garay, died in a Nazi concentration camp.

1932 Los Angeles T: 6, N: 6, D: 8.11.

	WON	LOST	MATCHES W	L
1. HUN	3	0	31	6
2. ITA	2	1	20	14
3. POL	1	2	10	26
4. USA	0	3	15	30

1. HUN—György Jekelfalussy-Piller, Endre Kabos Attila Petschauer, Ernő Nagy, Gyula Glykais, Aladár Gerevich
2. ITA—Renato Anselmi, Arturo De Vecchi, Emillo Salafia, Ugo Pignotti, Gustavo Marzi, Giulio Gaudini
3. POL—Adam Papée, Tadeusz Friedrich, Wladyslaw Segda, Leszek Lubicz-Nyzz, Władysław Dobrowolski, Marian Suski
4. USA—Peter Bruder, John Huffman, Norman Armitage, Nikolas Muray, Harold van Buskirk, Ralph Faulkner

Hungary won 56 bouts and lost only nine.

1936 Berlin T: 21, N: 21, D: 8.13.

	WON	LOST	MATCHES W	L
1. HUN	3	0	32	10
2. ITA	2	1	25	17
3. GER	1	2	14	25
4. POL	0	3	10	29
5. AUT				
5. FRA				
5. HOL				
5. USA				

1. HUN—Tibor Berczelly, László Rajcsányi, Pál Kovács, Aladár Gerevich, Imre Rajczy, Endre Kabos
2. ITA—Vincenzo Pinton, Giulio Gaudini, Aldo Masciotta, Gustavo Marzi, Aldo Montano, Athos Tanzini
3. GER—Richard Wahl, Julius Eisenecker, Erwin Casmir, August Heim, Hans Esser, Hans Jörger
4. POL—Antoni Sobik, Władysław Sagda, Władysław Dobrowolski, Adam Papée, Marian Suski, Teodor Zaczyk
5. AUT—Josef Losert, Hugo Weczerek, Karl Sudrich, Hubert Loisel, Karl Hanisch, Karl Kaschka
5. FRA—Marcel Faure, Maurice Gramain, Edward Gardère, Jean Piot, Roger Barisien, André Gardère
5. HOL—Ate Faber, Antonius Montfoort, Franciscus Mosman, Franciscus van Wieringen, Jacob Schriever
5. USA—Peter Bruder, Miguel de Capriles, Bela de Nagy, John Huffman, Samuel Stewart, Norman Armitage

The Hungarians won their first seven matches by scores of 13-3 or better, and then defeated Italy 9-6 to win the gold medal. Their final bout total was 106 wins and 16 losses. Leading Hungarian scorers were Berczelly (24-3), Kovács (21-2), Rajcsányi (20-4) and Gerevich (17-2).

1948 London T: 17, N: 17, D: 8.11.

	WON	LOST	MATCHES W	L
1. HUN	3	0	29	13
2. IT	2	1	24	24
3. USA	1	2	24	23
4. BEL	0	3	12	29
5. ARG				
5. FRA				
5. HOL				
5. POL				

1. HUN—Tibor Berczelly, Rudolf Kárpáti, Aladár Gerevich, Pál Kovács, László Rajcsányi, Bertalan Papp
2. ITA—Gastone Darè, Carlo Turcato, Vincenzo Pinton, Mauro Racca, Aldo Montano, Renzo Nostini
3. USA—Norman Armitage, George Worth, Tibor Nyilas, Dean Cetrulo, Miguel de Capriles, James Flynn
4. BEL—Robert Bayot, Georges de Bourguignon, Ferdinand Jassogne, Eugène Laermans, Marcel Nys, Edouard Yves
5. ARG—Manuel Agüero Ordóñez, José Luis D'Andrea Mohr, Edgardo Pomini, Jorge Cermesoni, Francesco Huergo, Daniel Sande
5. FRA—Jean-François Tournon, Jacques Parent, Maurice Gramain, Jacques Lefèvre, Jean Levavasseur, Georges Levèque
5. HOL—Henricus ter Weer, Antoon Hoevers, Willem van den Berg, Franciscus Mosman, Ludovicus Kuijpers
5. POL—Antoni Sobik, Boleslaw Banas, Teodor Zaczyk, Jerzy Wójcik, Jan Nawrocki

Berczelly had a 15-2 record, including four straight victories in the final 10-6 defeat of Italy. Hungary's total for the tournament was 65 wins and 20 losses.

1952 Helsinki T: 19, N: 19, D: 7.30.

	WON	LOST	MATCHES W	L
1. HUN	3	0	34	13
2. ITA	2	1	32	15
3. FRA	1	2	14	32
4. USA	0	3	13	33
5. AUT				
5. BEL				
5. GBR				
5. POL				

1. HUN—Bertalan Papp, László Rajcsányi, Rudolf Kárpáti, Aladár Gerevich, Pál Kovács, Tibor Berczelly
2. ITA—Vincenzo Pinton, Mauro Racca, Roberto Ferrari, Gastone Darè, Renzo Nostini, Giorgio Pellini
3. FRA—Jacques Lefèvre, Jean Laroyenne, Maurice Piot, Jean Levavasseur, Bernard Morel, Jean-François Tournon
4. USA—Norman Armitage, Miguel de Capriles, Tibor Nyilas, Alex Treves, George Worth, Allan Kwartler
5. AUT—Werner Plattner, Heinz Putzl, Hubert Loisel, Heinz Lechner, Paul Kerb
5. BEL—Marcel Vanderauwera, Gustave Balister, François Heyvaert, Robert Bayot, Georges de Bourguignon, Edouard Yves
5. GBR—Roger Tredgold, Olgierd Porebski, Robert Anderson, William Maurice Beatley, Ulrich Wendon
5. POL—Jerzy Twardokens, Leszek Suski, Jerzy Pawłowski, Wojciech Zabłocki, Zygmunt Pawlas

Great tension built up in the final contest as Hungary's string of 35 victories and four Olympic gold medals appeared in jeopardy when Italy took a 7-5 lead. Then Berczelly beat Nostini 5-0 and Kárpáti beat Ferrari 5-0 to even the match at 7-7. Gerevich, who had lost his other three bouts against the Italians, recovered to defeat Enzo Pinton 5-3 and give Hungary an insurmountable lead of 8-7, with a 14-touch advantage. Hungary's tournament totals were 111 wins and 25 losses.

1956 Melbourne T: 8, N: 8, D: 12.3.

	WON	LOST	MATCHES W	L
1. HUN	3	0	30	15
2. POL	2	1	23	22
3. SOV	1	2	22	25
4. FRA	0	3	17	30
5. ITA				

1. HUN—Attila Keresztes, Pál Kovács, Rudolf Kárpáti, Aladár Gerevich, Jenő Hámori, Dániel Magay
2. POL—Jerzy Pawłowski, Wojciech Zabłocki, Marian "Marek" Kuszewski, Zygmunt Pawlas, Ryszard Zub, Andrzej Piątkowski
3. SOV—Lev Kuznetsov, Yakov Rylsky, Yevhen Cherepovsky, David Tyshler, Leonid Bogdanov
4. FRA—Claude Gamot, Jacques Lefèvre, Bernard Morel, Jacques Roulot
5. ITA—Roberto Ferrari, Domenico Pace, Mario Ravagnan, Giuseppe Comini, Luigi Narduzzi, Gastone Darè

By 1956 the sabre contests were the only ones not using electronic scoring, which was finally introduced in 1992. Tensions were high during the match between Hungary and the USSR, since the Soviets had just invaded Hungary. The Hungarians were victorious, 9-7. After the Olympics Keresztes, Hámori, and Magay defected to the West. Keresztes and Hámori fenced for the United States in the 1964 Olympics.

1960 Rome T: 16, N: 16, D: 9.10.

1. HUN—Zoltán Horváth, Rudolf Kárpáti, Tamás Mendelényi, Pál Kovács, Gábor Delneky, Aladár Gerevich
2. POL—Andrzej Piątkowski, Emil Ochyra, Wojciech Zabłocki, Jerzy Pawłowski, Ryszard Zub, Marian "Marek" Kuszewski
3. ITA—Wladimiro Calarese, Gianpaolo Calanchini, Pierluigi Chicca, Mario Ravagnan, Roberto Ferrari
4. USA—Allan Kwartler, George Worth, Michael D'Asaro, Alfonso Morales, Tibor Nyilas, R. Richard Dyer
5. FRA—Marcel Parent, Claude Gamot, Jacques Lefèvre, Jacques Roulot, Claude Arabo
5. GER—Dieter Lohr, Jürgen Theuerkauff, Wilfried Wohler, Peter von Krockov, Walter Köstner
5. ROM—Dumitru Mustaţă, Cornel Pelmuş, Ion Szanto, Ladislau Rohony, Eméric Arus
5. SOV—Yevhen Cherepovsky, Umyar Mavlikhanov, Nugzar Asatiani, David Tyshler, Yakov Rylsky

Final: HUN 9-7 POL
3rd Place: ITA 9-6 USA

In the match for first place, Poland took a 3-0 lead. Then Hungary won five in a row, but Poland came

HUNGARY'S TEAM SABRE WINNING STREAK

1924	1928	1932	1936	1948	1952	1956	1960	1964
14 HOL 2	14 USA 2	14 MEX 2	16 DEN 0	9 EGY 3	15 POR 1	9 USA 1	9 BEL 3	9 ARG 2
11 CZE 5	13 GBR 3	13 USA 3	14 URU 2	15 ARG 1	15 SAA 1	12 FRA 4	9 ROM 3	9 ROM 0
	12 GER 4	9 ITA 2	15 GER 1	12 POL 3	9 DEN 0	9 SOV 4	9 ITA 6	
	12 FRA 4	9 POL 1	15 HOL 1	10 USA 6	13 FRA 3	9 POL 4	9 POL 7	
	14 POL 2		14 USA 2	9 BEL 1	13 BEL 3			
	9 ITA 7		13 GER 3	10 ITA 6	12 AUT 4			
	11 DEN 1		10 POL 1		13 FRA 3			
					13 USA 3			
					8 ITA 7			

back to tie it, 6-6. Finally Kárpáti beat Pawłowski 5-3 to secure the gold medal. Gerevich, 50 years old, won his sixth straight team sabre gold medal.

1964 Tokyo T: 13, N: 13, D: 10.23.
1. SOV—Yakov Rylsky, Nugzar Asatiani, Mark Rakita, Umyar Mavlikhanov, Boris Melnikov
2. ITA—Wladimiro Calarese, Cesare Salvadori, Gianpaolo Calanchini, Pierluigi Chicca, Mario Ravagnan
3. POL—Emil Ochyra, Jerzy Pawłowski, Ryszard Zub, Andrzej Piątkowski, Wojciech Zabłocki
4. FRA—Jean Ramez, Jacques Lefèvre, Claude Arabo, Marcel Parent, Robert Fraisse
5. HUN—Péter Bakonyi, Miklós Meszéna, Attila Kovács, Zoltán Horváth, Tibor Pézsa
6. GER—Dieter Wellmann, Klaus Allissat, Walter Köstner, Jürgen Theuerkauff, Percy Borucki
7. ROM—Attila Csipler, Octavian Vintilă, Tănase Mureşan, Ionel Drimbă
7. USA—Alfonso Morales, Robert Blum, Eugene [Jenő] Hamori, Attila Keresztes, Thomas Orley

Final: SOV 9-6 ITA
3rd Place: POL 860-859 FRA
5th Place: HUN 9-3 GER

In the semifinals Hungary's winning streak was finally stopped at 46 when it's team was upset by Italy, 9-7. It was Italy that had handed the Hungarians their last defeat 40 years earlier in Paris.

1968 Mexico City T: 12, N: 12, D: 10.21.
1. SOV/RUS—Vladimir Nazlymov, Eduard Vinokurov, Viktor Sidyak, Mark Rakita, Umyar Mavlikhanov
2. ITA—Wladimiro Calarese, Cesare Salvadori, Michele Maffei, Pierluigi Chicca, Rolando Rigoli
3. HUN—Tamás Kovács, Miklós Meszéna, János Kalmár, Péter Bakonyi, Tibor Pézsa
4. FRA—Marcel Parent, Claude Arabo, Bernard Vallée, Serge Panizza, Jean Ramez
5. POL—Jerzy Pawłowski, Józef Nowara, Franciszek Sobczak, Zygmunt Kawecki, Emil Ochyra
6. USA—Alex Orban, Alfonso Morales, Anthony Keane, Robert Blum, Thomas Balla
7. GBR—Alexander Leckie, Rodney Craig, David Acfield, Richard Oldcorn
7. GER—Percy Borucki, Walter Köstner, Paul Wischeidt, Klaus Allisat, Volker Duschner

Final: SOV 9-7 ITA
3rd Place: HUN 9-5 FRA
5th Place: POL 9-5 USA

1972 Munich T: 13, N: 13, D: 9.4.
1. ITA—Michele Maffei, Mario Aldo Montano, Cesare Salvadori, Mario Tullio Montano, Rolando Rigoli
2. SOV/RUS—Mark Rakita, Eduard Vinokurov, Viktor Bazhenov, Viktor Sidyak, Vladimir Nazlymov
3. HUN—Pál Gerevich, Tamás Kovács, Péter Marót, Tibor Pézsa, Péter Bakonyi
4. ROM—Dan Irimiciuc, Iosif Budahazi, Gheorghe Culcea, Constantin Nicolae, Octavian Vintilă
5. POL—Józef Nowara, Krzysztof Grzegorek, Zygmunt Kawecki, Jerzy Pawłowski, Janusz Majewski
6. CUB—Hilario Hipólito Vinent, Guzmán Salazar, Francisco de la Torre, Manuel Ortiz, Manuel Suárez
7. FRA—Regis Bonissent, Bernard Dumont, Bernard Vallée, Philippe Bena, Serge Panizza
7. GER—Walter Convents, Volker Duschner, Knut Höhne, Dieter Wellmann, Paul Wischeidt

Final: ITA 9-5 SOV
3rd Place: HUN 8-7 ROM
5th Place: POL 9-5 CUB

Maffei defeated all four Soviet fencers in the final, but it was Aldo Montano who won the decisive bout with Vinokurov, 5-1. Montano had previously been warned by the officials not to remove his mask before a decision had been announced. When he scored the winning hit the 205-pound Montano leaped up and down while his team manager and his cousin (and teammate), Tullio Montano, desperately held on to his helmet until the official call was made.

1976 Montreal T: 13, N: 13, D: 7.27.
1. SOV/RUS—Eduard Vinokurov, Viktor Krovopuskov, Mikhail Burtsev, Viktor Sidyak, Vladimir Nazlymov
2. ITA—Mario Aldo Montano, Michele Maffei, Angelo Arcidiacono, Tommaso Montano, Mario Tullio Montano
3. ROM—Dan Irimiciuc, Ioan Popa, Marin Mustaţă, Corneliu Marin, Alexandru Nilca
4. HUN—Péter Marót, Tamás Kovács, Imre Gedővári, Ferenc Hammang, Csaba Körmöczi
5. CUB—Manuel Ortiz, Francisco de La Torre, Guzmán Salazar, Ramon Hernández, Lázaro Mora
6. POL—Leszek Jabłonowski, Sylwester Królikowski, Jacek Bierkowski, Józef Nowara
7. USA—Paul Apostol, Peter Westbrook, Stephen Kaplan, Thomas Losonczy, Alex Orban
7. FRA—Philippe Bena, Regis Bonnissent, Bernard Dumont, Didier Flament, Patrick Quivrin

Final: SOV 9-4 ITA
3rd Place: ROM 9-4 HUN
5th Place: CUB 9-6 POL

1980 Moscow T: 8, N: 8, D: 7.29.
1. SOV—Mikhail Burtsev, Viktor Krovopuskov, Viktor Sidyak, Vladimir Nazlymov, Nikolai Alyokhin
2. ITA—Michele Maffei, Mario Aldo Montano, Marco Romano, Ferdinando Meglio
3. HUN—Imre Gedővári, Rudolf Nébald, Pál Gerevich, Ferenc Hammang, György Nébald
4. POL—Tadeusz Piguła, Leszek Jabłonowski, Jacek Bierkowski, Andrzej Kostrzewa
5. ROM—Ioan Pop, Marin Musață, Corneliu Marin, Ion Pantelimonescu, Alexandru Nilca
6. GDR—Rüdiger Müller, Hendrik Jung, Peter Ulbrich, Frank-Eberhard Höltje, Gerd May
7. CUB—Manuel Ortiz, Jesus Ortiz, José Laverdecia Montoya, Guzmán Salazar
8. BUL—Hristo Etropolski, Nikolai Marincheshki, Vassil Etropolski, Georgi Chomakov, Marin Ivanov

Final: SOV 9-2 ITA
3rd Place: HUN 9-6 POL
5th Place: ROM 9-6 GDR

1984 Los Angeles-Long Beach T: 8, N: 8, D: 8.9.
1. ITA—Marco Marin, Gianfranco Dalla Barba, Giovanni Scalzo, Ferdinando Meglio, Angelo Arcidiacono
2. FRA—Jean-François Lamour, Pierre Guichot, Hervé Granger-Veyron, Philippe Delrieu, Franck Ducheix
3. ROM—Marin Mustață, Ioan Pop, Alexandru Chiculita, Corneliu Marin, Vilmos Szabo
4. GER—Dieter Schneider, Jürgen Nolte, Freddy Scholz, Jürg Stratmann, Jörg Volkmann
5. CHN—Wang Ruiji, Chen Jinchu, Yang Shisheng, Liu Guozhen, Liu Yunhong
6. USA—Peter Westbrook, Steve Mormando, Phillip Reilly, Joel Glucksman, Michael Lofton

Final: ITA 9-3 FRA
3rd Place: ROM 8-7 GER
5th Place: CHN 9-7 USA

1988 Seoul T: 11, N: 11, D: 9.29.
1. HUN—Imre Bujdosó, László Csongrádi, Imre Gedővári, György Nébald, Bence Szabó
2. SOV—Andrei Alshan, Mikhail Burtsev, Sergei Koryazhkin, Serhei Mindyrhasov, Heorgy Pohosov
3. ITA—Massimo Cavaliere, Gianfranco Dalla Barba, Marco Marin, Ferdinando Meglio, Giovanni Scalzo
4. FRA—Philippe Delrieu, Franck Ducheix, Hervé Grange-Veyron, Pierre Guichot, Jean-François Lamour
5. POL—Marek Gniewkowski, Robert Kościelniakowski, Andrzej Kostrzewa, Janusz Olech, Tadeusz Piguła
6. GER—Felix Becker, Jörg Kempenich, Jürgen Nolte, Dieter Schneider, Stephan Thoennessen
7. USA—Robert Cottingham, Paul Friedberg, Michael Lofton, George Mormando, Peter Westbrook
8. BUL—Hristo Etropolski, Vassil Etropolski, Nikolai Marincheshki, Nikolai Mateyev, Georgi Chomakov

Final: HUN 867-864 SOV
3rd Place: ITA 864-863 FRA
5th Place: POL 9-4 GER

The glory years of Hungarian team sabre ended in 1964 and the mantle passed to the Soviets and Russians who have, since then, qualified for every Olympic final except the boycotted Games of Los Angeles. Prior to the 1988 Olympics, the Soviets had won three straight world championships. In Seoul the Hungarians survived with a 3-touch victory over Poland in the quarterfinals. The USSR took a 7-3 lead in the final, but Hungary fought back with four victories in a row and went on to win another 3-touch squeaker.

If the Hungarian triumph was a throwback to the 1950s, what happened in the bronze medal match brought back memories of the 1920s. Trailing 2-6, the French team protested the officiating decisions. A violent argument ensued and the French stalked off the piste, threatening to withdraw. After 30 minutes they were lured back. They rallied to tie the Italians 8-8, but lost by one touch.

1992 Barcelona T: 12, N: 12, D: 8.7.
1. SOV—Grigory Kiriyenko, Aleksandr Shirshov, Vadim Guttsayt, Stanislav Pozdnyakov, Heorgy Pohosov
2. HUN—Péter Abay, Imre Bujdosó, Csaba Köves, György Nébald, Bence Szabó
3. FRA—Franck Ducheix, Jean-Philippe Daurelle, Hervé Granger-Veyron, Pierre Guichot, Jean-François Lamour
4. ROM—Alexandru Chiculita, Victor Gaureanu, Daniel Grigore, Florin Lupeica, Vilmos Szabo
5. GER—Felix Becker, Jörg Kempenich, Jürgen Nolte, Jacek Huchwajda, Steffen Wiesinger
6. POL—Marek Gniewkowski, Norbert Jaskot, Jarsolaw Kisiel, Robert Koscielniakowski, Janusz Olech
7. CHN—Jia Guihua, Ning Xiankui, Yang Zhen, Jiang Yefei, Zheng Zhaokang
8. ITA—Marco Marin, Ferdinando Meglio, Giovanni Scalzo, Giovanni Sirovich, Tonhi Terenzi

Final: SOV 9-5 HUN
3rd Place: FRA 9-4 ROM
5th Place: GER 9-6 POL
7th Place: CHN 9-7 ITA

1996 Atlanta T: 11, N: 11, D: 7.24.
1. RUS—Grigory Kiriyenko, Sergei Sharikov, Stanislav Pozdnyakov
2. HUN—Bence Szabó, Csaba Köves, József Navarrete
3. ITA—Luigi Tarantino, Raffaello Caserta, Tonhi Terenzi
4. POL—Janusz Olech, Norbert Jaskot, Rafal Sznajder
5. FRA—Damien Touya, Franck Ducheix, Jean Daurelle
6. SPA—Antonio García Delgado, Fernando Medina Martínez, Raúl Peinador de Isidro
7. ROM—Florin Lupeica, Mihai Covaliu, Vilmos Szabo
8. GER—Felix Becker, Frank Bleckmann, Steffen Wiesinger

Final: RUS 45-25 HUN
3rd Place: ITA 45-37 POL
5th Place: FRA 45-41 SPA
7th Place: ROM 45-42 GER

The Russian team was never seriously challenged. They defeated Spain 45-34, Italy 45-28 and Hungary 45-25.

2000 Sydney T: 9, N: 9, D: 9.24.
1. RUS—Sergei Sharikov, Stanislav Pozdnyakov, Aleksei Frosin
2. FRA—Mathieu Gourdain, Damien Touya, Julien Pillet, Cédric Seguin
3. GER—Dennis Bauer, Alexander Weber, Wiradech Kothny

4. ROM—Mihai Covaliu, Florin Lupeica, Victor Gaureanu
5. HUN—Zsolt Nemcsik, Csaba Köves, Domonkos Ferjancsik, Péter Takács II
6. UKR—Vadym Huttsait, Volodymyr Lukashenko, Volodymyr Kaljusni
7. POL—Rafał Sznajder, Norbert Jaskot, Marcin Sobala
8. ITA—Luigi Tarantino, Raffaello Casserta, Tonhi Terenzi, Giampero Pastore

Final: RUS 45-32 FRA
3rd Place: GER 45-27 ROM
5th Place: HUN 45-43 UKR
7th Place: POL 45-39 ITA

Again the Russians were not seriously challenged, defeating Hungary 45-39, Romania 45-28 and France 45-32.

2004 Athens T: 9, N: 9, D: 8.19.

1. FRA—Julien Pillet, Damien Touya, Gaël Touya
2. ITA—Aldo Montano, Gianpiero Pastore, Luigi Tarantino
3. RUS—Sergei Sharikov, Aleksei Dyachenko, Stanislav Pozdnyakov, Aleksei Yakimenko
4. USA—Ivan Lee, Jason Rogers, Keeth Smart
5. HUN—Domonkos Ferjancsik, Kende Fodor, Balázs Lengyel, Zsolt Nemcsik
6. UKR—Volodymyr Kalyuzhnyi, Volodymyr Lukashenko, Oleh Shturbabin, Vladislav Tretiak
7. CHN—Chen Feng, Huang Yaojiang, Wang Jingzhi, Zhou Hanming
8. GRE—Marios Basmatzian, Jason Dourakos, Dimitris Kostakos, Konstantinos Manetas

Final: FRA 45-42 ITA
3rd Place: RUS 45-44 USA
5th Place: HUN 45-40 UKR
7th Place: CHN 45-42 GRE

Both semifinals were unusually close. In the first, Luigi Tarantino outscored Stanislav Pozdnyakov 6-2 in the final bout to give Italy a 45-42 come-from-behind victory over Russia. In the second semi, France and the United States were tied at 44, with the last touch to be contested by Damien Touya for France and Keeth Smart for the US. Touya and Smart charged simultaneously and both recorded touches. The referee did not award a point, but during the lunge Smart's sabre pierced Touya's right glove and hand. After a 10-minute timeout, and with a bandaged hand, Touya returned to the match and, after two more simultaneous touches, scored the final point. In the final, the French built a 25-18 lead, but Aldo Montano brought the Italians back into contention by outscoring Touya 11-5, and then bested Julien Pillet 7-4 to put Italy ahead 40-39 going into the final rotation. This bout matched the two heroes of the semifinals, Touya and Tarantino. Touya outpointed the Italian 6-2 and the French earned their first-ever Olympic team sabre title.

2008 Beijing T: 8, N: 8, D: 8.17.

1. FRA—Nicolas Lopez, Julien Pillet, Boris Sanson
2. USA—Tim Morehouse, Jason Rogers, Keeth Smart, James Williams
3. ITA—Aldo Montano, Diego Occhiuzzi, Gianpiero Pastore, Luigi Tarantino
4. RUS—Nikolay Kovalyov, Stanislav Pozdnyakov, Aleksey Yakimenko
5. BLR—Aleksandr Buykevich, Dmitry Lapkes, Valery Priyemko
6. CHN—Huang Yaojiang, Wang Jingzhi, Zhong Man, Zhou Hanming
7. HUN—Tamás Decsi, Balázs Lontay, Zsolt Nemcsik, Áron Szilágyi
8. EGY—Gamal Fathy, Tamim Ghazy, Mahmoud Samir, Shadi Talaat

Final: FRA 45-37 USA
3rd Place: ITA 45-44 RUS
5th Place: BLR 45-39 CHN
7th Place: HUN 45-25 EGY

The United States, eleventh at the last world championships, was not expected to contend for a medal. Facing reigning world champion Hungary in the first round, the Americans trailed 40-36 before 30-year-old Keeth Smart outscored Zsolt Nemcsik 9-4, giving the US a surprise 45-44 win. They then faced Russia, the 2005 world champions, in the semi-finals. Once again, the Americans trailed 40-35 going into the final match, and once again Smart delivered the decisive points, beating five-time world champion and 1996 gold medalist Stanislav Pozdnyakov 10-4 to earn another one-point victory.

In the final, defending Olympic champion and 2006 world champion France got off to a quick 5-1 lead and expanded their advantage to 40-28 going into the final match. Smart managed to make nine hits on Julien Pillet in the final bout, but could not wipe out all the deficit, and the US was left with silver.

Smart's path to Beijing had been difficult. Four years earlier, at the Athens Olympics, he had cost the US a place on the medal podium after giving up the final touches in two consecutive 44-45 losses. Discouraged, he left the sport for a year, during which both his parents died and he himself was diagnosed with a rare blood disorder. He eventually returned to training in 2005. Smart's sister, Erinn, was also a fencer and had earned a silver medal in the women's team foil event one day before the men's team sabre final.

DISCONTINUED EVENTS

ÉPÉE, TEAM

1906 Athens T: 6, N: 6, D: 4.26.

1. FRA—Pierre d'Hugues, Georges Dillon-Kavanagh, Mohr, Georges de la Falaise
2. GBR—William Desborough, Cosmo Duff Gordon, Charles Newton Robinson, Edgar Seligman
3. BEL—Constant Cloquet, Fernand de Montigny, Edmond Crahay, Philippe Le Hardy de Beaulieu

Final: FRA 9-9, 9-6 GBR

In the first round Germany was due to meet Great Britain. However, a misunderstanding of the schedule found the Germans asleep at their hotel at the time the match was to start. Quickly roused, the Germans rushed to the fencing grounds and were easily beaten, 9-2. The final resulted in a tie. The rematch was held immediately; France won, 9-6.

Cosmo Duff Gordon was 43 years old when he helped the British team earn second place at the 1906 Athens Games. But it was his involvement in an incident six years later that would burn his name into history books. On the night of April 15, 1912, Duff Gordon and his wife Lucille, a noted fashion designer, were passengers aboard the *Titanic* when the doomed ship struck an iceberg. Amid the panic, the Duff Gordons found an emergency lifeboat that was being prepared away from the throng. Along with Lady Duff Gordon's secretary, Miss Francatelli, they were hoisted aboard and the lifeboat was lowered into the water. Although the boat was big enough to accommodate forty people, there were only twelve inside: seven crew members, two American gentlemen, and the Duff Gordon party of three. What conversations passed among the twelve survivors is still a matter of dispute. What is certain is that, despite the fact that there was room for twenty-eight more people, they made no attempt to save any of the passengers who were drowning and freezing to death in the icy water. Indeed, they seemed to make a point of rowing away from the screams and wails of the victims.

After they were saved by the *Carpathia*, Duff Gordon gathered the seven crew members from the lifeboat and gave them each a check for £5, presumably to help them replace their lost kits (tools and uniforms). A group photo was taken and the crew members autographed Lady Duff Gordon's lifebelt. Upon their arrival in New York City, the Duff Gordons established themselves in a suite at the Ritz Hotel and immediately threw a dinner party, complete with champagne and caviar. But a few days later, word spread about the payment Duff Gordon had made to the crew members, and he was accused of having bribed the crew to row away from the sinking ship. The Duff Gordons found themselves booed when they tried to walk in the streets and many staff members of the Ritz refused to serve them.

The Duff Gordons returned to London, coincidentally on board another ill-fated ship: the *Lusitania*. As soon as they landed, they were confronted by newsboys calling out, "Read about the *Titanic* cowards," and selling newspapers whose headlines read, "Duff Gordon Scandal" and "Cowardly Baronet and his Wife Who Rowed Away from the Drowning." Less than two weeks later, Sir Cosmo and Lady Duff Gordon appeared before a Board of Trade inquiry into the sinking of the *Titanic*. The story was considered so sensational that those in attendance at their testimony included the Prime Minister's wife, Margot Asquith, and royalty from several European nations. The court absolved Duff Gordon of the charge of bribery, but it was clear that while in the lifeboat, he had been far more concerned with his wife's seasickness than with the hundreds of people dying nearby. When asked by an attorney for the Dockers' Union if he thought "it was natural not to think of rescuing the people," Duff Gordon replied that he still thought it was natural, although "I now see it would have been a splendid thing if it could have been done." Although he lived for another nineteen years, Cosmo Duff Gordon was never able to fully escape his public image as a coward.

1908 London T: 9, N: 9, D: 7.23.

1. FRA—Gaston Alibert, Bernard Gravier, Alexandre Lippmann, Eugène Olivier, Henri-Georges Berger, Charles Collignon, Jean Stern
2. GBR—Edgar Amphlett, C. Leaf Daniell, Cecil Haig, Robert Montgomerie, Martin Holt, Edgar Seligman
3. BEL—Paul Anspach, Fernand Bosmans, Fernand de Montigny, François Rom, Victor Willems, Désiré Beaurain, Ferdinand Feyerick
4. ITA—Marcello Bertinetti, Giuseppe Mangiarotti, Riccardo Nowak, Abelardo Olivier

Final: FRA 9-7 BEL
Pool for 2nd: GBR 9-8 DEN; GBR 9-5 BEL

1912 Stockholm T: 11, N: 11, D: 7.10.

	WON	LOST	TR
1. BEL	3	0	21
2. GBR	1	2	28
3. HOL	1	2	30
4. SWE	1	2	32
5. DEN			
5. GRE			
7. BOH/CZE			

1. BEL—Paul Anspach, Henri Anspach, Robert Hennet, Fernand de Montigny, Jacques Ochs, François Rom, Gaston Salmon, Victor Willems
2. GBR—Edgar Seligman, Robert Montgomerie, Percival Davson, Arthur Everitt, Sydney Martineau, Martin Holt
3. HOL—Adrianus de Jong, Willem Hubert van Blijenburgh, Jetze Doorman, Leonardus Nardus
4. SWE—Einar Sörensen, Gustaf Lindblom, Pontus von Rosen, Louis Sparre, Georg Branting, Eric Carlberg
5. DEN—Ejnar Levison, Hans Olsen, Ivan Osiier, Lauritz Østrup
5. GRE—Konstantinos Kotzias, Petros Manos, Georgios Petropoulos, Georgios Versis, Trifonos Triantafillakos
7. BOH/CZE—Vilém Goppold z Lobsdorfu, Jr., Josef Pfeiffer, František Kříž, Vilém Goppold z Lobsdorfu, Sr.

Jacques Ochs of the victorious Belgian team was a painter who went on to a successful career as an artist and museum director.

1920 Antwerp T: 11, N: 11, D: 8.20.

	WON	LOST	TIED	MATCHES W	MATCHES L
1. ITA	5	0	0	41	22
2. BEL	4	1	0	39	34

3. FRA	2	2	1	39	31
4. POR	2	2	1	30	35
5. SWI	1	4	0	33	41
6. USA	0	5	0	19	38
7. GBR					
7. HOL					

1. ITA—Nedo Nadi, Aldo Nadi, Abelardo Olivier, Tullio Bozza, Giovanni Canova, Andrea Marrazzi, Dino Urbani, Antonio Allocchio, Tommaso Constantino, Paolo Thaon di Revel
2. BEL—Ernest Gevers, Paul Anspach, Félix Goblet d'Alviella, Victor Boin, Joseph de Craecker, Léon Tom, Philippe Le Hardy de Beaulieu
3. FRA—Armand Massard, Alexandre Lippmann, Gustave Buchard, Georges Trombert, Georges Casanova, Gaston Amson, Émile Moreau
4. POR—António Mascarenhas de Menezes, Jorge de Paiva, Ruimondo Mayer, João Sassetti, Henrique Cunha da Silveira, Frederico Paredes, Manuel Queiroz
5. SWI—Henri Jacquet, Léopold Montagnier, Franz Wilhelm, Frédéric Fitting, Eugène Empeyta, Louis de Tribolet, John Albaret, Edouard Fitting
6. USA—William Russell, Raymond Dutcher, Henry Breckinridge, Arthur Lyon, Robert Sears, Harold Rayner
7. GBR—John Blake, George Burt, Martin Holt, Robert Montgomerie, Barry Notley, Edgar Seligman
7. HOL—Adrianus de Jong, Willem Hubert van Blijenburgh, George van Rossem, Salomon Zeldenrust, Henri Wijnoldij-Daniëls, Jetze Doorman

Two competitors worth noting were Nedo Nadi of Italy and Victor Boin of Belgium. Nadi, who won five gold medals in foil and sabre, was not as well known as an épéeist. His father, Beppe, considered the épée to be an "undisciplined" weapon, "the prostitution of fencing," and forbade the use of it in his salle. So Nedo would sneak out to enjoy the taboo sword. His insubordination paid off with a team épée gold medal in 1920. Boin's silver medal as part of the Belgian team was his third Olympic medal. His first two, however, were earned not in fencing but in water polo: a silver in 1908 and a bronze in 1912. Boin also enjoyed swimming, skating, flying, ice hockey, and motorcycle racing. He was founder of the International Association of Sports Journalists and President of the Belgian Olympic Committee.

1924 Paris T: 16, N: 16, D: 7.9.

			MATCHES	
	WON	LOST	W	L
1. FRA	3	0	29	16
2. BEL	2	1	24	22
3. ITA	1	2	21	26
4. POR	0	3	18	28
5. SPA				
5. USA				

1. FRA—Lucien Gaudin, Georges Buchard, Roger Ducret, André Labatut, Lionel Liottel, Alexandre Lippmann, Georges Tainturier
2. BEL—Paul Anspach, Joseph de Craecker, Charles Delporte, Fernand de Montigny, Ernest Gevers, Léon Tom
3. ITA—Giullo Basletta, Marcello Bertinetti, Giovanni Canova, Vincenzo Cuccia, Virgilio Mantegazza, Oreste Moricca
4. POR—Antonio Mascarenhas de Menezes, Jorge Paiva, Paulo d'Eca Leal, Rui Mayer, Henrique da Silveira, Mário de Noronha, Frederico Paredes, Antonio Pinto Leite
5. SPA—José Delgado y Hernández de Tejada, Félix de Pomes Soler, Diego Diez de Rivera y Figueroa, Fernando García Bilbao, Diego García-Montoro, Jesús López-Lara-Mallor, Carlos Miguel de los Reyes, Miguel Zabalza de la Fuente
5. USA—Henry Breckinridge, George Breed, George Calnan, Arthur Lyon, Allen Millner, William Russell, Leon Shore, Donald Waldhaus

1928 Amsterdam T: 18, N: 18, D: 8.5.

			MATCHES	
	WON	LOST	W	L
1. ITA	3	0	28	19
2. FRA	2	1	24	22
3. POR	1	2	21	26
4. BEL	0	3	20	26
5. HOL				
5. SPA				
5. USA				

1. ITA—Carlo Agostoni, Marcello Bertinetti, Giancarlo Cornaggia Medici, Renzo Minoli, Giulio Basletta, Franco Riccardi
2. FRA—Armand Massard, Georges Buchard, Gaston Amson, Emile Cornic, Bernard Schmetz, René Barbier
3. POR—Paulo d'Eca Leal, Mário de Noronha, Jorge Paiva, João Sassetti, Frederico Paredes, Henrique de Silveira
4. BEL—Émile Barbier, Balthazar de Beuckalaer, Charles Delporte, Charles Debeur, Léon Tom, Georges Dambois
5. CZE—Martin Harden, Josef Jungmann, František Kříž, Jan Tille, Miroslav Beznovska, Jan Çernohorský
5. HOL—Laurens Kuypers, Adrianus de Jong, Henri Wijnoldij Daniëls, William Driebergen, Alfred Labouchère, Karel van den Brandeler
5. SPA—José Delgado y Hernández de Tejada, Diego García Montoro, Diego Diez de Rivera y Figueroa, Félix de Pomes Soler, Fidel González Badía
5. USA—Arthur Lyon, George Calnan, Allen Milner, Harold Rayner, Henry Breckinridge, Edward Barnett

1932 Los Angeles T: 7, N: 7, D: 8.7.

			MATCHES	
	WON	LOST	W	L
1. FRA	3	0	30.5	17.5
2. ITA	2	1	27.5	20.5
3. USA	1	2	20.5	22.5
4. BEL	0	3	12.5	30.5

1. FRA—Philippe Cattiau, Georges Buchard, Bernard Schmetz, Jean Piot, Fernand Jourdant, Georges Tainturier
2. ITA—Carlo Agostoni, Giancarlo Cornaggia-Medici, Renzo Minoli, Franco Riccardi, Saverio Ragno
3. USA—George Calnan, Gustave Heiss, Frank Righeimer, Tracy Jaeckel, Curtis Shears, Miguel de Capriles
4. BEL—Raoul Henkaert, André Poplimont, Max Janlet, Balthazar de Beuckelaer, Albert Mund

1936 Berlin T: 21, N: 21, D: 8.8.

			MATCHES	
	WON	LOST	W	L
1. ITA	3	0	26	41
2. SWE	2	1	21	22
3. FRA	1	2	21	23
4. GER	0	3	11	23
5. POL				
5. POR				
5. USA				

1. ITA—Saverio Ragno, Alfredo Pezzana, Giancarlo Cornaggia-Medici, Edoardo Mangiarotti, Franco Riccardi, Giancarlo Brusati
2. SWE—Hans Granfelt, Sven Thofelt, Gösta Almgren, Gustaf Dyrssen, Hans Drakenberg, Birger Cederin
3. FRA—Michel Pécheux, Bernard Schmetz, Georges Buchard, Henri Dulieux, Paul Wormser, Philippe Cattiau
4. GER—Siegfried Lerdon, Joseph Uhlmann, Hans Esser, Eugen Geiwitz, Ernst Röthig, Otto Schröder
5. BEL—Raymond Stasse, Robert t'Sas, Charles Debeur, Hervé de Monceau, Jean Plumier, Marcel Heim
5. POL—Jerzy Staszewicz, Teodor Zaczyk, Rajmund Karwicki, Roman Kantor, Kazimierz Szempliński, Antoni Franz
5. POR—Henrique de Silveira, Paulo d'Eça Leal, António Mascarenhas de Menezes, João Sasseti, Gustavo Carinhas
5. USA—Frank Righeimer, Thomas Sands, Tracy Jaeckel, Gustave Heiss, Miguel de Capriles, Andrew Boyd

Two members of the Swedish team, Gustaf Dyrssen and Sven Thofelt, had previously won gold medals in modern pentathlon. Both men went on to serve as members of the International Olympic Committee.

1948 London T: 21, N: 21, D: 8.6.

	WON	LOST	MATCHES W	L
1. FRA	3	0	31	10
2. ITA	2	1	25	21
3. SWE	1	2	18	26
4. DEN	0	3	12	29
5. HUN				
5. LUX				
5. SWI				

1. FRA—Henri Guérin, Henri Lepage, Marcel Desprets, Michel Pécheux, Edouard Artigas, Maurice Huet
2. ITA—Luigi Cantone, Antonio Mandruzzato, Dario Mangiarotti, Edoardo Mangiarotti, Fiorenzo Marini, Carlo Agostoni
3. SWE—Per Carleson, Frank Cervell, Carl Forssel, Bengt Ljungquist, Sven Thofelt, H. Arne Tollbom
4. DEN—Mogens Lüchow, Erik Andersen, Ib Benjamin Nielsen, René Dybkaer, Jacob Lyng, Kenneth Flindt
5. BEL—Raymond Stasse, Léopold Hauben, Raymond Bru, Jean Radoux, Raoul Henkaert, Charles Debeur
5. HUN—Imre Hennyey, Pál Dunay, Béla Rerrich, Béla Mikla, Lajos Balthazár, Béla Bay
5. LUX—Fernand Leischen, Paul Anen, Émile Gretsch, Gustav Lamesch, Einy Putz
5. SWI—François Thiebaud, René Lips, Jean Hauert, Oswald Zappelli, Otto Rufenacht, Michel Chamay

France qualified for the final pool despite being upset 10-5 in the semifinal pool by Belgium. The French team was led by Michel Pécheux, a last-minute addition, who was 11-0 in the final pool and 23-3 total.

1952 Helsinki T: 19, N: 19, D: 7.26.

	WON	LOST	MATCHES W	L
1. ITA	3	0	32	11
2. SWE	2	1	26	17
3. SWI	1	2	18	24
4. LUX	0	3	9	33
5. DEN				
5. HUN				

1. ITA—Dario Mangiarotti, Edoardo Mangiarotti, Franco Bertinetti, Carlo Pavesi, Giuseppe Delfino, Roberto Battaglia
2. SWE—Bengt Ljundquist, Berndt Otto Rehbinder, Sven Fahlman, Per Carleson, Carl Forssell, Lennart Magnusson
3. SWI—Otto Rüfenacht, Paul Meister, Oswald Zappelli, Paul Barth, Willy Fitting, Mario Valota
4. LUX—Émile Gretsch, Fernand Leischen, Paul Anen, Léon Buck
5. DEN—Raimondo Carnera, Erik Swane-Lund, René Dybkaer, Mogens Lüchow, Ib Benjamin Nielsen, Jacob Lyng
5. HUN—Lajos Balthazár, Barnabás Berzsenyi, Béla Rerrich, József Sákovics, Imre Hennyey

The 1952 Olympics saw the downfall of defending champion France, eliminated in the second round after losses to Luxembourg and Hungary. Italy defeated Sweden 8-5 in the deciding match, despite the efforts of Bengt Ljundquist, who beat all four Italians. After earning two silver medals in fencing, Ljundquist returned to the Olympics in 1964 to represent Sweden in equestrian dressage.

1956 Melbourne T: 11, N: 11, D: 11.28.

	WON	LOST	MATCHES W	L
1. ITA	3	0	34	10
2. HUN	2	1	22	22
3. FRA	1	2	17	27
4. GBR	0	3	15	29
5. BEL				
5. SOV				

1. ITA—Giuseppe Delfino, Alberto Pellegrino, Edoardo Mangiarotti, Carlo Pavesi, Giorgio Anglesio, Franco Bertinetti
2. HUN—József Sákovics, Béla Rerrich, Lajos Balthazár, Ambrus Nagy, József Marosi, Barnabás Berzsenyi
3. FRA—Armand Mouyal, Claude Nigon, Daniel Dagallier, Yves Dreyfus, René Queyroux
4. GBR—R. René Paul, Michael Howard, Henry Hoskyns, Allan Jay
5. BEL—François Dehez, Roger Achten, Ghislain Delaunois, Marcel Vanderauwera, Jacques Debeur
5. SOV—Arnold Chernushevich, Valentin Chernikov, Lev Saitchuk, Revas Tsirekidze, Iosas Oudras

James Wolfensohn, a member of the Australian épée team in 1956, later became president of the World Bank.

1960 Rome T: 21, N: 21, D: 9.9.

1. ITA—Giuseppe Delfino, Alberto Pellegrino, Carlo Pavesi, Edoardo Mangiarotti, Fiorenzo Marini, Gianluigi Saccaro
2. GBR—Allan Jay, Michael Howard, John Pelling, Henry Hoskyns, Raymond Harrison, Michael Alexander
3. SOV—Guram Kostava, Bruno Habārovs, Arnold Chernushevich, Valentin Chernikov, Aleksandr Pavlovsky
4. HUN—József Marosi, Tamás Gábor, István Kausz, József Sákovics, Árpád Bárány
5. GER—Paul Gnaier, Fritz Zimmerman, Dieter Finger, Georg Neuber, Helmut Anschütz, Walter Kostner
5. LUX—Roger Theisen, Edouard Schmit, Robert Schiel, Rodolphe Kugeler, Edmond Gutenkauff

5. SWE—Hans Lagerwall, Göran Abrahamsson, Ling Vannerus, Berndt Rehbinder, Carl-Wilhem Engdahl, Orvar Lindwall
5. SWI—Hans Baessler, Amez Droz, Paul Meister, Charles Ribordy, Claudio Polledri, Michel Steininger

Final: ITA 9-5 GBR
3rd Place: SOV 9-5 HUN

The Italian squad included the last three individual épée champions: Mangiarotti (1952), Pavesi (1956), and Delfino (1960), as well as 21-year-old Gianluigi Saccaro, who fenced with a patch over his injured right eye. In Italy's semifinal match against the USSR, the usually subdued Delfino found himself trailing Chernikov 4-1 with 13 seconds left. He then scored three hits in 12 seconds to force an overtime bout, which he also won.

1964 Tokyo T: 18, N: 18, D: 10.21.

1. HUN—Győző Kulcsár, Zoltán Nemere, Tamás Gábor, István Kausz, Árpád Bárány
2. ITA—Gianluigi Saccaro, Giovanni Battista Breda, Gianfranco Paolucci, Giuseppe Delfino, Alberto Pellegrino
3. FRA—Claude Brodin, Yves Dreyfus, Claude Bourquard, Jack Guittet, Jacques Brodin
4. SWE—Ivar Genesjö, Orvar Lindwall, Hans Lagerwall, Göran Abrahamsson, Carl-Wilhem Engdahl
5. POL—Henryk Nielaba, Mikolaj Pomarnacki, Bogdan Gonsior, Bogdan Andrzejewski, Jerzy Pawłowski
6. GER—Franz Rompza, Max Geuter, Volkmar Würtz, Paul Gnaier, Haakon Stein
7. SOV—Bruno Habārovs, Guram Kostava, Yuri Smolyakov, Hryhory Kryss, Aleksei Nikanchikov
7. SWI—Claudio Polledri, Paul Meister, Walter Bar, Jean Gontier, Michel Steininger

Final: HUN 8-3 ITA
3rd Place: FRA 864-859 SWE
5th Place: POL 866-862 GER

Hungary broke the 44-year Italian-French domination of team épée, as Győző Kulcsár won all 20 of his bouts.

1968 Mexico City T: 20, N: 20, D: 10.25.

1. HUN—Csaba Fenyvesi, Zoltán Nemere, Pál Schmitt, Győző Kulcsár, Pál Nagy
2. SOV—Hryhory Kryss, Iosyf Vitebsky, Aleksei Nikanchikov, Yuri Smolyakov, Viktor Modzelevsky
3. POL—Bohdan Andrzejewski, Michal Butkiewicz, Bohdan Gonsior, Henryk Nielaba, Kazimierz Barburski
4. GER—Dieter Jung, Franz Rompza, Fritz Zimmerman, Max Geuter, Paul Gnaier
5. GDR—Bernd Uhlig, Klaus Dumke, Harry Fiedler, Hans-Peter Schulze
6. ITA—Gianfranco Paolucci, Claudio Francesconi, Giovanni Battista Breda, Gianluigi Saccaro, Antonio Albanese
7. FRA—François Jeanne, Claude Bourquard, Yves Boissier, Jacques Ladegaillerie, Jean-Pierre Allemand
7. GBR—Nicholas Halsted, E. Owen Bourne, Henry Hoskyns, W. Ralph Johnson, Peter Jacobs

Final: HUN 7-4 SOV
3rd Place: POL 9-6 GER
5th Place: GDR 9-6 ITA

For the first time in 56 years, Italy failed to finish among the top three.

1972 Munich T: 20, N: 20, D: 9.9.

1. HUN—István Osztrics, Sándor Erdős, Csaba Fenyvesi, Pál Schmitt, Győző Kulcsár
2. SWI—Peter Löetscher, Christian Kauter, Guy Evéquoz, Daniel Giger, François Suchanecki
3. SOV—Georgi Zažitski, Hryhory Kryss, Viktor Modzelevsky, Igor Valetov, Serhei Paramonov
4. FRA—François Jeanne, Jacques Brodin, Pierre Marchand, Jean-Pierre Allemand, Jacques La Degaillerie
5. ROM—Constantin Dutu, Costică Bărăgan, Anton Pongratz, Alexandru Istrate, Nicolae Iorgu
6. POL—Bohdan Andrzejewski, Jerzy Janikowski, Henryk Nielaba, Kazimierz Barburski, Bohdan Gonsior
7. NOR—Jan von Koss, Jeppe Norman, Ole Morch, Claus Morch
7. SWE—Hans Wieselgren, Carl Von Essen, Orvar Jönsson, Rolf Edling, Per Sundberg

Final: HUN 8-4 SWI
3rd Place: SOV 9-4 FRA
5th Place: ROM 9-3 POL

In July 2010 Pál Schmitt was elected President of Hungary, becoming the first Olympic champion to go on to be elected head of a national government. The first Olympic competitor to become an elected head of state was weightlifter Marcus Stephen of Nauru (who took part in the Games of 1992, 1996 and 2000), elected as Nauru's president in 2007.

1976 Montreal T: 19, N: 19, D: 7.29.

1. SWE—Hans Jacobson, Orvar Jonsson, Carl Von Essen, Leif Högström, Göran Flodström, Rolf Edling
2. GER—Alexander Pusch, Jürgen Hehn, Hanns Jana, Reinhold Behr, Volker Fischer
3. SWI—Jean-Blaise Evéquoz, Michel Poffet, Daniel Giger, Christian Kauter, François Suchanecki
4. HUN—Csaba Fenyvesi, Sándor Erdős, István Osztrics, Pál Schmitt, Győző Kulcsár
5. SOV—Aleksandr Abushakhmetov, Viktor Modzelevsky, Vasyl Stankovych, Aleksandr Bykov, Boris Lukomski
6. ROM—Ioan Popa, Anton Pongratz, Nicolae Iorgu, Paul Szabo
7. ITA—John Pezza, Nicola Granieri, Fabio Dal Zotto, Marcello Bertinetti, Giovan Battista Coletti
7. NOR—Nils Koppang, Jeppe Normann, Kjell Otto Moe, Bård Vonen, Ole Morch

Final: SWE 8-5 GER
3rd Place: SWI 9-3 HUN
5th Place: SOV 9-2 ROM

The world champion Swedish team received a setback in the first bout of the final match, when Göran Flodström was knocked out. Carl Von Essen was brought in as a replacement and won two crucial bouts, including one against Alexander Pusch, which took place while Flodström was being carried out on a stretcher.

1980 Moscow T: 11, N: 11, D: 7.31.
1. FRA—Philippe Riboud, Patrick Picot, Hubert Gardas, Michel Salesse, Philippe Boisse
2. POL—Piotr Jabkowski, Andrzej Lis, Mariusz Strzałka, Ludomir Chronowski, Leszek Swornowski
3. SOV—Boris Lukomsky, Aleksandr Abushakhmetov, Volodymyr Smirnov, Ashot Karagan, Aleksandr Mozhayev
4. ROM—Ioan Popa, Octavian Zidaru, Anton Pongratz, Costică Bărăgan, Petru Kuki
5. SWE—Johan Harmenberg, Rolf Edling, Leif Högström, Göran Malkar, Hans Jacobsen
6. CZE—Jaroslav Jurka, Jaromír Holub, Jiří Douba, Jiří Adam, Oldřich Kubišta
7. GBR—Steven Paul, John Llewellyn, Neal Mallett, Robert Bruniges
8. HUN—Ernő Kolczonay, István Osztrics, Lászlo Pető, Jenő Pap, Péter Takács

Final: FRA 8-4 POL
3rd Place: SOV 9-5 ROM
5th Place: SWE 9-2 CZE
7th Place: GBR 16-0 HUN forfeit

Led by Philippe Riboud's 16-2 effort, France pulled off a major upset and won the team épée gold medal for the first time in 32 years. Steven Paul of the British team also competed in the Olympics in 1984 and 1992. Ten years later he trained Pierce Brosnan for his fencing scenes in the James Bond film *Die Another Day* and served as Brosnan's double for the more technical shots.

1984 Los Angeles-Long Beach T: 16, N: 16, D: 8.11.
1. GER—Elmar Borrmann, Volker Fischer, Gerhard Heer, Rafael Nickel, Alexander Pusch
2. FRA—Philippe Boisse, Jean-Michel Henry, Olivier Lenglet, Philippe Riboud, Michel Salesse
3. ITA—Stefano Bellone, Sandro Cuomo, Cosimo Ferro, Roberto Manzi, Angelo Mazzoni
4. CAN—Jacques Cardyn, Jean-Marc Chouinard, Alain Cote, Michel Dessureault, Daniel Perreault
5. SWE—Jerri Bergström, Greger Forslöw, Kent Hjerpe, Jonas Rosén, Björne Väggö
6. CHN—Cui Yining, Pang Jin, Zhao Lizhong, Zong Xiangqing
7. KOR—Kim Bong-man, Kim Sung-moon, Lee Il-hee, Min Kyung-seun, Yoon Nam-jin
8. GBR—W. Ralph Johnson, John Llewellyn, Neal Mallett, Steven Paul, Jonathan Stanbury

Final: GER 8-5 FRA
3rd Place: ITA 8-2 CAN
5th Place: SWE 8-6 CHN
7th Place: KOR 869-862 GBR

1988 Seoul T: 18, N: 18, D: 9.30.
1. FRA—Frédéric Delpla, Jean-Michel Henry, Olivier Lenglet, Philippe Riboud, Éric Srecki
2. GER—Elmar Borrmann, Volker Fischer, Thomas Gerull, Alexander Pusch, Arnd Schmitt
3. SOV—Andrei Shuvalov, Pavel Kolobkov, Vladimir Reznitšenko, Mykhalo Tyshko, Igor Tikhomirov
4. ITA—Stefano Bellone, Andrea Bermond Das Ambrois, Sandro Cuomo, Angelo Mazzoni, Stefano Pantano
5. SWI—Patrice Gaille, André Kuhn, Zsolt Madarasz, Gérald Pfefferle, Michel Poffet
6. HUN—Lászlo Fabian, Ferenc Hegedűs, Ernő Kolczonay, Szabolcs Pásztor, Zoltán Székely
7. KOR—Cho Hee-jae, Lee Il-hee, Lee Sang-ki, Yang Dal-sik, Yoon Nam-jin
8. SWE—Johan Bergdahl, Jerni Bergström, Otto Drakenberg, Ulf Sandegren, Péter Vánky

Final: FRA 8-3 GER
3rd Place: SOV 8(65)-8(63) ITA
5th Place: SWI 8-4 HUN
7th Place: KOR 8(64)-8(60) SWE

In a rematch of the 1984 final, France was led by Lenglet (4-0) and Henry (3-0).

1992 Barcelona T: 12, N: 12, D: 8.6.
1. GER—Elmar Borrmann, Robert Felisiak, Uwe Proske, Vladimir Resnitschenko [Reznitšenko], Arnd Schmitt
2. HUN—Iván Kovács, Krisztián Kulcsár, Ferenc Hegedűs, Ernő Kolczonay, Gábor Totola
3. SOV—Andrei Shuvalov, Pavel Kolobkov, Sergei Kravchuk, Sergei Kostarev, Valery Zakharevich
4. FRA—Éric Srecki, Jean-Michel Henry, Olivier Lenglet, Jean-François Di Martino, Robert Leroux
5. ITA—Sandro Cuomo, Angelo Mazzoni, Stefano Pantano, Maurizio Randazzo, Sandro Resegotti
6. SPA—Fernando De La Peña Olivas, Ángel Fernández García, César González Llorens, Raúl Maroto López, Manuel Pereira Senabre
7. CAN—Jean-Marc Chouinard, Alain Coté, Allan Francis, Bogdan Nowosielski, Laurie Shong
8. SWE—Mats Ahlgren, Jerri Bergström, Tomas Lundblad, Ulf Sandegren, Péter Vánky

Final: GER 8-4 HUN
3rd Place: SOV 8(70)-8(66) FRA
5th Place: ITA 8(68)-8(66) SPA
7th Place: CAN 9-5 SWE

Days before the competition was to begin, the five members of the épée team of the ex-Soviet Union threatened to boycott unless they were paid the bonuses of about $1500 each that they had been promised for winning the 1991 world championship. A tentative agreement was reached, but the squad performed below expectations, losing 8-7 to Germany in the semifinals. One of the German team members was Vladimir Resnitschenko, who had earned a bronze medal in Seoul as a member of the Soviet team. Resnitschenko, a Russian from Estonia, gained German citizenship just in time to compete in Barcelona. Hungary defeated Germany 9-5 in pool play, but in the final the Germans dominated the Hungarians, outtouching them 59-44.

1996 Atlanta T: 11, N: 11, D: 7.23.
1. ITA—Sandro Cuomo, Angelo Mazzoni, Maurizio Randazzo
2. RUS—Aleksandr Beketov, Pavel Kolobkov, Valery Zakharevich
3. FRA—Jean-Michel Henry, Robert Leroux, Éric Srecki
4. GER—Elmar Borrmann, Arnd Schmitt, Mariusz Strzałka
5. EST—Kaido Kaaberma, Andrus Kajak, Meelis Loit
6. HUN—Géza Imre, Iván Kovács, Krisztián Kulcsár
7. SPA—Oscar Fernández Albarracín, César González Llorens, Raúl Maroto López
8. USA—Tamir Bloom, James Carpenter, Michael Marx

Final: ITA 45-43 RUS
3rd Place: FRA 45-42 GER
5th Place: EST 45-39 HUN
7th Place: SPA 45-32 USA

The Italian épée team was one of the least dominating winners of the 1996 Olympics. They fought three matches. In the first they beat the United States by one touch. In the semifinal, after trailing by seven points, they beat Germany by winning the coin toss. In the final, Italy was leading Russia 44-43 when Aleksandr Beketov aggressively attacked five-time Olympian Angelo Mazzoni. Beketov missed, but his handle smashed into Mazzoni's mask, twisting it into the Italian's face and cutting him on the brow and below the eye. The match was halted with six seconds left in order to clear the blood out of Mazzoni's eye. After a ten-minute break, the match resumed and three seconds later, Mazzoni scored the winning point with a quick stab.

2000 Sydney T: 11, N: 11, D: 9.18.
1. ITA—Angelo Mazzoni, Paolo Milanoli, Alfredo Rota, Maurizio Randazzo
2. FRA—Jean-François Di Martino, Hugues Obry, Éric Srecki
3. CUB—Carlos Pedroso Curiel, Iván Trevejo Pérez, Nelson Loyola Torriente
4. KOR—Lee Sang-ki, Lee Sang-yup, Yang Roy-sung
5. GER—Jörg Fiedler, Arnd Schmitt, Marc Steifensand, Daniel Strigel
6. BLR—Vitaly Zakharov, Andrey Murashko, Vladimir Pchenikin
7. HUN—Attila Fekete, Márk Marsi, Iván Kovács
8. AUS—Gerard Adams, Nick Heffernan, Luc Cartillier

Final: ITA 39-38 FRA
3rd Place: CUB 45-31 KOR
5th Place: GER 41-37 BLR
7th Place: HUN 45-39 AUS

The tournament was full of tension and drama as three of four quarterfinal matches were decided by a single point, as were one of the semifinals and the final. In one quarterfinal, Belarus trailed South Korea 23-36, but caught up to 44-44. Finally, Lee Sang-yup touched Vitaly Zakharov six seconds into overtime to allow the Koreans to advance. In another quarterfinal, France's Éric Srecki blew a six-point lead to Hungary's Iván Kovács, but then scored the deciding touch to win 43-42. In one semifinal, France defeated Cuba 45-36. In the other, South Korea led Italy 40-35 going into the final bout between Alfredo Rota and Lee Sang-yup. Rota outscored Lee 9-3 to give Italy a 44-43 victory. In the final, Éric Srecki gave France a 4-2 lead against Alfredo Rota and the French stayed in front all through the match. With the score 38-36, the last bout brought together Hugues Obry, the individual silver medalist and Rota. Rota scored twice and then the two let the clock run down, forcing sudden death. Eighteen seconds into the overtime, Rota touched Obry on the knee and Italy had successfully defended their Olympic championship.

2004 Athens T: 8, N: 8, D: 8.22.
1. FRA—Eric Boisse, Fabrice Jeannet, Jérôme Jeannet, Hugues Obry
2. HUN—Gábor Boczkó, Géza Imre, Iván Kovács, Krisztián Kulcsár
3. GER—Jörg Fiedler, Sven Schmid, Daniel Strigel
4. RUS—Sergei Kochetkov, Pavel Kolobkov, Igor Turchin
5. UKR—Dmitriy Kariuchenko, Maksym Khvorost, Bohdan Nikishin, Vitaliy Osharov
6. USA—Weston Kelsey, Cody Mattern, Soren Thompson, Joseph Viviani
7. CHN—Tuo Tong, Wang Lei, Xie Yongjun, Zhao Gang
8. EGY—Ibrahim Abdel Rahim, Yasser Mahmoud, Ahmed Nabil, Mohamed Saif El-Din Sabry

Final: FRA 43-32 HUN
3rd Place: GER 37-29 RUS
5th Place: UKR 45-33 USA
7th Place: CHN 45-26 EGY

Two-time defending Olympic champion Italy failed to qualify for the Olympics. This left France in the role of favorites, The French beat the United States 45-32 in the quarterfinals and edged out Germany 45-44 in the semifinals to reach the gold medal match against Hungary. The final was closely fought, with the French leading only 19-18 after six of the nine bouts. In the last bout, Fabrice Jeannet outscored Krisztián Kulcsár 16-9 to earn the French a clear victory.

2008 Beijing T: 9, N: 9, D: 8.15.
1. FRA—Fabrice Jeannet, Jérôme Jeannet, Ulrich Robeiri
2. POL—Robert Andrzejuk, Tomasz Motyka, Adam Wiercioch, Radosław Zawrotniak
3. ITA—Diego Confalonieri, Alfredo Rota, Matteo Tagliariol, Stefano Carozzo
4. CHN—Dong Guotao, Li Guojie, Wang Lei, Yin Lianchi
5. HUN—Gábor Boczkó, Géza Imre, Iván Kovács, Krisztián Kulcsár
6. VEN—Silvio Fernández Briceño, Francisco Limardo Gascón, Rubén Limardo Gascón
7. UKR—Dmytro Chumak, Maksym Khvorost, Vitaliy Medvediev, Bohdan Nikishyn
8. KOR—Jung Jin-sun, Kim Seung-gu, Kim Won-jin

Final: FRA 45-29 POL
3rd Place: ITA 45-35 CHN
5th Place: HUN 40-25 VEN
7th Place: UKR 41-39 KOR

Four years after winning gold medals with the French épée team, brothers Fabrice and Jérôme Jeannet returned to the Olympics, once again the gold medal favorites. In the intervening years France had won the épée world championship title three consecutive times, with Fabrice participating all three times, Jérôme in 2005 and 2007 and first-time Olympian Ulrich Robeiri helping in 2006.

The first big surprise of the competition came in the quarter-final round, when Hungary, the defending Olympic silver medalists, lost to China 45-43. France had fewer difficulties, beating Venezuela 45-33 to reach the semi-finals, where they faced 2007 world silver medalists Italy, led by Matteo Tagliariol, who had beaten Fabrice Jeannet for the individual épée gold medal five days earlier. This time Jérôme Jeannet outscored Tagliariol 5-1 in the first bout, and France never relinquished the lead, winning 45-39. In the other semi-final, Poland scored a dramatic 45-44 victory over China.

The French squad earned a convincing win over Poland in the final, with Fabrice outscoring his opponents 17-7, including seven of eleven points in the final bout.

MASTERS FOIL FENCING

1896 Athens C: 2, N: 2, D: 4.7.

		TG	TR
1. Leon Pyrgos	GRE	3	1
2. Jean Perronnet	FRA	1	3

Pyrgos, although a professional, was the first Greek winner of the modern Olympic Games.

1900 Paris C: 60, N: 8, D: 5.29.

				BARRAGE	
		W	L	W	L
1. Lucien Mérignac	FRA	6	1	1	0
2. Alphonse Kirchhoffer	FRA	6	1	0	1
3. Jean-Baptiste Mimiague	FRA	4	3	1	0
4. Antonio Conte	ITA	4	3	0	1
5. Jules Rossignol	FRA	3	4		
6. Léopold Ramus	FRA	2	5		
7. Italo Santelli	ITA	0	7		
8. Adolphe Rouleau	FRA	3	4		

Rouleau was placed last in the final pool because he withdrew from his bout with Mimiague "under the pretext of a sore thumb."

MASTERS ÉPÉE FENCING

1900 Paris C: 54, N: 4, D: 6.14.

1. Albert Ayat	FRA
2. Emile Bougnol	FRA
3. Henri Laurent	FRA
4. Hippolyte-Jacques Hyvernaud	FRA
5. Marie-Louis Damotte	FRA
6. Brassart	FRA
7. Lézard	FRA
8. Georges Jourdan	FRA

1904 not held

1906 Athens C: 3, N: 3, D: 4.27.

		W	L
1. Cyril Verbrugge	BEL	2	0
2. Carlo Gandini	ITA	1	1
3. Ioannis Raïssis	GRE	0	2

ÉPÉE FOR AMATEURS AND MASTERS

1900 Paris C: 8, N: 2, D: 6.15.

		W	L
1. Albert Ayat	FRA	7	0
2. Ramón Fonst Segundo	CUB	6	1
3. Léon Sée	FRA	4	3
4. Georges de la Falaise	FRA	3	4
5. Emile Bougnol	FRA	2	5
5. Hippolyte-Jacques Hyvernaud	FRA	2	5
5. Henri Laurent	FRA	2	5
5. Louis Perrée	FRA	2	5

This event brought together the first four finishers in the amateur and masters tournaments. Ayat won without receiving a hit and was awarded a prize of 3000 francs.

SABRE, THREE HITS

1906 Athens C: 21, N: 6, D: 5.1.

1. Gustav Casmir	GER
2. George van Rossem	HOL
3. Péter Tóth	HUN
4. Emil Schön	GER
5. Jenő Apáthy	HUN
6. Ernst Königsgarten	AUT

MASTERS SABRE FENCING

1900 Paris C: 29, N: 7, D: 6.27.

				BARRAGE	
		W	L	W	L
1. Antonio Conte	ITA	7	0		
2. Italo Santelli	ITA	6	1		
3. Milan Neralic	AUT	4	3		
4. François Delibes	BEL	3	4	1	0
5. Michaux	FRA	3	4	0	1
6. Xavier Anchetti	FRA	2	5	1	0
7. Zacharov	RUS	2	5	0	1
8. Hébrant	BEL	1	6		

1904 not held

1906 Athens C: 2, N: 2, D: 4.27.

1. Cyril Verbrugge	BEL
2. Ioannis Raïssis	GRE

SINGLE STICKS

1904 St. Louis C: 3, N: 1, D: 9.8.

		TG
1. Albertson Van Zo Post	USA	11
2. William Scott O'Connor	USA	8
3. William Grebe	USA	2

WOMEN

FOIL, INDIVIDUAL

1896–1920 not held

1924 Paris C: 25, N: 9, D: 7.4.

		W	L	TG	TR
1. Ellen Osiier	DEN	5	0	25	14
2. Gladys Davies	GBR	4	1	23	16
3. Grete Heckscher	DEN	3	2	22	16
4. Muriel Freeman	GBR	2	3	17	20
5. Yutha Barding	DEN	1	4	20	22
6. Gizella Tary	HUN	0	5	6	25

The first female Olympic fencing champion was 33-year-old Ellen Ottilia Osiier, who won all 16 of her bouts. She scored 80 touches and received only 34.

1928 Amsterdam C: 27, N: 11, D: 8.1.

		W	L	TG	TR
1. Helene Mayer	GER	7	0	35	9
2. Muriel Freeman	GBR	6	1	32	19
3. Olga Oelkers	GER	4	3	25	27
4. Erna Sondheim	GER	3	4	22	29
5. Gladys Daniell	GBR	2	5	23	27
6. Jenny Addams	BEL	2	5	23	30
6. Margit Dany	HUN	2	5	23	30
8. Johanna de Boer	HOL	2	5	23	33

Helene Mayer was only 14 years old when she won the German national championship in 1925. Three years later, when she was still only 17 years old, she swept through the Olympic tournament with surprising ease, winning 18 bouts and losing only two.

1932 Los Angeles C: 17, N: 11, D: 8.3.

						BARRAGE	
		W	L	TG	TR	TG	TR
1. Ellen Preis	AUT	8	1	44	27	5	3
2. Heather "Judy" Guinness	GBR	8	1	43	19	3	5
3. Erna Bogáthy Bogen	HUN	7	2	38	30		
4. Jenny Addams	BEL	6	3	37	29		
5. Helene Mayer	GER	5	4	38	27		
6. Johanna de Boer	HOL	5	4	30	35		
7. Gerda Munck	DEN	2	7	29	39		
8. Marion Lloyd	USA	2	7	26	42		
8. Grete Olsen	DEN	2	7	31	42		

Preis won by defeating Guinness 5-3 in both the final pool and the barrage. During the barrage, Judy Guinness pointed out to the officials two touches against her which the officials had failed to acknowledge. This act of fair play proved to be the margin of victory. Preis eventually competed in five Olympics. Bronze medalist Erna Bogen was the daughter of Albert Bogen, who won a silver medal in team sabre in 1912. She later married seven-time sabre gold medalist Aladár Gerevich. Their son, Pál, earned two bronze medals in team sabre in 1972 and 1980.

1936 Berlin C: 41, N: 17, D: 8.5.

		W	L	TG	TR
1. Ilona Elek	HUN	6	1	33	17
2. Helene Mayer	GER	5	2	33	19
3. Ellen Preis	AUT	5	2	32	20
4. Hedwig Hass	GER	5	2	30	23
5. Karen Lachmann	DEN	3	4	23	24
6. Jenny Addams	BEL	2	5	18	28
7. Ilona Vargha	HUN	2	5	17	31
8. Elisabeth Grasser	AUT	0	7	11	35

Helene Mayer returned to the Olympics in 1932, but shortly before the women's fencing competition, she learned that her boyfriend had drowned in a military training accident. Understandably distracted, she only placed fifth. Before leaving Germany, Mayer had arranged to stay on in Southern California after the Olympics as an exchange student at Scripps College. She planned to represent Germany at the 1936 Olympics, but in 1933 something happened that would radically change Mayer's life: Adolf Hitler and the Nazis took control of the German government. Helene Mayer was blonde, blue-eyed and stood 1.78 meters (5 feet 10 inches) tall. She was the perfect embodiment of the Nazis' conception of Aryan womanhood, except for one detail—her father, a doctor who had died before the Los Angeles Olympics, was Jewish. Mayer did not think of herself as Jewish, particularly after her father's death. But in April 1933, while still in California, she learned that her membership in the Offenbach Fencing Club, her home club back in Germany, had been withdrawn for racial reasons. Shortly thereafter, the German sponsorship for her exchange fellowship was also rescinded. American

Women's Foil, 1936

The award ceremony for the 1936 women's foil: (left to right) Ellen Preis (bronze), Ilona Elek (gold), and German Jew Helene Mayer (silver).

friends supported her and then she was offered a job teaching at Mills College in Oakland. Meanwhile the controversy about the Nazis' hosting of the 1936 Olympics was growing. Under pressure from the international community, the Germans decided to allow one Jewish athlete to represent Germany at the Berlin Games. They chose Helene Mayer. Mayer, who had always considered herself German rather than Jewish, welcomed the opportunity to regain the Olympic title. Also competing at Berlin were the defending Olympic champion, Ellen Preis and the European champion, Ilona Elek, who was also half-Jewish. In the final pool, Elek defeated Mayer 5-4 and Preis 5-3, losing only to Hedwig Hass. On the victory platform at the award ceremony, Helene Mayer hesitated momentarily and then raised her right arm high in the "Heil Hitler" salute. Mayer had hoped that her participation in the Olympics would allow her to regain the German citizenship that had been taken from her because of her father, but it was not to be. She won the 1937 world championship in Paris, beating both Elek and Preis, but when she traveled to Offenbach to visit her family, she learned that her victory had not been reported by the German press. She visited Offenbach once more the following year, but then she resigned herself to life in exile. In 1940 Mayer took out American citizenship and, in 1943, she helped teach the German language to US soldiers on their way to World War II. She returned to Germany in 1952 and died there of cancer the following year at the age of 42.

1948 London C: 39, N: 15, D: 8.2.

		W	L	TG	TR
1. Ilona Elek	HUN	6	1	31	15
2. Karen Lachmann	DEN	5	2	24	11
3. Ellen Müller-Preis	AUT	5	2	24	16
4. Maria Cerra	USA	5	2	23	16
5. Fritzi Filz	AUT	4	3	20	21
6. Margit Elek	HUN	1	6	10	26
7. Velleda Cessari	ITA	1	6	15	27
8. Mary Glen Haig	GBR	1	6	10	27

Ilona Elek's retention of her Olympic title after a 12-year interlude was a tremendous achievement in itself. But the manner in which she won added to the drama. In her next-to-last bout she trailed Maria Cerra 2-0 before scoring four straight hits. Then, with the winner earning the gold medal, she defeated Karen Lachmann 4-2 as well. Elek's sister, Margit, placed sixth.

1952 Helsinki C: 37, N: 15, D: 7.27.

					BARRAGE			
		W	L	TR	W	L	TG	TR
1. Irene Camber	ITA	5	2	22	1	0	4	3
2. Ilona Elek	HUN	5	2	21	0	1	3	4
3. Karen Lachmann	DEN	4	3	22	3	0	12	4
4. Janice Lee York	USA	4	3	25	2	1	8	7
5. Maxine Mitchell	USA	4	3	23	1	2	9	8
6. Renée Garilhe	FRA	4	3	24	0	3	2	12
7. Lylian Lecomte-Guyonneau	FRA	1	6	30				
8. Magdolna Kovács-Nyári	HUN	1	6	32				

The 45-year-old Elek appeared well on her way to her third gold medal when she won her first 20 bouts, including five in the final pool. But then she lost to Mitchell and then to Camber, 4-3. Forced into a barrage, she was again defeated by Camber, 4-3.

1956 Melbourne C: 23, N: 11, D: 11.29.

						BARRAGE	
		W	L	W	L	TG	TR
1. Gillian Sheen	GBR	6	1	26	20	4	2
2. Olga Orban	ROM	6	1	27	17	2	4
3. Renée Garilhe	FRA	5	2	26	14		
4. Janice Lee Romary York	USA	4	3	23	21		
5. Kate Delbarre	FRA	3	4	20	25		
6. Karen Lachmann	DEN	2	5	17	20		
7. Ellen Müller-Preis	AUT	1	6	20	25		
8. Bruna Colombetti	ITA	1	6	14	27		

Sheen, a 28-year-old London dental surgeon, barely qualified for the final by defeating world champion Lídia Dömölky of Hungary in a barrage to finish fourth in her semifinal pool. She lost 4-2 to Orban, but won the rest of her bouts to force a barrage. This time she defeated the Romanian, 4-2. Sheen remains the only British fencer ever to win a gold medal.

1960 Rome C: 56, N: 24, D: 9.1.

						BARRAGE			
		W	L	TG	TR	TG	TR	W	L
1. Heidi Schmid	GER	6	1	26	13				
2. Valentina Rastvorova	SOV/RUS	5	2	24	12				
3. Maria Vicol	ROM	4	3	23	18	2	0	8	5
4. Galina Gorokhova	SOV/RUS	4	3	22	19	1	1	7	6
5. Olga Szabó-Orban	ROM	4	3	20	20	0	2	4	8
6. Elżbieta Pawlas	POL	2	5	14	24				
7. María del Pilar Roldán	MEX	2	5	13	25				
8. Waltraut Ebert	AUT	1	6	14	27				

Heidi Schmid was a left-handed 21-year-old music teacher from Augsburg. She scored 18 wins against only two losses, one of which occurred after she had clinched the championship.

1964 Tokyo C: 39, N: 17, D: 10.15.

						BARRAGE			
		W	L	TG	TR	W	L	TG	TR
1. Ildikó Ujlaki-Rejtő	HUN	2	1	10	5	2	0	8	1
2. Helga Mees	GER	2	1	8	9	1	1	4	6
3. Antonella Ragno	ITA	2	1	9	7	0	2	3	8
4. Galina Gorokhova	SOV/RUS	0	3	6	12				

5. Katalin Juhász	HUN
6. Giovanna Masciotta	ITA
7. Bruna Colombetti	ITA
7. Catherine Rousselet	FRA

Ildikó Ujlaki-Rejtő was born deaf on May 11, 1937. When she began fencing at age 14 her coaches communicated their instructions on pieces of paper. A factory worker, she faced Helga Mees, a 27-year-old secretary from Saarbrücken, for the championship. Mees had already beaten Ujlaki-Rejtö twice, in the first round and in the final round, but in the barrage the Hungarian won, 4-0.

1968 Mexico City C: 38, N: 16, D: 10.20.

		W	L	TG	TR
1. Yelena Novikova	SOV/BLR	4	1	19	11
2. María del Pilar Roldán	MEX	3	2	17	14
3. Ildikó Ujlaki-Rejtő	HUN	3	2	14	16
4. Brigitte Gapais	FRA	2	3	15	15
5. Kerstin Palm	SWE	2	3	17	17
6. Galina Gorokhova	SOV/RUS	1	4	10	19
7. Giovanna Masciotta	ITA				
7. Heidi Schmid	GER				

Novikova, a tall 21-year-old student teacher, compiled a record of 15 wins and two losses. Silver medalist Roldán, a mother of two, came out of retirement to compete in the Olympics before a hometown crowd.

1972 Munich C: 44, N: 20, D: 9.3.

		W	L	TG	TR
1. Antonella Ragno-Lonzi	ITA	4	1	19	13
2. Ildikó Bóbis	HUN	3	2	17	14
3. Galina Gorokhova	SOV/RUS	3	2	16	14
4. Marie-Chantal Demaille	FRA	3	2	14	16
5. Yelena Belova Novikova	SOV/BLR	2	3	15	13
6. Kerstin Palm	SWE	0	5	9	20

1976 Montreal C: 48, N: 20, D: 7.24.

						BARRAGE	
		W	L	TG	TR	TG	TR
1. Ildikó Schwarczenberger-Tordasi	HUN	4	1	21	15	5	4
2. Maria Consolata Collino	ITA	4	1	24	12	4	5
3. Yelena Belova Novikova	SOV/BLR	3	2	21	19		
4. Brigitte Dumont-Gapais	FRA	2	3	17	17		
5. Cornelia Hanisch	GER	1	4	13	22		
6. Ildikó Bóbis	HUN		4	13	24		
7. Valentina Sidorova	SOV/RUS						
7. Ecaterina Stahl Iencic	ROM						

The reigning world champion, Ecaterina Stahl, ran up a 15-2 record before being eliminated in the prefinal round by Ildikó Schwarczenberger. The final pool turned into an exciting three-way affair. Collino defeated Schwarczenberger 5-1, which appeared to end the Hungarian's chance for a gold medal. Then Yelena Belova beat Collino on the last hit to put Schwarczenberger back into a tie for first place. In her final match, Belova faced Ildikó Bóbis, who had lost all of her other final pool matches. A win would put her into a triple barrage. However, Bóbis summoned all her skill and defeated Belova 5-4. Inspired by her teammate's effort, Schwarczenberger won the final hit against Collino to take the championship.

1980 Moscow C: 33, N: 14, D: 7.24.

		W	L	TG	TR
1. Pascale Trinquet	FRA	4	1	21	16
2. Magda Maros	HUN	3	2	23	17
3. Barbara Wysoczańska	POL	3	2	19	18
4. Ecaterina Stahl Iencic	ROM	2	3	19	21
5. Brigitte Latrille-Gaudin	FRA	2	3	20	22
6. Dorina Vaccaroni	ITA	1	4	14	22
7. Katarina Loksova	CZE				
7. Delfina Skapska	POL				

1984 Los Angeles-Long Beach C: 42, N: 18, D: 8.3.

1. Luan Jujie	CHN
2. Cornelia Hanisch	GER
3. Dorina Vaccaroni	ITA
4. Elisabeta Guzganu	ROM
5. Véronique Brouquier	FRA
6. Laurence Modaine	FRA
7. Sabine Bischoff	GER
8. Brigitte Gaudin Latrille	FRA

Final: Luan 8-3 Hanisch
3rd Place: Vaccaroni 8-5 Guzganu

Luan, a 25-year-old from Nanjing, finished the tournament with a record of 17 wins and 2 losses. Hanisch had entered the final at 16-1.

1988 Seoul C: 45, N: 19, D: 9.22.

1. Anja Fichtel	GER
2. Sabine Bau	GER
3. Zita-Eva Funkenhauser	GER
4. Zsuzsanna Jánosi	HUN
5. Tatyana Sadovskaya	SOV/RUS
6. Gertrúd Stefanek	HUN
7. Sun Hongyun	CHN
8. Yelena Glikina	SOV/RUS

Final: Fichtel 8-5 Bau
3rd Place: Funkenhauser 8-7 Jánosi

The final was a rematch of the 1986 world championship, in which then-18-year-old Fichtel defeated Bau 8-3. Kerstin Palm of Sweden, who finished twenty-ninth, became the first woman in any sport to compete in seven Olympics. Her first appearance was in 1964.

1992 Barcelona C: 46, N: 19, D: 7.30.

1. Giovanna Trillini	ITA
2. Wang Huifeng	CHN
3. Tatyana Sadovskaya	RUS
4. Laurence Modaine	FRA
5. Margherita Zalaffi	ITA
6. Reka Zsofia Szabo-Lazăr	ROM
7. Sabine Bau	GER
8. Fiona McIntosh	GBR

Final: Trillini—Wang 5-6, 5-3, 6-5
3rd Place: Sadovskaya—Modaine 5-1,1-5, 5-3

The 1992 tournament was unusually competitive. All four semifinalists qualified through *repêchage*. Trillini, although the defending world champion, lost four of her first nine bouts. In the semis, Wang defeated Modaine 5-0, 2-5, 5-3 and Trillini outlasted Sadovskaya 5-2, 3-5, 5-3. In the third match of the final Trillini led 3-1 with only 24 seconds remaining. But Wang was able to score twice and force a deciding point. However, it was Trillini who struck first to win the dramatic marathon.

1996 Atlanta C: 40, N: 18, D: 7.22.

1. Laura Badea	ROM
2. Valentina Vezzali	ITA
3. Giovanna Trillini	ITA
4. Laurence Modaine-Cessac	FRA
5. Monika Weber-Koszto (Monica Weber)	GER
6. Xiao Aihua	CHN
7. Ann Marsh	USA
8. Aida Mohamed	HUN

Final: Badea 15-10 Vezzali
3rd Place: Trillini 15-9 Modaine-Cessac

The most exciting match of the tournament came in the semifinals when defending world champion Laura Badea faced defending Olympic champion Giovanna Trillini. Trillini led 6-0 and 13-8 before Badea stormed back to win the next six hits and lead 14-13. Trillini tied the match and sent it into sudden-death overtime. Badea scored the winning touch after 14 seconds.

2000 Sydney C: 40, N: 21, D: 9.21.

1. Valentina Vezzali	ITA
2. Rita König	GER
3. Giovanna Trillini	ITA
4. Laura Badea-Carlescu	ROM
5. Aihua Xiao	CHN
6. Diana Bianchedi	ITA
7. Aida Mohamed	HUN
8. Reka Zsofia Szabo-Lazăr	ROM

Final: Vezzali 15-5 König
3rd Place: Trillini 15-9 Badea-Carlescu

World champion Valentina Vezzali faced only one difficult match. In the quarterfinals, she and Reka Szabó were tied 8-8 when time ran out. Vezzali scored the deciding touch 41 seconds into overtime. In her other four matches, Vezzali outscored her opponents 60-26. Rita König was a surprise finalist. On the way, she upset number two seed Sabine Bau 15-11 and number three seed Giovanna Trillini 15-10.

2004 Athens C: 25, N: 20, D: 8.18.

1. Valentina Vezzali	ITA
2. Giovanna Trillini	ITA
3. Sylwia Gruchała	POL
4. Aida Mohamed	HUN
5. Laura Badea-Carlescu	ROM
6. Gabriella Varga	HUN
7. Adeline Wuillème	FRA
8. Nam Hyun-hee	KOR

Final: Vezzali 15-11 Trillini
3rd Place: Gruchała 15-9 Mohamed

Teammates and friends, Valentina Vezzali and Giovanna Trillini both came from the small town of Jesi in eastern Italy. Prior to the Olympics, Trillini had won four Olympic gold medals and Vezzali had won three. The pair advanced to the final, where Trillini scored the only touch of the first round. By the end of the second round the two were tied 6-6, but Vezzali built a quick lead at the start of the third round and held off a late flurry by Trillini to win.

2008 Beijing C: 41, N: 24, D: 8.11.

1. Valentina Vezzali	ITA
2. Nam Hyun-hee	KOR
3. Margherita Granbassi	ITA
4. Giovanna Trillini	ITA
5. Edina Knapek	HUN
6. Yevgeniya Lamonova	RUS
7. Chieko Sugawara	JPN
8. Katja Wächter	GER

Final: Vezzali 6-5 Nam
3rd Place: Granbassi 15-12 Trillini

Two-time defending Olympic champion Valentina Vezzali had won two of the last three world championship titles, missing out only in 2006, when she beaten in the final by teammate Margherita Granbassi. Along with Giovanna Trillini, the three Italians had swept the top three spots at the 2007 world championships, Vezzali taking the title, with Granbassi in second and Trillini in third.

The only two threats to an Italian sweep seemed to be two-time world bronze medalist Aida Mohamed of Hungary and world third-ranked Nam Hyun-hee, who had finished fifth at each of the past two world championships.

Of the five, Mohamed was the first to fall, losing 15-5 to Russia's Yevgeniya Lamonova in the third round. Nam, Trillini, Granbassi and Vezzali all reached the semi-finals, where Nam defeated Trillini 15-10 and Vezzali steamrolled Granbassi 12-3.

Vezzali took a 3-0 lead in the final, but Nam fought back to a 3-3 tie, and then moved up to a 5-4 advantage with one minute remaining. Vezzali leveled the score and, with four seconds left, took the lead on a touch to earn her third consecutive gold medal.

FOIL, TEAM

1896–1956 not held

1960 Rome T: 12, N: 12, D: 9.3.

1. SOV—Tatyana Petrenko, Valentina Rastvorova, Lyudmila Shishova, Valentina Prudskova, Aleksandra Zabelina, Galina Gorokhova
2. HUN—Györgyi Szekely, Ildikó Ujlaki-Reijtő, Magdolna Kovács-Nyári, Katalin Juhász, Lídia Dömölky

3. ITA—Irene Camber, Velleda Cesari, Antonella Ragno, Bruna Colombetti, Claudia Pasini
4. GER—Heidi Schmid, Helga Mees, Helga Stroh, Helmi Höhle, Gudrun Theuerkauff, Rosemarie Weiss
5. FRA—Monique Leroux, Régine Veronnet, Françoise Mailliard, Renée Garilhe, Kate Delbarre
5. HOL—Nina Kleyweg, Daniel Van Rossem, Helena Kokkes, Elisa Botbjil
5. POL—Elżbieta Pawlas, Silwia Julito, Barbara Orzechowska, Genowefa Migas, Wanda Kaczmarczyk
5. ROM—Ecaterina Lazar, Eugenia Mateianu, Olga Szabó-Orban, Maria Vicol

Final: SOV 9-3 HUN
3rd Place: ITA 9-2 GER

The Soviets received their only scare in the quarterfinals, when they had to rally from a 3-8 deficit to defeat France by two touches. Their final win-loss total was 48-21.

1964 Tokyo T: 10, N: 10, D: 10.17.

1. HUN—Ildikó Ujiaki-Rejtő, Katalin Juhász-Nagy, Lídia Dömölky, Judit Mendelényi-Ágoston, Paula Marosi
2. SOV—Galina Gorokhova, Valentina Prudskova, Tatyana Samusenko [Petrenko], Lyudmila Shishova, Valentina Rastvorova
3. GER—Heidi Schmid, Helga Mees, Rosemarie Scherberger, Gudrun Theuerkauff
4. ITA—Antonella Ragno, Giovanna Masciotta, Irene Camber, Natalina Sanguineti, Bruna Colombetti
5. ROM—Olga Szabó-Orban, Ileana Gyulai, Ana Dersidan, Maria Vicol, Ecaterina Iencic
6. FRA—Catherine Rousselet, Marie-Chantal Depetris, Brigitte Gapais, Annick Level, Colette Revenu

Final: HUN 9-7 SOV
3rd Place: GER 9-5 ITA
5th Place: ROM 9-6 FRA

1968 Mexico City T: 10, N: 10, D: 10.24.

1. SOV—Aleksandra Zabelina, Yelena Novikova, Galina Gorokhova, Tatyana Samusenko [Petrenko], Svetlana Tširkova
2. HUN—Ildikó Bóbis, Lidia Sákovics, Ildikó Ujlaki-Rejtö, Mária Gulácsy, Paula Marosi
3. ROM—Ecaterina Stahl [Iencic], Ileana Drimbă [Gyulai], Olga Szabó-Orban, Maria Vicol, Ana Ene-Derşidan
4. FRA—Cathérine Ceretti, Brigitte Gapais, Marie-Chantal Depetris, Claudette Herbster, Annick Level
5. GER—Heidi Schmid, Helga Koch, Gudrun Theuerkauff, Monika Pulch, Helga Volz-Mees
6. ITA—Antonella Ragno, Giulia Lorenzoni, Giovanna Masciotta, Bruna Colombetti, Silvana Sconciafurno

Final: SOV 9-3 HUN
3rd Place: ROM 8(47)-8(45) FRA
5th Place: GER 8-7 ITA

1972 Munich T: 11, N: 11, D: 9.8.

1. SOV—Yelena Belova [Novikova], Alexandra Zabelina, Tatyana Samusenko [Petrenko], Galina Gorokhova, Svetlana Tširkova
2. HUN—Ildikó Ságiné-Rejtő [Ujlaki-Rejtő], Ildikó Schwarczenberger [Tordasi], Ildikó Matuscakné-Ronay, Maria Szolnoki, Ildikó Bóbis
3. ROM—Ileana Gyulai, Ana Pascu [Ene-Dersidan], Ecaterina Stahl [Iencic], Olga Szabó-Orban
4. ITA—Antonella Ragno-Lonzi, Giulia Lorenzoni, Reka Der Cipriani, Maria Consolata Collino, Giuseppina Bersani
5. GER—Gudrun Theuerkauff, Irmela Broniecki, Karin Giesselmann, Monika Pulch, Erika Bethmann
6. FRA—Marie-Chantal Demaille, Catherine Ceretti, Claudie Josland, Brigitte Dumont-Gapais
7. POL—Halina Balon, Krystyna Urbánska-Machnicka, Jolanta Bebel-Rzymowska, Kamila Skladanowska, Elżbieta Franke
7. USA—Ruth White, Natalia Clovis, Tanya Adamovich, Harriet King, Ann O'Donnell

Final: SOV 9-5 HUN
3rd Place: ROM 9-7 TA
5th Place: GER 8-7 FRA

The Soviet team compiled a record of 52 wins and 20 losses. They were led by Belova (17-3) and Zabelina (14-4).

1976 Montreal T: 13, N: 13, D: 7.28.

1. SOV—Yelena Belova [Novikova], Olga Kniazeva, Valentina Sidorova, Nailya Gilyazova, Valentina Nikonova
2. FRA—Brigitte Latrille, Brigitte Dumont-Gapais, Christine Muzio, Véronique Trinquet, Claudie Josland
3. HUN—Ildikó Schwarczenberger [Tordasi], Edit Kovács, Magda Maros, Ildikó Ságiné-Rejtö [Ujlaki-Rejtö], Ildikó Bóbis
4. GER—Karin Rutz, Cornelia Hanisch, Ute Kircheis, Brigitte Oertel, Jutta Höhne
5. ITA—Maria Consolata Collino, Giulia Lorenzoni, Doriana Pigliapoco, Susanna Batazzi, Carola Mangiarotti
6. POL—Jolanta Bebel-Rzymowska, Barbara Wysoczańska, Kamilla Mazurowska-Skladanowska, Krystyna Urbańska-Machnicka, Grażyna Staszak-Makowska
7. GBR—Wendy Agar, Susan Wrigglesworth, Hilary Cawthorne, Clare Halsted, Susan Green
7. ROM—Ileana Jenei [Gyulai, Drimbá], Marcela Moldovan, Ecaterina Stahl [Iencic], Ana Pascu [Ene-Derşidan], Magdalena Bartos

Final: SOV 9-2 FRA
3rd Place: HUN 9-4 GER
5th Place: ITA 9-7 POL

The USSR won almost without competition, with 50 wins and only 13 losses. Belova was 13-0 and Kniazeva 11-2. The final victory came on Belova's 29th birthday.

1980 Moscow T: 9, N: 9, D: 7.27.

1. FRA—Brigitte Latrille-Gaudin, Pascale Trinquet, Isabelle Boeri-Bégard, Véronique Brouquier, Christine Muzio
2. SOV—Valentina Sidorova, Nailya Gilyazova, Yelena Belova [Novikova], Irina Ushakova, Larissa Tsagarayeva
3. HUN—Ildikó Schwarczenberger [Tordasi], Magda Maros, Gertrud Stefanek, Zsuzsa Szöcz, Edit Kovács
4. POL—Delfina Skapska, Agnieszka Dubrawska, Jolanta Królikowska, Barbara Wysoczanska, Kamila Mazurowska Skladanowska
5. ITA—Dorina Vaccaroni, Anna Rita Sparaciari, Susanna Batazzi, Carola Mangiarotti, Clara Mochi
6. CUB—Margarita Rodríguez Vargas, Marlene Font Kindelán, María García Pascau, Clara Alfonso Freire, Mercedes del Risco Randich
7. GBR—Susan Wrigglesworth, Ann Brannon, Wendy Grant, Linda Martin, Hilary Cawthorne
8. GDR—Mandy Niklaus, Gabriele Janke, Sabine Hertrampf, Beate Schubert, Marion Schulze

Final: FRA 9-6 SOV
3rd Place: HUN 9-7 POL
5th Place: ITA 9-6 CUB

1984 Los Angeles-Long Beach T: 10, N: 10, D: 8.7.

1. GER—Christiane Weber, Cornelia Hanisch, Sabine Bischoff, Zita-Eva Funkenhauser, Ute Wessel

2. ROM—Aurora Dan, Monica Veber, Rozalia Oros, Marcela Zsak [Moldovan], Elisabeta Guzganu
3. FRA—Laurence Modaine, Pascale Trinquet-Hachin, Brigitte Gaudin [Latrille], Véronique Brouquier, Anne Meygret
4. ITA—Dorina Vaccaroni, Clara Mochi, Margherita Zalaffi, Lucia Traversa, Carola Cicconetti
5. CHN—Luan Jujie, Zhu Qingyuan, Li Huahua, Wu Qiuhua
6. USA—Vincent Bradford, Sharon Monplaisir, Susan Badders, Debra Waples, Jana Angelakis
7. GBR—Ann Brannon, Linda Martin, Fiona McIntosh, Elizabeth Thurley, Katie Arup
8. JPN—Mieko Miyahara, Azusa Oikawa, Miyuki Maekawa, Tomoko Oka

Final: GER 9-5 ROM
3rd Place: FRA 9-7 ITA
5th Place: CHN 9-5 USA

The decisive contest was the semifinal matchup between West Germany and Italy. Both sides registered eight wins, but in the final bout, Zita Funkenhauser managed three hits in her loss to Lucia Traversa, giving the West Germans a one touch advantage.

1988 Seoul T: 12, N: 12, D: 9.28.

1. GER—Sabine Bau, Anja Fichtel, Zita-Eva Funkenhauser, Anette Klug, Christiane Weber
2. ITA—Francesca Bortolozzi, Annapia Gandolfi, Lucia Traversa, Dorina Vaccaroni, Margherita Zalaffi
3. HUN—Zsuzsanna Jánosi, Edit Kovács, Gertrúd Stefanek, Zsuzsa Szöcs, Katalin Tuschák
4. SOV/RUS—Yelena Glikina, Yelena Grishina, Tatyana Sadovskaya, Marina Soboleva, Olga Voshchakina
5. CHN—Li Huahua, Luan Jujie, Sun Hongyun, Xiao Aihua, Zhu Qingyuan
6. USA—Caitlin Bilodeau, Elaine Cheris, Sharon Monplaisir, Mary O'Neill, Molly Sullivan
7. FRA—Brigitte Gaudin [Latrille], Gisèle Meygret, Laurence Modaine, Nathalie Pallet, Isabelle Spennato
8. KOR—Kim Jin-soon, Shin Sung-ja, Tak Jung-im, Yoon Jung-sook

Final: GER 9-4 ITA
3rd Place: HUN 9-2 SOV
5th Place: CHN 861-860 USA
7th Place: FRA 9-4 KOR

The West Germans whipped their five opponents, registering 45 wins against only 15 losses. Weber was 14-1 and Fichtel 12-2.

1992 Barcelona T: 12, N: 12, D: 8.4.

1. ITA—Diana Bianchedi, Francesca Bortolozzi, Giovanna Trillini, Dorina Vaccaroni, Margherita Zalaffi
2. GER—Sabine Bau, Annette Dobmeier, Anja Fichtel-Mauritz, Zita-Eva Funkenhauser, Monika Weber-Koszto [Koszto-Veber]
3. ROM—Laura Badea, Roxana Dumitrescu, Claudia Grigorescu, Reka Szabo, Elisabeta Tufan [Guzganu]
4. RUS—Yelena Glikina, Yelena Grishina, Tatyana Sadovskaya, Olga Velichko, Olga Voshchakina
5. FRA—Camille Couzi, Gisèle Meygret, Laurence Modaine, Julie-Anne Gross, Isabelle Spennato
6. CHN—E Jie, Liang Jun, Wang Huifeng, Xiao Aihua, Ye Lin
7. HUN—Gabriella Lantos, Ildikó Mincza, Zsuzsanna Némethné-Jánosi, Ildikó Pusztai, Gertrúd Stefanek
8. POL—Katarzyne Felusiak, Monika Maciejewska, Anna Sobczak, Barbara Szewczyk, Agnieszka Szuchnicka

Final: ITA 9-6 GER
3rd Place: ROM 860-855 RUS
5th Place: FRA 9-5 CHN
7th Place: HUN 9-7 POL

The Italians dominated the tournament, winning 45 matches and losing only 13. Bianchedi was 15-0 and Zalaffi 15-1. Anja Fichtel of the German team competed only six weeks after giving birth to a son.

1996 Atlanta T: 11, N: 11, D: 7.25.

1. ITA—Francesca Bortolozzi Borella, Giovanna Trillini, Valentina Vezzali
2. ROM—Laura Badea, Reka Zsofia Szabo-Lazăr, Roxana Scarlat
3. GER—Anja Fichtel-Mauritz, Monika Weber-Koszto, Sabine Bau
4. HUN—Aida Mohamed, Gabriella Romaczne Lantos, Zsuzsanna Néméthne-Jánosi
5. FRA—Adeline Wuilleme, Clothilde Magnan, Laurence Modaine-Cessac
6. RUS—Olga Sharkova, Olga Velitchko, Svetlana Boyko
7. CHN—Liang Jun, Wang Huifeng, Xiao Aihua
8. POL—Anna Rybicka, Barbara Szewczyk, Katarzyna Felusiak

Final: ITA 45-33 ROM
3rd Place: GER 45-42 HUN
5th Place: FRA 45-44 RUS
7th Place: CHN 45-32 POL

The Italian team faced their most difficult challenge in the semifinals against Hungary. Francesca Bortolozzi went to Atlanta as an alternate, embittered because she felt she had been unjustly rejected as a starter. But when Diana Bianchedi was injured during a fall from the piste during the individual competition, Bortolozzi was added to the team as a late substitute against Hungary. Bortolozzi stepped up as the final fencer with Italy trailing 36-40. It was Bortolozzi herself who had put Italy behind by losing to Nemethne-Janosi 1-7 and Lantos 4-9. But she was able to outscore Aida Mohamed 9-2 and save a 45-42 Italian victory. In the final, the three Italians took advantage of Romania's lack of depth by outscoring Roxana Scarlat 19-5.

2000 Sydney T: 9, N: 9, D: 9.23.

1. ITA—Diana Bianchedi, Giovanna Trillini, Valentina Vezzali
2. POL—Sylwia Gruchala, Magdalena Mroczkiewicz, Anna Rybicka, Barbara Wolnicka
3. GER—Sabine Bau, Rita König, Monika Weber-Koszto
4. USA—Ann Marsh, Felicia Zimmermann, Iris Zimmermann
5. RUS—Svetlana Boyko, Yekaterina Yusheva, Olga Sharkova-Sidorova
6. HUN—Edina Knapek, Gabriella Lantos, Aida Mohamed
7. CHN—Xiao Aihua, Meng Jie, Li Yuan, Zhang Lei
8. UKR—Lyudmyla Vasylyeva, Olena Koltsova, Olga Leleyko

Final: ITA 45-36 POL
3rd Place: GER 45-42 USA
5th Place: RUS 45-38 HUN
7th Place: CHN 45-40 UKR

Individual gold medalist Valentina Vezzali led the Italians to their third consecutive Olympic title. In the semifinals against the United States, she outscored her opponents 15-4 to provide the winning margin in a

45-38 victory. The only blemish in the Italian record since the last Olympics had been a 45-43 loss to Poland in the quarterfinals of the 1999 world championships. In Sydney, they avenged this glitch, winning 45-36, with Vezzali outscoring the Poles 28-8 to again provide the margin of victory.

2004 not held

2008 Beijing T: 8, N: 8, D: 8.16.

1. RUS—Svetlana Boyko, Yevgeniya Lamonova, Viktoriya Nikishina, Aida Shanayeva
2. USA—Emily Cross, Erinn Smart, Hanna Thompson
3. ITA—Margherita Granbassi, Ilaria Salvatori, Giovanna Trillini, Valentina Vezzali
4. HUN—Edina Knapek, Aida Mohamed, Virginie Újlaki, Gabriella Varga
5. GER—Carolin Golubytskyi, Anja Schache, Katja Wächter
6. CHN—Huang Jialing, Su Wanwen, Sun Chao, Zhang Lei
7. POL—Karolina Chlewi ska, Sylwia Gruchała, Magdalena Mroczkiewicz, Małgorzata Wojtkowiak
8. EGY—Eman El-Gammal, Shaimaa El-Gammal, Iman Shaban

Final: RUS 28-11 USA
3rd Place: ITA 32-23 HUN
5th Place: GER 34-28 CHN
7th Place: POL 45-14 EGY

The first big surprise of the tournament came in the first round, when the United States pulled off a 31-30 victory over reigning world champion Poland. The US hadn't done better than tenth place at any of the last three world championships and was not expected to be vying for a medal.

In the semi-final round, the Americans gave another surprise performance, beating number three seed Hungary 35-33 despite fourteen touches delivered by Aida Mohamed in the final bout against Erinn Smart.

The other semi-final match was a repeat of the 2006 world championship final, when Russia beat Italy 26-25. This time the two were tied 21-21 after regular time. Russia's Svetlana Boyko scored the final touch against reigning individual foil world champion Valentina Vezzali twelve seconds into overtime.

After the two close semi-finals, the final matches were rather less exciting. Russia and the US were tied 4-4 after the first three bouts, but then Russia scored sixteen of the next seventeen touches over the next five bouts, and went on to win 28-11. Italy took an early lead against Hungary in the bronze medal match and never relinquished the advantage.

One day after Erinn Smart earned a silver medal in this event, her brother, Keeth, won a silver medal as part of the US men's sabre team.

ÉPÉE, INDIVIDUAL

1896–1992 not held

1996 Atlanta C: 48, N: 24, D: 7.21.

1. Laura Flessel	FRA
2. Valérie Barlois	FRA
3. Gyongyi Szalay Horvathne	HUN
4. Margherita Zalaffi	ITA
5. Timea Nagy	HUN
6. Adrienn Hormay	HUN
7. Eva-Maria Ittner	GER
8. Ko Sung-jun	KOR

Final: Flessel 15-12 Barlois
3rd Place: Szalay Horvathne 15-13 Zalaffi

Laura Flessel and Valérie Barlois were both coached by Michel Salesse. Flessel was born on the Caribbean island of Guadeloupe and moved to Paris at the age of 18 to further her fencing career. In the final, Flessel took an 11-4 lead before Barlois scored six straight points. Flessel scored three in a row to bring the match to 14-10 and then won 15-12.

2000 Sydney C: 39, N: 22, D: 9.17.

1. Tímea Nagy	HUN
2. Gianna Hablützel-Bürki	SWI
3. Laura Flessel-Colovic	FRA
4. Tatyana Logunova	RUS
5. Valérie Barlois-Leroux	FRA
6. Zuleydis Ortíz Puente	CUB
7. Margherita Zalaffi	ITA
8. Claudia Bokel	GER

Final: Nagy 15-11 Hablützel-Bürki
3rd Place: Flessel-Colovic 15-6 Logunova

Tímea Nagy and Gianna Hablützel-Bürki were unlikely finalists in that neither one had ever won a major competition. Hablützel-Bürki had a wild ride to the final, winning three of her four matches by a single touch. Strange as it seems, her only clear victory was a 15-9 upset of number one seed Ildikó Mincza of Hungary. Nagy's breakthrough was a dramatic 15-14 semifinal upset of defending champion Laura Flessel. Hablützel-Bürki led 6-3 after the first period of the final. Nagy came back with four straight touches and finally pulled away in the last minute of the match. The 31-year-old Nagy began fencing at the age of 14 in order to impress a boy who fenced.

2004 Athens C: 38, N: 21, D: 8.15.

1. Tímea Nagy	HUN
2. Laura Flessel-Colovic	FRA
3. Maureen Nisima	FRA
4. Ildikó Mincza-Nébald	HUN
5. Imke Duplitzer	GER
6. Zhang Li	CHN
7. Kim Hee-jeong	KOR
8. Ioanna "Jeanne" Khristou	GRE

Final: Nagy 15-10 Flessel-Colovic
3rd Place: Nisima 15-12 Mincza-Nébald

The semifinals matched two fencers from Hungary and two from France. In the first, 1996 Olympic champion Laura Flessel-Colovic edged Ildikó Mincza-Nébald 15-14, while in the second, defending Olympic champion Tímea Nagy defeated Maureen Nisima by the same score. The final began with a flurry of action, as Nagy took a 9-7 lead after only two and a half minutes. Flessel-Colovic could never get closer and Nagy won 15-10.

2008 Beijing C: 25, N: 20, D: 8.13.

1. Britta Heidemann GER
2. Ana Maria Brânz ROM
3. Ildikó Mincza-Nébald HUN
4. Li Na CHN
5. Imke Duplitzer GER
6. Lyubov Shutova RUS
7. Laura Flessel-Colovic FRA
8. Emma Samuelsson SWE

Final: Heidemann 15-11 Brânz
3rd Place: Mincza-Nébald 15-11 Li

Reigning world champion and top seed Britta Heidemann swept through the competition, beating world silver medalist Li Na 15-13 in the semi-finals before facing 2008 European silver medalist Ana Maria Brânz in the final. Heidemann established a 5-0 advantage and never relinquished the lead, going on to win 15-11. A student at the University of Cologne, Heidemann first visited China in 1999 on a high school exchange program. She later focused on Chinese regional studies and became fluent in Mandarin.

ÉPÉE, TEAM

1896–1992 not held

1996 Atlanta T: 11, N: 11, D: 7.24.

1. FRA—Laura Flessel, Sophie Moressée-Pichot, Valérie Barlois
2. ITA—Elisa Uga, Laura Chiesa, Margherita Zalaffi
3. RUS—Karina Aznavuryan, Mariya Mazina, Yuliya Garayeva
4. HUN—Adrienn Hormay, Gyongyi Szalay Horvathne, Timea Nagy
5. EST—Heidi Rohi, Maarika Vosu, Oksana Jermakova
6. CUB—Milagros Palma González, Mirayda García Soto, Tamara Esteri Almeida
7. GER—Claudia Bokel, Eva-Maria Ittner, Katja Nass
8. USA—Elaine Cheris, Leslie Marx, Nhi Lan Le

Final: FRA 45-33 ITA
3rd Place: RUS 45-44 HUN
5th Place: EST 45-30 CUB
7th Place: GER 45-37 USA

Hungary had won four of the last five world championships, but they were upset in the semifinals by the Italians 45-32. The French women faced Russia in their semifinal. They fell behind 5-10, but gradually came back to tie the score at 30. Then Valérie Barlois outscored Yuliya Garayeva 10-3 and Laura Flessel sealed the victory at 45-39. The French fell behind again in the final. Italy was ahead 15-10 when Flessel outscored Elisa Uga 15-8. Then, with the score 30-28, the French won 15 of the next 20 points to win 45-33.

2000 Sydney T: 8, N: 8, D: 9.19.

1. RUS—Karina Aznavuryan, Tatyana Logunova, Mariya Mazina, Oksana Jermakova
2. SWI—Gianna Hablützel-Bürki, Sophie Lamon, Diana Romagnoli
3. CHN—Li Na, Qin Liang, Yang Shaoqi
4. HUN—Tímea Nagy, Ildikó Mincza, Gyöngyi Szalay
5. FRA—Valérie Barlois-Leroux, Laura Flessel-Colovic, Sangita Tripathi, Sophie Moresse-Pichot
6. GER—Katja Nass, Imke Duplitzer, Claudia Bokel
7. CUB—Tamara Esteri Almeida, Zuleydis Ortíz Puente, Mirayda García Soto
8. NOR—Margrete Mørch, Ragnhild Andenæs, Silvia Lesoil

Final: RUS 45-35 SWI
3rd Place: CHN 41-39 HUN
5th Place: FRA 45-33 GER
7th Place: CUB 45-32 NOR

Seeded fourth, the Russians won three dramatic victories. In their opening contest, they trailed Germany 32-36 going into the final round, but Tatyana Logunova outscored Imke Duplitzer 13-7 to give Russia a 45-43 victory. The semifinal with Hungary went into overtime with Ildikó Mincza being awarded priority, meaning that if no touch score was registered, Hungary would win. After three double touches, Logunova managed to score with only eight seconds left. In the final against Switzerland, the Russians jumped out to leads of 9-2 and 11-5, but then 15-year-old Sophie Lamon outscored Oksana Jermakova 10-5 to close the gap to 16-15. Lamon returned to the piste in the eighth round against Mariya Mazina with Russia leading 24-22. Lamon scored two quick touches to tie the match, but in the fourth minute Mazina pulled away to give Russia a 40-32 advantage. Logunova finished the job, outscoring Gianna Hablützel-Bürki 5-3 in 75 seconds.

2004 Athens T: 9, N: 9, D: 8.20.

1. RUS—Karina Aznavuryan, Tatyana Logunova, Anna Sivkova, Oksana Jermakova
2. GER—Claudia Bokel, Imke Duplitzer, Britta Heidemann
3. FRA—Sarah Daninthe, Laura Flessel-Colovic, Hajnalka Kiraly-Picot, Maureen Nisima
4. CAN—Monique Kavelaars, Julie Leprohon, Sherraine Schalm-MacKay
5. HUN—Adrienn Hormay, Ildikó Mincza-Nébald, Tímea Nagy, Hajnalka Tóth
6. CHN—Li Na, Shen Weiwei, Zhang Li, Zhong Weiping
7. KOR—Kim Hee-jeong, Go Jung-nam, Lee Keum-nam, Kim Mi-jung
8. GRE—Ioanna "Jeanne" Khristou, Dimitra Manganoudaki, Niki-Katerina Sidiropoulou

Final: RUS 34-28 GER
3rd Place: FRA 45-37 CAN
5th Place: HUN 32-31 CHN
7th Place: KOR 44-30 GRE

The defending Olympic and world champions, Russia faced Germany, the season's top-ranked team, in the final.

The Russians played defensively, scoring just eight touches in the first four rotations, while only allowing one touch to the Germans. The Russians led 20-16 going into the final bout, during which Tatyana Logunova outscored Britta Heidemann 14-12 to hold on for the victory.

2008 not held

SABRE, INDIVIDUAL

1896–2000 not held

2004 Athens C: 23, N: 19, D: 8.17.

1. Mariel Zagunis	USA
2. Tan Xue	CHN
3. Sada Jacobson	USA
4. Catalina Gheorghitoaia	ROM
5. Yelena Nechayeva	RUS
6. Leonore Perrus	FRA
7. Elena Jemayeva	AZR
8. Zhang Ying	CHN

Final: Zagunis 15-9 Tan
3rd Place: Jacobson 15-7 Gheorghitoaia

Initially, 19-year-old Mariel Zagunis did not qualify for the Olympics, as the two US berths went to sisters Sada and Emily Jacobsen. When Nigeria decided not to send its entrant, Jacqueline Esimaje, the spot went to the highest-ranked fencer not already qualified: Zagunis. Zagunis, whose parents, Robert and Cathy, had both been members of the 1976 US rowing team, grew stonger as the Olympic tournament proceeded. She defeated Catalina Gheorghitoaia 15-7 in the semifinals to advance to the final, where she met former world champion Tan Xue. Zagunis leaped to a 9-2 lead before Tan scored four straight points to narrow the margin. Zagunis regained control of the match, moving up to a 14-7 lead before securing the gold 15-9. Zagunis was the first American to win a gold medal in fencing since 1904.

2008 Beijing C: 39, N: 21, D: 8.9.

1. Mariel Zagunis	USA
2. Sada Jacobson	USA
3. Rebecca Ward	USA
4. Sofiya Velikaya	RUS
5. Tan Xue	CHN
6. Bao Yingying	CHN
7. Azza Besbes	TUN
8. Olena Khomrova	UKR

Final: Zagunis 15-8 Jacobson
3rd Place: Ward 15-14 Velikaya

The competition produced an early surprise when reigning world champion Yelena Netchayeva was eliminated 15-12 in her opening match against Poland's Irena Więckowska.

The American line-up included defending Olympic champion Mariel Zagunis, 2006 world champion and number-one-ranked Becca Ward and defending Olympic bronze medalist Sada Jacobson. All three reached the semi-finals, as did 2005 world silver medalist Sofiya Velikaya, after her 15-9 quarter-final victory over defending Olympic silver medalist and hometown favorite Tan Xue.

In the semi-finals, Jacobson defeated Velikaya 15-11 and Zagunis beat Ward by the same score.

Velikaya took a 6-1 lead in the bronze-medal bout, but Ward fought back, recording five straight touches at one point and leading briefly at 14-13 before Velikaya tied the match. Velikaya and Ward both attacked on the final point, forcing the referee to consult a video monitor before awarding the winning touch to Ward. The US sweep assured, Zagunis scored the first two points against Jacobson and never trailed, taking the final three points to win 15-8.

DISCONTINUED EVENT

SABRE, TEAM

2008 Beijing T: 8, N: 8, D: 8.14.

1. UKR—Olha Kharlan, Olena Khomrova, Halyna Pundyk, Olha Zhovnir
2. CHN—Bao Yingying, Huang Haiyang, Ni Hong, Tan Xue
3. USA—Sada Jacobson, Becca Ward, Mariel Zagunis
4. FRA—Solène Mary, Leonore Perrus, Anne-Lise Touya, Carole Vergne
5. RUS—Yekaterina Dyachenko, Yekaterina Fedorkina, Yelena Nechayeva, Sofiya Velikaya
6. POL—Bogna Jóźwiak, Aleksandra Socha, Irena Więckowska
7. CAN—Julie Cloutier, Olga Ovtchinnikova, Wendy Saschenbrecker, Sandra Sassine
8. SAF—Jyoti Chetty, Adele du Plooy, Shelley Gosher, Elvira Wood

Final: UKR 45-44 CHN
3rd Place: USA 45-38 FRA
5th Place: RUS 45-36 POL
7th Place: CAN 45-16 SAF

All three members of the US team had won medals in the individual sabre event five days earlier, and the team looked strong in the first round, outscoring South Africa 45-8. However, the Americans were less successful in their semi-final: reigning world silver medalists Ukraine out-touched them in six of nine bouts to win 45-39. China reached the final by beating reigning world champion France 45-38.

The gold medal match was an exciting back-and-forth affair, with Ukraine trailing 10-2 after the first two bouts. China maintained a significant advantage until the sixth bout, when Olena Khomrova outscored Bao Yingying 12-5, narrowing the deficit to 30-27. Trailing 36-40 going into the final bout, Olha Kharlan fought back to a 44-44 tie to set up a sensational finish. Karlan and Tan attacked at the same time on the final point. After consulting a video replay, the referee declined to give either athlete the winning point and ordered another duel Again both fencers attacked simultaneously, and both appeared to land a hit. But this time the referee ruled quickly, and the winning point went to Ukraine.

Chapter 12 **Field Hockey**

Field hockey is played on a field, or pitch, of artificial turf 100 yards (91.4 meters) long and 60 yards (55 meters) wide. There are eleven players on a team, including a goalie. Using sticks that are flat on one side and curved on the other, each team hits and dribbles the ball down the field and tries to shoot it past the goalie into a goal that is 7 feet (2.13 meters) high and 12 feet (3.66 meters) wide. The ball is small—slightly larger than a baseball. Only the flat side of the stick may be used to strike the ball. Except for the goalie, players may not touch the ball with their hands or their bodies. Matches are divided into two 35-minute halves. If play is suspended to deal with an injury, the missed time is added to the end of the second half. If the score is tied after 70 minutes, a 15-minute overtime period, divided into two halves, is played. In pool play ties after 85 minutes are allowed to stand, but, according to the rules since 2004, once the elimination rounds begin, ties are decided by sudden-death golden goal.

Some of the rules of field hockey are similar to those of soccer. However, there are certain rules that are specific to field hockey. All shots on goal must be taken within the striking circle, which extends in a semicircle 16 yards (14.6 meters) from the goal. Players are not allowed to shield the ball from an opponent with their bodies or with their sticks. Another novel aspect of field hockey is the bully, which is the equivalent of a face-off in ice hockey. The ball is placed on the ground between two players, one from each team. Each player taps the ground with his stick once. Then the players tap sticks together once and go for the ball.

Penalties can be called for (1) striking the ball with the rounded side of the stick, (2) taking part in the play while not holding a stick, (3) kicking, throwing, or otherwise propelling the ball without the stick, (4) wielding the stick in a dangerous manner or aiming the ball at an opponent, (5) interfering with an opponent's stick, (6) kicking, tripping, shoving, or striking an opponent, (7) obstructing play by running between an opponent and the ball or placing one's body or stick between an opponent and the ball. Generally these infractions are penalized by awarding a free hit to the opposing team. However, if the infraction is committed by a defender within the striking circle, the attacking team is awarded a penalty corner or a penalty stroke. A penalty corner is also awarded for a deliberate offense inside the 25-yard line or if the defensive team intentionally plays the ball over the goal line. In a penalty corner the ball is placed on the goal line ten yards from the nearest goal post. One attacking player hits the ball to a teammate standing just outside the striking circle line. All other players on both teams must wait beyond the striking circle or out of bounds and may not move until the ball is struck. Intentional fouls preventing a goal or illegal positioning on penalty corners are penalized by awarding the attacking team a penalty stroke. Penalty strokes are taken from seven yards out; the ball may be pushed or flicked, but not hit. The goalie may not move his feet until the ball has been played.

Currently, Olympic field hockey tournaments begin with preliminary pool play. The top two teams in each of the two pools advance to the semifinals, while the other teams play off for the remaining places. The men's tournament features twelve teams and the women's tournament ten teams.

MEN

1896–1906 not held

1908 London T: 6, N: 3, D: 10.31.

	W	L	T	GF	GA
1. GBR	3	0	0	24	3
2. GBR	1	1	0	4	9
3. GBR	1	1	0	5	6
3. GBR	0	1	0	1	3
5. GER	1	1	0	1	4
6. FRA	0	2	0	1	11

Final: ENG 8-1 IRL

1. GBR—England: Harvey Wood, Harry Freeman, Louis Baillon, John Robinson, Edgar Page, Alan Noble, Percy Rees, Gerald Logan, Stanley Shoveller, Reginald Pridmore, Eric Green
2. GBR—Ireland: Edward Holmes, Henry Brown, Walter Peterson, Jack Peterson William Graham, Walter Campbell, Henry Murphy, Charles Power, Richard Gregg, Edward Allman-Smith, Frank Robinson, Robert Kennedy
3. GBR—Scotland: John Burt, Hugh Neilson, Charles Foulkes, Hew Fraser, Alexander Burt, Alastair Denniston, Norman Stevenson, Ivan Laing, James Harper-Orr, Hugh Walker, William Orchardson
3. GBR—Wales: W. Bertrand Turnbull, Edward Richards, Llewellyn Evans, Charles Shephard, Richard Lyne, Frederick Connah, Frederick Phillips, Arthur Law, Philip Turnbull, James Williams, Wilfred Pallott
5. GER—Albert Stüdemann, Friedrich Rahe, Alfons Brehm, Elard Dauelsberg, Franz Diederichsen, Carl Ebert, Mauricio Galvao, Raulino Galvao, Fritz Möding, Friedrich Uhl, Jules Fehr
6. FRA—René Salarnier, L. Saulnier, F. Roux, R.P. Aublin, L. Gautier, R. Benoit, D. Baidet, D.M. Girard, L. Poupon, André Bonnal, C. Pattin, F. Versini

The English team outclassed the rest of the field. They defeated France 10-1, Scotland 6-1 and Ireland 8-1. Reggie Pridmore scored ten goals, only two less than the combined total of the five non-English teams. One participant of particular interest is Alastair Denniston of the Scottish team. In 1914 Denniston was recruited into British secret intelligence service because he was an expert in the German language. Over the next thirty years, he was one of the most important players in the closed world of cryptoanalysis. He was instrumental in continuing the work of code-cracking after World War I and leading operations during World War II. Despite Denniston's obsession with secrecy and security he successfully promoted the complete sharing of information with the United States.

1912 not held

1920 Antwerp T: 4, N: 4, D: 9.5.

	W	L	T	GF	GA
1. GBR	3	0	0	17	2
2. DEN	2	1	0	15	8
3. BEL	1	2	0	6	19
4. FRA	0	3	0	3	12

1. GBR—Harry Haslam, John Bennett, Charles Atkin, Harold Cooke, Eric Crockford, Cyril Wilkinson, William Smith, George McGrath, John MacBryan, Stanley Shoveller, Reginald "Rex" Crummack, Arthur Leighton, Harold Cassels, C. Sholto Marcon
2. DEN—Andreas Rasmussen, Hans Christian Herlak, Frans Faber, Erik Husted, Henning Holst, Hans Jörgen Hansen, Hans Adolf Bjerrum, Thorvald Eigenbrod, Svend Blach, Steen Due, Ejvind Blach, Paul Metz
3. BEL—Charles Delelienne, Maurice van den Bemden, Raoul Daufresne de la Chevalerie, René Strauwen, Fernand de Montigny, Adolphe Goemaere, Pierre Chibert, Andre Becquet, Raymond Keppens, Pierre Valcke, Jean van Nerom, Robert Gevers, Louis Diercxens, Charles Gniette
4. FRA—Paul Haranger, Robert Lelong, Pierre Estrabant, Georges Breuille, Jacques Morise, Edmond Loriol, Désiré Guard, Roland Bedel, André Bounal, Gaston Rogot, Pierre Rollin

1924 not held

1928 Amsterdam T: 9, N: 9, D: 5.26.

	W	L	T	GF	GA
1. IND	5	0	0	29	0
2. HOL	3	1	0	8	5
3. GER	3	1	0	11	3
4. BEL	3	2	0	8	12

Final: IND 3-0 HOL
3rd Place: GER 3-0 BEL

1. IND—Richard Allen, Leslie Hammond, Michael Rocque, Sayed Yusuf, Broome Eric Pinniger, Rex Norris, William Cullen, Frederic Seaman, Dhyan Chand, George Marthins, Maurice Gateley, Jaipal Singh, Shaukat Ali, Feroze Khan
2. HOL—Adrian Katte, Reindert de Waal, Albert Tresling, Jan Ankerman, Emile Duson, Johannes Brand, August Kop, Gerrit Jannink, Paulus van de Rovaert, Robert van der Veen, Hendrik Visser t'Hooft
3. GER—Georg Brunner, Heinz Wöltje, Werner Proft, Erich Zander, Theodor Haag, Werner Freyberg, Herbert Kemmer, Herbert Hobein, Bruno Boche, Herbert Müller, Friedrich Horn, Erwin Franzkowiak, Hans Haussmann, Karl-Heinz Irmer, Aribert Heymann, Kurt Haverbeck, Rolf Wollner, Gerd Strantzen, Heinz Förstendorf
4. BEL—Etienne Soubre, Johnny van der Straeten, Corneille Wellens, Lambert Adelot, Claude Baudoux, Adolphe Goemaere, André Seeldrayers, Charles Delheid, Louis Diercxens, Yvon Baudoux, Charles Koning, Freddy Cattoir, Louis de Deken, Emile Vercken, Auguste Goditiabois, Georges Grosjean, René Mallieux

Final: IND 3-0 HOL
3rd Place: GER 3-0 BEL

The first Indian hockey clubs were formed in Calcutta in 1885. In 1926 India played its initial international matches against New Zealand. But it was the 1928 Olympics in Amsterdam that established India as the world's number-one power in field hockey. Led by 22-year-old Dhyan Chand, an army captain from Uttar Pradesh who scored fifteen goals, the Indians whipped through the tournament without giving up a single goal. Chand eventually won three Olympic gold medals. In the twelve matches that he played in the Olympics, he scored 38 goals. Chand later became coach of the Indian national team. He was such a legend that he became known as the embodiment of hockey excellence. Thus Balbir Singh was known as the "Modern-Day Dhyan Chand" and Habib-ur-Rehman as the "Dhyan Chand of Pakistan."

1932 Los Angeles T: 3, N: 3, D: 8.11.

	W	L	T	GF	GA
1. IND	2	0	0	35	2
2. JPN	1	1	0	10	13
3. USA	0	2	0	3	33

1. IND—Richard Allen, Arthur Hind, Carlyle Tapsell, Leslie Hammond, Masud Minhas, Broome Eric Pinniger, Lal Shah Bokhari, Richard Carr, Gurmit Singh Kullar, Dhyan Chand, Roop Singh, Sayed Mohammed Jaffar, Muhammed Aslam, Frank Brewin, William Sullivan
2. JPN—Shumkichi Hamada, Akio Sohda, Sadayoshi Kobayashi, Katsumi Shibata, Yoshio Sakai, Eiichi Nakamura, Haruhiko Kon, Hiroshi Nagata, Kenichi Konishi, Toshio Usami, Junzo Inohara
3. USA—Harold Brewster, Samuel Ewing, Leonard O'Brien, Henry Greer, James Gentle, Horace Disston, Lawrence Knapp, Charles Shaeffer, Amos Deacon, William Boddington, David McMullin, Frederick Wolters, Roy Coffin

Following the Olympic triumph of 1928, interest in hockey spread rapidly throughout India. When it came time to raise money to send a team to the Los Angeles Olympics, a journalist representing the Indian Hockey Federation approached Mahatma Gandhi and asked him to issue an appeal to the masses. Gandhi's only reply was, "What's hockey?" Nevertheless, an Indian team did make it to Los Angeles, paying its way by playing exhibition matches in Europe on the way home. The Indians had no problems with the competition, defeating Japan, 11-1, and the United States, 24-1. In the latter game, which had the highest score ever achieved in an international match, Roop Singh scored ten goals and Dhyan Chand eight.

1936 Berlin T: 11, N: 11, D: 8.15.

	W	L	T	GF	GA
1. IND	5	0	0	38	1
2. GER	3	1	0	14	9
3. HOL	3	1	1	13	10
4. FRA	2	3	0	7	19

Final: IND 8-1 GER
3rd Place: HOL 4-3 FRA

1. IND—Richard Allen, Carlyle Tapsell, Mohomed Hussain, Baboo Narsoo Nimal, Earnest Cullen, Joseph Galibardy, Shabban Shahab-ud-Din, Syed Iqtidar Ali Shah Dara, Dhyan Chand, Roop Singh, Sayed Mohammed Jaffar, Cyril Michie, Paul Peter Fernandes, Joseph Phillip, Garewal Gurcharan Singh, Ahsan Mohomed Khan, Ahmed Sher Khan, Lionel Emmett, Mirza Nasir-ud-Din Masood
2. GER—Karl Dröse, Herbert Kemmer, Erich Zander, Alfred Gerdes, Erwin Keller, Heinrich Schmalix, Harald Huffmann, Werner Hamel, Kurt Weiss, Hans Scherbart, Fritz Messner, Tito Warnholtz, Detlef Okrent, Hermann auf der Heide, Heinrich Peter, Carl Menke, Heinz Raack, Paul Mehlitz, Ludwig Beisiegel, Karl Ruck, Erich Cuntz, Werner Kubitzki
3. HOL—Jan de Looper, Reindert de Waal, Max Westerkamp, Hendrik de Looper, Rudolf van der Haar, Antoine van Lierop, Pieter Gunning, Henri Schnitger, Ernst Willem van den Berg, Agathon de Roos, René Sparenberg, Carl Haybroek
4. FRA—Raymond Tixier, Guy Chevalier, Paul Imbault, Claude Graveraux, Félix Grimonprez, François Verger, Paul Sartorius, Anatole Vologe, Joseph Goubert, Claude Soulé, Claude Roques, Etienne Guibal, Michel Verkindere, Marcel Lachmann, Guy Hénon, Emmanuel Gonat, Jean Rouget, Charles Imbault, Robert Rousse

Final: IND 8-1 GER
3rd Place: HOL 4-3 FRA

As a British colony, India was forced to march behind the flag of Great Britain. But in the dressing room before their final match against Germany, the Indian team saluted the tricolor flag of the Indian National Congress. The Germans fought hard and trailed only 1-0 at halftime. But the Indians wore them down after the break, winning 8-1, with Dhyan Chand scoring six goals while playing barefoot.

1948 London T: 13, N: 13, D: 8.13.

	W	L	T	GF	GA
1. IND	5	0	0	25	2
2. GBR	3	1	1	21	4
3. HOL	4	2	1	17	11
4. PAK	4	2	1	25	7

Final: IND 4-0 GBR
3rd Place: HOL 1-1 PAK
3rd Place Replay: HOL 4-1 PAK

1. IND—Leo Pinto, Trilochan Singh, Randhir Singh Gentle, Keshava Datt, Amir Kumar, Maxie Vaz, Kishan Lal, Kunwar Digvijai Singh, Grahanandan Singh, Patrick Jansen, Lawrie Fernandes, Ranganandhan Francis, Akhtar Hussain, Leslie Claudius, Jaswant Rajput, Reginald Rodrigues, Latifur Rehman, Balbir Singh, Walter D'Souza, Gerry Glacken
2. GBR—David Brodie, George Sime, William Lindsay, Michael Walford, Frank Reynolds, F. Robin Lindsay, John Peake, W. Neil White, Robert Adlard, Norman Borrett, William Griffiths, Ronald Davies
3. HOL—Antonius Richter, Henri Derckx, Johan Drijver, Jenne Langhout, Hermanus Loggere, Edouard Tiel, Willem van Heel, Andries Boerstra, Pieter Bromberg, Jan Kruize, Rius Esser, Henricus Bouwman
4. PAK—M. Anwar Beg Moghal, Mohammad Niaz Khan, Mohammad Abdul Razzaq, Hameedullah Khan Burki, Abdul Ghafoor Khan, Shahrukh Shahzada, Masood Ahmed Khan, M. Shaikh, Syed Ali Iqtidar Shah Dara, Abdul Aziz Mali, Shaikh Rahmatullah, Sayed Mohamad Saleem, Shahzada Khurrum, Khawaja Mohammad Taqi, Mukhtar Bhatti, Abdul "Hamidi" Hamid, Milton D'Mello, Abdul Qayyum, Azizur-Rehman Khan, Mahmood-Ul Hasan

Final: IND 4-0 GBR
3rd Place: HOL 1-1 PAK

Ever since India first appeared on the international field hockey scene, Great Britain had studiously avoided playing the Indian team, apparently afraid of the embarrassment of losing to one of its colonies. However in 1948 India gained not only its independence from Britain, but also a chance to face its former mentor in what had now become the Indian national sport. The match for first place turned out to be no contest, as Great Britain, which had advanced to the final without giving up a goal, was itself shut out, 4-0.

1952 Helsinki T: 12, N: 12, D: 7.24.

	W	L	T	GF	GA
1. IND	3	0	0	13	2
2. HOL	2	1	0	3	6
3. GBR	2	1	0	4	4
4. PAK	1	2	0	7	3

Final: IND 6-1 HOL
3rd Place: GBR 2-1 PAK

1. IND—Ranganandhan Francis, Dharam Singh, Randhir Singh Gentle, Leslie Claudius, Keshava Datt, Govind Perumal, Raghbir Lal, Kunwar Digvijai Singh, Balbir Singh, Udham Singh, Muniswarmy Rajagopal, Chinadorai Deshmutu, Meldric St. Clair Daluz, Grahanandan Singh
2. HOL—Laurentz Mulder, Henri Derckx, Johan Drijver, Julius Ancion, Hermanus Loggere, Edouard Tiel, Willem van Heel, Rius Esser, Jan Hendrik Kruize, Andries Boerstra, Leonard Wery, Andries Dirk
3. GBR—Graham Dadds, Roger Midgley, Denys Carnill, John Cockett, Dennis Eagan, Anthony Robinson, Anthony Nunn, Robin Fletcher, Richard Norris, John Conroy, John Taylor, Derek Day, Neil Nugent
4. PAK—Qazi Waheed Qazi, Mohammad Niaz Khan, Asghar Ali Khan, Jack Britto, Syed Mansoor Hussain Atif, Habib Ali Kiddi, Mahmood-Ul Hasan, Abdul "Hamidi" Hamid, Abdul Aziz Mali, Habibur Rehman, Latifur Rehman, Latif Mir, Safdar Ali Babul, Mohammad Rafique Khan, Fazlur Rehman, Abdul Qayyum, Syed Azmat Ali

Final: IND 6-1 HOL
3rd Place: GBR 2-1 PAK

Nine of India's 13 goals were scored by Balbir Singh, a police inspector from Punjab.

1956 Melbourne T: 12, N: 12, D: 12.6.

	W	L	T	GF	GA
1. IND	5	0	0	38	0
2. PAK	3	1	1	10	4
3. GER	2	1	2	8	6
4. GBR	2	2	2	9	10
5. AUS	2	2	0	6	5
6. NZL	1	2	0	8	10

Final: IND 1-0 PAK
3rd Place: GER 3-1 GBR

1. IND—Shankar Laxman, Bakshish Singh, Randhir Singh Gentle, Leslie Claudius, Amir Kumar, Govind Perumal, Raghbir Lal, Gurdev Singh, Balbir Singh, Udham Singh, Raghbir Singh Bhola, Charles Stephen, Ranganandhan Francis, Balkrishnan Singh, Amit Singh Bakshi, Kaushik Haripal, Hardyal Singh
2. PAK—Syed Zakir Hussain, Muneer Ahmed Dar, Syed Mansoor Hussain Atif, Chaudhri Ghulam Rasool, Anwar Ahmed Khan, Qazi Mussarat Hussain, Noor Alam, Abdul "Hamidi" Hamid, Habibur Rehman, Naseer Ahmed Bunda, Motiullah, Latifur Rehman, Akhtar Hussain, Habib Ali Kiddi
3. GER—Alfred Lücker, Helmut Nonn, Günther Brennecke, Werner Delmes, Eberhard Ferstl, Hugo Dollheiser, Heinz Radzikowski, Wolfgang Nonn, Hugo Budinger, Werner Rosenbaum, Günther Ullerich
4. GBR—David Archer, John Strover, Denys Carnill, John Cockett, Francis Davis, Anthony Robinson, Frederick Hugh Scott, Neil Forster, David Thomas, John Conroy, Michael Doughty, Steven Johnson, Colin Dale, Geoffrey Cutter
5. AUS—Louis Hailey, Alan Barblett, Desmond Spackman, Kevin Carton, Keith Leeson, Dennis Kemp, Raymond Whiteside, Ian Dick, Melville Pearce, Eric Pearce, Gordon Pearce, Maurice Foley
6. NZL—David Goldsmith, Brian Johnston, Reginald Johansson, John Tynan, Murray Loudon, John Abrams, Archie Currie, Noel Hobson, Guy McGregor, Bruce Turner, Ivan Armstrong, Phillip Bygrave, William Schaefer

India began confidently with victories of 14-0 over Afghanistan and 16-0 over the United States. However they barely got by a roughhouse German team, 1-0, in the semifinal, and they won the final by the same score on a short corner hit by Gentle midway through the second half.

1960 Rome T: 16, N: 16, D: 9.9.

	W	L	T	GF	GA
1. PAK	6	0	0	25	1
2. IND	5	1	0	19	2
3. SPA	4	1	1	11	4
4. GBR	3	2	1	7	5
5. NZL	4	3	1	10	9
6. AUS	4	3	2	16	10
7. GER	2	3	0	11	4
7. KEN	2	2	2	11	5

Final: PAK 1-0 IND
3rd Place: SPA 2-1 GBR

1. PAK—Abdul Rashid, Bashir Ahmed, Syed Mansoor Hussain Atif, Ghulam Rasul, Anwar Ahmed Khan, Habib Ali Kiddi, Noor Alam, Abdul "Hamidi" Hamid, Abdul Waheed, Naseer Ahmed Bunda, Motiullah, Mushtaq Ahmed, Muneer Ahmed Dar, Khursheed Aslam
2. IND—Shankar Laxman, Prithipal Singh, Jaman Lal Sharma, Leslie Claudius, Joseph Antic, Mohinder Lal, Joginder Singh, John Peter, Jaswant Singh, Udham Singh, Raghbir Singh Bhola, Charanjit Singh, Govind Savant
3. SPA—Pedro Amat Fontanals, Francisco Caballer Soteras, Juan Ángel Calzado de Castro, José Colomer Rivas, Carlos del Coso Iglesias, José Antonio Dinarés Massagué, Eduardo Dualde Santos de Lamadrid, Joaquín Dualde Santos de Lamadrid, Rafael Egusquiza Basterra, Ignacio Macaya Santos de Lamadrid, Pedro Murúa Leguizamón, Pedro Roig Junyent, Luis María Usoz Quintana, Narciso Ventalló Surralles
4. GBR—Harold Cahill, John Neill, Denys Carnill, Charles Jones, F. Howard Davis, Neil Livingstone, Ian Taylor, John Hindle, Stuart Mayes, Frederick Hugh Scott, Derek Miller, Peter Croft, John Bell, Christopher Saunders-Griffiths, Patrick Austen
5. NZL—William Schaefer, John Abrams, Ian Kerr, Bruce Turner, John Cullen, John Ross Gillespie, Anthony Hayde, Guy McGregor, Noel Hobson, Mervyn McKinnon, Phillip Bygrave, James Barclay, Kelvin Percy, Murray Mathieson
6. AUS—Louis Hailey, William Spackman, Mervyn Crossman, John McBryde, Kevin Carton, Julian Pearce, Gordon Pearce, Michael Craig, Raymond Evans, Eric Pearce, Donald Currie, Phillip Pritchard, Graham Wood, Errol Bill, Barry Malcolm
7. GER—Wolfgang End, Helmut Nonn, Günther Ullerich, Dieter Krause, Werner Delmes, Eberhard Ferstl, Klaus Woller, Carsten Keller, Hugo Budinger, Norbert Schuler, Herbert Winters, Christian Buchting, Willi Brendel, Klaus Greinert
7. KEN—George Saudi, Anthony Vaz, Avtar Singh Sohal, Jagnandan Singh, Deol Surjeet Singh, Silvester Fernandes, Edgar Fernandes, Hilary Fernandes, Surjeet Singh Panesar, Sandhu Pritan Singh, John Simonian, Gurarian Kirpal Singh, Egbert Fernandes, Aloysius Mendonca, Krishan Aggarwal, Sehmi Cursarah Singh

Final: PAK 1-0 IND
3rd Place: SPA 2-1 GBR

The early rounds saw some surprising incidents. In the quarterfinal contest between Germany and Pakistan, the score was tied 1-1 with only a few minutes to play. A penalty was called against Ullerich of Germany for illegally blocking a shot with his hand. The referee, Asselmann of Belgium, ordered a bully, or face-off. When a bully is called, two players, one from each team, touch sticks three times and then go after the ball. Ullerich bullied off for the Germans, but only touched sticks twice. The referee caught him and ordered the

INDIA'S FIELD HOCKEY WINNING STREAK

1928			**1948**			**1956**		
IND	6-0	AUS	IND	8-0	AUS	IND	14-0	AFG
IND	9-0	BEL	IND	9-1	ARG	IND	16-0	USA
IND	5-0	DEN	IND	2-0	SPA	IND	6-0	SIN
IND	5-0	SWI	IND	2-1	HOL	IND	1-0	GER
IND	3-0	HOL	IND	4-0	GBR	IND	1-0	PAK
			IND	1-0	GER			
1932			**1952**			**1960**		
IND	11-1	JPN	IND	4-0	AUS	IND	10-0	DEN
IND	24-1	USA	IND	3-1	GBR	IND	4-1	HOL
			IND	6-1	HOL	IND	3-0	NZL
1936						IND	1-0	AUS
IND	4-0	HUN						
IND	7-0	USA						
IND	9-0	JPN						
IND	10-0	FRA						
IND	8-1	GER						

bully repeated. Again Ullerich struck before the third touch. This time the referee awarded a goal to Pakistan, a goal which gave Pakistan a 2-1 victory. The next day a consolation match was held between France and Belgium. With the score 0-0 and the French attacking, an Italian traffic policeman, on duty just outside the field, blew his whistle. The Belgians thought it was an umpire's whistle and stopped playing, whereupon the French team knocked the ball into the net for what proved to be the only goal of the game. Meanwhile India was forced into double overtime in the quarterfinals before they were able to defeat Australia, 1-0. But that was nothing compared to the Great Britain-Kenya match that followed. That contest went into six overtimes before Saunders of Great Britain scored to give the British a 2-1 victory after 127 minutes of play.

The semifinals were tense contests, with both Pakistan and India scoring early and holding on for 1-0 wins over Spain and Great Britain, respectively. Entering the final, India had a cumulative Olympic record of 30 wins and no losses, their teams having scored 197 goals while allowing only eight. Unintimidated, the Pakistanis attacked aggressively from the beginning. After 12 minutes Noor Alam of Pakistan took a pass from four-time Olympian Abdul Hamid and sent a cross pass to the top of the circle. Naseer Bunda flicked the ball into the corner of the net. Despite vigorous play on both sides, that was the only score of the match. The Pakistanis were ecstatic, and most observers were thrilled to have seen such a hard-fought match. But back in India the loss to Pakistan was considered a national tragedy, and plans were immediately made to regain the Olympic title in Tokyo in 1964.

1964 Tokyo T: 15, N: 15, D: 10.23.

	W	L	T	GF	GA
1. IND	7	0	2	22	5
2. PAK	7	1	0	20	4
3. AUS	5	3	0	20	10
4. SPA	4	2	3	18	9
5. GDR	4	0	5	17	5
6. KEN	4	3	1	10	13
7. HOL	4	3	1	21	7
7. JPN	3	4	0	7	11

Final: IND 1-0 PAK
3rd Place: AUS 3-2 SPA
5th Place: GDR 3-0 KEN

1. IND—Shankar Laxman, Prithipal Singh, Dharam Singh, Mohinder Lal, Charanjit Singh, Gurbux Singh, Joginder Singh, John Peter, Harbinder Singh, Kaushik Haripal, Darshan Singh, Jagjit Singh, Bandu Patil, Udham Singh, Ali Sayeed
2. PAK—Abdul Hamid, Munir Ahmed Dar, Syed Mansoor Hussain Atif, Saeed Anwar, Anwar Ahmed Khan, Mohammad Rasheed, Khalid Mahmood, Khawaja Mohammad Zakauddin, Mohammad Afzal Manna, M. Asad Malik, Motiullah, Tariq Niazi, Hayat Khan, Khursheed Azam, Khizan Nawaz Bajwa, Tariq Aziz
3. AUS—Paul Dearing, Donald McWatters, Brian Glencross, John McBryde, Julian Pearce, Graham Wood, Robin Hodder, Raymond Evans, Eric Pearce, Patrick Nilan, Donald Smart, Antony Waters, Mervyn Crossman, Desmond Piper
4. SPA—Carlos del Coso Iglesias, José Colomer Rivas, Julio Solaun Garteizgogeascoa, Juan Angel Calzado de Castro, José Antonio Dinarés Massagué, Narciso Ventalló Surralles, Ignacio Macaya Santos de Lamadrid, Jaime Amat Fontanals, Eduardo Dualde Santos de Lamadrid, Jorge Vidal Mitjans, Jaime Echevarria Arteche, Luis María Usoz Quintana, Pedro Amat Fontanals, Francisco Amat Fontanals
5. GDR—Rainer Stephan, Axel Thieme, Klaus Vetter, Horst Brennecke, Klaus Bahner, Horst Dahmlos, Reiner Hanschke, Rolf Westphal, Lothar Lippert, Dieter Ehrlich, Adolf Krause, Karl-Heinz Freiberger
6. KEN—John Simonian, Anthony Vaz, Avtar Singh Sohal, Surjeet Singh Panesar, Silvester Fernandes, Leo Fernandes, Edgar Simon Fernandes, Egbert Carmo Fernandes, Amar Singh Mangat, Aloysius Mendonca, Saude André George, Krishan Kumar Aggarwal, Tejparkash Singh Brar, Reynold D'Souza, Santokh Singh Matharu
7. HOL—Joost Boks, Jacob Leemhuis, Jan van Gooswilligen, Johan Fokker, Franciscus Fiolet, Theodorus Terlingen, Theo van Vroonhoven, Arie de Keyzer, Guillaum Zweerts, Jacob Voigt, Nicolaas "Nico" Spits, Jan Veentjer, John Elffers, Leendert Krol, Jan van Hooft, Johan Mijnarends, Eric van Rossem, Charles Coster van Voorhout
7. JPN—Hiroshi Miwa, Tsuneya Yuzaki, Akio Takashima, Katsuhiro Yuzaki, Tetsuya Wakabayashi, Toshihiko Yamaoka, Kenji Takizawa, Shigeo Kadku, Hiroshi Tanaka, Michio Okabe, Seiji Kihara, Junichi Yamaguchi, Kunio Iwahashi

India struggled through to the final, surviving 1-1 ties with East Germany and Spain. Pakistan, on the other hand, won seven straight matches. However, in the deciding contest, with five minutes gone in the second half, Munir Ahmad Dar of Pakistan was penalized for stopping a shot with his foot. Mohinder Lal converted the penalty shot for the only goal of the game.

1968 Mexico City T: 16, N: 16, D: 10.26.

	W	L	T	PF	PA
1. PAK	9	0	0	26	5
2. AUS	5	3	1	15	8
3. IND	7	2	0	23	7
4. GER	5	3	1	16	8
5. HOL	6	3	0	15	12
6. SPA	3	3	3	9	7
7. NZL	3	1	4	9	7
8. KEN	4	3	1	12	8

Final: PAK 2-1 AUS
3rd Place: IND 2-1 GER
5th Place: HOL 1-0 SPA
7th Place: NZL 2-0 KEN

1. PAK—Syed Zakir Hussain, Tanvir Ahmed Dar, Tariq Aziz, Saeed Anwar, Riaz Ahmed, Gulraiz Akhtar, Khalid Mahmood, Ashfaq Ahmed, Abdul Rashid Jr., Mohammad Asad Malik, Jahangir Butt, Riazuddin, Tariq Niazi
2. AUS—Paul Dearing, James Mason, Brian Glencross, Gordon Pearce, Julian Pearce, Robert Haigh, Donald Martin, Raymond Evans, Ronald Riley, Patrick Nilan, Donald Smart, Desmond Piper, Eric Pearce, Frederick Quinn

3. IND—Rajendra Absolem Christy, Gurbux Singh, Prithipal Singh, Balbir Singh II, Ajitpal Singh, Krishnamurty Perumal, Balbir Singh III, Balbir Singh I, Harbinder Singh, Inamur Rehman, Inder Singh, Munir Sait, Harmik Singh, Jagjit Singh, John Peter, Tarsem Singh, Gurbaksh Singh
4. GER—Wolfgang Rott, Günter Krauss, Utz Aichinger, Dirk Michel, Klaus Greinert, Ulrich Vos, Michael Krause, Norbert Schuler, Fritz Schmidt, Carsten Keller, Ulrich Sloma, Wolfgang Müller, Eckart Suhl, Friedrich-Wilhelm Josten, Jürgen Wein, Detlef Kittstein, Wolfgang Baumgart, Hermann End
5. HOL—Joost Boks, Theodorus Terlingen, Heiko Locker van Staveren, Charles de Lanoy Meijer, Johan Fokker, John Elffers, Frans Spits, Otto Boudewijn ter Haar, Charles Thole, Petrus Weemers, Arie de Keyzer, Aernout Brederode, Ewaldus Kist, Sebo Onno Ebbens, Theo van Vroonhoven, Gerardus Hijikema, Edo Buma
6. SPA—Carlos del Coso Iglesias, Antonio Nogués Dalmases, Julio Solaun Garteizgogeascoa, Francisco Fábregas Bosch, José Antonio Dinarés Massagué, Juan Amat Fontanals, Juan Quintana Bosch, José Salles Salva, Francisco Amat Fontanals, Pedro Amat Fontanals, Agustín Masana Díaz, José Colomer Rivas, Jorge Fábregas, Narciso Ventalló Surralles, Rafael Camina, Jorge Vidal Mitjans, Juan José Alvear Calleja
7. NZL—Ross McPherson, Roger Capey, Alan Patterson, Keith Thomson, Selwyn Maister, John Anslow, Bruce Judge, John Christensen, Alan Mcintyre, Barry Maister, Jan Borren, Edwin Salmon, John Hicks
8. KEN—John Simonian, Kirpal Bhardwaj, Avtar Singh Sohal, Harvinder Marwa, Surjeet Singh Panesar, Silvester Fernandes, Leo Fernandes, Santokh Singh Matharu, Davinder Deegan, Hilary Fernandes, Aloysius Mendonca, Mohamed Malik, Egbert Fernandes, Reynold Pereira

With the score tied 0-0 after 55 minutes in a preliminary match between India and Japan, a penalty stroke was awarded to India. The Japanese were so upset that they laid down their sticks and walked off the field, forfeiting the game. Earlier, India had lost to New Zealand, 2-1, the first time that India had given up more than one goal in an Olympic match. They lost their semifinal match to Australia by the same score. In the final, the winning goal was scored by Mohammad Asad Malik after 56 minutes of play. The Australian team included three brothers: Eric, Gordon, and Julian Pearce. A fourth Pearce brother, Mel, represented Australia in 1956.

1972 Munich T: 16, N: 16, D: 9.10.

	W	L	T	PF	PA
1. GER	8	1	0	21	5
2. PAK	6	2	1	19	7
3. IND	6	1	2	27	11
4. HOL	5	3	1	21	14
5. AUS	5	2	2	22	10
6. GBR	5	3	1	18	12
7. SPA	3	2	4	11	11
8. MAL	4	4	1	11	11

1. GER—Wolfgang Rott, Michael Peter, Dieter Freise, Michael Krause, Eduard Thelen, Horst Dröse, Carsten Keller, Ulrich Kiaes, Wolfgang Baumgart, Uli Vos, Peter Trump, Peter Kraus, Werner Kaessmann, Wolfgang Strödter, Detlef Kittstein, Rainer Seifert, Eckart Suhl, Fritz Schmidt
2. PAK—Saleem Sherwani, Akhtar-Ul Islam, Munawa-Uz Zaman, Saeed Anwar, Akhtar Rasool, Fazlur Rehman, Mudassar Asghar, Islahuddin Siddiqui, Abdul Rashid Jr., Mohammad Asad Malik, Shahnaz Sheikh, Riaz Ahmed, Iftikhar Syed, Mohammad Zahid, Jahangir Butt
3. IND—Manuel Frederick, Mukhbain Singh, Kindo Michael, Krishnamurtay Perumal, Ajitpal Singh, Harmik Singh, Ganesh Mollerapoovayya, Harbinder Singh, Kulwant Singh, Ashok Kumar, Harcharan Singh, Govinda Billimogaputtaswamy, Vairinder Singh, Cornelius Charles
4. HOL—Andre Bolhuis, Thijs Kaanders, Coen Kranenberg, Thies Kruize, Maarten Sikking, Frans Spits, Nico Spits, Bart Taminiau, Charles Thole, Piet Weemers, Jeroen Zweerts, Wouter Leefers, Flip van Lidth de Jeude, Paul Litjens, Marinus Dijkerman, Irving van Nes
5. AUS—Brian Glencross, Robert Haigh, Richard Charlesworth, Paul Dearing, Thomas Colder, James Mason, Terry McAskell, Patrick Nilan, Desmond Piper, Ronald Riley, Donald Smart, Gregory Browning, Robert Andrew, Graham Reid, Ronald Wilson, Wayne Hammond
6. GBR—D. Austin Savage, Paul Svehlik, Tony Ekins, Keith Sinclair, Bernard Cotton, N. Rui Saldanha, Richard Oliver, Michael Crowe, Michael Corby, Peter Marsh, John French, Dennis Hay, Terence Gregg, Peter Mills, Sheikh Mahmood Ahmad, Graham Evans, Christopher Langhorne
7. SPA—Luis Alberto Carrera, Jorge Fábregas Bosch, Francisco Segura Ruda, Juan Amat Fontanals, Francisco Fábregas Bosch, José Salles Salva, José Alusitza García, José Borrell, Francisco Amat Fontanals, Ramón Quintana Bosch, Juan Anbós Perarnau, Juan Quintana Bosch, Luis Towse Roura, Jorge Camina Borda, Antonio Nogués Dalmases, Agustin Churruca Otero
8. MAL—Khairuddin Bin Zainal, Belavantheran Francis, Sri Shanmuganathan Naganathy, Poh-meng Phang, Choon-hin Wong, Balasingam Singaram, Siow-ming Yang, Franco D'Cruz, Mahendran Murugesan, Harnahal Sewa Singh, Pathmarajah Ramalingam, Omar Razali Yeop, Sayed Samát, Sulaiman Saibot, Brian Santa Maria

The final was a bitter and violent contest, with Michael Krause of Germany scoring the only goal of the game from a penalty corner with ten minutes to play. The Pakistani team and their supporters in the stands were so angry at the officiating that they stormed the judges' table and poured water on René Frank, President of the International Hockey Federation. At the medal ceremony, several of the Pakistani players refused to face the German flag during the playing of the German national anthem. All 11 Pakistani finalists were banned for life by the International Olympic Committee, but reinstated in time for the 1976 Olympics.

1976 Montreal T: 11, N: 11, D: 7.30.

	W	L	T	GF	GA
1. NZL	3	1	2	9	9
2. AUS	4	3	0	16	8
3. PAK	4	1	1	20	11
4. HOL	5	2	0	14	8
5. GER	3	2	1	22	13
6. SPA	2	2	2	12	17
7. IND	4	3	0	16	12
8. MAL	2	5	0	4	11

Final: NZL 1-0 AUS
3rd Place: PAK 3-2 HOL
5th Place: GER 9-1 SPA
7th Place: IND 2-0 MAL

1. NZL—Paul Ackerley, Jeff Archibald, Tur Borren, Alan Chesney, John Christensen, Greg Dayman, Tony Ineson, Alan McIntyre, Barry Maister, Selwyn Maister, Trevor Manning, Arthur Parkin, Mohan Patel, Ramesh Patel
2. AUS—Robert Haigh, Richard Charlesworth, David Bell, Gregory Browning, Ian Cooke, Barry Dancer, Douglas Golder, Wayne Hammond, James Irvine, Malcolm Poole, Robert Proctor, Graham Reid, Ronald Riley, Trevor Smith, Terry Walsh
3. PAK—Saleem Sherwani, Mansoor-Ul Hasan, Munawar-Uz Zaman, Salim Nazim, Akhtar Rasool, Iftikhar Syed, Islahuddin Siddiqui, Mansoor Hasan, Abdul Rashid Jr., Shahnaz Sheikh, Samiullah Khan, Qamar Zia, Arshad Mahmood, Arshad Ali Chaudhri, Mudassar Asghar, Hanif Khan
4. HOL—Maarten Sikking, Andre Bolhuis, Tim Steens, Geert van Eijk, Theodoor Doyer, Coen Kranenburg, Rob Toft, Wouter Leefers, Hans Jorritsma, Hans Kruize, Jan Albers, Paul Litjens, Imbert Jebbink, Ron Steens, Bart Taminiau, Wouter Kan
5. GER—Wolfgang Rott, Klaus Ludwiczak, Michael Peter, Dieter Freise, Fritz Schmidt, Michael Krause, Horst Dröse, Werner Kaessmann, Uli Vos, Peter Caninenberg, Peter Trump, Hans Montag, Wolfgang Strödter, Heiner Dopp, Rainer Seifert, Ralf Lauruschkat
6. SPA—Luis Alberto Carrera, Juan Amat Fontanals, Jaime Arbós Serra, Juan Arbós Perarnau, Ricardo Cabot Durán, Juan Colomer, Francisco Codina, Agustin Churruca Otero, Francisco Fábregas Bosch, Jorge Fábregas Bosch, Agustín Masana Díaz, Juan Pellón Fernández, Ramón Quintana Bosch, José Salles Salva, Francisco Segura Ruda, Luis Towse Roura
7. IND—Ajitpal Singh, Vaduvelu Phillips, Baldev Singh, Ashok Diwan, Govinda Billimogaputtaswamy, Ashok Singh, Varinder Singh, Harcharan Singh, Mohinder Singh, Aslam Sher Khan, Syed Ali, Birbhadur Chattri, Chand Singh, Ajit Singh, Surjit Singh, Bhaskaran Vasudevan
8. MAL—Khairuddin Bin Zainal, Azraai Mohammed Zain, Sri Shanmuganathan Naganathy, Francis Anthonysamy, Kok-ming Lam, Mohindar Singh Amar, Choon-hin Wong, Balasingam Singaram, Palanisamy Nallasamy, Rama Krishnan Rengasamy, Mahendran Murugesan, Avtar Gill Singh, Antony D'Cruz, Fook-loke Poon, Pathmarajah Ramalingam, Soon-kooi Ow

New Zealand didn't exactly overwhelm their opposition; in fact, they didn't even outscore them. But they scored when it counted, including a penalty shot by Tony Ineson early in the second half that gave them a 1-0 victory over Australia in the final. This was the first Olympic tournament to be played on artificial turf. Ric Charlesworth of the Australian team gave up a promising career in cricket to concentrate on hockey and eventually competed in four Olympics. He also served as a member of parliament from Perth for ten years and coached the women's hockey team to victory at the 1996 and 2000 Olympics.

1980 Moscow T: 6, N: 6, D: 7.26.

	W	L	T	GF	GA
1. IND	4	0	2	43	9
2. SPA	4	1	1	36	7
3. SOV	4	2	0	32	2
4. POL	2	3	1	20	17
5. CUB	2	4	0	11	43
6. TAN	0	6	0	4	58

Final: IND 4-3 SPA
3rd Place: SOV 2-1 POL
5th Place: CUB 4-1 TAN

1. IND—Allan Schofield, Chettri Bir Bhadur, Dung Dung Sylvanus, Rajinder Singh, Davinder Singh, Gurmail Singh, Ravinder Pal Singh, Bhaskaran Vasudevan, Somaya Maneypandemuttana, Maharaj Krishon Kaushik, Charanjit Kumar, Mervyn Fernandis, Amarjit Rana Singh, Shahid Mohamed, Zafar Iqbal, Surinder Singh
2. SPA—José Miguel García Messeguer, Juan Amat Fontanals, Santiago Malgosa Morera, Rafael Garralda Garre, Francisco Fábregas Bosch, Juan Luis Coghen Alberdingk, Ricardo Cabot Durán, Jaime Arbós Serra, Carlos Roca Portolés, Juan Pellón Fernández, Miguel De Paz Pla, Miguel Chaves Sánchez, Juan Arbós Perarnau, Javier Cabot Durán, Paulino Monsalve Ballesteros, Jaime Zumalacárregui Benítez
3. SOV—Vladimir Pleshakov, Vyacheslav Lampeyev, Leonid Pavlovsky, Sos Airapetyan, Farit Zigangirov, Valery Belyakov, Sergei Klevtsov, Oleg Zagorodnev, Aleksandr Gusev, Sergei Pleshakov, Mikhail Nichepurenko, Minneula Azizov, Aleksandr Sytchev, Aleksandr Myasnikov, Viktor Deputatov, Aleksandr Goncharov
4. POL—Zygfryd Józefiak, Andrzej Mikina, Krystian Bąk, Wlodzimierz Stanislawski, Leszek Hensler, Jan Sitek, Jerzy Wybieralski, Leszek Tórz, Zbigniew Rachwalski, Henryk Horwat, Andrzej Myśliwiec, Leszek Andrzejczak, Jan Mielniczak, Mariusz Kubiak, Adan Dolatowski, Krysztof Glodowski
5. CUB—Angel Mora Parra, Severo Frometa Conte, Bernabé Izquierdo Martínez, Edgardo Vázquez Márquez, Hector Pedroso García, Manuel Varela Pérez, Raul García Cabrera, Jorge Mico Gutiérrez, Rodolfo Delgado Orbáñez, Lázaro Hernández Rangel, Juan Blanco Peñalver, Juan Caballero Pérez, Roberto Ramírez Hernández, Ángel Fontane Escobar, Ricardo Campos Hernández, Juan Ríos Álvarez
6. TAN—Leopold Gracias, Benedict Mendes, Soter Da Silva, Abraham Sykes, Yusuf Manwar, Jaypal Singh, Mohamed Manji, Rajabu Rajab, Jasbir Virdee, Islam Islam, Stephen D'Silva, Frederick Furtado, Taherali Hassanali, Anoop Mukundan, Patrick Toto, Julius Peter

The 1980 field hockey tournament was decimated by the boycott. Of the 11 teams that competed in Montreal in 1976, only Spain and India were represented in Moscow. Cuba and Tanzania were added to fill the field even though they had little experience with the sport. It was like old times for India, trouncing Tanzania 18-0 and Cuba 13-0. However, they had a tougher match with Poland, salvaging a 2-2 tie when Mervyn Fernandis scored a goal with five seconds to play. India also scraped through with a 2-2 tie against Spain. The two teams met again in the final. India took a 3-0 lead and held on to win, 4-3, despite the fact that Juan Amat of Spain scored three goals in twelve minutes.

1984 Los Angeles-Monterey Park T: 12, N: 12, D: 8.11.

	W	L	T	GF	GA
1. PAK	4	0	3	19	8
2. GER	4	2	1	14	6
3. GBR	5	1	1	13	8
4. AUS	5	2	0	19	8
5. IND	5	1	1	20	11
6. HOL	4	2	1	18	14
7. NZL	2	3	2	11	11
8. SPA	2	5	0	11	13

Final: PAK 2-1 GER
3rd Place: GBR 3-2 AUS
5th Place: IND 5-2 HOL
7th Place: NZL 1-0 SPA

1. PAK—Ghulam Moinuddin, Qazim Zia, Nasir Ali, Abdul Rashid, Ayaz Mahmood, Naeem Akhtar, Kaleemullah Khan, Manzoor Hussain, Hasan Sardar, Hanif Khan, Khalid Hameed, Shahid Ali Khan, Tauqeer Ahmed Dar, Ishtiaq Ahmed, Saleem Sherwani, M. Mushtaq Ahmad
2. GER—Christian Bassemir, Tobias Frank, Horst-Ulrich Hänel, Carsten Fischer, Karl-Joachim Hürter, Eckhard Schmidt-Opper, Reinhard Krull, Michael Peter, Stefan Blöcher, Andreas Keller, Thomas Reck, Markku Slawyk, Thomas Gunst, Heiner Dopp, Volker Fried, Dirk Brinkmann
3. GBR—Ian Taylor, Stephen Martin, Paul Barber, Robert Cattrall, Jonathan Potter, Richard Dodds, William McConnell, Norman "Billy" Hughes, David Westcott, Richard Leman, Stephen Batchelor, Sean Kerly, James Duthie, Kulbir Bhaura, Mark Precious
4. AUS—Richard Charlesworth, James Irvine, Colin Batch, David Bell, Adrian Berce, Grant Boyce, Craig Davies, Peter Haselhurst, Treva King, Terry Leece, Grant Mitton, Michael Nobbs, Nigel Patmore, Trevor Smith, Neil Snowden, Terry Walsh
5. IND—Romeo James, Manohar Topno, Vineet Kumar Sharma, Somaya Maneypandemuttana, Joaquim Carvaho, Rajinder Singh, Charanjit Kumar, Mervyn Fernandis, Hardeep Singh, Shahid Mohamed, Zafar Iqbal, Nila Komol Singh, Iqbaljit Grewal, Ravinder Pal Singh, Marcellusmark Gomes, Jalaludin Syed
6. HOL—Petrus Hermans, Arno den Hartog, Cees Jan Diepeveen, Henricus Pierik, Theodoor Doyer, Thomas van't Hek, Peter van Asbeck, Willem van Asbeck, Hans Kruize, Ties Kruize, Ronaldus Steens, Jan Hidde Kruize, Alexander Bos, Roderik Bouwman, René Klaassen, Maarten van Grimbergen
7. NZL—Jeffrey Archibald, Husmukh Bhikha, Christopher Brown, George Carnoutsos, Peter Daji, Laurence Gallen, Stuart Grimshaw, Trevor Laurence, Grant McLeod, Brent Miskimmin, Peter Miskimmin, Arthur Parkin, Ramesh Patel, Robin Wilson, Maurice Marquet, Graham Sligo
8. SPA—José Agut Bonsfills, Javier Cabot Durán, Juan Arbós Perarnau, Andrés Gómez Rodrígez, Juan Carlos Peón Melón, Jaime Arbós Serra, Ricardo Cabot Durán, Juan Malgosa Paloma, Carlos Roca Portolés, Mariano Bordas Mon, Ignaclo Cobos Vidal, Jorge Oliva Izquierdo, Miguel de Paz Pal, Ignacio Escudé Torrente, Santiago Malgosa Morera

Australia, unbeaten in two years and the winner of five straight international tournaments, seemed well on their way to their first Olympic championship when they were beaten 1-0 by a rough Pakistani team in a stunning semifinal upset. In the other semifinal, West Germany defeated Great Britain 1-0.

"PAKISTAN AVENGES MUNICH" read a banner hoisted in the stands as play began in the final match, a reference to the ugly 1972 final between Pakistan and West Germany. This time, in the blistering heat at East Los Angeles College, it was the Asian champions who prevailed. For the first time in Olympic history, the gold medal was decided in overtime, as Kaleemullah scored his only goal of the tournament in the twelfth minute.

In the bronze medal match, the demoralized Australians were upset again, this time by a surprising British team which had qualified for the Olympic tournament only as a result of the Soviet withdrawal.

1988 Seoul T: 12, N: 12, D: 10.1.

	W	L	T	GF	GA
1. GBR	5	1	1	18	8
2. GER	5	1	1	16	7
3. HOL	4	2	1	15	9
4. AUS	5	2	0	22	8
5. PAK	5	2	0	18	9
6. IND	3	3	1	16	15
7. SOV	3	3	1	9	12
8. ARG	2	5	0	15	22

Final: GBR 3-1 GER
3rd Place: HOL 2-1 AUS
5th Place: PAK 2-1 IND
7th Place: SOV 4-1 ARG

1. GBR—Ian Taylor, David Faulkner, Paul Barber, Jonathan Potter, Richard Dodds, Martyn Grimley, Stephen Batchelor, Richard Leman, James Kirkwood, Kulbir Bhaura, Sean Kerly, Robert Cliff, Imran Sherwani, Russell Garcia, Veryan Pappin, Stephen Martin
2. GER—Christian Schliemann, Tobias Frank, Horst-Ulrich Hänel, Carsten Fischer, Andreas Mollandin, Ekkhard Schmidt-Opper, Dirk Brinkmann, Heiner Dopp, Stefan Blöcher, Andreas Keller, Thomas Reck, Thomas Brinkmann, Hanns-Henning Fastrich, Michael Hilgers, Volker Fried, Michael Metz
3. HOL—Prank Leistra, Marc Benninga, Cees Jan Diepeveen, Maurits Crucg, Rene Klaassen, Hendrik Jan Kooijman, Marc Delissen, Jacques Brinkman, Gerrit Jan Schlatmann, Tim Steens, Floris Jan Bovelander, Patrick Faber, Ronald Jansen, Jan Hidde Kruize, Erik Parlevliet, Taco van den Honert
4. AUS—Craig Davies, Colin Batch, John Bestall, Warren Birmingham, Richard Charlesworth, Andrew Deane, Michael York, Mark Hager, Jay Stacy, Neil Hawgood, Peter Noel, Graham Reid, Roger Smith, Neil Snowden, David Wansbrough, Ken Wark
5. PAK—Mansoor Ahmed, Nasir Ali, Qazi Mohib-Ur Rehman, Aamir Zafar, Ishtiaq Ahmed, Naeem Akhtar, M. Qamar Ibrahim, Shahbaz Ahmed, Tariq Shaikh, Zahid Sharif, Khalid Hameed, Khalid Bashir, Naeem Amjad, Tahir Zaman, Musaddiq Hussain
6. IND—Rawat Rajinder Singh, Pargat Singh, Ashok Kumar, Mohinderpal Singh, Somaya Maneypandemuttana, Vivek Singh, Sujit Kumar, Subramani Baladadalaiash, Shahid Mohamed, Sebastian Jude Felix, Balwinder Singh, Mervyn Fernandis, Thoiba Singh, Gundeep Kumar, Jagbir Singh, Patterson Markphilip
7. SOV—Vladimir Pleshakov, Viktor Deputatov, Igor Yulchiyev, Sos Airapetyan, Vladimir Antakov, Vyacheslav Chechenov, Igor Atanov, Sergei Chakvorostov, Sergei Pleshakov, Mikhail Nichepurenko, Aleksandr Domashev, Igor Davydov, Aleksandr Myasnikov, Yevgeny Nechayev, Mikhail Bukatin
8. ARG—Otto Schmitt, Alejandro Siri, Miguel Altube, Marcelo Mascheroni, Marcelo Garraffo, Edgardo Pailos, Alejandro Doherty, Aldo Ayala, Carlos Geneyro, Gabriel Minadeo, Alejandro Verga, Fernando Ferrara, Emanuel Roggero, Franco Nicola, Martín Sordelli, Mariano Silva

As in 1984, the favored Australians swept through the preliminary round undefeated, only to be beaten in the semifinals. This time Great Britain spoiled the Australians' tournament when Sean Kerly broke a 2-2 tie with 1:22 to play. In the final, Britain faced West Germany, who had defeated them 2-1 in the preliminary round. But the Germans were frustrated by Britain's superb defensive play. Imran Sherwani, a newsagent from Stoke-on-Trent, scored two of Great Britain's three goals.

1992 Barcelona-Terrassa T: 12, N: 12, D: 8.8.

	W	L	T	GF	GA
1. GER	6	0	1	20	6
2. AUS	5	1	1	24	6
3. PAK	6	1	0	25	11
4. HOL	4	3	0	25	17
5. SPA	5	2	0	19	12
6. GBR	4	3	0	11	14
7. IND	3	4	0	7	12
8. NZL	1	6	0	11	18

Final: GER 2-1 AUS
3rd Place: PAK 4-3 HOL
5th Place: SPA 2-1 GBR
7th Place: IND 3-2 NZL

1. GER—Michael Knauth, Christopher Reitz, Jan Peter Tewes, Carsten Fischer, Christian Blunck, Stefan Saliger, Michael Metz, Christian Mayerhöfer, Sven Meinhardt, Andreas Keller, Michael Hilgers, Andreas Becker, Stefan Tewes, Klaus Michler, Volker Fried, Oliver Kurtz
2. AUS—Warren Birmingham, David Wansbrough, John Bestall, Lee Bodimeade, Ashley Carey, Stephen Davies, Damon Diletti, Lachlan Dreher, Lachlan Elmer, Michael Evans, Gregory Corbitt, Paul Lewis, Graham Reid, Jay Stacey, Kenneth Wark, Michael York
3. PAK—Shahid Ali Khan, Rana Mujahid Ali, Khalid Bashir, Anjum Saeed, Farhat Hussain Khan, Khawaja Mohammad Junaid, M. Qamar Ibrahim, Tahir Zaman, Mohammad Asif Akhlaq, Shahbaz Ahmed, Waseem Feroz, Mansoor Ahmed, Mohammad Ikhlaq, Mohammad Khalid, Musaddiq Hussain, Mohammad Shahbaz
4. HOL—Frank Leistra, Harrie Kwinten, Cees-Jan Diepeveen, Pieter van Ede, Bastiaan Poortenaar, Wouter van Pelt, Marc Delissen, Jacques Brinkman, Gisj Weterings, Stephan Veen, Floris Jan Bovelander, Hendrik Kooijman, Bart Looije, Maarten van Grimbergen, Leo Klein Gebbinck, Taco van den Honert
5. SPA—Santiago Grau Viola, Ignacio Escudé Torrente, Joaquín Malgosa Morera, Miguel Ortego Fernández, Juantxo García-Mauriño, Jaime Amat Durán, Jordi Avilés Cortés, Pere Jufresa Lluch, Jose Iglesias Bilbao, Xavier Escudé Torrente, Javier "Xavi" Arnau Creus, Víctor Pujol Sala, Juan Antonio Dinarés Quera, David Freixa Paloma, Pablo Usoz Ciriza, Ramón Jufresa Lluch
6. GBR—Sean Rowlands, Stephen Martin, Paul Bolland, Simon Nicklin, Jonathan Potter, Jason Laslett, Robert Hill, Stephen Batchelor, Russell Garcia, John Shaw, Robert Thompson, Sean Kerly, Robert Clift, Jason Lee, Donald Williams
7. IND—Cheppudira Poonacha, Jagdev Rai, Harpreet Singh, Sukhjit Singh, Shaqeel Ahmed, Mukesh Kumar Nandanoori, Sebastian Jude Felix, Jagbir Singh, Dhanraj Pillay, Didar Singh, Ashish Ballal, Pargat Powar, Ravi Nayakar, Darryl D'Souza, Lakra Ajit
8. NZL—Peter Daji, Brett Leaver, David Grundy, Scott Hobson, D. Grant McLeod, Peter Miskimmin, Paresh Patel, David Penfold, John Radovonich, Craig Russ, Gregory Russ, Umesh Parag, James Smith, Anthony Thornton, Scott Anderson, Ian Woodley

Germany qualified for the final by winning a difficult semifinal against Pakistan. Carsten Fischer, a medical doctor, scored from a penalty corner in the 13th minute of overtime to give the Germans a 2-1 victory. In the final, Germany faced Australia. The two teams had drawn 1-1 in pool play. The Germans were known for their methodical play, but they startled the Australians by attacking from the start and were rewarded when insurance broker Michael Hilgers scored after only 90 seconds. Hilgers added a second goal in the 59th minute. Gregory Corbitt brought Australia back to 2-1 with four minutes to play, but it was too little, too late. German midfielder Andreas Keller came from a remarkable hockey family. His grandfather Erwin earned a silver medal in 1936 and his father, Carsten, represented Germany in three Olympics and was a member of the 1972 gold-medal-winning squad. Andreas himself won silver in 1984 and 1988 before picking up his own gold. As if that weren't enough, Andreas' girlfriend, Anke Wild, earned a silver medal as a member of the 1992 German women's team.

The match for third place was an unusually exciting contest. With 15 minutes to play Holland held a seemingly safe 2-0 lead. But Pakistan scored four goals in the next 13 minutes. Although the Dutch scored once more, the bronze medal went to Pakistan, 4-3.

1996 Atlanta T: 12, N: 12, D: 8.2

	W	L	T	GF	GA
1. HOL	6	0	1	20	8
2. SPA	5	2	0	17	9
3. AUS	4	2	1	17	11
4. GER	3	3	1	13	9
5. KOR	3	2	2	18	17
6. PAK	3	3	1	14	12
7. GBR	2	1	4	13	13
8. IND	2	3	2	14	10

Final: HOL 3-1 SPA
3rd Place: AUS 3-2 GER
5th Place: KOR 3-1 PAK
7th Place: GBR 4-3 IND

1. HOL—Floris Jan Bovelander, Teun de Nooijer, Taco van den Honert, Wouter van Pelt, Remco van Wijk, Jacques Brinkman, Maurits Crucq, Marcus Delissen, Jeroen Delmee, Franciscus "Ronald" Jansen, Erik Jazet, Leo Klein Gebbink, Abraham "Bram" Lomans, Tycho van Meer, Stephan Veen, Augustinus Vogels
2. SPA—Ramón Jufresa Lluch, Oscar Barrena González, Joaquín Malgosa Morera, Jordi Arnau Creus, Juantxo García-Mauriño Sanchiz, Jaime Amat Durán, Juan Escarré Urueña, Víctor Pujol Sala, Ignacio Cobos Vidal, Xavier Escudé Torrente, Javier "Xavi" Arnau Creus, Ramón Sala Vallmonrat, Juan Antonio Dinarés Quera, Pablo "Pol" Amat Escudé, Pablo Usoz Ciriza, Antonio González Izquierdo
3. AUS—Stuart Carruthers, Baedon Choppy, Stephen Davies, Damon Diletti, Lachlan Dreher, Lachlan Elmer, Brendan Garard, Paul Gaudoin, Mark Hager, Paul Lewis, Grant Smith, Matthew Smith, Daniel Sproule, Jay Stacy, Kenneth Wark, Michael York
4. GER—Christoph Bechmann, Andreas Becker, Patrick Bellenbaum, Christian Blunck, Oliver Domke, Bjorn Emmerling, Carsten Fischer, Volker Fried, Michael Green, Michael Knauth, Christian Mayerhoefer, Sven Meinnhardt, Klaus Michler, Stefan Saliger, Jan Peter Tewes, Christopher Reitz
5. KOR—Cho Myung-jun, Han Beung-kook, Hong Kyung-suep, Jeon Jong-ha, Jeong Yong-kyun, Kang Keon-wook, Kim Jong-yi, Kim Yong-bae, Kim Yoon, Kim Young-kyu, Koo Jin-soo, Park Shin-heum, Shin Seok-kyo, Song Seung-tae, You Myung-keun, You Seung-jin
6. PAK—Mansoor Ahmed, Naveed Alam, Rana Mujahid Ali, Kamran Ashraf, Rahim Kahn, M. Danish Kaleem, Mohammad Khalid, Irfan Mahmood, Khalid Mahmood, Aleem Raza, Mohammad Sarwar, Malik Shafqat, Mohammad Shahbaz, Zaman Tahir, Mohammad Usman, Shahbaz Ahmed

7. GBR—Russell Garcia, Calum Giles, Daniel Hall, Julian Halls, Simon Hazlitt, Jason Laslett, David Luckes, Phillip McGuire, Simon Mason, Chris Mayer, John Shaw, Soma Singh, Kalbir Takher, Nicky Thompson, Jonathan Wyatt, Jason Lee
8. IND—Anil Alexander, Subbaiah Aljaparavanda, Baljit Singh Dhillon, Alloysius Edwards, Gavin Ferreira, Sanjeev Kumar, Mukesh Kumar Nandanoori, Dhanraj Pillay, Pargat Singh Powar, Mohamed Riaz, Baljeet Singh, Harpreet Singh, Rahul Singh, Ramandeep Singh, Dilip Tirkey, Sabu Varkey

The big surprise was the team from Spain, which opened the tournament with two unexpected wins: 1-0 over defending champion Germany and 3-0 over perennial power Pakistan. After placing first in pool A, Spain faced medal favorite Australia in the semifinals—and scored another upset, 2-1. Meanwhile, the Netherlands won pool B despite a 2-2 tie with Great Britain. The Dutch had a bleak history at this stage of Olympic tournaments, having qualified for the semifinals four times since 1972 and lost every time. This time they scored first against Germany and won 3-1. In the final Spain looked like they might continue their upset streak when Victor Pujol opened the scoring in the 45th minute. This seemed to shock the Dutch into action. Floris Jan Bovelander, playing in his 235th international match, tied the score from a penalty corner in the 52nd minute and then put the Netherlands ahead three minutes later with another penalty corner. Bram Lomans completed the scoring on yet another penalty corner shortly before time ran out.

In the bronze medal match, Australia, trailing Germany 2-1 with seven minutes to play, scored twice. The winning goal, struck by Baeden Choppy off a penalty corner with 79 seconds to play, deflected off Carsten Fischer and into the goal.

2000 Sydney T: 12, N: 12, D: 9.30.

	W	L	T	GF	GA
1. HOL	4	1	2	14	11
2. KOR	3	2	2	13	10
3. AUS	4	1	2	18	9
4. PAK	2	2	3	18	13
5. GER	4	1	2	17	8
6. GBR	2	3	2	10	21
7. IND	3	2	2	13	10
8. ARG	1	4	2	16	22

Final: HOL 3(5)-3(4) KOR
3rd Place: AUS 6-3 PAK
5th Place: GER 4-0 GBR
7th Place: IND 3-1 ARG

1. HOL—Jacques Brinkman, Jaap Derk Buma, Teun de Nooijer, Jeroen Delmee, Marten Eikelboom, Piet-Hein Geeris, Franciscus "Ronald" Jansen, Erik Jazet, Abraham "Bram" Lomans, Sander van der Weide, Wouter van Pelt, Diederik van Weel, Remco van Wijk, Stephan Veen, Guus Vogels, Pieter Windt
2. KOR—Han Hyung-bae, Hwang Jong-hyun, Jeon Hong-kwon, Jeon Jong-ha, Ji Seong-hwan, Kang Keon-wook, Kim Chel-hwan, Kim Jung-chul, Kim Kyung-seok, Kim Yong-bae, Kim Yoon, Lim Jong-chun, Lim Jung-woo, Seo Jong-ho, Song Seung-tae, Yeo Woon-kon
3. AUS—Michael Brennan, Adam Commens, Stephen Davies, Damon Diletti, Lachlan Dreher, Jason Duff, Troy Elder, James Elmer, Paul Gaudoin, Stephen Holt, Brent Livermore, Daniel Sproule, Jay Stacy, Craig Victory, Matthew Wells, Michael York
4. PAK—Sohail Abbas, Waseem Ahmad, Ahmad Alam, Muhammad Anis, Kamran Ashraf, Atif Bashir, Sameer Hussain, Tariq Imran, Kashif Javad, Mohammad Nadeem, Mohammed Qasim, Aleem Raza, Muhammad Sarwar, Mohammad Shafqat, Imran Yousaf, Irfan Yousaf
5. GER—Clemens Arnold, Christoph Bechmann, Philipp Crone, Oliver Domke, Christoph Eimer, Björn Emmerling, Michael Green, Florian Kunz, Christian Mayerhöfer, Björn Michel, Ulrich Moissl, Sascha Reinelt, Christopher Reitz, Christian Wein, Tibor Weißenborn, Matthias Witthaus
6. GBR—Tom Bertram, Guy Fordham, Brett Garrard, Calum Giles, David Hacker, Danny Hall, Julian Halls, Michael Johnson, David Luckes, Simon Mason, Craig Parnham, Mark Pearn, Ben Sharpe, Jimmy Wallis, Bill Waugh, Jonathan Wyatt
7. IND—Lajrus Barla, Samir Dad, Sukhbir Singh Gill, Ramandeep Singh, Jude Menezes, Riaz Nabi Mohammed, Mukesh Kumar Nandanoori, Dinesh Nayak, Dhanraj Pillay, Thirumal Valavan Selvaraj, Baljit Singh Saini, Gagan Ajit Singh, Deepak Thakur, Dilip Kumar Tirkey, Baljit Singh Dhillon
8. ARG—Mario Almada, Santiago Capurro, Mariano Chao, Juan Hourquebie, Jorge Lombi, Tomás MacCormik, Pablo Moreira, Germán Orozco, Fernando Oscaris, Ezequiel Paulón, Máximo Pellegrino, Carlos Retegui, Marco Riccardi, Matías Vila, Rodrigo Vila, Fernando Zylberberg

The Dutch team was heavily favored to defend their Olympic championship and they did pull it off, although it was just by the skin of their teeth. In pool play, they won only two of their five matches and were even held to a 0-0 draw by lowly Malaysia. When the Dutch were beaten 2-0 by Pakistan in their final qualifying match, it looked like they would finish third in their pool and fail to make it to the semifinals. But three hours later Great Britain upset European champion Germany and suddenly the disconsolate Dutch were back in the medal hunt. Their semifinal contest with Australia ended in a 0-0 tie and went to penalty shootout. The first nine players all converted their shots but then Dutch goalkeeper Ronald Jansen made a diving save of Brent Livermore's low flick and the home team was out and the Netherlands was on to the final. There they met South Korea, which had defeated Pakistan 1-0 in the semifinals. The Koreans shocked the Dutch when Song Seung-tae scored first, barely 8 minutes into the game. Eleven minutes later, Dutch captain Stephan Veen tied the score with a penalty stroke. Two minutes and twenty seconds into the second half, Veen put the Netherlands into the lead. With 7 minutes to play, Veen scored again and the game appeared to be settled. But the Koreans would not give up. Kim Kyung-seok scored from a penalty corner with 4 minutes 21 seconds left in regulation and, less than two minutes later, Korean captain Kang Keon-wook tied the score. Neither side scored in overtime and the game went to penalty shootout. Song Seung-tae, taking the third stroke, flicked wide left. When everyone else scored, the Netherlands ended up winning the championships after all.

2004 Athens T: 12, N: 12, D: 8.27.

	W	L	T	GF	GA
1. AUS	5	1	1	22	14
2. HOL	6	1	0	20	13
3. GER	4	1	2	21	12
4. SPA	3	2	2	20	13
5. PAK	5	2	0	26	10
6. NZL	4	3	0	19	18
7. IND	2	4	1	16	18
8. KOR	2	3	2	22	17

Final: AUS 2-1 HOL
3rd Place: GER 4-3 SPA
5th Place: PAK 4-2 NZL
7th Place: IND 5-2 KOR

1. AUS—Michael Brennan, Travis Brooks, Dean Butler, Liam de Young, Jamie Dwyer, Nathan Eglington, Troy Elder, Bevan George, Robert Hammond, Mark Hickman, Mark Knowles, Brent Livermore, Michael McCann, Stephen Mowlam, Grant Schubert, Matthew Wells
2. HOL—Matthijs Brouwer, Ronald Brouwer, Teun de Nooijer, Jeroen Delmée, Geert-Jan Derikx, Rob Derikx, Marten Eikelboom, Floris Evers, Erik Jazet, Karel Klaver, Jesse Mahieu, Rob Reckers, Taeke Taekema, Sander van der Weide, Klaas Veering, Guus Vogels
3. GER—Vogels Arnold, Christoph Bechmann, Sebastian Biederlack, Philipp Crone, Eike Duckwitz, Christoph Eimer, Björn Emmerling, Florian Kunz, Björn Michel, Sascha Reinelt, Justus Scharowsky, Christian Schulte, Tibor Weißenborn, Timo Wess, Matthias Witthaus, Christoph Zeller
4. SPA—Eduardo Aguilar Estrada, David Alegre Biosca, Ramón Alegre Biosca, Pablo "Pol" Amat Escudé, Javier Bruses Manresa, Juan Pablo Escarré Urueña, Alexandre Fábregas Carne, Francisco "Kiko" Fábregas Monegal, Santiago Freixa i Escudé, Rodrigo Garza Barbero, Bernardino Herrera Casanueva, Xavier Ribas Centelles, Albert Sala Moreno, Josep "Pep" Sánchez Galobardes, Víctor Manuel Sojo Jiménez, Eduard "Edi" Tubau Cutal
5. PAK—Sohail Abbas, Shakil Abbasi, Ahmed Alam, Wasim Ahmed, Salman Akbar, Ghazanfar Ali, Mudassar Ali Khan, Zeeshan Ashraf, Tariq Aziz, Rehan Butt, Dilawar Hussain, Kashif Jawwad, Adnan Maqsood, Muhammad Nadeem Ahmed, Shabbir Muhammad, Ali Raza
6. NZL—Gareth Brooks, Phillip Burrows, Dean Couzins, Dave Kosoof, Dion Gosling, Bevan Hari, Blair Hopping, Wayne McIndoe, James Nation, Umesh Parag, Mitesh Patel, Kyle Pontifex, Hayden Shaw, Darren Smith, Simon Towns, Paul Woolford
7. IND—Devesh Chauhan, Adnan D'Souza, Arjun Halappa, Dhanraj Pillay, Vikram Pillay, Viren Rasquinha, Adam Sinclair, Baljit Singh Dhillon, Gagan Ajit Singh, Harpal Singh, Prabhjot Singh, Sandeep Singh, Deepak Thakur Sonkhla, Dilip Kumar Tirkey, Ignace Tirkey, William Xalco
8. KOR—Ko Dong-sik, You Hyo-sik, Han Hyung-bae, Jeon Jong-ha, Seo Jong-ho, Jang Jong-hyun, Kim Jong-min, Kim Jung-chul, Lee Jung-seon, Lim Jung-woo, Kim Kyung-seok, Ji Seong-hwan, Kang Seong-jung, Song Seung-tae, Yeo Woon-kon, Kim Yong-bae

Spain and Germany led Group A, both winning three matches and drawing twice. In Group B, the two-time defending Olympic champions and 2002 and 2003 Champions Trophy winners, the Netherlands, dominated the round robin, winning every match. Their final pool contest was a 2-1 defeat of Australia, which finished second in the group to qualify for the semifinals. In the semifinals, the Netherlands beat Germany 3-2, and Michael McCann and Grant Schubert scored twice each to lead Australia to a 6-3 victory over Spain. The bronze medal match between Germany and Spain was tied 3-3 at the end of regulation. With five minutes left in overtime, Björn Michel, playing in his 333rd and final international match, scored a golden goal to win the match for Germany.

The gold medal match saw two penalty corners for each team in the first 15 minutes, none of which were successful. In the 29th minute, Matthijs Brouwer sent a pass to his cousin Ronald Brouwer, who sidestepped two defenders and Australian goalkeeper Stephen Mowlam to give the Netherlands a 1-0 lead. Three minutes into the second half, a rebound shot by Australian forward Travis Brooks evened the score, and regulation play ended with the score 1-1. Eight minutes into sudden death overtime, Australian striker Jamie Dwyer earned the winning goal, scored off of a penalty corner, to give Australia their first Olympic championship in men's field hockey. Dwyer was named World Hockey Player of the Year for 2004 by his fellow players from around the world.

There was one disappointed Australian in the stadium that night: former Australian coach Terry Walsh. Dropped by Australia following their bronze-medal finish in Sydney, he coached the Dutch team in Athens.

2008 Beijing T: 12, N: 12, D: 8.23.

	W	L	T	GF	GA
1. GER	5	0	2	14	7
2. SPA	5	2	0	12	8
3. AUS	4	1	2	32	12
4. HOL	4	2	1	19	13
5. GBR	3	1	2	15	9
6. KOR	2	3	1	15	16
7. NZL	3	2	1	14	11
8. PAK	2	4	0	13	17

Final: GER 1-0 SPA
3rd Place: AUS 6-2 HOL
5th Place: GBR 5-2 KOR
7th Place: NZL 4-2 PAK

1. GER—Sebastian Biederlack, Moritz Fürste, Tobias Hauke, Florian Keller, Oliver Korn, Niklas Meinert, Jan-Marco Montag, Max Müller, Juan Carlos Nevado, Max Weinhold, Tibor Weißenborn, Benjamin Weß, Timo Weß, Philip Witte, Matthias Witthaus, Christoph Zeller, Philipp Zeller
2. SPA—David Alegre Biosca, Ramón Alegre Biosca, Pablo "Pol" Amat Escudé, Eduard Arbós Borras, Francisco "Quico" Cortés Juncosa, Sergi Enrique Montserrat, Francisco "Kiko" Fábregas Monegal, Alexandre Fábregas i Carné, Juan Fernández La Villa, Santiago Freixa i Escudé, Rodrigo Garza Barbero, Xavier Ribas Centelles, Albert Sala Moreno, Víctor Manuel Sojo Jiménez, Eduard "Edi" Tubau Cutal

3. AUS—Des Abbott, Travis Brooks, Kiel Brown, Liam De Young, Luke Doerner, Jamie Dwyer, Bevan George, David Guest, Rob Hammond, Fergus Kavanagh, Mark Knowles, Stephen Lambert, Eli Matheson, Eddie Ockenden, Grant Schubert, Andrew Smith, Matthew Wells
4. HOL—Thomas Boerma, Ronald Brouwer, Matthijs Brouwer, Teun de Nooijer, Jeroen Delmeé, Geert-Jan Derikx, Rob Derikx, Laurence Docherty, Jeroen Hertzberger, Timme Hoyng, Rob Reckers, Taeke Taekema, Robert van der Horst, Sander van der Weide, Guus Vogels, Roderick Weusthof
5. GBR—Richard Alexander, Jon Bleby, Jonty Clarke, Matt Daly, Stephen Dick, Ben Hawes, Ashley Jackson, Glenn Kirkham, Rick Mantell, Simon Mantell, Ben Marsden, Alistair McGregor, Barry Middleton, Rob Moore, James Tindall, Alastair Wilson
6. KOR—Cha Jong-bok, Hong Eun-seong, Hyun Hye-sung, Jang Jong-hyeon, Kang Seong-jung, Kang Moon-kweon, Kim Chul, Kim Yong-bae, Kim Sam-seok, Kim Byung-hoon, Ko Dong-sik, Lee Nam-yong, Lee Myung-ho, Seo Jong-ho, Yeo Woon-kon, Yoon Sung-hoon, Yu Hyo-sik
7. NZL—Ryan Archibald, Gareth Brooks, Phillip Burrows, Simon Child, Benjamin Collier, Dean Couzins, Steven Edwards, Casey Henwood, Blair Hopping, Dave Kosoof, Shea McAleese, James Nation, Kyle Pontifex, Bradley Shaw, Hayden Shaw, Paul Woolford
8. PAK—Shakeel Abbasi, Nasir Ahmed, Waqar Akbar, Salman Akbar, Zeeshan Ashraf, Syed Abbas Haider Bilgrami, Rehan Butt, Muhammad Imran, Muhammad Javed, Adnan Maqsood, Muhammad Asif Rana, Shafqat Rasool, Muhammad Saqlain, Muhammad Waqas, Syed Imran Ali Warsi, Muhammad Zubair

Four years after the Athens Olympics, the favorites in the event remained largely unchanged. Each of the top four Athens finishers had won the prestigious Champions Trophy in the years leading up to Beijing: Spain in 2004, Australia in 2005, the Netherlands in 2006 and Germany in 2007. A little over a month before the Beijing Olympics, Australia won its ninth Champions title, beating Spain 4-1 in the final.

As expected, all four favorites made it through the round-robin stage. Australia won their first three matches by a combined score of 19-2 before tying the Netherlands 2-2 and Great Britain 3-3. Spain and Germany were drawn into the same group, with Germany winning their match 1-0.

The first semifinal match between Germany and the Netherlands was a tense affair, as neither team was able to score until the final four minutes of play. Holland's Timme Hoyng opened the scoring on a penalty corner, followed two minutes later by Germany's Philipp Zeller. After a scoreless 15-minute overtime the two teams went to penalty shoot-out, which ended 3-3. The match was finally decided by sudden-death penalties. Christopher Zeller scored first, giving Germany a 4-3 lead, and German goalkeeper Max Weinhold clinched the victory by stopping a shot by Dutch penalty corner specialist Taeke Taekema, who had scored 10 goals in the previous six games.

In the other semifinal, Australia scored in the first minute against Spain and were up 2-0 before Spain's Eduard Tubau scored twice in five minutes to tie the score. Santi Freixa put Spain ahead 3-2 on a penalty corner in the 68th minute to advance his team into the final.

After the intensity of the semifinal round, the final itself was less exciting. Zeller scored what would end up being the winning goal 16 minutes into the first half, and Germany spent the rest of the match warding off Spain's counterattacks. German striker Florian Keller joined his grandfather, father, brother and sister as an Olympic field hockey medalist.

The Beijing Games were the first Olympics in which former hockey powerhouse India failed to qualify.

WOMEN

1896–1976 not held

1980 Moscow T: 6, N: 6, D: 7.31.

	W	L	T	GF	GA
1. ZIM	3	0	2	13	4
2. CZE	3	1	1	10	5
3. SOV	3	2	0	11	5
4. IND	2	2	1	9	6
5. AUT	2	3	0	6	11
6. POL	0	5	0	0	18

1. ZIM—Sarah English, Ann Mary Grant, Brenda Phillips, Patricia McKillop, Sonia Robertson, Patricia Davies, Maureen George, Linda Watson, Susan Huggett, Gillian Cowley, Elizabeth Chase, Sandra Chick, Helen Volk, Christine Prinsloo, Arlene Boxhall, Anthea Stewart
2. CZE—Jarmila Kralicková, Berta Hruba, Iveta Sranková, Lenka Vymazalová, Jirina Krizová, Jirina Kadlecová, Jirina Čermaková, Marta Urbanová, Kveta Petricková, Marie Sykorová, Ida Hubacková, Milada Blazková, Jana Lahodová, Alena Kyselicová, Jirina Hajková, Viera Podhanyiová
3. SOV—Galina Inzhuvatova, Nelli Gorbyatkova, Valentina Zazdravnykh, Nadezhda Ovechkina, Natella Krasnikova, Natalya Bykova, Lidiya Glubokova, Galina Vyuzhanina, Natalya Buzunova, Lyailya Akhmerova, Nadezhda Filipova, Yelena Guryeva, Tatyana Yembakhtova,Tatyana Shvyganova, Alina Kham, Lyudmila Frolova
4. IND—Margaret Toscano, Sudha Chaudhry, Gangotri Bhandari, Rekha Mundphan, Rupa Kumari Saini, Varsha Soni, Eliza Nelson, Prem Maya Sonir, Naazleen Madraswalla, Selma D'Silva, Lorraine Fernandes, Harpreet Gill, Balwinder Kaur Bhatia, Geeta Sareen, Nisha Sharma, Hutoxi Bagli
5. AUT—Patricia Lorenz, Sabine Blemenschütz, Elisabeth Pistauer, Andrea Kozma, Brigitta Pecanka, Brigette Kindler, Friederike Stern, Regina Lorenz, Eleonore Pecanka, Ilse Stipanovsky, Andrea Porsch, Erika Csar, Dorit Ganster, Ulrike Kleinhansl, Eva Cambal, Jana Cejpek
6. POL—Malgorzata Gajewska, Bogumila Pajor, Jolanta Sekulak, Jolanta Blędowska, Lucyna Matuszna, Danuta Stanislawska, Wieslawa Rylko, Lidia Zgajewska, Maria Kornek, Malgorzata Lipska, Halina Koldras, Lucyna Siejka, Dorota Bielska, Dorota Zaleczna, Michalina Plekaniec, Jadwiga Koldras

When five of the six nations scheduled to compete in the inaugural women's field hockey tournament withdrew as part of the Jimmy Carter boycott, it set the stage for a true Cinderella story. As white-ruled Rhodesia,

Zimbabwe had been banned from the Olympics, but when the black majority took power, the ban was lifted. Desperate to fill the field, the Soviet Union and the International Olympic Committee contacted Zimbabwe five weeks before the start of the Games and offered to subsidize the sending of a team, the members of which were not selected until the weekend before the Olympics opened. Ironically, the team that represented Zimbabwe was all white. They were held to ties by Czechoslovakia and India, but they were the only team to avoid defeat. A 4-1 victory over Austria assured them of gold medals.

Sonia Robertson and Sandy Chick of the Zimbabwe team became the second set of identical twins ever to win Olympic gold medals – just four days after Bernd and Jörg Landvoigt won gold in the men's Pair-Oared Uncoxed Shell competition.

1984 Los Angeles-Monterey Park T: 6, N: 6, D: 8.10.

	W	L	T	GF	GA
1. HOL	4	0	1	14	6
2. GER	2	1	2	9	9
3. USA	2	2	1	9	7
4. AUS	2	2	1	9	7
5. CAN	2	2	1	9	11
6. NZL	0	5	0	2	12

1. HOL—Bernadette de Beus, Alette Pos, Margriet Zegers, Laurien Willemse, Marjolein Eijsvogel, Josephine Boekhorst, Carina Benninga, Alexandra le Poole, Francisca Hillen, Marieke van Doorm, Sophie von Weiler, Aletta van Manen, Irene Hendriks, Elisabeth Sevens, Martine Ohr, Anneloes Nieuwenhuizen
2. GER—Ursula Thielemann, Elke Drüll, Beate Deininger, Christina Moser, Hella Roth, Dagmar Breiken, Birgit Hagen, Birgit Hahn, Gabriele Appel, Andrea Lietz-Weiermann, Corinna Lingnau, Martina Koch, Gabriela Schley, Patricia Ott, Susanne Schmid, Sigrid Landgraf
3. USA—Gwen Cheeseman, Beth Anders, Kathleen McGahey, Anita Miller, Regina Buggy, Christine Larson-Mason, Beth Beglin, Marcella Place, Julie Staver, Diane Moyer, Sheryl Johnson, Charlene Morett, Karen Shelton, Brenda Stauffler, Leslie Milne, Judy Strong
4. AUS—Kym Ireland, Liane Tooth, Pamela Glossop, Susan Watkins, Lorraine Hillas, Robyn Leggatt, Sandra Pisani, Penny Gray, Robyn Holmes, Sharon Buchanan, Marian Aylmore, Colleen Pearce, Loretta Dorman, Julene Sunderland, Trisha Heberle, Evelyn Botfield
5. CAN—Laurie Lambert, Sharon Creelman, Jean Major, Laura Branchaud, Lynne Beecroft, Shelley Andrews, Darlene Stoyka, Phyllis Ellis, Karen Hewlett, Diane Virjee, Terry Wheatley, Lisa Bauer, Sheila Forshaw, Sharon Bayes, Zoe Mackinnon, Nancy Charlton
6. NZL—Lesley Murdoch, Barbara Tilden, Mary Clinton, Susan McLeish, Isobel Thomson, Sandra Mackie, Jillian Smith, Jane Goulding, Robyn Blackman, Jan Martin, Harina Kohere, Jennifer McDonald, Shirley Haig, Catherine Thompson, Lesley Elliott, Christine Arthur

The Australian women entered the final match of the round-robin tournament with a clear understanding of what they needed to accomplish. If they could beat the heavily favored Dutch team by two goals, they would earn gold medals. If they won by one goal or tied, they would finish second. If they lost by one goal they would win bronze medals, and if they lost by three goals, they would finish out of the money. The Dutch won 2-0, which meant that Australia and the US completed the tournament with identical records. Although the Australians had defeated the Americans 3-1, tournament rules stated that the bronze medals would be decided by a penalty stroke shoot-off, which took place 15 minutes after the last match. The US won easily, 10-5.

1988 Seoul T: 8, N: 8, D: 9.30.

	W	L	T	GF	GA
1. AUS	3	0	2	12	8
2. KOR	3	1	1	13	9
3. HOL	4	1	0	14	6
4. GBR	1	3	1	5	11
5. GER	3	2	0	9	9
6. CAN	1	3	1	8	11
7. ARG	2	3	0	6	7
8. USA	0	4	1	6	12

Final: AUS 2-0 KOR
3rd Place: HOL 3-1 GBR
5th Place: GER 4-2 CAN
7th Place: ARG 3-1 USA

1. AUS—Kathleen Partridge, Elspeth Clement, Liane Tooth, Loretta Dorman, Lorraine Hillas, Michelle Capes, Sandra Pisani, Deborah Bowman, Lee Capes, Kim Small, Sally Carbon, Jacqueline Pereira, Tracey Belbin, Rechelle Hawkes, Sharon Patmore, Maree Fish
2. KOR—Kim Mi-sun, Han Ok-kyung, Chang Eun-jung, Han Keum-sil, Choi Choon-ok, Kim Soon-duk, Chung Sang-hyun, Jin Won-sim, Hwang Keum-sook, Cho Ki-hyang, Seo Kwang-mi, Park Soon-ja, Kim Young-sook, Seo Hyo-sun, Lim Kye-sook, Chung Eun-kyung
3. HOL—Bernadette de Beus, Yvonne Buter, Willemien Aardenburg, Laurien Willemse, Marjolein Bolhuis-Eijsvogel, Elisabeth "Lisanne" Lejeune, Carina Benninga, Annemieke Fokke, Ingrid Wolff, Marieke van Doorn, Sophie von Weiler, Aletta van Manen, Eleoner "Noor" Holsboer, Helen van der Ben, Martine Ohr, Anneloes Nieuwenhuizen
4. GBR—Jillian Atkins, Wendy Banks, Gillian Brown, Karen Brown, Mary Nevill, Julie Cook, Victoria Dixon, Wendy Fraser, Barbara Hambly, Caroline Jordan, Violet McBride, Moira Macleod, Caroline Brewer, Jane Sixsmith, Kate Parker, Alison Ramsey
5. GER—Susanne Schmid, Carola Hoffmann, Heike Gehrmann, Dagmar Bremer, Gabriele Uhlenbruck, Viola Grahl, Bettina Blumenberg, Gabriele Appel, Martina Hallmen, Christine Ferneck, Silke Wehrmeister, Caren Jungjohann, Eva Hegener, Susanne Wollschläger, Gabriela Schowe
6. CAN—Sharon Bayes, Wendy Baker, Deb Covey, Lisa Lyn, Laura Branchaud, Sandra Levy, Kathryn Johnson, Shona Schleppe, Michelle Conn, Liz Czenczek Sheila Forshaw, Nancy Charlton, Sara Ballantyne, Sharon Creelman
7. ARG—Laura Mulhall, Cecilia Colombo, Marisa López, Alejandra Tucat, Victoria Carbó, Fabiana Ricchezza, Gabriela Liz, Gabriela Sánchez, Moira Brinnand, Marcela Hussey, Alejandra Palma, Verónica Bengochea, Andrea Alina Vergara, Gabriela Pazos, Andrea Fioroni
8. USA—Patricia Shea, Yolanda Hightower, Mary Koboldt, Marcia Pankratz, Cheryl Van Kuren, Diane Bracalente, Elizabeth Beglin, Marcell Von Schottenstein, Sandra Vander-Heyden, Tracey Fuchs, Sheryl Johnson, Sandra Costigan, Christy Morgan, Barbara Marois, Megan Donnelly, Donna Lee

When Australia defeated the Netherlands 3-2 in the semifinals, it marked the first time in 8 years that the

Dutch had failed to reach the final of an international tournament. Australia and South Korea played an exciting 5-5 draw to close the preliminary round. Australia tightened its defense for the final and successfully choked off the fast-paced offense of the Korean "Red Bees." Five minutes into the second half, Australian captain Debbie Bowman scored on a penalty stroke. Lee Capes added an insurance goal in the 58th minute.

1992 Barcelona-Terrassa T: 8, N: 8, D: 8.7.

	W	L	T	GF	GA
1. SPA	4	0	1	9	5
2. GER	3	1	1	10	5
3. GBR	3	2	0	12	10
4. KOR	2	3	0	12	9
5. AUS	3	2	0	9	3
6. HOL	3	2	0	6	5
7. CAN	1	4	0	3	10
8. NZL	0	5	0	3	17

Final: SPA 2-1 GER
3rd Place: GBR 4-3 KOR
5th Place: AUS 2-0 HOL
7th Place: CAN 2-0 NZL

1. SPA—María González Laguillo, Natalia Dorado Gómez, Virginia Ramírez Merino, María del Carmen Barea Cobos, Silvia Manrique Pérez, Nagore Gabellanes Marieta, María Rodríguez Suárez, Sonia Barrio Gutiérrez, Elisabeth Maragall Verge, Teresa Motos Iceta, Maider Tellería Goñi, Mercedes Coghen Alberdingk, Nuria Olivé Vancells, Ana Maiques Dern, María Martínez de Murguía
2. GER—Susanne Wollschläger, Bianca Weiss, Tanja Dickenscheid, Susanne Müller, Nadine Ernsting-Krienke, Simone Thomaschinski, Irma Kuhnt, Anke Wild, Franziska Hentschel, Kristina Peters, Eva Hagenbäumer, Britta Becker, Caren Jungjohann, Christine Ferneck, Heike Lätzsch, Katrin Kauschke
3. GBR—Joanne Thompson, Helen Morgan, Lisa Bayliss, Karen Brown, Mary Nevill, Gillian Atkins, Vickey Dixon, Wendy Fraser, Sandra Lister, Jane Sixsmith, Alison Ramsay, Jackie McWilliams, Tammy Miller, Mandy Nicholls, Kathryn Johnson, Susan Fraser
4. KOR—You Jae-sook, Han Gum-shil, Chang Eun-jung, Lee Seon-young, Lee Kui-joo, Son Jeong-im, Ro Young-mi, Kim Kyung-ae, Lee Eun-kyung, Jang Dong- sook, Kwon Chang-sook, Yang Hea-sook, Lee Kyoung-hei, Koo Mun-young, Lim Gae-sook, Jin Deok-sah
5. AUS—Kathleen Partridge, Christine Dobson, Liane Tooth, Alyson Annan, Juliet Haslam, Michelle Hager, Alison Peek, Lisa Powell, Lisa Naughton, Katie Starre, Sally Carbon-Bell, Jacqueline Pereira, Tracey Belbin, Rechelle Hawkes, Sharon Buchanan, Deborah Sullivan [Bowman]
6. HOL—Jacqueline Toxopeus, Carina Bleeker, Caroline van Nieuwenhuyze-Leenders, Annemieke Fokke, Cécile Vinke, Jeannette Lewin, Carina Benninga, Daniëlle Koenen, Ingrid Wolff, Mieketine Wouters, Martine Ohr, Florentine Steenberghe, Eleonor "Noor" Holsboer, Helen Lejeune-van de Ben, Wietske de Ruiter, Carole Thate
7. CAN—Deborah Whitten, Deb Covey, Rochelle Low, Tara Croxford, Sandra Levy, Sue Reid, Heather Jones, Candy Thomson, Bernadette Bowyer, Michelle Conn, Laurelee Kopeck, Joel Brough, Milena Gaiga, Sherri Field, Sharon Creelman
8. NZL—Elaine Jensen, Mary Clinton, Tina Bell, Christine Arthur, Shane Collins, Sapphire Cooper, Kylie Foy, Sue Duggan, Susan Furmage, Trudy Kilkolly, Anna Lawrence, Kieren O'Grady, Amanda Smith, Robyn Toomey, Kate Trolove

The victory of the Spanish women's field hockey team was one of the least likely of the Barcelona Games. Spain had no tradition to speak of in the sport and, although they had performed credibly in recent years, they were basically a fifth-place team. But they took advantage of their status as the host country by training continuously on the Olympic pitches at Terrassa for over five months prior to the Games. In pool play they came from behind to tie Germany 2-2, beat Canada 2-1, and then qualified for the semifinals by shocking the defending champions, Australia, 1-0 on a fourth-minute penalty corner by Silvia Manrique. In the semis they defeated South Korea when María Barea converted a penalty corner with two minutes left in overtime. The final was a rematch with Germany. Spain scored first as Barea smashed in a penalty corner in the eighth minute. High-scoring Franziska Hentschel evened the match four minutes later, but there were no more goals during regulation play. Thirteen minutes into overtime, Eli Maragall, the niece of the president of the Barcelona Olympic Organizing Committee, made a spectacular dive to deflect the ball into the net and earn the Spanish team its unexpected championship.

1996 Atlanta T: 8, N: 8, D: 8.1.

	W	L	T	GF	GA
1. AUS	7	0	1	27	5
2. KOR	4	2	2	19	12
3. HOL	3	3	2	15	15
4. GBR	4	2	2	12	11
5. USA	2	3	2	8	11
6. GER	2	4	1	10	11
7. ARG	2	4	1	7	21
8. SPA	0	6	1	5	17

Final: AUS 3-1 KOR
3rd Place: HOL 0(4)-0(3) GBR

1. AUS—Michelle Andrews, Alyson Annan, Louise Dobson, Renita Farrell, Juliet Haslam, Rechelle Hawkes, Clover Maitland, Karen Marsden, Jenny Morris, Jackie Pereira, Nova Peris-Kneebone, Katrina Powell, Lisa Powell, Danielle Roche, Kate Starre, Liane Tooth
2. KOR—Chang Eun-jung, Cho Eun-jung, Choi Eun-kyung, Choi Mi-soon, Jeon Young-sun, Jin Deok-san, Kim Myong-ok, Kwon Soo-hyun, Kwon Chang-sook, Lee Eun-kyung, Lee Eun-young, Lee Ji-young, Lim Jeong-sook, Oh Seung-shin, Woo Hyun-jung, You Jae-sook
3. HOL—Stella de Heij, Wietske de Ruiter, Fleur van de Kieft, Dillianne van den Boogaard, Suzan van der Wielen, Wilhelmina "Mijntje" Donners, Willemijn Duyster, Eleonoor Holsboer, Nicole Koolen, Ellen Kuipers, Jeannette Lewin, Suzanne Plesman, Florentine Steenberghe, Margje Teeuwen, Carole Thate, Jacqueline Toxopeus
4. GBR—Gillian Atkins, Anna Bennett, Karen Brown, Christine Cook, Christina Cullen, Mandy Davies, Susan Fraser, Kathryn Johnson, Tammy Miller, Joanne Mould, Mandy Nicholls, Pauline Robertson, Hilary Rose, Rhona Simpson, Jane Sixsmith, Joanne Thompson
5. USA—Pamela Bustin, Kristen Fillat, Tracey Fuchs, Laurel Martin, Kelli James, Katie Kauffman, Antoinette Lucas, Leslie Lyness, Diane Madl, Barbara Marois, Marcia Pankratz, Jill Reeve, Patricia Shea, Elizabeth Tchou, Cindy Werley, Andrea Wieland
6. GER—Vanessa van Kooperen-Schmoranzer, Britta Becker, Brigit Beyer, Melanie Cremer, Tanja Dickenscheid, Nadine Ernsting-Krienke, Eva Hagenbäumer, Franziska Hentschel, Katrin Kauschke, Irina Kuhnt, Heike Lätzsch, Kristina Peters, Philippa Suxdorf, Simone Thomaschinski, Susanne Wollschlager

7. ARG—María Magdalena Aicega Amicarelli, Mariana Arnal, Verónica Artica, Julieta Castellán, María Paula Castelli, Anabel Gambero Erdozain, Mariana González Oliva Gulla, Sofía Mackenzie, Karina Masotta, Vanina Oneto, Gabriela Pando, Jorgelina Rimoldi Puig, María Cecilia Rognoni, Gabriela Sánchez Grossi, Ayelén Stepnik, Silvina Corvalán Mayoral
8. SPA—Elena Carrión de la Lastra, Natalia Dorado Gómez, María Cruz González Alvarez, María del Carmen Barea Cobos, Silvia Manrique Pérez, Nagore Gabellanes Marieta, Teresa Motos Iceta, Sonia Barrio Gutiérrez, Mónica Rueda Guardeño, María del Mar Feito Acebo, Maider Tellería Goñi, Elena Urquízu Sáez, Lucía López Martínez, Begoña Larzabal Fernández, Sonia de Ignacio-Simó Casas, María Victoria González Laguillo

Australia and South Korea tied 3-3 in pool play before meeting again in the final. The Australians entered the championship match with a 38-game unbeaten streak. Alyson Annan put Australia ahead in the fourteenth minute with the game's first penalty corner, but Chang Eun-jung tied it before the end of the first half. Australia regained the lead at 43:31 on an Annan penalty stroke and Katrina Powell made it 3-1 with seven minutes to go.

Australian defender Nova Peris-Kneebone was the first Aborigine to earn an Olympic gold medal. Peris-Kneebone, who was also part Filipino and part Danish, was the first Australian mother to win an Olympic championship since Shirley Strickland de la Hunty forty years earlier. After the Atlanta Games, Peris-Kneebone switched to sprinting and won a gold medal at 200 meters at the 1998 Commonwealth Games.

2000 Sydney T: 10, N: 10, D: 9.29.

	W	L	T	GF	GA
1. AUS	7	0	1	25	5
2. ARG	5	3	0	18	12
3. HOL	3	3	2	14	18
4. SPA	1	3	4	5	9
5. CHN	2	4	1	6	12
6. NZL	2	3	2	10	17
7. GER	3	1	2	11	8
8. GBR	2	3	1	8	9

Final: AUS 3-1 ARG
3rd Place: HOL 2-0 SPA

1. AUS—Kate Allen, Alyson Annan, Lisa Carruthers Powell, Renita Farrell-Garard, Juliet Haslam, Rechelle Hawkes, Nikki Hudson, Rachel Imison, Clover Maitland, Claire Mitchell-Taverner, Jenny Morris, Alison Peek, Katrina Powell, Angie Skirving, Kate Starre, Julie Towers
2. ARG—María Magdalena Aicega Amicarelli, Mariela Andrea Antoniska, Inés Arrondo, Luciana "Lucha" Aymar, María Paz Ferrari, Anabel Gambero Erdozain, Agustina "Sole" García, María de la Paz Hernández, Laura Maiztegui, María de la Paz "Maripi" Hernández Margalot, María Mercedes "Mechi" Margalot, Karina Masotta, Vanina Oneto, Jorgelina Rimoldi Puig, María Cecilia Rognoni, Ayelén Stepnik, Paola Vukojicic
3. HOL—Minke Booij, Ageeth Boomgaardt, Julie Deiters, Wilhemina "Mijntje" Donners, Fátima Moreira de Melo, Suzan van der Wielen, Clarinda Sinnige, Hanneke Smabers, Minke Smabers, Margje Teeuwen, Carole Thate, Daphne Touw, Fleur van de Kieft, Dillianne van den Boogaard, Macha van der Vaart, Myrna Veenstra
4. SPA—María del Carmen Barea Cobos, Sonia Barrio Gutierrez, Nuria Camón Farell, Elena Carrion de la Lastra, Sonia de Ignacio-Simó Casas, María del Mar Feito Acebo, Erdoitza Goikoetxea Zornoza, Amanda González Gutiérrez, Begoña Larzabal Fernández, Lucia López Martínez, Carmen Martín González, Nuria Moreno de Pedrón, Silvia Muñoz Escudé, Cibeles Romero Misioner, Maider Telleria Goñi, Elena Urquizu Sáez
5. CHN—Xuemei Cai, Zhaoxia Chen, Hui Cheng, Xiaolan Hou, Junxia Huang, Lijie Liu, Fengyu Long, Yali Nie, Lihong Shen, Chunling Tang, Jiuyan Wang, Hongbing Yang, Huiping Yang, Yali Yu, Wanfeng Zhou
6. NZL—Tina Bell-Kake, Sandy Bennett, Helen Clarke, Jenny Duck, Kylie Foy, Skippy Hamahona, Anne-Marie Irving, Anna Lawrence, Caryn Paewai, Suzie Pearce, Rachel Petie, Moira Senior, Mandy Smith, Kate Trolove, Michelle Turner, Diana Weavers
7. GER—Friederike Barth, Britta Becker, Birgit Beyer, Caroline Casaretto, Tanja Dickenscheid, Nadine Ernsting-Krienke, Simone Gräßer, Franziska Gude, Katrin Kauschke, Natascha Keller, Denise Klecker, Heike Lätzsch, Inga Möller, Fanny Rinne, Marion Rodewald, Julia Zwehl
8. GBR—Kirsty Bowden, Melanie Clewlow, Christina Cullen, Fiona Greenham, Kath Johnson, Denise Marston-Smith, Mandy Nicholson, Carolyn Reid, Helen Richardson, Hilary Rose, Rhona Simpson, Jane Sixsmith, Jane Smith, Pauline Stott, Kate Walsh, Lucilla Wright

The Australian Hockyroos had won every major tournament since the 1992 Olympics, except the Champions Trophy in June 2000, during which coach Ric Charlesworth benched senior players during critical matches. The Australians got off to a sluggish start at the 2000 Olympics, defeating Great Britain 2-1 in a match that ended with both sides yelling at the umpires, and being held to a 1-1 tie by Spain. But then Australia shifted gears and it was all over for the rest of the world. They beat Argentina 3-1 and South Korea 3-0 to advance to the medal pool, where they defeated a stubborn New Zealand squad 3-0 and then blew away the Netherlands 5-0 and China 5-1. The final was more of the same: a repeat 3-1 victory over Argentina.

2004 Athens T: 10, N: 10, D: 8.26.

	W	L	T	GF	GA
1. GER	4	2	0	8	11
2. HOL	5	1	0	17	9
3. ARG	4	2	0	15	6
4. CHN	4	2	0	11	3
5. AUS	3	2	1	12	6
6. NZL	2	4	0	6	14
7. KOR	2	3	1	14	12
8. JPN	2	4	0	7	13

Final: GER 2-1 HOL
3rd Place: ARG 1-0 CHN
5th Place: AUS 3-0 NZL
7th Place: KOR 3-1 JPN

1. GER—Tina Bachmann, Caroline Casaretto, Nadine Ernsting-Krienke, Franziska Gude, Mandy Haase, Natascha Keller, Denise Klecker, Anke Kühn, Badri Latif, Heike Lätzsch, Sonja Lehmann, Silke Müller, Fanny Rinne, Marion Rodewald, Louisa Walter, Julia Zwehl

2. HOL—Minke Booij, Ageeth Boomgaardt, Chantal de Bruijn, Lisanne de Roever, Wilhemina "Mijntje" Donners, Sylvia Karres, Fatima Moreira de Melo, Eefke Mulder, Maartje Scheepstra, Janneke Schopman, Clarinda Sinnige, Minke Smabers, Jiske Snoeks, Macha van der Vaart, Miek van Geenhuizen, Lieve van Kessel
3. ARG—María Magdalena Aicega Amicarelli, Mariela Andrea Antoniska, Inés Arrondo, Luciana "Lucha" Aymar, Claudia Burkart, Marina Di Giacomo, Agustina "Sole" García, Mariana González Oliva Gulla, Alejandra Gulla, Mariné Russo, María de la Paz "Maripi" Hernández Margalot, María Mercedes "Mechi" Margalot, Vanina Oneto, María Cecilia Rognoni, Ayelén Stepnik, Paola Vukojicic
4. CHN—Chen Qiuqi, Chen Qunqing, Chen Zhaoxia, Cheng Hui, Fu Baorong, Gao Lihua, Hou Xiaolan, Huang Junxia, Li Shuang, Ma Yibo, Mai Shaoyan, Nie Yali, Qiu Yingling, Tang Chunling, Zhang Yimeng, Zhou Wanfeng
5. AUS—Katie Allen, Jessica Arrold, Carmel Bakurski, Toni Cronk, Louise Dobson, Suzie Faulkner, Peta Gallagher, Emily Halliday, Nikki Hudson, Rachel Imison, Bianca Netzler, Katrina Powell, Angie Skirving, Karen Smith, Julie Towers, Melanie Twitt
6. NZL—Stacey Carr, Helen Clarke, Tara Drysdale, Lizzy Igasan, Leisen Jobe, Beth Jurgeleit, Suzie Pearce-Muirhead, Emily Naylor, Meredith Orr, Jaimee Provan, Niniwa Roberts-Lang, Rachel Robertson, Kayla Sharland, Rachel Sutherland, Lisa Walton, Diana Weavers
7. KOR—Park Eun-kyung, Yoo Hee-joo, Park Jeong-sook, Lee Jin-hee, Kim Jin-kyoung, Kim Jung-a, Lim Ju-young, Oh Ko-woon, Ko Kwang-min, Park Mi-hyun, Kim Mi-seong, Lee Mi-seong, Kim Seong-eun, Lee Seon-ok, Park Yong-sook, Kim Yun-mi
8. JPN—Kaori Chiba, Rika Ishida, Sachimi Iwao, Akemi Kato, Chie Kimura, Akiko Kitada, Rika Komazawa, Tomomi Komori, Keiko Miura, Nami Miyazaki, Sakae Morimoto, Miyuki Nakagawa, Naoko Saito, Emi Sakurai, Rie Terazono, Yukari Yamamoto

The Germans were not expected to be serious contenders, as it appeared that four teams would battle for the medals: defending gold and silver medal winners Australia and Argentina, China and the Netherlands. China and the Netherlands did dominate their pools, both winning all four matches. China earned a 3-2 victory over Argentina, while Netherlands defeated Australia 1-0 to knock them out of the semifinals. Germany, meanwhile, opened with a 2-1 upset of Australia, but were then thrashed by Netherlands 4-1 and by South Africa 3-0. However, in their final match they edged South Korea 3-2 to unexpectedly squeak through to the semis.

Both semi-final matches were decided by penalty shootouts. In the first, Argentina trailed the Dutch 2-1 with less than three minutes to play, when María Magdalena Aicega scored a disputed goal from a penalty corner to send the match into overtime. When neither team scored again, Netherlands won the penalty shoot-out 4-2 after goalkeeper Clarinda Sinnige saved two penalty strokes. The match between China and Germany was scoreless through regulation time and two extra periods, as China failed to convert five penalty corners in the second half and another five in the first overtime period. Germany won the shoot-out 4-3 to register their second upset of the tournament. Argentina won the bronze medal match when Luciana Paula Aymar scored the only goal of the contest in the final minute of regulation time.

In the final, Anke Kühn opened the scoring on Germany's first penalty corner with a shot to the bottom right of the net at the 4:46 mark. In the twentieth minute, midfielder Franziska Gude gave Germany a 2-0 lead with a reverse hit during a scramble in front of the goal. The Netherlands failed to convert three penalty corners before the half and continued to trail by two until three minutes into the second half, when Maartje Scheepstra deflected into the goal a shot by captain Mijntje Donners. Despite their best efforts, the Dutch women were unable to score again, and Germany held on for the surprising win. The German team was the first in history to win an Olympic field hockey tournament despite being cumulatively outscored by their opponents.

2008 Beijing T: 12, N: 12, D: 8.22.

	W	L	T	GF	GA
1. HOL	7	0	0	21	5
2. CHN	4	2	1	17	8
3. ARG	4	1	2	18	13
4. GER	4	3	0	15	14
5. AUS	4	1	1	19	9
6. GBR	2	2	2	7	11
7. SPA	3	3	0	7	14
8. USA	1	2	3	11	11

Final: HOL 2-0 CHN
3rd Place: ARG 3-1 GER
5th Place: AUS 2-0 GBR
7th Place: SPA 3-2 USA

1. HOL—Marilyn Agliotti, Minke Booij, Eva de Goede, Lisanne de Roever, Wieke Dijkstra, Maartje Goderie, Ellen Hoog, Fátima Moreira de Melo, Eefke Mulder, Maartje Paumen, Sophie Polkamp, Janneke Schopman, Minke Smabers, Naomi van As, Miek van Geenhuizen, Lidewij Welten
2. CHN—Chen Zhaoxia, Chen Qiuqi, Cheng Hui, Fu Baorong, Gao Lihua, Huang Junxia, Li Shuang, Li Hongxia, Ma Yibo, Pan Fengzhen, Ren Ye, Song Qingling, Tang Chunling, Zhang Yimeng, Zhao Yudiao, Zhou Wanfeng
3. ARG—Magdalena Aicega Amicarelli, Luciana "Lucha" Aymar, María Noel Barrionuevo, Claudia Burkart, Agustina "Sole" García, Mariana González Oliva Gulla, Alejandra Gulla, María de la Paz "Maripi" Hernández Margalot, Giselle "Gisi" Kañevsky, Rosario Luchetti, María "Mechi" Margalot, Carla Rebecchi, Mariana Rossi, Mariné Russo, María Belén Succi, Paola Vukojicic
4. GER—Tina Bachmann, Janine Beermann, Pia Eidmann, Mandy Haase, Martina Heinlein, Eileen Hoffmann, Natascha Keller, Anke Kühn, Julia Müller, Janne Müller-Wieland, Kristina Reynolds, Fanny Rinne, Marion Rodewald, Katharina Scholz, Christina Schütze, Maike Stöckel
5. AUS—Jessica "Nic" Arnold, Teneal Attard, Madonna Blyth, Casey Eastham, Emily Halliday, Kate Hollywood, Nicole "Nikki "Hudson, Rachel Imison, Angela Lambert (Skirving), Shelly Liddelow, Kobie McGurk, Hope Munro, Megan Rivers, Kim Walker, Melanie Twitt (Wells), Sarah Young
6. GBR—Laura Bartlett, Jennie Bimson, Mel Clewlow, Charlotte Craddock, Chay Cullen, Alex Danson, Joanne Ellis, Joanne "Jo" Ellis, Michelle Ann Panter, Helen Richardson, Chloe Rogers,

Elizabeth Storry, Sarah Thomas, Rachel Walker, Kathrin Walsh, Lisa Wooding, Lucilla Wright

7. SPA—Silvia Bonastre Peremateu, Nuria Camón Farell, Gloria Comerma Broto, Montserrat "Montse" Cruz Funes, Marta Ejarque Guillamat, Raquel Huertas Soler, María López de Eguilaz Zubiria, Barbara Malda Salinas, Julia Menéndez Ortega, Silvia Muñoz Escudé, Georgina Oliva Isern, María Romagosa Romagosa, María Jesús Rosa Durán, Pilar Sánchez Cervi, Esther Termens Cañabate, Rocío Ybarra Solaun
8. USA—Kate Barber, Kayla Bashore, Lauren Crandall, Rachel Dawson, Kelly Doton, Katelyn Falgowski, Jesse Gey, Carrie Lingo, Angela Loy, Caroline Nichols, Lauren Powley, Dina Rizzo, Dana Sensenig, Keli Smith, Tiffany Snow, Amy Tran

The top five finishers in Athens—Germany, the Netherlands, Argentina, China and Australia—were the only teams to have reached the semifinals in a World Cup or Champions Trophy in the years leading up to the Beijing Olympics.

Of the five, the Netherlands seemed to have the best chance at the gold. Three months after losing to Germany in Athens 2-1, they beat their rivals 2-0 to win the 2004 Champions Trophy. They went on to win the 2005 Trophy and 2006 World Cup, defeating Australia both times, as well at the 2007 Trophy, beating Argentina. Germany won the Trophy in 2007 over China 3-2 in the final. Three months before the Olympics, Argentina, led by Luciana Aymar, crushed Germany 6-2 to win the 2008 Trophy.

The run-up to the Olympics was also marked by an odd controversy, when two members of the Spanish team failed doping tests after winning a qualifying match against Azerbaijan in Baku four months before the Olympics. The Spanish team appealed the test, saying that they believed their food or air-conditioning system had been tampered with. The International Hockey Federation decided not to impose any sanctions, and Azerbaijan lost an appeal to the Court of Arbitration of Sport.

The Dutch lived up to expectations, winning all five of their round-robin matches by a combined score of 14-3. The second qualifer from the group was decided in the final match between China and Australia. Australia fought back from a 2-0 deficit to tie the game 2-2, but China advanced on goal differential.

Germany led the second round-robin group despite a painful 4-0 loss to Argentina, which qualified second after tying its first two matches against the US and Great Britain.

China faced Germany in the first semifinal match, and held them to a 1-1 tie at the half. Germany scored in the first minute of the second half, but China answered three minutes later with a penalty corner to tie the game and then took the lead with twelve minutes left in regulation. Germany had a chance to take the game to overtime with a late penalty but were unable to convert.

Holland trounced Argentina in the other semifinal, taking a 4-0 lead on a hat trick by Maartje Paumen and a goal by Marilyn Agliotti before Argentina closed the gap for a final score of 5-3.

The Netherlands dominated the final, but China's goalkeeper Zhang Yimeng managed several spectacular saves to keep the game scoreless through the first half. The Dutch finally got on the scoreboard via a penalty corner by Naomi van As in the 51st minute and clinched the victory with a second goal by Lidewij Welten in the 62nd minute.

Chapter 13 **Football (Soccer)**

Football, also known as soccer, is played on a field 105 meters (114 yards, 2 feet, 5 inches) long and 68 meters (74 yards, 1 foot, 1 inch) wide. The goals are 8 feet (2.44 meters) high and 24 feet (7.32 meters) wide. Olympic matches must be played on natural turf. There are 11 players on each team including a goalie. Only two substitutions are allowed per match or three if the goalie is one of the players replaced. Substituted players may not return. The object of football is to move the ball down the field by dribbling and passing and to kick or head the ball into the goal. The ball must cross the goal line completely for a score to be counted. Except for the throw-ins after the ball goes out of bounds, only the goalie may touch the ball with his hands or arms and even the goalie may use his hands only within the penalty area, which extends 16.47 meters (18 yards) in front of the goal and is 40 meters (44 yards) wide. In addition, the goalie may not use his hands if the ball is *kicked* back to him by one of his teammates, although he may use his hands if it is *headed* back.

A player is considered offside if he is in the opponent's half of the field with less than two opposing players (including the goalie) between him and the goal at the time that the ball is kicked or headed. However, the referee may choose not to penalize a player for being offside if he believes that the player has not gained an advantage by being offside. This subjective distinction leads to endless arguments and protests. The offside infraction results in an indirect kick for the opposing team. A goal may not be scored on an indirect kick. A direct kick, which can result in a goal, is awarded for such fouls as tripping, holding, or kicking an opponent, charging an opponent from behind in a dangerous manner, or touching the ball with the hand or arm. When direct kick fouls occur within the penalty area, a penalty kick is awarded. The ball is placed 11 meters (36 feet 1 inch) in front of the net and a player is given a free shot against the goalie, who may not move his feet until the ball is kicked. When the ball crosses the endline after being touched last by a defending player the attacking team is awarded a corner kick. If a player commits a serious foul, he is shown a yellow card. A player who earns two yellow cards in the same match in ejected and may not be replaced. A player who commits a really serious foul, such as tackling from behind, intentionally using his hand to stop a ball entering the goal, spitting, or acting violently, is shown a red card and is immediately ejected.

Football matches consist of two 45-minutes halves. If play is suspended because of injury, the time lost is added to the end of each half. In the qualifying round of pool play, ties are allowed to stand. In the elimination rounds, if the score is tied after 90 minutes, a 30-minute overtime period, divided into two halves, is played. However, Olympic rules actually provide for sudden-death overtime. The first team to score in overtime is declared the winner. If the score is still tied after 120 minutes of play, the match is decided by a penalty shoot-out, five against five. If the shoot-out is tied, each team shoots once until the tie is broken.

Football is the most widely played sport in the world, and Olympic football has had trouble dealing with the immense popularity of the professional leagues. The growth of professional football after World War II meant that the best players were not eligible to compete in the Olympics—unless they lived in Communist countries. Beginning in 1952, Olympic tournaments featured the best players from the Communist nations defeating amateurs from the real football powers of Western Europe and South America. In 1984 some professional players were allowed to take part in the Olympics, but for European and South American teams, it was only those professionals who had not yet played in the World Cup—the quadrennial championship of soccer. In 1992, all professionals were considered eligible, provided they were less than 23 years old. Since 1996, for the Olympic tournament itself, each qualifying team may add to its squad three professionals regardless of age.

In 2012, the men's tournament will feature sixteen teams and the women's tournament twelve teams. The host nation qualifies automatically. The remaining teams are determined through regional tournaments. Olympic competition begins with pool play. The top teams qualify for a direct elimination tournament.

MEN

1896 not held

1900 Paris T: 3, N: 3, D: 9.23.

	W	L	GF	GA
1. GBR	1	0	4	0
2. FRA	1	1	6	6
3. BEL& GBR	0	1	2	6

1. GBR—Upton Park Football Club: J.H. Jones, C. Percy Buckenham, William Gosling, Alfred Chalk, J.E. Barridge, William Quash, Arthur Turner, F.G. Spackman, J. Nicholas, James Zealley, A. Haslam
2. FRA—Union des sociétés françaises de sports athlétiques: Lucien Huteau, Louis Bach, Pierre Allemane, Virgile Gaillard, Alfred Bloch, Maurice Macaire, Eugène Fraysse, Georges Garnier, Marcel Lambert, Grandjean, Fernand Canelle, Duparc, Gaston Peltier
3. BEL&GBR—University of Brussels: Marcel Leboutte, R. Kelecom, Ernest Moreau de Melen, Alphonse Renier, Georges Pelgrims, E. Neefs, Eric Thornton [GBR], Albert Delbecque, W. Spannoghe, van Heuckelum, Lucien Londot

1904 St. Louis T: 3, N: 2, D: 11.23.

	W	L	T	GF	GA
1. CAN	2	0	0	11	0
2. USA	1	1	1	2	7
3. USA	0	2	1	0	6

1. CAN—Galt Football Club: Ernest Linton, George Ducker, John Gourley, John Fraser, Albert Johnson, Robert Lane, Tom Taylor, Frederick Steep, Alexander Hall, Gordon McDonald, William Twaits
2. USA—Christian Brothers College: Louis Menges, Joseph Lydon, Thomas January, John January, Charles January, Peter Ratican, Warren Brittingham, Alexander Cudmore, Charles Bartliff, Oscar Brockmeyer, Raymond Lawlor
3. USA—St. Rose Parish School: Frank Frost, George Cooke, Henry Jameson, Joseph Brady, Martin Dooling, Dierkes, Cormic Cosgrove, O'Connell, Claude Jameson, Harry Tate, Thomas Cooke, Johnson

The St. Rose team managed to put one ball into the net. Unfortunately, it was into the goal they were defending.

1906 Athens T: 4, N: 2, D: 4.24.

	W	L	GF	GA
1. DEN	2	0	14	1
2. INT	1	1	4	5
3. GRE	0	2	0	8

Final: DEN 9-0 GRE (Athens)
2nd Place: INT 3-0 GRE (Thessaloniki)

1. DEN—Viggo Andersen, Peder Pedersen, Charles von Buchwald, Parmo Ferslev, Stefan Rasmussen, Aage Andersen, Oscar Nielsen, Carl Petersen, Holger Frederiksen, August Lindgren, Henry Rambusch, Hjalmar Herup
2. INT—Smyrna: Edwin Charnaud, Zareck Couyoumdzian, Edouard Giraud, Jacques Giraud, Henri Joly, Percy de la Fontaine, Donald Whittal, Albert Whittal, Godfrey Whittal, Harold Whittal, Edward Whittal
3. GRE—Thessaloniki Music Club: Georgios Vaporis, Nicolaos Pindos, Antonios Tegos, Nicolaos Pentzikis, Ioannis Kyrou, Georgios Sotiriadis, Vasilios Zarkadis, Dimitrios Mikhitsopoulos, Antonios Karangionidis, Ioannis Saridakis, Ioannis Abbot

The team from Smyrna was an international one, including players from Great Britain, France, Armenia and Greece. The five British players were all members of the Whittal family. Albert, Edward, and Godfrey were the sons of Edward Whittal; Donald and Harold were the sons of Edward's brother, Easton. A team from Athens defeated Thessaloniki 5-0 and then played Denmark in the final. After trailing 9-0 at halftime, the Athenians did not appear for the second half. They were ordered to play off against Smyrna and Thessaloniki for second place. They refused and were disqualified.

1908 London T: 6, N: 5, D: 10.24.

	W	L	GF	GA
1. GBR	3	0	18	1
2. DEN	2	1	26	3
3. HOL	1	1	2	4
4. SWE	0	2	1	14

Final: GBR 2-0 DEN
3rd Place: HOL 2-0 SWE

1. GBR—Horace Bailey, Walter Corbett, Herbert Smith, Kenneth Hunt, Frederick Chapman, Robert Hawkes, Arthur Berry, Vivian Woodward, Henry Stapley, Clyde Purnell, Harold Hardman
2. DEN—Ludwig Drescher, Charles von Buchwald, Harald Hansen, Harald Bohr, Christian Middelboe, Nils Middelboe, Oscar Nielsen, August Lindgren, Sofus Nielsen, Vilhelm Wolfhagen, Bjørn Rasmussen, Peter Marius Andersen, Johannes Gandil
3. HOL—Reinier Beeuwkes, Karel Heijting, Louis Otten, Johannes Sol, Johannes "Bok" de Korver, Emil Mundt, Jan-Herman Welcker, Everardus Snethlage, Gerard Reeman, Jan Snethlage, Jan Thomée, George de Bruyn Kops, Johannes "Jan" Kok
4. SWE—Oskar Bengtsson, Åke Fjästad, Teodor Malm, Sven Olsson, Hans Lindman, Olle Olsson, Sune Almkvist, Gustaf Bergström, Sven Ohlsson, Karl Ansén, Nils Andersson, Valter Lidén, Arvid Fagrell, Karl Gustafsson

France entered two teams, both of which were thrashed by Denmark. In the 17-1 defeat of the French "B" team, Sofus Nielsen of Denmark scored 10 goals.

1912 Stockholm T: 11, N: 11, D: 7.4.

	W	L	GF	GA
1. GBR	3	0	15	2
2. DEN	2	1	13	5
3. HOL	3	1	17	8
4. FIN	2	2	5	16
5. HUN	2	1	6	8
6. AUT	3	2	12	8
7. GER	1	2	18	8
7. ITA	1	2	4	8

Final: GBR 4-2 DEN
3rd Place: HOL 9-0 FIN

1. GBR—Ronald Brebner, Thomas Burn, Arthur Knight, Douglas McWhirter, Henry Littlewort, Joseph Dines, Arthur Berry, Vivian Woodward, Harold Walden, Gordon Hoare, Ivan "Ivor" Sharpe, Edward Hanney, E. Gordon Wright, Harold Stamper

2. DEN—Sofus Hansen, Nils Middleboe, Harald Hansen, Charles von Buchwald, Emil Jørgensen, Paul Berth, N.C. Oscar Nielsen, M. Axel Tufvesson, O. Anton Olsen, Sofus Nielsen, Vilhelm Wolfhagen, Hjalmar Christoffersen, Axel Petersen, Ivar-Lykke Seidelin-Nielsen, N. Poul Nielsen
3. HOL—Marius Göbel, David Wijnveldt, Pieter Bouman, Gerardus Fortgens, Constant Feith, Nicolaas de Wolf, Dirk Lotsij, Johannes Boutmij, Jan van Breda Kolff, Henri de Groot, Caesar ten Cate, Jan van der Sluis, Jan Vos, Nicolaas Bouvy, Johannes "Bok" de Korver
4. FIN—August Syrjäläinen, Hjalmar "Jalmari" Holopainen, Gösta Löfgren, Knut Lund, Eino Soinio, Viljo Lietola, Lauri Tanner, Bror Wiberg, Jarl "Lali" Öhman, Artur Nyssönen, Algoth Niska, August Wickström, Kaarlo Soinio
5. HUN—Gáspár Borbás, Imre Schlosser, Mihály Pataky, Sándor Bodnár, Béla Sebestyén, Antal Vágó, Jenő Károly, Gyula Biró, Imre Payer, Gyula Rumbold, László Domonkos, Kálmán Szury, Zoltán Blum, Miklós Fekete
6. AUT—Alois Müller, Leopold Neubauer, Johann Studnicka, Robert Merz, Ludwig Hussak, Robert Cimera, Karl Braunsteiner, Josef Brandstätter, Bernhard Graubard, Ladislaus Kurpiel, Otto Noll, Gustav Blaha, Franz Weber, Josef Kaltenbrunner, Leopold Grundwald
7. GER—Julius Hirsch, Eugen Kipp, Willi Worpitzky, Adolf Jäger, Karl Wegele, Hermann Bosch, Max Breunig, Georg Krogmann, Ernst Hollstein, Helmut Röpnack, Albert Weber, Gottfried Fuchs, Hans Reese, Walter Hempel, Karl Burger, Josef Glaser, Camillo Ugi, Karl Uhle, Fritz Förderer, Emil Oberle, Otto Thiel
7. ITA—Edoardo Mariani, Enrico Sardi, Felice Berardo, Franco Bontadini, Enea Zuffi, Pietro Leone, Giuseppe Milano, Carlo De Marchi, Renzo De Vecchi, Angelo Binaschi, Piero Campelli, Luigi Barbesino, Modesto Valle, Vittorio Morelli di Popolo

Great Britain was leading 2-1 in the final when Buchwald of Denmark was injured and had to be helped from the field. Denmark was forced to continue with only ten players, and Britain quickly capitalized by scoring two goals in three minutes. The Danes then adjusted to playing shorthanded, but it was too late and they lost, 4-2. In a consolation match against Russia, Gottfried Fuchs of Germany scored ten goals to match Sofus Nielsen's feat of four years earlier. Eleven of Britain's 15 tournament goals were scored by Harold Walden, who later became a popular music-hall comedian in West Yorkshire. When asked why he switched from football to the stage, Walden once explained, "With football it's 45 minutes each half, rain or snow, with a ten minute interval and a 'raspberry' from the crowd if you don't score." As a comedian "it's ten minutes each show . . . and a two hour interval in between. And there's a 'benefit' at the end of the week whether you score or not."

1920 Antwerp T: 14, N: 14, D: 9.2.

	W	L	GF	GA
1. BEL	3	0	8	1
—CZE	3	1	15	3
2. SPA	4	1	9	5
3. HOL	2	2	9	10
4. ITA	2	2	5	7
5. NOR	1	2	4	7
5. SWE	1	2	14	7
7. EGY	1	1	5	4

2nd Place: SPA 3-1 HOL

1. BEL—Jean De Bie, Armand Swartenbroeks, Oscar Verbeeck, Joseph Musch, Emile Hanse, André Fierens, Louis van Hege, Henri "Rik" Larnoe, Mathieu Bragard, Robert Coppée, Désiré Bastin, Félix Balyu, Fernand Nisot, Georges Hebdin
—CZE—Rudolf Klapka, Antonín Hojer, Miroslav Pospíšil, Karel Steiner, František Kolenatý, Karel "Káďa" Pešek, Antonín Perner, Emil Seifert, Josef Sedlášek, Antonin Janda, Václav Pilát, Jan Vaník, Otakar Mazal, Jan Plaček
2. SPA—Ricardo Zamora Martínez, Pedro Vallana Jeanguenat, Mariano Arrate Esnaola, José Samitier Vilalta, José María "Belauste" Belausteguigoitia Landaluce, Agustín Sancho Agustina, Ramón Eguiazábal Berroa, Félix Sesúmaga Ugarte, Patricio Arabolaza Aramburu, Rafael "Pichichi" Moreno Aranzadi, Domingo Gómez-Acedo Villanueva, Juan Artola Letamendía, Francisco Pagazaurtundúa González-Murrieta, Louis Otero Sánchez-Encinas, Joaquin Vázquez González, Ramón "Moncho" Gil Sequeiros, Sabino Bilbao Libano, M. Silverio Izaguirre Sorzabalbere
3. HOL—Richard MacNeill, Henri "Harry" Dénis, Bernard Verweij, Leonard Bosschart, Frederik Kuipers, Hermanus Steeman, Oscar van Rappard, Jan van Dort, Bernardus Groosjohan, Herman van Heijden, Jacob Bulder, Johannes "Jan" de Natris, Evert Bulder, Adrianus Bieshaar
4. ITA—Piero Campelli, Giovanni Giacone, Antonio Bruna, Renzo de De Vecchi, Virginio "Viri" Rosetta, Gracco De Nardo, Ettore Reynaudi, Mario Meneghetti, Giuseppe Parodi, Luigi Burlando, Rinaldo Roggero, Giustiniano Marucco, Pio Ferraris, Giuseppe Forlivesi, Cesare Lovati, Enrico Sardi, Adolfo Baloncieri, Emilio Badini, Guglielmo Brezzi, Aristodemo Emilio Santamaria, Alevildo de Marchi
5. NOR—Rolf Aas, Arne Andersen, Gunnar Andersen, Otto Aulie, Einar Gundersen, Asbjørn Hansen, Johny Helgesen, Per Holm, John Johnsen, Ellef Mohn, Michael Paulsen, Per Skou, Rolf Thorstvedt, Sigurd Wathne, Einar Wilhelms, Adolph Wold
5. SWE—Rune Bergström, Albin Dahl, Karl Gustafsson, Fritjof Hillén, Herbert Carlsson, M. Valdus Lund, Bertil Nordenskjöld, Albert Olsson, Mauritz Sandberg, Ragnar Wicksell, Robert Zander, Albert Öijermark
7. EGY—Kamel Taha, Mohamed El-Sayed, Abdel Salam Hamdy, Riad Shawki, Ali Fahmy El-Hassany, Galim Osman, Tawfik Abdalla, Hussein Hegazi, Hassan Ali Allouba, Sayed Abaza, Zaki Osman

The final matched the home team, Belgium, against the Czechoslovakians, who had outscored their opponents 15-1 on their way to the final. From the Belgian point-of-view, the football final was the highlight of the Antwerp Olympics. The stadium, built to accommodate 40,000 spectators, was filled to capacity two hours before kickoff. Not to be denied, a group of youthful fans dug a tunnel under an outside fence and soon every free space was overrun with supporters of the home team. A cordon of Belgian army troops was marched in to surround the field, ostensibly to prevent the crowd from spilling onto the pitch. The team from the recently created Czechoslovak Republic interpreted the soldiers' presence differently and found their conduct on the touch line "provocative and menacing." The Czechoslovaks also objected to the choice of John Lewis of England as the referee. In a pre-Olympic match in Prague, Lewis had been physically attacked by Czech supporters and it was thought, no doubt with some justification, that Lewis might not be able to judge the game objectively.

Ten minutes into the match, Robert Coppée converted a penalty. In the 28th minute Antwerp's own Rik Larnoe scored a second goal. With six minutes left in the first half, Lewis sent off Czech star Karel Steiner for rough play, whereupon the entire Czechoslovakian team walked off the field in protest and were disqualified.

Unfortunately, the battle for second place was run according to the complex and silly Bergvall system in which 1) the defeated quarterfinalists played a mini-tournament, the winner of which played against the loser of the final, 2) the two teams beaten by the winner before the final played each other, 3) the winner of parts one and two played to determine second and third place. The disqualification of Czechoslovakia threw this already complicated system into confusion. In addition, Sweden initally withdrew to protest poor officiating, but were lured back after a day's delay. Eventually Spain defeated Sweden and Italy to qualify for the second-place match against Holland.

Karel Pešek is the only Olympic athlete to have competed in both a winter and a summer sport at the same Olympics, having been a member of Czechoslovakia's football and ice hockey teams in Antwerp.

1924 Paris T: 22, N: 22, D: 6.9.

	W	L	T	GF	GA
1. URU	5	0	0	20	2
2. SWI	4	1	1	15	6
3. SWE	3	1	1	18	5
4. HOL	2	2	1	11	7
5. EGY	1	1	0	3	5
5. FRA	1	1	0	8	5
5. IRL	1	1	0	2	2
5. ITA	2	1	0	4	2

Final: URU 3-0 SWI
3rd Place: SWE 1-1 HOL, SWE 3-1 HOL

1. URU—Andrés Mazali, José "El Mariscal" Nasazzi Yarza, Pedro Arispe, José Andrade, José Vidal, Alfredo Ghierra, Santos Urdinarán, Héctor Scarone, Pedro Petrone, José Pedro Cea, Angel Romano, Humberto Tomassina, José Naya, Alfredo Zibechi, Antonio Urdinarán
2. SWI—Hans Pulver, Adolphe Reymond, Rudolf Ramseyer, August Oberhauser, Paul Schmiedlin, Aron Pollitz, Karl Ehrenbolger, Robert Pache, Walter Dietrich, Max Abegglen, Paul Fässler, Felix Bédouret, Adolphe Mengotti, Paul Sturzenegger, Edmond Kramer
3. SWE—Sigfrid "Sigge" Lindberg, Axel Alfredsson, Fritjof Hillén, Gunnar Holmberg, Sven Friberg, Harry Sundberg, Evert Lundqvist, Sven Rydell, Per Kaufeldt, Tore Keller, Rudolf Kock, Gustaf Carlson, Charles Brommesson, Thorsten Svensson, Albin Dahl, Konrad Hirsch, Sven Lindqvist, Sten Mellgren
4. HOL—Gejus van der Meulen, Henri Dénis, Hendrik Vermetten, Albert Oosthoek, Gerardus Krom, Gerardus Horstén, Johannes de Natris, Gerrit Visser, André Lefèvre, Ocker Formenoy, Marinus Sigmond, Bernard Verweij, Johannes Tetzner, Evert van Linge, Klaas Jan Breeuwer, Bernardus Groosjohan, Cornelius Pijl, Albert Snouck-Hurgronje, Johannes ter Beek
5. EGY—Abaza Sayed Fahmy, Abdel Hamid Moharren, Abdel Kader Mohammed, Ali Fahmi El-Hassany, Mohammed El-Mahdwy, Mahmoud Fouad, Ibrahim Yaghen, Abdel Salam Hamdy, Hussein Hegazi, Rizkalla Henein, Housny Khalil, Ismail El-Sayed, Ismail Mahmoud Hooda, Ahmed Mansour Hooda, Marey Mahmoud Moktar Mahmoud, Osman Gamil, Ali Mohamed Riad, Mohammed Rouston, Salim Ahmed, Shawky Riad, Kamel Taha
5. FRA—Henri Bard, Jean Batmale, Edouard Baumann, Pierre Bonnardel, Jean Boyer, Jacques Canthelou, Pierre Chayriguès, Pierre Chesnau, Maurice Cottenet, Edouard Crut, Jules Dewaquez, Marcel Domergue, René Dufour, Raymond Dubly, Ernest Gravier, Ernest Gross, Léon Huot, Gérard Isbecque, Albert Jourda, Antoine Parachini, Albert Renier, Paul Nicolas
5. IRL—Tom Aungier, Billy Cowzer, W. Ernest Crawford, Charlie Dowdall, Robert Duncan, Jimmy Dykes, John Farrell, Jimmy Ghent, Dennis Hannon, Tommy Healy, Frank Heaney, Joe Kendrick, Bertie Kerr, Pat Lee, Jack McCarthy, Alec McKay, Tom Muldoon, Tom Murphy, Jim Murray, Paddy O'Reilly, Sam Robinson, Bob Thomas
5. ITA—Giuseppe Aliberti, Mario Ardissone, Giuseppe Baldi, Adolfo Baloncieri, Ottavio Barbieri, Antonio Bruna, Luigi Burlando, Giampiero Combi, Leopoldo Conti, Giuseppe Della Valle, Giovanni De Prà, Renzo De Vecchi, Antonio Fayenz, Antonio Janni, Virgilio Levratto, Mario Magnozzi, Feliciano Monti, Virginio "Viri" Rosetta, Severino Rosso

The tournament opened with an upset as Italy defeated one of the favorites, Spain, 1-0, on a goal that was actually kicked through the net by the Spanish captain, Vallana. The Uruguayan team caught the fancy of the crowd with its 2-1 come-from-behind win over Holland in the semifinals. Holland lodged a protest, but it was denied. Then, when a Dutch referee was assigned to the final, it was Uruguay's turn to protest. Their protest was accepted, and the Dutch official was replaced by a Frenchman. The stadium was packed with 60,000 people for the final match and another 5000 were left outside, causing a crush that led to several injuries. The Swiss struggled vigorously but were unable to stop the Uruguayans, who led 1-0 at the break before winning 3-0.

Uruguayan goalkeeper Andrés Mazali is perhaps best known for his behavior just before the 1930 World Cup, when he broke a team curfew—supposedly to visit his wife—and was subsequently dropped from the team.

1928 Amsterdam T: 17, N: 17, D: 6.13.

	W	L	T	GF	GA
1. URU	4	0	1	12	5
2. ARG	3	1	1	25	8
3. ITA	3	1	1	25	11
4. EGY	2	2	0	12	19
5. BEL	1	1	0	8	9
5. GER	1	1	0	5	4
5. POR	1	1	0	3	3
5. SPA	1	1	1	9	9

Final: URU 1-1 ARG, URU 2-1 ARG
3rd Place: ITA 11-3 EGY

1. URU—Andrés Mazzali, José "El Mariscal" Nasazzi Yarza, Pedro Arispe, José Andrade, Lorenzo Fernández, Juan Piriz, Alvaro Gestido, Santos Urdinarán, Héctor Castro, Pedro Petrone, José Pedro Cea, Antonio Campolo, Adhemar Canavesi, Juan Arremón, René Borjas, Héctor Scarone, Roberto Figueroa
2. ARG—Ángel Bossio, Fernando Paternoster, Ludovico Bidoglio, Juan Evaristo, Luis Monti, Ángel Segundo Médici, Raimundo Orsi, Enrique Gainzarain, Manuel "Nolo" Ferreira, Domingo Tarasconi, Alfredo Carricaberry, Feliciano Perducca, Octavio Díaz, Roberto Cerro, Rodolfo Orlandini, Saúl Calandra
3. ITA—Giampiero Combi, Delfo Bellini, Umberto Caligaris, Alfredo Pitto, Fulvio Bernardini, Pietro Genovesi, Adolfo Baloncieri, Elvio Banchero, Angelo Schiavio, Mario Magnozzi, Virgilio Levratto, Giovanni De Prá, Virginio "Viri" Rosetta, Silvio Pietroboni, Antonio Janni, Enrico Rivolta, Gino Rossetti
4. EGY—Abdel Hamdi Hamdi, Sayed Fahmi Abaza, Mohammed Ahmad Shemais, Gaber Yaqoub El-Soury, Ali Fahmy El-Hassani, Abdel Halim Younis Hassan, Ismail El-Said Hooda, Aly Mohamed Riad, Ismail Mahmoud Houda, Hassan Moussa El-Azam, Mohamed Gamil El-Zubeir, Mohamed Ali Rostam, Mohamed Salem, Mohamed Ezz El-Din Gamal, Mahmoud Mokhtar Refaee, Ahmed Soliman
5. BEL—Jean De Bie, Georges Despae, Louis Versyp, Albert Ruyssevelt, Jean Diddens, Jacques Moeschal, Raymond Braine, Gerard de Vos, Pierre Braine, Florimond Van Halme, Gustave Boesman, Jacques Lavigne, Nicolas Hoydonckx, Jean Caudron
5. GER—Ernst Albrecht, Albert Beier, Ludwig Hofmann, Richard Hofmann, Josef Hornauer, Hans Kalb, Georg Knöpfle, Ludwig Leinberger, Josef Pöttinger, Heinrich Stuhlfauth, Henrich Weber
5. POR—Antonio Fernandes Roquete, Carlos Alves, Jorge Gomes Vieira, Raul Soares Figueiredo, Augusto Silva, César de Matos Rodrigues, Valdemar Mota Fonseca, José Manuel Soares Louro, Vitor Marcolino da Silva, Armando Martins, José Manuel Martins, João dos Santos
5. SPA—José Yermo Solaegui, Martín Marculeta Barbería, Luis Regueiro Pagola, Jacinto Quincoces López, José María Jauregui Lagunas, Luis "Kiriki" Iruretagoyena Ayestarán, Ángel Mariscal Ibeuba Beuba, Trino Arizcorreta Sein, Francisco Gamborena Hernandorena, Amadeo Labarta Rey, Pedro Vallana Jeanguenat, Domingo de Zaldua Anabitarte, José Legarreta Abaitua, Antero González de Audicana Inchaurraga, Ignacio "Cholín" Alcorta Hermoso, Francisco Bienzobas Ocariz, Robustiano "Robus" Bilbao Echevarría

In the semifinals, Argentina defeated Egypt 6-0 and Uruguay beat Italy 3-2. The first final ended in a draw and had to be replayed. In the second final, Hector Scarone scored the winning goal with 17 minutes to play.

As a point of interest, the complete name of the fourth member of the Spanish team was Jacinto Francisco Fernández de Quincoces y López de Arbina!

1932 not held

1936 Berlin T: 16, N: 16, D: 8.15.

	W	L	GF	GA
1. ITA	4	0	13	2
2. AUT	2	1	7	4
3. NOR	3	1	10	4
5. GBR	1	1	6	5
5. GER	1	1	9	2
5. JPN	1	1	3	10
5. PER	1	0	7	3

Final: ITA 2-1 AUT
3rd Place: NOR 3-2 POL

1. ITA—Bruno Venturini, Alfredo Foni, Pietro Rava, Giuseppe Baldo, Achille Piccini, Ugo Locatelli, Annibale Frossi, Libero Marchini, Sergio Bertoni, Carlo Biagi, Francesco Gabriotti, Luigi Scarabello,Giulio Cappelli, Alfonso Negro
2. AUT—Eduard Kainberger, Ernst Künz, Martin Kargl, Anton Krenn, Karl Wahlmüller, Max Hofmeister, Walter Werginz, Adolf Laudon, Klement Steinmetz, Karl Kainberger, Franz Fuchsberger, Franz Mandi, Josef Kitzmüller
3. NOR—Henry Johansen, Nils Eriksen, Øivind Holmsen, Frithjof Ulleberg, Jörgen Juve, Rolf Holmberg, Magdalon Monsen, Reidar Kvammen, Alf Martinsen, Odd Frantzen, Arne Brustad, Fredrik Horn, Sverre Hansen, Magnar Isaksen
4. POL—Spirydion Albański, Władysław Szczepaniak, Antoni Gałecki, Wilhelm Góra, Franciszek Cebulak, Ewald Dytko, Walerian Kisieliński, Michał Matyas, Teodor Peterek, Hubert God, Gerard Wodarz, Henryk Martyna, Józef Kotlarczyk, Jan Wasiewicz, Ryszard Piec, Walenty Musielak, Fryderyk "Fritz" Scherfke
5. GBR—Haydn Hill, Guy Holmes, Robert Fulton, John Gardiner, Bernard Joy, Daniel Pettit, James Crawford, Joseph Kyle, John Dodds, Maurice Edelston, Lester Finch
5. GER—Hans Jakob, Reinhold Münzenberg, Heinz Ditgens, Rudolf Gramlich, Ludwig Goldbrunner, Robert Bernard, Ernst Lehner, Otto Siffling, August Lenz, Adolf Urban, Wilhelm Simetsreiter
5. JPN—Rihei Sano, Sekiji Suzuki, Teizo Takeuchi, Matoo Tatsuhara, Oita, Yoshuku Kin, Matsunaga Ukon, Taigo Kawamoto, Takeshi Kamo, Shogo Kamo, Koichi Teneda
5. PER—Juan Valdivieso Padilla, Arturo Fernández Meyzán, José María Víctor Lavalle, Carlos Tovar Venegas, Segundo Castillo, Orestes Jordán Cánepa, Adelfo "El Bólido" Magallanes Campos, Jorge Alcalde Millos, Teodoro Fernández Meyzán, Carlos Alejandro Villanueva Martínez, José Morales

The stature of Olympic soccer, already weakened by the introduction of the World Cup in 1930 and the exclusion of the sport from the 1932 Olympic Games, received another blow when the 1936 tournament was marred by unruly incidents. First came the match between Italy and the United States, in which two Americans were injured. When the German referee, Weingartner, ordered Achille Piccini of Italy to leave the game, he refused to go. Several Italian players surrounded Weingartner, pinned his arms to his sides, and covered his mouth with their hands. The game continued with Piccini still in the lineup, and Italy won 1-0.

This unfortunate affair was nothing compared to what took place five days later, during the quarterfinal contest between Peru and Austria. Austria led 2-0 at the interval, but Peru tied the game with two goals in the last 15 minutes. A 15-minute overtime period was then played without further scoring, so a second overtime was ordered. By this time the small but vocal group of Peruvian spectators had become frantic with emotion. What followed depends on which continent is telling the story. Evidently, some Peruvian fans rushed onto the field while the game was still in progress and actually attacked one of the Austrian players. The Peruvian team took advantage of the chaos to score two quick goals and win the game, 4-2. Austria protested

Annibale Frossi, 1936
Annibale Frossi of Italy was a rare bespectacled football player.

immediately, and a Jury of Appeal, composed of five European men, ordered the match replayed two days later. The jury also decreed that the game be played behind locked doors with no spectators allowed. The Peruvians refused to show up, and the entire Peruvian Olympic contingent withdrew from the games, as did the Colombians, who supported their South American neighbors. Back in Lima, Peruvian demonstrators threw stones at the German consulate, while Peru's president, Oscar Benavides, denounced "the crafty Berlin decision." When German diplomats appealed to Benavides and pointed out that the decision had been made not by Germans but by officials of F.I.F.A., the International Football Federation, the president changed his position and blamed the demonstrations on Communists.

Meanwhile, back in Berlin, a bitterly contested final was fought between Italy and Austria. The first 45-minute half ended without a score. Midway in the second half, Annibale Frossi, Italy's right wing, scored the first goal of the game. Eleven minutes later Karl Kainberger, Austria's inside left, tied the score and the match went into overtime. A quick goal by Frossi proved decisive, and Italy won the gold medal, 2-1.

Frossi, who was affected by myopia, was one of the few football players to wear spectacles while playing.

1948 London T: 18, N: 18, D: 8.13.

	W	L	GF	GA
1. SWE	4	0	22	3
2. YUG	3	1	13	6
3. DEN	3	1	15	11
4. GBR	2	2	9	11
5. FRA	1	1	2	2
5. ITA	1	1	12	5
5. KOR	1	1	5	13
5. TUR	1	1	5	3

Final: SWE 3-1 YUG
3rd Place: DEN 5-3 GBR

1. SWE—Torsten Lindberg, Knut Nordahl, Erik Nilsson, Birger Rosengren, Bertil Nordahl, Sune Andersson, Kjell Rosén, Gunnar Gren, Gunnar Nordahl, Henry Carlsson, Nils Liedholm, Börje Leander
2. YUG—Ljubomir Lovrić, Miroslav Brozovič, Branisłav Stanović, Ziatko Čajkovski, Miodrag Jovanović, Zvonko Cimermanćic, Rajko Mitić, Stjepan Bobek, Željko Cajkovski, Bernard Vukas, Franjo Šoštarić, Prvoslav Mihajlović, Fränjo Wolfl, Kosta Tomašević
3. DEN—Ejgil Nielsen, Viggo Jensen, Knud Börge Overgaard, Axel Pilmark, Dion Ørnvold, Ivan Jensen, Johannes Plöger, Knud Lundberg, Carl Aage Praest, John Hansen, Jörgen Sörensen, Holger Seebach, Karl Aage Hansen
4. GBR—Ronald Simpson, Charles "Jack" Neale, Andrew Carmichael, John Roderick Hardisty, Eric Lee, Eric Fright, J. Alan Boyd, Andrew Aitken, Harold McIlvenny, John Rawlings, William Amor, Kevin McAlinden, George Manning, James McColl, Douglas McBain, Frank Donovan, Thomas Hopper, Denis Kelleher, F. Peter Kippax
5. FRA—Gaston Rouxel, Robert Krug, Bernard Bienvue, René Persillon, Marcel Colau, Georges Robert, Jean Heckel, Antoine Strappe, René Hebinger, Jacques Paluch, René Courbin
5. ITA—Giuseppe Casari, Guglielmo Giovannini, Adone Stellin, Tommaso Maestrelli, Maino Neri, Giacomo Mari, Emilio Cavigioli, Angelo Turconi, Francesco Pernigo, Valerio Cassani, Emilio Caprile

Football, 1948
An unusual play from the 1948 football (soccer) tournament. Henry Carlsson of Sweden scores a goal against Denmark that is caught by his teammate Gunnar Nordahl, who had dashed into the opposing goal to avoid an offside call.

5. KOR—Hong Duk-yung, Pak Kyoo-chung, Pak Dai-chong, Choi Soon-gon, Kim Kyoo-whan, Min Byung-dai, Woo Zung-whan, Bai Chong-hoo, Chung Nam-sik, Kim Yong-sik, Chung Kook-chin
5. TUR—Cihat Arman, Murat Alyuz, Vedu Tosuncuk, Naim Ozhaya, Bülent Eken, Hüseyin Saygun, Fikret Kercan, Erol Keskin, Gündüz Kilic, Lefter Küçükandonyadis, Sükrü Gülesin

By 1948 the best players of Western Europe and South America were turning professional, and Olympic soccer began to be dominated by the state-sponsored "amateur" teams of Eastern Europe. Sweden was the last non-Communist team to win an unboycotted Olympic football tournament until 1992. Their team included three brothers, Gunnar, Bertil, and Knut Nordahl, as well as three firemen, including Gunnar Nordahl.

1952 Helsinki T: 25, N: 25, D: 8.2.

	W	L	T	GF	GA
1. HUN	5	0	0	20	2
2. YUG	4	1	1	26	13
3. SWE	3	1	0	9	8
4. GER	2	2	0	8	8
5. AUT	1	1	0	5	6
5. BRA	2	1	0	9	6
5. DEN	2	1	0	7	6
5. TUR	1	1	0	3	8

Final: HUN 2-0 YUG
3rd Place: SWE 2-0 GER

1. HUN—Gyula Grosics, Jenő Buzánszky, Mihály Lantos, József Bozsik, Gyula Lóránt, József Zakariás, Nándor Hidegkuti, Sándor Kocsis, Péter Palotás, Ferenc Puskás, Zoltán Czibor, Jenő Dalnoki, Imre Kovács, László Budai II, Lajos Csordás
2. YUG—Vladimir Beara, Branislav Stanković, Tomislav Crnković, Zlatko Čajkovski, Ivan Horvat, Vujadin Boškov, Tihomir Ognjanov, Rajko Mitić, Bernard Vukas, Stjepan Bobek, Branko Zebec
3. SWE—Karl Svensson, Lennart Samuelsson, Erik Nilsson, Olof Ahlund, Bengt Gustavsson, Gösta Lindh, Sylve Bengtsson, Gösta Löfgren, Ingvar Rydell, Yngve Brodd, Gösta Sandberg, Holger Hansson
4. GER—Rudolf Schönbeck, Hans Eberle, Herbert Jäger, Kurt Sommerlatt, Herbert Schäfer, Alfred Post, Ludwig Hinterstocker, Georg Stollenwerk, Hans Zeitler, Willi Schröder, Kurt Ehrmann, Erich Gleixner, Matthias Mauritz, Karl Klug
5. AUT—Fritz Nikolai, Walter Kollmann, Anton Krammar, Anton Wolf, Josef Walter, Robert Fendler, Hermann Hochleitner, Franz Feldinger, Erich Stumpf, Herbert Grohs, Otto Gollnhuber
5. BRA—Carlos Alberto Martins Cavalheiro, Mauro Torres Homem Rodrigues, Waldir Villas Boas, Zózimo Alves Calazans, Adesio Alves Machado, Edison Campos Martins, Larry Pinto de Faria, Milton Pessanha, Evaldo "Vavá" Neto, Humberto Barbosa Tozzi, Jansen Moreira
5. DEN—Jorgen Johansen, Poul Erik Petersen, Svend Nielsen, Erik Terkelsen, Poul Andersen, Steen Blicher, Jorgen Hansen, Poul Eyvind Petersen, Jens Hansen, Knud Lundberg, Holger Seebach
5. TUR—Erdoğan Akin, Nekdet Sentürk, Ridvan Bolatli, Mustafa Ertan, Basri Dirimilili, Erküment Güder, Vasif Cetinel, Tekin Bilge, Yalçin Çaka, Muzaffer Tokac, Makit Gürdal

Entering the Olympics for the first time, the Soviet Union expected to win the gold medal. Within the football world, however, the focus was firmly on the Hungarian team, undefeated since May 1950 and composed of some of the greatest players of the era, including the legendary Ferenc Puskás.

The Soviet Union faced Yugoslavia in the second round and trailed 5-1 before scoring four goals in the last 15 minutes to send the game into overtime. A half hour of extra time failed to produce another score, so the match was replayed two days later. This time Yugoslavia overcame a 0-1 deficit to win 3-1. This was such a humiliating shock that the match was not mentioned in the Soviet press until after the death of dictator Josef Stalin the following year.

Meanwhile Hungary beat Italy 3-0, and then scored seven goals against Turkey in the quarter-finals and six against defending Olympic champion Sweden in the semi-finals. The final against Yugoslavia was a tense affair, with Puskás giving Hungary the lead in the 70th minute and Czibor clinching the gold medal in the final two minutes. Back home in Hungary the celebrations lasted a week, and each player was given a new car.

Later nicknamed the "Golden Team" or the "Mighty Magyars", the Hungarian national team became known as one of the best national teams of all time, defeating England 6-3 in a friendly match at Wembley the following year and remaining unbeaten until a controversial 2-3 loss to West Germany in the final of the 1954 World Cup in Switzerland.

1956 Melbourne T: 11, N: 11, D: 12.8.

	W	L	T	GF	GA
1. SOV	4	0	1	9	2
2. YUG	2	1	0	13	3
3. BUL	2	1	0	10	3
4. IND	1	2	0	10	3
5. AUS	1	1	0	4	4
5. GBR	1	1	0	10	6

Final: SOV 1-0 YUG
3rd Place: BUL 3-0 IND

1. SOV—Lev Yashin, Anatoly Bashashkin, Mikhail Ogonikov, Boris Kuznetsov, Igor Netto, Anatoly Maslyonkin, Boris Tatushin, Anatoly Issayev, Nikita Simonyan, Sergei Salnikov, Anatoly Ilyin, Vadym Tyshchenko, Aleksei Paramonov, Eduard Streltsov, Valentin Ivanov, Vladimir Ryshkin, Yosif Betsa, Boris Razinsky
2. YUG—Petar Radenković, Mladen Koščak, Nikola Radović, Ivan Šantek, Ljubisa Spajić, Dobroslav Krstić, Dragoslav Šekularac, Zlatko Papec, Sava Antić, Todor Veselinović, Muhamed Mujić, Blagoje Vidinic, Ibrahim Biogradić, Luka Lipošinović
3. BUL—Yosif Yosilov, Kiril Rakarov, Nikola Kovatschev, Stefan Stefanov, Manol Manolov, Gavril Stojanov, Dimiter Milanov, Georgy Dimitrov, Panayot Panayotov, Ivan Kolev, Todor Diyev, Georgy Naydenov, Miltscho Goranov, Krum Yanev
4. IND—Narayan Subramaniam, Syed Khaja Aziz, Shaikh Abdul Lateef, Mohamed Kempiah, Noor Muhamed, Ahmed Husain, Mohamed Kannayan, Neville Stephen D'Souza, Krishna Chandra Pal, Nikhil Kumar Nunday, Krishna Swamy Kittu, T. Abdul Rahman, Muhamed Abdus Salam, Pradip Kuma Banerjee, Tulsidas Balaram, Peter Ramaswamy Thangaraj, Samar Banerjee

5. AUS—Ronald Lord, Robert Bignell, John Pettigrew, George Arthur, William Sander, Bruce Morrow, Francis Loughran, Jack Lennard, Graham McMillan, Edward Smith, Alwyn Warren
5. GBR—Harry Sharratt, Donald Stoker, Leslie Thomas Farrer, Lawrence Topp, Stanley Prince, Herbert Dodkins, James Lewis, John Roderick Hardisty, John Laybourne, George Bromilow, Charles Twissell

The winning goal was headed in early in the second half by Anatoly Ilyin. The Soviet victory was preserved when a goal by Yugoslavia's Zlatko Papec was disallowed because of an offside infraction. Of the 18 men on the Soviet squad, only Ukrainian Vadym Tyshchenko was not from Russia.

1960 Rome T: 16, N: 16, D: 9.10.

	W	L	T	GF	GA
1. YUG	3	0	2	17	7
2. DEN	4	1	0	11	7
3. HUN	4	1	0	17	6
4. ITA	2	1	2	11	7

Final: YUG 3-1 DEN
3rd Place: HUN 2-1 ITA

1. YUG—Blagoje Vidinić, Novak Roganović, Fahrudin Jusufi, Zeljko Perušić, Vladimir Durković, Ante Žanetić, Andrija Anković, Zeljko Matuš, Milan Galić, Tomislav Knez, Borivoje Kostić, Milutin Soskić, Velimir Sombolac, Aleksandar Kozilna, Silvester Takać, Dusan Maravić
2. DEN—Henry From, Poul Andersen, Poul Jensen, Bent Hansen, Hans Nielsen, Flemming Nielsen, Poul Pedersen, Tommy Troelsen, Harald Nielsen, Henning Enoksen, Jörn Sörensen, John Danielsen
3. HUN—Gábor Török, Zoitán Dudás, Jenő Dalnoki, Ernő Solymosi, Pál Várhidi, Ferenc Kovács, Imre Sátori, János Göröcs, Flórián Albert, Pál Orosz, János Dunai, Lajos Faragó, Dezső Novák, Oszkár Vilezsál, Gyula Rákosi, László Pál, Tibor Pál
4. ITA—Luciano Alfieri, Tarcisio Burgnich, Mario Trebbi, Paride Tumburus, Sandro Salvadore, Giovanni Trappatoni, Giancarlo Cella, Giovanni Rivera, Ugo Tomeazzi, Giacomo Bulgarelli, Giorgio Rossano, Orazio Rancati, Giorgio Ferrini, Giovanni Fanello, Gilberto Noletti, Luciano Magistrelli

Three-time runner-up Yugoslavia shocked Denmark when their captain, Milan Galić, scored a goal from 30 meters out in the first minute of play. Ten minutes later, Zeljko Matuš made it 2-0 and it looked like a rout might be in the making. However, late in the first half, Galić was ejected for insulting a referee, and Yugoslavia played the rest of the game with only ten players. Nevertheless, they held on to their lead and prevailed 3-1. It is worth noting that Yugoslavia tied with Bulgaria in their preliminary pool and qualified for the semifinals only because they won a coin toss.

1964 Tokyo T: 14, N: 14, D: 10.23.

	W	L	T	GF	GA
1. HUN	5	0	0	22	6
2. CZE	5	1	0	19	5
3. GDR	4	1	1	12	4
4. EGY	2	3	1	18	16
5. GHA	1	1	1	5	8
5. JPN	1	2	0	5	9
5. ROM	2	1	0	5	4
5. YUG	1	2	0	8	8

Final: HUN 2-1 CZE
3rd Place: GDR 3-1 EGY

1. HUN—Antal Szentmihályi, Dezső Novák, Kálman Ihász, Gusztáv Szepesi, Árpád Orban, Ferenc Nógrádi, János Farkas, Tibor Csernai, Ferenc Bene, Imre Komora, Sándor Katona, József Gelei, Károly Polotai, Zoltán Varga
2. CZE—František Schmucker, Anton Urban, Karel Zdeněk Pičman, Josef Vojta, Vladimír Weiss, Ján Geleta, Jan Brumovský, Ivan Mráz, Karel Lichtnégl, Vojtech Masný, František Valošek, Anton Švajlen, Karel Knesl, Štefan Matlák, Karel Nepomucký, František Knebort, Ľudovít Cvetler
3. GDR—Hans Jürgen Heinsch, Peter Rock, Manfred Geisler, Herbert Pankau, Manfred Walter, Gerhard Körner, Hermann Stöcker, Otto Frässdorf, Henning Frenzel, Jürgen Nöldner, Eberhard Vogel, Horst Weigang, Klaus Urbanczyk, Bernd Bauchspiess, Klaus-Dieter Seehaus, Werner Unger, Wolfgang Barthels, Klaus Lisiewicz, Dieter Engelhardt
4. EGY—Reda Ahmed, Yaken Zaki, Amin Elisnawi, Mohamed Kotb, Raafat Attia, Mohamed Abdelat Elsherbini, Seddik Mohamed, Ibrahim Riad, Mohamed Badawi, Nabil Nosseir, K. Aly Etman, F. Aly Korshed, Darwish Amin, Rifaat Elfanagili, Ahmed Moust Gad, Kalil Shahin, Mahmoud Hassan, Taha Ismail, Farouk Mahmoud
5. GHA—Dodoo-Ankrah, Samuel Okai, Emmanuel Oblitey, Sam Acquah, Charles Addo-Odametey, Emmanuel Nkansah, Gyau Agyemang, Wilberforce Mfum, Edward Aggrey Fynn, Edward Acquah, Kofi Pare
5. JPN—Kenzo Yokoyama, Hiroshi Katayama, Yoshitada Yamaguchi, Ryozo Suzuki, Aritatsu Ogi, Mitsuo Kamata, Saburo Kawabuchi, Shigeo Yaegashi, Kunishige Kamamoto, Teruki Miyamoto, Masashi Watanabe
5. ROM—Ilie Datcu, Ilie Greavu, Bujor Hălmăgeanu, Emil Petru, Ion Nunweiler, Niculae Georgescu, Ion Pircălab, Gheorge Constantin, Ion Ionescu, Dan Coe, Carol Crăinicheanu
5. YUG—Ivan Curković, Mirsad Fazlagić, Svetozar Vujović, Rudolf Belin, Milan Cop, Jovan Miladinović, Spasoje Samardžić, Slaven Zambata, Ivan Osim, Lazar Radović, Dragan Dzajić

Most of the fireworks took place before the tournament even started. Beginning in 1952, so many nations began applying to compete in the Olympics that pre-Olympic soccer tournaments had to be held to decide the 16 Olympic teams. On May 24, 1964, one such qualifying match took place in Lima between Peru and Argentina. Argentina led 1-0, but with two minutes to play Peru scored to tie the game. However, the Uruguayan referee, Angel Eduardo Payos, nullified the goal because of rough play by the Peruvians. While the crowd of 45,000 booed its disapproval, two spectators leaped onto the field and attacked the referee. They were quickly arrested, which angered the crowd even more. Then Payos ordered the game suspended, claiming, with obvious justification, that police protection on the field was inadequate. The incensed crowd surged onto the field while the police hustled Payos and the players to safety. Some spectators began breaking windows and before long mounted police appeared and began herding the rioters toward the exits, many of which were, unfortunately, locked. Tear-gas grenades were fired by the police, while the Peruvian soccer fans responded by throwing stones and bottles and setting part of the stadium on fire. The fighting spilled into the streets of Lima, and before the night was out, 328 people had been killed and over 500 injured. Most of those killed had been trampled to death, but at least four persons were shot by police bullets. The Peruvian government declared a national "state of siege" and suspended the constitution. Meanwhile, demonstrators marched to the National Palace demanding an end to police brutality and the declaration of a tie in the match with Argentina. Neither demand was met. Argentina, by the way, went to Tokyo but lost both of their games.

When the Olympic tournament finally commenced, two of the 16 qualifying teams were missing. North Korea dropped out following a dispute with the IOC. Italy, the only Western European team to qualify for the Tokyo tournament, withdrew following accusations that several of its players were actually professionals. This charge was fairly hard to deny considering that three members of the Italian Olympic team were also members of the Inter-Milan team, which was the reigning European Cup champion. In fact, Sandro Mazzola scored two of the goals that defeated Real Madrid in the Cup final.

The Olympic tournament itself was not very impressive, particularly after all that had preceded it. However, the final between Hungary and Czechoslovakia was an exciting match. Hungary's first goal, scored at the beginning of the second half, was actually put through the net by Josef Vojta of Czechoslovakia, who inadvertently deflected a Hungarian pass past his own goalie. Thirteen minutes later, Hungarian center forward Ferenc Bene outran the Czech defense and blasted in a second goal, which proved to be decisive.

1968 Mexico City T: 16, N: 16, D: 10.26.

	W	L	T	GF	GA
1. HUN	5	0	1	18	3
2. BUL	3	1	2	16	10
3. JPN	3	3	0	10	9
4. MEX	3	3	0	10	9
5. FRA	2	2	0	9	8
5. GUA	2	2	0	6	4
5. ISR	2	1	1	9	7
5. SPA	2	1	1	4	2

Final: HUN 4-1 BUL
3rd Place: JPN 2-0 MEX

1. HUN—Károly Fatér, Dezső Novák, Lajos Dunai, Miklós Páncsics, Iván Menczel, Lajos Szűcs, Laszló Fazekas, Antal Dunai, László Nagy, Ernö Noskó, István Juhász, Lajos Kocsis, Istvan Básti, László Keglovich, István Sárközi
2. BUL—Stoyan Yordanov, Atanas Gerov, Georgi Hristakiev, Milko Gaidarski, Kiril Ivkov, Ivailo Georgiev, Tsvetan Veselinov, Yevgeny Yanchovski, Peter Zhekov, Atanas Hristov, Asparuh Nikodimov, Kiril Stankov, Todor Krustev, Mihail Gionin, Yancho Dimitrov, Georgi Tsetkov, Ivan Zafirov, Georgi Vasilev
3. JPN—Kenzo Yokoyama, Hiroshi Katayama, Yoshitada Yamaguchi, Mitsuo Kamata, Takaji Mori, Aritatsu Ogi, Teruki Miyamoto, Masashi Watanabe, Kunishige Kamamoto, Ikuo Matsumoto, Ryuichi Sugiyama, Masakatsu Miyamoto, Yasuyuki Kuwahara, Shigeo Yaegashi
4. MEX—Javier Vargas, Juan Manuel Alejándrez Rodríguez, Héctor Sanabria, Mario Pérez Guadarrama, Luis Regueiro, Luis Estrada, Vicente Pereda, Cesáreo Victorino, Javier Sánchez Galindo, J. Ignacio Basaguren García, Albino Morales, Humberto Medina, Héctor Pulido Rodríguez, Elías Muñoz Rios, Fernando Bustos Castañeda
5. FRA—Jean Lempereur, Freddy Zix, Michel Verhoeve, Gilbert Plante, Jean-Michel Larque, Jean Louis Hodoul, Daniel Perrigaud, Daniel Hortaville, Marc Case, Gerard Hallet, Henri Ribul
5. GUA—Alberto López Oliva, Llijon León de León, Roberto Camposeco Marques, Hugo Montoya, Armando Melgar, Jorge Roldán Popol, Hugo Torres Ocampo, Carlos Valdez, Hugo Peña Segura, David Stokes, Julio Rodolfo García Guzmán
5. ISR—Haim Levin, Menacham Bello, Zvi Rosen, Shaia Shwager, Shmuel Rosenthal, Rachamim Talbi, Giora Shpigal, Jehoshua Faygenbaum, Mordechai Shpiegler, Itzhak Druker, George Borba
5. SPA—Pedro Mora Mariné, Gregorio Benito Rubio, Francisco Espildora Muñoz, Miguel Ángel Ochoa Vaca, Isidro Sala Puigvedal, Juan Asensi Ripoll, Rafael Jaén Rodríguez, Juan Fernández Vilela, José Garzon Fito, José Grande Cereijo, Fernando Ortuño Blasco

Morocco qualified for the final tournament, but refused to participate against Israel. They were replaced by Ghana. The Ghana-Israel game, won by Israel 5-3, disintegrated into brawling, which continued back at the Olympic Village. A match between Czechoslovakia and Guatemala was also disrupted by fighting. The final pitted defending champion Hungary against Bulgaria, which qualified only after their tied quarterfinal game with Israel was decided by the toss of a coin. Bulgaria scored first on a header by Dimitrov, but four minutes before the end of the first half, Menczel of Hungary evened the score. A minute later Dunai of Hungary put in another goal. At this point the situation deteriorated drastically. Referee Diego De Leo, an Italian-born naturalized Mexican, ejected Dimitrov for rough play. Seconds later another Bulgarian, Kiril Ivkov, was thrown out. An angry teammate, Atanas Hristov, kicked the ball toward the referee, and he too was ejected. The Mexican crowd was none too pleased with the actions of Mr. De Leo. Having already disrupted the third-place game by throwing cushions onto the field, they used the same tactic to show their disapproval and cause delay in the final. The ejections effectively ended the contest, as Bulgaria was forced to play the second half with only eight players. Juhász of Hungary was eventually banished as well, but the Hungarians still outnumbered the Bulgarians 10-8 and won easily, 4-1.

1972 Munich T: 16, N: 16, D: 9.10.

	W	L	T	GF	GA
1. POL	6	0	1	21	5
2. HUN	5	1	1	18	5
3. GDR	4	2	1	23	9
3. SOV	5	1	1	17	6
5. DEN	3	2	1	11	10
5. GER	3	2	1	17	8
5. MEX	2	3	1	4	14
5. MOR	1	4	1	7	14

Final: POL 2-1 HUN
3rd Place: GDR 2-2 SOV

1. POL—Hubert Kostka, Zbigniew Gut, Jerzy Gorgoń, Zygmunt Anczok, Lesław Ćmikiewicz, Zygmunt Maszczyk, Jerzy Kraska, Kazimierz Deyna, Zygfryd Szołtysik, Włodzimierz Lubański, Robert Gadocha, Ryszard Szymczak, Antoni Szymanowski, Marian Ostafiński, Grzegorz Lato, Joachim Marx, Kazimierz Kmiecik
2. HUN—István Géczi, Péter Vépi, Miklós Páncsics, Péter Juhász, Lajos Szücs, Mihály Kozma, Antal Dunai, Lajos Kü, Béla Váradi, Ede Dunai, László Bálint, Lajos Kocsis, Kálmán Tóth, József Kovács, László Branikovits, Csaba Vidáts, Ádám Rothermel
3. GDR—Jürgen Croy, Manfred Zapf, Konrad Weise, Bernd Bransch, Jürgen Pommerenke, Jürgen Sparwasser, Hans-Jürgen Kreische, Joachim Streich, Wolfgang Seguin, Peter Ducke, Frank Ganzera, Lothar Kurbjuweit, Eberhard Vogel, Ralf Schulenberg, Reinhard Häfner, Harald Irmscher, Siegmar Wätzlich
3. SOV—Oleh Blokhin, Murtaz Khurtsilava, Yuri Istomin, Vladimir Kaplichnyi, Viktor Kolotov, Yevgeny Lovchev, Sergei Olshansky, Yevhen Rudakov, Vyacheslav Semenov, Gennady Yevryuzhikhin, Oganes Zanazanyan, Andrei Yakubik, Arkady Andriasyan
5. DEN—Mogens Therkildsen, Flemming Ahlberg, Svend Andersen, Per Rontved, Jorgen Rasmussen, Jack Hansen, Kresten Nygaard, Allan Simonsen, Max Rasmussen, Arvo Heino Hansen, Keld Bak, Leif Prinzlau, Hans Ewald Hansen
5. GER—Hans Jürgen Bradler, Heiner Baltes, Reiner Hollmann, Egon Schmitt, Friedheim Häbermann, Jürgen Kalb, Hermann Bitz, Ulrich Hoeness, Ottmar Hitzfeld, Bernd Nickel, Klaus Wunder, Ronald Worm, Rudi Seliger
5. MEX—Jesus Rico, José Luis Trejo Montoya, Juan Manuel Álvarez Álvarez, Enrique Martín del Campo, Alejandro Hernández, Fernando Blanco Garell, Manuel Manzo, Daniel Razo, Leonardo Cuéllar Rivera, Horacio Sánchez, Alejandro Peña, Alfredo Hernández
5. MOR—Mohamed Hazzaz, Mohamed Elfilali, Bouiamaa Benkhrif, Abdallah Tazi, Ahmed Faras, Mohamed Merzaq, Ahmed Belkorchi, Larbi Ihardane, Khalifa Elbakhti, Abdelali Zahraoui, Mustapha Yaghcha, Ghazouani Mouhoub, Ahmed Najah, Atati Zouita Mohamed, Abdelfattah Jafri

Hungary entered the final having lost only one of their last 21 Olympic matches going back to 1960. The game was played in torrential rain and near gale-force wind. Hungary led 1-0 at the interval, but when the teams switched sides for the second half Poland took advantage of having the wind at their backs and scored two goals to gain the victory.

1976 Montreal T: 13, N: 13, D: 7.31.

	W	L	T	GF	GA
1. GDR	4	0	1	10	2
2. POL	3	1	1	11	5
3. SOV	4	1	0	10	4
4. BRA	2	2	1	6	6
5. FRA	2	2	1	9	7
5. IRN	1	2	0	4	5
5. ISR	0	1	3	4	7
5. PRK	1	2	0	3	9

Final: GDR 3-1 POL
3rd Place: SOV 2-0 BRA

1. GDR—Jürgen Croy, Gerd Weber, Hans-Jürgen Dörner, Konrad Weise, Lothar Kurbjuweit, Reinhard Lauck, Gert Heidler, Reinhard Häfner, Hans-Jürgen Riediger, Benrd Bransch, Martin Hoffmann, Gerd Kische, Wolfram Löwe, Hartmut Schade, Dieter Riedel, Hans-Ullrich Grapenthin, Wilfried Gröbner
2. POL—Jan Tomaszewski, Antoni Szymanowski, Jerzy Gorgoń, Wojciech Rudy, Władysław Zmuda, Zygmunt Maszczyk, Grzegorz Lato, Henryk Kasperczak, Kazimierz Deyna, Andrzej Szarmach, Kazimienz Kmiecik, Piotr Mowlik, Henryk Wawrowski, Henryk Wieczorek, Lesław Ćmikiewicz, Jan Beniger, Roman Ogaza
3. SOV—Vladimir Astapovsky, Anatoly Konkov, Viktor Matviynko, Mykhalo Fomenko, Stefan Reshko, Volodymyr Troshkin, David Kipiani, Volodymyr Onyshenko, Viktor Kolotov, Volodymyr Veremiyev, Oleh Blokhin, Leonid Buryak, Vladimir Feodorov, Aleksandr Minayev, Viktor Zvyagintsev, Leonid Nazarenko, Aleksandr Prokhorov
4. BRA—Carlos Gallo, Rosemiro Corrêa de Souza, Roberto Franqueira, Edino Nazareth Filho, Léovegildo Lins Gama, Alberto Marques, Mario Emiliano, João Batista da Silva, Eudes Medeiros, Eriveito Martins, João dos Santos, Mauro de Campos, Julio da Silva Gurjol, Francisco Fraga da Silva, Jarbas Tomazoli Nunes, Edval da Costa, José Pessanha
5. FRA—Jean-Claude Larrieu, Henri Orlandini, Patrick Battiston, Claude Chazottes, Francis Meynieu, Michel Pottier, Alexandre Strassievitch, Henri Zambelli, Michel Couge, Jean Fernandez, Michel Platini, Francisco Rubio, Loic Amisse, Bruno Baronchelli, Eric Pecout, Olivier Rouyer, Jean Marc Schaer
5. IRN—Mansour Rashidi, Hassan Nazari, Andranik Eskandarian, Bijan Zolfagharnasab, Parviz Qelichkhani, Ali Parvin, Nasrollah Abdollahi, Nasser Nouraii,Hassan Rowshan, Ali-Reza Khorshidi, Hassan Nayebagha, Gholam Mazloomi, Hessem Mirfakhali, Ghafoor Jahani, Ali-Reza Azizi, Nasser Hejazi
5. ISR—Itzhak Vissoker, Abrahm Lev, Yaron Oz, Haim Bar, Moshe Shani, Itzak Peretz, Itzhak Shum, Elimeleh Leventhal, Rifaat Tourk, Gideon Damti, Josef Sorynow, Meir Nimni, Oded Nachness, Avraham Cohen, Joshua Gal, Ehud Ben-Tovim, Alon Ben-Dor
5. PRK—Jin In-chol, Kim Gwang-sok, Kim Il-nam, Kim Myong-song, Ma Jong-u, Pak Jong-hun, An Se-uk, Hong Song-nam, Cha Jong-sok, Kim Sung-gyu, Yang Song-guk, An Gil-wan, Li Hi-yon, Myong Dong-chan, Pak Kyong-won

Again the Olympic soccer final was played in heavy rain, and again it was dominated by the professional amateurs of Eastern Europe, including ten members of Poland's 1974 World Cup team. In the final match, East Germany scored two goals in the first 15 minutes and scored again with six minutes to play to secure the gold medal.

1980 Moscow T: 16, N: 16, D: 8.2.

	W	L	T	GF	GA
1. CZE	4	0	2	10	1
2. GDR	4	1	1	12	2
3. SOV	5	1	0	10	3
4. YUG	3	2	1	9	7
5. ALG	1	2	1	4	4
5. CUB	2	2	0	3	12
5. IRQ	1	1	2	4	5
5. KUW	1	1	2	4	5

Final: CZE 1-0 GDR
3rd Place: SOV 2-0 YUG

1. CZE—Stanislav Seman, Luděk Macela, Josef Mazura, Libor Radimec, Zdeněk Rygel, Petr Němec, Ladislav Vizek, Jan Berger, Jindřich Svoboda, Lubomír Pokluda, Werner Lička, Rostislav Václaviček, Jaroslav Netolička, Oldřich Rott, František Štambacher, František Kunzo
2. GDR—Bodo Rudwaleit, Artur Ullrich, Lothar Hause, Frank Uhlig, Frank Baum, Rüdiger Schnuphase, Frank Terletzki, Wolfgang Steinbach, Jürgen Bähringen, Werner Peter, Dieter Kühn, Norbert Trieloff, Matthias Liebers, Bernd Jakubowski, Wolf Rüdiger Netz, Matthias Müller
3. SOV—Rinat Dasayev, Tengiz Sulakvelidze, Aleksandr Chivadze, Vagiz Khidiyatullin, Oleg Romantsev, Sergei Shavlo, Sergei Andreyev, Volodymyr Bezsonov, Yuri Gavrilov, Fyodor Cherenkov, Valery Gazzayev, Vladimir Pilguy, Serhei Baltacha, Sergei Nikulin, Khoren Oganesyan, Aleksandr Prokopenko, Revaz Chelebadze
4. YUG—Dragan Pantelić, Nikica Cukrov, Ivan Gudelj, Miloš Hrstić, Milan Jovin, Nikica Klinčarski, Mišo Krstičević, Dževad Šećerbegović, Vladimir Matijević, Dušan Pešić, Tomislav Ivković, Boro Primorac, Srebrenko Repčić, Miloš Šestić, Zlatko Vujović, Zoran Vujović
5. ALG—Mourad Ahara, Mahmoud Guendouz, Bouzid Mahiduz, Chaabane Merzekane, Mohamed Kheddis, Rabah Madjer, Ali Fergani, Tadj Bensaoula, Lakhdar Belloumi, Salah Assad, Mohamed Rahmani, Salah Larbes, Djamel Menad, Abderrahmane Derouaz, Hocine Yahi, Mohamed Ouamar Ghrib
5. CUB—José Reinoso, Miguel López, Raimundo Frometa, Luis Sánchez, Luis Dreke, Roberto Espinosa, Andres Roldán, Amado Povea, Dagoberto Lara, Ramón Núñez Armas, Calixto Martínez, Roberto Pereira, Jorge Masso, Fermin Madera, Carlos Loredo, Luis Hernández
5. IRQ—Abdul Fatah Jassim, Adnan Derchal Hutar, Jamal Ali Hamza, Saad Jassih Mohammed, Hassan Farhan Hassoun, Alaa Ahmed Khdhayir, Adil Khohayrr Hafidh, Falah Hassan Jasim, Hadi Ahmed Basheer, Hussain Saeed Muhammed, Thamir Assoufi Elias, Ibrahim Ali Kadhum, Wathiq Aswad, Muhyi Nazar Asmraf Salman, Ali Kadhum Nasir, Kadom Shibib Abdulsada
5. KUW—Ahmad Al-Tarabulsi, Naeem Sa'ad Mubarak, Mahoub Mubarak, Jamal Alqabendi, Walid Al-Jasem Mubarak, Sa'ad Al-Houti, Fathi Marzouq, Jasem Sultan, Mujayed Alhaddad, Hamad Bohamad, Youssef Al-Suwayed, Ahmad Hasan, Humoud Al-Shemmari, Sami Alhashash, Faisal Al-Dakhil, Abdulnabi Alkhadi

Seven of the 16 qualifying teams withdrew as part of the anti-Soviet boycott and were replaced by lesser teams. The only goal of the final was scored by a substitute, Jindřich Svoboda, who entered the game with 19 minutes to play and put in a header six minutes later. For the third straight time, the Olympic final was played in a rainstorm.

1984 Los Angeles-Pasadena T: 16, N: 16, D: 8.11.

	W	L	T	GF	GA
1. FRA	4	0	2	13	6
2. BRA	5	1	0	9	5
3. YUG	5	1	0	16	10
4. ITA	3	3	0	5	5
5. CAN	1	2	1	5	4
5. CHI	1	1	2	2	2
5. EGY	1	2	1	5	5
5. GER	2	2	0	10	6

Final: FRA 2-0 BRA
3rd Place: YUG 2-1 ITA

1. FRA—Albert Rust, William Ayache, Michel Biband, Dominique Bijotat, François Brisson, Patrick Cubaynes, Patrice Garande, Philippe Jeannol, Guy Lacombe, Jean-Claude Lemoult, Jean-Philippe Rohr, Didier Sénac, Jean-Christoph Thouvenel, José Touré, Daniel Xuereb, Jean-Louis Zanon
2. BRA—Gilmar Rinaldi, Ronaldo Silva, Jorge Luiz Brum, Mauro Galvão, Ademir Roque Kaeser, André Luiz Ferreira, Paulo Santos, Carlos "Dunga" Verri, João Leiehardt Neto, Augilmar Oliveira, Silvio Paiva, Luiz Carlos Winck, Davi Cortez Silva, Antonio José Gil, Francisco "Chicão" Vidal, Milton Cruz
3. YUG—Ivan Pudar, Vlado Čapljić, Mirsad Baijić, Srečko Katanec, Marko Elsner, Ljubomir Radanović, Admir Smajić, Nenad Gračan, Milko Đurovski, Mehmed Baždarević, Borislav Cvetković, Tomislav Ivković, Jovica Nikolć, Stjepan Deverić, Branko Miljuš, Dragan Stojković, Mitar Mrkela
4. ITA—Franco Tancredi, Riccardo Ferri, Filippo Galli, Sebastiano Nela, Roberto Tricella, Pietro Vierchowod, Salvatore Bagni, Franco Baresi, Sergio Battistini, Antonio Sabato, Beniamino Vignola, Walter Zenga, Pietro Fanna, Daniele Massaro, Massimo Briaschi, Maurizio Iorio, Aldo Serena
5. CAN—Tino Lettieri, Bob Lenarduzzi, Bruce Wilson, Terry Moore, Ian Bridge, Randy Ragan, David Norman, Gerry Gray, Ken Garraway, Dale MItchell, Mike Sweeney, Igor Vrablic, Paul James, John Catliff
5. CHI—Eduardo Fournier Arriagada, Daniel Ahumada, Luis Mosquera, Alex Martínez, Leonel Contreras, Alejandro Hisis Araya, Alfredo Núñez, Jaime Vera Rodríguez, Fernando Santis, Sergio Marchant, Juvenal Olmos Rojas, Carlos Ramos, Jaime Baeza, Marco Figueroa Montero
5. EGY—Adel Elmaamour, Ali El Sayed Gadallah, Rabie Yassen, Mahmoud Saleh, Ibrahim Youssif, Yehia Sedky, Mostafa Ismail, Shawki Gharib, Magdy Abdelghani, Mahmoud Eikhatib, Emad Soleman, Taher Abouzied, Badreldin Hamed, Mohamad Helmy, Omar Elzeer, Alaa Morsy, Nagy Salem
5. GER—Bernd Franke, Manfred Bockenfeld, Roland Dickgiesser, Dieter Bast, Bernd Wehmeyer, Guido Buchwald, Jürgen Groh, Rudolf Bommer, Dieter Schatzschneiden, Andreas Brehme, Frank Mill, Alfred Schoen, Peter Lux, Uwe Rahn, Christian Schreier

For the first time, professional football players were allowed to take part in an Olympic tournament. In the case of European and South American teams, only those professionals who had not yet competed in World Cup competition were considered eligible. This, plus the absence of all of the 1980 medalists, due to the Soviet-bloc boycott, led to a lively and wide-open competition.

The final, played before a crowd of 101,799, was won by the French on two second-half goals, a header by François Brisson, ten minutes into the half and a follow shot by Daniel Xuereb less than eight minutes later.

1988 Seoul T: 16, N: 16, D: 10.1.

	W	L	T	GF	GA
1. SOV	5	0	1	14	6
2. BRA	5	1	0	12	4
3. GER	4	2	0	16	4
4. ITA	3	3	0	11	13
5. ARG	1	2	1	4	5
5. AUS	2	2	0	2	6
5. SWE	2	1	1	7	5
5. ZAM	2	1	1	10	6

Final: SOV 2-1 BRA
3rd Place: GER 3-0 ITA

1. SOV—Dimitri Kharin, Gela Ketashvili, Igor Sklyarov, Oleksei Cherednyk, Arvidas Janonis, Yevgeny Kuznetsov, Igor Ponomarev, Aleksandr Borodyuk, Igor Dobrovolsky, Volodymyr Lyuty, Yevgeny Yakovenko, Sergei Fokin, Volodymyr Tatarchuk, Oleksei Mykhaylychenko, Viktor Losev, Sergei Gorlukovich, Yuri Savichev, Arminas Narbekovas
2. BRA—Claudio Taffarel, Jorge "Jorginho" Campos, João Santos, Batista, Ricardo Gomes Raimundo, Ademir Roque Kaeser, Geovani Silva, Edmar dos Santos, Hamilton "Careca II" de Souza, Romário de Souza Faria, José Araujo, André Cruz, Luiz Winck, Aloisio Alves, Milton de Souza Filho, José Ferreira Neto, Sergio Luiz, Jorge Luís Andrade da Silva, José "Bebeto" Gama de Oliveira
3. GER—Oliver Reck, Michael Schulz, Armin Görtz, Wolfgang Funkel, Thomas Hörster, Olaf Janssen, Rudi Bommer, Holger Fach, Jürgen Klinsmann, Wolfram Wuttke, Frank Mill, Uwe Kamps, Roland Grahammer, Thomas Hässler, Christian Schreier, Fritz Walter, Ralf Sievers, Gerhard Kleppinger, Karlheinz Riedle
4. ITA—Stefano Tacconi, Roberto Cravero, Andrea Carnevale, Luigi De Agostini, Ciro Ferrara, Mauro Tassotti, Angelo Colombo, Luca Pellegrini, Massimo Brambati, Stefano Carobbi, Massimo Crippa, Giuliano Giuliani, Antonio Virdis, Ruggiero Rizzitelli, Roberto Galla, Giuseppe Iachini, Stefano Desideri, Massimo Mauro, Alberigo Evani
5. ARG—Luis Islas Ranieri, Rubén José Agüero, Mauro Airez, Carlos Alfaro Moreno, Claudio Cabrera, Jorge Comas Romero, Hernán Díaz, Néstor Fabbri, Daniel Hernández, Néstor Lorenzo, Fabián Cancelarich, Mario Lucca, Carlos Mayor, Pedro Monzón, Hugo Pérez, Alejandro Ruidíaz, Alejandro Russo, Dario Siviski
5. AUS—Jeffrey Olver, Gary Van Egmond, Graham Jennings, Charlie Yankos, Robert Dunn, Paul Wade, Frank Farina, Mike Petersen, Graham Arnold, John Kosmina, Oscar Crino, Alan Davidson, Andrew Koczka, Vlado Bozinoski, Robert Slater, David Mitchell, Scott Ollerenshaw, Michael Gibson
5. SWE—Sven Andersson, Sulo Vaattovaara, Peter Lönn, Göran Arnberg, Roland Nilsson, Jonas Thern, Leif Engqvist, Michael Andersson, Joakim Nilsson, Anders Limpar, Håkan Lindman, Bengt Nilsson, Martin Dahlin, Hans Eskilsson, Jan Hellström, Roger Ljung, Lars Eriksson, Ola Svensson, Anders Palmér, Stefan Rehn
5. ZAM—David Chabala, Peter Mwanza, Edmon Mumba, Samuel Chomba, James Chitalu, Derby Makinka, Johnson Bwalya, Charles Musonda, Beston Chambeshi, Webster Chikabala, Lucky Msiska, Kalusha Bwalya, Manfred Chabinga, Ashols Melu, Richard Mwanza, Pearson Mwanza, Wisdom Mumba Chansa, Stone Nyirenda, Eston Mulenga

The highlight of the preliminary round was the shocking 4-0 trouncing of Italy by unheralded Zambia. Both Brazil and the Soviet Union advanced to the final with come-from-behind overtime victories. The Soviets scored two goals in extra time to beat Italy, while the Brazilians defeated West Germany in a penalty kick shoot-out. Brazil's Romário, the leading scorer in the tournament with seven, scored the first goal of the final in the 30th minute. Eleven minutes into the second half, Igor Dobrovolsky evened the match with a penalty kick. The decisive goal—the result of a fast-breaking counterattack—was struck in the 14th minute of overtime by substitute Yuri Savichev of Moscow.

1992 Barcelona T: 16, N: 16, D: 8.8.

	W	L	T	GF	GA
1. SPA	6	0	0	14	2
2. POL	4	1	1	17	6
3. GHA	3	1	2	9	6
4. AUS	2	3	1	8	12
5. ITA	2	2	0	3	5
5. PAR	1	1	2	5	5
5. QAT	1	2	1	2	5
5. SWE	1	1	2	6	3

Final: SPA 3-2 POL
3rd Place: GHA 1-0 AUS

1. SPA—Albert Ferrer Llopis, Mikel Lasa Goikoetxea, Roberto Solozábal Villanueva, Juan López Martínez, David Villabona Etxaleku, José Amavisca Garate, Luis Enrique Martínez García, Josep Guardiola Sala, Abelardo Fernández Antuña, Antonio Jiménez Sistachs, Gabriel Vidal Nova, Francisco Soler Atencia, Miguel Hernández Sánchez, Rafael "Rafa" Bergés Marín, Antonio Pinilla Miranda, Francisco "Kiko" Narváez, Alfonso Pérez Muñoz
2. POL—Aleksander Kłak, Marcin Jałocha, Tomasz Łapiński, Marek Koźmiński, Tomasz Wałdoch, Dariusz Gęsior, Piotr Świerczewski, Dariusz Adamczuk, Grzegorz Mielcarski, Jerzy Brzęczek, Andrzej Juskowiak, Ryszard Staniek, Marek Bajor, Andnzej Kobylański, Mirosław Waligóra, Dariusz Koseła, Wojciech Kowalczyk
3. GHA—Anthony Mensah, Frank Amankwah, Isaac Asare, Mohammed Gargo, Joachin Acheampong, Alex Nyarko, Oli Rahman, Nii Lamptey, Kwame Ayew, Shamo Quaye, Samuel Osei Kuffour, Osei Kuffuor, Sammi Adjel, Mohammed Kalilu, Bernard Aryee, Simon Addo, Maxwell Konadu, Yaw Preko, Mamood Amadu, Ibrahim Dossey
4. AUS—John Filan, Milan Blagojevic, Dominic Longo, Nedjelko "Ned" Zelic, Shaun Murphy, Anthony Vidmar, Paul Okon, Zlatko Arambasic, George Slifkas, John Markovski, Damian Mori, Carl Veart, Stavros "Steve" Refenes, Anthony Popovic, David Seal, Gary Hasler, Stephen Corica, Bradley Maloney, Mark Bosnich
5. ITA—Francesco Antonioli, Mauro Bonomi, Giuseppe Favalli, Luca Luzardi, Salvatore Matrecano, Stefano Rossini, Rufo Verga, Demitrio Albertni, Dino Baggio, Eugenio Corini, Dario Marcolin, Gianluca Sordo, Renato Buso, Pasquale Rocco, Alessandro Melli, Roberto Muzzi
5. PAR—Rubén Ruiz Díaz, Andrés Duarte Villamayor, Juan Jara Martínez, Celso Ayala Gavilán, Carlos Gamarra Pavón, Francisco Ferreira Romero, Hugo Sosa Franco, Arsenio Benítez Zarza, Gustavo Neffa Rodríguez, Julio Yegros Torres, Juan Marecos Talavera, Ricardo Sanabria Acuña, Guido Alvarenga Torales, Francisco Arce Rolón, Harles Bourdier Molinas, Mauro Caballero López, Jorge Campos Velásquez
5. QAT—Ahmad Saleh, Hamad Al-Attev, Rashid Suwaid, Zamel Al-Kuwani, Al-Nasser Ali Al-Obaidly, Waleed Maayof, Mubarak Nooralla, Jumah Johar, Mahmoud Souf, Fahad Al-Kuwari, Adel Al-Mulla, Yousuf Mahmoud, Waleed Ibrahim, Abdulla Alabdulla, Mohd Al-Mohannadi, Rashid Al-Kuwari, Al-Aziz Hassan Jaloof, Khalid Al-Waheebi
5. SWE—Jan Ekholm, Magnus Johansson, Joachim Björklund, Filip Apelstav, Niclas Alexandersson, Håkan Mild, Patrik Andersson, Stefan Landberg, Christer Fursth, Jonny Rödlund, Tomas Brolin, Jesper Jansson, Björn Lilius, Pascal Simpson, Niklas Gudmundsson, Jonas Axeldahl

Prior to hosting the 1992 Games, Spain had taken part in 16 summer Olympics and won a grand total of four gold medals. In Barcelona, they earned 13. None was as dramatic and as satisfying as the final one—in the soccer tournament. The Spanish team cruised through to the finals without giving up a single goal in five matches. Their shutout streak came to an end at the close of the first half of the final when Wojciech Kowalczyk put Poland in the lead, 1-0. The Poles were still on top 15 minutes into the second half when Juan Carlos, the King of Spain, arrived in the stadium with his family. Four minutes later Abelardo Fernández tied the score with a header off a free kick by Josep Guardiola. Six minutes after that, Francisco Narváez, known as Kiko or Quico, put Spain into the lead. But Poland wasn't about to fold before 95,000 screaming Spanish fans. In the 76th minute, Ryszard Staniek tied the score again. It looked like the match would go into overtime. With 72 seconds left in regulation, Spain was awarded a corner kick. There was a flurry of activity in front of the goal. Luis Enrique took a shot that was blocked and rebounded to Kiko, who blasted the ball into the upper left corner of the net. The entire Spanish team fell back on defense and 52 seconds later the game was over.

1996 Atlanta-Athens T: 16, N: 16, D: 8.3.

	W	L	T	GF	GA
1. NGR	5	1	0	12	6
2. ARG	3	1	2	13	6
3. BRA	4	2	0	16	8
4. POR	2	2	2	6	10
5. FRA	2	1	1	6	4
6. SPA	2	1	1	5	7
7. MEX	1	1	2	2	3
8. GHA	1	2	1	6	8

Final: NGR 3-2 ARG
3rd Place: BRA 5-0 POR

1. NGR—Celestine Babayaro, Taribo West, Nwankwo Kanu, Uche Okechukwu, Emmanuel Amunike, Tijani Babangida, Wilson Oruma, Teslim Fatusi, Augustine "Jay Jay" Okocha, Victor Ikpeba Nosa, Abiodon Obafemi, Garba Lawal, Daniel Amokachi, Sunday Oliseh, Mobi Oparaku, Joseph Dosu
2. ARG—Carlos Bossio, Roberto Ayala, José Antonio Chamot, Javier Zanetti, Matías Almeyda, Roberto Sensini, Claudio López, Diego Simeone, Hernán Crespo, Ariel Ortega, Hugo Morales, Pablo Cavallero Rodríguez, M. Héctor Pineda, Pablo Paz Gallo, Christian Bassedas, Gustavo López Pablo, Marcelo Delgado, Marcelo Gallardo
3. BRA—Nelson Silva, José "Zé Maria" Ferreira, Aldair Nascimento Santos, Ronaldo Guiaro, Flávio da Conceição, Roberto Carlos da Silva, José "Bebeto" Gama Oliveira, Alexandre "Amaral" da Silva Mariano, Oswaldo "Juninho" Giroldo, Rivaldo Borba Ferreira, Sávio Bortolini Pimentel, Narciso dos Santos, André Luiz Moreira, José "Zé Elias" Moedin, Marcelo "Marcelinho Paulista" de Souza, Luiz "Luizão" Goulart, Ronaldo Nazario Lima
4. POR—Daniel "Dani" Carvalho, Paulo Costinha, Daniel Kenedy dos Santos, Rui Bento, Emilio Peixe, Roberto "Beto" Severo, Luis Andrade de Oliveira, José Dominguez, Nuno "Capucho" Rocha, Paulo Alves, Afonso Martins da Agra, Rui Jorge de Oliveira, Nuno do Espiríto Santo, José Vidigal, José Calado da Silva, Nuno "Gomes" Ribeiro, Hugo Porfirio, Carlos "Litos" Magalhães, Nuno Alfonso
5. FRA—Lionel Letizi, Martin Djetou, Jérôme Bonnissel, Florent Laville, Patrick Moreau, Claude Makelele, Vikash Dhorasoo, Florian Maurice, Antoine Sibierski, Robert Pires, Geoffray Toyes, Vincent Candela, Olivier Dacourt, Tony Vairelles, Sylvain Wiltord, Sylvain Legwinsky
6. SPA—Juan Luis Mora Palacios, Gaizka Mendieta Zabala, Agustín Aranzábal Alkorta, Francisco Vicente Navarro, Santiago Denia Sánchez, Oscar García Junyent, Raúl González Blanco, Roberto Fresnedoso Prieto, Sergio Corino Ramón, José Sáenz Marín, Iñigo Idiákez Barkaiztegi, Aitor Karanka de la Hoz, Fernando Morientes Sánchez, Iván de la Peña López, Jordi Lardín Cruz, José Suárez Rivas, Daniel García Lara
7. MEX—Claudio Suárez Sánchez, Germán Villa Castañeda, Duilio Davino Rodríguez, Raúl Lara Tovar, José García Torres, Manuel Sol Sañudo, Jorge Campos Navarrete, Luis García Postigo, Cuauhtémoc Blanco Bravo, Pável Pardo Segura, José de Jesús Arellano Alcócer, Enrique Alfaro Rojas, Juan Francisco Palencia Hernández, José Manuel Abundis Sandoval
8. GHA—Nii Aryee Welbeck, Stephen Baidoo, Joseph Addo, Afo Dodoo, Emmanuel Osei Kuffour, Mallam Yahya, Augustine Ahinful, Charles Akunnor, Emmanuel Duah, Felix Aboagye, Ohene Kennedy, Ebenezer Hagan, Christian Sabah, Prince Koranteng, Osei E. Kuffour, Simon Addo

The 1996 tournament was the first in which each team was allowed to add to its roster three professionals over the age of 23. Some teams, such as France and Spain, chose not to do so. None of these progressed past the quarterfinals.

The pre-Olympic favorites were South American powerhouses Brazil and Argentina. Nigeria, which had achieved great success at international youth tournaments, entered the Olympics in a state of chaos. After South African president Nelson Mandela criticized Nigerian dictator Sani Abacha for hanging nine political dissidents, Abacha refused to allow Nigeria to play in the African Nations Cup in South Africa. F.I.F.A. threatened to ban Nigeria from international competition, but eventually relented. The next few months were filled with endless wrangling about who should be included on the team. The final squad included only two players who played in Nigeria and gathering the squad for training was difficult. Nigeria's captain, Nwankwo Kanu arrived in Atlanta from Europe only three days before the team's opening match. Not surprisingly, Nigeria began sluggishly, struggling to victory over Hungary and Japan and losing 1-0 to Brazil on a goal by Ronaldo.

Fortunately, Nigeria's Dutch coach, Jon Bonfrère, who had resigned in April only to return at the request of the players, gave the team good advice: "Forget all the problems for one and a half hours and then, after the game, we can start with new problems."

The Nigerians came alive in the quarterfinals, defeating Mexico 2-0. In the semifinals they faced Brazil again. Brazil led at halftime 3-1. Even Nigeria's only goal had gone into the net off the foot of a Brazilian, Roberto Carlos. In the second half, Nigeria's Jay Jay Okocha missed a penalty shot. With 13 minutes to play, Brazil still led by two goals. A 20-meter shot by Victor Ikpeba cut the score to 3-2. In the final minute of regulation, Kanu controlled a loose ball, popped it up and whacked it into the goal. This put the match into sudden death overtime. In the fourth minute, a long pass bounced off Ikpeba's back and landed at Kanu's feet. He moved past defender Aldair and scored with a left footed shot.

In comparison to Nigeria's wild ride to the final, Argentina's road was smooth. After placing first in their preliminary group, they steamrolled Spain in the quarterfinals 4-0 and defeated Portugal 2-0 in the semifinals. Argentina did suffer one unexpected setback: returning to their hotel rooms one evening, eight of the Argentinian players discovered that they had been robbed.

Before a crowd of 86,117, Argentina took charge immediately. Less than two minutes into the final, Hernán Crespo sent a long cross from the right side to Claudio López, who headed the ball into the upper left corner of the goal from six meters out. In the 28th minute, Celestine Babayaro headed in a pass from Kanu to tie the score.

Five minutes after the start of the second half, Taribo West was called for pushing Ariel Ortega in the penalty area. Most observers thought this a phantom foul, but Italian referee Pierluigi Collina remained adamant. Crespo converted the penalty to put Argentina ahead 2-1. As in the semifinal, the Nigerians found themselves trailing with 17 minutes to play. A long throw in by Babayaro from the left side was headed on by Kanu. Sunday Oliseh swung at the ball but missed it completely. However, Daniel Amokachi, standing behind Oliseh, chipped the ball past Argentinian goalie Pablo Cavallero.

It looked like the game would go into overtime. With less than two minutes left on the clock, Nigeria gained a free kick when Javier Zanetti fouled substitute Emmanuel Amunike outside the left corner of the penalty area. Wilson Oruma took the kick. The Argentine defense set an offside trap, rushing forward in a line as Oruma struck the ball. It appeared that the trap worked, but the linesman and referee thought otherwise. Amunike, unmarked, volleyed the ball into the goal to give Nigeria a stunning victory.

2000 Sydney T: 16, N: 16, D: 9.30.

	W	L	T	GF	GA
1. CAM	4	0	2	11	8
2. SPA	4	2	0	12	6
3. CHI	4	2	0	14	6
4. USA	2	2	2	9	11
5. ITA	2	1	1	5	3
6. JPN	2	2	0	6	5
7. BRA	2	2	0	6	6
8. NGR	1	1	2	8	10

Final: CAM 2 (5)-2 (3) SPA
3rd Place: CHI 2-0 USA

1. CAM—Aaron Nguimbat, Albert Meyong Zé, Clement Beaud, Daniel Bekono, Daniel Ngom Kome, Geremi Njitap Fotso, Idriss Carlos Kameni, Joel Epalle, Laureano "Lauren" Etame-Mayer, Modeste Mbami, Nicolas Alnoudji, Patrice Abanda, H. Patrick Mboma, Patrick Suffo, Pierre Wome, Samuel Eto'o Fils, Serge Branco, Serge Mimpo
2. SPA—David Albelda Aliqués, Iván Amaya Carazo, Miguel Ángel Angulo Valderrey, Daniel Aranzubia Aguado, Joan Capdevila Méndez, Jordi Ferrón Forné, Gabriel García de la Torré, Ismael Ruiz Salmón, Jesús María Lacruz Gómez, Albert Luque Martos, Carlos Marchena López, José María "José Mari" Romero Poyón, Carles Puyol i Saforcada, Raúl Tamudo Montero, Unai Vergara Díez Caballero, Antonio "Toni" Velamazán Tejedor, Xavier "Xavi" Hernández Creus
3. CHI—Cristián Álvarez Valenzuela, Francisco Arrué Pardo, Pablo Contreras Fica, Sebastián González Valdés, David Henríquez Espinoza, Manuel Ibarra Valdez, Claudio Maldonado Rivera, Reinaldo Navia Amador, Rodrigo Núñez Ortiz, Rafael Olarra Guerrero, Luis Patricio Ormazábal Mozó, David Pizarro Cortés, Pedro Reyes González, Nelson Tapia Ríos, Rodrigo Tello Valenzuela, Iván Zamorano Zamora, Mauricio Rojas Toro
4. USA—Joshua Wolff, Benjamin Olsen, Bradley Friedel, Brian Dunseth, Chad McCarty, Christopher Albright, Conor Casey, Daniel Califf, Evan Whitfield, Frank Hejduk, Jeffrey Agoos, Joseph DiGiamarino, John O'Brien, Landon Donovan, Panayiotis "Pete" Vagenas, Ramiro Corrales, Sasha Victorine
5. ITA—Alessandro Grandoni, Andrea Pirlo, Bruno Cirillo, Christian Abbiati, Claudio Rivalta, Cristiano Zanetti, Gennaro Ivan Gattuso, Gianluca Zambrotta, Gianni Comandini, Ighli Vannucchi, Luca Mezzano, Marco Zanchi, Massimo Ambrosini, Massimo Margiotta, Matteo Ferrari, Nicola Ventola, Roberto Baronio
6. JPN—Atsuhiro Miura, Atsushi Yanagisawa, Hidetoshi Nakata, Junichi Inamoto, Koji Nakata, Masashi Motoyama, Naohiro Takahara, Naoki Matsuda, Ryuzo Morioka, Seigo Narazaki, Shunsuke Nakamura, Tomokazu Myojin, Tomoyuki Hirase, Tomoyuki Sakai, Tsuneyasu Miyamoto, Yuji Nakazawa
7. BRA—Alexsandro "Alex" de Souza, Álvaro Luiz De Aquino, Athirson Oliveira, Dermival "Baiano" Lima, Fabiano da Costa, Fábio Aurélio Rodrigues, Fábio Bilica da Silva, Helton Arruda, Lucas Severino, Luis Eduardo "Edu" Schmidt, Marcos Paulo Alves, Mozart Batista Junior, Roger Flores, Ronaldo "Ronaldinho Gaúcho" Moreira, Geovanni da Silva, Lucio da Costa
8. NGR—Azubuike Oliseh, Blessing Kaku, Bright Igbinadolor, Celestine Babayaro, Christopher Kanu, Furo Iyenemi, Garba Lawal, Gbenga Okunowo, Godwin Okpara, Gregg Etafia, Henry Onwuzuruike, Isaac Okoronkwo, Johnson Sunday, Julius Aghahowa, Pius Ikedia, Victor Agali, Yakubu Ayegbeni

Considered outsiders, the Cameroon team attracted little attention during pool play, beating Kuwait 3-2 and tying both the United States and the Czech Republic 1-1. But their quarterfinal performance against Brazil in

Brisbane was another story. Cameroon led 1-0 at halftime on an early goal by Patrick Mboma, but their hopes for an upset began to unravel with 15 minutes to go in regulation when their captain, Geremi Njitap was sent off when he picked up his second yellow card—for stalling on a throw-in. Two minutes into injury time, Aaron Nguimbat was also shown a red card and Cameroon was down to nine men. Two minutes later, with only seconds left, Ronaldinho scored on a free kick to equalize for Brazil and send the game into overtime. Playing two men short, it appeared that Cameroon's only chance was to survive the 30 minutes of overtime and hope that their 16-year-old goalkeeper, Carlos Kameni, who was playing in his first senior-level international match, could win the penalty shootout. However, with seven minutes remaining, Cameroon attacked and substitute Modeste Mbami scored the unexpected winning goal.

Three days later, in Melbourne, Cameroon faced Chile in the semifinals. The game was scoreless until the 78th minute when Kameni blocked a shot. The ball hit defender Patrice Abanda in the chest and bounced into the goal. Six minutes later, Patrick Mboma scored to put Cameroon back in the game. Then, with one minute left in regulation, Mboma was fouled in the penalty box by Pablo Contreras. Lauren Etame-Mayer converted the penalty and the Cameroonians moved on to Sydney for the final, which was played before a crowd of 98,212. Only 78 seconds into the match, Spain opened the scoring on a free kick by Xavier Hernández. Three minutes later, Carlos Kameni stopped a penalty kick by Miguel Angulo. But during first-half injury time, Gabri García de la Torre scored to give Spain a 2-0 lead at halftime. Eight minutes into the second half, a cross by Mboma deflected off the face of Spanish defender Iván Amaya and into the goal. Five minutes later, Samuel Eto'o tapped in another cross from Mboma to tie the game. Late in the half both Gabri and José Mari picked up red cards, forcing Spain to go into overtime with only nine players. Spain almost won anyway in the first minute of overtime when Joan Capdevila's free kick hit the outside of the post. Later, Eto'o did put the ball in the net, but was called for offside. So the Olympic championship was decided by penalty shootout. With the shootout score at 3-2 Cameroon, Spain's third shooter, Iván Amaya, hit the crossbar. Both Etame-Mayer and Pierre Wome converted their shots and Cameroon won 5-3. Back in Cameroon, President Paul Biya declared a national holiday to add to the informal one that had been celebrated by many Cameroonians in preparation for the final, which began at 2 a.m. local time.

2004 Athens T: 16, N: 16, D: 8.28.

	W	L	T	GF	GA
1. ARG	6	0	0	17	0
2. PAR	4	2	0	12	9
3. ITA	3	2	1	7	8
4. IRQ	3	3	0	9	8
5. MLI	1	1	2	5	4
6. KOR	1	1	2	8	8
7. AUS	1	2	1	6	4
8. CRC	1	2	1	4	8

Final: ARG 1-0 PAR
3rd Place: ITA 1-0 IRQ

1. ARG—Germán Lux, Roberto Ayala, Fabricio Coloccini, Gabriel Heinze, Javier Mascherano, Cristian "Kily" González Peret, Andrés D'Alessandro, Luis González, César Delgado Godoy, Carlos Martínez Tévez, Mauro Rosales, Nicolás Burdisso, Javier Saviola Fernández, Nicolás Medina, Clemente Rodríguez, Mariano González
2. PAR—Diego Barreto Cáceres, Julio César Manzur Caffarena, Carlos Gamarra Pavón, José Devaca, Celso Esquivel González, Aureliano Torres Román, Ernesto Cristaldo,Édgar Barreto Cáceres, Diego Figueredo Matiauda, Pablo Giménez, José Cardozo Otazú, Emilio Martínez, Fredy Bareiro Gamarra, Pedro Benítez, Julio César Enciso Ferreira, Julio González, Osvaldo Díaz
3. ITA—Ivan Pelizzoli, Emiliano Moretti, Matteo Ferrari, Daniele Bonera, Andrea Barzagli, Daniele De Rossi, Giampiero Pinzi, Angelo Palombo, Andrea Pirlo, Alberto Gilardino, Giuseppe Sculli, Giorgio Chiellini, Andrea Gasbarroni, Cesare Bovo, Marco Donadel, Simone Del Nero, Giandomenico Mesto
4. IRQ—Bassim Abbas Kati, Haidar Abdul Amir, Haidar Abdul Razzaq, Ali Nashat Akram, Saad Attiya Hafidh, Razzaq Farhan, Haidar Jabar, Mahdi Karim Ajeel, Younis Mahmoud Khalef, Ahmed Manajid Abbas, Emad Mohammed, Hawar Mulla Mohammed, Qusai Munir Aboudy, Nour Sabri, Salih Sadir, Ahmed Salah Alwan, Abdul Wahab Abu Al-Hail
5. MLI—Sheikh Bathily, Adama Tamboura, Boubacar Kone, Abdou Traoré, Moussa Coulibaly, Mamadi Berthe, Momo Sissoko, Tenema N'diaye, Dramane Traoré, Jimmy Kebe, Mamadou Diallo, Boucader Diallo, Rafan Sidibe, Mintou Doucoure, Sedonoude Abouta, Drissa Diakite
6. KOR—Cho Byung-kuk, Kim Chi-gon, Lee Chun-soo, Kim Do-heon, Kim Dong-jin, Cho Jae-jin, Kim Jung-woo, Nam Kung-do, Chung Kyung-ho, Park Kyu-seon, Yoo Sang-chul, Choi Sung-kuk, Choi Tae-uk, Choi Won-kwon, Park Yong-ho, Kim Young-kwang
7. AUS—Eugene Galekovic, Jade North, Shane Cansdell-Sherriff, Craig Moore, Adrian Madaschi, Ahmad Elrich, Luke Wilkshire, Tim Cahill, Carl Valeri, John Aloisi, Alex Brosque, Jon McKain, Brett Holman, Anthony Danze, Spase Dilevski, Ryan Griffiths
8. CRC—Neighel Drummond Morales, Pablo Salazar Sánchez, Míchael Umaña Corrales, Roy Myrie Medrano, José Villalobos Chan, Júnior Díaz Campbell, José Luis López Ramírez, Pablo Brenes Quesada, Carlos Hernández Valverde, Erick Scott Bernard, Álvaro Saborío Chacón, Whayne Wilson Harris, Warren Granados, Jairo Arrieta Obando

Although Argentina has always been one of the world's leading football powers, until 2004 it had never won an Olympic championship. In fact, Argentina had not won a team sport at the Olympics since the polo tournament in 1936, and no Argentinian had earned a gold medal in any sport since Tranquilo Cappozzo and Eduardo

Guerrero took the double sculls rowing event in 1952. Considering this history, the Argentinians swept through the 2004 tournament with remarkable ease. In group play, they began by overwhelming Serbia 6-0, and followed with a 2-0 shutout of Tunisia and a 1-0 defeat of Australia. In the quarterfinals, they cruised past Costa Rica 4-0 and in the semifinals they knocked off Italy 3-0. Paraguay advanced to the final against Argentina by winning their group despite a 2-1 loss to Ghana. In the quarterfinals, they took a 3-0 lead against South Korea and then survived two goals by Lee Chun-soo to hold on for a 3-2 victory. In the semifinals, the Paraguayans faced the team from Iraq, which was competing while its nation was at war. Thirty-four-year-old José Cardozo scored two first-half goals for Paraguay, which went on to win 3-1.

The bronze medal match between Iraq and Italy was a somber affair, coming just two days after Islamic extremists in Iraq announced that they had executed Italian journalist Enzo Baldoni. The Italian team wore black armbands, and Iraqi captain Abdul Wahab Abu Al-Hail presented his Italian counterpart, Andrea Pirlo, with a bouquet of white flowers before the game began. Italy scored in the eighth minute on a header by Alberto Gilardino. Despite several close attempts, Iraq proved unable to equalize.

Although Argentina went into the gold medal match as favorites, they had previously suffered two narrow defeats in Olympic finals. In 1928, they tied Uruguay 1-1. According to the rules of the time, the final was replayed and this time, Argentina lost 2-1. In the 1996 final, Argentina was upset when Nigeria scored two late goals to win 3-2. If the Argentinians might have felt haunted by history in Athens, at least their Olympic record was better than that of Paraguay, which first entered the Olympics in 1968 and had never earned a medal in any sport. Paraguay ran into trouble even before the final began, when José Cardozo, their top scorer, injured his knee during practice before the match and was unable to play. Argentina scored in the 18th minute on a cross by Mauro Rosales to 20-year-old Carlos Tévez, who maneuvered around two defenders before planting the ball into the back of the net. Paraguay became increasingly desperate as the match continued, earning seven yellow cards, as well as two ejections late in the second half. The Argentine players celebrated their victory by dancing in a circle to the music of Carlos Santana's "Smooth." Argentina was the first country in one hundred years to manage the impressive feat of winning every Olympic match in a competition without conceding a single goal.

2008 Beijing T: 16, N: 16, D: 8.23.

	W	L	T	GF	GA
1. ARG	6	0	0	11	2
2. NGR	4	1	1	10	4
3. BRA	5	1	0	14	3
4. BEL	3	3	0	7	10
5. ITA	2	1	1	8	3
6. IVC	2	2	0	6	6
7. HOL	1	1	2	4	4
8. CAM	1	1	2	2	3

Final: ARG 1-0 NGR
3rd Place: BRA 3-0 BEL

1. ARG—Lautaro Acosta, Sergio Agüero del Castillo, Éver Banega, Diego Buonanotte Rende, Ángel Di María Hernández, Federico Fazio, Fernando Gago, Ezequiel Garay, Ezequiel Lavezzi, Javier Mascherano, Lionel Messi, Fabián Monzón, Nicolás Pareja, Juan Riquelme, Sergio Romero, José Sosa, Óscar Ustari, Pablo Zabaleta Girod
2. NGR—Olubayo Adefemi, Dele Adeleye, Femi Ajilore, Efe Ambrose, Victor Anichebe, Onyekachi Apam, Emmanuel Ekpo, Promise Isaac, Monday James, Sani Kaita, Victor Obinna, Peter Odemwingie, Chinedu Ogbuke Obasi, Chibuzor Okonkwo, Solomon Okoronkwo, Ambruse Vanzekin
3. BRA—Alex da Silva, Alexandre "Pato" da Silva, Ânderson Luís de Abreu Oliveira, Breno Vinicius Rodrigues Borges, Diego Ribas da Cunha, Anderson "Hernanes" de Carvalho Andrade Lima, Ilson "Ilsinho" Pereira Dias, João "Jô" Alves de Assis Silva, Lucas Pezzini Leiva, Marcelo Vieira da Silva, Rafael Sóbis do Nascimento, Márcio Rafael "Rafinha" Ferreira de Souza, Ramires Santos do Nascimento, Renan Brito Soares, Ronaldo "Ronaldinho" de Assís Moreira, Thiago Neves Augusto, Thiago Emiliano da Silva
4. BEL—Logan Bailly, Laurent Ciman, Tom De Mul, Sepp De Roover, Stijn De Smet, Moussa Dembélé, Marouane Fellaini, Faris Haroun, Vincent Kompany, Yves Makabu-Kalambay, Maarten Martens, Kevin Mirallas, Landry Mulemo, Vadis Odjidja-Ofoe, Sebastien Pocognoli, Jeroen Simaeys, Anthony Vanden Borre, Thomas Vermaelen, Jan Vertonghe

Lionel Messi and Angel Di Maria, 2008
Celebrating Argentina's Victory.

5. ITA—Ignazio Abate, Robert Acquafresca, Salvatore Bocchetti, Antonio Candreva, Luca Cigarini, Andrea Coda, Andrea Consigli, Domenico Criscito, Paolo De Ceglie, Lorenzo De Silvestri, Daniele Dessena, Sebastian Giovinco, Claudio Marchisio, Riccardo Montolivo, Marco Motta, Antonio Nocerino, Tommaso Rocchi, Giuseppe Rossi, Emiliano Viviano
6. IVC—Vincent Angban, Brou Angoua, Mamadou Bagayoko, Soleymane Bamba, Sekou Cissé, Kafoumba Coulibaly, Ousman Diarrassouba, Franck Dja Djedje, Gervais Kouassi, Abraham Guie-Gnekl, Salomon Kalou, Hervé Kambou, Emmanuel Koné, Anthony Moura-Komenan, Antoine N'Gossan, Serge Wawa
7. HOL—Ryan Babel, Otman Bakkal, Roy Beerens, Jonathan de Guzmán, Royston Drenthe, Urby Emanuelson, Kew Jaliens, Calvin Jong-a-Pin, Hedwiges Maduro, Roy Makaay, Dirk Marcellis, Erik Pieters, Gerald Sibon, Evander Sno, Kenneth Vermeer, Gianni Zuiverloon
8. CAM—Albert Baning, Gustave Bebbe, Paul Bebey, Christian Bekamenga, André Bikey, Aurélien Chedjou, Alexis Enam, Antonio Ghomsi, Georges Mandjeck, Stéphane Mbia, Marc Mboua, Serge N'Gal, Nicolas N'Koulou, Alain Ollé, Alex Song, Franck Songo'o, Amour Tignyemb

Four years after sweeping through the 2004 Athens Olympic tournament, Argentina remained the leading youth national football team in the world, having won both the intervening under-20 World Cup titles. The Argentine line-up was led by 21-year-old Barcelona striker Lionel Messi, who was already emerging as one of the greatest strikers in the history of the sport, and 20-year-old striker Sergio Agüero, who helped Argentina defend their title at the 2007 U-20 World Cup, contributing six goals and earning the Most Valuable Player award.

Argentina and Brazil both won all three of their matches in their round-robin pools matches. Argentina opened by beating Ivory Coast 2-1, and then followed with a 1-0 defeat of Australia and a 2-0 shutout of Serbia. Brazil did not concede a single goal in their matches against Belgium (1-0), New Zealand (5-0) and China (3-0). The 2006 World Cup champion, Italy, qualified top of their group, after 3-0 wins over Honduras and South Korea and a scoreless tie with Cameroon. The fourth round-robin pool was headed by Nigeria.

Brazil defeated Cameroon 2-0 in the quarterfinals, with Rafael Sóbis and Marcelo scoring in overtime after a rough match that saw eight yellow cards given to Cameroon and five to Brazil.

Belgium played most of their quarterfinal match against Italy a man down after losing defender Thomas Vermaelen to a red card in the 17th minute. Trailing 2-1 at the half, Italy evened the score on a penalty by Giuseppe Rossi in the 74th minute, but five minutes later Moussa Dembélé scored to give Belgium a 3-2 win.

In Argentina's quarterfinal match against the Netherlands Messi gave the South Americans the early lead with a brilliant goal in the 14th minute; however, Otman Bakkal equalized in the 36th minute. There was no more scoring until 15 minutes into overtime, when Messi set up midfielder Ángel Di María to give the team a 2-1 victory. Nigeria rounded out the semifinal line-up, advancing on a 2-0 win over Ivory Coast.

The first semifinal, between Nigeria and Belgium, was one of the more lopsided of the competition. Nigeria's Olubayo Adefemi opened the scoring seventeen minutes into play, then came two goals in the second half from midfielder Chinedu Ogbuke and a fourth from defender Chibuzor Okonkwo. A late goal by Belgium put the final score at 4-1.

Brazil and Argentina faced each other in the much-anticipated second semifinal. Brazil, led by former FC Barcelona midfielder Ronaldinho, had yet to concede a goal in the tournament, and the game remained scoreless through the first half. Seven minutes into the second half Agüero scored on a pass from Di María, and again five minutes later after a pass from Messi. Brazil struggled to respond, a free kick by Ronaldinho ricocheted off the upright and a follow-up goal was disallowed due to an offside infraction. With 14 minutes remaining in regulation, Argentine captain Juan Riquelme hammered another nail into the coffin, scoring on a penalty. Brazil fell apart in the final ten minutes, losing two players to red cards on ugly fouls. After the victory, Agüero revealed that he and his girlfriend, the daughter of Argentine soccer legend Diego Maradona, were expecting a baby. "I'm very proud to have a son-in-law who can score two goals against Brazil and then gets fouled in the box for a penalty," Maradona said.

The final between Argentina and Nigeria was a repeat of the match-up for the 1996 Atlanta final, in which Nigeria had taken the gold medal with a 3-2 win. The 2008 match was held in stifling midday heat and the match was twice halted to allow the players to rehydrate. Nigeria's Chinedu Ogbuke, who had scored twice in the semifinal win over Belgium, was sidelined with a shin injury, and Nigeria were unable to score despite outshooting Argentina in the first half. Thirteen minutes into the second half Messi passed to Di María, who chipped the ball over goalkeeper Ambruse Vanzekin in what would turn out to be the only goal of the match.

WOMEN

1896–1992 not held

1996 Atlanta-Athens T: 8, N: 8, D: 8.1.

	W	L	T	GF	GA
1. USA	4	0	1	9	3
2. CHN	3	1	1	11	5
3. NOR	3	1	1	12	6
4. BRA	1	2	2	7	8
5. GER	1	1	1	6	6
6. SWE	1	2	0	4	5
7. JPN	0	3	0	2	9
8. DEN	0	3	0	2	11

Final: USA 2-1 CHN
3rd Place: NOR 2-0 BRA

1. USA—Briana Scurry, Cindy Parlow, Carla Overbeck, Tiffany Roberts, Brandi Chastain, Staci Wilson, Shannon MacMillan, Mariel "Mia" Hamm, Michelle Akers, Julie Foudy, Carin Gabarra, Kristine Lilly, Joy Fawcett, Tisha Venturini, Tiffeny Milbrett
2. CHN—Wang Liping, Fan Yunjie, Yu Hongqi, Chen Yufeng, Wei Haiying, Zhao Lihong, Shi Guihong, Shui Qingxia, Sun Wen, Xie Huilin, Wen Lirong, Gao Hong, Sun Qingmei, Liu Ying, Liu Ailing
3. NOR—Bente Nordby, Agnete Carlsen, Gro Espeseth, Nina Nymark Andersen, Merete Myklebust, Hege Riise, Anne Nymark Andersen, Marianne Pettersen, Linda Medalen, Brit Sandaune, Tina Svensson, Tone Haugen, Trine Tangeraas, Ann Kristen Aarønes, Reidun Seth
4. BRA—Margarete "Meg" Pioresan, Elissandra "Nenê" Cavalcanti, Suzy Bitencourt de Oliveiri, Roselane "Fanta" Motta, Márcia Taffarel, Elane dos Santos Rego, Delma "Pretinha" Gonçalves, Miraildes "Formiga" Mota, Mariela "Michael Jackson" dos Santos, Sisleide "Sissi" Lima do Amor, Roseli de Belo, Diedja Barreto, Marisa Pires Nogueira, Tânia Pereira Ribeiro, Nilda do Nascimento, Sônia "Acre" da Costa
5. GER—Manuela Goller, Jutta Nardenbach, Birgitt Austermuhl, Kerstin Stegemann, Doris Fitschen, Dagmar Pohlmann, Martina Voss, Bettina Wiegmann, Heidi Mohr, Silvia Neid, Patrizia Brocker, Sandra Minnert, Pia Wunderlich, Birgit Prinz, Renate Lingor
6. SWE—Annelie Nilsson, Cecilia Sandell, Åsa Jakobsson, Annika Nessvold, Kristin Bengtsson, Anna Pohjanen, Pia Sundhage, Malin Swedberg, Malin Andersson, Ulrika Kalte, Lena Videkull, Ulrika Karlsson, Camilla Svensson, Maria Kun, Julia Carlsson, Hanna Ljungberg
7. JPN—Junko Ozawa, Yumi Tomei, Rie Yamaki, Maki Haneta, Yumi Obe, Kae Nishina, Homare Sawa, Asako Takakura, Futaba Kioka, Akemi Noda, Tamaki Uchiyama, Nami Otake, Kaoru Kadohara, Miyuki Izumi, Shiho Onodera
8. DEN—Doerthe Larsen, Annette Laursen, Bonny Madsen, Kamma Bodil Thaasti Flæng, Rikke Holm, Christina Bendt Petersen, Birgit Melgaard Christensen, Lisbet Bagge Kolding, Helle Kristine Lund Jensen, Gitte Krogh, Lene Fleng Madsen, Lene Bjerning Terp, Anne Dot Eggers Nielsen, Merete Pedersen, Christina Bonde

For several years, Norway and the United States had been battling for supremacy in women's football. Since 1987 they had met 18 times. Norway led the series ten to seven with one tie. Their most notable encounters had been in the 1991 Women's World Cup final (USA 2, Norway 1) and the 1995 Women's World Cup semifinal (Norway 1, USA 0). The two teams met again in the semifinals of the inaugural Olympic tournament. Police officer Linda Medalen scored for Norway in the 18th minute and the Norwegians still led 1-0 with 16 minutes to play. Then Norwegian defender Gro Espeseth blocked a shot with her elbow. Despite protests from the American side, referee Sonia Denoncourt ordered play to continue. However, two minutes later she awarded the US a penalty kick on a phantom hand ball against Espeseth. Veteran Michelle Akers took the kick and drilled it into the net. After the expulsion of Norway's Agnete Carlsen for a rough tackle, the match went into sudden death overtime. In the sixth minute, US coach Tony Dicicco replaced Tiffeny Milbrett with her former University of Portland teammate Shannon MacMillan. Four minutes later MacMillan scored the winning goal on a perfect pass from Julie Foudy.

Earlier in the day, China had qualified for the final in equally dramatic fashion. Trailing upset-minded Brazil 2-1, China's Wei Huiying scored two goals in the last eight minutes of regulation to eke out a 3-2 victory.

The final was played four days later before a crowd of 76,481 at the University of Georgia in Athens about 65 miles outside of Atlanta. The United States and China had met in pool play and tied 0-0 in a match that was played after both had already qualified for the semifinals.

In the 19th minute of the final, Mia Hamm struck a hard shot that Chinese goalie Gao Hong deflected into the post. Shannon MacMillan collected the rebound and scored to put the US up 1-0. Thirteen minutes later, Sun Wen caught the US goalie out too far and chipped the ball over her head from twenty meters. A desperate dive by Brandi Chastain failed to keep the ball out of the net. US 1, China 1. The Chinese dominated the rest of the first half and the first fifteen minutes of the second half. But then the Americans took charge. After six minutes of intense pressure, US defender Joy Fawcett drove towards the right corner of the penalty area and then passed the ball in front of goalie Gao to onrushing Tiffeny Milbrett, who tapped the ball past the diving Gao. This would prove to be the last and winning goal.

Earlier in the year, a *Sports Illustrated* reporter had telephoned Briana Scurry at her apartment and asked her what she would do if the US won the gold medal. Half-asleep, Scurry replied that she would run naked down the streets of Athens, Georgia. Eight hours after the Olympic final ended, an honor-bound Scurry ventured out at 2 a.m. with a friend and a video camera. On a side street off Milledge Ave., Scurry, wearing only her gold medal, made a ten-meter dash and fulfilled her promise.

2000 Sydney T: 8, N: 8, D: 9.28.

	W	L	T	GF	GA
1. NOR	4	0	0	9	6
2. USA	3	1	1	9	5
3. GER	4	1	0	8	2
4. BRA	2	3	0	5	6
5. CHN	1	1	0	5	4
6. SWE	0	2	1	1	4
7. AUS	0	2	1	2	6
8. NGR	0	3	0	3	9

Final: NOR 3-2 USA (overtime)
3rd Place: GER 2-0 BRA

1. NOR—Kristin Bekkevold, Christine Bø Jensen, Gro Espeseth, Ragnhild Gulbrandsen, Solveig Gulbrandsen, Margunn Haugenes, Silje Jørgensen, Monica Knudsen, Gøril Kringen, Unni Lehn, Dagny Mellgren, Bente Nordby, Marianne Pettersen, Anita Rapp, Hege Riise, Brit Sandaune, Anne Tønnessen
2. USA—Brandi Chastain, Christine Pearce, Cindy Parlow, Joy Fawcett, Julie Foudy, Kate Sobrero, Kristine Lily, Lorrie Fair, Mariel "Mia" Hamm, Nikki Serlenga, Shannon MacMillan, Siri Mullinix, Tiffeny Milbrett
3. GER—Nicole Brandebusemeyer, Ariane Hingst, Bettina Wiegmann, Birgit Prinz, Claudia Müller, Doris Fitschen, Inka Grings, Jeannette Goette, Kerstin Stegemann, Maren Meinert, Melanie Hoffmann, Renate Lingor, Sandra Minnert, Silke Rottenberg, Stefanie Gottschlich, Steffi Jones, Tina Wunderlich
4. BRA—Juliana Cabral, Andréia Suntaque, Maria "Cidinha" Dias, Daniela Lima, Miraildes "Formiga" Mota, Kátia da Silva, Andréia "Maycon" dos Santos, Mônica Angélica de Paula, Elissandra "Nenê" Cavalcante, Delma "Pretinha" Gonçalves, Raquel Noronha, Rosana Augusto, Roseli de Belo, Simone Jatobá, Sisleide "Sissi" do Amor, Suzana da Silva, Tânia Maria Ribeiro
5. CHN—Jie Bai, Yunjie Fan, Hong Gao, Yan Jin, Ailling Liu, Ying Liu, Wei Pu, Wen Sun, Liping Wang, Lirong Wen, Huilin Xie, Ouying Zhang, Lihong Zhao
6. SWE—Caroline Jönsson, Cecilia Sandell, Hanna Ljungberg, Hanna Marklund, Jane Törnqvist, Karoline Westberg, Kristin Bengtsson, Linda Fagerström, Malin Andersson, Malin Moström, Malin Swedberg, Sara Johansson, Sara Larsson, Therese Sjögren, Tina Nordlund, Victoria Svensson
7. AUS—Alicia Ferguson, Alison Forman, Amy Wilson, Anissa Tann-Darby, Bridgette Starr, Bryony Duus, Cherly Salisbury, Dianne Alagich, Heather Garriock, Julie Murray, Kate McShea, Kelly Golebiowski, Sacha Wainwright, Sharon Black, Sunni Hughes, Tracey Wheeler
8. NGR—Anna Chiejine, Eberechi Opara, Florence Omagbemi, Gloria Usieta, Ifeanyichukwu Chiehene, Judith Chime, Kikelomo Ajayi, Maureen Mmadu, Mercy Akide, Nkiru Okosieme, Patience Avre, Perpetua Nkwocha, Rita Nwadike, Stella Mbachu, Yinka Kudaisi

For all their hard work, both Norway and the United States needed a bit of luck to make it to the final. The only goal in Norway's 1-0 semifinal victory over Germany came in the 80th minute when German defender Tina Wunderlich headed the ball back towards her own goal, not realizing that goalkeeper Silke Rottenberg had come forward to retrieve the ball herself. The ball went into the net. The United States, facing Brazil, also won their semifinal by a score of 1-0. The US goal came in the 60th minute when Tiffeny Milbrett knocked down goalie Maycon. Mia Hamm kicked the loose ball into the goal. Even Milbrett expected a foul to be called, but Swiss referee Nicole Petignant did not blow her whistle. It was Petignant who had handed the Americans the 1999 World Cup when she chose not to penalize US goalie Briana Scurry for moving too soon during the final penalty shootout with China. Norway and the US had met during pool play with the Americans winning 2-0. In the final, the US opened the scoring again, in the fifth minute, when Milbrett converted a pass from Hamm. Just before the end of the half, Gro Espeseth brought Norway even by heading in a corner kick from Hege Riise. In the 78th minute, US goalkeeper Siri Mullinix collided with defender Joy Fawcett, and Ragnhild Gulbrandsen was able to head the ball into an empty net. As the game moved into injury time, the Norwegians on the bench began to gather in preparation for their celebration. But with less than 30 seconds to play, Hamm made a cool cross into the box and 5-foot 2-inch Milbrett scored on a header. The game went into overtime. In the 12th minute, Fawcett tried to head away a Norwegian pass. The ball hit substitute Dagny Mellgren above the elbow. It bounced on the ground twice and Mellgren kicked it towards the goal. American goalie Mullinix touched the ball, but could not stop it from crossing the line and the Norwegians won on the golden goal.

2004 Athens T: 10, N: 10, D: 8.26.

	W	L	T	GF	GA
1. USA	5	0	1	12	4
2. BRA	4	2	0	15	4
3. GER	4	1	0	14	3
4. SWE	2	3	0	4	5
5. AUS	1	2	1	3	4
6. NGR	1	2	0	3	4
7. JPN	1	2	0	2	3
8. MEX	0	2	1	1	8

Final: USA 2-1 BRA
3rd Place: GER 1-0 SWE

1. USA—Briana Scurry, Christie Pearce-Rampone, Catherine "Cat" Reddick, Joy Fawcett, Kate Markgraf, Shannon Boxx, Alyson Wagner, Julie Foudy, Kristine Lilly, Mariel "Mia" Hamm, Abby Wambach, Heather Mitts, Lindsay Tarpley, Brandi Chastain, Angela Hucles, Cindy Parlow, Heather O'Reilly
2. BRA—Daniela "Costadaniela" Alves, Juliana Cabral, Renata "Kóki" da Costa, Roseli de Belo, Mônica de Paula, Andréia "Maycon" dos Santos, Rosana Augusto, Elaine "Baiuca" Moura, Delma "Pretinha" Gonçalves, Miraildes "Formiga" Mota, Grazielle Nascimento, Kelly da Silva, Aline Pellegrino, Tânia "Tânia Maranhão" Ribeiro, Cristiane Rozeira, Andréia Suntaque, Marta da Silva
3. GER—Silke Rottenberg, Kerstin Stegemann, Steffi Jones, Sonja Fuss, Ariane Hingst, Kerstin Garefrekes, Viola Odebrecht, Pia Wunderlich, Renate Lingor, Petra Wimbersky, Birgit Prinz, Sarah Günther, Martina Müller, Navina Omilade, Sandra Minnert, Isabell Bachor, Conny Pohlers

4. SWE—Malin Andersson, Kristin Bengtsson, Linda Fagerström, Caroline Jönsson, Sara Larsson, Hanna Ljungberg, Hanna Marklund, Malin Moström, Salina Olsson, Josefine Öqvist, Frida Östberg, Lotta Schelin, Therese Sjögran, Anna Sjöström, Victoria Svensson, Jane Törnqvist, Karolina Westberg
5. AUS—Cassandra Kell, Rhian Davies, Sacha Wainwright, Dianne Alagich, Cheryl Salisbury, Sally Shipard, Heather Garriock, Joanne Peters, Gillian Foster, Danielle Small, Sarah Walsh, Kylie Ledbrook, Lisa De Vanna, Karla Reuter, Thea Slatyer, Selin Kuralay
6. NGR—Precious Dede, Felicia Eze, Faith Ikidi, Yinka Kudaisi, Chima Nwosu, Efioanwan Ekpo, Maureen Mmadu, Perpetua Nkwocha, Stella Mbachu, Mercy Akide, Vera Okolo, Ajuma Ameh, Rita Nwadike, Blessing Igbojionu, Akudo Sabi, Nkechi Egbe
7. JPN—Nozomi Yamago, Hiromi Isozaki, Naoko Kawakami, Yasuyo Yamagishi, Aya Shimokozuru, Tomoe Sakai, Tomomi Miyamoto, Yayoi Kobayashi, Eriko Arakawa, Homare Sawa, Mio Otani, Kyoko Yano, Emi Yamamoto, Karina Maruyama, Miyuki Yanagita, Kozue Ando
8. MEX—María de Jesús Castillo Nicasio, Maribel Domínguez Castelán, Elizabeth Patricia Gómez Randall, Mónica González Canales, Nancy Gutiérrez Vásquez, Fatima Leyva Morán, Juana Evelyn López Luna, Alma Martínez Torres, Jennifer Marie Molina Shea, Iris Adriana Mora Vallejo, Patricia Pérez Peña, Luz del Rosario Saucedo, Rubí Marlene Sandoval Nungaray, Pamela Tajonar Alonso, Dioselina Valderrama Reyes, Monica Vergara Rubio, Teresa Guadalupe Worbis Aguilar

Defending Olympic champions Norway failed to qualify for the 2004 Olympics after losing to the United States in the quarterfinals of the 2003 FIFA Women's World Cup. Although the Olympic tournament began with round-robin group play, it served only to eliminate two of the ten teams, China and Greece. In the most dramatic of the quarterfinals, defending World Cup champion Germany fell behind Nigeria, but scored two goals in the last fifteen minutes to win 2-1. This set up a semifinal match between Germany and the United States, which had lost to the Germans 3-0 on home turf in the semifinals of the 2003 World Cup. This time, the Americans dominated most of the match and did not even give up a shot on goal until the 77th minute. Leading 1-0, the US seemed poised for victory when, in the third minute of second half injury time, Germany's Isabell Bachor took a shot that deflected off the hip of veteran American defender Joy Fawcett and into the goal. Four minutes into overtime, nineteen-year-old Heather O'Reilly faced an open net from a sharp angle and hit the post. Five minutes later, Mia Hamm drew the German defense and then passed to O'Reilly, who scored from six meters out. In the other semifinal, Brazil defeated Sweden 1-0 victory on a goal by forward Pretinha in the 64th minute.

The United States had beaten Brazil 2-0 in pool play. In the rematch in the final, Brazil dominated the first half, but it was the US that opened the scoring on a 24-meter drive by Lindsay Tarpley that curled inside the left post in the 39th minute. Pretinha evened the score for Brazil in the 73rd minute, and both she and 19-year-old Cristiane hit the post in the closing minutes of regulation. With eight minutes to go in the second overtime, Abby Wambach headed in the winning goal on a corner kick from Kristine Lilly. On January 19th, 2006, Lilly became the first football player, male or female, to represent her nation in 300 international matches.

2008 Beijing T: 12, N: 12, D: 8.21.

	W	L	T	GF	GA
1. USA	5	1	0	12	5
2. BRA	4	1	1	11	5
3. GER	4	1	1	7	4
4. JPN	2	3	1	11	10
5. CHN	2	1	1	5	4
6. SWE	2	2	0	4	5
7. NOR	2	2	0	5	7
8. CAN	1	2	1	5	6

Final: USA 1-0 BRA
3rd Place: GER 2-0 JPN

1. USA—Shannon Boxx, Rachel Buehler, Lori Chalupny, Lauren Cheney, Stephanie Cox, Tobin Heath, Angela Hucles, Natasha Kai, Carli Lloyd, Kathryn Sobrero-Markgraf, Heather Mitts, Heather O'Reilly, Christie Pearce-Rampone, Amy Rodriguez, Hope Solo, Lindsay Tarpley, Alyson Wagner
2. BRA—Andréia Suntaque, Andréia Rosa de Andrade, Bárbara do Monte Barbosa, Cristiane Rozeira de Souza Silva, Daniela Alves Lima, Érika Cristiano dos Santos, Ester Aperecida dos Santos, Fabiana da Silva Simões, Miraildes "Formiga" Maciel Mota, Francielle Manoel Alberto, Marta Vieira da Silva, Maurine Dorneles Gonçalves, Andréia "Maycon" dos Santos, Delma "Pretinha" Gonçalves, Renata Aparecida "Kóki" da Costa, Rosana dos Santos Augusto, Simone Gomes Jatobá, Tânia "Tânia Maranhão" Pereira Ribeiro
3. GER—Nadine Angerer, Fatmire Bajramaj, Melanie Behringer, Linda Bresonik, Kerstin Garefrekes, Ariane Hingst, Annike Krahn, Simone Laudehr, Renate Lingor, Anja Mittag, Célia Okoyino da Mbabi, Babett Peter, Conny Pohlers, Birgit Prinz, Sandra Smisek, Kerstin Stegemann
4. JPN—Kozue Ando, Eriko Arakawa, Miho Fukumoto, Ayumi Hara, Hiromi Isozaki, Azusa Iwashimizu, Tomoe Kato, Yukari Kinga, Karina Maruyama, Aya Miyama, Yuki Nagasato, Shinobu Ohno, Mizuho Sakaguchi, Homare Sawa, Rumi Utsugi, Miyuki Yanagita, Kyoko Yano
5. CHN—Bi Yan, Gu Yasha, Han Duan, Han Wenxia, Li Jie, Liu Huana, Liu Sa, Lou Jiahui, Pu Wei, Wang Dandan, Weng Xinzhi, Xu Yuan, Zhang Na, Zhang Ying, Zhang Yanru, Zhou Gaoping
6. SWE—Johanna Almgren, Maria Aronsson, Nilla Fischer, Linda Forsberg, Jessica Landström, Sara Larsson, Hedvig Lindahl, Josefine Öqvist, Frida Östberg, Anna Paulson, Charlotte Rohlin, Lotta Schelin, Caroline Seger, Stina Segerström, Therese Sjögran, Victoria Svensson, Sara Thunebro
7. NOR—Marit Fiane Christensen, Gunhild Følstad, Solveig Gulbrandsen, Isabell Herlovsen, Guro Knutsen, Marie Knutsen, Leni Larsen Kaurin, Lene Mykjåland, Siri Nordby, Trine Rønning, Marita Skammelsrud Lund, Erika Skarbø, Ane Stangeland Horpestad, Ingvild Stensland, Lene Storløkken, Elise Thorsnes, Melissa Wiik
8. CAN—Candace Chapman, Jonelle Filigno, Martina Franko, Robyn Gayle, Randee Hermus, Kara Lang, Karina LeBlanc, Diana Matheson, Erin McLeod, Jodi-Ann Robinson, Clare Rustad, Sophie Schmidt, Christine Sinclair, Melissa Tancredi, Brittany Timko, Amy Walsh, Rhian Wilkinson, Emily Zurrer

One year before the Beijing Olympics, all three Athens medalists—the US, Brazil and Germany—met in the final rounds of the FIFA Women's World Cup. Brazil handed the US a stinging 4-0 defeat in the semifinals but were toppled 2-0 in the final by Germany, which successfully defended its 2003 title without conceding a single goal. One month before the Olympics, leading US scorer Abby Wambach broke her left leg in a warm-up match against Brazil and was forced to withdraw.

The competition in Beijing opened with a challenging round-robin stage. Germany and Brazil were drawn into the same group and held each other to a scoreless draw in their first match. Each won both of their next two matches against Nigeria and North Korea to reach the quarterfinals. The US had a rough start in their pool, losing their first match 2-0 to Norway before beating Japan 1-0 and New Zealand 4-0 to advance, along with Norway and Japan. In the third of the three preliminary pools China opened with a 2-1 win over Sweden and led the group by tying with Canada 1-1 and beating Argentina 2-0.

The US and Germany both needed extra time to win their quarterfinal matches. The former tied 1-1 with Canada after regulation play, but substitute forward Tasha Kai scored their winning goal in the 11th minute of overtime. Germany and Sweden remained scoreless through 105 minutes of play. German forward Kerstin Garefrekes scored fifteen minutes into overtime, and Simone Laudehr followed with a second goal ten minutes later. Brazil and Japan also reached the semifinals: Brazil with a 2-1 win over Norway, and Japan after brushing aside China 2-0.

Brazil and Germany faced each other a second time in the semifinals. Germany's Birgit Prinz opened the scoring ten minutes into play, and the Germans held off Brazil until just before halftime, when playmaker Cristiane set up a low cross to Formiga, who scored from 20 yards (18 meters) out. Continuing to attack, Brazil scored twice in five minutes early in the second half with goals by Cristiane and 22-year-old twice FIFA World Player of the Year Marta. A second goal by Cristiane with fourteen minutes to play clinched the 4-1 victory and took Brazil into the final.

Japan's Shinobu Ohno opened the scoring in the other semifinal in the 17th minute with a point-blank shot past US goalkeeper Hope Solo. The US came back with two goals in the closing minutes of the first half, expanding their lead to 4-1 with ten minutes remaining before Japanese substitute Eriko Arakawa scored once more for Japan in stoppage time.

The final was a thrilling hard-fought match between Brazil and the US that saw numerous shots at goal but no goals in regulation time. The US had two clear opportunities in the final four minutes of play, both saved by Brazilian goalkeeper Bárbara. Six minutes into overtime, midfielder Carli Lloyd scored from just outside the box, giving the US a 1-0 advantage to which Brazil was unable to respond.

Chapter 14 **Gymnastics (Men)**

All-Around
Horizontal Bar (High Bar)
Parallel Bars
Long Horse Vault
Pommel Horse (Side Horse)
Rings
Floor Exercises
Team Combined Exercises
Trampoline
Discontinued Events

ABBREVIATIONS
HB= Horizontal bar
PB = Parallel bars
LHV = Long horse vault
SH = Side horse (pommel horse)
R = Rings
FE = Floor exercises
SHV = Side horse vault
CLSV = Combined long and side horse vaults
100 = 100-yard run
SP = Shot put
LJ = Long jump
RC = Rope climb
CLHJ = Combined long and high jump
PV = Pole vault
W = Weightlifting

There are three stages to Olympic gymnastics competitions: the team competition, followed by the individual All-Around competition, and finally the individual apparatus finals. In 2008 each team will enter six gymnasts. Traditionally each gymnast performed twice on each apparatus: once doing compulsory exercises and once optional exercises. The 2000 Olympics were the first in which compulsory exercises were eliminated. Gymnasts who are not part of a full-sized national squad take part in the team competition because the team competition also serves as the qualifying round for both the individual all-around competition and the apparatus finals.

The 24 gymnasts with the highest scores in the team competition advance to the All-Around final. However, since 2004, no more than two gymnasts per nation may compete in the all-around final. Prior to the break-up of the Soviet Union this restriction led to some awkward situations in which leading medal contenders were dropped to make room for lesser gymnasts.

The top eight scorers for each apparatus in the team competition qualify for the apparatus finals, although no more than two gymnasts per nation may compete in the final for any apparatus. Until 1992, scores from the team competition were carried over to the all-around and apparatus finals. For the Barcelona Games the rules were changed: the gymnasts now start again at zero.

Two judges rate a routine's degree of difficulty or *start value*, while six judges score its execution. The highest and lowest execution marks are dropped and the average of the four remaining marks is subtracted from the start value to determine the gymnast's score. In the case of a tie, the average of the four B-judge scores is used to

Borys Shakhlin, 1960
The Ukrainian won four golds, two silvers and a bronze medal at the Rome Games to add to the two gold medals he had won in 1956. In 1964 he added a gold, two silvers and a bronze.

determine the winner. If the score is still tied, the lowest score is dropped and the average taken until the tie is broken.

The top 12 teams at the most recent world championships are each allowed to enter six gymnasts. The nations that place 13th through 18th are allowed to enter two gymnasts each. Ten gymnasts from the next highest placed nations are also eligible. Four places are reserved for the host nation, special invitations and "unexpected cases."

Current rules require that gymnasts be at least 16 years old in the year of the Olympics.

The 1996 Olympics was the first since 1896 at which each men's individual event was won by a different gymnast. It was also the first ever at which each individual gold went to a different nation.

ALL-AROUND

1896 not held

1900 Paris C: 135, N: 9, D: 7.30.
Events: HB, PB, LHV, SH, R, FE, LJ, RC, CLHJ, PV, W

		PTS.
1. Gustave Sandras	FRA	302
2. Nöel Bass	FRA	295
3. Lucien Demanet	FRA	293
4. Pierre Payssé	FRA	290
4. Jules Rolland	FRA	290
6. Gustave Fabry	FRA	283
7. Joseph Martinez	FRA/ALG	277
8. Marcel Lalue	FRA	275
8. Mauvezain	FRA	275

Gustave Sandras, the first all-around gymnastics champion, worked in a dry cleaner's.

1904 St. Louis C: 119, N: 4, D: 7.2.

		PB	HB	CLSV	FT-IN. LJ	SP	TIME 100	TOTAL PTS.
1. Julius Lenhart	AUT	14.40	14.60	14.00	18-0	28-6	12.0	69.80
2. Wilhelm Weber	GER	14.17	13.93	13.50	18-1	30-1	12.0	69.10
3. Adolf Spinnler	SWI	14.53	14.53	14.43	16-2¼	29-7	12.4	67.99
4. Ernest Mohr	GER	12.90	13.00	13.00	18-8¼	30-0	11.4	67.90
5. Otto Wiegand	GER	14.20	13.12	13.50	17-6	30-4¾	12.0	67.82
6. Otto Steffen	USA	12.80	14.10	12.63	18-1	30-9½	12.0	67.03
7. Hugo Peitsch	GER	14.03	14.30	13.23	16-10¾	27-4¾	12.0	66.66
8. John Bissinger	USA	13.10	12.37	12.10	18-4¾	32-9½	11.4	66.57

1906 Athens C: 37, N: 8, D: 4.26.
Events: HB, PB, LHV, R, CLHJ

		PTS.
1. Pierre Payssé	FRA	97
2. Alberto Braglia	ITA	95
3. Georges Charmoille	FRA	94
4. Carl Ohms	GER	93
5. Vitaliano Masotti	ITA	92
6. Pissié	FRA	91

7. Nikolaos Aliprantis (GRE), Béla Eródy (HUN), Mario Gubiani (ITA), Bohumil Honzátko (BOH/CZE), Joseph Krämer (GER), Daniel Lavielle (FRA), Karl Schwartz (GER), Wilhelm Weber (GER)—90

1906 Athens C: 25, N: 8, D: 4.26.
Events: HB, PB, LHV, R, CLHJ, SH

		PTS.
1. Pierre Payssé	FRA	116
2. Alberto Braglia	ITA	115
3. Georges Charmoille	FRA	113
4. Carl Ohms	GER	112
5. Vitaliano Masotti	ITA	111
6. Béla Eródy	HUN	110
6. Mario Gubiani	ITA	110
6. Pissié	FRA	110
6. Wilhelm Weber	GER	110

This event combined the results of the five apparatuses in the previous event with the results of one more apparatus: the side or pommeled horse.

1908 London C: 97, N: 11, D: 7.15.
Events: HB, PB, SH, R, RC

		PTS.
1. Alberto Braglia	ITA	317.0
2. S. Walter Tysal	GBR	312.0
3. B. Louis Ségura	FRA	297.0
4. Curt Steuernagel	GER	273.5
5. Friedrich Wolf	GER	267.0
6. Samuel Hodgetts	GBR	266.0
7. Marcel Lalu	FRA	258.75
8. Robert Diaz	FRA	258.5

Between Olympics, Alberto Braglia of Modena found it difficult to earn a living and took to performing as "The Human Torpedo." He was declared a professional and drummed out of the Italian national gymnastics federation. However he regained his amateur status in time for the 1912 Olympics and successfully defended his championship. Afterwards he became a popular circus performer. In 1932 Braglia coached the Italian gymnastics team to a surprise victory at the Los Angeles Olympics.

1912 Stockholm C: 44, N: 9, D: 7.12.

		HB	PB	R	SH	TOTAL PTS.
1. Alberto Braglia	ITA	32.75	34.75	31.75	35.75	135.0
2. B. Louis Ségura	FRA	30.0	35.75	32.25	34.5	132.5
3. Adolfo Tunesi	ITA	30.25	35.0	30.5	35.75	131.5
4. Guido Boni	ITA	29.75	35.25	28.25	34.75	128.0
4. Giorgio Zampori	ITA	29.0	35.0	30.75	33.25	128.0
6. Pietro Bianchi	ITA	29.5	33.75	30.75	33.75	127.75
7. Marcel Lalue	FRA	29.25	35.5	30.5	31.75	127.0
7. Marco Torrès	FRA	30.25	35.0	31.0	30.75	127.0

1920 Antwerp C: 25, N: 7, D: 8.26.
Events: HB, PB, SH, R, FE

		PTS.
1. Giorgio Zampori	ITA	88.35
2. Marco Torrès	FRA	87.62
3. Jean Gounot	FRA	87.45
4. Félicien Kempeneers	BEL	86.25
5. Georges Thurnherr	FRA	86.00
6. Laurent Grech	FRA	85.65
7. Luigi Maiocco	ITA	85.38
8. Luigi Costigliolo	ITA	84.90

1924 Paris C: 72, N: 9, D: 7.20.

		HB		PB		LHV		SH		R		SHV		RC		TOTAL PTS.
1. Leon Štukelj	YUG/SLO	19.73	1	20.40	20	9.91	4	19.37	10	21.33	4	9.6	17	10.0	10	110.34
2. Robert Pražak	CZE	18.73	9	21.61	2	9.73	9	18.97	13	21.483	2	9.8	8	10.0	13	110.323
3. Bedřich Supčik	CZE	17.86	16	21.26	8	9.33	15	17.53	24	21.12	5	9.83	6	10.0	1	106.93
4. Ferdinando Mandrini	ITA	18.12	14	20.21	24	9.75	7	16.06	30	20.943	8	8.73	21	10.0	18	105.583
5. Miroslav Klinger	CZE	16.47	26	21.13	10	9.75	7	19.67	7	20.73	11	9.75	12	8.0	21	105.5
6. Ladislav Vácha	CZE	14.7	39	21.31	6	9.7	10	18.33	17	21.43	3	9.83	6	10.0	4	105.3
7. August Güttinger	SWI	18.886	8	21.63	1	9.08	17	19.6	8	17.57	37	8.41	29	10.0	3	105.176
8. Jean Gounot	FRA	19.043	6	20.15	25	9.0	18	17.3	27	19.73	19	9.93	2	10.0	6	105.153

Štukelj, a lawyer from Novo Mesto, eventually won three gold medals, one silver, and two bronze in his Olympic career, including a silver in the rings in 1936, when he was 37 years old. In 1992, when he was 93 years old, Štukelj attended the Opening Ceremony of the Barcelona Olympics and watched as athletes from Slovenia marched behind their own flag for the first time. Four years later, he was honored at the Atlanta Opening Ceremony and amazed the crowd by bounding onto the stage at the age of 97. He died November 8, 1999, four days before his 101st birthday.

1928 Amsterdam C: 88, N: 11, D: 8.10.

		HB		PB		LHV		SH		R		TOTAL PTS.
1. Georges Miez	SWI	57.5	1	49.75	30	28.25	4	57.75	2	54.25	8	247.5
2. Hermann Hänggi	SWI	56.5	4	54.25	3	27.125	18	59.25	1	49.5	36	246.625
3. Leon Štukelj	YUG/SLO	53.75	21	53.5	7	26.625	28	53.25	12	57.75	1	244.875
4. Romeo Neri	ITA	57.0	2	53.0	12	27.25	16	51.5	19	56.0	4	244.75
5. Josip Primožič	YUG/SLO	56.0	6	55.5	2	28.25	4	51.75	18	52.5	18	244.0
6. Mauri Nyberg-Noroma	FIN	54.0	16	53.5	7	26.75	26	54.5	7	55.0	5	243.75
6. Heikki Savolainen	FIN	54.5	13	51.75	17	27.25	16	56.5	3	53.75	12	243.75
8. Eugen Mack	SWI	56.75	3	51.0	21	28.75	1	54.25	9	52.5	18	243.25

At the Amsterdam Games, 23-year-old Georges Miez won three gold medals and one silver. Between 1924 and 1936 his Olympic total was four gold, three silver, and one bronze. Like Leon Štukelj, Miez lived a full life, finally dying in Lugano in 1999 at the age of 94.

1932 Los Angeles C: 24, N: 5, D: 8.12.

		HB		PB		LHV		SH		R		TOTAL PTS.
1. Romeo Neri	ITA	28.9	2	28.1	3	27.525	3	28.0	4	28.0	3	140.625
2. István Pelle	HUN	29.15	1	27.9	6	24.675	9	24.85	11	28.35	1	134.925
3. Heikki Savolainen	FIN	27.25	7	28.4	1	22.925	15	28.35	3	27.65	5	134.575
4. Mario Lertora	ITA	28.2	3	27.25	8	27.25	4	23.35	14	28.35	1	134.4
5. Savino Guglielmetti	ITA	28.2	3	28.4	1	28.325	1	22.6	16	26.85	6	134.375
6. Frank Haubold	USA	26.9	10	28.0	4	25.725	7	28.45	1	23.45	16	132.525
7. Oreste Capuzzo	ITA	27.5	6	27.3	7	23.7	10	26.15	9	27.8	4	132.45
8. Frederick Meyer	USA	27.1	9	26.45	14	27.55	2	28.4	2	22.15	19	131.65

1936 Berlin C: 111, N: 14, D: 8.11.

		HB		PB		LHV		SH		R		FE		TOTAL PTS.
1. Alfred Schwarzmann	GER	19.233	3	18.967	3	19.2	1	19.0	7	18.534	4	18.166	10	113.1
2. Eugen Mack	SWI	18.9	9	18.834	5	18.967	2	19.167	2	18.0	13	18.466	3	112.334
3. Konrad Frey	GER	19.267	2	19.067	1	17.666	20	19.333	1	17.733	18	18.466	3	111.532
4. Alois Hudec	CZE	18.834	10	18.966	4	17.867	18	17.966	26	19.433	1	18.133	11	111.199
5. Martti Uosikkinen	FIN	19.0	7	18.433	11	18.3	6	19.066	4	17.634	22	18.267	8	110.7
5. Michael Reusch	SWI	18.566	18	19.034	2	18.266	7	19.0	7	18.434	6	17.4	22	110.7
7. Matthias Volz	GER	18.8	11	17.033	38	18.467	3	18.766	10	18.667	3	18.366	5	110.099
8. Willi Stadel	GER	18.7	14	18.133	18	18.033	14	18.887	9	16.966	36	18.3	6	108.999

Schwarzmann was a baker from Nuremberg. Sixteen years later, he returned to the Olympics at the age of 40 and earned a silver medal on the horizontal bar.

1948 London C: 123, N: 16, D: 8.13.

		HB		PB		LHV		SH		R		FE		TOTAL PTS.
1. Veikko Huhtanen	FIN	39.2	3	39.3	2	38.4	6	38.7	1	37.8	11	36.3	34	229.7
2. Walter Lehmann	SWI	39.4	12	39.0	5	38.1	8	37.6	11	38.4	4	36.5	29	229.0
3. Paavo Aaltonen	FIN	38.4	12	38.8	7	39.1	1	38.7	1	37.3	17	36.5	29	228.8
4. Josef Stalder	SWI	39.7	1	39.1	3	36.9	33	37.7	8	38.3	5	37.0	16	228.7
5. Christian Kipfer	SWE	38.6	9	39.1	3	37.9	14	37.2	14	37.8	11	36.5	29	227.1
6. Emil Studer	SWI	38.8	4	37.8	21	38.0	10	37.7	8	38.3	5	36.0	41	226.6
7. Zdeněk Růžička	CZE	37.9	17	38.8	7	36.6	46	36.3	30	38.5	3	38.1	3	226.2
8. Kalevi Laitinen	FIN	38.1	14	38.1	16	38.0	10	36.9	19	37.4	16	37.15	13	225.65

1952 Helsinki C: 185, N: 29, D: 7.21.

		HB		PB		LHV		SH		R		FE		TOTAL PTS.
1. Viktor Chukarin	SOV/UKR	19.4	5	19.6	2	19.2	1	19.5	1	19.55	2	18.45	29	115.7
2. Grant Shaginyan	SOV/ARM	19.05	14	19.35	4	18.5	35	19.4	2	19.75	1	18.9	8	114.95
3. Josef Stalder	SWI	19.5	2	19.5	3	18.8	13	19.2	5	19.1	11	18.65	19	114.75
4. Valentin Muratov	SOV/RUS	19.2	9	19.25	8	18.7	19	18.3	32	19.35	5	18.85	11	113.65
5. Hans Eugster	SWI	19.15	11	19.65	1	18.95	5	18.55	25	19.4	3	17.7	66	113.4
6. Vladimir Belyakov	SOV/RUS	18.8	23	19.25	8	18.5	35	19.1	7	18.95	14	18.75	14	113.35
6. Yevgeny Korolkov	SOV/RUS	18.8	23	19.3	5	18.4	44	19.4	2	19.15	7	18.3	35	113.35
8. Jean Tschabold	SWI	19.35	6	19.3	5	18.7	19	19.05	8	18.75	23	18.15	41	113.3

Chukarin, a Ukrainian who had spent four years in a concentration camp during World War II, earned six medals at Helsinki—four gold and two silver. Of his years in the concentration camp, Chukarin said, "I had gone through a most severe ordeal, but I emerged with an enlightened soul cleansed of pettiness, conceit and uncertainty."

1956 Melbourne C: 63, N: 18, D: 12.6.

		HB		PB		LHV		SH		R		FE		TOTAL PTS.
1. Viktor Chukarin	SOV/UKR	19.25	4	19.2	1	18.6	7	19.1	3	19.0	7	19.1	2	114.25
2. Takashi Ono	JPN	19.6	1	19.1	3	18.5	16	19.2	2	19.05	5	18.75	8	114.2
3. Yuri Tytov	SOV/UKR	19.4	2	18.85	8	18.75	3	19.0	5	18.85	10	18.95	5	113.8
4. Masao Takemoto	JPN	19.3	3	19.1	3	18.65	6	18.9	7	19.1	3	18.5	16	113.55
5. Valentin Muratov	SOV/RUS	18.6	25	18.7	16	18.85	1	18.8	9	19.15	2	19.2	1	113.3
6. Helmut Bantz	GER	19.15	6	18.8	13	18.85	1	18.75	12	18.6	18	18.75	8	112.9
7. Albert Azaryan	SOV/ARM	18.95	8	19.0	5	18.55	11	18.75	12	19.35	1	17.95	40	112.55
8. Borys Shakhlin	SOV/UKR	18.75	13	18.85	8	18.7	4	19.25	1	18.7	15	18.25	28	112.5

Chukarin, by then a 35-year-old teacher, added to his medal collection three gold, one silver, and one bronze at Melbourne, for a remarkable total of 11 Olympic medals.

1960 Rome C: 130, N: 23, D: 9.7.

		HB		PB		LHV		SH		R		FE		TOTAL PTS.
1. Borys Shakhlin	SOV/UKR	19.55	2	19.4	1	19.2	3	19.35	1	19.5	2	18.95	7	115.95
2. Takashi Ono	JPN	19.6	1	19.4	1	19.3	1	19.15	4	19.45	3	19.0	4	115.9
3. Yuri Tytov	SOV/UKR	19.5	4	19.2	6	19.0	5	19.2	3	19.45	3	19.25	2	115.6
4. Shuji Tsurumi	JPN	19.25	8	19.15	8	19.0	5	19.1	6	19.2	9	18.85	13	114.55
5. Yukio Endo	JPN	19.45	6	19.2	6	19.05	4	18.85	10	19.0	12	18.9	10	114.45
5. Masao Takemoto	JPN	19.55	2	19.25	4	19.0	5	18.6	26	19.25	8	18.8	14	114.45
7. Nobuyuki Aihara	JPN	19.0	13	19.25	4	18.85	9	18.6	26	19.4	5	19.3	1	114.4
8. Miroslav Cerar	YUG/SLO	19.5	4	19.15	8	18.75	13	19.05	7	19.05	11	18.75	17	114.25

Borys Shakhlin, a Ukrainian from the small town of Ishin, won four gold medals, two silver, and one bronze at the Rome Games to add to the two gold medals he had won at Melbourne four years earlier.

1964 Tokyo C: 130, N: 30, D: 10.20.

		HB		PB		LHV		SH		R		FE		TOTAL PTS.
1. Yukio Endo	JPN	19.4	3	19.55	1	19.4	3	18.7	16	19.5	1	19.4	1	115.95
2. Vikton Lisitsky	SOV/RUS	19.25	6	19.5	2	19.5	1	18.75	13	19.1	9	19.3	2	115.4
2. Borys Shakhlin	SOV/UKR	19.55	1	19.25	9	19.35	4	18.9	7	19.4	4	18.95	14	115.4
2. Shuji Tsurumi	JPN	18.9	21	19.5	2	19.3	6	19.25	3	19.35	5	19.1	9	115.4
5. Franco Menichelli	ITA	19.25	6	19.3	6	19.05	24	18.8	10	19.45	2	19.3	2	115.15
6. Hanuhiro Yamashita	JPN	19.25	6	19.3	6	19.5	1	19.15	4	18.75	21	19.15	7	115.1
7. Miroslav Cerar	YUG/SLO	19.3	5	19.5	2	19.1	19	19.45	1	19.05	12	18.65	30	115.05
8. Takuji Hayata	JPN	19.1	12	19.15	10	19.15	16	18.9	7	19.45	2	19.15	7	114.9

1968 Mexico City C: 117, N: 28, D: 10.24.

		HB		PB		LHV		SH		R		FE		TOTAL PTS.
1. Sawao Kato	JPN	19.45	3	19.35	3	18.9	5	19.0	8	19.55	1	19.65	1	115.9
2. Mikhail Voronin	SOV/RUS	19.5	1	19.45	2	19.0	2	19.2	2	19.45	3	19.25	4	115.85
3. Akinori Nakayama	JPN	19.5	1	19.55	1	18.85	7	18.85	12	19.5	2	19.4	2	115.65
4. Eizo Kenmotsu	JPN	19.35	5	19.25	5	18.95	4	19.1	4	19.0	7	19.25	4	114.9
5. Takeshi Kato	JPN	19.1	11	19.3	4	19.05	1	18.65	21	19.4	4	19.35	3	114.85
6. Sergei Diomidov	SOV/RUS	19.3	6	18.9	23	18.9	5	19.0	8	19.05	6	18.95	9	114.1
7. Vladimir Klimenko	SOV/RUS	19.1	11	19.25	5	18.85	7	19.1	4	18.9	9	18.75	13	113.95
8. Yukio Endo	JPN	19.25	7	19.15	9	19.0	2	18.4	26	18.95	8	18.8	11	113.55

1972 Munich C: 113, N: 26, D: 8.30.

		HB		PB		LHV		SH		R		FE		TOTAL PTS.
1. Sawao Kato	JPN	19.525	2	19.275	1	19.0	2	18.9	3	19.15	4	18.8	6	114.65
2. Eizo Kenmotsu	JPN	19.3	3	19.1	4	19.0	2	19.15	1	19.05	5	18.975	3	114.575
3. Akinori Nakayama	JPN	19.275	4	19.275	1	18.75	7	18.75	7	19.25	1	19.025	1	114.325
4. Nikolai Andrianov	SOVIRUS	19.25	5	18.925	6	19.35	1	18.7	8	19.0	6	18.975	3	114.2
5. Shigeru Kasamatsu	JPN	19.25	5	18.825	10	18.625	10	19.075	2	18.9	7	19.025	1	113.7
6. Viktor Klimenko	SOV/RUS	18.755	18	19.275	1	18.8	6	18.875	4	18.7	13	18.675	9	113.075
6. Klaus Köste	GDR	18.975	11	19.1	4	18.875	4	18.4	17	18.85	9	18.875	5	113.075
8. Mitsuo Tsukahara	JPN	19.675	1	18.625	15	18.35	22	18.15	20	19.225	2	18.75	8	112.775

The 5-foot 3-inch, 125-pound Kato became the third repeat winner of the men's all-around championship, joining Alberto Braglia of Italy (1908 and 1912) and Viktor Chukarin of the Soviet Union (1952 and 1956).

1976 Montreal C: 90, N: 20, D: 7.21.

		HB		PB		LHV		SH		R		FE		TOTAL PTS.
1. Nikolai Andrianov	SOV/RUS	19.3	4	19.4	2	19.475	1	19.425	3	19.6	1	19.45	1	116.65
2. Sawao Kato	JPN	19.5	2	19.475	1	19.1	8	19.3	5	19.075	6	19.2	3	115.65
3. Mitsuo Tsukahara	JPN	19.525	1	19.375	3	19.45	2	19.2	7	19.0	9	19.025	7	115.575
4. Aleksandr Dityatin	SOV/RUS	19.0	11	19.05	5	19.275	6	19.35	4	19.5	2	19.35	2	115.525
5. Hiroshi Kajiyama	JPN	19.225	7	19.325	4	19.325	5	19.275	6	19.2	3	19.075	6	115.425
6. Andrzej Szajna	POL	19.1	9	19.05	5	19.35	4	18.95	10	19.075	6	19.1	5	114.625
7. Michael Nikolay	GDR	19.2	8	18.725	12	18.725	21	19.575	2	18.8	16	18.575	16	113.6
8. Imre Molnár	HUN	18.875	16	18.875	9	19.375	3	19.2	7	18.7	19	18.55	17	113.575

The 5-foot 5½-inch Andrianov, who had collected a complete set of medals in 1972, added seven more in Montreal—four gold, two silver, and one bronze.

1980 Moscow C: 65, N: 14, D: 7.24.

		HB		PB		LHV		SH		R		FE		TOTAL PTS.
1. Aleksandr Dityatin	SOV/RUS	19.8	2	19.7	2	19.875	1	19.8	3	19.875	1	19.6	3	118.65
2. Nikolai Andrianov	SOV/RUS	19.725	3	19.6	4	19.8	2	19.7	4	19.725	3	19.675	1	118.225
3. Stoyan Deltchev	BUL	19.825	1	19.675	3	19.725	5	19.65	6	19.775	2	19.35	6	118.0
4. Aleksandr Tkachyov	SOV/RUS	19.525	4	19.775	1	19.75	4	19.675	5	19.675	6	19.3	8	117.7
5. Roland Brückner	GDR	19.075	17	19.45	5	19.775	3	19.625	7	19.725	3	19.65	2	117.3
6. Michael Nikolay	GDR	19.475	6	19.35	7	19.575	11	19.875	2	19.525	8	18.95	13	116.75
7. Lutz Hoffmann	GDR	19.4	9	19.05	11	19.7	6	19.125	14	19.425	10	19.325	7	116.025
8. Jiří Tabák	CZE	19.225	11	18.975	15	19.675	7	18.675	22	19.6	7	19.525	4	115.675

Handsome Aleksandr Dityatin became the first person to win eight medals in one Olympic celebration. He gained three gold, four silver, and one bronze. Dityatin also became the first male gymnast to receive a ten in an Olympic competition, with his long horse vault. Four more tens were awarded in rapid succession to Stoyan Deltchev on the rings, Aleksandr Tkachyov on the horizontal bar, and Zoltán Magyar and Michael Nikolay on the side horse. Meanwhile, Nikolai Andrianov added two gold, two silver, and one bronze to his collection for a grand career total of 15 Olympics medals—seven gold, five silver, and three bronze. In 1994, Andrianov became the coach of Naoya Tsukahara, the son of his old rival, Mitsuo Tsukahara.

1984 Los Angeles C: 71, N: 19, D: 8.2.

		HB		PB		LHV		SH		R		FE		TOTAL PTS.
1. Koji Gushiken	JPN	19.9	3	19.8	3	19.875	1	19.525	10	19.85	2	19.75	3	118.7
2. Peter Vidmar	USA	19.95	2	19.8	3	19.725	4	19.85	2	19.75	4	19.6	8	118.675
3. Li Ning	CHN	19.6	9	19.675	7	19.775	3	19.9	1	19.8	3	19.825	1	118.575
4. Tong Fei	CHN	19.975	1	19.625	8	19.725	4	19.75	4	19.75	4	19.725	5	118.55
5. Mitchell Gaylord	USA	19.625	8	19.85	1	19.825	2	19.775	3	19.875	1	19.575	9	118.525
6. Bart Conner	USA	19.8	4	19.8	3	19.625	10	19.675	5	19.675	9	19.775	2	118.35
7. Xu Zhiqiang	CHN	19.6	9	19.775	6	19.725	4	19.65	6	19.725	6	19.75	3	118.225
8. Nobuyuki Kajitani	JPN	19.225	22	19.825	2	19.7	7	19.625	7	19.7	7	19.3	17	117.375

Twenty-seven-year-old Koji Gushiken, placed only fifth after the preliminaries, came from behind to edge Peter Vidmar in the closest Olympic All-Around competition in sixty years. "I'm neither a Christian nor a Buddhist," Gushiken later said, reflecting on the medal ceremony, "and suddenly I felt the existence of God. It was clear-cut and exceedingly beautiful."

Among the boycott missing was world champion and pre-boycott favorite Dmitri Bilozerchev of the USSR.

1988 Seoul C: 89, N: 23, D: 9.22.

		HB		PB		LHV		SH		R		FE		TOTAL PTS.
1. Vladimir Artemov	SOV/RUS	19.95	1	19.975	1	19.775	2	19.775	8	19.8	4	19.85	1	119.125
2. Valery Lyukin	SOV/KAZ	19.925	2	19.9	2	19.7	3	19.875	2	19.875	2	19.8	4	119.025
3. Dmitri Bilozerchev	SOV/RUS	19.575	13	19.9	2	19.8	1	19.95	1	19.975	1	19.775	5	118.975
4. Sven Tippelt	GDR	19.4	23	19.65	7	19.675	4	19.8	5	19.875	2	19.6	14	118.0
5. Marius Gherman	ROM	19.75	5	19.65	7	19.55	10	19.7	10	19.525	17	19.65	12	117.825
6. Kalofer Hristozov	BUL	19.55	14	19.725	5	19.3	24	19.675	13	19.8	4	19.7	8	117.75
6. Wang Chongsheng	CHN	19.775	4	19.5	24	19.65	5	19.7	10	19.625	14	19.5	21	117.75
8. György Guczoghy	HUN	19.425	19	19.625	12	19.525	13	19.8	5	19.775	7	19.525	19	117.675
8. Yukio Iketani	JPN	19.625	10	19.65	7	19.475	14	19.55	18	19.525	17	19.85	1	117.675

Dmitri Bilozerchev caused a sensation in 1983 when he became world champion at the tender age of 16. The following year he was kept out of the Olympics by the Soviet boycott, but he did win the Friendship Games for athletes from boycotting nations. In 1985 he won the European championships and seemed on target to defend his world title when his career was suddenly derailed. Bilozerchev, on unauthorized leave from training camp, drank too much champagne and, only ten days after receiving his driver's license, borrowed his father's car and went driving in a rainstorm. On the slippery Moscow streets he turned in front of a truck and lost control. His left leg was shattered into more than 40 pieces. He was injured so badly that amputation was seriously considered.

Abandoned by the Soviet sports community, Bilozerchev was determined to regain his world-class form. Unfortunately he renewed his training too early. Overcompensating for his still tender left leg, he injured his *right* leg and required surgery on his ankle in December 1986. Despite these setbacks, Bilozerchev managed to return to competition in time to win the 1987 world championship. Still only 21 years old, he was installed as the favorite for the 1988 Olympics. Bilozerchev performed brilliantly in Seoul. But in Olympic-level gymnastics it is necessary to make no mistakes. Bilozerchev made a big one. While performing on the horizontal bar, normally his best apparatus, he veered off center on a one-armed giant swing, lost his momentum, and landed on the bar. The resulting half-point penalty cost him the gold medal. Ready to take advantage of Bilozerchev's lapse was teammate Vladimir Artemov. Back home in the Soviet Union Artemov was known as "The Permanent Runner-Up" and "Always Second." Indeed he had made a career of finishing second: at the 1984 Friendship Games, the 1985 World Championships, and the 1986 Goodwill Games. He had placed third at the 1987 World Championships. In Seoul, however, Artemov was not to be denied.

Bilozerchev went on to win two gold medals in the apparatus finals. But in August 1989, he and teammate Vladimir Gogoladze were expelled from the Soviet team for going on a two-day drinking binge and for having "a corrupting influence on other members of the team." Artemov moved to the United States in 1990 and became a US citizen.

1992 Barcelona C: 93, N: 25, D: 7.31.

		HB		PB		LHV		SH		R		FE		TOTAL PTS.
1. Vitaly Scherbo	BLR	9.775	5	9.8	2	9.8	2	9.875	1	9.9	1	9.875	1	59.025
2. Hryhoriy Misyutin	UKR	9.9	1	9.8	2	9.825	1	9.775	7	9.8	2	9.825	2	58.925
3. Valeri Belenki	AZR	9.775	5	9.825	1	9.575	15	9.85	3	9.775	4	9.825	2	58.625
4. Andreas Wecker	GER	9.85	2	9.7	6	9.55	19	9.85	3	9.8	2	9.7	8	58.45
5. Li Xiaoshuang	CHN	9.6	13	9.65	9	9.625	8	9.75	8	9.7	5	9.825	2	58.15
6. Guo Linyao	CHN	9.65	11	9.675	7	9.55	19	9.8	5	9.6	12	9.65	12	57.925
7. Marius Gherman	ROM	9.7	9	9.675	7	9.725	4	9.675	16	9.4	27	9.525	26	57.7
8. Lee Joo-hyung	KOR	9.8	3	9.575	20	9.6	11	9.625	23	9.475	20	9.6	17	57.675

Two months before the Olympics, Igor Korobchinsky, the son of a Ukrainian coal miner, won the European championship and looked to be the favorite to repeat the win in Barcelona. He placed fifth out of 93 in the team competition in which the top 36 gymnasts advanced to the individual final. Unfortunately for Korobchinsky, three of the four gymnasts ahead of him were also from the Unified Team of the ex-Soviet Union and only three competitors per nation were allowed to advance. So, while James May of Great Britain, who qualified in 49th place, took part in the individual All-Around competition, Korobchinsky had to watch from the sidelines. What he saw was a superb and consistent performance by his teammate, 20-year-old Vitaly

Scherbo of Minsk. Two days later Scherbo won four straight apparatus finals to become the first gymnast in history to earn six gold medals in one Olympics. He added four bronze medals in 1996.

1996 Atlanta C: 112, N: 32, D: 7.24.

		HB		PB		LHV		SH		R		FE		TOTAL PTS.
1. Li Xiaoshuang	CHN	9.787	2	9.65	7	9.812	1	9.712	5	9.775	2	9.687	3	58.423
2. Aleksei Nemov	RUS	9.8	1	9.762	1	9.7	2	9.8	1	9.612	14	9.7	2	58.374
3. Vitaly Scherbo	BLR	9.787	2	9.712	4	9.687	4	9.662	9	9.587	17	9.762	1	58.197
4. Zhang Jingin	CHN	9.787	2	9.762	1	9.65	8	9.75	3	9.562	21	9.637	9	58.148
5. Shen Jian	CHN	9.675	15	9.7	5	9.662	5	9.65	12	9.637	12	9.537	21	57.861
6. Valeri Belenki	GER	9.637	19	9.625	8	9.6	10	9.762	2	9.612	14	9.612	13	57.848
7. John Roethlisberger	USA	9.725	6	9.475	25	9.575	12	9.662	9	9.65	9	9.675	5	57.762
8. Rustam Sharipov	UKR	9.65	18	9.75	3	9.4	24	9.637	14	9.65	9	9.625	10	57.712

After winning the 1995 world championship, Li Xiaoshuang was asked who he feared as a rival at the 1996 Olympics. Li replied, "Aleksei Nemov," pointedly dismissing defending Olympic champion Vitaly Scherbo, who had just finished second and who was sitting beside him. Li explained that an Olympic champion has to be strong on all six apparatuses and that Scherbo was weak on the rings. It was a harsh criticism. Scherbo had earned the gold medal on the rings at the 1992 Olympics, but surgery on both shoulders in 1994 had definitely diminished his strength for that one event. It turned out that Li's analysis was correct, but before his prophecy was fulfilled, it was not Scherbo, but Li himself who would meet disaster on the rings.

In the team compulsory competition, Li's right hand and arm slipped through the ring while he lowered to a cross. This debacle left him with a score of 8.35 and damaged China's chances for the gold medal. On the day of the individual final, however, Li was back in top form. After five rotations, he trailed Nemov by 48 hundredths of a point. While Li performed on the high bar, ultimately earning a score of 9.787, Nemov began his floor routine. A mental lapse caused Nemov to leave out a full twist at the end of his front tumbling pass. He tried to make up for it by adding an extra tumbling pass later in the routine, but the damage was done. Needing a 9.75 to stay ahead of Li, he only earned a 9.7.

2000 Sydney C: 36, N: 16, D: 9.20.

		HB		PB		LHV		SH		R		FE		TOTAL PTS.
1. Aleksei Nemov	RUS	9.787	2	9.755	1	9.650	7	9.775	1	9.687	5	9.800	1	58.474
2. Wei Yang	CHN	9.737	8	9.750	2	9.712	3	9.750	3	9.712	3	9.700	3	58.361
3. Oleksandr Beresh	UKR	9.800	1	9.750	3	9.675	5	9.762	2	9.550	19	9.675	4	58.212
4. Ivan Ivankov	BLR	9.762	5	9.700	10	9.500	16	9.725	6	9.762	1	9.575	10	58.024
5. Oleksandr Svitlychny	UKR	9.700	12	9.725	6	9.725	2	9.675	9	9.525	24	9.600	9	57.95
6. Blaine Wilson	USA	9.525	27	9.712	9	9.800	1	9.587	22	9.612	11	9.700	2	57.936
7. Aleksei Bondarenko	RUS	9.775	3	9.675	13	9.400	21	9.725	5	9.712	4	9.637	7	57.924
8. Yordan Yovchev	BUL	9.700	11	9.675	12	9.475	17	9.737	4	9.750	2	9.550	11	57.887

Since the last Olympics, Aleksei Nemov had battled through a series of injuries. Although he continued to perform well in the floor exercise, his chances of winning the all-around in Sydney were in doubt. As it turned out, he was in fine form, earning the highest score in the qualification round and then leading the final from start to finish. He later earned one gold medal and three bronze medals in the apparatus finals. Along with another bronze in the team event, he brought his career Olympic total to 4 gold, 1 silver and 6 bronze.

2004 Athens C: 98, N: 30, D: 8.14.

		HB		PB		LHV		SH		R		FE		TOTAL PTS.
1. Paul Hamm	USA	9.837	1	9.837	1	9.137	22	9.700	5	9.587	8	9.725	1	57.823
2. Kim Dae-eun	KOR	9.725	4	9.775	3	9.412	16	9.537	11	9.712	4	9.650	3	57.811
3. Yang Tae-young	KOR	9.475	11	9.712	7	9.700	3	9.650	7	9.725	3	9.512	11	57.774
4. Ioan Silviu Suciu	ROM	9.662	5	9.312	20	9.737	2	9.737	1	9.550	14	9.650	3	57.648
5. Rafael Martínez Barrena	SPA	9.475	11	9.700	8	9.612	10	9.687	6	9.575	10	9.500	13	57.549
6. Hiroyuki Tomita	JPN	9.662	5	9.637	12	9.625	7	9.737	1	9.762	1	9.062	21	57.485
7. Yang Wei	CHN	8.987	21	9.800	2	9.512	11	9.725	3	9.737	2	9.600	7	57.361
8. Marian Drăgulescu	ROM	9.337	15	9.437	18	9.850	1	9.525	12	9.562	13	9.612	6	57.323

Paul Hamm and his fraternal twin brother Morgan competed in their first Olympics in Sydney. At the time, Morgan reached the finals of the floor competition, while Paul finished 14th in the all-around. The following year, Paul became better known for an unfortunate incident during the 2001 World Championships, when he accidentally hit the bar with his face and was seriously injured. By 2003, Paul had surpassed his brother. At the 2003 World Championships, Paul became the first American male to win the all-around competition. He arrived in Athens as favorite for the gold, with his main competition expected to come from 2000 silver medalist Yang Wei, who had finished second behind Hamm at the 2003 world championships.

Hamm earned the highest score in the qualifying round, followed by Yang Tae-young. The final was composed of four groups of six athletes organized by qualifying rank, each group starting on a different apparatus, with the top-seeded group finishing on the high bar in the final rotation. Hamm took an early lead in the final by earning the highest score in his speciality, the floor exercise. By the midway point, Yang Wei had narrowed Hamm's lead to .038 points. During the fourth rotation, the vault, Hamm performed a Kasamatsu-1½ twist, but he disastrously missed his landing, staggering sideways off of two mats, almost tumbling into the judges' table and ending up on his rear. His score of 9.137 dropped him to 12th place. Hamm's coach, Miles Avery, tried to look at the bright side; he told Hamm that if he could score 9.8s on the last two apparatuses, he might be able to earn a bronze medal. Meanwhile, Yang Wei, performing on the parallel bars, moved into the lead. In the fifth round, Hamm responded with one of the best parallel bars routines of his career, sticking a peach, front uprise double back to earn the highest score of the rotation, 9.837, which moved him back up to fourth place, while Yang Wei on the high bar missed a grip, dropping his score to a miserable 8.987 and eliminating him from medal contention. Romania's Ioan Suciu, who had nailed a Kasamatsu-1½ twist on the vault to score 9.737, lost his balance on a handstand after a simple reverse pirouette on the parallel bars, dropping his score to 9.312 and eliminating his chance for a gold medal. Yang Tae-young was also in medal range, having scored 9.725 on the rings and 9.700 with a Kasamatsu-1½ vault. Unexpectedly, this left two South Koreans, 19-year-old Kim Dae-eun and Yang Tae-young, in the top two positions with one rotation remaining. As it would turn out, the scoring of Yang Tae-young's fifth round parallel bars routine would cause a major scandal.

Kim scored an impressive 9.650 on the floor. Needing to score above 9.512 to take the lead from Kim, Yang Tae-young nailed the most difficult element of his routine, a Stalder-Tkatchev, but finished one of his full pirouettes with a mixed grip instead of an elgrip, dropping his score to 9.475 and putting him in second place. Performing last, Paul Hamm delivered a near-perfect performance, nailing his dismount. "When I finished my routine," he would later explain, "I thought that I had taken the bronze medal." Deservedly proud of his clutch comeback, he celebrated with Coach Avery. But when Hamm's score, 9.837, was posted, it turned out that it was good enough not for bronze, but for gold. Hamm's winning margin of .012 points over Kim was the closest in Olympic history. The previous closest was Leon Štukelj's .017-point win over Robert Pražak in 1924.

Meanwhile, however, trouble was brewing. As soon as Yang Tae-young finshed his parallel bars routine and his score was posted, his coach, Lee Joo-hyung, recognized that something was wrong. Yang's Start Value for the routine, which had been listed as 10.0 during the qualifying round and the team final, was dropped to 9.9. Kim Dong-min, a Korean judge on the parallel bars, approached the head judge for the apparatus, George Beckford of the United States, and complained about the changed Start Value. Beckford merely replied that the 9.9 was correct and left it at that. Kim Dong-min then informed a member of the South Korean delegation, Yoo Jae-soo, what had happened and Yoo presented the problem to the two A-panel judges, Bultrago Reyes of Colombia and Benjamin Bango of Spain. Reyes and Bango reviewed their notes and discovered their error. They had mistakenly identified one of Yang's elements as a Morisue (double back to upper arms) instead of a Belle (giant to double back to upper arms), a difference of .10 points. Had the start value been accurate, Yang would have earned a total score of 57.874 and he would have won the gold medal.

The South Korean Olympic Committee then filed a protest with the International Gymnastics Federation (FIG), who refused to hear a protest against the judges' decision, citing the fact that the protest had been filed after the event had finished. According to FIG rules, protests must be filed immediately, during the competition, to be considered. Two days after the competition, the FIG Executive Committee reviewed the case and released a statement admitting that Yang's start value should have been 10.0. They suspended the three judges responsible for the error, but still refused to change the results. Under increasing media pressure and desperate for a resolution, FIG president Bruno Grandi wrote a letter to Paul Hamm, via the USOC, urging him to voluntarily give his gold medal to Yang. The USOC refused to forward the letter to Hamm, describing it as "a blatant and inappropriate attempt on the part of the FIG to once again shift responsibility for its own mistakes." The Koreans eventually lodged a protest with the Court of Arbitration for Sport (CAS), which upheld the FIG ruling on the basis that they did not have jurisdiction because the FIG decision had been consistent with its published rules that a protest had to filed during a competition.

In the end, the Korean Olympic Committee gave Yang a symbolic gold medal and the $20,000 prize awarded to gold medalists.

2008 Beijing C: 96, N: 35, D: 8.14.

		HB	PB	LHV	SH	R	FE	TOTAL PTS.
1. Yang Wei	CHN	14.775 (15)	16.100 (3)	16.550 (2)	15.275 (5)	16.625 (2)	15.250 (7)	94.575
2. Kohei Uchimura	JPN	15.400 (5)	15.975 (6)	16.300 (4)	13.275 (24)	15.200 (9)	15.825 (1)	91.975
3. Benoît Caranobe	FRA	14.875 (12)	15.050 (17)	16.600 (1)	14.875 (11)	15.175 (10)	15.350 (5)	91.925
4. Hiroyuki Tomita	JPN	15.675 (1)	16.000 (4)	15.700 (15)	15.425 (4)	13.850 (22)	15.100 (15)	91.750
5. Sergey Khorokhordin	RUS	15.050 (10)	15.700 (7)	15.300 (22)	15.100 (8)	15.400 (5)	15.150 (14)	91.700
6. Maksim Devyatovsky	RUS	15.100 (8)	15.325 (10)	15.225 (24)	15.200 (6)	15.625 (3)	15.225 (10)	91.700
7. Fabian Hambüchen	GER	15.400 (6)	15.275 (11)	15.975 (9)	14.375 (15)	15.025 (12)	15.625 (2)	91.675
8. Yang Tae-yeong	KOR	14.750 (16)	16.350 (1)	16.075 (7)	14.300 (16)	14.900 (13)	15.225 (12)	91.600

A year before the Beijing Olympics, Sydney 2000 silver medalist Yang Wei became the first men's all-around world champion to defend his title since Yugoslav gymnast Petar Sumi in 1926. Yang was known for selecting routines with high difficulty scores. At the 2007 world championships he had the highest start value in four of six events and had built a lead of more than 3.5 points going into the final event, the high bar. The cushion came in handy, giving him a final margin of 1.475 points despite a dramatic tumble during his final routine.

Yang was placed first in the Olympic qualifying round with 93.875 points, followed by 2007 world silver medalist Fabian Hambüchen and 2004 Olympic silver medalist Kim Dae-eun. In the final he was in eighth place after the first two routines, but moved up to second with a strong performance on the rings, behind defending Olympic bronze medalist Yang Tae-yeong. A solid vault put him into first place, and he extended his lead on the parallel bars. Yang Wei went into the final apparatus, the high bar, with a commanding lead over his Korean rival and began to celebrate immediately after completing his routine. When his score was finally posted it was his lowest of the competition, but it was still enough to secure the gold.

Nineteen-year-old Kohei Uchimura nearly ruined his medal chances after a disastrous performance on the pommel horse, in which he fell off twice and finished last of 24 athletes. However, his solid performances in the other routines kept him in the medal running. Reigning horizontal bar world champion Fabian Hambüchen fell off the bar and dropped out of medal contention.

Benoît Caranobe's bronze medal was a surprise to everyone, including himself, as the 27-year-old had never come close to winning an all-around medal. "I was not taking any notice of my scores or anyone else's scores. I only realized at the end that I had won a medal," he said.

HORIZONTAL BAR (HIGH BAR)

The horizontal bar stands 2.55 meters (8 feet 4½ inches) above the ground. It is 2.5 meters (8 feet 2½ inches) long and has a diameter of 28 millimeters (1⅒ inches).

1896 Athens C: 15, N: 4, D: 4.9.

1. Hermann Weingärtner	GER
2. Alfred Flatow	GER

1900 not held

1904 St. Louis C: 9?, N: 1, D: 10.28.

		PTS.
1. Anton Heida	USA	40
1. Edward Hennig	USA	40
3. George Eyser	USA	39

1908–1920 not held

1924 Paris C: 72, N: 9, D: 7.20.

		PTS.
1. Leon Štukelj	YUG/SLO	19.73
2. Jean Gutweniger	SWI	19.236
3. André Higelin	FRA	19.163
4. Antoine Rebetez	SWI	19.053
4. Georges Miez	SWI	19.053
6. Jean Gounot	FRA	19.043
7. François Gangloff	FRA	18.933
8. August Güttingen	SWI	18.886

1928 Amsterdam C: 86, N: 11, D: 8.10.

		PTS.
1. Georges Miez	SWI	19.17
2. Romeo Neri	ITA	19.00
3. Eugen Mack	SWI	18.92
4. Hermann Hänggi	SWI	18.83
4. Vittorio Lucchetti	ITA	18.83
6. Josip Primožič	YUG/SLO	18.67
7. Hans Grieder	SWI	18.58
7. August Güttinger	FRA	18.58

1932 Los Angeles C: 12, N: 6, D: 8.11.

		PTS.
1. Dallas Bixler	USA	18.33
2. Heikki Savolainen	FIN	18.07
3. Einari Teräsvirta	FIN	18.07
4. Veikko Pakarinen	FIN	17.27
4. István Pelle	HUN	17.27
6. Michael Schuler	USA	15.57
7. Miklós Péter	HUN	15.13
8. Mahito Haga	JPN	12.47

Dallas Bixler, performing in his home town impressed the judges with an innovative dismount: the reverse. He went on to serve 44 years as a gymnastics judge. Savolainen and Teräsvirta tied for second. While the judges discussed a method for deciding which one should get the silver medal, the two Finns talked it out and agreed that Savolainen should receive the silver and Teräsvirta the bronze. The judges abided by their decision.

1936 Berlin C: 111, N: 14, D: 8.11.

		PTS.
1. Aleksanteri Saarvala	FIN	19.367
2. Konrad Frey	GER	19.267
3. Alfred Schwarzmann	GER	19.233
4. Innozenz Stangl	GER	19.167
4. Heikki Savolainen	FIN	19.133
6. Veikko Pakarinen	FIN	19.067
7. Martti Uosikkinen	FIN	19.00
8. Walter Steffens	GER	18.966

1948 London C: 123, N: 16, D: 8.13.

		PTS.
1. Josef Stalder	SWI	19.85
2. Walter Lehmann	SWI	19.70
3. Veikko Huhtanen	FIN	19.60
4. Raymond Dot	FRA	19.40
4. Aleksanteri Saarvala	FIN	19.40
4. Lajos Sántha	HUN	19.40
4. Emil Studer	SWI	19.40
8. Einari Teräsvirta	FIN	19.35

1952 Helsinki C: 185, N: 29, D: 7.21.

		PTS.
1. Jack Günthard	SWI	19.55
2. Alfred Schwarzmann	GER	19.50
2. Josef Stalder	SWI	19.50
4. Heikki Savolainen	FIN	19.45
5. Viktor Chukarin	SOV/UKR	19.40
6. Jean Tschabold	SWI	19.35
7. Helmut Bantz	GER	19.25
7. Melchior Thalmann	SWI	19.25

1956 Melbourne C: 63, N: 18, D: 12.6.

		PTS.
1. Takashi Ono	JPN	19.60
2. Yuri Tytov	SOV/UKR	19.40
3. Masao Takemoto	JPN	19.30
4. Pavel Stolbov	SOV/RUS	19.25
4. Viktor Chukarin	SOV/UKR	19.25
6. Helmut Bantz	GER	19.15
7. John Beckner	USA	19.00
8. Albert Azaryan	SOV/ARM	18.95

1960 Rome C: 130, N: 28, D: 9.10.

		PTS.
1. Takashi Ono	JPN	19.60
2. Masao Takemoto	JPN	19.525
3. Borys Shakhlin	SOV/UKR	19.475
4. Yukio Endo	JPN	19.425
5. Miroslav Cerar	YUG/SLO	19.40
5. Yuri Tytov	SOV/UKR	19.40

1964 Tokyo C: 130, N: 24, D: 10.23.

		PTS.
1. Borys Shakhlin	SOV/UKR	19.625
2. Yuri Tytov	SOV/UKR	19.550
3. Miroslav Cerar	YUG/SLO	19.50
4. Viktor Lisitsky	SOV/RUS	19.325
5. Yukio Endo	JPN	19.050
6. Takashi Ono	JPN	19.00

1968 Mexico City C: 115, N: 27, D: 10.26.

		PTS.
1. Akinori Nakayama	JPN	19.55
1. Mikhail Voronin	SOV/RUS	19.55
3. Eizo Kenmotsu	JPN	19.375
4. Klaus Köste	GDR	19.225
5. Sergei Diomidov	SOV/RUS	19.15
6. Yukio Endo	JPN	19.025

1972 Munich C: 113, N: 26, D: 9.1.

		PTS.
1. Mitsuo Tsukahara	JPN	19.725
2. Sawao Kato	JPN	19.525
3. Shigeru Kasamatsu	JPN	19.45
4. Eizo Kenmotsu	JPN	19.35
5. Akinori Nakayama	JPN	19.225
6. Nikolai Andrianov	SOV/RUS	19.10

1976 Montreal C: 90, N: 20, D: 7.23.

		PTS.
1. Mitsuo Tsukahara	JPN	19.675
2. Eizo Kenmotsu	JPN	19.50
3. Henry Boërio	FRA	19.475
3. Eberhard Gienger	GER	19.475
5. Gennady Kryssin	SOV/RUS	19.25
6. Ferenc Donáth	HUN	19.20

Although Mitsuo Tsukahara achieved his greatest Olympic success on the horizontal bar, it was in a different event that he made gymnastics history. Tsukahara was the first gymnast to perform the vault sideways, starting with a cartwheel, hitting the horse in the middle of the move and then springing off into a backflip.

Mitsuo Tsukahara, 1976
Japan's innovative gymnast performs at the Montreal Games.

Considered daring when he introduced it, the Tsukahara vault became so commonplace that it was included in compulsory exercises for women.

1980 Moscow C: 65, N: 14, D: 7.25.

		PTS.
1. Stoyan Deltchev	BUL	19.825
2. Alexandr Dityatin	SOV/RUS	19.75
3. Nikolai Andrianov	SOV/RUS	19.675
4. Ralf-Peter Hemmann	GDR	19.525
4. Michael Nikolay	GDR	19.525
6. Sergio Suárez Aime	CUB	19.45

1984 Los Angeles C: 71, N: 19, D: 8.4.

		PTS.
1. Shinji Morisue	JPN	20.00
2. Tong Fei	CHN	19.975
3. Koji Gushiken	JPN	19.95
4. Timothy Daggett	USA	19.85
4. Lou Yun	CHN	19.85
4. Peter Vidmar	USA	19.85
7. Marco Piatti	SWI	19.80
8. Daniel Wunderlin	SWI	19.675

1988 Seoul C: 89, N: 23, D: 9.24.

		PTS.
1. Vladimir Artemov	SOV/RUS	19.90
1. Valery Lyukin	SOV/KAZ	19.90
3. Holgen Behrendt	GDR	19.80
3. Marius Gherman	ROM	19.80
5. Wang Chongsheng	CHN	19.775
6. Xu Zhiqiang	CHN	19.70
7. Curtis Hibbert	CAN	19.675
8. Andreas Wecker	GDR	19.50

1992 Barcelona C: 93, N: 25, D: 8.2.

		PTS.
1. Trent Dimas	USA	9.875
2. Hryhoriy Misyutin	UKR	9.837
2. Andreas Wecker	GER	9.837
4. Guo Linyao	CHN	9.812
5. Valeri Belenki	AZR	9.787
5. Yoshiaki Hatakeda	JPN	9.787
5. Daisuke Nishikawa	JPN	9.787
8. Li Jing	CHN	6.425

Twenty-one-year-old Trent Dimas was a highly unlikely Olympic champion. He had never qualified for an apparatus final in an international event and even in Barcelona he only placed sixth in the qualifying round. The performer before Dimas in the final, Li Jing, fell off the bar, and the judges' confusion as to how to score his routine caused an unexpected delay. As Dimas stood waiting for his turn, he was so nervous he was afraid he might fall over. But once he began, everything went right—for 30 seconds Trent Dimas performed the best routine of his life, culminating with a triple-back-somersault dismount and a perfect landing that he held for several seconds to make sure the judges were quite clear that he had hit it. The judges got the message. Dimas was the first American gymnast to win a gold medal in a non-boycotted Olympics since Dallas Bixler won the same event in 1932. He was also only the second Olympic champion ever who was a native of the state of New Mexico. The first was Cathy Carr, who won the 100-meter breaststroke in 1972. Dimas credited his love of cartoons with inspiring him to pursue gymnastics because "Gymnastics was the closest thing to being a superhero."

As for silver medalist Andreas Wecker, it took him 30 seconds to earn his medal, but five hours to produce a urine sample for drug testing.

1996 Atlanta C: 106, N: 32, D: 7.29.

		PTS.
1. Andreas Wecker	GER	9.85
2. Krasimir Dunev	BUL	9.825
3. Fan Bin	CHN	9.80
3. Aleksei Nemov	RUS	9.80
3. Vitaly Scherbo	BLR	9.80
6. Aleksei Voropayev	RUS	9.712
7. Jesús Caraballo Martínez	SPA	9.35
8. Lee Joo-hyung	KOR	8.525

Andreas Wecker's victory was considered highly controversial because his routine was relatively simple. But Wecker, the reigning world champion, knew what it took to please the judges. For example, he had his own tanning bed at home because, as he explained, "It certainly has an aesthetic effect if you're nicely tanned out there than if you're all white."

2000 Sydney C: 79, N: 28, D: 9.25.

		PTS.
1. Aleksei Nemov	RUS	9.787
2. Benjamin Varonian	FRA	9.787
3. Lee Joo-hyung	KOR	9.775
4. Aleksei Bondarenko	RUS	9.762
5. Oleksandr Beresh	UKR	9.750
6. Ilia Georgadze	GEO	9.625
7. Dieter Rehm	SWI	8.925
8. Naoya Tsukahara	JPN	8.825

Nemov and Varonian received the same score, but Nemov was given the edge based on the complicated tie-breaking system. Although Nemov had already won the all-around gold medal, his victory on the high bar was a surprise because he had never before placed higher than third on the apparatus in a major event.

2004 Athens C: 79, N: 29, D: 8.23.

		PTS.
1. Igor Cassina	ITA	9.812
2. Paul Hamm	USA	9.812
3. Isao Yoneda	JPN	9.787
4. Morgan Hamm	USA	9.787
5. Aleksei Nemov	RUS	9.762
6. Xiao Qin	CHN	9.737
7. Fabian Hambüchen	GER	9.700
8. Valeriy Honcharov	UKR	8.887

Four-time Olympic champion Aleksei Nemov performed a seemingly flawless routine, including six release moves, but took a step on his landing. He was given a score of 9.725, putting him in last place with seven competitors left. When the score was announced, the crowd immediately began a noisy protest, disrupting the competition with jeers and whistles and giving thumbs-down signs to the judges. After several minutes, two members of the judging panel, The Kin Kin of Malaysia and Chris Grabowecky of Canada, agreed to revise their scores, bringing Nemov up to a 9.762, but that did not change his placing. Consequently, this did not calm the crowd, which continued to loudly disrupt the competition until Nemov took the podium and pleaded for quiet. Even then, the disruption continued until the next performer, all-around champion Paul Hamm, approached the bar. Despite the unsettling atmosphere, Hamm executed an excellent routine, including three consecutive release moves. He did step slightly on his landing, but he earned a score of 9.812, putting him in the lead and prompting further protests from the crowd. Igor Cassina was next up and matched Hamm's score. Both the gold and bronze were decided on tie-breaks, with Cassina finishing first and Isao Yoneda winning bronze.

2008 Beijing C: 76, N: 27, D: 8.19.

		PTS.
1. Zou Kai	CHN	16.200
2. Jonathan Horton	USA	16.175
3. Fabian Hambüchen	GER	15.875
4. Igor Cassina	ITA	15.675
5. Takuya Nakase	JPN	15.450
6. Hiroyuki Tomita	JPN	15.225
7. Epke Zonderland	HOL	15.000
8. Yann Cucherat	FRA	14.825

Reigning world champion and three-time European champion Fabian Hambüchen led after the qualifying round, followed by defending Olympic champion Igor Cassina. Hambüchen opened with a solid 15.875 for his final routine but was passed by 20-year-old Zou Kai, who had won the floor exercise gold medal two days earlier. Kai's score held up for the gold despite a dynamic routine by Olympic newcomer Jonathan Horton, which came within 0.025 points of Zou.

PARALLEL BARS

The parallel bars are 1.95 meters (6 feet 4¾ inches) high and 3.5 meters (11 feet 5¾ inches) long. Their distance apart can be adjusted between 42 and 52 centimeters (16½ and 20½ inches).

1896 Athens C: 18, N: 5, D: 4.10.

1. Alfred Flatow	GER
2. Louis Zutter	SWI
3? Conrad Böcker	GER
3? Hermann Weingärtner	GER
5. Carl Schuhmann	GER

When Alfred Flatow returned to Germany after winning three events and placing second in another, he was banned from competition for two years because the Olympic Games was an unauthorized international event. Because he was Jewish, Flatow was deported by the Nazis to the concentration camp in Theresienstadt in 1942. He died there on December 28. In 1987, after a 47-year battle with local residents, the Berlin street leading to the Olympic Stadium was renamed Alfred und Gustav Felix Flatow-Allee in honor of Flatow and his gymnast cousin, who also died in Theresienstadt, starving to death January 29, 1945.

1900 not held

1904 St. Louis C:?, N: 1, D: 10.28.

		PTS.
1. George Eyser	USA	44
2. Anton Heida	USA	43
3. John Duha	USA	40

Eyser also won a gold in the long horse vault, two silvers in the pommel horse and combined competitions, and a bronze in the horizontal bar. His gymnastic feats were all the more impressive considering that his left leg was made of wood. His leg had been amputated after he was run over by a train.

1908–1920 not held

1924 Paris C: 72, N: 9, D: 7.20.

		PTS.
1. August Güttinger	SWI	21.63
2. Robert Pražak	CZE	21.61
3. Giorgio Zampori	ITA	21.45
4. Josef Wilhelm	SWI	21.40
5. Mario Lertora	ITA	21.33
6. Ladislav Vácha	CZE	21.31
7. Jaroslav Kos	CZE	21.28
8. Jean Gutweniger	SWI	21.26
8. Bedřich Šupčik	CZE	21.26

1928 Amsterdam C: 85, N: 11, D: 8.10.

		PTS.
1. Ladislav Vácha	CZE	18.83
2. Josip Primožič	YUG/SLO	18.50
3. Hermann Hänggi	SWI	18.08
4. Jan Gajdoš	CZE	17.92
4. André Lemoine	FRA	17.92
4. Bedřich Šupčik	CZE	17.92
7. Mario Lertora (ITA), Mauri Nyberg-Noroma (FIN),Leon Štukelj (YUG/SLO), Melchior Wetzel (SWI)		17.83

1932 Los Angeles C: 15, N: 6, D: 8.12.

		PTS.
1. Romeo Neri	ITA	18.97
2. István Pelle	HUN	18.60
3. Heikki Savolainen	FIN	18.27
4. Mauri Nyberg-Noroma	FIN	17.80
5. Mario Lertora	ITA	17.53
6. Alfred Jochim	USA	17.47
7. József Hegedűs	HUN	17.30
7. Miklós Péter	HUN	17.30

1936 Berlin C: 111, N: 14, D: 8.11.

		PTS.
1. Konrad Frey	GER	19.067
2. Michael Reusch	SWI	19.034
3. Alfred Schwarzmann	GER	18.967
4. Alois Hudec	CZE	18.966
5. Eugen Mack	SWI	18.834
6. Walter Bach	SWI	18.733
7. Heikki Savolainen	FIN	18.633
8. Eduard "Edi" Steinemann	SWI	18.500

1948 London C: 123, N: 16, D: 8.13.

		PTS.
1. Michael Reusch	SWI	19.75
2. Veikko Huhtanen	FIN	19.65
3. Christian Kipfer	SWI	19.55
3. Josef Stalder	SWI	19.55
5. Walter Lehmann	SWI	19.50
6. Heikki Savolainen	FIN	19.45
7. Paavo Aaltonen	FIN	19.40
7. Zdeněk Růžička	CZE	19.40

1952 Helsinki C: 185, N: 29, D: 7.21.

		PTS.
1. Hans Eugster	SWI	19.65
2. Viktor Chukarin	SOV/UKR	19.60
3. Josef Stalder	SWI	19.50
4. Grant Shaginyan	SOV/ARM	19.35
5. Ferdinand Daniš	CZE	19.30
5. Yevgeny Korolkov	SOV/RUS	19.30
5. Jean Tschalbold	SWI	19.30
8. Vladimir Belyakov	SOV/RUS	19.25
8. Valentin Muratov	SOV/RUS	19.25

1956 Melbourne C: 63, N: 18, D: 12.6.

		PTS.
1. Viktor Chukarin	SOV/UKR	19.20
2. Masami Kubota	JPN	19.15
3. Takashi Ono	JPN	19.10
3. Masao Takemoto	JPN	19.10
5. Albert Azaryan	SOV/ARM	19.00
6. Nobuyuki Aihara	JPN	18.90
6. Bengt Lindfors	FIN	18.90
8. Onni Lappalainen (FIN), Olavi Leimuvirta (FIN), Borys Shakhlin (SOV/UKR), Shinsaku Tsukawai (JPN), Yuri Tytov (SOV/UKR)		18.85

1960 Rome C: 130, N: 28, D: 9.10.

		PTS.
1. Borys Shakhlin	SOV/UKR	19.40
2. Giovanni Carminucci	ITA	19.375
3. Takashi Ono	JPN	19.35
4. Nobuyuki Aihara	JPN	19.275
5. Yuri Tytov	SOV/UKR	19.20
6. Masao Takemoto	JPN	19.125

1964 Tokyo C: 130, N: 29, D: 10.23.

		PTS.
1. Yukio Endo	JPN	19.675
2. Shuji Tsurumi	JPN	19.45
3. Franco Menichelli	ITA	19.35
4. Sergei Diomidov	SOV/UZB	19.225
5. Viktor Lisitsky	SOV/RUS	19.20
6. Miroslav Cerar	YUG/SLO	18.45

1968 Mexico City C: 117, N: 28, D: 10.26.

		PTS.
1. Akinori Nakayama	JPN	19.475
2. Mikhail Voronin	SOV/RUS	19.425
3. Vladimir Klimenko	SOV/RUS	19.225
4. Takeshi Kato	JPN	19.20
5. Eizo Kenmotsu	JPN	19.175
6. Václav Kubička	CZE	18.95

1972 Munich C: 113, N: 26, D: 9.1.

		PTS.
1. Sawao Kato	JPN	19.475
2. Shigeru Kasamatsu	JPN	19.375
3. Eizo Kenmotsu	JPN	19.25
4. Viktor Klimenko	SOV/RUS	19.125
5. Akinori Nakayama	JPN	18.875
6. Nikolai Andrianov	SOV/RUS	17.975

1976 Montreal C: 90, N: 20, D: 7.23.

		PTS.
1. Sawao Kato	JPN	19.675
2. Nikolai Andrianov	SOV/RUS	19.50
3. Mitsuo Tsukahara	JPN	19.475
4. Bernd Jäger	GDR	19.20
5. Miloslav Netušil	CZE	19.125
6. Andrzej Szajna	POL	18.95

1980 Moscow C: 65, N: 14, D: 7.25.

		PTS.
1. Aleksandr Tkachyov	SOV/RUS	19.775
2. Aleksandr Dityatin	SOV/RUS	19.75
3. Roland Brückner	GDR	19.65
4. Michael Nikolay	GDR	19.60
5. Stoyan Deltchev	BUL	19.575
6. Roberto Leon Richards-Aguiar	CUB	19.50

1984 Los Angeles C: 71, N: 19, D: 8.4.

		PTS.
1. Bart Conner	USA	19.95
2. Nobuyuki Kajitani	JPN	19.925
3. Mitchell Gaylord	USA	19.85
4. Tong Fei	CHN	19.825
5. Koji Gushiken	JPN	19.80
6. Li Ning	CHN	19.775
7. Jürgen Geiger	GER	19.60
7. Daniel Winkler	GER	19.60

In 1996, Bart Conner married fellow gymnastics gold medalist Nadia Comăneci.

1988 Seoul C: 89, N: 23, D: 9.24.

		PTS.
1. Vladimir Artemov	SOV/RUS	19.925
2. Valery Lyukin	SOV/KAZ	19.90
3. Sven Tippelt	GDR	19.75
4. Kalofer Hristozov	BUL	19.725
5. Marius Gherman	ROM	19.70
6. Curtis Hibbert	CAN	19.675
7. Sylvio Kroll	GDR	19.625
8. Boris Preti	ITA	19.60

1992 Barcelona C: 93, N: 25, D: 8.2

		PTS.
1. Vitaly Scherbo	BLR	9.90
2. Li Jing	CHN	9.812
3. Guo Linyao	CHN	9.80
3. Igor Korobchinsky	UKR	9.80
3. Masayuki Matsunaga	JPN	9.80
6. Jair Lynch	USA	9.712
7. Andreas Wecker	GER	9.612
8. Daisuke Nishikawa	JPN	9.575

Two-time world champion Li Jing was the favorite, but he didn't stick his double-pike dismount whereas Scherbo did. Because of the restriction of two finalists per nation, Jair Lynch made it to the final even though he placed only 16th in the qualifying round.

1996 Atlanta C: 107, N: 32, D: 7.29.

		PTS.
1. Rustam Sharipov	UKR	9.837
2. Jair Lynch	USA	9.825
3. Vitaly Scherbo	BLR	9.80
4. Aleksei Nemov	RUS	9.75
4. Zhang Jingin	CHN	9.75
6. Huang Liping	CHN	9.737
7. Lee Joo-hyung	KOR	9.687
8. Sergei Sharkov	RUS	9.65

Rustam Sharipov was born in Tajikistan and moved to Kharkov, Ukraine, at age 15 to further his gymnastics career. He competed with part of a screw embedded in his left foot—left behind after surgery in 1991. Jair Lynch was the first African-American to win a medal in Gymnastics.

2000 Sydney C: 81, N: 30, D: 9.25.

		PTS.
1. Li Xiaopeng	CHN	9.825
2. Lee Joo-hyung	KOR	9.812
3. Aleksei Nemov	RUS	9.800
4. Jung Jin-soo	KOR	9.787
5. Ivan Ivankov	BLR	9.775
6. Yann Cucherat	FRA	9.725
7. Xu Huang	CHN	9.650
8. Marius Urzica	ROM	8.887

Li Xiaopeng was the reigning Asian Games champion and Lee Joo-hyung the reigning world champion.

2004 Athens C: 81, N: 30, D: 8.23.

		PTS.
1. Valeriy Honcharov	UKR	9.787
2. Hiroyuki Tomita	JPN	9.775
3. Li Xiaopeng	CHN	9.762
4. Ivan Ivankov	BLR	9.762
5. Daisuke Nakano	JPN	9.762
6. Yann Cucherat	FRA	9.762
7. Paul Hamm	USA	9.737
8. Yernar Yerimbetov	KAZ	9.737

Defending Olympic champion and two-time defending world champion Li Xiaopeng was expected to win again in Athens. He did earn the highest score in the qualification round, but in the final his routine, although spectacular, was not smooth and he was given 9.762 points, the exact same score as the three gymnasts who preceded him. However, the 26-year-old European Championships silver medalist Valeriy Honcharov, who had temporarily quit gymnastics after the 2000 Olympics, had already earned a 9.787.

2008 Beijing C: 76. N: 27, D: 8.19.

1. Li Xiaopeng	CHN	16.450
2. Yoo Won-chul	KOR	16.250
3. Anton Fokin	UZB	16.200
4. Fabian Hambüchen	GER	15.975
5. Mitja Petkovšek	SLO	15.725
6. Huang Xu	CHN	15.700
7. Yang Tae-yeong	KOR	15.650
8. Nikolay Kryukov	RUS	15.150

After being sidelined for several years due to recurrent foot and ankle injuries, Sydney 2000 gold medalist Li Xiaopeng finally underwent surgery in early 2006. He came back to win the 2006 World Cup Final and was due to compete at the 2007 world championships when a fractured toe during a floor exercise put him back into rehabilitation.

Li recovered in time to compete in Beijing and was placed first in the qualifying round. Competing last in the final, he performed a near-perfect routine, scoring 16.450 points to move past 2006 world silver medalist Yoo Won-chul for the gold medal. This gave him a total of sixteen Olympic and world titles, more than any other gymnast in China.

LONG HORSE VAULT

According to current rules, finalists perform two vaults from different categories. The final score is an average of the scores of the two vaults.

1896 Athens C: 15, N: 4, D: 4.9.

1. Carl Schuhmann	GER
2. Louis Zutter	SWI
3. Hermann Weingärtner	GER

1900 not held

1904 St. Louis C: 7, N: 1, D: 10.28.

		PTS.
1. George Eyser	USA	36
1. Anton Heida	USA	36
3. William Merz	USA	31

1908–1920 not held

1924 Paris C: 70, N: 9, D: 7.20.

		PTS.
1. Frank Kriz	USA	9.98
2. Jan Koutny	CZE	9.97
3. Bohumil Mořkovsky	CZE	9.93
4. Leon Štukelj	YUG/SLO	9.91
5. Max Wandrer	USA	9.85
6. Ivan Porenta	YUG/SLO	9.76
7. Miroslav Klinger	CZE	9.75
7. Ferdinando Mandrini	ITA	9.75

1928 Amsterdam C: 85, N: 11, D: 8.10.

		PTS.
1. Eugen Mack	SWI	9.58
2. Emanuel Löffler	CZE	9.50
3. Stane Derganc	YUG/SLO	9.46
4. Georges Miez	SWI	9.42
4. Josip Primožič	YUG/SLO	9.42
6. Georges Leroux	FRA	9.33
7. August Güttinger	SWI	9.28
7. Ivan Porenta	YUG/SLO	9.28
7. Herman Witzig	USA	9.28

1932 Los Angeles C: 10, N: 4, D: 8.10.

		PTS.
1. Savino Guglielmetti	ITA	18.03
2. Alfred Jochim	USA	17.77
3. Edward Carmichael	USA	17.53
4. Einari Teräsvirta	FIN	17.53
5. Marcel Gleyre	USA	17.46
6. István Pelle	HUN	17.13
7. Miklós Péter	HUN	16.97
8. Mario Lertora	ITA	16.40

1936 Berlin C: 110, N: 14, D: 8.11.

		PTS.
1. Alfred Schwarzmann	GER	19.20
2. Eugen Mack	SWI	18.967
3. Matthias Volz	GER	18.467
4. Walter Bach	SWI	18.40
5. Walter Beck	SWI	18.367
6. Martti Uosikkinen	FIN	18.30
7. Michael Reusch	SWI	18.266
8. Georges Miez	SWI	18.234
8. Josef Walter	SWI	18.234

1948 London C: 123, N: 16, D: 8.13.

		PTS.
1. Paavo Aaltonen	FIN	19.55
2. Olavi Rove	FIN	19.50
3. János Mogyorósi-Klencs	HUN	19.25
3. Ferenc Pataki	HUN	19.25
3. Leo Sotornik	CZE	19.25
6. Veikko Huhtanen	FIN	19.20
7. Einari Teräsvirta	FIN	19.15
8. Walter Lehmann	SWI	19.05
8. Sulo Salmi	FIN	19.05

1952 Helsinki C: 185, N: 29, D: 7.21.

		PTS.
1. Viktor Chukanin	SOV/UKR	19.20
2. Masao Takemoto	JPN	19.15
3. Takashi Ono	JPN	19.10
3. Tadao Uesako	JPN	19.10
5. Hans Eugster	SWI	18.95
5. Theo Wied	GER	18.95
7. Iosef Berdiyev	SOV/RUS	18.90
7. Ernst Fivian	SWI	18.90

1956 Melbourne C: 63, N: 18, D: 12.6.

		PTS.
1. Helmut Bantz	GER	18.85
1. Valentin Muratov	SOV/RUS	18.85
3. Yuri Tytov	SOV/UKR	18.75
4. Borys Shakhlin	SOV/UKR	18.70
4. Theo Wied	GER	18.70
6. Masao Takemoto	JPN	18.65
7. John Beckner (USA), Jakob Kiefer (GER), Robert Klein (GER), Viktor Chukanin (SOV/UKR		18.60

A prisoner of war during World War II, Helmut Bantz helped train British gymnasts prior to the 1948 Olympics. He led the German team at the 1952 and 1956 Olympics and was 35 years old when he won his gold medal.

1960 Rome C: 130, N: 28, D: 9.10.

		PTS.
1. Takashi Ono	JPN	19.35
1. Borys Shakhlin	SOV/UKR	19.35
3. Vladimir Portnoy	SOV/RUS	19.225
4. Yuri Tytov	SOV/UKR	19.20
5. Yukio Endo	JPN	19.175
6. Shuji Tsurumi	JPN	19.15

1964 Tokyo C: 130, N: 29, D: 10.23.

		PTS.
1. Haruhiro Yamashita	JPN	19.60
2. Viktor Lisitsky	SOV/RUS	19.325
3. Hannu Rantakari	FIN	19.30
4. Shuji Tsurumi	JPN	19.225
5. Borys Shakhlin	SOV/UKR	19.20
6. Yukio Endo	JPN	19.075

Yamashita executed a handspring in a piked position, a vault that became known as a "yamashita." One of the judges, Dr. Widmer of Switzerland, was so impressed that he gave Yamashita a ten—the highest mark possible.

1968 Mexico City C: 116, N: 28, D: 10.26.

		PTS.
1. Mikhail Voronin	SOV/RUS	19.00
2. Yukio Endo	JPN	18.95
3. Sergei Diomidov	SOV/RUS	18.925
4. Takeshi Kato	JPN	18.775
5. Akinori Nakayama	JPN	18.725
6. Eizo Kenmotsu	JPN	18.65

1972 Munich C: 113, N: 26, D: 9.1.

		PTS.
1. Klaus Köste	GDR	18.85
2. Viktor Klimenko	SOV/RUS	18.825
3. Nikolai Andrianov	SOV/RUS	18.80
4. Sawao Kato	JPN	18.55
4. Eizo Kenmotsu	JPN	18.55
6. Peter Rohner	SWI	18.525

Performing a yamashita and a forward somersault, the 5-foot 4½-inch Köste won East Germany's first gold medal in men's gymnastics.

1976 Montreal C: 90, N: 20, D: 7.23.

		PTS.
1. Nikolai Andrianov	SOV/RUS	19.45
2. Mitsuo Tsukahana	JPN	19.375
3. Hiroshi Kajiyama	JPN	19.275
4. Dănut Grecu	ROM	19.20
5. Zoltán Magyar	HUN	19.15
5. Imre Molnár	HUN	19.15

1980 Moscow C: 65, N: 14, D: 7.25.

		PTS.
1. Nikolai Andrianov	SOV/RUS	19.825
2. Aleksandr Dityatin	SOV/RUS	19.80
3. Roland Brückner	GDR	19.775
4. Ralf-Peter Hemmann	GDR	19.75
5. Stoyan Deltchev	BUL	19.70
6. Jiří Tabák	CZE	19.525

1984 Los Angeles C: 71, N: 19, D: 8.4

		PTS.
1. Lou Yun	CHN	19.95
2. Mitchell Gaylord	USA	19.825
2. Koji Gushiken	JPN	19.825
2. Li Ning	CHN	19.82
2. Shinji Morisue	JPN	19.825
6. James Hartung	USA	19.80
7. Warren Long	CAN	19.70
8. Daniel Wunderlin	SWI	19.625

1988 Seoul C: 89, N: 23, D: 9.24.

		PTS.
1. Lou Yun	CHN	19.875
2. Sylvio Kroll	GDR	19.862
3. Park Jong-hoon	KOR	19.775
4. Dian Kolev	BUL	19.737
5. Holger Behrendt	GDR	19.65
6. Sergei Kharkov	SOV/RUS	19.60
7. Yukio Iketani	JPN	19.525
8. Vladimir Gogoladze	SOV/GEO	19.512

1992 Barcelona C: 93, N: 25, D: 8.2.

		PTS.
1. Vitaly Scherbo	BLR	9.856
2. Hryhoriy Misyutin	UKR	9.781
3. Yoo Ok-ryul	KOR	9.762
4. Li Xiaoshuang	CHN	9.731
5. Zoltán Supola	HUN	9.674
6. Sylvio Kroll	GER	9.662
7. Szilveszter Csollány	HUN	9.524
8. Yutaka Aihara	JPN	9.45

1996 Atlanta C: 106, C: 32, D: 7.29.

		PTS.
1. Aleksei Nemov	RUS	9.787
2. Yeo Hong-chul	KOR	9.756
3. Vitaly Scherbo	BLR	9.724
4. Ivan Ivanov	BUL	9.643
4. Li Xiaoshuang	CHN	9.643
6. Aleksei Voropayev	RUS	9.618
7. Igor Korobchinsky	UKR	9.568
8. Ivan Pavlovsky	BLR	9.493

After winning the Individual Event World Championships three months before the Olympics, Aleksei Nemov told the press that he thought Yeo Hong-chul deserved the victory. In Atlanta, Yeo led after the first jump, 9.837 to 9.762. But during his second try he overrotated a 2½ twist and bounded backwards when he landed. This handed the gold to Nemov, who was rewarded by letters from thousands of girls wanting to meet him.

2000 Sydney C: 80, N: 31, D: 9.25.

		PTS.
1. Gervasio Deferr Ángel	SPA	9.712
2. Aleksei Bondarenko	RUS	9.587
3. Leszek Blanik	POL	9.475
4. Aleksei Nemov	RUS	9.456
5. Sergei Fedorchenko	KAZ	9.399
6. Blaine Wilson	USA	9.362
7. Ioannis Melissanidis	GRE	9.262
8. Dieter Rehm	SWI	9.006

Spain's first gymnastics medalist, Gervasio Deferr of Barcelona was the only finalist to hit both of his landings.

2004 Athens C: 79, N: 30, D: 8.23.

		PTS.
1. Gervasio Deferr Ángel	SPA	9.737
2. Jevgēnijs Saproņenko	LAT	9.706
3. Marian Drăgulescu	ROM	9.612
4. Kyle Shewfelt	CAN	9.599
5. Filip Yanev	BUL	9.581
6. Róbert Gál	HUN	9.538
7. Li Xiaopeng	CHN	9.368
8. Aleksei Bondarenko	RUS	4.550

The competition got off to a dramatic start, when Aleksei Bondarenko of Russia, competing on his 26th birthday, crashed on his first vault, nearly landing on his head. After a stunned few seconds, Bondarenko attempted his second vault, but again crashed, this time falling on his side. Alhough he was able to walk away, he was later hospitalized for a fracture in his lower back. Three-time world champion Li Xiaopeng fell on his first vault, and although he recovered with a strong second vault, his medal hopes were gone. Two-time world champion silver medalist Jevgēnijs Saproņenko then took the lead with a handspring double front with a half turn, earning 9.712, and a round-off with two backflips, earning 9.700 points, for an average score of 9.706. Photogenic Gervasio Deferr, the defending Olympic champion, moved ahead of Saproneņko, earning 9.687 with a Yurchenko-2½ twist and 9.787 on a Tsukahara-2½ twist. Performing last, Marian Drăgulescu performed his signature move, which bears his name, a handspring double front with a half turn, which he performed nearly flawlessly to earn a 9.9, the highest score awarded in a world championship or Olympic competition since 1995. Having seemingly clinched the gold medal, Drăgulescu attempted an easier second vault, a Katsumatsu-1½ twist. However, he overshot his landing, bounced over the penalty stripe and put both hands to the mat. Considering the automatic deductions that he should have incurred, he was awarded the surprisingly high score of 9.325, winning the bronze medal despite having failed to land one of his vaults.

Gymnastics Canada immediately lodged a protest, arguing that it was mathematically impossible for Drăgulescu to have scored more than 9.1 on his second vault. Under the rules, of the five performance scores given, the high and low scores were thrown out and the rest must be within 0.2 points of each other if the score is 9.0 or over. In Drăgulescu's case, the scores were outside of the 0.2 range, and because two of his scores were 9.5, one of them was included in his final average, boosting it to 9.325. The Canadian protest was largely ignored by International Gymnastics Federation Technical Director, Adrian Stoica, who, like Drăgulescu, was from Romania. After submitting an appeal to the Court of Arbitration for Sport (CAS), Gymnastics Canada decided to abandon their protest given the small likelihood of the CAS reversing the decision. Six months after the controversy, four of the judges involved in the vault controversy were given one-year suspensions.

2008 Beijing C: 16, N: 13, D: 8.18.

		PTS.
1. Leszek Blanik	POL	16.537
2. Thomas Bouhail	FRA	16.537
3. Anton Golotsutskov	RUS	16.475
4. Marian Drăgulescu	ROM	16.225
5. Benoît Caranobe	FRA	16.062
6. Dmitry Kasperovich	BLR	16.050
7. Flavius Koczi	ROM	15.925
8. Isaac Botella Pérez de Landazabal	SPA	15.737

Three-time vault world champion Marian Drăgulescu came first in the qualifying round with 16.762 points, followed by 22-year-old Thomas Bouhail and reigning world champion Leszek Blanik. Drăgulescu maintained first place after scoring 16.800 on his first vault of the final and seemed to be on track for the gold medal, but fell on landing his second vault and dropped to fourth.

Blanik and Bouhail finished in a dead heat, both scoring 16.537 points on their two jumps, 9.537 points for execution and 7.0 for difficulty. Because Blanik's highest score of the two jumps (16.6 on his first vault) was higher than Bouhail's, the gold medal went to Blanik. "I don't know exactly why I won." Blanik said after the competition, "I guess it is a special rule for judges."

Bouhail had been a replacement on the French team, called to compete when Pierre-Yves Bény withdrew due to injury.

POMMEL HORSE (SIDE HORSE)

The pommel is 1.15 meters (3 feet 9¼ inches) high, 1.6 meters (5 feet 4 inches) long and 35 centimeters (13¾ inches) wide. The pommels are set between 40 and 45 centimeters (15¾ and 17¾ inches) apart.

1896 Athens C: 15, N: 4, D: 4.9.

1. Louis Zutter	SWI	
2. Hermann Weingärtner	GER	

1900 not held

1904 St. Louis C: 9?, N: 1, D: 10.28.

		PTS.
1. Anton Heida	USA	42
2. George Eyser	USA	33
3. William Merz	USA	29

1908–1920 not held

1924 Paris C: 70, N: 9, D: 7.20.

		PTS.
1. Josef Wilhelm	SWI	21.23
2. Jean Gutwenigen	SWI	21.13
3. Antoine Rebetez	SWI	20.73
4. Carl Widmer	SWI	20.50
5. Giuseppe Paris	ITA	20.10
6. Stane Derganc	YUG/SLO	19.93
7. Minoslav Klinger	CZE	19.67
8. August Güttinger	SWI	19.60

1928 Amsterdam C: 87, N: 11, D: 8.10.

		PTS.
1. Hermann Hänggi	SWI	19.75
2. Georges Miez	SWI	19.25
3. Heikki Savolainen	FIN	18.83
4. Eduard "Edi" Steinemann	SWI	18.67
5. August Güttinger	SWI	18.58
6. Georges Leroux	FRA	18.25
7. Mauri Nyberg-Noroma	FIN	18.17
7. Melchior Wetzel	SWI	18.17

1932 Los Angeles C: 10, N: 5, D: 8.11.

		PTS.
1. István Pelle	HUN	19.07
2. Omero Bonoli	ITA	18.87
3. Frank Haubold	USA	18.57
4. Frank Cumiskey	USA	18.23
5. Péter Boros	HUN	17.57
6. Alfred Jochim	USA	17.07
7. Heikki Savolainen	FIN	17.00
8. Veikko Pakarinen	FIN	16.63

1936 Berlin C: 110, N: 14, D: 8.11.

		PTS.
1. Konrad Frey	GER	19.333
2. Eugen Mack	SWI	19.167
3. Albert Bachmann	SWI	19.067
4. Martti Uosikkinen	FIN	19.066
5. Walter Steffens	GER	19.033
5. Walter Bach	SWI	19.033
7. Michael Reusch	SWI	19.00
7. Alfred Schwarzmann	GER	19.00

1948 London C: 123, N: 16, D: 8.13.

		PTS.
1. Paavo Aaltonen	FIN	19.35
1. Veikko Huhtanen	FIN	19.35
1. Heikki Savolainen	FIN	19.35
4. Luigi Zanetti	ITA	19.15
5. Guido Figone	ITA	19.10
6. Frank Cumiskey	USA	18.95
7. Michael Reusch	SWI	18.90
8. Aleksanteri Saarvala	FIN	18.85
8. Josef Stalder	SWI	18.85
8. Emil Studer	SWI	18.85

Between 1928 and 1952 Heikki Savolainen of Joensuu won two gold medals, one silver, and six bronze. When he received his last medal, as a member of the third-place Finnish team in Helsinki, Savolainen was 44 years old.

1952 Helsinki C: 185, N: 29, D: 7.21.

		PTS.
1. Viktor Chukarin	SOV/UKR	19.50
2. Yevgeny Korolkov	SOV/RUS	19.40
2. Grant Shaginyan	SOV/ARM	19.40
4. Mikhail Perelman	SOV/RUS	19.30
5. Josef Stalder	SWI	19.20
6. Hans Sauter	AUT	19.15
7. Vladimir Belyakov	SOV/RUS	19.10
8. Jean Tschabold	SWI	19.05

1956 Melbourne C: 63, N: 18, D: 12.6.

		PTS.
1. Borys Shakhlin	SOV/UKR	19.25
2. Takashi Ono	JPN	19.20
3. Viktor Chukarin	SOV/UKR	19.10
4. Josef Škvor	CZE	19.05
5. Yuri Tytov	SOV/UKR	19.00
6. Jaroslav Bim	CZE	18.95
7. Pavel Stolbov	SOV/RUS	18.90
7. Masao Takemoto	JPN	18.90

1960 Rome C: 130, N: 28, D: 9.10.

		PTS.
1. Eugen Ekman	FIN	19.375
1. Borys Shakhlin	SOV/UKR	19.375
3. Shuji Tsurumi	JPN	19.15
4. Takashi Mitsukuri	JPN	19.125
5. Yuri Tytov	SOV/UKR	18.95
6. Takashi Ono	JPN	18.525

1964 Tokyo C: 130, N: 29, D: 10.22.

		PTS.
1. Miroslav Cerar	YUG/SLO	19.525
2. Shuji Tsurumi	JPN	19.325
3. Yuri Tsapenko	SOV/RUS	19.20
4. Haruhiro Yamashita	JPN	19.075
5. Harald Wigaard	NOR	18.925
6. Takashi Mitsukuri	JPN	18.65

1968 Mexico City C: 114, N: 27, D: 10.26.

		PTS.
1. Miroslav Cerar	YUG/SLO	19.325
2. Olli Eino Laiho	FIN	19.225
3. Mikhail Voronin	SOV/RUS	19.20
4. Wilhelm Kubica	POL	19.15
5. Eizo Kenmotsu	JPN	19.05
6. Viktor Kilmenko	SOV/RUS	18.95

1972 Munich C: 113, N: 26, D: 9.1.

		PTS.
1. Viktor Klimenko	SOV/RUS	19.125
2. Sawao Kato	JPN	19.00
3. Eizo Kenmotsu	JPN	18.95
4. Shigeru Kasamatsu	JPN	18.925
5. Mikhail Voronin	SOV/RUS	18.875
6. Wilhelm Kubica	POL	18.75

1976 Montreal C: 90, N: 20, D: 7.23.

		PTS.
1. Zoltán Magyar	HUN	19.70
2. Eizo Kenmotsu	JPN	19.575
3. Nikolai Andrianov	SOV/RUS	19.525
3. Michael Nikolay	GDR	19.525
5. Sawao Kato	JPN	19.40
6. Aleksandr Dityatin	SOV/RUS	19.35

1980 Moscow C: 65, N: 14, D: 7.25.

		PTS.
1. Zoltán Magyar	HUN	19.925
2. Aleksandr Dityatin	SOV/RUS	19.80
3. Michael Nikolay	GDR	19.775
4. Roland Brückner	GDR	19.725
5. Aleksandr Tkachyov	SOV/RUS	19.475
6. Ferenc Donáth	HUN	19.40

1984 Los Angeles C: 71, N: 19, D: 8.4.

		PTS.
1. Li Ning	CHN	19.95
1. Peter Vidmar	USA	19.95
3. Timothy Daggett	USA	19.825
4. Tong Fei	CHN	19.75
5. Jean-Luc Cairon	FRA	19.70
6. Nobuyuki Kajitani	JPN	19.625
7. Benno Gross	GER	19.525
8. Josef Zellweger	SWI	19.50

1988 Seoul C: 89, N: 23, D: 9.24.

		PTS.
1. Dmitri Bilozerchev	SOV/RUS	19.95
1. Zsolt Borkai	HUN	19.95
1. Lubomir Geraskov	BUL	19.95
4. Koichi Mizushima	JPN	19.90
5. Valery Lyukin	SOV/KAZ	19.875
6. Daisuke Nishikawa	JPN	19.85
7. Sven Tippelt	GDR	19.80
8. Sylvio Kroll	GDR	19.775

1992 Barcelona C: 93, N: 25, D: 8.2.

		PTS.
1. Pae Gil-su	PRK	9.925
1. Vitaly Scherbo	BLR	9.925
3. Andreas Wecker	GER	9.887
4. Guo Linyao	CHN	9.875
5. M. Chris Waller	USA	9.825
6. Yoshiaki Hatakeda	JPN	9.775
7. Li Jing	CHN	9.25
7. Valeri Belenki	AZR	9.25

Pae's unusually long set amazed gymnastics fans, but three of the six judges gave Scherbo a higher mark, and the two ended up in a tie for first place. It was the fifth time that the pommels gold was shared and the third time in a row. Pae Gil-su won the world championship in 1993, but then, because of North Korea's political abnormalities and poverty, he did not compete again internationally for the next three years. He reemerged in April 1996 to win the Individual Event World Championships. He was allowed a wildcard entry at the 1996 Olympics but placed thirteenth and did not qualify for the final.

1996 Atlanta C: 103, N: 32, D: 7.28.

		PTS.
1. Donghua Li	SWI	9.875
2. Marius Urzică	ROM	9.825
3. Aleksei Nemov	RUS	9.787
4. Patrice Casimir	FRA	9.762
5. Yoshiaki Hatakeda	JPN	9.712
5. Huang Huadong	CHN	9.712
7. Eric Poujade	FRA	9.35
8. Fan Bin	CHN	9.30

Li Donghua was born in Chengdu, China, and began gymnastics at the age of seven. In 1984, when he was seventeen years old, he was seriously injured while training on the vault. His spleen and one kidney were removed, but he returned to the sport. In 1986 he tore both Achilles' tendons while performing a double layout salto on the floor exercise and spent several weeks in a wheelchair. The following year he won the Chinese championship on pommel horse, but in 1988 his life took an unexpected turn. On the streets of Beijing, a Swiss tourist named Esperanza Friedli asked him directions and the two fell in love. They were married in Chengdu in December and moved to Lucerne, Switzerland in March 1989. Li changed his name to Donghua Li to fit in with western custom, and he applied for Swiss citizenship. Swiss law required five years of residency before granting citizenship so, during what would normally have been the peak years of his athletic carrer, Li was unable to compete internationally.

Finally, in 1994, Li earned a Swiss passport and

entered his first international tounament—at the age of 27. The following year he won the gold medal on pommel horse at the 1995 world championships. By the time of the 1996 Olympics, Li, at 29, was the oldest gymnast in the Atlanta Games. In fact, he was more than five years older than any of the finalists. Li's chief rival, defending Olympic champion Pae Gil-su, performed an uninspired compulsory routine, and did not advance to the final. Li, on the other hand, used his superior form and technique to earn a well-deserved gold medal.

2000 Sydney C: 80, N: 29, D: 9.24.

		PTS.
1. Marius Urzică	ROM	9.862
2. Eric Poujade	FRA	9.825
3. Aleksei Nemov	RUS	9.800
4. Lee Jang-hyung	KOR	9.775
5. Pae Gil-su	PRK	9.762
6. Zoltán Supola	HUN	9.762
7. Oleksandr Beresh	UKR	9.712
8. Nikolai Kryukov	RUS	9.700

Marius Urzică won the pommel horse world championship in 1994, but did not win another major title until he triumphed at the European Championships four months before the 2000 Olympics.

2004 Athens C: 80, N: 30, D: 8.22.

		PTS.
1. Teng Haibin	CHN	9.837
2. Marius Urzică	ROM	9.825
3. Takehiro Kashima	JPN	9.787
4. Xu Huang	CHN	9.775
5. Víctor Cano Segura	SPA	9.762
6. Paul Hamm	USA	9.737
7. Rúnar Alexandersson	ICE	9.725
8. Hiroyuki Tomita	JPN	9.062

As expected, the 2004 competition was a battle among the reigning co-world champions, Teng Haibin and Takehiro Kashima, and the defending Olympic champion Marius Urzică, himself a three-time world champion. Urzică gave a dazzling performance, completing two full Russians on one pommel and a flaired spindle, and earning a score of 9.825 from the judges. Kashima performed next, moving into second place with 9.787, followed by China's Huang Xu who scored a 9.775 to move into third. Performing last, the 19-year-old Teng gave a beautiful routine with spectacular amplitude. His score of 9.837 earned him the gold medal.

2008 Beijing C: 76, N: 27, D: 8.17.

		PTS.
1. Xiao Qin	CHN	15.875
2. Filip Ude	CRO	15.725
3. Louis Smith	GBR	15.725
4. Yang Wei	CHN	15.450
5. Hiroyuki Tomita	JPN	15.375
6. Kim Ji-hun	KOR	15.175
7. Sasha Artemev	USA	14.975
8. José Luis Fuentes Bustamante	VEN	14.650

Three-time world champion Xiao Qin earned 16.000 points in the qualifying round, the highest score by far, followed by Venezuela's José Luis Fuentes with 15.525 points. Xiao had a slight break in form during his final routine, but his score was still enough to earn him the gold medal. "The longest holiday I've had in the last few years was three days, due to training," Xiao said after the competition. "Now I can finally take a rest."

The bronze medal was decided by a tie-breaker after Filip Ude and Louis Smith both scored 15.725 points. The silver medal went to Ude, who had a higher execution score by 9.325 to 9.025. Ude was the first Olympic gymnastics medalist for Croatia, while Smith was the first gymnast from Great Britain to earn an individual medal since Walter Tysall won the all-around silver medal in 1908.

RINGS

The rings are made of wood and are suspended 2.8 meters (9 feet 2¼ inches) above the mat.

1896 Athens C: 8, N: 3, D: 4.9.

1. Ioannis Mitropoulos	GRE
2. Hermann Weingärtner	GER
3. Petros Persakis	GRE
4. —	—
5. Carl Schuhmann	GER

The six judges split three for Mitropoulos and three for Weingärtner. Prince Georgios of Greece cast the tie-breaking vote for his countryman. Mitropoulos was the first Greek winner in the Olympic stadium and his victory was greeted with wild enthusiasm.

1900 not held

1904 St. Louis C: 10?, N: 1, D: 10.28.

		PTS.
1. Hermann Glass	USA	45
2. William Merz	USA	35
3. Emil Voigt	USA	32

1908–1920 not held

1924 Paris C: 70, N: 9, D: 7.20.

		PTS.
1. Francesco Martino	ITA	21.553
2. Robert Pražak	CZE	21.483
3. Ladislav Vácha	CZE	21.43
4. Leon Štukelj	YUG/SLO	21.33
5. Bedřich Šupčik	CZE	21.12
6. Bohumil Mořkovsky	CZE	21.083
7. Jan Koutny	CZE	21.053
8. Ferdinando Mandrini	ITA	20.943

1928 Amsterdam C: 87, N: 11, D: 8.10.

		PTS.
1. Leon Štukelj	YUG/SLO	19.25
2. Ladislav Vácha	CZE	19.17
3. Emanuel Löffler	CZE	18.83
4. Romeo Neri	ITA	18.67
5. Mauri Nyberg-Noroma	FIN	18.33
6. Bedřich Šupčik	CZE	18.25
7. Paul Krempel	USA	18.17
8. Jan Gajdoš	CZE	18.08
8. Georges Miez	SWI	18.08
8. Armand Solbach	FRA	18.08

1932 Los Angeles C: 14, N: 6, D: 8.12.

		PTS.
1. George Gulack	USA	18.97
2. William Denton	USA	18.60
3. Giovanni Lattuada	ITA	18.50
4. Richard Bishop	USA	18.47
5. Oreste Capuzzo	ITA	18.27
6. Franco Tognini	ITA	18.03
7. Heikki Savolainen	FIN	17.70
8. Toshihiko Sasano	JPN	17.47

Gulack had emigrated from Latvia to the United States in 1922.

1936 Berlin C: 111, N: 14, D: 8.11.

		PTS.
1. Alois Hudec	CZE	19.433
2. Leon Štukelj	YUG/SLO	18.867
3. Matthias Volz	GER	18.667
4. Alfred Schwarzmann	GER	18.534
5. Franz Beckert	GER	18.533
6. Michael Reusch	SWI	18.434
7. Jaroslav Kollinger	CZE	18.433
8. Heikki Savolainen	FIN	18.40

1948 London C: 123, N: 16, D: 8.13.

		PTS.
1. Karl Frei	SWI	19.80
2. Michael Reusch	SWI	19.55
3. Zdeněk Růžička	CZE	19.25
4. Walter Lehmann	SWI	19.20
5. Josef Stalder	SWI	19.15
5. Emil Studer	SWI	19.15
7. Vladimir Karas	CZE	19.10
8. Heikki Savolainen	FIN	19.05

1952 Heisinki C: 185, N: 29, D: 7.21.

		PTS.
1. Grant Shaginyan	SOV/ARM	19.75
2. Viktor Chukarin	SOV/UKR	19.55
3. Hans Eugster	SWI	19.40
3. Dmytro Leonkin	SOV/UKR	19.40
5. Valentin Muratov	SOV/RUS	19.35
6. Masao Takemoto	JPN	19.20
7. Attia Ali Alizaky (EGY), Ferenc Kemény (HUN), Yevgeny Korolkov (SOV/RUS), Berndt Lindfors (FIN)		19.15

1956 Melbourne C: 63, N: 18, D: 12.6.

		PTS.
1. Albert Azaryan	SOV/ARM	19.35
2. Valentin Muratov	SOV/RUS	19.15
3. Masami Kubota	JPN	19.10
3. Masao Takemoto	JPN	19.10
5. Nobuyuki Aihara	JPN	19.05
5. Takashi Ono	JPN	19.05
7. Viktor Chukarin	SOV/UKR	19.00
7. Shinsaku Tsukawaki	JPN	19.00

Albert Azaryan was a blacksmith who didn't take up gymnastics until he was 16 years old. He was the inventor of the Olympic cross, a variation of the iron cross, in which the gymnast twists sideways while maintaining a cross position. Most new moves in gymnastics are developed after extensive planning, experimentation, and practice. That was not the case with the Olympic cross. Azaryan was competing at the 1953 USSR championships. The Armenian team felt they were being underscored by the Russian judges. When the Armenian coach demanded an explanation, he was told that his gymnasts were not holding their crosses for the required three seconds. When Azaryan's turn came, he lowered into the cross position, turned to the judge on one side and asked, "Is this long enough?" Then he turned to the judge on the other side and asked the same question. Then he twisted sideways into what is now called an Olympic cross and asked one of the judges behind him, "Is this long enough?" Finally he twisted in the other direction and repeated his question to the other rear judge. The judges were not amused and awarded him a score of only 9.30. However, the Olympic cross had been born.

1960 Rome C: 130, N: 28, D: 9.10.

		PTS.
1. Albert Azaryan	SOV/ARM	19.725
2. Borys Shakhlin	SOV/UKR	19.50
3. Velik Kapsazov	BUL	19.425
3. Takashi Ono	JPN	19.425
5. Nobuyuki Aihara	JPN	19.40
6. Yuri Tytov	SOV/UKR	19.275

1964 Tokyo C: 130, N: 29, D: 10.22.

		PTS.
1. Takuji Haytta	JPN	19.475
2. Franco Menichelli	ITA	19.425
3. Borys Shakhlin	SOV/UKR	19.40
4. Viktor Leontyev	SOV/RUS	19.35
5. Shuji Tsurumi	JPN	19.275
6. Yukio Endo	JPN	19.25

1968 Mexico City C: 117, N: 28, D: 10.26.

		PTS.
1. Akinori Nakayama	JPN	19.45
2. Mikhail Voronin	SOV/RUS	19.325
3. Sawao Kato	JPN	19.225
4. Mitsuo Tsukahara	JPN	19.125
5. Takeshi Kato	JPN	19.05
6. Sergei Diomidov	SOV/RUS	18.975

1972 Munich C: 113, N: 26, D: 9.1.

		PTS.
1. Akinori Nakayama	JPN	19.35
2. Mikhail Voronin	SOV/RUS	19.275
3. Mitsuo Tsukahara	JPN	19.225
4. Sawao Kato	JPN	19.15
5. Eizo Kenmotsu	JPN	18.95
5. Klaus Köste	GDR	18.95

Sawao Kato, 1968
Kato won eight gold medals between 1968 and 1976.

1976 Montreal C: 90, N: 20, D: 7.23.

		PTS.
1. Nikolai Andrianov	SOV/RUS	19.65
2. Aleksandr Dityatin	SOV/RUS	19.55
3. Dănut Grecu	ROM	19.50
4. Ferenc Dónath	HUN	19.20
5. Eizo Kenmotsu	JPN	19.175
6. Sawao Kato	JPN	19.125

1980 Moscow C: 65, N: 14, D: 7.25.

		PTS.
1. Aleksandr Dityatin	SOV/RUS	19.875
2. Aleksandr Tkachyov	SOV/RUS	19.725
3. Jiří Tabak	CZE	19.60
4. Roland Brückner	GDR	19.575
5. Stoyan Deltchev	BUL	19.475
6. Dănut Grecu	ROM	10.85

1984 Los Angeles C: 71, N: 19, D: 8.4.

		PTS.
1. Koji Gushiken	JPN	19.85
1. Li Ning	CHN	19.85
3. Mitchell Gaylord	USA	19.825
4. Tong Fei	CHN	19.75
4. Peter Vidmar	USA	19.75
6. Kyoji Yamawaki	JPN	19.725
7. Emilian Nicula	ROM	19.50
8. Josef Zellweger	SWI	19.375

1988 Seoul C: 89, N: 23, D: 9.24.

		PTS.
1. Holger Behrendt	GDR	19.925
1. Dmitri Bilozerchev	SOV/RUS	19.925
3. Sven Tippelt	GDR	19.875
4. Kalofer Hristozov	BUL	19.825
4. Valery Lyukin	SOV/KAZ	19.825
6. Jury Chechi	ITA	19.80
7. Lou Yun	CHN	19.80
8. György Guczoghy	HUN	19.70

1992 Barcelona C: 93, N: 25, D: 8.2.

		PTS.
1. Vitaly Scherbo	BLR	9.937
2. Li Jing	CHN	9.875
3. Li Xiaoshuang	CHN	9.862
3. Andreas Wecker	GER	9.862
5. Valeri Belenki	AZR	9.825
6. Szilveszter Csollány	HUN	9.80
7. Yukio Iketani	JPN	9.762
8. Kalofer Hristozov	BUL	9 75

1996 Atlanta C: 103, N: 32, D: 7.28.

		PTS.
1. Jury Chechi	ITA	9.887
2. Dan Burincă	ROM	9.812
2. Szilveszter Csollány	HUN	9.812
4. Jordan Jovtchev	BUL	9.80
5. Fan Hongbin	CHN	9.762
5. Andreas Wecker	GER	9.762
7. Marius Toba	GER	9.737
7. Blaine Wilson	USA	9.737

Jury Chechi missed the 1992 Olympics when he ruptured his right Achilles' tendon twenty days before the Games began. Then he won four straight world championships and entered the Atlanta Olympics as the overwhelming favorite. Performing last in the final, he did not disappoint, and earned the highest score of any gymnast in the apparatus finals.

2000 Sydney C: 78, N: 29, D: 9.24.

		PTS.
1. Szilveszter Csollány	HUN	9.850
2. Dimosthenis Tampakos	GRE	9.762
3. Yordan Yovchev	BUL	9.737
4. Wei Yang	CHN	9.712
5. Ivan Ivankov	BLR	9.700
6. Marius Toba	GER	9.675
7. Norimasa Iwai	JPN	9.662
8. Roman Zozulya	UKR	9.637

Although 30-year-old Szilveszter Csollány had been competing internationally for ten years, his only major title had been at the 1998 European Championships.

2004 Athens C: 77, N: 28, D: 8.22.

1. Dimosthenis Tampakos	GRE	9.862
2. Yordan Yovchev	BUL	9.850
3. Jury Chechi	ITA	9.812
4. Hiroyuki Tomita	JPN	9.800
5. Matteo Morandi	ITA	9.800
6. Pierre-Yves Beny	FRA	9.800
7. Aleksandr Safoshkin	RUS	9.750
8. Andreas Schweizer	SWI	9.737

The competition for the Olympic gold was expected to be between Dimosthenis Tampakos and Yordan Yovchev, who tied for the rings title at the 2003 world championships. Five-time world champion and 1996 gold medalist Jury Chechi was only considered a medal contender. Competing first, defending silver medalist Tampakos delivered a calm, error-free performace with a double somersault dismount, earning a 9.862 points, the highest score in any event at the 2004 Olympics. Yordan Yovchev, competing in his fourth Olympics at the age of 31, followed with a strong performance, presenting his newest combination—inverted cross, lower toward a back lever, press to Maltese—and ending on a full-twist double, to move into second place with a score of 9.850. Performing last, Chechi rounded out the medals with a score of 9.812. Many observers felt that Tampakos, although he had performed admirably, was given the victory over Yovchev because he was a Greek competing in Greece.

2008 Beijing C: 70, N: 25, D: 8.18.

1. Chen Yibing	CHN	16.600
2. Yang Wei	CHN	16.425
3. Oleksandr Vorobiov	UKR	16.325
4. Andrea Coppolino	ITA	16.225
5. Danny Rodrigues	FRA	16.225
6. Matteo Morandi	ITA	16.200
7. G. Robert Stănescu	ROM	15.825
8. Yordan Yovchev	BUL	15.525

One year before the Olympics, 2006 world champion Chen Yibing successfully defended his world title, beating his main rival, 2005 world champion Yuri van Gelder of the Netherlands, by 0.075 points. The loss also prevented van Gelder from earning a berth at the Beijing Olympics because gymnasts from nations that did not qualify for the team competition could qualify only if they won an individual event at the most recent world championships.

Chen led the qualifying round with 16.525 points, followed by Athens silver medalist and five-time Olympian Yordan Yovchev. Chen's final routine was nearly flawless, earning him 16.600 points and the gold medal. All-around champion Yang Wei took silver, beating 2007 European champion Oleksandr Vorobiov, while Yovchev missed a handstand and finished last.

FLOOR EXERCISES

The floor exercise is performed on an area 40 feet by 40 feet (12.2 meters). The exercise, which for men is done without musical accompaniment, must last between 50 and 70 seconds and must include at least one forward and one backward tumbling pass, as well as a balance element on one arm or leg.

1896–1928 not held

1932 Los Angeles C: 25, N: 6, D: 8.8.

		PTS.
1. István Pelle	HUN	9.60
2. Georges Miez	SWI	9.47
3. Mario Lertora	ITA	9.23
4. Frank Haubold	USA	9.00
4. Romeo Neri	ITA	9.00
6. Heikki Savolainen	FIN	8.97
7. Alfred Jochim	USA	8.80
7. Martti Uosikkinen	FIN	8.80

1936 Berlin C: 110, N: 14, D: 8.11.

		PTS.
1. Georges Miez	SWI	18.666
2. Josef Walter	SWI	18.50
3. Konrad Frey	GER	18.466
3. Eugen Mack	SWI	18.466
5. Matthias Volz	GER	18.366
6. Willi Stadel	GER	18.30
6. Walter Steffens	GER	18.30
8. Martti Uosikkinen	FIN	18.267

1948 London C: 123, N: 16, D: 8.13.

		PTS.
1. Fenenc Pataki	HUN	19.35
2. János Mogyorósi-Klencs	HUN	19.20
3. Zdeněk Růžička	CZE	19.05
4. Raymond Dot	FRA	18.90
5. Elkana Grönne	DEN	18.825
6. Pavel Benetka	CZE	18.80
6. Leo Sotornik	CZE	18.80
8. Vladimir Karas	CZE	18.10

As a teenager in Budapest, Ferenc Pataki wanted to become an actor. His first role was a walk-on part in which he performed some acrobatic moves. His skill was immediately noticed and he was rerouted into gymnastics.

1952 Helsinki C: 185, N: 29, D: 7.21.

		PTS.
1. K. William Thoresson	SWE	19.25
2. Jerzy Jokiel	POL	19.15
2. Tadao Uesako	JPN	19.15
4. Takashi Ono	JPN	19.05
5. Onni Lappalainen	FIN	19.00
6. Kalevi Laitinen	FIN	18.95
6. Anders Lindh	SWE	18.95
8. Ferdinand Daniš	CZE	18.90
8. Grant Shaginyan	SOV/ARM	18.90
8. Robert Stout	USA	18.90

1956 Melbourne C: 63, N: 18, D: 12.6.

		PTS.
1. Valentin Muratov	SOV/RUS	19.20
2. Nobuyuki Aihara	JPN	19.10
2. Viktor Chukarin	SOV/UKR	19.10
2. K. William Thoresson	SWE	19.10
5. Yuri Tytov	SOV/UKR	18.95
6. Ferdinand Daniš	CZE	18.80
6. Mintscho Todorov	BUL	18.80
8. Helmut Bantz	GER	18.75
8. Takashi Ono	JPN	18.75

1960 Rome C: 130, N: 28, D: 9.10.

		PTS.
1. Nobuyuki Aihara	JPN	19.45
2. Yuri Tytov	SOV/UKR	19.325
3. Franco Menichelli	ITA	19.275
4. Takashi Mitsukuri	JPN	19.20
4. Takashi Ono	JPN	19.20
6. Jaroslav Štastny	CZE	19.05

1964 Tokyo C: 130, N: 29, D: 10.22.

		PTS.
1. Franco Menichelli	ITA	19.45
2. Yukio Endo	JPN	19.35
2. Viktor Lisitsky	SOV/RUS	19.35
4. Viktor Leontyev	SOV/RUS	19.20
5. Takashi Mitsukuri	JPN	19.10
6. Yuri Tsapenko	SOV/RUS	18.85

1968 Mexico City C: 117, N: 28, D: 10.26

		PTS.
1. Sawao Kato	JPN	19.475
2. Akinori Nakayama	JPN	19.40
3. Takeshi Kato	JPN	19.275
4. MItsuo Tsukuhara	JPN	19.05
5. Valery Karasyov	SOV/RUS	18.95
6. Eizo Kenmotsu	JPN	18.925

1972 Munich C: 113, N: 26, D: 9.1.

		PTS.
1. Nikolai Andrianov	SOV/RUS	19.175
2. Akinori Nakayama	JPN	19.125
3. Shigeru Kasamatsu	JPN	19.025
4. Eizo Kenmotsu	JPN	18.925
5. Klaus Köste	GDR	18.825
6. Sawao Kato	JPN	18.75

1976 Montreal C: 90, N: 20, D: 7.23.

		PTS.
1. Nikolai Andrianov	SOV/RUS	19.45
2. Vladimir Marchenko	SOV/RUS	19.425
3. Peter Kormann	USA	19.30
4. Roland Brückner	GDR	19.275
5. Sawao Kato	JPN	19.25
6. Eizo Kenmotsu	JPN	19.10

1980 Moscow C: 65, N: 14, D: 7.25.

		PTS.
1. Roland Brückner	GDR	19.75
2. Nikolai Andrianov	SOV/RUS	19.725
3. Aleksandr Dityatin	SOV/RUS	19.70
4. Jiří Tabák	CZE	19.675
5. Péter Kovács	HUN	19.425
6. Lutz Hoffmann	GDR	18.725

1984 Los Angeles C: 71, N: 19, D: 8.4.

		PTS.
1. Li Ning	CHN	19.925
2. Lou Yun	CHN	19.775
3. Koji Sotomura	JPN	19.70
3. Philippe Vatuone	FRA	19.70
5. Bart Conner	USA	19.675
6. Valerian Pintea	ROM	19.60
7. Peter Vidmar	USA	19.55
8. Koji Gushiken	JPN	19.45

Li Ning, a member of the Zhuang ethnic group, went home with more medals than any other athlete at the Los Angeles Olympics: 3 gold, 2 silver and 1 bronze. When he retired in 1989, he opened a sportswear factory and became an extremely successful entrepreneur.

1988 Seoul C: 89, N: 23, D: 9.24.

		PTS.
1. Sergei Kharkov	SOV/RUS	19.925
2. Vladimir Artemov	SOV/RUS	19.90
3. Yukio Iketani	JPN	19.85
3. Lou Yun	CHN	19.85
5. Li Ning	CHN	19.80
6. Boris Preti	ITA	19.775
7. Kalofer Hristozov	BUL	19.75
8. Curtis Hibbert	CAN	19.525

1992 Barcelona C: 93, N: 25, D: 8.2.

		PTS.
1. Li Xiaoshuang	CHN	9.925
2. Yukio Iketani	JPN	9.787
2. Hryhoriy Misyutin	UKR	9.787
4. Yoo Ok-ryul	KOR	9.775
5. Yutaka Aihana	JPN	9.737
6. Vitaly Scherbo	BLR	9.712
7. Andreas Wecker	GER	9.687
8. Li Chunyang	CHN	9.387

Since the previous Olympics this event had been dominated by Igor Korobchinsky and Vitaly Scherbo. Korobchinsky won at the 1989 European Championships, the 1989 World Championships, the 1991 World Championships, and the Individual Event World Championships in April 1992. Scherbo won at the 1990 European Championships, the 1990 World Cup, and the 1992 European Championships in May. However, in Barcelona Korobchinsky failed to make it to the finals despite placing fourth in the qualifying round; two of the three gymnasts ahead of him were also from the Unified Team of ex-Soviet republics. Scherbo did qualify for the final but was penalized one-tenth of a point when he stepped out of bounds on his mount. In the end it was 18-year-old Li Xiaoshuang of Wuchang who earned the gold medal by dazzling the judges with his backward triple salto tucked.

1996 Atlanta C: 108, N: 32, D: 7.28.

		PTS.
1. Ioannis Melissanidis	GRE	9.85
2. Li Xiaoshuang	CHN	9.837
3. Aleksei Nemov	RUS	9.80
4. Thierry Aymes	FRA	9.75
4. Ivan Ivanov	BUL	9.75
6. Yevgeny Podgorny	RUS	9.55
7. Vitaly Scherbo	BLR	9.275
8. Hryhoriy Misyutin	UKR	9.10

Nineteen-year-old Thessaloniki medical student Ioannis Melissanidis was an unexpected winner. In 1994 he became Greece's first world championship medalist by taking a silver. But since then his results had been undistinguished and he had not even qualified for the finals at the last two world championships. Part of Melissanidis' problem was that he stretched the normal protocol of the event by including elements of dance and attempting to "tell a story." In Atlanta, in the words of *International Gymnast,* the favorites, except for Li Xiaoshuang, showed "more stumbling than tumbling." When Melissanidis performed, the judges appeared to finally realize that his technical skills were solid and that his artistry did not distract from his performance, but rather supplemented it. The entire Greek men's gymnastics team, Melissonidis was his nation's first Olympics champion in the sport since 1896.

2000 Sydney C: 76, N: 26, D: 9.24.

		PTS.
1. Igors Vihrovs	LAT	9.812
2. Aleksei Nemov	RUS	9.800
3. Yordan Yovchev	BUL	9.787
4. Wei Yang	CHN	9.750
5. Li Xiaopeng	CHN	9.737
6. Marian Drăgulescu	ROM	9.712
7. Morgan Hamm	USA	9.262
8. Yevgeny Podgornyi	RUS	8.550

Aleksei Nemov had won the last two world championships and was the definite favorite, particularly after he won the all-around gold medal. However he was upset by unheralded Igors Vihrovs. Suffering from a sore left ankle, Vihrovs, Latvia's only gymnast, had withdrawn from the all-around competition in order to concentrate on his specialty. He was the first Olympic champion to represent the independent Latvia.

2004 Athens C: 77, N: 30, D: 8.22.

		PTS.
1. Kyle Shewfelt	CAN	9.787
2. Marian Drăgulescu	ROM	9.787
3. Yordan Yovchev	BUL	9.775
4. Gervasio Deferr Ángel	SPA	9.712
5. Paul Hamm	USA	9.712
6. Daisuke Nakano	JPN	9.712
7. Isao Yoneda	JPN	9.662
8. Morgan Hamm	USA	9.650

After winning four gold medals in the 2004 European Championships, 23-year-old Marian Drăgulescu was considered the clear favorite for gold. Drăgulescu recorded the highest qualifying score, 9.762 points, ahead of Gervasio Deferr, with 9.750, and 22-year-old world champion bronze medalist Kyle Shewfelt with 9.737. In the final, Drăgulescu began with an impressive mount, a layout full-out, punch front 1¼, but took a slight step on his tucked double-double dismount. Performing next, Shewfelt, who had missed the 2000 final by less than a tenth of a point when he stepped out of bounds, stuck every element of his routine and finished with his signature dismount, a four-element dash with a front and back layout. Shewfelt and Drăgulescu finished with identical scores of 9.787, but Shewfelt was awarded the gold medal based on deductions, in which the lowest jury deductions from the four B-jury judges are dropped until the tie is broken.

In 2006, Shewfelt played a fictional version of himself, "Kyle Manjak," in the Hungarian gymnastics film *White Palms.*

2008 Beijing C: 77, N: 28, D: 8.17.

		PTS.
1. Zou Kai	CHN	16.050
2. Gervasio Deferr Ángel	SPA	15.775
3. Anton Golotsutskov	RUS	15.725
4. Fabian Hambüchen	GER	15.650
5. Kohei Uchimura	JPN	15.575
6. Diego Hypólito	BRA	15.200
7. Marian Drăgulescu	ROM	14.850
8. Aleksandr Shatilov	ISR	14.125

Diego Hypólito was the clear gold-medal favorite in Beijing. The first male gymnast from South America to win a medal at the world championships, Hypólito won the world title in 2005, the silver in 2006 and gold again in 2007. Four months before the Olympics he was hospitalized with dengue fever, but recovered in time to compete in Beijing.

Hypólito came first in the qualifying round with 15.950 points, followed by 2004 Olympic silver medalist and 2006 world champion Marian Drăgulescu. Defending Olympic champion Kyle Shewfelt of Canada scored a modest 15.525 and failed to qualify for the final, but his performance was a remarkable comeback after he had fractured both legs while training for the 2007 world championships.

Hypólito seemed headed for the gold medal until he fell on the landing of his last pass. Drăgulescu also had trouble with his final routine, falling on his second tumbling pass to finish seventh. Twenty-year-old Zou Kai entered the final in sixth place, but performed a strong routine with a difficulty score of 6.7 points, the highest of the eight finalists, moving into first place. Performing last, 2007 world silver medalist and twice Olympic vault champion Gervasio Deferr edged out European champion Anton Golotsutskov for silver.

Kai dedicated his win to the people of his home province, Sichuan, which had been hit three months earlier by an 8.0 earthquake that left an estimated 87,000 people dead or missing.

TEAM COMBINED EXERCISES

According to current rules, each team has six members, three of whom perform each set of exercises. Each nation's final score is determined by combining the scores of the three performers on each apparatus in optional exercises. In 1996, six team members performed on each apparatus, but only the top five scores counted. For 1996, only those men or women whose scores contributed to the team total are included in the results charts. In 2012, twelve teams will take part in the qualifying round and the top eight will advance to the team final.

1896–1904 not held

1906 Athens T: 6, N: 5, D: 4.23.

	Total Points
1. NOR	19.00
2. DEN	18.00
3. ITA	16.71
4. ITA	16.60
5. GER	16.25
6. HUN	14.45

1. NOR—Carl-Albert Andersen, Oskar Bye, Conrad Carlsrud, Harald Eriksen, Osvald Falch, Christian Fjerdingen, Yngvar Fredriksen, Karl Haagensen, Harald Halvorsen, Petter Hol, Andreas Hagelund, Eugen Ingebretsen, Per Mathias Jespersen, Finn Münster, Fridtjof Olsen, Carl Pedersen, Rasmus Pettersen, Thorleif Petersen, Thorleif Røhn, Johan Stumpf
2. DEN—Carl Andersen, Halvor Birch, Harold Bukdahl, Kaj Gnudtzmann, Knud Holm, Erik Klem, Harald Klem, Louis Larsen, Jens Lorentzen, Robert Madsen, Carl Manicus-Hansen, Oluf Olsson, Kristian Pedersen, Hans Pedersen, Niels Petersen, Viktor Rasmussen, Marius Skram-Jensen, Marius Thuesen
3. ITA—Pistoia/Florence: Spartaco Nerozzi, Rodrigo Bertinotti, Vitaliano Masotti, Raffaello Giannoni, Quintilio Mazzoncini, Azeglio Innocenti, Filiberto Innocenti, Cino Civinini, Manrico Masetti
4. ITA—Roma: Dante Aloisi, Enrico Brignoli, Pierino Caccialupi, Guido Colavini, Romeo Giannotti, Mario Gubiani, Venceslao Rossi, Romolo Tuzzi, Amadeo Zinzi
5. GER—Bernhard Abraham, Otto Franke, George Hax, Cassius Hermes, Julius Keyl, Josef Krämer, Bruno Mahler, Carl Ohms, Adolf Schirmer, Karl Schwarz, Wilhelm Weber, Otto Wiegand
6. HUN—Béla Dáner, Arpád Erdös, Béla Erödi, Frigyes Gráf, Gyula Kakas, Nándor Kovács, Kálmán Szabó, Vilmos Szücs

1908 London T: 8, N: 8, D: 7.16.

	Total Points
1. SWE	438
2. NOR	425
3. FIN	405
4. DEN	378
5. FRA	319
6. ITA	316
7. HOL	297
8. GBR	196

1. SWE—K. Gösta Åsbrink, Carl Bertilsson, Andreas Cervin, Hjalmar Cedercrona, Rudolf Degermark, Carl Folcker, Sven Forssman, Erik Granfelt, Carl Hårleman, Nils Hellsten, Gunnar Höjer, Arvi Holmberg, Carl Holmberg, Oswald Holmberg, Hugo Jahnke, John Jarlén, Gustaf Johnsson, Rolf Johnsson, Nils Kantzow, Sven Landberg, Olle Lanner, Axel Ljung, Osvald Moberg, Carl Norberg, Erik Norberg, Tor Norberg, Axel Norling, Daniel Norling, Gösta Olson, Leonard Peterson, Sven Rosén, Gustav Rosenquist, Axel Sjöblom, Birger Sörvik, Haakon Sörvik, Karl-Johan Svensson [Sarland], Karl Gustaf Vinqvist, Nils Widforss
2. NOR—Arthur Amundsen, Carl-Albert Andersen, Otto Authén, Hermann Bolme, Trygve Böyesen, Oskar Bye, Conrad Carlsrud, Sverre Grøner, Harald Halvorsen, Harald Hansen, Petter Hol, Eugen Ingebretsen, Ole Iversen, Per Mathias Jespersen, Sigurd Johannessen, Nicolai Kiær, Karl Klæth, Thor Larsen, Rolf Lefdahl, Hans Lem, Anders Moen, Frithjof Olsen, Carl Pedersen, Paul Pedersen, Sigvard Sivertsen, Johannes Skrataas, Harald Smedvik, Andreas Strand, Olaf Syvertsen, Thomas Torstensen

3. FIN—Eino Forsström, Otto Granström, Johan Kemp, Iivari Kyykoski, Heikki Lehmusto, John Lindroth, Yrjö Linko, Edvand Linna, Matti Markkanen, Kaarle Mikkolainen, Veli Nieminen, Källe Paasia, Arvi Pohjanpää, Aarne Pohjonen, Eino Railio, Heikki Riipinen, Arno Saarinen, Einar Sahlstein, Aarne Salovaara, Karl Viktor Sandelin, Elias Sipilä, Viktor Smeds, Kaarlo Soinio, Kurt Stenberg, Väinö Tiiri, Magnus Wegelius
4. DEN—Carl Andersen, Hans Bredmose, Jens Chiewitz, Arvor Hansen, Christian Hansen, Ingvardt Hansen, Einar Hermann, Knud Holm, Poul Holm, Oluf Husted Nielsen, Charles Jensen, Gorm Jensen, Hendrik Johansen, Harald Klem, Robert Madsen, Viggo Meulengracht Madsen, Lucas Nielsen, Oluf Olsson, Niels Petersen, Nicolai Philipsen, Heindrik Rasmussen, Victor Rasmussen, Marius Thuesen, Niels Turin-Nielsen
5. FRA—Lucien Bogart, Albert Borizée, Henri de Breyne, Nicolas Constant, Charles Courtois, Louis Delattre, Antoine Delescluse, Louis Delescluse, Georges Demarle, Joseph Derov, Charles Desmarcheliers, Claude Desmarcheliers, Étienne Dharaney, Gérard Donnet, Émile Duhamel, A. Duponchel, Paul Durin, A. Eggremont, G. Guiot, L. Hennebicq, Henri Hubert, Daniel Hudels, E. Labitte, L. Léstienne, R. Lis, Victor Magnier, G. Nys, Joseph Parent, Louis Pappe, V. Polidori, Gustave Pottier, Antoine Pinoy, Louis Sandray, Émile Schmoll, Edouard Steffe, E. Vercruysse, Hugo Vergin, E. Vicogne, Jules Walmée, G. Warlouzer
6. ITA—Alfredo Accorsi, Nemo Agodi, Umberto Agliorini, Adriano Andreani, Vincenzo Blo, Flaminio Bottoni, Bruto Buozzi, Giovanni Bonati, Pietro Borsetti, Adamo Bozzani, Gastone Calabresi, Carlo Celada, Tito Collevati, Antonio Cotichini, Guido Cristofori, Stanislao Di Chiara, Giovanni Gasperini, Amadeo Marchi, Carlo Manchiandi, Ettore Massari, Roberto Nardini, Gaetano Preti, Decio Pavani, Gino Ravenna, Massimo Ridolfi, Gustavo Taddia, Giannetto Termanini, Ugo Savonuzzi, Gioacchino Vaccari
7. HOL—Cornelis Becker, Michel Biet, Jan de Boer, Reiner Blom, Jan Bolt, E. Brouwer, Constantijn van Daalen, Johann Flemer, Johannes Göckel, I. Goudeket, Dirk Janssen, Jan Jacob Kieft, Salomon Konijn, Herman van Leeuwen, Abraham Mok, Abraham de Oliveira, Johannes Posthumus, Johan Schmitt, Jonas Slier, Johannes Stikkelman, Henricus Thijsen, Gerardus Wesling
8. GBR—P.A. Baker, W.F. Barrett, R. Bonney, J.H. Catley, M. Clay, E. Clough, J. Cotterell, W. Cowy, G.C. Cullen, F. Denby, Herbert Drury, W. Fitt, H. Gill, A.S. Harley, Arthur Hawkins, William Hoare, J.A. Horridge, H.J. Huskinson, J.W. Jones, E. Justice, N.J. Keighley,R. Laycock, R. McGaw, J. McPhail, W. Manning, W.G. Merrifield, C.J. Oldaker, G. Parrott, E. Parsons, E.F. Richardson, J. Robertson, George Ross, D. Scott, J.E.F. Simpson, W.R. Skeeles, J. Speight, H. Stell, C.V. Suderman, William Titt, Charles Vigurs, E. Walton, H. Waterman, E.A. Watkins, John Whitaker, F. Whitehead

1912 Stockholm T: 5, N: 5, D: 7.11.

	Total Points
1. ITA	265.75
2. HUN	227.25
3. GBR	184.50
4. LUX	179.75
5. GER	162.00

1. ITA—Guido Boni, Giuseppe Domenichelli, Luciano Savorini, Guido Romano, Angelo Zorzi, Giorgio Zampori, Giovanni Mangiante, Lorenzo Mangiante, Adolfo Tunesi, Pietro Bianchi, Paolo Salvi, Alberto Braglia, Alfredo Gollini, Serafino Mazzarocchi, Francesco Loi, Carlo Fregosi
2. HUN—Lajos Kmetykó, József Bittenbinder, Imre Erdödy, Samu Fóti, Imre Gellért, Győző Haberfeld, Ottó Hellmich, István Herczeg, József Keresztessy, János Krizmanich, Elemér Pászti, Árpád Pédery, Jenő Rittich, Ferenc Szüts, Ödön Téry, Géza Tuli
3. GBR—Albert Betts, Harold Dickason, Samuel Hodgetts, Alfred Messenger, Edward Pepper, Charles Vigurs, Samuel Walker, John Whitaker, Sidney Cross, Bernard Franklin, Edward Potts, Reginald Potts, George Ross, Henry Oberholzer, Charles Simmons, Arthur Southern, Ronald McLean, Charles Luck, Herbert Drury, William MacKune, William Titt, William Cowhig, Leonard Hanson
4. LUX—Nicolas Adam, Charles Behm, André Bordang, François Hentges, Pierre Hentges, Michel Hemmerling, Jean-Baptiste Horn, Nicolas Kanivé, Nicolas Kummer, Marcel Langsam, Emile Lanners, Jean-Pierre Thommes, François Wagner, Antoine Wehren, Ferdinand Wirtz, Joseph Zuang
5. GER—Walter Engelmann, Adolf Seebass, Alfred Staats, Hans Roth, Arno Glockauer, Alexander Sperling, Kurt Reichenbach, Rudolf Körner, J. Erwin Buder, Wilhelm Brülle, Heinrich Pahner, Johannes Reuschle, Walter Jesinghaus, Eberhard Sorge, Karl Richter, M. Erich Worm, Karl Jordan, Hans Werner

Charles Simmons of the British team was the father of actress Jean Simmons.

1920 Antwerp T: 5, N: 5, D: 8.24.

	Total Points
1. ITA	359.855
2. BEL	346.765
3. FRA	340.100
4. CZE	305.255
5. GBR	299.115

1. ITA—Arnaldo Andreoli, Ettore Bellotto, Pietro Bianchi, Fernando Bonatti, Luigi Cambiaso, Luigi Contessi, Carlo Costigliolo, Luigi Costigliolo, Giuseppe Domenichelli, Roberto Ferrari, Carlo Fregosi, Romualdo Ghiglione, Ambrogio Levati, Francesco Loi, Vittorio Lucchetti, Luigi Maiocco, Ferdinando Mandrini, Lorenzo Mangiante, Antonio Marovelli, Michele Mastromarino, Giuseppe Paris, Manlio Pastorini, Ezio Roselli, Paolo Salvi, Giovanni Battista Tubino, Giorgio Zampori, Angelo Zorzi
2. BEL—Eugène Auwerkerken, Théophile Bauer, François Claessens, Augustus Cootmans, François Gibens, Albert Haepers, Domien Jacob, Félicien Kempeneers, Jules Labéeu, Hubert Lafortune, Auguste Landrieu, Charles Lannie, Constant Loriot, Nicolaas Moerloos, Ferdinand Minnaert, Louis Stoop, Jean van Guysse, Alphonse van Mele, François Verboven, Jean Verboven, Julien Verdonck, Joseph Verstraeten, Georges Vivex, Julianus Wagemans
3. FRA—Georges Berger, Émile Bouchès, René Boulanger, Alfred Buyenne, Eugène Cordonnier, Léon Delsarte, Lucien Démanet, Paul Joseph Durin, Georges Duvant, Fernand Fauconnier, Arthur Hermann, Albert Hersoy, André Higelin, Auguste Hoël, Louis Kempe, Georges Lagouge, Paulin Lemaire, Ernest Lespinasse, Émile Martel, Jules Pirard, Eugène Pollet, Georges Thurnherr, Marco Torrès, François Walker, Julien Wartelle, Paul Wartelle
4. CZE—Josef Bochníček, Ladislav Bubeníček, Josef Čada, Stanislav Indruch, Miroslav Klinger, Josef Malý, Zdeněk Opočenský, Josef Pagáč, František Pecháček, Robert Pražák, Václav Stolaž, Svatopluk Svoboda, Ladislav Vácha, František Vaněček, Jaroslav Velda, Václav Wirt
5. GBR—Sydney Andrew, Albert Betts, A.E. Cocksedge, J. Cotterell, William Cowhig, Sydney Cross, H.S. Dawswell, J.E. Dingley, S. Domville, H.W. Doncaster, R.E. Edgecombe, W. Edwards, Henry Finchett, Bernard Franklin, J. Harris, Samuel Hodgetts, Stanley Leigh, G. Masters, Ronald McLean, O. Morris, E.P. Ness, A.E. Page, A.O. Pinner, E. Pugh, H.W. Taylor, J.A. Walker, R.H. Zandell

1924 Paris T: 9, N: 9, D: 7.20.

	Total Points
1. ITA	839.058
2. FRA	820.528
3. SWI	816.661
4. YUG	762.101
5. USA	715.117
6. GBR	637.790
7. FIN	521.998
8. LUX	514.529

1. ITA—Fernando Mandrini 105.583 [4], Mario Letona 103.619 [10], Vittorio Lucchetti 102.803 [12], Francesco Martino 101.529 [16], Luigi Cambiaso 101.320 [17], Giuseppe Paris 101.169 [18], Giorgio Zampori 96.549 [26], Luigi Maiocco 92.486 [33]
2. FRA—Jean Gounot 105.153 [8], Léon Delsarte 104.739 [9], Albert Séguin 102.326 [15], Eugène Cordonnier 99.906 [21], François Gangloff 98.796 [23], Arthur Hermann 95.716 [27], André Higelin 92.133 [34], Joseph Huber 88.119 [39]
3. SWI—August Güttinger 105.176 [7], Jean Gutweniger 102.342 [14], Hans Grieder 99.646 [22], Georges Miez 98.796 [24], Josef Wilhelm 97.096 [25], Otto Pfister 95.746 [28], Carl Widmer 94.936 [32], Antoine Rebetez 89.583 [38])
4. YUG—Leon Štukelj 110.340 [1], Ivan Porenta 100.172 [20], Stane Zilič 95.523 [29], Stane Derganc 95.293 [30], Miha Osvald 91.066 [36], Slavko Hlastan 81.248 [44], Rastko Poljšak 77.665 [45], Josip Primožič 77.393 [47]
5. USA—Frank Kriz 100.293 [19], Alfred Jochim 95.090 [31], John Pearson 89.852 [37], Frank Safanda 86.953 [41], Curtis Rottman 82.946 [42], Rudolph Novak 77.593 [46], Max Wandrer 76.320 [48], John Mais 72.770 [53]
6. GBR—Stanley Leigh 91.266 [35], Harold Brown 87.059 [40], Henry Finchett 81.710 [43], Frank Hawkins 73.796 [49], Thomas Hopkins 72.350 [54], Edward Leigh 69.200 [55], Samuel Humphreys 64.656 [64], Albert Spencer 64.253 [65]
7. FIN—Jaakko Kunnas 73.473 [51], Otto Suhonen 72.843 [52], Aksell Roine 66.503 [56], Aarne Roine 65.46 [59], Mikko Hamalainen 65.23, Väinö Karonen 65.18 [63], Evert Kerttula 62.863 [66], Edward "Eetu" Kostamo 50.443 [70]
8. LUX—C. Quaino 73.569 [50], T. Jeitz 65.98 [57], E. Munhofen 65.556 [58], Mathias Erang 65.356 [60], A. Neumann 65.196 [62], J. Palzer 61.563 [67], P. Tolar 58.713 [68], M. Weishaupt 58.596 [69]

1928 Amsterdam T: 11, N: 11, D: 8.10.

	Total Points
1. SWI	1718.625
2. CZE	1712.25
3. YUG	1648.75
4. FRA	1620.75
5. FIN	1609.25
6. ITA	1599.125
7. USA	1519.125
8. HOL	1364.875

1. SWI—Georges Miez 247.500 [1], Hermann Hänggi 246.625 [2], Eugen Mack 243.250 [8], Melchior Wetzel 240.875 [12], Eduard "Edi" Steinemann 237.875 [15], August Güttinger 237.750 [16], Hans Grieder 234.125 [18], Otto Pfister 230.875 [24]
2. CZE—Ladislav Vácha 242.875 [9], Emanuel Löffler 242.500 [10], Jan Gajdoš 240.625 [13], Josef Effenberger 238.875 [14], Bedřich Šupčík 233.250 [20], Václav Vesely 227.625 [28], Jan Koutny 225.250 [31], Ladislav Tikal 217.750 [37]
3. YUG—Leon Štukelj 244.875 [3], Josip Primožič 244.000 [5], Anton Malej 228.875 [25], Eduard Antonijevič 228.000 [26], Boris Gregorka 221.000 [33], Ivan Porenta 220.250 [34], Stane Derganc 211.875 [43], Dragutin Ciotti 210.000 [45]
4. FRA—Armand Solbach 241.625 [11], Georges Leroux 235.750 [17], André Lemoine 232.000 [22], Jean Larrouy 226.500 [29], Étienne Schmitt 219.125 [35], Jean Gounot 216.750 [39], Antoine Chatelain 202.375 [54], Alfred Kraus 100.25 [DNF]
5. FIN—Heikki Savolainen 243.750 [6], Mauri Nyberg-Noroma 243.750 [6], Martti Uosikkinen 231.875 [23], Jaakko Kunnas 217.500 [38], Urho Korhonen 209.875 [46], Rafael Ylönen 188.750 [61], Kaiku Kinos 185.375 [62], Birger Stenman 179.750 [66]
6. ITA—Romeo Neri 244.750 [4], Mario Lertora 233.375 [19], Vittorio Lucchetti 228.000 [26], Fernando Mandrini 226.250 [30], Giuseppe Lupi 224.000 [32], Mario Tambini 212.500 [41], Giuseppe Paris 203.250 [53], Ezio Roselli 192.625 [58]
7. USA—Alfred Jochim 218.250 [36], Glenn Berry 212.750 [40], Frank Kriz 211.625 [44], Frank Haubold 209.375 [47], Harold Newhart 209.375 [47], John Pearson 208.75 [50], Herman Witzig 206.250 [51], Paul Krempel 203.625 [52]
8. HOL—Elias Melkman 199.500 [56], Pieter van Dam 199.375 [59], Mozes Jacobs 199.000 [60]. Israel Wijnschenk 182.625 [64], Willibrodus Pouw 182.125 [65], Klaas Boot 169.000 [71], Jacobus van der Vinden 169.000 [71], Hugo Licher 143.500 [85]

1932 Los Angeles T: 5, N: 5, D: 8.10.

	Total Points
1. ITA	541.850
2. USA	522.275
3. FIN	509.995
4. HUN	465.650
5. JPN	402.000

1. ITA—Romeo Neri 140.625 [1], Mario Lertora 134.400 [4], Savino Guglielmetti 134.375 [5], Oreste Capuzzo 132.450 [7]
2. USA—Frank Haubold 132.525 [6], Frederick Meyer 131.650 [8], Alfred Jochim 129.075 [11], Frank Cumiskey 129.025 [12]
3. FIN—Heikki Savolainen 134.575 [3], Mauri Nyberg-Noroma 129.800 [10], Veikko Pakarinen 122.700 [14], Einari Teräsvirta 122.700 [14]
4. HUN—István Pelle 134.925 [2], Miklós Péter 119.200 [17], Péter Boros 105.775 [20], József Hegedűs 105.750 [21]
5. JPN—Toshihiko Sasano 108.475 [19], Shigeo Honma 103.100 [22], Takashi Kondo 101.925 [23], Yoshitaki Takeda 88.500 [24]

1936 Berlin T: 14, N: 14, D: 8.11.

	Total Points
1. GER	657.430
2. SWI	654.802
3. FIN	638.468
4. CZE	625.763
5. ITA	615.133
6. YUG	598.366
7. HUN	591.930
8. FRA	580.266

1. GER—Alfred Schwarzmann 113.100 [1], Konrad Frey 111.532 [3], Matthias Volz 110.099 [7], Willi Stadel 108.999 [8], Franz Beckert 107.200 [15], Walter Steffens 106.500 [17]
2. SWI—Eugen Mack 112.334 [2], Michael Reusch 110.700 [5], Eduard "Edi" Steinemann 108.633 [10], Walter Bach 108.299 [11], Albert Bachmann 107.502 [13], Georges Miez 107.334 [14]
3. FIN—Martti Uosikkinen 110.700 [5], Heikki Savolainen 108.766 [9], Mauri Nyberg-Noroma 106.801 [16], Aleksanteri Saarvala 105.235 [19], Esa Seeste 103.934 [24], Veikko Pakarinen 103.032 [28]
4. CZE—Alois Hudec 111.199 [4], Jaroslav Kollinger 104.733 [23], Jan Sládek 103.399 [26], Jan Gajdoš 103.065 [27], Vratislav Petraček 101.966 [34], Jindřich Tintera 101.401 [38]
5. ITA—Savino Guglielmetti 107.699 [12], Oreste Capuzzo 102.500 [30], Egidio Armelloni 101.601 [36], Danilo Fioravanti 101.467 [37], Franco Tognini 101.266 [39], Nicolo Tronci 100.600 [41]

6. YUG—Konrad Gralc 103.632 [25], Josip Primožič 102.367 [31], Leon Štukelj 102.300 [32], Miroslav Forte 99.200 [46], Jože Vadnov 95.934 [56], Janoz Pristov 94.933 [61]
7. HUN—István Pelle 105.566 [18], Lajos Tóth 101.867 [35], Miklós Péter 99.034 [47], Gábor Kecskeméti 97.766 [51], István Sárkány 94.565 [64], József Sarlós 93.132 [71]
8. FRA—Armand Walter 98.933 [49], Armand Solbach 97.633 [52], Lucien Masset 97.233 [53], Robert Herold 96.168 [55], Antoine Schildwein 95.633 [59], Maurice Rousseau 94.666 [62]

1948 London T: 16, N: 16, D: 8.13.

	Total Points
1. FIN	1358.30
2. SWI	1356.70
3. HUN	1330.85
4. FRA	1313.85
5. ITA	1300.30
6. CZE	1292.10
7. USA	1252.50
8. DEN	1245.40

1. FIN—Veikko Huhtanen 229.70 [1], Paavo Aaltonen 228.80 [3], Kalevi Laitinen 225.65 [8], Olavi Rove 225.20 [10], Einari Teräsvirta 225.00 [12], Heikki Savolainen 223.95 [14]
2. SWI—Walter Lehmann 229.00 [2], Josef Stalder 228.70 [4], Christian Kipfer 227.10 [5], Emil Studer 226.60 [6], Robert Lucy 223.30 [15], Michael Reusch 222.00 [18]
3. HUN—Lajos Tóth 225.20 [10], Lajos Sántha 224.30 [13], László Baranyai 222.40 [16], Ferenc Pataki 221.30 [19], János Mogyorósi-Klencs 218.95 [27], Ferenc Varköi 218.70 [29]
4. FRA—Raymond Dot 220.80 [20], Michel Mathiot 220.40 [22], Lucien Masset 219.95 [24], André Weingand 219.80 [25], Antoine Schlindwein 216.50 [34], Alphonse Anger 216.40 [35]
5. ITA—Guido Figone 225.30 [9], Luigi Zanetti 219.00 [26], Savino Guglielmetti 217.20 [32], Domenico Grosso 214.10 [40], Quinto Vadi 214.00 [42], Danilo Fioravanti 210.70 [51]
6. CZE—Zdeněk Růžička 226.20 [7], Pavel Benetka 220.30 [23], Miroslav Málek 212.90 [47], Vladimir Karas 212.20 [48], Leo Sotornik 210.80 [50], František Wirth 209.70 [52]
7. USA—Edward Scrobe 213.90 [44], Vincent D'Autorio 211.30 [49], William Roetzheim 209.10 [53], Joseph Kotys 208.50 [55], Frank Cumiskey 205.15 [62], Raymond Sorensen 204.55 [63]
8. DEN—Paul Jessen 214.30 [38], Tage Gronne 213.50 [45], Freddy Jensen 208.35 [56], Arnold Thomsen 206.25 [58], Wilhelm Moller 201.75 [68], Poul Jensen 201.25 [70]

1952 Helsinki T: 29, N: 29, D: 7.21.

	Total Points
1. SOV	574.40
2. SWI	567.50
3. FIN	564.20
4. GER	561.20
5. JPN	556.90
6. HUN	555.80
7. CZE	555.55
8. USA	543.15

1. SOV—Viktor Chukarin 115.70 [1], Grant Shaginyan 114.95 [2], Valentin Muratov 113.65 [4], Yevgeny Korolkov 113.35 [6], Vladimir Belyakov 113.35 [6], Iosif Berdiyev 113.10 [10], Mikhail Perelman 112.50 [11], Dmytro Leonkin 103.75 [78]
2. SWI—Josef Stalder 114.75 [3], Hans Eugster 113.40 [5], Jean Tschabold 113.30 [8], Jack Günthard 111.60 [17], Melchior Thalmann 110.75 [25], Ernst Gebendinger 109.75 [39], Hans Schwarzentruber 108.40 [52], Ernst Fivian 107.95 [55]
3. FIN—Onni Lappalainen 111.85 [14], Berndt Lindfors 111.45 [19], Paavo Aaltonen 111.40 [20], Kaino Lempinen 110.60 [28], Heikki Savolainen 110.45 [29], Kalevi Laitinen 110.10 [35], Kalevi Viskari 109.80 [38], Olavi Rove 109.45 [42]
4. GER—Helmut Bantz 113.25 [9], Adalbert Dickhut 110.85 [24], Theo Wied 110.70 [26], Alfred Schwarzmann 110.65 [27], Hans Pfann 110.20 [33], Erich Wied 109.70 [40], Friedel Overwien 108.65 [48], Jakob Kiefer 91.70 [150]
5. JPN—Takashi Ono 112.20 [12], Tadao Uesako 111.65 [15], Masao Takemoto 111.65 [15], Akitomo Kaneko 111.30 [21], Tetsumi Nabeya 110.10 [35]
6. HUN—Lajos Santha 111.50 [18], Ferenc Pataki 110.90 [23], József Fekete 108.90 [46], Karoly Kocsis 108.65 [48], Ferenc Kemény 108.40 [52], Sándor Rétl 107.75 [57], Lajos Tóth 107.45 [58], János Mogyorósi-Klencs 106.80 [61]
7. CZE—Ferdinand Daniš 112.00 [13], Zdeněk Růžička 110.40 [30], Josef Svoboda 110.05 [37], Lee Sotornik 109.50 [41], Josef Skvor 109.10 [44], Jindřich Mikulec 108.95 [45], Vladimir Kejř 108.15 [54], Miloslav Kolejka 106.70 [63]
8. USA—Edward Scrobe 110.40 [30], Robert Stout 110.15 [34], William Roetzheim 107.05 [59], Donald Holder 103.50 [80], John Beckner 103.40 [81], Charles Simms 102.40 [89], Walter Blattmann 102.35 [90], Vincent D'Autorio 101.20 [100]

1956 Melbourne T: 7, N: 7, D: 12.6.

	Total Points
1. SOV	568.25
2. JPN	566.40
3. FIN	555.95
4. CZE	554.10
5. GER	552.45
6. USA	547.50
7. AUS	477.15

1. SOV—Vikton Chukarin 114.25 [1], Yuni Tytov 113.80 [3], Valentin Muratov 113.30 [5], Albert Azaryan 112.55 [7], Borys Shakhlin 112.50 [8], Pavel Stolbov 111.75 [14]
2. JPN—Takashi Ono 114.20 [2], Masao Takemoto 113.55 [4], Masami Kubota 112.50 [8], Nobuyuki Aihara 112.45 [10], Shinsaku Tsukawaki 112.20 [12], Akira Kono 111.55 [16]
3. FIN—Kalevi Suoniemi 112.35 [11], Berndt Lindfors 111.60 [15], Martti Mansikka 110.60 [20], Onni Lappalainen 110.45 [22], Olavi Leimuvirta 109.35 [27], Raimo Heinonen 108.10 [37]
4. CZE—Ferdinand Daniš 111.90 [13], Josef Škvor 110.85 [18], Vladimir Kejř 110.30 [23], Zdeněk Růžička 109.65 [26], Jaroslav Mikoška 109.35 [27], Jaroslav Bim 108.25 [26]
5. GER—Helmut Bantz 112.90 [6], Robert Klein 110.60 [20], Theo Wied 109.90 [25], Hans Pfann 109.15 [29], Erich Wied 107.50 [29], Jakob Kiefer 107.45 [42]
6. USA—John Beckner 111.00 [17], Jose Armando Vega 108.45 [31], Charles Simms 108.40 [32], Richard Beckner 108.30 [35], Abraham Grossfeld 107.75 [39], William Tom 107.35 [43]
7. AUS—Brian Blackburn 91.40 [58], Graham Bond 96,40 [54], David Gourlay 95.90 [55], John Lees 93.05 [56], Alexander Punton 85.75 [59], Bruce Sharp 92.95 [57]

1960 Rome T: 20, N: 20, D: 9.7.

	Total Points
1. JPN	575.20
2. SOV	572.70
3. ITA	559.05
4. CZE	557.15
5. USA	555.20
6. FIN	554.45
7. GDR & GER	553.35
8. SWI	551.45

1. JPN—Takashi Ono 115.90 [2], Shuji Tsurumi 114.55 [4], Yukio Endo 114.45 [5], Masao Takemoto 114.45 [5], Nobuyuki Aihara 114.40 [7], Takashi Mitsukuri 114.10 [9]
2. SOV—Borys Shakhlin 115.95 [1], Yuri Tytov 115.60 [3], Albert Azaryan 113.35 [11], Vladimir Portnoy 113.30 [12], Nikolai Miligulo 113.05 [13], Valery Kerdemelidi 111.95 [17]
3. ITA—Franco Menichelli 113.80 [10], Giovanni Carminucci 112.30 [14], Angelo Vicardi 110.90 [24], Pasquale Carminucci 110.40 [31], Orlando Polmonari 109.95 [38], Gianfranco Marzolla 109.05 [50]
4. CZE—Ferdinand Daniš 112.10 [15], Jaroslav Štastny 111.50 [18], Jaroslav Bim 111.00 [23], Pavel Gajdoš 110.60 [28], Josef Trmal 110.25 [33], Ladislav Pazdera 108.85 [54]
5. USA—Larry Banner 111.05 [21], John Beckner 110.85 [25], Donald Tonry 110.75 [27], Abraham Grossfeld 110.05 [36], Fred Orlofsky 109.45 [44], Garland O'Quinn 109.00 [53]
6. FIN—Otto Kestola 112.00 [16], Eugen Ekman 110.45 [30], Olavi Leimuvirta 110.25 [33], Kauko Heikkinen 109.85 [40], Raimo Heinonen 109.60 [42], Sakkari Olkkonnen 109.40 [45]
7. GDR&GER—Günter Lyhs 110.80 [26], Siegfried Füller 110.60 [28], Erwin Koppe 109.05 [50], Günter Nachtigall 108.75 [59], Karlheinz Friedrich 108.00 [67], Philipp Fürst 106.65 [76]
8. SWI—Ernst Fivian 111.05 [21], Max Benker 110.00 [37], Fritz Feuz 109.85 [40], André Brullmann 109.15 [47], Hans Schwarzentruber 109.15 [47], Edy Thomi 108.35 [63]

Masao Takemoto, a member of the Japanese team, had won a total of two silver medals and three bronze in 1952 and 1956, but he didn't win a gold medal until 1960, when he was 40 years old. He is the oldest gymnast in Olympic history to win a gold medal. In 1960 he also gained another silver medal on the horizontal bar.

1964 Tokyo T: 18, N: 18, D: 10.20.

	Total Points
1. JPN	577.95
2. SOV	575.45
3. GER&GDR	585.10
4. ITA	560.90
5. POL	559.50
6. CZE	558.15
7. USA	556.95
8. FIN	556.20

1. JPN—Yukio Endo 115.95 [1], Shuji Tsurumi 115.40 [2], Haruhiro Yamashita 115.10 [6], Takuji Hayata 114.90 [8], Takashi Mitsukuri 114.80 [9], Takashi Ono 114.40 [11]
2. SOV—Borys Shakhlin 115.40 [2], Viktor Lisitsky 115.40 [2], Viktor Leontyev 114.50 [10], Yuri Tsapenko 114.40 [11], Yuri Tytov 114.35 [13], Sergei Diomidov 114.20 [14]
3. GER&GDR—Siegfried Fülle 114.10 [15], Klaus Köste 112.75 [18], Erwin Koppe 112.45 [19], Peter Weber 112.35 [21], Philipp Fürst 112.35 [24], Günter Lyhs 111.70 [29]
4. ITA—Franco Menichelli 115.15 [5], Luigi Cimnaghi 112.35 [21], Giovanni Carminucci 111.80 [27], Pasquale Carminucci 110.70 [42], Angelo Vicardi 109.40 [63], Bruno Franceschetti 108.70 [75]
5. POL—Mikolaj Kubica 113.20 [16], Aleksander Rokosa 111.95 [25], Wilhelm Kubica 111.10 [35], Alfred Kucharczyk 111.05 [37], Jan Jankowicz 110.60 [45], Andrzej Konopka 108.70 [75]
6. CZE—Bohumil Mudřik 111.50 [30], Ladislav Pazdera 110.70 [42], Václav Kubička 110.65 [44], Přemysl Krbec 110.60 [45], Karel Kiečka 110.35 [52], Pavel Gajdoš 101.75 [106]
7. USA—Makoto Sakamoto 112.40 [20], Russell Mitchell 111.20 [32], Ronald Barak 110.95 [39], Larry Banner 110.05 [55], Gregor Weiss 109.90 [59], Arthur Shurlock 109.10 [68]
8. FIN—Eino Laiho 111.85 [26], Eugen Ekman 111.15 [34], Raimo Heinonen 110.95 [39], Hannu Rantakara 110.50 [48], Otto Kestola 109.95 [58], Kauko Heikkinen 109.35 [64]

1968 Mexico City T: 16, N: 16, D: 10.24.

	Total Points
1. JPN	575.90
2. SOV	571.10
3. GDR	557.15
4. CZE	557.10
5. POL	555.40
6. YUG	550.75
7. USA	548.90
8. GER	548.35

1. JPN—Sawao Kato 115.90 [1], Akinori Nakayama 115.65 [3], Eizo Kenmotsu 114.90 [4], Takeshi Kato 114.85 [5], Yukio Endo 113.55 [8], Misuo Tsukahara 111.50 [18]
2. SOV—Mikhail Voronin 115.85 [2], Sergei Diomidov 114.10 [6], Viktor Klimenko 113.95 [7], Valery Karasyov 113.25 [10], Viktor Lisitsky 112.60 [14], Valery Ilyinykh 111.90 [15]
3. GDR—Matthias Brehme 112.85 [12], Klaus Köste 111.85 [16], Siegfried Fülle 111.10 [21], Peter Weber 110.15 [26], Gerhard Dietrich 109.70 [34], Günter Beier 108.20 [51]
4. CZE—Václav Kubička 111.30 [19], Jiří Fejtek 111.20 [20], František Bocko 111.00 [22], Bohumil Mudřik 109.95 [28], Miloslav Netusil 109.40 [37], Václav Skoumal 109.30 [38]
5. POL—Wilhelm Kubica 113.15 [11], Mikolaj Kubica 112.80 [13], Sylwester Kubica 109.80 [31], Andrzej Gonera 109.25 [39], Aleksander Rokosa 108.85 [44], Jerzy Kruza 108.15 [53]
6. YUG—Miroslav Cerar 113.30 [9], Janez Brodnik 110,75 [23], Milenko Kersnič 109.85 [30], Milko Vratič 108.90 [42], Damir Anič 105.80 [75], Martin Šrot 104.80 [84]
7. USA—David Thor 110.60 [24], Fred Roethlisberger 109.70 [34], Stephen Hug 109.60 [36], Stephen Cohen 108.75 [46], Sidney Freudenstein 108.00 [57], Kanati Allen 105.45 [80]
8. GER—Heinz Häussler 108.80 [45], Helmut Tepasse 108.35 [50], Heiko Reinemer 108.20 [51], Hermann Hopfner 108.10 [55], Erich Hess 107.75 [60]

1972 Munich T: 16, N: 16, D: 8.29.

	Total Points
1. JPN	571.25
2. SOV	564.05
3. GDR	559.70
4. POL	551.70
5. GER	546.40
6. PRK	545.05
7. ROM	538.90
8. HUN	538.60

1. JPN—Sawao Kato 115.10 [1], Eizo Kenmotsu 114.75 [2], Shigeru Kasamatsu 114.40 [3], Akinori Nakayama 114.25 [4], Mitsuo Tsukahara 112.25 [11], Teruichi Okamura 111.20 [14]
2. SOV—Nikolai Andrianov 113.80 [5], Mikhail Voronin 112.95 [7], Viktor Kilmenko 112.65 [8], Edvard Mikayelyan 112.50 [9], Aleksandr Maleyev 110.70 [18], Vladimir Shukin 110.20 [20]
3. GDR—Klaus Köste 113.25 [6], Matthias Brehme 112.45 [10], Wolfgang Thüne 112.15 [12], Wolfgang Klotz 111.05 [16], Reinhard Rychly 109.95 [21], Jürgen Paeke 109.35 [28]
4. POL—Mikolaj Kubica 111.25 [13], Andrzej Szajna 111.15 [15], Sylwester Kubica 110.75 [16], Wilhelm Kubica 109.90 [22], Mieczyslaw Strzalka 106.45 [47], Jerzy Kruza 106.35 [49]
5. GER—Eberhard Gienger 109.75 [23], Walter Mössinger 109.70 [24], Günter Spies 108.70 [30], Bernd Effing 107.75 [37], Reinhard Ritter 106.80 [43], Heinz Häusslen 106.25 [51]

6. PRK—Li Song-sob 110.75 [16], Kim Song-yu 109.45 [25], Kim Song-il 108.25 [32], Shin Heung-do 107.75 [37], Ho Yun-hang 106.45 [47], Jo Jong-ryol 106.15 [53]
7. ROM—Petre Mihăiuc 109.30 [29], Dănut Grecu 108.10 [33], Gheorghe Păunescu 107.25 [41], Mircea Gheorghiu 105.00 [62], Nicolae Oprescu 104.60 [66], Constantin Petrescu 103.70 [73]
8. HUN—Imre Molnár 110.55 [19], Zoltán Magyar 108.70 [30], István Kiss 106.65 [45], Béla Herczeg 105.60 [56], Antal Kisteleki 105.30 [61], István Bérczi 104.95 [63]

1976 Montreal T: 12, N: 12, D: 7.20.

	Total Points
1. JPN	576.85
2. SOV	576.45
3. GDR	564.65
4. HUN	564.45
5. GER	557.40
6. ROM	557.30
7. USA	556.10
8. SWI	550.60

1. JPN—Sawao Kato 115.90 [2], Mitsuo Tsukahara 115.75 [3], Hiroshi Kajiyama 115.25 [5], Eizo Kenmotsu 115.15 [6], Hisato Igarashi 113.55 [15], Shun Fujimoto 84.55 [89]
2. SOV—Nikolai Andrianov 116.50 [1], Aleksandr Dityatin 115.15 [6], Gennady Kryssin 114.25 [8], Vladimir Manchenko 113.85 [11], Vladimir Tikhonov 112.15 [23]
3. GDR—Lutz Mack 113.00 [17], Bernd Jäger 112.95 [18], Michael Nikolay 112.90 [19], Roland Brückner 112.00 [24], Wolfgang Klotz 111.95 [25], Rainer Hanschke 111.50 [28]
4. HUN—Zoltán Magyar 114.25 [8], Imre Molnár 113.65 [13], Ferenc Donáth 113.60 [14], Béla Laufer 111.60 [26], Árpád Farkas 109.65 [40], Imre Bánrévi 109.15 [48]
5. GER—Eberhard Gienger 113.30 [16], Volke Rohrwick 112.20 [22], Edgar Jonek 111.25 [29], Werner Steinmetz 110.30 [34], Reinhard Dietze 108.80 [53], Reinhard Ritter 107.75[61]
6. ROM—Dănut Grecu 114.10 [10], Nicolae Oprescu 110.30 [34], Sorin Cepoi 109.95 [36], Ionel Checicheş 109.85 [37], Mihai Borş 109.75 [38], Ştefan Gal 109.15 [48]
7. USA—Wayne Young 111.55 [27], Kurt Thomas 111.05 [30], Peter Kormann 110.75 [31], Thomas Beach 110.55 [32], Marshall Avener 109.45 [43], Bart Conner 109.35 [46]
8. SWI—Robert Bretscher 112.35 [21], Ueli Bachmann 109.60 [41], Philippe Gaille 109.40 [44], Bernhard Locher 108.30 [55], Peter Rohner 108.25 [56], Armin Vock 81.45 [90]

The entire team competition came down to the horizontal bar routine of the Japanese star Mitsuo Tsukahara. A score above 9.5 would give Japan first place, while a score below 9.5 would turn over the gold medal to the USSR. Tsukahara came through in superb fashion and earned a 9.9 to ensure the fifth straight Japanese team victory.

Another hero of the Japanese gymnastics team was Shun Fujimoto. Fujimoto broke his leg at the knee while finishing his floor exercises routine. Not wanting to cause concern among his coaches or fellow team members during the tense competition with the Soviets, Fujimoto kept his injury to himself and went ahead with his side horse performance, earning a 9.5. Next up were the rings. Fujimoto completed a successful routine (9.7) and then faced a difficult moment—the dismount. Landing on his feet, he compounded his injury by dislocating his knee. The pain was intense: "My whole blood was boiling at my stomach." Fujimoto finally submitted himself to medical inspection and was convinced to withdraw from the remainder of the competition. Asked years later if he would have gone ahead on the rings if he had known how much pain he would experience, Fujimoto replied without hesitation: "No."

1980 Moscow T: 9, N: 9, D: 7.22.

	Total Points
1. SOV	598.60
2. GDR	581.15
3. HUN	575.00
4. ROM	572.30
5. BUL	571.55
6. CZE	569.80
7. CUB	563.20
8. FRA	559.20

1. SOV—Aleksandr Dityatin 118.40 [1], Nikolai Andrianov 118.15 [2], Eduard Azaryan 117.40 [4], Aleksandr Tkachyov 117.40 [4], Bohdan Makuts 116.95 [6], Vladimir Markelov 116.40 [9]
2. GDR—Roland Brückner 116.90 [7], Michael Nikolay 116.50 [8], Lutz Hoffmann 115.75 [13], Ralf-Peter Hemmann 115.70 [14], Andreas Bronst 114.85 [15], Lutz Mack 114.00 [20]
3. HUN—Ferenc Donáth 115.90 [11], Zoltán Magyar 115.85 [12], Péter Kovács 114.70 [18], György Guczoghy 113.85 [21], István Vamos 113.10 [27], Zoltán Kelemen 112.70 [33]
4. ROM—Dănut Grecu 114.85 [15], Kurt Szilier 114.80 [17], Aurelian Georgescu 113.75 [22], Sorin Cepoi 113.55 [25], Nicolae Oprescu 112.95 [28], Romulus Bucuroiu 112.75 [32]
5. BUL—Stoyan Delchev 117.50 [3], Dancho Yordanov 113.75 [22], Plamen Petkov 113.50 [26], Roumen Petkov 112.50 [34], Ognyan Bangiev 112.05 [39], Yanko Radanchev 111.60 [42]
6. CZE—Jiří Tabák 115.95 [10], Rudolf Babiak 114.10 [19], Dan Zoulík 113.70 [24], Miroslav Kučeřik 112.10 [38], Jan Migdau 111.95 [40], Jozef Konečný 111.35 [43]
7. CUB—Sergio Suárez Aime 112.50 [34], Roberto León Richards-Aguiar 112.45 [36], Miguel Arroyo 112.15 [37], Enrique Bravo 111.75 [41], Mario Castro 111.15[46], Jorge Roche 83.40 [65]
8. FRA—Michel Boutard 112.95 [28], Willi Moy 112.85 [30], Henry Boerio 111.35 [43], Joel Suty 111.25 [45], Yves Boquel 108.65 [59], Marc Touchais 108.10 [62]

1984 Los Angeles T: 9, N: 9, D: 7.31.

	Total Points
1. USA	591.40
2. CHN	590.80
3. JPN	586.70
4. GER	582.10
5. SWI	579.95
6. FRA	578.25
7. CAN	577.15
8. KOR	574.95

1. USA—Peter Vidmar 118.55 [1], Bart Conner 118.30 [4], Mitchell Gaylord 118.15 [6], Timothy Daggett 117.85 [8], James Hartung 117.75 [9], Scott Johnson 116.60 [16]
2. CHN—Li Ning 118.45 [2], Tong Fei 118.40 [3], Xu Zhiqiang 118.15 [6], Lou Yun 117.65 [10], Li Xiaoping 116.85 [12], Li Yuejiu 116.70 [15]
3. JPN—Koji Gushiken 118.20 [5], Nobuyuki Kajitani 116.95 [11], Noritoshi Hirata 116.80 [13], Shinji Morisue 116.60 [16], Koji Sotomura 116.05 [25], Kyoji Yamawaki 115.65 [29]

4. GER—Jürgen Geiger 116.75 [14], Daniel Winkler 116.40 [18], Andreas Japtok 116.20 [21], Benno Gross 116.05 [25], Volker Rohrwick 115.45 [32], Bernhard Simmelbauer 115.25 [36]
5. SWI—Josef Zellweger 116.40 [18], Markus Lehmann 116.30 [20], Daniel Wunderlin 116.10 [22], Marco Piatti 115.95 [27], Bruno Cavelti 114.60 [43], Urs Meister 113.25 [59]
6. FRA—Jean-Luc Cairon 116.10 [22], Joël Suty 115.50 [31], Philippe Vatuone 115.45 [32], Laurent Barbieri 115.30 [34], Jacques Def 114.85 [41], Michel Boutard 113.25 [59]
7. CAN—Philippe Chartrand 115.75 [28], Brad Peters 115.15 [37], Warren Long 115.05 [38], Daniel Gaudet 114.60 [43], Frank Nutzenberger 114.30 [49], Allan Reddon 114.05 [51]
8. KOR—Chang Tae-eun 115.30 [34], Han Chung-sik 115.05 [38], Lee Jeoung-sik 114.70 [42], Ju Young-sam 113.95 [52], Nam Seoung-gu 113.75 [56], Chae Kwang-suk 113.50 [57]

Competing at Pauley Pavilion on the campus of UCLA, the home arena for three of the six Americans (Vidmar, Gaylord and Daggett), the US team scored an emotional upset victory over the world champion Chinese.

1988 Seoul T: 12, N: 12, D: 9.20.

	Total Points
1. SOV	593.35
2. GDR	588.45
3. JPN	585.60
4. CHN	585.25
5. BUL	585.10
6. HUN	582.30
7. ROM	581.70
8. ITA	579.00

1. SOV—Vladimir Artemov 118.95 [1], Valery Lyukin 118.85 [2], Dmitri Bilozerchev 118.45 [3], Sergei Kharkov 118.40 [4], Vladimir Gogoladze 117.70 [6], Vladimir Novikov 117.50 [11]
2. GDR—Sylvio Kroll 117.85 [5], Sven Tippelt 117.60 [9], Ralf Büchner 117.20 [15], Holger Behrendt 116.95 [19], Ulf Hoffman 116.40 [29], Andreas Wecker 116.30 [30]
3. JPN—Yukio Iketani 117.65 [8], Koichi Mizushima 117.45 [12], Daisuke Nishikawa 117.25 [13], Toshiharu Sato 116.65 [26], Hiroyuki Konishi 115.80 [37], Takahiro Yamada 115.40 [43]
4. CHN—Wang Chongsheng 117.20 [15], Lou Yun 117.10 [17], Xu Zhiqiang 117.00 [18], Li Chunyang 116.15 [32], Guo Linxian 115.35 [45], Li Ning 114.95 [50]
5. BUL—Kalofer Hristozov 117.70 [6], Lubomir Geraskov 116.75 [21], Dimitar Taskov 116.75 [21], Dian Kolev 116.30 [30], Stoycho Gochev 115.95 [36], Petar Georgiev 115.60 [39]
6. HUN—György Guczoghy 117.25 [13], Csaba Fajkusz 116.75 [21], Zsolt Horváth 115.50 [41], Zsolt Borkai 115.40 [43], Jenő Paprika 114.70 [55], Balázs Tóth 77.05 [89]
7. ROM—Marius Gherman 117.55 [10], Marius Eugen Toba 116.75 [21], Nicolae Bejenaru 115.30 [46], Adrian Sandu 115.15 [48], Marian Rizan 114.85 [51], Valerian Pintea 105.55 [87]
8. ITA—Boris Preti 116.90 [20], Jury Chechi 116.55 [27], Paolo Bucci 115.70 [38], Riccardo Trapella 114.75 [53], Gabriele Sala 114.25 [61], Vittorio Allievi 112.65 [78]

1992 Barcelona T: 12, N: 12, D: 7.29.

	Total Points
1. SOV	585.450
2. CHN	580.375
3. JPN	578.250
4. GER	575.575
5. ITA	571.750
6. USA	571.725
7. ROM	571.150
8. KOR	570.850

1. SOV—Vitaly Scherbo 117.875 [1], Valeryi Belenki 117.500 [2], Hryhoriy Misyutin 116.975 [3], Igor Korobchinsky 116.500 [5], Aleksei Voropayev 115.125 [16], Rustam Sharipov 114.950 [22]
2. CHN—Li Xiaoshuang 116.450 [6], Li Chunyang 115.925 [7], Guo Linyao 115.900 [8], Li Jing 114.950 [22], Li Dashuang 114.875 [24], Li Ge 114.875 [24]
3. JPN—Yukio Iketani 115.450 [9], Yoshiaki Hatakeda 115.300 [10], Takashi Chinen 115.275 [13], Daisuke Nishikawa 115.100 [17], Yutaka Aihara 114.975 [21], Masayuki Matsunaga 114.325 [35]
4. GER—Andreas Wecker 116.875 [4], Sylvio Kroll 114.850 [26], Oliver Walther 114.425 [31], Ralf Büchner 114.400 [33], Sven Tippelt 113.775 [41], Mario Franke 113.175 [50]
5. ITA—Boris Preti 115.275 [13], Paolo Bucci 115.100 [17], Ruggero Rossato 114.175 [37], Gabriele Sala 113.075 [53], Gianmatteo Centazzo 112.125 [66], Alexandro Viligiardi 111.850 [71]
6. USA—M. Chris Waller 114.800 [27], John Roethlisberger 114.200 [36], Scott Keswick 113.725 [43], Trent Dimas 113.675 [44], Dominick Minicucci 112.950 [56], Jair Lynch 112.775 [60]
7. ROM—Marius Gherman 115.300 [10], Maria Rizan 114.725 [28], Adrian-Francisc Gal 113.325 [47], Nicolae Bejenaru 113.150 [51], Nicu Stroia 112.925 [57], Adrian Sandu 113.850 [59]
8. KOR—Yoo Ok-ryul 115.025 [19], Lee Joo-hyung 114.375 [34], Han Yoon-soo 113.825 [40], Jung Jin-soo 113.625 [45], Han Kwang-ho 112.350 [64], Yeo Hong-chul 110.525 [81]

1996 Atlanta T: 12, N: 12, D: 7.22.

	Total Points
1. RUS	576.778
2. CHN	575.539
3. UKR	571.541
4. BLR	571.381
5. USA	570.618
6. BUL	567.567
7. GER	567.405
8. KOR	567.054

1. RUS—Aleksei Nemov, Aleksei Voropayev, Dmitri Vasilenko, Sergei Sharkov, Nikolai Kryukov, Yevgeny Podgorny, Dmitri Trush
2. CHN—Li Xiaoshuang, Zhang Jingin, Shen Jian, Fan Bin, Huang Liping, Huang Huadong, Fan Hongbin
3. UKR—Rustam Sharipov, Alexandre Svetlichnyi, Vladimir Shamenko, Igor Korobchinsky, Yuri Yermakov, Oleg Kosiak, Hryhoriy Misyutin
4. BLR—Vitaly Scherbo, Andrei Kan, Vitaly Rudnitsky, Aleksandr Belanovsky, Alexander Shostak, Aleksey Sinkevich, Ivan Pavlovsky
5. USA—John Roethlisberger, Blaine Wilson, Kip Simons, Jair Lynch, John Macready, Chainey Umphrey, Mihai Bagiu
6. BUL—Jordan Jovtchev, Krasimir Dunev, Dimitar Lunchev, Ivan Ivanov, Kalofer Hristozov, Deyan Tordanov, Vassil Vetzev
7. GER—Andreas Wecker, Valeri Belenki, Oliver Walther, Jan-Peter Nikiferow, Karsten Oelsch, Uwe Billerbeck, Marius Toba
8. KOR—Lee Joo-hyung, Han Yoon-sho, Jung Jin-soo, Yeo Hong-chul, Cho Seong-min, Kim Dong-hwa, Kim Bong-hyun

At the 1995 world championships, the Russians made so many mistakes in the compulsory exercises that they entered the optional phase in eleventh place and only finished fourth overall. There was no such collapse at the Olympics. Led by Aleksei Nemov and Aleksei Voropayev, the Russians led China by almost a full point after compulsories and held their lead throughout the optionals.

2000 Sydney T: 12, N: 12, D: 9.18.

	Total Points
1. CHN	231.919
2. UKR	230.306
3. RUS	230.019
4. JPN	229.857
5. USA	228.983
6. ROM	227.543
7. KOR	
8. BLR	

1. CHN—Yang Wei, Zheng Lihui, Li Xiaopeng, Xing Aowei, Huang Xu, Xiao Junfeng
2. UKR—Oleksandr Beresh, Oleksandr Svitlychny, Roman Zozulya, Valery Honcharov, Valery Pereshkura, Ruslan Myezyentsev
3. RUS—Aleksei Nemov, Aleksei Bondarenko, Maksim Alekhin, Yevgeny Podgornyi, Nikolai Kryukov, Dmitri Drivin
4. JPN—Naoya Tsukahara, Kenichi Fujita,Yoshihiro Saito, Mutsumi Harada, Akihiro Kasamatsu, Norimasa Iwai
5. USA—Paul Hamm, Blaine Wilson, Stephen McCain, Morgan Hamm, Sean Townsend, John Roethlisberger
6. ROM—Marian Drăgulescu, Ioan Suciu, Rares Orzata, Florentin Pescaru, Marius Urzică
7. KOR—Cho Seong-min, Jung Jin-soo, Lee Joo-hyung, Kim Dong-hwa, Lee Jang-hyung, Yeo Hong-chul
8. BLR—Ivan Ivankov, Aleksei Sinkevich, Ivan Pavlovsky, Aleksandr Shostak, Vitaly Rudnitsky, Aleksandr Kruzhilov

After finishing second at three of the last four Olympics, the Chinese men finally broke through to the gold medal podium, leading the final from start to finish.

2004 Athens T: 12, N: 12, D: 8.14.

	Total Points
1. JPN	173.821
2. USA	172.933
3. ROM	172.384
4. KOR	171.847
5. CHN	171.257
6. RUS	169.808
7. UKR	168.244
8. GER	167.372

1. JPN—Takehiro Kashima, Hisashi Mizutori, Daisuke Nakano, Hiroyuki Tomita, Naoya Tsukahara, Isao Yoneda
2. USA—Jason Gatson, Morgan Hamm, Paul Hamm, Brett McClure, Blaine Wilson, Guard Young
3. ROM—Marian Drăgulescu, Ilie Daniel Popescu, Dan Nicolae Potra, Răzvan Şelariu, Ioan Silviu Suciu, Marius Urzică
4. KOR—Kim Dae-eun, Kim Dong-hwa, Kim Seung-il, Lee Sun-sung, Yang Tae-young
5. CHN—Huang Xu, Li Xiaopeng, Teng Haibin, Xiao Qin, Xing Aowei, Yang Wei
6. RUS—Aleksei Bondarenko, Maksim Devyatovsky, Anton Golotsutskov, Georgi Grebenkov, Aleksei Nemov, Aleksandr Safoshkin
7. UKR—Yevheniy Bohonosiuk, Valeriy Honcharov, Vadim Kuvakin, Ruslan Miezientsev, Andriy Mikhailichenko, Roman Zozulia
8. GER—Thomas Andergassen, Matthias Fahrig, Fabian Hambüchen, Robert Juckel, Sven Kwiatkowski, Sergei Pfeifer

The United States had a rocky lead-in to the qualifying round. One week before the competition, Paul Hamm, Blaine Wilson and Brett McClure were informed that one of the elements in their high bar routines had been devalued, and their start values had been downgraded from what they had been at the previous two world championships. The trio modified their routines to increase their start value, but Wilson fell while attempting the new routine, hitting his head on the mat. He followed with a clear 9.700 on the floor exercise, but withdrew from the competition before the pommels because of nausea and dizziness. The Japanese team included three-time Olympian Naoya Tsukhara, whose father Mitsuo was a five-time Olympic champion, Takehiro Kashima, the 2003 world champion in pommel horse and high bar, and 2003 all-around world bronze medalist Hiroyuki Tomita. The Japanese placed first in the qualifying round, followed by the United States, Romania and reigning world champion China.

The US took an early lead in the floor exercise, earning 29.137 points, with Romania in second followed closely by Japan and South Korea. China, the defending Olympic champion, trailed in seventh after both 2000 all-around silver medalists Yang Wei and Xing Aowei stepped out of bounds. On the pommel horse, the US maintained its lead, earning 29.050 points for a total of 58.187, while Romania narrowed the gap with a total of 57.973 points, Japan maintaining third with 57.386. China, despite finishing first on the pommel horse, could only rise to fifth place and struggled throughout the rest of the competition. The US finally lost momentum on the rings, slipping to third place behind Romania and Japan. The Romanians strengthened their lead in the vault, posting the highest score on the apparatus. Japan maintained their hold on second place, while the US held onto third.

Romania began to falter in the second-to-last rotation, the parallel bars, with Marian Drăgulescu leading with a poor 9.200, followed by a 9.537 from Dan Potra. A 9.725 by Marius Urzică helped them maintain first place, but the Japanese narrowed the lead to only .063 points with Kashima scoring 9.737. The Americans also delivered a strong performance on the parallel bars. Highlighted by Jason Gatson's 9.825, the US moved within .125 points of Romania. Romania's lead finally fell on the high bar, beginning with a mediocre 9.275 from Ioan Suciu and a poor 8.912 from Răzvan Şelariu. Led by Morgan Hamm's 9.762, the US passed the Romanians. With the gold within reach, the Japanese rallied, giving their strongest performance in the competition. Isao Yoneda and Takehiro Kashima scored

9.787 and 9.825 respectively. Last to perform was Hiroyuki Yomita, who needed a score of only 8.963 to move past the United States. Yomita performed nearly flawlessly, earning the highest score of the apparatus, 9.850 points, and giving Japan the gold with a clear 0.888 lead over the United States. It was Japan's first gymnastics team gold medal since the country won five consecutive gold medals between 1960 and 1976. Completing a true changing of the guard, the United States earned its first team medals in a non-boycotted Olympics since 1932 and Romania, long a power in women's gymnastics, won its first team medals ever in men's competition.

2008 Beijing T: 12, N: 12, D: 8.12.

	Total Points
1. CHN	286.125
2. JPN	278.875
3. USA	275.850
4. GER	274.600
5. KOR	274.375
6. RUS	274.300
7. ROM	274.175
8. FRA	272.875

1. CHN—Huang Xu, Chen Yibing, Li Xiaopeng, Xiao Qin, Yang Wei, Zou Kai
2. JPN—Hiroyuki Tomita, Takehiro Kashima, Koki Sakamoto, Makoto Okiguchi, Kohei Uchimura, Takuya Nakase
3. USA—Raj Bhavsar, Joey Hagerty, Jonathan Horton, Justin Spring, Kevin Tan, Sasha Artemev
4. GER—Philipp Boy, Fabian Hambüchen, Marcel Nguyen, Eugen Spiridonov, Thomas Andergassen, Robert Juckel
5. KOR—Kim Ji-hun, Yang Tae-yeong, Kim Su-myeon, Yu Won-cheol, Kim Dae-eun, Kim Seung-il
6. RUS—Konstantin Pluzhnikov, Sergey Khorokhordin, Yury Ryazanov, Nikolay Kryukov, Maksim Devyatovsky, Anton Golotsutskov
7. ROM—Marian Drăgulescu, Flavius Koczi, Răzvan Şelariu, Daniel Popescu, Adrian Bucur, G. Robert Stănescu
8. FRA—Thomas Bouhail, Benoît Caranobe, Yann Cucherat, Danny Rodrigues, Hamilton Sabot, Dimitri Karbanenko

Although they had finished a disappointing fifth at the Athens 2004 Olympics, the Chinese men's gymnastics team was still clearly in a league of its own. China had won seven of the past eight men's team world championship titles, beating defending Olympic champion Japan to win the 2007 title by a combined margin of 4.875 points, the widest of the past eight world championships.

China's line-up in Beijing included double (and reigning) all-around world champion Yang Wei, three-time (and reigning) pommel horse world champion Xiao Qin, double (and reigning) rings world champion Chen Yibing and double parallel bars world champion Li Xiaopeng.

As expected, China led the qualifying round, earning the highest combined scores in the pommel horse and rings and tying with Romania for the highest score on the vault.

In the final China, paired with Japan, trailed briefly by 0.05 points after the floor exercise, the team's weakest element. But the Chinese dominated the rest of the competition, recording both the top combined and the top individual scores in every other event, with Xiao achieving the highest total on the pommel horse (16.100), Chen on the rings (16.575), Huang Xu on the parallel bars (16.475), Li on the vault (16.775) and Zou Kai on the high bar (15.975).

The US stayed in second place throughout most of the competition, despite competing without defending Olympic all-around champion Paul Hamm and his twin brother Morgan, both forced to withdraw due to injury. The Americans actually took the overall lead by 0.825 points over China at the end of the third rotation, but struggled on their floor exercise and pommel horse rotations, slipping to third behind Japan.

TRAMPOLINE

The trampoline is 5.05 meters (16 feet 6¾ inches) wide and 1.155 meters (3 feet 9½ inches) high. The spring bed is made of nylon or string. The ceiling must be at least 8 meters (26 feet 3 inches) high, which gives a good idea of how high the trampolinists bounce. Bouncers try to land inside of a rectangle 108 centimeters (42½ inches) by 216 centimeters (85 inches).

Sixteen men and 16 women will take part in the 2012 Olympic trampoline competition. Athletes must turn at least 18 years old in the Olympic year. Competition begins with a qualifying round consisting of both compulsory and optional routines. The top eight comptitiors advance to the final which is a single optional routine in which each gymnast performs ten moves. There is no time limit for a routine. There are nine judges: five award points for execution, two decide a score for a routine's degree of difficulty and two oversee the competition. The highest and lowest execution scores are dropped and the three remaining scores are added to the single difficulty rating. In the final round, ties are broken by adding all five execution scores.

Trampolinists may perform in socks or gymnastics shoes.

1896–1996 not held

2000 Sydney C: 8, N: 8, D: 9.23.

		PTS.
1. Aleksandr Moskalenko	RUS	41.7
2. Ji Wallace	AUS	39.3
3. Mathieu Turgeon	CAN	39.1
4. David Martin	FRA	38.8
5. Dmitri Polyarush	BLR	38.1
6. Lee Brearley	GBR	37.9
7. Alan Villafuerte	HOL	27.6
8. Oleksandr Chernonos	UKR	7.5

Growing up in Pereyaslovka, Siberia, Aleksandr Moskalenko lived across the street from a trampoline coach. In 1990 he fractured his spine when a trampoline collapsed underneath him. That year he won the world championship anyway. He defended his title in 1992 and 1994 and then retired. But when trampolining was added to the Olympic program in late 1997, Moskalenko returned to training and won the world championship in 1999. Thirty years old at the time of the Sydney Olympics, he won easily. Moskalenko took advantage of an unusual power meal: pancakes and caviar. Mathieu Turgeon was a surprise medalist. He had only placed 15th at the last world championship, but received a wild card berth for the Olympics.

2004 Athens C: 16, N: 14, D: 8.21.

		PTS.
1. Yuriy Nikitin	UKR	41.5
2. Aleksandr Moskalenko	RUS	41.2
3. Henrik Stehlik	GER	40.8
4. Dmitry Polyarush	BLR	40.2
5. Aleksandr Rusakov	RUS	40.2
6. Nuno Merino	POR	40.1
7. Gary Smith	GBR	40.0
8. David Martin	FRA	39.9

Defending Olympic champion and five-time world champion Aleksandr Moskalenko performed an excellent routine with a difficulty score of 16.2. With the same difficulty score, 26-year-old Yuriy Nikitin executed his jumps with even more height and, in particular, more precise centering, to edge Moskalenko for the gold medal.

2008 Beijing C: 16, N: 13, D: 8.19.

		PTS.
1. Lu Chunlong	CHN	41.0
2. Jason Burnett	CAN	40.7
3. Dong Dong	CHN	40.6
4. Tetsuya Sotomura	JPN	39.8
5. Yuriy Nikitin	UKR	39.8
6. Dmitry Ushakov	RUS	38.8
7. Aleksandr Rusakov	RUS	38.5
8. Nikolay Kazak	BLR	38.1

The qualifying round was led by 19-year-old Olympic newcomer Lu Chunlong, who earned 41.2 points on his optional routine. Lu had never competed in a world championship but had won five World Cup gold medals.

Performing second in the final, Jason Burnett moved into first place with a routine that had the highest difficulty score of the competition: 16.8. Burnett's lead held up despite the efforts of the next five competitors, including 2005 world champion Aleksandr Rusakov, defending Olympic champion Yuri Nikitin, and reigning world silver medalist Dong Dong, who came within 0.1 points. Performing last, Lu started with a difficulty score far lower than Burnett (16.2) but earned the highest execution score of the final, 24.8, to take the gold medal.

Lu was the only gymnast to perform while whistling, using it as a breathing technique. "Other trampolinists also have their own way to adjust their breath." Lu said, "They do not make sound, but I do."

DISCONTINUED EVENTS

COMBINED COMPETITION (3 EVENTS)

1904 St. Louis C: 119, N: 3, D: 7.2.
Events: PB, HB, CLSV

		PTS.
1. Adolf Spinnler	SWI	43.49
2. Julius Lenhart	AUT	43.00
3. Wilhelm Weber	GER	41.60
4. Hugo Peitsch	GER	41.56
5. Otto Wiegand	GER	40.82
6. Otto Steffen	USA	39.53
7. William Andelfinger	USA	39.03
8. Andreas Kempf	USA	38.97

COMBINED COMPETITION (4 EVENTS)

1904 St. Louis C: 10?, N: 1, D: 10.28.
Events: PB, HB, SH, LHV

		PTS.
1. Anton Heida	USA	161
2. George Eyser	USA	152
3. William Merz	USA	135
4. John Duha	USA	—
5. Edward Hennig	USA	—

ROPE CLIMBING

1896 Athens C: 5, N: 4, D: 4.10.

1. Nikolaos Andriakopoulos	GRE	23.4
2. Thomas Xenakis	GRE	—
3. Fritz Hofmann	GER	—
4. Viggo Jensen	DEN	—
5. Launceston Elliot	GBR	—

The rope was 14 meters (45 feet 11 inches) high. Only the two Greeeks made it to the top. The other places were decided according to height achieved and style.

1900 not held

1904 St. Louis C: ?, N: 1, D: 10.28.

1. George Eyser	USA	7.0
2. Charles Krause	USA	7.2
3. Emil Voigt	USA	9.8

The rope was 25 feet (7.62 meters) high.

1906 Athens C: 17, N: 4, D: 4.26.

1. Georgios Aliprantis	GRE	11.4
2. Béla Erődy	HUN	13.8
3. Konstantinos Kozanitas	GRE	13.8
4. Georgios Georgantopoulos	GRE	14.0
5. Nicolaos Aliprantis	GRE	14.2
6. Konstantinos Pantzopoulos	GRE	14.8
7. G. Koemzopoulos	GRE	15.2
8. Petros Pavlides	GRE	15.6

The rope was 10 meters (32 feet 9¾ inches) high.

1908–1920 not held

1924 Paris C: 70, N: 9, D: 7.20.

1. Bedřich Šupčik	CZE	7.2
2. Albert Séguin	FRA	7.4
3. August Güttinger	SWI	7.8
3. Ladislav Vácha	CZE	7.8
5. Stane Žilič	YUG/SLO	8.0
6. Jean Gounot	FRA	8.4
6. Arthur Hermann	FRA	8.4
6. Frank Kriz	USA	8.4
6. Janez Porenta	YUG/SLO	8.4

Šupčik was Czechoslovakia's first Olympic champion.

1928 not held

1932 Los Angeles C: 5, N: 2, D: 8.10.

1. Raymond "Ben" Bass	USA	6.7
2. William Galbraith	USA	6.8
3. Thomas Connelly	USA	7.0
4. Miklós Péter	HUN	11.5
5. Péter Boros	HUN	11.6

The rope was 8 meters (26 feet 3 inches) high. Ben Bass was a submarine commander during World War II and rose to the rank of rear admiral. Galbraith and Connelly were also graduates from the US Naval Academy and all three medalists were trained by Navy coach Lou Mang.

CLUB SWINGING

1904 St. Louis C: 9?, N: 1, D: 10.28.

		PTS.
1. Edward Hennig	USA	13
2. Emil Voigt	USA	9
3. Ralph Wilson	USA	5

Hennig remained active in club swinging and won the American championship as late as 1951, when he was 71 years old.

1906–1928 not held

1932 Los Angeles C: 4, N: 2, D: 8.9.

		PTS.
1. George Roth	USA	8.97
2. Philip Erenberg	USA	8.90
3. William Kuhlmeier	USA	8.63
4. Francisco Alvarez	MEX	8.47

Unemployed and nearly starving in the midst of the Great Depression, Roth, who once went 15 days without eating, would go to the Olympic Village each day, collect some food, and sneak it home to his wife and baby girl in East Hollywood. He competed with one of his daughter's booties stuffed inside his own shoe for good luck. After receiving his gold medal before 60,000 cheering spectators, Roth walked out of the stadium and hitchhiked home.

SIDEHORSE VAULT

1924 Paris C: 70, N: 9, D: 7.20.

		PTS.
1. Albert Séguin	FRA	10.00
2. François Gangloff	FRA	9.93
2. Jean Gounot	FRA	9.93
4. Slavko Hlastan	YUG/SLO	9.86
5. Stane Derganc	YUG/SLO	9.85
6. Bedřich Šupčik	CZE	9.83
6. Ladislav Vácha	CZE	9.83
8. Eugene Cordonnier FRA), Mathias Erang (LUX), Frank Kriz (USA), Robert Prażak (CZE		9.80

TUMBLING

1932 Los Angeles C: 4, N: 2, D: 8.10.

		PTS.
1. Rowland Wolfe	USA	18.90
2. Edward Gross	USA	18.67
3. William Hermann	USA	18.37
4. István Pelle	HUN	15.43

Rowland "Flip" Wolfe of Dallas introduced the backflip with a double twist.

PARALLEL BARS—TEAM

1896 Athens T: 3, N: 2, D: 4.9.

1. GER—Conrad Böcker, Alfred Flatow, Gustav Felix Flatow, Georg Hilmar, Fritz Manteuffel, Karl Neukirch, Richard Röstel, Gustav Schuft, Carl Schuhmann, Hermann Weingärtner
2. GRE—Panhellenic Club of Athens: Sotirios Athanasopoulos, Nicolaos Andriakopoulos, Petros Persakis, Thomas Yenakis
3. GRE—National Gymnastic Club of Athens: Ioannis Chrysaphis, Ioannis Mitropoulos, Dimitrios Loundras, Philippos Karvelas

Dimitrios Loundras of the National Gymnastic Club was 10 years and 218 days old. He grew up to be an admiral in the Greek navy and served in both world wars.

HORIZONTAL BAR—TEAM

1896 Athens T: 1, N: 1, D: 4.9.

1. GER—Conrad Böcker, Alfred Flatow, Gustav Felix Flatow, Georg Hilmar, Fritz Manteuffel, Karl Neukirch, Richard Röstel, Gustav Schuft, Carl Schuhmann, Hermann Weingärtner

FREE EXERCISES AND APPARATUS—TEAM

1912 Stockholm T: 5, N: 5, D: 7.10.

	Total Points
1. NOR	114.25
2. FIN	109.25
3. DEN	106.25
4. GER	84.25
5. LUX	81.50

1. NOR—Isak Abrahamsen, Hans Beyer, Hartman Bjørnson, Alfred Engelsen, Bjarne Johnsen, Sigurd Jørgensen, Knud Knudsen, Alf Lie, Rolf Lie, Tor Lund, Petter Martinsen, Per Mathiesen, Jacob Opdahl, Nils Opdahl, Bjarne Pettersen, Frithjof Sælen, Øistein Schirmer, Georg Selenius, Sigvard Sivertsen, Robert Sjursen Rafro, Einar Strøm, Gabriel Thorstensen, Thomas Torstensen, Nils Voss
2. FIN—Kaarle Ekholm, Eino Forsström, Eero Hyvärinen, Mikko Hyvärinen, Tauno Ilmoniemi, Ilmari Keinänen, Jalmari Kivenheimo, Karl Lund, Aarne Pelkonen, K. Ilmari Pernaja, Arvid Rydman, K. Eino Saastamoinen, Aarne Salovaara, Heikki Sammallahti, Hannes Sirola, Klaus Uuno Suomela, Lauri Tanner, Väinö Tiiri, Kaarlo Vähämäki, Kalle Vasama
3. DEN—Axel Andersen, Hjalmar Andersen, Halvor Birch, Wilhelm Grimmelmann, Aage Hansen, Arvor Hansen, Christian Hansen, Charles Jensen, Poul Jørgensen, Hjalmar Johansen, Carl Krebs, Viggo Meulengracht-Madsen, Lukas Nielsen, Richard Nordstrøm, Oluf Olsson, Steen Olsen, Carl Pedersen, Kristian Petersen, Olaf Pedersen, Niels Petersen, Christian Svendsen
4. GER—Walter Engelmann, Adolf Seebass, Alfred Staats, Hans Roth, Arno Glockauer, Alexander Sperling, Kurt Reichenbach, Rudolf Körner, J. Erwin Buder, Wilhelm Brülle, Heinrich Pahner, Johannes Reuschle, Walter Jesinghaus, Eberhard Sorge, Karl Richter, M. Erich Worm, Karl Jordan, Hans Werner
5. LUX—Nicolas Adam, Charles Behm, André Bordang, Jean-Pierre Frantzen, François Hentges, Pierre Hentges, Michel Hemmerling, Jean-Baptiste Horn, Nicolas Kanivé, Émile Knepper, Nicolas Kummer, Marcel Langsam, Émile Lanners, Maurice Palgen, Jean-Pierre Thommes, François Wagner, Antoine Wehrer, Ferdinand Wirtz, Joseph Zuang

1920 Antwerp T: 2, N: 2, D: 8.27.

	Total Points
1. DEN	51.35
2. NOR	48.55

1. DEN—Georg Albertsen, Carl Andersen, Viggo Dibbern, Aage Frandsen, Hugo Helsten, Harry Holm, Herold Jansson, Robert Johnsen, Christian Juhl, Vilhelm Lange, Svend Meulengracht-Madsen, Peder Marcussen, Peder Møller, Niels Turin-Nielsen, Steen Lerche Olsen, Christian Pedersen, Stig Rønne, Harry Sørensen, Christian Thomas, Knud Vermehren
2. NOR—Alf Aaning, Karl Aas, Jørgen Andersen, Gustav Bayer, Jørgen Bjørnstad, Asbjørn Bodahl, Eilert Bøhm, Trygve Bøyesen, Ingolf Davidsen, Haakon Endreson, Jacob Erstad, Harald Færstad, Hermann Helgesen, Petter Hol, Otto Johannessen, Anker Johansen, Torbjørn Steen Kristoffersen, Henrik Nielsen, Jacob Opdahl, Arthur Rydstrøm, Frithjof Sælen, Bjørn Skjærpe, Wilhelm Steffensen, Olav Sundal, Reidar Tønsberg, Lauritz Wigand-Larsen

SWEDISH SYSTEM—TEAM

1912 Stockholm T: 3, N: 3, D: 7.8.

	Total Points
1. SWE	937.46
2. DEN	898.84
3. NOR	857.21

1. SWE—Per Bertilsson, Carl Ehrenfried Carlberg, Nils Daniel Granfelt, Curt Hartzell, Oswald Holmberg, Anders Hylander, Axel Janse, Anders Boo Kullberg, Sven Landberg, Per Nilsson, Benkt Rudolf Norelius, Axel Norling, Daniel Norling, Sven Rosén, Nils Silfverskiöld, Carl Silfverstrand, John Sörenson, Yngve Stiernspetz, Carl-Erik Svensson, Karl-Johan Svensson [Sarland], Knut Torell, Edvard Wennerholm, Claës Wersäll, David Wiman
2. DEN—Peter Andersen, Valdemar Bøggild, Søren Christensen, Ingvald Eriksen, Georg Falcke, Torkild Garp, Hans Trier Hansen, Johannes Hansen, Rasmus Hansen, Jens Kristian Jensen, Søren Jensen, Karl Kirk, Jens Kirkegaard, Olav Kjems, Carl Larsen, Jens Peter Laursen, Marius Lefevre, Poul Mark, Einar Olsen, Hans Pedersen, Hans Eilert Pedersen, Jens Thorup Pedersen, Peder Larsen Pedersen, Jørgen Christian Ravn, Aksel Sørensen, Martin Hansen Thau, Søren Thorborg, Kristen Vadgaard, Johannes Vinther
3. NOR—Arthur Amundsen, Jørgen Andersen, Trygve Bøyesen, Georg Brustad, Conrad Christensen, Oscar Engelstad, Marius Eriksen, Axel Henry Hansen, Peter Hol, Eugen Ingebretsen, Olaf Ingebretsen, Olof Jacobsen, Erling Jensen, Thor Jensen, Frithjof Olsen, Oscar Olstad, Edvin Paulsen, Carl Alfred Pedersen, Paul Pedersen, Rolf Robach, Sigurd Smebye, Torleif Torkildsen

1920 Antwerp T: 3, N: 3, D: 8.26.

	Total Points
1. SWE	1363.833
2. DEN	1324.833
3. BEL	1094.000

1. SWE—Fausto Acke (Padovini), Albert Andersson, K. Arvid Andersson-Holtman, Helge Bäckander, Bengt Bengtsson, Fabion Biörck, Carl-Erik Charpentier, Sture Ericsson, Konrad Granström, Helge Gustafson, Åke Häger, Ture Hedman, Sven Johnson, Sven-Olof Jonsson, Karl Lindahl, Edmund Lindmark, Bengt Mohrberg, Frans Persson, Klas Särner, Curt Sjöberg, Gunnar Söderlindh, John Sörenson, Erik Svensén, Gösta Törner

2. DEN—Johannes Birk, Frede Hansen, Frederik Hansen (Melvang), Kristian Hansen (Bøgesø), Hans Hovgaard Jakobsen, Aage Jørgensen, Alfred Jørgensen [Frökjærgaard], Alfred Jørgensen [Ollerup], Arne Jørgensen, Knud Kirkeløkke, Jens Lambæk, Kristjan Larsen, M. Kristian Madsen (Krogshede), Niels Erik Nielsen, Niels Kristian Nielsen, Dynes Sneptrup Pedersen, Hans Pedersen, Johannes Pedersen, Peder Dorf Pedersen, Rasmus Rasmussen, Hans Christian Sørensen (Drigstrup), Hans Laurids Sørensen, Søren Sørensen, Georg Vest, Aage Walther

3. BEL—Paul Arets, Léon Bronckaert, Léopold Clabots, Jean-Baptiste Claessens, Léon Darrien, Lucien Dehoux, Ernest Deleu, Émile Duboisson, Ernest Dureuil, Joseph Fiems, Marcel Hansen, Louis Henin, Omer Hoffman, Félix Logiest, Charles Maerschalcke, René Paenhuysen, Arnold Pierret, René Pinchart, Gaspard Pirotte, Augustien Pluys, Léopold Son, Édouard Taeymans, Pierre Thiriar, Henri Verhavert

Chapter 15 **Gymnastics (Women)**

All-Around
Side Horse Vault
Asymmetrical (Uneven) Bars
Balance Beam
Floor exercises
Combined Exercises
Rhythmic All-Around
Rhythmic Team
Trampoline
Discontinued Event

KEY TO ABBREVIATIONS
HV = Horse vault
AB = Asymmetrical (Uneven) bars
BB = Balance beam
FE = Floor exercises

Olga Korbut, 1972
In Munich, she captured hearts around the world with her dramatic cycle of success, failure, and success.

ALL-AROUND

1896–1948 not held

1952 Helsinki C: 134, N: 18, D: 7.23.

		HV		AB		BB		FE		TOTAL PTS.
1. Maria Gorochovskia	SOV/UKR	19.19	2	19.26	2	19.13	2	19.2	2	76.78
2. Nina Bocharova	SOV/UKR	19.03	6	18.99	4	19.22	1	18.7	10	75.94
3. Margit Korondi	HUN	18.4	22	19.4	1	19.02	3	19.0	3	75.82
4. Galina Minaicheva	SOV/RUS	19.16	3	18.89	8	18.66	10	18.96	6	75.67
5. Galina Urbanovich	SOV/RUS	19.1	5	18.62	12	18.93	5	18.99	4	75.64
6. Ágnes Keleti	HUN	18.1	41	19.16	3	18.96	4	19.36	1	75.58
7. Pelageya Danilova	SOV/RUS	18.62	12	18.99	7	18.76	9	18.6	11	75.03
8. Galina Shamrai	SOV/UZB	18.93	7	18.39	23	18.79	8	18.86	8	74.97

1956 Melbourne C: 65, N: 15, D: 12.7.

		HV		AB		BB		FE		TOTAL PTS.
1. Larysa Latynina	SOV/UKR	18.833	1	18.833	2	18.533	4	18.733	1	74.933
2. Ágnes Keleti	HUN	18.133	23	18.966	1	18.8	1	18.733	1	74.633
3. Sofia Muratova	SOV/RUS	18.666	5	18.8	3	18.433	10	18.566	4	74.466
4. Elena Leuştean	ROM	18.633	6	18.533	10	18.5	6	18.7	3	74.366
4. Olga Tass	HUN	18.733	3	18.633	6	18.466	7	18.533	7	74.366
6. Tamara Manina	SOV/RUS	18.8	2	18.333	16	18.633	2	18.466	9	74.233
7. Eva Bosáková (Věchtová	CZE	18.166	22	18.733	4	18.633	2	18.566	4	74.1
8. Helena Rakoczy	POL	18.5	7	18.7	5	18.133	16	18.366	14	73.7

The 1956 competition was dominated by 35-year-old Ágnes Keleti and 21-year-old Larysa Latynina. Keleti captured gold medals on three of the four apparatuses, but a lapse on the vault lost her the All-Around title to Latynina, a Ukrainian from Kherson. In 1952 and 1956 Keleti won a total of ten Olympic medals: five gold, three silver, and two bronze. Keleti, who was Jewish, had survived the Holocaust by buying the papers of a young Christian woman and lived in a small village working as a maid until World War II was over. After the 1956 Games, she decided not to return to Hungary, as did half of the Hungarian delegation. Instead she stayed in Australia and eventually settled in Israel.

1960 Rome C: 124, N: 27, D: 9.8.

		HV		AB		BB		FE		TOTAL PTS.
1. Larysa Latynina	SOV/UKR	18.966	3	19.433	2	19.066	3	19.566	1	77.031
2. Sofia Muratova	SOV/RUS	19.032	2	19.299	3	19.132	2	19.233	4	76.696
3. Polina Astakhova	SOV/UKR	18.766	4	19.633	1	18.233	28	19.532	2	76.164
4. Marharyta Nikolayeva	SOV/UKR	19.1	1	18.799	20	18.966	4	18.966	15	75.831
5. Sonia Iovan	ROM	18.732	6	19.266	4	18.6	11	19.199	5	75.797
6. Keiko Ikeda (Tanaka	JPN	18.432	18	19.266	4	18.932	5	19.066	12	75.696
7. Lidiya Ivanova (Kalinina	SOV/RUS	18.566	8	19.053	7	18.699	8	19.133	7	75.431
8. Věra Čáslavská	CZE	18.699	7	18.733	21	18.766	6	19.1	9	75.298

1964 Tokyo C: 86, N: 24, D: 10.21.

		HV		AB		BB		FE		TOTAL PTS.
1. Věra Čáslavská	CZE	19.5	1	19.432	1	19.366	1	19.266	3	77.564
2. Larysa Latynina	SOV/UKR	19.166	5	19.133	4	19.233	3	19.466	1	76.998
3. Polina Astakhova	SOV/UKR	19.032	7	19.333	2	19.2	5	19.4	2	76.965
4. Birgit Radochla	GDR	19.366	2	18.933	13	18.933	9	19.199	5	76.431
5. Hana Růžičková	CZE	18.866	18	19.033	7	19.232	4	18.966	10	76.097
6. Keiko Ikeda (Tanaka	JPN	18.999	9	18.766	16	19.166	6	19.1	7	76.031
7. Toshiko Aihara (Shirasu	JPN	19.233	3	19.099	5	18.599	29	19.066	8	75.997
8. Yelena Volchetskaya	SOV/BLR	19.233	3	18.633	24	18.966	7	18.933	13	75.765

Latynina collected six more Olympic medals to bring her career total to an unprecedented 18: nine gold, five silver, and four bronze. But in Tokyo she lost the All-Around title to a new star, Věra Čáslavská, a 22-year-old secretary from Prague. Latynina served as coach of the Soviet team from 1967 until 1977 when she was dismissed because, despite the fact that the Soviet women continued to win team titles, no Soviet gymnast could individually defeat Nadia Comăneci.

1968 Mexico City C: 101, N: 24, D: 10.23.

		HV		AB		BB		FE		TOTAL PTS.
1. Věra Čáslavská	CZE	19.75	1	19.5	1	19.45	2	19.55	2	78.25
2. Zinaida Voronina	SOV/RUS	19.4	5	19.25	4	18.8	15	19.4	4	76.85
3. Natalya Kuchinskaya	SOV/RUS	19.45	3	18.1	37	19.6	1	19.6	1	76.75
4. Larissa Petrik	SOV/BLR	19.2	8	18.95	11	19.0	5	19.55	2	76.7
4. Erika Zuchold	GDR	19.65	2	19.05	6	19.0	5	19.0	8	76.7
6. Karin Janz	GDR	19.2	8	19.3	2	19.05	4	19.0	8	76.55
7. Olga Karasyova	SOV/RUS	19.15	10	19.0	7	18.7	18	19.15	5	76.0
7. Bohumila Řimnáčová	CZE	18.7	24	19.3	2	18.85	10	19.15	5	76.0

The undisputed heroine of the Mexico City Olympics was defending All-Around champion Věra Čáslavská. In April 1968, Čáslavská had signed the "Manifesto of 2000 Words," which rejected Soviet involvement in Czechoslovakia. On August 21, she was at a training camp in Moravia when Soviet tanks rolled into Prague. Warned by friends that she was in danger of arrest, Čáslavská fled to the small town of Šumperk in the Jeseníky Mountains. With the Olympics only two months away, Čáslavská was in hiding, keeping in shape by swinging from tree limbs and practicing her floor exercise in a meadow. After three weeks, the government consented to let her join the rest of the Czechoslovak team in Mexico.

After one of Čáslavská's performances on the balance beam received a 9.6, the audience spent ten minutes booing, howling, and chanting "Ver-a, Ver-a," until finally her mark was upped to 9.8. The last performer in the final event, Čáslavská thrilled her admirers by performing her floor exercise to the tune of "The Mexican Hat Dance." She eventually earned four gold medals and two silver to add to the three gold and two silver she had won four years earlier in Tokyo. In the floor exercises she shared first place with Larissa Petrik of the Soviet Union, which meant that the two women stood together on the top platform at the medal ceremony and listened first to Czechoslovakia's national anthem and then to the USSR's. Political observers noted that Čáslavská bowed her head and turned away during the playing of the Soviet anthem. Twenty-four hours later Čáslavská topped off her week by marrying Czechoslovak 1500-meter champion Josef Odlozil. After a civil ceremony at the Czechoslovakian ambassador's house, the happy couple pushed their way through a mob of 10,000 people to get to the altar of the Roman Catholic church in Xocalo Square. The couple divorced in 1992. The following year, their teenage son, Martin, killed Odlozil during a fight at a pub.

Vera Čáslavská's personal odyssey in the years after her Olympic triumphs mirrored the political fortunes of her nation. Heroine of Mexico City she may have been, but the Communist authorities did not forget her public support of the "Manifesto of 2000 Words." They made absolutely sure that she would remain unemployed unless she repudiated the Manifesto. She refused. Every year, on January 3, Čáslavská appeared at the office of Antonin Himmel, the Czechoslovak sports minister, and asked for a coaching job with the national team. Every year he turned her down. Realizing that creative tactics were needed, she showed up for her 1975 appointment with a surprise under her coat. Fifteen years later she told *The New York Times* that she wore "an aerobics suit, high in the neck, very tight." When interviewed by France's *L'Equipe Magazine*, Čáslavská described her outfit as "an extremely low-cut T-shirt." Whatever the details, she explained to Himmel and twenty of his associates that she was dressed for work and would not leave until she was given a team to coach. Čáslavská was assigned to a local club on the condition that she not leave the country. Visiting journalists who asked for her were told that she was not available.

Then, in 1979, the president of Mexico, José López Portillo, asked if Čáslavská could come to Mexico and coach the national team. The Czechoslovakian government was desperate for access to Mexican oil and so Čáslavská was allowed to leave the country for the first time in eleven years. However, when she returned to Prague in 1981, she was again forbidden from meeting foreign visitors. Finally, in 1985, the wall around Čáslavská began to crack when IOC president Juan Antonio Samaranch insisted on presenting an award to Čáslavská and fellow Olympic champion and "2000 Words" signer Emil Zátopek.

Upon the collapse of the Communist regime in November 1989, Čáslavská's situation changed dramatically. Her 21-year-old defiance of the hated Communist government was suddenly an asset, as was her friendship with author Vaclav Havel, who was elected president of the new government. Čáslavská was appointed president of the Czech National Olympic Committee and later became a member of the International Olympic Committee. Cáslavská's life took another downward turn in 1997, after she convinced President Havel to pardon her son. The resultant public uproar led Cáslavská to resign her Olympic posts, withdraw from public life and take up life in a psychiatric home.

Věra Čáslavská and Josef Odlozil, 1968
The couple married during the Games at the home of the Czechoslovakian ambassador to Mexico.

At the time of the Mexico City Games, Zina Voronina, who finished second to Čáslavská in 1968, was married to the Soviet Union's leading gymnast, Mikhail Voronin. Between them they won ten medals at the 1968 Olympics. Voronina gave birth to a son, but returned to competition in time to win an All-Around bronze medal at the 1970 world championships. She was given a job as a coach but, plagued by alcoholism and an inablility to work with children, she was fired. Her husband divorced her and she lost custody of her son. While her 1968 teammmates were moving on to comfortable post-athletic lives, Zina Voronina was a manual laborer at a mechanical foundry. Eventually she lost this job too because of alcoholism.

1972 Munich C: 118, N: 23, D: 8.30.

		HV		AB		BB		FE		TOTAL PTS.
1. Lyudmila Turischeva	SOV/RUS	19.3	1	19.275	3	18.8	5	19.65	1	77.025
2. Karin Janz	GDR	19.275	2	19.475	1	18.825	4	19.3	3	76.875
3. Tamara Lazakovich	SOV/BLR	19.0	6	19.225	4	19.325	1	19.3	3	76.85
4. Erika Zuchold	GDR	19.275	2	19.30	2	18.8	5	19.075	6	76.45
5. Lyubov Burda	SOV/RUS	19.075	5	18.875	8	18.675	8	19.15	5	75.775
6. Angelika Hellmann	GDR	18.925	7	19.15	5	18.425	14	19.05	7	75.55
7. Olga Korbut	SOV/BLR	19.175	4	17.15	35	19.3	2	19.475	2	75.1
8. Elvira Saadi	SOV/UZB	18.8	9	18.7	15	18.625	10	18.95	9	75.075

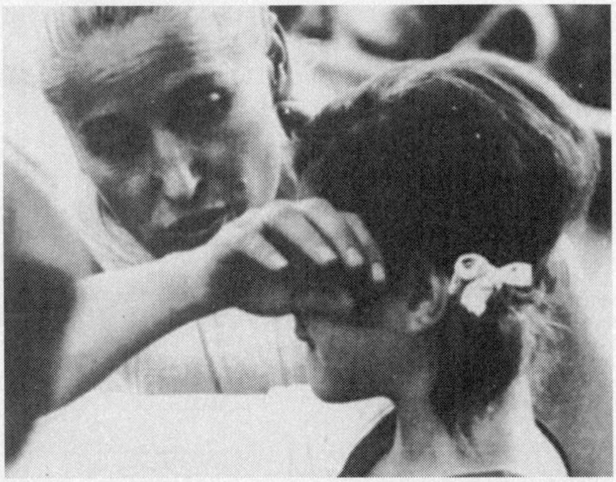

Věra Čáslavská had played a major role in popularizing women's gymnastics, but the real turning point came at the 1972 Munich Olympics. The All-Around championship was won by 19-year-old world champion Lyudmila Turischeva, and the silver medal went to Karin Janz of Berlin, who also took first place on the horse vault and the uneven parallel bars. But it was neither of these capable young women who focused the attention of the world on gymnastics. Instead it was the seventh-place finisher a 4-foot 11-inch, 85-pound 17-year-old from Grodno in Belarus—Olga Korbut.

Korbut was trained by the eccentric and sometimes physically abusive Renald Knysh, who kept a card file on all the young married couples in Grodno, particularly those whom he thought might produce future gymnasts. During the team competition Korbut caught the public's eye with a spectacular routine on the uneven parallel bars. By the end of the day it looked as if she had a good chance of pulling an upset and depriving Turischeva of the All-Around championship. This was the first time Korbut had competed in a major international event and she was unprepared for her sudden popularity. The crowd chanted "Olga" and people asked for her autograph. "It was amazing," she later recalled in her 1992 autobiography, *My Story*. "One day, I was nobody, and the next day, I was a *star*. It was almost more than I could take in." Two days later the individual final began and halfway through, Korbut moved into first place. But then disaster struck.

The crowd watched in silence as she started her performance on the uneven bars. She scuffed her feet on the mat as she mounted, then slipped off the bars during a later move; finally, she missed a simple kip to remount. The judges gave her a 7.5, and she was effectively eliminated from the race for All-Around champion. She returned to her seat to weep with disappointment.

Olga Korbut, 1972

Korbut is comforted by her coach in Munich after erring in the All-Around competition. A day later, she stood with her gold medal after the floor excercises with teammates Lyudmila Turischeva (left) and Tamara Lazakovich (right).

Twenty hours later Olga Korbut was back in the arena to compete for the championships on the four individual apparatuses. With hundreds of millions of people all over the world watching, Olga regained her form, finished second to Karin Janz on the uneven parallel bars, and won the gold medal for both the balance beam and the floor exercises. Even in the United States, with its widespread antipathy to the USSR, little Olga Korbut's dramatic cycle of success, failure, and success captured the national imagination. However, because the Soviet team was kept completely isolated, Olga herself was unaware of how popular she had become outside the arena itself. She would find out soon enough. When she returned to the Olympic Village she discovered that her room was filled with flowers, letters, and telegrams. The messages were in Russian, English, German, French, and Japanese. When she went for a walk in Munich, public buses stopped so that the riders could get out and ask for her autograph. When she went shopping for gifts to bring back to her family, she found it impossible to spend any money because all the shopkeepers insisted that she take whatever she wanted free of charge. Finally she had to buy a wig and a wide-brimmed hat to wear as a disguise in order to gain a bit of peace. When she returned home to Grodno she received so much fan mail—20,000 letters in one year—that the post office had to assign a special clerk to sort out her mail.

Bronze medal winner Tamara Lazakovich later spent several years in prison after being convicted of larceny. Lazakovich, who would sometimes drink a bottle of cognac the night before a competition, died of alcoholism in November 1992.

1976 Montreal C: 86, N: 18, D: 7.21.

		HV		AB		BB		FE		TOTAL PTS.
1. Nadia Comăneci	ROM	19.625	4	20.0	1	19.95	1	19.7	3	79.275
2. Nelli Kim	SOV/KAZ	19.85	1	19.725	2	19.3	5	19.8	2	78.675
3. Lyudmila Turischeva	SOV/RUS	19.75	2	19.575	9	19.475	3	19.825	1	78.625
4. Teodora Ungureanu	ROM	19.425	7	19.8	2	19.7	2	19.45	5	78.375
5. Olga Korbut	SOV/BLR	19.525	6	19.8	2	19.325	4	19.375	6	78.025
6. Gitta Escher	GDR	19.65	3	19.625	8	19.125	7	19.35	8	77.75
7. Márta Egervári	HUN	19.6	5	19.775	4	18.725	10	19.225	9	77.325
8. Marion Kische	GDR	19.325	10	19.7	6	18.55	14	19.375	6	76.95

Soviet women's gymnastics went through a period of turmoil and crisis between 1972 and 1976. Olga Korbut never did defeat Lyudmila Turischeva, and it must have been confusing, at the very least, to the Soviet champion to realize that no matter how successful she was, she could never achieve Olga's popularity. When the Soviet team made an exhibition tour of the United States, the leader of the group was Lyudmila Turischeva and the highlighted performer was their up-and-coming star Nelli Kim. But Americans showed little interest in Turischeva and Kim; instead they turned out by the thousands to see Olga Korbut, the Munchkin of Munich. It didn't take long for Olga to realize that huge profits were being made on her popularity, and she became more demanding of rewards for herself.

Back home, however, where heroes were measured by the number of medals they won and by their willingness to follow orders and be team players, Olga Korbut had become a thorn in the side of the Soviet bureaucracy. The situation was also hard on Turischeva, who had always toed the party line and yet was forced to play second fiddle to an inferior gymnast. As the winner of the 1976 USSR Olympic trials, Korbut even replaced Turischeva as team captain in Montreal.

However, the real threat to the competitive success of the Soviet team came not from internal dissension, but from a 4-foot 11-inch Romanian named Nadia Comăneci. Born in Onesti, Moldova, Nadia had been trained as a gymnast since the age of 6. In 1975 she dethroned her idol, five-time European champion Turischeva. At Montreal she was considered a slight favorite to take the All-Around championship even though she was only 14 years old. During the team competition she made Olympic history by receiving the first perfect scores of ten for her performances on the uneven bars and the balance beam. Before the Olympics were over, Nadia had been awarded seven 10s, while Nelli Kim had earned two perfect scores for her vault and floor exercise. Despite their superb performances, Korbut and Turischeva were left with tears of disappointment. Turischeva, in fact, won four medals, to bring her Olympic totals to four gold, two silver, and three bronze.

Nadia Comăneci did not have the charisma of Olga Korbut, but she was an incredible athlete who was absolutely unafraid of dangerous moves and seemingly oblivious to the millions of people watching her. The most difficult part of the Olympics for Nadia was the obligatory press conferences. Many journalists seemed to forget her age. When one asked what her greatest wish was, she replied, "I want to go home." When another asked if she had plans for retirement, Nadia reminded him, "I'm only 14."

In an attempt to lessen the dominance of the nations strongest in gymnastics, a ruling had been passed prior to the Olympics that only three gymnasts from each country could compete in the final round of 36. The absurdity of this decision was shown when Elvira Saadi, who had achieved the seventh highest score during the individual competitions, was eliminated because she was the fourth-best Soviet performer, while Monique Bolleboom of Holland was allowed to continue even though she ranked 62nd out of 86. Not surprisingly, Bolleboom finished last in the final round.

As for Olga Korbut, she married a famous Byelorussian singer and settled down as a housewife. Soviet sports officials punished her for her independent ways by not informing her of the frequent invitations she received to visit the United States and other Western nations. In 1986 she finally moved to the United States and became a coach. In the 1990s, at a time when many were complaining that gymnastics coaches were too hard on their pupils, Korbut complained that her American students were too spoiled to put in the hard work necessary to become champions. Indeed, Korbut, despite the affection that Americans had for her, had a great deal of trouble adapting to her new environment. In 2002 she was arrested for shoplifting $19.35 worth of food at a supermarket in Norcross, Georgia, and a couple months later, at the age of 47, she appeared on "Celebrity Boxing."

1980 Moscow C: 62, N: 16, D: 7.24.

		HV		AB		BB		FE		TOTAL PTS.
1. Yelena Davydova	SOV/RUS	19.8	1	19.80	3	19.7	5	19.85	3	79.15
2. Nadia Comăneci	ROM	19.675	4	19.725	6	19.8	1	19.875	1	79.075
2. Maxi Gnauck	GDR	19.625	5	19.925	1	19.65	6	19.875	1	79.075
4. Natalya Shaposhnikova	SOV/RUS	19.8	1	19.775	4	19.775	3	19.675	6	79.025
5. Nelli Kim	SOV/BLR	19.525	10	19.725	6	19.8	1	19.375	13	78.425
6. Emilia Eberle	ROM	19.4	14	19.85	2	19.3	11	19.85	3	78.4
7. Rodica Dunka	ROM	19.6	6	19.35	14	19.75	4	19.65	7	78.35
8. Steffi Kräker	GDR	19.725	3	19.775	4	19.175	12	19.525	10	78.2

The favorite in 1980 was defending world champion Yelena Mukhina of the USSR. However, sixteen days before the opening of the Moscow Olympics, Mukhina was practicing her floor exercise when she missed a one-and-a-half-turn salto with a 540-degree twist and broke her spine. Mukhina was paralyzed from the neck down. She was unable even to speak for six months.

In Mukhina's absence the contest for All-Around champion came down to the final apparatus. Performing fourth for the Soviet team, the 4-foot 10-inch (1.47-meter) 18-year-old Davydova was not expected to qualify for any final events, and at best was thought to be in the running for the All-Around bronze medal. In the final rotation, Maxi Gnauck was second among the nine gymnasts on the vault, but lost the lead after scoring only 9.70. Performing seventh on the bars, Davydova delivered a bold, confident routine. Her score, 9.95, put her in first place and gave her a lead that only Comăneci could hope to overtake, and then only if she also scored 9.95 on her final beam routine. The last time Comăneci had scored that high on the beam in an All-Around final was at the 1976 Olympics. Her average score was closer to 9.75.

With the arena in complete silence, Nadia went through an impressive routine with only two small errors, including a step back on landing. The 1980

Nadia Comăneci, 1980
The Romanian was already a veteran at the age of 18.

US Olympic book described the routine as "good but not great." The real controversy, however, began when the scores were being tallied. The Romanian head judge, Maria Simionescu, a friend of Comăneci's since 1969, refused to accept the final result and tried to get three other judges to increase their scores. The judges argued for 28 minutes before overruling Simionescu's complaint. Even then she refused to punch the score into the computer. A representative of the Moscow Organizing Committee had to do it while Simionescu looked on in rage. Finally Nadia's score flashed on the computer: 9.85. Davydova had won the gold medal.

These Olympics weren't a total loss for Comăneci, however. The next day she took first place in the beam and the floor exercise events, giving her an Olympic total of five gold medals, three silver and one bronze. Nineteen-eighty marked the first time that Soviet gymnasts failed to earn at least two of the medals in the All-Around event.

1984 Los Angeles C: 65, N: 16, D: 8.3.

		HV		AB		BB		FE		TOTAL PTS.
1. Mary Lou Retton	USA	19.95	1	19.7	4	19.6	3	19.925	1	79.175
2. Ecaterina Szabó	ROM	19.85	2	19.5	8	19.85	1	19.925	1	79.125
3. Simona Păuca	ROM	19.625	6	19.575	6	19.85	1	19.625	5	78.675
4. Julianne McNamara	USA	19.725	3	19.95	1	19.075	13	19.65	4	78.4
5. Laura Cutina	ROM	19.7	4	19.725	3	19.125	11	19.75	3	78.3
6. Ma Yanhong	CHN	19.3	15	19.95	1	19.55	4	19.05	13	77.85
7. Zhou Ping	CHN	19.525	7	19.4	9	19.175	10	19.375	8	77.775
8. Chen Yongyan	CHN	19.525	7	19.275	11	19.5	5	19.425	7	77.725

Mary Lou Retton, 1984
Retton became the first American to win the All-Around gold medal.

Ever since Olga Korbut had melted American hearts in 1972, US sports fans had wondered when a homegrown female gymnastics star would emerge. Considering that no American woman had ever won an individual Olympics gymnastics medal, the prospects did not look bright. However, the Soviet boycott of 1984 opened the door—and in walked a 16-year-old from Fairmont, West Virginia, named Mary Lou Retton. At 4 feet 8¾ inches and weighing 94 pounds, the powerful Italian-American represented a new breed of female gymnast—more muscular and athletic.

Retton had never taken part in a major international tournament before the Olympics, having missed the 1983 world championships because of a wrist injury. She almost missed the Olympics as well when she incurred a knee injury less than six weeks before the Games began. Torn cartilage removed during arthroscopic surgery saved the day.

In Los Angeles the battle for the All-Around gold medal developed into a tight contest between Retton and the Romanian champion Kati Szabó. With two rotations to go, Szabó led by .15 of a point. But Retton rose to the occasion, earning 10s for the floor exercise and the vault, and ensuring her place in sports history books, as well as in the pantheon of US cultural heroes. Aspiring gymnasts should take heart from the story of Retton's first competition when she was still a little girl. Like so many little girls around the world, Mary Lou watched Nadia Comăneci score her history-making 10s in 1976. Retton noticed that the scoreboard, unprepared for Comăneci's perfection, had registered "1.0" rather than "10.0." After performing on the first apparatus in her first meet (the uneven bars), 8-year-old Mary Lou Retton jumped with joy when the scoreboard flashed "1.0." Alas, it really was a 1.0. However, she refused to give up on gymnastics until her 1.0s turned to genuine 10.0s.

1988 Seoul C: 90, N: 23, D: 9.23.

		HV		AB		BB		FE		TOTAL PTS.
1. Yelena Shushunova	SOV/RUS	20.0	1	19.862	4	19.85	1	19.95	1	79.662
2. Daniela Silivaş	ROM	19.85	3	20.0	1	19.837	2	19.95	1	79.637
3. Svetlana Boginskaya	SOV/BLR	19.887	2	19.862	4	19.837	2	19.812	4	79.4
4. Gabriela Potorac	ROM	19.687	7	19.737	7	19.837	2	19.775	7	79.037
5. Natalija Lascenova	SOV/LAT	19.725	5	19.662	14	19.687	6	19.8	5	78.875
6. Aurelia Dobre	ROM	19.612	11	19.762	6	19.787	5	19.65	14	78.812
7. Dörte Thümmler	GDR	19.7	6	19.925	2	19.325	19	19.85	3	78.8
8. Dagmar Kersten	GDR	19.8	4	19.887	3	19.325	19	19.762	9	78.775

With two apparatuses left in the final, Silivaş led Shushunova by the slim margin of .025 of a point. The deficiencies in gymnastics judging quickly became apparent. Shushunova performed a flawless floor exercise and was awarded a perfect 10.0. Silivaş followed her onto the mat and gave an even better performance. But because Shushunova had already received the highest possible score, Silivaş had to settle for a tie despite her superiority. This meant that the competition came down to the final apparatus: the vault. Silivaş hopped slightly on landing. Although Soviet judge Nelli Kim gave her a scandalously low 9.8, Silivaş' total score was 9.95. Still, this left the door open for Shushunova. Like Mary Lou Retton four years earlier, if she could achieve a 10.0, she would win the All-Around title. Shushunova's vault, a full-twisting Yurchenko, was high and perfect and the gold was hers. However, like Los Angeles silver-medalist Kati Szabó, Silivaş came back two days later to win three of the four apparatus finals, while Shushunova, like Retton, won none.

Women's gymnastics is a breeding ground for media stars: Olga Korbut, Nadia Comăneci, Mary Lou Retton. Next in line for megastardom was the 1987 world champion, Aurelia Dobre of Romania. Besides being the best female gymnast in the world, she was charming, graceful and unusually beautiful. Only 14 years old at the time she won the world championship, Dobre was on track to become a bigger celebrity than her predecessors. But a knee injury forced her to submit to three operations, and the pressure to produce a winner led her coaches to ignore the advice of doctors and make her resume training before she was fully recovered. In Seoul she was already only a shadow of her former self. She placed sixth in the All-Around competition, went home without an individual medal and was ignored by the television cameras of the world. Three years later, however, Aurelia Dobre did earn a place in sports history when she became the first Olympic athlete to appear nude in *Playboy* magazine—even if it was only in the Dutch edition.

1992 Barcelona C: 92, N: 24, D: 7.30.

		HV		AB		BB		FE		TOTAL PTS.
1. Tatyana Gutsu	UKR	9.95	5	9.95	1	9.912	2	9.925	3	39.737
2. Shannon Miller	USA	9.975	1	9.925	2	9.925	1	9.9	7	39.725
3. Lavinia Miloşovici	ROM	9.975	1	9.9	4	9.85	9	9.962	1	39.687
4. Christina Bontaş	ROM	9.95	5	9.862	11	9.9	5	9.962	1	39.674
5. Svetlana Boginskaya	BLR	9.962	3	9.887	7	9.912	2	9.912	4	39.673
6. Gina Gogean	ROM	9.95	5	9.862	11	9.9	5	9.912	4	39.624
7. Tetiana Lysenko	UKR	9.962	3	9.9	4	9.875	7	9.8	18	39.537
8. Henrietta Ónodi	HUN	9.95	5	9.875	10	9.712	20	9.912	4	39.449

In the press, the women's individual All-Around was billed as a showdown between 1989 world champion Svetlana Boginskaya of Belarus and 1991 world champion Kim Zmeskal of the United States. Gymnastics aficionados knew better—not since Lyudmila Turischeva in 1972 had a world champion gone on to win at the Olympics. Tatyana Gutsu of Odessa, on the other hand, was peaking at the right time. The 15-year-old with white hair won the European Championship only two months before the Olympic competition. But in Barcelona, Gutsu fell off the beam during the team optionals and it looked like her chance for gold was finished. Although she qualified in ninth place, only three gymnasts from each country were allowed to advance to the final, and three of the eight ahead of Gutsu were also from the Unified Team of ex-Soviet republics. Not to worry—Unified Team officials announced that 15-year-old Roza Galiyeva of Uzbekistan had conveniently aggravated a knee injury, and overnight Gutsu was back in the hunt.

With three rotations completed in the final and only one to go, Gutsu and Lavinia Miloşovici were tied for first place with 29.787 points. Boginskaya was third with 29.761, and Shannon Miller, who looked so much like Gutsu that the two could have been sisters, was fourth with 29.750. The advantage was with Gutsu and Miller because they would perform on the high-scoring side horse while Miloşovici was on the bars and Boginskaya on the beam. Sure enough, it came down to the vaulters. Miller hit a beautiful Yurchenko-full and earned a 9.975. This meant that Gutsu, performing a full-twisting Yurchenko, needed a 9.939 to beat her. She hopped after landing her first vault and received a 9.25. And so, as in 1984 and 1988, the gold medal came down to one gymnast having to hit her vault. On her second attempt, Gutsu stuck her landing and was rewarded with a 9.5. By placing second, Shannon Miller became the first female United States gymnast to earn a silver medal in a non-boycotted Olympics.

Tatyana Gutsu added a silver on the uneven bars and a bronze for floor exercises, but for the fourth straight time the winner of the All-Around championship failed to earn a single gold in the apparatus finals. As a reward for winning the All-Around gold medal, Gutsu was given $3000. She turned over half of it to Roza Galiyeva.

1996 Atlanta C: 104, C: 28, D: 7.25.

		HV		AB		BB		FE		TOTAL PTS.
1. Lilia Podkopayeva	UKR	9.781	3	9.8	2	9.787	7	9.887	1	39.255
2. Gina Gogean	ROM	9.775	4	9.7	11	9.8	5	9.8	3	39.075
3. Simona Amanar	ROM	9.843	1	9.762	5	9.725	10	9.737	7	39.067
3. Lavinia Miloşovici	ROM	9.743	5	9.737	9	9.775	9	9.812	2	39.067
5. Mo Huilan	CHN	9.799	2	9.8	2	9.8	5	9.65	13	39.049
6. Dina Kochetkova	RUS	9.581	20	9.787	4	9.825	2	9.787	4	38.98
7. Rozalya Galiyeva	RUS	9.681	13	9.762	5	9.825	2	9.637	15	38.905
8. Shannon Miller	USA	9.724	6	9.75	8	9.862	1	9.475	29	38.811

Lilia Podkopayeva was a 5-year-old in Dovetsk, Ukraine, (home of "Serhei Bubka, coal mines and roses") when her grandmother introduced her to gymnastics. By 1995 Podkopayeva was world All-Around champion. Her grandmother died three weeks before the Olympics. Podkopayeva was used to playing to the crowd, but in Atlanta she discovered that the 32,000 pro-US spectators, although not openly hostile (like the 1980 Russian crowds), were indifferent to foreign competitors. Although the 17-year-old Podkopayeva initially found this unnerving, by the day of the individual event, she had learned to ignore the spectators and play to the judges instead.

After three rotations, and with only one remaining, there were still six gymnasts in contention for the medals. Mo Huilan and Dina Kochetkova were tied for first place with 29.399 points. Podkopayeva was third at 29.368. Then came three Romanians. Gina Gogean, who had undergone an appendectory less than six weeks before the competition began, was fourth with 29.3 points. Fifth was 1992 bronze medalist Lavinia Miloşovici (29.255) and sixth Simona Amanar (29.224). As the fourth highest scoring Romanian in the team competition, Amanar had not automatically qualified for the individual final. But team coach Octavien Belu took advantage of a new rule allowing teams to switch entrants and replaced Alexandra Marinescu with Amanar.

Kochetkova, Gogean and Amanar performed on the vault while Mo, Podkopayeva and Miloşovici moved to floor exercises. Kochetkova's faulty jumps dropped her out of the medals. Podkopayeva, performing a routine choreographed by prima ballerina Svetlana Dubova, earned a 9.887, the highest score by any gymnast on any apparatus. It was left to Mo to try to match Podkopayeva, but she bounced way out of bounds after a 2½ twist to punch front and the judges dropped her score so low that she ended up in fifth place.

Lilia Podkopayeva was the first defending world champion to win an Olympic title since Lyudmila Turischeva in 1972.

2000 Sydney C: 36, N: 15, D: 9.21.

		HV		AB		BB		FE		TOTAL PTS.
1. Simona Amanar	ROM	9.656	4	9.512	23	9.662	8	9.812	3	38.642
2. Maria Olaru	ROM	9.656	5	9.600	18	9.700	7	9.625	11	38.581
3. Xuan Liu	CHN	9.331	19	9.725	5	9.750	4	9.612	12	38.418
4. Yekaterina Lobaznyuk	RUS	9.693	3	9.700	9	9.425	13	9.575	13	38.393
5. Yun Yang	CHN	9.531	9	9.787	2	9.287	17	9.700	6	38.305
6. Yelena Zamoldchikova	RUS	9.731	1	9.725	6	9.700	6	9.122	29	38.268
7. Olha Roshchupkina	UKR	9.368	16	9.725	7	9.750	4	9.362	19	38.205
8. Lisa Skinner	AUS	9.168	29	9.650	12	9.625	9	9.750	4	38.193

DISQ (Drugs): Andreea Răducan (ROM) 38.893

Svetlana Khorkina entered the 2000 Olympics as the queen of international gymnastics. She had won the 1997 world championship, the 1998 European championship and, four months before the Olympics, she successfully defended her European championship. In addition, she had enhanced her image by appearing topless, at the age of 18, in the November 1997 issue of the Russian edition of *Playboy*. In Sydney, Khorkina led the qualification round, with 16-year-old Andreea Răducan second and fellow Romanian Simona Amanar third.

Khorkina began the final with the floor exercise and immediately took the lead with a 9.812, a floor exercise score that would ultimately be matched only by Amanar. Khorkina moved on to the vault and suddenly disaster struck. Khorkina had placed third on the vault in the qualifying round, but she appeared to mistime her leap and she ended up on her knees. Stunned, she missed the landing of her second vault too. Khorkina's third apparatus was her specialty, the uneven bars. Distraught, she fell off the bars at the exact point at which she had fallen during the team competition. Unbeknownst to Khorkina, there was confusion and controversy brewing back at the vault. Khorkina was only one of many gymnasts who had unexpectedly fallen during the vault. Annika Reeder of Great Britain actually had to be taken away in a wheelchair. During the warm-ups for the third rotation, 16-year-old Allana Slater of Australia noticed that there was something wrong with the height of the horse. "I thought it was too low," she explained. "Either that or I've grown quite a bit in the last two days." She told her coach, who told the officials, who measured the horse and discovered that, sure enough, it was 5 centimeters (1.97 inches) too low. It seemed that when the apparatus was shifted from the men's event to the women's, the workmen had missset the height and none of the Australian officials in charge of the competition had noticed. The eighteen gymnasts who had already vaulted were given the opportunity to revault, but for Khorkina it was too late because she had already recorded a second low score on the uneven bars.

Before the final, Maria Olaru of Romania had predicted that the medals would go to Răducan, Amanar and Olaru herself, in that order, and that was exactly what happened . . . or so it seemed. At 1.48 meters (4 feet 10 inches) and 37 kilograms (82 pounds), tiny Andreea Răducan was a popular champion, Romania's first all-around winner since Nadia Comăneci. But four days later, the gymnastics world was hit by a bombshell: Răducan had tested positive for a prohibited substance, pseudoephedrine. The Romanians claimed that their team doctor, Ioachim Oană, had given Răducan a cold medicine named Nurofen and that she was unaware that she had taken anything improper. This was probably true, but Oană had been around for a long time (since the days of Comăneci) and it was hard to imagine that he did not know what he was doing. Răducan was disqualified, although she was allowed to keep the medals she won in other events. Oană was banned for four years. Amanar ended up with her third career gold medal although, back in Romania, she presented this particular one to Andreea Răducan.

2004 Athens C: 98, N: 31, D: 8.19.

		HV		AB		BB		FE		TOTAL PTS.
1. Carly Patterson	USA	9.375	4	9.575	7	9.725	1	9.712	1	38.387
2. Svetlana Khorkina	RUS	9.462	1	9.725	1	9.462	4	9.562	5	38.211
3. Nan Zhang	CHN	9.325	6	9.462	15	9.662	2	9.600	3	38.049
4. Anna Pavlova	RUS	9.425	2	9.337	18	9.650	3	9.612	2	38.024
5. Nicoleta Daniela Şofronie	ROM	9.412	3	9.637	4	9.362	6	9.537	6	37.948
6. Irina Yarotska	UKR	9.200	14	9.650	3	9.400	5	9.437	9	37.687
7. Marine Debauve	FRA	9.162	18	9.512	12	9.262	8	9.425	10	37.361
8. Elena Gómez Servera	SPA	9.150	19	9.525	11	9.162	10	9.462	8	37.299

The favorite in the event was five-time Olympic medalist and five-time world champion Svetlana Khorkina. Despite two gold medals in the uneven bars and the 2003 all-around world championship title, the 25-year-old Khorkina had never won an Olympic all-around gold. In Sydney, she crashed when officials mistakenly set the vault too low and she declined to retake the vault when the error was discovered. In Athens, Khorkina's main competition came from 16-year-old Carly Patterson, of Allen, Texas, who finished behind Khorkina at the 2003 world championships. Patterson was the top qualifier with a total score of 38.337 points. Khorkina, who qualified in fifth with 37.836 points, had widely varied results, including the top score of the qualification round, 9.750 in the uneven bars, as well as a poor 9.137 on the balance beam.

In the final, Khorkina took an early lead after the vault, while Patterson placed fourth. Khorkina solidified her lead with a solid performance on the uneven bars, her strongest apparatus, to put herself 0.138 points ahead of Daniela Şofronie. Patterson made her move in the third event, the balance beam, sticking her landing to score 9.725. Both Şofronie and Khorkina wobbled in their balance beam routines, placing sixth and fourth, and dropping behind Patterson. Coming into the final apparatus, Patterson held a narrow .026 point lead over Khorkina. Khorkina took the floor first. Performing to the song "Acropolis Adieu," her routine emphasized grace over athletics, and earned her only 9.562 points from the judges. Competing last, Patterson performed a more energetic routine, emphasizing her jumps. Landing perfectly on all four of her passes, her score of 9.712 points secured the gold. She was the first American to win the all-around event in a non-boycotted Olympics.

After her win, Patterson retired from competition to focus on a singing career, appearing on the reality TV show "Celebrity Duets," where she sang alongside Cheech Marin, Lea Thompson and Jesse McCartney.

2008 Beijing C: 98, N: 35, D: 8.15.

		HV		AB		BB		FE		TOTAL PTS.
1. Anastasia "Nastia" Liukin	USA	15.025	7	16.650	2	16.125	1	15.525	1	63.325
2. Shawn Johnson	USA	15.875	1	15.275	10	16.050	2	15.525	1	62.725
3. Yang Yilin	CHN	15.175	5	16.725	1	15.750	6	15.000	5	62.650
4. Kseniya Semyonova	RUS	14.750	14	16.475	3	15.925	4	14.775	6	61.925
5. Steliana Nistor	ROM	15.025	8	15.975	4	15.550	8	14.500	10	61.050
6. Jiang Yuyuan	CHN	14.825	13	15.875	5	15.425	10	14.775	6	60.900
7. Anna Pavlova	RUS	15.275	4	14.525	18	15.975	3	15.050	4	60.825
8. Sandra Izbaşa	ROM	15.075	6	14.300	20	15.875	5	15.500	3	60.750

Nastia Liukin and Shawn Johnson were the two clear favorites in the all-around event. Liukin had won the 2005 and 2006 US nationals but had been narrowly edged out in the 2005 world championship all-around final, losing to teammate Chellsie Memmel by one thousandth of a point.

In 2007 Liukin struggled with a persistent ankle injury, which coincided with the rise of teammate and competitor Shawn Johnson. Born and raised in Des Moines, Iowa, Johnson won back-to-back US national titles in 2007 and 2008 and won the 2007 all-around world championship title, beating Steliana Nistor by 1.25 points. Two months before the Olympics she defeated Liukin at the US Olympic trials.

Johnson led the qualifying round in Beijing, posting the highest vault score of the round, 16.000, and equaling Liukin's score on the balance beam, 15.975. Liukin finished second, despite an ugly fall on her uneven bars dismount, while China's Yang Yilin was third after recording the highest uneven bars score, 16.650.

The top six qualifiers were placed in the same subgroup during the final, performing on the same apparatus in each rotation. Starting on the vault, Jiang Yuyuan attempted the highest starting score, 6.50, but fell on her landing, scoring only 14.825. Johnson also attempted a difficulty score of 6.50. She made a small step forward on her landing, but took the lead with a score of 15.875.

Yang and Liukin shone on the uneven bars, both attempting the most difficult routines on the apparatus. Liukin had a small step on her landing, earning 16.650 points, while Yang had a nearly flawless performance, moving into first place with a score of 16.725.

Performing first on the balance beam, Johnson scored a solid 16.050. Liukin moved into the lead with a score of 16.125 points, the highest of the round, while Yang scored 15.750 points. The top three, Liukin, Yang and Johnson, were separated by only 0.600 points going into the final apparatus, the floor exercise.

Yang had a misstep on her dance routine, scoring 15.000 and effectively dropping out of contention for the gold medal. Competing next, Liukin performed a smooth routine, scoring 15.525. Johnson needed a score of at least 16.025 to match Liukin, but her final score, also 15.525, kept her in second place, making Liukin the gold medal winner.

Born in Moscow, Liukin was raised in Texas by her father and coach Valeri, the 1988 Seoul Olympics all-around silver medalist and team and high bar gold medalist. "I wanted to go out and win this for my father," Liukin said. "It's just so cool that he was in the Olympics twenty years ago, and I wanted to bring home the all-around medal he almost won."

SIDE HORSE VAULT

Whereas the men vault across the length of the horse, the women attack it from the side. The horse is 1.2 meters (3 feet 11¼ inches) high and 1.63 meters (5 feet 4 inches) long. The runway is 25 meters long and the vaults are taken from a plywood springboard. The women's vault is the only gymnastics apparatus at which the competitors are given two attempts. The scores for the two vaults are averaged to produce a final score.

1896–1948 not held

1952 Helsinki C: 134, N: 18, D: 7.23.

		PTS.
1. Yekaterina Kalinchuk	SOV/RUS	19.20
2. Maria Horokhovska	SOV/UKR	19.19
3. Galina Minaicheva	SOV/RUS	19.16
4. Medeya Dzchugeli	SOV/GEO	19.13
5. Galina Urbanovich	SOV/RUS	19.10
6. Nina Bocharova	SOV/UKR	19.03
7. Karin Lindberg	SWE	18.79
7. Helena Rakoczy	POL	18.79

1956 Melbourne C: 65, N: 15, D: 12.5.

		PTS.
1. Larysa Latynina	SOV/UKR	18.833
2. Tamara Manina	SOV/RUS	18.80
3. Ann-Sofi Colling-Pettersson	SWE	18.733
3. Olga Tass	HUN	18.733
5. Sofia Muratova	SOV/RUS	18.666
6. Elena Leuştean	ROM	18.633
7. Natalia Kot	POL	18.50
7. Helena Rakoczy	POL	18.50

1960 Rome C: 124, N: 27, D: 9.9.

		PTS.
1. Marharyta Nikolayeva	SOV/UKR	19.316
2. Sofia Muratova	SOV/RUS	19.049
3. Larysa Latynina	SOV/UKR	19.016
4. Adolfina Tačová	CZE	18.783
5. Sonia Iovan	ROM	18.766
6. Polina Astakhova	SOV/UKR	18.716

Larysa Latynina, 1960

Between 1956 and 1964, Latynina won 18 medals (nine gold, five silver, and four bronze), more than any other athlete in Olympic history.

1964 Tokyo C: 82, N: 23, D: 10.22.

		PTS.
1. Vera Čáslavská	CZE	19.483
2. Larysa Latynina	SOV/UKR	19.283
2. Birgit Radochla	GDR	19.283
4. Toshiko Aihara (Shirasu	JPN	19.282
5. Yelena Volchetskaya	SOV/BLR	19.149
6. Ute Starke	GDR	19.116

1968 Mexico City C: 101, N: 24, D: 10.25.

		PTS.
1. Vera Čáslavská	CZE	19.775
2. Erika Zuchold	GDR	19.625
3. Zinaida Voronina	SOV/RUS	19.50
4. Maria Krajčírová	CZE	19.475
5. Natalya Kuchinskaya	SOV/RUS	19.375
6. Miroslava Skleničková	CZE	19.325

1972 Munich C: 118, N: 23, D: 8.31.

		PTS.
1. Karin Janz	GDR	19.525
2. Erika Zuchold	GDR	19.275
3. Lyudmila Turischeva	SOV/RUS	19.25
4. Lyubov Burda	SOV/RUS	19.225
5. Olga Korbut	SOV/BLR	19.175
6. Tamara Lazakovich	SOV/BLR	19.05

1976 Montreal C: 86, N: 18, D: 7.22.

		PTS.
1. Nelli Kim	SOV/KAZ	19.80
2. Carola Dombeck	GDR	19.65
2. Lyudmila Turischeva	SOV/RUS	19.65
4. Nadia Comăneci	ROM	19.625
5. Gitta Escher	GDR	19.55
6. Márta Egervári	HUN	19.45

1980 Moscow C: 62, N: 16, D: 7.25.

		PTS.
1. Natalya Shaposhnikova	SOV/RUS	19.725
2. Steffi Kräker	GDR	19.675
3. Melita Rühn	ROM	19.65
4. Yelena Davydova	SOV/RUS	19.575
5. Nadia Comăneci	ROM	19.35
6. Maxi Gnauck	GDR	19.30

1984 Los Angeles C: 65, N: 16, D: 8 .5.

		PTS.
1. Ecaterina Szabó	ROM	19.875
2. Mary Lou Retton	USA	19.85
3. Lavinia Agache	ROM	19.75
4. Tracee Talavera	USA	19.70
5. Zhou Ping	CHN	19.50
6. Kelly Brown	CAN	19.425
6. Brigitta Lehmann	GER	19.425
8. Chen Yongyan	CHN	19.30

Two nights after finishing second to Mary Lou Retton in the All-Around competition, Kati Szabó reestablished her dominance by winning three of the four apparatus finals. Szabó went home with 4 gold medals and 1 silver, a better haul than even Carl Lewis.

1988 Seoul C: 90, N: 23, D: 9.25.

		PTS.
1. Svetlana Boginskaya	SOV/BLR	19.905
2. Gabriela Potorac	ROM	19.83
3. Daniela Silivaş	ROM	19.818
4. Boriana Stoyanova	BUL	19.78
5. Brandy Johnson	USA	19.774
6. Dagmar Kersten	GDR	19.756
7. Wang Xiaoyan	CHN	19.73
8. Yelena Shushunova	SOV/RUS	19.712

Yelena Shushunova, who had dominated the event for three years, led after the preliminaries with a score of 10.0. However she muffed both vaults in the final, finishing her second attempt by landing on her knees. Svetlana Boginskaya placed third in the All-Around Competition. This was such a disappointment to her coach, Lyubov Miromanova, that it contributed to Miromanova committing suicide three days after the conclusion of the Seoul Games. Boginskaya would ultimately take part in three Olympics, earning three gold medals, one silver and one bronze.

1992 Barcelona C: 92, N: 24, D: 8.1.

		PTS.
1. Lavinia Miloşovici	ROM	9.925
1. Henrietta Ónodi	HUN	9.925
3. Tetiana Lysenko	UKR	9.912
4. Svetlana Boginskaya	BLR	9.899
5. Gina Gogean	ROM	9.893
6. Shannon Miller	USA	9.837
7. Eva Rueda Bravo	SPA	9.787
8. Kim Zmeskal	USA	9.593

1996 Atlanta C: 96, N: 28, D: 7.28.

		PTS.
1. Simona Amanar	ROM	9.825
2. Mo Hiulan	CHN	9.768
3. Gina Gogean	ROM	9.75
4. Rozalya Galiyeva	RUS	9.743
5. Svetlana Boginskaya	BLR	9.712
6. Dominique Dawes	USA	9.649
7. Yelena Grosheva	RUS	9.637
8. Shannon Miller	USA	9.35

2000 Sydney C: 8, N: 5, D: 9.24.

		PTS.
1. Yelena Zamolodchikova	RUS	9.731
2. Andreea Răducan	ROM	9.693
3. Yekaterina Lobaznyuk	RUS	9.674
4. Esther Moya Salvador	SPA	9.618
5. Laura Martínez Ruiz	SPA	9.612
6. Simona Amănar	ROM	9.537
7. Denisse López Sing	MEX	8.843

DISQ: Dong Fangxiao (CHN) 9.487

World champion Yelena Zamolodchikova failed to qualify for the final when, as the third best Russian, she only placed ninth in the preliminary round. One hour before the final, Russian leader Svetlana Khorkina withdrew from the event, allowing Zamolodchikova to take her place. Third after the first vault, Zamolodchikova scored a 9.75 on her second attempt to win the gold medal.

2004 Athens C: 84, N: 31, D: 8.22.

		PTS.
1. Monica Roşu	ROM	9.656
2. Annia Hatch	USA	9.481
3. Anna Pavlova	RUS	9.475
4. Yelena Zamolodchikova	RUS	9.412
5. Kang Yun-mi	PRK	9.381
6. Alona Kvasha	UKR	9.344
7. Wang Tiantian	CHN	9.081
8. Coralie Chacon	FRA	4.456

Competing three and a half months after she won the European championship, 17-year-old Monica Roşu earned the two highest scores of the competition, a 9.575 for a double-twist Tsukahara, followed by a 9.737 on a 2½ twist Yurchenko. Annia Hatch was competing in her first international event since she won a world championship bronze medal in the vault in 1996. Born in Guantánamo, Cuba, she retired in 1997 (on national televison), moved to the United States, married and became a coach in Connecticut. She came out of retirement in 2001 and became a US citizen later that year. By the time she earned her silver medal at the Athens Olympics, she was 26 years old.

2008 Beijing C: 15, N: 15, D: 8.17.

		PTS.
1. Hong Un-jong	PRK	15.650
2. Oksana Chusovitina	GER	15.575
3. Cheng Fei	CHN	15.562
4. Alicia Sacramone	USA	15.537
5. Ariella Kaeslin	SWI	15.050
6. Carlotta Giovannini	ITA	14.550
7. Jade Barbosa	BRA	14.487
8. Anna Pavlova	RUS	7.812

Three-time reigning world champion Cheng Fei finished first in the qualifying round and seemed poised for the gold medal. Her first vault of the final, 16.075, was the highest of the round, 0.325 points ahead of Alicia Sacramone, who had won vault medals at each of the last three world championships, silver in 2006 and bronze in 2005 and 2007. However, Cheng lost her balance on her final vault, landing on her knees and scoring 15.050 points.

In fifth place after incurring a 0.3 point penalty on her first vault for landing off-balance, North Korea's Hong Un-jong delivered a solid landing on her final vault, earning 15.750 points to move into first place. Thirty-three-year-old Oksana Chusovitina, the oldest female gymnast at the Beijing Olympics, finished second, slightly ahead of Cheng, whose start values, 6.5 points, were high enough to earn her the bronze medal. Sacramone finished out of medal contention despite landing both of her vaults cleanly. Russian hopeful Anna Pavlova had seemed to be in medal contention after the first vault of the final but her second vault was ruled invalid after she took off down the runway too early.

The silver medal was Chusovitina's first individual medal in five Olympics and her first since winning the all-around team gold medal with the Unified Team at the 1992 Barcelona Olympics. It was also her first time competing for Germany instead of her native Uzbekistan; she moved to Germany in 2002 so that her son Alisher could be treated for leukemia.

ASYMMETRICAL (UNEVEN) BARS

The two parallel uneven bars are 3.5 meters (11 feet 5¾ inches) long. The high bar must be between 2.2 and 2.4 meters (7 feet 2½ inches and 7 feet 10½ inches) above the floor. The low bar must be between 1.4 and 1.6 meters (4 feet 7 inches and 5 feet 3 inches) above the floor. The distance between the bars may be adjusted according to the size of the gymnast.

1896–1948 not held

1952 Helsinki C: 134, N: 18, D: 7.23.

		PTS.
1. Margit Korondi	HUN	19.40
2. Maria Horokhovska	SOV/UKR	19.26
3. Ágnes Keleti	HUN	19.16
4. Nina Bocharova	SOV/UKR	18.99
4. Pelageya Danilova	SOV/RUS	18.99
6. Edit Perényi-Weckinger	HUN	18.96
7. Galina Shamrai	SOV/UZB	18.93
8. Galina Minaicheva	SOV/RUS	18.89

1956 Melbourne C: 65, N: 15, D: 12.5.

		PTS.
1. Ágnes Keleti	HUN	18.966
2. Larysa Latynina	SOV/UKR	18.833
3. Sofia Muratova	SOV/RUS	18.80
4. Eva Bosáková (Věchtová	CZE	18.733
5. Helena Rakoczy	POL	18.70
6. Aliz Kertész	HUN	18.633
6. Olga Tass	HUN	18.633
8. Natalia Kot	POL	18.60

1960 Rome C: 124, N: 27, D: 9.9.

		PTS.
1. Polina Astakhova	SOV/UKR	19.616
2. Larysa Latynina	SOV/UKR	19.416
3. Tamara Lyukhina	SOV/RUS	19.399
4. Sofia Muratova	SOV/RUS	19.382
5. Keiko Ikeda (Tanaka	JPN	19.333
6. Sonia Iovan	ROM	19.099

The audience was so upset by the low scoring of Ikeda's final routine that they booed for ten minutes until Astakhova stepped up for her turn.

1964 Tokyo C: 82, N: 23, D: 10.22.

		PTS.
1. Polina Astakhova	SOV/UKR	19.332
2. Katalin Makray	HUN	19.216
3. Larysa Latynina	SOV/UKR	19.199
4. Toshiko Aihara (Shirasu	JPN	18.782
5. Vera Čáslavská	CZE	18.416
6. Tamara Zamotailova (Lyukhina	SOV/RUS	17.833

1968 Mexico City C: 101, N: 24, D: 10.25

		PTS.
1. Věra Čáslavská	CZE	19.65
2. Karin Janz	GDR	19.50
3. Zinaida Voronina	SOV/RUS	19.425
4. Bohumila Řimnáčová	CZE	19.35
5. Erika Zuchold	GDR	19.325
6. Miroslava Skleničková	CZE	18.20

1972 Munich C: 118, N: 23, D: 8.31.

		PTS.
1. Karin Janz	GDR	19.675
2. Olga Korbut	SOV/BLR	19.45
2. Erika Zuchold	GDR	19.45
4. Lyudmila Turischeva	SOV/RUS	19,425
5. Ilona Békési	HUN	19.275
6. Angelika Hellmann	GDR	19.20

1976 Montreal C: 86, N: 18, D: 7.22.

		PTS.
1. Nadia Comăneci	ROM	20.00
2. Teodora Ungureanu	ROM	19.80
3. Márta Egervári	HUN	19.775
4. Marion Kische	GDR	19.75
5. Olga Korbut	SOV/BLR	19.30
6. Nelli Kim	SOV/KAZ	19.225

1980 Moscow C: 62, N: 16, D: 7.25.

		PTS.
1. Maxi Gnauck	GDR	19.875
2. Emilia Eberle	ROM	19.85
3. Maria Filatova	SOV/RUS	19.775
3. Steffi Kräker	GDR	19.775
3. Melita Ruhn	ROM	19.775
6. Nelli Kim	SOV/BLR	19.725

1984 Los Angeles C: 65, N: 16, D: 8.5.

		PTS.
1. Ma Yanhong	CHN	19.95
1. Julianne McNamara	USA	19.95
3. Mary Lou Retton	USA	19.80
4. Miháela Stănulet	ROM	19.65
5. Romi Kessler	SWI	19.425
6. Zhou Ping	CHN	19.35
7. Noriko Mochizuki	JPN	19.325
8. Lavinia Agache	ROM	19.15

1988 Seoul C: 90, N: 23, D: 9.25.

		PTS.
1. Daniela Silivaş	ROM	20.00
2. Dagmar Kersten	GDR	19.987
3. Yelena Shushunova	SOV/RUS	19.962
4. Dörte Thümmler	GDR	19.90
5. Svetlana Boginskaya	SOV/BLR	19.899
6. Iveta Poloková	CZE	19.837
7. Aurelia Dobre	ROM	19.824
8. Phoebe Mills	USA	19.787

1992 Barcelona C: 92, N: 24, D: 8.1.

		PTS.
1. Lu Li	CHN	10.000
2. Tatyana Gutsu	UKR	9.975
3. Shannon Miller	USA	9.962
4. Kim Gwang-suk	PRK	9.912
4. Lavinia Miloşovici	ROM	9.912
4. Mirela Paşca	ROM	9.912
7. Cristina Fraguas Sánchez	SPA	9.900
8. Li Li	CHN	9.887

Lu Li, a 15-year-old from Changsha, in Hunan Province, stood only 4 feet 5½ inches (1.36 m) and weighed only 66 pounds (30 kg). She qualified for the final with only the sixth best score and then hit a perfect routine to earn tens from all six judges.

1996 Atlanta C: 98, N: 28, D: 7.28.

		PTS.
1. Svetlana Khorkina	RUS	9.85
2. Bi Wenjiing	CHN	9.837
2. Amy Chow	USA	9.837
4. Dominique Dawes	USA	9.80
5. Simona Amanar	ROM	9.787
5. Dina Kochetkova	RUS	9.787
5. Lilia Podkopayeva	UKR	9.787
8. Lavinia Miloşovici	ROM	9.75

The favorite, 17-year-old Svetlana Khorkina, lived up to expectations. She continued her policy of changing her routine for every competition. For the Olympics she included a spectacular Shaposhnikova-half turn in which she began by circling the bar and then switched axes to spin sideways.

2000 Sydney C: 8, N: 5, D: 9.24.

		PTS.
1. Svetlana Khorkina	RUS	9.862
2. Ling Jie	CHN	9.837
3. Yun Yang	CHN	9.787
4. Viktoriya Karpenko	UKR	9.775
5. Tatyana Zharganova	BLR	9.737
6. Olha Roshchupkina	UKR	9.725
7. Yelena Produnova	RUS	9.650
8. Elvire Teza	FRA	9.512

Svetlana Khorkina had won every major championship on the uneven bars for the last six years. At the Sydney Olympics however, she had fallen off the bars in both the team competition and the all-around final. In the apparatus final, she was back to her top form. She still had to wait for Ling Jie, who performed a near-perfect routine, but hopped slightly when she landed.

2004 Athens C: 85, N: 31, D: 8.22.

		PTS.
1. Émilie Le Pennec	FRA	9.687
2. Terin Humphrey	USA	9.662
3. Courtney Kupets	USA	9.637
4. Pyon Kwang-sun	PRK	9.600
5. Li Ya	CHN	9.562
6. Nicoleta Daniela Şofronie	ROM	9.462
7. Lin Li	CHN	9.200
8. Svetlana Khorkina	RUS	8.925

Only sixteen years old, Émilie Le Pennec was France's first Olympics gymnastics champion in 80 years. After completing a difficult routine with only minor problems, she was followed by 25-year-old Svetlana Khorkina. The two-time defending Olympic champion and five-time world champion lost her grip in the middle of her routine, failing to complete a swing through. Khorkina completed her routine, but left the stadium immediately after her score was posted.

2008 Beijing C: 84, N: 34, D: 8.18.

		PTS.
1. He Kexin	CHN	16.725
2. Anastasia "Nastia" Liukin	USA	16.725
3. Yang Yilin	CHN	16.650
4. Beth Tweddle	GBR	16.625
5. Anastasiya Koval	UKR	16.375
6. Kseniya Semyonova	RUS	16.325
7. Steliana Nistor	ROM	15.575
8. Dariya Zgoba	UKR	14.875

He Kexin made the final despite falling from the bar during her qualifying routine. She and 2005 world champion and reigning world silver medalist Nastia Liukin had identical scores in their final routines, 9.025 points for execution and 7.7 for difficulty. Instead of sharing gold, officials used a tie-breaking system whereby the highest and lowest marks for execution were progressively removed until a winner emerged. Yang Yilin, who qualified in first place, finished third with the same difficulty score as He and Liukin, but a lower score for execution.

"For me, it's not correct," FIG president Bruno Grandi said later. "When two people arrive on the same level, they are champions. But this competition doesn't belong to us. It is the IOC's." The rules for dual medals had been dropped in 1997 at the direction of the IOC.

He Kexin
He Kexin miraculously became two years older just before the 2008 Olympics.

BALANCE BEAM

The balance beam is 5 meters (16 feet 4¾ inches) long and 10 centimeters (4 inches) wide. It stands 1.2 meters (3 feet 11¼ inches) above the floor. Routines must last between 70 and 90 seconds.

1896–1948 not held

1952 Helsinki C: 134, N: 18, D: 7.23.

		PTS.
1. Nina Bocharova	SOV/UKR	19.22
2. Maria Horokhovska	SOV/UKR	19.13
3. Margit Korondi	HUN	19.02
4. Ágnes Keleti	HUN	18.96
5. Galina Urbanovich	SOV/RUS	18.93
6. Tsvetana Stancheva	BUL	18.86
6. Olga Tass	HUN	18.86
8. Galina Shamrai	SOV/UZB	18.79

1956 Melbourne C: 65, N: 15, D: 12.5.

		PTS.
1. Ágnes Keleti	HUN	18.80
2. Eva Bosáková (Věchtová	CZE	18.633
2. Tamara Manina	SOV/RUS	18.633
4. Larysa Latynina	SOV/UKR	18.533
4. Anna Marelkova	CZE	18.533
6. Elena Leuştean	ROM	18.50
7. Margit Korondi	HUN	18.466
7. Olga Tass	HUN	18.466
7. Lyudmila Yegorova	SOV/RUS	18.466

1960 Rome C: 124, N: 27, D: 9.9.

		PTS.
1. Eva Bosáková (Věchtová)	CZE	19.283
2. Larysa Latynina	SOV/UKR	19.233
3. Sofia Muratova	SOV/RUS	19.232
4. Marharyta Nikolayeva	SOV/UKR	19.183
5. Keiko Ikeda (Tanaka	JPN	19.132
6. Věra Čáslavská	CZE	19.083

Competing in her third Olympics, 28-years-old Eva Bosáková won her first gold medal. In 1963 she was the subject of the film *Something Different* by Vera Chytilová, which juxtaposed Bosáková's life as a gymnast with that of a housewife. Bosáková also toured the world as a member of the Czechoslovak Song and Dance Ensemble and she holds an unusual place in canine history as the first person to bring a Samoyed puppy into Czechoslovakia.

1964 Tokyo C: 83, N: 24, D: 10.23.

		PTS.
1. Věra Čáslavská	CZE	19.449
2. Tamara Manina	SOV/RUS	19.399
3. Larysa Latynina	SOV/UKR	19.382
4. Polina Astakhova	SOV/UKR	19.366
5. Hana Ružčková	CZE	19.349
6. Keiko Ikeda (Tanaka	JPN	19.216

1968 Mexico City C: 101, N: 24, D: 10.25.

		PTS.
1. Natalya Kuchinskaya	SOV/RUS	19.65
2. Věra Čáslavská	CZE	19.575
3. Larissa Petrik	SOV/BLR	19.25
4. Karin Janz	GDR	19.225
4. Linda Metheny	USA	19.225
6. Erika Zuchold	GDR	19.15

In 1987, Natalya Kuchinskaya, who was teaching gymnastics to children, told *Sovietsky Sport*: "Big sport is, in one sense, cruel. When you are riding high . . . everyone needs you; but when you leave the sporting arena, then they forget about you. In gymnastics, this blossoming out happens at 15 or 16 years old, when the girl is not yet fully formed as a person. Her head has been affected by applause, flowers and articles written in her praise . . . At 20 years, she finishes performing and attention to her evaporates, as if she did not exist. She becomes like everyone else, only a bit worse because the book that everyone has read she has not read—she had to hurry off to training; the film everyone has seen she has not seen—she was at a competition . . . It is not that I am against big-time sport, but I think you must try to safeguard children against its costs—serious injuries, excessive psychological pressure. It is necessary in the first place to preserve the person in the child while creating the gymnast."

1972 Munich C: 118, N: 23, D: 8.31.

		PTS.
1. Olga Korbut	SOV/BLR	19.40
2. Tamara Lazakovich	SOV/BLR	19.375
3. Karin Janz	GDR	18.975
4. Mónika Császár	HUN	18.925
5. Lyudmila Turischeva	SOV/RUS	18.80
6. Erika Zuchold	GDR	18.70

1976 Montreal C: 86, N: 18, D: 7.22.

		PTS.
1. Nadia Comăneci	ROM	19.95
2. Olga Korbut	SOV/BLR	19.725
3. Teodora Ungureanu	ROM	19.70
4. Lyudmila Turischeva	SOV/RUS	19.475
5. Angelika Hellmann	GDR	19.45
6. Gitta Escher	GDR	19.275

1980 Moscow C: 62, N: 16, D: 7.25.

		PTS.
1. Nadia Comăneci	ROM	19.80
2. Yelena Davydova	SOV/RUS	19.75
3. Natalya Shaposhnikova	SOV/RUS	19.725
4. Maxi Gnauck	GDR	19.70
5. Radka Zemanová	CZE	19.65
6. Emilia Eberle	ROM	19.40

1984 Los Angeles C: 65, N: 16, D: 8.5.

		PTS.
1. Simona Păuca	ROM	19.80
1. Ecaterina Szabó	ROM	19.80
3. Kathy Johnson	USA	19.65
4. Mary Lou Retton	USA	19.55
5. Ma Yanhong	CHN	19.45
6. Romi Kessler	SWI	19.35
7. Chen Yongyan	CHN	19.20
7. Anja Wilhelm	GER	19.20

1988 Seoul C: 90, N: 23, D: 9.25.

		PTS.
1. Daniela Silivaş	ROM	19.924
2. Yelena Shushunova	SOV/RUS	19.875
3. Phoebe Mills	USA	19.837
3. Gabriela Potorac	ROM	19.837
5. Svetlana Boginskaya	SOV/BLR	19.787
6. Diana Dudeva	BUL	19.724
7. Kelly Garrison-Steves	USA	19.649
8. Ulrike Klotz	GDR	18.125

Phoebe Mills of Northfield, Illinois, became the first female gymnast from the US to win an individual medal at an unboycotted Olympics.

1992 Barcelona C: 92, N: 24, D: 8.1.

		PTS.
1. Tetiana Lysenko	UKR	9.975
2. Lu Li	CHN	9.912
2. Shannon Miller	USA	9.912
4. Christina Bontaş	ROM	9.875
5. Svetlana Boginskaya	BLR	9.862
6. Elizabeth Okino	USA	9.837
7. Yang Bo	CHN	9.300
8. Lavinia Miloşovici	ROM	9.262

Lysenko, a 17-year-old from Kherson, became the first non-Romanian to win this event in 20 years.

1996 Atlanta C: 95, N: 28, D: 7.29.

		PTS.
1. Shannon Miller	USA	9.862
2. Lilia Podkopayeva	UKR	9.825
3. Gina Gogean	ROM	9.787
4. Dina Kochetkova	RUS	9.737
5. Olga Teslenko	UKR	9.625
6. Dominique Moceanu	USA	9.125
7. Rozalya Galiyeva	RUS	9.112
8. Alexandra Marinescu	ROM	8.462

Shannon Miller won five medals at the 1992 Olympics, two silver and three bronze, and then added two gold in

Atlanta to become the most decorated US gymnast ever. She was also the first American woman to win an individual gold medal in an unboycotted Olympics.

2000 Sydney C: 8, N: 5, D: 9.25.

		PTS.
1. Liu Xuan	CHN	9.825
2. Yekaterina Lobaznyuk	RUS	9.787
3. Yelena Produnova	RUS	9.775
4. Claudia Presacan	ROM	9.750
5. Tetyana Yarosh	UKR	9.712
6. Maria Olaru	ROM	9.700
7. Jie Ling	CHN	9.675
8. Elise Ray	USA	9.387

Liu Xuan's mother was a gymnast whose career was terminated by the Cultural Revolution, the extreme political movement that, among other things, prohibited sports. Liu herself was chosen for the Chinese national team when she was 13 years old and moved from Changsha to Beijing, after which she saw her parents once a year. Liu was 21 years old when she won her gold medal. A popular figure in China, she appeared in various advertising campaigns, served as "The Gold Lady" for the World Gold Association, and starred in the 2003 film *Far From Home* (*Wode Meili Xiangchou*).

After retiring in 2001, she obtained a degree in journalism and worked as a commentator, a gymnastics judge and an actress. In 2009 she signed with a leading Hong Kong broadcaster, landing a leading role in a television kung-fu series, and released a pop album entitled "Beautiful Faces."

2004 Athens C: 95, N: 31, D: 8.23.

		PTS.
1. Cătălina Ponor	ROM	9.787
2. Carly Patterson	USA	9.775
3. Alexandra Eremia	ROM	9.700
4. Anna Pavlova	RUS	9.587
5. Courtney Kupets	USA	9.375
6. Nan Zhang	CHN	9.237
7. Ya Li	CHN	9.050
8. Allana Slater	AUS	8.750

Favorite Cătălina Ponor, the 2003 world championship silver medalist and 2004 European champion, did not disappoint. Her routine, including a switch leap Kochetkova and a back dive with a quarter turn to a split handstand, earned 9.787, enough to hold off the challenge of the penultimate performer, all-around gold medalist Carly Patterson.

2008 Beijing C: 84, N: 35, D: 8.19.

		PTS.
1. Shawn Johnson	USA	16.225
2. Anastasia "Nastia" Liukin	USA	16.025
3. Cheng Fei	CHN	15.950
4. Anna Pavlova	RUS	15.900
5. Gabriela Drăgoi	ROM	15.625
6. Li Shanshan	CHN	15.300
7. Kseniya Afanasyeva	RUS	14.825
8. Koko Tsurumi	JPN	14.450

The 2007 world silver medalist, Li Shanshan finished first in the qualifying round, followed closely by 2005 and 2007 world champion Nastia Liukin. Li stumbled during her final routine, falling on a back handspring to earn a disappointing 15.300 points. Performing sixth of the eight finalists, Johnson nailed her routine, earning 16.225 points. Liukin avoided any major mistakes, but her score was not enough to move her past Johnson.

FLOOR EXERCISES

1896–1948 not held

1952 Helsinki C: 134, N: 18, D: 7.23.

		PTS.
1. Ágnes Keleti	HUN	19.36
2. Maria Horokhovska	SOV/UKR	19.20
3. Margit Korondi	HUN	19.00
4. Erzsébet Gulyás	HUN	18.99
4. Galina Urbanovich	SOV/RUS	18.99
6. Galina Minaicheva	SOV/RUS	18.96
7. Olga Tass	HUN	18.89
8. Galina Shamrai	SOV/UZB	18.86

1956 Melbourne C: 65, N: 15, D: 12.5.

		PTS.
1. Ágnes Keleti	HUN	18.733
1. Larysa Latynina	SOV/UKR	18.733
3. Elena Leuştean	ROM	18.70
4. Eva Bosáková (Věchtová	CZE	18.566
4. Sofia Muratova	SOV/RUS	18.566
4. Keiko Tanaka	JPN	18.566
7. Olga Tass	HUN	18.533
8. Doris Hedberg	SWE	18.50

1960 Rome C: 124, N: 27, D: 9.9.

		PTS.
1. Larysa Latynina	SOV/UKR	19.583
2. Polina Astakhova	SOV/UKR	19.532
3. Tamara Lyukhina	SOV/RUS	19.449
4. Eva Bosáková (Věchtová	CZE	19.383
5. Sofia Muratova	SOV/RUS	19.349
6. Sonia Iovan	ROM	19.232

1964 Tokyo C: 83, N: 24, D: 23.10.

		PTS.
1. Larysa Latynina	SOV/UKR	19.599
2. Polina Astakhova	SOV/UKR	19.50
3. Anikó Jánosi-Ducza	HUN	19.30

4. Birgit Radochla	GDR	19.299
5. Ingrid Föst	GDR	19.266
6. Věra Čáslavská	CZE	19.099

1968 Mexico City C: 101, N: 24, D: 10.20.

		PTS.
1. Věra Čáslavská	CZE	19.675
1. Larissa Petrik	SOV/BLR	19.675
3. Natalya Kuchinskaya	SOV/RUS	19.65
4. Zinaida Voronina	SOV/RUS	19.55
5. Olga Karasyova	SOV/RUS	19.325
5. Bohumila Řimnáčová	CZE	19.325

1972 Munich C: 118, N: 23, D: 10.25.

		PTS.
1. Olga Korbut	SOV/BLR	19.575
2. Lyudmila Turischeva	SOV/RUS	19.55
3. Tamara Lazakovich	SOV/BLR	19.45
4. Karin Janz	GDR	19.40
5. Lyubov Burda	SOV/RUS	19.10
5. Angelika Hellmann	GDR	19.10

1976 Montreal C: 86, N: 18, D: 7.22.

		PTS.
1. Nelli Kim	SOV/KAZ	19.85
2. Lyudmila Turischeva	SOV/RUS	19.825
3. Nadia Comăneci	ROM	19.75
4. Anna Pohludková	CZE	19.575
5. Marion Kische	GDR	19.475
6. Gitta Escher	GDR	19.45

Nelli Kim was born in Chimkent, Kazakhstan, to a Tatar mother and a Korean father. In the Olympics of 1976 and 1980 she won 5 gold medals and 1 silver. From the point of view of fame and fortune, Kim had the bad luck to compete at the same time as Nadia Comăneci. When, in 1976, Comăneci became the first gymnast to score a perfect ten, Kim was the second—and only other—to do so.

1980 Moscow C: 62, N: 16, D: 7.25.

		PTS.
1. Nadia Comăneci	ROM	19.875
1. Nelli Kim	SOV/BLR	19.875
3. Maxi Gnauck	GDR	19.825
3. Natalya Shaposhnikova	SOV/RUS	19.825
5. Emilia Eberle	ROM	19.75
6. Jana Labáková	CZE	19.725

1984 Los Angeles C: 65, N: 16, D: 8.5.

		PTS.
1. Ecaterina Szabó	ROM	19.975
2. Julianne McNamara	USA	19.95
3. Mary Lou Retton	USA	19.775
4. Zhou Qiurui	CHN	19.625
5. Romi Kessler	SWI	19.575
6. Ma Yanhong	CHN	19.45
7. Maiko Morio	JPN	19.375
8. Laura Cutina	ROM	19.15

When Ecaterina Szabó stepped up for her final Olympic routine, a power outage plunged the arena into darkness. When the lights were restored eight minutes later, the scoreboard showed that Szabó's closest rival, Julianne McNamara, had been awarded a 10 for her performance. This meant that Szabó would need a 10 as well to assure herself sole possession of first place. Unfazed by the delay or the pressure, she earned her 10 and, with it, her fourth gold medal.

Lyudmila Turischeva
The Russian great was doomed to play second fiddle to her wildly popular, though less successful, teammate Olga Korbut.

1988 Seoul C: 90, N: 23, D: 9.25.

		PTS.
1. Daniela Silivaş	ROM	19.937
2. Svetlana Boginskaya	SOV/BLR	19.887
3. Diana Dudeva	BUL	19.85
4. Deliana Vodenicharova	BUL	19.837
5. Beáta Storczer	HUN	19.675
6. Phoebe Mills	USA	19.662
7. Yelena Shushunova	SOV/RUS	19.575
8. Dörte Thümmler	GDR	19.525

Silivaş returned home from Seoul with three gold medals and two silver. Dudeva became the first Bulgarian woman to win an Olympic gymnastics medal.

1992 Barcelona C: 92, N: 24, D: 8.1.

		PTS.
1. Lavinia Miloşovici	ROM	10.000
2. Henrietta Ónodi	HUN	9.950
3. Christina Bontaş	ROM	9.912
3. Tatyana Gutsu	UKR	9.912
3. Shannon Miller	USA	9.912
6. Kim Zmeskal	USA	9.900
7. Oksana Chusovitina	UZB	9.812
8. Sylvia Mitova	BUL	9.400

Svetlana Boginskaya finished in a tie for first place in the qualifying round, but officials of the Unified Team replaced her in the final with world champion Oksana Chusovitina. In 2002, Lavinia Miloşovici appeared topless in a Japanese magazine, book and DVD. The Romanian Gymnastics Federation banned her from coaching in official competitions for five years, not because she posed partially nude, but because she did so while wearing clothing that bore the emblem of the Romanian federation.

1996 Atlanta C: 96, N: 28, D: 7.29.

		PTS.
1. Lilia Podkopayeva	UKR	9.887
2. Simona Amanar	ROM	9.850
3. Dominique Dawes	USA	9.837
4. Dominique Moceanu	USA	9.825
5. Dina Kochetkova	RUS	9.800
6. Mo Huilan	CHN	9.700
7. Gina Gogean	ROM	9.662
8. Ji Liya	CHN	9.637

Kerri Strug of the United States had the highest score in the qualifying round, but was forced to withdraw from the final because of an injury sustained in the team competition.

2000 Sydney C: 8, N: 5, D: 9.25.

		PTS.
1. Yelena Zamoldchikova	RUS	9.850
2. Svetlana Khorkina	RUS	9.812
3. Simona Amanar	ROM	9.712
4. Esther Moya Salvador	SPA	9.700
5. Yun Yang	CHN	9.637
6. Fangxiao Dong	CHN	9.537
6. Andreea Răducan	ROM	9.275
7. Lisa Skinner	AUS	9.012

DISQ: Dong Fangxiao (CHN) 9.537

Tiny Yelena Zamoldchikova had never placed higher than eighth in floor exercise in a major competition and she only earned the seventh highest score in the qualifying round. Yet when it came time for the final, she performed a popular American detective-themed routine and earned her second gold medal in two days.

2004 Athens C: 83, N: 30, D: 8.23.

		PTS.
1. Cătălina Ponor	ROM	9.750
2. Nicoleta Daniela Şofronie	ROM	9.562
3. Patricia Moreno Sánchez	SPA	9.487
4. Cheng Fei	CHN	9.412
5. Daiane dos Santos	BRA	9.375
6. Mohini Bhardwaj	USA	9.312
7. Kate Richardson	CAN	9.312
8. Alina Kozich	UKR	8.500

First on the floor, reigning world champion Daiane dos Santos gave an excellent acrobatic performance, including a layout Arabian double and a piked Arabian double, but went out of bounds on her first pass and stumbled on her second. Performing only a few minutes after she earned the gold medal on the balance beam, Cătălina Ponor showed her dominance in the floor exercise with a piked full-in back-out, a 2½ twist punch front layout and a double pike. Her winning margin of .188 points was the widest in the history of the event and the largest in any apparatus final, men's or women's, since Nadia Comăneci won the 1976 uneven bars by two-tenths of a point. Patricia Moreno's bronze made her the first Spanish woman to earn an Olympic gymnastics medal.

2008 Beijing C: 82, N: 34, D: 8.17.

		PTS.
1. Sandra Izbaşa	ROM	15.650
2. Shawn Johnson	USA	15.500
3. Anastasia "Nastia" Liukin	USA	15.425
4. Jiang Yuyuan	CHN	15.350
5. Yekaterina Kramarenko	RUS	15.025
6. Daiane dos Santos	BRA	14.975
7. Cheng Fei	CHN	14.550
8. Anna Pavlova	RUS	14.125

Three-time vault world champion and 2006 floor exercise world champion Cheng Fei led the qualifying round convincingly with 15.750 points, followed by reigning European champion Sandra Izbaşa with 15.475.

Reigning world champion Shawn Johnson was the first of the eight finalists to perform, earning 9.100 execution points on a routine with a difficulty of 6.4 points. Her score was unmatched by the next six finalists, including Cheng, who fell twice during her routine to finish second-to-last, and teammate Nastia Liukin, who earned higher execution scores across the board but finished behind Johnson due to her lower difficulty score (6.2). Competing last, Izbaşa executed a beautiful routine to the tune "Taniec Eleny" by Michał Lorenc, scoring 15.650 with the highest difficulty score of the final, 6.5 points, to earn the gold medal.

TEAM COMBINED EXERCISES

According to current rules, each nation's final score is determined by combining the scores of the top five performers on each apparatus.

1896–1924 not held

1928 Amsterdam T: 5, N: 5, D: 8.10.

	Total points
1. HOL	316.75
2. ITA	289.00
3. GBR	258.25
4. HUN	256.50
5. FRA	247.50

1. HOL—Petronella van Randwijk, Jacomina van den Berg, Anna Polak, Helena Nordheim, Alida van den Bos, Hendrika van Rumt, Anna van der Vegt, Elka de Levie, Jacoba Stelma, Estella Agsteribbe
2. ITA—Bianca Ambrosetti, Lavinia Gianoni, Luigina Perversi, Diana Pizzavini, Luigina Giavotti, Luisa Tanzini, Carolina Tronconi, Ines Vercesi, Rita Vittadini, Virginia Giorgi, Germana Malabarba, Clara Marangoni
3. GBR—Margaret Hartley, Edith Carrie Pickles, Annie Broadbent, Amy Jagger, Ada Smith, Lucy Desmond, Doris Woods, Jessie Kite, Isabel "Queenie" Judd, Marjorie "Midge" Moreman, Ethel Seymour, Hilda Smith
4. HUN—Mária Hámos, Aranka Hennyei, Anna Kael, Margit Pályi, Erzsébet Rudas, Nandorné Szeiler, Ilona Szöllösi, Judit Tóth, Rudolfné Herpich, Irén Hennyey, Margit Kövessy, Irén Rudas
5. FRA—Honorine Delescluse, Louise Delescluse, R. Oger, Georgette Meulebrouck, Mathilde Bataille, Galuelle Dhont, Valentine Héméryck, Jeanne Vanoverloop, Paulette Houteer, Berthe Verstraete, Geneviève Vankiersbilck, Antonie Straeteman

Four of the ten members of the Dutch team were Jewish. Helena Nordheim died in a Nazi gas chamber at Sobibor on July 2, 1943, along with her husband and 10-year-old daughter; Anna Polak and her 6-year-old daughter died July 23, 1943, also at Sobibor; Estella Agsterribe lost her life in a gas chamber at Auschwitz on September 17, 1943, along with her 6-year-old daughter and 2-year-old son. Alternate Judikje Simons also died with her son and daughter at Sobibor. The only Jewish member of the team to survive World War II was Elka de Leve.

1932 not held

1936 Berlin T: 8, N: 8, D: 8.12.

	Total points
1. GER	506.50
2. CZE	503.60
3. HUN	499.00
4. YUG	485.6
5. USA	471.60
6. POL	470.30
7. ITA	442.05
8. GBR	408.30

1. GER—Trudi Meyer 67.55 [1], Erna Bürger 67.45 [2], Käthe Sohnemann 67.05 [3], Isolde Frölian 65.75 [8], Anita Bärwirth 65.45 [9], Paula Pöhlsen 65.00 [12], Friedel Iby 63.75 [17], Julie Schmitt 62.10 [27]
2. CZE—Vlasta Foltová 66.45 [5], Vlasta Dekanová 65.95 [6], Zdeňka Veřmiřovská 65.90 [7], Matylda Pálfyová 64.10 [16], Anna Hřebřinová 62.70 [21], Božena Dobešová 62.65 [22], Marie Vetrovská 60.25 [28], Marie Bajerová 59.35 [45]
3. HUN—Margit Csillik 65.30 [11], Judit Tóth 64.70 [13], Margit Sándor-Nagy 64.55 [15], Gabriella Mészáros 63.05 [19], Eszter Volt 62.90 [20], Olga Törös 61.90 [30], Ilona Madary 61.25 [33], Margit Kalocsai 59.85 [41]
4. YUG—Dušica Radivojevič 62.30 [25], Lidica Rupnik 62.25 [26], Márta Pustišek 62.00 [28], Olga Rajkovič 62.00 [28], Drogana Djordjevič 61.20 [34], Angelina Kopurenko 60.75 [35], Katarina Hribar 60.60 [36], Maja Veršec 58.65 [46]
5. USA—Consetta Caruccio 66.85 [4], Jennie Caputo 65.45 [9], Irma Haubold 62.45 [23], Margaret Duff 60.50 [37], Ada Lunardoni 60.25 [38], Adelaide Meyer 56.55 [50], Mary Wright 55.10 [54], Marie Kibler 5.75 [injured]
6. POL—Klara Sierońska 64.65 [14], Márta Majowska 63.15 [18], Matylda Osadnik 62.45 [23], Wisława Noskiewicz 61.40 [32], Janina Skirlińska 60.20 [40], Alma Cichecka 59.70 [44], Julia Wojciechowska 57.87 [47], Stefania Krupowa 56.95 [49]
7. ITA—Ebore Canella 61.75 [31], Clara Bimbocci 59.75 [42], Elda Cividino 59.75 [42], Carmela Toso 57.60 [48], Pina Cipriotto 55.35 [52], Anny Avanzini 55.20 [53], Vittoria Avanzini 54.75 [55], Gianna Guaita 51.40 [59]
8. GBR—Mary Heaton 56.15 [51], Mary Kelly 53.70 [56], Lilian Ridgewell 53.00 [57], Doris Blake 52.45 [58], Brenda Crowe 49.00 [60], Clarice Hanson 49.00 [60], Marion Wharton 46.95 [62], Edna Gross 43.84 [63]

1948 London T: 11, N: 11, D: 8.14.

	Total points
1. CZE	445.45
2. HUN	440.55
3. USA	422.63
4. SWE	417.95
5. HOL	408.35
6. AUT	405.45
7. YUG	397.90
8. ITA	394.20

1. CZE—Zdenka Honsová 54.85 [1], Miloslava Misáková 53.40 [4], Vera Růžičková 53.00 [7], Božena Srncová 52.95 [8], Milena Mullerová 52.50 [10], Zdenka Veřmiřovská 50.00 [23], Olga Silhanová 49.95 [24], Marie Kovářová 49.60 [26]
2. HUN—Edit Perényi-Weckinger 54.25 [2], Mária Kova 53.40 [4], Irén Kárpáti-Karcsics 53.26 [6], Erzébet Gulyás-Köteles 52.25 [12], Erzsébet Balázs 52.10 [13], Olga Tass 51.45 [15], Anna Fehér 49.15 [28], Margit Sandor-Nagy 39.10 [74]
3. USA—Helen Schifano 51.70 [14], Clara Schroth 51.05 [17], Meta Elste 50.90 [18], Marian Barone 50.30 [19], Ladislava Bakanic 50.10 [20], Consetta Lenz [Caruccio] 49.10 [29], Anita Simonis 47.80 [39], Dorothy Dalton 47.65 [41]
4. SWE—Karin Lindberg 52.70 [9], Kerstin Bohman 51.40 [16], Ingrid Sandahl 51.00 [18], Göta Pettersson 50.10 [21], Gunnel Johansson 49.10 [29], Märta Andersson 49.05 [30], E. Ingrid Andersson 47.10 [47], Stina Haage 39.10 [74]
5. HOL—Jacoba Tonneman 52.50 [10], Helena Gerritsen 49.50 [27], Jacoba Wijnands 47.25 [44], Johanna Ros 45.75 [54], Anna van Geene 45.45 [57], Klassje Post 44.80 [62], Geertruida Heil-Bonnet 42.55 [67], Barendina Meijer-Haantjes 38.30 [78]

6. AUT—Gertrude Fesl 51.05 [17], Gretchen Hehenberger 50.00 [23], Gertrude Kolar 48.65 [36], Edeltraud Schramm 45.10 [60], Erika Enzenhofer 38.95 [76]
7. YUG—Vida Gerbeč 49.00 [34], Dragan Djordjevič 47.60 [42], Rusa Vojsk 47.20 [45], Draginja Djipalovič 47.15 [46], Tanja Žutič 45.25 [58], Dragica Basletič 42.70 [66], Zlatica Mijatovič 40.35 [72], Noda Cerne 24.70 [88]
8. ITA—Laura Micheli 53.65 [3], Elena Santoni 47.55 [43], Licia Macchini 46.30 [52], Wanda Nuti 45.75 [54], Liliana Torriani 45.10 [60], Renata Bianchi 43.25 [65], Norma Icardi 40.70 [70], Luciana Pezzoni 28.20 [85]

In gymnastics, as in other sports in which scoring is dependent on subjective judging, controversies and partisan decisions are commonplace. But a special level of incompetence was displayed by one of the judges in the 1948 women's gymnastics competition when, scoring on a scale of one through ten, she awarded one gymnast a 13.1. The major benefactors of the strange scoring standards of 1948 were the Czechoslovakians, who won the gold medal under dramatic circumstances. Shortly after the Czech team arrived in London, one of its members, 22-year-old Eliska Misáková, was taken ill and confined to an iron lung. The day of her team's appearance at the Olympics, she died of infantile paralysis. The Czech team, which included her older sister, Miloslava, went ahead with its performance and was awarded first place. When the Czech flag was raised for the medal ceremony, it was bordered with a black ribbon. After the Olympics, Marie Provaznikova, the leader of the Czech women's team and the president of the Women's Technical Commission, refused to return to Czechoslovakia because "there is no freedom of speech, of the press or of assembly." She was the first Olympic participant to defect, although hardly the last.

1952 Helsinki T: 18, N: 18, D: 7.24.

	Total points
1. SOV	527.03
2. HUN	520.96
3. CZE	503.32
4. SWE	501.83
5. GER	495.2
6. ITA	494.74
7. BUL	493.77
8. POL	483.72

1. SOV—Maria Gorochovskia 76.78 [1], Nina Bocharova 75.94 [2], Galina Minaicheva 75.67 [4], Galina Urbanovich 75.64 [5], Pelageya Danilova 75.03 [7], Galina Shamrai 74.97 [8], Yekaterina Kalinchuk 73.91 [13]
2. HUN—Margit Korondi 75.82 [3], Ágnes Keleti 75.58 [6], Edit Perényi-Weckinger 74.77 [10], Olga Tass 74.71 [11], Erzsébet Gulyás 74.61 [12], Mária Zalai-Kövi 73.87 [15], Andrea Bodó 71.67 [28], Irén Daruházi-Karcscics 70.87 [40]
3. CZE—Eva Věchtová 73.87 [14], Alena Chadimová 72.25 [20], Jana Rabasová 72.13 [21], Božena Srncová 72.08 [22], Hana Bobková 71.52 [31], Matylda Šinová 71.47 [33], Vera Vančurová 71.38 [34], Alena Reichová 70.40 [47]
4. SWE—Karin Lindberg 73.13 [17], Gun Röring 72.07 [23], Evy Berggren 71.07 [36], Göta Pettersson 70.97 [37], Ann-Sofi Colling-Pettersson 70.71 [44], Ingrid Sandahl 69.68 [57], Hjördis Nordin 69.28 [65], Vanja Blomberg 67.84 [83]
5. GER—Irma Walther 71.95 [24], Hanna Grages 71.77 [26], Elisabeth Ostermeier 70.91 [38], Wolfgard Voss 70.00 [53], Inge Sedlmaier 69.83 [54], Lydia Zeitlhofer 69.57 [60], Brigitte Kiesier 67.98 [80], Hilde Koop 63.40 [118]
6. ITA—Lidia Pitteri 71.60 [30], Miranda Cicognani 71.50 [32], Licia Macchini 71.24 [35], Liliana Scaricabarozzi 70.81 [41], Grazia Bozzo 70.77 [42], Luciana Reali 70.62 [45], Elisabetta Durelli 70.39 [48], Renata Bianchi 69.76 [55]
7. BUL—Tsvetana Stancheva 73.67 [16], Ivanka Doldzheva 72.81 [18], Saltirka Turpova 72.30 [19], Vasilka Stancheva 71.64 [29], Raina Grigorova 70.18 [49], Yordanka Yovkova 66.37 [98], Stoyanka Angelova 64.85 [110], Penka Prisadashka 62.91 [122]
8. POL—Stefania Świerzy 71.68 [27], Stefania Reindlowa 70.91 [38], Helena Rakoczy 70.74 [43], Zofia Kowalczyk 69.20 [67], Honorata Marcińczak 68.85 [69], Barbara Wilk-Ślizowska 68.14 [76], Dorota Horzonek, 67.57 [86], Ursula Lukomska 62.90 [123]

1956 Melbourne T: 9, N: 9, D: 12.7.

	Total points
1. SOV	444.800
2. HUN	443.500
3. ROM	438.200
4. POL	436.500
5. CZE	435.356
6. JPN	433.653
7. ITA	428.654
8. SWE	428.600

1. SOV—Larysa Latynina 74.933 [1], Sofia Muratova 74.466 [3], Tamara Manina 74.233 [6], Lyudmila Yegorova 73.533 [10], Polina Astakhova 72.700 [17], Lidiya Kalinina 72.033 [21]
2. HUN—Ágnes Keleti 74.633 [2], Olga Tass 74.366 [4], Margit Korondi 73.333 [12], Andrea Bodó 72.900 [14], Erzsébet Gulyás-Köteles 72.200 [18], Aliz Kertész 63.400 [61]
3. ROM—Elena Leuştean 74.366 [4], Sonia Iovan 72.900 [14], Georgeta Hurmuzache 72.733 [16], Emilia Vătăşoiu 72.100 [20], Elena Mărgărit 72.033 [21], Elena Săcalici 71.433 [30]
4. POL—Helena Rakoczy 73.700 [8], Natalia Kot 73.633 [9], Danuta Nowak-Stachow 71.800 [25], Dorota Jokiel 71.666 [27], Barbara Wilk-Ślizowska 70.533 [45], Lidia Szczerbska 70.300 [47]
5. CZE—Eva Bosákova [Věchtová] 74.100 [7], Hana Marejková 73.500 [11], Matylda Śinová 71.800 [25], Vera Drazdiková 71.333 [32], Alena Reichová 70.866 [39], Miroslava Brdičková 70.833 [40]
6. JPN—Keiko Tanaka 73.100 [13], Mitsuka Ikeda 71.900 [23], Kazuko Sogabe 71.833 [24], Shizuko Sakashita 71.500 [29], Kyoko Kubota 71.133 [34], Suzuko Seki 71.000 [35]
7. ITA—Miranda Cicognani 71.600 [28], Luciana Reali 70.933 [37], Rosella Cicognani 70.766 [42], Elisa Calsi 70.733 [43], Elena Lagorara 70.700 [44], Luciana Lagorara 69.700 [50]
8. SWE—Ann-Sofi Colling-Pettersson 71.40 [31], Eva Rönström 70.933 [37], Doris Hedberg 70.466 [46], Karin Lindberg 70.033 [48], Evy Berggren 69.966 [49], Maude Karlén 68.80 [53]

1960 Rome T: 17, N: 17, D: 9.8.

	Total points
1. SOV	382.320
2. CZE	373.323
3. ROM	372.053
4. JPN	371.422
5. POL	368.620
6. GDR	367.754
7. HUN	367.054
8. BUL	364.920

1. SOV—Larysa Latynina 77.031 [1], Sofia Muratova 76,696 [2], Polina Astakhova 76.164 [3], Marharyta Nikolayeva 75.831 [4], Lidiya Ivanova [Kalinina] 75.431 [7], Tamara Lyukhina 66.664 [89]
2. CZE—Věra Čáslavská 75.298 [8], Eva Bosáková [Věchtová] 75.197 [10], Ludmila Svédová 74.565 [13], Adolfina Tačová 74.564 [14], Matylda Matoušková [Šinová] 73.265 [26], Hana Růžicková 72.732 [33]
3. ROM—Sonia Iovan 75.797 [5], Elena Leuştean 74.865 [11], Emilia Liţă [Vătăşoiu] 74.264 [16], Atanasia Ionescu 73.564 [21], Uta Poreceau 73.197 [27], Elena Niculescu [Mărgărit] 70.563 [67]
4. JPN—Keiko Ikeda [Tanaka] 75.696 [6], Kiyoko Ono 75.398 [15], Kimiko Tsukada 73.398 [22], Toshiko Shirasu 73.298 [24], Ginko Abukawa 72.311 [43], Kazuko Sogabe 17.598(56]
5. POL—Natalia Kot 74.864 [12], Danuta Stachow 73.930 [17], Barbara Eustachiewicz 73.298 [24], Eryka Madra 72.764 [32], Gizela Niedurna 72.647 [37], Brygida Dziuba 71.898 [52]
6. GDR—Ingrid Föst 75.265 [9], Roselore Sonntag 72.964 [29], Ute Starke 72.798 [31], Gretel Schiener 72.697 [34], Renate Schneider 72.029 [48], Karin Boldermann 71.298 [59]
7. HUN—Judit Füle 73.831 [19], Anikó Jánosi-Ducza 73.398 [22], Klára Förstner 72.697 [34], Katalin Müller 72.530 [38], Olga Tass 72.397 [40], Maria Bencsik 72.030 [46]
8. BUL—Raina Grigorova 73.898 [18], Ivanka Doldzheva 72.332 [42], Saltirka Turpova 72.064 [45], Tsvetana Rangelova 71.996 [49], Elisaveta Mileva 71.964 [50], Stanka Pavlova 71.697 [54]

1964 Tokyo T: 10, N: 10, D: 10.21.

	Total points
1. SOV	380.890
2. CZE	379.989
3. JPN	377.889
4. GER & GDR	376.038
5. HUN	375.455
6. ROM	371.984
7. POL	371.287
8. SWE	367.888

1. SOV—Larysa Latynina 76.998 [2], Polina Astakhova 76.965 [3], Yelena Volchetskaya 75.765 [8], Tamara Zamotailova [Lyukhina] 75.398 [13], Tamara Manina 75.397 [14], Lyudmila Gromova 74.398 [30]
2. CZE—Věra Čáslavská 77.564 [1], Hana Růžicková 76.097 [5], Jaroslava Sedlačková 75.598 [11], Adolfina Tkačiková [Tačová] 75.331 [19], Mária Krajčirová 74.898 [21], Jana Posnerová 74.765 [23]
3. JPN—Keiko Ikeda [Tanaka] 76.031 [6], Toshiko Aihara [Shirasu] 75.997 [7], Kiyoko Ono 75.665 [9], Taniko Nakamura 75.198 [19], Ginko Chiba [Abukawa] 74.665 [24], Hiroko Tsuji 74.597 [25]
4. GER&GDR—Birgit Radochla 76.431 [4], Ute Starke 75.632 [10], Ingrid Föst 75.465 [12], Karin Mannewitz 74.363 [31], Christel Felgner 74.014 [35], Barbara Stolz 73.430 [44]
5. HUN—Anikó Jánosi-Ducza 75.33 [16], Katalin Makray 75.330 [18], Mária Tressel 74.932 [21], Gyöngyi Kovacs-Mák 74.597 [26], Katalin Müller 74.565 [27], Márta Erdösi-Talnai 74.23 [32]
6. ROM—Sonia Iovan 75.397 [14], Elena Popescu-Leuştean 75.130 [20], Elena Ceampelea 73.831 [37], Atanasia Ionescu 73.698 [41], Emilia Liţă [Vătăşoiu] 72.995 [48], Cristina Doboşan 72.497 [54]
7. POL—Gerda Brylka 74.563 [28], Małgorzata Wilczek 74.563 [28], Elżbieta Apostolska 73.831 [37], Dorota Miller 73.465 [43], Gizela Niedurny 72.365 [56], Barbara Eustachiewicz 72.197 [58]
8. SWE—Anna Marie Lundquist 73.798 [39], Laila Egman 73.764 [40], Ewa Rydell 73.599 [42], Ulla Lindstrom 72.898 [50], Anne-Marie Lambert 72.796 [52], Gerola Lindahl 72.763 [53]

Kiyoko Ono of the Japanese team later entered politics and served in the upper chamber of Japan's parliament.

1968 Mexico City T: 14, N: 14, D: 10.23.

	Total points
1. SOV	382.85
2. CZE	382.20
3. GDR	379.10
4. JPN	375.45
5. HUN	369.80
6. USA	369.75
7. FRA	361.75
8. BUL	355.10

1. SOV—Zinaida Voronina 76.85 [2], Natalya Kuchinskaya 76.75 [3], Larissa Petrik 76.70 [4], Olga Karasyova 76.00 [7], Lyudmila Turischeva 74.50 [24], Lyubov Burda 74.20 [25]
2. CZE—Věra Čáslavská 78.25 [1], Bohumila Řimnáčová 76.00 [7], Miroslava Skleničková 75.85 [9], Máriana Krajčirová 75.85 [9], Hana Lišková 75.65 [11], Jana Kubičková [Posnerová] 75.05 [15]
3. GDR—Erika Zuchold 76.70 [4], Karin Janz 76.55 [6], Maritta Bauerschmidt 75.45 [12], Ute Starke 74.65 [22], Marianne Noack 74.10 [27], Magdalena Schmidt 73.95 [29]
4. JPN—Kazue Hanyu 75.30 [13], Miyuki Matsuhisa 74.90 [17], Taniko Mitsukuri 74.85 [18], Chieko Oda 74.80 [19], Mitsuko Kandori 74.65 [22], Kayoko Hashiguchi 73.15 [33]
5. HUN—Ágnes Bánfai 75.10 [14], Anikó Jánosi-Ducza 74.80 [19], Katalin Schmitt-Makray 74.15 [26], Márta Erdösi-Tolnai 72.45 [35], Katalin Száll-Müller 72.15 [37], Ilona Békési 71.65 [38]
6. USA—Cathy Rigby 74.95 [16], Linda Metheny 74.00 [28], Joyce Tanac 73.65 [30], Kathy Gleason 73.60 [31], Colleen Mulvihill 73.05 [34], Wendy Cluff 71.80 [39]
7. FRA—Evelyne Letourneur 74.80 [19], Jacqueline Brisepierre 72.45 [35], Mireille Cayre 71.75 [40], Françoise Nourry 70.75 [46], Dominique Lauvard 70.15 [57], Nicole Bourdiau 69.05 [69]
8. BUL—Maria Karashka 73.30 [32], Vania Marinova 71.30 [44], Veselina Pasheva 70.45 [51], Neli Stoyanova 70.45 [51], Raina Atanasova 69.60 [65]

The Soviet team took a lead of .95 in the compulsories, stretched it to 2.25 points during the first rotation of optionals, and then held off a strong challenge from the Czechoslovak team. In 1994, Olga Karasyova appeared on German television and tearfully revealed that prior to the 1968 Olympics, she and other Soviet gymnasts were ordered to become pregnant in order to increase their level of male hormones. Then, after ten weeks, they submitted to abortions.

1972 Munich T: 19, N: 19, D: 9.28.

	Total points
1. SOV	380.50
2. GDR	376.55
3. HUN	368.25
4. USA	365.90
5. CZE	365.00
6. ROM	360.70
7. JPN	359.75
8. GER	357.95

1. SOV—Lyudmila Turischeva 76.85 [1], Olga Korbut 76.70 [3], Tamara Lazakovich 76.40 [4], Lyubov Burda 75.35 [6], Elvira Saadi 74.65 [8], Antonina Koshel 73.00 [20]
2. GDR—Karin Janz 76.85 [1], Erika Zuchold 76.00 [5], Angelika Hellmann 75.30 [7], Irene Abel 73.75 [13], Christine Schmitt 73.70 [14], Richarda Schmeisser 73.20 [17]

3. HUN—Ilona Békési 74.40 [9], Mónika Császár 73.85 [12], Krisztina Medveczky 73.60 [15], Anikó Kéry 73.40 [16], Márta Kelemen 73.00 [20], Zsuzsanna Nagy 71.45 [41]
4. USA—Cathy Rigby 74.25 [10], Kimberly Chace 73.05 [18], Roxanne Pierce 72.55 [25], Linda Metheny 72.50 [26], Joan Moore 72.50 [26], Nancy Thies 71.95 [35]
5. CZE—Mariana Némethová [Krajčirová] 74.00 [11], Zdena Dornáková 72.90 [23], Sona Brázdová 72.80 [24], Zdena Bujnáčková 72.50 [26], Hana Lišková 72.05 [33], Marcela Váchová 71.95 [35]
6. ROM—Elena Ceampelea 73.05 [18], Alma Goreac 72.25 [30], Anca Grigoraş 72.10 [31], Elisabeta Turcu 71.20 [44], Paula Ion 71.10 [46], Marcela Păunescu 70.50 [55]
7. JPN—Miyuki Matsuhisa 72.50 [26], Takato Hasegawa 72.00 [34], Elko Hirashima 71.95 [35], Kayoko Saka 71.80 [40], Kazue Hanyu 71.30 [43], Toshiko Miyamoto 70.000 [60]
8. GER—Uta Schorn 72.10 [31], Jutta Oltersdorf 71.95 [35], Andrea Niederheide 71.10 [46], Angelika Kern 70.95 [48], Ulrike Weyh 70.85 [50], Ingrid Santer 68.85 [76]

1976 Montreal T: 12, N: 12, D: 7.19.

	Total points
1. SOV	466.00
2. ROM	462.35
3. GDR	459.30
4. HUN	454.45
5. CZE	451.75
6. USA	448.20
7. GER	445.55
8. JPN	444.05

1. SOV—Nelli Kim 78.25 [2], Lyudmila Turischeva 78.25 [2], Olga Korbut 77.95 [5], Elvira Saadi 77.45 [7], Maria Filatova 77.05 [9], Svetlana Grozdova 77.05 [9]
2. ROM—Nadia Comăneci 79.05 [1], Teodora Ungureanu 78.05 [4], Mariana Constantin 76.75 [14], Anca Grigoraş 76.70 [15], Gabriela Truşcă 76.10 [18], Georgeta Gabor 75.70 [21]
3. GDR—Gitta Escher 77.60 [6], Marion Kische 77.20 [8], Kerstin Gerschau 77.00 [12], Angelika Hellmann 76.90 [13], Steffi Kräker 75.70 [21], Carola Dombeck 74.90 [33]
4. HUN—Márta Egervári 77.05 [9], Kriszta Medveczky 76.15 [17], Margit Tóth 76.05 [19], Éva Ovári 75.40 [25], Mária Lövei 75.15 [20], Márta Kelemen 74.65 [34]
5. CZE—Anna Pohludková 76.40 [16], Ingrid Holkovičova 75.60 [23], Jana Knopová 75.10 [28], Eva Porádková 75.05 [29], Drahomira Smoliková 75.05 [29], Alena Černáková 74.55 [40]
6. USA—Kimberly Chace 75.45 [24], Debra Willcox 75.05 [29], Leslie Wolfsberger 74.65 [34], Colleen Casey 74.50 [41], Carrie Englert 74.40 [42], Doris Howard 74.15 [46]
7. GER—Andrea Bieger 75.95 [20], Petra Kurbjuweit 74.60 [36], Jutta Oltersdorf 74.60 [36], Traudi Schubert 73.60 [55], Uta Schorn 73.55 [56], Beate Renschler 73.25 [59]
8. JPN—Satoko Okazaki 75.30 [26], Miyuki Hironaki 75.00 [32], Nobue Yamazaki 73.85 [50], Chieko Kikkawa 73.65 [53], Sakiko Nozawa 73.45 [57], Kyoko Mano 72.80 [65]

1980 Moscow T: 8, N: 8, D: 7.23.

	Total points
1. SOV	394.90
2. ROM	393.50
3. GDR	392.55
4. CZE	388.80
5. HUN	384.30
6. BUL	382.1
7. POL	376.25
8. PRK	364.05

1. SOV—Natalya Shaposhnikova 79.15 [2], Yelena Davydova 79.00 [5], Nelli Kim 78.95 [6], Maria Filatova 78.80 [7], Stella Zakharova 78.75 [8], Yelena Naimushina 78.40 [12]
2. ROM—Emilia Eberle 79.10 [3], Nadia Comăneci 79.05 [4], Rodica Dunca 78.50 [10], Melita Rühn 78.30 [13], Cristina Grigoraş 78.00 [15], Dumitrita Turner 77.25 [22]
3. GDR—Maxi Gnauck 79.35 [1], Katharina Rensch 78.55 [9], Steffi Kräker 78.50 [10], Birgit Süss 77.90 [17], Silvia Hindorff 77.35 [21], Karola Sube 77.20 [23]
4. CZE—Eva Marečková 78.05 [14], Jana Labáková 77.85 [18], Katarina Šarišská 77.55 [19], Dana Brydlová 77.05 [26], Anita Sauerová 76.05 [33], Radke Zemanova 76.05 [33]
5. HUN—Erika Csányi 77.50 [29], Erika Flander 77.20 [23], Márta Egervári 76.50 [27], Lenke Almási 76.25 [29], Éva Óvári 76.25 [29], Erzsébet Hanti 75.35 [37]
6. BUL—Silvia Topalova 77.20 [23], Galina Marinova 76.50 [27], Krassimira Toneva 76.25 [29], Kamelia Eftimova 75.60 [35], Dimitrinka Filipova 75.50 [36], Antoaneta Rahneva 74.35 [41]
7. POL—Lucja Matraszek-Chydzińska 76.15 [32] Malgorzata Majza 75.20 [38], Anita Jokiel 74.95 [39], Wieslawa Zelaskowska 74.30 [42], Agata Jaroszek 73.65 [43], Katarzyna Snopko 73.45 [45]
8. PRK—Choe Jong-sil 74.85 [40], Sin Myong-ok 72.50 [45], Kang Myong-suk 72.35 [48], Kim Chunson 71.40 [52], Choe Myong-hui 71.20 [54], Lo Ok-sil 70.50 [59]

1984 Los Angeles T: 16, N: 16, D: 8.1.

	Total points
1. ROM	392.20
2. USA	391.20
3. CHN	388.60
4. GER	379.15
5. CAN	378.90
6. JPN	376.75
7. GBR	373.85
8. SWI	373.50

1. ROM—Ecaterina Szabó 78.12 [2], Laura Cutina 78.40 [3], Simona Păuca 78.05 [7], Cristina Grigoraş 77.90 [8], Miháela Stănulet 77.70 [10], Lavinia Agache 77.60 [11]
2. USA—Mary Lou Retton 79.05 [1], Julianne McNamara 78.40 [3], Kathy Johnson 78.10 [6], Michelle Dusserre 77.55 [12], Tracee Talavera 77.10 [16], Pamela Bileck 76.80 [17]
3. CHN—Ma Yanhong 78.20 [5], Wu Jiani 77.75 [9], Chen Yongyan 77.35 [13], Zhou Ping 77.35 [13], Zhou Qiurui 76.50 [19], Huang Qun 76.30 [21]
4. GER—Elke Heine 76.55 [18], Anja Wilhelm 76.45 [20], Astrid Beckers 75.25 [29], Angela Golz 74.85 [31], Brigitta Lehmann 74.85 [31], Heike Schwarm 74.85 [31]
5. CAN—Andrea Thomas 75.85 [23], Bonnie Wittmeier 75.85 [23], Anita Botnen 75.55 [27], Gigi Zosa 75.40 [28], Jessica Tudos 74.75 [36], Kelly Brown 73.50 [50]
6. JPN—Maiko Morio 75.90 [22], Noriko Mochizuki 75.70 [26], Tokie Kawase 74.85 [31], Chihiro Oyagi 74.85 [31], Ayami Yukimori 73.90 [45], Sae Watanabe 73.75 [47]
7. GBR—Natalie Davies 75.05 [30], Amanda Harrison 74.55 [38], Kathleen Williams 74.45 [39], Hayley Price 74.05 [43], Lisa Young 74.05 [43], Sally Larner 73.60 [48]
8. SWI—Romi Kessler 77.35 [13], Susi Latanzio 74.40 [41], Natalie Seiler 74.15 [42], Monika Beer 73.20 [51], Bettina Ernst 73.20 [51], Marisa Jervella 72.55 [58]

As the winners of eight consecutive Olympic titles, the Soviet women's team would have been the overwhelming favorites in Los Angeles had they not been prevented from competing by their government's boycott.

In 2011 US gymnastics head coach Don Peters was accused of sexually abusing two athletes in the 1980s. Although the alleged abuse could not be prosecuted under California law because the statute of limitations had expired, Peters was banned for life by USA Gymnastics and his place in the Hall of Fame was revoked.

1988 Seoul T: 12, N: 12, D: 9.21.

	Total points
1. SOV	395.475
2. ROM	394.125
3. GDR	390.875
4. USA	390.575
5. BUL	390.550
6. CHN	388.400
7. CZE	386.150
8. HUN	385.625

1. SOV—Yelena Shushunova 79.675 [1], Svetlana Boginskaya 79.40 [3], Natalija Lascenova 78.90 [5], Svetlana Baitova 78.425 [13], Yelena Shevchenko 78.35 [14], Olha Strazheva 68.175 [85]
2. ROM—Daniela Silivaş 79.575 [2], Gabriela Potorac 78.925 [4], Aurelia Dobre 78.615 [6], Celestina Popa 78.575 [10], Eugenia Golea 77.875 [18], Camelia Voinea 77.775 [22]
3. GDR—Dagmar Kersten 78.65 [8], Dörte Thümmler 78.55 [11], Ulrike Klotz 78.275 [16], Gabriele Fähnrich 77.625 [25], Betti Schieferdecker 77.45 [30], Martina Jentsch 38.25 [87]
4. USA—Phoebe Mills 78.675 [6], Brandy Johnson 78.55 [11], Kelly Garrison-Staves 77.825 [21], Theresa Spivey 77.45 [30], Chelle Stack 77.40 [32], Melissa Marlowe 76.85 [46]
5. BUL—Diana Dudeva 78.65 [8], Deliana Vodenicharova 78.325 [15], Boriana Stoyanova 77.95 [17], Ivelina Raikova 77.85 [20], Maria Kartalova 77.25 [35], Khrabrina Khrabova 76.025 [62]
6. CHN—Chen Cuiting 77.875 [18], Fan Di 77.475 [28], Wang Wenjing 77.40 [32], Wang Huiying 77.35 [34], Ma Ying 77.025 [41], Wang Xiaoyan 76.925 [44]
7. CZE—Iveta Poloková 77.65 [23], Hana Říčná 77.175 [38], Alena Dřevjaná 76.975 [43], Ivona Krmelová 76.725 [49], Martina Velisková 76.60 [52], Jana Vejrková 76.175 [58]
8. HUN—Eszter Óváry 77.50 [26], Andrea Ladányi 77.25 [35], Beáta Storczer 77.25 [35], Zsuzsanna Csisztu 76.775 [47], Zsuzsanna Miskó 76.275 [56], Ágnes Miskó 38.15 [88]

The Soviet women overcame the embarrassment of losing the 1987 World Championships to the Romanians by easily continuing their Olympic undefeated streak.

Although the race for gold and silver was uneventful, controversy emerged in the battle for bronze when the East Germans found themselves facing unexpectedly stiff challenges from the US and Bulgaria. The problem arose during the compulsory round while the American women were performing on the uneven bars. It was the responsibility of the US alternate, Rhonda Faehn, to remove the springboard that competing gymnasts used to mount the bars. After Kelly Garrison-Steves had mounted, Faehn took hold of the springboard. But instead of climbing down from the podium, the competition platform, to the bench, she withdrew to the edge of the podium and watched Garrison-Steves go through her routine.

Ellen Berger, the East German president of the technical committee of the International Gymnastics Federation, immediately pointed out that Faehn's presence on the podium was an infraction of the rules and imposed a penalty of five tenths of a point. To apply this rarely enforced rule was petty, but technically correct. Unfortunately, as it turned out, the deduction cost the US the bronze medal—they lost it to the East Germans by three tenths of a point.

US coach Béla Karolyi was furious. He referred to Berger as a "cow" and called the ruling against the US "a Communist plot."

International politics undoubtedly influenced the controversial decision; however, the ruling probably involved another factor of a more personal nature. Four years earlier at the Los Angeles Olympics, Béla Karolyi had jumped the press barricade to embrace his pupil, Mary Lou Retton. Ellen Berger, who was the head of the technical committee at that meet as well, reminded Karolyi that he was not a member of the US coaching squad and was not allowed to be on the competition floor. She warned US team officials that if Karolyi appeared on the floor again, she would enforce the rules and deduct three-tenths of a point from Retton's score. When US head coach Don Peters told Karolyi of Berger's threat, he replied, "She doesn't have the guts to do it here with 10,000 screaming Americans."

Karolyi, who had been observed practicing his jump over the barricade the night before the competition, hopped over again on the night after he had been warned, when Retton completed the vault that won her the All-Around gold medal. Karolyi was right about Berger: she didn't penalize Retton three-tenths of a point, a penalty that would have cost her the gold medal, not in front of 10,000 screaming Americans. But four years later, Berger got her revenge on Karolyi and six young women were the victims.

1992 Barcelona T: 12, N: 12, D: 7.28.

	Total points
1. SOV	395.666
2. ROM	395.079
3. USA	394.704
4. CHN	392.941
5. SPA	391.428
6. HUN	388.602
7. AUS	387.502
8. FRA	386.052

1. SOV—Svetlana Boginskaya 79.287 [2], Tetiana Lysenko 79.122 [5], Rozalya Galiyeva 78.886 [8], Tatyana Gutsu 78.848 [9], Yelena Grudneva 78.411 [22], Oksana Chusovitina 78.111 [30]
2. ROM—Cristina Bontaş 79.211 [3], Lavinia Miloşovici 79.198 [4], Gina Gogean 78.886 [7], Vanda Hădărean 78.761 [11], Maria Neculişă 78.623 [17], Mirela Paşca 78.585 [19]

3. USA—Shannon Miller 79.311 [1], Elizabeth Okino 78.998 [6], Kim Zmeskal 78.749 [12], Kerri Strug 78.735 [14], Dominique Dawes 78.360 [26], Wendy Bruce 78.161 [28]
4. CHN—Yang Bo 78.737 [13], Lu Li 78.734 [15], Li Yifang 78.598 [18], Li Li 78.536 [20], He Xuemei 78.198 [27], Zhang Xia 77.773 [35]
5. SPA—Cristina Fraguas Sánchez 78.436 [21], Sonia Fraguas Sánchez 78.147 [29], Alicia Fernández 78.062 [31], Eva Rueda Bravo 78.035 [32], Ruth Rollán González 77.397 [42], Silvia Martínez Albalat 77.111 [49]
6. HUN—Henrietta Ónodi 78.698 [16], Andrea Molnár 78.386 [23], Bernadette Balázs 76.898 [54], Kinga Horváth 76.836 [55], Ildikó Balog 75.624 [81], Krisztina Molnár 67.859 [89]
7. AUS—Lisa Read 77.935 [33], Monique Allen 77.548 [39], Kylie Shadbolt 77.196 [46], Jane Warrilow 77.049 [51], Julie-Anne Monico 76.360 [68], Brooke Gysen 76.311 [69]
8. FRA—Marie Angeline Colson 77.661 [36], Virginie Machado 77.611 [37], Chloé Maigre 77.284 [43], Karine Boucher 76.573 [62], Karine Charlier 76.148 [71], Jenny Rolland 75.422 [84]

The Barcelona Olympics marked the tenth and final time that the republics of the former Soviet Union would compete as one team. Despite a spirited challenge from the Romanians, they kept their winning streak alive, earning their tenth straight set of gold medals. Ten years later, Gina Gogean revealed that, in 1992, Romanian officials had used a forged birth certificate to qualify her for the Olympics, when she was actually only 13 years old.

1996 Atlanta T: 12, N: 12, D: 7.23.

	Total points
1. USA	389.225
2. RUS	388.404
3. ROM	388.246
4. CHN	385.867
5. UKR	385.841
6. BLR	381.263
7. SPA	378.081
8. FRA	377.715

1. USA—Dominique Dawes, Kerri Strug, Dominique Morceanu, Shannon Miller, Jaycie Phelps, Amy Chow, Amanda Borden
2. RUS—Dina Kochetkova, Svetlana Khorkina, Rozalya Galiyeva, Yelena Grosheva, Yelena Dolgopolova, Yevgeniya Kuznetsova, Oksana Lyapina
3. ROM—Lavinia Miloşovici, Gina Gogean, Mirela Ţugurla, Alexandra Marinescu, Simona Amanar, Ionela Loaies
4. CHN—Mo Huilan, Mao Yanling, Qiao Ya, Ji Liya, Kui Yuanyuan, Bi Wenjiang, Liu Xuan
5. UKR—Svetlana Zelepoukina, Lilia Podkopayeva, Lioubov Sheremeta, Anna Mirgorodskaia, Oksana Knijnik, Olena Shaparna, Olga Teslenko
6. BLR—Yelena Piskun, Alena Polozkova, Svetlana Boginskaya, Lyudmila Vytukova, Olga Yurkina, Svetlana Tarasevich, Tatyana Zharganova
7. SPA—Mónica Martín Cid, Joana Juárez Roura, Mercedes Pacheco del Barrio, Elisabeth Valle Romero, Diana Plaza Martín, Verónica Castro Gómez
8. FRA—Isabelle Severino, Elvire Teza, Emilie Volle, Ludivine Furnon, Cécile Canqueteau, Laure Gely

Kerri Strug (centre) Dominique Morceanu and Shannon Miller, 1996
Strug, her leg in a cast, stands between teammates Morceanu and Miller after being awarded a gold medal in team gymnastics in 1996.

The Russian team built a slim lead of .127 in the compulsories, but the Americans, cheered on by 32,000 spectators, most of whom seemed unaware that non-US gymnasts were also performing, quickly took the lead in the optionals two nights later. After three rotations, the US had built a seemingly unsurmountable lead of .897. Several of the Russian gymnasts were already in tears as they moved to their final apparatus: floor exercise. The Americans concluded with the vault. The first four US performers, Phelps, Chow, Miller and Dawes, each earned solid scores. But 14-year-old Dominique Morceanu suffered two straight pratfalls. Her 9.2 looked droppable since the final American, Kerri Strug, was a vault specialist. Strug attempted a Yurchenko 1½ twist, a vault she had not missed in more than three months. Yet this time she missed it, landing short and falling back on her seat. Her score was only 9.162, but what was worse, Strug heard something snap and felt a terrific pain shoot up from her left ankle.

What happened next would transform Strug, who had always played a supporting role to other US stars, into a national heroine. At 18, Strug was 4 feet 9½ inches (1.46 meters) tall, weighed 87 pounds (39.5 kilograms) and spoke with a high-pitched and literally pre-pubescent voice. Strug had been trained by US team coach Béla Karolyi until Karolyi temporarily retired following the 1992 Olympics. Strug bounced through three coaches during the next three years before returning to Karolyi in 1995. She also struggled through more than her share of injuries, most notably a severely sprained lower back after a 1994 fall from the uneven bars.

Now, in Atlanta, Strug limped back to the sidelines. She was in great pain and, including the time while she waited for her score, she had only one and a half minutes to decide if she should pass her second vault and let Morceanu's 9.2 go on the US scorecard.

"I can't do it," said Strug. "I can't feel my leg."

Béla Karolyi replied, "We need a 9.6." Her teammates, not realizing the seriousness of her injury, urged Strug to shake it off and try the second vault. At the 1995 world championships, Strug had qualified for the vault final, but had withdrawn, citing an injury to her right ankle. This time, at the Olympics, she raced down the runway, made the jump, stuck the landing, hopped a couple times on her right foot and collapsed in agony. Score: 9.712. A few minutes later, wearing a soft cast, she was carried to the victory podium by Béla Karolyi.

The US television version, presented not live, but on tape delay, was that Strug, realizing her team needed one more high score to ensure victory, sacrificed herself for the common good. This was not untrue, but reality was more complicated than the television version. In the first place, the US didn't need Strug's second vault. Without it, they would have won anyway by .309. Karolyi and others would say that no one in the American camp knew this, particularly since Russia's Roza Galiyeva was still performing. But Galiyeva would have needed a 9.972 to give her team gold, a virtual impossibility considering that the competition's highest score on any apparatus had been a 9.887. In fact, Galiyeva earned a 9.5 that was dropped. If the US team didn't know that Strug's final vault was unnecessary, they were the only ones on the floor who didn't.

Strug's motivation was also more complex than mere patriotism. As a 14-year-old at the Barcelona Olympics, she had missed qualifying for the All-Around final by the slimmest of margins. Typical of her pre-Atlanta career, in Barcelona she was the fourth best American when only three from each nation were allowed to advance. One of Strug's goals in 1996 was to make it to the individual final. To do so, she needed to improve her vault score. Strug did qualify for the All-Around. She also qualified for two apparatus finals: floor exercise, in which she posted the highest score of any gymnast, and vault. Unfortunately, her ankle injury, which was reported to be a lateral sprain with two torn ligaments, forced her to withdraw from all three events.

Kerri Strug's undeniably courageous performance would, quite unexpectedly, earn her a small fortune in appearance fees. But she also paid a hard price for her act of courage. The ankle injury would turn out to be more serious that originally perceived. At one point, in 1997, she was actually sued by a company that arranged a gymnastics exhibition tour for her on the grounds that she had failed to disclose the full extent of her injury. In 1999, after running her first marathon, she told *Runner's World*, "Unfortunately, the ankle problem is just part of my life now."

Alexandra Marinescu of the Romanian team later revealed that she had been forced to lie about her age in order to compete. The minimum age was 15, however Marinescu was actually only 14 years old.

2000 Sydney T: 6, N: 6, D: 9.19.

	Total points
1. ROM	154.608
2. RUS	154.403
3. CHN	154.008
3. USA	152.933
4. SPA	152.113
5. UKR	151.846

1. ROM—Andreea Răducan, Simona Amanar, Maria Olaru, Loredana Boboc, Andreea Isarescu, Claudia Presacan
2. RUS—Svetlana Khorkina, Yekaterina Lobaznyuk, Yelena Produnova, Yelena Zamoldchikova, Anastassia Kolesnikova, Anna Chepeleva
3. CHN—Yun Yang, Fangxiao Dong, Xuan Liu, Jie Ling, Mandan Huang, Yuanyuan Kui
3. USA—Elise Ray, Amy Chow, Kristin Maloney, Dominique Dawes, Tasha Schwikert-Warren, Jamie Dantzscher
4. SPA—Esther Moya Salvador, Laura Martínez Ruiz, Sara Moro de Faes, Susana García Escrich, Marta Cusido Muntada, Paloma Moro López Menchero
5. UKR—Olha Roshchupkina, Viktoriya Karpenko, Halyna Tyryk, Tetyana Yarosh, Olha Teslenko, Alona Kvasha

DISQ: CHN—Yang Yun, Dong Fangxiao, Liu Xuan, Ling Jie, Huang Mandan, Kui Yuanyuan

Romania and Russia finished one-two at the 1997 world championships, the 1998 European championships and the 1999 world championships. The Russians finally broke through to the top podium at the 2000 European championships in May, as the Romanians fell back to third behind Ukraine. The Russians also finished first in the qualifying round at the Sydney Olympics. In the final, after a shaky start on the uneven bars, all of the Romanians put in solid performances, completing every routine on every apparatus with nothing worse than minor bobbles. When they were finished, the Russians and the Chinese still had two rotations to go. Both teams were slightly ahead of the Romanians, even though Russian captain Svetlana

Khorkina had fallen off the uneven bars, an apparatus for which she was the reigning world and Olympic champion. As the Romanians watched, two Russians, Yelena Zamolodchikova and Yekaterina Lobaznyuk, fell off the beam. Russia staged a comeback on the floor exercise and moved ahead of China into second place, but they were too far back to catch the Romanians.

Claudia Presacan of the Romanian team was involved in a minor scandal in 2002 when she and two other gymnasts, Lavinia Miloşovici and Corina Ungureanu appeared in a Japanese magazine, book and DVD posing naked and performing gymnastic routines semi-nude and wearing uniforms that included the emblem of the Romanian Gymnastics Federation. Vanda Hădărean, a member of the 1992 Romanian Olympic team, had already appeared nude in the August 2000 Romanian edition of *Playboy*.

Eight years after winning the bronze medal with China's gymnastics team, Dong Fangxiao came under suspicion during an investigation into the ages of China's 2008 female gymnastics team. Dong's accreditation information for the Beijing Olympics listed her birthday as 23 January 1986, which would have made her 14 years old in Sydney, two years below the minimum required age. In 2010, after an extensive investigation by the International Gymnastics Federation, the IOC nullified Dong's results, stripping China of the bronze medals and lifting the US to third place. Dong was also stripped of her sixth place result in the individual floor exercise and seventh place in the vault.

2004 Athens T: 12, N: 12, D: 8.17.

	Total points
1. ROM	114.283
2. USA	113.584
3. RUS	113.235
4. UKR	112.309
5. SPA	111.572
6. FRA	110.159
7. CHN	110.008
8. AUS	108.847

1. ROM—Oana Ban, Alexandra Eremia, Cătălina Ponor, Monica Roşu, Nicoleta Daniela Şofronie
2. USA—Mohini Bhardwaj, Annia Hatch, Terin Humphrey, Courtney Kupets, Carly Patterson
3. RUS—Lyudmila Yezhova, Svetlana Khorkina, Anna Pavlova, Yelena Zamolodchikova, Natalya Ziganshina
4. UKR—Mirabella Akhunu, Alina Kozich, Irina Krasnianska, Alona Kvasha, Olha Sherbatykh, Irina Yarotska
5. SPA—Tania Gener Cordero, Elena Gómez Servera, Mónica Mesalles Sallarés, Patricia Moreno Sánchez, Sara Moro de Faes
6. FRA—Coralie Chacon, Soraya Chaouch, Marine Debauve, Emilie Le Pennec, Camille Schmutz, Isabelle Severino
7. CHN—Cheng Fei, Fan Ye, Li Ya, Lin Li, Wang Tiantian, Zhang Nan
8. AUS—Karen Nguyen, Stephanie Moorhouse, Melissa Munro, Monette Russo, Lisa Skinner, Allana Slater

After their victory at the 2000 Olympics, Romania won the world championship in 2001, but were beaten by the United States in 2003 when the world championships were held in the US, in Anaheim, California. At the Athens Olympics, led by Monica Roşu's 9.625, Romania took a slight first rotation lead of .05 points over the United States. The Romanians struggled on the uneven bars, with a fifth-place total, and fell .338 points behind the Americans. Only a solid performance by Daniela Şofronie (9.562 points) kept them in the running. The Romanians regained their form on the balance beam, moving back into the lead by .124, as Cătălina Ponor and Alexandra Eremia achieved the apparatus' highest scores. The final apparatus was the floor exercise, where the Romanians were confident they could withstand the US, especially since the Americans had lower start values. Sure enough, led by Ponor's 9.750, the Romanians outscored the Americans by more than half a point to gain a clear victory.

2008 Beijing T: 12, N: 12, D: 8.13.

	Total points
1. CHN	188.900
2. USA	186.525
3. ROM	181.525
4. RUS	180.625
5. JPN	176.700
6. AUS	176.525
7. FRA	175.275
8. BRA	174.875

1. CHN—Cheng Fei, He Kexin, Jiang Yuyuan, Li Shanshan, Yang Yilin, Deng Linlin
2. USA—Shawn Johnson, Anastasia "Nastia" Liukin, Chellsie Memmel, Samantha Peszek, Alicia Sacramone, Bridget Sloan
3. ROM—Steliana Nistor, Sandra Izbaşa, Andreea Acatrinei, Andreea Grigore, Gabriela Drăgoi, Ana Tămârjan
4. RUS—Kseniya Afanasyeva, Svetlana Klyukina, Yekaterina Kramarenko, Anna Pavlova, Lyudmila Yezhova-Grebenkova, Kseniya Semyonova
5. JPN—Koko Tsurumi, Kyoko Oshima, Yu Minobe, Miki Uemura, Mayu Kuroda, Yuko Shintake
6. AUS—Georgia Bonora, Ashleigh Brennan, Lauren Mitchell, Olivia Vivian, Dasha Joura, Shona Morgan
7. FRA—Marine Debauve, Laetitia Dugain, Katheleen Lindor, Pauline Morel, Marine Petit, Rose-Eliandre Bellemare
8. BRA—Ana Silva, Daiane dos Santos, Daniele Hypólito, Ethiene Franco, Jade Barbosa, Laís Souza

One of the most publicized controversies of the Beijing Olympics involved the Chinese women's gymnastics team. Under the rules in force in 2008 (and still in force), gymnasts must turn sixteen in an Olympic year to be eligible to compete. Two weeks before the Opening Ceremony *The New York Times* reported that several newspaper and online accounts indicated that He Kexin and Jiang Yuyuan were underage. Gymnast registration lists and at least one newspaper account from *China Daily*, the country's official English-language paper, indicated He's age as fourteen, while an online list of junior gymnastics competitors listed Jiang's birth date as 1 October 1993, which would have made her only fifteen. An Associated Press report from 2007 included a speech by Chinese sports administrator Liu Peng praising "13-year-old uneven bar gymnast He Kexin." The official Chinese government sports website had listed He's birthday as 1 January 1994. But before the Olympics it was changed to 1 January 1992. A third gymnast, Yang Yilin, became implicated after state-run China Central Television (CCTV) posted a profile of her indicating that she too was fourteen. The websites were quickly taken down, but not before online security consultant Mike Walker posted backup versions on a public blog.

Officials with China's gymnastics federation responded by providing copies of each gymnast's ID card and passport, indicating their ages as sixteen or over. FIG (the International Gymnastics Federation) quickly issued a statement saying that the IOC had examined all gymnasts' passports and determined that none were underage. The abundant evidence indicating that these documents might have been forged was ignored.

Whatever the case, the differences between the two leading teams were stark. The Chinese team had an average height of 4 ft 9 in (1.45m) and an average weight of 77 pounds (35 kg), with the Americans on average three and a half inches (8.9 cm) taller and 30 pounds (13.5 kg) heavier.

Shrugging off the controversy, China finished first in the qualifying round, despite a fall by He Kexin on her final apparatus, the uneven bars. The US qualified in second place, with Shawn Johnson and Nastia Liukin contributing 62.725 and 62.375 points each, the highest individual scores of the competition.

China and the US were paired in the final, going head-to-head on the same apparatuses. The US took the lead after the first rotation, outscoring China 46.875 to 46.350 on the vault. China moved into first place after the uneven bars, with strong performances by He and Yang (16.850 and 16.800), although Liukin earned the highest score of the round, 16.900.

The US had an opportunity to retake the lead on the third apparatus, the balance beam, when Chinese team captain Cheng Fei fell during her first tumbling pass. Performing first for the US, Alicia Sacramone also fell while mounting the bar, scoring 15.100 on her routine and keeping the US in second place.

Trailing by one point going into the last rotation, the US needed three strong floor exercise routines to overtake China. Sacramone started off well, but fell on her second tumbling pass, and then stepped out of bounds, while Johnson and Liukin both stepped out of bounds as well. Competing last, Cheng Fei clinched the gold medal for China by scoring 15.450 points, the second-highest floor exercise score.

The IOC declined to launch their own investigation into the age of the Chinese gymnasts. Instead, a week after the competition, they asked FIG to do so. In October, FIG declared that the documentation provided by Chinese authorities was sufficient. Chinese officials blamed the age discrepancies on administrative errors.

RHYTHMIC ALL-AROUND

In rhythmic gymnastics, thin young women perform 75- to 90-second routines using various accessories: hoop, rope, clubs, ball, and ribbon. Only four of the five accessories are chosen for each Olympic competition. In 2012 they will be: ball, clubs, hoop and ribbon. The floor area is 12 meters square: the same as that used in artistic floor exercise. Each routine is scored by ten judges, five for composition and five for execution. Acrobatic feats, such as cartwheels, flips, and handsprings, are not allowed. The accessories, or apparatus as they are known officially, may be any color except gold, silver, and bronze. Competitors must be at least 15 years old. Their dress is strictly regulated. Gymnasts must wear leotards of non-transparent material without decoration or trim. The cut of the leotard must not go beyond the fold of the crotch, the neckline in the back cannot extend beyond the center point between the shoulder blades, and the neckline of the front must be "proper."

Nineteen of the 24 individual competitors are determined by the results of the most recent World Rhythmic Gymnastics Championships: two from each of the top five ranked teams and one each from the next ten ranked teams. The International Gymnastics Federation (FIG) chooses the other four wildcard entries.

1896–1960 not held

1984 Los Angeles C: 33, N: 20, D: 8.11.

		HOOP		ROPE		CLUBS		RIBBON		TOTAL PTS.
1. Lori Fung	CAN	14.525	3	14.425	4	14.6	2	14.4	2	57.95
2. Doina Stăiculescu	ROM	14.55	1	14.7	1	14.725	1	13.925	9	57.90
3. Regina Weber	GER	14.55	1	14.425	4	14.35	5	14.375	3	57.70
4. Alma Drăgan	ROM	14.475	4	14.5	2	14.525	3	13.875	11	57.375
5. Milena Reljin	YUG/SER	14.175	10	14.375	6	14.275	7	14.425	1	57.25
6. Marta Cantón Gutiérrez	SPA	14.275	7	14.2	9	14.35	5	14.125	4	56.95
7. Giulia Staccioli	ITA	14.45	5	14.25	8	14.25	8	13.825	14	56.775
8. Hiroko Yamasaki	JPN	14.3	6	14.35	7	14.175	10	13.85	12	56.675

There were few winners at the 1984 Olympics more unexpected than 21-year-old Lori Fung of Vancouver, Canada. Even with the absence of the boycotting nations, in particular the Bulgarians, Fung was a rank outsider, having finished 23rd at the 1983 World Championships. However, in the interim, she had studied hard in Romania with gold medal favorite Doina Stăiculescu. In Los Angeles, while others were dropping their balls, or having their ribbons disrupted by unpredictable currents from the air conditioning system, or suffering the exposure of their bra straps (an automatic deduction), Fung performed smoothly and went home with the gold medal.

1988 Seoul C: 35, N: 21, D: 9.30.

		HOOP		ROPE		CLUBS		RIBBON		TOTAL PTS.
1. Marina Lobach	SOV/BLR	15.0	1	15.0	1	15.0	1	15.0	1	60.00
2. Adriana Dunavska	BUL	15.0	1	15.0	1	14.95	2	15.0	1	59.95
3. Oleksandra Tymoshenko	SOV/UKR	15.0	1	15.0	1	14.875	3	15.0	1	59.875
4. Bianka Panova	BUL	15.0	1	15.0	1	14.775	4	14.95	4	59.725
5. María Isabel Lloret	SPA	14.725	5	14.75	5	14.7	6	14.725	6	58.90
6. Andrea Sinkó	HUN	14.65	7	14.75	5	14.725	5	14.65	8	58.775
7. Teresa Folga	POL	14.55	10	14.675	9	14.6	13	14.8	5	58.625
8. Diana Schmiemann	GER	14.6	8	14.65	11	14.7	6	14.65	8	58.60

Lobach, who had never before placed higher than fourth in a major international competition, was awarded a perfect score for each of her four routines in both the preliminary and the final. Nevertheless, she almost lost the gold medal when she came within one second of exceeding the time limit during her clubs performance. Fortunately, her pianist, Anatoly Vekshin, began playing faster at the end of the routine and Lobach finished just as the gong sounded.

Seventh-place finisher Teresa Folga of Kraków won the Miss Olympic Village beauty contest. In the words of the *Korea Herald,* Folga "outshined other contestants with her beautiful hair, slim and attractive body and eloquent conversation skills." She had been voted a similar prize by journalists attending the 1987 rhythmic world championships.

1992 Barcelona C: 43, N: 25, D: 8.8.

		HOOP		ROPE		CLUBS		BALL		TOTAL PTS.
1. Oleksandra Tymoshenko	UKR	14.812	1	14.85	1	14.85	1	14.525	2	59.037
2. Carolina Pascual Gracia	SPA	14.5	3	14.45	2	14.562	2	14.587	1	58.100
3. Oksana Skaldina	UKR	14.587	2	14.325	4	14.487	3	14.512	3	57.912
4. Carmen Acedo Jorge	SPA	14.337	4	14.262	6	14.275	5	14.35	4	57.225
5. Maria Petrova	BUL	14.225	6	14.312	5	14.325	4	14.225	6	57.087
6. Irina Deleanu	ROM	13.8	12	14.387	3	14.262	6	14.162	7	56.612
7. Joanna Bodak	POL	14.112	7	14.0	9	14.25	7	14.112	8	56.475
8. Lenk Oulehlová	CZE	14.0	9	14.175	7	13.862	10	14.1	9	56.137

Rhythmic gymnastics has a reputation as one of the joke sports of the Olympics, included in the program to please a limited constituency. The International Gymnastics Federation did not help matters when they approved an unusually ridiculous format for the 1992 Games. Rather than choosing the gymnasts with the highest scores in the qualifying round to advance to the final, they decided that the six best would qualify for the final, along with the top 12 for each apparatus. Because the medals were decided on the basis of total score with all four apparatus, this meant that nine of the 17 finalists were performing with only one to three apparatus and had no chance to win.

The competition had more than its share of controversy. Skaldina, convinced that Pascual had beaten her out for the silver medal only because the judges were trying to please the Spanish hosts, refused to acknowledge her rival at the medal ceremony. But Skaldina, although the defending world champion, was lucky to be at the Olympics at all. On June 8, she placed only fifth at the European Championships (won by Maria Petrova) and, with only two entrants allowed for each nation, it appeared that she would lose her spot to the up-and-coming Siberian Oksana Kostina. Three and a half months after the Olympics, Kostina won the world championships, but on February 11, 1993, she was killed in a car crash. She was 17 years old.

As for European champion Petrova, she would have placed fourth at the Olympics, but while she was performing with her hoop, her zipper broke and the back of her leotard popped open. Naturally she was penalized two-tenths of a point, which dropped her back to fifth place.

1996 Atlanta-Athens C: 37, N: 22, D: 8.1.

		ROPE		BALL		CLUBS		RIBBON		TOTAL PTS.
1. Yekaterina Serebryanskaya	UKR	9.95	1	9.95	1	9.95	1	9.833	1	39.683
2. Yanina Batyrshina	RUS	9.85	3	9.916	2	9.933	2	9.683	7	39.382
3. Yelena Vytrychenko	UKR	9.866	2	9.8	4	9.849	3	9.816	2	39.331
4. Amina Zarypova	RUS	9.783	4	9.866	3	9.832	4	9.783	3	39.264
5. Maria Petrova	BUL	9.733	5	9.783	5	9.733	5	9.75	4	38.999
6. Eva Serrano	FRA	9.683	7	9.7	7	9.7	6	9.733	6	38.816
7. Larisa Lukyanenko	BLR	9.466	10	9.75	6	9.7	6	9.75	4	38.666
8. Tatyana Ogryzko	BLR	9.583	8	9.682	8	9.599	9	9.666	8	38.530

The judging left most observers mystified and seemed to be based as much on career achievement as on actual performances at the Olympics. As three-time world champion Maria Petrova said after placing fifth despite four error-free exercises, "Our sport is more of a sport outside the competition hall. It's in the hallways; it's in the cafes; between the judges." The specific controversy in 1996 occurred when Vytrychenko, who had led the preliminary round, performed flawlessly in the final but was marked lower than Serebryanskaya and Batyrshina, both of whom had drops in their routines. The conspiracy against Vytrychenko got even worse in 2000 when, three months before the Olympics, she was ranked 18th in the preliminary round of the European Championships. An inquiry into the incident led the International Gymnastics Federation to suspend six judges for block voting.

Yanina Batyrshina, 1996
Batyrshina, winner of the silver medal in the 1996 rhythmic gymnastics competition.

2000 Sydney C: 10, N: 7, D: 10.1.

		ROPE		HOOP		BALL		RIBBON		TOTAL PTS.
1. Yuliya Barsukova	RUS	9.833	3	9.900	1	9.916	3	9.933	2	39.632
2. Yuliya Raskina	BLR	9.908	2	9.791	4	9.933	2	9.916	3	39.548
3. Alina Kabayeva	RUS	9.925	1	9.641	9	9.950	1	9.950	1	39.466
4. Olena Vitrychenko	UKR	9.825	5	9.833	3	9.875	4	9.875	4	39.408
5. Eva Serrano	FRA	9.841	4	9.850	2	9.841	5	9.858	5	39.390
6. Tamara Yerofeyeva	UKR	9.750	8	9.750	5	9.750	8	9.750	6	39.000
7. Dona Evmorfia	GRE	9.766	7	9.716	8	9.775	6	9.725	9	38.982
8. Valeria Vatkina	BLR	9.791	6	9.750	5	9.666	10	9.750	6	38.957

Uzbek-born Alina Kabayeva had won every major competition since 1998 and entered the Olympics as the prohibitive favorite. She earned the highest score in the qualification round and then opened the final with the highest score with the rope. But during her second routine, Kabayeva lost control of her hoop during a jump and then watched as it spun off the mat. Because she had to leave the mat to retrieve it, she incurred an automatic penalty of two tenths of a point that proved to be the margin that kept her out of first place despite her top scores with the last two apparatuses. Kabayeva's teammate, 21-year-old Yulia Barsukova, was the surprised and delighted beneficiary of Kabayeva's error.

2004 Athens C: 24, N: 19, D: 8.29.

		HOOP		BALL		CLUBS		RIBBON		TOTAL PTS.
1. Alina Kabayeva	RUS	26.800	2	27.350	1	27.150	1	27.100	1	108.400
2. Irina Chashchina	RUS	27.100	1	27.100	2	26.825	3	26.300	3	107.325
3. Anna Bezsonova	UKR	26.500	3	26.525	4	26.950	2	26.725	2	106.700
4. Aliya Yusupova	KAZ	25.500	4	26.600	3	26.325	5	25.550	5	103.975
5. Natalia Hodunko	UKR	25.500	4	25.800	5	26.375	4	26.125	4	103.800
6. Simona Peycheva	BUL	25.375	6	25.675	6	25.600	6	24.400	8	101.050
7. Inna Zhukova	BLR	25.000	8	25.300	7	25.200	7	25.075	6	100.575
8. Almudena Cid Tostado	SPA	25.125	7	25.000	8	24.900	8	23.425	10	98.450

After her disappointing bronze medal finish in Sydney, Alina Kabayeva went on to win the 2001 all-around world championship title ahead of compatriot Irina Chashchina. Both Kabayeva and Chashchina were subsequently stripped of their titles after testing positive for a banned diuretic, furosemide, at the 2001 Goodwill Games. Back in action by spring 2003, Kabayeva defended her world championship later that year. In the qualifying round at the 2004 Olympics, Kabayeva dropped three of her four apparatus, but still managed to qualify in first place. Chashchina placed a close second, with 2003 world championship silver medalist Anna Bezsonova third. In the final, Chashchina finished first in the hoop routine, with 27.1 points, to Kabayeva's 26.8. Despite finishing second in the ball routine, Chashchina held on to a narrow .05-point lead over Kabayeva, but slipped to second after the clubs. Kabayeva expanded her lead in the final ribbon routine, earning 27.1 points to finish more than a full point ahead of Chashchina. Unusually flexible, even by rhythmic gymnastics standards, Kabayeva, during her clubs routine, was able to stand on one leg while bending the other leg back over her shoulder and under her chin . . . and hold the club between her shoulder and her foot.

2008 Beijing C: 24, N: 18, D: 8.23.

		ROPE		HOOP		CLUBS		RIBBON		TOTAL PTS
1. Evgenia Kanaeva	RUS	18.850	(1)	18.850	(1)	18.950	(1)	18.850	(1)	75.500
2. Inna Zhukova	BLR	18.125	(3)	18.125	(3)	17.850	(3)	17.825	(4)	71.925
3. Anna Bessonova	UKR	17.975	(4)	17.775	(5)	17.900	(2)	18.225	(2)	71.875
4. Olga Kapranova	RUS	18.200	(2)	18.500	(2)	16.950	(8)	18.050	(3)	71.700
5. Aliya Yusupova	KAZ	17.825	(5)	17.625	(6)	17.650	(4)	16.700	(7)	69.800
6. Aliyə Qarayeva	AZE	17.750	(6)	18.075	(4)	17.225	(6)	16.625	(8)	69.675
7. Nataliya Hodunko	UKR	16.700	(8)	17.500	(7)	17.525	(5)	17.125	(5)	68.850
8. Almudena Cid Tostado	SPA	17.000	(7)	17.000	(9)	17.150	(7)	16.950	(6)	68.100

The 2005 world champion and reigning world bronze medalist, Olga Kapranova led after the first day of the qualifying round but was passed on the second day by 2008 European champion Evgenia Kanaeva, who posted the highest club and ribbon scores to qualify first.

In the final, the 18-year-old Kanaeva earned the top scores on all four apparatuses, including three 18.850s and an 18.950 score on the clubs, the highest score of the competition. Kapranova looked set for the silver medal before dropping a club on her third routine to finish just outside the medals. Inna Zhukova took silver despite also fumbling a club in her third routine, with reigning world champion Anna Bessonova in third, earning her second consecutive Olympic bronze medal.

One year after her amazing performance in Beijing, Kanaeva became the first rhythmic gymnast ever to earn six gold medals at a single world championship, winning gold in all four individual accessory events, as well as the individual and team all-around. Two years later she repeated the feat at the 2011 world championships in Montpellier, France.

RHYTHMIC TEAM

Team, or group, rhythmic gymnastics competitions consist of two apparatus sets. For 2012, for example, one apparatus set will be 5 balls, and the other 3 ribbons and 2 hoops. Each team has six members, five of whom peform in any given set. Each exercise must last between two and a quarter and two and a half minutes. In theory eight teams were supposed to participate in the Olympics: the host nation and the nations that finished first through seventh at the most recent world championships. At the 1995 world championships, China unexpectedly placed eighth, so the International Gymnastics Federation (FIG) made an exception and expanded the Olympic field to nine. In 2012, twelve teams are scheduled to compete: the top ten from the world championships and two wildcard entries. At the Olympics, the top six teams in the preliminary round advance to the final.

1896–1992 not held

1996 Atlanta-Athens T: 9, N: 9, D: 8.2.

	5 Hoops		3 Balls 2 Ribbons		Total Pts.
1. SPA	19.483	1	19.45	1	38.933
2. BUL	19.416	3	19.45	1	38.866
3. RUS	19.466	2	18.899	4	38.365
4. FRA	19.149	6	19.050	3	38.199
5. CHN	19.199	5	18.8	5	37.999
6. BLR	19.266	4	18.716	6	37.982
7. ITA					
8. GER					

1. SPA—Marta Baldó Marín, Nuria Cabanillas Provencio, Estela Giménez Cid, Lorena Guréndez García, Tania Lamarca Celada, Estíbaliz Martínez Yerro
2. BUL—Ina Delcheva, Valentina Kevlian, Maria Koleva, Maja Tabakova, Ivelina Taleva, Viara Vatachka
3. RUS—Yevgeniya Bochkaryeva, Olga Shtyrenko, Irina Dzhuba, Angelin Yushkova, Yuliya Ivanova, Yelena Krivoshey
4. FRA—Charlotte Camboulives, Carolina Chimot, Sylvie Didone, Audrey Grosclaude, Frédérique Léhon, Nadia Mimoun
5. CHN—Cai Yingying, Huang Ting, Huang Ying, Zheng Ni, Zheng Li
6. BLR—Natalya Budilyo, Olga Demskaya, Oksana Zhdanovich, Svetlana Luzanova, Galina Malachenko, Aleksiya Pohodina
7. ITA—Manuela Bocchini, Valentina Marino, Sara Pipi, Sara Pinciroli, Valentina Rovetta, Nicoletta Tinti
8. GER—Nicole Bittner, Katrin Hoffmann, Anne Jung, Dorte Schiltz, Luise Stablein, Katherina Wildermuth

There was little to separate the Spanish and Bulgarian teams. Bulgaria won the preliminary, but Spain received the highest scores in the final. Their margin of victory was attributed to the execution scores of their hoops routine.

2000 Sydney T: 8, N: 8, D: 9.30.

	Clubs		Hoop & Ribbon		Total Pts
1. RUS	19.800	1	19.700	2	39.500
2. BLR	19.800	1	19.700	2	39.500
3. GRE	19.550	3	19.733	1	39.283
4. GER	19.533	4	19.366	4	38.899
5. JPN	19.350	5	19.200	7	38.550
6. ITA	19.250	6	19.233	6	38.483
7. BUL	19.166	7	19.266	5	39.432
8. BRA	19.066	8	19.200	7	39.266

1. RUS—Irina Belova, Yelena Chalamova, Natalya Lavrova, Mariya Netesova, Vyera Shimanskaya, Irina Zilber
2. BLR—Tatyana Ananko, Tatyana Belan, Anna Glazkova, Irina Ilyenkova, Mariya Lazuk, Olga Puzhevich
3. GRE—Eirini Aindili, Evangelia Khristodoulou, Maria Georgatou, Zakharoula Kariami, Khariklia Pantazi, Anna Pollatou
4. GER—Friederike Arlt, Susan Benicke, Jeanine Fissler, Selma Neuhaus, Jessica Schumacher, Annika Seibel
5. JPN—Ayako Inada, Yukari Mizobe, Yukari Murata, Rie Nakashima, Masami Nakata, Madoka Okamon
6. ITA—Elena Amato, Eva D'Amore, Silvia Gregorini, Noemi Iezzi, Roberta Lucentini, Arianna Rusca
7. BUL—Gabriela Atanasova, Zhaneta Ilieva, Proletina Kalcheva, Eleonora Kezhova, Galina Marinova, Khristina Rangelova
8. BRA—Camila Amarante, Natalia Eidt, Flavia Faria, Alessandra Guidugli, Thalita Nakadomari, Dayane Silva

Russia and Belarus finished in a tie. The tie-breaker was to reinstate the high and low scores that are dropped in normal scoring. This brought back one judge's higher score for the execution of the Russians' clubs routine and another judge's higher score for their hoop and ribbon routine.

2004 Athens T: 10, N: 10, D: 8.28.

	Ribbons		3 Hoops 2 Balls		Total Pts.
1. RUS	25.300	1	25.800	1	51.100
2. ITA	24.150	2	25.300	2	49.450
3. BUL	23.400	4	25.300	3	48.600
4. BLR	23.500	3	24.500	4	48.000
5. GRE	22.600	6	23.925	5	46.525
6. CHN	23.100	5	23.400	6	46.500
7. SPA	22.400	7	22.950	7	45.350
8. BRA	21.900	8	22.500	8	44.400

1. RUS—Olesya Belugina, Olga Glatskikh, Tatyana Kurbakova, Nataliya Lavrova, Yelena Murzina, Yelena Posevina
2. ITA—Elisa Blanchi, Fabrizia D'Ottavio, Marinella Falca, Daniela Masseroni, Elisa Santoni, Laura Vernizzi
3. BUL—Zhaneta Ilieva, Eleonora Kezhova, Zornitsa Marinova, Kristina Rangelova, Galina Tancheva, Vladislava Tancheva
4. BLR—Natalya Aliaksandrava, Yavhenia Burlo, Hlafira Martsinovich, Zlatislava Nersesian, Alina Nikandrava, Maria Paplyka
5. GRE—Styliani Khristidou, Eleni Khronopoulou, Ilektra-Elli Efthymiou, Maria Kakiou, Varvara Magnisali, Stergiani Pantazi
6. CHN—Dai Yongjun, Hu Mei, Li Jia, Lu Yingna, Lu Yuanyang, Zhang Shuo
7. SPA—Sonia Abejón Esteban, Bárbara González Oteiza, Marta Linares García, Isabel Pagán Navarro, Carolina Rodríguez-Ballesteros, Nuria Velasco Pardo
8. BRA—Larissa Barata, Fernanda Cavalieri, Ana Maria Maciel, Tayanne Mantovaneli, Jennifer Oliveira, Dayane Camilo

The Russians arrived in Athens as the overwhelming favorites, having won the last three world championships and the last two European championships, not to mention the last Olympics. They finished first in the qualifying round and led the scoring for both routines in the final.

2008 Beijing T: 12, N: 12, D: 8.24.

	Ropes		Hoops/Clubs		Total Pts
1. RUS	17.750	(1)	17.800	(1)	35.550
2. CHN	17.575	(3)	17.650	(2)	35.225
3. BLR	17.625	(2)	17.275	(4)	34.900
4. ITA	17.000	(4)	17.425	(3)	34.425
5. BUL	16.750	(5)	16.800	(5)	33.550
6. ISR	16.050	(7)	16.050	(6)	32.100
7. AZE	16.075	(6)	15.500	(7)	31.575
8. UKR	15.975	(8)	15.125	(8)	31.100

1. RUS—Anna Gavrilenko, Margarita Aliychuk, Tatyana Gorbunova, Yelena Posevina, Dariya Shkurikhina, Nataliya Zuyeva
2. CHN—Lu Yuanyang, Cai Tongtong, Chou Tao, Sui Jianshuang, Sun Dan, Zhang Shuo
3. BLR—Zina Lunina, Alesya Babushkina, Anastasiya Ivankova, Glafira Martinovich, Kseniya Sankovich, Alina Tumilovich
4. ITA—Daniela Masseroni, Elisa Blanchi, Fabrizia D'Ottavio, Marinella Falca, Elisa Santoni, Anzhelika Savrayuk
5. BUL—Yolita Manolova, Tsveta Kuseva, Zornitsa Marinova, Maya Paunovska, Yoanna Tancheva, Tatyana Tongova
6. ISR—Olena Dvornichenko, Katia Pisetsky, Maria Savenkov, Rahel Vigdozchik, Veronika Vitenberg
7. AZE—Dina Qorina, Alina Trepina, Vəfa Hüseynova, Anastasiya Prosolova, Anna Bitiyeva, Valeriya Yegay
8. UKR—Krystyna Cherepienina, Olena Dmytrash, Alina Maksymenko, Vira Perederiy, Yuliya Slobodian, Vita Zubchenko

The Russians had won the last two Olympic titles and were the clear favorites to defend in Beijing, having won the previous five consecutive world championships and four European titles. Italy and Belarus were the only two other teams to have reached the podium in the four years since the Athens Olympics.

The Russian team made several mistakes in the qualifying round, but bounced back to earn the highest scores on both their final routines, earning their third consecutive Olympic championship. In third place behind Belarus after the ropes routine, China moved up to second with a strong performance in the hoops/clubs and the highest difficulty scores in both rotations.

TRAMPOLINE

1896–1996 not held

2000 Sydney C: 8, N: 8, D: 9.22.

		PTS.
1. Irina Karavayeva	RUS	38.9
2. Oksana Tsyhulyeva	UKR	37.7
3. Karen Cockburn	CAN	37.4
4. Yekaterina Khilko	UZB	36.6
5. Nataliya Karpenkova	BLR	35.8
6. Akiko Furu	JPN	35.3
7. Rusudan Khoperia	GEO	34.1
8. Ana Dogonadze	GER	5.0

Three-time world champion Irina Karavayeva was the overwhelming favorite. In the qualifying round, her score was matched by Anna Dogonadze, who had competed for the USSR and Georgia before marrying a German and obtaining German citizenship in 1998. In the final, Karavayeva performed as superbly as expected, while Dogonadze, after spending four days in bed with the flu, ran out of energy, flew off the trampoline and landed in last place.

This inaugural Olympic competition was graced with the presence of two important figures in trampolining history: George Nissen, the 86-year-old co-creator of the trampoline, and Judy Wills Cline, the sport's first world champion back in 1964.

2004 Athens C: 16, N: 14, D: 8.20.

		PTS.
1. Anna Dogonadze	GER	39.6
2. Karen Cockburn	CAN	39.2
3. Huang Shanshan	CHN	39.0
4. Natalya Chernova	RUS	38.6
5. Olena Movchan	UKR	37.6
6. Heather Ross-McManus	CAN	37.4
7. Haruka Hirota	JPN	37.2
8. Rea Lenders	HOL	24.3

Anna Dogonadze and defending Olympic champion Irina Karavayeva were good friends, which helped them survive an unfortunate incident at the 2001 world championships in Odense, Denmark. Dogonadze appeared to be the winner, but the final scores showed Karavayeva in first place, and she was awarded the gold medal, while Dogonadze was given the silver. A German judge noticed that one of the other judges had mistakenly keyed in a higher difficulty score for Karavayeva than she had actually deserved. Karavayeva offered to give her gold medal to Dogonadze, but the rules stated that results cannot be changed after the medals have been awarded. Bruno Grandi, the president of the International Gymnastics Federation, declared an exception to the rules and, a month later, in a special ceremony, the two gymnasts exchanged medals. In the qualifying round at the next Olympics, in Athens, Karavayeva bounced off the trampoline and was eliminated, finishing in 15th place. Dogonadze, who had endured a similar disaster at the previous Olympics, won the gold medal.

2008 Beijing C: 16, N: 13, D: 8.18.

		PTS.
1. He Wenna	CHN	37.8
2. Karen Cockburn	CAN	37.0
3. Yekaterina Khilko	UZB	36.9
4. Olena Movchan	UKR	36.6
5. Irina Karavayeva	RUS	36.2
6. Luba Golovina	GEO	36.1
7. Rosie MacLennan	CAN	35.5
8. Anna Dogonadze-Lilkendey	GER	18.9

Thirty-three-year-old Irina Karavayeva had won the 2000 Olympic gold medal and five world championship titles, including the two most recent ones. Known for attempting the highest difficulty scores in her competitions, Karavayeva lost points on execution in the qualifying round, finishing second behind newcomer He Wenna.

Twenty-six-year-old Yekaterina Khilko narrowly reached the final, edging Belarus' Tatyana Petrenya out of the final qualifying spot by 63.9 to 63.8. Khilko took the early lead in the final, earning 36.9 points with a difficulty score of 14.4. Defending Olympic champion Anna Dogonadze lost control during her routine, requiring a spotter to break her fall with a mat, and she dropped to last place. Two-time Olympic medalist Karen Cockburn moved into the lead with 37.0 points (despite being on significant pain medication after aggravating a knee injury that had twice required surgery). Karavayeva attempted the most difficult routine of the final, but was penalized for touching a side pad during her dismount, dropping her out of medal contention.

Performing last, He Wenna earned the highest execution points of the final, 23.3, and the second-highest difficulty score, 14.5, to move into first place. All three medalists performed at least one forward triple somersault with a half twist and multiple twisting double somersaults in tucked, piked and straight positions.

DISCONTINUED EVENT

TEAM EXERCISE WITH PORTABLE APPARATUS

1952 Helsinki T: 16, N: 16, D: 7.24.

	Total Points
1. SWE	74.2
2. SOV	73.0
3. HUN	71.6
4. GER	71.2
5. FIN	70.6
6. CZE	70.0
6. HOL	70.0
8. YUG	69.2

1. SWE—Karin Lindberg, Gun Röring, Evy Berggren, Göta Pettersson, Ann-Sofi Colling-Pettersson, Ingrid Sandahl, Hjördis Nordin, Vanja Blomberg
2. SOV—Maria Horokhovska, Nina Bocharova, Galina Minaicheva, Galina Urbanovich, Pelageya Danilova, Galina Shamrai, Medeya Dzchugeli, Yekaterina Kalinchuk
3. HUN—Margit Korondi, Ágnes Keleti, Edit Perényi-Weckinger, Olga Tass, Erzsébet Gulyás, Mária Zalai-Kövi, Andrea Bodó, Irén Daruházi-Karcscics
4. GER—Irma Walther, Hanna Grages, Elisabeth Ostermeier, Wolfgard Voss, Inge Sedelmeier, Lydia Zeitlhofer, Brigitte Kiesler, Hilde Koop
5. FIN—Raili Tuominen, Vappu Salonen, Arja Lehtinen, Raili Hoviniemi, Pirkko Vilppunen, Maila Nisula, Pirkko Pyykönen, Raija Simola
6. CZE—Eva Vechtová, Alena Chadimová, Jana Rabasová, Božena Srncová, Hana Bobková, Matylda Ăinová, Vera Vančurová, Alena Reichová
6. HOL—Helena Gerritsen, Huiberdina Krul van der Nolk van Gogh, Johanna Cox-Ladru, Catharina Selbach, Jacoba Kampen, Johanna Ros, Bertha Selbach, Anna Simon
8. YUG—Sonja Rožman, Tanja Žutić, Anka Drinić, Nada Spasić, Milica Rožman, Ada Smolnikar, Marija Ivandekić, Tereza Kočiš

1956 Melbourne T: 9, N: 9, D: 12.7.

	Total Points
1. HUN	75.2
2. SWE	74.2
3. POL	74.0
3. SOV	74.0
5. ROM	73.4
6. JPN	73.2
7. CZE	73.0
8. ITA	72.8

1. HUN—Ágnes Keleti, Margit Korondi, Olga Tass, Andrea Bodó, Aliz Kertész, Erzsébet Gulyás-Köteles

2. SWE—Ann-Sofi Colling-Pettersson, Karin Lindberg, Eva Rönström, Evy Berggren, Doris Hedberg, Maude Karlén
3. POL—Helena Rakoczy, Natalia Kot, Dorota Jokiel (Horzonek), Danuta Nowak-Stachow, Barbara Wilk-Ślizowska, Lidia Szczerbińska
3. SOV—Tamara Manina, Larysa Latynina, Sofia Muratova, Lidiya Kalinina, Polina Astakhova, Lyudmila Yegorova
5. ROM—Georgeta Hurmuzache, Sonia Iovan, Elena Leuştean, Elena Mărgăret, Elena Săcalici, Emilia Vătăşoiu
6. JPN—Mitsuka Ikeda, Keiko Tanaka, Kazuko Sogabe, Kyoko Kubota, Suzuko Seki, Shizuko Sakashita
7. CZE—Eva Bosáková, [Vechtová], Hana Marejková, Matylda Šinová, Vera Drazdiková, Alena Reichová, Miraslava Brdičková
8. ITA—Miranda Cicognani, Luciana Reali, Rosella Cicognani, Elisa Calsi, Elena Lagorara, Luciana Lagorara

Chapter 16 **Team Handball**

Team handball is an exciting, fast-paced sport that deserves greater popularity. It is a hybrid of basketball and soccer: the ball is moved down the court by passing and dribbling, as in basketball, but instead of being shot into a basket, it is thrown past a goalie and into a goal, as in soccer. There are seven players on a team. Besides goalies, the most common positions are big shooters (usually tall and good jumpers, like forwards in basketball), middle backcourt players (playmakers who direct the offense), wings (smaller, faster players who shoot from difficult angles), and circle runners (large and aggressive players who set screens and picks for other shooters as well as shooting themselves).

Unlike basketball, a player may take three steps before and after dribbling, but he or she may not hold the ball for more than three seconds without dribbling or passing.

A handball court is 40 meters (131 feet 2 inches) long and 20 meters (65 feet 7 inches) wide. The goals are three meters (9 feet 10 inches) wide and two meters (6 feet 7 inches) high. The goal area extends six meters (19 feet 8 inches) from the goal. No player other than the goalie may enter the goal area. However, a player may take off outside the goal area and leap toward the goal as long as he releases a shot before landing. Clearly, this is a sport made to order for American basketball players. Fortunately for the rest of the world, Americans have not yet discovered team handball and the cumulative record of United States men's teams in the Olympics is a dismal 4 wins, 26 losses, and 1 tie, while American women have won 4 and lost 14.

Penalty throws, usually awarded when a player is fouled in the act of shooting, are taken from 7 meters (22 feet 9 inches) out, with only the goalie between the shooter and the goal.

Games are divided into two 30-minute halves. In preliminary matches, ties are allowed to stand. Beginning with the semifinals, a ten-minute overtime period is played. If the game is still tied, the teams play for ten more minutes. If the score is still tied, the match is decided by penalty throws.

In 2012 twelve teams will participate in the men's Olympic tournament: the host nation, the world champion and the winners of four regional tournaments. The remaining six teams will be selected from tournaments for countries that have not yet qualified.

Team Handball, 1972
A typical scene from a handball match.

The teams are divided into two round-robin pools. The four leading teams from each pool advance to the quarter-finals.

MEN

1896–1932 not held

1936 Berlin T: 6, N: 6, D: 8.14.

	W	L	PF	PA
1. GER	5	0	96	19
2. AUT	4	1	60	29
3. SWI	2	3	33	52
4. HUN	1	4	25	64
5. ROM	1	2	19	27
6. USA	0	3	6	46

Final: GER 10-6 AUT
3rd Place: SWI 10-5 HUN
5th Place: ROM 10-3 USA

1. GER—Heinz Körvers, Arthur Knautz, Willy Bandholz, Hans Keiter, Wilhelm Brinkmann, Georg Dascher, Erich Hermann, Hans Theilig, Helmut Berthold, Alfred Klingler, Fritz Fromm, Carl Kreutzberg, Heinrich Keimig, Wilhelm Müller, Kurt Dossin, Rudolf Stahl, Hermann Hansen, Fritz Spengler, Edgar Reinhardt, Günther Ortmann, Wilhelm Baumann, Helmuth Braselmann

2. AUT—Alois Schnabel, Franz Bartl, Johann Tauscher, Otto Licha, Emil Juracka, Leopold Wohlrab, Jaroslav Volak, Alfred Schmalzer, Ludwig Schubert, Ferdinand Kiefler, Anton Perwein, Fritz Maurer, Franz Brunner, Fritz Wurmböck, Siegfried Purner, Hans Zehetner, Hans Houschka, Franz Bistricky, Franz Berghammer, Walter Reisp, Josef Krejci, Siegfried Powolny
3. SWI—Willy Gysi, Robert Studer, Erich Schmitt, Rolf Faes, Erland Herkenrath, Burkhard Gantenbein, Werner Meyer, Max Streib, Georg Mischon, Ernst Hufschmid, Eugen Seiterle, Edy Schmid, Max Blösch, Werner Scheurmann, Willy Schäfer, Willy Hufschmid, Rudolf Wirz
4. HUN—Antal Ujváry, János Koppány, István Serényi, Lajos Kutasi, Frigyes Rakosi, Lörinc Galgóczy, Ferenc Cziráki, Gyula Takács, Miklós Fodor, Endre Salgó, Sándor Cséffai, Tibor Máté, Antal Benda, Imre Páli, Ferenc Velkel, Sándor Szomori
5. ROM—Ştefan Zoller, Carol Haffer, Ludovic Haffer, Bruno Holtzträger, Ştefen Höchsmann, Robert Speck, Gheorghe Hertog, Frederic Halmen, Wilhelm Kirschmer, Wilhelm Heidel, Günter Schörsten, Peter Fasci, Ion Zikeli, Vilhelm Zaharias, Stadter Herman
6. USA—Henry Oehler, Charles Dauner, Alfred Roseco, Herbert Carl Oehmichen, Edmund Schallenberg, William Ahlemeyer, Gerald Yantz, Joe Kaylor, Willy Benz, Walter Bowden, Fred Leinweber, Edward John Hagen, Otto Oehler, Philip Schupp

Field handball was invented in Germany, so when the Germans were given the opportunity to add one sport to the 1936 Olympics, they chose handball. In 1936 the game was played outdoors with 11 men on a side. Not surprisingly, Germany dominated the tournament, defeating the United States 29-1, Hungary 22-0 and 19-6, and Switzerland 16-6. Austria put up the best fight, trailing only 8-6 with five minutes to play.

1948–1968 not held

1972 Munich T: 16, N: 16, D: 9.11.

	W	L	T	PF	PA
1. YUG	7	0	0	140	105
2. CZE	3	3	1	114	99
3. ROM	6	1	0	111	92
4. GDR	5	2	0	103	85
5. SOV	3	1	3	91	84
6. GER	2	4	1	98	106
7. SWE	2	2	3	93	92
8. HUN	2	5	0	126	119

Final: YUG 21-16 CZE
3rd Place: ROM 19-16 GDR
5th Place: SOV 17-16 GER
7th Place: SWE 19-18 HUN

1. YUG—Abaz Arslanagić, Zoran Živković, Miroslav Pribanić, Hrvoje Horvat, Đorđe Lavrnić, Zdravko Miljak, Slobodan Mišković, Branislav Pokrajac, Nebojša Popović, Milan Lazarević, Milorad Karalić, Albin Vidović, Zdenko Zorko, Petar Fajfrić
2. CZE—Ivan Satrapa, Vladimír Jarý, Jiří Kavan, Vladimír Haber, Jindřich Krepindl, Ladislav Beneš, Vincent Lafko, Peter Pospíšil, Jaroslav Konečný, Pavel Mikeš, Jaroslav Škarvan, František Králik, Andrej Lukošík, Zdeněk Škára, Arnošt Klimčík
3. ROM—Cornel Penu, Gavril Kicsid, Valentin Samungi, Ştefan Birtalan, Cristian Gaţu, Roland Gunesch, Simion Schöbel, Gheorghe Gruia, Constantin Tudosie, Alexandru Dincă, Werner Stöckl, Dan Mann Marin, Ghiţă Licu, Radu Voina, Adrian Cosma
4. GDR—Reiner Frieske, Peter Randt, Klaus Langhoff, Reiner Ganschow, Wolfgang Lakenmacher, Rainer Würdig, Jürgen Hildebrandt, Udo Röhrig, Wolfgang Böhme, Harry Zörnack, Josef Rose, Siegfried Voigt, Klaus Weiss, Rainer Zimmerman, Horst Jankhöfer, Peter Larisch
5. SOV—Nikolai Semenov, Mykhalo Ischenko, Aleksandr Panov, Vladimir Maksimov, Valentin Kulev, Vassily Ilyin, Anatoly Shevchenko, Yuri Klimov, Mikhail Lutsenko, Oleksander Reza Nov, Valery Gassi, Albert Oganezov, Yuri Lahutyn, Ivan Ussatiy, Yan Vilson
6. GER—Klaus Kater, Uwe Rathjen, Herwig Ahrendsen, Wolfgang Braun, Peter Bucher, Diethard Finkelmann, Klaus Lange, Herbert Lübking, Heiner Möller, Hans-Peter Neuhaus, Herbert Rogge, Herbert Wehnert, Hans-Jürgen Bode, Jochen Feldhoff, Josef Karrer, Klaus Westebbe
7. SWE—Sten Olsson, Frank Ström, Björn Andersson, Dan Eriksson, Lennart Eriksson, Johan Fischerström, Benny Johansson, Jan Jonsson, Michael Koch, Thomas Persson, Göran Hård af Segerstad, Berth Söderberg
8. HUN—József Horváth, Sándor Kaló, Károly Vass, István Varga, István Szabó, István Marosi, Sándor Vass, Lajos Simó, János Adorján, Sándor Takács, János Stiller, László Szabó

With the Olympics back in Germany, team handball was returned to the schedule, but this time there were seven men on a side and the matches were played indoors. The decisive match was the second-round contest between Yugoslavia and world champion Romania. With 15 minutes to play, Milan Lazarević scored to give Yugoslavia a 10-9 lead. Four minutes later Djoko Lavrnić scored again, and Yugoslavia had the first two-goal lead of the game. They built their lead to 14-11 and survived two late goals to win, 14-13. The final against Czechoslovakia was anticlimatic; Yugoslavia led 12-5 at halftime and 18-8 with 13 minutes to play.

1976 Montreal T: 11, N: 11, D: 7.28.

	W	L	T	PF	PA
1. SOV	5	1	0	130	92
2. ROM	3	1	1	106	90
3. POL	4	1	0	101	89
4. GER	4	2	0	115	97
5. YUG	5	1	0	131	112
6. HUN	2	3	0	111	103
7. CZE	2	2	1	10	103
8. DEN	2	4	0	113	127

Final: SOV 19-15 ROM
3rd Place: POL 21-18 GER
5th Place: YUG 21-19 HUN
7th Place: CZE 25-21 DEN

1. SOV—Mykhalo Ishchenko, Anatoly Fedyukin, Vladimir Maksimov, Serhei Kushniryuk, Vassily Ilyin, Vladimir Kravzov, Yuri Klimov, Yuri Lahutyn, Aleksandr Anpilogov, Yevgeny Chernyshov, Valery Gassy, Mykola Tomyn, Yuri Kidyayev, Oleksander Rezanov
2. ROM—Cornel Penu, Gavril Kicsid, Cristian Gaţu, Cezar Drăgăniţă, Radu Voina, Roland Gunesch, Alexandru Fölker, Ştefan Birtalan, Adrian Cosma, Constantin Tudosie, Nicolae Munteanu, Werner Stöckl, Mircea Grabovschi, Ghiţă Licu
3. POL—Andrzej Szymczak, Piotr Cieśla, Zdzisław Antczak, Zygfryd Kuchta, Jerzy Klempel, Janusz Brzozowski, Ryszard Przybysz, Jerzy Melcer, Andrzej Sokołowski, Jan Gmyrek, Henryk Rozmiarek, Alfred Kałuziński, Włodzimierz Zieliński, Mieczysław Wojczak
4. GER—Manfred Hofmann, Jürgen Hahn, Günter Böttcher, Kurt Klühspies, Peter Kleibrink, Walter Oepen, Horst Spengler, Gerd Becker, Bernhard Busch, Joachim Deckarm, Rudolf Rauer, Arno Ehret, Heiner Brand, Peter Jaschke

5. YUG—Abaz Arslanagić, Vlado Bojović, Zdravko Rađenović, Milorad Karalić, Radislav Pavićević, Zvonimir Serdarušić, Hrvoje Horvat, Branislav Pokrajac, Radivoj Krivokapić, Predrag Timko, Zdravko Miljak, Zdenko Zorko, Nebojša Popović, Željko Nimš
6. HUN—Béla Bartalos, Ferenc Buday, Péter Kovács, István Varga, Mihály Süvöltős, István Szilágyi, József Kenyeres, László Janovszki, Károly Vass, Ernő Gubányi, Zsolt Kontra, Gábor Verőci
7. CZE—Ján Packa, František Šulc, Ivan Satrapa, Vladimír Jarý, Jiří Kavan, Štefan Katušák, Vladimír Haber, Jindřich Krepindl, Jiří Hanzl, Jaroslav Papiernik, Jozef Dobrotka, Bohumil Čepák, Jiří Liška, Pavel Mikeš
8. DEN—Kay Jorgensen, Palle Jensen, Anders Dahl-Nielsen, Lars Bock, Jürgen Frandsen, Claus From, Thomas Pazyj, Bent Larsen, Soren Andersen, Morten Christensen, Henrik Jacobsgaard, Johnny Pechnik, Thor Munkager, Jesper Petersen

Again Romania entered the Olympics as defending world champions and again they were unable to win the tournament. They survived the preliminary pool undefeated to qualify for the final. The other pool was won by the Soviet Union despite a 20-18 loss to Yugoslavia, which was unlucky to finish fifth considering they lost only one match—to West Germany, 18-17. The USSR took control of the final early, led 10-6 at halftime, and was never behind.

1980 Moscow T: 12, N: 12, D: 7.30.

	W	L	T	PF	PA
1. GDR	5	0	1	131	114
2. SOV	4	2	0	156	98
3. ROM	5	1	0	139	106
4. HUN	3	1	2	114	108
5. SPA	3	2	1	126	129
6. YUG	4	2	0	156	116
7. POL	3	2	1	146	119
8. SWI	2	4	0	132	121

Final: GDR 23-22 SOV
3rd Place: ROM 20-18 HUN
5th Place: SPA 24-23 YUG
7th Place: POL 23-22 SWI

1. GDR—Siegfried Voigt, Günter Dreibrodt, Peter Rost, Klaus Gruner, Hans-Georg Beyer, Dietmar Schmidt, Hartmut Krüger, Lothar Döring, Ernst Gerlach, Frank-Michael Wahl, Ingolf Wiegert, Wieland Schmidt, Rainer Höft, Hans-Georg Jaunich
2. SOV—Mykhalo Ishchenko, Viktor Makhorin, Serhei Kushniryuk, Aleksandr Karshakevich, Vladimir Kravzov, Vladimir Belov, Anatoly Fedyukin, Aleksandr Anpilogov, Yevgeny Chernyshov, Aleksei Zhuk, Mykola Tomyn, Yuri Kidyayev, Vladimir Repyev, Voldemaras Novickis
3. ROM—Nicolae Munteanu, Marian Dumitru, Iosif Boroş, Maricel Voinea, Vasile Stîngă, Radu Voina, Cezar Drăgăniţă, Cornel Durău, Ştefan Birtalan, Alexandru Fölker, Neculai Vasilcă, Lucian Vasilache, Adrian Cosma, Claudiu Ionescu
4. HUN—Béla Bartalos, László Szabó, Péter Kovács, Sándor Vass, János Fodor, István Szilágyi, József Kenyeres, László Jánovszki, Ambrus Lele, Ernő Gubányi, Zsolt Kontra, Alpár Jegenyés, Árpád Pál, Miklós Kovacsics
5. SPA—José María Pagoaga Larrañaga, Juan Javier Cabanas López, Jesús María Albisu Andrade, Vicente Calabuig Saus, Juan de la Puente Bordonaba, Rafael López de León, José Novoa Behovide, Juan José Uría Bazterrica, Agustín Millán García, Francisco López Balcells, Eugenio Serrano Gispert, Gregorio López Pelayo, Juan Pedro de Miguel Rubio, Juan Francisco Muñoz Melo
6. YUG—Zlatan Arnautović, Momir Rnić, Enver Koso, Drago Jovović, Stjepan Obran, Jasmin Mrkonja, Peter Mahne, Pavle Jurina, Goran Nerić, Jovica Cvetković, Velibor Nenadić, Adnan Dizdar, Mile Isaković, Jovica Elezović
7. POL—Andrzej Kącki, Zbigniew Gawlik, Piotr Czaczka, Marek Panas, Jerzy Klempel, Janusz Brzozowski, Zbigniew Tłuczyński, Grzegorz Kosma, Daniel Waszkiewicz, Ryszard Jedliński, Henryk Rozmiarek, Alfred Kałuziński, Jerzy Garpiel, Mieczysław Wojczak
8. SWI—Edi Wickli, Ernst Zuellig, Robert Jehle, Roland Brand, Max Schaer, Peter Haag, Walter Müller, Rudolf Weber, Hans Huber, Konrad Affolter, Hanspeter Lutz, Ugo Jametti, Peter Jehle, Martin Ott

The final was a particularly exciting match, as neither team ever led by more than two goals. As the clock ran down, East Germany led 20-19, but Aleksandr Anpilogov of the USSR made a penalty shot with 22 seconds to play and the game went into overtime. Anpilogov also scored the first goal of the ten-minute extra period, but the Soviet Union was held scoreless for the next eight and a half minutes while the Germans took a 23-21 lead. Anpilogov scored the final goal of the game with 51 seconds left to play. East Germany's last point was put in by 23-year-old Hans-Georg Beyer, whose older brother, Udo, was winning the bronze medal in the shot put at the exact same time. Two days later, their sister, Gisela, finished fourth in the discus. Last-place finisher Kuwait had a tough tournament, including losses of 44-10 to Yugoslavia and 38-11 to the USSR.

1984 Los Angeles-Inglewood T: 12, N: 12, D: 8.11.

	W	L	T	PF	PA
1. YUG	5	0	1	141	93
2. GER	5	1	0	131	113
3. ROM	5	1	0	143	110
4. DEN	4	2	0	134	122
5. SWE	4	2	0	145	134
6. ICE	3	2	1	126	122
7. SWI	3	3	0	101	119
8. SPA	2	4	0	122	124

Final: YUG 18-17 GER
3rd Place: ROM 23-19 DEN
5th Place: SWE 26-24 ICE
7th Place: SWI 18-17 SPA

1. YUG—Zlatan Arnautović, Momir Rnić, Veselin Vuković, Milan Kalina, Jovica Elezović, Zdravko Zovko, Branko Štrbac, Pavle Jurina, Veselin Vujović, Slobodan Kuzmanovski, Mirko Bašić, Dragan Mladenović, Zdravko Rađenović, Mile Isaković
2. GER—Andreas Thiel, Arnulf Meffle, Rüdiger Neitzel, Martin Schwalb, Dirk Rauin, Michael Paul, Thomas Happe, Erhard Wunderlich, Thomas Springel, Klaus Wöller, Jochen Fraatz, Siegfried Roch, Ulrich Roth, Uwe Schwenker, Michael Roth
3. ROM—Nicolae Munteanu, Marian Dumitru, Iosif Boroş, Maricel Voinea, Vasile Stîngă, Gheorghe Dogărescu, Gheorghe Covaciu, Cornel Durău, Alexandru Fölker, Neculai Vasilcă, Alexandru Buligan, Vasile Oprea, Mircea Bedivan, Adrian Simion
4. DEN—Mogens Jeppesen, Jens Erik Roepstorff, Anders Dahl-Nielsen, Erik Veje Rasmussen, Keld Nielsen, Klaus Sletting Jensen, Morten Stig Christensen, Carsten Haurum, Hans Henrik Hattesen, Jörgen Gluver, Peter Michael Fenger, Poul Sörensen, Michael Strom, Per Skaarup

5. SWE—Claes Hellgren, Per Öberg, Danny Augustsson, Göran Bengtsson, Christer Magnusson, Per Carlén, Pär Jilsén, Lennarth Ebbinge, Björn Jilsén, Mats Lindau, Sten Sjögren, Rolf Hertzberg, Peter Olofsson, Mats Olsson
6. ICE—Einar Thorvardson, Thorglis Mathiesen, Thorbergur Adalsteinsson, Bjarni Gudmundsson, Jakob Sigurdsson, Sigurdur Gunnarsson, Atli Hilmarsson, Gudmundur Gudmundsson, Kristjan Arason, Thörbjorn Jensson, Jens Einarsson, Sigurdur Sveinsson, Brynjar Kvaran, Alfred Gislason, J. Steinar Birgisson
7. SWI—Martin Ott, Martin Glaser, Jürgen Baetschmann, Peter Weber, Max Schaer, Heinz Karrer, Roland Gassmann, René Barth, Norwin Platzer, Peter Hürlimann, Uwe Mall, Peter Jehle, Max Delhees, Markus Brau
8. SPA—Pedro García Ramírez, Juan Javier Cabanas López, Juan Francisco Muñoz Melo, Javier Reino García, Juan de la Puente Bordonaba, Cecilio Alonso Suárez, José Novoa Behovide, Juan José Uría Bazterrica, Julián Ruiz Gómez, Eugenio Serrano Gispert, Lorenzo Rico Díaz, Rafael López de León, Jaime Puig Rofés, Juan Pedro de Miguel Rubio

West Germany was admitted to the Olympic tournament only after four of the qualifying teams withdrew as part of the Soviet-bloc boycott. Yet the Germans were able to complete their preliminary pool undefeated and advance to the final. There they met the Yugoslavs, who had survived an early 22-22 tie against Iceland and then beaten Romania 19-18 in a crucial matchup of the preOlympic favorites. The West Germans never held a lead after the first 12 minutes of the final, but they still clung to a 15-15 tie with 6 minutes remaining. Then Yugoslavia scored three unanswered goals and held on to win 18-17. Yugoslav coach Branislav Pokraja was one of the players on the 1972 team that won Yugoslavia's other Olympic championship.

1988 Seoul T: 12, N: 12, D: 10.1.

	W	L	T	PF	PA
1. SOV	6	0	0	162	107
2. KOR	4	2	0	152	149
3. YUG	4	1	1	143	132
4. HUN	3	3	0	125	120
5. SWE	4	2	0	133	109
6. CZE	3	3	0	127	130
7. GDR	4	2	0	140	129
8. ICE	2	3	1	125	133

Final: SOV 32-25 KOR
3rd Place: YUG 27-23 HUN
5th Place: SWE 27-18 CZE
7th Place: GDR 31-29 ICE

1. SOV—Andrei Lavrov, Aleksandr Tuchkin, Aleksandr Rymanov, Aleksandr Karshakevich, Yuri Nesterov, Georgy Sviridenko, Andrei Tyumentsev, Mikhail Vasilyev, Yuri Shevtsov, Vyacheslav Atavin, Voldemaras Novickis, Igor Chumak, Konstantin Sharovarov
2. KOR—Yoon Tae-il, Kim Jae-hwan, Sin Young-suk, Park Do-hun, Park Young-dae, Koh Suk-chang, Roh Hyun-suk, Oh Young-ki, Choi Suk-jae, Kang Jae-won, Lee Sang-hyo, Lim Jin-suk
3. YUG—Momir Rnić, Zlatko Saračević, Iztok Puc, Goran Perkovac, Irfan Smajlagić, Zlatko Portner, Veselin Vujović, JJožef Holpert, Mirko Bašić, Alvaro Načinović, Slobodan Kuzmanovski, Ermin Velić
4. HUN—László Hoffmann, József Bordás, Péter Kovács, Mihály Kovács, János Fodor, László Marosi, Mihály Iváncsik, Jakab Sibalin, László Szabó, Géza Tóth, Ottó Csicsai, Imre Biró, János Gyurka, Tibor Oross
5. SWE—Mats Olsson, Peder Järphag, Magnus Wislander, Johan Eklund, Ola Lindgren, Per Carlén, Erik Hajas, Per Carlsson, Björn Jilsén, Pär Jilsén, Sten Sjögren, Mats Fransson, Steffan Olsson, Claes Hellgren
6. CZE—Michal Barda, Jozef Škandík, Miroslav Bajgar, Libor Sovadina, Jiří Kotrč, Milan Brestovanský, Milan Folta, František Štika, Tomáš Bártek, Zdeněk Vaněk, Petr Baumruk, Karel Jindřichovský, Jan Novák, Peter Mesiarik
7. GDR—Peter Hofmann, Stephan Hauck, Peter Pysall, Frank-Michael Wahl, Holger Winselmann, Bernd Metzke, Andreas Neitzel, Rüdiger Borchardt, Jens Fiedler, Mike Fuhrig, Matthias Hahn, Wieland Schmidt, Holger Schneider
8. ICE—Einar Thorvardarson, Thorgilsóttar Mathiesen, Jakob Sigurđsson, Bjarki Sigurđsson, Karl Thráinsson, Sigurđur Gunnarsson, Alfređ Gíslason, Guđmundur Guđmundsson, Páll Ólafsson, Kristján Arason, Geir Sveinsson, Brynjar Kvaran, Sigurđur Sveinsson, Atli Hilmarsson, Guđmundur Hrafnkelsson

The Soviet team, whose players averaged almost 6 feet 4 inches, swept through the tournament. Their closest match was a 22-18 victory over Sweden.

1992 Barcelona T: 12, N: 12, D: 8.8.

	W	L	T	PF	PA
1. SOV	7	0	0	166	137
2. SWE	6	1	0	165	130
3. FRA	5	2	0	157	143
4. ICE	3	3	1	140	146
5. SPA	4	2	0	133	119
6. KOR	3	3	0	135	153
7. HUN	3	3	0	125	127
8. ROM	1	4	1	126	138

Final: SOV 22-20 SWE
3rd Place: FRA 24-20 ICE
5th Place: SPA 36-21 KOR
7th Place: HUN 23-19 ROM

1. SOV—Andrei Lavrov, Igor Chumak, Igor Vassiliyev, Yuri Gavrilov, Andrei Barbashinsky, Sergei Bebeshko, Valery Gopin, Vasily Kudinov, Mikhail Yakimovich, Oleg Grebnev, Oleg Kiselyev, Talant Dujshebaev
2. SWE—Mats Olsson, Tomas Svensson, Magnus Wislander, Ola Lindgren, Per Carlén, Erik Hajas, Magnus Cato, Axel Sjöblad, Robert Andersson, Pierre Thorsson, Steffan Olsson, Magnus Andersson, Robert Hedin, Anders Bäckegren, Patrik Liljestrand, Tommy Suoraniemi
3. FRA—Philippe Médard, Frédéric Perez, Pascal Mahé, Philippe Debureau, Frédéric Volle, Denis Lathoud, Eric Quintin, Philippe Gardent, Thierry Perreux, Laurent Munier, Jackson Richardson, Stéphane Stoecklin, Denis Tristant, Jean-Luc Thiébaut, Alain Portes, Gaël Monthurel
4. ICE—Gunnar Andrésson, Guđmunđur Hrafnkelsson, Bergsveinn Bergsveinsson, Birgir Sigurđsson, Jakob Sigurđsson, Váldimar Grimsson, Gunnar Gunnarsson, Sigurđur Bjarnason, Konrád Olavsson, Héđinn Gilsson, Geir Sveinsson, Einar Gunnar Sigurđsson, Július Jónasson
5. SPA—Jaume Fort Mauri, Lorenzo Rico Díaz, Juan Javier Cabanas López, Juan Muñoz Melo, Ricardo Marín Marín, Mateo Garralda Larumbe, Ignacio Urdangarin Liebaert, Enric Masip Borrás, Juan Alemany Marín, Aitor Etxaburu Castro, Luis García López, Aleix Franch Alfós, Fernando Bolea Alonso, Ángel Hermida García, David Barrufet Bofill, Alberto Urdiales Márquez

6. KOR—Choi Suk-jai, Lee Ki-ho, Cho Bum-yun, Park Do-hun, Lim Jin-suk, Cho Young-shin, Back Sang-suh, Cho Chi-hyo, Lee Sun-soon, Kang Jae-won, Moon Byung-wook, Shim Jae-hong, Lee Kyu-chang, Jung Kang- wook, Youn Kyung-shin
7. HUN—János Szathmári, Imre Bíró, Attila Borsos, László Sótonyi, László Marosi, Mihály Iváncsik, Jakab Sibalin, Igor Zubjuk, József Éles, Ferenc Füzesi, Richárd Mezei, Attila Horváth, Ottó Csicsai, Sándor Györffy, István Csoknyai
8. ROM—Alexandru Buligan, Sorin Toacsen, Valentin Zaharia, Marian Dumitru, Alexandru Dedu, Robert Licu, Rudi Prisăcaru, Dumitru Berbece, Ion Mocanu, Adi Popovici, Gheorghe-Titel Raduta, Maricel Voinea, Ionel Radu, Costica Neagu, Mitică Bontaş

The final was a tight match all the way. Eight and a half minutes into the second half, Sweden led 14-12. Then the aggressive man-to-man defense of the ex-Soviet Union took its toll, holding the Swedes to only one goal over the next nine minutes and moving ahead 17-15. Still, the defending world champions refused to fold. With three and a half minutes to play, Erik Hajas scored on a fast break and the ex-Soviet's lead was cut to 20-19. However, Sweden was unable to come up with another goal until four seconds before the end and the game ended at 22-20. During the Olympics, Spanish star Inaki Urdangarin met Princess Christina, daughter of King Juan Carlos of Spain. The couple married in 1997.

1996 Atlanta T: 12, N: 12, D: 8.4.

	W	L	T	PF	PA
1. CRO	6	1	0	183	168
2. SWE	6	1	0	182	141
3. SPA	5	2	0	161	147
4. FRA	4	3	0	190	165
5. RUS	4	2	0	166	132
6. EGY	3	3	0	138	132
7. GER	4	2	0	144	128
8. SWI	2	4	0	142	138

Final: CRO 27-26 SWE
3rd Place: SPA 27-25 FRA
5th Place: RUS 29-26 EGY
7th Place: GER 23-16 SWI

1. CRO—Vladimir Jelčić, Goran Perkovac, Irfan Smajlagić, Božidar Jović, Alvaro Načinović, Vladimir Šujster, Bruno Gudelj, Nenad Kljaić, Iztok Puc, Zoran Mikulić, Venio Losert, Patrik Ćavar, Valner Franković, Slavko Goluža, Valter Matošević, Zlatko Saračević
2. SWE—Andreas Larsson, Erik Hajas, Johan Pettersson, Magnus Andersson, Magnus Wislander, Martin Frändesjö, Mats Olsson, Ola Lindgren, Per Carlén, Pierre Thorsson, Robert Andersson, Robert Hedin, Staffan Olsson, Stefan Lövgren, Thomas Sivertsson, Tomas Svensson
3. SPA—Aitor Etxaburu Castro, Alberto Urdiales Márquez, Demetrio Lozano Jarque, Fernando Hernández Casado, Ignacio Urdangarin Liebaert, Jaume Fort Mauri, Jesüs Fernández Oceja, Jesús Fernández Oceja, Jesús Olalla Iraeta, Jordi Núñez Carretero, José Hombrados Ibáñez, Juan Pérez Márquez, Mateo Garralda Larumbe, Salvador Guijosa Castillo, Salvador Esquer Bisbal, Talant Dujshebaev, Raúl González Gutiérrez
4. FRA—Eric Amalou, Gregory Anquetil, Stéphane Cordinier, Yohan Delattre, Christian Gaudin, Stéphane Joulin, Guéric Kervadec, Denis Lathoud, Pascal Mahé, Bruno Martini, Gaël Monthurel, Raoul Prandi, Jackson Richardson, Philippe Schaaf, Stéphane Stoecklin, Frédéric Volle
5. RUS—Aleksei Frantsuzov, Andrei Lavrov, Dmitry Filippov, Dmitri Torgovanov, Igor Lavrov, Lev Voronin, Oleg Grebnev, Oleg Kiselyov, Oleg Kuleshov, Pavel Sukosyan, Sergei Pogorelov, Valery Gopin, Vasily Kudinov, Vyacheslav Gorpishin
6. EGY—Ahmed El-Awady, Ahmed El-Attar, Ahmed Ali, Hossam Abdalla, Mahmoud Soliman, Gohar Mohamed, Yaser Mahmoud, Khaled Mahmoud, Ayman El-Alfy, Mohamed Bakir El-Nakib, Amro El-Geioushy, Ashraf Mabrouk, Ayman Soliman, Ahmed Belal, Saber Hussein, Sameh Abdelwaress
7. GER—Andreas Thiel, Christian Scheffler, Christian Schwarzer, Daniel Stephan, Henning Fritz, Holger Löhr, Jan Fegter, Jan Holpert, Karsten Kohlhaas, Klaus-Dieter Petersen, Markus Baur, Martin Schmidt, Martin Schwalb, Stefan Kretzschmar, Thomas Knorr, Volker Zerbe
8. SWI—Alex Vasilakis, Carlos Lima, Christian Meisterhans, Daniel Spengler, Marc Baumgartner, Matthias Zumstein, Nicolas Christen, René Barth, Robbie Kostadinovich, Rolf Dobler, Roman Brunner, Stefan Schärer, Urs Schärer

Sweden beat Croatia 27-18 in pool play, but the Croats, having already qualified for the semifinals, rested four of their key players. The two teams met again four days later in the final. This time Croatia jumped out to a 6-1 lead after ten minutes. They held Sweden at bay for the next forty minutes and still led 23-18 with 8½ minutes to play. But then, over the next four minutes, the Swedes scored four straight goals to close the score to 23-22. For the rest of the match the two teams traded goals, with Croatia retaining at least a one point lead throughout. With 21 seconds to play and Croatia leading 26-25, Nenad Kljajić, the son of coach Velimir Kljajić, scored from the left side to ice the victory. It was an emotional triumph for the Croatian players, five of whom had represented Yugoslavia at the 1988 Olympics—three years before Croatia broke free of Yugoslavia in a bloody civil war. Indeed, this was Croatia's first gold medal since gaining independence.

2000 Sydney T: 12, N: 12, D: 9.30.

	W	L	T	PF	PA
1. RUS	7	1	0	219	195
2. SWE	7	1	0	240	197
3. SPA	5	3	0	222	206
4. YUG	4	4	0	204	203
5. GER	5	2	1	203	180
6. FRA	4	3	1	192	177
7. EGY	4	4	0	197	194
8. SLO	2	5	1	209	223

Final: RUS 28-26 SWE
3rd Place: ESP 26-22 YUG
5th Place: GER 25-22 FRA
7th Place: EGY 34-28 SLO

1. RUS—Aleksandr Tuchkin, Andrei Lavrov, Denis Krivoshlykov, Dmitri Filipov, Dmitri Kuzelev, Dmitri Torgovanov, Eduard Kokcharov, Igor Lavrov, Lev Voronin, Oleg Khodkov, Pavel Sukosyan, Sergei Pogorelov, Stanislav Kulinchenko, Vasily Kudinov, Vyacheslav Gorpishin

2. SWE—Andreas Larsson, Johan Pettersson, Ljubomir Vranjes, Magnus Andersson, Magnus Wislander, Martin Boquist, Martin Frändesjö, Mathias Franzen, Ola Lindgren, Peter Gentzel, Pierre Thorsson, Staffan Olsson, Stefan Lövgren, Tomas Sivertsson, Tomas Svensson
3. SPA—Alberto Urdiales Márquez, Andrei Xepkin, Antonio Ortega Pérez, Antonio Ugalde García, David Barrufet Bofill, Demetrio Lozano Jarque, Enric Masip Borrás, Ignacio Urdangarin Liebaert, Jesús Olalla Iraeta, Jordi Nuñez Carretero, Juan Pérez Márquez, Mateo Garralda Larube, Rafael Guijosa Castillo, Talant Dujshebaev, Xavier O'Callaghan Ferrer
4. YUG—Aleksandar Knežević, Arpad Sterbik, Dejan Perić, Dragan Škrbić, Goran Đukanović, Igor Butulija, Ivan Lapčević, Nebojša Golić, Nedeljko Jovanović, Nenad Peruničić, Petar Kapisoda, Ratko Nikolić, Ratko Đurković, Vladan Matić, Žikica Milosavljević
5. GER—Bernd Roos, Bogdan Wenta, Christian Schwarzer, Daniel Stephan, Florian Kehrmann, Frank von Behren, Henning Fritz, Jan Holpert, Jörg Kunze, Klaus-Dieter Petersen, Markus Baur, Mike Bezdicek, Stefan Kretzschmar, Sven Lakenmacher, Volker Zerbe
6. FRA—Andrej Golic, Bertrand Gille, Bruno Martini, Cédric Burdet, Christian Gaudin, Didier Dinart, Grégory Anquetil, Guéric Kervadec, Guillaume Gille, Jackson Richardson, Jérôme Fernandez, Marc Wiltberger, Olivier Girault, Patrick Cazal, Stéphane Joulin
7. EGY—Ahmed Belal, Amro El-Geioushy, Ashraf Awaad, Ayman El-Alfy, Hany El-Fakharany, Hazem Awaad, Saber Hussein, Hussein Said, Hussein Zaky, Magdy Abou El-Magd, Mohamed Bakir El-Nakib, Gohar Mohamed, Sherif Moemen, Marwan Ragab, Mohamed Sharaf El-Din
8. SLO—Aleš Pajovič, Andrej Kastelič, Beno Lapajne, Branko Bedekovič, Gregor Cvijič, Iztok Puc, Jani Likaveč, Renato Vugrineč, Roman Pungartnik, Rolando Pušnik, Tettey-Sowah Banfro, Tomaž Tomšič, Uroš Šerbec, Zoran Jovičič, Zoran Lubej

The Sydney men's handball tournament showcased the ongoing rivalry between Sweden and Russia. The Russians defeated the Swedes 23-21 in the final of the 1997 world championship. Sweden gained revenge in the 1999 world championship final by a score of 25-24 and then beat the Russians again in the final of the 2000 European championship, this time in overtime, 32-31. At the Olympics, Sweden went undefeated in pool play, although in three of the five games they trailed at halftime and their victories over France and Spain were by only one point each. Meanwhile, in the other preliminary pool, Russia was upset by Germany, but finished first in the pool anyway when the Germans lost to Egypt. Sweden advanced to the final by defeating Egypt 27-23 and Spain 32-25, while Russia beat Slovenia 33-22 and Yugoslavia 29-26. So, once again, the Swedes and the Russians faced off in a championship match. The first half was so evenly matched that neither side ever led by more than one point. At halftime it was 14-13 Sweden. The Swedes increased their lead to 16-14, but then the Russians scored seven straight goals, including two each by Dmitri Torgovanov, Aleksandr Tuchkin and Eduard Kokcharov. Ljubomir Vranjes led a Swedish comeback that brought the score to 24-23 Russia with nine minutes to play. Russia's goalie, 38-year-old Andrei Lavrov, made a series of late saves to halt the Swedish momentum. Russia scored three goals in a row and held on to win 28-26. Lavrov, competing in his fourth Olympics, won his third gold medal, while Sweden lost their third straight Olympic final.

2004 Athens T: 12, N: 12, D: 8.29.

	W	L	T	GF	GA
1. CRO	8	0	0	238	211
2. GER	5	3	0	216	181
3. RUS	4	4	0	214	216
4. HUN	5	3	0	219	210
5. FRA	7	1	0	221	176
6. GRE	3	5	0	188	220
7. SPA	5	3	0	242	222
8. KOR	2	6	0	221	238

Final: CRO 26-24 GER
3rd Place: RUS 28-26 HUN
5th Place: FRA 33-15 GRE
7th Place: SPA 31-24 KOR

1. CRO—Ivano Balić, Davor Dominiković, Mirza Džomba, Slavko Goluža, Nikša Kaleb, Blaženko Lacković, Valter Matošević, Vlado Šola, Denis Špoljarić, Goran Šprem, Petar Metličić, Venio Losert, Igor Vori, Drago Vuković, Vedran Zrnić
2. GER—Markus Baur, Mark Dragunski, Henning Fritz, Pascal Hens, Jan-Olaf Immel, Torsten Jansen, Florian Kehrmann, Stefan Kretzschmar, Klaus-Dieter Petersen, Christian Ramota, Christian Schwarzer, Daniel Stephan, Frank von Behren, Christian Zeitz, Volker Zerbe
3. RUS—Mikhail Chipurin, Aleksandr Gorbatikov, Vyacheslav Gorpishin, Vitaly Ivanov, Eduard Kokcharov, Aleksei Kostygov, Denis Krivoshlykov, Vasily Kudinov, Oleg Kuleshov, Andrei Lavrov, Sergei Pogorelov, Aleksei Rastvortsev, Dmitri Torgovanov, Aleksandr Tuchkin
4. HUN—Gábor Császár, Nándor Fazekas, Gyula Gál, Gergely Harsányi, Ferenc Ilyés, Gergely Ivancsik, Balázs Laluska, Péter Lendvay, Richárd Mezei, Tamás Mocsai, László Nagy, István Pásztor, Carlos Pérez, János Szathmári, Ivo Diaz
5. FRA—Joel Abati, Grégory Anquetil, Cédric Burdet, Didier Dinart, Jérôme Fernandez, Guillaume Gille, Bertrand Gille, Olivier Girault, Michaël Guigou, Nikola Karabatić, Guéric Kervadec, Daniel Narcisse, Thierry Omeyer, Yohann Ploquin, Jackson Richardson
6. GRE—Alexis Alvanos, Spyros Balomenos, Giorgos Khalkidis, Gregor Khatsatourian, Jiotsa Khrysopoulos, Nikolaos Grammatikos, Dimitrios Kaffatos, Savvas Karypidis, Nikolaos Kokolodimitrakis, Andreas Troupis, Dimitrios Tzimourtos, Alexandros Vasilakis, Enagelos Voglis, Georgios Zaravinas, Sasa Zivoulovic
7. SPA—David Barrufet Bofill, Jon Belaustegui Ruano, Manuel Colón Rodríguez, Talant Dujshebaev, Alberto Entrerríos Rodríguez, Juan García Lorenzana, Mateo Garralda Larumbe, Fernando Hernández Casado, José Javier Hombrados, Demetrio Lozano Jarque, Xavier O'Callaghan Ferrer, Antonio Carlos Ortega Pérez, Juan Pérez Márquez, Iker Romero Fernández, Rolando Uríos Fonseca
8. KOR—Lee Chang-woo, Park Chan-yong, Lim Duk-jun, Lee Jae-woo, Yoon Kyung-min, Yoon Kyung-shin, Han Kyung-tai, Park Min-chul, Ji Seung-hyun, Choi Seung-wook, Kim Sung-heon, Kim Tea-wan, Lee Tea-young, Paek Won-chul, Oh Yun-suk

After winning the 1996 Olympic gold medal, Croatian handball took a deep plunge. The Croatian team did not even qualify for the 2000 Olympics and was considered one of the worst teams in Europe. In 2003, however, the Croatians achieved a major turnaround, winning the world championship by defeating Germany 34-31 in the final. Meanwhile, Germany went on to win the 2004 European Championship, despite competing without star player Stefan Kretzschmar, who was recovering from a groin injury. In the preliminary rounds in Athens, Croatia dominated Group A, winning all five matches, with Spain placing second. In Group B, France went undefeated, while Hungary surprised Germany 30-29 to finish second in the group. In the quarterfinals, Hungary defeated South Korea 30-25 and Croatia dominated Greece 33-27. That evening, in a matchup of medal favorites, Germany and Spain fought an exciting contest in which neither team ever led by more than two goals. Finally, after two overtime periods, the Germans won a penalty shootout 2-0 to gain a 32-30 victory. In another tight match, Russia defeated France 26-24. In the first semifinal, Croatia led 18-16 at the end of the first half, and then maintained a lead of between three and six points for most of the second half, finally winning 33-31. In the second semifinal, Germany trailed Russia 10-12 after 38 minutes, but outscored the Russians 11-3 the rest of the way to win 21-15.

The gold medal contest between Germany and Croatia was a rematch of the 2003 world championship final. This time, the Germans, led by Christian Schwarzer and Stefan Kretzschmar, opened an 8-5 lead after 16 minutes and led 12-11 at the half. They were still ahead by three goals, 16-13, seven minutes into the second half, but a pair of goals by right back Petar Metličić evened the score. Four goals by Mirza Džomba and three by Niška Kaleb helped give Croatia a 24-21 lead with three minutes to play. Although Kretzschmar scored twice for Germany in the final minute, Croatia held on to win 26-24.

2008 Beijing T: 12, N: 12, D: 8.24.

	W	L	T	GF	GA
1. FRA	7	0	1	228	185
2. ICE	4	2	2	242	234
3. SPA	5	3	0	246	234
4. CRO	4	4	0	218	199
5. POL	5	2	1	235	214
6. RUS	3	4	1	216	214
7. DEN	3	3	2	225	211
8. KOR	3	5	0	198	224

Final: FRA 28-23 ICE
3rd Place: SPA 35-29 CRO
5th Place: POL 29-28 RUS
7th Place: DEN 37-26 KOR

1. FRA—Michaël Guigou, Luc Abalo, Nikola Karabatić, Joël Abati, Daouda Karaboue, Cédric Burdet, Christophe Kempe, Didier Dinart, Daniel Narcisse, Jérôme Fernandez, Thierry Omeyer, Bertrand Gille, Cédric Paty, Guillaume Gille, Olivier Girault
2. ICE—Sturla Ásgeirsson, Arnór Atlason, Logi Geirsson, Snorri Guðjónsson, Hreidar Guðmundsson, Róbert Gunnarsson, Björgvin Gustavsson, Ásgeir Örn Hallgrímsson, Ingimundur Ingimundarson, Sverre Jakobsson, Alexander Petersson, Guðjón Valur Sigurðsson, Sigfús Sigurðsson, Ólafur Stefánsson
3. SPA—David Barrufet Bofill, Jon Belaustegui Ruano, David Davis Cámara, Alberto Entrerríos Rodríguez, Raúl Entrerríos Rodríguez, Rubén Garabaya Arenas, Juan García Lorenzana, José Javier Hombrados Ibáñez, Demetrio Lozano Jarque, Cristian Malmagro Viaña, Carlos Prieto Martos, Albert Rocas Comas, Iker Romero Fernández, Víctor Tomás González
4. CRO—Mirko Alilović, Ivano Balić, Davor Dominiković, Domagoj Duvnjak, Mirza Džomba, Zlatko Horvat, Blaženko Lacković, Venio Losert, Petar Metličić, Goran Šprem, Renato Sulić, Tonči Valčić, Igor Vori, Ljubo Vukić, Drago Vuković
5. POL—Karol Bielecki, Mateusz Jachlewski, Bartłomiej Jaszka, Mariusz Jurasik, Bartłomiej "Bartosz" Jurecki, Michał Jurecki, Krzysztof Lijewski, Marcin Lijewski, Paweł Piwko, Artur Siódmiak, Sławomir Szmal, Grzegorz Tkaczyk, Tomasz Tłuczyński, Marcin Wichary
6. RUS—Samvel Aslanyan, Aleksandr Chernovyanov, Timur Dibirov, Yegor Yevdokimov, Vasily Filippov, Oleg Grams, Konstantin Igropulo, Vitaly Ivanov, Aleksey Kamanin, Eduard Koksharov, Aleksey Kostygov, Dmitry Kovalyov, Denis Krivoshlykov, Aleksey Rastvortsev
7. DEN—Lasse Boesen, Joachim Boldsen, Klavs Bruun Jørgensen, Lars Christiansen, Mikkel Hansen, Peter Henriksen, Kasper Hvidt, Jesper Jensen, Lars Jørgensen, Michael Knudsen, Hans Lindberg, Kasper Nielsen, Jesper Nøddesbo, Kasper Søndergaard, Bo Spellerberg
8. KOR—Jo Chi-hyo, Han Gyeong-tae, Jeong Yik-yeong, Jung Su-young, Gang Il-gu, Kim Tae-wan, Ko Kyung-soo, Lee Jae-u, Lee Tae-yeong, Baeg Won-cheol, Park Chan-yong, Park Jung-geu, Yun Gyeong-min, Yun Gyeong-sin

France had been the most consistent handball team over the previous four years, winning bronze at the 2005 world championships, gold at the 2006 European championships and bronze at the 2008 European championships.

Led by Yugoslav-born Nikola Karabatić, who spoke six languages and was voted the 2007 World Handball Player of the Year, France won four of their five pool matches, tying with reigning world silver medalist Poland 30-30 in their final match to lead Group A. Poland finished second in the group despite a 29-30 loss to Spain.

The real surprise occurred in Group B, where tiny Iceland (population 317,000) opened with a 33-31 victory over Athens bronze medalist Russia, and then followed with a 33-29 victory over reigning world champion Germany. Iceland, which had finished 11th at the 2008 European championships and 9th at the 2004 Olympics, ended the round-robin stage in a three-way point tie with South Korea and reigning European Champion Denmark, but was placed third in the group because of tie-breakers.

Led by 35-year-old Ólafur Stefánsson, Iceland kept up their momentum in the quarterfinals, upsetting Poland 32-20 to reach the semifinals. France advanced with a 27-24 victory over Russia; defending Olympic champion Croatia knocked out Denmark 26-24, and 2005 world champions Spain made it to the semifinals by beating South Korea 29-24.

France and Croatia played a close semifinal match, with the lead changing four times and neither side moving more than three points ahead. It was tied 22-22 in the 52nd minute, but then France scored three consecutive goals and held off Croatia for a 25-23 win.

Iceland came out strongly in their match against Spain, scoring the first five goals. Spain evened the score twice in the first half, but Iceland blew open the match with a 6-2 spurt early in the second half, going on to win. Iceland's President Ólafur Ragnar Grímsson described the victory as "the biggest moment in Icelandic sports history," and added that "nobody will do anything tomorrow."

After the excitement of the semifinals, the gold medal match started slowly. It was tied 2-2 after the first eight minutes, before France broke through with a 5-0 streak midway through the first half and held on to their five-point lead through the rest of the match.

The silver medal was Iceland's first-ever handball medal and equaled their best Olympic result of all time: a 1956 silver medal in the triple jump by Vilhjálmur Einarsson.

WOMEN

In 2012 twelve teams will participate in the women's Olympic tournament: the host nation, the world champion and the winners of four regional tournaments. The remaining six teams will be selected from tournaments for countries that have not yet qualified. The teams are divided into two round-robin pools. The four leading teams from each pool advance to the quarterfinals.

1896–1972 not held

1976 Montreal T: 6, N: 6, D: 7.28.

	W	L	T	PF	PA
1. SOV	5	0	0	92	40
2. GDR	3	1	1	89	47
3. HUN	3	1	1	85	55
4. ROM	2	3	0	73	83
5. JPN	1	4	0	72	115
6. CAN	0	5	0	35	106

1. SOV—Natalya Sherstyuk, Rafiga Shabanova, Lyubov Berezhnaya, Zinaida Turchyna, Tetyana Makarets, Mariya Litoshenko, Lyudmyla Bobrus, Tetyana Hluschenko, Lyudmila Shubina, Halyna Zakharova, Aldona Česaityte, Nina Lobova, Lyudmyla Panchuk, Larysa Karlova
2. GDR—Hannelore Zober, Gabriele Badorek, Evelyn Matz, Roswitha Krause, Christina Rost, Petra Uhlig, Christina Voss, Liane Michaelis, Silvia Siefert, Marion Tietz, Kristina Richter, Eva Paskuy, Waltraud Kretzschmar, Hannelore Burosch
3. HUN—Ágota Bujdosó, Márta Pacsai-Megyeri, Borbála Tóth Harsányi, Katalin Tóth Harsányi-Laki, Amália Sterbinszky, Ilona Nagy, Klára Horváth-Csík, Rozália Tomann-Lelkes, Mária Vanya-Vadász, Éva Angyal, Mária Berzsenyi, Marianna Nagy, Zsuzsanna Pethő-Kézi
4. ROM—Elisabeta Ionescu, Rozalia Şoş, Simona Arghir, Georgeta Lăcustă, Doina Furcoi, Niculina Sasu, Cristina Petrovici, Constantina Pițigoi, Doina Cojocaru, Magdalena Mikloş, Maria Bosi, Viorica Ionică, Maria Lackovics, Iuliana Hobincu
5. JPN—Shoko Wada, Hiroko Kosahara, Natsue Shimada, Terumi Kurata, Mikiko Kato, Hitomi Matsushita, Emiko Yamashita, Kuriko Komori, Eiko Kawada, Mihoko Hozumi, Nanami Kino, Tokuko Kubo
6. CAN—Danielle Chenard, Louise Hurtubise, Denise Lemaire, Francine Boulay-Parizeau, Joanes Rail, Nicole Génier, Lucie Balthazar, Hélène Tétreault, Manon Charette, Monique Prud'homme, Louise Beaumont, Mariette Houle, Nicole Robert, Johanne Valois

1980 Moscow T: 6, N: 6, D: 7.29.

	W	L	T	PF	PA
1. SOV	5	0	0	99	52
2. YUG	3	1	1	107	67
3. GDR	3	1	1	91	58
4. HUN	1	3	1	65	74
5. CZE	1	3	1	65	78
6. CON	0	5	0	46	159

1. SOV—Natalya Tymoshkina [Sherstyuk], Larysa Karlova, Iryna Palchykova, Zinaida Turchyna, Tetyana Kocherhina [Makarets], Lyudmyla Poradnyk [Bobrus], Larissa Savkina, Aldona Nenėnienė [Česaityte], Yulia Safina, Olha Zubaryeva, Valentyna Lutayeva, Lyubov Odynokova [Berezhnaya], Sigita Strečen
2. YUG—Ana Titlić, Slavica Jeremić, Zorica Vojinović, Radmila Drljača, Katica Ileš, Mirjana Ognjenović, Svetlana Anastasovska, Radmila Savić, Svetlana Kitić, Mirjana Đurica, Biserka Višnjić, Vesna Radović, Jasna Merdan, Vesna Milosević
3. GDR—Hannelore Zober, Katrin Krüger, Evelyn Matz, Roswitha Krause, Christina Rost, Petra Uhlig, Claudia Wunderlich, Sabine Röther, Kornelia Kunisch, Marion Tietz, Kristina Richter, Waltraud Kretzschmar, Birgit Heinecke, Renate Rudolph
4. HUN—Mária Berzsenyi, Erzsébet Németh-Csajbók, Rozália Tomann-Lelkes, Éva Bozó-Csulik, Amália Sterbinszky, Klára Horváth-Csík, Marianna Nagy, Ilona Samus-Mihályka, Mária Vanya-Vadász, Erzsébet Nyári-Balogh, Eva Angyal, Györgyi Őri-Győrvári, Piroska Budai, Klára Bonyhádi
5. CZE—Mária Končeková, Elena Boledovičová, Daniela Nováková, Katerina Lamrichová, Alena Horalová, Jolana Nemethová, Viola Pavlasová, Piroska Polačeková, Jana Kuťková, Věra Datínská, Milena Foltýnová, Elena Brezanyová, Petra Komínková
6. CON—Madeleine Mitsotso, Pascaline Bobeka, Angelik Abebame, Nicole Oba, Henriette Koula, Solange Koulinka, Isabelle Azanga, Micheline Okemba, Viviane Okoula, Germaine Djimbi, Yolande Kada-Gango, Pemba Lopez, Julienne Malaki, Yvonne Makouala

The USSR faced their only threat against Hungary when they led 12-11 with just five minutes to play. The Soviets then scored four straight goals and won, 16-12. Roswitha Krause of the bronze-medal-winning East German team had won a silver medal in the freestyle swimming relay 12 years earlier in Mexico City.

1984 Los Angeles-Fullerton T: 6, N: 6, D: 8.9.

	W	L	T	PF	PA
1. YUG	5	0	0	143	102
2. KOR	3	1	1	125	119
3. CHN	2	2	1	112	115
4. GER	2	3	0	91	100
4. USA	2	3	0	114	123
6. AUT	0	5	0	91	117

1. YUG—Jasna Ptujec, Mirjana Ognjenović, Zorica Pavićević, Ljubinka Janković, Svetlana Anastasovska, Svetlana Dašić-Kitić, Emilija Erčić, Alenka Cuderman, Svetlana Mugoša-Antić, Mirjana Đurica, Biserka Višnjić, Slavica Đukić, Jasna Kolar-Merdan, Ljiljana Mugoša, Dragica Đurić

2. KOR—Son Mi-na, Kim Kyung-soon, Lee Soon-ei, Jeong Hyoi-soon, Kim Mi-sook, Han Hwa-soon, Kim Ok-hwa, Kim Choon-yei, Jeung Soon-bok, Yoon Byung-soon, Lee Young-ja, Sung Kyung-hwa, Youn Soo-kyung
3. CHN—Wu Xingjiang, He Jianping, Zhu Juefeng, Zhang Weihong, Gao Xiumin, Wang Linwei, Liu Liping, Zhang Peijun, Sun Xiulan, Liu Yumei, Li Lan, Wang Mingxing, Chen Zhen
4. GER—Elke Blumauer, Maike Becker, Corinna Kunze, Silvia Schmitt, Roswitha Mroczynski, Sabine Erbs, Dagmar Stelberg, Kerstin Jönsson, Astrid Hühn, Petra Platen, Claudia Sturm, Sabrina Koschella, Vanadis Putzke
4. USA—Pamela Boyd, Carol Lindsey, Reita Clanton, Sherry Winn, Theresa Contos, Carmen Forest, Sandra De La Riva, Janice Trombly, Mary Phyllis Dwight, Cynthia Stinger, Melinda Hale, Leora "Sam" Jones, Penelope Stone
6. AUT—Ulrike Huber, Ulrike Popp, Martina Neubauer, Karin Prokop, Susanne Unger, Milena Gschiessl-Foltýnová, Maria Sykora, Silvia Steinbauer, Karin Hillinger, Elisabeth Zehetner, Gabriele Gebauer, Vesna Radović, Teresa Zielewicz, Gudrun Neunteufel, Monika Unger

Yugoslavia were seriously challenged only in their opening match when they defeated West Germany 20-19 after Mirjana Djurica converted a penalty with 1:06 to play. During the Yugoslavs' 33-20 drubbing of the US, 27-year-old Jasna Kolar-Merdan scored an Olympic record 17 goals.

1988 Seoul-Suwon T: 8, N: 8, D: 9.29.

	W	L	T	PF	PA
1. KOR	4	1	0	120	106
2. NOR	3	1	1	115	91
3. SOV	3	1	1	112	85
4. YUG	2	3	0	88	96
5. CZE	4	1	0	141	102
6. CHN	2	3	0	128	106
7. USA	1	4	0	104	123
8. IVC	0	5	0	65	164

1. KOR—Song Ji-hyun, Han Hyun-sook, Kim Choon-rye, Kim Myung-soon, Lee Ki-soon, Kim Hyun-mee, Kim Mi-sook, Suk Min-hee, Son Mi-na, Lim Mi-kyung, Kim Kyung-soon, Sung Kyung-hwa
2. NOR—Vibeke Johnsen, Cathrine Svendsen, Heidi Sundal, Hanne Hegh, Susann Goksør, Hanne Hogness, Karin Singstad, Trine Haltvik, Berit Digre, Ingrid Steen, Karin Pettersen, Annette Skotvoll, Kristin Midthun, Marte Eliasson, Kjerstin Andersen
3. SOV—Natalya Matryuk, Larysa Karlova, Svitlana Mankova, Zinaida Turchyna, Olha Semenova, Maryna Bazhanova, Natalya Morskova, Tetyana Horb, Yevhenia Tovstohan, Natalya Rusnachenko, Olena Nemashkalo, Tatyana Dzhandzhgava, Natalya Anissimova, Elina Guseva, Natalya Lapitskaya
4. YUG—Mirjana Krstić, Slavica Rinčić, Dragana Pešić, Svetlana Anastasovski-Obućina, Zita Galic, Ljubinka Janković, Svetlana Mičić, Ljiljana Marković, Mirjana Đurica, Nataša Kolega, Slavica Đukić, Ljiljana Mugoša, Svetlana Mugoša-Antić, Desanka Stojanović, Dragica Đurić
5. CZE—Anna Hradská, Irena Tomašovičová, Daniela Trandžíková-Nováková, Gabriela Sabadošová, . Júlia Kolečániová, Zuzana Budayová, Alena Damitšová, Petra Lupačová, Mária Ďurišinová, Monika Hejtmánková, Lenka Pospíšilová, Jana Stašová, Božena Mažgutová, Marta Pösová
6. CHN—Zhang Hong, He Jianping, Zhang Weihong, Wang Ming-xing, Chen Zhen, Li Lirong, Li Jie, Sun Xiulan, Xue Jinhua, Dai Jianfen, Wang Tao, Lu Guanghong
7. USA—Kathy Callaghan, Amy Gamble, Margaret Gallagher, Sherry Winn, Karyn Palgut, Portia Lack, Sandra De La Riva, Kim Clarke, Cynthia Stinger, Angie Raynor, Leora Jones, Carol Peterka, Penelope Stone, Laura Coenen
8. IVC—Elisabeth Kouassi, Wandou Guehi, Koko Elleingand, Emilie Djoman, Zomou Awa, Alimata Douamba, Mahoula Kramou, Clementine Blé, Adjoua N'Dri, Dounbia Bah, Julienne Vodoungbo, Hortense Konan, Gouna Irie, Brigitte Guigui

The Korean women, who had finished eleventh at the 1986 world championships, clinched their gold medal with a stunning, emotion-charged 21-19 upset of the USSR.

1992 Barcelona T: 8, N: 8, D: 8.8.

	W	L	T	PF	PA
1. KOR	4	0	1	136	107
2. NOR	3	2	0	100	111
3. SOV	4	1	0	124	100
4. GER	2	3	0	131	111
5. AUT	2	1	1	90	79
6. USA	1	3	0	72	102
7. SPA	1	3	0	76	85
8. NGR	0	4	0	73	107

Final: KOR 28-21 NOR
3rd Place: SOV 24-20 GER
5th Place: AUT 26-17 USA
7th Place: SPA 26-17 NGR

1. KOR—Moon Hyang-ja, Jang Ri-ra, Nam Eun-young, Lee Ho-youn, Lee Mi-young, Hong Jeong-ho, Lim O-kyung, Min Hye-sook, Park Jeong-lim, Oh Sung-ok, Kim Hwa-sook, Park Kap-sook, Ca Jae-kyung
2. NOR—Annette Skotvoll, Tonje Sagstuen, Hanne Hogness, Heidi Sundal, Cathrine Svendsen, Susann Goksør, Siri Eftedal, Ingrid Steen, Karin Pettersen, Kristine Duvholt, Heidi Tjugum, Mona Dahle, Hege Frøseth, Henriette Henriksen
3. SOV—Svetlana Bogdanova, Natalya Deryugina, Galina Onoprienko, Maryna Bazhanova, Natalya Morskova, Lyudimila Gudz, Svetlana Pryakhina, Galina Borzenkova, Tetyana Horb, Tatyana Dzhandzhgava, Elina Guseva, Natalya Anisimova, Larissa Kiseleva
4. GER—Sabine Adamik, Andrea Stolletz, Bianka Urbanke, Birgit Wagner, Kerstin Mühlner, Carola Ciszewski, Silvia Schmitt, Andrea Bölk, Michaela Erler, Sybille Gruner, Anja Krüger, Silke Fittinger, Eike Bram, Elena Leonte, Rita Köster, Gabriele Palme
5. AUT—Natali Rusnatchenko, Marianna Racz, Jadranka Jez, Kerstin Jönsson, Karin Prokop, Edith Matei, Nicole Peissl, Liliana Topea, Jasna Kolar-Merdan, Stanka Bozovic, Iris Morhammer, Barbara Strass, Slavica Đukić, Teresa Zurowski
6. USA—Laurie Fellner, Angie Raynor, Patricia Neder, Laura Coenen, Karyn Palgut, Portia Lack, Sharon Cain, Kim Clarke, Dannette Leininger, Cynthia Stinger, Leora Jones, Carol Peterka, Barbara Schnaf
7. SPA—Montserrat Marín López, Eugenia Sánchez Bravo, Amaia Ugartemendia Sagarzazu, Esperanza Tercero Rolando, Paloma Arranz Santamarta, Mercedes Fuentes Valmaña, Karmele Makazaga Urrutia, Cristina Gómez Arquer, Begoña Sánchez Santos, Raquel Vizcaíno Torre, Dolores Ruiz de Assín Jorda, Blanca Martín-Calero Gutiérrez-Cortines, Rita Hernández Martín, Montserrat Puche Díaz
8. NGR—Barbara Diribe, Immaculate Nwaogu, Agustina Nkechi Abi, Bridget Yamala Egwolosan, Eunice Idausa, Mary Soronadi, Mary Nwachukwu, Justina Anyiam, Auta Olivia Sana, Angela Ajodo, Chiaka Ihebom, Mary Ihedioha, Ngozi Opara, Justina Akpulo, Victoria Umunna

Norway was an unlikely finalist. Although they placed second in Seoul, they were admitted to the 1992 Olympic tournament only as a replacement for Yugoslavia, which was banned by the IOC at the last minute. In their first match in Barcelona, the Norwegians were crushed 27-16 by defending champion South Korea. Still, they managed to qualify for the semifinals, where they upset the team from the former Soviet Union 24-23 when Siri Eftedal scored with three seconds to play. The other semi was won by the Koreans 26-25 over Germany. Midway through the first half of the final, Norway was leading 7-5 when the momentum shifted completely. Over the next 15 minutes, South Korea outscored Norway 11-1 to take a 16-8 halftime lead. The Koreans allowed the Norwegians only two more goals in the first 12½ minutes of the second half and Norway was never able to cut the deficit to less than five points.

1996 Atlanta T: 8, N: 8, D: 8.3.

	W	L	T	PF	PA
1. DEN	5	0	0	149	114
2. KOR	4	1	0	155	122
3. HUN	3	2	0	126	127
4. NOR	2	3	0	116	109
5. CHN	2	2	0	99	109
6. GER	1	3	0	96	101
7. ANG	1	3	0	73	105
8. USA	0	4	0	87	114

Final: DEN 37-33 KOR (overtime)
3rd Place: HUN 20-18 NOR
5th Place: CHN 28-26 GER
7th Place: ANG 24-23 USA

1. DEN—Anja Andersen, Camilla Andersen, Heidi Astrup, Tina Nielsen Bøttzau, Marianne Florman Christensen, Conny Hamann, Anja Byrial Hansen, Anette Hoffmann-Møberg, Tonje Kjærgaard, Janne Kolling, Susanne Munk Lauritsen, Gitte Madsen, Lene Rantala, Gitte Sunesen, Anne Dorthe Tanderup
2. KOR—Cho Eun-hee, Han Sun-hee, Hong Jeong-ho, Huh Soon-young, Kim Cheong-shim, Kim Eun-mi, Kim Jeong-mi, Kim Mi-sim, Kim Rang, Kwag Hye-jeong, Lee Sang-eun, Lim O-kyung, Moon Hyang-ja, Oh Seong-ok, Oh Yong-ran, Park Jeong-rim
3. HUN—Anikó Meksz, Beatrix Kökény, Andrea Farkas, Anikó Kántor, Anikó Nagy, Anna Szántó, Auguszta Mátyás, Beáta Hoffmann, Beáta Siti, Erzsébet Kocsis, Eszter Mátéfi, Éva Erdős, Helga Németh, Ildikó Pádár, Katalin Szilágyi
4. NOR—Heidi Tjugum, Tonje Larsen, Kjersti Grini, Kristine Duvholt, Susann Goksør, Kari Solem, Mona Dahle, Ann-Cathrin Eriksen, Hege Kvitsand, Trine Haltvik, Kristine Moldestad, Annette Skotvoll, Mette Davidsen, Sahra Hausmann, Hilde Østbø
5. CHN—Che Zhihong, Chen Bangping, Chen Haiyun, Cong Yanxia, Jia Shujun, Li Jianfang, Shi Wei, Wang Tao, Yu Geli, Zhai Chao, Zhang Li, Zhang Limei, Zhao Ying
6. GER—Andrea Bölk, Bianca Urbanke, Christine Lindemann, Csilla Elekes, Eike Bram, Emilia Luca, Eva Kiss-Györi, Franziska Heinz, Grit Jurack, Heike Murrweiss, Kathrin Blacha, Marlies Waelzer, Melanie Schliecker, Michaela Erler, Michaela Schanze, Miroslava Ritskiavitchius
7. ANG—Anica Neto, Maria Gonçalves, Filomena Trindade, Domingas Cordeiro, Maura Faial, Aña Bela Joaquim, Elisa "Lili" Webba-Torres, Palmira de Almeida, Luzia Maria Bezerra, Justina Praça, Lia Paulo, Maria Joaquim, Elisa Peres
8. USA—Cheryl Abplanalp, Dawn Allinger, Sharon Cain, Kim Clarke, Laura Coenen, Kristen Danihy, Jennifer Demby Horton, Lisa Eagen, Laurie Fellner, Chryssandra Hires, Tami Jameson, Toni Jameson, Dannette Leininger, Dawn Marple, Patricia Neder, Carol Peterka

Two-time defending champion South Korea was expected to receive a stiff challenge from Denmark and that was exactly what happened. The Koreans appeared too strong for the Danes in the first half, opening a 16-10 gap before settling for a 17-13 lead at the break. Denmark finally tied the score at 23 on a fast break goal by Gitte Madsen with 11:19 to play after a pass from Anja Andersen, and then took their first lead at 8:35 when Andersen fed Anette Hoffman on another fast break. South Korea regained the lead, but the Danes fought back to tie the game again at 29. It appeared the match would go into overtime, but with one second to play, Kim Eun-mi fouled Andersen. Up to this point in the tournament, Andersen had converted ten of twelve penalty shots. With the game on the line, Andersen took her shot—and goalie Oh Yong-ran blocked it with her foot. While the Koreans mobbed Oh, the Danes returned to their bench in shock.

These moods would be short lived. Surprisingly, it was Denmark who took charge of the ten-minute overtime, scoring the first three goals and ultimately outscoring the Koreans 8-4.

2000 Sydney T: 10, N: 10, D: 10.1.

	W	L	T	PF	PA
1. DEN	6	1	0	214	165
2. HUN	4	2	1	202	187
3. NOR	6	1	0	174	137
4. KOR	5	2	0	216	177
5. AUT	4	3	0	220	173
6. FRA	3	4	0	180	177
7. ROM	2	4	1	176	191
8. BRA	1	6	0	180	238

Final: DEN 31-27 HUN
3rd Place: NOR 22-21 KOR
5th Place: AUT 33-32 FRA
7th Place: ROM 38-33 BRA

1. DEN—Anette Hoffmann-Møberg, Anja Nielsen, Camilla Andersen, Christina Roslyng, Janne Kolling, Karin Mortensen, Karen Brodsgaard, Katrine Fruelund, Lene Rantala, Lotte Kiærskou, Maja Grønbek Grønbæk, Mette Vestergaard, Rikke Petersen-Schmidt, Tina Bøttzau, Tonje Kjaergaard
2. HUN—Ágnes Farkas, Andrea Farkas, Anikó Kántor, Anikó Nagy, Anita Kulcsár, Beáta Siti, Beatrix Balogh, Beatrix Kökény, Bojana Radulovics, Dóra Lőwy, Ildikó Pádár, Katalin Pálinger, Krisztina Pigniczki-Sepsi, Rita Deli, Judit Simics-Zsemberi
3. NOR—Ann Cathrin Eriksen, Birgitte Saettem, Cecilie Leganger, Elisabeth Hilmo, Else-Marthe Sørlie, Heidi Tjugum, Jeanette Nilsen, Kjersti Grini, Kristine Duvholt, Marianne Rokne, Mia Hundvin, Monica Sandve, Susann Goksør-Bjerkrheim, Tonje Larsen, Trine Haltvik

4. KOR—Choi Hyun-jung, Chung Eun-hee, Han Sun-hee, Huh Soon-young, Huh Soon-young, Kim Hyang-ki, Kim Hyun-ok, Kim Jin-soon, Lee Jung-young, Lee Nam-soo, Lee Sang-eun, Moon Kyeong-ha, Oh Seong-ok, Oh Yong-ran, Park Chung-hee
5. AUT—Ausrele Fridrikas, Barbara Strass, Doris Meltzer, Iris Morhammer, Laura Fritz, Nataliya Rusnachenko, Sorina-Gratiela Teodorovic, Stanka Bozovic, Stephanie Ofenböck, Svetlana Mugoša-Antić, Tatjana Logvin, Tatyana Dzhandzhgava
6. FRA—Christelle Joseph-Mathieu, Isabelle Cendier Ajaguin, Isabelle Wendling, Joanne Dudziak, Laisa Lerus, Leïla Lejeune-Duchemann, Myriam Korfanty, Nathalie Selambarom, Nodjialem Myaro, Raphaëlle Tervel, Sandrine Mariot-Delerce, Stéphanie Cano, Stéphanie Ludwig, Valérie Nicolas, Véronique Pecqueux-Rolland
7. ROM—Aurelia Stoica, Valeria Motogna-Beşe, Cristina Vărzaru, Cristina Dogaru-Cucuian, Elena Napăr, Gabriela Doina Tănaşe, Lidia Drăgănescu, Luminită Huţupan-Dinu, Mihaela Ignat, Nicolaeta Alina Dobrin, Ramona Farcău-Maier, Steluţa Luca, Talida Tolnai, Victorina Bora
8. BRA—Alessandra Medeiros da Oliveira, Aline "Chicôria" da Silva, Chana Masson, Dilane Roese, Idalina "Daly" Borges Mesquita, Lucila Vianna da Silva, Margareth "Meg" Lobo Montão, Maria "Zezé" de Sales, Rosana Ferreira de Aleluia, Sandra Silva de Oliveira, Valéria de Oliveira, Viviane Rodrigues Jacques

The first day of competition saw an unusual occurrence: for the first time in Olympic history, a married couple played against each other. Three months before the Sydney Games, Camilla Andersen of Denmark and Mia Hundvin of Norway became "registered partners" in Copenhagen. (They separated in 2003.) As expected, Norway won the match and then won their three other pool games as well. In the other preliminary pool, South Korea won each of their four games by at least seven goals. Both South Korea and Norway had easy quarterfinal matches, with the Koreans defeating Brazil 35-24 and the Norwegians beating Romania 28-16. The other two quarterfinals went into overtime, as Hungary came from behind to edge Austria 28-27 and Denmark beat back a tenacious French team 28-26. The following evening's semifinal matches were both surprisingly easy upsets. First Denmark beat South Korea 31-29 in a match that was not really as close as the final score. Then Hungary disposed of Norway 28-23.

If the semifinals were short on suspense, the final made up for it. Denmark jumped out to a 5-2 lead. Hungary caught up at 8-8 and moved ahead with 11:28 left in the first half. The Danes regained the lead with 4:08 to go, but at halftime the score was Hungary 16 Denmark 14. In the second half, the Hungarians boosted their lead to 22-16 and 23-17, but with 13:21 left in the game, Anette Hoffmann Moberg and Janne Kolling led a Danish comeback. They drew even at 23-23 with 9:40 to go. The two sides traded goals until it was 26-26 with 4 minutes to play. Over a two-minute period, first Camilla Andersen and then Hoffmann Moberg scored two goals apiece to give the Danes a four-goal lead that they held to the end to successfully defend their Olympic championship.

2004 Athens T: 10, N: 10, D: 8.29.

	W	L	T	GF	GA
1. DEN	6	0	1	224	182
2. KOR	5	1	1	229	196
3. UKR	6	1	0	165	152
4. FRA	3	4	0	179	182
5. HUN	5	2	0	215	178
6. SPA	1	5	1	165	196
7. BRA	2	5	0	178	192
8. CHN	2	5	0	182	175

Final: DEN 38-36 KOR
3rd Place: UKR 21-18 FRA
5th Place: HUN 38-29 SPA
7th Place: BRA 26-25 CHN

1. DEN—Kristine Andersen, Karen Brødsgaard, Line Daugaard, Katrine Fruelund, Trine Jensen, Rikke Hørlykke Jørgensen, Lotte Kiærskou, Henriette Rønde Mikkelsen, Karin Ørnhøj Mortensen, Louise Bager Nørgaard, Rikke Petersen-Schmidt, Rikke Skov, Camilla Thomsen, Josephine Touray, Mette Vestergaard Larsen
2. KOR—Myoung Bok-hee, Kim Cha-youn, Lee Gong-joo, Kim Hyun-ok, Choi Im-jeong, Moon Kyeong-ha, Lim O-kyeong, Moon Pil-hee, Lee Sang-eun, Oh Seong-ok, Jang So-hee, Huh Soon-young, Woo Sun-hee, Oh Yong-ran, Huh Young-sook
3. UKR—Natalia Borysenko, Iryna Honcharova, Larysa Zaspa, Hanna Burmistrova, Tetiana Shinkarenko, Maryna Verheliuk, Olena Yatsenko, Hanna Siukalo, Olena Radchenko, Olena Tsyhitsa, Halina Markushevska, Liudmyla Shevchenko, Natalia Liapina, Anastasia Borodina, Oksana Raikhel
4. FRA—Joanne Dudziak, Isabelle Cendier Ajaguin, Estelle Vogein, Leïla Lejeune-Duchemann, Sandrine Delerce, Melinda Jacques, Nodjialem Myaro, Véronique Pecqueux-Rolland, Sophie Herbrecht, Stéphanie Cano, Isabelle Wendling, Myriam Korfanty, Delphine Guehl, Raphaëlle Tervel, Valérie Nicolas
5. HUN—Beáta Bohus-Megyerbíró, Anita Kulcsár, Zsuzsanna Lovász-Pavlik, Zsuzsanna Palffy, Krisztina Pigniczki-Sepsi, Eszter [?] Siti, Timea Tóth, Ágnes Farkas, Anita Görbicz, Bernadett Ferling, Bojana Radulović, Erika Kirsner, Ibolya Mehlmann, Irina Sirina, Katalin Pálinger
6. SPA—Patricia Alonso Jiménez, Vanessa Amorós Quiles, Maite Teresa Andreu Rodríguez, Diana Box Alonso, Susana Fraile Celaya, Soraya García Leite, Cristina Gómez Arquer, Cristina López Quiros, Elisabeth López Valledor, Marta Mangué Gonzalez, Noelia Oncina Moreno, Isabel Ortuño Torrico, Susana Pareja Ibarra, Montserrat Puche Díaz, María Eugenia Sánchez Bravo
7. BRA—Fabiana "Dara" Carvalho Carneiro Diniz, Alexandra "Alê" do Nascimento, Milene "Mi" Lima Figueiredo, Fabiana "Fabi Magra" Kuestener, Aline "Para" de Conceição da Silva, Aline Silva dos Santos, Aline "Chicôria" da Silva, Ana Amorim, Chana Masson, Daniela "Dani" de Oliveira Piedade, Darly Zogbi de Paula, Idalina "Daly" Borges Mesquita, Lucila Vianna da Silva, Margareth "Meg" Lobo Montão, Viviane Rodrigues Jacques
8. CHN—Fan Jie, Yu Geli, Zhai Chao, Liu Yun, Li Bing, Zhang Li, Wang Min, Wang Shasha, Chen Ji, Wu Yanan, Liu Xiaomei, Lei Sufen, Li Weiwei, Sun Laimiao

In the 2003 world championships final, France overcame a seven-point deficit in the last seven minutes of regulation, and then upset Hungary in overtime. The two were considered the favorites at the Olympics, but the field was comparatively open. Ukraine finished at the top of Group A in the preliminary round, winning all four of their matches, incuding a come-from-behind 23-22 upset of Hungary. In Group B, South Korea and Denmark both won three matches and tied with each other 29-29. The quarterfinals saw three close matches. After Ukraine beat Spain 25-23, France and Hungary faced each other . . . prematurely. Hungary led 20-17 with 14 minutes to play, but the French scored four straight goals to move ahead. The score was 22-22 with less than five minutes in regulations, when France, in two minutes, put in three goals, two of them by Veronique Pecqueux-Rolland, and finally won 25-23. South Korea survived a late rush by Brazil to win the third quarterfinal 26-24, and in the last quarterfinal, Denmark, after allowing China to close an 8-point gap to one point midway through the second half, revived to win 32-28.

In the first semifinal, South Korea built a 30-23 lead over France with less than eight minutes to play, but the French would not give up and scored five consecutive goals to close the gap to two. However, the Koreans held on to win 32-31. In the second semi, Denmark rolled over Ukraine 29-20, as Danish left back Katrine Fruelund led the way with nine goals.

The final was surprisingly similar to the 1996 Olympic final, in which Denmark and South Korea went into overtime, except that this time the match was even more tense. In Athens, the Danes and the Koreans were never more than two points apart during the first half, which ended in a 14-14 tie. South Korea came out strong in the second half, opening a 19-16 lead with three goals by Huh Soon-young. Katrine Fruelund and Kristine Andersen led a Danish comeback with three and four goals respectively, moving Denmark ahead 25-22 with five minutes to play. However, the Koreans evened the score in the closing minutes, and when Danish goalkeeper Karin Mortensen made a dramatic save with three seconds left to keep the score at 25-25, the match went into overtime. South Korea led 29-27 with less than three minutes to play in the first overtime, but Frueland and Lotte Kiærskou scored to force a second overtime. This time, the Danes opened with two goals, but the Koreans came back with four in a row, including three straight by Moon Pil-hee. Frueland scored twice in the final minute of the second overtime, which ended in a 34-34 tie, The match then advanced to a penalty shootout. Denmark made all four of their penalty shots, while Mortensen blocked two shots by South Korea, giving Denmark a 38-36 victory and their third consecutive Olympic championship.

2008 Beijing T: 12, N: 12, D: 8.23.

	W	L	T	GF	GA
1. NOR	8	0	0	248	185
2. RUS	6	1	1	229	210
3. KOR	5	2	1	247	207
4. HUN	3	4	1	211	227
5. FRA	4	4	0	218	217
6. CHN	3	5	0	188	216
7. ROM	4	3	0	214	182
8. SWE	2	5	0	166	188

Final: NOR 34-27 RUS
3rd Place: KOR 33-28 HUN
5th Place: FRA 31-23 CHN
7th Place: ROM 34-30 SWE

1. NOR—Ragnhild Aamodt, Karoline Dyhre Breivang, Marit Malm Frafjord, Kari Aalvik Grimsbø, Gro Hammerseng, Katrine Lunde Haraldsen, Kari Mette Johansen, Tonje Larsen, Kristine Lunde, Else-Marthe Sørlie Lybekk, Tonje Nøstvold, Katja Nyberg, Linn-Kristin Riegelhuth, Gøril Snorroeggen
2. RUS—Yekaterina Andryushina, Inna Bliznova, Yelena Dmitriyeva, Anna Kareyeva, Yekaterina Marennikova, Yelena Polyonova, Irina Poltoratskaya, Lyudmila Postnova, Oksana Romenskaya, Nataliya Shipilova, Mariya Sidorova, Inna Suslina, Emiliya Turey, Yana Uskova
3. KOR—An Jeong-hwa, Bae Min-hee, Choi Im-jeong, Hong Jeong-ho, Heo Sun-yeong, Kim Cha-yeon, Kim Nam-sun, Kim On-a, Lee Min-hui, Mun Pil-hui, Oh Seong-ok, Oh Yeong-ran, Park Jeong-hui, Song Hai-rim
4. HUN—Bernadett Bódi, Rita Borbás, Bernadett Ferling, Anita Görbicz, Orsolya Herr, Ágnes Hornyák, Mónika Kovacsicz, Katalin Pálinger, Krisztina Pigniczki, Piroska Szamoránsky, Gabriella Szűcs, Zsuzsanna Tomori, Tímea Tóth, Orsolya Vérten
5. FRA—Camille Ayglon, Paule Baudouin, Stéphanie Cano, Sophie Herbrecht, Nina Kamto Njitam, Alexandra Lacrabère, Amandine Leynaud, Valérie Nicolas, Véronique Pecqueux-Rolland, Mariama Signate, Raphaëlle Tervel, Maakan Tounkara, Christine Vanparys-Torres, Isabelle Wendling
6. CHN—Huang Dongjie, Huang Hong, Li Bing, Li Weiwei, Liu Guini, Liu Xiaomei, Liu Yun, Sun Laimiao, Wang Min, Wang Shasha, Wei Qiuxiang, Wu Wenjuan, Wu Yanan, Yan Meizhu, Zhang Geng
7. ROM—Carmen Amarei, Mihaela Ani Senocico, Aurica Motogna-Beşe, Florina Bârsan, Aurelia Stoica-Brădeanu, Luminită Huţupan-Dinu, Neli Ardean-Elisei, Narcisa Lecuşanu, Ramona Farcău, Laura Meiroşu, Cristina Georgiana Neagu, Adriana Nechita-Olteanu, Tereza Pâslaru, Ionela Gâlcă-Stanca, Talida Tolnai
8. SWE—Johanna Ahlm, Therese Bengtsson, Matilda Boson, Jessica Enström, Sara Eriksson, Tina Flognman, Madeleine Grundström, Isabelle Gulldén, Sara Holmgren, Therese Helgesson, Linnéa Torstenson, Frida Toveby, Teresa Utkovic, Johanna Wiberg, Annika Fredén

After three consecutive Olympic championships, Denmark's reign over women's handball had ended abruptly. After finishing 11th at the 2006 European championships, the team failed to qualify for the 2007 world championships, leaving them unable to earn a berth at the Beijing Olympics. Thereafter the tournament favorites were twice (and reigning) world champions Russia and 2006 European champions and world silver medalists Norway.

Both countries swept through their respective round-robin groups easily, with Norway winning all five of their matches by a combined goal differential of 48 points. Russia opened with a 29-29 tie against Athens silver medalists South Korea and went on to win their next four matches with a goal differential of 23 points to top Group B.

After lopsided quarterfinal wins by Norway and South Korea (over Sweden and China, respectively) and a 34-30 Hungarian victory over Romania, the most exciting quarterfinal match by far was between Russia and France. Trailing by two points near the end of regulation time, Russia scored three of the last four goals to take the teams to overtime. After the first overtime finished in another dead heat, Russia clawed ahead by a single point in the second overtime, holding off France for a 32-31 win.

The semifinal match between South Korea and Norway was another close contest. The lead changed hands four times in regulation time. Trailing by two points going into the final minute, the Koreans scored once, and then leveled the match at 28 with 25 seconds on the clock. In the final seconds of the match, Norway's Gro Hammerseng ran the length of the court to score just as the final whistle blew, putting Norway ahead 29-28. The South Korean team staged a courtside protest for more than twenty minutes but the results were allowed to stand. Russia had an easier time in the other semifinal, leading Hungary 14-9 at the half and holding off a number of late attacks to win 22-20.

The final was a complete rout, with Norway going on an 8-1 scoring blitz early in the first half. A panicked timeout by Russia failed to change the momentum, and Norway maintained an 18-13 lead at the half, widening the gap to 30-21 with ten minutes remaining. With the gold medal secure, Norway eased up at the end, finishing 34-27.

The Norwegian team featured two of the only ten publicly gay Olympians at the Beijing Olympics, lesbian couple Hammerseng and Katja Nyberg.

Chapter 17 **Judo**

MEN	WOMEN
Extra-Lightweight—60 kg	Extra-Lightweight—48 kg
Half-Lightweight—66 kg	Half-Lightweight—52 kg
Lightweight—73 kg	Lightweight—57 kg
Half-Middleweight—81 kg	Half-Middleweight—63 kg
Middleweight—90 kg	Middleweight—70 kg
Half-Heavyweight—100 kg	Half-Heavyweight—78 kg
Heavyweight—over 100 kg	Heavyweight—over 78 kg
Discontinued Event	

JUDO TERMS

Scoring

Ippon	10 points
Waza-ari	7 points
Yuko	5 points
Koka	3 points

Penalties

Hansokumake (= ippon)	Disqualification
Keikoku (= waza-ari)	Warning
Chui (= yuko)	Caution
Shido (= koka)	Note

Throws

Ashi-guruma	Leg wheel
De-ashi-barai	Advanced foot sweep
Harai-goshi	Sweeping hip throw
Harai-goshi-gaeshi	Sweeping hip counter
Kibisu-gaeshi	Heel trip reversal
Kochiki-taoshi	Leg grab shoulder throw
Ko-soto-gake	Minor outer hook
Ko-soto-gari	Minor outer reap
Ko-uchi-gari	Minor inner reap
Ko-uchi-maki-komi	Minor inner wrap around throw
Kuchiki-taoshi	Single leg takedown
Morote-gari	Double wheel leg grab
Morote-seoi-nage	Two arm shoulder throw
O-soto-gari	Major outer reaping throw
O-soto-gaeshi	Major outer counter
O-uchi-gari	Major inner reaping throw
Sasae-tsurikomi-ashi	Pull throw foot sweep
Seoi-nage	Shoulder throw
Seoi-otoshi	Shoulder drop
Sode-tsurikomi-goshi	Sleeve lift pulling hip
Sukui-nage	Scoop throw
Sumi-otoshi	Corner drop
Tai-otoshi	Body drop
Tani-otoshi	Valley drop throw
Tate-shiho-gatame	Horizontal four quarters hold
Tomoe-nage	Whirl throw
Uchi-mata	Inner thigh throw
Uchi-mata-gaeshi	Inner thigh counter
Uchi-mata-makikomi	Inner thigh wrap around
Uchi-mata-sukashi	Slip through inner thigh throw

Holds

Juji-gatame	Arm lock
Kami-shiho-gatame	Upper four quarters hold
Kesa-gatame	Sash hold
Kuzure-kami-shiho-gatame	Variant on upper four quarters hold
Kuzure-kesa-gatame	Broken scarf hold
Ushiro-kesa-gatame	Reverse scarf hold
Yoke-shiho-gatame	Side four quarters hold

Other Terms

Awasewaza	Ippon by two waza-ari
Katsu	A system of resuscitation
Kinsa	Slight superiority or close decision
Shime-waza	Strangulation or choking techniques
Yusei-gachi	Win by superiority scores or officials' decision

Judo matches are held on rectangular vinyl-covered foam mats called tatamis. The contest area is 9 to 10 meters (29 feet 6 inches to 32 feet 10 inches) square.

A judo match is won by a score of "ippon" which ends the match. A match which goes to full term without an ippon is decided by lesser scores. In the case of a tie, the majority decision of the referee and the two judges awards the match to the competitor who has displayed superiority.

Ippon can be scored by a clean, forceful throw; by holding the opponent mainly on his back for 30 seconds, under control, but not necessarily immobile; or by submission to a strangle, a choke or a lock applied against the elbow. Waza-ari is scored by a throw not quite good enough for ippon or by a 25-second hold-down. Yuko and koka can be scored for inferior throws or by 20- and 10-second hold-downs respectively. A second waza-ari in a match counts as ippon, but any amount of yukos is inferior to one waza-ari and any amount of kokas is inferior to one yuko.

In 1964 preliminary matches lasted ten minutes and final matches 15 minutes. In 1972 and 1976, the matches were six and ten minutes, and in 1980 and 1984 five and seven minutes. Since 1988, all men's matches have lasted five minutes. Women's matches are four minutes long. Olympic judo competitions are divided into two direct-elimination pools. The winner of each pool advances to the final. All those who lost to the pool winner take part in a *repêchage.* The winners of the two *repêchage* pools are awarded bronze medals.

Judokas must have short fingernails and toenails and they must be free of body odour. Derogatory remarks and gestures are forbidden. The word judo in Japanese means "the way of gentleness."

A combination of various jujitsu styles, judo was invented in the 1880s by Jigoro Kano who, in 1909, was appointed the first Asian member of the International Olympic Committee. The first world championship was held in Tokyo in 1956.

MEN

EXTRA-LIGHTWEIGHT
(60 kg–132.25 lbs)

1896–1976 not held

1980 Moscow C: 29. N: 29, D: 8.1.

		FINAL MATCH
1. Thierry Rey	FRA	Ko-soto-gari 7:00
2. Rafael Rodríguez Carbenell	CUB	
3. Tibor Kincses	HUN	
3. Aramby Yemizh	SOV/RUS	
5. John Holliday	GBR	
5. Pavel Petrikov	CZE	
7. Samir Elnajjar	SYR	
7. Reino Fagerlund	FIN	

In 1996 Thierry Rey was involved in a controversial incident when it was announced that he was the father of the first grandchild of France's president, Jacques Chirac. The controversy was not that Chirac's daughter, Claude, had given birth out-of-wedlock, but that she defied tradition by giving the child her own last name rather than that of the father.

1984 Los Angeles C: 27, N: 27, D: 8.4.

		FINAL MATCH
1. Shinji Hosokawa	JPN	Yoke-shiho-gatame 1:09
2. Kim Jae-yup	KOR	
3. Neil Eckersley	GBR	
3. Edward Liddie	USA	
5. Guy Delvingt	FRA	
5. Felice Mariani	ITA	

Hosokawa needed only 23 seconds to take Kim to the mat in the final.

1988 Seoul C: 37, N: 37, D: 9.25.

		FINAL MATCH
1. Kim Jae-yup	KOR	Shido 5:00
2. Kevin Asano	USA	
3. Shinji Hosokawa	JPN	
3. Amiran Totikashvili	SOV/GEO	
5. Patrick Roux	FRA	
5. Sheu Tsay-chwan	TAI	

Three years after losing to Hosokawa at the Los Angeles Olympics, Kim won the 1987 world championship by throwing Hosokawa after just 27 seconds. It was expected that the two would meet again in the Seoul final, but in the semifinals Hosokawa lost a controversial split decision to Kevin Asano. Kim thrilled the hometown crowd by showings up for the medal ceremony wearing not a sports suit but a traditional Korean outfit.

To qualify for the Olympic Games, Kim needed to lose 13 pounds in 20 days. He did this by limiting himself to one meal a day: a bowl of porridge with raw fish slices.

Kim, who was recovering from an injury to his backbone, had actually lost the Korean Olympic trials to Yun Hyun. However, the Korea Judo Association chose Kim as its representative anyway. After his victory in Seoul, Kim told the press, "I apologize to Yun and his mother. My gold medal is won together by them and me." In honor of his Olympic championship, Kim (unlike Yun and his mother) was rewarded with a lifetime pension of $16,600 a year by Korea's National Sports Promotion Foundation.

1992 Barcelona C: 43, N: 43, D: 8.2.

		FINAL MATCH
1. Nazim Guseynov	AZR	Sasae-tsuri-komi-ashi 5:00
2. Yun Hyun	KOR	
3. Tadanori Koshino	JPN	
3. Richard Trautmann	GER	
5. Philippe Pradayrol	FRA	
5. József Wágner	HUN	
7. Dashgombo Battulga	MGL	
7. Willis García García	VEN	

1996 Atlanta C: 34, N: 34, D: 7.26.

		FINAL MATCH
1. Tadahiro Nomura	JPN	Morote-seoi-nage 4:33
2. Girolamo Giovinazzo	ITA	
3. Dorjpalan Narmandakh	MGL	
3. Richard Trautmann	GER	
5. Natik Bagirov	BLR	
5. Nikolai Oyegin	RUS	
7. Nigel Donohue	GBR	
7. Giori Vazagashvili	GEO	

Tadahiro Nomura was the nephew of 1972 half-middleweight champion Toyokazu Nomura. Tadahiro qualified for the Japanese team by upsetting 1993 world champion Ryoji Sonda in the Olympic trials. He was considered the Japanese judoka least likely to achieve success in Atlanta. As Nomura would later relate, "At the airport, the photographers pushed me aside." In the round of 16 at the Olympics, Nomura upset reigning world champion Nikolai Oyegin when, while trailing with eight seconds to go, he executed a wild mid-air somersaulting hip throw. Nomura had to come from behind against Giovinazzo as well. With the score tied, Giovinazzo received a warning for non-combativity. He responded by attempting a leg sweep. Nomura dodged the attack, countered low, pulled on Giovinazzo's sleeves and flipped him over with a shoulder throw.

2000 Sydney C: 34, N: 34, D: 9.16.

		FINAL MATCH
1. Tadahiro Nomura	JPN	Sumi-otoshi 0:14
2. Jung Bu-Kyung	KOR	
3. Manolo Poulot Ramos	CUB	
3. Aidyn Smagulov	KYG	
5. Bazarbek Donbay	KAZ	
5. Alisher Mukhtarov	UZB	
7. Brandan Greczkowski	USA	
7. Elchin Ismayilov	AZR	

Defending champion Tadahiro Nomura needed a total of only 4 minutes 24 seconds to defeat his first three opponents and qualify for the semifinals. His semifinal opponent, Manolo Poulot spent even less time on the mat, disposing of his first three victims in 3 minutes 19 seconds. The Nomura-Poulot match was an epic struggle with Nomura holding off a comeback by Poulot to win with a yuko. The final was an anti-climax, as Nomura beat Jung Bu-kyung with a sumi-otoshi body drop after only 14 seconds. It was the quickest finals victory in Olympic history. The previous record, 27 seconds, had been set by Nomura's uncle in 1972.

2004 Athens C: 33, N: 33, D: 8.14.

		FINAL MATCH
1. Tadahiro Nomura	JPN	Penalty 5:00
2. Nestor Khergiani	GEO	
3. Choi Min-ho	KOR	
3. Khashbaatar Tsagaanbaatar	MGL	
5. Masoud Hadj Akhondzade	IRN	
5. Kenji Uematsu Treviño	SPA	
7. Oliver Gussenberg	GER	
7. Revazi Zintiridis	GRE	

Two-time defending Olympic champion Tadahiro Nomura arrived in Athens hoping to make up for a disappointing preliminary round loss to Anis Lounifi of Tunisia that left him with a bronze medal at the 2003 world championships. Nomura dominated the Olympic competition, recording an ippon in the round of 16 with a perfect throw of Oliver Gussenberg of Germany, and needing just 14 seconds to defeat Miguel Albarracín of Argentina in the quarterfinal round. In the semifinals, Nomura toppled Khashbaatar Tsagaanbaatar using a o-soto-gari technique to move into the final, where he narrowly outpointed Nestor Khergiani on cautions when no points were awarded on technique. Nomura's win made him the first-ever judoka to earn three consecutive gold medals.

2008 Beijing C: 33, N: 33, D: 8.9.

		FINAL MATCH
1. Choi Min-ho	KOR	Morote-gari (2:14)
2. Ludwig Paischer	AUT	
3. Ruben Houkes	HOL	
3. Rishod Sobirov	UZB	
5. Dimitri Dragin	FRA	
5. Gal Yekutiel	ISR	
7. Craig Fallon	GBR	
7. Frazer Will	CAN	

Three-time Olympic champion Tadahiro Nomura failed to qualify for the Japanese national team, leaving reigning world champion Ruben Houkes and reigning European champion Ludwig Paischer the pre-competition favorites.

Paischer defeated 2005 world champion Craig Fallon in the second round and advanced to the gold-medal match by beating North Korea's Kim Kyong-jin and France's Dimitri Dragin. Houkes made it to the semifinals, where he faced 2004 bronze medalist Choi Min-ho. Choi needed only four seconds to throw Houkes and advance to the final.

Choi and Paischer grappled several times over the first two minutes of the gold-medal match, before Choi took Paischer down with a leg grab. Choi, the 2003 world champion, won all five of his matches by ippon.

HALF-LIGHTWEIGHT

(66 kg—145.5 lbs [1980-1996 65 kg—143 lbs])

1896–1976 not held

1980 Moscow C: 29, N: 29, D: 7.31.

		FINAL MATCH
1. Nikolai Solodukhin	SOV/RUS	Shido 7:00
2. Tsendying Damdin	MGL	
3. Iliyan Nedkov	BUL	
3. Janusz Pawlowski	POL	
5. Yves Delvingt	FRA	
5. Torsten Reissmann	GDR	
7. Wolfgang Biedron	SWE	
7. Jaroslav Kříž	CZE	

Damdin spent most of the final backpedaling and was finally charged with a shido that proved decisive.

1984 Los Angeles C: 34, N: 34, D: 8.5.

		FINAL MATCH
1. Yoshiyuki Matsuoka	JPN	Seoi-nage 7:00
2. Hwang Jung-oh	KOR	
3. Marc Alexandre	FRA	
3. Josef Reiter	AUT	
5. Stephen Gawthorpe	GBR	
5. Sandro Rosati	ITA	

1988 Seoul C: 42, N: 42, D: 9.26.

		FINAL MATCH
1. Lee Kyung-keun	KOR	Yusei-gachi 5:00
2. Janusz Pawłowski	POL	
3. Bruno Carabetta	FRA	
3. Yosuke Yamamoto	JPN	
5. Tamás Bujkó	HUN	
5. Brent Cooper	NZL	

Like all members of the Korean judo team, Lee's training included periodic midnight visits to a cemetery, where he was forced to sit alone for an hour before being returned to his dormitory to watch videotapes of his potential opponents. Lee's path to the gold medal included a controversial semifinal split decision over Bruno Carabetta. Lee's father, Lee Kyung-do, was a student at Hiroshima Technical High School when the atomic bomb was dropped in 1945. He suffered burns and radioactive injuries, but competed in the 1960 Asian Games as a judoka.

In 2008, Bujkó was gruesomely murdered outside a metro station in north-west London. The attacker, a waiter at a five-star hotel near Buckingham Palace, threw acid in his face, then stabbed and beat him to death in front of a crowd of horrified bystanders. The two men had clashed six months earlier at the attacker's former home, which Bujkó had moved into. The killer was sentenced to life in prison.

1992 Barcelona C: 46, N: 46, D: 8.1.

		FINAL MATCH
1. Rogerio Sampaio Cardoso	BRA	O-soto-gari 5:00
2. József Csák	HUN	
3. Israel Hernández Planas	CUB	
3. Udo Quellmalz	GER	
5. Philip Laats	BEL	
5. Francisco Lorenzo Aparicio	SPA	
7. Kim Sang-moon	KOR	
7. Kenji Maruyama	JPN	

1996 Atlanta C: 35, N: 35, D: 7.25.

		FINAL MATCH
1. Udo Quellmalz	GER	Yusei-gachi 5:00
2. Yukimasa Nakamura	JPN	
3. Carlos Henrique Guimãres	BRA	
3. Israel Hernández Planas	CUB	
5. József Csák	HUN	
5. Philip Laats	BEL	
7. Ivan Netov	BUL	
7. Giorgi Revazishvili	GEO	

Udo Quellmalz, 1996
Quellmalz is thrown into the air by his teammates after his victory in the 1996 half lightweight judo tournament.

Udo Quellmalz breezed through his first four matches, winning each on ippon and needing only a total of 5 minutes 36 seconds to do it. The final was a rematch of the 1995 world championships final in which Quellmalz defeated Yukimasa Nakamura with 13 seconds remaining. Their Olympic confrontation ended scoreless despite close calls on both sides. The judges split 2-1 in favor of Quellmalz.

2000 Sydney C: 35, N: 35, D: 9.17.

		FINAL MATCH
1. Huseyin Özkan	TUR	Uchi-mata-makikomi 2:46
2. Larbi Benboudaoud	FRA	
3. Girolamo Giovinazzo	ITA	
3. Georgi Vazagashvili	GEO	
5. Arash Miresmaeili	IRN	
5. Patrick van Kalken	HOL	
7. Han Ji-hwan	KOR	
7. Yukimasa Nakamura	JPN	

The final was a rematch of the 1999 world championship, which was won by Larbi Benboudaoud. This time, Benboudaoud was leading after a penalty and a koka when, midway through the match, Huseyin Özkan suddenly counterattacked and threw Benboudaoud with a uchi-mata-makikomi. Although Turkey had previously won 32 gold medals, Özkan, who was born in Chechnya and moved to Turkey in 1993, was the first Turk to win an Olympic championship in a sport other than wrestling or weightlifting.

2004 Athens C: 31, N: 31, D: 8.15.

		FINAL MATCH
1. Masato Uchishiba	JPN	Sumi-otoshi 1:46
2. Jozef Krnáč	SLV	
3. Georgi Georgiev	BUL	
3. Yordanis Arencibia Verdecia	CUB	
5. Óscar Peñas García	SPA	
5. David Margoshvili	GEO	
7. Jorge Lencina	ARG	
7. João da Pina	POR	

The clear favorite for gold was two-time reigning world champion Arash Miresmaeili, a 22-year-old who was Iran's first judo world champion. Miresmaeili caused a stir when he arrived at his pre-match weigh-in more than two kilograms (four pounds) over the weight limit and was disqualified. Miresmaeli was later quoted by the Iranian News Agency as saying that he had deliberately failed to make weight to avoid his first-round opponent, Israeli judoka Ehud Vaks. When he returned to Iran, Miresmaeli was given $125,000 and a ticket to Mecca. With Miresmaeili out of the competition, the field was open. Competing in his first Olympics, 23-year-old Masato Uchishiba advanced quickly, winning all his matches through ippon. Uchishiba used a leg trip technique to defeat Magomed Dzhafarov of Russia to advance to the semifinals, where he toppled Georgi Georgiev in 43 seconds. In the final, Uchishiba grappled with Jozef Krnáč, getting him off-balance in less than two minutes and scooping him to the floor to win the gold medal. Uchishiba nearly missed the competition entirely, having seriously considered retirement in 2003 after failing to qualify for that year's world championships in Osaka.

2008 Beijing C: 33, N: 33, D: 8.10.

		FINAL MATCH
1. Masato Uchishiba	JPN	Tate-shiho-gatame (1:08)
2. Benjamin Darbelet	FRA	
3. Yordanis Arencibia Verdecia	CUB	
3. Pak Chol-min	PRK	
5. Alim Gadanov	RUS	
5. Mirali Sharipov	UZB	
7. Giovanni Casale	ITA	
7. Ameen El-Hady	EGY	

There were several early exits among the gold-medal favorites in the half-lightweight class. Three-time (and reigning) European champion Zaza Kedelashvili of Georgia lost his first match in overtime to world number-two-ranked Miklós Ungvári of Hungary, while the twice reigning world champion, Brazil's João Derly, was eliminated in his second match by 2008 European champion bronze medalist Pedro Dias of Portugal. Dias and Ungvári both fell in their following matches.

Defending Olympic champion Masato Uchishiba advanced to the gold-medal match, beating Iran's Arash Miresmaeili in the quarterfinals. Miresmaeili had caused controversy in 2004 when he purposely failed to make weight to avoid fighting Israeli Ehud Vaks.

Uchishiba faced 2003 European champion Benjamin Darbelet in the final, throwing him to the ground just seconds into the match. Darbelet twisted enough to keep the throw from ending the match, but thirty seconds later Uchishiba put him into a painful armlock, forcing him to concede. Uchishiba and Darbelet had trained together several times in the run-up to the Olympics and had become regular drinking buddies.

Reigning world silver medalist Yordanis Arencibia earned his second consecutive Olympic bronze medal by throwing European bronze medalist Alim Gadanov.

In September 2011 Uchishiba was fired from his job as judo coach at Kyushu University of Nursing and Social Welfare after allegations of sexual harassment. Three months later he was charged with raping a teenage girl.

LIGHTWEIGHT

(73 kg—164 lbs [1980–1996 71 kg—156.5 lbs])

1896–1960 not held

1964 Tokyo C: 25, N: 18, D: 10.20.
(68 kg—150 lbs)

		FINAL MATCH
1. Takehide Nakatani	JPN	Awasewaza 1:15
2. Eric Hänni	SWI	
3. Aron Bogolubovs	SOV/LAT	
3. Oleg Stepanov	SOV/RUS	

5. Chang Won-ku (TAI), Paul Maruyama (USA), Park Chung-sam (KOR), Gerhard Zotter (AUT)

1968 not held

1972 Munich C: 29, N: 29, D: 9.4.
(63 kg—139 lbs)

		FINAL MATCH
1. Takao Kawaguchi	JPN	Kami-shiho-gatame 0:39
3. Kim Yong-ik	PRK	
3. Jean-Jacques Mounier	FRA	
5. Wolfram Koppen	GER	
5. Hector Rodríguez Torres	CUB	
7. Cheng Chi-hsiang	TAI	
7. Ferenc Szabó	HUN	

DISQ (Drugs): Bakhaavaa Buidaa (MGL)

Buidaa lost a silver medal when he became the first person in judo history to fail a drug test. He tested positive for excess caffeine. Buidaa was so unschooled in judo tradition that he wrapped his belt around his waist only once instead of twice.

1976 Montreal C: 32, N: 32, D: 7.26.
(63 kg—139 lbs)

		FINAL MATCH
1. Hector Rodríguez Torres	CUB	Uchi-mata 10:00
2. Chang Eun-kyung	KOR	
3. Felice Mariani	ITA	
3. József Tuncsik	HUN	
5. Erich Pointner	AUT	
5. Marian Standowicz	POL	
7. Brad Farrow	CAN	
7. José Pinto Gomes	POR	

Surprisingly, two-time world champion Yoshiharu Minami was eliminated in his first match by Yves Delvingt of France. The final was a rugged contest, which was interrupted at one point to allow Rodríguez's ribs to be wrapped up by a doctor. Rodríguez told reporters that he began practicing judo to protect himself from his six older brothers.

The Australian representative in this event, Warren Richards, was later involved in an unusual incident. When the Olympics came to Sydney in 2000, Richards, as one of Australia's 1800 living Olympians, was invited to carry the torch as part of the Torch Relay. He accepted and sent in money to pay for a torch replica to keep as a souvenir. It was then discovered that Richards resided in the maximum security section of Sydney's Long Bay Jail, where his was serving a 12-year sentence for smuggling heroin. His invitation was withdrawn and his payment returned.

1980 Moscow C: 30, N: 30, D: 7.30.

		FINAL MATCH
1. Ezio Gamba	ITA	Yusei-gachi 7:00
2. A. Neil Adams	GBR	
3. Ravdan Davaadalai	MGL	
3. Karl-Heinz Lehmann	GDR	
5. Edward Alksnin	POL	
5. Christian Dyot	FRA	
7. Kim Byong-gun	PRK	
7. Michael Picken	AUS	

European champion Neil Adams needed less than four minutes to defeat his first three opponents, but in the final he lost a unanimous decision to his 21-year-old nemesis, Ezio Gamba. Gamba was the only Italian judoka to resist the anti-Soviet boycott. He took a leave of absence from the army and traveled to Moscow on his own. The most noteworthy confrontation between Gamba and Adams occurred at the 1977 European Championships when Gamba, in a desperate attempt to avoid submission, bit Adams on the backside. A shocked Adams won anyway but, Adams later recalled, "I still wonder how far Gamba would have gone if I had continued holding him down. I'm just glad I wasn't lying on top of him the other way around."

1984 Los Angeles C: 30, N: 30, D: 8.6.

		FINAL MATCH
1. Ahn Byeong-keun	KOR	Seoi-nage 7:00
2. Ezio Gamba	ITA	
3. Kerrith Brown	GBR	
3. Luis Onmura	BRA	
5. Glenn Beauchamp	CAN	
5. Hidetoshi Nakanishi	JPN	

Defending Olympic champion Ezio Gamba needed only 4 minutes and 1 second to demolish his first four opponents, but he ran out of steam in the final and was beaten by Ahn Byeong-keun. Earlier, Ahn had defeated world champion Hidetoshi Nakanishi, who had suffered a broken rib in his opening match.

1988 Seoul C: 41, N: 41, D: 9.27.

		FINAL MATCH
1. Marc Alexandre	FRA	Kouchi-gari 5:00
2. Sven Loll	GDR	
3. Michael Swain	USA	
3. Georgy Tenadze	SOV/GEO	
5. Bertalan Hajtós	HUN	
5. Steffen Stranz	GER	

DISQ (Drugs): Kerrith Brown (GBR)

Alexandre scored by knocking down Loll at 3:55 with a well-timed foot hook. Initially Kerrith Brown of Great Britain was awarded a bronze medal by virtue of his *repêchage* victory over world champion Michael Swain. However, he tested positive for Furosemide, a proscribed diuretic. When asked how he felt about backing into a bronze medal, Swain was philosophical. "I didn't want to win it this way," he said, "but I can always lie to my grandchildren."

1992 Barcelona C: 44, N: 44, D: 7.31.

		FINAL MATCH
1. Toshihiko Koga	JPN	Yusei-gachi 5:00
2. Bertalan Hajtós	HUN	
3. Jeoung Hun	KOR	
3. Shay Oren Smadga	ISR	
5. Bruno Carabetta	FRA	
5. Stefan Dott	GER	
7. Wiesław Błach	POL	
7. Khaliun Boldbaatar	MGL	

Hajtos qualified for the final with four straight ippons, but in the final he lost to two-time world champion Toshihiko Koga in a decision that shocked and outraged the crowd. Bronze medalist Chung Se-hoon died in March 1996 during a crash diet to make weight in the half-lightweight division. Chung had already lost 8 kilograms (17 pounds 10 ounces) when he experienced a heart attack while sitting in a sauna. He died on his way to the hospital.

1996 Atlanta C: 35, N: 35, D: 7.24.

		FINAL MATCH
1. Kenzo Nakamura	JPN	Yusei-gachi 5:00
2. Kwak Dae-sung	KOR	
3. Christophe Gagliano	FRA	
3. James Pedro	USA	
5. Khaliun Boldbaatar	MGL	
5. Sebastian Pereira	BRA	
7. Martin Schmidt	GER	
7. Andrei Shturbabin	UZB	

Kenzo Nakamura was the youngest of three brothers competing at the 1996 Olympics and the only one who had never won a world championship. He qualified for the Japanese team by defeating world champion Daisuke Hideshima at the Olympic trials. In the Atlanta final, Kwak Dae-sung was seven seconds away from victory when he was called for overly defensive play and the match ended in a tie. The judges awarded Nakamura a split decision.

2000 Sydney C: 34, N: 34, D: 9.18.

		FINAL MATCH
1. Giuseppe Maddaloni	ITA	Uchi-mata-sukashi 3:25
2. Tiago Camilo	BRA	
3. Anatoly Laryukov	BLR	
3. Vadims Zeljonnijs	LAT	
5. Jimmy Pedro	USA	
5. Choi Yong-sin	KOR	
7. Michel Almeida	POR	
7. Ferrid Kheder	FRA	

Although he did not win a medal, the sensation of the division was unheralded Choi Yong-sin, who upset two of the favorites. First he defeated world champion Jimmy Pedro when the American was penalized for an illegal grip with 46 seconds to go in their opening bout. Later Choi threw defending Olympic champion Kenzo Nakamura after 1 minute 25 seconds, before finally succumbing to 18-year-old Tiago Camilo. In the final, two-time European champion Giuseppe Maddaloni floored Camilo with a sukashi.

2004 Athens C: 33, N: 33, D: 8.16.

		FINAL MATCH
1. Lee Won-hee	KOR	Ko-uchi-maki-kmoi 4:51
2. Vitaly Makarov	RUS	
3. Leandro Guilheiro	BRA	
3. Jimmy Pedro	USA	
5. Victor Bivol	MOL	
5. Daniel Fernandes	FRA	
7. David Kevkhishvili	GEO	
7. João Neto	POR	

With a record 48 consecutive victories, including 43 by ippon, reigning world champion Lee Won-hee was the clear favorite for gold in Athens. His first match was against 2000 bronze medalist Anatoly Laryukov, whom he defeated with a yuko after a difficult match. In the round of sixteen, Lee faced rival Jimmy Pedro, the 1999 world champion and four-time Olympian who had come out of retirement in late 2003 to break Lee's 48-win streak in the final of the Korean Open. Lee scored a waza-ari sixteen seconds into the bout, and then finished the match at 3:37. Pedro moved into the *repêchage*, where he advanced to a bronze medal. Meanwhile, Lee fought Victor Bivol in the semifinals. Bivol scored an early point against Lee, but was taken down five seconds later. In the final, Lee scored a decisive victory over 2001 world champion Vitaly Makarov, culminating with an ippon throw in the final nine seconds of the match.

2008 Beijing C: 32, N: 32, D: 8.11.

		FINAL MATCH
1. Elnur Mammadli	AZE	Kibisu-gaeshi (0:13)
2. Wang Gi-chun	KOR	
3. Rasul Bokiyev	TJK	
3. Leandro Guilheiro	BRA	
5. Ali Maloumat	IRN	
5. Dirk Van Tichelt	BEL	
7. Hennadiy Bilodid	UKR	
7. Yusuke Kanamaru	JPN	

The gold-medal match was a repeat of the 2007 world championship final in Rio de Janeiro between Wang Gi-chun and Elnur Mammadli, which Wang had won. This time around the 20-year-old Mammadli needed only thirteen seconds to throw 19-year-old Wang with a leg grab. It was Azerbaijan's first-ever Olympic judo gold medal. Wang had earned his place in the national team by beating defending Olympic champion Lee Won-hee at the South Korean Olympic trials.

Rasul Bokiyev beat reigning European champion Dirk Van Tichelt in the repêchage round to win Tajikistan's first Olympic medal of any kind, while Leandro Guilheiro earned his second consecutive Olympic bronze medal by defeating Ali Maoumat by ippon.

HALF-MIDDLEWEIGHT

(81 kg—178.6 lbs [1980-1996 78 kg—172 lbs])

1896–1968 not held

1972 Munich C: 29, N: 29, D: 9.3.
(70 kg—154 lbs)

		FINAL MATCH
1. Toyokazu Nomura	JPN	Seoi-nage 0:27
2. Antoni Zajkowski	POL	
3. Dietmar Hötger	GDR	
3. Anatoly Novikov	SOV/UKR	
5. Engelbert Doerbandt	GER	
5. Antal Hetényi	HUN	
7. Wang Jong-she	TAI	
7. Reto Zinsli	SWI	

Nomura disposed of his five opponents in a total of ten minutes and 49 seconds.

1976 Montreal C: 29, N: 29, D: 7.29.
(70 kg—154 lbs)

		FINAL MATCH
1. Vladimir Nevzorov	SOV/RUS	Tai-otoshi 10.00
2. Koji Kuramoto	JPN	
3. Marian Talaj	POL	
3. Patrick Vial	FRA	
5. Lee Chang-sun	KOR	
5. Vaccinuf Morrison	GBR	
7. Juan Carlos Rodríguez	SPA	
7. John Van Hoek	AUS	

Nevzorov was from the Republic of Adygheya in the Caucasus Mountains.

1980 Moscow C: 29, N: 29, D: 7.29.

		FINAL MATCH
1. Shota Khabareli	SOV/GEO	O-uchi-gari 7:00
2. Juan Ferrer La Hera	CUB	
3. Harald Heinke	GDR	
3. Bernard Tchoullyan	FRA	
5. Mircea Frățică	ROM	
5. Ignacio Sanz Paz	SPA	
7. Georgi Petrov	BUL	
7. Slavko Sikirić	YUG/BSH	

Noticeably missing because of the anti-Soviet boycott was four-time world champion Shozo Fuji of Japan.

1984 Los Angeles C: 38, N: 38, D: 8.7.

		FINAL MATCH
1. Frank Wieneke	GER	Seoi-nage 4:04
2. A. Neil Adams	GBR	
3. Mircea Frățică	ROM	
3. Michel Nowak	FRA	
5. Filip Lesčak	YUG/SLO	
5. Hiromitsu Takano	JPN	

Wieneke's sudden victory over Adams was a shocking upset. At the 3:50 mark, Adams glanced at the clock and thought, "Three minutes to go and you're Olympic champion." Wieneke launched a weak right-handed attack, which Adams easily repelled. But then Wieneke noticed Adams relax momentarily, so he quickly executed a left shoulder throw. The former world champion was down on the mat and the contest was over. It was the first time in his entire career that Adams had lost a match by ippon.

1988 Seoul C: 41, N: 41, D: 9.28.

		FINAL MATCH
1. Waldemar Legień	POL	Seoi-nage 4:44
2. Frank Wieneke	GER	
3. Torsten Bréchôt	GDR	
3. Bashir Varayev	SOV/RUS	
5. Kevin Doherty	CAN	
5. Pascal Tayot	FRA	

Wieneke was defeated by the same shoulder throw that he had used to win four years earlier.

1992 Barcelona C: 42, N: 42, D: 7.30.

		FINAL MATCH
1. Hidehiko Yoshida	JPN	Uchi-mata 3:35
2. Jason Morris	USA	
3. Bertrand Damaisin	FRA	
3. Kim Byung-joo	KOR	
5. Lars Adolfsson	SWE	
5. Johan Laats	BEL	
7. Alexandru Ciupe	ROM	
7. Bashir Varayev	RUS	

Yoshida defeated all six of his opponents by ippon. The total time for all his matches was 16 minutes and 21 seconds.

1996 Atlanta C: 34, N: 34, D: 7.23.

		FINAL MATCH
1. Djamel Bouras	FRA	Yusei-gachi 5:00
2. Toshihiko Koga	JPN	
3. Cho In-chul	KOR	
3. Soso Liparteliani	GEO	
5. Stefan Dott	GER	
5. Darío Gastón García Aguilar	ARG	
7. Flávio Canto	BRA	
7. Irakli Uznadze	TUR	

The final was a sluggish defensive affair dependent on penalty calls. Koga, the 1992 lightweight Olympic champion, was leading when a penalty for inactivity with 12 seconds to go forced a decision. All three votes went to Bouras, who became the first French Muslim to win an Olympic gold medal. At the 1997 World Judo Championships, Bouras tested positive for the anabolic steroid nandrolone and served a fifteen-month suspension.

2000 Sydney C: 36, N: 36, D: 9.19.

		FINAL MATCH
1. Makoto Takimoto	JPN	Seoi-nage 5:00
2. Cho In-chul	KOR	
3. Aleksey Budolin	EST	
3. Nuño Delgado	POR	
5. Djamel Bouras	FRA	
5. Alvaro Paseyro	URU	
7. Kwak Ok-chol	PRK	
7. Kazem Sarikhani	IRN	

One of the less-heralded Japanese judokas in Sydney, 25-year-old Makoto Takimoto defeated Alvaro Paseyro by decision to earn a semifinal shot at defending champion Djamel Bouras. He gained the margin of victory over Bouras by taking him down with a leg sweep. In the final, Takimoto defeated 1996 bronze medalist Cho In-chul by scoring two yukos, throwing Cho after two minutes and staggering him with a leg sweep two minutes after that.

Krisztián Tölgyesi, who failed to advance out of his preliminary pool, went on to work as a car mechanic after his athletic career ended. In 2008 he was arrested in Budapest after police found several home-made bombs and detonators in his car. Tölgyesi, whose parents were members of a neo-Nazi white supremacist group, confessed to having made the bombs from instructions obtained on the Internet, intending to detonate them during Hungary's independence day celebrations.

2004 Athens C: 32, N: 32, D: 8.17.

		FINAL MATCH
1. Ilias Iliadis	GRE	Seoi-otoshi 2:06
2. Roman Hontiuk	UKR	
3. Flávio Canto	BRA	
3. Dmitri Nosov	RUS	
5. Robert Krawczyk	POL	
5. Mehman Akif Azizov	AZR	
7. Kwon Young-woo	KOR	
7. Florian Wanner	GER	

Seventeen-year-old Ilias Iliadis sprang onto the international judo scene just three months before the Olympics when he won the European championship. Born in Georgia under the name Jarji Zviadauri, Ilias was adopted by Greek national judo coach, Nikolos Iliadis, which allowed him to move to Greece to train and compete. In Athens, Iliadis advanced easily to the quarterfinals, where he faced Kwon Young-woo in a closely-fought match. The pair entered sudden death play, during which Kwon lost on a penalty point. Meanwhile, Roman Hontiuk earned a surprise victory over world champion Florian Wanner in the quarterfinals, immobilizing Wanner for 25 seconds to earn an ippon victory. In the semifinals, Iliadis beat Dmitri Nosov, who had earned a bronze medal at the 2003 European Championships, while Hontiuk defeated world championship bronze medalist Robert Krawczyk. In the final, Iliadis threw Hontiuk thirteen seconds into the bout, and then scored again on a takedown, before finishing the match with a shoulder throw to ippon.

2008 Beijing C: 35, N: 35, D: 8.12.

		FINAL MATCH
1. Ole Bischof	GER	Ko-uchi-gari (5:00)
2. Kim Jae-beom	KOR	
3. Tiago Camilo	BRA	
3. Roman Hontiuk	UKR	
5. Damdinsürengiin Nyamkhüü	MGL	
5. Guillaume Elmont	HOL	
7. Euan Burton	GBR	
7. Robert Krawczyk	POL	

The 2005 European champion, 28-year-old Ole Bischof dispatched reigning world champion Tiago Camilo in the Pool A semifinals with two waza-ari moves. Bischof then beat defending Olympic silver medalist Roman Hontiuk by points in the pool final to reach the gold-medal match.

There he faced 2005 Asian Games champion Kim Jae-beom, who had reached the final by beating 2005 world champion Guillaume Elmont with a winning hold in the final five seconds of overtime. Bischof recorded the only score of the final with just over a minute remaining to earn the gold medal. He was coached by 1984 gold medalist Frank Wieneke.

MIDDLEWEIGHT

(90 kg—198.5 lbs [1980–1996 86 kg—189.5 lbs])

1896–1960 not held

1964 Tokyo C: 25, N: 20, D: 10.21.
(80 kg—176 lbs)

		FINAL MATCH
1. Isao Okano	JPN	Yoke-shiho-gatame 1:36
2. Wolfgang Hofmann	GER	
3. James Bregman	USA	
3. Kim Eui-tae	KOR	

5. Lionel Grossain (FRA), Rodolfo Pérez (ARG), Lhoffei Shiozawa (BRA), Petrus Snijders (HOL)

In the quarterfinal match between Okano and Grossain, the referee failed to notice that Grossain had been rendered unconscious by shime-waza. When the Japanese coach called his attention to the Frenchman's condition, Okano revived his opponent through the use of katsu. In his book *Vital Judo,* Okano described his state of mind during major competitions: "By . . . the second or third bout of the tournament, the athlete becomes conscious of an imaginary membrane separating him from all outside things, including the spectators . . . Surrounded by that imaginary membrane, I found my mind alert and cool. I was like an animal standing alone. Voices and shouts from the crowd had no effect on me. Winning and losing were the only important things.

"When I reached the semifinal or final stage, a tension of an entirely different kind welled up inside me. I was entirely enclosed in a veil of transparency; I felt that I could see through everything. The opponent was nothing but a physical object. The sense of doing battle with myself became clearer in my mind. I sensed a unity with all of the spectators. When I won . . . the world seemed to belong to me, and the single moment of intensely concentrated meaning is unforgettable."

1968 not held

1972 Munich C: 35, N: 35, D: 9.2.
(80 kg—176 lbs)

		FINAL MATCH
1. Shinobu Sekine	JPN	Yusei-gachi 10:00
2. Oh Seung-lip	KOR	
3. Jean-Paul Coché	FRA	
3. Brian Jacks	GBR	
5. Guram Gogalauri	SOV/GEO	
5. Lutz Lischka	AUT	
7. Gerd Egger	GER	
7. Petr Jákl	CZE	

Sekine, the All-Japan open category champion, actually lost to Oh in the preliminary pool. But he was able to fight his way into the final through *repêchage,* or second-chance matches, and won by a split decision, to the great relief of all the Japanese who were present.

1976 Montreal C: 32, N: 32, D: 7.28.
(80 kg—176 lbs)

		FINAL MATCH
1. Isamu Sonoda	JPN	O-uchi-gari 10:00
2. Valery Dvoynikov	SOV/UKR	
3. Slavko Obadov	YUG/SER	
3. Park Young-chul	KOR	
5. José Luis de Frutos Molinero	SPA	
5. Fred Marhenke	GER	
7. Paul Buganey	AUS	
7. Suheyl Yesilnur	TUR	

Policeman Isamu Sonoda upset three-time world champion Shozo Fuji in the All-Japan championships, which served as Japan's Olympic qualifying tournament.

1980 Moscow C: 27, N: 27, D: 7.28.

		FINAL MATCH
1. Jürg Röthlisberger	SWI	Harai-goshi 7:00
2. Isaac Azcuy Oliva	CUB	
3. Aleksandrs Jackevičš	SOV/LAT	
3. Detlef Ultsch	GDR	
5. Walter Carmona	BRA	
5. Bertil Ström	SWE	
7. Peter Donnelly	GBR	
7. Henri-Richard Lobe	CAM	

The final was twice delayed mid-contest because of a controversy concerning the size of Röthlisberger's jacket. After a five-minute argument, the referee ordered Röthlisberger to change his jacket. He did so and the fight resumed. But the referee stopped the contest again, declaring that the second jacket was also unacceptable. Röthlisberger changed back into his original jacket, which had miraculously transformed into the proper size, and the match continued.

1984 Los Angeles C: 29, N: 29, D: 8.8.

		FINAL MATCH
1. Peter Seisenbacher	AUT	Ashi-guruma 2:26
2. Robert Berland	USA	
3. Walter Carmona	BRA	
3. Seiki Nose	JPN	
5. Fabien Canu	FRA	
5. Densign White	GBR	

Seisenbacher, a 24-year-old goldsmith, was the first Austrian ever to win a major judo championship. He dispatched his five opponents in an elapsed time of 11 minutes and 5 seconds.

1988 Seoul C: 36, N: 36, D: 9.29.

		FINAL MATCH
1. Peter Seisenbacher	AUT	Yusei-gachi 5:00
2. Vladimir Shestakov	SOV/RUS	
3. Akinobu Osako	JPN	
3. Ben Spijkers	HOL	
5. Fabien Canu	FRA	
5. Densign White	GBR	

At age 28, Seisenbacher became the first judoka in Olympic history to retain his title. A curious incident occurred in the *repêchage* rounds. After Ben Spijkers defeated Densign White, the two longtime rivals embraced and left the mat arm in arm. This was a breach of the strict protocols of judo and the judges ordered them to return for a more formal farewell. Spijkers and White bowed properly—and again walked off arm in arm. This time the officials waived the rules, to the delight of the crowd.

One of the Olympics' nastier competitors was James Waithe, who represented Barbados and reached the second round. In October 2009 he was arrested after police stumbled upon a massive cocaine production facility at an apartment he owned. Waithe had been the drug gang's "enforcer", torturing its debtors with a variety of sadistic techniques, including putting a man's hand in an electric toaster. In May 2011 he was given an indefinite prison sentence with a minimum of nine years.

1992 Barcelona C: 33, N: 33, D: 7.29.

		FINAL MATCH
1. Waldemar Legień	POL	Uchi-mata 5:00
2. Pascal Tayot	FRA	
3. Nicolas Gill	CAN	
3. Hirotaka Okada	JPN	
5. Adrian Croitoru	ROM	
5. Axel Lobenstein	GER	
7. Daniel Kistler	SWI	
7. Yang Jong-ock	KOR	

Legień moved up in weight class and won his second gold medal. He got off to a quick start in Barcelona, defeating Michael Oduor of Kenya in 8 seconds and Yahya Mufarrich of Bulgaria in 12. But that was slow work compared to the record set by Cuba's Andrés Franco. In the second round Franco dispatched Illus Isako of Zaire with a morote-gari in only 3 seconds.

1996 Atlanta C: 33, N: 33, D: 7.22.

		FINAL MATCH
1. Jeon Ki-young	KOR	Morote-seoi-nage 4:11
2. Armen Bagdasarov	UZB	
3. Mark Huizinga	HOL	
3. Marko Spittka	GER	
5. Adrian Croitoru	ROM	
5. Hidehiko Yoshida	JPN	
7. Nicolas Gill	CAN	
7. Oleg Maltsev	RUS	

Two-time world champion Jeon Ki-young overwhelmed surprise finalist Armen Bagdasarov, finally finishing him off with a two arm shoulder throw.

2000 Sydney C: 32, N: 32, D: 9.20.

		FINAL MATCH
1. Mark Huizinga	HOL	Uchi-mata-gaeshi 3:22
2. Carlos Honorato	BRA	
3. Frédéric Demontfaucon	FRA	
3. Ruslan Mashurenko	UKR	
5. Keith Morgan	CAN	
5. Rasul Salimov	AZR	
7. Fernando González Pérez	SPA	
7. Brian Olson	USA	

Gidehiko Yoshida, the 1992 half-middleweight champion, retired in 1997, but came back after two years and won the 1999 middleweight world championship. He looked strong in Sydney, but 43 seconds into his quarterfinal match against Carlos Honorato, he fell on his elbow and dislocated his arm. Adding a victory over Frédéric Demontfaucon, Honorato advanced to the final. In the other half of the draw, Marc Huizinga's first opponent was Cuban Yosvane Despaigne, who had eliminated Huizinga early in both the 1997 and 1999 world championships. This time Huizanga, trailing after four minutes, threw Despaigne to gain the victory. In the final, Huizinga floored Honorato halfway through the match and then finished him with a leg throw.

2004 Athens C: 32, N: 32, D: 8.18.

		FINAL MATCH
1. Zurab Zviadauri	GEO	O-soto-gaeshi 3:03
2. Hiroshi Izumi	JPN	
3. Mark Huizinga	HOL	
3. Khasanbi Taov	RUS	
5. Winston Gordon	GBR	
5. Hwang Hee-tae	KOR	
7. Eduardo Costa	ARG	
7. Daniel Kelly	AUS	

Defending Olympic champion Mark Huizinga was outpointed in the second round by reigning world champion Hwang Hee-tae. Hwang advanced to the semifinals, but was defeated by Hiroshi Izumi, who caught him off guard with a shoulder throw with nine seconds left in the match. Izumi had also beaten world championship bronze medalist Siarhei Kukharenka of Belarus with an o-soto-gari ippon just 10 seconds into his first-round match. In the final, Izumi struggled to find an opening against two-time world champion silver medalist Zurab Zviadauri. Izumi was given a penalty for passivity after two and a half minutes, before Zviadauri caught him off guard, picked him up and threw him to the ground for an ippon victory. Zviadauri was the second Georgian-born judoka to win gold in two days. His younger cousin, Ilias Iliadis, won the half-middleweight gold for Greece the day before.

2008 Beijing C: 31, N: 31, D: 8.13.

		FINAL MATCH
1. Irakli Tsirekidze	GEO	Koka (5:00)
2. Amar Benikhlef	ALG	
3. Sergei Aschwanden	SWI	
3. Hesham Misbah	EGY	
5. Yves-Matthieu Dafreville	FRA	
5. Ivan Pershin	RUS	
7. Andrey Kazusenok	BLR	
7. Eduardo Santos	BRA	

Defending Olympic champion and current world silver medalist Ilias Iliadis of Greece was drawn against reigning European champion and 2000 Olympic gold medalist Mark Huizinga in the opening round. Huizinga advanced on ippon, but lost his second match to two-time European champion Sergei Aschwanden.

Reigning world champion Irakli Tsirekidze advanced to the gold-medal match, beating 2006 European champion Ivan Pershin in the pool final. Tsirekidze faced surprise finalist Amar Benikhlef in the final, narrowly defeating him by scoring koka after 53 seconds.

HALF-HEAVYWEIGHT
(100 kg—220.5 lbs [1980–1996 95 kg—209 lbs])

1896–1968 not held

1972 Munich C: 30, N: 30, D: 9.1.
(93 kg—205 lbs)

		FINAL MATCH
1. Shota Chochoshvili	SOV/GEO	Yusei-gachi 10:00
2. David Starbrook	GBR	
3. Paul Barth	GER	
3. Chiaki Ishii	BRA	
5. Helmut Howiller	GDR	
5. James Wooley	USA	
7. Pierre Albertini	FRA	
7. Terry Farnsworth	CAN	

Two-time world champion Fumio Sasahara of Hokkaido, Japan, was unexpectedly thrown and defeated by 22-year-old Shota Chochoshvili of Tbilisi, Georgia. Chochoshvili then lost a split decision to Dave Starbrook, the operator of a newspaper, tobacco, and sweet shop in Hackney. The two met again in the finals, and this time Chochoshvili prevailed with a unanimous decision.

1976 Montreal C: 35, N: 35, D: 7.27.
(93 kg—205 lbs)

		FINAL MATCH
1. Kazuhiro Ninomiya	JPN	Keikoku 10:00
2. Ramaz Kharshiladze	SOV/GEO	
3. Jürg Röthlisberger	SWI	
3. David Starbrook	GBR	
5. Jo Jae-gi	KOR	
5. Dietmar Lorenz	GDR	
7. An Ung-nam	PRK	
7. Abdoulaye Djiba	SEN	

Ninomiya, who won three of his four preliminary fights in one minute or less, had to lose more than 25 pounds to make the weight limit.

1980 Moscow C: 23, N: 23, D: 7.27.

		FINAL MATCH
1. Robert Van de Walle	BEL	Tani-otoshi 7:00
2. Tengiz Khubuluri	SOV/GEO	
3. Dietmar Lorenz	GDR	
3. Henk Numan	HOL	
5. István Szepesi	HUN	
5. Rolando José Tornes Babastro	CUB	
7. Daniel Radu	ROM	
7. Jean-Luc Rouge	FRA	

1984 Los Angeles C: 22, N: 22, D: 8.9.

		FINAL MATCH
1. Ha Hyoung-zoo	KOR	Yusei-gachi 7:00
2. Douglas Vieira	BRA	
3. Bjarni Friđriksson	ICE	
3. Günter Neureuther	GER	
5. Yuri Fazi	ITA	
5. Joseph Meli	CAN	

1988 Seoul C: 21, N: 21, D: 9.30.

		FINAL MATCH
1. Aurélio Miguel	BRA	Chui 5:00
2. Marc Meiling	GER	
3. Dennis Stewart	GBR	
3. Robert van de Walle	BEL	
5. Jacek Beutler	POL	
5. Jiří Sosna	CZE	

Incredibly, Miguel won all five of his matches without scoring a single point. He gained two victories by judges' decision and three, including the final, when his opponents were penalized for excessive passivity. Nineteen-eighty Olympic champion Robert van de Walle earned a bronze in 1988 at the age of 34.

1992 Barcelona C: 34, N: 34, D: 7.28.

		FINAL MATCH
1. Antal Kovács	HUN	Uchi-mata 5:00
2. Raymond Stevens	GBR	
3. Theo Meijer	HOL	
3. Dmitri Sergeyev	RUS	
5. Paweł Nastula	POL	
5. Indrek Pertelson	EST	
7. Yasuhiro Kai	JPN	
7. Robert van de Walle	BEL	

The 20-year-old Kovács was a surprising and gracious winner. "I was lucky," he told reporters after defeating Stevens. "I have a partner back home who is very similar in his build and style."

1996 Atlanta C: 32, N: 32, D: 7.21.

		FINAL MATCH
1. Paweł Nastula	POL	Kuzure-kesa-gatame 1:33
2. Kim Min-soo	KOR	
3. Aurélio Miguel	BRA	
3. Stéphane Traineau	FRA	
5. Antal Kovács	HUN	
5. Bernardus "Ben" Sonnemans	HOL	
7. Alejandro Bender	ARG	
7. Yoshio Nakamura	JPN	

World champion Paweł Nastula made quick work of the opposition with only 1988 Olympic champion Aurélio Miguel going the distance. Nastula's other four matches lasted a total of 8 minutes 48 seconds. In the final he downed Kim with a shoulder throw and then kept him down for thirty seconds with a scarf hold.

2000 Sydney C: 33, N: 33, D: 9.21.

		FINAL MATCH
1. Kosei Inoue	JPN	Uchi-mata 2:09
2. Nicolas Gill	CAN	
3. Yury Stepkin	RUS	
3. Stéphane Traineau	FRA	
5. Luigi Guido	ITA	
5. Ariel Ze'evi	ISR	
7. Mário Sabino	BRA	
7. Iveri Zhikurali	GEO	

The reigning world champion, Kosei Inoue put on the most dominating performance in Olympic history. His five victories lasted a total of only 7 minutes 43 seconds and the longest, a quarterfinal defeat of Ariel Ze'evi, was over in 2 minutes 39 seconds. In the final, the score was tied 1-1 when Inoue suddenly put Nicolas Gill on his back with a right uchi-mata. On the victory podium, Inoue held aloft a framed photograph of his mother, who had died of a brain hemorrhage in June 1999.

One of the bronze medal matches ended in controversy when officials ruled that Stéphane Traineau's takedown of Ze'evi had taken place out of bounds, but then reversed their decision.

2004 Athens C: 33, N: 33, D: 8.19.

		FINAL MATCH
1. Igor Makarov	BLR	Sukui-nage 5:00
2. Jang Sung-ho	KOR	
3. Michael Jurack	GER	
3. Ariel Ze'evi	ISR	
5. Elco van der Geest	HOL	
5. Mövlud Miraliyev	AZR	
7. Ghislain Lemaire	FRA	
7. Askhat Zhitkeyev	KAZ	

The clear favorite in the competition was defending Olympic champion and three-time defending world champion Kosei Inoue. Inoue had an unexpectedly difficult start, struggling to beat Hungary's Anatal Kovacs on yuko before moving to the quarterfinals, where he faced Elco van der Geest, the 2002 European champion. Leading on points from two incomplete throws, Van der Geest scored a major upset with a shoulder throw with 12 seconds left in the match. It was Inoue's first defeat in a major international competition in four years. Van der Geest was defeated in the semifinals by 25-year-old Igor Makarov, the 2003 world championship bronze medalist, who moved on to the final, where he faced Jang Sung-ho, the 1999 world championship silver medalist. Makarov threw Jang with a waza-ari in the second minute to score one point. Jang managed an incomplete throw of Makarov with 20 seconds left in the match, but lost on points. Makarov's victory earned him Belarus' first Olympic gold medal in judo.

2008 Beijing C: 32, N: 32, D: 8.14.

		FINAL MATCH
1. Naidangiin Tüvshinbayar	MGL	Sode-tsurikomi-goshi (5:00)
2. Askhat Zhitkeyev	KAZ	
3. Henk Grol	HOL	
3. Mövlud Mirəliyev	AZE	
5. Przemysław Matyjaszek	POL	
5. Lovan Zhorzholiani	GEO	
7. Dániel Hadfi	HUN	
7. Jang Seong-ho	KOR	

Naidangiin Tüvshinbayar and Askhat Zhitkeyev were both surprise qualifiers for the gold-medal match. Tüvshinbayar's previous best result had been a fifth place at the 2006 Asian Games, while Zhitkeyev's sole major international win had been at the Asian Championships in 2004.

Tüvshinbayar was drawn against 2004 heavyweight gold medalist and twice world champion Keiji Suzuki in the first round, advancing on a double leg grab for ippon after a minute-and-a-half. Zhitkeyev's biggest challenge came in his pool final, when he faced 2008 European champion Henk Grol, who had beaten reigning world champion Luciano Corrêa of Brazil in the first round. Grol was leading on points when both combatants tried a winning ippon throw, which the judges awarded to Zhitkeyev.

The final went the full five minutes, with 24-year-old Tüvshinbayar winning a clear victory. Both finalists made sports history: Zhitkeyev as Kazakhstan's first Olympic judo medalist and Tüvshinbayar as Mongolia's first-ever Olympic gold medalist. Until his victory Mongolia held the record as the country that had won the most total medals (16) without earning a single gold.

HEAVYWEIGHT

(Over 100 kg-220.5 lbs [1980-1996 Over 95 kg—209 lbs])

1896–1960 not held

1964 Tokyo C: 15, N: 13, D: 10.22.
(Over 80 kg—176 lbs)

		FINAL MATCH
1. Isao Inokuma	JPN	Kinsa 15.00
2. A. Douglas Rogers	CAN	
3. Parnaoz Chikviladze	SOV/GEO	
3. Anzor Kiknadze	SOV/GEO	
5. Kim Jong-dal	KOR	

Inokuma and Rogers were used to practicing together in Japan, so the final was a relatively quiet affair. The referee, Charles Palmer of Great Britain, became so annoyed by their passivity that he threatened to disqualify both men and deprive them of medals. The lightest entrant in the heavyweight division, Inokuma weighed only 192 pounds (87 kilograms), compared to Rogers' 260 pounds (118 kilograms). Inokuma was once asked why he had never married. He replied, "To marry, you have to be kind." Inokuma went on to become the president of a major construction company, but committed suicide in 2001 after the business fell into financial troubles.

1968 not held

1972 Munich C: 21, N: 21, D: 8.31.
(Over 93 kg—205 lbs)

		FINAL MATCH
1. Willem Ruska	HOL	Harai-goshi 1:43
2. Klaus Glahn	GER	
3. Motoki Nishimura	JPN	
3. Givi Onashvili	SOV/GEO	
5. Jean-Claude Brondani	FRA	
5. Douglas Nelson	USA	
7. Tijive Bankassou	MOR	
7. M'Bagnik Mebodj	SEN	

1976 Montreal C: 20, N: 20, D: 7.26.
(Over 93 kg—205 lbs)

		FINAL MATCH
1. Serhei Novikov	SOV/UKR	O-soto-gari 1:19
2. Günther Neureuther	GER	
3. Allen Coage	USA	
3. Sumio Endo	JPN	
5. Gunsem Jalaa	MGL	
5. Keith Remfry	GBR	
7. Abdoulaye Kote	SEN	
7. Radomir Kovačević	YUG/SER	

Because there was no seeding system, the two favorites, Sumio Endo and Serhei Novikov, met in the very first round. It was a dull match without any scoring, won by Novikov by decision. A most unusual sight was the *repêchage* match between the 5-foot 6½-inch, 259-pound (1.69 meter, 117.5 kilogram) Sumio Endo and 7-foot 0-inch, 350-pound (2.13 meter, 159 kilogram) Pak Jong-gil of North Korea. Endo, the defending world champion, was the victor.

1980 Moscow C: 18, N: 18, D: 7.27.

		FINAL MATCH
1. Angelo Parisi	FRA	Ippon 6:14
2. Dimitar Zapryanov	BUL	
3. Radomir Kovačević	YUG/SER	
3. Vladimír Kocman	CZE	
5. Kim Myong-gyu	PRK	
5. Paul Radburn	GBR	
7. Wojciech Reszko	POL	

Born in Italy, Parisi was a former member of the British team who married a Frenchwoman and changed citizenship. Because of the anti-Soviet boycott, neither of the two Japanese world champions, Sumio Endo and Yasuhiro Yamashita, could compete.

1984 Los Angeles C: 16, N: 16, D: 8.10.

		FINAL MATCH
1. Hitoshi Saito	JPN	Shido 7:00
2. Angelo Parisi	FRA	
3. Mark Berger	CAN	
3. Cho Yong-chul	KOR	
5. Radomir Kovačević	YUG/SER	
5. Douglas Nelson	USA	

The 320-pound (145 kilogram) Saito made quick work of his first three opponents. Mark Berger lasted 17 seconds, Isidore Silas of Cameroon 29 seconds, and Radomir Kovačević 44 seconds. In the final, Parisi held firm, so firm in fact that he was penalized once too often for inactivity, and lost the match.

1988 Seoul C: 26, N: 26, D: 10.1.

		FINAL MATCH
1. Hitoshi Saito	JPN	Keikoku 5:00
2. Henry Stöhr	GDR	
3. Cho Yong-chul	KOR	
3. Grigory Verichev	SOV/RUS	
5. István Dubovsky	HUN	
5. Dimitar Zaprianov	BUL	

Saito, down to a trim 315 pounds (143 kilograms), won his second Olympic championship by incurring only two warnings for inactivity to Stöhr's three.

1992 Barcelona C: 28, N: 28, D: 7.27.

		FINAL MATCH
1. David Khakhaleishvili	GEO	Tani-otoshi 1:04
2. Naoya Ogawa	JPN	
3. Imre Csősz	HUN	
(See hu.wikipedia.org/wiki/Csősz_Imre)		
3. David Douillet	FRA	
5. Frank Moreno García	CUB	
5. Harry Van Barneveld	BEL	
7. Damon Keeve	USA	
7. Ernesto Pérez Lobo	SPA	

The 1989 world champion, Naoya Ogawa, tore through his first four opponents in 7 minutes 53 seconds. In the final, however, it was Ogawa who was thrown twice in the first minute.

1996 Atlanta C: 34, N: 34, D: 7.20.

		FINAL MATCH
1. David Douillet	FRA	Uchi-mata 5:00
2. Ernesto Pérez Lobo	SPA	
3. Frank Möller	GER	
3. Harry van Barneveld	BEL	
5. Liu Shenggang	CHN	
5. Naoya Ogawa	JPN	
7. Sergei Kosorotov	RUS	
7. Harris Papaioannou	GRE	

Judo fans anticipated a hot battle between defending Olympic champion David Khakhaleishvili and defending world champion David Douillet. But Khakhaleishvili never left the starting gate. On the morning of the competition he travelled from the Olympic Village to the judo venue for the pre-tournament weigh-in only to discover that the weigh-in was actually at the Village. He rushed back, but the weigh-in was over and he was disqualified. The incident was particularly frustrating considering that heavywights don't actually have to make weight.

In the semifinals, Douillet faced Naoya Ogawa, the man who had beaten him in the semifinals four years earlier. This time, in what Douillet termed, "the final before the final," Douillet managed a narrow victory. The real final was easier for him. He dominated Ernesto Pérez early and then won with an inner thigh throw.

2000 Sydney C: 32, N: 32, D: 9.22.

		FINAL MATCH
1. David Douillet	FRA	Uchi-mata-gaeshi 5:00
2. Shinichi Shinohara	JPN	
3. Indrek Pertelson	EST	
3. Tamerlan Tmenov	RUS	
5. Ruslan Sharapov	BLR	
5. Selim Tataroğlu	TUR	
7. Song Pan	CHN	
7. Ernesto Pérez Lobo	SPA	

Two months after his victory at the Atlanta Olympics, David Douillet was involved in a motorcycle accident that left him with leg, collarbone and shoulder injuries. He was able to recover in time to win the 1997 world championship, however that triumph was not without controversy. In the final against Shinichi Shinohara, the referee, in front of a French crowd in Paris, assessed a disputed penalty against Shinohara that gave hometown favorite Douillet the winning point. Douillet missed the 1999 world championships because of a back injury and actually had to take off 15 months before returning to training in February 2000. In the meantime, Shinohara, beginning in 1998, won 38 straight matches, including a sweep of the world championships, leading right up to the Olympics. In Sydney, Shinohara survived one challenging bout with Angel Sánchez of Cuba, but basically he and Douillet advanced to the final without difficulty. However, their confrontation would end in controversy once again. Eighty seconds into the match, Douillet attempted a leg sweep, but Shinohara countered and the two went tumbling to the mat with Douillet doing a somersault and landing on his back. One judge ruled ippon for Shinohara, giving him the match, but the other judge and the referee scored a yuko for Douillet. The bout continued until Douillet broke a tie with 46 seconds to go. The Japanese protested, but as soon as the referee and the judges left the competition area, no change could be made. Sill, as a matter of principle, the Japanese filed a formal complaint. A panel of the International Judo Federation reviewed the video coverage of the match and, four weeks after the end of the Olympics, they ruled that neither Shinohara nor Douillet should have been awarded a point, but the result was allowed to stand.

2004 Athens C: 33, N: 33, D: 8.20.

		FINAL MATCH
1. Keiji Suzuki	JPN	De-ashi-barai 1:17
2. Tamerlan Tmenov	RUS	
3. Dennis van der Geest	HOL	
3. Indrek Pertelson	EST	
5. Paolo Bianchessi	ITA	
5. Sayed Mahmoud Reza Miran Fashandi	IRN	
7. Selim Tataroğlu	TUR	
7. Andreas Tölzer	GER	

For Keiji Suzuki, making the Japanese Olympic team was more challenging than the Olympics themselves. The reigning world champion in the non-Olympic open division, Suzuki had to defeat heavyweight world champion Yasuyuki Muneta in the All-Japan Open in April to earn his place in Athens. Specializing in the uchi-mata leg throw, Suzuki won his first match against Andreas Tölzer with a waza-ari, and then defeated Charalampos Papaioannou of Greece with an uchi-mata ippon. In the quarterfinals, Suzuki overcame a half point deficit against Yury Rybak of Belarus, using his uchi-mata to earn an ippon victory with one minute left. He advanced to the semis, where he took the lead against Paolo Bianchessi with a yuko before completing another uchi-mata throw to reach the final. In the final, Suzuki faced Tamerlan Tmenov, the five-time European Champion and 2000 Olympic bronze medalist. Suzuki used a quick foot sweep to take down Tmenov 77 seconds into the match.

2008 Beijing C: 34, N: 34, D: 8.15.

		FINAL MATCH
1. Satoshi Ishii	JPN	Yuko (5:00)
2. Abdullo Tangriyev	UZB	
3. Oscar Braison	CUB	
3. Teddy Riner	FRA	
5. Lasha Gujejiana	GEO	
5. Mohammad Reza Rodaki	IRN	
7. João Schlittler	BRA	
7. Tamerlan Tmenov	RUS	

Santoshi Ishii qualified for the Olympics by beating 2004 Olympic champion Keiji Suzuki at the Japanese national championships. The 21-year-old had been crowned world junior champion in 2004 and gone on to win the silver medal at the 2006 Asian Games. Ishii dispatched 2004 silver medalist and reigning European champion Tamerlan Tmenov in the pool semifinals and double world bronze medalist Lasha Gujejiana in the pool final. He finished his first four matches with four perfect ippon scores.

Lasha Gujejiana and Ricardo Blas Jr, 2008
Georgia's Lasha Gujejiana (bottom) tries to throw Ricardo Blas Jr. the heaviest athlete in Olympic history (AP Photo-Charles Dharapak)

Nineteen-year-old reigning world champion Teddy Riner had been an early gold-medal favorite, but lost his pool final to Abdullo Tangriyev.

Ishii took an early lead in the final, and then clinched the gold medal with a yuko when Tangriyev was penalized for passivity.

The competition also featured the heaviest competitor of the modern Olympic Games, Ricardo Blas, Jr. of Guam. Nicknamed "The Little Mountain," Blas weighed in at 463 lbs (210 kg). Despite his size advantage, Blas lost to Gujejiana in his first bout after incurring a penalty for stalling and lost his repêchage bout against Dan McCormick of the United States after stepping out of bounds. Blas' father, also a judoka, had competed at the 1988 Olympics.

After winning the gold medal, Ishii left judo to pursue a career in mixed martial arts (MMA). He made his MMA debut in 2009, losing by unanimous decision to 1992 Olympic gold medalist Hidehiko Yoshida. Two years later he announced he was returning to judo.

DISCONTINUED EVENT

OPEN

1964 Tokyo C: 9, N: 9, D: 10.23.

		FINAL MATCH
1. Antonius Geesink	HOL	Kesa-gatame 9:22
2. Akio Kaminaga	JPN	
3. Theodore Boronovskis	AUS	
3. Klaus Glahn	GER	

Anton Geesink's victory was a shocking blow to the Japanese, even though he was two-time world champion and the clear favorite. In 1961 the 6-foot 6-inch, 267-pound judo instructor from Utrecht had become the first non-Japanese to win a world championship. Geesink won his semifinal fight with Boronovskis in only 12 seconds. Although he failed to gain the gold medal, Kaminaga set an Olympic speed record that would last for 28 years when he threw Thomas Ong of the Philippines in four seconds in the *repêchage* round. Ten minutes earlier, Ong had been thrown in six seconds by John Ryan of Ireland.

The American representative in this event, Ben Nighthorse Campbell, was later elected to the US Congress and, in 1998, he became the first American Indian to chair the Indian Affairs Committee of the US Senate.

1968 not held

1972 Munich C: 29, N: 29, D: 9.9.

		FINAL MATCH
1. Willem Ruska	HOL	Yoke-shiho-gatame 3:58
2. Vitaly Kusnetzov	SOV/RUS	
3. Jean-Claude Brondani	FRA	
3. Angelo Parisi	GBR	
5. Klaus Glahn	GER	
5. Alfred Douglas Rogers	CAN	
7. Tijini Benkassou	MOR	
7. Chiaki Ishii	BRA	

Having previously swept to victory in the heavyweight class, Ruska became the only person ever to win two Olympic gold medals in judo in the same year. In the open division, Ruska lost an early unanimous decision to Kusnetzov, but was able to pin him when they met again in the final.

1976 Montreal C: 30, N: 30, D: 7.31.

		FINAL MATCH
1. Haruki Uemura	JPN	Kuzure-kami-shiho-gatame 7:28
2. Keith Remfry	GBR	
3. Jo Jae-gi	KOR	
3. Shota Chochoshvili	SOV/GEO	
5. Jorge Portelli	ARG	
5. Jean-Luc Rouge	FRA	
7. Günther Neureuther	GER	
7. Pak Jong-gil	PRK	

1980 Moscow C: 21, N: 21, D: 8.2.

		FINAL MATCH
1. Dietmar Lorenz	GDR	Yusei-gachi 7:00
2. Angelo Parisi	FRA	
3. Arthur Mapp	GBR	
3. András Ozsvár	HUN	
5. Serhei Novikov	SOV/UKR	
5. Dambajan Tsend-Auish	MGL	
7. Pavel Drăgoi	ROM	

Lorenz, a car mechanic and army officer, had the rare distinction of being a sixth Dan red-and-white belt judoka. At 1.80 meters (5 feet 11 inches), he was also the shortest entrant in the open category.

1984 Los Angeles C: 15, N: 15, D: 8.11.

		FINAL MATCH
1. Yasuhiro Yamashita	JPN	Yoke-shiho-gatame 1:05
2. Mohamed Ali Rashwan	EGY	
3. Mihai Cioc	ROM	
3. Arthur Schnabel	GER	
5. Laurent del Colombo	FRA	
5. Xu Guoqing	CHN	

Yasuhiro Yamashita (left) and Hitoshi Saito, 1984
Yamashita prepares to throw Saito in the 1984 All-Japan Judo championship. Three and a half months later, they both won gold medals at the Los Angeles Olympics.

In October of 1977, Yasuhiro Yamashita lost by decision in the final of the Japanese Student Championships. Furious with himself for not fighting "like a warrior," he vowed never to allow such a lapse to occur again. In the next seven years Yamashita would suffer not a single loss, including 194 matches at national and international-level competition. All but five of his victories were by ippon. Included in that unbeaten string were four world championship titles. But one goal, his greatest goal, had eluded him—an Olympic gold medal.

When Japan joined the U.S-led boycott of the 1980 Moscow Olympics, Yamashita appeared on national television pleading, with tears in his eyes, for a reversal of that decision. A week later Yamashita was held to a draw by Sumio Endo, who fell on top of Yamashita's left leg, breaking his ankle.

By the time 1984 rolled around, all this was forgotten and Yamashita seemed as sure a bet for a gold medal as anyone in Los Angeles. But in his second match, a victory over Arthur Schnabel, Yamashita tore a muscle in his right calf, causing him great pain and forcing him to walk with a limp. His next opponent, Laurent del Colombo, attacked Yamashita's right leg and scored a throw for Koka. Ten seconds later del Colombo was flat on his back with the 5-foot 11-inch, 280-pound Yamashita on top of him. The match was quickly over.

In the final, Yamashita, described by one disgruntled opponent as "a refrigerator with a head on top," faced Mohamed Ali Rashwan, a 28-year-old building contractor from Alexandria. Yamashita scored a quick and easy victory, and was immediately overcome by his emotions. So sore was his leg that Rashwan had to help him onto the top step at the medal ceremony.

Afterwards, Rashwan told reporters, "I did not attack his right side because this is against my principles. I would not want to win this way." Rashwan was applauded for his good sportsmanship and news of his deed spread far and wide. On September 26, 1985, Rashwan was awarded the Fair Play Trophy by the International Committee for Fair Play. However, this inspiring tale of the true Olympic spirit has an odd twist to it. Videotapes of the Olympic final clearly show that Rashwan *did* try to attack Yamashita's injured leg. In fact, it was his first move, a mere ten seconds after the match began.

Yasuhiro Yamashita was known for his gentlemanly manner and his kind smile. However he once explained, "when I was training for competition, I had to smile. If I showed my real feelings of determination on my face, no one would practice with me."

WOMEN

The first women's world championship was held in New York City in 1980, thanks to the persistence of Rusty Kamokogi, who had gained fame by winning the New York state championship by cutting her hair, taping her breasts and pretending to be a man. Women's matches last for four minutes.

EXTRA-LIGHTWEIGHT
(48 kg—106 lbs)

1896–1988 not held

1992 Barcelona C: 22, N: 22, D: 8.2.

		FINAL MATCH
1. Cécile Nowak	FRA	Kochiki-taoshi 4:00
2. Ryoko Tamura	JPN	
3. Amarilys Savón Carmenate	CUB	
3. Hülya Şenyurt	TUR	
5. Karen Briggs	GBR	
5. Salima Souakri	ALG	
7. Yolanda Soler Grajera	SPA	
7. María Villapol Blanco	VEN	

The division was dominated by Cécile Nowak and Karen Briggs, who had met in the final of the 1991 world championship and the last three European championships, with Nowak winning each time. It was assumed that the two would meet again in the Olympic final, but in her semifinal bout against 16-year-old Ryoko Tamura, Briggs dislocated her shoulder and ended up without a medal. Hülya Şenyurt was the first Turkish woman to win an Olympic medal.

1996 Atlanta C: 23, N: 23, D: 7.26.

		FINAL MATCH
1. Kye Sun-hui	PRK	Harai-goshi-gaeshi 5:00
2. Ryoko Tamura	JPN	
3. Amarilys Savón Carmenate	CUB	
3. Yolanda Soler Grajera	SPA	
5. Sarah Nichilo	FRA	
5. Salima Souakri	ALG	
7. Tatyana Moskvina	BLR	
7. Małgorzata Roszkowska	POL	

This event saw one of the most stunning upsets of the 1996 Olympics. Since losing to Cécile Nowak in the 1992 Olympic final, Ryoko Tamura had gone undefeated for four years. The 4-foot 9½-inch (1.46-meter) Tamura was hugely popular in Japan, where her success had spawned an interest in women's judo. She was known as "Yawara-chan" because of her resemblance to a popular comic book character. Tamura entered the final with an 84-match winning streak. Her opponent was a complete unknown: 16-year-old Kye Sun-hui of

North Korea. For political and economic reasons, North Korea had withdrawn from international competitions for the last three years, including all Olympic qualifying events. The International Judo Federation awarded North Korea one wildcard entry to the Olympics and the Koreans gave that spot to Kye. Kye had never heard of Ryoko Tamura and had never seen her fight until she watched a couple of her matches on a video monitor prior to the final. Kye startled Tamura by attacking from the start and the double world champion was unable to establish her rhythm. With 22 seconds left, Kye scored with a leg hook and then added an insurance point when Tamura, on her knees, was penalized for "false attack."

The US entrant in the extra-lightweight division was actress Hillary Wolf, who was best known for playing Macaulay Culkin's sister in *Home Alone.* She competed again in 2000 as a half-lightweight.

2000 Sydney C: 23, N: 23, D: 9.16.

		FINAL MATCH
1. Ryoko Tamura	JPN	Uchi-mata 0:36
2. Lyubov Bruletova	RUS	
3. Anna-Maria Gradante	GER	
3. Ann Simons	BEL	
5. Cha Hyon-hyang	PRK	
5. Shunxin Zhao	CHN	
7. Sarah Nichilo-Rosso	FRA	
7. Amarilys Savón Carmenate	CUB	

Once again, Ryoko Tamura entered the Olympics having gone undefeated since the last Olympics. By this time, she had appeared in advertising campaigns for thirteen different companies, there were 350 Internet websites devoted to her, and no Japanese athlete bore the weight of her nation's expectations more than Tamura. "My goal at Sydney?" she said. "At best a gold, at worst a gold." Her most serious opponent was expected to be Amarilys Savón, whom she had defeated at the last two Olympics, and in the final of the last two world championships. However Savón was upset in her second bout by European championship runner-up Lyubov Bruletova. Tamura survived a near-upset herself in the semifinals when she was awarded a decision over North Korean Cha Hyon-hyang. As a contest, the final was an anticlimax, as Tamura used an uchi-mata to score ippon after only 36 seconds. Tamura was mobbed by photographers and cameramen who broke down the barrier separating the athletes from the media. She was kept up doing live television interviews until 3 a.m., when she was finally able to lock herself into her room at the Olympic Village. Alone at least, she burst into tears and then placed her gold medal on her pillow and fell asleep.

2004 Athens C: 21, N: 21, D: 8.14.

		FINAL MATCH
1. Ryoko Tani (Tamura)	JPN	O-uchi-gari 5:00
2. Frédérique Jossinet	FRA	
3. Gao Feng	CHN	
3. Julia Matijass	GER	
5. Alina Alexandra Dumitru	ROM	
5. Maria Karagiannopoulou	GRE	
7. Ye Gue-rin	KOR	
7. Anna Zemla-Krajewska	POL	

Between Olympics, defending champion Ryoko Tamura married baseball player Yoshitomo Tani, who also represented Japan at the Athens Games. The 28-year-old judoka, now known as Ryoko Tani, was injured less than a month before the Games in a freak training accident, when she fell backwards with her big toe caught between judo mats. Despite the injury, Tani, competing in her fourth Olympics, was the overwhelming favorite, with an unprecedented six consecutive world championship titles to her name. Tani swept through the competition, advancing to the final with a decisive ippon victory over Alina Alexandra Dumitru. In the gold medal match, Tani needed the full five minutes to defeat Frédérique Jossinet on points, scoring a koka in the first 12 seconds and following with a yuko 22 seconds later, before finishing the match with a waza-ari in the final 15 seconds to become the first woman to win consecutive judo gold medals.

2008 Beijing C: 23, N: 23, D: 8.9.

		FINAL MATCH
1. Alina Alexandra Dumitru	ROM	O-soto-gari (1:20)
2. Yanet Bermoy Acosta	CUB	
3. Paula Belén Pareto	ARG	
3. Ryoko Tani (Tamura)	JPN	
5. Lyudmila Bogdanova	RUS	
5. Pak Ok-song	PRK	
7. Éva Csernoviczki	HUN	
7. Ana Hormigo	POR	

Aged 32, Ryoko Tani had already won two Olympic gold medals and seven world championship titles. Her most recent defeat in a major international championship had been in the 1996 Olympic final, which she lost to Kye Sun-hui.

In Beijing she advanced to the semifinals, where she faced four-time European champion Alina Alexandra Dumitru. Neither of them was able to mount a successful attack, and the match was halted several times as both combatants received multiple warnings.. Tani ultimately lost the match after receiving a final caution 33 seconds from the end.

The final was more exciting, as Dumitru threw Yanet Bermoy with a sudden right leg sweep for ippon one minute and twenty seconds into the match.

Tani earned a bronze medal in the *repêchage* round, overcoming Lyudmila Bogdanova with a hip throw. It was Tani's fifth consecutive Olympic medal. In July 2010 she was elected to Japan's legislative upper house. She was still in training for the 2012 London Olympics at the time, but a few months later she announced her retirement from sports.

North Korea's Pak Ok-song was initially declared the winner of the second *repêchage* round, but a review of the match revealed that a late point by Paula Pareto had not been added to the scoreboard. The judges reversed the call, declaring Pareto the rightful winner.

HALF-LIGHTWEIGHT

(52 kg—114.61 lbs)

1896–1988 not held

1992 Barcelona C: 25, N: 25, D: 8.1.

		FINAL MATCH
1. Almudena Muñoz Martínez	SPA	Tani-otoshi 4:00
2. Noriko Mizoguchi	JPN	
3. Li Zhongyun	CHN	
3. Sharon Rendle	GBR	
5. Jessica Gal	HOL	
5. Alessandra Giungi	ITA	
7. C. Carolina Mariani Ambrueso	ARG	
7. Paula Saldanha	POR	

Muñoz was the beneficiary of a series of "hometown" decisions that pleased the Spanish crowd but shocked judo aficionados. Particularly surprising was the result of her third-round match against tournament favorite Sharon Rendle. The referee declared Rendle the winner, but the judges overruled the decision, leaving even Muñoz with a look of surprise on her face.

1996 Atlanta C: 21, N: 21, D: 7.25.

		FINAL MATCH
1. Marie-Clarie Restoux	FRA	Ushiro-goshi 5:00
2. Hyun Sook-hee	KOR	
3. Noriko Sugawara	JPN	
3. Legna Verdecia Rodríguez	CUB	
5. Larysa Krause	POL	
5. Almudena Muñoz Martínez	SPA	
7. C. Carolina Mariani Ambrueso	ARG	
7. Marisa Pedulla	USA	

A last-minute substitute at the 1995 world championships, Marie-Clarie Restoux surprised everyone by winning the gold medal. Restoux, who grew up in the tiny village of Palisson (population: 50) in Charentes, was more of a known quantity at the Olympics ten months later, but it did her opponents little good. In the final she defeated Hyun Sook-hee, who had beaten her twice in the pre-Olympic season.

2000 Sydney C: 23, N: 23, D: 9.17.

		FINAL MATCH
1. Legna Verdecia Rodríguez	CUB	Seoi-otoshi 2:19
2. Noriko Narazaki (Sugawara)	JPN	
3. Yuxiang Liu	CHN	
3. Kye Sun-hui	PRK	
5. Ioana Maria Dinea	ROM	
5. Deborah Gravenstijn	HOL	
7. María "Miren" León Ruiz	SPA	
7. Salima Souakri	ALG	

Before the competitions even began, this event was hit by a bizarre controversy. At the practice weigh-in two hours before the official weigh-in, Debbie Allan, the 1999 European champion from Great Britain, met the qualifying standard. But at the official weigh-in she was 400 grams (14.1 ounces) overweight. Examination of the three practice scales revealed that all three had been tampered with—tissue had been placed underneath the platforms to make the results appear lighter than they really were. Given less than an hour to shed the weight, Allan cut off her shoulder-length hair and stripped naked before climbing back onto the scale. Unfortunately, she was still 50 grams (1.8 ounces) too heavy and was disqualified. The ensuing argument between judo officials and other members of the British team almost led to the blanket disqualification of the entire British squad.

The Olympic final turned out to be a rematch of the final of the 1999 world championship, in which Noriko Narazaki defeated Legna Verdecia by penalty. This time Narazaki almost threw Verdecia after 50 seconds, but the Cuban survived and then, just past the halfway mark, she surprised Narazaki with a shoulder drop to score ippon. Verdecia, who was 27 years old, had not won a major title since the 1993 world championships.

One of the bronze medals was won by North Korea's Kye Sun-hui, who had earned a gold medal in the extra-lightweight division in 1996. In Sydney, Kye was cheered on by hundreds of *South* Korean fans, who, in the spirit of solidarity, sang traditional North Korean songs in her honor.

2004 Athens C: 24, N: 24, D: 8.15.

		FINAL MATCH
1. Xian Dongmei	CHN	Yoke-shiho-gatame 1:06
2. Yuki Yokosawa	JPN	
3. Amarilys Savón Carmenate	CUB	
3. Ilse Heylen	BEL	
5. Annabelle Euranie	FRA	
5. Salima Souakri-Dahmani	ALG	
7. Ioana Maria Dinea-Aluaş	ROM	
7. Georgina Singleton	GBR	

After a decade competing in the lightweight category against six-time world champion Ryoko Tamura, two-time

Olympic bronze medalist Amarilys Savón moved up to the half-lightweight division. Savón, who had lost twelve times to Tamura, including twice in a world championship final, immediately went on to win the 2003 world championship in her new division. In Athens, Savón advanced easily to the semifinals, where she built a lead over Yuki Yokosawa with a partial takedown. With only four seconds left in the match, Yokosawa took advantage of a momentary lapse in concentration, grabbing Savón's collar and flipping her to the ground to earn a suprise ippon victory. In the final, Yokosawa faced 29-year-old Xian Dongmei of Guangdong Province, who had beaten her easily in their only previous match, in March. Yokosawa appeared to have the advantage on the mat until Xian hooked her leg inside from behind and flipped Yokosawa on her back, scoring an ippon victory after only 66 seconds. When asked how she would celebrate her gold medal when she returned home, Xian replied, "I really do not know . . . Judo is the only thing I know."

2008 Beijing C: 22, N: 22, D: 8.10.

		FINAL MATCH
1. Xian Dongmei	CHN	Kuchiki-taoshi (5:00)
2. An Kum-ae	PRK	
3. Soraya Haddad	ALG	
3. Misato Nakamura	JPN	
5. Sholpan Kaliyeva	KAZ	
5. Kim Gyeong-ok	KOR	
7. Ana Carrascosa Zaragoza	SPA	
7. Ilse Heylen	BEL	

After winning the gold medal in Athens in 2004 Xian Dongmei retired from competition and became a mother. She returned to competition in 2007, winning back-to-back World Cup competitions in early 2008.

Xian received a bye in the first round of the Beijing competition and won her first three matches by ippon, beating reigning European champion and world number-one-ranked Ana Carrascosa in her first match and then reigning world silver medalist Telma Monteiro. Xian used a move from Chinese wrestling to take out three-time African champion Soraya Haddad in the semifinals, spinning under Haddad's arm and flipping her onto her back.

In the final Xian faced 2006 Asian Games champion An Kum-ae, outscoring her by yuko. Haddad beat Sholpan Kaliyeva in the *repêchage* round, becoming Africa's first female Olympic judo medalist.

After her victory Xian revealed that she had seen her 18-month-old daughter just once in the previous year, keeping in touch only via phone calls and internet video chats.

LIGHTWEIGHT

(57 kg—125.68 lbs)

1896–1988 not held

1992 Barcelona C: 23, N: 23, D: 7.31.
(56 kg—123 lbs)

		FINAL MATCH
1. Míriam Blasco Soto	SPA	Ko-soto-gake 4:00
2. Nicola Fairbrother	GBR	
3. Driulys González Morales	CUB	
3. Chiyori Tateno	JPN	
5. Kate Donahoo	USA	
5. Nicole Flagothier	BEL	
7. Catherine Arnaud	FRA	
7. Maria Gontowicz Szalas	POL	

Twenty-eight-year-old Miriam Blasco was the defending world champion. A popular figure in Spain, when she appeared the enthusiastic audience loudly chanted her name. Two minutes into the final she earned a yuko on a counterattack and then survived a near-strangulation when the referee called a break.

1996 Atlanta C: 22, N: 22, D: 7.24.

		FINAL MATCH
1. Driulys González Morales	CUB	Seoi-nage 5:00
2. Jung Sun-yong	KOR	
3. Isabel Fernández Gutiérrez	SPA	
3. Marie-Isabelle "Marisabel" Lomba	BEL	
5. Nicola Fairbrother	GBR	
5. Liu Chuang	CHN	
7. Zulfiya Garipova	RUS	
7. Zülfiyya Hüseynova	AZR	

Driulys González won the gold medal only two months after fracturing her cervical vertebra.

2000 Sydney C: 23, N: 23, D: 9.18.

		FINAL MATCH
1. Isabel Fernández Gutiérrez	SPA	O-uchi-gari 5:00
2. Driulys González Morales	CUB	
3. Kie Kusakabe	JPN	
3. Mária Pekli	AUS	
5. Cinzia Cavazzuti	ITA	
5. Jun Shen	CHN	
7. Barbara Harel	FRA	
7. Zülfiyya Hüseynova	AZR	

The final was another battle in the ongoing duel between defending Olympic champion Driulys González and 1996 bronze medalist Isabel Fernández. Fernández had defeated González at the 1997 world championships, but González had won back the title in 1999, beating Fernández in the final. She entered the Sydney Olympics with an overall 5-2 advantage over Fernández. The Spaniard struggled through two victories by judges' decisions over Kie Kusakabe and Mária

Pekli to earn another rematch with González. The final was a cautious, defensive affair that Fernández won by a penalty.

2004 Athens C: 23, N: 23, D: 8.16.

		FINAL MATCH
1. Yvonne Bönisch	GER	Uchi-mata 5:00
2. Kye Sun-hui	PRK	
3. Deborah Gravenstijn	HOL	
3. Yurisleidy Lupetey Cobas	CUB	
5. Isabel Fernández Gutiérrez	SPA	
5. Barbara Harel	FRA	
7. Cinzia Cavazzuti	ITA	
7. Natalya Yukhareva	RUS	

The final pitted 23-year-old Yvonne Bönisch of Germany against 1996 gold medalist and two-time world champion Kye Sun-hui of North Korea. The 25-year old Kye, who had beaten Bönisch when they last met in the final of the 2003 world championships, had made history as the first judoka to win international titles in three different weight classes. In the final, both competitors were given penalties for passivity. Then Bönisch took the lead with an incomplete throw in the second minute. Kye attempted several throws, but could not make up the points difference. Bönisch's gold medal was the first for Germany in women's judo.

2008 Beijing C: 22, N: 22, D: 8.11.

		FINAL MATCH
1. Giulia Quintavalle	ITA	O-soto-gari (5:00)
2. Deborah Gravenstijn	HOL	
3. Ketleyn Quadros	BRA	
3. Xu Yan	CHN	
5. Barbara Harel	FRA	
5. Mária Pekli	AUS	
7. Bernadett Baczkó	HUN	
7. Aiko Sato	JPN	

Several gold medal contenders fell in the early rounds of the women's lightweight tournament. Defending Olympic champion Yvonne Bönisch was outscored by Olympic newcomer Giulia Quintavalle in the first round, while four-time world champion and 1996 Olympic gold medalist Kye Sun-hui lost to 2006 European champion Barbara Harel in the quarterfinals. Quintavalle, whose best previous result had been fifth at the 2007 world championships, beat Harel in the semifinals to reach the gold-medal match.

Quintavalle took an early lead over Athens bronze medalist Deborah Gravenstijn in the final, scoring on a throw with just under two minutes remaining in the match. Gravenstijn was unable to respond and remained scoreless throughout the five-minute bout.

HALF-MIDDLEWEIGHT

(63 kg—138.9 lbs)

1896–1988 not held

1992 Barcelona C: 29, N: 29, D: 7.30.
(61kg—134.5 lbs)

		FINAL MATCH
1. Catherine Fleury	FRA	Yusel-gachi 4:00
2. Yael Arad	ISR	
3. Yelena Petrova	RUS	
3. Zhang Di	CHN	
5. Frauke Eickhoff	GER	
5. Koo Hyun-sook	KOR	
7. Xiomara Griffith Mahon	VEN	
7. Begoña Gómez Martín	SPA	

In the semifinals, world champion Frauke Eickoff faced Yael Arad, who was attempting to become Israel's first Olympic medalist. Two minutes and twenty-one seconds into the bout the referee signaled an ippon, ending the fight. Eickoff leaped to her feet, her arms raised in victory. Then the referee pointed to Arad, indicating that it was she who had scored. Twenty years after eleven members of the Israeli Olympic team had been killed by terrorists, Arad, a native-born Israeli, had earned her nation's first medal.

In the final, Arad faced Catherine Fleury, who had won the European and world championships in 1989, but had not made it to a major final since. The contest ended without a single point being scored. The two judges split and the referee gave the nod to Fleury.

1996 Atlanta C: 24, N: 24, D: 7.23.

		FINAL MATCH
1. Yuko Emoto	JPN	Uchi-mata 1:55
2. Gella Vandecaveye	BEL	
3. Jenny Gal	HOL	
3. Jung Sung-sook	KOR	
5. Yael Arad	ISR	
5. Ilknur Kobaş	TUR	
7. Sara Álvarez Menéndez	SPA	
7. Xiomara Griffith Mahon	VEN	

At the 1995 world championships held in Chiba, Japan, Yuko Emoto of Asahikawa, Hokkaido, was eliminated in 11 seconds. At the Olympics she defeated defending gold medalist Cathy Fleury, defending silver medalist Yael Arad, European champion Jenny Gal, and finally, with an impressive inner thigh sweep, Gella Vandecaveye.

2000 Sydney C: 22, N: 22, D: 9.19.

		FINAL MATCH
1. Séverine Vandenhende	FRA	Yusei-gachi 4:00
2. Li Shufang	CHN	
3. Jung Sung-sook	KOR	
3. Gella Vandecaveye	BEL	
5. Jenny Gal	ITA	
5. Anja von Rekowski	GER	
7. Saida Dhahri	TUN	
7. Vânia Ishii	BRA	

Séverine Vandenhende qualified for the final by throwing all four of her opponents. Li Shufang, on the other hand, won her last two bouts, against three-time European champion Gella Vandecaveye and Jennifer Gal, without scoring a single point. She finally scored one by penalty early in the final, but Vandenhende matched her and then forced a second penalty for false attack with 11 seconds to go to earn the victory.

2004 Athens C: 22, N: 22, D: 8.17.

		FINAL MATCH
1. Ayumi Tanimoto	JPN	Yoke-shiho-gatame 1:17
2. Claudia Heill	AUT	
3. Driulys González Morales	CUB	
3. Urška Žolnir	SLO	
5. Marie-Hélène Chisholm	CAN	
5. Daniela Krukower	ARG	
7. Lucie Decosse	FRA	
7. Hong Ok-song	PRK	

In the second round, 22-year-old Urška Žolnir knocked out three-time Olympic medalist Driulys González, before defeating 1996 silver medalist Gella Vandecaveye of Belgium in the quarterfinals. Meanwhile, world champion Daniela Krukower advanced to the semifinals by throwing Lucie Decosse in overtime. Krukower faced 23-year-old Ayumi Tanimoto, who had advanced easily through the competition with a series of ippons, pinning Saida Dhahri of Tunisia in the first round and then knocking out Diana Maza of Ecuador with an uchimata leg throw only 15 seconds into her second match. Tanimoto advanced to the semifinal by taking out Canadian judoka Marie-Hélène Chisholm with a back sweep. In the semis, Tanimoto threw Krukower to the mat and pinned her shoulder to win an ippon in 1:24. She faced Claudia Heill in the final, toppling the Austrian with a shoulder throw and pinning her for 20 seconds to win the gold medal.

In March 2011 Heill was killed after falling from a sixth-story window in Vienna. Police found no evidence of foul play and attributed the death to suicide, although no note was found. Heill had been working as a junior coach and TV commentator and had seemed upbeat in the days before her death.

2008 Beijing C: 25, N: 25, D: 8.12.

		FINAL MATCH
1. Ayumi Tanimoto	JPN	Uchi-mata (1:26)
2. Lucie Décosse	FRA	
3. Elisabeth Willeboordse	HOL	
3. Won Ok-im	PRK	
5. Driulys González Morales	CUB	
5. Claudia Heill	AUT	
7. Isis Barreto Rodríguez	VEN	
7. Urška Žolnir	SLO	

Defending Olympic champion Ayumi Tanimoto won each of her matches leading up to the final by ippon, including a pool final match against three-time world champion and four-time Olympic medalist Driulys González.

For the gold medal Tanimoto faced long-time rival Lucie Décosse, who had defeated her in four of their previous five encounters, including the 2005 world championship final. "She was the opponent I trained for," Tanimoto said later. "I've known her since Juniors. She always beats me."

This time, less than a minute-and-a-half into the match, Tanimoto countered a foot sweep attack with a sudden inner thigh throw to gain the gold medal.

MIDDLEWEIGHT

(70 kg—154.35 lbs)

1896–1988 not held

1992 Barcelona C: 21, N: 21, D: 7.29.
(66 kg-145.5 lbs)

		FINAL MATCH
1. Odalys Revé Jiménez	CUB	Uchi-mata 4:00
2. Emanuela Pierantozzi	ITA	
3. Kate Howey	GBR	
3. Heidi Rakels	BEL	
5. Claire Lecat	FRA	
5. Alexandra Schreiber	GER	
7. Grace Jividen	USA	
7. Laura Martinel Acuña	ARG	

Two-time world champion Emanuela Pierantozzi needed only seven seconds to defeat Alexandra Schreiber in the semifinals. In the final she faced Odalys Revé, whom she had beaten in the 1991 world championship final. However, in the Olympic final it was Revé who dominated the match. When asked afterward to describe the bout, she replied, "The final was very fast—so fast I can't remember what happened."

1996 Atlanta C: 20, N: 20, D: 7.22.

		FINAL MATCH
1. Cho Min-sun	KOR	Yoke-shiho-gatame 4:42
2. Aneta Szczepańska	POL	
3. Wang Xianbo	CHN	
3. Claudia Zwiers	HOL	
5. Alice Dubois	FRA	
5. Odalys Revé Jiménez	CUB	
7. Liliko Ogasawara	USA	
7. Rowena Sweatman	GBR	

Two-time world champion Cho Min-sun was never seriously challenged. She won all five of her matches by ippon in an elapsed time of 12 minutes 44 seconds.

2000 Sydney C: 23, N: 23, D: 9.20.

		FINAL MATCH
1. Sibelis Veranes Morell	CUB	Tani-otoshi 4:00
2. Kate Howey	GBR	
3. Cho Min-sun	KOR	
3. Ylenia Scapin	ITA	
5. Ursula Martín Oñate	SPA	
5. Ulla Werbrouck	BEL	
7. Edith Bosch	HOL	
7. Yvonne Wansart	GER	

In the final, 1999 world champion Sibelis Veranes faced 1997 world champion Kate Howey. Veranes scored waza-ari with a leg throw after only 23 seconds and then fought defensively for the rest of the match to preserve the victory.

2004 Athens C: 23, N: 23, D: 8.18.

		FINAL MATCH
1. Masae Ueno	JPN	Sode-tsurikomi-goshi 3:10
2. Edith Bosch	HOL	
3. Annett Böhm	GER	
3. Qin Dongya	CHN	
5. Catherine Arlove	AUS	
5. Catherine Jacques	BEL	
7. Cecilia Blanco García	SPA	
7. Kim Ryon-mi	PRK	

Two-time world champion Masae Ueno got off to a slow start in the competition, falling behind in her opening match against Celita Schutz of the United States, when she incurred a passivity penalty, before going on to pin Schutz at 3:36. Ueno managed a points victory over Rasa Sraka of Slovakia in her second contest, but she was off-balance for much of the match. Ueno finally found her rhythm in the quarterfinals, defeating Catherine Jacques with an inner leg sweep one minute into the match. In the semifinals, she dominated Catherine Marie Joelle, winning in 1:24 with an o-soto-gari. Ueno faced Edith Bosch in the final. The short and stocky Ueno, who had a 22 cm (8½ in) disadvantage against Bosch, used her lower center of gravity to launch a number of attacks and throws, eventually surprising Bosch with an over-the-hip throw just after the third minute, scoring an ippon to win.

2008 Beijing C: 22, N: 22, D: 8.13.

		FINAL MATCH
1. Masae Ueno	JPN	Kuchiki-taoshi (0:46)
2. Anaisis Hernández Sarria	CUB	
3. Edith Bosch	HOL	
3. Ronda Rousey	USA	
5. Annett Böhm	GER	
5. Leire Iglesias Armiño	SPA	
7. Yuri Alvear Orejuela	COL	
7. Anett Mészáros	HUN	

Reigning Olympic champion Masae Ueno swept through her pool, winning each of her first three matches by ippon. She beat 2005 world champion Edith Bosch in the pool final, a repeat of the 2004 Olympic final, countering an arm throw from Bosch with an inner thigh sweep to win on points. In the gold medal match Ueno needed only 46 seconds to beat Anaisis Hernández, pulling out Hernández's legs and putting her into a submission hold.

HALF-HEAVYWEIGHT
(78 kg—172 lbs)

1896–1988 not held

1992 Barcelona C: 22, N: 22, D: 7.28.
(72 kg—158.5 lbs)

		FINAL MATCH
1. Kim Mi-jung	KOR	Yusei-gachi 4:00
2. Yoko Tanabe	JPN	
3. Irene de Kok	HOL	
3. Laetitia Meignan	FRA	
5. Josie Horton	GBR	
5. Regina Schüttenhelm	GER	
7. A. Katarina Hakånsson	SWE	
7. Katarzyna Juszczak	POL	

Kim, the defending world champion, won her first bout in five seconds and her second in ten seconds. Her four victories leading to the final took a total of only six minutes.

1996 Atlanta C: 21, N: 21, D: 7.21.

		FINAL MATCH
1. Ulla Werbrouck	BEL	Uchi-mata-sukashi 4:58
2. Yoko Tanabe	JPN	
3. Diadenis Luna Castellanos	CUB	
3. Ylenia Scapin	ITA	
5. Tatyana Belyayeva	UKR	
5. Estha Essombe	FRA	
7. Hannah Ertel	GER	
7. Svetlana Galante	RUS	

Ulla Werbrouck left the 1992 Olympics with a broken knee and her leg in a cast. She was unable to compete for a year. In the 1996 final she scored early and forced Yoko Tanabe into an increasingly desperate attempt to catch up. Finally she won with a counterattack with two seconds to go. Although Belgium had been competing in the Olympics since 1900 (only missing the 1904 Games) Werbrouck was the first Belgian woman to win a gold medal in any sport in the Summer Games. Werbrouck set an impressive career record at the European Championships, earning a medal thirteen straight times between 1989 and 2001.

2000 Sydney C: 23, N: 23, D: 9.21.

		FINAL MATCH
1. Tang Lin	CHN	Yusei-gachi 4:00
2. Céline Lebrun	FRA	
3. Emanuela Pierantozzi	ITA	
3. Simona Richter	ROM	
5. Diadenis Luna Castellanos	CUB	
5. Heidi Rakels	BEL	
7. Edinanci da Silva	BRA	
7. Lee So-yeon	KOR	

Two-time world champion Noriko Anno of Japan was upset in her first match by Emanuela Pierantozzi. Because Pierantozzi lost her next match, Anno's Olympics was over after only four minutes on the mat. The final ended in controversy. European champion Céline Lebrun and late entrant Tang Lin ended with equal points. Australian judge Manfred Hausler raised his flag for Lebrun, but judge Huang Yu-san of Taiwan and Korean-American referee Chi Joon voted for Tang. Lebrun had won two scoreless decisions to make it to the final.

2004 Athens C: 21, N: 21, D: 8.19.

		FINAL MATCH
1. Noriko Anno	JPN	Sode-tsurikomi-goshi 4:38
2. Liu Xia	CHN	
3. Yurisel Laborde Duanes	CUB	
3. Lucia Morico	ITA	
5. Céline Lebrun	FRA	
5. Anastasia Matrosova	UKR	
7. Lee So-yeon	KOR	
7. Edinanci da Silva	BRA	

Noriko Anno had an uneven record, having won four world championships in two weight classes, but also having been eliminated in the first round of both the 1996 and 2000 Olympics. In Athens, Anno received a bye in the first round, and survived her first match by pinning Keivi Mayerlin Pinto of Venezuela. In the quarterfinals she defeated Lucia Morico. Anno faced defending silver medalist Céline Lebrun in the semifinals, with the match going into sudden death overtime before Anno advanced with a leg throw. In the final, Anno and Liu Xia seemed fairly evenly matched, until Anno stepped in with her left leg for an over the hip sleeve throw with 22 seconds left in the match to earn an ippon victory.

2008 Beijing C: 21, N: 21, D: 8.14.

		FINAL MATCH
1. Yang Xiuli	CHN	Koka (5:00)
2. Yalennis Castillo Ramírez	CUB	
3. Jeong Gyeong-mi	KOR	
3. Stéphanie Possamaï	FRA	
5. Esther San Miguel Busto	SPA	
5. Edinanci da Silva	BRA	
7. Pürevjargalyn Lkhamdegd	MGL	
7. Heide Wollert	GER	

Three months before the Beijing Olympics, two-time reigning world champion Yurisel Laborde of Cuba defected to the United States, walking out of her hotel on the last day of the Pan American Judo Championships in Miami, Florida. Laborde applied for political asylum a week later, pointing to the difficult lives of Cuban athletes. "I played for twelve years on the national team," she said. "I was twice the champion of the world, and I couldn't have a home or a car."

Laborde's replacement, Yalennis Castillo, had no international record, but made it to the final, where she faced 2006 Asian Games bronze medalist Yang Xiuli. The final was a passive affair in which neither challenger managed to score a point in five minutes of regulation and five minutes of overtime. The gold medal was ultimately decided by a panel of judges and was given to Yang for initiating the most attacks.

HEAVYWEIGHT
(Over 78 kg—172 lbs)

1896–1988 not held

1992 Barcelona C: 21, N: 21, D: 7.27.
(Over 72 kg—158.5 lbs)

		FINAL MATCH
1. Zhuang Xiaoyan	CHN	Kami-shiho-gatame 2:42
2. Estela Rodríguez Villanueva	CUB	
3. Natalina Lupino	FRA	
3. Yoko Sakaue	JPN	
5. Beata Maksymowa	POL	
5. Claudia Weber	GER	
7. Svetlana Gundarenko	RUS	
7. Éva Gránicz	HUN	

Zhuang won four of her five bouts using kami-shiho-gatame.

1996 Atlanta C: 20, N: 20, D: 7.20.

		FINAL MATCH
1. Sun Fuming	CHN	Seoi-nage 5:00
2. Estela Rodríguez Villanueva	CUB	
3. Christine Cicot	FRA	
3. Johanna Hagn	GER	
5. Svetlana Gundarenko	RUS	
5. Beata Maksymowa	POL	
7. Edinanci Silva	BRA	
7. Shon Hyun-me	KOR	

Estela Rodríguez tested positive for the banned diuretic furosemide, which is used to hide the presence of steroids and other prohibited substances. However the IOC let her off with a reprimand and she was allowed to keep her silver medal.

One of the more unusual stories of the Atlanta Games concerned 19-year-old Edinanci Silva who was forced to undergo extraordinary measures to ensure that she passed gender and doping tests. Although clearly a woman, Silva, upon reaching puberty, discovered that she had testicles. Three months before the 1996 Olympics, according to Brazilian newspaper accounts, Silva underwent an operation to remove her testicles as well as to reduce the size of her clitoris. In Atlanta Silva won two of her four matches and placed seventh.

2000 Sydney C: 24, N: 24, D: 9.22.

		FINAL MATCH
1. Yuan Hua	CHN	Yusei-gachi 4:00
2. Daima Beltrán Guisado	CUB	
3. Kim Seon-young	KOR	
3. Mayumi Yamashita	JPN	
5. Christine Cicot	FRA	
5. Sandra Köppen	GER	
7. Priscila Marques	BRA	
7. Irina Rodina	RUS	

World champion Beata Maksymow of Poland was upset in her opening match by Colleen Rosensteel of the United States. When Rosensteel herself was beaten in her next bout, Maksymow was automatically eliminated from the competition. Both Yuan Hua and Daima Beltrán steamrolled their way into the final. Yuan defeated her three opponents in a total of 4 minutes 15 seconds, while Beltrán needed only 4 minutes 26 seconds to beat four rivals. The final itself was cautious and tactical with each woman scoring a single penalty point. Yuan earned a unanimous decision.

2004 Athens C: 22, N: 22, D: 8.20.

		FINAL MATCH
1. Maki Tsukada	JPN	Ushiro-kesa-gatame 1:50
2. Daima Beltrán Guisado	CUB	
3. Tea Donguzashvili	RUS	
3. Sun Fuming	CHN	
5. Maryna Prokofieva	UKR	
5. Insaf Yahyaoui	TUN	
7. Giovanna José Blanco Bazon	VEN	
7. Choi Sook-le	KOR	

After receiving a bye in the first round, 2003 world champion silver medalist Maki Tsukada scored an ippon against Jessica Malone of Australia only 21 seconds into their match. In the quarterfinals she pinned reigning European champion Maryna Prokofieva, and in the semis, after a hard-fought struggle, she did the same to Tea Donguzashvili. In the other semifinal, the favorite in the event, reigning world champion and 1996 gold medalist Sun Fuming, was beaten by 2000 silver medalist Daima Beltrán. In the final, Beltrán threw Tsukada in the second minute, earning half a point, and tried to pin her down for the win, but Tsukada gained the upper hand and held Beltrán for 25 seconds to earn the victory.

2008 Beijing C: 21, N: 21, D: 8.15.

		FINAL MATCH
1. Tong Wen	CHN	Seoi-nage (4:52)
2. Maki Tsukada	JPN	
3. Idalys Ortíz Boucurt	CUB	
3. Lucija Polavder	SLO	
5. Dorjgotovyn Tserenkhand	MGL	
5. Kim Na-yeong	KOR	
7. Anne-Sophie Mondière	FRA	
7. Samah Ramadan	EGY	

The clear heavyweight gold medal favorites were defending Olympic champion Maki Tsukada and three-time reigning world champion Tong Wen. As expected, the two met in the final, a repeat of the 2007 world championship final.

Tsukada took the lead two minutes into the match with a foot sweep to score a yuko. Tong narrowed the gap with a koka point and then unleashed a shoulder throw in the final sixteen seconds of the match to score ippon. Tong celebrated by lifting her coach in the air. "I said 'I've won' and she replied 'Yes you did Fatty,'" said Tong. "We have been together twelve years. She is like a mother to me and I'm like her daughter. This was our dream and we achieved it."

Two years after her Olympic victory Tong was banned for two years by the International Judo Federation and stripped of her 2009 world championship title after testing positive for clenbuterol. Tong blamed the positive test on eating too many pork chops, pointing to the fact that clenbuterol is used to prevent animals like pigs from getting fat, as well as by athletes to build up muscle. In 2011 Tong's ban was overturned by the Court of Arbitration for Sport due to "procedural failure" in the laboratory tests, and her 2009 title was reinstated. Six months later Tong won her fifth straight world championship title.

Chapter 18 **Modern Pentathlon**

MEN
Individual
Discontinued Event

WOMEN
Individual

One of the highlights of the ancient Olympics for over 900 years was the pentathlon, in which athletes would run a short distance, jump, throw a javelin, throw a discus, and wrestle. Baron Pierre de Coubertin, the founder of the modern Olympics, created the modern pentathlon and managed to get it included in the Olympic program for 1912.

The basic premise behind the modern pentathlon is that a soldier is ordered to deliver a message. He starts out on the back of an unfamiliar horse, but is forced to dismount and fight a duel with swords. He escapes, but is trapped and has to shoot his way out with a pistol. Then he swims across a river, and finally he finishes his assignment by running a long distance through the woods.

In 1912, from 1924 to 1980, and in 1988, the modern pentathlon competition was held over a period of five days with one event each day. In 1920, 1984, and 1992 it lasted four days. Faced with the sport's elimination from the Olympic program, the International Modern Pentathlon Union radically altered the format by scheduling all five events in one day.

Between 1912 and 1952 the scoring was based on an athlete's placing in each of the five events. Since 1956, the modern pentathlon has been scored like the decathlon, with a set of charts assigning a point total to each performance.

According to current regulations, the pentathletes begin by firing 20 shots with an air pistol at a target 10 meters away. A bull's-eye earns ten points. A total score of 172 out of 200 points is worth 1000 pentathlon points.

Every target point above or below is worth plus or minus 12 pentathlon points.

In the fencing competition the athletes use épée swords. Each athlete fences for one touch against every other athlete. If no touch is made within one minute, both fencers are credited with a loss. A total score of 70 percent victories is equal to 1000 pentathlon points.

The swimming event is a freestyle race over 200 meters. A time of 2 minutes 30 seconds is worth 1000 pentathlon points. For women 2 minutes 40 seconds equals 1000 points. For each third of a second above or below that time four points are subtracted or added.

The riding portion of the contest is a show-jumping competition with horses picked by lot twenty minutes before the competition begins. The track is 400 meters long and must include fifteen obstacles including one double and one triple. Competitors begin with 1200 points and lose 28 points for a knockdown, 40 points for refusal to jump, 40 points for falling off, and 4 points per second for being over the time limit.

Eduard Zenovka and Aleksandr Parygin, 1996
Zenovka stumbles just before the finish, as Parygin slips past for the win.

The competition concludes with a 3000-meter cross-country run. Happily, a handicapped start system, used in 1984 and 1988, was revived in 1996. The runners' starting order is based on their total score for the first four events. The leader starts first; the others start sometime later, with four points equaling a one-second delay.

Thirty six men and 36 women will take part at the 2012 Olympics with a limit of two each per nation.

MEN

INDIVIDUAL

1896–1908 not held

1912 Stockholm C: 32, N: 10, D: 7.12.

		SHOOTING	SWIMMING	FENCING	RIDING	RUNNING	TOTAL
1. Gustaf "Gösta" Lilliehöök	SWE	3	10	5	4	5	27
2. K. Gösta Åsbrink	SWE	1	4	15	7	1	28
3. Georg de Laval	SWE	2	3	10	3	12	30
4. Åke Grönhagen	SWE	18	5	1	1	10	35
5. George Patton	USA	21	7	4	6	3	41
6. Sidney Stranne	SWE	11	9	3	8	11	42
7. Karl Mannström	SWE	14	14	16	2	9	55
8. Edmund Bernhardt	AUT	26	2	6	12	14	60

Silver medalist Gösta Åsbrink had earned a gold medal in team gymnastics at the 1908 Olympics. The fifth-place finisher was a 26-year-old army lieutenant, George S. Patton, Jr. who later went on to considerable fame as a general during World War II. Ironically, Patton might have won the event had he not been such a poor marksman, placing a mediocre 21st in a field of 32 in the shooting competition. Patton claimed that he was penalized for missing the target completely when in fact the bullet had gone through a previously-made hole. If he had been been able to prove his case, he would have won the gold medal. However, there is no evidence at all to support his contention. During his training for the Olympics, Patton followed a diet of raw steak and salad. On the final day of the competion, he prepared for the cross-country run by receiving an injection of opium.

If Lilliehöök had taken five more seconds to finish the 4000-meter cross-country run, he would have lost the gold medal.

1920 Antwerp C: 23, N: 8, D: 8.27.

		SHOOTING	SWIMMING	FENCING	RIDING	RUNNING	TOTAL
1. Gustaf Dyrssen	SWE	62	2	6	2	18	
2. Erik de Laval	SWE	1	13	5	1	3	23
3. Gösta Runö	SWE	4	1	16	5	1	27
4. Bertil Uggla	SWE	13	5	10	13	5	46
5. Marius Christensen	DEN	12	7	3	7	18	47
6. Harold Rayner	USA	5	12	13	14	4	48
7. Emil Hagelberg	FIN	10	3	21	9	8	51
8. Robert Sears	USA	3	8	9	11	20	51

1924 Paris C: 38, N: 11, D: 7.17.

		SHOOTING	SWIMMING	FENCING	RIDING	RUNNING	TOTAL
1. Bo Lindman	SWE	9	1	3	4	1	18
2. Gustaf Dyrssen	SWE	20	4	1	3	11.5	39.5
3. Bertil Uggla	SWE	7	21	5	5	7	45
4. Ivan Duranthon	FRA	4	18	17.5	11	4	54.5
5. Harry Avellan	FIN	17	6	17.5	1	14	55.5
6. Helge Jensen	DEN	2	19	11.5	9.5	19	61
7. George Vokins	GBR	24	11	10	8	11.5	64.5
8. Christiaan Tonnet	HOL	22	12	13.5	16	2	65.5

1928 Amsterdam C: 37, N: 14, D: 8.4.

		SHOOTING	SWIMMING	FENCING	RIDING	RUNNING	TOTAL
1. Sven Thofelt	SWE	6	2	4	21	14	47
2. Bo Lindman	SWE	15	5	22	3	5	50
3. Helmuth Kahl	GER	10	9	2	19	12	52
4. Ingvar Berg	SWE	3	11	36	7	1	58
5. Heinz Hax	GER	1	15	21	20	2	59
6. David Turquand-Young	GBR	24	7	15	9	10	65
7. Hermann Hölter	GER	16	8	11	21	13	69
7. Christiaan Tonnet	HOL	8	24	27	6	4	69

Sven Thofelt later won medals in team épée fencing in 1936 and, 20 years after his modern pentathlon gold, in 1948. Thofelt founded the Modern Pentathlon Union in 1949 and served as its president for 23 years. When his sport was threatened with exclusion from the Olympics in 1992, Thofelt, then 88 years old, defended modern pentathlon by saying, "The sport is an education in itself. It trains the mind as much as the body, and should be experienced by all leaders of men . . . Riding and fencing are wholly in the head, the body being only an instrument of the mind. Shooting is a test of character and will, of steadiness. Only the swimming and running are wholly physical."

1932 Los Angeles C: 25, N: 10, D: 8.6.

		SHOOTING	SWIMMING	FENCING	RIDING	RUNNING	TOTAL
1. Johan Oxenstierna	SWE	4	14	2	5	7	32
2. Bo Lindman	SWE	1	2.5	19	9	4	35.5
3. Richard Mayo	USA	2	4.5	1	14	17	38.5
4. Sven Thofelt	SWE	15	1	9	1	13	39
5. Willy Remer	GER	12	10	4	13	8	47
6. Conrad Miersch	GER	10	10	5	17	6	48
7. Elemér Somfay	HUN	20	4.5	6	12	10	52.5
8. C. Percy Legard	GBR	6	18	10	18	1	53

After taking a few practice shots in the woods just before the competition was to begin, Oxenstierna was confronted by an angry policeman who threatened to arrest him. Since the competition was about to begin, the police officer agreed to wait. He watched Oxenstierna shoot, realized he was not a criminal, and let him go.

1936 Berlin C: 42, N: 16, D: 8.6.

		SHOOTING	SWIMMING	FENCING	RIDING	RUNNING	TOTAL
1. Gotthardt Handrick	GER	2.5	2	4	9	14	31.5
2. Charles Leonard	USA	15	10	1	6	7.5	39.5
3. Silvano Abba	ITA	1	15.5	10	14	5	45.5
4. Sven Thofelt	SWE	8.5	5.5	6	3	24	47
5. Nándor Orbán	HUN	4	12.5	21	2	16	55.5
6. Hermann Lemp	GER	31	3.5	11	1	21	67.5
7. Alfred Starbird	USA	8.5	8.5	23	20	7.5	67.5
8. Rezső von Bartha	HUN	27	12.5	3	12	22	76.5

In the pistol-shooting portion of the competition, Lieutenant Charles Leonard of St. Petersburg, Florida, became the first person in the history of the event to achieve a perfect score of 200.

Modern Pentathlon, 1936
Competitors take aim at targets shaped like humans.

1948 London C: 45, N: 16, D: 8.4.

		SHOOTING	SWIMMING	FENCING	RIDING	RUNNING	TOTAL
1. William "Willie" Grut	SWE	1	1	5	1	8	16
2. George Moore	USA	2	3	21	17	4	47
3. Gösta Gärdin	SWE	6	17	10	11	5	49
4. Lauri Vilkko	FIN	17	38	4	3	2	64
5. Olavi Larkas	FIN	26	3	7	19	16	71
6. Bruno Riem	SWI	19	9	1	36	9	74
7. Fritz Hegner	SWI	24	13	3	7	29	79
8. Richard Gruenther	USA	13	12	14	24	19	81

Captain William Grut, a 33-year-old artillery officer, accomplished the most decisive victory in the history of the modern pentathlon, finishing first in three of the five events. Six months earlier, at the Winter Olympics in St. Moritz, Grut had finished second in a demonstration event called the "winter pentathlon," consisting of downhill skiing, cross-country skiing, shooting, fencing, and an equestrian course.

1952 Helsinki C: 51, N: 19, D: 7.25.

		SHOOTING	SWIMMING	FENCING	RIDING	RUNNING	TOTAL
1. Lars Hall	SWE	1	7	15	1	8	32
2. Gábor Benedek	HUN	8	2	9	18	2	39
3. István Szondy	HUN	3	4	12	5	17	41
4. Igor Novikov	SOV/ARM	24	13	4	4	10	55
5. Frederick Denman	USA	9	11	6	17	19	62
5. Olavi Mannonen	FIN	2	37	10	9	4	62
7. Lauri Vilkko	FIN	1	8	38	11	5	63
8. W. Thad McArthur	USA	29	3	23	12	1	68

Twenty-five-year old Lars Hall was the first non-military winner of the modern pentathlon. A carpenter from Karlskrona, Hall had two lucky breaks. The horse that he drew for the equestrian competition was discovered to be lame. The horse that he was assigned as a substitute turned out to be the best horse in Finland, and Hall's only challenge was to keep from falling off as the horse raced through the course. Two days later, Hall arrived 20 minutes late for the pistol-shooting, but was saved from disqualification due to a Soviet protest that was still being sorted out.

Lars Hall, 1952
Lars Hall with fellow Swedish modern pentathlon Olympic champions Gustaf Dyrssen, Bo Lindman, Johan Gabriel Oxenstierna, and Willie Grut.

1956 Melbourne C: 40, N: 16, D: 11.28.

		SHOOTING		SWIMMING		FENCING		RIDING		RUNNING		TOTAL
1. Lars Hall	SWE	1034	4	889	4	720	24	1030	2	1159	8	4833
2. Olavi Mannonen	FIN	997.5	5	815	8	880	5	920	15	1162	7	4774
3. Väinö Korhonen	FIN	885	9	963	2	880	5	905	16	1117	12	4750
4. Igor Novikov	SOV/ARM	802.5	14	815	8	920	2	935	6	1192	4	4714
5. George Lambert	USA	1070	1	667	17	900	4	975	7	1081	15	4693
6. Gábor Benedek	HUN	860	11	889	4	920	2	855	18	1126	10	4650
7. William André	USA	887.5	5	889	4	860	8	870	17	1123	11	4629
8. Aleksandr Tarassov	SOV/RUS	810	13	778	10	880	5	825	21	1186	5	4479

1960 Rome C: 60, N: 23, D: 8.31.

		SHOOTING		SWIMMING		FENCING		RIDING		RUNNING		TOTAL
1. Ferenc Németh	HUN	1009	31	977	2	880	10	990	6	1168	7	5024
2. Imre Nagy	HUN	1048	19	1000	1	840	23	935	18	1165	8	4988
3. Robert Beck	USA	1039	24	977	2	940	3	1010	4	1015	24	4981
4. András Balczó	HUN	1037	20	885	6	760	36	1075	1	1216	2	4973
5. Igor Novikov	SOV/ARM	982	33	839	9	860	15	1035	2	1246	1	4962
6. Nikolai Tatarinov	SOV/RUS	1138	5	747	19	820	27	885	28	1168	6	4758
7. Stanisław Przybylski	POL	1111	13	747	20	860	16	815	39	1198	3	4731
8. Jack Daniels	USA	1024	27	793	12	900	6	1015	3	985	26	4717

1964 Tokyo C: 37, N: 15, D: 10.15.

		SHOOTING		SWIMMING		FENCING		RIDING		RUNNING		TOTAL
1. Ferenc Török	HUN	1070	15	1000	1	960	10	960	23	1126	5	5116
2. Igor Novikov	SOV/ARM	1040	26	856	5	1020	3	1055	5	1096	6	5067
3. Albert Mokeyev	SOV/RUS	970	33	748	15	1060	1	1045	7	1216	1	5039
4. Peter Macken	AUS	1070	19	640	21	1020	4	1035	8	1132	3	4897
5. Viktor Mineyev	SOV/AZR	1040	24	820	9	960	13	1050	6	1024	15	4894
6. James Moore	USA	1070	16	676	20	960	12	990	15	1195	2	4891
7. Imre Nagy	HUN	1040	30	892	2	960	9	940	28	1042	11	4874
8. Bo-Herman Jansson	SWE	1100	3	748	16	780	28	1075	1	1057	10	4760

Török was elected a member of parliament in Hungary's post-Communist government.

1968 Mexico City C: 48, N: 18, D: 10.17.

		SHOOTING		SWIMMING		FENCING		RIDING		RUNNING		TOTAL
1. Björn Ferm	SWE	1100	5	885	8	934	11	1075	2	970	5	4964
2. András Balczó	HUN	1010	22	931	6	934	12	1054	5	1024	2	4953
3. Pavlo Lednyov	SOV/UKR	1070	8	839	15	934	9	1060	4	892	16	4795
4. Karl-Heinz Kutschke	GDR	1070	10	632	41	846	26	1126	1	1090	1	4764
5. Borys Onyshchenko	SOV/UKR	995	28	885	8	912	15	1054	5	910	13	4756
6. Raoul Gueguen	FRA	1040	14	954	5	912	13	1000	10	850	20	4756
7. István Moná	HUN	1010	20	1040	2	868	22	943	23	847	22	4714
8. Jeremy "Jim" Fox	GBR	1010	21	862	12	890	18	1006	9	895	15	4663
DISQ (Drugs):												
Hans-Gunnar Liljenwall	SWE	4664										

Björn Ferm, a 24-year-old economics student, kept busy during the 12-hour fencing competition by reading detective stories. When it came down to the final cross-country run, he needed to beat 14 minutes 30 seconds to win the gold medal. Ferm struggled through the unfamiliar rarefied air and crossed the finish line with only four seconds to spare. An ugly incident had marred the riding event. Hans-Jürgen Todt of West Germany drew a beautiful but stubborn horse named Ranchero, which balked three times at one of the obstacles. After completing the course, Todt, disconsolate at seeing his years of training gone to waste because of bad luck, attacked the horse and had to be pulled away by his teammates.

1972 Munich C: 59, N: 21, D: 8.31.

		SHOOTING		SWIMMING		FENCING		RIDING		RUNNING		TOTAL
1. András Balczó	HUN	1060	17	1057	2	956	12	1060	25	1279	3	5412
2. Borys Onyshchenko	SOV/UKR	945	42	1076	1	1066	2	1128	11	1120	21	5335
3. Pavlo Lednyov	SOV/UKR	1060	14	1019	3	1022	4	1092	18	1135	14	5328
4. Jeremy "Jim" Fox	GBR	1100	2	1019	3	868	22	1024	32	1300	1	5311
5. Vladimir Shmelyov	SOV/RUS	920	47	962	7	1022	5	1176	6	1222	6	5302
6. Björn Ferm	SWE	1100	4	943	10	978	7	1112	13	1150	10	5283
7. Heiner Thade	GER	1065	12	962	7	956	13	1012	37	1150	9	5145
8. Risto Hurme	FIN	950	40	981	5	1044	3	1068	24	1051	33	5094

Five-time world champion András Balczó finally won an Olympic individual gold medal at the age of 34. Tied for third place after four events, Balczó, a typewriter mechanic, set off on the cross-country course at a terrific pace and staggered home a winner. Quite an uproar developed when it was discovered through drug tests that 14 pentathletes had taken the tranquilizers Valium and Librium before going out on the shooting range. These drugs were banned by the International Modern Pentathlon Union, but were considered acceptable by the International Olympic Committee. For this reason no disqualifications were made.

In 1988 András Balczó was chosen to be one of the leaders of Hungary's first pro-democracy network of activist groups.

1976 Montreal C: 47, N: 15, D: 7.22.

		SHOOTING		SWIMMING		FENCING		RIDING		RUNNING		TOTAL
1. Janusz Pyciak-Peciak	POL	1066	23	928	5	1044	3	1164	17	1318	3	5520
2. Pavlo Lednyov	SOV/UKR	1032	32	1096	1	1022	6	1092	30	1243	10	5485
3. Jan Bártu	CZE	1100	1	976	3	1044	5	1184	13	1162	22	5466
4. Daniele Masala	ITA	1090	14	832	13	1066	2	1244	2	1201	17	5433
5. Adrian Parker	GBR	1100	1	712	30	868	29	1240	7	1378	1	5298
6. John Fitzgerald	USA	1036	25	952	4	1000	9	1232	8	1066	42	5286
7. Jorn Steffensen	DEN	1100	1	856	9	1044	4	1066	38	1213	14	5281
8. Boris Mosolov	SOV/RUS	1036	25	856	9	934	20	1212	9	1162	22	5200

Pyciak-Peciak was only in fifth place after four events, but he ran a strong 4000 meters and finished with 12 seconds to spare in 12:29.70.

1980 Moscow C: 43, N: 19, D: 7.24.

		SHOOTING		SWIMMING		FENCING		RIDING		RUNNING		TOTAL
1. Anatoly Starostin	SOV/RUS	1068	13	1000	4	1110	2	1216	10	1174	8	5566
2. Tamás Szombathelyi	HUN	1100	2	1026	2	1088	3	1144	24	1144	11	5502
3. Pavlo Lednyov	SOV/UKR	1026	21	1026	2	1022	15	1104	31	1204	4	5382
4. Svante Rasmuson	SWE	936	40	922	7	1000	17	1332	2	1183	6	5373
5. Tibor Maracskó	HUN	980	32	964	6	956	27	1208	12	1171	9	5279
6. Janusz Pyciak-Peciak	POL	1070	12	844	13	978	25	1172	14	1204	5	5266
7. Lennart Pettersson	SWE	1050	18	922	7	1088	6	1156	19	1027	32	5243
8. Milan Kadlec	CZE	1084	8	792	20	1088	4	1088	34	1177	7	5229

Following his victory at the 1986 world championships, Starostin was one of 15 pentathletes who failed a doping test for sedatives and were banned from competition for 30 months.

1984 Los Angeles-Irvine C: 52, N: 18, D: 8.1.

		SHOOTING		SWIMMING		FENCING		RIDING		RUNNING		TOTAL
1. Daniele Masala	ITA	1100	1	956	4	1300	8	978	10	1135	20	5469
2. Svante Rasmuson	SWE	1070	13	1022	2	1304	4	912	24	1148	16	5456
3. Carlo Massullo	ITA	1100	2	758	27	1220	20	1066	2	1262	2	5406
4. Richard Phelps	GBR	1100	3	912	5	1304	5	780	43	1295	1	5391
5. Michael Storm	USA	1040	23	888	12	1288	9	1088	1	1041	30	5325
6. Paul Four	FRA	1040	20	978	3	1204	21	1066	2	999	35	5287
7. Ivar Sisniega	MEX	1070	9	912	5	1320	2	780	43	1200	7	5282
8. Jorge Quesada	SPA	1060	16	890	9	1172	25	1000	8	1159	14	5281

The 1984 Olympics saw two important changes in the organization of the modern pentathlon competition. First, the event was compressed into four days instead of five. In order to discourage the pentathletes from taking sedatives and beta-blockers to steady their nerves before shooting, the shooting portion of the competition was moved to the morning of the final day, five hours before the cross country run.

The second change was instituted to create a more dramatic finish. Instead of starting the runners in random order, the leader after four events, in this case Daniele Masala, started first. The other runners were given a handicap time depending on how many points behind they were, with 3 points equaling one second. Thus Svante Rasmuson had to wait 8⅔ seconds before he started and Paul Four 15⅓ seconds. By the time Carlo Massullo hit the course in fifth place, Masala had been running 1 minute 10⅔ seconds. The new method meant that even though the scoring was the same, the first person across the finish line was actually the winner.

The finish was indeed a dramatic one. Rasmuson caught Masala with 100 meters to go and appeared headed for victory. But 20 meters from the finish, the exhausted Swedish medical student stumbled on the soft dirt after rounding the final sharp left turn. Rasmuson staggered into a potted plant which was being used to brighten up the course boundary, and Masala ran by to take the gold medal.

"Have you ever been so tired you can't even control your body?" Rasmuson asked later. Then he added "I hate soft dirt."

1988 Seoul C: 65, N: 26, D: 9.22.

		SHOOTING		SWIMMING		FENCING		RIDING		RUNNING		TOTAL
1. János Martinek	HUN	1066	6	990	2	1264	15	868	45	1216	6	5404
2. Carlo Massullo	ITA	1010	19	881	13	1204	32	1044	8	1240	4	5379
3. Vakhtang Yagorashvili	SOV/GEO	980	24	915	8	1344	2	978	16	1150	19	5367
4. Attila Mizsér	HUN	1010	20	847	18	1196	33	934	26	1294	1	5281
5. Christophe Ruer	FRA	968	28	779	30	1348	1	934	29	1213	7	5242
6. Richard Phelps	GBR	964	29	898	11	1304	8	868	47	1195	11	5229
7. László Fábián	HUN	876	47	1051	1	1304	8	802	53	1168	17	5201
8. Joël Bouzou	FRA	1004	22	983	3	1172	37	868	46	1171	10	5190

In 1988, thanks to improved drug-testing procedures, the competition was able to revert to its traditional five-day format. Martinek began the cross-country course 9⅔ seconds after Yagorashvili, passed him at the halfway mark and pulled away to a convincing victory, finishing 9 seconds ahead of Massullo.

1992 Barcelona C. 66, N: 30, D: 7.29.

		SHOOTING		SWIMMING		FENCING		RIDING		RUNNING		TOTAL
1. Arkadiusz Skrzypaszek	POL	1000	2	1252	21	1120	11	1147	23	1040	13	5559
2. Attila Mizsér	HUN	898	7	1208	40	1135	7	1213	9	992	27	5446
3. Eduard Zenovka	RUS	830	21	1300	7	1240	1	1255	3	736	56	5361
4. Anatoly Starostin	RUS	864	13	1236	32	1120	9	1117	31	1010	22	5347
5. Roberto Bomprezzi	ITA	847	16	1148	56	1105	12	1216	8	1010	24	5326
6. Håkan Norebrink	SWE	847	17	1272	14	1030	37	1072	39	1100	3	5321
7. Marian Gheorghe	ROM	878	8	1252	22	955	50	1108	35	1100	1	5293
8. Graham Brookhouse	GBR	762	44	1304	6	1015	40	1141	24	1070	5	5292

Between Olympics the International Modern Pentathlon Union decided that, since the riding portion of the sport was so volatile it often caused leading contenders to be knocked out of serious contention on the first day, it would be more dramatic if the riding test was the final event rather than the first. As an attempt to attract media attention, this experiment (which had been tried once before in 1928) failed. After Barcelona, the Union voted to return to the handicapped start system that had been used successfully in 1984 and 1988. However, the 1992 format did in fact produce a dramatic shift on the final day.

After four events Eduard Zenovka led world champion Arkadiusz Skrzypaszek by 106 points. But the 23-year-old Zenovka had a history of falling off horses and landing on his head. Indeed, he had already lost two major titles this way. Sure enough, having already chalked up 120 penalty points over the first nine obstacles, his horse stumbled at the tenth obstacle, dumping Zenovka, who lost his riding helmet and then breached the rules by heading on to the next obstacle before remembering to retrieve it. He fell again at the triple jump, although this time he kept his helmet on and doffed it to the VIP box after he remounted. Zenovka also lost 124 points when he exceeded the time limit of 1 minute 43 seconds by over a minute. By this time, he was lucky to hold on for a bronze medal.

Zenovka's sports misfortunes were nothing compared to the tragedy that would strike him on February 11, 1993. That night he was involved in a car crash that killed his passenger, world champion rhythmic gymnast Oksana Kostina. Zenovka, who was critically injured in the incident (and lost a kidney), was charged with drunken driving.

1996 Atlanta-Conyers C: 32, N: 22, D: 7.30.

		SHOOTING		SWIMMING		FENCING		RIDING		RUNNING		TOTAL
1. Aleksandr Parygin	KAZ	1072	11	970	1	1196	27	1040	8	1273	6	5551
2. Eduard Zenovka	RUS	1084	9	820	14	1268	14	1016	11	1342	1	5530
3. János Martinek	HUN	1000	22	910	5	1248	16	1100	1	1243	11	5501
4. Dmitri Svatkovsky	RUS	1012	20	880	7	1248	18	1010	12	1339	2	5489
5. Igor Warabida	POL	1072	11	790	18	1208	24	1100	3	1282	5	5452
6. Ákos Hanzély	HUN	1084	9	940	3	1236	21	947	20	1228	12	5435
7. Imre Tiidemann	EST	1144	2	820	14	1212	23	950	19	1288	3	5414
8. Cesare Toraldo	ITA	1108	7	880	7	1296	7	1040	9	1078	26	5402

The first one-day modern pentathlon competition began at 7 a.m. and concluded almost 13 hours later. After four events, Cesare Toraldo was in first place. Aleksandr Parygin, in second, began with a handicap of

15⅛ seconds and János Martinek, in third, with a handicap of 22 seconds. Barcelona bronze medalist Eduard Zenovka was in sixth place 45⅛ seconds back while two-time defending world champion Dimitri Svatkovsky, in ninth place, gave up 58 seconds.

While Toraldo faded from contention, Zenovka gradually moved up and took the lead. Parygin tried to keep pace, but with 100 meters to go, he threw up his hands in frustration. Then, much to his surprise, he found one last burst of energy and drew level with Zenovka. Ten meters from the finish line, it was Zenovka who was drained of his last ounce of strength. In desperation he leaned towards the line, stumbled and fell. He struggled to his feet and crossed the finish—7 seconds behind Parygin and 9½ seconds ahead of Martinek. Svatkovsky ran a strong race, but missed a medal by 4½ seconds.

The dramatic finish was a shot in the arm for modern pentathlon, which had been in danger of being dropped from the Olympics. However, the incompetence of the organizers had the opposite effect. The riding and cross-country took place at the Georgia International Horse Park, 37 miles (59.5 kilometers) from the venue for the first three disciplines. Potential spectators, who had purchased tickets for the entire event, arrived to discover security roadblocks that prevented access to the Horse Park. There were no shuttle buses from the parking lot to the competition venue and the only way to reach the venue was to walk 5 miles (8 kilometers) in blazing heat. The situation was little better for the athletes themselves. When they reached the jumping arena, they discovered that the only shady spot for them to stand while waiting was underneath an oak tree.

2000 Sydney C: 24, N: 19, D: 9.30.

		SHOOTING		SWIMMING		FENCING		RIDING		RUNNING		TOTAL
1. Dmitri Svatkovsky	RUS	1048	14	880	5	1224	7	1070	1	1154	4	5376
2. Gabor Balogh	HUN	1108	6	920	4	1221	9	980	11	1124	8	5353
3. Pavel Dovgal	BLR	1168	1	760	17	1254	4	1070	2	1086	12	5338
4. Sébastien Deleigne	FRA	1048	13	880	5	1190	17	1010	7	1198	1	5326
5. Vadim Tkachuk	UKR	1144	3	840	9	1138	21	1070	3	1082	13	5274
6. Chad Senior	USA	1060	12	960	2	1278	2	890	18	1068	14	5256
7. Andrejus Zadneprovskis	LIT	1000	19	840	9	1257	3	955	13	1184	2	5236
8. Olivier Clergeau	FRA	1096	8	1000	1	1163	20	1040	5	918	21	5217

Dmitri Svatkovsky started badly, placing only fourteenth in shooting and falling 120 points off the pace. He was still in only fifth place with only one event to go, at which point the scores stood: Clergeau—4299, Bulgarian-born American Velizar Illiev—4299, Dovgal—4252, Balogh—4229 and Svatkovsky—4222. Svatkovsky started running 19 seconds after Clergeau and Iliev, but picked off the leaders one by one and won by 5½ seconds. Two-time world champion Sébastien Deleigne would have won a silver medal if teammate Olivier Clergeau had conceded a touch to him in the fencing competition. However the two chose to fight fairly, Deleigne lost the touch—and forty points—and finished fourth instead of second.

2004 Athens C: 32, N: 21, D: 8.26.

		SHOOTING		SWIMMING		FENCING		RIDING		RUNNING		TOTAL
1. Andrei Moiseyev	RUS	1036	16	1000	1	1376	1	1032	19	1036	11	5480
2. Andrejus Zadneprovskis	LIT	1000	22	916	2	1308	6	1088	12	1116	1	5428
3. Libor Capalini	CZE	1084	13	776	19	1336	2	1116	6	1080	6	5392
4. Deniss Čerkovskis	LAT	1096	9	916	2	1252	17	1004	21	1088	3	5356
5. Dmitri Meliakh	BLR	1168	1	692	30	1332	5	1144	3	1004	15	5340
6. Michal Michalík	CZE	1108	6	888	6	1260	15	1144	3	932	28	5332
7. Eric Walther	GER	952	29	832	11	1336	3	1116	6	1084	4	5320
8. Gábor Balogh	HUN	1036	16	804	15	1240	21	1172	1	1044	9	5296

Andrei Moiseyev was not one of the favorites in 2004, having placed only seventh in the world championships three months earlier. The 25-year-old policeman from Rostov-on-Don was a swimmer for eleven years until his local pool closed. Shooting was his weakest event. He hoped for a score of 180 out of 200, but only achieved a 175. Meanwhile, Dmitri Meliakh took the early lead by matching the Olympic record of 186 target points. He was followed closely by Rustem Sabirkhuzin of Russia and Qian Zhenhua of China, who tied for second at 185. Sabirkhuzin moved into the lead after the fencing competition, while Moiseyev earned 22 fencing victories against only 9 defeats to close within eight point of his teammate. In the swimming event, Moiseyev finished more than three seconds ahead of second-place finisher Libor Capalini to open a 108-point lead over Marcin Horbacz of Poland in second place. Horbacz's medal hopes ended after his horse refused a jump six times in the riding competition, earning him a mere 112 points and dropping him to last place. Despite placing only 19th in the riding event, Moiseyev maintained a 44-point lead, with Michal Michalík moving into second place, and Meliakh jumping from eighth to third. Given an 11-second headstart in the 3,000-meter run, Moiseyev held onto first place. The 2004 world champion, Andrejus Zadneprovskis, used his running speed to move up from fifth and earn the silver medal.

2008 Beijing C: 36, N: 22, D: 8.21.

		SHOOTING		SWIMMING		FENCING		RIDING		RUNNING		TOTAL
1. RUS	Andrei Moiseyev	1168	5	1024	1	1332	6	1060	15	1048	27	5632
2. LIT	Edvinas Krungolcas	1156	7	904	5	1272	23	1144	4	1072	25	5548
3. LIT	Andrejus Zadneprovskis	1120	17	760	24	1336	5	1168	2	1140	13	5524
4. CHN	Qian Zhenhua	1204	2	1024	1	1272	22	1032	19	984	34	5516
5. GER	Steffen Gebhardt	1132	15	832	13	1280	19	1128	5	1108	19	5480
6. CZE	Michal Michalík	1192	3	784	21	1260	24	1172	1	1052	26	5460
7. UKR	Pavlo Tymoshchenko	1156	9	908	4	1252	28	1048	17	1072	24	5436
8. MEX	Óscar Soto Carrillo	988	31	880	7	1236	30	1160	3	1156	9	5420

Andrei Moiseyev had had a steady record in the years after winning the gold medal in Athens, earning a bronze medal at the 2005 world championship and silver at the 2006 European championship. A month before the Beijing Olympics Moiseyev won the 2008 European title, beating reigning world champion Ilya Frolov.

Reigning world silver medalist David Svoboda of the Czech Republic set an Olympic record of 191 points in the shooting round, but was passed by 2005 world champion Qian Zhenhua for first place after the fencing round. Moiseyev, who had tied with Qian for first place in the fencing, moved into the lead after the third round and took a 13-second head start into the final cross-country race. Moiseyev came only 27th in the running phase, but held on to successfully defend his Olympic title. Qian was still in second place after four events but dropped to fourth behind 2006 world champion Edvinas Krungolcas and 2006 world bronze medalist Andrejus Zadneprovskis during the running phase.

Moiseyev was only the second modern pentathlete in Olympic history to win back-to-back gold medals, the first being Lars Hall in 1952 and 1956.

DISCONTINUED EVENT

TEAM

1952 Helsinki T: 15, N: 15, D: 7.25.

		SHOOTING		SWIMMING		FENCING		RIDING		RUNNING		TOTAL
1. HUN	Gábor Benedek István Szondy Aladár Kovácsi	21	2	16	1	45	4	46	5	38	3	166
2. SWE	Lars Hall Torsten Lindqvist Claes Egnell	18	1	16	1	68	8	29	2	51	6	182
3. FIN	Olavi Mannonen Lauri Vilkko Olavi Rokka	38	4	90	10	30	1	27	1	28	1	213
4. USA	Frederick Denman W. Thad McArthur Guy Troy	27	3	50	5	41	2	49	6	48	4	215
5. SOV	Igor Novikov Pavel Rakityansky Aleksandr Dehayev	76	6	69	6	81	11	37	4	30	2	293
6. BRA	Eduardo Leal Medeiros Aloysio Alves Borges Eric Tinoco Marques	94	11	42	3	70	9	34	3	73	9	313
7. CHI	Nilo Floody Buxton Hernán Fuentes Besoaín Luis Carmona Barrales	77	7	42	3	42	3	90	11	81	11	336
8. ARG	Luis Riera Carlos Velázquez Jorge Cáceres Monié	53	15	98	12	52	5	75	9	77	10	355

Lars Hall
The only repeat winner of the modern pentathlon (1952 and 1956) and a member of the second-place Swedish team in 1952.

1956 Melbourne T: 12, N: 12, D: 11.28.

		SHOOTING		SWIMMING		FENCING		RIDING		RUNNING		TOTAL
1. SOV	Igor Novikov Aleksandr Tarassov Ivan Deryuhin	2457.5	3	2194	2	2850	1	2880	1	3579	1	13,690.5
2. USA	George Lambert William André Jack Daniels	3020	1	2008	4	2560	2	2780	2	3114	5	13,482
3. FIN	Olavi Mannonen Väinö Korhonen Berndt Katter	2512.5	2	2008	4	2520	4	2755	3	3390	3	13,185.5
4. HUN	Gábor Benedek János Bódy Antal Moldrich	1727.5	4	2566	1	2460	5	2660	4	3141	4	12,554.5
5. MEX	José Pérez Mier Antonio Almada Félix David Romero Vargas	1700	5	2008	4	2560	2	2640	5	2073	8	10,981
6. ROM	Cornel Vena Dumitru Tintea Victor Teodorescu	1160	8	2194	2	2160	6	2195	8	2904	6	10,613
7. GBR	Donald Cobley Thomas Hudson George Norman	335	11	1574	7	1340	8	2560	6	3417	2	9226
8. AUS	Neville Sayers Sven Coomer George Nicoll	1060	9	1264	8	2040	7	2220	7	2241	7	8825

1960 Rome T: 17, N: 17, D: 8.31.

		SHOOTING		SWIMMING		FENCING		RIDING		RUNNING		TOTAL
1. HUN	Ferenc Németh Imre Nagy András Balczó	3094	5	2740	1	2480	6	3000	1	3549	2	14,863
2. SOV	Igor Novikov Nikolai Tatarinov Hanno Selg	3087	6	2326	5	2460	7	2845	4	3591	1	14,309
3. USA	Robert Beck Jack Daniels George Lambert	3228	4	2402	3	2580	2	3000	2	2982	7	14,192
4. FIN	Kurt Lindeman Berndt Katter Eero Lohi	2929	13	2480	2	2580	3	2705	7	3171	5	13,865
5. POL	Stanisław Przybylski Kazimierz Paszkiewicz Kazimierz Mazur	3315	3	1804	11	2660	1	2535	12	3432	3	13,746
6. SWE	Per-Erik Ritzén Sture Ericson Björn Thofelt	3078	8	2352	4	2360	9	2585	11	2841	10	13,216
7. GBR	Patrick Harvey Donald Cobley Peter Little	3060	9	1700	15	2400	8	2670	8	3273	4	13,103
8. MEX	Antonio Almada Félix Sergio Escobedo Garduño José Pérez Mier	3393	1	2184	6	2540	4	2625	9	2103	16	12,845

1964 Tokyo T: 11, N: 11, D: 10.15.

		SHOOTING		SWIMMING		FENCING		RIDING		RUNNING		TOTAL
1. SOV	Igor Novikov Albert Mokeyev Viktor Mineyev	3050	11	2385	3	3040	1	3150	2	3336	1	14,961
2. USA	James Moore David Kirkwood Paul Pesthy	3240	3	2262	4	2640	5	2915	6	3132	3	14,189
3. HUN	Ferenc Török Imre Nagy Otto Török	3150	8	2590	1	2380	9	2885	7	3168	2	14,173
4. SWE	Bo-Herman Jansson Rolf Junefelt Hans-Gunnar Liljenwall	3240	4	2057	6	2460	8	3200	1	3099	4	14,056
5. AUS	Peter Macken Donald McMiken Duncan Page	3210	5	1770	7	2880	2	2990	4	2853	6	13,703
6. GER & GDR	Wolfgang Gödicke Uwe Adler Elmar Frings	3130	9	1729	8	2800	4	2955	5	2985	5	13,599
7. FIN	Jorma Hotanen Keijo Vanhala Karl Kaaja	3120	10	2221	5	2560	6	2885	8	2754	9	13,540
8. JPN	Yoshihide Fukutome Shigeaki Uchino Shigeki Mino	3210	6	1524	10	2860	3	2865	9	2943	6	13,402

1968 Mexico City T: 15, N: 15, D: 10.17.

		SHOOTING		SWIMMING		FENCING		RIDING		RUNNING		TOTAL
1. HUN	András Balczó István Móna Ferenc Török	2940	5	3130	1	2714	1	2877	6	2664	4	14,325
2. SOV	Pavlo Lednyov Borys Onyshchenko Stasys Šaparnis	3135	1	2558	2	2648	5	3141	1	2766	2	14,248
3. FRA	Raoul Gueguen Lucien Guiguet Jean-Pierre Giudicelli	2855	8	2168	11	2626	6	2931	4	2709	3	13,289
4. USA	James Moore Robert Beck M. Thomas Lough	3030	2	2324	7	2670	4	2844	7	2412	9	13,280
5. FIN	Seppo Aho Martti Ketelä Jorma Hotanen	2890	6	2558	2	2384	13	2799	8	2607	5	1,3238
6. GDR	Karl-Heinz Kutschke Jörg Tscherner Wolfgang Lüderitz	2485	12	2194	10	2626	6	3093	2	2769	1	13,167
7. JPN	Toshio Fukui Yuso Makihira Katsuaki Tashiro	2980	4	2428	5	2428	9	2796	9	2451	6	13,083
8. GBR	Jeremy "Jim" Fox Barry Lillywhite Robert Phelps	2790	9	2324	9	2670	2	2952	3	2157	11	12,893

DISQ (Drugs): SWE (Björn Ferm, Hans-Gunnar Liljenwal, Hans Jacobson) 14,188

The Swedish team finished third with 14,188 points, but was disqualified when one of its members, Hans-Gunnar Liljenvall, failed the drug test for alcohol. It was a common practice for pentathletes to steady their nerves with a bit of alcohol before the shooting contest, but Liljenvall, who finished eighth individually, was found to have a blood alcohol concentration well above the acceptable limit, despite the fact that he claimed he had only drunk two beers. He was the first Olympic athlete to be disqualified for doping.

1972 Munich T: 19, N: 19, D: 8.31.

		SHOOTING		SWIMMING		FENCING		RIDING		RUNNING		TOTAL
1. SOV	Borys Onyshchenko Pavlo Lednyov Vladimir Shmelyov	2925	13	3060	1	3110	1	3396	2	3477	2	15,968
2. HUN	András Balczó Zsigmond Villányi Pál Bakó	2975	10	2820	2	2736	2	3280	5	3537	1	15,348
3. FIN	Risto Hurme Veikko Salminen Martti Ketelä	3010	6	2580	4	2670	3	3300	3	3252	9	14,812
4. USA	Charles Richards John Fitzgerald Scott Taylor	3115	3	2280	10	2450	10	3564	1	3393	5	14,802
5. SWE	Björn Ferm Bo-Herman Jansson Hans-Gunnar Liljenwal	3125	2	2640	3	2428	11	3236	7	3279	8	14,708
6. GER	Heiner Thade Walter Esser Hole Rössler	3010	7	2520	7	2626	4	3232	8	3294	7	14,682
7. FRA	Michel Gueguen Jean-Pierre Giudicelli Raoul Gueguen	2990	8	2320	9	2538	8	3252	6	3459	3	14,559
8. POL	Ryszard Wach Janusz Pyciak-Peciak Stanisław Skwira	2955	11	2420	8	2362	13	3296	4	3252	10	14,285

1976 Montreal T: 14, N: 14, D: 7.22.

		SHOOTING		SWIMMING		FENCING		RIDING		RUNNING		TOTAL
1. GBR	Adrian Parker R. Daniel Nightingale Jeremy "Jim" Fox	3212	3	2256	8	2648	8	3492	5	3951	1	15,559
2. CZE	Jan Bártu Bohumil Starnovsky Jiří Adam	2962	10	2783	1	3000	1	3400	8	3306	12	15,451
3. HUN	Tamás Kancsal Tibor Maracskó Szvetiszláv Sasics	2772	12	2773	2	2758	5	3528	4	3564	5	15,395
4. POL	Janusz Pyciak-Peciak Krzysztof Trybusiewicz Zbigniew Pacelt	3170	6	2132	11	2912	3	3544	3	3585	2	15,343
5. USA	John Fitzgerald Michael Burley Robert Nieman	3140	7	2535	4	2296	12	3768	1	3546	7	15,285
6. ITA	Daniele Masala Pier Paolo Cristofori Mario Medda	3194	4	2256	8	2670	6	3428	7	3483	8	1,5031
7. FIN	Risto Hurme Jussi Pelli Heikki Hulkkonen	2794	11	2597	3	2802	4	3228	10	3579	3	15,000
8. SWE	Hans Lager Bengt Lager Gunnar Jacobson	3268	1	2318	7	2340	11	3468	6	3552	6	14,946

In 1976 the noble sport of modern pentathlon was wracked by controversy. First of all, Captain Orben Greenwald, a member of the US team, was prevented from competing when his team manager, Lieutenant-Colonel Donald Johnson of the US Modern Pentathlon Training Center, courtmartialed him for insubordination. Although the charge was thrown out as soon as an investigation was begun, Greenwald was refused accreditation when he arrived in Montreal.

The real shock came on the second day of competition, during the fencing tournament. The favored Soviet team was fencing against the team from Great Britain, when the British pentathletes noticed something odd about the defending silver medalist, Army Major Borys Onyshchenko. In his fight against Adrian Parker, the automatic light registered a hit for the Ukrainian even though he didn't appear to have touched his opponent. Veteran Jeremy Fox was next to be drawn against Onyshchenko. When he too lost a hit without being touched, it became obvious that something was wrong with Onyshchenko's épée The weapon was taken away to be examined by the Jury of Appeal. Onyshchenko continued with a different sword, but an hour or so later the news came that he had been disqualified.

Evidently Onyshchenko, desperate for victory in his final international competition, had wired his sword with a well-hidden push-button circuit breaker which enabled him to register a hit whenever he wanted. It is unknown how long Onyshchenko had been using this trick, but his fencing scores, which were already high, showed a marked upward surge beginning in 1970. He was spirited away from the Olympic Village almost immediately and was never seen outside the USSR again. He was forever after known as Borys Dis-Onyshchenko.

Onyshchenko's disqualification eliminated the Soviets from the team competition, leaving an open field. After four events the British team was in fifth place, 547 points behind Czechoslovakia. But running was their specialty, and Parker, the first runner of the day, inspired the others to victory by completing the 4000-meter course in 12 minutes 9 seconds, the fastest time ever recorded in Olympic competition. Strong performances by Nightingale and Fox assured Britain of the unexpected victory. Strong performances by Danny Nightingale and Jim Fox assured Britain of the unexpected victory.

1980 Moscow T: 12, N: 12, D: 7.24.

		SHOOTING		SWIMMING		FENCING		RIDING		RUNNING		TOTAL
1. SOV	Anatoly Starostin Pavlo Lednyov Yevgeny Lipeyev	3194	2	2896	2	2956	7	3552	4	3528	1	16,126
2. HUN	Tamás Szombathelyi Tibor Maracskó László Horváth	3088	5	3042	1	3000	6	3428	9	3354	4	15,912
3. SWE	Svante Rasmuson Lennart Pettersson George Horvath	3022	8	2714	3	3220	1	3640	1	3249	7	15,845
4. POL	Janusz Pyciak-Peciak Jan Olesiński Marek Bajan	3208	1	2506	5	2646	8	3576	3	3498	2	15,634
5. FRA	Paul Four Joël Bouzou Alain Cortes	3070	6	2600	4	3088	3	3464	8	3123	10	15,345
6. CZE	Milan Kadlec Jan Bártů Bohumil Starnovský	3154	3	2298	8	3044	5	3504	5	3339	6	15,339
7. FIN	Heikki Hulkkonen Jussi Pelli Pekka Santanen	2851	11	2480	6	3132	2	3384	10	3240	8	15,087
8. GBR	R. Daniel Nightingale Peter Whiteside Nigel Clark	2946	10	2246	10	2824	9	3584	2	3462	3	15,062

1984 Los Angeles-Irvine T: 17, N: 17, D: 8.1.

		SHOOTING		SWIMMING		FENCING		RIDING		RUNNING		TOTAL
1. ITA	Daniele Masala Carlo Massullo Pierpaolo Cristofori	3240	1	2560	4	3716	4	2912	4	3632	1	16,066
2. USA	Michael Storm Robert Gregory Losey Dean Glenesk	3188	2	2604	3	3700	6	2802	7	3274	8	15,568
3. FRA	Paul Four Didier Boube Joël Bouzou	2994	9	2626	2	3484	11	3044	1	3417	7	15,565
4. SWI	Andy Jung Peter Steinmann Peter Minder	3090	5	2516	5	3564	10	2956	2	3217	9	15,343
5. MEX	Ivar Sisniega Campbell Alejandro Yrizar Barranco Marcelo Hoyo	3056	7	2450	7	3704	5	2648	9	3425	6	15,283
6. GER	Achim Bellmann Michael Rehbein Christian Sandow	3058	6	2494	6	3736	3	2296	14	3444	5	15,028
7. GBR	Richard Phelps Michael Mumford Stephen Sowerby	2605	15	2362	9	3764	2	2626	10	3537	2	14,894
8. SPA	Jorge Quesada Molina Eduardo Burguete Babi Federico Galera Fernández	3106	4	2208	11	3568	9	2516	12	3493	4	14,891

1988 Seoul T: 19, N: 19, D: 9.22.

		SHOOTING		SWIMMING		FENCING		RIDING		RUNNING		TOTAL
1. HUN	János Martinek Attila Mizsér László Fábián	2952	5	2888	1	3764	4	2604	14	3678	1	15,886
2. ITA	Carlo Massullo Daniele Masala Gianluca Tiberti	2998	3	2392	8	3732	8	3110	1	3339	7	15,571
3. GBR	Richard Phelps Dominic Mahony Graham Brookhouse	2986	4	2439	7	3764	4	2604	14	3483	3	15,276
4. FRA	Christophe Ruer Joël Bouzou Bruno Génard	2884	6	2473	6	3780	3	2714	11	3417	4	15,268
5. SOV	Vakhtang Yagorashvili German Yuferov Anatoly Avdeyev	2376	14	2735	2	3992	1	2802	7	3309	8	15,214
6. CZE	Milan Kadlec Tomáš Fleissner Jiří Prokopius	3050	2	2361	9	3508	14	2758	9	3366	6	15,043
7. SWI	Peter Steinmann Andy Jung Peter Burger	2832	8	2541	5	3616	13	2472	17	3402	5	14,863
8. MEX	Ivar Sisniega Campbell Alejandro Yrizar Barranco Marcelo Hoyo	2730	11	2361	9	3648	11	2560	16	3486	2	14,785

1992 Barcelona T: 17, N: 17, D: 7.29.

		SHOOTING		FENCING		SWIMMING		RIDING		RUNNING		TOTAL
1. POL	Maciej Czyżowicz Akradiusz Skrzypaszek Dariusz Goździak	2575	2	3420	1	3632	16	3369	8	3022	2	16,018
2. RUS	Anatoly Starostin Dmitri Svatkovsky Eduard Zenovka	2490	7	3345	2	3760	4	3573	2	2756	8	15,924
3. ITA	Gianluca Tiberti Carlo Massullo Roberto Bomprezzi	2388	12	3330	3	3640	13	3252	9	3150	1	15,760
4. USA	Rob Stull James Haley J. Michael Gostigian	2507	5	3195	5	3812	1	3240	10	2895	6	15,649
5. HUN	László Fábián Attila Kálnoki Kis Attila Mizsér	2796	1	3000	11	3696	9	3489	5	2590	13	15,571
6. GBR	Graham Brookhouse Richard Phelps Dominic Mahony	2490	7	2835	14	3756	5	3480	6	3010	3	15,571
7. FRA	Joel Bouzou Christophe Ruer Sébastien Deleigne	2388	11	3120	8	3704	6	3546	3	2683	11	15,441
8. SWE	Per-Olov Danielsson Håkan Norebrink Per Nyqvist	2422	10	3105	10	3668	10	3237	11	2996	4	15,428

The same disastrous ride that dropped Eduard Zenovka from first to third in the individual event allowed Poland to upset the Russians in the team event.

WOMEN

INDIVIDUAL

1896–1996 not held

2000 Sydney C: 24, N: 19, D: 10.1.

		SHOOTING		SWIMMING		FENCING		RIDING		RUNNING		TOTAL
1. Stephanie Cook	GBR	1072	8	760	18	1138	12	1040	8	1308	1	5318
2. Emily DeRiel	USA	1156	1	800	9	1182	7	1070	1	1102	3	5310
3. Kate Allenby	GBR	1036	12	920	5	1191	5	1040	5	1086	4	5273
4. Mary Beth Iagorashvili	USA	964	18	960	1	1205	3	1040	6	960	13	5129
5. Paulina Boenisz	POL	1060	9	800	9	1121	17	1040	7	1078	5	5099
6. Jama Shubenok	BLR	1084	6	840	7	1142	11	1010	9	1010	11	5086
7. Elizaveta Suvorova	RUS	1096	5	960	1	1117	18	827	18	1076	6	5076
8. Jeļena Rubļevska	LAT	964	19	960	1	1110	20	955	12	1062	8	5051

Stephanie Cook and Emily DeRiel were teammates on the women's modern pentathlon team at Oxford University. In the inaugural Olympic competition in Sydney, DeRiel outscored Cook in each of the first four events, but Cook was such a superior cross-country runner that she remained the favorite. She started the 3000 meters in eighth place, 49 seconds behind DeRiel. She picked off the seven women ahead of her one by one, passing teammate Kate Allenby 750 meters from the finish and finally De Riel with about 300 meters to go. Of the 22 athletes who ran the cross-country course, only one came within 50 seconds of Cook's time. The three pentathletes were among the best-educated set of medalists in Olympic history. Cook was a doctor who earned degrees at both Cambridge and Oxford. DeRiel graduated from Yale and then received a master's degree at Oxford in medieval English literature. Allenby was a graduate student in philosophy at the University of Surrey.

2004 Athens C: 32, N: 21, D: 8.27.

		SHOOTING		SWIMMING		FENCING		RIDING		RUNNING		TOTAL
1. Zsuzsanna Vörös	HUN	1120	3	916	5	1296	4	1124	9	992	18	5448
2. Jeļena Rubļevska	LAT	988	15	1028	1	1160	21	1116	14	1088	4	5380
3. Georgina Harland	GBR	808	30	832	12	1308	2	1144	6	1252	1	5344
4. Claudia Corsini	ITA	964	18	972	2	1236	11	1116	13	1036	12	5324
5. Kim Raisner	GER	1072	8	832	12	1264	6	1116	12	1028	13	5312
6. Sylwia Czwojdzińska	POL	1084	6	860	7	1224	14	1116	16	992	19	5276
7. Viktoria Tereshchuk	UKR	1060	11	692	29	1244	9	1116	15	1144	2	5256
8. Kate Allenby	GBR	964	18	972	2	1272	5	1004	25	1024	14	5236

The world champion in 1999, Zsuzsa Vörös had a disappointing performance at the Sydney Olympics, placing only fifteenth. She arrived at the 2004 Olympics as the favorite, having won the last two world championships, including the most recent just three months before the Athens Games. Opening with a third place in the shooting competition, Vörös moved into first place after a 19-12 performance in fencing. Thereafter, she never relinquished the lead. After finishing fourth in swimming, Vörös led Kate Allenby by 124 points, with Jeļena Rubļevska in third, another 32 points back. Vörös expanded her lead to 164 points by surviving riding, the event that had led to her downfall four years earlier. Rubļevska edged back into second place, four points ahead of Claudia Corsini and eight ahead of Sylwia Czwojdzińska. Vörös enjoyed a 41-second headstart over Rubļevska in the 3,000-meter run, giving her time to grab a Hungarian flag while coming down the home stretch. Rubļevska took silver, while world top-ranked Georgina Harland finished her comeback from a nearly disastrous 30th-place finish in the shooting event by passing eleven women in the final race to earn the bronze medal.

2008 Beijing C: 36, N: 23, D: 8.22.

		SHOOTING		FENCING		SWIMMING		RIDING		RUNNING		TOTAL
1. Lena Schöneborn	GER	1060	20	1072	1	1280	10	1172	4	1208	9	5792
2. Heather Fell	GBR	1156	6	880	11	1328	3	1144	11	1244	5	5752
3. Viktoriya Tereshchuk	UKR	1072	17	928	5	1316	5	1088	21	1268	2	5672
4. Anna Arkhipenko	BLR	1180	3	856	14	1128	33	1172	5	1304	1	5640
5. Chen Qian	CHN	1060	19	880	11	1260	15	1200	3	1212	8	5612
6. Paulina Boenisz	POL	1132	10	904	9	1192	27	1096	20	1240	6	5564
7. Katy Livingston	GBR	1072	18	808	18	1292	7	1172	6	1204	10	5548
8. Aya Medany	EGY	1144	9	928	5	1292	8	1004	30	1176	11	5544

Reigning world silver medalist Lena Schöneborn took a 60-point lead after the second round, having won 28 of 35 fencing bouts. A former swimmer, the 23-year-old Schöneborn finished only tenth in the swimming round, but managed to hold on to the lead through the next two rounds, despite a ninth-place finish in the running phase. She finished 40 points ahead of 2007 European silver medalist Heather Fell to win the gold medal. Two-time reigning world champion Amelie Cazé of France finished ninth after struggling in the shooting and running phases.

Nineteenth-place finisher Sheila Taormina of the United States made Olympic history by becoming the first woman to qualify for the Olympics in three different sports. Taormina had won an Olympic gold medal in the 1996 women's 4 × 200-meter freestyle relay and had competed in the triathlon at the 2000 and 2004 Olympics. She struggled in the first two rounds in the modern pentathlon, finishing 28th in shooting and last in fencing, but came back to set an Olympic record of 2:08.86 in the swimming round and finished first in the riding phase.

Chapter 19 **Rowing**

MEN
Single Sculls
Double Sculls
Quadruple Sculls
Pair-Oared Shell Without Coxswain
Four-Oared Shell Without Coxswain
Eight-Oared Shell With Coxswain
Lightweight: Double Sculls
Lightweight: Four-Oared Shell Without Coxswain
Discontinued Events

WOMEN
Single Sculls
Double Sculls
Quadruple Sculls
Pair-Oared Shell Without Coxswain
Eight-Oared Shell With Coxswain
Lightweight: Double Sculls
Discontinued Events

There are two kinds of rowing events. In sculling events, each rower pulls two oars. In sweep events, each rower pulls one oar. In races in which a coxswain calls the strokes for the rowers, the coxswain must weigh at least 55 kg (121 lbs) for men's races and 50 kg (110 lbs) for women's races. If the coxswain is underweight, up to 5 kg of dead weight may be added to the boat. In

Vyacheslav Ivanov, 1964
The Soviet rower took gold in single sculls in 1956, 1960 and 1964.

1996, lightweight events were included in the Olympics for the first time. Men in lightweight events may weigh no more than 72.5 kg (160 lbs), women no more than 59 kg (130 lbs). In men's races, lightweight crews must average no more than 70 kg (154.3 lbs); in women's races, the average must be no more than 57 kg (125.7 lbs).

Since 1964 rowing contests have begun with qualifying tests. The fastest qualifiers advance directly to the semifinals or final, while the rest take part in a *repêchage*, or second-chance round (*repêchage* being the French word for "fishing again"). The top six semifinalists take part in the final, while the other six take part in a "petit-final," to determine 7th through 12th places.

In 1900 the course was 1750 meters long, in 1904 3218 meters (2 miles), in 1908 2414 meters (1.5 miles), and in 1948, 1883 meters. In 1906 the courses varied. In all other years, all races have been 2000 meters long. Each lane is 13.5 meters (44 feet 3½ inches) wide. The water must be at least 3.5 meters (11 feet 5¾ inches) deep.

MEN

SINGLE SCULLS

1896 not held

1900 Paris C: 12, N: 2, D: 8.26.

1. Hermann Barrelet	FRA	7:35.6
2. André Gaudin	FRA	7:41.6
3. Saint-George Ashe	GBR	8:15.6
4. Robert d'Heilly	FRA	8:16.0

DNF: Louis Prével (FRA)

1904 St. Louis C: 4, N: 1, D: 7.30.

1. Frank Greer	USA	10:08.5
2. James Juvenal	USA	—
3. Constance Titus	USA	—
4. David Duffield	USA	—

Greer won by two lengths.

1906 Athens C: 2, N: 1, D: 4.27.

1. Gaston Delaplane	FRA	5:53.4
2. Joseph Larran	FRA	6:07.2

1908 London-Henley-on-Thames C: 9, N: 6, D: 7.31.

1. Henry Blackstaffe	GBR	9:26.0
2. Alexander McCulloch	GBR	—
3. Bernhard von Gaza	GER	
3. Károly Levitzky	HUN	

The 40-year-old Blackstaffe, who worked as a butcher, was twice the age of McCulloch, his opponent in the final. Yet he was able to finish more strongly and win by one and a quarter lengths.

1912 Stockholm C: 13, N: 11, D: 7.19.

1. William Kinnear	GBR	7:47.3
2. Polydore Veirman	BEL	7:56.0
3. Everard Butler	CAN	—
3. Hugo Kuusik	RUS/EST	—

Wally Kinnear of Laurencekirk was Scotland's second gold medal winner (the first was 1908 400 meters champion Wyndham Halswelle).

1920 Antwerp-Vilvoorde C: 10, N: 10, D: 8.29.

1. John Kelly, Sr.	USA	7:35.0
2. Jack Beresford	GBR	7:36.0
3. Darcy Hadfield	NZL	
4. Frits Eyken	HOL	

Jack Kelly, who once won 126 straight races, was barred from competing in London's famous Diamond Sculls race at Henley because the Vesper Boat Club of Philadelphia, of which he was a member, had been accused of professionalism. Kelly got his revenge a few weeks later in the Olympics, when he defeated the Diamond Sculls winner, Jack Beresford, in the final. The two men were so exhausted after the race that they were unable to shake hands. Nevertheless, Kelly managed to recover sufficiently to win a second gold medal in the double sculls 30 minutes later. Kelly had two illustrious offspring. His son John, Jr., who competed in four Olympics himself, brought his father great joy when he won the Diamond Sculls at Henley in 1947 and 1949. His daughter was Grace Kelly, the famous film actress who later became Princess of Monaco.

Jack Kelly

Kelly, father of Princess Grace of Monaco, won three rowing gold medals in 1920 and 1924.

1924 Paris C: 8, N: 8, D: 7.17.

1. Jack Beresford	GBR	7:49.2
2. William Garrett Gilmore	USA	7:54.0
3. Josef Schneider	SWI	8:01.1

DNF: Arthur Bull (AUS)

In 1924 the system of *repêchage* was introduced, in which the second-place finishers in the preliminary heats were allowed a row-off for a place in the final. This was a break for Beresford, who lost to Gilmore in the opening round. Qualifying through the *repêchage,* Beresford turned the tables on Gilmore in the final and won by two and a half lengths. Despite his defeat, Gilmore had fond memories of the race. "During the last 200 meters," he later wrote, "when the sun seemed to get hotter with every stroke and I was making a supreme effort to grasp victory, a kindly breeze swept across the Seine, carrying a strong but pleasant scent from a perfumery which was not within sight. It was truly so strong that it first gagged me, but in a moment I was rowing on as if in a flowing river of the perfume itself."

1928 Amsterdam-Sloten C: 15, N: 15, D: 8.10.

1. Henry Pearce	AUS	7:11.0
2. Kenneth Myers	USA	7:20.8
3. Theodore Collet	GBR	7:29.8
4. Lambertus Gunther	HOL	7:31.6
5. Joseph Wright	CAN	
6. Josef Straka, Sr.	CZE	
7. Edouard Candeveau	SWI	
8. Victor Saurin	FRA	

"Bobby" Pearce, a third-generation sculling champion from Sydney, faced an unexpected challenge in the middle of his quarterfinal race against Victor Saurin when a family of ducks passed single-file in front of his boat. Pearce let them pass and then sculled to a popular victory. He had hoped that his Olympic win would allow him to row in the Diamond Sculls at Henley, but he was refused admission because he was a carpenter. Back in Sydney he was unable to find work due to the Depression. When Lord Dewar, the Canadian whisky manufacturer, learned of Pearce's plight, he offered him a job as a salesman. This new position made Pearce eligible for Henley, since he was no longer a laborer. In 1931 he went to London and won the Diamond Sculls by six lengths. Although he moved to Hamilton, Ontario, in Canada, Pearce represented Australia again in 1932 and won a second gold medal.

1932 Los Angeles-Long Beach C: 5, N: 5, D: 8.13.

1. Henry Pearce	AUS	7:44.4
2. William Miller	USA	7:45.2
3. Guillermo Douglas	URU	8:13.6
4. Leslie Southwood	GBR	8:33.6

1936 Berlin-Grünau C: 20, N: 20, D: 8.14.

1. Gustav Schäfer	GER	8:21.5
2. Josef Hasenöhrl	AUT	8:25.8
3. Daniel Barrow	USA	8:28.0
4. Charles Campbell	CAN	8:35.0
5. Ernst Rufli	SWI	8:38.9
6. Pascual José Giorgio	ARG	8:57.5
7. Roger Verey	POL	
7. Humphrey Lloyd Warren	GBR	

The Olympic final was Schäfer's 51st consecutive victory.

1948 London-Henley-on-Thames C: 14, N: 14, D: 8.9.

1. Mervyn Wood	AUS	7:24.4
2. Eduardo Risso Salaverría	URU	7:38.2
3. Romolo Catasta	ITA	7:51.4
4. Tranquilo Cappozzo	ARG	
4. John Kelly, Jr.	USA	
4. Jean Sepheriades	FRA	
7. Anthony Rowe	GBR	

The unusually handsome Wood was dubbed "The Cary Grant of Scullers" by US journalists. A policeman who specialized in fingerprint analysis, Wood celebrated his victory by smoking his pipe for the first time in five months.

1952 Helsinki C: 18, N: 18, D: 7.23.

1. Yuri Tyukalov	SOV/RUS	8:12.8
2. Mervyn Wood	AUS	8:14.5
3. Teodor Kocerka	POL	8:19.4
4. T. Anthony Fox	GBR	8:22.5
5. Ian Stephen	SAF	8:31.4

1956 Melbourne-Ballarat C: 12, N: 12, D: 11.27.

1. Vyacheslav Ivanov	SOV/RUS	8:02.5
2. Stuart Mackenzie	AUS	8:07.7
3. John Kelly, Jr.	USA	8:11.8
4. Teodor Kocerka	POL	8:12.9

Mackenzie, who worked as a chicken-sexer on his father's farm, seemed to have the race well in hand, but Ivanov made a sensational spurt with 200 meters to go and won going away. He earned two more gold medals in 1960 and 1964. In 1959 Mackenzie became the first person to win both the single and double sculls at Henley. Jack Kelly, Jr. was elected president of the United States Olympic Committee in 1985, but died of a heart attack while jogging only 22 days later.

1960 Rome-Lake Albano C: 13, N: 13, D: 9.3.

1. Vyacheslav Ivanov	SOV/RUS	7:13.96
2. Achim Hill	GDR	7:20.21
3. Teodor Kocerka	POL	7:21.26
4. James Hill	NZL	7:23.98
5. Harry Parker	USA	7:29.26
6. Savino Rebek	ITA	7:31.09

1964 Tokyo C: 13, N: 13, D: 10.15.

1. Vyacheslav Ivanov	SOV/RUS	8:22.51
2. Achim Hill	GDR	8:26.24
3. Gottfried Kottmann	SWI	8:29.68
4. Alberto Demiddi	ARG	8:31.51
5. Murray Watkinson	NZL	8:35.57
6. Donald Spero	USA	8:37.53
7. Robert Groen	HOL	
8. Leif Gotfredsen	CAN	

Ivanov staged another one of his famous finishing bursts, gaining 11 seconds on Hill in the last 500 meters. Actually he made such a tremendous effort that he blacked out before the finish line. In his book, *Winds of Olympic Lakes*, Ivanov wrote, "I don't remember how long it was before consciousness gradually returned . . . I mustered the last ounce of my strength, raised my head and couldn't believe it: there was clear water ahead of me and nobody in front of me in those last 50 meters to the finish. I wondered whether it was a case of delirium and that I was having hallucinations . . . I managed to find an extra bit of strength, picked up the oars and crossed the line first."

1968 Mexico City-Xochimilco C: 17, N: 17, D: 10.19.

1. Henri Jan Wienese	HOL	7:47.80
2. Jochen Meissner	GER	7:52.00
3. Alberto Demiddi	ARG	7:57.19
4. John Van Blom	USA	8:00.51
5. Achim Hill	GDR	8:06.09
6. Kenneth Dwan	GBR	8:13.76
7. Zdzisław Bromek	POL	
8. Niels Secher	DEN	

1972 Munich-Oberschleissheim C: 18, N: 18, D: 9.2.

1. Yuri Malishev	SOV/RUS	7:10.12
2. Alberto Demiddi	ARG	7:11.53
3. Wolfgang Güldenpfennig	GDR	7:14.45
4. Udo Hild	GER	7:20.81
5. James Dietz	USA	7:24.81
6. Melchior Bürgin	SWI	7:31.99
7. Seán Drea	IRL	
8. Yordan Vulchev	BUL	

1976 Montreal C: 15, N: 15, D: 7.25.

1. Pertti Karppinen	FIN	7:29.03
2. Peter Michael Kolbe	GER	7:31.67
3. Joachim Dreifke	GDR	7:38.03
4. Seán Drea	IRL	7:42.53
5. Mykhalo Dovgan	SOV/UKR	7:57.39
6. Ricardo Ibarra	ARG	8:03.05
7. James Dietz	USA	
8. Edward Hale	AUS	

Karppinen, a 6-foot 7-inch fireman from Parsio, won Finland's first rowing gold medal by coming from behind to upset world champion Kolbe and co-favorite Dreifke.

1980 Moscow C: 14, N: 14, D: 7.27.

1. Pertti Karppinen	FIN	7:09.61
2. Vassily Yakusha	SOV/AZR	7:11.66
3. Peter Kersten	GDR	7:14.88
4. Vladek Lacina	CZE	7:17.57
5. Hans Svensson	SWE	7:19.38
6. Hugh Matheson	GBR	7:20.28
7. Bernard Destraz	SWI	
8. Konstantinos Kontomanolis	GRE	

1984 Los Angeles-Lake Casitas C: 16, N: 16, D: 8.5.

1. Pertti Karppinen	FIN	7:00.24
2. Peter Michael Kolbe	GER	7:02.19
3. Robert Mills	CAN	7:10.38
4. John Biglow	USA	7:12.00
5. Ricardo Ibarra	ARG	7:14.59
6. Konstantinos Kontomanolis	GRE	7:17.03
7. Gary Reid	NZL	
8. Raimund Haberl	AUT	

Kolbe, now a ball-bearing salesman in Norway and the winner of four world championships, took the early lead. But Karppinen, as usual, came from behind, caught Kolbe after 1750 meters and then powered ahead in the last 25 meters to match Vyacheslav Ivanov's record of three single sculls gold medals.

1988 Seoul C: 22, N: 22, D: 9.24.

1. Thomas Lange	GDR	6:49.86
2. Peter Michael Kolbe	GER	6:54.77
3. Eric Verdonk	NZL	6:58.66
4. Hamish McGlashan	AUS	7:01.43
5. Kajetan Broniewski	POL	7:03.67
6. Andrew Sudduth	USA	7:11.45
7. Pertti Karpinnen	FIN	
8. Jüri Jaanson	SOV/EST	

Lange, a 24-year-old medical student from Halle, was the defending world champion. He overhauled Kolbe at 1300 meters and pulled away to win by a wide margin. Kolbe earned his third silver medal at age 35.

1992 Barcelona-Banyoles C: 22, N: 22, D: 8.1.

1. Thomas Lange	GER	6:51.40
2. Václav Chalupa, Jr.	CZE	6:52.93
3. Kajetan Broniewski	POL	6:56.82
4. Eric Verdonk	NZL	6:57.45
5. Jüri Jaanson	EST	7:12.92
6. Sergio Fernández González	ARG	7:15.53
7. Joaquín Gómez Gurza	MEX	
8. Harald Faderbauer	AUT	

Lange followed up his 1988 Olympic victory by winning the world championship in 1989 and 1991. He missed the 1990 world championship after his father, a high-ranking member of the Communist Party, committed suicide following the collapse of Communism in East Germany.

1996 Atlanta-Lake Lanier C: 21, N: 21, D: 7.27. WB: 6:37.03 (Jüri Jaanson)

1. Xeno Müller	SWI	6:44.85
2. Derek Porter	CAN	6:47.45
3. Thomas Lange	GER	6:47.72
4. Iztok Čop	SLO	6:51.71
5. Václav Chalupa, Jr.	CZE	6:55.65
6. Fredrik Bekken	NOR	6:59.51
7. Robert Waddell	NZL	
8. Aly Ibrahim	EGY	

Derek Porter led for the first 1500 meters, but Xeno Müller rowed the last 500 meters in an amazing 1:36.56, passing first Thomas Lange and then Porter for a clear victory. The peripatetic Müller grew up in Switzerland, Germany, Spain and France (where he first took up rowing at age 13), before attending Brown University in the United States. By 1996, Müller had become so Americanized that at the medal ceremony, he automatically placed his hand over his heart in the American fashion during the playing of the national anthem—the Swiss national anthem.

2000 Sydney-Penrith Lakes C: 24, N: 24, D: 9.23. WB: 6:36.68 (Rob Waddell)

1. Rob Waddell	NZL	6:48.90
2. Xeno Müller	SWI	6:50.55
3. Marcel Hacker	GER	6:50.83
4. Derek Porter	CAN	6:51.10
5. Ivo Yanakiev	BUL	6:57.32
6. Jüri Jaanson	EST	6:59.15
7. Gerard Egelmeers	HOL	
8. Don Smith	USA	

DISQ (Drugs): Andris Reinholds (LAT)

Rob Waddell's rowing career was disrupted by a heart condition, atrium fibrillation, which caused him to lose energy mid-race. After an attack occurred while he was competing as a member of a coxless fours crew at the 1995 world championships, Waddell decided to withdraw from team events, so as not to damage the chances of his teammates. Instead, he switched to single sculls. In 1997 he began taking anti-arrhythmic medication and his results improved. He won the 1998 and 1999 world championships. But three months before the 2000 Olympics, his two-year undefeated streak ended when defending Olympic champion Xeno Müller beat him in Vienna. At the Olympics, Waddell recorded the fastest time in both the heats and the semifinals. In the final, he and Müller pulled away from the others by the halfway mark and dueled for 1500 meters before Waddell pulled away to win by eight meters. Andris Reinholds finished second in the B final, but tested positive for steroids.

2004 Athens-Schinias C: 29, N: 29, D: 8.21. WB: 6:36.33 (Marcel Hacker)

1. Olaf Tufte	NOR	6:49.00
2. Jüri Jaanson	EST	6:51.42
3. Ivo Yanakiev	BUL	6:52.80
4. Santiago Fernández	ARG	6:55.17
5. Václav Chalupa, Jr.	CZE	6:59.13
6. Tim Maeyens	BEL	7:01.74
7. Marcel Hacker	GER	
8. André Vonarburg	SWI	

Olaf Tufte began his sports career in motocross and did not switch to rowing until he was eighteen years old. Only three months later, he competed in the coxless fours event at the 1994 Junior World Championships. He represented Norway in the same event at the 1996 Olympics and then earned a silver medal in double sculls at the Sydney 2000 Games. The following season he concentrated on single sculls and won the world championship in 2001, a feat he repeated in 2003. Tufte was expected to be challenged by his good friend Marcel Hacker, who earned a bronze medal at the 2000 Olympics, won the world championship in 2001 and arrived at the Athens Olympics as the reigning world record holder. Tufte and Hacker also faced two powerful veterans, Jüri Jaanson and Václav Chalupa, both of whom were competing in their fifth Olympics. Jaanson also had a single sculls world chamiponship to his credit . . . from 1990, while Chalupa was a silver medal winner from the 1992 Olympics.

The big surprise in 2004 came in the second of three semifinal races when Hacker finished third behind Tufte and Ivo Yanakiev and failed to advance to the A final. In the final, Chalupa took the early lead, but by the halfway point Tufte had edged ahead, with Jaanson close behind. Jaanson took the lead briefly with 500 meters remaining, but then Tufte pulled away at the end to gain a clear victory. Meanwhile, Marcel Hacker's winning time of 6:47.26 in the B final would have been good enough for the gold medal had he qualified for the A final.

2008 Beijing C: 32, N: 32, D: 8.16. WB: 6:35.40 (Mahé Drysdale)

1. Olaf Tufte	NOR	6:59.83
2. Ondřej Synek	CZE	7:00.63
3. Mahé Drysdale	NZL	7:01.56
4. Tim Maeyens	BEL	7:03.40
5. Alan Campbell	GBR	7:04.47
6. Lassi Karonen	SWE	7:07.64
7. Marcel Hacker	GER	
8. Mindaugas Griskonis	LIT	

Defending Olympic champion Olaf Tufte was expected to be challenged by three-time world champion Mahé Drysdale. Drysdale, however, came down with a stomach bug a week before the competition and almost didn't make it to the final, finishing third in his semifinal race behind Ondřej Synek. Besides Drysdale, Synek was the only other person to have won a medal in each of the past three world championships.

DOUBLE SCULLS

1896–1900 not held

1904 St. Louis T: 3, N: 1, D: 7.30.

1. USA	John Mulcahy, William Varley	10.03.2
2. USA	James McLoughlin, John Hoben	—
3. USA	Joseph Ravanack, John Wells	—

Mulcahy and Varley, representing New York's Atalanta Boat Club, won by two lengths.

1906–1912 not held

1920 Antwerp-Vilvoorde T: 5, N: 5, D: 8.29.

1. USA	John Kelly, Sr., Paul Costello	7:09.0
2. ITA	Erminio Dones, Pietro Annoni	7:19.0
3. FRA	Alfred Pié, Gaston Giran	7:21.0

1924 Paris T: 5, N: 5, D: 7.17.

1. USA	Paul Costello, John Kelly, Sr.	6:34.0
2. FRA	Marc Detton, Jean-Pierre Stock	6:38.0
3. SWI	Rudolf Bosshard, Heinrich Thoma	—
4. BRA	Edmundo Castello Branco, Carlos Castello Branco	

1928 Amsterdam-Sloten T: 10, N: 10, D: 7.17.

1. USA	Paul Costello, Charles McIlvaine	6:41.4
2. CAN	Joseph Wright, Jack Guest	6:51.0
3. AUT	Leo Losert, Viktor Flessl	6:48.8
4. GER	Horst Hoeck, Gerhard Voigt	6:48.2
5. HOL	Henri Cox, Constant Pieterse	6:52.8
6. SWI	Rudolf Bosshard, Maurice Rieder	6:53.4

Costello won his third straight double sculls gold medal with relative ease. He and McIlvaine were never seriously challenged and won the final against Wright and Guest by five lengths.

1932 Los Angeles-Long Beach T: 5, N: 5, D: 8.13.

1. USA	Kenneth Myers, William Garrett Gilmore	7:17.4
2. GER	Herbert Buhtz, Gerhard Boetzelen	7:22.8
3. CAN	Charles Pratt, Noël de Mille	7:27.6
4. ITA	Orfeo Paroli, Mario Moretti	7:49.2

Veteran Olympians Myers and Gilmore were 36 and 37 years old, respectively.

1936 Berlin-Grünau T: 12, N: 12, D: 8.14.

1. GBR	Jack Beresford, Leslie Southwood	7:20.8
2. GER	Willy Kaidel, Joachim Pirsch	7:26.2
3. POL	Roger Verey, Jerzy Ustupski	7:36.2
4. FRA	André Giriat, Robert Jacquet	7:42.3
5. USA	John Houser, William Dugan	7:44.8
6. AUS	William Dixon, Herbert Turner	7:45.1

A few weeks before the Olympics, British coach Eric Phelps, who was also coaching the German scullers, advised Beresford and Southwood to use a lighter boat and to follow the same training regimen he had devised for the Germans. He also warned his countrymen that Kaidel and Pirsch would launch their final sprint at the 1800-meter mark. Beresford and Southwood ordered a new, lighter boat, but the boat disappeared on its way to Berlin. It was finally located in a railway siding in Hamburg and transported to the anxious British pair.

Beresford and Southwood were beaten by Kaidel and Pirsch in the first round, but qualified for the final through *repêchage*. In the first match-up, Southwood observed that the Germans were able to gain a stroke at the start because the starter, Victor de Bisschop of Belgium, could not see around the large megaphone he was using. In the final the Brits employed a bit of gamesmanship themselves. First they deliberately false-started. Then they caused a further delay by taking off their sweaters. Then, instead of waiting for the starter, they watched Kaidel and Pirsch and took off when they did. The Germans led from the start, but the British pair caught them at 1800 meters, rowed neck and neck for 100 meters, and then pulled away to win by two and a half lengths.

The 37-year-old Beresford was competing in his fifth Olympic Games. Each time he won a medal: in 1920 a silver in the single sculls; in 1924 a gold in the same event; in 1928 a silver in the eights; in 1932 a gold in the coxswainless fours; and finally, in 1936, this third gold, in the double sculls. Considering that he and Southwood won the Double Sculls Challenge Cup at Henley in 1939, it is quite possible that Beresford would have won a sixth medal had not World War II intervened. His father, Julius, won a silver medal in the coxed fours in 1912.

1948 London-Henley-on-Thames T: 15, N: 15, D: 8.9.

1. GBR	Richard Burnell, Bertie Bushnell	6:51.3
2. DEN	Ebbe Parsner, Aage Larsen	6.55.3
3. URU	Juan Rodríguez Iglesias	7:12.4

Bushnell and Burnell were competing on their home course at Henley. Burnell's father, Charles, won a gold medal in the eights race in 1908, also at Henley. Richard Burnell was a rowing correspondent for *The Times* of London and *The Sunday Times* for 44 years.

1952 Helsinki T: 16, N: 16, D: 7.23.

1. ARG	Tranquilo Cappozzo, Eduardo Guerrero	7:32.2
2. SOV/UKR	Heorhi Zhylin, Ihor Yemchuk	7:38.3
3. URU	Miguel Seijas Cuestas, Juan Rodríguez Iglesias	7:43.7
4. FRA	Jacques Maillet, Achille Giovannoni	7:46.8
5. CZE	Antonín Malinković, Jiří Vykoukal	7:53.8

6. AUS: John Rogers, Murray Riley, BEL: Robert George, Joseph Van Stichel, ITA: Silvio Bergamini, Lodovico Sommaruga

1956 Melbourne-Ballarat T: 8, N: 8, D: 11.27.

1. SOV/RUS	Aleksandr Berkutov, Yuri Tyukalov	7:24.0
2. USA	Bernard Paul Costello, James Gardiner	7:32.2
3. AUS	Murray Riley, Mervyn Wood	7:37.4
4. GER	Thomas Schneider, Kurt Hipper	7:41.7

It is hard to imagine an Olympic pair with a more dubious post-Olympic career than bronze medal winners and fellow police officers Mervyn Wood and Murray Riley. Wood rose to the position of New South Wales police commissioner in 1977. In 1989 he was charged with two counts of "perverting the course of justice." The charges were eventually dropped, but Wood's reputation was sufficiently controversial that in 2000 he was one of only a handful of Australian Olympians who was not invited to carry the Olympic torch. Another one was Wood's 1956 double sculls partner, Murray Riley. One of Sydney's most notorious criminals, beginning in 1966 he was convicted of various charges of fraud, counterfeiting and drug-related offenses. The Sydney Olympics found him in prison in England.

1960 Rome-Lake Albano T: 16, N: 16, D: 9.3.

1. CZE	Václav Kozák, Pavel Schmidt	6:47.50
2. SOV/RUS	Aleksandr Berkutov, Yuri Tyukalov	6:50.49
3. SWI	Ernst Hürlimann, Rolf Larcher	6:50.59
4. FRA	René Duhamel, Bernard Monnereau	6:52.22
5. HOL	Peter Bakker, Jacobus Rentmeester	6:53.86
6. BEL	Gérard Higny, Jean Lemaire	6:56:40

Václav Kozák was a 23-year-old noncommissioned officer. His partner was 30-year-old Pavel Schmidt, a psychiatrist from Bratislava.

1964 Tokyo T: 13, N: 13, D: 10.15.

1. SOV/RUS	Oleg Tyurin, Boris Dubrovsky	7:10.66
2. USA	Seymour Cromwell, James Storm	7:13.16
3. CZE	Vladimír Andrs, Pavel Hofmann	7:14.23
4. SWI	Melchior Bürgin, Martin Studach	7:24.97
5. GER	Helmut Lebert, Josef Steffes-Mies	7:30.03
6. FRA	René Duhamel, Bernard Monnereau	7:41.80
7. GBR	Arnold Cook, Peter Webb	
8. HOL	Max Alwin, Peter Bots	

1968 Mexico City-Xochimilco T: 13, N: 13, D: 10.19.

1. SOV/RUS	Anatoly Sass, Aleksandr Timoshinin	6:51.82
2. HOL	Leendert van Dis, Henricus Droog	6:52.80
3. USA	William Maher, John Nunn	6:54.21
4. BUL	Atanas Schelev, Yordan Valtschev	6:58.48
5. GDR	Hans-Ulrich Schmied, Manfred Haake	7:04.92
6. GER	Wolfgang Glock, Udo Hild	7:12.20
7. BRA	Harri Klein, Edgard Gijsen	
8. ROM	Alexandru Aposteanu, Octavian Pavelescu	

1972 Munich-Oberschleissheim T: 18, N: 18, D: 9.2.

1. SOV/RUS	Aleksandr Timoshinin, Gennady Korshikov	7:01.77
2. NOR	Frank Hansen, Svein Thögersen	7:02.58
3. GDR	Joachim Böhmer, Hans-Ulrich Schmied	7:05.55
4. DEN	Niels Secher, Jörgen Engelbrecht	7:14.19
5. GBR	Timothy Crooks, Patrick Delafield	7:16.29
6. CZE	Josef Straka, Jr., Vladek Lacina	7:17.60
7. HOL	Jan Bruyn, Paul Veenemans	
8. SWI	Hans Ruckstuhl, Ulrich Isler	

Timoshinin and Korshikov took the lead shortly before the halfway mark and held on to win in the closest double sculls finish in Olympic history.

1976 Montreal T: 13, N: 13, D: 7.25.

1. NOR	Frank Hansen, Alf Hansen	7:13.20
2. GBR	Christopher Baillieu, Michael Hart	7:15.26
3. GDR	Hans-Ulrich Schmied, Jürgen Bertow	7:17.45
4. SOV/RUS	Yevgeny Barbakov, Gennady Korshikov	7:18.87
5. GER	Peter Becker, Gerhard Kroschewski	7:22.15
6. FRA	Jean-Noël Ribot, Jean-Michel Izart	7:50.18
7. ITA	Umberto Ragazzi, Silvio Ferrini	
8. USA	William Belden, Lawrence Klecatsky	

Two years after Frank Hansen won the silver medal in the double sculls at the Munich Olympics, he asked his younger brother, Alf, to become his new partner. Together they took first place at the 1975 world championships and then went on to win the Olympics the following year. Frank, 30, was an electrician; Alf, 28, worked for the telephone company.

1980 Moscow T: 9, N: 9, D: 7.27.

1. GDR	Joachim Dreifke, Klaus Kröppelien	6:24.33
2. YUG/SER	Zoran Pančić, Milorad Stanulov	6:26.34
3. CZE	Žděněk Pecka, Václav Vochoska	6:29.07
4. GBR	R. James Clark, Christopher Baillieu	6:31.13
5. SOV	Aleksandr Fomchenko, Yevgeny Duleyev	6:35.34
6. POL	Wiesław Kujda, Piotr Tobolski	6:39.66
7. SPA	Ramón Oyarzábal, José Luis Corta Elizondo	
8. FRA	Marc Boudoux, Didier Gallet	

1984 Los Angeles-Lake Casitas T: 11, N: 11, D: 8.5.

1. USA	Bradley Lewis, Paul Enquist	6:36,87
2. BEL	Pierre-Marie Deloof, Dirk Crois	6:38.19
3. YUG/SER	Zoran Pančić, Milorad Stanulov	6:39.59
4. GER	Andreas Schmelz, Georg Agrikola	6:40.41
5. ITA	Francesco Esposito, Ruggero Verroca	6:44.29
6. CAN	Tim Storm, Peter MacGowan	6:46.68
7. AUT	Wilfried Auerbach, Thomas Linemayr	
8. FIN	Reina Karppinen, Aarne Lindroos	

Starting in last place, Lewis and Enquist passed Deloof and Crois 300 meters from the finish and pulled away for a clear victory. The story of their victory is vividly told in Lewis' memoir *Assault on Lake Casitas.*

1988 Seoul C: 17, N: 17, D: 9.24.

1. HOL	Ronald Florijn, Nicolaas Rienks	6:21.13
2. SWI	Beat Schwerzmann, Ueli Bodenmann	6:22.59
3. SOV	Oleksander Marchenko, Vassily Yakusha	6:22.87
4. GER	Christian Händle, Ralf Thienel	6:24.97
5. GDR	Uwe Mund, Uwe Heppner	6:26.20
6. DEN	Per Rasmussen, Bjarne Eltang	6:26.98
7. SPA	José Manuel Bermúdez García, Manuel Vera Vásquez	
8. BUL	Vasil Radev, Daniel Yordanov	

Florijn and Rienks fashioned a startling upset by rowing a powerful middle 1000 meters and then holding off the equally surprising Swiss. Rienks competed in every Olympics between 1984 and 2000, adding a bronze in the 1992 double sculls and a gold in the 1996 eights.

1992 Barcelona-Banyoles C: 19, N: 19, D: 8.1.

1. AUS	Stephen Hawkins, Peter Antonie	6:17.32
2. AUT	Arnold Jonke, Christoph Zerbst	6:18.42
3. HOL	Henk-Jan Zwolle, Nicolaas Rienks	6:22.82
4. EST	Priit Tasane, Roman Lutochkin	6:23.34
5. POL	Andrzej Marszałek, Andrzej Krzepiński	6:24.32
6. SPA	Miguel Álvarez Villar, José Merín Hierro	6:26.96
7. CAN	Donald Dickison, Todd Hallert	
8. GER	Jens Köppen, Christian Händle	

Antonie and Hawkins were by far the lightest pair in the competition, and Hawkins, at 75 kg (165 lbs) was the lightest of all. They took the lead from the Dutch in the second quarter of the final and fought off a late challenge from the Austrians to earn a surprise victory.

1996 Atlanta-Lake Lanier T: 19, N: 19, D: 7.27. WB: 6:06.14 (Henk-Jan Zwolle, Nicolaas Rienks)

1. ITA	Davide Tizzano, Agostino Abbagnale	6:16.98
2. NOR	Kjetil Undset, Steffen Skår Størseth	6:18.42
3. FRA	Frédéric Kowal, Samuël Barathay	6:19.85
4. DEN	Lars Christensen, Martin Haldbo Hansen	6:24.77
5. AUT	Arnold Jonke, Christoph Zerbst	6:25.17
6. GER	Sebastian Mayer, Roland Opfer	6:29.32
7. CAN	Michael Forgeron, Todd Hallett	
8. AUS	Peter Antonie, Jason Day	

Tizzano and Abbagnale led from start to finish. At the 1988 Olympics they had been members of the winning quadruple sculls team.

2000 Sydney-Penrith Lakes T: 16, N: 16, D: 9.23. WB: 6:04.37 (Luka Špik, Iztok ˇCop)

1. SLO	Luka Špik, Iztok Čop	6:16.63
2. NOR	Olaf Tufte, Fredrik Bekken	6:17.98
3. ITA	Giovanni Calabrese, Nicola Sartori	6:20.49
4. GER	Sebastian Mayer, Stefan Röhnert	6:23.58
5. HUN	Tibor Pető, Ákos Haller	6:27.04
6. POL	Adam Korol, Marek Kolbowicz	6:32.11
7. FRA	Frédéric Kowal, Adrien Hardy	
8. USA	Henry Nuzum, Mike Ferry	

As a single sculler, Iztok Čop finished fourth at the 1996 Olympics, fourth at the 1997 world championships and fourth at the 1998 world championships. Exasperated, he switched to double sculls. After only four weeks of training together, Čop and Luka Špik easily won the 1999 world championship. At the Olympics, they led from start to finish.

2004 Athens-Schinias T: 14, N: 14, D: 8.21. WB: 6:04.37 (Luka Špik, Iztok Čop)

1. FRA	Sébastien Vieilledent, Adrien Hardy	6:29.00
2. SLO	Luka Špik, Iztok Čop	6:31.72
3. ITA	Rossano Galtarossa, Alessio Sartori	6:32.93
4. EST	Leonid Gulov, Tõnu Endrekson	6:35.30
5. CZE	Milan Doleček, Ondrej Synek	6:35.81
6. USA	Aquil Abdullah, Henry Nuzum	6:36.86
7. NOR	Nils-Torolv "Nito" Simonsen, Morten Adamsen	
8. GBR	Matthew Wells, Matthew Langridge	

The clear favorites in the event were defending gold medalists Luka Špik and Iztok Čop, reigning world champions Sébastien Vieilledent and Adrien Hardy, and world champion silver medalists Rossano Galtarossa and Alessio Sartori. Galtarossa and Sartori recorded the fastest time in both the qualifying round and the semi-finals. They captured an early lead in the final, opening a gap of 1.7 seconds in front of Vieilledent and Hardy. The French pair pulled ahead in the final 500 meters and achieved the largest double sculls margin of victory in 44 years.

2008 Beijing T: 14, N: 14, D: 8.16. WB: 6:03.25 (Jean-Baptiste Macquet, Adrien Hardy)

1. AUS	David Crawshay, Scott Brennan	6:27.77
2. EST	Tõnu Endrekson, Jüri Jaanson	6:29.05
3. GBR	Matthew Wells, Stephen Rowbotham	6:29.10
4. NZL	Robert Waddell, Nathan Cohen	6:30.79
5. FRA	Jean-Baptiste Macquet, Adrien Hardy	6:33.36
6. SLO	Luka Špik, Iztok Čop	6:33.96
7. BLR	Denis Migal, Stanislav Shcherbachenya	
8. BEL	Bart Poelvoorde, Christophe Raes	

The gold medal was expected to be a toss-up between Luka Špik and Iztok Čop, the 2005 and 2007 world champions, and 2006 world champions Jean-Baptiste Macquet and Adrien Hardy, (the latter also being defending Olympic champion).

As it turned out, the final was dominated by Australians David Crawshay and Scott Brennan, neither of whom had ever placed higher than sixth in a world championship final. In Beijing they led throughout the race and won by more than a second. Brennan had been a member of the Australian quadruple sculls crew that finished seventh in Athens, and after that disappointing finish he wrote a letter to himself that said, "In four years time I don't just want to win, I want to wipe the floor." His coach kept the letter for four years, giving it to him just before the final. "I honestly can't believe it just happened," an emotional Brennan said after the race, "It's all a blur, a very exhausting blur."

The men's double sculls also featured the first-ever Olympic rowing team from Iraq, Hamzah Jebur and Haidar Nozad. The pair had trained on the Tigris river in Baghdad, facing suicide bombers, gunshots and bodies dumped in the water. The pair finished last in each of their races but remained upbeat. "It is great for rowing, even just to participate," Jebur said in an interview, "I will never be upset."

QUADRUPLE SCULLS

1896–1972 not held

1976 Montreal T: 11, N: 11, D: 7.25.

1. GDR	Wolfgang Güldenpfennig, Rüdiger Reiche, Karl-Heinz Bussert, Michael Wolfgramm	6:18.65
2. SOV	Yevgeny Duleyev, Yuri Yakomov, Aivars Lazdenieks, Vytautas Butkus	6:19.89
3. CZE	Jaroslav Helebrand, Václav Vochoska, Žderněk Pecka, Vladek Lacina	6:21.77
4. GER	Norbert Kothe, Helmut Krause, Michael Gentsch, Helmut Wolber	6:24.81
5. BUL	Yordan Vulchev, Mincho Nikolov, Hristo Zhelov, Eftim Gerzilov	6:32.04
6. USA	Peter Cortes, Kenneth Foote, Neil Halleen, John van Blom	6:34.33
7. FRA	Roland Weill, Roland Thibaut, Patrick Monrineau, Charles Imbert	
8. SWI	Hans Ruckstuhl, Denis Oswald, Jürg Weitnauer, Reto Wyss	

Martin Winter of the East German team had to undergo an emergency appendectomy and was replaced at the last minute by Bussert. The sudden change caused the team some problems in the opening round, and they lost to the USSR. But by the final they were all straightened out and won a hard-fought race. Winter finally won his gold medal in 1980.

1980 Moscow T: 12, N: 12, D: 7.27.

1. GDR	Frank Dundr, Karsten Bunk, Uwe Heppner, Martin Winter	5:49.81
2. SOV	Yuri Shapochka, Yevgeny Barbakov, Valery Kleshnev, Mykola Dovhan	5:51.47
3. BUL	Mincho Nikolov, Lubomir Petrov, Ivo Roussev, Bogdan Dobrev	5:52.38
4. FRA	Christian Marquis, Jean Raymond Peltier, Charles Imbert, Roland Weill	5:53.45
5. SPA	Joan Solano Bustamante, Jesús González Guisande, Manuel Vera Vásquez, Julio Oliver Cañadas, Julio Oliver	6:01.19
6. YUG	Milan Arezina, Darko Zibar, Dragan Obradovič, Nikola Stefanovič	6:10.76
7. POL	Andrzej Skowroński, Zbigniew Andruszkiewicz, Ryszard Burak, Stanisław Wierzbicki	
8. HOL	Victor Scheffers, Jeroen Vervoort, Robert Robbers, Ronald Vervoort	

1984 Los Angeles-Lake Casitas T: 10, N: 10, D: 8.5.

1. GER	Albert Hedderich, Raimund Hörmann, Dieter Wiedenmann, Michael Dürsch	5:57.55
2. AUS	Paul Reedy, Gary Gullock, Timothy McLaren, Anthony Lovrich	5:57.98
3. CAN	Douglas Hamilton, Michael Hughes, J. Philip Monckton, Bruce Ford	5:59.07
4. ITA	Piero Poli, Renato Gaeta, Antonio Dell'Aquila, Stefano Lari	6:00.94
5. FRA	Marc Boudoux, Serge Fornara, Pascal Body, Pascal Dubosquelle	6:01.35
6. SPA	Luis Miguel Oliver Cañadas, Jesús González Guisande, Manuel Vera Vásquez, Julio Oliver Cañadas	6:04.99
7. USA	Curtis Fleming, Gregg Montesi, Ridgely Johnson, Bruce Beall	
8. NOR	Pål Sandli, Espen Thorsen, Vetle Vinje, Ivan Enstad	

Six weeks before the 1980 Olympics, the West German crew, prevented by the anti-Soviet boycott from taking part in the Games themselves, defeated the East German crew that went on to win in Moscow. The West Germans, a pipefitter, a butcher, a bank clerk and a machinist, stayed together for four more years and, in Los Angeles in 1984, staged a furious come-from-behind sprint to defeat the Australians in a photo-finish.

1988 Seoul T: 13, N: 13, D: 9.25.

1. ITA	Piero Poli, Gianluca Farina, Davide Tizzano, Agostino Abbagnale	5:53.37
2. NOR	Lars Bjønness, Vetle Vinje, Rolf Bernt Thorsen, Alf Hansen	5:55.08
3. GDR	Steffen Bogs, Steffen Zühlke, Heiko Habermann, Jens Köppen	5:56.13
4. SOV	Pavlo Krupko, Oleksander Zaskalko, Sergei Kiniakin, Yuri Zelikovich	5:57.18
5. AUS	Richard Powell, Brenton Terrell, Paul Reedy, Peter Antonie	5:59.15
6. GER	Christoph Galandi, Oliver Grüner, Georg Agrikola, Andreas Reinke	5:59.59
7. POL	Sławomir Cieślakowski, Andrzej Krzepiński, Mirosław Mruk, Tomasz Świątek	
8. HOL	Robbert Bakker, Hans Kelderman, Juergen Nelis, Hermanus Van der Eerenbeemt	

Alf Hansen, the Norwegian stroke, had won gold in the double sculls in 1976. He added a silver in the quadruple twelve years later at age 40. During the celebration by the Italians, team member Davide Tizzano was thrown into the water and lost his gold medal in the muddy bottom of the Han River. A Korean diver, working as a security guard at the regatta course, retrieved it after a 50-minute search.

1992 Barcelona-Banyoles T: 15, N: 15, D: 8.2.

1. GER	André Willms, Andreas Hajek, Stephan Volkert, Michael Steinbach	5:45.17
2. NOR	Lars Bjønness, Rolt Bernt Thorsen, Kjetil Undset, Per Albert Saetersdal	5:47.09
3. ITA	Gianluca Farina, Rossano Galtarossa, Alessandro Corona, Filippo Soffici	5:47.33
4. SWI	Ueli Bodenmann, Alexander Ruckstuhl, Beat Schwerzmann, Marc-Sven Nater	5:47.39
5. HOL	Hans Kelderman, Ronald Florijn, Koos Maasdijk, Rutger Arisz	5:48.92
6. FRA	Fiorenzo Di Giovanni, Fabrice LeClerc, Yves Lamarque, Samuel Barathay	5:54.80
7. SOV	Valery Dosenko, Sergei Kinyakin, Nikolai Chuprina, Girts Vilks	
8. USA	Kier Pearson, John Riley, Robert Kaehler, John "Chip" McKibben	

The Germans gained a decisive victory, but it was the Norwegians who won the admiration of the spectators by using a wooden boat and wooden oars while everyone else used molded glass fiber reinforced with carbon fiber and bonded with epoxy resin.

1996 Atlanta-Lake Lanier T: 14, N: 14, D: 7.28. WB: 5:37.68 (ITA—Paradiso, Sartori, Galtarossa, Corona)

1. GER	André Steiner, Andreas Hajek, Stephan Volkert, André Willms	5:56.93
2. USA	Tim Young, Brian Jamieson, Eric Mueller, Jason Gailes	5:59.10
3. AUS	Janusz Hooker, Duncan Free, Ronald Snook, Boden Hanson	6:01.65
4. ITA	Massimo Paradiso, Alessio Sartori, Rossano Galtarossa, Alessandro Corona	6:02.12
5. SWI	Rene Benguerel, Michael Erdlen, Ueli Bodenmann, Simon Stürm	6:04.52
6. SWE	Johan Flodin, Pontus Ek, Fredrik Hultén, Henrik Nilsson	6:07.75
7. UKR	Oleksandr Marchenko, Oleksandr Zaskalo, Mykola Chupryna, Leonid Shaposhnikov	
8. RUS	Igor Kravtsov, Nikolai Spinev, Georgy Nikitin, Vladimir Sokolov	

With three of four members returning from the victorious 1992 squad, the Germans built a lead of 3.79 after 1500 meters and held on to defend their title. The big surprise was the Italians, who had won the last two world championships, but finished out of the medals at the Olympics.

2000 Sydney-Penrith Lakes T: 13, N: 13, D: 9.24. WB: 5:37.68 (ITA—Paradiso, Sartori, Galtarossa, Corona)

1. ITA	Agostino Abbagnale, Alessio Sartori, Rossano Galtarossa, Simone Raineri	5:45.56
2. HOL	Jochem Verbernem, Dirk Lippits, Diederik Simon, Michiel Bartman	5:47.91
3. GER	Marco Geisler, Andreas Hajek, Stephan Volkert, André Willms	5:48.64
4. AUS	Peter Hardcastle, Jason Day, Stuart Reside, Duncan Free	5:50.32
5. SWI	Simon Stürm, Christian Stofer, Michael Erdlen, André Vonarburg	5:54.88
6. UKR	Oleksandr Marchenko, Oleh Lykov, Oleksandr Zaskal'ko, Leonid Shaposhnikov	5:55.12
7. USA	M. Sean Hall, Nicholaas Peterson, Ian McGowan, Jake Wetzel	
8. POL	Karol Lazar, Sławomir Kruszkowski, Adam Bronikowski, Michał Wojciechowski	

The German crew led at the halfway mark, but faded, leaving the Italians with a clear lead over the Dutch, which they held to the finish. Agostino Abbagnale won his third career gold medal.

2004 Athens-Schinias T: 13, N: 13, D: 8.22. WB: 5:37.68 (Paradiso, Sartori, Galtarossi, Corona)

1.	RUS	Sergei Fyodorovtsev, Igor Kravtsov, Aleksei Svirin, Nikolai Spinev	5:56.85
2.	CZE	David Kopřiva, Tomáš Karas, Jakub Hanák, David Jirka	5:57.43
3.	UKR	Serhiy Hrin, Serhiy Bilushchenko, Oleh Lykov, Leonid Shaposhnikov	5:58.87
4.	POL	Adam Bronikowski, Marek Kolbowicz, Sławomir Kruszkowski, Adam Korol	5:58.94
5.	GER	André Willms, Stephan Volkert, Marco Geisler, Robert Sens	6:07.04
6.	BLR	Valery Radzevich, Stanislav Shcharbachenia, Pavel Shurmei, Andrey Plyashkov	6:09.33
7.	AUS	Scott Brennan, David Crawshay, Duncan Free, Shaun Coulton	
8.	SWI	Simon Stürm, Christian Stofer, Olivier Gremaud, Florian Stofer	

Germany seemed the obvious favorites, having won the last three world championships. In fact, the same crew of four that was competing in the Olympics had won the most recent world championship by more than three seconds. They got off to a quick start in the final, but were soon passed by the Czechs and the Russians, with Ukraine closing the gap in fourth place. By the halfway point, Germany had slipped out of medal position. The Russians began to pull ahead in the last 500 meters, opening a lead of half a boat length and holding off a last-minute attack by the Czechs to take the gold.

2008 Beijing T: 13, N: 13, D: 8.17. WR: 5:37.31 (POL–Wasielewski, Kolbowicz, Jeliński, Korol)

1.	POL	Konrad Wasielewski, Marek Kolbowicz, Michal Jeliński, Adam Korol	5:41.33
2.	ITA	Luca Agamennoni, Simone Venier, Rossano Galtarossa, Simone Raineri	5:43.57
3.	FRA	Jonathan Coeffic, Pierre-Jean Peltier, Julien Bahain, Cédric Berrest	5:44.34
4.	AUS	Chris Morgan, James McRae, Brendan Long, Daniel Noonan	5:44.68
5.	USA	Matt Hughes, Sam Stitt, Jamie Schroeder, Scott Gault	5:47.64
6.	GER	Stephan Krüger, René Bertram, Hans Gruhne, Christian Schreiber	5:50.96
7.	RUS	Nikita Morgachev, Sergey Fyodorovtsev, Igor Salov, Nikolay Spinev	
8.	UKR	Serhiy Hryn, Volodymyr Pavlovskiy, Oleh Lykov, Serhiy Biloushchenko	

The four members of the Polish team had won the past three world championship titles. As expected, they had little difficulty in the final, taking the lead from the start and easily holding off Italy. France finished strongly at the end to edge out Australia for the bronze.

PAIR-OARED SHELL WITHOUT COXSWAIN

1896–1900 not held

1904 St. Louis T: 3, N: 1, D: 7.30.

1.	USA	Robert Farnam, Joseph Ryan	10:57.0
2.	USA	John Mulcahy, William Varley	—
3.	USA	John Joachim, Joseph Buerger	—

Farnam and Ryan, representing the Seawanhaka Boat Club of Brooklyn, New York, won by about four lengths.

1906 not held

1908 London-Henley-on-Thames T: 4, N: 3, D: 7.31.

1.	GBR	Reginald Fenning, Gordon Thomson	9:41.0
2.	GBR	George Fairbairn, Philip Verdon	—
3.	CAN	Frederick Toms, Norwey Jackes	
3.	GER	Martin Stahnke, Willy Düskow	

Fenning and Thomson won by two and a half lengths. Both finalists represented the Leander Club.

1912–1920 not held

1924 Paris T: 3, N: 3, D: 7.17.

1.	HOL	Anthonie Beijnen, Wilhelm Rösingh	8:19.4
2.	FRA	Maurice Bouton, Georges Piot	8:21.6

DNS: GBR: Gordon Killick, Charles Southgate

Twenty years after his Olympic triumph, Anthonie Beijnen played an unusual role in the Dutch resistance to the Nazis. A wealthy man, he allowed his home in Beusichem to be used by the German Wehrmacht, while secretly hiding British soldiers in his attic and helping them escape. Beijnen also listened in on the conversations of the German officers and passed on the information to the Allies.

1928 Amsterdam-Sloten T: 8, N: 8, D: 8.10.

1.	GER	Bruno Müller, Kurt Moschter	7:06.4
2.	GBR	Terence O'Brien, Robert Archibald Nisbet	7:08.6
3.	USA	Paul McDowell, John Schmitt	7:20.4
4.	ITA	Romeo Sisti, Nino Bolzoni	7:24.4
5.	SWI	Alois Reinhard, Wilhelm Müller	7:29.1
6.	HOL	Carel van Wankum, Hendrik van Suylekom	7:30.2

1932 Los Angeles-Long Beach T: 6, N: 6, D: 8.13.

1.	GBR	Hugh Edwards, Lewis Clive	8:00.0
2.	NZL	Cyril Stiles, Frederick Thompson	8:02.4
3.	POL	Henryk Budziński, Janusz Mikołajczak	8:08.2
4.	HOL	Godfried Röel, Pieter Roelofsen	8:08.4
5.	FRA	Fernand Vandernotte, Marcel Vandernotte	

Hugh "Jumbo" Edwards won two gold medals in one day, following up his victory in the coxless pairs with another in the coxless fours. During World War II Edwards used his rowing ability to save his life. While serving as a squadron leader with the Royal Air Force's Coastal Command in 1943, he was forced to ditch his plane in the Atlantic Ocean. He rowed a dinghy four miles through a minefield to safety. He was the only member of the plane's crew to survive. Edwards' Olympic partner, Lewis Clive, was killed in the Spanish Civil War on August 2, 1938, at the age of 27.

1936 Berlin-Grünau T: 13, N: 13, D: 8.14.

1. GER	Willi Eichhorn, Hugo Strauss	8:16.1
2. DEN	Richard Olsen, Harry Larsen	8:19.2
3. ARG	Horacio Podestá, Julio Curatella	8:23.0
4. HUN	Károly Győry, Tibor Mamusich	8:25.7
5. SWI	Wilhelm Klopfer, Karl Müller	8:33.0
6. POL	Ryszard Borzuchowski, Edward Kobyliński	8:41.9

1948 London-Henley-on-Thames T: 12, N: 12, D: 8.6.

1. GBR	W. Ranald "Ran" Laurie	7:21.1
2. SWI	Hans Kalt, Josef Kalt	7:23.9
3. ITA	Felice Fanetti, Bruno Boni	7:31.5

Jack Wilson and Ran Laurie were best friends who joined the Colonial Service and were sent to the Sudan. Returning to London on leave in 1938, they entered the Henley Regatta and took first place. Then they went back to the Sudan and didn't touch an oar for ten years. In May 1948 they returned to Britain on another leave and decided to take up rowing again. After six weeks' training they entered the Henley Regatta and won again. This gained them an invitation to represent Great Britain at the Olympics, and they were granted six months' leave to prepare. Rowing on their favorite course at Henley, "the Desert Rats," as they were known, took the lead after 1150 meters and fought off a late challenge from the Kalt brothers to secure the gold medal. Laurie was the father of Hugh Laurie, the actor and comedian best known for playing the title role in the hospital drama series *House.*

1952 Helsinki T: 16, N: 16, D: 7.23.

1. USA	Charles Logg, Thomas Price	8:20.7
2. BEL	Michel Knuysen, Robert Baetens	8:23.5
3. SWI	Kurt Schmid, Hans Kalt	8:32.7
4. GBR	David Callender, Christopher Davidge	8:37.4
5. FRA	Jean-Pierre Souche, René Guissart	8:48.8

Logg and Price, of Rutgers University, were the Cinderella pair of 1952. Neither man had sat in a pair-oared shell until two months before the Olympics, and the 19-year-old Price had only started rowing in January.

1956 Melbourne-Ballarat T: 9, N: 9, D: 11.27.

1. USA	James Fifer, Duvall Hecht	7:55.4
2. SOV/RUS	Igor Buldakov, Viktor Ivanov	8:03.9
3. AUT	Alfred Sageder, Josef Kloimstein	8:11.8
4. AUS	Peter Adrian Raper, Maurice Grace	8:22.2

Eighteen-year-old Viktor Ivanov was so thrilled when he was presented with his silver medal that he jumped up and down with joy—and dropped the medal into Lake Wendouree. He immediately dived to the bottom of the water, but came back up empty-handed. After the Games were over he was given a replacement medal by the IOC.

Duvall Hecht had been a Marine combat pilot during the Korean War. In 1976, Hecht, then a marketing director for a securities firm in Southern California, launched a business that would turn into a new industry: Books on Tape. Hecht was the first to hire professional actors to record unabridged books and rent the tapes by mail order.

1960 Rome-Lake Albano T: 18, N: 18, D: 9.3.

1. SOV/RUS	Valentin Boreyko, Oleg Golovanov	7:02.01
2. AUT	Alfred Sageder, Josef Kloimstein	7:03.69
3. FIN	Veli Lehtelä, Toimi Pitkänen	7:03.80
4. GDR	Jochen Neuling, Heinz Weigel	7:08.81
5. USA	Ted Frost, Robert Rogers	7:17.08
6. YUG/SER	Nikola Čupin, Antun Ivanković	7:20.91

1964 Tokyo T: 14, N: 14, D: 10.15.

1. CAN	George Hungerford, Roger Jackson	7:32.94
2. HOL	Steven Blaisse, Ernst Venemans	7:33.40
3. GER	Michael Schwan, Wolfgang Hottenrott	7:38.63
4. GBR	James Lee Nicholson, Stewart Farquharson	7:42.00
5. DEN	Peter Fich Christiansen, Hans Jørgen Boye	7:48.13
6. FIN	Toimi Pitkänen, Veli Lehtelä	8:05.74
7. SWI	Peter Bolligen, Nicolas Gobet	
8. POL	Czesław Nawrot, Alfons Ślusarski	

Sent to Tokyo as reserves for the Canadian eights team, Hungerford and Jackson were allowed to enter the coxless pairs as compensation. Given only six weeks to get used to each other, they had their first race together ever in the opening round of the Olympics. To compound their problems, Hungerford had not yet recovered from an attack of mononucleosis. In the final they stroked to a one-and-a-half-length lead at the 1500-meter mark and hung on desperately to win Canada's only victory of the 1964 Olympics. Hungerford and Jackson were considered such long shots that no Canadian journalists were present for their race. The two young men celebrated their victory by drinking seven Cokes each. The shell that they used had been loaned to them by the University of Washington; it was the same shell that had been used by Fifer and Hecht when they won the gold medal in 1956.

1968 Mexico City-Xochimilco T: 18, N: 18, D: 10.19.

1. GDR	Jörg Lucke, Hans-Jürgen Bothe	7:26.56
2. USA	Lawrence Hough, Philip "Tony" Johnson	7:26.71
3. DEN	Peter Fich Christiansen, Ib Ivan Larsen	7:31.84
4. AUT	Dieter Ebner, Dieter Losert	7:41.80
5. SWI	Fred Rüssli, Werner Zwimpfer	7:46.79
6. HOL	Roelof Luynenburg, Rudolf Stokvis	—
7. AUS	David Ramage, Paul Guest	
8. POL	Alfons Ślusarski, Jerzy Broniec	

An exciting nip-and-tuck battle saw the favored team of Hough and Johnson take the lead with 500 meters to go, only to have Lucke and Bothe pass them in the last ten meters.

1972 Munich-Oberscheissheim T: 20, N: 20, D: 9.2.

1. GDR	Siegfried Brietzke, Wolfgang Mager	6:53.16
2. SWI	Heinrich Fischer, Alfred Bachmann	6:57.06
3. HOL	Roelof Luynenburg, Rudolf Stokvis	6:58.70
4. CZE	Lubomír Zapletal, Petr Lakomý	6:58.77
5. POL	Alfons Ślusarski, Jerzy Broniec	7:02.74
6. ROM	Ilie Oanţă, Dumitru Grumezescu	7:42.90
7. GER	Erwin Haas, Lutz Ulbricht	
8. SOV/RUS	Vladimir Polyakov, Nikolai Vasiliev	

In 1968 a comedian named Heinz Quermann appealed over radio and TV for tall young people in East Germany to register with the rowing section of the Leipzig Sports Club. Among the respondents were two 16-year-olds, Siegfried Brietzke and Wolfgang Mager. When they began to achieve competitive success they became known as the "Quermann pair."

1976 Montreal T: 15, N: 15, D: 7.25.

1. GDR	Jörg Landvoigt, Bernd Landvoigt	7:23.31
2. USA	Calvin Coffey, Michael Staines	7:26.73
3. GER	Peter Vanroye, Thomas Strauss	7:30.03
4. YUG	Žlatko Celent, Duško Mrduljaš	7:34.17
5. BUL	Valentin Stoyev, Georgi Georgiev	7:37.42
6. CZE	Miroslav Knapek, Vojtěch Caska	7:51.06
7. SOV/EST	Gennadi Kinko, Tiit Helmja	
8. FIN	Leo Ahonen, Kari Hanska	

The Landvoigt twins were 25-year-old steelworkers from Potsdam. The US team, besides being the only American rowers to win medals at Montreal, were also noteworthy for their unusual combination of names—Coffey and Staines.

1980 Moscow T: 15, N: 15, D: 7.27.

1. GDR	Bernd Landvoigt, Jörg Landvoigt	6:48.01
2. SOV/RUS	Yuri Pimenov, Nikolai Pimenov	6:50.50
3. GBR	A. Charles Wiggin, Malcolm Carmichael	6:51.47
4. ROM	Constantin Postoiu, Valer Toma	6:53.49
5. CZE	Miroslav Vrastil, Miroslav Knapek	7:01.54
6. SWE	Anders Larson, Anders Wilgotson	7:02.52
7. IRL	Patrick Gannon, William Ryan	
8. FRA	Jean-Claude Roussel, Dominique Lecointe	

The medal ceremony presented a bizarre sight, as the gold-medal-winning Landvoigt twins stood beside the silver-medal-winning Pimenov twins.

1984 Los Angeles-Lake Casitas T: 14, N: 14, D: 8.5.

1. ROM	Petru Iosub, Valer Toma	6:45.39
2. SPA	Fernando Climent Huerta, Luis María Lasúrtegui Berridi	6:48.47
3. NOR	Hans Magnus Grepperud, Sverre Loken	6:51.81
4. GER	Thomas Möllenkamp, Axel Wöstmann	6:52.53
5. ITA	Marco Romano, Pasquale Aiese	6:55.88
6. USA	David De Ruff, John Strotbeck	6:58.46
7. HOL	Sjoerd Hoekstra, Joost Adema	
8. BRA	Ronaldo Carvalho, Ricardo Carvalho	

1988 Seoul T: 18, N: 18, D: 9.24.

1. GBR	Andrew Holmes, Steven Redgrave	6:36.84
2. ROM	Dragoş Neagu, Dănuţ Dobre	6:38.06
3. YUG/SLO	Bojan Prešern, Sadik Mujkič	6:41.01
4. BEL	Alain Lewuillon, Wim Van Belleghem	6:45.47
5. GDR	Carl Ertel, Uwe Gasch	6:48.86
6. SOV/BLR	Igor Zyboronko, Valery Vyrvich	6:51.11
7. GER	Frank Dietrich, Michael Twittmann	
8. FRA	Laurent Lacasa, Alex Perahia	

Holmes and Redgrave had already earned gold medals in the coxed fours in 1984. In Seoul they led from start to finish to win the coxless pairs. Twenty-three hours later they placed third in the coxed pairs.

1992 Barcelona-Banyoles T: 18, N: 18, D: 8.1.

1. GBR	Steven Redgrave, Matthew Pinsent	6:27.72
2. GER	Peter Höltzenbein, Colin von Ettingshausen	6:32.68
3. SLO	Iztok Čop, Denis Žvegelj	6:33.43
4. FRA	Michel Andrieux, Jean-Christophe Rolland	6:36.34
5. BEL	Jaak van Driessche, Luc Goiris	6:38.20
6. USA	Peter Sharis, John Pescatore	6:39.23
7. NOR	Snorre Lorgen, Sverke Lorgen	
8. HOL	Sjors van Iwaarden, Kai Compagner	

Steve Redgrave became only the third British athlete—and the first in 72 years—to earn gold medals in three consecutive Olympics. The other two were water polo players Paul Radmilovic and Charles Smith.

1996 Atlanta-Lake Lanier T: 18, N: 18, D: 7.27. WB: 6:18.37 (Steven Redgrave, Matthew Pinsent)

1. GBR	Steven Redgrave, Matthew Pinsent	6:20.09
2. AUS	David Weightman, Robert Scott	6:21.02
3. FRA	Michel Andrieux, Jean-Christophe Rolland	6:22.15
4. ITA	Marco Penna, Walter Bottega	6:28.61
5. NZL	Toni Dunlop, David Schaper	6:29.24
6. CRO	Marko Banović, Ninoslav Saraga	6:30.48
7. USA	Michael Peterson, Jonathan Holland	
8. BEL	Luc Goiris, Jaak van Driessche	

Redgrave, the school dropout, and Pinsent, graduate of Eton and Oxford, successfully defended their Olympic title in their 100th race together. They built a lead of 2.85 seconds at the halfway mark and won without worry.

2000 Sydney-Penrith Lakes T: 15, N: 15, D: 9.22. WB: 6:18.37 (Steven Redgrave, Matthew Pinsent)

1. FRA	Michel Andrieux, Jean-Christophe Rolland	6:32.97
2. USA	Ted Murphy, Sebastian Bea	6:33.80
3. AUS	Matthew Long, James Tomkins	6:34.26
4. GBR	Edward Coode, Gregory Searle	6:34.38
5. YUG	Đorđe Višacki, Nikola Stojić	6:38.70
6. SAF	Ramon di Clemente, Donovan Cech	6:43.10
7. CAN	Phil Graham, Henry Hiering	
8. CRO	Oliver Martinov, Ninoslav Saraga	

Steve Redgrave and Matthew Pinsent, 1996
The British duo won the coxless pairs in 1992 and 1996.

Michel Andrieux and Jean-Christophe Rolland had been rowing together for eleven years except for one year, 1998, which they took off to marry and begin families. Tomkins and Long stormed into the early lead and held on through the halfway mark. With 750 meters to go, Andrieux shouted out the code that signaled the start of their attack: "Victor-Matthias," the names of their infant sons. They swept past the three boats ahead of them and were already in first place at 1500 meters. A late surge by Murphy and Bea earned them surprise silver medals.

2004 Athens-Schinias T: 13, N: 13, D: 8.21. WB: 6:14.27 (Matthew Pinsent, James Cracknell)

1. AUS	Drew Ginn, James Tomkins	6:30.76
2. CRO	Siniša Škelin, Nikša Škelin	6:32.64
3. SAF	Donovan Cech, Ramon di Clemente	6:33.40
4. NZL	Nathan Twaddle, George Bridgewater	6:34.24
5. SER	Nikola Stojić, Mladen Stegić	6:39.74
6. GER	Tobias Kühne, Jan Herzog	6:46.50
7. GBR	Toby Garbett, Richard Dunn	
8. ITA	Giuseppe De Vita, Dario Lari	

Drew Ginn and James Tomkins won the 1999 world championship with ease and looked to be on track for gold medals when the Olympics came to Australia. Unfortunately, a back injury kept Ginn from competing. Paired with a new partner, Matthew Long, Tompkins gained a bronze medal. Back together, Ginn and Tompkins won the 2003 world championship. In the final of the 2004 Olympics, they took the early lead and held on throughout the race, while brothers Siniša and Nikša Škelin held off Donovan Cech and Ramon di Clemente for silver. The three pairs finished in the same order as they did in the final of the 2003 world championships. Tompkins was taking part in his fifth Olympics, having won gold in the coxless fours in 1992 and 1996. Ginn was also a member of Australia's 1996 "Oarsome Foursome."

2008 Beijing T: 14, N: 14, D: 8.16. WR: 6:14.27 (Matthew Pinsent, James Cracknell)

1. AUS	Drew Ginn, Duncan Free	6:37.44
2. CAN	David Calder, Scott Frandsen	6:39.55
3. NZL	Nathan Twaddle, George Bridgewater	6:44.19
4. GER	Tom Lehmann, Felix Drahotta	6:47.40
5. SAF	Shaun Keeling, Ramon di Clemente	6:47.83
6. USA	Tyler Winklevoss, Cameron Winklevoss	7:05.58
7. SER	Goran Jagar, Nikola Stojić	
8. CZE	Jakub Makovička, Václav Chalupa, Jr.	

After winning the Athens gold medal with seven-time world champion James Tomkins, Drew Ginn teamed up with long-time friend Duncan Free in 2006. The two went on to win the world championship that year, beating reigning world champions Nathan Twaddle and George Bridgewater. They successfully defended their title in 2007, again defeating Twaddle and Bridgewater.

Despite being the clear favorites in Beijing the Australian pair almost didn't get to compete together, as in the week leading up to the competition Ginn struggled with a nerve problem in his lower back, which nearly forced him to withdraw. Ginn missed five days of practice, but was well enough to compete. The pair won both their preliminary races by wide margins. In the final, Canadians Dave Calder and Scott Frandsen took a slight lead at the start but were soon passed by the Australian pair, who went on to finish nearly a boat length in front.

Sixth-place finishers Tyler and Cameron Winklevoss are better known for their long-running legal battle with Mark Zuckerberg, creator of the popular social media site Facebook, whom they accused of stealing their idea for the website while classmates at Harvard. Their story was popularized in the 2010 movie *The Social Network*. In 2011, after seven years of lawsuits, the Winklevoss twins agreed to a $65 million settlement.

FOUR-OARED SHELL WITHOUT COXSWAIN

1896–1900 not held

1904 St. Louis T: 3, N: 1, D: 7.30.

1. USA—Century Boat Club, St. Louis: Arthur Stockhoff, August Erker, George Dietz, Albert Nasse	9:05.8
2. USA—Mound City Rowing Club, St. Louis: Frederick Suerig, Martin Fromanack, Charles Aman, Michael Begley	—
3. USA—Western Rowing Club, St. Louis: Gustav Voerg, John Freitag, Louis Helm, Frank Dummerth	—

The Century team won by two lengths.

1906 not held

1908 London-Henley-on-Thames T: 4, N: 3, D: 7.31.

1. GBR/AUS—Magdalen College Boat Club, Oxford: C. Robert Cudmore (AUS), James Gillan, Duncan MacKinnon, Robert Somers-Smith 8:34.0
2. GBR—Leander Club: Philip Filleul, Harold Barker, Reginald Fenning, Gordon Thomson —
3. CAN—Argonauts Rowing Club, Toronto: Gordon Balfour, Becher Gale, Charles Riddy, Geoffrey Taylor
3. HOL—Amstel Amsterdam: Hermanus Höfte, Albertus Wielsma, Johan Burk, Bernardus Croon

Two members of the Magdalen team, Somers-Smith and McKinnon, were killed in action during World War I.

1912–1920 not held

1924 Paris T: 4, N: 4, D: 7.17.

1. GBR—Charles Eley, James Macnabb, Robert Morrison, Terence Sanders 7:08.6
2. CAN—Cohn Finlayson, Archibald Black, George Mackay, William Wood 7:18.0
3. SWI—Emile Albrecht, Alfred Probst, Eugen Sigg-Bächthold, Hans Walter —
4. FRA—Théo Cremnitz, Jean Camuset, Henri Bonzano, Albert Bonzano —

All four members of the British crew attended Eton and Trinity College, Cambridge.

1928 Amsterdam-Sloten T: 6, N: 6, D: 8.10.

1. GBR—John Lander, Michael Warriner, Richard Beesly, Edward Bevan 6:36.0
2. USA—Charles Karle, William Miller, George Heales, Ernest Bayer 6:37.0
3. ITA—Cesare Rossi, Pietro Freschi, Umberto Bonadè, Paolo Gennari 6:37.6
4. GER—Henry Zänker, Wolfgang Goedecke, Günther Roll, Werner Zschieke DNS

The semifinal race between Great Britain and Germany saw a dramatic finish. The Germans led by half a length with 50 meters to go, when Zschieke, their stroke, suddenly collapsed and fell forward on his oar. His teammates stopped rowing and watched the British crew shoot past to victory. In the final, the British team, which was from Trinity College, Cambridge, trailed the US crew for almost the entire race, caught them with 20 yards to go and spurted ahead to a half-length win.

1932 Los Angeles-Long Beach T: 5, N: 5, D: 8.13.

1. GBR—John "Felix" Badcock, Hugh Edwards, Jack Beresford, Rowland George 6:58.2
2. GER—Karl Aletter, Ernst Gaber, Walter Flinsch, Hans Maier 7:03.0
3. ITA—Antonio Ghiardello, Francesco Cossu, Giliante D'Este, Antonio Provenzani 7:04.0
4. USA—John McCosker, George Mattson, Thomas Pierie, Edgar Johnson 7:14.2

1936 Berlin-Grünau T: 9, N: 9, D: 8.14.

1. GER—Rudolf Eckstein, Anton Rom, Martin Karl, Wilhelm Menne 7:01.8
2. GBR—Thomas Bristow, Alan Barrett, Peter Jackson, John Duncan Sturrock 7:06.5
3. SWI—Hermann Betschart, Hans Homberger, Alex Homberger, Karl Schmid 7:10.6
4. ITA—Antonio Ghiardello, Luigi Luscardo, Aldo Pellizzoni, Francesco Pittaluga 7:12.4
5. AUT—Rudolf Höpfler, Camillo Winkler, Wilhelm Pichler, Johann Binder 7:20.5
6. DEN—Knud Olsen, Keld Karise, Bjørner Drøger, Emil Boje Jensen 7:26.3

1948 London-Henley-on-Thames T: 10, N: 10, D: 8.9.

1. ITA—Giuseppe Moioli, Elio Morille, Giovanni Invernizzi, Franco Faggi 6:39.0
2. DEN—Helge Halkjaer, Aksel Bonde Hansen, Helge Schröder, Ib Storm Larsen 6:43.5
3. USA—Frederick John Kingsbury, Stuart Griffing, Gregory Gates, Robert Perew 6:47.7
4. GBR—Peter Kirkpatrick, Hedley Rushmere, Thomas Christie, Anthony Butcher —
5. HOL—Henrik van Suylekom, Sietze Haarsma, Johannes Dekker, Johannes van den Berg —
6. SAF—Edward Ramsay, Anthony Ikin, David Mayberry, Charles Kietzman —

1952 Helsinki T: 17, N: 17, D: 7.23.

1. YUG/CRO—Duje Bonačić, Velimir Valenta, Mate Trojanović, Petar Šegvić 7:16.0
2. FRA—Pierre Blondiaux, Jacques Guissart, Marc Bouissou, Roger Gautier 7:18.9
3. FIN—Veikko Lommi, Kauko Wahlsten, Oiva Lommi, Lauri Nevalainen 7:23.3
4. GBR—Harry Almond, John Jones, James Crowden, George Cadbury 7:25.2
5. POL—Edward Schwarzer, Zbigniew Schwarzer, Henryk Jagodziński, Zbigniew Żarnowiecki 7:28.2

1956 Melbourne-Ballarat T: 12, N: 12, D: 11.27.

1. CAN—Archibald McKinnon, Lorne Loomer, Walter D'Hondt, Donald Arnold 7:08.8
2. USA—John Welchli, John McKinlay, Arthur McKinlay, James McIntosh 7:18.4
3. FRA—René Guissart, Yves Delacour, Gaston Mercier, Guy Guillabert 7:20.9
4. ITA—Giuseppe Moioli, Attilio Cantoni, Giovanni Zucchi, Abbondio Marcelli 7:22.5

The Canadian crew consisted of four small-town boys from the University of British Columbia, three of whom had only been rowing for a year. In the final they were so nervous that they almost missed the water with their first stroke and were left behind. However, they were able to catch up by the halfway mark and pull away to a five-length victory. The four Canadians returned to the Olympics four years later in Rome and won silver medals as part of the eights crew.

1960 Rome-Lake Albano T: 16, N: 16, D: 9.3.

1. USA—Arthur Ayrault, Theodore "Ted" Nash, John Sayre, Richard Wailes 6:26.26
2. ITA—Tullio Baraglia, Renato Bosatta, Giancarlo Crosta, Giuseppe Galante 6:28.78
3. SOV/RUS—Igor Akhremchik, Yuri Bachurov, Valentin Morkoykin, Anatoly Tarabrin 6:29.62
4. CZE—Jindřich Blažek, Miroslav Jiška, René Libal, Jaroslav Starosta 6:34.30
5. GBR—J. Michael Beresford, Christopher Davidge, Colin Porter, John Vigurs 6:36.18
6. SWI—Paul Kölliker, Gottfried Kottmann, Kurt Schmid, Rolt Streuli 6:38.81

1964 Tokyo T: 14, N: 14, D: 10.15.

1. DEN—John Hansen, Björn Haslöv, Erik Petersen, Kurt Helmudt 6:59.30
2. GBR—John Russell, Hugh Arthur Wardell-Yerburgh, William Barry, John James 7:00.47
3. USA—Geoffrey Picard, Richard Lyon, Theodore Mittet, Theodore Nash 7:01.37
4. HOL—Sjoerd Wartena, Jaap Enters, Herman Boelen, Spike Castelein 7:09.98
5. ITA—Romano Sgheiz, Fulvio Balatti, Giovanni Zucchi, Luciano Sgheiz 7:10.05
6. GER—Günter Schrörs, Horst Effertz, Albrecht Müller, Manfred Misselhorn 7:10.33
7. SOV/LIT—Tselestinas Yutsis, Eugenius Levitskas, Ionas Mateyunas, Pavilas Liutkaitis
8. AUT—Dieter Ebner, Horst Kuttelwascher, Dieter Losert, Manfred Kraushar

1968 Mexico City-Xochimilco T: 11, N: 11, D: 10.19.

1. GDR—Frank Forberger, Dieter Grahn, Frank Rüle, Dieter Schubert 6:39.18
2. HUN—Zoltán Melis, György Sarlós, József Csermely, Antal Melis 6:41.64
3. ITA—Renato Bosatta, Tullio Baraglia, Pier Angelo Conti Manzini, Abramo Albini 6:44.01
4. SWI—Roland Altenburger, Nicolas Noël Gobet, Franz Rentsch, Alfred Meister 6:45.78
5. USA—Peter Raymond, Raymond Wright, Charles Hamlin, Lawrence Terry 6:47.70
6. GER—Thomas Hitzbleck, Manfred Weinreich, Volkhart Buchter, Jochen Heck 7:08.22
7. ROM—Pavel Cichi, Dumitru Ivanov, Emanoil Stratan, Anton Chirlacopschi
8. MEX—Roberto Retolaza Romero, Arcadio Padilla Romero, Jesús Toscano Palacios, David Trejo Sánchez

1972 Munich-Oberschleissheim T: 20, N: 20, D: 9.2.

1. GDR—Frank Forberger, Frank Rüle, Dieter Grahn, Dieter Schubert 6:24.27
2. NZL—Dick Tonks, Dudley Storey, Ross Collinge, Noel Mills 6:25.64
3. GER—Joachim Ehrig, Peter Funnekötter, Franz Held, Wolfgang Plottke 6:28.41
4. SOV/RUS—Anatoly Tkachuk, Igor Kashurov, Aleksandr Motin, Vitaly Sapronov 6:31.92
5. ROM—Emeric Tuşa, Adalbert Agh, Mihai Naumencu, Francisc Papp 6:35.60
6. DEN—Willy Poulsen, Peter Fich Christiansen, Egon Peterson, Rolf Andersen 6:37.28
7. GBR—Frederick Smallbone, Leonard Robertson, R. James Clark, William Mason
8. BUL—Biser Boyadzhiev, Borislav Vasilev, Nikolai Kolev, Metodi Halvadzhiiski

Forberger, Rüle, Grahn, and Schubert had been rowing together for 11 years. In winning their second Olympic title, the Dresden four completed six years of unbeaten rowing in which they also won two world championships and two European championships. The lead changed hands six times in their exciting final race with the crew from New Zealand.

1976 Montreal T: 15, N: 15, D: 7.25.

1. GDR—Siegfried Brietzke, Andreas Decker, Stefan Semmler, Wolfgang Mager 6:37.42
2. NOR—Ole Nafstad, Arne Bergodd, Finn Tveter, Rolf Andreassen 6:41.22
3. SOV—Raul Arnemann, Nikolai Kuznetsov, Valery Dolinin, Anushavan Gassan-Dzhalilov 6:42.52
4. NZL—Robert Murphy, Grant McAuley, Desmond Lock, David Lindstrom 6:43.23
5. CAN—Brian Dick, Philip Monckton, Andrew van Ruyven, Ian Gordon 6:46.11
6. GER—Bernhard Foelkel, Klaus Roloff, Wolfgang Horak, Johann Gabriel Konertz 6:47.44
7. BUL—Dimiter Vulov, Dimiter Yanakiev, Todor Mrunkov, Rumen Hristov
8. USA—Anthony Brooks, James Moroney, Gary Piantedosi, Hugh Stevenson

1980 Moscow T: 11, N: 11, D: 7.27.

1. GDR—Jürgen Thiele, Andreas Decker, Stefan Semmler, Siegfried Brietzke 6:08.17
2. SOV/RUS—Aleksei Kamkin, Valery Dolinin, Aleksandr Kulagin, Vitaly Yeliseyev 6:11.81
3. GBR—John Beattie, Ian McNuff, David Townsend, Martin Cross 6:16.58
4. CZE—Vojtěch Caska, Jiři Prudil, Josef Neštický Lubomir Zapletal 6:18.63
5. ROM—Daniel Voiculescu, Carolică Ilieş, Petru Iosub, Nicolae Simion 6:19.45
6. SWI—Jürg Weitnauer, Bruno Saile, Hans-Konrad Trümpler, Stefan Netzle 6:26.46
7. FRA—Jean-Pierre Bremer, Nicolas Lourdaux, Bernard Bruand, Dominique Basset
8. POL—Mirosław Jarzembowski, Mariusz Trzciński, Henryk Trzciński, Marek Niedziałkowski

Siegfried Brietzke became the fourth of eight male rowers to win gold medals in three different Olympics, joining company with Paul Costello, Jack Beresford, and Vyacheslav Ivanov. Their number was joined in 1984 by Pertti Karppinen, in 1992 by Steve Redgrave and in 2000 by Matthew Pinsent and Agostino Abbagnale. In 1980, the East Germans dominated rowing so thoroughly that they won 11 of 14 finals. Every one of their 54 oarsmen and women went home with a medal.

1984 Los Angeles-Lake Casitas T: 10, N: 10, D: 8.5.

1. NZL—Leslie O'Connell, Shane O'Brien, Conrad Robertson, Keith Trask 6:03.48
2. USA—David Clark, Jonathan Smith, Philip Stekl, Alan Forney 6:06.10

3. DEN—Michael Jessen, Lars Nielsen, Per Rasmussen, Erik Christiansen 6:07.72
4. GER—Norbert Kesslau, Volker Grabow, Jörg Puttlitz, Guido Grabow 6:09.27
5. SWI—Bruno Saile, Jürg Weitnauer, Hans-Konrad Trümpler, Stefan Netzle 6:09.50
6. SWE—Anders Wilgotson, Hans Svensson, Lars-Åke Lindqvist, Anders Larson 6:11.71
7. CAN—Timothy Turner, Edward Gibson, David Johnson, Stephen Beatty
8. AUS—David Doyle, James Lowe, Duncan Fisher, John Bentley

1988 Seoul T: 15, N: 15, D: 9.25.

1. GDR—Roland Schröder, Thomas Greiner, Ralf Brudel, Olaf Förster 6:03.11
2. USA—Raoul Rodriguez, Thomas Bohrer, David Krmpotich, Richard Kennelly 6:05.53
3. GER—Norbert Kesslau, Volker Grabow, Jörg Puttlitz, Guido Grabow 6:06.22
4. GBR—Mark Buckingham, Stephen Peel, Simon Berrisford, Peter Mulkerrins 6:06.74
5. ITA—Sergio Caropreso, Carlo Gaddi, Pasquale Marigliano, Valter Molea 6:09.55
6. SOV/RUS—Ivan Vysotsky, Sergei Smirnov, Yuri Pimenov, Nikolai Pimenov 11:03.77
7. NZL—Campbell Clayton-Greene, Geoffrey Cotter, William Coventry, Neil Gibson
8. FRA—Pascal Bahuaud, Dominique Lecointe, Jean-Jacques Martigne, Olivier Pons

The unusual time registered by the Soviet team was a result of one of their seats breaking in the middle of the race.

1992 Barcelona-Banyoles T: 14, N: 14, D: 8.2.

1. AUS—Andrew Cooper, Michael McKay, Nicholas Green, James Tomkins 5:55.04
2. USA—William Burden, Jeffrey McLaughlin, Thomas Bohrer, Patrick Manning 5:56.68
3. SLO—Janez Klemenčič, Sašo Mirjanič, Milan Janša, Sadik Mujkič 5:58.24
4. GER—Armin Weyrauch, Matthias Ungemach, Dirk Balster, Markus Vogt 5:58.39
5. HOL—Bart Peters, Niels van der Zwan, Jaap Krijtenburg, Sven Schwarz 5:59.14
6. NZL—Scott Brownlee, Christopher White, Patrick Peoples, Campbell Clayton-Greene 6:02.13
7. GBR—Salih Hassan, John Garrett, Gavin Stewart, Richard Stanhope
8. ITA—Luca Sartori, Rocco Pecoraro, Carmine La Mura, Riccardo Dei Rossi

Known as the "Oarsome Foursome," the Australian crew from Melbourne burst on the scene when they won the 1990 world championship. In the Olympic final they built up a two-and-a-half-second lead with 500 meters to go and then hung on for the victory.

Andrew Cooper, 1992

Cooper of the victorious coxless four team pays the price of fame during a 1992 parade in honour of Australia's medalists.

1996 Atlanta-Lake Lanier T: 14, N: 14, D: 7.27. WB: 5:47.89 (ITA—Molea, Dei Rossi, Leonardo, Mornati)

1. AUS—Drew Ginn, James Tomkins, Nicholas Green, Michael McKay 6:06.37
2. FRA—Gilles Bosquet, Daniel Fauche, Bertrand Vecten, Olivier Moncelet 6:07.03
3. GBR—Rupert Obholzer, Jonathon Searle, Gregory Searle, Timothy Foster 6:07.28
4. SLO—Denis Žvegelj, Janez "Jani" Klemenčič, Milan Janša, Sadik Mujkič 6:07.87
5. ROM—Claudiu Marin, Dorin Alupei, Dimitrie Popescu, Vasile Măstăcan 6:08.97
6. ITA—Valter Molea, Riccardo Dei Rossi, Raffaello Leonardo, Carlo Mornati 6:10.60
7. CRO—Siniša Skelin, Sead Marušić, Igor Boraska, Tihomir Franković
8. NOR—Halvor Sannes Lande, Odd-Even Bustnes, Olaf Tufte, Morten Bergesen

The Oarsome Foursome took a two-year break after the 1992 Olympics. Regrouped for the 1995 world championships, they placed only fifth. Andrew Cooper retired and Drew Ginn replaced him in time for the 1996 Olympics. In the meantime, Italy had won the last two world championships and was considered the favorite in Atlanta. In the final, Romania took the early lead with Italy close behind. At the halfway point, Italy was first and Romania second, but then the Italians crumpled, eventually finishing last. The Romanians held on a little longer, but they too faded in the final quarter. Australia, third at 1000 meters, were left in the lead and held off the strong closing French.

Collectors of unusual names of Olympians should take note of the second member of the Norwegian crew.

2000 Sydney-Penrith Lakes T: 13, N: 13, D: 9.23. WB: 5:46.12 (NOR—Undset, Bjørvig, Størseth, Simonsen)

1. GBR—James Cracknell, Steven Redgrave, Timothy Foster, Matthew Pinsent 5:56.24
2. ITA—Valter Molea, Riccardo Dei Rossi, Lorenzo Carboncini, Carlo Mornati 5:56.62
3. AUS—James Stewart, Benjamin Dodwell, Geoffrey Stewart, Boden "Bo" Hanson 5:57.61
4. SLO—Janez Klemenčić, Milan Janša, Rok Kolander, Matej Prelog 5:58.34
5. USA—Michael Wherley, Eric Mueller, James Koven, Wolfgang Moser 6:02.34
6. NZL—David Schaper, Scott Brownlee, Toni Dunlop, Robert Hellstrom 6:09.13
7. FRA—Daniel Fauche, Antoine Beghin, Laurent Beghin, Gilles Bosquet
8. YUG—Filip Filipić, Ivan Smiljanić, Boban Ranković, Mladen Stegić

The British crew was undefeated for three years until they unexpectedly placed fourth at the Lucerne meet three months before the Olympics. It was the first time in eleven years that Steve Redgrave had finished out of the top three in a international event. Now 38 years old, Redgrave had been taking insulin for diabetes since 1997. The British led the final from start to finish, although they were hard-pressed by the Italians right up until the end. With this race, Redgrave became the first male rower to win gold medals 16 years apart and only the fourth athlete in any sport to earn gold medals in five different Olympics.

2004 Athens-Schinias T: 13, N: 13, D: 8.21. WB: 5:41.35 (GER—Thormann, Dienstbach, Stueer, Heidicker)

1. GBR—Steven Williams, James Cracknell, Edward Coode, Matthew Pinsent 6:06.98
2. CAN—Cameron Baerg, Thomas Herschmiller, Jacob Wetzel, Barney Williams 6:07.06
3. ITA—Lorenzo Porzio, Dario Dentale, Luca Agamennoni, Raffaello Leonardo 6:10.41
4. AUS—David McGowan, Robert Jahrling, Thomas Laurich, David Dennis 6:13.06
5. NZL—Donald Leach, Mahé Drysdale, Carl Meyer, Eric Murray 6:15.47
6. POL—Jarosław Godek, Mariusz Daniszewski, Artur Rozalski, Rafał Smoliński 6:22.43
7. GER—Jochen Urban, Sebastian Thormann, Philipp Stueer, Bernd Heidicker
8. CZE—Jakub Makovička, Jan Schindler, Petr Vitásek, Karel Neffe, Jr.

Great Britain's crew included two members of the defending Olympic champion crew, Matthew Pinsent and James Cracknell, as well as 2001 world champion Steven Williams and two-time world champion Edward Coode. Coode was added to the crew after Alex Partridge suffered a cracked rib during training one month before the Olympics. Their main competition came from reigning world champion Canada.

The final was a heated battle between the two favorites, with three lead changes and the smallest margin of victory in the history of the event. Great Britain capitalized on a fast start by opening a small gap over the first 1000 meters, but Canada stayed close and pushed into the lead, holding a slight edge with 500 meters remaining. In the final 300 meters, Great Britain steadily moved ahead and took a lead of half a boat length. The Canadians launched their final attack in the last 100 meters, pulling even with Great Britain at the end. The two teams finished so close that there were several seconds of stunned silence until the results were flashed up, and the British saw that they had won by eight hundredths of a second. It was the fourth straight Olympics in which Pinsent had earned a gold medal.

2008 Beijing T: 13, N: 13, D: 8.16. WR: 5:41.35 (GER—Thormann, Dienstbach, Stueer, Heidicker)

1. GBR	Tom James, Steve Williams, Pete Reed, Andrew Triggs Hodge	6:06.57
2. AUS	Matt Ryan, James Marburg, Cameron McKenzie-McHarg, Francis Hegerty	6:07.85
3. FRA	Julien Després, Benjamin Rondeau, Germain Chardin, Dorian Mortelette	6:09.31
4. SLO	Tomaž Pirih, Rok Rozman, Rok Kolander, Miha Pirih	6:11.62
5. CZE	Jan Gruber, Michal Horvath, Milan Bruncvik, Karel Neffe, Jr.	6:16.56
6. GER	Jochen Urban, Richard Schmidt, Urs Käufer, Gregor Hauffe	6:19.63
7. NZL	Carl Meyer, James Dallinger, Eric Murray, Hamish Bond	
8. HOL	Geert Cirkel, Matthijs Vellenga, Jan-Willem Gabriëls, Gijs Vermeulen	

Great Britain had won the last two Olympic gold medals and six of the last eight world championship titles. Led by returning 2004 gold medalist Steve Williams, the crew won the 2005 and 2006 world championships before finishing fourth in 2007, behind New Zealand, Italy and the Netherlands.

The Australians led throughout most of the final, but were passed at the end by the Britsh team, who made a dramatic sprint over the final 500 meters. "It's almost like when you close your eyes before you crash, and hope for the best," Britain's Andrew Hodge said after the race. "That's what I did, closed my eyes and hoped for the best."

EIGHT-OARED SHELL WITH COXSWAIN

1896 not held

1900 Paris T: 5, N: 5, D: 8.26.

1. USA	6:07.8
2. BEL	6:13.8
3. HOL	6:23.0
4. GER&BEL	6:33.0

1. USA—Vesper Boat Club, Philadelphia: Louis Abell, Harry DeBaecke, William Carr, John Exley, John Geiger, Edwin Hedley, James Juvenal, Roscoe Lockwood, Edward Marsh
2. BEL—Royal Club Nautique de Gand: Marcel van Crombrugghe, Maurice Hemelsoet, Oscar de Cook, Maurice Verdonck, Prospère Bruggeman, Oscar de Somville, Frank Odberg, Jules de Bisschop, Alfred Van Landeghem
3. HOL—Minerva Amsterdam: Walter Thijssen, Ruud Leegstra, Johannes van Dijk, Henricus Tromp, Hendrik Offerhaus, Roelof Klein, François Brandt, Walter Middleberg, Hermanus Brockmann
4. GER&BEL—Germania, Hamburg: Oscar Gossler, Walther Katzenstein, Ernst Jencquel, Theodor Laurezzari, Waldemar Tietgens, Arthur Warncke, Edgar Katzenstein, Gustav Gossler, unknown Belgian boy (final), Alexander Gleichmann von Oven (semi-final)

1904 St. Louis T: 2, N: 2, D: 7.30.

1. USA	7:50.0
2. CAN	—

1. USA —Vesper Boat Club, Philadelphia: Louis Abell, Joseph Dempsey, Michael Gleason, Frank Schell, James Flanigan, Charles Armstrong, Harry Lott, Frederick Cresser, John Exley
2. CAN—Argonaut Rowing Club, Toronto: Joseph Wright, Donald MacKenzie, William Wadsworth, George Strange, Philip Boyd, George Reiffenstein, William Rice, Arthur Bailey, Thomas Loudon

1906 not held

1908 London-Henley-on-Thames T: 6, N: 5, D: 7.31.

1. GBR	7:52.0
2. BEL	—
3. CAN	
3. GBR	

1. GBR—Leander Club: Albert Gladstone, Frederick Kelly, Banner Johnstone, Guy Nickalls, Charles Burnell, Ronald Sanderson, Raymond Etherington-Smith, Henry Bucknall, Gilchrist Maclagan
2. BEL—Royal Club Nautique de Gand: Oscar Taelman, Marcel Morimont, Rémy Orban, Georges Mijs, François Vergucht, Polydore Veirman, Oscar de Somville, Rodolphe Poma, Alfred Van Landeghem
3. CAN—Argonaut Rowing Club, Toronto: Irvine Robertson, Joseph Wright, Julius Thomson, Walter Lewis, Gordon Balfour, Becher Gale, Charles Riddy, Geoffrey Taylor, Douglas Kertland
3. GBR—Cambridge University Boating Club: Frank Jerwood, Eric Powell, Oswald Carver, Edward Williams, Henry Goldsmith, Harold Kitching, John Burn, Douglas Stuart, Richard Boyle

The Leander eight won by two lengths.

1912 Stockholm T: 11, N: 8, D: 7.19.

1. GBR	6:15.7
2. GBR	6.19.2
3. GER	

1. GBR—Leander Club: Edgar Burgess, Sidney Swann, Leslie Wormald, Ewart Horsfall, James Gillan, Arthur Garton, Alister Kirby, Philip Fleming, Henry Wells
2. GBR—New College, Oxford: William Fison, William Parker, Thomas Gillespie, Beaufort Burdekin, Frederick Pitman, Arthur Wiggins, Charles Littlejohn, Robert Bourne, John Walker
3. GER—Berliner Ruderverein von 1876: Otto Liebing, Max Bröske, Max Vetter, Willi Bartholomae, Fritz Bartholomae, Werner Dehn, Rudolf Reichelt, Hans Mathiae, Kurt Runge

Sidney Swann of the Leander crew was the only one of the 18 finalists who had not attended Oxford University.

1920 Antwerp-Vilvoorde T: 8, N: 8, D: 8.29.

1. USA	6:05.0
2. GBR	6:05.8
3. NOR	
4. FRA	

1. USA—Virgil Jacomini, Edwin Graves, William Jordan, Edward Moore, Alden Sanborn, Donald Johnston, Vincent Gallagher, Clyde King, Sherman Clark
2. GBR—Ewart Horsfall, Guy Nickalls, Richard Lucas, Walter James, John Campbell, Sebastian Earl, Ralph Shove, Sidney Swann, Robin Johnstone
3. NOR—Theodor Nag, Conrad Olsen, Adolf Nilsen, Håkon Ellingsen, Thore Michelsen, Arne Mortensen, Karl Nag, Tollef Tollefsen, Thoralf Hagen
4. FRA—Albert Diebold, Charles Hahn, Frédéric Grossmann, Robert Fleig, Henri Barbenès, Frédéric Fleig, Charles Schlewer, Émile Ruhlmann, Émile Barberolle

The winning crew represented the US Naval Academy. They trailed from the start and caught the British crew from the Leander Club 50 meters from the finish. Regatta officials first awarded the bronze medals to the Swiss team because they had recorded the third fastest time in the preliminary heats when they lost to Great Britain. But after a protest, it was decided that the semifinal losers, Norway and France, should row off for third place; however, this race was never held. Most Olympic historians credit Norway with third place, since their semifinal time was faster than that of France.

1924 Paris T: 10, N: 10, D: 7.17.

1. USA	6:33.4
2. CAN	6:49.0
3. ITA	
4. GBR	

1. USA—Leonard Carpenter, Howard Kingsbury, Daniel Lindley, John Miller, James Rockefeller, Frederick Sheffield, Benjamin Spock, Alfred Wilson, Laurence Stoddard

2. CAN—Arthur Bell, Robert Hunter, William Langford, Harold Little, John Smith, Warren Snyder, Norman Taylor, William Wallace, Ivor Campbell
3. ITA—Antonio Cattalinich, Francesco Cattalinich, Simeon Cattalinch, Giuseppe Crivelli, Latino Galasso, Pietro Ivanov, Bruno Sorich, Carlo Toniatti, Vittorio Gliubich
4. GBR—Reginald Bare, Edward Chandler, H.C. Debenham, Hugh Dulley, S. Ian Fairbairn, A.F. Long, H.L. Morphy, Charles Rew, J.S. Godwin

Bill Havens was a member of the Yale University team that won the right to represent the United States. However, he chose not to make the trip to Paris because his wife was expecting their first child. That child, a boy named Frank, was born five days after the closing of the 1924 Olympics. Twenty-eight years later, the Havens family finally got their Olympic gold medal when Frank won the 10,000 meters Canadian canoeing singles event in Helsinki.

One Yale crew member who did compete in 1924 and win was a gangly 6-foot 4-inch junior named Ben Spock. After graduating from medical school, Spock became a pediatrician. In 1945 he finished writing a book called *The Common Sense Book of Baby and Child Care,* which eventually sold over 45 million copies in more than 30 languages and gained its author international fame as "Dr. Spock, the baby expert." In 1972 he was the presidential candidate of the People's Party. Spock died March 15, 1998, at the age of 94.

1928 Amsterdam-Sloten T: 11, N: 11, D: 8.10.

1. USA	6:03.2
2. GBR	6:05.6
3. CAN	
4. POL	
5. GER	
6. ITA	

1. USA—Marvin Stalder, John Brinck, Francis Frederick, William Thompson, William Dally, James Workman, Hubert Caldwell, Peter Donlon, Donald Blessing
2. GBR—James Hamilton, Guy Oliver Nickalls, John "Felix" Badcock, Donald Gollan, Harold Lane, Gordon Killick, Jack Beresford, Harold West, Arthur Sulley
3. CAN—Frederick Hedges, Frank Fiddes, John Hand, Herbert Richardson, Jack Murdock, Athol Meech, Edgar Norris, William Ross, John Donnelly
4. POL—Otto Gordziałkowski, Stanisław Urban, Andrzej Sołtan, Marian Wodziański, Janusz Ślązak, Waclaw Michalski, Jósef Łaszewski, Henryk Niezabitowski, Jerzy Skolimowski
5. GER—Karl Aletter, Ernst Gaber, Willi Reichert, Erwin Hoffstätter, Hermann Herbold, Gustav Maier, Robert Huber, Hans Maier, Fritz Bauer
6. ITA—Medardo Lamberti, Arturo Moroni, Vittore Stocchi, Guglielmo Carubbi, Amilcare Canevari, Medardo Galli, Giulio Lamberti, Benedetto Borella, Angelo Polledri

The United States was represented by the crew from the University of California at Berkeley. *New York Times* correspondent Wythe Williams described the work of coxswain Don Blessing as "one of the greatest performances of demonical howling ever heard on a terrestrial planet . . . He gave the impression of a terrier suddenly gone mad. But such language and what a vocabulary! . . . One closed his eyes and waited for the crack of a cruel whip across the backs of the galley slaves." After they had won the Olympic championship, the galley slaves, following custom, grabbed their tormentor and threw him into the middle of Sloten Canal.

1932 Los Angeles-Long Beach T: 8, N: 8, D: 8.13.

1. USA	6:37.6
2. ITA	6:37.8
3. CAN	6:40.4
4. GBR	6:40.8

1. USA—Edwin Salisbury, James Blair, Duncan Gregg, David Dunlap, Burton Jastram, Charles Chandler, Harold Tower, Winslow Hall, Norris Graham
2. ITA—Vittorio Cioni, Mario Balleri, Renato Bracci, Dino Barsotti, Roberto Vestrini, Guglielmo Del Bimbo, Enrico Garzelli, Renato Barbieri, Cesare Milani
3. CAN—Earl Eastwood, Joseph Harris, Stanley Stanyar, Harry Fry, Cedric Liddell, William Thoburn, Donald Boal, Albert Taylor, George MacDonald
4. GBR—Lewis Luxton, Donald McCowen, Harold Rickett, Charles Sergell, William Sambell, Thomas Askwith, Kenneth Payne, David Haig-Thomas, John Ranking

The US team from the University of California and the Italian team from the University of Pisa staged a dramatic battle, which the Californians won by a foot with their very last stroke. Lewis Luxton of the British crew later served as chairman of the Shell oil company.

1936 Berlin-Grünau T: 14, N: 14, D: 8.14

1. USA	6:25.4
2. ITA	6:26.0
3. GER	6:26.4
4. GBR	6:30.1
5. HUN	6:30.3
6. SWI	6:35.8

1. USA—Herbert Morris, Charles Day, Gordon Adam, John White, James McMillin, George Hunt, Joseph Rantz, Donald Hume, Robert Moch
2. ITA—Guglielmo Del Bimbo, Dino Barsotti, Oreste Grossi, Enzo Bartolini, Mario Checcacci, Dante Secchi, Ottorino Quaglierini, Enrico Garzelli, Cesare Milani
3. GER—Alfred Rieck, Helmut Radach, Hans Kuschke, Heinz Kaufmann, Gerd Völs, Werner Löckle, Hans-Joachim Hannemann, Herbert Schmidt, Wilhelm Mahlow
4. GBR—Annesley Kingsford, Thomas Askwith, McAlister Pender Lonnon, Desmond Kingsford, John Cherry, John Couchman, Hugh Mason, W. Ranald "Ran" Laurie, John Duckworth
5. HUN—Pál Domonkos, Sándor Korompay, Hugó Ballya, Imre Kapossy, Antal Szendey, Gábor Alapy, Frigyes Hollósi-Jung, László Szabó, Ervin Kereszthy
6. SWI—Werner Schweizer, Fritz Feldmann, Rudolf Homberger, Oskar Neuenschwander, Hermann Betschart, Hans Homberger, Alex Homberger, Karl Schmid, Rolf Spring

An exciting blanket finish was won by the crew of the University of Washington, which moved up from fifth place at the halfway mark.

1948 London-Henley-on-Thames T: 12, N: 12, D: 8.9.

1. USA	5:56.7
2. GBR	6:06.9
3. NOR	6:10.3

1. USA—Ian Turner, David Turner, James Hardy, George Ahlgren, Lloyd Butler, David Brown, Justus Smith, John Stack, Ralph Purchase
2. GBR—Christopher Barton, Michael Lepage, Guy Richardson, Ernest Paul Bircher, Paul Massey, Charles Brian Lloyd, David Meyrick, Alfred Mellows, Jack Dearlove
3. NOR—Kristoffer Lepsöe, Torstein Kråkenes, Hans Egil Hansen, Halfdan Gran Olsen, Harald Kråkenes, Leif Naess, Thor Pedersen, Carl Henrik Monssen, Sigurd Monssen

The victorious University of California at Berkeley crew had barely qualified for the Olympics, winning the US tryouts by a mere one-tenth second over the University of Washington. But when they got to London they discovered that their most difficult challenge was behind them, as they won all three of their races by at least ten seconds.

1952 Helsinki T: 14, N: 14, D: 7.23.

1. USA	6:25.9
2. SOV	6:31.2
3. AUS	6:33.1
4. GBR	6:34.8
5. GER	6:42.8

1. USA—Franklin Shakespeare, William Fields, James Dunbar, Richard Murphy, Robert Detweiler, Henry Proctor, Wayne Frye, Edward Stevens, Charles "Dave" Manring
2. SOV—Yevgeny Brago, Vladimir Rodimushkin, Aleksei Komarov, Igor Borisov, Slava Amiragov, Leonid Gissen, Yevgeny Samsonov, Vladimir Krukov, Igor Polyakov
3. AUS—Robert Tinning, Ernest Chapman, Nimrod Greenwood, Mervyn Finlay, Edward Pain, Phillip Cayzer, Thomas Chessel, David Anderson, Geoffrey Williamson
4. GBR—David Macklin, Alastair MacLeod, Nicholas Clack, Roger Sharpley, Edward Worlidge, Charles Lloyd, William Windham, David Jennens, John Hinde
5. GER—Anton Reinartz, Michael Reinartz, Roland Freiloff, Heinz Zünkler, Peter Betz, Stefan Reinartz, Hans Betz, Toni Siebenhaar, Hermann Zander

The winning crew was from the US Naval Academy.

1956 Melbourne-Ballarat T: 10, N: 10, D: 11.27.

1. USA	6:35.2
2. CAN	6:37.1
3. AUS	6:39.2
4. SWE	6:48.1

1. USA—Thomas Charlton, David Wight, John Cooke, Donald Beer, Caldwell Esselstyn, Charles Grimes, Richard Wailes, Robert Morey, William Becklean
2. CAN—Philip Kueber, Richard McClure, Robert Wilson, David Helliwell, Donald Pretty, William McKerlich, Douglas McDonald, Lawrence West, Carlton Ogawa
3. AUS—Michael Aikman, David Boykett, Angus Benfield, James Howden, Garth Manton, Walter Howell, Adrian Monger, Bryan Doyle, Harold Hewitt
4. SWE—Olof Larsson, Lennart Andersson, Kjell Hansson, Rune Ivar Andersson, Sture Lennart Hanson, Gösta Eriksson, Ivar Aronsson, Sven Gunnarsson, Bertil Göransson

The United States, represented by the Yale crew, finished third to Australia and Canada in the opening round, but qualified for the semifinal through *repêchage.* No Olympic eights had ever been won by a team that lost its opening race, but the Yale crew broke this tradition to give the United States its eighth straight win in the event.

1960 Rome-Lake Albano T: 14, N: 14, D: 9.3.

1. GER	5:57.18
2. CAN	6:01.52
3. CZE	6:04.84
4. FRA	6:06.57
5. USA	6:08.06
6. ITA	6:12.73

1. GER—Klaus Bittner, Karl-Heinz Hopp, Hans Lenk, Manfred Rulffs, Frank Schepke, Kraft Schepke, Walter Schröder, Karl-Heinrich von Groddeck, Willi Padge
2. CAN—David Anderson, Donald Arnold, Walter D'Hondt, Nelson Kuhn, John Lecky, Archibald McKinnon, William McKerlich, Glen Mervyn, Sohen Biln
3. CZE—Bohumil Janoušek, Jan Jindra, Jiří Lundak, Stanislav Lusk, Václav Pavkovič, Ludek Pojezny, Jan Švéda, Josef Vĕntus, Miroslav Koniček
4. FRA—Christian Puibaraud, Jean Bellet, Emile Clerc, Jean Ledoux, Gaston Mercier, Bernard Meynadier, Joseph Moroni, Michel Viaud, Alain Bouffard
5. USA—Joseph Baldwin, Peter Bos, Mark Moore, Lyman Perry, Warren Sweetser, Gayle Thompson, Robert Wilson, Howard Winfree, William Long
6. ITA—Paolo Amorini, Vasco Cantarello, Giancarlo Casalini, Luigi Prato, Vincenzo Prina, Nazzareno Simonato, Luigi Spozio, Armido Torri, Giuseppe Pira

The US winning streak was finally broken by a combined crew from Ratzeburg and Ditmarsia Kiel rowing clubs. The Germans led from the start and were never headed.

1964 Tokyo T: 14, N: 14, D: 10.15.

1. USA	6:18.23
2. GER	6:23.29
3. CZE	6:25.11
4. YUG	6:27.15
5. SOV	6:30.69
6. ITA	6:42.78
7. FRA	
8. AUS	

1. USA—Joseph Amlong, Thomas Amlong, Harold Budd, Emory Clark Stanley Cwiklinski, Hugh Foley, William Knecht, William Stowe, Robert Zimonyi
2. GER—Klaus Aeffke, Klaus Bittner, Karl-Heinrich von Groddeck, Hans-Jurgen Wallbrecht, Klaus Behrens, Jürgen Schröder, Jürgen Plagemann, Horst Meyer, Thomas Ahrens

3. CZE—Petr Čermák, Jiří Lundák, Jan Mrvik, Július Toček, Josef Věntus, Luděk Pojezný, Bohumil Janoušek, Richard Nový, Miroslav Koníček
4. YUG—Boris Klavora, Jadran Barut, Jože Berc, Vjekoslav Skalak, Marko Mandič, Alojz Colja, Pavao Martić, Lucijan Kelva, Zdenko Balaš
5. SOV—Juozas Jagelavičius, Yuri Suslin, Piatras Karla, Vytautas Briedis, Volodymyr Sterlyk, Zigmas Jukna, Antanas Bagdonavičius, Ričardas Vaitkevičius, Yuri Lorentson
6. ITA—Dario Giani, Sergio Tagliapetra, Gianpietro Gilardi, Francesco Glorioso, Pietro Polti, Giuseppe Schiavon, Orlando Savarin, Sereno Brunello, Ivo Stefanoni
7. FRA—André Fevret, Pierre Maddaloni, André Sloth, Joseph Moroni, Robert Dumontois, Jean Pierre Grimaud, Bernard Meynadier, Michel Viaud, Alain Bouffard
8. AUS—David Ramage, David Boykett, Terence Davies, Robert Lachel, Paul Guest, Martin Tomanovits, Brian Vear, Graeme McCall, Kevin Wickham

The Vesper Club of Philadelphia, the first noncollegiate eight to represent the United States in 60 years, scored a one-and-a-quarter-length upset victory over the crew from Ratzeburg, Germany. The Vesper coxswain was Bob Zimonyi, a 46-year-old accountant who had defected after being a member of the 1956 Hungarian squad. Zimonyi's first Olympic appearance had been in the coxed fours of 1948.

1968 Mexico City-Xochimilco T: 12, N: 12, D: 10.19.

1. GER	6:07.00
2. AUS	6:07.98
3. SOV	6:09.11
4. NZL	6:10.43
5. CZE	6:12:17
6. USA	6:14.34
7. GDR	
8. HOL	

1. GER—Horst Meyer, Dirk Schreyer, Rüdiger Henning, Wolfgang Hottenrott, Lutz Ulbricht, Egbert Hirschfelder, Jörg Siebert, Nikolaus "Nico" Ott, Günther Tiersch
2. AUS—Alfred Duval, Michael Morgan, Joseph Fazio, Peter Dickson, David Dougals, John Ranch, Gary Pearce, Robert Shirlaw, Alan Grover
3. SOV—Zigmas Jukna, Antanas Bagdonavičius, Volodymyr Sterlyk, Juozas Jagelavičius, Aleksandr Martyshkin, Vytautas Briedis, Valentyn Kravchuk, Viktor Suslin, Yuri Lorentson
4. NZL—Alan Webster, Wybo Veldman, Alistair Dryden, John Hunter, Mark Brownlee, John Gibbons, Thomas Just, Gilbert Cawood, Robert Page
5. CZE—Vladimír Jánoš, Zdeněk Kuba, Oldřich Svojanovský, Karel Kolesa, Pavel Svojanovský, Jan Wallisch, Otakar Mareček, Petr Čermák, Jiří Pták
6. USA—Stephen Brooks, Curtis Canning, Andrew Larkin, Scott Steketee, Franklin Hobbs, Jacques Fiechter, Cleve Livingston, David Higgins, Paul Hoffman
7. GDR—Günter Bergau, Klaus-Dieter Bähr, Claus Wilke, Peter Gorny, Reinhard Zerfowski, Peter Hein, Manfred Schneider, Peter Prompe, Karl-Heinz Danielowski
8. HOL—Maarten Kloosterman, Pieter Bon, Eric Nieche, Jaap Reesink, Gerard van Enst, Jan Steinhauser, Izak "Erik" Wesdorp, Jan van Laarhoven, Arthur Koning

The victorious Ratzeburg crew used a shell that was 75 pounds lighter than the shells of the other teams.

1972 Munich-Oberschleissheim T: 15, N: 15, D: 9.2.

1. NZL	6:08.94
2. USA	6:11.61
3. GDR	6:11.67
4. SOV/RUS	6:14.48
5. GER	6:14.91
6. POL	6:29.35
7. HUN	
8. AUS	

1. NZL—Anthony Hurt, Wybo Veldman, Dick Joyce, John Hunter, Lindsay Wilson, Athol Earl, Trevor Coker, Gary Robertson, Simon Dickie
2. USA—Lawrence Terry, Fritz Hobbs, Peter Raymond, Timothy Mickelson, Eugene Clapp, William Hobbs, Cleve Livingston, Michael Livingston, Paul Hoffman
3. GDR—Hans-Joachim Borzym, Jörg Landvoigt, Harold Dimke, Manfred Schneider, Hartmut Schreiber, Manfred Schmorde, Bernd Landvoigt, Heinrich Mederow, Dietmar Schwarz
4. SOV/RUS—Aleksandr Riazankin, Viktor Dementiev, Sergei Koliaskin, Aleksandr Shitov, Valery Bissarnov, Boris Vorobiev, Vladimir Savelov, Aleksandr Martyshkin, Viktor Mikheyev
5. GER—Reinhard Wendemuth, Frithjof Henckel, Norbert Kindlmann, Wolfgang Hottenrott, Hans-Ulrich Buchholz, Günter Petermann, Bernd Truschinski, Winfried Ringwald, Manfred Klein
6. POL—Jerzy Ulczyński, Marian Siejkowski, Krzysztof Marek, Jan Młodzikowski, Grzegorz Stellak, Marian Drażdżewski, Ryszard Giło, Sławomir Maciejowski, Ryszard Kubiak
7. HUN—Zoltán Melis, András Pályl, Antal Gelley, Béla Zsitnik Jr., László Romvári, Péter Kokas, Imre Dávid, Ágoston Bányai, Róbert Örlschléger
8. AUS—John Clark, Michael Morgan, Bryan Curtin, Richard Curtin, Robert Paver, Kerry Jelbart, Gary Pearce, Malcolm Shaw, Alan Grover

The New Zealand team raised the $45,000 needed to support their training and trip to Munich by holding a series of bingo games, as well as a raffle for a "dream kitchen."

1976 Montreal T: 13, N: 13, D: 7.25.

1. GDR	5:58.29
2. GBR	6:00.82
3. NZL	6:03.51
4. GER	6:06.15
5. AUS	6:09.75
6. CZE	6:14.29
7. SOV	
8. CAN	

1. GDR—Bernd Baumgart, Gottfried Döhn, Werner Klatt, Hans-Joachim Lück, Dieter Wendisch, Roland Kostulski, Ulrich Karnatz, Karl-Heinz Prudöhl, Karl Heinz Danielowski
2. GBR—Richard Lester, John Yallop, Timothy Crooks, Hugh Matheson, David Maxwell, R. James Clark, Frederick Smallbone, Leonard Robertson, Patrick Sweeney
3. NZL—Ivan Sutherland, Trevor Coker, Peter Dignan, Lindsay Wilson, Athol Earl, Dave Rodger, Alexander "Alec" McLean, Anthony Hurt, Simon Dickie
4. GER—Reinhard Wendemuth, Bernd Truschinski, Frank Schütze, Frithjof Henckel, Wolfram Thiem, Volker Sauer, Otmar Kaufhold, Wolf-Dieter Oschlies, Helmut Latz

5. AUS—Islay Lee, Ian Clubb, Timothy Conrad, Robert Paver, Gary Eubergang, Athol MacDonald, Peter Shakespear, Brian Richardson, Stuart Carter
6. CZE—Pavel Konvička, Václav Mls, Josef Plamínek, Josef Pokorný, Karel Mejta Jr., Josef Neštický, Lubomir Zapletal, Miroslav Vraštil, Jiří Pták
7. SOV—Aleksandr Shitov, Antanas Chikotas, Vassily Potapov, Aleksandr Plyushkin, Anatoly Nemtyrev, Igor Konnov, Anatoly Ivanov, Vladimir Vasilyev, Vladimir Zharov
8. CAN—Edgar Smith, Dirk Gidney, George Tintor, James Henniger, Patrick Croskerry, Melvin La Forme, Ronald Burak, Alexander Manson, Robert Choquette

The East German team included a butcher, a plumber, a gardener, a mechanic, and a student.

1980 Moscow T: 9, N: 9, D: 7.27.

1. GDR	5:49.05
2. GBR	5:51.92
3. SOV	5:52.66
4. CZE	5:53.75
5. AUS	5:56.74
6. BUL	6:04.05
7. HUN	
8. CUB	

1. GDR—Bernd Krauss, Hans-Peter Koppe, Ulrich Kons, Jörg Friedrich, Jens Doberschütz, Ulrich Karnatz, Uwe Dühring, Bernd Höing, Klaus-Dieter Ludwig
2. GBR—Duncan McDougall, Allan Whitwell, J. Henry Clay, Christopher Mahoney, Andrew Justice, John Pritchard, Malcolm McGowan, Richard Stanhope, Colin Moynihan
3. SOV—Viktor Kokoshyn, Andrei Tyshchenko, Jonas Pinskus, Jonas Normantas, Andrei Lugin, Oleksander Mantsevych, Igor Maistrenko, Hryhoriy Dmytrenko, Oleksander Tkachenko
4. CZE—Pavel Pevný, Lubomír Janko, Ctirad Jungmann, Karel Neffe, Karel Mejta Jr., Dušan Vičik, Milan Doleček, Milan Kyselý, Jiří Pták
5. AUS—Islay Lee, Stephen Handley, William Dankbaar, Andrew Withers, Timothy Willoughby, James Lowe, Timothy Young, Brian Richardson, David England
6. BUL—Dimitar Yanakiev, Todor Mrunkov, Bozhidar Rogelov, Ivan Botev, Yani Ignatóv, Mikhail Petrov, Petar Patzev, Vesselin Shterev, Ventzislav Kunchev
7. HUN—Ferenc Kiss, Péter Tóvári, Róbert Sass, Attila Strochmayer, András Kormos, Zoltán Sztárcsevics, Kálmán Toronyi, László Kiss, Miklós Bálint
8. CUB—Wenceslao Borroto Torres, Ismael Carbonell Same, Juan Alfonso Armenteros, Juan Bueno Despaigne, Francisco Mora Molina, Hermenegildo Palacio Cantero, Jorge Álvarez Galvez, Antonio Riaño González, Enrique Carrillo Barnal

1984 Los Angeles-Lake Casitas T: 7, N: 7, D: 8.5.

1. CAN	5:41.32
2. USA	5:41.74
3. AUS	5:43.40
4. NZL	5:44.14
5. GBR	5:47.01
6. FRA	5:49.52
7. CHI	6:07:03

1. CAN—Patrick Turner, Kevin Neufeld, Mark Evans, Grant Main, Paul Steele, J. Michael Evans, Dean Crawford, Blair Horn, Brian McMahon
2. USA—Walter Lubsen, Andrew Sudduth, John Terwilliger, Christopher Penny, Thomas Darling, Earl Borchelt, Charles Clapp, Bruce Ibbetson, Robert Jaugstetter
3. AUS—Craig Muller, Clyde Hefer, Samuel Patten, Timothy Willoughby, Ian Edmunds, James Battersby, Ion Popa, Stephen Evans, Gavin Thredgold
4. NZL—Nigel Atherfold, David Rodger, Roger White-Parsons, George Keys, Gregory Johnston, Christopher White, Andrew Stevenson, Michael Stanley, Andrew Hay
5. GBR—Duncan McDougal, Christopher Mahoney, Salih Hassan, Clive Roberts, David Adam Clift, John Pritchard, Malcolm McGowan, Allan Whitwell, Colin Moynihan
6. FRA—Alain Duprat, Dominique Lecointe, Thierry Louvet, Patrick Vibert-Vichet, Jacques Taborski, Jean-Jacques Martigne, Olivier Pons, Bernard Chevalier, Jean-Pierre Huguet-Balent
7. CHI—Mario Castro, Carlos Neyra, Zibor Llanos, Giorgio Vallebuona, Alejandro Rojas, Víctor Contreras, Rodolfo Pereira, Marcelo Rojas, Rodrigo Abasolo

A bizarre incident enlivened the eights competition. One hundred meters after the start of the *repêchage*, the oarlock gate of the number 6 rower on the French crew broke and he lost his oar. This was not unusual in itself, but upon examination it was discovered that the gate had been intentionally filed down so that it would snap under pressure. A similar act of sabotage had occurred two weeks earlier at the junior championships in Sweden. That time the victims had been a US women's crew. In Los Angeles, the French were allowed to participate in the final along with the six qualifiers. Thus all seven of the original entrants went on to the final despite having to endure two preliminary races and a *repêchage*.

The final had been expected to be a hot contest among New Zealand, the US and Australia. But the Canadians led from start to finish, holding off a late sprint by the Americans. At the 1984 Olympics, each of the eight men's rowing titles was won by a different nation.

1988 Seoul T: 10, N: 10, D: 9.25.

1. GER	5:46.05
2. SOV	5:48.01
3. USA	5:48.26
4. GBR	5:51.59
5. AUS	5:53.73
6. CAN	5:54.26
7. ITA	
8. BUL	

1. GER—Thomas Möllenkamp, Matthias Mellinghaus, Eckhardt Schultz, Ansgar Wessling, Armin Eichholz, Thomas Domian, Wolfgang Maennig, Bahne Rabe, Manfred Klein
2. SOV—Veniamin But, Mykhalo Komarov, Vassily Tikhanov, Aleksandr Dumchev, Pavlo Hurkovsky, Viktor Diduk, Viktor Omelyanovych, Andrei Vassilyev, Aleksandr Lukianov
3. USA—Michael Teti, John Smith, Edward Patton, John Rusher, Peter Nordell, Jeffrey McLaughlin, W. Douglas Burden, John Pescatore, Seth Bauer
4. GBR—Richard Stanhope, Anton Obholzer, Peter Beaumont, Gavin Stewart, Terence Dillon, Salih Hassan, Stephen Turner, Nicholas Burfitt, Simon Jeffries

5. AUS—James Galloway, Hamish McGlashan, Andrew Cooper, Michael Mckay, Mark Doyle, James Tomkins, Ion Popa, Stephen Evans, Dale Caterson
6. CAN—Don Telfer, Kevin Neufeld, Jason Dorland, Andrew Crosby, Paul Steele, Gerald Main, James "Jamie" Schaffer, John Wallace, Robert McMahon
7. ITA—Antonio Baldacci, Ettore Bulgarelli, Piero Carletto, Giuseppe Di Palo, Renato Gaeta, Dino Lucchetta, Giovanni Suarez, Annibale Venier, Franco Zucchi
8. BUL—Rumen Aleksiev, Emil Bondev, Yuri Dyulgurov, Ivo Gulov, Dimitar Kamburski, Ventzislav Kanchev, Ivan Stanev, Dimitar Tonchev, Nikola Zlatanov

1992 Barcelona-Banyoles T: 14, N: 14, D: 8.2.

1. CAN	5:29.53
2. ROM	5:29.67
3. GER	5:31.00
4. USA	5:33.18
5. AUS	5:33.72
6. GBR	5:39.92
7. DEN	
8. SAF	

1. CAN—John Wallace, Bruce Robertson, Michael Forgeron, Darren Barber, Robert Marland, Michael Rascher, Andrew Crosby, Derek Porter, Terrence Paul
2. ROM—Ioan Vizitiu, Dănuț Dobre, C. Gabriel Marin, Iulică Ruican, Viorel Talapan, Vasile Năstase, Valentin Robu, Vasile Măstăcan, Marin Gheorghe
3. GER—Frank Richter, Thorsten Streppelhoff, Detlef Kirchhoff, Armin Eichholz, Bahne Rabe, Hans Sennewald, Ansgar Wessling, Roland Baar, Manfred Klein
4. USA—Michael Teti, Christian Sahs, James Munn, Jeffrey Klepacki, Robert Shepherd, Malcolm Baker, Richard Kennelly, John Parker, Michael Moore
5. AUS—Simon Spriggs, Peter Murphy, Wayne Diplock, Jaime Fernandez, Ben Dodwell, Samuel Patten, Boden "Bo" Hanson, Boden Hanson, Robert Scott, David Colvin
6. GBR—Martin Cross, Timothy Foster, Richard Phelps, James Walker, Benjamin Hunt-Davis, Stephen Turner, Rupert Obholzer, Johnathan Singfield, Adrian Ellison
7. DEN—Jens Pørneki, Jørgen Tramm, Thomas Larsen, Lars Christensen, Carsten Hassing, Jesper Thusgård Kristiansen, Martin Hansen, Kent Skovsager, Stephen Masters
8. SAF—Martin Walsh, Rogan Clarke, Grant Hillary, Andrew Gordon-Brown, Erich Mauff, Timothy Lahner, Robin McCall, Ivan Pentz, Andrew Lonmon-Davis

Germany had won all three world championships since the last Olympics, but it was the Canadians and the surprising Romanians who fought for the gold medal. Romania took the early lead, but Canada edged ahead by the halfway mark and held on to win by less than a foot in the closest rowing final in Olympic history. Spain's coxswain, 11-year-old Carlos Front, was the youngest competitor in the Summer Games since 1900.

1996 Atlanta-Lake Lanier T: 10, N: 10, D: 7.28. WB: 5:23.90 (HOL—Zwolle, Simon, Bartman, Maasdijk, van der Zwan, van Steenis, Florijn, Rienks, Duyster)

1. HOL	5:42.74
2. GER	5:44.58
3. RUS	5:45.77
4. CAN	5:46.54
5. USA	5:48.45
6. AUS	5:58.82
7. ROM	
8. GBR	

1. HOL—Henk-Jan Zwolle, Diederik Simon, Michiel Bartman, Koos Maasdijk, Niels van der Zwan, Niels van Steenis, Ronald Florijn, Nico Rienks, Jeroen Duyster
2. GER—Frank Richter, Mark Kleinschmidt, Wolfram Huhn, Marc Weber, Detlef Kirchhoff, Thorsten Streppelhoff, Ulrich Viefers, Roland Baar, Peter Thiede
3. RUS—Anton Chermashentsev, Andrey Glukhov, Dmitri Rozinkevich, Vladimir Volodenkov, Nikolai Aksyonov, Roman Monchenko, Pavel Melnikov, Sergei Matveyev, Aleksandr Lukianov
4. CAN—Gregory Stevenson, Philip Graham, Henry Hering, Mark Platt, Darren Barber, Andrew Crosby, Scott Brodie, Adam Parfitt, Patrick Newman
5. USA—Doug Burden, Bob Kaehler, Porter Collins, Edward Murphy, James "Jamie" Koven, Jonathan Brown, Donald Smith, Fredric Honebein, Steven Segaloff
6. AUS—James Stewart, Geoffrey Stewart, Robert Jahrling, Nicholas Porzig, Jaime Fernandez, Benjamin Dodwell, Robert Walker, Richard Wearne, Brett Hayman
7. ROM—C. Gabriel Marin, Andrei Bănică, Cornel Nemțoc, Dorin Alupei, Viorel Talapan, Neculai Țaga, Valentin Robu, Iulică Ruican, Marin Gheorghe
8. GBR—Matthew Parish, James Walker, Alexander Story, Richard Hamilton, Roger Brown, Peter Bridge, Benjamin Hunt-Davis, Graham Smith, Garry Herbert

The Dutch crew stayed close to the Germans for the first half of the final and then drew away evenly for the rest of the race. Russian coxswain Aleksandr Lukianov had won his first medal, a gold, twenty years earlier in the coxed fours event.

2000 Sydney-Penrith Lakes T: 9, N: 9, D: 9.24. WB: 5:22.80 (HOL—Middag, Fontein, Van der Zwan, Van Dongen, Derksen, Kind, Van Leeuwne, Rienks, Van Ooijen)

1. GBR	5:33.08
2. AUS	5:33.88
3. CRO	5:34.85
4. ITA	5:35.37
5. USA	5:39.16
6. ROM	5:43.89
7. CAN	
8. HOL	

1. GBR—Andrew Lindsay, Benjamin Hunt-Davis, Simon Dennis, Louis Attrill, Luka Grubor, Kieran West, Fred Scarlett, Stephen Trapmore, Rowley Douglas
2. AUS—Christian Ryan, Alastair Gordon, Nicholas Porzig, Robert Jahrling, Michael McKay, Stuart Welch, Daniel Burke, Jaime Fernandez, Brett Hayman
3. CRO—Igor Francetić, Tihomir Franković, Tomislav Smoljanović, Nikša Skelin, Siniša Škelin, Krešimir Čuljak, Igor Boraska, Branimir Vujević, Silvijo Petriško
4. ITA—Gioacchino Cascone, Franco Berra, Mario Palmisano, Marco Penna, Valerio Pinton, Raffaello Leonardo, Alessandro Corona, Luca Ghezzi, Gaetano Iannuzzi
5. USA—Bryan Volpenhein, Robert Kaehler, Porter Collins, Thomas Welsh, David Simon, Christian Ahrens, Garrett Miller, Jeffrey Klepacki, Peter Cipollone

6. ROM—Costel Mutescu, Vasile Măstăcan, Cornel Nemtoc, Florian Tudor, Viorel Talapan, Andrei Bănică, Gheorghe Pîrvan, Dorin Alupei, Dumitru Răducanu
7. CAN—Michael Belenkie, Bryan Donnelly, Matt Swick, Thomas Herschmiller, Lawrence Varga, Morgan Crooks, David Calder, Adam Parfitt, Chris Taylor
8. HOL—Adriaan Middag, Johannes "Peter" van der Noort, Cornelis "Niels" van der Zwan, Gerritjan Eggenkamp, Gerardus "Geert-Jan" Derksen, Gijs Kind, Geert Cirkel, Nicolaas "Nico" Rienks, Merijn van Oijen

The US crew had won the last three world championships, but they were not in contention at the Olympics. The British crew moved ahead almost immediately and led by two seconds after 1500 meters. The Australians, in fourth place with 500 meters to go, staged a furious challenge, but the Brits held on for the victory.

2004 Athens-Schinias T: 9, N: 9, D: 8.22. WB: 5:22.80 (HOL—Middag, Fontein, Van der Zwan, Van Dongen, Derksen, Kind, Van Leeuwne, Rienks, Van Ooijen)

1. USA	5:42.48
2. HOL	5:43.75
3. AUS	5:45.38
4. GER	5:49.43
5. CAN	5:51.66
6. FRA	5:53.31
7. ITA	
8. POL	

1. USA—Jason Read, Wyatt Allen, Christian Ahrens, Joseph Hansen, Matthew Deakin, Daniel Beery, Beau Hoopman, Bryan Volpenhein, Peter Cipollone
2. HOL—Diederik Simon, Gijsbert Vermeulen, Jan-Willem Gabriëls, Daniël Mensch, Gerardus "Geert-Jan" Derksen, Gerritjan Eggenkamp, Matthijs Vellenga, Michiel Bartman, Chun Wei Cheung
3. AUS—Stefan Szczurowski, Stuart Reside, Stuart Welch, James Stewart, Geoffrey Stewart, Boden "Bo" Hanson, Michael McKay, Stephen Stewart, Michael Toon
4. GER—Sebastian Schulte, Stephan Koltzk, Jörg Diessner, Thorsten Engelmann, Jan-Martin Bröer, Enrico Schnabel, Ulf Siemes, Michael Ruhe, Peter Thiede
5. CAN—Scott Frandsen, Kevin Light, Benjamin Rutledge, Kyle Hamilton, Adam Kreek, Andrew Hoskins, Joseph Stankevicius, Jeffrey Powell, Brian Price
6. FRA—Bastien Ripoll, Bastien Gallet, Jean-Baptiste Macquet, Julien Peudecoeur, Donatien Mortelette, Anthony Perrot, Jean-David Bernard, Laurent Cadot, Christophe Lattaignant
7. ITA—Sergio Canciani, Aldo Tramontano, Marco Penna, Pierpaolo Frattini, Valerio Pinton, Niccolo Mornati, Carlo Mornati, Luca Ghezzi, Gaetano Iannuzzi
8. POL—Bogdan Zalewski, Piotr Buchalski, Rafał Hejmej, Dariusz Nowak, Mikołaj Burda, Wojciech Gutorski, Sebastian Kosiorek, Michał Stawowski, Daniel Trojanowski

The final was a rematch of the 2003 world championships, in which Canada defeated the United States by one second. In an unusually competitive first-round heat, the Americans pulled ahead of Canada in the final 500 meters to advance directly to the final, as both teams set world best times (5:19.85 and 5:20.46). In the final, the Americans attacked early, opening a gap of more than three seconds by the midway point and never relinquishing the lead. The Netherlands began to move up at the end, passing Australia for the silver, while Canada slipped to fifth behind Germany.

The US crew was led by Jason Read, a trained firefighter and paramedic who had worked search and rescue for victims of the September 11, 2001, attack on the World Trade Center in New York City.

2008 Beijing T: 8, N: 8, D: 8.17. WR: 5:19.85 (USA—Read, Allen, Ahrens, Hansen, Deakin, Beery, Hoopman, Volpenhein, Cipollone)

1. CAN	5:23.89
2. GBR	5:25.11
3. USA	5:25.34
4. HOL	5:29.26
5. POL	5:31.42
6. AUS	5:35.10
7. CHN	
8. GER	

1. CAN Kevin Light, Benjamin Rutledge, Andrew Byrnes, Jacob Wetzel, Malcolm Howard, Dominic Seiterle, Adam Kreek, Kyle Hamilton, Brian Price
2. GBR Alex Partridge, Thomas Stallard, Thomas Lucy, Richard EgingtonJoshua West, Alastair Heathcote, Matthew Langridge, Colin Smith, Acer Nethercott
3. USA Beau Hoopman, Matthew Schnobrich, Micah Boyd, Wyatt Allen, Daniel Walsh, Steven Coppola, Joshua Inman, Bryan Volpenhein, Marcus McElhenne
4. HOL Meindert Klem, Rogier Blink, Olivier Siegelaar, Jozef Klaassen, David Kuiper, Mitchel Steenman, Olaf van Andel, Diederik Simon, Peter Wiersum
5. POL Sebastian Kosiorek, Michal Stawowski, Patryk Brzeziński, Sławomir Kruszkowski, Wojciech Gutorski, Marcin Brzeziński, Rafał Hejmej, Mikołaj Burda, Daniel Trojanowski
6. AUS David Dennis, Samuel Loch, James Chapman, Thomas Laurich, Jeremy Stevenson, James Tomkins, Sam Conrad, Stephen Stewart, Marty Rabjohns
7. CHN Qu Xiaoming, Wang Jingfeng, Liu Zhen, Zhang Shunyin, Zheng Chuanqi, Zhou Yinan, Zhang Yongqiang, Wang Xiangdang, Zhang Dechang, He Yi
8. GER Florian Eichner, Sebastian Schmidt, Matthias Flach, Philipp Naruhn, Jörg Lehnigk, Florian Menningen, Kristof Wilke, Andreas Penker, Peter Thiede, Jochen Urban

A year before the Olympics, Canada had beaten defending world champion Germany for the 2007 world championship title, winning by a margin of 2.27 seconds. In Beijing the Canadian team won their first-round heat 7.26 seconds ahead of Poland and got off to a strong start in the final, building a 2.5-second gap by the halfway point and holding off a late challenge from Great Britain.

LIGHTWEIGHT: DOUBLE SCULLS

1896–1992 not held

1996 Atlanta-Lake Lanier T: 19, N: 19, D: 7.28. WB: 6:15.58 (Anthony Edwards, Bruce Hick)

1.	SWI	Markus Gier, Michael Gier	6:23.47
2.	HOL	Maarten van der Linden, Pepijn Aardewijn	6:26.48
3.	AUS	Anthony Edwards, Bruce Hick	6:26.69
4.	SPA	José María de Marco Pérez, Juan Carlos Sáez Bernardos	6:28.09
5.	AUT	Wolfgang Sigl, Walter Rantasa	6:30.85
6.	SWE	Mattias Tichy, Anders Christensson	6:34.78
7.	POL	Robert Sycz, Grzegorz Wdowiak	
8.	ITA	Marco Audisio, Michelangelo Crispi	

The Gier brothers, 29-year-old Michael and 26-year-old Markus, had been training together for eight years and sharing an apartment in Rorschach, Switzerland. By the time of the 1996 Olympics, they were getting on each other's nerves so badly that they agreed to stop competing together as soon as the Games were over. This discord did not prevent them from outclassing the field. They passed the early leaders, Edwards and Hick, shortly after the midway point and won easily.

2000 Sydney-Penrith Lakes T: 19, N: 19, D: 9.24. WB: 6:14.57 (Tomasz Kucharski, Robert Sycz)

1.	POL	Tomasz Kucharski, Robert Sycz	6:21.75
2.	ITA	Elia Luini, Leonardo Pettinari	6:23.47
3.	FRA	Pascal Touron, Thibaud Chapelle	6:24.85
4.	GER	Ingo Euler, Bernhard Rühling	6:26.54
5.	SWI	Markus Gier, Michael Gier	6:28.52
6.	JPN	Hitoshi Hase, Daisaku Takeda	6:29.74
7.	AUS	Haimish Karrasch, Bruce Hick	
8.	GRE	Vasilios Polymeros, Panagiotis Miliotis	

Tomasz Kucharski and Robert Sycz won the world championship in 1997 and 1998, but in 1999 they failed to make weight and did not compete. They ran into a similar problem at the Sydney Games. They were, collectively, one kilogram overweight. However, this time they were able to go for a run and lose the weight. Kucharski and Sycz went straight to the lead and then surged at 1300 meters and none of the other teams could close the gap.

2004 Athens-Schinias T: 21, N: 21, D: 8.22. WB: 6:10.80 (Elia Luini, Leonardo Pettinari)

1.	POL	Tomasz Kucharski, Robert Sycz	6:20.93
2.	FRA	Frédéric Dufour, Pascal Touron	6:21.46
3.	GRE	Vasilios Polymeros, Nikolaos Skiathitis	6:23.23
4.	DEN	Mads Rasmussen, Rasmus Quist	6:23.92
5.	HUN	Zsolt Hirling, Tamás Varga	6:24.69
6.	JPN	Kazushige Ura, Daisaku Takeda	6:24.98
7.	USA	Steven Tucker, Gregory Ruckman	
8.	SPA	Rubén Álvarez Hoyos, Juan Zunzunegui Guimerans	

After winning gold medals in Sydney in 2000, Tomasz Kucharski and Robert Sycz had gone on to place second in the next three world championship finals—each time behind 2000 silver medalists Leonardo Pettinari and Elia Luini. However, prior to the Athens Games, Pettinari incurred a rib stress fracture and it quickly became apparent that the heavily-favored Italians would not be contenders. In their opening heat, they finished more than four seconds behind the Greek pair, Vasilios Polymeros and Nikolaos Skiathitis. Kucharski and Sycz also lost their heat, but they made it through the *repêchage* and into the semifinals, where they recorded the fastest time of the round, 6:14.91. Meanwhile, Pettinari and Luini could do no better than fifth place and did not qualify for the final. With the Italian threat gone, Kucharski and Sycz controlled the final, taking the lead early and holding it throughout the race.

2008 Beijing T: 20, N: 20, D: 8.17. WR: 6:10.02 (Mads Rasmussen, Rasmus Quist)

1.	GBR	Zachary Purchase, Mark Hunter	6:10.99
2.	GRE	Dimitris Mougios, Vasilios Polymeros	6:11.72
3.	DEN	Mads Rasmussen, Rasmus Quist	6:12.45
4.	ITA	Marcello Miani, Elia Luini	6:16.15
5.	CHN	Zhang Guolin, Sun Jie	6:16.69
6.	CUB	Eider Batista Vargas, Yunior Pérez Aguilera	6:19.96
7.	NZL	Storm Uru, Peter Taylor	
8.	POR	Pedro Fraga, Nuno Mendes	

Zac Purchase and Mark Hunter won both their preliminary races by a wide margin and controlled the final from the start, finishing a boat-length ahead of Dimitris Mougios and Vasilios Polymeros. The medal podium order was the exact reverse of the 2007 world championships, with two-time reigning world champions Mads Rasmussen and Rasmus Quist in third place.

LIGHTWEIGHT: FOUR-OARED SHELL WITHOUT COXSWAIN

1896–1992 not held

1996 Atlanta-Lake Lanier T: 17, N: 17, D: 7.28. WB: 5:52.34 (ITA—Re, Pettinari, Zasio, Gaddi)

1.	DEN—Niels Lauland Henriksen, Thomas Poulsen, Eskild Ebbesen, Victor Feddersen	6:09.58
2.	CAN—Jeffrey Lay, David Boyes, Gavin Hassett, Brian Peaker	6:10.13
3.	USA—David Collins, Jeffrey Pfaendtner, Marc Schneider, William Carlucci	6:12.29
4.	IRL—Derek Holland, Samuel Lynch, Neville Maxwell, Anthony O'Connor	6:13.51
5.	GER—Tobias Rose, Martin Weis, Michael Buchheit, Bernhard Stomporowski	6:14.79
6.	AUS—Haimish Karrasch, Gary Lynagh, David Belcher, Simon Burgess	6:18.16
7.	FRA—Stéphane Barre, Xavier Dorfmann, Stéphane Guerinot, Henri-Pierre Dall'acqua	
8.	ITA—Andrea Re, Leonardo Pettinari, Ivano Zasio, Carlo Gaddi	

The Irish crew led early and the Canadians controlled the middle of the race, but the experienced Danish team came from behind to win by less than half a length.

2000 Sydney-Penrith Lakes T: 14, N: 14, D: 9.24. WB: 5:45.60 (DEN—Ebert, Poulsen, Ebbesen, Feddersen)

1. FRA—Laurent Porchier, Jean-Christophe Bette, Yves Hocdé, Xavier Dorfmann	6:01.68
2. AUS—Simon Burgess, Anthony Edwards, Darren Balmforth, Robert Richards	6:02.09
3. DEN—Søren Madsen, Thomas Ebert, Eskild Ebbesen, Victor Feddersen	6:03.51
4. ITA—Salvatore Amitrano, Franco Sancassani, Catello Amarante, Carlo Gaddi	6:03.77
5. SAF—Mark Rowand, Ross Hawkins, Roger Tobler, Michael Hasselbach	6:07.67
6. USA—Marc Schneider, Gregory Ruckman, Paul Teti, Thomas Auth	6:10.09
7. CAN—Iain Brambell, Chris Davidson, Gavin Hassett, Jonathan Beare	
8. HOL—Joris Trooster, Jeroen Spaans, Simon Kalkman, Robert van der Vooren	

The Danish crew continued to dominate the event after the 1996 Olympics, winning the next three world championships. But then, in May 2000, Thomas Poulsen injured his knee and had to withdraw from the team. He was replaced by Søren Madsen, who was actually more powerful than Poulsen, but the team lost the rhythm they had developed over the years. In the Olympic final, the Danes took the early lead, but faded to third place at the halfway mark and just managed to hold off the Italians for bronze. Meanwhile, the Australian crew, spurred on by a crowd of more than 20,000, drove into the lead and tried desperately to resist the challenge of the French crew. However the French edged ahead fifty meters from the finish line and won by less than half a second. When asked at what point he started to think they could win, Laurent Porchier replied, "In 1997," the year the French almost beat Denmark at the world championships.

2004 Athens-Schinias T: 13, N: 13, D: 8.22. WB: 5:45.60 (DEN—Poulsen, Ebert, Ebbesen, Feddersen)

1. DEN—Thor Kristensen, Thomas Ebert, Stephan Mølvig, Eskild Ebbesen	6:01.39
2. AUS—Glen Loftus, Anthony Edwards, Benjamin Cureton, Simon Burgess	6:02.79
3. ITA—Lorenzo Bertini, Catello Amarante, Salvatore Amitrano, Bruno Mascarenhas	6:03.74
4. HOL—Gerard van der Linden, Ivo Snijders, Karel Dormans, Joeri de Groot	6:03.79
5. CAN—Iain Brambell, Jonathan Mandick, Gavin Hassett, Jonathan Beare	6:05.10
6. IRL—Richard Archibald, Eugene Coakley, Niall O'Toole, Paul Griffin	6:09.96
7. SER—Veljko Urošević, Nenad Babović, Goran Nedeljković, Miloš Tomić	
8. RUS—Aleksandr Zyuzyn, Sergei Bukreyev, Valery Sarychev, Aleksandr Savkin	

Denmark, two-time defending world champions and the clear favorites in Athens, got out to an early lead in the final, with Italy in second and Australia a close third. The Australians pulled even with the Italians at the halfway point, but slipped back into third with 500 meters left. The Danish crew held onto their narrow lead through the final 500 meters, while the Australians surged at the end to take silver. Denmark's Eskild Ebbesen was a member of the Danish crew that won the inaugural lightweight coxless fours championship at the 1996 Olympics.

2008 Beijing T: 13, N: 13, D: 8.17. WR: 5:45.60 (DEN—Ebert, Poulsen, Ebbesen, Feddersen)

1. DEN	Thomas Ebert, Morten Jørgensen, Mads Andersen, Eskild Ebbesen	5:47.76
2. POL	Łukasz Pawłowski, Bartłomiej Pawełczak, Miłosz Bernatajtys, Paweł Rańda	5:49.39
3. CAN	Iain Brambell, Jon Beare, Mike Lewis, Daniel Parsons	5:50.09
4. FRA	Franck Solforosi, Guillaume Raineau, Jean-Christophe Bette, Fabien Tilliet	5:51.22
5. GBR	Richard Chambers, James Lindsay-Fynn, Paul Mattick, James Clarke	5:52.12
6. HOL	Gerard van der Linden, Marshall Godschalk, Ivo Snijders, Paul Drewes	5:54.06
7. ITA	Jiri Vlcek, Catello Amarante, Salvatore Amitrano, Bruno Mascarenhas	
8. CHN	Huang Zhongming, Wu Chongkui, Zhang Lin, Tian Jun	

Led by double Olympic gold medalist Eskild Ebbesen and 2004 gold medalist Tomas Ebert, Denmark led from start to finish in the final. Reigning world champion Great Britain stayed in medal contention until the final 500 meters, before slipping to fifth place behind twice (and reigning) world silver medalists France.

The Canadian crew dedicated their bronze medals to coach Bent Jensen, who was undergoing chemotherapy treatment for pancreatic cancer. Jensen had coached Denmark to the last two Olympic gold medals and made arrangements to come to Beijing to watch the final from the team boathouse.

DISCONTINUED EVENTS

PAIR-OARED SHELL WITH COXSWAIN

1900 Paris T: 7, N: 3, D: 8.26.

1. HOL&FRA—Minerva Amsterdam: François Antoine Brandt, Roelof Klein, unknown French boy [Hermanus Brockmann]	7:34.2
2. FRA—Société Nautique de la Maine: Lucien Martinet, Waleff, coxswain unknown	7:34.4
3. FRA—Rowing Club Castillon: Carlos Deltour, Antoine Védrenne, Paoli	7:57.2
4. FRA—Cercle Nautique de Reims: Mathieu Pierre, Ferlin, coxswain unknown	8:01.0

This event was the source of one of the modern Olympics' most enduring mysteries: who is the youngest person ever to compete in the Olympics?

François Antoine Brandt and Roelof Klein had expected to win the championship with ease and were surprised when they were beaten by 8.6 seconds in their qualifying heat by the team of Martinet and Waleff. However the reason for their loss was clear. Whereas the Dutch pair used a normal coxswain, Dr. Hermanus Brockmann, who weighed 60 kilograms (132 pounds), the French teams all used children as coxes. For the final, the Dutch decided that they would have to do the same. They found a local boy who had been discarded by the French because he was too heavy (33 kilograms—72¾ pounds). After putting their new cox in their boat, Brandt and Roelf found that he was too light to force the rudder under water, so they attached a 5-kilo lead weight to the rudder.

Warned that the French boats might row a team race against them, with one boat cutting in front early and interfering with their progress, Brandt and Roelof sprinted into the lead as soon as the race began. They held the lead throughout, and crossed the finish line less than a meter ahead of the fast-closing Martinet and Waleff.

The young French cox stayed around long enough to be photographed with his new Dutch friends, but then he vanished into the city. Despite persistent and inventive efforts on the part of Tony Bijkerk and other Olympic historians, the boy's identity has never been found. For many years it was assumed that this boy was the youngest competitor in Olympic history. However after careful study of his photograph, it would appear that he was older than Greek gymnast Dimitrious Loundras, who took part in the 1896 team parallel bars event when he was ten years old. In addition, if Brandt and Klein's cox was discarded for being too heavy, it is quite possible that other coxswains in the race were not only lighter, but younger.

Roelof Klein and François Brandt, 1900

The Dutch rowers chose a local Parisian boy to be their coxswain in the coxed pair final. They won the race. After this photograph was taken, the boy returned to the streets of Paris. He may be the youngest winner in Olympic history. Unfortunately, his name and age remain a mystery.

1904 not held

1906 Athens T: 8, N: 5, D: 4.27.

1000 Meters

1. ITA—Bucintoro, Venice: Enrico Bruna, Emilio Fontanella, Giorgio Cesana 4:23.0
2. ITA—Barion, Bari: Luigi Diana, Francesco Civera, Emilio Cesarana 4:30.0
3. FRA—Société Nautique de la Basse Seine, Paris: Gaston Delaplane, Charles Delaporte, Marcel Frébourg —
4. FRA—Société Nautique de Bayonne: Adolphe Bernard, Joseph Halcet, Jean-Baptiste Mathieu —
5. BEL&GRE—Royal Club Nautique de Gand: Max Orban, Rémy Orban, Theofilakos Psiliakos

1906 Athens T: 7, N: 5, D: 4.27.

1606 Meters

1. ITA—Bucintoro, Venice: Enrico Bruna, Emilio Fontanella, Giorgio Cesana 7:32.4
2. BEL&GRE—Royal Club Nautique de Gand: Max Orban, Rémy Orban, Theofilakos Psiliakos 8:00.0
3. FRA—Société Nautique de Bayonne: Adolphe Bernard, Joseph Halcet, Jean-Baptiste Mathieu 8:08.6
4. DEN—Hannibal Østergård, Henning Rasmussen, Harald Steinthal

Psiliakos was a young Greek who offered to cox for the Belgian pair.

1908–1912 not held

1920 Antwerp-Vilvoorde T: 4, N: 4, D: 8.29.

1. ITA—Ercole Olgeni, Giovanni Scatturin, Guido De Filip 7:56.0
2. FRA—Gabriel Poix, Maurice Bouton, Ernest Barberolle 7:57.0
3. SWI—Édouard Candeveau, Alfred Felber, Paul Piaget —

1924 Paris T: 5, N: 5, D: 7.17.

1. SWI—Édouard Candeveau, Alfred Felber, Émile Lachapelle 8:39.0
2. ITA—Ercole Olgeni, Giovanni Scatturin, Gino Sopracordevole 8:39.1
3. USA—Leon Butler, Harold Wilson, Edward Jennings —
4. FRA—Eugène Constant, Raymond Talleux, Marcel Lepan —

The final was, by all accounts, a thrilling race, and was won by the Swiss by only two feet.

1928 Amsterdam-Sloten T: 6, N: 6, D: 8.10.

1. SWI—Hans Schöchlin, Karl Schöchlin, Hans Bourquin 7:42.6
2. FRA—Armand Marcelle, Edouard Marcelle, Henri Préaux 7:48.4
3. BEL—Léon Flament, François de Coninck, Georges Anthony
4. ITA—Renzo Vestrini, Roberto Vestrini, Cesare Milani

1932 Los Angeles-Long Beach T: 4, N: 4, D: 8.13.

1. USA—Joseph Schauers, Charles Kieffer, Edward Jennings 8:25.8
2. POL—Jerzy Braun, Janusz Ślązak, Jerzy Skolimowski 8:31.2
3. FRA—Anselme Brusa, André Giriat, Pierre Brunet 8:41.2
4. BRA—José Ramalho, Estevan Strata, Francisco Bricio 8:53.2

1936 Berlin-Grünau T: 12, N: 12, D: 8.14.

1. GER—Gerhard Gustmann, Herbert Adamski, Dieter Arend 8:36.9
2. ITA—Almiro Bergamo, Guido Santin, Luciano Negrini 8:49.7
3. FRA—Georges Tapie, Marceau Fourcade, Noël Vandernotte 8:54.0
4. DEN—Raymond Larsen, Carl Berner, Aage Jensen 8:55.8
5. SWI—Georges Gschwind, Hans Appenzeller, Rolf Spring 9:10.9
6. YUG—Ivo Fabris, Elko Mrduljaš, Line Ljubičić 9:19.4

1948 London-Henley-on-Thames T: 9, N: 9, D: 8.9.

1. DEN—Finn Pedersen, Tage Henriksen, Carl-Ebbe Andersen 8:00.5
2. ITA—Giovanni Steffe, Aldo Tarlao, Alberto Radi 8:12.2
3. HUN—Antal Szendey, Béla Zsitnik Sr., Róbert Zimonyi 8:25.2
4. FRA—Ampelio Sartor, Aristide Sartor, René Crezen
4. YUG—Vladeta Ristić, Milan Horvatin, Duško Đorđević

1952 Helsinki T: 15, N: 15, D: 7.23.

1. FRA—Raymond Salles, Gaston Mercier, Bernard Malivoire 8:28.6
2. GER—Heinz-Joachim Manchen, Helmut Heinhold, Helmut Noll 8:32.1
3. DEN—Svend Pedersen, Poul Svendsen, Jörgen Frandsen 8:34.9
4. ITA—Giuseppe Ramani, Aldo Tarlao, Luciano Marion 8:38.4
5. FIN—Veijo Mikkolainen, Toimi Pitkänen, Érkki Lyijynen 8:40.8

The French coxswain, Bernard Malivoire, was 14 years old.

1956 Melbourne-Ballarat T: 8, N: 8, D: 11.27.

1. USA—Arthur Ayrault, Conrad "Conn" Findlay, A. Kurt Seiffert 8:26.1
2. GER—Karl-Heinrich von Groddeck, Horst Arndt, Rainer Borkowsky 8:29.2
3. SOV—Ihor Yemchuk, Heorhi Zhylin, Vladimir Petrov 8:31.0
4. POL—Henryk Jagodziński, Zbigniew Szwarcer, Berthold Mainka 8:31.5

1960 Rome-Lake Albano T: 18, N: 18, D: 9.3.

1. GER—Bernhard Knubel, Heinz Renneberg, Klaus Zerta 7:29.14
2. SOV—Antanas Bagdonavičius, Zigmas Jukna, Igor Rudakov 7:30.17
3. USA—Richard Draeger, Conrad "Conn" Findlay, H. Kent Mitchell 7:34.58
4. DEN—Jens Behrendt Jensen, Knud Nielsen, Sven Lysholt Hansen 7:39.20
5. ITA—Giancarlo Piretta, Renzo Ostino, Vincenzo Bruno 7:40.92
6. ROM—Ştefan Kureska, Gheorghe Riffelt, Mircea Roger 7:49.57

German coxswain Klaus Zerta was 13 years old. Except for the unknown coxswain in 1900, Zerta is the youngest male in Olympic history to win a gold medal.

1964 Tokyo T: 16, N: 16, D: 15.

1. USA—Edward Ferry, Conrad "Conn" Findlay, H. Kent Mitchell 8:21.23
2. FRA—Jacques Morel, Georges Morel, Jean-Claude Darouy 8:23.15
3. HOL—Jan Bos, Herman Rouwé, Frederik Hartsuiker 8:23.42
4. SOV/RUS—Nikolai Safronov, Leonid Rakovschik, Igor Rudakov 8:24.85
5. CZE—Václav Chalupa, Jiři Palko, Zdeněk Mejstřík 8:36.21
6. POL—Kazimierz Naskręcki, Marian Siejkowski, Stanisław Kozera 8:40.00
7. GDR—Günter Bergau, Peter Gorny, Karl-Heinz Danielowski
8. AUT—Alfred Sageder, Josef Kloimstein, Peter Salzbacher

1968 Mexico City-Xochimilco T: 18, N: 18, D: 10.19.

1. ITA—Primo Baran, Renzo Sambo, Bruno Cipolla 8:04.81
2. HOL—Herman Suselbeek, Hadriaan van Nes, Roderick Rijnders 8:06.80
3. DEN—Jörn Krab, Harry Jörgensen, Preben Krab 8:08.07
4. GDR—Helmut Wollmann, Wolfgang Gunkel, Klaus-Dieter Neubert 8:08.22
5. USA—William Hobbs, Richard Edmunds, Stewart MacDonald 8:12.60
6. GER—Bernhard Hiesinger, Rolf Hartung, Lutz Benter 8:41.51
7. SWI—Urs Frankhauser, Urs Bitterli, Beat Wirz
8. BUL—Georgi Atanasov, Georgi Nikolov, Veselin Stayevski

1972 Munich-Oberschleissheim T: 21, N: 21, D: 9.2.

1. GDR—Wolfgang Gunkel, Jörg Lucke, Klaus-Dieter Neubert 7:17.25
2. CZE—Oldřich Svojanovský, Pavel Svojanovský, Vladimír Petříček 7:19.57
3. ROM—Ştefan Tudor, Petre Ceapura, Ladislau Lovrenschi 7:21.36
4. GER—Heinz Mussmann, Bernd Krause, Stefan Kuhnke 7:21.52
5. SOV/RUS—Vladimir Yeshinov, Nikolai Ivanov, Yuri Lorentson 7:24.44
6. POL—Wojciech Repsz, Wiesław Długosz, Jacek Rylski 7:28.92
7. NOR—Rolf Andreassen, Arne Bergodd, Thor Egil Olsen
8. GBR—David Maxwell, Michael Hart, Alan Inns

1976 Montreal T: 17, N: 17, D: 7.25.

1. GDR—Harald Jährling, Friedrich-Wilhelm Ulrich, Georg Spohr 7:58.99
2. SOV/RUS—Dmitri Bekhterev, Yuri Shurkalov, Yuri Lorentson 8:01.82
3. CZE—Oldřich Svojanovský, Pavel Svojanovský, Ludvík Vébr 8:03.82
4. BUL—Rumen Hristov, Tsvetan Petkov, Tosho Kishev 8:11.27
5. ITA—Primo Baran, Annibale Venier, Franco Venturini 8:15.97

6. POL—Ryszard Stadniuk, Grzegorz Stellak, Ryszard Kubiak 8:23.02
7. GBR—A. Neil Christie, James Macleod, David Webb
8. GER—Winfried Ringwald, Klaus Jaeger, Holgen Hocke

1980 Moscow T: 11, N: 11, D: 7.20.
1. GDR—Harald Jährling, Friedrich-Wilhelm Ulrich, Georg Spohr 7:02.54
2. SOV—Viktor Pereverzev, Gennady Kryuchkin, Aleksandr Lukyanov 7:03.35
3. YUG/CRO—Duško Mrduljaš, Zlatko Celent, Josip Reić 7:04.92
4. ROM—Petre Ceapura, Gabriel Bularda, Ladislau Lovrenschi 7:07.17
5. BUL—Tsvetan Petkov, Rumen Hristov, Todor Kishev 7:09.21
6. CZE—Josef Plaminek, Milan Škopek, Oldřich Hejdušek 7:09.41
7. ITA—Antonio Dell'Aquila, Giuseppe Abbagnale, Giuseppe Di Capua
8. FRA—Serge Fornara, Hervé Bourquel, Jean-Pierre Huguet-Balent

1984 Los Angeles-Lake Casitas T: 12, N: 12, D: 8.5.
1. ITA—Carmine Abbagnale, Giuseppe Abbagnale, Giuseppe Di Capua 7:05.99
2. ROM—Dimitrie Popescu, Vasile Tomoiagă, Dumitru Răducanu 7:11.21
3. USA—Kevin Still, Robert Espeseth, Douglas Herland 7:12.81
4. BRA—Valter Hime Soares, Angelo Rosio Neto, Nilton Silva Alonco 7:17.07
5. CAN—Harold Backer, Anthony Zasada, Ian Barkley 7:18.98
6. GER—Hermann Gress, Dieter Göpfert, Rudolf Ziegler 7:25.16
7. YUG—Dario Vidošević, Zlatko Celent, Mirko Ivančić
8. GBR—Adrian Genziani, William Lang, Alan Inns

The coxswain for the bronze-medal-winning US team was 32-year-old Doug Herland, who stood 4 feet 9 inches tall and weighed 103 pounds. Herland was born with broken hips, broken ribs and a broken collarbone as a result of osteogenesis imperfecta—brittle bone disease. He broke bones twice a year for the first eight years of his life. Herland discovered rowing at Pacific Lutheran U. in Tacoma, Washington, where he earned a degree in social psychology. He went on to a career in social work, counseling handicapped and mentally retarded children, and establishing a rowing team for the disabled in Michigan.

The coxswain for the 11th place Belgian pair was the youngest competitor at the 1984 Olympics, 12-year-old Philippe Cuelenaere.

1988 Seoul T: 14, N: 14, D: 9.25.
1. ITA—Carmine Abbagnale, Giuseppe Abbagnale, Giuseppe Di Capua 6:58.79
2. GDR—Mario Streit, Detlef Kirchhoff, René Rensch 7:00.63
3. GBR—Andrew Holmes, Steven Redgrave, Patrick Sweeney 7:01.95
4. ROM—Dimitrie Popescu, Vasile Tomolağa, Ladislau Lovrenchi 7:02.60
5. BUL—Emil Groitzov, Atanas Andreyev, Stefan Stoykov 7:03.04
6. SOV/RUS—Andrei Korikov, Roman Kazantsev, Andrei Lipsky) 7:06.07
7. CZE—Jan Kabrhel, Jiří Pták, Milan Škopek
8. YUG—Roman Ambrožič, Milan Janša, Sašo Mirjanič

The Abbagnale brothers of Pompeii transmuted a furious start into their second Olympic championship. Their younger brother, Agostino, a member of the Italian quadruple sculls team, also went home with a gold medal.

1992 Barcelona-Banyoles T: 16, N: 16, D: 8.2.
1. GBR—Jonathon Searle, Gregory Searle, Garry Herbert 6:49.83
2. ITA—Carmine Abbagnale, Giuseppe Abbagnale, Giuseppe Di Capua 6:50.98
3. ROM—Dimitrie Popescu, Nicolaie Taga, Dumitru Răducanu 6:51.58
4. GER—Thomas Woddow, Michael Peter, Peter Thiede 6:56.98
5. CUB—Ismael Carbonell Same, Arnaldo Rodríguez Silva, Roberto Ojeda González 6:58.26
6. FRA—Patrick Berthou, Laurent Lacasa, Emmanuel Bunoz 7:03.01
7. POL—Piotr Basta, Tomasz Mruczkowski, Bartosz Sroga
8. USA—Aaron Pollok, John Moore, Stephen Shellans

The Abbagnale brothers had won seven world championships and two Olympic championships and they had not been beaten since 1986. The Searle brothers, on the other hand, although respected rowers, had only taken up the coxed pairs in April 1992. But it was the Searles who recorded the fastest times in both the preliminary round and the semifinals. In the final the Abbagnales followed their usual strategy of setting a blistering pace. They led by almost four seconds at the halfway mark. The Searles, lying in third place, picked up speed with 750 meters to go and passed the stunned Italians in the final hundred meters. Greg Searle later admitted to a "pang of guilt" when he looked over at the Italians and saw that they looked "suddenly very old . . . I could tell how devastated they were and utterly gutted." The Abbagnales and Di Capua rowed over and offered their congratulations, and Greg Searle "was very touched by their graciousness and chivalry."

FOUR-OARED SHELL WITH COXSWAIN

1900 Paris T: 10, N: 4, D: 8.26, 8.29.

First Final
1. FRA—Cercle de l'Aviron de Roubaix: Emile Delchambre, Jean Cau, Henri Bouchaert, Henri Hazebroucq, Charlot 7:11.0
2. FRA—Club Nautique de Lyon: Charles Perrin, Daniel Soubeyran, Emile Wegelin, Georges Lumpp, coxswain unknown 7:18.0
3. GER—Favorite Hammonia, Hamburg: Hugo Rüster, Wilhelm Carstens, Julius Körner, Adolf Möller, Max Ammermann [Gustav Moths] 7:18.2

Second Final
1. GER—Germania Ruder Club, Hamburg: Oscar Gossler, Walther Katzenstein, Waldemar Tietgens, Gustav Gossler, Carl Gossler 5:59.0

2. HOL—Minerva Amsterdam: Gerhard Lotsy, Coenraad Hiebendaal, Paulus Lotsy, Johannes Terwogt, Hermanus Brockmann — 6:03.0
3. GER—Ludwigshafener Ruder Verein: Carl Lehle, Ernst Feller, Hermann Wilker, Otto Fickeisen, Franz Kröwerath — 6:05.0

Incompetence on the part of regatta officials resulted in the unusual development of two separate finals in the 1900 Olympics in this event. At first it was declared that the winners of three heats would qualify for the final as would the second-place finisher in heat 3, which included four of the ten entrants. When it was discovered that the losers in heats 2 and 3 had recorded faster times than the winner of heat 1, the officials announced that an extra qualifying heat would have to be run. However, they were unable to notify all of the crews, so the extra heat was cancelled. It was then decided that the three heat winners would be joined in the final by the three fastest losers. But since the course was laid out for only four boats, the heat winners protested and refused to participate in the final. So the first final was run off with only Roubaix of the original qualifiers in the water. The result was obviously ridiculous, so a second final was announced for the three heat winners. Participants in both finals were awarded prizes.

1904 not held

1906 Athens T: 8, N: 5, D: 4.24.

1. ITA—Bucintoro, Venice: Enrico Bruna, Emilio Fontanella, Riccardo Zardinoni, Giuseppe Poli, Giorgio Cesana — 8:13.0
2. FRA—Société Nautique de la Basse Seine, Paris: Gaston Delaplane, Charles Delaporte, Léon Delignières, Paul Échard, Marcel Frébourg — —
3. FRA—Société Nautique de Bayonne: Adolphe Bernard, Joseph Halcet, Jean-Baptiste Laporte, Pierre Sourbé, Jean-Baptiste Mathieu — —
4. DEN—Dansk Idræts Forbund: Knud Bay, Emanuel Saugmann, Frederick Bielefeldt, Henning Rasmussen, Hannibal Østergård — —
5. GRE—Panhellenios Gymnastikos Syllogos: Nikolaos Vianginis, Parmenios Nomikis, Dimitrios Kountouris, Georgios Tsakonas, Khristos Brisimitzakis — —
6. GRE—Peraikos Syndesmos: Nikolaos Zamanos, Georgios Georgitseas, N. Petros, Panagiotis Saousopoulos, Demetrios Pediadis — —
7. INT—Omilos Ereton Smyrnis: Donald Whittal, Nikolaos Petropoulos, Petros Paulidis, Ioannis Gounaris, Nikolaos Mardelis — —

DNF: GRE—Nautikos Omilos: Khristos Liambeis, Khristos Rangos, Menelaos Sakorafos, Georgios Boumboulis, Konstantinos Athanasiadis

1908 not held

1912 Stockholm T: 11, N: 9, D: 7.19.

1. GER—Ludwigshafener Ruderverein: Albert Arnheiter, Hermann Wilker, Rudolf Fickeisen, Otto Fickeisen, Otto Maier — 6:59.4
2. GBR—Thames Rowing Club: Julius Beresford, Karl Vernon, Charles Rought, Bruce Logan, Geoffrey Carr — —
3. DEN—Polytehnic Roklub: Erik Bisgaard, Rasmus Frandsen, Mikael Simonsen, Poul Thymann, Ejgil Clemmensen — —
3. NOR—Kristiana Roklub: Henry Larsen, Mathias Torstensen, Theodor Klem, Håkon Tønsager, Ejnar Tønsager — —

The German crew won by two lengths

1920 Antwerp-Vilvoorde T: 8, N: 8, D: 8.29.

1. SWI—Wilhelm Brüderlin, Max Rudolf, Paul Rudolf, Hans Walter, Paul Staub — 6:54.0
2. USA—Kenneth Myers, Carl Klose, Franz Federschmidt, Erich Federschmidt, Sherman Clark — 6:58.0
3. NOR—Birger Var, Theodor Klem, Henry Larsen, Per Gulbrandsen, Thoralf Hagen — —

1924 Paris T: 10, N: 10, D: 7.17.

1. SWI—Emile Albrecht, Alfred Probst, Eugen Sigg-Bächthold, Hans Walter, Emile Lachapelle — 7:18.4
2. FRA—Eugène Constant, Louis Gressier, Georges Lecointe, Raymond Talleux, Marcel Lepan — 7:21.6
3. USA—Robert Gerhardt, Sidney Jelinek, Edward Mitchell, Henry Welsford, John Kennedy — 7:23.0
4. ITA—Renato Berninzone, Marcello Casanova, Gastone Cerato, Jean Cipollina, Massimo Ballestrero — —

DNF: HOL—Johannes Brandsma, Jacob Brandsma, Dirk Fortuin, Jean van Silfhout, Louis Dekker

1928 Amsterdam-Sloten T: 11, N: 11, D: 8.10.

1. ITA—Valerio Peretin, Giliante D'Este, Nicolo Vittori, Giovanni Delise, Renato Petronio — 6:47.8
2. SWI—Ernst Haas, Joseph Meyer, Otto Bucher, Karl Schwegler, Fritz Bösch — 7:03.4
3. POL—Franciszek Bronikowski, Edmund Jankowski, Leon Birkholc, Bernard Ormanowski, Bolesław Drewek — 7:12.8
4. GER—Karl Golzo, Hans Nickel, Karl Hoffmann, Werner Kleine, Alfred Krohn — 7:26.4
5. BEL—Maurice Delplanck, Théo Wambeke, Alphonse Dewette, Charles van Son, Jean Bauwens — 7:30.2

1932 Los Angeles-Long Beach T: 7, N: 7, D: 8.13.

1. GER—Hans Eller, Horst Hoeck, Walter Meyer, Joachim Spremberg, Karl-Heinz Neumann — 7:19.0
2. ITA—Bruno Vattovaz, Giovanni Plazzer, Riccardo Divora, Bruno Parovel, Giovanni Scherl — 7:19.2
3. POL—Jerzy Braun, Janusz Ślązak, Stanisław Urban, Edward Kobyliński, Jerzy Skolimowski — 7:26.8
4. NZL—Noel Pope, Somers Cox, Charles Saunders, John Solomon, Delmont Gullery — 7:32.6

A spectacular finish saw the Germans win by a mere one foot.

1936 Berlin-Grünau T: 16, N: 16, D: 8.14.

1. GER—Hans Maier, Walter Volle, Ernst Gaber, Paul Söllner, Fritz Bauer 7:16.2
2. SWI—Hermann Betschart, Hans Homberger, Alex Homberger, Karl Schmid, Rolf Spring 7:24.3
3. FRA—Fernand Vandernotte, Marcel Vandernotte, Marcel Cosmat, Marcel Chauvigné, Noël Vandernotte 7:33.3
4. HOL—Martinus Schoorl, Hotse Sjoerd Bartlema, John Regout, Simon de Wit, Gerard Hallie 7:34.7
5. HUN—Miklós Mihó, Vilmos Éden, Ákos Inotay, Alajos Szilassy-Szymiczek, László Molnár 7:35.6
6. DEN—Hans Mikkelsen, Ibsen Sörensen, Flemming Jensen, Svend Aage Sörensen, Aage Jensen 7:40.4

Coxswain for the French bronze medalists was 12-year-old Noël Vandernotte, whose father, Fernand, and uncle, Marcel, were also members of the crew. Noël also coxed for the pair-oared shell.

1948 London-Henley-on-Thames T: 16, N: 16, D: 8.9.

1. USA—Warren Westlund, Robert Martin, Robert Will, Gordon Giovanelli, Allen Morgan 6:50.3
2. SWI—Rudolf Reichling, Erich Schriever, Emile Knecht, Pierre Stebler, André Moccand 6:53.3
3. DEN—Erik Larsen, Börge Nielsen, Henry Larsen, Harry Knudsen, Jörgen Ib Olsen 6:58.6
4. FRA—Jean Pieddeloup, René Lotti, Gaston Maquat, Jean-Pierre Souche, Marcel Boigegrain; HUN—Miklós Zágon, Lajos Nagy, Béla Nyilasi, Tibor Nádas, Róbert Zimonyi; ITA—Reginaldo Polloni, Francesco Gotti, Renato Macario, Riccardo Cerutti, Dominico Cambieri

Two members of Cuba's rowing team, Manuel Lorenzo Puig and Tirso del Junco, participated in the unsuccessful US-backed Bay of Pigs invasion of Cuba in 1961. Puig was captured and executed by Cuban government forces.

1952 Helsinki T: 17, N: 17, D: 7.23.

1. CZE—Karel Mejta Sr., Jiří Havlis, Jan Jindra, Stanislav Lusk, Miroslav Koranda 7:33.4
2. SWI—Enrico Bianchi, Karl Weidmann, Heinrich Scheller, Emile Ess, Walter Leiser 7:36.5
3. USA—Carl Lovested, Alvin Ulbrickson, Richard Wahlström, Matthew Leanderson, Albert Rossi 7:37.0
4. GBR—Roderick Macmillan, Graham Fisk, Laurence Guest, Peter de Giles, Paul Massey 7:41.2
5. FIN—Kurt Grönholm, Paul Stråhlman, Birger Karlsson, Karl-Erik Johansson, Antero Tukiainen 7:43.8

1956 Melbourne-Ballarat T: 10, N: 10, D: 11.27.

1. ITA—Alberto Winkler, Romano Sgheiz, Angelo Vanzin, Franco Trincavelli, Ivo Stefanoni 7:19.4
2. SWE—Olof Larsson, Gösta Eriksson, Ivar Aronsson, Sven Ever Gunnarsson, Bertil Göransson 7:22.4
3. FIN—Kauko Hänninen, Reino Poutanen, Veli Lehtelä, Toimi Pitkänen, Matti Niemi 7:30.9
4. AUS—Gordon Cowey, Kevin McMahon, Reginald Libbis, Ian Allen, John Jenkinson 7:31.1

1960 Rome-Lake Albano T: 21, N: 21, D: 9.3.

1. GER—Gerd Cintl, Horst Effertz, Klaus Rieckemann, Jürgen Litz, Michael Obst 6:39.12
2. FRA—Robert Dumontois, Claude Martin, Jacques Morel, Guy Nosbaum, Jean-Claude Klein 6:41.62
3. ITA—Fulvio Balatti, Romano Sgheiz, Franco Trincavelli, Giovanni Zucchi, Ivo Stefanoni 6:43.72
4. SOV/RUS—Oleg Aleksandrov, Igor Khokhlov, Boris Fyodorov, Valentin Zanin, Igor Rudakov 6:45.67
5. AUS—Graeme Allen, Maxwell Annett, John Hudson, Roland Waddington, Lionel Robberds 6:45.80
6. HUN—Tibor Bedekovics, Csaba Kovács, László Munteán, Pál Wágner, Gyula Lengyel 6:51.65

1964 Tokyo T: 16, N: 16, D: 10.15.

1. GER—Peter Neusel, Bernhard Britting, Joachim Werner, Egbert Hirschfelder, Jürgen Oelke 7:00.44
2. ITA—Renato Bosatta, Emilio Trivini, Giuseppe Galante, Franco De Pedrina, Giovanni Spinola 7:02.84
3. HOL—Alex Mullink, Jan van de Graaf, Frederick van de Graaf, Robert van de Graaf, Marius Klumperbeek 7:06.46
4. FRA—Yves Fraisse, Claude Pache, Gérard Jacquesson, Michel Dumas, Jean Claude Darouy 7:13.92
5. SOV/RUS—Anatoly Tkatchuk, Vitaly Kurdchenko, Boris Kuzmin, Anatoly Luzgin, Vladimir Yevseyev 7:16.05
6. POL—Szczepan Grajczyk, Marian Leszczyński, Ryszard Lubicki, Andrzej Nowaczyk, Jerzy Pawłowski 7:28.15
7. USA—Paul Gunderson, Harry Pollock, Thomas Pollock, James Tew, Edward Washburn
8. NZL—Darien Boswell, Alistair Dryden, Peter Masfen, Robert Page, Dudley Storey

1968 Mexico City-Xochimilco T: 13, N: 13, D: 10.19.

1. NZL—Richard Joyce, Dudley Storey, Ross Hounsell Collinge, Warren Cole, Simon Dickie 6:45.62
2. GDR—Peter Kremtz, Roland Göhler, Manfred Gelpke, Klaus Jakob, Dieter Semetzky 6:48.20
3. SWI—Denis Oswald, Hugo Waser, Peter Bolliger, Jakob Grob, Gottlieb Fröhlich 6:49.04
4. ITA—Romano Sgheiz, Emilio Trivini, Giuseppe Galante, Luciano Sgheiz, Mariano Gottifredi 6:49.54
5. USA—Luther Jones, William Purdy, Anthony Martin, Aspinwall Gardner Cadwalader, John Hartigan 6:51.41
6. SOV—Anatoly Mentyrev, Nikolai Surov, Oleksei Myschyn, Arkady Kudinov, Viktor Mikheyev 7:00.00
7. ROM—Reinhold Batschi, Petre Ceapura, Ştefan Tudor, Francisc Papp, Ladislau Lovrenchi
8. ARG—Hugo Aberastegui, José Robledo, Juan Gómez, Guillermo Segurado, Rolando Locatelli

The winning New Zealand crew had never competed together before the Olympics.

1972 Munich-Oberschleissheim T: 14, N: 14, D; 9.2.

1. GER—Peter Berger, Hans-Johann Färber, Gerhard Auer, Alois Bierl, Uwe Benter 6:31.85
2. GDR—Dietrich Zander, Reinhard Gust, Eckhard Martens, Rolf Jobst, Klaus-Dieter Ludwig 6:33.30
3. CZE—Otakar Mareček, Karel Neffe, Vladimir Jánoš, František Provaznik, Vladimír Petříček 6:35.64
4. SOV—Volodymyr Sterlyk, Vladimir Soloviev, Aleksandr Lyubaturov, Yuri Shamayev, Igor Rudakov 6:37.71
5. USA—David Sawyer, Charles Ruthford, Chadwick Rudolph, Michael Vespoli, Stewart MacDonald 6:41.86

6. NZL—Warren Cole, Christopher Nilsson, John Clark, David Linstrom, Peter Lindsay 6:42.55
7. HOL—Wim Grothuis, Evert Kroes, Jan Woudenberg, Johan ter Haar, Cornelis de Korver
8. SWI—Hanspeter Leuthi, Urs Frankhauser, Franz Rentsch, Denis Oswald, Rolf Stadelmann

1976 Montreal T: 14, N: 14, D: 7.25.

1. SOV/RUS—Vladimir Yeshinov, Nikolai Ivanov, Mikhail Kuznetsov, Aleksandr Klepikov, Aleksandr Lukianov 6:40.22
2. GDR—Andreas Schulz, Rüdiger Kunze, Walter Diessner, Ullrich Diessner, Johannes Thomas 6:42.70
3. GER—Hans-Johann Färber, Ralph Kubail, Siegfried Fricke, Peter Niehusen, Hartmut Wenzel 6:46.96
4. CZE—Otakar Mareček, Karel Neffe, Milan Suchopár, Vladimir Jánoš, Vladimir Petřiček 6:50.15
5. BUL—Lachezar Boychev, Nacho Minchev, Ivan Botev, Kiril Kirchev, Nenko Dobrev 6:52.88
6. NZL—Vivian Haar, Daniel Keane, Timothy Logan, Ian Boserio, David Simmons 7:00.17
7. IRL—Michael Ryan, James Muldoon, William Ryan Christy O'Brien, Liam Redmond
8. POL—Jerzy Broniec, Adam Tomasiak, Jerzy Ulczyński, Ryszard Burak, Włodzimierz Chmielewski

1980 Moscow T: 12, N: 12, D: 7.27.

1. GDR—Dieter Wendisch, Ullrich Diessner, Walter Diessner, Gottfried Döhn, Andreas Gregor 6:14.51
2. SOV/LAT—Artürs Garonskis, Dimants Krišjānis, Dzintars Krišjānis, Žoržs Tikmers, Juris Bērziņš 6:19.05
3. POL—Grzegorz Stellak, Adam Tomasiak, Grzegorz Nowak, Ryszard Stadniuk, Ryszard Kubiak 6:22.52
4. SPA—Manuel Bermúdez García, Isidro Martín Solano, Salvador Verges Soler, Luis Lasúrtegui Berridi, Javier Sabriá Pitarch 6:26.23
5. BUL—Hristo Aleksandrov, Vilhem Germanov, Georgi Petkov, Stoyan Stoyanov, Nenko Dobrev 6:28.13
6. SWI—Daniel Homberger, Peter Rahn, Roland Stocker, Peter Stocker, Karl Graf 6:30.26
7. GBR—Leonard Robertson, Gordon Rankine, Colin Seymour, John Roberts, Alan Inns
8. BRA—Laildo Machado, Wandir Kuntze, Walter Soares, Henrique Johann, Manoel Novo

1984 Los Angeles-Lake Casitas T: 8, N: 8, D: 8.5.

1. GBR—Martin Cross, Richard Budgett, Andrew Holmes, Steven Redgrave, Adrian Ellison 6:18.64
2. USA—Thomas Kiefer, Gregory Springer, Michael Bach, Edward Ives, John Stillings 6:20.28
3. NZL—Kevin Lawton, Donald Symon, Barrie Mabbott, Ross Tong, Brett Hollister 6:23.68
4. ITA—Giovanni Sergi Sergas, Giovanni Suarez, Gino Iseppi, Giuseppe Carando, Siro Meli 6:26.44
5. CAN—David Ross, Timothy Christian, Richard Doey, Nicholas Toulmin, Paul Tessier 6:28.78
6. GER—Heribert Karches, Georg Konermann, Wolfram Theim, Wolfgang Maennig, Manfred Klein 6:34.23
7. BRA—Andre Berezin, Luiz Santos, Denis Marinho, Laildo Machado, Manoel Novo
8. JPN—Satoru Miyoshi, Tadashi Abe, Shunsuke Kawamoto, Hideaki Maeguchi, Akihiro Koike

1988 Seoul T: 14, N: 14, D: 9.24.

1. GDR—Frank Klawonn, Bernd Eichwurzel, Bernd Niesecke, Karsten Schmeling, Hendrik Reiher 6:10.74
2. ROM—Dimitrie Popescu, Ioan Snep, Valentin Robu, Vasile Tomoiagă, Ladislau Lovrenchi 6:13.58
3. NZL—George Keys, Ian Wright, Gregory Johnston, Christopher White, Andrew Bird 6:15.78
4. GBR—D. Adam Cliff, John Maxey, John Garrett, Martin Cross, H. Vaughan Thomas 6:18.08
5. USA—John Terwilliger, Christopher Huntington, Thomas Darling, John Walters, Mark Zembsch 6:18.47
6. YUG—Sead Marušić, Lazo Pivač, Zlatko Celent, Vladimir Banjanac, Dario Varga 6:23.28
7. GER—Roland Baar, Wolfgang Klapheck, Christoph Korte, Andreas Lütkefels, Martin Ruppel
8. CZE—Milan Doleček, Oldřich Hejdušek, Petr Hlídek, Dušan Macháček, Michal Šubrt

1992 Barcelona-Banyoles T: 12, N: 12, D: 8.1.

1. ROM—Viorel Talapan, Iulică Ruican, Dimitrie Popescu, Neculai Ţaga, Dumitru Răducanu 5:59.37
2. GER—Uwe Kellner, Ralf Brudel, Thoralf Peters, Karsten Finger, Hendrik Reiher 6:00.34
3. POL—Jacek Streich, Wojciech Jankowski, Tomasz Tomiak, Maciej Łasicki, Michał Cieślak 6:03.27
4. USA—James Neil, Teo Bielefeld, M. Sean Hall, John Rusher, Timothy Evans 6:06.03
5. FRA—Yannick Schulte, Philippe Lot, Daniel Fauché, Jean-Paul Vergne, Jean Pierre Huguet-Balent 6:06.82
6. SOV—Veniamin But, Igor Bortnitsky, Vladimir Romanishin, Gennady Kryuchkin, Pyotr Petrinich 6:12.13
7. CRO—Sead Marušić, Marko Banović, Ninoslav Saraga, Aleksandar Fabijanić, Goran Puljko
8. CHN—Feng Feng, Sun Senlin, Huang Xiaoping, Xu Wuling, Li Jianxin

SIX-MAN NAVAL ROWING BOATS

1906 Athens T: 4, N: 2, D: 4.24

2000 Meters

1. ITA—Varese: Giuseppe Russo, P. Toio, R. Taormina, G. Tarantino, E. Bellotti, Angelo Formaciari, Giovanni Battista Tanio 10:45.0
2. GRE—Spetsai: Demetrios Balourdos, Spyros Vesalas, Nikolaos Dekavalas, Demetrios Dais, Nikolaos Karsouvas, Pavlos Kypraios Kipraios, Konstantinos Misonginis —
3. GRE—Hydra: Demetrius Grous, P. Lomvardos, Georgios Maroulis, Demetrios Souranis, Nikolaos Photinakis, Dionysius Khristeas, Petros Mexis —
4. GRE—Psara: Dimitrios Mavronas, Emilios Vafeas, Aristides Spalieris, Nikolaos Valsamakis, Emilios Paravolos, A. Kordonis, Spyros Lomvardos —

SEVENTEEN-MAN NAVAL ROWING BOATS

1906 Athens T: 5, N: 2, D: 4.24.

3000 Meters

1. GRE	16:35.0
2. GRE	17:09.6
3. ITA	—
4. GRE	—
5. GRE	—

1. GRE—Poros: Ioannis Georgas, Khristos Tsirigotakis, Ioannis Agrimis, Konstantinos Kephalas, Demetrios Kakousis, Ioannis Pilouris, Pavlos Karangonidis, Demetrios Piaditis, Ioannis Lafiotis, Isidoros Mikhas, Mikhail Mouratis, Mikhail Sokos, Andreas Drivas, Argos Milonas, Ioannis Kaisarevs, Ioannis Loukas, Petros Velliotis
2. GRE—Hydra: Petros Ptemeas, Ioannis Dolas, Ioannis Gripaios, Ioannis Tsirakis, Evangelos Khaldaios, Konstantinos Niotis, Konstantinos Papagiannoulis, Nikolaos Stergiou, S. Lemonis, Ioannis Papapanagiotou, Evangelos Kanakaris, Georgios Nikoloutsos, Xenophon Stellas, Samatios Diomataras, Mikhail Katsoulis, Ioannis Fasilis, Ioannis Milakas
3. ITA—Varese: G. Cingottu, F. Pieraccini, G. Pizzo, Augusto Graffigna, L. Frediani, Alberto Ruggia, F. Mennella, S. Messina, Antonio Mautrere, Ezio Germignani, Angelo Sartini, Sebastiano Randazzo, Angelo Buoni, Alphonso Nordio, P. Oddone, G. Zannino, E. Rossi
4. GRE —Psara: Athanasios Kalyvas, Athanasios Lafis, Argos Khalukiopoulos, Vasilios Falangas, Pavlos Tzetzos, Konstantinos Perimenis, Nikolaos Khalas, Elios Tzannidis, Anastasious Maniatis, Khristos Koutoulangas, Pavlos Tzannos, Georgios Barous, Georgios Vogiatzakos, Konstantinos Karakatsanis, Nikolaos Karagiannis, Nikolaos Blioziotis, Petros Freskalakis
5. GRE—Spetsia: Georgios Papazis, Pavlos Alsanis, Aristides Drakakis, Anastasios Stavrianos, Nikolaos Filippidis, Georgios Khasapis, Vasilios Katekhis, Antonios Pitsilos, Konstantinos Pagoulatos, N. Vasileiadis, Ioannis Melakhroinos, Evangelos Oikonomou, Georgios Fouskas, D. Ringas, I. Kottas, Nikolaos Maurakis, Eleios Marinos

FOUR-OARED INRIGGERS WITH COXSWAIN

1912 Stockholm T: 6, N: 4, D: 7.18.

1. DEN—Ejler Allert, Jørgen Hansen, Carl Møller, Carl Pedersen, Poul Hartmann	7:44.6
2. SWE—Ture Rosvall, William Bruhn-Möller, Conrad Brunkman, Herman Dahlbäck, Wilhelm Wilkens	7:56.9
3. NOR—Claus Høyer, Reidar Holter, Magnus Herseth, Frithjof Olstad, Olaf Bjørnstad	—

WOMEN

All women's races are rowed on a 2000-meter course. Before 1988, they were rowed at 1000 meters.

SINGLE SCULLS

1896–1972 not held

1976 Montreal C: 11, N: 11, D: 7.24.

1. Christine Scheiblich	GDR	4:05.56
2. Joan Lind	USA	4:06.21
3. Yelena Antonova	SOV/RUS	4:10.24
4. Rositsa Spasova	BUL	4:10.86
5. Ingrid Munneke	HOL	4:18.71
6. Mariann Ambrus	HUN	4:22.59
7. Annick Anthoine	FRA	
8. Christel Agrikola	GER	

1980 Moscow C: 11, N: 11, D: 7.26.

1. Sanda Toma	ROM	3:40.69
2. Antonina Makhina	SOV/RUS	3:41.65
3. Martina Schröter	GDR	3:43.54
4. Rositsa Spasova	BUL	3:47.22
5. Beryl Mitchell	GBR	3:49.71
6. Beata Dziadura	POL	3:51.45
7. Frances Cryan	IRL	
8. Mariann Ambrus	HUN	

1984 Los Angeles-Lake Casitas C: 16, N: 16, D: 8.4.

1. Valeria Račilă	ROM	3:40.68
2. Charlotte Geer	USA	3:43.89
3. Ann Haesebrouck	BEL	3:45.72
4. Andrea Schreiner	CAN	3:45.97
5. Lise Marianne Justesen	DEN	3:47.79
6. Beryl Mitchell	GBR	3:51.20
7. Stephanie Foster	NZL	
8. Josephine Compaan	HOL	

1988 Seoul C: 13, N: 13, D: 9.25.

1. Jutta Behrendt	GDR	7:47.19
2. Anne Marden	USA	7:50.28
3. Magdalena Georgieva	BUL	7:53.65
4. Harriet van Ettekoven	HOL	7:57.29
5. Marioara Popescu	ROM	7:59.44
6. Inger Pors	DEN	7:59.77
7. Antonia Svaier	GRE	
8. Natalya Kvasha	SOV/UKR	

Defending world champion Magdalena Georgieva pushed to a 2.86-second lead at the 1500-meter mark, but then blew up and faded to third, leaving the victory to 1986 world champion Jutta Behrendt of Berlin.

1992 Barcelona-Banyoles C: 15, N: 15, D: 8.2.

1. Elisabeta Lipă (Oleniuc)	ROM	7:25.54
2. Annelies Bredael	BEL	7:26.64
3. Silken Laumann	CAN	7:28.85
4. Anne Marden	USA	7:29.84
5. Maria Brandin	SWE	7:37.55
6. Corine Le Moal	FRA	7:41,85
7. Antonia Svaier	GRE	
8. Irene Eijs	HOL	

Having won the 1991 world championship by over three seconds, 27-year-old Silken Laumann of Mississauga, Ontario, was considered the overwhelming favorite for Barcelona. But on May 16, 1992, 73 days before she was scheduled to race for the first time at the Olympics, Laumann was the victim of a horrific accident. In a poorly supervised warm-up area in Essen,

Germany, her shell was rammed by the shell of the German coxless pair, Peter Holtzenbein and Cohn von Ettingshausen. A piece of wood ripped through Laumann's lower right leg, fracturing the bone, cutting the muscles in her calf and causing extensive nerve and tissue damage. The wound was so gruesome that both Holtzenbein and Ettingshausen, after helping to save Laumann, fainted.

Doctors told Laumann she would need at least six months to recover. But Laumann insisted that she wanted to compete again at the Olympics. In 1984, rowing with her sister, she had earned a bronze medal in double sculls. In 1988 she placed seventh in the same event. For 1992 her goal was to finish ahead of at least one other rower. Miraculously, after five operations, she made it to Barcelona, although she walked with a cane and was advised to avoid standing up for more than fifteen minutes at a time.

With Laumann out of contention, the favorite's mantle fell to Elisabeta Lipă, who made her living working for the Romanian version of the CIA. Lipă did not disappoint, leading from start to finish and earning her fifth Olympic medal.

Meanwhile, Laumann was performing new miracles every couple of days. First she finished second in her qualifying heat behind Anne Marden. Then she won her semifinal race. In the final, Laumann held on to third place for three quarters of the race. Then she was passed by Marden, but Laumann pulled ahead of her again in the last 100 meters to earn a bronze medal.

1996 Atlanta-Lake Lanier C: 17, N: 17, D: 7.27. WB: 7:17.09 (Silken Laumann)

1. Ekaterina Khodatovich	BLR	7:32.21
2. Silken Laumann	CAN	7:35.15
3. H. Trine Hansen	DEN	7:37.20
4. Maria Brandin	SWE	7:42.58
5. Guinevere Batten	GBR	7:45.08
6. Ruth Davidon	USA	7:46.47
7. Annelies Bredael	BEL	
8. Rumyana Neykova	BUL	

Ekaterina Khodatovich was one of the last products of the Soviet Union's talent identification system. In 1987 the Olympic School of Rowing in Minsk sent out letters to all the secondary schools in rural Belarus asking teachers and school officials to lookout for "tall, healthy country girls." Fifteen-year-old Katya Khodatovich from the small village of Osecheno, north of Minsk, was 1.85 meters (6 feet ¾ inch) tall and healthy. Although she had never rowed before, Khodatovich moved to Minsk. Within three years she was junior world champion in single sculls. At the 1992 Olympics, she earned a bronze medal as a member of the Unified Team's quadruple sculls crew. Four years later, at the Atlanta Games, she fended off a mid-race challenge from Silken Laumann and powered to a length and a half victory.

2000 Sydney-Penrith Lakes C: 19, N: 19, D: 9.23. WB: 7:11.68 (Ekaterina Karsten [Khodatovich])

1. Ekaterina Karsten (Khodatovich)	BLR	7:28.14
2. Rumyana Neykova	BUL	7:28.15
3. Katrin Rutschow-Stomporowski	GER	7:28.99
4. Yuliya Aleksandrova	RUS	7:36.57
5. Georgina Douglas	AUS	7:37.88
6. Sonia Waddell	NZL	7:43.71
7. Mayra González Borroto	CUB	
8. Agnieszka Tomczak	POL	

After earning the gold medal at the 1996 Olympics, Ekaterina Khodatovich added the 1997 world championship and then took a year off to marry German Wilfred Karsten and to give birth to a baby girl. She returned to competition in 1999 and won the world championship by a whopping three seconds. At the 2000 Olympics, Karsten fell victim to the flu and struggled through the early rounds. In the final, she and Rumyana Neykova appeared to finish in a dead-heat. The judges' decision-making process took three times as long as the race itself. Eventually they decided that Karsten had won by 12 thousandths of a second. The Bulgarians protested, but their complaint was rejected.

2004 Athens-Schinias C: 24, N: 24, D: 8.21. WB: 7:07.71 (Rumyana Neykova)

1. Katrin Rutschow-Stomporowski	GER	7:18.12
2. Ekaterina Karsten (Khodatovich)	BLR	7:22.00
3. Rumyana Dzhadzharova-Neykova	BUL	7:23.10
4. Miroslava Knapková	CZE	7:25.14
5. Sonia Waddell-Scown	NZL	7:31.66
6. Nuria Domínguez Asensio	SPA	7:49.11
7. Irina Fedotova	RUS	
8. Frida Svensson	SWE	

The three medalists from the Sydney Olympics, Ekaterina Karsten, Rumyana Neykova and Katrin Rutschow, continued to dominate the single sculls in the years leading to the next Olympics. Rutschow won the 2001 world championship, with Karsten in third place, while Neykova took the year off to have a baby. She came back to earn the world championship in both 2002 and 2003, beating Karsten by more than four seconds the first time (with Rutschow in third) and Rutschow by more than three seconds the second time (with Karsten third). The three defending medalists all won their respective qualifying heats by large margins. In the semis, Katrin Rutschow gave an impressive performance, finishing almost six seconds ahead of her nearest competitor, while Karsten edged out Neykova by .15 seconds in the second semi. In the final, Rutschow opened a slight lead at the halfway point and expanded it over the rest of the race. Both Rutschow and Neykova retired after the Athens Games, but Karsten went on to win the next three world championships, in 2005, 2006 and 2007.

2008 Beijing C: 26, N: 26, D: 8.16. WB: 7:07.71 (Rumyana Neykova)

1. Rumyana Neykova	BUL	7:22.34
2. Michelle Guerette	USA	7:22.78
3. Ekaterina Karsten (Khodatovich)	BLR	7:23.98
4. Zhang Xiuyun	CHN	7:25.48
5. Miroslava Knapková	CZE	7:35.52
6. Julia Michalska	POL	7:43.44
7. Frida Svensson	SWE	
8. Gabriella Bascelli	ITA	

Competing in her fifth Olympics, 36-year-old Ekaterina Karsten had won each of the three world championships held since the Athens Games. She breezed through the first two rounds and beat 35-year-old Rumyana Neykova in the semifinals… but only by less than half a second.

Twice world silver medalist Mirka Knapková set the early pace in the final, but was soon passed by Neykova, who held off a fast-charging Michelle Guerette to win her first Olympic gold medal. Like Karsten, Neykova was taking part in her fifth Olympics.

DOUBLE SCULLS

1896–1972 not held

1976 Montreal T: 10, N: 10, D: 7.24.

1. BUL	Svetla Otsetova, Zdravka Yordanova	3:44.36
2. GDR	Sabine Jahn, Petra Boesler	3:47.86
3. SOV/LIT	Leonora Kaminskaitė, Genovaitė Ramoškienė	3:49.93
4. NOR	Solfrid Johansen, Ingunn Brechan	3:52.18
5. USA	Jan Palchikoff, Diane Braceland	3:58.25
6. CAN	Cheryl Howard, Beverley Cameron	4:06.23
7. HOL	Andrea Vissers, Helie Klaasse	
8. CZE	Miluse Neffova, Zuzana Prokesova	

1980 Moscow T: 7, N: 7, D: 7.26.

1. SOV	Yelena Khloptseva, Larissa Popova [Aleksandrova]	3:16.27
2. GDR	Cornelia Linse, Heidi Westphal	3:17.63
3. ROM	Olga Homeghi, Valeria Răcilă-Roşca	3:18.91
4. BUL	Svetla Otsetova, Zdravka Yordanova	3:23.14
5. POL	Hanna Jarkiewicz, Janina Klucznik	3:27.25
6. HUN	Ilona Bata, Pétervári-Langhoffer	3:35.70
7. GBR	Sue Hanscombe, Astrid Ayling	

1984 Los Angeles-Lake Casitas T: 8, N: 8, D: 8.4.

1. ROM	Marioara Popescu, Elisabeta Oleniuc	3:26.75
2. HOL	Greet Hellemans, Nicolette Hellemans	3:29.13
3. CAN	Danièle Laumann, Silken Laumann	3:29.82
4. SWE	Carina Gustavsson, Marie Carlsson	3:30.79
5. NOR	Haldis Lenes, Solfrid Johansen	3:32.09
6. USA	Cathleen Thaxton, Julia Geer	3:32.33
7. AUT	Ingeborg Niedermayer, Vera Sommerbauer	
8. GBR	Eleanor "Nonie" Ray, Sally Bloomfield	

1988 Seoul T: 10, N: 10, D: 9.24.

1. GDR	Birgit Peter, Martina Schröter	7:00.48
2. ROM	Elisabeta Lipă [Oleniuc], Veronica Cogeanu	7:04.36
3. BUL	Violeta Ninova, Stefka Madina	7:06.03
4. SOV	Marina Zhukova, Marya Omelyanovych	7:12.67
5. CHN	Guo Mei, Cao Mianying	7.18.69
6. USA	Monica Havelka, Cathleen Tippett	7:21.28
7. CAN	Silken Laumann, Kay Worthington	
8. SWE	Maria Brandin, Carina Gustafsson	

1992 Barcelona-Banyoles T: 13, N: 13, D: 8.1.

1. GER	Kerstin Köppen, Kathrin Boron	6:49.00
2. ROM	Veronica Cochelea [Cogeanu], Elisabeta Lipă [Oleniuc]	6:51.47
3. CHN	Gu Xiaoli, Lu Huali	6:55.16
4. NZL	Philippa Baker, Brenda Lawson	6:56.81
5. GBR	Annabel Eyres, Alison Gill	7:06.62
6. SOV	Sariya Zakirova, Inna Frolova	7:09.45
7. BUL	Daniela Oronova, Galina Kamenova	
8. AUS	Jennifer Luff, Gillian Campbell	

1996 Atlanta-Lake Lanier T: 14, N: 14, D: 7.27. WB: 6:42.02 (Kerstin Köppen, Kathrin Boron)

1. CAN	Marnie McBean, Kathleen Heddle	6:56.84
2. CHN	Cao Mianying, Zhang Xiuyun	6:58.35
3. HOL	Irene Eijs, Eeke van Nes	6:58.72
4. AUS	Marina Hatzakis, Bronwyn Roye	7:01.26
5. GER	Jana Thieme, Manuela Lutze	7:04.14
6. NZL	Philippa Baker, Brenda Lawson	7:09.92
7. NOR	Kristine Bjerknes, Kristine Klaveness	
8. UKR	Tetyana Ustyuzhanina, Olena Reutova	

Marnie McBean and Kathleen Heddle were known as the "odd couple" of rowing because McBean was so gregarious and Heddle so shy. In 1992 they won the coxless pairs event and then joined the Canadian eights crew to earn a second gold medal. Heddle retired after the Barcelona Games, but two years later she rejoined McBean. This time they switched to double sculls and quadruple sculls. In the 1996 double sculls final they took the lead early, but were never able to shake Cao and Zhang and Eijs and van Nes. Nevertheless, they struggled through the finish line without ever having given up the lead. McBean and Heddle were the first Canadians in any sport to win three gold medals. The next day they added a bronze in the quadruple sculls. In 1998, Marnie McBean became the first woman to earn either an Olympic or world championship medal in each of the six open weight classes.

2000 Sydney-Penrith Lakes T: 10, N: 10, D: 9.23. WB: 6:41.98 (Jana Thieme, Kathrin Boron)

1. GER	Jana Thieme, Kathrin Boron	6:55.44
2. HOL	Pieta van Dishoeck, Eeke van Nes	7:00.36
3. LIT	Birutė Šakickienė, Kristina Poplavskaja	7:01.71
4. USA	Carol Skricki, Ruth Davidon	7:02.61

5. ROM	Elisabeta Lipă [Oleniuc], Veronica Cochelea [Cogeanu]	7:05.05
6. AUS	Marina Hatzakis, Bronwyn Roye	7:05.35
7. SWI	Caroline Lüthi, Bernadette Wicki	
8. FRA	Céline Garcia, Gaëlle Buniet	

The victory of Boron and Thieme was never in doubt. They won the 1999 world championship by four seconds and did even better at the Olympics. For Kathrin Boron, it was her third gold medal. The first was in the 1992 double sculls and the second in the 1996 quadruple sculls.

2004 Athens-Schinias T: 10, N: 10, D: 8.21. WB: 6:38.78 (Georgina Evers-Swindell, Caroline Evers-Swindell)

1. NZL	Georgina Evers-Swindell, Caroline Evers-Swindell	7:01.79
2. GER	Peggy Waleska, Britta Oppelt	7:02.78
3. GBR	Sarah Winckless, Elise Laverick	7:07.58
4. BUL	Anet-Jacqueline Buschmann, Miglena Markova	7:13.97
5. ROM	Camelia Macoviciuc-Mihalcea, Simona Strimbeschi	7:17.58
6. UKR	Natalia Huba, Svitlana Maziy	7:21.78
7. FRA	Caroline Delas, Gaëlle Buniet	
8. ITA	Elisabetta Sancassani, Gabriella Bascelli	

The two-time defending world champions and holders of the world's best time, 25-year-old identical twins Georgina and Caroline Evers-Swindell arrived at the Athens Games with a three-year winning streak. In the final, they opened a comfortable two-length lead over the first 1500 meters, followed by Peggy Waleska and Britta Oppelt, who began to attack in the final 500 meters. The Germans steadily narrowed the lead, but the Evers-Swindell sisters held them off by just under a second to take gold.

2008 Beijing T: 10, N: 10, D: 8.16. WB: 6:38.78 (Georgina Evers-Swindell, Caroline Evers-Swindell)

1. NZL	Georgina Evers-Swindell, Caroline Evers-Swindell	7:07.32
2. GER	Annekatrin Thiele, Christiane Huth	7:07.33
3. GBR	Elise Laverick, Anna Bebington	7:07.55
4. CHN	Li Qin, Tian Liang	7:15.85
5. USA	Megan Kalmoe, Ellen Tomek	7:17.53
6. CZE	Miroslava Knapková, Gabriela Vařeková	7:25.09
7. UKR	Kateryna Tarasenko, Yana Dementieva	
8. AUS	Catriona Oliver-Sens, Sonia Mills	

Defending Olympic champions Georgina and Caroline Evers-Swindell had won medals at each of the past three world championships: gold in 2005, bronze in 2006 and silver in 2007. The pair won their first-round race easily, beating Germany's Annekatrin Thiele and Christiane Huth.

The final was a thrilling sprint to the finish between the New Zealand and German pairs. The result was so close that neither side knew who the winner was until the results flashed on the scoreboard thirty seconds after the finish: the Evers-Swindell sisters had successfully defended their Olympic title by one-hundredth of a second. Reigning world champions Li Qin and Tian Liang set the early pace but faded to fourth at the end, while British pair Elise Laverick and Anna Bebington made up three seconds on the leaders to finish a close third.

QUADRUPLE SCULLS

1896–1984 not held

1988 Seoul T: 10, N: 10, D: 9.25.

1. GDR—Kerstin Förster, Kristina Mundt, Beate Schramm, Jana Sorgers	6:21.06
2. SOV—Iryna Kalimbet, Svitlana Maziy, Inna Frolova, Antonina Dumcheva	6:23.47
3. ROM—Anişoara Bălan, Anişoara Minea, Veronica Cogeanu, Elisabeta Lipă [Oleniuc]	6:23.81
4. BUL—Pavlina Hristova, Galia Anohrieva, Iskra Velinova, Krasimira Tocheva	6:24.10
5. CZE—Hana Krejčová, Ľubica Kurhajcová, Blanka Mikysková, Irena Soukupová	6:41.86
6. BEL—Marie-Anne Vandermoere, Ann Haesebrouck, Lucia Focque, Annelies Bredael	6:43.79
7. HOL—Josephine Compaan, Marjan Pentenga, Nicolette Wessel, Marijke Zeekant	
8. HUN—Erika Bertényi, Ildikó Cserey, Anikó Kapócs, Katalin Sarlós	

1992 Barcelona-Banyoles T: 9, N: 9, D: 8.2.

1. GER—Kerstin Müller, Sybille Schmidt, Birgit Peter, Kristina Mundt	6:20.18
2. ROM—Constanța Pipotă, Doina Ignat, Veronica Cochelea [Cogeanu], Anişoara Dobre Bălan	6:24.34
3. SOV—Ekaterina Khodatovich, Antonina Zelikovich, Tatyana Ustyuzhanina, Yelena Khloptseva	6:25.07
4. HOL—Laurien Vermulst, Marjan Pentenga, Anita Meiland, Harriet van Ettekoven	6:32.40
5. USA—Kristine Karlson, Alison Townley, Serena Eddy-Moulton, Michelle Knox-Zaloom	6:32.65
6. CZE—Ľubica Novotníková [Kurhajcová], Michaela Burešova, Hana Kafková, Irena Soukupová	6:35.99
7. CHN—Feng Lili, Yang Hong, Lu Huali, Gu Xiaoli	
8. DEN—Berit Christoffersen, Lene Pedersen, H. Trine Hansen, Ulla Hansen	

1996 Atlanta-Lake Lanier T: 10, N: 10, D: 7.28. WB: 6:10.80 (GER—Sorgers, Rutshow, Boron, Köppen)

1. GER—Jana Sorgers, Katrin Rutschow, Kathrin Boron, Kerstin Köppen	6:27.44
2. UKR—Olena Ronzhina, Inna Frolova, Svitlana Maziy, Diana Miftakhutdinova	6:30.36
3. CAN—Laryssa Biesenthal, Marnie McBean, Diane O'Grady, Kathleen Heddle	6:30.38
4. DEN—Inger Pors, Ulla Hansen, Sarah Lauritzen, Dorthe Pedersen	6:30.92
5. CHN—Cao Mianying, Zhang Xiuyun, Liu Xirong, Gu Xiaoli	6:31.10
6. HOL—Irene Eijs, Meike van Driel, Petronella "Nelleke" Penninx, Eeke van Nes	6:35.54
7. RUS—Irina Fedotova, Oksana Dorodnova, Larisa Merk, Magarita Bogdanova	
8. USA—Andrea Thies, Cecile Tucker, Catherine Symon, Julia Chilicki	

The German crew won as expected, but the next four teams were less than four meters apart as they crossed the finish line. The Ukrainians edged the Canadians for silver by about 10 centimeters (4 inches).

2000 Sydney-Penrith Lakes T: 9, N: 9, D: 9.24. WB: 6:10.80 (GER—Sorgers, Rutshow, Boron, Köppen)

1. GER—Manja Kowalski, Meike Evers, Manuela Lutze, Kerstin Kowalski	6:19.58
2. GBR—Guinevere Batten, Gillian Lindsay, Katherine Grainger, Miriam Batten	6:21.64
3. RUS—Oksana Dorodnova, Irina Fedotova, Yuliya Levina, Larisa Merk	6:21.65
4. UKR—Dina Myftakhutdinova, Tetyana Ustyuzhanina, Svitlana Maziy, Olena Ronzhyna	6:25.71
5. USA—Hilary Gehman, Jennifer Dore, Laurel Korholz, Kelly Salchow	6:30.26
6. DEN—Bianca Carstensen, Katrin Gleie, Sarah Lauritzen, Dorthe Pedersen	6:31.30
7. AUS—Kerry Knowler, Monique Heinke, Julia Wilson, Sally Robbins	
8. CHN—Lijuan Liu, Jing Han, Guangxia Sun, Lin Liu	

The German victory was not unexpected considering that German quad sculls crews had won every Olympic title since the event was added to the program and all but one world championship (1993) since 1984. The British silver medal, on the other hand, was a surprise, as no British women's crew had ever placed better than fifth in an Olympic event. They just edged ahead of the Russians at the finish line.

2004 Athens-Schinias T: 8, N: 8, D: 8.22. WB: 6:10.80 (GER—Sorgers, Rutshow, Boron, Köppen)

1. GER—Kathrin Boron, Meike Evers, Manuela Lutze, Kerstin El-Qalqili (Kowalski)	6:29.29
2. GBR—Alison Mowbray, Deborah Flood, Frances Houghton, Rebecca Romero	6:31.26
3. AUS—Dana Faletic, Rebecca Sattin, Kerry Hore, Amber Bradley	6:34.73
4. RUS—Yuliya Levina, Larisa Merk, Anna Sergeyeva, Oksana Dorodnova	6:36.49
5. USA—Michelle Guerette, Hilary Gehman, Kelly Salchow, Danika Holbrook-Harris	6:39.67
7. DEN—Dorthe Pedersen, Sarah Lauritzen, Christina Rindom, Majbrit Nielsen	
8. BLR—Mariya Brel, Tatsyana Narelik, Olga Berezhneva, Mariya Varona	

DISQ (Drugs): UKR (Olena Morozova (Ronzhyna), Tetiana Kolesnikova, Olena Olefirenko, Yana Dementieva) 6:34.31

Led by three-time gold medalist and seven-time world champion Kathrin Boron, the German crew swept through to the final, where they took an early lead and easily held off a late attack by Great Britain to earn their fifth straight gold medal in the Olympic quad sculls event. The Ukrainian crew finished in third place and was awarded bronze medals. However, one of the crew members, Olena Olefirenko, tested positive for the stimulant ethamivan, an ingredient in a medication she had openly stated that she had taken. Although the International Rowing Federation ruled that Olifirenko herself was not at fault because she had only taken medicine given to her by the Ukrainian team doctor, the Ukrainian crew was disqualified and their medals passed to the Australian crew.

2008 Beijing T: 8, N: 8, D: 8.17. WR: 6:10.80 (GER—Sorgers, Rutshow, Boron, Köppen)

1. CHN	Tang Bin, Jin Ziwei, Xi Aihua, Zhang Yangyang	6:16.06
2. GBR	Annabel Vernon, Deborah Flood, Frances Houghton, Katherine Grainger	6:17.37
3. GER	Britta Oppelt, Manuela Lutze, Kathrin Boron, Stephanie Schiller	6:19.56
4. UKR	Svitlana Spiriukhova, Tetiana Kolesnikova, Olena Olefirenko, Nataliya Lialchuk	6:20.02
5. USA	Lia Pernell, Lindsay MeyerJennifer Kaido, Margot Shumway	6:25.86
6. AUS	Zoe Uphill, Amber Bradley, Kerry Hore, Amy Ives	6:30.05
7. RUS	Oksana Dorodnova, Yuliya Levina, Larisa Merk, Yuliya Kalinovskaya	
8. CAN	Rachelle De Jong, Anna-Marie de Zwager, Janine Hanson, Krista Guloien	

Led by 2004 silver medalists Debbie Flood and Frances Houghton, Great Britain had won the past three world championship titles. Their main challenge was expected to come from Germany, who had won the last five Olympic titles and had finished behind Britain at the 2007 world championships in Munich.

The British team took the early lead and was still in front after 1500 meters. However, the Chinese, who had come third at the last world championships, zipped by them in the sprint to the finish and won by half a length. It was China's first-ever Olympic rowing championship.

PAIR-OARED SHELL WITHOUT COXSWAIN

1896–1972 not held

1976 Montreal T: 11, N: 11, D: 7.24.

1. BUL	Siika Kelbecheva, Stoyanka Gruicheva	4:01.22
2. GDR	Angelika Noack, Sabine Dähne	4:01.64
3. GER	Edith Eckbauer, Thea Einöder	4:02.35
4. SOV/UKR	Nataliya Horodilova, Anna Karnaushenko	4:03.27
5. CAN	Patricia Smith, Elisabeth Craig	4:08.09
6. ROM	Marlena Predescu, Marinela Maxim	4:15:44
7. USA	Susan Morgan, Laura Staines	
8. POL	Anna Karbowiak, Małgorzata Kowalska	

1980 Moscow T: 6, N: 6, D: 7.26.

1. GDR	Ute Steindorf, Cornelia Khier	3:30.49
2. POL	Małgorzata Dłużewska, Czesława Kościańska	3:30.95
3. BUL	Siika Barbulova [Kelbecheva], Stoyanka Kurbatova [Gruicheva]	3:32.39
4. ROM	Florica Dospinescu [Petcu], Elena Oprea	3:35.14
5. SOV/RUS	Larissa Zavarzina, Galina Stepanova	4:12.53

Despite the fact that there were only six entrants, regatta officials insisted that two elimination heats and a *repêchage* be run in order to trim the field in the final to five.

1984 Los Angeles-Lake Casitas T: 6, N: 6, D: 8.4.

1. ROM	Rodica Arba [Puşcatu], Elena Horvat [Oprea]	3:32.60
2. CAN	Elizabeth Craig, Patricia Smith	3:36.06
3. GER	Ellen Becker, Iris Völkner	3:40.50
4. HOL	Harriet van Ettekoven, Lynda Cornet	3:44.01
5. USA	Barbara Kirch, Charlene "Chari" Towne	3:44.35
6. GBR	Katherine Panter, Ruth Howe	3:48.53

1988 Seoul T: 10, N: 10, D: 9.24.

1. ROM	Rodica Arba [Puşcatu], Olga Homeghi	7:28.13
2. BUL	Radka Stoyanova, Lalka Berberova	7:31.95
3. NZL	Nicola Payne, Lynley Hannen	7:35.68
4. GDR	Kerstin Spittler, Katrin Schröder	7:40.47
5. SOV	Sarmite Stone, Marina Smorodina	7:53.19
6. USA	Barbara Kirch, Mara Keggi	7:56.27
7. CAN	Jennifer-Kirsten Barnes, Sarah Ann Ogilvie	
8. GBR	Alison Bonner, Kim Thomas	

Arba and Homeghi were the overwhelming favorites, having won 40 straight races since 1986, including two world championships. In addition, they both had extensive Olympic experience. Arba, besides being the defending champion in the pairs, had won a bronze medal in the eights in 1980. Homeghi too took home a bronze in 1980 and a gold in 1984; hers were in the double sculls and coxed fours. In Seoul they were unchallenged in the pairs. Twenty-four hours later they both added silvers to their medal haul as part of the Romanian eights crew.

1992 Barcelona-Banyoles T: 13, N: 13, D: 8.1.

1. CAN	Marnie McBean, Kathleen Heddle	7:06.22
2. GER	Stefani Werremeier, Ingeburg Schwerzmann [Althoff]	7:07.96
3. USA	Anna Seaton, Stephanie Pierson	7:08.11
4. FRA	Christine Gosse, Isabelle Danjou	7:08.70
5. GBR	Joanne Turvey, Miriam Batten	7:17.28
6. BUL	Violeta Zareva, Teodora Zareva	7:32.67
7. ROM	Doina Snep [Bălan], Doina Robu	
8. UKR	Anna Motrechko, Yelena Ronzhina	

Marnie McBean was 16 years old when she was inspired by the performances of Canadian rowers at the 1984 Olympics. She took her first step in the sport by looking up Rowing in the Toronto phone directory and then calling a local club, the Argonaut. Her partner, Kathleen Heddle, didn't start rowing until age 18, when she was recruited by a coach while she was a student at the University of British Columbia, in 1983.

1996 Atlanta-Lake Lanier T: 13, N: 13, D: 7.27. WB: 6:57.42 (Marnie McBean, Kathleen Heddle)

1. AUS	Megan Still, Kate Slatter	7:01.39
2. USA	Melissa "Missy" Schwen, Karen Kraft	7:01.78
3. FRA	Christine Gossé, Hélène Cortin	7:03.82
4. GER	Katherin Haacker, Stefani Werremeier	7:08.49
5. CAN	Emma Robinson, Anna van der Kamp	7:12.27
6. RUS	Albina Ligachova, Vera Pochitayeva	DISQ
7. CHN	Liang Xiling, Jing Yanhua	
8. HOL	Elien Meijer, Anneke Venema	

Still and Slatter and Schwen and Kraft spent the winter of 1995-1996 training together at the Australian Institute of Sport in Canberra. In the Olympic final, the Australian pair built a lead of 1.63 seconds at 1000 meters and then fought off the closing rush of the Americans. Four weeks to the hour after earning an Olympic silver medal, Missy Schwen gave up her kidney to be transplanted into her brother, Michael.

2000 Sydney-Penrith Lakes T: 10, N: 10, D: 9.23. WB: 6:56.27 (Emma Robinson, Theresa Luke)

1. ROM	Georgeta Damian, Doina Ignat	7:11.00
2. AUS	Rachael Taylor, Kate Slatter	7:12.56
3. USA	Melissa "Missy" Ryan [Schwen], Karen Kraft	7:13.00
4. CAN	Emma Robinson, Theresa Luke	7:15.48
5. SAF	Helen Fleming, Colleen Orsmond	7:16.84
6. GER	Lenka Wech, Claudia Barth	7:20.08
7. RUS	Albina Ligacheva, Vyera Pochitayeva	
8. UKR	Nina Proskura, Yevgeniya Andryeyeva	

Doina Ignat earned a silver medal in the quad sculls in 1992 and added a gold medal in the eights in 1996. However, two days after returning to Bucharest from the Atlanta Olympics, her apartment was robbed and the gold medal was stolen. Ignat, a police officer, vowed to win another one. In fact, she and partner Georgeta Damian won two, as both were also members of the victorious Romanian eights crew. Rachael Taylor also had trouble with her silver medal. During a rowdy late-night celebration, she lost it in a taxi cab. Fortunately, when her plight was publicized, a Sydney taxi driver found the medal underneath his back seat.

2004 Athens-Schinias T: 10, N: 10, D: 8.21. WB: 6:53.80 (Georgeta Andrunache (Damian), Viorica Susanu)

1. ROM	Georgeta Andrunache (Damian), Viorica Susanu	7:06.55
2. GBR	Katherine Grainger, Catherine Bishop	7:08.66
3. BLR	Yuliya Bichyk, Natalya Gelakh	7:09.86
4. CAN	Darcy Marquardt, Buffy-Lynne Alexander-Williams	7:13.33
5. GER	Maren Derlien, Sandra Goldbach	7:20.20
6. NZL	Juliette Haigh, Nicola Coles	7:23.52
7. CHN	Cong Huanling, Feng Xueling	
8. BUL	Milka Tancheva, Anna Chuk	

After winning two gold medals in 2000, Georgeta Andrunache (formerly Damian) paired with Viorica Susanu and went on to win two world championships in the coxless pairs. In the 2003 world championships, however, they were beaten by two pairs, Katherine Grainger and Catherine Bishop, and Yuliya Bichyk and Natalya Gelakh. In the Olympic final, Darcy Marquardt and Buffy-Lynne Alexander-Williams jumped out to the early lead, but Andrunache and Susanu soon passed them, built a healthy lead by the midway point and were never seriously threatened.

2008 Beijing T: 10, N: 10, D: 8.16. WR: 6:53.80 (Georgeta Andrunache (Damian), Viorica Susanu)

1. ROM	Georgeta Damian-Andrunache, Viorica Susanu	7:20.60
2. CHN	Wu You, Gao Yulan	7:22.28
3. BLR	Yuliya Bichik, Nataliya Gelakh	7:22.91
4. GER	Lenka Wech, Maren Derlien	7:25.73
5. NZL	Juliette Haigh, Nicola Coles	7:28.80
6. GBR	Louisa Reeve, Olivia Whitlam	7:33.61
7. USA	Portia McGee, Anna Mickelson-Cummins	
8. FRA	Inène Pascal-Pretre, Stéphanie Dechand	

Georgeta Andrunache and Viorica Susanu took two years off after winning the 2004 Olympic championship, and then came back to earn bronze at the 2007 world championships in Munich, finishing behind Yuliya Bichik and Nataliya Gelakh of Belarus and Nicole Zimmerman and Elke Hipler of Germany.

In the 2008 Olympic final Andrunache and Susanu led at the halfway point and held on for the win, while China's Wu You and Gao Yulan moved up two places in the last 500 meters to beat Bichik and Gelakh to the silver medals.

It was Susanu's fourth Olympic gold medal and Andrunache's fifth, which made her the second female rower in Olympic history to win five gold medals. "I'm very happy with the gold," Andrunache said after the race. "Now my boyfriend will understand why I didn't spend so much time with him last year."

EIGHT-OARED SHELL WITH COXSWAIN

1896–1972 not held

1976 Montreal T: 8, N: 8, D: 7.24.

1. GDR	3:33.32
2. SOV	3:36.17
3. USA	3:38.68
4. CAN	3:39.52
5. GER	3:41.06
6. ROM	3:44.79
7. POL	
8. HOL	

1. GDR—Viola Goretzki, Christiane Knetsch, Ilona Richter, Brigitte Ahrenholz, Monika Kallies, Henrietta Ebert, Helma Lehmann, Irina Müller, Marina Wilke
2. SOV—Lyubov Talalayeva, Nadezhda Roshchina, Klavdia Koženkova, Elena Zubko, Olha Kolkova, Nelli Tarakanova, Nadiya Rozhon, Olha Huzenko, Olha Pukhovska
3. USA—Jacqueline Zoch, Anita DeFrantz, Carolyn "Carie" Graves, Marion Greig, Anne Warner, Margaret "Peggy" McCarthy, Carol Brown, Gail Ricketson, Lynn Silliman
4. CAN—Carol Eastmore, Rhonda Ross, Nancy Higgins, Mazina DeLure, Susan Antoft, Wendy Pullan, Christine Neuland, Gail Cort, Illoana Smith
5. GER—Waltraud Roick, Erika Endriss, Monika Zipplies, Birgit Kiesow, Hiltrud Gürtler, Isolde Eisele, Marianne Weber, Eva Dick, Ingrid Huhn-Wagner
6. ROM—Elena Oprea, Florica Petcu, Filigonia Tol, Aurelia Marinescu, Georgeta Militaru, Iuliana Munteanu, Elena Avram, Marioara Constantin, Aneta Matei
7. POL—Anna Brandysiewicz, Bogusława Kozłowska, Barbara Wenta-Wojciechowska, Danuta Konkalec, Róża Data, Mieczysława Franczyk, Maria Stadnicka, Aleksandra Kaczyńska, Dorota Zdanowska
8. HOL—Karin Abma, Joke Dierdorf, Barbara Dejong, Annette Schortingshuis, Marleen Van Ry, Maria Kusters, Liesbeth Pascal, Louise "Loes" Schutte, Evelien Koogie

In 1986, Anita DeFrantz of the 1976 third-place US team became the first black woman to be selected for membership on the International Olympic Committee. She was elected to the IOC's executive board in 1992.

1980 Moscow T: 6, N: 6, D: 7.26.

1. GDR	3:03.32
2. SOV	3:04.29
3. ROM	3:05.63
4. BUL	3:10.03
5. GBR	3:13.85

1. GDR—Martina Boesler, Kersten Neisser, Christiane Köpke [Knetsch], Birgit Schütz, Gabriele Kühn [Lohs], Ilona Richter, Marita Sandig, Karin Metze, Marina Wilke
2. SOV—Olha Pyvovarova, Nina Umanets, Nadiya Pryshchepa, Valentina Zhulina, Tetyana Stetsenko, Olena Tereshyna, Nina Preobrazhenska, Mariya Pazyun, Nina Frolova
3. ROM—Angelica Aposteanu, Marlena Zagoni [Predescu], Rodica Frîntu, Florica Bucur, Rodica Puşcatu, Ana Iliuță, Maria Constantinescu, Elena Bondar, Elena Dobrițoiu
4. BUL—Daniela Stavreva, Stefka Koleva, Todorka Vassileva, Snezhka Hristeva, Roumiana Kostova, Veneta Karamandtzukova, Mariana Mincheva, Valentina Aleksandrova, Stanka Georgieva
5. GBR—Gillian Hodges, Joanna Toch, Penelope Sweet, Linda Clark, Elizabeth Paton, Rosemary Clugston, Nicola Boyes, Beverly Jones, Pauline Wright

1984 Los Angeles-Lake Casitas T: 6, N: 6, D: 8.4.

1. USA	2:59.80
2. ROM	3:00.87
3. HOL	3:02.92
4. CAN	3:03.64
5. GBR	3:04.51
6. GER	3:09.92

1. USA—Shyril O'Steen, Harriet Metcalf, Carol Bower, Carolyn "Carie" Graves, Jeanne Flanagan, Kristine Norelius, Kristen Thorsness, Kathryn Keeler, Elizabeth "Betsy" Beard
2. ROM—Doina Bălan, Mărioara Trașcă, Aurora Plesca, Aneta Mihaly, Adriana Chelariu, Mihaela Armăşescu, Camelia Diaconescu, Lucia Sauca, Viorica Ioja
3. HOL—Nicolette Hellemans, Lynda Cornet, Harriet van Ettekoven, Greet Hellemans, Marieke van Drogenbroek, Anne Marie Quist, Catharina Neelissen, Willemien Vaandrager, Martha Laurijsen
4. CAN—Christine Clarke, Lisa Robertson, Katherine Lichty, Carol Colgan, Catherine Lund, Kay Worthington, Gail Cort, Joan Gillingham, Lesley Anderson-Herweck

5. GBR—Alexa Forbes, Katherine McNicol, Kathryn Holroyd, Belinda Holmes, Sarah Hunter-Jones, Astrid Ayling, Ann Callaway, Gillian Hodges, Susan Bailey
6. GER—Elke Riesenkönig, Claudia Horning, Iris Völkner, Ellen Becker, Sabine Hinkelmann, Heike Neu, Kerstin Rehders, Angelika Beblo, Heidrun Barth

1988 Seoul T: 7, N: 7, D: 9.25.

1. GDR	6:15.17
2. ROM	6:17.44
3. CHN	6:21.83
4. SOV	6:22.35
5. BUL	6:25.02
6. USA	6:26.66
7. GER	

1. GDR—Annegret Strauch, Judith Zeidler, Kathrin Haacker, Ute Wild, Anja Kluge, Beatrix Schröer, Ramona Balthasar, Uta Stange, Daniela Neunast
2. ROM—Doina Bălan, Mărioara Trașcă, Veronica Necula, Herta Anitas, Adriana Bazon [Chelariu], Mihaela Armăşescu, Rodica Arba [Puşcatu], Olga Homeghi, Ecaterina Oancia
3. CHN—Zhou Xiuhua, Zhang Yali, He Yanwen, Han Yaqin, Zhang Xianghua, Zhou Shouying, Yang Xiao, Hu Yadong, Li Ronghua
4. SOV—Margarita Teselko, Marina Znak, Nadezhda Sugako, Sandra Brazauskaitė, Olena Pukhayeva, Sariya Zakirova, Natalya Fedorenko, Lidiya Averyanova, Aušra Gudeliūnaitė
5. BUL—Teodora Zareva, Violeta Zareva, Neviana Ivanova, Olia Stoichkova, Todorka Vassileva, Rita Todorova, Mariana Stoyanova, Daniela Oronova, Greta Georgieva
6. USA—Juliet Thompson, Christine Campbell, Abigail Peck, Margaret Mallery, Susan Broome, Stephanie Maxwell, Anna Seaton, Alison Townley, Elizabeth Beard
7. GER—Ingeburg Althoff, Meike Holländer, Elke Markwort, Gabriele Mehl, Kerstin Peters, Cerstin Petersmann, Katrin Petersmann, Kerstin Rehders, Ana Schäfer

1992 Barcelona-Banyoles T: 8, N: 8, D: 8.2.

1. CAN	6:02.62
2. ROM	6:06.26
3. GER	6:07.80
4. SOV	6:09.68
5. CHN	6:12.08
6. USA	6:12.25
7. GBR	
8. CZE	

1. CAN—Kirsten Barnes, Brenda Taylor, Megan Delehanty, Shannon Crawford, Marnie McBean, Kay Worthington, Jessica Monroe, Kathleen Heddle, Lesley Thompson
2. ROM—Doina Snep [Bălan], Doina Robu, Ioana Olteanu, Viorica Lepădatu, Iulia Bobeică, Veronica Necula, Adriana Bazon [Chelariu], Maria Pădurariu, Elena Georgescu
3. GER—Annegret Strauch, Sylvia Dördelmann, Kathrin Haacker, Dana Pyritz, Cerstin Petersmann, Ute Wagner [Stange], Christiane Harzendorf, Judith Zeidler, Daniela Neunast
4. SOV—Svetlana Fil, Marina Znak, Irina Gribko, Sarmīte Stone, Marina Suprun, Natalya Stasyuk, Natalya Grigoryeva, Yekaterina Kotko, Yelena Medvedeva
5. CHN—Lin Zhiai, Ma Linqin, Pei Jiayun, He Yanwen, Liu Xirong, Liang Xiling, Cao Mianying, Zhou Shouying, Li Ronghua
6. USA—Christina Brown, Shannon Day, Elizabeth "Betsy" McCagg, Mary McCagg, Sarah Gengler, Tracy Rude, Kelley Jones, Diana Olson, Yasmin Farooq
7. GBR—Fiona Freckleton, Philippa Cross, Dorothy Blackie, Susan Smith, Katherine Grose, Rachel Hirst, Kareen Marwick, Kathrine Brownlow, Alison Paterson
8. CZE—Lenka Zavadilová, Eliška Jandová, Renata Beránková, Martina Šefčíková, Sabina Telenská, Michaela Vávrová, Hana Žáková, Hana Dariusová, Lenka Kováčová

1996 Atlanta-Lake Lanier T: 8, N: 8, D: 7.28. WB: 5:58.50 (ROM—Tănase, Cochelea [Cogeanu], Gafencu, Spîrcu, Olteanu, Lipă [Oleniuc], Popescu [Ciobanu], Ignat, Georgescu)

1. ROM	6:19.73
2. CAN	6:24.05
3. BLR	6:24.44
4. USA	6:26.19
5. AUS	6:30.10
6. HOL	6:31.11
7. GBR	
8. GER	

1. ROM—Anca Tănase, Veronica Cochelea [Cogeanu], Liliana Gafencu, Doina Spîrcu, Ioana Olteanu, Elisabeta Lipă [Oleniuc], Marioara Popescu [Ciobanu], Doina Ignat, Elena Georgescu
2. CAN—Heather McDermid, Tosha Tsang, Maria Maunder, Alison Korn, Emma Robinson, Anna van der Kamp, Jessica Monroe, Theresa Luke, Lesley Thompson
3. BLR—Natalya Lavrinenko, Aleksandra Pankina, Natalya Volchek, Tamara Davydenko, Valentina Skrabatun, Yelena Mikulich, Natalya Stasyuk, Marina Znak, Yaroslava Pavlovich
4. USA—Anne Kakela, Mary McCagg, Laurel Korholz, Catriona Fallon, Elizabeth "Betsy" McCagg, Monica Tranel Michini, Amy Fuller, Jennifer Dore, Yasmin Farooq
5. AUS—Jennifer Luff, Georgina Douglas, Amy Safe, Anna Ozolins, Karina Wieland, Alison Davies, Carmen Klomp, Bronwyn Thompson, Kaylynn Hick
6. HOL—Femke Boelen, Marleen van der Velden, Astrid van Koert, Marieke Westerhof, Rita de Jong, Tessa Knaven, Muriel van Schilfgaarde, Jissy de Wolf
7. GBR—Annamarie Stapleton, Lisa Eyre, Dorothy Blackie, Catherine "Kate" Pollitt, Miriam Batten, Catherine Bishop, Joanne Turvey, Alison Gill, Suzie Ellis
8. GER—Ina Justh, Antje Rehaag, Kathleen Naser, Andrea Gesch, Dana Pyritz, Micaela Schmidt, Anja Pyritz, Ute Schell, Daniela Neunast

With this race, Romania's Elisabeta Lipă became the first rower in Olympic history to win six medals (three gold, two silver and one bronze).

2000 Sydney-Penrith Lakes T: 7, N: 7, D: 9.24. WB: 5:57.02 (ROM—Damian, Susanu, Olteanu, Chiriță, Dumitrache, Spîrcu, Popescu, Ignat, Georgescu)

1. ROM	6:06.44
2. HOL	6:09.39
3. CAN	6:11.58
4. BLR	6:13.57
5. AUS	6:15.16
6. USA	6:16.87

1. ROM—Georgeta Damian, Viorica Susanu, Ioana Olteanu, Veronica Cochelea (Cogeanu), Maria Dumitrache, Elisabeta Lipă [Oleniuc], Liliana Gafencu, Doina Ignat, Elena Georgescu
2. HOL—Anneke Venema, Carin ter Beek, Petronella "Nelleke" Penninx, Pieta van Dishoeck, Eeke van Nes, Tessa Appeldoorn, Marieke Westerhof, Elien Meijer, Martijntje Quik

3. CAN—Heather McDermid, Heather Davis, Dorota Urbaniak, Theresa Luke, Emma Robinson, Alison Korn, Laryssa Biesenthal, Buffy-Lynne Alexander, Lesley Thompson
4. BLR—Irina Bazilevskaya, Marina Kuzmar, Olga Berezhneva, Marina Znak, Yuliya Bichik, Inessa Zakharevskaya, Nataliya Gelakh, Olga Tratsevskaya, Valentyna Khokhleva
5. AUS—Victoria Roberts, Alison Davies, Jodi Winter, Bronwyn Thompson, Rachael Kininmonth, Kristina Larsen, Emily Martin, Jane Robinson, Katie Foulkes
6. USA—Katherine Maloney, Linda Miller, Amy Martin, Elizabeth "Betsy" McCagg, Torrey Falk, Amy Fuller, Sarah Jones, Lianne Nelson, Rajanya Shah
7. GBR—Alison Sanders, Rowan Carroll, Elise Laverick, Francesca Zino, Alison Trickey, Alexandra Beever, Catherine "Kate" MacKenzie, Lisa Eyre, Charlotte Miller

The favored Romanians won by almost a boat length. Elisabeta Lipăă became the first rower to win seven medals and the first woman to earn gold medals sixteen years apart. Teammate Veronica Cochelea brought her career medal total to six: 2 gold, 3 silver and 1 bronze. Doina Ignat, who had already won her second gold medal in the coxless pairs, caused something of a stir when, after crossing the finish line in the eights, she pointed to the sky and cried out, "Death to our enemies." Lesley Thompson, the coxswain for the Canadian team, was 41 years old.

2004 Athens-Schinias T: 7, N: 7, D: 8.22. WB: 5:57.02 (ROM—Damian, Susanu, Olteanu, Chiriță, Dumitrache, Spîrcu, Popescu, Ignat, Georgescu)

1. ROM	6:17.70
2. USA	6:19.56
3. HOL	6:19.85
4. CHN	6:21.71
5. GER	6:21.99
6. AUS	6:31.65

1. ROM—Rodica Florea, Viorica Susanu, Aurica Chiriță-Bărăscu, Ioana Papuc, Liliana Gafencu, Elisabeta Lipă (Oleniuc), Georgeta Andrunache (Damian), Doina Ignat, Elena Nedelcu (Georgescu)
2. USA—Katie Johnson, Samantha Magee, Mary Whipple, Megan Dirkmaat, Alison Cox, Anna Mickelson, Laurel Korholz, Caryn Davies, Lianne Nelson-Bennion
3. HOL—Froukje Wegman, Marlies Anne Smulders, Ester Workel, Nienke Hommes, Hurnet Dekkers, Annemarieke van Rumpt, Annemiek de Haan, Sarah Siegelaar, Helen Tanger
4. CHN—Yu Fei, Luo Xiuhua, Cheng Ran, Yan Xiaoxia, Wu You, Yang Cuiping, Gao Yanhua, Jin Ziwei, Zheng Na
5. GER—Elke Hipler, Britta Holthaus, Maja Tucholke, Anja Pyritz, Susanne Schmidt, Nicole Zimmermann, Silke Günther, Lenka Wech, Annina Ruppel
6. AUS—Sarah Outhwaite, Jodi Winter, Catriona Oliver, Monique Heinke, Julia Wilson, Sally Robbins, Vicky Roberts, Kyeema Doyle, Katie Foulkes

The field in Athens was relatively evenly-matched. It included two-time defending Olympic champion Romania, 2002 world champion the United States, and the reigning world champion, Germany. The three met in the same qualifying heat, which the US won, setting a world best time of 5:56.55 in the process. In the final, the US took a narrow lead over Romania, with Australia, Germany and China all close behind. Romania moved into the lead near the halfway point and held off the US at the end, while a surge from the Netherlands pushed them ahead of China and Germany to take the bronze medals. Although still in medal contention with 400 meters remaining, the Australian squad slipped to last place after rower Sally Robbins succumbed to exhaustion and stopped rowing. This was a repeat of the 2002 World Championships quad sculls final, in which Robbins had stopped rowing in the final 400 meters, dropping Australia from first to fourth.

The Romanian crew was led by Elisabeta Lipă, who increased her medal count to five gold, two silver and one bronze, the most in rowing history. Her teammate, Georgeta Andrunache, had already won the coxless pairs event the day before. She became the first rower to twice earn two gold medals in one Olympics.

2008 Beijing T: 7, N: 7, D: 8.17. WR: 5:55.50 (USA—Sickler, Cooke, Goodale, Shoop, Mickelson, Francia, Lind, Davies, Whipple)

1. USA	6:05.34
2. HOL	6:07.22
3. ROM	6:07.25
4. CAN	6:08.04
5. GBR	6:13.74
6. AUS	6:14.22
7. GER	

1. USA—Erin Cafaro, Lindsay Schoop, Anna Goodale, Eleanor Logan, Anna Mickelson-Cummins, Susan Francia, Caroline Lind, Caryn Davies, Mary Whipple
2. HOL—Femke Dekker, Marlies Smulders, Nienke Kingma, Roline Repelaer van Driel, Annemarieke van Rumpt, Helen Tanger, Sarah Siegelaar, Annemiek de Haan, Ester Workel
3. ROM—Constanța Burcică (Pipotă), Viorica Susanu, Rodica Şerban (Florea), Eniko Barabas, Simona Strimbeschi-Muşat, Ioana Papuc, Georgeta Andrunache (Damian), Doina Ignat, Elena Georgescu
4. CAN—Heather Mandoli, Andréanne Morin, Sarah Bonikowsky, Ashley Brzozowicz, Romina Stefancic, Buffy Alexander-Williams, Darcy Marquardt, Jane Rumball, Lesley Thompson
5. GBR—Carla Ashford, Beth Rodford, Louisa Reeve, Alice Freeman, Natasha Page, Sarah Winckless, Jessica Eddie, Catherine Greves, Caroline O'Connor
6. AUS—Pauline Frasca, Brooke Pratley, Sally Kehoe, Natalie Bale, Elizabeth Kell, Kate Hornsey, Sarah Outhwaite-Tait, Sarah Heard, Elizabeth Patrick
7. GER—Christina Hennings, Katrin Reinert, Nina Wengert, Nadine Schmutzler, Lenka Wech, Maren Derlien, Nicole Zimmermann, Elke Hipler, Annina Ruppel

After finishing second at the Athens 2004 Olympics, the US women's eight crew returned to win back-to-back world championship titles in 2006 and 2007, beating their rivals, three-time Olympic champions Romania, by more than a second in the 2007 final.

The US led the Beijing final from the start and never gave up the advantage, while the Netherlands, fourth with 500 meters to go, surged at the end to edge Romania out of second place.

LIGHTWEIGHT: DOUBLE SCULLS

1896–1992 not held

1996 Atlanta-Lake Lanier T: 16, N: 16, D: 7.28. WB: 6:50.63 (Berit Christoffersen, Lene Andersson)

1. ROM	Constanța Burcică, Camelia Macoviciuc	7:12.78
2. USA	Teresa Z. Bell, Lindsay Burns	7:14.65
3. AUS	Rebecca Joyce, Virgina Lee	7:16.56
4. ITA	Lisa Bertini, Martina Orzan	7:16.83
5. DEN	Berit Christoffersen, Lene Andersson	7:18.20
6. HOL	Laurien Vermulst, Ellen Meliesie	7:21.92
7. CAN	Colleen Miller, Wendy Wiebe	
8. GER	Michelle Darvill, Ruth Kaps	

Colleen Miller and Wendy Wiebe had won the last three world championships, but Wiebe was weakened by illness. They never found their form at the Olympics and did not qualify for the A final.

2000 Sydney-Penrith Lakes T: 18, N: 18, D: 9.24. WB: 6:50.63 (Berit Christoffersen, Lene Andersson)

1. ROM	Constanța Burcică, Angela Alupei	7:02.64
2. GER	Valerie Viehoff, Claudia Blasberg	7:02.95
3. USA	Christine Collins, Sarah Garner	7:06.37
4. AUS	Sally Newmarch, Virginia Lee	7:12.04
5. SWI	Kim Plugge, Pia Vogel	7:15.57
6. HOL	Kirsten van der Kolk, Marit van Eupen	7:17.89
7. FRA	Benedicte Luzuy, Christelle Fernandez-Schulte	
8. POL	Elżbieta Kuncewicz, Ilona Mokronowska	

Constanța Burcică, with new partner Angela Alupei, defended her Olympic title by coming from behind to beat Viehoff and Blasberg by less than two meters.

2004 Athens-Schinias T: 18, N: 18, D: 8.22. WB: 6:50.63 (Berit Christoffersen, Lene Andersson)

1. ROM	Constanța Burcică, Angela Alupei	6:56.05
2. GER	Daniela Reimer, Claudia Blasberg	6:57.33
3. HOL	Kirsten van der Kolk, Marit van Eupen	6:58.54
4. AUS	Sally Newmarch, Amber Halliday	6:59.91
5. CHN	Xu Dongxiang, Li Qian	7:02.05
6. POL	Magdalena Kemnitz, Ilona Mokrownowska	7:04.48
7. USA	Lisa Schlenker, Stacey Borgman	
8. CAN	Mara Jones, Fiona Milne	

Defending Olympic champions Constanța Burcică and Angela Alupei faced reigning world champions Daniela Reimer and Claudia Blasberg, and 2002 world champion Amber Halliday, now rowing with Sally Newmarch. All three pairs won their qualifying heats, with Halliday and Newmarch setting a world best time of 6:49.40. In third place midway through the final, the Romanian pair surged past the Australians and the Germans to take the lead and the victory, which, for Burcică, was her third in a row.

2008 Beijing T: 17, N: 17, D: 8.17. WR: 6:49.77 (Xu Dongxiang, Yu Hua)

1. HOL	Kirsten van der Kolk, Marit van Eupen	6:54.74
2. FIN	Sanna Stén, Minna Nieminen	6:56.03
3. CAN	Melanie Kok, Tracy Cameron	6:56.68
4. GER	Berit Carow, Marie-Louise Dräger	6:56.72
5. CHN	Xu Dongxiang, Yu Hua	7:01.90
6. GRE	Khrysa Biskitzi, Alexandra Tsiavou	7:04.61
7. DEN	Katrin Olsen, Juliane Rasmussen	
8. AUS	Amber Halliday, Marguerite Houston	

After winning the bronze medals together at the 2004 Athens Olympics, Kristen van der Kolk and Marit van Eupen went their separate ways. Van Eupen focused on the lightweight single sculls, winning three consecutive world titles in 2005, 2006 and 2007, while Van der Kolk left competition to have a daughter. The pair reunited in 2008.

In Beijing they won their first-round heat, beating reigning world champions Amber Halliday and Marguerite Houston, and their semifinal heat finishing ahead of reigning world silver medalists Sanna Stén and Minna Nieminen. In the final, Van der Kolk and van Eupen started slowly, but perfectly timed their final charge over the last 500 meters, pulling ahead of Stén and Nieminen by half a boat-length for the win. Canadian pair Melanie Kok and Tracy Cameron earned bronze ahead of Berit Carow and Marie-Louise Dräger in a photo finish.

DISCONTINUED EVENTS

QUADRUPLE SCULLS WITH COXSWAIN

1976 Montreal T: 9, N: 9, D: 7.19.

1. GDR—Anke Borchmann, Jutta Lau, Viola Poley, Roswietha Zobelt, Liane Weigelt	3:29.99
2. SOV—Anna Kondrachina, Mira Bryunina, Larissa Aleksandrova, Galina Yermolayeva, Nadezhda Chernyshova	3:32.49
3. ROM—Ioana Tudoran, Maria Micşa, Felicia Afrăsiloaie, Elisabeta Lazăr, Elena Giurcă	3:32.76
4. BUL—Iskra Velinova, Verka Aleksieva, Troyanka Vasileva, Svetla Gincheva, Stanka Georgieva	3:34.13
5. CZE—Anna Marešová, Marie Bartáková, Jarmila Patková, Hana Kavková, Alena Svobodová	3:42.53
6. DEN—Kirsten Thomsen, Else Maersk-Kristensen, Judith Andersen, Karen Nielsen, Kirsten Plum-Jensen	3:46.99
7. USA—Karen McCloskey, Lisa Hansen, Elizabeth "Betsy" Hills, Claudia Schneider, Irene Moreno	
8. HUN—Ilona Bata, Kamilla Kosztolányi, Valéria Gyimesi, Ágnes Szijj, Erzsébet Nagy	

1980 Moscow T: 7, N: 7, D: 7.26.

1. GDR—Sybille Reinhardt, Jutta Ploch, Jutta Lau, Roswietha Zobelt, Liane Buhr [Weigelt] 3:15.32
2. SOV—Antonina Pustovit, Yehena Matievskaya, Olga Vasilchenko, Nadezhda Lyubimova, Nina Cheremisina 3:15.73
3. BUL—Mariana Serbezova, Roumeliana Boneva, Dolores Nakova, Ani Bakova, Stanka Georgieva 3:16.10
4. ROM—Marta Macoviciuc, Aneta Mihaly, Sofia Banovici, Mariana Zaharia, Elena Giurcă 3:16.82
5. POL—Bogusława Tomasiak, Mariola Abrahamczyk, Maria Kobylińska, Aleksandra Kaczyńska, Maria Dzieża 3:20.95
6. HOL—Ineke Donkervoort, Lily Meeuwisse, Greet Hellemans, Josephine Compaan, Monique Pronk 3:22.64

1984 Los Angeles-Lake Casitas T: 7, N: 7. D: 8.4.

1. ROM—Maricia Ţăran, Anişoara Sorohan, Ioana Badea, Sofia Corban [Banovici], Ecaterina Oancia 3:14.11
2. USA—Anne Marden, Lisa Rohde, Joan Lind, Virginia Gilder, Kelly Rickon 3:15.57
3. DEN—Hanne Eriksen, Birgitte Hanel, Charlotte Koefoed, Bodil Steen Rasmussen, Jette Hejli Sörensen 3:16.02
4. GER—Anne Dickmann, Regina Kleine-Kuhlmann, Ute Kumitz, Sabine Reuter, Kathrien Plückhahn 3:16.81
5. FRA—Evelyne Imbert, Lydie Dubedat, Christine Gosse, Hélène Ledoux, Patricia Couturier 3:17.87
6. ITA—Raffaella Memo, Alessandra Borio, Donata Minorati, Antonella Corazza, Roberta Del Core 3:21.48

FOUR-OARED SHELL WITHOUT COXSWAIN

1992 Barcelona-Banyoles T: 9, N: 9, D: 8.1.

1. CAN—Kirsten Barnes, Brenda Taylor, Jessica Monroe, Kay Worthington 6:30.85
2. USA—Shelagh Donohoe, Cynthia Eckert, Amy Fuller, Carol Freeney 6:31.86
3. GER—Antje Frank, Gabriele Mehl, Birte Siech, Annette Hohn 6:32.34
4. CHN—Liu Xirong, He Yanwen, Cao Mianying, Zhou Shouying 6:32.50
5. ROM—Victoria Lepădatu, Iulia Bobeică, Adriana Bazon [Chelariu], Maria Păduraru 6:37.24
6. AUS—Jodie Dobson, Emmelia Snook, Megan Still, Kate Slatter 6:41.72
7. FRA—Frédérique Heligon, Chantal Lafon, Christine Jullien, Hélène Cortin
8. GBR—Alison Barnett, Kim Thomas, Suzanne Kirk, Gillian Lindsay

FOUR-OARED SHELL WITH COXSWAIN

1976 Montreal T: 8, N: 8, D: 7.24.

1. GDR—Karin Metze, Bianka Schwede, Gabriele Lohs, Andrea Kurth, Sabine Hess 3:45.08
2. BUL—Ginka Gyurova, Liliana Vaseva, Reni Yordanova, Mariika Modeva, Kapka Georgieva 3:48.24
3. SOV/RUS—Nadezhda Sevostyanova, Lyudmila Krokhina, Galina Mishenina, Anna Pasokha, Lidiya Krylova 3:49.38
4. ROM—Elena Oprea, Florica Petcu, Filigonia Tol, Aurelia Marinescu, Aneta Matei 3:51.17
5. HOL—Liesbeth Vosmaer-De Bruin, Henriette "Hette" Borrias, Myrian van Rooyen, Angelina "Ans" Gravesteijn, Monique Pronk 3:54.36
6. USA—Pamela Behrens, Catherine Menges, Nancy Storrs, Julia Geer, Mary Kellogg 3:56.50
7. CAN—Linda Schaumleffel, Dolores Young, Monica Draeger, Joy Fera, Barbara Mutch
8. GBR—Gillian Webb, Pauline Bird, Clare Grove, Diana Bishop, Pauline Wright

1980 Moscow T: 6, N: 6, D: 7.26.

1. GDR—Ramona Kapheim, Silvia Fröhlich, Angelika Noack, Romy Saalfeld, Kirsten Wenzel 3:19.27
2. BUL—Ginka Gyurova, Mariika Modeva, Rita Todorova, Iskra Velinova, Nadezhda Filipova 3:20.75
3. SOV/RUS—Mariya Fadeyeva, Galina Sovetnikova, Marina Studneva, Svetlana Semyonova, Nina Cheremisina 3:20.92
4. ROM—Georgeta Maşca [Militaru], Florica Silaghi, Maria Tănasă, Valeria Cătescu, Aneta Matei 3:22.08
5. AUS—Anne Chirnside, Verna Westwood, Pamela Westendorf, Sally Harding, Susanne Palfreyman 3:26.37

1984 Los Angeles-Lake Casitas T: 9, N: 9, D: 8.4.

1. ROM—Florica Lavric, Maria Fricioiu [Tănasă], Chira Apostol, Olga Bularda [Homeghi], Viorica Ioja 3:19.30
2. CAN—Marilyn Brain, Angela Schneider, Barbara Armbrust, Jane Tregunno, Lesley Thompson 3:21.55
3. AUS—Robyn Grey-Gardner, Karen Brancourt, Susan Chapman, Margot Foster, Susan Lee 3:23.29
4. USA—Abigail Peck, Patricia Spratlen, Janet Harville, Elizabeth Miles, Valerie McClain-Ward 3:23.58
5. HOL—Marieke van Drogenbroek, Anne Marie Quist, Catharina Neelissen, Willemien Vaandrager, Martha Laurijsen 3:23.97
6. GER—Heike Neu, Sabine Hinkelmann, Kerstin Rehders, Angelika Beblo, Heidrun Barth 3:29.03
7. GBR—Teresa Millar, Jean Genchi, Joanna Toch, Kathryn Ball, Kathryn Talbot
8. CHN—Huang Meixia, Yang Xiao, Shi Meiping, Chen Changfeng, Zhang Liming

1988 Seoul T: 10, N: 10, D: 9.24.

1. GDR—Martina Walther, Gerlinde Doberschütz, Carola Hornig, Birte Siech, Sylvia Rose 6:56.00
2. CHN—Zhang Xianghua, Hu Yadong, Yang Xiao, Zhou Shouying, Li Ronghua 6:58.78
3. ROM—Mărioara Traşcă, Veronica Necula, Herta Anitas, Doina Bălan, Ecaterina Oancia 7:01.13
4. BUL—Teodora Zareva, Violeta Zareva, Miglena Mihaleva, Svetla Durchova, Greta Georgieva 7:02.27
5. USA—Jennifer Corbet, Sarah Gengler, Elizabeth Bradley, Cynthia Eckert, Kimberly Santiago 7:09.12
6. GBR—Fiona Johnston, Katherine Grose, Joanne Gough, Susan Smith, Alison Norrish 7:10.80
7. CAN—Heather Clarke, Patricia Smith, Lesley Thompson, E. Jane Tregunno, Jennifer Walinga
8. POL—Grażyna Błąd, Elżbieta Jankowska, Zyta Jarka, Elwira Lorenz, Czesława Szczepińska

Chapter 20 **Sailing**

MEN	WOMEN	DISCONTINUED EVENTS
Windsurfer	Windsurfer	
Laser	Laser	
Finn	Elliott 6m	
470		
49er		
Star		

Beginning in 1996, the point system reverted to one point per place (i.e.: 1st place: 1; 2nd place: 2; 3rd place: 3, etc.). At the conclusion of the final race in 1996 and 2000, each yacht was allowed to drop its two worst scores. If less than nine races were completed, only one score was dropped. The remaining points were added, and the yacht with the lowest total won. Between 1936 and 1992 each yacht always dropped its single worst score. The Olympic competitions reverted to this single score drop in 2004, except for the 49er class. Since 2008 all classes have used the single score drop. In 2008 a final medal race was added for the top ten boats, in which the score order counts double (i.e. 1st place: 2 points; 2nd place: 4; etc.)

Ten minutes before the starting gun for a race the yachts are called to the starting line. The intervening minutes are generally devoted to jockeying for position, and penalties are often assessed. Traditionally, during a race the yachts have followed a triangular course designated by marks that must be passed on a required side. In 1996 a trapezoidal course was introduced for certain classes. A yacht is considered to have finished a race when any part of its hull or equipment or crew in a normal position crosses the finish line.

For 2012 the mixed sailing classes were done away with, and the total number of sailing events reduced to ten: six for men and four for women.

Jacques Lebrun, 1932
Winner of the Finn class.

SAILING TERMS

Abeam—In a line at a right angle from another yacht's body.
Aft—In or near the back or stern part of a yacht.
Astern—To the rear of a yacht.
Bearing away—Altering course away from the wind until a yacht begins to jibe.
Clear astern—A yacht is clear astern of another yacht when its hull and equipment are behind an imaginary line projected abeam from the aftermost point of the other yacht's hull and equipment. The other yacht is clear ahead.
Close-hauled—A yacht is close-hauled when sailing by the wind as close as it can lie with advantage in working to windward.
Hull—The body or frame of a yacht, not including its masts, sails, and rigging.
Jibing—A yacht begins to jibe at the moment when, with the wind aft, the foot of its mainsail crosses its center line, and completes the jibe when the mainsail has filled on the other tack.
Leeward—The leeward side of a yacht is the one on which it is carrying its mainsail. The opposite side is the windward side.
Leeward yacht—When neither of two yachts on the same tack is clear astern, the one on the leeward side of the other is the leeward yacht. The other yacht is the windward yacht.
Luffing—Altering course toward the wind.
Mark—An object that a yacht must round or pass on a required side.
Mast abeam—A windward yacht is mast abeam when its helmsman's line of sight abeam is in front of the leeward yacht's mainmast.
On a tack—A yacht is on a tack except when if is tacking or jibing.
Overlap—Two yachts overlap when neither is clear astern, or when, although one is clear astern, an intervening yacht overlaps both of them.
Port—The lefthand side of a yacht, looking forward.
Room—The space needed by a yacht to maneuver in a seamanlike manner in the prevailing conditions.
Starboard—The righthand side of a yacht, looking forward.
Tacking—A yacht is tacking from the moment it is beyond facing directly into the wind until it is borne away to a close-hauled course.
Windward—See leeward.

MEN

WINDSURFER

The 2008 competition will utilize the Neil Pryde RS:X, a 2.86-meter (9 foot 4½ inch) long board weighing 15.5 kilograms (34 pounds) and topped with a 9.5 square meter sail.

1896–1980 not held

1984 Los Angeles-Long Beach C: 38, N: 38, D: 8.8.
Windglider

		PTS.
1. Stephan van den Berg	HOL	27.7
2. Randall Scott Steele	USA	46.0
3. A. Bruce Kendall	NZL	46.4
4. Gildas Guillerot	FRA	52.4
5. Klaus Maran	ITA	54.4
6. Gregory Hyde	AUS	55.7
7. Dirk Meyer	GER	67.2
8. Björn Eybl	AUT	80.0

The inaugural windsurfer competition used the Windglider, a board 12 feet 9 inches (3.9 meters) long and 25½ inches (65 centimeters) wide which carried 70 square feet of sail.

1988 Seoul-Pusan C: 45, N: 45, D: 9.27.
Lechner Division II

		PTS.
1. A. Bruce Kendall	NZL	35.4
2. Jan Boersma	NLA	42.7
3. Michael Gebhardt	USA	48.0
4. Bart Verschoor	HOL	53.4
5. Robert Nagy	FRA	61.7
6. Francesco Wirz	ITA	63.0
7. Jorge García Velazco	ARG	70.1
8. Carlos Iniesta Mira	SPA	81.7

The Division II board chosen for the competition was a 12-foot-long (3.65 meters), round-bottomed sailboard with a 78.6-square-foot (7.25 square meters) sail. The boardsailors faced heavy winds which, on the fifth day, gusted up to 25 knots and stirred up waves of almost 2 meters. In that race, only 19 of the 43 starters completed the course. These conditions should have favored the heavier boardsailors. However, the winner, Bruce Kendall, weighed only 143 pounds. The 24-year-old Kendall did run into problems on land: listening to rock music on a Walkman while skateboarding, he fell off and badly grazed his hand. New Zealand team officials ordered him to stay off his skateboard until after the Olympics.

At a pre-Olympic regatta in Athens, Greece, in 2002, Kendall was involved in a bizarre and unfortunate accident, when the inflatable chase boat he was piloting collided with US windsurfer Kimberly Birkenfeld. Birkenfeld suffered severe brain injury and spinal cord injury and spent a month in a coma. In 2007 Birkenfeld sued Kendall for $15 million, but an Australian Court of Appeals limited the amount payable to $430,000.

1992 Barcelona C: 43, N: 43, D: 8.2.
Lechner Division II

		PTS.
1. Franck David	FRA	70.7
2. Michael Gebhardt	USA	71.1
3. Lars Kleppich	AUS	98.7
4. A. Bruce Kendall	NZL	105.7
5. Christoph Sieber	AUT	110.1
6. Asier Fernández de Bobadilla	SPA	117.0
7. Stephan van den Berg	HOL	117.7
8. Amit Inbar	ISR	118.1

Franck David, a 22-year-old from the island of Arz (population 200), in Brittany, needed to finish three places ahead of Mike Gebhardt in the tenth and final race to win the gold medal or he had to win the race and have Gebhardt place no better than third. David took an early lead and held it to the end. Gebhardt on the other hand, fell back to seventh place, fought his way up to third, but couldn't catch Bruce Kendall in second place.

Among the more unusual quirks of fate that have decided Olympic championships was one that hit Mike Gebhardt. Prior to the Olympics there had been numerous complaints from boardsailers and other members of the yachting community that the Parc de Mar venue, which was in the harbor of Barcelona, was polluted with garbage and waste that included everything from dead rats to floating refrigerators. Under pressure from the International Yacht Racing Union, Barcelona authorities assigned four garbage vessels to collect the waste daily. Unfortunately for Gebhardt, they didn't get it all. During the last lap of the seventh race, a plastic garbage bag got caught on his board and he was passed by six boardsailers before he could dislodge it. Had Gebhardt been able to stave off even one of those six, he would have won the gold medal.

Trash was not the only danger that boardsailors faced in Barcelona. The day before competition began, Murray McCaig of Canada was bicycling in the Olympic Village when he pulled out to pass a slow-moving bus and was hit by a police car. He came away with a broken leg and was unable to compete.

1996 Atlanta-Savannah C: 46, N: 46, D: 7.29.
Mistral

		PTS.
1. Nikolaos Kaklamanakis	GRE	17
2. Carlos Espínola Lorenzo	ARG	19
3. Gal Fridman	ISR	21
4. Aaron McIntosh	NZL	27
5. Jean-Max de Chavigny	FRA	37
6. Michael Gebhardt	USA	41
7. João Rodrigues	POR	42
8. Brendan Todd	AUS	48

Nikolaos Kaklamanakis was the reigning world champion and had won the pre-Olympic regatta on the Olympic course in 1995.

2000 Sydney C: 36, N: 36, D: 9.24.
Mistral

		PTS.
1. Christoph Sieber	AUT	38
2. Carlos Espínola Lorenzo	ARG	43
3. Aaron McIntosh	NZL	48
4. Lars Kleppich	AUS	61
5. Yuanguo Zhou	CHN	64
6. Nikolaos Kaklamanakis	GRE	64
7. Amit Inbar	ISR	79
8. Przemysław Miarczyński	POL	84

Unheralded Christoph Sieber won three of the first five races and entered the final day's two races with a six-point lead over Carlos Espinola. Sieber finished fifth in race 10 and Espinola eleventh, his second-worst placing of the competition. This meant that Sieber only needed to finish in the top ten in the final race to win the gold medal. Sailing conservatively, he placed seventh. Sieber credited his success to the strength he built up during winter weight training in the snow with Austrian skiing star Hermann Maier.

2004 Athens-Helliniko C: 34, N: 34, D: 8.25.
Mistral

		PTS.
1. Gal Fridman	ISR	42
2. Nikos Kaklamanakis	GRE	52
3. Nick Dempsey	GBR	53
4. Ricardo Winicki Santos	BRA	54
5. Przemysław Miarczyński	POL	73
6. João Rodrigues	POR	78
7. Zhou Yuanguo	CHN	84
8. Lars Kleppich	AUS	84

The sentimental favorite was Greece's 1996 gold medal winner, Nikos Kaklamanakis, who was chosen, at the last minute, to light the Olympic Flame at the Opening Ceremony, when the first choice, sprinter Kostas Kenteris avoided a doping test. At the 2004 Olympics, Kaklamanakis was seriously challenged by his training partner, Gal Fridman, who had taken the bronze behind him back in 1996. Going into the eleventh and final race, Ricardo Santos was in first place, followed by Fridman and Kaklamanakis. However, Santos came apart at the end of the race and finished in 17th place, leaving him not only without the gold, but without any medal at all. Fridman finished second to snatch the overall victory. His gold medal was the first ever for Israel, which had been competing in the Olympics since 1952. Meanwhile, Nick Dempsey won three of the last five races, including the last one, to edge Santos for the bronze.

2008 Beijing-Qingdao C: 35, N: 35, D: 8.20.
Neil Pryde RS:X

		PTS.
1. Thomas Ashley	NZL	52
2. Julien Bontemps	FRA	53
3. Shahar Zubari	ISR	58
4. Nick Dempsey	GBR	60
5. Ricardo Winicki Santos	BRA	77
6. King Yin Chan	HKG	84
7. Wang Aichen	CHN	95
8. Nikos Kaklamanakis	GRE	97

Going into the final race Julien Bontemps led by a single point ahead of Tom Ashley, who had won the world championship at home in New Zealand seven months before the Olympics, and defending Olympic bronze medalist Nick Dempsey. Nine points behind in fourth place lay reigning world bronze medalist Shahar Zubari, who had defeated 2004 Olympic champion Gal Fridman at the Israeli national trials to earn a berth at the Beijing Olympics.

Bontemps dropped his sail at the first mark, falling well behind leader King Yin Chan and the rest of the field. The two-time windsurfing world champion came back hard to finish fourth, one place behind Ashley, who took the gold medal by a single point. Zubari came from behind to finish second, edging out Dempsey for the bronze medal.

LASER

The Laser was designed in 1969 by Bruce Kirby of the United States. It is 4.24 meters (13 feet 11 inches) long and weighs 59 kilograms (130 pounds). The sail covers 76 square feet, the same as that of the Finn.

1896–1992 not held

1996 Atlanta-Savannah C: 56, N: 56, D: 7.31.

		PTS.
1. Robert Scheidt	BRA	26
2. Ben Ainslie	GBR	37
3. Peer Moberg	NOR	46
4. Michael Blackburn	AUS	48
5. Stefan Warkalla	GER	54
6. John Harrysson	SWE	55
7. Vasco Serpa	POR	74
8. Thomas Johanson	FIN	78

Robert Scheidt led Ben Ainslie by two points going into the final race. This led to aggressive pre-race manouveuring. Ainslie stayed close to Scheidt and tried to lure him into fouling. After four false starts, race officials raised the black flag, indicating that any and all boats that crossed the starting line early would be disqualified. At the fifth try, Scheidt took off for the line. If the gun went off before he reached it, Ainslie would be left behind and his chances of finishing ahead of the Brazilian would be slim. The 19-year-old Ainsley followed Scheidt—and both of them crossed the starting line prematurely. The double disqualification gave the victory to Scheidt.

2000 Sydney C: 43, N: 43, D: 9.29.

		PTS.
1. Ben Ainslie	GBR	42
2. Robert Scheidt	BRA	44
3. Michael Blackburn	AUS	60
4. Serge Kats	HOL	72
5. Andreas Geritzer	AUT	78
6. Gustavo Lima	POR	83
7. Maciej Grabowski	POL	86
8. Diego Negri	ITA	91

The dramatic finish of the 1996 Olympic competition was just the beginning of an intense, but friendly rivalry between Robert Scheidt and Ben Ainslie. Scheidt won the 1997 world championship, but Ainslie defeated Scheidt at the 1999 world championships. The Brazilian came back to win the next world championship six months before the Sydney Olympics. As in 1996, the Olympic gold medal came down to the final race. This time Scheidt led Ainslie by seven points. Because of Scheidt's superior second-worst score, Ainslie knew that the only way he could win was to prevent Scheidt from placing 21st or better. He began by harassing Scheidt at the start line and successfully forcing Scheidt to commit an infraction that required a 720° penalty turn. Once they left the line, Ainslie blocked Scheidt's wind and repeatedly prevented him from passing. By the first windward mark, the two were 90 seconds behind the rest of the field and more than three minutes behind the leaders. Increasingly desperate, Scheidt gybed and crashed into Ainslie's boat. Bursting free, he began to move up the field until he was in 22nd place. If Scheidt could pass Stanley Tan of Singapore, he would finish first overall. But Tan just beat him to the finish line. Scheidt filed two protests against Ainslie, one for interference at the start and the other for interference when they clashed physically. The first was rejected for being filed too late. The judges spent three hours considering the other protest and ended up ruling in favor of Ainslie and disqualifying Scheidt. Ainslie, despite his quiet and shy demeanor, had gained revenge by using hard-nosed and rough—but legal—tactics.

2004 Athens-Helliniko C: 42, N: 42, D: 8.22.

		PTS.
1. Robert Scheidt	BRA	55
2. Andreas Geritzer	AUT	68
3. Vasilij Žbogar	SLO	76
4. Paul Goodison	GBR	81
5. Gustavo de Lima	POR	88
6. Karl Suneson	SWE	104
7. Hamish Pepper	NZL	108
8. Mark Mendelblatt	USA	111

The final race was delayed twice, once due to low wind conditions after the racers failed to make the first mark in the alloted time, and again when the wind shifted 15 degrees. When the race finally did commence, 1996 gold medalist and seven-time Laser world champion Robert Scheidt moved up to sixth place, well ahead of any of the other potential medalists, to earn his third Olympic medal.

2008 Beijing-Qingdao C: 43, N: 43, D: 8.19.

		PTS.
1. Paul Goodison	GBR	63
2. Vasilij Žbogar	SLO	71
3. Diego Romero	ITA	75
4. Gustavo de Lima	POR	76
5. Andrew Murdoch	NZL	81
6. Rasmus Myrgren	SWE	83
7. Julio Alsogaray	ARG	92
8. Jean Bernaz	FRA	104

After winning the 2005 world championship title, double Olympic gold medalist Robert Scheidt switched focus to the Star class, leaving the 2008 Olympic Laser competition wide open. Four-time European champion Paul Goodison, who in 2004 had missed an Olympic medal by five points, took the lead after the fourth race. Then he gradually pulled ahead over the next five races, building up an 18-point lead over Rasmus Myrgren going into the final medal race.

All Goodison had to do to secure the gold medal was to avoid finishing last, while at the same time preventing a first-place finish by Myrgren. Goodison engaged Myrgren in a match race at the back of the fleet, blocking them both from the lead. The tactic worked perfectly, as Goodison finished second-to-last to clinch the gold medal, while Myrgren finished last, dropping to fifth place.

"I need to thank Goodison," silver medalist Vasilij Žbogar said after the race, "I was lucky because the second place Swedish guy was very close to Goodison, so Goodison was watching him, and keeping him behind. Pity for him, but it left just three of us for two medals."

FINN

The Finn class uses a centerboard dinghy and a one-man crew. It is 4.5 meters (14 feet 9 inches) long and weighs 126 kilograms (278 pounds). The spread of the mainsail is 10.68 square meters (115 square feet). Boats are assigned at random, although since 1976 a helmsman may provide his own sail and mast. The Finn was designed in 1949 by Rickard Sarby of Finland—hence its name. Between 1920 and 1948 other types of centerboard dinghys were used.

1896–1912 not held

1920 Antwerp-Ostende, Amsterdam T: 2, N: 1, D: 9.3.
12-Foot Dinghy

	PTS.
1. HOL Johannes Hin, Cornelis Hin, Franciscus Hin	4
2. HOL Arnoud van der Biesen, Petrus Beukers	5

The first two races were staged off Ostende, 100 kilometers from Antwerp, on July 7 and 8. The results of the second race were voided because a buoy changed position and a dispute broke out about the course. Because both teams were from the Netherlands, the final two races were rescheduled for September 3—in Holland. Other than the 1956 equestrian events, this was the only time in history that an official event was contested outside the host country.

1924 Paris C: 17, N: 17, D: 7.13.

		PTS.
1. Léon Huybrechts	BEL	2
2. Henrik Robert	NOR	7
3. Hans Dittmar	FIN	8
4. Santiago Amat Cansino	SPA	8
5. Johannes Hin	HOL	10
6. Clarence Hammar	SWE	11
7. H. Gordon Fowler	GBR	12
8. Frederico Guilherme-Burnay	POR	15

The Official Report of 1924 attributes to Huybrechts a sixth sense that allowed him to anticipate changes in wind direction. Second, third, and fourth place were decided by an extra race.

1928 Amsterdam C: 23, N: 20, D: 8.9.

1. Sven Thorell	SWE
2. Henrik Robert	NOR
3. Bertil Broman	FIN
4. Willem de Vries Lentsch	HOL
5. Egon Beyn	GER
6. Tito Nordio	ITA
7. Jens Andersen	DEN
8. H. Gordon Fowler	GBR
8. Harold Gaydon	GBR

Thorell won four of eight races and also placed second twice, while Robert had three firsts. Broman earned the bronze with two firsts and two seconds to de Vries Lentsch's two firsts and one second.

1932 Los Angeles C: 11, N: 11, D: 8.11.

		PTS.
1. Jacques Lebrun	FRA	87
2. Adriaan Maas	HOL	85
3. Santiago Amat Cansino	SPA	76
4. Edgar Behr	GER	74
5. Reginald Dixon	CAN	72
6. G. Colin Ratsey	GBR	69
7. Charles Lyon	USA	66
8. Silvio Treleani	ITA	62

When the official results were announced following the eleventh and final race, Adriaan Maas was declared the winner with 87 points. He was followed by Jacques Lebrun with 79 points. But the decision was not final. After placing fourth in the ninth race, Lebrun had been disqualified and his protest had been rejected by the race judge. Lebrun appealed, and the day after the last race a protest committee reversed the judge's decision. Lebrun's reinstatement added eight points to his total and subtracted two from Maas'. During World War II Lebrun distinguished himself by helping to hide the treasures of the Louvre from the Nazis.

1936 Berlin-Kiel C: 25, N: 25, D: 8.12.

		PTS.
1. Daniel Kagchelland	HOL	163
2. Werner Krogmann	GER	150
3. Peter Scott	GBR	131
4. Erich Wichmann-Harbeck	CHI	130
5. Giuseppe Fago	ITA	115
6. Jacques Lebrun	FRA	109
7. Tibor Heinrich	HUN	102
8. Willy Pieper	SWI	99

Bronze medalist Peter Scott was the son of explorer Robert Falcon Scott, who died near the South Pole when Peter was an infant. In 1941 Scott created the camouflage scheme that was eventually used by most of the Allied forces in World War II. After the war, Scott, who had previously been an ardent hunter of geese and ducks, renounced his former ways and became a wildfowl protection activist. Co-founder of the World Wildlife Fund, he was known as "the patron saint of conservation."

1948 London-Torbay C: 21, N: 21, D: 8.12.

		PTS.
1. Paul Elvstrøm	DEN	5543
2. Ralph Evans	USA	5408
3. Jacobus de Jong	HOL	5204
4. Richard Sarby	SWE	4603
5. Paul McLaughlin	CAN	4535
6. Félix Sienra Castellanos	URU	4079
7. Jean-Jacques Herbulot	FRA	4068
8. Pierre van der Haeghen	BEL	3660

Twenty-year-old Paul Elvstrøm began his Olympic career quietly, failing to finish the first day's race. After five races, the competition appeared to be a tight contest between Evans, McLaughlin, and Sarby. All the others were more than 800 points behind. Elvstrøm was in eighth place. But on the sixth day the young Dane finished first, 23 seconds ahead of Herbulot, and the extra 301 points that he gained propelled Elvstrøm into third place, 564 points behind Evans. This meant that Evans could clinch the gold medal by finishing third on the final day. However, he landed in fifth place, three minutes away from his goal, while Elvstrøm took first place again, three minutes and seven seconds ahead of de Jong; the 301-point bonus for winning provided the margin of victory in the final standings.

1952 Helsinki C: 28, N: 28, D: 7.28.

		PTS.
1. Paul Elvstrøm	DEN	8209
2. Charles Currey	GBR	5449
3. Richard Sarby	SWE	5051
4. Jacobus de Jong	HOL	5033
5. Wolfgang Erndl	AUT	4273
6. Morits Skaugen	NOR	4073
7. Adelchi Pelaschiar	ITA	4068
8. Paul McLaughlin	CAN	4033

Elvstrøm won three of the first four races and gained so many points that he had earned the gold medal without having to race the last day. He entered anyway and won again. His other placings were a fifth, a third, and a fourth.

1956 Melbourne C: 20, N: 20, D: 12.5.

		PTS.
1. Paul Elvstrøm	DEN	7509
2. André Nelis	BEL	6254
3. John Marvin	USA	5953
4. Jürgen Vogler	GER	4199
5. Richard Sarby	SWE	3990
6. Eric Bongers	SAF	3912
7. Adelchi Pelaschiar	ITA	3409
8. Bruce Kirby	CAN	3213

Elvstrøm finished first in the opening race, fell to eighth and 15th in the next two, and then won each of the last four races.

1960 Rome-Naples C: 35, N: 35, D: 9.7.

		PTS.
1. Paul Elvstrøm	DEN	8171
2. Aleksander Tšutšelov	SOV/EST	6520
3. André Nelis	BEL	5934
4. Ronald Jenyns	AUS	5758
5. Reinaldo Conrad	BRA	5176
6. Ralph Roberts	NZL	5140
7. Ian Bruce	CAN	5133
8. Kenneth Albury	BAH	5092

Elvstrøm, now 32 years old, chalked up three firsts, one second, and two fifths to clinch his fourth gold medal without having to enter the final race. This time Elvstrøm, who was not in perfect health, declined to start.

1964 Tokyo-Fujisawa C: 33, N: 33, D: 10.21.

		PTS.
1. Wilhelm Kuhweide	GER	7638
2. Peter Barrett	USA	6373
3. Henning Wind	DEN	6190
4. Peter Mander	NZL	5684
5. Hubert Raudaschl	AUT	5405
6. Colin Ryrie	AUS	5273
7. Joerg Bruder	BRA	4956
8. Panagiotis Kouligas	GRE	4546

In 1964 East and West Germany entered a combined team. However, a dispute developed as to which side should be represented in the Finn class. At the last moment the International Yacht Racing Union interceded and authorized the West German helmsman, Willi Kuhweide. Kuhweide sailed well throughout the regatta and won the gold medal by placing second, first, fourth, sixth, fifth, third, and first.

1968 Mexico City-Acapulco C: 36, N: 36, D: 10.21.

		PTS.
1. Valentyn Mankin	SOV/UKR	11.7
2. Hubert Raudaschl	AUT	53.4
3. Fabio Albarelli	ITA	55.1
4. Ronald Jenyns	AUS	67.0
5. Panagiotis Kouligas	GRE	71.0
6. Jan Winquist	FIN	72.0
7. Arne Akerson	SWI	77.0
8. Philippe Soria	FRA	80.0

Mankin had a consistent series, placing third, fifth, first, first, second, second, and first. Silver medalist Hubert Raudaschl would ultimately enter the record books as the first person in history to compete in nine Olympics. The son of a boatbuilder in the village of St. Gilgen in Austria's Salzkammergut lake district, Raudaschl attended the 1960 Rome Games as an alternate and then began his streak in 1964, when he finished fifth in the Finn class. In addition to his 1968 silver medal, he earned a second silver in the 1980 Star class. In the 1996 Star competition Raudaschl placed fifteenth at the age of 53.

1972 Munich-Kiel C: 35, N: 35, D: 9.8.

		PTS.
1. Serge Maury	FRA	58.0
2. Ilias Hatzipavlis	GRE	71.0
3. Viktor Potapov	SOV/RUS	74.7
4. John Bertrand	AUS	76.7
5. Thomas Lundqvist	SWE	81.0
6. Kim Weber	FIN	85.7
7. Hans-Christian Schröder	GDR	91.0
8. György Fináczy	HUN	94.0

1976 Montreal-Kingston C: 28, N: 28, D: 7.27.

		PTS.
1. Jochen Schümann	GDR	35.4
2. Andrei Balashov	SOV/RUS	39.7
3. John Bertrand	AUS	46.4
4. Claudio Biekarck	BRA	54.7
5. Kent Carlson	SWE	66.4
6. Anastassios Boudouris	GRE	77.0
7. David Howlett	GBR	77.7
8. Sanford Riley	CAN	83.0

Schümann and Balashov entered the final race in a tie for first place. Schümann pulled away on the last day and finished 40 seconds ahead of his rival.

John Bertrand made sailing history in 1983 when he broke the 132-year-old US monopoly of the America's Cup with his yacht, *Australia II*.

1980 Moscow-Tallinn C: 21, N: 21, D: 7.29.

		PTS.
1. Esko Rechardt	FIN	36.7
2. Wolfgang Mayrhofer	AUT	46.7
3. Andrei Balashov	SOV/RUS	47.4
4. Claudio Blekarck	BRA	53.0
5. Jochen Schümann	GDR	54.4
6. Kent Carlson	SWE	63.7
7. Ryszard Skarbiński	POL	71.1
8. Mark Neeleman	HOL	76.0

1984 Los Angeles-Long Beach C: 28, N: 28, D: 8.8.

		PTS.
1. Russell Coutts	NZL	34.7
2. John Bertrand	AUS	37.0
3. Terry Neilson	CAN	37.7
4. Joaquín Blanco Roca	SPA	60.7
5. Wolfgang Gerz	GER	66.1
6. Chris Pratt	AUS	68.0
7. Michael McIntyre	GBR	70.7
8. Jorge Zarif Neto	BRA	78.7

The decisive moment in the Finn class competition came in the very first race when Bertrand, who finished first, was disqualified for touching Coutts' bow while attempting to port-tack. This provided Coutts with his eventual margin of victory. Coutts was almost disqualified himself at the final weigh-in when his clothing was found to be one pound overweight. However, a third weigh-in, for which Coutts carefully arranged each garment, found him just below the 20 kg maximum. In 1995, Coutts was the skipper of *Black Magic 1* when it won the America's Cup. Coutts won the Cup again in 2000. Then he switched to a Switzerland-based team and won a third time in 2003. He is one of only three skippers to win the America's Cup three times, the other two being Charlie Barr and Harold Vanderbilt.

1988 Seoul-Pusan C: 33, N: 33, D: 9.27.

		PTS.
1. José Luis Doreste Blanco	SPA	38.1
2. Peter Holmberg	VIR	40.4
3. John Cutler	NZL	45.0
4. Stuart Childerley	GBR	50.7
5. Lasse Hjortnaes	DEN	51.0
6. Thomas Schmid	GER	72.1
7. Roy Heiner	HOL	78.4
8. Oleg Khopyorsky	SOV/RUS	81.0

Doreste, whose younger brother, Luis, won a gold medal in the 470 class in 1984, survived a close and bitter contest that wasn't decided until the last race. Doreste, who was disqualified in the fourth race, accused his opponents of trying to win "in the jury room" rather than on the water. Peter Holmberg won the first-ever medal for the US Virgin Islands and would have earned the gold had he not drifted a few feet over the line at the start of the fourth race.

In the fifth race, Lawrence Lemieux of Canada was in second place when he noticed Joseph Chan, the 470 crew from Singapore, struggling in the water 25 yards from his capsized boat. Chan had injured his back and was being swept away by the powerful currents. Lemieux turned around and saved Chan, who was too exhausted to heave himself into the Canadian's boat. The International Olympic Committee gave Lemieux a special award for his act of gallantry. Lemieux, baffled by the attention he received, reminded reporters of what might have happened if he had ignored Chan. "I'm not *that* intense," he said.

1992 Barcelona C: 28, N: 28, D: 8.3.

		PTS.
1. José María van der Ploeg García	SPA	33.4
2. Brian Ledbetter	USA	54.7
3. Craig Monk	NZL	64.7
4. Stuart Childerley	GBR	68.1
5. Fredrik Lööf	SWE	68.7
6. Otmar Müller von Blumencron	SWI	70.0
7. Xavier Rohart	FRA	75.0
8. Hans Spitzauer	AUT	79.4

Van der Ploeg, a native of Barcelona, secured his victory after six races and didn't take part in the seventh. Hank Lammens of Canada won the second race, but was disqualified because he forgot to pack a life jacket. Without the disqualification he would have placed fourth; instead, he ended up 13th.

1996 Atlanta-Savannah C: 31, N: 31, D: 7.29.

		PTS.
1. Mateusz Kusznierewicz	POL	32
2. Sébastien Godefroid	BEL	45
3. Roy Heiner	HOL	50
4. Hans Spitzauer	AUT	54
5. Fredrik Lööf	SWE	57
6. Paul McKenzie	AUS	67
7. José María van der Ploeg García	SPA	69
8. Ian Ainslie	SAF	72

In fourth place after four races, 21-year-old Mateusz Kusznierewicz put together a string of first, second, first and first to win with a day to spare.

2000 Sydney C: 25, N: 25, D: 9.30.

		PTS.
1. Iain Percy	GBR	35
2. Luca Devoti	ITA	46
3. Fredrik Lööf	SWE	47
4. Mateusz Kusznierewicz	POL	48
5. Xavier Rohart	FRA	55
6. Russ Silvestri	USA	64
7. Sébastien Godefroid	BEL	65
8. Ali Enver Adakan	TUR	66

In 1999, Iain Percy won the European Championships and the pre-Olympic regatta on the Olympic course. At the Olympics itself, Percy finished second in the first race and then first in the second race to take an overall lead that he would never relinquish. He went into the penultimate race with an 11-point lead over Fredrik Lööf. Lööf needed to place in the top five to stay in contention for the gold medal, so Percy concentrated on blocking Lööf's wind and generally obstructing him within the rules. When Lööf ended up in eleventh place, Percy was able to sit out the final race. In that contest, Luca Devoti crossed the finish line just ahead of Lööf to secure the silver medal.

2004 Athens-Helliniko C: 25, N: 25, D: 8.21.

		PTS.
1. Ben Ainslie	GBR	38
2. Rafael Trujillo Villar	SPA	51
3. Mateusz Kusznierewicz	POL	53
4. Karlo Kuret	CRO	61
5. Aimilios Papathanasiou	GRE	72
6. Anthony Nossiter	AUS	93
7. Sébastien Godefroid	BEL	96
8. Guillaume Florent	FRA	96

Three-time world champion and Olympic Laser gold medalist Ben Ainslie was disqualified from the second race after a protest by Guillaume Florent. Ainslie responded by finishing in the top four in each of the next eight races, winning half and building up enough of a lead that a 14th place finish in the final race still gave him the gold ahead of friend and training partner Rafael Trujillo. To reach his optimum weight for the Olympics, Ainslie put on 33 lbs. (15 kilograms) through a combination of consuming 5,000 calories a day and pursuing daily weightlifting sessions.

2008 Beijing-Qingdao C: 26, N: 26, D: 8.17.

		PTS.
1. Ben Ainslie	GBR	23
2. Zachary Railey	USA	45
3. Guillaume Florent	FRA	58
4. Daniel Birgmark	SWE	58
5. Chris Cook	CAN	67
6. Jonas Høgh Christensen	DEN	70
7. Gašper Vinčec	SLO	72
8. Ivan Kljaković-Gašpić	CRO	76

Two-time Olympic champion Ben Ainslie was the clear favorite in the one-man dinghy class. Seven months before the Beijing Olympics he won the 2008 Gold Cup in Victoria, Australia, his fifth career Gold Cup win. In China the 31-year-old won three of the eight preliminary races and finished second in two others.

Ainslie was leading the medal race when it was called off due to dying wind conditions. Twenty-four hours later he took the lead in the refixed race, finishing thirteen seconds in front to claim his third straight gold medal.

Silver medalist Zach Railey was a surprise addition to the podium; he had come 19th at the 2007 world championship and 28th at the 2008 Gold Cup. The 24-year-old first-time Olympian finished one minute back in sixth place but held on for the silver medal.

After the Beijing Olympics, Ainslie was named the ISAF World Sailor of the Year for the third time.

470

The 470 class, designed by Andre Cornu in the early 1970s, was given its name because it measures 4.70 meters (15 ft. 5 in.) in length. The 470 is a two-handed dinghy with a beam of 1.7 meters (5 ft. 7 in.). Originally a mixed event, the 470 was divided into separate competitions for men and for women in 1988.

1896–1972 not held

1976 Montreal-Kingston T: 28, N: 28, D: 7.27.

		PTS.
1. GER	Frank Hübner, Harro Bode	42.4
2. SPA	Antonio Gorostegui Ceballos, Pedro Millet Soler	49.7
3. AUS	Ian Brown, Ian Ruff	57.0
4. SOV/RUS	Viktor Potapov, Aleksandr Potapov	57.0
5. NZL	Mark Paterson, Brett Bennett	59.7
6. GBR	Philip Crebbin, Derek Clark	69.4
7. SWI	Jean-Claude Vuithier, Laurent Quellet	71.7
8. FRA	Marc Laurent, Roger Surmin	79.4

1980 Moscow-Tallinn T: 14, N: 14, D: 7.29.

		PTS.
1. BRA	Marcos Rizzo Soares, Eduardo Penido	36.4
2. GDR	Jörn Borowski, Egbert Swensson	38.7
3. FIN	Jouko Lindgren, Georg Tallberg	39.7
4. HOL	Henk Van Gent, Jan Van Den Hondel	49.4
5. POL	Leon Wrobel, Tomasz Stocki	53.0
6. SPA	Gustavo Doreste Blanco, Alfredo Rigau Llauger	54.1
7. ITA	Ernesto Treves, Silvio Necchi	57.7
8. SWE	Lars Bengtsson, Stefan Bengtsson	60.0

Gold medal winners Soares and Penido, wind surfers from Rio de Janeiro, were only 19 and 20 years old, respectively. Had Borowski and Swensson crossed the finish line two seconds sooner in the final race, they would have taken the championship away from the Brazilians. Borowski was the son of Paul Borowski, who won medals in the Dragon class in 1968 and 1972.

1984 Los Angeles-Long Beach T: 28, N: 28, D: 8.8.

		PTS.
1. SPA	Luis Doreste Blanco, Roberto Molina Carrasco	33.7
2. USA	Stephan Benjamin, Christopher Steinfeld	43.0
3. FRA	Thierry Peponnet, Luc Pillot	49.4
4. GER	Wolfgang Hunger, Joachim Hunger	50.1
5. ITA	Thomaso Chieffi, Enrico Chieffi	57.0
6. FIN	Peter von Koskull, Johan von Koskull	67.4
7. GBR	Catherine Foster, Peter Newlands	70.0
8. ISR	Shimshon Brokman, Eitan Friedlander	70.0

The unheralded Spanish duo, born in the Canary Islands and residents of Barcelona, earned their gold medals without having to take part in the final race.

1988 Seoul-Pusan T: 29, N: 29, D: 9.27.

		PTS.
1. FRA	Thierry Peponnet, Luc Pillot	34.7
2. SOV/EST	Tõnu Tõniste, Toomas Tõniste	46.0
3. USA	John Shadden, Charlie McKee	51.0
4. SPA	Fernando León Boissier, Francisco Sánchez Luna	55.0
5. GER	Wolfgang Hunger, Joachim Hunger	58.7
6. NZL	Peter Evans, Simon Mander	62.7
7. ITA	Sandro Montefusco, Paolo Montefusco	68.7
8. CAN	Nigel Cochrane, Gordon McIlquham	71.7

The previously unknown Tõniste twins from Estonia won the fourth and fifth races and finished second in the sixth race to take the overall lead. All they had to do to win gold medals was place ahead of Peponnet and Pillot in the final race, which was sailed in near-gale conditions. The Tõnistes were in the lead with less than a lap to go when they suffered a severe capsize and were forced to retire.

1992 Barcelona T: 37, N: 37, D: 8.3.

		PTS.
1. SPA	Jordi Calafat Esterlich, Francisco Sánchez Luna	50.0
2. USA	Morgan Reeser, Kevin Burnham	66.7
3. EST	Tõnu Tõniste, Toomas Tõniste	68.7
4. FIN	Petri Leskinen, Mika Aarnikka	69.7
5. NOR	Herman Johannessen, Pål McCarthy	71.7
6. GBR	Paul Brotherton, Andrew Hemmings	76.4
7. NZL	Craig Greenwood, Jon Bilger	80.4
8. GER	Wolfgang Hunger, Rolf Schmidt	82.4

Calafat and Sánchez won three of the first four races and coasted to victory. When they crossed the finish line in the last race, the were so excited they they stood up and capsized.

1996 Atlanta-Savannah T: 36, N: 36, D: 8.1.

		PTS.
1. UKR	Yevhan Braslavets, Ihor Matviyenko	40
2. GBR	John Merricks, Ian Walker	60
3. POR	Vitor Rocha, Nuno Barreto	62
4. FIN	Petri Leskinen, Mika Aarnikka	65
5. RUS	Dmitri Beryozkin, Yevgeny Durmatnov	66
6. FRA	Jean-François Berthet, Gwenaël Berthet	72
7. ARG	Martín Billoch, Martín Rodríguez Castells	73
8. USA	Morgan Reeser, Kevin Burnham	74

2000 Sydney T: 29, N: 29, D: 9.28.

		PTS.
1. AUS	Mark Turnbull, Tom King	38
2. USA	Paul Foerster, Robert Merrick	42
3. ARG	Javier Conte, Juan de la Fuente	57
4. GBR	Joe Glanfield, Nicholas Rogers	58
5. POR	Alvaro Marinho, Miguel Nunes	67
6. UKR	Ihor Matviyenko, Yevhen Braslavets	72
7. NZL	Peter Nicholas, Simon Cooke	76
8. GRE	Andreas Kosmatopoulos, Konstantinos Tringonis	78

Tom King and Mark Turnbull were considered longshots until they won the 470 world championship in May 2000. They moved into the lead at the Olympic regatta after winning the eighth race. In the final race, they needed to place fifth or higher to stay ahead of Paul Foerster and Robert Merrick. After an awkward start, they moved up quickly and finished second to the Americans, who won the last two races.

2004 Athens-Helliniko T: 27, N: 27, D: 8.21.

		PTS.
1. USA	Paul Foerster, Kevin Burnham	71
2. GBR	Nick Rogers, Joe Glanfield	74
3. JPN	Kazuto Seki, Kenjiro Todoroki	90
4. SWE	Johan Molund, Martin Andersson	94
5. FRA	Gildas Philippe, Nicolas le Berre	97
6. HOL	Sven Gunther Coster, Kalle Coster	101
7. POR	Álvaro Marinho, Miguel Nunes	103
8. BRA	Alexandre Paradeda, Bernardo Arndt	104

Leading after ten races, Paul Foerster and Kevin Burnham needed to keep Nick Rogers and Joe Glanfield from gaining three places on them in the final race. Ignoring all of the other competitors, the Americans placed themselves windward of the British pair two and a half minutes before the start and, for the rest of the race, never let them break away. Foerster and Burnham finished the race in 23rd place, but that was one place ahead of the only boat they cared about, that of Rogers and Glanfield.

2008 Beijing-Qingdao T: 29, N: 29, D: 8.18.

		PTS.
1. AUS	Nathan Wilmot, Malcolm Page	44
2. GBR	Nick Rogers, Joe Glanfield	75
3. FRA	Nicolas Charbonnier, Olivier Bausset	78
4. HOL	Sven Erik Coster, Kalle Coster	78
5. SPA	Onán Barreiros Rodríguez, Aarón Sarmiento Padilla	87
6. ITA	Gabrio Zandonà, Andrea Trani	91
7. JPN	Tetsuya Matsunaga, Taro Ueno	97
8. POR	Álvaro Marinho, Miguel Nunes	102

The past four world championship titles had alternated between two crews: Australia's Nathan Wilmot and Malcolm Page in 2005 and 2007 and Great Britain's Nic Asher and Elliot Willis in 2006 and 2008. Despite Asher and Willis's two world championship titles, the British berth was taken by veteran duo and defending Olympic silver medalists Nick Rogers and Joe Glanfield.

Wilmot and Page had built up an insurmountable 22-point lead over the first ten races but still came out strongly in the medal race, leading around every mark to win the gold by 31 points, the widest margin of victory in the history of the event. Rogers and Glanfield finished third in the race to win their second consecutive silver medals.

49ER

Designed in Australia, the 49er is a 16-foot (4.88-meter) double-handed, high-performance dinghy. It has a huge sail area of 639 square feet (59 square meters) and can sail faster than the wind. The 49er is built of fiberglass and carbon fiber and weighs 375 pounds (124.7 kilograms) fully rigged. The wings can be adjusted according to the weight of the crew. The 49er is the only class that is decided by sixteen fleet races rather than eleven.

1896–1996 not held

2000 Sydney T: 17, N: 17, D: 9.25.

		PTS.
1. FIN	Jyrki Järvi, Thomas Johanson	55
2. GBR	Ian Barker, Simon Hiscocks	60
3. USA	Charlie McKee, Jonathan McKee	64
4. SPA	Javier de la Plaza Zubizarreta, Santiago López-Vázquez Navarro	79
5. GER	Marcus Baur, Philip Barth	81
6. AUS	Chris Nicholson, Daniel Phillips	86
7. POR	Alfonso Domingos, Diogo Cayolla	93
8. NZL	Daniel Slater, Nathan Handley	99

Thomas Johanson and Jyrki Järvi were ranked only 21st in the world, but they had placed third at the world championships in Mexico six months before the Olympics. In Sydney they overtook the McKee brothers for the overall lead after the thirteenth race and then clinched the gold medal with one race to spare.

2004 Athens-Helliniko T: 19, N: 19, D: 8.26.

		PTS.
1. SPA	Iker Martínez Lizardey, Xavier Fernández Gaztañaga	67
2. UKR	Rodion Luka, Heorhiy Leonchuk	72
3. GBR	Chris Draper, Simon Hiscocks	77
4. NOR	Christoffer Sundby, Frode Bovim	88
5. USA	Timothy Wadlow, Peter Spaulding	92
6. BRA	André Otto "Bochecha" da Fonseca, Rodrigo Duarte	104
7. AUS	Chris Nicholson, Gary Boyd	105
8. FIN	Thomas Johanson, Jukka Piirainen	111

After fifteen of the sixteen regatta races, all of the top six teams were still in contention for a medal. Going into the final race with a nine-point lead, the reigning world champions, Iker Martínez and Xavier Fernández, secured the gold with a seventh-place finish, while Rodion Luka and Heorhiy Leonchuk placed third to earn the silver ahead of 2003 world champions Chris Draper and Simon Hiscocks.

2008 Beijing-Qingdao T: 19, N: 19, D: 8.17.

		PTS.
1. DEN	Jonas Warrer, Martin Kirketerp	61
2. SPA	Iker Martínez Lizardey, Xavier Fernández Gaztañaga	64
3. GER	Jan Peter Peckolt, Hannes Peckolt	66
4. ITA	Piero Sibello, Gianfranco Sibello	66
5. AUS	Nathan Outteridge, Ben Austin	73
6. USA	Tim Wadlow, Christopher Rast	89
7. BRA	André da Fonseca, Rodrigo Duarte	99
8. AUT	Nico Delle Karth, Nikolaus Resch	99

The final medal race was held in strong winds and heavy rain. Every crew capsized at least once, and two boats failed to finish, including US pair Tim Wadlow and Christopher Rast, who entered the final race in the lead by three points.

Danish pair Jonas Warrer and Martin Kirketerp broke their mast before the start of the race and borrowed a boat from the Croatian team at the last minute in order to compete. The Danes finished seventh in the race and were initially the gold medalists ahead of defending Olympic champions Iker Martínez and Xavier Fernández. Protests from the Italian and Spanish contingents caused the final results to be delayed nearly twenty-four hours, but the medals were ultimately allowed to stand.

STAR

The Star is a 6.9-meter (22-foot 8-inch) long shallow keelboat with a 285-square-foot (44.9 square meters) sail. It weighs 676 kilograms (1490 pounds) and has a two-person crew. The Star was designed by Francis Sweisguth of Long Island, New York, in 1910.

1896–1928 not held

1932 Los Angeles T: 7, N: 7, D: 8.12.

		PTS.
1. USA	Gilbert Gray, Andrew Libano	46
2. GBR	G. Colin Ratsey, Peter Jaffe	35
3. SWE	Gunnar Asther, Daniel Sundén-Cullberg	28
4. CAN	Henry Wylie, Henry Simmonds	27
5. FRA	Jean-Jacques Herbulot, Jean Peytel	26
6. HOL	Jan Maas, Adriaan Maas	14
7. SAF	Arent Van Soelen, Cecil Goodricke	7

The *Jupiter*, skippered by 30-year-old Gilbert Gray of New Orleans, won five of the seven races.

1936 Berlin-Kiel T: 12, N: 12, D: 8.10.

		PTS.
1. GER	Peter Bischoff, Hans-Joachim Weise	80
2. SWE	Arvid Laurin, Uno Wallentin	64
3. HOL	Willem de Vries-Lentsch, Adriaan Maas	63
4. GBR	Keith Grogno, William Wolpy	56
5. USA	William Waterhouse, Woodbridge Metcalf	51
6. NOR	Øivind Christensen, Sigurd Herbern	44
7. FRA	Jean-Jacques Herbulot, Pierre de Montaut	41
8. TUR	Harun Ulman, Behzat Baydar	38

Bischoff matched Gray's feat of winning five of seven races. The Germans had clinched the gold medals after the sixth race, but raced the next day anyway and won again.

1948 London-Torbay T: 17, N: 17, D: 8.12.

		PTS.
1. USA	Hilary Smart, Paul Smart	5828
2. CUB	Carlos de Cárdenas Culmell, Carlos de Cárdenas Pla	4949
3. HOL	Adriaan Maas, Edward Stutterheim	4731
4. GBR/BAH	Durward Knowles, Sloan Farrington	4372
5. ITA	Agostino Straulino, Nicolo Rode	4370
6. POR	Joaquim Mascarenhas de Fiúza, Júlio de Sousa Leite Gourinho	4292
7. AUS	Alexander Sturrock, Len Fenton	3828
8. CAN	Norman Gooderham, A. Gerald Fairhead	2635

Paul Smart was a 56-year-old lawyer from New York. His 23-year-old son, Hilary, was a student at Harvard. The silver medal-winning Cárdenases were also father and son.

1952 Helsinki T: 21, N: 21, D: 7.28.

		PTS.
1. ITA	Agostino Straulino, Nicolò Rode	7635
2. USA	John Reid, John Price	7126
3. POR	Joaquim Mascarenhas de Fiúza, Francisco Rebelo de Andrade	4903
4. CUB	Carlos de Cárdenas Culmell, Carlos de Cárdenas Pla	4535
5. BAH	Durward Knowles, Sloan Farrington	4405
6. FRA	Edouard Chabert, Jean-Louis Dauris	3866
7. SWE	Bengt Melin, Björn Carlsson	3785
8. HOL	Adriaan Maas, Edward Stutterheim	3510

The Italians and the Americans engaged in a private battle, winning all seven races and generally leaving the others far behind. Straulino skippered the Merope to three firsts and four seconds. The US pair placed first four times and third once, but also finished seventh in the second race and eighth on the final day.

1956 Melbourne T: 12, N: 12, D: 12.5.

		PTS.
1. USA	Herbert Williams, Lawrence Low	5876
2. ITA	Agostino Straulino, Nicolò Rode	5649
3. BAH	Durward Knowles, Sloan Farrington	5223
4. POR	Duarte de Almeida Bello, José Bustorff Silva	3825
5. FRA	Philippe Chancerel, Michel Parent	3126
6. CUB	Carlos de Cárdenas Culmell, Jorge de Cárdenas Plá	2714
7. GBR	B. Bruce Banks, Stanley Potter	2387
8. SOV/ RUS	Timir Pinegin, Fyodor Shutkov	1778

Skippered by 48-year-old Sussex-born Herbert Williams of Evanston, Illinois, the *Kathleen* placed first, fifth, second, first, second, second, second.

1960 Rome-Naples T: 26, N: 26, D: 9.7.

		PTS.
1. SOV/RUS	Timir Pinegin, Fyodor Shutkov	7619
2. POR	José Quina, Mário Quina	6665
3. USA	William Parks, Robert Halperin	6269
4. ITA	Agostino Straulino, Carlo Rolandi	6047
5. SWI	Hans Bryner, Ulrich Bucher	5716
6. BAH	Durward Knowles, Sloan Farrington	5282
7. GER	Bruno Splieth, Eckart Wagner	4745
8. YUG/SLO	Mario Fafangel, Janko Kosmina	3977

This was the first Soviet victory in Olympic yachting, a sport which had previously been considered the domain of capitalists. Oddly enough, the Soviet craft, the *Tornado,* had been built in Old Greenwich, Connecticut.

1964 Tokyo-Fujisawa T: 17, N: 17, D: 10.21.

		PTS.
1. BAH	Durward Knowles, C. Cecil Cooke	5664
2. USA	Richard Stearns, Lynn Williams	5585
3. SWE	Pelle Pettersson, Holger Sundström	5527
4. FIN	Peder Tallberg, Henrik Tallberg	5402
5. SOV/RUS	Timir Pinegin, Fyodor Shutkov	4305
6. GER	Bruno Splieth, Karsten Meyer	4175
7. CAN	David Miller, William West	3565
8. POR	Manuel Duarte, Pinto Fernando	3330

Forty-six-year-old Durward Knowles was competing in his fifth Olympics. If Stearns and Williams had finished six seconds faster in the last race, they would have won the gold medal.

1968 Mexico City-Acapulco T: 20, N: 20, D: 10.21.

		PTS.
1. USA	Lowell North, Peter Barrett	14.4
2. NOR	Peder Lunde, Jr., Per Olav Wiken	43.7
3. ITA	Franco Cavallo, Camilo Gargano	44.7
4. DEN	Paul Elvström, Poul Mik-Meyer	50.4
5. BAH	Durward Knowles, Percival Knowles	63.4
6. AUS	David Forbes, Richard Williamson	68.7
7. BRA	Erik Schmidt, Axel Schmidt	74.4
8. SWI	Edwin Bernet, Rolf Amrein	75.0

North and Barrett secured first place after six races, but won the seventh race anyway. Lowell North founded and developed North Sails, the most successful sail designer and manufacturer in the world.

1972 Munich-Kiel T: 18, N: 18, D: 9.8.

		PTS.
1. AUS	David Forbes, John Anderson	28.1
2. SWE	Pelle Pettersson, Stellan Westerdahl	44.0
3. GER	Wilhelm Kuhweide, Karsten Meyer	44.4
4. BRA	Jorge Bruder, Jan Willem Aten	52.7
5. ITA	Flavio Scala, Mauro Testa	58.4
6. POR	Antonio Correia, Ulrich Anjos	68.4
7. GBR	Stuart Jardine, John Wastall	68.7
8. HUN	András Gosztonyi, György Holovits	74.0

The Australians were assured of first place after the sixth race. At the same time that John Anderson was winning a gold medal in the Star class, his identical twin brother, Tom, was winning a gold medal in the Dragon class on a different course.

1976 not held

1980 Moscow-Tallinn T: 13, N: 13, D: 7.29.

		PTS.
1. SOV	Valentyn Mankin, Aleksandrs Muzičenko	24.7
2. AUT	Hubert Raudaschl, Karl Ferstl	31.7
3. ITA	Giorgio Gorla, Alfio Peraboni	36.1
4. SWE	Peter Sundelin, Håkan Lindström	44.7
5. DEN	Jens Håkon Christensen, Morten Nielsen	45.7
6. HOL	Boudewijn Binkhorst, Jacob Vandenberg	49.4
7. SPA	Antonio Gorostegui Ceballos, José María Benavides Accibar	72.7
8. GDR	Wolf-Eberhard Richter, Olaf Engelhardt	83.7

Forty-one-year-old Valentyn Mankin gained his third gold medal, having won the Finn class in 1968 and the Tempest in 1972. He is the only yachtsman to have earned gold medals in three different classes. He also won a silver in the 1976 Tempest. The Austrians could have won with a fourth-place finish in the last race, but they could do no better than ninth. Most damaging to the Austrians was the third race, in which they were disqualified after finishing first.

1984 Los Angeles-Long Beach T: 19, N: 19, D: 8.8.

		PTS.
1. USA	William E. Buchan, Stephen Erickson	29.7
2. GER	Joachim Griese, Michael Marcour	41.4
3. ITA	Giorgio Gorla, Alfio Peraboni	43.5
4. SWE	Kent Carlson, Henrik Eyermann	43.7
5. AUT	Hubert Raudaschl, Karl Ferstl	53.4
6. GRE	Ilias Hatzipavlis, Leonidas Pelekanakis	67.0
7. SPA	Antonio Gorostegui Ceballos, José Luis Doreste Blanco	74.0
8. HOL	Hans Binkhorst, Wilem van Walt Meijer	76.0

After six races, the gold medal was still up for grabs among the four leaders. Buchan, a 49-year-old building contractor from Seattle, Washington, got off to a poor start and he and Erickson found themselves discussing how to protect third place. But a sudden wind shift, coupled with a mistake by Gorla, who missed a mark and had to go around the buoy again, opened the way for the Americans, who shot through for their third victory of the regatta. As Buchan would later say, "In five minutes we went from nothing to silver to gold. I've been sailing these little suckers for 35 years, and I've never felt the speed I had. I still don't know how I did it." Buchan's son, Carl, won a gold medal in the Flying Dutchman class.

1988 Seoul-Pusan T: 21, N: 21, D: 9.27.

		PTS.
1. GBR	Michael Mcintyre, P. Bryn Vaile	45.7
2. USA	Mark Reynolds, Hal Haenel	48.0
3. BRA	Torben Grael, Nelson Falcão	50.0
4. SWE	Mats Johansson, Mats Hansson	56.7
5. ITA	Giorgio Gorla, Alfio Peraboni	63.1
6. CAN	D. Ross MacDonald, D. Bruce MacDonald	63.7
7. AUS	Colin Beashel, Gregory Torpy	66.4
8. SOV/RUS	Viktor Sohovyov, Aheksandr Zybin	68.4

McIntyre and Vaile were in fourth place after six races. To earn gold medals they needed to win the final race, with Reynolds and Haenel placing worse than fifth and Grael and Falcão worse than fourth. As it happened, the Brazilians could manage only eighth place; the Americans suffered a broken mast and failed to finish. Meanwhile, McIntyre and Vaile successfully fought off a challenge from the Australian pair to win by 11 seconds. Regarding his upset victory, McIntyre, a car-phone sales manager from West Dean, near Salisbury, said, "In my wildest dreams I thought we could win, but not in any other state of mind."

The skipper of the 19th place Bahamian boat was 1964 Olympic champion Durwood Knowles, who, at age 70, was the third-oldest competitor in any sport in the history of the Olympics. He was also one of only five people to take part in eight Olympics.

1992 Barcelona T: 26, N: 26, D: 8.2.

		PTS.
1. USA	Mark Reynolds, Hal Haenel	31.4
2. NZL	Roderick Davies, Donald Cowie	58.4
3. CAN	D. Ross MacDonald, Eric Jespersen	62.7
4. HOL	Mark Neeleman, Jos Schrier	64.0
5. SWE	Hans Wallén, Bobbie Loshe	65.0
6. GER	Hans Vogt, Jörg Fricke	69.7
7. AUS	Colin Beashel, David Giles	71.4
8. GRE	Iakovos Kiseoglou, Dimitris Boukis	84.0

Reynolds and Haenel made up for their disappointment of four years earlier by finishing second, first, third, first, third, and eleventh to clinch the victory without having to compete in the final race. Rod Davies, the skipper of the New Zealand boat, had won a gold medal in the 1984 Soling class while representing the United States.

1996 Atlanta-Savannah T: 25, N: 25, D: 7.29.

		PTS.
1. BRA	Marcelo Ferreira, Torben Grael	25
2. SWE	Bobbie Lohse, Hans Wallen	29
3. AUS	Colin Beashel, David Giles	32
4. GRE	Anastassios Bountouris, Dimitrios Boukis	45
5. NZL	Roderick Davis, Donald Cowie	46
6. ITA	Enrico Chieffi, Roberto Sinibaldi	52
7. SPA	José Luis Doreste Blanco, F. Javier Hermida Freijomil	57
8. USA	Mark Reynolds, Hal Haenel	58

Beashel and Giles had a slight lead over Grael and Ferreira going into the final day's two races, but a ninth-place finish and a premature start dropped them back to third.

2000 Sydney T: 16, N: 16, D: 9.30.

		PTS.
1. USA	Magnus Liljedahl, Mark Reynolds	34.0
2. GBR	Ian Walker, Mark Covell	35.0
3. BRA	Marcelo Ferreira, Torben Grael	39.0
4. BER	Lee White, Peter Bromby	45.3
5. CAN	Kai Bjorn, D. Ross MacDonald	48.0
6. HOL	Jos Schrier, Mark Neeleman	50.0
7. AUS	Colin Beashel, David Giles	51.0
8. SPA	José María van der Ploeg García, Rafael Trujillo Villar	55.0

Competing in his fifth Olympics, Torben Grael, along with his partner Marcelo Ferreira, led for almost the entire regatta and entered the final race with a five-point lead over both Walker and Covell and Reynolds and Liljedahl. The Americans had staged an impressive comeback. Back in eleventh place after five races, they climbed up to third overall with two races to go. The start of the final race saw an unexpected development. Gavin Brady of New Zealand drew six boats across the line, including the Brazilians and the Americans. Of the six, only Reynolds and Liljedahl turned around and restarted. Grael, apparently unaware of his infraction, kept going, was disqualified and lost the gold medal. Reynolds managed to catch up quickly and crossed the finish line in second place—31 seconds ahead of Walker—and won the gold medal by one point. Walker and Covell had both lost their original partners in tragic accidents. Walker's partner in winning the 470 silver in 1996 was John Merricks. Walker and Merricks were passengers in a mini-van in Italy in 1997 when the driver lost control. Merricks, in the passenger seat, was killed. In December 1998, Covell's helmsman, Glyn Charles, was swept overboard by a huge wave during a race in the Tasman Sea. Walker and Covell began sailing together in 1999.

2004 Athens-Helliniko T: 17, N: 17, D: 8.28.

		PTS.
1. BRA	Torben Grael, Marcelo Ferreira	42
2. CAN	D. Ross MacDonald, Mike Wolfs	51
3. FRA	Xavier Rohart, Pascal Rambeau	54
4. SWI	Flavio Marazzi, Enrico De Maria	70
5. USA	Paul Cayard, Phil Trinter	71
6. GBR	Iain Percy, Steven Mitchell	73
7. ITA	Francesco Bruni, Guido Vigna	75
8. BER	Peter Bromby, Lee White	82

Considering that they faced seven world champions in the other sixteen boats, Torben Grael and Marcelo Ferreira dominated the competition with surprising ease, moving into first place on the second day of competition and securing the gold with a race to spare. It was Grael's second gold medal and fifth medal overall, the most in Olympic sailing history.

2008 Beijing-Qingdao T: 16, N: 16, D: 8.21.

		PTS.
1. GBR	Iain Percy, Andrew "Bart" Simpson	45
2. BRA	Robert Scheidt, Bruno Prada	53
3. SWE	Fredrik Lööf, Anders Ekström	53
4. POL	Mateusz Kusznierewicz, Dominik Życki	59
5. SWI	Flavio Marazzi, Enrico De Maria	59
6. FRA	Xavier Rohart, Pascal Rambeau	69
7. GER	Marc Aurel Pickel, Ingo Borkowski	70
8. POR	Afonso Domingos, Bernardo Santos	72

Swedish pair Fredrik Lööf and Anders Ekström had a narrow two-point lead going into the medal race, followed by British crew Iain Percy and Andrew Simpson and three-time world champion medalists Robert Scheidt and Bruno Prada.

Lööf and Ekström were in third place at the second mark, but fell off the pace at the end to finish last, leaving Percy and Simpson with the victory. The Brazilian and Swedish boats finished tied on points but the silver medal went to Scheidt and Prada for their higher placing in the final race.

Percy and Simpson's partnership dated back 25 years to early childhood. "On the days when it was too windy to go sailing, we would sit and play Lego together," Percy recalled, "We've been best mates ever since."

Silver medalist Robert Scheidt earned his fourth straight Olympic medal, including gold medals in the one-person Laser event in 1996 and 2004. He switched to the Star class in 2005, after winning his eighth solo world title. Scheidt's girlfriend, Gintarė Volungevičiūtė, had won silver in the Laser Radial class two days earlier.

WOMEN

The first women to take part in Olympic yachting were Frances Clytie Rivett-Carnac of Great Britain, who crewed for her husband in the uncontested 7-meter class in 1908 and Dorothy Wright of Great Britain who crewed for her husband in the 7-meter class in 1920. The first woman to skipper an Olympic boat was Virginie Hériot of France, who won a gold medal in the 8-meter class in 1928.

WINDSURFER

The 2008 competition will utilize the Neil Pryde RS:X, a 2.86-meter (9 foot 4½ inch) long board weighing 15.5 kilograms (34 pounds) and topped with an 8.5 square meter sail.

1896–1988 not held

1992 Barcelona C: 24, N: 24, D: 8.2.
Lechner Division II

		PTS.
1. Barbara Kendall	NZL	47.8
2. Zhang Xiaodong	CHN	65.8
3. Dorien de Vries	HOL	68.7
4. Maud Herbert	FRA	78.0
5. Lanee Butler	USA	95.7
6. Penny Way	GBR	99.4
7. Alessandra Sensini	ITA	101.4
8. Jorunn Horgen	NOR	102.7

Seven months before the Olympics, Barbara Kendall was thrown from a power boat, and the boat's propeller severed a tendon and broke the scaphoid bone in her wrist. Barbara Kendall's older brother Bruce won the sailboard gold medal in 1988. Zhang Xiaodong was the first Asian athlete to earn an Olympic yachting medal.

1996 Atlanta-Savannah C: 27, N: 27, D: 7.29.
Mistral

		PTS.
1. Lee Lai-shan	HKG	16
2. Barbara Kendall	NZL	24
3. Alessandra Sensini	ITA	28
4. Li Ke	CHN	29
5. Jorunn Horgen	NOR	31
6. Dorota Staszewska	POL	38
7. Penny Wilson	GBR	44
8. Maud Herbert	FRA	46

Lee Lai-shan, affectionately known in Hong Kong as "San-San," was the eighth of ten children. When her father died, she was sent to live with her uncle on the island of Cheung Chau. Her uncle owned a sailing shop and introduced Lee to windsurfing when she was twelve

Lee Lai-shan, 1996
All smiles after winning the sailboard competition.

years old. She first competed at the Olympics in Barcelona and was disappointed with her eleventh place finish. The following year however, she caused a sensation by winning both the European and world championships. She was the first Hong Kong athlete to become world champion in an Olympic sport. As for the Olympics themselves, athletes from Hong Kong had been entering various sports since 1952, but none had brought home a medal. At the 1996 Games, Lee produced a remarkably consistent series—third, second, second, second, fourth, second, seventh and first, and won the gold medal without having to compete in the final race.

2000 Sydney C: 29, N: 29, D: 9.24.
Mistral

		PTS.
1. Alessandra Sensini	ITA	15
2. Amelie Lux	GER	15
3. Barbara Anne Kendall	NZL	19
4. Lanee Butler	USA	57
5. Jessica Crisp	AUS	59
6. Lee Lai-shan	HKG	59
7. Chujun Zhang	CHN	60
8. María del Carmen Vaz Pardal	SPA	72

Tiny Amelie Lux, a late addition to the German team, surprised the field by winning the first race and holding on to the lead through eight races by finishing fourth or better in every race. Despite her consistency, she was unable to shake world champion Alessandra Sensini or 1992 Olympic champion Barbara Kendall. Sensini won race nine to take her first overall lead, but she faltered in race ten, allowing Lux to go into the last race with 13 points, while Sensini had 14 and Kendall 16. This meant that either Lux or Sensini could capture the gold medal by winning the final race. The two pulled away from the others and staged an exciting private duel. Sensini led most of the way, but her lead was only two seconds at the penultimate mark. She then held on to win by seven seconds. Last across the finish line in every race was Endra Ha-Tiff of the Seychelles. However, Ha-Tiff was grateful just to be competing. Five weeks before the Olympics, she was taking part in a warm-up regatta in Sydney Harbour when she was almost hit by a ferry in what could easily have been a fatal accident. A shaken Ha-Tiff survived the encounter with only a scraped knee.

2004 Athens-Helliniko C: 26, N: 26, D: 8.25.
Mistral

		PTS.
1. Faustine Merret	FRA	31
2. Yin Jian	CHN	33
3. Alessandra Sensini	ITA	34
4. Lee Lai-shan	HKG	42
5. Barbara Anne Kendall	NZL	58
6. Jessica Crisp	AUS	74
7. Amelie Lux	GER	87
8. Blanca Manchón Domínguez	SPA	95

The favorite in Athens was defending Olympic champion and reigning world champion Alessandra Sensini. However, throughout the regatta, she was in a tight battle with Faustine Merret and Yin Jian. Merret took the lead after the third race, but Sensini caught her in race six and moved ahead by one point after race seven. Then Yin, winning her third straight race, took a one-point lead over both Sensini and Merret after the eighth race. She was still ahead after race nine, but Yin's ninth-place finish in the tenth race allowed Sensini to enter the final race two points ahead of Merret and five ahead of Yin. In the final race, a seventh-place finish dropped Sensini to bronze, while Merret earned the gold medal by finishing in second place behind Yin.

2008 Beijing-Qingdao C: 27, N: 27, D: 8.20.
Neil Pryde RS:X

		PTS.
1. Yin Jian	CHN	39
2. Alessandra Sensini	ITA	40
3. Bryony Shaw	GBR	45
4. Marina Alabau Neira	SPA	54
5. Jessica Crisp	AUS	66
6. Barbara Kendall	NZL	75
7. Zofia Klepacka	POL	82
8. Olha Maslivets	UKR	83

Defending Olympic silver medalist Yin Jian got off to a strong start, winning the first three races and finishing third in the next two. Yin's biggest challenger was three-time Olympic medalist Alessandra Sensini, who had won two of the past three world championship titles, including the most recent in Auckland, New Zealand, in January 2008.

Sensini took a commanding lead in the medal race and was never seriously challenged, finishing well ahead of the pack. Needing at least a third-place finish for the overall win, Yin moved up from fifth place, passing Olha Maslivets and Marina Alabau to finish third, and clinching the gold medal by a single point.

LASER RADIAL

1896–2004 not held

2008 Beijing-Qingdao C: 28, N: 28, D: 8.19.

		PTS.
1. Anna Tunnicliffe	USA	37
2. Gintarė Volungevičiūtė	LIT	42
3. Xu Lijia	CHN	50
4. Sarah Blanck	AUS	62
5. Sarah Steyaert	FRA	77
6. Nathalie Brugger	SWI	90
7. Jo Aleh	NZL	90
8. Evi Van Acker	BEL	91

Born in northern England, Anna Tunnicliffe moved to the United States with her family at the age of 12. Despite a steady downward trend in her world championship results—third in 2005, fourth in 2006, fifth in 2007 and sixth in 2008—she won the Olympic test event in Qingdao in August 2007 and beat 2005 world champion Paige Railey two months later at the US Trials to earn a berth in Beijing.

Tunnicliffe held a seven-point lead going into the medal race, but false-started and was forced to circle back and restart. She battled her way back from second-to-last to finish second behind Lithuania's Gintarė Volungevičiūtė, who earned the silver medal.

470

1896–1984 not held

1988 Seoul-Pusan T: 21, N: 21, D: 9.27.

		PTS.
1. USA	Allison Jolly, Lynne Jewell	26.7
2. SWE	Marit Söderström, Birgitta Bengtsson	40.0
3. SOV/UKR	Larysa Moskalenko, Iryna Chunykhovska	45.4
4. FIN	Bettina Lemström, Annika Lemström	47.0
5. GER	Susanne Meyer, Katrin Adlkofer	56.4
6. AUS	Nicola Green, Karyn Davis	57.0
7. GDR	Susanne Theel, Silke Preuss	57.4
8. FRA	Florence Lebrun, Sophie Berge	81.7

Söderström and Jolly had faced each other six times in world championships prior to 1988, with Söderström winning four. However, Jolly's two victories came, significantly, in the Olympic years of 1980 and 1984. In the inaugural women-only competition in Seoul, Jolly and Jewell took two firsts, two seconds, and a third. But because they were disqualified in the fifth race for tacking too close, they needed to finish fourteenth or better in the final race to earn gold medals. Despite the treacherous weather conditions, this did not seem a difficult task. However, in the middle of the race they dropped off a large wave. As a result, the wire connecting the jib to the halyard broke and their jib sail sagged down the jib wire.

"There goes the gold," said Jolly, as they dropped back from fourth place to fifteenth. "We've got to fight!" answered Jewell, who, despite 30 knots of wind and 10-foot waves, spent the next 5 minutes repairing the jib with a small piece of spare twine. With the sail back in place, they managed to finish ninth.

1992 Barcelona T: 17, N: 17, D: 8.3.

		PTS.
1. SPA	Theresa Zabell Lucas, Patricia Guerra Cabrera	29.7
2. NZL	Leslie Egnot, Jan Shearer	36.7
3. USA	Jennifer "JJ" Isler, Pamela Healy	40.7
4. SOV	Larysa Moskalenko, Alena Pakholchik	43.0
5. JPN	Yumiko Shige, Alicia Kinoshita	53.7
6. FRA	Florence Lebrun, Odile Barre	65.7
7. ITA	Maria Quarra, Anna Maria Barabino	68.7
8. GER	Peggy Hardwiger, Christina Pinnow	71.7

Eight out of 17 boats—almost half the field—were disqualified in the first race for starting prematurely, including all of the eventual medalists. Zabell and Guerra moved into the lead after winning the fourth race, applied more pressure by winning the sixth race, and insured their victory with a seventh place in the final race. Egnot and Shearer moved up from fourth to second by winning the last race, their third win of the regatta. Theresa Zabell was born in Ipswich and maintained dual Spanish and British citizenship.

1996 Atlanta-Savannah T: 22, N: 22, D: 8.1.

		PTS.
1. SPA	Theresa Zabell Lucas, Begoña Via-Dufresne Pereña	25
2. JPN	Yumiko Shige, Alicia Kinoshita	36
3. UKR	Ruslana Taran, Olena Pakholchik	38
4. USA	Kris Stookey, Louise Van Voorhis	47
5. GER	Susanne Bauckholt, Kathrin Adlkofer	49
6. DEN	Susanne Ward, Lise Michaela Ward	56
7. ITA	Federica Salva, Emanuela Sossi	64
8. AUS	Jennifer Lidgett, Addy Bucek	64

Zabell and Dufresne moved into first place midway through the regatta and won the last two races to secure the victory.

2000 Sydney T: 19, N: 19, D: 9.28.

		PTS.
1. AUS	Belinda Stowell, Jennifer Armstrong	33
2. USA	Jennifer "JJ" Isler, Pease Glaser	47
3. UKR	Olena Panholchik, Ruslana Taran	48
4. ISR	Anat Fabrikant, Shany Kedmy	50
5. GER	Nicola Birkner, Wibke Bülle	54
6. SPA	Natalia Vía-Dufresne Pereña, Sandra Azón Canalda	55
7. ITA	Emanuela Sossi, Federica Salvao	60
8. JPN	Yumiko Shige, Yurie Alicia Kinoshita	66

Ruslana Taran and Olena Panholchik won every major title between the Atlanta and Sydney Olympics: three world championships and three European championships. But when their coach, Viktor Kobalenko, moved to Australia, their results began to slip. Conversely, Kobalenko's arrival in Australia boosted the performances of Jenny Armstrong and Belinda Stowell. Armstrong and Stowell were the first Australian women to win sailing medals, although neither of them was born in Australia. Stowell came from Zimbabwe, while Armstrong represented New Zealand at the 1992 Olympics, placing fourth in the Europe class.

2004 Athens-Helliniko T: 20, N: 20, D: 8.21.

		PTS.
1. GRE	Sofia Bekatorou, Aimilia Tsoulfa	38
2. SPA	Natalia "Juana" Vía-Dufresne Pereña, Sandra Azón Canalda	62
3. SWE	Therese Torgersson, Vendela Zachrisson	63
4. SLO	Vesna Dekleva, Klara Maučec	65
5. USA	Katie McDowell, Isabelle Kinsolving	84
6. DEN	Susanne Ward, Michaëla Ward-Meehan	89
7. GBR	Christina Bassadone, Katherine Hopson	91
8. RUS	Vlada Iliyenko, Natalya Gaponovich	94

Three-time world champions and hometown favorites Sofia Bekatorou and Aimilia Tsoulfa swept through the competition, winning five races and adding three second place finshes to secure the gold medals by 24 points with a race to spare.

2008 Beijing-Qingdao T: 19, N: 19, D: 8.18.

		PTS.
1. AUS	Elise Rechichi, Tessa Parkinson	43
2. HOL	Marcelien de Koning, Lobke Berkhout	53
3. BRA	Fernanda Oliveira, Isabel Swan	60
4. ISR	Nike Kornecki, Vered Buskila	66
5. ITA	Giulia Conti, Giovanna Micol	75
6. GBR	Christina Bassadone, Saskia Clark	82
7. CZE	Lenka Šmídová, Lenka Mrzilková	83
8. AUT	Sylvia Vogl, Caro Flatscher	84

Marcelien de Koning and Lobke Berkhout had won three consecutive world championship titles, from 2005 to 2007, before dropping to fourth place at the 2008 world championships in Melbourne, Australia. Their odds for a medal improved after reigning world champions Erin Maxwell and Isabelle Kinsolving lost at the US Olympic trials to Amanda Clark and Sarah Mergenthaler, who had never cracked the top ten at a major international tournament.

Reigning world bronze medalists Elise Rechichi and Tessa Parkinson built up a virtually unbeatable 18-point lead over the Dutch pair in the first ten races and only needed to avoid a last place in the medal race (and a first-place finish by Holland) to ensure the gold medal. They finished second-to-last, winning the gold medal by ten points.

ELLIOT 6M

Making its debut at the 2012 Olympics, the Elliott 6m is a three-person keelboat. Designed by New Zealander George Elliott in 2000, the boat was modified in 2008 to allow sailing in a greater wind range. The modified Elliott 6 is 6 meters (19 feet 8 inches) long, has a mainsail of 15.9 square meters (52 square feet) and carries a symmetrical spinnaker, which is considered more suitable for match racing.

For the women's match racing event, the competition will consist of an opening round-robin series followed by a series of knockout rounds. In match racing, the first boat across the line wins the match.

DISCONTINUED EVENTS

1900 YACHTING

Olympic historians are of differing opinions as to which events at the 1900 Paris Games should be considered official Olympic events. The thorniest of these issues concerns the yachting events. The 1900 regatta was irregular in several ways. To begin with, the winners were awarded cash prizes in an era when the Olympics were supposed to be the domain of amateurs. However, cash prizes were also offered in the archery and shooting competitions. In the second place, there were two separate finals in most of the yachting classes. In the 10-20 ton class, there were actually three finals. There is no other instance in Olympic history in which more than one final was planned for an event. Even if the awarding of cash prizes and the double and triple finals can be excused, there is one more problem with the 1900 yachting contests: they were handicap races. The final time of each crew was adjusted according to the weight of its boat. In the case of the 20+ ton class, for example, the British boat *Brynhild* recorded a time 31 minutes slower than the British boat *Cicely*, but was placed second because it was assigned a handicap of 31 minutes 20 seconds. Handicap events have never been accepted in the Olympics. For this reason, in this author's opinion, the 1900 yachting events should not be viewed as part of the Olympics. Those readers who are nonetheless curious about these events should read, "A Review of Olympic Yachting—1900" by Ian Buchanan in *The Unofficial Report of the 1900 Olympic Games* by Bill Mallon (McFarland & Company, Inc.; Box 611; Jefferson, North Carolina 28640; USA).

EUROPE

The Europe is a single-handed dinghy, 11 feet (3.35 meters) long and weighing only 44.9 kilograms (99 pounds). It is sometimes known as the "small Finn." It was designed by Alois Roland of Belgium in 1960.

1992 Barcelona C: 24, N: 24, D: 8.3.

		PTS.
1. Linda Andersen	NOR	48.7
2. Natalia Vía-Dufresne Pereña	SPA	57.4
3. Julia Trotman	USA	62.7
4. Jennifer Armstrong	NZL	65.0
5. Dorte Jensen	DEN	65.7
6. Krista Kruuv	EST	67.1
7. Martine van Leeuwen	HOL	67.7
8. Arianna Bogatec	ITA	69.0

Trotman won the first race and placed second in the second race. She was first across the line in the third race, but was disqualified for a premature start. She was still in first place overall after five races, but was disqualified again in the sixth race and had to settle for bronze. Andersen started prematurely once, but also won the third and fourth race.

1996 Atlanta-Savannah C: 28, N: 28, D: 7.31.

		PTS.
1. Kristine Roug	DEN	24
2. Margriet Matthijsse	HOL	30
3. Courtenay Becker-Dey	USA	39
4. Shirley Robertson	GBR	41
5. Sharon Ferris	NZL	73
6. Sibylle Powarzynski	GER	75
7. Linda Konttorp	NOR	81
8. Serena Amato	ARG	81

The world champion in both 1994 and 1995, Kristine Roug finished in the top three in the first six races and protected her lead in the last five.

2000 Sydney C: 27, N: 27, D: 9.29.

		PTS.
1. Shirley Robertson	GBR	37
2. Margriet Matthijsse	HOL	39
3. Serena Amato	ARG	51
4. Neus Garriga	SPA	61
5. Sari Multala	FIN	61
6. Min Dezillie	BEL	68
7. Lenka Šmidová	CZE	75
8. Larissa Nevierov	ITA	75

Scottish sailor Shirley Robertson needed to finish fourth or better in either of the last two races to secure the gold medal. She could do no better than sixteenth in race 10, so it came down to a final race duel with Margriet Matthijsse, who had come back from a slow start in the regatta to win races 9 and 10. Matthijsse won race 11 as well. Only fifth halfway through the race, Robertson moved up one place and then one more to finish with 30 seconds to spare.

2004 Athens-Helliniko C: 25, N: 25, D: 8.22.

		PTS.
1. Siren Sundby	NOR	47
2. Lenka Šmídová	CZE	65
3. Signe Livbjerg	DEN	74
4. Sarah Blanck	AUS	75
5. Sari Multala	FIN	85
6. Serena Amato	ARG	86
7. Shen Xiaoying	CHN	88
8. Sarah Macky	NZL	91

Reigning world champion Siren Sundby recorded five first-place finishes, including three in a row, on her way to the gold medal, despite a disqualification in the third race of the regatta. In the sixth race, Sundby was involved in another protest, against Lenka Šmídová, but this time Šmídová was hit with the disqualification. In the final race, Sundby needed only to finish in the top 21 of the 25 racers to secure the gold. She placed 12th.

DRAGON

1948 London-Torbay T: 12, N: 12, D: 8.12.

		PTS.
1. NOR	Thor Thorvaldsen, Sigve Lie, Håkon Barfod	4746
2. SWE	Folke Bohlin, Hugo Jonsson, Gösta Brodin	4621
3. DEN	William Berntsen, Ole Berntsen, Klaus Baess	4223
4. GBR	William Eric Strain, George Brown, James Wallace	3943
5. ITA	Giuseppe Canessa, Bruno Bianchi, Luigi DeManincor	3366
6. FIN	Rainer Packalen, Niilo Orama, Aatos Hirvisalo	3057
7. ARG	Roberto Sieburger, Jorge del Río Sálas, Jorge Salas Chávez	2843
8. HOL	Cornelis Jonker, Abraham Dudok van Heel, Willem van Duyl	2508

1952 Helsinki T: 17, N: 17, D: 7.28.

		PTS.
1. NOR	Thor Thorvaldsen, Sigve Lie, Håkon Barfod	6130
2. SWE	Per Gedda, Sidney Boldt-Christmas, Erland Almkvist	5556
3. GER	Theodor Thomsen, Erich Natusch, Georg Nowka	5352
4. ARG	Roberto Sieburger, Jorge del Río Sálas, Horacio Campi	5339
5. DEN	Ole Berntsen, William Berntsen, Aage Birch	4460
6. HOL	Willem van Duyl, Abraham Dudok van Heel, Michiel Dudok van Heel	4041
7. BRA	Wolfgang Richter, Peter Mangels, Francisco Felici Italo Osoldi	2884
8. POR	João Tito, Carlos Lourenco, Alberto Graca	2782

1956 Melbourne T: 16, N: 16, D: 12.5.

		PTS.
1. SWE	Folke Bohlin, Bengt Palmquist, Leif Wikström	5723
2. DEN	Ole Berntsen, Cyril Andresen, Christian von Bülow	5723
3. GBR	Graham Mann, Ronald Backus, Jonathan Janson	4547
4. ARG	Jorge Salas Chávez, Arnoldo Pekelharing, Boris Belada	4225
5. AUS	Graham Drane, Brian Carolan, James Carolane	3769
6. ITA	Sergio Sorrentino, Piero Gorgatto, Adelchi Pelaschiar	3404
7. NOR	Thor Thorvaldsen, Carl Otto Svae, Björn Guibrandsen	3253
8. CAN	David Howard, Herald Howard, Donald Tytler	3186

The Swedes came from behind to win the last two races and tie the Danes at 5723 points. Sweden was then awarded first place because they won three races to Denmark's one.

1960 Rome-Naples T: 27, N: 27, D: 9.7.

		PTS.
1. GRE	Crown Prince Konstantinos, Odysseus Eskitzoglou, Georgios Zaimis	6733
2. ARG	Jorge Salas Chávez, Héctor Calegaris, Jorge del Río Sálas	5715
3. ITA	Antonio Cosentino, Antonio Ciciliano, Giulio De Stefano	5704
4. NOR	Øivind Christensen, Arild Amundsen, Carl Otto Svae	5403
5. CAN	Samuel McDonald, Lynn Watters, Gordon Norton	5177
6. DEN	Aage Birch, Paul Jörgensen, Niels Markussen	4715
7. GBR	Graham Mann, Jonathan Janson, Ian Hannay	4604
8. GER	Hans Ravenborg, Günther Benecke, Peter Rebien	4329

Twenty-year-old Crown Price Konstantinos received the traditional victory dunking by being pushed into the water by his mother, Queen Frederika.

One member of the Philippine crew, which finished twenty-fourth, was Francisco González, who gained dubious notoriety four years later when he shot the pilot of a commercial airplane in Northern California, causing the death of forty-four people, including himself. González had taken out a $100,000 flight insurance policy before boarding the flight.

1964 Tokyo-Fujisawa T: 23, N: 23, D: 10.21.

		PTS.
1. DEN	Ole Berntsen, Christian von Bülow, Ole Poulsen	5854
2. GDR	Peter Ahrendt, Ulrich Mense, Wilfried Lorenz	5826
3. USA	Lowell North, Charles Rogers, Richard Deaver	5523
4. GBR	Edwin Parry, Jeremy Harris, Peter Reade	5090
5. BER	Edmund Cooper, Eugene Simmons, Conrad Soares	5055
6. ITA	Sergio Sorrentino, Sergio Furlan, Annibale Pelaschiar	4636
7. BAH	Godfrey Kelly, Basil Kelly, Robert Eardley	4294
8. GRE	Odysseus Eskitzoglou, Georgios Zaimis, Themistoklis Magoulas	4188

The East Germans finished 16 seconds short of a gold medal in the final race.

1968 Mexico City-Acapulco T: 23, N: 23, D: 10.21.

		PTS.
1. USA	G. Shelby "Buddy" Friedrichs, Barton Jahncke, Gerald Schreck	6.0
2. DEN	Aage Birch, Poul Höj Jensen, Niels Markussen	26.4
3. GDR	Paul Borowski, Karl-Heinz Thun, Konrad Weichert	32.7
4. CAN	Stephen Tupper, David Miller, Timothy Irwin	64.1
5. AUS	John Cuneo, Thomas Anderson, John Ferguson	65.0
6. SWE	Gunnar Broberg, Lennart Eisner, Sven Hanson	71.4
7. GER	Klaus Oldendorff, Peter Stuicken, Axel May	74.0
8. FRA	Michel Briand, Michel Alexandre, Pierre Blanchard	81.4

The US crew won four of the seven races and also finished second twice and sixth once. Friedrichs was a stock broker, Jahncke a shipping executive and Schreck the owner of a sail loft.

1972 Munich-Kiel T: 23, N: 23, D: 9.8.

		PTS.
1. AUS	John Cuneo, Thomas Anderson, John Shaw	13.7
2. GDR	Paul Borowski, Konrad Weichert, Karl-Heinz Thun	41.7
3. USA	Donald Cohan, Charles Horter, John Marshall	47.7
4. GER	Franz Heilmeler, Richard Kuchler, Konrad Glas	47.7
5. NZL	Ronald Watson, Noel Everett, Fraser Beer	51.0
6. SWE	Jörgen Sundelin, Peter Sundelin, Ulf Sundelin	67.4
7. DEN	Poul Höj Jensen, Frank Höj Jensen, Gunnar Dahlgaard	68.0
8. FIN	Kurt Nyman, Göran Schauman, Aleksander Bielaczyc	68.7

Skippered by 44-year-old optician John Cuneo, the Australian yacht won the first three races of a competition that was cut short after six races due to inclement weather.

5.5-METER

1952 Helsinki T: 16, N: 16, D: 7.28.

		PTS.
1. USA	Britton Chance, Sumner White, Edgar White, Michael Schoettle	5751
2. NOR	Peder Lunde, Sr., Vibeke Lunde, Börre Falkum-Hansen	5325
3. SWE	Folke Wassén, Magnus Wassén, Carl-Erik Ohlson	4554
4. POR	Duarte de Almeida Bello, Fernando Pinto Coelho Bello, Júlio de Sousa Leite Gourinho	4450
5. ARG	Rodolfo Vollenweider, Tomás Galfrascoli, Ludovico Kempter	3982
6. GBR	Robert Perry, John Dillon, Neil Cochran-Patrick	3727
7. SAF	Leslie Horsfield, Joseph Ellis-Brown, Eric Benningfield	3338
8. FIN	Hans Dittmar, Aarne Castrén, Johan Stadigh	3292

Britton Chance was an extremely well-respected professor of biophysics and physical biochemistry, most noted for his research into how oxygen is used by the body to provide energy.

1956 Melbourne T: 10, N: 10, D: 12.5.

		PTS.
1. SWE	Lars Thörn, Hjalmar Karlsson, Sture Stork	5527
2. GBR	Robert Perry, Neil Cochran-Patrick, John Dillon, David Bowker	4050
3. AUS	Alexander Sturrock, Deveraux Mytton, Douglas Buxton	4022
4. USA	Ferdinand Schoettle, Victor Sheronas, John Bryant, Robert Stinson	3971
5. NOR	Peder Lunde, Sr., Odd Harsheim, Halfdan Ditlev-Simonsen, Jr.	3807
6. FRA	Albert Cadot, Jean-Jacques Herbulot, Dominque Perroud	1779
7. ITA	Massimo Oberti, Antonio Carattino, Carlo Spirito, Antonio Cosentino	1677
8. SOV/RUS	Konstantin Aleksandrov, Konstantin Melgunov, Lev Alekseyev	1598

1960 Rome-Naples T: 19, N: 19, D: 9.7.

		PTS.
1. USA	George O'Day, James Hunt, David Smith	6900
2. DEN	William Berntsen, Steen Christensen, Sören Hancke	5678
3. SWI	Henri Copponex, Pierre Girard, Manfred Metzger	5122
4. ARG	Roberto Sieburger, Enrique Sieburger, Carlos Sieburger	4402
5. SWE	Bengt Sjösten, Claes Turitz, Göran Witting	4277
6. GBR	Robin Aisher, George Nicholson, John Ruggles	3807
7. NOR	Finn Ferner, Odd Harsheim, Knut Wang	3765
8. BAH	Robert Symonette, Basil Kelly, George Roy Ramsey	3024

George O'Day of Brookline, Massachusetts, designed 32 classes of sailboats. He served as assistant helmsman of the victorious America's Cup yachts of 1962 and 1967.

1964 Tokyo-Fujisawa T: 15, N: 15, D: 10.21.

		PTS.
1. AUS	William Northam, James Sargeant, Peter O'Donnell	5981
2. SWE	Lars Thörn, Sture Stork, Ernst Arne Karlsson	5284
3. USA	John McNamara, Francis Scully, Joseph Batchelder	5106
4. ITA	Agostino Straulino, Bruno Petronio, Massimo Minervini	4738
5. GER	Fritz Kopperschmidt, Herbert Reich, Eckart Wagner, Uwe Mares	3057
6. FIN	Johann Gullichsen, Karl Peter Frazer, Juhani Salovaara	3039
7. CAN	Samuel McDonald, John Woodward, G. Bernard Skinner	2955
8. NOR	Crown Prince Harald, Eirik Johannessen, Stein Foyen	2860

Former motorcycle speedway rider Bill Northam was a 59-year-old grandfather of five when he skippered the yacht *Barrenjoey* to a gold medal.

1968 Mexico City-Acapulco T: 14, N: 14, D: 10.21.

		PTS.
1. SWE	Ulf Sundelin, Jörgen Sundelin, Peter Sundelin	8.0
2. SWI	Louis Noverraz, Bernhard Dunand, Marcel Stern	32.0
3. GBR	Robin Aisher, Adrian Jardine, Paul Anderson	39.8
4. GER	Rudolf Harmstorf, Karl-August Stolze, Harald Stein	47.4
5. ITA	Giuseppe Zucchinetti, Antonio Carattino, Domenico Carattino	51.1
6. CAN	Stanley Leibel, Ernest Weiss, Jack Hasen	68.0
7. AUS	William Solomons, James Hardy, Gilbert Kaufman	69.4
8. USA	Gardner Cox, Stephen Colgate, Stuart Walker	74.7

The Sundelin brothers, from the small resort town of Ektorp, won five of the seven races, finishing fourth and fifth in the other two. Silver medalist Louis Noverraz was 66 years old.

6-METER

1908 London-Ryde T: 5, N: 4, D: 7.29.

1. GBR	Gilbert Laws, Thomas McMeekin, Charles Crichton
2. BEL	Léon Huybrechts, Louis Huybrechts, Henri Weewauters
3. FRA	Henri Arthus, Louis Potheau, Pierre Rabot
4. GBR	John Leuchars, William Leuchars, Frank Smith
5. SWE	Karl Sjögren, Birger Gustafsson, Jonas Jonsson

There were three races. Two were won by Laws and one by Léon Huybrechts.

1912 Stockholm-Nynas T: 6, N: 5, D: 7.22.

		PTS.
1. FRA	Gaston Thubé, Amédée Thubé, Jacques Thubé	10
2. DEN	Hans Meulengracht Madsen, Steen Herschend, Sven Thomsen	10
3. SWE	Harald Sandberg, Erik Sandberg, Otto Aust	1
4. SWE	Olof Mark, Edvin Hagberg, E. Jonas Jonsson	1
5. FIN	Ernst Estlander, Torsten Sandelin, Gunnar Stenbäck	0
5. NOR	Edvard Christensen, Hans Ferdinand Christiansen, Eigil Kragh Christiansen	0

1920 Antwerp T: 2, N: 2, D: 7.9.

1. NOR	Andreas Brecke, Paal Kaasan, Ingolf Rød	
2. BEL	Léon Huybrechts, John Klotz, Charles van den Bussche	

1924 Paris-Le Havre T: 9, N: 9, D: 7.26.

		PTS.
1. NOR	Eugen Lunde, Christopher Dahl, Anders Lundgren	2
2. DEN	Wilhelm Vett, Knud Degn, Christian Nielsen	5
3. HOL	Johan Carp, Johannes Guépin, Jan Vreede	5
4. SWE	Nils Rinman, Olle Rinman, Magnus Hellström	12
5. BEL	Leon Huybrechts, John Klotz, Léopold Standaert	16
5. FRA	Georges Herpin, Henri Louit, Pierre Moussié	16

Eugen Lunde spawned one of the most successful families in Olympic history. His son, Peder, won a silver medal in 1952 in the 5.5 meter class; his grandson Peder, Jr., won gold in the 1960 Flying Dutchman and silver in the 1968 Star class; and his great-granddaughter, Jeanette, represented Norway in downhill skiing at the 1994 Winter Olympics.

1928 Amsterdam T: 13, N: 13, D: 8.9.

1. NOR	Crown Prince Olav, Johan Anker, Erik Anker, Haakon Bryhn
2. DEN	Niels Otto Möller, Aage Höy-Petersen, Peter Schlütter, Svend Linck
3. EST	Nikolai Vekšin, William von Wirén, Eberhard Vogdt, Andreas Fählmann, Georg Fählmann
4. HOL	Hendrik Pluijgers, Carl Huisken, Willem Schouten, Hendrik Fokker
5. BEL	Léon Huybrechts, Arthur Sneyers, Frits Mulder, Ludovic Franck, Willy van Rompaey
6. USA	Herman "Swede" Whiton, Conway Olmstead, Willets Outerbridge, James Thompson, Frederick Morris
7. SWE	Harry Hansson, Georg Lindahl, Yngve Lindquist, Hakon Reuter
8. FRA	Ph. de Rothschild, H. Allard, R. Gofflet, J.P. Rovanet

During World War II, Crown Prince Olav became a symbol of Norwegian resistance to the Nazis. His reign as King Olav V was a popular one and lasted from 1957 until his death in 1991.

US sailor Jim Thompson went on to lead a fascinating and mysterious life. After enlisting in the US Army during World War II, Thompson joined the Office of Strategic Services, the precursor to the CIA. He worked with the French resistance movement in North Africa before being sent to Bangkok. After the war he remained in Thailand, founding a textile company and hiring local weavers to revitalize the dying Thai silk industry. He became known as the "silk king," amassing a fortune and an exquisite collection of South-east Asian art, which he displayed in a six-building mansion he built along the Klong River.

On Easter Sunday 1967 the 61-year-old Thompson was holidaying with friends at a Malaysian resort. After attending church the group returned to their hotel for an afternoon siesta; Thompson remained on the veranda while his friends rested. At about 3:30pm, his friends heard the sound of someone—they assumed Thompson—leaving the bungalow. He was never seen again. The next day a search was organized, involving Malaysian and British troops, bloodhounds, local tribesmen, an area Boy Scout troop and even local psychics and medicine men. No trace of the missing man was ever found. The disappearance was made more mysterious by the fact that Thompson had been trained in jungle survival; that, despite being a chain smoker and gallstone sufferer, he had left without his cigarettes or medicine; and that no kidnapping or ransom note was ever found.

1932 Los Angeles T: 3, N: 3, D: 8.12.

		PTS.
1. SWE	Tore Holm, Martin Hindorff, Olle Åkerlund, Åke Bergqvist	18
2. USA	Frederick Conant, Robert Carlson, Temple Ashbrook, Charles Smith, Donald Douglas, Emmett Davis	12
3. CAN	Philip Rogers, Gerald Wilson, Gardner Boultbee, Kenneth Glass	4

The Swedes won all six races.

1936 Berlin-Kiel T: 12, N: 12, D: 8.10.

		PTS.
1. GBR	Charles Leaf, Christopher Boardman, Miles Bellville, Russell Harmer, Leonard Martin	67
2. NOR	Magnus Konow, Karsten Konow, Fredrik Meyer, Vadjuv Nyquist, Alt Tveten	66
3. SWE	Sven Salén, Dagmar Salén, Lennart Ekdahl, Martin Hindorff, Torsten Lord	62
4. ARG	Julio Sieburger, Claudio Bincaz, Germán Frers, Edlef Hosmann, Jorge Linck	52
5. ITA	Renato Cosentino, Giuliano Oberti, Massimo Oberti, Giovanni Stampa, Giuseppe Volpi	50
6. GER	Hans Lubinus, Dietrich Christensen, Kurt Frey, Theodor Thomsen, Haimar Wedemeyer	49
7. FIN	Curt Mattson, Yngve Pacius, Ragnar Stenbaeck, Holger Sumelius, Lars-Gunnar Winqvist	43
8. HOL	Johan Carp, Ansco Dokkum, Cornelis Jonker, Herman Looman, Ernst Moltzer	42

1948 London-Torbay T: 11, N: 11, D: 8.12.

		PTS.
1. USA	Herman "Swede" Whiton, Alfred Loomis, James Weekes, James Smith, Michael Mooney	5472
2. ARG	Enrique Sieburger Sr., Emilio Homps, Rufino Rodríguez de la Torre Newton, Rodolfo Rivademar, Julio Sieburger	5120
3. SWE	Tore Holm, Torsten Lord, Martin Hindorff, Karl Ameln, Gösta Salén	4033
4. NOR	Magnus Konow, Anders Evensen, Lars Musaeus, Håkon Solem, Ragnar Hargreaves	3217
5. GBR	James Douglas Hume, James Howden Hume, Brian Hardie, Henry Hardie, Harry Hunter	2879
6. BEL	Ludovic Franck, Emile Hayoit, Willy Huybrechts, Henri van Riel, Willy van Rompaey	2752

7. SWI	Henri Copponex, P. Bonnet, R. Fehlmann, André Firmenich, Emile Lachapelle, Louis Noverraz, Charles Stern, Marcel Stern	2594
8. ITA	Giovanni Reggio, Giorgio Audizio, Renato Costentino, Giuseppe Croce, G. De Luca, Luigi Poggi, Enrico Poggi	2099

1952 Helsinki T: 11, N: 11, D: 7.28.

		PTS.
1. USA	Herman "Swede" Whiton, Eric Ridder, Julian Roosevelt, Everard Endt, John Morgan, Emelyn Whiton	4870
2. NOR	Finn Ferner, Johan Ferner, Erik Heiberg, Carl Mortensen, Tor Arneberg	4648
3. FIN	Ernst Westerlund, Paul Sjöberg, Ragnar Jansson, Adolf Konto, Rolf Turkka	3944
4. SWE	Sven Salén, Martin Hindorff, Torsten Lord, Jacob Lars Lundström, Karl Ameln	3773
5. ARG	Enrique Sieburger Sr., Rufino Rodríguez de la Torre Newton, Werner von Foerster, Horacio Monti, Hércules Morini	3393
6. SWI	Louis Noverraz, André Firmenich, Charles Stern, Marcel Stern, François Chapot	3020
7. CAN	Norman Gooderham, Kenneth Bradfield, William Copehand, William Macintosh, Donald Tytler	3013
8. ITA	Enrico Poggi, Antonio Cosentino, Pietro Reggio, Giusto Spigno, Andrea Ferrari	2560

Herman Whiton and the *Llanoria* repeated their 1948 triumph, winning the final race by 81 seconds. Finland's bronze-medal-winning yacht, *Ralia,* was the same boat that Sweden had used four years earlier to gain the bronze medal in London. The Swedes had named it *Ali Baba.*

6-METER, 1907 RATING

1920 Antwerp T: 4, N: 2, D: 7.10.

		PTS.
1. BEL	Émile Cornellie, Florimond Cornellie, Frédéric-Albert Bruynseels	5
2. NOR	Ejnar Torgersen, Leif Erichsen, Annan Knudsen	7
3. NOR	Henrik Agersborg, Trygve Pedersen, Einar Berntsen	9
4. BEL	Louis Depière, Raymond Bauwens, Willy Valcke	9

FLYING DUTCHMAN

The Flying Dutchman class is a centerboard dinghy with a crew of two, one of whom is attached to the boat by a rope and a trapeze. This allows him to lean far outside the craft without falling overboard. The boat is 6.05 meters (19 feet 10 inches) long and weighs 165 kilograms (364 pounds). The Flying Dutchman was designed in 1951 by Conrad Gulcher and U. van Essen of Holland.

1960 Rome-Naples T: 31, N: 31, D: 9.7.

		PTS.
1. NOR	Peder Lunde, Jr., Björn Bergvall	6774
2. DEN	Hans Fogh, Ole Erik Petersen	5991
3. GER	Rolf Mulka, Ingo von Bredow, Achim Kadelbach	5882
4. ZIM	David Butler, Christopher Bevan	5792
5. HOL	Gijsbertus Verhagen, Gerardus Lautenschutz	5452
6. SOV/RUS	Aleksandr Shelkovnikov, Viktor Pilchin	5123
7. GBR	William "Slotty" Dawes, James Ramus	4954
8. NZL	Murray Rae, Ronald Watson	4641

Eighteen-year-old Peder Lunde came from an illustrious sailing family. His grandfather Eugen won a gold medal in the six-meter class in 1924, and his father and mother Peder and Vibeke, won silver medals in the 5.5-meter class in 1952. Young Peder also gained a Star class silver medal in 1968.

1964 Tokyo-Fujisawa T: 21, N: 21, D: 10.21.

		PTS.
1. NZL	Helmer Pedersen, Earle Wells	6255
2. GBR	F. Keith Musto, Arthur "Tony" Morgan	5556
3. USA	Harry Melges, William Bentsen	5158
4. DEN	Ole Erik Petersen, Hans Fogh	4500
5. SOV/RUS	Aheksandr Shelkovnikov, Viktor Pilchin	4375
6. HOL	Gijsbertus Verhagen, Nicolaas de Jong	4214
7. FRA	Marcel-André Buffet, Alain-François Lehoerff	3864
8. AUT	Karl Geiger, Werner Fischer	3706

Pedersen and Wells got off to a slow start, placing 16th the first day and failing to finish the second race. After that they picked up three firsts, a third, and a fourth.

1968 Mexico City-Acapulco T: 30, N: 30, D: 10.21.

		PTS.
1. GBR	Rodney Pattison, Iain Macdonald-Smith	3.0
2. GER	Ullrich Libor, Peter Naumann	43.7
3. BRA	Reinaldo Conrad, Burkhard Cordes	48.4
4. AUS	Carl Ryves, James Sargeant	49.1
5. NOR	Bjorn Lofteröd, Odd Lofteröd	52.4
6. FRA	Bertrand Cheret, Bruno Trouble	68.0
7. CAN	Roger Green, Stewart Green	79.0
8. NZL	Geoffrey Smale, Ralph Roberts	84.0

Submarine lieutenant Rod Pattison and solicitor's clerk Iain Macdonald-Smith finished first in the opening race, but were disqualified for interference. Undeterred by what they considered an unjust decision, the two men guided their boat *Superdocious* to five straight victories. Sailing cautiously on the final day, they still placed second to win the competition by a wide margin.

1972 Munich-Kiel T: 29, N: 29, D: 9.8.

		PTS.
1. GBR	Rodney Pattisson, Christopher Davies	22.7
2. FRA	Yves Pajot, Marc Pajot	40.7
3. GER	Ullrich Libor, Peter Naumann	51.1
4. BRA	Reinaldo Conrad, Burkhard Cordes	62.4

5. YUG	Anton Grego, Simo Nikoli	63.7
6. SOV	Vladimir Leontyev, Valery Zubanov	67.7
7. DEN	Hans Fogh, Elrik Brock	74.4
8. AUS	Mark Bethwaite, Timothy Alexander	75.7

Pattisson and Davies won four of the first six races and didn't bother to start on the final day.

1976 Montreal-Kingston T: 20, N: 20, D: 7.27.

		PTS.
1. GER	Jörg Diesch, Eckart Diesch	34.7
2. GBR	Rodney Pattisson, Julian Brooke Houghton	51.7
3. BRA	Reinaldo Conrad, Peter Eicker	52.1
4. CAN	Hans Fogh, Evert Bastet	57.1
5. SOV	Vladimir Leontyev, Valery Zubanov	59.4
6. USA	Norman Freeman, John Mathias	65.7
7. SPA	Alejandro Abascal García José María Benavides Accibar	66.0
8. FRA	Yves Pajot, Marc Pajot	72.0

For the third straight time, Rod Pattison was first across the finishing line in the opening race. However, he fell off badly in the last three races, placing 18th, 12th, and 11th. The Diesch brothers were ten points ahead after six races. On the way to the starting line for the final race they discovered that their centerboard was cracked. They returned to shore, obtained permission to replace the board, made the repair, and still arrived on time to compete. They placed fifth, good enough to take the gold medal.

1980 Moscow-Tallinn T: 15, N: 15, D: 7.29.

		PTS.
1. SPA	Alejandro Abascal García, Miguel Noguer Castellvi	19.0
2. IRL	David Wilkins, James Wilkinson	30.0
3. HUN	Szabolcs Detre, Zsolt Detre	45.7
4. GDR	Wolfgang Haase, Wolfgang Wenzel	51.4
5. SOV	Vladimir Leontyev, Valery Zubanov	51.7
6. DEN	Jörgen Bojsen Möller, Jacob Bojsen Möller	54.5
7. HOL	Jan Erik Vollebregt, Sjoerd Vollebregt	54.7
8. BRA	Reinaldo Conrad, Manfred Kaufmann	63.4

Helmsman Alejandro Abascal, a 28-year-old physicist, won without having to take part in the final race. He and medical student Miguel Noguer had three firsts, a second, and two fourths in the first six races.

1984 Los Angeles-Long Beach T: 17, N: 17, D: 8.8.

		PTS.
1. USA	Jonathan McKee, William Carl Buchan	19.7
2. CAN	Terry McLaughlin, Evert Bastet	22.7
3. GBR	Jonathan Richards, Peter Allam	48.7
4. DEN	Jörgen Bojsen Möller, Jacob Bojsen Möller	52.4
5. GER	Jörg Diesch, Eckart Diesch	56.7
6. BRA	Alan Adler, Marcus Tenke	61.7
7. ITA	Mario Celon, Claudio Celon	78.7
8. ISR	Yoel Sela, Eldad Amir	79.4

McLaughlin entered the last race with a three-point lead over McKee, after winning three of the first six races. But the intense jockeying for position found the Canadians over the line at the start, forcing them to go back and re-start. McKee and Buchan, son of Star class winner Bill Buchan, needed to finish two places ahead of McLaughlin and Bastet, which is exactly what they did, placing sixth to the Canadians' eighth.

1988 Seoul-Pusan T: 22, N: 22, D: 9.27.

		PTS.
1. DEN	Jörgen Bojsen Möller, Christian Grönborg	31.4
2. NOR	Ole Petter Pollen, Erik Bjorkum	37.4
3. CAN	Frank McLaughlin, John Millen	48.4
4. ISR	Yoel Sela, Eldad Amir	59.7
5. NZL	Murray Jones, Gregory Knowles	60.0
6. GBR	Roger Yeoman, Neal McDonald	72.7
7. BRA	Alan Adler, Marcus Temke	76.4
8. GER	Albert Batzill, Peter Lang	79.0

The three medal-winning crews trained together in north Jutland, Denmark, an area chosen by Bojsen Möller because the rough ocean conditions were similar to those in Pusan. The Danes clinched first place before the final race.

Sela and Amir almost became Israel's first Olympic medalists. Unfortunately for them, the second race fell on the Jewish high holiday of Yom Kippur. Israeli Olympic officials made it clear that any of their athletes who competed on Yom Kippur would be withdrawn from competition and sent home, a punishment which they did in fact mete out to the Israeli men's 470 crew. Sela and Amir would have won medals had they taken part in the second race and placed higher than eleventh, a result which they bettered in five of their six races.

1992 Barcelona T: 23, N: 23, D: 8.2.

		PTS.
1. SPA	Luis Doreste Blanco, Domingo Manrique	29.7
2. USA	Paul Foerster, Stephen Bourdow	32.7
3. DEN	Jörgen Bojsen Möller, Jens Bojsen Möller	37.7
4. NZL	Murray Jones, Gregory Knowles	68.0
5. GER	Albert Batzill, Peter Lang	70.4
6. SWE	Mats Nyberg, Johan Lindell	78.4
7. NOR	Ole Petter Pollen, Knut Frostad	80.7
8. SWI	Jan Eckert, Piet Eckert	81.7

Foerster and Bourdow won three straight races (the second, third, and fourth), but were still beaten by the more consistent pair of Doreste and Manrique. Doreste had won the 470 class in Los Angeles in 1984.

TORNADO

The Tornado is a two-man catamaran. The vessel is 6.1 meters (20 feet) long and has a sail area of 235 square feet (21.85 square meters). It was designed in England in 1966.

1976 Montreal-Kingston T: 14, N: 14, D: 7.28.

		PTS.
1. GBR	Reginald White, John Osborn	18.0
2. USA	David McFaull, Michael Rothwell	36.0
3. GER	Jörg Spengler, Jörg Schmall	37.7
4. AUS	Brian Lewis, Warren Rock	44.4
5. SWE	Peter Kolni, Jörgen Kolni	57.4
6. SWI	Walter Steiner, Albert Schiess	63.4
7. CAN	Larry Woods, Michael de la Roche	69.7
8. ITA	Franco Pivoli, Cesare Biagi	71.7

Forty-year-old Reg White and his 30-year-old brother-in-law, John Osborn, won four of the first six races; they were able to sit out the final day

1980 Moscow-Tallinn T: 11, N: 11, D: 7.29.

		PTS.
1. BRA	Alexandre Welter, Lars Sigurd Björkström	21.4
2. DEN	Peter Due, Per Kjergard	30.4
3. SWE	Göran Marström Jörgen Ragnarsson	33.7
4. SOV	Viktor Potapov, Aleksandr Zõbin	35.1
5. HOL	Willem Van Walt Meijer, Govert Brasser	39.0
6. FIN	Pekka Narko, Juha Siira	47.7
7. AUT	Hubert Porkert, Hermann Kupfrier	67.7
8. GDR	Uwe Steingross, Jörg Schramme	82.0

1984 Los Angeles-Long Beach T: 20, N: 20, D: 8.8.

		PTS.
1. NZL	Rex Sellers, Christopher Timms	14.7
2. USA	Randy Smyth, Jay Glaser	37.0
3. AUS	Chris Cairns, John Anderson	50.4
4. DEN	Paul Elvstrøm, Inge Trine Elvstrøm	51.1
5. BER	Alan Burland, Christopher Nash	53.5
6. GBR	Robert White, David Campbell-James	53.7
7. BRA	Lars Grael, Glein Haynes	74.7
8. FRA	Yves Loday, Bernard Pichery	81.0

This was expected to be a dramatic showdown between Smyth and Cairns. Meanwhile, the sentimental favorite was four-time Finn class Olympic champion Paul Elvstrøm, who came out of retirement to compete with his daughter, Trine. With all the attention focused on these three, Rex Sellers, a 33-year-old lobster fisherman, slipped through for a decisive victory. Sellers and Timms compiled a record of two firsts, three seconds and a third to clinch the gold medal after the sixth race When asked if he would be back to take part in the final race anyway, Sellers replied, "If we're still standing after tonight's celebration." The New Zealand boat was not at the starting line the next day.

1988 Seoul-Pusan T: 23, N: 23, D: 9.27.

		PTS.
1. FRA	Jean-Yves Le Déroff, Nicolas Hénard	16.0
2. NZL	Rex Sellers, Christopher Timms	35.4
3. BRA	Lars Grael, Clinio Freitas	40.1
4. AUT	Norbert Petschel, Christian Claus	46.0
5. ITA	Giorgio Zuccoli, Luca Santella	60.1
6. NOR	Per Arne Nilsen, Carl Johannessen	67.7
7. SOV	Yuri Konovalov, Sergei Kravsov	70.0
8. GBR	Robert White, Jeremy Newman	70.1

Le Déroff and Hénard, sailing instructors from Brest, took three firsts and two seconds in the first five races, then sailed a cautious fifth to secure the gold medals without having to participate in the final race In fifteenth place was Paul Elvstrøm of Denmark, competing in his eighth Olympics at the age of 60.

1992 Barcelona T: 22, N: 22, D: 8.2.

		PTS.
1. FRA	Yves Loday, Nicolas Hénard	40.4
2. USA	Randy Smyth, Keith Notary	42.0
3. AUS	Mitchell Booth, John Forbes	44.4
4. NZL	Rex Sellers, Brian Jones	51.7
5. CAN	David Sweeney, Kevin Smith	62.7
6. HOL	Ron van Teylingen, Paul Manuel	65.4
7. AUT	Andreas Hagara, Roman Hagara	65.5
8. BRA	Lars Schmidt Grael, Clinio Freitas	69.7

After six races, Smyth and Notary led with 25 points. They were followed by Booth and Forbes with 34.4 and Loday and Hénard with 37.4. The Americans were leading the final race, but light winds made for a slow race. In yachting, at least one boat has to cross the finish line within the time limit (in this case four hours) for the race to count. Smyth and Notary were still ten or fifteen minutes away when the time limit expired The race was resailed the following day. This time it was won by Sellers and Jones, with Loday and Hénard in second. The American pair needed a ninth place finish to secure the gold medals, but could only manage eleventh Booth and Forbes also had a shot at gold. They needed to place third, but missed by ten seconds and ended up fifth.

1996 Atlanta-Savannah T: 19, N: 19, D: 7.30.

		PTS.
1. SPA	José Luis Ballester Tuliesa, Fernando León Boissier	30
2. AUS	Mitchell Booth, Andrew Landenberger	42
3. BRA	Lars Grael, Henrique "Kiko" Pellicano	43
4. AUT	Andreas Hagara, Florian Schneeberger	44
5. ITA	Walter Pirinoli, Marco Pirinoli	44
6. FRA	Frédéric Le Peutrec, Franck Citeau	46
7. GER	Roland Gäbler, Frank Parlow	48
8. USA	John Lovell, Charlie Ogletree	48

2000 Sydney T: 16, N: 16, D: 9.24.

		PTS.
1. AUT	Hans Peter Steinacher, Roman Hagara	16
2. AUS	Darren Dundock, John Forbes	25
3. GER	René Schwall, Roland Gäbler	38
4. FRA	Pierre Pennec, Yann Guichard	43
5. NZL	Christopher Dickson, Glen Sowry	46
6. GBR	Adam May, Hugh Styles	53
7. USA	Charlie Ogletree, John Lovell	57
8. PUR	Enrique Figueroa Suárez, Pedro Colón Hernández	58

Light weather specialists Roman Hagara and Hans Peter Steinacher chalked up 5 firsts, 2 seconds, a third and a fourth to earn gold medals with two races to spare.

2004 Athens-Helliniko T: 17, N: 17, D: 8.28.

		PTS.
1. AUT	Roman Hagara, Hans Peter Steinacher	34.0
2. USA	John Lovell, Charles Ogletree	45.0
3. ARG	Santiago Lange, Carlos Espínola Lorenzo	54.0
4. FRA	Olivier Backes, Laurent Voiron	57.0
5. HOL	Mitchell Booth, Herbert Dercksen	61.0
6. AUS	Darren Bundock, John Forbes	62.0
7. PUR	Enrique Figueroa Suárez, Jorge Hernández	72.0
8. SPA	Fernando Echavarri Erasun, Iván Pastor La Fuente Antón Paz Blanco	74.8

Leading by just three points going into the final race, 2000 Olympic champions Roman Hagara and Hans Peter Steinacher used their light wind prowess to pull away in the final minutes and successfully defend their title.

2008 Beijing-Qingdao T: 15, N: 15, D: 8.21.

		PTS.
1. SPA	Fernando Echavarri Erasum, Antón Paz Blanco	44
2. AUS	Darren Bundock, Glenn Ashby	49
3. ARG	Santiago Lange, Carlos Espínola Lorenzo	56
4. CAN	Oskar Johansson, Kevin Stittle	61
5. HOL	Mitch Booth, Pim Nieuwenhuis	64
6. GBR	Leigh McMillan, Will Howden	68
7. ITA	Francesco Marcolini, Edoardo Bianchi	74
8. GER	Johannes Polgar, Florian Spalteholz	74

The previous four world championship titles had been traded between two crews: Spain's Fernando Echavarri and Antón Paz had won in 2005 and 2007 and Australia's Darren Bundock and Glenn Ashby in 2006 and 2008.

Echavarri and Paz led Bundock and Ashby by three points going into the medal race. This was held in heavy wind and rain, and two of the ten boats failed to finish. The Spaniards held off their rivals, finishing one place ahead of them to earn the gold medals.

YNGLING

Pronounced "ING-ling", the Yngling class was designed in 1968 by Jan Herman Linge of Norway for his 14-year-old son. The three-person keelboat was designed as a smaller, lighter and more easily handled boat than the previous Soling class.

2004 Athens-Helliniko T: 16, N: 16, D: 8.20.

		PTS.
1. GBR	Shirley Robertson, Sarah Webb, Sarah Ayton	39
2. UKR	Ruslana Taran, Hanna Kalinina, Svitlana Matevusheva	50
3. DEN	Dorte Jensen, Helle Jespersen, Christina Børregaard Otzen	54
4. HOL	Annelies Thies, Annemieke Bes, Petronella de Jong	56
5. FRA	Anne le Helley, Elodie Lesaffre, Marion Deplanque	57
6. GER	Kristin Wagner, Anna Höll, Veronika Lochbrunner	76
7. NZL	Sharon Ferris, Joanna White, Kylie Jameson	77
8. RUS	Yekaterina Skudina, Tatyana Lartseva, Diyana Krutskikh	79

Competing in her fourth Olympics, Shirley Robertson, who won the Europe class at the 2000 Sydney Games, led the British team to gold with a day to spare.

2008 Beijing-Qingdao T: 15, N: 15, D: 8.17.

		PTS.
1. GBR	Sarah Ayton, Sarah Webb, Philippa "Pippa" Wilson	24
2. HOL	Mandy Mulder, Annemieke Bes, Merel Witteveen	31
3. GRE	Sofia Bekatorou, Sofia Papadopoulou, Virginia Kravarioti	48
4. GER	Ulli Schümann, Ute Höpfner, Julia Bleck	56
5. FRA	Anne le Helley, Catherine Lepesant, Julie Gerecht	56
6. RUS	Yekaterina Skudina, Diana Krutskikh, Nataliya Ivanova	56
7. USA	Sally Barkow, Carrie Howe, Deborah Capozzi	61
8. CHN	Song Xiaqun, Yu Yanli, Li Xiaoni	63

After winning the inaugural women's Yngling Olympic championship at the 2004 Athens Games under skipper Shirley Robertson, Great Britain's Sarah Webb and Sarah Ayton reunited and brought in newcomer Pippa Wilson. The trio, nicknamed "Three Blondes in a Boat," won back-to-back world championship titles in 2007 and 2008.

At the Beijing Olympics the British crew finished in the top five in all but one of their preliminary races, but entered the medal race only one point ahead of the Dutch team, who had won three of the eight races. However, they made no mistakes in the final race, finishing seven seconds ahead of the second-place German boat, while the Dutch finished fourth to take silver. Fifth-place finisher Australia, disqualified for failing to weigh in before the final medal race, dropped to tenth place overall.

6.5-METER

1920 Antwerp T: 2, N: 2, D: 7.9.

		PTS.
1. HOL	Robbert Carp, Petrus Wernink, Bernard Carp	2
2. FRA	Albert Weil, Félix Picon, Robert Monier	4

TEMPEST

1972 Munich-Kiel T: 21, N: 21, D: 9.8.

		PTS.
1. SOV/UKR	Valentyn Mankin, Vitaly Dyrdyra	28.1
2. GBR	Alan Warren, David Hunt	34.4
3. USA	Glen Foster, Peter Dean	47.7
4. SWE	John Albrechtson, Ingvar Hansson	57.4
5. HOL	Bernard Staartjes, Kees Kuppershoek	58.7
6. NOR	Peder Lunde, Jr., Aksel Gresvig	70.0
7. BRA	Mario Buckup, Peter Ficker	73.7
8. IRL	David Wilkins, Sean Whitaker	74.7

Funeral director Alan Warren and his partner, David Hunt, provided a light touch to the Kiel Regatta. Their six-year-old keelboat, *Gift 'Orse,* was damaged in transit and performed poorly at the Olympics. After the final race, Warren and Hunt took some acetone and a flare and set their boat on fire. "She went lame on us," said Warren, "so we decided the poor, old 'orse should be cremated." "My skipper has style," added Hunt, "but not that much. I tried to persuade him to burn with the ship, but he wouldn't agree."

1976 Montreal-Kingston T: 16, N: 16, D: 7.27.

		PTS.
1. SWE	John Albrechtson, Ingvar Hansson	14.0
2. SOV/UKR	Valentyn Mankin, Vladyslav Akimenko	30.4
3. USA	Dennis Conner, Conn Findlay	32.7
4. GER	Uwe Mares, Wolf Stadler	42.1
5. ITA	Giuseppe Milone, Roberto Mottola	55.4
6. DEN	Claes Thunbo Christensen, Finn Thunbo Christensen	62.7
7. CAN	Allan Leibel, Lorne Leibel	65.1
8. HOL	Ben Staartjes, Abram Ekels	78.7

Bronze medalist Conn Findlay also won two gold medals and one bronze medal in the coxed pair rowing events of 1956–1964. His skipper, Dennis Conner, won the America's Cup in 1980, lost it in 1983, won it back in 1987, and defended it in a catamaran in 1988.

SWALLOW

1948 London-Torbay T: 14, N: 14, D: 8.12.

		PTS.
1. GBR	Stewart Morris, David Bond	5625
2. POR	Duarte de Almeida Bello, Fernando Pinto Coelho Bello	5579
3. USA	Lockwood Pine, Owen Tory	4352
4. SWE	Stig Hedberg, Lars Matton	3342
5. DEN	Johan Rathje, Nolly Petersen	2935
6. ITA	Dario Salata, Achille Roncoroni	2893
7. CAN	John Robertson, Richard Townsend	2807
8. NOR	Øivind Christensen, Knut Bengtson	2768

The Swallow class was the same size as the Star, but with a smaller sail area (200 square feet rather than 285). Morris and Bond came within 15 seconds of losing the gold medal in the final race. During World War II, Stewart Morris helped design an air defence system for aircraft carriers that was later adopted as the standard for British carriers.

7-METER

1908 London-Ryde T: 1, N: 1, D: 7.28.

1. GBR Charles Rivett-Carnac, S.S. Norman Bingley, Richard Dixon, Frances Clytie Rivett-Carnac

1912 not held

1920 Antwerp T: 2, N: 2, D: 7.9.

		PTS.
1 GBR	Cyril Wright, Dorothy Wright, Robert Coleman, William Maddison	4
2. NOR	Niels Nielsen, Johan Faye, Christian Dick, Sten Abel	5

8-METER

1908 London-Ryde T: 5, N: 3, D: 7.29.

1. GBR	Blair Cochrane, Arthur Wood, Hugh Sutton, John Rhodes, Charles Campbell
2. SWE	Carl Hellström, Edmund Thormählen, Eric Wallerius, Erik Sandberg, Harald Wallin
3. GBR	Philip Hunloke, Collingwood Hughes, Frederick Hughes, George Ratsey, William Ward
4. NOR	Johan Anker, Einar Hvoslef, Hagbert Steffens, Magnus Konow, Eilert Falch Lund
5. SWE	John Carlsson, Edvin Hagberg, Hjalmar Lönnroth, Karl Ljungberg, August Olsson

1912 Stockholm-Nynas T: 7, N: 4, D: 7.22.

		PTS.
1. NOR	Thoralf Glad, Thomas Valentin Aas, Andreas Brecke, Torleiv Corneliussen, Christian Jebe	14
2. SWE	Bengt Heyman, Emil Henriques, Herbert Westermark, Nils Westermark, Alvar Thiel	3
3. FIN	Bertil Tallberg, Arthur Ahnger, Emil Lindh, Gunnar Tallberg, Georg Westling	3
4. FIN	Axel Gustaf Estlander, Curt Andstén, Jarl Andstén, Carl-Oscar Girsén, Bertil Justén	2
5. RUS	Ventseslav Kuzmichev, Yevgeny Kuhn, Pavel Pavlov, Viktor Markov, Yevgeny Lomach	0
5. RUS	Herman von Adlerberg, Johan Farber, Vladimir Ilyevich, Vladimir Lurasov, Nikolay Podgornov	0
5. SWE	Fritz Sjöqvist, Johan Sjöqvist, Ragnar Gripe, Theodor Grönfors, Erik Hagström	0

1920 Antwerp T: 3, N: 2, D: 7.9.

		PTS.
1. NOR	Magnus Konow, Reidar Marthiniussen, Ragnar Vik, Thorleif Christoffersen	3
2. NOR	Jens Salvesen, Lauritz Schmidt, Fin Schiander, Nils Thomas, Ralph Tschudi	6

		PTS.
3. BEL	Albert Grisar, Willy de l'Arbre, Georges Hellebuyck, Léopold Standaert, Henri Weewauters	9

1924 Paris-Le Havre T: 5, N: 5, D: 7.26.

		PTS.
1. NOR	August Ringvold, Sr., Rick Bockelie, Harald Hagen, Ingar Nielsen, August Ringvold, Jr.	2
2. GBR	Edwin Jacob, Thomas Riggs, Walter Riggs, Ernest Roney, H. Gordon Fowler	5
3. FRA	Louis Bréguet, Pierre Ganthier, Robert Girardet, André Guerrier, Georges Mollard	5
4. BEL	Fernand Carlier, Maurice Passelecq, Emmanuel Pauwels, Victor Vandersleyen, Paul van Halteren	8
5. ARG	Rolando Aguirre Barreyro, César Gérico, Juan Carlos Milberg Bossi, Bernardo Milhas, M. Roberto Uriburu Peró	—

1928 Amsterdam T: 8, N: 8, D: 8.9.

1. FRA	Virginie Hériot, Donatien Bouché, André Lesauvage, Jean Lesieur, Charles de la Sablière, André Derrien
2. HOL	Lambertus Doedes, Maarten de Wit, Johannes van Hoolwerff, Gerardus de Vries Lentsch, Hendrik Kersken, Cornelis van Staveren
3. SWE	Johan Sandblom, Philip Sandblom, Carl Sandblom, Tore Holm, Clarence Hammar, Wilhelm Törsleff
4. ITA	Francesco Giovanelli, Guido Giovanelhi, Marcantonio de Beaumont-Bonelli, Carlo Alberto d'Alberti, Edoardo Moscatelli, Mario Bruzzone
4. NOR	Jens Salvesen, Magnus Konow, W. Wilhelmsen, Bernhard Lund
6. USA	Owen Churchill, Benjamin Weston, Manfred Curry, Frank Hekma, Nicholas Barry Hekma
7. GBR	Philip Falle, Ernest Roney, Esmond Roney, Thomas Riggs, Thomas Skinner, Mrs. M. H. Roney
8. ARG	Carlos Serantes Saavedra, Miguel Bosch Marín, Horacio Seeber Demaría

Virginie Hériot, France's first female Olympic champion, skippered an all-male crew. She died of a heart attack on August 28, 1932, while sailing. She was 42 years old.

1932 Los Angeles T: 2, N: 2, D: 8.9.

		PTS.
1. USA	Owen Churchill, John Biby, William Cooper, Carl Dorsey, Robert Sutton, Alan Morgan, Pierpont Davis, Alphonse Burnand, Thomas Webster, John Huettner, Richard Moore, Kenneth Carey	8
2. CAN	Ronald Maitland, Ernest Cribb, Harry Jones, Peter Gordon, Hubert Wallace, George Gyles	4

Helmsman Owen Churchill made sure that all eleven members of his crew and alternate crew participated in at least one race so that each would be awarded a gold medal. The ship they used, the *Angelita,* was discovered in a boatyard in Santa Cruz, California, in 1981. It was then restored and honored as the flagship of the 1984 Olympics with the 88-year-old Churchill at its helm. In 1940 Owen Churchill patented the first rubber swim fin. His fins were used by American and British frogmen during World War II and he continued to collect royalties on his invention until his death in 1985.

1936 Berlin-Kiel T: 12, N: 10, D: 8.10.

		PTS.
1. ITA	Giovanni Reggio, Bruno Bianchi, Luigi De Manincor, Domenico Mordini, Luigi Poggi, Enrico Poggi	55
2. NOR	Olav Ditlev-Simonsen, John Ditlev-Simonsen, Hans Struknaes, Lauritz Schmidt, Nordahl Wallem, Jacob Tullin Thams	53
3. GER	Hans Howaldt, Alfred Krupp von Bohlen und Halbach, Felix Scheder-Bieschin, Eduard Mohr, Otto Wachs, Fritz Bischoff	53
4. SWE	Marcus Wallenberg, Tore Holm, Wilhelm Moberg, Detlow von Braun, Per Gedda, Bo Westerberg	51
5. FIN	Gunnar Grönblom, Sven Grönblum, Hilding Silander, Oscar Sumelius, Olof Wallin, Walter Kjellberg	37
6. GBR	Kenneth Preston, Francis Preston, Robert Steele, Joseph Compton, John Eddy	36
7. ARG	Rufino Rodríguez de la Torre Newton, Mario Ortiz Sauze, Luis Aguirre Barreyro, Guillermo Peralta Ramos Grondona	25
8. DEN	Niels Hansen, Hans Tholstrup, Otto Danielsen, Carl Berntsen, Vagn Kastrup, Niels Schibbye	22

The Germans led after six races, but finished only sixth on the final day. Norway was awarded second place after winning a sail-off against Germany two days later. Jacob Thams of the Norwegian crew had won the ski-jump in the first Winter Olympics at Chamonix in 1924. Alfred Krupp of the German crew was the owner and director of the infamous Krupp armaments works. He was convicted as a war criminal at the Nuremberg trials after World War II.

8-METER, 1907 RATING

1920 Antwerp T: 1, N: 1, D: 7.9.

1. NOR August Ringvold, Sr., Thorleif Holbye, Tell Waghe, Kristoffer Olsen, Bruun Jacobsen

SOLING

The Soling is a three-man keelboat. It is 8.2 meters (26 feet 11 inches) long and weighs 1035 kilograms (2282 pounds). It was designed in 1965 by Jan Herman Linge of Norway.

In 1992 the Soling competition switched to a new format. The six boats that led the overall standing after six fleet races advanced to a round-robin pool in which each crew sailed once against every other crew. The top four crews in the pool advanced to direct-elimination semifinals. In 1992 the semifinals, the final, and the contest for third place were decided on a best two-out-of-three basis. In 1996, the rules were altered slightly. Competition began with ten fleet races. The round-robin pool was eliminated. Instead, the top two qualifiers advanced to the semifinals while the other four qualifiers participated in a quarterfinal round. In 1996 all match races were best three out of five. In 2000 there were six fleet races and the top twelve boats advanced to the match race stage.

1972 Munich-Kiel T: 26, N: 26, D: 9.8.

		PTS.
1. USA	Harry "Buddy" Melges, William Bentsen, William Allen	8.7
2. SWE	Stig Wennerström, Lennart Roslund, Bo Knape, Stefan Krook	31.7
3. CAN	David Miller, John Ekels, Paul Cote	47.1
4. FRA	Jean-Marie le Guillou, Bernard Drubay, Jean-Yves Pellerin	53.0
5. GBR	John Oakeley, Charles Reynolds, Barry Dunning	54.7
6. BRA	Axel Schmidt-Preben, Patrick Matte Mascarenhas, Erik Schmidt-Preben	64.7
7. SOV/RUS	Timir Pinegin, Valentin Zamotaikin, Rais Galimov	65.0
8. POL	Zygfryd Perlicki, Józef Blaszczyk, Stanisław Stefański	75.0

The competition was limited to six races because of bad weather. Paul Elvstrøm, attempting to become the first person in history to win gold medals at five different Olympics, became infuriated and disillusioned by a bumping incident with the French crew, packed up his boat and drove home in a huff after the fifth race, finishing 13th overall. Crown Prince Harald of Norway placed tenth. Less illustrious, but more successful, was helmsman Buddy Melges of Zenda, Wisconsin, who guided his boat to three firsts, a second, a third, and a fourth on his way to the gold medal. In 1992 Melges coskippered the victorious *America 3* in the America's Cup. He was the first helmsman to win both an Olympic championship and the America's Cup.

Paul Cote of the Canadian crew had already earned a place in history in a non-sporting arena. In 1971 Cote was part of a group of five people who formed the "Don't Make a Wave Committee," whose purpose was to sail a boat to Amchitka Island in Alaska where the United States military was planning to test a 5.2 megaton nuclear bomb. As the committee grew, a new name was chosen for the group: Greenpeace. A Greenpeace boat, the *Phyllis Cormack*, did sail into the zone, although Cote, who was training for the Olympics, was not a member of the crew.

1976 Montreal-Kingston T: 24, N: 24, D: 7.27.

		PTS.
1. DEN	Poul Jensen, Valdemar Bandolowski, Erik Hansen	46.7
2. USA	John Kolius, Walter Glasgow, Richard Hoepfner	47.4
3. GDR	Dieter Below, Michael Zachries, Olaf Engelhard	47.4
4. SOV/RUS	Boris Budnikov, Valentin Zamotaikin, Nikolai Polyakov	48.7
5. HOL	Geert Bakker, Harald de Vlaming, Pieter Keijzer	58.0
6. GER	Wilhelm Kuhweide, Karsten Meyer, Axel May	60.7
7. FRA	Patrick Haegeli, Patrick Oeuvrard, Bruno Trouble	64.0
8. CAN	Glen Dexter, Alexander "Sandy" Macmillan, Andreas Josenhans	68.7

The 1976 Soling regatta was so close that the Danish team didn't know they had won until they returned to their berth and saw a large crowd waiting for them. Had they finished seven seconds slower in the final race they would have had to settle for bronze medals instead of gold. Instead, they swept past the French boat before the finish line to place fifth, and the extra 1.7 points provided their margin of victory.

1980 Moscow-Tallinn T: 9, T: 9, D: 7.29.

		PTS.
1. DEN	Poul Jensen, Valdemar Bandolowski, Erik Hansen	23.0
2. SOV/RUS	Boris Budnikov, Aleksandr Budnikov, Nikolai Pohyakov	30.4
3. GRE	Anastassios Boudouris, Anastassios Gavrilis, Aristidis Rapanakis	31.1
4. GDR	Dieter Below, Bernd Klenke, Michael Zachries	37.4
5. HOL	Geert Bakker, Steven Bakker, Dick Coster	45.0
6. BRA	Vicente D'Avila Brun, Gastao D'Avila Brun, Roberto Luiz Souza	47.1
7. SWI	Jean-François Corminboeuf, Roger-Claude Guignard, Robert Perret	71.7
8. SWE	Jan Andersson, Göran Andersson, Bertil Larsson	75.7

The three Danes defended their championship by winning the last two races, with the Soviet boat in second place both times

1984 Los Angeles-Long Beach T: 22, N: 22, D: 8.8.

		PTS.
1. USA	Robert Haines, Edward Trevelyan, Roderick Davis	33.7
2. BRA	Torben Grael, Daniel Adler, Ronaldo Senfft	43.4
3. CAN	Hans Marius Fogh, John Kerr, Steve Calder	49.7
4. GBR	Christopher Law, Edward Leask, Jeremy Richards	54.7
5. NOR	Dag Halfdan Usterud, Stein Lund Halvorsen, Börre Skui	57.7
6. GRE	Anastassios Boudouris, Dimitrios Deligiannis, George Spiridis	59.2
7. AUS	Gary Sheard, Timothy Dorning, Dean Gordon	62.4
8. GER	Wilhelm Kuhweide, Axel May, Eckhard Loll	71.0

The US team won without having to compete in the final race. Bronze medalist Hans Marius Fogh was competing in his sixth Olympics, having won a silver medal in 1960 while representing Denmark in the Flying Dutchman class.

1988 Seoul-Pusan T: 20, N: 20, D: 9.27.

		PTS.
1. GDR	Jochen Schümann, Thomas Flach, Bernd Jäkel	11.7
2. USA	John Kostecki, William Baylis, Robert Billingham	14.0
3. DEN	Jesper Bank, Jan Dupont Mathiasen, Steen Secher	52.7
4. GBR	Lawrie Smith, Edward Leask, Jeremy Richards	67.1
5. BRA	José Paulo Dias, José Augusto Dias, Christoph Bergman	67.4

6. FRA	Michel Kermarec, Stanislas Dripaux, Xavier Phelippon	68.4
7. NZL	Thomas Dodson, Simon Daubney, Aran Hansen	74.4
8. SWE	Lennart Persson, Eje Öberg, Tony Wallin	77.7

This exciting competition pitted two-time world champion John Kostecki against 1976 Finn gold medalist Jochen Schümann. Earlier in the year, Schümann had defeated Kostecki at the European championships. In Seoul, both men took three firsts and two seconds. Schümann won because his sixth best finish was a third to Kostecki's fourth. In the final race, the East German had to place second. Schümann started poorly, but moved up from ninth place to second by the start of the final leg, then held his position to finish.

1992 Barcelona T: 24, N: 24, D: 8.4.

		FINAL MATCHES
1. DEN	Jesper Bank, Steen Secher, Jesper Seier	2-0
2. USA	Kevin Mahaney, James Brady, Doug Kern	
3. GBR	Lawrie Smith, Robert Cruikshank, Simon "Ossie" Stewart	2-1
4. GER	Jochen Schümann, Thomas Flach, Bernd Jäkel	
5. SWE	Magnus Holmberg, Björn Alm, Johan Barne	
6. SPA	Fernando León Boissier, Crown Prince Felipe, Alfredo Vázquez Jiménez	
7. CAN	R. Paul Thomson, R. Stuart Flinn, Philip Gow	
8. NZL	Simon Daubney, Russell Coutts, Graham Fleury	

The American crew led the round-robin pool with four wins and one loss, with the Danes in second place. Both of them won their semifinal match-ups in straight races. In the first race of the final, Bank came from behind to beat Mahaney by less than a boatlength. Just before the start of the second race, Mahaney's boat touched the Danish boat and the Americans were forced to sail a 270-degree penalty turn that left them 26 seconds behind before they entered the course. Bank did not waste his advantage and the race was never in doubt. One member of the Spanish crew was Prince Felipe, heir to the Spanish throne. His full title was Crown Prince Felipe Juan Pablo Alfonso de Todos los Santos Borbón Schleswig-Borbón Sonderburg Glucksburg.

1996 Atlanta-Savannah T: 22, N: 22, D: 8.2.

		FINAL MATCHES
1. GER	Jochen Schümann, Thomas Flach, Bernd Jäkel	3-0
2. RUS	Georgi Shayduko, Dmitri Shabanov, Igor Skalin	
3. USA	Geoffrey Madrigali, James Barton, J. Kent Massey	3-1
4. GBR	Andrew Beadsworth, Barry Parkin, Adrian George Stead	
5. CAN	William Abbott, Joanne Abbott, Bradley Boston	
6. DEN	Stig Westergaard, Jan Eli Andersen, Jens Bojsen-Møller	
7. UKR	Serhiy Pichugin, Serhiy Khayndrava, Volodymyr Korotkov	
8. SPA	Luis Doreste Blanco, Domingo Manrique Peñate, David Vera San Luis	

Eight years after their last Soling victory, Schümann, Flach and Jäckel finished first in the fleet competition, defeated the British crew 3-0 in the semifinals and then easily swept the final races against the Russian crew. Schümann earned his third gold medal, twenty years after winning his first in the 1976 Finn class.

2000 Sydney T: 16, N: 16, D: 9.30.

		FINAL MATCHES
1. DEN	Jesper Bank, Henrik Blakskjær, Thomas Jacobsen	4-3
2. GER	Jochen Schümann, Gunnar Bahr, Ingo Borkowski	
3. NOR	Herman Johannessen, Paul Davis, Espen Stokkeland	3-1
4. HOL	Roy Heiner, Peter van Niekerk, Dirk de Ridder	
5. NZL	Roderick Davis, Donald Cowie, Alan Smith	
6. RUS	Georgy Shayduko, Oleg Khopersky, Andrey Kirylyuk	
7. SWE	Hans Wallén, Johan Barne, Magnus Augustson	
8. AUS	Neville Wittey, Joshua Grace, David Edwards	

Eight of the sixteen boats included sailors who had already earned at least one Olympic medal. Norway, New Zealand and the Netherlands led the fleet racing and qualified directly for the match race quarterfinals. But the quarterfinals, in which the top four qualified for the semifinals, turned out to be a complicated affair. Jochen Schümann and Jesper Bank, winners of the last two Soling gold medals, each won four of five matches and moved on, but the determination of the other two semifinalists was controversial. Norway, New Zealand and the Netherlands all won two races. The initial tie-breaking rules left the three still tied. The Jury of Appeal ruled that the Norwegians and the New Zealanders qualified for the semifinals because they had finished first and second in the fleet racing. The Dutch protested the decision, claiming that the wording of the rules was vague and only applied to the winner of the fleet racing. The jury agreed and ordered a one match sail-off between Roy Heiner of the Netherlands and Rod Davis of New Zealand. Davis almost lost before he started when he narrowly avoided being crushed by a passenger ferry. In the end, Heiner won by almost two lengths. When the semifinals were finally held, Schümann defeated Heiner 3-1 and Bank beat Johannessen 3-1. Schümann took a 3-2 lead in the final. Bank forced a decisive seventh match, which he then won when Schümann was ordered to take a penalty turn just before the finish line.

10-METER

1912 Stockholm T: 4, N: 3, D: 7.22.

			PTS.
1.	SWE	Carl Hellström, Erik Wallerius, Harald Wallerius, Humbert Lundén, Herman Nyberg, Harry Rosenswärd, Paul Isberg, Filip Ericsson	14
2.	FIN	Harry Wahl, Waldemar Björkstén, Jacob Carl Björnström, Bror Brennar, Allan Franck, Emil Lindh, Johan Pekkalainen	4
3.	RUS	Yossif Shomaker, Yesper Beloselsky, Ernest Brasche, Karl Lindholm, Nikolay Pusnitsky, Aleksandr Rodionov, Filipp Strauch	4
4.	SWE	Björn Bothén, Bertil Bothén, Fred Wilhelm Forsberg, Erland Lindén, Erik Waller	0

10-METER, 1907 RATING

1920 Antwerp T: 1, N: 1, D: 7.9.

1. NOR Erik Herseth, Sigurd Holter, Ingar Nielsen, Ole Sørensen, Gunnar Jamvold, Petter Jamvold, Claus Juell

10-METER 1919 RATING

1920 Antwerp T: 1, N: 1, D: 7.9.

1. NOR Acher Arentz, Willy Gilbert, Robert Giertsen, Arne Sejersted, Halfdan Schjøtt, Trygve Schjøtt, Otto Falkenberg

12-METER

1908 London-Firth of Clyde T: 2, N: 1, D: 8.13.

1. GBR Thomas Glen-Coats, John Downes, John Buchanan, James Bunten, Arthur Downes, David Dunlap, John Mackenzie, Albert Martin, T. Gerald Tait, R.B. Aspin
2. GBR Charles MacIver, James Kenion, James Baxter, William Davidson, J.A. Gardiner, John Jellico, Thomas Littledale, Charles MacLeod Robertson, John Spence, Cecil MacIver

This was the only event in Olympic history to be staged in Scotland, and in fact it was won in two straight races by a crew of Scotsmen.

1912 Stockholm-Nynas T: 3, N: 3, D: 7.21.

			PTS.
1.	NOR	Alfred Larsen, Johan Anker, Nils Bertelsen, Halfdan Hansen, Magnus Konow, Petter Andreas Larsen, Eilert Falch-Lund, Fritz Staib, Arnfinn Heje, Gustav Thaulow	14
2.	SWE	Hugo Clason, Nils Persson, Richard Sällström, Nils Lamby, Kurt Bergström, Dick Bergström, Erik Lindqvist, Per Bergman, Sigurd Kander, Folke Johnson	6
3.	FIN	Ernst Krogius, Max Alfthan, Erik "Pekka" Hartvall, Jarl Hulldén, Sigurd Juslén, Eino Sandelin, John Silen	2

12-METER, 1907 RATING

1920 Antwerp T: 1, N: 1, D: 7.9.

1. NOR Henrik Østervold, Jan Østervold, Ole Østervold, Hans Naess, Laurits Christiansen, Halvor Møgster, Rasmus Birkeland, Halvor Birkeland, Kristian Østervold

12-METER, 1919 RATING

1920 Antwerp T: 1, N: 1, D: 7.9.

1. NOR Johan Friele, Olav Ørvig, Arthur Allers, Christen Wiese, Martin Borthen, Egill Reimers, Kaspar Hassel, Thor Ørvig, Erik Ørvig

SHARPIE—12 SQUARE METERS

1956 Melbourne T: 13, N: 13, D: 12.5.

			PTS.
1.	NZL	Peter Mander, John Cropp	6086
2.	AUS	Rolland Tasker, John Scott	6086
3.	GBR	Jasper Blackall, Terence Smith	4859
4.	ITA	Mario Capio, Emilio Massino	3928
5.	SAF	John Sully, Alfred Evans	2917
6.	GER	Rolf Mulka, Ingo von Bredow	2840
7.	SOV	Boris Iliine, Aleksandr Chumakov	2479
8.	FRA	Roger Tiriau, Claude Flahault	2058

Rolly Tasker and John Scott appeared to have won the final race and the gold medal, but a protest by the French led to their disqualification, leaving the Australians tied on points with New Zealand's Mander and Cropp. The New Zealand pair was awarded first place because they had won three races while the Australians had won only two.

30 SQUARE METERS

1920 Antwerp T: 1, N: 1, D: 7.9.

1. SWE Gösta Lundqvist, Rolf Steffenburg, Gösta Bengtson

40 SQUARE METERS

1920 Antwerp T: 2, N: 1, D: 79

			PTS.
1.	SWE	Tore Holm, Yngve Holm, Axel Rydin, Georg Tengwall	4
2.	SWE	Gustav Svensson, Ragnar Svensson, Percy Almstedt, Erik Mellbin	6

Chapter 21 **Shooting**

MEN	WOMEN
Rapid-Fire Pistol	Sport Pistol
Free Pistol	Air Pistol
Air Pistol	Small Bore Rifle, Three Positions
Small-Bore Rifle, Prone	Air Rifle
Small-Bore Rifle, Three Positions	Trap
Air Rifle	Skeet
Trap	Discontinued Event
Double Trap	
Skeet	
Discontinued Events	

International shooting competitions have employed a wide variety of tie-breaking rules, including shoot-offs (designated by slash lines in the following charts) and by the positions of the bullets on the target. Current practice in case of ties is to award the victory to whichever shooter recorded the highest score in the final series. Ties for medal spots are decided by shootout.

Every few years someone conquers a target and achieves a perfect score. At this point the officials of the International Shooting Union alter the target by decreasing the size of the bull's-eye and the rings. It is for this reason that the world records for various events sometimes go down instead of up.

Sexual integration of Olympic shooting began in 1968. In 1984, however, some of the events were divided into separate men's and women's competitions. By 1996 the sexes were completely segregated once again.

Another major change was instituted in 1988. For the first time, a final round was created in which the six or eight leading scorers from the preliminary round shoot off against each other while standing on the firing line at the same time. Scores in the final are added to the preliminary scores to determine the winner.

MEN

RAPID-FIRE PISTOL

Since 1948 the rapid-fire pistol event has consisted of two 30-shot courses at five silhouettes 25 meters away. The shooter, using a .22 caliber pistol, has eight seconds to fire at each of the five targets. Then the targets reappear, and he has six seconds to fire. Finally he must attempt shots at each of the targets within four seconds. This set of 15 shots is repeated four times. Since 2008 the top six in the preliminary round advance to the final round. In the final, four sets of five shots are taken with a four-second time limit.

1896 Athens C: 4, N: 3, D: 4.11.

		PTS.
1. Ioannis Frangoudis	GRE	344
2. Georgios Orfanidis	GRE	249
3. Holger Nielsen	DEN	—

DNF: Sidney Merlin (GBR)

1900–1904 not held

1906 Athens C: 22, N: 7, D: 4.25.
(25 Meters)

		BULL'S-EYES/PTS.
1. Konstantinos Skarlatos	GRE	29/133
2. Johann Hübner von Holst	SWE	27/115
3. Vilhelm Carlberg	SWE	26/115
4. Gerald Merlin	GBR	26/111
5. Sándor Török	HUN	25/104
6. Léon Moreaux	FRA	23/104
7. Sidney Merlin	GBR	23/103
7. Ludwig Ternajgo	AUT	23/103

This event was contested with dueling pistols. The target was the silhouette of a human dummy dressed in a frock-coat. The bull's-eye was the middle of the thorax.

1908 not held

1912 Stockholm C: 42, N: 10, D: 6.29.

		PTS.
1. Alfred Lane	USA	287
2. Paul Palén	SWE	286
3. Johan Hübner von Holst	SWE	283
3. John Dietz	USA	283
5. C. Ivan Törnmark	SWE	280
6. Eric Carlberg	SWE	278
7. Georg de Laval	SWE	277
8. Walter Winans	USA	276

1920 Antwerp-Beverloo C: 38, N: 14, D: 8.3.

		PTS.
1. Guilherme Paraense	BRA	274
2. Raymond Bracken	USA	272
3. Fritz Zulauf	SWI	269

1924 Paris C: 55, N: 17, D: 6.28.

		PTS.
1. Henry Bailey	USA	18
2. Vilhelm Carlberg	SWE	18
3. Lennart Hannelius	FIN	18
4. Lorenzo Amaya Toledo	ARG	18
5. Matías Osinalde	ARG	18
6. André de Castelbajac	FRA	18
7. Unio Sarlin	FIN	18
8. Einar Liberg	NOR	18

The 1924 match consisted of three series of six shots at six silhouettes in ten seconds. Eight of the 55 competitors achieved perfect scores and, according to the rules of the day, shot off another round of six shots, but this time within eight seconds. All eight shooters had perfect scores, so a second shoot-off string was ordered. This time three of the shooters missed. The third round saw Osinalde fall by the wayside, the fourth round Amaya, and the fifth round Hannelius. Bailey and Carlberg had now each hit 48 straight targets. A sixth shoot-off was called, and again the two men had perfect scores. Bailey, a 31-year-old gunnery sergeant in the US Marine Corps, fired first in the seventh shoot-off. After calling for the silhouettes, he attempted to fire his first shot. But his .22 autoloader malfunctioned and the cartridge stuck in the breech. Rather than give up, Bailey coolly pulled the spent case out with his fingers, closed the breech, and got off five shots in what remained of his eight seconds. All five shots hit their targets. Carlberg, who had already won three gold medals, three silver, and one bronze since the 1906 games, was either unnerved or gracious, for he missed two of his next six shots and Bailey won the match.

1928 not held

1932 Los Angeles C: 18, N: 7, D: 8.12.

		PTS.
1. Renzo Morigi	ITA	36
2. Heinz Hax	GER	36
3. Domenico Matteucci	ITA	36
4. Walter Boninsegni	ITA	35
4. José González Delgado	SPA	35
4. Arturo Villanueva	MEX	35

The first three series of six shots were shot at eight seconds each. Those with perfect scores took another six shots in six seconds. The eleven survivors shot again at four seconds. Six men were still perfect and shot another round in three seconds. Boninsegni, Delgado, and Villanueva each missed once, leaving Hax, Morigi, and Matteucci still in the contest. The next round required shooting six shots at six turning silhouettes in two seconds. Major Morigi amazed the crowd, which consisted mostly of Los Angeles policemen, by hitting all six targets, the last one after it had already started to turn away.

1936 Berlin C: 53, N: 22, D: 8.7.

		PTS.
1. Cornelius van Oyen	GER	30/6
2. Heinz Hax	GER	30/5
3. Torsten Ullman	SWE	30/4/4
4. Angelos Papadimas	GRE	30/4/1
5. Helge Mueller	SWE	30/3
6. Walter Boninsegni	ITA	29/6/3
7. Kazimierz Suchorzewski	POL	29/6/1
8. Haralds Marvē	LAT	29/3

1948 London C: 59, N: 22, D: 8.4. WR: 570 (Carlos Enrique Díaz Sáenz Valiente)

		PTS.
1. Károly Takács	HUN	580 WR
2. Carlos Enrique Díaz Sáenz Valiente	ARG	571
3. Sven Lundqvist	SWE	569
4. Torsten Ullman	SWE	564
5. Leonard Ravilo	FIN	563/36
6. Väinö Heusala	FIN	563/34
7. Lajos Börzsönyi	HUN	562
8. Birger Bühring-Andersen	NOR	559

Károly Takács was a member of the Hungarian world champion pistol shooting team in 1938 when, while serving as a sergeant in the army, a grenade exploded in his right hand—his pistol hand—and shattered it completely. Undaunted, Takács taught himself to shoot with his left hand and ten years later, at the age of 38, he qualified for the Hungarian Olympic team in the rapid-fire pistol

Károly Takács, 1948

Takács was a champion shooter when his right hand, his pistol hand, was shattered by a grenade. Ten years later, in 1948, he won his first Olympic gold medal—using his left hand.

event. In London, the favorite, world champion and world record holder, Carlos Enrique Díaz Sáenz Valiente, asked Takács why he was in London. Takács replied, "I'm here to learn." Takács won the gold medal and beat the world record by ten points. During the medal ceremony Díaz Sáenz Valiente, who finished second, turned to Takács and said, "You have learned enough."

1952 Helsinki C: 53, N: 28, D: 7.28. WR: 582 (Huelet Benner)

		PTS.
1. Károly Takács	HUN	579
2. Szilárd Kun	HUN	578
3. Gheorghe Lichiardopol	ROM	578
4. Carlos Enrique Díaz Sáenz Valiente	ARG	577
5. Pentti Linnosvuo	FIN	577
6. Panait Calcai	ROM	575
7. William McMillan	USA	575
8. Vassily Frolov	SOV/RUS	573

1956 Melbourne C: 35, N: 22, D: 12.5. WR: 589 (Carlos Enrique Díaz Sáenz Valiente)

		PTS.
1. Stefan Petrescu	ROM	587 OR
2. Yevgeny Cherkasov	SOV/RUS	585
3. Gheorghe Lichiardopol	ROM	581
4. Pentti Linnosvuo	FIN	581
5. Oscar Cervo Rosando	ARG	580
6. Szilárd Kun	HUN	578
7. Kalle Sievänen	FIN	576
8. Károly Takács	HUN	575

1960 Rome C: 57, N: 35, D: 9.9. WR: 592 (Aleksandr Kropotin, Aleksandr Zabelin)

		PTS.
1. William McMillan	USA	587/147 EOR
2. Pentti Linnosvuo	FIN	587/139 EOR
3. Aleksandr Zabelin	SOV/RUS	587/135 EOR
4. Hansrüdi Schneider	SWI	586
5. Stefan Petrescu	ROM	585
6. Gavril Maghiar	ROM	583
7. Czesław Zając	POL	582
8. Jiří Hrneček	CZE	582

On May 21, 1980, Bill McMillan was working as a weapons training coordinator for the San Diego County Sheriff's Department in California when a shooting instructor trainee mistakenly fired in the wrong direction. Two bullets from a .357 Magnum went through a wall and a glass window and hit McMillan in the upper right side of his chest. McMillan was unconscious for two weeks and, four years after competing in his sixth Olympics, lost the use of this shooting hand.

1964 Tokyo C: 53, N: 34, D: 10.19. WR: 595 (Aleksandr Kropotin)

		PTS.
1. Pentti Linnosvuo	FIN	592 OR
2. Ion Tripşa	ROM	591
3. Lubomír Nácovský	CZE	590
4. Hans Albrecht	SWI	590
5. Szilárd Kun	HUN	589
6. Marcel Roşca	ROM	588
7. Igor Bakalov	SOV/RUS	588
8. Kanji Kubo	JPN	587

Pentti Linnosvuo became only the second shooter to win gold medals in both the rapid-fire and free pistol events. Alfred Lane won both in the same year (1912), while Linnosvuo's victories were eight years apart.

Two different participants in this event were inspired to defect following the Games. First Bela Gabor, who finished 23rd, sought asylum at the West German Embassy rather than return to his native Hungary. Then last place finisher Ma Chin-shan, a retired army officer from Taiwan, took refuge in the Ginza office of the General Council of Chinese Merchants of Tokyo, requesting that he be allowed to return to mainland China to live with his parents whom he had not seen since World War II. To this day, Ma remains the only Olympic athlete to defect *to* a Communist country.

1968 Mexico City C: 56, N: 34, D: 10.23. WR: 596 (Virgil Atanasiu)

		PTS.
1. Józef Zapędzki	POL	593 OR
2. Marcel Roşca	ROM	591/147
3. Renart Suleimanov	SOV/RUS	591/146/148
4. Christian Düring	GDR	591/146/147
5. Erich Masurat	GER	590
6. Gerhard Dommrich	GDR	589
7. Lubomír Nácovský	CZE	588
8. Giovanni Liverzani	ITA	588

1972 Munich C: 62, N: 38, D: 9.1. WR: 598 (Giovanni Liverzani)

		PTS.
1. Józef Zapędzki	POL	595 OR
2. Ladislav Falta	CZE	594
3. Victor Torshin	SOV/RUS	593
4. Paul Buser	SWI	592
5. Jaime González Chas	SPA	592
6. Giovanni Liverzani	ITA	591
7. Dencho Denev	BUL	590
8. Gerhard Petritsch	AUT	590

The 43-year-old Zapędzki was a major in the Polish army when he won his second gold medal. After the competition he visited nearby Dachau and laid a wreath at the grave of his father, who had been killed by the Nazis thirty years earlier.

1976 Montreal C: 48, N: 30, D: 7.23. WR: 598 (Giovanni Liverzani)

		PTS.
1. Norbert Klaar	GDR	597 OR
2. Jürgen Wiefel	GDR	596
3. Roberto Ferraris	ITA	595
4. Afanasijs Kuzmins	SOV/LAT	595
5. Corneliu Ion	ROM	595
6. Erwin Glock	GER	594
7. Gerhard Petritsch	AUT	594
8. Marin Stan	ROM	594

Bill McMillan of the United States, competing in his sixth Olympics, scored only one point below his gold-medal-winning performance of 1960. However, the quality of marksmanship had improved so much in 16 years that he was able to finish in only a tie for 16th place in 1976. The winner, Norbert Klaar, was a 26-year-old car mechanic from the small industrial town of Wittenberge on the river Elbe. He shot a perfect 300 in the second course.

1980 Moscow C: 40, N: 26, D: 7.25. WR: 598 (Giovanni Liverzani, Corneliu Ion)

		PTS.
1. Corneliu Ion	ROM	596/148/147/148
2. Jürgen Wiefel	GDR	596/148/147/147
3. Gerhard Petritsch	AUT	596/146
4. Vladas Turla	SOV/LIT	595
5. Roberto Ferraris	ITA	595
6. Afanasijs Kuzmins	SOV/LAT	595
7. Marin Stan	ROM	595
8. Rafael Rodríguez Avila	CUB	594

1984 Los Angeles-Chino C: 55, N: 31, D: 8.2. WR: 599 (Igor Puzyrev)

		PTS.
1. Takeo Kamachi	JPN	595
2. Corneliu Ion	ROM	593
3. Rauno Bies	FIN	591/146
4. Delival Nobre	BRA	591/141
5. Yang Chung-yul	KOR	590
6. Alfred Radke	GER	590
7. Park Jong-gil	KOR	590
8. Bernardo Tovar Ante	COL	590

Competing in his fourth Olympics, Takeo Kamachi finally won a medal at the age of 48.

1988 Seoul C: 32, N: 23, D: 9.23. WR: 697 (Ralf Schumann)

		PTS.
1. Afanasijs Kuzmins	SOV/LAT	698 WR
2. Ralf Schumann	GDR	696
3. Zoltán Kovács	HUN	693
4. Alberto Sevieri	ITA	693
5. Adam Kaczmarek	POL	691
6. Bernardo Tobar Ante	COL	690
7. John McNally	USA	690
8. Dirk Köhler	GER	689

When he was 22 years old, Afanasijs Kuzmins had a dream that he had won an Olympic gold medal. As a result, he kept going in the sport until his dream came true—19 years later. Kuzmins shot a 598 in the qualifying round to lead by 1 point, then achieved a perfect score in the final.

1992 Barcelona-Mollet del Vallès C: 30, N: 23, D: 7.30. WR: 891 (Ralf Schumann)

		PTS.
1. Ralf Schumann	GER	885
2. Afanasijs Kuzmins	LAT	882/97
3. Vladimir Vokhmyanin	KAZ	882/96
4. Krzysztof Kucharczyk	POL	880
5. John McNally	USA	781
6. Miroslav Ignatyuk	UKR	779
7. Adam Kaczmarek	POL	778
8. Bernardo Tovar Ante	COL	776

Since 1986 Ralf Schumann had earned a medal in all 30 of his starts. Twenty-one times he finished first, four times second, and five times third. He was the defending world champion and the world record holder. But because he was upset in Seoul by Afanasijs Kuzmins, he was still missing an Olympic gold medal. In Barcelona he took a three-point lead in the qualifying round and held it through the semifinal and final.

1996 Atlanta-Wolf Creek C: 23, N: 19, D: 7.24. WR: 699.7 (Ralf Schumann)

		PTS.
1. Ralf Schumann	GER	698.0
2. Emil Milev	BUL	692.1
3. Vladimir Vokhmyanin	KAZ	691.5
4. Krzysztof Kucharczyk	POL	690.5
5. Meng Gang	CHN	687.1
6. Ghenadie Lisoconi	MOL	687.0
7. Lajos Pálinkás	HUN	685.9
8. Daniel Leonhard	GER	683.6

Ralf Schumann, now 34 years old, easily defended his championship by taking a six-point lead in the preliminary round. He later explained that his most difficult challenge at the Olympics was not winning the gold medal, but urinating on demand for the post-competition drug test.

2000 Sydney C: 20, N: 17, D: 9.21. WR: 699.7 (Ralf Schumann)

		PTS.
1. Sergei Alifirenko	RUS	687.6
2. Michel Ansermet	SWI	686.1
3. Iulian Raicea	ROM	684.6
4. Emil Milev	BUL	684.5
5. Ralf Schumann	GER	683.3
6. Oleg Khvatsovas	BLR	682.4
7. Krzysztof Kucharczyk	POL	682.2
8. Afanasijs Kuzmins	LAT	681.3

Alifirenko, Ansermet and Raicea entered the final round tied at 587. Ansermet fell behind with an 8.7 on his second shot. Raicea led Alifirenko by .5 after three shots, but missed the ten ring with four of his next six shots while Alifirenko remained consistent and won by

1.5 points. For the 41-year-old Alifirenko, as important as it was to win the gold medal, it was equally satisfying to finally defeat Ralf Schumann, whose portrait Alifirenko kept in his training room.

2004 Athens-Markopoulo C: 17, N: 14, D: 8.21. WR: 699.7 (Ralf Schumann)

		PTS.
1. Ralf Schumann	GER	694.9
2. Sergei Polyakov	RUS	692.7
3. Sergei Alifirenko	RUS	692.3
4. Oleh Tkachov	UKR	688.7
5. Iulian Raicea	ROM	687.6
6. Chen Yongqiang	CHN	683.8
7. Zhang Penghui	CHN	
7. Leuris Pupo Requejo	CUB	

Ralf Schumann had gone to the 2000 Sydney Olympics as the favorite to become the first shooter to win the same event three times. However, he shot poorly (for him) and ended up with only the third highest score. After registering only eight points for one shot, he filed a protest, claiming that the electronic scoring system had malfunctioned. When it was proven that this was not the case, he was penalized two points for lodging an unsuccessful appeal and lost his chance at a medal. Four years later, Schumann again arrived at the Olympics as the favorite. He, Sergei Polyakov and defending Olympic champion Sergei Alifirenko all completed the qualifying round tied at 592 points. Polyakov led Schumann by .3 points after the first series of the final, but Schumann moved ahead on the final series to finally win his third gold, having missed the 10-point ring on only one of his final ten shots.

Ralf Schumann, 2004
In Athens, Schumann won the rapid-fire pistol event for the third time.

2008 Beijing C: 19, N: 14, D: 8.16. WR: 794.0 (Christian Reitz)

		PTS.	
1. Oleksandr Petriv	UKR	780.2	OR
2. Ralf Schumann	GER	779.5	
3. Christian Reitz	GER	779.3	
4. Leonid Ekimov	RUS	778.2	
5. Keith Sanderson	USA	776.6	
6. Roman Bondaruk	UKR	774.7	
7. Leuris Pupo Requejo	CUB		
8. Aleksei Klimov	RUS		

First-time Olympian Keith Sanderson finished first in the preliminary round, setting a 60-shot Olympic record of 583 points. Three-time Olympic champion Ralf Schumann and his 21-year-old teammate Christian Reitz, the International Shooting Sport Federation (ISSF) world number one-ranked shooter, both scored 579 points in the preliminary round, advancing to the final in the final two spots. Reigning world champion Zhang Penghui was disqualified for raising his arm too soon.

Sanderson struggled in the final round, scoring the lowest of the six finalists and dropping out of medal contention. Schumann recorded the highest score in the final, 200.5, but was unable to make up his one-point deficit from the first round, finishing second behind outsider Oleksandr Petriv, who scored 200.2 points in the final to set an Olympic record of 780.2 points.

The 34-year-old Petriv explained his plans for the future, "All my friends keep asking me, 'When are you going to marry?' Perhaps, now that my dream has come true and I have achieved my goal, I will dedicate more time to this problem."

FREE PISTOL

The free pistol event is a leisurely affair in which the shooter has two hours in which to fire 60 shots at a target 50 meters (55 yards) away. The 10-ring, or bull's-eye, of the target is only two inches in diameter. The final consists of 10 shots with 75 seconds for each shot.

1896 Athens C: 5, N: 3, D: 4.11.

		PTS.
1. Sumner Paine	USA	442
2. Holger Nielsen	DEN	285
3. Ioannis Frangoudis	GRE	—
4. Leonidas Morakis	GRE	—
5. Georgios Orfanidis	GRE	—

Sumner Paine was working in Paris when his brother John showed up as a representative of the Boston Athletic Association team that was on its way to the

Olympic Games. In the words of Sumner Paine: "I came home from luncheon one day and found my brother, Lieutenant Paine, sitting in my office. I had not the slightest idea that he was on this side of the pond." John convinced his brother to join him, so the two, not knowing the events or conditions, loaded up with eight guns and 3500 rounds of ammunition (they used only 96) and took the next train to Athens. After John won the military pistol event, he agreed to withdraw from the free pistol contest, which Sumner then won.

In 1901 Sumner Paine returned home early one day and discovered his wife with his daughter's music teacher, who was in "a state of partial undress." Paine chased the teacher out of the house and, using the .32 caliber pistol that he usually carried with him, fired four shots. Paine was jailed and charged with assault. However he was released when it was determined that Paine, who was after all an expert marksman, could have easily killed the music teacher if he had wanted to. One hundred years after Sumner Paine's Olympic triumph, his great-granddaughter, Cecile Tucker, represented the United States in the 1996 women's quadruple sculls rowing event.

1900 Paris C: 20, N: 4, D: 8.1.

		PTS.
1. C. Karl Röderer	SWI	503
2. Achille Paroche	FRA	466
3. Konrad Stäheli	SWI	453
4. Louis Richardet	SWI	448
5. Louis Duffoy	FRA	442
6. Dirk Boest Gips	HOL	437
7. Friedrich Luthi	SWI	435
7. Léon Moreau	FRA	435

1904 not held

1906 Athens C: 28, N: 8, D: 4.26.
25 Meters

		PTS.
1. Maurice Lecoq	FRA	258
2. Léon Moreaux	FRA	249
3. Aristides Rangavis	GRE	244
4. Louis Richardet	SWI	241
5. Johan Hübner von Holst	SWE	239
6. Cesare Liverziani	ITA	238
7. Hermann Martin	FRA	236
8. Alexandros Theofilakis	GRE	235

1906 Athens C: 21, N: 8, D: 4.23.
50 Meters

		PTS.
1. Georgios Orfanidis	GRE	221
2. Jean Fouconnier	FRA	219
3. Aristides Rangavis	GRE	218
4. Konrad Stäheli	SWI	206
5. Konstantinos Skarlotos	GRE	206
6. Maurice Lecoq	FRA	205
7. Ludwig Ternajgo	AUT	199
8. Cesare Liverziani	ITA	199

1908 London C: 43, N: 7, D: 7.10.

		PTS.
1. Paul Van Asbroeck	BEL	490
2. Réginald Storms	BEL	487
3. James Gorman	USA	485
4. Charles Axtell	USA	480
5. Jesse Wallingford	GBR	467
6. André Barbillat	FRA	466
7. Walter Ellicott	GBR	458
8. Irving Calkins	USA	457

1912 Stockholm C: 54, N: 12, D: 7.1.

		PTS.
1. Alfred Lane	USA	499
2. Peter Dolfen	USA	474
3. Charles Stewart	GBR	470
4. Georg de Laval	SWE	470
5. Erik Boström	SWE	468
6. Horatio Poulter	GBR	461
7. Henry Sears	USA	459
8. Nikolai Panin (Kolomenkin)	RUS	457

Alfred Lane of New York City was only 20 years old when he went to Stockholm and won three gold medals. Eight years later in Antwerp he added two more gold medals and one bronze. Eighth-place finisher Kolomenkin, a ten-time Russian pistol champion, was also a well-known figure skater who had won a gold medal in the special figures event of 1908.

1920 Antwerp-Beverloo C: 36, N: 13, D: 8.2.

		PTS.
1. Karl Frederick	USA	496
2. Afrânio da Costa	BRA	489
3. Alfred Lane	USA	481
4. Lauritz Larsen	DEN	475
5. Niels Larsen	DEN	470
6. Anders Andersson	SWE	467
7. Paul Van Asbroeck	BEL	466
8. Iason Sappas	GRE	464

Da Costa used a new Colt .22 that had been loaned to the Brazilian team by the US team, and ammunition given to him by Alfred Lane.

1924–1932 not held

1936 Berlin C: 43, N: 19, D: 8.7. WR: 547 (Torsten Ullman)

		PTS.
1. Torsten Ullman	SWE	559 WR
2. Erich Krempel	GER	544
3. Charles Juchault des Jammonières	FRA	540
4. Marcel Bonin	FRA	538
5. Tapio Vartiovaara	FIN	537
6. Elliott Jones	USA	536
7. Georges Stathis	GRE	532
8. Aatto Nuora	FIN	532

Earlier in the day Ullman had won a bronze medal in the rapid-fire pistol event.

1948 London C: 50, N: 22, D: 8.2. WR: 559 (Torsten Ullman)

		PTS.
1. Edwin Vásquez Cam	PER	545
2. Rudolf Schnyder	SWI	539/60/21
3. Torsten Ullman	SWE	539/60/16
4. Huelet "Joe" Benner	USA	539/58
5. Beat Rhyner	SWI	536
6. Angel León de González	SPA	534
7. Ambrus Balogh	HUN	532
8. Marcel La Fortune	BEL	530

Vásquez is the only Peruvian ever to win an Olympic gold medal.

1952 Helsinki C: 48, N: 28, D: 7.25. WR: 559 (Torsten Ullman)

		PTS.
1. Huelet "Joe" Benner	USA	553 OR
2. Angel León de González	SPA	550
3. Ambrus Balogh	HUN	549
4. Konstantin Martazov	SOV/RUS	546
4. Lev Vainshtein	SOV/RUS	546
6. Torsten Ullman	SWE	543
7. Klaus Lahti	FIN	541
8. Beat Rhyner	SWI	539

1956 Melbourne C: 33, N: 22, D: 11.30. WR: 566 (Anton Yasinsky)

		PTS.
1. Pentti Linnosvuo	FIN	556/26 OR
2. Makhmud Umarov	SOV/RUS	556/24 OR
3. Offutt Pinion	USA	551
4. Choji Hosaka	JPN	550/24
5. Anton Yasinsky	SOV/RUS	550/20
6. Torsten Ullman	SWE	549
7. Åke Lindblom	SWE	542
8. Leonard Tolhurst	AUS	541

1960 Rome C: 67, N: 40, D: 9.6. WR: 566 (Anton Yasinsky)

		PTS.
1. Aleksei Gushchin	SOV/RUS	560 OR
2. Makhmud Umarov	SOV/RUS	552/26
3. Yoshihisa Yoshikawa	JPN	552/20
4. Torsten Ullman	SWE	550
5. Stanisław Romik	POL	548
6. Alfred Späni	SWI	546
7. Vladimír Kudrna	CZE	545
8. Horst Kadner	GDR	544

Fourth-place finisher Ullman was now 52 years old.

1964 Tokyo C: 52, N: 42, D: 10.18. WR: 566 (Anton Yasinsky)

		PTS.
1. Väinö Markkanen	FIN	560 EOR
2. Franklin Green	USA	557
3. Yoshihisa Yoshikawa	JPN	554/26
4. Johann Garreis	GDR	554/24
5. Anthony Chivers	GBR	552
6. Antonio Vita Segura	PER	550
7. Leif Larsson	SWE	549
8. Thomas Smith	USA	548

1968 Mexico City C: 69, N: 42, D: 10.18. WR: 566 (Anton Yasinsky)

		PTS.
1. Grigory Kossykh	SOV/RUS	562/30 OR
2. Heinz Mertel	GER	562/26 OR
3. Harald Vollmar	GDR	560
4. Arnold Vitarbo	USA	559
5. Paweł Małek	POL	556
6. Helmut Artelt	GDR	555
7. Nelson Oñate Temprana	CUB	555
8. Neagu Bratu	ROM	554

1972 Munich C: 59, N: 37, D: 8.28. WR: 572 (Grigory Kossykh)

		PTS.
1. Ragnar Skanåker	SWE	567 OR
2. Dan luga	ROM	562
3. Rudolf Dollinger	AUT	560
4. Rajmund Stachurski	POL	559
5. Harald Vollmar	GDR	558
6. Hynek Hromada	CZE	556
7. Kornél Marosvári	HUN	555
8. Grigory Kossykh	SOV/RUS	555

This was the first of Ragnar Skanåker's seven consecutive Olympic appearances.

1976 Montreal C: 47, N: 32, D: 7.18. WR: 572 (Grigory Kossykh, Harald Vollmar)

		PTS.
1. Uwe Potteck	GDR	573 WR
2. Harald Vollmar	GDR	567
3. Rudolf Dollinger	AUT	562
4. Heinz Mertel	GER	560
5. Ragnar Skanåker	SWE	559
6. Vincenzo Tondo	ITA	559
7. Grigory Kossykh	SOV/RUS	559
8. Dencho Denev	BUL	557

1980 Moscow C: 33, N: 19, D: 7.20. WR: 577 (Moritz Minder, Paavo Palokangas)

		PTS.
1. Aleksandr Melentyev	SOV/KYR	581 WR
2. Harald Vollmar	GDR	568
3. Ljubcho Diakov	BUL	565
4. Soh Gil-san	PRK	565
5. Seppo Saarenpää	FIN	565
6. Sergei Pyzhyanov	SOV/RUS	564
7. Ragnar Skanåker	SWE	563
8. Paavo Palokangas	FIN	561

1984 Los Angeles-Chino C: 56, N: 38, D: 7.29. WR: 581 (Aleksandr Melentyev)

		PTS.
1. Xu Haifeng	CHN	566
2. Ragnar Skanåker	SWE	565
3. Wang Yifu	CHN	564
4. Jürgen Hartmann	GER	560
5. Vincenzo Tondo	ITA	560
6. Philippe Cola	FRA	559
7. Hector De Lima Carrillo	VEN	558
8. Paavo Palokangas	FIN	558

To Xu Haifeng, a former "barefoot doctor" and chemical fertilizer salesman, went the honor of not only being the first gold-medal winner of the 1984 Olympics, but also of becoming the first representative of China to win an Olympic medal. He defeated 50-year-old Ragnar Skanåker, who added a silver medal to the gold he had won twelve years earlier.

1988 Seoul C: 43, N: 31, D: 9.18. WR: 666 (Igor Basinsky)

		PTS.
1. Sorin Babii	ROM	660
2. Ragnar Skanåker	SWE	657
3. Igor Basinsky	SOV/BLR	657
4. Tanyu Kiriakov	BUL	656
5. Gernot Eder	GDR	654
6. Gyula Karácsony	HUN	654
7. Arndt Kaspar	GER	651
8. Wang Yifu	CHN	651

Babii trailed Basinsky by 4 points following the preliminary round, with 54-year-old Skanåker another 2 points back in fourth place. Basinsky seemed rattled in the final and scored only 87 points to Babii's 94 and Skanåker's 93. Skanåker was more than twice as old as the other top five finishers.

1992 Barcelona-Mollet del Vallès C: 44, N: 29, D: 7.26. WR: 671 (Sergei Pyzhyanov)

		PTS.
1. Konstantin Lukashik	BLR	658
2. Wang Yifu	CHN	657/92
3. Ragnar Skanåker	SWE	657/91
4. Darius Young	USA	655
5. Sorin Babii	ROM	653
6. István Ágh	HUN	652/91
7. Xu Haifeng	CHN	652/87
8. Tanyu Kiriakov	BUL	618

The final was a tight contest. Tanyu Kiriakov, who had won a gold medal in the air pistol event in 1988, scored a 567 in the qualifying round, as did 16-year-old Konstantin Lukashik of Grodno. One shot behind were 54-year-old Darius Young and 58-year-old Ragnar Skanåker, followed by the two Chinese shooters, Wang Yifu and 1984 Olympic champion Xu Haifeng with 565. Xu and Kiriakov were the first to fall from contention. After his sixth shot, an 8, dropped him four points off the pace, Kiriakov slammed his pistol against the rest, altering the sight. Unable to shoot properly afterward, he stalked off the range. Meanwhile, Skanåker caught Lukashik after the first shot, moved ahead with his third and led by two points midway through the ten-shot final. Lukashik pulled even again with his sixth shot. With four shots to go, Wang, Young, and 1988 Olympic champion Sorin Babii were all just two points behind the leaders. Lukashik inched one point ahead of Skanåker in the ninth round. With one shot remaining, the score stood: Lukashik—649, Skanåker—648 and Wang—648. A ten would have won the match for any of them. However, all three scored nines, with Wang gaining the silver medal because of his higher total in the final.

1996 Atlanta-Wolf Creek C: 45, N: 28, D: 7.23. WR: 675.3 (Tanyu Kiriakov)

		PTS.
1. Boris Kokorev	RUS	666.4
2. Igor Basinsky	BLR	662.0
3. Roberto Di Donna	ITA	661.8
4. Konstantin Lukachik	BLR	660.1
5. Vigilio Fait	ITA	659.8
6. Wang Yifu	CHN	659.3
7. Martin Tenk	CZE	657.7
8. Sergio Sánchez Gómez	GUA	657.1

After winning his gold medal, 37-year-old Boris Kokorev revealed a long-held secret. "When I was young," he confessed, "my mother used to give me pocket money to buy my lunch at school. But I always went straight to the shooting range and spent it there. She always wondered why I ate so much in the evening when I got home. I have never told her what I did, but now that I have won the gold medal, I think she will forgive me."

Igor Basinsky, an army major, jumped from fourth to second with his final shot.

2000 Sydney C: 36, N: 27, D: 9.19. WR: 676.2 (William Demarest)

		PTS.
1. Tanyu Kiriakov	BUL	666.0
2. Igor Basinsky	BLR	663.3
3. Martin Tenk	CZE	662.5
4. Vladimir Goncharov	RUS	662.2
5. Dilshod Mukhtarov	UZB	662.0
6. Wang Yifu	CHN	659.0
7. Roberto Di Donna	ITA	657.3
8. Vladimir Gushcha	KAZ	655.8

Tanyu Kiriakov was leading Igor Basinsky by 2.9 points when he misfired his fifth shot of the final and only scored a 7.2. His lead dropped to .4, but Kiriakov regrouped and pulled away to win his second gold medal twelve years after he earned his first.

2004 Athens-Markopoulo C: 42, N: 31, D: 8.17. WR: 676.2 (William Demarest)

		PTS.
1. Mikhail Nestruyev	RUS	663.3
2. Jin Jong-oh	KOR	661.5
3. Kim Jong-sou	PRK	657.7
4. Norayr Bakhtamyan	ARM	654.8
5. Boris Kokorev	RUS	654.6
6. Vladimir Isachenko	KAZ	654.5
7. Tanyu Kiriakov	BUL	654.3
8. Isidro Lorenzo González	SPA	652.0

In second place, two points behind Jin Jong-oh after the qualifying round, Mikhail Nestruyev moved into the lead after outscoring Jin by 3.8 points in the final.

Jin's downfall came on his seventh shot, when he earned only 6.9 points, a disaster that he blamed on the automatic sensor of the pistol's trigger. Nestruyev's win took place three days after he had missed the gold medal in the air pistol on his final shot.

2008 Beijing C: 45, N: 32, D: 8.12. WR: 676.2 (William Demarest)

		PTS.
1. Jin Jong-o	KOR	660.4
2. Tan Zongliang	CHN	659.5
3. Vladimir Isakov	RUS	658.9
4. Oleg Omelchuk	UKR	658.9
5. Pavol Kopp	SVK	657.6
6. Tanyu Kiryakov	BUL	656.8
7. Damir Mikec	SER	655.8
8. Tomoyuki Matsuda	JPN	

DISQ (Drugs): Kim Jong-su (PRK) 660.2

Competing three days after winning the silver medal in the air pistol event, defending Olympic silver medalist Jin Jong-o completed the preliminary round in a four-way tie for second place with 563 points, two points behind leader Tan Zongliang, the 2006 world champion.

Jin moved into the lead early in the final, shooting 97.4 to earn the gold medal. Defending Olympic bronze medalist Kim Jong-su moved into second place on his last shot but was disqualified after testing positive for propanolol, a banned beta-blocker. Kim blamed the positive test on a traditional Korean medicine called gusimhwan. The tie between Vladimir Isakov and Oleg Omelchuk was decided by shoot-off, with Isakov scoring 9.1 points to Omelchuk's 6.5.

AIR PISTOL

Competition in the qualification round consists of 60 shots at a distance of 10 meters with a time limit of 1 hour and 45 minutes. The top eight shooters take part in a 10-shot final series with 75 seconds allowed for each shot. The bull's-eye has a diameter of 11.5 mm (.45 in).

1896–1984 not held

1988 Seoul C: 44, N: 29, D: 9.24. WR: 692.3 (Igor Basinsky)

		PTS.
1. Tanyu Kiriakov	BUL	687.9
2. Erich Buljung	USA	687.9
3. Xu Haifeng	CHN	684.5
4. Sorin Babii	ROM	683.3
5. Igor Basinsky	SOV/BLR	683.2
6. Miroslav Růžička	CZE	681.4
7. Jerzy Pietrzak	POL	678.3
8. Boris Kokorev	SOV/RUS	677.3

US Army shooting instructor Erich Buljung equaled the 60-shot world record of 590 in the preliminary round. In the 10-shot final, however, his 5-point lead gradually evaporated until Kiriakov trailed by only 0.7 points after nine shots. On the final shot Kiriakov outscored Buljung 9.8 to 9.1 to finish in a tie. The Bulgarian was awarded the gold medal on the basis of his higher point total in the final round.

1992 Barcelona-Mollet del Vallès C: 45, N: 30, D: 7.28. WR: 695.1 (Sergei Pyzhyanov)

		PTS.
1. Wang Yifu	CHN	684.8
2. Sergei Pyzhyanov	RUS	684.1/100.1
3. Sorin Babii	ROM	684.1/98.1
4. Xu Haifeng	CHN	681.5
5. Sakari Paasonen	FIN	680.1/98
6. Jerzy Pietrzak	POL	680.1/93
7. Tanyu Kiriakov	BUL	679.7
8. Robert Di Donna	ITA	678.5

Babii set an Olympic record of 586 in the qualifying round. He was followed by Wang at 585 and Pyzhyanov at 584. The Romanian led by 1.7 points after six rounds in the final, but then he began to falter. With one shot remaining, Wang crept to within one-tenth of a point of Babii: 675.2 to 675.1. Babii fired first and scored only 8.9 points. Wang, normally a quick shooter himself, was about to fire when he heard the surprised reaction to Babii's shot. Wang peeked at the score and lowered his gun. For years Wang had lived with the reputation of being a poor performer at major competitions. In the words of Xie Bian of *China Sports* magazine, "His repeated failures hung over his head, turning him from an easygoing man into a somewhat melancholy one." Wang raised his pistol, but again lowered it. "You must overcome yourself," he told himself, "this is the chance of a lifetime." With exquisite concentration, he aimed again and finally fired. His 9.7 earned him the gold medal. Pyzhyanov, meanwhile, scored 9.9 to tie Babii and gain the silver medal due to his higher point total in the final.

Wang Yifu's wife, Zhang Qiuping, finished tenth in the women's small-bore rifle, three positions event.

1996 Atlanta-Wolf Creek C: 50, N: 32, D: 7.20. WR: 695.1 (Sergei Pyzhyanov)

		PTS.
1. Roberto Di Donna	ITA	684.2
2. Wang Yifu	CHN	684.1
3. Tanyu Kiriakov	BUL	683.8
4. Sergei Pyzhyanov	RUS	683.5
5. Jerzy Pietrzak	POL	682.7
6. Tan Zongliang	CHN	682.0
7. Igor Basinsky	BLR	681.8
8. Friedhelm Sack	NAM	680.2

This was one of those rare shooting events in which the three favorites really did take home the medals, although it ended in spectacular fashion. To begin with, the final was unexpectedly halted in the midst of the ninth round when a fallen tree hit a power line and disabled the electronic scoring system. The competition resumed after a delay of several minutes. With one round to go, defending champion Wang Yifu held a seemingly insurmountable lead of 3.8 points. But Wang, who had been ill for several days, appeared to black out on his feet. His final shot went awry and earned him only 6.5 points. This left him two tenths of a point behind Roberto Di Donna, who scored 10.5 on his last shot. Wang sank into a chair in shock, and was being comforted by his wife and his coach when he suddenly fainted. He was carried away on a stretcher. Unfortunately, the stretcher bearers did not know the location of the medical aid center and wandered about aimlessly before finding it. Fortunately, Wang recovered sufficiently to take part in the free pistol event three days later, although he was clearly still suffering. One observant Chinese journalist noted that during the free pistol competition, in which he placed sixth, Wang inhaled from an oxygen bottle eight times and, because of a headache, massaged his head 21 times.

2000 Sydney C: 42, N: 29, D: 9.16. WR: 695.1 (Sergei Pyzhyanov)

		PTS.
1. Franck Dumoulin	FRA	688.9
2. Wang Yifu	CHN	686.9
3. Igor Basinsky	BLR	682.7
4. Mikhail Nestruyev	RUS	682.3
5. Stéphane Gagne	FRA	682.0
6. Roberto Di Donna	ITA	680.5
7. João Costa	POR	679.4
8. Tanyu Kiryakov	BUL	676.8

Franck Dumoulin endured a rough year in 1999. First he mistakenly shot himself in the left hand. Then he shattered his leg and broke his arm in a motorcycle accident and he found himself in a wheelchair less than one year before the Olympics. Dumoulin and Wang Yifu entered the final tied at 590. Dumoulin's first shot was only an 8.5 and he immediately fell behind by 1.5 points. Wang was still ahead after the fourth shot, but in the fifth round Dumoulin outscored Wang 10.3 to 8.9 and maintained a lead until the end. Part of Dumoulin's mental training was to maintain a stable position by holding in his mind an image of the Eiffel Tower and thinking about its solidity and stability.

2004 Athens-Markopoulo C: 47, N: 35, D: 8.14. WR: 695.1 (Sergei Pyhzyanov)

		PTS.
1. Wang Yifu	CHN	690.0
2. Mikhail Nestruyev	RUS	689.8
3. Vladimir Isakov	RUS	684.3
4. Tanyu Kiriakov	BUL	683.4
5. Jin Jong-oh	KOR	682.9
6. Kim Hyon-ung	PRK	682.0
7. Norayr Bakhtamyan	ARM	681.9
8. Kim Jong-su	PRK	681.2

The competition for gold was a duel between reigning world champion Mikhail Nestruyev and Wang Yifu, who was competing in his sixth Olympics and who had won either gold or silver in the air pistol event in the last three Olympics. Nestruyev set an Olympic record of 591 points in the qualification round, with Wang, now 43 years old, a single point behind. Wang made up the difference with his first shot of the final, but Nestruyev quickly moved back ahead and held onto a slim lead through the sixth of the final's ten rounds. Wang finally took over first place in the seventh round, but only by three-tenths of a point. In the eighth round he scored only 8.9 points to Nestruyev's 10.2 to fall behind again. In the ninth round it was Nestruyev's turn to slip up, scoring only 9.3 points, while Wang hit a 10.3. Thus the two entered the final round in an exact tie. Wang's last shot was a 9.9, while Nestruyev scored only 9.7. It was Wang's sixth Olympic medal.

2008 Beijing C: 48, N: 35, D: 8.9. WR: 695.1 (Sergei Pyzhyanov)

		PTS.
1. Pang Wei	CHN	688.2
2. Jin Jong-o	KOR	684.5
3. Jason Turner	USA	682.0
4. Brian Beaman	USA	682.0
5. Leonid Ekimov	RUS	680.5
6. Walter Lapeyre	FRA	680.3
7. Jakkrit Panichpatikum	THA	679.0
8. Vigilio Fait	ITA	580.0

DISQ (Drugs): Kim Jong-su (PRK) 683.0

After winning the 2004 Olympic gold medal, six-time Olympic pistol medalist Wang Yifu retired and became the head coach of the Chinese national shooting team. Under Wang's guidance, Pang Wei took over the mantle of gold-medal favorite, winning the 2006 world championship.

The 22-year-old Pang led the qualifying round and posted the highest score in the final round to win the gold by a wide margin. North Korea's Kim Jong-su placed third after two strong final shots but was disqualified after testing positive for a banned beta-blocker.

SMALL-BORE RIFLE, PRONE

The small-bore rifle, prone match is shot at a distance of 50 meters with a .22 rimfire rifle. Originally the 10-ring bull's-eye was .89 inches in diameter. When high scores became too common, it was scaled down in 1958 to .487 inches. Currently, the diameter is 10.4mm (.409 inches)—smaller than a thumbnail. The shooter must keep his wrist at least six inches above the ground. He is given one hour and 15 minutes in which to take 60 shots and is also allowed 15 sighting shots, which can only be taken between the strings of ten record shots. The final consists of 10 shots with a time limit of 45 seconds per shot.

1896–1906 not held

1908 London C: 19, N: 5, D: 7.11.

		PTS.
1. Arthur Carnell	GBR	387
2. Harold Humby	GBR	386
3. George Barnes	GBR	385
4. Michael Matthews	GBR	384
5. Edward Amoore	GBR	383
6. William Pimm	GBR	379
7. Albert Taylor	GBR	376
8. Harold Hawkins	GBR	374

In his book *British Olympians,* Ian Buchanan relates the story of the unfortunate Philip Plater of Great Britain. The rules of the competition limited each nation to 12 entries. When the entry form of George Barnes was misplaced, Plater was entered in his place. Barnes' entry form was subsequently found, but on the day of the match, confusion reigned. Thinking that only 11 British shooters had fired, Plater was allowed to start even though there were only 30 minutes remaining. Plater set a world record of 391 and was initially recognized as the Olympic champion. Then it was discovered that all 12 members of the official British team had shot before Plater. Several days later Plater was declared an illegal entrant and his performance was expunged from the records.

1912 Stockholm C: 41, N: 9, D: 7.4.

		PTS.
1. Frederick Hird	USA	194
2. William Milne	GBR	193
3. Harold Burt	GBR	192
4. Edward Lessimore	GBR	192
5. Francis Kemp	GBR	190
6. Robert Murray	GBR	190
7. William Leushner	USA	189
8. Erik Boström	SWE	189

1920 not held

1924 Paris C: 66, N: 19, D: 6.23.

		PTS.
1. Pierre Coquelin de Lisle	FRA	398 WR
2. Marcus Dinwiddie	USA	396
3. Josias Hartmann	SWI	394
4. Erik Sætter-Lassen	DEN	393
4. Anders Peter Nielsen	DEN	393
4. Johannes Theslöf	FIN	393
7. Viktor Knutsson	SWE	392
7. Jakob Reich	SWI	392

Silver medalist Marcus Dinwiddie was a 17-year-old schoolboy from Washington, D.C. His record score of 396 out of 400 held up for most of the match, until the 23-year-old Coquelin de Lisle hit a sensational set of 100, 100, 99, and 99. Following his victory, Coquelin de Lisle sent the following succinct cable to his mother: "Am Olympic champion. World record beaten. Will arrive Tuesday morning."

1928 not held

1932 Los Angeles C: 26, N: 9, D: 8.13.

		PTS.
1. Bertil Rönnmark	SWE	294/296
2. Gustavo Huet Bobadilla	MEX	294/290
3. Zoltán Soós-Ruszka Hradetzky	HUN	293
4. Mario Zorzi	ITA	293
5. Gustaf Andersson	SWE	292
5. William Harding	USA	292
5. Karl Larsson	SWE	292
5. Francisco Real	POR	292

Antal Barát Limberkovits of Hungary fired one bull's-eye which he had unfortunately aimed at the wrong target. He called out his mistake to the officials, who ruled the shot a complete miss. Had he not made this error and had he not been so honest, Limberkovits would have won the gold medal.

1936 Berlin C: 66, N: 25, D: 8.8.

		PTS.
1. Willy Røgeberg	NOR	300 WR
2. Ralph Berzsenyi	HUN	296
3. Władysław Karaś	POL	296
4. Martin Gison	PHI	296
5. José Trindade Mello	BRA	296
6. Jacques Mazoyer	FRA	296
7. Gustavo Huet Bobadilla	MEX	296
8. Bertil Rönnmark	SWE	295

The 30-year-old Røgeberg fired the first perfect score ever recorded in international competition. Fourth-place finisher Gison was captured by the Japanese during World War II and forced to take part in the infamous Bataan death march. He survived and was able to compete in the 1948 Olympics in London.

1948 London C: 71, N: 26, D: 8.3.

		PTS.	
1. Arthur Cook	USA	599/43	WR
2. Walter Tomsen	USA	599/42	WR
3. Jonas Jonsson	SWE	597/44	
4. Halvor Kongsjorden	NOR	597/39	
5. Thore Skredegaard	NOR	597/39	
6. E. Guillermo Baldwin Ponte	PER	596/39	
7. Jaako Ravila	FIN	596/39	
8. Willy Rögeberg	NOR	596/37	

Cook and Tomsen each missed the 10-ring only once in 60 shots, but Cook was awarded first place because he had fired one shot more than Tomsen within the ⅜-inch inner bull's-eye.

1952 Helsinki C: 58, N: 32, D: 7.29. WR: 400 (T. Manttari)

		PTS.	
1. Iosif Sîrbu	ROM	400/33	EWR
2. Boris Andreyev	SOV/RUS	400/28	EWR
3. Arthur Jackson	USA	399/28	
4. Gilmour Boa	CAN	399/28	
5. Erich Spörer	GER	399/25	
6. Otto Horber	SWI	398/29	
7. Veikko Leskinen	FIN	398/28	
8. Severino Moreira	BRA	398/22	

Sârbu was Romania's first Olympic champion.

1956 Melbourne C: 44, N: 25, D: 12.5. WR: 598 (Gilmour Boa)

		PTS.
1. Gerald Ouellette	CAN	600
2. Vassily Borissov	SOV/RUS	599
3. Gilmour Boa	CAN	598
4. Otakar Hořínek	CZE	598
5. Iosif Sîrbu	ROM	598
6. Sándor Krebs	HUN	598
7. Erling Kongshaug	NOR	598
8. Severino Moreira	BRA	597

After he had done poorly in the three-position small-bore event, Ouellette and his teammate Gilmour Boa decided that they should both use Boa's rifle for the prone competition, even though this meant that they both had to shoot within the same two-and-a-half-hour time limit. Boa went first and, coached by Ouellette, matched his world record of 598. Then, with half the time remaining, it was Ouellette's turn. Coached by Boa, who encouraged the Windsor, Ontario, tool designer to take two breaks to ease the pressure, Ouellette shot 60 straight bull's-eyes for a perfect score. Unfortunately, his score was not accepted as a world record because the Australian officials had set the targets one and a half meters too close. Ouellette's second appearance in the Olympics didn't come until 12 years later, when he finished sixth in the three-position event in Mexico City.

1960 Rome C: 85, N: 46, D: 9.10. WR: 595 (János Holup)

		PTS.
1. Peter Kohnke	GER	590
2. James Hill	USA	589
3. Enrico Forcella Pelliccioni	VEN	587
4. Vasily Borisov	SOV/RUS	586
5. Arthur Skinner	GBR	586
6. Yukio Inokuma	JPN	586
7. Daniel Puckel	USA	585
8. Martsel Koen	BUL	585

Eighteen-year-old Peter Kohnke of Bremervörde was the youngest of the 85 entrants in the prone event.

1964 Tokyo C: 73, N: 43, D: 10.16. WR: 595 (János Holup, Rudolf Bortz)

		PTS.	
1. László Hammerl	HUN	597	WR
2. Lones Wigger	USA	597	WR
3. Tommy Pool	USA	596	
4. Gilmour Boa	CAN	595	
5. Nicolae Rotaru	ROM	595	
6. Akihiro Rinzaki	JPN	594	
7. Karl Wenk	GER	594	
8. Traian Cogut	ROM	593	

Gerald Ouellette, 1956

Ouellette shot 60 straight bull's eyes to win the 1956 small-bore rifle, prone event.

László Hammerl was a 22-year-old medical student from Budapest. He was awarded the victory on the basis of a tie-breaking rule which stated that whoever had the highest score in the final string of ten shots was the winner.

1968 Mexico City C: 86, N: 45, D: 10.19. WR: 598 (David Boyd, Alfons Meyer)

		PTS.
1. Jan Kůrka	CZE	598 EWR
2. László Hammerl	HUN	598 EWR
3. Ian Ballinger	NZL	597
4. Nicolae Rotaru	ROM	597
5. John Palin	GBR	596
6. Jean Loret	FRA	596
7. Bjørn Bakken	NOR	595
8. Gary Anderson	USA	595

This time Hammerl lost the gold medal because of the same tie-breaking rule from which he had benefitted four years earlier. Eulalia Rolińska of Poland and Gladys de Seminario of Peru had the distinction of being the first women to compete in Olympic shooting. They finished 22nd and 31st, respectively.

1972 Munich C: 101, N: 59, D: 8.28. WR: 598 (David Boyd, Alfons Meyer, Jan Kurka, László Hammerl, Peter Gorewski, Wolfram Waibel, Manfred Fiess, Esa Kervinen)

		PTS.
1. Li Ho-jun	PRK	599 WR
2. Victor Auer	USA	598
3. Nicolae Rotaru	ROM	598
4. Giuseppe de Chirico	ITA	597
5. Jiří Vogler	CZE	597
6. Jaime Santiago	PUR	597
7. Lones Wigger	USA	597
8. László Hammerl	HUN	597

After his victory, Li was asked by reporters to what he attributed his brilliant performance. He replied, "I thought I was shooting at my enemies. Our Prime Minister, Kim-Il Sung, told us prior to our departure to shoot as if we were fighting our enemies. And that's exactly what I did." This attitude was considered to be unsportsmanlike, and so a second press conference was called at which Li claimed he had been misquoted. Second-place finisher Vic Auer was a North Hollywood TV scriptwriter who had written for *Death Valley Days, Gunsmoke,* and *Bonanza.*

1976 Montreal C: 76, N: 49, D: 7.19. WR: 599 (Li Ho-jun, Karel Bulan, Mircea Ilca)

		PTS.
1. Karlheinz Smieszek	GER	599 EWR
2. Ulrich Lind	GER	597
3. Gennady Lushchikov	SOV/RUS	595
4. Anton Müller	SWI	595
5. Walter Frescura	ITA	594
6. Arne Sörensen	CAN	593
7. Henning Clausen	DEN	593
8. Desanka Pešut	YUG/SER	592

Smieszek, a 27-year-old insurance agent, was a surprise winner who had never before won a major shooting title.

1980 Moscow C: 56, N: 33, D: 7.21. WR: 599 (Li Ho-jun, Karel Bulan, Mircea Ilca, Karlheinz Smieszek, Alister Allan, Lones Wigger)

		PTS.
1. Károly Varga	HUN	599 EWR
2. Hellfried Heilfort	GDR	599 EWR
3. Petar Zapryanov	BUL	598
4. Krzysztof Stefaniak	POL	598
5. Timo Hagman	FIN	597
6. Aleksandr Mastianin	SOV/RUS	597
7. Nonka Matova	BUL	597
8. Walter Frescura	ITA	597

Varga broke his shooting hand playing soccer two days before the competition and had to wear a bandage while he shot. After winning the gold medal he explained that the injury had actually helped him, because it forced him to squeeze the trigger more delicately.

1984 Los Angeles-Chino C: 71, N: 46, D: 7.30. WR: 600 (Alister Allan, Ernest Vande Zande, Edward Etzel, Donald Durbin)

		PTS.
1. Edward Etzel	USA	599 EOR
2. Michel Bury	FRA	596
3. Michael Sullivan	GBR	596
4. Alister Allan	GBR	595
5. Francesco Nanni	SMR	594
6. Hans Strand	SWE	594
7. John Duus	NOR	594
8. Ulrich Lind	GER	593

Ed Etzel of Morgantown, West Virginia, completed his 60 shots in only 40 minutes and was the first of the 71 shooters to finish. Francesco Nanni's fifth place finish made him the most successful Olympic athlete ever from the tiny nation of San Marino (pop. 22,000).

1988 Seoul C: 55, N: 33, D: 9.19. WR: 704.9 (Petr Kürka)

		PTS.
1. Miroslav Varga	CZE	703.9
2. Cha Young-chul	KOR	702.8
3. Attila Záhonyi	HUN	701.9
4. Pavel Soukeník	CZE	701.2
5. Alister Allan	GBR	700.9
6. Xu Xiaoguang	CHN	700.6
7. Bernd Rücker	GER	700.5
8. Michael Ashcroft	CAN	698.5

Miroslav Varga of Plzeň needed only 28 minutes to achieve a perfect score of 600 in the qualifying round. His speed turned out to be well advised, as a thunderstorm swept in a few minutes later, darkening the sky and impairing the vision of the remaining shooters. In the final, Cha drew within 0.2 points with two shots remaining, but Varga shot a pair of 10.6s to hold him off. Cha's closing in on Varga caused great excitement among the Korean spectators, who clapped and cheered after each of Cha's shots even though other shooters were still firing. This was an unprecedented breach of etiquette on the part of the crowd.

1992 Barcelona-Mollet del Vallès C: 52, N: 34, D: 7.29. WR: 703.5 (Jens Harskov)

		PTS.
1. Lee Eun-chul	KOR	702.5
2. Harald Stenvaag	NOR	701.4
3. Stevan Pletikosić	YUG/SER	701.1/104.1
4. Hubert Bichler	GER	701.1/103.1
5. Michel Bury	FRA	700.0
6. Juha Hirvi	FIN	699.5/102.5
7. Peter Gabrielsson	SWE	699.5/102.5
8. Hrachya Petikyan	ARM	699.2

Bichler led the qualifying round with a score of 598, but all of the other seven finalists were only one point back, at 597. Lee passed Bichler in the sixth round and held his lead to the end. Bichler, in second place with one shot remaining, fell to fourth after missing the ten-ring for the second straight time. Stenvaag, on the other hand, went from sixth place halfway through the final to second at the end.

1996 Atlanta-Wolf Creek C: 52, N: 36, D: 7.25. WR: 703.5 (Jens Harshov)

		PTS.	
1. Christian Klees	GER	704.8	WR
2. Sergei Belyayev	KAZ	703.3	
3. Jozef Gönci	SLV	701.9	
4. Jorge González Rodríguez	SPA	701.7	
5. Milan Mach	CZE	700.9	
6. Sergei Martynov	BLR	699.6	
7. Lee Eun-chul	KOR	699.1	
8. Bill Meek	USA	698.9	

Christian Klees shot a perfect 600 in the preliminary round and then kept his composure to set a finals world record.

2000 Sydney C: 53, N: 37, D: 9.21. WR: 704.8 (Christian Klees)

		PTS.
1. Jonas Edman	SWE	701.3
2. Torben Grimmel	DEN	700.4
3. Sergei Martynov	BLR	700.3
4. Maik Eckhardt	GER	699.8
5. Václav Bečvář	CZE	699.7
6. Artem Khadzhibekov	RUS	699.2
7. Igor Pirekeyev	TRM	699.2
8. Philippe Joualin	FRA	699.0

Jonas Edman shot 599 out of 600 in the qualifying round and then maintained his lead throughout the final to register an unexpected victory.

2004 Athens-Markopoulo C: 46, N: 34, D: 8.20. WR: 704.8 (Christian Klees)

		PTS.
1. Matthew Emmons	USA	703.3
2. Christian Lusch	GER	702.2
3. Sergei Martynov	BLR	701.6
4. Jozef Gönci	SLV	700.5
5. Marco De Nicolo	ITA	699.7
6. Maik Eckhardt	GER	697.6
7. Michael Babb	GBR	696.8
8. Jia Zhanbo	CHN	696.6

Reigning world champion Matthew Emmons finished the qualifying round with 599 points, giving him a one-point lead over Christian Lusch and Jozef Gönci. After eight rounds in the final, Emmons led Lusch by only three tenths of a point. Then he scored 10.6 with each of his last two shots to secure the victory. In fifth place after the qualifying round, Sergei Martynov moved up to third by earning the top score in the final, 105.6 points, to gain his second straight bronze medal. In April, Emmons discovered that someone had sabotaged his rifle with a screwdriver. After that, he began competing with a rifle borrowed from his training partner, Amber Darland, and this was the gun he used to win the gold medal. "I owe her a real nice dinner when we get back," he noted after the medal ceremony.

2008 Beijing C: 56, N: 37, D: 8.15. WR: 704.8 (Christian Klees, Warren Potent)

		PTS.
1. Artur Aivazian	UKR	702.7
2. Matthew Emmons	USA	701.7
3. Warren Potent	AUS	700.5
4. Vebjørn Berg	NOR	699.1
5. Konstantin Prikhodchenko	RUS	699.0
6. Valerian Sauveplane	FRA	698.8
7. Juha Hirvi	FIN	698.5
8. Sergey Martynov	BLR	698.3

Competing in his third Olympics, Armenian-born Artur Aivazian led the preliminary round with 599 points, two points ahead of defending Olympic champion Matt Emmons. Emmons outshot Aivazian 104.7 points to 103.7 in the final but could not close the gap, as Aivazian scored at least ten points on each of his ten shots in the final to take gold.

Forty-six year old Warren Potent, the oldest of the six finalists, recorded the best score in the final round, 105.5 points, to earn bronze. Four months before the competition, at the pre-Olympic test event in Beijing, Warren had equalled Christian Klees's world record of 704.8 points.

SMALL-BORE RIFLE, THREE POSITIONS

In the small-bore rifle, three-position event, each entrant shoots 40 shots prone, 40 kneeling, and 40 standing, with a .22 rifle at a target 50 meters away. The target is the same as that used in the prone event. The time limits are 45 minutes for the prone round, 1 hour 15 minutes standing and 1 hour kneeling. In the final the top eight qualifiers take ten shots in the standing position. The time limit is 75 seconds per shot.

1896–1948 not held

1952 Helsinki C: 44, N: 25, D: 7.29. WR: 1167 (Karl Steigelmann)

		PRONE	KNEELING	STANDING	TOTAL PTS.
1. Erling Kongshaug	NOR	397	387	380	1164/53
2. Vilho Ylönen	FIN	397	394 WR	373	1164/53
3. Boris Andreyev	SOV/RUS	400 WR	387	376	1163
4. Ernst Huber	SWI	397	390	375	1162
5. Pyotr Avilov	SOV/RUS	395	385	382	1162
6. Iosif Sîrbu	ROM	400 WR	383	378	1161
7. Uno Berg	SWE	396	388	374	1158
8. K.V. Kullervo Leskinen	FIN	398	390	369	1157

1956 Melbourne C: 44, N: 28, D: 12.4. WR: 1176 (Ole Jensen)

		PRONE	KNEELING	STANDING	TOTAL PTS.
1. Anatoly Bogdanov	SOV/RUS	396	392	384	1172 OR
2. Otakar Hořinek	CZE	393	395	384	1172 OR
3. Nils Johan Sundberg	SWE	397	396	374	1167
4. Vasily Borisov	SOV/RUS	395	391	377	1163
5. Vilho Ylönen	FIN	394	386	381	1161
6. Gilmour Boa	CAN	400 WR	391	368	1159
7. Iosif Sîrbu	ROM	397	392	368	1157
8. Anders Kvissberg	SWE	394	389	373	1156

1960 Rome C: 75, N: 40, D: 9.8. WR: 1149 (Klaus Zähringer)

		PRONE	KNEELING	STANDING	TOTAL PTS.
1. Viktor Shamburkin	SOV/RUS	394	386	369	1149 EWR
2. Marat Niyazov	SOV/TRM	384	388	373	1145
3. Klaus Zähringer	GER	394	381	364	1139
4. Dušan Houdek	CZE	387	386	366	1139
5. Jerzy Nowicki	POL	394	378	365	1137
6. Esa Kervinen	FIN	392	381	364	1137
7. Daniel Puckel	USA	390	385	361	1137
8. János Holup	HUN	394	384	356	1134

1964 Tokyo C: 53, N: 33, D: 10.20. WR: 1157 (Gary Anderson)

		PRONE	KNEELING	STANDING	TOTAL PTS.
1. Lones Wigger	USA	398	394	372	1164 WR
2. Velichko Velichkov	BUL	396	384	372	1152
3. László Hammerl	HUN	397	387	367	1151
4. Harry Köcher	GDR	394	389	365	1148
5. Jerzy Nowicki	POL	396	389	362	1147
6. Tommy Pool	USA	393	392	362	1147
7. Ion Olărescu	ROM	393	391	360	1144
8. Kurt Müller	SWI	390	386	367	1143

US Army Captain Lones Wigger of Carer, Montana, had never shot before a large crowd. Teammate Gary Anderson advised him not to be afraid of the crowd but to feel a part of it. Wigger set a world record in the prone event, but lost on a tie-breaker. Four days later he set another world record in the three-position event, but this time he finished 12 points ahead of his nearest opponent. Eight years later, at the Munich Olympics, Wigger won another gold medal in the 300-meter free rifle event.

1968 Mexico City C: 62, N: 35, D: 10.21. WR: 1165 (Gary Anderson)

		PRONE	STANDING	KNEELING	TOTAL PTS.
1. Bernd Klingner	GER	394	367	396 WR	1157
2. John Writer	USA	395	370	391	1156
3. Viktor Parkhimovich	SOV/BLR	395	366	393	1154
4. John Foster	USA	394	369	390	1153
5. José González Soto	MEX	397	376	379	1152
6. Gerald Ouellette	CAN	396	364	391	1151
7. Peter Kohnke	GER	395	368	388	1151
8. Kurt Müllor	SWI	390	373	388	1151

1972 Munich C: 69, N: 41, D: 8.30. WR: 1165 (Gary Anderson, Oleg Lapkin)

		PRONE	STANDING	KNEELING	TOTAL PTS.
1. John Writer	USA	395	381 WR	390	1166 WR
2. Lanny Bassham	USA	390	375	392	1157
3. Werner Lippoldt	GDR	393	372	388	1153
4. Petr Kovářík	CZE	397	368	388	1153
5. Vladimir Agishev	SOV/RUS	392	369	391	1152
6. Andrzej Sieledcow	POL	395	369	387	1151
7. Gottfried Kustermann	GER	397	364	388	1149
8. Nicolae Rotaru	ROM	397	361	390	1148

1976 Montreal C: 57, N: 35, D: 7.21. WR: 1167 (Lones Wigger)

		PRONE	STANDING	KNEELING	TOTAL PTS.
1. Lanny Bassham	USA	397	373	392	1162
2. Margaret Murdock	USA	398	376	388	1162
3. Werner Seibold	GER	397	377	386	1160
4. Srećko Pejović	YUG/SER	391	379	386	1156
5. Sven Johansson	SWE	394	367	391	1152
6. Li Ho-jun	PRK	390	373	389	1152
7. Zdravko Milutinović	YUG/SER	394	394	389	1152
8. Aleksandr Mitrofanov	SOV/RUS	394	369	388	1151

After finishing second in 1972, Lanny Bassham, a soldier from Fort Worth, Texas, became convinced that his technical skill had to be supplemented by mental training. He went to the Montreal Olympics as the favorite. His US teammate was Margaret Murdock, a 33-year-old nurse from Topeka, Kansas. In 1970 Murdock had won the standing event at the world championships while she was four months' pregnant. At the 1976 Olympics, Bassham and Murdock finished in a tie at 1162. Bassham was awarded the gold medal because he had scored three 100s to Murdock's two. Bassham felt that the tie-breaker was a silly rule, and at the medal ceremony he pulled Murdock up to the first-place platform and they stood together for the playing of the US national anthem. Murdock was probably less upset about the tie-breaking rule, since it was the same rule that had allowed her to gain a place on the US team when she and John Writer finished with the same scores at the US tryouts. Bassham later started a mental management business to help people become better shooters and make more money. Murdock was the first woman to win an Olympic shooting medal.

1980 Moscow C: 39, N: 21, D: 7.23. WR: 1172 (Nonka Matova)

		PRONE	STANDING	KNEELING	TOTAL PTS.
1. Viktor Vlasov	SOV/RUS	398	378	397	1173 WR
2. Bernd Hartstein	GDR	399	374	393	1166
3. Sven Johansson	SWE	398	379	388	1165
4. Mauri Röppänen	FIN	397	379	388	1164
4. Aleksandr Mitrofanov	SOV/RUS	397	378	389	1164
6. Nonka Matova	BUL	396	377	390	1163
7. Hellfried Heilfort	GDR	394	378	390	1162
8. Eugeniusz Pędzisz	POL	397	368	391	1156

1984 Los Angeles-Chino C: 51, N: 29, D: 8.1. WR: 1173 (Viktor Vlasov, Vladimir Lvov)

		PRONE	STANDING	KNEELING	TOTAL PTS.
1. Malcolm Cooper	GBR	397	381	395	1173 EWR
2. Daniel Nipkow	SWI	396	381	386	1163
3. Alister Allan	GBR	392	378	392	1162
4. Kurt Hillenbrand	GER	396	369	389	1154
5. Bo Arne Lilja	DEN	394	375	384	1153
6. Glenn Dubis	USA	396	368	387	1151
7. Jean-Pierre Amat	FRA	393	375	382	1150
7. Peter Heinz	GER	394	375	381	1150

1988 Seoul C: 47, N: 25, D: 9.22. WR: 1283.4 (Petr Kürka)

		PRONE	STANDING	KNEELING	FINAL	TOTAL PTS.
1. Malcolm Cooper	GBR	400 EWR	387	393	99.3	1279.3
2. Alister Allan	GBR	399	386	396	94.6	1275.6
3. Kirill Ivanov	SOV/RUS	399	382	392	102.0	1275.0
4. Klaus Jorn Christensen	DEN	399	387	391	96.6	1273.6
5. Glenn Dubis	USA	400 EWR	386	388	99.5	1273.5
6. Grachya Petikyan	SOV/ARM	394	387	392	99.2	1272.2
7. Harald Stenvaag	NOR	395	389	389	98.7	1271.7
8. Goran Maksimović	YUG/SER	399	383	391	98.5	1271.5

One week before the competition began, a clumsy technician from the BBC knocked over Cooper's rifle and cracked the stock. Fortunately the defending Olympic champion was able to repair it with the help of a Soviet gunsmith.

1992 Barcelona-Mollet del Vallès C: 42, N: 24, D: 7:31 WR: 1276.7 (Rajmond Debevec)

		PRONE	STANDING	KNEELING	FINAL	TOTAL PTS.
1. Hrachya Petikyan	ARM	399	383	387	98.4	1267.4
2. Robert Foth	USA	395	386	388	97.6	1266.6
3. Ryohei Koba	JPN	393	387	391	94.9	1265.9
4. Juha Hirvi	FIN	398	384	390	92.8	1264.8
5. Harald Stenvaag	NOR	397	381	388	98.6	1264.6
6. Rajmond Debevec	SLO	394	387	386	95.6	1262.6
7. Peter Gabrielsson	SWE	398	379	391	93.1	1261.1
8. Zsolt Vári	HUN	398	379	387	94.6	1258.6

Hirvi led the qualifying round at 1172. He was followed by Koba at 1171, and Petikyan and Foth at 1169. But Hirvi put himself out of contention with the first shot of the final when he scored only 5.0 points. The lead changed hands eight times in the final, with Petikyan taking over for the first time after the seventh shot. With one shot remaining, the score could hardly have been closer: Foth—1257.4, Petikyan—1257.3, and Koba— 1257.1. It was Petikyan who came through in the end, scoring a 10.1 to Foth's 9.2 and Koba's 8.8. The sacrifices of Olympic athletes know no limits. After the competition was over, Koba revealed to the press that during his final weeks of training he had given up not only alcohol but karaoke singing as well.

1996 Atlanta-Wolf Creek C: 45, N: 30, D: 7.27. WR: 1287.9 (Rajmond Debevec)

		PRONE	STANDING	KNEELING	FINAL	TOTAL PTS.
1. Jean-Pierre Amat	FRA	396	387	392	98.9	1273.9
2. Sergei Belyayev	KAZ	399	382	394	97.3	1272.3
3. Wolfram Waibel	AUT	394	389	387	99.6	1269.6
4. Goran Maksimović	YUG/SER	394	387	392	95.8	1268.8
5. Jozef Gönci	SLV	393	382	391	101.7	1267.7/10.0
6. Rob Harbison	USA	394	388	388	97.7	1267.7/ 8.5
7. Václav Bečvář	CZE	398	381	389	96.0	1264.0
8. Sergei Martynov	BLR	397	377	392	97.9	1263.9

Competing in his fourth Olympics, Jean-Pierre Amat finally earned his first medal—a bronze in air rifle—and then took the three-position gold five days later. Amat and Sergei Belyayev were tied at 117 after the prelminary round. Amat led by only one tenth of a point after eight rounds, but was steadier with his last two shots.

2000 Sydney C: 44, N: 29, D: 9.23. WR: 1287.9 (Rajmond Debevec)

		PRONE	KNEELING	STANDING	TOTAL PTS.
1. Rajmond Debevec	SLO	397	392	388	1275.1
2. Juha Hirvi	FIN	394	393	384	1270.5
3. Harald Stenvaag	NOR	399	393	383	1268.6
4. Artyom Khadzhibekov	RUS	398	393	382	1268.2
5. Artur Aivazian	UKR	396	391	383	1266.6
6. Christian Bauer	GER	399	387	383	1266.0
7. Yevgeny Aleynikov	RUS	393	389	384	1265.5
8. Jozef Gönci	SLV	399	390	376	1261.3

Rajmond Debevec was twice chosen international shooter of the year and he was the reigning world record holder in both the three positions and air rifle events. Yet, even though he had already competed in three Olympics, the 37-year-old had never won an Olympic medal. He came out of the qualifying round with a two-point lead over Harald Stenvaag. The only shooter to outscore him in the final was Juha Hirvi, who moved from fourth place to second.

2004 Athens-Markopoulo C: 40, N: 29, D: 8.22. WR: 1287.9 (Rajmond Debevec)

		PRONE	KNEELING	STANDING	FINAL	TOTAL PTS.
1. Jia Zhanbo	CHN	398	386	387	93.5	1264.5
2. Michael Anti	USA	398	385	382	98.1	1263.1
3. Christian Planer	AUT	396	381	390	95.8	1262.8
4. Rajmond Debevec	SLO	397	384	385	96.6	1262.6
5. Artyom Khadzhibekov	RUS	397	374	393	97.6	1261.6
6. Thomas Farnik	AUT	395	383	387	96.4	1261.4
7. Artur Aivazian	UKR	396	380	390	95.0	1261.0
8. Matthew Emmons	USA	399	387	383	88.4	1257.4

With a healthy three-point lead going into the final shot, Matthew Emmons, who had won the prone event two days earlier, accidentally aimed and fired at the wrong target, earning zero points and dropping to eighth place. His mistake moved Jia Zhanbo into first place. Emmons was not the only American to make a mistake. Michael Anti lost *his* chance for the gold medal when, during the qualification round, he was penalized two points for accidentally firing too many shots from the kneeling position.

Emmons's blunder did come with a silver lining. After the competition, Czech shooter Kateřina Kůrková came over to offer her condolences. The pair started dating and married in 2007.

2008 Beijing C: 49, N: 31, D: 8.17. WR: 1287.9 (Rajmond Debevec)

		PRONE	KNEELING	STANDING	FINAL	TOTAL PTS.
1. Qiu Jian	CHN	394	392	387	99.5	1272.5
2. Yuriy Sukhorukov	UKR	398	392	384	98.4	1272.4
3. Rajmond Debevec	SLO	399	391	386	95.7	1271.7
4. Matt Emmons	USA	399	387	389	95.3	1270.3
5. Thomas Farnik	AUT	391	394	386	97.9	1268.9
6. Mario Knögler	AUT	395	389	386	98.4	1268.4
7. Valerian Sauveplane	FRA	396	392	384	95.1	1267.1
8. Vebjørn Berg	NOR	398	391	383	94.5	1266.5

Four years after snatching defeat from the jaws of victory by shooting at the wrong target in Athens, American shooter Matt Emmons looked ready to redeem himself. Two days after winning silver in the prone rifle event, Emmons earned 1175 points in the three-position rifle qualifying round, one point behind leader Rajmond Debevec, the 2000 Olympic champion.

Emmons scored 90.9 points on his first nine shots of the final, well ahead of the other finalists. Needing only 6.7 points to win the gold medal, Emmons' gun went off before he had fully prepared. The misfire earned him only 4.4 points, dropping him out of medal contention for the second straight Olympics. "As I was starting to get on the trigger, the gun just went off," Emmons explained. "I was like, 'Uh, that's not going to be good.'"

With Emmons out of contention the gold medal went to China's Qiu Jian, who finished a tenth of a point ahead of Yuriy Sukhorukov of the Ukraine. "It was accidental, these things happen in sport," said Sukhorukov. "I once shot a zero in a World Cup in Russia. I feel sorry for him."

AIR RIFLE

In the qualifying round 60 shots are taken at a distance of 10 meters with a time limit of 1 hour 45 minutes. The center ring is ½ millimeter across. The final consists of 10 shots with a 75-second time limit per shot.

1896–1980 not held

1984 Los Angeles-Chino C: 52, N: 35, D: 8.3. WR: 590 (Harald Stenvaag)

		PTS.
1. Philippe Héberlé	FRA	589
2. Andreas Kronthaler	AUT	587
3. Barry Dagger	GBR	587
4. Nicolas Berthelot	FRA	585
5. Peter Heinz	GER	583
5. John Rost	USA	583
7. Harald Stenvaag	NOR	582
7. Itzhak Yonassi	ISR	582

Defending world champion Philippe Héberlé, a 21-year-old fire fighter from Belfort, was also two-time crossbow world champion. During a pre-Olympic tournament at the Olympic site in Chino in April 1984, Héberlé was impressed by the stifling heat. Back home in France he simulated the Olympic conditions by employing a large gas heater to raise the temperature at his practice site. When the French shooting team returned to Los Angeles they decided to avoid the Olympic villages, which were far from the shooting venue. Instead, they rented nine motor homes and set up shop in a campground where they used fishing rods and crossbows to satisfy their taste for fish, rabbits, and ducks.

1988 Seoul C: 46, N: 29, D: 9.20. WR: 699.1 (Tapio Saeynevirta)

		PTS.
1. Goran Maksimović	YUG/SER	695.6
2. Nicolas Berthelot	FRA	694.2
3. Johann Riederer	GER	694.0
4. Robert Foth	USA	692.5
5. Harald Stenvaag	NOR	692.0
6. Attila Záhonyi	HUN	691.4
7. An Byung-kyun	KOR	690.7
8. Andreas Wolfram	GDR	689.8

1992 Barcelona-Mollet del Vallès C: 44, N: 28, D: 7.27. WR: 699.4 (Rajmond Debevec)

		PTS.
1. Yuri Fedkin	RUS	695.3
2. Franck Badiou	FRA	691.9
3. Johann Riederer	GER	691.7
4. Jean-Pierre Amat	FRA	691.6
5. Goran Maksimović	YUG/SER	690.6
6. Thomas Farnik	AUT	690.2
7. Robert Foth	USA	689.4
8. Chae Keun-bae	KOR	687 8

1996 Atlanta-Wolf Creek C: 44, N: 31, D: 7.22. WR: 699.4 (Rajmond Debevec)

		PTS.
1. Artyom Khadzhibekov	RUS	695.7
2. Wolfram Waibel	AUT	695.2
3. Jean-Pierre Amat	FRA	693.1
4. Yevgeny Aleynikov	RUS	692.9
5. Leif Steinar Rolland	NOR	692.5
6. Rajmond Debevec	SLO	692.1
7. Rob Harbison	USA	691.8
8. Milan Bakeš	CZE	690.5

Five weeks before the Olympics, Artem Khadzhibekov shot 701.5 at the Russian national championships, although his score did not qualify as a world record because it was not made in an international competition. Khadzhibekov trailed Wolfram Waibel by two points after the preliminary round, but took the lead with his fifth shot of the final.

2000 Sydney C: 46, N: 32, D: 9.18. WR: 700.6 (Jason Parker)

		PTS.
1. Cai Yalin	CHN	696.4
2. Artyom Khadzhibekov	RUS	695.1
3. Yevgeny Aleynikov	RUS	693.8
4. Anatoly Klimenko	BLR	693.4
5. Jason Parker	USA	693.1
6. Nedžad Fazlija	BSH	692.7
7. Leif Steinar Rolland	NOR	692.2
8. Artur Aivazian	UKR	692.0

Cai Yalin was described by Chinese team manager Feng Jianyhong as "very quiet and shy, small and skinny. He's like a pale-faced scholar." Cai led the qualifying round and was never headed in the final.

2004 Athens-Markopoulo C: 47, N: 33, D: 8.16. WR: 702.5 (Jason Parker)

		PTS.
1. Zhu Qinan	CHN	702.7 WR
2. Li Jie [I]	CHN	701.3
3. Jozef Gönci	SLV	697.4
4. Cheon Min-ho	KOR	696.6
5. Maik Eckhardt	GER	696.3
6. Je Sung-tae	KOR	696.3
7. Abhinav Bindra	IND	694.6
8. Jason Parker	USA	694.5

Reigning world champion and world record holder Jason Parker seemed the favorite for gold, but placed only eighth in the qualifying round. Zhu Qinan and Li Jie finished first and second, with 599 and 598 points respectively. Zhu earned 103.7 points in the final to break Parker's world record.

2008 Beijing C: 51, N: 37, D: 8.11. WR: 703.5 (Gagan Narang)

		PTS.
1. Abhinav Bindra	IND	700.5
2. Zhu Qinan	CHN	699.7
3. Henri Häkkinen	FIN	699.4
4. Alin Moldoveanu	ROM	698.9
5. Konstantin Prikhodchenko	RUS	698.4
6. Péter Sidi	HUN	698.4
7. Stevan Pletikosić	SER	697.7
8. Sergei Kruglov	RUS	697.0

Reigning world champion Abhinav Bindra finished fourth in the qualifying round, two points behind leader Henri Häkkinen of Finland. World record holder Gagan Narang narrowly failed to qualify, finishing ninth.

Bindra earned more than ten points on each of his shots in the final, clinching the gold medal with a final shot of 10.8 points. Häkkinen scored 9.7 points on his final shot, dropping to third place behind defending Olympic champion Zhu Qinan. Bindra's gold medal was the first individual gold medal for India in Olympic history. The 25-year-old was showered with gifts, including some $300,000 in cash, congratulations from India's President and Prime Minister and a free lifetime pass from the Indian Railway service.

TRAP

In the trap or clay pigeon event, saucers approximately four inches in diameter are flung into the air at various angles. The targets now used in competition are not made of clay, but of pitch and chalk. The shooter is allowed two shots with a 12-gauge shotgun at each saucer (or bird). According to current rules, after 125 targets, the top six shooters advance to the final, in which they shoot at 25 targets, with a single shot per target.

1896 not held

1900 Paris C: 31, N: 4, D: 7.17.

		PTS.
1. Roger de Barbarin	FRA	17
2. René Guyot	FRA	17
3. Justinien, Count Clary	FRA	17
4. César Bettex	FRA	16
5. Hilaret	FRA	15
6. Edouard Geynet	FRA	13
7. Jules Charpentier (FRA), Charles, Baron de Jaubert, (FRA), Joseph Labbé (FRA), Sidney Merlin (GBR), André, Baron de Schonen (GER), Sion (FRA)		12

Roger de Barbarin was described as a man with "a piercing gaze and a delicate black moustache."

There were two members of the 2004 Chinese Olympic shooting team named Li Jie. One earned the air rifle silver medal; the other finished sixth in the running target event.

1904 St. Louis not held

1906 Athens C: 12, N: 4, D: 4.26.

		PTS.
1. Gerald Merlin	GBR	24/4
2. Ioannis Peridis	GRE/CYP	24/3
3. Sidney Merlin	GBR	23
4. Maurice Faure	FRA	22
5. Konstantinos Thanopoulos	GRE/CYP	16
6. Ioannis Drosopoulos	GRE	14
7. Sándor Török	HUN	12
8. Demetrios Petropoulos	GRE	7

Merlin defeated Peridis on the fourth shot of a sudden-death shoot-out.

1908 London C: 31, N: 6, D: 8.11.

		PTS.
1. Walter Ewing	CAN	72
2. George Beattie	CAN	60
3. Alexander Maunder	GBR	57
4. Anastasios Metaxas	GRE	57
5. Charles Palmer	GBR	55
5. Arthur Westover	CAN	55
7. Mylie Fletcher	CAN	53
7. Richard Hutton	GBR/IRL	53
7. John Wilson	HOL	53

1912 Stockholm C: 61, N: 11, D: 7.4.

		PTS.
1. James Graham	USA	96
2. Alfred Göldel-Bronikoven	GER	94
3. Harry Blau	RUS/LAT	91
4. Harold Humby	GBR	88
4. Anastasios Metaxas	GRE	88
4. Albert Preuss	GER	88
4. Gustaf Adolf Schnitt	FIN	88
4. Franz von Zedlitz und Leipe	GER	88

1920 Antwerp-Beverloo C: 53, N: 9, D: 7.24.

		PTS.
1. Mark Arie	USA	95
2. Frank Troeh	USA	93
3. Frank Wright	USA	87
4. Frederick Plum	USA	87
5. Horace Bonser	USA	87
6. Robert Montgomery	CAN	86
7. Johannes Nordahl-Lunde	NOR	85
7. Henri Quersin	BEL	85

1924 Paris C: 44, N: 14, D: 7.8.

		PTS.
1. Gyula Halasy	HUN	98/8 OR
2. Konrad Huber	FIN	98/7 OR
3. Frank Hughes	USA	97
4. James Montgomery	CAN	97
5. Louis d'Heur	BEL	96/8
6. George Beattie	CAN	96/7
6. Samuel Sharman	USA	96/7
6. Samuel Vance	CAN	96/7

1928–1948 not held

1952 Helsinki C: 40, N: 22, D: 7.26.

		PTS.
1. George Généreux	CAN	192
2. Knut Holmqvist	SWE	191
3. Hans Liljedahl	SWE	190
4. František Čapek	CZE	188
5. Konrad Huber	FIN	188
6. Ioannis Koutsis	GRE	187
7. Galliano Rossini	ITA	187
8. Italo Bellini	ITA	186

George Généreux, of Saskatoon, Saskatchewan, was only 17 years old when he won the Olympic championship. Holmqvist needed to score a perfect 25 on his last round to tie Généreux, but he missed his next to last shot.

1956 Melbourne C: 32, N: 18, D: 12.1.

		PTS.
1. Galliano Rossini	ITA	195 OR
2. Adam Smelczyński	POL	190
3. Alessandro Ciceri	ITA	188/24
4. Nikolai Mogilevsky	SOV/RUS	188/23
5. Yuri Nikandrov	SOV/UKR	188/22
6. František Čapek	CZE	187
7. Knut Holmqvist	SWE	178
8. Hans Liljedahl	SWE	177

1960 Rome C: 66, N: 38, D: 10.9.

		PTS.
1. Ion Dumitrescu	ROM	192
2. Galliano Rossini	ITA	191
3. Sergei Kalinin	SOV/RUS	190
4. James Clark	USA	188
5. Hans Aasnes	NOR	185
5. Joseph Wheater	GBR	185
7. Adam Smelczyiński	POL	184
8. Claude Foussier	FRA	183
8. Karni Singh	IND	183

1964 Tokyo-Tokorozawa C: 51, N: 28, D: 10.17.

		PTS.
1. Ennio Mattarelli	ITA	198 OR
2. Pāvels Seničevs	SOV/LAT	194/25
3. William Morris	USA	194/24
4. Galliano Rossini	ITA	194/23
5. Ion Dumitrescu	ROM	193
5. Juan Enrique Lira Vergara	CHI	193
7. J. Robert Braithwaite	GBR	192
8. Joachim Marscheider	GDR	191

1968 Mexico City C: 59, N: 34, D: 10.19. WR: 198 (Ennio Mattarelli)

		PTS.
1. J. Robert Braithwaite	GBR	198 EWR
2. Thomas Garrigus	USA	196/25/25
3. Kurt Czekalla	GDR	196/25/23
4. Pāvels Seničevs	SOV/LAT	196/22
5. Pierre Candelo	FRA	195
6. Adam Smelczyński	POL	195
7. Aleksandr Alipov	SOV/RUS	195
8. John Primrose	CAN	194

The 43-year-old Braithwaite missed two of his first 13 shots, but then hit the last 187 in a row. A veterinary surgeon from Preston, near Liverpool, Bob Braithwaite took up clay pigeon shooting because he could no longer stand to shoot real birds and animals and see them suffer.

1972 Munich C: 57, N: 33, D: 8.29. WR: 198 (Ennio Mattarelli, Robert Braithwaite, Silvano Basagni)

		PTS.
1. Angelo Scalzone	ITA	199 WR
2. Michel Carrega	FRA	198
3. Silvano Basagni	ITA	195
4. Burckhardt Hoppe	GDR	193
5. Johnny Påhlsson	SWE	193
6. James Poindexter	USA	192
7. John Primrose	CAN	192
8. Marcos Olsen	BRA	191

1976 Montreal C: 44, N: 29, D: 7.20. WR: 199 (Angelo Scalzone, Michel Carrega)

		PTS.
1. Donald Haldeman	USA	190
2. Armando da Silva Marques	POR	189
3. Ubaldesco Baldi	ITA	189
4. Burckhardt Hoppe	GDR	186
5. Aleksandr Androshkin	SOV/RUS	185
6. Adam Smelczyński	POL	183
7. John Primrose	CAN	183
8. Bernard Blondeau	FRA	182

The low scores were due to poor weather conditions. In a sport where contestants are known to calm their nerves with alcohol or tranquilizers, it came as a shock when 65-year-old Paul Cerutti of Monaco was disqualified after it was found that he had been taking amphetamines. The stimulants did him little good anyway. He finished 43rd out of a field of 44.

1980 Moscow C: 34, N: 22, D: 7.22. WR: 199 (Angelo Scalzone, Michel Carrega)

		PTS.
1. Luciano Giovannetti	ITA	198
2. Rustam Yambulatov	SOV/UZB	196/24/25
3. Jörg Damme	GDR	196/24/24
4. Josef Hojný	CZE	196/23
5. Eladio Vallduvi Casals	SPA	195
6. Aleksandr Asanov	SOV/KAZ	195
7. Silvano Basagni	ITA	194
8. Burckhardt Hoppe	GDR	192

The 34-year-old Giovannetti celebrated his victory by tossing his cap into the air and shooting a hole through it.

1984 Los Angeles-Chino C: 70, N: 42, D: 7.31. WR: 200 (Daniel Carlisle)

		PTS.
1. Luciano Giovannetti	ITA	192/24
2. Francisco Boza Dibos	PER	192/23
3. Daniel Carlisle	USA	192/22
4. Timo Nieminen	FIN	191
5. Michel Carrega	FRA	190
6. Eli Ellis	AUS	190
7. Terry Rumbel	AUS	189
8. Johnny Påhlsson	SWE	189

Giovannetti, a gun-shop owner from Pistoia, finished strongly to become the first repeat winner in Olympic trap shooting. On May 22, 1990, bronze medalist Dan Carlisle broke an obscure world record by shooting down 3,172 clay targets in one hour.

1988 Seoul C: 49, N: 28, D: 9.20. WR: 224 (Miroslav Bednařík)

		PTS.
1. Dmytro Monakov	SOV/UKR	222/8
2. Miroslav Bednařík	CZE	222/7
3. Franz Peeters	BEL	219/16
4. Francisco Boza Dibos	PER	219/15
5. Bean van Limbeek	HOL	219/7
6. Kazumi Watanabe	JPN	216
7. Urmas Saaliste	SOV/EST	194
8. A. Matti Nummela	FIN	194

Monakov, the defending world champion, and Bednařík, the 1986 world champion, both completed the semifinals with a score of 197 and then shot perfect rounds in the final. This necessitated a sudden-death shoot-off. But first Monakov and Bednařík had to wait for the three-way shoot-off for third place. When their turn came, Monakov and Bednařík both hit their first seven shots, but the Czechoslovak missed his eighth bird, and when Monakov made his, the contest was over. Less than a year later, Bednařík was killed in a motorcycle accident. He was 24 years old.

1992 Barcelona-Mollet del Vallès C: 54, N: 36, D: 8.2. WR: 224 (Jörg Damme)

		PTS.
1. Petr Hrdlička	CZE	219/1
2. Kazumi Watanabe	JPN	219/0
3. Marco Venturini	ITA	218/23/9
4. Jörg Damme	GER	218/23/8
5. Pavel Kubec	CZE	218/22
6. Jay Waldron	USA	217
7. José Bladas Torras	SPA	194/25
8. Zhang Bing	CHN	194/24

Hrdlička won the match when Watanabe missed the first shot of the shoot-out. The shoot-out for third place, on the other hand, wasn't decided until the ninth target.

1996 Atlanta-Wolf Creek C: 58, N: 41, D: 7.21. WR: 150 (Marcello Tittarelli)

		PTS.
1. Michael Diamond	AUS	149
2. Joshua Lakatos	USA	147/28
3. Lance Bade	USA	147/27
4. John Maxwell	AUS	146/7
5. Zhang Bing	CHN	146/6
6. Vladimír Slamka	SLV	145
7. Manuel Vieira da Silva	POR	122
8. George Leary	CAN	121

Michael Diamond was a 24-year-old liquor store clerk from Goulburn. Lakatos and Bade, who engaged in an extended shootout for the silver medal, were longtime friends and training partners. Marcello Tittarelli of Italy shot a perfect 150 in Suhl, Germany, on June 11, but could do no better than 20th place at the Olympics six weeks later.

2000 Sydney C: 41, N: 29, D: 9.17. WR: 150 (Marcello Tittarelli)

		PTS.
1. Michael Diamond	AUS	147
2. Ian Peel	GBR	142
3. Giovanni Pellielo	ITA	140
4. Khaled Al-Mudhaf	KUW	139
5. Marco Venturini	ITA	138/5
6. David Kostelecký	CZE	138/4
7. Danilo Caro Guarnieri	COL	115
8. Christophe Vicard	FRA	115

Michael Diamond dedicated his second gold medal to his father, Lon, who coached Michael for twenty years, but died three months before the Sydney Olympics. Diamond's margin of victory was the largest since the last time the Olympics was held in Australia 44 years earlier.

2004 Athens-Markopoulo C: 35, N: 26, D: 8.15. WR: 150 (Marcello Tittarelli)

		PTS.
1. Aleksei Alypov	RUS	149
2. Giovanni Pellielo	ITA	146
3. Adam Vella	AUS	145
4. Ahmed Al-Maktoum	UAE	144
5. Lance Bade	USA	143
6. Khaled Al-Mudhaf	KUW	141
7. Francisco Boza Dibos (SMR), Francisco Boza (PER), Derek Burnett (IRL), Stéphane Clamens (FRA), Michael Diamond (AUS), Olaf Kirchstein (GER)		119

Aleksei Alypov finished the qualifying round in first place by two points, missing only one of 125 targets. He followed with a perfect final round to take the gold. Defending champion Michael Diamond almost didn't make it to Athens to defend his title because he missed the Australian Shooting Trials after his firearms license was suspended pending a trial for assaulting his girlfriend.

The charges were later dropped and Diamond won a shoot-out to make the team. However he missed six shots in the qualifying round and failed to make the final.

2008 Beijing C: 35, N: 25, D: 8.10. WR: 149 (Karsten Bindrich)

		PTS.
1. David Kostelecký	CZE	146 OR
2. Giovanni Pellielo	ITA	143
3. Aleksei Alipov	RUS	142/3
4. Michael Diamond	AUS	142/2
5. Josip Glasnović	CRO	140/2
6. Erminio Frasca	ITA	140/1
7. Karsten Bindrich	GER	119
8. Mansher Singh	IND	117
9. Erik Varga	SVK	117

The pre-competition favorite, two-time Olympic champion Michael Diamond, finished fifth in the qualifying round, two points behind defending Olympic champion Aleksei Alipov and outside medal hopeful David Kostelecký of the Czech Republic.

Competing in heavy rain, Kostelecký shot a perfect 25 targets in the final round to earn the gold medal with 146 total points, an Olympic record. Thirty-eight-year-old Giovanni Pellielo, a police officer from Vercelli, Italy, won his second consecutive silver medal, while Alipov outshot Diamond 3-2 to take bronze.

DOUBLE TRAP

Competitiors shoot from each of five stations. The saucers, 11 centimeters (4.33 inches) in diameter, are launched two at a time from one of three machines so that the shooters cannot be sure of the angle or direction of the target. The preliminary round consists of 150 targets. The top six shooters advance to the final and shoot at an additional 50 targets.

1896–1904 not held

1906 Athens C: 10, N: 4, D: 4.26.

		PTS.
1. Sidney Merlin	GBR	15
2. Anastasios Metaxas	GRE	13
3. Gerald Merlin	GBR	12
4. Ioannis Peridis	GRE/CYP	11
5. Maurice Faure	FRA	9
6. Jean Fouconnier	FRA	8
6. Vasileios Stais	GRE	8
6. Konstantinos Thanopoulos	GRE/CYP	8

Sidney and Gerald Merlin were cousins who were born in Greece and lived in Athens.

1908–1992 not held

1996 Atlanta-Wolf Creek C: 35, N: 25, D: 7.24. WR: 191 (Joshua Lakatos)

		PTS.
1. Russell Mark	AUS	189
2. Albano Pera	ITA	183/7
3. Zhang Bing	CHN	183/6
4. Park Chul-sung	KOR	183/2
5. Richard Faulds	GBR	180
6. Huang I-chien	TAI	178
7. Li Bo	CHN	138/5
8. David Alcoriza	USA	138/1

Russell Mark and Huang I-chien were tied at 141 after the preliminary round. Mark hit 48 of 50 targets in the final—three more than anyone else, while Huang scored a disastrous 37.

2000 Sydney C: 25, N: 20, D: 9.20. WR: 194.0 (Daniele Di Spigno)

		PTS.
1. Richard Faulds	GBR	187/3
2. Russell Mark	AUS	187/2
3. Fehaid Al-Deehani	KUW	186
4. Conny Persson	SWE	184
5. Roland Gerebics	HUN	180
6. Lance Bade	USA	179
7. Waldemar Schanz	GER	136
8. Marco Innocenti	ITA	135

Two Australian shooters won gold medals at the 1996 Olympics: Michael Diamond and Russell Mark. The two roomed together four years later in Sydney. On September 17, Diamond successfully defended his Olympic trap title. Three days later, Mark entered the double trap final two points ahead of Fehaid Al-Deehani, Conny Persson and Richard Faulds. Mark made his first 38 shots in the 50-shot final, but then he missed twice. Still, he had a seemingly safe lead. However, at the 23rd pair, he missed both shots and Faulds was able to force a shoot-off. Mark shot first and missed one of the two targets. With a chance to win, Faulds also missed one target. In the next round, Mark again missed one target. Given an unexpected reprieve, Faulds hit both targets and won. A month before the Olympics, Mark had invited Faulds to train with him. "I think I might have taught him too much," commented Mark ruefully.

Al-Deehani was the first Kuwaiti to earn an Olympic medal.

2004 Athens-Markopoulo C: 25, N: 19, D: 8.17. WR: 194 (Daniele Di Spigno)

		PTS.
1. Ahmed Al-Maktoum	UAE	189
2. Rajyavardhan Rathore	IND	179
3. Wang Zheng	CHN	178
4. Hu Binyuan	CHN	177/2
5. Håkan Dahlby	SWE	177/1
6. Waldemar Schanz	GER	175
7. Daniele Di Spigno	ITA	134
8. Fehaid Al-Deehani	KUW	134

Sheikh Ahmed bin Hashr Al-Maktoum, a member of Dubai's ruling family, earned the first medal of any kind for the United Arab Emirates, building a six-point lead in the qualifying round and expanding his lead in the final. Al-Maktoum did not take up the sport until the age of 34, after a successful sporting career in squash, including winning the UAE national championship. Silver medal winner Rajyavardhan Rathore, known as "Chilly" for his calm disposition, was a major in the Indian army.

2008 Beijing C: 19, N: 14, D: 8.12. WR: 194 (Daniele DiSpigno, Ronjan Sondhi)

		PTS.
1. Glenn Eller	USA	190 OR
2. Francesco D'Aniello	ITA	187
3. Hu Binyuan	CHN	184
4. Jeffrey Holguin	USA	182
5. Russell Mark	AUS	181
6. Richard Faulds	GBR	180
7. Ahmed Al-Maktoum	UAE	136/5
8. William Chetcuti	MLT	136/3

Three-time Olympian and US Army marksman Glenn Eller earned 145 points in the qualifying round, four points ahead of Italy's Francesco D'Aniello. Eller missed both his first two targets in the final round but recovered to shoot 45 of 50 final targets, win the gold medal and set an Olympic record.

D'Aniello and reigning world silver medalist Hu Binyuan both scored 46 points in the final round to round out the podium. In third place after the qualifying round, fellow US Army marksman Jeff Holguin dropped to fourth place after shooting only 42 final targets. Many athletes complained about the polluted air in Beijing, but Russell Mark was not one of them. He commented, "The smog helps us. I can see the orange disks better in the sky."

SKEET

Skeet shooting is similar to trap shooting in that the shooter, using a 12-gauge shotgun, fires at a flung four-and-a-third-inch clay saucer. However, in the skeet match, the rifle must be held at the hip until the target is launched. The birds may be thrown up to three seconds after they are called. Whereas trap birds are sent out from ground level, in skeet they are released from two towers, one high, one low. The competition begins with a 125-shot preliminary round. The shooters with the six highest scores advance to the 25-shot final. According to current rules, ties for medal positions are decided by shoot-offs.

1896–1964 not held

1968 Mexico City C: 52, N: 30, D: 10.22. WR: 198 (J. Faber, Konrad Wirnhier)

		PTS.
1. Yevgeny Petrov	SOV/RUS	198/25 EWR
2. Romano Garagnani	ITA	198/24/25 EWR
3. Konrad Wirnhier	GER	198/24/23 EWR
4. Yuri Tsuranov	SOV/RUS	196
5. Pedro Gianella Merino	PER	194
6. Nicolas Atalah	CHI	194
7. Jorge Jottar Mereb	CHI	194
8. Panagiotis Xanthakos	GRE	194

1972 Munich C: 63, N: 37, D: 9.2. WR: 200 (Yevgeny Petrov, Yuri Tsuranov)

		PTS.
1. Konrad Wirnhier	GER	195/25
2. Yevgeny Petrov	SOV/RUS	195/24
3. Michael Buchheim	GDR	195/23
4. Joseph Neville	GBR	194
5. Roberto Castrillo García	CUB	194
6. Klaus Reschke	GDR	193
7. Élie Pénot	FRA	193
8. Paskhalis "Lakis" Georgiou	GRE/CYP	192

World champion Yuri Tsuranov of the USSR was so upset by a judge's call against him that he walked off the field. The jury decided to penalize him three birds for leaving, but permitted him to continue the round. He ended, up three points shy of a tie for first place and finished ninth instead.

Ben Pons, who finished in 31st place, had already completed a successful career as a race car driver.

1976 Montreal C: 68, N: 41. D: 7.24. WR: 200 (Yevgeny Petrov, Yuri Tsuranov, Jariel Zhgentii, Hans Kjeld Rasmussen, Wieslaw Gawlikowski)

		PTS.
1. Josef Panáček	CZE	198 EOR
2. Eric Swinkels	HOL	198 EOR
3. Wiesław Gawlikowski	POL	196
4. Klaus Reschke	GDR	196
5. Franz Schitzhofer	AUT	195
6. Edgardo Zachrisson	GUA	194
7. Juan Ávalos Carballo	SPA	194
8. Jean Petitpied	FRA	194

1980 Moscow C: 46, N: 25, D: 7.26. WR: 199 (Joseph Clemmons)

		PTS.
1. Hans Kjeld Rasmussen	DEN	196/25/25
2. Lars-Göran Carlsson	SWE	196/25/24
3. Roberto Castrillo García	CUB	196/25/23
4. Pavel Pulda	CZE	196/24
5. Celso Giardini	ITA	196/24
6. Guillermo Torres Rodríguez	CUB	195
7. Francisco Pérez Giménez	SPA	195
8. Ari Westergård	FIN	195

Because too many perfect scores had been achieved, the rules were changed to make the match speedier and more difficult.

1984 Los Angeles-Chino C: 69, N: 41, D: 8.4. WR: 200 (Matthew Dryke, Jan Hula)

		PTS.
1. Matthew Dryke	USA	198 EOR
2. Ole Riber Rasmussen	DEN	196/25
3. Luca Scribani Rossi	ITA	196/23
4. Johannes Pierik	HOL	194
5. Anders Berglind	SWE	194
6. Norbert Hofmann	GER	194
7. Jorge Molina	COL	194
8. Ian Hale	AUS	193

As a teenager, Matt Dryke performed as a trick shooter, shooting through washers and shooting speed skeet while riding a unicycle. Although he never gave up trick and fancy shooting, he also became involved in competitive shooting, entering the Olympics as the world record holder and prohibitive favorite. Spurred on by an enthusiastic crowd which unnerved other competitors, Dryke did not disappoint his supporters. In 1989 Dryke received a two-year suspension when he tested positive for cocaine.

1988 Seoul C: 52, N: 31, D: 9.24. WR: 224 (Matthew Dryke, Luca Scribani Rossi, Ole Riber Rasmussen)

		PTS.
1. Axel Wegner	GDR	222
2. Alfonso de Iruarrizaga	CHI	221
3. Jorge Guardiola Hay	SPA	220/24
4. Daniel Carlisle	USA	220/23
5. Zhang Weigang	CHN	219
6. Jürgen Raabe	GDR	219
7. Luca Scribani Rossi	ITA	196
8. Firmo Emilio Roberti Buabud	ARG	196

Guardiola was awarded the bronze medal by virtue of his higher score over Carlisle in the final.

1992 Barcelona-Mollet del Vallès C: 60, N: 38, 0: 7.28. WR: 225 (Hennie Dompeling, Axel Wegner)

		PTS.
1. Zhang Shan	CHN	223
2. Juan Giha Yarur	PER	222/24/3
3. Bruno Rossetti	ITA	222/24/2/10
4. Ioan Toman	ROM	222/24/2/9
5. José María Colorado González	SPA	222/23
6. Matthew Dryke	USA	221
7. Luca Scribani Rossi	ITA	197/24
8. Erik Swinkels	HOL	197/23

Zhang Shan, a 24-year-old from Nanchong, in Sichuan province, caused a sensation when she became the first female shooter to win a mixed competition at the Olympics. Unfortunately, the International Shooting Union had already decided to bar women from future skeet competitions, so Zhang was not allowed to defend her title in 1996.

1996 Atlanta-Wolf Creek C: 54, N: 34, D: 7.26. WR: 150 (Jan-Henrik Heinrich, Andrea Benelli)

		PTS.
1. Ennio Falco	ITA	149
2. Mirosław Rzepkowski	POL	148
3. Andrea Benelli	ITA	147/6
4. Ole Riber Rasmussen	DEN	147/5
5. Nikolai Tioply	RUS	146
6. Boriss Timofejevs	LAT	145
7. Andrei Inešin	EST	121/12
8. Juan Miguel Rodríguez Martínez	CUB	121/11

Andrea Benelli equalled the world record on June 11, but it was his teammate, Ennio Falco, who was almost perfect at the Olympics. In 1988 and 1992 the Sultanate of Brunei participated in the Olympics, but sent only officials—no athletes. Sensitive to criticism that they were using the Olympics for their own pleasure, the National Olympic Committee of Brunei solved the problem by entering an athlete in the 1996 skeet event: the sultan's nephew: Prince Abdul Hakeem. Abdul Hakeem caused something of a sensation in 1993 when he reputedly sent his private jet from Glasgow to London to purchase a jar of his favorite brand of mustard. He arrived in Atlanta with two $35,000 gold-inlay Kriegoffs shotguns. He ended up in a tie for 49th place.

2000 Sydney C: 49, N: 37, D: 9.23. WR: 150 (Jan-Henrik Heinrich, Andrea Benelli)

		PTS.
1. Mykola Milchev	UKR	150
2. Petr Málek	CZE	148
3. James Graves	USA	147
4. Hennie Dompeling	HOL	146/4
5. Andrea Benelli	ITA	146/3
6. Nasser Al-Attiya	QAT	145
7. Sergey Yakshin	KAZ	122
8. Antonis Andreou	CYP	122

Mykola Milchev registered a perfect score of 125 in the qualifying round and then made every shot in the final as well.

2004 Athens-Markopoulo C: 41, N: 32, D: 8.22. WR: 150 (Valeri Shomin)

		PTS.
1. Andrea Benelli	ITA	149/5
2. Marko Kemppainen	FIN	149/4
3. Juan Miguel Rodríguez Martínez	CUB	147/10
4. Nasser Al-Attiya	QAT	147/9
5. Shawn Dulohery	USA	147/5
6. Harald Jensen	NOR	145
7. Michael Nielsen	DEN	122
8. Georgios Akhilleos (CYP), Todd Graves (USA), Mykola Milchev (UKR), Abdullah Al-Rashidi (KUW), Jan Sychra (CZE), Anthony Terras (FRA), Erik Watndal (NOR)		121

Marko Kemppainen had a perfect qualifying round, hitting all 125 targets to match the world record. Andrea Benelli, who missed one target in the qualifying round, went 25 for 25 in the final, tying Kemppainen at 149. The gold went down to a shoot-off. Both men missed one of two targets in the second round. Kemppainen missed another in the third round, but Benelli hit both to gain the victory. The bronze medal was also decided by a shoot-off.

2008 Beijing C: 41, N: 30, D: 8.16. WR: 150 (Vincent Hancock, Tore Brovold)

		PTS.
1. Vincent Hancock	USA	145/4 OR
2. Tore Brovold	NOR	145/3 OR
3. Anthony Terras	FRA	144/3
4. Antonis Nikolaidis	CYP	144/2
5. Giorgos Akhilleos	CYP	143
6. Qu Ridong	CHN	142
7. Jin Di	CHN	118
7. Juan Aramburu Amorena	SPA	118
7. Abdullah Al-Rashidi	KUW	118

One month before the Beijing Olympics Norway's Tore Brovold shot 150 points at the European Championships in Nicosia, Cyprus, equalling the world record set by Vincent Hancock in 2007.

The 19-year-old Hancock led the qualifying round with 121 points, one ahead of Brovold. Hancock hit his first 19 targets in the final round but missed the 20th, while Brovold shot clean to tie with him for first place with 145 points, an Olympic record. All three medals were decided by shoot-off, with Hancock outshooting Brovold 4-3 and Anthony Terras outshooting Antonis Nikolaidis 3-2.

Reigning world champion Giorgos Akhilleos finished fifth, while defending Olympic champion Andrea Benelli scored only 113 points in the preliminary round and failed to qualify for the final.

DISCONTINUED EVENTS

MILITARY REVOLVER

1896 Athens C: 16, N: 4, D: 4.10.
(25 Meters)

		PTS.
1. John Paine	USA	442
2. Sumner Paine	USA	380
3. Nikolaos Dorakis	GRE	205
4. Ioannis Frangoudis	GRE	—
5. Holger Nielsen	DEN	—

The Paine brothers set a precedent for family involvement in the Olympics by taking first and second.

1900–1904 not held

1906 Athens C: 31, N:9, D: 4.24.
(20 Meters)

		PTS.
1. Louis Richardet	SWI	253
2. Alexandros Theofilakis	GRE	250
3. Georgios Skotadis	GRE	240
4. Konrad Stäheli	SWI	240
5. Léon Moreaux	FRA	239
6. Ludwig Ternajgo	AUT	235
7. Matthias Triantafilades	GRE	235
8. Anastasios Metaxas	GRE	233

1906 Athens C: 31, N: 9, D: 4.23.
(20 Meters—Model 1873—74)

		PTS.
1. Jean Fouconnier	FRA	219
2. Raoul de Boigne	FRA	216
3. Hermann Martin	FRA	215
4. Maurice Lecoq	FRA	211
5. Ludwig Ternajgo	AUT	208
6. Aristides Rangavis	GRE	201
7. Louis Richardet	SWI	199
8. Aristides Kronis	GRE	198

The 1906 contest required the use of a Gras-type revolver first made in France in 1873.

FREE PISTOL, TEAM

1900 Paris T: 4, N: 4, D: 8.1.
(50 Meters)

	TOTAL PTS.
1. SWI—C. Karl Röderer, Konrad Stäheli, Louis Richardet, Friedrich Lüthi, Paul Probst	2271
2. FRA—Achille Paroche, Louis Duffoy, Léon Moreaux, Trinité, Maurice Lecoq	2203
3. HOL—Dirk Boest Gips, Henrik Sillem, Antoine Bouwens, Solko van den Bergh, Anthony Sweijs	1876
4. BEL—Alban Rooman, Émile Thèves, Victor Robert, Pierre Eichhorn, Charles Lebègue	1823

1904–1906 not held

1908 London T: 7, N: 7, D: 7.11.
(50 Yards)

	TOTAL PTS.
1. USA—James Gorman, Irving Calkins, John Dietz, Charles Axtell	1914
2. BEL—Paul Van Asbroeck, Réginald Storms, Charles Paumier du Verger, René Englebert	1863
3. GBR—Jesse Wallingford, Geoffrey Coles, Henry Lynch-Staunton, Walter Ellicott	1817
4. FRA—André Barbillat, André Regaud, Léon Moreaux, Jean Depassis	1750
5. SWE—Vilhelm Carlberg, Eric Carlberg, Johan Hübner von Holst, Frans-Albert Schartau	1732
6. HOL—Jacob van der Kop, Gerard van den Bergh, Jan Johannes de Blécourt, Petrus ten Bruggen Cate	1632
7. GRE—Frangiskos Mavrommatis, Alexandros Theofilakis, Ioannis Theofilakis, Georgios Orfanidis	1576

1920 Antwerp-Beverloo T: 13, N: 13, D: 8.2.
(50 Meters)

	TOTAL PTS.
1. USA—Karl Frederick, Alfred Lane, James Snook, Michael Kelly, Raymond Bracken	2372
2. SWE—Anders Andersson, Casimir Reuterskiöld, Gunnar Gabrielsson, Sigvard Hultcrantz, Anders Johnson	2289
3. BRA—Afrânio da Costa, Guilherme Parãense, , Sebastião Wolf, Dario Barbosa, Fernando Soledade	2264
4. GRE—Iason Sappas, Ioannis Theofilakis, Alexandros Theofilakis, Georgios Moraitinis, Alexandros Vrasivanopoulos	2240
5. BEL—Paul Van Asbroeck, Conrad Adriaenssens, Arthur Balbaert, Joseph Haesaerts, François Heyens	2229
6. FRA—Joseph Pecchia, Jules Maujean, Léon Johnson, Émile Boitout, André Regaud	2225
7. ITA—Riccardo Ticchi, Alfredo Galli, Roberto Preda, Giancarlo Boriani, Raffaele Frasca	2224
8. DEN—Niels Larsen, Lars Jørgen Madsen, Otto Plantener, Carl Pedersen, Christian Andersen	2159

The targets were supposed to be 50 meters from the shooting line. However, after each participant had taken fifteen shots it was discovered that the Brazilians' targets were only 45 meters away, while the US shooters were 54 meters away from their targets. Both teams started over.

Dr. James H. Snook of the gold-medal-winning US team gained national notoriety in June of 1929 after he was arrested for first-degree murder. Snook, then a 48-year-old professor of veterinary medicine at Ohio State University, confessed to killing his 25-year-old mistress, Theora Hix, by beating her with a hammer following an overly violent sexual act that took place at the local rifle range. He was put to death in an electric chair eight months later.

MILITARY REVOLVER, TEAM

1912 Stockholm T: 5, N: 5, D: 7.2.
(50 Meters)

	TOTAL PTS.
1. USA—Alfred Lane, Henry Sears, Peter Dolfen, John Dietz	1916
2. SWE—Georg de Laval, Eric Carlberg, Vilhelm Carlberg, Erik Boström	1849
3. GBR—Horatio Poulter, Hugh Durant, Albert Kempster, Charles Stewart	1804
4. RUS—Nikolai Panin [Kolomenkin], Grigory Shesterikov, Pavel Voyloshnikov, Nikolai Melnitsky	1801
5. GRE—Frangiskos Mavrommatis, Ioannis Theofilakis, Konstantinos Skarlatos, Alexandros Theofilakis	1731

MILITARY PISTOL, TEAM

1920 Antwerp-Beverloo T: 9, N: 9, D: 8.3.
(30 Meters)

	TOTAL PTS.
1. USA—Louis Harant, Alfred Lane, Karl Frederick, James Snook, Michael Kelly	1310
2. GRE—Alexandros Theofilakis, Ioannis Theofilakis, Georgios Moraitinis, Alexandros Vrasivanopoulos, Iason Sappas	1285
3. SWI—Fritz Zulauf, Joseph Jehle, Gustave Amoudruz, Hans Egli, Domenico Giambonini	1270
4. BRA—Guilherme Parãense, Afrânio da Costa, Sebastião Wolf, Dario Barbosa, Fernando Soledade	1261
5. FRA—Joseph Pecchia, Jules Maujean, Léon Johnson, Émile Boitout, André Regaud	1239
6. SPA—José Benito López, Luis Calvet Sandoz, Antonio Bonilla Sanmartín, Antonio Vásquez de Aldana, José María Miró Trepat	1224
7. BEL—Paul Van Asbroeck, Norbert Van Molle, Philippe Cammaerts, Robert Andrieux, Joseph Bastin, Léon Louis de Coster	1221
8. POR—Herminio Rebelo, António Dos Santos, António Damiao, António da Silva Martins, Dario Cannas	1184

DUELING PISTOL

1906 Athens C: 24, N; 7, D: 4.24.
(20 Meters)

		PTS.
1. Léon Moreaux	FRA	242
2. Cesare Liverziani	ITA	233
3. Maurice Lecoq	FRA	231
4. Konstantinos Skarlatos	GRE	221
5. Ludwig Ternajgo	AUT	218
6. Frangiskos Mavrommatis	GRE	214
7. Aristides Rangavis	GRE	214
8. Jean Fouconnier	FRA	210

The participants in the two dueling pistol events of 1906 shot at dummies dressed in frock coats. The bulls-eye was the middle of the thorax.

DUELING PISTOL, TEAM

1912 Stockholm T: 7, N: 7, D: 6.29, 7.3.

(30 Meters)

	TOTAL PTS.
1. SWE—Vilhelm Carlberg, Eric Carlberg, Johan Hübner von Holst, Paul Palén	120/1145
2. RUS—Amos Kash, Nikolai Melnitsky, Pavel Voyloshnikov, Georgi Panteleymonov	118/1091
3. GBR—Hugh Durant, Albert Kempster, Charles Stewart, Horatio Poulter	117/1107
4. USA—Alfred Lane, Reginald Sayre, Walter Winans, John Dietz	117/1097
5. GRE—Konstantinos Skarlatos, Ioannis Theofilakis, Frangiskos Mavrommatis, Georgios Petropoulos	115/1057
6. FRA—Edmond Sandoz, Charles de Jaubert, Georges de Créqui-Montfort de Courtivron, Maurice Faure	113/1041
7. GER—Bernhard Wandolleck, Gerhard Bock, Georg Meyer, Heinrich Hoffmann	102/ 890

FREE RIFLE

1896 Athens C: 20, N: 3, D: 4.12.

(300 meters)

		PTS.
1. Georgios Orfanidis	GRE	1583
2. Ioannis Frangoudis	GRE	1312
3. Viggo Jensen	DEN	1305
4. Anastasios Metaxas	GRE	1102
5. Pantelis Karasevdas	GRE	1039

1900 Paris C: 30, N: 6, D: 8.5.

(300 Meters, Three Positions)

		PRONE	KNEELING	STANDING	TOTAL PTS.
1. Emil Kellenberger	SWI	324	314	292	930
2. Anders Peter Nielsen	DEN	330	314	277	921
3. Paul Van Asbroeck	BEL	329	289	299	917
3. Ole Østmo	NOR	312	308	297	917
5. Lars Jørgen Madsen	DEN	301	299	305	905
6. Charles Paumier du Verger	BEL	302	297	298	897
7. Achille Paroche	FRA	332	287	268	887
8. Franz Böckli	SWI	289	300	294	883

(300 Meters, Standing)

		PTS.
1. Lars Jørgen Madsen	DEN	305
2. Ole Østmo	NOR	299
3. Charles Paumier du Verger	BEL	298
4. Paul Van Asbroeck	BEL	297
5. Franz Böckli	SWI	294
6. Emil Kellenberger	SWI	292
7. Jules Bury	BEL	282
7. Alfred Grütter	SWI	282

(300 Meters, Kneeling)

		PTS.
1. Konrad Stäheli	SWI	324
2. Emil Kellenberger	SWI	314
2. Anders Peter Nielsen	DEN	314
4. Paul Van Asbroeck	BEL	308
5. Maximiliaan Ravenswaaij	HOL	306
6. Uilke Vuurman	HOL	303
7. Franz Böckli	SWI	300
8. Lars Jørgen Madsen	DEN	299

(300 Meters, Prone)

		PTS.
1. Achille Paroche	FRA	332
2. Anders Peter Nielsen	DEN	330
3. Ole Østmo	NOR	329
4. Léon Moreaux	FRA	325
5. Emil Kellenberger	SWI	324
6. Henrik Sillem	HOL	317
7. Auguste Cavadini	FRA	316
8. Paul Van Asbroeck	BEL	312
8. Uilke Vuurman	HOL	312

1904 not held

1906 Athens C: 35, N: 9, D: 4.28.

(300 Meters, Any Position)

		PTS.
1. Marcel Meyer de Stadelhofen	SWI	243
2. Konrad Stäheli	SWI	238
3. Léon Moreaux	FRA	234
4. Gudbrand Skatteboe	NOR	230
5. Albert Helgerud	NOR	230
6. Julius Braathe	NOR	224
7. Raoul de Boigne	FRA	224
8. Jean Fouconnier	FRA	223

1908 London C: 49, N: 8, D: 7.9.

(1000 Yards)

		PTS.
1. Joshua "Jerry" Millner	GBR/IRL	98
2. Kellogg Casey	USA	93
3. Maurice Blood	GBR/IRL	92
4. Richard Barnett	GBR/IRL	92
5. Thomas "Ted" Ranken	GBR	92
6. Thomas Caldwell	GBR	91
6. S. Harry Kerr	CAN	91
6. John Sellars	GBR/IRL	91

The target for this long-range event was six feet by ten feet, with a 36-inch bull's-eye. At 61, Colonel Millner remains the oldest winner of an individual event in any sport in Olympic history. Millner devoted much of his life to breeding red setters and in 1924 published the book *The Irish Setter, its History and Training.*

FREE RIFLE, THREE POSITIONS

This event required 120 shots from 300 meters at a 39-inch target with a bull's-eye less than four inches in diameter. In other words, it was like shooting a bullet through an apple three football fields away.

1908 London C: 51, N: 10, D: 7.11. WR: 1004 (Charles Paumier de Verger)

		PRONE	KNEELING	STANDING	TOTAL PTS.
1. Albert Helgerud	NOR	340	292	277	909
2. Harry Simon	USA	365	294	228	887
3. Ole Sæther	NOR	327	284	272	883
4. Gustav-Adolf Sjöberg	SWE	338	285	251	874
5. Johan "Janne" Gustafsson	SWE	324	283	265	872
6. Julius Braathe	NOR	303	291	257	851
7. Axel Jansson	SWE	312	296	235	843
8. Léon Johnson	FRA	303	282	250	835

1912 Stockholm C. 84, N: 9, D: 7.2. WR: 1078 (Konrad Stäheli)

		PRONE	KNEELING	STANDING	TOTAL PTS.
1. Paul Colas	FRA	362	342	283	987
2. Lars Jørgen Madsen	DEN	330	333	318	981
3. Niels Larsen	DEN	355	334	273	962
4. Carl Hugo Johansson	SWE	341	326	292	959
5. Gudbrand Skatteboe	NOR	343	308	305	956
6. Bernhard Larsson	SWE	341	339	274	954
7. Albert Helgerud	NOR	354	317	281	952
8. Tonnes Björkman	SWE	340	322	285	947

1920 Antwerp-Beverloo C: 70, N: 14, D: 7.31. WR: 1078 (Konrad Stäheli)

		PRONE	KNEELING	STANDING	TOTAL PTS.
1. Morris Fisher	USA	347	361	288	996
2. Niels Larsen	DEN	328	341	320	989
3. Østen Østensen	NOR	347	324	309	980
4. Carl Osburn	USA	353	347	280	980
5. Gudbrand Skatteboe	NOR	351	330	294	975
5. Lloyd Spooner	USA	341	328	306	975
7. Mauritz Eriksson	SWE	347	333	294	974
7. Voitto Kolho	FIN	357	316	301	974

Sergeant Morris Fisher, who played the violin for relaxation, found himself too nervous to take the first shot in the standing position. After 20 minutes of standing at the firing line, aiming but not taking a shot, his coach ordered him to shoot even if he missed the target. Fisher shot wide but within the scoring rings, and then went on to win the match.

Most of the shooters actually used a seated position for the kneeling portion of the competition.

1924 Paris C: 73, N: 19, D: 6.27.
(600 Meters)

		PTS.
1. Morris Fisher	USA	95
2. Carl Osburn	USA	95
3. Niels Larsen	DEN	93
4. Walter Stokes	USA	92
5. Ludovic Augustin	HAI	91
6. Albert Courquin	FRA	90
6. Ludovic Valborge	HAI	90
8. Carl Hugo Johansson	SWE	88

Fisher earned two gold medals in 1924 to go with the three he had won in 1920.

1928–1936 not held

1948 London C: 46, N: 13, D: 8.6. WR: 1124 (E. Kivistik)

		PRONE	KNEELING	STANDING	TOTAL PTS.
1. Emil Grünig	SWI	390	375	355	1120
2. Pauli Janhonen	FIN	387	376	351	1114
3. Willy Rögeberg	NOR	382	373	357	1112
4. Kurt Johansson	SWE	383	374	347	1104
5. Kullervo Leskinen	FIN	389	368	346	1103
6. Olavi Elo	FIN	379	359	357	1095
7. Halvor Kongsjorden	NOR	384	373	336	1093
8. Holger Erbén	SWE	380	367	344	1091

1952 Helsinki C 32, N: 18, D: 7.27. WR: 1124 (E. Kivistik)

		PRONE	KNEELING	STANDING	TOTAL PTS.
1. Anatoly Bogdanov	SOV/RUS	388	376	359	1123 OR
2. Robert Bürchler	SWI	389	381 WR	350	1120
3. Lev Vainshtein	SOV/RUS	378	376	355	1109
4. August Hollenstein	SWI	384	370	354	1108
5. Vilho Ylönen	FIN	379	377	351	1107
6. Robert Sandager	USA	384	371	349	1104
7. Holger Erbén	SWE	347	376	379	1102
8. Walther Fröstell	SWE	335	375	389	1099

1956 Melbourne C: 20, N: 14, D: 12.1. WR: 1143 (Anatoly Bogdanov)

		PRONE	KNEELING	STANDING	TOTAL PTS.
1. Vasily Borissov	SOV/RUS	396 WR	383	359	1138 OR
2. Allan Erdman	SOV/RUS	392	385	360	1137
3. Vilho Ylönen	FIN	387	382	359	1128
4. Jorma Taitto	FIN	392	379	349	1120
5. Constantin Antonescu	ROM	386	374	341	1101
6. Nils Johan Sundberg	SWE	384	367	343	1094
7. Anders Kvissberg	SWE	389	362	342	1093
8. James Smith	USA	381	368	333	1082

1960 Rome C: 39, N: 22, D: 9.5. WR: 1145 (Anatoly Bogdanov)

		PRONE	KNEELING	STANDING	TOTAL PTS.
1. Hubert Hammerer	AUT	390	379	360	1129
2. Hans Spillman	SWI	397	377	353	1127
3. Vasily Borissov	SOV/RUS	383	381	363	1127
4. Vilho Ylönen	FIN	389	381	356	1126
5. Moisei Itkis	SOV/UKR	380	379	365	1124
6. Vladimír Stibořík	CZE	383	380	360	1123
7. John Foster	USA	380	384	357	1121
8. Sándor Krebs	HUN	386	373	359	1118

1964 Tokyo C: 30, N: 18, D: 10.15. WR: 1150 (August Hollenstein)

		PRONE	KNEELING	STANDING	TOTAL PTS.
1. Gary Anderson	USA	382	384	377	1153 WR
2. Shota Kveliashvili	SOV/GEO	389	389	366	1144
3. Martin Gunnarsson	USA	389	380	367	1136
4. Aleksandrs Gerasimjonoks	SOV/LAT	396	376	363	1135
5. August Hollenstein	SWI	382	381	372	1135
6. Esa Kervinen	FIN	392	383	358	1133
7. Kurt Müller	SWI	392	385	354	1121
8. Harry Köcher	GDR	392	378	360	1130

Gary Anderson was a theological student from Axtell, Nebraska.

1968 Mexico City C: 30, N: 16, D: 10.23. WR: 1156 (Gary Anderson)

		PRONE	KNEELING	STANDING	TOTAL PTS.
1. Gary Anderson	USA	394	389	374	1157 WR
2. Vladimir Kornev	SOV/RUS	398 WR	384	369	1151
3. Kurt Müller	SWI	395	379	374	1148
4. Shota Kveliashvili	SOV/GEO	394	383	365	1142
5. Erwin Vogt	SWI	398 WR	384	358	1140
6. Hartmut Sommer	GER	389	384	358	1140
7. John Foster	USA	386	386	368	1140
8. Péter Sándor	HUN	394	376	368	1138

Anderson, by now a 29-year-old army lieutenant and Presbyterian minister, told reporters that he intended to keep up his involvement in shooting "because I think it's important for a minister to be actively involved in what people are doing." He later became executive director of the National Rifle Association.

1972 Munich C: 33, N: 20, D: 9.2. WR: 1157 (Gary Anderson)

		PRONE	KNEELING	STANDING	TOTAL PTS.
1. Lones Wigger	USA	394	382	379 WR	1155
2. Borys Melnyk	SOV/UKR	394	387	374	1155
3. Lajos Papp	HUN	394	391	364	1149
4. Uto Wunderlich	GDR	393	388	368	1149
5. Karel Bulan	CZE	394	382	370	1146
6. Jaakko Minkkinen	FIN	396	386	364	1146
7. Lanny Bassham	USA	389	387	368	1144
8. Valentin Kornev	SOV/RUS	391	387	365	1143

FREE RIFLE, THREE POSITIONS, TEAM

1900 Paris T: 6, N: 6, D: 8.5.
(300 Meters)

	TOTAL PTS.
1. SWI—Emil Kellenberger, Franz Böckli, Konrad Stäheli, Louis Richardet, Alfred Grütter	4399
2. NOR—Ole Østmo, Hellmer Hermandsen, Tom Seeberg, Ole Sæther, Olaf Frydenlund	4290
3. FRA—Achille Paroche, Léon Moreaux, Auguste Cavadini, Maurice Lecoq, René Thomas	4278
4. DEN—Anders Nielsen, Lars Jørgen Madsen, Viggo Jensen, Laurids Worslund Jensen-Kjaer, Axel Kristensen	4265
5. HOL—Marcus Ravenswaaij, Uilke Vuurman, Henrik Sillem, Antonius Bouwens, Solko van den Bergh	4221
6. BEL—Paul Van Asbroeck, Charles Paumier du Verger, Jules Bury, Edouard Myin, Joseph Baras	4166

1906 Athens T: 4, N: 4, D: 4.28.
(300 Meters)

	TOTAL PTS.
1. SWI—Konrad Stäheli, Jean Reich, Louis Richardet, Marcel Meyer de Stadelhofen, Alfred Grütter	4617
2. NOR—Gudbrand Skatteboe, Julius Braathe, Albert Helgerud, John Møller, Ole Holm	5055
3. FRA—Léon Moreaux, Maurice Lecoq, Raoul de Boigne, Jean Fouconnier, Maurice Faure	4511

1908 London T: 9, N: 9, D: 7.11.
(300 Meters)

	Total Pts.
1. NOR	5055
2. SWE	4711
3. FRA	4652
4. DEN	4543
5. BEL	4509
6. GBR	4355
7. HOL	4130
B. FIN	3962

1. NOR—Albert Helgerud, Ole Sæther, Gudbrand Skatteboe, Olaf Sæther, Julius Braathe, Einar Liberg
2. SWE—Gustaf Adolf Jonsson, Per-Olaf Àrvidsson, Axel Jansson, Gustav-Adolf Sjöberg, Claës Rundberg, Johan "Janne" Gustafsson
3. FRA—Léon Johnson, Eugène Balme, André Parmentier, Albert Courquin, Maurice Lecoq, Raoul de Boigne
4. DEN—Niels Andersen, Lars Jørgen Madsen, Ole Olsen, Christian Christensen, Christian Petersen, Hans Christian Schultz
5. BEL—Charles Paumier du Verger, Paul Van Asbroeck, Ernest Ista, Henri Sauveur, Joseph Geens, Edouard Poty
6. GBR—Jesse Wallingford, Harold Hawkins, Charles Churcher, Thomas Raddall, John Bostock, Robert Brown
7. HOL—Gerard van den Bergh, Christiaan Brosch, Cornelis van Altenburg, Antoine de Gee, Uilke Vuurman, Pieter Brussaard

B. FIN—Frans Nässling, Gustaf Nyman, Heikki Huttunen, Voitto Kolko, Emil Nassling, Huvi Tuiskunen

1912 Stockholm T: 7, N: 7, D: 7.4.
(300 Meters)

	Total Pts.
1. SWE	5655
2. NOR	5605
3. DEN	5529
4. FRA	5471
5. FIN	5323
6. SAF	4897
7. RUS	4892

1. SWE—Mauritz Eriksson, Carl Hugo Johansson, Erik Blomqvist, Carl Björkman, Bernhard Larsson, Gustaf Adolf Jonsson
2. NOR—Gudbrand Skatteboe, Ole Sæther, Østen Østensen, Albert Helgerud, Olaf Sæther, Elnar Liberg
3. DEN—Ole Olsen, Lars Jørgen Madsen, Niels Larsen, Niels Andersen, Laurits Larsen, Jens Madsen Hajslund
4. FRA—Paul Colas, Louis Percy, Léon Johnson, Pierre Gentil, Raoul de Boigne, Auguste Marion
5. FIN—Voitto Kolho, Heikki Huttunen, Gustaf "Kustaa" Nyman, Emil Holm, Huvi Tuiskunen, Vilho Vauhkonen
6. SAF—George Harvey, Robert Bodley, Robert Patterson, Arthur Smith, Ernest Keeley, George Whelan
7. RUS—Pavel Valdayne, Teotan Lebedev, Alexander Tillo, Konstantin Kalinin, Dmitri Kuskov, Pavel Leche

1920 Antwerp-Beverloo T: 14, N: 14, D: 7.31.
(300 Meters)

	Total Pts.
1. USA	4876
2. NOR	4748
3. SWI	4698
4. FIN	4668
5. DEN	4644
6. SWE	4591
7. FRA	4487
8. HOL	4383

1. USA—Morris Fisher, Carl Osburn, Lloyd Spooner, Willis Lee, Dennis Fenton
2. NOR—Østen Østensen, Gudbrand Skatteboe, Albert Helgerud, Olaf Sletten, Otto Olsen
3. SWI—Fritz Kuchen, Gustave Amoudruz, Werner Schneeberger, Ulrich Fahrner, Bernhard Siegenthaler
4. FIN—Voitto Kolho, Vilho Vauhkonen, Kalle Lappalainen, Veil Nieminen, Magnus Wegelius
5. DEN—Niels Larsen, Lars Jørgen Madsen, Peter Geltzer Petersen, Niels Laursen, Anton Andersen
6. SWE—Mauritz Eriksson, Carl Hugo Johansson, Erik Blomqvist, Viktor Knutsson, Leon Lagerlöf
7. FRA—Achille Paroche, Georges Roes, André Parmentier, Paul Colas, Albert Regnier
8. HOL—Gerard van den Bergh, Antoine Bouwens, Jan Brussaard, Hermanus Bouwens, Cornelis van Dalen

1924 Paris T: 18, N: 18, D: 6.27.
(400+600+800 Meters)

	Total Pts.
1. USA	676
2. FRA	646
3. HAI	646
4. SWI	635
5. FIN	628
6. DEN	626
7. SWE	623
8. NOR	594

1. USA—Morris Fisher, Walter Stokes, Joseph Crockett, Raymond "Chan" Coulter, Sidney Hinds
2. FRA—Emile Rumeau, Albert Courquin, Pierre Hardy, Georges Roes, Paul Colas
3. HAI—Ludovic Augustin, Astrel Rolland, Ludovic Valborge, Destin Destine, Eloi Metullus
4. SWI—Jakob Reich, Arnold Rösli, Willy Schnyder, Conrad Stucheli, Albert Tröndle
5. FIN—Aarne Valkama, Vilho Nieminen, Voitto Kolho, Heikki Huttunen, Johannes Theslöf
6. DEN—Niels Larsen, Lars Jörgen Madsen, Anders Nielsen, Erik Saetter-Lassen, Peter Geltzer Petersen
7. SWE—Carl Hugo Johansson, Ivar Wester, Mauritz Eriksson, Olle Ericsson, Gustaf Anderson
8. NOR—Ludvig Larsen, Olaf Johansson, Willy Rogeberg, Halvard Angaard, Otto Olsen

France defeated Haiti in the shoot-off for second place. Lieutenant Sidney Hinds shot a perfect 50 for the US team, a performance that was all the more remarkable considering that he was accidentally shot in the foot in the middle of the competition, when the Belgian rifleman beside him knocked his rifle to the ground in the midst of an argument with an official.

MILITARY RIFLE

1896 Athens C: 42, N: 7, D: 4.9.
(200 Meters)

		PTS.
1. Pantelis Karasevdas	GRE	2320
2. Paulos Pavlidis	GRE	1978
3. Nikolaos Trikoupes	GRE	1713
4. Anastasios Metaxas	GRE	1701
5. Georgios Orfanidis	GRE	1698
6. Viggo Jensen	DEN	1640
7. Georgios Diamantis	GRE	1456
8. Albert Baumann	SWI	1294

1900–1904 not held

1906 Athens C: 31, N: 8, D: 4.24.
(200 Meters, Standing or Kneeling: 1873-1874 Gras Model)

		PTS.
1. Léon Moreaux	FRA	187
2. Louis Richardet	SWI	187
3. Jean Reich	SWI	183
4. John Møller	NOR	175
5. Maurice Faure	FRA	173
6. Gerald Merlin	GBR	169
7. Sidney Merlin	GBR	166
8. Georgios Orfanidis	GRE	165

1906 Athens C: 46, N: 11, D: 4.23.
(300 Meters, Standing or Kneeling)

		PTS.
1. Louis Richardet	SWI	238
2. Jean Reich	SWI	234
3. Raoul de Boigne	FRA	232
4. Léon Moreaux	FRA	231
5. Maurice Lecoq	FRA	224
6. Julius Braathe	NOR	223
7. Marcel Meyer de Stadelhofen	SWI	222
8. Gudbrand Skatteboe	NOR	221

1908 not held

1912 Stockholm C: 91, N: 12, D: 7.1.
(300 Meters, Three Positions)

		PTS.
1. Sándor Prokopp	HUN/SLV	97
2. Carl Osburn	USA	95/99
3. Embret Skogen	NOR	95/91
4. Nicolaos Levidis	GRE	95/70
5. Nils Romander	SWE	94
6. Arthur Fulton	GBR	92
7. Rezső Velez	HUN	92
8. Carl Flodström	SWE	91

1912 Stockholm C: 85, N: 12, D: 7.1.
(600 Meters, Any Position)

		PTS.
1. Paul Colas	FRA	94/91
2. Carl Osburn	USA	94/90
3. John Jackson	USA	93/90
4. Allan Briggs	USA	93/89
5. Phillip Plater	GBR	90
6. Verner Jernström	SWE	88
7. Harcourt Ommundsen	GBR	88
8. Charles Burdette	USA	87

1920 Antwerp-Beverloo C: 49, N: 12, D: 7.29–30.
(300 Meters, Prone)

		PTS.
1. Otto Olsen	NOR	60
2. Léon Johnson	FRA	59/58
3. Fritz Kuchen	SWI	59/57
4. Vilho Vauhkonen	FIN	59/56
5. Achille Paroche	FRA	59/56
6. Erik Blomqvist	SWE	58
6. Mauritz Eriksson	SWE	58
6. Albert Helgerud	NOR	58
6. Carl Hugo Johansson	SWE	58
6. Olaf Sletten	NOR	58
6. Lloyd Spooner	USA	58

1920 Antwerp-Beverloo C: 48, N: 12, D: 7.29–30.
(300 Meters, Standing)

		PTS.
1. Carl Osburn	USA	56
2. Lars Jørgen Madsen	DEN	55
3. Lawrence Nuesslein	USA	54/56
4. Erik Sætter-Lassen	DEN	54/52
5. Joseph Janssens	BEL	54/47
6. Riccardo Ticchi	ITA	54/44
7. Anders Peter Nielsen	DEN	53
7. Anders Petersen	DEN	53
7. Lloyd Spooner	USA	53

1920 Antwerp-Beverloo C: 46, N: 11, D: 7.29–30.
(600 Meters, Prone)

		PTS.
1. Carl Hugo Johansson	SWE	59/58
2. Mauritz Eriksson	SWE	59/56/6
3. Lloyd Spooner	USA	59/56/5
4. Ioannis Theofilakis	GRE	59/55
5. Erik Blomqvist	SWE	58
5. Joseph Jackson	USA	58
5. Olaf Sletten	NOR	58
8. Povl Gerlow	DEN	57
8. Joseph Lawless	USA	57
8. Erik Ohlsson	SWE	57

MILITARY RIFLE, TEAM

1908 London T: 8, N: 8, D: 7.11.
(200 +500 +600 +800 +900 +1000 Yards)

	Total Pts.
1. USA	2531
2. GBR	2497
3. CAN	2439
4. FRA	2227
5. SWE	2213
6. NOR	2192
7. GRE	1999
8. DEN	1909

1. USA—William Leushner, William Martin, Charles Winder, Kellogg Casey, Albert Eastman, Charles Benedict
2. GBR—Harcourt Ommundsen, Fleetwood Varley, Arthur Fulton, Philip Richardson, William Padgett, John Martin
3. CAN—William Smith, Charles Crowe, Bruce Williams, Dugald McInnes, William Eastcott, S. Harry Kerr
4. FRA—Raoul de Boigne, Albert Courquin, Eugène Balme, Daniel Merillon, Léon Hecht, André Parmentier
5. SWE—Claës Rundberg, Ossian Jörgensen, Johan "Janne" Gustafsson, Per-Olof Arvidsson, Axel Jansson, Gustaf Adolf Jonsson
6. NOR—Ole Sæther, Einar Liberg, Gudbrand Skatteboe, Albert Helgerud, Mathias Glomnes, Jørgen Bruu
7. GRE—Ioannis Theofilakis, Frangiskos Mavrommatis, Alexandros Theofilakis, Georgios Orfanidis, Mathias Triantarilades, Deukalion Rediadis
8. DEN—Niels Andersen, Christian Christensen, Lorents Jensen, Niels Laursen, Julius Hillemann-Jensen, Ole Olsen

The Russians had sent word that they were going to enter a team, but when they finally arrived the competition was long over. It turned out that Russia was still operating on the Julian calendar, whereas the rest of the world was using the Gregorian calendar; the two calendars were 13 days apart.

1912 Stockholm T: 10, N: 10, D: 6.29.
(200 +400 +500 +600 Meters)

	Total Pts.
1. USA	1687
2. GBR	1602
3. SWE	1570
4. SAF	1531
5. FRA	1515
6. NOR	1473
7. GRE	1445
8. DEN	1419

1. USA—Cornelius Burdette, Allan Briggs, Harry Adams, John Jackson, Carl Osburn, Warren Sprout
2. GBR—Harcourt Ommundsen, Henry Burr, Edward Skilton, James Reid, Edward Parnell, Arthur Fulton
3. SWE—Mauritz Eriksson, Verner Jernström, Carl Björkman, Tönnes Björkman, Bernhard Larsson, C. Hugo Johansson
4. SAF—George Harvey, Robert Bodley, Arthur Smith, Ernest Keeley, Charles Jeffreys, Robert Patterson
5. FRA—Louis Percy, Paul Colas, Raoul de Boigne, Pierre Gentil, Léon Johnson, Maxime Landin
6. NOR—Ole Christian Degnes, Arne Sunde, Ole Jensen, Hans Nordvik, Olav Husby, Mathias Glomnes
7. GRE—Frangiskos Mavrommatis, Alexandros Theofilakis, Ioannis Theofilakis, Nikolaos Levidis, Iakovos Theofilas, Spiridon Mostras
8. DEN—Niels Andersen, Lars Jørgen Madsen, Hans Schultz, Niels Larsen, Jens Madsen Hajslund, Rasmus Friis

1920 Antwerp-Beverloo T: 15, N: 15, D: 7.29.
(300 Meters, Standing)

	Total Pts.
1. DEN	266
2. USA	255
3. SWE	255
4. ITA	251
5. FRA	249
6. NOR	242
7. FIN	235
8. SW	234

1. DEN—Erik Sætter-Lassen, Lars Jørgen Madsen, Anders Petersen, Anders Peter Nielsen, Niels Larsen
2. USA—Lawrence Nuesslein, Carl Osburn, Lloyd Spooner, Willis Lee, Thomas Brown

3. SWE—Olle Ericsson, Walfrid Hellman, Mauritz Eriksson, Carl Hugo Johansson, Leonard Lagerlöf
4. ITA—Riccardo Ticchi, Camillo Isnardi, Luigi Favretti, Giancarlo Boriani, Sem De Ranieri
5. FRA—Léon Johnson, Achille Paroche, Émile Rumeau, André Parmentier, Georges Roes
6. NOR—Østen Østensen, Otto Olsen, Olaf Sletten, Albert Helgerud, Gudbrand Skatteboe
7. FIN—Kalle Lapalainen, Vilho Vauhkonen, Magnus Wegelius, Voitto Kolho, Nestori Toivonen
8. SWI—Fritz Kuchen, Albert Tröndle, Arnold Rösli, Walter Lienhard, Caspar Widmer

1920 Antwerp-Beverloo T: 15, N: 15, D: 7.29.

(300 Meters, Prone)

	Total Pts.
1. USA	289
2. FRA	283
3. FIN	281
4. SWI	281
5. SWE	281
6. NOR	280
7. SPA	278
8. SAF	276

1. USA—Carl Osburn, Lloyd Spooner, Morris Fisher, Willis Lee, Joseph Jackson
2. FRA—Léon Johnson, Achille Paroche, Émile Rumeau, André Parmentier, Georges Roes
3. FIN—Vilho Vauhkonen, Kalle Lappalainen, Veli Nieminen, Magnus Wegelius, Voitto Kolho
4. SWI—Fritz Kuchen, Albert Tröndle, Arnold Rösli, Walter Lienhard, Caspar Widmer
5. SWE—C. Hugo Johansson, Mauritz Eriksson, Erik Blomqvist, Thure Holmberg, Verner Jernström
6. NOR—Østen Østensen, Otto Olsen, Olaf Stetten, Albert Helgerud, Jacob Onsrud
7. SPA—José Bento López, Antonio Bonilla Sanmartín, Domingo Rodríguez Somoza, Luis Calvet Sandoz, Antonio Moreira Montero
8. SAF—Robert Bodley, George Lishman, David Smith, Mark Paxton, Frederick Morgan

1920 Antwerp-Beverloo T: 14, N: 14, D: 7.29–30, 8.2.

(600 Meters, Prone)

	Total Pts.
1. USA	287/283/284
2. SAF	287/283/279
3. SWE	287/275
4. NOR	282
5. FRA	280
6. SWI	279
7. GRE	270
8. FIN	268

1. USA—Dennis Fenton, Willis Lee, Lloyd Spooner, Ollie Schriver, Joseph Jackson
2. SAF—Robert Bodley, Ferdinand Buchanan, George Harvey, Frederick Morgan, David Smith
3. SWE—Carl Hugo Johansson, Mauritz Eriksson, Erik Blomqvist, Erik Ohlsson, Gustaf Adolf Jonsson
4. NOR—Østen Østensen, Otto Olsen, Olaf Sletten, Albert Helgerud, Jakob Onsrud
5. FRA—Léon Johnson, Achille Paroche, Émile Rumeau, André Parmentier, Georges Roes
6. SWI—Fritz Kuchen, Albert Tröndle, Arnold Rösli, Walter Lienhard, Caspar Widmer
7. GRE—Andreas Vikhos, Ioannis Theofilakis, Alexandros Theofilakis, Konstantinos Kefalas, Emmanuel Peristerakis
8. FIN—Veli Nieminen, Voitto Kolho, Vilho Vauhkonen, Magnus Wegelius, Kalle Lappalainen

1920 Antwerp-Beverloo T: 14, N: 14, D: 7.29.

(300 +600 Meters, Prone)

	Total Pts.
1. USA	573
2. NOR	565
3. SWI	563
4. FRA	563
5. SAF	560
6. SWE	558
7. GRE	553
8. CZE	536

1. USA—Joseph Jackson, Willis Lee, Ollie Schriver, Lloyd Spooner, Carl Osburn
2. NOR—Otto Olsen, Østen Østensen, Olaf Sletten, Albert Helgerud, Jakob Onsrud
3. SWI—Werner Schneeberger, Joseph Jehle, Weibel, Fritz Kuchen, Eugene Addor
4. FRA—Léon Johnson, Achille Paroche, Émile Rumeau, André Parmentier, Georges Roes
5. SAF—David Smith, Robert Bodley, Ferdinand Buchanan, George Harvey, Frederick Morgan
6. SWE—Erik Blomqvist, Mauritz Eriksson, C. Hugo Johansson, Bror Andreasson, Gustaf Adolf Jonsson
7. GRE—Alexandros Theofilakis, Ioannis Theofilakis, Konstantinos Kefalas, Vasilios Xilinakis, Emmanuel Peristerakis
8. CZE—Rudolf Jelen, Josef Sucharda, Václav Kindl, Josef Linert, Antonín Brych

SMALL-BORE RIFLE

1908 London C: 22, N: 5, D: 7.11.

(25 Yards, Moving Target)

		PTS.
1. John Fleming	GBR	24
2. Michael Matthews	GBR	24
3. William Marsden	GBR	24
4. Edward Newitt	GBR	24
5. Phillip Plater	GBR	22
6. William Pimm	GBR	21
7. William Milne	GBR	21
8. Otto von Rosen	SWE	18

(25 Yards, Disappearing Target)

		PTS.
1. William Styles	GBR	45
2. Harold Hawkins	GBR	45
3. Edward Amoore	GBR	45
4. William Mime	GBR	45
5. John Mime	GBR	45
6. Arthur Wilde	GBR	45
7. Vilhelm Carlberg	SWE	45
8. Harold Humby	GBR	45

1912 Stockholm C: 36, N: 8, D: 7.5.
(25 Meters, Disappearing Target)

		PTS.
1. Vilhelm Carlberg	SWE	242
2. Johan Hübner von Holst	SWE	233
3. Gideon Ericsson	SWE	231
4. Joseph Pepe	GBR	231
5. Robert Murray	GBR	228
6. Axel Gyllenkrok	SWE	227
7. William Pimm	GBR	225
8. Frederick Hird	USA	221

1920 Antwerp-Beverloo C: 50, N: 10, D: 8.2.
(50 Meters, Standing)

		PTS.
1. Lawrence Nuesslein	USA	391
2. Arthur Rothrock	USA	386
3. Dennis Fenton	USA	385
4. Sigvard Holtcrantz	SWE	382
5. P. Erik Ohlsson	SWE	381
6. Anton Olsen	NOR	379
7. Lars Jørgen Madsen	DEN	378
8. Erik Sætter-Lassen	DEN	378

SMALL-BORE RIFLE, TEAM

1908 London T: 3, N: 3, D: 7.11.
(50 +100 Yards)

	TOTAL PTS.
1. GBR—Michael Matthews, Harold Humby, William Pimm, Edward Amoore	771
2. SWE—Vilhelm Carlberg, Frans-Albert Schartau, Johan Hübner von Holst, Eric Carlberg	737
3. FRA—Paul Colas, André Regaud, Léon Lécuyer, Henri Bonnefoy	710

1912 Stockholm T: 4, N: 4, D: 7.5.
(25 Meters, Disappearing Target)

	TOTAL PTS.
1. SWE—Johan Hübner von Holst, Eric Carlberg, Vilhelm Carlberg, Gustaf Boivie	925
2. GBR—William Pimm, Joseph Pepe, William Milne, William Styles	917
3. USA—Frederick Hird, Warren Sprout, W. Neil McDonnell, William Leushner	881
4. GRE—Ioannis Theofilakis, Iakovos Theofilas, Frangiskos Mavrommatis, Nikolaos Levidis	716

1912 Stockholm T: 6, N: 6, D: 7.3.
(50 Meters, Prone)

	TOTAL PTS.
1. GBR—Edward Lessimore, William Pimm, Joseph Pepe, Robert Murray	762
2. SWE—Arthur Nordenswan, Eric Carlberg, Ruben Örtegren, Vilhelm Carlberg	748
3. USA—Warren Sprout, William Leushner, Frederick Hird, Carl Osburn	744
4. FRA—Léon Johnson, Pierre Gentil, André Regaud, Maxime Landin	714
5. DEN—Povl Gerlow, Lars Jørgen Madsen, Frants Nielsen, Hans Denver	708
5. GRE—Ioannis Theofilakis, Iakovos Theofilas, Frangiskos Mavrommatis, Nikolaos Levidis	708

1920 Antwerp-Beverloo T: 10, N: 10, D: 8.2.
(50 Meters, Standing)

	TOTAL PTS.
1. USA—Lawrence Nuesslein, Arthur Rothrock, Dennis Fenton, Willis Lee, Ollie Schriver	1899
2. SWE—Sigvard Hultcrantz, Erik Ohlsson, Leonard Lagerlöf, Olle Ericsson, Ragnar Stare	1873
3. NOR—Anton Olsen, Albert Helgerud, Sigvart Johansen, Olaf Sletten, Østen Østensen	1866
4. DEN—Lars Jørgen Madsen, Erik Sætter-Lassen, Anders Peter Nielsen, Otto Wegener, Christian Møller	1862
5. FRA—Léon Johnson, Achille Paroche, Émile Rumeau, André Parmentier, Georges Roes	1847
6. BEL—Paul Van Asbroeck, Norbert Van Molle, Phillippe Cammaerts, Victor Robert, Louis Andrieu	1785
7. ITA—Alfredo Galli, Raffaele Frasca, Pier-Francesco "Peppy" Campus, Franco Micheli, Riccardo Ticchi	1777
8. SAF—George Lisham, Frederick Morgan, George Harvey, Robert Bodley, Mark Paxton	1755

RUNNING DEER SHOOTING, SINGLE SHOT

1908 London C: 15, N: 4, D: 7.9.

		PTS.
1. Oscar Swahn	SWE	25
2. Thomas "Ted" Ranken	GBR	24
3. Alexander Rogers	GBR	24
4. Maurice Blood	GBR	23
5. Albert Kempster	GBR	22
6. James Cowan	GBR	21
6. William Lane-Joynt	GBR	21
6. Walter Winans	USA	21

In 1908, Oscar Swahn was already 60 years old when he won his *first* Olympic gold medal, taking a total of two gold and one bronze. In 1912 he won one gold and one bronze, and in Antwerp, in 1920, at the age of 72, he won his first silver medal as part of the Swedish double-shot running deer team. He died in 1927.

1912 Stockholm C: 34, N: 7, D: 7.1.

		PTS.
1. Alfred Swahn	SWE	41/20
2. Åke Lundeberg	SWE	41/17
3. Nestori Toivonen	FIN	41/11
4. Karl Larsson	SWE	39
4. Sven August Lindskog	SWE	39
4. Oscar Swahn	SWE	39
7. Heinrich Elbogen	AUT	38
8. Adolf Cederström	SWE	37
8. William Leuschner	USA	37

Oscar Swahn finished in a three-way tie for fourth place in Stockholm, but his 32-year-old son Alfred earned the gold medal after a three-way shoot-off. Alfred's Olympic career was even more successful than his father's. Between 1908 and 1924 he won nine medals—three gold, three silver, and three bronze.

1920 Antwerp-Beverloo C: 22, N: 4, D: 7.27.

		PTS.
1. Otto Olsen	NOR	43
2. Alfred Swahn	SWE	41/20
3. Harald Natvig	NOR	41/19
4. Yrjö Kolho	FIN	40
5. Robert Tikkanen	FIN	40
6. Frederic Landelius	SWE	39
7. Laurence Nuesslein	USA	38
8. Oscar Swahn	SWE	37

1924 Paris C: 32, N: 8, D: 7.3.

		PTS.
1. John Boles	USA	40
2. Cyril Mackworth-Praed	GBR	39
3. Otto Olsen	NOR	39
4. Otto Hultberg	SWE	39
5. Martti Liuttula	FIN	37
6. Alfred Swahn	SWE	37
7. Einar Liberg	NOR	36
8. Harold Natvig	NOR	36

Twenty-eight years after he earned three medals at the Paris Games, Cyril Mackworth-Praed took part in the Olympics for a second time, placing eleventh in the trap event at Helsinki at the age of 60. Mackworth-Praed was a noted ornithologist who spent 40 years compiling his six-volume *African Handbook of Birds.*

Oscar Swahn

Seventy-two-year-old Swahn, the oldest competitor—and medalist—in Olympic history.

TEAM RUNNING DEER SHOOTING, SINGLE-SHOT

1908 London T: 2, N: 2, D: 7.10.

	TOTAL PTS.
1. SWE—Alfred Swahn, Arvid Knöppel, Oscar Swahn, Ernst Roseil	86
2. GBR—Charles Nix, William Lane-Joynt, Walter Ellicott, Thomas "Ted" Ranken	85

1912 Stockholm T: 5, N: 5, D: 7.4.

	TOTAL PTS.
1. SWE—Oscar Swahn, Åke Lundeberg, Alfred Swahn, Per-Olof Arvidsson	151
2. USA—Walter Winans, William Leushner, William Libbey, W. Neil McDonnell,	132
3. FIN—Nestori Toivonen, Iivar Väänänen, Axel Londen, Ernst Rosenqvist	123
4. AUT—Peter Paternelli, Adolf Michel, Heinrich Ellbogen, Eberhard Steinböck	115
5. RUS—Vasily Skrotsky, Dmitri Barkov, Haralds "Harry" Blaus, Aleksandr Dobrzhansky	108

1920 Antwerp-Beverloo T: 4, N: 4, D: 7.26.

	TOTAL PTS.
1. NOR—Harald Natvig, Otto Olsen, Ole Lilloe-Olsen, Einar Liberg, Hans Nordvik	178
2. FIN—Nestori Toivonen, Yrjö Kolho, Magnus Wegelius, Robert Tikkanen, Kalle Lappalainen	159
3. USA—Thomas Brown, Lawrence Nuesslein, Lloyd Spooner, Carl Osburn, Willis Lee	158
4. SWE—Alfred Swahn, Per Kinde, Bengt Lagercrantz, Oscar Swahn, Karl Larsson	153

1924 Paris T: 6, N: 6, D: 7.3.

	TOTAL PTS.
1. NOR—Ole Lilloe-Olsen, Einar Liberg, Harald Natvig, Otto Olsen	160
2. SWE—Alfred Swahn, Fredrik Landelius, Otto Hultberg, G. Mauritz Johansson	154
3. USA—John Boles, Walter Stokes, Raymond "Chan" Coulter, Dennis Fenton	148
4. GBR—Cyril Mackworth-Praed, Alexander Rogers, John Faunthorpe, John O'Leary	136
5. FIN—Karl Magnus Wegelius, Martti Liuttula, Jalo Urho Autonen, Robert Tikkanen	130
6. HUN—Gusztáv Szomjas, Rezső Velez, Elemér Takács, László Szomjas	97

RUNNING DEER SHOOTING, DOUBLE-SHOT

1908 London C: 15, N: 4, D: 7.10.

		PTS.
1. Walter Winans	USA	46/44
2. Thomas "Ted" Ranken	GBR	46/41
3. Oscar Swahn	SWE	38
4. Maurice Blood	GBR	34
5. Albert Kempster	GBR	34
6. Walter Ellicott	GBR	33
6. Alexander Rogers	GBR	33
8. Ernst Rosell	SWE	33

Walter Winans was born to American parents living in Russia. He spent most of his life in England. He was not allowed to compete until he had sworn allegiance to the US Consul General in London.

1912 Stockholm C: 20, N: 6, D: 7.3.

		PTS.
1. Åke Lundeberg	SWE	79
2. Edward Benedicks	SWE	74
3. Oscar Swahn	SWE	72
4. Per-Olof Arvidsson	SWE	68
4. Alfred Swahn	SWE	68
6. Sven August Lindskog	SWE	67
7. Erik Sökjer-Petersén	SWE	65
8. Emil Lindewald	SWE	64

1920 Antwerp-Beverloo C: 23, N: 4, D: 7.27.

		PTS.
1. Ole Lilloe-Olsen	NOR	82
2. Fredrik Landelius	SWE	77
3. Einar Liberg	NOR	71

1924 Paris C: 31, N: 8, D: 7.3.

		PTS.
1. Ole Lilloe-Olsen	NOR	76
2. Cyril Mackworth-Praed	GBR	72
3. Alfred Swahn	SWE	72
4. Fredrik Landelius	SWE	70
5. Einar Liberg	NOR	70
6. Robert Tikkanen	FIN	69
7. John Boles	USA	64
8. Karl Magnus Wegelius	FIN	64

TEAM RUNNING DEER SHOOTING, DOUBLE-SHOT

1920 Antwerp-Beverloo T: 4, N: 4, D: 7.26.

	TOTAL PTS.
1. NOR—Ole Lilloe-Olsen, Thorstein Johansen, Harald Natvig, Einar Liberg, Hans Nordvik	343
2. SWE—Fredrik Landelius, Alfred Swahn, Oscar Swahn, Bengt Lagercrantz, Edvard Benedicks	336
3. FIN—Robert Tikkanen, Magnus Wegelius, Nestori Toivonen, Yrjö Kolho, Vilho Vauhkonen	285
4. USA—Lloyd Spooner, Willis Lee, Lawrence Nuesslein, Carl Osburn, Thomas Brown	282

1924 Paris T: 6, N: 6, D: 7.3.

	TOTAL PTS.
1. GBR—Cyril Mackworth-Praed, Allen Whitty, Herbert Perry, Philip Neame	263
2. NOR—Ole Lilloe-Olsen, Otto Olsen, Harald Natvig, Einar Liberg	262
3. SWE—Alfred Swahn, G. Mauritz Johansson, Fredrik Landelius, Axel Ekblom	250
4. FIN—Karl Magnus Wegelius, Jalo Urho Autonen, Martti Liuttula, Robert Tikkanen	239
5. USA—Raymond "Chan" Coulter, Walter Stokes, John Boles, Dennis Fenton	233
6. CZE—Miloslav Hlaváč, Josef Sucharda, Rudolf Jelen, Josef Hosa	204

Philip Neame of the British team earned the Victoria Cross for bravery shown at Neuve Chapelle in 1914. He is the only person to be awarded the Victoria Cross and win an Olympic gold medal. In 1933 Neame was badly mauled by a tiger while hunting. As a lieutenant general in 1941, he led British, Australian and Indian troops in Libya against General Erwin Rommel's first offensive. Neame was captured by the Germans, but escaped in 1943.

RUNNING DEER SHOOTING, SINGLE-AND DOUBLE-SHOT

1952 Helsinki C: 14, N: 7, D: 7.29. WR: 398 (Rolf Bergersen)

		PTS.
1. John Larsen	NOR	413 WR
2. Per Olof Sköldberg	SWE	409
3. Tauno Mäki	FIN	407
4. Rolf Bergersen	NOR	399
5. B. Thorleif Kockgård	SWE	397
6. Yrjö Miettinen	FIN	392
7. Petr Nikolayev	SOV	385
8. Vladimir Sevryugin	SOV	383

1956 Melbourne C: 11, N: 6, D: 12.4.

		PTS.
1. Vitaly Romanenko	SOV/UKR	441 OR
2. Per Olof Sköldberg	SWE	432
3. Vladimir Sevryugin	SOV	429
4. Miklós Kovács	HUN	417
5. Miklós Kocsis	HUN	416
6. Rolf Bergersen	NOR	409
7. Benkt Austrin	SWE	405
8. John Larsen	NOR	390

RUNNING TARGET

Between 1972 and 1988 the running target or running boar event consisted of 60 shots at 50 meters. The target, a life-size reproduction of a wild boar with a two-inch 10-ring, crossed a ten-meter gap. The boar did 30 fast runs at two and a half seconds and 30 slow runs at five seconds. In 1992 the boar was replaced by a regular target with two bull's-eyes, each 5 millimeters wide.

1972 Munich C: 28, N: 16, D: 9.1. WR: 566 (Göte Gåård)

		PTS.
1. Yakiv Zheleznyak	SOV/UKR	569 WR
2. Helmut Bellingrodt Wolf	COL	565
3. John Kynoch	GBR	562
4. Valery Postoianov	SOV/RUS	560
5. Christoph-Michael Zeisner	GER	554
6. Göte Gåård	SWE	553
7. Günther Danne	GER	551
8. Karl-Axel Karlsson	SWE	551

1976 Montreal C: 27, N: 16, D: 7.23. WR: 577 (Helmut Bellingrodt, Valery Postoianov)

		PTS.
1. Aleksandr Gazov	SOV/BLR	579 WR
2. Aleksandr Kedyarov	SOV/BLR	576
3. Jerzy Greszkiewicz	POL	571
4. Thomas Pfeffer	GDR	571
5. Wolfgang Hamberger	GER	567
6. Helmut Bellingrodt Wolf	COL	567
7. Karl Karlsson	SWE	565
8. Louis Theimer	USA	564

1980 Moscow C: 19, N: 11, D: 7.24. WR: 581 (Thomas Pfeffer)

		PTS.
1. Igor Sokolov	SOV/RUS	589 WR
2. Thomas Pfeffer	GDR	589
3. Aleksandr Gazov	SOV/BLR	587
4. András Doleschall	HUN	584
5. Tibor Bodnár	HUN	584
6. Jorma Lievonen	FIN	584
7. Giovanni Mezzani	ITA	582
8. Hans-Jürgen Helbig	GDR	579

1984 Los Angeles-Chino C: 23, N: 15, D: 7.31. WR: 595 (Igor Sokolov)

		PTS.
1. Li Yuwei	CHN	587
2. Helmut Bellingrodt Wolf	COL	584
3. Huang Shiping	CHN	581
4. Uwe Schröder	GER	581
5. David Lee	CAN	580
6. Kenneth Skoglund	NOR	576
7. Jorma Lievonen	FIN	576
8. Ezio Cini	ITA	576

1988 Seoul C: 23, N: 16, D: 9.23. WR: 691 (Sergei Lusov, Nikolai Lapin)

		PTS.
1. Tor Heiestad	NOR	689
2. Huang Shiping	CHN	687
3. Hennady Avramenko	SOV/UKR	686
4. Ján Kermiet	CZE	679
5. András Doleschall	HUN	588
6. Attila Solti	HUN	588
7. Thomas Pfeffer	GDR	587
8. Christian Stützinger	GER	586

Heiestad was a 26-year-old farm mechanic from Oslo.

1992 Barcelona-Mollet del Vallès C: 24, N: 15, D: 8.1. WR: 679 (Luboš Račanský)

		PTS.
1. Michael Jakosits	GER	673
2. Anatoly Asrabayev	RUS	672
3. Luboš Račanský	CZE	670
4. Andrei Vasilyev	BLR	667/91
5. József Sike	HUN	667/91
6. Jens Zimmermann	GER	667/89
7. Kim Man-chol	PRK	573
8. Su Qingquan	CHN	573

1996 Atlanta-Wolf Creek C: 20, N: 14, D: 7.26. WR: 687.9 (Yang Ling)

		PTS.
1. Yang Ling	CHN	685.8
2. Xiao Jun	CHN	679.8
3. Miroslav Januš	CZE	678.4
4. József Sike	HUN	677.1
5. Dmitri Lykine	RUS	676.7
6. Krister Holmberg	FIN	672.4
7. Jens Zimmermann	GER	672.2
8. Attila Solti	GUA	667.0

Yang Ling, who set a world record on June 6, 1996, was easily the class of the field. The night before the competition, he prepared himself by reading a book about kung fu.

2000 Sydney C: 18, N: 12, D: 9.22. WR: 687.9 (Yang Ling)

		PTS.
1. Yang Ling	CHN	681.1
2. Oleg Moldovan	MOL	681.0
3. Zhiyuan Niu	CHN	677.4
4. Pasi Wedman	FIN	672.1
5. Dmitri Lykin	RUS	671.7
6. Manfred Kurzer	GER	671.3
7. Igor Kolesov	RUS	667.5
8. Miroslav Januš	CZE	666.8

Yang Ling successfully defended his Olympic championship, but it did not come easily. Yang scored 581 points in the qualifying round to Oleg Moldovan's 580. Moldovan's first two shots of the final, a 10.7 and a 10.6, put him ahead of Yang, but Yang regained the lead immediately. After the sixth shot, Yang was leading by 1.8 points, but Moldovan came from behind to move ahead by two tenths of a point with only one shot remaining. Moldovan shot a respectable 10.1, but Yang rose to the occasion and hit a 10.4 to win by one tenth of a point.

2004 Athens-Markopoulo C: 19, N: 12, D: 8.19. WR: 687.9 (Yang Ling)

		PTS.
1. Manfred Kurzer	GER	682.4
2. Aleksandr Blinov	RUS	678.0
3. Dmitri Lykin	RUS	677.1
4. Emil Andersson	SWE	676.8
5. Michael Jakosits	GER	676.7
6. Li Jie [2]	CHN	675.8

7. Andrei Kazak	BLR	575
7. Vladyslav Prianishnikov	UKR	575
7. Adam Saathoff	USA	575

Manfred Kurzer set a world record in the qualifying round, earning 590 points. Taking a six-point lead into the final, Kurzer won the gold medal despite recording the worst score of the six finalists, 92.4 points. Meanwhile, Aleksandr Blinov jumped from fifth place to second after leading the final with 100 points.

TRAP (CLAY PIGEON) SHOOTING, TEAM

1908 London T: 4, N: 3, D: 7.11.

	Total Pts.
1. GBR	407
2. CAN	405
3. GBR	372
4. HOL	174

1. GBR—Alexander Maunder, James Pike, Charles Palmer, John Postans, Frank Moore, Peter Easte
2. CAN—Walter Ewing, George Beattie, Arthur Westover, Mylie Fletcher, George Vivian, Donald McMackon
3. GBR—George Whitaker, Gerald Skinner, John Butt, William Morris, Harold Creasey, Richard Hutton
4. HOL—John Wilson, Franciscus van Voorst tot Voorst, Cornelis Viruly, Eduardus van Voorst tot Voorst, Rudolf van Pallandt, Romain "Reindert" de Fauvage

1912 Stockholm T: 6, N: 6, D: 7.1.

	Total Pts.
1. USA	532
2. GBR	511
3. GER	510
4. SWE	243
5. FIN	233
6. FRA	90

1. USA—James Graham, Charles Billings, Ralph Spotts, John Hendrickson, Frank Hall, Edward Gleason
2. GBR—Harold Humby, William Grosvenor, Alexander Maunder, George Whitaker, John Butt, Charles Palmer
3. GER—Franz von Zedlitz und Leipe, Horst-Goeldel-Bronikoven, Erich, Count von Bernstorff-Gyldensteen, Erich von Bernstorff-Bronikoven, Erland Koch, Albert Preuss, Alfred Goeldel-Bronikoven
4. SWE—Åke Lundeberg, Alfred Swahn, Johann Ekman, Victor Wallenberg, E. Hjalmar Frisell, Carl Wollert
5. FIN—C. Edvard Bacher, Robert Huber, Gustaf Adolf Schnitt, Emil Johannes Collan, Karl Fazer, Axel Londen
6. FRA—André Fleury, Henri de Castex, Georges de Créqui-Montfort de Courtivron, Charles de Jaubert, René Texier, Edouard Creuze de Lesser

1920 Antwerp-Beverloo T: 8, N: 8, D: 7.23.

	Total Pts.
1. USA	547
2. BEL	503
3. SWE	500
4. GBR	488
5. CAN	474
6. HOL	222
7. FRA	210
7. NOR	210

1. USA—Mark Arie, Frank Troeh, Horace Bonser, Forest McNeir, Frank Wright, Jay Clark
2. BEL—Albert Bosquet, Joseph Cogels, Émile Dupont, Henri Quersin, Louis van Tilt, Édouard Fesinger
3. SWE—Erik Lundqvist, Per Kinde, Fredric Landelius, Alfred Swahn, Karl Richter, Erik Sökjer-Petersén
4. GBR—Harold Humby, William Grosvenor, Walter Ellicot, George Whitaker, Ernest Pocock, Charles Palmer
5. CAN—George Beattie, Samuel Vance, William Hamilton, Robert Montgomery, James Oliver, William McLaren
6. HOL—Romain "Reindert" de Fauvage, Cornelis van der Vliet, M. Pieter Waller, Émile Jurgens, Franciscus Jurgens, Eduardus van Voorst tot Voorst
7. FRA—André Fleury, Marcel Lafitte, Henri de Castex, Augustin Berjat, René Texier, Jean de Lareinty-Tholozan
7. NOR—Oluf Wesmann-Kjær, Johannes Nordahl-Lunde, Harald Natvig, Thorstein Johansen, Hans Nordvik, Ole Lilloe-Olsen

1924 Paris T: 12, N: 12, D: 7.7.

	Total Pts.
1. USA	363
2. CAN	360
3. FIN	360
4. SWE	354
5. BEL	354
6. AUT	347
7. NOR	336
8. GBR	328

1. USA—Frank Hughes, Samuel Sharman, William Silkworth, Frederick Etchen
2. CAN—George Beattie, James Montgomery, Samuel Vance, John Black, Samuel Newton, William Barnes
3. FIN—Konrad Huber, Robert Huber, Werner Ekman, Robert Tikkanen
4. SWE—Erik Lundqvist, Fredrik Landelius, Alfred Swahn, Magnus Hallman
5. BEL—Albert Bosquet, Louis d'Heur, Emile Dupont, Jacques Mouton
6. AUT—Heinrich Bartosch, August Baumgartner, Hans Schödl, Erich Zoigner
7. NOR—Ole Lilloe-Olsen, Oluf Wesmann-Kjaer, Eivind Holmsen, Martin Stenersen
8. GBR—John O'Leary, Enoch Jenkins, Herbert Larsen, Cyril Mackworth-Praed

WOMEN

SPORT PISTOL

The sport pistol competition is fired at a distance of 25 meters. The qualifying round is divided into two 30-shot stages: precision and rapid-fire. Five minutes are allowed for the precision stage. In the rapid-fire stage shots are taken at a turning target with three seconds per shot. The bull's-eye in the precision stage is 5 centimeters (1.97 inches) across. The rapid-fire bull's-eye is 10 centimeters (4 inches) across. The final consists of four series of five shots, with three seconds per shot.

1896–1980 not held

1984 Los Angeles-Chino C: 30, N: 21, D: 7.29. WR: 592 (G. Korsun)

		PTS.
1. Linda Thom	CAN	585/198
2. Ruby Fox	USA	585/197
3. Patricia Dench	AUS	583/196
4. Liu Haiying	CHN	583/195
5. Kristina Fries	SWE	581
6. Wen Zhifang	CHN	578
7. Débora Srour	BRA	578
8. Maria Macovei	ROM	577

Linda Thom was a 40-year-old chef and caterer from Ottawa.

1988 Seoul C. 35, N: 24, D: 9.19. WR: 695 (Nino Salukvadze)

		PTS.
1. Nino Salukvadze	SOV/GEO	690
2. Tomoko Hasegawa	JPN	686
3. Jasna Šekarić	YUG/SER	686
4. Lieselotte Breker	GER	685
5. Agnes Ferencz	HUN	685
6. Kristina Fries	SWE	685
7. Evelyne Manchon	FRA	684
8. Marina Dobrancheva	SOV/RUS	682

Nineteen-year-old Nino Salukvadze of Soviet Georgia also won a silver medal in the air pistol event.

1992 Barcelona-Mollet del Vallès C: 41, N: 29, D: 7.27. WR: 693 (Nino Salukvadze)

		PTS.
1. Marina Logvinenko (Dobrancheva)	RUS	684
2. Li Duihong	CHN	680
3. Dorjsurengiin Mönkhbayar	MGL	679
4. Mirela Skoko	CRO	677
5. Nino Salukvadze	GEO	676
6. Jasna Šekarić	YUG/SER	676
7. Lynne-Marie Freh	AUS	675
8. Julita Macur	POL	674

Silver medalist Li Duihong had been one of the favorites in 1988 until she tested positive for drugs and was slapped with a two-year suspension. Li's twin sister, Li Shuanghong, placed ninth in the air pistol event.

1996 Atlanta-Wolf Creek C: 37, N: 24, D: 7.26. WR: 696.2 (Diana Yorgova)

		PTS.
1. Li Duihong	CHN	687.9
2. Diana Yorgova	BUL	684.8
3. Marina Logvinenko (Dobrancheva)	RUS	684.2
4. Boo Soon-hee	KOR	683.9
5. Otryadyn Gündegmaa	MGL	681.3
6. Jasna Šekarić	YUG/SER	680.4
7. Nino Salukvadze	GEO	677.6
8. Julita Macur	POL	677.4

Diana Yorgova outscored Marina Logvinenko 10.5 to 9.5 on the final shot to overtake her for the silver medal. Gold medal winner Li Duihong was a lieutenant colonel in the army. At the medal ceremony, she cried straight through the playing of the Chinese national anthem. Back in Daqing in Heilongjiang Province, Li's father did what he always did when she won a shooting championship: he lit a string of firecrackers and hung them over his doorway.

2000 Sydney C: 42, N: 28, D: 9.22. WR: 696.2 (Diana Yorgova)

		PTS.
1. Maria Grozdeva	BUL	690.3
2. Tao Luna	CHN	689.8
3. Lolita Yevglevskaya	BLR	686.0
4. Yuliya Sinyak	BLR	685.9
5. Michiko Fukushima	JPN	684.8
6. Otryadyn Gündegmaa	MGL	680.9
7. Yoko Inada	JPN	679.6
8. Yeqing Cai	CHN	678.8

Tao Luna had already won a gold medal in the air pistol event, when she entered the final of the sport pistol with a one-point lead over Maria Grozdeva, who had earned bronze medals in the air pistol event at the last two Olympics. Grozdeva caught Tao after seven shots, picked up six tenths of a point with each of her next two shots and hit a 9.9 with her last shot to secure the gold medal.

2004 Athens-Markopoulo C: 37, N: 26, D: 8.18. WR: 695.9 (Tao Luna)

		PTS.
1. Maria Grozdeva	BUL	688.2
2. Lenka Hyková	CZE	687.8
3. Irada Ashumova	AZR	687.3
4. Chen Ying	CHN	686.2
5. Dorjsurengiin Mönkhbayar	GER	684.6
6. Otryadyn Gündegmaa	MGL	683.4
7. Seo Joo-hyung	KOR	680.8
8. Nino Salukvadze	GEO	678.3

For the second Olympics in a row, Maria Grozdeva had to come from behind to earn the gold medal. Three points behind Hyková and Ashumova (tied at 588) after the qualifying round, Grozdeva still trailed Ashumova by three points midway through the ten-shot final. However the Azeri shooter opened the door for Grozdeva with a 7.6 on her sixth shot, and Grozveda posted the highest total in the final, 103.2 points, to successfully defend her Olympic title. Three days earlier, in the air pistol final, Ashumova had been tied for first place with two shots remaining, only to slip up and fall to eighth.

2008 Beijing C: 41, N: 28, D: 8.13. WR: 796.7 (Maria Grozdeva)

		PTS.
1. Chen Ying	CHN	793.4
2. Otryadyn Gündegmaa	MGL	792.2
3. Dorjsurengiin Mönkhbayar	GER	789.2

4. Fei Fengji	CHN	787.9
5. Mariya Grozdeva	BUL	786.6
6. Jo Yong-suk	PRK	783.4
7. Tanyaporn Prucksakorn	THA	777.7
8. Luisa Maida Leiva	ESA	774.0

Two-time reigning Olympic champion Mariya Grozdeva was hoping to become the first person to win the same shooting event three times in a row, but finished fifth in the qualifying round, seven points behind Mongolia's Otryadyn Gündegmaa, the 2006 world bronze medalist. Reigning world champion and hometown favorite Chen Ying qualified third, five points behind Otryadyn.

Otryadyn suffered a pistol malfunction during the third of her four five-shot series in the final round. She was allowed to reshoot, but her final score, 202.2 points, dropped her behind Chen, whose 208.4 was the highest score in the final and enough to win the gold medal. Dorjsurengiin Mönkhbayar equalled the bronze medal she won for Mongolia in 1992, this time for Germany.

After the Olympics Chen discovered that her mother had been receiving chemotherapy treatment for breast cancer for three months, but had kept the news from her daughter to avoid distracting her.

Appearing in her fourth Olympics, 56-year-old Elizabeth "Libby" Callahan became the oldest US female competitor in Olympic history; she finished 25th.

AIR PISTOL

Forty shots are taken from a distance of 10 meters with a time limit of 75 minutes. The bull's-eye has a diameter of 11.5 millimeters (.45 inches). The top eight qualifiers take part in a 10-shot final with 75 seconds per shot.

1896–1984 not held

1988 Seoul C: 37, N: 26, D: 9.21. WR: 489 (Jasna Šekarić)

		PTS.
1. Jasna Šekarić	YUG/SER	489.5 WR
2. Nino Salukvadze	SOV/GEO	487.9
3. Marina Dobrancheva	SOV/RUS	485.2
4. Anne Goffin	BEL	480.2
5. Anke Völker	GDR	479.3
6. Liu Halying	CHN	476.9
7. Lieselotte Breker	GER	476.0
8. Christine Strahalm	AUT	472.6

Salukvadze, who had won the sport pistol championship 2 days earlier, set a world record of 390 in the preliminary round. However, this left her only one point up on defending world champion Jasna Šekarić, who outshot her on seven of the first eight shots of the final to set a world record of her own. The battle for the bronze medal looked like it would be a tight contest between Breker and Dobrancheva. However, when the final began, Breker failed to get off her first shot before the time limit elapsed. She was forced to take a zero for the shot, which put her out of the running.

Jasna Šekaric, 1988
Yugoslavia's most successful female athlete.

1992 Barcelona-Mollet del Vallès C: 47, N: 31, D: 8.1. WR: 492.4(Lieselotte Breker)

		PTS.
1. Marina Logvinenko (Dobrancheva)	RUS	486.4/99.4
2. Jasna Šekarić	YUG/SER	486.4/97.4
3. Maria Grozdeva	BUL	481.6
4. Wang Lina	CHN	479.7
5. Cris Kajd	SWE	478.9
6. Mariá Fernández Julián	SPA	478.5
7. Daniela Dumitraşcu	ROM	478.1
8. Mirosława Sagun	POL	477.8

Defending Olympic champion Jasna Šekarić took a two-point lead into the final and was still ahead by

.8 points after the ninth of ten rounds. However, in the final round, Logvinenko, who had won the sport pistol event five days earlier, outshot Šekarić 10.6 to 9.8. This left the two shooters with the exact same score, but because Logvinenko had a higher score in the final, the Rostov-on-Don native earned her second gold medal.

1996 Atlanta-Wolf Creek C: 41, N: 26, D: 7.21. WR: 492.4 (Liselotte Breker)

		PTS.
1. Olga Klochneva	RUS	490.1
2. Marina Logvinenko (Dobrancheva)	RUS	488.5/10.1
3. Maria Grozdeva	BUL	488.5/9.9
4. Jasna Šekarić	YUG/SER	487.1
5. Nino Salukvadze	GEO	484.0
6. Galina Belyeyeva	KAZ	481.7
7. Yuliya Bondareva	KAZ	479.3
8. Lolita Milchina	BLR	479.1

In Atlanta, Olga Klochneva of Samara, Russia, had her own group of fans rooting for her—a group of Americans. In 1992, in Samara, Klochneva met a couple of Baptist missionaries from Largo, Florida, and became a Christian. The following year she visited Largo and was made an honorary citizen of the city.

2000 Sydney C: 45, N: 32, D: 9.17. WR: 493.5 (Ren Jie)

		PTS.
1. Tao Luna	CHN	488.2
2. Jašna Šekarić	YUG/SER	486.5
3. Annemarie Forder	AUS	484.0
4. Svetlana Smirnova	RUS	483.7
5. Michiko Fukushima	JPN	483.7
6. Dina Aspandiyarova	KAZ	483.7
7. Olga Kuznetsova (Klochneva)	RUS	482.4
8. Yoko Inada	JPN	481.2

Tao Luna led the qualifying round by two points and was never headed in the final. Annemarie Forder delighted the Australian crowd by coming from behind to snatch the bronze medal with her final shot. Five days after the air pistol competition, Tao added a silver medal in the sport pistol event.

2004 Athens-Markopoulo C: 41, N: 30, D: 8.15. WR: 493.5 (Ren Jie)

		PTS.
1. Olena Kostevych	UKR	483.3/10.2
2. Jasna Šekarić	SER	483.3/9.4
3. Maria Grozdeva	BUL	482.3/10.4
4. Ren Jie	CHN	482.3/9.7
5. Natalya Paderina	RUS	481.9/10.0
6. Dorjsurengiin Mönkhbayar	GER	481.9/9.3
7. Cornelia Frölich	SWI	481.5
8. Irada Ashumova	AZR	481.4

Reigning world champion Olena Kostevych qualified for the final three points behind the top qualifier, three-time world champion and 1988 gold medalist Jasna Šekarić. The final was so close that with seven shots down and only three to go, only 1.6 points separated Natalya Paderina in first place from Šekarić in eighth. After the eighth round, the contest was even closer, with Kostevych and Irada Ashumova in first place 1.3 points ahead of Cornelia Frölich in eighth. Šekarić hit a 10.6 in the ninth round to close within two tenths of a point of Kostevych, and then caught her on the final shot to force a one-shot shoot-off for the gold medal. Kostevych won 10.2 to 9.4. Third place and fifth place were also decided by tie-breakers.

2008 Beijing C: 44, N: 30, D: 8.10. WR: 493.5 (Ren Jie)

		PTS.
1. Guo Wenjun	CHN	492.3
2. Nataliya Paderina	RUS	489.1
3. Nino Salukvadze	GEO	487.4
4. Viktoriya Chayka	BLR	482.0
5. Mirosława Sagun	POL	481.3
6. Jasna Šekarić	SER	480.9
7. Mira Nevansuu	FIN	480.5
8. Tsogbadrakhyn Mönkhzul	MGL	479.6

Reigning world champion Nataliya Paderina led the qualifying round with 391 points, an Olympic record, followed by 2006 Asian Games silver medalist Guo Wenjun with 390. Guo led the final round, scoring 102.3 points to move into the lead.

Nino Salukvadze's bronze medal was her first since her Olympic debut in 1988, when she won gold in the sport pistol and silver in the air pistol. Her achievement of winning a medal 20 years after her previous one was an Olympic record for women.

SMALL-BORE RIFLE, THREE POSITIONS

The rules are the same as for the men's competition with the exception that 20 shots, rather than 40, are taken at each position. Also, there is no time limit for each position, but rather an overall time limit of 2 hours 15 minutes.

1896–1980 not held

1984 Los Angeles-Chino C: 27, N: 17, D: 8.2. WR: 592 (Marlies Helbig)

		PRONE	STANDING	KNEELING	TOTAL PTS.
1. Wu Xiaoxuan	CHN	197	187	197	581
2. Ulrike Holmer	GER	197	191	190	578
3. Wanda Jewell	USA	194	189	195	578
4. Gloria Parmentier	USA	199	187	190	576
5. Anne Grethe Jeppesen	NOR	196	190	188	574
6. Jin Dongxiang	CHN	193	183	195	571
7. Biserka Vrbek	YUG/CRO	196	181	192	569
8. Mirjana Jovović	YUG/BSH	196	182	191	569

Wu, who also won a bronze medal in the air rifle event, told reporters the secret of her success at the Olympics: "I just concentrated on the music of our national anthem and shot."

1988 Seoul C: 37, N: 21, D: 9.21. WR: 691.6 (Vessela Letcheva)

		PRONE	STANDING	KNEELING	FINAL	TOTAL PTS.
1. Sylvia Sperber	GER	200	193	197	95.6	685.6
2. Vessela Letcheva	BUL	199	192	192	100.2	683.2
3. Valentina Cherkasova	SOV/RUS	198	193	195	95.4	681.4
4. Katja Klepp	GDR	199	187	198	96.5	680.5
5. Sharon Bowes	CAN	196	194	194	96.5	680.5
6. Anna Malukhina	SOV/RUS	198	191	196	93.4	678.4
7. Launi Meili	USA	197	190	195	94.5	676.5
8. Anita Karlsson	SWE	198	193	192	93.4	676.4

After finishing eleventh in the air rifle event in 1984, Sylvia Sperber retired from the sport even though she was only 19 years old. She returned to competition three years later. In 1988 she equaled the world record in the air rifle, took a silver in that event at Seoul, and then, three days later, earned a gold in the three-position competition.

1992 Barcelona-Mollet del Vallès C 36, N: 21, D: 7.30. WR: 684.9 (Vessela Lecheva)

		PRONE	STANDING	KNEELING	FINAL	TOTAL PTS.
1. Launi Meili	USA	200	194	193	97.3	684.3
2. Nonka Matova	BUL	200	190	194	98.7	682.7
3. Małgorzata Książkiewicz	POL	195	191	199	96.5	681.5
4. Éva Fórián	HUN	199	189	194	97.5	679.5
5. Suzana Skoko	CRO	196	191	193	98.7	678.7
6. Vessela Letcheva	BUL	199	187	195	97.0	678.0
7. Sharon Bowes	CAN	198	189	193	93.6	673.6
8. Éva Joó	HUN	198	191	191	93.6	673.6

In 1988 Launi Meili entered the final of the air rifle event tied for first place. Then she succumbed to nerves and dropped to seventh place. Four years later in Barcelona Meili took a two-point lead into the final of the small-bore event. This time, despite her nervousness, she shot a solid final round and earned the gold medal.

1996 Atlanta-Wolf Creek C: 38, N: 21, D: 7.24. WR: 689.7 (Vessela Letcheva)

		PRONE	STANDING	KNEELING	FINAL	TOTAL PTS.
1. Aleksandra Ivošev	YUG/SER	199	193	195	99.1	686.1
2. Irina Gerasimyonok	RUS	196	194	195	95.1	680.1
3. Renata Mauer	POL	200	192	197	90.8	679.8
4. Kirsten Obel	GER	200	194	190	95.2	679.2
5. Nonka Matova	BUL	197	191	196	94.8	678.8
6. Kong Hyun-ah	KOR	198	191	194	92.8	675.8
7. Elizabeth Bourland	USA	195	194	194	91.0	674.0
8. Tetyana Nesterova	UKR	197	191	193	92.3	673.3

Renata Mauer led the qualifying round by two points, but scored less than eight points with three of her first seven shots in the final. She fell to fifth place before coming back to earn the bronze medal.

2000 Sydney C: 42, N: 28, D: 9.20. WR: 689.7 (Vessela Letcheva, Wang Xian)

		PRONE	KNEELING	STANDING	TOTAL PTS.
1. Renata Mauer-Różańska	POL	198	195	192	684.6
2. Tatyana Goldobina	RUS	198	196	191	680.9
3. Mariya Feklistova	RUS	194	196	192	679.9
4. Sonja Pfeilschifter	GER	200	197	188	678.5
5. Hong Shan	CHN	198	197	185	676.9
6. Anni Bissø	DEN	199	193	192	675.6
7. Olga Dovgun	KAZ	197	198	188	674.2
8. Melissa Mulloy	USA	197	190	193	673.7

Renata Mauer-Różańska, Tatyana Goldobina and two-time world champion Sonja Pfeilschifter entered the final tied at 585. Pfeilschifter took a narrow early lead, then Mauer-Różańska moved ahead for two rounds and then Goldobina took over first place at the halfway point. After the sixth of ten shots, the score was: Goldobina—59.3, Mauer-Różańska—59.2 and Pfeilschifter—59.2. The pressure was intense and Pfeilschifter proceeded to hit two 7s and two 9s while Goldobina shot three straight 8s before finshing with a 10.6. Mauer-Różańska, the only one of three to remain focused, closed with a string of 10.3, 10.5, 10.2 and 9.4 to earn a clear victory. Shooting is not a sport that allows most participants to train full-time. Mauer-Różańska was an economist, while Pfeilschifter, despite being chosen International Shooter of the Year twice, worked as a seamstress for an upholstery company.

2004 Athens-Markopoulo C: 33, N: 22, D: 8.20. WR: 689.7 (Vessela Letcheva, Wang Xian)

		PRONE	KNEELING	STANDING	FINAL	TOTAL PTS.
1. Lyubov Galkina	RUS	199	191	197	101.4	688.4 OR
2. Valentina Turisini	ITA	197	193	195	100.9	685.9
3. Wang Chengyi	CHN	196	195	193	101.4	685.4
4. Olga Dovgun	KAZ	200	193	195	96.9	684.9
5. Lee Hye-jin	KOR	196	197	191	97.0	681.0
6. Sonja Pfeilschifter	GER	198	192	192	97.6	679.6
7. Barbara Lechner	GER	197	189	194	97.6	677.6
8. Natalia Kalnysh	UKR	194	187	198	98.2	677.2

Olga Dovgun led favorite Lyubov Galkina by one point after the qualifying round, but scored only 7.9 points with her first shot of the final to Galkina's 10.4. The two were still tied after six rounds, but Galkina hit 10.4 and 10.6 with her next two shots to Dovgun's 8.7 and 9.4. Galkina pulled away to the victory, while Dovgun fell short of a medal.

2008 Beijing C: 43, N: 28, D: 8.14. WR: 698.0 (Sonja Pfeilschifter)

		PRONE	KNEELING	STANDING	FINAL	TOTAL PTS.
1. Du Li	CHN	196	194	194	101.3	690.3 OR
2. Kateřina Emmons (Kůrková)	CZE	197	195	194	101.7	687.7
3. Eglis Yaima Cruz Farfan	CUB	199	196	193	99.6	687.6
4. Lyubov Galkina	RUS	197	194	194	102.4	687.4
5. Jamie Beyerle	USA	198	197	191	100.9	686.9
6. Olga Dovgun	KAZ	200	196	192	98.3	686.3
7. Lidija Mihajlović	SER	199	196	191	100.0	686.0
8. Wu Liuxi	CHN	199	194	192	100.9	685.9

Better known for her performances in the air rifle, including the 2004 Olympic gold medal and the 2006 world championship title, China's Du Li led the qualifying round, one point ahead of Eglis Cruz. Du scored 101.3 points in the final round to win the gold in an Olympic record. Kateřina Emmons edged past Cruz by a tenth of a point to take silver, five days after winning the gold medal in the air-rifle event. Defending Olympic champion and reigning world champion Lyubov Galkina scored the highest final-round total but could not overcome her deficit from the preliminary round, finishing fourth.

AIR RIFLE

The shooters have 74 minutes to fire 40 shots at a target 10 meters away. The bull's-eye is only .5 millimeters (.02 inches) in diameter. The eight finalists take 10 more shots with a time limit of 75 seconds per shot.

1896–1980 not held

1984 Los Angeles-Chino C: 33, N: 20, D: 7.31. WR: 395 (Anna Malukhina, Marbles Helbig)

		PTS.
1. Pat Spurgin	USA	393
2. Edith Gufler	ITA	391
3. Wu Xiaoxuan	CHN	389
4. Sharon Bowes	CAN	388
5. Yvette Courault	FRA	386
6. Gisela Sailer	GER	385
7. Siri Landsem	NOR	384
8. Sirpa Ylönen	FIN	383

Just before the competition began, a friend gave Pat Spurgin the following advice: "Just be like a duck." After winning the gold medal, the surprisingly poised 18-year-old from Billings, Montana, explained that to be like a duck meant, "Sit still on the surface, but paddle like hell underneath."

1988 Seoul C: 45, N: 29, D: 9.18. WR: 504.0 (Vessela Letcheva)

		PTS.
1. Irina Shilova	SOV/BLR	498.5
2. Sylvia Sperber	GER	497.5
3. Anna Malukhina	SOV/RUS	495.8
4. Zhang Qiuping	CHN	494.7
5. Pirjo Peltola	FIN	493.6
6. Launi Meili	USA	493.3
7. Sharon Bowes	CAN	493.1
8. Gabriele Bühlmann	SWI	493.0

The favorite in this event, the first to be decided at the Seoul Olympics, was world champion, world record holder, and two-time Female Shooter of the Year, Vessela Letcheva of Bulgaria. Lecheva was the focus of heavy media attention in South Korea, where she was considered unusually beautiful. Unnerved by the pressure of celebrity, she finished in a tie for seventeenth place. A few minutes later, a Korean shooting official found Letcheva wailing and beating her head against a restroom wall. Three days later she came from behind to earn a silver medal in the three-position event.

1992 Barcelona-Mollet del Vallès C: 45, N: 28, D: 7.26. WR: 500.8 (Valentina Cherkasova)

		PTS.
1. Yeo Kab-soon	KOR	498.2
2. Vessela Letcheva	BUL	495.3
3. Aranka Binder	YUG/SER	495.1
4. Dagmar Bílková	CZE	494.9
5. Valentina Cherkasova	SOV/RUS	494.6
6. Lee Eun-ju	KOR	492.6
7. Éva Fórián	HUN	492.4
8. Mirjana Horvat (Jovović)	BSH	491.6

The first gold medal of the 1992 Olympics was won by an unknown 18-year-old, Yeo Kab-soon, who was competing in her first international match. An extra level of tension was added to the final when Binder of Yugoslavia and Horvat of Bosnia were placed next to each other on the firing line. The two had been roommates when both competed for Yugoslavia, but now they represented two nations at war. After the competition ended, they embraced, but Binder declined to take part in the post-competition medalists' press conference.

1996 Atlanta-Wolf Creek C: 49, N: 30, D: 7.20. WR: 501.5 (Vessela Letcheva)

		PTS.
1. Renata Mauer	POL	497.6
2. Petra Horneber	GER	497.4
3. Aleksandra Ivošev	YUG/SER	497.2
4. Valerie Bellenque	FRA	496.6
5. Olga Pogrebniak	BLR	496.4
6. Marta Nedvědová	CZE	495.1
7. Éva Joó	HUN	494.5
8. Lesya Leskiv	UKR	494.2

Petra Horneber led from start to almost finish. She took a two-point lead into the final and was still ahead by 1.7 points after the ninth round of the final. But she misfired her final attempt and scored only 8.8 points. Beside her, Renata Mauer then took her last shot and won with a 10.7

In 46th place was Lida Fariman. Competing while wearing a traditional *chador* cloak, she was the first woman to represent Iran at the Olympics in 20 years, since the Iranian women's foil team competed at the 1976 Montreal Olympics.

2000 Sydney C: 49, N: 35, D: 9.16. WR: 503.5 (Gabriele Bühlmann)

		PTS.
1. Nancy Johnson	USA	497.7
2. Kang Cho-hyun	KOR	497.5
3. Jing Gao	CHN	497.2
4. Lyubov Galkina	RUS	496.7
5. Sonja Pfeilschifter	GER	495.9
6. Jayme Dickman	USA	495.3
7. Choi Dae-young	KOR	493.1/10.4
8. Anjali Ramakanta Vedpathak	IND	493.1/ 9.8

Seventeen-year-old Kang Cho-hyun took up shooting over the objections of her father, who had lost both legs in a hand grenade explosion during the Vietnam War. Nancy Johnson had wanted to try archery, but because there was no range near her home in Downers Grove, Illinois, at the age of fifteen she tried shooting instead. At seventeen she was forced to give up the sport because of nerve damage to her arms and legs, but she started training again anyway a few months later. Kang led the qualifying round, with Johnson and the six other finalists two and three points behind. It was Johnson who rose to the challenge. Halfway through the final she drew within one tenth of a point of Kang. In round 6, they both scored 10.2. Round 7 went to Kang 10.3 to 10.2. Round 8 they both shot 9.7. In round 9 Johnson drew even by scoring 10.7 to Kang's 10.5. Actually, Johnson did not know the exact score because she was afraid that the bright lights of the scoreboard would affect her shooting. With her final shot, Johnson scored 9.9 points. Kang followed with a 9.7 and the gold and silver medals were decided. Gao Jing earned the bronze medal by scoring 10.4 or higher with each of her last five shots.

2004 Athens-Markopoulo C: 44, N: 31, D: 8.14. WR: 504.9 (Du Li)

		PTS.
1. Du Li	CHN	502.0
2. Lyubov Galkina	RUS	501.5
3. Kateřina Kůrková	CZE	501.1
4. Zhao Yinghui	CHN	500.8
5. Tatyana Goldobina	RUS	499.5
6. Sonja Pfeilschifter	GER	498.7
7. Laurence Brize	FRA	497.9
8. Suma Shirur	IND	497.2

Lyubov Galkina set an Olympic record in the qualifying round, scoring 399 points. One point ahead of Du Li going into the final, Galkina held on to a slim lead throughout the first nine rounds of the final. With one shot remaining, she still led by four tenths of a point. Galkina's final shot, a 9.7, was her lowest score of the final. Meanwhile, the 22-year-old Du earned 10.6 points with her final shot to earn the first gold medal of the Athens Olympics.

2008 Beijing C: 47, N: 31, D: 8.9. WR: 505.0 (Sonja Pfeilschifter)

		PTS.
1. Kateřina Emmons (Kůrková)	CZE	503.5 OR
2. Lyubov Galkina	RUS	502.1
3. Snježana Pejčić	CRO	500.9
4. Jamie Beyerle	USA	499.8
5. Du Li	CHN	499.6
6. Olga Dovgun	KAZ	498.1
7. Marie-Laure Gigon	FRA	497.3
8. Sylwia Bogacka	POL	495.7

The 2004 Olympic bronze medalist, Kateřina Emmons recorded a perfect score of 400 points in the qualifying round. Three shooters scored 399 points: defending Olympic silver medalist Lyubov Galkina, Olympic newcomer Snježana Pejčić, and defending Olympic champion and reigning world champion Du Li.

Emmons led the final round with 103.5 points, and her Olympic-record-setting total score of 503.5 points earned her the first gold medal of the Beijing Olympics. Galkina scored the second-highest final-round score, 103.1, to take silver, while Du scored 100.6, the second-lowest of the final, to drop to fifth.

Emmons competed as Kateřina Kůrková at the 2004 Olympics, where she met American shooter Matt Emmons. The pair married in 2007.

TRAP

In the trap event, saucers 11 centimeters (4⅜ inches) in diameter are flung into the air at various angles. The shooter is allowed two shots with a 12-gauge shotgun at each saucer (or bird). According to the rules for women, after 75 targets, the top six shooters advance to the final, in which they shoot at 25 targets.

1896–1996 not held

2000 Sydney C: 17, N: 15, D: 9.18. WR: 95 (Satu Pusila)

		PTS.
1. Daina Gudzinevičiūtė	LIT	93
2. Delphine Racinet	FRA	92
3. Gao E	CHN	90
4. Anne Focan	BEL	88
5. Susanne Kiermayer	GER	86
6. Yelena Tkach	RUS	81
7. Emanuela Felici	SMR	64
8. Pia Hansen	SWE	64

Outsider Daina Gudzinevičiūtė, a 34-year-old lawyer, led the qualifying round by three points and then survived a spirited comeback by Delphine Racinet, who shot a perfect 25 in the final.

2004 Athens-Markopoulo C: 17, N: 16, D: 8.16. WR: 97 (Yelena Tkach)

		PTS.
1. Suzanne Balogh	AUS	88
2. María Quintanal Zubizarreta	SPA	84
3. Lee Bo-na	KOR	83
4. Whitly Loper	USA	82
5. Susanne Kiermayer	GER	79
6. Sue Nattrass	CAN	76
7. Emanuela Felici	SMR	60
8. Taeko Takeba	JPN	59

The qualifying round was held in blustery conditions, which wreaked havoc among the medal favorites. Defending Olympic champion Daina Gudzinevičiūtė and world top-ranked Gao E both failed to qualify for the final, finishing in 14th place and last place respectively.

Ranked only twentieth in the world, 31-year-old Suzanne Balogh led after the qualifying round with 66 points and scored 22 points in the final to take the gold. Working as an agricultural protection officer in Orange, New South Wales, Balogh had to travel four hours to Sydney to train on weekends.

2008 Beijing C: 20, N: 20, D: 8.11. WR: 96 (Zuzana Štefečeková)

		PTS.
1. Satu Mäkelä-Nummela	FIN	91 OR
2. Zuzana Štefečeková	SVK	89
3. Corey Cogdell	USA	86/1
4. Yukie Nakayama	JPN	86/1
5. Daina Gudzinevičiūtė	LIT	86/2
6. Yelena Struchayeva	KAZ	86/1
7. Deborah Gelisio	ITA	66
8. Susanne Kiermayer	GER	65

Several medal favorites failed to make the final, including 2006 world champion and six-time Olympian Sue Nattrass of Canada, who finished 11th, 2007 world champion Liu Yingzi of China (12th) and world number-three-ranked Daniela Del Din of San Marino (15th).

World record holder Zuzana Štefečeková and Satu Mäkelä-Nummela both scored 70 points in the qualifying round, but Mäkelä-Nummela outshot Štefečeková by two points in the final to take the gold and set an Olympic record. The bronze medal was decided by a four-way shoot-off, won by 21-year-old Alaskan Corey Cogdell, who had honed her skill by hunting wild game as a child.

SKEET

The competition begins with a 75-shot preliminary round. The shooters with the six highest scores advance to the 25-shot final.

1896–1996 not held

2000 Sydney C: 13, N: 11, D: 9.21. WR: 99 (Svetlana Demina)

		PTS.
1. Zemfira Meftakhetdinova	AZR	98
2. Svetlana Demina	RUS	95
3. Diána Igaly	HUN	93/4
4. Tash Lonsdale	AUS	93/3
5. Cindy Shenberger	USA	92/6
6. Yerdzhanik Avetisyan	RUS	92/5
7. Kim Rhode	USA	69
8. Shan Zhang	CHN	69

Zemfira Meftakhetdinova had a hard time training for the Olympics. The only shooting range in her hometown of Baku was shut down in 1990 when martial law was imposed in Azerbaijan. After that, Meftakhetdinova was only able to train by making one or two trips a year to Istanbul or Dubai. She and her trainer flew to Australia three weeks before the Olympics in order to prepare for the competition. Meftakhetdinova was haunted by her experience at the 1998 World Cup, where she set a world record in the opening round and then missed seven of 25 targets in the final to end up in fourth place. For the next six months she would wake up in the middle of the night and ask herself, "How could I have done that?" In Sydney, she took a two-point lead into the final . . . and then shot a perfect 25 to earn the gold medal.

2004 Athens-Markopoulo C: 12, N: 11, D: 8.19. WR: 99 (Svetlana Demina)

		PTS.
1. Diána Igaly	HUN	97
2. Wei Ning	CHN	93/2
3. Zemfira Meftakhetdinova	AZR	93/1
4. Lauryn Mark	AUS	92
5. Kimberly Rhode	USA	91
6. Connie Smotek	USA	90
7. Ri Hyon-ok	PRK	68
8. Chiara Cainero	ITA	67

Diána Igaly finished the qualifying round one point ahead of defending Olympic champion Zemfira Meftakhetdinova, 72 to 71. Igaly scored a perfect 25 points in the final to earn the gold medal, while Meftakhetdinova and Wei tied at 93 points, Wei winning the shoot-off for silver. The three medalists had won the past three world championships, Meftakhetdinova in 2001, Igaly in 2002 and Wei in 2003.

2008 Beijing C: 19, N: 19, D: 8.14. WR: 99 (Danka Barteková)

		PTS.
1. Chiara Cainero	ITA	93/2 OR
2. Kimberly Rhode	USA	93/1/2 OR
3. Christine Brinker	GER	93/1/1 OR
4. Nathalie Larsson	SWE	92
5. Sutiya Jiewchaloemmit	THA	92
6. Wei Ning	CHN	91
7. Antri Eleftheriou	CYP	67
8. Danka Barteková	SVK	67

The women's skeet competition was held in pouring rain. Reigning world silver medalist Chiara Cainero led the qualifying round with 72 points, followed by Thailand's Sutiya Jiewchaloemmit with 71, and three shooters tied with 70, including two-time double trap gold medalist Kim Rhode and reigning world champion Christine Brinker. Cainero, Rhode and Brinker all tied for first place with 93 points, so the medals were decided by shoot-off. Cainero earned gold after making her first two shots, when Brinker and Rhode both missed their second target. Rhode won silver in the second round of shoot-offs.

DISCONTINUED EVENT

DOUBLE TRAP

Competitiors shoot from each of five stations. The targets, 11 centimeters (4.33 inches) in diameter, are launched two at a time from one of three machines so that the shooters cannot be sure of the angle or direction of the target. The preliminary round consists of 120 targets. The top six shooters advance to the final and shoot at an additional 40 targets.

1996 Atlanta-Wolf Creek C: 21, N: 14, D: 7.23. WR: 149 (Deborah Gelisio, Xu Xiang)

		PTS.
1. Kimberly Rhode	USA	141
2. Susanne Kiermayer	GER	139/2
3. Deserie Huddleston	AUS	139/1
4. Theresa "Terry" DeWitt	USA	137
5. Riitta-Mari Murtoniemi	FIN	133
6. Yoshiko Kira	JPN	132
7. Annmaree Roberts	AUS	103/7
8. Gao E	CHN	103/6

Kim Rhode of El Monte, California, won the gold medal just one week after her 17th birthday. She was in first place after the qualifying round, but fell behind early in the final. She regained the lead by hitting 19 of her last 20 targets including the last ten in a row.

2000 Sydney C: 17, N: 12, D: 9.19. WR: 149 (Deborah Gelisio, Xu Xiang)

		PTS.
1. Pia Hansen	SWE	148
2. Deborah Gelisio	ITA	144
3. Kimberly Rhode	USA	139
4. Lin Yi-chun	TAI	134/14
5. Cynthia Meyer	CAN	134/13
6. Cindy Gentry	USA	130
7. Anne Focan	BEL	99
8. Yafei Zhang	CHN	98

Thirty-four-year-old Pia Hansen won easily, leading the qualifying round with 112 points to Deborah Gelisio's 107 and Kim Rhode's 103 and then hitting 36 of 40 targets in the final to win by four points. Hansen's technique would lead to a change in the rules of trap shooting. Traditionally, trap shooters would call for release of the targets, wait to see the clays and then shoot. Hansen would call and shoot immediately, hitting the clays almost as soon as they left the trap. After seeing Hansen's success, others copied her technique, leading to danger from ricochets and flying debris. The International Shooting Federation changed the rules to allow the clays to be released on a variable time delay.

2004 Athens-Markopoulo C: 15, N: 12, D: 8.18. WR: 150 (Zhang Yafei)

		PTS.
1. Kimberly Rhode	USA	146
2. Lee Bo-na	KOR	145
3. Gao E	CHN	142/2
4. Li Qingnian	CHN	142/1
5. Megumi Inoue	JPN	140
6. Nadine Stanton	NZL	137
7. Lin Yi-chun	TAI	106
7. Susan Trindall	AUS	106

To help Kim Rhode prepare for the 2004 Olympics, the Oak Tree Gun Hill in the Santa Clarita Valley of Southern California built an exact replica of the range to be used in the Athens Games. Rhode and Lee Bo-na emerged from the qualifying round in a tie. They were still tied after 26 of 40 shots in the final, but in the fourteenth round Lee missed one target, while Rhode hit both and went on to win by one point. Gao E won a shoot-off against teammate Li Qingnian to take bronze. Rhode earned a unique place in the record books, becoming both the first and the last woman to win the double trap competition, which was eliminated from the Olympic program after the Athens Games.

Chapter 22 **Swimming (Men)**

50-Meter Freestyle	200-Meter Individual Medley
100-Meter Freestyle	400-Meter Individual Medley
200-Meter Freestyle	10,000-Meter Open Water
400-Meter Freestyle	4 × 100-Meter Freestyle Relay
1500-Meter Freestyle	4 × 200-Meter Freestyle Relay
100-Meter Backstroke	4 × 100-Meter Medley Relay
200-Meter Backstroke	4 × 100-Meter Medley Relay
100-Meter Breaststroke	Discontinued Events
200-Meter Breaststroke	
100-Meter Butterfly	
200-Meter Butterfly	

Olympic pools must be 50 meters long. Olympic swimming competitions begin with a preliminary round. In races shorter than 400 meters, the swimmers with the sixteen fastest times advance to the semifinals. In races 400 meters or longer and in the relays, the eight fastest times qualify directly for the final. Between 1968 and 1996 all semifinal rounds were eliminated. In most events, a B final is held to determine places 9 through 16. The swimmer with the fastest qualifying time is assigned lane 4, the second-fastest lane 5, the third-fastest lane 3, the fourth-fastest lane 6, and so on until the slowest finalist, who is assigned lane 8.

The false-start rule in swimming is a bit odd. The first false start in a race is excused and the violator is not noted. However, anyone who commits a false start after the first one is immediately disqualified even if the first false start was committed by someone else. The International Federation of Amateur Swimming (FINA) also employs a rather questionable procedure for drug testing. Unlike most other sports, all medalists are not required to be tested. Instead, the subjects for testing are picked at random. At the 1992 Olympics, two of the top four finishers were tested and one of the next four. This rule led to controversy when it was revealed that certain Chinese women swimmers, who appeared to be taking banned substances, were not tested. Under pressure from coaches and the media, the federation agreed—in the middle of the meet—to require testing of gold medalists. After the Barcelona Olympics, FINA returned to its policy of random testing.

50-METER FREESTYLE

In freestyle events swimmers may use any style whatsoever. Some part of the swimmer must touch the wall at the end of each lap of the pool before heading back the other way; some part of the swimmer must also touch the wall at the finish.

Mark Spitz, 1972
Spitz won a record seven gold medals at the Munich Olympics, to go with the two he had earned four years earlier.

1896–1900 not held

1904 St. Louis C: 9, N: 2, D: 9.6.
(50 Yards—45.72 Meters)

			SWIM-OFF
1. I. Zoltán Halmay	HUN	28.2	28.0
2. J. Scott Leary	USA	28.2	28.6
3. Charles Daniels	USA	—	
4. David Gaul	USA	—	
5. Leo "Budd" Goodwin	USA	—	
6. Raymond Thorne	USA	—	

Halmaj defeated Leary by a foot. However, the US judge declared that Leary had won. A brawl broke out and went on for some time. Finally it was decided to call the race a dead heat and to have the two men swim again. After two false starts, Halmaj was off quickly and won easily.

1906–1984 not held

1988 Seoul C: 71, N: 44, D: 9.24. WR: 22.23 (Thomas Jager)

1. Matthew Biondi	USA	22.14 WR
2. Thomas Jager	USA	22.36
3. Gennady Prigoda	SOV/RUS	22.71
4. Daniel "Dano" Halsall	SWI	22.83
5. Stefan Volery	SWI	22.84
6. Vladimir Tkashenko	SOV/UKR	22.88
7. Frank Henter	GER	23.03
8. Andrew Baildon	AUS	23.15

Prior to the Olympics, friendly rivals Tom Jager and Matt Biondi had faced each other 14 times at 50 meters. Jager, a psychology graduate from UCLA, had won 10 of those confrontations, including the ones at the 1986 world championships and the 1988 Olympic trials. In fact, Biondi hadn't beaten Jager in two years. However, Biondi entered the final on a roll. Although his personal best in competition was a 22.33 set in 1986, he had beaten that time 50 times at the US Olympic training camp. And in Seoul he had already won five medals, including three gold. In the final, Biondi was able to keep up with Jager's typically fast start and then power his way to the finish in world record time. Biondi would ulitmately win eleven Olympic medals (8 gold, 2 silver, 1 bronze), but the one he earned in the 1988 50 meters was his most prized. All of Matt Biondi's medals are on display at the National Italian-American Sports Hall of Fame in Chicago.

Peter Williams, a South African competing in the United States for the University of Indiana, was not allowed to take part in the Games. In April, Williams had clocked a 22.18 in a time trial without competitors. His time was not allowed as a world record, not because it was achieved outside of competition, but because Williams was a citizen of South Africa. Steve Crocker also did not compete, due to the rule limiting each nation to two entrants. Crocker's time of 22.65 at the US trials, had he been given the opportunity to repeat it in Seoul, would have been good enough for the bronze medal. On the other hand, so would Dano Halsall's Olympic preliminary time of 22.61 or Gennady Prigoda's of 22.57.

1992 Barcelona C: 75, N: 51, D: 7.30. WR: 21.81 (Thomas Jager)

1. Aleksandr Popov	RUS	21.91 OR
2. Matthew Biondi	USA	22.09
3. Thomas Jager	USA	22.30
4. Christophe Kalfayan	FRA	22.50
4. Peter Williams	SAF	22.50
6. Mark Foster	GBR	22.52
7. Gennady Prigoda	RUS	22.54
8. Nils Rudolph	GER	22.73

In the run-up to the Barcelona Olympics, it was widely assumed that this race would be a battle between two close friends: 26-year-old Matt Biondi and 27-year-old Tom Jager. Between the two of them, Biondi and Jager had recorded 23 of the 24 fastest times in history. One or the other of them had held the world record for the past 6½ years, with Jager having set the current record on March 24, 1990. Biondi was the defending Olympic champion. That was the way it looked the day the Olympics began. But by the morning of the 50-meter final, the outlook appeared completely different. Two days earlier, 20-year-old Aleksandr Popov had won the 100-meter freestyle, leaving a stunned Biondi back in fifth place. On May 30, the fast-improving Popov had set a European record in the 50 free of 22.31. Exactly two months later he led the qualifying round with a time of 22.21, just ahead of Biondi's 22.32. In the final Popov got off to a quick start and was never headed.

1996 Atlanta C: 64, N: 57, D: 7.25. WR: 21.81 (Thomas Jager)

1. Aleksandr Popov	RUS	22.13
2. Gary Hall, Jr.	USA	22.26
3. Fernando Scherer	BRA	22.29
4. Jiang Chengji	CHN	22.33
5. Brendon Dedekind	SAF	22.59
6. David Fox	USA	22.68
7. Francisco Sánchez Betancourd	VEN	22.72
8. Ricardo Busquets Healey	PUR	22.73

Three days after beating Gary Hall to defend his 100-meter title, Aleksandr Popov did the same at 50 meters. The race was even after forty meters, but Popov powered ahead in the final strokes. One month later, Popov was stabbed by an Azeri watermelon vendor on the streets of Moscow. The knife penetrated 15 centimeters (6 inches) into his stomach, grazed his lung and barely missed his kidney. By 1997 Popov had recovered sufficiently to win the European championship at both 50 and 100 meters. At the 1998 world championhip he placed first in the 100 and second in the 50.

2000 Sydney C: 77, N: 71, D: 9.22. WR: 21.64 (Aleksandr Popov)

1. Anthony Ervin	USA	21.98
1. Gary Hall, Jr.	USA	21.98
3. Pieter van den Hoogenband	HOL	22.03
4. Lorenzo Vismara	ITA	22.11
5. Bartołomiej "Bartosz" Kizierowski	POL	22.22
6. Aleksandr Popov	RUS	22.24
7. Mark Foster	GBR	22.41
8. Oleksandr Volynets	UKR	22.51

Any doubts about Aleksandr Popov's chances to defend his Olympic title again were put to rest when on June 16, three months before the Sydney Games, he swam a 21.64 to break Tom Jager's 10-year-old world record. Two months later, Gary Hall, Jr., who had never before broken 22 seconds, did so three times at the US Olympic trials, culminating in a final time of 21.76. Although Hall had not been stabbed like Popov, he had survived a rough couple years that included a three-month suspension in 1998 after testing positive for marijuana and the 1999 discovery that he had diabetes. Bart Kizierowski led the qualifying round at 22.05. In the first semifinal, Hall beat teammate Anthony Ervin

22.07 to 22.13 and in the second semi Pieter van den Hoogenband, who had already won the 200- and 100-meter freestyles, edged Popov 22.11 to 22.17. Popov was out of the picture in the final, but the Americans finished in a deadheat for first. Ervin, whose father was African-American, was the first black swimmer to represent the United States at the Olympics. Hall, Ervin and Kizierowski all trained together as part of the Sprint Team 2000 group in Phoenix, Arizona.

The slowest participant in the 50 free was Samson Ndayishimiye of Rwanda, who completed his lap in 38.76 seconds. Ndayishimiye had trained in a 20-meter hotel pool and was thrilled just to swim in a pool that was clean.

In May 2005 Ervin sold his gold medal on eBay for $17,100, which he donated to UNICEF to help the victims of the 2004 Asian tsunami.

2004 Athens C: 83, N: 74, D: 8.20. WR: 21.64 (Aleksandr Popov)

1. Gary Hall, Jr.	USA	21.93
2. Duje Draganja	CRO	21.94
3. Roland Schoeman	SAF	22.02
4. Stefan Nystrand	SWE	22.08
5. Jason Lezak	USA	22.11
6. Brett Hawke	AUS	22.18
7. Oleksandr Volynets	UKR	22.26
8. Salim Iles	ALG	22.37

After a disappointing sixth place finish at the 2000 Olympics, world record holder Aleksandr Popov proved he was still a threat by sweeping the 50- and 100-meter freestyle events at the 2003 world championships. He also won the European championship three months before the 2004 Olympics. In Athens, however, Popov failed to reach the final, finishing 18th in the qualifying round with a time of 22.58. Gary Hall successfully defended his Olympic title, edging by a mere one-hundredth of a second his friend and training partner Duje Draganja, who had competed in the 100-meter butterfly less than a half-hour earlier. It was Hall's ninth Olympic medal and his fifth gold. At the age of 29, Hall was the oldest male swimmer to represent the United States at the Olympics since 1924. He also matched his father's feat of competing in three Olympics.

2008 Beijing C: 97, N: 90, D: 8.16. WR: 21.28 (Eamon Sullivan)

1. César Cielo Filho	BRA	21.30 OR
2. Amaury Leveaux	FRA	21.45
3. Alain Bernard	FRA	21.49
4. Ashley Callus	AUS	21.62
5. Ben Wildman-Tobriner	USA	21.64
6. Eamon Sullivan	AUS	21.65
7. Roland Schoeman	SAF	21.67
8. Stefan Nystrand	SWE	21.72

The 50-meter freestyle was expected to be a battle between reigning European champion Alain Bernard and world-record-holder Eamon Sullivan. In early 2008 the two had lowered the world record four times in a period of a month and a half, with Sullivan recording the latest time, 21.28, at the Australian Olympic trials.

As it turned out, 21-year-old César Cielo Filho was the one to beat. Cielo broke Aleksandr Popov's 16-year-old Olympic record in his first heat, finishing in 21.47, and proceeded to do the same in both the semifinal (21.34) and final (21.30) races, touching 0.15 seconds ahead of Amaury Leveaux. Cielo's gold medal was Brazil's first-ever for swimming.

A year after earning his gold medal, Cielo won both the 50- and 100-meter freestyle events at the 2009 world championships in Rome, becoming the third swimmer to achieve the feat and breaking the 100-meter freestyle world record in the process.

100-METER FREESTYLE

1896 Athens-Piraeus C: 10, N: 4, D: 4.11.

1. Alfréd Hajós (Arnold Guttmann)	HUN	1:22.2 OR
2. Otto Herschmann	AUT	1:22.8

The first Olympic swimming contests were held outdoors in open water, in and around the Bay of Zea, near Piraeus, and were watched by 20,000 people on the shore. The weather had turned unusually cold, and on the morning of the competition the temperature in the water dropped to 55 degrees Fahrenheit (13 degrees centigrade). The course was marked by a series of hollowed out pumpkins that floated on top of the water. The eventual winner of two of the three races, the 100 meters and the 1200 meters, was Alfréd Hajós, an 18-year-old from Budapest. Hajós recalled the experience of climbing into the water from the boat that had carried the 13 swimmers to the starting point: "The icy water almost cut into our stomachs. Until 70 meters it was a neck-and-neck race, but then I got my second wind and won the competition. My time wasn't anything to brag about."

Hajós was 13 years old when he felt compelled to become a good swimmer after his father drowned in the Danube River. In 1895 he won the 100-meter title at the unofficial European championships in Vienna. In 1902 he was a member of the first Hungarian national football team. Hajós went on to become a successful architect, winning a prize in the architectural division of the Olympic Art Contest in 1924. He was born Arnold Guttmann, but, following the fashion among Eastern

Alfréd Hajós, 1896

The winner of the 100-meter freestyle also survived 55°F water and 12-foot waves to win the 1500-meter freestyle in 1896. He later recalled, "My will to live completely overcame my desire to win."

European Jews of the time, he competed under a pseudonym. Later he legally changed his name to Hajós. His younger brother, Henrik, won a gold medal in 1906 as a member of Hungary's 4 × 200-meter freestyle relay team.

Otto Herschmann, who was also Jewish, earned a silver medal in the team sabre fencing event in 1912.

1900 not held

1904 St. Louis C: 8 or 9, N: 2, D: 9.5.
(100 yards)

1. I. Zoltán Halmay	HUN	1:02.8
2. Charles Daniels	USA	—
3. J. Scott Leary	USA	—
4. David Gaul	USA	—
5. David Hammond	USA	—
6. Leo "Budd" Goodwin	USA	—

Including the Intercalated Games of 1906, in which he won one gold medal and one silver, Zoltán Halmaj earned a total of nine Olympic medals: three gold, five silver, and one bronze.

1906 Athens C: 17, N: 10, D: 4.25. WR: 1:05.8 (Zoltán Halmaj)

1. Charles Daniels	USA	1:13.0
2. I. Zoltán Halmay	HUN	—
3. Cecil Healy	AUS	—
4. Paul Radmilovic	GBR	—
5. John Henry Derbyshire	GBR	—
6. József Onódy	HUN	—
7. Marquard Schwartz	USA	—
8. Hjalmar Johansson	SWE	—

Daniels defeated Halmaj by one meter with all the others far behind.

1908 London C: 34, N: 12, D: 7.20. WR: 1:05.8 (Zoltán Halmaj)

1. Charles Daniels	USA	1:05.6 WR
2. I. Zoltán Halmay	HUN	1:06.2
3. Harald Julin	SWE	1:08.0
4. Leslie Rich	USA	—

In 1908, 23-year-old Charles Daniels of New York City closed out his Olympic career, having won five gold medals, one silver, and two bronze, including the Intercalated Games of 1906.

1912 Stockholm C: 34, N: 12, D: 7.10. WR: 1:02.4 (Kurt Bretting)

1. Duke Paoa Kahanamoku	USA	1:03.4
2. Cecil Healy	AUS	1:04.6
3. Kenneth Huszagh	USA	1:05.6
4. Kurt Bretting	GER	1:05.8
5. Walter Ramme	GER	1:06.4

DNS: William Longworth (AUS)

Duke Paoa Kahinu Mokoe Hulikohola Kahanamoku was born in Honolulu on August 24, 1890. He was named after his father, who was named after the Duke of Edinburgh, who visited Hawaii in 1869. In Stockholm, Kahanamoku impressed the European spectators with his powerful, smooth stroking, and quickly became one of the most popular figures at the Games. His first-round time of 1:02.6 was more than two seconds faster than any of the other swimmers. He won his second round heat in a leisurely 1:03.8, the fastest time of the round. Because of a misunderstanding, the three US representatives, Kahanamoku, Kenneth Huszagh, and Perry McGillivray, failed to show up for the semifinals on Sunday evening July 7. Holding the final without them seemed absurd, so the three were allowed to take part in an extra heat on Tuesday, with the stipulation that to qualify for the final the winner would have to beat the time of Billy Long-worth, who had finished third in the first heat in 1:06.2. If this happened, then the second-place finisher in the special heat would also advance to the final. Not wanting to take any chances, Duke Kahanamoku equaled Kurt Bretting's world record of 1:02.4, allowing Huszagh to qualify as well. In the final, the following day, Kahanamoku took the time to look back and survey the field at the halfway mark. Noting that he had a comfortable lead, he eased up a bit and still won by two yards.

Silver medalist Cecil Healy was killed in the battle of the Somme on August 29, 1918. Healy, who also won a gold medal in the 4 × 200-meter freestyle relay, is the only Australian Olympic champion to have died on a battlefield.

1920 Antwerp C: 31, N: 15, D: 8.24/8.29. WR: 1:01.4 (Duke Paoa Kahanamoku)

First Final

1. Duke Paoa Kahanamoku	USA	1:00.4 WR
2. Pua Kela Kealoha	USA	1:02.2
3. William Harris	USA	1:03.2
4. William Herald	AUS	—

DISQ: Norman Ross (USA) 1:03.8

Duke Paoa Kahanamoku, 1920

The winner of the 1912 and 1920 100-meter freestyle, Kahanamoku also finished second in 1924, at the age of 33.

Second Final

1. Duke Paoa Kahanamoku	USA	1:01.4
2. Pua Kela Kealoha	USA	1:02.6
3. William Harris	USA	1:03.0
4. William Herald	AUS	1:03.8

Kahanamoku equaled his own world record of 1:01.4 in the semifinals, and then set a new record of 1:00.4 in the final, to celebrate his 30th birthday. However, Herald claimed that he had been fouled by Ross. Ross was disqualified and the race was ordered reswum. The order of the finish was exactly the same the second time, except that Ross, who had won the 1500-meter championship the day after the first 100-meter final, and the 800 meters the day before the second final, did not take part.

Kahanamoku eventually competed in three Olympics, winning three gold medals and two silver. Later he appeared in minor roles in 28 Hollywood films. He also played a major role in introducing the sport of surfing around the world. In 1917, in Honolulu, he guided his 16-foot surfboard on a 1¾-mile ride that would become a legend in surfing history. On June 14, 1925, Kahanamoku was relaxing on the beach in Corona del Mar, California, when a luxury yacht capsized, killing 17 people. The death toll would have been higher, but Duke used his surfboard to save the lives of eight of the yacht's passengers.

1924 Paris C: 30, N: 15, D: 7.20. WR: 57.4 (P. John Weissmuller)

1. P. John Weissmuller	USA	59.0 OR
2. Duke Paoa Kahanamoku	USA	1:01.4
3. Samuel Kahanamoku	USA	1:01.8
4. Arne Borg	SWE	1:02.0
5. Katsuo Takaishi	JPN	1:03.0
6. Orvar Trolle	SWE	

Johnny Weissmuller was born to German Swabian parents in Freidorf in what is now Romania on June 2, 1904. His family emigrated to the United States in 1908. His father worked as a coal miner before moving to Chicago, where he died of tuberculosis before his son had started on the path to fame and fortune. His mother worked as a cook in a restaurant while Johnny helped out by earning money as a bellhop and elevator operator at a hotel. On July 9, 1922. Johnny made swimming history by becoming the first person to swim 100 meters in less than one minute. On February 17, 1924. he lowered his time from 58.6 to 57.4, establishing a world record that would last for ten years. At the start of the 100-meter final at the Paris Olympics, Weissmuller found himself with 34-year-old defending champion Duke Kahanamoku on one side of him and Duke's 19-year-old brother, Sam, on the other side. Weissmuller was worried that the two Hawaiians had planned to swim a team race against him, but as they stood above the water Duke turned to him and said, "Johnny, good luck. The most important thing in this race is to get the American flag up there three times. Let's do it." And they did, with Weissmuller starting quickly and winning easily. That day he also won a gold medal in the 4 × 200-meter relay and a bronze medal in water polo. Two days earlier he had won the 400-meter freestyle. Johnny Weissmuller was one of the most popular participants at the 1924 Olympics, delighting the tough Parisian crowd not only with his superb swimming, but also with a comedy diving act, which he put on several times between races with his partner, Stubby Kruger. After Weissmuller's 100 meters victory, the crowd of 7000 stood and called for him for two or three minutes, until it was announced that he would appear again later in the afternoon.

1928 Amsterdam C: 30, N: 17, D: 8.11. WR: 57.4 (P. John Weissmuller)

1. P. John Weissmuller	USA	58.6 OR
2. István Bárány	HUN	59.8
3. Katsuo Takaishi	JPN	1:00.0
4. George Kojac	USA	1:00.8
5. Walter Laufer	USA	1:01.0
6. Walter Spence	CAN	1:01.4
7. Alberto Zorrilla	ARG	1:01.6

Coming out of the midrace turn in the 100 meters final at Amsterdam, Weissmuller inadvertently gulped a mouthful of water and almost blacked out. He lost two yards, but regained his composure and went on to win the fourth of his five Olympic gold medals. A couple of years later Weissmuller was training for the 1932 Olympics, when he received an offer of $500 a week to work for the BVD Underwear Company, advertising swimsuits. Out in Hollywood he was noticed while swimming at a club on Sunset Boulevard and was invited to try out for the part of Tarzan. Needless to say, he got the part, and in 1932 Weissmuller made his film debut in *Tarzan, the Ape Man.* The first of four Olympic medalists to play the part of Tarzan in the movies (the others being Buster Crabbe, Herman Brix, and Glenn Morris), Weissmuller acted in 11 more Tarzan films in the next 16 years. Another activity he engaged in more than once was getting married, which he did five times.

In 1958 Johnny Weissmuller was taking part in a celebrity golf tournament in Havana during a period in which Fidel Castro's guerrilla troops were doing battle with the soldiers of the Batista government. Weissmuller was on his way to the golf course with some friends and a couple of bodyguards, when rebel soldiers suddenly appeared out of the bushes and surrounded their car. The guerrillas disarmed the guards and pointed their rifles at the decadent Yankee imperialists. But Weissmuller had the proper solution to an otherwise difficult situation. Slowly raising himself to his full height, he beat his chest with his fists and let out an enormous yell. After a moment of stunned silence, the revolutionaries broke into smiles of delight and began calling out, "Tarzan! Tarzan! *Bienvenido!* Welcome to Cuba!" Dropping their weapons, they crowded around Johnny, shaking his hand and asking for his autograph. After a few minutes Weissmuller and his party were not only not kidnapped, but they were actually given a rebel escort to the golf course.

A note for trivia buffs—Question: in which film did Johnny Weissmuller say, "Me Tarzan, you Jane."? Answer: none. He did say, "Tarzan; Jane." For years he tried to correct the misquotation, but finally gave up.

1932 Los Angeles C: 22, N: 10, D: 8.7. WR: 57.4 (P. John Weissmuller)

1. Yasuji Miyazaki	JPN	58.2
2. Tatsugo Kawaishi	JPN	58.6
3. Albert Schwartz	USA	58.8
4. Manuella Kalili	USA	59.2
5. Zenjiro Takahashi	JPN	59.2
6. Raymond Thompson	USA	59.5

The 1932 men's swimming contests were highlighted by the fantastic performances of the Japanese, who stunned the Americans by winning the relay and by taking first and second in four of the five individual events. The first of these victories was recorded by 15-year-old Yasuji Miyazaki, who brought his schoolbooks with him to Los Angeles so that he wouldn't fall too far behind in his studies. Miyazaki had set an Olympic record of 58.0 in the semifinals. It is worth noting that the Japanese swimmers were the first Olympic athletes to inhale oxygen before and after their races.

1936 Berlin C: 45, N: 23, D: 8.9. WR: 56.4 (Peter Fick)

1. Ferenc Csík	HUN	57.6
2. Masanori Yusa	JPN	57.9
3. Shigeo Arai	JPN	58.0
4. Masaharu Taguchi	JPN	58.1
5. Helmut Fischer	GER	59.3
6. Peter Fick	USA	59.7
7. Arthur Lindegren	USA	59.9

Between 1912 and 1944 there were only three world record holders for the 100-meter freestyle: Duke Kahanamoku (1912–1922), Johnny Weissmuller (1922–1934), and Peter Fick (1934–1944). After the first round it appeared that the final would be a contest between Fick and the three Japanese, Taguchi recording the fastest time of 57.5 (an Olympic record), followed by Fick's 57.6. The semifinals were won by Taguchi and Yusa in 57.9 and 57.5, respectively, with Fick looking unusually off form. However, the final

Johnny Weissmuller, 1936

Weissmuller won five gold medals in 1924 and 1928 and then gained international fame as Tarzan (here to Maureen O'Sullivan's Jane).

provided a major upset. While the Japanese and Americans raced against each other, a 22-year-old Hungarian medical student named Ferenc Csík sneaked up in the outside lane to win the race in his fastest time ever. Although there was no question of who had finished first, there was a good deal of controversy regarding the remaining places. Photos of the finish led observers to believe that the actual order was 2—Taguchi, 3—Yusa, 4—Fick, 5—Arai, 6—Fischer, 7—Lindegren.

Dr. Csík died in an air raid on March 29, 1945, while administering first aid to a wounded man.

1948 London C: 41, N: 20, D: 7.31. WR: 55.4 (Alan Ford)

1. Walter Ris	USA	57.3 OR
2. Alan Ford	USA	57.8
3. Géza Kádas	HUN	58.1
4. Keith Carter	USA	58.3
4. Alexandre Jany	FRA	58.3
6. Per-Olof Olsson	SWE	59.3
7. Zoltán Szilárd	HUN	59.6
8. Taha El Gamal	EGY	1:00.5

Alex Jany led at the 50-meter turn, but he was passed in the next 25 meters by Ford, Kádas, and Ris. In the last ten meters Wally Ris of Iowa surged past the others to take first place. On March 18, 1944, Alan Ford had made history by becoming the first person to swim 100 yards in less than 50 seconds.

1952 Helsinki C: 61, N: 33, D: 7.27. WR: 55.4 (Alan Ford)

1. Clarke Scholes	USA	57.4
2. Hiroshi Suzuki	JPN	57.4
3. Göran Larsson	SWE	58.2
4. Toru Goto	JPN	58.5
5. Géza Kádas	HUN	58.6
6. Rex Aubrey	AUS	58.7
7. Aldo Eminente	FRA	58.7
8. Ronald Gora	USA	58.8

Scholes set an Olympic record of 57.1 in his preliminary heat.

Australian competitor Frank O'Neill, who failed to advance out of his qualifying round, went on to marry Patricia Cavendish, a British aristocrat. In 2000, after returning home from an extended visit to the Sydney Olympics, O'Neill found his wife had decided to change her will, leaving her entire fortune (then estimated at $80 million, or £52 million) to her pet chimpanzee Kalu.

1956 Melbourne C: 34, N: 19, D: 11.30. WR: 54.8 (Richard Cleveland)

1. Jon Henricks	AUS	55.4 OR
2. John Devitt	AUS	55.8
3. Gary Chapman	AUS	56.7
4. Logan Reid Patterson	USA	57.2
5. Richard Hanley	USA	57.6
6. William Woolsey	USA	57.6
7. Atsushi Tani	JPN	58.0
8. Aldo Eminente	FRA	58.1

Jon Henricks was the first favorite to win the 100-meter freestyle since Johnny Weissmuller. His victory in the final was his 56th win at that distance in 57 starts over a three-year period. When asked the secret of his success, Henricks, who was as feisty as his good friend and fellow Olympic champion Dawn Fraser, once replied, "You see that goddamn pool there—well, if you want to get to the top of it, dive in and start swimming. You do that for three, four or five years, and every time you stop swimming your coach bawls you out. You get a crazy ear disease from these tropical waters, but you've still got to keep on swimming. You get your head shaved to make you look like a zombie so that you will cut down water resistance, and you shave your legs for the same reason. You get invitations to a party and you write back regretting you are unable to attend owing to a prior engagement. That's a lie, of course, the only prior engagement is at the pool, going up and down, up and down, then up and down again. You finish going up and down and it's time to do some weightlifting—or maybe go to sleep while your coach goes out playing golf or fishing." Henricks is credited with being the first swimmer to shave the hair on his body before a race. He did so at the instigation of his father, who described Jon as "hairy as a goat."

1960 Rome C: 51, N: 34, D: 8.26. WR: 54.6 (John Devitt)

1. John Devitt	AUS	55.2 OR
2. Lance Larson	USA	55.2 OR
3. Manuel Dos Santos	BRA	55.4
4. R. Bruce Hunter	USA	55.6
5. Gyula Dobai	HUN	56.3
6. Richard Pound	CAN	56.3
7. Aubrey Burer	SAF	56.3
8. Per-Ola Lindberg	SWE	57.1

Two leading contenders were absent from the final. An emergency appendectomy six days before the US trials prevented Jeff Farrell from qualifying as one of the three American representatives, and defending champion Jon Henricks was eliminated in the semifinals as a result of intestinal problems developed on the way from Australia to Rome.

Dos Santos led the final at the turn, but Larson and Devitt passed him at 70 meters and finished in a near dead heat. Devitt congratulated Larson and left the pool in disappointment. Confusion developed, however, when the judges met to discuss their verdict. Of the three judges assigned the task of determining who had finished first, two voted for Devitt and one for Larson. However the second-place judges also voted 2-1 for Devitt. In other words, of the six judges involved, three thought Devitt had won and three thought Larson had won. When the electronic timers were consulted, it turned out that Larson had registered 55.1 seconds and Devitt 55.2. The unofficial electronic timer also showed Larson winning—by four inches, 55.10 to 55.16. Despite this evidence, the chief judge, Hans Runströmer of Germany, who did not have any say in the matter according to the official rules, ordered Larson's time changed to 55.2 and gave the decision to Devitt. Four years of protests failed to change the result.

John Devitt and Lance Larson, 1960
Larson, in lane four, appears to touch first at the finish of the 1960 100-meter freestyle. Yet John Devitt, in lane three (above), was awarded the gold medal.

1964 Tokyo C: 66, N: 33, D: 10.12. WR: 52.9 (Alain Gottvallès)

1. Donald Schollander	USA	53.4 OR
2. Robert McGregor	GBR	53.5
3. Hans-Joachim Klein	GER	54.0
4. Gary Ilman	USA	54.0
5. Alain Gottvallès	FRA	54.2
6. Michael Austin	USA	54.5
7. Gyula Dobai	HUN	54.9
8. Uwe Jacobsen	GER	56.1

The fastest times of the qualifying rounds, 54.0 and 53.9, were recorded by Gary Ilman, with Don Schollander close behind at 54.3 and 54.0. In the final, however, Ilman ran into a wave just after the turn and momentarily lost his concentration. Schollander finished strongly, passed McGregor in the last five meters, and won by about six inches. Schollander, who was born in Charlotte, North Carolina, and raised in Lake Oswego, Oregon, was trained by George Haines in Santa Clara, California. Before the Tokyo Games were over, the 18-year-old Schollander had become the first swimmer to win four gold medals at one Olympics.

A minor controversy developed over the awarding of the bronze medal. The judges were split as to whether Ilman or Klein had finished third. Both were clocked in the same time. The Japanese had thoughtfully provided electronic timers for the swimming events and, even though they were not used officially, they were consulted by the judges. It turned out that Ilman and Klein had stopped the clock at the exact same hundredth of a second, but that Klein had finished one one-thousandth of a second sooner. After 35 minutes of consultation, the judges decided that even if the electronic timing was unofficial, it had provided sufficient cause to award third place to Klein.

Three years after winning the gold medal, Schollander was tapped to join the Skull and Bones secret society at Yale, the same year that future US President George W. Bush was chosen.

1968 Mexico City C: 64, N: 35, D: 10.19. WR: 52.6 (Kenneth Walsh, Zachary Zorn)

1. Michael Wenden	AUS	52.2 WR
2. Kenneth Walsh	USA	52.8
3. Mark Spitz	USA	53.0

4. Robert McGregor	GBR	53.5
5. Leonid Ilyichov	SOV/RUS	53.8
6. Georgi Kulikov	SOV/LAT	53.8
7. Luis Nicolao Yanuzzi	ARG	53.9
8. Zachary Zorn	USA	53.9

Zac Zorn had equaled Ken Walsh's world record at the US Olympic trials, and the Americans went to Mexico City as heavy favorites. But they hadn't counted on 18-year-old Michael Wenden of Liverpool, New South Wales. Wenden had arrived in Mexico City hoping to qualify for the final, but when he clocked 53.0 in a trial meet, he began to think he had a shot at the bronze medal. Wenden's heat time of 53.6 was seven-tenths of a second faster than anyone else's, and his semifinal time of 52.9 was a half-second better than the rest. In the final, Zac Zorn, weakened by a week-long illness, went all-out for the first 50 meters and reached the turn almost a full body length ahead of the other swimmers. But he had exhausted himself, and eventually faded to last place. Wenden, on the other hand, swam the race of his life to score the most decisive 100-meter victory in 40 years.

1972 Munich C: 48, N: 30, D: 9.3. WR: 51.47 (Mark Spitz)

1. Mark Spitz	USA	51.22 WR
2. Jerry Heidenreich	USA	51.65
3. Vladimir Bure	SOV/RUS	51.77
4. John Murphy	USA	52.08
5. Michael Wenden	AUS	52.41
6. Igor Grivennikov	SOV/RUS	52.44
7. Michel Rousseau	FRA	52.90
8. Klaus Steinbach	GER	52.92

Mark Spitz had three goals at the Munich Games. The first was to prove himself better than Don Schollander by becoming the first swimmer to win five gold medals in one Olympics. The second was to become the first athlete in any sport to win six gold medals in one Olympics. The third goal was to go one better and win seven gold medals. It was this final goal that Mark Spitz was having doubts about on September 1. He had already won five gold medals. A sixth gold medal seemed assured, since the final race of the Olympics, the medley relay, looked to be a certain US victory. But about the 100-meter freestyle, Spitz was not so certain. Jerry Heidenreich had been swimming very well lately and had to be considered a serious threat. Spitz's father, Arnold, had constantly stressed to his son from an early age the motto "Swimming isn't everything, winning is." For Mark Spitz, it would have been better to enter four events and win all four than to enter seven events and win only six.

When he heard rumors that Spitz was thinking of withdrawing from the 100 freestyle, Spitz's coach, Sherm Chavoor, who was in Munich as the coach of the US women's team, rushed over to see his student. Chavoor successfully convinced Spitz that he would be perceived as "chicken" if he avoided a confrontation with Heidenreich. Finding this an unacceptable option, Spitz decided against withdrawing.

The heats were swum on the morning of September 2, and the semifinals seven hours later. In both races Spitz held back and finished behind defending champion Michael Wenden and slower than Jerry Heidenreich. In the final the following night, Spitz surprised Heidenreich when he departed from his usual tactics by going out at full speed rather than saving his strength for the second lap, as he usually did. Spitz reached the turn with a clear lead. With 15 yards to go, Spitz suddenly lost his rhythm, but he pulled himself together and reached the wall a half-stroke ahead of the onrushing Heidenreich.

Bronze medal winner Vladimir Bure was the father of ice hockey star Pavel Bure. The younger Bure led the Russian ice hockey team at the 1998 Winter Olympics.

1976 Montreal C: 41, N: 28, D: 7.25. WR: 50.59 (James Montgomery)

1. James Montgomery	USA	49.99 WR
2. Jack Babashoff	USA	50.81
3. Peter Nocke	GER	51.31
4. Klaus Steinbach	GER	51.68
5. Marcello Guarducci	ITA	51.70
6. Joe Bottom	USA	51.79
7. Vladimir Bure	SOV/RUS	52.03
8. Andrei Krylov	SOV/RUS	52.15

Jim Montgomery won his semifinal heat in 50.39 to break his own world record. In the final he not only set another record, but he also became the first person to break the 50-second barrier for 100 meters. Three weeks later in Philadelphia, Jonty Skinner brought the record down to 49.44. Skinner was not allowed to compete in the Olympics because he was from South Africa. He later became a coach at the University of Alabama.

1980 Moscow C: 39, N: 27, D: 7.27. WR: 49.44 (Jonty Skinner)

1. Jörg Woithe	GDR	50.40
2. Per Holmertz	SWE	50.91
3. Per Johansson	SWE	51.29
4. Sergei Kopliakov	SOV/BLR	51.34
5. Raffaele Franceschi	ITA	51.69
6. Serhei Krasyuk	SOV/UKR	51.80
7. René Ecuyer	FRA	52.01
8. Graeme Brewer	AUS	52.22

Woithe recorded his best time ever, 50.21, in the semifinals. Three days after the boycotted Olympic final, the US Outdoor National was won in 50.19 by Rowdy Gaines, who had twice clocked 49.61. Chris Cavanaugh was second in 50.26.

1984 Los Angeles C: 68, N: 44, D: 7.31. WR: 49.36 (Ambrose "Rowdy" Gaines)

1. Ambrose "Rowdy" Gaines	USA	49.80	OR
2. Mark Stockwell	AUS	50.24	
3. Per Johansson	SWE	50.31	
4. Michael Heath	USA	50.41	
5. Daniel "Dano" Halsall	SWI	50.50	
6. Stéphan Caron	FRA	50.70	
6. Alberto Mestre Sosa	VEN	50.70	
8. Dirk Korthals	GER	50.93	

In 1980, Rowdy Gaines, then at the peak of his career, had been expected to win four gold medals. His dreams of triumph and glory were shattered by the US boycott. He decided to stick it out until 1984 and qualified for the 100-meter freestyle by finishing second to Mike Heath at the US trials. This time Gaines felt much less confident of victory. He even prepared a loser's speech in which he would graciously praise those swimmers who had beaten him. In the afternoon, between the qualifying heats and the final, a nervous Gaines tried to relax by watching "The Newlywed Game" and Woody Woodpecker cartoons on television. Only a talk with fellow swimmer Tracy Caulkins calmed him down temporarily.

But standing on the starting block before the race, Gaines, who, at 25, was older than 66 of his 67 rivals in Los Angeles, was trembling like a leaf. However, he still had the presence of mind to recall some important advice from his coach, Richard Quick. Quick had noticed that the starter for the men's swimming events, Frank Silvestri of Panama, was very quick to pull the trigger, so quick in fact that the US team had protested against him at the 1983 Pan-American Games.

With this in mind, Gaines was ready for Silvestri and was first off the blocks, while leading contenders Mark Stockwell and Mike Heath were left behind. Gaines maintained his lead for the entire race, earning the first of his three gold medals. The Australians filed an official protest, but it was disallowed.

1988 Seoul C: 77, N: 51, D: 9.22. WR: 48.42 (Matthew Biondi)

1. Matthew Biondi	USA	48.63	OR
2. Christopher Jacobs	USA	49.08	
3. Stéphan Caron	FRA	49.62	
4. Gennady Prigoda	SOV/RUS	49.75	
5. Yuri Bashkatov	SOV/MOL	50.08	
6. Andrew Baildon	AUS	50.23	
7. Per Johansson	SWE	50.35	
8. Tommy Werner	SWE	50.54	

Six-foot-six-inch Matt Biondi had already recorded the 10 fastest 100-meter times in history, so his victory in Seoul was not surprising. Still, it was his first gold medal in an individual event and made up for his disappointment in losing the 100-meter butterfly by one one-hundredth of a second. When he climbed out of the Olympic pool after his victory, Biondi fulfilled a commercial contract by announcing to the TV cameras, "I'm going to Disneyland." And then, "I'm going to Disney World." The IOC ordered NBC-TV to destroy the tape of Biondi's statement, which they did quickly. Silver medalist Chris Jacobs was a former cocaine and alcohol addict who gave up drugs and drink two years before the Games.

1992 Barcelona C: 75, N: 52, D: 7.28. WR: 48.42 (Matthew Biondi)

1. Aleksandr Popov	RUS	49.02
2. Gustavo Borges	BRA	49.43
3. Stéphan Caron	FRA	49.50
4. Jon Olsen	USA	49.51
5. Matthew Biondi	USA	49.53
6. Tommy Werner	SWE	49.63
7. Christian-Alexander Tröger	GER	49.84
8. Gennady Prigoda	RUS	50.25

Aleksandr Popov was a backstroker when coach Gennady Touretsky converted him to freestyle, using underwater tapes of Matt Biondi for training. In the Olympics Popov, who had won the 1991 European championship in 49.18, would face the real Matt Biondi. At the time, Biondi had recorded nine of the ten fastest times in history and he hadn't lost a major race at 100 meters in eight years. He hadn't gone below 49 seconds since 1988, but he had won the United States trials in 49.17.

In Barcelona it was Popov who led the qualifying round at 49.27. In the final Biondi turned first, followed by Prigoda and Borges, while Popov held back in sixth place. Then Popov cut loose with a superb back 50—the first sub-25-second back 50 in history (24.99)—and won a clear victory. The race for second place was not so clear. Gustavo Borges, a 19-year-old student at the University of Michigan, appeared to touch second, but his name did not appear on the scoreboard because the touch pad in his lane malfunctioned. Officials studied a videotape of the finish and concluded that Borges had placed fourth.

A disappointed Borges was sitting crying by the warm-up pool when he was informed that he was actually second—the officials had mistakenly studied Biondi's finish, not that of Borges.

The results of the final left little doubt that the 100 free is a tall man's race. Three of the top five finishers—Borges, Caron, and Biondi—were 6 feet 7 inches tall, while Popov was 6 feet 6 inches and Olsen 6 feet 4 inches. Tommy Werner, in sixth place, was a mere 6 feet 3½ inches, which was no doubt his undoing.

Way, way back in the pack in the qualifying round, Ahmed Imthiyaz became the first athlete from the

Maldive Islands not to finish last at the Olympics when he finished next to last in the first heat. Unfortunately, the swimmer he beat was also from the Maldive Islands.

1996 Atlanta C: 60, N: 54, D: 7.22. WR: 48.21 (Aleksandr Popov)

1. Aleksandr Popov	RUS	48.74
2. Gary Hall, Jr.	USA	48.81
3. Gustavo Borges	BRA	49.02
4. Pieter van den Hoogenbrand	HOL	49.13
5. Fernando Scherer	BRA	49.57
6. Pavlo Khnykin	UKR	49.65
7. Ricardo Busquets Healey	PUR	49.68
8. Francisco Sánchez Betancourd	VEN	49.84

Undefeated in major meets since the last Olympics, Aleksandr Popov was the overwhelming favorite to defend his Olympic title. As Popov put it: " On a good day, nobody can beat me; on a bad day nobody can beat me." Actually, it was the closest men's 100-meter freestyle finish since the John Devitt-Lance Larson controversy of 1960, with Popov inching ahead of Gary Hall in the last fifteen meters. At the post-race press conference, a US reporter asked Popov to name his favorite actor or actress. "This is an American question," snapped Popov. "I don't dream about actors and actresses. They should dream about me. I'm reality; they are not." Popov was the first repeat winner of the 100 free since Johnny Weissmuller.

2000 Sydney C: 73, N: 66, D: 9.20. WR: 48.21 (Aleksandr Popov)

1. Pieter van den Hoogenband	HOL	48.30
2. Aleksandr Popov	RUS	48.69
3. Gary Hall, Jr.	USA	48.73
4. Michael Klim	AUS	48.74
5. Neil Walker	USA	49.09
6. Lars Frölander	SWE	49.22
7. Denis Pimankov	RUS	49.36
8. Chris Fydler	AUS	49.44

When the Sydney Olympics opened on September 15, the world record of 48.21 was held by Aleksandr Popov. The following evening, in the final of the 4 × 100-meter freestyle relay, Michael Klim broke Popov's six-year-old record with a time of 48.18. Three days after that, in the 100 meters semifinals, it was medical student Pieter van den Hoogenband who became the first person to break 48 seconds when he won the second semi in 47.84. In the first semi, Klim edged Popov 48.80 to 48.84. Expectations for the final were high, as Popov had defeated van den Hoogenband at the European Championships only two months before the Olympics. Indeed, of the eight finalists, five had already won gold medals and only Denis Pimankov had never won a medal of any color. Klim led at the turn, followed closely by Gary Hall, Jr., van den Hoogenband and Neil Walker, with Popov in sixth place. Van den Hoogenband pulled away to win, while Popov, by finishing second, earned his ninth career medal (4 gold and 5 silver).

Van den Hoogenband, Popov, Hall and Klim had expected to receive a lot of media attention, but another swimmer found himself an unexpected celebrity. With the encouragement of the International Olympic Committee, the International Swimming Federation allowed each nation to enter two swimmers even if they did not meet the official qualifying times. In the small West African nation of Equatorial Guinea, three trial races were held in a 20-meter hotel pool. Two of them were won by 22-year-old Eric Moussambani, who did not start swimming until January 2000. Because he could not afford the fee to use the hotel pool, he was only able to practice once a week for one hour at 6am on Sundays. He arrived in Sydney expecting to compete in the 50-meter freestyle, but his coach ordered him to enter the 100 meters, a distance Moussambani had never attempted. So, on the morning of September 19, Moussambani found himself on the starting line of heat one of the 100 meters, alongside two other extreme outsiders, Karim Bare of Niger and Farkhod Oripov of Tajikistan. Bare jumped into the pool too soon and was disqualified. Oripov, thinking the race had started, also dove in, and he too was disqualified. Moussambani, who had the presence of mind to stay on the podium until the gun went off, was left to swim the race alone. Swimming with his head above the water, he managed to complete the first 50 meters in 40.97 seconds, but he had expended almost all of his strength and the second 50 turned into an adventure. His speed, not great to begin with, diminished dramatically. He flailed and thrashed and, ten meters from the finish line, he stopped moving forward. Swim officials began to wonder if they should intevene, but then Moussambani heard the crowd shouting encouragement and he called up an extra burst of energy and made it to the wall. His time, 1:52.72, was more than 50 seconds slower than the next slowest swimmer, Dawood Yosuf Mohamed Jassim of Brunei. In fact, it was more than seven seconds slower than van den Hoogenband's winning time in the *200* meters. Relieved, Moussambani shyly waved to the crowd and went into the changing room and cried. It was not until the next day that he discovered that he had become, literally, an overnight celebrity. Encouraged by the kindness shown him by the other swimmers, among others, Moussambani decided to stick with the sport. At the 2001 world championships, he wisely limited himself to the 50 meters and finished in 31.88 seconds, almost six seconds faster than a swimmer from Antigua.

2004 Athens C: 72, N: 62, D: 8.18. WR: 47.84 (Pieter van den Hoogenband)

1. Pieter van den Hoogenband	HOL	48.17
2. Roland Schoeman	SAF	48.23
3. Ian Thorpe	AUS	48.56
4. Ryk Neethling	SAF	48.63
5. Filippo Magnini	ITA	48.99
6. Duje Draganja	CRO	49.23
7. Salim Iles	ALG	49.30
7. Andrei Kapralov	RUS	49.30

Defending Olympic champion Pieter van den Hoogenband had traded victories with Russia's Aleksandr Popov, with van den Hoogenband beating Popov by more than a second in the 2002 European Championships and Popov outtouching van den Hoogenband by a quarter second at the 2003 world championships. Van den Hoogenband recorded the fastest time of the qualifying round in Athens, 48.70 seconds, and then finished second in his semifinal heat behind Roland Schoeman. In the other semi, Ian Thorpe, the silver medalist in the 200 meters at the Sydney Olympics, edged out Aleksandr Popov–but not for first place. Thorpe took the last berth in the final, eliminating Popov from the competition. In the final, Schoeman and Ryk Neethling grabbed the early lead, but van den Hoogenband moved into second place at the turn and then surged past Schoeman to successfully defend his Olympic title.

2008 Beijing C: 64, N: 55, D: 8.14. WR: 47.50 (Alain Bernard)

1. Alain Bernard	FRA	47.21
2. Eamon Sullivan	AUS	47.32
3. César Cielo Filho	BRA	47.67
3. Jason Lezak	USA	47.67
5. Pieter van den Hoogenband	HOL	47.75
6. Lyndon Ferns	SAF	48.04
7. Matt Targett	AUS	48.20
8. Stefan Nystrand	SWE	48.33

Nicknamed "The Hovercraft," Alain Bernard became the favorite in the 100-meter freestyle event after breaking Pieter van den Hoogenband's nearly eight-year-old world record twice in two days to win the 2008 European championships in March. Bernard's main challenger was 50-meter freestyle world-record-holder Eamon Sullivan, who had come within 0.02 seconds of Bernard's 100-meter world record at the Australian Olympic trials less than a month later.

Two days before the 100-meter freestyle event in Beijing, Sullivan swam a 47.24 in the first leg of the 4 × 100-meter freestyle relay event. Bernard responded with a 47.20 in his 100-meter semi-final round, a record that lasted only five minutes before Sullivan bested it with a 47.05 to win his semifinal.

Swimming side-by-side in the final, the two stayed close throughout the race, with Bernard finally pulling ahead over the last 15 meters. Thirty-two-year-old veteran Jason Lezak moved up from fifth place in the second half to tie with César Cielo Filho for the bronze medal.

200-METER FREESTYLE

1896 not held

1900 Paris C: 26, N: 10, D: 8.12. WR (220 yards): 2:38.2 (Frederick Lane)

1. Frederick Lane	AUS	2:25.2 OR
2. I. Zoltán Halmay	HUN	2:31.4
3. Karl Ruberl	AUT	2:32.0
4. Robert Crawshaw	GBR	2:45.6
5. Maurice Hochepied	FRA	2:53.0
6. F. Stapleton	GBR	2:55.0
7. Jules Clévenot	FRA	2:56.2
8. Julius Frey	GER	2:58.2

The unusually fast times were due to the fact that the 1900 swimming races were held in the River Seine and swum *with* the current. Freddy Lane was unusually small for a swimmer: 5 feet 6 inches tall (1.68 m) and 133 pounds (60 kg). In honor of his victories in Paris, Lane was awarded a 50-pound bronze statue of a horse and another of a peasant girl. Lane managed to haul the statues back to Australia where he displayed them in his home (he used the peasant girl as a hat rack) until they were destroyed by a fire in 1968 when he was 88 years old. Two years after his Olympic triumphs, on July 24, 1902, Lane became the first person to swim 100 yards in one minute.

1904 St. Louis C: 4, N: 2, D: 9.6 WR (220 yards): 2:28.6 (Frederick Lane)

(220 Yards)

1. Charles Daniels	USA	2:44.2
2. Francis Gailey	AUS	2:46.0
3. Emil Rausch	GER	2:56.0
4. Edgar Adams	USA	—

1906–1964 not held

1968 Mexico City C: 57, N: 27, D: 10.24. WR: 1:54.3 (Donald Schollander)

1. Michael Wenden	AUS	1:55.2 OR
2. Donald Schollander	USA	1:55.8
3. John Nelson	USA	1:58.1
4. Ralph Hutton	CAN	1:58.6
5. Alain Mosconi	FRA	1:59.1
6. Robert Windle	AUS	2:00.9
7. Semyon Belits-Geiman	SOV/RUS	2:01.5

DNS: Stephen Rerych (USA)

Michael Wenden won his second gold medal, while Don Schollander added a silver to his five golds. Both swimmers were stretched to the limit by their high-altitude ordeal. Schollander had to be given oxygen while Wenden actually lost consciousness in the pool and almost drowned. He was saved by teammate Robert Windle. Afterward Schollander announced his retirement, telling reporters, "I'm finished with water—in fact I may not take a bath or a shower for another two years." As for Wenden, he returned to Australia a hero and had to face the shock of suddenly being a public person. His advice to future gold medalists? "Seek advice about an appropriate business manager and maintain close contact with a psychologist."

1972 Munich C: 46, N: 31, D: 8.29. WR: 1:53.5 (Mark Spitz)

1. Mark Spitz	USA	1:52.78 WR
2. Steven Genter	USA	1:53.73
3. Werner Lampe	GER	1:53.99
4. Michael Wenden	AUS	1:54.40
5. Frederick Tyler	USA	1:54.96
6. Klaus Steinbach	GER	1:55.65
7. Vladimir Bure	SOV/RUS	1:57.24
8. Ralph Hutton	CAN	1:57.56

Spitz trailed Genter with 50 meters to go, but came from behind to win his third gold medal in two days. Genter's performance was remarkable for the fact that he underwent surgery in Munich for a partially collapsed lung and had been released from the hospital only the day before the race. On the victory platform Spitz waved his shoes at the crowd and the cameras. Called before an IOC committee, he successfully convinced them that he had been motivated by exuberance rather than commercialism.

1976 Montreal C: 55, N: 33, D: 7.19. WR: 1:50.32 (Bruce Furniss)

1. Bruce Furniss	USA	1:50.29 WR
2. John Naber	USA	1:50.50
3. Jim Montgomery	USA	1:50.58
4. Andrei Krylov	SOV/RUS	1:50.73
5. Klaus Steinbach	GER	1:51.09
6. Peter Nocke	GER	1:51.71
7. Gordon Downie	GBR	1:52.78
8. Andrei Bogdanov	SOV/RUS	1:53.33

Furniss moved ahead in the last 50 meters to edge Naber, who had won the 100-meter backstroke an hour earlier. Because of drug testing and interviews, Furniss and Naber were not able to return to the pool for their warm-down until hours after the race ended. By this time, the stands were empty and they were alone. After a few minutes, they began to pick up speed and, before they knew it, they were racing each other again. "It showed," Furniss later recalled, "you didn't need 20,000 people to be there."

1980 Moscow C: 42, N: 25, D: 7.21. WR: 1:49.16 (Ambrose "Rowdy" Gaines)

1. Sergei Kopliakov	SOV/BLR	1:49.81 OR
2. Andrei Krylov	SOV/RUS	1:50.76
3. Graeme Brewer	AUS	1:51.60
4. Jörg Woithe	GDR	1:51.86
5. Ron McKeon	AUS	1:52.60
6. Paolo Revelli	ITA	1:52.76
7. Thomas Lejdström	SWE	1:52.94
8. Fabrizio Rampazzo	ITA	1:53.25

On August 1, the US Outdoor National was won by Rowdy Gaines in 1:50.02.

1984 Los Angeles C: 56, N: 36, D: 7.29. WR: 1:47.55 (Michael Gross)

1. Michael Gross	GER	1:47.44 WR
2. Michael Heath	USA	1:49.10
3. Thomas Fahrner	GER	1:49.69
4. Jeffrey Float	USA	1:50.18
5. Alberto Mestre Sosa	VEN	1:50.23
6. Frank Drost	HOL	1:51.62
7. Marco Dell'Uomo	ITA	1:52.20
8. Peter Dale	AUS	1:53.84

Standing 6 feet 7 inches and with a "wingspan" of 6 feet 11 inches, Michael Gross of Offenbach gained the nickname "The Albatross." In the 200-meter freestyle, Gross overwhelmed his opposition, winning by two bodylengths (two very long bodylengths) and becoming the first West German ever to win an Olympic swimming title.

1988 Seoul C: 63, N: 41, D: 9.19. WR: 1:47.44 (Michael Gross)

1. Duncan Armstrong	AUS	1:47.25 WR
2. Anders Holmertz	SWE	1:47.89
3. Matthew Biondi	USA	1:47.99
4. Artur Wojdat	POL	1:48.40
5. Michael Gross	GER	1:48.59
6. Steffen Zesner	GDR	1:48.77
7. Troy Dalbey	USA	1:48.86
8. Thomas Fahrner	GER	1:49.19

A talent-rich field lined up for the final. Michael Gross was the world record holder at 200 meters, the defending Olympic champion, and the two-time defending world champion. Matt Biondi, the world record holder in the 100-meter freestyle, had clocked the fastest non-Gross time of the year. Artur Wojdat, the world record holder in the 400-meter freestyle, had registered the best time of the preliminaries: 1:48.02. Anders Holmertz, although barely qualifying for the Olympic final, had swum the fastest time of 1987 in winning the European championship.

Few people paid any attention to Duncan Armstrong of Brisbane. More should have, though—his qualifying time of 1:48.66 bettered his two-year-old pre-Olympic best by 1.3 seconds. Armstrong, who was ranked forty-sixth in the world at the time, appeared to be peaking at the right time.

Armstrong was coached by Lawrie Laurence, who had coached Jon Sieben to an upset victory over Michael Gross in the 200-meter butterfly at the 1984 Olympics. Following the preliminaries of the Seoul 200-meter freestyle, Lawrence devised a special strategy for Armstrong in the final. He was assigned to lane 6 (as Sieben had been four years earlier) with Biondi beside him in lane 5. Because Biondi could be counted on to lead for the first 150 meters, Lawrence advised Armstrong to conserve energy by swimming as close to Biondi's lane as possible, drafting in the wake of the powerful American. Armstrong followed the strategy to perfection. As he explained later, "I just sucked into his trough and bodysurfed the first 100 meters." Placed third at the final turn, he passed Holmertz and then slingshotted away from Biondi with 25 meters to go. His time of 1:47.25 ended Michael Gross' 5-year reign as world record holder.

1992 Barcelona C: 55, N: 39, D: 7.26. WR: 1:46.69 (Giorgio Lamberti)

1. Yevgeny Sadovyi	RUS	1:46.70	OR
2. Anders Holmertz	SWE	1:46.86	
3. Antti Kasvio	FIN	1:47.63	
4. Artur Wojdat	POL	1:48.24	
5. Vladimir Pyshnenko	RUS	1:48.32	
6. Joseph Hudepohl	USA	1:48.36	
7. Steffen Zesner	GER	1:48.84	
8. Douglas Gjertsen	USA	1:50.57	

Laid low by flu, world champion and world record holder Giorgio Lamberti failed to qualify for the Italian team except in the 100 free. Lightly regarded at 200 meters prior to the Olympics, Yevgeny Sadovyi of Volgograd almost broke Lamberti's world record in the qualifying round when he swam a 1:46.74. In the final he came even closer, winning the first of his three gold medals, while Holmertz picked up his second straight silver medal. Antti Kasvio, in third place, became the first Finnish swimmer in 72 years to earn an Olympic medal. Both of his parents swam in the Olympics in the 1960s

1996 Atlanta C: 43, N: 36, D: 7.20. WR: 1:46.69 (Giorgio Lamberti)

1. Danyon Loader	NZL	1:47.63
2. Gustavo Borges	BRA	1:48.08
3. Daniel Kowalski	AUS	1:48.25
4. Pieter van den Hoogenband	HOL	1:48.36
5. Anders Holmertz	SWE	1:48.42
6. Massimiliano Rosolino	ITA	1:48.50
7. Joshua Davis	USA	1:48.54
8. Paul Palmer	GBR	1:49.39

Swimming in the fourth heat of the preliminary round, Jani Sievinen of Finland and Paul Palmer of Great Britain deadheated at 1:49.05. It turned out that this put them in a tie for eighth place overall. A swim-off was ordered to determine which of the two would advance to the final. Again Sievinen and Palmer tied, this time with a time of 1:48.89. Sievinen, who was scheduled to compete in the 400-meter individual medley the next day, declined to participate in a second swim-off.

For the third Olympics in a row, Anders Holmertz led in the final, only to be passed late in the race. This time it was ponytailed Dan Loader who overtook the Swede just before the final turn. Loader was the first swimmer from New Zealand to win a gold medal in an individual event.

2000 Sydney C: 51, N: 44, D: 9.18. WR: 1:45.51 (Ian Thorpe)

1. Pieter van den Hoogenband	HOL	1:45.35	EWR
2. Ian Thorpe	AUS	1:45.83	
3. Massimiliano Rosolino	ITA	1:46.65	
4. Joshua Davis	USA	1:46.73	
5. Paul Palmer	GBR	1:47.95	
6. James Salter	GBR	1:48.74	
7. Richard Say	CAN	1:48.76	
8. Grant Hackett	AUS	1:49.46	

On Friday, September 16, Ian Thorpe won two gold medals, setting world records in both the 400-meter freestyle and as a member of Australia's 4 × 100-meter relay team. Australian sports fans were expecting more of the same in the 200 meters, an event in which Thorpe already held the world record. But then came the semifinals on Saturday. In the first semi, Pieter van den Hoogenband swam a 1:45.35 to break Thorpe's world record. Thorpe came roaring back in the second semi, winning in 1:45.37. The stage was set for a great final the following night and the two favorites lived up to expectations. Van den Hoogenband held a slight lead at the halfway point, but he and Thorpe reached the 150-meter turn in a deadheat. Up to this point, Josh Davis had managed to keep up with the big two, but down the final stretch, as Davis put it, "They've got a second gear. I've just got that hold-on-for-dear-life gear." Van den Hoogenband and Thorpe pulled away, but, much to the shock of the predominantly Australian crowd, it was the Dutchman who really pulled away, matching exactly the record he had set in the semifinals. He went on to win another gold medal in the 100 free, as well as two bronze medals, one in the 4 × 200-meter relay and the other in the 50 free.

2004 Athens C: 59, N: 53, D: 8.16. WR: 1:44.06 (Ian Thorpe)

1. Ian Thorpe	AUS	1:44.71 OR
2. Pieter van den Hoogenband	HOL	1:45.23
3. Michael Phelps	USA	1:45.32
4. Klete Keller	USA	1:46.13
5. Grant Hackett	AUS	1:46.56
6. Richard Say	CAN	1:47.55
7. Simon Burnett	GBR	1:48.02
8. Emiliano Brembilla	ITA	1:48.40

The field included the four fastest men in the history of the event: defending Olympic champion Pieter van den Hoogenband, two-time world champion and current world record holder Ian Thorpe, former world record holder Grant Hackett, and 200-meter butterfly world champion and world record holder Michael Phelps. Van den Hoogenband recorded the fastest time of the semifinals (1:46.00), while Thorpe (1:46.65) edged out Phelps (1:47.08) and Hackett in the other. In a near repeat of the 2000 final, Thorpe trailed van den Hoogenband throughout the race, but this time it was the Australian who pulled away at the end, setting an Olympic record in the process.

2008 Beijing C: 57, N: 49, D: 8.12. WR: 1:43.86 (Michael Phelps)

1. Michael Phelps	USA	1:42.96	WR
2. Park Tae-hwan	KOR	1:44.85	
3. Peter Vanderkaay	USA	1:45.14	
4. Jean Basson	SAF	1:45.97	
5. Paul Biedermann	GER	1:46.00	
6. Dominik Meichtry	SWI	1:46.95	
7. Yoshihiro Okumura	JPN	1:47.14	
8. Robbie Renwick	GBR	1:47.47	

Competing at the 2004 Olympics at the age of nineteen, Michael Phelps had entered six individual events and earned five individual gold medals. In the only event he did not win, the 200-meter freestyle, he finished third.

Four years later, Phelps had won both intervening world championships, breaking Ian Thorpe's world record and becoming the first swimmer to crack the 1:44 barrier. Phelps held back in the preliminary rounds of the 2008 Olympic competition, finishing second and third in his heats, but came out strongly in the final, leading by a full body length halfway through the second lap. He finished nearly two seconds ahead of Park Tae-hwan, lowering his own world record by 0.90 seconds and becoming the first swimmer to complete the distance in under 1:43.

The event was the third of Phelps' eventual eight gold medals at the 2008 Olympics.

400-METER FREESTYLE

1896 Athens-Piraeus C: 3, N: 2, D: 4.11.
(500 Meters)

1. Paul Neumann	AUT	8:12.6
2. Antonios Pepanos	GRE	9:57.6
3. Eustathios Korafas	GRE	—

1900 not held

1904 St. Louis C: 4, N: 2, D: 9.7. WR (440 yards): 5:22.2
(440 Yards)

1. Charles Daniels	USA	6:16.2
2. Francis Gailey	AUS	6:22.0
3. Otto Wahle	AUT/POL	6:39.0
4. Leo "Budd" Goodwin	USA	—

For more than a century, Frank Gailey was mistakenly listed in official records as an American. Born in Brisbane, Gailey sailed to the United States in February 1904 and joined the Olympic Club of San Francisco. He competed in four events at the St Louis Olympics—winning three silver medals and one bronze—and returned to Australia soon after. Gailey later returned to the US and became a naturalized citizen, settling in Southern California, where he managed orange groves.

1906 Athens C: 13, N: 5, D: 4.27. WR (440 yards): 5:19.0

1. Otto Scheff	AUT	6:24.0
2. Henry Taylor	GBR	6:26.0
3. John Arthur Jarvis	GBR	—
4. Alajos Bruckner	HUN	—
5. Paul Radmilovic	GBR	—
6. Cecil Healy	AUS	—

1908 London C: 25, N: 10, D: 7.16. WR (440 yards): 5:19.0

1. Henry Taylor	GBR	5:36.8
2. Francis Beaurepaire	AUS	5:44.2
3. Otto Scheff	AUT/POL	5:46.0
4. William Foster	GBR	—

Henry Taylor, a cotton mill worker from Oldham, Lancashire, won the first of his three gold medals at the London Games. Including the Intercalated Games of 1906 and the Olympics of 1912 and 1920, Taylor earned a total of four gold medals, one silver, and three bronze. This race also marked the first appearance of Frank Beaurepaire, who was still winning Olympic medals in 1924 at the age of 33. Beaurepaire missed the 1912 Olympics when he was suspended for professionalism. His crime? As part of his job as a physical education teacher, he lectured on swimming and lifesaving.

1912 Stockholm C: 26, N: 13, D: 7.14. WR: 5:23.0 (Frank Beaurepaire)

1. George Hodgson	CAN	5:24.4 OR
2. John Hatfield	GBR	5:25.8
3. Harold Hardwick	AUS	5:31.2
4. Cecil Healy	AUS	5:37.8
5. Béla Las-Torres	HUN	5:42.0

Hodgson, a student at McGill University, had won the 1500 meters four days earlier. Bronze medalist Harold Hardwick was a multitalented athlete who won the Australian professional heavyweight boxing championship in 1915.

1920 Antwerp C: 22, N: 11, D: 8.28. WR: 5:14.6 (Norman Ross)

1. Norman Ross	USA	5:26.8
2. Ludy Langer	USA	5:29.0
3. George Vernot	CAN	5:29.6
4. Fred Kahele	USA	—

DNF: Francis Beaurepaire (AUS)

Twenty-four-year-old Norman Ross also won gold medals in the 1500-meter freestyle and in the 4 × 200-meter relay. He later achieved success as a radio music announcer in Chicago.

1924 Paris C: 23, N: 13, D: 7.18. WR: 4:54.7 (Arne Borg)

1. P. John Weissmuller	USA	5:04.2 OR
2. Arne Borg	SWE	5:05.6
3. Andrew "Boy" Charlton	AUS	5:06.6
4. Åke Borg	SWE	5:26.0
5. John Hatfield	GBR	5:32.0
6. Lester Smith	USA	

This was a thrilling race in which no more than five feet separated Weissmuller and Borg at any time. At 100 meters, Borg led by six inches. At the halfway mark, it was Weissmuller by nine inches, and at 300 meters, Borg touched first by three inches. Weissmuller finally drew away 20 meters from the finish and won by four feet.

Arne and Åke Borg were twin brothers.

1928 Amsterdam C: 26, N: 17, D: 8.9. WR: 4:50.3 (Arne Borg)

1. Alberto Zorrilla	ARG	5:01.6 OR
2. Andrew "Boy" Charlton	AUS	5:03.6
3. Arne Borg	SWE	5:04.6
4. Clarence "Buster" Crabbe	USA	5:05.4
5. Austin Clapp	USA	5:16.0
6. Raymond Ruddy	USA	5:25.0

Charlton and Borg were so intent on their personal duel that they failed to notice Zorrilla creep up in the outside lane and move ahead in the last 50 meters. In 1931, Zorrilla won the European ballroom dancing championship.

1932 Los Angeles C: 19, N: 10, D: 8.10. WR: 4:47.0 (Jean Taris)

1. Clarence "Buster" Crabbe	USA	4:48.4 OR
2. Jean Taris	FRA	4:48.5
3. Tsutomu Oyokota	JPN	4:52.3
4. Takashi Yokoyama	JPN	4:52.5
5. Noboru Sugimoto	JPN	4:56.1
6. Andrew "Boy" Charlton	AUS	4:58.6

Takashi Yokoyama set Olympic records of 4:53.2 and 4:51.4 in the opening round and the semifinals, but the final turned out to be a duel between world record holder Jean Taris and local favorite Buster Crabbe. Taris sprinted to an early lead and reached the halfway mark two lengths ahead. By 300 meters, Crabbe had cut the gap to one length. He continued to edge closer, finally drawing even 25 meters from the finish. The excitement was so great that swimmers and ushers rushed

Buster Crabbe, 1932

Crabbe came from behind to win the 1932 400-meter freestyle by one tenth of a second, in a thrilling finish. He attracted the attention of Hollywood producers, who later cast him as Tarzan, Buck Rogers, and Flash Gordon.

over from all parts of the stadium, while Johnny Weissmuller, sitting in the front row, leaped a fence to get a closer view of the finish. Crabbe touched the wall inches ahead of Taris. "That one-tenth of a second changed my life," Crabbe later recalled. "It was then that [the Hollywood producers] discovered latent histrionic abilities in me."

It seems that Paramount Studios, jealous of MGM's success with Johnny Weissmuller, wanted an Olympic star of its own. So scouts visited the Olympic Village, rounded up twenty likely candidates, and brought them to the studio for a screen test. As Crabbe described it later, "They take the twenty of us to wardrobe and issue each guy a G-string, and put us in front of a camera. Nobody knew what to do. The director said, 'Here, throw a spear.' So we each threw a spear. 'Here, throw this big rock.' So we each picked up this paper-maché rock and tried to make our muscles bulge throwing it. Then we went back to the Olympic Village and forgot about it." Seven days later, Crabbe won the gold medal. Three days after that, the Paramount scouts reappeared and brought him back to the studio. Crabbe went on to great fame as an actor; he was best known for his roles as Tarzan, Buck Rogers, and Flash Gordon. He died on April 23, 1983, at the age of 74.

1936 Berlin C: 34, N: 16, D: 8.12. WR: 4:38.7 (Jack Medica)

1. Jack Medica	USA	4:44.5 OR
2. Shumpei Uto	JPN	4:45.6
3. Shozo Makino	JPN	4:48.1
4. Ralph Flanagan	USA	4:52.7
5. Hiroshi Negami	JPN	4:53.6
6. Jean Taris	FRA	4:53.8
7. Robert Leivers	GBR	5:00.9

Jack Medica of Seattle staged a thrilling last-lap spurt to overtake Uto ten meters from the finish.

1948 London C: 41, N: 21, D: 8.4. WR: 4:35.2 (Alexandre Jany)

1. William Smith	USA	4:41.0 OR
2. James McLane	USA	4:43.4
3. John Marshall	AUS	4:47.4
4. Géza Kádas	HUN	4:49.4
5. György Mitró	HUN	4:49.9
6. Alexandre Jany	FRA	4:51.4
7. Jack Hale	GBR	4:55.9
8. Alfredo Yantorno	ARG	4:58.7

Bill Smith had been stricken with typhoid when he was six years old, and took up swimming to rebuild his body.

1952 Helsinki C: 51, N: 29, D: 7.30. WR: 4:26.9 (John Marshall)

1. Jean Boiteux	FRA	4:30.7 OR
2. Ford Konno	USA	4:31.3
3. Per-Olof Östrand	SWE	4:35.2
4. Peter Duncan	SAF	4:37.9
5. John Wardrop	GBR	4:39.9
6. Wayne Moore	USA	4:40.1
7. James McLane	USA	4:40.3
8. Hironashin Furuhashi	JPN	4:42.1

Boiteux, whose mother, Bibienne, represented France in the freestyle relay in 1924 and 1928, held off a late challenge from Ford Konno to win a surprise gold medal. As soon as Boiteux touched the wall, an older Frenchman in a beret rushed forward, leaped fully clothed into the water, and embraced the new champion. Reporters gathered around to find out who he was. "Coach?" "Manager?" they asked in various languages. Beaming with pride and overcome with emotion, the man in the beret held his arms up and uttered one word: "Papa!"

1956 Melbourne C: 32, N: 19, D: 12.4. WR: 4:26.7 (Ford Konno)

1. I. Murray Rose	AUS	4:27.3 OR
2. Tsuyoshi Yamanaka	JPN	4:30.4
3. George Breen	USA	4:32.5
4. Kevin O'Halloran	AUS	4:32.9
5. Hans Zierold	GDR	4:34.6
6. Garry Winram	AUS	4:34.9
7. Koji Nonoshita	JPN	4:38.2
8. Angelo Romani	ITA	4:41.7

Murray Rose was a 17-year-old vegetarian who became known as "The Seaweed Streak." Since his diet could not be provided for in the Olympic Village, Rose's parents moved him out and took care of his nutrition. His three gold medals at the Melbourne Games made a lot of Australians think twice about their diet.

1960 Rome C: 40, N: 25, D: 8.31. WR (440 yards): 4:15.9 (John Konrads)

1. I. Murray Rose	AUS	4:18.3 OR
2. Tsuyoshi Yamanaka	JPN	4:21.4
3. John Konrads	AUS	4:21.8
4. Ian Black	GBR	4:21.8
5. Alan Somers	USA	4:22.0
6. Murray McLachlan	SAF	4:26.3
7. Eugene Lenz	USA	4:26.8
8. Makoto Fukui	JPN	4:29.6

By 1960, both Murray Rose and Tsuyoshi Yamanaka had moved to Los Angeles and become students at the University of Southern California. In Rome, Alan Somers set an Olympic record of 4:19.2 in the qualifying round, but was unable to reproduce his time in the final. Although four years had passed since the last

Jean Boiteux, 1952
Boiteux, winner of the 1952 400-meter freestyle, helps his proud father out of the pool after the latter had leaped in to congratulate him.

Olympics, Rose and Yamanaka repeated their one-two finish, with the exact same distance separating them.

1964 Tokyo C: 49, N: 27, D: 10.15. WR: 4:12.7 (Donald Schollander)

1. Donald Schollander	USA	4:12.2 WR
2. Frank Wiegand	GDR	4:14.9
3. Allan Wood	AUS	4:15.1
4. Roy Saari	USA	4:16.7
5. John Nelson	USA	4:16.9
6. Tsuyoshi Yamanaka	JPN	4:19.1
7. Russell Phegan	AUS	4:20.2
8. Semyon Belits-Geiman	SOV/RUS	4:21.4

Schollander swam the last 100 meters in 1:01.7 to win his third gold medal.

1968 Mexico City C: 37, N: 20, D: 10.23. WR: 4:06.5 (Ralph Hutton)

1. Michael Burton	USA	4:09.0 OR
2. Ralph Hutton	CAN	4:11.7
3. Alain Mosconi	FRA	4:13.3
4. Gregory Brough	AUS	4:15.9
5. Graham White	AUS	4:16,7
6. John Nelson	USA	4:17.2
7. Hans-Joachim Fassnacht	GER	4:18.1
8. Brent Berk	USA	4:26.0

The day before the qualifying heats, Mike Burton woke up feeling nauseated; later he fainted in an elevator in the Olympic Village. The next day he "took it easy" and qualified in 4:19.3. He took charge of the final before the halfway mark and won going away, covering the last 100 meters in 1:01.6. Three days later, Burton won a second gold medal in the 1500 meters.

1972 Munich C: 43, N: 28, D: 9.1. WR: 4:00.11 (Kurt Krumpholz)

1. Bradford Cooper	AUS	4:00.27 OR
2. Steven Genter	USA	4:01.94
3. Tom McBreen	USA	4:02.64
4. Graham Windeatt	AUS	4:02.93
5. Brian Brinkley	GBR	4:06.69
6. Bengt Gingsjö	SWE	4:06.75
7. Werner Lampe	GER	4:06.97

DISQ (Drugs): Richard DeMont (USA) 4:00.26

Rick DeMont was a 16-year-old from San Rafael, California. Allergic to wheat and fur, he had been taking medication for asthma since he was four years old. When DeMont qualified for the US Olympic team, he was asked to fill out a standard medical form in which he listed all medications that he took. The team physicians of most other nations took this information from their athletes, found out the component parts of the various drugs from the *Physician's Desk Reference (PDR)* or similar works, and compared them to the list of banned drugs issued by the IOC for the 1972 Olympics. If any forbidden drugs were being used, the physicians came up with acceptable substitutes for their athletes. Unfortunately the US team physicians were not so well organized. Evidently they never even looked at

Rick DeMont, 1972

Sixteen-year-old Rick DeMont (center) finished first in the 1972 400-meter freestyle, but was disqualified for taking an asthma drug he did not know was on the prohibited list.

the forms. Instead, they just told the athletes not to take any drugs within 48 hours of competing without first clearing it with a doctor.

The night before the 400 meters competition, Rick DeMont woke up wheezing between 1 a.m. and 2 a.m., and took a tablet of Marax, unaware that it contained the banned drug ephedrine. At 8 a.m. he took another tablet. He swam his heat at about noon and qualified easily. Since his prescription said to take one tablet every six hours, he might have taken one more dose of Marax later in the day. The final began at 6:40 p.m. DeMont started slowly, saving his strength. In last place after 100 meters and sixth after 200, he picked up speed in the second half of the race. Swimming the last 100 meters in 58.22 seconds, he defeated Cooper by one-hundredth of a second, the smallest margin possible. After the race, DeMont, along with the other two medalists, was taken away for dope testing. At the awards ceremony there was no indication of any problem.

Two days later, on Sunday, DeMont, who was the world record holder at 1500 meters, took part in the preliminary round of that event, qualifying without being pressed. The next morning, however, he was informed that he had failed the drug test after the 400 meters and therefore would not be allowed to take part in the final of the 1500 meters. A distraught DeMont watched from the stands.

Over the next couple of days, hearings were held, affidavits were filed, and confusion reigned. At one point, DeMont's pharmacist in California received a call from a US doctor in Munich asking him, among other things, what Marax contained. Apparently, not one US team physician had bothered to take a copy of the *PDR* to Germany. The IOC ordered DeMont disqualified and issued a stern reprimand to the US officials in charge. Put on the defensive, team physicians tried to blame the swimming coaches, DeMont's family doctor, even the teenager himself. Yet DeMont had made no attempt to hide the fact that he took Marax. He didn't even know it was forbidden. When team officials had entered his room at the Olympic Village on Sunday to confiscate his drugs, the bottle of Marax was sitting in plain view.

By 1976 US swim officials had learned their lesson. Before the Montreal Olympics, the 51 members of the US team were questioned carefully about their medications, and it was learned that 16 of them were unknowingly using banned drugs. Substitutes were found for those 16, but all of this was far too late to help Rick DeMont, who had become the first American since Jim Thorpe to be forced to return his gold medal.

In 1996 DeMont filed suit against the United States Olympic Committee for breach of fiduciary duty, libel and negligence. In the suit, DeMont claimed that back in 1972 the IOC Medical Commission actually voted to allow DeMont to keep his gold medal on the condition that the US doctors publicly accept partial responsibility for DeMont's use of Marax. According to the lawsuit, when the US Olympic Committee refused, the IOC withdrew the offer and stripped DeMont of his medal. In 2001, DeMont agreed to withdraw the lawsuit in exchange for the USOC's public acknowledgement that he had in fact informed team doctors that he was using Marax for his asthma. In the meantime, DeMont had become a swimming coach. One of his students, Chrissy Ahmann Leighton, won two relay gold medals at the 1992 Olympics. She gave one of them to DeMont with the words, "Hold on to this until you get yours."

1976 Montreal C: 47, N: 29, D: 7.22. WR: 3:53.08 (Brian Goodell)

1. Brian Goodell	USA	3:51.93 WR
2. Timothy Shaw	USA	3:52.54
3. Volodymyr Raskatov	SOV/UKR	3:55.76
4. Djan Madruga Garrido	BRA	3:57.18
5. Stephen Holland	AUS	3:57.59
6. Sándor Nagy	HUN	3:57.81
7. Vladimir Mikheyev	SOV/RUS	4:00.79
8. Stephen Badger	CAN	4:02.83

Brian Goodell had already won the 1500 meters gold medal two days earlier. United States dominance in the 400-meter freestyle was so great that Volodymyr Raskatov's pre-Olympic European record of 3:58.02 would not have qualified him for the final at the US trials. Silver medalist Tim Shaw also won a silver medal in water polo in 1984.

1980 Moscow C: 28, N: 16, D: 7.24. WR: 3:50.49 (Peter Szmidt)

1. Vladimir Salnikov	SOV/RUS	3:51.31	OR
2. Andrei Krylov	SOV/RUS	3:53.24	
3. Ivar Stukolkin	SOV/EST	3:53.95	
4. Djan Madruga Garrido	BRA	3:54.15	
5. Daniel Machek	CZE	3:55.66	
6. Sándor Nagy	HUN	3:56.83	
7. Max Metzker	AUS	3:56.87	
8. Ronald McKeon	AUS	3:57.00	

Twenty-year-old Vladimir Salnikov of Leningrad was one of several Soviet swimmers who had been training in the United States when President Jimmy Carter made his first speech threatening a boycott of the Moscow Olympics unless Soviet troops pulled out of Afghanistan. However, Soviet coach Sergei Vaitsekhovsky was quick to thank American swimmers and coaches for the subsequent Soviet successes at the Olympics. "The Americans," he explained, "surprised us by not keeping any of their training secrets from us, which means there must still be some decent people left in the world."

Peter Szmidt of Canada set a world record of 3:50.49 in the 400 meters just before the Moscow Games began. At the US Outdoor National on July 31, Mike Bruner finished first in 3:52.19, followed by Brian Goodell in 3:52.99.

1984 Los Angeles C: 36, N: 25, D: 8.2. WR: 3:48.32 (Vladimir Salnikov)

1. George DiCarlo	USA	3:51.23	OR
2. John Mykkanen	USA	3:51.49	
3. Justin Lemberg	AUS	3:51.79	
4. Stefan Pfeiffer	GER	3:52.91	
5. Franck Iacono	FRA	3:54.58	
6. Darjan Petrič	YUG/SLO	3:54.88	
7. Marco Dell'Uomo	ITA	3:55.44	
8. Ronald McKeon	AUS	3:55.48	

In the absence of world record holder and defending Olympic champion Vladimir Salnikov, the gold medal was won by 21-year-old George DiCarlo, who led from the start and held on to break Salnikov's Olympic record. But the real stir in the 400-meter freestyle came a few minutes later. For the 1984 Games a consolation final had been added to determine places 9 through 16. It was here that Thomas Fahrner of West Germany saw a chance to redeem himself for the blunder he had committed in the preliminary round. Hoping to qualify just fast enough to gain an outside lane for the final, Fahrner took it easy and found himself shut out completely with only the ninth fastest qualifying time. In the consolation race, Fahrner gave it everything he had, bettering his personal best by almost two seconds and breaking DiCarlo's short-lived Olympic record with a time of 3:50.91.

1988 Seoul C: 49, N: 33, D: 9.23. WR: 3:47.38 (Artur Wojdat)

1. Uwe Dassler	GDR	3:46.95	WR
2. Duncan Armstrong	AUS	3:47.15	
3. Artur Wojdat	POL	3:47.34	
4. Matthew Cetlinski	USA	3:48.09	
5. Mariusz Podkościelny	POL	3:48.59	
6. Stefan Pfeiffer	GER	3:49.96	
7. Kevin Boyd	GBR	3:50.16	
8. Anders Holmertz	SWE	3:51.04	

All eight finalists had to break Thomas Fahrner's Olympic record just to qualify for the final. Holmertz took the early lead with Cetlinski and Wojdat close behind, Dassler in fourth, and Armstrong last. There were no changes in position for the first 200 meters. At 225 meters Cetlinski passed Holmertz and stayed in front until the 350 mark. Then he was caught by Wojdat, who sprinted home to break his own world record. Wojdat finished third. He was no match for the incredible closing rushes of Dassler and Armstrong, who swam the last 100 meters in 55.55 and 55.02,

Uwe Dassler, 1988
Dassler, winner of the 400-meter freestyle.

respectively. Dassler beat Armstrong by one foot with Wojdat another foot behind. Dassler improved his personal record by two seconds; Armstrong bettered his pre-Olympic best by five seconds.

1992 Barcelona C: 46, N: 31, D: 7.29. WR: 3:46.47 (Kieren Perkins)

1. Yevgeny Sadovyi	RUS	3:45.00 WR
2. Kieren Perkins	AUS	3:45.16
3. Anders Holmertz	SWE	3:46.77
4. Artur Wojdat	POL	3:48.10
5. Ian Brown	AUS	3:48.79
6. Sebastian Wiese	GER	3:49.06
7. Stefan Pfeiffer	GER	3:49.75
8. Danyon Loader	NZL	3:49.97

Just as he had four years earlier in Seoul, Anders Holmertz took the early lead and was still on world record pace after 300 meters. But as fast as he was going, Holmertz was never much more than a meter ahead of either Yevgeny Sadovyi or Kieren Perkins. Sadovyi had already won two golds in the 200-meter freestyle and the 4 × 200-meter relay. Perkins had broken Uwe Dassler's world record at the Australian Olympic trials in April. The two passed Holmertz almost in tandem, with Sadovyi holding his edge the whole way as both he and Perkins swam the last 100 meters in 54.62 seconds to blast Perkins' world record. All of the finalists set personal bests except Wojdat and Pfeiffer. Sadovyi beat his by 4 seconds. Almost as thrilling for Sadovyi as his victory was the fact that after the race he was interviewed for Russian television by his idol, Vladimir Salnikov, whom he had never met.

This was the first time in 80 years that swimmers from the United States had competed but failed to qualify for the final.

1996 Atlanta C: 34, N: 30, D: 7.23. WR: 3:43.80 (Kieren Perkins)

1. Danyon Loader	NZL	3:47.97
2. Paul Palmer	GBR	3:49.00
3. Daniel Kowalski	AUS	3:49.39
4. Emiliano Brembilla	ITA	3:49.87
5. Anders Holmertz	SWE	3:50.68
6. Massimiliano Rosolino	ITA	3:51.04
7. Jörg Hoffmann	GER	3:52.15
8. Jacob Carstensen	DEN	3:54.45

Three months before the Olympics, it seemed obvious that the gold medal would go to world champion and world record holder Kieren Perkins of Australia. But Perkins finished only third in the Australian trials and failed to qualify. The favorite's mantle passed on to Tom Dolan of the United States, who had recorded the fastest time of the pre-Olympic season (3:48.99). But Dolan, competing two days after winning the 400-meter individual medley, could only do 3:53.91 in the freestyle preliminary and didn't make it to the final. As usual, Anders Holmertz sprinted out to the early lead and held it for about 290 meters. Then he was passed by Dan Loader, who had won the 200-meter freestyle three days earlier, and by Paul Palmer. Loader pulled away steadily over the last two laps.

In the first preliminary heat, Omar Dallal of Jordan recorded a time of 4:41.12—almost 29 seconds slower than any of the 33 other swimmers. However, Dallal did better his previous best—and the Jordanese national record—by 15.86 seconds.

2000 Sydney C: 46, N: 40, D: 9.16. WR: 3:41.33 (Ian Thorpe)

1. Ian Thorpe	AUS	3:40.59 WR
2. Massimiliano Rosolino	ITA	3:43.40
3. Klete Keller	USA	3:47.00
4. Emiliano Brembilla	ITA	3:47.01
5. Dragoş Coman	ROM	3:47.38
6. Chad Carvin	USA	3:47.58
7. Grant Hackett	AUS	3:48.22
8. Ryk Neethling	SAF	3:48.52

It was the first night of competition at the Sydney Olympics and Australians were ready to root on one of their biggest favorites, 17-year-old Ian Thorpe. Thorpe had set world records at 200 meters three times and at 400 meters while qualifying first in the heats. Thorpe, with his size 17 feet and his 75" arm span, looked a bit like a large fish, and swam like one as well. He led the final from the start and pulled away to win with ease, setting another world record in the process. Less than an hour later, Thorpe anchored the Australian 4 × 100-meter relay team to victory in world record time. The following year, Thorpe earned six gold medals at the 2001 world championships.

2004 Athens C: 47, N: 43, D: 8.14. WR: 3:40.08 (Ian Thorpe)

1. Ian Thorpe	AUS	3:43.10
2. Grant Hackett	AUS	3:43.36
3. Klete Keller	USA	3:44.11
4. Larsen Jensen	USA	3:46.08
5. Massimiliano Rosolino	ITA	3:46.25
6. Yuri Prylukov	RUS	3:46.69
7. Spyridon Gianniotis	GRE	3:48.77
8. Takeshi Matsuda	JPN	3:48.96

The defending Olympic champion, world record holder and three-time world champion in the event, Ian Thorpe nearly didn't make it to Athens. On the blocks at the Australian Olympic trials, he lost his balance, fell into the pool and was disqualified. Thorpe was awarded an Olympic berth anyway when Craig Stevens, who had earned the second qualifying time, stepped aside, under intense public pressure, to focus on his main event, the 1500-meter freestyle. Stevens' decision sparked a controversy after it came out that he had been paid A$130,000 (US$114,000) by an Australian news program.

Thorpe's main challenger in Athens was Grant Hackett, the last man to have beaten him at 400 meters (in 1997). Hackett had also finished behind him in the 2001 and 2003 world championships. Thorpe took the lead in the final, but was passed by Klete Keller at 150 meters, before reclaiming the lead at the halfway point. Hackett stayed close to Thorpe, but was unable to close the gap and finished with silver.

2008 Beijing C: 36, N: 26, D: 8.10. WR: 3:40.08 (Ian Thorpe)

1. Park Tae-hwan	KOR	3:41.86
2. Zhang Lin	CHN	3:42.44
3. Larsen Jensen	USA	3:42.78
4. Peter Vanderkaay	USA	3:43.11
5. Oussama Mellouli	TUN	3:43.45
6. Grant Hackett	AUS	3:43.84
7. Yuri Prilukov	RUS	3:43.97
8. Nikita Lobintsev	RUS	3:48.29

At the 2007 world championships 17-year-old Park Tae-hwan had come from behind in the last 50 meters to upset Grant Hackett. A year-and-a-half later, in Beijing, Park pulled out to an early lead in the final, and then held off Zhang for the gold medal, while Hackett faded to sixth over the last two laps. Park was the first swimmer from South Korea to win an Olympic medal.

1500-METER FREESTYLE

1896 Athens-Piraeus C: 9, N: 4, D: 4.11.
(1200 Meters)

1. Alfréd Hajós (Arnold Guttmann)	HUN	18:22.2
2. Ioannis Andreou	GRE	21:03.4

The competitors had to battle not only each other, but also horribly cold weather and 12-foot waves. Alfréd Hajós, the eventual winner, gave the following graphic description of the race:

"Three small boats took us out to the open sea, which was quite rough. My body had been smeared with a half-inch-thick layer of grease, for I was more cunning after the 100 meters event, and tried to protect myself against the cold. We jumped into the water at the start of a pistol, and from that point on the boats left the competitors to the mercy of the waves, rushing back to the finish line, to inform the jury of the successful start.

"I must say that I shivered from the thought of what would happen if I got a cramp from the cold water. My will to live completely overcame my desire to win. I cut through the water with a powerful determination and only became calm when the boats came back in my direction, and began to fish out the numbed competitors who were giving up the struggle. At that time I was already at the mouth of the bay. The roar of the crowd increased . . . I won ahead of the others with a big lead."

1900 Paris C: 16, N: 6, D: 8.12.
(1000 Meters)

1. John Arthur Jarvis	GBR	13:40.2
2. Otto Wahle	AUT	14:53.6
3. I. Zoltán Halmay	HUN	15:16.4
4. Max Hainle	GER	15:22.6
5. Louis Martin	FRA	16:30.4
6. Jean Leuillieux	FRA	16:53.2
7. Maurice Hochepied	FRA	16:53.4
8. Verbecke	FRA	17:13.8

John Jarvis, a Leicester house painter, was described by a contemporary source as "fat all over, which literally hangs in some parts. His breasts fall like a woman's, but he has powerful shoulders and tremendous thighs."

1904 St. Louis C: 7, N: 4, D: 9.6. WR: 24:36.2
(1 Mile—1609.34 Meters)

1. Emil Rausch	GER	27:18.2
2. Géza Kiss	HUN	28:28.2
3. Francis Gailey	AUS	28:54.0
4. Otto Wahle	AUT	—

DNF: Edgar Adams (USA), Louis deBreda Handley (USA), John Meyers (USA)

1906 Athens C: 24, N: 10, D: 4.24. WR: 23:16.8 (Barney Kieran)

1. Henry Taylor	GBR	28:28.0
2. John Arthur Jarvis	GBR	30:07.6
3. Otto Scheff	AUT/POL	30:53.4
4. Max Pape	GER	32:34.6
5. Emil Rausch	GER	32:40.6
6. Ernst Bahnmeyer	GER	33:29.4
7. Oskar Schiele	GER	33:52.4
8. Leopold Mayer	AUT	34:41.0

1908 London C: 19, N: 8, D: 7.25.

1. Henry Taylor	GBR	22:48.4 WR
2. Thomas Battersby	GBR	22:51.2
3. Francis Beaurepaire	AUS	22:56.2

DNF: Otto Scheff (AUT/POL)

Battersby led from the start and wasn't overtaken by Taylor until less than 200 meters remained. Taylor's time was the first internationally acknowledged world record for the 1500-meter freestyle. An English swimmer with the unusually appropriate name of Lewis Moist was eliminated in the semifinals.

1912 Stockholm C: 19, N: 11, D: 7.10. WR: 22:48.4 (Henry Taylor)

1. George Hodgson	CAN	22:00.0 WR
2. John Hatfield	GBR	22:39.0
3. Harold Hardwick	AUS	23:15.4

DNF: Malcolm Champion (NZL), Béla Las-Torres (HUN)

Until the 1984 Games, George Hodgson of Montreal was the only Canadian to win an Olympic swimming championship. In the first round he set a world record of 22:23.0. He bettered this time in the final, setting a 1000-meter world record of 14:37.0 on the way. After completing 1500 meters, he continued on to swim the mile, setting three world records in one race. Four days later, he also won the 400-meter race. His 1500-meter record lasted for 11 years.

1920 Antwerp C: 23, N: 12, D: 8.25. WR: 22:00.0 (George Hodgson)

1. Norman Ross	USA	22:23.2
2. George Vernot	CAN	22:36.4e
3. Francis Beaurepaire	AUS	23:04.0e
4. Fred Kahele	USA	23:59.1e
5. Eugene Bolden	USA	24:04.3e

Ross allowed Vernot to set the early pace, then took charge midway and went on to win by 12 meters.

1924 Paris C: 22, N: 12. D: 7.15. WR: 21:15.0 (Arne Borg)

1. Andrew "Boy" Charlton	AUS	20:06.6 WR
2. Arne Borg	SWE	20:41.4
3. Francis Beaurepaire	AUS	21:48.4
4. John Hatfield	GBR	21:55.6
5. Katsuo Takaishi	JPN	22:10.4
6. Åke Borg	SWE	

The son of a bank manager in Manly, Boy Charlton became an Australian cultural icon when, at the age of 16, he defeated the great Swedish swimmer, Arne Borg, in a heavily publicized 440-yard race in Sydney in early 1924. Borg added to the sensation of Charlton's victory by rowing his conqueror the length of the pool in a dinghy and hailing him as a champion. A few months later, Charlton sailed for Paris, accompanied by his coach, a local war veteran named Tom Adrian, as well as the rest of the Australian team. Unfortunately, Adrian suffered from what was then known as shell shock and what is now known as post-traumatic stress syndrome. As the steamer headed west, Adrian became increasingly moody. Finally he threw himself overboard. He was fished out safely, but he was never the same again, and there was great apprehension that Charlton's performance would be adversely affected. Instead, the teenager seemed more determined than ever, winning his preliminary heat in 21:20.8. Arne Borg, "The Swedish Sturgeon," came right back in the next heat to break his own world record in a time of 21:11.4. However, in the final, it was Charlton who prevailed, bettering Borg's two-day-old record by more than a minute.

1928 Amsterdam C: 19, N: 13, D: 8.6. WR: 19:07.2 (Arne Borg)

1. Arne Borg	SWE	19:51.8 OR
2. Andrew "Boy" Charlton	AUS	20:02.6
3. Clarence "Buster" Crabbe	USA	20:28.8
4. Raymond Ruddy	USA	21:05.0
5. Alberto Zorrilla	ARG	21:23.8
6. Garnet Ault	CAN	21:46.0

Arne Borg led from start to finish to win his only Olympic gold medal. Borg was an extremely popular athlete in Sweden and abroad. Once he was called up for military service, but ignored the notice in order to take a tour of Spain. Imprisoned upon his return to Sweden, he received so many gifts of food and wine during his incarceration that he gained 17 pounds before he was finally released. Between 1921 and 1929, Borg set 32 world records at distances from 300 yards to one mile. His 1500 meters world record of 19:07.2, set in Bologna on September 2; 1927, remained unbroken for almost 11 years. He set the record despite having just lost four teeth in a water polo match against France.

1932 Los Angeles C: 15, N: 8, D: 8.13. WR: 19.07.2 (Arne Borg)

1. Kuzuo Kitamura	JPN	19:12.4 OR
2. Shozo Makino	JPN	19:14.1
3. James Cristy	USA	19:39.5
4. Noel Philip Ryan	AUS	19:45.1
5. Clarence "Buster" Crabbe	USA	20:02.7
6. Jean Taris	FRA	20:09.7

Fourteen-year-old Kuzuo Kitamura pulled away from his 17-year-old teammate, Shozo Makino, in the final 300 meters. Kitamura, the youngest male ever to win an Olympic gold medal in an individual event in any sport, grew up to become the Japanese representative to the International Labor Organization.

1936 Berlin C: 21, N: 10, D: 8.15. WR: 19:07.2 (Arne Borg)

1. Noboru Terada	JPN	19:13.7
2. Jack Medica	USA	19:34.0
3. Shumpei Uto	JPN	19:34.5
4. Sunao Ishiharada	JPN	19:48.5
5. Ralph Flanagan	USA	19:54.8
6. Robert Leivers	GBR	19:57.4
7. Heinz Arendt	GER	19:59.0

Terada took the lead at the gun and drew away slowly but steadily to win by 25 meters.

1948 London C: 39, N: 21, D: 8.7. WR: 18:58.8 (Tomikatsu Amano)

1. James McLane	USA	19:18.5
2. John Marshall	AUS	19:31.3
3. György Mitró	HUN	19:43.2
4. György Csordás	HUN	19:54.2
5. Marijan Stipetič	YUG/SER	20:10.7
6. Forbes Norris	USA	20:18.8
7. Donald Bland	GBR	20:19.8
8. William Heusner	USA	20:45.4

Seventeen-year-old Jimmy McLane studied the technique of rival John Marshall and discovered that Marshall stayed close to the lane line on his breathing side. Swimming in the next lane, McLane took advantage of this quirk on each lap that found him on Marshall's right side. McLane swam as close to Marshall as he could and kept exactly one body length ahead of him so that the splashing from his powerful kick distracted the Australian. After the Olympics, the two became teammates at Yale.

Arne Borg
Known as "the Swedish Sturgeon", Borg earned silver in the 1924 1500-meter freestyle, then followed it with gold in 1928.

1952 Helsinki C: 37, N: 22, D: 8.2. WR: 18:19.0 (Hironashin Furuhashi)

1. Ford Konno	USA	18:30.3 OR
2. Shiro Hashizume	JPN	18:41.4
3. Tetsuo Okamoto	BRA	18:51.3
4. James McLane	USA	18:51.5
5. Joseph Bernardo	FRA	18:59.1
6. Yasuo Kitamura	JPN	19:00.4
7. Peter Duncan	SAF	19:12.1
8. John Marshall	AUS	19:53.4

Ford Konno of Hawaii caught up with Hashizume after 1200 meters and pulled away to a decisive victory, covering the last 100 meters in 1:11.7.

1956 Melbourne C: 20, N: 11, D: 12.7. WR: 17:59.5 (I. Murray Rose)

1. I. Murray Rose	AUS	17:58.9
2. Tsuyoshi Yamanaka	JPN	18:00.3
3. George Breen	USA	18:08.2
4. Murray Garretty	AUS	18:26.5
5. William Slater	CAN	18:38.1
6. Jean Boiteux	FRA	18:38 3
6. Yukiyoshi Aoki	JPN	18:38.3
8. Garry Winram	AUS	19:06.2

George Breen set a world record of 17:52.9 in the third heat of the qualifying round. After 800 meters in the final, he, Rose, and Yamanaka were neck and neck. Then Rose began to surge ahead. He had built up a six-meter lead with only 100 meters to go, when Yamanaka began to sprint. He drew to within a yard of Rose, while the Australian crowd screamed at their young hero until he was finally alerted to the danger behind him. One last push earned Rose his third gold medal. Rose later recalled, "For years there was still some resentment in Australia toward the Japanese. I knew the crowd was watching us closely. Then, simultaneously, we both smiled, fell over the lane lines and warmly embraced. Behind us we heard the crowd cheering. But the true significance of our race and what happened afterward was on the front page of every newspaper the next day. One of the captions read, 'The war is finally over.'"

1960 Rome C: 30, N: 19. D: 9.3. WR: 17:11.0 (John Konrads)

1. John Konrads	AUS	17:19.6 OR
2. I. Murray Rose	AUS	17:21.7
3. George Breen	USA	17:30.6
4. Tsuyoshi Yamanaka	JPN	17:34.7

5. József Katona	HUN	17:43.7
6. Murray McLachlan	SAF	17:44.9
7. Alan Somers	USA	18:02.8
8. Richard Campion	GBR	18:22.7

John Konrads' family fled Latvia in 1944, when John was two years old. They wanted to emigrate to the United States, but were rejected because their family was too large. Instead, they settled in Australia. John started swimming as therapy after being hospitalized with a minor case of polio. In Rome, Konrads swam stroke for stroke with George Breen for 1050 meters before drawing away. Konrads' sister, Ilsa, won a silver medal in the 4 × 100-meter freestyle relay.

1964 Tokyo C: 31, N: 21, D: 10.17. WR: 16:58.7 (Roy Saari)

1. Robert Windle	AUS	17:01.7 OR
2. John Nelson	USA	17:03.0
3. Allan Wood	AUS	17:07.7
4. William Farley	USA	17:18.2
5. Russell Phegan	AUS	17:22.4
6. Sueaki Sasaki	JPN	17:25.3
7. Roy Saari	USA	17:29.2
8. József Katona	HUN	17:30.8

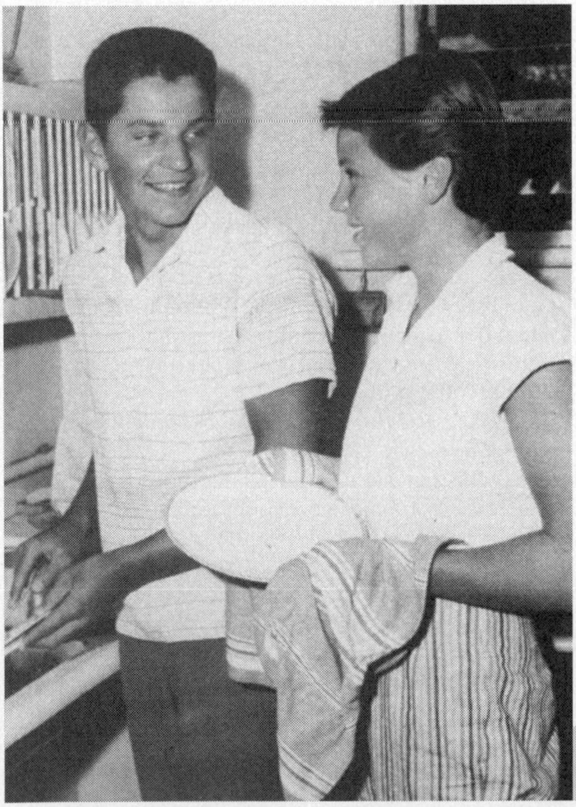

John and Ilsa Konrads, 1960
The Australian siblings both won swimming medals in Rome.

Noticeably absent was Murray Rose, who had been refused a place on the Australian team because he wouldn't return home for the Australian National Championships in February, unaware that they also served as Olympic tryouts. Rose presented his own version of a tryout on August 2, when he set a world record of 17:01.8. This embarrassed the officials of the Australian Swimming Union, but they refused to make an exception to the rules they had laid down. In Tokyo, Windle opened a 12-meter lead at the halfway mark and held on for the victory.

1968 Mexico City C: 21, N: 16, D: 10.26. WR: 16:08.5 (Michael Burton)

1. Michael Burton	USA	16:38.9 OR
2. John Kinsella	USA	16:57.3
3. Gregory Brough	AUS	17:04.7
4. Graham White	AUS	17:08.0
5. Ralph Hutton	CAN	17:15.6
6. Guillermo Echevarría Pérez	MEX	17:36.4
7. Juan Alanís	MEX	17:46.6
8. John Nelson	USA	18:05.1

The son of a truck driver, Mike Burton began his swimming career when, at the age of thirteen, he was hit head-on by a truck while bicycling. After spending eight weeks in the hospital with a dislocated hip and torn ligaments in his right leg, he was told that swimming was the only sport he could pursue.

1972 Munich C: 42, N: 30, D: 9.4. WR: 15:52.91 (Richard DeMont)

1. Michael Burton	USA	15:52.58 WR
2. Graham Windeatt	AUS	15:58.48
3. Douglas Northway	USA	16:09.25
4. Bengt Gingsjö	SWE	16:16.01
5. Graham White	AUS	16:17.22
6. Mark Treffers	NZL	16:18.84
7. Bradford Cooper	AUS	16:30.49
8. Guillermo García Castillo	MEX	16:36.03

Burton led for the first 600 meters, then Windeatt took over. By the 1200-meter mark, Burton was back in the lead for good, and dipped just below Rick DeMont's world record to win the third gold medal of his career.

1976 Montreal C: 31, N: 20, D: 7.20. WR: 15:06.66 (Brian Goodell)

1. Brian Goodell	USA	15:02.40 WR
2. Bobby Hackett	USA	15:03.91
3. Stephen Holland	AUS	15:04.66
4. Djan Madruga Garrido	BRA	15:19.84
5. Vladimir Salnikov	SOV/RUS	15:29.45
6. Max Metzker	AUS	15:31.53
7. Paul Hartloff	USA	15:32.08
8. Zoltán Wladár	HUN	15:45.97

The 1976 1500 meters final quickly evolved into a three-man race, with all three medalists ultimately breaking the world record. Bobby Hackett of Yonkers, New York, took the early lead and held it for 950 meters, at which point he was passed by Steve Holland. Holland was still in front after 1300 meters, but then Brian Goodell of Mission Viejo, California, stormed past both Hackett and Holland, taking the lead 150 meters from the finish and pulling away with a time of 57.73 seconds over the last 100 meters.

1980 Moscow C: 18, N: 11, D: 7.22. WR: 15:02.40 (Brian Goodell)

1. Vladimir Salnikov	SOV/RUS	14:58.27 WR
2. Aleksandr Chayev	SOV/RUS	15:14.30
3. Max Metzker	AUS	15:14.49
4. Rainer Strohbach	GDR	15:15.29
5. Borut Petrič	YUG/SLO	15:21.78
6. Rafael Escalas	SPA	15:21.88
7. Zoltán Wladár	HUN	15:26.70
8. Eduard Petrov	SOV/UKR	15:28.24

Vladimir Salnikov won three gold medals at the 1980 Olympics, but the big one was in the 1500 meters. In the final, on July 22, Salnikov became the first swimmer to break the 15-minute barrier, a feat that had been eagerly anticipated since Brian Goodell came within two and a half seconds at the previous Olympics.

1984 Los Angeles C: 27, N: 19, D: 8.4. WR: 14:54.76 (Vladimir Salnikov)

1. Michael O'Brien	USA	15:05.20
2. George DiCarlo	USA	15:10.59
3. Stefan Pfeiffer	GER	15:12.11
4. Rainer Henkel	GER	15:20.03
5. Franck Iacono	FRA	15:26.96
6. Stefano Grandi	ITA	15:28.58
7. David Shemilt	CAN	15:31.28
8. Wayne Shillington	AUS	15:38.18

Mike O'Brien, a 6-foot 6-inch 18-year-old, took the lead from DiCarlo after 600 meters and pulled away for an unchallenged victory. At the Friendship Games in Moscow three weeks later, Vladimir Salnikov took first place with a time of 15:03.51.

1988 Seoul C: 35, N: 22, D: 9.25. WR: 14:54.76 (Vladimir Salnikov)

1. Vladimir Salnikov	SOV/RUS	15:00.40
2. Stefan Pfeiffer	GER	15:02.69
3. Uwe Dassler	GDR	15:06.15
4. Matthew Cetlinski	USA	15:06.42
5. Mariusz Podkościelny	POL	15:14.76
6. Rainer Henkel	GER	15:18.19
7. Kevin Boyd	GBR	15:21.16
8. Darjan Petrič	YUG/SLO	15:37.12

Between 1977 and 1986 Vladimir Salnikov won 61 consecutive finals at 1500 meters. He broke the 15-minute mark four times. No one else did it even once. Then, at the 1986 world championships, Salnikov finished fourth. The following year, at the European championships, he failed to qualify for the final. It appeared that he was over the hill and ready for retirement. But Salnikov refused to give up. Trained by his wife, Marina, he mounted a comeback aimed at regaining his Olympic title in Seoul. The coaches of the Soviet team were dubious and refused to select him as a member of the national team. However, the Soviet Minister of Sport intervened and announced that if Vladimir Salnikov thought he deserved to represent the USSR in the 1988 Olympics, then the coaches must find a place for him. Still, Salnikov was not considered a serious medal contender. *Time* magazine summed up the consensus: "Salnikov's long day as the world's freestyle champion has passed. He can expect nothing more in Seoul than to see the last of his records fall in front of him."

But in the preliminary round, Salnikov served notice that he was still a threat. His qualifying time of 15:07.83 was second only to that of Matt Cetlinski. In the final, Cetlinski, in lane 4, took the early lead. Salnikov, beside him in lane 5, stayed close behind him in second place. Then, after 675 meters, Salnikov surged ahead, extending his lead steadily until the final 100 meters when Stefan Pfeiffer managed to close the gap somewhat. At 28, Salnikov was the oldest Olympic swimming champion in 56 years.

At 11:30 that night, after all the photos and interviews and ceremonies and congratulations were over, Vladimir Salnikov walked into the cafeteria at the athletes' village, hoping to grab a late snack. There were about 250 or 300 athletes and coaches in the room, representing a wide variety of nations and sports. As word spread that Salnikov had entered, the athletes and coaches spontaneously stopped eating, rose, and gave him a standing ovation.

1992 Barcelona C: 30, N: 24, D: 7.31. WR: 14:48.40 (Kieren Perkins)

1. Kieren Perkins	AUS	14:43.48 WR
2. Glen Housman	AUS	14:55.29
3. Jörg Hoffmann	GER	15:02.29
4. Stefan Pfeiffer	GER	15:04.28
5. Ian Wilson	GBR	15:13.35
6. Igor Majcen	SLO	15:19.12
7. Lawrence Frostad	USA	15:19.41
8. Viktor Andreyev	RUS	15:33.94

When Kieren Perkins was nine years old he ran through a sliding glass door while playing with his brother. His left calf was badly slashed and he needed 86 stitches. His doctor prescribed swimming to help heal the muscle. In 1990, when Perkins was only 16 years old, he became the third person to break 15 minutes. The following year, at the world championships in Perth, he pushed Jörg Hoffman to a world record of 14:50.36, touching only .22 seconds later. On April 5, 1992, at the Australian Olympic trials, Perkins broke that record with a time of 14:48.40. In the Olympic final, Perkins ripped through the first 100 meters in 55.30 seconds and the first 400 meters in 3:51.59. He pulled away steadily and won by more than 20 meters, setting another world record in the process.

1996 Atlanta C: 34, N: 26, D: 7.26. WR: 14:41.66 (Kieren Perkins)

1. Kieren Perkins	AUS	14:56.40
2. Daniel Kowalski	AUS	15:02.43
3. Graeme Smith	GBR	15:02.48
4. Emiliano Brembilla	ITA	15:08.58
5. Ryk Neethling	SAF	15:14.63
6. Masato Hirano	JPN	15:17.28
7. Jörg Hoffmann	GER	15:18.86
8. Aleksei Akatyev	RUS	15:21.68

Much was expected of defending champin Kieren Perkins going into the Olympic season. But at the Australian Olympic trials he missed qualifying in the 400 meters and finished second to Daniel Kowalski at 1500 meters. Then, in Atlanta, he barely qualified for the final by a quarter second. However, once he made it to the final, it was another story. Just as he had four years earlier, Perkins swam the first 100 meters in 55.30 and was never headed. The battle for second went down to the wire with Kowalski nipping Scotland's Graeme Smith by about 9 centimeters (3½ inches).

2000 Sydney C: 41, N: 32, D: 9.23. WR: 14:41.66 (Kieren Perkins)

1. Grant Hackett	AUS	14:48.33
2. Kieren Perkins	AUS	14:53.59
3. Christophe Thompson	USA	14:56.81
4. Aleksey Filipets	RUS	14:56.88
5. Ryk Neethling	SAF	15:00.48
6. Erik Vendt	USA	15:08.61
7. Ihor Chervynskiy	UKR	15:08.80
8. Heiko Hell	GER	15:19.87

There was never any doubt that this would be a battle between two-time defending champion Kieren Perkins and world champion Grant Hackett, who had defeated Perkins at 1500 meters four straight times. Hackett was the pre-Olympic favorite, but once the Games started, he seemed off-form, finishing seventh in the 400 free, eighth in the 200 free and missing making the Australian squad for the final of the 4 × 200-meter freestyle relay. Perkins, on the other hand, led the qualifying round with a time of 14:58.34—his first sub-15-minute 1500 since the 1996 Olympics. However, after meeting privately with his family, Hackett's spirits rose and, when the afternoon of the final arrived, he was ready. Hackett took the lead immediately. Perkins kept within striking distance for 800 meters, but then began to lose ground slowly but steadily. With 450 meters to go, Hackett pulled away and the race for gold was over. The Saturday afternoon race was a huge event in Australia, earning a 96.1 per cent audience share when it was broadcast live on television.

Perkins was the first person to win medals in the 1500-meter event at three *consecutive* Olympics (Francis Beaurepaire had won bronze medals at the 1908, 1920 and 1924 Games).

2004 Athens C: 34, N: 28, D: 8.21. WR: 14:34.56 (Grant Hackett)

1. Grant Hackett	AUS	14:43.40
2. Larsen Jensen	USA	14:45.29
3. David Davies	GBR	14:45.95
4. Yuri Prylukov	RUS	14:52.48
5. Spyridon Gianniotis	GRE	15:03.69
6. Graeme Smith	GBR	15:09.71
7. Dragoş Coman	ROM	15:10.21
8. Craig Stevens	AUS	15:13.66

As part of his preparation for the Olympics, Larsen Jensen, the 18-year-old son of almond farmers, wrote his target time—14 minutes 45 seconds—and his projected split times, on post-it notes throughout his apartment, including on the bottom of his toilet lid. Although Jensen achieved his goal in the final, it wasn't fast enough for the gold, as defending Olympic champion, three-time world champion and world record holder Grant Hackett, leading Jensen by only a sixth of a second with 100 meters left, swam the last 50 meters in 28.28 seconds to pull away to victory. Hackett had been battling bronchial asthma throughout the year, requiring 15 courses of antibiotics. After the Olympics, he discovered that he had competed with a partially collapsed lung, which had diminished his total lung capacity by 25%.

2008 Beijing C: 35, N: 27, D: 8.17. WR: 14:34.56 (Grant Hackett)

1. Oussama Mellouli	TUN	14:40.84
2. Grant Hackett	AUS	14:41.53
3. Ryan Cochrane	CAN	14:42.69
4. Yuri Prilukov	RUS	14:43.21
5. Larsen Jensen	USA	14:48.16
6. David Davies	GBR	14:52.11
7. Zhang Lin	CHN	14:55.20
8. Sun Yang	CHN	15:05.12

Two-time defending Olympic champion, four-time world champion and reigning world record holder in the 1500-meter freestyle, Grant Hackett was attempting to become the first man to win the same individual swimming event at three consecutive Olympics. The only two previous competitors to have done this were Dawn Fraser of Australia, winner of the 100-meter freestyle in 1956, 1960 and 1964, and Hungary's Krisztina Egerszegi, who won the 200-meter backstroke in 1988, 1992 and 1996.

Ryan Cochrane set an Olympic record of 14:40.84 seconds in his first-round heat, but Hackett lowered it to 14:38.92 two heats later. The two traded the lead during the first 1200 meters of the final, before Oussama Mellouli sprinted into the lead, holding off a late surge by Hackett to win Tunisia's first-ever Olympic swimming medal.

Born in Tunis and educated in Marseilles, France, Mellouli gained his first major international title at the 2007 world championships in Melbourne, Australia, coming from behind to win the 800-meter freestyle title. He also earned a silver in the 400-meter freestyle. However, his results were nullified after an in-competition drug test from 2006 turned up positive for amphetamines. Mellouli, who was studying at the University of Southern California at the time, admitted to having taken an Adderall pill to finish writing a term paper. Because of his admission, the Court of Arbitration for Sport reduced his ban from two years to 18 months, allowing him to compete at the 2008 Olympics.

"I've been waiting for this moment for two years," Mellouli said after his victory, "It's been two years since I haven't gone back to my hometown. I'm going to see my dad, my friends, my brothers and sisters."

100-METER BACKSTROKE

Swimmers begin backstroke races in the water, facing the starting wall, with both hands holding starting grips.

Their feet, including the toes, must be submerged. Swimmers may remain completely submerged for the first 15 meters of a race. After that, some part of the swimmer must be above the surface of the water, except during turns. Swimmers must swim on their backs, but they are permitted to rotate up to, but not including, 90 degrees from horizontal. Before 1991, backstrokers had to touch the wall with their hands during turns. Now it is possible to do a flip turn. During turns, a swimmer may turn his or her shoulders to the vertical. Once the body has left the position on the back, no kick or arm pull can be made that is independent of the continuous turning action. The swimmer must touch the wall with some part of the body and must return to a position on the back upon leaving the wall.

1896–1900 not held

1904 St. Louis C: 6, N: 2, D: 9.6.
(100 Yards)

1. Walter Brack	GER	1:16.8
2. Georg Hoffmann	GER	—
3. Georg Zacharias	GER	—
4. William Orthwein	USA	—

AC: David Hammond (USA), Edwin Swatek (USA)

1906 not held

1908 London C: 21, N: 11, D: 7.17. WR: 1:25.0

1. Arno Bieberstein	GER	1:24.6 WR
2. Ludvig Dam	DEN	1:26.6
3. Herbert Haresnape	GBR	1:27.0
4. Gustav Aurisch	GER	—

1912 Stockholm C: 18, N: 7, D: 7.13. WR: 1:15.6 (Otto Fahr)

1. Harry Hebner	USA	1:21.2
2. Otto Fahr	GER	1:22.4
3. Paul Kellner	GER	1:24.0
4. András Baronyi	HUN	1:25.2
5. Otto Gross	GER	1:25.8

Hebner set an Olympic record of 1:20.8 in the semifinals.

1920 Antwerp C: 13, N: 6, D: 8.23. WR: 1:15.6 (Otto Fahr)

1. Warren Paoa Kealoha	USA	1:15.2
2. Ray Kegeris	USA	1:16.8
3. Gérard Blitz	BEL	1:19.0
4. Percy McGillivray	USA	1:19.4
5. Harold Kruger	USA	—

Seventeen-year-old Warren Kealoha set a world record of 1:14.8 in the preliminary round.

1924 Paris C: 20, N: 11, D: 7.8. WR: 1:12.4 (Warren Kealoha)

1. Warren Paoa Kealoha	USA	1:13.2 OR
2. Paul Wyatt	USA	1:15.4
3. Károly Bartha	HUN	1:17.8
4. Gérard Blitz	BEL	1:19.6
5. Austin Rawlinson	GBR	1:20.0
6. Giyo Saito	JPN	

1928 Amsterdam C: 19, N: 12, D: 8.9. WR: 1:09.0 (George Kojac)

1. George Kojac	USA	1:08.2 WR
2. Walter Laufer	USA	1:10.0
3. Paul Wyatt	USA	1:12.0
4. Toshio Irie	JPN	1:13.6
5. Ernst Küppers	GER	1:13.8
6. John Besford	GBR	1:15.4

George Kojac was born in New York City and learned to swim in the East River.

1932 Los Angeles C: 16, N: 9, D: 8.12. WR: 1:08.2 (George Kojac)

1. Masaji Kiyokawa	JPN	1:08.6
2. Toshio Irie	JPN	1:09.8
3. Kentaro Kawazu	JPN	1:10.0
4. Robert Zehr	USA	1:10.9
5. Ernst Küppers	GER	1:11.3
6. Robert Kerber	USA	1:12.8

Kiyokawa served as vice-president of the International Olympic Committee from 1979 until 1983.

1936 Berlin C: 30, N: 17, D: 8.14. WR: 1:04.8 (Adolf Kiefer)

1. Adolf Kiefer	USA	1:05.9 OR
2. Albert VandeWeghe	USA	1:07.7
3. Masaji Kiyokawa	JPN	1:08.4
4. Taylor Drysdale	USA	1:09.4
5. Kiichi Yoshida	JPN	1:09.7
6. Yasuhiko Kojima	JPN	1:10.4
7. Percival Oliver	AUS	1.10.7

1948 London C: 39, N: 24, D: 8.6. WR: 1:04.0 (Allen Stack)

1. Allen Stack	USA	1:06.4
2. Robert Cowell	USA	1:06.5
3. Georges Vallerey, Jr.	FRA	1:07.8
4. Mario Chávez	ARG	1:09.0
5. Clemente Mejía Avila	MEX	1:09.0
6. Johannes Wild	SAF	1:09.1
7. W. John Brockway	GBR	1:09.2
8. Albert Kinnear	GBR	1:09.6

Allen Stack was already in the water awaiting the start of the final when he pulled up his swim trunks. The cord broke and his trunks began to slip off. Fortunately he was allowed to leave the pool and change his trunks.

1952 Helsinki C: 38, N: 25, D: 8.1. WR: 1:03.6 (Allen Stack)

1. Yoshinobu Oyakawa	USA	1:05.4 OR
2. Gilbert Bozon	FRA	1:06.2
3. Jack Taylor	USA	1:06.4
4. Allen Stack	USA	1:07.6
5. Pedro Galvão	ARG	1:07.7
6. Robert Wardrop	GBR	1:07.8
7. Boris Škanata	YUG/SER	1:08.1
8. Nicolaas Meiring	SAF	1:08.3

1956 Melbourne C: 25, N: 14, D: 12.6. WR: 1:02.1 (Gilbert Bozon)

1. David Theile	AUS	1:02.2 OR
2. John Monckton	AUS	1:03.2
3. Frank McKinney	USA	1:04.5
4. Robert Christophe	FRA	1:04.9
5. John Hayres	AUS	1:05.0
6. Graham Sykes	GBR	1:05.6
7. Albert Wiggins	USA	1:05.8
8. Yoshinobu Oyakawa	USA	1:06.9

1960 Rome C: 37, N: 27, D: 8.31. WR(110 yards): 1:01.5 (John Monckton)

1. David Theile	AUS	1:01.9 OR
2. Frank McKinney	USA	1:02.1
3. Robert Bennett	USA	1:02.3
4. Robert Christophe	FRA	1:03.2
5. Leonid Barbier	SOV/UKR	1:03.5
6. Wolfgang Wagner	GDR	1:03.5
7. John Monckton	AUS	1:04.1
8. Veiko Siimar	SOV/EST	1:04.6

After the 1956 Olympics, David Theile of Brisbane dropped out of swimming for two years so that he could concentrate on his medical studies. Yet he was able to come back better than ever to defend his championship. John Monckton was even with Theile at 50 meters but misjudged the turn and hit the wall with his head.

1964 not held

1968 Mexico City C: 37, N: 26, D: 10.22. WR: 58.4 (Roland Matthes)

1. Roland Matthes	GDR	58.7 OR
2. Charles Hickcox	USA	1:00.2
3. Ronald Mills	USA	1:00.5
4. Larry Barbiere	USA	1:01.1
5. James Shaw	CAN	1:01.4
6. Bob Schoutsen	HOL	1:01.8
7. Reinhard Blechert	GER	1:01.9
8. Franco Del Campo	ITA	1:02.0

Roland Matthes of Erfurt, Thuringia, was 16 years old when he set his first backstroke world record on September 11, 1967. In the next six years he would break records in the 100-meter and 200-meter backstroke 16 times. He also won four Olympic gold medals, two silver, and two bronze. In 1978 Matthes married Olympic champion Kornelia Ender. Their first child, Franziska, was born later that year, the product of parents who, between them, had earned eight gold medals, six silver medals, and two bronze. The couple divorced in 1982.

1972 Munich C: 39, N: 27, D: 8.29. WR: 56.3 (Roland Matthes)

1. Roland Matthes	GDR	56.58 OR
2. Michael Stamm	USA	57.70
3. John Murphy	USA	58.35
4. Mitchell Ivey	USA	58.48
5. Igor Grivennikov	SOV/RUS	59.50
6. Lutz Wanja	GDR	59.80
7. Jürgen Krüger	GDR	59.93
8. Tadashi Honda	JPN	1:00.41

1976 Montreal C: 41, N: 29, D: 7.19. WR: 56.30 (Roland Matthes)

1. John Naber	USA	55.49 WR
2. Peter Rocca	USA	56.34
3. Roland Matthes	GDR	57.22
4. Carlos Berrocal	PUR	57.28
5. Lutz Wanja	GDR	57.49
6. Bob Jackson	USA	57.69
7. Mark Kerry	AUS	57.94
8. Mark Tonelli	AUS	58.42

When John Naber was 9 years old he visited Olympia, in Greece, and told his parents that someday he would become an Olympic champion. Eleven years later, now 6 feet 6 inches tall and 195 pounds, Naber fulfilled his vow. In 1974 he had ended Roland Matthes' seven-year winning streak. Matthes was still the holder of the world record, but an appendectomy six weeks before the 1976 Olympics hurt his chances for defending his title. Naber set a world record of 56.19 in the semifinals and then set another one 24 hours later to win the first of his four gold medals.

1980 Moscow C: 33, N: 23, D: 7.21. WR: 55.49 (John Naber)

1. Bengt Baron	SWE	56.53
2. Viktor Kuznetsov	SOV/RUS	56.99
3. Volodymyr Dolhov	SOV/UKR	57.63
4. Miloslav Rol'ko	CZE	57.74
5. Sándor Wladár	HUN	57.84
6. A. Frederik Eefting	HOL	57.95
7. Mark Tonelli	AUS	57.98
8. Gary Abraham	GBR	58.38

The victory of 18-year-old Bengt Baron of Finspång, Sweden, was so unexpected that even he was stunned. "I just can't understand how I did it," he told reporters afterward. His pre-Olympic best had been 57.77. Silver medalist Viktor Kuznetsov served a suspension after testing positive for steroids in 1978. Ten days after the Olympic final, the US Outdoor National championship was won by Peter Rocca in a time of 56.64, with Bob Jackson second at 56.78.

Baron went on to become the President and CEO of Absolut Vodka.

1984 Los Angeles C: 45, N: 31, D: 8.3. WR: 55.19 (Richard Carey)

1. Richard Carey	USA	55.79
2. David Wilson	USA	56.35
3. Mike West	CAN	56.49
4. Gary Hurring	NZL	56.90
5. Mark Kerry	AUS	57.18
6. Bengt Baron	SWE	57.34
7. Donald "Sandy" Goss	CAN	57.46
8. Hans Kroes	HOL	58.07

Rick Carey won the second of his three gold medals. This time he pleased his critics by smiling and celebrating his victory despite his disappointment at not setting a world record. Three weeks later, the Friendship Games were won by Dirk Richter in a time of 55.67.

1988 Seoul C: 52, N: 38, D: 9.24. WR: 54.91 (David Berkoff)

1. Daichi Suzuki	JPN	55.05
2. David Berkoff	USA	55.18
3. Igor Polyansky	SOV/RUS	55.20
4. Sergei Zabolotnov	SOV/UZB	55.37
5. Mark Tewksbury	CAN	56.09
6. Frank Baltrusch	GDR	56.10
7. Frank Hoffmeister	GER	56.19
8. Sean Murphy	CAN	56.32

On March 15, 1988, Rick Carey's 4½-year-old world record finally fell to Igor Polyansky, who swam 55.17 in Tallinn, Estonia. Polyansky dropped the record to 55.16 the following night and then to 55.00 four months later in Moscow. But on August 13, David Berkoff, competing in the US Olympic trials, broke Polyansky's record twice: 54.95 in the prelims and 54.91 in the final. Berkoff, a Harvard senior from Willow Grove, Pennsylvania, caused a sensation with his submarine start. Using a dolphin kick borrowed from the butterfly stroke, Berkoff swam 32 kicks underwater, exploding to the surface after 35 meters. Berkoff was not the first to use the technique, but he was the first world-class backstroker to stay under for so long.

In the preliminaries at Seoul, Berkoff swam a 54.51 to set the sixth world record in less than six and a half months. In the final, however, Berkoff got off to a slow start. After 30 meters, Berkoff, Suzuki, and Polyansky were all still underwater. When Berkoff popped up last, 5 meters later, he was in first place, but not by nearly the margin he had expected. Suzuki, who had been practicing the submerged start daily for seven years (three years longer than Berkoff) caught Berkoff with 10 meters to go and won by about 10 inches (25 centimeters). Suzuki had placed eleventh at the 1984 Olympics and competed only once a year at the international level. He appeared truly stunned by his victory. After the medal ceremony he told reporters, "I did not expect to win the gold medal. I can't believe it's true, yet I find myself in this interview."

FINA banned the submarine start immediately after the Seoul Olympics, ruling that any backstroker still underwater after 10 meters would be disqualified. This ruling was later amended to 15 meters.

1992 Barcelona C: 52, N: 37, D: 7.30. WR: 53.93 (Jeffrey Rouse)

1. Mark Tewksbury	CAN	53.98 OR
2. Jeffrey Rouse	USA	54.04
3. David Berkoff	USA	54.78
4. Martín López-Zubero Purcell	SPA	54.96
5. Vladimir Selkov	RUS	55.49
6. Franck Schott	FRA	55.72
7. Rodolfo Falcón Cabrera	CUB	55.76
8. Dirk Richter	GER	56.26

At the 1991 world championships, Jeff Rouse beat Mark Tewksbury by .06 seconds. At the Olympics, Tewksbury came from behind to turn the tables by the exact same slim margin. Before the Olympics, the Canadian had never swum faster than 55.19.

1996 Atlanta C: 50, N: 43, D: 7.23. WR: 53.86 (Jeffrey Rouse)

1. Jeffrey Rouse	USA	54.10
2. Rodolfo Falcón Cabrera	CUB	54.98
3. Neisser Bent Vázquez	CUB	55.02
4. Martín López-Zubero Purcell	SPA	55.22
5. William "Tripp" Schwenk	USA	55.30
6. Emanuele Merisi	ITA	55.53
7. Ralf Braun	GER	55.56
8. Franck Schott	FRA	55.76

Jeff Rouse was ranked number one in the world every year since 1989, but in the two biggest races in that period he finished second. In the 1992 Olympic final he was beaten when Mark Tewksbury swam the race of his life. At the 1994 world championships, Rouse jammed his turn and was beaten by a surprised Martín López-Zubero. For these two fractions of a second, some commentators labeled Rouse a choker. Meanwhile Rouse's coach, Skip Kenny, blamed himself for the Barcelona loss because he had not devoted enough time to teaching Rouse to make the final stroke to the wall. In Atlanta one could have been excused for not knowing there had ever been a problem. Rouse blasted into the lead and no one came close to catching him. Rodolfo Falcón, seventh at the turn, came from behind to edge teammate Neisser Bent for the silver medal. Bent, meanwhile, bettered his pre-Olympic record by 1.33 seconds.

2000 Sydney C: 55, N: 48, D: 9.18. WR: 53.60 (Lenny Krayelburg)

1. Lenny Krayzelburg	USA	53.72
2. Matthew Welsh	AUS	54.07
3. Stev Theloke	GER	54.82
4. Josh Watson	AUS	55.01
5. Bartołomiej "Bartosz" Kizierowski	POL	55.04
6. Neil Walker	USA	55.14
7. Steffen Driesen	GER	55.27
8. Eithan Urbach	ISR	55.74

Lenny Krayzelburg grew up in Odessa, Ukraine, the only Jewish student in a school of 2000. His parents feared for the future of Lenny and his younger sister. They did not want their son to be drafted into the Soviet army and they had endured enough anti-Semitism to realize that his career choices would be limited. So, in 1988, they left their home, arriving in West Hollywood, California, in March 1989. Struggling with their new life, Lenny worked as a lifeguard at a swimming pool to help his family. His high school had no swim team and no university showed interest in Krayzelburg's times. He enrolled at Santa Monica College, a two-year junior college. The coach there, Stu Blumkin, recognized Krayzelburg's potential and helped him transfer to the University of Southern California. By 1998 Krayzelburg was the world champion in both the 100- and 200-meter backstroke and in 1999 he set world records in both events. The clear favorite in Sydney, Krayzelburg was pushed hard by Matt Welsh, but with fifteen meters to go, Krayzelburg pulled away. He later explained that he had benefitted from the best of two worlds. "Growing up in Russia and being in the Soviet system during Communism . . . you learn things that stay with you a very long time. The work ethic, the discipline. The great thing about America is it gives you an opportunity if you're willing to take advantage and sacrifice."

2004 Athens C: 44, N: 38, D: 8.16. WR: 53.60 (Lenny Krayzelburg)

1. Aaron Peirsol	USA	54.06
2. Markus Rogan	AUT	54.35
3. Tomomi Morita	JPN	54.36
4. Lenny Krayzelburg	USA	54.38
5. Matthew Welsh	AUS	54.52
6. László Cseh	HUN	54.61
7. Steffen Driesen	GER	54.63
8. Marco di Carli	GER	55.27

Reigning world champion Aaron Peirsol came to Athens as the favorite in the event and dominated the competition, recording the fastest semifinal time, 54.34, ahead of Markus Rogan's 54.42. In the final, Matt Welsh led Peirsol at the turn, but Peirsol surged ahead at the end to take gold, while Rogan moved up from last place at the turn to outtouch Morita for silver. Peirsol had been trained and mentored by former Olympic champion and world record holder Lenny Krayzelburg. Krayzelburg, who had fought back from two surgeries on his left shoulder and one on his left knee to earn a spot on the US team, missed a medal by two-hundredths of a second.

2008 Beijing C: 45, N: 36, D: 8.12. WR: 52.89 (Aaron Peirsol)

1. Aaron Peirsol	USA	52.54	WR
2. Matt Grevers	USA	53.11	
3. Hayden Stoeckel	AUS	53.18	
3. Arkady Vyachanin	RUS	53.18	
5. Ashley Delaney	AUS	53.31	
6. Liam Tancock	GBR	53.39	
7. Aschwin Wildeboer Faber	SPA	53.51	
8. Junichi Miyashita	JPN	53.99	

The Olympic record was lowered three times in the preliminary rounds, first by 23-year-old Matt Grevers in his first-round heat (53.41), then by Arkady Vyachanin (53.06) and Hayden Stoeckel (52.97) in the two semifinal heats.

In the end, however, it was defending Olympic champion and world record holder Aaron Peirsol who dominated the final. Swimming in lane 2, Peirsol trailed by half a second at the midway point, but surged over the last fifty meters, lowering his world record by 0.35 seconds and leading an American 1-2 in the event. Vyachanin and Stoeckel finished in a dead heat at 53.18 seconds to tie for bronze.

In 2011 Peirsol announced his retirement from competition. He had won five Olympic gold medals, two silver medals and ten world championships during his nearly decade-long career.

200-METER BACKSTROKE

1896 not held

1900 Paris C: 16, N: 6, D: 8.12.

1. Ernst Hoppenberg	GER	2:47.0
2. Karl Ruberl	AUT	2:56.0
3. Johannes Drost	HOL	3:01.0
4. Johannes Bleomen	HOL	3:02.2
5. Thomas Burgess	FRA	3:12.0
6. de Romand	FRA	3:38.0
7. Paolo Bussetti	ITA	3:45.0
8. Erik Eriksson	SWE	3:56.4

1904–1960 not held

1964 Tokyo C: 34, N: 21, D: 10.13. WR: 2:10.9 (Thomas Stock)

1. Jedward Graef	USA	2:10.3 WR
2. Gary Dilley	USA	2:10.5
3. Robert Bennett	USA	2:13.1
4. Shigeo Fukushima	JPN	2:13.2
5. Ernst-Joachim Küppers	GER	2:15.7
6. Viktor Mazanov	SOV/RUS	2:15.9
7. Ralph Hutton	CAN	2:15.9
8. Peter Reynolds	AUS	2:16.6

1968 Mexico City C: 30, N: 21, D: 10.25. WR: 2:07.5 (Roland Matthes)

1. Roland Matthes	GDR	2:09.6 OR
2. Mitchell Ivey	USA	2:10.6
3. Jack Horsley	USA	2:10.9
4. Gary Hall	USA	2:12.6
5. Santiago Esteva Escoda	SPA	2:12.9
6. Leonid Dobroskokin	SOV/RUS	2:15.4
7. Joachim Rother	GDR	2:15.8
8. Franco Del Campo	ITA	2:16.5

1972 Munich C: 36, N: 25, D: 9.2. WR: 2:02.8 (Roland Matthes)

1. Roland Matthes	GDR	2:02.82 EWR
2. Michael Stamm	USA	2:04.09
3. Mitchell Ivey	USA	2:04.33
4. Bradford Cooper	AUS	2:06.59
5. Alexander "Tim" McKee	USA	2:07.29
6. Lothar Noack	GDR	2:08.67
7. Zoltán Verrasztó	HUN	2:10.09
8. Jean-Paul Berjeau	FRA	2:11.77

1976 Montreal C: 33, N: 23, D: 7.24. WR: 2:00.64 (John Naber)

1. John Naber	USA	1:59.19 WR
2. Peter Rocca	USA	2:00.55
3. Dan Harrigan	USA	2:01.35
4. Mark Tonelli	AUS	2:03.17
5. Mark Kerry	AUS	2:04.07
6. Miloslav Rol'ko	CZE	2:05.81
7. Robert Rudolf	HUN	2:07.30
8. Zoltán Verrasztó	HUN	2:08.23

With this race, John Naber won his fourth gold medal and became the first backstroker to break the two-minute barrier for 200 meters.

1980 Moscow C: 25, N: 16, D: 7.26. WR: 1:59.19 (John Naber)

1. Sándor Wladár	HUN	2:01.93
2. Zoltán Verrasztó	HUN	2:02.40
3. Mark Kerry	AUS	2:03.14
4. Vladimir Shemetov	SOV/RUS	2:03.48
5. A. Frederik Eefting	HOL	2:03.92
6. Michael Söderlund	SWE	2:04.10
7. Douglas Campbell	GBR	2:04.23
8. Paul Moorfoot	AUS	2:06.15

Three days after the Moscow final, Steve Barnicoat won the US Outdoor National in 2:01.06. Second place went to Peter Rocca in 2:01.34.

1984 Los Angeles C: 34, N: 25, D: 7.31. WR: 1:58.86 (Richard Carey)

1. Richard Carey	USA	2:00.23
2. Frédéric Delcourt	FRA	2:01.75

3. Cameron Henning	CAN	2:02.37
4. Ricardo Prado	BRA	2:03.05
5. Gary Hurring	NZL	2:03.10
6. Nicolai Klapkarek	GER	2:03.95
7. Ricardo Aldabe	SPA	2:04.53
8. David Orbell	AUS	2:04.61

After setting an Olympic record of 1:58.99 in the prelims, Rick Carey of Mt. Kisco, New York, an extremely self-critical perfectionist, assumed that he would be able to break his own world record in the final. He won the race, but fell far short of the record. Afterwards he expressed nothing but disappointment, anger and dejection. He ignored the cheers of the crowd and the congratulations of his opponents. At the medal ceremony he hung his head and again ignored the audience, pausing only once on the way out to kiss his mother. This behavior led to such a torrent of harsh criticism from the US press that Carey felt compelled to issue a formal apology which concluded, "I found it very difficult to smile when my performance didn't live up to my expectations. By not breaking the world record I felt I had not only let myself down, but also the crowd . . . But, please, don't get the impression that I didn't appreciate winning. What everyone saw was purely an emotional reaction—or over-reaction—to Rick Carey's imperfection." Ironically, at the Friendship Games in Moscow three weeks later, Carey's world record was broken by Sergei Zabolotnov in a time of 1:58.41.

1988 Seoul C: 44, N: 32, D: 9.22. WR: 1:58.14 (Igor Polyansky)

1. Igor Polyansky	SOV/RUS	1:59.37
2. Frank Baltrusch	GDR	1:59.60
3. Paul Kingsman	NZL	2:00.48
4. Sergei Zabolotnov	SOV/UZB	2:00.52
5. Dirk Richter	GDR	2:01.67
6. Jens-Peter Berndt	GER	2:01.84
7. Daniel Veatch	USA	2:02.26
8. Rogerio Romero	BRA	2:02.28

Polyansky hailed from Novosibirsk in western Siberia, where his mother was a librarian and his father worked in a meat factory. He had dominated this event since 1985, losing only once to Zabolotnov at the 1987 European championships. In Seoul, Polyansky, Zabolotnov, and Baltrusch swam first, second, and third for the first 150 meters. Then Zabolotnov faded and Baltrusch came on with a rush, but Polyansky held on for the victory.

1992 Barcelona C: 44, N: 34, D: 7.28. WR: 1:56.57 (Martín López-Zubero Purcell)

1. Martín López-Zubero Purcell	SPA	1:58.47 OR
2. Vladimir Selkov	RUS	1:58.87
3. Stefano Battistelli	ITA	1:59.40
4. Hajime Itoi	JPN	1:59.52
5. William "Tripp" Schwenk	USA	1:59.73
6. Tino Weber	GER	1:59.78
7. Tamás Deutsch	HUN	2:00.06
8. Stefaan Maene	BEL	2:00.91

Martín López-Zubero was born in Jacksonville, Florida, raised in Jacksonville, Florida, attended the University of Florida, and won the United States Summer National Championship. But at the Olympics he competed for Spain because his father was Spanish. Martín's older brother, David, who was also born and raised in the United States, won Spain's first swimming medal when he placed third in the 100-meter butterfly in 1980. As expected, Vladimir Selkov set the early pace, while López-Zubero conserved his energy in fifth place for the first half of the race. Hajime Itoi led briefly at 150 meters, then faded. López-Zubero passed Selkov 25 meters from the finish and won going away.

1996 Atlanta C: 39, N: 33, D: 7.26. WR: 1:56.57 (Martín López-Zubero Purcell)

1. Bradley Bridgewater	USA	1:58.54
2. William "Tripp" Schwenk	USA	1:58.99
3. Emanuele Merisi	ITA	1:59.18
4. Bartosz Sikora	POL	2:00.05
5. Hajime Itoi	JPN	2:00.10
6. Martín López-Zubero Purcell	SPA	2:00.74
7. Mirko Mazzari	ITA	2:01.27
8. Rodolfo Falcón Cabrera	CUB	2:08.14

Brad Bridgewater and Tripp Schwenk were schoolboy rivals growing up in Florida. Back then Schwenk, who was two years older, always won. By 1996, however, it was Bridgewater who was on top. In March he upset Schwenk by 24 hundredths of a second at the US Olympic trials. Four and a half months later he beat Schwenk again at the Olympics, this time by 45 hundredths of a second.

2000 Sydney C: 44, N: 38, D: 9.21. WR: 1:55.87 (Lenny Krazelburg)

1. Lenny Krayzelburg	USA	1:56.76 OR
2. Aaron Peirsol	USA	1:57.35
3. Matthew Welsh	AUS	1:57.59
4. Örn Arnarson	ICE	1:59.00
5. Emanuele Merisi	ITA	1:59.01
6. Răzvan Florea	ROM	1:59.05
7. Rogério Romero Aoki	BRA	1:59.27
8. Goran Kožulj	CRO	1:59.38

Lenny Krayzelburg had not been beaten in two years when, two months before the Olympics, he was upset by 17-year-old Aaron Peirsol. In the Olympic final, however, Krayzelburg led from start to finish to earn the second of his three gold medals. Örn Arnarson was the first Icelandic swimmer to make it to an Olympic final.

2004 Athens C: 36, N: 30, D: 8.19. WR: 1:54.74 (Aaron Peirsol)

1. Aaron Peirsol	USA	1:54.95 OR
2. Markus Rogan	AUT	1:57.35
3. Răzvan Florea	ROM	1:57.56
4. James Goddard	GBR	1:57.76
5. Tomomi Morita	JPN	1:58.40
6. Simon Dufour	FRA	1:58.49
7. Gregor Tait	GBR	1:59.28
8. Blaž Medvešek	SLO	2:00.06

As the world record holder and two-time defending world champion, Aaron Peirsol was the clear favorite. In fact, Peirsol did dominate the event, qualifying in 1:57.33, more than half a second ahead of the next fastest qualifier, James Goddard, and recording the fastest time of the semifinal, 1:55.14, more than two seconds ahead of Goddard.

In the final, Peirsol won easily, setting an Olympic record and finishing 2.4 seconds ahead of Markus Rogan in second place. As he got out of the pool and began to celebrate, Peirsol, who three days earlier had publically criticized the judges for not disqualifying breaststroker Kosuke Kitajima, saw his name dropped from the scoreboard and his time replaced with a "DQ." The judges had disqualified Peirsol for continuing to kick after turning on his stomach during the final tumbleturn. But, before the Americans could protest, the International Swiming Federation (FINA) reversed the decision, stating that the chief inspector for turns, Felix Mikhailov of Russia, who filled out the disqualification form, had failed to describe the violation in either of FINA's official languages, English or French. Two hours later, after appeals by both Austria and Great Britain, FINA issued a second statement that there was no valid technical reason for the disqualification. Rogan, himself, opposed the appeal. "Aaron is one of my best friends," he explained. "Nothing is as beautiful as friendship."

2008 Beijing C: 40, N: 31, D: 8.15. WR: 1:54.32 (Ryan Lochte, Aaron Peirsol)

1. Ryan Lochte	USA	1:53.94	WR
2. Aaron Peirsol	USA	1:54.33	
3. Arkady Vyachanin	RUS	1:54.93	
4. Markus Rogan	AUT	1:55.49	
5. Ryosuke Irie	JPN	1:55.72	
6. Hayden Stoeckel	AUS	1:56.39	
7. Răzvan Florea	ROM	1:56.52	
8. Gregor Tait	GBR	1:57.00	

Three days after successfully defending his 100-meter backstroke gold medal, Aaron Peirsol sought to become the second swimmer in Olympic history to sweep both backstroke events in consecutive Olympics—after Roland Matthes, who did so in 1968 and 1972.

Peirsol had been unbeaten in the event since 2001, but his streak came to an end at the 2007 world championships in Melbourne when teammate Ryan Lochte beat him by 0.48 seconds to win the title, breaking Peirsol's world record in the process. Peirsol outswam Lochte by 0.02 seconds at the US Olympic trials, equaling the world record time of 1:54.32 and setting the stage for an exciting 2008 Olympic final.

As expected, each of them finished first in their respective first-round and semifinal heats. In the final Arkady Vyachanin led over the first 150 meters, trailed closely by Peirsol and Lochte. With fifty meters remaining Peirsol surged into the lead, but Lochte pulled ahead in the final lap, touching in under the world record time to win the gold medal and block Peirsol's attempt at Olympic history.

100-METER BREASTSTROKE

The most rigidly defined of swimming strokes, the breaststroke requires swimmers to follow several rules:

1. All leg and arm movements must be made simultaneously. Alternating movements are not allowed.
2. Both shoulders must be kept in line with the water.
3. The hands must be pushed forward together and from the breast, and must be brought back on or under the surface of the water. They must not be brought back beyond the line of the hips.
4. Only the backward and out frog-leg kick is allowed.
5. At turns and at the finish, both hands must touch the wall simultaneously.
6. Except for the start and the first stroke and kick after each turn, a part of the head must break the surface of the water during each stroke and kick cycle.

The breaststroke has always been the most controversial stroke because of ongoing arguments as to what constitutes legal or illegal technique. In the early 1930s some US swimmers discovered a "loophole" in the rules then in force and began bringing their arms back *above* the surface of the water, which saved precious time and energy. In 1952, this new technique, known as the butterfly, was officially recognized as the fourth Olympic swimming style and given its own set of competitions, separate from the breaststroke.

Classical breaststroke enthusiasts, rid at last of the upstart butterfly stroke, were not allowed even a moment to breathe a sigh of relief, thanks to the

Japanese, who discovered another loophole—underwater swimming. Swimming *below* the surface of the water turned out to be faster than swimming on the surface, so in 1956 underwater swimming was banned from breaststroke competitions.

1896–1964 not held

1968 Mexico City C: 39, N: 24, D: 10.19. WR: 1:06.2 (Nikolai Pankin)

1. Donald McKenzie	USA	1:07.7 OR
2. Vladimir Kosinsky	SOV/RUS	1:08.0
3. Nikolai Pankin	SOV/RUS	1:08.0
4. José Sylvio Fiolo	BRA	1:08.1
5. Yevhen Mykhaylov	SOV/UKR	1:08.4
6. Ian O'Brien	AUS	1:08.6
7. Alberto Forelli	ARG	1:08.7
8. Egon Henninger	GDR	1:09.7

1972 Munich C: 44, N: 31, D: 8.30. WR: 1:05.8 (Nikolai Pankin)

1. Nobutaka Taguchi	JPN	1:04.94 WR
2. Thomas Bruce	USA	1:05.43
3. John Hencken	USA	1:05.61
4. Mark Chatfield	USA	1:06.01
5. Walter Kusch	GER	1:06.23
6. José Sylvio Fiolo	BRA	1:06.24
7. Nikolai Pankin	SOV/RUS	1:06.36
8. David Wilkie	GBR	1:06.52

In the first semifinal John Hencken set a world record of 1:05.68. Less than ten minutes later, Nobutaka Taguchi broke that record with a time of 1:05.43 in the second semifinal. The following evening, in the final, Taguchi overtook Tom Bruce in the last 25 meters and set yet another world record.

1976 Montreal C: 32, N: 22, D: 7.20. WR: 1:03.88 (John Hencken)

1. John Hencken	USA	1:03.11 WR
2. David Wilkie	GBR	1:03.43
3. Arvydas Juozaitis	SOV/LIT	1:04.23
4. Graham Smith	CAN	1:04.26
5. Giorgio Lalle	ITA	1:04.37
6. Walter Kusch	GER	1:04.38
7. Duncan Goodhew	GBR	1:04.66
8. Chris Woo	USA	1:05.13

John Hencken, a 22-year-old graduate of Stanford University with a degree in electrical engineering, equaled his own world record of 1:03.88 in the preliminary round, and broke it with a time of 1:03.62 in the semifinals. Hard pressed by David Wilkie in the final, he set another record of 1:03.11.

1980 Moscow C: 26, N: 20, D: 7.22. WR: 1:02.86 (Gerald Mörken)

1. Duncan Goodhew	GBR	1:03.44
2. Arsens Miskarovs	SOV/LAT	1:03.82
3. Peter Evans	AUS	1:03.96
4. Aleksandr Fedorovsky	SOV/RUS	1:04.00
5. János Dzvonyár	HUN	1:04.67
6. Lindsay Spencer	AUS	1:05.04
7. Pablo Restrepo	COL	1:05.91

DISQ: Albán Vermes (HUN)

Jeered at by his schoolmates as an adolescent because a fall from a tree on his school's assault course at age ten had left him bald, and also because he was dyslexic, Duncan Goodhew vowed that he would become an Olympic champion. Although his stepfather, a retired air vice-marshal, refused to attend the Games because his government opposed British participation, Goodhew's mother was in the audience to watch her son's dream come true. Despite all the noise in the stadium, Goodhew "seemed to hear her voice above all the others."

Duncan Goodhew, 1980

Mocked by his schoolmates because an accident left him bald and because he was dyslexic, Duncan Goodhew fought back by winning a gold medal in the 1980 100-meter breaststroke.

At the US Outdoor National a week later, Steve Lundquist clocked 1:02.88 and Bill Barrett 1:02.93. The world record of 1:02.86 had been set by Gerald Mörken of West Germany in 1977.

1984 Los Angeles C: 52, N: 37, D: 7.29. WR: 1:02.13 (John Moffet)

1. Steve Lundquist	USA	1:01.65 WR
2. Victor Davis	CAN	1:01.99
3. Peter Evans	AUS	1:02.97
4. Adrian Moorhouse	GBR	1:03.25
5. John Moffet	USA	1:03.29
6. Brett Stocks	AUS	1:03.49
7. Gerald Mörken	GER	1:03.95
8. Raffaele Avagnano	ITA	1:04.11

At the US Olympic trials on June 25, John Moffet had defeated Steve Lundquist for the first time, and taken away his world record for good measure. Competing in the Olympics five weeks later, Moffet led all qualifiers with an Olympic record of 1:02.16. Unfortunately, pushing off the wall at the 50-meter turn, Moffet badly tore a muscle in his right thigh. As the seriousness of his injury became apparent, doctors injected his leg with xylocaine and taped his thigh. But his chances for Olympic victory were fading fast. In the ready room before the final, Moffet took Lundquist aside and said, "If something goes haywire with my leg, win the gold for the USA." Lundquist did just that, fighting off a determined challenge from Victor Davis and regaining his world record.

Steve Lundquist, 1984
In the 100-meter breaststroke, Lundquist reclaimed the world record and, with it, the gold medal.

1988 Seoul C: 61, N: 45, D: 9.19. WR: 1:01 .65 (Steve Lundquist)

1. Adrian Moorhouse	GBR	1:02.04
2. Károly Güttler	HUN	1:02.05
3. Dmitri Volkov	SOV/RUS	1:02.20
4. Victor Davis	CAN	1:02.38
5. Tamás Debnár	HUN	1:02.50
6. Richard Schroeder	USA	1:02.55
7. Gianni Minervini	ITA	1:02.93
8. Christian Poswiat	GDR	1:03.43

When he was 12 years old, Adrian Moorhouse of Bingley, Yorkshire, watched on television as David Wilkie won a gold medal in the 200-meter breaststroke. Moorhouse thought to himself, "I want one of those."

Eight years later at the Los Angeles Olympics swimming aficionados thought that he had a very good chance of winning "one of those" in the 100-meter event. However, he finished a disappointing fourth and went home to England without a medal. While he was still in Los Angeles he received a telegram from his former Sunday school teacher, Geoff Carter. It read, "Very bad luck, all proud of you. There will be a next time." Moorhouse kept the telegram and four years later took it with him to Seoul. This time he entered the competition as the clear favorite, having recorded the fastest time in the world in 1986, 1987, and pre-Olympic 1988.

In the preliminaries, Moorhouse was the fastest qualifier, with a time of 1:02.19. In the final, Dmitri Volkov turned first, with Moorhouse 1.3 seconds back in sixth place. Moorhouse expected Volkov to die by the 75-meter mark. When he didn't, Moorhouse realized for the first time that "maybe the Olympics mean something to him too." In fact, Volkov was, in his own words, "washed out" by the 75-meter mark, but he managed to stay in front for another 15 meters.

When Moorhouse reached the finish, he wasn't sure whether he had beaten Volkov for the gold. He hadn't even noticed Károly Güttler two lanes away. When he looked back at the scoreboard, Moorhouse discovered that he had edged out Güttler by only one one-hundredth of a second. As elated as he was, Moorhouse cringed with guilt for having "stolen" the gold from Güttler. Actually, the Hungarian, who was not considered a medal contender, was ecstatic at having earned an unexpected silver.

After the medal ceremony, Moorhouse tucked the four-year-old telegram from his Sunday school teacher into the box that contained his gold medal.

1992 Barcelona C: 59, N: 45, D: 7.26. WR: 1:01.29 (Norbert Rózsa)

1. Nelson Diebel	USA	1:01.50 OR
2. Norbert Rózsa	HUN	1:01.68
3. Philip Rogers	AUS	1:01.76
4. Akira Hayashi	JPN	1:01.86
5. Vassily Ivanov	RUS	1:01.87
6. Dmitri Volkov	RUS	1:02.07
7. Nicholas Gillingham	GBR	1:02.32
8. Adrian Moorhouse	GBR	1:02.33

After his parents separated when he was 12 years old, Nelson Diebel, who was already a hyperactive child, spent several years getting into trouble. He drank alcohol, smoked marijuana, partied excessively, got into fights, and was thrown out of schools. He was, in his own words, "a rebel without a clue." Fortunately, at the Peddie School, a private high school in Hightstown, New Jersey, he was coached by Chris Martin, who turned Diebel into a serious swimmer. When he was 17 years old, Diebel placed an impressive and very encouraging fifth at the 1988 United States Olympic trials. Three days later Diebel tried to dive into the Peddie pool from the railing above the stands, twenty feet above the pool. He slipped and landed on concrete. He broke the fall with his hands and broke his wrists. Reasonably under control four years later, he won the 1992 United States Olympic trials in a time of 1:01.40. The favorite in the Olympics was Norbert Rózsa, the world champion and world record holder. However, Rózsa did not appear to be in top form in Barcelona. He barely qualified for the final, edging fellow Hungarian Károly Güttler by .03 seconds. In the final, Volkov and Ivanov led at the turn, with Diebel, Rózsa, and Rogers close behind. Immediately, the Russians began to fade while the others maintained their positions all the way to the finish.

1996 Atlanta C: 45, N: 41, D: 7.20. WR: 1:00.95 (Károly Güttler)

1. Frédéric Deburghgraeve	BEL	1:00.65
2. Jeremy Linn	USA	1:00.77
3. Mark Warnecke	GER	1:01.33
4. Károly Güttler	HUN	1:01.49
5. Philip Rogers	AUS	1:01.64
6. Kurt Grote	USA	1:01.69
7. Zeng Qiliang	CHN	1:02.01
8. Stanislav Lopukhov	RUS	1:02.13

At the 1992 Olympics, Fred Deburghgraeve slipped at the start of the 100-meter breaststroke and finished in 34th place. He was so discouraged by his Barcelona results that he quit swimming for six months and went to work at a brewery. By 1996, however, Deburghgraeve was the favorite. He set a world record of 1:00.60 in the qualifying round. He led from the start in the final and was entering the last half lap when he felt Jeremy Linn pull alongside him. Through the din of the crowd, Deburghgraeve heard his coach, Ronald Gaastra gave a special whistle that told him to go faster. Deburghgraeve made it to the wall before Linn could catch him. Deburghgraeve was Belgium's first Olympic swimming champion. Linn bettered his pre-Olympic best time by 1.17 seconds.

2000 Sydney C: 60, N: 60, D: 9.17. WR: 1:00.36 (Roman Sludnov)

1. Domenico Fioravanti	ITA	1:00.46 OR
2. G. Edward Moses	USA	1:00.73
3. Roman Sludnov	RUS	1:00.91
4. Kosuke Kitajima	JPN	1:01.34
5. Daniel Málek	CZE	1:01.50
6. Morgan Knabe	CAN	1:01.58
7. Brett Petersen	SAF	1:01.63
8. Remo Lütolf	SWI	1:01.88

On June 15, 2000, Roman Sludnov broke Frédéric Deburghgraeve's four-year-old world record and it was assumed that he would battle for the gold medal with Ed Moses, who had come within eight hundredths of a second of Sludnov's time at the US Olympic trials less than four weeks later. However it was European champion Domenico Fioravanti who recorded the fastest times in both the qualifying round (1:01:32) and the semifinals (1:00:84). In the final, Moses took the early lead and turned first. Fioravanti drew even at 75 meters and won the lunge for the wall. He was Italy's first swimming champion. On June 29, 2001, Sludnov made up for his Olympic disappointment by becoming the first breaststroker to break one minute when, in Moscow, he stopped the clock at 59.97.

2004 Athens C: 60, N: 55, D: 8.15. WR: 59.30 (Brendan Hansen)

1. Kosuke Kitajima	JPN	1:00.08
2. Brendan Hansen	USA	1:00.25
3. Hugues Duboscq	FRA	1:00.88
4. Mark Gangloff	USA	1:01.17
5. Vladislav Polyakov	KAZ	1:01.34
6. James Gibson	GBR	1:01.36
7. Darren Mew	GBR	1:01.66
8. Oleh Lisohor	UKR	1:02.42

One month before the start of the Athens Games, Brendan Hansen caused a sensation at the US Olympic trials by setting world records in both the 100- and 200-meter breaststroke. The stage was set for a showdown between Hansen and the reigning world champion, butcher's son Kosuke Kitajima, who had held both the world records that Hansen broke. In Athens, Kitajima recorded the fastest time of the qualifying round, setting an Olympic record of 1:00.03. Hansen responded with a semifinal time of 1:00.01. In the final, Kitajima jumped out to a quick lead, but had been overtaken slightly by Hansen at the halfway point. Kitajima retook the lead off the turn and held it the rest of the way. The competition took place on Hansen's 23rd birthday.

2008 Beijing C: 64, N: 52, D: 8.11. WR: 59.13 (Brendan Hansen)

1. Kosuke Kitajima	JPN	58.91 WR
2. Alexander Dale Oen	NOR	59.20
3. Hugues Duboscq	FRA	59.37
4. Brendan Hansen	USA	59.57
5. Brenton Rickard	AUS	59.74
6. Roman Sludnov	RUS	59.87
7. Ihor Borysyk	UKR	1:00.20
8. Mark Gangloff	USA	1:00.24

Kosuke Kitajima had swept both breaststroke events at the 2004 Athens Olympics and was looking to do the same in 2008. His biggest challenge was expected to come from two-time reigning world champion and world record holder Brendan Hansen, who had beaten Kitajima in each of the past two world championship finals.

Reigning European champion Alexander Dale Oen set an Olympic record of 59.41 in his first round heat and lowered it to 59.16 to qualify for the final. Kitajima recorded the second-fastest qualifying time, while Hansen qualified fifth.

Kitajima trailed Oen after the first 50 meters, but pulled away in the second half of the race to defend his Olympic gold medal, and break Hansen's world record.

200-METER BREASTSTROKE

1896–1906 not held

1908 London C: 27, N: 10. D: 7.18.

1. Frederick Holman	GBR	3:09.2 WR
2. William Robinson	GBR	3:12.8
3. Pontus Hanson	SWE	3:14.6
4. Ödön Toldi	HUN	3:15.2

Twenty-five meters from the finish, the 23-year-old Holman overtook Robinson, who was 38 years old.

1912 Stockholm C: 24, N: 11, D: 7.10. WR: 3:00.8 (Félicien Coubert)

1. Walter Bathe	GER	3:01.8 OR
2. Wilhelm Lützow	GER	3:05.0
3. Paul Malisch	GER	3:08.0
4. Percy Courtman	GBR	3:08.8

DNF: Thor Henning (SWE)

The appropriately named Walter Bathe won without being seriously threatened. Two days later he won the 400-meter breaststroke.

1920 Antwerp C: 24, N: 11. D: 8.29. WR: 2:56.6 (Percy Courtman)

1. Håkan Malmrot	SWE	3:04.4
2. Thor Henning	SWE	3:09.2
3. Arvo Aaltonen	FIN	3:12.2
4. Jack Howell	USA	—
5. Ivan Stedman	AUS	—

DNF: Per Cederblom (SWE)

1924 Paris C: 28, N: 16, D: 7.17. WR: 2:50.4 (Erich Rademacher)

1. Robert Skelton	USA	2:56.6
2. Joseph de Combe	BEL	2:59.2
3. William Kirschbaum	USA	3:01.0
4. Bengt Linders	SWE	3:02.2
5. Robert Wyss	SWI	3:05.6
6. Thor Henning	SWE	

Skelton set an Olympic record of 2:56.0 in the opening round.

1928 Amsterdam C: 21, N: 13, D: 8.8. WR: 2:48.0 (Erich Rademacher)

1. Yoshiyuki Tsuruta	JPN	2:48.8 OR
2. Erich Rademacher	GER	2:50.6
3. Teófilo Yldefonso	PHI	2:56.4
4. Erwin Sietas	GER	2:56.6
5. Eric Harling	SWE	2:56.8
6. Walter Spence	CAN	2:57.2

1932 Los Angeles C: 18, N: 11, D: 8:13. WR: 2:44.0 (Leonard Spence)

1. Yoshiyuki Tsuruta	JPN	2:45.4
2. Reizo Koike	JPN	2:46.6
3. Teófilo Yldefonso	PHI	2:47.1
4. Erwin Sietas	GER	2:48.0
5. Jikirum Adjaluddin	PHI	2:49.2
6. Shigeo Nakagawa	JPN	2:52.8

Koike defeated Tsuruta 2:44.9 to 2:45.4 in the first semifinal. The defending champion repeated his time exactly in the final, but this time it was good enough to win.

1936 Berlin C: 25, N: 11, D: 8.15. WR: 2:37.2 (Jack Kasley)

1. Tetsuo Hamuro	JPN	2:41.5 OR
2. Erwin Sietas	GER	2:42.9
3. Reizo Koike	JPN	2:44.2

4. John Herbert Higgins	USA	2:45.2
5. Saburo Ito	JPN	2:47.6
6. Joachim Balke	GER	2:47.8
7. Teófilo Yldefonso	PHI	2:51.1

1948 London C: 32, N: 20, D: 8.7. WR: 2:30.0 (Joseph Verdeur)

1. Joseph Verdeur	USA	2:39.3 OR
2. Keith Carter	USA	2:40.2
3. Robert Sohl	USA	2:43.9
4. John Davies	AUS	2:43.7
5. Antun "Tone" Cerer	YUG/SLO	2:46.1
6. Willy Otto Jordan	BRA	2:48.4
7. Ahmed Kandil	EGY	2:47.5
8. Bjorn Bonte	HOL	2:47.6

Joe Verdeur was known as "The Rubber Man" because he was double-jointed in the shoulders. The first seven finishers all used the butterfly stroke. The judges awarded Bob Sohl the bronze medal even though his official time was slower than that of Davies.

1952 Helsinki C: 40, N: 27, D: 8.2. WR: 2:27.3 (Herbert Klein)

1. John Davies	AUS	2:34.4 OR
2. Bowen Stassforth	USA	2:34.7
3. Herbert Klein	GER	2:35.9
4. Nobuyasu Hirayama	JPN	2:37.4
5. Takayoshi Kajikawa	JPN	2:38.6
6. Jiro Nagasawa	JPN	2:39.1
7. Maurice Lusien	FRA	2:39.8
8. Ľudovít Komadel	CZE	2:40.1

John Davies believed, contrary to popular theory at the time, that the key to winning was to swim even lap times rather than go all out at the beginning or save energy for a finishing burst. Four years earlier he had lost out on a bronze medal when the lane judges overruled the timers. In Helsinki, he would take no chances. Two and a half seconds behind after 100 meters, Davies patiently held his pace. He passed the fading Klein and then just outtouched Stassforth. Davies later graduated from UCLA and became a United States citizen and an entertainment lawyer. Davies represented Universal Studios and Walt Disney Productions when the two media groups sued Sony Corporation about the right of homeviewers to make videotape copies of movies shown on television. In 1986 Davies was appointed a United States district judge. In 1993, forty years after his Olympic celebrity, Davies was in the news again when he presided over the trial of Los Angeles police officers Laurence Powell and Stacey Koon in the case of the videotaped beating of Rodney King. Coincidentally, one of the witnesses in the trial was another gold medalist, 1964 shot putter Dallas Long.

1956 Melbourne C: 21, N: 17, D: 12.6. WR: 2:31.0 (Masaru Furukawa)

1. Masaru Furukawa	JPN	2:34.7 OR
2. Masahiro Yoshimura	JPN	2:36.7
3. Kharis Yunichev	SOV/RUS	2:36.8
4. Terry Gathercole	AUS	2:38.7
5. Ihor Zasyeda	SOV/UKR	2:39.0
6. Knud Gleie	DEN	2:40.0
7. Manuel Sanguily	CUB	2:42.0

DISQ: Hughes Broussard (FRA)

For the first time, the butterfly stroke and the breaststroke were separated into two different events. Differences in interpretation of what was a breaststroke and what wasn't led to six disqualifications. The most controversial was the ousting of Herbert Klein of Germany, who won the second heat. He was accused of using a scissors kick and of dipping his right shoulder. Furukawa was one of the least visible Olympic champions, since his unusual technique kept him underwater 75 percent of the time.

1960 Rome C: 42, N: 30, D: 8.30. WR: 2:36.5 (Terry Gathercole)

1. William Mulliken	USA	2:37.4
2. Yoshihiko Osaki	JPN	2:38.0
3. Wieger Mensonides	HOL	2:39.7
4. Egon Henninger	GDR	2:40.1
5. Roberto Lazzari	ITA	2:40.1
6. Terry Gathercole	AUS	2:40.2
7. Andrzej Kłopotowski	POL	2:41.2
8. Paul Hait	USA	2:41.4

The slower times in 1960 were the result of the banning of underwater swimming in 1957, five months after Masaru Furukawa's Olympic victory. Bill Mulliken's win was considered a major upset, since his pre-Olympic best had been 2:40.9. In the semifinals he set an Olympic record of 2:37.2.

1964 Tokyo C: 33, N: 20, D: 10.15. WR: 2:28.2 (Chester Jastremski)

1. Ian O'Brien	AUS	2:27.8 WR
2. Heorhy Prokopenko	SOV/UKR	2:28.2
3. Chester Jastremski	USA	2:29.6
4. Aleksandr Tutakayev	SOV/GEO	2:31.0
5. Egon Henninger	GDR	2:31.1
6. Osamu Tsurumine	JPN	2:33.6
7. Wayne Anderson	USA	2:35.0
8. Vladimir Kosinsky	SOV/RUS	2:38.1

Seventeen-year-old Ian O'Brien didn't catch Prokopenko until five meters from the finish. In winning, he improved his personal best by more than 4 seconds.

1968 Mexico City C: 36. N: 23, D: 10.22. WR: 2:27.4 (Vladimir Kosinsky)

1. Felipe Muñoz Kapamas	MEX	2:28.7
2. Vladimir Kosinsky	SOV/RUS	2:29.2
3. Brian Job	USA	2:29.9
4. Nikolai Pankin	SOV/RUS	2:30.3
5. Yevhen Mykhaylov	SOV/UKR	2:32.8
6. Egon Henninger	GDR	2:33.2
7. Philip Long	USA	2:33.6
8. Osamu Tsurumine	JPN	2:34.9

The 1968 Olympics was ten days old and the host country had yet to win a gold medal when 17-year-old Felipe "Pepe" Muñoz stood at the edge of the pool before the start of the final of the 200-meter breaststroke. He was also known as "Tibio" (lukewarm) because his father was from Aguascalientes (hot waters) and his mother from Rio Frío (cold river). Muñoz was not the favorite, that role falling to world record holder Vladimir Kosinsky, but there was hope that the Mexican would gain a medal, and since he had registered the fastest time of the heats (2:31.1), maybe, just maybe, a miracle might happen.

At the halfway mark Muñoz was in fourth place behind Kosinsky, Henninger, and Job. But then, in the most dramatic fashion possible, Muñoz began to gain on the leaders. Coming off the final turn, with 50 meters to go, he was only inches behind Kosinsky. The excitement in the stadium reached a fever pitch as 8000 cheering Mexicans voiced the hopes of the hundreds of thousands more who were watching on television. Twenty-five meters from the finish Muñoz caught Kosinsky, and in the last few meters he moved ahead, touching the wall a half-second ahead of the Soviet champion. Before he could make a move of his own, Muñoz was hoisted out of the pool and carried, dripping wet and in tears, around the arena. His American coach, Ron Johnson, was thrown into the pool despite the fact that his broken hand was encased in plaster.

1972 Munich C: 40, N: 27, D: 9.2. WR: 2:22.79 (John Hencken)

1. John Hencken	USA	2:21.55 WR
2. David Wilkie	GBR	2:23.67
3. Nobutaka Taguchi	JPN	2:23.88
4. Richard Colella	USA	2:24.28
5. Felipe Muñoz Kapamas	MEX	2:26.44
6. Walter Kusch	GER	2:26.55
7. Igor Cherdakov	SOV/UKR	2:27.15
8. Klaus Katzur	GDR	2:27.44

Hencken's superiority was never in doubt, as he led from start to finish.

1976 Montreal C: 26, N: 18, D: 7.24. WR: 2:18.21 (John Hencken)

1. David Wilkie	GBR	2:15.11 WR
2. John Hencken	USA	2:17.26
3. Richard Colella	USA	2:19.20
4. Graham Smith	CAN	2:19.42
5. Charles Keating	USA	2:20.79
6. Arvydas Juozaitis	SOV/LIT	2:21.87
7. Nikolai Pankin	SOV/RUS	2:22.21
8. Waiter Kusch	GER	2:22.36

In 1976, 12 of the 13 men's swimming events were won by swimmers from the United States. The only exception was the 200-meter breaststroke. In that race, double world champion David Wilkie of Scotland became the first British male to win an Olympic swimming title in 68 years.

1980 Moscow C: 19, N: 14, D: 7.26. WR: 2:15.11 (David Wilkie)

1. Robertas Žulpa	SOV/LIT	2:15.85
2. Albán Vermes	HUN	2:16.93
3. Arsens Miskarovs	SOV/LAT	2:17.28
4. Gennady Utenkov	SOV/RUS	2:19.64
5. Lindsay Spencer	AUS	2:19.68
6. Duncan Goodhew	GBR	2:20.92
7. Peter Berggren	SWE	2:21.65
8. Jörg Walter	GDR	2:22.39

1984 Los Angeles C: 47, N: 35, D: 8.2. WR: 2:14.58 (Victor Davis)

1. Victor Davis	CAN	2:13.34 WR
2. Glenn Beringen	AUS	2:15.79
3. Etienne Dagon	SWI	2:17.41
4. Richard Schroeder	USA	2:18.03
5. Ken Fitzpatrick	CAN	2:18.86
6. Pablo Restrepo	COL	2:18.96
7. Alexandre Yokochi	POR	2:20.69
DISQ: Marco Del Prete (ITA)		

World record holder Victor Davis took command before the 50-meter turn, kept a clear lead throughout the race, and then poured it on in the final 50 meters to set another world record and win by the largest margin in an Olympic breaststroke final in 60 years. Victor Davis died on Nov. 13, 1989, after being struck by a car following an altercation outside a bar. He was 25 years old. His ashes were scattered at sea along with a quart of water from lane 5 of the University of Southern California pool, where he had won his Olympic gold medal.

1988 Seoul C: 54, N: 40, D: 9.23. WR: 2:13.34 (Victor Davis)

1. József Szabó	HUN	2:13.52
2. Nicholas Gillingham	GBR	2:14.12
3. Sergio López Miró	SPA	2:15.21
4. Michael Barrowman	USA	2:15.45
5. Valery Lozyk	SOV/UKR	2:16.16
6. Vadim Alekseyev	SOV/KAZ	2:16.70
7. Jonathan Cleveland	CAN	2:17.10
8. Péter Szabó	HUN	2:17.12

The two Szabós (not related) and Barrowman all practiced the new "wave-action" breaststroke taught by Hungarian coach József Nagy.

1992 Barcelona C: 54, N: 41. D: 7.29. WR: 2:10.60 (Michael Barrowman)

1. Michael Barrowman	USA	2:10.16 WR
2. Norbert Rózsa	HUN	2:11.23
3. Nicholas Gillingham	GBR	2:11.29
4. Sergio López Miró	SPA	2:13.29
5. Károly Güttler	HUN	2:13.32
6. Philip Rogers	AUS	2:13.59
7. Kenji Watanabe	JPN	2:14.70
8. Akira Hayashi	JPN	2:15.11

There were no surprises in this race. Mike Barrowman had dominated the event since the last Olympics and owned the five fastest times in history. He led from start to finish and set his sixth world record. All the finalists except López and Güttler set personal bests. When Barrowman returned to his home in Potomac, Maryland, his neighbors had painted the front lawn gold.

1996 Atlanta C: 34, N: 29, D: 7.24. WR: 2:10.16 (Michael Barrowman)

1. Norbert Rózsa	HUN	2:12.57
2. Károly Güttler	HUN	2:13.03
3. Andrei Korneyev	RUS	2:13.17
4. Nicholas Gillingham	GBR	2:14.37
5. Philip Rogers	AUS	2:14.79
6. Marek Krawszyk	POL	2:14.84
7. Eric Wunderlich	USA	2:15.69
8. Kurt Grote	USA	2:16.05

European champion Andrei Korneyev took the lead immediately and was on world record pace after 100 meters. He was still in front at the final turn, but then he began to fade. Rózsa and Güttler shot past him to give Hungary a one-two finish. Four days later it was announced that Korneyev had tested positive for the stimulant bromantan. He was disqualified and Nick Gillingham, at 29 the oldest swimmer in the field, was moved up to the bronze medal position. But the following week the Court of Arbitration for Sport lifted the ban on bromantan and Korneyev was reinstated.

2000 Sydney C: 47, N: 41, D: 9.20. WR: 2:10.16 (Michael Barrowman)

1. Domenico Fioravanti	ITA	2:10.87
2. Terence Parkin	SAF	2:12.50
3. David Rummolo	ITA	2:12.73
4. Regan Harrison	AUS	2:12.88
5. Daniel Málek	CZE	2:13.20
6. Kyle Salyards	USA	2:13.27
7. Johann Bernard	FRA	2:13.31
8. Ryan Mitchell	AUS	2:14.00

Three days after winning the 100-meter breaststroke, Domenico Fioravanti added the 200-meter gold by taking the lead on the second lap and pulling away steadily for the rest of the race. Silver medalist Terence Parkin was 100 percent deaf since birth, so a strobe light was used to communicate to him the start of the race.

2004 Athens C: 46, N: 38, D: 8.18. WR: 2:09.04 (Brendan Hansen)

1. Kosuke Kitajima	JPN	2:09.44 OR
2. Dániel Gyurta	HUN	2:10.80
3. Brendan Hansen	USA	2:10.87
4. Paolo Bossini	ITA	2:11.20
5. Vladislav Polyakov	KAZ	2:11.76
6. Mike Brown	CAN	2:11.94
7. Scott Usher	USA	2:11.95
DISQ: Jim Piper (AUS)		

One month before the Olympics, Brendan Hansen shattered reigning world champion Kosuke Kitajima's world record of 2:09.42. In Athens, Kitajima held off Hansen to win the 100-meter breaststroke. Three days later, in the 200, Kitajima led from start to finish to earn his second gold medal.

2008 Beijing C: 52, N: 38, D: 8.14. WR: 2:07.51 (Kosuke Kitajima)

1. Kosuke Kitajima	JPN	2:07.64 OR
2. Brenton Rickard	AUS	2:08.88
3. Hugues Duboscq	FRA	2:08.94
4. Michael Brown	CAN	2:09.03
5. Dániel Gyurta	HUN	2:09.22
6. Scott Spann	USA	2:09.76
7. Loris Facci	ITA	2:10.57
8. Paolo Bossini	ITA	2:11.48

Three days after successfully defending his gold medal in the 100-meter breaststroke, reigning Olympic and world champion Kosuke Kitajima was the clear favorite in the 200-meter event. At a meet in Tokyo on June 8 2008, exactly two months before the Opening Ceremony of the 2008 Olympics, he had knocked 0.99 seconds off the previous world record for the distance.

The 25-year-old recorded an Olympic record of 2:08.61 in his semifinal heat, and won the final easily, pulling away to win by more than a second. He was the first swimmer to complete the double in the breaststroke events at two consecutive Olympics.

100-METER BUTTERFLY

As in the breaststroke, butterfly swimmers must keep their shoulders in line with the surface of the water, they must move their arms and legs simultaneously, and they must not swim underwater, except for the first stroke after the start and after each turn. Unlike the breaststroke, butterfly rules allow swimmers to bring back their arms over the water and to kick their legs and feet up and down, as long as the movement of left and right arms or legs is simultaneous.

1896–1964 not held

1968 Mexico City C: 47, N: 23, D: 10.21. WR: 55.6 (Mark Spitz)

1. Douglas Russell	USA	55.9 OR
2. Mark Spitz	USA	56.4
3. Ross Wales	USA	57.2
4. Volodymyr Nemshilov	SOV/UKR	58.1
5. Satoshi Maruya	JPN	58.6
6. Yuri Suzdaltsev	SOV/RUS	58.8
7. Lutz Stoklasa	GER	58.9
8. Robert Cusack	AUS	59.8

Mark Spitz and Doug Russell had raced against each other nine times in the 100-meter butterfly, and the result was always the same: Russell would take the early lead and then Spitz would finish strongly to win. In Mexico City, though, the two Californians separately and secretly decided to reverse their tactics. This allowed Russell to come from behind and defeat Spitz for the first time.

1972 Munich C: 39, N: 26, D: 8.31. WR: 54.56 (Mark Spitz)

1. Mark Spitz	USA	54.27 WR
2. Bruce Robertson	CAN	55.56
3. Jerôme Heidenreich	USA	55.74
4. Roland Matthes	GDR	55.87
5. David Edgar	USA	56.11
6. Byron MacDonald	CAN	57.27
7. Hartmut Flöckner	GDR	57.40
8. Neil Rogers	AUS	57.90

Spitz won his fourth gold medal of the Munich Games.

1976 Montreal C: 43, N: 29, D: 7.21. WR: 54.27 (Mark Spitz)

1. Matthew Vogel	USA	54.35
2. Joseph Bottom	USA	54.50
3. Gary Hall	USA	54.65
4. Roger Pyttel	GDR	55.09
5. Roland Matthes	GDR	55.11
6. Clay Evans	CAN	55.81
7. Hideaki Hara	JPN	56.34
8. Neil Rogers	AUS	56.57

1980 Moscow C: 34, N: 29, D: 7.23. WR: 54.15 (Pär Arvidsson)

1. Pär Arvidsson	SWE	54.92
2. Roger Pyttel	GDR	54.94
3. David López-Zubero Purcell	SPA	55.13
4. Kees Vervoorn	HOL	55.25
5. Yevgeny Seredin	SOV/RUS	55.35
6. Gary Abraham	GBR	55.42
7. Xavier Savin	FRA	55.66
8. Aleksei Markovsky	SOV/RUS	55.70

On August 2, William Paulus won the US Outdoor National championship in 54.34. Second was Matt Gribble in 54.51. On July 22, in Canada, West Germany's Michael Gross recorded a 54.69.

1984 Los Angeles C: 53, N: 39, D: 7.30. WR: 53:38 (P. Pablo Morales)

1. Michael Gross	GER	53.08 WR
2. P. Pablo Morales	USA	53.23
3. Glenn Buchanan	AUS	53.85
4. Rafael Vidal Castro	VEN	54.27
5. Andrew Jameson	GBR	54.28
6. Anthony Mosse	NZL	54.93
7. Andreas Behrend	GER	54.95
8. Bengt Baron	SWE	55.14

In a race that was so fast that the top six finishers all set national records, Michael Gross rocketed past Pablo Morales ten meters from the finish to win his second gold medal and set his second world record of the 1984 Olympics.

1988 Seoul C: 51, N: 36, D: 9.21. WR: 52.84 (P. Pablo Morales)

1. Anthony Nesty	SUR	53.00 OR
2. Matthew Biondi	USA	53.01
3. Andrew Jameson	GBR	53.30
4. Jonathan Sieben	AUS	53.33
5. Michael Gross	GER	53.44
6. Jay Mortenson	USA	54.07
7. Thomas Ponting	CAN	54.09
8. Vadym Yaroshchuk	SOV/UKR	54.60

Favorite Matt Biondi led from the start. Ten meters from the finish, he was still in first place by 2 feet. But as he neared the touch pad, he was caught between strokes and elected to kick in the last few feet instead of taking an extra stroke. However, he was farther away than he thought and his miscalculation allowed 20-year-old Anthony Nesty of Suriname to slip by and win by less than an inch.

The top four finishers all set personal records. Nesty had placed fifth at the 1986 world championships and had the fourth best time of 1987. Still, his victory was a shocker. Suriname, a small tropical nation (population: 380,000) on the east coast of South America, had never before produced an Olympic medalist. Suriname had only one Olympic-size pool, so Nesty, who was born in Trinidad, had gone to live and train in the United States and to study at the University of Florida.

Nesty, a retiring sort, returned to Suriname a hero. After leaving the airport, his motorcade was stopped by a crowd of people in Onverwacht who insisted on giving him $3000. The government chipped in with a larger sum. In addition, the local stadium was renamed for him and a stamp was issued in his honor, as were gold and silver commemorative coins. Anthony Nesty was also the first black swimmer to win an Olympic gold (Holland's Enith Brigitha was the first to win an Olympic medal: bronze in the 1976 100-meter freestyle event).

As for Biondi, he was left to ponder his narrow loss. After the race he mused, "One one hundredth of a second—what if I had grown my fingernails longer?" Biondi successfully channeled his anger and disappointment and went on to win five gold medals.

1992 Barcelona C: 69, N: 48, D: 7.27. WR: 52.84 (P. Pablo Morales)

1. P. Pablo Morales	USA	53.32
2. Rafał Szukała	POL	53.35
3. Anthony Nesty	SUR	53.41
4. Pavlo Khnykin	UKR	53.81
5. Melvin Stewart	USA	54.04
6. Marcel Gery	CAN	54.18
7. Martín López-Zubero Purcell	SPA	54.19
8. Vladislav Kulikov	RUS	54.26

In 1984, Pablo Morales went to the Olympics as the world record holder and the favorite to win a gold medal. He did swim fast enough to break his world record, but Michael Gross swam even faster. Morales earned a gold medal in the medley relay, two silvers in the 100-meter butterfly and the 200-meter individual medley, and he finished fourth in the 200-meter butterfly. Not a bad haul for a 19-year-old, but he didn't go home with the individual golds that were expected of him. On June 23, 1986, Morales won back the world record and by 1988 he was again the butterfly favorite for the Olympics. But at the United States Olympic trials, with only two Americans qualifying for each event, Morales placed third in both butterfly finals. When the Olympic 100-meter butterfly final came on television, Morales couldn't bring himself to watch it and left the room. He retired from swimming and entered law school at Cornell University.

In the summer of 1991, Morales' mother, Blanca, died of cancer. In November, Morales returned to competitive swimming, after a three-and-a-half-year absence. In March he won the US Olympic trials, and as his 1986 mark of 52.84 had not been beaten, he was the reigning world record holder for the third straight Olympics. Morales led the qualifying round with a time of 53.59, with Rafal Szukala close behind at 53.60. In the final, Morales was slow to leave the starting platform, but by the turn he was leading Pavel Khnykin by three-tenths of a second. In the closing meters, Szukala, sixth at the turn, rapidly closed in on Morales, but it was the 27-year-old American who touched first.

During the playing of the United States national anthem at the medal ceremony, Morales thought of his mother and how, when he was a boy, the two of them used to watch Bud Greenspan's Olympic documentaries on television. They told stories of courage and triumph over adversity. "When I was up on the victory stand," Morales told reporters, "I was thinking that my mother would want to be here to experience this, and I know that she was with me in spirit. This was my time at last."

1996 Atlanta C: 58, N: 52, D: 7.24. WR: 52.32 (Denis Pankratov)

1. Denis Pankratov	RUS	52.27 WR
2. Scott Miller	AUS	52.53
3. Vladislav Kulikov	RUS	53.13
4. Jiang Chengji	CHN	53.20
5. Rafał Szukała	POL	53.29
6. Michael Klim	AUS	53.30
7. Stephen Clarke	CAN	53.33
8. Pavlo Khnykin	UKR	53.58

Scott Miller set an Olympic record of 52.89 in his preliminary heat, but in the final it was the favorite, Denis Pankratov of Volgograd, who dominated the race, breaking his own world record. When Vladislav Kulikov touched the wall and looked back at the scoreboard to see where he had finished, he thought he saw an "8" next to his name. Then he removed his goggles and discovered, much to his delight, that the "8" was actually a "3."

2000 Sydney C: 62, N: 53, D: 9.22. WR: 51.81 (Michael Klim)

1. Lars Frölander	SWE	52.00
2. Michael Klim	AUS	52.18
3. Geoff Huegill	AUS	52.22
4. Ian Crocker	USA	52.44
5. Michael Mintenko	CAN	52.58
5. Takashi Yamamoto	JPN	52.58
7. Anatoly Polyakov	RUS	53.13
7. Thomas Rupprath	GER	53.13

The hometown crowd was expecting a one-two finish by Australians Michael Klim and Geoff Huegill. Klim had earned seven medals at the last world championships in 1998. On December 12, 1999, he set the existing world record in the 100-meter butterfly and at the Sydney Olympics he had already won two relay gold medals. Klim and Huegill had split their last six meetings in the 100 butterfly and in each of the last three they had been separated no more than two hundredths of a second. Meanwhile, Lars Frölander had won the last three European championships and placed second at the 1994 world championships and at the 1998 world championships, where he trailed Klim and beat Huegill. Klim and Huegill recorded the fastest times in the Olympic qualifying round, while Frölander was back in fifth. In the first semifinal, Huegill set an Olympic record of 51.96. Klim won the second semi in 52.63, with Frölander third. In the final, Klim turned first, followed by Huegill and Frölander. Klim tried to hold on against Frölander's finishing kick, but, in Klim's words, in the last meters, "a grand piano fell from the ceiling and landed square on my back." Frölander blew by the Australians and reached the wall first. Competing in his third Olympics, the 26-year-old Swede had won his first individual medal.

2004 Athens C: 59, N: 51, D: 8.20. WR: 50.76 (Ian Crocker)

1. Michael Phelps	USA	51.25 OR
2. Ian Crocker	USA	51.29
3. Andriy Serdinov	UKR	51.36
4. Thomas Rupprath	GER	52.27
5. Igor Marchenko	RUS	52.32
6. Gabriel Mangabeira	BRA	52.34
7. Duje Draganja	CRO	52.46
8. Geoff Huegill	AUS	52.56

Born and raised in the Rodgers Forge neighborhood just outside Baltimore, Maryland, Michael Phelps started swimming at the age of seven as an outlet for his abundant energy, training at the North Baltimore Aquatic Club under coach Bob Bowman.

By the age of fifteen he had qualified for the 2000 Olympics, where he finished fifth in the 200-meter butterfly. His real breakthrough came at the 2003 world championships, where, at the age of 18, he made history by breaking five world records at a single competition, while winning four gold medals. In the 100-meter butterfly, he finished second behind Ian Crocker, who became the first person to swim the event in under 51 seconds, breaking Phelps' previous world record time by nearly half a second to finish in 50.98 seconds. At the 2004 US Olympic trials, less than six weeks before the Olympic final, Crocker beat Phelps again, and again lowered the world record, this time to 50.76.

In Athens, Crocker started quickly and reached the turn first. He held on until the final stroke when Phelps, who was fifth at the turn, barely reached the wall first to earn his fifth gold medal of the Games. In third place was Andriy Serdinov, who held the world record for approximately five minutes during the 2003 world championships, having broken Michael Klim's time of 51.81 seconds during the semifinals, before Phelps swam faster in the next semifinal.

After the race, Phelps announced his decision to give his berth in the 4 × 100-meter medley relay to Crocker, citing his wish to see his teammate win a gold medal.

2008 Beijing C: 65, N: 51, D: 8.16. WR: 50.40 (Ian Crocker)

1. Michael Phelps	USA	50.58 OR
2. Milorad Čavić	SER	50.59
3. Andrew Lauterstein	AUS	51.12
4. Ian Crocker	USA	51.13
5. Jason Dunford	KEN	51.47
6. Takuro Fujii	JPN	51.50
7. Andriy Serdinov	UKR	51.59
8. Ryan Pini	PNG	51.86

The 100-meter butterfly was the only race Michael Phelps contested at the 2008 Olympics for which he did not already hold the world record. That honor went to defending Olympic silver medalist Ian Crocker, who had beaten Phelps at the 2005 world championships. Phelps had come back to defeat Crocker for the 2007 world title. By the time the two reached the Olympic final, Phelps had already won six gold medals at the 2008 Games, each one in world-record time.

American-born Milorad Čavić, competing in his third Olympics, set an Olympic record of 50.76 in the first round and led the field halfway through the final, with Phelps trailing in seventh place. In a sensational finish, Phelps surged over the final 50 meters, making up a deficit of more than half a second to touch in a virtual tie with Čavić that was too close to call by the naked eye.

The results of swimming races are determined not by a photo, but by the pressure applied to touchpads. Omega, the official timekeeper of the Olympics (and one of Phelps' sponsors) announced that Phelps had won by 4.7 mm (⅕in.). Serbian officials made a token protest of the result, but it was dismissed after a frame-by-frame review. A week later, Omega released a digital

100-meter butterfly, 2008

Michael Phelps (left) edges Milorad Čavić to win the 100-meter butterfly photo sequence of the finish, explaining that swimming touchpads require 3 kg (6.6 lb) of pressure to activate. "Any less and waves would set it off," Omega timer Silvio Chianese told the press. "You can't just put your fingertips on the pad, you really have to push it." So even if Čavić, who was gliding at the end, reached the touchpad first, it was Phelps who first pushed it.

But Čavić was far from a sore loser. "If you ask me if I'm disappointed," he said, "it's a miracle that I'm here. I retired 1½ years ago. In my heart I'm enjoying the experience. For me it's an incredible feeling to have come this far."

The gold medal was Phelps' seventh at the 2008 Olympics, matching Mark Spitz's record at the 1972 Olympics. It was the only one of his eventual 2008 gold medals in which he did not also break the world record.

200-METER BUTTERFLY

1896–1952 not held

1956 Melbourne C: 19, N: 14, D: 12.1. WR: 2:16.7 (William Yorzyk)

1. William Yorzyk	USA	2:19.3 OR
2. Takashi Ishimoto	JPN	2:23.8
3. György Tumpek	HUN	2:23.9
4. Jack Nelson	USA	2:26.6
5. John Marshall	AUS	2:27.2
6. Eulalio Ríos Alemán	MEX	2:27.3
7. Brian Wilkinson	AUS	2:29.7
8. Alexandru Popescu	ROM	2:31.0

William Yorzyk's huge margin of victory was about six and a half meters. In 1984 Yorzyk, then a 57-year-old anesthesiologist, swam the 200-yard butterfly in 2:11.0—faster than he did in his athletic heyday.

1960 Rome C: 34, N: 23, D: 9.2. WR: 2:13.2 (Michael Troy)

1. Michael Troy	USA	2:12.8 WR
2. Neville Hayes	AUS	2:14.6
3. J. David Gillanders	USA	2:15.3
4. Federico Dennerlein	ITA	2:16.0
5. Haruo Yoshimuta	JPN	2:18.3
6. Kevin Berry	AUS	2:18.5
7. Valentin Kuzmin	SOV/RUS	2:18.9
8. Kenzo Izutsu	JPN	2:19.4

1964 Tokyo C: 32, N: 19, D: 10.18. WR: 2:06.9 (Kevin Berry)

1. Kevin Berry	AUS	2:06.6 WR
2. Carl Robie	USA	2:07.5
3. Frederick Schmidt	USA	2:09.3
4. Philip Riker	USA	2:11.0
5. Valentin Kuzmin	SOV/RUS	2:11.3
6. Yoshinori Kadonaga	JPN	2:12.6
7. Brett Hill	AUS	2:12.8
8. Daniel Sherry	CAN	2:14.6

Even though Kevin Berry held the world record in the 200-meter butterfly, he still had to earn a living. In 1964 he was working as a dishwasher at the Angus Steak House in Sydney when a reception was held there to honor Australia's Olympic team. Berry washed dishes, changed his clothes, attended the luncheon, and then went to the back of the restaurant and returned to his dishwashing. In the Tokyo final, Berry overtook Robie after 130 meters and broke his own world record.

1968 Mexico City C: 29, N: 18, D: 10.24. WR: 2:05.7 (Mark Spitz)

1. Carl Robie	USA	2:08.7
2. Martin Woodroffe	GBR	2:09.0
3. John Ferris	USA	2:09.3
4. Valentin Kuzmin	SOV/RUS	2:10.6
5. Peter Feil	SWE	2:10.9
6. Folkert Meeuw	GER	2:11.5
7. Viktor Sharygin	SOV/RUS	2:11.9
8. Mark Spitz	USA	2:13.5

Having won five gold medals at the 1967 Pan American Games, Mark Spitz brashly predicted that he would win six golds at the 1968 Olympics in Mexico City. Instead, he fell far short of his expectations. He did gain two gold medals, but they were in relays rather than individual events. After finishing third in the 100-meter freestyle, he placed second in his specialty, the 100-meter butterfly, thus losing his place on the medley relay team to the winner, Douglas Russell. Spitz's last appearance of the 1968 Olympics was in the 200-meter butterfly, in which he was the world record holder. Along with John Ferris, Spitz managed to lead the qualifiers in 2:10.6. But in the final it was clear that his confidence had been shattered. Exhausted by a long week of races, he was never in contention and finished far back in last place.

Carl Robie, on the other hand, was in tip-top shape. Four years earlier he had been the favorite, but was beaten by Kevin Berry. In Mexico City, with the attention on Spitz, Robie was able to relax and hold off a late challenge from Martin Woodroffe to gain the victory.

1972 Munich C: 29, N: 20, D: 8.28. WR: 2:01.53 (Mark Spitz)

1. Mark Spitz	USA	2:00.70 WR
2. Gary Hall, Sr.	USA	2:02.86
3. Robin Backhaus	USA	2:03.23
4. Jorge Delgado Panchana, Jr.	ECU	2:04.60
5. Hans Fassnacht	GER	2:04.69
6. András Hargitay	HUN	2:04.69
7. Hartmut Flöckner	GDR	2:05.34
8. Folkert Meeuw	GER	2:05.57

It seemed only fitting that Mark Spitz's first race of the 1972 Olympics should be the same one as his last race at the 1968 Games—the 200-meter butterfly. Here was a chance for Spitz to redeem himself immediately for his disappointing performances four years earlier. Not surprisingly Spitz was more than a bit nervous as he stood on the starting block before the final, but once he was in the water his victory was never in doubt. Afterward he leaped out of the water with his arms held high. The four-year psychological burden had been lifted, and Mark Spitz was on his way to becoming the first person in history to win seven gold medals in one Olympics.

1976 Montreal C: 38, N: 25, D: 7.18 WR: 1:59.63 (Roger Pyttel)

1. Michael Bruner	USA	1:59.23 WR
2. Steven Gregg	USA	1:59.54
3. Bill Forrester	USA	1:59.96
4. Roger Pyttel	GDR	2:00.02
5. Michael Kraus	GER	2:00.46
6. Brian Brinkley	GBR	2.01.49
7. Jorge Delgado Panchana, Jr.	ECU	2:01.95
8. Aleksandr Manachinsky	SOV/UKR	2:04.61

1980 Moscow C: 25, N: 19, D: 7.20. WR: 1:59.23 (Mike Bruner)

1. Serhei Fesenko	SOV/UKR	1:59:76
2. Philip Hubble	GBR	2:01.20
3. Roger Pyttel	GDR	2:01.39
4. Peter Morris	GBR	2:02.27
5. Mikhail Gorelik	SOV/RUS	2:02.44
6. Kees Vervoorn	HOL	2:02.52
7. Pår Arvidsson	SWE	2:02.61
8. Stephen Poulter	GBR	2:02.93

This was one event in which the boycotting Americans were sorely missed. In 1972 and 1976 US swimmers had swept all three medals, and they probably could have done it again in 1980. At the US Outdoor National on July 30, Craig Beardsley of Harrington Park, New Jersey, set a world record of 1:58.21 in his qualifying heat. He won the final in 1:58.46, followed by Mike Bruner in 1:59.13 and Bill Forrester in 1:59.40. Eighth-place finisher Steve Gregg clocked 2:00.98—faster than the silver medal winner in Moscow ten days earlier.

1984 Los Angeles C: 35, N: 28, D: 8.3. WR: 1:57.05 (Michael Gross)

1. Jonathan Sieben	AUS	1:57.04 WR
2. Michael Gross	GER	1:57.40
3. Rafael Vidal Castro	VEN	1:57.51
4. P. Pablo Morales	USA	1:57.75
5. Anthony Mosse	NZL	1:58.75
6. Thomas Ponting	CAN	1:59.37
7. Peter Ward	CAN	2:00.39
8. Patrick Kennedy	USA	2:01.03

With two gold medals already under his belt, Michael Gross entered his best event, the 200-meter butterfly, as the clear favorite. He expected stiff challenges from Pablo Morales and Rafael Vidal and that's exactly what he got. But over in lane 6, something completely unexpected happened. Seventeen-year-old Jon Sieben, from the Brisbane suburb of Coorparoo, seventh at the halfway mark and fourth with 50 meters to go, shot past the favorites to out-touch Gross and gain the victory, the world record, and one of the most surprising upsets in Olympic swimming history. Sieben's time of 1:57.04 was over four seconds faster than his pre-Olympic best of 2:01.17. Sieben was so excited by his victory that it was not until an hour later that he realized that he had broken the world record.

The rabidly pro-US crowd gave Sieben a standing ovation, and the outcome was so delightful that the defeated favorites expressed pleasure more than disappointment. Gross, who had refused to appear before reporters following his two gold-medal races, and whose disdain for pomp and press had earned him the nickname "The American" in West Germany, sat beside Sieben after the 200 butterfly preferring to praise the young Australian rather than talk about himself.

1988 Seoul C: 40, N: 29, D: 9.24. WR: 1:56.24 (Michael Gross)

1. Michael Gross	GER	1:56.94 OR
2. Benny Nielsen	DEN	1:58.24
3. Anthony Mosse	NZL	1:58.28
4. Thomas Ponting	CAN	1:58.91
5. Melvin Stewart	USA	1:59.19
6. David Wilson	AUS	1:59.20
7. Jon Kelly	CAN	1:59.48
8. Anthony Nesty	SUR	2:00.80

Michael Gross had dominated this event since 1981, winning two world championships, four European championships, and setting four world records. The only stain on his record was his unexpected loss to Jon Sieben at the 1984 Olympics. In Seoul, Gross placed fifth in the two events he had won in Los Angeles: the 200-meter freestyle and the 100-meter butterfly. But in the 200 butterfly, he lived up to the expectations, leading from start to finish and winning by a body length.

1992 Barcelona C: 46, N: 32, D: 7.30. WR: 1:55.69 (Melvin Stewart)

1. Melvin Stewart	USA	1:56.26 OR
2. Danyon Loader	NZL	1:57.93
3. Franck Esposito	FRA	1:58.51
4. Rafał Szukała	POL	1:58.89
5. Keiichi Kawanaka	JPN	1:58.97
6. Denis Pankratov	RUS	1:58.98
7. Robert Pinter	ROM	1:59.34
8. Martin Roberts	AUS	1:59.64

"Disneyland with a halo" was the way Melvin Stewart described the place where he grew up: Heritage USA, the Christian theme park created by television evangelist Jim Bakker and his wife, Tammy Faye. His father was the athletic director at the Heritage Academy and Melvin himself once worked as a bellhop in the park hotel. Since the 1988 Olympics, Stewart had dominated the 200-meter butterfly, setting a world record at the 1991 world championships and winning every other meet of importance. In Barcelona, Stewart lived up to expectations, leading from start to finish. Danyon Loader, on the other hand, was on nobody's list of favorites but improved his pre-Olympic personal best by 3.36 seconds to earn the silver medal.

1996 Atlanta C: 42, N: 36, D: 7.22. WR: 1:55.22 (Denis Pankratov)

1. Denis Pankratov	RUS	1:56.51
2. Thomas Malchow	USA	1:57.44
3. Scott Goodman	AUS	1:57.48
4. Franck Esposito	FRA	1:58.10
5. Scott Miller	AUS	1:58.28
6. Denys Sylantyev	UKR	1:58.37
7. James Hickman	GBR	1:58.47
8. Péter Horváth	HUN	1:59.12

Denis Pankratov had dominated the 200-meter butterfly since the last Olympics, and yet he entered the 1996 Olympics feeling he had something to prove. In February he had broken the short-course world records at both 100 and 200 meters at a meet in Paris, but the records were not ratified because incompetent French officials had run out of bottles for the urine test for drugs. Although Pankratov had personally asked three times to be tested, the rumor spread in Russia that he had refused to be tested. Stung by this unjust criticism, Pankratov was determined to prove himself in Atlanta. In the preliminary round he recorded only the fourth best time, but in the final he won easily. Relaxing as the competition continued, he set a world record two days later at 100 meters.

2000 Sydney C: 46, N: 40, D: 9.19. WR: 1:55.18 (Tom Malchow)

1. Thomas Malchow	USA	1:55.35 OR
2. Denys Sylantyev	UKR	1:55.76
3. Justin Norris	AUS	1:56.17
4. Anatoly Polyakov	RUS	1:56.34
5. Michael Phelps	USA	1:56.50
6. Stephen Parry	GBR	1:57.01
7. Denis Pankratov	RUS	1:57.97
8. Franck Esposito	FRA	1:58.39

After setting the world record on June 17, Tom Malchow was the clear favorite to win the Olympic title three months later. He broke the Olympic record in the qualifying round and again in the semifinals. In the final he followed his game plan perfectly. Fifth after 50 meters and third after 100 meters, he took the lead in the final lap . . . and set another Olympic record. In fifth place was 15-year-old Michael Phelps. Six months later, Phelps broke Malchow's world record to become, at 15 years 9 months, the youngest man to set a swimming world record. On July 27, 2003, Phelps became the first man to set world records in two different individual events (the 100-meter butterfly and the 200-meter individual medley) on the same day.

2004 Athens C: 39, N: 34, D: 8.17. WR: 1:53.93 (Michael Phelps)

1. Michael Phelps	USA	1:54.04 OR
2. Takashi Yamamoto	JPN	1:54.56
3. Steve Parry	GBR	1:55.52
4. Paweł Korzeniowski	POL	1:56.00
5. Ioan Ştefan Gherghel	ROM	1:56.10
6. Wu Peng	CHN	1:56.28
7. Nikolai Skvortsov	RUS	1:57.14
8. Thomas Malchow	USA	1:57.48

Two-time defending world champion and world record holder Michael Phelps was never seriously threatened. He was almost a half second under his world record split at the halfway point, but could not quite keep up the pace, and settled for an Olympic record. One hour later, Phelps led the US to victory in the 4 × 200-meter freestyle relay. Phelps' older sister Whitney had represented the United States in the 200-meter butterfly at the 1994 world championships.

2008 Beijing C: 44, N: 39, D: 8.13. WR: 1:52.09 (Michael Phelps)

1. Michael Phelps	USA	1:52.03 WR
2. László Cseh, Jr.	HUN	1:52.70
3. Takeshi Matsuda	JPN	1:52.97
4. Moss Burmester	NZL	1:54.35
4. Wu Peng	CHN	1:54.35
6. Paweł Korzeniowski	POL	1:54.60
7. Kaio Almeida	BRA	1:54.71
8. Nikolai Skvortsov	RUS	1:55.14

Michael Phelps, 2008
Michael Phelps with gold medals and sponsor

The 200-meter butterfly was Michael Phelps' signature event. He had held the world record in the event since 2001, lowering it five times, and had not been beaten in competition since 2002.

Phelps was in the lead at the halfway point and held off a late surge by László Cseh despite a mishap in which his goggles started filling up with water. "At the end, I really couldn't see," Phelps said afterwards, "I was looking for the 'T' on the bottom of the pool. It got to the point where I was counting strokes and hoping I would hit the wall just about right."

The victory was Phelps' fourth of the 2008 Olympics, and his tenth career gold medal, surpassing the tally of Olympic legends Paavo Nurmi, Carl Lewis, Mark Spitz and Larysa Latynina, all of whom won nine.

200-METER INDIVIDUAL MEDLEY

In individual medley races the order of strokes is butterfly, backstroke, breaststroke, and freestyle.

1896–1964 not held

1968 Mexico City C: 46, N: 27, D: 10.20. WR: 2:10.6 (Charles Hickcox)

1. Charles Hickcox	USA	2:12.0 OR
2. Gregory Buckingham	USA	2:13.0
3. John Ferris	USA	2:13.3
4. Juan Bello	PER	2:13.7
5. George Smith	CAN	2:15.9
6. John Gilchrist	CAN	2:16.6
7. Michael Holthaus	GER	2:16.8
8. Péter Lázár	HUN	2:18.3

Charlie Hickcox won the first of his three gold medals.

1972 Munich C: 39, N: 26, D: 9.3. WR: 2:09.3 (Gunnar Larsson, Gary Hall)

1. Gunnar Larsson	SWE	2:07.17 WR
2. Alexander "Tim" McKee	USA	2:08.37
3. Steven Furniss	USA	2:08.45
4. Gary Hall	USA	2:08.49
5. András Hargitay	HUN	2:09.66
6. Mikhail Suharev	SOV/RUS	2:11.78
7. Juan Bello	PER	2:11.87
8. Hans Ljungberg	SWE	2:13.56

Larsson and McKee duplicated their one-two finish in the 400-meter individual medley, as the first four finishers all broke the world record. McKee celebrated his medal by slipping past security guards and performing a one-and-a-half somersault dive off the 10-meter platform.

1976–1980 not held

1984 Los Angeles C: 45, N: 34, D: 8.4. WR: 2:02.45 (Alex Baumann)

1. Alex Baumann	CAN	2:01.42 WR
2. P. Pablo Morales	USA	2:03.05
3. Neil Cochran	GBR	2:04.38
4. Robin Brew	GBR	2:04.52
5. Steve Lundquist	USA	2:04.91
6. Andrew Phillips	JAM	2:05.60
7. Nicolai Klapkarek	GER	2:05.88
8. Ralf Diegel	GER	2:06.66

Baumann won his second gold medal of the Los Angeles Games, setting a world record, as he had in the 400 individual medley five days earlier. The victor at the Friendship Games, with a time of 2:02.51, was Jens-Peter Berndt of East Germany, who defected to the US less than five months later and competed for West Germany in 1988.

1988 Seoul C: 56, N: 35, D: 9.25. WR: 2:00.56 (Tamás Darnyi)

1. Tamás Darnyi	HUN	2:00.17 WR
2. Patrick Kühl	GDR	2:01.61
3. Vadym Yaroshchuk	SOV/UKR	2:02.40
4. Mikhail Zubkov	SOV/RUS	2:02.92
5. Peter Bermel	GER	2:03.81
6. Robert Bruce	AUS	2:04.34
7. Raik Hannemann	GDR	2:04.82
8. Gary Anderson	CAN	2:06.35

When Tamás Darnyi was 15 years old, he lost the vision in his left eye after being hit by an icy snowball during some horseplay three years earlier. He underwent seven operations to repair a detached retina. Although the surgery did not restore his sight, it did give him sensitivity to light. Beginning in 1985 Darnyi won every major title in both individual medal events. In Seoul, the 21-year-old Budapest native was in third place after 150 meters. Then, as expected, he pulled away with a 27.73 freestyle leg to win his second gold medal and set his second world record.

1992 Barcelona C: 56, N: 41, D: 7.31. WR: 1:59.36 (Tamás Darnyi)

1. Tamás Darnyi	HUN	2:00.76
2. Gregory Burgess	USA	2:00.97
3. Attila Czene	HUN	2:01.00
4. Jani Sievinen	FIN	2:01.28
5. Christian Gessner	GER	2:01.97
6. Ronald Karnaugh	USA	2:02.18
7. Matthew Dunn	AUS	2:02.79
8. Gary Anderson	CAN	2:04.30

Tamás Darnyi had not lost an individual medley race since 1984 and he was not about to start at the Olympics. Fourth after 150 meters, he swam a 27.53 freestyle leg to earn his fourth gold medal.

The second-fastest time of the pre-Olympic season

had been recorded by Ron Karnaugh of Maplewood, New Jersey, the son of a retired truck driver. Because Karnaugh's family couldn't afford to travel to Barcelona, the 23,000 people of Maplewood raised the funds to send them. During the Parade of Nations at the Opening Ceremony, Ron's father, Peter, caught his eye and took his photograph. On the way back to his seat, Peter Karnaugh was stricken by a heart attack and died. Six days later Ron swam in the Olympic final. He led after 50 meters, held on to third place until the final leg, and then faded to sixth.

1996 Atlanta C: 39, N: 31, D: 7.25. WR: 1:58.16 (Jani Sievinen)

1. Attila Czene	HUN	1:59.91 OR
2. Jani Sievinen	FIN	2:00.13
3. Curtis Myden	CAN	2:01.13
4. Marcel Wouda	HOL	2:01.45
5. Matthew Dunn	AUS	2:01.57
6. Gregory Burgess	USA	2:02.56
7. Thomas Dolan	USA	2:03.89
8. Xavier Marchand	FRA	2:04.29

Curtis Myden led after 50 meters, but Attila Czene, swimming in lane one, burst into the lead as soon as the backstroke leg began. He was still one second ahead of Myden after 150 meters. Jani Sievinen, who had won 39 straight finals in the 200-meter individual medley, swam a strong freestyle leg to power past Myden, but he fell about 40 centimeters (16 inches) short of catching Czene. Like all swimmers, Attila Czene was required to meet a qualifying time in order to participate in the Olympics. In Czene's case, it was a 2:00.88 recorded at a meet in Budapest held June 6-8. Except, as it was revealed several weeks after the Atlanta Games, the Budapest meet never actually happened. It seems that Hungarian swimming officials had neglected to keep track of their athletes' times and had failed to arrange an official meet to allow them to meet the qualifying standards. So they did the next best thing: they invented a meet, complete with qualifying times, failed times and even disqualifications. Half of the 22-person Hungarian Olympic team qualified at this phantom meet, although Czene was the only medal winner among them.

2000 Sydney C: 56, N: 49, D: 9.21. WR: 1:58.16 (Jani Sievinen)

1. Massimiliano Rosolino	ITA	1:58.98 OR
2. Thomas Dolan	USA	1:59.77
3. Thomas Wilkens	USA	2:00.87
4. Attila Czene	HUN	2:01.16
5. Marcel Wouda	HOL	2:01.48
6. Christian Keller	GER	2:02.02
7. Xavier Marchand	FRA	2:02.23
8. Jani Sievinen	FIN	2:02.49

Massi Rosolino had already won a silver medal in the 400-meter freestyle and a bronze medal in the 200-meter freestyle when he swam in the 200-meter individual medley. Marcel Wouda led after the butterfly leg with Dolan fifth and Rosolino seventh. Defending champion Attila Czene moved ahead in the backstroke, while Dolan moved up to second and Rosolino to third. Rosolino surged ahead on the breaststroke leg and then pulled away over the final lap. In Sydney, Rosolino told the media that he was proud to have won without drugs and that his drug was "spaghetti with all sauces." However, two weeks later, the news broke that Rosolino was one of 61 Italian athletes who had tested positive for elevated levels of human growth hormone. Although a government investigation was begun, it was halted for reasons of "privacy."

2004 Athens C: 49, N: 41, D: 8.19. WR: 1:55.94 (Michael Phelps)

1. Michael Phelps	USA	1:57.14 OR
2. Ryan Lochte	USA	1:58.78
3. George Bovell	TRI	1:58.80
4. László Cseh	HUN	1:58.84
5. Thiago Pereira	BRA	2:00.11
6. Takahiro Mori	JPN	2:00.60
7. Vytautas Janušaitis	LIT	2:01.28
8. Jiro Miki	JPN	2:02.16

World champion and world record holder Michael Phelps stormed to his fourth gold medal of the Athens Olympics.

2008 Beijing C: 46, N: 41, D: 8.15. WR: 1:54.80 (Michael Phelps)

1. Michael Phelps	USA	1:54.23 WR
2. László Cseh, Jr.	HUN	1:56.52
3. Ryan Lochte	USA	1:56.53
4. Thiago Pereira	BRA	1:58.14
5. Ken Takakuwa	JPN	1:58.22
6. James Goddard	GBR	1:59.24
7. Keith Beavers	CAN	1:59.43
8. Liam Tancock	GBR	2:00.76

Michael Phelps led the final from start to finish, defending his Olympic title and lowering his own world record by 0.57 seconds. It was Phelps' sixth straight gold medal at the 2008 Olympics, each won in world record time. Ryan Lochte took the bronze medal less than thirty minutes after winning the gold medal in the 200-meter backstroke.

400-METER INDIVIDUAL MEDLEY

1896–1960 not held

1964 Tokyo C: 30, N; 18, D: 10.14. WR: 4:48.6 (Richard Roth)

1. Richard Roth	USA	4:45.4 WR
2. Roy Saari	USA	4:47.1
3. Gerhard Hetz	GER	4:51.0
4. Carl Robie	USA	4:51,4
5. John Gilchrist	CAN	4:57.6
6. Johannes Jiskoot	HOL	5:01.9
7. György Kosztolánczy	HUN	5:01.9
8. Terence Buck	AUS	5:03.0

Three days before the competition, world record holder Dick Roth was stricken with an acute attack of appendicitis. Japanese doctors recommended an immediate operation, but Roth refused. Since he also refused to take drugs, they packed him in ice instead. Willing the pain to subside temporarily, the 17-year-old Californian took the lead 70 meters from the finish and won the final in world record time. After successful careers as a rancher and entrepeneur, Roth wrote the 1999 book *No, It's Not Hot in Here: A Husband's Guide to Understanding Menopause.*

1968 Mexico City C: 35, N: 22, D: 10.23. WR: 4:39.0 (Charles Hickcox)

1. Charles Hickcox	USA	4:48.4
2. Gary Hall	USA	4:48.7
3. Michael Holthaus	GER	4:51.4
4. Gregory Buckingham	USA	4:51.4
5. John Gilchrist	CAN	4:56.7
6. Reinhard Merkel	GER	4:59.8
7. Andrei Dunayev	SOV/RUS	5:00.3
8. Rafael Hernández Rojas	MEX	5:04.3

Hickcox and Hall swam side by side, almost neck and neck for the entire race.

1972 Munich C: 32, N: 24, D: 8.30. WR: 4:30.81 (Gary Hall)

1. Gunnar Larsson	SWE	4:31.98 OR
2. Alexander "Tim" McKee	USA	4:31.98 OR
3. András Hargitay	HUN	4:32.70
4. Steven Furniss	USA	4 35.44
5. Gary Hall, Sr.	USA	4 37 38
6. Bengt Gingsjö	SWE	4:37.96
7. Graham Windeatt	AUS	4:40.39
8. Wolfram Sperling	GDR	4:40.66

Both Larsson and McKee were credited with the Olympic record, but Larsson was declared the winner by two one-thousandths of a second, 4:31.981 to 4:31.983. As a result of this race, the rules were changed to declare a deadheat any swimming contest in which the swimmers were tied to hundredths of a second. McKee went on to work for a marketing firm but then, in 1982, he gave up his job—and took a 50 percent pay cut—to become a lifeguard in Miami Beach. Bronze medalist András Hargitay had almost drowned in the Danube River at the age of nine. "After that," he recalled, "my mother ordered me to learn how to swim, and this is what's come of it."

1976 Montreal C: 31, N: 22, D: 7.25. WR: 4:26.00 (Zóltan Verrasztó)

1. Rod Strachan	USA	4:23.68 WR
2. Alexander "Tim" McKee	USA	4:24.62
3. Andrei Smirnov	SOV/RUS	4:26.90
4. András Hargitay	HUN	4:27.13
5. Graham Smith	CAN	4:28.64
6. Steven Furniss	USA	4.29.23
7. Andrew Ritchie	CAN	4:29.87
8. Hans-Joachim Geisler	GER	4:34.95

1980 Moscow C: 23, N: 17, D: 7.27. WR: 4:20.05 (Jesse Vassallo)

1. Oleksander Sydorenko	SOV/UKR	4:22.89 OR
2. Serhei Fesenko	SOV/UKR	4:23.43
3. Zóltan Verrasztó	HUN	4:24.24
4. András Hargitay	HUN	4:24.48
5. Djan Madruga Garrido	BRA	4:26.81
6. Miloslav Rolko	CZE	4:26.99
7. Leszek Górski	POL	4:28.89
8. Daniel Machek	CZE	4:29.86

Three days after the Olympic final, the US Outdoor National was won by world record holder Jesse Vassallo in 4:21.51.

1984 Los Angeles C: 23, N: 19, D: 7.30. WR: 4:17.53 (Alex Baumann)

1. Alex Baumann	CAN	4:17.41 WR
2. Ricardo Prado	BRA	4:18.45
3. Robert Woodhouse	AUS	4:20.50
4. Jesus "Jesse" Vassallo	USA	4:21.46
5. Maurizio Divano	ITA	4:22.76
6. Jeffrey Kostoff	USA	4:23.28
7. Stephen Poulter	GBR	4:25.80
8. Giovanni Franceschi	ITA	4:26.05

Born in Prague, 4-year-old Alex Baumann was in New Zealand with his family when Soviet tanks rolled into Czechoslovakia in 1968. Baumann's parents refused to return to their homeland, eventually settling instead in Sudbury, Ontario. Proud to be a Canadian, Baumann appeared at the Olympics sporting a maple-leaf tattoo (and a diamond-stud earring)—and earned Canada's first swimming gold medal since 1912. Baumann was unable to meet with reporters after the race because he required almost two hours to produce a urine sample for the drug-testing. In the middle of his third beer, medical officials discovered that he was under age and forced him to switch to soft drinks.

In Moscow three weeks later, Jens-Peter Berndt of East Germany clocked 4:18.29 to win at the Friendship Games.

1988 Seoul C: 34, N: 24, D: 9.21. WR: 4:15.42 (Tamás Darnyi)

1. Tamás Darnyi	HUN	4:14.75 WR
2. David Wharton	USA	4:17.36
3. Stefano Battistelli	ITA	4:18.01
4. József Szabó	HUN	4:18.15
5. Patrick Kühl	GDR	4:18.44
6. Jens-Peter Berndt	GER	4:21.71
7. Luca Sacchi	ITA	4:23.23
8. Peter Bermel	GER	4:24.02

This race was billed as a showdown between world record holder Tamás Darnyi, who was blind in one eye, and former world record holder David Wharton, who was born severely hearing-impaired. However, Darnyi built such a large lead during the backstroke leg that the second half of the contest was anticlimactic.

1992 Barcelona C: 32, N: 25, D: 7.27. WR: 4:12.36 (Tamás Darnyi)

1. Tamás Darnyi	HUN	4:14.23 OR
2. Eric Namesnik	USA	4:15.57
3. Luca Sacchi	ITA	4:16.34
4. David Wharton	USA	4:17.26
5. Christian Gessner	GER	4:17.88
6. Patrick Kühl	GER	4:19.66
7. Sergei Marinyuk	MOL	4:22.93
8. Takahiro Fujimoto	JPN	4:23.86

Namesnik led after 200 meters, but Darnyi, unbeaten in eight years, forged ahead at the end of the breastroke leg and pulled away to a clear victory.

1996 Atlanta C: 27, N: 23, D: 7.21. WR: 4:12.30 (Tom Dolan)

1. Thomas Dolan	USA	4:14.90
2. Eric Namesnik	USA	4:15.25
3. Curtis Myden	CAN	4:16.28
4. Matthew Dunn	AUS	4:16.66
5. Marcel Wouda	HOL	4:17.71
6. Luca Sacchi	ITA	4:18.31
7. Marcin Maliński	POL	4:20.50
8. Sergei Marinyuk	MOL	4:21.15

The final featured three swimmers from the University of Michigan: Marcel Wouda of the Netherlands and American rivals Eric Namesnik and Tom Dolan. Curtis Myden led after the butterfly with Dolan and Namesnik close behind. Halfway through the race, Dolan and Namesnik were exactly tied at 2:02.87. Namesnik moved ahead by 44 hundredths of a second during the breaststroke leg and was still a tiny bit ahead at the final turn. But it was world champion and world record holder Dolan, a sufferer of exercise-induced asthma, who pulled away to win by about 60 centimeters (2 feet).

Sergei Marinyuk finished seventh in 1992. When he returned to Kishinev, Moldova, there was no money to support the maintenance of swimming pools, so Marinyuk retired and became a taxi driver. Five months later he was held up at gunpoint and decided that he might be better off finding a way to continue swimming. He moved to Santa Clara, California, and found a job coaching children. In 1996, at the age of 27, he made it to the final again.

2000 Sydney C: 45, N: 39, D: 9.17. WR: 4:12.30 (Tom Dolan)

1. Thomas Dolan	USA	4:11.76 WR
2. Erik Vendt	USA	4:14.23
3. Curtis Myden	CAN	4:15.33
4. Alessio Boggiatto	ITA	4:15.93
5. Terence Parkin	SAF	4:16.92
6. Justin Norris	AUS	4:17.87
7. Cezar Bădiță	ROM	4:20.91
8. Shinya Taniguchi	JPN	4:20.93

In March 2000, Tom Dolan suffered his first loss in seven years in the 400-meter individual medley when he was beaten by fellow American Tom Wilkens. At the US Olympic trials, Dolan, weakened by a high fever and antibiotics, had to come from behind to qualify. Five hours before the Olympic final less than six weeks later, Dolan had trouble breathing and sought help in the medical tent of the Athletes' Village. He spent an hour attached to an oxygen tank and sweating profusely. Yet when the race began, Dolan was back in form. He took the lead in the first lap of the backstroke leg and pulled away steadily, eventually breaking his own six-year-old world record.

2004 Athens C: 36, N: 26, D: 8.14. WR: 4:08.41 (Michael Phelps)

1. Michael Phelps	USA	4:08.26 WR
2. Erik Vendt	USA	4:11.81
3. László Cseh	HUN	4:12.15
4. Alessio Boggiatto	ITA	4:12.28
5. Oussama Mellouli	TUN	4:14.49
6. Ioannis Kokkodis	GRE	4:18.60
7. Jiro Miki	JPN	4:19.97
8. Travis Nederpelt	AUS	4:20.08

The first of five individual events in which Michael Phelps was competing (he qualified for six but dropped the 200-meter backstroke), the 400-meter medley was one of three events in which the 19-year-old prodigy held the world record. In Athens, Phelps broke his own record and won by the largest margin in the event's history.

2008 Beijing C: 29, N: 22, D: 8.10. WR: 4:05.25 (Michael Phelps)

1. Michael Phelps	USA	4:03.84	WR
2. László Cseh, Jr.	HUN	4:06.16	
3. Ryan Lochte	USA	4:08.09	
4. Alessio Boggiatto	ITA	4:12.16	
5. Luca Marin	ITA	4:12.47	
6. Gergő Kiss	HUN	4:12.84	
7. Brian Johns	CAN	4:13.38	
8. Thiago Pereira	BRA	4:15.40	

Swimming in his first event at the 2008 Olympics, Michael Phelps entered the 400-meter individual medley as defending Olympic champion, reigning world champion and world record holder. (He had held the world record since 2002, lowering it six times, most recently at the US Olympic trials in June.)

The battle for silver was expected to be between Ryan Lochte and 2005 world champion László Cseh. Lochte had finished behind Phelps at both the 2007 world championships and the 2008 US Olympic trials, while Cseh had won the past three consecutive European championships.

Phelps, Lochte and Cseh each won their preliminary heats, with Phelps setting an Olympic record of 4:07.82 in his. The three rivals traded the lead during the first two legs of the final, with Phelps slightly ahead at the 200-meter mark. The rest of the race was a formality, as Phelps pulled ahead to finish more than two seconds ahead of Cseh, lowering his world record by 1.41 seconds.

Phelps would go on to win eight gold medals at the 2008 Olympics.

10,000-METER OPEN WATER

The 10,000-meter open water event includes 25 athletes, no more than two from each nation. The top ten finishers from the last world championships automatically qualify for the Olympics, along with the top nine finishers at a pre-Olympic Marathon Swim Qualifier. One swimmer qualifies from each of the five FINA continents, with one spot held for the host nation, if it has not already qualified by other means.

1896–2004 not held

2008 Beijing-Shunyi C: 25, N: 24, D: 8.21.

1. Maarten van der Weijden	HOL	1:51:51.6
2. David Davies	GBR	1:51:53.1
3. Thomas Lurz	GER	1:51:53.6
4. Valerio Cleri	ITA	1:52:07.5
5. Yevgeny Drattsev	RUS	1:52:08.9
6. Petar Stoychev	BUL	1:52:09.1
7. Brian Ryckeman	BEL	1:52:10.7
8. Mark Warkentin	USA	1:52:13.0

Making its Olympic debut, the so-called "marathon swim" consisted of four 2.5 kilometer (1.5 mile) rectangular loops around the Olympic rowing basin in Shunyi.

The favorites in the event were two-time reigning world champion Vladimir Dyatchin of Russia and 2004 and 2006 world champion Thomas Lurz. The two had staged an epic battle through jellyfish-infested waters in Melbourne for the 2007 world title, with Dyatchin winning by a margin of just 0.06 seconds over the 10,000-meter race despite suffering lacerations 10 in. (25 cm) long due to a jellyfish sting. The following year, Dyatchin again won the world title, this time beating Britain's David Davies by three-tenths of a second, with Lurz finishing third.

Davies and Lurz shared the lead throughout most of the Olympic race, as Dyatchin struggled to keep pace. Dyatchin finished in eleventh place, but was disqualified after receiving a red card for excessive physical contact during the final lap. Davies opened a lead of eight body lengths in the final 500 meters, but was unable to keep the lead, as 27-year-old Maarten van der Weijden slipped ahead in the last 100 meters to win by 1.5 seconds. The completely spent Davies had to be carried away by stretcher.

Van der Weijden had been diagnosed with leukemia in 2001 and underwent chemotherapy and a stem cell transplant. He came back to compete at the 2003 world championships and in 2008 he won the 25-kilometer world championship title. "I think the leukemia taught me to think step by step," Van der Weijden said. "When you're lying in the hospital bed and feeling so much pain and feeling so tired, you don't want to think about next week or next month, you're only thinking about the next hour … That was almost the same strategy I chose here to wait for my chance in the pack."

4 × 100-METER FREESTYLE RELAY

Swimmers who took part in preliminary rounds of relays but not in the final are listed in brackets.

1896–1960 not held

1964 Tokyo T: 13, N: 13, D: 10.14. WR: 3:36.1 (USA—Clark, McDonough, Ilman, Townsend)

1. USA	Stephen Clark, Michael Austin, Gary Ilman, Donald Schollander, [Lary Schulhof]	3:32.2 WR
2. GER& GDR	Horst Löffler, Frank Wiegand, Uwe Jacobsen, Hans-Joachim Klein	3:37.2
3. AUS	David Dickson, Peter Doak, John Ryan, Robert Windle	3:39.1
4. JPN	Kunihiro Iwasaki, Tadaharu Goto, Tatsuo Fujimoto, Yukiaki Okabe, [Katsuki Ishihara]	3:40.5

5. SWE	Bengt-Olof Nordvall, E. Lester Eriksson, Jan Lundin, Per-Ola Lindberg	3:40.7
6. SOV/ RUS	Viktor Mazanov, Vladimir Shuvalov, Viktor Semchenkov, Yuri Sumtsov, [Vladimir Berezin]	3:42.1
7. GBR	Robert Lord, John Martin-Dye, Peter Kendrew, Robert McGregor	3:42.6

DISQ: FRA—Alain Gottvallès, Gérard Gropaiz, Pierre Canavèse, Jean-Pascal Curtillet, [Robert Christophe]

Steve Clark had failed to qualify for the US team in any individual events, but he made up for it by winning three gold medals in the relays. His lead-off leg in the 4 × 100-meter freestyle relay equaled Alain Gottvallès' 100-meter world record of 52.9 seconds and also earned him the right to swim the freestyle leg of the medley relay.

1968 Mexico City T: 16, N: 16, D: 10.17. WR: 3:32.5 (USA—Zorn, Rerych, Walsh, Schollander)

1. USA	Zachary Zorn, Stephen Rerych, Mark Spitz, Kenneth Walsh, [William Johnson, David Johnson, Michael Wall, Donald Schollander]	3:31.7 WR
2. SOV	Semyon Belits-Geiman, Viktor Mazanov, Georgi Kulikov, Leonid Ilyichev, [Sergei Gusev]	3:34.2
3. AUS	Gregory Rogers, Robert Windle, Robert Cusack, Michael Wenden	3:34.7
4. GBR	Michael Turner, David Hembrow, Robert McGregor, Anthony Jarvis	3:38.4
5. GDR	Frank Wiegand, Udo Poser, Horst-Günther Gregor, Lothar Gericke	3:38.8
6. GER	Wolfgang Kremer, Olaf von Schilling, Peter Schorning, Hans Fassnacht	3:39.0
7. CAN	Glen Finch, George Smith, Ralph Hutton, John Gilchrist	3:39.2
8. JPN	Kunihiro Iwasaki, Masayuki Ohsawa, Satoru Nakano, Teruhiko Kitani	3:41.5

1972 Munich T: 13, N: 13, D: 8.28. WR: 3:28.8 (USA, Los Angeles Swim Club—Havens, Weston, Frawley, Heckl)

1. USA	David Edgar, John Murphy, Jerôme Heidenreich, Mark Spitz, [David Fairbank, Gary Conelly]	3:26.42 WR
2. SOV	Vladimir Bure, Viktor Mazanov, Viktor Aboimov, Igor Grivennikov, [Georgy Kulikov]	3:29.72
3. GDR	Roland Matthes, Wilfried Hartung, Peter Bruch, Lutz Unger, [Udo Poser]	3:32.42
4. BRA	Ruy Aquino Oliveira, Paulo Zanetti, Paulo Becskehazy, José Diaz-Aranha	3:33.14
5. CAN	Bruce Robertson, Brian Phillips, Timothy Bach, Robert Kasting	3:33.20
6. GER	Klaus Steinbach, Werner Lampe, Rainer Jacob, Hans Fassnacht, [Gerhard Schiller, Hans-Günther Vosseler, Kersten Meier]	3:33.90
7. FRA	Gilles Vigne, Alain Mosconi, Alain Hermitte, Michel Rousseau	3:34.13
8. SPA	Jorge Comas López, Antonio Culebras Juliana, Enrique Melo Ramón, José Pujol Simón	3:38.21

The US "reserve" team of Dave Fairbank, Gary Conelly, Jerry Heidenreich, and Dave Edgar clocked 3:28.84 in the qualifying round to equal the world record. Six hours later, in the final, Fairbank and Conelly were replaced by John Murphy and Mark Spitz, and a new world record was set. It was Spitz's second gold medal of the evening.

1976–1980 not held

1984 Los Angeles T: 23, N: 23, D: 8.2. WR: 3:19.26 (USA—Cavanaugh, Leamy, McCagg, Gaines)

1. USA	Christopher Cavanaugh, Michael Heath, Matthew Biondi, Ambrose "Rowdy" Gaines, [Thomas Jager, Robin Leamy]	3:19.03 WR
2. AUS	Gregory Fasala, Neil Brooks, Michael Delany, Mark Stockwell	3:19.68
3. SWE	Thomas Lejdström, Bengt Baron, Mikael Örn, Per Johansson, [Richard Milton, Michael Söderlund]	3:22.69
4. GER	Dirk Korthals, Andreas Schmidt, Alexander Schowtka, Michael Gross, [Nicolai Klapkarek]	3:22.98
5. GBR	David Lowe, Roland Lee, Paul Easter, Richard Burrell	3:23.61
6. FRA	Stéphan Caron, Laurent Neuville, Dominique Bataille, Bruno Lesaffre	3:24.63
7. CAN	David Churchill, Blair Hicken, Alex Baumann, Donald "Sandy" Goss, [Levente Mady]	3:24.70
8. ITA	Marcello Guarducci, Marco Colombo, Metello Savino, Fabrizio Rampazzo, [Raffaele Franceschi]	3:24.97

1988 Seoul T: 22, N: 22, D: 9.23. WR: 3:17.08 (USA—McCadam, Heath, Wallace, Biondi)

1. USA	Christopher Jacobs, Troy Dalbey, Thomas Jager, Matthew Biondi, [Brent Lang, Douglas Gjertsen, Shaun Jordan]	3:16.53 WR
2. SOV	Gennady Prigoda, Yuri Bashkatov, Nikolai Yevseyev, Vladimir Tkachenko, [Raimundas Mažuolis, Aleksei Borislavsky]	3:18.33
3. GDR	Dirk Richter, Thomas Flemming, Lars Hinneburg, Steffen Zesner	3:19.82
4. FRA	Stéphan Caron, Christophe Kalfayan, Laurent Neuville, Bruno Gutzeit	3:20.02
5. SWE	Per Johansson, Tommy Werner, Joakim Holmquist, Göran Titus, [Richard Milton]	3:21.07
6. GER	Michael Gross, Thomas Fahrner, Björn Zikarsky, Peter Sitt, [Torsten Wiegel]	3:21.65
7. GBR	Michael Fibbens, Mark Foster, Roland Lee, Andrew Jameson	3:21.71
8. ITA	Roberto Gleria, Giorgio Lamberti, Fabrizio Rampazzo, Andrea Ceccarini	3:22.93

As usual, the US won this event with a world record. This time the USSR, by placing their fastest swimmers first, managed to keep pace with the Americans for 300 meters. But as soon as anchor Matt Biondi hit the water the race ceased to be close. Biondi, already credited with the seven fastest relay splits in history, swam a 47.81 to earn the third of his five gold medals.

1992 Barcelona T: 18, N: 18, D: 7.29. WR: 3:16.53 (USA—Jacobs, Dalbey, Jager, Biondi)

1. USA	Joseph Hudepohl, Matthew Biondi, Thomas Jager, Jon Olsen, [Shaun Jordan, Joel Thomas]	3:16.74
2. SOV	Pavlo Khnykin, Gennady Prigoda, Yuri Bashkatov, Aleksandr Popov, [Vladimir Pyshnenko, Veniamin Tayanovich]	3:17.56
3. GER	Christian-Alexander Tröger, Dirk Richter, Steffen Zesner, Mark Pinger, [Andreas Szigat, Bengt Zikarsky]	3:17.90
4. FRA	Christophe Kalfayan, Franck Schott, Frédéric Lefèvre, Stéphan Caron, [Ludovic Dépickère, Bruno Gutzeit]	3:19.16
5. SWE	Tommy Werner, Håkan Karlsson, Fredrik Letzler, Anders Holmertz, [Göran Titus]	3:20.10
6. BRA	José Souza-Junior, Gustavo Borges, Emmanuel Fortes Nascimento, Cristiano Michelena	3:20.99
7. GBR	Roland Lee, Mark Foster, Michael Fibbens, Paul Howe	3:21.75
8. AUS	Christopher Fydler, Andrew Baildon, Thomas Stachewicz, Darren Lange	3:22.04

The United States continued its streak of winning this event every time it has been held, but for the first time the Americans failed to break the world record. Matt Biondi moved the United States from fourth place to first on the second leg. Tom Jager held the lead, and then Jon Olsen fended off Aleksandr Popov's 47.83 final leg.

1996 Atlanta T: 19, N: 19, D: 7.23. WR: 3:15.11 (USA—Fox, Hudepohl, Olsen, Hall Jr.)

1. USA	Jon Olsen, Josh Davis, Bradley Schumacher, Gary Hall, Jr., [David Fox, Scott Tucker]	3:15.41 OR
2. RUS	Roman Yegorov, Aleksandr Popov, Vladimir Predkin, Vladimi Pyshnenko, [Denis Pimankov, Konstantin Ushkov]	3:17.06
3. GER	Christian Tröger, Bengt Zikarsky, Björn Zikarsky, Mark Pinger, [Alexander Lüderitz]	3:17.20
4. BRA	Fernando Scherer, Alexandre Massura, André Cordeiro, Gustavo Borges	3:18.30
5. HOL	Mark Hermanus Veens, Pie Geelen, Martin van der Spoel, Pieter van den Hoogenband	3:19.02
6. AUS	Michael Klim, Matthew Dunn, Scott Logan, Chris Fydler, [Ian Vander Wal, Scott Logan]	3:20.13
7. SWE	Lars Frölander, Fredrik Letsler, Anders Holmertz, Christer Wallin, [Johan Wallberg]	3:20.16
8. GBR	Nicholas Shackell, Alan Rapley, Mark Stevens, Michael Fibbens	3:21.52

After the first leg, the United States was in fourth place behind Brazil, Germany and Australia and only one hundredth of a second ahead of Russia. Aleksandr Popov, swimming second, moved the Russian team from fifth to first, with Germany second after 200 meters and the US third. They remained in that order after 300 meters, but the closeness of the race was deceptive: Russia and Germany had already used their fastest swimmers while the US had saved their best for last. Gary Hall's 47.45 anchor was the fastest relay leg in history and the US kept alive its 4 × 100-meter freestyle relay streak.

2000 Sydney T: 23, N: 23, D: 9.16. WR: 3:15.11 (USA—Fox, Hudepohl, Olsen, Hall Jr.)

1. AUS	Michael Klim, Christopher Fydler, Ashley Callus, Ian Thorpe, [Todd Pearson, Adam Pine]	3:13.67 WR
2. USA	Anthony Ervin, Neil Walker, Jason Lezak, Gary Hall, Jr., [Scott Tucker, Joshua Davis]	3:13.86
3. BRA	Fernando Scherer, Gustavo Borges, Carlos Jayme, Edvaldo Silva Filho	3:17.40
4. GER	Torsten Spanneberg, Christian-Alexander Tröger, Stephan Kunzelmann, Stefan Herbst, [Lars Conrad]	3:17.77
5. ITA	Lorenzo Vismara, Klaus Lanzarini, Massimiliano Rosolino, Simone Cercato, [Mauro Gallo]	3:17.85
6. SWE	Stefan Nystrand, Lars Frölander, Mattias Ohlin, Johan Nyström	3:19.60
7. FRA	Frédérick Bousquet, Romain Barnier, Hugo Viart, Nicolas Kintz	3:21.00
8. RUS	Andrei Kapralov, Denis Pimankov, Aleksandr Popov, Dmitri Chernyshev, [Leonid Khokhlov]	DQ

The United States had won this event each of the seven times it had been included in the Olympic program. The Australians were determined to break that streak, particularly as the race was held on the first night of competition. Michael Klim got the home team off to a perfect start by setting a world record of 48.18. The second American, Neil Walker caught Chris Fydler two thirds of the way through the second leg, but Fydler regained the lead just before he touched the wall. During the third leg, Jason Lezak grabbed the lead in the first lap, but Ashley Callus fought back and put Australia back in the lead. The anchor swimmers were Gary Hall for the United States and Ian Thorpe for Australia. Less than an hour earlier, Thorpe had won the final of the 400-meter freestyle. He barely had time to change into his warmup uniform for the medal ceremony and then back into a bodysuit, a process that ended up requiring four helpers and ten minutes. Hall passed Thorpe in the first lap and turned six tenths of a second ahead of the Australian. But the 17-year-old Thorpe poured it on and, with the arena reverberating with the screaming of Australian supporters, he caught Hall less then 20 meters from the finish and with each of his last six strokes he edged ahead to give Australia the victory by less than half a meter.

2004 Athens T: 16, N: 16, D: 8.15. WR: 3 :13.67 (AUS—Klim, Fydler, Callus, Thorpe)

1. SAF	Roland Schoeman, Lyndon Ferns, Darian Townsend, Ryk Neethling	3:13.17 WR
2. HOL	Johan Kenkhuis, Mitja Zastrow, Klaas-Erik Zwering, Pieter Van Den Hoogenband [Mark Veens]	3:14.36
3. USA	Ian Crocker, Michael Phelps, Neil Walker, Jason Lezak, Gabriel Woodward, Nathaniel Dusing, Gary Hall, Jr.]	3:14.62

4. RUS	Andrei Kapralov, Yevgeny Lagunov, Denis Pimankov, Aleksandr Popov, [Ivan Usov]	3:15.75
5. ITA	Lorenzo Vismara, Filippo Magnini, Michele Scarica, Christian Galenda, [Alessandro Calvi]	3:15.75
6. AUS	Michael Klim, Todd Pearson, Eamon Sullivan, Ian Thorpe, [Ashley Callus, Jonathan Van Hazel]	3:15.77
7. FRA	Romain Barnier, Julien Sicot, Fabien Gilot, Frédérick Bousquet, [Amaury Leveaux]	3:16.23
8. GER	Jens Schreiber, Lars Conrad, Torsten Spanneberg, Stefan Herbst [Stephan Kunzelmann, Christian Keller]	3:17.18

Unheralded South Africa, which had placed eighth at the 2003 world championships, recorded the fastest time in the qualifying round, 3:13.84, to finish nearly two seconds ahead of the United States. In the final, South Africa's Roland Schoeman opened up a full body length lead with a 48.17 opening leg. By the end of the second leg, a 48.13 by Lyndon Ferns, South Africa was .36 seconds under world record pace. Darian Townsend recorded a 48.96 penultimate leg before Ryk Neethling recorded the fastest split for the team, 47.91 seconds, to break the world record by a half second. It was South Africa's first-ever gold medal in men's swimming.

2008 Beijing T: 16, N: 16, D: 8.11. WR: 3:12.46 (USA—Phelps, Walker, Jones, Lezak)

1. USA	Michael Phelps, Garrett Weber-Gale, Cullen Jones, Jason Lezak, [Nathan Adrian, Benjamin Wildman-Tobriner, Matt Grevers]	3:08.24 WR
2. FRA	Amaury Leveaux, Fabien Gilot, Frédéric Bousquet, Alain Bernard [Grégory Mallet, Boris Steimetz]	3:08.32
3. AUS	Eamon Sullivan, Andrew Lauterstein, Ashley Callus, Matt Targett, [Leith Brodie, Patrick Murphy]	3:09.91
4. ITA	Alessandro Calvi, Christian Galenda, Marco Belotti, Filippo Magnini, [Michele Santucci]	3:11.48
5. SWE	Petter Stymne, Lars Frölander, Stefan Nystrand, Jonas Persson	3:11.92
6. CAN	Brent Hayden, Joel Greenshields, Colin Russell, Rick Say	3:12.26
7. SAF	Lyndon Ferns, Darian Townsend, Roland Schoeman, Ryk Neethling	3:12.66
8. GBR	Simon Burnett, Adam Brown, Benjamin Hockin, Ross Davenport	3:12.87

The US squad had won the past two world championships and had held the relay world record since 2006. Their biggest challenge was expected to come from France, whose anchor, Alain Bernard, had set a 100-meter freestyle world record to win the 2008 European championship.

The US quartet of Nathan Adrian, Cullen Jones, Ben Wildman-Tobriner and Matt Grevers lowered the world record to 3:12.23 in the qualifying round. Only Jones also swam in the final.

Australia's Eamon Sullivan lowered Bernard's world record in the final, swimming a 47.24 in the lead-off leg, followed by Michael Phelps in 47.51, a personal best and an American record. Garrett Weber-Gale put the US in front in the second leg, but France's Fréd Bousquet took the lead in the third leg, giving Bernard a half-second advantage going into the final 100 meters. Still trailing Bernard at the final turn, 32-year-old US anchor Jason Lezak relentlessly narrowed the gap, pulling even with 10 meters to go and edging ahead by eight-hundredths of a second to give the US the win, as the top five teams all swam under the world record time.

Lezak's anchor leg, 46.06, was the fastest relay split in the event's history, and helped the US break the world record by 4.22 seconds. The victory also kept alive Phelps' goal of winning eight gold medals at a single Olympics.

4 × 200-METER FREESTYLE RELAY

1896–1904 not held

1906 Athens T: 6, N: 6, D: 4.28.
(4 × 250 Meters)

1. HUN	József Ónody, Henrik Hajós (Guttmann), Géza Kiss, I. Zoltán Halmay	16:52.4
2. GER	Ernst Bahnmeyer, Oscar Schiele, Emil Rausch, Max Pape	17:16.2
3. GBR	William Henry, John Henry Derbyshire, Henry Taylor, John Arthur Jarvis	—
4. USA	Frank Bornamann, Joseph Spencer, Maquard Schwartz, Charles Daniels	—
5. SWE	Harald Julin, Gustaf Wretman, Charles Norelius, Nils Regnell	—

DNF: AUT—Edmund Bernhardt, Leopold Mayer, Simon Orlik, Otto Scheff

At 46 years 302 days, William Henry of the British team is the oldest person ever to have won a swimming medal.

1908 London T: 6, N: 6, D: 7.24.

1. GBR	John Henry Derbyshire, Paul Radmilovic, William Foster, Henry Taylor	10:55.6 WR
2. HUN	József Munk, Imre Zachár, Béla Las-Torres, I. Zoltán Halmay	10:59.0
3. USA	Harry Hebner, Leo "Budd" Goodwin, Charles Daniels, Leslie Rich	11:02.8
4. AUS& NZL	Francis Beaurepaire, Fred Springfield, Reginald "Snowy" Baker, Theodore Tartakover	—

The Hungarians seemed to have the race well in hand, when Halmaj suddenly began to lose consciousness during the last 50 meters. He struggled to the finish line, but had to be hauled from the pool before he drowned. William Foster, at age 18 years 2 weeks, remains Great Britain's youngest gold medalist in any sport.

1912 Stockholm T: 5, N: 5, D: 7.15. WR: 10:55.6 (GBR—Derbyshire, Radmilovic, Foster, Taylor)

1. AUS& NZL	Cecil Healy, Malcolm Champion, Leslie Boardman, Harold Hardwick	10:11.2 WR
2. USA	Kenneth Huszagh, Perry McGillivray, Harry Hebner, Duke Paoa Kahanamoku	10:20.2
3. GBR	William Foster, T. Sydney Battersby, John Hatfield, Henry Taylor	10:28.6
4. GER	Oskar Schiele, Georg Kunisch, Kurt Bretting, Max Ritter	10:37.0

1920 Antwerp T: 7, N: 7, D: 8.29. WR: 10:11.2 (AUS&NZL—Healy, Champion, Boardman, Hardwick)

1. USA	Perry McGillivray, Pua Kela Kealoha, Norman Ross, Duke Paoa Kahanamoku	10:04.4 WR
2. AUS	Henry Hay, William Herald, Ivan Stedman, Francis Beaurepaire, [Keith Kirkland]	10:25.4
3. GBR	Leslie Savage, Edward Percival Peter, Henry Taylor, Harold Annison	10:37.2
4. SWE	Robert Andersson, Frans Möller, Orvar Trolle, Arne Borg	10:50.2
5. ITA	Mario Massa, Agostino Frassinetti, Antonio Quarantotto, Gilio Bisagno	—

1924 Paris T: 13, N: 13, D: 7.20. WR: 10:04.4 (USA—McGillivray, Kealoha, Ross, Kahanamoku)

1. USA	J. Wallace O'Connor, Harrison Glancy, Ralph Breyer, P. John Weissmuller, [Richard Howell]	9:53.4 WR
2. AUS	Maurice "Moss" Christie, Ernest Henry, Francis Beaurepaire, Andrew "Boy" Charlton, [Ivan Stedman]	10:02.2
3. SWE	Georg Werner, Orvar Trolle, Åke Borg, Arne Borg, [Thor Henning, Gösta Persson]	10:06.8
4. JPN	Torahiko Miyahata, Katsuo Takaishi, Kazuo Noda, Kazuo Onoda	10:15.2
5. GBR	John Thomson, Albert Dicken, Harold Annison, Edward Percival Peter, [Leslie Savage]	10:29.4
6. FRA	Guy Middleton, Henri Padou, Edouard Vanzeveren, Emile Zeibig	

1928 Amsterdam T: 13, N: 13, D: 8.11. WR: 9:53.4 (USA—O'Connor, Glancy, Breyer, Weissmuller)

1. USA	Austin Clapp, Walter Laufer, George Kojac, P. John Weissmuller, [Paul Samson, David Young]	9:36.2 WR
2. JPN	Hiroshi Yoneyama, Nobuo Arai, Tokuhei Sada, Katsuo Takaishi	9.41.4
3. CAN	F. Munroe Bourne, James Thompson, Garnet Ault, Walter Spence	9:47.8
4. HUN	András Wanie, Rezső Wanie, Géza Szigritz-Tarródy, István Bárány	9:57.0
5. SWE	Aulo Gustafsson, Sven Pettersson, Eskil Lundahl, Arne Borg	10:01.8
6. GBR	Reginald Sutton, Joseph Whiteside, Edward Percival Peter, Albert Dicken	10:15.8
7. SPA	José González Esplugas, Estanislao Artal Garriga, Ramón Artigas Rigal, Francisco Segala Torres	—

Johnny Weissmuller completed his Olympic career by winning his fifth gold medal.

1932 Los Angeles T: 7, N: 7, D: 8.9. WR: 9:36.2 (USA—Clapp, Laufer, Kojac, Weissmuller)

1. JPN	Yasuji Miyazaki, Masonori Yusa, Takashi Yokoyama, Hisakichi Toyoda	8:58.4 WR
2. USA	Frank Booth, George Fissler, Maiola Kalili, Manuella Kalili	9:10.5
3. HUN	András Wanie, László Szabados, András Székely, István Bárány	9:31.4
4. CAN	George Larson, George Burrows, Walter Spence, F. Munro Bourne	9:36.3
5. GBR	Joseph Whiteside, Robert Leivers, Martyn ffrench-Williams, Reginald Sutton	9:45.8
6. ARG	Carlos Kennedy, Leopoldo Tahier, Roberto Peper, Alfredo Rocca	10:13.1
7. BRA	Manoel Lourenço Silva, Isaac Dos Santos Moraes, Manoel Rocha Villar, Benevenuto Martins Nunes	10:36.5

1936 Berlin T: 18, N: 18, D: 8.11. WR: 8:52.2 (JPN—Yusa, Makino, Isharada, Negami)

1. JPN	Masanori Yusa, Shigeo Sugiura, Masaharu Taguchi, Shigeo Arai	8:51.5 WR
2. USA	Ralph Flanagan, John Macionis, Paul Wolf, Jack Medica, [Ralph Gilman, Charles Hutter]	9:03.0
3. HUN	Árpád Lengyel, Oszkár Abay-Nemes, Ödön Gróf, Ferenc Csík	9:12.3
4. FRA	Alfred Nakache, Christian Talli, René Cavalero, Jean Taris	9:18.2
5. GER	Werner Plath, Wolfgang Heimlich, Hermann Heibel, Helmut Fischer	9:19.0
6. GBR	Martyn ffrench-Williams, Romund Gabrielsen, Robert Leivers, Norman Wainwright	9:21.5
7. CAN	F. Munroe Bourne, Robert Hamerton, Robert Hooper, Robert Pirie	9:27.5
8. SWE	Björn Borg, Sten Olov Bolldén, Sven Petterson, Gunnar Werner	9:37.5

1948 London T: 14, N: 14, D: 8.3. WR: 8:51.5 (JPN—Yusa, Sugiura, Taguchi, Arai)

1. USA	Walter Ris, James McLane, Wallace Wolf, William Smith, [Robert Gibe, William Dudley, Edwin Gilbert, Eugene Rogers]	8:46.0 WR
2. HUN	Elemér Szathmáry, György Mitró, Imre Nyéki, Géza Kádas	8:48.4
3. FRA	Joseph Bernardo, Henri Padou, René Cornu, Alexandre Jany	9:08.0
4. SWE	Martin Lundén, Per-Olof Östrand, Olle Johansson, Per-Olof Olsson	9:09.1
5. YUG	Ivan Illič, Čiril Pelhan, Ivan "Janko" Puhar, Branko Vidović	9:14.0
6. ARG	Horacio White, José Durañona, Juan Garay, Alfredo Yantorno, [Augusto Cantón]	9:19.2
7. MEX	Ramón Bravo Prieto, Angel Maldonado Campos, Apolonio Diaz Castillo, Alberto Isaac Ahumada	9:20.2
8. BRA	Sergio Alencar Rodrigues, Willy Jordan, Rof Kestener Egon, Aram Boghossian	9:31.0

1952 Helsinki T: 17, N: 17, D: 7.29, WR: 8:29.4 (USA, Yale University—Moore, McLane, Sheff, Thoman)

1. USA	Wayne Moore, William Woolsey, Ford Konno, James McLane, [Wallace Wolf, Donald Sheff, Frank Dooley, Burwell Jones]	8:31.1 OR
2. JPN	Hiroshi Suzuki, Yoshihiro Hamaguchi, Toru Goto, Teijiro Tanikawa	8:33.5

3. FRA	Joseph Bernardo, Aldo Eminente, Alexandre Jany, Jean Boiteux	8:45.9
4. SWE	Lars Svanteson, Göran Larsson, Per-Olof Östrand, Olle Johansson, [Rolf Olander]	8:46.8
5. HUN	László Gyöngyösi, György Csordás, Géza Kádas, Imre Nyéki, [Gusztáv Kettesi]	8:52.6
6. GBR	Frank Botham, Ronald Burns, Thomas Welsh, John Wardrop	8:52.9
7. SAF	Graham Johnston, Dennis Ford, John Durr, Peter Duncan	8:55.1
8. ARG	Federico Zwanck, Marcelo Trabucco, Pedro Galvão, Alfredo Yantorno	8:56.9

Knowing that they would lose under normal circumstances, the Japanese reversed the usual order of their swimmers, putting the fastest man first and the slowest last. They did build up a big lead, but Ford Konno closed the gap and Jimmy McLane pulled away in the final 100 meters.

1956 Melbourne T: 11, N: 11, D: 12.3. WR: 8:24.5 (SOV—Nikitin, Strushanov, Nikolayev, Sorokin)

1. AUS	Kevin O'Halloran, John Devitt, I. Murray Rose, John Henricks, [Gary Chapman, Graham Hamilton, Murray Garretty]	8:23.6 WR
2. USA	Richard Hanley, George Breen, Willam Woolsey, Ford Konno, [Perry Jecku, Richard Tanabe], Tim Jecko	8:31.5
3. SOV	Vitaly Sorokin, Vladimir Strushanov, Gennady Nikolayev, Boris Nikitin	8:34.7
4. JPN	Manabu Koga, Atsushi Tani, Koji Nonoshita, Tsuyoshi Yamanaka	8:36.6
5. GER& GDR	Hans Köhler, Hans-Joachim Reich, Hans Zierold, Horst Bleeker	8:43.4
6. GBR	Kenneth Williams, Ronald Roberts, Neil McKechnie, John Wardrop	8:45.2
7. ITA	Federico Dennerlein, Paolo Galletti, Guido Elmi, Anthony Romani	8:46.2
8. SAF	William Steuart, Anthony Briscoe, Dennis Ford, Peter Duncan	8:49.5

1960 Rome T: 15, N: 15, D: 9.1. WR (880 yards): 8:16.6 (AUS—Henricks, Dickson, Konrads, Rose)

1. USA	George Harrison, Richard Blick, Michael Troy, F. Jeffrey Farrell, [William Darnton, Thomas Winters, Stephen Clark]	8:10.2 WR
2. JPN	Makoto Fukui, Hiroshi Ishii, Tsuyoshi Yamanaka, Tatsuo Fujimoto	8:13.2
3. AUS	David Dickson, John Devitt, I. Murray Rose, John Konrads, [John RIgby, Allan Wood]	8:13.8
4. GBR	Hamilton Milton, John Martin-Dye, Richard Campion, Ian Black	8:28.1
5. FIN	Ilkka Suvanto, Karl Haavisto, Stig-Olof Grenner, Harri Käyhko	8:29.7
6. SWE	Sven-Göran Johansson, Lars-Erik Bengtsson, Bengt Nordvall, Per-Ola Lindberg, [Bengt-Olov Almsted]	8:31.0
7. GER& GDR	Frank Wiegand, Gerhard Hetz, Hans Zierold, Hans Klein	8:31.8
8. SOV	Igor Lushkovski, Gennady Nikolayev, Vitaly Sorokin, Boris Nikitin, [Sergei Tovstoplet]	8:32.2

1964 Tokyo T: 15, N: 15, D: 10.18. WR: 8:01.8 (USA—Mettler, Wall, Lyons, Schollander)

1. USA	Stephen Clark, Roy Saari, Gary Ilman, Donald Schollander, [William Mettler, David Lyons, Michael Wall, R. Edward Townsend]	7:52.1 WR
2. GDR& GER	Horst-Günter Gregor, Gerhard Hetz, Frank Wiegand, Hans-Joachim Klein	7:59.3
3. JPN	Makoto Fukui, Kunihiro Iwasaki, Toshio Shoji, Yukiaki Okabe	8:03.8
4. AUS	David Dickson, Allan Wood, Peter Doak, Robert Windle, [John Konrads, John Ryan]	8:05.5
5. SWE	Mats Svensson, E. Lester Eriksson, Hans Rosendahl, Jan Lundin	8:08.0
6. FRA	Jean-Pascal Curtillet, Pierre Canavese, Francis Luyce, Alain Gottvallès	8:08.7
7. SOV/ RUS	Semyon Belits-Geiman, Vladimir Berezin, Aleksandr Paramonov, Yevgeny Novikov	8:15.1
8. ITA	Sergio De Gregorio, Bruno Bianchi, Giovanni Orlando, Pietro Bascaini	8:18.1

Don Schollander, 1964

In Tokyo, Schollander became the first swimmer to earn four golds at one Olympics.

With this race Steve Clark earned his third gold medal, and Don Schollander became the first swimmer in Olympic history to win four gold medals in one Olympics.

1968 Mexico City T: 16, N: 16, D: 10.21 WR: 7:52.1 (USA—Clark, Saari, Ilman, Schollander; USA, Santa Clara Swim Club—Ilman, Spitz, Wall, Schollander)

1. USA	John Nelson, Stephen Rerych, Mark Spitz, Donald Schollander, [William Johnson, David Johnson, Andrew Strenk, Michael Wall]	7:52.33
2. AUS	Gregory Rogers, Graham White, Robert Windle, Michael Wenden	7:53.77
3. SOV	Vladimir Bure, Semyon Belits-Geiman, Georgi Kulikov, Leonid Ilyichev	8:01.66
4. CAN	George Smith, Ronald Jacks, John Gilchrist, Ralph Hutton	8:03.22
5. FRA	Michel Rousseau, Gérard Letast, Francis Luyce, Alain Mosconi	8:03.77
6. GER	Hans Fassnacht, Olaf von Schilling, Volkert Meeuw, Wolfgang Kremer	8:04.33
7. GDR	Frank Weigand, Horst-Günter Gregor, Alfred Müller, Jochen Herbst	8:06.00
8. SWE	Hans Ljungberg, Karl Larson, Sven Ferm, Erik Eriksson	8:12.11

1972 Munich T: 14, N: 14, D: 8.31. WR: 7:43.3 (USA—Spitz, Heidenreich, Tyler, McBreen)

1. USA	John Kinsella, Frederick Tyler, Steven Genter, Mark Spitz, [Gary Conelly, Thomas McBreen, Michael Burton]	7:35.78 WR
2. GER	Klaus Steinbach, Werner Lampe, Hans-Günter Vosseler, Hans-Joachim Fassnacht, [Gerhard Schiller, Folkert Meeuw]	7:41.69
3. SOV	Igor Grivennikov, Viktor Mazanov, Georgi Kulikov, Vladimir Bure, [Viktor Aboimov, Aleksandr Samsonov]	7:45.76
4. SWE	Bengt Gingsjö, Hans Ljungberg, Anders Bellbring, Gunnar Larsson	7:47.37
5. AUS	Michael Wenden, Graham Windeatt, Robert Nay, Bradford Cooper, [Robert Featherstone, Graham White]	7:48.66
6. GDR	Wilfried Hartung, Peter Bruch, Udo Poser, Lutz Unger, [Roger Pyttel]	7:49.11
7. CAN	Bruce Robertson, Brian Phillips, Ian MacKenzie, Ralph Hutton, [Dean Buckboro]	7:53.61
8. GBR	Brian Brinkley, John Mills, Michael Bailey, Colin Cunningham	7:55.59

One hour after winning the 100-meter butterfly, Mark Spitz was back in the water to swim the anchor leg for the 4 × 200-meter freestyle relay team. Steve Genter's third leg of 1:52.72 gave the US a big lead. Spitz took over from there to gain his fifth gold medal and fifth world record in four days.

1976 Montreal T: 18, N: 18, D: 7.21. WR: 7:30.54 (USA, Long Beach Swim Club—Favero, Shaw, S. Furniss, B. Furniss)

1. USA	Michael Bruner, Bruce Furniss, John Naber, James Montgomery, [Douglas Northway, Timothy Shaw]	7:23.22 WR
2. SOV	Volodymyr Raskatov, Andrei Bogdanov, Sergei Kopliakov, Andrei Krylov, [Andrei Smirnov, Vladimir Mikheyev]	7:27.97
3. GBR	Alan McClatchey, David Dunne, Gordon Downie, Brian Brinkley	7:32.11
4. GER	Klaus Steinbach, Peter Nocke, Werner Lampe, Hans-Joachim Geisler [Andreas Schmidt]	7:32.27
5. GDR	Roger Pyttel, Wilfried Hartung, Rainer Strohbach, Frank Pfütze	7:38.92
6. HOL	Abdul Ressand, René van der Kuil, André in het Veld, Henk Elzerman	7:42.56
7. SWE	Pär Arvidsson, Peter Petterson, Anders Bellbring, Bengt Gingsjö	7:42.84
8. ITA	Marcello Guarducci, Roberto Pangaro, Paolo Barelli, Paolo Revelli	7:43.39

The US team of Doug Northway, Tim Shaw, Mike Bruner, and Bruce Furniss set a world record of 7:30.33 in the qualifying round. That night, Northway and Shaw were replaced by John Naber and Jim Montgomery, and another world record was set.

1980 Moscow T: 13, N: 13, D: 7.23. WR: 7:20.82 (USA—B. Furniss, Forrester, Hackett, Gaines)

1. SOV	Sergei Kopliakov, Vladimir Salnikov, Ivar Stukolkin, Andrei Krylov, [Sergei Rusin, Sergei Krasyuk, Yuri Presekin]	7:23.50
2. GDR	Frank Pfütze, Jörg Woithe, Detlev Grabs, Rainer Strohbach	7:28.60
3. BRA	Jorge Lutz Fernandes, Marcus Laborne Mattioli, Cyro Marques, Djan Madruga Garrido	7:29.30
4. SWE	Michael Söderlund, Pelle Wikström, Per-Alvar Magnusson, Thomas Lejdström, [Anders Rutkvist, Per-Ola Quist]	7:30.10
5. ITA	Paolo Revelli, Raffaele Franceschi, Andrea Ceccarini, Fabrizio Rampazzo, [Federic Silvestri]	7:30.37
6. GBR	Douglas Campbell, Philip Hubble, T. Martin Smith, Andrew Astbury, [Mark Taylor, Kevin Lee]	7:30.81
7. AUS	Graeme Brewer, Mark Tonelli, Mark Kerry, Ronald McKeon, [Max Metzker]	7:30.82
8. FRA	Fabien Noel, Mark Lazzaro, Dominique Petit, Paskal Laget	7:36.08

1984 Los Angeles T: 14, N: 14, D: 7.30. WR: 7:20.40 (GER—Fahrner, Schmidt, Schowtka, Gross)

1. USA	Michael Heath, David Larson, Jeffrey Float, L. Bruce Hayes, [Geoffrey Gamberino, Richard Saeger]	7:15.69 WR
2. GER	Thomas Fahrner, Dirk Korthals, Alexander Schowtka, Michael Gross, [Rainer Henkel]	7:15.73
3. GBR	Neil Cochran, Paul Easter, Paul Howe, Andrew Astbury	7:24.78
4. AUS	Peter Dale, Justin Lemberg, Ronald McKeon Graeme Brewer, [Thomas Stachewicz]	7:25.63
5. CAN	Donald "Sandy" Goss, Wayne Kelly, Peter Szmidt, Alex Baumann, [Benoit Clément]	7:26.51
6. SWE	Michael Söderlund, Tommy Werner, Anders Holmertz, Thomas Lejdström, [Mikael Orn]	7:26.53
7. HOL	Hans Kroes, Peter Drost, Edsard Schlingemann, Frank Drost	7:26.72
8. FRA	Stephan Caron, Dominique Bataille, Michel Pou, Pierre Andraca	7:30.16

The 1984 gold medal for prescience went to sportswriter Craig Neff of *Sports Illustrated* who predicted in the magazine's souvenir program: "In what should be a heartstopping 4 × 200 free relay, the West Germans will likely lose their world record and the gold medal to the U.S—but just barely."

The world record went quickly in the qualifying round when the US "B" team of Geoffrey Gamberino, David Larson, Bruce Hayes and Richard Saeger swam a 7:18.87. In the final, Gamberino and Saeger were replaced by Mike Heath and Jeff Float. Normally the US coaches would have had Heath swim the anchor leg, since he was the fastest man on the team. But the presence of Michael Gross as the West German anchor called for a change of strategy. It was decided to swim Heath first and build up as big a lead as possible before Gross hit the water. The unenviable task of fighting off the brilliant German swimmer was given to 21-year-old Bruce Hayes, an experienced anchor man. This was the only event for which Hayes had qualified, so much of his training concentrated on practicing his finishing touch.

Swimming the third leg for the US was Jeff Float, who had lost 80% of his hearing in his right ear and 60% in his left ear when he contracted viral meningitis at the age of 13 months. So great was the roar of the crowd during the final as Float lengthened the US lead against Alexander Schowtka that, for the first time in his life, he heard the crowd cheering him on. When Float touched the wall at the end of his leg, he handed over to Hayes a three-yard lead. But Gross went out so powerfully that he caught Hayes after only 50 meters, and passed him after 100. Hayes was shocked that Gross had appeared by his side so quickly, but he didn't panic. Instead he kept the pressure on. Gross came out of the final turn with a two-foot lead, but then Hayes began gaining on the world record holder. As they reached for the wall it was impossible to tell who had won. All eyes turned to the scoreboard. Almost immediately, the number "1" appeared next to "USA," setting off a wildly emotional celebration.

Michael Gross, whose 1:46.89 split was the fastest ever recorded, was, as always, as gracious in defeat as in victory. "I just ran out of gas," he said. "That was a really hot race. It was an honorable defeat."

1988 Seoul T: 16, N: 16, D: 9.21. WR: 7:13.10 (GER—Sitt, Henkel, Fahrner, Gross)

1. USA	Troy Dalbey, Matthew Cetlinski, Douglas Gjertsen, Matthew Biondi, [Craig Oppel, Daniel Jorgensen]	7:12.51 WR
2. GDR	Uwe Dassler, Sven Lodziewski, Thomas Flemming, Steffen Zesner, [Lars Hinneburg]	7:13.68
3. GER	Erik Hochstein, Thomas Fahrner, Rainer Henkel, Michael Gross, [Peter Sitt, Stefan Pfeiffer]	7:14.35
4. AUS	Thomas Stachewicz, Ian Brown, Jason Plummer, Duncan Armstrong, [Martin Roberts]	7:15.23
5. ITA	Roberto Gleria, Giorgio Lamberti, Massimo Trevisan, Valerio Giambalvo, [Fabrizio Rampazzo]	7:16.00
6. SWE	Anders Holmertz, Tommy Werner, Michael Söderlund, Christer Wallin, [Henrik Jangvall]	7:19.10
7. FRA	Michel Pou, Franck Iacono, Olivier Fougeroud, Ludovic Dépickère, [Stéphan Caron, Laurent Neuville]	7:24.69
8. CAN	Turlough O'Hare, Donald "Sandy" Goss, Donald Haddow, Gary Vandermeulen, [Darren Ward]	7:24.91

The United States entered this race in the unaccustomed role of underdog to the world record-holding West Germans and the world champion East Germans. Anders Holmertz put Sweden in the lead after the first leg. At the halfway mark, Italy was in front, thanks to a powerful swim by Giorgio Lamberti. At that point East Germany was in second place, West Germany in fourth, and the US in fifth. Thomas Hemming gave the GDR a bodylength lead over the US with one lap to go. Then Matt Biondi took over. Two hours earlier he had missed a gold medal in the 100-meter butterfly by one one-hundredth of a second and now he was tired of losing. He passed Steffen Zesner after 75 meters, recorded the fastest relay split in history (1:46.44), and won by a bodylength.

The following night, US team member Troy Dalbey caused a scandal when he stole a 65-pound decorative lion's mask from a hotel bar. He was arrested along with teammate Doug Gjertsen, but both swimmers were subsequently released after they apologized to the Korean people.

1992 Barcelona T: 18, N: 18, D: 7.27. WR: 7:12.51 (USA—Dalbey, Cetlinski, Gjertsen, Biondi)

1. RUS	Dmitri Lepikov, Vladimir Pyshnenko, Veniamin Tayanovich, Yevgeny Sadovyi, [Aleksei Kudryavtsev, Yuri Mukhin]	7:11.95 WR
2. SWE	Christer Wallin, Anders Holmertz, Tommy Werner, Lars Frölander	7:15.51
3. USA	Joseph Hudepohl, Melvin Stewart, Jon Olsen, Douglas Gjertsen, [Scott Jaffe, Daniel Jorgenson]	7:16.23
4. GER	Peter Sitt, Steffen Zesner, Andreas Szigat, Stefan Pfeiffer, [Christian Tröger]	7:16.58
5. ITA	Roberto Gleria, Giorgio Lamberti, Massimo Trevisan, Stefano Battistelli, [Emanuele Idini, Piermaria Siciliano]	7:18.10
6. GBR	Paul Palmer, Steven Mellor, Stephen Akers, Paul Howe	7:22.57
7. BRA	Gustavo Borges, Emmanuel Fortes Nascimento, Teofilo Laborne Ferreira, Cristiano Michelena	7:24.03

DISQ: AUS—Ian Brown, Deane Pieters, Kieren Perkins, Duncan Armstrong, [Martin Roberts]

The United States' winning streak in the 4 × 200 was finally stopped at seven. The well-prepared Russian team passed the Swedes during the third leg, allowing Yevgeny Sadovyi an easy race to the finish to pick up the second of his three gold medals.

1996 Atlanta T: 17, N: 17, D: 7.21. WR: 7:11.95 (SOV—Lepikov, Pyshnenko, Tayanovich, Sadovyi)

1. USA	Joshua Davis, Joe Hudepohl, Bradley Schumacher, Ryan Berube, [Jon Olsen]	7:14.84
2. SWE	Christer Wallin, Anders Holmertz, Lars Frölander, Anders Lyrbring	7:17.56
3. GER	Almo Heilmann, Christian Keller, Christian Tröger, Steffen Zesner, [Konstantin Dubrovin, Oliver Lampe]	7:17.71
4. AUS	Daniel Kowalski, Michael Klim, Malcolm Allen, Matthew Dunn, [Kieren Perkins, Glen Housman, Ian Vander Wal]	7:18.47
5. GBR	Paul Palmer, Andrew Clayton, Mark Stevens, James Salter	7:18.74
6. ITA	Massimiliano Rosolino, Emanuele Idini, Emanuele Merisi, Piermaria Siciliano, [Emiliano Brembilla]	7:19.92
7. HOL	Marcel Wouda, Mark van der Zijden, Martin van der Spoel, Pieter van den Hoogenband, [Tim Hoeijmans]	7:21.96
8. FRA	Yann de Fabrique, Lionel Poirot, Bruno Orsoni, Christophe Bordeau	7:24.85

US dominance in the 4 × 200 appeared to be a thing of the past when American teams finished third at the 1992 Olympics and fourth at the 1994 world championships. Not so. Lead-off Josh Davis gave the US a one-second lead, but Michael Klim (1:48.04) and Anders Holmertz (1:47.03) brought Australia and Sweden back into the hunt at the halfway mark. Bradley Schumacher handed over a lead of eleven hundredths of a second over Sweden to Ryan Berube, who pulled away to an easy victory.

2000 Sydney T: 16, N: 16, D: 9.19. WR: 7:08.79 (AUS—Thorpe, Kirby, Hackett, Klim)

1. AUS	Ian Thorpe, Michael Klim, Todd Pearson, William Kirby, [Grant Hackett, Daniel Kowalski]	7:07.05 WR
2. USA	Scott Goldblatt, Joshua Davis, James Rauch, Klete Keller, [Chad Carvin, Nathaniel Dusing]	7:12.64
3. HOL	Martijn Zuijdweg, Johan Kenkhuis, Marcel Wouda, Pieter van den Hoogenband, [Mark van der Zijden]	7:12.70
4. ITA	Andrea Beccari, Matteo Pelliciari, Emiliano Brembilla, Massimiliano Rosolino, [Klaus Lanzarini, Simone Cercato]	7:12.91
5. GBR	Edward Sinclair, Paul Palmer, Marc Spackman, James Salter, [Andrew Clayton]	7:12.98
6. GER	Stefan Pohl, Christian Keller, Stefan Herbst, Christian-Alexander Tröger, [Heiko Hell, Michael Kiedel]	7:20.19
7. CAN	Mark Johnston, Michael Mintenko, Richard Say, Yannick Lupien, [Brian Johns]	7:21.92
8. RUS	Dmitri Chernyshev, Andrei Kapralov, Sergei Lavrenov, Aleksei Filipets, [Aleksei Yegorov]	7:24.37

The result was never in doubt, as the powerful Australian team was only competing against their own world record. The battle for second place was more exciting, as US anchor Klete Keller slipped back from second to fifth before surging in the final lap to gain the silver medal. For the Netherlands, anchor Pieter van den Hoogenband swam the fastest relay leg in history, 1:44.88, to help teammate Marcel Wouda earn his first medal after competing in three Olympics and seven events.

2004 Athens T: 16, N: 16, D: 8.17. WR: 7:04.66 (AUS—Hackett, Klim, Kirby, Thorpe)

1. USA	Michael Phelps, Ryan Lochte, Peter Vanderkaay, Klete Keller Scott Goldblatt, Dan Ketchum	7:07.33
2. AUS	Grant Hackett, Michael Klim, Nicholas Sprenger, Ian Thorpe, [Todd Pearson, Anthony Matkovich, Craig Stevens]	7:07.46
3. ITA	Emiliano Brembilla, Massimiliano Rosolino, Simone Cercato, Filippo Magnini, [Matteo Pelliciari, Federico Cappellazzo]	7:11.83
4. GBR	Simon Burnett, Gavin Meadows, David O'Brien, Ross Davenport, [David Carry]	7:12.60
5. CAN	Brent Hayden, Brian Johns, Andrew Hurd, Richard Say, [Mark Johnston]	7:13.33
6. GER	Jens Schreiber, Heiko Hell, Lars Conrad, Christian Keller, [Johannes Oesterling, Stefan Herbst]	7:16.51
7. FRA	Amaury Leveaux, Fabien Horth, Nicolas Kintz, Nicolas Rostoucher	7:17.43
8. GRE	Apostolos Antonopoulos, Dimitrios Manganas, Andreas Zisimos, Nikolaos Xylouris	7:23.02

One year after the winning the Olympic championship in Sydney, the Australian team broke their own world record and won the world championship title, which they successfully defended in 2003. In Athens, however, the Australians faced a strong American team, led by Michael Phelps, who gave the US a one-second lead after the first leg, which it carried into the final leg after Peter Vanderkaay recorded the best 200 meters time of his life. In one of the more exciting finishes, Ian Thorpe began to steadily close the gap behind Klete Keller in the final lap, but Keller managed to hold him off by .13 seconds at the touch.

2008 Beijing T: 16, N: 16, D: 8.13. WR: 7:03.24 (USA—Phelps, Lochte, Keller, Vanderkaay)

1. USA	Michael Phelps, Ryan Lochte, Ricky Berens, Peter Vanderkaay, [Dave Walters, Erik Vendt, Klete Keller]	6:58.56 WR
2. RUS	Nikita Lobintsev, Yevgeny Lagunov, Danila Izotov, Aleksandr Sukhorukov, [Mikhail Polishchuk]	7:03.70
3. AUS	Patrick Murphy, Grant Hackett, Grant Brits, Nicholas Ffrost, [Kirk Palmer, Leith Brodie]	7:04.98
4. ITA	Marco Belotti, Emiliano Brembilla, Massimiliano Rosolino, Filippo Magnini, [Nicola Cassio]	7:05.35
5. CAN	Colin Russell, Brian Johns, Brent Hayden, Andrew Hurd, [Richard Say, Adam Sioui]	7:05.77

6. GBR	David Carry, Andrew Hunter, Robert Renwick, Ross Davenport	7:05.92
7. JPN	Yoshihiro Okumura, Sho Uchida, Yasunori Mononobe, Hisato Matsumoto	7:10.31
8. SAF	Jean Basson, Darian Townsend, Jan Venter, Sebastien Rousseau	7:13.02

Less than one hour after winning the 200-meter butterfly event, Phelps swam the first leg of the 200-meter freestyle relay. His leg gave the US a lead of nearly two-and-a-half seconds, which they expanded to more than five seconds before the finish. Their final time, 6:58.56 seconds, was the first in history under seven minutes and cut 4.68 seconds off their previous world record. It was Phelps' eleventh career gold medal (including six from the 2004 Olymipcs). By the end of the 2008 Olympics he had increased that total to 14: the most by any athlete in Olympic history.

"He is just a normal person," Russia's Aleksandr Sukhorukov said of Phelps after the race, "but maybe from a different planet."

4 × 100-METER MEDLEY RELAY

In medley relays, the order of strokes is backstroke, breaststroke, butterfly, and freestyle.

1896–1956 not held

1960 Rome T: 18, N: 18, D: 9.1. WR: 4:09.2 (USA, Indianapolis Athletic Club—McKinney, Jastremski, Troy, Sintz)

1. USA	Frank McKinney, Paul Hait, Lance Larson, F. Jeffrey Farrell, [Robert Bennett, David Gillanders, Stephen Clark]	4:05.4 WR
2. AUS	David Theile, Terry Gathercole, Neville Hayes, Geoffrey Shipton, [Julian Carroll, William Burton, Kevin Berry]	4:12.0
3. JPN	Kazuo Tomita, Koichi Hirakida, Yoshihiko Osaki, Keigo Shimizu, [Kazuo Watanabe, Katsuki Ishikara]	4:12.2
4. CAN	Robert Wheaton, Stephen Rabinovitch, Cameron Grout, Richard Pound	4:16.8
5. SOV	Leonid Barbier, Leonid Kolesnikov, Grigory Kiselyov, Igor Lushkovski	4:16.8
6. ITA	Guiseppe Avellone, Roberto Lazzari, Federico Dennerlein, Bruno Bianchi	4:17.2
7. GBR	Graham Sykes, Christopher Walkden, Ian Black, Stanley Clarke	4:17.6
8. HOL	Johannes Jiskoot, Wieger Mensonides, Gerrit Korteweg, Ronald Kroon	4:18.2

The US "reserve" team of Bob Bennett, Paul Hait, Dave Gillanders, and Steve Clark set a world record of 4:08.2 in the qualifying round. Only Hait also took part in the final, in which a new US team set another world record.

1964 Tokyo T: 14, N: 14, D: 10.16. WR: 4:00.1 (USA—McGeagh, Craig, Richardson, Clark)

1. USA	H. Thompson Mann, William Craig, Frederick Schmidt, Stephen Clark, [Richard McGeagh, Virgil Luken, Walter Richardson, Robert Bennett]	3:58.4 WR
2. GDR& GER	Ernst-Joachim Küppers, Egon Henninger, Horst-Günther Gregor, Hans-Joachim Klein	4:01.6
3. AUS	Peter Reynolds, Ian O'Brien, Kevin Berry, David Dickson, [Peter Tonkin]	4:02.3
4. SOV	Viktor Mazanov, Heorhy Prokopenko, Valentin Kuzmin, Vladimir Schuvalov, [Aleksandr Tutakayev, Viktor Semchenkov]	4:04.2
5. JPN	Shigeo Fukushima, Kenji Ishikawa, Isao Nakajima, Yukiaki Okabe	4:06.6
6. HUN	József Csikány, Ferenc Lenkei, József Gulrich, Gyula Dobai	4:08.5
7. ITA	Chiaffredo Rora, Gian Corrado Gross, Giampiero Fossati, Pietro Boscaini	4:10.3
8. GBR	Geoffrey Thwaites, Neil Nicholson, Brian Jenkins, Robert McGregor	4:11.4

Backstroker Thompson Mann led off for the United States with a world record of 59.6, the first time that the one minute barrier had ever been broken for the 100-meter backstroke. The German and Soviet teams caught up by the halfway mark, but Fred Schmidt put the victory away for the United States with a 56.8 butterfly leg, and Steve Clark sealed it with a 52.4 anchor.

1968 Mexico City T: 18, N: 18, D: 10.26. WR: 3:56.5 (GDR—Matthes, Henninger, Gregor, Wiegand)

1. USA	Charles Hickcox, Donald McKenzie, Douglas Russell, Kenneth Walsh, [Ronald Mills, Chester Jastremski, Carl Robie, Donald Schollander]	3:54.9 WR
2. GDR	Roland Matthes, Egon Henninger, Horst-Günther Gregor, Frank Wiegand	3:57.5
3. SOV	Yuri Hromak, Vladimir Kossinsky, Volodymyr Nemshilov, Leonid Ilyichev, [Viktor Mazanov, Nikolai Pankin, Yuri Suzdatsev, Sergei Gusev]	4:00.7
4. AUS	Karl Byrom, Ian O'Brien, Robert Cusack, Michael Wenden	4:00.8
5. JPN	Yasuo Tanaka, Nobutaka Taguchi, Satoshi Maruya, Kunihiro Iwasaki	4:01.8
6. GER	Reinhard Blechert, Gregor Betz, Lutz Stoklasa, Wolfgang Kremer	4:05.4
7. CAN	James Shaw, William Mahony, Toomas Arusoo John Gilchrist	4:07.3
8. SPA	Santiago Esteva Escoda, José Durán Noguera, Arturo Lang-Lenton León, José Chicoy Massa	4:08.8

Roland Matthes opened with a backstroke world record of 58.0, but Doug Russell's butterfly leg put the United States in the lead to stay.

1972 Munich T: 17, N: 17, D: 9.4. WR: 3:50.4 (USA—Campbell, Dahlberg, Spitz, Heidenreich)

1. USA	Michael Stamm, Thomas Bruce, Mark Spitz, Jerôme Heidenreich, [Mitchell Ivey, John Hencken, Gary Hall, Sr., David Fairbank]	3:48.16 WR
2. GDR	Roland Matthes, Klaus Katzur, Hartmut Flöckner, Lutz Unger	3:52.12
3. CAN	Eric Fish, William Mahony, Bruce Robertson, Robert Kasting, [William Kennedy]	3:52.26
4. SOV/RUS	Igor Grivennikov, Nikolai Pankin, Viktor Sharygin, Vladimir Bure, [Viktor Stulikov, Viktor Aboimov]	3:53.26
5. BRA	Rómulo Duncan Arantes, José Sylvio Fiolo, Sergio Waismann, José Roberto Diniz-Aranha	3:57.89
6. JPN	Tadashi Honda, Nobutaka Taguchi, Yasuhiro Komazaki, Jiro Sasaki	3:58.23
7. GBR	Colin Cunningham, David Wilkie, John Mills, Malcolm Windeatt	3:58.82
8. HUN	László Cseh, Sándor Szabó, István Szentirmay, Attila Császári, [András Hargitay]	3:59.07

Once again, Roland Matthes opened with a world record performance, but then the Americans took over, as Mark Spitz, swimming the butterfly leg, won his seventh gold medal.

1976 Montreal T: 14, N: 14, D: 7.22. WR: 3:48.16 (USA—Stamm, Bruce, Spitz, Heidenreich)

1. USA	John Naber, John Hencken, Matthew Vogel, James Montgomery, [Peter Rocca, Christopher Woo, Joseph Bottom, Jack Babashoff]	3:42.22 WR
2. CAN	Stephen Pickell, Graham Smith, Clay Evans, Gary MacDonald, [Bruce Robertson]	3:45.94
3. GER	Klaus Steinbach, Walter Kusch, Michael Kraus, Peter Nocke, [Peter Lang, Dirk Braunleder]	3:47.29
4. GBR	James Carter, David Wilkie, John Mills, Brian Brinkley, [Gary Abraham, Duncan Goodhew, Kevin Burns]	3:49.56
5. SOV	Igor Omelchenko, Arvydas Juozaitis, Yevgeny Seredin, Andrei Krylov, [Nikolai Pankin, Andrei Bogdanov]	3:49.90
6. AUS	Mark Kerry, Paul Jarvie, Neil Rogers, Peter Coughlan	3:51.54
7. ITA	Enrico Bisso, Giorgio Lalle, Paolo Barelli, Marcello Guarducci	3:52.92
8. JPN	Tadashi Honda, Nobutaka Taguchi, Hideaki Hara, Tsuyoshi Yanagidate	3:54.74

In the qualifying round, Americans Peter Rocca, Chris Woo, Joe Bottom, and Jack Babashoff set a world record of 3:47.28. The 1976 US team was so strong that they were able to field a completely different foursome in the final and set yet another world record.

1980 Moscow T: 11, N: 11, D: 7.24. WR: 3:42.22 (USA—Naber, Hencken, Vogel, Montgomery)

1. AUS	Mark Kerry, Peter Evans, Mark Tonelli, Neil Brooks, [Glen Patching]	3:45.70
2. SOV	Viktor Kuznetsov, Arsens Miskarovs, Yevgeny Seredin, Sergei Kopliakov, [Vladimir Shmetov, Aleksandr Fedorovsky, Aleksei Markovsky, Sergei Krasyuk]	3:45.92
3. GBR	Gary Abraham, Duncan Goodhew, David Lowe, T. Martin Smith, [Paul Marshall, Mark Taylor]	3:47.71
4. GDR	Dietmar Göhring, Jörg Walter, Roger Pyttel, Jörg Woithe, [Frank Kühn]	3:48.25
5. FRA	Frédéric Delcourt, Olivier Borios, Xavier Savin, René Ecuyer	3:49.19
6. HUN	Sándor Wladár, János Dzvonyár, Zoltán Verrasztó, Gábor Mészáros	3:50.29
7. HOL	A. Frederik Eefting, Albert Boonstra, Kees Vervoorn, Cees Jan Winkel	3:51.81
8. BRA	Rómulo Duncan Arantes, Sérgio Pinto Ribeiro, Claudio Mamede Kestener, Jorge Luiz Fernandes, [Ciro Marques Delgado]	3:53.23

Australian anchorman Neil Brooks swam a stirring 49.86 to overtake 200-meter freestyle gold medalist Sergei Kopliakov and give Australia an upset victory. While most teams choose aggressive-sounding names for a nickname—like the Mean Machine or the Fearsome Foursome—the Australian 4×100-meter medley relay team christened themselves the Quietly Confident Quartet.

1984 Los Angeles T: 21, N: 21, D: 8.4. WR: 3:40.42 (USA—Carey, Lundquist, Gribble, Gaines)

1. USA	Richard Carey, Stephen Lundquist, P. Pablo Morales, Ambrose "Rowdy" Gaines, [David Wilson, Richard Schroeder, Michael Heath, Thomas Jager]	3:39.30 WR
2. CAN	Michael West, Victor Davis, Thomas Ponting, Donald "Sandy" Goss	3:43.23
3. AUS	Mark Kerry, Peter Evans, Glenn Buchanan, Mark Stockwell, [Jonathan Sieben, Neil Brooks]	3:43.25
4. GER	Stefan Peter, Gerald Mörken, Michael Gross, Dirk Korthals, [Andreas Behrend, Alexander Schowtka]	3:44.26
5. SWE	Bengt Baron, Peter Berggren, Thomas Lejdström, Per Johansson, [Michael Söderlund, Peter Berggren]	3:47.13
6. GBR	Neil Harper, Adrian Moorhouse, Andrew Jameson, Richard Burrell, [David Lowe]	3:47.39
7. SWI	Patrick Ferland, Etienne Dagon, Théophile David, Daniel "Dano" Halsall	3:47.93

DISQ: JPN—Daichi Suzuki, Shigehiro Takahashi, Taihel Saka, Hiroshi Sakamoto

Rick Carey opened with an Olympic backstroke record of 55.41 and the rest of the race was never close.

1988 Seoul T: 25, N: 25, D: 9.25. WR: 3:38.28 (USA—Carey, Moffet, Morales, Biondi)

1. USA	David Berkoff, Richard Schroeder, Matthew Biondi, Christopher Jacobs, [Jay Mortenson, Thomas Jager]	3:36.93 WR
2. CAN	Mark Tewksbury, Victor Davis, Thomas Ponting, Donald "Sandy" Goss	3:39.28
3. SOV	Igor Polyansky, Dmitri Volkov, Vadym Yaroshchuk, Gennady Prigoda, [Sergei Zabolotnov, Valery Lozik, Konstantin Petrov, Nikolai Yevseyev]	3:39.96
4. GER	Frank Hoffmeister, Alexander Mayer, Michael Gross, Björn Zikarsky, [Mark Warnecke]	3:42.98
5. JPN	Daichi Suzuki, Hironobu Nagahata, Hiroshi Miura, Shigeo Ogata	3:44.36
6. AUS	Carl Wilson, Ian Mcadam, Jonathan Sieben, Andrew Baildon	3:45.85
7. HOL	Hans Kroes, Ronald Dekker, Frank Drost, Patrick Dybiona	3:46.85

DISQ: GBR—Neil Harper, Adrian Moorhouse, Andrew Jameson, Mark Foster, [Gary Binfield, Roland Lee]

David Berkoff opened with a sizzling 54.56 backstroke leg and the US never looked back. Matt Biondi left Seoul with five gold medals, one silver, and one bronze. The West German team celebrated the end of the meet by walking to the blocks dressed in lederhosen. At the 1986 world championships they had appeared in togas made of bedsheets.

1992 Barcelona T: 23, N: 23, D: 7.31. WR: 3:36.93 (USA— Berkoff, Schroeder, Biondi, Jacobs)

1. USA	Jeffrey Rouse, Nelson Diebel, P. Pablo Morales, Jon Olsen, [David Berkoff, Hans Dersch, Melvin Stewart, Matthew Biondi]	3:36.93 EWR
2. SOV	Vladimir Selkov, Vasily Ivanov, Pavlo Khnykin, Aleksandr Popov, [Vladislav Kulikov, Dmitri Volkov, Vladimir Pyshnenko]	3:38.56
3. CAN	Mark Tewksbury, Jonathan Cleveland, Marcel Gery, Stephen Clarke, [Thomas Ponting]	3:39.66
4. GER	Tino Weber, Mark Warnecke, Christian Kelley, Mark Pincer, [Bengt Zikarsky]	3:40.19
5. FRA	Franck Schott, Stéphane Vossart, Bruno Gutzeit, Stéphan Caron, [Franck Esposito, Christophe Kalfayan]	3:40.51
6. HUN	Tamás Deutsch, Norbert Rózsa, Peter Horváth, Béla Szabados	3:42.03
7. AUS	Thomas Stachewicz, Philip Rogers, Jonathan Sieben, Christopher Fydler	3:42.65
8. JPN	Hajime Itoi, Akira Hayashi, Keiichi Kawanaka, Tsutomu Nakano	3:43.25

A day after he was out-touched by Mark Tewksbury in the 100-meter backstroke final, Jeff Rouse led off with a world record of 53.86 seconds. The United States extended its win streak in this event to eight in a row. By swimming in the preliminary round, Matt Biondi earned a gold medal, bringing his career medal total to eleven: 8 gold, 2 silver, 1 bronze.

1996 Atlanta T: 25, N: 25, D: 7.26. WR: 3:36.93 (USA—Berkoff, Schroeder, Biondi, Jacobs; USA—Rouse, Diebel, Morales, Olsen)

1. USA	Jeffrey Rouse, Jeremy Linn, Mark Henderson, Gary Hall,Jr., [William "Tripp" Schwenk, Kurt Grote, John Hargis, Joshua Davis]	3:34.84 WR
2. RUS	Vladimir Selkov, Stanislav Lopukhov, Denis Pankratov, Aleksandr Popov, [Roman Ivanovsky, Vladislav Kulikov, Roman Yegorov]	3:37.55
3. AUS	Steven Dewick, Philip Rogers, Scott Miller, Michael Klim, [Toby Haenen]	3:39.56
4. GER	Ralf Braun, Mark Warnecke, Christian Keller, Björn Zikarsky, [Stev Theloke, Oliver Lampe]	3:39.64
5. JPN	Keitaro Konnai, Akira Hayashi, Takashi Yamamoto, Shunsuke Ito	3:40.51
6. HUN	Tamás Deutsch, Károly Güttler, Péter Horváth, Attila Czene, [Attila Zubor]	3:40.84
7. POL	Mariusz Siembida, Marek Krawczyk, Rafał Szukała, Bartołomiej "Bartosz" Kizierowski	3:41.94
8. ISR	Ethan Urbach, Vadim Alekseyev, Dan Kutler, Yoav Bruck	3:42.90

The outcome of the race was never in doubt. Jeff Rouse and Jeremy Linn gave the US a lead of 2.92 seconds. Although Denis Pankratov swam the fastest butterfly relay leg in history (51.55), he made little headway on Mark Henderson. Gary Hall outswam Aleksandr Popov 48.18 to 48.81 and the US once again broke the world record.

2000 Sydney T: 23, N: 23, D: 9.23. WR: 3:34.84 (USA—Rouse, Linn, Henderson, Hall, Jr.)

1. USA	Lenny Krayzelburg, Ed Moses, Ian Crocker, Gary Hall, Jr., [Neil Walker, Tommy Hannan, Jason Lezak]	3:33.73 WR
2. AUS	Matthew Welsh, Regan Harrison, Geoff Huegill, Michael Klim, [Joshua Watson, Ryan Mitchell, Adam Pine, Ian Thorpe]	3:35.27
3. GER	Stev Theloke, Jens Kruppa, Thomas Rupprath, Torsten Spanneberg	3:35.88
4. HOL	Klaas-Erik Zwering, Marcel Wouda, Joris Keizer, Pieter van den Hoogenband, [Mark Veens]	3:37.53
5. HUN	Péter Horváth, Károly Güttler, Zsolt Gáspár, Attila Zubor	3:39.09
6. CAN	Chris Renaud, Morgan Knabe, Michael Mintenko, Craig Hutchison, [Shamek Pietucha, Yannick Lupien]	3:39.88
7. FRA	Simon Dufour, Hugues Duboscq, Franck Esposito, Frédérick Bousquet	3:40.02
8. GBR	Neil Willey, Darren Mew, James Hickman, Simon Brinn	3:40.19

The United States broke the world record their swimmers had set at the last Olympics. Ed Moses' 59.84 was the fastest breaststroke leg in history and Geoff Huegill's 51.33 split for Australia was the fastest ever butterfly leg.

2004 Athens T: 16, N: 16, D: 8.21. WR: 3:31.54 (USA—Peirsol, Hansen, Crocker, Lezak)

1. USA	Aaron Peirsol, Brendan Hansen, Ian Crocker, Jason Lezak, [Lenny Krayzelburg, Mark Gangloff, Michael Phelps, Neil Walker]	3:30.68 WR
2. GER	Steffen Driesen, Jens Kruppa, Thomas Rupprath, Lars Conrad, [Helge Meeuw]	3:33.62
3. JPN	Tomomi Morita, Kosuke Kitajima, Takashi Yamamoto, Yoshihiro Okumura	3:35.22
4. RUS	Arkady Vyachanin, Roman Sludnov, Igor Marchenko, Aleksandr Popov, [Yevgeny Korotyshkin, Andrei Kapralov]	3:35.91
5. FRA	Simon Dufour, Hugues Duboscq, Franck Esposito, Frédérick Bousquet	3:36.57
6. UKR	Pavlo Illichov, Oleh Lisohor, Andriy Serdinov, Yuriy Yehoshin, [Valeriy Dymo, Denys Sylantyev]	3:36.87
7. HUN	László Cseh, Richárd Bodor, Zsolt Gáspár, Attila Zubor	3:37.46
8. GBR	Gregor Tait, James Gibson, James Hickman, Matthew Kidd	3:37.77

After winning the 100-meter butterfly one day earlier, Michael Phelps ceded his spot in the final to teammate Ian Crocker, saying he wanted to see Crocker win a gold medal. The US lineup was the same as the one that had broken the world record while winning the 2003 world championship. In Athens, the US victory was never in doubt, with Aaron Peirsol leading off by breaking the 100-meter backstroke world record with a 53.45 split. Crocker bettered his 100-meter butterfly world record time with a 50.2-second third leg.

2008 Beijing T: 16, N: 16, D: 8.17. WR: 3:30.68 (USA—Peirsol, Hansen, Crocker, Lezak)

1. USA	Aaron Peirsol, Brendan Hansen, Michael Phelps, Jason Lezak, [Matt Grevers, Mark Gangloff, Ian Crocker, Garrett Weber-Gale]	3:29.34 WR
2. AUS	Hayden Stoeckel, Brenton Rickard, Andrew Lauterstein, Eamon Sullivan, [Ashley Delaney, Christian Sprenger, Adam Pine, Matthew Targett]	3:30.04
3. JPN	Junichi Miyashita, Kosuke Kitajima, Takuro Fujii, Hisayoshi Sato	3:31.18
4. RUS	Arkady Vyachanin, Roman Sludnov, Yevgeny Korotyshkin, Yevgeny Lagunov [Nikolai Skvortsov, Andrei Grechin]	3:31.92
5. NZL	Daniel Bell, Glenn Snyders, Corney Swanepoel, Cameron Gibson	3:33.39
6. GBR	Liam Tancock, Christopher Cook, Michael Rock, Simon Burnett	3:33.69
7. SAF	Gerhard Zandberg, Cameron van der Burgh, Lyndon Ferns, Darian Townsend	3:33.70

DISQ: ITA—Mirco Di Tora, Loris Facci, Mattia Nalesso, Filippo Magnini, Alessandro Terrin

The 4 × 100-meter medley relay had been dominated by the US since its introduction in 1960, with the US winning gold every time it participated and setting or equaling the world record each time.

Aaron Peirsol got the Americans off to a strong start, building a half-second lead over the backstroke leg. The team dropped to third place behind Japan and Australia during the breaststroke, but Michael Phelps surged back into the lead with his butterfly leg. Jason Lezak held off 100-meter freestyle world record holder Eamon Sullivan to clinch the 12th US gold medal in the event, lowering the world record by 0.66 seconds.

The relay victory completed Phelps' extraordinary medal sweep at the 2008 Olympics, in which he won eight gold medals over nine days, and set seven world records. Phelps' seventeen total races covered a distance of 3.3 kilometers (2.05 miles).

Phelps was the first Olympic athlete ever to win fourteen career gold medals, surpassing the previous record of nine set by Paavo Nurmi in the 1920s and tied by Soviet gymnast Larysa Latynina, Mark Spitz and Carl Lewis. Phelps' sixteen total medals was the most ever by a male athlete, second only to Soviet gymnast Larisa Latynina, who won eighteen medals between 1956 and 1964.

Despite spending most of his time in the pool, Phelps did have his brushes with controversy. After the 2004 Olympics he was arrested on a drunken driving charge and was sentenced to 18 months probation and community service. In November 2008 Phelps was photographed while smoking a marijuana pipe at a party at the University of South Carolina. Although the photo was taken out of competition, Phelps was suspended by USA Swimming for three months.

DISCONTINUED EVENTS

100-METER FREESTYLE FOR SAILORS

1896 Athens-Piraeus C: 3, N: 1, D: 4.11.

1. Ioannis Malokinis	GRE	2:20.4
2. Spiridon Khazapis	GRE	—
3. Dimitrios Drivas	GRE	—

This rather specialized event was limited to members of the Greek navy.

880-YARD FREESTYLE

1904 St. Louis C: 6, N: 4, D: 9.7.

1. Emil Rausch	GER	13:11.4
2. Francis Gailey	AUS	13.23.4
3. Géza Kiss	HUN	—
4. Edgar Adams	USA	—
5. Otto Wahle	AUT	—
6. H. Jamison Handy	USA	—

4000-METER FREESTYLE

1900 Paris C: 29, N: 7, D: 8.19.

1. John Arthur Jarvis	GBR	58:24.0
2. I. Zoltán Halmay	HUN	1:08:55.4
3. Louis Martin	FRA	1:13:08.4
4. Thomas Burgess	GBR	1:15:07.6
5. Eduard Meijer	HOL	1:16:37.2
6. Fabio Magnoni	ITA	1:18:25.4
7. E. Martin	FRA	1:26:32.2

In 1911, fourth place finisher Thomas Burgess became the second person to swim the English Channel—36 years after Matthew Webb did it first.

400-METER BREASTSTROKE

1904 St. Louis C: 4, N: 2, D: 9.7.
(440 Yards—402.33 Meters)

1. Georg Zacharias	GER	7:23.6
2. Walter Brack	GER	—
3. H. Jamison Handy	USA	—
4. Jörg Hoffmann	GER	—

Jam Handy later became known as swimming's most prolific inventor. He was the first person to paint lines on the bottom of a pool to help swimmers keep to a straight course, the first swimmer to use alternating armstrokes in the backstroke, and the first person to use modern breathing techniques. At the age of 80, he was still able to swim more laps than his age.

1906–1908 not held

1912 Stockholm C: 17, N: 10, D: 7.12.

1. Walter Bathe	GER	6:29.6 OR
2. Thor Henning	SWE	6:35.6
3. Percy Courtman	GBR	6:36.4
4. Paul Malisch	GER	6:37.0

DNF: Wilhelm Lützow (GER)

1920 Antwerp C: 20, N: 10, D: 8.25.

1. Håkan Malmrot	SWE	6:31.8
2. Thor Henning	SWE	6:45.2
3. Arvo Aaltonen	FIN	6:48.0
4. Jackson Howell	USA	6:51.0
5. Per Cederblom	SWE	7:08.0

200-METER TEAM SWIMMING

1900 Paris T: 4, N: 2, D: 8.12.

		PTS.
1. GER	1—Ernst Hoppenberg 2:35.0, 2—Max Hainle 2:36.0, 3—Gustav Lexau 2:42.0, 8—Ernest Luhrsen 2:55.0	32
2. FRA	Tritons Lillois: 7—Maurice Hochepied 2:53.0, 10—Victor Hochepied 2:56.4, 11—J. Bertrand 3:00.0, 13—Verbecke 3:01.6, 18—V ictor Cadet 3:18.0	51
3. FRA	Pupilles de Neptune de Lille: 5— René Tartara 2:48.6, 6—Louis Martin 2:51.4, 9—Désiré Merchez 2:55.4, 14—Georges Leuillieux 3:02.0	61
4. FRA	Libellule de Paris: 4—Jules Clévenot 2:45.0, 12—Féret 3:00.4, 15—Gasaigne 3:02.0, 16—Rosier 3:04.4, 17—Pelloy 3:06.0	64

This was not a relay, but a team race in which 20 men were entered. Each team was assigned points according to the places in which its individual members finished. The German team, which was from Berlin, and the Neptune de Lille team only entered four swimmers, so their non-competing fifth swimmers were considered to have tied for ninteenth place. A British team had also been entered, but was misinformed as to the starting time and arrived after the race was over. The results of this event are provided courtesy of Bill Mallon, who patiently sorted through the complex and bizarre rules that were used.

200-METER OBSTACLE RACE

1900 Paris C: 12, N: 5, D: 8.12.

1. Frederick Lane	AUS	2:38.4
2. Otto Wahle	AUT	2:40.0
3. Peter Kemp	GBR	2:47.4
4. Karl Ruberl	AUT	2:51.2
5. F. Stapleton	GBR	2:55.0
6. William Henry	GBR	2:58.0
7. Maurice Hochepied	FRA	2:58.0
8. Verbecke	FRA	3:08.4

This quaint event required the participants to struggle past three sets of obstacles. First they had to climb over a pole, then they had to scramble over a row of boats, and finally they had to swim *under* another row of boats. Freddy Lane grew up around boats in Sydney's harbor and put this experience to good use in the obstacle race. Rather than clamber over the middle of the boats, he crossed them at the stern, where the going was smoother. Lane was probably better known for his victory in the unimpeded 200-meter freestyle.

UNDERWATER SWIMMING

1900 Paris C: 14, N: 4, D: 8.12.

		M	TIME	PTS.
1. Charles de Vendeville	FRA	60	1:08.4	188.4
2. André Six	FRA	60	1:05.4	185.4
3. Peder Lykkeberg	DEN	28.50	1:30.0	147.0
4. de Romand	FRA	47.50	50.2	145.0
5. Tisserand	FRA	30.75	48.0	109.5
6. Hans Aniol	GER	36.95	30.0	103.9
7. Menault	FRA	32.50	38.4	103.4
8. Louis Marc	FRA	34	32.0	100.0

Two points were awarded for each meter swum and one point for each second that the swimmer was able to stay under water.

PLUNGE FOR DISTANCE

1904 St. Louis C: 5, N: 1, D: 9.5.

		M	FT.-IN.
1. William Dickey	USA	19.05	62-6
2. Edgar Adams	USA	17.53	57-6
3. Leo "Budd" Goodwin	USA	17.37	57-0
4. Newman Samuels	USA	16.76	55-0
5. Charles Pyrah	USA	14.02	46-0

In the plunge for distance, the contestants began with a standing dive, then remained motionless for 60 seconds or until their heads broke the surface of the water, whichever came first. Then the length of their dives was measured. Charles Pyrah held the US record at 63 feet, but was "completely out of form" according to the local newspapers. It was most unfortunate that the great British plungers John Arthur Jarvis and W. Taylor did not make the trip to St. Louis. Jarvis won the 1904 Amateur Swimming Association plunging championship with a plunge of 75 feet 4 inches (22.96 meters), while Taylor was the national record holder at 78 feet 9 inches (24 meters). In 1933 Frank Parrington plunged 86 feet 8 inches (26.40 meters). The ASA championship was discontinued after 1946.

Chapter 23 Swimming (Women)

50-Meter Freestyle	100-Meter Butterfly
100-Meter Freestyle	200-Meter Butterfly
200-Meter Freestyle	200-Meter Individual Medley
400-Meter Freestyle	400-Meter Individual Medley
800-Meter Freestyle	10,000-Meter Open Water
100-Meter Backstroke	4 × 100-Meter Freestyle Relay
200-Meter Backstroke	4 × 200-Meter Freestyle Relay
100-Meter Breaststroke	4 × 100-Meter Medley Relay
200-Meter Breaststroke	

50-METER FREESTYLE

1896–1984 not held

1988 Seoul C: 50, N: 33, D: 9.25. WR: 24.98 (Yang Wenyi)

1. Kristin Otto	GDR	25.49 OR
2. Yang Wenyi	CHN	25.64
3. Katrin Meissner	GDR	25.71
3. Jill Sterkel	USA	25.71
5. Leigh Ann Fetter	USA	25.78
6. Tamara Costache	ROM	25.80
7. Catherine Plewinski	FRA	25.90
8. Karen Van Wirdum	AUS	26.01

At the 1982 world championships, 6-foot 1-inch Kristin Otto of Leipzig won three gold medals. At the 1986 world championships she won four gold medals and at the 1987 European championships she won five. Incredibly, Otto was able to improve on her record by earning an unprecedented six golds in Seoul. Her final victory, and the one that was least expected, came in the 50-meter freestyle. Otto, who had been expected to win three to five gold medals four years earlier, until East Germany announced its boycott of the Los Angeles Games, was unanimously voted the outstanding competitor of the 1988 Olympics by an IOC panel. East German documents declassified in 1994 revealed that Otto had been put on a steady diet of prohibited drugs, notably testosterone, throughout her career.

Jill Sterkel, who tied for third place, became the first female swimmer to win medals 12 years apart. In 1976 she had earned a gold as a member of the US freestyle relay team.

1992 Barcelona C: 50, N: 35, D: 7.31. WR: 24.98 (Yang Wenyi)

1. Yang Wenyi	CHN	24.79 WR
2. Zhuang Yong	CHN	25.08
3. Angelina Martino	USA	25.23
4. Catherine Plewinski	FRA	25.36
5. Jennifer Thompson	USA	25.37
6. Natalya Meshcheryakova	MOL	25.47
7. Simone Osygus	GER	25.74
8. Inge de Bruijn	HOL	25.84

For four years after Yang Wenyi set her world record, on April 11, 1988, she did not live up to expectations. The favorite at the 1988 Olympics, she finished second to Kristin Otto. At the 1989 Pan Pacific Championships, she was second to Jenny Thompson. At the 1991 world championships, she dropped to fourth place. In the qualifying round at the 1992 Olympics, she dropped even further to sixth place. But in the final that evening, the 5-foot 10-inch Yang was first into the water, held her lead to the end, and broke her world record. All of the finalists except Thompson and Osygus beat or tied their personal bests.

1996 Atlanta C: 55, N: 47, D: 7.26. WR: 24.51 (Le Jingyi)

1. Amy Van Dyken	USA	24.87
2. Le Jingyi	CHN	24.90
3. Sandra Völker	GER	25.14
4. Angelina Martino	USA	25.31
5. Leah Martindale	BAR	25.49
6. Linda Olofsson	SWE	25.63
7. Shan Ying	CHN	25.70
8. Natalya Meshcheryakova	RUS	25.88

Dawn Fraser, 1960

Poolside in Rome, where she would claim the second of her three 100-meter freestyle titles. Fraser's triple has been matched by only one other swimmer, Hungary's Krisztina Egerszegi.

Before the Olympics began, 23-year-old Amy Van Dyken was considered mildly interesting to the US public because she had qualified for five events despite her struggle with exercise-induced asthma. Over a period of seven days she would be transformed into a major star. Her Olympic odyssey began with a fourth-place finish in the 100-meter freestyle, after which she collapsed on the deck with upper thigh cramps. Two nights later she won a gold medal as a member of the US 4 × 100 freestyle relay team. The following evening she scored a dramatic upset victory in the 100-meter butterfly, defeating Liu Limin of China by one one-hundredth of a second. The next evening she earned a third gold medal in the 4 × 100 medley relay. Two nights later, in the 50-meter freestyle, Van Dyken had the chance to become the first American woman in any sport to win four gold medals in one Olympics. But she would have to face world champion and world record holder Le Jingyi.

Van Dyken would leave nothing to chance. Between the preliminaries and the final, she reshaved her legs. "Everyone thinks I'm crazy for shaving every day," she would later explain," but that extra shave just might mean two or three hundredths faster." In the Ready Room, Van Dyken planted herself in front of Le and stared at her. When Le tried to avoid her, Van Dyken changed positions and continued to stare.

It was clear from past experience that Le would jump into the early lead and Van Dyken would close the gap. That is exactly what happened, with Van Dyken gaining the victory with her final stroke. As it turned out, the margin of victory was decided in the first second of the race. Van Dyken dove into the pool seven hundredths of a second sooner than Le and won the race by three hundredths of a second. Or maybe the last reshave made the difference after all.

The slowest swimmer in the preliminary heats was Nishma Gurung of Nepal, whose time of 41.45 was 7 seconds slower than any of the 54 other participants and was the equivalent of twenty meters behind the time of top qualifier Le Jingyi—in a fifty-meter race. One other swimmer worth noting was finalist Natalya Meshcheryakova, who, with the encouragement of her husband, gold medal swimmer Vladimir Pyshnenko, appeared in the Russian edition of *Playboy* just prior to the Atlanta Games. In 1997, both Meshcheryakova and Pyshnenko were suspended when they tested positive for anabolic steroids.

2000 Sydney C: 74, N: 66, D: 9.23. WR: 24.39 (Inge de Bruijn)

1. Inge de Bruijn	HOL	24.32
2. Therese Alshammar	SWE	24.51
3. Dara Torres	USA	24.63
4. Amy Van Dyken	USA	25.04
5. Martina Moravcová	SLV	25.24
6. Sandra Völker	GER	25.27
7. Alison Sheppard	GBR	25.45
8. Sumika Minamoto	JPN	25.65

Back in 1991, Inge de Bruijn won a silver medal in the 100-meter freestyle at the world championships. But the following year she missed qualifying for the Olympic final. De Bruijn stopped progressing and, although she qualified for the 1996 Olympics, she chose not to compete. However as she watched the Atlanta Games on television, she realized she had made a terrible mistake. De Bruijn apprenticed herself to American coach Paul Bergen and began a comeback. By 1998, she was ranked number one in the world in the 50-meter freestyle and at the 1999 European championships she won the 50-meter freestyle and the 100-meter butterfly and finished second in the 100-meter freestyle. But then she really peaked in 2000. Between May 27 and July 22, she tied or broke the world record in the 50-meter freestyle three times, the 100-meter butterfly twice and the 100-meter freestyle once. She also set two world records in a non-Olympic event, the 50-meter butterfly. At the Olympics she continued her streak, winning both the 100-meter butterfly and the 100-meter freestyle and setting world records in both events. She also picked up a silver medal in the 4 × 100-meter relay. De Bruijn's final event was the 50-meter freestyle. She set a world record of 24.13 seconds in the semifinals and then won her third gold medal in the final.

Because de Bruijn was 27 years old at the time of the Sydney Olympics, and she was achieving her best times at a relatively advanced age, there were grumbling that she must be taking performance-enhancing drugs. However she passed every doping test she ever took. And if de Bruijn's success at 27 was surprising, what was one to make of bronze medal-winner Dara Torres? Torres had earned relay medals in 1984, 1988 and 1992. Then she quit swimming and, for the next seven-years, pursued careers as a model (she was the first athlete to appear in *Sports Illustrated*'s annual swimsuit issue) a television commentator and as an infomercial spokeswoman. She unretired in 1999 and won her first medals (three bronzes) in individual events at the Sydney Olympics—at the age of 33. In fact, Torres became the oldest woman to earn a medal in swimming and the first swimmer to win medals in four different Olympics.

The first heat of the qualifying round saw the participation of two unusual athletes: Paula Barila Bolopa of Equatorial Guinea and Fatema Hameed Gerashi of Bahrain. Like her better-known Equatorial Guinean teammate, Eric Moussambani, Barila Bolopa had no formal training and had never swum in a full-size pool. She completed her 50-meter lap in 63.97 seconds: ten seconds more than it took Inge de Bruijin to win the *100*-meter race, not to mention more than 28 seconds slower than the second slowest swimmer in the 50 free, Aissatou Barry of Guinea.

As for Hameed, she was the youngest athlete at the 2000 Olympics: 12 years old. Before arriving in Sydney, Hameed had never swum in front of men. Understandably nervous before thousands of people on the morning of her race, she wobbled on the starting block rather than remaining still and was disqualified.

2004 Athens C: 73, N: 66, D: 8.21. WR: 24.13 (Inge de Bruijn)

1. Inge de Bruijn	HOL	24.58
2. Malia Metella	FRA	24.89
3. Lisbeth Lenton	AUS	24.91
4. Therese Alshammar	SWE	24.93
5. Kara Lynn Joyce	USA	25.00
6. Michelle Engelsman	AUS	25.06
7. Jenny Thompson	USA	25.11
8. Flávia Delaroli	BRA	25.20

Between Olympics, defending champion Inge de Bruijn was rarely seen in international competition. But when she did show up, she was unbeatable. De Bruijn won both world championships, in 2001 and 2003, the latter by an impressive six-tenths of a second. Both de Bruijn and 19-year-old Libby Lenton arrived in Athens with seasonal bests of 24.70 seconds. Recording a 24.66, de Bruijn led the qualifying round by four-tenths of a second. In the second semifinal, she defeated Lenton 24.56 to 24.90. Both sprinters duplicated their times almost exactly in the final. However, Malia Metella, a native of French Guiana in South America, outtouched Lenton to gain the silver medal. De Bruijn's victory came three days before her 31st birthday.

2008 Beijing C: 90, N: 82, D: 8.17. WR: 23.97 (Libby Trickett)

1. Britta Steffen	GER	24.06 OR
2. Dara Torres	USA	24.07
3. Cate Campbell	AUS	24.17
4. Lisbeth "Libby" Trickett (Lenton)	AUS	24.25
5. Marleen Veldhuis	HOL	24.26
6. Kara Lynn Joyce	USA	24.63
7. Hinkelien Schreuder	HOL	24.65
8. Aleksandra Gerasimenya	BLR	24.77

50-meter freestyle, 2008

41-year-old Dara Torres became the oldest swimmer to earn an Olympic medal (photo-Mark J. Terrill, AP)

Forty-one-year-old Dara Torres recorded the fastest qualifying time and swam the final in lane 4. At the halfway point she was in the lead, but was edged out at the last moment by 24-year-old Britta Steffen, who touched one-hundredth of a second faster. Torres's time, 24.07, was a personal best and an American record.

With this, her fifth Olympic appearance, Torres made history as the oldest female swimmer ever to compete in the Games. Born in Beverly Hills in 1967, she retired for the first time in 1992, to pursue a modeling career. After returning to win five medals at the 2000 Sydney Olympics she retired again, this time to focus on starting a family. She gave birth to a daughter, Tessa, in 2006 and in 2007 returned once again to competition, winning the US Nationals and the 2008 US Olympic Trials.

For Steffen, this victory, two days after her win in the 100-meter freestyle, completed her sweep of the freestyle sprint events at the 2008 Olympics. Bronze medalist Cate Campbell celebrated her sixteenth birthday three months before the Olympics. Neither of them had been born when Torres won her first Olympic gold medal.

100-METER FREESTYLE

1896–1908 not held

1912 Stockholm C: 27, N: 8, D: 7.12. WR: 1:20.6 (Daisy Curwen)

1. Sarah "Fanny" Durack	AUS	1:22.2
2. Wilhelmina Wylie	AUS	1:25.4
3. Jennie Fletcher	GBR	1:27.0
4. Margarete "Grete" Rosenberg	GER	1:27.2
5. Annie Speirs	GBR	1:27.4

DNS: Daisy Curwen (GBR)

Fanny Durack, Mina Wylie and Jennie Fletcher, 1912
The medalists in the first women's swimming contest, the 1912 100-meter freestyle.

Fanny Durack's biggest struggle came before the Olympics. The men who were in charge of naming the Australian team thought it an absurd waste of time and money to send women to Stockholm. Eventually the New South Wales Ladies' Amateur Swimming Association voted to let Durack and her friend and rival, Mina Wylie, go, but only if they paid their own way. A fund was raised to send Durack, and Wylie's family and friends covered her expenses. In the fourth heat of the second round, Durack swam a 1:19.8 to break Daisy Curwen's world record. In the semifinals she defeated Curwen herself, who then went straight to the hospital for an emergency appendectomy. Durack led the final from start to finish and won easily despite running into the side wall of the pool. At one time Fanny Durack held every world record in women's swimming, from 100 yards to one mile. Bronze medalist Jennie Fletcher came from a poor family in Leicester. She worked 72 hours a week at a textile factory and had little free time to train.

1920 Antwerp C: 16, N: 9, D: 8.25. WR: 1:16.2 (Sarah "Fanny" Durack)

1. Ethelda Bleibtrey	USA	1:13.6 WR
2. Irene Guest	USA	1:17.0
3. Frances Schroth	USA	1:17.2
4. Constance Jeans	GBR	1:22.8
5. Violet Walrond	NZL	—
6. Jane Gylling	SWE	—

DNF: Charlotte Boyle (USA)

Bleibtrey broke the world record in the third heat with a time of 1:14.4, then broke the record again in winning the final. Eventually she won all three swimming events for women at Antwerp. The year before the Antwerp Olympics, Bleibtrey caused a sensation in New York when she was arrested for "nude swimming"—she had removed her stockings before entering the ocean. In later years, she was a co-founder of the United States Olympians Association.

1924 Paris C: 16, N: 7, D: 7.20. WR: 1:12.8 (Gertrude Ederle)

1. Ethel Lackie	USA	1:12.4
2. Mariechen Wehselau	USA	1:12.8
3. Gertrude Ederle	USA	1:14.2
4. Constance Jeans	GBR	1:15.4
5. Irene Tanner	GBR	1:20.8
6. Maria Vierdag	HOL	

The US sweep was particularly impressive considering the absurd restrictions imposed on the female swimmers by the US Olympic Committee. American officials, concerned about protecting their teenaged swimmers from the immoral temptations of Paris, housed the young ladies way outside the city and forced them to spend five to six hours a day traveling to and from the Olympic pool. In the first heat, Mariechen Wehselau of Honolulu set a world record of 1:12.2. Lackie and Ederle won the next two heats in 1:12.8 and 1:12.6. In the final race, Wehselau held a two-yard lead at the 50-meter turn, with Ederle second and Lackie third. But 17-year-old Ethel Lackie of Chicago put on a fantastic spurt in the last 25 meters to edge Wehselau for first place.

Two years later Gertrude Ederle, the 19-year-old daughter of a New York City butcher, carved herself a permanent place in the history books with a swimming feat that shocked the world. Just after seven a.m. on the morning of August 6, 1926, she set off from France in an attempt to become the first woman to swim the English Channel. That day, the London *Daily News* ran an editorial which haughtily announced, "Even the most uncompromising champion of the rights and capacities of women must admit that in contests of physical skill, speed and endurance they must remain forever the weaker sex." Such overblown male chauvinism was buried in an avalanche of feminist joy when Ederle reached the English coast at Kingsdown in a time of 14 hours 31 minutes—almost two hours faster than the *men's* record for the Channel swim.

Ederle returned home to a tickertape parade attended by an estimated 2,000,000 people. A slew of personal appearances followed, but this period involved a series of setbacks. By 1933 she had suffered a nervous breakdown, become deaf as a result of her Channel swim, and received a serious back injury that forced her to wear a cast for four and a half years. Not one to wallow in self-pity, Ederle went right ahead with her life and eventually began teaching swimming to deaf children.

1928 Amsterdam C: 24. N: 11, D: 8.11. WR: 1:10.0 (Ethel Lackie)

1. Albina Osipowich	USA	1:11.0 OR
2. Eleanor Garatti	USA	1:11.4
3. M. Joyce Cooper	GBR	1:13.6
4. Jean McDowell	GBR	1:13.6
5. Susan Laird	USA	1:14.6
6. Charlotte Lehmann	GER	1:15.2

Three judges voted that Joyce Cooper touched first for the bronze medal while two voted for Jean McDowell.

1932 Los Angeles C: 20, N: 10, D: 8.8. WR: 1:06.6 (Helene Madison)

1. Helene Madison	USA	1:06.8 OR
2. Willemijntje den Ouden	HOL	1:07.8
3. Eleanor Saville (Garatti)	USA	1:09.3
4. Josephine McKim	USA	1:09.3
5. Frances Bult	AUS	1:09.9
6. Jennie Maakal	SAF	1:10.8

If ever there was a sure bet for a gold medal, it was 5-foot 10½-inch, 154-pound Helene Madison, a 19-year-old from Seattle, Washington, who was invariably referred to by the press as "shapely." During a 16½-month period in 1930–31, Madison broke all 16 world records for the distances between 100 yards and 1 mile. However, the results of the semifinals in Los Angeles raised serious doubts as to whether she could actually win the final. The first semifinal was won by 14-year-old Willy den Ouden in the surprisingly fast time of 1:07.6. In the second semi, Helene Madison went all out for the first 50 meters and then huffed home to win in 1:09.9, a time that would have placed her only fifth in the first semi. The American coaches advised Madison to change her tactics and save herself for the second half of the final race. This proved to be advice well worth taking, as Madison forged to a full-length lead between 50 and 75 meters before bumping into the lane divider. A final burst of speed provided her with a comfortable margin of victory.

Joyce Cooper of Great Britain was most unlucky to be drawn in the first semifinal. Her times of 1:09.0 and 1:09.2 would have been good enough for third place in the final.

After the Olympics it appeared that Helene Madison was headed for a very glamorous life, but things didn't work out that way. In 1933 she played a minor role in the film *The Warrior's Husband*. Then she tried to earn a living as a nightclub entertainer, a swimming instructor, and a department store clerk. In 1935 she became a probationary nurse at a Seattle hospital, but she failed to earn a registered nurse's certificate. She was also frustrated in her personal life. Married and divorced three times, she was living alone with her Siamese cat when she died of throat cancer in 1970 at the age of 56.

Josephine McKim, who placed fourth in 1932, acted in three films, including a bit part as the little mermaid in *Bride of Frankenstien* (1935).

1936 Berlin C: 33, N: 14, D: 8.10. WR: 1:04.6 (Willemijntje den Ouden)

1. Hendrika "Rie" Mastenbroek	HOL	1:05.9 OR
2. Jeannette Campbell	ARG	1:06.4
3. Gisela Arendt	GER	1:06.6
4. Willemijntje den Ouden	HOL	1:07.6
5. Catherina Wagner	HOL	1:08.1
6. Olive McKean	USA	1:08.4
7. Katherine Rawls	USA	1:08.7

Six months before the Berlin Games, Willy den Ouden swam a phenomenal 1:04.6, setting a world record that would last for 20 years. But in the preliminary rounds of the Olympics, it was her 17-year-old teammate, Rie Mastenbroek, who recorded the fastest times. In the final Mastenbroek was fifth at the 50-meter turn and was still behind Arendt and Campbell (whose parents were Scottish) with only ten meters to go. But her furious finishing strokes gave her a dramatic victory. Over the next five days Mastenbroek won two more gold medals and one silver medal.

1948 London C: 34, N: 14, D: 8.2. WR: 1:04.6 (Willemijntje den Ouden)

1. Greta Andersen	DEN	1:06.3
2. Ann Curtis	USA	1:06.5
3. Marie-Louise Vaessen	HOL	1:07.6
4. Karen-Margrete Harup	DEN	1:08.1
5. Ingegärd Fredin	SWE	1:08.4
6. Irma Schumacher	HOL	1:08.4
7. Elisabeth Ahlgren	SWE	1:08.8
8. Fritze Carstensen	DEN	1:09.1

Greta Andersen got her start in competitive sports when her brother charged his friends to watch 13-year-old Greta wrestle and beat older boys. Several years after her Olympic triumph, Andersen became a professional and swam the English Channel six times, culminating in an England-to-France record of 13 hours 14 minutes, which she set in 1964 at the age of 36.

1952 Helsinki C: 41, N: 19, D: 7.28. WR: 1:04.6 (Willemijntje den Ouden)

1. Katalin Szőke	HUN	1:06.8
2. Johanna Termeulen	HOL	1:07.0
3. Judit Temes	HUN	1:07.1
4. Joan Harrison	SAF	1:07.1
5. Joan Alderson	USA	1:07.1
6. Irma Heijting-Schuhmacher	HOL	1:07.3
7. Marilee Stepan	USA	1:08.0
8. Angela Barnwell	GBR	1:08.6

The 1952 100-meter freestyle race saw a thrilling finish in which the lead changed hands three times in the last ten meters and the first six women finished within two feet of each other. Judit Temes, who had set an Olympic record of 1:05.5 in the first round, pushed to the front after 90 meters, but then Joan Harrison moved ahead. The South African swimmer had the unfortunate experience of finishing out of the medals despite the fact that she appeared to be in first place with only five meters to go. The eventual winner, 16-year-old Katalin Szőke, had been well-known in Hungary for quite some time. Her mother had introduced her to swimming when she was only six months old, and she became known as "Kati, the World's First Waterproof Baby." She was able to stay afloat unaided before she was two years old. Szőke's father, Márton Homonnai, was a member of Hungary's gold medal water polo team in 1932 and 1936 and her husband, Kalman Markovits, was a member of Hungary's gold medal water polo team in 1952 and 1956.

1956 Melboume C 35, N: 16, D: 12.1. WR: 1:02.4 (Lorraine Crapp)

1. Dawn Fraser	AUS	1:02.0 WR
2. Lorraine Crapp	AUS	1:02.3
3. Faith Leech	AUS	1:05.1
4. Joan Rosazza	USA	1:05.2
5. Virginia Grant	CAN	1:05.4
6. Shelley Mann	USA	1:05.6
7. Marrion Roe	NZL	1:05.6
8. Natalie Myburgh	SAF	1:05.8

Dawn Fraser was the youngest of eight children born to working-class parents in Balmain, an industrial suburb of Sydney. On February 21, 1956, Fraser broke Willy den Ouden's 20-year-old world record and upset Lorraine Crapp to win the Australian championship in a time of 1:04.5. Dawn was not that impressed by her feat and told reporters that she could do a lot better. At the time some people may have considered Fraser to be excessively cocky, but it turned out that she was absolutely right. In fact, the quality of women's freestyle swimming was going through a period of rapid change. In the next eight months the 100 meters record was lowered five more times, twice by Cockie Gastelaars of the Netherlands, once more by Dawn Fraser, and, finally, twice in the month of October by Lorraine Crapp.

With Gastelaars out of the Games because of the Dutch Olympic boycott, there was no question that the battle for the gold medal would be between Crapp and Fraser. In the first heat of the first round, Crapp swam a 1:03.4 to lower the Olympic record by over two seconds. In the fifth heat Fraser lowered it further with a 1:02.4. The two Australian teenagers then won their semifinal races, Fraser in 1:03.0 and Crapp in 1:03.1. The day before the women's final, the Australian men had scored a sweep in the 100-meter freestyle, and with Faith Leech recording the third fastest time in each of the first two rounds, it looked as if the Australian women might match the accomplishments of their male counterparts.

The night before the race Dawn Fraser went to bed early, prayed for the strength to win, and then thought through the race, particularly the turn, before she finally dropped off to sleep. Before long she was stricken by a nightmare, which she later described quite graphically in her autobiography, *Below the Surface*. "The gun went off," she began, "but I had honey on my feet and it was hard to pull them away from the starting block. I finally fought free and dived high ... It seemed a long time before I hit the water, and the water wasn't water; it was spaghetti. I fought with it and kept going up and down in the one place, like a yo-yo. The spaghetti strands tangled and tied my feet, and I was swimming with my arms alone. Of course I fouled up the turn and took a few mouthfuls, and I woke up gasping and fighting in a sea of spaghetti."

She must have been somewhat relieved the next day to discover that the pool was in fact filled with water, although she was still incredibly nervous, since she had never before swum in an international meet. Fraser and Crapp pulled away from the others after only 25 meters. Fraser completed the turn first, but Crapp caught up with her with 25 meters to go; the two reached the finish without knowing which one had won. They were so far ahead of the others that they were able to turn around and watch their teammate, Faith Leech, win the battle for third place. After her victory was announced, Dawn Fraser borrowed a ladder from a TV crew and climbed into the stands to share tears of joy with her parents, and to savor a moment which they had all dedicated to Dawn's dead brother, Don, who had introduced her to swimming when she was a child. Starting with that day in Melbourne, Dawn Fraser was the world record holder at 100 meters for the next 15 years.

1960 Rome C: 32, N: 19, D: 8.29. WR: (110 yards) 1:00.2 (Dawn Fraser)

1. Dawn Fraser	AUS	1:01.2 OR
2. S. Christine Von Saltza	USA	1:02.8
3. Natalie Steward	GBR	1:03.1
4. Carolyn Wood	USA	1:03.4
5. Csilla Dobai-Madarász	HUN	1:03.6
6. Erica Terpstra	HOL	1:04.3
7. Cornelia "Cocki" van Engelsdorp Gastelaars	HOL	1:04.7
8. Marie Stewart	CAN	1:05.5

Undefeated at 100 meters since the last Olympics, Dawn Fraser made news by becoming the second woman to defend an Olympic swimming title (the first was Martha Norelius, who won the 400 meters freestyle gold medal in 1924 and 1928). But she made bigger news the following day with her defiance of Australian officials. Thinking she had the day off, she had stayed up late, celebrating. In the morning a routine meeting of the Australian women's swim team turned into a violent argument, which didn't end until Fraser had smacked teammate Jan Andrew in the face with a pillow. Fraser spent the rest of the morning shopping for a wedding dress (which she didn't use) and sightseeing in Rome. She returned to the Olympic Village in time for lunch and had just finished a big plate of spaghetti when Roger Pegram, the manager of the Australian swimming team, approached her and ordered her to get dressed so that she could swim the butterfly leg of the medley relay qualifying heat. Stating that she was stuffed and unprepared, Fraser refused to swim and returned to her room for a nap. Eventually Alva Colquhoun volunteered to take her place, but for the remainder of their stay in Rome, the Australian women punished Fraser by "sending her to Coventry." In others words, they refused to speak a single word to her or to each other as long as Fraser was in the room.

1964 Tokyo C: 44, N: 22, D: 10.13. WR: 58.9 (Dawn Fraser)

1. Dawn Fraser	AUS	59.5 OR
2. Sharon Stouder	USA	59.9
3. Kathleen Ellis	USA	1:00.8
4. Erica Terpstra	HOL	1:01.8
5. Marion Lay	CAN	1:02.2
6. Csilla Dobai-Madarász	HUN	1:02.4
7. Ann Hagberg	SWE	1:02.5
8. Lynette Bell	AUS	1:02.7

On October 27, 1962, Dawn Fraser, swimming in Melbourne, became the first woman to break the one-minute barrier for 100 meters when she covered the longer distance of 110 yards in 59.9 seconds. By February 29, 1964, she had cut her time down to 58.9, and it was almost eight years before anyone would do better. But in March, tragedy struck. She was driving home from a football social with three passengers, her mother, her sister, and a friend, when her car skidded and crashed into a parked truck. Her mother was killed, her sister was knocked unconscious, and Dawn herself spent six weeks with her neck in plaster because of a chipped vertebra.

Seven months later Dawn Fraser was, remarkably, back in form for the Olympics. By this time she was 27 years old, an old-timer by swimming standards who was known to her teammates as "Granny." She had by no means lost her rebellious spirit, however. Ordered by team officials to skip the opening-day ceremonies, she sneaked in anyway and enjoyed the parade and festivities. She tied her own Olympic record of 1:00.6 (set in the 1960 relay) in the first round and then swam a 59.9 in the semifinals. Entering the final she was sure that her only serious challenger would be 15-year-old Sharon Stouder of Glendora, California. Fraser took the lead immediately, but Stouder swam a tremendous race and caught her at the 70-meter mark. Fraser was not to be denied, though, and she called on an extra reserve of strength to pull away once again. Stouder's time of 59.9 made her the first woman other than Dawn Fraser to break one minute. Later Fraser committed the final indiscretion of her career, when she led a middle-of-the-night raid to steal a "souvenir" flag from the entrance to the Emperor's palace. She was arrested, but the charges were dropped and the Emperor gave her the flag as a gift. However, the Australian Swimming Union slapped her with a ten-year suspension which was lifted after four years. The escapade in no way detracted from her status as a national heroine, since most Australians were less interested in her out-of-the-pool antics than they were in the fact that she had become the first Olympic swimmer of either sex to win the same event three times. In 1988, Fraser was elected to the parliament of New South Wales, but was defeated when she ran for reelection.

In 2009 the 71-year-old Fraser was attacked at her home in Queensland, Australia. A man grabbed her throat and threatened to kill her, whereupon Fraser grabbed his hair and ear, kneed him in the groin and made him lie on the ground until the police arrived. As she said later, "I got him with the replacement knee. It's pretty sore today but I have a titanium knee, so it must have hurt him."

1968 Mexico City C: 57, N: 27, D: 10.19. WR: 58.9 (Dawn Fraser)

1. Jan Henne	USA	1:00.0
2. Susan Pedersen	USA	1:00.3
3. Linda Gustavson	USA	1:00.3
4. Marion Lay	CAN	1:00.5
5. Martina Grunert	GDR	1:01.0
6. Alexandra Jackson	GBR	1:01.0
7. Mirjana Šegrt	YUG/SER	1:01.5
8. Judit Turóczy	HUN	1:01.6

1972 Munich C: 46, N: 23, D: 8.29. WR: 58.5 (Shane Gould)

1. Sandra Neilson	USA	58.59 OR
2. Shirley Babashoff	USA	59.02
3. Shane Gould	AUS	59.06
4. Gabriele Wetzko	GDR	59.21
5. Heidemarie Reineck	GER	59.73
6. Andrea Eife	GDR	59.91
7. Magdolna Patoh	HUN	1:00.02
8. Enith Brigitha	HOL	1:00.09

Following the Australian sweeps of 1956, the number of entrants per nation per event was reduced from three to two. This restriction was dropped after 1960, then reinstated after the US sweeps of 1968. It was dropped again in 1976, but reinstated once more in 1984 as a result of the East German sweeps of 1976 and 1980. In 1972 the Australian favorite, Shane Gould, lost her first freestyle race in two years when she was beaten by two Southern California high school students, Sandy Neilson and Shirley Babashoff. Neilson led all the way, but Babashoff had to come from seventh place at the turn to nip Gould for the silver. The one-two victory gave confidence to the US swimmers, who had been wearing T-shirts that read, "All that glitters is not Gould."

1976 Montreal C: 45, N: 25, D: 7.19. WR: 55.73 (Kornelia Ender)

1. Kornelia Ender	GDR	55.65 WR
2. Petra Priemer	GDR	56.49
3. Enith Brigitha	HOL	56.65
4. Kim Peyton	USA	56.81
5. Shirley Babashoff	USA	56.95
6. Claudia Hempel	GDR	56.99
7. Jill Sterkel	USA	57.06
8. Jutta Weber	GER	57.26

At Munich in 1972, the East German women swimmers failed to win a single gold medal, yet four years later in Montreal they were able to finish first in 11 of 13 events. This extraordinary transformation actually began at the 1973 world swimming championships in Belgrade, Yugoslavia, where the East German women appeared wearing the latest model of their skin-tight, semi-see-through Lycra suits. Some people began to raise a protest, until it was revealed that the suits had actually been invented and manufactured in West Germany. By 1976 the Americans in particular were also accusing the East German women of appearing too muscular and masculine, of being shot up with anabolic steroids, and of being "all work and no play" types, who would be unable ever to bear children.

Although there is no doubt that steroids and other drugs were being used by virtually all East German women swimmers, whether they knew it or not, East Germany's success also depended on the enormous emphasis that country placed on legitimate sports science. While US and Soviet scientists were busy conquering space and designing weapons systems, the East Germans were studying athletes—taking blood tests and muscle biopsies, checking oxygen levels, and testing for nutritional needs. The scandalous "Belgrade suits" of 1973 soon became commonplace throughout the world. Likewise, the East Germans were years ahead in studies of such things as lactic acid buildup during training.

Kornelia Ender, 1976
Reaping the benefits—legitimate and otherwise—of the East German sports science machine.

At the age of 13, Kornelia Ender of Bitterfeld won three silver medals at the 1972 Olympics. The following year, in East Berlin, she broke Shane Gould's world record in the 100-meter freestyle. In the three years preceding the 1976 Olympics, Ender broke the world record for that event nine times. Two months before the Montreal Games, the 5-foot 10-inch, 154-pound Ender announced her engagement to backstroker Roland Matthes. She set her tenth 100 meters world record in the Olympic final, her second gold medal of the Games. After the Olympics were over Kornelia Ender was reunited with her grandmother, who had left East Germany in 1961 and moved to Kansas. After the fall of the Berlin Wall, in 1989, Ender revealed that during her competitive career, she was given frequent injections without being told what they contained.

Enith Brigitha of the Netherlands was the first black swimmer to win an Olympic medal.

1980 Moscow C: 30, N: 22, D: 7.21. WR: 55.41 (Barbara Krause)

1. Barbara Krause	GDR	54.79 WR
2. Caren Metschuck	GDR	55.16
3. Ines Diers	GDR	55.65
4. Olga Klevakina	SOV/RUS	57.40
5. Cornelia van Bentum	HOL	57.63
6. Natalya Strunnikova	SOV/RUS	57.83
7. Guylaine Berger	FRA	57.88
8. Agnota Eriksson	SWE	57.90

In 1980 the East German women duplicated their 1976 feat of winning 11 of 13 events. But this time, with the US and Canada out of the Games, they were able to take 15 other medals as well, which meant that they averaged two out of three medals per event.

Like Kornelia Ender, Barbara Krause was introduced to swimming as therapy for orthopedic problems. One of East Germany's leading swimmers in 1976, she was forced to sit out the Montreal Games because team doctors miscalculated her dose of forbidden drugs and she would have failed the doping test at the Olympics. As she followed the competition from her home, she made the decision to continue swimming for four more years so that she could take part in the 1980 Olympics. With only 30 starters in the 100-meter freestyle, the smallest field since 1932, it was decided to skip the semifinals and simply allow the swimmers with the eight fastest times in the heats to qualify directly for the final, a practice which has since been institutionalized. Barbara Krause won the third heat in 54.98 to lower her own world record and to become the first woman to break the 55-second barrier. In the final she was hard-pressed by her East German teammates, but she led all the way and set yet another world record.

1984 Los Angeles C: 45, N: 30, D: 7.29. WR: 54.79 (Barbara Krause)

1. Nancy Hogshead	USA	55.92
1. Carrie Steinseifer	USA	55.92
3. Annemarie Verstappen	HOL	56.08
4. Cornelia van Bentum	HOL	56.43
5. Michele Pearson	AUS	56.83
6. June Croft	GBR	56.90
7. Susanne Schuster	GER	57.11
8. Angela Russel	AUS	58.09

In 1972, when Gunnar Larsson and Tim McKee were both timed at 4:31.98 in the final of the men's 400-meter individual medley, the timing was taken to thousandths of a second and Larsson was declared the winner. Because of possible technical problems, it was decided that hundredths of a second would have to do in the future. So, in 1984, when Hogshead and Steinseifer registered the same time in the 100-meter freestyle, a dead-heat was declared and each was awarded a gold medal, the first double gold medal in Olympic swimming history. In 1981, while a student at Duke University, Nancy Hogshead was brutally raped in an attack that left her with a fractured skull and broken ribs. She used competitive swimming as a means to purge her anger. Three years later Hogshead left Los Angeles with three gold medals and one silver.

1988 Seoul C: 57, N: 35, D: 9.19. WR: 54.73 (Kristin Otto)

1. Kristin Otto	GDR	54.93
2. Zhuang Yong	CHN	55.47
3. Catherine Plewinski	FRA	55.49
4. Manuela Stellmach	GDR	55.52
5. Silvia Poll Ahrens	CRC	55.90
6. Karin Brienesse	HOL	56.15
7. Dara Torres	USA	56.25
8. Cornelia van Bentum	HOL	56.54

Twenty-two-year-old Kristin Otto won the first of her six gold medals.

1992 Barcelona C: 48, N: 34, D: 7.26. WR: 54.48 (Jennifer Thompson)

1. Zhuang Yong	CHN	54.64 OR
2. Jennifer Thompson	USA	54.84
3. Franziska van Almsick	GER	54.94
4. Nicole Haislett	USA	55.19
5. Catherine Plewinski	FRA	55.72
6. Le Jingyi	CHN	55.89
7. Simone Osygus	GER	55.93
8. Karin Brienesse	HOL	56.59

On March 1, 1992, Jenny Thompson, swimming in the qualifying round of the United States Olympic trials, broke Kristin Otto's world record by a quarter of a second. She was the first non-East German to set a world record in the 100-meter freestyle in 20 years. In the qualifying round at the Olympics, she set an Olympic record of 54.69. But in the final it was not Thompson but Seoul silver medalist Zhuang Yong who led from start to finish. Zhuang immediately became the focus of a growing suspicion that the Chinese women swimmers were taking steroids and other prohibited substances. With her deep voice, heavy muscles, and bad acne, she fit the profile of a steroid user. Opposing coaches were particularly upset when Zhuang was not tested for drugs after her victory. FINA's policy was to test randomly only two of the top four finishers, whereas other sports tested all medalists.

Zhuang did pass a doping test five days later, but she was unable to escape international scepticism. The Chinese press attacked American journalists in no uncertain terms. In the words of the *Beijing Daily*: "With the inherent arrogance and bias of hegemonists, they continued to provoke gold-medal winners Zhuang Yong and Qian Hong [100-meter butterfly] by doing their utmost to blacken their feat." Interviewed two years later, Zhuang revealesome of the details of her training regimen, which she likened to "real torture." She trained 364 days a year for eight hours every day. She was not allowed to watch television, date or visit her family. Often she and other members of the Chinese national team would swim while dressed in street clothes including shoes.

1996 Atlanta C: 48, N: 44, D: 7.20. WR: 54.01 (Le Jingyi)

1. Le Jingyi	CHN	54.50 OR
2. Sandra Völker	GER	54.88
3. Angelina Martino	USA	54.93
4. Amy Van Dyken	USA	55.11
5. Franziska van Almsick	GER	55.59
6. Sarah Ryan	AUS	55.85
7. Mette Jacobsen	DEN	56.01
8. Karin Brienesse	HOL	56.12

Angel Martino touched first at 50 meters, but was unable to hold off the finishing charges of Le Jingyi and Sandra Völker. At the 1994 world championships, Chinese swimmers won 12 of the 16 women's races. Suspicions of illegal drug use forced FINA to step up out-of-competition testing and Chinese dominance vanished. At the 1996 Olympics, Le was the only Chinese swimmer to earn a gold medal. After the awards ceremony, Angel Martino immediately presented her bronze medal to a childhood friend, Trisha Henry, who was serving as an Olympic volunteer despite undergoing chemotherapy for ureter cancer.

2000 Sydney C: 54, N: 49, D: 9.21. WR: 53.80 (Inge de Bruijn)

1. Inge de Bruijn	HOL	53.83
2. Therese Alshammar	SWE	54.33
3. Dara Torres	USA	54.43
3. Jenny Thompson	USA	54.43
5. Martina Moravcová	SLV	54.72
6. Karina Muller	SAF	55.19
7. Sumika Minamoto	JPN	55.53
8. Wilma van Hofwegen-van Rijn	HOL	55.58

Inge de Bruijn swam a 53.77 in the semifinals and then pulled away in the second half of the final to win the second of her three gold medals. The two US entrants, Jenny Thompson and Dara Torres, both trained with coach Richard Quick at Stanford University. However they got along so poorly that Quick had to work with them separately at different times. As it happened, Thompson and Torres finished in a deadheat for third place and, at the medal ceremony, were forced to share the bronze medal podium that had been intended for one person. With this race, Jenny Thompson became the first female swimmer to earn nine Olympic medals.

2004 Athens C: 50, N: 44, D: 8.19. WR: 53.66 (Lisbeth "Libby" Lenton)

1. Jodie Henry	AUS	53.84
2. Inge de Bruijn	HOL	54.16
3. Natalie Coughlin	USA	54.40
4. Malia Metella	FRA	54.50
5. Kara Lynn Joyce	USA	54.54
6. Nery Mantey Niangkouara	GRE	54.81
7. Martina Moravcová	SLV	55.12
8. Yelena Popchenko	BLR	55.24

Nineteen-year-old Libby Lenton caused a sensation at the Australian Olympic Trials on March 31, 2004, when, in the semifinals, she broke the world record that Inge de Bruijn had set at the 2000 Olympics. Yet in the final of that meet, Lenton was beaten by 20-year-old Jodie Henry. In Athens, it was de Bruijn who led the qualifying round with a 54.43, but in the semifinals, Henry set a world record of 53.52. The surprise of the semis was Lenton failing to qualify for the final by nine hundredths of a second. In the final, Henry was the slowest out of the blocks, and trailed in fifth place at the turn before charging past de Bruijn to take the second of three gold medals she would earn at the 2004 Games.

In the opening heat of the preliminary round, Gloria Koussihouede of Benin finished in the leisurely time of 1:30.96. This was the slowest time recorded at the Olympics since Ireland's Marguerite Dockrell swam a 1:31.6 . . . in 1928.

2008 Beijing C: 48, N: 41, D: 8.15. WR: 52.88 (Libby Trickett)

1. Britta Steffen	GER	53.12 OR
2. Lisbeth "Libby" Trickett (Lenton)	AUS	53.16
3. Natalie Coughlin	USA	53.39
4. Hanna-Maria Seppälä	FIN	53.97
5. Jeanette Ottesen	DEN	54.06
6. Zhu Yingwen	CHN	54.21
6. Marleen Veldhuis	HOL	54.21
8. Francesca Halsall	GBR	54.29

Reigning world champion and world record holder Libby Trickett nearly failed to make the final, mistiming her swim in her semifinal race to finish ninth overall when only the top eight qualified. She had already left for the warm-down pool when she learned that Chinese swimmer Pang Jiaying had been disqualified for starting too soon, opening up one more qualifying spot.

Swimming in lane 8, alongside previous world record holder Britta Steffen, Trickett was under the world record pace at the turn. However, she could not keep it up, and Steffen reeled her in during the last lap.

200-METER FREESTYLE

1896–1964 not held

1968 Mexico City C: 39, N: 23, D: 10.22. WR: 2:06.7 (Deborah Meyer)

1. Deborah Meyer	USA	2:10.5 OR
2. Jan Henne	USA	2:11.0
3. Jane Barkman	USA	2:11.2
4. Gabriele Wetzko	GDR	2:12.3
5. Mirjana Šegrt	YUG/SER	2:13.3
6. Claude Mandonnaud	FRA	2:14.9
7. Lynette Bell	AUS	2:15.1
8. Ol'ga Kozičová	CZE	2:16.0

This was Debbie Meyer's second gold medal of the 1968 Olympics.

1972 Munich C: 33, N: 17, D: 9.1. WR: 2:05.21 (Shirley Babashoff)

1. Shane Gould	AUS	2:03.56 WR
2. Shirley Babashoff	USA	2:04.33
3. Keena Rothhammer	USA	2:04.92
4. Ann Marshall	USA	2:05.45
5. Andrea Eife	GDR	2:06.27
6. Hansje Bunschoten	HOL	2:08.40
7. Anthonia "Anke" Rijnders	HOL	2:09.41
8. Karin Tuelling	GDR	2:11.70

Between July 1971 and January 1972, Shane Gould set world records in all five internationally recognized freestyle distances: the 100, 200, 400, 800, and 1500 meters. In the 1972 Olympics, the 15-year-old phenomenon swam 12 races in eight days, logging 4200 meters of competitive swimming. In the 200 meters final Gould built up a large lead in the first 100 meters. World record holder Shirley Babashoff almost cut the gap in half, but could get no further. Shane Gould closed out the Munich Olympics with three gold medals, one silver, and one bronze. A year later, tired of the sacrifices required of a champion swimmer, Gould announced her retirement at the age of 16 and disappeared from public life for 25 years. At 18 she married a controlling and ultimately violent man seven years her senior and moved to a farm in western Australia where she raised four children. Her only competitive activities involved horses and, in 1994 and 1995, she won the Western Australia State Open Ploughing Competition. When she expressed an interest in entering the Australian Masters' Swimming Championship, her husband hit her and knocked her unconscious. They divorced in 1997 and, by the time of the 2000 Sydney Olympics, Gould had reconciled herself to her role as one of Australia's sporting icons.

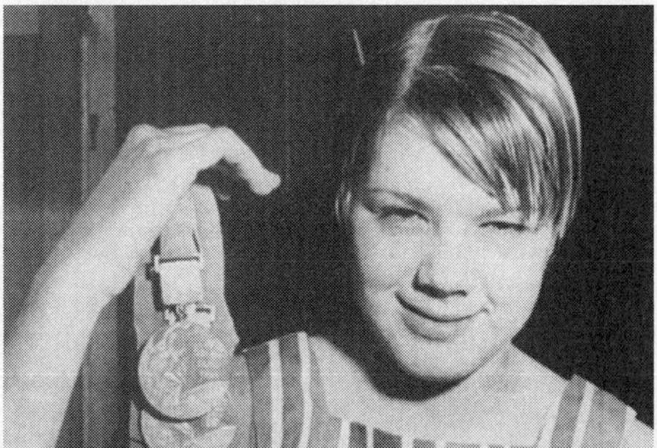

Debbie Meyer, 1968
Sweet 16 and bedecked with three gold medals.

1976 Montreal C: 40, N: 22, D: 7.22. WR: 1:59.78 (Kornelia Ender)

1. Kornelia Ender	GDR	1:59.26 WR
2. Shirley Babashoff	USA	2:01.22
3. Enith Brigitha	HOL	2:01.40
4. Annelies Maas	HOL	2:02.56
5. Gail Amundrud	CAN	2:03.32
6. Jennifer Hooker	USA	2:04.20
7. Claudia Hempel	GDR	2:04.61
8. Irina Vlasova	SOV/RUS	2:05.63

Kornelia Ender equaled her own world record to win the 100-meter butterfly, then returned to face Shirley Babashoff in the very next race, the 200-meter freestyle. Babashoff had defeated Ender in the 200 at the 1975 world championships, but Ender had chopped almost three seconds off her time in the following year. Babashoff took the early lead and held it for the first 100 meters, but Ender moved ahead over the next length of the pool and won going away to earn her second gold medal in 27 minutes. She thus became the first female swimmer to win four gold medals at one Olympics.

1980 Moscow C: 22, N: 14, D: 7.24. WR: 1:58.23 (Cynthia Woodhead)

1. Barbara Krause	GDR	1:58.33 OR
2. Ines Diers	GDR	1:59.64
3. Carmela Schmidt	GDR	2:01.44
4. Olga Klevakina	SOV/RUS	2:02.29
5. Regina "Reggie" de Jong	HOL	2:02.76
6. June Croft	GBR	2:03.15
7. Natalya Strunnikova	SOV/RUS	2:03.74
8. Irma Aksyonova	SOV/RUS	2:04.00

Krause staged a phenomenal comeback to win her second gold medal. Trailing Ines Diers by over a second after 150 meters, she swam the last 50 meters in 28.47 to win by a comfortable margin. Eight days later, world record holder Cynthia Woodhead won the US Outdoor National championship in 1:59.44.

1984 Los Angeles C: 36, N: 25, D: 7.30. WR: 1:57.75 (Kristin Otto)

1. Mary Wayte	USA	1:59.23
2. Cynthia "Sippy" Woodhead	USA	1:59.50
3. Annemarie Verstappen	HOL	1:59.69
4. Michele Pearson	AUS	1:59.79
5. Cornelia van Bentum	HOL	2:00.59
6. June Croft	GBR	2:00.64
7. Ina Beyermann	GER	2:01.89
8. Anna McVann	AUS	2:02.87

On May 23, at the East German trials, Kristin Otto had set a world record of 1:57.75. She was followed by Birgit Meineke in 1:58.75.

1988 Seoul C: 44, N: 29, D: 9.21. WR: 1:57.55 (Heike Friedrich)

1. Heike Friedrich	GDR	1:57.65 OR
2. Silvia Poll Ahrens	CRC	1:58.67
3. Manuela Stellmach	GDR	1:59.01
4. Mary Wayte	USA	1:59.04
5. Natalya Trefilova	SOV/RUS	1:59.24
6. Mitzi Kremer	USA	2:00.23
7. Stephanie Ortwig	GER	2:00.73
8. Cecile Prunier	FRA	2:02.88

The prohibitive favorite, world champion and world record holder Heike Friedrich, let Wayte and Kremer set the pace for the first half of the race, then stormed ahead for an easy bodylength victory over Silvia Poll, Costa Rica's first Olympic medallist. The 6-foot 3½-inch (1.91-meter), blonde-haired Poll was the daughter of German-born parents who had moved to Costa Rica from Nicaragua when she was 8 years old.

1992 Barcelona C: 37, N: 26, D: 7.27. WR: 1:57.55 (Heike Friedrich)

1. Nicole Haislett	USA	1:57.90
2. Franziska van Almsick	GER	1:58.00
3. Kerstin Kielgass	GER	1:59.67
4. Catherine Plewinski	FRA	1:59.88
5. Luminița Liliana Dobrescu	ROM	2:00.48
6. Suzu Chiba	JPN	2:00.64
7. Olha Kirichenko	UKR	2:00.90
8. Lu Bin	CHN	2:02.10

The final was a straight duel between 19-year-old Nicole Haislett of St. Petersburg, Florida, and 14-year-old Franziska van Almsick, who had led the qualifying round with a time of 1:57.90. In the final, van Almsick went out very fast for the first 50 meters, then calmed down without letting up pressure. Haislett, swimming beside her, noticed that the inexperienced German girl was swimming right next to the lane line. Haislett moved into her wake and saved precious energy drafting off her for much of the race. Haislett pulled even with van Almsick ten meters from the finish and then edged ahead to win by about six inches.

1996 Atlanta C: 42, N: 35, D: 7.21. WR: 1:56.78 (Franziska van Almsick)

1. Claudia Poll Ahrens	CRC	1:58.16
2. Franziska van Almsick	GER	1:58.57
3. Dagmar Hase	GER	1:59.56
4. Trina Jackson	USA	1:59.57
5. Susan O'Neill	AUS	1:59.87
6. Cristina Teuscher	USA	2:00.79
7. Julia Greville	AUS	2:01.46
8. Luminița Liliana Dobrescu	ROM	2:01.63

One of the last products of the East German sports system, Franziska van Almsick's swimming potential was discovered when she was five years old. Fortunately she was only eleven when the Berlin Wall fell and so she was untainted by revelations regarding East German doping practices. When she was fourteen years old, van Almsick earned four medals (2 silver, 2 bronze) at the 1992 Olympics. In Germany, with her youthful good looks, she skyrocketed to major celebrity status. Soon she signed millions of dollars worth of sponsorship agreements and replaced Steffi Graf in Opel commercials. She even hosted her own television talk show. Her private life was followed as closely as those of movie stars. Many Germans were scandalized when, at the age of fifteen, van Almsick acquired a 25-year-old boyfriend, fellow swimmer Steffen Zesner.

Van Almsick's coronation as international queen of swimming was supposed to come at the 1994 world championships in Rome, but she was upstaged by the apparently drug-enhanced Chinese squad. However, the big Franzi story in Rome was the surprising developments involving her speciality: the 200-meter freestyle. Van Almsick attempted to conserve her energy in the preliminary round, but miscalculated and placed ninth—with only the top eight advancing to the final. The eighth-fastest qualifier was van Almsick's German teammate, veteran Dagmar Hase. Hase withdrew from the final, claiming she wanted to save herself for the 400-meter freestyle. Although she denied that she had been bought off by van Almsick's sponsors, Hase was given a free two-week vacation by Lufthansa, the German airline. Whatever Hase's motivations, van Almsick took full advantage of her reprieve. Not only did she win the gold medal, she also broke Heike Friedrich's 8-year-old world record. By a bizarre coincidence, Dagmar Hase placed ninth in the 400-meter preliminaries while fellow German Jana

Henke placed eighth. Henke did not withdraw in favor of Hase.

A year later, at the 1995 European championships, van Almsick again placed ninth in the 200 meters preliminaries. This time she was relegated to the B final, which she won in a time that was 2.85 seconds faster than the winner of the A final, fellow German Kerstin Kielgass. Van Almsick did manage to win five gold medals at the European championships.

In Atlanta, van Almsick took no chances, leading the qualifying round with a time of 1:59.40. So both she and Dagmar Hase made it to the 1996 Olympic final, but there they faced a formidable challenge in the person of Claudia Poll, whose sister, Silvia, had earned Costa Rica's first Olympic medal in 1988, also at 200 meters. At 1.90 meters (6 feet 2¾ inches), Poll was by far the tallest competitior in the event and was, in fact, the tallest female swimmer at the Olympics. Van Almsick took the early lead. Poll caught her after 80 meters and slowly but steadily increased her lead to win by about 27 centimeters (11 inches). Poll was mobbed by the small but emotional Costa Rican contingent that included her sister, her mother and two aunts who had traveled from Germany to support their niece. But this celebration was nothing to compare to the one that took place when Costa Rica's first Olympic champion returned to San José. The entire nation shut down and an estimated 1,500,000 people—almost half of Costa Rica's population—thronged the streets to honor their heroine.

Claudia Poll did cause one minor controversy. She competed while wearing three corporate logos on her swimming cap, including one for Pepsi, rival of the official Olympic sponsor Coca-Cola. At the medal ceremony she unzipped her suit to reveal a t-shirt bearing the same three logos. This was a clear breach of the Olympic Charter, but Poll was let off with a warning. Poll won two bronze medals at the 2000 Olympics, but then, in February 2002, she tested positive for steroids and was handed a four-year suspension, which was later reduced to two years. She competed in the 2004 Olympics, but failed to reach the final.

2000 Sydney C: 40, N: 35, D: 9.19. WR: 1:56.78 (Franziska van Almsick)

1. Susan O'Neill	AUS	1:58.24
2. Martina Moravcová	SLV	1:58.32
3. Claudia Poll	CRC	1:58.81
4. Nadyezhda Chemezova	RUS	1:58.86
4. Kerstin Kielgass	GER	1:58.86
6. Nataliya Baranovskaya	BLR	1:59.28
7. Camelia Potec	ROM	1:59.46
8. Wang Luna	CHN	1:59.55

Extremely popular with the hometown crowd, Susie O'Neill was competing in her third Olympics and had already won four medals before 2000. In Sydney she swam in seven events, of which the 200-meter freestyle was the second. Martina Moravcová took the early lead in the final, but O'Neill moved ahead after 75 meters and increased her lead until the final turn. However, in the last lap, O'Neill began to fade and the field closed in on her. Nonetheless, she was able to hold on and beat Moravcová by about 13 centimeters.

2004 Athens C: 41, N: 36, D: 8.17. WR: 1:56.64 (Franziska van Almsick)

1. Camelia Potec	ROM	1:58.03
2. Federica Pellegrini	ITA	1:58.22
3. Solenne Figues	FRA	1:58.45
4. Paulina Barzycka	POL	1:58.62
5. Franziska van Almsick	GER	1:58.88
6. Dana Vollmer	USA	1:58.98
7. Pang Jiaying	CHN	1:59.16
8. Josefin Lillhage	SWE	1:59.20

Swimming in lane four, 16-year-old Federica Pellegrini held off Solenne Figues in lane five in the closing meters, but failed to notice European Champion Camelia Potec move ahead in lane one to take the gold. Potec had finished eleventh in the qualifying round and was the second-slowest qualifier for the final.

2008 Beijing C: 46, N: 37, D: 8.13. WR: 1:55.52 (Laure Manaudou)

1. Federica Pellegrini	ITA	1:54.82	WR
2. Sara Isakovič	SLO	1:54.97	
3. Pang Jiaying	CHN	1:55.05	
4. Katherine Hoff	USA	1:55.78	
5. Camelia Potec	ROM	1:56.87	
6. Caitlin McClatchey	GBR	1:57.65	
7. Bronte Barratt	AUS	1:57.83	
7. Ophélie Etienne	FRA	1:57.83	

Defending Olympic silver medalist Federica Pellegrini set a world record of 1:55.45 in her first-round heat, surpassing the Olympic records set by Pang Jiaying and Sara Isakovič in the two previous heats.

Swimming in lane 3, Pellegrini took the lead in the first 100 meters of the final and held off Isakovič and Pang to finish in 1:54.82; all three medalists beat the new world record time. After the race Pellegrini revealed that she had worn two swimsuits . . . to prevent embarrassment if the first one had broken. The win came a week after her 20th birthday.

400-METER FREESTYLE

1896–1912 not held

1920 Antwerp C: 16, N: 7, D: 8.28. WR (300 meters): 4:43.6 (Ethelda Bleibtrey)

(300 Meters)

1. Ethelda Bleibtrey	USA	4:34.0 WR
2. Margaret Woodbridge	USA	4:42.8
3. Frances Schroth	USA	4:52.0
4. Constance Jeans	GBR	4:52.4
5. Eleanor Uhl	USA	—
6. Jane Gylling	SWE	—
7. Violet Walrond	NZL	—

Bleibtrey set a world record of 4:41.4 in her preliminary heat and then set another record in the final. Between August 23 and August 29, Bleibtrey swam in five races in three events and broke the world record in every one.

1924 Paris C: 18, N: 8, D: 7.15. WR: 5:53.2 (Gertrude Ederle)

1. Martha Norelius	USA	6:02.2 OR
2. Helen Wainwright	USA	6:03.8
3. Gertrude Ederle	USA	6:04.8
4. Doris Molesworth	GBR	6:25.4
DNF: Gwitha Shand(NZL)		
6. Irene Tanner(GBR)		

Fifteen-year-old, Stockholm-born Martha Norelius pulled away from Wainwright and Ederle in the final 15 meters. In the 1924 Olympics five swimmers took part in each final, while sixth place was awarded to the non-finalist who recorded the fastest time in the semi-finals.

1928 Amsterdam C: 14, N: 9, D: 8.6. WR: 5:49.6 (Martha Norelius)

1. Martha Norelius	USA	5:42.8 WR
2. Maria Braun	HOL	5:57.8
3. Josephine McKim	USA	6:00.2
4. Sarah "Cissie" Stewart	GBR	6:07.0
5. Frederica van der Goes	SAF	6:07.2
6. Irene Tanner	GBR	6:11.6

Norelius swam a 5:45.4 opening heat to break her own world record, and defended her title by winning the final easily, again in world record time. Norelius dominated women's swimming from 1922 to 1929. Her father represented Sweden in gymnastics in 1912. Norelius later married Canada's 1928 double sculls silver medalist, Joe Wright.

1932 Los Angeles C: 14, N: 9, D: 8.13. WR: 5:31.0 (Helene Madison)

1. Helene Madison	USA	5:28.5 WR
2. Lenore Kight	USA	5:28.6
3. Jennie Maakal	SAF	5:47.3
4. M. Joyce Cooper	GBR	5:49.7
5. Yvonne Godard	FRA	5:54.4
6. Norene Forbes	USA	6:06.0

Helene Madison and Lenore Kight pulled away from the others immediately and went through most of the race with Madison one foot ahead. Kight moved into the lead at 325 meters, but Madison drew even at the final turn. In the end, Madison was able to touch the last wall inches ahead of Kight and thus win her third gold medal. That evening, Madison celebrated by dancing at the Coconut Grove with Clark Gable.

1936 Berlin C: 20, N: 10, D: 8.15. WR: 5:16.0 (Willemijntje den Ouden)

1. Hendrika "Rie" Mastenbroek	HOL	5:26.4 OR
2. Ragnhild Hveger	DEN	5:27.5
3. Lenore Wingard (Kight)	USA	5:29.0
4. Mary Lou Petty	USA	5:32.2
5. Piedade Coutinho Azevedo	BRA	5:35.2
6. Kazue Koijma	JPN	5:43.1
7. Grete Frederiksen	DEN	5:45.0
8. Catharine Wagner	HOL	5:46.0

On race day, fifteen-year-old Ragnhild Hveger received a box of chocolates from her supporters. She shared them with the other swimmers, but passed by seventeen-year-old Rie Mastenbroek. Mastenbroek took this as a deliberate snub and vowed to take revenge. Hveger led throughout the final, but Mastenbroek fought back in the final 25 meters to gain a one-meter victory and win her third gold medal. During her final sprint, Mastenbroek thought, "This is better than a piece of chocolate." She also earned a silver medal in the 100-meter backstroke. Mastenbroek was the first woman to win four medals in one Olympics. She donated one of her gold medals to raise funds for the construction of a village for disabled people. Between 1936 and 1942 Hveger broke 42 individual world records. From 1938 until 1953 she was the official world record holder in the 200, 400, 800, and 1500 meters. She retired in 1945, but came back in 1952 to finish fifth in the 400 in the Helsinki Olympics at the age of 31.

1948 London C: 19, N: 11, D: 8.7. WR: 5:00.1 (Ragnhild Hveger)

1. Ann Curtis	USA	5:17.8 OR
2. Karen-Margrete Harup	DEN	5:21.2
3. Catherine Gibson	GBR	5:22.5
4. Fernande Caroen	BEL	5:25.3
5. Brenda Helser	USA	5:26.0
6. Piedade Silva Tavares	BRA	5:29.4
7. Fritze Carstensen	DEN	5:29.4
8. Nancy Lees	USA	5:32.9

1952 Helsinki C: 34, N: 17, D: 8.2. WR: 5:00.1 (Ragnhild Hveger)

1. Valéria Gyenge	HUN	5:12.1 OR
2. Éva Novák	HUN	5:13.7
3. Evelyn Kawamoto	USA	5:14.6
4. Carolyn Green	USA	5:16.5
5. Ragnhild Andersen-Hveger	DEN	5:16.9
6. Éva Székely	HUN	5:17.9
7. Ana María Schultz	ARG	5:24.0
8. Greta Andersen	DEN	5:27.0

Ragnhild Hveger's 1940 world record was still in the books when, as Ragnhild Andersen-Hveger, she prepared for the start of the 1952 Olympic 400 meters final, the same event in which she had won a silver medal 16 years earlier. In Helsinki she led for the first 275 meters, but couldn't keep up the pace.

1956 Melbourne C: 26, N: 13, D: 12.7. WR: 4:47.2 (Lorraine Crapp)

1. Lorraine Crapp	AUS	4:54.6 OR
2. Dawn Fraser	AUS	5:02.5
3. Sylvia Ruuska	USA	5:07.1
4. Marley Shriver	USA	5:12.9
5. Rypszima Székely	HUN	5:14.2
6. Sandra Morgan	AUS	5:14.3
7. Héda Frost	FRA	5:15.4
8. Valéria Gyenge	HUN	5:21.0

On August 25, 1956, 17-year-old Lorraine Crapp became the first woman to swim 400 meters in less than five minutes when she broke Ragnhild Hveger's 16-year-old world record with a time of 4:50.8. In that same race she also bettered the world records for 200 meters, 220 yards, and 440 yards. Two and a half months later at the Olympics, Dawn Fraser kept up with her teammate for 100 meters, but then Crapp drew clear to win by almost eight seconds.

1960 Rome C: 22, N: 13. D: 9.1. WR: 4:44.5 (S. Christine Von Saltza)

1. S. Christine Von Saltza	USA	4:50.6 OR
2. Jane Cederqvist	SWE	4:53.9
3. Catharina "Tineke" Lagerberg	HOL	4:56.9
4. Ilsa Konrads	AUS	4:57.9
5. Dawn Fraser	AUS	4:58.5
6. A. Nancy Rae	GBR	4:59.7
7. Cornelia Schimmel	HOL	5:02.3
8. Bibbi Segerstrom	SWE	5:02.4

Sixteen-year-old Chris Von Saltza moved quickly into the lead, built up a five-second gap after 300 meters, and was too far ahead to be affected by the late surge of Jane Cederqvist. Von Saltza had won the first of her three gold medals. In her post-athletic life, Von Saltza spent 25 years as a systems engineer for IBM before starting her own consulting firm specializing in midrange computer performance. Third- and fourth-place finishers Lagerberg and Konrads were the world record holders at 800 meters and 1500 meters, respectively, neither of which was an Olympic distance at the time.

Chris Von Saltza, 1960
Three gold medals in her only Olympics.

1964 Tokyo C: 30, N: 16, D: 10.18. WR: 4:39.5 (Marilyn Ramenofsky)

1. Virginia Duenkel	USA	4:43.3 OR
2. Marilyn Ramenofsky	USA	4:44.6
3. Terri Stickles	USA	4:47.2
4. Dawn Fraser	AUS	4:47.6
5. Jane Hughes	CAN	4:50.9
6. Elizabeth Long	GBR	4:52.0
7. Kim Herford	AUS	4:52.9
8. Gun Lilja	SWE	4:53.0

Seventeen-year-old Ginny Duenkel of West Orange, New Jersey, was favored to win a gold medal in the 100-meter backstroke, but with less than ten meters to go she made a critical error: she looked to the side to check the position of her opponents. The finish was so close that the mistake was the difference between her third-place finish and second or even first. Fortunately for Duenkel, she had another chance four days later. In the 400-meter freestyle she took the lead after 175 meters and pulled away, slowly but steadily.

1968 Mexico City C: 30, N: 17, D: 10.20. WR: 4:24.5 (Debbie Meyer)

1. Debbie Meyer	USA	4:31.8 OR
2. Linda Gustavson	USA	4:35.5
3. Karen Moras	AUS	4:37.0
4. Pamela Kruse	USA	4:37.2
5. Gabriele Wetzko	GDR	4:40.2
6. María Teresa Ramírez Gómez	MEX	4:42.2
7. Angela Coughlan	CAN	4:51.9
8. Ingrid Morris	SWE	4:53.8

At the US Olympic trials, 16-year-old Debbie Meyer set world records in the 200, 400, and 800. The rarefied air of Mexico City prevented her from duplicating that feat, but she did win all three races, starting with the 400 meters.

1972 Munich C: 29, N: 17, D: 8.30. WR: 4:21.2 (Shane Gould)

1. Shane Gould	AUS	4:19.04 WR
2. Novella Calligaris	ITA	4:22.44
3. Gudrun Wegner	GDR	4:23.11
4. Shirley Babashoff	USA	4:23.59
5. Jenny Wylie	USA	4:24.07
6. Keena Rothhammer	USA	4:24.22
7. Hansje Bunschoten	HOL	4:29.70
8. Anthonia "Anke" Rijnders	HOL	4:31.51

Shane Gould came back from her loss in the 100 meters the previous day to win her second gold medal.

1976 Montreal C: 34, N: 22, D: 7.20. WR: 4:11.69 (Barbara Krause)

1. Petra Thümer	GDR	4:09.89 WR
2. Shirley Babashoff	USA	4:10.46
3. Shannon Smith	CAN	4:14.60
4. Rebecca Perrott	NZL	4:14.76
5. Kathryn Heddy	USA	4:15.50
6. Brenda Borgh	USA	4:17.43
7. Annelies Maas	HOL	4:17.44
8. Sabine Kahle	GDR	4:20.42

On June 3, 1976, Barbara Krause broke Shirley Babashoff's world record by over three seconds. However, two weeks later she suffered an attack of angina and had to be dropped from the East German squad. Fifteen-year-old Petra Thümer, who had finished second to Krause in the East German championships, rose to the occasion at the Olympics. She built up most of her lead during the second 100 meters and then fought off Babashoff's attempts to close the gap. Thümer's time would have won her a silver medal in the 1968 men's 400-meter race and a gold in 1964.

1980 Moscow C: 19, N: 12, D: 7.22. WR: 4:06.28 (Tracey Wickham)

1. Ines Diers	GDR	4:08.76 OR
2. Petra Schneider	GDR	4:09.16
3. Carmela Schmidt	GDR	4:10.86
4. Michelle Ford	AUS	4:11.65
5. Irina Aksyonova	SOV/RUS	4:14.40
6. Annelies Maas	HOL	4:15.79
7. Regina "Reggie" de Jong	HOL	4:15.95
8. Olga Klevakina	SOV/RUS	4:19.18

This was one race that was definitely affected by the anti-Soviet boycott. Missing was world record holder Tracey Wickham of Australia as well as Kim Linehan and Cynthia "Sippy" Woodhead of the United States, who clocked 4:07.77 and 4:08.17, respectively, at the US national championships on July 31. In their absence, the East Germans had a field day. Petra Schneider led for over 300 meters, but 16-year-old Ines Diers finished strongly to win. Before the Moscow Games were over Diers had won five medals: two gold, two silver and one bronze.

1984 Los Angeles C: 25, N: 17, D: 7.31. WR: 4:06.28 (Tracey Wickham)

1. Tiffany Cohen	USA	4:07.10 OR
2. Sarah Hardcastle	GBR	4:10.27
3. June Croft	GBR	4:11.49
4. Kimberly Linehan	USA	4:12.26
5. Anna McVann	AUS	4:13.95
6. Jolande van der Meer	HOL	4:16.05
7. Birgit Kowalczik	GER	4:16.33
8. Julie Daigneault	CAN	4:16.41

Eighteen-year-old Tiffany Cohen led from start to finish and won by five meters, registering the fastest women's 400-meter time since Tracey Wickham set her world record in 1978.

1988 Seoul C: 30, N: 21, D: 9.22. WR: 4:05.45 (Janet Evans)

1. Janet Evans	USA	4:03.85 WR
2. Heike Friedrich	GDR	4:05.94
3. Anke Möhring	GDR	4:06.62
4. Tami Bruce	USA	4:08.16
5. Janelle Elford	AUS	4:10.64
6. Isabelle Arnould	BEL	4:11.73
7. Stephanie Ortwig	GER	4:13.05
8. Natalya Trefilova	SOV/RUS	4:13.92

When Heike Friedrich was only 15 years old, she won five gold medals at the 1985 European championships. The following year she added four golds at the world championships. By the time of the 1988 Olympics, she was still undefeated in major international competition, having won 13 consecutive finals. She added a fourteenth victory in Seoul when she finished first in the 200-meter freestyle. But the following night she finally met her match in Janet Evans, a 17-year-old student at appropriately named El Dorado High School in Placentia, California.

Despite her small size and unorthodox windmill stroke, Evans was a natural-born swimmer. She was swimming laps at the age of two, literally before she was out of diapers. By the time she was 3 years old she had already mastered the butterfly and breaststroke. During her early years of competition other swimmers snickered and laughed at her diminutive stature, but the laughter stopped in 1987 when, at the age of 15, the 95-pound Evans broke the world record at 800 meters and 1500 meters, the 1500 record having stood the onslaught of larger swimmers for more than seven and a half years and the 800 for almost nine. On December 20, 1987, she eclipsed Tracey Wickham's nine-year-old record at 400 meters.

In the Olympic final, Evans took the early lead, but Friedrich and East German teammate Anke Möhring, both strong finishers, stayed right by her shoulder. Friedrich, who had planned to win the race with a world record of 4:05, pushed the pace in the third 100, leaving Möhring behind. But Evans refused to be passed. However, with 100 meters to go, her lead was down to 1 foot (30.5 centimeters).

Then, surprisingly, it was Evans who pulled away in the final two laps by swimming the second half of the race faster than she had the first half. It was the first "negative split" of her career and it earned her the second of her three gold medals.

1992 Barcelona C: 33, N: 24, D: 7.28. WR: 4:03.85 (Janet Evans)

1. Dagmar Hase	GER	4:07.18
2. Janet Evans	USA	4:07.37
3. Hayley Lewis	AUS	4:11.22
4. Erika Hansen	USA	4:11.50
5. Kerstin Kielgass	GER	4:11.52
6. Isabelle Arnould	BEL	4:13.75
7. Malin Nilsson	SWE	4:14.10
8. Suzu Chiba	JPN	4:15.71

Janet Evans entered the Olympics with a six-year win streak covering 18 national and international meets. Dagmar Hase, on the other hand, was a backstroke specialist who entered the 400-meter freestyle at the German Olympics trials in May because it was held after her other races were already completed. She won in a personal best of 4:12.60. The Olympics would be the first major meet at which she swam the 400 free. In her mind, Hase conceded the gold medal to Evans, but thought herself capable of a silver or bronze. Evans set a hard pace, hoping to burn off the rest of the field, but Hase was able to keep within striking distance. By 300 meters, Evans had managed to stretch her lead to a body length. Hase crept closer, executed an excellent final turn, and then powered ahead over the last lap. She caught Evans with 15 or 20 meters to go and won by a foot (30 centimeters).

1996 Atlanta C: 39, N: 34, D: 7.22. WR: 4:03.85 (Janet Evans)

1. Michelle Smith	IRL	4:07.25
2. Dagmar Hase	GER	4:08.30
3. Kirsten Vlieghuis	HOL	4:08.70
4. Kerstin Kielgass	GER	4:09.83
5. Claudia Poll Ahrens	CRC	4:10.00
6. Carla Louise Geurts	HOL	4:10.06
7. Eri Yamanoi	JPN	4:11.68
8. Cristina Teuscher	USA	4:14.21

If someone had predicted in 1993 that Irish swimmer Michelle Smith would win more gold medals in individual events at the next Olympics than any athlete from any nation in any sport, they would have been considered crazy. To begin with, no swimmer from Ireland had ever won an Olympic medal. In fact, Ireland did not have a single Olympic-size pool. Second, no woman from Ireland had ever won a medal in any sport. Third, no Irish athlete had ever won more than one gold medal at a single Olympics. And, finally, Smith herself had compiled a mediocre record at the Olympics. In 1988, when she entered four events, her best placing was seventeenth in the 200-meter back stroke. At the 1992 Olympics she swam in three events. Her highlight was a 26th place in the 400-meter individual medley. And yet, at the 1996 Atlanta Games, Michelle Smith came away with three gold medals and one bronze. The story of Smith's rapid transformation from anonymity to celebrity is a painful and contentious one.

One fact is not in dispute: Smith was a hard worker. Determined to fulfill her potential, she left Ireland and trained instead in Canada and Texas. At the Barcelona Olympics, her performances were unimpressive, but it was there that she met the man who would become her husband and coach: Dutch discus thrower Erik de Bruin. De Bruin was a discus thrower who had represented the Netherlands at the 1984 and 1988 Olympics. In 1993 de Bruin became the subject of controversy when he failed a doping test that showed excessive levels of testosterone as well as traces of human chorionic gonadatropine, a hormone produced by pregnant women. De Bruin contested the test result and the Dutch athletics federation supported him. But the IAAF overruled the Dutch and de Bruin was suspended for four years, effectively ending his career. In 1993 de Bruin also gave an interview to the Dutch newspaper *De Volkskrant* in which he said, "Who says doping is unethical? Who decides what is unethical? Sport is by definition dishonest. Some people are naturally gifted; others have to work hard. Some people are not going to make it without extra help." The interview would later come back to haunt both de Bruin and Smith.

In 1993, Michelle Smith was ranked 90th in the

world in the 400-meter individual medley. The following year, under de Bruin's tutelage, she knocked 8.63 seconds off her personal best and her ranking jumped to seventeenth. Even more impressive, at the 1994 world championships, she qualified for a major final for the first time in her career and finished fifth in the 200-meter butterfly.

It was in 1995 that insiders in the swimming community began to be suspicious of Smith's performances. At the European championships, she won gold medals in the 200-meter butterfly and the 200-meter individual medley and finished second in the 400-meter individual medley. In the longer event she dropped her time by another 5.08 seconds. This sudden improvement late in her career, combined with de Bruin's drug suspension, raised eyebrows. De Bruin made matters worse by sneaking into the drug testing area using the credentials of a Belgian coach and filing protests about the testing procedure. It would later come out that FINA, the international swimming federation, had expressed concern to the Irish Amateur Swimming Association about their inability, through most of 1995, to track down Smith and administer out-of-competition drug tests.

Michelle Smith's first event at the Atlanta Olympics was the 400-meter individual medley. She cut another 3.63 seconds off her personal record—bringing her three-year improvement to 17.34 seconds—and won the gold medal handily. Her victory caused a sensation back in Ireland and overnight Smith, who spoke Gaelic fluently, became the most popular female athlete in the country.

The Irish team handbook for the 1996 Olympics listed Smith as being entered in four events: the two individual medley races and the two butterfly events. When the official entry lists were published on July 19, a fifth event had been added: the 200-meter freestyle. But after Smith's victory the next day in the 400 individual medley, it was announced that she would also enter the 400-meter freestyle. The United States, supported by Germany and the Netherlands, protested her entry, contending that Smith's qualifying time had been made July 6, one day after the deadline for qualifying times. There was no disputing the fact, but Irish officials claimed the late race was the result of a mistake made by the Atlanta Committee for the Olympic Games (ACOG), the hapless group in charge of organizing the 1996 Olympics. It seems that ACOG sent out a directive that new entries and changes could be made as late as July 20. FINA caught this error and sent letters to all swimming federations informing them that the real date was July 5. FINA rejected Michelle Smith's entry in the 400-meter freestyle; however the Irish team appealed the verdict to the Court of Arbirtation for Sport (CAS). The CAS is an international organization created to resolve just such disputes. In fact, the Michelle Smith case was the very first Olympic dispute to be referred to the CAS. The Court of Arbitration for Sport ruled in favor of Smith. It was only after the Olympics that it was revealed that the date of Smith's race was only one of several irregularities. It turned out that the "race," which was held in Florida, was actually an unsanctioned time trial; that electronic touch pads were not used; and that de Bruin coached Smith from poolside throughout her swim.

Another thing that disturbed Smith's opponents was the qualifying time itself: 4:08.64, the fastest time of the year and a whopping 17.54 seconds faster that Smith's previous recorded best in the 400 free. Although Smith would later claim that she once clocked a 4:21 in a short course (25-meter) race—in 1988—the fact remained that, at the age of 26, she had never competed internationally in the 400-meter freestyle.

Smith recorded the second fastest time of the preliminary round (4:09.00), only one one-hundredth of a second slower than leader Kerstin Kielgass. The controversy surrounding Smith's entry was complicated by the fact that the US favorite in the event, triple gold medalist Janet Evans, placed ninth in the preliminaries and missed qualifying for the final. Had Smith not been in the race, Evans would have qualified. Repeatedly pressed by journalists to comment on drug allegations against Smith, Evans refused to support the allegations but finally conceded, "I have heard that question posed in the last few weeks about this particular swimmer . . . It's a topic of conversation on the pool deck." Out of this innocuous statement, Smith supporters would, for the next two years, portray Evans as a vicious, bad-spirited, sore loser. All allegations of drug use would be portrayed as a conspiracy on the part of the US media.

In the final, Carla Louise Geurts led for the first 200 meters. Then Smith threw in a 61.10 third 100 and stormed into a large lead. Defending champion Dagmar Hase closed the gap in the final 50 meters, but Smith scored a clear victory. Two nights later she won a third gold medal in the 200-meter individual medley and later she added a bronze in the 200-meter butterfly to complete what Smith called "the best week of my life."

When Michelle Smith flew back to Dublin, she was met at the airport by Ireland's president, Mary Robinson and a local folk group and sang a song composed in her honor: "The Great Michelle, our golden girl, the princess of our tide." In Smith's home village of

Rathcoole, southwest of Dublin, the celebration, which had already been going on for days, reached a level that was greater than the one for the Pope's visit in 1979.

Smith should have been basking in universal glory, but the suspicions of drug use would not go away and she found it difficult to land the sponsorship contracts that would normally be offered a triple gold medalist. When word leaked in early 1997 that drug testers were again complaining that Smith was not available, the controversy flared again. The situation became so tense that Irish journalists and swimming officials who expressed doubts about the legitimacy of Smith's performances were attacked for being anti-patriotic "begrudgers."

Smith won two gold medals and two silvers at the 1997 European championships, but that would be the last of her career highlights. At dawn on January 10, 1998, two drug testers, Al and Kay Guy, showed up at the home of Michelle and Erik de Bruin in County Kilkenny. They were told that Michelle could not submit to a drug test because she had to meet someone at the airport. The Guys explained that that would not be a problem: they would accompany her to the airport and whenever she was ready to produce a urine sample Kay Guy would accompany her. Eventually the de Bruins agreed to have Smith produce at home. When she was finally ready, Kay Guy, following normal procedures, joined Smith while she sat on the toilet. However, because Smith was wearing a bulky sweater, Guy could not see what she was doing. The sample was sealed and labeled and taken away. When it was analyzed by a laboratory in Barcelona, it was shown to contain a level of alcohol that would be fatal if consumed by a human. FINA concluded that the sample had been manipulated, that alcohol had been added as a masking agent, and they suspended Smith for four years. Smith appealed the ban to the Court of Arbitration for Sport. On June 8, 1999, the Court ruled that the lethal level of alcohol in Smith's urine sample could only have been added by Smith herself and upheld the ban, ending Smith's career. The Irish public split 50/50 for and against Smith while the swimmers who finished behind Smith in Atlanta were left to wonder what might have been.

One of the challenges to the legitimacy of Smith's performances had been that she was too old to compete naturally in the 400-meter freestyle, an event that has traditionally been won by younger swimmers. For the record, coincidentally, two other women in the 1996 Olympic final, Dagmar Hase and Kerstin Kielgass, were born in the same month as Smith: December 1969. What raised suspicion about Smith was not that she was 26 years old, but that, unlike Hase and Kielgass, she suddenly began improving at the age of 24.

2000 Sydney C: 39, N: 31, D: 9.17. WR: 4:03.85 (Janet Evans)

1. Brooke Bennett	USA	4:05.80
2. Diana Munz	USA	4:07.07
3. Claudia Poll	CRC	4:07.83
4. Janelle Atkinson	JAM	4:08.79
5. Nadyezhda Chemezova	RUS	4:10.37
6. Hannah Stockbauer	GER	4:10.38
7. Carla Geurts	HOL	4:12.36
8. Hua Chen	CHN	4:13.11

Diana Munz edged Brooke Bennett at the US Olympic trials to cap a 13-month comeback after fracturing her vertebrae when the VW bug in which she was a passenger was hit by a truck. In the Olympic final, Bennett sought to overcome her lack of a finishing kick by taking the early lead and grinding out a steady pace for the entire race. Her strategy worked perfectly as she bettered her personal record by moving up from fourth to second in the last 150 meters. Janelle Atkinson was the first Jamaican swimmer to qualify for an Olympic final.

2004 Athens C: 38, N: 31, D: 8.15. WR: 4:03.85 (Janet Evans)

1. Laure Manaudou	FRA	4:05.34
2. Otylia Jędrzejczak	POL	4:05.84
3. Kaitlin Sandeno	USA	4:06.19
4. Camelia Potec	ROM	4:06.34
5. Ai Shibata	JPN	4:07.51
6. Sachiko Yamada	JPN	4:10.91
7. Linda Mackenzie	AUS	4:10.92
8. Rebecca Cooke	GBR	4:11.35

European Champion Laure Manaudou recorded the fastest qualifying time and led throughout the final, followed closely by Otylia Jędrzejczak, who was unable to close the distance. Manaudou was the first French woman to win a swimming gold medal. Manaudou went on to win both the 2005 and 2007 world championships, and caused a stir in 2007 when she decided to move to Turin, Italy, to be with her boyfriend, Italian swimmer Luca Marin. A few weeks later she was injured in a freak accident after a meet in Rome, breaking a bone in her left foot when two of her Italian teammates threw her into the pool as a prank.

2008 Beijing C: 41, N: 34, D: 8.11. WR: 4:01.53 (Federica Pellegrini)

1. Rebecca Adlington	GBR	4:03.22
2. Katherine Hoff	USA	4:03.29
3. Joanne Jackson	GBR	4:03.52
4. Coralie Balmy	FRA	4:03.60
5. Federica Pellegrini	ITA	4:04.56
6. Camelia Potec	ROM	4:04.66
7. Bronte Barratt	AUS	4:05.05
8. Laure Manaudou	FRA	4:11.26

The favorites in the event seemed to be defending Olympic champion and two-time reigning world champion Laure Manaudou and reigning European champion and world record holder Federica Pellegrini. The two had been embroiled in a tabloid scandal over the previous two years involving their romantic relationships with Italian swimmer Luca Marin.

Manaudou led for the first 150 meters, but then faded, while 19-year-old Katie Hoff moved into the lead. At the 300-meter mark Hoff was still in front by more than a second, followed by Coralie Balmy, Pellegrini and another 19-year-old, Becky Adlington. Adlington, an 800-meter specialist, caught Hoff, and the two swam the final lap neck and neck, with Adlington touching just ahead for the victory. She was the first female British swimming gold medalist since Anita Lonsbrough won the 200-meter breaststroke in 1960.

800-METER FREESTYLE

1896–1964 not held

1968 Mexico City C: 26, N: 16, D: 10.24. WR: 9.10.4 (Deborah Meyer)

1. Deborah Meyer	USA	9:24.0 OR
2. Pamela Kruse	USA	9:35.7
3. María Teresa Ramírez Gómez	MEX	9:38.5
4. Karen Moras	AUS	9:38.6
5. Patricia Caretto	USA	9:51.3
6. Angela Coughlan	CAN	9:56.4
7. Denise Langford	AUS	9:56.7
8. Laura Vaca Hernández	MEX	10.02.5

Debbie Meyer was never really challenged as she became the first swimmer to win three individual gold medals in one Olympics. The only excitement of the race came when 15-year-old Maria Teresa Ramírez came from behind to nip Karen Moras for the bronze medal, bringing joy to the Mexican crowd.

1972 Munich C: 36, N: 19, D: 9.3. WR: 8:53.83 (Jo Harshbarger)

1. Keena Rothhammer	USA	8:53.68 WR
2. Shane Gould	AUS	8:56.39
3. Novella Calligaris	ITA	8:57.46
4. Ann Simmons	USA	8:57.62
5. Gudrun Wegner	GDR	8:58.89
6. Jo Harshbarger	USA	9:01.21
7. Hansje Bunschoten	HOL	9:16.69
8. Narelle Moras	AUS	9:19.06

Calligaris led for 500 meters, but then Rothhammer, fourth at the halfway mark, took the lead and pulled away.

1976 Montreal C: 19, N: 11, D: 7.25. WR: 8:39.63 (Shirley Babashoff)

1. Petra Thümer	GDR	8:37.14 WR
2. Shirley Babashoff	USA	8:37.59
3. Wendy Weinberg	USA	8:42.60
4. Rosemary Milgate	AUS	8:47.21
5. Nicole Kramer	USA	8:47.33
6. Shannon Smith	CAN	8:48.15
7. Regina Jäger	GDR	8:50.40
8. Jennifer Turrall	AUS	8:52.88

On June 4, 1976, Petra Thümer set a world record of 8:40.68, but 17 days later Shirley Babashoff bettered that time by a second. This was Babashoff's last chance for an individual gold medal so she withdrew from the 400-meter individual medley in order to save her strength for her long-distance showdown with Thümer, who had beaten her at 400 meters five days earlier. Shannon Smith led for 300 meters, but then Thümer took over. Babashoff trailed right behind her, but every time she drew closer, Thümer would draw away again. In the end Thümer had her second world record and Babashoff had her sixth Olympic silver medal.

There is no question that Petra Thümer, like all East German swimmers in 1976, had been taking anabolic steroids. If she and the other East Germans hadn't, they would have been kicked off the team. Of all the foreign athletes who suffered because of the East German cheating, none was affected as greatly as Shirley Babashoff. Babashoff left Montreal with one gold medal (in the freestyle relay) and four silver medals. If the East Germans had been disqualified,

Shirley Babashoff, 1976

Cornering the market on silver with five second-place finishes in individual events and one more in a relay in her two Olympics.

Babashoff would have won five gold medals, a feat that has still never been achieved in the Summer Olympics by an American woman.

1980 Moscow C: 14, N: 9, D: 7.27. WR: 8:24.62 (Tracey Wickham)

1. Michelle Ford	AUS	8:28.90 OR
2. Ines Diers	GDR	8:32.55
3. Heike Dähne	GDR	8:33.48
4. Irina Aksyonova	SOV/RUS	8:38.05
5. Oksana Komissarova	SOV/RUS	8:42.04
6. Pascale Verbauwen	BEL	8:44.84
7. Ines Geissler	GDR	8:45.28
8. Olena Ivanova	SOV/UKR	8:46.45

Eighteen-year-old Michelle Ford took the lead after 250 meters and pulled away to break the East German gold medal monopoly. Missing were world record holder Tracey Wickham of Australia and US champion Kim Linehan whose best time was 8:24.70 and who clocked an 8:27.86 two days after the Olympic final.

1984 Los Angeles C: 20, N: 14, D: 8.3. WR: 8:24.62 (Tracey Wickham)

1. Tiffany Cohen	USA	8:24.95 OR
2. Michele Richardson	USA	8:30.73
3. Sarah Hardcastle	GBR	8:32.60
4. Anna McVann	AUS	8:37.94
5. Carla Lasi	ITA	8:42.45
6. Jolande van der Meer	HOL	8:42.86
7. Monica Olmi	ITA	8:47.32
8. Karen Ward	CAN	8:48.12

Challenged only by the memory of Tracey Wickham's six-year-old world record, Tiffany Cohen added the 800 gold to the one she had won in the 400 three days earlier.

1988 Seoul C: 27, N: 19, D: 9.24. WR: 8:17.12 (Janet Evans)

1. Janet Evans	USA	8:20.20 OR
2. Astrid Strauss	GDR	8:22.09
3. Julie McDonald	AUS	8:22.93
4. Anke Möhring	GDR	8:23.09
5. Tami Bruce	USA	8:30.86
6. Janelle Elford	AUS	8:30.94
7. Isabelle Arnould	BEL	8:37.47
8. Antoaneta Strumenlieva	BUL	8:41.05

As they stood on the blocks waiting for the start of the final, Janet Evans and her East German rivals presented an odd sight. Astrid Strauss measured 6 feet 1½ inches (1.87 meters) and weighed 181 pounds (82 kilograms). Teammate Anke Möhring was 5 feet 11¼ inches (1.81 meters) and 152 pounds (69 kilograms). Between them stood the favorite, Evans, 5 feet 5¼ inches (1.66 meters) and a mere 101 pounds (45.8 kilograms). Her main challengers were thought to be Möhring, the former world record holder, and Julie McDonald, the fastest qualifier and the last person to beat Evans, a year earlier in Brisbane. However, it was Strauss who gave Evans the best run for her money, improving her personal best by 4.43 seconds. But even she was 10 feet (2.74 meters) behind at the finish, as Janet Evans won the last of her three Seoul gold medals.

1992 Barcelona C: 25, N: 18, D: 7.30. WR: 8:16.22 (Janet Evans)

1. Janet Evans	USA	8:25.52
2. Hayley Lewis	AUS	8:30.34
3. Jana Henke	GER	8:30.99
4. Philippa Langrell	NZL	8:35.57
5. Irene Dalby	NOR	8:37.12
6. Olga Šplíchalová	CZE	8:37.66
7. Erika Hansen	USA	8:39.25
8. Isabelle Arnould	BEL	8:41.86

Janet Evans had not lost an 800-meter race in five years. Although her time was slower than in the last Olympics, her margin of victory was larger. She led from start to finish and won by eight meters.

1996 Atlanta C: 28, N: 22, D: 7.25. WR: 8:16.22 (Janet Evans)

1. Brooke Bennett	USA	8:27.89
2. Dagmar Hase	GER	8:29.91
3. Kirsten Vlieghuis	HOL	8:30.84
4. Kerstin Kielgass	GER	8:31.06
5. Irene Dalby	NOR	8:38.34
6. Janet Evans	USA	8:38.91
7. Carla Louise Geurts	HOL	8:40.43
8. Sarah Hardcastle	GBR	8:41.75

On July 31, 1995, Janet Evans' eight-year win streak at 800 meters was finally snapped when she placed fourth at the US Summer Nationals. The winner was 15-year-old Brooke Bennett of Plant City, Florida, who used to keep a poster of Evans in her bedroom. A year later, in the Olympic final, Bennett moved into a clear lead after 70 meters and steadily pulled away to win by two seconds.

2000 Sydney C: 26, N: 21, D: 9.22. WR: 8:16.22 (Janet Evans)

1. Brooke Bennett	USA	8:19.67 OR
2. Yana Klochkova	UKR	8:22.66
3. Kaitlin Sandeno	USA	8:24.29
4. Flavia Rigamonti	SWI	8:25.91
5. Hannah Stockbauer	GER	8:30.11
6. Hua Chen	CHN	8:30.58
7. Jana Henke	GER	8:31.97
8. Sachiko Yamada	JPN	8:37.39

One month before the Olympics, Brooke Bennett won the US Olympic trials in 8:23.92, the fastest time in the world in eleven years. Bennett opened her Sydney performance by earning a gold medal in the 400-meter freestyle. Five days later, she successfully defended her 800-meter title by taking the lead in the first lap and increasing it steadily for the rest of the race. Yana Klochkova won the silver medal to add to the two gold medals she had already won in the individual medley events.

2004 Athens C: 29, N: 24, D: 8.20. WR: 8:16.22 (Janet Evans)

1. Ai Shibata	JPN	8:24.54
2. Laure Manaudou	FRA	8:24.96
3. Diana Munz	USA	8:26.61
4. Kalyn Keller	USA	8:26.97
5. Erika Villaecija García	SPA	8:29.04
6. Rebecca Cooke	GBR	8:29.37
7. Jana Henke	GER	8:33.95
8. Simona Păduraru	ROM	8:37.02

There was such a turnover in the 800-meter freestyle that none of the eight finalists at the 2003 world championships made it to the Olympic final one year later. Five days after winning the 400-meter freestyle, Laure Manaudou was the favorite in the 800 free and set the pace in the final, opening a body length lead in the first 100 meters. Ai Shibata gradually chipped away at Manaudou's lead, finally cathching her after 700 meters and then edging ahead in the final length to take gold. Shibata was the first female Japanese freestyle medalist.

2008 Beijing C: 35, N: 29, D: 8.16. WR: 8:16.22 (Janet Evans)

1. Rebecca Adlington	GBR	8:14.10 WR
2. Alessia Filippi	ITA	8:20.23
3. Lotte Friis	DEN	8:23.03
4. Camelia Potec	ROM	8:23.11
5. Li Xuanxu	CHN	8:26.34
6. Kylie Palmer	AUS	8:26.39
7. Yelena Sokolova	RUS	8:29.79
8. Cassandra Patten	GBR	8:32.35

Five days after winning gold in the 400-meter freestyle, 19-year-old Becky Adlington pulled away in the 800-meter freestyle final, finishing more than six seconds ahead of reigning European champion Alessia Filippi. Her time, 8:14.10, broke the 19-year-old world record, set by Janet Evans in 1989, by more than two seconds. Adlington was the first British swimmer to win more than one gold medal at a single Olympics since Henry Taylor won three in 1908.

100-METER BACKSTROKE

1896–1920 not held

1924 Paris C: 10, N: 5, D: 7.20. WR: 1:22.4 (Sybil Bauer)

1. Sybil Bauer	USA	1:23.2 OR
2. Phyllis Harding	GBR	1:27.4
3. Aileen Riggin	USA	1:28.2
4. Florence Chambers	USA	1:30.8
5. Jarmila Müllerová	CZE	1:31.2
6. Ellen King	GBR	

Sybil Bauer of Chicago was the world record holder in all women's backstroke events when she completely outclassed her opposition at the Paris Olympics. She was still undefeated when she died of intestinal cancer on January 31, 1927, at the age of 23. Bronze medalist Aileen Riggin became the first person to win medals in both swimming and diving.

1928 Amsterdam C: 12, N: 7, D: 8.11 WR: 1:22.0 (Willy van den Turk)

1. Maria Braun	HOL	1:22.0
2. Ellen King	GBR	1:22.2
3. M. Joyce Cooper	GBR	1:22.8
4. Marion Gilman	USA	1:24.2
5. Eleanor Holm	USA	1:24.4
5. Lisa Lindstrom	USA	1:24.4
7. Elizabeth Stockley	NZL	1:25.8

Ellen King of Scotland equaled the world record in the first heat. In the second heat, 17-year-old local favorite Zus Braun broke the world record with a time of 1:21.6.

1932 Los Angeles C: 12, N: 7, D: 8.11. WR: 1:18.2 (Eleanor Holm)

1. Eleanor Holm	USA	1:19.4
2. Philomena "Bonny" Mealing	AUS	1:21.3
3. E. Valerie Davies	GBR	1:22.5
4. Phyllis Harding	GBR	1:22.6
5. Joan McSheehy	USA	1:23.2
6. M. Joyce Cooper	GBR	1:23.4

DNS: Maria Phillipsen-Braun (HOL)

Defending champion Zus Braun qualified for the final, but received an insect bite that developed into blood poisoning and forced her to withdraw—at least that was the official story. She claimed that the day before the final she was standing on her seat watching Buster Crabbe win the 400-meter freestyle when someone stabbed her in the left leg and by the next day she had such a high fever that she could not compete. Braun speculated that she had been attacked by gamblers who had bet against her. In Braun's absence, eighteen-year-old Eleanor Holm, the daughter of a Brooklyn fire captain, inched ahead after 25 meters, held off the challenge of Bonny Mealing, and pulled away in the last 25 meters. Holm had set an Olympic record of 1:18.3 in her qualifying heat.

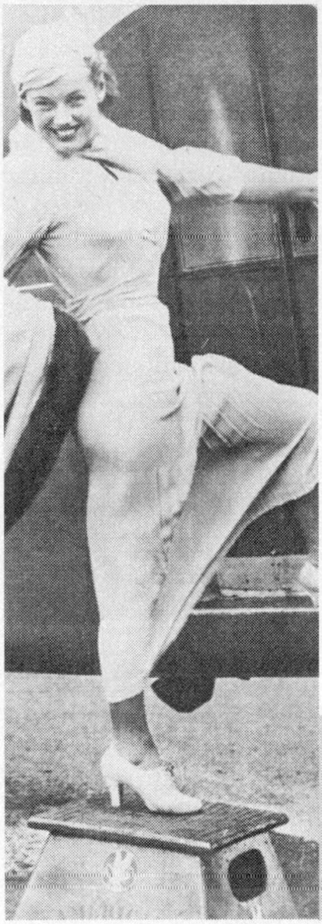

Eleanor Holm
Holm won the 100-meter backstroke in 1932 and was on her way to Berlin to defend her title when she was overtaken by a major scandal.

1936 Berlin C: 21, N: 12, D: 8.13. WR: 1:15.8 (Hendrika "Rie" Mastenbroek)

1. Dina "Nida" Senff	HOL	1:18.9
2. Hendrika "Rie" Mastenbroek	HOL	1:19.2
3. Alice Bridges	USA	1:19.4
4. Edith Motridge	USA	1:19.6
5. Tove Bruunstrøm Madsen	DEN	1:20.4
6. Lorna Frampton	GBR	1:20.6
7. Phyllis Harding	GBR	1:21.5

Life had been very full for Eleanor Holm between Olympics. While in Hollywood she had met singer and orchestra leader Art Jarrett, who was a fellow alumnus of Erasmus Hall High School back in Brooklyn. Five months later, on September 2, 1933, they were married in Beverly Hills. For the next three years Holm led a very active social life and joined her husband singing in nightclubs. But she always kept in shape. In 1935 she set a world record for the 100-meter backstroke, and in 1936 she also broke the record for 200 meters. On February 27, 1936, her 100-meter record was broken by Rie Mastenbroek. However, when Eleanor Holm boarded the S.S. *Manhattan* on July 15 for the nine-day voyage to Germany, along with about 350 other members of the US Olympic team, she was still the favorite to defend her championship, and there was little hint of the outrageous scandal that was about to bring an abrupt end to her amateur career.

Now on her way to her third Olympics, married and used to a flashy and independent life-style, Eleanor did not take too well to the third-class accommodations and strict regulations that had been arranged by the American Olympic Committee. She felt more comfortable in the first-class section, which happened to be where the American officials were staying, as well as the press. On Friday, July 17, Mr. Maybaum of the United States Lines, which owned the S.S. *Manhattan,* invited Eleanor to attend a party he was throwing that night in the A-deck bar and lounge. She was the only team member invited. Quick to accept, she stayed up until six a.m., matching drinks with the sportswriters. She had to be helped back to her cabin.

The next day there was much joking and wisecracking among the non-Olympic first-class passengers about the "training techniques" of the US team. Embarrassed US Olympic officials issued Holm a warning, but she was defiant and continued to drink in public off and on for the next few days. When advised by friends to moderate her behavior, she reminded them that she was "free, white, and 22."

On July 23, while the ship made a prolonged stopover in Cherbourg, France, with the passengers confined to ship, Holm attended an afternoon and evening champagne party. At about ten-thirty p.m. the official team chaperone, Ada Taylor Sackett, discovered Eleanor staggering along the deck, accompanied by a young man. After returning to her cabin, which she shared with two other swimmers, Holm stuck her head out the porthole and began shouting obscenities. Her roommates, Olive McKean and Mary Lou Petty, pulled her back inside and convinced her to go to sleep. At midnight Mrs. Sackett returned with the team doctor, J. Hubert Lawson, and the ship's doctor. Dr. Lawson found Holm "in a deep slumber which approached a state of coma." His diagnosis: "Acute alcoholism." The physical examination failed to awaken her. Members of the American Olympic Committee met to discuss the charges against Holm, which also included shooting craps. (She never denied the charges and later boasted that she had won "a couple hundred dollars" just before the final party.)

At six a.m. team manager Herbert Holm (no relation) woke Eleanor and informed her that the American Olympic Committee had voted to remove her from the team. She went to the stateroom of Avery

Brundage, president of the AOC, and pleaded her case through a crack in the door. It was to no avail. More than half of the US team members signed a petition asking for Eleanor's reinstatement and the press split was about the same.

The news of Eleanor Holm's expulsion caused a sensation when the S.S. *Manhattan* docked in Hamburg, particularly when word began to spread about the details of the case. When her final appeal was denied, Holm lashed back at the American officials, pointing out that they had held cocktail parties every night and that they had ignored the athletes. Joseph Goebbels' Nazi propaganda periodical, *Der Angriff,* took the side of the AOC, editorializing, "She probably didn't believe they could disqualify her, but she thought wrong. It wasn't herself who mattered. It was the others—and discipline. For that no sacrifice is too great, no matter how many tears are shed."

Eleanor Holm didn't get to participate in the 1936 Olympics, but that didn't prevent her from having a good time in Berlin. The Nazis quickly forgave her lack of discipline and entertained her as a special visitor. "I had such fun!" she told *Sports Illustrated* 36 years later. "I enjoyed the parties, the *Heil Hitlers,* the uniforms, the flags . . . Göring was fun. He had a good personality. So did the one with the club foot [Goebbels]. Göring gave me a sterling-silver swastika. I had a mold made of it and I put a diamond Star of David in the middle." Holm issued a public challenge to whoever won the Olympic championship to face her in a swim-off, but when the day came for the final of the women's 100-meter backstroke, Eleanor Holm, who hadn't been beaten in seven years, was sitting in the stands instead of swimming in the pool.

As it happened, the competition, although it did not get as much press attention as all that had preceded it, was not without its own element of sensation. Sixteen-year-old Nida Senff surprised the experts by recording the fastest preliminary times, 1:16.6. and 1:17.1. In the final she was away quickly and had opened up a two-meter lead by the halfway mark. But she missed touching the wall and had to go back. This dropped her to sixth place out of seven, but she sped on, regained the lead with 20 meters to go, and won with a very little bit to spare. She might have lost anyway had not world record holder Rie Mastenbroek become entangled in the lane ropes. Of the four events which Mastenbroek entered in 1936, this was the only one she didn't win.

As for Eleanor Holm, she became more popular than ever. In 1938 she divorced Art Jarrett and also acted in her only film, co-starring as Jane in *Tarzan's Revenge* with 1936 decathlon champion Glenn Morris. The following year she married impresario Billy Rose. The pair divorced in 1954 following a spicy case, which became known as "The War of the Roses" and which was filled with titillating accusations of sexual "misbehavior" on both sides. She later became an interior decorator and retired to Miami Beach. However she never lost her feistiness. In 1999, Holm was invited to the White House for a reception in honor of Women in Sports. Standing beside President Bill Clinton, who had just survived a sex-related scandal of his own, the 85-year-old Holm looked up at him and said, "Mr. President, you're really a good-looking dude."

1948 London C: 24, N: 16, D: 8.5. WR: 1:10.9 (Cornelia Kint)

1. Karen-Margrete Harup	DEN	1:14.4 OR
2. Suzanne Zimmerman	USA	1:16.0
3. Judith Davies	AUS	1:16.7
4. Ilona Novák	HUN	1:18.4
5. Hendrika van der Horst	HOL	1:18.8
6. Dirkje van Ekris	HOL	1:18.9
7. Muriel Mellon	USA	1:19.0
8. Greta Galliard	HOL	1:19.1

Eliminated in the semifinals was French swimmer and journalist Monique Berlioux who later became Director of the International Olympic Committee.

1952 Helsinki C: 20, N: 14, D: 7.31. WR: 1:10.9 (Cornelia Kint)

1. Joan Harrison	SAF	1:14.3
2. Geertje Wielema	HOL	1:14.5
3. Jean Stewart	NZL	1:15.8
4. Johanna de Korte	HOL	1:15.8
5. Barbara Stark	USA	1:16.2
6. Gertrud Herrbruck	GER	1:18.0
7. Margaret McDowell	GBR	1:18.4
DISQ: Hendrika van der Hurst (HOL)		

Joan Harrison's upset victory was so unexpected that Alex Bulley, the South African team manager, fainted from excitement when he realized she had won. Wielema set an Olympic record of 1:13.8 in her opening heat.

1956 Melbourne C: 23, N: 14, D: 12.5. WR: 1:10.9 (Cornelia Kint)

1. Judith Grinham	GBR	1:12.9 OR
2. Carin Cone	USA	1:12.9
3. Margaret Edwards	GBR	1:13.1
4. Helga Schmidt	GER	1:13.4
5. Maureen Murphy	USA	1:14.1
6. Julie Hoyle	GBR	1:14.3
7. Sara Barber	CAN	1:14.3
8. Gerganyia Beckitt	AUS	1:14.7

Seventeen-year-old Judy Grinham, of Neasden, got off to a bad start and was only fifth at the turn. She caught

Cone with ten meters left and thought, "If I can just touch first, it wouldn't matter if I dropped dead immediately afterwards." Grinham did touch first, but she also survived.

1960 Rome C: 30, N: 19, D: 9.3. WR: 1:09.2 (Lynn Burke)

1. Lynn Burke	USA	1:09.3 OR
2. Natalie Steward	GBR	1:10.8
3. Satoko Tanaka	JPN	1:11.4
4. Laura Ranwell	SAF	1:11.4
6. Rose-Marie "Rosy" Piacentini	FRA	1:11.4
6. Sylvia Lewis	GBR	1:11.8
7. Maria van Velsen	HOL	1:12.1
8. Nadine Delache	FRA	1:12.4

On September 22, 1939, Holland's Cor Kint swam a 1:10.9 to slash two seconds off the world record. Kint's time remained unapproachable for almost 21 years, until the summer of 1960. On July 10, Ria van Velsen equaled Kint's record. A week later Lynn Burke finally broke it. At the US Olympic trials in August she set two more world records.

1964 Tokyo C: 31, N: 17, D: 10.14. WR: 1:08.3 (Virginia Duenkel)

1. Kathleen Ferguson	USA	1:07.7 WR
2. Christine Caron	FRA	1:07.9
3. Virginia Duenkel	USA	1:08.0
4. Satoko Tanaka	JPN	1:08.6
5. Nina Harmar	USA	1:09.4
6. Linda Ludgrove	GBR	1:09.5
7. Eileen Weir	CAN	1:09.8
8. Jill Norfolk	GBR	1:11.2

The 1964 final matched six past and present world record holders at various backstroke distances: Caron, Duenkel, Tanaka, Ferguson, Ludgrove, and Norfolk. Sixteen-year-old Kiki Caron had set a 100 meters world record of 1:08.6 on June 14, but that was broken by Ginny Duenkel on September 28. In the Olympic final, however, it was 16-year-old 200 meters record holder Cathy Ferguson who edged ahead just before the finish to gain her second world record and her first gold medal.

1968 Mexico City C: 40, N: 23, D: 10.23. WR: 1:06.4 (Karen Muir)

1. Kaye Hall	USA	1:06.2 WR
2. Elaine Tanner	CAN	1:06.7
3. Jane Swagerty	USA	1:08.1
4. Kendis Moore	USA	1:08.3
5. Andrea Gyarmati	HUN	1:09.1
6. Lynette Watson	AUS	1:09.1
7. Sylvie Canet	FRA	1:09.3
8. Glenda Stirling	NZL	1:10.6

Sixteen-year-old world record holder Karen Muir was excluded from Olympic competition because she was from South Africa, which had been banned from the Olympics since 1964 because of its government's racial policies. In Muir's absence, the favorite was 17-year-old Elaine Tanner of Vancouver, who had the fastest times of the qualifying rounds, setting Olympic records of 1:07.6 and 1:07.4 in the heats and semifinals. But as Canada's main gold medal hope, she carried a heavy burden. "Usually, before a race, she explained afterward, "you're concentrating on strategy, the other swimmers, the race. But at Mexico all I could think about was the twenty million people who were expecting me to win." Another finalist was 17-year-old Kaye Hall of Tacoma, Washington, who had been beaten by Tanner several times and as recently as the semifinals the previous day. Tanner and Hall swam neck and neck for 50 meters. but Hall surged ahead at the turn, and even though Tanner produced her best time ever, she couldn't catch the inspired American teenager.

1972 Munich C: 37, N: 21, D: 9.2. WR: 1:05.6 (Karen Muir)

1. Melissa Belote	USA	1:05.78 OR
2. Andrea Gyarmati	HUN	1:06:26
3. Susan Atwood	USA	1:06.34
4. Karen Moe	USA	1:06.69
5. Wendy Cook	CAN	1:06.70
6. Enith Brigitha	HOL	1:06.82
7. Christine Herbst	GDR	1:07.27
8. Silke Pielen	GER	1:07.36

This was the first of Melissa Belote's three gold medals. She had orginally turned to the backstroke because it was the only stroke that kept the chlorine out of her eyes. Belote attributed her fine performance in Munich to the fact that she felt relaxed and unpressured since she was not expected to win.

1976 Montreal C: 34, N: 21, D: 7.21. WR: 1:01.51 (Ulrike Richter)

1. Ulrike Richter	GDR	1:01.83 OR
2. Birgit Treiber	GDR	1:03.41
3. Nancy Garapick	CAN	1:03.71
4. Wendy Hogg-Cook	CAN	1:03.93
5. Cheryl Gibson	CAN	1:05.16
6. Nadiya Stavko	SOV/UKR	1:05.19
7. Antje Stille	GDR	1:05.30
8. Diane Edelijn	HOL	1:05.53

The order of finish for the first four places was exactly the same as it had been a year earlier at the 1975 world championships in Cali, Colombia. Seventeen-year-old Ulrike Richter had broken the 100 meters world record nine times in the three years preceding the Montreal Olympics.

1980 Moscow C: 26, N: 18, D: 7.23. WR: 1:01.51 (Ulrike Richter)

1. Rica Reinisch	GDR	1:00.86 WR
2. Ina Kleber	GDR	1:02.07
3. Petra Riedel	GDR	1:02.64
4. Carmen Bunaciu	ROM	1:03.81
5. Carine Verbauwen	BEL	1:03.82
6. Larissa Gorchakova	SOV/RUS	1:03.87
7. Monique Bosga	HOL	1:04.47
8. Manuela Carosi	ITA	1:05.10

Fifteen-year-old Rica Reinisch had quite a successful week at the Moscow Olympics. First she equaled Ulrike Richter's four-year-old 100-meter backstroke world record of 1:01.51 while swimming the opening leg for East Germany's victorious medley relay team. Two days later she broke Richter's record by clocking 1:01.50 in her elimination heat. In the final, 24 hours later, Reinisch took the lead early on the way to her third world record. Four days later, in the 200-meter backstroke final, she earned her third gold medal and her fourth world record.

The following year Reinisch was hospitalized with chronically inflamed ovaries, the result of being given steroids during puberty by her coach. With sterility a real threat if she continued to compete, Reinisch retired. In 1994, Reinisch was one of the first East German athletes to speak publicly about her experiences with doping. "What makes me sad," she lamented, "is that I will never know how good I could have been."

1984 Los Angeles C: 31, N: 21, D: 7.31. WR: 1:00.86 (Rica Reinisch)

1. Theresa Andrews	USA	1:02.55
2. Elizabeth "Betsy" Mitchell	USA	1:02.63
3. Jolanda de Rover	HOL	1:02.91
4. Carmen Bunaciu	ROM	1:03.21
5. Aneta Patrascoiu	ROM	1:03.29
6. Svenja Schlicht	GER	1:03.46
7. Beverley Rose	GBR	1:04.16
8. Carmel Clark	NZL	1:04.47

On August 24, at the Friendship Games in Moscow, East Germany's Ina Kleber set a world record of 1:00.59.

1988 Seoul C: 41, N: 30, D: 9.22. WR: 1:00.59 (Ina Kleber)

1. Kristin Otto	GDR	1:00.89
2. Krisztina Egerszegi	HUN	1:01.56
3. Cornelia Sirch	GDR	1:01.57
4. Elizabeth "Betsy" Mitchell	USA	1:02.71
5. Beth Barr	USA	1:02.78
6. Silvia Poll Ahrens	CRC	1:03.34
7. Nicole Livingstone	AUS	1:04.15
8. Marion Aizpors	GER	1:04.19

Kristin Otto won the second of her six gold medals and, an hour later, earned her third in the 4 × 100-meter freestyle relay. One curiosity of note occurred among the lower-ranked swimmers. Olympic rules provided for a "B" final to be swum by the ninth through sixteenth fastest qualifiers. Manuela Carosi of Italy and Karen Lord of Australia tied for sixteenth place and were forced to swim off for the final spot in the "B" final. Again they finished in a dead heat and had to return to the water for a second swimoff. They were exactly even at 50 meters, but Carosi finally won, 1:04.62 to 1:04.75. To her credit, Carosi finished third in the "B" final, her fourth race of the day, with her best time yet: 1:03.80.

1992 Barcelona C: 45, N: 31, D: 7.28. WR: 1:00.31 (Krisztina Egerszegi)

1. Krisztina Egerszegi	HUN	1:00.68 OR
2. Tünde Szabó	HUN	1:01.14
3. Lea Loveless	USA	1:01.43
4. Nicole Stevenson (Livingstone)	AUS	1:01.78
5. Elizabeth "Janie" Wagstaff	USA	1:01.81
6. Joanne Meehan	AUS	1:02.07
7. Nina Zhivanevskaya	UKR	1:02.36
8. Yoko Koikawa	JPN	1:03.23

Egerszegi set an Olympic record of 1:00.85 in her qualifying heat and then broke the record again in the final to win the second of her three gold medals in Barcelona.

1996 Atlanta C: 36, N: 30, D: 7.22. WR: 1:00.16 (He Cihong)

1. Elizabeth Botsford	USA	1:01.19
2. Whitney Hedgepeth	USA	1:01.47
3. Marianne Kriel	SAF	1:02.12
4. Mai Nakamura	JPN	1:02.33
5. Chen Yan	CHN	1:02.50
6. Antje Buschschulte	GER	1:02.52
7. Nicole Stevenson (Livingston)	AUS	1:02.70
8. Miki Nakao	JPN	1:02.78

The preliminary round saw the elimination of world champion and world record holder He Cihong of China, who could do no better than 26th place. World championship runner-up Nina Zhivanevskoya missed qualifying for the final by five hundredths of a second. She won the B final with a time of 1:02.38. The A final was won by 15-year-old Beth Botsford with 25-year-old schoolteacher Whitney Hedgepeth close behind. Of the top six finishers, all but Mai Nakamura set personal bests.

2000 Sydney C: 46, N: 39, D: 9.18. WR: 1:00.16 (He Cihong)

1. Diana Mocanu	ROM	1:00.21 OR
2. Mai Nakamura	JPN	1:00.55
3. Nina Zhivanevskaya	SPA	1:00.89
4. Roxana Maracineanu	FRA	1:01.10
5. Noriko Inada	JPN	1:01.14
6. Barbara "B. J." Bedford	USA	1:01.47
7. Dyana Calub	AUS	1:01.61
8. Louise Ørnstedt	DEN	1:02.02

Mai Nakamura started fast, reached the turn first and was still in first place after 75 meters. Sixteen-year-old Diana Mocanu surged past Nakamura ten meters from the wall and won with the best time since He Cihong's dubious 1994 world record. Although Mocanu had finished second in both backstroke events at the European championships in July, her victory caused a sensation back in her hometown of Braila, where the few people who had followed her career had hoped for "an honorable place in the final." In fact, she was the first Romanian swimmer to win an Olympic gold medal. In honor of her win, Mocanu, who also won the 200-meter backstroke, was given a car. Unfortunately, not only did her family not have a garage, but not one person in her family had a driver's license.

2004 Athens C: 44, N: 35, D: 8.16. WR: 59.58 (Natalie Coughlin)

1. Natalie Coughlin	USA	1:00.37
2. Kirsty Coventry	ZIM	1:00.50
3. Laure Manaudou	FRA	1:00.88
4. Reiko Nakamura	JPN	1:01.05
5. Nina Zhivanevskaya	SPA	1:01.12
6. Antje Buschschulte	GER	1:01.39
7. Louise Ørnstedt	DEN	1:01.51
8. Haley Cope	USA	1:01.76

After failing to make the US Olympic team in 2000, Natalie Coughlin refused to watch the Games on television. The following year, she won the world championship in the 100-meter backstroke. At the 2002 US National Championships, she won five individual events and became the first woman to swim the 100-meter backstroke in under a minute. In 2003, Coughlin's roller-coaster career dipped again as she came down with a high fever at the world championships and failed to reach the final. In Athens, Coughlin was back in perfect shape. She set an Olympic record of 1:00.17 in the semifinals, and then held off a late surge by Kirsty Coventry to win the final.

2008 Beijing C: 48, N: 37, D: 8.12. WR: 58.97 (Natalie Coughlin)

1. Natalie Coughlin	USA	58.96
2. Kirsty Coventry	ZIM	59.19
3. Margaret Hoelzer	USA	59.34
4. Gemma Spofforth	GBR	59.38
5. Anastasiya Zuyeva	RUS	59.40
6. Reiko Nakamura	JPN	59.72
7. Laure Manaudou	FRA	1:00.10
8. Hanae Ito	JPN	1:00.18

Four years after winning the 100-meter backstroke gold in Athens, Natalie Coughlin was once again the favorite. She had finished third at the 2005 world championships but had come back in 2007 to win the championship title in a world record time. A month before the Beijing Olympics, at the US Olympic Trials, she lowered the record again, becoming the first woman to swim the distance in under 59 seconds.

As in 2004, Coughlin's biggest challenger in the event was defending Olympic silver medalist and 2005 world champion Kirsty Coventry. Coventry set an Olympic record in her first-round heat and lowered Coughlin's world record to 58.77 in the semifinals.

In the final Coughlin got off to the fastest start, held off Coventry and never relinquished the lead, thus becoming the first woman in Olympic history to win back-to-back 100-meter breaststroke gold medals. Her time of 58.96 was a personal best.

200-METER BACKSTROKE

1896–1964 not held

1968 Mexico City C: 30, N: 19, D: 10.25. WR: 2:23.8 (Karen Muir)

1. Lillian "Pokey" Watson	USA	2:24.8 OR
2. Elaine Tanner	CAN	2:27.4
3. Kaye Hall	USA	2:28.9
4. Lynette Watson	AUS	2:29.5
5. Wendy Burrell	GBR	2:32.3
6. Gašparac Gašparač	YUG/SER	2:33.5
7. Maria Corominas	SPA	2:33.9
8. Bendicte Duprez	FRA	2:36.6

1972 Munich C: 37, N: 20, D: 9.4. WR: 2:20.64 (Melissa Belote)

1. Melissa Belote	USA	2:19.19 WR
2. Susan Atwood	USA	2:20.38
3. Donna Gurr	CAN	2:23.22
4. Annegret Kober	GER	2:23.35
5. Christine Herbst	GDR	2:23.44
6. Enith Brigitha	HOL	2:23.70
7. Deborah Palmer	AUS	2:24.65
8. Leslie Cliff	CAN	2:25.80

Melissa Belote swam a 2:20.58 in the heats to break her own world record. She broke it again in the final eight hours later to win her third gold medal in three days.

1976 Montreal C: 31, N: 18, D: 7.25. WR: 2:12.47 (Birgit Treiber)

1. Ulrike Richter	GDR	2:13.43 OR
2. Birgit Treiber	GDR	2:14.97
3. Nancy Garapick	CAN	2:15.60
4. Nadiya Stavko	SOV/UKR	2:16.28
5. Melissa Belote	USA	2:17.27
6. Antje Stille	GDR	2:17.55
7. Klavdia Studennikova	SOV/UKR	2:17.74
8. Wendy Hogg-Cook	CAN	2:17.95

The 200-meter backstroke had seen five different world record holders in the two and a half years prior to the Montreal Olympics: Belote, Richter, Garapick, Treiber, and Stille. All five started in the Olympic final. As it turned out, there was little drama; Ulrike Richter led from start to finish to gain her third gold medal.

1980 Moscow C: 21, N: 13, D: 7.27. WR: 2:11.95 (Linda Jezek)

1. Rica Reinisch	GDR	2:11.77 WR
2. Cornelia Polit	GDR	2:13.75
3. Birgit Treiber	GDR	2:14.14
4. Carmen Bunaciu	ROM	2:15.20
5. Yolande van der Straeten	BEL	2:15.58
6. Carine Verbauwen	BEL	2:16.66
7. Lisa Forrest	AUS	2:16.75
8. Larissa Gorchakova	SOV/RUS	2:17.72

Reinisch improved her personal best from 2:15.59 in only eight weeks.

1984 Los Angeles C: 27, N: 18, D: 8.4. WR: 2:09.91 (Cornelia Sirch)

1. Jolanda de Rover	HOL	2:12.38
2. Amy White	USA	2:13.04
3. Patrascoiu Pătrăşcoiu	ROM	2:13.29
4. Georgina Parkes	AUS	2:14.37
5. Tori Trees	USA	2:15.73
6. Svenja Schlicht	GER	2:15.93
7. Carmen Bunaciu	ROM	2:16.15
8. Carmel Clark	NZL	2:17.89

1988 Seoul C: 32, N: 23, D: 9.25. WR: 2:08.60 (Betsy Mitchell)

1. Krisztina Egerszegi	HUN	2:09.29 OR
2. Kathrin Zimmerman	GDR	2:10.61
3. Cornelia Sirch	GDR	2:11.45
4. Cynthia "Beth" Barr	USA	2:12.39
5. Nicole Livingstone	AUS	2:13.43
6. Andrea Hayes	USA	2:15.02
7. Jolanda de Rover	HOL	2:15.17
8. Svenja Schlicht	GER	2:15.94

Two-time world champion Cornelia Sirch led the qualifying round with an Olympic record of 2:10.46. But 14-year-old Krisztina Egerszegi, emboldened by her silver medal in the 100-meter backstroke, felt for the first time that she was capable of beating the East Germans. This despite the fact that, at 99 pounds, the Budapest native was 42 pounds lighter than any of her opponents in the final. Sirch took the early lead with Egerszegi right beside her. After the turn at 100 meters, Egerszegi suddenly sprinted ahead and continued to pull away for the remainder of the race. Discouraged, Sirch was also passed by teammate Kathrin Zimmerman, who had to beat her four-year-old personal best to do it.

1992 Barcelona C: 43, N: 30, D: 7.31. WR: 2:06.62 (Krisztina Egerszegi)

1. Krisztina Egerszegi	HUN	2:07.06 OR
2. Dagmar Hase	GER	2:09.46
3. Nicole Stevenson (Livingstone)	AUS	2:10.20
4. Lea Loveless	USA	2:11.54
5. Anna Simcic	NZL	2:11.99
6. Tünde Szabó	HUN	2:12.94
7. Sylvia Poll Ahrens	CRC	2:12.97
8. Leigh Habler	AUS	2:13.68

Krisztina Egerszegi, by now a seasoned 17-year-old, swam the second-fastest time in history, 2:07.34, in the qualifying round to break her own Olympic record. In the final she took the early lead and won by four meters to earn her third gold medal of the 1992 Games. This brought her career total to 4 golds and 1 silver, all in individual events.

1996 Atlanta C: 33, N: 28, D: 7.25. WR: 2:06.62 (Krisztina Egerszegi)

1. Krisztina Egerszegi	HUN	2:07.83
2. Whitney Hedgepeth	USA	2:11.98
3. Cathleen Rund	GER	2:12.06
4. Anke Scholz	GER	2:12.90
5. Miki Nakao	JPN	2:13.57
6. Anna Simcic	NZL	2:14.04
7. Lorenza Vigarani	ITA	2:14.56
8. Nina Zhivanevskaya	RUS	2:14.59

With this race, Krisztina Egerszegi secured several places in the record books. She became the first woman swimmer to earn five gold medals in individual events. She became only the second swimmer to win the same event three times (Dawn Fraser was the first). Her margin of victory, 4.15 seconds, was the greatest in a women's 200-meter event in any discipline. It is also worth noting that in addition to adding a bronze medal in the 400-meter individual medley, Egerszegi's backstroke leadoff time in the 4 × 100-meter medley relay—1:01.15—was faster than the winning time in the 100-meter backstroke final.

2000 Sydney C: 35, N: 29, D: 9.22. WR: 2:06.62 (Krisztina Egerszegi)

1. Diana Mocanu	ROM	2:08.16
2. Roxana Maracineanu	FRA	2:10.25
3. Miki Nakao	JPN	2:11.05
4. Tomoko Hagiwara	JPN	2:11.21
5. Amanda Adkins	USA	2:12.35
6. Nina Zhivanevskaya	SPA	2:12.75
7. Antje Buschschulte	GER	2:13.31
8. Kelly Stefanyshyn	CAN	2:14.57

Diana Mocanu, who had won the 100-meter backstroke four days earlier, was seventh after 50 meters and second after 100 meters. Then she passed early leader Roxanna Maracineanu and pulled away to a clear victory. Like Mocanu, Maracineanu was born in Romania.

However her family moved to France when Roxana was nine years old.

2004 Athens C: 34, N: 27, D: 8.20. WR: 2:06.62 (Krisztina Egerszegi)

1. Kirsty Coventry	ZIM	2:09.19
2. Stanislava Komarova	RUS	2:09.72
3. Reiko Nakamura	JPN	2:09.88
3. Antje Buschschulte	GER	2:09.88
5. Margaret Hoelzer	USA	2:10.70
6. Louise Ørnstedt	DEN	2:11.15
7. Katherine Sexton	GBR	2:12.11
8. Aya Terakawa	JPN	2:12.90

Born in Harare, Kirsty Coventry became the first Zimbabwean swimmer to compete in the final of an Olympic competition when she earned the silver medal in the 100-meter backstroke. Four days later, Coventry led the 200 from start to finish, easily holding off Stanislava Komarova to complete her medal set, having earned bronze in the 200-meter medley the day after her 100 backstroke silver. When Coventry returned to Zimbabwe, the nation's dictator, Robert Mugabe, held a party in her honor and gave her $50,000 cash, referring to it as "some pocket money."

2008 Beijing C: 34, N: 24, D: 8.16. WR: 2:06.09 (Margaret Hoelzer)

1. Kirsty Coventry	ZIM	2:05.24	WR
2. Margaret Hoelzer	USA	2:06.23	
3. Reiko Nakamura	JPN	2:07.13	
4. Anastasiya Zuyeva	RUS	2:07.88	
5. Elizabeth Beisel	USA	2:08.23	
6. Elizabeth Simmonds	GBR	2:08.51	
7. Meagen Nay	AUS	2:08.84	
8. Belinda Hocking	AUS	2:10.12	

Kirsty Coventry and Margaret Hoelzer had been roommates at Auburn University in Alabama and had been friendly rivals since 2005, when Coventry beat Hoelzer by 1.52 seconds to win the world championship title. Two years later Hoelzer beat Coventry by 0.38 seconds to take the 2007 title. Their friendly rivalry heated up in early 2008 when Coventry set a 200-meter backstroke world record, breaking the long-standing record set by Krisztina Egerszegi in 1991. Five months later Hoelzer lowered the record to 2:06.09 at the US Olympic trials.

Coventry set an Olympic record in her first-round heat. In the final, she took the lead after the first 100 meters and finished almost a second ahead of Hoelzer, shaving 0.85 seconds off Hoelzer's world record. Coventry earned four medals at the 2008 Olympics, bringing her career total to two gold, four silver and one bronze. On her return to Zimbabwe she was once again rewarded with a suitcase stuffed with cash, this time $100,000 in US dollars.

A few weeks after the 2008 Olympics, Margaret Hoelzer spoke publicly about being sexually abused as a child by the father of a friend; she later became a spokesperson for the National Children's Advocacy Center. Her grandfather, Helmut Hölzer, a German engineer who worked on the V-2 rocket and was a pioneer in analog computing, was brought to the US after World War II as part of Operation Paperclip, in which the US recruited Nazi scientists.

100-METER BREASTSTROKE

1896–1964 not held

1968 Mexico City C: 33, N: 20, D: 10.19. WR: 1:14.2 (Catie Ball)

1. Đurđica Bjedov	YUG/CRO	1:15.8 OR
2. Halina Prozumenshchykova	SOV/UKR	1:15.9
3. Sharon Wichman	USA	1:16.1
4. Uta Frommater	GER	1:16.2
5. Catherine Ball	USA	1:16.7
6. Kyoe Nakagawa	JPN	1:17.0
7. Svetlana Babanina	SOV/RUS	1:17.2
8. Ana María Norbis Palmieri	URU	1:17.3

Catie Ball of Jacksonville, Florida, set her fifth 100-meter breaststroke world record seven weeks before the opening of the 1968 Olympics. But in Mexico City she succumbed to a viral infection and lost ten pounds. She competed anyway, but could finish only fifth. Twenty-one-year-old Djurdjica Bjedov is the only representative of Yugoslavia ever to have won an Olympic swimming championship. Previous to the Olympics her main claim to fame had been finishing third in a 200-meter heat at the 1966 European championships.

1972 Munich C: 40, N: 23, D: 9.2. WR: 1:14.2 (Catie Ball)

1. Catherine Carr	USA	1:13.58 WR
2. Halina Stepanova (Prozumenshchykova)	SOV/UKR	1:14.99
3. Beverley Whitfield	AUS	1:15.73
4. Ágnes Kiss-Kaczander	HUN	1:16.26
5. Judy Melick	USA	1:17.16
5. Verena Eberle	GER	1:17.16
7. Britt-Marie Smedh	SWE	1:17.19
8. Dorothy Harrison	GBR	1:17.49

1976 Montreal C: 38, N: 23, D: 7.24. WR: 1:11.93 (Carola Nitschke)

1. Hannelore Anke	GDR	1:11.16
2. Lyubov Rusanova	SOV/RUS	1:13.04
3. Marina Koshevaia	SOV/RUS	1:13.30
4. Carola Nitschke	GDR	1:13.33
5. Gabriele Askamp	GER	1:14.15
6. Maryna Yurchenya	SOV/UKR	1:14.17
7. Margaret Kelly	GBR	1:14.20
8. Karla Linke	GDR	1:14.21

In the fifth heat of the opening round, 18-year-old

Hannelore Anke of Aue set a new world record of 1:11.11. Nine hours later in the semifinals, she lowered the record to 1:10.86. In the final, two nights later, Anke's slowest performance of the Games was good enough for an easy gold medal.

At the 1977 European Championships, Carola Nitschke was awarded a gold medal in the 4 × 100-meter breaststroke. Since the age of thirteen, she had been taking the anabolic steroid Oral-Turinabol. She also received injections of the male hormone testosterone. Two years later she tried to train without drugs, but was unable to match her elite-level times. In 1998 Nitschke became the first doped athlete to return her medals and ask that her name be removed from the record books.

1980 Moscow C: 25, N: 19, D: 7.26. WR: 1:10.20 (Ute Geweniger)

1. Ute Geweniger	GDR	1:10.22
2. Elvira Vasilkova	SOV/RUS	1:10.41
3. Susanne Nielsson	DEN	1:11.16
4. Margaret Kelly	GBR	1:11.48
5. Eva-Marie Håkansson	SWE	1:11.72
6. Susannah Brownsdon	GBR	1:12.11
7. Lina Kačiušytė	SOV/LIT	1:12.21
8. Monica Bonon	ITA	1:12.51

Sixteen-year-old Ute Geweniger clocked a 1:10.11 in the fourth heat to break her own world record. In the final she was only fifth at the turn. Three days later, Tracy Caulkins set a US record of 1:10.40.

1984 Los Angeles C: 30, N: 21, D: 8.2. WR: 1:08.51 (Ute Geweniger)

1. Petra van Staveren	HOL	1:09.88 OR
2. Anne Ottenbrite	CAN	1:10.69
3. Cathérine Poirot	FRA	1:10.70
4. Tracy Caulkins	USA	1:10.88
5. Eva-Marie Håkansson	SWE	1:11.14
6. Hiroko Nagasaki	JPN	1:11.33
7. Susan Rapp	USA	1:11.45
8. Jean Hill	GBR	1:11.82

Three weeks after the Olympic final, 15-year-old Sylvia Gerasch of East Germany set a world record of 1:08.29 at the Friendship Games. Second place went to fellow East German Ute Geweniger in 1:08.59, and third to Larissa Belokon of the Soviet Union in 1:09.63.

1988 Seoul C: 42, N: 27, D: 9.23. WR: 1:07.91 (Silke Hörner)

1. Tania Dangalakova (Bogomilova)	BUL	1:07.95 OR
2. Antoaneta Frenkeva	BUL	1:08.74
3. Silke Hörner	GDR	1:08.83
4. Allison Higson	CAN	1:08.86
5. Yelena Volkova	SOV/RUS	1:09.24
6. Tracey McFarlane	USA	1:09.60
7. Huang Xiaomin	CHN	1:10.53
8. Annett Rex	GDR	1:10.67

In 1987 Tania Dangalakova, the reigning European champion in the 200-meter breaststroke, made a move not uncommon among 23-year-old female swimmers: she put aside her competitive career to have a baby. But the following year she did something highly unusual: she staged a successful comeback. In the preliminary round she set an Olympic record of 1:08.35. This time was matched two heats later by the overwhelming favorite, Silke Hörner. Hörner, the world record holder at 100 meters, had won the 200-meter gold medal with a world record two days earlier. In the 100-meter final Hörner swam the first 50 meters in 31.58, faster than world record pace. Dangalakova was right behind her. Prior to her pregnancy, Dangalakova had had a reputation for swimming a fast first half and then dying badly for the remainder of the race. In fact that is exactly what she did in the 200-meter final. This time, however, it was Hörner who struggled to the finish line while Dangalakova took the lead at 80 meters and went on to become Bulgaria's first Olympic swimming champion. She was so overcome by emotion after her victory that she collapsed in tears and was unable to speak to the press.

1992 Barcelona C: 43, N: 31, D: 7.29. WR: 1:07.91 (Silke Hörner)

1. Yelena Rudkovskaya	BLR	1:08.00
2. N. Anita Nall	USA	1:08.17
3. Samantha Riley	AUS	1:09.25
4. Guylaine Cloutier	CAN	1:09.71
5. Jana Dörries	GER	1:09.77
6. Gabriella Csépe	HUN	1:10.19
7. Manuela Dalla Valle	ITA	1:10.39
8. Daniela Brendel	GER	1:11.05

The 19-year-old daughter of a Minsk trolley car driver, Rudkovskaya led from start to finish. The first name of silver medallist Anita Nall is really Nadia. While baby Anita was emerging from her mother's womb, her father and the obstetrician were watching Nadia Comăneci earn perfect tens on television at the 1976 Olympics.

1996 Atlanta C: 46, N: 38, D: 7.21. WR: 1:07.46 (Penelope Heyns)

1. Penelope Heyns	SAF	1:07.73
2. Amanda Beard	USA	1:08.09
3. Samantha Riley	AUS	1:09.18
4. Svitlana Bondarenko	UKR	1:09.21
5. Vera Lischka	AUT	1:09.24
6. Guylaine Cloutier	CAN	1:09.40
7. Ágnes Kovács	HUN	1:09.55
8. Brigitte Becue	BEL	1:09.79

At the 1994 world championships Samantha Riley swam a 1:07.69 to break the seven-year-old world record. In February 1996 it was announced that Riley, a popular sports figure in Australia, had tested positive for the banned narcotic analgesic dextropropozyphene. Apparently her coach, Scott Volker, gave her a painkilling pill to fight a headache. Riley was threatened with a two-year ban but, after the intervention of IOC president Juan Antonio Samaranch, she was let off with a warning, while Volker was suspended for one year. In the meantime, a bigger threat to Riley's chances for a gold medal arrived in the form of Penny Heyns, who broke Riley's world record at the South African trials with a time of 1:07.46. Heyns was a psychology student at the University of Nebraska. Heyns and Riley were expected to receive a stiff challenge from fast-improving Amanda Beard, who was only fourteen years old.

In the preliminary round, Heyns set another world record: 1:07.02. That evening she led from the start, but made a mistake at the turn, gliding when she should have taken an extra stroke. Beard was known for her powerful back 50, so Heyns had to fight hard to keep her lead. She did not know she had won until Beard told her. Penny Heyns was South Africa's first Olympic champion in any sport since backstroker Joan Harrison in 1952.

In the first heat of the preliminary round, Reaksmey Hem of Cambodia finished in 1:44.68, more than 8½ seconds slower than the previous slowest time in the history of the event. It is worth noting that Hem was twelve years old.

2000 Sydney C: 43, N: 37, D: 9.18. WR: 1:06.52 (Penelope Heyns)

1. Megan Quann	USA	1:07.05
2. Leisel Jones	AUS	1:07.49
3. Penelope Heyns	SAF	1:07.55
4. Sarah Poewe	SAF	1:07.85
5. Ágnes Kovács	HUN	1:08.09
6. Masami Tanaka	JPN	1:08.37
7. Tarnee White	AUS	1:09.09
8. Sylvia Gerasch	GER	1:09.86

Between July 17 and August 28, 1999, Penny Heyns broke the world record in the 100-meter breaststroke three times and in the 200-meter breaststroke four times. However, 16 year-old Megan Quann of Puyallup, Washington, was convinced that the year 2000 was hers. She swam 100,000 meters a week. On her closet door, she kept a list of all the leading breaststrokers. As she beat the best time of one, Quann would cross out her name. Eventually the only one left was Penny Heyns and her world record. Beginning at the age of fourteen, Quann practiced a detailed system of visualization in which she closed her eyes, started her stopwatch and imagined every stroke of her race until she touched the wall and checked her stopwatch again. Often she also visualized the announcement of her victory and the award ceremony. She repeated the exercise over and over again the night before the Olympic final. The next evening, Heyns and fellow South African Sarah Poewe led at the turn with Quann third and Australian favorite Leisel Jones fifth. Heyns began struggling with 25 meters to go and Quann shot past to win, just as she had pictured it so many times.

In eighth place was Sylvia Gerasch, who was competing in her first Olympics at the age of 31. Back when she was 15 years old, Gerasch was one of the favorites for the 1984 Olympics, but her nation, East Germany, boycotted the Games. Two weeks later, Gerasch broke the world record. She broke it again in winning the 1986 world championships. But then she failed to qualify for the next three Olympics, most painfully in 1992, when she missed by only three hundredths of a second. In the meantime, her swim club expelled her for being too old and she took a job in a bank. Then in 2000, she won the German Olympic trials. Besides making the final in the 100-meter breaststroke in Sydney, Gerasch placed fourth in the medley relay.

2004 Athens C: 48, N: 43, D: 8.16. WR: 1:06.37 (Leisel Jones)

1. Luo Xuejuan	CHN	1:06.64 OR
2. Brooke Hanson	AUS	1:07.15
3. Leisel Jones	AUS	1:07.16
4. Amanda Beard	USA	1:07.44
5. Sarah Poewe	GER	1:07.53
6. Tara Kirk	USA	1:07.59
7. Svitlana Bondarenko	UKR	1:08.19
DISQ: Qi Hui (CHN)		

At the age of sixteen, Luo Xuejuan of Hongzhou defeated Leisel Jones to win the 2001 world championship. Two years later, at the next world championships in Barcelona, Jones set a world record of 1:06.37 in the semifinals. But in the final, Luo won again, while Amanda Beard nipped Jones for the silver medal. In Athens, Luo led at the turn and was never headed. Luo announced her retirement in 2007, at the age of 23, due to a potentially fatal heart problem.

2008 Beijing C: 49, N: 39, D: 8.12. WR: 1:05.09 (Leisel Jones)

1. Leisel Jones	AUS	1:05.17	OR
2. Rebecca Soni	USA	1:06.73	
3. Mirna Jukic	AUT	1:07.34	
4. Yuliya Yefimova	RUS	1:07.43	
5. Megan Quann-Jendrick	USA	1:07.62	
6. Tarnee White	AUS	1:07.63	
7. Sun Ye	CHN	1:08.08	
8. Asami Kitagawa	JPN	1:08.43	

The heavy favorite in Beijing was defending Olympic bronze medalist and two-time reigning world champion

Leisel Jones. The 22-year-old, who also held the world record, set an Olympic record of 1:05.64 in her first-round heat and recorded the fastest qualifying time of the semifinals.

Jones was under the world record pace at the halfway point but was unable to lower the record, instead setting another Olympic record of 1:05.17. Trailing in fifth place at the turn, Rebecca Soni moved up over the final 50 meters to finish second. She had not originally been scheduled to race the 100-meter breaststroke, but was added to the start list after teammate Jessica Hardy tested positive for clenbuterol at the US Olympic trials and was dropped from the team.

200-METER BREASTSTROKE

1896–1920 not held

1924 Paris C: 15, N: 8, D: 7.18. WR: 3:20.4 (Irene Gilbert)

1. Lucy Morton	GBR	3:33.2
2. Agnes Geraghty	USA	3:34.0
3. Gladys Carson	GBR	3:35.4
4. Vivan Pettersson	SWE	3:37.6
5. Irene Gilbert	GBR	3:38.0
6. Laure "Laury" Koster	LUX	3:39.2
7. Hjördis Töpel	SWE	3:47.6

The first qualifying heat was won by Marie Baron of Holland in 3:22.6, with Agnes Geraghty second in 3:27.6. Baron was disqualified, however, for making a faulty turn. Geraghty led the final for 150 meters, but she couldn't withstand the surprising closing rush of 26-year-old Lucy Morton.

1928 Amsterdam C: 21, N: 12, D: 8.9. WR: 3:11.2 (Lotte Mühe)

1. Hildegard Schrader	GER	3:12.6
2. Mietje "Marie" Baron	HOL	3:15.2
3. Lotte Mühe	GER	3:17.6
4. Else Jacobsen	DEN	3:19.0
5. Margaret Hoffman	USA	3:19.2
6. Brita Hazelius	SWE	3:23.0

Lotte Mühe broke Marie Baron's world record on July 15, but three weeks later in Amsterdam it was her teammate, 18-year-old Hilde Schrader, who was in control. Her opening heat time of 3:11.6 bettered the Olympic record by 16 seconds. In the semifinals Schrader equaled Mühe's world record. The final was her slowest race, but with good reason: the straps of her bathing suit broke. She was able to finish, but after the race she had to stay in the water until her suit could be fixed.

1932 Los Angeles C: 11, N: 7, D: 8.9. WR: 3:03.4 (Else Jacobsen)

1. Clare Dennis	AUS	3:06.3 OR
2. Hideko Maehata	JPN	3:06.4
3. Else Jacobsen	DEN	3:07.1
4. Margery Hinton	GBR	3:11.7
5. Margaret Hoffman	USA	3:11.8
6. Anne Govednik	USA	3:16.0
7. Jane Cadwell	USA	3:18.2

On August 6, Clare Dennis, a 16-year-old from Sydney, set an Olympic record of 3:08.2 in winning her preliminary heat. After the race, she was approached by the American swimmer Buster Crabbe. Crabbe advised her to begin the final by taking three strokes underwater before surfacing after her dive. He also urged her to demoralize her opponents by touching first at each turn. Three days later, Dennis followed Crabbe's instructions to the letter. Mere inches separated Dennis and Jacobsen for the first 175 meters. Jacobsen wilted slightly at the end, enabling the fast-finishing Maehata to beat her by a foot for second place.

1936 Berlin C: 23, N: 12, D: 8.11. WR: 3:00.4 (Hideko Maehata)

1. Hideko Maehata	JPN	3:03.6
2. Martha Geneger	GER	3:04.2
3. Inge Sørensen	DEN	3:07.8
4. Johanna "Hanni" Hölzner	GER	3:09.5
5. Johanna Waalberg	HOL	3:09.5
6. Doris Storey	GBR	3:09.7
7. Jeannette Kastein	HOL	3:12.8

The year 1936 saw the first Olympic appearance of the controversial butterfly stroke, in which the swimmer recovers her arms above the water rather than under. The first woman to try the stroke in the Olympics was Maria Lenk of Brazil who was eliminated in the semifinals. Silver medallist Martha Geneger was 14 years old, while bronze medallist Inge Sörensen was only 12 years and 24 days old. Sörensen is the youngest athlete ever to win an Olympic medal in an individual event.

By contrast, Hideko Maehata, who set an Olympic record of 3:01.9 in her preliminary heat, was an elderly 22. Maehata brought a small piece of paper with a prayer on it to the starting platform. She read it one last time before the final and then ate it. Maehata was the first Asian woman to win an Olympic gold medal. The Japanese radio call of the race gained a special place in history because the NHK announcer became so excited that he kept shouting, "Go Maehata! Go Maehata!" and forgot to describe the progress of the race.

1948 London C: 22, N: 14, D: 8.3. WR: 2:49.2 (Petronella van Vliet)

1. Petronella van Vliet	HOL	2:57.2
2. Beatrice "Nancy" Lyons	AUS	2:57.7
3. Éva Novák	HUN	3:00.2
4. Éva Székely	HUN	3:02.5
5. Adriana de Groot	HOL	3:06.2
6. Elizabeth Church	GBR	3:06.1
7. Antonia Hom	HOL	3:07.5
8. Jytte Hansen	DEN	3:08.1

De Groot was awarded fifth place despite the fact that her official time was slower than that of Church.

1952 Helsinki C: 34, N: 19, D: 7.29. WR: 2:48.5 (Éva Novák)

1. Éva Székely	HUN	2:51.7 OR
2. Éva Novák	HUN	2:54.4
3. Helen Orr "Elenor" Gordon	GBR	2:57.6
4. Klára Killermann	HUN	2:57.6
5. Jytte Hansen	DEN	2:57.8
6. Maria Havrysh	SOV/UKR	2:58.9
7. Ulla-Britt Eklund	SWE	3:01.8
8. Petronella Garritsen	HOL	3:02.1

Like 100-meter freestyle winner Katalin Szöke, 25-year-old Éva Székely was married to a member of the 1952 champion Hungarian water polo team. Husband Dezső Gyarmati also won water polo gold medals in 1956 and 1964. In 1972, their daughter Andrea earned medals in the backstroke and butterfly. Székely was the first female butterfly stroker to win a gold medal. Following the 1952 Olympics, the breaststroke and butterfly were separated into two different events.

1956 Melbourne C: 14, N: 10, D: 11.30. WR: 2:46.4 (Adelaide den Haan)

1. Ursula Happe	GER	2:53.1 OR
2. Éva Székely	HUN	2:54.8
3. Eva-Maria ten Elsen	GDR	2:55.1
4. Vinka Jeričević	YUG/CRO	2:55.8
5. Klára Killermann	HUN	2:56.1
6. Helen Orr "Elenor" Gordon	GBR	2:56.1
7. Mary Sears	USA	2:57.2
8. Christine Gosden	GBR	2:59.2

World record holder Ada den Haan was unable to compete because the Netherlands withdrew from the 1956 Games to protest the Soviet invasion of Hungary.

1960 Rome C: 29, N: 19, D: 9.27. WR: 2:50.2 (Wiltrud Urselmann)

1. Anita Lonsbrough	GBR	2:49.5 WR
2. Wiltrud Urselmann	GER	2:50.0
3. Barbara Göbel	GDR	2:53.6
4. Adelaide den Haan	HOL	2:54.4
5. Margareta Kok	HOL	2:54.6
6. Anne Warner	USA	2:55.4
7. Patty Kempner	USA	2:55.5
8. Dorrit Kristensen	DEN	2:55.7

In 1957 underwater stroking was banned from breaststroke competitions, which explains why the world record was slower in 1960 than it was in 1956. Nineteen-year-old Anita Lonsbrough, a clerk for the Huddersfield Corporation in Yorkshire, faced a problem not uncommon to amateur athletes in Great Britain. Far from being appreciative of the free publicity that her swimming exploits brought them, her employers actually docked her wages whenever she took time off for training. In Rome she slept for twelve hours before the final. On the starting block she became hypnotized by a fly on the water. All she could think about was that she had to miss the fly when she dived in. Lonsbrough's victory was the result of iron nerves and perfect tactics. She trailed Urselmann by two seconds at the halfway mark, then she gradually closed the gap, catching the tiring German with 25 meters to go. Urselmann surprised Lonsbrough with a final spurt, but Lonsbrough held on for the victory.

1964 Tokyo C: 26, N: 15, D: 10.12. WR: 2:45.4 (Halyna Prozumenshchykova)

1. Halyna Prozumenshchykova	SOV/UKR	2:46.4 OR
2. Claudia Kolb	USA	2:47.6
3. Svetlana Babanina	SOV/RUS	2:48.6
4. Stella Mitchell	GBR	2:49.0
5. Jill Slattery	GBR	2:49.6
6. Bärbel Grimmer	GDR	2:51.0
7. Klena Bimolt	HOL	2:51.3
8. Ursula Küper	GDR	2:53.9

Prozumenshchykova, a 15-year-old schoolgirl from Sevastopol, let Babanina set the pace for 100 meters and then surged ahead to win the USSR's first gold medal in swimming.

1968 Mexico City C: 21, N: 20, D: 10.23. WR: 2:38.5 (Catie Ball)

1. Sharon Wichman	USA	2:44.4 OR
2. Đurđica Bjedov	YUG/CRO	2:46.4
3. Halyna Prozumenshchykova	SOV/UKR	2:47.0
4. Alla Grebennikova	SOV/RUS	2:47.1
5. Catherine Jamison	USA	2:48.4
6. Svetlana Babanina	SOV/RUS	2:48.4
7. Chieno Shibata	JPN	2:51.5
8. Ana María Norbis Palmieri	URU	2:51.9

Prozumenshchykova was leading after 175 meters when she suddenly ran out of energy and barely hung on for third place. She had to be administered oxygen as soon as the race was over. Sharon Wichman's victory meant that the gold medals in the first ten Olympic women's 200-meter breaststroke competitions had been won by swimmers from eight different nations.

1972 Munich C: 39, N: 22, D: 8.29. WR: 2:38.5 (Catie Ball)

1. Beverley Whitfield	AUS	2:41.71 OR
2. Dana Schoenfield	USA	2:42.05
3. Halyna Stepanova (Prozumenshchykova)	SOV/UKR	2:42.36
4. Claudia Clevenger	USA	2:42.88
5. Petra Nows	GER	2:43.41
6. Ágnes Kiss-Kaczander	HUN	2:43.41
7. Lyudmila Porubaiko	SOV/RUS	2:44.48
8. Éva Kiss	HUN	2:45.12

As usual, Halyna Prozumenshchykova took the early lead and eventually opened a four-meter gap. But just as she had done four years earlier, the Soviet swimmer, now Halyna Stepanova, "died" in the final 50 meters and faded to third place. Meanwhile, 18-year-old Bev Whitfield, in last place after 50 meters and fourth place after 150 meters, sprinted home to pass Stepanova and stave off a final challenge from Schoenfield. As she climbed out of the pool, Whitfield called out to her teammates, "For once I kept my cool. This is the greatest feeling in the world."

1976 Montreal C: 38, N: 21, D: 7.21. WR: 2:34.99 (Karla Linke)

1. Marina Koshevaia	SOV/RUS	2:33.35 WR
2. Maryna Yurchenya	SOV/UKR	2:36.08
3. Lyubov Rusanova	SOV/RUS	2:36.22
4. Hannelore Anke	GDR	2:36.49
5. Karla Linke	GDR	2:36.97
6. Carola Nitschke	GDR	2:38.27
7. Margaret Kelly	GBR	2:38.37
8. Deborah Rudd	GBR	2:39.01

Koshevaia moved up from fifth to first during the third 50 meters and then pulled away to the most decisive women's breaststroke victory in Olympic history.

1980 Moscow C: 25, N: 19, D: 7.23. WR: 2:28.36 (Lina Kačiušytė)

1. Lina Kačiušytė	SOV/LIT	2:29.54 OR
2. Svetlana Varganova	SOV/RUS	2:29.61
3. Yulia Bogdanova	SOV/RUS	2:32.39
4. Susanne Nielsson	DEN	2:32.75
5. Irena Fleissnerová	CZE	2:33.23
6. Ute Geweniger	GDR	2:34.34
7. Bettina Löbel	GDR	2:34.51
8. Sylvia Rinka	GDR	2:35.38

Svetlana Varganova led for almost the entire race while Lithuanian Lina Kačiušytė improved from last place at 50 meters to fourth place at the halfway mark and second place two and a half seconds behind Varganova, with 50 meters to go. An impressive finishing spurt earned 17-year-old Kačiušytė the gold medal.

1984 Los Angeles C: 23, N: 16, D: 7.30. WR: 2:28.36 (Lina Kačiušytė)

1. Anne Ottenbrite	CAN	2:30.38
2. Susan Rapp	USA	2:31.15
3. Ingrid Lempereur	BEL	2:31.40
4. Hiroko Nagasaki	JPN	2:32.93
5. Sharon Kellett	AUS	2.33.60
6. Ute Hasse	GER	2:33.82
7. Susannah Brownsdon	GBR	2:35.07
8. Kimberly Rhodenbaugh	USA	2:35.51

The term "accident-prone" was meant for people like Anne Ottenbrite of Whitby, Ontario. Fortunately for Ottenbrite, all of her accidents had been relatively minor. Having previously survived bloody encounters with a plateglass window and a potato processor, on May 21st she dislocated her right kneecap while showing off a new pair of shoes. Unable to take part in the Canadian trials, she was placed on the team anyway. During her brief stay in Los Angeles before the Olympics began, Ottenbrite suffered a whiplash injury to her neck when the van in which she was traveling crashed into the back of another car. Relaxing back at the Olympic Village, she strained a thigh muscle while playing a video game. Despite all of these mishaps, the 18-year-old Ottenbrite moved ahead of Hiroko Nagasaki after the midway point of the Olympic final and held off the closing rushes of Rapp and Lempereur to win a gold medal. Ottenbrite's victory was a mild surprise, but the real shocker was the performance of 15-year-old Ingrid Lempereur, who bettered her pre-Olympic personal best by 6.36 seconds.

At the Friendship Games on August 20th, Larissa Belokon finished first in 2:29.13.

1988 Seoul C: 43, N: 27, D: 9.21. WR: 2:27.27 (Allison Higson)

1. Silke Hörner	GDR	2:26.71 WR
2. Huang Xiaomin	CHN	2:27.49
3. Antoaneta Frenkeva	BUL	2:28.34
4. Tania Dangalakova (Bogomilova)	BUL	2:28.43
5. Yulia Bocharova	SOV/UKR	2:28.54
6. Ingrid Lempereur	BEL	2:29.42
7. Allison Higson	CAN	2:29.60
8. Manuela Dalla Valle	ITA	2:29.86

Hörner, whose hobby was collecting palm trees in her Leipzig apartment, took the lead from Dangalakova in the third quarter of the race and recaptured the world record she had lost to Higson four months earlier. It was Hörner's third world record at 200 meters.

1992 Barcelona C: 39, N: 28, D: 7.27. WR: 2:25.35 (N. Anita Nall)

1. Kyoko Iwasaki	JPN	2:26.65 OR
2. Lin Li	CHN	2:26.85
3. N. Anita Nall	USA	2:26.88

4. Yelena Rudkovskay	BLR	2:28.47
5. Guylaine Cloutier	CAN	2:29.88
6. Nathalie Giguère	CAN	2:30.11
7. Manuela Dalla Valle	ITA	2:31.21
8. Alicja Pęczak	POL	2:31.76

On March 2, 1992, Anita Nall, then 15 years old, broke the world record at the United States Olympic trials not once but twice. In the morning she swam 2:25.92 in her qualifying heat and then followed up with a 2:25.35 in the final. Nall won her Olympic heat in 2:27.77, but, much to her surprise, right beside her was 5-foot 1-inch, 99-pound Kyoko Iwasaki in 2:27.78. Six days earlier, on the same day that Nall celebrated her 16th birthday, Iwasaki turned 14 years old. In the final, Nall immediately went into the lead, while Iwasaki lingered in sixth place after 50 meters before moving up to third at the halfway mark, and second with a lap to go. She passed the fading world record holder in the closing meters, as did Lin Li. Iwasaki beat her pre-Olympic personal best by 4.43 seconds while Lin improved hers by 3.94 seconds. Iwasaki is the youngest swimmer ever to win an Olympic gold medal. When she returned to her hometown of Numazu in Shizuoka Prefecture, she was greeted by a crowd of 70,000 people.

1996 Atlanta C: 40, N: 33, D: 7.23. WR: 2:24.76 (Rebecca Brown)

1. Penelope Heyns	SAF	2:25.41 OR
2. Amanda Beard	USA	2:25.75
3. Ágnes Kovács	HUN	2:26.57
4. Samantha Riley	AUS	2:27.91
5. Masami Tanaka	JPN	2:28.05
6. Nadine Neumann	AUS	2:28.34
7. Brigitte Becue	BEL	2:28.36
8. Christin Petelski	CAN	2:31.45

The 200-meter breaststroke was almost a repeat of the 100-meter final two days earlier. Penny Heyns, who set an Olympic record in the preliminary round, built a solid lead. Amanda Beard closed the gap in the last fifty meters, but fell just short of catching her. Heyns was the first swimmer to win both breaststroke events in the same Olympics.

2000 Sydney C: 35, N: 29, D: 9.21. WR: 2:23.64 (Penelope Heyns)

1. Ágnes Kovács	HUN	2:24.35
2. Kristy Kowal	USA	2:24.56
3. Amanda Beard	USA	2:25.35
4. Qi Hui	CHN	2:25.36
5. Olga Bakaldina	RUS	2:25.47
6. Sarah Poewe	SAF	2:25.72
7. Masami Tanaka	JPN	2:26.98
8. Luo Xuejuan	CHN	2:27.33

Ágnes Kovács broke the Olympic record in both the preliminary round and in the semifinals. The final was eerily similar to the final of the 1998 world championships, which were also held in Australia. In that race, Kovács' friend, Kristy Kowal, led the Hungarian by 43 hundredths of a second at 100 meters before Kovács came from behind to win with Kowal taking second. In the Olympic final Kowal again led Kovács by 43 hundredths of a second at 100 meters (with Qi Hui between them in second place). This time Kovács did not catch Kowal until halfway through the last lap, but the two finished one-two again. Amanda Beard, who had qualified for the final in eighth place, came from behind to snatch the bronze from Qi as they reached for the wall.

2004 Athens C: 31, N: 28, D: 8.19. WR: 2:22.44 (Amanda Beard)

1. Amanda Beard	USA	2:23.37
2. Leisel Jones	AUS	2:23.60
3. Anne Poleska	GER	2:25.82
4. Masami Tanaka	JPN	2:25.87
5. Ágnes Kovács	HUN	2:26.12
6. Qi Hui	CHN	2:26.35
7. Mirna Jukic	AUT	2:26.36
8. Brooke Hanson	AUS	2:26.39

The Olympic final was the latest instalment of the ongoing duel between Amanda Beard and Leisel Jones. Beard had already medaled in the 200-meter breaststroke at the last two Olympics when she defeated Jones 2:26.31 to 2:26.42 at the 2002 Pan Pacific Championships. The following year, Beard matched Qi Hui's world record of 2:22.99 to win the world championship, with Jones taking second place. On July 10, 2004, barely a month before the Olympics, Jones broke this record with a 2:22.96 at a meet in Brisbane, Australia. However, two days later, Beard lowered the world record again, winning the US Olympic trials in 2:22.44. In Athens, Jones led from the start, while Beard tried to stay close enough to the Australian to exploit her late-race strength. Still almost a second behind Jones with 50 meters to go, Beard caught her in the closing meters and just reached the wall first.

2008 Beijing C: 40, N: 34, D: 8.15. WR: 2:20.54 (Leisel Jones)

1. Rebecca Soni	USA	2:20.22 WR
2. Leisel Jones	AUS	2:22.05
3. Sara Nordenstam	NOR	2:23.02
4. Mirna Jukic	AUT	2:23.24
5. Yuliya Yefimova	RUS	2:23.76
6. Annamay Pierse	CAN	2:23.77
7. Rie Kaneto	JPN	2:25.14
8. Megumi Taneda	JPN	2:25.23

Competing three days after winning the 100-meter breaststroke gold medal, defending Olympic silver medalist and two-time reigning world champion Leisel Jones looked set to win her second individual gold medal at the 2008 Olympics.

Jones took the initial lead in the final and led by 0.23 seconds at the halfway point. But then 21-year-old Rebecca Soni, the daughter of Hungarian immigrants, closed the gap and pushed ahead during the last lap, finishing more than a body length in front and setting a world record.

100-METER BUTTERFLY

1896–1952 not held

1956 Melbourne C: 12, N: 8, D: 12.5. WR: 1:10.5 (Aartje Voorbij)

1. Shelly Mann	USA	1:11.0 OR
2. Nancy Ramey	USA	1:11.9
3. Mary Sears	USA	1:14.4
4. Mária Littomeritzky	HUN	1:14.9
5. Beverly Bainbridge	AUS	1:15.2
6. Jutta Langenau	GDR	1:17.4
7. Elizabeth Whittall	CAN	1:17.9
8. Sara Barber	CAN	1:18.4

Shelley Mann, 1956
Mann overcame polio to win the inaugural Olympic 100-meter butterfly event, leading an American sweep.

With world record holder Atie Voorbij absent because of the Dutch boycott, the inaugural women's butterfly event was swept by the Americans. Crippled by polio at the age of six, Shelly Mann began swimming to regain strength in her arms and legs.

1960 Rome C: 25, N: 16, D: 8.30. WR: 1:09.1 (Nancy Ramey)

1. Carolyn Schuler	USA	1:09.5 OR
2. Marianne Heemskerk	HOL	1:10.4
3. Janice Andrew	AUS	1:12.2
4. Sheila Watt	GBR	1:13.3
5. Aartje Voorbij	HOL	1:13.3
6. Zinaida Belovetskaya	SOV/RUS	1:13.3
7. Kristina Larsson	SWE	1:13.6

DNF: Carolyn Wood (USA)

Fourteen-year old Carolyn Wood had beaten Carolyn Schuler at the US trials. A close second after 70 meters of the Olympic final, Wood swallowed too much water, became confused, and stopped swimming.

1964 Tokyo C: 31, N: 16, D: 10.16 WR (110 yards): 1:05.1 (Ada Kok)

1. Sharon Stouder	USA	1:04.7 WR
2. Ada Kok	HOL	1:05.6
3. Kathleen Ellis	USA	1:06.0
4. Ella Pyrhönen	FIN	1:07.3
5. Donna De Varona	USA	1:08.0
6. Heike Hustede	GER	1:08.5
7. Elko Takahashi	JPN	1:09.1
8. Mary Stewart	CAN	1:10.0

Fifteen-year-old Sharon Stouder won 3 gold medals and 1 silver at the Tokyo Games.

1968 Mexico City C: 28, N: 21, D: 10.21. WR: 1:04.5 (Ada Kok)

1. Lynette McClements	AUS	1:05.5
2. Ellie Daniel	USA	1:05.8
3. Susan Shields	USA	1:06.2
4. Ada Kok	HOL	1:06.2
5. Andréa Gyarmati	HUN	1:06.8
6. Heike Hustede	GER	1:06.9
7. Toni Hewitt	USA	1:07.5
8. Helga Lindner	GDR	1:07.6

Lyn McClements was a 17-year-old stenographer from Perth. Her daughter, Jacqueline McKenzie, represented Australia as a swimmer at the 1992 Olympics.

1972 Munich C: 30, N: 21, D: 9.1. WR: 1:03.9 (Mayumi Aoki)

1. Mayumi Aoki	JPN	1:03.34 WR
2. Roswitha Beier	GDR	1:03.61
3. Andrea Gyarmati	HUN	1:03.73
4. Deena Deardurff	USA	1:03.95
5. Dana Shrader	USA	1:03.98
6. Ellie Daniel	USA	1:04.08
7. Gudrun Beckmann	GER	1:04.15
8. Noriko Asano	JPN	1:04.25

Andrea Gyarmati was the daughter of 1952 breaststroke gold medallist Éva Székely and Dezsõ Gyarmati, who won three gold medals in water polo. In the semifinals she set a world record of 1:03.80. But in the final, Aoki moved up from seventh place at the mid-race turn to recapture the record.

1976 Montreal C: 39, N: 26, D: 7.2. WR: 1:00.13 (Kornelia Ender)

1. Kornelia Ender	GDR	1:00.13 EWR
2. Andrea Pollack	GDR	1:00.98
3. Wendy Boglioli	USA	1:01.17
4. Camille Wright	USA	1:01.41
5. Rosemarie Gabriel (Kother)	GDR	1:01.56
6. Wendy Quirk	CAN	1:01.75
7. Lelei Fonoimoana	USA	1:01.95
8. Tamara Shelofastova	SOV/RUS	1:02.74

At 7:48 p.m. on July 22, 1976, Kornelia Ender won the 100-meter butterfly final in world record time. At 8:03 she descended from the victory platform and went to the dressing room. At 8:08 she returned to the pool for the final of the 200-meter freestyle. At 8:13 she was racing through the water again, and by 8:15 she had won her second gold medal in 27 minutes.

1980 Moscow C: 24, N: 18, D: 7.24. WR: 59.26 (Mary T. Meagher)

1. Caren Metschuck	GDR	1:00.42
2. Andrea Pollack	GDR	1:00.90
3. Christiane Knacke	GDR	1:01.44
4. Ann Osgerby	GBR	1:02.21
5. Lisa Curry	AUS	1:02.40
6. Agneta Mårtensson	SWE	1:02.61
7. María del Milagro París	CRC	1:02.89
8. Janet Osgerby	GBR	1:02.90

The 1980 women's 100-meter butterfly was the symbol of the dual crises that the Olympic Movement faced between 1976 and 1984: exploitation of the Olympics by governments with political agendas and systematic use of forbidden, performance-enhancing drugs. At the US Outdoor National on August 2, world record holder Mary T. Meagher clocked a time of 59.41 and Tracy Caulkins 1:00.75. Neither of these medal favorites was allowed to compete in the Olympics because of the anti-Soviet boycott. In their absence, all three medals were won by East German women who took prohibited drugs.

In 1989, Christiane Knacke became one of the first East German athletes to speak publically about the way her nation's sporting system really worked. When she was thirteen years, Knacke—and every member of her family—were forced to sign a form agreeing not to have any contact with the "capitalist foreigners of the West." By this time, her coach was already giving her pills that he said contained "vitamin E and protein." On August 28, 1977, at the age of fifteen, Knacke became the first woman to break the one minute barrier in the 100-meter butterfly. Her coach, Rolf Gläsen now added to her regime a daily dose of ten to fifteen steroid pills. She also received shots of cortisone and procaine and, twice a week, intravenous drips of an unknown liquid. In less than a year Knacke grew from 50 kilograms (110 pounds) to 65 kilograms (143 pounds). She was preparing for the 1978 world championships when she was unexpectedly sent to a sports medicine institute near Dresden. There she and 400-meter freestyle champion Petra Thümer apent 137 days being "cleansed" because they had been given too many drugs. It was then that the 16-year-old Knacke became seriously worried that what her coach was giving her was truly dangerous.

Shortly after winning the bronze medal in Moscow, Knacke underwent the first of three operations to repair damage done to her elbow by anabolic steroids. Her bones had turned to "crystal." In 1998, Knacke was co-plaintiff in a lawsuit against former East German coaches and two doctors accused of damaging the health of their athletes. In the course of the trial, Rolf Gläser publically apologized to Knacke, and Knacke became the first Olympic athlete to volunteer to return her medal because she had been doped.

The British representatives, Ann and Janet Osgerby, were 17-year-old twins from Chorley, Lancashire. Ann was 20 minutes older and 0.69 seconds faster.

1984 Los Angeles C: 35, N: 23, D: 8.2. WR: 57.93 (Mary T. Meagher)

1. Mary T. Meagher	USA	59.26
2. Jenna Johnson	USA	1:00.19
3. Karin Seick	GER	1:01.36
4. Annemarie Verstappen	HOL	1:01.56
5. Michelle MacPherson	CAN	1:01.58
6. Janet Tibbits	AUS	1:01.78
7. Cornelia van Bentum	HOL	1:01.94
8. Ina Beyermann	GER	1:02.11

In 1980, 15-year-old Mary T. Meagher of Louisville, Kentucky, was the world record holder in both butterfly events and the favorite to win two gold medals in Moscow until the anti-Soviet boycott forced her to stay home. The following year she lowered her world record by a phenomenal 1.33 seconds. She never approached that time again, but neither did anyone else. In Los Angeles in 1984, Meagher set an Olympic record of 59.05 in the preliminaries and then overcame a fast start by teammate Jenna Johnson to win the first of her three gold medals.

Lisa Curry of Australia won the "B" final in 1:01.25, a time that would have earned her the bronze medal if she had qualified for the final.

1988 Seoul C: 40, N: 28, D: 9.23. WR: 57.93 (Mary T. Meagher)

1. Kristin Otto	GDR	59.00 OR
2. Birte Weigang	GDR	59.45
3. Qian Hong	CHN	59.52
4. Catherine Plewinski	FRA	59.58
5. Janel Jorgensen	USA	1:00.48
6. Cornelia van Bentum	HOL	1:00.62
7. Mary T. Meagher	USA	1:00.97
8. Wang Xiaohong	CHN	1:01.15

Kristin Otto won her fourth gold medal of the Seoul Games. Birte Weigang is the daughter of Horst Weigang, who won a bronze medal as the goalkeeper for East Germany's 1964 football team.

1992 Barcelona C: 49, N: 34, D: 7.30. WR: 57.93 (Mary T. Meagher)

1. Qian Hong	CHN	58.62 OR
2. Christine Ahmann-Leighton	USA	58.74
3. Catherine Plewinski	FRA	59.01
4. Wang Xiaohong	CHN	59.10
5. Susan O'Neill	AUS	59.69
6. Summer Sanders	USA	59.82
7. Franziska van Almsick	GER	1:00.70
8. Rie Shito	JPN	1:01.16

For nine years after Mary T. Meagher set her world record of 57.93 on August 18, 1981, no one broke the 59-second barrier again, not even Meagher herself. Finally, at the Asian Games in Beijing on September 27, 1990, two Chinese swimmers, Wang Xiaohong and Qian Hong, swam 58.87 and 58.89, respectively. The next sub-59 100-meter butterfly didn't come until the 1992 US Olympic trials, when Crissy Ahmann-Leighton beat a strong field in 58.61. At the Olympics, Ahmann-Leighton burst into the lead immediately and led Wang and Qian by half a body length at the turn. But it was Qian who had the strongest finish and managed to outtouch AhmannLeighton by about eight inches (20 centimeters).

1996 Atlanta C: 42, N: 35, D: 7.23. WR: 57.93 (Mary T. Meagher)

1. Amy Van Dyken	USA	59.13
2. Liu Limin	CHN	59.14
3. Angelina Martino	USA	59.23
4. Hitomi Kashima	JPN	1:00.11
5. Susan O'Neill	AUS	1:00.17
6. Ayari Aoyama	JPN	1:00.18
7. Cai Huijue	CHN	1:00.46
8. Mette Jacobsen	DEN	1:00.76

Amy van Dyken earned the second of her four gold medals. The finish was so close that no one was able to tell who won until the electronically-derived results were flashed on the scoreboard.

2000 Sydney C: 49, N: 39, D: 9.17. WR: 56.64 (Inge de Bruijn)

1. Inge de Bruijn	HOL	56.61 WR
2. Martina Moravcová	SLV	57.97
3. Dara Torres	USA	58.20
4. Petria Thomas	AUS	58.49
5. Jenny Thompson	USA	58.73
6. Junko Onishi	JPN	59.13
7. Susan O'Neill	AUS	59.27
8. Diana Mocanu	ROM	59.43

At the 1999 Pan Pacific Championships in Sydney, Jenny Thompson swam 57.88 to break Mary T. Meagher's 18-year-old world record. Thompson seemed to be on target to win at the Olympics, but in 2000 her performances were overshadowed by the reemergence of Inge de Bruijn, who broke Thompson's record twice, swimming 56.69 on May 27 and 56.64 on July 22. De Bruijn continued her record-setting spree in Sydney, setting Olympic records in both the preliminary round and the semifinals and then winning the final in world-record time. Her margin of victory, 1.36 seconds, was the largest in the event's history. Martina Moravcová's silver medal honored her successful recovery from thyroid surgery for Graves' disease and Dara Torres' bronze medal was the culmination of her comeback after seven years away from the sport. Diana Mocanu finished last in the final, but she was competing only 23 minutes after winning her heat in the 100-meter backstroke, an event in which she later won the gold medal.

2004 Athens C: 38, N: 30, D: 8.15. WR: 56.61 (Inge de Bruijn)

1. Petria Thomas	AUS	57.72
2. Otylia Jędrzejczak	POL	57.84
3. Inge de Bruijn	HOL	57.99
4. Jess Schipper	AUS	58.22
5. Jenny Thompson	USA	58.72
6. Martina Moravcová	SLV	58.96
7. Yelena Popchenko	BLR	59.06
8. Junko Onishi	JPN	59.83

Petria Thomas edged Otylia Jędrzejczak 58.27 to 58.72 to win the 2001 world championship. In 2003 Thomas was unable to defend her title due to shoulder surgery, having dislocated her shoulder while awkwardly reaching for her alarm clock. It was Thomas' third shoulder reconstruction. Throw in an ankle reconstruction in 2001 and abdominal surgery in 2002, and Thomas earned the nickname "the Bionic Butterfly." In Athens, Thomas faced not only Jędrzejczak, but defending Olympic champion and world record holder Inge de Bruijn, and 2003 world champion and 10-time Olympic medalist Jenny Thompson. Thomas led the qualifying round at 57.47 seconds, while de Bruijn had the fastest semifinal time, 57.50 seconds. In the final, De Bruijn took a quick lead and was ahead of her own world record pace at the turn. Thomas and Jędrzejczak pushed ahead of her in the final stretch, with Thomas touching first to take gold.

2008 Beijing C: 49, N: 38, D: 8.11. WR: 56.61 (Inge de Bruijn)

1. Lisbeth "Libby" Trickett (Lenton)	AUS	56.73
2. Christine Magnuson	USA	57.10
3. Jessicah Schipper	AUS	57.25
4. Zhou Yafei	CHN	57.84
5. Tao Li	SIN	57.99
6. Jemma Lowe	GBR	58.06
7. Gabriella Silva	BRA	58.10
8. Inge Dekker	HOL	58.54

Libby Trickett and Jess Schipper had finished 1-2 at each of the two previous world championships, Schipper winning in 2005 and Trickett in 2007. In the Olympic final, Trickett led from the start, holding off a late challenge by Christine Magnuson.

200-METER BUTTERFLY

1896–1964 not held

1968 Mexico City C: 21, N: 16, D: 10.24. WR (220 yards): 2:21.0 (Ada Kok)

1. Ada Kok	HOL	2:24.7 OR
2. Helga Lindner	GDR	2:24.8
3. Ellie Daniel	USA	2:25.9
4. Toni Hewitt	USA	2:26.2
5. Heike Hustede	GER	2:27.9
6. Diane Giebel	USA	2:31.7
7. Margaret Auton	GBR	2:33.2
8. Yasuko Fujii	JPN	2:34.3

Six-foot, 183-pound Ada Kok, "The Gentle Giant," had experienced nothing but disappointment in the Olympics. Because of her world records and her general domination of international competitions, she had been expected to win gold medals, but in Tokyo she had to settle for two silver medals in the 100-meter butterfly and the medley relay. Four years later, in Mexico City, Kok was part of the Dutch medley relay team that finished seventh. Then, in the 100-meter butterfly, she finished a disappointing fourth. This left her one last chance for an Olympic victory—the 200-meter butterfly. Her chances seemed slim after her previous defeats, but she recorded the fastest time of the eliminations. In the final she was third at the final turn behind Heike Hustede and Helga Lindner, but Kok's powerful finish gave her a popular and well-deserved victory.

1972 Munich C: 24, N: 17, D: 9.4. WR: 2:16.62 (Karen Moe)

1. Karen Moe	USA	2:15.57 WR
2. Lynn Colella	USA	2:16.34
3. Ellie Daniel	USA	2:16.74
4. Rosemarie Kother	GDR	2:17.11
5. Noriko Asano	JPN	2:19.50
6. Helga Lindner	GDR	2:20.47
7. Gail Neall	AUS	2:21.88
8. Mayumi Aoki	JPN	2:22.84

Karen Moe let Daniel and Kother set the pace for 150 meters and then took the lead after the final turn. Moe went on to coach women's swimming at the University of California-Berkeley for fourteen years and was serving as assistant athletics director when she was terminated in 2004 after complaining about the treatment of women in the athletics department. Moe sued for gender discrimination and won a settlement of more than $3.5 million.

1976 Montreal C: 32, N: 19, D: 7.19. WR: 2:11.22 (Rosemarie Gabriel [Kother])

1. Andrea Pollack	GDR	2:11.41 OR
2. Ulrike Tauber	GDR	2:12.50
3. Rosemarie Gabriel (Kother)	GDR	2:12.86
4. Karen Thornton (Moe)	USA	2:12.90
5. Wendy Quirk	CAN	2:13.68
6. Cheryl Gibson	CAN	2:13.91
7. Tamara Shelofastova	SOV/RUS	2:14.26
8. Natalia Popova	SOV/RUS	2:14.50

1980 Moscow C: 21, N: 14, D: 7.21. WR: 2:07.01 (Mary T. Meagher)

1. Ines Geissler	GDR	2:10.44 OR
2. Sybille Schönrock	GDR	2:10.45
3. Michelle Ford	AUS	2:11.66
4. Andrea Pollack	GDR	2:12.13
5. Dorota Brzozowska	POL	2:14.12
6. Ann Osgerby	GBR	2:14.83
7. Agneta Mårtensson	SWE	2:15.22
8. Alla Grishchenkova	SOV/RUS	2:15.70

Geissler led at 50 meters and 100 meters, while Schönrock was first to touch at 150. In the end, the 17-year-old Geissler reached the wall in time to win the closest of victories. However neither woman's time came close to the performance of 15-year-old Mary T. Meagher of Cincinnati, who set a world record of 2:06.37 at the US Outdoor National nine days after the Olympic final.

1984 Los Angeles C: 29, N: 18, D: 8.4. WR: 2:05.96 (Mary T. Meagher)

1. Mary T. Meagher	USA	2:06.90 OR
2. Karen Phillips	AUS	2:10.56
3. Ina Beyermann	GER	2:11.91
4. Nancy Hogshead	USA	2:11.98
5. Samantha Purvis	GBR	2:12.33
6. Naoko Kume	JPN	2:12.57
7. Sonja Hausladen	AUT	2:15.38
8. Cornelia van Bentum	HOL	2:17.39

Mary T. Meagher led from start to finish and won by seven meters. Her time of 2:06.90 was her fastest since her 1981 world record and gave her the seven fastest times ever. Silver medallist Karen Phillips bettered her pre-Olympic best time by four seconds.

1988 Seoul C: 28, N: 21, D: 9.25. WR: 2:05.96 (Mary T. Meagher)

1. Kathleen Nord	GDR	2:09.51
2. Birte Weigang	GDR	2:09.91
3. Mary T. Meagher	USA	2:10.80
4. Stela Pura	ROM	2:11.28
5. Trina Radke	USA	2:11.55
6. Kiyomi Takahashi	JPN	2:11.62
7. Wang Xiaohong	CHN	2:12.34
8. Cornelia van Bentum	HOL	2:13.17

Mary T. Meagher entered the Olympics as the defending champion, the holder of the 11 fastest times in history and the fastest time of the year (2:09.13 at the US trials). But, like most of the US swimmers in 1988, she was unable to match her trials time and suffered only her third 200-meter butterfly loss in nine years. Twenty-two-year-old Kathleen Nord of Magdeburg overcame teammate Birte Weigang in the last 50 meters to earn the victory.

1992 Barcelona C: 32, N: 23, D: 7.31. WR: 2:05.96 (Mary T. Meagher)

1. Summer Sanders	USA	2:08.67
2. Wang Xiaohong	CHN	2:09.01
3. Susan O'Neill	AUS	2:09.03
4. Mika Haruna	JPN	2:09.88
5. Rie Shito	JPN	2:10.24
6. Ina "Angie" Wester-Krieg	USA	2:11.46
7. Mette Jacobsen	DEN	2:11.87
8. Ilaria Tocchini	ITA	2:13.78

The defending world champion, 19-year-old Summer Sanders, generally started fast and tried to hold on for the victory. Already in the Barcelona Olympics she had lost both individual medley finals after leading with a lap to go. This time Sanders held back in third place while Susie O'Neill set off at breakneck speed, followed closely by Wang Xiaohong. With one lap left, Sanders was still one-half second behind O'Neill, who did not begin swimming the 200-meter butterfly until 1991, but the Australian was running out of gas. With each stroke Sanders clawed closer, finally moving ahead in the final meters, while Wang out-touched O'Neill by an inch to take the silver. The race was so fast that the first seven finishers all set personal records.

1996 Atlanta C: 34, N: 28, D: 7.26. WR: 2:05.96 (Mary T. Meagher)

1. Susan O'Neill	AUS	2:07.76
2. Petria Thomas	AUS	2:09.82
3. Michelle Smith	IRL	2:09.91
4. Qu Yun	CHN	2:10.26
5. Liu Limin	CHN	2:10.70
6. Jessica Deglau	CAN	2:11.40
7. Mika Haruna	JPN	2:11.93
8. Trina Jackson	USA	2:11.96

Competing in her sixth event in six days, Susie O'Neill led from start to finish. Teammate Petria Thomas improved her personal record by 2½ seconds to catch fading Michelle Smith at the end.

2000 Sydney C: 36, N: 27, D: 9.20. WR: 2:05.81 (Susan O'Neill)

1. Misty Hyman	USA	2:05.88 OR
2. Susan O'Neill	AUS	2:06.58
3. Petria Thomas	AUS	2:07.12
4. Mette Jacobsen	DEN	2:08.24
5. Otylia Jędrzejczak	POL	2:08.48
6. Kaitlin Sandeno	USA	2:08.81
7. Yuko Nakanishi	JPN	2:09.66
8. Maki Mita	JPN	2:10.72

Defending Olympic champion Susie O'Neill was the overwhelming favorite to win again in 2000. Not only had she not been beaten in the 200-meter butterfly for six years, but at the Australian Olympic trials on May 17, she swam a 2:05.81 to break Mary T. Meagher's 1981 world record—the oldest swimming record in the books. On top of that, O'Neill was on a roll: the day before the butterfly final, she had won the gold medal in the 200-meter freestyle. If she could win the 200 free, there was no reason to doubt that she could also prevail in the 200-meter butterfly, which was her stronger event. Most observers were conceding the silver medal to O'Neill's teammate, Petria Thomas, who finished second to O'Neill at both the 1996 Olympics and the 1998 world championships. Third place in those world championships had gone to American Misty Hyman. But Hyman had had a rough two years. She had developed an innovative underwater sideways "fish kick" that she used for up to 30 meters after each turn. In 1998 FINA limited the use of the "fish kick" to 15 meters. Once she had adjusted to the new rule, Hyman faced a new problem. Prior to the US Olympics trials she had to overcome a "multi-layered sinus infection" that aggravated her asthma and left her on the verge of quitting. Hyman recovered in time to win the trials, but she was not considered a medal contender. Then when she arrived in Sydney, she became ill and slept for almost 20 hours.

However, when the time came for the competition to begin, it was Hyman who recorded the fastest preliminary time, 2:07.87, bettering her 3-year-old personal best by 1.21 seconds. In the semifinals, her time was only fourth best, so on the night of the final, the excited crowd of 17,500 had every reason to expect an

O'Neill-Thomas sweep. As expected, Thomas led after 50 meters before Hyman moved ahead. She led O'Neill by six-tenths of a second at the final turn, but Hyman had a history of fading in the final lap, whereas O'Neill was known for her strong finish. In the semifinals, O'Neill's time for the last 50 meters had been seven tenths of a second faster than Hyman's. But this time Hyman did not fade and actually increased her lead. Hyman was so shocked that she had to look back at the scoreboard three times before she realized she had won. The spectators were stunned into silence and Hyman could be heard to call out, "Oh my God!" eleven times.

2004 Athens C: 32, N: 26, D: 8.18. WR: 2:05.78 (Otylia Jędrzejczak)

1. Otylia Jędrzejczak	POL	2:06.05
2. Petria Thomas	AUS	2:06.36
3. Yuko Nakanishi	JPN	2:08.04
4. Kaitlin Sandeno	USA	2:08.18
5. Felicity Galvez	AUS	2:09.28
6. Mette Jacobsen	DEN	2:10.01
7. Paola Cavallino	ITA	2:10.14
8. Éva Risztov	HUN	2:10.58

World record holder and reigning world champion Otylia Jędrzejczak was the favorite in the event, but was expected to be challenged by Petria Thomas, who had won the 100-meter butterfly three days earlier. Thomas took the lead, building a full body-length advantage by the halfway point, but Jędrzejczak caught her in the final 50 meters to take the gold. After the race, Jędrzejczak auctioned her gold medal on the Internet, donating the proceeds ($82,000) to a children's hospital in Warsaw.

In October 2005, Jędrzejczak was involved in a car accident while attempting to pass several trucks on a two-lane road. She swerved into a ditch and hit a tree, killing her 19-year-old brother. Jędrzejczak herself sustained spinal and head injuries, but returned to competition and won the European championship in August 2006.

2008 Beijing C: 34, N: 26, D: 8.14. WR: 2:05.40 (Jessicah Schipper)

1. Liu Zige	CHN	2:04.18	WR
2. Jiao Liuyang	CHN	2:04.72	
3. Jessicah Schipper	AUS	2:06.26	
4. Otylia Jędrzejczak	POL	2:07.02	
5. Yuko Nakanishi	JPN	2:07.32	
6. Aurore Mongel	FRA	2:07.36	
7. Elaine Breeden	USA	2:07.57	
8. Kathleen Hersey	USA	2:08.23	

Liu Zige and Jiao Liuyang recorded the two fastest qualifying times and dominated the final, moving past reigning world champion Jess Schipper for a 1-2 finish. Liu improved her personal best by nearly two-and-a-half seconds and lowered the world record by 1.22 seconds. The 19-year-old was almost completely unknown before the Beijing Olympics, having competed only once in an international meet—at the 2005 world championship.

200-METER INDIVIDUAL MEDLEY

In individual medley races the order of strokes is butterfly, backstroke, breaststroke, and freestyle.

1896–1964 not held

1968 Mexico City C: 39, N: 26, D: 10.20. WR: 2:23.5 (Claudia Kolb)

1. Claudia Kolb	USA	2:24.7 OR
2. Susan Pedersen	USA	2:28.8
3. Jan Henne	USA	2:31.4
4. Sabine Steinbach	GDR	2:31.4
5. Yoshimi Nishigawa	JPN	2:33.7
6. Marianne Seydel	GDR	2:33.7
7. Larissa Zakharova	SOV	2:37.0

DISQ: Shelagh Ratcliffe (GBR)

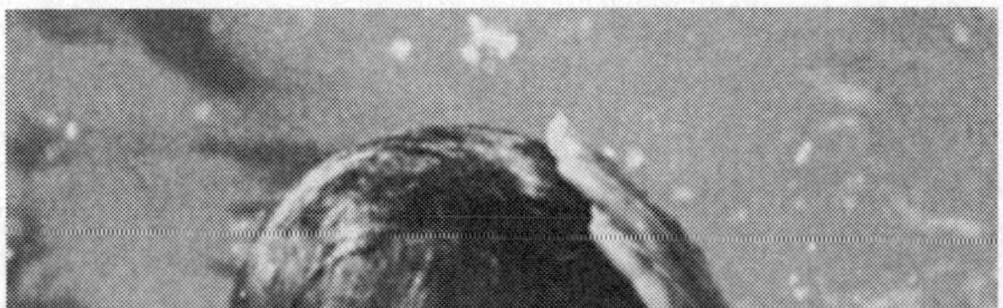

Claudia Kolb, 1968
A silver medalist at 14, dominant in winning the 200 and 400-meter individual medleys in Mexico City at 18.

When she was 14 years old, Claudia Kolb of Santa Clara, California, earned a surprise silver medal in the 200-meter breaststroke. Four years later she overwhelmed her opposition to win both the 200-meter and 400-meter individual medleys.

1972 Munich C: 44, N: 26, D: 8.28. WR: 2:23.5 (Claudia Kolb)

1. Shane Gould	AUS	2:23.07 WR
2. Kornelia Ender	GDR	2:23.59
3. Lynn Vidali	USA	2:24.06
4. Jennifer Bartz	USA	2:24.55
5. Leslie Cliff	CAN	2:24.83
6. Evelyn Stolze	GDR	2:25.90
7. Yoshimi Nishigawa	JPN	2:26.35
8. Carolyn Woods	USA	2:27.42

Lynn Vidali led by over a second after 150 meters, but Shane Gould used her freestyle strength to catch her 20 meters later and win the first of her three gold medals. As she walked out for the medal ceremony, Australian swimming great Dawn Fraser handed Gould a worn out toy kangaroo that she had held while being presented one of her medals. In second place was 13-year-old Kornelia Ender, who won the first of her eight Olympic medals.

1976–1980 not held

1984 Los Angeles C: 27, N: 21, D: 8.3. WR: 2:11.73 (Ute Geweniger)

1. Tracy Caulkins	USA	2:12.64 OR
2. Nancy Hogshead	USA	2:15.17
3. Michele Pearson	AUS	2:15.92
4. Lisa Curry	AUS	2:16.75
5. Christiane Pielke	GER	2:17.82
6. Manuela Dalla Valle	ITA	2:19.69
7. Petra Zindler	GER	2:19.86
8. Katrine Bomstad	NOR	2:20.48

Tracy Caulkins won the second of her three gold medals.

1988 Seoul C: 36, N: 24, D: 9.24. WR: 2:11.73 (Ute Geweniger)

1. Daniela Hunger	GDR	2:12.59 OR
2. Yelena Dendeberova	SOV/RUS	2:13.31
3. Noëmi Lung	ROM	2:14.85
4. Judith "Jodie" Clatworthy	AUS	2:16.31
5. Marianne Muis	HOL	2:16.40
6. Aneta Pătrăşcoiu	ROM	2:16.70
7. Lin Li	CHN	2:17.42
8. Whitney Hedgepeth	USA	2:17.99

Sixteen-year-old Daniela Hunger of Berlin overcame Dendeberova in the final 50 meters.

1992 Barcelona C: 43, N: 31, D: 7.30. WR: 2:11.73 (Ute Geweniger)

1. Lin Li	CHN	2:11.65 WR
2. Summer Sanders	USA	2:11.91
3. Daniela Hunger	GER	2:13.92
4. Yelena Dendeberova	RUS	2:15.47
5. Ellinora Overton	AUS	2:15.76
6. Marianne Limpert	CAN	2:17.09
7. Nancy Sweetnam	CAN	2:17.13
8. Ewa Synowska	POL	2:18.85

The final was a terrific duel between Lin Li of Nantung, in Jiangsu Province, and Summer Sanders of Roseville, California. At the 1991 world championships, Lin had come from behind to edge Sanders by .66 seconds. This time the race was even closer. Sanders used her butterfly strength (the next day she won the gold medal in the 200-meter butterfly) to take a lead of .42 seconds after 50 meters. Lin moved ahead on the backstroke lap, but Sanders regained the lead with the breaststroke. Lin exploited Sanders' freestyle weakness to inch ahead again with 30 meters to go. Sanders made one last challenge in the race to the wall, but Lin held on to win, by about 16 inches. Her time of 2:11.65 broke Ute Geweniger's 11-year-old world record.

1996 Atlanta C: 43, N: 39, D: 7.24. WR: 2:11.65 (Lin Li)

1. Michelle Smith	IRL	2:13.93
2. Marianne Limpert	CAN	2:14.35
3. Lin Li	CHN	2:14.74
4. Joanne Malar	CAN	2:15.30
5. Ellinora Overton	AUS	2:16.04
6. Allison Wagner	USA	2:16.43
7. Minouche Smit	HOL	2:16.73
8. Louise Karlsson	SWE	2:17.25

Michelle Smith led at the halfway mark, fell back to fourth after the breaststroke leg, and then forged ahead in the last 25 meters to win her third gold medal.

2000 Sydney C: 36, N: 28, D: 9.19. WR: 2:09.72 (Wu Yanyan)

1. Yana Klochkova	UKR	2:10.6 OR
2. Beatrice Coadă-Câşlaru	ROM	2:12.57
3. Cristina Teuscher	USA	2:13.32
4. Marianne Limpert	CAN	2:13.44
5. Joanne Malar	CAN	2:13.70
6. Oksana Verevka	RUS	2:13.88
7. Gabrielle Rose	USA	2:14.82
8. Tomoko Hagiwara	JPN	2:15.64

This event had seen more than its share of ugliness in the run-up to the 2000 Olympics. In 1998, the 1996 Olympic champion, Michelle Smith, was banned from competition for tampering with a drug test. Wu Yanyan of China set the world record in 1997 and then won the 1998 world championship. But at the Chinese Olympic trials in May 2000, she tested positive for steroids and she too was suspended.

Yana Klochkova had already won the 400-meter individual medley in world record time when, three days later, she surprised herself by winning the 200 IM with relative ease.

2004 Athens C: 30, N: 27, D: 8.17. WR: 2:09.72 (Wu Yanyan)

1. Yana Klochkova	UKR	2:11.14
2. Amanda Beard	USA	2:11.70
3. Kirsty Coventry	ZIM	2:12.72
4. Ágnes Kovács	HUN	2:13.58
5. Teresa Rohmann	GER	2:13.70
6. Lara Carroll	AUS	2:13.74
7. Katharine Hoff	USA	2:13.97
8. Beatrice Coadă-Câşlaru	ROM	2:15.40

Yana Klochkova was the clear favorite, having won nearly every Olympic, world and European individual medley title since 1999. The one exception was a surprise loss to Maggie Bowen of the United States in the final of the 2001 200-meter world championships. Three days after successfully defending her 400-meter gold, Klochkova became the first woman to sweep the Olympic individual medleys twice.

2008 Beijing C: 38, N: 29, D: 8.13. WR: 2:08.92 (Stephanie Rice)

1. Stephanie Rice	AUS	2:08.45 WR
2. Kirsty Coventry	ZIM	2:08.59
3. Natalie Coughlin	USA	2:10.34
4. Katherine Hoff	USA	2:10.68
5. Alicia Coutts	AUS	2:11.43
6. Asami Kitagawa	JPN	2:11.56
7. Julia Wilkinson	CAN	2:12.43
8. Kasia Baranowska	POL	2:13.36

World record holder Stephanie Rice completed her sweep of the 2008 individual medley events, holding off twice world silver medalist Kirsty Coventry for the second time in four days. Natalie Coughlin took bronze one day after beating Coventry in the 100-meter backstroke event.

As in the 400-meter event, Coventry managed to swim under the world record time in the final, but still finished second to Rice.

400-METER INDIVIDUAL MEDLEY

1896–1960 not held

1964 Tokyo C: 22, N: 12, D: 10.17. WR: 5:14.9 (Donna De Varona)

1. Donna De Varona	USA	5:18.7 OR
2. Sharon Finneran	USA	5:24.1
3. Martha Randall	USA	5:24.2
4. Veronika Holletz	GDR	5:25.6
5. Linda McGill	AUS	5:28.4
6. Elisabeth Heukels	HOL	5:30.3
7. Anita Lonsbrough	GBR	5:30.5
8. Márta Egerváry	HUN	5:38.4

Donna De Varona, 1964
After winning two gold medals at the Tokyo Games, De Varona went on to become a sports commentator and an activist for women in sports.

Donna De Varona was a popular and much-photographed winner. She later became a television sports commentator as well as an activist for women in sports. She was a cofounder of the Women Sports Foundation and chair of the 1999 Women's World Cup Organizing Committee. Linda McGill, who placed fifth, later gained reknown as an endurance swimmer. She crossed from France to England in 9 hours 59 minutes and she was the first person to swim around Hong Kong.

1968 Mexico City C: 28, N: 19, D: 10.25. WR: 5:04.7 (Claudia Kolb)

1. Claudia Kolb	USA	5:08.5 OR
2. Lynn Vidali	USA	5:22.2
3. Sabine Steinbach	GDR	5:25.3
4. Susan Pedersen	USA	5:25.8
5. Shelagh Ratcliffe	GBR	5:30.5
6. Marianne Seydel	GDR	5:32.0
7. Tui Shipston	NZL	5:34.6
8. Laura Vaca Hernández	MEX	5:35.7

Claudia Kolb won by 20 meters, the most decisive women's swimming victory in 40 years.

1972 Munich C: 38, N: 26, D: 8.31. WR: 5:04.7 (Claudia Kolb)

1. Gail Neall	AUS	5:02.97 WR
2. Leslie Cliff	CAN	5:03.57
3. Novella Calligaris	ITA	5:03.99
4. Jennifer Bartz	USA	5:05.56
5. Evelyn Stolze	GDR	5:06.80
6. Mary Montgomery	USA	5:09.98
7. Lynn Vidali	USA	5:13.06
8. Nina Petrova	SOV/RUS	5:15.68

Gail Neall, from the Sydney suburb of Gordon, took the lead on the second lap and held it all the way through the backstroke and breaststroke legs. At the beginning of the freestyle, Leslie Cliff made her move and pulled ahead at the final turn. Neall fought back and drew even again with 30 meters to go. The two matched strokes for ten meters. Then Neall pushed ahead to gain the victory and break Claudia Kolb's four-year-old world record. A surprise winner, Neall bettered her personal best by seven seconds.

1976 Montreal C: 20, N: 11, D: 7.24. WR: 4:48.79 (Birgit Treiber)

1. Ulrike Tauber	GDR	4:42.77 WR
2. Cheryl Gibson	CAN	4:48.10
3. Rebecca Smith	CAN	4:50.48
4. Birgit Treiber	GDR	4:52.40
5. Sabine Kahle	GDR	4:53.50
6. Donnalee Wennerstrom	USA	4:55.34
7. Joann Baker	CAN	5:00.19
8. Monique Rodahl	NZL	5:00.21

Eighteen-year-old Ulrike Tauber of Karl-Marx-Stadt (Chemnitz), who was given steroids from 1974 until 1980, bettered the world record by a phenomenal 6.02 seconds.

1980 Moscow C 16, N: 11, D: 7.26. WR: 4:38.44 (Petra Schneider)

1. Petra Schneider	GDR	4:36.29 WR
2. Sharron Davies	GBR	4:46.83
3. Agnieszka Czopek	POL	4:48.17
4. Grit Slaby	GDR	4:48.54
5. Ulrike Tauber	GDR	4:49.18
6. Sonya Dangalakova	BUL	4:49.25
7. Olga Klevakina	SOV/RUS	4:50.91
8. Magdalena Białas	POL	4:53.30

Once again the 400-meter individual medley was completely dominated by one swimmer. This time it was an easy win and new world record for 17-year-old Petra Schneider, who had been trained in part by her older teammate Ulrike Tauber. At the 1977 European Championships in Sweden, Sharron Davies and other British swimmers heard deep baritone voices on the other side of a wall. Thinking it was Swedish workmen spying on them while they changed, they protested to the authorities in charge. But what they heard was not workmen—it was the East German swimmers. Petra Schneider later revealed that she was secretly given a reward of 20,000 East German marks for her gold medal. Davies, on the other hand, was stripped of her amateur status after she accepted $40 from a television program.

In the United States on July 30, Tracy Caulkins clocked 4:40.61 at the Outdoor National to bolster her position as the fastest non-drugged female medley swimmer in the world.

1984 Los Angeles C: 18, N: 13, D: 7.29. WR: 4:36.10 (Petra Schneider)

1. Tracy Caulkins	USA	4:39.24
2. Suzanne Landells	AUS	4:48.30
3. Petra Zindler	GER	4:48.57
4. Susan Heon	USA	4:49.41
5. Nathalie Gingras	CAN	4:50.55
6. Donna McGinnis	CAN	4:50.65
7. Gaynor Stanley	GBR	4:52.83
8. Katrine Bomstad	NOR	4:53.28

Since 1978 Tracy Caulkins of Nashville, Tennessee, had set five world records, over 60 US records and had won 48 US national titles, twelve more than any other swimmer. All that was missing from her sterling career was an Olympic championship. That void was filled when she led the 400-meter individual medley from start to finish, winning by almost 15 meters.

1988 Seoul C: 30, N: 22, D: 9.19. WR: 4:36.10 (Petra Schneider)

1. Janet Evans	USA	4:37.76
2. Noëmi Lung	ROM	4:39.46
3. Daniela Hunger	GDR	4:39.76
4. Yelena Dendeberova	SOV/RUS	4:40.44
5. Kathleen Nord	GDR	4:41.64
6. Judith "Jodie" Clatworthy	AUS	4:45.86
7. Lin Li	CHN	4:47.05
8. Donna Procter	AUS	4:47.51

Janet Evans took command on the backstroke leg and won the first of her four gold medals.

1992 Barcelona C: 32, N: 21, D: 7.26. WR: 4:36.10 (Petra Schneider)

1. Krisztina Egerszegi	HUN	4:36.54
2. Lin Li	CHN	4:36.73
3. Summer Sanders	USA	4:37.58
4. Hayley Lewis	AUS	4:43.75
5. Hideko Hiranaka	JPN	4:46.24
6. Daniela Hunger	GER	4:47.57
7. Eri Kimura	JPN	4:47.78
8. Ewa Synowska	POL	4:53.32

Sanders, who later won the 200-meter butterfly, led by a body length after the butterfly leg. Egerszegi, who later won both backstroke golds, sailed past Sanders in the backstroke leg and moved ahead by more than two meters. The breaststroke was the great equalizer. Sanders recaptured the lead while Lin turned the race into a three-woman contest. Sanders, a weak freestyler, could not hold on. Egerszegi took the lead for good in the final lap and then held off Lin by a foot. Egerszegi and Lin swam the fastest times since Petra Schneider's 1982 world record.

1996 Atlanta C: 31, N: 24, D: 7.20. WR: 4:36.10 (Petra Schneider)

1. Michelle Smith	IRL	4:39.18
2. Allison Wagner	USA	4:42.03
3. Krisztina Egerszegi	HUN	4:42.53
4. Sabine Herbst	GER	4:43.78
5. Emma Johnson	AUS	4:44.02
6. Beatrice Coadă	ROM	4:44.91
7. Lourdes Becerra Portero	SPA	4:45.17
8. Whitney Metzler	USA	4:46.20

Allison Wagner of Gainesville, Florida, could be excused if she was disheartened by her experiences in international swimming. At the 1994 world championship in Rome, she finished second in both individual medley races. She lost the gold medal in the 200 IM to China's Lu Bin, who tested positive for steroids four weeks later. In the 400 IM she was beaten by another Chinese swimmer, Dai Guohong, who disappeared from competition a year later. In Atlanta, Wagner was deprived of an Olympic gold medal by Michelle Smith, who was ultimately suspended for tampering with a drug test.

2000 Sydney C: 28, N: 24, D: 9.16. WR: 4:34.79 (Chen Yan)

1. Yana Klochkova	UKR	4:33.59 WR
2. Yasuko Tajima	JPN	4:35.96
3. Beatrice Coadă-Câşlaru	ROM	4:37.18
4. Kaitlin Sandeno	USA	4:41.03
5. Nicole Hetzer	GER	4:43.56
6. Madeleine Crippen	USA	4:44.63
7. Joanne Malar	CAN	4:45.17
8. Jennifer Reilly	AUS	4:45.99

Yana Klochkova led from start to finish. Yasuko Tajima stayed close for the first half of the race, but could not keep up on the breaststroke leg as Klochkova pulled away to break Chen Yan's three-year-old world record.

2004 Athens C: 25, N: 21, D: 8.14. WR: 4:33.59 (Yana Klochkova)

1. Yana Klochkova	UKR	4:34.83
2. Kaitlin Sandeno	USA	4:34.95
3. Georgina Bardach	ARG	4:37.51
4. Éva Risztov	HUN	4:39.29
5. Joanna Maranhão	BRA	4:40.00
6. Nicole Hetzer	GER	4:40.20
7. Nam Yoo-sun	KOR	4:50.35
8. Vasiliki Angelopoulou	GRE	4:50.85

Yana Klochkova, 2004
Klochkova won both 200-meter and 400-meter individual medley events in 2000 and 2004.

Competing one week after her 22nd birthday, defending Olympic champion, two-time defending world champion and world record holder Yana Klochkova was seriously, and unexpectedly, challenged by Kaitlin Sandeno of Los Angeles. Sandeno kept pace with Klochkova throughout the race, pulling ahead briefly at the final turn, before Klochkova swam the last 50 meters in 29.93 seconds to secure the gold. Sandeno's time of 4:34.95 bettered her personal best by 5.44 seconds.

2008 Beijing C: 37, N: 27, D: 8.10. WR: 4:31.12 (Katie Hoff)

1. Stephanie Rice	AUS	4:29.45 WR
2. Kirsty Coventry	ZIM	4:29.89
3. Katherine Hoff	USA	4:31.71
4. Elizabeth Beisel	USA	4:34.24
5. Alessia Filippi	ITA	4:34.34
6. Hannah Miley	GBR	4:39.44
7. Yana Martynova	RUS	4:40.04
8. Li Xuanxu	CHN	4:42.13

A month before the Olympics, two-time reigning world champion Katie Hoff set a world record at the US Olympic trials. However, in Beijing it was the previous world record holder, Stephanie Rice, who came out strongly in the final, moving almost four seconds ahead of world record pace at the halfway mark. Kirsty Coventry, swimming in lane one, closed the gap, but Rice held on for the victory, as both of them smashed Hoff's world record. Three days later Rice won the 200-meter individual medley event, again finishing just ahead of Coventry.

10,000-METER OPEN WATER

1896-2004 not held

2008 Beijing C: 25, N: 23, D: 8.20.

1. Larisa Ilchenko	RUS	1:59:27.7
2. Keri-Anne Payne	GBR	1:59:29.2
3. Cassandra Patten	GBR	1:59:31.0
4. Angela Maurer	GER	1:59:31.9
5. Ana da Cunha	BRA	1:59:36.8
6. Swann Oberson	SWI	1:59:36.9
7. Poliana Okimoto	BRA	1:59:37.4
8. Jana Pechanová	CZE	1:59:39.7

Three-time world champion Larisa Ilchenko spent most of the race trailing double world silver medalist Cassie Patten and her teammate Keri-Anne Payne. The 19-year-old Ilchenko made her move in the final straightaway, pulling ahead over the last 100 meters to win the gold.

Sixteenth place finisher Natalie du Toit had an inspiring path to the Olympics. As a teenager she had narrowly missed a spot on South Africa's Sydney 2000 Olympic team. A year later she was hit by a car while riding her scooter and lost her left leg below the knee. She continued swimming, winning five gold medals and one silver at the 2004 Paralympics. She qualified for the Beijing Olympics after finishing fourth at the 2008 world championships.

Du Toit was the first amputee to compete at the Olympics since gymnast George Eyser won three gold medals, two silver and one bronze at the 1904 Olympics. Eyser competed with a wooden leg.

4 × 100-METER FREESTYLE RELAY

Swimmers who took part in preliminary heats but not in finals are listed in brackets.

1896–1908 not held

1912 Stockholm T: 4, N: 4, D: 7.15.

1. GBR	Isabella Moore, Jennie Fletcher, Annie Speirs, Irene Steer	5:52.8 WR
2. GER	Wally Dressel, Louise Otto, Hermine Stindt, Margareta Rosenberg	6:04.6
3. AUT	Margareta Adler, Klara Milch, Josefine Sticker, Berta Zahourek	6:17.0
4. SWE	Greta Carlsson, Margareta Johansson, Sonja Jonsson, Vera Thulin	—

Australia's two women swimmers, Fanny Durack and Mina Wylie, finished first and second in the individual race. They wanted to compete in the relay and offered to swim two legs each, but their proposal was rejected.

1920 Antwerp T: 3, N: 3, D: 8.29

1. USA	Margaret Woodbridge, Frances Schroth, Irene Guest, Ethelda Bleibtrey	5:11.6 WR
2. GBR	Hilda James, Constance Jeans, Charlotte Radcliffe, Grace McKenzie	5:40.8
3. SWE	Aina Berg, Emy Machnow, Carin Nilsson, Jane Gylling	5:43.6

1924 Paris T: 6, N: 6, D: 7.18.

1. USA	Gertrude Ederle, Euphrasia Donnelly, Ethel Lackle, Marlechen Wehselau	4:58.8 WR
2. GBR	Florence Barker, Grace McKenzie, Irene Vera Tanner, Constance Jeans	5:17.0
3. SWE	Aina Berg, "Wivan" Pettersson, Gunhild "Gulli" Ewerlund, Hjördis Töpel	5:35.6
4. DEN	Vibeke Möller, Hedevig Rasmussen, Karen Maud Rasmussen, Agnete Olsen	5:42.4
5. FRA	Ernestine Lebrun, Gilberte Mortier, Bibienne Pellegry, Marguerite Protin	5:43.4
6. HOL	Mietje Baron, Alida Bolten, Geertruida Klapwijk, Maria Vierdag	5:45.8

1928 Amsterdam T: 7, N: 7, D: 8.9.

1. USA	Adelaide Lambert, Eleanor Garatti, Albina Osipowich, Martha Norelius, [Josephine McKim, Susan Laird]	4:47.6 WR
2. GBR	M. Joyce Cooper, Sarah "Cissie" Stewart, Irene Tanner, Ellen King	5:02.8
3. SAF	Kathleen Russell, Rhoda Rennie, Marie Bedford, Frederica van der Goes	5:13.4
4. GER	Charlotte Lehmann, Irene Erkens, Herta Wunder, Irmintraut Schneider	5:14.4
5. FRA	Bibienne Pellegry, Anne Dupire, Marguerite Ledoux, Claire Horrent, [Georgina Roty]	5.32.0

DISQ: HOL—Elisabeth Smits, Geertje Baumeister, Maria Vierdag, Maria Braun

1932 Los Angeles T:5, N: 5, D: 8.12. WR: 4:47.6 (USA—Lambert, Garatti, Osipowich, Norelius)

1. USA	Josephine McKim, Helen Johns, Eleanor Saville [Garatti], Helene Madison	4:38.0 WR
2. HOL	Maria Vierdag, Maria Oversloot, Cornelia Laddé, Willemijntje den Ouden	4:47.5
3. GBR	E. Valerie Davies, Helen Varcoe, M. Joyce Cooper, Edna Hughes	4:52.4
4. CAN	Irene Pirie, Irene Mullen, Ruth Kerr, Elizabeth Edwards	5:05.7
5. JPN	Kazue Kojima, Hatsuko Morioka, Misao Yokota, Yukie Arata	5:06.7

1936 Berlin T: 9, N: 9, D: 8.14. WR: 4:32.8 (HOL—Selbach, Mastenbroek, Wagner, den Ouden)

1. HOL	Johanna "Jopie" Selbach, Catharina "Tini" Wagner, Willemijntje "Willy" den Ouden, Hendrika "Rie" Mastenbroek	4:36.0 OR
2. GER	Ruth Halbsguth, Leni Lohmar, Ingeborg Schmitz, Gisela Arendt, [Ursula Pollack]	4:36.8
3. USA	Katherine Rawls, Bernice Lapp, Mavis Freeman, Olive McKean, [Elizabeth Ryan]	4:40.2
4. HUN	Ilona Ács, Ágnes Biró, Véra Harsányi, Magdolna Lenkei	4:48.0
4. CAN	Mary McConkey, Irene Milton-Pirie, Margaret Stone, Phyllis Dewar	4:48.0
6. GBR	Margaret Jeffery, Zilpha Grant, Edna Hughes, Olive Wadham	4:51.0
7. DEN	Ragnhild Hveger, Tove Brunnström Madsen, Elvi Svendsen, Eva Arendt	4:51.4

Germany led for 200 meters before den Ouden gave Holland the lead. The race was still in doubt with 20 meters to go, at which point Mastenbroek sprinted to victory.

1948 London T: 11, N: 11, D: 8.6. WR: 4:27.6 (DEN—Arndt, Kraft, Ove-Peterson, Hveger)

1.	USA	Marie Corridon, Thelma Kalama, Brenda Helser, Ann Curtis	4:29.2 OR
2.	DEN	Eva Riise, Karen-Margrete Harup, Greta Andersen, Fritze Carstensen, [Elvi Carlsen Svendsen]	4:29.6
3.	HOL	Irma Schuhmacher, Margot Marsman, Marie-Louise Vaessen, Johanna Termeulen	4:31.6
4.	GBR	Patricia Nielsen, Margaret Wellington, Lillian Preece, Catherine Gibson	4:34.7
5.	HUN	Mária Littomeritzky, Judit Temes, Ilona Novák, Éva Székely	4:44.8
6.	BRA	Eleonora Schmitt, Maria Leão da Costa, Talita de Alencar Rodrigues, Piedade Silva Tavares	4:49.1
7.	FRA	Josette Arène, Gisèle Vallerey, Colette Thomas, Ginette Jany, [Marie Foucher-Cretau]	4:49.8

DISQ: SWE—Gisela Thidholm, Elisabeth Ahlgren, Marianne Lundquist, Ingegärd Fredin

Ann Curtis swam a spectacular anchor leg to give the United States a come-from-behind victory over Denmark. She was timed in 1:04.4, which unofficially bettered Willy den Ouden's 12-year-old world record for the 100 meters. However, marks set during relays do not qualify for world records unless they are accomplished on the first leg.

1952 Helsinki T: 13, N: 13, D: 8.1. WR: 4:27.2 (HUN— Littomeritzky, Novák, Székely, Szöke)

1.	HUN	Ilona Novák, Judit Temes, Éva Novák Katalin Szőke, [Mária Littomericzky]	4:24.4 WR
2.	HOL	Marie-Louise Linssen [Vaessen], Koosje van Voorn, Johanna Termeulen, Irma Heijting-Schuhmacher	4:29.0
3.	USA	Jacqueline La Vine, Marilee Stepan, Joan Alderson, Evelyn Kawamoto	4:30.1
4.	DEN	Rita Larsen, Mette Ove-Peterson, Greta Andersen, Ragnhild Andersen-Hveger	4:36.2
5.	GBR	Phyllis Linton, Jean Botham, Angela Barnwell, Lillian Preece	4:37.8
6.	SWE	Marianne Lundquist, Anita Andersson, Maud Berglund, Ingegärd Fredin	4:39.0
7.	GER	Elisabeth Rechlin, Vera Schäferkordt, Kati Jansen, Gisela Jacobs [Arendt]	4:40.3
8.	FRA	Gaby Tanguy, Maryse Morandini, Ginette Jany, Josette Arène	4:44.1

Judit Temes, Eva Novák and Katalin Szőke swam legs of 1:05.8, 1:05.1, and 1:05.7, respectively, each of which was a full second faster than Szöke's time when she won the 100-meter freestyle final four days earlier.

1956 Melbourne T: 10, N: 10, D: 12.6. WR: 4:19.7 (AUS—Crapp, Fraser, Leech, Gibson)

1.	AUS	Dawn Fraser, Faith Leech, Sandra Morgan, Lorraine Crapp, [Margeret Gibson]	4:17.1 WR
2.	USA	Sylvia Ruuska, Shelly Mann, Nancy Simons, Joan Rosazza, [Elizabeth Brey, Kathryn Knapp, Marley Shriver]	4:19.2
3.	SAF	Jeanette Myburgh, Susan Roberts, Natalie Myburgh, Moira Abernathy	4:25.7
4.	GER	Ingrid Künzel, Hertha Haase, Katharine Jansen Birgit Klomp	4:26.1
5.	CAN	Helen Stewart, Gladys Priestley, Sara Barber, Virginia Grant	4:28.3
6.	SWE	Anita Hellström, Birgitta Wängberg, Anna Larsson, Kate Jobson	4:30.0
7.	HUN	Mária Littomeritzky, Katalin Szöke, Judit Temes, Valéria Gyenge	4:31.1
8.	GBR	Frances Hogben, Judith Grinham, Margaret Girvan, Fearne Ewart	4:35.8

The Australians got off to a bad start when the starter's gun went off a second time by mistake and lead-off swimmer Dawn Fraser, thinking a false start had been called, stopped swimming. When she realized that the other swimmers had kept going, she caught up quickly and touched off with a two-second lead. The Americans gradually caught up, but Lorraine Crapp's anchor leg of 1:03.1 sealed the victory.

1960 Rome T: 12, N: 12, D: 9.3. WR (440 yards): 4:16.2 (AUS—Fraser, Colquhoun, Konrads, Crapp)

1.	USA	Joan Spillane, Shirley Stobs, Carolyn Wood, S. Christine Von Saltza, [Donna De Varona, Susan Doerr, Sylvia Ruuska, Molly Botkin]	4:08.9 WR
2.	AUS	Dawn Fraser, Ilsa Konrads, Lorraine Crapp, Alva Colquhoun, [Sandra Morgan, Ruth Everuss]	4:11.3
3.	GDR& GER	Christel Steffin, Heidi Pechstein, Gisela Weiss, Ursula Brunner	4:19.7
4.	HUN	Anna Temesvári, Mária Frank, Kátalin Boros, Csilla Dobai-Madarász	4:21.2
5.	GBR	Natalie Steward, Beryl Noakes, Judith Samuel, Christine Harris	4:24.6
6.	SWE	Inger Thorngren, Karin Larsson, Kristina Larsson, Birte Segerström	4:25.1
7.	ITA	Paola Saini, Annamaria Cecchi, Rosanna Contardo, Maria Christina Pacifici, [Daniela Beneck]	4:26.8
8.	SOV	Irina Liakhovskaya, Ulvi Voog, Galina Sosnova, Marina Shamal	4:29.0

In 1956 Lorraine Crapp had been one of Australia's heroines, winning two gold medals and one silver. But in 1960 she had other things on her mind. The night before the Australian team left for Rome she had secretly married Bill Thurlow, one of the doctors associated with the Australian swimmers. Thurlow traveled to Rome on his own and rented an apartment. After the lights were put out at the Olympic Village, Crapp would sneak out and spend the night with her husband. When Australian officials became suspicious of her early morning absences, Crapp admitted her deception. Unfortunately, the officials overreacted. Instead of simply giving her permission to sleep outside the Village as many other married athletes did, they punished her by restricting her movements and keeping watch on her. Demoralized, Crapp swam a lackluster third leg in the freestyle relay, losing a crucial five yards and 2.7 seconds to Carolyn Wood.

1964 Tokyo T: 10, N: 10, D: 10.15. WR: 4:07.6 (USA—Allsup, Stickles, Seidel, Bricker)

1. USA	Sharon Stouder, Donna De Varona, Lillian "Pokey" Watson, Kathleen Ellis, [Jeanne Hallock, Ericka Bricker, Lynne Allsup, Patience Sherman]	4:03.8 WR
2. AUS	Robyn Thorn, Janice Murphy, Lynette Bell, Dawn Fraser, [Jan Turner]	4:06.9
3. HOL	Paulina van der Wildt, Catharina Beumer, Wilhelmina van Weerdenburg, Erica Terpstra	4:12.0
4. HUN	Judit Turóczy, Éva Erdélyi, Katalin Takács, Csilla Dobai-Madarász, [Mária Frank]	4:12.1
5. SWE	Ann-Charlott Lilja, Katrin Andersson, Ulla Jäfvert, Ann-Christine Hagberg	4:14.0
6. GDR& GER	Martina Grunert, Gertrude "Traudi" Beierlein, Rita Schumacher, Heidi Pechstein	4:15.0
7. CAN	Mary Stewart, Patricia Thompson, Helen Kennedy, Marion Lay	4:15.9
8. ITA	Paola Saini, Maria Christina Pacifici, Mara Sacchi, Daniela Beneck	4:17.2

1968 Mexico City T: 15, N: 15, D: 10.26. WR: 4:01.1 (USA, Santa Clara Swim Club—Gustavson, Watson, Carpinelli, Henne)

1. USA	Jane Barkman, Linda Gustavson, Susan Pedersen, Jan Henne	4:02.5 OR
2. GDR	Gabriele Wetzko, Roswitha Krause, Uta Schmuck, Martina Grunert, [Gabriele Perthes]	4:05.7
3. CAN	Angela Coughlan, Marilyn Corson, Elaine Tanner, Marion Lay	4:07.2
4. AUS	Janette Steinbeck, Susan Eddy, Lynette Watson, Lynette Bell, [Julie McDonald]	4:08.7
5. HUN	Edit Kovács, Magdolna Patóh, Andrea Gyarmati, Judit Turóczy	4:11.0
6. JPN	Shigeko Kawanishi, Yoshimi Nishigawa, Yasuko Fujii, Miwako Kobayashi, [Yumiko Ono]	4:13.6
7. GBR	Shelagh Ratcliffe, Fiona Kellock, Susan Williams, Alexandra Jackson	4:18.0

DISQ: FRA—Marie Kersaudy, Simone Hanner, Daniele Dorleans, Claude Mandonnaud

1972 Munich T: 16, N: 16, D: 8.30. WR: 3:58.11 (USA—Peyton, Neilson, Barkman, Babashoff)

1. USA	Sandra Neilson, Jennifer Kemp, Jane Barkman, Shirley Babashoff, [Kimberley Peyton, Lynn Skrifvars, Ann Marshall]	3:55.19 WR
2. GDR	Gabriele Wetzko, Andrea Eife, Elke Sehmisch, Kornelia Ender, [Sylvia Eichner]	3:55.55
3. GER	Jutta Weber, Heidemarie Reineck, Gudrun Beckmann, Angela Steinbach	3:57.93
4. HUN	Andréa Gyarmati, Judit Turóczy, Edit Kovács, Magdolna Patoh	4:00.39
5. HOL	Enith Brigitha, Anke Rijnders, Hansje Bunschoten, Josien Elzerman	4:01.49
6. SWE	Anita Zarnowiecki, Eva Andersson, Diana Olsson, Irwi Johansson	4:02.69
7. CAN	Wendy Cook, Judy Wright, Mary-Beth Rondeau, Leslie Cliff	4:03.83
8. AUS	Deborah Palmer, Leanne Francis, Sharon Booth, Shane Gould, [Debra Cain]	4:04.82

Until August 18, 1972, no women's relay team had broken the four-minute barrier. On that day Neilson, Barkman, Babashoff, and Kim Peyton of the United States recorded a time of 3:58.11. Twelve days later, in the qualifying heats of the Olympics, the East Germans tied that mark. That evening, in the final, the record took another battering. Sandy Neilson took a quarter-second lead over Gabriele Wetzko, and the remaining American swimmers held on with great determination, withstanding a continuous challenge from the East Germans that lasted until the final touch.

1976 Montreal T: 14, N: 14, D: 7.25. WR: 3:48.80 (GDR, Sports Club Dynamo—Krause, Seltman, Gabriel, Pollack)

1. USA	Kim Peyton, Wendy Boglioli, Jill Sterkel, Shirley Babashoff, [Jennifer Hooker]	3:44.82 WR
2. GDR	Kornelia Ender, Petra Priemer, Andrea Pollack, Claudia Hempel	3:45.50
3. CAN	Gail Amundrud, Barbara Clark, Rebecca Smith, Anne Jardin, [Deborah Clarke]	3:48.81
4. HOL	Ineke Ran, Linda Faber, Annelies Maas, Enith Brigitha	3:51.67
5. SOV	Lyubov Kobzova, Irina Vlasova, Marina Kliuchnikova, Larissa Tsareva	3:52.69
6. FRA	Guylaine Bergen, Sylvie Le Noach, Caroline Carpentier, Chantal Schertz	3:56.73
7. SWE	Pia Martensson, Ylva Persson, Diana Olsson, Ida Hansson, [Gunilla Lundberg]	3:57.25
8. GER	Jutta Weber, Marion Platten, Regina Nissen, Beate Jasch, [Gudrun Beckmann]	3:58.33

The freestyle relay was the last women's swimming event of the Montreal Olympics. In the first 12 events, the East Germans had won 11 gold medals, the Soviet Union had won one, and the United States had won none. With 100-meter gold medalist Kornelia Ender swimming the first leg, East Germany took a 1.16-second lead. East Germany's second swimmer was 100-meter silver medallist Petra Priemer. But Wendy Boglioli swam a 55.81 leg to draw the United States 0.35 seconds closer. Jill Sterkel followed with a blistering 55.78, passing Andrea Pollack and giving the United States a lead of 0.40 seconds. Shirley Babashoff's 56.28 assured the United States of a gold medal at last. Babashoff finished her Olympic career with two gold medals, both in the freestyle relay, and six silver medals.

1980 Moscow T: 9, N: 9, D: 7.27. WR: 3:43.43 (USA—Caulkins, Elkins, Sterkel, Woodhead)

1.	GDR	Barbara Krause, Caren Metschuck, Ines Diers, Sarina Hülsenbeck, [Carmela Schmidt]	3:42.71 WR
2.	SWE	Carina Ljungdahl, Tina Gustafsson, Agneta Mårtensson, Agneta Eriksson, [Birgitta Jonsson, Helena Peterson]	3:48.93
3.	HOL	Cornelia van Bentum, Wilma van Velsen, Regina “Reggie” de Jong, Annelies Maas	3:49.51
4.	GBR	Sharron Davies, Kaye Lovatt, Jacquelina Willmott, June Croft	3:51.71
5.	AUS	Lisa Curry, Karen van de Graaf, Rosemary Brown, Michele Pearson	3:54.16
6.	MEX	Isabel Reuss, Dagmar Erdman, Teresa Rivera, Helen Plaschinski	3:55.41
7.	BUL	Dobrinka Mincheva, Rumiana Nikolova, Ani Kostova, Sonya Dangalakova	3:56.34
8.	SPA	Natalia Más Masdefiol, Margarita Armengol Fuster, Laura Flaque Centellas, Gloria Casado Bermejo	3:58.73

Although there were only nine teams, two qualifying heats were held to determine which eight teams would advance to the final. In the second heat the Soviet Union was disqualified for an improper changeover, which made it much easier to decide who the finalists would be. The East Germans won easily. If the United States had entered a team they probably would have finished second, based on times from the same period.

1984 Los Angeles T: 12, N: 12, D: 7.31. WR: 3:42.71 (GDR—Krause, Metschuck, Diers, Hülsenbeck)

1.	USA	Jenna Johnson, Carolyn Steinseifer, Dara Torres, Nancy Hogshead, [Gillian Sterkel, , Mary Wayte]	3:43.43
2.	HOL	Anna Maria Verstappen, Elles Voskes, Dirkje “Desi” Reijers, Cornelia van Bentum, [Wilhelmina van Velsen]	3:44.40
3.	GER	Iris Zscherpe, Susanne Schuster, Christiane Pielke, Karin Seick	3:45.56
4.	AUS	Michele Pearson, Angela Russel, Anna McVann, Lisa Curry, [Janet Tibbits]	3:47.79
5.	CAN	Pamela Rai, Carol Klimpel, Cheryl McArton, Jane Kerr, [Maureen New]	3:49.50
6.	GBR	June Croft, Nicola Fibbens, Debra Gore, Annabelle Cripps	3:50.12
7.	SWE	Maria Kardum, Agneta Eriksson, Petra Hilder, Karin Furuhed, [Malin Rundgren]	3:51.24
8.	FRA	Carole Amoric, Sophie Kamoun, Véronique Jardin, Laurence Bensimon	3:52.15

1988 Seoul T: 15, N: 15, D: 9.22. WR: 3:40.57 (GDR—Otto, Stellmach, Schulze, Friedrich)

1.	GDR	Kristin Otto, Katrin Meissner, Daniela Hunger, Manuela Stellmach, [Sabina Schulze, Heike Friedrich]	3:40.63 OR
2.	HOL	Marianne Muis, Mildred Muis, Cornelia van Bentum, Karin Brienesse, [Diana van der Plaats]	3:43.39
3.	USA	Mary Wayte, Mitzi Kremer, Laura Walker, Dara Torres, [Paige Zemina, Jill Sterkel]	3:44.25
4.	CHN	Xia Fujie, Yang Wenyi, Lou Yaping, Zhuang Yong	3:44.69
5.	SOV	Yelena Dendeberova, Svetlana Issakova, Natalya Trefilova, Svitlana Kopchykova, [Inna Abramova]	3:44.99
6.	CAN	Kathleen Bald, Patricia Noall, Andrea Nugent, Jane Kerr, [Kristen Topham, Allison Higson]	3:46.75
7.	GER	Stephanie Ortwig, Marion Aizpors, Christiane Pielke, Karin Seick, [Katja Ziliox]	3:46.90
8.	DEN	Gitta Jensen, Pia Sørensen, Mette Jacobsen, Annette Moldrup Jorgensen	3:49.25

1992 Barcelona T: 13, N: 13, D: 7.28. WR: 3:40.57 (GDR—Otto, Stellmach, Schulze, Friedrich)

1.	USA	Nicole Haislett, Dara Torres, Angelina Martino, Jennifer Thompson, [Ashley Tappin, Christine Ahmann-Leighton]	3:39.46 WR
2.	CHN	Zhuang Yong, Lu Bin, Yang Wenyi, Le Jingyi, [Zhao Kun]	3:40.12
3.	GER	Franziska van Almsick, Simone Osygus, Daniela Hunger, Manuela Stellmach, [Kerstin Kielgass, Annette Hadding]	3:41.60
4.	SOV	Natalya Meshcheryakova, Svetlana Leshukova, Yelena Dendeberova, Yelena Shubina, [Yevganya Yarmakova]	3:43.68
5.	HOL	Diana van der Plaats, Mildred Muis, Marianne Muis, Karin Brienesse, [Inge de Bruijn]	3:43.74
6.	DEN	Gitta Jensen, Matte Jacobsen, Berit Puggaard, Matte Nielsen, [Annette Poulsen]	3:47.81
7.	SWE	Eva Nyberg, Louise Karlsson, Ellenor Svensson, Malin Nilsson, [Linda Olofsson]	3:48.47
8.	CAN	Marianne Limpert, Nicole Dryden, Andrea Nugent, Allison Higson	3:49.37

Zhuang set an Olympic record of 54.51 on the leadoff leg—in fact, it was the second-fastest time in history. Torres and Martino closed the gap for the United States. By the time Jenny Thompson took off for her anchor leg, she was only a stroke behind the Chinese team. She then swam a sizzling 54.01, the fastest relay leg in history, to win the race and break the six-year-old world record.

1996 Atlanta T: 19, N: 19, D: 7.22. WR: 3:37.91 (CHN—Le J., Shan, Le Y., Lu)

1.	USA	Angelina Martino, Amy Van Dyken, Catherine Fox, Jennifer Thompson, [Lisa Jacob, Melanie Valerio]	3:39.29 OR
2.	CHN	Le Jingyi, Chao Na, Nian Yun, Shan Ying	3:40.48
3.	GER	Sandra Völker, Simone Osygus, Antje Buschschulte, Franziska van Almsick, [Meike Freitag]	3:41.48
4.	HOL	Marianne Muis, Minouche Smit, Willemina van Hofwegen, Karine Brienesse, [Manon Masseurs]	3:42.40
5.	SWE	Linda Olofsson, Louise Jöhncke, Louise Karlsson, Johanna Sjöberg	3:44.91
6.	AUS	Sarah Ryan, Julia Greville, Lise Mackie, Susan O’Neill, [Anna Windsor]	3:45.31
7.	CAN	Shannon Shakespeare, Julie Howard, Andrea Moody, Marianne Limpert	3:46.27

DISQ: RUS—Yelena Nazemnova, Svetlana Leshukova, Natalya Meshcheryakova, Natalya Sorokina

Le Jingyi gave China a half second lead after 100

meters, but Amy Van Dyken's 53.91 second leg put the United States in front for good. Catherine Fox was the first Vietnamese-American Olympic medalist.

2000 Sydney T: 13, N: 13, D: 9.16. WR: 3:37.91 (CHN—Le J., Shan, Le Y., Lu)

1. USA	Amy Van Dyken, Dara Torres, Courtney Shealy, Jennifer Thompson, [Ashley Tappin, Erin Phenix]	3:36.61 WR
2. HOL	Manon van Rooijen, Wilma van Hofwegen-van Rijn, Thamar Henneken, Inge de Bruijn, [Chantal Groot]	3:39.83
3. SWE	Louise Jöhncke, Therese Alshammar, Johanna Sjöberg, Anna-Karin Kammerling, [Josefin Lillhage, Malin Svahnström]	3:40.30
4. GER	Antje Buschschulte, Katrin Meissner, Franziska van Almsick, Sandra Völker [Britta Steffen, Daniela Samulski, Kerstin Kielgass]	3:40.31
5. GBR	Karen Pickering, Alison Sheppard, Rosalind Brett, Susan Rolph	3:40.54
6. AUS	Susan O'Neill, Sarah Ryan, Elka Graham, Giaan Rooney, [Mel Dodd]	3:40.91
7. CAN	Marianne Limpert, Shannon Shakespeare, Laura Nicholls, Jessica Deglau	3:42.92
8. ITA	Cecilia Vianini, Luisa Striani, Sara Parise, Cristina Chiuso	3:44.49

The United States fielded a veteran team. Dara Torres was 33 years old, Amy Van Dyken and Jenny Thompson were both 27, while Courtney Shealy was the youngest at 23. Both Torres and Thompson were swimming in their third 4 × 100-meter relay final. Inge de Bruijn swam the anchor leg for the Netherlands and brought the Dutch from sixth to second with the fastest relay leg in history: 53.41 seconds.

2004 Athens T: 16, N: 16, D: 8.14. WR: 3:36.00 (GER—Meissner, Dallmann, Völker, van Almsick)

1. AUS	Alice Mills, Lisbeth Lenton, Petria Thomas, Jodie Henry, [Sarah Ryan]	3:35.94 WR
2. USA	Kara Lynn Joyce, Natalie Coughlin, Amanda Weir, Jennifer Thompson, [Colleen Lanne, Lindsay Benko, Maritza Correia]	3:36.39
3. HOL	Chantal Groot, Inge Dekker, Marleen Veldhuis, Inge de Bruijn, [Annabel Kosten]	3:37.59
4. GER	Antje Buschschulte, Petra Dallmann, Daniela Götz, Franziska van Almsick	3:37.94
5. FRA	Solenne Figues, Céline Couderc, Aurore Mongel, Malia Metella	3:40.23
6. GBR	Melanie Marshall, Kathryn Evans, Karen Pickering, Lisa Chapman, [Alison Sheppard]	3:40.82
7. SWE	Josefin Lillhage, Maria Johanna Sjöberg, Therèse Alshammar, Anna-Karin Kammerling	3:41.22
8. CHN	Cheng Jiaru, Xu Yanwei, Yang Yu, Zhu Yingwen	3:42.90

Led by 100-meter freestyle world record holder Libby Lenton and former world record holder Jodie Henry, the Australians were given a good chance to end the US streak of three Olympic championships. The Australian anchor, Henry took off four-tenths of a second behind American veteran Jenny Thompson. Henry had nearly caught up by the turn and then pushed into the lead in the final 50 meters, completing her leg in 52.95 seconds.

Maritza Correia, who swam in the preliminary round, was the first black woman to qualify for the US Olympic swimming team.

2008 Beijing T: 15, N: 15, D: 8.10. WR: 3:33.62 (HOL—Dekker, Kromowidjojo, Heemskerk, Veldhuis)

1. HOL	Inge Dekker, Ranomi Kromowidjojo, Femke Heemskerk, Marleen Veldhuis, [Hinkelien Schreuder, Manon van Rooijen]	3:33.76 OR
2. USA	Natalie Coughlin, Lacey Nymeyer, Kara Lynn Joyce, Dara Torres, [Julia Smit, Emily Silver]	3:34.33
3. AUS	Cate Campbell, Alice Mills, Melanie Schlanger, Lisbeth "Libby" Trickett (Lenton), [Shayne Reese]	3:35.05
4. CHN	Zhu Yingwen, Tang Yi, Xu Yanwei, Pang Jiaying	3:35.64
5. GER	Britta Steffen, Meike Freitag, Daniela Götz, Antje Buschschulte	3:36.85
6. FRA	Céline Couderc, Alena Popchanka, Ophélie Etienne, Malia Metella, [Hanna Shcherba-Lorgeril]	3:37.68
7. GBR	Francesca Halsall, Caitlin McClatchey, Jessica Sylvester, Melanie Marshall, [Julia Beckett]	3:38.18
8. CAN	Julia Wilkinson, Erica Morningstar, Geneviève Saumur, Audrey Lacroix	3:38.32

Five months before the Olympics, the Dutch squad set a world record to win the 2008 European championship.

Germany's Britta Steffen set an Olympic record of 53.38 seconds in the lead-off leg, but her team could not maintain the advantage, eventually slipping to fifth place. Swimming third, Femke Heemskerk put the Netherlands in front, and anchor Marleen Veldhuis held off 41-year-old Dara Torres to secure the victory. Torres became the oldest swimmer of either gender to earn an Olympic medal

4 × 200-METER FREESTYLE RELAY

1896–1992 not held

1996 Atlanta T: 21, N: 21, D: 7.25. WR: 7:55.47 (GDR—Stellmach, Strauss, Möhring, Friedrich)

1. USA	Trina Jackson, Cristina Teuscher, Sheila Taormina, Jennifer Thompson, [Lisa Jacob, Ashley Whitney, Annette Salmeen]	7:59.87 OR
2. GER	Franziska van Almsick, Kerstin Kielgass, Anke Scholz, Dagmar Hase, [Simone Osygus, Meike Freitag]	8:01.55
3. AUS	Julie Greville, Nicole Stevenson, Emma Johnson, Susan O'Neill, [Lisa Mackie]	8:05.47
4. JPN	Eri Yamanoi, Naoko Imoto, Aiko Miyake, Suzu Chiba	8:07.46
5. CAN	Marianne Limpert, Shannon Shakespeare, Andrea Schwartz, Jessica Deglau, [Joanne Malar, Sophie Simard]	8:08.16

6. HOL	Carla Louise Geurts, Patricia Stokkers, Minouche Smit, Kerstin Vlieghuis, [Karin Brienesse]	8:08.48
7. ROM	L. Liliana Dobrescu, Loredana Zisu, Ioana Diaconescu, Carla Negrea	8:10.02
8. CHN	Nian Yun, Wang Luna, Chen Yan, Shan Ying, [Pu Yiqi]	8:15.38

Franziska van Almsick opened with a 1:58.14—a time that would have earned her the gold medal in the 200-meter freestyle had she managed it four days earlier. Christina Teuscher's 1:58.86 second leg put the United States in a lead that they never relinquished. Anchor Jenny Thompon earned her fifth gold medal, all in relays. Sheila Taormina switched from swimming to triathlon in 1998, qualified for the 2000 Olympics and placed sixth.

2000 Sydney T: 15, N: 15, D: 9.20. WR: 7:55.47 (GDR—Stellmach, Strauss, Möhring, Friedrich)

1. USA	Samantha Arsenault, Diana Munz, Lindsay Benko, Jenny Thompson, [Julia Stowers, Kim Black]	7:57.80 OR
2. AUS	Susan O'Neill, Giaan Rooney, Kirsten Petria Thomas, [Elka Graham, Jacinta van Lint]	7:58.52
3. GER	Franziska van Almsick, Antje Buschschulte, Sara Harstick, Kerstin Kielgass, [Britta Steffen, Meike Freitag]	7:58.64
4. ROM	Camelia Potec, Simona Paduraru, Ioana Diaconescu, Beatrice Coadă-Câşlaru [Carmen Herea]	8:01.63
5. CAN	Marianne Limpert, Shannon Shakespeare, Joanne Malar, Jessica Deglau, [Katie Brambley, Jennifer Button]	8:02.65
6. GBR	Nicola Jackson, Karen Legg, Janine Belton, Karen Pickering, [Claire Huddart]	8:03.69
7. ITA	Sara Parise, Cecilia Vianini, Luisa Striani, Sara Goffi	8:04.68
8. FRA	Solenne Figuès, Laëtitia Choux, Laetitia Choux, Katarin Quelennec, Alicia Bozon	8:05.99

Susie O'Neill led off for Australia and put the home team in the lead with the other favorites, Germany and the United States, in third and sixth. Diana Munz's 1:59.19 second leg brought the US up to second place. Lindsay Benko closed the gap to 25 hundredths of a second. The American anchor, Jenny Thompson, caught Australia's Petria Thomas after 50 meters and gradually pulled away. Meanwhile, Germany's Kerstin Kielgass swam the fastest leg of the race, 1:57.90, but could not quite catch Thomas. With this race, Jenny Thompson became the first female swimmer to win seven career gold medals.

2004 Athens T: 16, N: 16, D: 8.18. WR: 7:55.47 (GDR—Stellmach, Strauss, Möhring, Friedrich)

1. USA	Natalie Coughlin, Carly Piper, Dana Vollmer, Kaitlin Sandeno, [Lindsay Benko, Rhiannon "Rhi" Jeffrey, Rachel Komisarz]	7:53.42 WR
2. CHN	Zhu Yingwen, Xu Yanwei, Yang Yu, Pang Jiaying, [Li Ji]	7:55.97
3. GER	Franziska van Almsick, Petra Dallmann, Antje Buschschulte, Hannah Stockbauer, [Janina Kristin Götz, Sara Harstick]	7:57.35
4. AUS	Alice Mills, Elka Graham, Shayne Reese, Petria Thomas, [Linda Mackenzie, Giaan Rooney]	7:57.40
5. GBR	Melanie Marshall, Georgina Lee, Caitlin McClatchey, Karen Pickering, [Joanne Jackson]	7:59.11
6. SPA	Tatiana Rouba Beniarz, Melissa Caballero Ayasse, Arantxa Ramos Plasencia, Erika Villaecija García	8:02.11
7. BRA	Joanna Maranhão, Monique Ferreira, Mariana Brochado, Paula Baracho	8:05.29
8. SWE	Josefin Lillhage, Ida Mattsson, Malin Svahnström, Lotta Wänberg, [Maria Johanna Sjöberg]	8:08.34

Natalie Coughlin swam a leadoff leg of 1:57.74, a time that would have won the individual 200-meter freestyle the day before. This gave the United States a body-length lead and the US team was never remotely challenged. They shattered by more than two seconds the 17-year-old world record held by East Germany.

2008 Beijing T: 16, N: 16, D: 8.14. WR: 7:50.09 (USA—Coughlin, Vollmer, Nymeyer, Hoff)

1. AUS	Stephanie Rice, Bronte Barratt, Kylie Palmer, Linda MacKenzie, [Felicity Galvez, Angie Bainbridge, Melanie Schlanger, Lara Davenport]	7:44.31 WR
2. CHN	Yang Yu, Zhu Qianwei, Tan Miao, Pang Jiaying, [Tang Jingzhi]	7:45.93
3. USA	Allison Schmitt, Natalie Coughlin, Caroline Burckle, Katherine Hoff, [Christine Marshall, Kimberly Vandenberg, Julia Smit]	7:46.33
4. ITA	Renata Spagnolo, Alessia Filippi, Flavia Zoccari, Federica Pellegrini, [Alice Carpanese]	7:49.76
5. FRA	Coralie Balmy, Ophélie Etienne, Aurore Mongel, Camille Muffat, [Alena Popchanka, Céline Couderc]	7:50.66
6. HUN	Ágnes Mutina, Evelyn Verrasztó, Eszter Dara, Zsuzsanna Jakabos	7:55.53
7. JPN	Haruka Ueda, Misaki Yamaguchi, Maki Mita, Emi Takanabe	7:57.56
8. SWE	Josefin Lillhage, Gabriella Fagundez, Ida Marko-Varga (Mattsson), Petra Granlund	7:59.83

A day after completing her sweep of the individual medley races, Australia's Stephanie Rice swam the lead-off leg in the 4 × 200-meter freestyle relay. She finished close behind France's Coralie Balmy, but Bronte Barratt put Australia into the lead in the second leg, and her team was never seriously challenged after that, finishing 5.78 seconds under the world record. In fourth place at the halfway point, the US moved up to finish third behind China. It was the first time the US had lost the event since its introduction at the 1996 Olympics.

4 × 100-METER MEDLEY RELAY

In medley relays the order of strokes is backstroke, breaststroke, butterfly, and freestyle.

1896–1956 not held

1960 Rome T: 13, N: 13, D: 9.2. WR: 4:44.6 (USA—Cone, Bancroft, Collins, Von Saltza)

1. USA	Lynn Burke, Patricia Kempner, Carolyn Schuler, S. Christine Von Saltza, [Anne Warner, Carolyn Wood, Joan Spillane]	4:41.1 WR
2. AUS	Marilyn Wilson, Rosemary Lassig, Janice Andrew, Dawn Fraser, [Amber Gergay Beckett, Ilsa Konrads]	4:45.9
3. GDR& GER	Ingrid Schmidt, Ursula Küper, Bärbel Fuhrmann, Ursel Brunner	4:47.6
4. HOL	Maria van Velsan, Adelaide den Haan, Marianne Heemskerk, Erica Terpstra, [Catharina Lagerberg]	4:47.6
5. GBR	Sylvia Lewis, Anita Lonsbrough, Sheila Watt, Natalie Steward, [Jean Oldroyd]	4:47.6
6. HUN	Magdolna Dávid, Klára Bartos-Killermann, Márta Egerváry, Csilla Dobai-Madarász	4:53.7
7. JPN	Satoko Tanaka, Yoshiko Takamatsu, Shizue Miyabe, Yoshiko Sato	4:56.4
8. SOV	Larissa Viktorova, Lyudmila Korobova, Zinaida Belovskaya, Marina Shamal, [Valentina Poznyak]	4:58.1

US leadoff swimmer Lynn Burke finished her leg in 1:09.0 to break the 100-meter backstroke world record for the fourth time in seven weeks. The race was no contest after that, with the United States winning by seven meters. Burke and Von Saltza were best friends who trained together and lived together in the home of Von Saltza's parents in Saratoga, California. They were both coached by George Haines. They dieted together, cut their hair the same way, and, in Rome, they won gold medals together. Von Saltza went home with three and Burke with two.

1964 Tokyo T: 9, N: 9, D: 10.18. WR: 4:34.6 (USA—Ferguson, Goyette, Ellis, Randall)

1. USA	Kathleen Ferguson, Cynthia Goyette, Sharon Stouder, Kathleen Ellis, [Nina Harmar, Judith Reeder, Susan Pitt, Lillian "Pokey" Watson]	4:33.9 WR
2. HOL	Kornelia Winkel, Klena Bimolt, Ada Kok, Erica Terpstra, [Aartje Lasterie]	4:37.0
3. SOV	Tatyana Savelyeva, Svetlana Babanina, Tetyana Devyatova, Natalya Ustinova	4:39.2
4. JPN	Satoko Tanaka, Noriko Yamamoto, Eiko Takahashi, Michiko Kihara	4:42.0
5. GBR	Jill Norfolk, Stella Mitchell, Mary Anne Cotterill, Elizabeth Long, [Linda Ludgrove]	4:45.8
6. CAN	Eileen Weir, Marion Lay, Mary Stewart, Helen Kennedy	4:49.9

DISQ: GDR&GER—Ingrid Schmidt, Bärbel Grimmer, Heike Hustede, Martina Grunert; HUN: Mária Balla, Zsuzsa Kovács, Márta Egerváry, Csilla Dobai-Madarász

Cathy Ferguson gave the United States the lead after the first leg, but Svetlana Babanina, swimming two seconds faster than the official world record, touched first at 200 meters. Sharon Stouder then pulled away by a commanding margin, which Kathy Ellis added to. Stouder finished the Olympics with three gold medals and one silver, Ellis with two gold and two bronze.

1968 Mexico T: 16, N: 16, D: 10.17. WR: 4:28.1 (USA—Hall, Ball, Daniel, Pedersen)

1. USA	Kaye Hall, Catherine Ball, Eleanor Daniel, Susan Pedersen, [Jane Swagerty, Susanne Jones, Susan Shields, Jan Henne]	4:28.3 OR
2. AUS	Lynette Watson, Judith Playfair, Lynette McClements, Janet Steinbeck, [Lynette Bell]	4:30.0
3. GER	Angelika Kraus, Uta Frommater, Heike Hustede, Heidemarie Reineck	4:36.4
4. SOV	Tinatin Lekveishvili, Alla Grebennikova, Tetyana Devyatova, Lidiya Hrebets, [Larissa Zakharova]	4:37.0
5. GDR	Martina Grunert, Eva Wittke, Helga Lindner, Uta Schmuck	4:38.0
6. GBR	Wendy Burrell, Dorothy Harrison, Margaret Auton, Alexandra Jackson	4:38.3
7. HOL	Jacobje Buter, Klena Bimolt, Ada Kok, Petronella Bos	4:38.7
8. HUN	Mária Lantos, Edit Kovács, Andréa Gyarmati, Judit Turóczy	4:42.9

The United States led Australia by 0.7 seconds at 100 meters, 0.3 at 200, and 0.5 at 300 before Susan Pedersen pulled away from Janet Steinbeck for the victory.

1972 Munich T: 16, N: 16, D: 8.30. WR: 4:25.34 (USA—Atwood, Vidali, Daniel, Barkman)

1. USA	Melissa Belote, Catherine Carr, Deena Deardurff, Sandra Neilson, [Susan Atwood, Judith Melick, Dana Shrader, Shirley Babashoff]	4:20.75 WR
2. GDR	Christine Herbst, Renate Vogel, Roswitha Beier, Kornelia Ender, [Gabriele Wetzko]	4:24.91
3. GER	Silke Pielen, Verena Eberle, Gudrun Beckmann, Heidemarie Reineck, [Annegret Kober, Edeltraud Koch, Jutta Weber]	4:26.46
4. SOV	Tinatin Lekveishvili, Halina Stepanova (Prozumenshchykova), Iryna Ustymenko, Tatyana Zolotnickaia	4:27.81
5. HOL	Enith Brigitha, Alice te Riet, Anthonia "Anke" Rijnders, Hansje Bunschoten, [J. Friederike Buys]	4:29.99
6. JPN	Suzuko Matsumura, Yoko Yamamoto, Mayumi Aoki, Yoshimi Nishigawa	4:31.56

7. CAN	Wendy Cook, Sylvia Dockerill, Marylin Corson, Leslie Cliff	4:31.56
8. SWE	Diana Olsson, Britt-Marie Smedh, Eva Wikner, Anita Zarnowiecki	4:32.61

1976 Montreal T: 17, N: 17, D: 7.18. WR: 4:13.41 (GDR, Sports Club Dynamo—Seltman Nitschke, Pollack, Krause)

1. GDR	Ulrike Richter, Hannelore Anke, Andrea Pollack, Kornelia Ender, [Birgit Treiber, Carola Nitschke, Rosemarie Gabriel]	4:07.95 WR
2. USA	Linda Jezek, Lauri Siering, Camille Wright, Shirley Babashoff, [Lelei Fonoimoana, Wendy Boglioli]	4:14.55
3. CAN	Wendy Hogg, Robin Corsiglia, Susan Sloan, Anne Jardin, [Deborah Clarke]	4:15.22
4. SOV	Nadiya Stavko, Maryna Yurchenya, Tamara Shelofastova, Larissa Tsareva	4:16.05
5. HOL	Diane Edelijn, Wijda Mazaneeuw, Josina Damen, Enith Brigitha, [Ineke Ran]	4:19.03
6. GBR	Joy Beasley, Margaret Kelly, Susan Jenner, Deborah Hill	4:23.25
7. JPN	Yoshimi Nishigawa, Toshiko Haruoka, Yasue Hatsuda, Sachiko Yamazaki	4:23.47
8. AUS	Michelle Devries, Judith Hudson, Linda Hanel, Jennifer Tate	4:25.91

The first women's swimming event to be decided in 1976, the medley relay was won with an awesome display by the chemically augmented East German swimmers. Richter, Anke, Pollack, and Ender each recorded the fastest time for her leg.

1980 Moscow T: 10, N: 10, D: 7.20. WR: 4:07.95 (GDR—Richter, Anke, Pollack, Ender)

1. GDR	Rica Reinisch, Ute Geweniger, Andrea Pollack, Caren Metschuck, [Sarina Hulsenbeck]	4:06.67 WR
2. GBR	Helen Jameson, Margaret Kelly, Ann Osgerby, June Croft	4:12.24
3. SOV	Yelena Kruglova, Elvira Vasilkova, Alla Grishchenkova, Natalya Strunnikova, [Irina Aksyonova, Olga Klevakina]	4:13.61
4. SWE	Annika Uvehall, Eva-Marie Håkansson, Agneta Mårtensson, Tina Gustafson	4:16.91
5. ITA	Laura Foralosso, Sabrina Seminatore, Cinzia Savi-Scarponi, Monica Vallarin	4:19.05
6. AUS	Elizabeth "Lisa" Forrest, Lisa Curry, Karen Van De Graaf, Rosemary Brown	4:19.90
7. ROM	Carmen Bunaciu, Brigitte Prass, Mariana Parachiv, Irinel Pănulescu	4:21.27
8. BUL	Sonya Dangalakova, Tania Bogomilova, Ani Moneva, Dobrinka Mincheva	4:22.38

Rica Reinisch opened with a world-record-equaling backstroke leg and Ute Geweniger followed with 100 meters of breaststroking that bettered the official world record. Pollack and Metschuck recorded the fastest times of their respective legs, and the East Germans were on their way again.

In 1998, after suspicions of universal East German use of steroids were confirmed, Maggie Kelly of the 1980 British 4 × 100-meter medley team was asked what she thought of the campaign to retroactively disqualify the East Germans and promote the British squad to first place in the record books. "Someone said it would be nice for our kids if we were listed as winners in the record books," she replied. "My three kids would be more interested in my getting their boiled eggs right."

1984 Los Angeles T: 13, N: 13, D: 8.3. WR: 4:05.79 (GDR—Kleber, Geweniger, Geissler, Meineke)

1. USA	Theresa Andrews, Tracy Caulkins, Mary T. Meagher, Nancy Hogshead, [Elizabeth "Betsy" Mitchell, Susan Rapp, Jenna Johnson, Carolyn Steinseifer]	4:08.34
2. GER	Svenja Schlicht, Ute Hasse, Ina Beyermann, Karin Seick	4:11.97
3. CAN	Reema Abdo, Anne Ottenbrite, Michelle MacPherson, Pamela Rai	4:12.98
4. GBR	Beverley Rose, Jean Hill, Nicola Fibbens, June Croft	4:14.05
5. ITA	Manuela Carosi, Manuela Dalla Valle, Roberta Lanzarotti, Silvia Persi	4:17.40
6. SWI	Eva Gysling, Patricia Brülhart, Carole Brook, Marie-Thérèse Armentero	4:19.02

DISQ: JPN—Naomi Sekido, Hiroko Nagasaki, Naoko Kume, Kaori Yanase; SWE—Anna-Karin Eriksson, Eva-Marie Håkansson, Agneta Eriksson, Maria Kardum

US team members Caulkins, Meagher and Hogshead each won three gold medals in Los Angeles. Their main competition in the medley relay had been expected to come from the Dutch team, which was disqualified for jumping too soon during an exchange in the preliminary round. Three weeks after the Olympic final, the East German Friendship Games team of Ina Kleber, Sylvia Gerasch, Ines Geissler and Birgit Meineke set a world record of 4:03.69. The Soviets were second in 4:08.13.

1988 Seoul T: 18, N: 18, D: 9.24. WR: 4:03.69 (GDR—Kleber, Gerasch, Geissler, Meineke)

1. GDR	Kristin Otto, Silke Hörner, Birte Weigang, Katrin Meissner, [Cornelia Sirch, Manuela Stellmach]	4:03.74 OR
2. USA	Elizabeth Barr, Tracey McFarlane, Janel Jorgensen, Mary Wayte, [Elizabeth "Betsy" Mitchell, Mary T. Meagher, Dara Torres]	4:07.90
3. CAN	Loraine Melien, Allison Higson, Jane Kerr, Andrea Nugent, [Keltie Duggan, Patricia Noall]	4:10.49
4. AUS	Nicole Livingstone, Lara Hooiveld, Fiona Alessandri, Karen Van Wirdum	4:11.57
5. HOL	Jolanda de Rover, Linda Moes, Cornelia van Bentum, Karin Brienesse	4:12.19
6. BUL	Bistra Gospodinova, Tania Dangalakova (Bogomilova), Neviana Miteva, Natasha Hristova	4:12.36
7. GER	Svenja Schlicht, Britta Dahm, Gabi Rehaa, Marion Aizpors	4:12.89
8. ITA	Lorenza Vigarani, Manuela Dalla Valle, Ilaria Tocchini, Silvia Persi	4:13.85

1992 Barcelona T: 17, N: 17, D: 7.30. WR: 4:03.69 (GDR—Kleber, Gerasch, Geissler, Meineke)

1. USA	Lea Loveless, N. Anita Nall, Christine Ahmann-Leighton, Jennifer Thompson, [Elizabeth "Janie" Wagstaff, Megan Kleine, Summer Sanders, Nicole Haislett]	4:02.54 WR
2. GER	Dagmar Hase, Jana Dörries, Franziska van Almsick, Daniela Hunger, [Daniela Brendel, Bettina Ustrowski, Simone Osygus]	4:05.19
3. SOV	Nina Zhivanevskaya, Yelena Rudkovskaya, Olga Kirichenko, Natalya Meshcheryakova, [Yelena Shubina]	4:06.44
4. CHN	Lin Li, Lou Xia, Qian Hong, Le Jingyi, [He Cihong]	4:06.78
5. AUS	Nicole Stevenson (Livingstone), Samantha Riley, Susan O'Neill, Lisa Curry-Kenny, [Joanne Meehan]	4:07.01
6. CAN	Nicole Dryden, Guylaine Cloutier, Kristin Topham, Andrea Nugent	4:09.26
7. JPN	Yoko Koikawa, Kyoko Iwasaki, Yoko Kando, Suzu Chiba	4:09.92
8. HOL	Ellen Elzerman, Kira Bulten, Inge de Bruijn, Marianne Muis	4:10.87

The team from the United States led from start to finish and broke the eight-year-old world record.

1996 Atlanta T: 24, N: 24, D: 7.24. WR: 4:01.67 (CHN—He, Dai, Liu, Le J.)

1. USA	Elizabeth Botsford, Amanda Beard, Angel Martino, Amy van Dyken, [Whitney Hedgepeth, Kristine Quance, Jennifer Thompson, Catherine Fox]	4:02.88
2. AUS	Nicole Stevenson (Livingstone), Samantha Riley, Susan O'Neill, Sarah Ryan, [Helen Denman, Angela Kennedy]	4:05.08
3. CHN	Chen Yan, Han Xue, Cai Huijue, Shan Ying	4:07.34
4. SAF	Marianne Kriel, Penelope Heyns, Amanda Loots, Helene Muller	4:08.16
5. CAN	Julie Howard, Guylaine Cloutier, Sarah Evanetz, Shannon Shakespeare	4:08.29
6. GER	Antje Buschschulte, Kathrin Dumitru, Franziska van Almsick, Sandra Völker	4:09.22
7. RUS	Nina Zhivanevskaya, Yelena Makarova, Yelena Nazemnova, Natalya Meshcheryakova, [Svetlana Pozdeyeva]	4:10.56
8. ITA	Lorenza Vigarani, Manuela Dalle Valle, Ilaria Tocchini, Cecilia Vianini	4:10.59

As it did in 1964, 1984 and 1992, the United States used one set of four swimmers in the preliminaries and a fresh set in the final, during which the Americans led from start to finish.

2000 Sydney T: 18, N: 18, D: 9.23. WR: 4:01.67 (CHN—He, Dai, Liu, Le J.)

1. USA	Barbara "B.J." Bedford, Megan Quann, Jennifer Thompson, Dara Torres [Courtney Shealy, Staciana Stitts, Ashley Tappin, Amy Van Dyken]	3:58.30 WR
2. AUS	Dyana Calub, Leisel Jones, Petria Thomas, Susan O'Neill, [Giaan Rooney, Tarnee White, Sarah Ryan]	4:01.59
3. JPN	Mai Nakamura, Masami Tanaka, Junko Onishi, Sumika Minamoto	4:04.16
4. GER	Antje Buschschulte, Sylvia Gerasch, Franziska van Almsick, Katrin Meissner	4:04.33
5. SAF	Charlene Wittstock, Sarah Poewe, Mandy Loots, Karina Muller	4:05.15
6. CAN	Kelly Stefanyshyn, Christin Petelski, Jen Button, Marianne Limpert, [Michelle Lischinsky, Laura Nicholls]	4:07.55
7. GBR	Katy Sexton, Heidi Earp, Susan Rolph, Karen Pickering	4:07.61
8. CHN	Zhan Shu, Qi Hui, Liu Limin, Han Xue	4:07.83

The US swimmers recorded the fastest time for each leg and became the first team to break the four-minute barrier. Jenny Thompson won her eighth career gold medal (all in relays), a women's swimming record. Like Thompson, Dara Torres earned her ninth career medal (4 gold, 1 silver, 4 bronze).

Charlene Wittstock, who swam the lead leg for South Africa, went on to marry Prince Albert of Monaco, the five-time bobsled Olympian and son of Grace Kelly and Prince Rainier.

2004 Athens T: 16, N: 16, D: 8.21. WR: 3:58.30 (USA—Bedford, Quann, Thompson, Torres)

1. AUS	Giaan Rooney, Leisel Jones, Petria Thomas, Jodie Henry, [Brooke Hanson, Jessicah Schipper, Alice Mills]	3:57.32 WR
2. USA	Natalie Coughlin, Amanda Beard, Jennifer Thompson, Kara Lynn Joyce, [Haley Cope, Tara Kirk, Rachel Komisarz, Amanda Weir]	3:59.12
3. GER	Antje Buschschulte, Sarah Poewe, Franziska van Almsick, Daniela Götz	4:00.72
4. CHN	Chen Xiujun, Luo Xuejuan, Zhou Yafei, Zhu Yingwen, [Zhan Shu, Qi Hui]	4:03.35
5. JPN	Reiko Nakamura, Masami Tanaka, Junko Onishi, Tomoko Nagai, [Noriko Inada]	4:04.83
6. HOL	Stefanie Luiken, Madelon Baans, Inge de Bruijn, Marleen Veldhuis, [Chantal Groot]	4:07.36
7. SPA	Nina Zhivanevskaya, Sara Pérez Sala, María Peláez Navarrete, Tatiana Rouba Beniarz	4:07.61

DISQ: GBR—Katherine Sexton, Kirsty Balfour, Georgina Lee, Kathryn Evans, [Sarah Price, Melanie Marshall]

Natalie Coughlin swam a 59.68 leadoff lead, the second-fastest 100-meter backstroke in history, and Amanda Beard increased the US lead to 1.68 seconds at the halfway point. However, the Australians closed with Petria Thomas, who had won the 100-meter butterfly, and Jodie Henry, who had won the 100-meter freestyle. Thomas swept into the lead, and Henry brought the Australia home almost a second below the world record. With this race, Jenny Thompson, who swam the butterfly leg for the United States, gained her twelfth career medal (8 gold, 3 silver and 1 bronze), ten of which came in relay events.

2008 Beijing T: 16, N: 16, D: 8.17. WR: 3:55.74 (AUS—Seebohm, Jones, Schipper, Lenton)

1. AUS	Emily Seebohm, Leisel Jones, Jessicah Schipper, Lisbeth "Libby" Trickett (Lenton), [Tarnee White, Felicity Galvez, Shayne Reese]	3:52.69 WR
2. USA	Natalie Coughlin, Rebecca Soni, Christine Magnuson, Dara Torres, [Margaret Hoelzer, Megan Jendrick, Elaine Breeden, Kara Lynn Joyce]	3:53.30
3. CHN	Zhao Jing, Sun Ye, Zhou Yafei, Pang Jiaying, [Xu Tianlongzi]	3:56.11
4. GBR	Gemma Spofforth, Kate Haywood, Jemma Lowe, Francesca Halsall	3:57.50
5. RUS	Anastasiya Zuyeva, Yuliya Yefimova, Nataliya Sutyagina, Anastasiya Aksenova [Kseniya Moskvina]	3:57.84
6. JPN	Reiko Nakamura, Asami Kitagawa, Yuka Kato, Haruka Ueda, [Hanae Ito]	3:59.54
7. CAN	Julia Wilkinson, Annamay Pierse, Audrey Lacroix, Erica Morningstar	4:01.35

DISQ: SWE (Sarah Sjöström, Joline Höstman, Anna-Karin Kammerling, Josefin Lillhage)

The Australian line-up included the reigning world record holders in the 100-meter freestyle (Libby Trickett), 200-meter butterfly (Jessicah Schipper) and 100-meter breaststroke (Leisel Jones). Along with backstroke swimmer Emily Seebohm, the squad had won the 2007 world championships in world record time.

Five days after winning the 100-meter backstroke Natalie Coughlin swam the fastest lead-off leg, followed closely by Britain's Gemma Spofforth. By the end of the second leg Australia had moved into the lead by nearly a full second, and the team held on for the victory, bettering their own world record by 3.05 seconds.

Swimming the anchor leg less than an hour after winning silver in the 50-meter freestyle, 41-year-old Dara Torres narrowed the gap on Trickett but was unable to overtake her, finishing 0.61 seconds back in second place. The medal was Torres' twelfth over five Olympics, including four gold, four silver and four bronze.

Chapter 24 **Synchronized Swimming**

WOMEN
Duet
Team
Discontinued Event

Synchronized swimming was introduced to the Olympics in 1984 with a solo event and a duet event. Both of these events were dropped after the 1992 Olympics and were replaced in 1996 by a team event with nine swimmers on each team. The duet event was reinstated in 2000. Twenty-four pairs take part in the duet competition. Each duet performs a technical routine lasting up to 2 minutes 20 seconds and a free routine of up to 3 minutes 30 seconds. The top ten duets advance to the final and perform their free routine again. Eight nations contest the team event, in which there is only a final—no preliminary round. The teams perform a technical routine, lasting up to 2 minutes 50 seconds and a free routine, lasting 4 minutes.

The technical routine accounts for 50 percent of the total score and the free routine for 50 percent. Routines are scored by ten judges on a scale of 0 (failed) to 10.0 (very good). Five judges score a routine for technical merit and five for artistic impression. The technical merit score is derived by weighing execution of strokes and figures (40 percent), synchronization within the team and with the music (20 percent for duets and 30 percent for teams), and difficulty of strokes and figures (40 percent for duets and 30 percent for teams). The artistic impression score weighs choreography (60 percent) with music interpretation (20 percent) and manner of presentation (20 percent). The final score for each routine is determined by dropping the highest and lowest score for both technical merit and artistic impression, and averaging the remaining scores for each.

Figures range from simple moves like the somersault back tuck to difficult moves such as the castle and the Eiffel Tower twist spin. Synchronized swimming has a reputation as a somewhat silly sport, but in fact it is more physically demanding than many other sporting endeavors, such as shooting, dressage, or playing right field in a baseball game.

Olga Brusnikina (left) and Maria Kisseleva, 2000
A fusion of karate and ballet earned the Russian pair the gold in Sydney.

DUET

1896–1980 not held

1984 Los Angeles T: 18, N: 18, D: 8.9.

1. Candace Costie, Tracie Ruiz	USA	195.584
2. Sharon Hambrook, Kelly Kryczka	CAN	194.234
3. Saeko Simura, Miwako Motoyoshi	JPN	187.992
4. Caroline Holmyard, Carolyn Wilson	GBR	184.050
5. Edith Boss, Karin Singer	SWI	180.109
6. Catrien Eijken, Marijke Engelen	HOL	179.058
7. Pascale Besson, Muriel Hermine	FRA	176.709
8. Claudia Novelo, Pilar Ramírez Laguna	MEX	176.409

1988 Seoul T: 15, N: 15, D: 10.1.

1. Michelle Cameron, Carolyn Waldo	CAN	197.317
2. Sarah Josephson, Karen Josephson	USA	197.284
3. Miyako Tanaka, Mikako Kotani	JPN	190.159
4. Karine Schuler, Anne Capron	FRA	184.792
5. Edith Boss, Karin Singer	SWI	183.950
6. Maria Cherniaeva, Tatyana Titova	SOV/RUS	182.667
7. Nicola Shearn, Lian Goodwin	GBR	179.075
8. Lourdes Candin Sánchezi, Sonia Cárdenas Saavedra	MEX	176.833

Cameron and Waldo achieved a narrow victory, thanks to a superb performance in the compulsory figures and patriotic judging on the part of Canadian judge Joyce Corner. During the freestyle routine, Corner was the only one of seven judges to give Cameron and Waldo a higher mark than the Josephson twins. Had the scores of the Canadian and American judges been dropped, rather than the highest and lowest scores, the final placings would have been reversed.

1992 Barcelona T: 18, N: 18, D: 8.7.

1. Karen Josephson, Sarah Josephson	USA	192.175
2. Penny Vilagos, Victoria Vilagos	CAN	189.394
3. Fumiko Okuno, Aki Takayama	JPN	186.868
4. Anna Kozlova, Olga Sedkova	RUS	184.083
5. Marianne Aeschbacher, Anne Capron	FRA	181.795
6. Kerry Shacklock, Laila Vakil	GBR	179.366
7. Marjolijn Both, Tamara Zwart	HOL	179.345
8. Guan Zewen, Wang Xiaojie	CHN	177.843

Both the Josephsons and the Vilagoses were identical twin sisters. The Josephsons were undefeated since the 1988 Olympics, having won 15 straight meets. The Vilagoses came back after five years away from competition to prepare for the 1992 Olympics. It was the first time two sets of twins took gold and silver since the Landvoigt and Pimenov twins won the men's coxless pairs rowing at the 1980 Games.

1996 not held

2000 Sydney T: 24, N: 24, D: 9.26.

1. Olga Brusnikina, Maria Kisseleva	RUS	99.580
2. Miya Tachibana, Miho Takeda	JPN	98.650
3. Virginie Dedieu, Myriam Lignot	FRA	97.437
4. Anna Kozlova, Tuesday Middaugh	USA	96.990
5. Claire Carver-Dias, Fanny Letourneau	CAN	95.984
6. Maurizia Cecconi, Alessia Lucchini	ITA	95.387
7. Min Li, Yuanyuan Li	CHN	94.784
8. Gemma Mengual Civil, Paola Tirados Sánchez	SPA	94.520

Olga Brusnikina first attracted attention when, at the age of 14, she performed a mesmerizing solo routine at the 1993 world junior synchro championships that earned her a standing ovation. By 1999 she was the senior world champion, a title she successfully defended in 2000. Meanwhile, she won the World Cup and the world championships in both the duet and team competitions. Less than two months before the Olympics, Brusnikina amd Maria Kisseleva won the European Championships, only to lose it when Kisseleva tested positive for ephedrine. The normal penalty for an ephedrine violation is a three-month suspension, but the Russian federation let her off with one month . . . and she was back in time for the Olympics. Once there, the result was never in doubt. Brusnikina and Kisseleva's karate-themed free routine, performed to Japanese drums, earned straight 10's for artistic interpretation and technical merit scores of 10 from four of the five judges.

2004 Athens T: 24, N: 24, D: 8.25.

1. Anastasiya Davydova, Anastasiya Yermakova	RUS	99.334
2. Miya Tachibana, Miho Takeda	JPN	98.417
3. Alison Bartosik, Anna Kozlova	USA	96.918
4. Gemma Mengual Civil, Paola Tirados Sánchez	SPA	96.251
5. Virginie Dedieu, Laure Thibaud	FRA	95.584
6. Fanny Létourneau, Courtenay Stewart	CAN	95.334
7. Beibei Gu, Xiaohuan Zhang	CHN	93.668
8. Beatrice Spaziani, Lorena Zaffalon	ITA	93.250

After losing to Miya Tachibana and Miho Takeda in their senior international debut at the 2001 world championships, the Russian duo of Anastasiya Davydova and Anastasiya Yermakova dominated the world scene, winning the 2002 European championship and World Cup, the 2003 world championship, and the 2004 Olympic qualifying tournament and European championship. Performing a lively final routine to "Don Quixote," the Russians scored a nearly flawless 49.917, earning perfect 10s from all five judges for artistic impression and three perfect 10s for technical merit.

2008 Beijing T: 24, N: 24, D: 8.20.

1. Anastasiya Davydova, Anastasiya Yermakova	RUS	99.251
2. Andrea Fuentes Fache, Gemma Mengual Civil	SPA	98.334
3. Saho Harada, Emiko Suzuki	JPN	97.167
4. Jiang Tingting, Jiang Wenwen	CHN	96.334
5. Christina Jones, Andrea Nott	USA	95.500
6. Marie-Pierre Boudreau-Gagnon, Isabelle Rampling	CAN	95.084
7. Beatrice Adelizzi, Giulia Lapi	ITA	93.751
8. Daria Yushko, Kseniya Sydorenko	UKR	92.668

Anastasiya Davydova and Anastasiya Yermakova had been undefeated in international competition since 2001 and had no difficulty defending their Olympic title. The pair scored 49.334 points in the technical round, leading Spain by 0.500 points. Their free routine, performed to the "Peer Gynt Suite," earned them another 49.917 points, including perfect 10s from all five technical merit judges.

The top eight finishers were the same as in the 2007 world championships.

TEAM

1896–1992 not held

1996 Atlanta T: 8, N: 8, D: 8.2.

1. USA	99.720
2. CAN	98.367
3. JPN	97.753
4. RUS	97.260

5. FRA	96.076
6. ITA	94.253
7. CHN	94.124
8. MEX	93.836

1. USA—Suzannah Bianco, Tammy Cleland, Rebekah Dyroen-Lancer, Emily LeSueur, Heather Pease, Jill Savery, Nathalie Schneyder, Heather Simmons-Carrasco, Jill Sudduth, Margot Thien
2. CAN—Christine Larsen, Karen Clark, Sylvie Fréchette, Janice Bremner, Karen Fonteyne, Valerie Hould-Marchand, Erin Woodley, Cari Read, Lisa Alexander
3. JPN—Miya Tachibana, Akiko Kawase, Rei Jimbo, Miho Takeda, Kaori Takahashi, Raika Fujii, Junko Tanaka, Riho Nakajima, Miho Kawabe
4. RUS—Yelena Azarova, Yelena Antonova, Olga Brusnikina, Maria Kisseleva, Galina Maksimova, Olga Novokshchenova, Yulia Pankratova, Olga Sedakova, Anna Yuriyayeva
5. FRA—Marianne Aeschbacher, Virginie Dedieu, Julie Fabre, Myriam Lignot, Delphine Marechal, Charlotte Massardier, Magali Rathier, Eva Riffet
6. ITA—Giada Ballan, Serena Bianchi, Giovanna Burlando, Mara Brunetti, Manuela Carnini, Brunella Carrafelli, Maurizia Cecconi, Paola Celli, Roberta Farinelli, Letizia Nuzzo
7. CHN—Long Yan, Li Min, Li Yuanyuan, Wu Chunlan, Chen Xuan, Guo Cui, Fu Yuling, Pan Yan
8. MEX—Olivia González Pérez, Wendy Aguilar Martínez, Aline Reich Rincón, Ingrid Reich Rincón, Lilián Leal Ramírez, N. Patricia Vila Islas, Berenice Guzmán Cano, Ariadna Medina Martínez, Erika Leal Ramírez

As entertainment, the inaugural team synchronized swimming event passed the test, but as a sporting competition, it left a lot to be desired. The eight teams finished in exactly the same positions as they did at the 1994 world championships, and at the Olympics the only change between the technical and free routines was that Italy moved up from eighth place to sixth. The only drama concerned the French team, which had planned for their free routine a portrayal of the arrival of Jewish women at a Nazi concentration camp, their selection for execution and their final walk to the gas chambers. Less than two months before the Olympics, Guy Drut, the Minister of Youth and Sport (and 1976 gold medal winner in the 110-meter hurdles), vetoed the routine as inappropriate.

2000 Sydney T: 8, N: 8, D: 9.29.

1. RUS	99.146
2. JPN	98.860
3. CAN	97.357
4. FRA	96.467
5. USA	96.104
6. ITA	95.177
7. CHN	94.593
8. AUS	89.493

1. RUS—Yelena Azarova, Yelena Antonova, Olga Brusnikina, Maria Kisseleva, Olga Novokshchenova, Yelena Soya, Yulia Vasilyeva, Olga Vasyukova
2. JPN—Raika Fujii, Yoko Isoda, Rei Jimbo, Miya Tachibana, Miho Takeda, Yoko Yoneda, Yuko Yoneda, Juri Tatsumi, Ayano Egami
3. CAN—Claire Carver-Dias, Erin Chan, Catherine Garceau, Fanny Létourneau, Kirstin Normand, Jacinthe Taillon, Reidun Tatham, Lyne Beaumont
4. FRA—Cinthia Bouhier, Virginie Dedieu, Charlote Fabre, Myriam Glez, Rachel le Bozec, Myriam Lignot, Charlotte Massardier, Magali Rathier
5. USA—Carrie Barton, Tammy Cleland-McGregor, Anna Kozlova, Kristina Lum, Elicia Marshall, Tuesday Middaugh, Heather Pease-Olson, Kim Wurzel, Bridgett Finn
6. ITA—Giada Ballan, Serena Bianchi, Mara Brunetti, Chiara Cassin, Maurizia Cecconi, Alice Dominici, Alessia Lucchini, Clara Porchetto, Giovanna Burlando
7. CHN—Hou Yingli, Jin Na, Li Min, Li Rouping, Li Yuanyuan, Wang Fang, Xia Ye, Zhang Xiaohuan, Li Zhen
8. AUS—Tracey Davis, Kelly Geraghty, Amanda Laird, Katrine Orpwood, Rachel Ren, Cathryn Wightman, Naomi Young, Dannielle Liesch, Irena Olevsky

The first seven places were the same as they were at the 1998 world championships, except that the United States fell from third to fifth. The only change from the technical routine to the free routine was that Italy passed China for sixth place. The Russians performed their free routine to Modest Mussorgsky's *Night on the Bare Mountain.*

2004 Athens T: 8, N: 8, D: 8.27.

1. RUS	99.501
2. JPN	98.501
3. USA	97.418
4. SPA	96.751
5. CAN	95.251
6. CHN	94.584
7. ITA	94.084
8. GRE	92.750

1. RUS—Yelena Azarova, Olga Brusnikina, Anastasiya Davydova, Anastasiya Yermakova, Mariya Gromova, Elvira Khasyanova, Mariya Kiselyeva, Olga Novokshchenova, Anna Shorina
2. JPN—Michiyo Fujimaru, Saho Harada, Naoko Kawashima, Kanako Kitao, Emiko Suzuki, Miya Tachibana, Miho Takeda, Juri Tatsumi, Yoko Yoneda
3. USA—Alison Bartosik, Tamara Crow, Erin Dobratz, Rebecca Jasontek, Anna Kozlova, Sara Lowe, Lauren McFall, Stephanie Nesbitt, Kendra Zanotto
4. SPA—Raquel Corral Aznar, Andrea Fuentes Fache, Tina Fuentes Fache, Gemma Mengual Civil, Anastasia Montero Pacheco, Irina Rodríguez Álvarez, Alicia Sanz Rodriguez, Saray Ione Serrano Alfonso, Paola Tirados Sánchez
5. CAN—Nicole Cargill, Erin Chan, Jessica Chase, Jessika Dubuc, Marie-Pierre Gagné, Fanny Létourneau, Shayna Nackoney, Anouk Renière-Lafrenière, Courtenay Stewart
6. CHN—Chen Yu, Gu Beibei, He Xiaochu, Hou Yingli, Hu Ni, Li Zhen, Wang Na, Wu Man, Zhang Xiaohuan
7. ITA—Monica Cirulli, Costanza Fiorentini, Joey Paccagnella, Elisa Plaisant, Sara Savoia, Beatrice Spaziani, Federica Stefanelli, Lorena Zaffalon, Laura Zanazza
8. GRE—Aglaia-Savina Anastasiou, Maria Khristodoulou, Eleftheria Ftouli, Eleni Georgiou, Efrosyni Gouda, Apostolia Ioannou, Evgenia Koutsoudi, Olga Pelekanou, Khristina Thalassinidou

The Russian team continued their domination after the 2000 Olympics, winning every international tournament in the four years between Olympics. Despite having to restart their routine after 17 seconds due to a music malfunction, the Russians gave a confident and acrobatic performance, earning perfect 10s for artistic impression from all of the judges for a score of 49.834. The first seven places mirrored exactly the results of the 2003 world championships.

2008 Beijing T: 8, N: 8, D: 8.23.

1. RUS	99.500
2. SPA	98.251
3. CHN	97.334
4. CAN	95.668
5. USA	95.334
6. JPN	95.334
7. AUS	82.167
8. EGY	80.833

1. RUS—Anastasiya Davydova, Anastasiya Yermakova, Mariya Gromova, Nataliya Ishchenko, Elvira Khasyanova, Olga Kuzhela, Svetlana Romashina, Anna Shorina, Yelena Ovchinnikova
2. SPA—Alba Cabello Rodilla, Raquel Corral Aznar, Andrea Fuentes Fache, Thais Henríquez Torres, Laura López Valle, Gemma Mengual Civil, Irina Rodríguez Álvarez, Paola Tirados Sánchez
3. CHN—Gu Beibei, Jiang Tingting, Jiang Wenwen, Liu Ou, Luo Xi, Sun Qiuting, Wang Na, Zhang Xiaohuan, Huang Xuechen
4. CAN—Marie-Pierre Boudreau-Gagnon, Jessika Dubuc, Marie-Pierre Gagné, Dominika Kopcik, Éve Lamoureux, Tracy Little, Élise Marcotte, Jennifer Song
5. USA—Brooke Abel, Janet Culp, Kate Hooven, Christina Jones, Andrea Nott, Annabelle Orme, Jillian Penner, Kim Probst, Becky Kim
6. JPN—Ai Aoki, Saho Harada, Naoko Kawashima, Hiromi Kobayashi, Erika Komura, Ayako Matsumura, Emiko Suzuki, Masako Tachibana, Yumiko Ishiguro
7. AUS—Eloise Amberger, Coral Bentley, Sarah Bombell, Myriam Glez, Erika Leal Ramírez, Tarren Otte, Samantha Reid, Bethany Walsh, Tamika Domrow
8. EGY—Reem Abdalazem, Aziza Abdelfattah, Hagar Badran, Dalia El-Gebaly, Shaza El-Sayed, Youmna Khallaf, Mai Mohamed, Nouran Saleh

The Russian team remained the best in the world, having never lost a major international event since 1996, a streak that included eight world championship titles, four World Cup titles, six European titles and the past two Olympic championships. After winning the 2007 world championships, scoring near-perfect 99.000s in both the technical and free events, the team disappeared from competition to work on a new routine.

The Russians scored 49.50 points for their technical routine, opening a 0.583 lead over Spain. Performing to "Living Sea" by Paulo Oliveira (based on the theme from *Pirates of the Caribbean*) in the free routine, the Russians earned a perfect score of 50.000, winning their third straight Olympic championship. It was also the third consecutive Olympics at which Russia won both the team and duet synchronized events.

DISCONTINUED EVENT

SOLO

1984 Los Angeles C: 17, N: 17, D: 8.12.

1. Tracie Ruiz	USA	198.467
2. Carolyn Waldo	CAN	195.300
3. Miwako Motoyoshi	JPN	187.050
4. Marijke Engelen	HOL	182.632
5. Gudrun Hänisch	GER	182.017
6. Caroline Holmyard	GBR	182.000
7. Muriel Hermine	FRA	180.534
8. Karin Singer	SWI	178.383

This event, which was added to the Olympic program only two months before the Games began, was won by 21-year-old world champion Tracie Ruiz of Bothell, Washington, whose father was Hawaiian and mother a Norwegian-German mixture. Her Latin surname came from her stepfather.

1988 Seoul C: 46, N: 18, D: 9.30.

1. Carolyn Waldo	CAN	200.150
2. Tracie Ruiz-Conforto	USA	197.633
3. Mikako Kotani	JPN	191.850
4. Muriel Hermine	FRA	190.100
5. Karin Singer	SWI	185.600
6. Nicola Shearn	GBR	181.933
7. Khristina Falasinidi	SOV/GEO	180.650
8. Gerlind Scheller	GER	175.983

The rules for 1988 permitted each nation three entrants, but only one swimmer per nation was allowed to advance to the final. Carolyn Waldo of Beaconsfield, Quebec, used the compulsory figures to build an insurmountable lead over Ruiz-Conforto, who had defeated Waldo in a pre-Olympic competition in Seoul in June.

1992 Barcelona C: 21, N: 21, D: 8.6.

1. Kristen Babb-Sprague	USA	191.848
1. Sylvie Fréchette	CAN	191.717
3. Fumiko Okuno	JPN	187.056
4. Olga Sedakova	RUS	185.106
5. Anne Capron	FRA	182.449
6. Christina Thalassinidou (Khristina Falasinidi)	GRE	180.244
7. Kerry Shacklock	GBR	179.839
8. Marjolijn Both	HOL	179.354

When Tracie Ruiz-Conforto of the United States and Carolyn Waldo of Canada retired following the 1988 Olympics, their places were taken by Kristen Babb-Sprague and Sylvie Fréchette, respectively. Babb-Sprague was forced to begin learning synchronized swimming at the age of three. She entered her first competition when she was six. By the time she won her first United States

A thrilling moment in the 1988 solo synchronized swimming competition.

championship in 1989, when she was 20 years old, she was suffering from extreme pain in her lower back. It turned out that her frontal abdominal muscles were so overdeveloped from a lifetime of synchronized swimming that her oblique stomach muscles were unable to develop. The only cure was to let her muscles atrophy and then rebuild them in a more balanced manner. Babb-Sprague stayed away from the pool for over eight months, but returned to competition in time to win the 1990 United States championship.

While Babb-Sprague was learning her sport in Walnut Creek, California, Sylvie Fréchette was struggling to find pools in which to practice in Montreal. In 1990, the city of Montreal built a pool complex with state-of-the-art synchro equipment, including underwater cameras and sound system. It was destroyed by fire two weeks after it opened.

In 1991, Fréchette defeated Babb-Sprague at both the world championships and the World Cup, and she went into the Olympics as the favorite. One week before the Barcelona Opening Ceremony, Fréchette returned from a day of training to the condominium she shared with her boyfriend, television sports commentator Sylvain Lake. She found Lake dead, a victim of suicide by carbon monoxide poisoning. She went to Barcelona in shock, but determined to compete.

According to the rules then in force, the competition included a round of figures that counted for 50 percent of the final score. Fréchette, who was strong in figures, hoped to pick up some valuable points to offset the gains that Babb-Sprague was expected to make with her free routine. The figures competition, in which each swimmer performs four required movements, is usually the dullest part of synchronized swimming. But this time, just after Fréchette completed her albatross spin up 180 degrees, something unexpected happened. The exact details depend on whether you believe the Canadian version or the American version.

One thing is certain: One of the five judges, Ana Maria da Silveira of Brazil, gave Fréchette a score of 8.7, then announced that she had made a mistake and tried to change it. She was not allowed to make the change and the score of 8.7 stood. The Canadian team filed a protest. They claimed that da Silveira had intended to give Fréchette a 9.7 rather than an 8.7 but had pushed the wrong button. Noticing her mistake immediately, she tried to change the score, but had trouble with the touch pad and pressed the wrong button again. In desperation, she caught the attention of the assistant referee, Nakaka Saito, who was Japanese. Because they had trouble communicating in English, Saito did not understand what da Silveira was trying to tell her. By the time da Silveira was able to alert the referee, Judith McGowan of the United States, the 8.7 had already been displayed to the public as the official score. The rules stated that once a score was made public, it could not be changed.

The Americans conceded that da Silveira had tried to change her score, but challenged her motivation and timing. In figures competition the performers all wear black costumes and a white cap and their names are not announced to the judges until after they have recorded their scores. The Americans theorized that da Silveira had not realized that the woman she was grading was the favorite and had awarded her an 8.7. When she saw Fréchette's name flashed on the scoring screen, and saw that the other judges had given her scores of 9.2, 9.4, 9.5, and 9.6, da Silveira was embarrassed and tried to upgrade the score. McGowan disputed the Canadian claim that da Silveira's intended score was 9.7, stating that it was lower. Indeed, even though the 8.7 was Fréchette's lowest score of the figures competition, a 9.7 would have been the highest score by any judge for any figure by any performer.

A Jury of Appeal—which did not call da Silveira as a witness—voted 11-2 to retain the 8.7. The two dissenting votes came from the Canadian members. The whole controversy would have faded away except for what happened the next day during the free routines. Babb-Sprague came out of the figures with a lead of .251 points. Fréchette then performed an unusually strong free routine and picked up .120 points, leaving her .131 points short of Babb-Sprague, who thus won the gold medal. Had da Silveira's albatross spin score been changed to 9.7, Frechette would have won by .212 points. Even if da Silveira's revised score had been 9.4, the average of the other judges' scores, Fréchette still would have won by .041 points.

In post-Olympic interviews back in Brazil, da Silveira, a university professor, refused to reveal what score she had intended, except to imply that it was higher than 9.0. She also expressed doubt that her mistake actually influenced the final score because she felt that during the free routines, some judges inflated their scores for Fréchette to compensate for the previous day's error.

Babb-Sprague was married to professional baseball player Ed Sprague, who happened to play for the Toronto Blue Jays. Kristen flew straight from Barcelona to Toronto to watch Ed play. Whenever Ed came to bat, Canadian fans booed. All Canadian animosity for Ed Sprague dissolved when he helped the Blue Jays win the World Series, but the dispute did not end. Richard Pound, a powerful Canadian member of the executive board of the International Olympic Committee, led the crusade to overturn the official results. With the very existence of synchronized swimming as an Olympic sport on the line, FINA capitulated, and in October 1993 they awarded Fréchette a belated gold medal, although Babb-Sprague was allowed to retain hers as well.

Chapter 25 Table Tennis

MEN	WOMEN
Singles	Singles
Team	Team
Discontinued Event	Discontinued Event

Table tennis, also known as ping-pong, is played on a table 9 feet (2.74 meters) long and 5 feet (1.525 meters) wide. The playing surface is 2 feet 6 inches (76 centimeters) above the floor. The table is divided by a net 6 inches (15.25 centimeters) high. The ball is made of celluloid or a similar plastic material. After the 2000 Olympics, the size of the ball was changed from 1½ inches (38 millimeters) in diameter to 1.57 inches (40 millimeters) and the weight from .88 ounces (2.5 grams) to .95 ounces (2.7 grams). The racket may be any size, shape, or weight. Rackets are made of wood reinforced with fibrous material and covered with rubber.

According to rules in force since 2004, players take turns serving two serves at a time rather than the traditional five. The rules for a proper serve are quite strict. The server must begin by placing the ball on the open palm of his or her free hand, above the level of the playing surface and behind the end line. The server must toss the ball straight up, without adding spin, at least 6.3 inches (16 centimeters) in the air. As soon as the ball starts falling, the server may hit it. The serve must touch first on the server's side of the table and then pass over the net before touching the receiver's side. For each return after the service, the ball must be hit straight over the net before it touches the table. In doubles matches, the ball must touch first the right half of the server's side and then the right half of the receiver's side. During a rally, players on the same team must alternate hitting the ball. At each change of service in doubles matches, the receiver becomes the server and the server's partner becomes the receiver.

According to these rules, the first player or pair to score 11 points wins the game. However, if the players or pairs are tied at 10, one side must win by 2 points. When the score reaches 10-10, the service changes after each serve instead of after each two serves. A match is won when a player or pair wins four games.

Singles tournaments follow a single-elimination format. In 2012, the singles players seeded 33 to 64 will play in the opening round. The 16 winners will join the players seeded 17 to 32 in the second round. The winners of that round will advance to the third round and play against the top 16 seeded players. The tournament continues through quarterfinals, semifinals and finals.

The top 24 ranked players in the world automatically qualify for the Olympics, although there is a limit of two players per nation. Asia and Europe each qualify 11 more players, Africa and Latin America six each and North America and Oceania three each. The host nation also receives an automatic entry, one player is chosen through Tripartite Commission Invitation and two players qualify through a world qualification tournament. Twelve more men and 12 more women may be added to participate in the team tournament only.

In 2008, the men's and women's doubles event were replaced with men's and women's team events.

MEN

SINGLES

1896–1984 not held

1988 Seoul C: 64, N: 35, D: 10.1.

		MATCHES		GAMES	
		W	L	W	L
1. Yoo Nam-kyu	KOR	11	0	33	3
2. Kim Ki-taik	KOR	10	1	31	12
3. Erik Lindh	SWE	10	1	30	12
4. Tibor Klampár	HUN	8	3	26	17
5. Jiang Jialiang	CHN	10	1	31	6
6. Chen Longcan	CHN	8	3	27	12
7. Jörgen Persson	SWE	8	3	28	14
8. Jan-Ove Waldner	SWE	8	3	26	13

Final: Yoo—Kim 17-21, 21-19, 21-11, 23-21
3rd Place: Lindh—Klampár 14-21, 21-17, 21-17, 21-16
5th Place: Jiang—Chen 21-12, 21-16, 21-17
7th Place: Persson—Waldner 21-15, 21-16, 21-17

The inaugural men's table tennis tournament was highlighted by the shocking upsets of all five of the top-seeded players, none of whom advanced to the semifinals. In the round of 16, number four ranked Andrzej Grubba of Poland was beaten by the fifth seed, Jörgen Persson, who was in turn eliminated in the quarterfinals by Asian Games champion Yoo Nam-kyu. The quarterfinals also saw the defeat of number two seed Jan-Ove Waldner and number three Chen Longcan, who lost five-game cliffhangers to underdogs Kim Ki-taik and Tibor Klampár. But the biggest stunner was the demise of two-time world champion Jiang Jialiang. Jiang, a national hero of movie-star proportions, was beaten in four games by tenth-ranked Erik Lindh. In the semifinals, Yoo and Kim, responding to a wildly enthusiastic crowd, prevailed in straight games to set up a much-appreciated all-Korean final.

1992 Barcelona C: 64, N: 32, D: 8.6.

		MATCHES		GAMES	
		W	L	W	L
1. Jan-Ove Waldner	SWE	7	0	18	1
2. Jean-Philippe Gatien	FRA	6	1	15	9
3. Kim Taek-soo	KOR	5	1	12	8
3. Ma Wenge	CHN	5	1	14	4
5. Ding Yi	AUT	4	1	11	3
5. Jörgen Persson	SWE	4	1	9	4
5. Jörg Rosskopf	GER	4	1	10	4
5. Wang Tao	CHN	4	1	11	4

Final: Waldner—Gatien 21-10, 21-18, 25-23

At his best, such as at the 1989 world championships, Jan-Ove Waldner was unbeatable. But often Waldner played far from his best. At the 1988 Olympics, he was a medal favorite, but finished only eighth. At the 1992 European Championships, only 3½ months before the Olympics, he was also eliminated in the quarterfinals. In Barcelona, however, Waldner played better than he ever had, losing only one game to Jörg Rosskopf and crushing his remaining opponents in straight sets.

1996 Atlanta C: 64, N: 40, D: 8.1.

		MATCHES		GAMES	
		W	L	W	L
1. Liu Guoliang	CHN	7	0	18	5
2. Wang Tao	CHN	6	1	17	6
3. Jörg Rosskopf	GER	6	1	16	6
4. Petr Korbel	CZE	5	2	13	11
5. Kim Taek-soo	KOR	4	1	11	4
5. Jean-Michel Saive	BEL	4	1	9	3
5. Vladimir Samsonov	BLR	4	1	11	4
5. Wenguang "Johnny" Huang	CAN	4	1	10	4

Final: Liu—Wang 21-12, 22-24, 21-19, 15-21, 21-6
3rd Place: Rosskopf—Korbel 21-17, 19-21, 21-18, 21-19

Number one ranked Kong Linghui was beaten in the round of 16 by Kim Taek-soo. In the semifinals, China's number three player, Liu Guoliang, beat Jörg Rosskopf 21-17, 18-21, 21-18, 21-18. Liu owed his victory to sparring partner Zhang Yong, whose specialty was to play in the style of Rosskopf as well as other left-handed western players. In the final Liu faced Wang Tao, who happened to be his close friend and mentor. Wang had survived a quarterfinal scare against Vladimir Samsonov, falling behind 16-21, 16-21 before winning the last three games 21-10, 21-15, 21-15 in a match that was interrupted twice by power failures. Liu and Wang split the first four games of the gold medal match. In the final game, Liu jumped out to a 12-1 lead and Wang lost heart. Defending champion Jan-Ove Waldner was eliminated in the round of 16 by Johnny Huang, but came back the following year to win the world championship without losing a game.

2000 Sydney C: 64, N: 35, D: 9.25.

1. Kong Linghui	CHN
2. Jan-Ove Waldner	SWE
3. Liu Guoliang	CHN
4. Jörgen Persson	SWE
5. Jörg Rosskopf	GER
5. Liu Guozheng	CHN
5. Vladimir Samsonov	BLR
5. Werner Schlager	AUT

Final: Kong—Waldner 21-16, 21-19, 17-21, 14-21, 21-13
3rd Place: Liu—Persson 21-18, 19-21, 21-14, 21-13

In 1999, Olympic champion Liu Guoliang defeated countryman Ma Lin to win the world championship. But then it was revealed that Liu had tested positive for excessive epitestosterone. He failed another test in February 2000. The International Table Tennis Federation (ITTF) then asked an IOC-approved laboratory in Germany to analyze the samples. Finally, a month before the Sydney Olympics, the ITTF ruled that there was no evidence that there was "an external source of epitestosterone and therefore no proof of doping." Liu was seeded third in Sydney behind Kong Linghui and Vladimir Samsonov. Kong made it straight through to the final, but it was not easy. He was taken to five games by Lucjan Blaszczyk of Poland and then by Werner Schlager, who led Kong 2 games to 1. Samsonov and Liu were not as lucky as Kong because they had to face 34-year-old Jan-Ove Waldner. In the quarterfinals, Waldner defeated Samsonov 20-22, 18-21, 21-14, 21-18, 21-19 and in the semifinals he beat Liu 21-19, 21-16, 21-19. Kong won the first two sets of the final and the first four points of the third game. But Waldner fought back and, with the score tied at 17, he took the next four points and the game. When Waldner won the fourth game, as well, it was Kong's turn to reestablish control. He took a 10-1 lead and, although Waldner closed the gap to 15-12, he could get no closer, as Kong won six of the last seven points to secure the victory after 62 minutes.

2004 Athens C: 64, N: 39, D: 8.23.

1. Ryu Seung-min	KOR
2. Wang Hao	CHN
3. Wang Liqin	CHN
4. Jan-Ove Waldner	SWE
5. Timo Boll	GER
5. Chu Yan Leung	HKG
5. Chuan Chih-yuan	TAI
5. Lai Chak Ko	HKG

Final: Ryu—Wang 11-3, 9-11, 11-9, 11-9, 11-13, 11-9
3rd Place: Wang—Waldner 10-12, 11-3, 11-8, 11-7, 11-9

Ranked third in the world, Ryu Seung-min struggled in the early rounds. In the round of 16, he was pushed to the limit by Chiang Peng-lung of Taiwan, finally prevailing 11-6, 11-6, 7-11, 8-11, 11-3, 6-11, 11-4. In his quarterfinal match against Chu Yan Leung, he lost the first two games before winning the last four. Ryu faced veteran Jan-Ove Waldner in the semifinals and won 11-9, 9-11, 11-9, 11-5, 11-5. Meanwhile, Wang Hao defeated his top-seeded compatriot, Wang Liqin, in the semifinals 11-8, 11-5, 6-11, 11-9, 11-3. In the final, Ryu Seung-min took the first set easily, but Wang came back with his unusual penhold topspin backhand to win the second set. Ryu won the next two sets and had a chance to win the match in the fifth set with a match point at 10-9, but Wang saved the point and went on to win the game. In game six, Ryu took an 8-4 lead, but Wang fought back to 9-9, before Ryu secured the victory. He was the first non-Chinese athlete to earn a gold medal in table tennis since 1992. After his victory, Ryu told the press, "My girlfriend has shared difficult times we have had together, but getting a gold medal will help our relationship."

The 2004 competition also included the athlete with the shortest name in Olympic history: North Korea's O Il.

2008 Beijing C: 77, N: 44, D: 8.23.

1. Ma Lin	CHN
2. Wang Hao	CHN
3. Wang Liqin	CHN
4. Jörgen Persson	SWE
5. Ko Lai Chak	HKG
5. O Sang-eun	KOR
5. Zoran Primorac	CRO
5. Ruiwu Tan	CRO

Final: Ma—Wang 11-9, 11-9, 6-11, 11-7, 11-9
3rd Place: Wang—Persson 13-11, 11-2, 11-5, 11-9

Three days after winning the team event, Ma Lin, Wang Hao and Wang Liqin began their assault on the individual event.

As expected, the three swept through their preliminary rounds easily, reaching the semifinals along with 1991 world champion and Olympic veteran Jörgen Persson. Aged 42, Persson had competed in all six Olympics since table tennis was introduced, but had never won a medal.

After Ma had dispatched Persson 11-9, 11-9, 9-11, 11-7, 11-9, world number-one-ranked Wang Hao fought his way to a tough victory over teammate Wang Liqin, winning the first three games 11-5, 11-9, 11-9, then losing the next two 10-12, 3-11, before winning the sixth game 11-8 to reach the final.

Despite having won four World Cup titles, the most by any player in history, Ma Lin had built a reputation for crumbling at the decisive moment; at the world championships in 2007 he lost to Wang Liqin after leading 3-1 in games.

Ma won the first two games in the Olympic final 11-9, 11-9 before Wang came back to win the third. But Ma held on, winning the next two 11-7, 11-9 to clinch the gold medal. The Wangs had finished in the same order as at the 2004 Athens Olympics but this time at the top of the medal table. It was China's first-ever sweep of the men's individual event, and it completed their clean sweep of all four table tennis events at the 2008 Olympics, having won all eight possible medals, including six individual medals and two team medals.

TEAM

The men's and women's team events include sixteen teams each, including six based on continental rankings, the host country, and the remaining nine based on ITTF team rankings. Each team consists of three players, but a team of two players will be allowed if the third is injured or disqualified. Contests are won based on the best three of five matches, and consist of two singles matches followed by one doubles match, and followed, if necessary, by one or two singles matches to determine the winner. Whichever team-mate does not participate in the first two singles matches must participate in the doubles match. The competition consists of a round-robin stage, with teams divided into four groups of four. The two best teams from each group advance to the single-elimination round.

1896–2004 not held

2008 Beijing T: 16, N: 16, D: 8.18.

1. Wang Hao, Ma Lin, Wang Liqin	CHN
2. Timo Boll, Dmitrij Ovtcharov, Christian Süss	GER
3. O Sang-eun, Yu Seung-min, Yoon Jae-young	KOR
4. Weixing Chen, Robert Gardos, Werner Schlager	AUT
5. Cheung Yuk, Ko Lai Chak, Li Ching	HKG
5. Yo Kan, Seiya Kishikawa, Jun Mizutani	JPN
7. Andrej Gaćina, Zoran Primorac, Ruiwu Tan	CRO
7. Chang Yen-shu, Chiang Peng-lung, Chuan Chih-yuan	TAI

Final: CHN 3–0 GER
3rd Place: KOR 3–1 AUT

The Chinese men's team featured the three top-ranked players in the world: defending Olympic silver medalist Wang Hao, two-time reigning world champion Wang Liqin and 2004 Olympic doubles gold medalist Ma Lin. Cheered on by a loud, mostly Chinese crowd, the trio steamrolled through the tournament, beating every opponent they faced in three straight matches.

In pool play, the Chinese team won 27 games and lost only 5. They then defeated South Korea in the semifinals. Their final opponents, the Germans, had advanced thanks to via a hard-fought 3-2 win over Japan that included three matches that went the full five games.

In the final, Ma played the first singles match against 19-year-old Dmitrij Ovtcharov, beating him handily 11-4, 11-8, 11-7. Then Wang Hao defeated Timo Boll 11-7, 8-11, 11-4, 11-7. Wang Liqin and Ma lost their first doubles game 11-13 to Christian Süss and Boll but came back to win the next three 11-5, 11-8, 11-7 to finish out the tournament.

DISCONTINUED EVENT

DOUBLES

1988 Seoul T: 32, N: 23, D: 9.30.

		MATCHES		GAMES	
		W	L	W	L
1. CHN	Chen Longcan, Wei Qingguang	10	0	20	3
2. YUG	Ilija Lupulesku, Zoran Primorac	8	2	17	8
3. KOR	Ahn Jae-hyung, Yoo Nam-kyu	9	1	18	3
4. KOR	Kim Ki-taik, Kim Wan	7	3	16	7
5. CHN	Jiang Jialiang, Xu Zengcai	9	1	18	5
6. POL	Andrzej Grubba, Leszak Kucharski	7	3	15	7
7. SWE	Erik Lindh, Jörgen Persson	7	3	14	6
8. SWE	Mikael Appelgren, Jan-Ove Waldner	6	4	14	10

Final: Chen/Wei—Lupulesku/Primorac 20-22, 21-8, 21-9
3rd Place: Ahn/Yoo—Kim/Kim 21-13, 21-16
5th Place: Jiang/Xu—Grubba/Kucharski 21-7, 21-12
7th Place: Lindh/Persson—Appelgren/Waldner 21-10, 21-14

The final match was a replay of the 1987 world championship final. The result was also the same, with Chen and Wei defeating Lupulesku and Primora two games to one.

1992 Barcelona T: 30, N: 23. D: 8.4.

		MATCHES		GAMES	
		W	L	W	L
1. CHN	Lu Lin, Wang Tao	6	0	15	6
2. GER	Steffen Fetzner, Jörg Rosskopf	5	1	14	3
3. KOR	Kang Hee-chan, Lee Chul-seung	3	1	7	6
3. KOR	Kim Taek-soo, Yoo Nam-kyu	3	1	8	3
5. CHN	Ma Wenge, Yu Shentong	3	1	8	4
5. FRA	Damien Eloi, Jean-Philippe Gatien	3	1	7	4
5. RUS	Andrei Mazunov, Dmitri Mazunov	3	1	6	4
5. YUG/SER	Slobodan Grujić, Ilija Lupulesku	3	1	6	4

Final: Lu/Wang—Fetzner/Rosskopf 26-24, 18-21, 21-18, 13-21, 21-14

At 9 a.m. on August 4, two hours before the men's doubles final, Wang Tao and Lu Lin appeared at the Olympic Village bus stop, ready to take the shuttle bus to the Estació del Nord competition site. The bus never came. In a panic, they began jogging to the sports complex, finally hailing a taxi to take them the rest of the way. They arrived just in time for the match and found the stands filled with wildly enthusiastic German fans. In the first game, Wang and Lu fell behind 15-20 before winning 26-24. In the second game they led 18-12, only to see Fetzner and Rosskopf reel off nine straight points to even the match. The two teams traded games, to make it 2-2. The deciding game was also tied at 10-10, but then Wang and Lu took command and outscored the German pair 11-4 the rest of the way.

1996 Atlanta T: 31, N: 25, D: 7.30.

		MATCHES		GAMES	
		W	L	W	L
1. CHN	Kong Linghui, Liu Guoliang	6	0	15	1
2. CHN	Lu Lin, Wang Tao	5	1	13	5
3. KOR	Lee Chul-seung, Yoo Nam-kyu	5	1	12	3
4. GER	Steffen Fetzner, Jörg Rosskopf	4	2	9	6
5. FRA	Damien Eloi, Jean-Philippe Gatien	3	1	16	3
5. JPN	Koji Matsushita, Hiroshi Shibutani	3	1	6	3
5. KOR	Kang Hee-chan, Kim Taek-soo	2	1	16	3
5. SWE	Jörgen Persson, Jan-Ove Waldner	3	1	16	5

Final: Kong/Liu—Lu/Wang 21-8, 13-21, 21-19, 21-11
3rd Place: Lee/Yoo—Fetzner/Rosskopf 21-18, 21-13, 22-20

At the 1995 world championships, Kong Linghui defeated Liu Guoliang to win the singles title. At the Olympics the following year, the two teamed up to gain the doubles title by beating veterans Wang Tao and Lu Lin. The winning pair were never seriously threatened in any of their matches.

2000 Sydney T: 36, N: 29, D: 9.23.
1. CHN Wang Liqin, Yan Sen
2. CHN Kong Linghui, Liu Guoliang
3. FRA Jean-Philippe Gatien, Patrick Chila
4. KOR Lee Chul-seung, Yoo Seung-min
5. TAI Chang Yen-shu, Chiang Peng-lung
5. FRA Christophe Legout, Damien Eloi
5. AUT Karl Jindrak, Werner Schlager
5. KOR Kim Taek-soo, Oh Sang-eun

Final: Wang/Yan—Kong/Liu 22-20, 17-21, 21-19, 21-18
3rd Place: Gatien/Chila—Lee/Yoo 22-20, 21-23, 21-19, 21-10

Wang Liqin and Yan Sen dominated the tournament, losing only two games in four matches. The final was a rematch of the 1999 world championship, which was won by Kong Linghui and Liu Guoliang in five games. This time, although each game was close, Wang and Yan prevailed in four games.

2004 Athens T: 32, N: 25, D: 8.21.
1. CHN Chen Qi, Ma Lin
2. HKG Ko Lai-Chak, Li Ching
3. DEN Michael Maze, Finn Tugwell
4. RUS Dmitri Mazunov, Aleksei Smirnov
5. KOR Lee Chul-seung, Ryu Seung-min
5. POL Lucjan Błaszczyk, Tomasz Krzeszewski
5. SER Slobodan Grujić, Aleksandar Karakašević
5. SWE Jörgen Persson, Jan-Ove Waldner

Final: Chen/Ma—Ko/Li 11-6, 11-9, 7-11, 11-8, 8-11, 11-5
3rd Place: Maze/Tugwell—Mazunov/Smirnov 11-3, 11-8, 12-14, 3-11, 11-9, 11-8

It was a testament to the depth of China's talent that, four months before the Games, Chinese coaches dropped from the Olympic squad the defending Olympic champions and two-time defending world champions, Wang Liquin and Yan Sen. The Chinese berths were given to two-time Olympic finalists Kong Linghui and Wang Hao, and top seeds Ma Lin and Chen Qi. At the beginning of 2004, Ma was involved in a "dating scandal," dating, according to the Chinese table tennis system, being a threat to training. Ma's 19-year-old girlfriend, Bai Yang, and Fan Yin, the 17-year-old girlfriend of singles star Wang Hao, were removed from the national team for dating, while Ma and Wang, because of their high rankings, were allowed to stay on the team.

Kong and Wang were eliminated in the quarterfinals by Jörgen Persson and Jan-Ove Waldner, both of whom had competed in every Olympic tournament since the sport was added to the program in 1988. Ma and Chen advanced to the final with a hard-fought 11-9, 10-12, 11-7, 8-11, 13-11, 13-11 semifinal win over Michael Maze and Finn Tugwell. In the final, Ma and Chen overcame nervousness in the third and fifth games to defeat Ko Lai-Chak and Li Ching. Ko and Li had been members of the Chinese national team, but they left in 2000 for Hong Kong, which has its own Olympic team even though it is part of China.

WOMEN

SINGLES

1896–1984 not held

1988 Seoul C: 48, N: 28, D: 10.1.

		MATCHES		GAMES	
		W	L	W	L
1. Chen Jing	CHN	9	0	27	2
2. Li Huifen	CHN	8	1	26	4
3. Jiao Zhimin	CHN	8	1	24	9
4. Marie Hrachová	CZE	6	3	20	12
5. Flyura Bulatova	SOV/RUS	8	1	24	8
6. Valentina Popova	SOV/RUS	6	3	18	9
7. Bettine Vriesekoop	HOL	7	2	21	9
8. Hong Cha-ok	KOR	5	4	16	15

Final: Chen—Li 21-17, 21-16, 21-23, 15-21, 21-15
3rd Place: Jiao—Hrachová 21-18, 21-19, 21-17
5th Place: Bulatova—Popova 21-16, 21-11, 22-20
7th Place: Vriesekoop—Hong 21-19, 21-16, 25-23

The table tennis world was shocked and somewhat suspicious when Chinese officials announced that their Olympic team would include secondary stars Li Huifen and Chen Jing instead of the number one ranked player in the world, He Zhili, and number three ranked Dai Lili. It turned out that He was being punished for refusing to throw a match to another Chinese player during the 1987 world championship, which she then won. She eventually married a Japanese man and moved to Osaka. Chen's coach, Xi Enting, summed up the Olympic prospects of his 21-year-old protégé by saying, "I think there are two possible outcomes: one is that she [Chen] will become famous overnight and the other is that she will yield to the pressure, perform poorly and receive a lasting blow to her confidence."

As it turned out, Chen and Li crushed their opposition. Chen advanced to the final without losing a single game, while Li lost only one. Meanwhile, rumors spread in the Korean press that Li had won her semifinal contest over top seed Jiao Zhimin because Jiao had been ordered to throw the match. Jiao was hounded by the Korean media wherever she went because of interest in her "politically incorrect" romance with South Korean doubles champion Ahn Jae-hyung.

Despite the circus and scandal surrounding the women's singles tournament, the final was an exciting, hard-fought battle, won three games to two by Chen, who thus escaped "a lasting blow to her confidence."

As for Jiao Zhimin and Ahn Jae-hyung, they did in fact get married and settle in Seoul, where their first child was born three years to the day after the Opening Ceremony of the 1988 Olympics.

1992 Barcelona C: 62, N: 38. D: 8.5.

		MATCHES		GAMES	
		W	L	W	L
1. Deng Yaping	CHN	7	0	18	1
2. Qiao Hong	CHN	6	1	16	5
3. Hyun Jung-hwa	KOR	5	1	12	5
3. Li Bun-hui	PRK	4	1	11	5
5. Chai Po-wa	HKG	4	1	9	4
5. Chen Zihe	CHN	4	1	10	3
5. Emilia Ciosu	ROM	3	1	9	3
5. Yu Sun-bok	PRK	4	1	9	5

Final: Deng—Qiao 21-6, 21-8, 15-21, 23-21

The biggest obstacle in Deng Yaping's career was not her opponents, but her height. When she was 9 years old she won a provincial junior championship but was denied a place on the provincial team because she was too short. In 1988, when she was 15 years old, Deng won the national championship, but was refused a spot on the national team because she was too short. The national coaching staff finally gave in and, in 1989, Deng, still only 16 years old, teamed with Qiao Hong to win the doubles title at the world championships. In 1991, by which time she had topped out at 4 feet 10½ inches (1.49 meters), Deng defeated Li Bun-hui of North Korea to win the singles world championship. At the Olympics she obliterated everyone she faced. In the final her opponent was her doubles partner, Qiao Hong. Two days earlier, Deng and Qiao had won the doubles tournament. But with cash awards and other favors at stake, the Deng-Qiao match was a serious affair. Deng won the first two games easily. Then Qiao caught fire, won one game and almost won a second, but Deng won 6 of the last 8 points and prevailed, 23-21.

1996 Atlanta C: 63, N: 37, D: 7.31.

		MATCHES		GAMES	
		W	L	W	L
1. Deng Yaping	CHN	7	0	18	3
2. Chen Jing	TAI	6	1	17	5
3. Qiao Hong	CHN	6	1	15	4
4. Liu Wei	CHN	5	2	14	8
5. Chan Tan-Lui	HKG	4	1	9	5
5. Kim Hyon-hui	PRK	4	1	9	4
5. Chire Koyama	JPN	4	1	9	6
5. Nicole Struse	GER	4	1	9	5

Final: Deng—Chen 21-14, 21-17, 20-22, 17-21, 21-5
3rd Place: Qiao—Liu 21-17, 15-21, 21-19, 21-11

Eleven of the 63 participants were born in China including six of the eight quarterfinalists. None of the "Overseas Corps," as they were known in China, was more controversial than Chire Koyama, formerly known as He Zhili. After moving to Japan in 1989, she became a Japanese citizen and began representing her new nation in 1992. At the 1994 Asian Games in Hiroshima, Koyama defeated Qiao Hong in the semifinals and then defeated 1992 Olympic champion Deng Yaping in the final. Many Chinese were furious with Koyama and she was pilloried in the Chinese press as a "traitor" who engaged in "unpatriotic behavior." The 1995 world championships were held in Tianjin, China. Koyama withdrew rather than play before a potentially hostile crowd. In her absence, Deng defeated Qiao in the final.

In Atlanta, the round of 16 was enlivened by a controversial call. Chai Po Wa of Hong Kong was trailing North Korea's Kim Gyon-hui two games to one. The fourth game was tied 20-20 when Chai missed. She slammed the table with her hand in frustration. The Cuban umpire, Dagoberto Egoyucue, penalized Chai for "bad behavior" thus ending the match. Hong Kong officials vigorously protested the call, but US referee Wendell Dillion let it stand.

The big match of the quarterfinals was the confrontation between Chire Koyama and Qiao Hong. The Chinese gained satisfaction as Qiao won 21-18, 21-19, 21-16 despite the fact that Koyama led in each game. In the semifinals, Qiao faced yet another member of the "Overseas Corps," 1988 Olympic champion Chen Jing, who was representing Taiwan. Chen prevailed 21-9, 23-21, 21-17 and advanced to the final for a confrontation with defending champion Deng Yaping.

Deng won the first two games 21-14 and 21-17. The third game was tied at 15, when play was delayed due to a disruption in the stands. In order to appease China, the IOC ruled that Taiwan must compete as "Chinese Taipei" and could not use the national flag of Taiwan. This did not stop one fan from displaying his own Taiwanese flag. Since this was a contravention of IOC rules, police arrived to remove the fan. Another Taiwanese supporter punched a policeman in the mouth and both fans were hauled away. When play resumed, Chen took charge and won the game 22-20 and the next game 21-17. However, in the fifth game, Deng broke open a 2-2 tie by scoring nine straight points and Chen was never able to recover. Deng won 21-5 and earned her fourth gold medal.

2000 Sydney C: 63, N: 37, D: 9.24.

1. Wang Nan	CHN
2. Li Ju	CHN
3. Chen Jing	TAI
4. Jing Jun-hong	SIN
5. Chire Koyama	JPN
5. Mihaela Ştеff	ROM
5. Qianhong Gotsch	GER
5. Ryu Ji-hae	KOR

Final: Wang—Li 21-12, 12-21, 19-21, 21-17, 21-18
3rd Place: Chen—Jing 18-21, 21-14, 21-15, 21-10

China dominated women's table tennis once again as twelve different nations were represented by Chinese-born players. Seven of the eight top seeds were Chinese-born as were six of the eight quarterfinalists. In the semifinals, world champion Wang Nan defeated 1988 Olympic Champion Chen Jing 12-21, 22-20, 21-17, 21-15. At the final, a banner read, "China is sure to win." This was literally true, as Wang's opponent was her doubles partner, Li Ju, with whom she had won the gold medal two days earlier. Down two games to one, Wang came from behind to take the last two games. As the Olympic champion in one of her nation's most popular sports, Wang reaped the rewards of the "New China." On the one hand, she was appointed a delegate from Liaoning Province to the Chinese Party Congress, and on the other hand she appeared in advertisements for sanitary napkins.

2004 Athens C: 64, N: 35, D: 8.22.

1. Zhang Yining	CHN
2. Kim Hyang-mi	PRK
3. Kim Kyung-ah	KOR
4. Li Jiawei	SIN
5. Tamara Boroš	CRO
5. Wang Nan	CHN
5. Tie Yana	HKG
5. Zhang Xueling	SIN

Final: Zhang—Kim 11-8, 11-7, 11-2, 11-2
3rd Place: Kim—Li 9-11, 11-8, 11-7, 11-5, 11-8

The favorites for gold were defending Olympic champion and three-time defending world champion Wang Nan and upstart Zhang Yining, who had lost to Wang in all three world championships, but had beaten her at the 2002 Asian Games. The much-anticipated confrontation between Wang and Zhang was not to be, as Wang was eliminated in the quarterfinals in five games by Chinese-born Li Jiawei, representing Singapore. The following day, Wang and Zhang joined together to earn gold medals in the doubles event. Meanwhile, back in the singles tournament, Zhang swept into the final, losing only two of eighteen games on the way. Zhang's opponent in the final was Kim Hyang-mi of North Korea, who had upset China's Niu Jianfeng in four games in the round of 16, and then staged a dramatic comeback in her semifinal contest with Li Jiawei, finally winning 8-11, 11-6, 0-11, 8-11, 11-8, 11-6, 11-9. Zhang had no difficulty with Kim in the final, winning four straight games in 26 minutes.

2008 Beijing C: 77, N: 42, D: 8.22.

1. Zhang Yining	CHN
2. Wang Nan	CHN
3. Guo Yue	CHN
4. Li Jia Wei	SIN
5. Feng Tian Wei	SIN
5. Tie Ya Na	HKG
5. Chen Wang	USA
5. Xue "Nieves" Wu	DOM

Final: Zhang—Wang 8-11, 13-11, 11-8, 11-8, 11-3
3rd Place: Guo—Wei 11-6, 14-12, 9-11, 7-11, 11-3, 11-4

The top three seeds in the tournament were all Chinese, and all had won the gold medal in the team event just days earlier. Not surprisingly, all three advanced to the semifinals, along with Beijing-born Li Jia Wei, who moved to Singapore as a teenager to train, eventually becoming a Singaporean citizen.

Li faced defending singles and doubles Olympic champion Zhang Yining in the first semifinal match. Li won the first game 11-9, but Zhang came back to win the next four 11-8, 12-10, 11-8, 11-5 to reach the final. Reigning world champion Guo Yue and 2000 Olympic singles and doubles champion Wang Nan faced off in the second semi, trading the first four games before Wang won the last two to advance.

Wang won the first game of the final 11-8 before the 26-year-old Zhang hit her stride, winning the next four 13-11, 11-8, 11-8, 11-3 to successfully defend her singles gold medal. The bronze medal match was even after four games; but then Guo won the next two 11-3, 11-4 to seal the sweep. Not only were all three medalists Chinese, all eight top finishers were born in China.

TEAM

1896–2004 not held

2008 Beijing T: 16, N: 16, D: 8.17.

1. Guo Yue, Wang Nan, Zhang Yining	CHN
2. Feng Tian Wei, Li Jia Wei, Wang Jue Gu	SIN
3. Dang Ye-seo, Kim Gyeong-a, Park Mi-young	KOR
4. Al Fukuhara, Haruna Fukuoka, Sayaka Hirano	JPN
5. Lau Sui Fei, Lin Ling, Tie Ya Na	HKG
5. Gao Jun, Crystal Huang, Chen Wang	USA
7. Veronika Heine, Qiangbing Li, Jia Liu	AUT
7. Daniela Dodean, Iulia Necula, Elizabeta Samara	ROM

Final: CHN 3–0 SIN
3rd Place: KOR 3–0 JPN

The Chinese team consisted of 2004 Olympic singles and doubles champion Zhang Yining, 2000 Olympic singles and doubles champion Wang Nan, and reigning singles world champion Guo Yue. In addition, they were the top three seeds in the women's singles.

The trio lived up to expectations, sweeping through their preliminary pool undefeated, beating every competitor in three straight matches and winning 27 of 29 games. They trounced the Hong Kong team in the semifinals in nine straight games, giving up only 52 points.

In the other semifinal, Singapore fought to a 3-2 win over South Korea. In the first singles match Singapore's Feng Tian Wei beat Dang Ye-seo in a three-game sweep. In the second singles match, Korean Kim Gyeong-a, down two games to one, came from behind to defeat Li Jia Wei. Then, after Singapore had won the doubles match, Dang evened the contest up again with a three-game victory over Wang Jue Gu. In the deciding match, Feng beat Park Mi-young in four games.

In the final (in which all six players were Chinese-born) both Wang Nan and Zhang Yining lost the first game of their singles matches, but then won the next three. Guo and Zhang closed out the tournament by beating Wang and Li 11-8, 11-5, 11-6. This was Singapore's second-ever Olympic medal, 48 years after Howe Liang "Tiger" Tan won silver in the lightweight weightlifting event.

Gao Jun of the US team had earned a silver medal in doubles while representing China . . . in 1992.

DISCONTINUED EVENT

DOUBLES

1988 Seoul T: 15, N: 15, D: 9.30.

		MATCHES W	MATCHES L	GAMES W	GAMES L
1. KOR	Hyun Jung-hwa, Yang Young-ja	10	0	20	2
2. CHN	Chen Jing, Jiao Zhimin	8	1	17	4
3. YUG	Jasna Fazlić, Gordana Perkučin	7	3	15	7
4. JPN	Mika Hoshino, Kiyomi Ishida	4	5	10	11
5. CZE	Marie Hrachová, Renata Kasalová	7	2	14	7
6. SOV	Flyura Bulatova, Olena Kovtun	6	4	13	10
7. HOL	Mirjam Kloppenburg, Bettine Vriesekoop	5	4	10	11
8. HUN	Csilla Bátorfi, Edit Urbán	4	6	11	14

Final: Hyun/Yang—Chen/Jiao 21-19, 16-21, 21-10
3rd Place: Fazlić/Perkučin—Hoshino/Ishida 21-14, 11-21, 21-16
5th Place: Hracová/Kasalová—Bulatova/Kovtun 21-10, 8-21, 21-19
7th Place: Kloppenburg/Vriesekoop—Bátorfi/Urbán 21-18, 21-23, 21-17

Hyun and Yang took an 11-2 lead in the decisive third game of the final, which they went on to win 21-10. Bronze medalists Fazlić and Perkucin were from Bosnia and Serbia, respectively. By 1992 their nation, Yugoslavia, had splintered and they found themselves on different teams. They were allowed to compete as a pair anyway because Fazlić's husband was Serbian, but they were upset in pool play by Kloppenburg and Vriesekoop.

1992 Barcelona T: 31, N: 25, D: 8.3.

		MATCHES W	MATCHES L	GAMES W	GAMES L
1. CHN	Deng Yaping, Qiao Hong	6	0	15	4
2. CHN	Chan Zihe, Gao Jun	5	1	13	5
3. PRK	Li Bun-hui, Yu Sun-bok	4	1	10	4
3. KOR	Hong Cha-ok, Hyun Jung-Hwa	3	1	8	4
5. HKG	Chai Po-wa, Chan Tan-lui	3	1	7	3
5. HOL	Mirjam Hooman (Kloppenburg), Bettina Vriesekoop	3	1	7	4
5. KOR	Hong Soon-hwa, Lee Jung-im	3	1	7	4
5. RUS	Irina Palina, Yelena Timina	3	1	6	4

Final: Deng/Qiao—Chan/Gao 21-13,14-21, 21-14, 21-19

The final was delayed for ten minutes because Qiao twisted her ankle just before entering the arena. Two days later, Deng and Qiao faced each other in the singles final.

1996 Atlanta T: 31; N: 24; D: 7.29.

		MATCHES W	MATCHES L	GAMES W	GAMES L
1. CHN	Deng Yaping, Qiao Hong	5	0	13	4
2. CHN	Liu Wei, Quai Yunping	5	1	13	5
3. KOR	Park Hae-jung, Ryu Hi-jae	5	1	13	5
4. KOR	Kim Moo-kyo, Park Young-ae	4	2	11	6
5. HKG	Chai Po-Wa, Chan Tan-Liu	2	2	4	5
5. JPN	Chire Koyama, Taeko Todo	3	1	6	5
5. RUS	Irina Palina, Yelena Timina	3	1	7	3
5. TAI	Chen Chiu-Tan, Chen Jing	2	2	7	6

Final: Deng/Qiao—Liu/Quai 18-21, 25-23, 22-20, 21-14
3rd Place: Park/Ryu—Kim/Park 21-16, 21-8, 14-21, 21-13

In the quarterfinals, defending champions Deng Yaping and Qiao Hong faced a stiff challenge from former Chinese players Chen Jing and Chen Chiu-Tan. The Chens took the first game 21-18, but Deng and Qiao won the next two 21-16 and 21-19. In the fourth game, Chen and Chen staved off a match point before winning 24-22. In the fifth game it was Deng and Qiao who fought off two match points and then went on to win 23-21.

Deng Yaping and Qiao Hong faced Liu Wei and Quai Yunping in the final of the 1993 world championships, the 1994 Asian Games and the 1995 world championships. Liu and Quai won the first two, Deng and Qiao the third. The two pairs met again in the Olympic final. The match was comparatively dull with both teams stalling so much that even the umpire became annoyed. Liu and Quai won the first game, and almost won the second, but Deng and Qiao recovered and won three straight games to retain their Olympic title.

2000 Sydney T: 34, N: 25, D: 9.22.
1. CHN Li Ju, Wang Nan
2. CHN Sun Jin, Yang Ying
3. KOR Kim Moo-kyo, Ryu Ji-hae
4. HUN Csilla Bátorfi, Krisztina Tóth
5. CRO Eldijana Aganović, Tamara Boroš
5. KOR Lee Eun-sil, Suk Eun-mi
5. AUS Miao Miao, Shirley Zhou
5. ROM Mihaela Şteff, Otilia Bădescu

Final: Li/Wang—Sun/Yang 21-18, 21-11, 21-11
3rd Place: Moo-kyo/Ji-hae—Bátorfi/Tóth 21-18, 21-19, 22-24, 19-21, 21-19

Favorites Wang Nan and Li Ju were almost undone in the semifinal before they managed to outlast Kim Moo-kyo and Ryu Ji-hye 17-21, 21-15, 15-21, 21-14, 24-22. The final was a rematch of the 1999 world championships, which Wang and Li also won in straight games.

2004 Athens T: 34, N: 26, D: 8.20.
1. CHN Wang Nan, Zhang Yining
2. KOR Suk Eun-mi, Lee Eun-sil
3. CHN Guo Yue, Niu Jianfeng
4. KOR Kim Bok-rae, Kim Kyung-ah
5. CRO Tamara Boroš, Cornelia Vaida
5. HKG Ah Sim Song, Tie Yana
5. JPN Ai Fujinuma, Aya Umemura
5. PRK Kim Hyang-mi, Kim Hyon-hui

Final: Wang/Zhang—Suk/Lee 11-9, 11-7, 11-6, 11-6
3rd Place: Guo/Niu—Kim/Kim 11-7, 5-11, 11-4, 11-9, 7-11, 9-11, 11-9

After winning the Olympic tournament in 2000, Wang Nan and her partner, Li Ju, added the world championship in 2001. Wang won the 2003 world championship as well, but this time with a new partner, Zhang Yining, who was her rival in singles. In a repeat of the 2003 world championship final, Wang and Zhang toppled top-seeded compatriots Guo Yue and Niu Jianfeng, this time in the Olympic semifinals, 11-7, 13-11, 9-11, 13-11, 6-11, 13-11. In the final, Wang and Zhang steamrolled Suk Eun-mi and Lee Eun-sil in four games.

Chapter 26 **Taekwondo**

MEN
Olympic Flyweight—58kg
Olympic Featherweight—68kg
Olympic Welterweight—80kg
Olympic Heavyweight—over 80kg

WOMEN
Olympic Flyweight—49kg
Olympic Featherweight—57kg
Olympic Welterweight—67kg
Olympic Heavyweight—over 67kg

With its roots in ancient Korean martial arts, taekwondo was created in 1957. The first world championship was held in 1973. Taekwondo was included as a demonstration sport at the 1988 and 1992 Olympics.

Men's taekwondo matches consist of three three-minute rounds with one-minute breaks between rounds. Women engage in three two-minute rounds. A contestant can win by knocking down an opponent for ten seconds or by winning the most points. Points are scored by delivering strikes to specific areas on the opponent's body. There are four scoring areas: head, abdomen and the sides of the body. Contestants wear body protectors and the scoring areas are marked on the protectors. Hits below the waist are forbidden. Strikes must be made with the foot below the ankle or by the knuckles of the index and middle fingers. Points may be deducted because of penalties. Full point penalties, called *gam-jeom,* include such infractions as deliberately attacking an opponent's back, attacking an opponent's face with the hands or throwing an opponent. Half-point penalties, or *kyong-go,* include holding, pushing, grabbing, turning your back to an opponent or feigning injury. Half-point penalties do not count unless a second one is called. If a contest is tied, a fourth, sudden-death round is contested. If no point is scored in the fourth round, the refereeing officials decide the winner based on the performances in the sudden-death round.

Taekwondo tournaments are single elimination until the gold and silver medals are decided. The bronze medal is decided by a more complicated formula. Contestants who lost to the finalists before the semifinals compete in a two-pool single elimination mini-tournament. The two survivors join the two losing semifinalists in the bronze-medal semifinals.

There are actually eight taekwondo weight categories each for men and women. However, one of the conditions for allowing the sport into the Olympics was that only four weight categories would be allowed, so special weight divisions were created for the Olympics. In 2012 there will be sixteen competitors in each weight division for both men and women. Although there are four weight categories for each sex, each nation's entry is limited to two men and two women.

Tae means "to kick or smash with the foot," *kwon* means "to destroy with the fist," and *do* means "the art or way of."

MEN

OLYMPIC FLYWEIGHT
(58 kg—128 lbs)

1896–1996 not held

2000 Sydney C: 14, N: 14, D: 9.27.

1. Michalis Mouroutsos	GRE
2. Gabriel Esparza Pérez	SPA
3. Huang Chih-hsiung	TAI
4. Gabriel Taraburelli	ARG
5. József Salim	HUN
5. Younes Sekkat	MOR
7. Naser Buftain	KUW
7. Roberto Cruz	PHI

Final: Mouroutsos 4-2 Esparza
3rd Place: Huang 3-0 Taraburelli

European champion Michalis Mouroutsos upset Huang Chih-hsiung in the second round. In the final, the score was tied 1-1 when Mouroutsos outscored Esparza 3-1 in the last round.

2004 Athens C: 16, N: 16, D: 8.26.

1. Chu Mu-yen	TAI
2. Oscar Salazar Blanco	MEX
3. Tamer Bayoumi	EGY
4. Juan Antonio Ramos Sánchez	SPA
5. Yulis Gabriel Mercedes Reyes	DOM
5. Quốc Huân Nguyễn	VIE
7. Oleksandr Shaposhnyk	UKR
7. Ezedin Salem	LBA

Final: Chu 5-1 Salazar
3rd Place: Bayoumi 7-1 Ramos

Reigning world champion Chu Mu-yen's closest match came in the semifinal round, when he edged out Tamer Bayoumi 5-4, after Bayoumi had ousted defending Olympic champion Michalis Mouroutsos 8-2. On the other side of the bracket, Oscar Salazar advanced to the final by outscoring his three opponents 24-3. In the final, Chu took control after a scoreless first round by scoring three unanswered points in the second round. He then clinched the gold medal with two points in the third round to one for Salazar. Chu's victory came just 20 minutes after Chen Shih-hsin won Taiwan's first-ever gold medal in any sport by taking the women's taekwondo flyweight category. Chu began his post-competition press conference with the words, "I am from Taiwan," a reference to the fact that, under pressure from China, the IOC forced his country to compete in the Olympics as "Chinese Taipei."

In 2005, Chu was blackmailed by members of a fraud ring after making friends with a woman in an Internet chat room. The criminals recorded conversations between Chu and the woman, and threatened to release them and harm his family. Chu paid the gang $33,000 before going to the police and making a public apology on television.

2008 Beijing C: 16, N: 16, D: 8.20.

1. Guillermo Pérez Sandoval	MEX
2. Yulis Mercedes Reyes	DOM
3. Chu Mu-yen	TAI
3. Rohullah Nikpai	AFG
5. Chutchawal Khawlaor	THA
5. Juan Antonio Ramos Sánchez	SPA
7. Michael Harvey	GBR
7. Pedro Póvoa	POR

Final: Pérez 1-1 (Superiority) Mercedes
3rd Place: Chu 4-2 Khawlaor
3rd Place: Nikpai 4-1 Ramos

Yulis Mercedes upset defending Olympic champion Chu Mu-yen and reigning world champion Juan Antonio Ramos on his way to the final. Mercedes won each bout 3-2, beating Chu on a late point in the third round and dispatching Ramos with a back kick to the body with six seconds left in overtime.

Mercedes faced long-time friend and rival Guillermo Pérez in the gold medal match. Pérez, the reigning world silver medalist, scored early in the second round before Mercedes came back to score on a back kick in the final seconds of regulation time, sending the athletes to a two-minute tie-breaking round. Pérez was ultimately declared the winner by superiority after neither fighter was able to score.

Born in Uruapan, Mexico, Pérez took up taekwondo at the age of five after being inspired by Bruce Lee. He was the first male gold medalist from Mexico since Ernesto Canto and Raúl González swept the 20- and 50-kilometer walk events at the 1984 Olympics.

Twenty-one-year-old Rohullah Nikpai made history in the bronze medal match, beating Ramos 4-1 to win the first Olympic medal for Afghanistan in any sport. "I hope this will send a message of peace to my country after 30 years of war," Nikpai said after the match, "I won the medal for my country."

The other bronze went to Chu, who defeated Chutchawal Khawlaor 4-2.

OLYMPIC FEATHERWEIGHT
(68 kg—150 lbs)

1896–1996 not held

2000 Sydney C: 14, N: 14, D: 9.28.

1. Steven Lopez	USA
2. Sin Joon-sik	KOR
3. Hadi Saei Bonehkohal	IRN
4. Tuncay Caliskan	AUT
5. Aziz Acharki	GER
5. Carlo Massimino	AUS
7. Aslander Dzitiev	RUS
7. Claudio Nolano	ITA

Final: Lopez 1-0 Sin
3rd Place: Bonehkohal 4-2 Caliskan

Taekwondo's introduction as an official sport brought great excitement to supporters of the discipline, but lurking in the background of the inaugural tournament was controversy regarding the judging. Specifically, there were rumors that, on behalf of Korean competitors, referees and judges were "lopping off branches," which is to say that leading non-Korean rivals would be eliminated in preliminary matches. Conversely, there was the possibility that other referees and judges, as a reaction to Korean pressure, would favor non-Korean competitors. This controversy came to a head in the men's Olympic featherweight division. In the gold medal match, Steven Lopez, the son of Nicaraguan immigrants from Sugar Land, Texas, faced South Korea's Sin Joon-sik, who had defeated three-time world champion Hadi Saei Bonehkohal on his way to the final. Sin scored with a spinning hook kick to the head in the first round. Lopez tied the score with a back kick with one minute left in the final round. Referee Flavio Pérez of Columbia then awarded the match to Lopez by deducting a point from Sin's score because he had incurred two half-point penalties along the way. The problem was that Olympic referees had been instructed to decide ties by sudden death. Pérez was suspended for a year, but the result was allowed to stand.

2004 Athens C: 16, N: 16, D: 8.27.

1. Hadi Saei Bonehkohal	IRN
2. Huang Chih-hsiung	TAI
3. Song Myeong-Seop	KOR
4. Diogo da Silva	BRA

5. Gabriel Sagastume Ríos	GUA
5. Tamer Hussein	EGY
7. Carlo Molfetta	ITA
7. Tuncay Caliskan	AUT

Final: Bonehkohal 4-3 Huang
3rd Place: Song 12-7 Silva

After winning the 2003 Olympic qualifying tournament, South Korea's Lee Won-jae was considered the favorite. However he failed to make his nation's Olympic team, leaving the field wide open. In the semifinals, 2000 bronze medalist Hadi Saei Bonehkohal narrowly beat Song Myeong-seob 9-9 after Song was given a penalty. Earlier in the year, Bonehkohal had donated his Olympic bronze, as well as other medals, to be auctioned to raise money for the survivors of the December 26, 2003, earthquake that devastated his hometown of Bam. In the Olympic final, Bonehkohal edged out 62-kilo world champion Huang Chih-hsiung 4-3 after two points were deduced from Huang's score due to penalties. The Iranian government gave Bonehkohal $125,000 for his win.

Less than four months after the Olympics, silver medalist Huang was elected to the Taiwanese parliament.

2008 Beijing C: 15, N: 15, D: 8.21.

1. Son Tae-jin	KOR
2. Mark Lopez	USA
3. Sung Yu-chi	TAI
3. Servet Tazegül	TUR
5. Peter López Santos	PER
5. Daniel Manz	GER
7. Nesar Ahmad Bahave	AFG
7. Dennis Bekkers	HOL

Final: Son 3-2 Lopez
3rd Place: Tazegül 1-0 López
3rd Place: Sung 4-3 Manz

Twenty-six-year-old Mark Lopez, the 2005 world champion, cruised into the final, after winning both his preliminary matches by at least two points and beating training partner and 2001 world silver medalist Peter López (no relation) 2-1 in the semifinal.

Reigning lightweight world champion Sung Yu-chi also qualified easily for the semifinal round, where he faced 20-year-old Son Tae-jin of South Korea. Son had been eliminated in the first round of the 2007 world championships, finishing 65th, but came back four months later to win the 2007 world qualification tournament.

Sung and Son fought an exciting match, both scoring twice in the first round, twice in the second, and twice in the third round before Son landed a decisive body kick with 18 seconds remaining to win 7-6.

In the final, Son took a 2-0 lead with two roundhouse kicks before Lopez scored on a side kick in the second round. Son earned a one-point penalty for passivity, evening the score 1-1 going into the final round. The fighters traded kicks to take the score to 2-2, but Son scored a kick in the final seconds of the match to win the gold.

Lopez was one of three siblings competing for the US in taekwondo at the 2008 Olympics—his older brother, Steven, earned a bronze medal in the welterweight division and his younger sister, Diana, did the same in the featherweight category—all coached by their older brother Jean. (They had fallen into the sport by chance: their father, Julio, signed up the eight-year-old Jean, thinking he was getting him into karate.) This was the first time three siblings had competed for the US in the same Olympic sport since the Tritschler brothers competed in gymnastics in 1904. However the Lopez trio had made sports history at the 2005 world championships, becoming the first three siblings in any sport to claim three world titles at the same competition.

The featherweight division also featured 22-year-old Logan Campbell of New Zealand, who was drawn against Sung in the first round, losing 4-0. In 2009 Logan caused controversy because of the method he chose to raise funds for his 2012 Olympic bid: opening a brothel (legal in New Zealand since 2003).

OLYMPIC WELTERWEIGHT

(80 kg—176 lbs)

1896–1996 not held

2000 Sydney C: 14, N: 14, D: 9.29.

1. Angel Matos Fuentes	CUB
2. Faissal Ebnoutalib	GER
3. Victor Estrada Garibay	MEX
4. Roman Livaja	SWE
5. Warren Hansen	AUS
5. N'Guessan Sébastien Konan	IVC
7. Mohammed Alfararjeh	JOR
7. Felipe Soto Alvárez	CHI

Final: Matos 3-1 Ebnoutalib
3rd Place: Estrada 2-1 Livaja

Angel Matos dedicated his victory to his mother, who died on the day of the Opening Ceremony. The Sydney taekwondo tournament was plagued by judging controversies. In the first round of the men's Olympic welterweight competition, Australia's Warren Hansen was awarded a 6-5 victory over Muhammed Dahmani of Denmark. The Danes claimed that the referee had been influenced by the pro-Australian crowd. Dahmani refused to leave the mat and was escorted from the arena by federation officials.

2004 Athens C: 16, N: 16, D: 8.28.

1. Steven Lopez	USA
2. Bahri Tanrıkulu	TUR
3. Youssef Karami	IRN
4. Rashad Ahmadov	AZR
5. Víctor Estrada Garibay	MEX
5. Hichem Hamdouni	TUN
7. Raid Rasheed	IRQ
7. Donald Geisler	PHI

Final: Lopez 3-0 Tanrıkulu
3rd Place: Karami 9-8 Ahmadov

With no clear favorite, the field included 2000 Olympic featherweight champion and 78-kilo world champion Steven Lopez, reigning 84-kilo world champion Youssef Karami and former world champion Bahri Tanrikulu. Lopez defeated 2000 bronze medalist Victor Estrada 4-2 in the quarterfinals. Lopez's most challenging match came against Karami in the semifinal, which he won 7-6. Meanwhile, in the other semifinal, Rashad Ahmadov staged a five-minute sit-in after losing a 6-6 decision to Tanrikulu. Tied 1-1 after the first round of the final, Lopez scored two more points, while Tanrikulu gained a point and lost two to passivity.

2008 Beijing C: 16, N: 16, D: 8.22.

1. Hadi Saei Bonehkohal	IRN
2. Mauro Sarmiento	ITA
3. Steven Lopez	USA
3. Zhu Guo	CHN
5. Rashad Ahmadov	AZE
5. Aaron Cook	GBR
7. Deepak Bista	NEP
7. N'Guessan Sébastien Konan	IVC

Final: Saei 6-4 Sarmiento
3rd Place: Lopez 3-2 Ahmadov
3rd Place: Zhu 4-1 Cook

Two-time defending Olympic champion and four-time world champion Steven Lopez was drawn against Bahri Tanrikulu of Turkey in their first match, a rematch of the 2004 Athens Olympic final. Lopez came from behind to score four points in the third round, advancing 3-0 after both fighters received one-point penalties.

Lopez was upset in the quarterfinals by 25-year-old Mauro Sarmiento, who came back from a 2-0 deficit to score on a kick in the third round. Lopez received a controversial one-point penalty in the third round for lifting his shin, which was ruled an illegal kick, tying the score 1-1 and sending the fighters to sudden-death overtime, which Sarmiento won. The US team protested but were denied. It was Lopez' first defeat in five years.

Sarmiento advanced to the final by beating 17-year-old reigning junior world champion Aaron Cook 6-5 in the semifinals.

Sarmiento's opponent in the final was the 2004 Olympic featherweight champion, Hadi Saei. Sarmiento took a 4-2 lead after the first round, scoring two points with a solid kick to the head. Saei came back to tie the score 4-4 after the second round and scored on two kicks in the third round to win his second Olympic title.

OLYMPIC HEAVYWEIGHT
(Over 80 kg—Over 176 lbs)

1896–1996 not held

2000 Sydney C: 12, N: 12, D: 9.30.

1. Kim Kyong-hun	KOR
2. Daniel Trenton	AUS
3. Pascal Gentil	FRA
4. Khaleed Al-Dosri	SAU
5. Milton Castro Herrera	COL
5. Colin Daley	GBR
7. Carlos Delgado Dávila	NIC
7. Marcus Thoren	SWE

Final: Kim 5-2 Trenton
3rd Place: Gentil (withdrawal) Al-Dosri

The critical match took place in the semifinals when the two favorites, Pascal Gentil and Kim Kyong-hun faced off. Kim won 6-2. The French filed a formal protest, but a jury rejected the appeal.

2004 Athens C: 16, N: 16, D: 8.29.

1. Moon Dae-sung	KOR
2. Alexandros Nikolaidis	GRE
3. Pascal Gentil	FRA
4. Ibrahim Kamal	JOR
5. Adilkhan Sagyndykov	KAZ
5. Abdel Kader Zrouri	MOR
7. Jon García Aguado	SPA
7. Julián Rojas Rivera	COL

Final: Moon KO1 (2:10) Nikolaidis
3rd Place: Gentil 6-2 Kamal

Moon Dae-sung was leading local favorite Alexandros Nikolaidis 1-0 when, two minutes into the first round of the final, Moon caught Nikolaidis with a high left-leg roundhouse kick to the face for a knockout. As Moon later described the moment, "My left leg is not very strong and I had to protect it. But, suddenly, Nikolaidis' face came into it."

2008 Beijing C: 16, N: 16, D: 8.23.

1. Cha Dong-min	KOR
2. Alexandros Nikolaidis	GRE
3. Arman Chilmanov	KAZ
3. Chika Chukwumerije	NGR
5. Akmal Ergashev	UZB
6. Kristopher Moitland	CRC
6. Abdelkader Zrouri	MOR
8. Daba Modibo Keita	MLI
8. Liu Xiaobo	CHN

DISQ: Ángel Matos Fuentes (CUB)
Final: Cha 5-4 Nikolaidis
3rd Place: Chukwumerije 4-3 Ergashev

Making his Olympic debut, Cha Dong-min swept through the preliminary rounds, beating 2000 welterweight gold medalist Ángel Matos 1-0 in the semifinal round to reach the final.

The gold medal match was overshadowed by a dramatic turn of events in the second bronze medal match between Matos and world bronze medalist Arman Chilmanov. Leading 3-2 with 1:02 left in the second round, Matos fell to the mat after being hit by Chilmanov. After one minute of allowed injury time, Swedish referee Chakir Chelbat disqualified the still-seated Matos for taking too long. Matos angrily questioned the call . . . and then proceeded to kick Chelbat in the face and spit on the floor before being escorted out by security. Matos was disqualified and he and his coach Leodis González were given lifetime bans from international competition.

In the final, defending Olympic silver medalist Alexandros Nikolaidis scored first on a head shot before Cha came back with a body kick and a head shot of his own, pulling ahead 4-3 going into the third round. Nikolaidis evened the score with a body kick, but Cha scored the winning hit with 18 seconds left. Cha's victory came one day before his 22nd birthday.

WOMEN

OLYMPIC FLYWEIGHT
(49 kg—108 lbs)

1896–1996 not held

2000 Sydney C: 12, N: 12, D: 9.27.

1. Lauren Burns	AUS
2. Urbia Meléndez Rodríguez	CUB
3. Chi Shu-ju	TAI
4. Hanne Høegh Poulsen	DEN
5. Döndü Güvenc	TUR
5. Águeda Pérez López	MEX
7. Likeleli Alinah Thamae	LES
8. Juana Wangsa Putri	INA
8. Nguyen Thi Xuan Mai	VIE

Final: Burns 4-2 Meléndez
3rd Place: Chi 4-0 Poulsen

On her way to the final, Lauren Burns, a 26-year-old vegetarian, gained a controversial victory over world champion Chi Shu-ju. The bout ended in 3-3 tie, but British referee Kevin Hornsey awarded the advantage to Burns.

2004 Athens C: 15, N: 15, D: 8.26.

1. Chen Shih-hsien	TAI
2. Yanelis Labrada Diaz	CUB
3. Yaowapa Boorapolchai	THA
4. Gladys Mora Romero	COL
5. Euda Carías Morales	GUA
5. Ivett Gonda	CAN
7. Sangina Baidya	NEP
8. Dalia Contreras Rivero	VEN
8. Nevena Lukic	AUT

Final: Chen 6-4 Labrada
3rd Place: Boorapolchai 2-2 (Superiority) Mora

With reigning world champion Lee Ji-hye out of the competition after South Korea chose not to enter the flyweight division, the field was wide open. Chen Shih-hsien won her first two matches without giving up a single point, and then defeated Ivett Gonda 3-2 in the semifinals. In the final, Chen and Yanelis Labrada were tied 2-2 after the first round, but Chen pulled ahead 5-3 in the second round and held on to win Taiwan's first-ever Olympic gold medal in any sport. At the medal ceremony, the Taiwanese were not permitted to use their national flag or anthem. Instead, the Taiwanese Olympic flag was flown, to the tune of "Song of the National Flag."

Chen had taken up taekwondo at the age of five, and by 17 she had won two world cup tournaments. But the pressure of competition led her to abandon her sport and her family for two years, at one point finding work as a betel nut vendor. She returned to her family at the age of 20 and resumed training with her father. She was 26 years old when she earned her gold medal.

2008 Beijing C: 16, N: 16, D: 8.20.

1. Wu Jingyu	CHN
2. Buttree Puedpong	THA
3. Dalia Contreras Rivero	VEN
3. Daynellis Montejo Poll	CUB
5. Milka Alango	KEN
5. Yang Shu-chun	TAI
7. Trần Thị Ngọc Trúc	VIE
7. Hanna Zajc	SWE

Final: Wu 1-(-1) Puedpong
3rd Place: Montejo 3-2 Yang
3rd Place: Contreras 1-0 Alango

Reigning world champion Wu Jingyu beat her first opponent, Milka Akinyi of Kenya, 7-0, and her second, Sweden's Hanna Zajc, 8-1. Wu faced reigning world bronze medalist Yang Shu-chun in the semifinal, taking the lead with a looping head kick and a midsection kick in the first round. Yang scored one point in the second round but Wu closed out the match 4-1 to advance to the gold medal bout.

Wu's opponent in the final was seventeen-year-old Buttree Puedpong. Puedpong had made it to the final after being declared the winner in a tied semifinal bout against Dalia Contreras in which neither athlete was able to score in overtime. Wu took the lead in the first round of the final, scoring on a chest kick. She narrowly missed a high kick to the head in the second round, but Puedpong was deducted a point in the third round for passivity.

OLYMPIC FEATHERWEIGHT

(57 kg—126 lbs)

1896–1996 not held

2000 Sydney C: 12, N: 12, D: 9.28.

1. Jung Jae-eun	KOR
2. Trần Hiếu Ngân	VIE
3. Hamide Bikçin	TUR
4. Virginia Lourens	HOL
5. Cristiana Corsi	ITA
5. Jasmin Strachan	PHI
7. Areti Athanasopoulos	GRE
7. Hsu Chih-ling	TAI

Final: Jung 2-0 Trần
3rd Place: Bikçin 7-5 Lourens

Although she lost to former world champion Jung Jae-eun in the final, Trần Hiếu Ngân became the first Vietnamese athlete to earn an Olympic medal. Trần, whose father had died two months before the Olympics, came from the small fishing village of Tuy Hòa, where her family ran a sweet shop.

2004 Athens C: 15, N: 15, D: 8.27.

1. Jang Ji-won	KOR
2. Nia Abdallah	USA
3. Iridia Salazar Blanco	MEX
4. Sonia Reyes Sáez	SPA
5. Cristiana Corsi	ITA
5. Nootcharin Sukkhongdumnoen	THA
7. Margarita Mkrtchyan	RUS
7. Mariam Bah	IVC

Final: Jang 2-1 Abdallah
3rd Place: Salazar 3-2 Reyes

The winner of the Olympic qualifying tournament, Jang Ji-won was expected to reach the final, and she did not disappoint, defeating world champion silver medalist Iridia Salazar 2-1. The surprise was her opponent in the final, 20-year-old Nia Abdallah, who earned an 8-5 semifinal victory over Nootcharin Sukkongdumnoen. Jang had little difficulty earning the gold, winning 2-1 despite losing two points for passivity, as Adballah was unable to score until the final round.

2008 Beijing C: 15, N: 15, D: 8.21.

1. Lim Su-jeong	KOR
2. Azize Tanrikulu	TUR
3. Diana Lopez	USA
3. Martina Zubčić	CRO
5. Veronica Calabrese	ITA
5. Su Li-wen	TAI
7. Robin Cheong	NZL
7. Elaine Teo	MAL

Final: Lim 1-0 Tanrikulu
3rd Place: Lopez 3-2 Calabrese
3rd Place: Zubčić 5-4 Su

Competing one day after her 22nd birthday, South Korea's Lim Su-jeong narrowly won her first match, beating Taiwan's Su Li-wen 1-0. In the next two rounds she had an easier time, defeating New Zealand's Robin Cheong 4-1 and Italy's Veronica Calabrese 5-1 to make it to the final.

The 2005 world champion, Diana Lopez, had been expected to reach the final, but was defeated 2-1 in the quarterfinals by Azize Tanrikulu, the sister of defending Olympic welterweight silver medalist Bahri Tanrikulu. Tanrikulu came from behind in her semifinal match, scoring four points against Martina Zubčić in the third round to win 5-3.

Lim lost a point for passivity in the first round of the final, but evened the score with a body kick in the second round. She clinched the gold medal with a back kick in the final 20 seconds to win 1-0. Both bronze medals were decided in overtime.

OLYMPIC WELTERWEIGHT

(67 kg—148 lbs)

1896–1996 not held

2000 Sydney C: 12, N: 12, D: 9.29.

1. Lee Sun-hee	KOR
2. Trude Gundersen	NOR
3. Yoriko Okamoto	JPN
4. Sarah Stevenson	GBR
5. Mirjam Müskens	HOL
5. Kirsimarja Koskinen	FIN
7. He Lumin	CHN
7. Barbara Kunkel	USA

Final: Lee 6-3 Gundersen
3rd Place: Okamoto 6-5 Stevenson

Lee Sun-hee won all three of her matches with relative ease, although the final had to be stopped briefly in the first round when Trude Gundersen kicked Lee in the throat.

2004 Athens C: 15, N: 15, D: 8.28.

1. Luo Wei	CHN
2. Elisavet Mystakidou	GRE
3. Hwang Kyung-sun	KOR
4. Heidy Juárez Guzmán	GUA
5. Ineabelle Díaz Santana	PUR
5. Mary Antoinette Rivero	PHI
7. Verina Wihongi	NZL
7. Nina Solheim	NOR

Final: Luo 7-6 Mystakidou
3rd Place: Hwang 5-2 Juárez

The final was a fierce battle, with Luo Wei of Beijing taking a 2-1 lead after the first round, before Elisavet Mystakidou came back in the second to pull ahead 4-3. In the final round, the pair tied briefly at 5 before Luo pulled ahead 7-6 to take the gold.

2008 Beijing C: 16, N: 16, D: 8.22.

1. Hwang Kyung-sun	KOR
2. Karine Sergerie	CAN
3. Gwladys Epangue	FRA
3. Sandra Šarić	CRO
5. Tina Morgan	AUS
5. Asunción Ocasio Rodríguez	PUR
7. Maitha Al-Maktoum	UAE
7. Vanina Sánchez Berón	ARG

Final: Hwang 2-1 Sergerie
3rd Place: Šarić 5-1 Ocasio
3rd Place: Epangue 4-1 Morgan

Defending Olympic bronze medalist Hwang Kyung-sun had defeated Gwladys Epangue in the final of the last two world championships. The pair also fought in the final of the 2007 world qualification tournament, with Epangue coming out ahead. As it turned out, the rivals faced each other in the semifinals instead of the final. With the score tied after regulation time, the 22-year-old Hwang was the first to score in overtime to win 2-1.

Hwang's opponent in the final was reigning lightweight world champion Karine Sergerie. Both finalists competed with injuries, Hwang having twisted her knee in her quarterfinal match against Epangue, and Sergerie having broken her toe in her first-round match. The final started out slowly, with Hwang trailing 1-0 after the first round. She evened the score with 30 seconds left in the second round, and then clinched the gold medal with a back kick with 35 seconds remaining.

OLYMPIC HEAVYWEIGHT

(Over 67 kg—Over 148 lbs)

1896–1996 not held

2000 Sydney C: 12, N: 12, D: 9.30.

1. Chen Zhong	CHN
2. Nataliya Ivanova	RUS
3. Dominique Bosshart	CAN
4. Nataša Vezmar	CRO
5. Mounia Bourguigue	MOR
5. Adriana Carmona Gutiérrez	VEN
7. Myriam Baverel	FRA
7. Ireane Ruiz Arévalo	SPA

Final: Chen 8-3 Ivanova
3rd Place: Bosshart 11-8 Vezmar

At the 1998 Asian Games, Chen Zhong was involved in an unusual incident when she and her coaches refused to leave the mat for almost an hour to protest her loss to a South Korean fighter. There were no such problems in Sydney, as the high-scoring Chen outscored her four opponents 27-12.

2004 Athens C: 15, N: 15, D: 8.29.

1. Chen Zhong	CHN
2. Myriam Baverel	FRA
3. Adriana Carmona Gutiérrez	VEN
4. Natália Silva	BRA
5. Nadin Dawani	JOR
5. Dominique Bosshart	CAN
7. Yoriko Okamoto	JPN
7. Daniela Castrignano	ITA

Final: Chen 12-5 Baverel
3rd Place: Carmona 7-4 Silva

Chen Zhong successfully defended her Olympic title by overwhelming Myriam Baverel in the final, opening a 2-1 lead in the first round and widening it to 6-3 by the second, before doubling her score in the third and final round.

2008 Beijing C: 16, N: 16, D: 8.23.

1. María del Rosario Espinoza	MEX
2. Nina Solheim	NOR
3. Natália Falavigna	BRA
3. Sarah Stevenson	GBR
5. Nona Abd Rabo	EGY
5. Karolina Kedzierska	SWE
7. Khaoula Ben Hamza	TUN
7. Che Chew Chan	MAL

Final: Espinoza 3-1 Solheim
3rd Place: Falavigna 5-2 Kedzierska
3rd Place: Stevenson 5-1 Abd Rabo

Still only twenty-five years old, Chen Zhong was the two-time defending Olympic gold medalist and the reigning heavyweight world champion. The 6-foot (1.83 meter) former basketball player defeated defending Olympic bronze medalist Adriana Carmona 3-1 in the first round.

Chen faced 2001 world champion and 2005 world silver medalist Sarah Stevenson in the quarterfinals, taking a 1-0 lead after the second round. Stevenson landed a head kick in the final round, worth two points, but the kick was ruled too soft to count, and Chen was declared the winner. After a protest by the British delegation, the judges reversed the ruling, awarding Stevenson two additional points and sending her to the semifinals on a 2-1 win. It was the first time that a match result had been overturned since taekwondo became an Olympic sport in 2000.

Stevenson lost her semifinal match 4-1 to middleweight world champion María del Rosario Espinoza. In the other semifinal, Nina Solheim advanced on judges' decision after a 2-2 match against 2005 world champion Natália Falavigna.

Espinoza dominated the final, scoring an early point in the first round and three more in the third round, ending with a 3-1 victory (after incurring a one-point deduction).

Silver medalist Solheim was born in South Korea, but at the age of seven months she and her twin sister Mona were adopted by Norwegian parents.

Chapter 27 **Tennis**

MEN	**WOMEN**	**MIXED**
Singles	Singles	Doubles
Doubles	Doubles	

A tennis court is 78 feet (23.77 meters) long and 27 feet (8.23 meters) wide. For doubles play the width is extended 4½ feet (1.37 meters) on each side for a total width of 36 feet (10.97 meters). The court is divided by a net, the height of which is 3 feet (.914 meters) at the center. The lines at the ends of the court are called *baselines*. On each side of the net, 21 feet (6.4 meters) from it and parallel to it, is drawn a *service line*. A *center service line* is drawn perpendicular to the net, midway between the side lines and extending from the net to the service line. Thus, the forecourt on each side of the net is divided into *service courts*.

A tennis ball must be white or yellow. It must be between 2½ inches (6.35 centimeters) and 2⅝ inches (6.67 centimeters) in diameter and must weigh between 2 ounces (56.7 grams) and 2¹⁄₁₆ ounces (58.5 grams). Tennis balls must meet an official bounce test: when dropped onto concrete from a height of 100 inches (254 centimeters), a ball must bounce between 53 inches (135 centimeters) and 58 inches (147 centimeters).

The frame of a tennis racket may not exceed 29 inches (73.66 centimeters) in length, including the handle, and 12½ inches (31.75 centimeters) in width. The strung surface of the racket may not exceed 15½ (39.37 centimeters) in length and 11½ inches (29.21 centimeters) in width.

In tennis, a point is scored by a player whose opponent is unable to return the ball within the baseline and the sidelines on his or her opponent's side of the court. When a player has no points, the score is called love. When a player wins a point, the score is called 15. When the player scores a second point the score is called 30. A third point is scored 40 and if the player scores a fourth point, he or she wins a game. However, a player is awarded a game only if he has scored two more points than his opponent. If both players have won three points, the score is called deuce. The next point scored by a player is called advantage for that player. If the same player wins the next point, that player wins the game. If the other player wins the next point, the score returns to deuce, and play continues until one player wins two points in a row after the score of deuce. Players alternate service after each game.

The first player to win six games wins a set, except that a player must win by a margin of two games over his opponent. In Olympic tournaments, if both players win six games, a tie-break game is played. The first player to score seven points wins the tie-break, but the player must win by a margin of two points. Tiebreaker scores are represented in the charts by the losing player's score in parenthesis. No tie-break game is played in the third set of a three-set match or the fifth set of a five-set match. Instead, the set continues until one player wins by two games. Since 2008, all matches are won by the first player or pair to win two sets, except in men's finals, which is run on a best three sets of five basis. In mixed doubles, which is being reinstated in 2012 after an 88-

Steffi Graf, 1988

Graf earned a "Golden Slam" by following her Grand Slam achievement with an Olympic victory.

year gap, if the two pairs split the first two sets, the match goes straight to a tie-breaker with the first to score ten points winning.

The server must start with both feet behind the baseline, throw the ball in the air, and strike it before it touches the ground. The first service of a game is made from the right side of the court, with subsequent services made from alternating sides thereafter. The ball must pass over the net and hit the ground in the service court diagonally opposite. A service that fails to do so is called a fault. Two faults in a row, known as a double fault, results in a point for the server's opponent. If a served ball hits the net and then lands fair, it is called a let and is treated as if it never happened.

The rules for doubles matches are the same as those for singles, with some minor differences. The sidelines are wider (see above), although the service court is the same as in singles. Partners alternate serving games. The first player on a team serves an entire game. The next time that it is the team's turn to serve, the other player on the team serves an entire game. The serving pair switches sides after each point, while the players on the receiving team take turns receiving the service.

Olympic tournaments are run on a straight single-elimination basis: one lost match and you are out. In the singles events, the top sixteen players are seeded and in the doubles events, the top eight teams are seeded.

The top 54 players in the world qualify for the Olympics, based on rankings as of June 11, 2012, although no nation may enter more than four singles players and two doubles teams each for men and women. The International Tennis Federation chooses six more players and then works with the IOC to choose two more for each event.

In the following charts, players who participated in the quarterfinals or semifinals but did not win a match are not included unless they were actually awarded medals.

MEN

SINGLES

1896 Athens C: 13, N: 7, D: 4.11.

1. John Pius Boland	GBR/IRL
2. Dionysios Kasdaglis	EGY
3. Konstantinos Paspatis	GRE
3. Momčilo Tapavica	HUN/SER
5. Aristides Akratopoulos	GRE
5. Evangelis Rallis	GRE

Final: Boland—Kasdaglis, 6-2, 6-2

John Pius Boland was a student at Christ's College, Oxford when he invited a Greek friend, Thrasyvoalos Manaos, to speak at the Oxford Union on the subject of the upcoming Olympic Games. During the Easter holidays, Boland traveled to Athens as a spectator. One night at dinner, he met a Greek from Alexandria named Dionysios Kasdaglis, who convinced Boland to enter the tennis tournament, and he was enrolled the following morning, the day before play began. Boland competed while wearing leather-soled shoes with heels. He won three matches and then found himself in the final against none other than his new friend Kasdaglis. Because it was Kasdaglis who had arranged to have him enter in the first place, Boland considered forfeiting, but decided that this would be improper because "the game was of an international character." Later in life Boland became a renowned barrister, Member of Parliament, author, and ardent proponent of both Irish independence and the Irish language.

He died, appropriately enough, on St. Patrick's Day, 1958.

1900 Paris C: 13, N: 3, D: 7.11.

1. H. Laurence "Laurie" Doherty	GBR
2. Harold Mahoney	GBR/IRL
3. Reginald Doherty	GBR
3. Arthur Norris	GBR
5. Paul Lecaron	FRA
5. Basil Spalding de Garmendia	USA

Final: H. Doherty—Mahoney, 6-4, 6-2, 6-3

The Doherty brothers were scheduled to play one another in the semifinals, but refused to do so in a minor tournament. Reginald stepped aside and agreed to let his younger brother advance to the final. Between them, Reggie and Laurie won 9 Wimbledon singles championships between 1897 and 1906.

1904 St. Louis C: 27, N: 2, D: 9.3.

1. Beals Wright	USA
2. Robert LeRoy	USA
3. Alonzo Bell	USA
3. Edgar Leonard	USA

5. William Blatherwick (USA), Charles Cresson (USA), John Neely (USA), Sempronius Russ (USA).

Final: Wright—LeRoy, 6-4, 6-4

1906 Athens C 18, N: 6, D: 4.26.

1. Maxime Décugis	FRA
2. Maurice Germot	FRA
3. Zdenek "Jánský" Žemla	BOH/CZE
4. Gerardus Scheurleer	HOL
5. Karel Beukema	HOL
5. Georgios Simiriotis	GRE

Final: Decugis—Germot, 6-1, 7-9, 6-1, 6-1

Guus Kessler of the Netherlands entered the tournament, "won" his first three matchs by walkover and advanced to the semifinal round, where he lost to Decugis 6-0, 6-0.

1908 London C: 31, N: 9, D: 7.11.
1. Josiah Ritchie GBR
2. Otto Froitzheim GER
3. Wilberforce Eaves GBR
4. John Richardson SAF
5. Charles Brown (CAN), George Caridia (GBR), Charles Dixon (GBR), Maurice Germot (FRA)
Final: Ritchie—Froitzheim, 7-5, 6-3, 6-4
3rd Place: Eaves—Richardson, 6-2, 6 2, 6 3

Major Ritchie was 37 years old when he defeated the 24-year-old Froitzheim.

1908 London C: 7, N: 2, D: 5.11.
Indoor Courts
1. Arthur "Wentworth" Gore GBR
2. George Caridia GBR
3. Josiah Ritchie GBR
4. Wilberforce Eaves GBR
Final: Gore—Caridia, 6-3, 7-5, 6-4

Wentworth Gore played in every Wimbledon tournament that was held between 1888 and 1927. He is the oldest person to win a Wimbledon singles championship (aged 41, in 1909) and the oldest singles finalist (aged 44, in 1912).

1912 Stockholm C: 49, N: 12, D 7.5.
1. Charles Winslow SAF
2. Harold Kitson SAF
3. Oscar Kreuzer GER
4. Ladislav "Rázný" Žemla BOH/CZE
5. Louis Heyden (GER), Otto von Müller (GER), Ludwig, Count von Salm-Hoogstraeten (AUT), Arthur Zborzil (AUT)
Final: Winslow—Kitson, 7-5, 4-6,10-8, 8-6
3rd Place: Kreuzer—Žemla, 6-2, 3-6, 6-3, 6-1

The level of competition at the 1912 Olympics was somewhat disappointing, due to the fact that the Swedish organizers scheduled the tournament at the same time as the Wimbledon championships.

1912 Stockholm C: 22, N: 6, D: 5.12.
Indoor Courts
1. André Gobert FRA
2. Charles Dixon GBR
3. Anthony Wilding AUS/NZL
4. F. Gordon Lowe GBR
5. George Caridia GBR
5. Arthur Lowe GBR
5. Gunnar Setterwall SWE
Final: Gobert—Dixon, 8-6, 6-4, 6-4
3rd Place: Wilding—F.G. Lowe, 4-6, 6-2, 7-5, 6-0

Because it was held before Wimbledon, the covered courts tournament attracted a higher-quality field than the lawn court event. Tony Wilding, who won the singles title at Wimbledon four straight years (1910-1913), was upset in four sets in the semifinals by Charles Dixon. Wilding was killed in action in Belgium while fighting in World War I.

1920 Antwerp C: 41, N: 14, D: 8.23.
1. Louis Raymond SAF
2. Ichiya Kumagai JPN
3. Charles Winslow SAF
4. O. Noel Turnbull GBR
5. Manuel Alonso Areyzaga (SPA), George Dodd (SAF), F. Gordon Lowe (GBR), Sune Malmström (SWE)
Final: Raymond—Kumagai, 5-7, 6-4, 7-5, 6-4
3rd Place: Winslow—Turnbull, WO

The second round included one marathon match between Gordon Lowe of Great Britain and Anthanasios Zerlendtis of Greece, that lasted for almost six hours over a two-day period. At one point, the ballboys, bored by the prolonged cautious rallying, left the court and went to lunch, forcing Lowe and Zerlendtis to suspend play. Eventually Lowe won, 14-12, 6-8, 5-7, 6-4, 6-4. Lowe was subsequently eliminated in the fourth round after another five-set battle against Winslow. Raymond almost didn't make it into the final, having survived his semifinal match with Turnbull 2-6, 1-6, 6-2, 6-2, 6-1.

1924 Paris C: 82, N: 27, D: 7.20.
1. Vincent Richards USA
2. Henri Cochet FRA
3. Hubert "Umberto" De Mopurgo ITA
4. Jean Borotra FRA
5. Toshio Harada (JPN), Samuel Jacob (IND), René Lacoste (FRA), Richard Norris Williams (USA)
Final: Richards—Cochet, 6-4, 6-4, 5-7, 4-6, 6-2
3rd Place: de Morpurgo—Borotra, 1-6, 6-1, 8-6, 4-6, 7-5

1928–1984 not held

1988 Seoul C: 64, N: 32, D: 9.30.
1. Miloslav Mečíř CZE/SLV
2. Timothy Mayotte USA
3. Stefan Edberg SWE
3. Bradley Gilbert USA
5. Paolo Canè (ITA), Martín Jaite (ARG), Michiel Schapers (HOL), Carl-Uwe Steeb (GER)
Final: Mečíř—Mayotte, 3-6, 6-2, 6-4, 6-2

The critical match of the tournament took place in the semifinals when Wimbledon champion Stefan Edberg faced Slovak Miloslav Mečíř. Edberg, who had won the 1984 Olympic demonstration tournament, had defeated Mečíř in the Wimbledon semifinals in July 4-6, 2-6, 6-4, 6-3, 6-4. But in Seoul it was Mečíř who came from behind to win 3-6, 6-0, 1-6, 6-4, 6-2. Tim Mayotte advanced to the final by losing only one set in five matches, but was no match for Mečíř's hypnotic precision stroking.

1992 Barcelona C: 64, N: 36, D: 8.8.
1. Marc Rosset SWI
2. Jordi Arrese CastañéSPA
3. Andrei Cherkasov RUS
3. Goran Ivanišević CRO
5. Leonardo Lavalle Moreno (MEX), Jaime Oncins (BRA), Emilio Sánchez-Vicario (SPA), Fabrice Santoro (FRA)
Final: Rosset—Arresse, 7-6 (7-2), 6-4, 3-6, 4-6, 8-6

The best professionals in the world showed up for the Olympic tournament. As usual, the top 16 players were seeded so that they wouldn't meet until the later rounds. The organizers needn't have bothered. Of the top 11 seeded players, only one, Goran Ivanišević, made it as far as the quarterfinals. The rest were beaten early by the brutal heat, the slow clay surface, and the patriotic emotions of their unheralded opponents. The first to go was second seed Stefan Edberg of Sweden, who fell in the very first round in straight sets to Russia's Andrei Cherkasov. Tenth seeded Thomas Muster also lost his first match. In the second round, sixth seed Michael Chang of the United States was beaten by Jaime Oncins, seventh seed Guy Forget of France lost in straight sets to Magnus Larsson of Sweden, eighth seed Michael Stich of Germany lost to countryman Carl-Uwe Steeb, ninth seed Wayne Ferreira of South Africa was crushed 6-4, 6-0, 6-2 by Marc Rosset, and eleventh seed Sergi Bruguera of Spain was put away by Holland's third-string player Mark Koevermans.

Tennis fans had barely recovered from these surprises when the third round brought the really big upsets. Fifth seed Boris Becker of Germany lost to Fabrice Santoro, third seed Pete Sampras of the United States lost in five sets to Andrei Cherkasov, and in the biggest shocker of all, giant killer Marc Rosset sent top seed Jim Courier of the United States packing, 6-4, 6-2, 6-1.

The way seemed clear for Ivanišević, who was proud to be a member of Croatia's first Olympic team at a time when his nation was at war with Yugoslavia. But Ivanišević was worn out after four straight sweltering five-set matches. In the semifinals, he too fell to Rosset—his friend and sometime doubles partner.

And so, rather remarkably, the final was contested by Marc Rosset, who was ranked 44th in the world, and Barcelona-born-and-bred Jordi Arresse, who was ranked 30th. Arresse, Spain's third-string player, had almost been dropped from the team to make way for a hotter player, Carlos Costa, but Costa refused to take Arresse's place. What the final lacked in star quality, it made up for in drama. Rosset took the first two sets, but Arresse, encouraged by an extremely partisan Catalan crowd, won the next two sets. Rosset opened a 4-1 lead in the final set, but Arresse fought back to even the score at 4-4. Both players held their services until it was 7-6 Rosset. Arresse was up 40-15 on his next serve, when, five hours after the match began, Rosset shocked the crowd by winning the next four points and with them the set, the match, and the gold medal. The 21-year-old Rosset had never before made it as far as the quarterfinals of a major tournament and only did so twice more in his entire career.

In 1998 Rosset had a close call when he decided to stay on in New York to practice after a first-round elimination in the US Open. The flight he was originally booked on, Swissair Flight 111, crashed into the Atlantic Ocean, killing everyone on board.

1996 Atlanta-Stone Mountain C: 64, N: 36, D: 8.3.

1. Andre Agassi	USA
2. Sergi Bruguera Torner	SPA
3. Leander Paes	IND
4. Fernando Meligeni	BRA

5. Wayne Ferreira (SAF), Renzo Furlan (ITA), Andrei Olhovsky (RUS), MaliVai Washington (USA)
Final: Agassi—Bruguera, 6-2, 6-3, 6-1
3rd Place: Paes—Meligeni, 3-6, 6-2, 6-4

Emmanuel "Mike" Agassi represented Iran as a boxer at the 1948 and 1952 Olympics, losing his first fight both times. A member of Iran's Armenian minority, Agassi emigrated to the United States, settling first in Chicago and then in Las Vegas. He was obsessed with turning one of his four children into a tennis star. After traumatizing the three oldest, he hit the jackpot with the youngest, Andre. By the time he was three years old, Andre, with a racket taped to his hand, was volleying with his father. He turned professional at the age of sixteen and made it to the semifinals of the 1988 French and US Opens when he was eighteen. He scored a breakthrough victory by winning at Wimbledon in 1992, but then his career floundered again. Nonetheless, his image—long hair, earring, baggy pants—caught the public imagination and, despite his erratic results, Agassi became quite wealthy.

By 1996, Agassi had signed a $100 million contract with Nike. He flew around in his own jet, hobnobbed with celebrities and was going steady with actress Brooke Shields. (They would later marry and divorce.) By the time the Atlanta Olympics rolled around, Agassi was in another of his slumps. However, despite his glitzy lifestyle, Agassi was firmly committed to representing the United States. While other tennis stars, such as Pete Sampras, Boris Becker and Michael Chang, chose to skip the Olympics, Agassi saw it as a patriotic opportunity. His road to the final was not a smooth one. Agassi needed to win two tiebreakers to beat Jonas Björkman of Sweden; he lost the opening set to Andrea Gaudenzi of Italy and he struggled against Wayne Ferreira before prevailing 7-5, 4-6, 7-5. As it turned out, the final was his easiest match, lasting only 77 minutes. Agassi was on the top of his game and Bruguera, a clay court specialist, was unable to cope.

By taking the bronze medal, Leander Paes became the first Indian to earn a medal in an individual event since wrestler Kashaba Jadhav in 1952.

2000 Sydney C: 64, N: 32, D: 9.28.

1. Yevgeny Kafelnikov RUS
2. Tommy Haas GER
3. Arnaud Di Pasquale FRA
4. Roger Federer SWI
5. Karim Alami (MOR), Juan Carlos Ferrero Donat (SPA), Gustavo Kuerten (BRA), Max Mirnyi (BLR)

Final: Kafelnikov—Haas, 7-6(4), 3-6, 6-2, 4-6, 6-3
3rd Place: Di Pasquale—Federer, 7-6 (7-5), 6-7(7-9), 6-3

Yevgeny Kafelnikov was so discouraged by the quality of his play in the preceding months that he considered skipping the Olympics. Yet he had a good record playing in Australia, having won the Australian Open in 1999 and finishing second in January 2000. So he gave it a shot. In fact, Kafelnikov swept through the early rounds in Sydney, qualifying for the final by winning all five of his matches in straight sets. In the other half of the table, nothing was going to form. Six of the eight seeded players lost in the first round and the other two lost to Tommy Haas, who was ranked 49th in the world. And it was Haas who gave Kafelnikov his only real challenge. The first set alone lasted 70 minutes as both players broke the others' service twice. Haas scored the first three points of the tie breaker, but Kafelnikov prevailed 7-4. The two traded sets until Kafelnikov finally won 7-6, 3-6, 6-2, 4-6, 6-3, three hours and 35 minutes after the match began.

2004 Athens C: 64, N: 32, D: 8.22.

1. Nicolás Massú Fried CHI
2. Mardy Fish USA
3. Fernando González Ciuffardi CHI
4. Taylor Dent USA
5. Tomáš Berdych (CZE), Carlos Moyá Llompart (SPA), Mikhail Yuzhny (RUS), Sébastien Grosjean (FRA)

Final: Massú—Fish, 6-3, 3-6, 2-6, 6-3, 6-4
3rd Place: González—Dent, 6-4, 2-6, 16-14

The early rounds of the competition included a number of major upsets, beginning with the first-round elimination in straight sets of fourth-seed Tim Henman of Great Britain by Jiří Novák of the Czech Republic. In the second round, another Czech, world 74th-ranked Tomáš Berdych, stunned top-seed Roger Federer of Switzerland, who had beaten American Andy Roddick in the Wimbledon final less than six weeks before the Olympics. Fifth-seed Juan Carlos Ferrero of Spain also went down in the second round, defeated in a close match by Mardy Fish. In a third round surprise, second-seed Andy Roddick fell in straight sets to 16th-seed Fernando González. In the quarterfinals, 10th-seed Nicolás Massú, who had a 0-7 record on hard courts for the year before arriving in Athens, eliminated third-seed Carlos Moyá 6-2. 7-5.

So many of the favorites had been eliminated by the semifinals that Massú found himself the highest-seeded player still left in the competition. He defeated Taylor Dent 7-6, 6-1. In the other semi, Mardy Fish, who had never advanced past the third round in a grand slam event, beat Fernando González 3-6, 6-3, 6-4. González won the bronze medal 6-4, 2-6, 16-14, in a match that lasted three hours and 25 minutes. The gold medal match was even more exciting, coming one day after Massú and González, in the doubles event, had won Chile's first-ever gold medal in any sport in a 3½-hour final. An exhausted Massú won the first set of the singles final but lost the next two, before coming back to win in five sets. Massú's win gave Chile its second-ever gold medal in as many days, prompting massive celebrations in the Chilean capital of Santiago. When Massú and González returned to Chile, they were cheered by a crowd of thousands en route to breakfast with Chilean President Ricardo Lagos.

Nicolás Massú, 2004
Before 2004, no athlete from Chile had ever won a gold medal in any sport. Yet in Athens, Massú won both men's tennis events.

Massú accidentally left behind both of his gold medals in his room at the Olympic Village when he left Athens. Fortunately, they were found by Chile's swimming coach, Rodrigo Banados, who called Massú immediately.

2008 Beijing C: 64, N: 33, D: 8.17.

1. Rafael Nadal Parera SPA
2. Fernando González Ciuffardi CHI
3. Novak Đoković SER
4. James Blake USA
5. Roger Federer SWI
5. Paul-Henri Mathieu FRA
5. Jürgen Melzer AUT
5. Gaël Monfils FRA

Final: Nadal–González 6-3, 7-6 (2), 6-3
3rd Place: Đoković–Blake 6-3, 7-6 (4)

The 2008 Olympic tournament included the five top-ranked singles players in the world: Roger Federer, Rafael Nadal, Novak Đoković (a.k.a. Djokovic), Nikolay Davidenko of Russia and David Ferrer of Spain. Of the five, by far the most attention was focused on two players: world number-one-ranked Roger Federer and world number two Rafael Nadal.

Competing in his third Olympics, Federer had been the top-ranked tennis player in the world for the preceding four-and-a-half years, the longest streak in tennis history, but had never won an Olympic medal.

The 22-year-old Nadal had made his first Olympic appearance in Athens in 2004 as a little-known doubles player. He rose to become the second-ranked player in the world on July 25 2005, and held that position until the Beijing Olympics. The 2008 season had been a particularly good one for Nadal. In early June he beat Federer to win his fourth straight French Open, equaling Björn Borg's all-time record. One month later, he beat Federer again, this time to win his first Wimbledon crown, breaking Federer's five-year run of wins there.

Federer and Nadal both cruised through the first and second rounds. Ferrer was the first of the top five seeds to be knocked out, losing his first-round match in straight sets to Janko Tipsarević of Serbia. Davidenko and defending Olympic champion Nicolás Massú of Chile were eliminated in the second round, Davidenko losing 7-5, 6-3 to France's Paul-Henri Mathieu and Massú falling 7-6 (0), 6-1 to David Nalbandian of Argentina.

Federer faced the Czech Tomáš Berdych in the third round, the same player who had defeated him in the second round of the 2004 Olympics; this time Federer prevailed 6-3, 7-6 (4). The biggest upset of the tournament came in the quarterfinals, when Federer was knocked James Blake 6-4, 7-6 (2).

With Federer out, Nadal had little difficulty through the rest of the tournament. He rolled over Austria's Jürgen Melzer 6-0, 6-4 in the quarterfinals and defeated world number three Đoković 6-4, 1-6, 6-4 in the semifinals.

Nadal's opponent in the final was 2004 bronze medalist Fernando González. Playing in top form, Nadal took control from the start, winning the first set 6-3 and taking a commanding lead after five unforced errors from González in the second set tie-breaker. Nadal sealed the victory after four match points in the final set. It was Nadal's 38th win in 39 matches and made him the first player ranked in the top five to win an Olympic gold medal.

One day after his Olympic victory, Nadal formally gained the ATF world number one ranking, ending Federer's reign at the top.

DOUBLES

1896 Athens T: 5, N: 5, D: 4.11.

1.	GBR/IRL & GER	John Pius Boland, Fredrich "Fritz" Traun
2.	EGY & GRE	Dionysios Kasdaglis, Demetrios Petrokokkinos
3.	AUS & GBR	Edwin Flack, George Robertson

Final: Boland/Traun—Kasdaglis/Petrokokkinos, 5-7, 6-3, 6-3

Fritz Traun travelled to Athens to take part in the 800-meter run and then joined the tennis tournament for fun. He and Boland became friends during the singles competition and teamed up for doubles when Traun's partner fell ill. When the Union Jack was run up the pole to honor Boland's half of the victory, he objected vehemently, pointing out that the Irish had a flag of their own. The officials apologized and agreed to have an Irish flag prepared.

At the Closing Ceremony, Britain's George Robertson greatly pleased the crowd by reading an ode which he had written in ancient Greek in Pindaric meter to honor the Olympic Games. Although Robertson admired Greek culture, he had nothing but disdain for the French. Writing after the Games in the *Fortnightly Review,* he blamed the French for "the mismanagement of the international arrangements." He also criticized their athletic development. "Their successes," wrote Robertson, "'were confined to bicycling and fencing . . . the former a kind of exercise, by many scarcely admitted to the domain of sport." Robertson blamed the French failures on "a certain impatience and lack of necessary physique."

1900 Paris T: 8, N: 3, D: 7.11.

1.	GBR	Reginald Doherty, H. Laurence "Laurie" Doherty
2.	USA & FRA	Basil Spalding de Garmendia, Maxime Décugis
3.	FRA	André Prévost, Georges de la Chapelle
3.	GBR/IRL & GBR	Harold Mahoney, Arthur Norris

Final: Doherty/Doherty—de Garmendia/Decugis, 6-1, 6-1, 6-0

The Doherty brothers won the Wimbledon doubles championship a record 8 times between 1897 and 1905.

1904 St. Louis T: 15, N: 2, D: 9.3.

1.	USA	Edgar Leonard, Beals Wright
2.	USA	Alonzo Bell, Robert LeRoy
3.	USA	Joseph Wear, Allen West
3.	USA	Clarence Gamble, Arthur Wear

5. Charles Cresson, Sempronius Russ (USA); Ralph McKittrick, Dwight Davis (USA); Hugh McKittrick Jones, Harold Kauffman (USA)

Final: Leonard/Wright—Bell/LeRoy, 6-4, 6-4, 6-2

Dwight Davis donated the cup for what would become the most prestigious tournament for national teams: the Davis Cup.

Reginald and Laurie Doherty, 1900
The British brothers won the doubles title.

1906 Athens T: 7, N: 5, D: 4.25.
1. FRA Maxime Décugis, Maurice Germot
2. GRE Xenophon Kasdaglis, Ioannis Ballis
3. BOH/CZE Zdeněk "Jánský" Žemla, Ladislav "Rázný Žemla
4. GRE Georgios Simiriotis, Nikolaos Zarifis

Final: Décugis/Germot—Kasdaglis/Ballis, 6-3, 9-7, 3-6, 6-0, 6-0
3rd Place: Z. Žemla/L. Žemla—Simiriotis/Zarifis, 6-2, 6-3

1908 London T: 12, N: 7, D: 7.11.
1. GBR George Hillyard, Reginald Doherty
2. GBR&GBR/IRL Josiah Ritchie, James Parke
3. GBR Clement Cazalet, Charles Dixon
4. GBR Walter Crawley, Kenneth Powell
4. SAF Vincent Gauntlett, Harold Kitson

Final: Hillyard/Doherty—Ritchie/Parke, 9-7, 7-5, 9-7

Hillyard and Doherty fended off seven match points in the fourth set of their semifinal contest against Cazalet and Dixon before prevailing 5-7, 2-6, 6-4, 17-15, 6-4. Hillyard was 44 years old at the time of his Olympic victory.

1908 London T: 5, N: 2, D: 5.9.
Indoor Courts
1. GBR Arthur "Wentworth" Gore, H. Roper Barrett
2. GBR George Simond, George Caridia
3. SWE Gunnar Setterwall, Wollmar Boström
4. GBR Josiah Ritchie, Lionel Escombe

Final: Gore/Barrett—Simond/Caridia, 6-2, 2-6, 6-3, 6-3
3rd Place: Setterwall/Boström—Ritchie/Escombe, 4-6, 6-3, 1-6, 6-0, 6-3

1912 Stockholm T: 22, N: 10, D: 7.5.
1. SAF Charles Winslow, Harold Kitson
2. AUT F. Felix Piepes, Arthur Zborzil
3. FRA Albert Canet, Édouard Mény de Marangue
4. BOH/CZE Ladislav "Rázny" Žemla, Jaroslav Just
5. Robert Spies, Ludwig Maria Heyden (GER); Michel Mikhail Sumarokov-Elston, Aleksandr Alenitsyn (RUS); Charles Wennergren, Carl-Olof Nylén (SWE)

Final: Winslow/Kitson—Piepes/Zborzil, 4-6, 6-1, 6-2, 6-2
3rd Place: Canet/Mény—L. Žemla/Just, 13-11, 6-3, 8-6

1912 Stockholm T: 8, N: 3, D: 5.11.
Indoor Courts
1. FRA Andre Gobert, Maurice Germot
2. SWE Gunnar Setterwall, J. Carl Kempe
3. GBR Charles Dixon, Alfred Beamish
4. GBR Arthur "Wentworth" Gore, H. Roper Barrett
5. GBR F. Gordon Lowe, Arthur Lowe

Final: Gobert/Germot—Setterwall/Kempe, 6-4, 12-14, 6-2, 6-4
3rd Place: Dixon/Beamish—Gore/Barrett, 6-2, 0-6, 10-8, 2-6, 6-3

1920 Antwerp T: 22, N: 11, D: 8.24.
1. GBR O. Noel Turnbull, Maxwell Woosnam
2. JPN Ichiya Kumagai, Seiichiro Kashio
3. FRA Max Décugis, Pierre Albarran
4. FRA François "Jean-François" Blanchy, Jacques "Toto" Brugnon
5. Mino Balbi Di Robecco, Cesare Colombo (ITA); Jack Nielsen, Conrad Langaard (NOR); Brian Norton, Louis Raymond (SAF); George Dodd, Cecil Blackbeard (SAF)

Final: Turnbull/Woosnam—Kumagai/Kashio, 6-2, 5-7, 7-5, 7-5
3rd Place: Décugis/Albarran—Blanchy/Brugnon, WO

Max Woosnam was an all-around athlete who captained the English football (soccer) team in 1922, captained the Cambridge University cricket team and, in tennis, captained the British Davis Cup team.

1924 Paris T: 39, N: 24, D: 7.21.
1. USA Vincent Richards, Frank Hunter
2. FRA Jacques "Toto" Brugnon, Henri Cochet
3. FRA Jean Borotra, René Lacoste
4. SAF John Condon, Ivie John Richardson
5. Henning Müller, Charles Wennergren (SWE); Richard Norris Williams, Watson Washburn (USA); José Alonso Areyzaga, Manuel Alonso Areyzaga (SPA); Syed Mohammed "S.M." Hadi, David Rutnam (IND)

Final: Richards/Hunter—Brugnon/Cochet, 4-6, 6-2, 6-3, 2-6, 6-3
3rd Place: Borotra/Lacoste—Condon/Richardson, 6-3, 10-8, 6-3

Richards and Hunter, the reigning champions of Wimbledon, won an arduous five-set semifinal match against Borotra and Lacoste, 6-2, 6-3, 0-6, 5-7, 6-3. They won the final by taking four of the last five games. Brugnon, Cochet, Borotra, and Lacoste, known as the Four Musketeers, won 6 straight Davis Cup titles for France between 1927 and 1932. Once, while playing in the United States, René Lacoste coveted an alligator skin bag. His coach offered to buy it for him—if he won the tournament. Lacoste lost in the final, but the story made its way back to France, where the alligator was transformed into a crocodile. Lacoste himself became known as the "crocodile" and it was the crocodile that would become the emblem of the clothing line that he created.

1928–1984 not held

1988 Seoul T: 31, N: 31, D: 10.1.

1. USA Kenneth Flach, Robert Seguso
2. SPA Emilio Sánchez Vicario, Sergio Casal Martínez
3. CZE Miloslav Mečíř, Milan Srejber
3. SWE Stefan Edberg, Anders Järryd
5. Darren Cahill, John Fitzgerald (AUS); Morten Christensen, Michael Tauson (DEN); Guy Forget, Henri Leconte (FRA); Goran Ivaniševíc, Slobodan Živojinović (YUG)

Final: Flach/Seguso—Sánchez/Casal, 6-3, 6-4, 6-7 (5-7), 6-7(1-7), 9-7

Flach and Seguso led two sets to zero and 5-3 in the third set tie-breaker. But Sánchez and Casal pulled out the next 4 points to take the set, then won another tie-breaker in the fourth set. In the fifth set the Americans led 5-4 with Flach serving. But the gritty Spaniards fought back again, breaking service and moving ahead 6-5. Flach and Seguso fell behind 15-30, but came back to win the game, break Casal's serve, and move up 7-6. Again Sánchez and Casal broke Flach's serve to tie the match. Then Sánchez lost his service and, finally, Seguso served out the game at love and the match was over after 3 hours and 42 minutes.

1992 Barcelona T: 30, N: 30, D: 8.7.

1. GER Boris Becker, Michael Stich
2. SAF Wayne Ferreira, Piet Norval
3. ARG Javier Frana Maggi, Christian Miniussi Ventureira
3. CRO Goran Ivanišević, Goran Prpić
5. Ramesh Krishnan, Leander Paes (IND); George Cosac, Dinu Pescariu (ROM); Sergio Casal Martínez, Emilio Sánchez Vicario (SPA); Jakob Hlasek, Marc Rosset (SWI)

Final: Becker/Stich—Ferreira/Norval, 7-6, 4-6, 7-6, 6-3

Ferreira and Norval were the first South Africans to stand on the medal platform since South Africa was banned from the Olympics after the 1960 Games. Their victory preceded that of long-distance runner Elana Meyer by less than five hours.

1996 Atlanta-Stone Mountain T: 3, N: 31, D: 8.2.

1. AUS Todd Woodbridge, Mark Woodforde
2. GBR Neil Broad, Timothy Henman
3. GER Marc-Kevin Göllner, David Prinosil
4. HOL Jacco Eltingh, Paul Haarhuis
5. Saša Hiršzon, Goran Ivanišević (CRO); Jiří Novák, Daniel Vacek (CZE); Ellis Ferreira, Wayne Ferreira (SAF); Sergi Bruguera Torner, Tomás Carbonell Lladó (SPA)

Final: Woodbridge/Woodforde—Broad/Henman, 6-4, 6-4, 6-2
3rd Place: Göllner/Prinosil—Eltingh/Haarhuis, 6-2, 7-5

The obvious favorites were Mark Woodforde and Todd Woodbridge, known as The Woodies, who had won the last four Wimbledon titles. They did win at the Olympics, but not before overcoming two unexpected obstacles. First Woodbridge was involved in an altercation with a female security guard at the entrance to the Olympic Village. He was arrested, pleaded no contest and fined $100. The Woodies faced a more serious challenge in the semifinals against Jacco Eltingh and Paul Haarhuis. The Woodies won the first game 6-2, but the Dutch pair took the second 7-5. The Australians led 9-8 in the third set with Woodbridge serving at 40-love. Eltingh and Haarhuis fought off three match points and won the game. At 11-12, with Woodforde serving, the Woodies fell behind 15-40. They survived two match points, won the game and finally won the set 18-16.

2000 Sydney T: 29, N: 29, D: 9.27.

1. CAN Sebastien Lareau, Daniel Nestor
2. AUS Todd Woodbridge, Mark Woodforde
3. SPA Alex Corretja Verdegay, Alberto Costa Casal
4. SAF David Adams, John-Laffnie De Jager
5. Mark Knowles, Mark Merklein (BAH); Max Mirnyi, Vladimir Voltchkov (BLR); Tommy Haas, David Prinosil (GER); Dominik Hrbatý, Karol Kučera (SLV)

Final: Lareau/Nestor—Woodbridge/Woodforde, 5-7, 6-3, 6-4, 7-6 (7-2)
3rd Place: Corretja/Costa—Adams/De Jager, 2-6, 6-4, 6-3

It would have been an emotionally satisfying outcome if Mark Woodforde and Todd Woodbridge, winners of 61 tournaments, could close out their career with an Olympic victory in front of an Australian crowd. They did come close, but it was not to be. The Woodies did make it to the final, winning all three of their matches in straight sets. In the final, they faced Daniel Nestor and Sebastian Lareau who, a year earlier, had decided to drop their regular partners, neither of whom were Canadians, and join together so that they would be ready for the Olympics. In the quarterfinals of the Wimbledon tournament, the Woodies beat Nestor and Lareau in five sets. In Sydney, the Canadians swept into the finals by outscoring their opponents 48 games to 19. The Woodies took the first set 7-5, but Nestor and Lareau refused to fold. With Nestor in control, the Canadians succeeded with 85% of their first serves, including 92% in the fourth set. The match ended with Woodbridge double-faulting twice.

2004 Athens T: 30, N: 24, D: 8.21.

1. CHI Fernando González Ciuffardi, Nicolás Massú Fried
2. GER Nicolas Kiefer, Rainer Schüttler
3. CRO Mario Ančić, Ivan Ljubičić
4. IND Mahesh Bhupathi, Leander Paes
5. Michael Llodra, Fabrice Santoro (FRA); Jonathan Erlich, Andi Ram (ISR); Bob Bryan, Michael Bryan (USA); Wayne Black, Kevin Ullyett (ZIM)

Final: González/Massú—Kiefer/Schüttler, 6-2, 4-6, 3-6, 7-6 (9-7), 6-4
3rd Place: Ančić/Ljubičić—Bhupathi/Paes, 7-6 (7-5), 4-6, 16-14

Fernando González and Nicolás Massú advanced easily to the quarterfinals, where they defeated the top-seeded pair, twin brothers Bob and Mike Bryan, 7-5, 6-4. They followed with a 7-5, 4-6, 6-4 semifinal victory over Mario Ančić and Ivan Ljubičić. In the final, González and

Massú won the first set against Nicolas Kiefer and Rainer Schüttler, but lost the next two sets. In the critical fourth set, González and Massú were down 2-6 in the tie-breaker, but saved four match points and won 9-7. The Chileans fell behind 1-3 in the final set before breaking through for a 5-4 lead and then needed three match points to complete the victory. The match, which began at 11 p.m., ended at 2:39 a.m. Neither González nor Massú had ever won a doubles title before. At the medal ceremony, they were chatting with each other and did not hear their names announced. Bronze medal winner Ivan Ljubičić had to direct them to the medal platform.

Although Chile had been competing at the Olympics since 1912, this was the nation's first gold medal in any sport.

2008 Beijing T: 32, N: 24, D: 8.16.

1. SWI	Roger Federer, Stanislas Wawrinka
2. SWE	Simon Aspelin, Thomas Johansson
3. USA	Robert Bryan, Michael Bryan
4. FRA	Arnaud Clément, Michaël Llodra
5. AUS	Chris Guccione, Lleyton Hewitt
5. IND	Mahesh Bhupathi, Leander Paes
5. POL	Mariusz Fyrstenberg, Marcin Makowski
5. RUS	Igor Andreyev, Nikolay Davidenko

Final: Federer/Wawrinka–Aspelin/Johansson 6-3, 6-4, 6-7 (4), 6-3
3rd Place: Bryan/Bryan–Clément/Llodra 3-6, 6-3, 6-4

Roger Federer had been the top-ranked singles tennis player for more than four years but had never won an Olympic medal. Paired with world number-ten-ranked Stanislas Wawrinka, the pair steamrolled through the tournament, winning each of their first four matches in straight sets.

The Swiss duo defeated top-seeded American twins Bob and Mike Bryan in the semifinals 7-6 (6), 6-4. In the other semifinal, Sweden's Simon Aspelin and Thomas Johansson fought Arnaud Clément and Michaël Llodra of France in an epic match that lasted a record 59 games over four-and-three-quarter hours, the longest three-set match in Olympic history. Aspelin and Johansson eventually pulled ahead to win 7-6 (6), 4-6, 19-17.

Federer and Wawrinka won the first two sets of the final before Aspelin and Johansson came alive to take the third set. Federer served for the match at 5-3 in the fourth set, and Johansson's return went wide, sealing the Swiss victory at 6-3, 6-4, 6-7 (4), 6-3. A jubilant Federer told reporters after the match, "In singles, you're all alone on the court. You win, you sit down. This is quite a surreal moment. It's a joy sharing this victory with somebody else."

Charlotte Cooper, 1900
Cooper became the first female Olympic champion when she won the tennis tournament in Paris in 1900.

WOMEN

SINGLES

1896 not held

1900 Paris C: 6, N: 4, D: 7.11.

1. Charlotte Cooper	GBR
2. Hélène Prévost	FRA
3. Marion Jones	USA
3. Hedwiga Rosenbaumóvá	BOH/CZE

Final: Cooper—Prévost, 6-1, 6-4

Charlotte "Chattie" Cooper had already won three of her five Wimbledon titles when she traveled to Paris for the Olympics. She was the first female champion of the modern Games. Hélène Prévost's father, André, placed third in the men's doubles competition. Jones and Rosenbaumóvá were awarded third place even though neither of them won a match.

1904 St. Louis not held

1906 Athens C: 6, N: 2, D: 4.26.

1. Esmée Simiriotis	GRE
2. Sophia Marinou	GRE
3. Euphrosine Paspati	GRE
4. Aspasia Matsa	GRE

Final: Simiriotis—Marinou, 2-6, 6-3, 6-3
3rd Place: Paspati—Matsa, 6-0, 6-4

1908 London C: 5, N: 1, D: 7.11.

1. Dorothea "Dolly" Lambert Chambers	GBR
2. P. Dora Boothby	GBR
3. R. Joan Winch	GBR

Final: Lambert Chambers—Boothby, 6-1, 7-5

Due to numerous withdrawals, only four matches were contested, and Lambert Chambers won three of them. Boothby advanced to the final without playing a single game. Both Lambert Chambers and 1900 winner Charlotte Cooper were born and raised in Ealing, Middlesex. Between 1903 and 1914 Lambert Chambers won 7 Wimbledon singles titles. In 1911 she won the shortest championship match in Wimbledon history, defeating Dora Boothby 6-0, 6-0 in 25 minutes.

1908 London C: 7, N: 2, D: 5.11.
Indoor Courts

1. Gladys Eastlake-Smith	GBR
2. Alice Greene	GBR
3. Märtha Adlerstråhle	SWE
4. Elsa Wallenberg	SWE

Final: Eastlake-Smith—Greene, 6-2, 4-6, 6-0
3rd Place: Adlerstråhle—Wallenberg, 1-6, 6-3, 6-2

1912 Stockholm C: 8, N: 4, D: 7.4.

1. Marguerite Broquedis	FRA
2. Dorothea "Dora" Köring	GER
3. Anna "Molla" Bjurstedt	NOR
4. Edith Arnheim Lasch	SWE
5. Margareta Cederschiöld	SWE

Final: Broquedis—Köring, 4-6, 6-3, 6-4
3rd Place: Bjurstedt—Arnheim, 6-2, 6-2

1912 Stockholm C: 8, N: 3, D: 5.11.
Indoor Courts

1. Edith Hannam	GBR
2. Sofie Castenschiold	DEN
3. Mabel Parton	GBR
4. Sigrid Fick	SWE

Final: Hannam—Castenschiold, 6-4, 6-3
3rd Place: Parton—Fick, 6-3, 6-3

According to the Official Report of the 1912 Games, in the third-place match, "the difficult screws of [Mrs. Parton] were altogether too much for the Swedish representative."

1920 Antwerp C: 18, N: 7, D: 8.24.

1. Suzanne Lenglen	FRA
2. E. Dorothy Holman	GBR
3. Kathleen "Kitty" McKane	GBR
4. Sigrid Fick	SWE

5. Elisabeth d'Ayen (FRA), Lily Strömberg (SWE)
Final: Lenglen—Holman, 6-3, 6-0
3rd Place: McKane—Fick, 6-2, 6-0

Defending Wimbledon champion Suzanne Lenglen was one of the greatest women tennis players of all time. Between 1919 and 1926, she lost only one match. At the 1925 Wimbledon tournament, she played fourteen sets and lost only five games. In the ten sets that it took her to win the 1920 Olympic singles title, she lost only four games. The first major tennis star to turn professional, Lenglen died of pernicious anemia July 4, 1938 at the age of 39.

1924 Paris C: 31, N: 14, D: 7.20.

1. Helen Wills	USA
2. Julie "Didi" Vlasto	FRA
3. Kathleen "Kitty" McKane	GBR
4. Germaine Golding	FRA

5. Elia María "Lili" González Álvarez (SPA), Marion Jessup (USA), Anna "Molla" Bjurstedt-Mallory (NOR), Dorothy Shepherd-Barron (GBR)
Final: Wills—Vlasto, 6-2, 6-2
3rd Place: McKane—Golding, 5-7, 6-3, 6-0

In the semifinals McKane won her first set against Vlasto, 6-0, and was leading the second set 3-0 when a disruption occurred which turned the contest around. The match on the center court having just concluded, the Parisian crowd moved over to court number 3 to watch McKane and Vlasto. The umpire, Louis Raymond of South Africa, was calling the score in English and continued to do so, despite increasingly agitated requests from the audience that the score be announced in French. After things settled down, McKane had lost her touch and Vlasto was able to win 13 of the next 16 games to gain a 0-6, 7-5, 6-1 victory. However Vlasto was no match for the 18-year-old sensation Helen Wills, who succeeded Suzanne Lenglen as the queen of tennis. Known as "Miss Poker Face" because of her expressionless demeanor, Wills won eight Wimbledon titles. Although Lenglen avoided Wills and even withdrew from the 1924 Olympics, the two did play once on February 16, 1926, on Lenglen's home court in Cannes. Lenglen won 6-3, 8-6 but never took her chances with Wills again. Molla Bjürstedt-Mallory went on to win a record eight US singles titles.

1928–1984 not held

1988 Seoul C: 48, N: 26, D: 10.1.

1. Stefanie Graf	GER
2. Gabriela Sabatini	ARG
3. Zina Garrison	USA
3. Manuela Maleeva	BUL

5. Rafaella Reggi (ITA), Larissa Savchenko (SOV/LAT), Pamela Shriver (USA), Natalya Zvereva (SOV/BLR)

Final: Graf—Sabatini, 6-3, 6-3

In 1984 Steffi Graf, then 15 years old, won the Olympic demonstration tournament despite being its youngest entrant. By 1987 she was ranked number one in the world, and in 1988 she won the Australian Open, the French Open, Wimbledon, and, less than a week before the Olympics, the US Open, to become only the fifth player in history to win tennis' Grand Slam. She arrived in Seoul with a 5-month, 35-match winning streak. Her most difficult challenge came in the quarterfinals when she trailed Larissa Savchenko 3-1 in the third set. Graf then won five straight games to close out the match. In the final she faced Gabriela Sabatini, the only player to beat her in 1988. But this time Graf kept Sabatini on the defensive and won in straight sets. Between August 17, 1987, and March 10, 1991, Graf was ranked number one in the world for 186 weeks in a row. When she retired in 1999, her career win-loss record was 902-115. Her winning percentage, 88.7, was second in history only to Chris Evert's 90.0. Graf earned $21.8 million in prize money alone. In 2001 she married fellow gold medal winner Andre Agassi.

1992 Barcelona C: 64, N: 33, D: 8.7.

1. Jennifer Capriati	USA
2. Stefanie Graf	GER
3. Maria Jose "Mary Joe" Fernández	USA
3. Arantxa Sánchez Vicario	SPA

5. Sabine Applemans (BEL), Anke Huber (GER), Manuela Fragnière-Maleeva (SWI), Conchita Martínez Bernat (SPA)

Final: Capriati—Graf, 3-6, 6-3, 6-4

Three of the four top-ranked players, Monica Seles of Yugoslavia, Gabriela Sabatini of Argentina, and Martina Navratilova of the United States, were declared ineligible for the Olympics because they refused to take part in the Federation Cup. This left an easy road to gold for either defending champion Steffi Graf or local favorite Arantxa Sánchez Vicario. But it wasn't so easy after all, thanks to 16-year-old prodigy Jennifer Capriati. Capriati turned professional when she was 13 years old. At 14 she became the youngest semifinalist in the history of the French Open and the youngest player to win a match at Wimbledon. At 15 she was the youngest semifinalist in Wimbledon history. She was also making $5 million a year even though she had never made it to a Grand Slam final. By the time the Olympics rolled around, there were rumors that Capriati was burning out from stress. Maybe she was, but not fast enough for Sánchez Vicario and Graf. In the semifinals Capriati silenced a boisterous Spanish crowd by beating Sánchez Vicario 6-3, 3-6, 6-1. In the final she faced Graf, who had obliterated her first five opponents in straight sets and who had beaten Capriati the four times they met previously.

The fifth game of the first set lasted 32 points as Graf fought off 9 break points before holding her serve and going on to win the set. Most Graf opponents would have collapsed at that point. Instead, Capriati came back to win the second set and break Graf in the first game of the third set. Graf broke right back in the next game. But after trailing 3-4, Capriati won the last three games to gain the upset victory.

A year later, Capriati did in fact burn out. She dropped out of tennis at the age of 17, was treated at a private psychiatric facility, and in May 1994 she was arrested for possession of marijuana. She returned to tennis in 1996 and in 2001 she won her first Grand Slam titles.

1996 Atlanta-Stone Mountain C: 64, N: 34, D: 8.2.

1. Lindsay Davenport	USA
2. Arantxa Sánchez Vicario	SPA
3. Jana Novotná	CZE
4. Maria Jose "Mary Joe" Fernández	USA

5. Kimiko Date (JPN), Iva Majoli (CRO), Conchita Martínez Bernat (SPA), Monica Seles (USA)

Final: Davenport—Sánchez Vicario, 7-6 (8-6), 6-2

3rd Place: Novotná—Fernandez, 7-6 (8-6), 6-4

Although she was seeded ninth, 6-foot 2½ inch (1.88 meters) Lindsay Davenport had never advanced past the quarterfinals of a major tournament. She did, however, have Olympic bloodlines: her father, Wink, had represented the United States in volleyball in 1968. As it turned out, Davenport would lose only one set in six matches. The quarterfinals saw the elimination of the two top seeds. Monica Seles was beaten by Jana Novotná 7-5, 3-6, 8-6 and Conchita Martínez lost to Mary Joe Fernandez 3-6, 6-2, 6-3. In the semifinals, Davenport faced Fernandez, who happened to be her best friend. The morning of the match, the two breakfasted together, just as they had each morning for the past two weeks. When they met at the net following Davenport's 6-2, 7-6 (8-6) victory, Davenport apologized to Fernandez. In the other semifinal, Arantxa Sánchez Vicario defeated Novotná 6-4, 1-6, 6-3.

Davenport and Sánchez Vicario had played each other five times prior to the Olympic final and Sánchez Vicario had won every time. The first set went to tiebreaker. Davenport led 6-4. Sánchez Vicario drew even. Davenport won the next point and then benefited from a piece of luck that turned the match. At 7-6 in the tiebreaker, Davenport hit a two-handed backhand that struck the top of the net and dribbled over. Sánchez Vicario had said beforehand that whoever won the first set would win the match and she was right. Davenport gained confidence and dominated the second set, winning 6-2.

Virág Csurgó of Hungary, ranked 192nd in the world was only entered in the doubles event. On the morning of July 24, she was helping warm up a teammate when she was informed that one of the singles entrants had failed to appear and Csurgó could take her place if she showed up for the first round match—in five minutes. Wearing her practice shorts and a t-shirt, Csurgó hurried over to the court and actually defeated Aleksandra Olsya of Poland 6-2, 9-5. In the second round she was beaten by Kimiko Date 6-2, 6-3.

2000 Sydney C: 64, N: 33, D: 9.27.

1. Venus Williams	USA
2. Yelena Dementieva	RUS
3. Monica Seles	USA
4. Jelena Dokić	AUS

5. Amanda Coetzer (SAF), Arantxa Sánchez Vicario (SPA), Barbara Schett (AUT), Dominique Van Roost (BEL)

Final: Williams—Dementieva, 6-2, 6-4
3rd Place: Seles—Dokic, 6-1, 6-4

Twenty-year-old Venus Williams entered the Olympics with a 26-game winning streak that included victories at Wimbledon and the US Open. In the quarterfinals she faced the last woman to beat her, Arantxa Sánchez Vicario. Williams won 3-6, 6-2, 6-4 and then defeated Monica Seles in the semifinals 6-1, 4-6, 6-3. In the final, Williams had an easier time with Yelena Dementieva to extend her winning streak to 32.

2004 Athens C: 32, N: 32, D: 8.21.

1. Justine Henin-Hardenne	BEL
2. Amélie Mauresmo	FRA
3. Alicia Molik	AUS
4. Anastasiya Myskina	RUS

5. Mary Pierce (FRA), Francesca Schiavone (ITA), Ai Sugiyama (JPN), Svetlana Kuznetsova (RUS)

Final: Henin-Hardenne—Mauresmo, 6-3, 6-3
3rd Place: Molik—Myskina, 6-3, 6-4

Ranked number one in the world, Justine Henin spent the four months before the Athens Olympics battling a viral infection that sapped her strength and caused her to sleep 18 hours a day. She arrived in Athens having played in only one tournament in four months. Henin managed to sweep through the competition easily, not losing a set until her semifinal match against third-seeded Anastasiya Myskina, which she won 7-5, 5-7, 8-6, after trailing the final set 1-5. In the final, Henin overwhelmed world number-two Amélie Mauresmo and never faced a break point, winning in just 78 minutes. Henin celebrated her win with a sport she had picked up during her illness–skydiving.

2008 Beijing C: 64, N: 33, D: 8.17.

1. Elena Dementieva	RUS
2. Dinara Safina	RUS
3. Vera Zvonareva	RUS
4. Li Na	CHN
5. Jelena Janković	SER
5. Sybille Bammer	AUT
5. Serena Williams	USA
5. Venus Williams	USA

Final: Dementieva–Safina 3-6, 7-5, 6-3
3rd Place: Zvonareva–Li 6-0, 7-5

Three of the four semifinalists were Russian. The exception was China's Li Na, ranked 42nd in the world. Li had ridden a wave of hometown support through the early stages of the tournament, taking out third seed Svetlana Kuznetsova 7-6 (5), 6-4 in the first round and knocking out 2000 Olympic champion Venus Williams 7-5, 7-5 in the quarterfinals. Li's impressive run finally came to an end in the semifinal round, where she was beaten 7-6 (7), 7-5 by world number six Dinara Safina.

The other semifinal featured world number eleven Vera Zvonareva and 2000 Olympic silver medalist Elena Dementieva, who had beaten eight-time Grand Slam champion Serena Williams 3-6, 6-4, 6-3 to reach the semifinals. Dementieva advanced to the final by defeating Zvonareva 6-3, 7-6 (3).

Safina struggled in the final, committing 17 double-faults, while Dementieva recovered from an error-filled 3-6 loss in the first set, holding off a break point at 5-5 in the second set to win 7-5 before closing out the match 6-3 in the third set.

Zvonareva earned the bronze medal 6-0, 7-5 over Li Na to complete the Russian sweep. Zvonareva had only made the singles draw after teammate Maria Sharapova withdrew due to a shoulder injury.

Russia was the first country to sweep a tennis event since Great Britain swept women's singles in 1908.

DOUBLES

1896–1912 not held

1920 Antwerp T: 9, N: 5, D: 8.24.

1. GBR	Winifred McNair, Kathleen "Kitty" McKane
2. GBR	W. Geraldine Beamish, E. Dorothy Holman
3. FRA	Suzanne Lenglen, Elisabeth d'Ayen
4. BEL	Marie Storms, Fernande Arendt
5. BEL	Marthe Dupont-Trasenster, Anne Chaudoir

Final: McNair/McKane—Beamish/Holman, 8-6, 6-4
3rd Place: Lenglen/d'Ayen—Storms/Arendt, WO

Kitty McKane withdrew from her singles semifinal in order to conserve her energy for a doubles semi against Lenglen and d'Ayen. It turned out to be a wise decision, as she and 43-year-old Winifred McNair were stretched to the limit to defeat the French pair 2-6, 6-3, 8-6. McKane won a complete set of medals in Antwerp and then added another silver and bronze at the 1924 Olympics. In 1926 McKane and her husband, Leslie Godfree, became the only married couple in history to win the Wimbledon mixed doubles title. McKane was also a four-time All-England singles champion—in badminton.

1924 Paris T: 11, N: 8, D: 7.19.

1. USA Hazel Wightman, Helen Wills
2. GBR Phyllis Covell, Kathleen "Kitty" McKane
3. GBR Dorothy Shepherd-Barron, Evelyn Colyer
4. FRA Marguerite Billout [Broquedis], Yvonne Bourgeois
5. SWE Sigrid Fick, Lily von Essen

Final: Wightman/Wills—Covell/McKane, 7-5, 8-6
3rd Place: Shepherd-Barron/Colyer—Billout/Bourgeois, 6-1, 6-2

Hazel Wightman also won the gold medal in mixed doubles. In 1990 she became the first tennis player to appear on a US postage stamp. Despite her successes as a player, Wightman's greatest contribution to the world of tennis was the creation, in 1923, of the Wightman Cup, the women's equivalent of the Davis Cup. Despite her successes as a player, Wightman's greatest contribution to the world of tennis was the creation of the Wightman Cup, which was held between 1923 and 1989.

Dorothy Shepherd-Barron's son, John, invented the world's first automatic cash machine, commonly known as an ATM.

1928–1984 not held

1988 Seoul T: 14, N: 14 D: 9.30.

1. USA Pamela Shriver, Zina Garrison
2. CZE Jana Novotná, Helena Suková
3. AUS Elizabeth Smylie, Wendy Turnbull
3. GER Stefanie Graf, Claudia Kohde-Kilsch
5. Carling Bassett-Seguso, Jill Hetherington (CAN); Nathalie Tauziat, Isabelle Demongeot (FRA); Etsuko Inoue, Kumiko Okamoto (JPN); Larissa Savchenko, Natalya Zvereva (SOV)

Final: Shriver/Garrison—Novotná/Suková, 4-6, 6-2,10-8

With Garrison serving at 9-8 in the final set, she and Shriver lost 5 match points, including two double faults. Finally, on the sixth try, the Americans won when Novotná hit long on a service return.

A first-round match between Carling Bassett-Seguso and Jill Hetherington of Canada and Mercedes Paz and Gabriela Sabatini of Argentina earned a place in the record books because it included the longest set in Olympic history. The Canadians won 7-6, 5-7, 20-18.

1992 Barcelona T: 32, N: 32, D: 8.8.

1. USA Beatriz "Gigi" Fernández, Maria Jose "Mary Joe" Fernández
2. SPA Conchita Martínez Bernat, Arantxa Sánchez Vicario
3. AUS Rachel McQuillan, Nicole Provis
3. SOV Leila Meskhi, Natalya Zvereva
5. Mercedes Paz, Patricia Tarabini (ARG); Jana Novotná, Andrea Strnadová (CZE); Isabelle Demongeot, Nathalie Tauziat (FRA); Elna Reinach, Mariaan De Swardt (SAF)

Final: Fernandez/Fernandez—Martínez/Sánchez, 7-5, 2-6, 6-2

The final saw 13 service breaks in 28 games. Although Mary Joe and Gigi Fernandez were not related, they did share something besides the same surname: they were both born in the Caribbean. Mary Joe was born in the Dominican Republic to a Cuban mother and a Spanish father. The family moved to the United States when Mary Joe was six months old. Gigi was born in Puerto Rico and settled in the United States when she was 20 years old.

1996 Atlanta-Stone Mountain T: 28, N: 28, D: 8.3.

1. USA Beatriz "Gigi" Fernández, Maria Jose "Mary Joe" Fernández
2. CZE Jana Novotná, Helena Suková
3. SPA Conchita Martínez Bernat, Arantxa Sánchez Vicario
4. HOL Manon Bollegraf, Brenda Schultz-McCarthy
5. Jill Hetherington, Patricia Hy-Boulais (CAN); Valda Lake, Clare Wood (GBR); Martina Hingis, Patty Schnyder (SWI); Benjamas Sangaram, Tamarine Tanasugarn (THA)

Final: Fernandez/Fernandez—Novotná/Suková, 7-6 (8-6), 6-4
3rd Place: Martínez/Sánchez Vicario—Bollegraf/Schultz-McCarthy, 6-1, 6-3

Originally, Mary Joe Fernandez was not included in the US squad because she was the fifth-ranked American and only four players per nation were allowed to enter the Olympics. However, because she was a defending champion, the International Tennis Federation awarded her a wildcard entry. Fernandez and Fernandez won all four of their matches in straight sets. In the final, Jana Novotná was stricken by a pulled stomach muscle and had to have her waist taped in the middle of the match. At one point she was even reduced to serving underhand.

2000 Sydney T: 31, N: 31, D: 9.28.

1. USA Serena Williams, Venus Williams
2. HOL Kristie Boogert, Miriam Oremans
3. BEL Els Callens, Dominique Van Roost
4. BLR Olga Barabanschikova, Natasha Zvereva
5. Julie Halard-Décugis, Amélie Mauresmo (FRA); Petra Mandula, Katalin Marosi-Aracama (HUN); Benjamas Sangaram, Tamarine Tanasugarn (THA); Milagros Sequera, María Alejandra Vento (VEN)

Final: Williams/Williams—Boogert/Oremans, 6-1, 6-1
3rd Place: Callens/Van Roost—Barabanschikova/Zvereva, 4-6, 6-4, 6-1

The Williams sisters had won the 1999 French and US Opens and, two months before the Olympics, the Wimbledon title. In Sydney they lost one set to Yelena Likhovtseva and Anastasia Myskina of Russia, but otherwise cruised through the tournament. Venus was the first woman since Helen Wills to win both the singles and doubles titles and the victory that she and Serena achieved over Kristie Boogert and Miriam Oremans was the most decisive in an Olympic final since the men's doubles in 1900.

2004 Athens T: 32, N: 21, D: 8.22.
1. CHN Li Ting, Sun Tiantian
2. SPA Conchita Martínez Bernat, Virginia Ruano Pascual
3. ARG Paola Suárez, Patricia Tarabini
4. JPN Shinobu Asagoe, Ai Sugiyama
5. Alicia Molik, Rennae Stubbs (AUS); Yan Zi, Zheng Jie (CHN); Nathalie Dechy, Sandrine Testud (FRA); Martina Navratilova, Lisa Raymond (USA)

Final: Li/Sun—Martínez/Ruano, 6-3, 6-3
3rd Place: Suárez/Tarabini—Asagoe/Sugiyama, 6-3, 6-3

Eighth-seeded Li Ting and Sun Tiantian knocked out defending champion Venus Williams and her partner Chanda Rubin 7-5, 1-6, 6-3 in the first round, ending a four-match pre-Olympic losing streak. Two straight-set matches brought them to the semifinals, where they beat Paola Suárez and Patricia Tarabini 6-2, 2-6, 9-7. In the final, Li and Sun took advantage of a sub-standard performance by second-seeded Conchita Martínez and Virginia Ruano and won in straight sets. Neither Li nor Sun ever won another major tournament.

2008 Beijing T: 31, N: 21, D: 8.17.
1. USA Serena Williams, Venus Williams
2. SPA Anabel Medina Garrigues, Virginia "Vivi" Ruano Pascual
3. CHN Yan Zi, Zheng Jie
4. UKR Alona Bondarenko, Kateryna Bondarenko
5. RUS Svetlana Kuznetsova, Dinara Safina
5. USA Lindsay Davenport, Liezel Horn-Huber
5. ITA Flavia Pennetta, Francesca Schiavone
5. RUS Yelena Vesnina, Vera Zvonareva

Final: Williams/Williams–Medina/Ruano 6-2, 6-0
3rd Place: Yan/Zheng–Bondarenko/Bondarenko 6-2, 6-2

Venus and Serena Williams had been unable to defend their 2000 doubles gold medal at the 2004 Olympics because Serena was recovering from an injury to her left knee. By 2008, Serena was back in top form. A month before the Olympics the sisters not only finished 1-2 in the singles tournament at Wimbledon, they also won the doubles title, their first since 2002.

The Williams sisters faced Ukrainian pair Alona and Kateryna Bondarenko in the semifinals, making it the first all-sister tennis match-up in Olympic history. Venus and Serena lost the first set 4-6 before coming back 6-4, 6-1 to reach the final. In the other semifinal, Spanish pair Anabel Medina and Virginia Ruano beat Yan Zi and Zhang Jie 6-4, 7-6 (5).

Venus and Serena had a surprisingly easy time in the final, defeating Medina and Ruano 6-2, 6-0 to win their second Olympic title.

MIXED DOUBLES

1896 not held

1900 Paris T: 6, N: 4, D: 7.11.
1. GBR Charlotte Cooper, Reginald Doherty
2. FRA & GBR/IRL Hélène Prévost, Harold Mahoney
3. BOH/CZE & GBR Hedwiga Rosenbaúmá, Archibald Warden
3. USA & GBR Marion Jones, H. Laurence "Laurie" Doherty

Final: Cooper/R. Doherty—Prévost/Mahoney, 6-2, 6-4

1904 not held

1906 Athens T: 5, N: 2, D: 4.26.
1. FRA Marie Décugis, Max Décugis
2. GRE Sophia Marinou, Georgios Simiriotis
3. GRE Aspasia Matsa, Xenophon Kasdaglis

Final: Décugis/Décugis—Matsa/Kasdaglis, 6-3, 7-5

Max and Marie Decugis were husband and wife. First they beat Marinou and Simiriotis 8-6, 6-3 and then Matsa and Kasdaglis 6-3, 7-5. The jury awarded second place to Marinou and Simiriotis, although the reason why remains a mystery.

1908 not held

1912 Stockholm T: 6, N: 4, D: 7.5.
1. GER Dorothea "Dora" Köring, Heinrich Schomburgk
2. SWE Sigrid Fick, Gunnar Setterwall
3. FRA Marguerite Broquedis, Albert Canet
4. SWE Annie Holmström, Thorsten Grönfors

Final: Köring/Schomburgk—Fick/Setterwall, 6-4, 6-0

Shortly after the final match began, Mrs. Fick inadvertently smashed her partner in the face rather severely. In the words of the Official Report for 1912: "This little accident seemed to put Setterwall off his game, for his play fell off tremendously."

1912 Stockholm T: 8, N: 3, D: 5.12.
Indoor Courts
1. GBR Edith Hannam, Charles Dixon
2. GBR F. Helen Aitchison, H. Roper Barrett
3. SWE Sigrid Fick, Gunnar Setterwall
4. SWE Margareta Cederschiöld, J. Carl Kempe
5. GBR Mabel Parton, Theodore Mavrogordato

Final: Hannam/Dixon—Aitchison/Barrett, 4-6, 6-3, 6-2
3rd Place: Fick/Setterwall—Cederschiöld/Kempe, WO

1920 Antwerp T: 15, N: 7, D: 8.24.
1. FRA Suzanne Lenglen, Max Décugis
2. GBR Kathleen "Kitty" McKane, Maxwell Woosnam
3. CZE Milada Skrbková, Ladslav "Rázný" Žemla
4. DEN Amory Folmer-Hansen, Erik Tegner
5. Anne Chaudoir, Albert Lammens (BEL); Marie Storms, S. Joseph Halot (BEL)

Final: Lenglen/Décugis—McKane/Woosnam, 6-4, 6-2
3rd Place: Skrbková/Žemla—Folmer-Hansen/Tegner, 8-6, 6-4

1924 Paris T: 21, N: 14, D: 7.21.
1. USA Hazel Wightman, Richard Norris Williams
2. USA Marion Jessup, Vincent Richards
3. HOL Cornelia "Kea" Bouman, Hendrik Timmer
4. GBR Kathleen "Kitty" McKane, John Gilbert
5. P. Edith Covell, Leslie Godfree (GBR); Sigrid Fick, Henning Müller (SWE; Mary Wallis, Edwin McCrea (IRL)

Final: Wightman/Williams—Jessup/Richards, 6-2, 6-3
3rd Place: Bouman/Timmer—McKane/Gilbert, WO

Dick Williams was 21 years old in 1912 when, with his father Charles, he boarded the *Titanic* in Cherbourg and headed for New York. After the ship hit an iceberg, Williams watched as his father was killed by the collapse of a huge funnel. He dived into the freezing water and, wearing a fur coat, swam fifty feet to a collapsible lifeboat. Along with about 25 to 30 others, he clung to the boat for six hours. When the *Carpathia* finally arrived to save them, only eleven were still alive. The rest had frozen to death. The *Carpathia* doctor wanted to amputate both of Williams' legs to avoid gangrene, but Williams refused. Instead, he exercised daily and recovered. He returned to the US the following year as a member of the 1913 Davis Cup team. During World War I, Williams joined the US Army and served with distinction, earning the Croix de Guerre and the Legion of Honor.

With all this behind him, the stress of playing in the Olympics must not have fazed Williams. He sprained his ankle in the semifinals and suggested to his partner, Hazel Wightman, that they withdraw from the final. She refused. "She told me to stay at the net," Williams later recalled, "and she'd cover everything else. I didn't move much, but Hazel ran everywhere and won the match and the medals for us."

1928-2008 not held

This event will be reinstated in 2012.

Chapter 28 **Triathlon**

The triathlon begins with a 1500-meter open water swim. The competitors then cycle for 40 kilometers and conclude with a 10,000-meter run.

The first swim-bike-run triathlon was held in San Diego, California, on September 25, 1974. The first official world championship took place in Avignon, France in 1989.

Triathletes are required to wear swimming caps. If the water temperature is below 14 degrees Celsius, they must also wear wetsuits. If it is above 20 degrees Celsius, wetsuits are forbidden. Between 14 and 20 degrees, wetsuits are optional. During the cycling leg, the competitors must wear helmets, as well as something that covers their torsos. While running, they must wear shoes and, again, their torsos must be covered. Nudity and "indecent exposure" are forbidden, even during the rapid transition period between swimming and cycling. The 50 entrants in both the men's and women's event qualify through world rankings, although each nation is limited to three competitors per event.

In the charts below the times given are those for the individual legs only, and do not include the transitions.

MEN

1896–1996 not held

2000 Sydney C: 52, N: 27, D: 9.17.

		SWIM		BIKE		RUN		TOTAL
1. Simon Whitfield	CAN	17:56.59	(28)	58:54.40	(25)	30:53.73	(1)	1:48:24.02
2. Stephan Vuckovic	GER	18:14.19	(33)	58:33.90	(14)	31:09.89	(2)	1:48:37.58
3. Jan Rehula	CZE	17:45.39	(14)	58:54.00	(24)	31:21.25	(3)	1:48:46.64
4. Dmitry Gaag	KAZ	17:49.39	(18)	58:49.70	(19)	31:42.48	(4)	1:49:03.57
5. Iván Raña Fuentes	SPA	17:49.09	(17)	58:51.50	(21)	31:48.09	(5)	1:49:10.88
6. Miles Stewart	AUS	17:55.49	(26)	58:41.50	(15)	31:54.43	(8)	1:49:14.52
7. Olivier Marceau	FRA	17:52.19	(24)	57:52.60	(2)	32:53.94	(20)	1:49:18.03
8. Reto Hug	SWI	17:55.59	(27)	58:54.90	(26)	31:51.50	(7)	1:49:21.30

When Simon Whitfield was younger, he decided that someday he wanted to be included in the *Encyclopedia Britannica*. He realized that for an athlete to be included, he would have to be the best in the world in something. Whitfield, who had joint Canadian-Australian citizenship, was not one of the favorites at the Olympics. He was ranked 13th in the world and had not won a triathlon in a year. But while training at the Olympic Village, he was amazed at how fit he felt.

Conrad Stoltz of South Africa and world champion Olivier Marceau of France broke away from the field during the fifth of six bike laps and opened up a lead of almost a minute. On that same lap, a 15-man crash occurred and Whitfield was forced to put his foot down and skid to a stop. He began the 10-kilometer run in 24th place. Stoltz faded quickly (and ended up in 20th place), while Marceau held on for six kilometers, before being passed by Stephan Vuckovic. By this time it was clear that the medals would go to Vuckovic, Whitfield and Jan Rehula. Whitfield caught Vuckovic, but with 1000 meters to go, the German opened up a lead of almost 25 meters. Whitfield cut the gap in half and then began his final sprint with 450 meters left. He passed Vuckovic about 200 meters from the finish line and won easily. The first five places went to the five triathletes who recorded the fastest running times.

2004 Athens C: 49, N: 25, D: 8.26.

		SWIM		BIKE		RUN		TOTAL
1. Hamish Carter	NZL	18:19	(33)	1:00:24	(1)	31:46	(4)	1:51:07.73
2. Bevan Docherty	NZL	18:13	(17)	1:00:32	(4)	31:51	(5)	1:51:15.60
3. Sven Riederer	SWI	18:17	(25)	1:00:28	(2)	32:11	(7)	1:51:33.26
4. Greg Bennett	AUS	18:19	(29)	1:01:13	(7)	31:34	(2)	1:51:41.58
5. Frédéric Belaubre	FRA	18:04	(7)	1:00:39	(6)	32:34	(12)	1:52:00.53
6. Andreas Raelert	GER	18:07	(12)	1:01:23	(11)	32:30	(9)	1:52:35.62
7. Rasmus Henning	DEN	18:19	(28)	1:01:13	(7)	32:32	(10)	1:52:37.32
8. Olivier Marceau	SWI	18:18	(26)	1:00:28	(2)	33:20	(19)	1:52:44.36

With 500 meters to go in the 2003 world championships, Bevan Docherty of New Zealand and Ivan Raña of Spain were running side by side, and it became clear that one of them would win the gold medal. The two friends shook hands and sprinted to the finish line, with Docherty winning by one second. In Athens, Raña was out of form and placed only 23rd. Instead, Docherty's main competition came from his countryman, Hamish Carter. Carter had been one of the favorites at the 2000 Olympics, and at those Games he was well-placed in fifth after the bike leg. But he had a poor run and finished in 26th place.

The course in Athens included an unusually difficult bike route, with two steep hills on each of the five laps. At the end of the bike leg, Sven Riederer and Frédéric Belaubre led, with Carter, Docherty and Olivier Marceau close behind. The key breakaway came one lap into the running leg, when Docherty and Carter pulled away, with Riederer in close pursuit. Riederer faded late in the race, while Docherty and Carter stayed even until the final kilometer. Then Carter pulled ahead and held off his teammate over the last 100 meters. Docherty commented, "Who better to lose a gold medal to than Hamish?" Carter retired in 2007, saying, "Winning an Olympic gold medal spoils you as an athlete because if you win a race after that, it pales."

2008 Beijing C: 55, N: 31, D: 8.19.

		SWIM		BIKE		RUN		TOTAL
1. Jan Frodeno	GER	18:14	(16)	59:01	(34)	30:46	(1)	1:48:53.28
2. Simon Whitfield	CAN	18:18	(22)	58:56	(23)	30:48	(2)	1:48:58.47
3. Bevan Docherty	NZL	18:23	(31)	58:51	(16)	30:57	(3)	1:49:05.59
4. Javier Gómez Noya	SPA	18:08	(8)	59:06	(38)	31:03	(4)	1:49:13.92
5. Iván Raña Fuentes	SPA	18:22	(29)	58:52	(19)	31:14	(5)	1:49:22.03
6. Daniel Unger	GER	18:25	(37)	58:49	(13)	31:35	(6)	1:49:43.78
7. Hunter Kemper	USA	18:04	(4)	59:06	(38)	31:40	(7)	1:49:48.75
8. Rasmus Henning	DEN	18:18	(21)	58:57	(29)	31:48	(9)	1:49:57.47

Reigning world champion Javier Gómez had finished at the top of the world rankings in each of the previous two years and had only narrowly missed out on winning the world championship in 2007, having been passed at the line by Germany's Daniel Unger.

Shane Reed of New Zealand recorded the fastest swim leg, but had dropped to 38th by the end of the bike portion and was never a medal contender. Luxembourg's Dirk Bockel and Axel Zeebroek of Belgium led by nearly a minute after the bike leg, but their lead also disappeared as they eventually dropped to 25th and 13th.

In twelfth place going into the final running phase, 2000 Olympic champion Simon Whitfield worked his way into the lead, followed closely by Gómez, defending Olympic silver medalist and reigning world silver medalist Bevan Docherty, and the relatively unknown Jan Frodeno.

Frodeno produced a burst of speed in the final straight, moving past Whitfield into the lead just a few meters from the line. Competing in his first Olympics, the 6ft.-3in. (1.94-m.) Frodeno's best previous results in major events had been second place at the 2007 European Championship and sixth at the world championships the same year. His Olympic victory came a day after his twenty-seventh birthday.

"I had very little pressure going into this," Frodeno said afterwards. "Internationally, very few other people knew who I even was."

Frodeno grew up in South Africa between the ages of 11 and 23 and discovered triathlon while watching the 2000 Olympics on television.

Whitfield caused some controversy for using a domestique: a teammate whose sole purpose was to help Whitfield win. Whitfield's teammate, Colin Jenkins, raced only during the swimming and cycling phases, allowing Whitfield to profit from his slipstream, and then dropped to last place. Whitfield split his $15,000 silver medal bonus with Jenkins.

WOMEN

1896–1996 not held

2000 Sydney C: 48, N: 24, D: 9.16.

		SWIM		BIKE		RUN		TOTAL
1. Brigitte McMahon	SWI	19:16.88	(8)	1:05:14.50	(8)	35:13.64	(2)	2:00:40.52
2. Michellie Jones	AUS	19:21.68	(18)	1:05:13.20	(5)	35:25.77	(3)	2:00:42.55
3. Magali Messmer	SWI	19:14.88	(5)	1:05:18.70	(13)	35:49.45	(4)	2:01:08.83
4. Joanna Zeiger	USA	19:16.08	(7)	1:05:14.90	(9)	36:01.86	(5)	2:01:25.74
5. Loretta Harrop	AUS	19:13.58	(4)	1:05:20.40	(14)	36:24.14	(7)	2:01:42.82
6. Sheila Taormina	USA	18:36.48	(1)	1:05:59.00	(15)	37:18.83	(13)	2:02:45.91
7. Isabelle Mouthon-Michellys	FRA	19:19.38	(15)	1:05:06.10	(1)	37:35.93	(14)	2:02:53.41
8. Christine Hocq	FRA	19:18.58	(13)	1:05:12.00	(3)	37:44.22	(15)	2:03:01.90

The inaugural Olympic triathlon was viewed by an estimated 200,000 spectators lining the route, as local fans anticipated an Australian victory. Considering that Australian women had won at least two medals at each of the last four world championships, their expectations were not unfounded. Five months before the Olympics, the Sydney World Cup was held on the Olympic course. In that race, local favorite Michellie Jones beat Brigitte McMahon by ten seconds with Magali Messmer third. As it would turn out, the same three women would make it to the medal podium at the Olympics. Sheila Taormina completed the swimming leg with a 36-second lead, which was not surprising since she had won a gold medal in swimming at the last Olympics. Jones hit the running course in first place, with McMahon in 13th place, but only ten seconds back. The two ran shoulder-to shoulder in the final stage of the race, but about 200 meters from the finish, McMahon pulled away to win by two seconds.

In 2005, McMahon tested positive for EPO and was thrown off the Swiss national team. She was facing a two-year ban from competition when she retired.

2004 Athens C: 50, N: 25, D: 8.25.

		SWIM		BIKE		RUN		TOTAL
1. Kate Allen	AUT	20:38	(44)	1:09:33	(12)	33:48	(1)	2-04:43.45
2. Loretta Harrop	AUS	18:37	(1)	1:08:40	(2)	36:47	(13)	2-04:50.17
3. Susan Williams	USA	19:02	(9)	1:08:41	(1)	36:41	(10)	2-05:08.92
4. Kathleen Smet	BEL	19:42	(23)	1:09:04	(5)	36:05	(6)	2-05:35.89
5. Nadia Cortassa	ITA	20:36	(39)	1:09:32	(9)	34:56	(2)	2-05:45.35
6. Michelle Dillon	GBR	20:37	(42)	1:09:29	(6)	35:08	(3)	2-06:00.77
7. Ana Burgos Acuña	SPA	20:36	(41)	1:09:32	(9)	35:10	(4)	2-06:02.36
8. Vanessa Fernandes	POR	19:20	(11)	1:10:46	(25)	35:25	(5)	2-06:15.39

In only 28th place after the bike leg, the largely unknown Kate Allen started the running portion more than two and a half minutes behind leader Loretta Harrop. Setting a blistering pace, Allen passed more than half the field and surged past Harrop 200 meters from the finish to take the gold. Allen was so far back in the field that she had no idea she was close to a medal until her coach yelled the news to her late in the running leg. Born in Geelong, Australia, Allen was backpacking in Europe in 1995 when she met Austrian triathlete Marcel Diechter. Allen competed in her first triathlon six months later, married Diechter in 1999, and gained dual Austrian citizenship in 2002. She was 34 years old at the time of her Olympic victory.

2008 Beijing C: 55, N: 30, D: 8.18.

		SWIM		BIKE		RUN		TOTAL
1. Emma Snowsill	AUS	19:51	(5)	1:04:20	(15)	33:17	(1)	1:58:27.66
2. Vanessa Fernandes	POR	19:53	(9)	1:04:18	(13)	34:21	(2)	1:59:34.63
3. Emma Moffatt	AUS	19:55	(12)	1:04:12	(4)	34:46	(4)	1:59:55.84
4. Laura Bennett	USA	19:49	(1)	1:04:23	(17)	35:10	(7)	2:00:21.54
5. Juri Ide	JPN	19:50	(4)	1:04:24	(18)	35:05	(5)	2:00:23.77
6. Nicola Spirig	SWI	20:17	(36)	1:03:54	(1)	35:20	(9)	2:00:30.48
7. Daniela Ryf	SWI	19:56	(13)	1:04:17	(10)	35:31	(10)	2:00:40.20
8. Andrea Hewitt	NZL	19:54	(10)	1:04:15	(8)	35:38	(12)	2:00:45.99

Only 22 years old, Vanessa Fernandes had already become a consistently successful triathlete. After finishing eighth at the 2004 Olympics, she won silver at the 2006 world championships, finished first in the 2006 and 2007 world rankings and won the 2007 world title. In May 2008 she earned her 20th world cup victory, an all-time record.

Fernandes' biggest challenge at the Beijing Olympics was expected to come from Emma Snowsill, winner of the world championships in 2003, 2005 and 2006. Only 5ft. 3in. (1.6 m.) tall and weighing only 106 lbs (48 kg), Snowsill had finished behind Fernandes at the past two Beijing world cups, and the 2007 world championship.

Snowsill stayed in the lead pack through the swimming and biking legs, followed closely by Fernandes. Towards the end of the running phase Snowsill made her move, breaking away from the pack and quickly building a significant lead. She held on to finish more than a minute ahead of Fernandes despite taking time to celebrate with fans down the final stretch.

Snowsill had nearly quit the sport in 2002 after her boyfriend, Luke Harrop, also a triathlete, was struck and killed in a hit-and-run accident while on a training ride. Luke was the brother of 2004 Olympic silver medalist Loretta Harrop, and it was Loretta who encouraged Snowsill to continue training.

Chapter 29 **Volleyball**

MEN
Beach Volleyball: Men
WOMEN
Beach Volleyball: Women

Volleyball was invented in 1895 by an American named William Morgan. Volleyball matches are decided on the basis of the best three out of five games. Prior to 2000, a team won a game when it scored 15 points, provided the margin was two or more points. If the score was tied at 15, the first team to score 17 points was declared the winner. Points could only be scored by the serving team. If the defensive team won a rally, it gained the serve. In 1996, in the fifth and deciding game, a team could score a point on every play even if the other team was serving.

Since 2000, the team winning a rally scores a point whether they are serving or not. The first four sets are played to 25 and the final set to 15. A team must win by two points and service changes when the receiving team wins a rally.

Each team begins each point with three players near the net and three players in the backcourt. After the serve, all players may leave their positions. Prior to 2000, a new position was created: the libero. The libero is a defensive specialist whose play is restricted to the back row and who may not serve or block or hit a ball that is higher than the top of the net. A team wins a point when the ball strikes the floor on the opponent's side of the court or when the opposing team hits the ball out of bounds. On each play, a team may touch the ball no more than three times before sending it over the net, although when a player blocks a shot at the net, it does not count as a touch. A player may not touch the ball twice in a row except that a blocker may touch the ball after an attempted block. Rules in force through 1992 prohibited players from touching the ball with parts of their body below the waist. Since 1996, players have been allowed to use any part of their bodies, including their feet. Players may not touch the net while hitting the ball, trying to hit the ball, or pretending to try to hit the ball.

Players on a team rotate counter-clockwise after gaining the serve. Each team is permitted six substitute players per set, not including the libero, who may be substituted freely. If a substitute player is later removed from the game, he or she may not return and he or she may only be replaced by the same player for whom he was substituted.

A volleyball court is 18 meters (59 feet) long and 9 meters (29 feet 6 inches) wide. The court is divided by a center line above which is a one-meter (39-inch) net, the top of which is 2.43 meters (7 feet 11½ inches) above the floor for men and 2.24 meters (7 feet 4¼ inches) for women. The net is between 9.5 and 10 meters (32 to 32.6 feet) long. A volleyball is between 65 and 67 centimeters (25 and 27 inches) in circumference and weighs between 260 and 280 grams (9 and 10 ounces).

Twelve teams take part in each tournament: the top three teams from the most recent World Cup, five winners of continental tournaments, three teams from World Olympic Qualifying Tournaments, and the host nation.

MEN

1896–1960 not held

1964 Tokyo T: 10, N: 10, D: 10.23.

	MATCHES		GAMES			
	W	L	W	L	PF	PA
1. SOV	8	1	25	5	415	279
2. CZE	8	1	26	10	486	399
3. JPN	7	2	22	12	475	372
4. ROM	6	3	19	15	432	394
5. BUL	5	4	20	16	464	429
6. HUN	4	5	18	18	449	474
7. BRA	3	6	13	23	410	474
8. HOL	2	7	11	24	378	482

1. SOV—Ivans Bugajenkovs, Nikolai Burobin, Yuri Chesnokov, Vascha Kacharava, Valery Kalatschikhin, Vitaly Kovalenko, Stanislavs Lugailo, Georgy Mondzolevsky, Yuri Poyarkov, Eduard Sibiryakov, Yuri Venherovsky, Dmitri Voskoboynikov
2. CZE—Milan Čuda, Bohumil Golián, Zdenek Humhal, Petr Kop, Josef Labuda, Josef Musil, Karel Paulus, Boris Perušič, Pavel Schenk, Václav Šmidl, Josef Šorm, Ladislav Toman
3. JPN—Yutaka Demachi, Tsutomu Koyama, Sadatoshi Sugahara, Naohiro Ikeda, Yasutaka Sato, Toshiaki Kosedo, Tokihiko Higuchi, Masayuki Minami, Takeshi Tokutomi, Teruhisa Moriyama, Yuzo Nakamura, Katsutoshi Nekoda
4. ROM—Gheorghe Fieraru, Horatiu Nicolau, Aurel Drăgan, Iuliu Szöcs, William Schreiber, Mihai Grigorovici, Davila Plocon, Nicolae Bărbută, Eduard Derzsei, Mihai Chezan, Constantin Ganciu, Mihai Coste
5. BUL—Dimitar Karov, Yvan Gochev, Georgi Konstantinov, Petko Panteleev, Peter Kruchmarov, Simeon Srandev, Lachezar Stoyanov, Boris Gyuderov, Kiril Ivanov, Slavcho Slavov, Georgi Spasov, Angel Koritarov
6. HUN—Béla Czafik, Vilmos Iváncsó, Csaba Lantos, Gábor Bodó, István Molnár, Otto Prouza, Ferenc Tüske, Tibor Flórián, László Gálos, Antal Kangyerka, Mihály Tatár, Ferenc Jánosi

7. BRA—João Claudio Franca, Jose Schwart da Costa, Hernando Leao de Oliveira, Emanuel de Victor Newdon, Carlos Albano Feitosa, Marco Antônio Volpi, Carlos Artur Nuzman, José de Oliveira Ramalho, Décio de Azevedo, Victor Barcellos Borges
8. HOL—Jacob Korsloot, Jurjaan Kodlen, Johannes Tinkhof, Jan Martinus Oosterbaan, Robert Groenhuijzen, Pieter Swieter, Johan van Wijnen, Jacques de Vink, Dingeman van der Stoep, Jacques Ewalds, Johannes van der Hoek, Franklin Constandse

The USSR was awarded first place on the basis of a better ratio of points for and points against. The Soviets lost to Japan, but won their crucial match against Czechoslovakia, 15-9, 15-8, 5-15, 10-15, 15-7.

1968 Mexico City T: 10, N: 10, D: 10.26.

	MATCHES		GAMES			
	W	L	W	L	PF	PA
1. SOV	8	1	26	8	464	326
2. JPN	7	2	24	6	430	253
3. CZE	7	2	22	15	454	412
4. GDR	6	3	22	12	449	373
5. POL	6	3	18	11	370	280
6. BUL	4	5	16	17	379	385
7. USA	4	5	15	18	382	414
8. BEL	2	7	6	24	239	417

1. SOV—Eduard Sibiryakov, Yuri Poyarkov, Valery Kravchenko, Volodymyr Byeiyayev, Yevhen Lapinsky, Oleg Antropov, Vasilijus Matusevas, Viktor Mykhaichuk, Volodymyr Ivanov, Ivans Bugajenkovs, Boris Tereschuk, Georgy Mondzolevsky
2. JPN—Masayuki Minami, Katsutoshi Nekoda, Mamoru Shiragami, Isao Koizumi, Yasuaki Mitsumori, Jungo Morita, Tadayoshi Yokota, Seiji Oko, Tetsuo Sato, Kenji Shimaoka, Kenji Kimura
3. CZE—Antonin Procházka, Jiří Svoboda, Lubomir Zajiček, Josef Musil, Josef Smolka, Vladimir Petlák, Petr Kop, František Sokol, Bohumil Golian, Zdeněk Groessl, Pavel Schenk, Drahomír Koudelka
4. GDR—Horst Peter, Eckhardt Tielscher, Siegfried Schneider, Manfred Heine, Rainer Tscharke, Eckehard Pietzsch, Arnold Schulz, Rudi Schumann, Jürgen Kessel, Walter Toussaint, Jürgen Freiwald, Wolfgang Webner
5. POL—Stanisław Zduńczyk, Aleksander Skiba, Jerzy Szymczyk, Edward Skorek, Zbigniew Jasiukiewicz, Tadeusz Siwek, Zdzisław Ambroziak, Stanislaw Gościniak, Romuald Paszkiewicz, Hubert Wagner, Wojciech Rutkowski, Zbigniew Zarzycki
6. BUL—Alexander Trenev, Dimitar Zlatanov, Gramen Prinov, Peter Krutschmarov, Alexander Aleksandrov, Zdravko Simeonov, Milio Milev, Dimitar Karov, Kiri Slavov, Dinio Atanasov, Angel Koritarov, Stoyan Stoev
7. USA—Daniel Patterson, Pedro Velasco, John Henn, Robert "Butch" May, Larry Rundle, D. Michael Bright, Horrace Smith "Smitty" Duke, John Alstrom, Jon Stanley, Thomas Haine, Rudolph Suwara, Winthrop "Wink" Davenport
8. BEL—Jozef Mol, Paul Mesdagh, Fernand Walder, William Bossaerts, Bernard Valiant, Roger Maes, Ronald Vandewal, Hugo Huybrechts, Roger Vandergoten, Benno Saelens, Berto Poosen, Leo Dierckx

The Soviet team was upset by the United States in their opening contest. Shaken out of their complacency, they went on to win the rest of their matches easily, with only a brief five-set scare from the East Germans. They beat Japan 4-15, 15-13, 15-9, 15-13, in the decisive match.

1972 Munich T: 12, N: 12, D: 9.9.

	MATCHES		GAMES			
	W	L	W	L	PF	PA
1. JPN	7	0	21	3	348	192
2. GDR	5	2	16	8	295	256
3. SOV	6	1	19	6	340	296
4. BUL	4	3	15	14	386	347
5. ROM	4	3	9	15	300	286
6. CZE	4	3	15	9	321	274
7. KOR	3	4	10	13	284	270
8. BRA	2	5	12	16	316	373

Final: JPN—GDR 11-15, 15-2, 15-10, 15-10
3rd Place: SOV—BUL 15-11, 15-8, 15-13
5th Place: ROM—CZE 8-15, 15-7, 15-10, 16-14
7th Place: KOR—BRA 18-16, 15-7, 15-5

1. JPN—Kenji Kimura, Yoshihide Fukao, Jungo Morita, Seiji Oko, Tadayoshi Yokota, Katsutoshi Nekoda, Yasuhiro Noguchi, Kenji Shimaoka, Yuzo Nakamura, Tetsuo Nishimoto, Masayuki Minami, Tetsuo Sate
2. GDR—Siegfried Schneider, Arnold Schulz, Wolfgang Webner, Eckehard Pietzsch, Rudi Schumann, Wolfgang Weise, Horst Hagen, Horst Peter, Wolfgang Löwe, Rainer Tscharke, Wolfgang Maibohm, Jürgen Maune
3. SOV—Victor Borsch, Vyacheslav Domani, Vladimir Patkin, Leonid Zaiko, Yuri Starunski, Aleksandr Saprykine, Vladimir Kondra, Efim Chulak, Vladimir Poutiatov, Valery Kravchenko, Yevhen Lapinsky, Yuri Poyarkov
4. BUL—Dimitar Karov, Brunko Iliev, Aleksander Trenev, Ivan Ivanov, Dimitar Zlatanov, Zdravko Simeonov, Tsano Tsanov, Kiril Slavov, Emil Vulchev, Emile Trenev, Luchezar Stoyanov, Ivan Dimitrov
5. ROM—Gabriel Udisteanu, Gyula Bartha, Corneliu Oros, Laurentiu Dumănoiu, William Schreiber, Marian Stamate, Mircea Codoi, Romeo Enescu, Cristian Ion, Stelian Moculescu, Viorel Bălas
6. CZE—Drahomír Koudelka, Vladimír Petlák, Štefan Pipa, Pavel Schenk, Zdeněk Groessl, Jaroslav Stančo, Miroslav Nekola, Milan Vapenka, Lubomir Zajićek, Jaroslav Penč, Milan Vápenka, Lubomír Zajíček, Jaroslav Penc, Milan Řezníček, Jaroslav Tomáš
7. KOR—Jin Jun-tak, Kim Chung-han, Lee Yong-kwan, Kim Kun-bong, Lee Sun-koo, Choi Jong-ok, Park Kee-won, Kim Kyui-hwan, Chung Dong-kee, Kang Man-soo
8. BRA—João Jens, Jorge Delano Couto, Antônio Moreno, Luiz Coelho Zech, José Marcelino, Mário Procopio, Paulo "Bebeto" de Freitas, Décio Cattaruzzi, Alexandre Celso Kalache

1976 Montreal T: 9, N: 9, D: 7.30.

	MATCHES		GAMES			
	W	L	W	L	PF	PA
1. POL	6	0	18	9	377	293
2. SOV	4	1	14	3	247	162
3. CUB	4	2	14	7	280	212
4. JPN	2	3	8	8	157	204
5. CZE	4	2	14	7	282	234
6. KOR	2	4	10	14	245	295
7. BRA	2	3	8	11	216	228
8. ITA	0	5	2	15	125	148

Final: POL—SOV 11-15, 15-13, 12-15, 19-17, 15-7
3rd Place: CUB—JPN 15-8, 15-9, 15-8
5th Place: CZE—KOR 15-9, 10-1515-2, 15-9
7th Place: BRA—ITA 15-8, 15-6, 15-8

1. POL—Włodzimierz Stefański, Bronisław Bebel, Lech Łasko, Edward Skorek, Tomasz Wójtowicz, Wiesław Gawłowski, Mirosław Rybaczewski, Zbigniew Lubiejewski, Ryszard Bosek, Sadalski Sadalski, Zbigniew Zarzycki, Marek Karbarz

2. SOV—Anatoly Polishuk, Vyacheslav Zaitsev, Efim Chulak, Vladimir Dorohov, Aleksandr Ermilov, Pavels Selivanovs, Oleg Molyboha, Vladimir Kondra, Yuris Starunski, Vladimir Chernyshev, Vladimir Ulanov, Aleksandr Savin, Yuri Chesnokov, Vladimir Patkin
3. CUB—Leonel Marshall Steward, Victoriano Sarmientos Bios, Ernesto Martínez Hernández, Víctor García Campos, Carlos Salas Pérez, Raúl Vilches More, Jesús Savigne Savigne, Lorenzo Martínez Cordero, Diego Lapera Sotolongo, Antonio Rodríguez Aguirre, Alfredo Figueredo Ricardo, Jorge Pérez Vento
4. JPN—Takeshi Maruyema, Katsutoshi Nekoda, Katsumi Oda, Tetsuo Nishimoto, Yasunori Yasuda, Yoshihide Fukao, Shoichi Yanagimoto, Mikiyesu Tanaka, Tadayoshi Yokota, Seiji Oko, Kenji Shimaoka, Tetsuo Sate
5. CZE—Miroslav Nekola, Jaroslav Penc, Štefan Pipa, Vladimír Petlák, Josef Mikunda, Jaroslav Stančo, Vlastimil Lenert, Milan Šlambor, Pavel Řeřábek, Josef Vondrka, Drahomír Koudelka, Jaroslav Tomáš
6. KOR—Jo Jae-hak, Jeong Mun-gyeong, Gang Man-su, Kim Chung-han, Kim Geon-bong, Lee In, Lee Hui-won, Lee Chun-pyo, Lee Seon-gu, Lee Yong-gwan, Im Ho-dam, Park Gi-won
7. BRA—Paulo "Bebeto" de Freitas, Sérgio Danilas, Alexandre Abeid, Elói de Oliveira Neto, Antônio Moreno, Berhard Rajzman, William da Silva, Alexandre Celso Kalche, José Guimaraes, Jean Luc "Suíço" Rosat, Fernando "Fernandão" de Ávila
8. ITA—Andrea Nannini, Paolo Montorsi, Stefane Sibani, Giorgio Goldoni, Francesco Dall Olio, Fabrizio Nassi, Rodolfo Giovenzana, Andrea Nencini, Mario Mattioli, Giovanni Lanfranco, Erasmo Salemme, Marco Negri

The USSR and Poland reached the final match by completely different routes. The Soviet team, whose members averaged 6 feet 4¼ inches, swept through its four preliminary matches without losing a single set. Poland, on the other hand, was extended to five sets in three of their five victories, including a tense 13-15, 10-15, 15-6, 15-9, 20-18 win over Cuba. The Poles, however, were well prepared for such marathons—their daily training regimen required each player to jump 392 times over a four-and-a-half-foot barrier while wearing 20- to 30-pound weights on his legs and body. The turning point in the two-and-a-half-hour final came in the fourth set, with the Soviet Union leading two sets to one and 15-14—one point short of the gold medal. With the contest in the balance, 6-foot 7-inch Tomasz Wójtowicz smashed a long spike from behind the ten-foot line that saved the day. Eighteen serves later the Poles won the set, 19-17.

1980 Moscow T: 10, N: 10, D: 8.1.

	MATCHES		GAMES			
	W	L	W	L	PF	PA
1. SOV	6	0	18	2	297	190
2. BUL	4	2	13	8	263	241
3. ROM	4	2	13	9	290	230
4. POL	3	3	12	11	303	271
5. BRA	4	2	13	8	267	214
6. YUG	3	3	13	13	310	302
7. CUB	2	4	11	13	298	280
8. CZE	1	5	7	17	253	335

Final: SOV—BUL 15-7, 15-13, 14-16, 15-11
3rd Place: ROM—POL 15-10, 9-15, 15-13, 15-9
5th Place: BRA—YUG 14-16, 15-9, 8-15, 15-10, 15-8
7th Place: CUB—CZE 14-16, 15-7, 15-10, 15-6

1. SOV—Yuri Panchenko, Vyacheslav Zaitsev, Aleksandr Savin, Vladimir Dorokhov, Aleksandr Yermilov, Pavels Selivanovs, Oleg Moliboga, Vladimir Kondra, Vladimir Chernyshev, Fedir Lashchenov, Valery Krivov, Viljar Loor
2. BUL—Stoyan Gunchev, Hristo Stoyanov, Dimitar Zlatanov, Dimitar Dimitrov, Petke Petkov, Mitko Todorov, Kaspar Simeonov, Emil Vulchev, Hristo Iliev, Yordan Angelov, Tsano Tsanov, Stefan Dimitrov
3. ROM—Corneliu Oros, Laurenţiu Dumănoiu, Dan Gîrleanu, Nicu Stoian, Sorin Macavei, Constantin Sterea, Nicolae Pop, Günther Enescu, Valter Korneliu Chifu, Marius Chata-Chiţiga
4. POL—Robert Malinowski, Maciej Jarosz, Wiesław Czaja, Lech Łasko, Tomasz Wójtowicz, Wiesław Gawłowski, Wojciech Drzyzga, Boguslaw Kanicki, Ryszard Bosek, Włodzimierz Nalazek, Leszek Molenda
5. BRA—João Graneiro, Mário "Xandó" de Oliveira Neto, Antônio "Badalhoca" Gueiros Ribeiro, José Montanaro, Antônio Moreno, Renan dal Zotto, William da Silva, Amauri Ribeiro, Bernardo Rocha Rezende, Jean Luc "Suíço" Rosat, Deraldo Wanderley, Bernard Rajzman
6. YUG—Vladimir Bogoevski, Vladimir Trifunović, Aleksandar Tasevski, Zdravko Kuljić, Goran Srbinovski, Ivica Jelić, Boro Jović, Radovan Malević, Miodrag Mitić, Ljubomir Travica, Mladen Kasić, Slobodan Lozancić
7. CUB—Diego Lapera Sotolongo, Victor García Campos, Luis Oviedo Ponilla, Ernesto Martínez Hernández, Ricardo Leyva, Jorge Garbey Castillo, Raúl Vilches More, Carlos Salas Pérez, Antonio Pérez Vento Machado, Leonel Marshall Steward, Sr., Carlos Ruiz Lafargue, José David Suárez
8. CZE—Igor Prieložný, Pavel Valach, Vlado Sirvoň, Ján Repák, Josef Novotný, Jaroslav Šmíd, Vlastimil Lenert, Nicu Stoian, Ján Cifra, Pavel Řeřábek, Josef Pick, Cyril Krejčí

The team from Libya had a particularly difficult tournament, losing all five matches and all 15 sets, and scoring only 30 points while giving up 225.

1984 Los Angeles-Long Beach T: 10, N: 10, D: 8.11.

	MATCHES		GAMES			
	W	L	W	L	PF	PA
1. USA	5	1	15	4	258	159
2. BRA	4	2	13	8	267	214
3. ITA	4	2	15	7	280	231
4. CAN	3	3	10	9	221	212
5. KOR	5	1	15	8	312	253
6. ARG	2	4	11	13	282	307
7. JPN	4	2	13	8	271	245
8. CHN	1	5	4	15	200	261

Final: USA—BRA 15-6, 15-6, 15-7
3rd Piece: ITA—CAN 15-11, 15-12, 15-8
5th Place: KOR—ARG 15-13, 9-15, 15-9, 15-7
7th Place: JPN—CHN 16-14, 15-9, 15-6

1. USA—Douglas "Dusty" Dvorak, David Saunders, Stephen Salmons, Paul Sunderland, Richard Duwelius, Stephen Timmons, Craig Buck, Marc Waldie, Christian Marlowe, Aldis Berzins, Patrick Powers, Charles "Karch" Kiraly
2. BRA—Bernardo "Bernardinho" Rezende, Mário "Xandó" de Oliveira Neto, Antônio "Badalhoca" Gueiros Ribeiro, José Montanaro, Ruy Campos Nascimento, Renan dal Zotto, William Carvalho Silva, Amauri Ribeiro, Marcus Vinícius Freire Simões, Domingos Lampariello Neto, Bernard Rajzman, Fernando "Fernandão" de Ávila
3. ITA—Marco Negri, Pier Paolo Lucchetta, Gian Carlo Dametto, France Bertoli, Francesco Dall'Olio, Piero Rebaudengo, Giovanni Errichiello, Guido De Luigi, Fabio Vullo, Giovanni Lanfranco, Paolo Vecchi, Andrea Lucchetta

4. CAN—Glenn Hoag, Terry Danyluk, John Barrett, Dave Jones, Paul Gratton, Al Coulter, Tom Jones, Don Saxton, Randy Wagner, Alex Ketyzynski, Rick Bacon, Garth Pischke
5. KOR—Lee Jeng-kyung, Kang Doo-tae, Chang Yoon-chang, Lee Yong-sun, Lee Bum-joo, Yang Jin-wung, Moon Yong-kwan, Yoo Joong-tak, Kim Ho-chul, No Jin-su, Kang Man-soo, Chung Euy-tak
6. ARG—Daniel Castellani, Esteban Martínez, Carlos Wagenpfeil, Alejandro Díz, Hugo Conte, Waldo Kantor, Raúl Quiroga, Jon Uriarte, Alcides Cuminetti, Leonardo Wiernes
7. JPN—Koshi Sobu, Eiji Shimomura, Kazuya Mitake, Eizabura Mitsuhashi, Hiroaki Okuno, Yasushi Furukawa, Shuji Yamada, Mikiyasu Tanaka, Kimio Sugimoto, Minoru Iwata, Akihiro Iwashima, Shunichi Kawai
8. CHN—Yan Jianming, Song Jinwei, Yu Juemin, Zhai Jixin, Zhang Yousheng, Yang Liqun, Cao Ping, Shen Keqin, Zuo Yue, Xiao Jinsong, Zhao Duo, Liu Changcheng

Considering that volleyball was invented in the United States (by William G. Morgan in Holyoke, Massachusetts, in 1895), the US had been remarkably unsuccessful in international competition, qualifying for the Olympics only once since it became an official sport in 1964. However, the long drought ended in 1984. The US team went to Los Angeles with a 24-match winning streak, including four straight victories over the world champion Soviet team, all of which took place in the USSR. The streak was ended in the fourth match of the tournament when an inspired Brazilian team beat the Americans 15-12, 15-11, 15-2. But five nights later, in the final, the US turned the tables on the Brazilians, overwhelming them in straight sets.

1988 Seoul T: 12 N: 12 D: 10.2.

	MATCHES		GAMES			
	W	L	W	L	PF	PA
1. USA	7	0	21	4	366	211
2. SOV	5	2	18	7	332	282
3. ARG	4	3	14	12	325	317
4. BRA	4	3	16	13	374	342
5. HOL	5	2	16	9	314	272
6. BUL	3	4	10	12	259	270
7. SWE	3	4	14	16	350	388
8. FRA	3	4	12	13	312	300

Final: USA—SOV 13-15, 15-10, 15-4, 15-8
3rd Place: ARG—BRA 15-10, 15-17, 15-8, 12-15, 15-9
5th Place: HOL—BUL 15-6, 15-8, 15-10
7th Place: SWE—FRA 12-15, 15-5, 8-15, 15-12, 15-12

1. USA—Troy Tanner, David Saunders, Jonathan Root, Robert Ctvrtlik, R. Douglas Partle, Stephen Timmons, Craig Buck, Scott Fortune, Ricci Luyties, Jeffery Stork, Eric Sato, Charles "Karch" Kiraly
2. SOV—Yuri Panchenko, Andrei Kuznetsov, Vyacheslav Zaitsev, Igor Runev, Vladimir Shkurikhin, Yevgeny Krasilnikov, Raimonds Vilde, Valery Losev, Yuri Sapega, Oleksander Sorokolit, Yaroslav Antonov, Yuri Cherednik
3. ARG—Claudio Zulianello, Daniel Castellani, Esteban Martínez, Alejandro Diz, Daniel Colla, Carlos Javier Weber, Hugo Conte, Waldo Kantor, Raúl Quiroga, Jon Uriarte, Esteban de Palma, Juan Carlos Cuminetti
4. BRA—Mauricio Cemargo Lima, Wagner Rocha, Paulo Roese, José Montanaro, Paulo "Paulão" Jukoski da Silva, Renan dal Zotto, William da Silva, Amauri Ribeiro, Antônio "Carlão" Aguiar Gouveia, Domingos Lampariello Neto, Leonídio de Pra Filho, André "Pampa" Falbo Ferreira
5. HOL—Martin Teffer, Pieter-Jan Leeuwerink, Ronald Boudrie, Jan-Marcus Posthuma, Ronald Zoodsma, Ronald Zwerver, Avital Selinger, Edwin Benne, Teunis Buys, Peter Blange, Marco Brouwers, Karl Grabert
6. BUL—Kostedin Mitev, Petyo Draguiev, Borislav Kyossev, Ljubomir Ganev, Ilian Kaziiski, Dimo Tonev, Petko Petkov, Plamen Hristov, Sava Kovachev, Nayden Naydenov, Milcho Milanov, Tzvetan Florov
7. SWE—Urban Lennartsson, Jannis Keimazidis, Jan Hedengård Karlsson, Tomas Hoszek, Anders Lundmark, Per-Anders Sääf, Bengt Gustafson, Håkan Björne, Lars Nilsson, Peter Tholse, Patrik Johanssen
8. FRA—Philippe Blain, Hervé Mazzon, Eric N'Gapeth, Eric Bouvier, Christophe Meneau, Jean-Marc Jurkovitz, Laurent Tillie, Olivier Rossard, Patrick Duflos, Alain Fabiani, Philippe-Marie Salvan

The US team faced a stiff challenge from Argentina in the preliminary round, losing the first two sets before coming from behind to win the last three, exactly as they had in the 1987 Pan Am Games. In the final, the Americans confronted their number one rivals—and drinking buddies—the team from the USSR. The two teams had already played nine matches in 1988 with the US winning seven. In the Olympic final, the Americans, all of whom grew up in Southern California, wore down the Soviets in the first two sets, then overwhelmed them in the last two.

The bronze medal match between Argentina and Brazil was an epic struggle that lasted 3 hours and 10 minutes. The starting lineup for the Dutch team, which placed fifth, *averaged* 6 feet 7⅝ inches (2.02 meters).

1992 Barcelona T: 12, N: 12, D: 8.9.

	MATCHES		GAMES			
	W	L	W	L	PF	PA
1. BRA	8	0	24	3	395	263
2. HOL	4	4	14	14	355	316
3. USA	6	2	20	13	445	400
4. CUB	5	3	17	11	356	311
5. ITA	6	2	21	8	400	301
6. JPN	3	5	13	20	396	448
7. SOV	4	4	17	15	399	394
8. SPA	3	5	13	21	396	453

Final: BRA—HOL 15-12, 15-8, 15-5
3rd Place: USA—CUB 12-15, 15-13, 15-7, 15-11
5th Place: ITA—JPN 15-2, 15-7, 15-13
7th Place: SOV—SPA 16-14, 12-15, 15-8, 5-15, 15-12

1. BRA—Marcelo Teles Negrão, Jorge Souza de Brito, Giovane Farinazzo Gavio, Paulo "Paulão" Jukoski da Silva, Maurício Camargo Lima, Janelsen Carvalho Santos, Douglas Chiarotti, Antônio "Carlão" Aguiar Gouveia, Talmo Curto de Oliveira, André "Pampa" Falbo Ferreira, Alexandre "Tande" Ramos Samuel, Amauri Ribeiro
2. HOL—Martin Teffer, Henk-Jan Held, Ronald Boudrie, Jan-Marcus Posthuma, Ronald Zwerver, Avital Selinger, Edwin Benne, Peter Blange, Marko Klok, Roelof van der Meulen, Martin van der Horst, Ronald Zoodsma
3. USA—Robert Ctvrtlik, Stephen Timmons, Scott Fortune, Jeffery Stork, Eric Sato, Carlos Briceno, Nick Becker, Bryan Ivie, Brent Hilliard, Robert Samuelson, R. Douglas Partie

4. CUB—Freddy Brooks Bongó, Joël Despaigne Charles, Idalberto Valdes Pedro, Lazaro Beltran Rizo, Félix Millán Casanova, Rodolfo Sánchez Sánchez, Raúl Diago Izquierdo, Abel Sarmientos Bios, Osvaldo Hernández Chambert, Lázaro Marín Ortega, Nicolás Vives Coffigne, Ihosvany Hernández Riera
5. ITA—Andrea Gardini, Paolo Tofoli, Roberto Masciarelli, Claudio Marco Galli, Marco Bracci, Lorenzo Bernardi, Luca Cantagalli, Andrea Zorzi, Andrea Lucchetta, Andrea Giani, Fabio Vullo, Michele Pasinato
6. JPN—Takashi Narita, Katsumi Kawano, Yuichi Nakagaichi, Akihiko Matsuda, Masafumi Oura, Tatsuya Ueta, Masaji Ogino, Katsuyuki Minami, Shigeru Aoyama, Junichi Kuriuzawa, Hideyuki Otake, Masayuki Izumikawa
7. SOV—Oleg Shatunov, Aleksandr Shadchin, Ruslan Olikhver, Igor Runov, Andrei Kuznetsov, Yevgeny Krasilnikov, Yuri Korovyansky, Dmitri Fomin, Konstantin Ushakov, Yuri Cherednik, Sergei Gorbunov, Pavel Shishkin
8. SPA—Juan Robles Ania, Venancio Costa Monge, Francisco Sánchez Jover, Jesús Sánchez Jover, José Maroto Díaz, Ángel Alonso Nieto, Benjamín Vicedo Mayor, Héctor López Izquierdo, Francisco Hervás Tirada, Rafael Pascual Cortés, Ernesto Rodríguez Gómez

An unusual incident took place in the opening match between the United States and Japan. The Japanese were leading two games to one and 14-13 in the fourth game, when the umpire, Laert de Souza of Brazil, issued a yellow card to United States middle blocker Bob Samuelson for arguing a call. Because Samuelson had already received a yellow card earlier in the game, he should have been ejected from the match and Japan should have been awarded a point—a point that would have given Japan the victory. But referee Ramis Samedov of Azerbaijan didn't want to end a match on a penalty point and instead waved for play to continue. The Americans fought off match point and went on to win in five games. Japan protested and the next day the International Volleyball Federation control committee voted unanimously to award the victory to Japan. Samuelson suffered from alopecia universalis, a condition that left him bald. As a show of solidarity, the other eleven members of the United States team showed up for their next match with their heads completely shaved. The Americans won their next five matches, but were well beaten by Brazil in the semifinals.

In fact, Brazil raced through the entire tournament without being seriously challenged. The same could not be said of their opponents in the final, the team from the Netherlands. The Dutch placed only fourth in their preliminary pool of six teams, losing to Cuba, Brazil, and the team from the ex-Soviet Union. But in the quarterfinals they stunned tournament favorite Italy, 15-9, 12-15, 8-15, 15-2, 17-16. The Dutch beat the Cubans in straight games in the semifinals, but were outclassed by Brazil in the final.

The Dutch team, which averaged 6 feet 7 inches, would have set the record for the tallest team in Olympic history had not their average been brought down by 5-foot 9-inch Avital Selinger, the coach's son. Ten of their 12 members were at least 2 meters (6 feet 6¾) tall.

1996 Atlanta T: 12, N: 12, D: 8.4.

	MATCHES		GAMES			
	W	L	W	L	PF	PA
1. HOL	7	1	21	6	375	269
2. ITA	7	1	23	5	406	179
3. YUG	5	3	16	14	374	336
4. RUS	3	5	11	15	305	337
5. BRA	5	3	17	10	367	331
6. CUB	5	3	15	12	373	330
7. BUL	4	4	15	16	378	396
8. ARG	3	5	15	18	362	404

Final: HOL—ITA 15-12, 9-15, 16-14, 9-15, 17-15
3rd Place: YUG—RUS 15-8, 7-15, 15-8, 15-9
5th Place: BRA—CUB 15-12, 16-14, 16-14
7th Place: BUL—ARG 15-10, 15-10, 7-15, 7-15, 20-18

1. HOL—Misha Latuhihin, Hendrik Jan Held, Engelbrecht Rodenburg, Guido Görtzen, Richard Schuil, Ronald Zwerver, Sebastiaan van de Goor, Jan Posthuma, Roelof van der Meulen, Peter Blangé, Robert Grabert, Mike van de Goor
2. ITA—Andrea Gardini, Marco Meoni, Pasquale Gravina, Paolo Tofoli, Samuele Papi, Andrea Sartoretti, Marco Bracci, Lorenzo Bernardi, Luca Cantagalli, Andrea Zorzi, Andrea Giani, Vigor Bovolenta
3. YUG—Đorđe Đurić, Žarko Petrović, Vladimir Batez, Željko Tanasković, Dejan Brđović, Đula Mešter, Slobodan Kovač, Nikola Grbić, Vladimir Grbić, Rajko Jokanović, Goran Vujević
4. RUS—Oleg Shatunov, Vadym Khamutskich, Sergei Orlenko, Ruslan Olikhver, Aleksei Kazakov, Dmitri Fomin, Sergei Tetyukin, Pavel Shichkin, Konstantin Uchakov, Stanislav Dineikin, Igor Shulepov, Valery Goryushev
5. BRA—Marcelo Teles Negrão, Cássio Leandro Pereira, Giovane Farinazzo Gavio, Paulo "Paulão" Juroski da Silva, Maurício Camargo Lima, Fábio "Pinha" Marcelino, Antônio "Carlao" Aguiar Gouveia, Max Pereira, Nalbert Bitencourt, Alexandre "Tande" Ramos Samuel, Gílson Bernardo, Carlos Schwanke
6. CUB—Freddy Brooks Bongó, Nicolás Vives Coffigne, Ricardo Vantes Rodríguez, Joël Despaigne Charles, Rodolfo Sánchez Sánchez, Raúl Diago Izquierdo, Osvaldo Hernández Chambert, Alain Roca Borrero, Ihosvany Hernández Riera, Angel Beltrán Mariño, Alexis Batle Arredondo, Lázaro Marín Ortega
7. BUL—Martin Stoev, Ludmil Naydenov, Lubomir Ganev, Dimo Tonev, Nikolay Yeliazkov, Plamen Khristo, Petar Uzunov, Nayden Naydenov, Nikolay Ivanov, Ivaylo Gavrilov, Evgeni Ivanov, Plamen Konstantinov
8. ARG—Marcos Milinkovic, Jorge Elgueta, Sebastian Jabif, Leandro Maly, Guillermo Quaini, Carlos Javier Weber, Fernando Borrero, Alejandro Romano, Sebastián Firpo, Pablo Pereira, Guillermo Martínez, Eduardo Rodríguez

There was little doubt that the final would match Italy and the Netherlands. Italy had dominated men's volleyball for seven years, but lacked an Olympic championship because they were upset by the Dutch in the 1992 quarterfinals. Italy then defeated the Netherlands in the final of the 1993

European Championship, the 1994 world championship, the 1995 European championship and the 1995 World Cup. Three weeks before the 1996 Olympics, the Dutch finally beat the Italians, winning the final of the World League tournament 17-15, 15-12, 10-15, 10-15, 22-20.

The two teams met in the preliminary round at the Olympics with Italy winning easily, 15-8, 15-8, 15-13. They faced each other yet again in the final. After splitting the first four games, they played a tense fifth set. The score was tied at every point from 8 to 14. Italy earned match point at 15-14, but the Dutch scored three times in a row to frustrate Italy's Olympic dreams again.

Yugoslavia had never won a volleyball medal. They won their first three games. Then their captain, Dejan Brdović, rushed home when his 14-month-old son died of a brain tumor. Yugoslavia lost to the Netherlands and Italy, but then upset Brazil in the quarterfinals. After losing to the Italians in four sets in the semifinals, the Yugoslavs beat Russia in four sets to earn an emotion-filled place on the medal platform.

2000 Sydney T: 12, N: 12, D: 10.1.

	MATCHES		GAMES			
	W	L	W	L	PF	PA
1. YUG	6	2	21	11	765	707
2. RUS	6	2	19	13	739	714
3. ITA	7	1	21	8	725	629
4. ARG	3	5	11	18	643	716
5. HOL	6	2	20	8	678	594
6. BRA	6	2	19	9	674	606
7. CUB	4	4	16	13	669	595
8. AUS	2	6	7	19	505	621

Final: YUG—RUS 25-22, 25-22, 25-20
3rd Place: ITA—ARG 25-16, 25-15, 25-18
5th Place: HOL—BRA 25-21, 25-20, 25-22
7th Place: CUB—AUS 25-23, 25-11, 25-15

1. YUG—Vladimir Batez, Slobodan Boškan, Andrija Gerić, Nikola Grbić, Vladimir Grbić, Slobodan Kovač, Đula Mešter, Vasa Mijić, Ivan Miljković, Goran Vujević, Igor Vušurović
2. RUS—Igor Shulepov, Valery Goryushev, Aleksandr Gerasimov, Roman Yakovlev, Aleksey Kazakov, Vadym Khamutskich, Aleksey Kuleshov, Yevgeny Mitkov, Ruslan Olikhver, Ilya Savelyev, Sergey Tetyukhin, Konstantin Ushakov
3. ITA—Alessandro Fei, Andrea Gardini, Andrea Giani, Andrea Sartoretti, Luigi Mastrangelo, Marco Bracci, Marco Meoni, Mirko Corsano, Paolo Tofoli, Pasquale Gravina, Samuele Papi, Simone Rosalba
4. ARG—Jerónimo Bidegain, Hugo Conte, Sebastián Firpo, Christian Lares, Leandro Maly, Pablo Meana, Marcos Milinkovic, Leandro Patti, Pablo Pereira, Juan Pablo Porello, Alejandro Spajic, Carlos Javier Weber
5. HOL—Albert Cristina, Sebastiaan van de Goor, Guido Görtzen, Joost Kooistra, Martijn Dieleman, Johannes Martinus van der Horst, Mike van de Goor, Peter Blangé, Reinder Nummerdor, Richard Schuil
6. BRA—Alexandre "Tande" Ramos Samuel, Andre Heller, Dante Guimarães Santos do Amaral, Douglas Chiarotti, Gilberto "Giba" de Godoy Filho, Gilmar "Kid" Nascimento Teixeira, Giovane Farinazzo Gávio, Gustavo Endres, Marcelo Elgarten, . Maurício Camargo Lima, Max Pereira, Nalbert Bitencourt
7. CUB—Alain Roca Borrero, Alexeis Argilagos Segura, Angel Denis Díaz, Ihosvany Hernández Riera, Ivan Benito Ruiz Cuesta, Leonel Marshall Borges, Nicolás Vives Coffigne, Osvaldo Hernández Chambert, Pavel Pimienta Allen, Ramón Gato Moya, Raúl Diago Izquierdo, Yosenki García Díaz
8. AUS—Benjamin Hardy, Benjamin Loft, Daniel Howard, Daniel Ronan, David Beard, Hidde van Beest, Mark Williams, Nathan Jakavicius, Russell Wentworth, Scott Newcomb, Spiros Marazios, Steve Keir

Italy entered the tournament as the three-time defending world champion. They went through pool play undefeated and beat Australia in four sets in the quarterfinals. However, in the semifinals the Italians were knocked out by Yugoslavia in straight sets 27-25, 34-32, 25-14. Brazil was even more dominant in their preliminary pool, winning all five matches and losing only one set. But in the quarterfinals, they fell to Argentina 17-25, 25-21, 25-19, 27-25. Russia qualified for the final by defeating Argentina 27-25, 32-30, 21-25, 25-11. In their opening match of pool play, Russia had beaten Yugoslavia in four sets. In fact, Yugoslavia lost their second match as well, falling to Italy. But then the Yugoslavians caught fire. They finished pool play with three wins and knocked out the Netherlands in a five-set cliff hanger before their semifinal defeat of Italy. The final turned out to be an anticlimax as Yugoslavia beat Russia in straight sets.

2004 Athens T: 12, N: 12, D: 8.29.

	MATCHES		GAMES			
	W	L	W	L	PF	PA
1. BRA	7	1	22	8	734	635
2. ITA	5	3	20	11	724	679
3. RUS	5	3	17	13	685	671
4. USA	4	4	14	16	670	685
5. ARG	3	3	13	12	568	558
5. GRE	3	3	14	12	585	568
5. POL	3	3	10	12	487	496
5. SER	4	2	13	9	530	505

Final: BRA–ITA 25-15, 24-26, 25-20, 25-22
3rd Place: RUS–USA 25-22, 27-25, 25-16

1. BRA—Nalbert Bitencourt, Dante Guimarães Santos do Amaral, Sérgio "Escadinha" dos Santos, Gustavo Endres, Ricardo "Ricardinho" Garcia, Giovane Farinazzo Gávio, Gilberto "Giba" de Godoy Filho, André Heller, Maurício Camargo Lima, André Nascimento, Anderson Rodrigues, Rodrigo "Rodrigão" Santana
2. ITA—Matej Cernic, Alberto Cisolla, Paolo Cozzi, Alessandro Fei, Andrea Giani, Luigi Mastrangelo, Samuele Papi, Damiano Pippi, Andrea Sartoretti, Ventzislav Simeonov, Paolo Tofoli, Valerio Vermiglio
3. RUS—Pavel Abramov, Sergey Baranov, Stanislav Dineykin, Aleksey Kazakov, Vadim Khamutskikh, Taras Khtey, Aleksandr Kosaryev, Aleksei Kuleshov, Sergei Tetyukhin, Konstantin Ushakov, Aleksei Verbov, Andrei Yegorchev

4. USA—Lloy Ball, Kevin Barnett, Brook Billings, Phillip Eatherton, Gabriel Gardner, Thomas Hoff, Ryan Millar, William Priddy, Clayton Salmon, Clayton Stanley, Erik Sullivan, Donald Suxho
5. ARG—Jerónimo Bidegain, Santiago Darraidou, Jorge Alberto Elgueta, Hernán Ferraro, Gastón Giani, Diego Gutiérrez, Pablo Meana, Marcos Milinkovic, Leandro Patti, Pablo Peralta, Gustavo Porporatto, Alejandro Spajic
5. GRE—Tontor-Zlatko Baev, Marios Giourdas, Theodoros Khatziantoniou, Konstantinos Khristofidelis, Vasileios Kournetas, Andrei Kravarik, Ilias Lappas, Sotirios Pantaleon, Konstantinos Prousalis, Nikolaos Roumeliotis, Georgios Stefanou, Antonios Tsakiropoulos
5. POL—Michał Bąkiewicz, Piotr Gabrych, Arkadiusz Gołaś, Piotr Gruszka, Krzysztof Ignaczak, Łukasz Kadziewicz, Dawid Murek, Radosław Rybak, Andrzej Stelmach, Sebastian Świderski, Robert Szczerbaniuk, Paweł Zagumny
5. SER—Vladan Đorđević, Andrija Gerić, Nikola Grbić, Vladimir Grbić, Ivan Ilić, Milan Marković, Đula Mešter, Vasa Mijić, Ivan Miljković, Aleksandar Mitrović, Milan Vašić, Goran Vujević

The clear favorites in Athens were the Brazilians, who had won the 2002 world championship, the 2003 World Cup, and the 2004 World League titles. In pool play, Brazil did lose a four-set match to the United States, but only after they had already clinched first place in the pool. In the other pool, Serbia and Montenegro came back from a opening-match loss to Poland to sweep their remaining four games and finish first. However, they were knocked out in the quarterfinals by Russia 29-27, 23-25, 27-25, 28-26. In the semifinals, the Brazilians, playing for keeps, defeated the United States in straight sets, 25-16, 25-17, 25-23. Meanwhile, second-ranked Italy, which had finished second to Brazil in the 2003 World Cup and the 2004 World League, advanced to the final by beating Argentina 22-25, 25-22, 26-24, 28-26 in the quarterfinals and Russia 25-16, 25-17, 25-16 in the semifinals. The Italians managed to win the second set of the final, but it was the Brazilians who prevailed. Brazilian setter Mauricio Lima, appearing in his fifth Olympics, earned his second gold medal twelve years after he won his first at the 1992 Barcelona Games.

2008 Beijing T: 12, N: 12, D: 8.24.

	MATCHES		GAMES			
	W	**L**	**W**	**L**	**PF**	**PA**
1. USA	8	0	24	9	773	673
2. BRA	6	2	20	8	687	602
3. RUS	6	2	22	11	774	707
4. ITA	5	3	17	14	700	679
5. BUL	3	3	11	12	530	535
5. CHN	2	4	9	16	493	567
5. POL	4	2	14	9	543	515
5. SER	2	4	11	13	543	545

Final: USA—BRA 20-25, 25-22, 25-21, 25-23
3rd Place: RUS—ITA 25-22, 25-19, 25-23

1. USA—Scott Touzinsky, Clayton Stanley, Riley Salmon, Sean Rooney, Reid Priddy, Ryan Millar, David Lee, Richard Lambourne, Thomas Hoff, Kevin Hansen, Gabriel Gardner, Lloy Ball
2. BRA—Sérgio "Escadinha" Dutra dos Santos, Rodrigo "Rodrigão" Santana, Anderson de Oliveira Rodrigues, Bruno "Bruninho" Mossa de Rezende, André da Silva Nascimento, André Heller, Gilberto "Giba" Amauri de Godoy Filho, Samuel Fuchs, Gustavo Endres, Murilo Endres, Marcelo "Marcelinho" Elgarten, Dante Guimarães Santos do Amaral
3. RUS—Aleksandr Volkov, Aleksey Verbov, Sergey Tetyukhin, Semyon Poltavsky, Aleksey Ostapenko, Maksim Mikhaylov, Aleksey Kuleshov, Aleksandr Kosaryev, Aleksandr Korneyev, Vadim Khamuttskikh, Sergey Grankin, Yury Borozhko
4. ITA—Hristo Zlatanov, Valerio Vermiglio, Alessandro Paparoni, Marco Meoni, Luigi Mastrangelo, Matteo Martino, Mauro Gavotto, Alessandro Fei, Mirko Corsano, Alberto Cisolla, Vigor Bovolenta, Emanuele Birarelli
5. BUL—Andrey Zhekov, Boyan Yordanov, Khristo Tsvetanov, Ivan Tasev, Kostadin Stoykov, Teodor Salparov, Vladimir Nikolov, Plamen Konstantinov, Matey Kaziyski, Evgeni Ivanov, Krasimir Gaydarski, Todor Aleksiev
5. CHN—Yuan Zhi, Yu Dawei, Sui Shengsheng, Shi Hairong, Shen Qiong, Ren Qi, Jiao Shuai, Jiang Fudong, Guo Peng, Fang Yingchao, Cui Jianjun, Bian Hongmin
5. POL—Paweł Zagumny, Paweł Woicki, Mariusz Wlazły, Michał Winiarski, Martin Wika, Sebastian Świderski, Daniel Pliński, Marcin Możdżonek, Łukasz Kadziewicz, Krzysztof Ignaczak, Piotr Gruszka, Krzysztof Gierczyński
5. SER—Saša Starović, Marko Samardžić, Marko Podraščanin, Vlado Petković, Miloš Nikić, Ivan Miljković, Nikola Kovačević, Bojan Janić, Nikola Grbić, Andrija Gerić, Dejan Bojović, Novica Bjelica

The men's volleyball competition was marked by a shocking tragedy on the first day of competition, when the father-in-law of US men's coach Hugh McCutcheon was murdered by a deranged knife-wielding man while visiting the Beijing Drum Tower, a popular historic tourist site. Todd and Barbara Bachman, along with their Chinese tour guide, were attacked and stabbed by a former metal-worker from Hangzhou, who then killed himself by jumping off a 130-ft. (39.6 m) balcony. The Bachmans' daughter, 2004 volleyball Olympian Elisabeth "Wiz" McCutcheon, was with them at the time but was unhurt. Todd Bachman died of his wounds, while Barbara and the Chinese guide survived, Barbara after eight hours of surgery. Hugh McCutcheon missed the US team's first three matches to sit with his wife at her mother's hospital bed.

United by the tragedy, the US team won all five of their preliminary matches, dedicating their opening game to the family, a 3-2 win over Venezuela. They were the only team to finish pool play without a single loss. In the other round-robin pool, three teams finished with a 4-1 record: Brazil, Russia and Poland. Brazil had the strongest pre-Olympics record, having won both the 2006 world championship and the 2007 world cup, with Poland taking silver in 2006 and Russia taking silver in 2007.

The US continued their impressive performance in the knockout rounds, fighting to a 20-25, 25-23, 21-25, 25-18, 15-12 victory over Serbia in the quarterfinals and beating Russia 25-22, 25-21, 25-27, 22-25, 15-13 in the semis.

The US faced defending Olympic champion Brazil in the final, losing the opening set 20-25. Led by top scorer Clayton Stanley, the team came back to narrowly win the next two sets 25-22 and 25-21. Down two points in the fourth set, the US came from behind to win 25-23, ending the emotional two-and-a-half week run.

"On the one hand, I mourn the loss of my father-in-law greatly and my heart aches for my wife and our family for the loss," coach McCutcheon said after the victory. "On the other hand, I am extremely proud and happy for my team and USA Volleyball as an organization and the thing we've been able to achieve over these four years. Those are the two emotions I have. They are conflicted, obviously, but I cannot change what happened in either sphere."

Tokyo, 1964
The famous 1964 Japanese women's volleyball team in action.

WOMEN

1896–1960 not held

1964 Tokyo T: 6 N: 6 D: 10.23.

	MATCHES		GAMES			
	W	L	W	L	PF	PA
1. JPN	5	0	15	1	238	93
2. SOV	4	1	12	3	212	97
3. POL	3	2	10	6	180	162
4. ROM	2	3	6	9	140	172
5. USA	1	4	3	12	98	213
6. KOR	0	5	0	15	94	225

1. JPN—Masae Kasai, Emiko Miyamoto, Kinuko Tanida, Yuriko Handa, Yoshiko Matsumura, Sata Isobe, Katsumi Matsumure, Yoko Shinozaki, Setsuko Sasaki, Yuko Fujimoto, Masako Kondo, Ayano Shibuki
2. SOV—Nelli Abramova, Astra Biltauere, Lyudmila Buldakova, Lyudmilla Hureyeva, Valentina Kamenek, Marita Katusheva, Ninel Lukanina, Valentyna Myshak, Tatyana Roshchina,. Inna Ryskal, Antonina Ryzchova, Tamara Tikhonina
3. POL—Krystyna Czajkowska, Maria Golimowska, Krystyna Jakubowska, Danuta Kordaczuk-Wagner, Krystyna Krupa, Józefa Ledwig, Jadwiga Marko, Jadwiga Rutkowska, Maria Śliwka, Zofia Szcześniewska
4. ROM—Ana Mocanu, Cornelia Lăzeanu, Natalia Todorovschi, Doina Ivănescu, Doina Popescu, Sonia Colceru, Lia Vanea, Alexandrina Chezan, Ileana Enculescu, Elisabeta Goloşie, Marina Stanca, Doina Coste
5. USA—Jean Gaertner, Gail O'Rourke, Linda Murphy, Louisa Galloway, Verneda Thomas, Mary Perry, Mary Peppler, Nancy Owen, Patricia Bright, Jane Ward, Sharon Peterson, Barbara Harwerth
6. KOR—Suh Choon-kang, Moon Kyung-sook, Ryoo Choonja, Kim Kil-ja, Oh Soon-ok, Chung Jong-uen, Choi Don-hi, Hong Nam-sun, Oh Chung-ja, Yoon Jung-sook, Kwak Ryong-ja, Lee Keun-soo

Ten of the 12 members of the Japanese team came from the Nichibo spinning mill in Kaizuku, near Osaka. Their coach, the notorious Hirofumi Daimatsu, was the manager of the office supplies procurement department at the mill. Daimatsu was famous for his draconian methods: hitting the young women on the head, kicking them on their hips, insulting them, goading them, making them practice a minimum of six hours a day, seven days a week, 51 weeks a year. He was the first coach to introduce the rolling receive, in which a player dives to the ground, hits the ball, rolls over, and returns quickly to her feet.

Japanese sports fans looked forward with great anticipation to the Olympic volleyball tournament. Their great hopes almost met with disaster when the North Korean team withdrew over a political dispute, leaving the competition one team short of the six required to conduct an official tournament. The Japanese solved the problem by giving the South Korean Olympic Committee team 1,000,000 yen to send a team. The Japanese were never seriously challenged. The only time they lost a set (15-13, to Poland) was because Daimatsu pulled some of his better players when he saw that the Soviet coach was watching. The final Japanese victory over the USSR gained an 80 percent audience rating on Japanese television.

After the game, the team captain, 31-year-old Masae Kasai, was invited to the official residence of Japan's prime minister, Eisaku Sato. She confessed to Sato that she wanted to marry, but that her rigorous training schedule had prevented her from meeting any men. Sato promised to help her and subsequently introduced Kasai to Kazuo Nakamura, whom she later married. As for Daimatsu, he quit coaching and joined an advertising agency. In 1968 he was elected to the House of Councilors, the upper house of the Japanese Parliament. He served until 1974 and died of a heart attack in 1978.

1968 Mexico City T: 8, N: 8 D: 10.26.

	MATCHES		GAMES			
	W	L	W	L	PF	PA
1. SOV	7	0	21	3	333	194
2. JPN	6	1	19	3	318	147
3. POL	5	2	15	11	324	304
4. PER	3	4	12	15	306	327
5. KOR	3	4	11	14	276	305
6. CZE	3	4	11	15	307	307
7. MEX	1	6	7	18	215	228
8. USA	0	7	4	21	196	353

1. SOV—Lyudmila Buldakova, Lyudmila Mikhailovskaya, Vera Lantratova, Vera Galushka, Tatyana Sarycheva, Tatyana Ponyayeva, Nina Smoleyeva, Inna Ryskal, Galina Leontyeva, Roza Salikhova, Valentina Vinogradova (Kamenek)
2. JPN—Setsuko Yoshika, Suzue Takayama, Toyoko Iwahara, Yukiyo Kojima, Sachiko Fukunaka, Kunie Shishikura, Setsuko Inoue, Sumie Oinuma, Keiko Hama
3. POL—Krystyna Czajkowska, Józefa Ledwig, Elżbieta Porzec, Wanda Wiecha, Zofia Szcześniewska, Krystyna Jakubowska, Lidia Żmuda-Chmielnicka, Barbara Niemczyk, Halina Aszkiełowicz, Krystyna Krupa, Jadwiga Marko-Książek, Krystyna Ostromęcka
4. PER—Esperanza Jiménez Pérez, Teresa Nuñez Laos, Irma Cordero Bonilla, Olga Asato Hichiva, Aida Reyna Flores, Alicia Sánchez Ríos, Luisa Fuentes Quijandria, Ana María Ramírez Toledo, Norma Velarde Alvarez
5. KOR—Moon Kyung-sook, Park Kum-sook, Suh Hee-sook, Lee Eun-ok, Hwang Kyu-ok, Lee Hyang-seem, Yang Jin-soo, Kim Young-ja, Kim Oe-sun, An Kyoung-Ja
6. CZE—Pavlína Štefková, Elena Poláková, Karla Šašková, Jitka Senečká, Vera Strunčová, Vera Hrabáková, Júlia Bendeová, Anna Mifková, Irena Tichá, Hana Vlasáková, Eva Široká, Hilda Mazúrová
7. MEX—Isabel Nogueira, Carolina Mendoza, Rogelia Romo, Yolanda Reynoso, María del Carmen Rodríguez, Gloria Inzua, Alicia Cárdenas, Gloria Caseles, Patricia Nava, Trinidad Macías, Blanca García, Eloisa Cabada
8. USA—Jane Ward, Nancy Owen, Fanny Hopeau, Barbara Perry, Ninja Jorgensen, Barbara "Micki" McFadden, Sharon Peterson, Patricia Bright, Laurie Lewis, Marilyn McReavy, Mary Perry, Kathryn Heck

The crucial match between the Japanese and the Soviets was won by the USSR, 15-10, 16-14, 3-15, 15-9. After his team had been booed during its game against Czechoslovakia, the Soviet coach was asked if his players had been affected by the crowd's hostility. He replied, "'If my athletes cannot stand such distractions, they are not professionals and should be left home." Reminded that the Olympics were for amateurs only, the embarrassed coach claimed he had been misquoted.

1972 Munich T: 8, N: 8, D: 9.7.

	MATCHES		GAMES			
	W	L	W	L	PF	PA
1. SOV	5	0	15	5	270	206
2. JPN	4	1	14	3	244	131
3. PRK	3	2	10	6	211	154
4. KOR	2	3	7	9	169	189
5. HUN	3	2	10	10	256	252
6. CUB	2	3	8	10	181	252
7. CZE	1	4	6	12	191	241
8. GER	0	5	0	15	131	228

Final: SOV—JPN 15-11, 4-15, 15-11, 9-15, 15-11
3rd Place: PRK—KOR 15-7, 15-9, 15-9
5th Piece: HUN—CUB 13-15, 16-14, 14-16, 15-5, 15-11
7th Piece: CZE—GER 15-13, 15-4, 16-14

1. SOV—Inna Ryskal, Vera Douiounova (Galushka), Tatyana Tretyakova (Ponyayeva), Nina Smoleyeva, Roza Salikhova, Lyudmila Buldakova, Tatyana Gonobobleva, Lyubov Turina, Galina Leontyeva, Tatyana Sarycheva
2. JPN—Sumie Oinuma, Noriko Yamashita, Seiko Shimakage, Makiko Furukawa, Takako Lida, Katsumi Matsumura, Michiko Shiokawa, Takako Shirai, Mariko Okamato, Keiko Hama, Yaeko Yamazaki, Toyoko Iwahara
3. PRK—Ri Chun-ok, Kim Myong-suk, Kim Zung-bok, Kang Ok-sun, Kim Yeun-ja, Hwang He-suk, Jang Ok-Rim, Paek Myong-suk, Ryom Chun-ja, Kim Su-dae, Jong Ok-jin
4. KOR—Kim Young-ja, Lee In-sook, Lee Soon-bok, Jo Hea-chung, Yu Kyung-hwa, Kim Eun-hee, Lee Jung-ja, Yu Jung-hyae, Yoon Young-nae
5. HUN—Éva Szalay Sebők, Judit Kiss-Gerhard, Emerencia Király Siry, Ilona Makláry-Buzek, Judit Hazsik Fekete, Ágnes Torma, Mária Gál, Katalin Eichler-Schadek, Judit Schlégl-Blaumann, Emöke Énekes, Zsuzsanna Török Bokros
6. CUB—Mercedes Pérez Hernández, Ana Díaz Martínez, Margarita Mayeta Hierrezuelo, Mercedes Pomares Primelles, Nurys Sebey Deroncelo, Claritza Herrera Michelena, Miriam Herrera León, Mercedes Roca Arias, Claudina Villaurrutia García
7. CZE—Irena Svobodová, Ludmila Vindušková, Jana Semecká, Dorota Jelínková, Anna Mifková, Jana Vápenková, Elena Moskalová, Hilda Mazúrová, Mária Mališová, Hana Vlasáková
8. GER—Ingrid Lorenz, Annedore Richter, Ursula Westphal, Birgit Pörner, Margret Stender, Annette Ellerbracke, Ulrike Ruschenburg, Marianne Lepa, Gertrude "Traute" Schäfer, Erika Heucke, Regina Pütz

The final was so closely fought that at one point in the fourth set there were 24 service changes in a row without a single point being scored. During the tournament, a German woman named Ingeborg Schell filed a civil suit against the Japanese coach, Joji Kojima, for using "inhuman methods for making his team fit."

1976 Montreal T: 8, N: 8, D: 7.30.

	MATCHES		GAMES			
	W	L	W	L	PF	PA
1. JPN	5	0	15	0	225	84
2. SOV	4	1	12	7	248	211
3. KOR	3	2	10	11	260	259
4. HUN	2	3	7	11	192	234
5. CUB	3	2	12	9	267	250
6. GDR	1	4	8	14	237	286
7. PER	2	3	9	12	239	250
8. CAN	0	5	6	15	198	292

Final: JPN—SOV 15-7, 15-8, 15-2
3rd Piece: KOR—HUN 12-15, 15-12, 15-10, 15-6
5th Place: CUB—GDR 15-12, 15-12, 15-8
7th Plece: PER—CAN 15-9, 12-15, 15-4, 15-7

1. JPN—Takeko Iida, Mariko Okamoto, Echiko Maeda, Noriko Matsuda, Takaka Shirai, Kiyomi Kato, Yuko Arakida, Katsuko Kanesaka, Mariko Yoshida, Shoko Takayanagi, Hiromi Yano, Juri Yokoyama
2. SOV—Anna Rostova, Lyudmila Shchetinina, Liliya Osadcha, Natalya Kushnir, Olha Kozakova, Nina Smoleyeva, Lyubov Rudovska, Larissa Bergen, Inna Ryskal, Lyudmila Chernyshova, Zoya Yusova, Nina Muradyan
3. KOR—Lee Soon-bok, Yu Jung-hye, Byon Kyung-ja, Lee Soo-nok, Baik Myung-sun, Chang Hee-sook, Ma Kum-Ja, Yun Young-nae, Yu Kyung-hwa, Park Mi-kum, Jung Soo-nok, Jo Hea-jung
4. HUN—Zsuzsanna Szloboda, Gyöngyi Bardi, Éva Biszku, Zsuzsanna Biszku, Lucia Bánhegyi, Gabriella Feketé Csapó, Ágnes Hubai Gajdos, Judit Schlégl-Blaumann, Ágnes Torma, Katalin Schadek Eichler, Emerencia Király Siry, Éva Szalay Sebők
5. CUB—Mercedes Pérez Hernández, Imilsis Téllez Quesada, Ana Díaz Martínez, Mercedes Pomares Primelles, Lucila Urgelles Savon, Mercedes Roca Arias, Miriam Herrera León, Claudina Villaurrutia García, Melania Tartabull Carrasco, Nelly Barnet Wilson, Ana María García Crespo, Evelina Borroto Donner
6. GDR—Karla Roffeis, Johanna Strotzer, Cornelia Rickert, Christine Walther, Ingrid Mierzwiak, Helga Offen, Barbara Czekalla, Jutta Balster, Anke Westendorf, Hannelore Meincke, Monika Meissner, Gudrun Gärtner
7. PER—Mercedes González la Torre, María "Gaby" Cárdeñas, Teresa Nuñez Laos, Irma Cordero Bonilla, Ana Cecilia Carrillo, Luisa Merea, Delia Córdova, Silvia Quevedo, Luisa Fuentes Quijandria, María Cecilia del Risco, María Cervera, María Ostolaza
8. CAN—Carole Bishop, Barbara Dalton, Kathleen Girvan, Patricia Olson, Regyna Armonas, Anne Ireland, Mary Dempster, Claire Lloyd, Elizabeth Baxter, Constance Lebrun, Deborah Heeps, Audrey Vandervelden

The Japanese team dominated the tournament so completely that only once did an opponent (South Korea) reach double figures in a single game.

1980 Moscow T: 8, N: 8, D: 7.29.

	MATCHES		GAMES			
	W	L	W	L	PF	PA
1. SOV/	5	0	15	3	254	172
RUS	3	2	11	11	277	271
3. BUL	3	2	12	9	257	225
4. HUN	2	3	10	12	234	279
5. CUB	3	2	10	7	219	166
6. PER	1	4	7	12	189	257
7. BRA	1	4	7	12	210	248
8. ROM	2	3	7	13	221	243

Final: SOV—GDR 15-12, 11-15, 15-13, 15-7
3rd Place: BUL—HUN 15-5, 13-15, 6-15, 15-4, 15-8
5th Place: CUB—PER 15-9, 15-7, 12-15, 15-5
7th Place: BRA—ROM 15-8, 15-12, 15-12

1. SOV/RUS—Nadezhda Radzevich, Natalya Razumova, Olga Solovova, Yelena Akhaminova, Yelena Andreyuk, Irina Makagonova, Lyubov Kozyreva, Svetlana Nikishina, Lyudmila Chernyshova, Svetlana Badulina, Lidiya Loginoya
2. GDR—Ute Kostrzewa, Andrea Heim, Annette Schultz, Christine Mummhardt, Heike Lehmann, Barbara Czekalla, Karla Roffeis, Martina Schmidt, Anke Westendorf, Karin Püschel, Brigitte Fetzer, Katharina Bullin
3. BUL—Tania Dimitrova, Valentina Ilieva, Galina Stancheva, Silva Petrunova, Anka Hristolova, Vorka Borisova, Margarita Gherasimova, Roumiana Kaicheva, Maya Georgieva, Tania Gogova, Tzvetana Bozhurina, Rossitza Dimitrova
4. HUN—Julianna Simon Szalonna, Éva Szalay Sebők, Gyöngyi Gerevich (Bardi), Ágnes Balajczá Juhász, Lucia Bánhegyi Radó, Gabriella Feketé Csapó, Emöke Szegedi Varghá, Emerencia Király Siry, Ágnes Torma, Erzsébet Varga Pálinkás, Gabriella Lengyel, Bernadett Kőszegi
5. CUB—Mercedes Pérez Hernández, Imilsis Téllez Quesada, Ana Díaz Martínez, Mercedes Pomares Primelles, Mavis Guilarte Fernández, Erenia Díaz Sánchez, Maura Alfonso Dreke, Josefina Capote Travieso, Nelly Barnet Wilson, Ana María García Crespo, Lucila Urgelles Savon
6. PER—Carmen Pimentel, María "Gaby" Cárdeñas, Raquel Chumpitaz, Ana Cecilia Carrilo, María Cecilia del Risco, Cecilia Tait Villacorta, Silvia León, Aurora Heredia, Gina Torrealva, Natalia María Málaga Dibos
7. BRA—Denise Porto Mattioli, Ivonette das Neves, Lenice Peluso Oliveira, Regina Vilela Santos, Fernanda Emerick Silva, Paula Rodrigues Mello, Maria Castanheira Trade, Eliana Maria Aleixo, Maria Castanheira, Jacqueline Silva, Vera Helena Mossa Leme, Rita Cassia Teixeira
8. ROM—Mariana Ionescu, Gabriela Coman, Doina Săvoiu, Victoria Georgescu, Ileana Dobrovschi, Victoria Banciu, Irina Petculet, Corina Georgescu, Iuliana Enescu, Ioana Liteanu, Corina Crivăţ, Elena Piron

1984 Los Angeles-Long Beach T: 8 N: 8, D: 8.7.

	MATCHES		GAMES			
	W	L	W	L	PF	PA
1. CHN	4	1	13	3	234	148
2. USA	4	1	12	6	239	218
3. JPN	4	1	12	5	222	154
4. PER	2	3	7	11	192	229
5. KOR	3	2	12	7	240	194
6. GER	2	3	6	9	160	184
7. BRA	1	4	6	12	212	236
8. CAN	0	5	0	15	88	225

Final: CHN—USA 16-14, 15-3, 15-9
3rd Place: JPN—PER 13-15, 15-4, 15-7, 15-10
5th Place: KOR—GER 15-10, 15-10, 15-2
7th Place: BRA—CAN 15-9, 15-3, 15-8

1. CHN—Lang Ping, Liang Yan, Zhu Ling, Hou Yuzhu, Yang Xilan, Jiang Ying, Li Yanjun, Yang Xiaojun, Zheng Meizhu, Zhang Rongfang
2. USA—Paula Weishoff, Susan Woodstra, Rita Crockett, Laura Jean "Laurie" Flachmeier, Carolyn Becker, Flora Hyman, Rose Magers, Julie Vollertsen, Deborah Green, Kimberly Ruddins, Jeanne Beauprey, Linda Chisholm
3. JPN—Yumi Egami, Kimie Morita, Yoko Mitsuya, Miyoko Hirose, Kyoko Ishida, Yoko Kagabu, Norie Hiro, Kayoko Sugiyama, Sachiko Otani, Keiko Miyajima, Emiko Odaka, Kumi Nakada
4. PER—Carmen Pimentel, Rosa Gisella García, Isabel Heredia, Gabriela Pérez del Solar, María Cecilia del Risco, Cecilia Tait Villacorta, Luisa Cervera Cevedon, Denise Fajardo García, Miriam Gallardo, Gina Torrealva, Natalia María Málaga Dibos

5. KOR—Lee Eun-kyung, Lee Un-yim, Lee Young-sun, Kim Jeong-sun, Han Kyung-ae, Lee Myung-hee, Kim Ok-soon, Park Mi-hee, Lim Hae-suk
6. GER—Ruth Holzhausen, Gudrun Witte, Beate Bühler, Regina Vossen, Sigrid Terstegge, Andrea Seuvigny, Renate Riek, Marina Staden, Almut Kemperdick, Teresia Place-Brandel, Ute Hankers
7. BRA—Vera Helena Mossa Leme, Fernanda Da Silva, Monica De Silva, Maria Isabel Salgado, Heloisa Roese, Regina Pereira Uchoa, Jacqueline Silva, Ana Maria Richa, Sandra Lima, Eliana Miranda da Costa, Luiza Pinheiro Machado, Ana Ida Alvarez Vieira
8. CAN—Diane Ratnik, Suzanne Smith, Tracy Mills, Joyce Gamborg, Audrey Vandervelden, Monica Hitchcock, Karen Fraser, Rachel Beliveau, Lise Martin, Caroline Cote, Barbara Broen, Josée Lebel

The Chinese had defeated the US in seven of eight pre-Olympic matches, but when the two teams faced each other for the first time in Los Angeles, in a preliminary match, the more experienced Americans came out on top 15-13, 7-15, 16-14, 15-12. Four nights later they met again to decide the championship. As the Chinese team entered the arena, their star spiker, Lang Ping, noticed a television monitor displaying a freeze-frame of the US coach and three of his players wearing gold medals around their necks. Lang stopped, pointed out the image to her teammates and said, "Let's pluck the medals from their necks." The Chinese team then put on a brilliant, almost flawless performance to defeat the US in straight sets.

1988 Seoul T: 8, N: 8, D: 9.29.

	MATCHES		GAMES			
	W	L	W	L	PF	PA
1. SOV	4	1	14	5	268	190
2. PER	4	1	14	9	303	269
3. CHN	3	2	11	7	217	202
4. JPN	2	3	10	12	256	265
5. GDR	3	2	10	9	238	246
6. BRA	1	4	7	14	235	276
7. USA	2	3	9	13	257	263
8. KOR	1	4	8	13	224	277

Final: SOV—PER 10-15, 12-15, 15-13, 15-7, 17-15
3rd Place: CHN—JPN 15-13, 15-6, 15-6
5th Plece: GDR—BRA 15-9, 15-4, 11-15, 15-11
7th Place: USA—KOR 15-4, 12-15, 13-15, 15-9, 15-8

1. SOV—Valentina Ogiyenko, Yelena Volkova, Irina Smirnova, Tatyana Sidorenko, Irina Parkhomchuk, Olha Shkurnova, Marina Nikulina, Yelena Ovchinnikova, Olga Krivosheyeva, Marina Kumysh, Tatyana Kravnova, Svetlana Korytova
2. PER—Cenaida Uribe Medina, Rosa Gisella García, Gabriela Pérez del Solar, Isabel Heredia, Cecilia Tait Villacorta, Luisa Cervera Cevedon, Denise Fajardo García, Alejandra de la Guerra, Gina Torrealva, Natalia María Málaga Dibos
3. CHN—Li Guojun, Hou Yuzhu, Yang Xilan, Su Huijuan, Jiang Ying, Cui Yongmei, Yang Xiaojun, Zheng Meizhu, Wu Dan, Li Yueming
4. JPN—Yumi Maruyama, Kayoko Sugiyama, Reiko Takizawa, Miyako Yameashita, Akemi Sugiyama, Ichiko Sato, Norie Hiro, Kumi Nakada, Motoko Obayashi, Yukiko Takahashi, Sachiko Fujita, Noriyuki Muneuchi
5. GDR—Steffi Schmidt, Susanne Lahme, Monika Beu, Ariane Radfan, Kathrin Langschwager, Maike Arlt, Brit Wiedemann, Ute Steppin, Grit Jensen, Dörte Stüdemann, Heike Jensen, Ute Langenau
6. BRA—Kerly Santos, Ana Moser, Vera Helena Mossa Leme, Eliana Miranda da Costa, Ana Maria Richa, Maria Castanheira Trade, Ana Claudia Ramos, Márcia Cunha, Ana Lúcia Barros, Sandra Suruagy, Fernanda Venturini, Simone Storm
7. USA—Melissa McLinden, Angela Rock, Elizabeth Masakayan, Kimberly Oden, Kimberly Ruddins, Caren Kemner, Tammy Webb, Deitre Collins, Laurel Kessel, Prikeba "Keba" Phipps, Liane Sato, Jayne McHugh
8. KOR—Park Mi-hee, Kim Angela Rock, Kyung-hee, Kim Kyung-hee, Lim Hye-sook, Yoo Young-mi, Nam Soon-ok, Yoon Chung-hye, Park Bok-rye, Kim Yoon-hye, Ji Kyung-hee

Final: SOV—PER 10-15, 12-15, 15-13, 15-7, 17-15
3rd Place: CHN—JPN 15-13, 15-6, 15-6
5th Plece: GDR—BRA 15-9, 15-4, 11-15, 15-11
7th Place: USA—KOR 15-4, 12-15, 13-15, 15-9, 15-8

In 1948 Edwin Vásquez Cam of Peru won a gold medal in free pistol shooting. In the forty years that followed, no Peruvian was able to earn another Olympic title. But in 1988 the Peruvian people caught gold medal fever, pinning their hopes on their popular women's volleyball team. The team members were so well known that they were referred to always by their first names: Rosa, Gina, Natalia, Denisse, 6 foot 4½ inch (1.94 meters) Gabriela, and the media favorite, Cecilia.

With Cuba boycotted out of the Games, Peru's leading rivals were Japan, which had never finished out of the medals; the Soviet Union, which had never placed worse than second; and China, which had won each year's major tournament from 1981 through 1986 before faltering in 1987. So important was women's volleyball in China that when a new coach had to be chosen, the four leading contenders debated on national television.

In the very first match of the tournament, Japan defeated the USSR in five sets, the final set going to 19-17. Prior to 1988 the Soviets had lost only two of 27 Olympic contests—both to Japan. Three days later, Peru, trailing China 9-14 in the fifth set, scored 7 straight points to win the match. In their next match the Peruvians spotted the US two sets, then came roaring back for another five-set victory. In the first semifinal, the USSR obliterated the Chinese 15-0, 15-9, 15-2. The second semi saw Peru take the first two sets from Japan 15-9, 15-6, then lose the next two 6-15, 10-15, before sealing the victory 15-13.

The final took place at 6:30 a.m., Peru time, with almost the entire nation glued to the nearest television set. The Peruvian women won the first two sets 15-10, 15-12, and led the third 12-6. At this point, with most of the 6500 spectators cheering wildly for Peru, the Soviet coach, Nicolai Karpol, called timeout and made three substitutions. When play resumed, the momentum had shifted. The Soviets outscored the Peruvians 9-1 to win the set. They then took the next set 15-7 and led 6-0 in the fifth set. But Peru would not give in. They fought back to tie the score at 7. The USSR moved ahead again, 10-7. Again Peru came from behind to tie. They even took the lead at 15-14. Both sides fought off match points. Finally, the Soviets won 17-15. The Soviet women were so drained, physically and emotionally, that medical personnel had to be rushed onto the court to revive them for the medal ceremony.

Four of the six Soviet starters, as well as coach Karpol, were members of the Uralochka factory team of Sverdlovsk.

1992 Barcelona T: 8, N: 8, D: 8.7.

	MATCHES		GAMES			
	W	L	W	L	PF	PA
1. CUB	5	0	15	5	268	238
2. SOV	3	2	12	7	270	194
3. USA	4	2	16	9	327	280
4. BRA	3	3	11	13	291	299
5. JPN	3	2	10	9	253	224
6. HOL	1	4	6	14	215	278
7. CHN	1	3	8	9	219	198
8. SPA	0	4	0	1	248	180

Final: CUB—SOV 16-14, 12-15, 15-12, 15-13
3rd Place: USA—BRA 15-8, 15-6, 15-13
5th Place: JPN—HOL 15-0, 11-15, 15-13, 15-10
7th Place: CHN—SPA 15-1, 15-3, 15-3

1. CUB—Tania Ortiz Calvo, Marlenis Costa Blanco, Mireya Luis Hernández, Lilia Izquierdo Aguirre, Idalmis Gato Moya, Regla Bell McKenzie, Regla Torres Herrera, Norka Latamblet Daudinot, Mercedes Calderón Martínez, Magalys Carvajal Rivera
2. SOV—Valentina Makovetskaya (Ogiyenko), Natalya Morozova, Marina Pankova (Nikulina), Yelena Batukhtina, Irina Ilchenko (Smirnova), Yevgeniye Artamonova, Yelena Chebukina (Ovchinnikova), Svetlana Korytova
3. USA—Tonya "Tee" Sanders, Yoko Zetterlund, Kimberly Oden, Lori Endicott, Paula Weishoff, Caren Kemner, Tammy Liley, Elaina Oden, Janet Cobbs, Tara Cross-Battle, Liane Sato, Ruth Lawanson
4. BRA—Ana Moser, Hilma Caldeira, Ana Ida Alvarez Vieira, Ana Paula Rodrigues Connelly, Ana Flavia Sanglard, Cristina Lopes, Leila Barros, Ana Lúcia Barros, Marcia Cunha, Fernanda Venturini, Helia "Fofao" de Souza
5. JPN—Ichiko Sato, Kumi Nakada, Michiyo Ishikake, Chieko Nakanishi, Motoko Obayashi, Yukiko Takahashi, Ikuyo Namura, Mika Yamauchi, Asako Tajimi, Tomoko Yoshihara, Kiyoko Fukuda, Kazumi Nakamura
6. HOL—Sandra Wiegers, Erna Brinkman, Jacintha Boersma, Vera Koenen, Irena Machovcak, Aafke Hament, Marjolein de Jong, Henriette Weersing, Kirsten Gleis, Helena Crielaard, Alida "Linda" Moons
7. CHN—Lai Yawen, Li Guojun, Zhou Hong, Ma Fang, Wang Yi, Su Huijuan, Chen Fengqin, Su Liqun, Sun Yue, Wu Dan, Gao Lin, Li Yueming
8. SPA—Virginia Cardona Tapia, Ana Tostado Domingo, Rita Oraá Larrazábal, Inmaculada Torres Cerezo, Laura de la Torre Tur, Marta Gens Barberá, Olga Martín Rubio, Asunción Domenech Domínguez, Inmaculada González Casado, Estela Domínguez Cerviño, María del Mar Rey Abad, Carmen Miranda Martínez

The Cuban team was the overwhelming favorite and they did not disappoint. They were, however, hard-pressed by the United States in the semifinals. With the match tied at two games each and the United States leading 9-8 in the deciding game, Cuba scored five straight points and went on to win 15-11. In the final, every game was close right up to the end, but the Cubans were able to score when it counted most, converting the last two points of games one, three and four.

1996 Atlanta T: 12, N: 12, D: 8.3.

	MATCHES		GAMES			
	W	L	W	L	PF	PA
1. CUB	6	2	19	9	362	292
2. CHN	7	1	22	7	408	310
3. BRA	7	1	23	6	404	267
4. RUS	5	3	18	11	382	296
5. HOL	5	3	17	12	364	326
6. KOR	3	5	13	15	341	340
7. USA	5	3	16	12	344	331
8. GER	2	6	10	18	295	355

Final: CUB—CHN 14-16, 15-12, 17-16, 15-6
3rd Place: BRA—RUS 15-13, 4-15, 16-14, 8-15, 15-13
5th Place: HOL—KOR 15-9, 15-9, 15-13
7th Place: USA—GER 17-16, 15-6, 5-15, 15-6

1. CUB—Yumilka Ruiz Loaces, Marlenis Costa Blanco, Mireya Luis Hernández, Lilia Izquierdo Aguirre, Idalmis Gato Moya, Raisa O'Farril Bolaños, Regla Bell McKenzie, Regla Torres Herrera, Taismary Agüero Leiva, Ana Ivis Fernández Valle, Magalys Carvajal Rivera, Mirka Francis Vasconcelos
2. CHN—Lai Yawen, Li Yan, Cui Yongmei, Zhu Yunying, Wu Yongmei, Wang Yi, He Qi, Pan Wenli, Liu Xiaoning, Wang Ziling, Sun Yue, Wang Lina
3. BRA—Ana Moser, Ana Ida Alvarez Vieira, Ana Paula Rodrigues Connelly, Leila Barros, Hilma Caldeira, Virna Dias, Márcia Cunha, Ericléia "Filó" Bodziak, Ana Flávia Sanglard, Fernanda Venturini, . Helia "Fofao" de Souza, Sandra Suruagy
4. RUS—Valentina Ogyenko, Natalya Morozova, Marina Nikulina, Yelena Batukhtina, Irina Ilchenko, Yelena Godina, Tatyana Menshova, Yevgeniya Artamonova, Yelizaveta Tishchenko, Yuliya Timonova, Tatyana Gracheva, Lyubov Sokolova
5. HOL—Jenny Catharine "Jerine" Fleurke, Johanna "Saskia" van Hintum, Erna Brinkman, Jacintha "Cintha" Boersma, Irena Machovcak, Marjolein de Jong, Henriette Weersing, Marrit Leenstra, Elles Leferink, Claudia van Thiel, Emmy Henriëtte "Riëtte" Fledderus, Ingrid Visser
6. KOR—Yoo Yon-kyung, Chang Yoon-hee, Lee Soo-jung, Kang Hye-mi, Chung Sun-hye, Kim Nam-soon, Park Soo-jeong, Hong Ji-yeon, Lee In-sook, Eoh Yeon-soon, Chang So-yun, Choi Kwang-hee
7. USA—Tonya "Tee" Williams (Sanders), Yoko Zetterlund, Paula Weishoff, Caren Kemner, Lori Endicott, Kristin Klein, Beverly Oden, Tammy Liley, Elaina Oden, Danielle Scott, Tara Cross-Battle, Elaine Youngs
8. GER—Susanne Lahme, Tanja Hart, Constance Radfan, Sylvia Roll, Ute Steppin, Karin Horninger, Ines Pianka, Christina Schultz, Claudia Wilke, Nancy Celis, Grit Naumann (Jensen), Hanka Pachale

China's women's volleyball program had gone steadily downhill since its 1984 gold medal, hitting bottom with an embarrassing eighth place finish at the 1994 world championship. Then the Chinese came up with a creative solution: they brought back the captain of the 1984 squad, Lang Ping, to take over as coach. Lang, who had spent most of the last nine years living in Albuquerque, New Mexico, would be the only female volleyball coach at the Olympics. In Atlanta, China swept to the final undefeated, although they were taken to five sets by a determined team from South Korea. Defending champion Cuba had dominated women's volleyball, following up their 1992 Olympic triumph by winning every major tournament since then. But in the preliminary round, the Cubans appeared sluggish, losing to both Brazil and Russia. Nevertheless, they crushed the United States in the quarterfinals and won a contentious semifinal battle with Brazil 4-15, 15-8, 10-15, 15-13, 15-12 after which fighting broke out between the two teams both on and off the court. The final was less controversial. After giving up the first set, the more experienced Cubans won the big points in the bext two sets and breezed to victory in the fourth. Their success did little good for Cuban coach Eugenio George Laffita. He was fired nineteen days later after he publicly complained about inadequate training facilities.

2000 Sydney T: 12, N: 12, D: 9.30.

	MATCHES		GAMES			
	W	L	W	L	PF	PA
1. CUB	7	1	23	8	729	600
2. RUS	7	1	23	10	763	678
3. BRA	7	1	23	4	646	503
4. USA	5	3	18	12	653	608
5. CHN	4	4	14	14	639	611
6. GER	3	5	12	17	622	660
7. CRO	4	4	13	16	665	655
8. KOR	3	5	13	18	679	719

Final: CUB—RUS 25-27, 32-34, 25-19, 25-18, 15-7
3rd Place: BRA—USA 25-18, 25-22, 25-21
5th Place: CHN—GER 25-19, 25-19, 22-25, 25-18
7th Place: CRO—KOR 25-18, 24-26, 25-22, 25-21

1. CUB—Ana Ivis Fernández Valle, Marlenys Costa Blanco, Mireya Luis Hernández, Mirka Francia Vasconcelos, Regla Bell MacKenzie, Regla Torres Herrera, Taismary Agüero Leiva, Yumilka Ruíz Luaces
2. RUS—Anastasiya Belikova, Yelizaveta Tishchenko, Inessa Sargsyan, Lyubov Shashkova (Sokolova), Natalia Morozova, Olga Potashova, Tatyana Gracheva, Yekaterina Gamova, Yelena Godina, Yelena Tyurina, Yelena Vasilevskaya, Yevgenia Artamonova
3. BRA—Elisangela Oliveira, Erika Coimbra, Helia "Fofao" de Souza, Janina Conceicão, Karin Rodrigues, Katia Lopes, Kely Fraga, Leila Gomes, Raquel Silva, Ricarda Lima, Virna Dias, Walewska Oliveira
4. USA—Allison Weston, Charlene Tagaloa, Danielle Scott, Demetria Sance, Heather Brown, Kerri Walsh, Logan Tom, Mickisha Hurley, Robyn Ahmow, Sarah Noriega, Stacy Sykora, Tara Cross-Battle
5. CHN—Chen Jing, Gui Chaoran, He Qi, Li Shan, Li Yan, Qiu Aihua, Sun Yue, Wang Lina, Wu Dan, Wu Yongmei, Yin Yin, Zhu Yunying
6. GER—Angelina Grün, Anja-Nadin Pietrek, Beatrice Dömeland, Christina Benecke, Christina Schultz, Hanka Pachale, Judith Flemig, Judith Sylvester, Kerstin Tzscherlich, Susanne Lahme, Sylvia Roll, Tanja Hart
7. CRO—Barbara Jelić, Beti Rimac, Biljana Gligorović, Elena Čebukina, Gordana Jurčan, Ingrid Šišković, Marija Anzulović, Marijana Ribičić, Nataša Leto, Patricia Daničić, Vesna Jelić
8. KOR—Chang So-yun, Choi Kwang-hee, Chung Sun-hye, Eoh Yeon-soon, Kang Hye-mi, Kim Guy-hyun, Koo Ki-lan, Ku Min-jung, Lee Myung-hee, Lee Yun-hui, Park Mee-kyung, Park Soo-jeong

Favorites Cuba and Russia were drawn together in pool play with the Russians winning 20-25, 25-21, 21-25, 25-12, 15-13. Brazil dominated the other pool, going undefeated and losing only one game. Cuba and Brazil met in the semifinals, as they had at the last Olympics. Their Sydney encounter was less violent, but no less dramatic. Brazil won the first set 29-27 and led the second set 16-9 when the Cubans took nine straight points and went on to win 25-19. The Brazilians won the third set 25-21, but then Cuba took change and prevailed 25-19 and 15-9. In the other semifinal, Russia finally subdued a tenacious US team 25-15, 23-25, 25-15, 26-28, 15-8. The final was as close as expected. Cuba led the first set 24-21, but the Russians came from behind to win it 27-25. The second set saw both teams fight off four game points before Russia won 34-32. Down two sets to none, the Cubans finally asserted their superiority, taking the last three sets 25-19, 25-18 and 15-7 to gain an unprecedented third Olympic title in a row.

2004 Athens T: 12, N: 12, D: 8.28.

	MATCHES		GAMES			
	W	L	W	L	PF	PA
1. CHN	7	1	23	8	727	622
2. RUS	5	3	19	13	721	672
3. CUB	5	3	19	16	735	750
4. BRA	6	2	21	10	720	623
5. ITA	4	2	16	6	491	406
5. JPN	2	4	6	13	408	418
5. KOR	3	3	9	10	409	427
5. USA	2	4	13	13	572	579

Final: CHN–RUS 28-30, 25-27, 25-20, 25-23, 15-12
3rd Place: CUB–BRA 25-22, 25-22, 14-25, 25-27

1. CHN—Feng Kun, Yang Hao, Liu Yanan, Li Shan, Zhou Suhong, Zhao Ruirui, Zhang Yuehong, Chen Jing, Song Nina, Wang Lina, Zhang Na, Zhang Ping
2. RUS—Irina Tebenikhina, Yelena Batukhtina-Tyurina, Lyubov Sokolova-Shashkova, Yevgeniya Artamonova, Yelizaveta Tishchenko, Olga Chukanova, Yekaterina Gamova, Marina Sheshenina, Yelena Plotnikova, Olga Nikolayeva
3. CUB—Zoila Barros Fernández, Rosir Calderon Díaz, Nancy Carillo de la Paz, Ana Ivis Fernández Valle, Mayvelis Martínez Aldúm, Liana Mesa Luaces, Aniara Muñoz Carrazana, Yaima Ortíz Charro, Daimí Ramírez Echevarría, Yumilka Ruíz Luaces, Marta Sánchez Salfran, Dulce Téllez Palacio
4. BRA—Ana Beatriz "Bia" das Chagas, Fabiana Claudino, Érika Coimbra, Elisângela de Oliveira, Arlene Xavier, Hélia "Fofão" de Souza, Virna Dias, Welissa "Sassá" Gonzaga, Valeska "Valeskinha" Menezes, Walewska de Oliveira, Marianne "Mari" Steinbrecher, Fernanda Venturini

5. ITA—Simona Rinieri, Elisa Togut, Manuela Leggeri, Jenny Barazza, Nadia Centoni, Paola Paggi, Francesca Piccinini, Manuela Secolo, Eleonora Lo Bianco, Antonella del Core, Francesca Ferretti, Paola Cardullo
5. JPN—Tomoko Yoshihara, Ikumi Narita, Miki Sasaki, Kanako Omura, Yoshie Takeshita, Miyuki Takahashi, Sachiko Sugiyama, Ai Otomo, Kana Oyama, Megumi Kurihara, Saori Kimura
5. KOR—Jung Dae-young, Kang Hye-mi, Nam Jie-youn, Choi Kwang-hee, Kim Mi-jin, Ku Min-jung, Kim Sa-nee, Kim Se-young, Han Song-yi, Chang So-yun, Pak Sun-mi
5. USA—Prikeba "Keba" Phipps, Danielle Scott, Tayyiba Haneef, Lindsey Berg, Stacy Sykora, Elisabeth Bachman, Heather Bown, Ogonna Nnamani, Robyn Ah Mow-Santos, Nancy Metcalf, Tara Cross-Battle, Logan Tom

After winning their third straight Olympic championship in Sydney, Cuba's dominance in women's volleyball finally began to ebb, as the Cubans slipped to fifth in the 2002 world championships and sixth in the 2003 World Cup. The former was won by Italy and the latter by China, which won all eleven of its matches at the World Cup. In Athens, the Chinese lost in five sets to Cuba, but finished first in their pool anyway. In the other pool, World Cup runner-up Brazil won four of their matches in straight sets and beat Italy in five sets. In the quarterfinals, China and Russia both advanced to the semifinals on straight sets, China 25-20, 25-22, 25-20 over Japan and Russia 25-17, 25-15, 25-22 over South Korea. Cuba fought off Italy 25-23, 14-25, 22-25, 25-14, 15-12, and Brazil defeated the United States 25-22, 25-20, 22-25, 25-27, 15-6. In the first semifinal, Russia staged a dramatic comeback against Brazil, dropping the first two sets 18-25 and 21-25, before winning the last three 25-22, 28-26 and 16-14. In the fourth set, the Russians survived five match points before winning. In the second semifinal, China beat Cuba in the first two sets, 25-22 and 25-20, but the Cubans came back to win the third and fourth sets 25-17 and 25-23. The Chinese then put an end to the Cuban gold-medal streak with a 15-10 victory in the tie-breaking set. The final was another exciting match. Russia took two hard-fought sets 30-28 and 27-25, but China fought back to take the third set 25-20. In the fourth set, the Russians led 23-21, but the Chinese earned four consecutive points to win 25-21. Then they led the fifth set from the start. The Russians closed to 12-11, but China won 15-12 to earn gold.

2008 Beijing T: 12, N: 12, D: 8.23.

	MATCHES		GAMES			
	W	L	W	L	PF	PA
1. BRA	8	0	24	1	622	409
2. USA	6	2	19	14	712	682
3. CHN	5	3	19	11	701	612
4. CUB	6	2	19	9	630	609
5. ITA	4	2	14	7	467	419
5. JPN	2	4	7	14	429	464
5. RUS	3	3	10	9	419	389
5. SER	2	4	6	13	410	426

Final: BRA—USA 25-15, 18-25, 25-13, 25-21
3rd Place: CHN—CUB 25-16, 21-25, 25-13, 25-20

1. BRA—Marianne Steinbrecher, Hélia "Fofão" Rogério de Souza Pinto, Paula Marques Pequeno, Walewska Moreira de Oliveira, Thaísa Daher de Menezes, Valeska "Valeskinha" dos Santos Menezes, Welissa "Sassá" de Souza Gonzaga, Fabiana "Fabi" Alvim de Oliveira, Fabiana Marcelino Claudino, Sheilla Tavares de Castro, Jaqueline Pereira de Carvalho, Carolina Demartini de Albuquerque
2. USA—Kim Willoughby, Logan Tom, Stacy Sykora, Danielle Scott-Arruda, Ogonna Nnamani, Jennifer Joines, Tayyiba Haneef, Kimberly Glass, Nicole Davis, Heather Bown, Lindsey Berg, Robyn Ah Mow-Santos
3. CHN—Zhou Suhong, Zhao Ruirui, Zhang Na, Yang Hao, Xue Ming, Xu Yunli, Wei Qiuyue, Wang Yimei, Ma Yunwen, Liu Yanan, Li Juan, Feng Kun
4. CUB—Yusidey Silié Frómeta, Yanelis Santos Allegne, Rachel Sánchez Pérez, Yumilka Ruíz Luaces, Daimi Ramírez Echevarría, Yaima Ortíz Charro, Liana Mesa Luaces, Yusleynis Herrera Álvarez, Nancy Carillo de la Paz, Kenia Carcaces Opón, Rosir Calderon Díaz, Zoila Barros Fernández
5. ITA—Manuela Secolo, Francesca Piccinini, Serena Ortolani, Eleonora Lo Bianco, Martina Guiggi, Simona Gioli, Francesca Ferretti, Paola Croce, Nadia Centoni, Paola Cardullo, Jenny Barazza, Tai Aguero
5. JPN—Yoshie Takeshita, Miyuki Takahashi, Asako Tajimi, Sachiko Sugiyama, Yuko Sano, Yuka Sakurai, Kanako Omura, Megumi Kurihara, Saori Kimura, Yuki Kawai, Miyuki Kano, Erika Araki
5. RUS—Marina Sheshenina, Lyubov Sokolova-Shashkova, Aleksandra Pasynkova, Yuliya Merkulova, Yekaterina Kabeshova, Lena Godina, Yekaterina Gamova, Olga Fateyeva, Yevgeniya Artamonova-Estes, Mariya Borodakova, Nataliya Alimova, Marina Akulova
5. SER—Jovana Vesović, Stefana Veljković, Maja Ognjenović, Jelena Nikolić, Brižitka Molnar, Sanja Malagurski, Nataša Krasmanović, Ivana Đerisilo, Vesna Čitaković, Suzana Ćebić, Jovana Brakočević

Although the top-ranked team in the world coming into the Beijing Olympics, Brazil had been frustrated at the past two major international tournaments, finishing second behind Russia at the 2006 world championships and losing to Italy in the 2007 world cup final.

The Brazilians rolled through their round-robin pool, beating all five opponents in straight sets, including both Russia and Italy. Cuba topped the other round-robin pool, also with a 5-0 streak, beating the US 3-0 and defending Olympic champion China 3-2.

The US finished second in the pool after being shocked by the news that the father of 2004 Olympian Elisabeth "Wiz" Bachman had been stabbed to death while sightseeing in Beijing on the first day of competition and her mother hospitalized in the same attack. The team dedicated their first match, an emotional 3-1 win over Japan, to Wiz and her family.

The US faced Italy in the quarterfinals, losing the first set 20-25 before coming back in the second set 25-21.

The two teams traded the next two sets 19-25, 25-18, before the US clinched the victory 15-6 in the fifth set.

The US upset Cuba in the semifinal, winning in straight sets 25-20, 25-16, 25-17. Brazil did the same in the other semifinal match, beating China 27-25, 25-22, 25-14.

Brazil won the first set of the final 25-15, but the US came back to win the second set 25-18. It was the first time in the tournament that Brazil had lost a set, and the team responded by winning the next one 25-13. The US fought to a 21-21 tie in the fourth set before Brazil hit four straight points to clinch their first-ever women's volleyball gold medal.

The US team was coached by Lang Ping, who had led China to victory in the gold medal match against the US at the 1984 Olympics.

BEACH VOLLEYBALL

The principles of beach volleyball are basically the same as those of normal volleyball, but there are significant differences. To begin with, there are two players on a team, the court is made of sand, and the players wear less clothing. Since 2008, all matches have been played best of three sets. The first two sets will be played to 21 and the third set to 15. However a team must win a set by at least two points. Twenty-four men's pairs and 24 women's pairs take part in the Olympic tournaments: the sixteen highest ranked teams in the world, five winners of continental tournaments, two teams from a World Olympic Qualifying tournament and the host nation. The teams are split into six pools of four, with the top two teams from each pool advancing to single-elimination playoffs, along with the four best third-place teams.

MEN

1896–1992 not held

1996 Atlanta-Jonesboro T: 24, N: 19, D: 7.28.

1. USA Charles "Karch" Kiraly, Kent Steffes
2. USA Michael Dodd, Michael Whitmarsh
3. CAN John Child, Mark Heese
4. POR Luis Miguel Barbosa Maia, João Carlos Pereira Brenha Alves
5. SPA F. Javier Bosma Mínguez, Sixto Jiménez Galán
5. USA Carl Henkel, Christopher "Sinjin" Smith
7. CUB Francisco Álvarez Cutiño, Juan Miguel Rosell Milanés
7. NOR Jan Kvalheim, Björn Maaseide

Final: Kiraly/Steffes—Dodd/Whitmarsh 12-5, 12-8
3rd Place: Child/Heese—Maia/Brenha 12-5, 12-8

The Olympic tournament was preceded by a controversy about the method for choosing the three US teams. The best US pairs played in the tour organized by the Association of Volleyball Professionals (AVP). However, the International Volleyball Federation (FIVB), supported by the United States Olympic Committee, insisted that one US team qualify by participating in a rival FIVB tour. The other two teams qualified through Olympic trials. The FIVB team was 39-year-old beach volleyball legend Sinjin Smith and his partner, 26-year-old Carl Henkel. The number one AVP team was 35-year-old Karch Kiraly, who had already won two gold medals in indoor volleyball, and his 28-year-old partner, Kent Steffes. The second AVP team was 38-year-old Mike Dodd and 34-year-old Mike Whitmarsh. The AVP teams, resentful of their treatment by the FIVB, aimed for an all-AVP final. They got it, but it wasn't easy. In the fourth round, Kiraly and Steffes faced Smith and Henkel in what would turn out to be an epic confrontation. Not only was the all-AVP final on the line, but Kiraly and Smith were ex-partners who had achieved great success together in the early 1980s. Smith and Henkel took a 12-8 lead, but Kiraly and Steffes scored five unanswered points. Smith and Henkel moved ahead again 14-13 and 15-14 and Kiraly and Steffes were forced to fight off four match points. They scored twice to put the score at 16-15. Then it was Smith and Henkel's turn to stop four match points. On the fifth try, Kiraly and Steffes finally won 17-15. The rest of the tournament was anticlimatic. Kiraly and Steffes beat Child and Hesse 15-11 in the semifinals and Dodd and Whitmarsh 12-5, 12-8 in the final.

2000 Sydney T: 24, N: 17, D: 9.26.

1. USA Dain Blanton, Eric Fonoimoana
2. BRA José Marco "Zé Marco" Ferreira, Ricardo Santos
3. GER Jörg Ahmann, Axel Häger
4. POR L. Miguel Maia, João Brenha
5. John Child, Mark Heese (CAN); F. Javier Bosma Mínguez, Fabio Diez Steinaker (SPA); Martin Laciga, Paul Laciga (SUI); Kevin Wong, Robert Heidger, Jr. (USA)

Final: Blanton/Fonoimoana—Ferreira/Santos 12-11, 12-9
3rd Place: Ahmann/Häger—Maia/Brenha 12-9, 12-6

Eric Fonoimoana's sister had placed seventh in the 100-meter butterfly at the 1976 Olympics. Eric was a star youth player in both soccer and volleyball, but settled on the latter because, in California, it was easier to make money in beach volleyball than soccer. He and partner Dain Blanton barely made it to the Olympics. Qualifications were based on points accumulated during a series of 15 tournaments. They were behind the team of Karch Kiraly and Adam Johnson when Kiraly injured his shoulder and had to stop competing. Blanton and Fonoimoana needed to reach the semifinals of the last tournament, a month before the Olympics, to pass Kiraly and Johnson in the standings. Otherwise, Johnson would qualify and get to choose a new partner. Blanton and Fonoimoana made it to the semifinals by defeating number one ranked Emanuel Rego and José Loiola of Brazil. On Bondi Beach in Sydney, the spirited American pair argued with officials and opponents, but played the best volleyball of their careers. In the round of 16, they trailed Jorre Kjemperud and Vegard Høidalen of Norway 1-5, before clawing their way back to win 15-13. After easily disposing of fellow Americans Rob Heidger and Kevin Wong 15-3, they faced a difficult semifinal matchup with Luis Maia and João Brenha. The Portuguese pair was leading 11-10, when the Australian referee penalized Foinamoana for stalling and added a point to Maia and Brenha's score. This woke up the Americans. Blanton hit two service aces in a row and they went on to win 15-12. In the final, Blanton and Foinamoana had to play Zé Marco and Ricardo, against whom they had a career record of 0-4. The Brazilians took charge early in the first set, leading 10-7 and 11-8. But the Americans fought off four set points and then came from behind to win 12-11. With the momentum seemingly shifted, Blanton and Foinamoana led from the start of the second set. Zé Marco and Ricardo refused to fold and closed the gap to 10-9, before the Americans scored two more points. Seeded ninth, Samoan-American Foinamoana and African-American Blanton were unlikely champions, but even more sursprising were the winners of the bronze medal match, Jörg Ahmann and Axel Hager, who were only seeded sixteenth.

2004 Athens T: 24, N: 17, D: 8.25.

1. BRA Ricardo Santos, Emanuel Rego
2. SPA F. Javier Bosma Mínguez, Pablo Herrera Allepuz
3. SWI Patrick Heuscher, Stefan Kobel
4. AUS Julien Prosser, Mark Williams
5. John Child, Mark Heese (CAN); Christoph Dieckmann, Andreas Scheuerpflug (GER); Martin Laciga, Paul Laciga (SWI); Daxton Holdren, Stein Metzger (USA)

Final: Santos/Rego–Bosma/Herrera 21-16, 21-15
3rd Place: Heuscher/Kobel–Prosser/Williams 19-21, 21-17, 15-13

Known as "The Block Machine" because of his efficiency at the net, Ricardo Santos earned a silver medal at the 2000 Olympics and then tried out two new partners before settling on Emanuel Rego, who had placed ninth at the last two Olympics. They won the world championship in 2003 and arrived at the Athens Olympics ranked first in the world. Santos and Rego dominated the competition, winning fourteen sets in their seven matches and losing only three, although they were hard-pressed in the semifinals by Patrick Heuscher and Stefan Kobel. After splitting the first two sets, Ricardo and Emanuel trailed 9-10 in the deciding set before coming from behind to win 15-12. In the final against Javier Bosma and Pablo Herrera, the Brazilian pair never trailed and won 21-16, 21-15.

2008 Beijing T: 24, N: 18, D: 8.22.

1. USA Todd Rogers, Phillip Dalhausser
2. BRA Márcio Barroso Araújo, Fábio de Jesus Magalhães
3. BRA Ricardo Costa Santos, Emanuel Scheffler Rego
4. GEO Renato "Geor" da Rocha Gomes, Jorge "Gia" Ferreira Terceiro
5. AUT Florian Gosch, Alexander Horst
5. GER David Klemperer, Eric Koreng
5. HOL Reinder Nummerdor, Richard Schuil
5. USA Jacob Gibb, Sean Rosenthal

Final: Rogers/Dalhausser—Márcio/Fábio 23-21, 17-21, 15-4
3rd Place: Ricardo/Emanuel—Gomes/Terceiro 21-15, 21-10

The favorites in the event were defending Olympic champions Emanuel Rego and Ricardo Santos, who had topped the International Volleyball Federation (FIVB) rankings every year since 2003. Rego's and Santos's main challengers were expected to be US pair Todd Rogers and Phil Dalhausser. The Americans had beaten Rego and Ricardo in the semifinal of the 2007 world championship, going on to win the title.

Dalhausser and Rogers got off to a rough start in the tournament, losing their first round-robin match in straight sets to Latvian duo Aleksandrs Samoilovs and Mārtiņš Pļaviņš. They came back to win their next two matches to finish first in their pool. Rego and Santos had an easier time of it, winning all three of their preliminary matches in straight sets.

In the semifinals, Dalhausser and Rogers faced Brazilian-born pair Renato Gomes and Jorge Terceiro, who had been recruited to play for Georgia, renaming themselves Geor and Gia for the occasion. Rogers and Dalhausser won 21-11, 21-13.

Rego and Santos faced compatriots and 2005 world champions Márcio Araújo and Fábio Magalhães in the other semifinal, and the latter pair won 22-20, 21-18.

In the final, Rogers and Dalhausser fought to a 23-21 win in the first set, but Araújo and Magalhães came back to take the second set 21-17. Rogers and Dalhausser dominated the third set, cruising to a 15-4 win to earn the gold medals.

WOMEN

1896–1992 not held

1996 Atlanta-Jonesboro T: 18, N: 13, D: 7.27.
1. BRA Sandra Pires, Jacqueline Silva
2. BRA Mônica Rodrigues, Adriana Samuel
3. AUS Natalie Cook, Kerri Pottharst
4. USA Barbra Fontana Harris, Linda Hanley
5. JPN Sachiko Fujita, Yukiko Takahashi
5. USA Holly McPeak, Nancy Reno
7. AUS Liane Fenwick, Anita Spring-Palm
7. GER Beate Bühler, Danja Müsch

Final: Pires/Silva—Rodrigues/Ramos 12-11, 12-6
3rd Place: Cook/Pottharst—Harris/Hanley 12-11, 12-7

Jackie Silva represented Brazil in indoor volleyball at the 1980 and 1984 Olympics. She turned to beach volleyball in 1986. By the time her new sport was introduced into the Olympics ten years later, Silva was 34 years old and, along with her protégé, 23-year-old Sandra Pires, the two-time defending world champion. At the Olympics, Silva and Pires faced only one close call: a 15-13 third round victory over Liane Fenwick and Anita Spring. Although Brazil had been participating in the Olympics since 1920, the two beach volleyball pairs were the first Brazilian women to win medals.

2000 Sydney T: 24, N: 15, D: 9.25.
1. AUS Natalie Cook, Kerri Pottharst
2. BRA Adriana Behar, Shelda Bede
3. BRA Sandra Tavares (Pires), Adriana Samuel
4. JPN Yukiko Takahashi, Mika Saiki
5. Tania Gooley, Pauline Manser (AUS); Laura Bruschini, Annamaria Solazzi (ITA); Holly McPeak, Misty May (USA); Jennifer Johnson-Jordan, Annett Davis (USA)

Final: Cook/Pottharst—Behar/Bede 12-11, 12-10
3rd Place: Tavares/Ramos—Takahashi/Saiki 12-4, 12-6

After earning bronze medals at the 1996 Olympics, Kerri Pottharst and Natalie Cook broke up and switched partners. But they came back together in 1999. Cook hired a "success coach" who convinced the pair to walk on hot coals and broken glass to build their self-confidence. They also surrounded themselves in gold. Cook even found gold toothpaste and gold shampoo. Playing before a wildly supportive crowd at Bondi Beach, Cook and Pottharst faced defending Olympic champion Sandra Pires and her new partner, 1996 silver medalist Adriana Samuel, in the semifinals and beat them with surprising ease, 15-6. The final was not so easy. The Australian pair had previously played against Adriana Behar and Shelda 17 times and lost 14 times. The Brazilians stormed to a 10-6 lead in the first set and twice served for game at 11-8. But Cook and Pottharst saved both set points, tied the score at 11 and then won the set when Cook's serve hit the net and dribbled over. In the second set, Adriana Behar and Shelda again led early, 7-3, 8-5 and 10-8. The Australians scored twice to tie the game at 10-10. Pottharst scored an ace to put them ahead. Then Adriana shot wide and the pro-Australian crowd of 10,000 erupted in joy.

2004 Athens T: 24, N: 17, D: 8.25.
1. USA Kerri Walsh, Misty May
2. BRA Adriana Behar, Shelda Bede
3. USA Holly McPeak, Elaine Youngs
4. AUS Natalie Cook, Nicole Sanderson
5. Ana Paula Rodrigues Connelly, Sandra Tavares (Pires) (BRA); Guylaine Dumont, Annie Martin (CAN); Stephanie Pohl, Okka Rau (GER); Daniela Gattelli, Lucilla Perrotta (ITA)

Final: Walsh/May–Behar/Bede 21-17, 21-11
3rd Place: McPeak/Youngs–Cook/Sanderson 21-18, 15-21, 15-9

Both Kerri Walsh and Misty May competed at the 2000 Olympics. Walsh was a member of the US indoor volleyball team, while May made it to the quarterfinals in the beach event with partner Holly McPeak. Walsh and May teamed up in 2001 and won the 2003 world championship in Rio de Janeiro, defeating Adriana Behar and Shelda Bede 21-19, 21-19 in the final. They also won 90 straight matches between July 2003 and June 2004, before being upset by Americans Annett David and Jennifer Johnson Jordan. At the Olympics, there were no upsets, as Walsh and May won all seven of their matches without losing a single set. Their final victory was a repeat of the 2003 world championships, with Walsh and May beating Adriana and Shelda in straight sets.

Misty May's father, Butch May, was a member of the 1968 US Olympic volleyball team, and her cousin on her mother's side, Taylor Dent, placed fourth in the men's tennis singles event in Athens. May grew up on the beach in Santa Monica, California, where her parents ran a pizza stand.

2008 Beijing T: 24, N: 17, D: 8.21.
1. USA Misty May-Treanor, Kerri Walsh
2. CHN Tian Jia, Wang Jie
3. CHN Xue Chen, Zhang Xi
4. BRA Talita Antunes da Rocha, Renata Trevisan Ribeiro
5. AUS Tamsin Barnett, Natalie Cook
5. AUT Stefanie Schwaiger, Doris Schwaiger
5. BRA Ana Paula Rodrigues Connelly, Larissa França
5. USA Nicole Branagh, Elaine Youngs

Final: May/Walsh—Tian/Wang 21-18, 21-18
3rd Place: Xue/Zhang—Talita/Renata 21-19, 21-17

After winning the 2004 Olympic title, Misty May and Kerri Walsh continued to dominate women's beach volleyball, defending their world championship title in 2005 and 2007 and entering the 2008 Olympic tournament with a 101-match win streak going back to June 2007. The only team to have beaten them at an International Volleyball Federation (FIVB) match in the 2007 season was Chinese pair Tian and Wang. They had lost to Walsh and May at the 2007 world championships, and placed second behind them in the FIVB rankings for the past two years.

As they had in 2004, May and Walsh won every one of their matches in straight sets, beating Brazilians Ana Paula Rodrigues and Larissa França 21-18, 21-15 in the quarterfinals and then defeating their countrywomen Talita Antunes and Renata Ribeiro 21-12, 21-14 to qualify for the gold medal match.

Played in a downpour, the final was a repeat of the 2007 world championship final between Walsh and May and Tian and Wang. Tian and Wang led 18-17, but May and Walsh scored the last four points to take the first set. In the second set May and Walsh took the early lead before the Chinese pair pulled ahead 9-8. But their advantage was short-lived, and May and Walsh went on to win the set 21-18, becoming the first beach volleyball pair to successfully defend an Olympic championship.

Chapter 30 **Water Polo**

Water polo is played with seven players on a team including a goalkeeper. Between 1960 and 1980, matches consisted of four five-minute quarters. In 1984 the quarters were extended to seven minutes. Since 2008 the quarters have been eight minutes long. Ties are not broken in the preliminary round. In the medal round, if there is a tie after regulation play, play continues with two three-minute overtime periods. If the score is still even, a penalty shootout will determine the winner. Prior to 2008, three-minute overtime periods were used to determine the winner. A goal is scored when the entire ball passes over the goal line, between the goal posts, and underneath the crossbar. A goal may be scored using any part of the body except a clenched fist. As in basketball, there is a shot clock: each team must take a shot at the goal within 30 seconds of taking possession of the ball. If they fail to do so, the opposing team takes possession.

The field of play in water polo is 30 meters (32 yards 2 feet, 5 inches) from goal line to goal line. The width is 20 meters (21 yards 2 feet 7½ inches). The goal posts are 3 meters (9 feet 10 inches) apart; the underside of the crossbar is 90 centimeters (2 feet 11½ inches) above the surface of the water. The water must be at least 1.8 meters (5 feet 10⅞ inches) deep and preferably 2 meters (6 feet 6¾ inches) deep. The water temperature must be between 25 and 27 degrees centigrade (77 and 80.6 degrees Fahrenheit).

An offside rule is enforced: no offensive player may cross the line two meters in front of the goal unless he is preceded by the ball.

Water polo is a rough sport filled with a variety of fouls and accompanying officials' whistles. *Ordinary* (or common) *fouls* include holding on to the goal posts, holding the entire ball underwater, hitting the ball with a clenched fist (the goalkeeper is exempted within five meters of the goal), touching the ball with both hands at the same time (again the goalkeeper is exempted), impeding the free movement of an opponent who is not holding the ball, pushing an opponent, and wasting time. An ordinary foul is punished by awarding the opposing team a free throw from the point of the foul. If a foul is committed by a defending player within the two-meter area, the free throw is taken from the two-meter line.

Exclusion fouls include interfering with a free throw, intentionally splashing water in an opponent's face, holding an opponent, kicking or striking an opponent, using foul language, showing disrespect for a referee or other official, and committing an act of brutality. Exclusion fouls are punished by the awarding of a free throw and by the exclusion of the guilty player from the match for 20 seconds or until a goal is scored or his own team regains possession.

Penalty fouls include committing a foul within five meters of the goal a player is defending if a referee rules that the foul prevented a probable goal, committing an act of brutality within five meters of the goal, and toppling the goal cage to prevent a probable score. A penalty throw is taken from behind the five-meter line and any player on a team may be chosen to take the shot. At the 1996 Olympics, 78 percent of penalty throws were successful. If a missed penalty throw rebounds off the goal or the goalkeeper, it is considered in play and the match continues.

Twelve teams take part in the men's tournament and eight teams in the women's. The teams are divided into two round-robin pools with every team playing every other team in their pool. The top team in each pool advances directly to the semifinals, while the second and third place teams compete in the quarterfinals for the right to continue to the semifinals.

The twelve men's teams qualify according to the following formula: the winner of the Water Polo World League; the top three teams in the most recent World Championships; one each from five continental tournaments, including the host team as an automatic representative; the top three teams from an Olympic Games Qualifying Tournament involving teams that have not already qualified.

The formula for the eight women's teams is: the five winners of continental championships, including the host team, and three teams from an Olympic Games Qualifying tournament.

MEN

1896 not held

1900 Paris T: 7, N: 4, D: 8.12.

	W	L	PF	PA
1. GBR	3	0	29	3
2. BEL	2	1	9	8
3. FRA	1	1	4	12
4. FRA	0	1	1	5

Final: GBR 7-2 BEL

1. GBR—Osborne Swimming Club, Manchester: Arthur Robertson, Thomas Coe, Eric Robinson, Peter Kemp, George Wilkinson, John Henry Derbyshire, William Lister, William Henry, Robert Cranshaw, John Jarvis, F. Stapleton, Victor Lindberg
2. BEL—Swimming and Water Polo Club, Brussels: Albert Michant, Fernand Fayaerts, Henri Cohen, Victor de Behr, Oscar Grégoire, Victor Sonnemans, Jean de Backer, Guillaume Séron, Georges Romas, A. R. Upton
3. FRA—Libellule de Paris: Henri Peslier, Thomas Burgess, Alphonse Decuyper, Pesloy, Paul Vasseur, Jules Clévenot, Louis Laufray
3. FRA—Pupilles de Neptune de Lille: Louis Martin, Eugène Coulon, Fardelle, Désiré Merchez, Gellé, Camelin, Fiolet, Louis Marc

Final: GBR 7-2 BEL

In the final, the British limited the number of shots they took in order not to humiliate their opponents by running up the score.

1904–1906 not held

1908 London T: 4, N: 4, D: 7.22.

	W	L	PF	PA
1. GBR	1	0	9	2
2. BEL	2	1	18	14
3. SWE	0	1	4	8
4. HOL	0	1	1	8

Final: GBR 9-2 BEL

1. GBR—Charles Smith, George Nevinson, George Cornet, Thomas Thould, George Wilkinson, Paul Radmilovic, Charles Forsyth
2. BEL—Albert Michant, Herman Meyboom, Victor Boin, Joseph Pletincx, Fernand Feyaerts, Oscar Grégoire, Herman Donners
3. SWE—Torsten Kumfeldt, Axel Runström, Harald Julin, Pontus Hansen, Gunnar Wennerström, Robert Andersson, Erik Bengvall
4. HOL—Johan Rühl, Johan Cortlever, Jan Hulswit, Eduard Meijer, Karel Meijer, Pieter Ooms, Bouke Benehga

Paul Radmilovic of the British team eventually took part in five Olympics as a swimmer and water polo player, and also competed in the 1906 Intercalated Games.

1912 Stockholm T: 6, N: 6, D: 7.13.

	W	L	PF	PA
1. GBR	3	0	21	8
2. SWE	3	1	22	11
3. BEL	3	2	22	21
4. AUT	1	3	10	25
5. HUN	0	2	9	11
6. FRA	0	2	3	11

Final: GBR 8-0 AUT

1. GBR—Charles Smith, George Cornet, Charles Bugbee, Arthur Hill, George Wilkinson, Paul Radmilovic, Isaac Bentham
2. SWE—Torsten Kumfeldt, Harald Julin, Max Gumpel, Pontus Hanson, Wilhelm Andersson, Robert Andersson, Erik Bergqvist
3. BEL—Albert Durant, Herman Donners, Victor Boin, Joseph Pletinckx, Oscar Grégoire, Herman Meyboom, Félicien Courbet, Jean Hoffman, Pierre Nijs
4. AUT—Rudolf Buchfelder, Richard Manuel, Walter Schachtitz, Otto Scheff, Josef Wagner, Ernst Kovács, Hermann Buchfelder
5. HUN—Sándor Ádám, László Beleznai, Tibor Fazekas, Jenő Hégner Tóth, Károly Rémi, János Wenk, Imre Zachár
6. FRA—Gustave Prouvost, Gaston Vanlaere, Georges Rigal, Paul Louis Beulque, Jean Rodier, Jean Thorailler, Henri Decoin, Paul Vasseur

Great Britain's closest call was a 7-5 overtime victory over Belgium. George Wilkinson won his third Olympic championship.

1920 Antwerp T: 12, N: 12, D: 8.27.

	W	L	PF	PA
1. GBR & GBR [IRL]	3	0	19	4
2. BEL	4	1	27	9
3. SWE	4	1	35	9
4. USA	2	3	16	19

Final: GBR 3-2 BEL

1. GBR & GBR [IRL]—Charles Smith, Noel Purcell, Christopher Jones, Charles Bugbee, William Dean, Paul Radmilovic, William Peacock
2. BEL—Albert Durant, Paul Gailly, Pierre Nijs, Joseph Pletinckx, Maurice Blitz, René Bauwens, Gérard Blitz, Pierre de Win
3. SWE—Theodor Nauman, Pontus Hanson, Max Gumpel, Torsten Kumfeldt, Viihelm Anderson, Nils Backlund, Robert Andersson, Erik Andersson, Harald Julin, Enik Bergqvist
4. USA—Preston Steiger, Sophus Jensen, Michael McDermott, Clement Browne, Herbert Vollmer, Harry Hebner, James Carson, William Vosburgh, Herbert Taylor, Perry McGillivray, Norman Ross

The victory of the team from the United Kingdom was not a popular one. After the final match Belgian spectators attacked the British and Irish players, who had to be taken away under the protection of armed guards. Paul Radmilovic, who scored the winning goal in the final, earned his third gold medal in water polo. He won a fourth gold medal in the 1908 4 x 200-meter relay and later competed in water polo in 1924 and 1928.

1924 Paris T: 13, N: 13, D: 7.20.

	W	L	PF	PA
1. FRA	4	0	16	6
2. BEL	4	1	18	10
3. USA	3	2	13	11
4. SWE	3	3	27	12
5. HUN	2	2	17	17
6. CZE	2	2	11	15
7. HOL	1	2	12	10

Final: FRA 3-0 BEL

1. FRA—Paul Dujardin, Noël Delberghe, Georges Rigal, Henri Padou, Robert Desmettre, Albert Mayaud, Albert Delborgies
2. BEL—Albert Durant, Joseph Pletincx, Pierre Dewin, Gérard Blitz, Joseph Cludts, Georges Fleurix, Paul Gailly, Jules Thiry, Pierre Vermetten, Joseph de Combe, Maurice Blitz
3. USA—Frederick Lauer, Oliver Horn, George Mitchell, George Schroth, Herbert Vollmer, P. John Weissmuller, Arthur Austin, John Norton, J. Wallace O'Connor
4. SWE—Theodor Nauman, Gösta Persson, Vilhelm Anderson, Martin Norberg, Erik Andersson, Nils Backlund, Cletus Anderson, Hilmer Wictorin
5. HUN—István Barta, Tibor Fazekas, Márton Homonnai, Alajos Keserű, Lajos Homonnai, János Wenk, Ferenc Keserü, József Vértesy
6. CZE—Václav Ankrt, František Franěk, Ferenc Keserű, Hugo Klempfner, Josef Tomášek, Jiři Reitman, Béla Nemenyi, Jan Hora, František Vacin, Jaroslav Hummelhans
7. HOL—Gérard Bohlander, Frederik Wilhelm "Willy" Bohlander, Willem Bokhoven, Jan den Boer, Jakob "Sjaak" Köhler, Karel Struijs, Antonie "Han" van Senus

The French victory over Belgium came as a great surprise. The Parisian crowd was so excited that, after the playing of the "Marseillaise," they demanded that the Belgian national anthem be played as well. Belgium's loss dropped them into a playoff pool for second place. After defeating Sweden 4-2, they beat the United States, 2-1. However, the Americans lodged a protest, which was allowed. The match was replayed, and the Belgians won again, 2-1.

1928 Amsterdam T: 14, N: 14, D: 8.11.

	W	L	PF	PA
1. GER	3	0	18	10
2. HUN	3	1	26	8
3. FRA	5	1	4	7
4. GBR	2	2	15	21
5. BEL	1	1	14	6
5. HOL	1	1	14	6

Final: GER 5-2 HUN

1. GER—Erich Rademacher, Otto Cordes, Emil Benecke, Fritz Gunst, Joachim Rademacher, Karl Bähre, Max Amann, Johannes Blank
2. HUN—István Barta, Sánder Ivády, Alajos Keserű, Márton Homonnai, Ferenc Keserű, József Vértesy, Olivér Halassy
3. FRA—Paul Dujardin, Jules Keignaert, Henri Padou, Emile Bulteel, Achille Tribouillet, Henri Cuvelier, Albert Vandeplancke, Ernest Rogez, Albert Thévenon
4. GBR—Edward Temme, Paul Radmilovic, Edward Percival Peters, Nicholas Beamen, John "Jack" Budd, Leslie Ablett, Richard Hodgson, John Hatfield, William Quick
5. BEL—Jules Brandeleer, René Bouwens, Joseph Malissart, Gérard Blitz, Pierre Coppieters, Louis van Gheem, Henri de Pauw, Fernand Visser, André Mélardy
5. HOL—Abraham van Olst, Jean van Silfhout, Antonie "Han" van Senus, Jakob "Sjaak" Köhler, Cornelis "Cees" Leenheer, Jan Scholte, Johannes Jacobus "Ko" Köhler

Germany defeated Hungary in overtime after the regulation periods ended in a 2-2 tie.

1932 Los Angeles T: 5, N: 5, D: 8.13.

	W	L	T	PF	PA
1. HUN	3	0	0	31	2
2. GER	2	1	1	23	13
3. USA	2	1	1	20	12
4. JPN	0	3	0	0	38

1. HUN—György Bródy, Sándor Ivády, Márton Homonnai, Olivér Halassy, József Vértesy, Janös Németh, Ferenc Keserű, Alajos Keserű, István Barta, Miklós Sárkány
2. GER—Erich Rademacher, Fritz Gunst, Otto Cordes, Emil Benecke, Joachim Rademacher, Heiko Schwartz, Hans Schulze, Hans Eckstein
3. USA—Herbert Wildman, F. Calvert Strong, Charles Finn, C. Harold McAllister, Philip Daubenspeck, Austin Clapp, Wallace O'Connor
4. JPN—Takashige Matsumoto, Akira Fujita, Shuji Doi, Iwao Tokito, Yasutaro Sakagami, Takaji Takebayashi, Tosuke Sawami, Seibei Kimura

The team from Brazil, having lost 7-3 to Germany, gave a cheer for their conquerors, climbed out of the pool, and physically attacked the Hungarian referee, Béla Komjadi. They didn't let up until the police arrived. Needless to say, the entire Brazilian team was suspended and their remaining games were forfeited.

1936 Berlin T: 16, N: 16, D: 8.15.

	W	L	T	PF	PA
1. HUN	8	0	1	57	5
2. GER	8	0	1	56	10
3. BEL	4	3	2	17	17
4. FRA	4	5	0	21	37
5. HOL	3	1	5	23	28
6. AUT	5	3	1	31	18
7. SWE	3	6	0	29	18
8. GBR	2	4	3	28	46

1. HUN—György Bródy, Kálmán Hazai, Márton Homonnai, Olivér Halassy, Jenő Brandi, János Németh, Mihály Bozsi, György Kutasi, Miklós Sárkány, Sándor Tarics, István Molnár
2. GER—Paul Klingenburg, Bernhard Baier, Gustav Schürger, Fritz Gunst, Josef Hauser, Hans Schneider, Hans Schulze, Fritz Stolze, Heinrich Krug, Alfred Kienzle, Helmuth Schwenn
3. BEL—Henri Disy, Joseph de Combe, Henri Stoelen, Fernand Isselé, Albert Castelyns, Gérard Blitz, Pierre Coppieters, Henri de Pauw, Edmond Michiels
4. FRA—Georges Delporte, Paul Lambert, Maurice Lefebvre, Henri Padou, Roger van de Castelle, André Busch, René Joder
5. HOL—Johannes van Woerkom, Jean van Oostrom Soede, Rudolf den Hamer, Gerard Regter, Hans Maier, Cornelius van Aelst, Alexander Franken, Herman Veenstra, Jan van Hateren
6. AUT—Franz Wenninger, Karl Seitz, Karl Steinbach, Sebastian Ploner, Franz Schönfels, Alfred Lergetporer, Wilhelm Hawlik, Erwin Blasl, Otto Müller, Anton Kunz, Peter Riedl
7. SWE—Åke Nauman, Bertil Berg, Tore Ljungqvist, Gösta Persson, Erik Holm, Georg Svensson (Sollermar), Göte Andersson, Tore Lindzén, Runar Sandström
8. GBR—Alfred North, David Grogan, William Martin, Robert Mitchell, Leslie Ablett, David McGregor, Ernest Blake

Hungary and Germany tied 2-2, but Hungary was awarded first place on the basis of a greater goal differential.

Olivér Halassy played on three Hungarian Olympic water polo teams, despite the fact that one of his legs had been amputated below the knee following a streetcar accident when he was 11. On September 10, 1946, at the age of 37, Halassy was murdered by a Soviet soldier while walking down the street in Budapest.

1948 London T: 18, N: 18, D: 8.7.

	W	L	T	PF	PA
1. ITA	8	0	2	47	24
2. HUN	6	3	1	45	27
3. HOL	6	1	3	65	23
4. BEL	2	2	6	32	25
5. SWE	6	3	1	31	14
6. FRA	4	2	4	32	24
7. EGY	1	4	5	26	35
8. SPA	2	8	0	26	33

1. ITA—Pasquale Buonocore, Emilio Bulgarelli, Cesare Rubini, Geminio Ognio, Ermenegildo Arena, Aldo Ghira, Gianfranco Pandolfini, Mario Maioni, Tullio Pandolfini

2. HUN—Endre Györffi, Miklós Holop, Dezső Gyarmati, Károly Szittya, Oszkár Csuvik, István Szivós, Dezső Lemhényi, László Jeney, Dezső Fábián, Jenő Brandi
3. HOL—Johannes Rohner, Cornelis Korevaar, Cornelius Braasem, Hans Stam, Albert Ruimschotel, Rudolph van Feggelen, Frits Smol, Pieter Salomons, Hendrikus Keetelaar
4. BEL—Théo-Léo de Smet, Georges Leenheere, Emile d'Hooge, Paul Rigaumont, Fernand Isselé, Willy Simons, Alphonse Martin
5. SWE—Rune Öberg, Erik Holm, Rolf Julin, Roland Spångberg, Arne Jutner, Olle Johansson, Åke Julin, Folke Eriksson, Knut Gadd, Olle Ohlsson
6. FRA—François Debonnet, Maurice Lefebvre, Robert Le Bras, Marco Diener, Robert Himgi, Roger Dewasch, Jacques Berthe, Raymond Massol, Jacques Viaene, Emile Bermyn, Marcel Spilliaert
7. EGY—Ahmed Nessim, Taha El Gamal, Mohamed Khadry, Mohamed Haraga, Dorri El Said, Mohamed Abdel Aziz Khalifa, Samir Gharbo, Mohamed Hemmat
8. SPA—Juan Serra Llobet, José Pujol Coma, Carlos Falt Mont, Carlos Martí Arenas, Francisco Castillo Caupana, Agustín Mestres Rivas Valentín Sabate Mas, Angel Sabata Figa

1952 Helsinki T: 21, N: 21, D: 8.2.

	W	L	T	PF	PA
1. HUN	7	0	3	60	21
2. YUG/CRO	7	0	3	46	16
3. ITA	8	2	0	53	29
4. USA	5	6	0	43	41
5. HOL	7	2	1	45	22
6. BEL	6	3	1	37	35
7. SOV	4	4	2	43	34
8. SPA	3	7	0	33	41

1. HUN—László Jeney, György Vizvári, Dezső Gyarmati, Kálmán Markovits, Antal Bolváni, István Szivós, György Kárpáti, Róbert Antal, Dezső Fábián, Károly Szittya, Dezső Lemhényi, István Hasznos, Miklós Martin
2. YUG/CRO—Zdravko Kovačić, Veljko Bakašun, Ivo Štakula, Ivo Kurtini, Boško Vuksanović, Zdravko Ježić, Lovro Radonjić, Marko Brainović, Vlado Ivković
3. ITA—Raffaello Gambino, Vincenzo Polito, Cesare Rubini, Carlo Peretti, Ermenegildo Arena, Maurizio Mannelli, Renato De Sanzuane, Renato Traiolo, Geminio Ognio, Salvatore Gionta, Lucio Ceccarini
4. USA—Harry Bisbey, James Norris, Edward Jaworski, Norman Lake, William Kooistra, Peter Stange, Norman Dornblaser, John Spargo, Robert Hughes, Maroni Burns
5. HOL—Marcus van Gelder, Gerrit Bijsma, Cornelis Korevaar, Cornelius Braasem, Frits Smol, Rudolph van Geggelen, Johannes Cabout
6. BEL—Théo-Léo de Smet, Alphonse Martin, Joseph Smits, André Laurent, Marcel Heyninck, Roland Sierens, Johan van den Steen, François Maesschalck, Georges Leenheere, Joseph Reynders
7. SOV—Boris Goikhman, Yevgeny Semenov, Yuri Teplov, Lev Kokorin, Valentin Prokopov, Aleksandr Liferenko, Pyotr Mshvenieradze, Yuri Schlyapin, Vitaly Ushakov
8. SPA—Leandro Ribera Abad, Ricardo Conde Rosales, Josep Bazán Vilaldach, Roberto Queralt Alantorn, Antonio Subirana Castillejos, Agustín Mestres Rivas, José Abellán Pallani, Francisco Castillo Caupano

Holland defeated Yugoslavia 3-2 in a game of the semifinal round. However the Yugoslavs protested two decisions of the Belgian referee, and the match was ordered replayed. This time Yugoslavia won, 2-1, and advanced to the final round, in which they tied Hungary, 2-2, but lost because of a lower goal differential. One of the Hungarian players was Dezso Gyarmati, who eventually won medals in five different Olympics (1948-1964.) His wife, Éva Székely, was a breaststroker who won a gold medal in 1952 and a silver in 1956.

1956 Melbourne T: 10, N: 10, D: 12.7.

	W	L	T	PF	PA
1. HUN	7	0	0	32	6
2. YUG/CRO	6	1	1	28	13
3. SOV	5	3	0	23	20
4. ITA	4	3	0	21	16
5. USA	2	5	1	18	25
6. GER	1	5	1	18	25
7. GBR	3	2	0	25	20
8. ROM	3	3	0	30	17

1. HUN—Ottó Boros, István Hevesi, Dezső Gyarmati, Kálmán Markovits, Antal Bolvári, Mihály Mayer, György Kárpáti, László Jeney, István Szivós, Tivadar Kanizsa, Ervin Zádor
2. YUG/CRO—Zdravko Kovačić, Ivo Cipci, Hrvoje Kačić, Marijan Žužej, Zdravko Ježić, Lovro Radonjić, Tomislav Franjkovič, Vladimir Ivkovič
3. SOV—Boris Goikhman, Viktor Ageyev, Yuri Schlyapin, Vyacheslav Kurennoi, Pyotr Breus, Pyotr Mshvenieradze, Nodar Gvakharia, Mikhail Ryzhak, Valentin Prokopov, Boris Markarov
4. ITA—Enzo Cavazzoni, Cesare Rubini, Angelo Marciani, Paolo Pucci, Federico Dennerlein, Giuseppe D'Altrui, Alfonso Buonocore, Cosimo Antonelli, Luigi Mannelli, Maurizio D'Achille
5. USA—Robert Horn, William Ross, Robert Frojen, Wallace Wolf, Ronald Severa, James Gaughran, William Kooistra, Kenneth Hahn, Robert Hughes, Sam Kooistra
6. GER—Karl Neuse, Alfred Obschernikat, Wilfried Bode, Hans-Joachim Schneider, Wilhelm Sturin, Hans-Günther Hilker, Friedhelm Osselmann, Emil Bildstein, Erich Pennekamp, Hans Werner Seher
7. GBR—Arthur Grady, Gerald Worsell, John "Jack" Jones, Peter Pass, Ronald Turner, Terence Miller, E. Clifford Spooner, John Ferguson, Robert Knights
8. ROM—Alexandru Marinescu, Zoltan Hospodar, Aurel Zahan, Gavril Nagy, Francisc Simon, Ivan Bordi, Alexandru Szabo, Alexandru Bădiță, Iosif Deutsch

On November 4, 1956, 200,000 Soviet troops invaded Hungary to put down a major revolt against Communist rule. The bitter feelings between the Hungarians and Soviets carried over into the Olympics, which were held less than three weeks later. Hostilities culminated in the water polo match between the two countries on December 6. Although the players on the two teams had previously been on friendly terms, the game quickly turned into a brawl and was halted by the referee before completion, with Hungary leading 4-0. Hungary was credited with a victory; however the police had to be called in to prevent a riot, as the 5500 spectators wanted to punish the Soviets further.

1960 Rome T: 16, N: 16, D: 9.3.

	W	L	T	PF	PA
1. ITA	8	0	1	37	15
2. SOV	6	2	1	35	26
3. HUN	5	2	2	45	22
4. YUG	7	2	0	31	15
5. ROM	4	3	2	34	26
6. GER	4	5	0	42	48
7. USA	4	5	0	42	48
8. HOL	1	7	1	32	38

1. ITA—Dante Rossi, Giuseppe D'Aitrui, Eraldo Pizzo, Gianni Lonzi, Franco Lavoratori, Rosario Parmegiani, Danio Bardi, Brunello Spinelli, Salvatore Gionta, Amadeo Ambron, Giancarlo Guerrini
2. SOV—Leri Gogoladze, Givi Chikvanaya, Vyacheslav Kurennoi, Anatoly Kartashov, Yuri Grigorovsky, Pyotr Mshvenieradze, Vladimir Semyonov, Boris Goikhman, Yevgeny Salzyn, Viktor Ageyev, Vladimir Novikov
3. HUN—Ottó Boros, István Hevesi, Mihály Mayer, Dezső Gyarmati, Tivadar Konizsa, Zoltán Dömötör, László Felkai, László Jeney, András Katona, Kálmán Markovits, Péter Rusorán, György Kárpáti, János Konrád, András Bodnár
4. YUG—Milan Muškatirović, Hrvoje Kačić, Zlatko Šimenc, Zdravko Ježić, Marijen Žužej, Ante Nardeli, Mirko Sandić, Božidar Stanišić Drajoljub Siljak
5. ROM—Mircea Stefănescu, Alexandru Bădită, Aurel Zohan, Gavril Blajek, Alexandru Szabo, Anatol Grinţescu, Stefan Kroner
6. GER—Hans Hoffmeister, Hans-Joachim Schneider, Hans Schepers, Bernd Straesser, Lajos Nagy, Friedhelm Osselmann, Dieter Seiz, Emil Bildstein, Jürgen Honig
7. USA—Robert Horn, Marvin Burns, Ronald Severa, Ronald Crawford, Frederick Tisue, Wallace Wolf, Robert Volmer, Gordon Hall, Charles Bittick, Charles McIlroy
8. HOL—Lambertus Kniest, Harry Lamme, Frederik van der Zwan, Harro Ran, Abraham Leenards, Henri Vriend, Alfred van Dorp, Johannes Muller, Hendrik Hermsen

1964 Tokyo T: 13, N: 13, D: 10.18.

	W	L	T	PF	PA
1. HUN	6	0	2	43	17
2. YUG	7	0	2	42	16
3. SOV	5	2	1	20	13
4. ITA	4	4	0	17	19
5. ROM	4	3	1	36	28
6. GDR	3	5	0	26	26
7. BEL	2	6	0	28	43
8. HOL	4	5	0	37	47

1. HUN—Miklos Ambrus, László Felkai, János Konrád, Zoltán Dömötör, Tivadar Kanizsa, Péter Rusorán, György Kárpáti, Ottó Boros, Mihály Mayer, Dénes Pócsik, András Bodnár, Dezső Gyarmati
2. YUG—Milan Muškatirović, Ivo Trumbić, Vinka Rosić, Zlatko Šimenc, Božidar Stanišić, Ante Nardelli, Zoran Janković, Mirko Sandić, Ozren Bonačič, Frane Nonković, Kanlo Stipanić
3. SOV—Igor Grabovsky, Vladimir Kuznetsov, Boris Grishin, Boris Popov, Nikolai Kaleshnikov, Zenon Bortkevich, Nikolai Kuznetsov, Viktor Ageyev, Leonid Osipov, Vladimir Semyonov, Eduard Yegorov
4. ITA—Dante Rossi, Giuseppe D'Altrui, Eraldo Pizzo, Gianni Lonzi, Franco Lavoratori, Rosario Parmegiani, Mario Cevasco, Eugenio Merello, Alberto Spinola, Danio Bardi, Giancarlo Guerrini, Federico Dennerlein
5. ROM—Mircea Ştefănescu, Anatol Grinţescu, Alexandru Szabo, Ştefan Kroner, Nicolae Firoiu, Gruia Novac, Cornel Mărculescu, Emil Mureşan, Aurel Zahan, Iosif Kulineac
6. GDR—Peter Schmidt, Hubert Höhne, Siegfried Ballerstedt, Edgar Thiele, Klaus Schulze, Jürgen Thiel, Klaus Schlenkrich, Heinz Mäder, Dieter Vohs, Jürgen Kluge, Heinz Wittig
7. BEL—Bruno De Hesselle, Frank D'Osterlinck, Roger De Wilde, Jacques Cafrier, André Laurent, Karel De Vis, Jose de Vis, Nicolas Dumont, Johan Van Den Steen, Léon Pickers, Joseph Stappers
8. HOL—Hendrik Hermsen, Abraham Leenards, Willem van Springelen, Gerardus Wormgoor, Alfred van Dorp, Henri Vriend, Nicolaas van der Voet, Willem Vriend, Johan Muller, Jan Bultman, Lambertus Kniest

Thirty-seven-year-old Dezső Gyarmati brought his medal total to three gold, one silver, and one bronze. The Hungarians' narrow victory was the result of a 4-4 tie with Yugoslavia, in which they scored their final goal with only 25 seconds to play. After that they won because of a greater goal differential in the final round. A minor controversy developed when Hungary and Italy complained that the shallow pool (5 feet 10 inches deep) allowed the taller Yugoslav players to stand with their heads above the water.

1968 Mexico City T: 15, N: 15, D: 10.26.

	W	L	T	PF	PA
1. YUG	7	1	1	86	35
2. SOV	6	2	0	62	36
3. HUN	6	2	0	54	26
4. ITA	6	2	1	57	38
5. USA	5	2	1	49	43
6. GDR	6	2	1	78	30
7. HOL	5	3	1	53	39
8. CUB	3	4	1	38	51

1. YUG—Karlo Stipanić, Ivo Trumbić, Ozren Bonačić, Uroš Marović, Ronald Lopatni, Zoran Janković, Miroslav Poljak, Dejan Dabović, Đorđe Perišić, Mirko Sandić, Zdravko Hebel
2. SOV—Vadim Gulyayev, Givi Chikvanaya, Boris Grishin, Aleksandr Dolgushin, Oleksei Barkalov, Yuri Grigorovsky, Vladimir Semyonov, Aleksandr Shidiovsky, Vyacheslav Skok, Leonid Osipov, Oleg Bovin
3. HUN—Endre Molnár, Mihály Mayer, Istvan Szivós, János Konrád, László Felkai, Ferenc Konrád, Dénes Pócsik, Andrós Bodnár, Zoltán Dömötör, János Steinmetz
4. ITA—Alberto Alberani Samaritani, Eraldo Pizzo, Mario Cevasco, Gianni Lonzi, Enzo Barlocco, Franco Lavoratori, Gianni De Magistris, Alessandro Ghibellini, Giancarlo Guerrini, Paolo Ferrando, Eugenio Merello
5. USA—Anton Van Dorp, David Ashleigh, Russell Webb, Ronald Crawford, Stanley Cole, Bruce Bradley, L. Dean Willeford, Barry Weitzenberg, Gary Sheerer, John Parker, Steven Barnett
6. GDR—Hans-Georg Fehn, Klaus Schlenkrich, Jürgen Thiel, Siegfried Ballerstedt, Peter Rund, Jürgen Schüler, Jürgen Kluge, Veit Herrmanns, Manfred Herzog, Hans-Ulrich Lange, Peter Schmidt
7. HOL—Feike de Vries, Hans Wouda, Louis Geutjes, Johannes Hoogveld, Alfred van Dorp, Hans Parrell, Nicolaas van der Voet, Adrianus Moolhuijzen, Bartolomeus Bongers, Andreas Hermsen, Evert Kroon
8. CUB—Oscar Periche Cordet, Waldimiro Arcos Riera, Miguel Angel García Torres, Rolando Valdés González, Rubén Junco Borrell, Guillermo Martínez Ginoris, Ibrahim "Chepe" Rodríguez González, Osvaldo García del Poso, Roberto Rodríguez Reyes, Guillermo Cañete Reyes, Jesús Pérez Leal

In the final match, Yugoslavia defeated the USSR 13-11 in overtime, despite seven goals by Oleksei Barkalov, including two in the last 35 seconds of regulation. Australia had been accepted as one of the 16 teams to take part in the tournament. However, the Australian Olympic Committee considered it a waste of money to send their team to Mexico City. The players paid their own way, but were not allowed to compete.

1972 Munich T: 16, N: 16, D: 9.4.

	W	L	T	PF	PA
1. SOV	7	0	2	52	25
2. HUN	6	0	3	45	24
3. USA	7	1	2	55	41
4. GER	2	2	5	36	31
5. YUG	5	4	1	55	48
6. ITA	3	4	2	48	42
7. HOL	6	1	2	43	31
8. ROM	5	4	1	62	45

1. SOV—Vadim Gulyayev, Anatoly Akimov, Aleksandr Dreval, Aleksandr Dolgushin, Vladimir Shmudsky, Aleksandr Kabanov, Oleksei Barkalov, Aleksandr Shidlovsky, Nikolai Melnikov, Leonid Osipov, Vyacheslav Sobchenko
2. HUN—Endre Molnár, András Bodnár, István Görgényi, Zoltán Kásás, Tamás Faragó, László Sárosi, István Szivós, István Magas, Dénes Pócsik, Ferenc Konrád, Tibor Cservenyák
3. USA—James Slatton, Stanley Cole, Russell Webb, Barry Weitzenberg, Gary Sheerer, Bruce Bradley, Peter Asch, James Ferguson, Steven Barnett, John Parker, Eric Lindroth
4. GER—Gerd Olbert, Hermann Haverkamp, Peter Teicher, Kurt Küpper, Günter Wolf, Ingulf Nossek, Ludger Weeke, Kurt Schuhmann, Jürgen Stiefel, Hans Georg Simon, Hans Hoffmeister
5. YUG—Karlo Stipanić, Ratko Rudić, Ozren Bonačić, Uroš Marović, Ronald Lopatni, Zoran Janković, Siniša Belamarić, Dušan Antunović, Đorđe Perišić, Mirko Sandić, Milos Marković
6. ITA—Alberto Alberani, Eraldo Pizzo, Roldano Simeoni, Mario Cevasco, Allessandro Ghibellini, Gianni De Magistris, Guglielmo Marsili, Silvio Baracchini, Franco Lavoratori, Sante Marsili, Ferdinando Lignano
7. HOL—Evert Kroon, Hans Wouda, Jan Evert Veer, Hans Hoogveld, Willem Hermsen, Hans Parrel, Antoon Schmidt, Martinus Bras, Anton Buunk, Gijze Stroboer, Willem van de Schilde
8. ROM—Serban Huber, Bogdan Mihăilescu, Gheorghe Zamfirescu, Gruia Novac, Dinu Popescu, Claudiu Rusu, Iosif Kuliniac, Cornel Rusu, Viorel Rus, Radu Lazăr, Cornel Frățilă

The tournament included a bloody match between Yugoslavia and Cuba, and a contest between Hungary and Italy in which eight players were suspended within one 38-second span.

1976 Montreal T: 12, N: 12, D: 7.27.

	W	L	T	PF	PA
1. HUN	7	0	1	45	32
2. ITA	4	1	3	47	33
3. HOL	5	1	2	32	27
4. ROM	2	2	4	44	39
5. YUG	1	2	5	46	34
6. GER	2	5	1	24	28
7. CUB	5	1	2	56	31
8. SOV	4	2	2	47	28

1. HUN—Endre Molnár, István Szivós Jr., Tamás Faragó, László Sárosi, György Horkai, Gábor Csapó, Attila Sudár, György Kenéz, György Gerendás, Ferenc Konrád, Tibor Cservenyák
2. ITA—Alberto Alberani, Roldano Simeoni, Silvio Baracchini, Sante Marsili, Marcello Del Duca, Gianni De Magistris, Alessandro Ghibellini, Luigi Castagnola, Riccardo De Magistris, Vincenzo D'Angelo, Umberto Panerai
3. HOL—Evert Kroon, Nicolaas Landeweerd, Jan Evert Veer, Hans van Zeeland, Anton Buunk, Pieter de Zwarte, Hans Smits, Hendrik Toonen, Gijze Stroboer, Ilja Mohandas "Andy" Hoepelman, Alex Boegschoten
4. ROM—Florin Slăvei, Cornel Rusu, Gheorghe Zamfirescu, Adrian Nastasiu, Dinu Popescu, Claudiu Rusu, Ilie Slăvei, Liviu Răducanu, Viorel Rus, Adrian Schervan, Doru Spinu
5. YUG—Milos Marković, Ozren Bonačić, Uroš Marović, Predrag Manojlović, Đuro Savinović, Damir Polić, Siniša Belamarić, Dušan Antunović, Dejan Dabović, Boško Lozica, Zoran Kačić
6. GER—Günter Kilian, Ludger Weeke, Hans-Georg Simon, Jürgen Stiefel, Roland Freund, Wolfgang Mechler, Martin Jellinghaus, Werner Obschernikat, Horst Kilian, Peter Röhle, Günter Wolf
7. CUB—Oscar Periche Cordet, Osvaldo García del Poso, Ramon Peña Silva, Lázaro Costa Méndez, David Rodríguez Rodríguez, Nelson Domínguez Avila, Jorge Rizo Perera, Eugenio Almenteros Pérez, Jesús Pérez Leal, Gerardo Rodríguez Peñalver, Oriel Domínguez Ávila
8. SOV—Anatoly Klebanov, Sergei Kotenko, Aleksandr Dreval, Aleksandr Dolgushin, Vitaly Romanchuk, Aleksandr Kabanov, Aleksei Barkalov, Nikolai Melnikov, Nuzgari Mshvenieradze, Vladimir Iselidze, Aleksandr Za

The Soviet team was so humiliated by their failure to qualify for the final round of six that they tried to withdraw from the losers' round for seventh to 12th places, claiming that five of their players were too ill to compete. After forfeiting one game against Cuba, FINA officials convinced them to continue with the tournament.

1980 Moscow T: 12, N: 12, D: 7.29.

	W	L	T	PF	PA
1. SOV	8	0	0	58	31
2. YUG	5	1	2	58	42
3. HUN	5	2	1	51	44
4. SPA	4	4	0	43	42
5. CUB	2	3	3	50	49
6. HOL	2	5	1	42	48
7. AUS	5	2	1	45	39
8. ITA	4	3	1	40	35

1. SOV—Yevgeny Sharonov, Sergei Kotenko, Vladimir Akimov, Yevgeny Grishin, Mait Riisman, Aleksandr Kabanov, Oleksei Barkalov, Erkin Shagayev, Georgy Mshvenieradze, Mikhail Ivanov, Vyacheslav Sobchenko
2. YUG—Luka Vezilić, Zoran Gopčević, Damir Polić, Ratko Rudić, Zoran Mustur, Zoran Roje, Milivoj Bebić, Slobodan Trifunović, Boško Lozica, Predrag Manojlović, Milorad Krivokapić
3. HUN—Andre Molnár, István Szivós Jr., Attila Sudár, György Gerendás, György Horkai, Gábor Csapó, István Kiss, István Udvardi, László Kuncz, Tamás Faragó, Károly Hauszler
4. SPA—Manuel Delgado Ollo, Gaspart Ventura Messeguer, Antonio Esteller Serrahima, Federico Sabriá Miracle, Manuel Estiarte Duocastella, Pedro Robert Font, Jorge Alonso Íñiguez, José Alcázar Pérez, Antonio Aguilar Chastellain, Jorge Carmona Espinosa, Salvador Franch Martínez

5. CUB—Oscar Periche Cordet, Orlando Cowley del Barrio, Bárbaro Díaz Cervantes, Lázaro Costa Méndez, Pedro Rodríguez Rodríguez, Nelson Domínguez Avila, Jorge Rizo Perera, Arturo Ramos Hernández, Carlos Benítez Suárez, Gerardo Rodríguez Peñalver, Oriel Dominguez Avila
6. HOL—Wouly de Bie, Nicolaas Landeweerd, Jan Evert Veer, Hans van Zeeland, Anton Buunk, Eric Noordegraaf, Stanislaus van Belkum, Adrianus van Mil, Richard Nieuwenhuizen, Jan Jaap Korevaar, Rudolf Misdorp
7. AUS—Michael Turner, David Neesham, Robert Bryant, Peter Montgomery, Julian Muspratt, Andrew Kerr, Anthony Folson, Charles Turner, Martin Callaghan, Randall Goff, Andrew Steward
8. ITA—Alberto Alberani, Roldano Simeoni, Alfio Misaggi, Sante Marsili, Massimo Fondelli, Gianni De Magistris, Antonello Steardo, Paolo Ragosa, Romeo Collina, D'Angelo Vincenzo, Umberto Panerai

The USSR clinched first place with a tension-packed 8-7 victory over Yugoslavia. Between 1928 and 1980, Hungarian water polo teams won medals in twelve consecutive Olympics.

1984 Los Angeles T: 12, N: 12, D: 8.10.

	W	L	T	PF	PA
1. YUG	6	0	1	72	44
2. USA	6	0	1	65	43
3. GER	4	2	1	74	46
4. SPA	3	2	2	73	67
5. AUS	2	3	2	58	58
6. HOL	2	5	0	45	65
7. ITA	4	1	2	75	52
8. GRE	3	2	2	66	65

1. YUG—Milorad Krivokapić, Deni Lušić, Zoran Petrović, Božo Vuletić, Veselin Djuho, Zoran Roje, Milivoj Beblć, Perica Bukić, Goran Sukno, Tomislav Paskvalin, Igor Milanović, Dragan Andrić
2. USA—Craig Wilson, Kevin Robertson, Gary Figueroa, Peter Campbell, Douglas Burke, Joseph Vargas, Jon Svendsen, John Siman, Andrew McDonald, Terry Schroeder, Jodocus David "Jody" Campbell, Timothy Shaw
3. GER—Peter Röhle, Thomas Loebb, Frank Otto, Rainer Hoppe, Armando Fernandez, Thomas Huber, Jürgen Schröder, Rainer Osselmann, Hagen Stamm, Roland Freund, Dirk Theismann, Santiago Chalmovsky, Werner Obschernikat
4. SPA—Leandro Ribera Perpiñá, José Morillo Lobo, Félix Fernández Salcines, Alberto Canal Chonros, Manuel Estiarte Duocastella, Pedro Robert Font, Rafael Aguilar Morillo, Jorge Signes Portit, Antonio Aguilar Chastellain, Jorge Carmona Espinosa, Jordi Sans Juan, Jorge Neira Tost
5. AUS—Michael Turner, Richard Pengelley, Robert Bryant, Peter Montgomery, Russell Sherwell, Andrew Kerr, Raymond Mayers, Charles Turner, Martin Callaghan, Christopher Wybrow, Russell Basser, Julian Muspratt, Glenn Townsend
6. HOL—Wouly de Bie, Nicolaas Landeweerd, Eric Noordegraaf, Eduard van Es, Anton Buunk, Richard Nieuwenhuizen, Stanislaus van Belkum, Adrianus van Mil, Johan Aantjes, Anton Heiden, Remco Pielstroom, Roald van Noert, Rudolf Misdorp
7. ITA—Roberto Gandolfi, Alfio Misaggi, Andrea Pisano, Antonello Steardo, Maria Fiorillo, Gianni De Magistris, Marco Galli, Marco D'Altrui, Marco Baldineti, Vicenzo D'Angelo, Romeo Collino, Stefano Postiglione, Umberto Panerai
8. GRE—Ioannis Vossos, Spyros Capralos, Sotirios Stathakis, Andreas Gounas, Kiriakos Giannopoulos, Aristidis Kefalogiannis, Anastasios Papanastasiou, Dimitrios Seletopoulos, Antonios Aronis, Markellos Sitarenios, George Mavrotas, Xenofon Moudatsios, Stavros Giannopoulos

Trailing 5-2 with less than three minutes remaining in the third quarter of their final match against the US, Yugoslavia patiently rallied to tie the game 5-5 with three minutes left in the final period. Tenacious defense allowed the relatively inexperienced Yugoslavians to hold on until the end. The two teams finished with identical records but Yugoslavia won the tournament as a result of a greater goal differential in the medal round.

1988 Seoul T: 12, N: 12, D: 10.1.

	W	L	T	PF	PA
1. YUG	6	1	0	83	55
2. USA	5	2	0	71	56
3. SOV	4	2	1	84	51
4. GER	5	2	0	83	65
5. HUN	3	2	2	72	57
6. SPA	4	2	1	66	55
7. ITA	3	2	2	66	53
8. AUS	3	4	0	53	59

Final: YUG 9-7 USA (overtime)
3rd Place: SOV 14-13 GER

1. YUG—Aleksandar Šoštar, Deni Lušić, Dubravko Šimenc, Perica Bukić, Veselin Djuho, Dragan Andrić, Mirko Vičević, Igor Gočanin, Mislav Bezmalinović, Tomislav Paškvalin, Igor Milanović, Goran Radjenović, Renco Posinković
2. USA—Craig Wilson, Kevin Robertson, James Bergeson, George Campbell, Douglas Kimball, Craig Klass, Alan Mouchawar, Jeffrey Campbell, Gregory Boyer, Terry Schroeder, Jodocus David "Jody" Campbell, Christopher Duplanty, Michael Evans
3. SOV—Yevgeny Sharonov, Nurlan Mendygaliev, Yevgeny Grishin, Aleksandr Kolotov, Sergei Naumov, Viktor Berendyuha, Sergei Kotenko, Dmitri Apanasenko, Georgy Mshvenieradze, Mikhail Ivanov, Sergei Markoch, Mykola Smyrnov, Mikhail Giorgadze
4. GER—Peter Röhle, Dirk Jacoby, Frank Otto, Uwe Sterzik, Armando Fernandez, Andreas Ehrl, Ingo Borgmann, Rainer Osselmann, Hagen Stamm, Thomas Huber, Dirk Theismann, René Reimann, Werner Obschernikat
5. HUN—Péter Kuna, Gábor Bujka, Gábor Schmiedt, Zsolt Petővár y, István Pintér, Tibor Keszthelyi, Balázs Vincze, Zoltán Mohi, Tibor Pardi, László Tóth, András Györgyösi, Zoltán Kósz, Imre Tóth
6. SPA—Jesús Rollán Prada, Miguel Chillida Santiesteban, Marco Antonio González Junquera, Miguel Pérez Ibern, Manuel Estiarte Duocastella, Pedro Robert Font, Jorge Payá Rodríguez, José Antonio Rodriguez, Jordi "Chiqui" Sans Juan, Salvador Gómez Agüera, Mariano Moya San Martín, Jorge Neira Tost, Pedro García Aguado
7. ITA—Paolo Trapanese, Alfio Misaggi, Andrea Pisano, Antonello Steardo, Alessandro Campagna, Paolo Caldarella, Mario Fiorilla, Francesco Porzio, Stefano Postiglione, Riccardo Empestini, Massimiliano Ferretti, Marco D'Altrui, Gianni Averaima
8. AUS—Glenn Townsend, Richard Pengelley, Christopher Harrison, Troy Stockwell, Andrew Wightman, Andrew Kerr, Raymond Mayers, Geoffrey Clark, John Fox, Christopher Wybrow, Simon Asher, Andrew Taylor, Donald Cameron

Yugoslavia and the United States played each other eight times in the two and a half months before the Olympics; the US won five matches, Yugoslavia three. They met again to open the preliminary round in Seoul. The US won again, this time 7-6 on a goal by Jim Bergeson with 5 seconds to play.

Ten days later, the American and Yugoslavian teams, both of which returned five players from their 1984 Olympic squads, matched up yet again in a replay of the Los Angeles final. In fact, as the championship game developed, there were certain eerie and, for the US, unfortunate similarities between the two contests. Just as they had four years earlier, the US team took a 5-2 lead in the third quarter. Then, just as it had four years earlier, the US play became tentative and the Yugoslavians fought back to tie the score 5-5. This time they also took the lead 6-5, although the US scored one more goal to break a 10-minute drought with 2:12 to play. The game ended 6-6.

Following the rather unsatisfactory conclusion of the 1984 Olympics, in which the gold medal was determined by goal differential, the FINA decided to change the rules to allow six-minute overtime periods in the medal round. In fact, the 1986 world championship was decided when Yugoslavia's Igor Milanović defeated the USSR by scoring a goal with three-tenths of a second remaining in the *fourth* overtime period.

In Seoul no such marathon was needed. Yugoslavia scored three unanswered goals in the first 3:35 of overtime and held on for a 9-7 victory. The Yugoslavian players *averaged* 6 feet 6 inches (1.98 meters) tall.

1992 Barcelona T: 12, N: 12, D: 8.9.

	W	L	T	PF	PA
1. ITA	5	0	2	59	50
2. SPA	5	1	1	67	48
3. SOV	6	1	0	66	45
4. USA	4	2	1	48	38
5. HUN	4	1	2	69	64
6. GER	1	3	3	52	56
7. CUB	2	5	0	66	72
8. AUS	3	2	2	58	53

Final: ITA 9-8 SPA (overtime)
3rd Place: SOV 8-4 USA

1. ITA—Francesco Attolico, Alessandro Bovo, Alessandro Campagna, Paolo Caldarella, Mario Fiorillo, Francesco Porzio, Massimiliano Ferretti, Marco D'Altrui, Ferdinando Gandolfi, Amedeo Pomillo, Giuseppe Porzio, Carlo Silipo, Gianni Averaimo
2. SPA—Daniel Ballart Sans, Manuel Estiarte Duocastella, Pedro García Aguado, Salvador Gómez Agüera, Marco Antonio González, Rubén Michavila Jover, Miguel Oca Gaia, Sergio Pedrerol Cavallé, Josep Picó Lladó, Jesús Rollán Prada, Ricardo Sánchez Alarcón, Jordi "Chiqui" Sans Juan, Manuel Silvestre Sánchez
3. SOV—Dmitri Apanasenko, Andrei Belofastov, Yevgeny Sharonov, Dmitri Gorshkov, Vladimir Karabutov, Aleksandr Kolotov, Andrei Kovalenko, Nikolai Kozlov, Sergei Markoch, Sergei Naumov, Aleksandr Ogorodnikov, Aleksandr Chigir, Aleksei Vdovin
4. USA—Jeffrey Campbell, Christopher Duplanty, Michael Evans, Kirk Everist, Erich Fischer, Charles Harris, Christopher Humbert, Douglas Kimbell, Craig Klass, Alexis Rousseau, , Terry Schroeder, John Vargas, Craig Wilson
5. HUN—Péter Kuna, Gábor Schmiedt, Zsolt Petőváry, Balázs Vincze, László Tóth, András Györgyösi, Imre Tóth, Tibor Benedek, István Dóczi, Gábor Nemes, Imre Péter, Frank Tóth, Zsolt Varga
6. GER—Frank Otto, Uwe Sterzik, Ingo Borgmann, Hagen Stamm, Dirk Theismann, René Reimann, Piotr Bukowski, Raúl de la Peña Vega, Jörg Dresel, Torsten Dresel, Carsten Kusch, Guido Reibel, Peter Röhle
7. CUB—Juan Barreras Benítez, Norge Blay García, Pablo Cuesta Zulueta, Jorge del Valle Gutiérrez, Marcelo Derouville de la Cruz, Bárbaro Díaz Cervantes, Lázaro Fernández Bueno, Juan Hernández Olivera, Juan Hernández Silveira, Guillermo Martínez Luis, Iván Pérez Vargas, José Ramos Soler, Ernesto García Piñero
8. AUS—Glenn Townsend, Troy Stockwell, Andrew Wightman, Raymond Mayers, Geoffrey Clark, John Fox, Christopher Wybrow, Simon Asher, Daniel Marsden, Gregory McFadden, Guy Newman, Mark Oberman, Paul Oberman

Final: ITA 9-8 SPA (overtime)
3rd Place: SOV 8-4 USA

In the run-up to the Olympics it was assumed the final would be a showdown between Yugoslavia, the two-time defending Olympic champion, and Spain, seven of whose members were native Barcelonans. Yugoslavia had defeated Spain 8-7 in the final of the 1991 world championships and 11-10 in the final of the 1991 European championships. But two days before the Opening Ceremony of the Barcelona Games, the International Olympic Committee supported United Nations sanctions against Yugoslavia by banning the militarily aggressive nation from the Olympics. Individual athletes from Yugoslavia could compete under the banner of "Independent Olympic Participants," but Yugoslavia was not allowed to take part in team sports, such as water polo.

Surprisingly, it was the team from Italy that provided the challenge to Spain that had been expected to come from Yugoslavia. To say that the Italians and the Spanish were evenly matched is to put it mildly. They first met in pool play and tied 9-9. Four days later they faced each other again in the final.

In the semifinals, Spain had beaten the United States 6-4, while Italy had upset the predominantly Russian team from the ex-Soviet Union 9-8 on a penalty throw by Alessandro Campagna with 2:04 to play. The Yugoslav team may not have been present at the final, but the Yugoslavian system was very much in evidence: both head coaches, Dragan Matutinović of Spain and Ratko Rudić of Italy, were from Croatia, which had declared its independence from Yugoslavia in June of 1991. Rudić had played for the Yugoslavian Olympic team in 1980 and had coached Yugoslavia to gold medals in 1984 and 1988.

Italy scored first and pulled away to a 4-1 lead late in the second period and a 6-3 lead with two minutes to play in the third period. They were still ahead 7-6 with time running out when Miguel Oca scored for Spain with 34 seconds to play. Two three-minute overtime periods were ordered. There were no scores for the first five minutes, but, with 42 seconds left, Italy's Mario

Fiorillo fouled Jordi Sans. Spain's star, four-time Olympian Manuel Estiarte, converted the penalty throw. The predominantly Spanish crowd went wild, but their joy was short-lived. Nine seconds later, Jordi Sans was excluded and Italy capitalized on their one-man advantage when Massimiliano Ferretti evened the score with a backhand shot with 20 seconds on the clock.

During the break before the next overtime period, nerves were raw, and scuffling broke out between the two teams. Back in 1920 a tense tied match between Italy and Spain had ended abruptly during the second overtime period when the Italian team left the pool in a protest against the referee. Seventy-two years later, the Italian team had no intention of repeating the incident. Back into the pool the two teams went. There was no scoring in the third overtime period—or the fourth or the fifth. It appeared that the sixth overtime period would go the same way, when Massimiliano Ferretti passed to Ferdinando Gandolfi in the left corner and, with 32 seconds to play, Gandolfi shot the ball past Spanish goalie Jesús Rollán. Spain set up one last play, but Oca's shot with five seconds left hit the crossbar, and the 46-minute marathon was finally over. Ratko Rudić had won his third straight Olympic championship.

1996 Atlanta T: 12, N: 12, D: 7.28.

	W	L	T	PF	PA
1. SPA	6	2	0	58	48
2. CRO	5	3	0	71	58
3. ITA	7	1	0	85	72
4. HUN	6	2	0	83	73
5. RUS	4	3	1	77	72
6. GRE	3	5	0	60	66
7. USA	5	3	0	67	57
8. YUG	3	4	1	75	80

Final: SPA 7-5 CRO
3rd Place: ITA 20-18 HUN (overtime)
5th Place: RUS 10-8 GRE (overtime)
7th Place: USA 12-8 YUG

1. SPA—José María Abarca Platas, Ángel Andreo Gabán, Daniel Ballart Sans, Manuel Estiarte Duocastella, Pedro García Aguado, Salvador Gómez Agüera, Iván Moro Fernández, Miguel Oca Gaia, Jorge Payá Rodríguez, Sergi Pedrerol Cavallé, Jesús Rollán Prada, Jordi "Chiqui" Sans Juan, Carles Sans López
2. CRO—Maro Balić, Perica Bukić, Damir Glavan, Igor Hinić, Vjekoslav Kobešćak, Joško Kreković, Ognjen Kržić, Dubravko Šimenc, Siniša Skolneković, Ratko Štritof, Tino Vegar, Renato Vrbićić, Zdeslav Vrdoljak
3. ITA—Alberto Angelini, Francesco Attolico, Fabio Bencivenga, Alessandro Bovo, Alessandro Calcaterra, Roberto Calcaterra, Marco Gerini, Alberto Ghibellini, Luca Giustolisi, Amedeo Pomilio, Francesco Postiglione, Carlo Silipo, Leonardo Sottani
4. HUN—Tibor Benedek, Tamás Dala, Rajmund Fodor, András Gyöngyösi, Tamás Kásás, Zoltán Kósz, Péter Kuna, Attila Monostori, Zsolt Németh, Frank Tóth, László Tóth, Zsolt Varga, Balázs Vincze
5. RUS—Maksim Apanasenko, Dmitri Dugin, Sergei Garbuzov, Dmitri Gorshkov, Sergei Ivlev, Vladimir Karabutov, Ilya Konstantinov, Nikolai Kozlov, Nikolai Maksimov, Aleksei Panfili, Yuri Smolovoy, Aleksandr Yeryshov, Sergei Yevstigneyev
6. GRE—Georgios Afroudakis, Thomas Chatzis, Theodoros Chatzitheodorou, Simeon Georgaras, Filippos Kaiafas, Theodoros Kalakonas, Theodoros Lorantos, Konstantinos Loudis, Georgios Mavrotas, Anastasios Papanastasiou, Evangelos Patras, Georgios Psychos, Gerasimos Voltyrakis
7. USA—Gavin Arroyo, Troy Barnhart, Christopher Duplanty, Michael Evans, Kirk Everist, Daniel Hackett, Christopher Humbert, Kyle Kopp, Jeremy Laster, John McNair, Chris Oeding, Alexis Rousseau, Wolfgang Wigo
8. YUG—Aleksandar Cirić, Viktor Jelenić, Dragan Jovanović, Igor Milanović, Ranko Perović, Aleksandar Šapić, Dejan Savić, Aleksandar Šoštar, Vaso Subotić, Milan Tadić, Petar Trbojević, Veljko Uskoković, Mirko Vičević, Zeljko Vičević, Vlada Vujasinović, Nenad Vukanić, Predrag Zimonjić

There was little doubt that the final would match Italy and Hungary. Since the last Olympics, the two teams had met in the final of all but one major event. At the 1993 World Cup, Italy beat Hungary 8-7. At the 1993 European championship, the Italians prevailed 11-9. Hungary slumped at the 1994 world championship, finishing in fifth place, so Italy beat Spain instead. At the 1995 European championship, Italy defeated Hungary 10-8. Hungary finally came out on top at the 1995 World Cup, edging Italy 11-10.

Both Italy and Hungary swept through their preliminary pools undefeated and then won their quarterfinal matches. All was going according to form. But there were other teams that, although they placed only third in their pools, were driven by extra emotions. Ever since the painful day four years earlier when they lost the Olympic final in triple overtime, the seven returning players of the Spanish team had dreamed of redeeming themselves at the next Olympics. The feeling was particularly strong in 35-year-old Manuel Estiarte, who was competing in his fifth Olympics.

In the semifinals, Spain faced Hungary. Hungary had beaten Spain 8-7 in the preliminary round. With 18 minutes gone in the semifinal and ten minutes to go, Hungary led 5-3. Over the next 8½ minutes Spain scored four times and kept the Hungarians scoreless to take a 7-5 lead. Hungary scored one more goal, but it was too little too late and it was Spain that advanced to the final.

Before they left home, the Croatian team set their goals: second most important—win a medal; first most important—beat Yugoslavia. Two of the Croatian players, Dubravko Šimenc and Perica Bukić, had won gold medls while playing for Yugoslavia, but now they wanted to gain revenge against the country that had caused death and destruction to their nation. They got their chance in the quarterfinals and won a tension-charged match 8-6. In the semifinals, Croatia played heavily favored Italy. Italy had beaten the Croats 10-8 in pool play. But the second time around, Joško Kreković converted a penalty shot with 10.4 seconds left in overtime and Croatia was on its way to the final.

In the final, Spain erased a 3-1 halftime deficit to pull even 5-5 at the end of the third period. They scored twice in the fourth quarter. With ten seconds to play, Manuel Estiarte took the ball and held it until time ran out. "I've been dreaming of this moment all my life," he explained. "The last ten seconds of the Olympic final, I have the ball and Spain wins the gold medal. I waited five Olympics, but it finally happened."

Italy and Hungary did get to play each other for a medal. Just because it was bronze instead of gold didn't stop the two rivals from giving it their all—to say the least. After trailing by four goals with six minutes to play, Italy stormed back to lead 16-15 as the seconds ticked down. When Hungary missed a final opportunity, the Italian reserves leaped into the water to celebrate—only to discover that there was still two tenths of a second left on the clock. Consequently, Hungary was awarded a penalty shot, which their captain, Zsolt Varga, converted to send the match into overtime. During the six-minute overtime, three Hungarians and four Italians fouled out and both head coaches were ejected from the deck. Eventually Italy won 20-18. As a matter of fact, Croatia's coach, Bruno Silić, was banned from the deck for the final because of a suspension incurred during the semifinal. He watched the game from the stands and tried to communicate with his players by cellular phone, but a cameraman caught him in the act and he was forced to stop.

2000 Sydney T: 12, N: 12, D: 10.1.

	W	L	T	PF	PA
1. HUN	6	2	0	78	57
2. RUS	6	1	1	76	58
3. YUG	6	1	1	63	36
4. SPA	3	4	1	51	58
5. ITA	6	1	1	66	52
6. USA	3	5	0	69	68
7. CRO	5	2	1	68	56
8. AUS	1	5	2	53	61

Final: HUN 13-6 RUS
3rd Place: YUG 8-3 SPA
5th Place: ITA 10-8 USA
7th Place: CRO 10-8 AUS

1. HUN—Tibor Benedek, Péter Biros, Rajmund Fodor, Tamás Kásás, Gergely "Gergő" Kiss, Zoltán Kósz, Tamás Márcz, Tamás Molnár, Barnabas Steinmetz, Zoltán Szécsi, Bulcsú Székely, Zsolt Varga, Attila Vári
2. RUS—Aleksandr Yeryshov, Dmitry Dugin, Dmitry Gorshkov, Dmitry Stratan, Irek Zinnurov, Marat Zakirov, Nikolay Kozlov, Nikolay Maksimov, Revaz Chomakhidze, Roman Balashov, Sergey Garbuzov, Yury Yatsev
3. YUG—Aleksandar Šapić, Aleksandar Šoštar, Aleksandar Cirić, Danilo Ikodinović, Dejan Savić, Jugoslav Vasović, Nenad Vukanić, Nikola Kuljača, Petar Trbojević, Predrag Zimonjić, Veljko Uskoković, Viktor Jelenić, Vladimir "Vlada" Vujasinović
4. SPA—Daniel Ballart Sans, Manuel Estiarte Duocastella, Pedro García Aguado, Salvador "Chava" Gómez Agüera, Gabriel Hernández Paz, Gustavo Marcos Herrero, Daniel Moro Fernández, Ivan Moro Fernández, Sergio Pedrerol Cavallé, Jesús Rollán Prada, Javier Sánchez Toril del Pino, Jordi "Chiqui" Sans Juan
5. ITA—Alberto Angelini, Alberto Ghibellini, Alessandro Calcaterra, Amedeo Pomilio, Antonio Vittorioso, Carlo Silipo, Fabio Bencivenga, Francesco Attolico, Francesco Postiglione, Leonardo Binchi, Leonardo Sottani, Roberto Calcaterra, Stefano Tempesti
6. USA—Bradley Schumacher, Craig "Chi" Kredell, Christopher Humbert, Christopher Oeding, Daniel Hackett, Gavin Arroyo, Kyle Kopp, Robert Lynn, Ryan Bailey, Sean Kern, Sean Nolan, Anthony Azevedo, Wolfgang Wigo
7. CRO—Alen Bošković, Dubravko Šimenc, Elvis Fatović, Frano Vićan, Igor Hinić, Ivo Ivaniš, Mile Smodlaka, Ognjen Kržić, Ratko Štritof, Samir Barač, Siniša Školneković, Višeslav Sarić, Vjekoslav Kobešćak
8. AUS—Sean Boyd, Eddie Denis, Andriy Kovalenko, Daniel Marsden, Craig Miller, Timothy Neesham, Mark Oberman, Rod Owen-Jones, Rafael Sterk, Nathan Thomas, Grant Waterman, Thomas Whalan, Gavin Woods

Traditionally the world's leading waterpolo power, Hungary had won medals at nine straight Olympics, from 1948 through 1980. But the Hungarians boycotted the 1984 Los Angeles Olympics and, on the Olympic stage, they were unable to recover—until 2000. Actually they got off to a rocky start, losing two of five games in pool play, 8-7 to Croatia and 10-9 to Yugoslavia. The Hungarians defeated Italy 8-5 in the quarterfinals in an encounter that was filled with extracurricular excitement. Italy's Croatian-born coach, Ratko Rudić, accused the Turkish and Greek referees of improper rulings against Italy and objected so vociferously that a policeman had to intervene. Rudić was suspended for "bringing the sport of water polo in disrepute" and four of his players were suspended as well. Both semifinals were tension-packed. Hungary defeated Yugoslavia 8-7 on a goal by Gergely "Gergő" Kiss with 5:34 to play. The other semifinal, between Russia and Spain, was tied 7-7 at the end of regulation. After six minutes of overtime, the match moved on to sudden-death overtime. After numerous misses and saves, Dmitri Gorchkov finally scored for Russia from five meters out after 9 minutes 55 seconds. Forty-four years after the dramatic Hungarian-Soviet encounter the last time the Olympics were held in Australia, Hungary and Russia met again, but this time without political overtones. The final itself was completely anti-climatic as the Russians, exhausted by their semifinal marathon, were never in the game. Hungary led 8-2 at halftime and won 13-6.

Manuel Estiarte of Spain, at age 39, became the first water polo player to compete in six Olympics. The leading goal scorer in 1980, 1984, 1988 and 1992, Estiarte scored ten goals at the Sydney Games to bring his career total to 127 in 44 games.

2004 Athens T: 12, N: 12, D: 8.29.

	W	L	T	PF	PA
1. HUN	7	0	0	59	39
2. SER	6	2	0	58	42
3. RUS	5	3	0	55	45
4. GRE	4	3	0	51	40
5. GER	4	2	1	51	44
6. SPA	3	4	0	44	44
7. USA	4	3	0	47	50
8. ITA	4	3	0	58	40

Final: HUN 8-7 SER
3rd Place: RUS 6-5 GRE
5th Place: GER 6-4 SPA
7th Place: USA 9-8 ITA

1. HUN—Tibor Benedek, Péter Biros, Rajmund Fodor, István Gergely, Tamás Kásás, Gergely "Gergő" Kiss, Norbert Madaras, Tamás Molnár, Ádám Steinmetz, Barnabás Steinmetz, Zoltán Szécsi, Tamás Varga, Attila Vári
2. SER—Aleksandar Ćirić, Vladimir Gojković, Danilo Ikodinović, Viktor Jelenić, Predrag Jokić, Slobodan Nikić, Aleksandar Šapić, Dejan Savić, Denis Šefik, Petar Trbojević, Vanja Udovičić, Vladimir "Vlada" Vujasinović
3. RUS—Roman Balashov, Revaz Chomakhidze, Aleksandr Fedorov, Sergei Garbuzov, Dmitri Gorshkov, Nikolai Kozlov, Nikolai Maksimov, Andrei Rekechinsky, Dmytro Stratan, Aleksandr Yeryshov, Vitaly Yurchik, Marat Zakirov, Irek Zinnurov
4. GRE—Georgios Afroudakis, Khristos Afroudakis, Nikolaos Deligiannis, Theodoros Kalakonas, Theodoros Khatzitheodorou, Konstantinos Loudis, Dimitrios Mazis, Georgios Reppas, Stefanos Santa, Anastasios Schizas, Argyris Theodoropoulos, Ioannis Thomakos, Antonios Vlodakis
5. GER—Steffen Dierolf, Lukasz Kieloch, Tobias Kreuzmann, Sören Mackeben, Heiko Nossek, Jens Pohlmann, Marc Torsten Politze, Thomas Schertwitis, Fabian Schrödter, Alexander Tchigir, Patrick Weissinger, Tim Wollthan, Michael Zellmer
6. SPA—Ángel Luis Andreo Gabán, Daniel Ballart Sans, Javier García Gadea, Salvador "Chava" Gómez Agüera, Gabriel Hernández Paz, Gustavo Marcos Herrero, Guillermo Molina Ríos, Daniel Moro Fernández, Iván Moro Fernández, Sergio Pedrerol Cavallé, Iván Pérez Vargas, Jesús Rollán Prada, Javier Sánchez Toril del Pino
7. USA—Omar Amr, Anthony Azevedo, Ryan Bailey, Layne Beaubien, Brandon Brooks, Genai Kerr, Daniel Klatt, Brett Ormsby, Jeffrey Powers, Christopher Segesman, Jesse Smith, Wolfgang Wigo, Adam Wright
8. ITA—Alberto Angelini, Fabio Bencivenga, Leonardo Binchi, Fabrizio Buonocore, Alessandro Calcaterra, Roberto Calcaterra, Maurizio Felugo, Goran Fiorentini, Marco Gerini, Francesco Postiglione, Bogdan Rath, Carlo Silipo, Stefano Tempesti

The Hungarian team arrived in Athens as the favorites. The defending Olympic champions, they won the 2003 world championship, edging Greece 9-8 in the semifinals and beating Italy 11-9 in overtime in the final. In the World League Superfinal, less than four weeks before the 2004 Olympics, Hungary defeated Serbia and Montenegro 12-8 in the final. Hungary and Serbia faced off again on the first day of the Olympic tournament, with the Hungarians winning 6-4. Both teams won all four of their remaining pool matches, allowing Hungary to advance directly to the semifinals and Serbia to the quarterfinals. In the other preliminary pool, the Greeks lost their opening match with Germany 4-5, but won the rest of their matches to finish first. Meanwhile, Egypt finished last in the group, scoring 18 goals in five matches while allowing 67.

In the quarterfinals, Russia easily defeated Germany, 12-5, while Aleksandar Šapić scored twice in one minute in the fourth quarter to give Serbia a 7-5 victory over Spain. In the semifinals, Hungary, which had beaten Russia 7-6 in pool play, defeated the Russians again, this time by a score of 7-5. In the other semi, Serbia beat Greece easily, 7-3.

Revaz Chomakhidze scored four goals for Russia in the bronze medal match against Greece, with Marat Zakirov scoring a late goal to seal a 6-5 victory for the Russians.

Serbia got off to a strong start in the gold medal match, with defender Aleksandar Ćirić scoring in the first 30 seconds. Šapić and Viktor Jelenić also scored to give Serbia a 3-0 lead after only three minutes of play. Hungary responded with three straight goals, including one on a penalty by Gergely "Gergő" Kiss, the top scorer at the 2000 Olympics. The score was tied 5-5 at halftime, but Serbia regained the lead with two unanswered goals in the third quarter. Then the Hungarians took charge, holding Serbia scoreless for the final thirteen minutes. Tamás Kásás put in two goals to tie the match again and then contributed an assist, as Kiss scored his fourth goal of the match to give Hungary an 8-7 victory.

2008 Beijing T: 12, N: 12, D: 8.24.

	W	L	T	PF	PA
1. HUN	6	0	1	85	55
2. USA	5	2	0	57	50
3. SER	5	3	0	70	57
4. MNE	3	3	2	63	56
5. SPA	5	2	0	68	52
6. CRO	4	3	0	71	49
7. GRE	4	4	0	74	81
8. AUS	3	3	1	70	65

Final: HUN 14-10 USA
3rd Place: SER 6-4 MNE
5th Place: SPA 11-9 CRO
7th Place: GRE 9-8 AUS

1. HUN—Tibor Benedek, Péter Biros, Štefan-István Gergely, Norbert Hosnyánszky, Tamás Kásás, Gábor Kis, Gergő Kiss, Norbert Madaras, Tamás Molnár, Zoltán Szécsi, Dániel Varga, Dénes Varga, Tamás Varga
2. USA—Anthony Azevedo, Ryan Bailey, Layne Beaubien, Brandon Brooks, Peter Hudnut, Tim Hutten, James "J.W." Krumpholz, Rick Merlo, Merrill Moses, Jeffrey Powers, Jesse Smith, Peter Varellas, Adam Wright
3. SER—Aleksandar Ćirić, Filip Filipović, Živko Gocić, Branko Peković,

Duško Pijetlović, Andrija Prlainović, Nikola Rađen, Aleksandar Šapić, Dejan Savić, Denis Šefik, Slobodan Soro, Vanja Udovičić, Vlada Vujasinović
4. MNE—Draško Brguljan, Vladimir Gojković, Aleksandar Ivović, Mlađan Janović, Nikola Janović, Predrag Jokić, Vjekoslav Pasković, Zdravko Radić, Miloš Šćepanović, Milan Tičić, Veljko Uskoković, Nikola Vukčević, Boris Zloković
5. SPA—Iñaki Aguilar Vicente, Ángel Luis Andreo Gabán, Iván Gallego Vela, Javier García Gadea, Mario José García Rodríguez, David Martín Lozano, Marc Minguell Alférez, Guillermo Molina Ríos, Iván Pérez Vargas, Felipe Perrone Rocha, Ricardo Perrone Rocha, Svilen Piralkov, Xavier Valles Trias
6. CRO—Samir Barac, Miho Bošković, Damir Burić, Andro Bušlje, Teo Đogaš, Igor Hinić, Maro Joković, Aljoša Kunac, Pavo Marković, Josip Pavić, Mile Smodlaka, Frano Vićan, Zdeslav Vrdoljak
7. GRE—Khristos Afroudakis, Georgios Afroudakis, Nikolaos Deligiannis, Konstantinos Kokkinakis, Dimitrios Mazis, Dimitrios Miteloudis, Emmanouil Mylonakis, Georgios Ntoskas, Georgios Reppas, Anastasios Skhizas, Argyris Theodoropoulos, Ioannis Thomakos, Antonios Vlontakis
8. AUS—Jamie Beadsworth, Richie Campbell, Pietro Figlioli, Trent Franklin, Rhys Howden, Robert Maitland, Anthony Martin, Sam McGregor, Timothy Neesham, James Stanton, Rafael Sterk, Thomas Whalan, Gavin Woods

Hungary had won the past two Olympic championships, but had struggled in other international competitions, finishing second at every major tournament since the 2004 Olympics, each time losing in the final by a single point. It lost to the Serbian and Montenegrin team at both the 2005 world championships and 2006 world cup, and then to Serbia, competing without the newly-independent Montenegro, at the 2006 European championship final. In the 2007 world championship final the Hungarians were beaten in overtime by Croatia.

Reigning European champion Montenegro (competing at the Olympics for the first time as an independent country) held Hungary to a 10-10 tie in the latter's first match of pool play. However, Hungary went on to win their next four matches to finish first in their group, advancing directly to the semifinals.

Ranked ninth in the world, the United States was the surprise leader of the second round-robin group, after beating world champion Croatia 7-5. Croatia finished second in the group, thanks to an 11-8 win over Serbia, while Serbia suffered a narrow 13-12 loss to Italy on the last day of pool play to finish third.

Serbia beat Spain 9-5 in the first quarterfinal, while Montenegro advanced on a 7-6 win over Croatia, whose members had all grown out their moustaches as a sign of team unity. ("We will shave now," said Croatia's Maro Joković after the defeat.)

Both the semifinal matches were rematches from the preliminary round. Hungary and Montenegro met again, with the Montenegrins taking a 6-3 lead in the second quarter. However Hungary took control and outscored them 8-3 the rest of the way. The US faced Serbia, who had beaten them 4-2 in the round-robin stage. This time the Americans took a 5-4 lead just before the half and built it into a 10-5 win, to move on the Olympic final for the first time in twenty years. "Tonight was for the 99 times they have beaten us," said Tony Azevedo, who scored three goals.

Serbia played the bronze medal match without two of their best players, top scorer Aleksandar Šapić and goalkeeper Denis Šefik. Šapić had been flown back to Belgrade for knee surgery, while Šefik was out with a broken hand—injuries rumored to have resulted from a fight following their semifinal loss to the US. Down to 11 players, Serbia opened up a 6-1 lead over Montenegro, holding on to win 6-4.

The US matched Hungary goal for goal in the first half of the final, with Hungary taking a 9-8 lead in the final second of the half. The US evened the score 9-9 early in the third quarter before Hungary took control, scoring five goals to cruise to a clear victory.

WOMEN

The first women's water polo match was played in Harlem, Netherlands, in 1906. The first world championships were held in 1978. Although the sport made its official Olympic debut in 2000, two Dutch teams did play an exhibition match at the 1920 Antwerp Olympics.

1896–1996 not held

2000 Sydney T: 6, N: 6, D: 9.23.

	W	L	T	PF	PA
1. AUS	6	1	0	46	29
2. USA	4	2	1	45	39
3. RUS	3	3	1	46	39
4. HOL	3	4	0	35	36
5. CAN	2	2	2	42	42
6. KAZ	0	6	0	31	60

Final: AUS 4-3 USA
3rd Place: RUS 4-3 HOL
5th Place: CAN 9-8 KAZ

1. AUS—Naomi Castle, Joanne Fox, Bridgette Gusterson, Simone Hankin, Yvette Higgins, Kate Hooper, Bronwyn Mayer, Gail Miller, Melissa Mills, Debbie Watson, Liz Weekes, Danielle Woodhouse, Taryn Woods
2. USA—Robin Beauregard, Ellen Estes, Courtney Johnson, Ericka Lorenz, Heather Moody, Maureen O'Toole, Bernice Orwig, Nicolle Payne, Heather Petri, Kathy Sheehy, Coralie Simmons, Julie Swail, Brenda Villa
3. RUS—Galina Rytova, Irina Tolkunova, Maria Koroleva, Marina Akobia, Nataliya Kutuzova, Sofia Konukh, Svetlana Kuzina, Tatyana Petrova, Yekaterina Anikeyeva, Yekaterina Vasilyeva, Yelena Smurova, Yelena Tokun, Yuliya Petrova

4. HOL—Heleen Boering, Danielle de Bruijn, Edmee Hiemstra, Karin Kuipers, Ingrid Leijendekker, Patricia Megens, Marjan op den Velde, Mirjam Overdam, Heleen Peerenboom, Karla Plugge, Carla Quint, Gillian van den Berg, Ellen van der Weijden-Bast
5. CAN—Marie-Luc Arpin, Isabelle Auger, Johanne Begin, Cora Campbell, Melissa Collins, Marie-Claude Deslieres, Valerie Dionne, Ann Dow, Sue Gardiner, Waneek Horn-Miller, Sandra Lize, Josée Marsolais, Jana Salat
6. KAZ—Rezeda Aleyeva, Anastassiya Boroda, Irina Borodavko, Svetlana Buravova, Natalya Galkina, Yekaterina Gerzanich, Tatyana Gubina, Natalya Ignatyeva, Assel Jakayeva, Svetlana Koroleva, Olga Lechshuk, Larissa Olkhina, Yuliya Pyresseva

The struggle to convince the IOC to admit women's water polo into the Olympics was so exasperating that at one point, in 1995, upon hearing that an IOC delegation would be arriving at the Sydney airport, Australian players met them wearing swimsuits and carrying signs of protest. The IOC finally relented in 1998.

The tournament itself could not have been more exciting. After the conclusion of the round-robin preliminary pool, every one of the matches was decided by a single goal. Both the United States and Australia had to come from behind in the semifinals to qualify for the final. The Americans trailed the Netherlands 3-5 in the first half, but shut out the Dutch for the rest of the match, while scoring three goals. Goalie Bernice Orwig preserved the victory by stopping a point-blank shot by Carla Quint in the final minute. The Australians survived an even closer call. They trailed Russia 4-6 going into the fourth quarter and were still a goal down with 90 seconds to play. Then Naomi Castle tied the score. With 43 seconds left on the clock, Bridgett Gusterson made an over-the-shoulder shot that gave the Australians the win.

The final, played before an enthusiastic crowd of 17,000, was hard-fought and close all the way. The US led 2-1 at halftime, but Bronwyn Mayer tied the score for Australia early in the third period. With 1 minute 50 seconds left in the final period, and the US down a player after a foul, Naomi Castle put Australia ahead with a shot from the left side. Australian Taryn Woods committed a foul with 26 seconds to play, giving the Americans a one-player advantage. With only 13 seconds left, Brenda Villa of the United States shot from the right side and the ball dribbled into the goal. It looked like the game would go into overtime. But with 1.3 seconds on the clock, US captain Julie Swail was called for a foul against Yvette Higgins. The Americans thought the foul had taken place inside the 7-meter line, which would have required the Australians to make a pass before shooting. Higgins, positioned outside the 7-meter line, called for the ball and, unguarded, rifled a shot past two surprised defenders and the goalie and into the net. Despite the controversial ending, both teams were so thrilled to play in the Olympics, that both the post-match press conference and the medal ceremony were scenes of universal celebration.

2004 Athens T: 8, N: 8, D: 8.26.

	W	L	T	GF	GA
1. ITA	5	1	0	44	33
2. GRE	3	2	1	39	36
3. USA	3	2	0	31	27
4. AUS	2	2	1	29	28
5. RUS	3	2	0	37	40
6. HUN	1	4	0	35	40
7. CAN	2	2	0	26	22
8. KAZ	0	4	0	20	35

Final: ITA 10-9 GRE
3rd Place: USA 6-5 AUS
5th Place: RUS 12-11 HUN
7th Place: CAN 10-4 KAZ

1. ITA—Carmela Allucci, Alexandra Araujo, Silvia Bosurgi, Francesca Conti, Elena Gigli, Melania Grego, Giusy Malato, Tania Di Mario, Martina Miceli, Maddalena Musumeci, Cinzia Ragusa, Noemi Toth, Emanuela Zanchi
2. GRE—Dimitra Asilian, Georgia Ellinaki, Eftykhia Karagianni, Angeliki Karapataki, Stavroula Kozompoli, Georgia Lara, Kyriaki Liosi, Antiopi Melidoni, Antonia Moraiti, Evangelia Moraitidou, Anthoula Mylonaki, Katarina Oikonomopoulou, Antigoni Roumpesi
3. USA—Robin Beauregard, Margaret Dingeldein, Ellen Estes, Jacqueline Frank, Natalie Golda, Ericka Lorenz, Heather Moody, Thalia Munro, Heather Petri, Kelly Rulon, Amber Stachowski, Brenda Villa
4. AUS—Belinda Brooks, Jemma Brownlow, Naomi Castle, Nikita Cuffe, Joanne Fox, Kate Gynther, Kelly Heuchan, Emma Knox, Elise Norwood, Melissa Rippon, Rebecca Rippon, Bronwyn Mayer-Smith, Jodie Stuhmcke
5. RUS—Svetlana Bogdanova, Sofiya Konukh, Tatyana Petrova, Yekaterina Salimova, Natalya Shepelina, Yekaterina Shishova, Yelena Smurova, Olga Turova, Yekaterina Vasilyeva, Valentina Vorontsova, Mariya Yaina, Galina Zlotnikova, Anastasiya Zubkova
6. HUN—Rita Drávucz, Anett Györe, Dóra Kisteleki, Anikó Pelle, Ágnes Primász, Mercedes Stieber, Krisztina Szremkó, Andrea Tóth II, Ágnes Valkay, Erzsébet Valkay, Zsuzsanna Tiba, Krisztina Zantleitner, Ildikó Sós Zirigh
7. CAN—Marie-Luc Arpin, Johanne Bégin, Cora Campbell, Melissa Collins, Andrea Dewar, Valérie Dionne, Ann Dow, Susan Gardiner, Marianne Illing, Whynter Lamarre, Rachel Riddell, Christine Robinson, Jana Salat
8. KAZ—Yekaterina Gariyeva, Marina Gritsenko, Tatyana Gubina, Nataliya Ignatyeva, Svetlana Korolyeva, Nataliya Krasilnikova, Larisa Mikhaylova, Galina Rytova, Irina Tolkunova, Asel Dzhakayeva, Anna Zubkova

The field was so evenly matched that none of the eight teams was able to win all three of their preliminary round matches. In Group A, Australia, dealing with the retirement of the majority of its team after winning the 2000 Olympics, edged out Italy 6-5 to take first place despite having to overcome a three-goal second-half deficit to tie Greece 7-7. In the other group, the United States, which had gone undefeated in winning the 2003 world championship, placed first and advanced directly to the semifinals despite a surprise 5-4 loss to Canada.

The quarterfinals saw Greece upset Russia 7-4, thanks to ten saves by goalkeeper Georgia Ellinaki. In the other quarterfinal match, Italy trailed Hungary 4-5 in the third quarter, but outscored the Hungarians 4-0 the rest of the way to win 8-5. The first semifinal was a rematch of the 2003 world championship final, in which the US beat Italy 8-6. This time, the Americans led 4-2 in the final quarter, but Italy scored three unanswered goals to pull ahead 5-4. The US evened the score on a goal by Ellen Estes with 1:11 remaining, but a late offensive foul gave the Italians the ball in the closing seconds, and Manuela Zanchi scored the winning goal with two seconds left on the clock. In the other semifinal, Greece, playing in front of a raucous hometown crowd, powered to a 4-1 lead over defending champion Australia after less than six minutes, and went on to win 6-2.

In the bronze medal match, the United States took a 5-1 lead, but Australia fought back to tie the score. Finally, with 2:20 remaining, Ellen Estes scored the winning goal for the US.

The gold medal match turned out to be a sensational one. Italy had easily defeated Greece in pool play, 7-2, but the final was another matter. The lead seesawed throughout the match, and regulation time ended with the teams tied at 7. In overtime, Kyriaki Liosi (with her fifth goal of the match) and Katarina Oikonomopoulou gave Greece a 9-7 lead, but Italy regained the tie with nine seconds left on the clock, thanks to goals by Melania Grego and Tania Di Mario. Grego scored the only goal of the second overtime on a lob with 2:04 left to clinch the victory for Italy.

2008 Beijing T: 8, N: 8, D: 8.21.

	W	L	T	GF	GA
1. HOL	4	2	0	57	53
2. USA	3	1	1	50	44
3. AUS	4	1	1	57	53
4. HUN	2	2	1	46	40
5. CHN	2	3	0	54	52
6. ITA	2	2	1	46	49
7. RUS	1	3	0	38	40
8. GRE	0	4	0	22	39

Final: HOL 9-8 USA
3rd Place: AUS 12-11 HUN
5th Place: CHN 10-7 ITA
7th Place: RUS 12-6 GRE

1. HOL—Frederike "Mieke" Cabout, Daniëlle de Bruijn, Rianne Guichelaar, Biurakn Hakhverdian, Noeki Klein, Simone Koot, Alette Sijbring, Yasemin Smit, Lefke van Belkum, Gillian van den Berg, Marieke van der Ham, Ilse van der Meijden
2. USA—Elizabeth Armstrong, Patricia Cardenas, Kameryn Craig, Natalie Golda, Alison Gregorka, Brittany Hayes, Jaime Hipp, Heather Petri, Jessica Steffens, Moriah Van Norman, Brenda Villa, Lauren Wenger, Elsie Windes
3. AUS—Gemma Beadsworth, Nikita Cuffe, Suzannah Fraser, Taniele Gofers, Kate Gynther, Amy Hetzel, Bronwen Knox, Emma Knox, Alicia McCormack, Melissa Rippon, Rebecca Rippon, Jenna Santoromito, Mia Santoromito
4. HUN—Fruzsina Brávik, Rita Drávucz, Anett Györe, Patrícia Horváth, Dóra Kisteleki, Anikó Pelle, Ágnes Primász, Mercedes Stieber, Krisztina Szremkó, Orsolya Takács, Ágnes Valkai, Krisztina Zantleitner, Ildikó Sós Zirigh
5. CHN—Gao Ao, He Jin, Liu Ping, Ma Huanhuan, Qiao Leiying, Sun Huizi, Sun Yating, Sun Yujun, Tan Ying, Teng Fei, Wang Yi, Wang Ying, Yang Jun
6. ITA—Silvia Bosurgi, Chiara Brancati, Elisa Casanova, Tania Di Mario, Teresa Frassinetti, Elena Gigli, Martina Miceli, Maddalena Musumeci, Francesca Pavan, Cinzia Ragusa, Federica Rocco, Erzsébet Valkai, Emanuela Zanchi
7. RUS—Olga Belyayeva, Nadezhda Glyzina, Oleksandra Karpovich, Sofiya Konukh, Yekaterina Pantyulina, Yekaterina Prokofyeva, Yevgeniya Protsenko, Nataliya Shepelina, Yelena Smurova, Yevgeniya Soboleva, Olga Turova, Valentina Vorontsova, Alena Vylegzhanina
8. GRE—Stavroula Antonakou, Alexandra Asimaki, Georgia Ellinaki, Angeliki Gerolymou, Sofia Iosifidou, Voula Kozomboli, Georgia Lara, Kiki Liosi, Evi Moraitidou, Katerina Oikonomopoulou, Antigoni Roumbesi, Christina Tsoukala, Maria Tsouri

The United States entered the tournament as the reigning world champions and number-one-ranked team in the world. In 2007 they had outscored their opponents 56-36 in the world championship tournament, beating 2005 world champions Hungary in the semifinals and 2006 world cup winners Australia in the final.

The US led Group A in the preliminary round, beating China and Russia and tying defending Olympic champion Italy. Italy also defeated China and Russia, but finished second on goal differential.

Hungary and Australia led Group B after both teams beat the Netherlands and Greece and tied against each other 7-7. Hungary topped the group thanks to a better goal differential.

Ranked ninth in the world, the Netherlands barely made it out of the first qualifying round, finishing third in their group. They faced Italy in the quarterfinals, finishing regulation time tied 8-8. The match went to penalty shots after neither team was able to score in overtime, with the Dutch winning 5-3.

Still the obvious underdogs, the Netherlands faced Hungary in the semifinals. Hungary led 2-1 after the first quarter, but the Netherlands came back to score three goals in the second quarter, taking a 4-3 lead going into the second half. The Dutch matched Hungary goal for goal in the second half, finishing 8-7 to reach the Olympic final for the first time.

The US and Australia had a close match in the other semifinal. Tied 4-4 at the half, the US stormed to a three-point lead in the third quarter, but then watched their lead evaporate in the fourth. The teams were tied 8-8 with one minute remaining, when three-time

Olympian Brenda Villa scored on a power play to give the US a 9-8 win.

The Netherlands got off to a quick start in the final, scoring four times in the first three minutes, including three goals by Daniëlle de Bruijn. The US rallied to tie the match 5-5 at halftime. De Bruijn scored twice more in the third quarter to retake the lead, but the US fought back once again to even the score at 8-8 late in the final quarter. With 26 seconds left on the clock, de Bruijn scored on a power play—her seventh goal of the match—giving the Netherlands a 9-8 victory.

Chapter 31 **Weightlifting**

MEN
Bantamweight—56 kg
Featherweight—62 kg
Lightweight—69 kg
Middleweight—77 kg
Light Heavyweight—85 kg
Middle Heavyweight—94 kg
Heavyweight—105 kg
Super Heavyweight—
Unlimited Weight
Discontinued Events

WOMEN
Flyweight—48 kg
Featherweight—53 kg
Lightweight—58 kg
Middleweight—63 kg
Light Heavyweight—69 kg
Heavyweight—75 kg
Super Heavyweight—
Unlimited Weight

Each contestant is allowed three attempts at each type of lift. The *snatch* is performed by lifting the bar from the floor to above the head in one movement and holding it there for two seconds. The *clean and jerk,* or *jerk,* is a two-part lift. First the weight is brought up to the clavicle (collarbone) or the chest and then, using the combined strength of arms and legs, it is raised overhead until the arms are vertically extended. The *press,* which was discontinued following the 1972 Olympics, required the lifter to bring the bar to his shoulders, wait two seconds for the judges' approval, and then lift the bar overhead using only the arms. A competitor is allowed 60 seconds from the time his or her name is called until the beginning of the attempt. If a competitor makes two consecutive attempts, he or she is allowed two minutes between attempts. When a tie occurs, the lifter with the lower bodyweight is declared the winner. Until 1992 a lifter who completed a successful lift within 10 kilograms of the world record was allowed a fourth attempt, which did not count as part of the competition, but could count as a world record. In order to distance itself from a period tainted by drug abuse, the International Weightlifting Federation changed all weight categories following the 1992 Olympics, thus wiping out all world and Olympic records and starting "clean." Another cleansing occurred after the 1996 Olympics. New weight categories were instituted in 1998, thus allowing yet another cleansing.

Weightlifters qualify for the Olympics not as individuals, but as members of a national team, based on the results of the two most recent world championships. Each nation is allowed a set number of entrants according to its ranking. The allocations are:

Leonid Zhabotynsky, 1968
The gold medalist in both 1964 and 1968 in the Super-Heavyweight division, Zhabotynsky reveled in the role of "The World's Strongest Man."

National Ranking	Men	National Ranking	Women
1-6	6	1-9	4
7-12	5	10-16	3
13-18	4	17-21	2
19-24	3		

In addition, 48 men and 34 women qualify through regional championships and as wildcard entries.

MEN

BANTAMWEIGHT
(56 kg—123 lbs [1996: 59 kg—130.07 lbs])

1896–1936 not held

1948 London C: 19, N: 14, D: 8.9. WR: 300 kg (Joseph Di Pietro)

		PRESS	SNATCH	JERK	TOTAL KG
1. Joseph De Pietro	USA	105.0 OR	90.0	112.5	307.5 WR
2. Julian Creus	GBR	82.5	95.0 OR	120.0	297.5
3. Richard Tom	USA	87.5	90.0	117.5	295.0
4. Lee Kyu-hyuk	KOR	77.5	92.5	120.0	290.0
5. Mahmoud Namjou	IRN	82.5	82.5	122.5 OR	287.5
6. Marcel Thévenet	FRA	90.0	80.0	110.0	280.0
7. Rosaire Smith	CAN	82.5	85.0	110.0	277.5
8. Maurice Crow	NZE	77.5	85.0	110.0	272.5

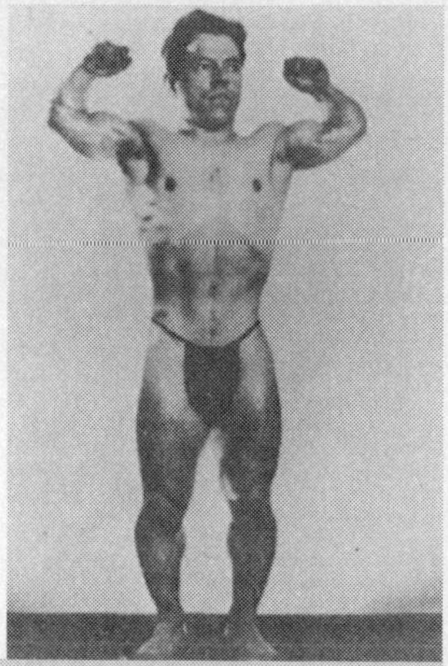

Joe De Pietro
The arms of 4-foot 10-inch weightlifter De Pietro were so short he could barely raise the bar above his head. Yet he was still able to win the 1948 Bantamweight gold medal.

Joe De Pietro's height was variously reported as 4 feet 8 inches or 4 feet 10 inches. Whichever figure is correct, his arms were so short that he was barely able to raise the bar above his head.

1952 Helsinki C: 19, N: 18, D: 7.25. WR: 317.5 kg (Mahmoud Namjou)

		PRESS	SNATCH	JERK	TOTAL KG
1. Ivan Udodov	SOV/RUS	90.0	97.5 OR	127.5 OR	315.0 OR
2. Mahmoud Namjou	IRN	90.0	95.0	122.5	307.5
3. Ali Mirzaii	IRN	95.0	92.5	112.5	300.0
4. Kim Hae-nam	KOR	80.0	95.0	120.0	295.0
5. Kamal Mahmoud Mahgoub	EGY	75.0	95.0	122.5	292.5
6. Pedro Landero	PHI	90.0	87.5	115.0	292.5
7. Maurice Megennis	GBR	82.5	85.0	112.5	280.0
8. Lon Mohamed Noor	SIN	77.5	85.0	112.5	275.0

1956 Melbourne C: 16, N: 13, D: 11.23. WR: 335 kg (Vladimir Stogov)

		PRESS	SNATCH	JERK	TOTAL KG
1. Charles Vinci	USA	105.0 EOR	105.0 OR	132.5	342.5 WR
2. Vladimir Stogov	SOV/RUS	105.0 EOR	105.0 OR	127.5	337.5
3. Mahmoud Namjou	IRN	100.0	102.5	130.0	332.5
4. Yu In-ho	KOR	90.0	95.0	135.0 OR	320.0
5. Kim Hae-nam	KOR	85.0	95.0	127.5	307.5
6. Yoshio Nanbu	JPN	87.5	97.5	120.0	305.0
7. Reginald Gaffley	SAF	97.5	90.0	117.5	305.0
8. Yukio Furuyama	JPN	90.0	87.5	125.0	302.5

As weigh-in time approached, the 4-foot 10-inch Vinci was one and a half pounds overweight. After an hour of running and sweating he was still seven ounces over the limit with 15 minutes to go. Fortunately, a severe last-minute haircut did the trick, and Vinci went on to win the gold medal.

1960 Rome C: 22, N: 18, D: 9.7. WR: 345 kg (Vladimir Stogov)

		PRESS	SNATCH	JERK	TOTAL KG
1. Charles Vinci	USA	105.0 EOR	107.5 EWR	132.5	345.0 EWR
2. Yoshinobu Miyake	JPN	97.5	105.0	135.0 EOR	337.5
3. Esmaiil Elmkhan	IRN	97.5	100.0	132.5	330.0
4. Shigeo Kogure	JPN	90.0	102.5	130.0	322.5
5. Marian Jankowski	POL	92.5	100.0	130.0	322.5
6. Imre Földi	HUN	100.0	90.0	130.0	320.0
7. Yu In-ho	KOR	90.0	95.0	130.0	315.0
8. Husain Hasan	IRO	87.5	100.0	125.0	312.5

1964 Tokyo C: 24, N: 18, D: 10.11. WR: 352.5 kg (Yoshinobu Miyake)

		PRESS	SNATCH	JERK	TOTAL KG
1. Aleksei Vakhonin	SOV/RUS	110.0	105.0	142.5 OR	357.5 WR
2. Imre Földi	HUN	115.0 OR	102.5	137.5	355.0
3. Shiro Ichinoseki	JPN	100.0	110.0 OR	137.5	347.5
4. Henryk Trębicki	POL	105.0	102.5	135.0	342.5
5. Yang Mu-shin	KOR	97.5	107.5	135.0	340.0
6. Yukio Furuyama	JPN	105.0	100.0	130.0	335.0
7. Yu In-ho	KOR	97.5	100.0	137.5	335.0
8. Martin Dias	GUY	100.0	102.5	132.5	335.0

Vakhonin, a 4-foot 10¾-inch, 29-year-old coal miner, set a world record in the jerk that was not allowed because he was, by then, overweight. The lift did count as an *Olympic* record, however. The same treatment was given to Ichinoseki's snatch record. Foldi, who had sweated down from a featherweight, was handicapped in the snatch because one of his fingers was missing and another was paralyzed. Vakhonin disappeared from international competition prior to the 1968 Olympics after being accused of "conduct unbecoming a Master of Sport."

1968 Mexico City C: 20, N: 19, D: 10.13. WR: 367.5 kg (Gennady Chetin)

		PRESS	SNATCH	JERK	TOTAL KG
1. Mohammad Nasiri Seresht	IRN	112.5	105.0	150.0 WR	367.5 EWR
2. Imre Földi	HUN	122.5 OR	105.0	140.0	367.5 EWR
3. Henryk Trębicki	POL	115.0	107.5	135.0	357.5
4. Gennady Chetin	SOV/RUS	110.0	102.5	140.0	352.5
5. Shiro Ichinoseki	JPN	110.0	107.5	132.5	350.0
6. Fernando Baez Cruz	PUR	120.0	92.5	132.5	345.0
7. Atanas Kirov	BUL	105.0	100.0	130.0	335.0
8. Chaiya Sukchinda	THA	100.0	105.0	125.0	330.0

Mohammad Nasiri, from the Kurdish city of Sanandaj, followed a precise ritual before each of his lifts. He would turn his back to the bar, pray for thirty seconds, turn towards the bar and yell loudly, "Ya Ali," as a sign of submission to Imam Ali, the first leader of Shi'a Islam. This was an expression used by Iranians before attempting something extraordinary. Nasiri had learned this technique from 1952 and 1956 medalist Mahmoud Namjou.

In Mexico City Nasiri found himself ten kilograms behind Imre Földi with only the jerk remaining. Because he was ten ounces (300 grams) lighter than Földi, he only needed to tie the Hungarian's total to win. But this meant jerking 150 kilograms—nine kilograms more than his own world record. Nasiri opened with a successful lift of 142.5 kg. and then called for 150 kg. This was a weight so far ahead of its time that it would not be matched at the Olympics for twelve years. Even 24 years later, at the Barcelona Olympics, only two lifters would be able to break the 150 kg. barrier. Nasiri finished his prayer and then roared out "Ya Ali" not once but three times. He lifted the weight up to his shoulders, yelled "Ya Ali" once more and brought it over his head. Earlier in the competition Nasiri had had three lifts declared invalid by split decisions of the judges. After his world record lift, he sent a message to the Russian and Japanese judges who had voted against him by refusing to drop the weight after it had been declared legal.

In 1972 Nasiri earned a silver medal and then completed his collection with a bronze in the flyweight division in 1976.

1972 Munich C: 24, N: 20, D: 8.28. WR: 375 kg (Gennady Chetin)

		PRESS	SNATCH	JERK	TOTAL KG
1. Imre Földi	HUN	127.5 OR	107.5	142.5	377.5 WR
2. Mohammad Nasiri Seresht	IRN	127.5 OR	100.0	142.5	370.0
3. Gennady Chetin	SOV/RUS	120.0	107.5	140.0	367.5
4. Henryk Trębicki	POL	122.5	107.5	135.0	365.0
5. Atanas Kirov	BUL	117.5	105.0	140.0	362.5
6. George Vasiliades	AUS	115.0	102.5	137.5	355.0
7. Hiroshi Ono	JPN	115.0	105.0	135.0	355.0
8. Georgi Todorov	BUL	110.0	100.0	140.0	350.0

Tenth-place finisher Koji Miki of Japan set an Olympic snatch record of 112.5 kg and then broke the world record with an extra lift of 114 kg. Polish-born Zeev Friedman, who finished twelfth, was one of the 11 Israelis who were murdered at the Games by Palestinian terrorists.

1976 Montreal C: 24 N: 19, D: 7.19. WR: 260 kg (Atanas Kirov)

		SNATCH	JERK	TOTAL KG
1. Norair Nurikian	BUL	117.5 OR	145.0	262.5 WR
2. Grzegorz Cziura	POL	115.0	137.5	252.5
3. Kenkichi Ando	JPN	107.5	142.5	250.0
4. Leszek Skorupa	POL	112.5	137.5	250.0
5. Imre Földi	HUN	105.0	140.0	245.0
6. Bernhard Backfisch	GER	105.0	137.5	242.5
7. Carlos Lastre Alfonso	CUB	105.0	135.0	240.0
8. Fazlollah Dehkhoda	IRN	105.0	135.0	240.0

Imre Földi became the only weightlifter to take part in five Olympics.

1980 Moscow C: 21, N: 17, D: 7.21. WR: 272.5 kg (Daniel Núñez Aguiar)

		SNATCH	JERK	TOTAL KG
1. Daniel Núñez Aguiar	CUB	125.0 WR	150.0	275.0 WR
2. Yurik Sarkisian	SOV/ARM	112.5	157.5 WR	270.0
3. Tadeusz Dembończyk	POL	120.0	145.0	265.0
4. Andreas Letz	GDR	115.0	150.0	265.0
5. Yang Eui-yong	PRK	112.5	150.0	265.0
6. Imre Stefanovics	HUN	115.0	145.0	260.0
7. Gheorghe Maftei	ROM	105.0	142.5	247.5
8. Petre Pavel	ROM	105.0	140.0	245.0

Dembończyk was awarded the bronze medal as a result of a post-competition weigh-in. In 1983 Núñez tested positive for excess testosterone and was banned for two years

1984 Los Angeles-Westchester C: 20, N: 18, D: 7.30. WR: 300 kg (Naim Süleymanoğlu)

		SNATCH	JERK	TOTAL KG
1. Wu Shude	CHN	120.0	147.5	267.5
2. Lai Runming	CHN	125.0 EOR	140.0	265.0
3. Masahiro Kotaka	JPN	112.5	140.0	252.5
4. Takashi Ichiba	JPN	110.0	140.0	250.0
5. Kim Chil-bong	KOR	105.0	140.0	245.0
6. Dionisio Muñoz Berrio	SPA	110.0	132.5	242.5
7. Arvo Ojalehto	FIN	105.0	137.5	242.5
8. Albert Hood	USA	112.5	130.0	242.5

One of the most popular weightlifters at the Los Angeles Olympics was fourth place finisher Takashi Ichiba, who entertained the audience by performing a back flip *before* each lift.

Few boycotting athletes in 1984 were more missed than world record holder Naim Süleymanoğlu, the 16-year-old boy wonder from Bulgaria. At the Friendship Games in September, Süleymanoğlu defeated Oksen Mirzoyan of the USSR 297.5 kg to 295.0 kg. In 1986 Süleymanoğlu, a member of Bulgaria's Turkish minority, defected after a competition in Melbourne, Australia, and moved to Turkey.

1988 Seoul C: 23, N: 17, D: 9.19. WR: 300 kg (Naim Süleymanoğlu)

		SNATCH	JERK	TOTAL KG
1. Oksen Mirzoian	SOV/ARM	127.5 OR	165.0 OR	292.5 OR
2. He Yingqiang	CHN	125.0	162.5	287.5
3. Liu Shoubin	CHN	127.5 OR	140.0	267.5
4. Dirdja Wihardja	INA	112.5	142.5	255.0
5. Takeshi Ichiba	JPN	107.5	145.0	252.5
6. Kim Kwi-shik	KOR	110.0	142.5	252.5
7. Joaquín Valle Montero	SPA	112.5	135.0	247.5
8. Giovanni Scarantino	ITA	110.0	135.0	245.0

DISQ (Drugs): Mitko Grablev (BUL) 297.5

1992 Barcelona C: 22, N: 17, D: 7.27. WR: 300 kg (Naim Süleymanoğlu)

		SNATCH	JERK	TOTAL KG
1. Chun Byung-kwan	KOR	132.5 OR	155.0	287.5
2. Liu Shoubin	CHN	130.0	147.5	277.5
3. Luo Jianming	CHN	125.0	152.5	277.5
4. Laurent Fombertasse	FRA	112.5	147.5	260.5
5. Katsuhiko Sakuma	JPN	120.0	135.0	255.0
6. Tibor Karczag	HUN	115.0	140.0	255.0
7. Kim Yong-chol	PRK	110.0	145.0	255.0
8. Marek Gorzelniak	POL	115.0	140.0	255.0

Chun did not make his first clean and jerk attempt until all the other lifters had completed theirs.

1996 Atlanta C: 20, N: 19, D: 7.21. WR: 307.5 kg (Tang Ningsheng)

		SNATCH	JERK	TOTAL KG
1. Tang Ningsheng	CHN	137.5 OR	170.0 EWR	307.5 WR
2. Leonidas Sampanis	GRE	137.5 OR	167.5	305.0
3. Nikola Peshalov	BUL	137.5 OR	165.0	302.5
4. Hiroshi Ikehata	JPN	132.5	165.0	297.5
5. William Vargas Trujillo	CUB	135.0	162.5	297.5
6. Xu Dong	CHN	132.5	162.5	295.0
7. Yurik Sarkisian	AUS	125.0	155.0	280.0
8. Zoltán Farkas	HUN	130.0	150.0	280.0

Tang ran into an unexpected obstacle when his uniform ripped. Zoltán Farkas, who had competed in the "B" group, loaned Tang his outfit and Tang won the gold medal with his final lift. All of Tang's six lifts were successful.

2000 Sydney C: 22, N: 19, D: 9.16. WR: 302.5 kg (Halil Mutlu)

		SNATCH	JERK	TOTAL KG
1. Halil Mutlu	TUR	137.5 WR	167.5 WR	305.0 WR
2. Wu Wenxiong	CHN	125.0	162.5	287.5
3. Zhang Xiangxiang	CHN	125.0	162.5	287.5
4. Wang Shin-yuan	TAI	125.0	160.0	285.0
5. Sergio Álvarez Boulet	CUB	120.0	155.0	275.0
6. Adrian Ioan Jigău	ROM	122.5	152.5	275.0
7. Vitaly Derbenev	BLR	125.0	150.0	275.0
8. Yang Chin-yi	TAI	120.0	150.0	270.0

DISQ (Drugs): Ivan Ivankov (BUL) 292.5

Undefeated since winning the gold medal in the flyweight division at the 1996 Olympics, Halil Mutlu was considered one of the surest bets in any sport in 2000. He came through by breaking his own world record in both the snatch and the clean and jerk. When Ivan Ivankov was disqualified after testing positive for the diuretic furosemide, Mutlu ended up with a winning margin of 17.5 kg, the largest in the history of the division.

With a final total of 157.5 kg—less than Mutlu's jerk weight, Martinho de Araujo of East Timor finished far behind the other lifters. However, with his nation involved in a war of independence against Indonesia, de Araujo found his training equipment destroyed and he was forced to create a makeshift bar by sticking a pole in buckets of wet cement.

2004 Athens C: 17, N: 15, D: 8.15. WR: 305.0 kg (Halil Mutlu)

		SNATCH	JERK	TOTAL KG
1. Halil Mutlu	TUR	135.0	160.0	295.0
2. Wu Meijin	CHN	130.0	157.5	287.5
3. Sedat Artuç	TUR	125.0	155.0	280.0
4. Vitaly Dzerbenyev	BLR	127.5	152.5	280.0
5. Oscar Figueroa Mosquera	COL	125.0	155.0	280.0
6. Adrian Ioan Jigău	ROM	120.0	155.0	275.0
7. László Tancsics	HUN	122.5	150.0	272.5
8. Jadi Setiadi	INA	117.5	145.0	262.5

After winning the 2001 world championship, world record holder and defending Olympic champion Halil Mutlu was forced to take a year off after tearing a rotator cuff and rupturing a biceps tendon. But he came back in 2003 to win the world championship in the 62-kilogram category. For the Olympics, Mutlu dropped back into the 56-kilogram category—but just barely, weighing in at 55.93 kilograms. Mutlu's main challenge came from Wu Meijin, who, in Mutlu's absence, had won both previous 56-kilogram world championships. Mutlu needed only three lifts to win the gold medal, raising first 130 kilos and then 135 kilos in the snatch, and then clinching gold by calmly lifting 160 kilos in the clean and jerk, also on his first attempt. He was only the fourth weightlifter in Olympic history to earn three consecutive gold medals.

In 2005 Mutlu was slapped with a two-year ban from competition after testing positive for the steroid nandrolone.

2008 Beijing C: 19, N: 16, D: 8.10. WR: 305 kg (Halil Mutlu)

		SNATCH	JERK	TOTAL KG
1. Long Qingquan	CHN	132.0	160.0	292.0
2. Hoàng Anh Tuấn	VIE	130.0	160.0	290.0
3. Eko Irawan	INA	130.0	158.0	288.0
4. Yang Chin-yi	TAI	128.0	157.0	285.0
5. Cha Kum-chol	PRK	128.0	155.0	283.0
6. Sergio Álvarez Boulet	CUB	120.0	152.0	272.0
7. Wang Shin-yuan	TAI	115.0	150.0	265.0
8. Amirul Ibrahim	MAL	121.0	144.0	265.0

Making his international debut, Long Qingquan took the lead after raising 132 kg (291 lbs) in the snatch, a junior world record. Reigning world champion Cha Kum-chol of North Korea nearly bombed out, barely clearing 128 kg on his final attempt. Long matched two-time world bronze medalist Hoàng Anh Tuấn in the jerk, lifting 160 kg to clinch the gold medal with a combined 292 kg, also a junior world record.

The eighteen-year-old Long had spent only three months training with China's national team before the Olympics. "I'm not very well disciplined," he told reporters after the event," I devote a lot of time to electronic games, so usually I'm not under a lot of pressure."

FEATHERWEIGHT

(62 kg—135.5 lbs [1920-1992: 60 kg—132 lbs; 1996: 64 kg—141.1 lbs])

1896–1912 not held

1920 Antwerp C: 14, N: 11, D: 8.29.

		ONE-HAND SNATCH	ONE-HAND JERK	TWO-HAND JERK	TOTAL KG
1. François de Haes	BEL	60.0	65.0	95.0	220.0
2. Alfred Schmidt	EST	55.0	65.0	90.0	210.0
3. Eugène Ryther	SWI	55.0	65.0	90.0	210.0
4. Luigi Gatti	ITA	50.0	55.0	90.0	195.0
5. Ludvik Wágner	CZE	50.0	65.0	80.0	195.0
6. Gustav Eriksson	SWE	47.5	65.0	80.0	192.5
7. Lionel de Haes	BEL	45.0	60.0	85.0	190.0
7. Karl Kõiv	EST	45.0	60.0	85.0	190.0

The rules of 1920 required each lifter to perform the one-hand jerk with whichever arm was not used in the one-arm snatch. The competitions were held in the cold and darkness of a canvas shelter on a surface of loose cinder. Schmidt was awarded second place after jerking 925 kg in a lift-off against Ryther. Frans De Haes was a native of Antwerp and a Flemish nationalist whose victory became the focal point of political bickering. He died of influenza in May 1923.

1924 Paris C: 21, N: 11, D: 7.21.

		ONE-HAND SNATCH	ONE-HAND JERK	TWO-HAND PRESS	TWO-HAND SNATCH	TWO-HAND JERK	TOTAL KG
1. Pierino Gabetti	ITA	65.0 OR	77.5	72.5	82.5	105.0 OR	402.5
2. Andreas Stadler	AUT	65.0 OR	75.0	65.0	75.0	105.0 OR	385.0
3. Arthur Reinmann	SWI	57.5	70.0	80.0	75.0	100.0	382.5
4. Maurice Martin	FRA	60.0	62.5	75.0	82.5	100.0	380.0
5. Wilhelm Rosinek	AUT	57.5	75.0	67.5	70.0	105.0 OR	375.0
6. Gustav Ernesaks	EST	60.0	80.0 OR	67.5	72.5	92.5	372.5
7. Alfred Baxter	GBR	55.0	65.0	70.0	75.0	105.0 OR	370.0
8. Edgar Juillerat	SWI	55,0	70.0	67.5	75.0	100.0	367.5

Mehmet Djemal Bey of Turkey, who finished 14th, was only 13 years old.

1928 Amsterdam C: 21, N: 13, D: 7.29.

		PRESS	SNATCH	JERK	TOTAL KG
1. Franz Andrysek	AUT	77.5	90.0 OR	120.0 OR	287.5 OR
2. Pierino Gabetti	ITA	80.0	90.0 OR	112.5	282.5
3. Hans Wölpert	GER	92.5 WR	82.5	107.5	282.5
4. Giuseppe Conca	ITA	92.5 WR	80.0	105.0	277.5
5. Arthur Reinmann	SWI	82.5	82.5	110.0	275.0
6. Andreas Stadler	AUT	72.5	80.0	115.0	267.5
7. Henri Baudrand	FRA	77.5	80.0	107.5	265.0
8. Mehmet Djemal Bey	TUR	85.0	75.0	102.5	262.5
8. Josef Vacek	CZE	80.0	82.5	100.0	262.5

1932 Los Angeles C: 6, N: 4, D: 7.31.

		PRESS	SNATCH	JERK	TOTAL KG
1. Raymond Suvigny	FRA	82.5	87.5	117.5	287.5 EOR
2. Hans Wölpert	GER	85.0	87.5	110.0	282.5
3. Anthony Terlazzo	USA	82.5	85.0	112.5	280.0
4. Helmut Schäfer	GER	77.5	77.5	112.5	267.5
5. Attilio Bescepè	ITA	82.5	77.5	102.5	262.5
6. Richard Bachtell	USA	70.0	80.0	102.5	252.5

An eating binge on the way to Los Angeles forced Suvigny to lose ten pounds in one week in order to make the weight limit.

1936 Berlin C: 21, N: 13, D: 8.2. WR: 297.5 kg (Max Walther)

		PRESS	SNATCH	JERK	TOTAL KG
1. Anthony Terlazzo	USA	92.5 EOR	97.5 OR	122.5	312.5 WR
2. Saleh Mohammed Soliman	EGY	85.0	95.0	125.0 OR	305.0
3. Ibrahim Hassan Shams	EGY	80.0	95.0	125.0 OR	300.0
4. Anton Richter	AUT	80.0	97.5 OR	120.0	297.5
5. Georg Liebsch	GER	92.5 EOR	90.0	107.5	290.0
6. Attilio Bescapè	ITA	87.5	90.0	110.0	287.5
7. John Terry	USA	75.0	92.5	120.0	287.5
8. Max Walther	GER	75.0	90.0	115.0	280.0

Tony Terlazzo was born in Italy and raised in Hoboken, New Jersey.

1948 London C: 23, N: 18, D: 8.9. WR: 320 kg (Arvid Anderson)

		PRESS	SNATCH	JERK	TOTAL KG
1. Mahmoud Fayyad	EGY	92.5	105.0 WR	135.0 WR	332.5 WR
2. Rodney Wilkes	TRI	97.5	97.5	122.5	317.5
3. Mohammad Jaafar Salmasi	IRN	100.0 OR	97.5	115.0	312.5
4. Nam Su-il	KOR	92.5	92.5	122.5	307.5
5. Rodrigo Del Rosario	PHI	97.5	92.5	117.5	307.5
6. Kotaro Ishikawa	USA	92.5	95.0	120.0	307.5
7. Johan Runge	DEN	95.0	90.0	120.0	305.0
8. Max Heral	FRA	85.0	95.0	120.0	300.0

1952 Helsinki C: 22, N: 21, D: 7.25. WR: 332.5 kg (Mahmoud Fayad)

		PRESS	SNATCH	JERK	TOTAL KG
1. Rafael Chimishkyan	SOV/GEO	97.5	105.0 EOR	135.0 EOR	337.5 WR
2. Nikolai Saksonov	SOV/RUS	95.0	105.0 EOR	132.5	332.5
3. Rodney Wilkes	TRI	100.0	100.0	122.5	322.5
4. Rodrigo Del Rosario	PHI	105.0 OR	92.5	120.0	317.5
5. Said Khalifa Gouda	EGY	85.0	102.5	125.0	312.5
6. Chay Weng Yew	SIN	87.5	97.5	127.5	312.5
7. Bálint Nagy	HUN	85.0	97.5	125.0	307.5
8. Mohsen Tabatabaie	IRN	90.0	97.5	120.0	307.5

1956 Melbourne C: 21, N: 19, D: 11.23. WR: 350 kg (Rafael Chimishkyan)

		PRESS	SNATCH	JERK	TOTAL KG
1. Isaac Berger	USA	107.5	107.5 OR	137.5 OR	352.5 WR
2. Yevgeny Minayev	SOV/RUS	115.0 WR	100.0	127.5	342.5
3. Marian Zieliński	POL	105.0	102.5	127.5	335.0
4. Rodney Wilkes	TRI	100.0	105.0	125.0	330.0
5. Hiroyoshi Shiratori	JPN	97.5	100.0	127.5	325.0
6. Georg Miske	GDR	100.0	95.0	125.0	320.0
7. Tan Ser Cher	SIN	92.5	92.5	130.0	315.0
8. Lee Kyung-sob	KOR	90.0	95.0	132.5	312.5

Born in Tel Aviv, Ike Berger was the 19-year-old son of a rabbi from Brooklyn.

1960 Rome C: 28, N: 25, D: 9.7. WR: 372.5 kg (Isaac Berger)

		PRESS	SNATCH	JERK	TOTAL KG
1. Yevgeny Minayev	SOV/RUS	120.0 EWR	110.0 OR	142.5 OR	372.5 EWR
2. Isaac Berger	USA	117.5	105.0	140.0	362.5
3. Sebastiano Mannironi	ITA	107.5	110.0 OR	135.0	352.5
4. Kim Hae-nam	KOR	105.0	105.0	135.0	345.0
5. Yukio Furuyama	JPN	107.5	102.5	135.0	345.0
6. Hosni Abbas	EGY	102.5	95.0	140.0	337.5
7. Tun Kywe	BUR	100.0	100.0	127.5	327.5
8. Alberto Nogar	PHI	97.5	100.0	127.5	325.0

The competition took ten hours and didn't end until four a.m., when Berger twice failed to jerk 152.5 kg. Minayev had lost to Berger six straight times prior to the Olympics. In Rome, he made all nine of his lifts.

1964 Tokyo C: 22, N: 20, D: 10.12. WR: 387.5 kg (Yoshinobu Miyake)

		PRESS	SNATCH	JERK	TOTAL KG
1. Yoshinobu Miyake	JPN	122.5 OR	122.5 OR	152.5 WR	397.5 WR
2. Isaac Berger	USA	122.5 OR	107.5	152.5 WR	382.5
3. Mieczysław Nowak	POL	112.5	115.0	150.0	377.5
4. Hiroshi Fukuda	JPN	120.0	115.0	140.0	375.0
5. Sebastiano Mannironi	ITA	112.5	112.5	145.0	370.0
6. Kim Hae-nam	KOR	115.0	112.5	140.0	367.5
7. Rudolf Kozłowski	POL	110.0	107.5	140.0	357.5
8. Hosni Abbas	EGY	105.0	100.0	137.5	342.5

Yoshinobu Miyake, who had won the Bantamweight silver medal in 1960, was a 24-year-old lieutenant in the National Self-Defense Force. Only 5 feet tall, he came from a poor family in Miyagi prefecture in northern Japan. His parents sold some pigs to raise the money to see their son compete in the Olympics.

1968 Mexico City C: 28, N: 22, D: 10.14. WR: 397.5 kg (Yoshinobu Miyake)

		PRESS	SNATCH	JERK	TOTAL KG
1. Yoshinobu Miyake	JPN	122.5 EOR	117.5	152.5 EWR	392.5
2. Dito Shanidze	SOV/GEO	120.0	117.5	150.0	387.5
3. Yoshiyuki Miyake	JPN	122.5 EOR	115.0	147.5	385.0
4. Jan Wojnowski	POL	117.5	115.0	150.0	382.5
5. Mieczysław Nowak	POL	117.5	110.0	147.5	375.0
6. Nasrollah Dehnavi	IRN	117.5	107.5	140.0	365.0
7. Young Moo-shin	KOR	110.0	115.0	140.0	365.0
8. Manuel Mateos de la Rosa	MEX	120.0	100.0	140.0	360.0

Yoshiyuki Miyake was six years younger than his brother Yoshinobu.

1972 Munich C: 13, N; 11, D: 8.29. WR: 402.5 kg (Dito Shanidze)

		PRESS	SNATCH	JERK	TOTAL KG
1. Norair Nurikian	BUL	127.5 OR	117.5	157.5 WR	402.5 EWR
2. Dito Shanidze	SOV/GEO	127.5 OR	120.0	152.5	400.0
3. János Benedek	HUN	125.0	120.0	145.0	390.0
4. Yoshinobu Miyake	JPN	120.0	120.0	145.0	385.0
5. Kurt Pittner	AUT	125.0	112.5	145.0	382.5
6. Rolando Chang Pérez	CUB	120.0	115.0	142.5	377.5
7. Mieczysław Nowak	POL	120.0	110.0	145.0	375.0
8. Peppino Tanti	ITA	120.0	107.5	140.0	367.5

This division saw the rare appearance of an athlete from Albania. Ymer Pampuri, a circus clown, broke the Olympic record in the press and actually led the competition after the first round due to his lower bodyweight. However, the snatch and the jerk were not practiced in Albania and he could do no better than 12th and tenth in those disciplines. Pampuri wound up in ninth place.

1976 Montreal C: 17, N: 13, D: 7.20. WR: 285 kg (Georgi Todorov)

		SNATCH	JERK	TOTAL KG
1. Nikolai Kolesnikov	SOV/RUS	125.0 OR	160.0 OR	285.0 EWR
2. Georgi Todorov	BUL	122.5	157.5	280.0
3. Kazumasa Hirai	JPN	125.0 OR	150.0	275.0
4. Takashi Saito	JPN	110.0	152.5	262.5
5. Edward Weitz	ISR	110.0	152.5	262.5
6. Davoud Maleki	IRN	115.0	145.0	260.0
7. Pedro Fuentes la Fuente	CUB	112.5	145.0	257.5
8. Om Jong-guk	PRK	110.0	145.0	255.0

Kolesnikov set a jerk world record of 161.5 kg on his fourth attempt.

1980 Moscow C: 18, N: 14, D: 7.22. WR: 297.5 kg (Viktor Mazin)

		SNATCH	JERK	TOTAL KG
1. Viktor Mazin	SOV/RUS	130.0 OR	160.0 EOR	290.0 OR
2. Stefan Dimitrov	BUL	127.5	160.0 EOR	287.5
3. Marek Seweryn	POL	127.5	155.0	282.5
4. Antoni Pawlak	POL	120.0	150.0	275.0
5. Julio Loscos Rodríguez	CUB	125.0	150.0	275.0
6. František Nedvěd	CZE	122.5	150.0	272.5
7. Víctor Pérez Ramírez	CUB	117.5	152.5	270.0
8. Gelu Radu	ROM	115.0	150.0	265.0

1984 Los Angeles-Westchester C: 21, N: 17, D: 7.31. WR: 315 kg (Stefan Topurov)

		SNATCH	JERK	TOTAL KG
1. Chen Weiqiang	CHN	125.0	157.5	2B2.5
2. Gelu Radu	ROM	125.0	155.0	280.0
3. Tsai Wen-yee	TAI	125.0	147.5	272.5
4. Kaoru Wabiko	JPN	120.0	150.0	270.0
5. Yosuke Muraki	JPN	120.0	147.5	267.5
6. Lee Myeong-su	KOR	117.5	150.0	267.5
7. Sorie Enda Nasution	INA	115.0	152.5	267.5
8. Uolevi Kahelin	FIN	112.5	155.0	267.5

Chen Weiqiang (left) and Tsai Wen-Yee, 1984

Weightlifters Chen and Tsai become the first athletes from China and Taiwan to share an Olympic medal platform after taking the gold and bronze medals respectively, in the 60kg category in 1984.

Silver medalist Gelu Radu was the only medalist at the 1983 world championships to take part in the 1984 Olympics. The medal ceremony for this event held a special drama as it marked the first time that the platform was shared by athletes from China and Taiwan. Chen and Tsai shook hands and spoke kindly of each other. At 19, Chen was the youngest weightlifting champion in Olympic history.

At the Friendship Games in Varna, Bulgaria, in September, Stefan Topurov of Bulgaria broke his own world record with a combined lift of 322.5 kg. He was followed by two Soviet lifters, Yurik Sarkisyan at 315 kg and Anton Kodzhabashev at 295 kg. At the 1983 world championships, Topurov had jerked 180 kg to become the first person in history to lift three times his own bodyweight.

1988 Seoul C: 17, N: 14, D: 9.20. WR: 335 kg (Naim Süleymanoğlu)

		SNATCH	JERK	TOTAL KG
1. Naim Süleymanoğlu	TUR	152.5 WR	190.0 WR	342.5 WR
2. Stefan Topurov	BUL	137.5	175.0	312.5
3. Ye Huanming	CHN	127.5	160.0	287.5
4. Min Joon-ki	KOR	125.0	155.0	280.0
5. Yosuke Muraki	JPN	127.5	150.0	277.5
6. Giannis Sidriopoulos	GRE	120.0	145.0	265.0
7. Kazushige Oguri	JPN	117.5	142.5	260.0
8. Tolentino Murillo	COL	120.0	140.0	260.0

He was born Naim Suleimanov in the small mountain village of Ptichar in the region of Bulgaria with the highest concentration of ethnic Turks. His father, a zinc miner, was 5 feet tall. His mother, who worked in a hot house, was 4 feet 7½ inches. Naim himself topped out just shy of 5 feet. Short though he may have been, he was also strong. In a nation where weightlifters are heroes, he was quickly discovered by Bulgarian sports officials.

Naim Süleymanoğlu, 1988
The Turkish government paid the Bulgarian government over $1,000,000 to allow featherweight weightlifter Süleymanoğlu to compete for Turkey in 1988.

He first competed internationally in a junior championship and, at the age of 14, came within 5½ pounds of breaking the adult world record for combined lifts. At 15 he set his first world record and at 16 he became the second lifter to clean and jerk three times his bodyweight. In recognition of his achievements, the Bulgarian government gave Suleimanov his own apartment and a monthly stipend. However, in 1984, at the same time that he was being well treated, the government also began a crackdown on the Turkish minority. In December, Suleimanov returned from a training camp to his parents' hometown of Momchilgrad (they had moved there when he was 3) to discover that a major demonstration by Turks had been violently suppressed by Bulgarian authorities. The anti-Turkish campaign intensified. Mosques were closed, Moslem holidays and burials were banned, and the use of the Turkish language was outlawed, as was the wearing of Turkish clothes. Violators were imprisoned and even executed.

In 1985, Suleimanov attended a ten-day training camp in Melbourne, Australia. There he was approached by Bulgarian defectors of Turkish descent who offered to help him defect. The 18-year-old declined, but told them that if the Bulgarian government changed his name to a non-Islamic one, as they had done to other Turks, he would reconsider. When he returned to Bulgaria his passport was confiscated and he was issued a new one bearing the name Naum Shalamanov. One day he opened up a newspaper and read a faked interview that quoted him as saying that he was proud to retake his "true Bulgarian name." Suleimanov was peppered with letters from Bulgarian Turks who believed the "interview," and accused him of selling his soul.

In December 1986, Suleimanov, by now a two-time world champion, returned to Melbourne for the World Cup competition. When the tournament was over, he joined the rest of the Bulgarian team for a banquet at the Leonda restaurant in the Melbourne suburb of Hawthorn. At one point he excused himself to go to the men's room—and never returned. After hiding out for four days, he presented himself to the Turkish consulate and asked for asylum. He was flown to London where he was met by a private jet belonging to Turkey's prime minister, Turgut Ozal. Upon arrival at the airport in Turkey, Suleimanov kissed the tarmac and became an instant national hero.

Olympic rules state that if an athlete changes nationality, he must wait three years to take part in international competition unless he receives a waiver from the country he has left. The Bulgarian government granted this waiver in 1988 after receiving over $1,000,000 from the Turkish government, as well as an assurance from Suleimanov (who by now had assumed the Turkish equivalent of his original name—Naim Süleymanoğlu) that he would suspend his public criticisms of their policies.

In Seoul, Süleymanoğlu lived up to all expectations. He broke the snatch world record with his second lift, then broke it again with his third. He repeated his double world record in the clean and jerk. His combined total was larger than that of the winner in the lightweight division, and his best lifts in both the snatch and jerk were greater than those of Paul Anderson when he won the heavyweight division in 1956. At that time, Anderson weighed 303 pounds. Süleymanoğlu in 1988 weighed 132.

1992 Barcelona C: 31, N: 26, D: 7.28. WR: 342.5 kg (Naim Süleymanoğlu)

		SNATCH	JERK	TOTAL KG
1. Naim Süleymanoğlu	TUR	142.5	177.5	320.0
2. Nikola Peshalov	BUL	137.5	167.5	305.0
3. He Yingqiang	CHN	130.0	165.0	295.0
4. Neno Terziiski	BUL	130.0	165.0	295.0
5. Leonidis Valerios	GRE	132.5	162.5	295.0
6. Ro Hyon-il	PRK	127.5	160.0	287.5
7. Attila Czanka	HUN	127.5	157.5	285.0
8. Li Jae-son	PRK	130.0	150.0	280.0

When Naim Süleymanoğlu completed his last lift at the 1988 Olympics, he literally kissed the bar good-bye. He was ready to retire. But retirement was easier said than done. When he stepped off the airplane that had carried him from Seoul to the Turkish capital of Ankara, there were an estimated one million people waiting to greet him. Speaking from Kizilay Plaza to a national television audience, he announced, "This is not my gold medal! This is the Turkish people's medal!" Süleymanoğlu, Turkey's first gold medalist in 20 years, graduated from being a major hero to being a symbol of his nation. Retirement was out of the question. His story became so widely known around the world that the plight of Bulgaria's Turkish minority became an international issue. The Bulgarian government was forced to allow one-third of the nation's 900,000 Turks to emigrate to Turkey.

Süleymanoğlu defeated Bulgaria's Nikola Peshalov at the 1989 world championships and then, citing a back injury, he did announce his retirement. At the 1990 world championships, Süleymanoğlu watched Peshalov win with a total of only 297.5 kilograms. This was too painful for Süleymanoğlu. He reentered training and won back his world title in 1991. Still, it was hard for him to maintain the discipline necessary to stay on top. When he was a teenager, girls had teased him because he was so short. Now he was pursued by numerous women and he fathered a child out of wedlock. The Turkish tabloids followed his every move and photographers surrounded him whenever he appeared in public. At the 1992 European championships, three months before the Olympics, Peshalov tied Süleymanoğlu at 312.5 kilograms and won because of a lower bodyweight. It was Suleymanoğlu's first defeat in 8½ years. It served as a serious wake-up call.

In Barcelona, Süleymanoğlu and Peshalov repeated their European snatch totals of 142.5 kg and 137.5 kg, but the clean-and-jerk was a different story. Peshalov, who had jerked 175 kilograms at the Euros, could do no better than 167.5 at the Olympics. When Peshalov was finished lifting, Süleymanoğlu coolly hoisted 170 kilograms and the contest was over. He made one more successful lift for good measure and then passed his final attempt.

Among the secondary contenders was Marcus Samuel, definitely one of the top ten lifters in his weight category, a legitimate qualifier for the Olympics. Unfortunately, Samuel hailed from the Pacific island of Nauru, a nation so small (population: 9000) that it didn't have a national Olympic committee. So Samuel did what he had to do: he acquired citizenship in a "big" country—Western Samoa (population 195,000). In Barcelona, Samuel lifted a total of 275 kilograms and placed a creditable ninth. In 1994, thanks to his accomplishments, Nauru was admitted as the 196th—and smallest—nation in the Olympic movement. In 2007, Samuel was named President of Nauru. He is the first non-royal Olympic athlete to go on to lead a nation.

1996 Atlanta C: 36, N: 26, D: 7.22. WR: 330.0 kg (Naim Suleymanoğlu)

		SNATCH	JERK	TOTAL KG
1. Naim Süleymanoğlu	TUR	147.5	187.5 WR	335.0 WR
2. Valerios Leonidis	GRE	145.0	187.5 WR	332.5
3. Xiao Jiangang	CHN	145.0	177.5	322.5
4. Yorgos Tzelilis	GRE	145.0	177.5	322.5
5. Adrián Popa	HUN	135.0	172.5	307.5
6. Ilian Iliev	BUL	142.5	162.5	305.0
7. Mücahit Yağci	TUR	135.0	167.5	302.5
8. Zoltán Kecskés	HUN	135.0	167.5	302.5

The 1996 featherweight competition was a classic sports event: an eagerly anticipated duel that actually exceeded expectations. By this time, Naim Süleymanoğlu was a hero of heroes in Turkey. In the words of television sports director Barboros Talis, "If he comes to a roadblock when he is driving, it is removed for him. If he eats in a restaurant, no one will ask him to pay. If he drives beyond the speed limit, police officers wave him on ahead." He owned 21 houses. It was said that if Süleymanoğlu succeeded in his quest to become the first weightlifter to win three gold medals, the

Turkish government would award him a 22nd house, as well as ten kilograms of gold.

When Süleymanoğlu won the 1992 Olympic gold medal, Russian-born Valerios Leonidis was in fifth place, 25 kg behind. When Süleymanoğlu won the 1993 world championship, Leonidis was fifth again, but this time he was only 10 kg back. Beginning in 1994, Leonidis emerged as Süleymanoğlu's main challenger in every major meet. At the European championships that year, Süleymanoğlu defeated Leonidis by 7.5 kg. At the 1994 world championship, his margin of victory was down to 5 kg. At the 1995 European championships, Leonidis closed the gap to 2.5 kg. At the 1995 world championships, Leonidis finally matched Süleymanoğlu's total, but lost anyway because he was 200 grams heavier. In Atlanta however, it would be Leonidis who would have the weight advantage (680 grams) in case of a tie. Momentum was clearly on Leonidis' side.

Leonidis may have had the momentum, but Süleymanoğlu, who smoked fifty cigarettes a day "to find my inner peace," had still been beaten only once in thirteen years.

In the Georgia World Congress Center, Süleymanoğlu's Turkish supporters gathered on one side of the stands, while Leonidis' Greek fans settled in directly opposite. Back in Turkey and Greece, two nations with a long history of conflict, it was after midnight, but the populations were wide-awake. The showdown earned the second highest rating in Greek television history.

In the snatch, Leonidis opened by lifting 140 kg. Süleymanoğlu countered with a first lift of 145 kg, which Leonidis then matched. Süleymanoğlu missed at 147.5 kg, but made it with a second attempt. Leonidis tried the same weight but missed. Halfway through the contest, Süleymanoğlu led by 2.5 kg.

Both men began to clean and jerk at 180 kg. and both succeeded. Süleymanoğlu considered moving on to 182.5 kg, but then upped it to 185. The world record was 183 kg. He lifted the weight and held it. Leonidis countered with a successful lift of 187.5 kg—another world record. At this point, with one lift remaining for both men, Leonidis was in first place based on lower bodyweight. Süleymanoğlu attacked 187.5 kg—and succeeded. Leonidis had no choice but to try 190 kg, ten kilograms more than his personal best. He raised the bar to his chest, but was unable to put it over his head. Süleymanoğlu had made Olympic history with his third gold medal. In the stands, the Turkish and Greek supporters, who had been taunting each other for more than two hours, forgot their differences and rose together to give both lifters a standing ovation.

2000 Sydney C: 21, N: 21, D: 9.17. WR: 325.0 kg (Nikolai Peshalov)

		SNATCH	JERK	TOTAL KG
1. Nikolai Peshalov	CRO	150.0	175.0	325.0 EWR
2. Leonidas Sampanis	GRE	147.5	170.0	317.5
3. Gennady Oleshchuk	BLR	142.5	175.0	317.5
4. Le Maosheng	CHN	140.0	175.0	315.0
5. Seyed Mahdi Panzvan Langroudi	IRN	140.0	162.5	302.5
6. Hiroshi Ikehata	JPN	135.0	165.0	300.0
7. Vladimir Popov	MOL	135.0	160.0	295.0
8. Elkhan Suleymanov	AZR	130.0	162.5	292.5

DISQ (Drugs): Sevdalin Minchev (BUL) 317.5

Naim Süleymanoğlu, at age 33, tried to win his fourth gold medal, but missed all three of his attempts to snatch 145 kilograms. Nikolai Peshalov had earned a silver medal in 1992 and a bronze in 1996 while competing for Bulgaria. Croatia then purchased Peshalov from Bulgaria, although they refused to pay up until Peshalov proved himself a medal contender by placing fifth at the 1999 world championships.

2004 Athens C: 20, N: 18, D: 8.16. WR: None Recognized

		SNATCH	JERK	TOTAL KG
1. Shi Zhiyong	CHN	152.5	172.5	325.0
2. Le Maosheng	CHN	140.0	172.5	312.5
3. Israel José Rubio Rivero	VEN	132.5	162.5	295.0
4. Armen Ghazaryan	ARM	135.0	160.0	295.0
5. Gustar Junianto	INA	132.5	160.0	292.5
6. Samson N'Dicka-Matam	FRA	127.5	160.0	287.5
7. Umurbek Bazarbayev	TRM	130.0	157.5	287.5
8. Sunarto	INA	125.0	160.0	285.0

DISQ (Drugs): Leonidas Sampanis (GRE) 312.5

After winning the world championship in the 62-kilogram weight category, Halil Mutlu dropped his weight for the Olympics to compete at 56 kilograms,

Leonidas Sampanis, 2004

The stamp was withdrawn after his disqualification.

leaving world championship silver medalist Shi Zhiyong the favorite for Athens. Shi built a commanding lead in the snatch, lifting 152.5 kilograms, half a kilo short of his world record, on his second attempt at the weight. In the clean and jerk, Shi cleared 172.5 kilos with his second lift, and celebrated with a backflip. This forced his compatriot and main challenger, Le Maosheng, to attempt 185 kilos, 2½ kilos over his world jerk record, for the gold. Le barely managed to lift the bar off the ground on his last two attempts and settled for silver.

In order to make the weight category, Shi Zhiyong was forced to lose nearly nine pounds (four kilograms) in three days. "I have not eaten for three days and my weight has come down by four kilos," said Shi. "It is not well known the amount of effort, work and sacrifice involved in weightlifting."

Leonidas Sampanis of Greece originally finished third, but was disqualified after testing positive for elevated levels of testosterone. Strange as it may seem, Sampanis' positive doping test caused ripples of excitement in the world of philately. The day after Sampanis was awarded a bronze medal, the Greek postal service issued a stamp in his honor. The stamp was quickly withdrawn after Sampanis' doping test was announced, and soon became a collector's item.

2008 Beijing C: 17, N: 15, D: 8.11. WR: 326 kg (Zhang Jie)

		SNATCH	JERK	TOTAL KG
1. Zhang Xiangxiang	CHN	143.0	176.0	319.0
2. Diego Fernando Salazar Quintero	COL	138.0	167.0	305.0
3. Triyatno	INA	135.0	163.0	298.0
4. Antoniu Buci	ROM	130.0	165.0	295.0
5. Phaisan Hansawong	THA	132.0	162.0	294.0
6. Lázaro Maikel Ruiz	CUB	132.0	162.0	294.0
7. Tolkunbek Hudaybergenov	TRM	126.0	162.0	288.0
8. Mohamed Abd El-Baki	EGY	129.0	159.0	288.0

Zhang Xiangxiang earned a bronze medal in the bantamweight division at the Sydney Olympics at the age of seventeen. Two years later he won the junior world championship, but was soon forced to retire after bungled treatment for a back injury almost cost him his life. While he was being injected with a pain killer, his nerves and spinal cord were damaged and his respiratory system was paralysed. Unable to exhale, he lapsed into a coma for four days. Zhang returned to the sport after a two-year hiatus and qualified for the Chinese national team after two-time world champion Qiu Le was injured at the 2007 world championships.

In Beijing, Zhang cleared 143 kg (315.3 lbs) to take the lead after the snatch, and then produced the biggest clean and jerk lift, 176 kg (388 lbs) to win the gold. In second place after the snatch, reigning world silver medalist Im Yong-su missed all three of his clean and jerk attempts.

Bronze medalist Triyatno came from a poor farming family in southern Sumatra and took up weightlifting as a way to travel around the world.

LIGHTWEIGHT

(69kg—152 lbs [1920-1992: 67.5 kg—148.75 lbs; 1996: 70 kg—154.32 lbs])

1896–1912 not held

1920 Antwerp C: 12, N: 10, D: 8.29.

		ONE-HAND SNATCH	ONE-HAND JERK	TWO-HAND JERK	TOTAL KG
1. Alfred Neuland	EST	72.5	75.0	110.0	257.5
2. Louis Williquet	BEL	60.0	75.0	105.0	240.0
3. Florimond Rooms	BEL	55.0	70.0	105.0	230.0
4. Giulio Monti	ITA	55.0	70.0	105.0	230.0
5. Fernand Arnout	FRA	60.0	60.0	100.0	220.0
5. Martin Olofsson	SWE	55.0	70.0	95.0	220.0
7. Jean Vaquette	FRA	55.0	65.0	95.0	215.0
8. Johny Grun	LUX	52.5	67.5	90.0	210.0
8. Willem Nimwegen	HOL	55.0	65.0	90.0	210.0

1924 Paris C: 22, N: 12, D: 7.22.

		ONE-HAND SNATCH	ONE-HAND JERK	TWO-HAND PRESS	TWO-HAND SNATCH	TWO-HAND JERK	TOTAL KG
1. Edmond Décottignies	FRA	70.0	92.5	77.5	85.0	115.0 OR	440.0
2. Anton Zwerina	AUT	75.0 OR	80.0	77.5	82.5	112.5	427.5
3. Bohumil Durdis	CZE	70.0	82.5	72.5	90.0	110.0	425.0
4. Leopold Treffny	AUT	65.0	85.0	77.5	85.0	112.5	425.0
5. Joseph Jaquenoud	SWI	65.0	85.0	77.5	85.0	105.0	417.5
6. Eduard Vanaaseme	EST	65.0	77.5	85.0	80.0	107.5	415.0
7. August Scheffer	HOL	62.5	80.0	80.0	82.5	110.0	415.0
8. Felix Bichsel	SWI	70.0	95.0 WR	65.0	75.0	105.0	410.0

1928 Amsterdam C: 18 , N: 12, D: 7.29. WR: 325 kg (Kurt Helbig)

		PRESS	SNATCH	JERK	TOTAL KG
1. Hans Haas	AUT	90.0 OR	97.5	135.0 OR	322.5
1. Kurt Helbig	GER	85.0	102.5 OR	135.0 OR	322.5
3. Fernand Arnout	FRA	85.0	97.5	120.0	302.5
4. Albert Aeschmann	SWI	87.5	90.0	120.0	297.5
5. Willi Reinfrank	GER	85.0	90.0	120.0	295.0
6. Jules Meese	FRA	90.0 OR	87.5	115.0	292.5
7. Anton Hangel	AUT	77.5	90.0	120.0	287.5
8. Gastone Pierini	ITA	90.0 OR	82.5	110.0	282.5

1932 Los Angeles C: 6, N: 4, D: 7.31. WR: 325 kg (Kurt Helbig)

		PRESS	SNATCH	JERK	TOTAL KG
1. René Duverger	FRA	97.5 OR	102.5 EOR	125.0	325.0 EWR
2. Hans Haas	AUT	82.5	100.0	125.0	307.5
3. Gastone Pierini	ITA	92.5	90.0	120.0	302.5
4. Pierino Gabetti	ITA	85.0	95.0	120.0	300.0
5. Arne Sundberg	USA	77.5	90.0	117.5	285.0
6. Walter Zagurski	USA	82.5	90.0	112.5	285.0

1936 Berlin C: 16, N: 12, D: 8.2. WR: 337.5 kg (Anwar Mohammed Mesbah)

		PRESS	SNATCH	JERK	TOTAL KG
1. Robert Fein	AUT	105.0 OR	100.0	137.5	342.5 WR
1. Anwar Mohammed Mesbah	EGY	92.5	105.0 OR	145.0 OR	342.5 WR
3. Karl Jansen	GER	95.0	100.0	132.5	327.5
4. Karl Schwitalle	GER	95.0	100.0	127.5	322.5
5. John Terpak	USA	97.5	100.0	125.0	322.5
6. El Sayed Ibrahim Masoud	EGY	90.0	100.0	132.5	322.5
7. René Duverger	FRA	97.5	95.0	125.0	317.5
8. Robert Mitchell	USA	85.0	97.5	130.0	312.5

Originally Mesbah was awarded sole possession of first place because he had weighed three and a half ounces less than Fein at the precompetition weigh-in. The Austrians lodged a protest, which was upheld, and both men received gold medals. Seven Jewish athletes won gold medals at the 1936 Nazi-run Olympics. Of the seven, the only ones who represented nations other than Hungary were Robert Fein and US basketball player Sam Balter.

1948 London C: 22, N: 17, D: 8.10. WR: 367.5 kg (Stanley Stanczyk)

		PRESS	SNATCH	JERK	TOTAL KG
1. Ibrahim Hassan Shams	EGY	97.5	115.0 OR	147.5 OR	360.0 OR
2. Attia Hamouda	EGY	105.0	110.0	145.0	360.0 OR
3. James Halliday	GBR	90.0	110.0	140.0	340.0
4. John Terpak	USA	102.5	102.5	135.0	340.0
5. John Stuart	CAN	107.5 OR	100.0	125.0	332.5
6. Kim Suk-young	KOR	95.0	100.0	135.0	330.0
7. La See-yun	KOR	90.0	100.0	125.0	330.0
8. Joseph Pittman	USA	100.0	95.0	127.5	322.5

Shams won a dramatic confrontation with his teammate Hamouda. After Shams missed a jerk of 145 kg, Hamouda successfully lifted the same weight on his final attempt. This forced Shams, who had set the world jerk record nine years earlier, to add 2.5 kg to the bar if he hoped to tie Hamouda and win as a result of his lower bodyweight. With the audience in complete silence, Shams approached the bar twice and then turned away. The third time, he seized the bar quickly and, in a flash, had it up to his shoulders and over his head for the victory. Shams' 1939 snatch of 116.5 kg stood as a world record until the 1952 Olympics. His 153.5 kg jerk of the same year was still on the books in 1957.

1952 Helsinki C: 24, N: 22, D: 7.26. WR: 367.5 kg (Stanley Stanczyk)

		PRESS	SNATCH	JERK	TOTAL KG
1. Tamio "Tommy" Kono	USA	105.0	117.5 WR	140.0	362.5 OR
2. Yevgeny Lopatin	SOV/RUS	100.0	107.5	142.5	350.0
3. Verne Barberis	AUS	105.0	105.0	140.0	350.0
4. Kim Chang-hee	KOR	100.0	105.0	140.0	345.0
5. Hassan Ferdows	IRN	102.5	107.5	135.0	345.0
6. Abd El Khadr El Touni	EGY	105.0	107.5	130.0	342.5
7. Johan Runge	DEN	105.0	97.5	127.5	330.0
8. Ging Hwie Thio	INA	105.0	92.5	130.0	327.5

Tommy Kono was a sickly child who suffered from asthma. His parents tried the usual traditional Japanese cures, such as bear kidneys, burned birds, and powdered snakes. "I used to wish with all my might for good health," he said. During World War II he and his family were forced to leave their home in Sacramento, California, and move to the Tule Lake detention camp for Japanese-Americans. It was there that 14-year-old Tommy was introduced to weightlifting. He caught on quickly and began what was to become an amazing career, which included two Olympic gold medals and one silver, and 21 world records set in four different divisions. His ability to move up and down in weight division without losing strength allowed him to fill in wherever the US team needed him; thus each of his three Olympic medals was won in a different category. He accomplished this by following an unusual system of dieting. If he needed to add weight, he would eat six or seven meals a day. If he needed to shed a few pounds, he would restrict himself to "only" three meals a day. In 1954 Kono won the Mr. World contest, and in 1955 and 1957 he was chosen Mr. Universe. He balanced his muscle-man image by washing and ironing his own clothes and doing his own cooking and cleaning. Yet another talent of Tommy Kono was his mental control—always an important factor in weightlifting. One of his many victims was Fyodor Bogdanovsky, who always lost to Kono, often performing well below his capabilities. Bogdanovsky once said, "When Kono looks at me from the wings, he works on me like a python on a rabbit."

Tommy Kono, 1956
Kono won three Olympic medals in three different weight categories in 1952, 1956 and 1960. His mental control led one rival to comment, "When Kono looks at me from the wings, he works on me like a python on a rabbit."

1956 Melbourne C: 18, N: 17, D: 11.24. WR: 382.5 kg (Nicolai Kostilev)

		PRESS	SNATCH	JERK	TOTAL KG
1. Ihor Rybak	SOV/UKR	110.0	120.0 OR	150.0 OR	380.0 OR
2. Rafael Khabutdinov	SOV/RUS	125.0 OR	110.0	137.5	372.5
3. Kim Chang-hee	KOR	107.5	112.5	150.0 OR	370.0
4. Kenji Onuma	JPN	110.0	110.0	147.5	367.5
5. Henrik Tamraz	IRN	115.0	105.0	145.0	365.0
6. Jan Czepułkowski	POL	120.0	105.0	135.0	360.0
7. Ivan Abadzhiev	BUL	102.5	117.5	137.5	357.5
8. Nil Tun Maung	BUR	110.0	105.0	137.5	352.5

1960 Rome C: 33, N: 29, D: 9.8. WR: 390 kg (Viktor Bushuyev)

		PRESS	SNATCH	JERK	TOTAL KG
1. Viktor Bushuyev	SOV/RUS	125.0 EOR	122.5 OR	150.0	397.5 WR
2. Tan Howe Liang	SIN	115.0	110.0	155.0 OR	380.0
3. Abdul Wahid Aziz	IRQ	117.5	115.0	147.5	380.0
4. Marian Zieliński	POL	115.0	110.0	150.0	375.0
5. Waldemar Baszanowski	POL	105.0	117.5	147.5	380,0
6. Mihály Huszka	HUN	110.0	107.5	147.5	365.0
7. Werner Dittrich	GDR	107.5	115.0	140.0	362.5
7. Zdenek Otáhal	CZE	115.0	107.5	140.0	362.5

Tan Howe Liang of Singapore and Abdul Wahid Aziz of Iraq are the only athletes from their respective countries to have won an Olympic medal.

1964 Tokyo C: 20, N: 18, D: 10.13. WR: 430 kg (Waldemar Baszanowski)

		PRESS	SNATCH	JERK	TOTAL KG
1. Waldemar Baszanowski	POL	132.5	135.0 OR	165.0 OR	432.5 WR
2. Vladimir Kaplunov	SOV/RUS	140.0 EWR	127.5	165.0 OR	432.5 WR
3. Marian Zieliński	POL	140.0 EWR	120.0	160.0	420.0
4. Anthony Garcy	USA	127.5	125.0	160.0	412.5
5. Zdenek Otáhal	CZE	130.0	117.5	152.5	400.0
6. Hiroshi Yamazaki	JPN	120.0	120.0	157.5	397.5
7. Parviz Jalayer	IRN	120.0	120.0	155.0	395.0
8. Alfred Kornprobst	GER	122.5	112.5	150.0	385.0

One of the greatest weightlifters of all time, Waldemar Baszanowski defeated Vladimir Kaplunov because he was ten and a half ounces lighter than his rival. Nine months later, at the European championships in Sofia, Bulgaria, the men tied again, and again Baszanowski was awarded first place as a result of his lower bodyweight.

1968 Mexico City C: 20, N: 17, D: 10.15. WR: 440 kg (Waldemar Baszanowski)

		PRESS	SNATCH	JERK	TOTAL KG
1. Waldemar Baszanowski	POL	135.0	135.0 EOR	167.5 OR	437.5 OR
2. Parviz Jalayer	IRN	125.0	132.5	165.0	422.5
3. Marian Zieliński	POL	135.0	125.0	160.0	420.0
4. Nobuyuki Hatta	JPN	135.0	127.5	155.0	417.5
5. Won Shin-hee	KOR	127.5	125.0	162.5	415.0
6. János Bagócs	HUN	132.5	122.5	157.5	412.5
7. Takeo Kimura	JPN	125.0	120.0	160.0	405.0
8. Kostadin Tilev	BUL	132.5	115.0	150.0	397.5

1972 Munich C: 22, N: 20, D: 8.30. WR: 450 kg (Waldemar Baszanowski)

		PRESS	SNATCH	JERK	TOTAL KG
1. Mukharby Kirzhinov	SOV/RUS	147.5	135.0 EOR	177.5 WR	460.0 WR
2. Mladen Kuchev	BUL	157.5 WR	125.0	167.5	450.0
3. Zbigniew Kaczmarek	POL	145.0	125.0	167.5	437.5
4. Waldemar Baszanowski	POL	142.5	130.0	162.5	435.0
5. Nasrollah Dehnavi	IRN	150.0	125.0	160.0	435.0
6. Jenő Ambrózi	HUN	142.5	120.0	165.0	427.5
7. Won Shin-hee	KOR	132.5	130.0	165.0	427.5
8. Masao Kato	JPN	140.0	120.0	165.0	425.0

1976 Montreal C: 23, N: 19, D: 7.21. WR: 312.5 kg (Mukharby Kirzhinov)

		SNATCH	JERK	TOTAL KG
1. Petro Korol	SOV/UKR	135.0 EOR	170.0	305.0 OR
2. Daniel Senet	FRA	135.0 EOR	165.0	300.0
3. Kazimierz Czarnecki	POL	130.0	165.0	295.0
4. Gunter Ambrass	GDR	125.0	170.0	295.0
5. Yatsuo Shimaya	JPN	127.5	165.0	292.5
6. Roberto Urrutia	CUB	130.0	162.5	292.5
7. Werner Schraut	GER	127.5	162.5	290.0
8. Roland Chavigny	FRA	130.0	155.0	285.0

DISQ (Drugs): Zbigniew Kaczmarek (POL) 307.5

Kaczmarek finished first but was subsequently disqualified after a test revealed that he had taken steroids.

1980 Moscow C: 20, N: 16, D: 7.23. WR: 337.5 kg (Yanko Russev)

		SNATCH	JERK	TOTAL KG
1. Yanko Russev	BUL	147.5 OR	195.0 WR	342.5 WR
2. Joachim Kunz	GDR	145.0	190.0	335.0
3. Mincho Pachov	BUL	142.5	182.5	325.0
4. Daniel Senet	FRA	147.5 OR	175.0	322.5
5. Gunter Ambrass	GDR	140.0	180.0	320.0
6. Zbigniew Kaczmarek	POL	140.0	177.5	317.5
7. Raúl González Millado	CUB	145.0	172.5	317.5
8. Virgil Dociu	ROM	140.0	170.0	310.0

1984 Los Angeles-Westchester C: 19, N: 17, D: 8.1. WR: 352.5 kg (Andreas Behm)

		SNATCH	JERK	TOTAL KG
1. Yao Jingyuan	CHN	142.5	177.5	320.0
2. Andrei Socaci	ROM	142.5	170.0	312.5
3. Jouni Grönman	FIN	140.0	172.5	312.5
4. Dean Willey	GBR	140.0	170.0	310.0
5. Choji Taira	JPN	132.5	172.5	305.0
6. Yasushige Sasaki	JPN	140.0	162.5	302.5
7. Basil Stellios	AUS	137.5	165.0	302.5
8. Ma Jianping	CHN	130.0	167.5	297.5

First place at the Friendship Games went to 1980 Olympic champion Yanko Russev with a combined total of 337.5 kg. Second was his Bulgarian teammate Alexandr Varbanov at 335 kg.

1988 Seoul C: 29, N: 25, D: 9.21. WR: 355 kg (Mikhail Petrov)

		SNATCH	JERK	TOTAL KG
1. Joachim Kunz	GDR	150.0	190.0	340.0
2. Israil Militosyan	SOV	155.0 OR	182.5	337.5
3. Li Jinhe	CHN	147.5	177.5	325.0
4. Marek Severyn	POL	145.0	172.5	317.5
5. Ergun Batmaz	TUR	145.0	172.5	317.5
6. Xiao Minglin	CHN	132.5	172.5	305.0
7. István Kerek	HUN	132.5	170.0	302.5
8. Christos Constandinidis	GRE	137.5	162.5	300.0

DISQ (Drugs): Angel Genchev (BUL) 362.5

Bulgaria entered the 1988 Olympic weightlifting tournament expecting to win four or five gold medals and an equal number of silver medals. At first things appeared to be going well: Sevdalin Marinov won the flyweight division, Mitko Grablev won the bantamweight division, Stefan Topurov took second in the featherweight division, Angel Genchev won the lightweight division, and Borislav Gidikov won the middleweight division. Then disaster struck: Grablev was disqualfied when he tested positive for a diuretic used as a masking agent for steroids. Two days later Genchev was disqualified for the same reason. Clearly the Bulgarians had underestimated the sophistication of the Olympic drug-testing equipment. After the announcement of the results of Genchev's drug test, the Bulgarian Weightlifting Federation withdrew the rest of their team from competition.

With Genchev disqualified, the gold medal was awarded to 29-year-old Joachim Kunz, who had not won a major championship in four years.

In 1992 Angel Genchev was convicted of rape and sent to prison for two years. However he was released early, not for good behavior, but so that he could represent Bulgaria at the 1994 world championships. In his first competition since his Olympic disgrace, Genchev earned a bronze medal.

1992 Barcelona C: 18, N: 16, D: 7.29. WR: 355 kg (Mikhail Petrov)

		SNATCH	JERK	TOTAL KG
1. Israil Militosyan	ARM	155.0 EOR	182.5	337.5
2. Yoto Yotov	BUL	150.0	177.5	327.5
3. Andreas Behm	GER	145.0	175.0	320.0
4. Abdelmanaane Yahiaoui	ALG	140.0	175.0	315.0
5. Jouni Grönman	FIN	135.0	170.0	305.0
6. Eyne Acevedo Tabares	COL	130.0	170.0	300.0
7. Im Sang-ho	PRK	135.0	165.0	300.0
8. Timothy McRae	USA	135.0	162.5	297.5

Militosyan's older cousin Vartan won a silver medal in the middleweight division in 1976. Israil himself earned a silver medal in 1988. After beating Yotov at the 1989 world championships, Militosyan lost to Yotov at the European championships of 1990, 1991, and 1992, as well as at the 1991 world championships. When he finally broke this string of second places in Barcelona, he and cousin Vartan, who was also his coach, shared a tearful embrace. Militosyan had dedicated his performance to the memories of his sister, brother, and uncle, who were killed in an earthquake that destroyed his hometown of Gumari three months after the 1988 Olympics.

1996 Atlanta C: 27, N: 22, D: 7.23. WR: 352.5 kg (Kim Myong-nam)

		SNATCH	JERK	TOTAL KG
1. Zhan Xugang	CHN	162.5 WR	195.0 WR	357.5 WR
2. Kim Myong-nam	PRK	160.0	185.0	345.0
3. Attila Feri	HUN	152.5	187.5	340.0
4. Plamen Zhelyazkov	BUL	155.0	180.0	335.0

5. Abdelmanaame Yahiaoui	ALG	150.0	185.0	335.0
6. Israil Militosyan	ARM	152.5	182.5	335.0
7. Wan Jianhui	CHN	152.5	180.0	332.5
8. Idalberto Aranda Quintero	CUB	145.0	187.5	332.5

After winning the 1995 world championship, Zhan Xugang of Hangzhou was usurped at the 1996 Asian Games by North Korea's Kim Myong-nam, who set world records in both the snatch and clean and jerk. In Atlanta, 3½ months later, it was Zhan who set world records in both disciplines.

2000 Sydney C: 17, N: 14, D: 9.20. WR: 357.5 kg (Galabin Boevski)

		SNATCH	JERK	TOTAL KG
1. Galabin Boevski	BUL	162.5	195.0	357.5 EWR
2. Georgi Markov	BUL	165.0 WR	187.5	352.5
3. Sergey Lavrenov	BLR	157.5	182.5	340.0
4. Zhang Guozheng	CHN	152.5	185.0	337.5
5. Rudik Petrosyan	ARM	147.5	187.5	335.0
6. Valerios Leonidis	GRE	145.0	185.0	330.0
7. Lee Bae-young	KOR	142.5	187.5	330.0
8. Kim Hak-bong	KOR	147.5	182.5	330.0

During the Sydney Olympics, three Bulgarian lifters failed doping tests. According to the rules, this meant that the entire Bulgarian team was expelled. However, Boevski and Markov had already competed and, because they did not test positive, they were allowed to keep their medals. In March 2004, on the other hand, both Boevski and Markov were found guilty of tampering with their urine samples at the 2003 world championships. Boevski was banned for eight years and Markov for eighteen months. In October 2011 Boevski ran into more trouble when he was arrested at São Paolo's international aiport after trying to board a plane to Spain carrying 9 kg (19.8 lbs) of cocaine in his luggage.

2004 Athens C: 17, N: 16, D: 8.18. WR: 357.5 kg (Galabin Boevski)

		SNATCH	JERK	TOTAL KG
1. Zhang Guozheng	CHN	160.0	187.5	347.5
2. Lee Bae-young	KOR	152.5	190.0	342.5
3. Nikolai Peshalov	CRO	150.0	187.5	337.5
4. Turan Mirzayev	AZR	147.5	185.0	332.5
5. Vencelas Dabaya Tientcheu	CAM	145.0	182.5	327.5
6. Sergei Lavrenyev	BLR	147.5	170.0	317.5
7. Romuald Ernault	FRA	142.5	165.0	307.5
8. Yukio Peter	NRU	135.0	167.5	302.5

Two-time defending world champion Zhang Guozheng took the lead with his first lift in the snatch, 152.5 kilograms, then raised it to 157.5 kg, and finally 160 kg. He strengthened his lead in the clean and jerk by lifting 187.5 kilograms on his first attempt, but failed twice at 192.5. Lee Bae-young had a chance to match Zhang's total weight, which would have given him the gold due to lower total bodyweight, but he missed his final attempt at 195 kg. Three-time Olympic medalist Nikolai Peshalov earned a surprise bronze medal despite missing four of his six lift attempts.

After the win Zhang said, "I won because of determination and endurance. Athletes can endure bitterness and pain five times more than others."

2008 Beijing C: 30, N: 26, D: 8.12. WR: 357.5 kg (Galabin Boevski)

		SNATCH	JERK	TOTAL KG
1. Liao Hui	CHN	158.0	190.0	348.0
2. Vencelas Dabaya	FRA	151.0	187.0	338.0
3. Tigran G. Martirosyan	ARM	153.0	185.0	338.0
4. Yordanis Borrero Suárez	CUB	148.0	180.0	328.0
5. Turan Mirzayev	AZR	146.0	181.0	327.0
6. Kim Chol-jin	PRK	146.0	180.0	326.0
7. Afgan Bayramov	AZR	145.0	175.0	320.0
8. Sitthisak Suphalak	THA	147.0	171.0	318.0

Twenty-one-year-old Liao Hui beat defending Olympic champion and reigning world champion Zhang Guozheng for a spot on the Chinese Olympic team. At the Beijing Games, Liao missed his first attempts in both the snatch and clean and jerk, but took the lead after the snatch portion. Former European champion Vencelas Dabaya attempted 197 kg (434.3 lbs) on his final lift, which would have given him the gold medal, but couldn't manage the weight. Dabaya took silver ahead of junior world champion Tigran Martirosyan based on lower bodyweight.

Defending Olympic silver medalist Lee Bae-young and 2005 world champion Shi Zhiyong both failed to finish. Lee, after snatching 155 kg, tore a calf muscle in his left leg during the clean and jerk, while Shi snatched 152 kg before incurring a waist injury.

Liao went on to win gold at the 2009 and 2010 world championships, but was stripped of his 2010 results—including two world records—and banned from competition for four years after testing positive for the anabolic steroid boldebolin.

MIDDLEWEIGHT

(77kg—169.75 lbs [1920–1992: 75 kg—165 lbs; 1996: 76 kg—167.55 lbs])

1896–1912 not held

1920 Antwerp C: 10, N: 7, D: 8.30.

		ONE-HAND SNATCH	ONE-HAND JERK	TWO-HAND JERK	TOTAL KG
1. Henri Gance	FRA	65.0	75.0	105.0	245.0
2. Pietro Bianchi	ITA	60.0	70.0	105.0	235.0
2. Albert Pettersson	SWE	55.0	75.0	105.0	235.0
4. Tinus Ringelberg	HOL	55.0	65.0	105.0	225.0
5. Paul Ledran	FRA	55.0	65.0	100.0	220.0
6. Christian Jensen	DEN	55.0	60.0	100.0	215.0
7. Marcel Marchand	BEL	55.0	55.0	95.0	205.0
8. Pieter Belmer	HOL	0.0	65.0	100.0	165.0

Both Bianchi and Pettersson hoisted 107.5 kg in a lift-off, using a two-handed jerk. They then drew lots to determine who would be awarded the silver medal rather than bronze. Bianchi won.

1924 Paris C: 25, N: 13, D: 7.22.

		ONE-HAND SNATCH	ONE-HAND JERK	TWO-HAND PRESS	TWO-HAND SNATCH	TWO-HAND JERK	TOTAL KG
1. Carlo Galimberti	ITA	77.5	95.0 OR	97.5 WR	95.0	127.5 WR	492.5
2. Alfred Neuland	EST	82.5 WR	90.0	77.5	90.0	115.0	455.0
3. Jaan Kikkas	EST	70.0	87.5	80.0	85.0	127.5 WR	450.0
4. Hamed Samy	EGY	72.5	77.5	97.5 WR	85.0	115.0	447.5
5. Albert Aeschmann	SWI	67.5	87.5	82.5	87.5	117.5	442.5
6. Roger François	FRA	72.0	80.0	87.5	87.5	117.5	442.5
7. Rupert Eidler	AUT	65.0	90.0	82.5	85.0	115.0	437.5
8. Pierre Vibert	FRA	72.5	75.0	80.0	85.0	115.0	432.5

1928 Amsterdam C: 23, N: 15, D: 7.29. WR: 320 kg (Carlo Galimberti)

		PRESS	SNATCH	JERK	TOTAL KG
1. Roger François	FRA	102.5	102.5	130.0	335.0 WR
2. Carlo Galimberti	ITA	105.0 WR	97.5	130.0	332.5
3. August Scheffer	HOL	97.5	105.0 OR	125.0	327.5
4. Franz Zinner	GER	87.5	100.0	135.0 OR	322.5
5. Gaston Le Pût	FRA	92.5	95.0	125.0	312.5
6. Wilhelm Hofmann	GER	90.0	95.0	120.0	305.0
7. Houssein Mouktah	EGY	95.0	92.5	120.0	302.5
8. Jan Van Rompaey	BEL	92.5	85.0	115.0	292.5

1932 Los Angeles C: 7, N: 6, D: 7.31. WR: 342.5 kg (Rudolf Ismayr)

		PRESS	SNATCH	JERK	TOTAL KG
1. Rudolf Ismayr	GER	102.5	110.0 OR	132.5	345.0 WR
2. Carlo Galimberti	ITA	102.5	105.0	132.5	340.0
3. Karl Hipfinger	AUT	90.0	107.5	140.0 OR	337.5
4. Roger François	FRA	102.5	102.5	130.0	335.0
5. Stanley Kratkowski	USA	82.5	102.5	120.0	305.0
6. Julio Juaneda	ARG	75.0	90.0	120.0	285.0
7. Sam Termine	USA	87.5	105.0	0.0	192.5

1936 Berlin C: 16, N: 12, D: 8.5. WR: 385 kg (Khadr Sayed El Touni)

		PRESS	SNATCH	JERK	TOTAL KG
1. Khadr Sayed El Touni	EGY	117.5 WR	120.0 WR	150.0 OR	387.5 WR
2. Rudolf Ismayr	GER	107.5	102.5	142.5	352.5
3. Adolf Wagner	GER	97.5	112.5	142.5	352.5
4. Anton Hangel	AUT	95.0	110.0	137.5	342.5
5. Stanley Kratkowski	USA	95.0	107.5	135.0	337.5
6. Hans Valla	AUT	102.5	102.5	130.0	335.0
7. Carlo Galimberti	ITA	100.0	102.5	130.0	332.5
8. Pierre Alleene	FRA	90.0	105.0	135.0	330.0

Twenty-one-year-old Khadr Sayed El Touni was one of the sensations of the 1936 Olympics. Not only did he outclass his opponents in the Middleweight division, but he actually lifted 15 kilograms more than the winner of the Light Heavyweight division. El Touni died of electrocution in 1956 while making a home repair.

Khadr Sayed El Touni, 1936
El Touni (center), the 1936 middleweight weightlifting champion, lifted 15 kilograms more than the light heavyweight winner.

1948 London C: 24, N: 18, D: 8.10. WR: 405 kg (Stanley Stanczyk)

		PRESS	SNATCH	JERK	TOTAL KG
1. Frank Spellman	USA	117.5	120.0	152.5	390.0 OR
2. Peter George	USA	105.0	122.5 OR	155.0 OR	382.5
3. Kim Sung-jip	KOR	122.5 OR	112.5	145.0	380.0
4. Khadr Sayed El Touni	EGY	120.0	117.5	142.5	380.0
5. Gérard Gratton	CAN	112.5	107.5	140.0	360.0
6. Pierre Bouladoux	FRA	102.5	110.0	142.5	355.0
7. Orlando Garrido Luloaga	CUB	112.5	107.5	135.0	355.0
8. G. William Watson	GBR	100.0	110.0	140.0	350.0

Peter George's only chance to win the gold medal was to clean and jerk 165 kg: 11 kilograms more than Stanley Stanczyk's world record. After pacing back and forth for twelve tense minutes, the 19-year-old George rubbed his hands with a block of chalk. Suddenly he crushed the chalk to dust and approached the bar. With great deliberation and concentration, he took hold of the weight, prepared his body, and hoisted the bar to his shoulders. The audience burst into applause, but quieted down quickly as George prepared for the second part of the lift. He pushed the bar overhead, but staggered and dropped it and had to settle for second place. Kim Sung-jip was Korea's first Olympic medalist.

1952 Helsinki C: 21, N: 20, D: 7.26. WR: 405 kg (Stanley Stanczyk)

		PRESS	SNATCH	JERK	TOTAL KG
1. Peter George	USA	115.0	127.5 OR	157.5 OR	400.0 OR
2. Gérard Gratton	CAN	122.5 EOR	112.5	155.0	390.0
3. Kim Sung-jip	KOR	122.5 EOR	112.5	147.5	382.5
4. Ismail Ragab	EGY	115.0	117.5	150.0	382.5
5. Moustafa Laham	LEB	115.0	112.5	142.5	370.0
6. Åke Hedberg	SWE	102.5	105.0	150.0	357.5
7. Angel Sposato	ARG	107.5	110.0	140.0	357.5
8. Jalal Mansouri	IRN	110.0	107.5	140.0	357.5

1956 Melbourne C: 16, N: 15, D: 11.24. WR: 415 kg (Fyodor Bogdanovsky)

		PRESS	SNATCH	JERK	TOTAL KG
1. Fyodor Bogdanovsky	SOV/RUS	132.5 OR	122.5	165.0 OR	420.0 WR
2. Peter George	USA	122.5	127.5 EOR	162.5	412.5
3. Ermanno Pignatfi	ITA	117.5	117.5	147.5	382.5
4. Jan Bochenek	POL	120.0	112.5	150.0	382.5
5. Kim Sung-jip	KOR	125.0	110.0	145.0	380.0
6. Krzysztof Beck	POL	122.5	112.5	145.0	380.0
7. Ebrahim Peyravi	IRN	107.5	117.5	147.5	372.5
8. Adrien Gilbert	CAN	112.5	115.0	142.5	370.0

History repeated itself when defending champion Peter George, now a dentist in the US Army, needed a world-record jerk to take first place. He attempted 170 kg, but couldn't make the weight. Nonetheless, his record of one gold and two silver medals is most impressive.

1960 Rome C: 27, N: 20, D: 9.8. WR: 430 kg (Tamio "Tommy" Kono)

		PRESS	SNATCH	JERK	TOTAL KG
1. Aleksandr Kurynov	SOV/RUS	135.0	132.5 OR	170.0 WR	437.5 WR
2. Tamio "Tommy" Kono	USA	140.0 OR	127.5	160.0	427.5
3. Győző Veres	HUN	130.0	120.0	155.0	405.0
4. Marcel Paterni	FRA	127.5	120.0	152.5	400.0
5. Krzysztof Beck	POL	135.0	117.5	147.5	400.0
6. Mohammad Amitehrani	IRN	117.5	120.0	155.0	392.5
7. Koh Yung-chang	KOR	115.0	120.0	150.0	385.0
8. Roland Lortz	GER	115.0	112.5	155.0	382.5

Tommy Kono, having already won gold medals as a Lightweight in 1952 and as a Light Heavyweight in 1956, decided to compete in the Middleweight division in 1960 because he had heard that Kurynov was "a very tough opponent." He heard right. The 26-year-old Soviet aviation engineer pulled off the victory and topped it with a world-record clean and jerk on his final attempt.

1964 Tokyo C: 19, N: 17, D: 10.14. WR: 445 kg (Viktor Kurentsov)

		PRESS	SNATCH	JERK	TOTAL KG
1. Hans Zdražila	CZE	130.0	137.5 OR	177.5 WR	445.0 EWR
2. Viktor Kurentsov	SOV/BLR	135.0	130.0	175.0	440.0
3. Masashi Ouchi	JPN	140.0 EOR	135.0	162.5	437.5
4. Lee Jong-sup	KOR	130.0	127.5	175.0	432.5
5. Sadahiro Miwa	JPN	120.0	132.5	170.0	422.5
6. Mihály Huszka	HUN	135.0	125.0	160.0	420.0
7. Rolf Maier	FRA	130.0	122.5	165.0	417.5
8. Veliko Konarov	BUL	130.0	130.0	155.0	415.0

1968 Mexico City C: 20, N: 17, D: 10.16. WR: 482.5 kg (Viktor Kurentsov)

		PRESS	SNATCH	JERK	TOTAL KG
1. Viktor Kurentsov	SOV/BLR	152.5 OR	135.0	187.5 WR	475.0 OR
2. Masashi Ouchi	JPN	140.0	140.0 OR	175.0	455.0
3. Károly Bakos	HUN	137.5	132.5	170.0	440.0
4. Russell Knipp	USA	147.5	122.5	167.5	437.5
5. Lee Chun-sik	KOR	140.0	132.5	165.0	437.5
6. Werner Dittrich	GDR	140.0	130.0	165.0	435.0
7. Miroslav Kolarik	CZE	140.0	127.5	162.5	430.0
8. Frederick Lowe	USA	132.5	127.5	170.0	430.0

In 1964 Kurentsov had entered the Olympics as the holder of the world record. However, in Tokyo he suffered an attack of nervousness and completed only four of his nine lifts. Four years later, at the next Olympics, he was a new man. Between lifts he calmly lay on a bed backstage reading Tolstoi. His winning margin was the largest in the Middleweight division since El Touni's great performance in 1936.

1972 Munich C: 26, N: 22, D: 8.31. WR: 482.5 (Viktor Kurentsov)

		PRESS	SNATCH	JERK	TOTAL KG
1. Yordan Bikov	BUL	160.0	140.0	185.0	485.0 WR
2. Mohamed Trabulsi	LEB	160.0	140.0	172.5	472.5
3. Anselmo Silvino	ITA	155.0	140.0	175.0	470.0
4. Ondrej Hekel	CZE	150.0	142.5 OR	170.0	462.5
5. Franklin Zielecke	GDR	150.0	140.0	170.0	460.0
6. Gábor Szarvas	HUN	150.0	135.0	175.0	460.0
7. András Stark	HUN	152.5	137.5	170.0	460.0
8. Russell Knipp	USA	160.0	127.5	170.0	457.5

Vladimir Kanygin of the USSR set an Olympic record in the press of 165 kg, but he failed at all three attempts at the snatch and was disqualified.

1976 Montreal C: 17, N: 14, D: 7.22. WR: 345 kg (Yordan Mitkov)

		SNATCH	JERK	TOTAL KG
1. Yordan Mitkov	BUL	145.0 OR	190.0 OR	335.0 OR
2. Vartan Militosyan	SOV/ARM	145.0 OR	185.0	330.0
3. Peter Wenzel	GDR	145.0 OR	182.5	327.5
4. Wolfgang Hübner	GDR	142.5	177.5	320.0
5. Arvo Ala-Pöntiö	FIN	137.5	177.5	315.0
6. András Stark	HUN	140.0	175.0	315.0
7. Ondrej Hekel	CZE	140.0	172.5	312.5
8. Daniel Zayas	CUB	140.0	170.0	310.0

DISQ (Drugs): Dragomir Cioroslan (ROM) 320.0

1980 Moscow C: 16, N: 14, D: 7.24. WR: 355 kg (Assen Zlatev)

		SNATCH	JERK	TOTAL KG
1. Assen Zlatev	BUL	160.0 OR	200.0 OR	360.0 WR
2. Oleksander Pervy	SOV/UKR	157.5	200.0 OR	357.5
3. Nedelcho Kolev	BUL	157.5	187.5	345.0
4. Julio Echenique González	CUB	145.0	182.5	327.5
5. Dragomir Cioroslan	ROM	140.0	182.5	322.5
6. Tapio Kinnunen	FIN	142.5	177.5	320.0
7. Bertil Sollevi	SWE	137.5	172.5	310.0
8. Newton Burrowes	GBR	130.0	172.5	302.5

After the formal competition was over, Zlatev jerked 205.5 kg. for a new world record.

1984 Los Angeles-Westchester C: 21, N: 17, D: 8.2. WR: 370.0 kg (Alexandr Varbanov)

		SNATCH	JERK	TOTAL KG
1. Karl-Heinz Radschinsky	GER	150.0	190.0	340.0
2. Jacques Demers	CAN	147.5	187.5	335.0
3. Dragomir Cioroslan	ROM	147.5	185.0	332.5
4. David Morgan	GBR	145.0	185.0	330.0
5. Li Shunzhu	CHN	147.5	175.0	322.5
6. Mohammed Yaseen Mohammed	IRQ	140.0	180.0	320.0
7. Antonio Pignone	AUS	147.5	170.0	317.5
8. Park Chun-jong	KOR	137.5	175.0	312.5

In 1983 Demers was arrested for smuggling steroid tablets into Canada, although his trial was delayed until after the Olympics. Demers qualified for the Canadian team again in 1988, but was dropped before the Games when he tested positive for steroids despite having injected someone else's clean urine into his bladder. In 1985 Radschinsky was arrested in West Germany for possessing steroids with intent to sell. He was subsequently convicted and fined $19,000.

At the Friendship Games in September, Zdravko Stoichkov of Bulgaria set a world record of 377.5 kg. In second place was Vladimir Kuznetsov of the USSR at 362.5 kg.

1988 Seoul C: 25, N: 20, D: 9.22. WR: 380 kg (Aleksandr Varbanov)

		SNATCH	JERK	TOTAL KG
1. Borislav Gidikov	BUL	167.5 OR	207.5 OR	375.0 OR
2. Ingo Steinhöfel	GDR	165.0	195.0	360.0
3. Aleksandr Varbanov	BUL	157.5	200.0	357.5
4. Cai Yanshu	CHN	157.5	190.0	347.5
5. Andrei Socaci	ROM	152.5	195.0	347.5
6. Waldemar Kosiński	POL	152.5	180.0	332.5
7. Dean Willey	GBR	152.5	180.0	332.5
8. Roberto "Tony" Urrutia	USA	150.0	177.5	327.5

DISQ (Drugs): Kalman Csengeri (HUN) 350.0

In 1990, Gidikov was banned from competing for eighteen months after he tested positive for steroids.

1992 Barcelona C: 34, N: 27, D: 7.30. WR: 382.5 kg (Aleksandr Varbanov)

		SNATCH	JERK	TOTAL KG
1. Fedor Kassapu	MOL	155.0	202.5	357.5
2. Pablo Lara Rodríguez	CUB	155.0	202.5	357.5
3. Kim Myong-nam	PRK	162.5	190.0	352.5
4. Andrzej Kozłowski	POL	160.0	192.5	352.5
5. Ingo Steinhöfel	GER	155.0	192.5	347.5
6. Raúl Mora Licea	CUB	150.0	195.0	345.0
7. Włodzimierz Chlebosz	POL	155.0	185.0	340.0
8. Lu Gang	CHN	150.0	185.0	335.0

Fedor Kassapu grew up on a poor collective farm near the small village of Cotovsk. His home had no running water and he developed strength early by carrying water for his family of 12 from a well a quarter of a mile away. He won the gold medal with a full-out effort on his final lift. He tied Lara, but was eight ounces (250 grams) lighter than the Cuban. In May 1995 Kassapu tested positive for the steroid mesterolone and was banned for life.

1996 Atlanta C: 24, N: 21, D: 7.24. WR: 372.5 kg (Pablo Lara Rodríguez)

		SNATCH	JERK	TOTAL KG
1. Pablo Lara Rodríguez	CUB	162.5	205.0	367.5
2. Yoto Yotov	BUL	160.0	200.0	360.0
3. Jon Chol-ho	PRK	162.5	195.0	357.5
4. Viktor Mitrou	GRE	162.5	195.0	357.5
5. Lin Shoufeng	CHN	157.5	195.0	352.5
6. Ingo Steinhöfel	GER	160.0	187.5	347.5
7. Sergei Filimonov	RUS	160.0	185.0	345.0
8. Hovhannes Barsegian	ARM	155.0	190.0	345.0

Khachatur Kyapanaksian of Armenia led the field midway after snatching 165 kg. However he missed all three attempts at the clean and jerk. Two-time defending world champion Pablo Lara had missed a gold medal in 1992 because of bodyweight. In Atlanta he was in fourth place after the snatch, but his clear superiority in the jerk gave him an easy, overdue victory. Yoto Yotov moved up from seventh place after the snatch to earn the silver medal.

2000 Sydney C: 17, N: 15, D: 9.22. WR: 372.5 kg (Zlatan Vanev)

		SNATCH	JERK	TOTAL KG
1. Zhan Xugang	CHN	160.0	207.5 EWR	367.5
2. Viktor Mitrou	GRE	165.0	202.5	367.5
3. Arsen Melikyan	ARM	167.5	197.5	365.0
4. Sergei Filimonov	KAZ	167.5	195.0	362.5
5. Ilirjan Suli	ALB	162.5	192.5	355.0
6. Jon Chol-Ho	PRK	162.5	190.0	352.5
7. Ingo Steinhöfel	GER	160.0	190.0	350.0
8. Dmytro Hnidenko	UKR	160.0	190.0	350.0

On April 26, 2000, Bulgarians Zlatan Vanev and Plamen Zhelyakov finished one-two at the European Championships. They arrived in Sydney as medal favorites, but before they could compete, the entire Bulgarian team was expelled after three of their lifters failed doping tests. This might have left the field open to world champion Saelem Nayef Badr of Qatar (formerly known as Petar Tanev of Bulgaria), but he and another Bulgarian-turned-Qatari withdrew at the last moment, claiming food poisoning. Arsen Melikyan was in first place after the snatch, with Viktor Mitrou, who had escaped from Albania to Greece in 1991, in third place and 1996 lightweight gold medalist Zhan Xugang fourth. Second place belonged to Sergei Filimonov who had competed in the B group. In the clean and jerk, Mitrou lifted 202.5 kg. with his final attempt, but Zhan cleared 207.5 kg to match Mitrou's total and win because he weighed 28 grams less than Mitrou. The unfortunate Mitrou had a long history of losing medals because of higher bodyweight. He lost the 1996 Olympic bronze medal, the 1998 world championship bronze medal and the 1999 world championship gold medal for same reason.

2004 Athens C: 25, N: 22, D: 8.19. WR: 377.5 kg (Plamen Jeliazkov)

		SNATCH	JERK	TOTAL KG
1. Taner Sağır	TUR	172.5	202.5	375.0
2. Sergei Filimonov	KAZ	172.5	200.0	372.5
3. Oleg Perepechenov	RUS	170.0	195.0	365.0
4. Reyhan Arabacıoğlu	TUR	165.0	195.0	360.0
5. Viktor Mitrou	GRE	160.0	200.0	360.0
6. Mohamed Hossein Barkhah	IRN	160.0	197.5	357.5
7. Attila Feri	HUN	155.0	200.0	355.0
8. Ivan Stoitsov	BUL	155.0	200.0	355.0

Taner Sağır and Sergei Filimonov both broke the Olympic record with their snatch lifts, 172.5 kilos, one kilogram less than Filimonov's snatch world record. Sağır moved into the lead with his first attempt in the clean and jerk, lifting 200 kg, and clinched gold after Filimonov missed his third lift, an attempt at 205 kilos. Despite having lifted competitively since the age of nine, 19-year-old Sağır's only previous senior competition had been the 2004 European championship, which he won four months before the Olympics.

Two-time Olympic defending champion Zhan Xugang missed all three snatch attempts and did not finish the competition.

2008 Beijing C: 28, N: 25, D: 8.13. WR: 377.5 kg (Plamen Jeliazkov)

		SNATCH	JERK	TOTAL KG
1. Sa Jae-hyok	KOR	163.0	203.0	366.0
2. Li Hongli	CHN	168.0	198.0	366.0
3. Gevorg Davtyan	ARM	165.0	195.0	360.0
4. Kim Gwang-hun	KOR	155.0	200.0	355.0
5. Oleg Perepechenov	RUS	162.0	192.0	354.0
6. Iván Cambar	CUB	157.0	196.0	353.0
7. Ara Khachatryan	ARM	162.0	191.0	353.0
8. Krzysztof Szramiak	POL	161.0	191.0	352.0

Sa Jae-hyok trailed in third place behind Li Hongli and Gevorg Davtyan after the snatch portion, but moved into the lead after lifting 203 kg (447.5 lbs) in the clean and jerk. The 2005 world champion, Li lifted the same total weight but finished second due to his greater bodyweight. Defending Olympic champion Taner Sagir failed all three of his snatch attempts and was eliminated.

LIGHT HEAVYWEIGHT

(85kg—187.4 lbs [1920–1992: 82.5 kg—181.5 lbs; 1996: 83 kg—182.98 lbs])

1896–1912 not held

1920 Antwerp C: 11, N: 9, D: 8.31.

		ONE-HAND SNATCH	ONE-HAND JERK	TWO-HAND JERK	TOTAL KG
1. Ernest Cadine	FRA	70.0	90.0	135.0	295.0
2. Fritz Hünenberger	SWI	75.0	90.0	112.5	277.5
3. Erik Pettersson	SWE	62.5	92.5	112.5	267.5
4. Erik Carlsson	SWE	67.5	75.0	120.0	262.5
5. Maurice Devène	FRA	65.0	70.0	115.0	250.0
6. Gino Mattiello	ITA	60.0	70.0	105.0	235.0
7. Jan Welter	HOL	65.0	70.0	95.0	230.0
8. Jaroslav Dvořák	CZE	55.0	65.0	107.5	227.5
8. Lionel van den Roye	BEL	57.5	65.0	105.0	227.5

1924 Paris C: 20, N: 12, D: 7.23.

		ONE-HAND SNATCH	ONE-HAND JERK	TWO-HAND PRESS	TWO-HAND SNATCH	TWO-HAND JERK	TOTAL KG
1. Charles Rigoulot	FRA	87.5 OR	92.5	85.0	102.5	135.0 EOR	502.5
2. Fritz Hünenberger	SWI	80.0	107.5 WR	80.0	97.5	125.0	490.0
3. Leopold Friedrich	AUT	75.0	95.0	95.0	95.0	130.0	490.0
4. Karl Freiberger	AUT	75.0	95.0	92.5	95.0	130.0	487.5
5. Carlos Bergara	ARG	80.0	85.0	92.5	97.5	127.5	482.5
6. Mario Giambelli	ITA	77.5	95.0	82.5	95.0	130.0	480.0
7. Anton Schärer	SWI	75.0	85.0	100.0	95.0	120.0	475.0
8. Jaroslav Skobla	CZE	70.0	95.0	92.5	85.0	127.5	470.0

Rigoulot later became a successful race car driver. During World War II he was deemed a national hero after he was jailed for hitting a Nazi officer.

1928 Amsterdam C: 15, N: 10, D: 7.29. WR: 350 kg (Jakob Vogt)

		PRESS	SNATCH	JERK	TOTAL KG
1. El Sayed Mohammed Nosseir	EGY	100.0 EOR	112.5 OR	142.5 WR	355.0 WR
2. Louis Hostin	FRA	100.0 EOR	110.0	142.5 WR	352.5
3. Johannes Verheijen	HOL	95.0	105.0	137.5	337.5
4. Václav Pšenička	CZE	100.0 EOR	105.0	130.0	335.0
4. Jakob Vogt	GER	100.0 EOR	105.0	130.0	335.0
6. Karl Freiberger	AUT	95.0	95.0	132.5	322.5
7. Karl Bierwirth	GER	95.0	95.0	125.0	315.0
7. Pierre Vibert	FRA	95.0	95.0	125.0	315.0
7. Josef Zemann	AUT	75.0	105.0	135.0	315.0

El Sayed Nosseir caused quite a sensation with his pre-lift ritual of raising his arms and head to the sky and calling out for Allah's assistance. A minor incident occurred during the award ceremony when the band struck up the Austrian national anthem by mistake instead of the French "Marseillaise." There were chuckles throughout the crowd, but the French were not amused.

1932 Los Angeles C: 4, N: 3, D: 7.31. WR: 365 kg (Jakob Vogt)

		PRESS	SNATCH	JERK	TOTAL KG
1. Louis Hostin	FRA	102.5 OR	112.5 EOR	150.0 OR	365.0 EWR
2. Svend Olsen	DEN	102.5 OR	107.5	150.0 OR	360.0
3. Henry Duey	USA	92.5	105.0	132.5	330.0
4. William Good	USA	95.0	97.5	130.0	322.5

Hostin was so confident of victory that he traded jokes with the referee while he was lifting.

1936 Berlin C: 14, N: 9, D: 8.3. WR: 375 kg (Fritz Haller)

		PRESS	SNATCH	JERK	TOTAL KG
1. Louis Hostin	FRA	110.0 OR	117.5 OR	145.0	372.5 OR
2. Eugen Deutsch	GER	105.0	110.0	150.0 EOR	365.0
3. Ibrahim Wasif	EGY	100.0	110.0	150.0 EOR	360.0
4. Helmut Opschruf	GER	97.5	110.0	147.5	355.0
5. Nicolas Scheitler	LUX	105.0	105.0	140.0	350.0
6. Fritz Haller	AUT	97.5	110.0	142.5	350.0
7. William Good	USA	100.0	105.0	145.0	350.0
8. Mohammed Ahmed Geissa	EGY	95.0	110.0	142.5	347.5

Eugen Deutsch was originally disqualified for missing all three of his snatch attempts. An hour later the Jury of Appeal validated one of his snatches, giving him the silver medal and causing resentment among many non-German observers.

1948 London C: 16, N: 13, D: 8.11. WR: 425 kg (Grigory Novack)

		PRESS	SNATCH	JERK	TOTAL KG
1. Stanley Stanczyk	USA	130.0 OR	130.0 OR	157.5 OR	417.5 OR
2. Harold Sakata	USA	110.0	117.5	152.5	380.0
3. Gösta Magnusson	SWE	110.0	120.0	145.0	375.0
4. Jean Debuf	FRA	107.5	112.5	150.0	370.0
5. Osvaldo Forte	ARG	105.0	115.0	147.5	367.5
6. James Varaleau	CAN	112.5	112.5	140.0	365.0
7. Juhani Vellamo	FIN	100.0	115.0	140.0	355.0
8. Rassoul Raiisi	IRN	110.0	110.0	135.0	355.0

Stanczyk made a great impression on the audience, not only because of his superior lifting, but because of his outstanding sportsmanship. With his third snatch he attempted a new world record of 132.5 kg. He successfully hoisted the weight and the judges signaled a fair lift. However, Stanczyk shook his head and tapped his leg to indicate that his knee had scraped the floor, thus invalidating his lift. Despite this miss, his eventual winning margin of 37.5 kg. was the largest in any division in Olympic history.

Stanley Stanczyk was a well-known figure in weightlifting circles, but the man who really achieved fame was silver medalist Harold Sakata. After completing a successful career as a professional wrestler (using the name Tosh Togo), Sakata became an actor. He reached international stardom in the role of Oddjob in the James Bond film *Goldfinger.* As for Stanczyk, he operated a bowling alley for 27 years and had a 27-year average of his own of 190.

1952 Helsinki C: 22, N: 19, D: 7.27. WR: 425 kg (Grigory Novack)

		PRESS	SNATCH	JERK	TOTAL KG
1. Trofim Lomakin	SOV/RUS	125.0	127.5	165.0 OR	417.5 EOR
2. Stanley Stanczyk	USA	127.5	127.5	160.0	415.0
3. Arkady Vorobyev	SOV/RUS	120.0	127.5	160.0	407.5
4. Mohammad Hassan Rahnavardi	IRN	120.0	122.5	160.0	402.5
5. Jean Debuf	FRA	117.5	122.5	160.0	400.0
6. Issy Bloomberg	SAF	127.5	115.0	150.0	392.5
7. Osvaldo Forte	ARG	112.5	115.0	155.0	382.5
8. Clyde Emrich	USA	120.0	115.0	145.0	380.0

The 1952 Light Heavyweight competition was an excellent three-way contest which unfortunately got caught up in the Cold War. The United States fired the first salvo when they lodged a protest after American Clyde Emrich had a press of 120 kg disallowed. After much fussing and arguing by US officials, Emrich went ahead and made the weight at his next attempt. Then Stanczyk was given credit for a press of 127.5 kg and the Soviets claimed that he had leaned back too far for a legal press. The judges voted 2–1 in Stanczyk's favor. When Vorobyev lost consciousness during his last press attempt, the Americans accused the Russians of drugging their lifters. At the end of the press, Stanczyk led Lomakin by 2.5 kg. Lomakin and Vorobyev both snatched 127.5 kg at their first attempt, while Stanczyk achieved the weight only at his last try. However, both Soviet lifters failed twice at 132.5 kg. So, with only the jerk left, Stanczyk still led Lomakin by 2.5 kg. All three leaders successfully jerked 160 kg. Both Stanczyk and Lomakin missed at 165 kg, but Lomakin had one more attempt left to him. This time he made the weight and moved into first place.

Then came Vorobyev's turn. He decided to go for broke and called for 170 kg—a world record. Vorobyev approached the bar, took hold of it, raised it a couple inches and dropped it again. An argument immediately broke out as to whether his action should be counted as an official attempt. Vorobyev shut out the commotion and prepared himself for another try. When he turned again to the bar, silence returned. He heaved the weight onto his chest and thrust it into the air at arm's length. "Although my muscles strained to the very limit," Vorobyev later wrote, "my heart was singing. I had done it! I had won!" The audience roared with excitement. But then Vorobyev staggered and dropped the bar just as the referee called out, "Release." One judge ruled that it had been a valid lift, but the other two rejected it. Forty minutes of arguing ensued, until finally the results were announced: Lomakin first, Stanczyk second, Vorobyev third.

Vorobyev returned to the dressing room in a deep depression and began slowly to undress. Suddenly his coach burst into the room and told him that he had been awarded one more attempt. But Vorobyev was unprepared. He needed more time to compose himself and warm up, but the officials had already started the

Harold Sakata, 1948
The Light Heavyweight silver medalist gained greater fame as Oddjob in the James Bond film *Goldfinger*.

clock. Forced to hurry back to the platform, he was unable to handle the weight a second time and fell backward, with the bar pinning him to the floor. The Soviets continued to argue that Vorobyev had been forced to hold his previous lift for more than two seconds, but the results were allowed to stand.

1956 Melbourne C: 10, N: 9, D: 11.26. WR: 435 kg (Tamio "Tommy" Kono)

		PRESS	SNATCH	JERK	TOTAL KG
1. Tamio "Tommy" Kono	USA	140.0 OR	132.5 OR	175.0 WR	447.5 WR
2. Vasilijs Stepanovs	SOV/LAT	135.0	130.0	162.5	427.5
3. James George	USA	120.0	130.0	167.5	417.5
4. Jalal Mansouri	IRN	132.5	122.5	162.5	417.5
5. Philip Caira	GBR	127.5	122.5	155.0	405.0
6. Václav Pšenička	CZE	125.0	120.0	155.0	400.0
7. Marcel Paterni	FRA	132.5	115.0	147.5	395.0
8. John Powell	AUS	120.0	117.5	145.0	382.5

James George used a fourth lift to set a snatch world record of 137.5 kg.

1960 Rome C: 24, N: 21, D: 9.9. WR: 457.5 kg (Rudolf Plukfelder)

		PRESS	SNATCH	JERK	TOTAL KG
1. Ireneusz Paliński	POL	130.0	132.5 EOR	180.0 WR	442.5
2. James George	USA	132.5	132.5 EOR	165.0	430.0
3. Jan Bochenek	POL	130.0	120.0	170.0	420.0
4. Géza Tóth	HUN	125.0	125.0	167.5	417.5
5. Jouni Kailajärvi	FIN	130.0	125.0	162.5	417.5
6. Peter Tachev	BUL	130.0	125.0	160.0	415.0
7. Minoru Kubota	JPN	125.0	120.0	155.0	400.0
8. Willy Claes	BEL	125.0	112.5	155.0	392.5

1964 Tokyo C: 24, N: 21, D: 10.16. WR: 477.5 kg (Gyözö Veres)

		PRESS	SNATCH	JERK	TOTAL KG
1. Rudolf Plukfelder	SOV/UKR	150.0	142.5 OR	182.5	475.0 OR
2. Géza Tóth	HUN	145.0	137.5	185.0 OR	467.5
3. Győző Veres	HUN	155.0 OR	135.0	177.5	467.5
4. Jerzy Kaczkowski	POL	145.0	135.0	167.5	455.0
5. Gary Cleveland	USA	152.5	135.0	167.5	455.0
6. Lee Hyung-woo	KOR	145.0	132.5	175.0	452.5
7. Kaarlo Kangasniemi	FIN	150.0	135.0	165.0	450.0
8. Karl Arnold	GDR	140.0	132.5	167.5	435.0

Thirty-six-year-old Plukfelder is the oldest weightlifter to win an Olympic gold medal.

1968 Mexico City C: 26, N: 22, D: 10.17. WR: 485 kg (Vladimir Byelyayev)

		PRESS	SNATCH	JERK	TOTAL KG
1. Boris Selitsky	SOV/RUS	150.0	147.5 OR	187.5 OR	485.0 EWR
2. Volodymyr Byelyayev	SOV/UKR	152.5	147.5 OR	185.0	485.0 EWR
3. Norbert Ozimek	POL	150.0	140.0	182.5	472.5
4. Győző Veres	HUN	150.0	140.0	182.5	472.5
5. Karl Arnold	GDR	155.0 EOR	137.5	175.0	467.5
6. Hans Zdražila	CZE	135.0	147.5 OR	180.0	462.5
7. Jouni Kailajärvi	FIN	140.0	130.0	175.0	445.0
8. Lee Jong-sup	KOR	135.0	130.0	175.0	440.0

1972 Munich C: 24, N: 21, D: 9.2. WR: 527.5 kg (Valery Shary)

		PRESS	SNATCH	JERK	TOTAL KG
1. Leif Jenssen	NOR	172.5 OR	150.0 OR	185.0	507.5 OR
2. Norbert Ozimek	POL	165.0	145.0	187.5	497.5
3. György Horváth	HUN	160.0	142.5	192.5 OR	495.0
4. Bernhard Radtke	GDR	162.5	145.0	185.0	492.5
5. Khristos Iakovou	GRE	170.0	137.5	182.5	490.0
6. Kaarlo Kangasniemi	FIN	150.0	145.0	185.0	480.0
7. Rolf Milser	GER	165.0	132.5	180.0	477.5
8. Juhani Avellan	FIN	140.0	145.0	182.5	467.5

The two Soviet representatives, world champion Boris Pavlov and world record holder Valery Shary, were so intent on beating each other that they started pressing at too high a weight. Both men missed all three attempts and were disqualified. Representing Israel was 28-year-old David Berger, originally of Shaker Heights, Ohio. Three days later, Berger was one of the 11 Israelis who were killed by terrorists.

1976 Montreal C: 17, N: 14, D: 7.24. WR: 372.5 kg (Trendafil Stoichev)

		SNATCH	JERK	TOTAL KG
1. Valery Shary	SOV/BLR	162.5 OR	202.5 OR	365.0 OR
2. Trendafil Stoichev	BUL	162.5 OR	197.5	360.0
3. Péter Baczako	HUN	157.5	187.5	345.0
4. Nicolaos Iliadis	GRE	150.0	190.0	340.0
5. Juhani Avellan	FIN	145.0	185.0	330.0
6. Stefan Jacobsson	SWE	147.5	170.0	317.5
7. Sueo Fujishiro	JPN	140.0	175.0	315.0
8. Gerd Kennel	GER	135.0	177.5	312.5

DISQ (Drugs): Blagoi Blagoev (BUL) 362.5

1980 Moscow C: 19, N: 17, D: 7.26. WR: 390 kg (Yurik Vardanyan)

		SNATCH	JERK	TOTAL KG
1. Yurik Vardanyan	SOV/ARM	177.5 WR	222.5 WR	400.0 WR
2. Blagoi Blagoev	BUL	175.0	197.5	372.5
3. Dušan Poliačik	CZE	160.0	207.5	367.5
4. Jan Lisowski	POL	150.0	205.0	355.0
5. Krassimir Drăndarov	BUL	155.0	200.0	355.0
6. Pawel Rabczewski	POL	155.0	195.0	350.0
7. Detlef Blasche	GDR	152.5	192.5	345.0
8. Juhani Avellan	FIN	150.0	182.5	332.5

Vardanyan's total would have earned him a gold medal in either of the next two higher weight classes.

1984 Los Angeles-Westchester C: 19, N: 16, D: 8.4. WR: 400 kg (Yurik Vardanyan)

		SNATCH	JERK	TOTAL KG
1. Petre Becheru	ROM	155.0	200.0	355.0
2. Robert Kabbas	AUS	150.0	192.5	342.5
3. Ryoji Isaoka	JPN	150.0	190.0	340.0
4. Newton Burrowes	GBR	147.5	180.0	327.5
5. Ebraheem Elbakh	EGY	145.0	177.5	322.5
6. Lee Kang-seong	KOR	140.0	182.5	322.5
7. Yvan Darsigny	CAN	142.5	180.0	322.5
8. Allister Nalder	NZL	142.5	175.0	317.5

On September 15, at the Friendship Games, Yurik Vardanyan broke his own 4-year-old world record with combined lifts of 405 kg. Second place went to Asen Zlatev of Bulgaria with 380 kg and third to László Király of Hungary with 370 kg.

1988 Seoul C: 22, N: 20, D: 9.24. WR: 405 kg (Yurik Vardanyan)

		SNATCH	JERK	TOTAL KG
1. Israil Arsamakov	SOV/RUS	167.5	210.0	377.5
2. István Messzi	HUN	170.0	200.0	370.0
3. Lee Hyung-kun	KOR	160.0	207.5	367.5
4. David Morgan	GBR	165.0	200.0	365.0
5. Krzystzof Siemion	POL	162.5	195.0	357.5
6. Ryoji Isaoka	JPN	155.0	195.0	350.0
7. FaustoTosi	ITA	155.0	185.0	340.0
8. Ali Eroğlü	TUR	145.0	185.0	330.0

Israil Arsamakov of Grozny never competed again after his Olympic victory, retiring at the age of 26.

1992 Barcelona C: 31, N: 26, D: 8.3. WR: 405 kg (Yurik Vardanyan)

		SNATCH	JERK	TOTAL KG
1. Pyrros Dimas	GRE	167.5	202.5	370.0
2. Krzysztof Siemion	POL	165.0	205.0	370.0
—Ibragim Samadov	RUS	167.5	202.5	370.0
3. Ibragim Samadov	RUS	167.5	202.5	370.0
4. Chon Chol-ho	PRK	165.0	200.0	365.0
5. Plamen Bratoitchev	BUL	167.5	197.5	365.0
6. Lino Elías Ocaña	CUB	160.0	205.0	365.0
7. Marc Huster	GER	160.0	202.5	362.5
8. José Heredia Ledea	CUB	165.0	197.5	362.5

This was one of the two closest weightlifting contests in Olympic history and also one of the most controversial. In 1991 the Soviet Union collapsed and broke into 15 different independent nations. The International Olympic Committee decided that although the three Baltic nations, Estonia, Latvia, and Lithuania, could organize separate teams for the 1992 Olympics, the remaining 12 ex-Soviet republics would be required to enter a combined squad known as the Unified Team. Unfortunately, in weight-lifting the Unified Team was not very unified. The head coach, two-time gold medalist Vassily Alekseyev, was Russian, and he definitely had his prejudices. The overwhelming favorite in the light-heavyweight division was 1990 world champion Altymurat Orazdurdiyev of Turkmenistan. The second entrant from the Unified Team was the 1991 world champion, Ibragim Samadov of Chechnya in Russia. Fifteen minutes before the official weigh-in, Alekseyev informed Orazdurdiyev that he would not be allowed to compete because he would "get in the way" of Samadov. Orazdurdiyev pleaded with Alekseyev and even offered to lose to Samadov and settle for a silver medal. Alekseyev ignored him.

Samadov already felt great pressure. When he received his gold medal at the world championships he didn't smile because he was dissatisfied with his performance. He was that hard on himself. In addition, his family back in Grozny was dependent on the modest income he earned from his weightlifting successes. Now the pressure on Samadov increased enormously.

At the European championships in April, in the absence of Orazdurdiyev, Samadov had won with a total of 370 kilograms. Close behind him were Krzysztof Siemion and Pyrros Dimas at 367.5 kilograms. Dimas was a member of the Greek ethnic minority in Albania and competed for Albania as recently as the 1990 European championships. In February 1991, Dimas and his brother slipped across the border into Greece and were granted Greek citizenship almost immediately.

Although Chon Chol-ho of North Korea was in the gold medal hunt right until his last failed attempt, the real competition was among Samadov, Siemion, and Dimas. With ties decided by lower bodyweight, everyone was aware that Samadov outweighed the other two by five grams (one-sixth of an ounce)—not much, but enough to mean that he needed to lift a higher total than his rivals. Trailing by 2.5 kilograms after the snatch, Siemion pulled even by successfully lifting 205 kilograms after Dimas and Samadov had cleared 202.5 There then followed a series of unsuccessful attempts at 207.5 kilograms. Chon missed twice, Dimas missed twice, Siemion missed once, and Samadov missed once. Everything came down to Samadov's final lift. He cleaned the bar, but couldn't pull off the jerk. A disappointed Samadov placed third because of his higher bodyweight. Since Dimas and Siemion shared the same weight, the gold medal was decided by a new tie-breaking rule: whichever lifter reached his final total first was declared the winner. In this case it was Dimas, whose 202.5 kg lift preceded Siemion's 205. The Greek contingent in the stands exploded with joy: no Greek had won a weightlifting gold since Dimitris Tophalo triumphed at the Intercalated Games in Athens in 1906.

But the excitement was not over. At the award ceremony, Dimas and Siemion happily received their medals. Not so Samadov. Frustrated with himself and emotionally distraught, Samadov refused to lean forward to allow the bronze medal to be put around his neck. When he finally took it in his hand, he dropped it onto the platform and walked away. IOC officials were outraged at this breach of protocol. They disqualified Samadov, announced that he would not be listed as the bronze-medal winner in the official results, and ordered him to leave the Olympic Village. Samadov came to his senses the next day and apologized, but the IOC refused to reverse its ruling, and the International Weightlifting Federation banned him for life.

Back in Greece after the Olympics, Dimas and the other 1992 Greek gold medalist, hurdler Voula Patoulidou, were treated to a hero's reception. Sixty thousand people packed into the Kallimarmaron Panathenian Stadium that had been used for the 1896 Olympics, while another thirty thousand crowded around outside. Dimas' father, Victor, summed up the mood: "We have almost reached the sky," he said, "on the wings of happiness."

1996 Atlanta C: 20, N: 18, D: 7.26. WR: 387.5 kg (Pyrros Dimas)

		SNATCH	JERK	TOTAL KG
1. Pyrros Dimas	GRE	180.0 WR	212.5 WR	392.5 WR
2. Marc Huster	GER	170.0	212.5 WR	382.5
3. Andrzej Cofalik	POL	170.0	202.5	372.5
4. Kiril Kounev	AUS	170.0	200.0	370.0
5. Vadim Vacarciuc	MOL	165.0	202.5	367.5
6. Sergo Chakhoian	ARM	170.0	195.0	365.0
7. Dursun Sevinç	TUR	165.0	197.5	362.5
8. Krastu Milev	BUL	160.0	200.0	360.0

At the 1993 world championships, Pyrros Dimas defeated Marc Huster by 2.5 kg. In 1994, Dimas missed all three attempts in the clean and jerk and Huster won the world championship with a total of 382.5 kg. At the 1995 world championships, Dimas came back to edge Huster on lower bodyweight. In Atlanta, Dimas snatched 180 kg. for a world record, creating an almost insurmountable lead. He made all six lifts. Only increments of 2.5 kg or more are recognized for competition purposes, but for world records, smaller increments are allowed. So even though Dimas' last lift counted as 212.5 kg in Olympic record books, he actually jerked 213 kg to break his own world record. Huster, conceding the gold medal to Dimas, finished the competition by jerking 213.5 kg for another world record.

2000 Sydney C: 20, N: 18, D: 9.23. WR: None Recognized

		SNATCH	JERK	TOTAL KG
1. Pyrros Dimas	GRE	175.0	215.0	390.0
2. Marc Huster	GER	177.5	212.5	390.0
3. Georgi Asanidze	GEO	180.0	210.0	390.0
4. Krzysztof Siemion	POL	167.5	212.5	380.0
5. Gagik Khachatryan	ARM	175.0	205.0	380.0
6. Sergo Chakhoyan	AUS	175.0	202.5	377.5
7. Khristos Spyrou	GRE	170.0	205.0	375.0
8. Ernesto Quiroga Aldama	CUB	165.0	210.0	375.0

It would be tempting to treat Pyrros Dimas and Marc Huster as bitter rivals, except that they were actually good friends who even vacationed together. In addition to their one-two finish at the 1996 Olympics, they placed first and second at the 1998 world championships. It would have happened again at the 1999 world championships, but the two were upset by Iran's Shakin Nasirinia. In Sydney, Nasirinia dislocated his right elbow on his first attempt and had to withdraw. Dimas was almost eliminated too. Opening the snatch at 175 kg, he was distracted by a yell and a cellphone and ran out of time on his first attempt. He missed his second try, but regained his concentration and made the third. Nonetheless, he completed the first half of the competition ten kilograms below his goal and found himself in fourth place behind Georgi Asanidze, Huster and Sergo Chakhoyan. Dimas jerked 210 kg on his first attempt. By the time of his second turn, he knew that if he cleared 215 kg, he would win. He cleared it easily. As in 1992, Dimas won a three-way tie based on bodyweight. He weighed 16 grams less than Huster and 64 grams less than Asanidze.

2004 Athens C: 21, N: 19, D: 8.21. WR: None Recognized

		SNATCH	JERK	TOTAL KG
1. Georgi Asanidze	GEO	177.5	205.0	382.5
2. Andrei Rybakou	BLR	180.0	200.0	380.0
3. Pyrros Dimas	GRE	175.0	202.5	377.5
4. Georgios Markoulas	GRE	167.5	205.0	372.5
5. Yuan Aijun	CHN	167.5	205.0	372.5
6. Aliaksandr Anishchanka	BLR	170.0	200.0	370.0
7. Tigran Martirosyan	ARM	167.5	200.0	367.5
8. Song Jong-shik	KOR	160.0	200.0	360.0

Three-time Olympic champion Pyrros Dimas returned to competition after three years' retirement, three knee surgeries and a recent wrist injury. Georgi Asanidze had tied Dimas in 2000, but placed third because of his bodyweight. The European champion in 2002, Asanidze dropped to twelfth place at the 2004 Euros, four months before the Athens Olympics, lifting only 360 kg total. In Athens, Asanidze was back in form. He led Dimas after the snatch, but both trailed Andrei Rybakou, who had competed earlier in the day in the B category. In the clean and jerk, Dimas managed 202.5 kg on his first lift, but missed his next two attempts and finished third. Asanidze secured the gold with his second lift. Rybakou was the first B group lifter in twenty years to earn a medal, and only the second ever.

2008 Beijing C: 21, N: 19, D: 8.15. WR: 393 kg (Andrei Rybakov)

		SNATCH	JERK	TOTAL KG
1. Lu Yong	CHN	180.0	214.0	394.0 WR
2. Andrei Rybakov	BLR	185.0 OR	209.0	394.0 WR
3. Tigran V. Martirosyan	ARM	177.0	203.0	380.0
4. Vladimir Sedov	KAZ	180.0	200.0	380.0
5. Jadier Valladares	CUB	169.0	203.0	372.0
6. Benjamin Hennequin	FRA	162.0	205.0	367.0
7. Mansurbek Chashemov	UZB	165.0	202.0	367.0
8. Kendrick Farris	USA	160.0	202.0	362.0

Defending Olympic silver medalist and two-time reigning world champion Andrei Rybakov took the lead after lifting 185 kg (407.8 lbs) in the snatch, and then set a total world record of 394 kg (868.6 lbs) with his final clean and jerk attempt.

Twenty-two-year-old Lu Yong lifted 214 kg on the second of his three clean and jerk attempts, equalling Rybakov's world record and giving Lu the gold medal based on his bodyweight advantage. The Chinese delegation were already celebrating the win when the jury panel overruled the judges' decision, declaring the lift ineligible. Lu returned to the stage and successfully completed the lift on his final attempt.

MIDDLE HEAVYWEIGHT

(94 kg—207.25 lbs [1952–1992: 90 kg—198.25 lbs; 1996: 91 kg—200.62 lbs])

1896–1948 not held

1952 Helsinki C: 20, N: 20, D: 7.27. WR: 427.5 kg (Norbert Schemansky)

		PRESS	SNATCH	JERK	TOTAL KG
1. Norbert Schemansky	USA	127.5	140.0 WR	177.5 WR	445.0 WR
2. Grigory Novak	SOV/RUS	140.0 OR	125.0	145.0	410.0
3. Lennox Kilgour	TRI	125.0	120.0	157.5	402.5
4. Mohammed Ibrahim Saleh	EGY	110.0	125.0	162.5	397.5
5. Firouz Pejhan	IRN	112.5	120.0	155.0	387.5
6. Kenneth McDonald	AUS	107.5	125.0	152.5	385.0
7. Francisco Rensonnet	ARG	107.5	112.5	150.0	370.0
8. Theunis Jonck	SAF	112.5	110.0	145.0	367.5

The 5-foot 3½-inch, 195-pound Novak was hampered by a leg injury, but it is very doubtful that he could have beaten Detroit's Norbert Schemansky, who upped his own world record by 38½ pounds. Schemansky eventually became the only weightlifter to win four Olympic medals—including a bronze in the Heavyweight division in 1964 at the age of 40. When asked if he followed a special diet during his competitive years, Schemansky once replied, "Hamburgers. Pizza. Beer."

1956 Melbourne C: 15, N: 14, D: 11.26. WR: 460 kg (Arkady Vorobyov)

		PRESS	SNATCH	JERK	TOTAL KG
1. Arkady Vorobyov	SOV/RUS	147.5 WR	137.5	177.5 EOR	462.5 WR
2. David Sheppard	USA	140.0	137.5	165.0	442.5
3. Jean Debuf	FRA	130.0	127.5	167.5	425.0
4. Mohammad Hassan Rahnavardi	IRN	140.0	127.5	157.5	425.0
5. Ivan Veselinov	BUL	132.5	120.0	155.0	407.5
6. Tan Kim Bee	MAL	117.5	122.5	155.0	395.0
7. Lennox Kilgour	TRI	127.5	117.5	145.0	390.0
8. Leonard Treganowan	AUS	122.5	117.5	150.0	390.0

A former deep-sea diver, Vorobyov made up for his disappointment in the controversial 1952 Light Heavyweight competition. He later became a doctor, wrote several textbooks on weightlifting, and served as coach of the Soviet team.

1960 Rome C: 20, N: 17, D: 9.9. WR: 470 kg (Arkady Vorobyov)

		PRESS	SNATCH	JERK	TOTAL KG
1. Arkady Vorobyov	SOV/RUS	152.5	142.5 OR	177.5 EOR	472.5 WR
2. Trofim Lomakin	SOV/RUS	157.5 WR	130.0	170.0	457.5
3. Louis Martin	GBR	137.5	137.5	170.0	445.0
4. John Pulskamp	USA	140.0	125.0	167.5	432.5
5. François Vincent	FRA	130.0	132.5	160.0	422.5
6. Vladimir Savov	BUL	110.0	137.5	165.0	412.5
7. Czesław Białas	POL	130.0	122.5	157.5	410.0
8. Leonardo Masu	ITA	135.0	117.5	155.0	407.5

Vorobyov later gained notoriety as the first coach to distribute anabolic steroids to members of the Soviet national team.

1964 Tokyo C: 19, N: 18, D: 10.17. WR: 480 kg (Louis Martin)

		PRESS	SNATCH	JERK	TOTAL KG
1. Vladimir Golovanov	SOV/RUS	165.0 OR	142.5 EOR	180.0	487.5 WR
2. Louis Martin	GBR	155.0	140.0	180.0	475.0
3. Ireneusz Paliński	POL	150.0	135.0	182.5 OR	467.5
4. William March	USA	155.0	135.0	177.5	467.5
5. Lazăr Baroga	ROM	145.0	135.0	180.0	460.0
6. Árpád Nemessányi	HUN	140.0	142.5 EOR	177.5	460.0
7. Jouni Kailajärvi	FIN	145.0	127.5	180.0	452.5
8. Peter Tachev	BUL	145.0	130.0	170.0	445.0

1968 Mexico City C: 29, N: 22, D: 10.18. WR: 522.5 kg (Kaarlo Kangasniemi)

		PRESS	SNATCH	JERK	TOTAL KG
1. Kaarlo Kangasniemi	FIN	172.5 OR	157.5 WR	187.5	517.5 OR
2. Jaan Talts	SOV/EST	160.0	150.0	197.5 WR	507.5
3. Marek Gołąb	POL	165.0	145.0	185.0	495.0
4. Bo Johansson	SWE	165.0	145.0	182.5	492.5
5. Jaakko Kailajärvi	FIN	145.0	150.0	190.0	485.0
6. Árpád Nemessányi	HUN	150.0	145.0	187.5	482.5
7. Philip Grippaldi	USA	155.0	137.5	185.0	477.5
8. Vítězslav Ortságh	CZE	157.5	130.0	175.0	462.5

1972 Munich C: 23, N: 15, D: 9.3. WR: 562.5 kg (David Rigert)

		PRESS	SNATCH	JERK	TOTAL KG
1. Andon Nikolov	BUL	180.0	155.0	190.0	525.0 OR
2. Atanas Shopov	BUL	180.0	145.0	192.5	517.5
3. Hans Bettembourg	SWE	182.5	145.0	185.0	512.5
4. Philip Grippaldi	USA	170.0	140.0	195.0	505.0
5. Patrick Holbrook	USA	162.5	145.0	197.5 EOR	505.0
6. Nicolo Ciancio	AUS	170.0	145.0	190.0	505.0
7. Juan Curbelo Molina	CUB	172.5	140.0	182.5	495.0
8. Jaakko Kailajärvi	FIN	150.0	150.0	187.5	487.5

The clear favorite, world record holder David Rigert of Chakhti, set an Olympic record in the press of 187.5 kg. However, he failed at all three of his attempts to snatch 160 kg, despite the fact that he held the world record of 167.5 kg. Rigert was so upset that he literally pulled his hair out and banged his head against a wall. He was finally restrained by his colleagues, but the next day he threw another fit and had to be sent home. Gold-medal-winner Andon Nikolov was a former troublemaker who was introduced to weightlifting in reform school.

1976 Montreal C: 19, N: 16, D: 7.25. WR: 400 kg (David Rigert)

		PRESS	JERK	TOTAL KG
1. David Rigert	SOV/KAZ	170.0 OR	212.5 OR	382.5 OR
2. Lee James	USA	165.0	197.5	362.5
3. Atanas Shopov	BUL	155.0	205.0	360.0
4. György Rehus	HUN	157.5	192.5	350.0
5. Peter Petzold	GDR	152.5	192.5	345.0
6. Alberto Blanco Fernández	CUB	152.5	192.5	345.0
7. Yvon Cousin	FRA	152.5	180.0	332.5
8. Guðmundur Sigurðsson	ICE	145.0	187.5	332.5

DISQ (Drugs): Philip Grippaldi (USA) 355.0

Rigert, the heaviest man to snatch twice his bodyweight, had no reason to lose any hair this time in Montreal, as his excellent lifting gave him a comfortable victory.

1980 Moscow C: 18, N: 16, D: 7.27. WR: 400 kg (David Rigert)

		PRESS	JERK	TOTAL KG
1. Péter Baczakó	HUN	170.0 EOR	207.5	377.5
2. Rumen Aleksandrov	BUL	170.0 EOR	205.0	375.0
3. Frank Mantek	GDR	165.0	205.0	370.0
4. Dalibor Řehák	CZE	165.0	200.0	365.0
5. Witold Walo	POL	160.0	200.0	360.0
6. Lubomír Şršeň	CZE	160.0	207.5	357.5
7. Vasile Groapă	ROM	160.0	195.0	355.0
8. Nicolaos Iliadis	GRE	150.0	195.0	345.0

David Rigert reverted to his form of eight years earlier when he started snatching at 170 kg, failed at all three attempts, and was eliminated.

1984 Los Angeles-Westchester C: 26, N: 21, D: 8.5. WR: 420 kg (Blagoi Blagoev)

		SNATCH	JERK	TOTAL KG
1. Nicolae "Nicu" Vlad	ROM	172.5 OR	220.0 OR	392.5 OR
2. Dumitru Petre	ROM	165.0	195.0	360.0
3. David Mercer	GBR	157.5	195.0	352.5
4. Peter Immesberger	GER	155.0	195.0	350.0
5. Hwang Woo-won	KOR	152.5	197.5	350.0
6. Nikos Iliadis	GRE	155.0	195.0	350.0
7. Henri Junch Hoeg	DEN	152.5	195.0	347.5
8. José Garcés	MEX	150.0	192.5	342.5

Handsome Nicu Vlad was known in Romania as "The Apollo of the Barbells." Vlad's total was good enough to win the heavyweight division. At the Friendship Games in Varna on September 16, Viktor Solodov set a world record of 422.5 kg. In second place, at 400 kg, was Blagoi Blagoev, the man whose record Solodov broke. Vlad went on to win a silver medal in the first heavyweight division in 1988 and a bronze as a heavyweight in 1996.

1988 Seoul C: 29, N: 23, D: 9.25. WR: 422.5 kg (Viktor Solodov)

		SNATCH	JERK	TOTAL KG
1. Anatoly Khrapaty	SOV/KAZ	187.5 OR	225.0 OR	412.5 OR
2. Nail Mukhamedyarov	SOV/UZB	177.5	222.5	400.0
3. Sławomir Zawada	POL	180.0	220.0	400.0
4. Andrzej Piotrowski	POL	165.0	200.0	365.0
5. Attila Buda	HUN	175.0	185.0	360.0
6. David Mercer	GBR	157.5	200.0	357.5
7. Roland Feldhofter	GER	150.0	200.0	350.0
8. Keith Boxell	GBR	157.5	192.5	350.0

1992 Barcelona C: 23, N: 19, D: 8.1. WR: 422.5 kg (Viktor Solodov)

		SNATCH	JERK	TOTAL KG
1. Kakhi Kakhiachvili	GEO	177.5	235.0 EWR	412.5 EOR
2. Sergei Syrtsov	UZB	190.0 OR	222.5	412.5 EOR
3. Sergiusz Wołczaniecki	POL	172.5	220.0	392.5
4. Kim Byung-chan	KOR	170.0	210.0	380.0
5. Ivan Tchakarov	BUL	170.0	207.5	377.5
6. Emillo Lara Rodríguez	CUB	165.0	210.0	375.0
7. Peter May	GBR	160.0	195.0	355.0
8. Harvey Goodman	AUS	157.5	192.5	350.0

Trailing by 10 kilograms with one attempt remaining, Kakhiachvili called for the world record weight of 235 kilograms. He made it—a remarkable achievement in an era of serious drug testing—and defeated Syrtsov because of his lower bodyweight, a difference of 20 grams (seven-tenths of an ounce).

1996 Atlanta C: 25, N: 22, D: 7.27. WR: 412.5 kg (Aleksei Petrov)

		SNATCH	JERK	TOTAL KG
1. Aleksei Petrov	RUS	187.5 WR	215.0	402.5
2. Leonidas Kokas	GRE	175.0	215.0	390.0
3. Oliver Caruso	GER	175.0	215.0	390.0
4. Sunay Bulut	TUR	177.5	212.5	390.0
5. Igor Alekseyev	RUS	182.5	205.0	387.5
6. Carlos Hernández Calderón	CUB	175.0	207.5	382.5
7. Oleh Chumak	UKR	167.5	212.5	380.0
8. Plamen Bratoychev	BUL	175.0	205.0	380.0

At the age of 19, Aleksei Petrov won the 1994 world championship by an impressive 15 kg. The following year he increased his margin of victory to 20 kg. But following the 1995 competition he tested positive for steroids and in March 1996 he was slapped with a lifetime ban. Supported by the Russian Weightlifting Federation and the Russian Olympic Committee, Petrov appealed. A former girlfriend came forward and confessed to slipping steroids into his food prior to his trip to the world championships. Petrov's suspension was lifted and two months later he won the Olympic gold medal.

2000 Sydney C: 19, N: 17, D: 9.24. WR: None Recognized

		SNATCH	JERK	TOTAL KG
1. Akakios "Kakhi" Kakiashvilis (Kakhi Kakiachvili)	GRE	185.0 WR	220.0	405.0 OR
2. Szymon Kołecki	POL	182.5	222.5	405.0 OR
3. Aleksey Petrov	RUS	180.0	222.5	402.5
4. Kouroush Bagheri	IRN	187.5	215.0	402.5
5. Vadim Vacarciuc	MOL	177.5	220.0	397.5
6. Zoltán Kovács	HUN	180.0	217.5	397.5
7. Bunyamin Sudas	TUR	177.5	215.0	392.5
8. Julio César Luna Fermín	VEN	177.5	215.0	392.5

Kakhi Kakiashvilis won his third gold medal in an unusual manner. Leading 18-year-old Szymon Kolecki by 2.5 kg after the snatch, and with a lower bodyweight, Kakiashvilis opened the clean and jerk with the relatively low 220 kg. Kolecki countered with 222.5 kg and then waited to see what weight Kakiashvilis would choose for his second attempt. When the Greek kept passing, Kolecki, who held the clean and jerk world record of 232.5 kg, tried 227.5 and missed. As it turned out, Kakiashvilis was hiding an injury that would have prevented him from making a heavier lift and Kolecki, had he known this, could have won with a relatively easy 225 kg.

2004 Athens C: 25, N: 18, D: 8.23. WR: None Recognized

		SNATCH	JERK	TOTAL KG
1. Milen Dobrev	BUL	187.5	220.0	407.5
2. Khadzhimurat Akkayev	RUS	185.0	220.0	405.0
3. Eduard Tyukin	RUS	182.5	215.0	397.5
4. Shahin Nasirinia	IRN	172.5	220.0	392.5
5. Julio César Luna Fermín	VEN	170.0	220.0	390.0
6. Hakan Yılmaz	TUR	175.0	215.0	390.0
7. Bakhyt Akhmetov	KAZ	180.0	210.0	390.0
8. Anatoly Mushik	UKR	175.0	212.5	387.5

Both Khadzhimurat Akkayev and reigning world champion Milen Dobrev snatched 180 kilograms and 185 kilograms. But when the weight was raised to 187.5 kg, Akkayev missed, while Dobrev succeeded. This proved to be the difference in the competition, as both lifted 220 kg in the clean and jerk. Meanwhile, three-time Olympic champion and hometown favorite Kakhi Kakiashvilis made only one successful lift in the snatch (180 kg), added extra weights in the clean and jerk to try to catch up quickly, and was eliminated after failing to lift 220 kg three times.

2008 Beijing C: 18, N: 14, D: 8.17. WR: 412 kg (Akakios Kakhiasvilis)

		SNATCH	JERK	TOTAL KG
1. Ilya Ilyin	KAZ	180.0	226.0	406.0
2. Szymon Kołecki	POL	179.0	224.0	403.0
3. Khadzhimurat Akkayev	RUS	185.0	217.0	402.0
4. Arsen Kasabiev	GEO	176.0	223.0	399.0
5. Nizami Paşayev	AZR	181.0	215.0	396.0
6. Yoandry Hernández Coba	CUB	178.0	215.0	393.0
7. Asghar Ebrahimi	IRN	180.0	212.0	392.0
8. Roman Konstantinov	RUS	175.0	212.0	387.0

Competing with the lesser-known competitors in Group B due to a low starting weight, Khadzhimurat Akkayev lifted 217 kg (478.4 lbs) on his third and final clean and jerk, giving him a total he expected would be good enough for gold.

Competing in Group A, 2006 world champion Ilya Ilin surpassed this, lifting 226 kg (498.2 lbs) on his final attempt. European champion Szymon Kołecki attempted to lift 228 kg (502.6 lbs) but failed, finishing in second place.

"My coach is a jerk," an angry Akkayev said after the competition, "If I had competed in Group A, I would have won the gold."

HEAVYWEIGHT

(105kg—231.5 lbs [1972–1992: 110 kg—242.5 lbs; 1996: 108 kg—238.1 lbs])

1896–1968 not held

1972 Munich C: 26, N: 19, D: 9.22. WR: 590 kg (Valery Yakubovsky)

		PRESS	SNATCH	JERK	TOTAL KG
1. Jaan Talts	SOV/EST	210.0 OR	165.0	205.0	580.0 OR
2. Aleksandr Kraichev	BUL	197.5	162.5	202.5	562.5
3. Stefan Grützner	GDR	185.0	162.5	207.5	555.0
4. Helmut Losch	GDR	190.0	152.5	205.0	547.5
5. Roberto Vezzani	ITA	192.5	147.5	205.0	545.0
6. János Hanzlik	HUN	190.0	157.5	195.0	542.5
7. Kauko Kangasniemi	FIN	175.0	165.0	197.5	537.5
8. Rainer Dörrzapf	GER	170.0	165.0	187.5	522.5

1976 Montreal C: 22, N: 18, D: 7.26. WR: 417.5 kg (Valentin Hristov)

		SNATCH	JERK	TOTAL KG
1. Yuri Zaitsev	SOV/RUS	165.0	220.0 OR	385.0
2. Krustiu Semerdzhiev	BUL	170.0 OR	215.0	385.0
3. Tadeusz Rutkowski	POL	167.5	210.0	377.5
4. Pierre Gourrier	FRA	157.5	215.0	372.5
5. Jürgen Ciezki	GDR	162.5	210.0	372.5
6. Javier González Ramos	CUB	160.0	205.0	365.0
7. Leif Nilsson	SWE	157.5	207.5	365.0
8. Rudolf Strejček	CZE	162.5	200.0	362.5

DISQ (Drugs): Valentin Hristov (BUL) 400.0, Mark Cameron (USA) 375.0

The case of Valentin Hristov is an illuminating study in the culture of steroid taking. A week before the Olympic competition he tested negative for prohibited drugs, proving that he had not taken any steroids for at least five weeks. After winning the Olympic contest, he tested positive. He had taken steroids in the few days preceding the Olympics even though steroids give no immediate boost and are effective only when taken regularly for an extended period of time. Apparently, the importance of taking of steroids was, for Hristov, as much psychological as physical.

1980 Moscow C: 13, N: 13, D: 7.29. WR: 420 kg (Leonid Taranenko)

		SNATCH	JERK	TOTAL KG
1. Leonid Taranenko	SOV/BLR	182.5	240.0 WR	422.5 WR
2. Valentin Hristov	BUL	185.0 OR	220.0	405.0
3. György Szalai	HUN	172.5	217.5	390.0
4. Leif Nilsson	SWE	167.5	212.5	380.0
5. Vinzenz Hörtnagl	AUT	170.0	202.5	372.5
6. Stefan Tasnadi	ROM	165.0	195.0	360.0
7. Donald Mitchell	AUS	162.5	190.0	352.5
8. Dimitrios Zarzavatsidis	GRE	155.0	192.5	347.5

Twelve years after his Moscow victory, Taranenko won a silver medal in the super-heavyweight division.

1984 Los Angeles-Westchester C: 15, N: 12, D: 8.7. WR: 440 kg (Vyacheslav Klokov)

		SNATCH	JERK	TOTAL KG
1. Norberto Oberburger	ITA	175.0	215.0	390.0
2. Stefan Tasnadi	ROM	167.5	212.5	380.0
3. Guy Carlton	USA	167.5	210.0	377.5
4. Frank Seipelt	GER	160.0	207.5	367.5
5. Albert Squires	CAN	165.0	200.0	365.0
6. Richard Eaton	USA	152.5	200.0	352.5
7. Ioannis Gerontas	GRE	152.5	197.5	350.0
8. Olaf Peters	GER	157.5	190.0	347.5

DISQ (Drugs): Göran Pettersson (SWE) 360.0

On September 17, 1984, Olympic champion Leonid Taranenko lifted a world record 442.5 kg to win at the Friendship Games. Second was Soviet teammate Yuri Zakharevich with 427.5 kg, and third Yanko Georgiev of Bulgaria with 412.5 kg.

1988 Seoul C: 20, N: 15, D: 9.27. WR: 452.5 kg (Yuri Zakharevich)

		SNATCH	JERK	TOTAL KG
1. Yuri Zakharevich	SOV/RUS	210.0 WR	245.0 WR	455.0 WR
2. József Jacsó	HUN	190.0	237.5	427.5
3. Ronny Weller	GDR	190.0	235.0	425.0
4. Michael Schubert	GDR	190.0	235.0	425.0
5. Aleksandr Popov	SOV/RUS	187.5	232.5	420.0
6. Norberto Oberburger	ITA	187.5	227.5	415.0
7. Stanisław Małysa	POL	180.0	215.0	395.0
8. Frank Seipelt	GER	170.0	217.5	387.5

In 1983 Yuri Zakharevich dislocated his left elbow while attempting a snatch world record. Doctors rebuilt his elbow using synthetic tendons. He returned to competition in 1984 and won the next four European championships as well as the next three world championships. In Seoul he broke the snatch world record twice as well as the record for combined total.

1992 Barcelona C: 24, N: 20, D: 8.3. WR: 455.0 kg (Yuri Zakharevich)

		SNATCH	JERK	TOTAL KG
1. Ronny Weller	GER	192.5	240.0	432.5
2. Artur Akoyev	RUS	195.0	235.0	430.0
3. Stefan Botev Khristov	BUL	190.0	227.5	417.5
4. Nicu Vlad	ROM	190.0	215.0	405.0
5. Dariusz Osuch	POL	175.0	222.5	397.5
6. Frank Seipelt	GER	170.0	220.0	390.0
7. Flavio Villavicenia Cabrera	CUB	170.0	217.5	387.5
8. Pavlos Saltsidis	GRE	175.0	210.0	385.0

In December 1989, Ronny Weller was driving down a poorly lit street with his girlfriend when he lost control of his car and crashed into a tree. When he awoke from a coma several days later, he learned that his girlfriend had been killed and he himself had fractured his skull, as well as other parts of his body. His rehabilitation was slow. He finally returned to training in March 1991, and seven months later he finished second to Artur Akoyev at the world championships.

The same month that Weller began training again, Stefan Botev emigrated from Bulgaria to Australia. In May 1992, he was told that he would have to compete for Bulgaria one more time before he could represent Australia. The same thing happened to Nicu Vlad, who left Romania for Australia in January 1991, but was forced to compete for Romania. Vlad, who had intended to compete in the first heavyweight division, was entered in the heavyweight division instead because his Olympic qualifying mark had come during a regional meet at that weight. Giving up more than 11½ pounds to all of his main rivals, Vlad finished out of the medals. Weller won the competition by making all six of his lifts.

Mehmed Skender of Bosnia finished 20th and last among those who didn't fail all their lifts, but Skender's preparations were not the same as those of the other lifters. Six weeks before the Olympics, Skender, a telephone repairman, was crouching in a trench, firing a machine gun at the Yugoslav army that was invading his hometown of Zenica, northwest of Sarajevo. Having survived on one meal of rice and macaroni a day, he became ill as soon as he arrived in the Olympic Village and was exposed to meat and rich foods. Before the Games were even over, he rushed back to his family in Zenica.

1996 Atlanta C: 23, N: 18, D: 7.29. WR: 435 kg (Timur Taimazov)

		SNATCH	JERK	TOTAL KG
1. Timur Taimazov	UKR	195.0	235.0 WR	430.0
2. Sergei Syrtsov	RUS	195.0	225.0	420.0
3. Nicolae "Nicu" Vlad	ROM	197.5	222.5	420.0
4. Vladimir Emelyanov	BLR	187.5	220.0	407.5
5. Cui Wenhua	CHN	190.0	215.0	405.0
6. Wesley Barnett	USA	175.0	220.0	395.0
7. Ara Vardanian	ARM	180.0	215.0	395.0
8. Dariusz Osuch	POL	177.5	215.0	392.5

After earning a silver medal in the first heavyweight division at the 1992 Olympics, Timur Taimazov moved up to heavyweight and won the world championship in 1993 and 1994. He missed the 1995 season because of a wrist injury. In his absence, fellow Ukrainian Ihor Razoronov won the world championship. The two were expected to vie for the gold medal in Atlanta. But during the warm-ups, Razoronov injured his back and was taken to the hospital while the competition began. Taimazov was in third place after the snatch, but his first jerk of 227.5 kg was more than his opponents could handle. With the gold medal secure, he set a clean and jerk world record of 236 kg.

2000 Sydney C: 21, N: 18, D: 9.25. WR: None Recognized

		SNATCH	JERK	TOTAL KG
1. Hossein Tavakoli	IRN	190.0	235.0	425.0
2. Alan Tsagaev	BUL	187.5	235.0	422.5
3. Said Saif Asaad	QAT	190.0	230.0	420.0
4. Ihor Razoronov	UKR	192.5	227.5	420.0
5. Yevgeny Tschiguychev	RUS	190.0	225.0	415.0
6. Alexandru Bratan	MOL	190.0	220.0	410.0
7. Florin Vlad	ROM	180.0	225.0	405.0
8. Grzegorz Kleszcz	POL	185.0	220.0	405.0

When Denys Gotfrid won the 1999 world championship in Athens, the Greek organizers could not find a copy of the Ukrainian national anthem so, at the award ceremony, they played the theme from *2001: A Space Odyssey* instead. Gotfrid was sure that the Australians would get it right at the Olympics, but although he was in second place after the snatch, he missed all three of his jerk attempts and was eliminated. In fact, 8 of the 21 entrants failed to complete successful lifts in both the snatch and jerk. Hossein Tavakoli was in only sixth place after the snatch, but after jerking 230 kg and missing once at 235 kg, he held his last attempt and scored an unexpected victory. Silver medalist Alan Tsagaev, who was born in Russia but competed for Bulgaria, was only cleared to compete the day of the competition. The entire Bulgarian weightlifting squad was expelled after three of their lifters failed drug tests. But the Bulgarians paid the International Weightlifting Federation a $50,000 fine and the Court of Arbitration for Sport gave Tsagaev the go-ahead to take part. The bronze medal went to Said Saif Asaad, formerly known as Angel Popov. In 1999, the emirate of Qatar, desirous of Olympic success, purchased eight weightlifters from Bulgaria, granted them Qatari citizenship and allowed them to continue training in Bulgaria. Popov was one of the eight and the only one to win a medal in Sydney.

2004 Athens C: 22, N: 19, D: 8.24. WR: None Recognized

		SNATCH	JERK	TOTAL KG
1. Dmitri Berestov	RUS	195.0	230.0	425.0
2. Ihor Razoronov	UKR	190.0	230.0	420.0
3. Gleb Pisarevskiy	RUS	190.0	225.0	415.0
4. Alexandru Bratan	MOL	192.5	222.5	415.0
5. Ramūnas Vyšniauskas	LIT	187.5	222.5	410.0
6. Alan Naniyev	AZR	190.0	220.0	410.0
7. Matthias Steiner	AUT	182.5	222.5	405.0
8. Aleksandr Urinov	UZB	185.0	215.0	400.0

DISQ (Drugs): Ferenc Gyurkovics (HUN) 420.0

After beating out 2001 world champion Vladimir Smortchkov for a place on the Russian team, Dmitri Berestov won the gold after clearing his first five lifts, including an Olympic record-breaking 195 kilograms in the snatch. The silver medal was originally awarded to Ferenc Gyurkovics due to lower bodyweight after he tied with Ihor Razoronov, but Gyurkovics was disqualified after testing positive for the anabolic steroid oxandrolone.

In July 2006, Berestov, too, was handed a two-year ban after failing a drug test.

2008 Beijing C: 19, N: 15, D: 8.18. WR: 430 kg (Denys Gotfrid)

		SNATCH	JERK	TOTAL KG
1. Andrei Aramnou	BLR	200.0 WR	236.0 WR	436.0 WR
2. Dmitri Klokov	RUS	193.0	230.0	423.0
3. Dmitri Lapikov	RUS	190.0	230.0	420.0
4. Marcin Dołęga	POL	195.0	225.0	420.0
5. Bakhyt Akhmetov	KAZ	190.0	225.0	415.0
6. Albert K'uzilovi	GEO	182.0	227.0	409.0
7. Sergei Istomin	KAZ	181.0	225.0	406.0
8. Robert Dołęga	POL	184.0	221.0	405.0

DISQ (Drugs): Ihor Razoronov (UKR) 410.0

Twenty-year-old reigning world champion Andrei Aramnou didn't miss a single lift attempt, breaking three world records on his way to winning the Olympic gold medal.

In second place after the snatch portion, 2006 world champion Marcin Dołęga missed his last two clean and jerk attempts at 228 kg (502.6 lbs), which dropped him to fourth place behind 2005 world champion Dmitri Klokov and 2006 world silver medalist Dmitri Lapikov.

Ihor Razoronov originally finished sixth, but was disqualified after he tested positive for the steroid nandrolone.

SUPER HEAVYWEIGHT

(Heavyweight 1896–1968, Unlimited Weight)

Historically, the minimum weights for athletes in this category have been:

1920–1948	82.5 kg–181.5 lbs
1952–1968	90 kg–198.25 lbs
1972–1992	110 kg–242.5 lbs
1996	108 kg–238.1 lbs
2000–2004	105 kg–231.5 lbs

1896 Athens C: 6, N: 5, D: 4.7.

Two-Hand Lift

		KG
1. Viggo Jensen	DEN	111.5
2. Launceston Elliot	GBR	111.5
3. Sotirios Versis	GRE	90.0
4. Georgios Papasideris	GRE	90.0
4. Carl Schuhmann	GER	90.0
6. Momcsilló Tapavicza	HUN/YUG	80.0

The first instance of an Olympic judging controversy occurred in the two-handed lift. Jensen and Elliot tied at 111.5 kg, but the Dane was awarded first place as a result of his better style, Elliot having moved one foot while lifting. Jensen was quite a versatile athlete. In addition to winning the two-handed weightlifting competition, he also finished second in the one-hand lift, third in the three-position free rifle, and fourth in the shot put and rope climb events.

1896 Athens C: 4, N: 3, D: 4.7.

One-Hand Lift

		KG
1. Launceston Elliot	GBR	71.0
2. Viggo Jensen	DEN	57.0
3. Alexandros Nikolopoulos	GRE	57.0
4. Sotirios Versis	GRE	40.0

Elliot, who lived in India until age 13, was Great Britain's first Olympic champion. He was named after the Tasmanian city where he was conceived.

1900 not held

1904 St. Louis C: 4, N: 2, D: 9.3.

Two-Hand Lift

		KG
1. Perikles Kakousis	GRE	111.70
2. Oscar Osthoff	USA	84.37
3. Frank Kungler	USA	79.61
4. Oscar Olson	USA	67.81

1904 St. Louis C: 3, N: 1, D: 9.3.

All-Around Dumbbell Contest

1. Oscar Osthoff	USA	48 points
2. Frederick Winters	USA	45 points
3. Frank Kungler	USA	10 points

Launceston Elliot
Winner of the one-hand lift in 1896.

The all-around dumbbell contest, won by Oscar Osthoff of Milwaukee, consisted of nine different types of lifts as well as an optional section.

1906 Athens C: 10, N: 6, D: 4.27.

Two-Hand Lift

		KG
1. Dimitrios Tofalos	GRE	142.4
2. Josef Steinbach	AUT	136.5
3. Alexandre Maspoli	FRA	129.5
3. Heinrich Rondi	GER	129.5
3. Heinrich Schneidereit	GER	129.5
6. Perikles Kakousis	GRE	121.5
7. Tullio Camillotti	ITA	108.5
7. Stephanos Christopoulos	GRE	108.5
7. Marcel Dubois	BEL	108.5
7. Ioannis Varanakis	GRE	108.5

Josef Steinbach caused a stir when he objected to the rule in the two-hand lift which required that the bar be raised straight to the shoulders before being brought overhead. Steinbach wanted to use the continental style, which allowed him to rest the weight at his waist before moving it to his shoulders. After Tofalos had won the competition and the jury had departed, Steinbach walked back to the bar and, using the forbidden style, lifted it easily over his head. The sportsmanlike Greek crowd, unaware of the rules, thought that Steinbach had been cheated of victory.

Tofalos, the son of a count, had been run over by a wagon as a young boy. His upper arm was crushed and doctors wanted to amputate it, but Tofalos' father wouldn't allow it. Dimitrios recovered the use of his arm even though it was two and a half inches shorter than his uninjured arm. After winning at the Olympics, Tofalos turned professional and eventually went to America, where he entered vaudeville and became a wrestler. In a match against world champion Frank Gotch, Tofalos got caught in one of Gotch's famous toeholds, but refused to submit. His stubbornness cost him six months in the hospital with a dislocated hip. Tofalos became a US citizen in 1921 and remained a popular figure in professional wrestling and physical culture circles for the rest of his life.

1906 Athens C: 12, N: 7, D: 4.27.

One-Hand Lift

		KG
1. Josef Steinbach	AUT	73.75
2. Tullio Camillotti	ITA	73.75
3. Heinrich Schneidereit	GER	70.75
4. Alexandre Maspoli	FRA	70.75
5. Carl Svensson	SWE	65.45
6. Heinrich Rondi	GER	65.45
6. Ioannis Varanakis	GRE	65.45
8. Marcel Dubois	BEL	60.40

A successful lift was not recorded unless the weight was lifted with *each* hand.

1908–1912 not held

1920 Antwerp C: 6, N: 5, D: 8.31.

	ONE-HAND	ONE-HAND SNATCH	TWO-HAND JERK	TOTAL JERK	KG
1. Filippo Bottino	ITA	70.0	75.0	120.0	265.0
2. Joseph Aizin	LUX	65.0	75.0	120.0	260.0
3. Louis Bernot	FRA	65.0	75.0	115.0	255.0
4. Ejnar Jensen	DEN	60.0	75.0	115.0	250.0
5. Richard Brunn	SWE	60.0	80.0	110.0	250.0
6. Joseph Duchâteau	FRA	65.0	72.5	110.0	247.5

1924 Paris C: 19, N: 12, D: 7.24.

		ONE-HAND SNATCH	ONE-HAND JERK	TWO-HAND PRESS	TWO-HAND SNATCH	TWO-HAND JERK	TOTAL KG
1. Giuseppe Tonani	ITA	80.0	95.0	112.5	100.0	130.0	517.5
2. Franz Aigner	AUT	80.0	97.5 OR	112.5	95.0	130.0	515.0
3. Harald Tammer	EST	75.0	95.0	90.0	97.5	140.0 OR	497.5
4. Louis Dannoux	FRA	80.0	95.0	87.5	100.0	135.0	497.5
5. Karlis Leilands	LAT	77.5	87.5	100.0	100.0	132.5	497.5
6. Filippo Bottino	ITA	77.5	85.0	110.0	97.5	125.0	495.0
7. Kaljo-Feliks Raag	EST	80.0	92.5	90.0	97.5	130.0	490.0
8. Claudlus Dutrieve	FRA	75.0	82.5	90.0	100.0	120.0	467.5

Places three through five were determined by a two-hand jerk lift-off.

1928 Amsterdam C: 17, N: 11, D: 7.29.

		PRESS	SNATCH	JERK	TOTAL KG
1. Josef Strassberger	GER	122.5 OR	107.5	142.5	372.5 WR
2. Arnold Luhäär	EST	100.0	110.0 OR	150.0 OR	360.0
3. Jaroslav Skobla	CZE	100.0	107.5	150.0 OR	357.5
4. Karlis Leilands	LAT	110.0	105.0	140.0	355.0
5. Josef Leppelt	AUT	105.0	110.0 OR	140.0	355.0
5. Rudolf Schilberg	AUT	115.0	105.0	135.0	355.0
7. Giuseppe Tonani	ITA	117.5	97.5	137.5	352.5
8. Hermann Volz	GER	97.5	110.0 OR	132.5	340.0

1932 Los Angeles C: 6, N: 4, D: 7.30. WR: 400 kg (El Sayed Mohammed Nosseir)

		PRESS	SNATCH	JERK	TOTAL KG
1. Jaroslav Skobla	CZE	112.5	115.0	152.5 OR	380.0 OR
2. Václav Pšenička	CZE	112.5	117.5 OR	147.5	377.5
3. Josef Strassberger	GER	125.0 OR	110.0	142.5	377.5
4. Marcel Dumoulin	FRA	95.0	107.5	140.0	342.5
5. Albert Manger	USA	100.0	92.5	122.5	315.0
6. Howard Turbyfill	USA	77.5	95.0	132.5	305.0

Twenty-four years later, Skobla's son Jiří won the bronze medal in the shot put at Melbourne.

1936 Berlin C: 13, N: 9, D: 8.5. WR: 407.5 kg (Václav Pšenička)

		PRESS	SNATCH	JERK	TOTAL KG
1. Josef Manger	GER	132.5 OR	122.5	155.0	410.0 WR
2. Václav Pšenička	CZE	122.5	125.0	155.0	402.5
3. Arnold Luhäär	EST	115.0	120.0	165.0 OR	400.0
4. Ronald Walker	GBR	110.0	127.5 OR	160.0	397.5
5. Hussein Mokhtar	EGY	112.5	122.5	160.0	395.0
6. Josef Zemann	AUT	110.0	122.5	155.0	387.5
7. Paul Wahl	GER	115.0	110.0	150.0	375.0
8. Rudolf Schilberg	AUT	125.0	107.5	140.0	372.5

1948 London C: 16, N: 14, D: 8.11. WR: 455 kg (John Davis)

		PRESS	SNATCH	JERK	TOTAL KG
1. John Davis	USA	137.5 OR	137.5 OR	177.5 WR	452.5 OR
2. Norbert Schemansky	USA	122.5	132.5	170.0	425.0
3. Abraham Charité	HOL	127.5	125.0	160.0	412.5
4. Alfred Knight	GBR	117.5	117.5	155.0	390.0
5. Hanafi Mustafa	EGY	120.0	115.0	150.0	385.0
6. Niels Petersen	DEN	115.0	112.5	155.0	382.5
7. Robert Allart	BEL	122.5	110.0	145.0	377.5
8. Pieter Taljaard	SAF	117.5	112.5	145.0	375.0

With his fourth attempt, Davis set a snatch world record of 142.5 kg.

1952 Helsinki C: 13, N: 11, D: 7.27. WR: 482.5 kg (John Davis)

		PRESS	SNATCH	JERK	TOTAL KG
1. John Davis	USA	150.0 OR	145.0 OR	165.0	460.0 OR
2. James Bradford	USA	140.0	132.5	165.0	437.5
3. Humberto Selvetti	ARG	150.0 OR	120.0	162.5	432.5
4. Heinz Schattner	GER	130.0	130.0	162.5	422.5
5. William David Baillie	CAN	145.0	122.5	152.5	420.0
6. Norberto Ferreira	ARG	140.0	115.0	155.0	410.0
7. R. Harold Cleghorn	NZL	130.0	117.5	152.5	400.0
8. Franz Hölbl	AUT	115.0	117.5	155.0	387.5

John Davis of Brooklyn was never bested in Olympic competition in either the press, the snatch, or the jerk, and was undefeated in all competitions between 1938 and 1953. An enthusiastic singer, he once made a record that sold 71 copies. Fourth-place finisher Schattner was a circus performer. He began his act by hoisting a weightlifting bar attached to two enormous globes. Once they were above his head, the globes opened to reveal his wife and son.

1956 Melbourne C: 9, N: 9, D: 11.26. WR: 519.5 kg (Paul Anderson)

		PRESS	SNATCH	JERK	TOTAL KG
1. Paul Anderson	USA	167.5	145.0 EOR	187.5 OR	500.0 OR
2. Humberto Selvetti	ARG	175.0 OR	145.0 EOR	180.0	500.0 OR
3. Alberto Pigaiani	ITA	150.0	130.0	172.5	452.5
4. Firouz Pejhan	IRN	147.5	132.5	170.0	450.0
5. Elno Mäkinen	FIN	127.5	137.5	167.5	432.5
6. William David Baillie	CAN	147.5	122.5	162.5	432.5
7. Franz Hölbl	AUT	142.5	125.0	157.5	425.0
8. Richard Jones	NZL	125.0	122.5	150.0	397.5

Twenty-two-year-old Paul Anderson of Toccoa, Georgia, travelled to Moscow in 1955 as an unknown substitute at a Soviet-American dual meet. He caused a sensation by breaking the world press record by 20 pounds with his first-ever lift in international competition. At the Olympics the following year, what had been expected to be an easy victory for Anderson, developed instead into a dramatic showdown between Anderson, who had developed a strep throat, and 1952's bronze medalist, Humberto Selvetti of Argentina. Selvetti surprised the audience by taking the lead in the press with a lift of 175 kg, after Anderson had missed twice at 172.5 kg. When it came time for the jerk, Selvetti was still ahead by 7.5 kg. Anderson watched as Selvetti successfully jerked 170 kg and 180 kg before missing at 185. Anderson, deciding to go straight for the victory, called for 187.5 kg for his first attempt. He failed. He tried it a second time, but missed again. Now he was down to one last lift that would determine if he would finish first or last. Straining heroically, Anderson balanced the weight above his head and finished the competition with a weight total of 500 kg, exactly the same as that of Humberto Selvetti. Paul Anderson was a huge man who weighed in at 303¼ pounds (137.9 kg) after losing 60 pounds to get in shape for the Olympics. Ironically though, he won his gold medal because his bodyweight was actually *less* than that of Selvetti, who was a mammoth 316½ pounds (143.5 kg). On June 17, 1957, at an exhibition in Toccoa, Anderson lifted on his back a table carrying 6,270 pounds (2844 kg). Anderson was a devout Christian who operated a home for delinquent and orphaned children until his death on August 15, 1994.

Super-Heavyweight Medalists, 1956
Paul Anderson (center), who weighed 303¼ lbs, was awarded first place because he weighed *less* than Humberto Selvetti (left).

1960 Rome C: 18, N: 15, D: 9.10. WR: 533 kg (Paul Anderson)

		PRESS	SNATCH	JERK	TOTAL KG
1. Yuri Vlasov	SOV/UKR	180.0 OR	155.0 OR	202.5 WR	537.5 WR
2. James Bradford	USA	180.0 OR	150.0	182.5	512.5
3. Norbert Schemansky	USA	170.0	150.0	180.0	500.0
4. Mohamed Mahmoud Ibrahim	EGY	140.0	137.5	177.5	455.0
5. Eino Mäkinen	FIN	140.0	142.5	172.5	455.0
6. William David Baillie	CAN	147.5	132.5	170.0	450.0
7. Alberto Pigaiani	ITA	152.5	127.5	170.0	450.0
8. Václav Syrovy	CZE	145.0	125.0	172.5	435.0

Although Vlasov's main opponents were the two veterans Bradford and Schemansky, most of the audience was aware of a third, invisible opponent—Paul Anderson, who had turned professional, but whose world record was still on the books. Vlasov assured himself the gold medal and an Olympic record with his first jerk of 185 kg. He followed with a 195, then stunned the crowd by jerking 202.5 kg and setting two world records (jerk and total lifts) with one lift.

After his Olympic victory, Vlasov quit lifting and turned to his great love—writing fiction and poetry. But he had trouble selling his work. He was also cast in the role of Pierre Bezukhov in the Soviet epic film *War and Peace.* However, at the last minute director Sergei Bondarchuk took the role for himself. Unable to support himself as a creative artist, Vlasov returned to weightlifting and began preparations for the Tokyo Olympics.

1964 Tokyo C: 21, N: 18, D: 10.18. WR: 580 kg (Yuri Vlasov)

		PRESS	SNATCH	JERK	TOTAL KG
1. Leonid Zhabotynsky	SOV/UKR	187.5	167.5 OR	217.5 WR	572.5 OR
2. Yuri Vlasov	SOV/UKR	197.5 WR	162.5	210.0	570.0
3. Norbert Schemansky	USA	180.0	165.0	192.5	537.5
4. Gary Gubner	USA	175.0	150.0	187.5	512.5
5. Károly Ecser	HUN	175.0	147.5	185.0	507.5
6. Mohamed Mahmoud Ibrahim	EGY	162.5	145.0	187.5	495.0
7. Ivan Veselinov	BUL	165.0	135.0	190.0	490.0
8. Hwang Ho-dong	KOR	162.5	135.0	185.0	482.5

Zhabotynsky, a 341-pound Ukrainian, scored a major upset when he came from behind to defeat teammate Yuri Vlasov by breaking Vlasov's world jerk record on his final attempt. A half hour earlier, Zhabotynsky had lulled Vlasov into a false sense of security by going up to him and conceding defeat. For his second jerk attempt, Zhabotynsky called for 217.5 kilograms. He raised it as far as his knees and then dropped it. He shook his head and slunk off the platform. When Vlasov was finished, Zhabotynsky returned for his final attempt and successfully hoisted the 217.5 kilograms with a minimum of trouble. When Vlasov realized that he had been made the victim of a dishonest trick, he was furious. "I was choked with tears," he later wrote. "I flung the silver medal through the window . . . I had always revered the purity, the impartiality of contests of strength. That night, I understood that there is a kind of strength that has nothing to do with justice."

In 1989, Vlasov, by then an outspoken critic of the Soviet sports system, with its emphasis on victory at any cost, was elected to the Council of People's Deputies. On May 30 of that year, he stunned the Communist government when he attacked the KGB in a speech that was broadcast live throughout the nation. Vlasov was elected to the State Duma in 1993, but lost a bid for reelection two years later. In 1996, he ran for president of Russia on an anti-Semitic nationalist platform, but received only 220,000 votes.

1968 Mexico City C: 17, N: 14, D: 10.19. WR: 590 kg (Leonid Zhabotynsky)

		PRESS	SNATCH	JERK	TOTAL KG
1. Leonid Zhabotynsky	SOV/UKR	200.0 OR	170.0 OR	202.5	572.5 EOR
2. Serge Reding	BEL	195.0	147.5	212.5	555.0
3. Joseph Dube	USA	200.0 OR	145.0	210.0	555.0
4. Manfred Rieger	GDR	175.0	155.0	202.5	532.5
5. Rudolf Mang	GER	177.5	152.5	195.0	525.0
6. Mauno Lindroos	FIN	157.5	145.0	192.5	495.0
7. Kalevi Lahdenranta	FIN	160.0	147.5	185.0	492.5
8. Donald Oliver	NZL	147.5	142.5	200.0	490.0

Zhabotynsky, now up to 359 pounds, reveled in his role of "World's Strongest Man." At the opening ceremony in Mexico City he astonished the crowd by carrying the huge Soviet flag one-handed. In the competition, he was so sure of victory that he passed his last two attempts in the jerk, upsetting the audience, which had hoped to see him try for a world record.

1972 Munich C: 13, N: 11, D: 9.6. WR: 645 kg (Vassily Alekseyev)

		PRESS	SNATCH	JERK	TOTAL KG
1. Vassily Alekseyev	SOV/RUS	235.0 OR	175.0 OR	230.0 OR	640.0 OR
2. Rudolf Mang	GER	225.0	170.0	215.0	610.0
3. Gerd Bonk	GDR	200.0	155.0	217.5	572.5
4. Jouko Leppä	FIN	205.0	157.5	210.0	572.5
5. Manfred Rieger	GDR	190.0	162.5	205.0	557.5
6. Petr Pavlásek	CZE	192.5	165.0	200.0	557.5
7. Kalevi Lahdenranta	FIN	190.0	165.0	200.0	555.0
8. Fernando Bernal Salas	CUB	190.0	147.5	207.5	545.0

Vassily Alekseyev came to international attention on January 24, 1970, when he broke the world record for the press, the jerk, and the three-lift total. On March 18 of the same year, he became the first person to lift a combined total of 600 kg. Six months later, while competing in Columbus, Ohio, he broke the 500-pound barrier for the jerk. Since Alekseyev only operated on the metric system, he was somewhat confused when his successful lift brought him so much attention. At Munich, the 30-year-old champion checked in at 337 pounds. The competition was no competition as Alekseyev racked up a convincing 30 kg winning margin. In 1962 he married a woman named Olympiada.

1976 Montreal C: 11, N: 8, D: 7.27. WR: 442.5 kg (Vassily Alekseyev)

		SNATCH	JERK	TOTAL KG
1. Vassily Alekseyev	SOV/RUS	185.0 OR	255.0 WR	440.0
2. Gerd Bonk	GDR	170.0	235.0	405.0
3. Helmut Losch	GDR	165.0	222.5	387.5
4. Jan Nagy	CZE	160.0	227.5	387.5
5. Bruce Wilhelm	USA	172.5	215.0	387.5
6. Gerardo Fernández Tabares	CUB	165.0	200.0	365.0
7. Robert Edmond	AUS	157.5	190.0	347.5
8. Jan-Olof Nolsjo	SWE	152.5	185.0	337.5

DISQ (Drugs): Petř Pavlásek (CZE) 387.5

Once again, Alekseyev, now 34 years old and over 345 pounds, was unchallenged. Between 1970 and 1977 he set 79 world records, a number that is particularly significant when one considers that he allegedly received from the Soviet government a prize of $700 to $1500 every time he broke a world record. He was unbeaten from 1970 until 1978.

1980 Moscow C: 12, N: 8, D: 7.30. WR: 445 kg (Vassily Alekseyev)

		SNATCH	JERK	TOTAL KG
1. Sultan Rakhmanov	SOV/UZB	195.0 OR	245.0	440.0 EOR
2. Jürgen Heuser	GDR	182.5	227.5	410.0
3. Tadeusz Rutkowski	POL	180.0	227.5	407.5
4. Rudolf Strejček	CZE	182.5	220.0	402.5
5. Bohuslav Braum	CZE	180.0	217.5	397.5
6. Francisco Méndez Polo	CUB	175.0	220.0	395.0
7. Robert Skolimowski	POL	175.0	210.0	385.0
8. Talal Najjar	SYR	157.5	205.0	362.5

Competing for the first time since he was injured during the 1978 world championship, Alekseyev failed three times to snatch 180 kg and was eliminated. Thirty-year-old Sultan Rakhmanov, whose mother was Ukrainian and whose father was an Uzbek, made six perfect lifts to score a decisive victory.

1984 Los Angeles-Westchester C: 9, N: 7, D: 8.8. WR: 465 kg (Aleksandr Gunyashev)

		SNATCH	JERK	TOTAL KG
1. Dean Lukin	AUS	172.5	240.0	412.5
2. Mario Martinez	USA	185.0	225.0	410.0
3. Manfred Nerlinger	GER	177.5	220.0	397.5
4. Ioannis Tsintsaris	GRE	162.5	185.0	347.5
5. Bartholomew Oluoma	NGR	150.0	187.5	337.5
6. Mosad Mosbah	EGY	150.0	180.0	330.0

DISQ (Drugs): Stefan Laggner (AUT) 385.0

Vassily Alekseyev, 1976
The Super Heavyweight champion in 1972 and 1976 keeps in shape during the off-season.

Dean Lukin was a 305-pound millionaire tuna fisherman from Port Lincoln, South Australia.

1988 Seoul C: 17, N: 13, D: 9.29. WR: 472.5 kg (Aleksandr Kurlovich)

		SNATCH	JERK	TOTAL KG
1. Aleksandr Kurlovich	SOV/BLR	212.5 OR	250.0	462.5 OR
2. Manfred Nerlinger	GER	190.0	240.0	430.0
3. Martin Zawieja	GER	182.5	232.5	415.0
4. Mario Martinez	USA	175.0	232.5	407.5
5. Petr Hudeček	CZE	175.0	225.0	400.0
6. Reda El Batoty	EGY	175.0	217.5	392.5
7. Charles Garzarella	AUS	162.5	207.5	370.0
8. Paulos Saltsidis	GRE	160.0	207.5	367.5

In December 1984, Aleksandr Kurlovich was arrested by customs officials in Montreal and charged with importing anabolic steroids with intent to sell. He pleaded guilty and paid a fine of $450. The USSR Weightlifting Federation banned him from competition for two years. In 1987 he returned to win the world championship.

Although he failed to make a single successful lift, Jiří Zubrický of Czechoslovakia set a record anyway: at 363½ pounds (164.95 kg), he was the heaviest weightlifter to take part in the Olympics.

1992 Barcelona C: 20, N: 16, D: 8.4. WR: 475.0 kg (Leonid Taranenko)

		SNATCH	JERK	TOTAL KG
1. Aleksandr Kurlovich	BLR	205.0	245.0	450.0
2. Leonid Taranenko	BLR	187.5	237.5	425.0
3. Manfred Nerlinger	GER	180.0	232.5	412.5
4. Ernesto Agüero Shell	CUB	182.5	230.0	412.5
5. Mitko Mitev	BUL	180.0	220.0	400.0
6. Jiří Zubrický	CZE	170.0	222.5	392.5
7. Erdinç Aslan	TUR	170.0	220.0	390.0
8. Mario Martinez	USA	170.0	215.0	385.0

Kurlovich made six straight successful lifts to earn his second gold medal. On January 28, 1995, Kurlovich tested positive for the steroid methandienone. He was banned from competition for one year, but returned in time for the 1996 Olympics in which he placed fifth. American Mark Henry broke Jiří Zubrický's record as the heaviest weightlifter in history when he weighed in at 366¾ pounds (166.4 kg). He finished in tenth place.

1996 Atlanta C: 18, N: 15, D: 7.30. WR: 457.5 kg (Aleksandr Kurlovich)

		SNATCH	JERK	TOTAL KG
1. Andrei Chemerkin	RUS	197.5	260.0 WR	457.5 EWR
2. Ronny Weller	GER	200.0	255.0	455.0
3. Stefan Botev Khristov	AUS	200.0	250.0	450.0
4. Kim Tae-hyun	KOR	190.0	247.5	437.5
5. Aleksandr Kurlovich	BLR	195.0	230.0	425.0
6. Manfred Nerlinger	GER	185.0	237.5	422.5
7. Pavlos Saltsidis	GRE	185.0	235.0	420.0
8. Tibor Stark	HUN	187.5	227.5	415.0

This was an exciting, record-setting competition, beginning with the weigh-in, when Mark Henry broke his own record as the heaviest weightlifter ever: 406½ pounds (184.42 kg). Stefan Botev was in first place after the snatch, ahead of Ronny Weller by lower bodyweight and defending world champion Andrei Chenerkin by 2.5 kg. During the clean and jerk portion of the competition, the lead would change eight times. Chemerkin began with 240 kg. Botev followed with 242.5 and Weller with 245. Chemerkin opened the second round with a lift of 250 kg. Botev matched this weight and moved ahead of Chemerkin because of his lower bodyweight (he was a good 41.51 kg lighter than Chemerkin). Then Weller hoisted 252.5 kg to take over first place by 2.5 kg.

With the world jerk record at 253.5 kg (set by Chemerkin in 1995), all three contenders were forced to attempt record weights in the final round. Botev tried 255 and failed, ending his quest for the gold medal. Weller also tried 255, but he was able to hold it. He was so excited that he leaped into the air, lost control and fell on his back. Then he pulled off his shoes and threw them into the stands. Chemerkin paid no attention to these displays of exuberance. He asked for 260 kg and, with a tremendous effort, lifted it over his head and held it.

2000 Sydney C: 24, N: 21, D: 9.26. WR: 465.0 kg (Ronny Weller)

		SNATCH	JERK	TOTAL KG
1. Hossein Rezazadeh	IRN	212.5 WR	260.0	472.5 WR
2. Ronny Weller	GER	210.0	257.5	467.5
3. Andrey Chemerkin	RUS	207.5	257.5	462.5
4. Jaber Salem	QAT	202.5	260.0	460.0
5. Kim Tae-hyun	KOR	205.0	255.0	460.0
6. Viktors Ščerbatihs	LAT	200.0	260.0	452.5
7. Paweł Najdek	POL	202.5	250.0	425.0
8. Tibor Stark	HUN	185.0	240.0	425.0

DISQ (Drugs): Ashot Danielyan (ARM) 465.0

The battle for the title of World's Strongest Man was expected to be a duel between the last two Olympic champions, Andrei Chemerkin and Ronny Weller, with European Champion Ashot Danielyan thrown in. Danielyan broke the snatch world record with a lift of 207.5 kg. Weller followed with another record: 210 kg. Then Hossein Rezazadeh, the pre-Olympic world record holder for the snatch, stepped up and successfully lifted 212.5 kg for the third world record in ten minutes. After Rezazadeh jerked 260 kg, the others were forced to go higher in an attempt to overcome him. Both Danielyan and Weller missed at 262.5 kg. Chemerkin called for 272.5 kg, but did not come close to clearing it. Danielyan was later disqualified when he tested positive for the steroid stanozolol. At the age of 22, Hossein Rezazadeh was the youngest winner ever of the super-heavyweight class.

2004 Athens C: 17, N: 15, D: 8.25. WR: 472.5 kg (Hossein Rezazadeh)

		SNATCH	JERK	TOTAL KG
1. Hossein Rezazadeh	IRN	210.0	262.5	472.5 EWR
2. Viktors Ščerbatihs	LAT	205.0	250.0	455.0
3. Velichko Cholakov	BUL	207.5	240.0	447.5
4. Hennadiy Krasilnikov	UKR	200.0	240.0	440.0
5. Oleksiy Kolokoltsev	UKR	195.0	242.5	437.5
6. Paweł Najdek	POL	190.0	240.0	430.0
7. Shane Hamman	USA	192.5	237.5	430.0
8. An Yong-kwon	KOR	202.5	225.0	427.5

As the defending Olympic champion, two-time defending world champion and world record holder, Hossein Rezazadeh was the overwhelming favorite in Athens. Rezazadeh was so popular in Iran that his 2003 wedding was broadcast live on television. At the 2004 Olympics, he made all three of his snatch attempts and then lifted 263.5 kilograms to break his own world record in the clean and jerk, and match his world record total. Germany's Ronny Weller, trying for his fifth medal in as many Olympics, injured himself on his second snatch, and dropped out of the competition.

2008 Beijing C: 14, N: 12, D: 8.19. WR: 472.5 kg (Hossein Rezazadeh)

		SNATCH	JERK	TOTAL KG
1. Matthias Steiner	GER	203.0	258.0	461.0
2. Yevgeny Chigishev	RUS	210.0	250.0	460.0
3. Viktors Ščerbatihs	LAT	206.0	242.0	448.0
4. Artem Udachyn	UKR	207.0	235.0	442.0
5. Ihor Shymechko	UKR	201.0	232.0	433.0
6. Rashid Sharifi	IRN	196.0	230.0	426.0
7. Grzegorz Kleszcz	POL	185.0	234.0	419.0
8. Almir Velagic	GER	188.0	225.0	413.0

A month before the 2008 Olympics, two-time defending Olympic champion and world record holder Hossein Rezazadeh announced his retirement from weightlifting, citing his doctor's advice that he should avoid "heavy and stressful activity".

With Rezazadeh out of the running, the super heavyweight favorite was defending Olympic silver medalist Viktors Ščerbatihs. Besides being the reigning world champion and four-time European champion, he was also a member of Latvia's parliament and had taken time off from his parliamentary duties to train for the Olympics.

Ščerbatihs was in third place after the snatch portion, trailing 2005 world silver medalist Yevgeny Chigishev and 2006 world silver medalist Artem Udachyn. In fourth place after missing his last snatch attempt, Austrian-born Matthias Steiner started with 246 kg (542.3 lbs) on his first clean and jerk lift, and then upped it to 248 kg (546.7 lbs) on his second.

Chigishev successfully lifted 250 kg (551.1 lbs) on his third and final lift, forcing Steiner to add 10 kg (22 lbs) to his final attempt, which he completed successfully to take the gold medal by a single kilogram. Steiner dedicated his medal to his late wife Susann, who had died in a car accident in 2007.

Ščerbatihs missed his last two clean and jerk attempts to finish third. "Being a member of parliament and a weightlifter at the same time is almost incompatible," he complained after the event, "You can't combine these two ways of living, it's either you lift or you work for parliament."

DISCONTINUED EVENTS

FLYWEIGHT

([1972–1992: 52kg—114.61 lbs] 1996: 54 kg—119.05 lbs)

1972 Munich C: 17, N: 13, D: 8.31. WR: 342.5 kg (Sándor Holczreiter)

		PRESS	SNATCH	JERK	TOTAL KG
1. Zygmunt Smalcerz	POL	112.5 OR	100.0	125.0	337.5
2. Lajos Szücs	HUN	107.5	95.0	127.5	330.0
3. Sándor Holczreiter	HUN	112.5 OR	92.5	122.5	327.5
4. Tetsuhide Sasaki	JPN	105.0	97.5	120.0	322.5
5. Gyi Aung	BUR	95.0	105.0 WR	120.0	320.0
6. Pak Dong-geun	PRK	97.5	90.0	130.0 OR	317.5
7. Chaiya Sukchinda	THA	100.0	92.5	120.0	312.5
8. Ion Hortopan	ROM	97.5	95.0	117.5	310.0

Charlie Depthios of Indonesia took an extra lift at the end of the competition and set a world jerk record of 132.5 kg.

1976 Montreal C: 23, N: 18, D: 7.18. WR: 242.5 kg (Aleksandr Voronin)

		SNATCH	JERK	TOTAL KG
1. Aleksandr Voronin	SOV/RUS	105.0	137.5 OR	242.5 EWR
2. György Kőszegi	HUN	107.5 OR	130.0	237.5
3. Mohammad Nasiri Seresht	IRN	100.0	135.0	235.0
4. Masatomo Takeuchi	JPN	105.0	127.5	232.5
5. Francisco Casamayor Fals	CUB	100.0	127.5	227.5
6. Stefan Leletko	POL	95.0	125.0	220.0
7. Boleslav Pachol	CZE	95.0	122.5	217.5
8. Daniel Núñez Aguiar	CUB	92.5	122.5	215.0

At 4 feet 8¼ inches, Voronin, an electrician from Kerekoo, was the shortest man in the competition. Taking an extra lift after winning the gold medal, he set a world jerk record of 141 kg.

1980 Moscow C: 18, N: 15, D: 7.20. WR: 247.5 kg (Aleksandr Voronin)

		SNATCH	JERK	TOTAL KG
1. Kanybek Osmanaliev	SOV/KYR	107.5	137.5 EOR	245.0 OR
2. Ho Bong-choi	PRK	110.0 OR	135.0	245.0
3. Han Gyong-si	PRK	110.0 OR	135.0	245.0
4. Béla Oláh	HUN	110.0 OR	135.0	245.0
5. Stefan Leletko	POL	105.0	135.0	240.0
6. Ferenc Hornyák	HUN	107.5	130.0	237.5
7. Francisco Casamayor Fals	CUB	102.5	130.0	232.5
8. Adjya Jugdernamjil	MGL	97.5	117.5	215.0

This unusually close contest was won by Osmanaliev as a result of his lower bodyweight. Han and Oláh had registered the same bodyweight, but Han was awarded third place when the two lifters were reweighed *after* the competition and Han was 100 grams (3½ ounces) lighter. Han set a world snatch record of 113 kg on his fourth attempt.

1984 Los Angeles-Westchester C: 20, N: 15, D: 7.29. WR: 262.5 kg (Neno Terziiski)

		SNATCH	JERK	TOTAL KG
1. Zeng Guoqiang	CHN	105.0	130.0	235.0
2. Zhou Peishun	CHN	107.5	127.5	235.0
3. Kazushito Manabe	JPN	102.5	130.0	232.5
4. Hidemi Miyashita	JPN	107.5	122.5	230.0
5. Mamen Suryaman	INA	102.5	125.0	227.5
6. Bang Hyo-mun	KOR	100.0	125.0	225.0
7. José Díaz López	PAN	95.0	125.0	220.0
8. Levent Erdogan	TUR	95.0	120.0	215.0

DISQ (Drugs): Mahmood Tarha (LEB) 230.0

No sport was as hard-hit by the 1984 Soviet-bloc boycott as weightlifting. Missing from the competition in the ten weight categories were all ten of the defending world champions, 29 of the 30 medalists at the last world championships, and 94 of the top 100 ranked lifters.

Zeng was awarded first place because he weighed 100 grams (3½ ounces) less than Zhou. Zeng, at 19 years of age, is the youngest weightlifting gold medalist in Olympic history. Tarha, in fourth place, was disqualified because he tested positive for anabolic steroids. At the Friendship Games, held in Varna, Bulgaria, for weightlifters from boycotting nations, the gold medal went to world record holder Neno Terziiski of Bulgaria with a total of 252.5 kg.

1988 Seoul C: 24, N: 18, D: 9.18. WR: 267.5 kg (He Zhuoqiang)

		SNATCH	JERK	TOTAL KG
1. Sevdalin Marinov	BUL	120.0 WR	150.0 OR	270.0 WR
2. Chun Byung-kwan	KOR	112.5	147.5	260.0
3. He Zhuoqiang	CHN	112.5	145.0	257.5
4. Zhang Shoulie	CHN	115.0	142.5	257.5
5. Jacek Gutowski	POL	112.5	135.0	247.5
6. I. Traian Cihărean	ROM	110.0	130.0	240.0
7. Béla Oláh	HUN	107.5	130.0	237.5
8. Kazushito Manabe	JPN	105.0	125.0	230.0

Despite He Zhuoqiang's having set a world record three months before the Olympics, Marinov had dominated the division since 1985, when he won the world championship at age 17. In 1995 Marinov failed a doping test for steroids.

1992 Barcelona C: 17, N: 13 , D: 7.27. WR: 272.5 kg (Ivan Ivanov)

		SNATCH	JERK	TOTAL KG
1. Ivan Ivanov	BUL	115.0	150.0 EOR	265.0
2. Lin Qisheng	CHN	115.0	147.5	262.5
3. I. Traian Cihărean	ROM	112.5	140.0	252.5
4. Ko Kwang-ku	KOR	112.5	140.0	252.5
5. Halil Mutlu	TUR	112.5	135.0	247.5
6. Gil Nam-su	PRK	100.0	135.0	235.0
7. HuHumberto Fuentes Rodríguez	VEN	100.0	130.0	230.0
8. Jośe Ibáñez Puig	SPA	100.0	127.5	227.5

Ivan Ivanov, one of four Ivan Ivanovs on the 1992 Bulgarian Olympic team, had won the last three world championships.

Albania made its first appearance at the Olympics in 1972. Then the Albanians set a record by boycotting the next four Olympics. In 1992 Albania returned to the Games, after 20 years away. Their first scheduled competitor was Genc Barkici, a flyweight weightlifter who had placed fifth at the European championships three months earlier. Unfortunately, Barkici got his finger caught in a door at the arena the day of the competition and he was forced to withdraw.

Both Ivan Ivanov and Traian Cihărean tested positive for steroids at the 2000 Sydney Olympics, Cihărean before the Games began and Ivanov after appearing to win a medal.

1996 Atlanta C: 22, N: 19, D: 7.20. WR: 290.0 kg (Halil Mutlu)

		SNATCH	JERK	TOTAL KG
1. Halil Mutlu	TUR	132.5 WR	155.0 OR	287.5 OR
2. Zhang Xiangsen	CHN	130.0	150.0	280.0
3. Sevdalin Minchev	BUL	125.0	152.5	277.5
4. Lan Shizhang	CHN	125.0	150.0	275.0
5. I. Traian Cihărean	ROM	120.0	145.0	265.0
6. Ivan Ivanov	BUL	112.5	145.0	257.5
7. Ko Kwang-ku	KOR	115.0	140.0	255.0
8. Juan Carlos Fernández Garzón	COL	110.0	145.0	255.0

Like his idol Naim Süleymanoğlu, 1.50 meter (4-foot 11-inch) Halil Mutlu was born in Bulgaria, but emigrated to Turkey.

FIRST HEAVYWEIGHT

([1980–1992:100 kg—220.46 lbs; 1996: 99 kg—218.26 lbs])

1980 Moscow C: 17, N: 13, D: 7.28. WR: 402.5 kg (David Rigert)

		SNATCH	JERK	TOTAL KG
1. Ota Zaremba	CZE	180.0 OR	215.0	395.0 OR
2. Igor Nikitin	SOV/RUS	177.5	215.0	392.5
3. Alberto Blanco Fernández	CUB	172.5	212.5	385.0
4. Michael Hennig	GDR	165.0	217.5 OR	382.5
5. János Sólyomvári	HUN	175.0	205.0	380.0
6. Manfred Funke	GDR	170.0	207.5	377.5
7. Anton Baraniak	CZE	165.0	210.0	375.0
8. László Varga	HUN	172.5	195.0	367.5

1984 Los Angeles-Westchester C: 16, N: 14, D: 8.6. WR: 440 kg (Yuri Zakharevich)

		SNATCH	JERK	TOTAL KG
1. Rolf Milser	GER	167.5	217.5 EOR	385.0
2. Vasile Groapă	ROM	165.0	217.5 EOR	382.5
3. Pekka Niemi	FIN	160.0	207.5	367.5
4. Kevin Roy	CAN	160.0	197.5	357.5
5. Ken Clark	USA	155.0	197.5	352.5
6. Franz Langthaler	AUT	162.5	187.5	350.0
7. Richard Shanko	USA	155.0	195.0	350.0
8. Jean-Marie Kretz	FRA	150.0	192.5	342.5

International weightlifting competitions are separated into two sessions. In the afternoon the less-distinguished lifters take part in the "B" session and in the evening the leading contenders lift in the "A" session. The top lifter in the 100-kg division "B" session was 31-year-old Pekka Niemi. Since no "B" lifter had ever won a medal in an international meet, Niemi skipped the evening session and went instead to the Los Angeles Coliseum to watch the track and field events. Niemi was playing with an Electronic Messaging System computer terminal in the press section when a German TV reporter said, "Let's see what you did." Niemi pushed some buttons and on the screen appeared the news that he had finished third. Meanwhile, back at the weightlifting venue at Loyola Marymount University, the medal ceremony was being delayed while officials unsuccessfully searched for Niemi or anyone else from the Finnish delegation. Finally they went ahead with the presentation with the bronze medal platform empty. When Niemi called home to share the good news, he learned that his family had learned of his good fortune on Finnish television before he himself had found out in Los Angeles. The next day Niemi received his medal at a special ceremony, after which he patiently signed 200 autographs. In 1985, Niemi was arrested in Finland for purchasing steroids on the black market.

Six weeks later, at the Friendship Games, Pavel Kuznetsov of the Soviet Union won first place with a lift total of 427.5 kg. Second was Andor Szanyi of Hungary at 390 kg.

1988 Seoul C: 21, N: 17, D: 9.26. WR: 440 kg (Yuri Zakharevich)

		SNATCH	JERK	TOTAL KG
1. Pavel Kuznetsov	SOV/RUS	190.0 OR	235.0 OR	425.0 OR
2. Nicolae "Nicu" Vlad	ROM	185.0	217.5	402.5
3. Peter Immesberger	GER	175.0	220.0	395.0
4. János Bökfi	HUN	180.0	212.5	392.5
5. Francis Tournefier	FRA	170.0	215.0	385.0
6. Denis Garon	CAN	160.0	222.5	382.5
7. Hwang Woo-won	KOR	162.5	220.0	382.5
8. Franz Langthaler	AUT	172.5	205.0	377.5

DISQ (Drugs): Andor Szanyi (HUN) 407.5

Kuznetsov was a graduate of the Vladimir Polytechnical Institute with a degree in weaving technology.

1992 Barcelona C: 25, N: 21, D: 8.2. WR: 440 kg (Yuri Zakharevich)

		SNATCH	JERK	TOTAL KG
1. Vikkor Tregubov	RUS	190.0 EOR	220.0	410.0
2. Timur Taimazov	UKR	185.0	217.5	402.5
3. Waldemar Malak	POL	185.0	215.0	400.0
4. Francis Tournefier	FRA	170.0	217.5	387.5
5. Petar Stefanov	BUL	170.0	210.0	380.0
6. Andrei Danisov	ISR	175.0	202.5	377.5
7. Udo Guse	GER	167.5	210.0	377.5
8. Yoshimitsu Nishimoto	JPN	165.0	207.5	372.5

Bronze medalist Waldemar Malak was killed in a car accident three months after the Olympics, on November 14. He was 22 years old.

1996 Atlanta C: 28, N: 25, D: 7.28. WR: 417.5 kg (Sergei Syrtsov)

		SNATCH	JERK	TOTAL KG
1. Akakios "Kakhi" Kakhiashvilis (Kakhi Kakhiachvili)	GRE	185.0	235.0 WR	420.0 WR
2. Anatoly Khrapaty	KAZ	187.5	222.5	410.0
3. Denys Gotfrid	UKR	187.5	215.0	402.5
4. Stanislav Rybalchenko	UKR	182.5	212.5	395.0
5. Vyacheslav Rubin	RUS	175.0	215.0	390.0
6. Dmitri Smirnov	RUS	175.0	215.0	390.0
7. Igor Sadykov	GER	177.5	207.5	385.0
8. Aghvan Grigorian	ARM	172.5	207.5	380.0

In 1992, Kakhi Kakhiachvili, representing Georgia (and the "Unified Team,") won the middle heavyweight gold medal by weighing 20 grams less than Sergei Syrtsov. At the 1995 world championships he again defeated Syrtsov by lower bodyweight, but by this time he had a new name—Akakios Kakiashvilis, a new nation—Greece (his mother was Greek) and a new division—first heavyweight. In Atlanta Syrtsov moved up in weight and Kakhiashvilis faced a new challenger: Anatoly Khrapaty. Khrapaty led Kakhiashvilis by 2.5 kg after the snatch. Kakhiashvilis moved ahead with a first jerk of 220 kg. Khrapaty hoisted 222.5 kg to regain the lead, but Kakhiashvilis responded with a lift of 225 kg. Khrapaty failed with a final attempt at 227.5 kg. With the gold medal secure, Kakhiashvilis delighted the crowd by trying—and successfully lifting—235 kg to break Khrapaty's 2½-month-old world record of 228 kg.

Kakhiashvilis became only the second athlete in Olympic history to earn gold medals while representing two distictly different countries. The first was rugby player Daniel Carroll who represented Australia in 1908 and the United States in 1920.

In 1996, all of the top nine lifters in the first heavyweight division had originally competed for the former Soviet Union. In Atlanta, they represented seven different countries.

WOMEN

The first world championships for women were held in Daytona Beach, Florida, in 1987.

FLYWEIGHT
(48 kg—106 lbs)

1896–1996 not held

2000 Sydney C: 12, N: 9, D: 9.17. WR: 197.5 kg (Liu Xiuhua)

		SNATCH	JERK	TOTAL KG
1. Tara Nott	USA	82.5	102.5	185.0
2. Raema Lisa Rumbewas	INA	80.0	105.0	185.0
3. Sri Indriyan	INA	82.5	100.0	182.5
4. Win Kay Thi	BUR	80.0	100.0	180.0
5. Robin Goad	USA	77.5	100.0	177.5
6. Kaori Niyanagi	JPN	75.0	100.0	175.0
7. Eva Giganti	ITA	77.5	92.5	170.0
8. Sabryna Richard	FRA	70.0	87.5	157.5

DISQ (Drugs): Izabela Dragneva (BUL) 190.0

Tara Nott was an unlikely Olympic champion in that she did not become interested in competitive weightlifting until she was 23 years old and she had only placed ninth at the last world championships. When she qualified for the US team, she said that if she earned a bronze medal at the Olympics she would be "in shock." However, a strong performance and a series of unexpected twists propelled Nott to the top. Liu Xiuhua of China set a world record of 197.5 kg three months before the Sydney Games, but in order to counteract Chinese dominance in the sport, each nation was only allowed to enter four of the seven weight classes. The Chinese chose to drop Liu. The world champion was Donka Mincheva of Bulgaria. But Mincheva had an appendectomy one month before the Olympics and, although she did compete, she was unable to make a single lift and was eliminated. The gold medal was awarded to another Bulgarian, Izabeta Dragneva. But then Dragneva tested positive for the diuretic furosemide and her medal was taken away. Nott was informed by cellphone that she had been elevated to Olympic champion and that a makeshift medal presentation ceremony would be held at the Olympic Village 90 minutes later. Such ceremonies were considered an embarrassment to both the IOC and the International Weightlifting Federation, so this one was scheduled to take place at the same time as the women's super-heavyweight final. Nott's friend, Cheryl Haworth, was competing in that event and Nott chose to root her on rather than attend the ceremony, which thus took place without her.

In fifth place was 30-year-old Robin Goad, the only woman to take part in both the inaugural women's world championships in 1987 and the inaugural Olympic championships thirteen years later. Maria Jorge of Brazil finished in ninth place at the age of 43. She came from a poor family, washed clothes for a living and did not take up weightlifting until she was 34 years old.

The honor of the first woman to compete in weightlifting in the Olympics went to 16-year-old Dika Toua of Papua New Guinea. Unnerved by the excitement of the moment, she dropped her first snatch attempt of 45 kg, but then returned and lifted the bar with ease.

2004 Athens C: 15, N: 14, D: 8.14. WR: 207.5 kg (Wang Mingjuan)

		SNATCH	JERK	TOTAL KG
1. Nurcan Taylan	TUR	97.5 WR	112.5	210.0 WR
2. Li Zhuo	CHN	92.5	112.5	205.0
3. Aree Wiratthaworn	THA	85.0	115.0	200.0
4. Namecrakpam Kunjarani Devi	IND	82.5	107.5	190.0
5. Izabela Dragneva	BUL	82.5	105.0	187.5
6. Chen Han-tung	TAI	80.0	102.5	182.5
7. Blessed Udoh	NGR	75.0	105.0	180.0
8. Choe Un-sim	PRK	82.5	95.0	177.5

DISQ (Drugs) Aye Khine Nan (BUR) 190.0

The favorite was Li Zhuo, who beat out two-time world champion Wang Mingjuan for a place on the Chinese team. Twenty-year-old Nurcan Taylan, the 2004

European champion in the 53-kilogram division, broke Li's world record with a second lift of 95kg, and then lifted 97.5 kg to take a 5-kilogram lead into the clean and jerk. Taylan jerked 112.5 kilograms with her final attempt, forcing Li to try 120 kg, 3.5 kg more than her world record. Li made two attempts at the weight but was unsuccessful.

Taylan was the first Turkish woman to win a gold medal. She was rewarded with $273,000 and a phone call from Turkish Prime Minister Recep Tayyip Erdoğan. In September 2004, the Turkish women's weightlifting coach, Mehmet Ustundag, was arrested and charged with sexual harassment and molestation of three members of the women's Turkish weightlifting team. Taylan, the only team member to speak out in support of the coach, stirred up further controversy by accusing her teammates of being lesbians.

2008 Beijing C: 14, N: 11, D: 8.9. WR: 217 (Yang Lian)

		SNATCH	JERK	TOTAL KG
1. Chen Xiexia	CHN	95.0	117.0 OR	212.0 OR
2. Sibel Özkan	TUR	88.0	111.0	199.0
3. Chen Wei-ling	TAI	84.0	112.0	196.0
4. Im Jeong-hwa	KOR	86.0	110.0	196.0
5. Pensiri Laosirikul	THA	85.0	110.0	195.0
6. Hiromi Miyake	JPN	80.0	105.0	185.0
7. Mélanie Noel	FRA	80.0	97.0	177.0
8. Misaki Oshiro	JPN	80.0	92.0	172.0

Reigning world champion Chen Xiexia dominated both rounds, successfully completing the six heaviest lifts of the competition. Chen so far outclassed the rest of the field that her starting totals—90 kg (198.4 lbs) in the snatch and 113 kilograms (249.1 pounds) in the clean and jerk—would have been enough for the gold medal.

Defending Olympic champion Nurcan Taylan crashed out after failing three attempts at 84 kg (185.1 lbs) in the snatch.

FEATHERWEIGHT

(53 kg—117 lbs)

1896–1996 not held

2000 Sydney C: 10, N: 10, D: 9.18. WR: 217.5 kg (Meng Xianjuan)

		SNATCH	JERK	TOTAL KG
1. Yang Xia	CHN	100.0 WR	125.0 WR	225.0 WR
2. Li Feng-Ying	TAI	97.5	115.0	212.5
3. Winarni Binti Slamet	INA	90.0	112.5	202.5
4. Franca Gbodo	NGR	85.0	110.0	195.0
5. Win Swe Swe	BUR	85.0	110.0	195.0
6. Thing Baijan Sanamacha Chanu	IND	85.0	110.0	195.0
7. Mari Nakaga	JPN	77.5	105.0	182.5
8. Marioara Munteanu	ROM	82.5	97.5	180.0

Yang Xia and Li Feng-Ying both grew up in Hunan Province in China. However Li married the national weightlifting coach of Taiwan and changed citizenship. They both broke Meng Xianjuan's snatch world record, but it was Yang who finished best at 100 kg. Li held the clean and jerk world record of 121.5 kg, but Yang topped it twice with lifts of 122.5 kg and 125 kg. Yang was a member of the Tujia ethnic minority.

2004 Athens C: 8, N: 8, D: 8.15. WR: 225 kg (Yang Xia)

		SNATCH	JERK	TOTAL KG
1. Udomporn Polsak	THA	97.5	125.0	222.5
2. Raema Lisa Rumbewas	INA	95.0	115.0	210.0
3. Mabel Mosquera Mena	COL	87.5	110.0	197.5
4. Marioara Munteanu	ROM	85.0	105.0	190.0
5. Anastasiya Novikova	BLR	87.5	102.5	190.0
6. Dika Toua	PNG	75.0	102.5	177.5
7. Virginie Lachaume	FRA	75.0	100.0	175.0

DISQ (Drugs): Thing Baijan Sanamacha Chanu (IND) 190.0

Reigning world champion Udomporn Polsak missed only one of six attempts, taking the lead after the snatch and winning easily to become the first Thai woman to earn an Olympic gold medal.

2008 Beijing C: 9, N: 9, D: 8.10. WR: 226 kg (Qiu Hongxia)

		SNATCH	JERK	TOTAL KG
1. Prapawadee Jaroenrattanatarakoon	THA	95.0	126.0 OR	221.0
2. Yoon Jin-hee	KOR	94.0	119.0	213.0
3. Anastasiya Novikova	BLR	95.0	118.0	213.0
4. Raema Lisa Rumbewas	INA	91.0	115.0	206.0
5. Yudelquis Maridalin Contreras	DOM	93.0	111.0	204.0
6. Melanie Roach	USA	83.0	110.0	193.0
7. Julia Rohde	GER	82.0	103.0	185.0
8. Dika Toua	PNG	80.0	104.0	184.0

After failing to make the Thai Olympic team in 2004 and placing second at the 2005 world championships and 2006 Asian Games, Junpim Kuntatean was told by a fortune teller that if she changed her name she would win an Olympic gold medal. Kuntatean took the advice, changing her name in 2007 to Prapawadee Jaroenrattanatarakoon ("Good Girl, Prosperous").

Jaroenrattanatarakoon and reigning world silver medalist Anastasiya Novikova finished the snatch portion tied at 95 kg (209.4 lbs) after both missed their final lift attempts.

Jaroenrattanatarakoon successfully lifted 120 kg (264.5 lbs) on her first clean and jerk attempt, and then moved up to 126 kg (277.7 lbs) with her second lift, an Olympic record. She tried a world record weight of 130 kg (286.6 lbs) on her final attempt, but couldn't complete the lift. Reigning world bronze medalist Yoon Jin-hee equalled Novikova's total weight on her final lift, and took silver on account of her lower bodyweight.

2008 Women Featherweight
Prapawadee Jaroenrattanatarakoon

At 31 letters, Prapawadee Jaroenrattanatarakoon set the record for the longest name of any Olympic champion. It was so long that it did not fit on the digital scoreboard in Beijing . . . so she was listed as "J."

LIGHTWEIGHT
(58 kg—128 lbs)

1896–1996 not held

2000 Sydney C: 17, N: 16, D: 9.18. WR: 235.0 kg (Chen Yanqing)

		SNATCH	JERK	TOTAL KG
1. Soraya Jiménez Mendivil	MEX	95.0	127.5	222.5
2. Ri Song-hui	PRK	97.5	122.5	220.0
3. Khassaraporn Suta	THA	92.5	117.5	210.0
4. Maryse Turcotte	CAN	90.0	115.0	205.0
5. Aleksandra Klejnowska	POL	90.0	112.5	202.5
6. Khin Moe New	BUR	90.0	110.0	200.0
7. Nataliya Skakun	UKR	85.0	112.5	197.5
8. Anna Batsyushko	BLR	90.0	107.5	197.5

Because China was only allowed to enter four lifters in Sydney and there were seven weight classes, world champion and world record holder Chen Yanqing did not take part in the competition. This left the favorite's role to Ri Song-hui, but she was given an unexpected challenge by Soraya Jiménez, whose pre-Olympic best was only 197.5 kg. Ri led by 2.5 kg after the snatch and expanded her lead to 5 kg after she and Jiménez had taken their first attempts. But then something strange happened. Ri appeared late for her second attempt, 122.5 kg, and had just laid her hands on the bar when time ran out and she was given a no-lift. The North Koreans argued that Ri had been detained by a competition marshal, but the International Weightlifting Federation ruled that the North Koreans had simply misjudged how much time was left. Ri reappeared and lifted 122.5 kg. But that was ruled her final attempt. Jiménez called for 127.5 kg, 15 kilograms more than her best lift at the 1999 world championships, and, after a great strain, she held it. Bronze medalist Khassaraporn Suta was the first Thai athlete to earn a medal in a sport other than boxing.

2004 Athens C: 14, N: 13, D: 8.16. WR: 240.0 kg (Wang Li)

		SNATCH	JERK	TOTAL KG
1. Chen Yanqing	CHN	107.5	130.0	237.5
2. Ri Song-hui	PRK	102.5	130.0	232.5
3. Wandee Kameaim	THA	102.5	127.5	230.0
4. Aylin Daşdelen	TUR	100.0	125.0	225.0
5. Aleksandra Klejnowska	POL	97.5	122.5	220.0
6. Pak Hyon-suk	PRK	95.0	122.5	217.5
7. Alexandra Escobar Guerrero	ECU	95.0	120.0	215.0
8. Patmawati	INA	95.0	117.5	212.5

The Chinese team was so deep in the 58-kilogram category that it included the world record holder, Wang Li, the 2002 world champion, Song Zhijuan, the 2003 world champion, Sun Caiyan, and the 2003 Asian Games champion Zhou Yan. Team officials did not select any of them for the 2004 Olympics. Instead, they turned to 25-year-old Chen Yanqing of Suzhou, who had retired for more than two years after not being chosen for the Chinese Olympic team in 2000. Chen's victory in Athens was an exact repeat of her last major international win, the 1999 world championships, which was also held in Athens and which she also won by beating Ri Song-hui by 5 kilograms.

2008 Beijing C: 12, N: 11, D: 8.11. WR: 251.0 kg (Chen Yanqing)

		SNATCH	JERK	TOTAL KG
1. Chen Yanqing	CHN	106.0	138.0 OR	244.0 OR
2. Marina Shainova	RUS	98.0	129.0	227.0
3. O Jong-ae	PRK	95.0	131.0	226.0
4. Wandee Kameaim	THA	98.0	128.0	226.0
5. Alexandra Escobar Guerrero	ECU	99.0	124.0	223.0
6. Romela Begaj	ALB	98.0	118.0	216.0
7. Aleksandra Klejnowska	POL	95.0	120.0	215.0
8. Roxana Cocoş	ROM	89.0	115.0	204.0

Reigning Olympic champion and world record holder Chen Yanqing had little difficulty defending her title. She lifted 100 kg (220.4 lbs) on her first snatch attempt and went on to set an Olympic record of 138 kg (304.2 lbs) on her final clean and jerk lift, also setting an Olympic record of 244 kilograms (537.9 pounds) for her total weight.

North Korea's O Jong-ae briefly set an Olympic record of 131 kg (288.8 lbs) with her third clean and jerk lift, but was edged out for the silver medal by 2007 world silver medalist Marina Shainova on her final lift. O beat defending Olympic bronze medalist Wandee Kameaim to finish third because of lower bodyweight.

MIDDLEWEIGHT
(63 kg—139 lbs)

1896–1996 not held

2000 Sydney C: 9, N: 9, D: 9.18. WR: 240.0 kg (Chen Yui-lien)

		SNATCH	JERK	TOTAL KG
1. Chen Xiamin	CHN	112.5 WR	130.0	242.5 WR
2. Valentina Popova	RUS	107.5	127.5	235.0
3. Ioanna Khatzioannou	GRE	97.5	125.0	222.5
4. Saipin Detsaeng	THA	102.5	120.0	222.5
5. Kim Yong-ok	PRK	90.0	115.0	205.0
6. Amanda Phillips	AUS	82.5	107.5	190.0
7. Josefa Pérez Carmona	SPA	85.0	102.5	187.5
8. Nora Köppel	ARG	80.0	102.5	182.5

Chen Xiaomin of southern Guangdong province won her first world championship in 1993 at the age of 16. She dominated the light-heavyweight class until 1997, when she was suspended for doping. The announcement of her return and her drop in weight class scared away the competition and only eight other women entered the middleweight class in Sydney.

2004 Athens C: 9, N: 8, D: 8.18. WR: 247.5 kg (Liu Xia)

		SNATCH	JERK	TOTAL KG
1. Natalia Skakun	UKR	107.5	135.0	242.5
2. Hanna Batsyushko	BLR	115.0 WR	127.5	242.5
3. Tatsiana Stukalava	BLR	100.0	122.5	222.5
4. Hayet Sassi	TUN	95.0	120.0	215.0
5. Kim Soo-kyung	KOR	92.6	122.5	215.0
6. Thị Thiết Nguyễn	VIE	95.0	110.0	205.0
7. Leila Françoise Lassouani	ALG	85.0	115.0	200.0

DNF: Anastasia Tsakiri (GRE)

Hanna Batsyushko took the lead by breaking her own world snatch record with a lift of 115 kilograms. In the clean and jerk, Batsyushko needed two attempts to clear 120 kilograms. World champion Natalia Skakun put the pressure on by lifting 125 kg on her first attempt. Batsyushko responded by successfully lifting 127.5 kg with her final attempt. Skakun raised 135 kg with her second lift, giving her the gold based on lower bodyweight.

2008 Beijing C: 19, N: 18, D: 8.12. WR: 257.5 kg (Liu Haixia)

		SNATCH	JERK	TOTAL KG
1. Pak Hyon-suk	PRK	106.0	135.0	241.0
2. Irina Nekrasova	KAZ	110.0	130.0	240.0
3. Lu Ying-chi	TAI	104.0	127.0	231.0
4. Christine Girard	CAN	102.0	126.0	228.0
5. Nguyễn Thị Thiết	VIE	100.0	125.0	225.0
6. Kim Su-gyeong	KOR	98.0	127.0	225.0
7. Ruth Kasirye	NOR	103.0	121.0	224.0
8. Luz Acosta Valdez	MEX	103.0	120.0	223.0

With weightlifting powerhouse China limited to four female weightlifters, reigning world champion and world record holder Liu Haixia was passed over for the 2008 Chinese Olympic team.

This made reigning world silver medalist Svetlana Tsarukayeva the favorite in the middleweight event. However, starting off at 107 kg (235.8 lbs), she failed all three snatch attempts and was eliminated. Trailing by 4 kg (8.8 lbs) going into the clean and jerk, reigning world bronze medalist Pak Hyon-suk missed her first two attempts at 135 kg (297.6 lbs) and faced elimination. She completed the lift on her third try, though, edging Irina Nekrasova by one kilogram to win the gold medal.

"I am overjoyed by the fact that I have brought joy to our dear general [Kim Jong-Il]," said an unsmiling Pak after the competition.

Taiwan's Lu Ying-chi was pleasantly surprised by her bronze medal after her coach lied and told her she was trailing in seventh place to help ease her nerves.

LIGHT HEAVYWEIGHT
(69 kg—152.5 lbs)

1896–1996 not held

2000 Sydney C: 15, N: 13, D: 9.19. WR: 255.0 kg (Lin Weining)

		SNATCH	JERK	TOTAL KG
1. Lin Weining	CHN	110.0	132.5	242.5
2. Erzsébet Márkus	HUN	112.5 WR	130.0	242.5
3. Malleswari Karnam	IND	110.0	130.0	240.0
4. Milena Trendafilova	BUL	100.0	132.5	232.5
5. Daniela Kerkelova	BUL	100.0	132.5	232.5
6. Irina Kasimova	RUS	100.0	130.0	230.0
7. Pawina Thongsuk	THA	100.0	125.0	225.0
8. Beata Prei	POL	100.0	125.0	225.0

Erzsébet Márkus set a world record in the snatch, but still led Lin Weining and Malleswari Karnam by only 2.5 kg. Malleswari and Márkus both jerked 130 kg with their second attempt, but then Lin opened with a successful lift of 132.5 kg to put her ahead of Márkus because of her lower bodyweight. When Malleswari and Márkus missed at 137.5 kg, the medals were decided. Malleswari was the first Indian woman ever to win an Olympic medal. She had won world championships in 1994 and 1995, but the Olympics was her first appearance in the light-heavyweight class. She had been informed that she was going to the Olympics only four days before the team left India.

2004 Athens C: 11, N: 10, D: 8.19. WR: 270.0 kg (Liu Chunhong)

		SNATCH	JERK	TOTAL KG
1. Liu Chunhong	CHN	122.5	152.5 WR	275.0 WR
2. Eszter Krutzler	HUN	117.5	145.0	262.5
3. Zarema Kasayeva	RUS	117.5	145.0	262.5
4. Slaveyka Ruzhinska	BUL	115.0	135.0	250.0
5. Vanda Maslovska	UKR	110.0	135.0	245.0
6. Milena Trendafilova	BUL	105.0	132.5	237.5
7. Madeleine Yamechi	CAM	105.0	130.0	235.0
8. Ubaldina Valoyes	COL	105.0	127.5	232.5

At the 2003 world championships, 18-year-old Liu Chunhong set world records in both the snatch and the jerk, on her way to a 270 kg–262.5 kg victory over Eszter Krutzler. The following year, at the Athens Olympics, Krutzler matched her world championships total, while Liu increased both her snatch and jerk by 2.5 kilograms. After jerking 147.5 kilograms with her first attempt, Liu was allowed to try 153 kg in order to break her clean and jerk world record, which she did. Because Olympic results are calculated only in 2.5 kilogram increments, the official results listed her lift as only 152.5 kg.

2008 Beijing C: 10, N: 9, D: 8.13. WR: 276.0 kg (Oksana Slivenko)

		SNATCH	JERK	TOTAL KG
1. Liu Chunhong	CHN	128.0 WR	158.0 WR	286.0 WR
2. Oksana Slivenko	RUS	115.0	140.0	255.0
3. Nataliya Davydova	UKR	115.0	135.0	250.0
4. Leydi Solís Arboleda	COL	105.0	135.0	240.0
5. Abir Khalil	EGY	105.0	133.0	238.0
6. Tulia Ángela Medina Alcalde	COL	106.0	124.0	230.0
7. Anna Batyushko	BLR	105.0	120.0	225.0
8. Rika Saito	JPN	87.0	122.0	209.0

Two-time reigning world champion and world record holder Oksana Slivenko was considered a pre-competition contender, but was left behind by defending Olympic champion Liu Chunhong.

Liu opened with a lift of 120 kg (264.6 lbs) in the snatch, setting world records with her next two lifts, 125 kg (275.6 lbs) and 128 kg (282.2 lbs). Backed by a noisy, mostly-Chinese crowd, Liu successfully completed all three clean-and-jerk attempts, setting a world record of 158 kg (348.3 lbs) and breaking the total world record by 10 kg (22 lbs).

After the competition Liu revealed that an intense training regimen had allowed her to spend only six days with her parents in the four years since she won the Athens gold medal.

HEAVYWEIGHT

(75 kg—165.5 lbs)

1896–1996 not held

2000 Sydney C: 11, N: 11, D: 9.20. WR: 257.5 kg (Sun Tianni)

		SNATCH	JERK	TOTAL KG
1. María Isabel Urrutia Ocoró	COL	110.0	135.0	245.0
2. Ruth Ogbeifo	NGR	105.0	140.0	245.0
3. Kuo Yi-hang	TAI	107.5	137.5	245.0
4. Kim Soon-hee	KOR	105.0	135.0	240.0
5. Gyöngyi Likerecz	HUN	105.0	122.5	227.5
6. Svetlana Khabirova	RUS	102.5	125.0	227.5
7. Cara Heads-Lane	USA	102.5	120.0	222.5
8. Wanda Rijo Contreras	DOM	95.0	120.0	215.0

Maria Isabel Urrutia first competed in the Olympics in 1988—as a discus thrower. She won her first weightlifting world championship in 1990. By the time women's weightlifting was added to the Olympic program in 2000, Urrutia was already 35 years old. After her final lift, she was tied with Ruth Ogbeifo and Kuo Yi-hang, but was in first place because of her lower bodyweight and undoubtedly thankful for every gram of the 15 kilograms she had lost to qualify for the heavyweight division. The competition was not over until Kuo and Kim Soon-hee missed at 140 kg and Ogbeifo at 142.5 kg. As the first South American woman to win an Olympic championship and the first Colombian champion of either sex, Urrutia beame a major celebrity back home, particularly as she came from a poor familly. One year after the Olympics, Urrutia was suspended when she tested positive for both the anabolic steroid nandrolone and the stimulant ephedrine. Yet her popularity was unaffected and, only five months later, she was elected to congress.

2004 Athens C: 16, N: 15, D: 8.20. WR: 270.0 kg (Sun Ruiping)

		SNATCH	JERK	TOTAL KG
1. Pawina Thongsuk	THA	122.5	150.0	272.5 WR
2. Natalya Zabolotnaya	RUS	125.0	147.5	272.5 WR
3. Valentyna Popova	RUS	120.0	145.0	265.0
4. Gyöngyi Likerecz	HUN	115.0	142.5	257.5
5. Khristina Ioannidi	GRE	112.5	142.5	255.0
6. Tatyana Khromova	KAZ	117.5	135.0	252.5
7. Kim Soon-hee	KOR	112.5	137.5	250.0
8. Tulia Ángela Medina Alcalde	COL	112.5	132.5	245.0

The gold medal in Athens was up for grabs after Chinese world record holder Shang Shichun was stripped of her 2003 world championship title, and her world record, and banned for two years after failing a drug test. The parents of Pawina Thongsuk encouraged her to pursue weightlifting, but they died before it became an Olympic sport. Pawina lived with the Thai weightlifting team from the age of sixteen. The light heavyweight world champion in 2002, she was 25 when she competed in the Athens Games. The 2003 European champion, Natalya Zabolotnaya, led Pawina by 2.5 kg after the snatch. In the clean and jerk, Zabolotnaya began with a successful lift of 142.5 kilograms. Pawina started with 145 kg and moved ahead because of her lower bodyweight. Zabolotnaya then cleared 147.5 kg, but Pawina moved ahead again with a 150-kilogram clearance. Both lifters missed their final attempt.

2008 Beijing C: 12, N: 11, D: 8.15. WR: 286.0 kg (Svetlana Podebedova)

		SNATCH	JERK	TOTAL KG
1. Cao Lei	CHN	128.0 OR	154.0 OR	282.0 OR
2. Alla Vazhenina	KAZ	119.0	147.0	266.0
3. Nadezhda Yevstyukhina	RUS	117.0	147.0	264.0
4. Irina Kulesha	BLR	118.0	137.0	255.0
5. Lidia Valentín Pérez	SPA	115.0	135.0	250.0
6. Damaris Gabriela Aguirre Aldaz	MEX	109.0	136.0	245.0
7. Ubaldina Valoyes Cuesta	COL	110.0	134.0	244.0
8. Jeane Lassen	CAN	105.0	135.0	240.0

Two-time world champion Cao Lei led throughout the competition, successfully completing her first five lifts, and setting three Olympic records in the process, including one for a total lift of 282 kg (621.7 lbs). The gold medal secure, Cao attempted to break the world record for total lift on her final clean and jerk attempt, but was unable to complete the lift.

The 24-year-old Cao dedicated her medal to her mother, who had passed away shortly before the Olympics. Cao was not told of her mother's death until after the funeral so as not to distract her from training.

Twelfth-place finisher Elizabeth Poblete of Chile made worldwide headlines in 2009 when she unexpectedly gave birth to a baby boy while straining during an attempted training lift. The 22-year-old Poblete had been feeling unwell, but had not been aware she was pregnant. The baby was rushed to an intensive care unit, but sadly died a few days later.

SUPER HEAVYWEIGHT

(Over 75 kg—165.5 lbs)

1896–1996 not held

2000 Sydney C: 11, N: 11, D: 9.22. WR: 285.0 kg (Ding Meiyuan)

		SNATCH	JERK	TOTAL KG
1. Ding Meiyuan	CHN	135.0 WR	165.0 WR	300.0 WR
2. Agata Wróbel	POL	132.5	162.5	295.0
3. Cheryl Haworth	USA	125.0	145.0	270.0
4. Carmenza Delgado Castillo	COL	115.0	145.0	260.0
5. Helen Idahosa	NGR	110.0	140.0	250.0
6. Monique Riesterer	GER	112.5	132.5	245.0
7. Mun Kyung-ae	KOR	110.0	135.0	245.0
8. Olivia Baker	NZL	105.0	130.0	235.0

The contest for World's Strongest Woman was a straight duel between 21-year-old Ding Meiyuan and 19-year-old Agata Wróbel, who had finished first and second at the 1999 world championships, 27.5 kg ahead of the rest of the field. Wróbel broke her own snatch world record with a third-attempt lift of 132.5 kg. Ding had two tries left. She missed her first attempt at 135, but succeeded with the second. The pre-Olympic clean and jerk record was 161 kg. Both Wróbel and Ding bettered this with second round lifts of 162.5 kg. When Ding closed with a successful 165, the championship was decided. The bronze medal went to 17-year-old Cheryl Haworth who, at 139.38 kilograms (307¼ pounds), was the heaviest woman ever to take part in the Olympics.

2004 Athens C: 12, N: 11, D: 8.21. WR: 302.5 kg (Tang Gonghong)

		SNATCH	JERK	TOTAL KG
1. Tang Gonghong	CHN	122.5	182.5 WR	305.0 WR
2. Jang Mi-ran	KOR	130.0	172.5	302.5
3. Agata Wróbel	POL	130.0	160.0	290.0
4. Viktória Varga	HUN	127.5	155.0	282.5
5. Viktoria Shaimardanova	UKR	130.0	150.0	280.0
6. Cheryl Haworth	USA	125.0	155.0	280.0
7. Olha Korobka	UKR	125.0	155.0	280.0
8. Vasiliki Kasapi	GRE	125.0	152.5	277.5

In eighth place after failing at two of her snatch attempts, Tang Gonghong trailed Jang Mi-ran by 7.5 kilograms. Tang also missed her first clean and jerk attempt at 172.5 kilograms, before clearing the weight on her second try. With only one lift left, Tang was forced to attempt 182.5 kg, a weight she had lifted only once before in practice. After raising the bar to her chest, she held it for ten seconds, and then lifted it over her head and held it again to earn the gold medal, breaking her own world record in the process.

Olha Korobka, who placed seventh, broke Cheryl Haworth's record as the heaviest woman ever to compete in the Olympics. In Athens, Korobka tipped the scales at 156.14 kilograms (344¼ pounds).

2008 Beijing C: 11, N: 10, D: 8.16. WR: 319.0 kg (Mu Shuangshuang)

		SNATCH	JERK	TOTAL KG
1. Jang Mi-ran	KOR	140.0 WR	186.0 WR	326.0 WR
2. Olha Korobka	UKR	124.0	153.0	277.0
3. Mariya Grabovetskaya	KAZ	120.0	150.0	270.0
4. Ele Opeloge	SAM	119.0	150.0	269.0
5. Mariam Usman	NGR	115.0	150.0	265.0
6. Cheryl Haworth	USA	115.0	144.0	259.0
7. Yuliya Dovgal	UKR	118.0	140.0	258.0
8. Deborah Lovely	AUS	113.0	135.0	248.0

Defending Olympic silver medalist Jang Mi-ran was the overwhelming favorite in the event, having won the past three world championships. China's Mu Shuangshuang had lifted the same total weight as Jang at all three world championships, finishing second each time due to a higher total bodyweight. Limited to entering four of the six women's weightlifting events, China chose not to send Mu, leaving Jang in a class of her own.

Jang set world records in both the snatch and the clean and jerk, as well as a new total world record of 326 kg (718.7 lbs). She was so dominant that Olha Korobka, in second place, skipped her final lift, finishing a full 49 kg (108 lbs) behind Jang.

After the event Jang revealed that she missed competing against her closest rival. "I thought [Mu] would attend these games so I was very surprised to not see her name in the start list," she said. "If I have the opportunity to compete with her in the next Olympics I will definitely feel less lonely."

Chapter 32 **Freestyle Wrestling**

MEN
Bantamweight—55 kg
Featherweight—60 kg
Lightweight—66 kg
Welterweight—74 kg
Middleweight—84 kg
Heavyweight—96 kg
Super Heavyweight—120 kg
Discontinued Events

WOMEN
Flyweight—48kg
Lightweight—55kg
Middleweight 63kg
Heavyweight—72kg

Wilfried Dietrich and Chris Taylor, 1972
Thirty-nine-year-old Dietrich (bottom) throwing 412-lb Taylor during the 1972 Super Heavyweight freestyle wrestling tournament.

International amateur wrestling has undergone a number of format changes. Beginning in 1984, matches of two three-minute rounds replaced matches of three three-minute rounds. In 1992 contests were reduced to one five-minute round. For 2000 and 2004 matches returned to the format of two three-minute rounds.

Since 2008 each match is divided into three two-minute periods, and a winner declared for each period. The first wrestler to win two periods wins the match. As a match progresses, contestants score technical points as a result of successful holds, actions, positions of advantage and near-throws. A match is terminated as the result of a fall or if one wrestler achieves a six-point difference, two holds of three points, or one hold of five points. A fall is declared when a wrestler holds an opponent so that both of his shoulders are against the mat. If a period ends in a tie by points, the winner is determined by successively considering the number of cautions, the value of holds and the last technical point scored. If a freestyle wrestling period ends in a scoreless tie, a 30-second overtime is held, with the first technical point scored determining the winner.

If at the end of a freestyle overtime period neither of the wrestlers has scored a point, the referee, the judge, and the mat chairman choose the winner by majority vote.

Before 2008, when the match ended without a fall or a 10-point lead, the wrestler with the most points was declared the winner if he had scored at least three points. Through 1984, in the case of a tie, the victory was awarded to the contestant who achieved the highest-scoring move or who scored the last point. In 1988 a three-minute sudden-death overtime period was introduced. In 2008 a thirty-second overtime period was used if neither wrestler had earned three points. Until 1984 scoring was done with negative or "penalty" points rather than positive points.

Olympic wrestling tournaments have used a variety of formats over the years. Since 2008, the competition has used direct elimination, with pairings drawn at random. All wrestlers losing against the two finalists compete in a repêchage group, with the winners of the two final *repêchage* matches both receiving a bronze medal.

In each division, the top eight finishers in the most recent world championships qualify for the Olympics. The remainder take part in a series of Olympic Qualification Tournaments.

Wrestling is the only sport with a maximum weight limit.

CLASSIFICATION POINTS:

winner–5 loser–0
victory by:
1) fall
2) injury
3) withdrawal
4) default
5) disqualification

winner–4 loser–0
1) victory by technical superiority (six-point difference), with the loser scoring no technical points

winner–4 loser–1
1) victory by technical superiority (six-point difference), with the loser scoring technical points

winner–3 loser–0
1) victory by points, with the loser scoring no technical points
2) victory declared by decision of the officiating team when neither wrestler has scored a technical point

winner–3 loser–1
1) victory by points, with the loser scoring technical points
2) victory declared by decision of the officiating team after a tie in which both wrestlers score technical points
3) victory declared by decision of the officiating team when neither wrestler scores three technical points

Point Values of Actions and Holds

Par terre position—The defending wrestler begins on his hands and knees; the attacking wrestler begins with both hands on top of his opponent's back.

Danger position—A wrestler is considered to be in a "danger position" when the line of his back or shoulders forms an angle of less than 90 degrees to the mat when he uses the upper part of his body to avoid a fall.

Grand amplitude hold—In the standing position a grand amplitude hold is called when a wrestler causes his opponent to lose all contact with the ground, sweeps him through the air, and brings him down to the mat in a danger position. In the *par terre* position, a grand amplitude hold occurs when a wrestler lifts his opponent from the ground and causes him to land belly-down (3 points) or in a danger position (5 points).

One point to the wrestler who:
(1) brings his opponent to the mat from behind and holds him down with three points of contact (two arms and one knee, or two knees and one arm)
(2) applies a correct hold but does not place his opponent in danger
(3) overcomes, holds, and controls his opponent on the mat, by passing behind him
(4) while attacking, has his opponent flee the hold or the mat, or whose opponent refuses to start, commits illegal actions or acts of brutality
(5) holds his opponent in a position of danger for five seconds or longer
(6) while in the *par terre* position, after being controlled or brought to the mat, raises himself up to the standing position.

Two points to the wrestler who:
(1) applies a correct move in the *par terre* position and places his opponent in a position of danger or in a fall position
(2) while attacking, causes his opponent to roll onto his shoulders
(3) while attacking, has an opponent flee the hold by jumping off the mat
(4) while being attacked, is prevented from completing a hold because his opponent uses an illegal hold
(5) while attacked, causes his opponent's shoulder to touch the mat in the course of his opponent's move.

Three points to the wrestler who:
(1) performs a hold in a standing position that brings his opponent into a danger position by direct projection
(2) raises his opponent from the ground and puts him in a danger position
(3) executes a grand amplitude hold that does not place his opponent in a danger position.

Five points to the wrestler who:
(1) performs a grand amplitude hold from the standing position and brings his opponent to a danger position
(2) from the *par terre* position, lifts his opponent oft the ground with a grand amplitude move and projects him into a danger position.

MEN

BANTAMWEIGHT
(55 kg—121¼ lbs)

1896–1900 not held

1904 St. Louis C: 7, N: 1, D: 10.15.
(56.70 kg—125 lbs)

		FINAL MATCH
1. Isidor "Jack" Niflot	USA	Fall 1:58
2. August Wester	USA	
3. Louis Strebler	USA	

1906 not held

1908 London C: 13, N: 3, D: 7.20.
(54 kg—119 lbs)

		FINAL MATCH
1. George Mehnert	USA	Fall 11:45; Fall 3:57
2. William Press	GBR	
3. Aubert Côté	CAN	Fall 3:55; Fall 8:50
4. Fitzlloyd Tomkins	GBR	

5. Frank Davis (GBR), Bruce Sansom (GBR), George Saunders (GBR)

Mehnert, a 26-year-old from Newark, New Jersey, had won the Flyweight championship in St. Louis four years earlier. Côté mortgaged his farm in Quebec to pay his way to London. When he returned with a medal, the Canadian Olympic Committee agreed to reimburse him.

1912–1920 not held

1924 Paris C: 12, N: 8, D: 7.14.
(56 kg—123½ lbs)

1. Kustaa Pihlajamäki	FIN
2. Kaarlo Mäkinen	FIN
3. Bryant Hines	USA
4. Gaston Ducayla	FRA

Pihlajamäki won the first of his three Olympic medals (two gold, one silver). His cousin, Hermanni, also won a gold and a bronze in freestyle wrestling.

1928 Amsterdam C: 8, N: 8, D: 8.1.
(56 kg—123½ lbs)

1. Kaarlo Mäkinen	FIN
2. Edmond Spapen	BEL
3. James Trifunov	CAN
4. Harold Sansum	GBR
5. Robert Hewitt	USA

Sansum was awarded fourth place even though he lost all three of his matches.

1932 Los Angeles C: 8, N: 8, D: 8.3.
(56 kg—123½ lbs)

1. Robert Pearce	USA
2. Ödön Zombori	HUN
3. Aatos Jaskari	FIN
4. Joseph Reid	GBR
5. Georgios Zervinis	GRE
6. Julien Depuichaffray	FRA

Pearce was the first in a long line of Olympic champion wrestlers from the state of Oklahoma.

1936 Berlin C: 14, N: 14, D: 8.5.
(56 kg—123½ lbs)

		ROUND ELIMINATED	PEN. PTS.	FINAL ROUND
1. Ödön Zombori	HUN	–	4	0
2. Ross Flood	USA	–	2	3
3. Johannes Herbert	GER	5	5	
4. Herman Tuvesson	SWE	5	6	
5. Aatos Jaskari	FIN	4	7	
6. Ahmet Çakiryildiz	TUR	4	7	
7. Marcello Nizzola	ITA	3	5	
8. Cesar Gaudard	SWI	3	6	
8. Auguste Laporte	BEL	3	6	

1948 London C: 15, N: 15, D: 7.31.
(57 kg—125½ lbs)

		ROUND ELIMINATED	PEN. PTS.	FINAL ROUND
1. Nasuh Akar	TUR	–	2	0
2. Gerald Leeman	USA	–	3	3
3. Charles Kouyos	FRA	5	7	
4. Joseph Trimpont	BEL	5	7	
5. Lajos Bencze	HUN	4	5	
5. Raymond Cazaux	GBR	4	5	
5. Sayad Hafez	EGY	4	5	
5. Erik Persson	SWE	4	5	

1952 Helsinki C: 20, N: 20, D: 7.23.
(57 kg—125½ lbs)

		ROUND ELIMINATED	PEN. PTS.	FINAL ROUND
1. Shohachi Ishii	JPN	–	4	2
2. Rashid Mamedbekov	SOV/AZR	–	3	4
3. Khashaba Jadav	IND	–	4	6
4. Edvin Westerby	SWE	5	7	
5. Cemil Saribacak	TUR	4	5	
6. Lajos Bencze	HUN	4	5	
7. Ferdinand Schmitz	GER	4	6	
8. Eigil Johansen	DEN	3	5	
8. M. Mehdi Yaghoubi	IRN	3	5	

A talented judoka, Ishii was forced to give up judo when US occupation forces banned the sport after World War II. Ishii switched to wrestling and won Japan's first post-war gold medal. Khashaba Jadav was India's first medalist in an individual event. In fact, until 1996, Jadav was the *only* individual medalist from the world's second most populous nation. When he returned to India, Jadav was accompanied during the final 40 kilometers of his journey to his home village of Goleshwar by his fellow villagers and a procession of 151 bullock carts. However he was soon forgotten by his nation and died in humble obscurity.

1956 Melbourne C: 14, N: 14, D: 12.1.
(57 kg—125½ lbs)

		ROUND ELIMINATED	PEN. PTS.	FINAL ROUND
1. Mustafa Dağistanli	TUR	–	4	1
2. M. Mehdi Yaghoubi	IRN	–	4	2
3. Mykhalo Shakhov	SOV/UKR	5	6	
4. Lee Sang-kyoon	KOR	5	7	
5. Minoru Iizuka	JPN	4	5	
6. Alfred Kämmerer	GDR	3	5	
7. Din Zahur	PAK	3	6	
8. Adolfo Díaz	ARG	3	7	
8. Tarakeshwar Pandey	IND	3	7	

1960 Rome C: 19, N: 19, D: 9.6.
(57 kg—125½ lbs)

		ROUND ELIMINATED	PEN. PTS.	FINAL ROUND
1. Terrence McCann	USA	–	5	2
2. Nezhdet Zalev	BUL	–	2	4
3. Tadeusz Trojanowski	POL	–	4	6
4. Tadashi Asai	JPN		5	6
5. Tanuo Jaskari	FIN	5	7	
6. Mykhalo Shakhov	SOV/UKR	5	8	
7. M. Mehdi Yaghoubi	IRN	4	6	
8. Luigi Chinazzo	ITA	4	8	

Terry McCann later became executive director of

Toastmasters International, an organization devoted to teaching and improving public speaking skills.

1964 Tokyo C: 20, N: 20, D: 10.14.
(57 kg—125½ lbs)

		ROUND ELIMINATED	PEN. PTS.	FINAL ROUND
1. Yojiro Uetake	JPN	–	3	2
2. Hüseyin Akbaş	TUR	–	5	4
3. Aydyn Ali Ibragimov	SOV/AZR	–	3	6
4. David Auble	USA	5	6	
5. Choi Young-kil	KOR	5	7	
6. Bishamber Singh	IND	5	8	
7. János Varga	HUN	4	7	
8. Abdollah Khodabande	IRN	3	6	

After winning Japan's national high school championship, Yojiro Uetake moved to the United States and enrolled at Oklahoma State University. He won all 58 of his collegiate matches. Midway through his undergraduate career he returned to his hometown of Tokyo and won the Olympic gold medal. He stayed at Oklahoma State as an assistant coach and repeated as Olympic champion in 1968 despite wrestling the final with a separated left shoulder.

In the 1990s, bronze medalist Aydyn Ali Ibragimov was involved in a bizarre crime in which twelve works of art, including rare drawings by Albrecht Dürer and Rembrandt, were stolen from the National Fire Arms Museum in Baku, Azerbaijan, and offered for sale to pay for a kidney transplant for a former Japanese wrestler. Ibragimov's wife was sentenced to a term in federal prison in the United States, but Ibragimov himself disappeared.

1968 Mexico City C: 21, N: 21, D: 10.20.
(57 kg—125½ lbs)

		ROUND ELIMINATED	PEN. PTS.	FINAL ROUND
1. Yojiro Uetake	JPN	–	5.5	
2. Donald Behm	USA	7	6.5	
3. Abutaleb Talebi Gorgori	IRN	7	7.5	
4. Ali Aliyev	SOV/RUS	7	8.5	
5. Ivan Shavov	BUL	6	7.5	
6. Zbigniew Żedzicki	POL	5	8	
7. Bishamber Singh	IND	5	8.5	
8. Sukhbaatar Bazaryn	MGL	4	7	

1972 Munich C: 28, N: 28, D: 8.31.
(57 kg—125½ lbs)

		ROUND ELIMINATED	PEN. PTS.	FINAL ROUND
1. Hideaki Yanagida	JPN	–	4	1
2. Richard Sanders	USA	–	4	3
3. László Klinga	HUN	7	8.5	
4. Prem Premnath	IND	7	9	
5. Ivan Shavov	BUL	6	7	
6. Horst Mayer	GDR	6	7.5	
7. Ramezan Kheder	IRN	6	8	
8. Jorge Ramos Caron	CUB	5	6	

Silver medalist Richard Sanders, a bartender from Portland, Oregon, had long hair, a beard, and a mustache, and wore a bead necklace. Sanders was notorious for waiting until the last moment to cut enough weight to meet the limit. Once, on the way to a dual meet in the Soviet Union, he had to spend much of the flight jogging up and down the aisle. Seven weeks after the Olympics, Sanders was killed in an automobile accident while touring in Europe. He was 23 years old.

1976 Montreal C: 21, N: 21, D: 7.31.
(57 kg—125½ lbs)

		ROUND ELIMINATED	PEN. PTS.	FINAL ROUND
1. Vladimir Yumin	SOV/RUS	–	7	2
2. Hans-Dieter Brüchert	GDR	–	3.5	4
3. Masao Arai	JPN	–	4.5	6
4. Miho Dukov	BUL	6	8	
5. Ramezan Kheder	IRN	6	8	
6. Migd Khoilogdorj	MGL	6	8	
7. George Khatziioannidis	GRE	5	8.5	
8. Zbigniew Żedzicki	POL	4	6	

1980 Moscow C: 16, N: 16, D: 7.31.
(57 kg—125½ lbs)

		ROUND ELIMINATED	PEN. PTS.	FINAL ROUND
1. Serhei Bilohlazov	SOV/UKR	–	0	0
2. Li Ho-pyong	PRK	–	6	5
3. Dugarsuren Ouinbold	MGL	–	2	7
4. Ivan Tzochev	BUL	5	7	
5. Aurel Neagu	ROM	4	6	
6. Wieslaw Kończak	POL	4	7	
7. Karim Salman Muhsin	IRQ	4	8	
8. Sándor Németh	HUN	4	9	

Serhei Bilohlazov, the twin brother of Flyweight winner Anatoly Bilohlazov (see p. 1138), threw five of his six opponents and defeated Ouinbold by disqualification, after leading in points 15–0. He outpointed his six victims, 58–3.

1984 Los Angeles-Anaheim C: 16, N: 16, D: 8.11.
(57 kg—125½ lbs)

		FINAL MATCH
1. Hideaki Tomiyama	JPN	8–3
2. Barry Davis	USA	
3. Kim Eui-kon	KOR	7–4
4. Orlando Cáceres	PUR	
5. Rohtas Singh	IND	3–2
6. Zoran Sorov	YUG/MAC	
7. Guanbunima	CHN	
8. Ibrahim Akgun	TUR	

With his 85-year-old grandfather in the audience for good luck, and with defending Olympic and world champion Serhei Bilohlazov prevented from competing because of the Soviet-bloc boycott, two-time world champion Hideaki Tomiyama outclassed the field.

1988 Seoul C: 25, N: 25, D: 10.1.
(57 kg—125½ lbs)

		FINAL MATCH
1. Serhei Bilohlazov	SOV/UKR	5–1
2. Askari Mohammadian	IRN	
3. Noh Kyung-sun	KOR	9–8 9:00
4. Ahmet Ak	TUR	
5. Valentin Ivanov	BUL	5–3
6. Béla Nagy	HUN	
7. Haltma Battul	MGL	3–1
8. Ryo Kanehama	JPN	

Six-time world champion Serhei Bilohlazov regained his Olympic title without being seriously challenged.

1992 Barcelona C: 18, N: 18, D: 8.7.
(57 kg—125½ lbs)

		FINAL MATCH
1. Alejandro Puerto Díaz	CUB	5–0
2. Sergei Smal	BLR	
3. Kim Yong-sik	PRK	3–2
4. Remzi Musaoğlu	TUR	
5. Rumen Pavlov	BUL	Fall 0:44
6. Kendall Cross	USA	
7. Jürgen Scheibe	GER	Injury
8. Robert Dawson	CAN	

Puerto shut out five of his opponents and defeated Cross 10–6.

1996 Atlanta C: 21, N: 21, D: 7.30.
(57 kg—125½ lbs)

		FINAL MATCH
1. Kendall Cross	USA	5-3
2. Giuvi Sissaouri	CAN	
3. Yong Ri-sam	PRK	3-0
4. Harun Doğan	TUR	
5. Shaban Trstena	MAC	4-3 2:41
6. Mohammad Talaie	IRN	
7. Aleksandr Guzov	BLR	3-2
8. Damir Zakhartdinov	UZB	

Kendall Cross faced his stiffest opposition before the Olympics. In 1992 he qualified for the Olympics by scoring an upset victory over world championship silver medalist Brad Penrith. Cross finished sixth in Barcelona. It was yet another American, Terry Brands, who dominated the division in the following years, winning the world championship in both 1993 and 1995. In 1996, Cross and Brands met in the US trials final: best two out of three. The winner would go to the Olympics; the loser would watch on television. In their first match, Brands overwhelmed Cross 7-2. But, five hours later, Cross won the second encounter 7-6 and then, an hour after that, won the tiebreaker 8-7.

Between the trials and the Olympics, Cross spent 75 percent of his time practicing to fight one man: Giuvi Sissaouri, a Georgian-born Canadian. Sissaouri had lost a controversial final at the 1995 world championships in Atlanta when, while leading Terry Brands 3-0 with 25 seconds to go, he was disqualified for stalling.

For three months, Cross' coach, Zeke Jones, pretended to be Sissaouri, studying tapes of his fights and copying his style. Sure enough, it was Cross and Sissaouri who fought their way to the final. Cross put his preparation to good use. "Everything he tried," Cross would later describe, "I was one second ahead of him because I knew what was coming." Only 35 seconds into the match, Sissaouri was trying to set up Cross for a counterattack when he left himself briefly vulnerable. Cross used a double-over hook to score an unexpected three points. Thirty seconds later he added two more points and then defended for the last four minutes.

2000 Sydney C: 20, N: 20, D: 10.1.
(58 kg—128 lbs)

		FINAL MATCH
1. Alireza Dabir	IRN	3-0
2. Yevgen Buslovych	UKR	
3. Terry Brands	USA	3-2
4. Damir Zakhartdinov	UZB	
5. David Pogosian	GEO	Disq
6. Martin Berberian	ARM	
7. Murad Ramazanov	RUS	
8. Aleksandr Guzov	BLR	

Alireza Dabir of Iran and Harum Doğan of Turkey had faced off in the final of the last two world championships. In 1998, Dabir was declared the winner—when the tournament was held in Iran—and in 1999 Doğan was given the victory—when the tournament was held in Turkey. It was anyone's guess who would emerge victorious when the two met in neutral Sydney; however the match-up never took place. Dabir qualified for the final as expected, but Doğan did not make it out of the elimination pool. Indeed, the Turkish wrestling team arrived at the Olympics in turmoil, caught in a political clash between secularists and religious fundamentalists who opposed the creation of a women's team. Doğan, a member of the antisecularist side, refused to wear the national team outfit and, after losing to Damir Zakhartdinov refused to participate in his final pool match.

Oyunbileg Purevbaatar of Mongolia won the match for fifth place but was disqualified when he tested positive for the diuretic furosemide.

2004 Athens C: 22, N: 22, D: 8.28.
(55 kg—121 lbs)

		FINAL MATCH
1. Mavlet Batyrov	RUS	9-1
2. Stephen Abas	USA	
3. Chikara Tanabe	JPN	7-0
4. Amiran Kardanov	GRE	
5. Li Zhengyu	CHN	6-4
6. Kim Hyo-sub	KOR	
7. Oleksandr Zakharuk	UKR	
8. O Song-nam	PRK	

Twenty-year-old Mavlet Batyrov of Dagestan was scheduled to face his older brother Adam in the final of the Russian trials, but Adam stepped aside to allow Mavlet to go to the Olympics. In his elimination pool, Batyrov upset world champion Dilshod Mansurov of Uzbekistan 3-1. He won his four other Olympic matches by a combined score of 40-2.

2008 Beijing C: 19, N: 19, D: 8.19.
(55 kg—121 lbs)

		FINAL MATCH
1. Henry Cejudo	USA	2-2, 3-0
2. Tomohiro Matsunaga	JPN	
3. Besik Kudukhov	RUS	
3. Radoslav Velikov	BUL	
5. Dilshod Mansurov	UZB	
5. Namiq Sevdiyev	AZE	
7. Rizvan Gadzhiyev	BLR	
8. Besarion Gochashvili	GEO	

3rd Place: Kudukhov—Mansurov 1-0, 2-0
3rd Place: Velikov—Sevdiyev 0-2, 3-1, 1-0

Henry Cejudo and Tomohiro Matsunaga were both surprise qualifiers for the gold medal final, having finished 31st and 26th respectively at the 2007 world championships.

The 21-year-old Cejudo upset 2006 world champion Radoslav Velikov 7-6 in overtime in his first match and survived a 10-10 decision over Namiq Sevdiyev to reach the final. Meanwhile Matsunaga defeated two-time world champion Dilshod Mansurov 4-3 in the quarterfinals, and then faced reigning world champion and 2004 Olympic silver medalist Besik Kudukhov in the semifinals, pinning Kudukhov for a fall three-and-a-half minutes into the match.

In the final, Matsunaga scored first on a leg drive before Cejudo gained two points for a back exposure. Matsunaga evened the score 2-2, but Cejudo won the period for having scored a two-point move. Cejudo scored three points on a high crotch takedown in the second period to clinch the gold medal.

The sixth of seven children, Cejudo was born in South Central Los Angeles to a pair of undocumented immigrants from Mexico. He was raised by his mother, Nelly Rico, in New Mexico and Arizona, as his father was in and out of prison. Introduced to wrestling by his brother, Angel, Cejudo was the first US wrestler to win the national title while still in high school. He dedicated his gold medal to his mother.

FEATHERWEIGHT
(60 kg—132 lbs)

1896–1900 not held

1904 St. Louis C: 9, N: 1, D: 10.15.
(61.23 kg—135 lbs)

		FINAL MATCH
1. Benjamin Bradshaw	USA	Dec 15:00
2. Theodore McLear	USA	
3. Charles Clapper	USA	

1906 not held

1908 London C: 12, N: 2, D: 7.22.
(60.3 kg—132½ lbs)

		FINAL MATCH
1. George Dole	USA	Fall 9:28; Dec 15:00
2. James Slim	GBR	
3. William McKie	GBR	
4. William Tagg	GBR	

5. Arthur Goddard (GBR), James Webster (GBR), James White (GBR)

Dole, a 5-foot 3½-inch (1.61 meters) student from Yale, was the only non-British wrestler in the Featherweight division.

1912 not held

1920 Antwerp C: 11, N: 7, D: 8.27.

		FINAL MATCH
1. Charles Ackerly	USA	Dec
2. Samuel Gerson	USA	
3. Philip Bernard	GBR	
4. Randhir Shinde	IND	

Ackerly, former captain of the Cornell University team, and Gerson, former captain of the University of Pennsylvania team, had each defeated the other once in collegiate competition. Ackerly won the tie-breaker at the AAU championships and then won again across the seas in Antwerp. Thirty-two years later Gerson organized the US Olympians, an alumni association for former members of US Olympic teams.

1924 Paris C: 17, N: 12, D: 7.14.
(61 kg—134½ lbs)

1. Robin Reed	USA
2. Chester Newton	USA
3. Katsutoshi Naito	JPN
4. Sigfrid Hansson	SWE

Reed and Newton were longtime bitter rivals from Portland, Oregon. At the Pacific Northwest regional tryouts for the 1924 Olympic team, Reed won four different weight divisions all the way up to 192 pounds (87 kg). One of the greatest US wrestlers ever, he eventually retired undefeated.

1928 Amsterdam C: 9, N: 9, D: 8.1.
(61 kg—134½ lbs)

		FINAL MATCH
1. Allie Morrison	USA	Injury
2. Kustaa Pihlajamäki	FIN	
3. Hans Minder	SWI	
4. René Rottenfluc	FRA	

1932 Los Angeles C: 10, N: 10, D: 8.3.
(61 kg—134½ lbs)

1. Hermanni Pihlajamäki	FIN
2. Edgar Nemir	USA
3. Einar Karlsson	SWE
4. Joseph Taylor	GBR
5. Ioannis Farmakidis	GRE
6. Jean Chasson	FRA

Hermanni Pihlajamäki, who also won a bronze medal in the lightweight division in 1936, was the cousin of Kustaa Pihlajamäki, who succeeded him as Olympic champion.

1936 Berlin C: 15, N: 15, D: 8.4.
(61 kg—134½ lbs)

		ROUND ELIMINATED	PEN. PTS.	FINAL ROUND
1. Kustaa Pihlajamäki	FIN	–	1	
2. Francis Millard	USA	6	5	
3. Gösta Jönsson	SWE	6	5	
4. John Vernon Pettigrew	CAN	5	7	
5. Ferenc Tóth	HUN	4	6	
6. Mitsuzo Mizutani	JPN	4	7	
7. Marco Gavelli	ITA	3	5	
8. Yasar Erkan (TUR), Nevil Hall (SAF), Norman Morrell (GBR)		3	7	

Kustaa Pihlajamäki of Nurmo was 34 years old when he won his second gold medal—twelve years after his first Olympic triumph in the 1924 bantamweight division.

1948 London C: 17, N: 17, D: 7.31.
(63 kg—139 lbs)

		ROUND ELIMINATED	PEN. PTS.	FINAL ROUND
1. Gazanfer Bilge	TUR	–	0	1
2. Ivar Sjölin	SWE	–	2	3
3. Adolf Müller	SWI	6	5	
4. Paavo Hietala	FIN	5	6	
4. Ferenc Tóth	HUN	5	6	
6. Harold "Hal" Moore	USA	4	5	
7. Antoine Raeymaeckers	BEL	4	6	
8. Abdel Hamid Yacout	EGY	4	7	
8. Arnold Parsons	GBR	4	7	

Bilge was rewarded by the Turkish government with a house and 20,000 liras ($7,142). This made him ineligible for the 1952 Olympics, but he was able to parlay his rewards into a fortune as a bus mogul. In 1963 Bilge was imprisoned after he shot Adil Atan, a business rival who had won a bronze medal as a Light Heavyweight wrestler in 1952.

1952 Helsinki C: 21, N: 21, D: 7.23.
(63 kg—139 lbs)

		ROUND ELIMINATED	PEN. PTS.	FINAL ROUND
1. Bayram Şit	TUR	–	2	1
2. Nasser Givehchi	IRN	–	4	4
3. Josiah Henson	USA	–	5	6
4. Keshav Mangave	IND	5	6	
5. Risaburo Tominaga	JPN	5	7	
6. Rauno Mäkinen	FIN	4	5	
7. Albert Bernard	CAN	4	6	
7. Abdel Essawi	EGY	4	6	

1956 Melbourne C: 13, N: 13, D: 12.1.
(63 kg—139lbs)

		ROUND ELIMINATED	PEN. PTS.	FINAL ROUND
1. Shozo Sasahara	JPN	–	4	1
2. Joseph Mewis	BEL	–	3	4
3. Erkki Penttilä	FIN	–	4	6
4. Myron Roderick	USA	4	5	
5. Bayram Şit	TUR	4	5	
6. Nasser Givehchi	IRN	4	7	
6. Linar Salimullin	SOV/UKR	4	7	
8. Ram Sarup	IND	3	6	

Sasahara later served as vice-president of both FILA, the international wrestling federation, and of the Japanese Olympic Committee. In 1998 he was mayor of the Olympic Village at the Nagano Winter Games.

1960 Rome C: 25, N: 25, D: 9.6.
(63 kg—139 lbs)

		ROUND ELIMINATED	PEN. PTS.	FINAL ROUND
1. Mustafa Dağistanli	TUR	–	4	1
2. Stancho Kolev Ivanov	BUL	–	3	3
3. Vladimir Rubashvili	SOV/GEO	6	7	
4. Tamiji Sato	JPN	6	7	
5. Joseph Mewis	BEL	5	8	
6. Mohamed Akhtar	PAK	5	9	
7. Abraham Geldenhuys	SAF	4	6	
8. Azohadi Khaden	IRN	4	9	

A native of Carsamba in Samsun province, Mustafa Dağistanli had already won a gold medal in the bantamweight division in 1956.

1964 Tokyo C: 21, N: 21, D: 10.14.
(63 kg—139 lbs)

		ROUND ELIMINATED	PEN. PTS.	FINAL ROUND
1. Osamu Watanabe	JPN	–	2	2
2. Stancho Kolev Ivanov	BUL	–	5	5
3. Nodar Khokhashvili	SOV/GEO	–	5	5
4. Robert "Bobby" Douglas	USA	5	6	
5. Mohammed Ebrahimi	AFG	5	7	
6. M. Ebrahim Seifpour Saadabadi	IRN	5	8	
7. Rainer Schilling	GER	4	6	
8. Mario Tovar González	MEX	4	7	

Watanabe's 1-0 win over Khokhashvili was his 186th consecutive victory. He didn't give up a single point in any of his six Olympic matches. Kolev was awarded the silver medal because he weighed less than Khokhashvili.

1968 Mexico City C: 23, N: 23, D: 10.20.
(63 kg—139 lbs)

		ROUND ELIMINATED	PEN. PTS.	FINAL ROUND
1. Masaaki Kaneko	JPN	–	1.5	3.5
2. Enyu Todorov	BUL	–	2	4.5
3. S. Shamseddin Seyyedabbasi	IRN	–	2.5	5
4. Nicolaos Karypidis	GRE	5	6.5	
5. Petre Coman	ROM	5	8	
6. Yeikan Tedeyev	SOV/RUS	4	6	
7. Vehbi Akdag	TUR	4	6.5	
7. Ismall Al Karaghouli	IRQ	4	6.5	

1972 Munich C: 26, N: 26, D: 8.31.
(62 kg—136½ lbs)

		ROUND ELIMINATED	PEN. PTS.	FINAL ROUND
1. Zagalav Abdulbekov	SOV/RUS	–	3.5	2
2. Vehbi Akdag	TUR	–	5.5	5
3. Ivan Krustev	BUL	–	5	5
4. Kiroshi Abe	JPN	6	6	
5. S. Shamseddin Seyyedabbasi	IRN	5	5.5	
6. Petre Coman	ROM	5	6	
7. Joseph Burge House	GUA	5	7	
8. Gerhard Weisenberg	GER	4	8	

1976 Montreal C: 17, N: 17, D: 7.31.
(62 kg—136½ lbs)

		ROUND ELIMINATED	PEN. PTS.	FINAL ROUND
1. Yang Jung-mo	KOR	–	1	3
2. Zevegin Oidov	MGL	–	3	4
3. Eugene Davis	USA	–	8	5
4. Mohsen Farahvashi	IRN	6	10	
5. Ivan Yankov	BUL	5	8	
6. Sergei Timofeyev	SOV/RUS	4	7	
7. Kenkichi Maekawa	JPN	4	8	
8. Helmut Strumpf	GDR	4	9	

Yang Jung-mo was South Korea's first Olympic gold medal winner.

1980 Moscow C: 13, N: 13, D: 7.29.
(62 kg—136½ lbs)

		ROUND ELIMINATED	PEN. PTS.	FINAL ROUND
1. Magomedgasan Abushev	SOV/RUS	–	2.5	1.5
2. Miho Dukov	BUL	–	5.5	3
3. Georges Khatziioannidis	GRE	–	5	7.5
4. Raúl Cascaret Fonseca	CUB	5	6.5	
5. Aurel Suteu	ROM	5	8.5	
6. Ulzibayar Nasanjargal	MGL	4	6	
7. Brian Aspen	GBR	3	6.5	
8. Zoltán Szalontai	HUN	3	7.5	

1984 Los Angeles-Anaheim C: 16, N: 16, D: 8.9.
(62 kg—136½ lbs)

		FINAL MATCH
1. Randall Lewis	USA	24–11 4:52
2. Kosei Akaishi	JPN	
3. Lee Jung-keun	KOR	11–6
4. Christopher Brown	AUS	
5. Martin Herbster	GER	11–4
6. Antonio La Bruna	ITA	
7. Selman Kaygusuz	TUR	
8. Gerard Santoro	FRA	

Randy Lewis of Rapid City, South Dakota, had a much more difficult time getting into the Olympics than he did once he got there. In 1980 Lewis made the US team, but the boycott prevented him from competing. In 1984, at the US Olympic trials, Lewis defeated world championship silver medalist Lee Roy Smith. But Smith filed a protest which was upheld and a re-wrestle was ordered. Smith emerged victorious when Lewis defaulted because of an injured knee. Lewis, supported by US coach Dan Gable, filed a protest of his own. An arbitrator ordered that the final 50 seconds of the original match be re-wrestled. This time Lewis won. The next day, only two days before the Los Angeles opening ceremonies, Lewis defeated Rick Delegatta to finally secure his participation in the Olympics.

Lewis outscored his first four opponents 52–4 to advance to the final, where he overwhelmed Akaishi in the first two minutes of the second period.

1988 Seoul C: 28, N: 28, D: 9.29.
(62 kg—136½ lbs)

		FINAL MATCH
1. John Smith	USA	4–0
2. Stepan Sarkisyan	SOV/ARM	
3. Simeon Shterev	BUL	5–2
4. Akbar Fallah	IRN	
5. Jörg Helindach	GER	5–4
6. Avirmed Enhe	MGL	
7. Giovanni Schillaci	ITA	5–0
8. Gary Bohay	CAN	

John Smith, the 1987 world champion, qualified for the US Olympic team by twice defeating Randy Lewis, the same man who had prevented John's older brother, Lee Roy, from qualifying in 1984. In Seoul, Smith suffered a fractured nose in his second match with Simeon Shterev. He also wrestled with an abscessed left ear, which had to be drained daily. In the final, Smith demoralized Sarkisyan early in the first round by slipping free of the Armenian's best leghold.

1992 Barcelona C: 21, N: 21, D: 8.7.
(62 kg—136½ lbs)

		FINAL MATCH
1. John Smith	USA	6–0
2. Asgari Mohammadian	IRN	
3. Lázaro Reinoso Martínez	CUB	4–0
4. Rossen Vassilev	BUL	
5. Gazikhan Azizov	RUS	11–5
6. Musa Ilhan	AUS	
7. Martin Müller	SWI	Fall 3:39
8. Shin Sang-kew	KOR	

John Smith continued to dominate the 62-kilogram division, winning all three world championships between Olympics, but he almost didn't qualify for the Barcelona Games. At the United States Olympic Wrestle-Off, his 56-match win streak was snapped when he was beaten 4-2 by John Fisher in the first match of a two-out-of-three contest. Smith came back to win the last two matches 3-1 and 6-5. Smith struggled at the Olympics as well. His first two matches were close victories, 3-2 over Ismail Faikoğlu of Turkey and 2-1 over Kim Gwang-chol of North Korea. He even lost one match, 3-1 in overtime, to Lazaro Reinoso. But because Smith had beaten Gazikhan Azizov 17-1 and Azizov had beaten Reinoso, Smith won his pool and made it to the final, where he controlled the contest from the start and earned his second gold medal.

1996 Atlanta C: 21, N: 21, D: 8.1.
(63 kg—139 lbs)

		FINAL MATCH
1. Thomas Brands	USA	7-0
2. Jang Jae-sung	KOR	
3. Elbrus Tedeyev	UKR	3-1
4. Takahiro Wada	JPN	
5. Magomed (Gazikhan) Azizov	RUS	WO
6. Giovanni Schillaci	ITA	
7. Martin Calder	CAN	9-1
8. Ramil Islamov	UZB	

Tom Brands and his twin brother Terry of Sheldon, Iowa, were both world champions with reputations for viciousness. Speaking of his wrestling philosophy, Tom declared, "If I could, I'd tear limbs off to win. When I get on top of an opponent, I want to rip out his arm and hand back a bloody stump." Terry didn't make it to the 1996 Olympics, but Tom did. In Atlanta Tom had to defeat two world champions. First up was Sergei Smal of Belarus, who had beaten Brands in their two previous encounters. This time Brands won 5-0. In the semifinals he defeated defending world champion Magomed Azizov 4-1. In the end, Brands won the gold medal by outscoring his four opponents 19-1.

2000 Sydney C: 19, N: 19, D: 9.30.
(63 kg—139 lbs)

		FINAL MATCH
1. Murad Umakhanov	RUS	3-2
2. Serafim Barzakov	BUL	
3. Jang Jae-sung	KOR	12-2 (2:23)
4. Mohammad Talaei	IRN	
5. Arshak Hayrapetian	ARM	Injury
6. Carlos Ortiz Castillo	CUB	
7. Shamil Afandiyev	AZR	
8. Stefan Fernyak	SLV	

Seven weeks after he placed second in the bantamweight division at the 1998 European Championships, Mourad Umakhanov's life was shattered by tragedy. While he was participating in the Russian national championships in Nalchik, a balcony collapsed, killing fifteen people, including Umakhanov's older brother, Shamil. Umakhanov's career flagged, but by 2000 he was back in form, capturing the European title as a featherweight in a tournament that included a semifinal pin of Serafin Barzakov. The two met again in the Olympic final five months later. With the score tied 2-2 and only 15 seconds left in regulation time, Umakhanov scored the winning point with a leg lift.

One unfortunate competitor was Cary Kolat of the United States. In 1997, Kolat was fighting Abbas Haj Kenari in the world championship final when the Iranian, in an attempt to break Kolat's momentum, began untying and retying his shoelaces. Kolat lost the match, but the incident led to two changes in the rules, one requiring wrestlers to tape their laces and the other allowing officials to penalize wrestlers one point for stalling. At the 1998 world championships, Kolat defeated Serafim Barzakov, but his victory was overturned after a protest. Once again this led to a rule change in which all protested matches would be re-wrestled. In the semifinals of the 1999 world championships, Kolat defeated Elbrus Tedeyev of Ukraine. A Ukrainian protest was upheld, the match was redone and Kolat lost in overtime. In his opening match at the 2000 Olympics, Kolat defeated former world champion Mohammad Talaei 3-1—or so it appeared. The Iranians protested, their protest was upheld and in the rematch . . . Kolat lost 5-4.

2004 Athens C: 22, N: 22, D: 8.29.
(60 kg—132 lbs)

		FINAL MATCH
1. Yandro Quintana	CUB	4-0
2. Masoud Jokar	IRN	
3. Kenji Inoue	JPN	6-5 6:45
4. Vasyl Fedoryshyn	UKR	
5. David Pogosian	GEO	WO
6. Giuvi "Gia" Sissaouri	CAN	
7. Jung Young-ho	KOR	
8. Lubos Cikel	AUT	

Yandro Quintana, the 2003 world champion silver medalist, swept through the competition, giving up only one point in his semifinal match against two-time European silver medalist Vasyl Fedoryshyn, before easily winning his final match against Masoud Jokar.

2008 Beijing C: 19, N: 19, D: 8.19.
(60 kg—132 lbs)

		FINAL MATCH
1. Mavlet Batyrov	RUS	1-0, 2-1
2. Vasyl Fedoryshyn	UKR	
3. Seyed Mohammadi	IRN	
3. Kenichi Yumoto	JPN	
5. Bazar Bazarguruev	KGZ	
5. Zəllmxan Hüseynov	AZE	
7. Murad Ramazanov	MAC	
8. Yandro Quintana Rivalta	CUB	

3rd Place: Mohammadi—Hüseynov 2-0, 3-1
3rd Place: Yumoto—Bazarguruev 1-0, 2-0

After winning the 2004 Olympic title in the 55-kilogram weight class, Mavlet Batyrov moved up to the 60-kilogram division and proceeded to win the 2006 European championship and 2007 world title. In Beijing, Batyrov beat defending Olympic champion Yandro Quintana 1-0, 1-1, 4-0 in the second round and 2006 world champion Seyed Mohammadi 1-0, 1-0 in the semifinals.

Batyrov's opponent in the final was three-time European champion Vasyl Fedoryshyn. Batyrov scored an early point to win the first period. Fedoryshyn moved ahead in the second period with a quick back move, but Batyrov clinched the victory late in the period, pushing Fedoryshyn out of the ring to score two points.

LIGHTWEIGHT
(66 kg—145½ lbs)

1896–1900 not held

1904 St. Louis C: 10, N: 1, D: 10.15.
(65.77 kg—145½ lbs)

		FINAL MATCH
1. Otto Roehm	USA	Dec 15:00
2. Rudolph Tesing	USA	
3. Albert Zirkel	USA	

1906 not held

1908 London C: 11, N: 2, D: 7.24.
(66.6 kg—147 lbs)

		FINAL MATCH
1. George de Relwyskow	GBR	Dec 15:00; Dec 15:00
2. William Wood	GBR	
3. Albert Gingell	GBR	Fall 6:44; Fall 3:20
4. George MacKenzie	GBR	

De Relwyskow had already won a silver medal in the Middleweight division when he took first place against the lightweights.

1912 not held

1920 Antwerp C: 10, N: 7, D: 8.27.
(67.5 kg—149 lbs)

		FINAL MATCH
1. Kaarle "Kalle" Anttila	FIN	Dec
2. Gottfrid Svensson	SWE	
3. Peter Wright	GBR	
4. Auguste Thijs	BEL	

1924 Paris C: 16, N: 10, D: 7.14.

1. Russell Vis	USA
2. Volmari Vikström	FIN
3. Arvo Haavisto	FIN
4. George Gardner	GBR
5. William Montgomery	CAN
5. Emile Pouvroux	FRA

1928 Amsterdam C: 11, N: 11, D: 8.1.

1. Osvald Käpp	EST
2. Charles Pacôme	FRA
3. Eino Leino	FIN
4. Birger Nilsen	NOR
5. Carlo Tesdorf Jörgensen	DEN
6. Clarence Berryman	USA

1932 Los Angeles C: 8, N: 8, D: 8.3.

1. Charles Pacôme	FRA
2. Károly Kárpáti	HUN
3. Gustaf Klarén	SWE
4. Melvin Clodfelter	USA
5. Kustaa Pihlajamäki	FIN

In the 1928 final, Pacôme, a law student, had lost a controversial decision to Osvald Käpp. Four years later in Los Angeles, the two met again in the first round. This time Pacôme won on points. Three more victories later, he was awarded the gold medal.

1936 Berlin C: 17, N: 17, D: 8.4.

		ROUND ELIMINATED	PEN. PTS.	FINAL ROUND
1. Károly Kárpáti	HUN	–	3	1
2. Wolfgang Ehrl	GER	–	4	2
3. Hermanni Pihlajamäki	FIN	–	4	6
4. Charles Delporte	FRA	5	6	
5. Harley De Witt Strong	USA	4	5	
6. Paride Romagnoli	ITA	4	7	
7. Eiichi Kazama	JPN	4	5	
8. Adalbert Toots	EST	4	7	

Kárpáti was born Károly Klein, but changed his name to Kárpáti to hide the fact that he was Jewish. Because he was an Olympic champion, Kárpáti was not sent to a Nazi concentration camp until 1943. At the camp in Nadvirna, Poland, Kárpáti threw a German soldier off a bridge and into a stream. The commanding officer did not punish Kárpáti. However when he resisted again at a different camp, he was beaten badly. Kárpáti survived the war, changed his name back to Klein and became a successful coach in Hungary.

1948 London C: 18, N: 18, D: 7.31.
(67 kg—147½ lbs)

		ROUND ELIMINATED	PEN. PTS.
1. Celal Atik	TUR	–	1
2. Gösta Frändfors	SWE	6	6
3. Hermann Baumann	SWI	6	8
4. Garibaldo Nizzola	ITA	6	10
5. William Koll	USA	4	6
6. Kim Suk-young	KOR	4	7
6. Sulo Leppänen	FIN	4	7
8. Lászlo Bakós	HUN	3	5

Atik won five of his six bouts by falls and defeated Leppanen on points.

1952 Helsinki C: 23, N: 23, D: 7.23.
(67 kg—147½ lbs)

		ROUND ELIMINATED	PEN. PTS.	FINAL ROUND
1. Olle Anderberg	SWE	–	1	2
2. Jay Thomas Evans	USA	–	2	4
3. Jahanbakht Towfigh	IRN	–	4	6
4. Armenak Yaltyryan	SOV/UKR	5	7	
5. Risto Talosela	FIN	5	7	
6. Heinrich Nettesheim	GER	4	6	
6. Takeo Shimotori	JPN	4	6	
8. Jan Cools	BEL	4	7	
8. Godfrey Pienaar	SAF	4	7	

1956 Melbourne C: 19, N: 19, D: 12.1.
(67 kg—147½ lbs)

		ROUND ELIMINATED	PEN. PTS.
1. Emamali Habibi Goudarzi	IRN	–	4
2. Shigeru Kasahara	JPN	5	6
3. Alimberg Bestayev	SOV/RUS	6	6
4. Gyula Tóth	HUN	5	5
5. Jay Thomas Evans	USA	4	5
5. Garibaldo Nizzola	ITA	4	5
7. Mario Tovar González	MEX	4	7
8. Muhammad Ashraf	PAK	4	7

1960 Rome C: 24, N: 24, D: 9.6.
(67 kg—147½ lbs)

		ROUND ELIMINATED	PEN. PTS.	FINAL ROUND
1. Shelby Wilson	USA	–	5	1
2. Volodymyr Synyavsky	SOV/UKR	–	5	3
3. Enyu Dimov	BUL	6	6	
4. Bong Chang-won	KOR	6	8	
4. Mostafa Tajik	IRN	6	8	
6. Garibaldo Nizzola	ITA	5	7	
7. Martti Peltoniemi	FIN	5	8	
8. Kazuo Abe	JPN	4	8	
8. Raymond Lougheed	CAN	4	8	
8. Hayrullah Sahin	TUR	4	8	

Shelby Wilson of Ponca City, Oklahoma, won the gold medal without registering a single fall.

1964 Tokyo C: 22, N: 22, D: 10.14.
(70 kg—154½ lbs)

		ROUND ELIMINATED	PEN. PTS.	FINAL ROUND
1. Enyu Vulchev (Dimov)	BUL	–	5	1
2. Klaus-Jürgen Rost	GER	–	5	3
3. Iwao Horiuchi	JPN	5	6	
4. Mahmut Atalay	TUR	5	6	
5. Abdollah Movahhed Ardabili	IRN	5	7	
6. Zarbeg Beriashvili	SOV/GEO	4	6	
6. Chung Dong-goo	KOR	4	6	
6. Gregory Ruth	USA	4	6	

1968 Mexico City C: 26, N: 26, D: 10.20.
(70 kg—154½ lbs)

		ROUND ELIMINATED	PEN. PTS.	FINAL ROUND
1. Abdollah Movahhed Ardabili	IRN	–	4	1
2. Enyu Vulchev (Dimov)	BUL	–	4	3
3. Danzandarja Sereeter	MGL	6	7.5	
4. Wayne Wells	USA	6	8	
5. Zarbeg Beriashvili	SOV/GEO	5	6	
6. Udey Chand	IND	5	6	
7. Iwao Horiuchi	JPN	5	8	
8. Klaus-Jürgen Rost	GER	5	9.5	

1972 Munich C: 25, N: 25, D: 8.31.
(68 kg—149½ lbs)

		ROUND ELIMINATED	PEN. PTS.	FINAL ROUND
1. Danny Gable	USA	–	1.5	2
2. Kikuo Wada	JPN	–	4.5	3
3. Ruslan Ashuraliyev	SOV/RUS	–	4.5	6
4. Tsedendamba Natsagdorj	MGL	5	6	
5. Ali Şahin	TUR	5	6	
6. Udo Schröder	GDR	5	8	
7. Włodzimierz Cieślak	POL	5	8.5	
8. József Rusznyák	HUN	4	7	

Twenty-three-year-old Dan Gable of Waterloo, Iowa, trained seven hours a day, every day, for three years prior to the Munich Olympics. Even as a teenager, he trained so relentlessly that he would mow the lawn by running while wearing a rubber suit and arm and leg weights. Between 1963 and 1973 he compiled a record of 299 wins, 6 losses and 3 draws. Gable became an extremely successful collegiate coach, leading the University of Iowa to fifteen US national championships, including a record nine in a row between 1977 and 1986. In 1984 he served as the coach of the US Olympic freestyle wrestling team.

1976 Montreal C: 24, N: 24, D: 7.31.
(68 kg—149½ lbs)

		ROUND ELIMINATED	PEN. PTS.	FINAL ROUND
1. Pavlo Pinigin	SOV/UKR	–	6	3.5
2. Lloyd "Butch" Keaser	USA	–	1	3.5
3. Yasaburo Sugawara	JPN	–	6	5
4. Doncho Zhekov	BUL	6	8.5	
5. José Ramos Cardoso	CUB	5	7	
6. Tsedendamba Natsagdorj	MGL	5	7	
7. Rami Miron	ISR	5	9	
8. Eberhard Probst	GDR	4	6.5	

Pinigin outpointed Keaser 12–1 in the final match. In 2003, the Science and Technology Board of the Yakutia State Committee for Geology named a goldfield in Pinigin's honor.

1980 Moscow C. 18, N: 18, D: 7.29.
(68 kg—149½ lbs)

		ROUND ELIMINATED	PEN. PTS.	FINAL ROUND
1. Saipulla Absaidov	SOV/RUS	–	1	1
2. Ivan Yankov	BUL	–	5	4
3. Shaban Sejdiu	YUG/MAC	–	2	7
4. Jagmander Singh	IND	5	6	
5. Eberhard Probst	GDR	5	7.5	
6. Octavian Dusa	ROM	4	7	
7. Ali Hussain Faris	IRQ	4	8	
8. Pekka Rauhala	FIN	4	9.5	

Absaidov outscored his five opponents 59–1, with only Yankov lasting the full nine minutes.

1984 Los Angeles-Anaheim C: 22, N: 22, D: 8.11.
(68 kg—149½ lbs)

		FINAL MATCH
1. You In-tak	KOR	5–5
2. Andrew Rein	USA	
3. Jukka Rauhala	FIN	Injury 3:02
4. Masakazu Kamimura	JPN	
5. Zsigmond Kelevitz	AUS	11–3
6. Fevzi Seker	TUR	
7. Erwin Knosp	GER	
8. René Neyer	SWI	

You scored an early 3-point arm throw which eventually gave him the victory. In the second period he suffered a lower back spasm requiring two injury time-outs. He had to be helped onto the victory podium and supported by security personnel during the playing of the Korean national anthem.

1988 Seoul C: 30, N: 30, D: 10.1.
(68 kg—149½ lbs)

		FINAL MATCH
1. Arsen Fadzayev	SOV/RUS	6–0
2. Park Jang-soon	KOR	
3. Nate Carr	USA	5–1
4. Kosei Akaishi	JPN	
5. David McKay	CAN	4–1
6. Jukka Rauhala	FIN	
7. Alexander Leipold	GER	14–10
8. Angel Yasenov	BUL	

Fadzayev, undefeated in international competition and a four-time world champion, overwhelmed each of his six opponents. Park qualified for the final by gaining a controversial 3–2 victory over Carr, which led to the suspension of the officials in charge of the match.

1992 Barcelona C: 21, N: 21, D: 8.5.
(68 kg—149½ lbs)

		FINAL MATCH
1. Arsen Fadzayev	RUS	13–1
2. Valentin Getzov	BUL	
3. Kosei Akaishi	JPN	4–0
4. Ali Akbarnejad	IRN	
5. Fatih Özbaş	TUR	3–1
6. Ko Young-ho	KOR	
7. Townsend Saunders	USA	6–3
8. Christopher Wilson	CAN	

Fadzayev gave up only three points in his five matches.

1996 Atlanta C: 19, N: 19, D: 7.30.
(68 kg—149½ lbs)

		FINAL MATCH
1. Vadim Bogiyev	RUS	1-1 8:00
2. Townsend Saunders	USA	
3. Zaza Zazirov	UKR	8-6
4. Yosmany Sánchez Larrude	CUB	
5. Arayik Gevorgyan	ARM	0-0 8:00
6. Hwang Sang-ho	KOR	
7. Küllo Kõiv	EST	7-2
8. Ahmad Alaosta	SYR	

Vadim Bogiyev's first opponent was his former coach, two-time defending champion Arsen Fadzayev, who was now representing Uzbekistan. Bogiyev won 3-1. In the final he faced defensive specialist Townsend Saunders, whose wife Tricia was a world champion wrestler. Bogiyev scored the only point in regulation on a take down with only seven seconds to go. In overtime, Saunders gut-wrenched Bogiyev, but Bogiyev slapped his hand on the mat before his elbow touched, thus limiting Saunders' score to a single point. The victory went to Bogiyev because he had received only two passivity calls to Saunders' three.

2000 Sydney C: 20, N: 20, D: 10.1.
(69 kg—152 lbs)

		FINAL MATCH
1. B. Daniel Igali	CAN	7-4
2. Arsen Gitinov	RUS	
3. Lincoln McIlravy	USA	3-1
4. Sergei Demchenko	BLR	
5. Yosmany Sánchez Larrude	CUB	6-3
6. Ivan Diaconu	MOL	
7. Arayik Gevorgian	ARM	
8. Almaz Askarov	KYR	

Daniel Igali was born and raised in the village of Eniwari in Bayelsa State in southeastern Nigeria. His father, an accountant, had four wives and 21 children. As Igali put it, "With the wives, enough for two football teams and reserves." Igali was a member of the Ijaw tribe, for whom traditional wrestling was part of their culture. In 1994, Igali represented Nigeria at the Commonwealth Games in Victoria, Canada. He placed 11th and then made a difficult decision: he chose to stay in Canada. Among the many Canadians who helped him was Maureen Matheny, an elementary-school principal who became his surrogate mother. Igali gained Canadian citizenship and represented Canada in the 1998 world championships, where he placed fourth. Matheny and her husband had hoped to accompany Igali to the next year's world championships in Ankara, Turkey, but Maureen was hospitalized with the return of a cancer she had been fighting for years. In the Ankara final, Igali upset American Lincoln McIlravy 3-2 to become the world champion. When he returned to Vancouver, Igali went straight to the hospital, showed Maureen Matheny his medal and gave her a kiss. Five days later, she died . . . but she did not leave Daniel Igali's life.

At the Sydney Olympics, Igali faced one tough battle after another. He made it out of the elimination pool only by winning the judges' decision after his match with Amir Tavakolian of Iran ended in a 2-2 tie. Igali's quarterfinal bout with Yosmany Sánchez was tied 1-1 after regulation, but Igali won in overtime. The following morning, he faced his semifinal opponent: Linclon McIlravy. Trailing 2-3, Igali tied the score with 12 seconds left in regulation and then won in overtime. Igali went back to his room and took a nap before the final. He dreamt that Maureen Matheny walked into the room, sat down across from him and repeated the last words she had said to him before she died: "I am so proud of you." "I thanked God," Igali later wrote, "for giving my angel a day pass to watch over her adopted son." Two hours later, an invigorated Igali defeated Arsen Gitinov 7-4 to win the gold medal.

2004 Athens C: 20, N: 20, D: 8.28.
(66 kg—145½ lbs)

		FINAL MATCH
1. Elbrus Tedeyev	UKR	5-1
2. Jamill Kelly	USA	
3. Makhach Murtazaliyev	RUS	2-1 9:00
4. Leonid Spiridonov	KAZ	
5. Kazuhiko Ikematsu	JPN	6-4
6. Apostolos Taskoudis	GRE	
7. Ömer Çubukçu	TUR	
8. Serafim Barzakov	BUL	

Born in the Ossetia region of Russia, Elbrus Tedeyev moved to Ukraine in 1992, at the age of seventeen, and was trained by Ukrainian coaches. He won the world championship at 62 kilograms in 1995 and 1999, both times after apparent losses were reversed on appeal. He won again in 2002, this time without controversy. The 62-kilogram bronze medalist at the 1996 Olympics, Tedeyev placed only eleventh at the Sydney Games. In the 2004 Olympic final, he faced an unlikely opponent, Jamill Kelly, who had finished in 28th place at the 2003 world championships. Kelly had never won a major tournament, in high school, college or after, until he won the US national title four months before the Olympics. In Athens, Kelly barely made it out of the semifinals, where he went into sudden death overtime against European champion Makhach Murtazaliyev. After a flurry of action at the edge of the mat, the judges reviewed the videotape replay and gave the winning points to Murtazaliyev. The US coaches appealed, and federation officials, after viewing the tape themselves, reversed the call. In the final, Tedeyev scored in the first minute, built a 5-0 lead and won 5-1.

2008 Beijing C: 21, N: 21, D: 8.20.
(66 kg—145½ lbs)

		FINAL MATCH
1. Ramazan Şahin	TUR	2-2, 2-1, 2-2
2. Andriy Stadnik	UKR	
3. Sushil Kumar	IND	
3. Otar Tushishvili	GEO	
5. Geandry Garzón Caballero	CUB	
5. Leonid Spiridonov	KAZ	
7. Irbek Farniyev	RUS	
8. Buyanjavyn Batzorig	MGL	

3rd Place: Kumar—Spirodonov 2-1, 0-1, 1-0
3rd Place: Tushishvili—Garzón 3-1, 1-1

Reigning world and European champion Ramazan Şahin faced Cuba's Geandry Garzón in their first match, a repeat of the 2007 world championship final. Şahin beat Garzón 1-0, 7-4, and then went on to defeat two-time junior world champion Mehdi Taghavi and 2006 world silver medalist Otar Tushishvili.

Şahin faced 2006 world bronze medalist Andriy Stadnik in the final. Şahin scored first, rolling Stadnik for two points, before Stadnik came back with two takedowns to level the score at 2-2 and take the period for scoring the final point. Şahin came back to win the next period 2-1 and take the match to a third, tie-breaking period. Trailing 2-0, Şahin scored two points on an exposure and held off Stadnik to win the gold medal.

Stadnik's wife, Mariya, had won the bronze medal four days earlier in the women's 48-kilogram weight class.

WELTERWEIGHT
(74 kg—163 lbs)

1896–1900 not held

1904 St. Louis C: 10, N: 1, D: 10.15.
(71.67 kg—158 lbs)

		FINAL MATCH
1. Charles Erickson	USA	Dec 15:00
2. William Beckmann	USA	
3. Jerry Winholtz	USA	

Erickson was a member of the Norwegian Turnverein of Brooklyn.

1906–1920 not held

1924 Paris C: 13, N: 7, D: 7.14.
(72 kg—158½ lbs)

1. Hermann Gehri	SWI
2. Eino Leino	FIN
3. Otto Müller	SWI
4. Guy Lookabough	USA
5. William Johnson	USA

1928 Amsterdam C: 11, N: 11, D: 8.1.
(72 kg—158½ lbs)

1. Arvo Haavisto	FIN
2. Lloyd Appelton	USA
3. Maurice Letchford	CAN
4. Jean Jourlin	FRA
5. T. Harry Morris	AUS

1932 Los Angeles C: 9, N: 9, D: 8.3.
(72 kg—158½ lbs)

1. Jack VanBebber	USA
2. Daniel MacDonald	CAN
3. Eino Leino	FIN
4. Jean Földeak	GER
5. Gyula Zombori	HUN

While waiting for his final match, Van Bebber learned that the start time had been moved up an hour and he was due on the mat—six miles away—in less than an hour. After walking for two miles, he was given a ride to the arena by a passing driver who recognized him as a member of the Los Angeles Athletic Club.

1936 Berlin C: 16, N: 16, D: 8.4.
(72 kg—158½ lbs)

		ROUND ELIMINATED	PEN. PTS.	FINAL ROUND
1. Frank Lewis	USA	–	3	3
2. Ture Andersson	SWE	–	4	3
3. Joseph Schleimer	CAN	–	3	6
4. Jean Jourlin	FRA	5	5	
5. Willy Angst	SWI	5	7	
6. Josef Paar	GER	4	5	
7. Julien Beke	BEL	3	6	
7. Huseyin Erçetin	TUR	3	6	
7. John O'Hara	AUS	3	6	

Frank Lewis of Cushing, Oklahoma, was awarded first place even though he was thrown by Andersson in the fourth round. Bronze medalist Joe Schleimer was forced to pay his own way to Berlin. This was not an easy task, considering that he was unemployed. He was able to contribute one-third of his expenses, but the rest came from a fund organized by the Toronto German Club and the local Catholic church.

1948 London C: 16, N: 16, D: 7.31.
(73 kg—161 lbs)

		ROUND ELIMINATED	PEN. PTS.	FINAL ROUND
1. Yaşar Doğu	TUR	–	0	1
2. Richard Garrard	AUS	–	2	5
3. Leland Merrill	USA	–	3	4
4. Jean-Baptiste Leclerc	FRA	4	6	
5. Kálmán Sóvári	HUN	4	7	
6. Frans Westergren	SWE	3	5	
7. Willy Angst	SWI	3	6	
7. Harry Peace	CAN	3	6	
7. Whang Byung-kwan	KOR	3	6	
7. Abbas Zandi	IRN	3	6	

1952 Helsinki C: 20, N: 20, D: 7.23.
(73 kg—161 lbs)

		ROUND ELIMINATED	PEN. PTS.	FINAL ROUND
1. William Smith	USA	–	2	4
2. Per Berlin	SWE	–	3	4
3. Abdollah Mojtabavi	IRN	–	4	4
4. Alberto Longarela	ARG	4	5	
5. Mohamed Hassan Moussa	EGY	4	6	
5. Ladislav Sekal	CZE	4	6	
5. Tsuguo Yamazaki	JPN	4	6	
8. Aleksanteri Keisala	FIN	4	7	

Twenty-three-year-old Bill Smith of Cedar Falls, Iowa, was so surprised by his victory that at the medal ceremony he mounted the third-place stand instead of the winner's pedestal.

1956 Melbourne C: 15, N: 15, D: 12.1.
(73 kg—161 lbs)

		ROUND ELIMINATED	PEN. PTS.	FINAL ROUND
1. Mitsuo Ikeda	JPN	–	3	2
2. Ibrahim Zengin	TUR	–	4	3
3. Vakhtang Balavadze	SOV/GEO	–	4	6
4. Per Berlin	SWE	4	5	
4. Nabi Sorouri	IRN	4	5	
4. Coenraad de Villiers	SAF	4	5	
7. Mitjus Petkov	BUL	4	6	
8. Ernest Fischer	USA	3	7	
8. Alfred Tischendorf	GDR	3	7	

1960 Rome C: 23, N: 23, D: 9.6.
(73 kg—161 lbs)

		ROUND ELIMINATED	PEN. PTS.	FINAL ROUND
1. Douglas Blubaugh	USA	–	0	1
2. Ismail Ogan	TUR	–	4	4
3. Muhammed Bashir	PAK	–	5	7
4. Gaetano De Vescovi	ITA	5	7	
4. Emamali Habibi Goudarzi	IRN	5	7	
4. Yutaka Kaneko	JPN	5	7	
7. Coenraad de Villiers	SAF	4	7	
8. Åke Carlsson	SWE	4	8	

Doug Blubaugh of Ponca City, Oklahoma, qualified for the US team by beating his former Oklahoma State teammate Phil Kinyon, after four scoreless draws. In fact, Blubaugh and Kinyon had drawn ten straight matches before Blubaugh finally won a decision. In Rome he tore through the opposition, winning five of his seven bouts by throws and one by default. Only Ogan lasted the full 12 minutes.

1964 Tokyo C: 22, N: 22, D: 10.14.
(78 kg—172 lbs)

		ROUND ELIMINATED	PEN. PTS.	FINAL ROUND
1. Ismail Ogan	TUR	–	4	4
2. Guliko Sagaradze	SOV/GEO	–	4	4
3. Mohammad Ali Sanatkaran	IRN	–	4	4
4. Petko Dermendzhiev	BUL	5	8	
5. Yasuo Watanabe	JPN	4	6	
6. Philip Oberlander	CAN	4	6	
7. Muhammad Afzal	PAK	4	7	
8. Madho Singh	IND	4	8	

Ogan was awarded first place because he weighed 2 kg (4.4 lbs) less than Sagaradze. Sanatkaran was relegated to third place because his two draws came in the final round.

1968 Mexico City C: 19, N: 19, D: 10.20.
(78 kg—172 lbs)

		ROUND ELIMINATED	PEN. PTS.	FINAL ROUND
1. Mahmut Atalay	TUR	–	4.5	1
2. Daniel Robin	FRA	–	5	3
3. Dagvasuren Purev	MGL	5	6	
4. Ali Mohammad Momeni	IRN	5	6.5	
5. Tatsuo Sasaki	JPN	5	6.5	
6. Yuri Schakmuradov	SOV/AZR	5	8	
7. Stephen Combs	USA	5	8	
7. Angel Sotirov	BUL	5	8	

In 1968, Daniel Robin won silver medals in both the freestyle and Greco-Roman competitions.

1972 Munich C: 25, N: 25, D: 8.31.

		ROUND ELIMINATED	PEN. PTS.	FINAL ROUND
1. Wayne Wells	USA	–	2	2
2. Jan Karlsson	SWE	–	4	4
3. Adolf Seger	GER	–	5	6
4. Yancho Pavlov	BUL	6	7.5	
5. Mansour Barzegar	IRN	5	7	
5. Wolfgang Nitschke	GDR	5	7	
5. Daniel Robin	FRA	5	7	
8. Miklós Urbanovics	HUN	4	6.5	

Wells was a lawyer from Norman, Oklahoma.

1976 Montreal C: 21, N: 21, D: 7.31.

		ROUND ELIMINATED	PEN. PTS.	FINAL ROUND
1. Jiichiro Date	JPN	–	0	1
2. Mansour Barzegar	IRN	–	2	5
3. Stanley Dziedzic	USA	–	2	6
4. Ruslan Ashuraliyev	SOV/RUS	5	7.5	
5. Marin Pircalabu	ROM	5	9	
6. Fred Hempel	GDR	5	10	
7. Jarmo Overmark	FIN	4	7	
8. Kiro Ristov	YUG/SER	4	8	

Date threw six of his seven opponents and outpointed Dziedzic 10–5.

1980 Moscow C: 18, N: 18, D: 7.30.

		ROUND ELIMINATED	PEN. PTS.	FINAL ROUND
1. Valentin Angelov	BUL	–	2	2
2. Jamtsyin Davajav	MGL	–	6	4
3. Daniel Karabin	CZE/SLV	–	7.5	6
4. Anatoly Pinigin	SOV/UKR	6	8.5	
5. Ryszard Ścigalski	POL	5	7	
6. Rajander Singh	IND	4	7	
7. István Fehér	HUN	4	9	
8. Riccardo Niccolini	ITA	4	9	

Angelov earned his gold medal by gaining five victories in one day. The big surprise was his win against Pinigin. Pinigin took Angelov to the mat twice in the first minute, but the Bulgarian came back to register a fall after 1:59. In the final match Angelov won on points, 6–5, over Davajav.

1984 Los Angeles-Anaheim C: 22, N: 22, D: 8.10.

		FINAL MATCH
1. David Schultz	USA	4–1
2. Martin Knosp	GER	
3. Šhaban Sejdiu	YUG/MAC	5–1
4. Rajender Singh	IND	
5. Naomi Higuchi	JPN	7–3
6. Han Myung-woo	KOR	
7. Marc Mongeon	CAN	
8. Pekka Rauhala	FIN	

The only defending world champion freestyle wrestler to take part in the 1984 Olympics, Dave Schultz won one match by a fall and his other five by a combined score of 42–2. Twenty-four hours after Schultz was awarded his gold medal, his younger brother, Mark, won the middleweight division. Dave retired from competition in 1987 but then began a successful comeback in 1993. He placed fifth at the 1995 world championships, and when the Olympic year of 1996 began he was ranked first in the United States. However, on January 26, he was shot to death by John du Pont, one of the major sponsors of the US freestyle wrestling team.

1988 Seoul C: 30, N: 30, D: 9.30.

		FINAL MATCH
1. Kenneth Monday	USA	5–2 6:42
2. Adlan Varayev	SOV/RUS	
3. Rakhmad Sukra Sofilyadi	BUL	8–3
4. Lodoin Enkhbayer	MGL	
5. Pekka Rauhala	FIN	Injury 3:00
6. Ayatollah Vagozari	IRN	
7. Yoon Kyung-Jae	KOR	Injury
8. Uwe Westendorf	GDR	

Kenny Monday of Tulsa, Oklahoma, qualified for the final by pinning one opponent and outscoring six others 34–2. For the gold medal, he faced defending world champion Adlan Varayev, who had beaten him in two of their three previous meetings. Neither man scored for over 4 minutes. Then, with 1:45 remaining, Monday took a 1–0 lead with a single-leg pick. Forty-five seconds later Varayev scored with a double-leg takedown to move ahead 2–1. With 17 seconds left, Monday evened the match with a crotch lift reversal. Forty seconds into the sudden death overtime, Monday caught the tiring Varayev in a bodylock, lifted him into the air, and slammed him to the mat for a 3-point takedown. Monday was the first black wrestler to win an Olympic gold medal.

1992 Barcelona C: 18, N: 18, D: 8.6.

		FINAL MATCH
1. Park Jang-soon	KOR	1–0
2. Kenneth Monday	USA	
3. Amirreza Khadem Azghadi	IRN	1–0 6:32
4. Mahomed Salam Gadzhiyev	RUS	
5. Krzysztof Walencik	POL	
6. Gary Holmes	CAN	
7. János Nagy	HUN	Injury
8. Lodoin Enkhbayer	MGL	

Park outpointed his pool opponents 25–3; Monday outpointed his 14–0. Both men wrestled cautiously in the final. As the clock ticked down, Monday attacked. Park countered and scored a one-point takedown with 15 seconds left in the match. In the end Monday gave up only that single point in five matches, but he had to settle for second place. Toshihiko Hara of Japan qualified for the match for fifth place, but refused to take part and was disqualified. Walencik and Holmes were awarded their places without a final match.

1996 Atlanta C: 22, N: 22, D: 8.1.

		FINAL MATCH
1. Buvaysa Saytiev	RUS	5-0
2. Park Jang-soon	KOR	
3. Takuya Ota	JPN	5-3
4. Plamen Paskalev	BUL	
5. Alexander Leipold	GER	WO
6. Kenneth Monday	USA	
7. Viktor Peicov	MOL	
8. Mahomed Salam Gadzhiyev	AZR	

Although he was the defending world champion, Buvaysa Saytiev of Khasavyurt, Chechnya, won the Olympic title with surprising ease. He defeated 1995 lightweight world champion Alexander Leipold 3-1 and 1988 Olympic champion Kenny Monday 6-1, before downing defending Olympic champion Park Jang-soon 5-0. Saytiev's cumulative score in his four matches was 22-2.

2000 Sydney C: 20, N: 20, D: 9.30.
(76 kg—167½ lbs)

		FINAL MATCH
1. Brandon Slay	USA	Disq
2. Moon Eui-jae	KOR	Fall 2:21
3. Adem Bereket	TUR	
4. Gennady Laliyev	KAZ	Injury
5. Ruslan Khinchagov	UZB	
6. Alik Muzayev	UKR	
7. Nasir Gadzhyanov	MAC	
8. Marcin Jurecki	POL	

DISQ (drugs): Alexander Leipold (GER)

Buvaysa Saytiev, the defending Olympic champion, entered the 2000 Olympics undefeated in international competition. But in the second match of his preliminary pool, Saytiev was upset by Brandon Slay, who scored a takedown 33 seconds into overtime. Slay squeezed through the quarterfinals on a judges' decision after tying Gennady Laliyev 2-2. Then he defeated Adem Bereket, a Chechen representing Turkey, 3-1 in the semifinals. In the other semifinal, Alexander Leipold, who was competing in his fourth Olympics, pinned Moon Eui-jae with ten seconds left in overtime while trailing 0-1. Leipold won the final 4-0, scoring his first three points on penalties called against Slay. On the medal platform, 31-year-old Leipold leaned over, patted 24-year-old Slay on the head and said, "Brandon, you have two more Olympic Games left. I think you can make the gold medal." As it turned out, Slay only had to wait three weeks for his gold medal. Leipold tested positive for the anabolic steroid nandrolone and was stripped of his Olympic title. Slay, Moon and Bereket were presented their new medals in a made-for-television event staged in front of the NBC-TV studios in New York City.

Not all Olympic champions are star athletes from the very beginning. Brandon Slay entered his first wrestling tournament when he was six years old. In his first match, an older boy pummeled him so badly that Slay ran off the mat crying in the middle of the bout and hid in the bathroom. His father coaxed him back and his opponent, Brandon Brown, pinned him after 30 seconds. Slay secluded himself in a corner, where he was approached by Brown. The older boy explained that the first match is always the hardest and he taught Slay some moves. Slay kept at it and lost all of his first season's matches except for one forfeit. By his third season, however, Slay was Texas state champion . . . and Brandon Brown became his best friend.

2004 Athens C: 20, N: 20, D: 8.29.
(74 kg—163 lbs)

		FINAL MATCH
1. Buvaysa Saytiev	RUS	7-0
2. Gennady Laliyev	KAZ	
3. Iván Fundora	CUB	3-1 7:13
4. Krystian Brzozowski	POL	
5. Joe Williams	USA	WO
6. Daniel Igali	CAN	
7. Salvatore Rinella	ITA	
8. Arayik Gevorgyan	ARM	

Except for his unexpected loss to Brandon Slay at the Sydney Olympics, Buvaysa Saytiev had dominated the division since 1995, winning five world championships, five European championships and the 1996 Olympic title. At the 2003 world championships, Saytiev had been hard-pressed by Murad Gaidarov of Belarus. Their final ended in a 2-2 tie after overtime, and Saytiev was given the victory based on classification points. In Athens, the two met again in the quarterfinals. Again the two were tied 2-2 after regulation time, but this time Saytiev was awarded a controversial point after only six seconds in sudden death overtime. After the match, Saytiev and Gaidarov were involved in a fracas in the mixed zone where athletes meet reporters, which had to be broken up by police. Gaidarov was disqualified, while Saytiev won his next two matches 8-0 (against Krystian Brzozowski) and 7-0 to win the gold.

2008 Beijing C: 21, N: 21, D: 8.20.
(74 kg—163 lbs)

		FINAL MATCH
1. Buvaisa Saytiev	RUS	0-1, 1-0, 3-1
2. Soslan Tigiyev	UZB	
3. Murad Gaydarov	BLR	
3. Kiril Terziev	BUL	
5. Iván Fundora Zaldivar	CUB	
5. Stefan Gheorghiţă	ROM	
7. Ben Askren	USA	
8. Arsen Gitinov	KGZ	

3rd Place: Gaydarov—Gheorghiţă 2-1, 3-1
3rd Place: Fundora—Terziev fall (3:58)

Thirty-three-year-old Buvaisa Saytiev had earned two Olympic gold medals, six world championships and six European championships, but was left off Russia's 2007 world championship squad after a disappointing eighth-place finish at the 2006 world championships. However, he earned a spot at the 2008 Olympics by defeating reigning world and European champion Makhach Murtazaliev at the Russian Olympic trials.

Saytiev reached the final after a dramatic win in the semifinals, pinning Bulgaria's Kiril Terziev to the mat one minute forty-nine seconds into the match. In the final, Saytiyev lost the first period to underdog Soslan Tigiyev on a takedown, but came back to win the second period with a go-behind point, and then clinched the gold medal in the third period by scoring on a low single and back exposure.

MIDDLEWEIGHT
(84 kg—185¼ lbs)

1896–1906 not held

1908 London C: 12, N: 3, D: 7.22.
(73 kg—161 lbs)

		FINAL MATCH
1. Stanley Bacon	GBR	Dec; Dec
2. George de Relwyskow	GBR	
3. Frederick Beck	GBR	WO
4. Carl Georg Andersson	SWE	
5. Edgar Bacon (GBR), Aubrey Coleman (GBR)		

Bacon was 5 feet 3½ inches tall. After George de Relzyskow was declared the winner over Carl Andersson, Swedish officials protested the decision (to no avail) and Andersson refused to take part in the bronze medal match.

1912 not held

1920 Antwerp C: 18, N: 12, D: 8.27.
(75 kg—165½ lbs)

		FINAL MATCH
1. Eino Leino	FIN	Dec
2. Väinö Penttala	FIN	
3. Charles Johnson	USA	
4. Angus Frantz	USA	
5. Otto Borgström (SWE), Pierre Derkinderen (BEL), Gudmund Grimstad (NOR), Frits Janssens (BEL)		

Eino Leino won the first of his four Olympic medals. In 1924 he earned a silver medal in the welterweight division. He added a bronze as a lightweight in 1928 and another bronze in 1932 as a welterweight.

1924 Paris C: 14, N: 9, D: 7.14.
(79 kg—174 lbs)

1. Fritz Hagmann	SWI
2. Pierre Ollivier	BEL
3. Viho Pekkala	FIN
4. Jaako Penttilä	FIN
5. Robert Christoffersen	DEN
5. Noel Rhys	GBR

1928 Amsterdam C: 9, N: 9, D: 8.1.
(79 kg—174 lbs)

1. Ernst Kyburz	SWI
2. Donald Stockton	CAN
3. Samuel Rabin	GBR
4. Ralph Hammond	USA
5. Andries Praeg	SAF

1932 Los Angeles C: 7, N: 7, D: 8.3.
(79 kg—174 lbs)

1. Ivar Johansson	SWE
2. Kyösti Luukko	FIN
3. Jözsef Tunyogi	HUN
4. Robert Hess	USA
5. Sumiyuki Kotani	JPN
6. Emile Poilvé	FRA

This was the first of Johansson's three Olympic gold medals. Four days later he won the Greco-Roman Welterweight division and four years later, in Berlin, he was victorious as a Greco-Roman middleweight.

1936 Berlin C: 15, N: 15, D: 8.4.
(79 kg—174 lbs)

		ROUND ELIMINATED	PEN. PTS.	FINAL ROUND
1. Emlle Poilvé	FRA	–	1	0
2. Richard Voliva	USA	–	3	3
3. Ahmet Kireççi	TUR	5	6	
4. Ernst Krebs	SWI	5	7	
5. Jaroslav Sysel	CZE	4	6	
6. Kyösti Luukko	FIN	4	7	
7. Ercole Gallegati	ITA	3	5	
8. János Riheczky	HUN	3	5	

Poilvé registered five throws in six matches, as well as a second-round decision over Luukko.

1948 London C: 16, N: 16, D: 7.31.
(79 kg—174 lbs)

		ROUND ELIMINATED	PEN. PTS.	FINAL ROUND
1. Glen Brand	USA	–	2	0
2. Adil Candemir	TUR	–	4	3
3. Erik Lindén	SWE	5	5	
4. Carel Reitz	SAF	4	5	
5. Paavo Sepponen	FIN	4	5	
6. André Brunaud	FRA	4	7	
7. Maurice Vachon	CAN	3	5	
8. Bruce Arthur	AUS	3	6	

Twenty-four-year-old Glen Brand of Clarion, Iowa, was awarded first place after he threw Candemir in the fourth round and then decisioned Lindén in Round 5. In seventh place was Maurice Vachon, who became a well-known professional wrestler using the name Mad Dog Vachon.

1952 Helsinki C: 17, N: 17, D: 7.23.
(79 kg—174 lbs)

		ROUND ELIMINATED	PEN. PTS.	FINAL ROUND
1. David Tsimakuridze	SOV/GEO	–	4	2
2. Gholam Reza Takhti	IRN	–	2	3
3. György Gurics	HUN	–	5	6
4. Gustav Gocke	GER	5	6	
5. Haydar Zafer	TUR	4	5	
6. León Genuth	ARG	4	7	
6. Carel Reitz	SAF	4	7	
8. Bengt Lindblad	SWE	3	5	

1956 Melbourne C: 15, N: 15, D: 12.1.
(79 kg—174 lbs)

		ROUND ELIMINATED	PEN. PTS.	FINAL ROUND
1. Nikola Stanchev	BUL	–	4	1
2. Daniel Hodge	USA	–	4	3
3. Georgy Skhirtladze	SOV/GEO	–	4	6
4. Ismet Atli	TUR	5	5	
5. Kazuo Katsuramoto	JPN	4	6	
5. Johann Sterr	GER	4	6	
7. Bengt Lindblad	SWE	3	7	
7. Abbas Zandi	IRN	3	7	

Stanchev was the first Bulgarian to win an Olympic gold medal.

1960 Rome C: 19, N: 19, D: 9.6.
(79 kg—174 lbs)

		ROUND ELIMINATED	PEN. PTS.	FINAL ROUND
1. Hasan Güngör	TUR	–	4	
2. Georgy Skhirtladze	SOV/GEO	5	6	
3. Hans Yngve Antonsson	SWE	5	6	
4. Edward De Witt	USA	5	7	
5. Prodan Gardzhev	BUL	4	6	
5. Géza Hollósi	HUN	4	6	
5. Madho Singh	IND	4	6	
8. Takashi Nagal	JPN	4	7	

1964 Tokyo C: 16, N: 16, D: 10.14.
(87 kg—192 lbs)

		ROUND ELIMINATED	PEN. PTS.	FINAL ROUND
1. Prodan Gardzhev	BUL	–	5	2
2. Hasan Güngör	TUR	–	5	2
3. Daniel Brand	USA	5	6	
4. Mansour Mehdizadeh	IRN	5	6	
5. Géza Hollósi	HUN	4	6	
5. Tatsuo Sasaki	JPN	4	6	
7. Günther Bauch	GDR	4	9	
7. Faiz Muhammad	PAK	4	9	

Güngör was deprived of a second gold medal because he outweighed Gardzhev by 1 kg (2.2 lbs).

1968 Mexico City C: 22, N: 22, D: 10.20.
(87 kg—192 lbs)

		ROUND ELIMINATED	PEN. PTS.
1. Borys Hurevych	SOV/UKR	–	4.5
2. Jigjid Munkhbat	MGL	7	6.5
3. Prodan Gardzhev	BUL	7	7.5
4. Thomas Peckham	USA	7	8
5. Hüseyin Gürsoy	TUR	6	7
6. Peter Döring	GDR	4	6
7. Ronald Grinstead	GBR	4	8
8. Shigeru Endo	JPN	4	8.5

Hurevych finished the tournament with draws against Munkhbat and Gardzhev. He had earlier served as the model for the sculpture "We Shall Beat Swords into Ploughshares" by Yerhen Vuchetych that stands in front of the United Nations building in New York City.

1972 Munich C: 24, N: 24, D: 8.31.
(82 kg—181 lbs)

		ROUND ELIMINATED	PEN. PTS.
1. Levan Tediashvili	SOV/GEO	–	4.5
2. John Peterson	USA	6	6
3. Vasile Iorga	ROM	6	7
4. Horst Stottmeister	GDR	6	7
5. Tatsuo Sasaki	JPN	5	6
6. Peter Neumair	GER	5	7
7. Kurt Elmgren	SWE	4	6
8. Jan Wypiórczyk	POL	4	7

1976 Montreal C: 18, N: 18, D: 7.31.
(82 kg—181 lbs)

		ROUND ELIMINATED	PEN. PTS.	FINAL ROUND
1. John Peterson	USA	–	2	0.5
2. Viktor Novozhilov	SOV/RUS	–	5.5	5
3. Adolf Seger	GER	–	6.5	6.5
4. Mehinet Uzun	TUR	6	7.5	
5. Ismail Abilov	BUL	5	7.5	
6. Henryk Mazur	POL	4	6	
7. István Kovács	HUN	4	6	
8. Masaru Motegi	JPN	4	8	

In 1972 John Peterson of Comstock, Wisconsin, won a silver medal, while his brother, Ben, a light heavyweight, won a gold. Four years later in Montreal they reversed medals.

1980 Moscow C: 14, N: 14, D: 7.31.
(82 kg—181 lbs)

		ROUND ELIMINATED	PEN. PTS.	FINAL ROUND
1. Ismail Abilov	BUL	–	1	1
2. Magomedhan Aratsilov	SOV/RUS	–	3	3
3. István Kovács	HUN	–	4	8
4. Henryk Mazur	POL	5	8.5	
5. Abdula Memedi	YUG/MAC	4	7	
6. Zevegying Duvchin	MGL	4	8	
7. Gunter Busarello	AUT	3	7	
8. Mohammad Eloulabi	SYR	3	7.5	

Abilov outpointed his five opponents 50–5. Only Aratsilov lasted nine minutes, losing a fifth-round 8–4 decision to the 29-year-old Bulgarian champion.

1984 Los Angeles-Anaheim C: 16, N: 16, D: 8.11.
(82 kg—181 lbs)

		FINAL MATCH
1. Mark Schultz	USA	13–0 1:59
2. Hideyuki Nagashima	JPN	
3. Christopher Rinke	CAN	5–2
4. Reiner Trik	GER	
5. Kim Tae-woo	KOR	10–3
6. Kenneth Reinsfield	NZL	
7. Iraklis Deskoulidis	GRE	
8. Luciano Ortelli	ITA	

With all of the top four 82 kg wrestlers boycotted out of the Olympics, the favorites' role fell to Resit Karabacek of Turkey and Mark Schultz, younger brother of 74 kg champion Dave Schultz. As it happened, Karabacek and Schultz met in the first round. Only 30 seconds into the match Karabacek, who had never before been pinned, was thrown by a single leg counter and the match was over. As Karabacek writhed in agony, having suffered a fractured left elbow, Schultz happily paraded around the mat, showing no interest in his opponent's condition. After escorting Karabacek to the hospital, Turkish officials filed a protest, claiming that Schultz had used an illegal hold. Their protest was upheld and Karabacek, who was unable to continue, was declared the winner by disqualification. However, because the protest was filed more than 30 minutes after the match ended, Schultz was not disqualified from the tournament. An extra judge was assigned to scrutinize the Schultz brothers during the remainder of the competition. Mark Schultz then put together four straight victories to match his brother's gold medal.

1988 Seoul C: 29, N: 29, D: 10.1.
(82 kg—181 lbs)

		FINAL MATCH	
1. Han Myung-woo	KOR	4–0	
2. Necmi Gencalp	TUR		
3. Josef Lohyňa	CZE/SLV	Passivity 7:54	
4. Aleksandr Tambovtsev	SOV/RUS		
5. Puntsag Suhbat	MGL	Injury	
6. Mark Schultz	USA		
7. Atsushi Ito	JPN	5–4	6:29
8. Hans Gstöttner	GDR		

1992 Barcelona C: 19, N: 19, D: 8.7.
(82 kg—181 lbs)

		FINAL MATCH
1. Kevin Jackson	USA	1–0 6:54
2. Elmadi Jabrailov	RUS	
3. Rasoul Khadem Azghadi	IRN	6–0
4. Hans Gstöttner	GER	
5. Josef Lohyňa	CZE/SLV	2–2 10:05
6. Sebahattin Öztürk	TUR	
7. Nicolae Ghita	ROM	4–1
8. Francisco Iglesias Serna	SPA	

In the final, 1991 world champion Kevin Jackson faced 1989 world champion Elmadi Jabrailov of Chechnya. They were evenly matched and regulation time ended in a scoreless tie. Forty-six seconds into sudden-death overtime, Jabrailov secured a deep leg attack. As Jackson scrambled to counterattack, the wrestlers moved out of bounds. The referee, Todor Grudev of Bulgaria, signaled for the action to continue. Jabrailov's team coach, two-time gold medalist Ivan Yarygin, immediately protested that his man had controlled Jackson and deserved a point, and with it the match and the gold medal. The match was resumed after several minutes and after another minute of fighting, Jackson won with a one-point double-leg takedown. Jackson called out, "Gold medal! Gold medal!" and began celebrating with his supporters. Meanwhile, to say that Jabrailov was disheartened would be an understatement. He cried and screamed and was inconsolable. When it came time for the medal ceremony, Jabrailov had to be pushed onto the podium. He accepted his silver medal, but refused to put it around his neck. Although Jabrailov held nothing against Jackson personally and did not hesitate to congratulate him, the Russian's supporters whipped the crowd into a frenzy and the "Star-Spangled Banner" was drowned out by whistling and booing. The International Wrestling Federation rejected a formal protest on the basis that the official video of the disputed non-point was inconclusive.

1996 Atlanta C: 21, N: 21, D: 7.31.
(82 kg—181 lbs)

		FINAL MATCH
1. Khadzhimurad Magomedov	RUS	2-1 8:00
2. Yang Hyun-mo	KOR	
3. Amirreza Khadem Azghadi	IRN	0-0 8:00
4. Sebahattin Öztürk	TUR	
5. Magomed Ibragimov	AZR	WO
6. Elmadi Jabrailov	KAZ	
7. Lesley Gutches	USA	3-0
8. Ariel Ramos Wilson	CUB	

A curious incident occurred in the second round when Barcelona silver medalist Elmadi Jabrailov of Kazakhstan faced the 1994 world champion, Tucuman Jabrailov of Moldova. The two were brothers from Chechnya who chose not to represent Russia because of its war against Chechnya. Elmadi won the high-scoring but unusually friendly encounter 10-8.

Tucuman and Elmadi Jabrailov, 1996
Brothers Tucuman and Elmadi Jabrailov go to the mat in the 1996 Light Middleweight freestyle wrestling tournament.

2000 Sydney C: 20, N: 20, D: 10.1.
(85 kg—187½ lbs)

		FINAL MATCH
1. Adam Saytiev	RUS	Fall 3:41
2. Yoel Romero Palacios	CUB	
3. Magamed Ibragimov	MAC	4-1
4. Amirreza Khadem Azghadi	IRN	
5. Charles Burton	USA	Injury
6. Yang Hyun-mo	KOR	
7. Gábor Kapuvári	HUN	
8. Nicolae Ghiță	ROM	

As expected, Adam Saytiev and Yoel Romero dominated the tournament. On the way to the final, Saytiev outscored his four opponents 23-1 and Romero shut out his four opponents 18-0. However, Saytiev, whose brother, Buvaysa, had won the welterweight gold in 1996, overwhelmed Romero 7-1 before pinning him 40 seconds into the second round. A Chechen, Saytiev had to be talked into wearing a Russian singlet at the 1999 world championships.

2004 Athens C: 20, N: 20, D: 8.28.
(84 kg—185 lbs)

		FINAL MATCH
1. Cael Sanderson	USA	3-1
2. Moon Eui-jae	KOR	
3. Sazhid Sazhidov	RUS	5-3
4. Yoel Romero Palacios	CUB	
5. Majid Khodaei	IRN	3-0
6. Lazaros Loizidis	GRE	
7. Taras Danko	UKR	
8. Shamil Aliev	TJK	

One of the most important decisions of the competition took place before the Olympic Games had begun, when Russia chose reigning world champion Sazhid Sazhidov to compete in Athens, over defending Olympic champion Adam Satiyev. In the semifinals, Moon Eui-jae crushed Sazhidov 10-2, while Cael Sanderson edged out Yoel Romero 3-2, Sanderson's first win against Romero in three career matches. Sanderson had gained fame as a college wrestler at Iowa State University, compiling a record of 159-0 to become the first wrestler in NCAA history to remain undefeated for four years. In the Olympic final, Moon gained a 1-0 advantage early in the second period before Sanderson rallied in the final minute and a half, rolling Moon for two points and scoring on a single-leg takedown to win.

2008 Beijing C: 20, N: 20, D: 8.21.
(84 kg—185 lbs)

		FINAL MATCH
1. Revaz Mindorashvili	GEO	2-3, 3-0, 4-0
2. Yusup Abdusalomov	TJK	
3. Taras Danko	UKR	
3. Georgy Ketoyev	RUS	
5. Serhat Balcı	TUR	
5. Davyd Bichinashvili	GER	
7. Novruz Temrezov	AZE	
8. Harutyun Yenokyan	ARM	

3rd Place: Danko—Balcı 1-0, 2-0
3rd Place: Ketoyev—Bichinashvili 3-0, 1-2, 2-2

The 2005 world champion, Revaz Mindorashvili pinned reigning world champion and two-time reigning European champion Georgy Ketoyev in the semifinals. He then faced reigning world silver medalist Yusup Abdusalomov in the gold medal match, losing the first period 2-3 to the Russian-born Abdusalomov. Mindorashvili rallied with seven unanswered points over the next two periods, including three takedowns to win the second period and two pushouts and a takedown in the third period.

HEAVYWEIGHT

(96 kg—211¾ lbs)

1896-1968 not held

1972 Munich C: 17, N: 17, D: 8.31.
(100 kg—220 lbs)

		ROUND ELIMINATED	PEN. PTS.	FINAL ROUND
1. Ivan Yarygin	SOV/RUS	–	0	0
2. Khorloo Baianmunkh	MGL	–	1	5
3. József Csatári	HUN	–	2	7
4. Vasil Todorov	BUL	5	7.5	
5. Enache Panait	ROM	5	9	
6. Ryszard Długosz	POL	4	7	
7. Abolfazl Anvari	IRN	4	9	
8. Julio Tamussin	ITA	3	6.5	

In an inspired performance, 23-year-old Ivan Yarygin pinned all seven of his opponents. Only Baianmunkh was able to last more than three minutes with the Soviet strongman. Yarygin spent a total of only 17 minutes and eight seconds on the mat in his seven matches.

1976 Montreal C: 15, N: 15, D: 7.31
(100 kg—220 lbs)

		ROUND ELIMINATED	PEN. PTS.	FINAL ROUND
1. Ivan Yarygin	SOV/RUS	–	2	1.5
2. Russell Hellickson	USA	–	3.5	4
3. Dimo Kostov	BUL	–	4.5	6.5
4. Petr Drozda	CZE	5	8	
5. Khorloo Baianmunkh	MGL	4	5.5	
6. Kazuo Shimizu	JPN	4	8	
7. Hans Stratz	GER	3	7	
8. Daniel Verník Grunmann	ARG	3	8	

In 1974 Yarygin was beaten in the European championships by Harald Büttner of East Germany. He was immediately removed from the Soviet team and replaced by veteran Vladimir Gulyutkin, who proceeded to win the 1974 world championship. But at the 1975 world championships, Büttner pinned Gulyutkin in 57 seconds and Yarygin was brought back after a year's absence from international competition. At the 1976 European championships, held in Leningrad three months before the Olympics, Yarygin was back to his old ways, overpowering each of his opponents. In Montreal, Yarygin faced Büttner in the very first round and defeated him 13–5. Yarygin's fifth and final victory was his most difficult, a 19–13 verdict over Russ Hellickson of Oregon, Wisconsin, who had moved up from Light Heavyweight to Heavyweight after losing five straight matches to Levan Tediashvili.

1980 Moscow C: 15, N: 15, D: 7.30.
(100 kg—220 lbs)

		ROUND ELIMINATED	PEN. PTS.	FINAL ROUND
1. Illya Mate	SOV/UKR	–	2	1
2. Slavcho Chervenkov	BUL	–	3	3.5
3. Július Strnisko	CZE	–	4	7.5
4. Harald Büttner	GDR	5	6.5	
5. Tomasz Busse	POL	5	7	
6. Vasile Puşcaşu	ROM	4	6	
7. Bárbaro Morgan	CUB	3	7.5	
8. Khorloo Baianmunkh	MGL	3	8	

1984 Los Angeles-Anaheim C: 11, N: 11, D: 8.11.
(100 kg—220 lbs)

		FINAL MATCH
1. Louis Banach	USA	Fall 1:01
2. Joseph Atiyeh	SYR	
3. Vasile Puşcaşu	ROM	4-3
4. Hayri Sezgin	TUR	
5. Tamon Honda	JPN	Injury
6. Georgios Pikilidis	GRE	
7. Kartar Singh Dhillon	IND	
8. Wayne Brightwell	CAN	

Lou Banach, twin brother of light-heavyweight gold medalist Ed Banach, pinned four of his five opponents, all within two minutes. Only Wayne Brightwell lasted the full six minutes. Joseph Atiyeh, a student at Louisiana State University, was the first representative of Syria ever to win an Olympic medal. He later became a bingo hall operator.

1988 Seoul C: 22, N: 22, D: 9.30.
(100 kg—220 lbs)

		FINAL MATCH
1. Vasile Puşcaşu	ROM	1–0
2. Leri Khabelov	SOV/GEO	
3. William Scherr	USA	Fall 3:31
4. Uwe Neupert	GDR	
5. Georgi Karaduchev	BUL	Fall 1:32
6. Bold Javhlantugs	MGL	
7. Noel Loban	GBR	Injury
8. Joe Byung-eun	KOR	

Puşcaşu, competing in his third Olympics at the age of 32, upset two-time world champion Khabelov by engineering a single-leg takedown with 19 seconds left in regulation time.

1992 Barcelona C: 18, N: 18, D: 8.5.
(100 kg—220 lbs)

		FINAL MATCH
1. Leri Khabelov	GEO	2–1
2. Heiko Balz	GER	
3. Au Kayali	TUR	2–0
4. Kim Tae-woo	KOR	
5. Andrzej Radomaki	POL	2–0
6. Subhash Verma	IND	
7. Mark Coleman	USA	2–0
8. Sándor Kiss	HUN	

Four-time world champion Leri Khabelov qualified for the final by outscoring his first five opponents 24–1. Heiko Balz, the other finalist, didn't give up a single point in his five preliminary matches, while scoring 15 points. Khabelov led 1–0, and then 2–0. Balz picked up a point with a little over a minute remaining, but was unable to score again.

1996 Atlanta C: 19, N: 19, D: 7.31.
(100 kg—220 lbs)

		FINAL MATCH
1. Kurt Angle	USA	1-1 8:00
2. Abbas Jadidi	IRN	
3. Arawat Sabejew	GER	7-4
4. Sergei Kovalevsky	BLR	
5. Marek Garmulewicz	POL	WO
6. Konstantin Aleksandrov	KYR	
7. Saghid Murtazaliyev	UKR	3-1
8. Oleg Ladik	CAN	

In 1993, Abbas Jadidi won the world championship at 90 kilograms but lost his gold medal and was suspended for two years when he failed the drug test. He returned to competition in 1995 at 100 kilograms and finished third at the world championships, which were won by Kurt Angle.

Abbas and Angle met in the Olympic final and struggled to a 1-1 tie. According to the rules, ties were to be decided in favor of the wrestler with the least number of passivity cautions. But both men received two cautions, so the decision went to a vote by two officials and the referee. The vote could have gone either way, so there was great suspense as the verdict was awaited. Referee Aduuch Baskhuu of Mongolia, following protocol, stood between Jadidi and Angle, holding each by the hand. Jadidi tried to raise his hand in victory, but Baskhuu held him down and then raised Angle's hand.

While a tearful Angle, carrying an American flag, paraded in front of chanting US fans, Jadidi dropped to his knees and pleaded with international wrestling officials (and later the US press) to review the tapes of the match and reconsider the decision. They did not comply. Angle briefly became a national hero. In 1998 he horrified wrestling afficianados by signing a contract with the entertainment-oriented World Wrestling Federation.

2000 Sydney C: 19, N: 19, D: 9.30.
(97 kg—213¾ lbs)

		FINAL MATCH
1. Saghid Murtazaliyev	RUS	6-0
2. Islam Bayramukov	KAZ	
3. Eldar Kurtanidze	GEO	4-1
4. Marek Garmulewicz	POL	
5. Aftantil Xanthopoulos	GRE	Injury
6. Alireza Heidari	IRN	
7. Aleksandr Shemarov	BLR	
8. George Torchinava	HOL	

After finishing seventh in the heavyweight division at the 1996 Olympics, Saghid Murtazaliyev moved to Dagestan and began competing for Russia. The reigning world and European champion, Murtazaliyev received his stiffest challenge in the elimination round when 37-year-old Melvin Douglas of the United States forced him into overtime. In January 2002 Murtazaliyev almost died when he was stabbed near the heart during a fight outside a Moscow nightclub.

2004 Athens C: 22, N: 22, D: 8.29.
(96 kg—211 lbs)

		FINAL MATCH
1. Khadzhimurat Gatsalov	RUS	4-1
2. Magomed Ibragimov	UZB	
3. Ali Reza Heidari	IRN	3-2 7:47
4. Daniel Cormier	USA	
5. Rüstam Ağayev	AZR	Fall 0:58
6. Wang Yuanyuan	CHN	
7. Aleksandr Shemarov	BLR	
8. Eldar Kurtanidze	GEO	

What appeared to be the most important match came early in the tournament when Eldar Kurtanidze of Georgia and law student Ali Reza Heidari were drawn in the same group. The two rivals had faced each other in the final of the previous two world championships, with Kurtanidze winning both times. Kurtanidze had also defeated Heidari in the quarterfinals of the 2000 Olympics. But in Athens, Heidari pulled off a 3-2 victory to eliminate Kurtanidze from medal contention. Heidari advanced to the semifinals with a 5-0 victory over Rüstam Ağayev, but was upset 4-6 by Magomed Ibragimov. Two-time European champion, Khadzhimurat Gatsalov defeated Ibragimov in a lop-sided final. Ibragimov was no relation to the Ibragimov who earned a bronze as a middleweight in 2000.

2008 Beijing C: 18, N: 18, D: 8.21.
(96 kg—211 lbs)

		FINAL MATCH
1. Sharvani Muradov	RUS	1-0, 1-0
2. Taymuraz Tigiyev	KAZ	
3. Giorgi Gogshelidze	GEO	
3. Xetaq Qazyumov	AZE	
5. Michel Batista Martínez	CUB	
5. Heorhiy Tibilov	UKR	
7. Kurban Kurbanov	UZB	
8. Gergely Sandor Kiss	HUN	

3rd Place: Gogshelidze—Batista 1-0, fall (2:58)
3rd Place: Qazyumov—Tibilov 5-0, 2-0

The semifinal match between Giorgi Gogshelidze and Taymuraz Tigiyev had to be halted twice, once in the first period, when Gogshelidze needed treatment for a facial wound caused by an attempted eye gouge by Tigiyev, and once in the second period, when Gogshelidze appeared to punch Tigiyev in the face.

The final was considerably less violent, as 2007 European champion Sharvani Muradov scored on a single-leg takedown in the first period, and then ran out the clock in the second period as Tigiyev failed to score a point.

Muradov had defeated defending Olympic champion and three-time reigning world champion Khadzhimurat Gatsalov to earn a spot on the Russian Olympic team.

SUPER HEAVYWEIGHT
(Heavyweight 1904–1968)

A maximum weight limit—286 lbs (130 kg)—was imposed for the first time at the 1988 Olympics. Since 2004 it has been changed to 120 kg.

1896–1900 not held

1904 St. Louis C: 5, N: 1, D: 10.15.

		FINAL MATCH
1. Bernhoff Hansen	USA	Fall 2:00
2. Frank Kugler	USA	
3. Frederick Warmbold	USA	

Hansen, a representative of the Norwegian Turnverein of Brooklyn, needed only 7:30 to pin his three opponents. In 1904 anyone over 158 pounds (71.67 kilograms) was considered a heavyweight. Currently, a 158-pound wrestler would compete in the Welterweight division.

1906 not held

1908 London C: 11, N: 3, D: 7.23.

		FINAL MATCH
1. George "Con" O'Kelly	GBR/IRL	Fall 13:27; Fall 3:35
2. Jacob Gundersen	NOR	
3. Edward Barrett	GBR/IRL	
4. Edward Nixson	GBR	
5. Lawrence Bruce	GBR	

Shortly before the Olympic Games, Barrett had defeated O'Kelly for the British Heavyweight championship. But at the Olympics the 221-pound (100.24 kilograms) O'Kelly came up against Barrett in the third round and pinned him after 2:14. Gundersen put up a tougher battle, and it took O'Kelly 17:02 to keep him on the mat for the required two falls.

1912 not held

1920 Antwerp C: 8, N: 5, D: 8.27.

		FINAL MATCH
1. Robert Roth	SWI	Dec
2. Nathaniel Pendleton	USA	
3. Frederick Meyer	USA	
3. Ernst Nilsson	SWE	

Silver medalist Nat Pendleton became an actor. Between 1924 and 1947 he appeared in 109 films including *Horse Feathers* (1932) and *The Thin Man* (1934). He also played the part of hospital attendant Joe Wayman nine times in the Dr Kildare and Dr Gillespie movie series.

1924 Paris C: 12, N: 6, D: 7.14.

1. Harry Steel	USA
2. Henri Wernli	SWI
3. Andrew McDonald	GBR
4. Ernst Nilsson	SWE
5. Johan Richthoff	SWE
6. Edmond Dame	FRA

1928 Amsterdam C: 7, N: 7, D: 8.1.

1. Johan Richthoff	SWE
2. Aukusti Sihvola	FIN
3. Edmond Dame	FRA
4. Edward George	USA
5. Henri Wernli	SWI

Edward "Don" George later became a professional wrestling champion.

1932 Los Angeles C: 3, N: 3, D: 8.3.

		PEN. PTS.
1. Johan Richthoff	SWE	2
2. John Riley	USA	3
3. Nikolaus Hirschl	AUT	6

Richthoff was 34 years old when he successfully defended his Olympic title.

1936 Berlin C: 11, N: 11, D: 8.4.

		ROUND ELIMINATED	PEN. PTS.	FINAL ROUND
1. Kristjan Palusalu	EST	–	2	
2. Josef Klapuch	CZE	4	4	
3. Hjalmar Nyström	FIN	5	5	
4. Nils Åkerlindh	SWE	4	4	
5. Robert Herland	FRA	4	6	
6. Werner Bürki	SWI	4	7	
7. Georg Gehring	GER	3	5	
8. George Chiga	CAN	3	6	

The 27-year-old Palusalu, one of the quiet heroes of the Berlin Games, achieved a rare double by winning the Heavyweight title in both freestyle and Greco-Roman. In 1991, Palusalu was voted the greatest Estonian athlete in history.

1948 London C: 9, N: 9, D: 7.31.

		ROUND ELIMINATED	PEN. PTS.	FINAL ROUND
1. Gyula Bóbis	HUN	–	2	0
2. Bertil Antonsson	SWE	–	3	2
3. Joseph Armstrong	AUS	–	4	6
4. Sadik Esen	TUR	4	7	
5. Josef Růžička	CZE	3	5	
5. Abolghasem Sakhdari	IRN	3	5	
7. Richard Hutton	USA	3	6	

Bóbis began wrestling as a flyweight and kept moving up in division as he grew, until, at the age of 38, he won the Olympic gold medal as a heavyweight.

1952 Helsinki C: 13, N: 13, D: 7.23.

		ROUND ELIMINATED	PEN. PTS.	FINAL ROUND
1. Arsen Mekokishvili	SOV/RUS	–	2	2
2. Bertil Antonsson	SWE	–	2	3
3. Kenneth Richmond	GBR	–	4	6
4. Irfan Atan	TUR	4	5	
5. William Kerslake	USA	4	6	
6. Taisto Kangasniemi	FIN	4	6	
7. Natale Vecchi	ITA	4	7	
7. Willi Waltner	GER	4	7	

When Ken Richmond entered the ring he was one of the most recognized men in the world, even though no one knew his name. Richmond's muscular body was famous because he was the one who struck the gong at the beginning of J. Arthur Rank films. Richmond almost pinned Mekokishvili in the second minute of their third-round bout, but the 256-pound (116.12 kilograms) Georgian broke loose and regained the offensive to win a split decision. The following day Mekokishvili won another split decision from Bertil Antonsson to secure the gold medal.

Bill Kerslake, who placed fifth, was the co-inventor of the first ion thruster for space propulsion and served as chairman of the technical committee of the American Institute of Aeronautics and Astronautics.

1956 Melbourne C: 11, N: 11, D: 12.1.

		ROUND ELIMINATED	PEN. PTS.	FINAL ROUND
1. Hamit Kaplan	TUR	–	1	2
2. Yusein Mehmedov	BUL	–	3	3
3. Taisto Kangasniemi	FIN	–	3	6
4. Ray Mitchell	AUS	4	7	
4. Kenneth Richmond	GBR	4	7	
6. Ivan Vykhrystyuk	SOV/UKR	3	5	
7. William Kerslake	USA	3	6	

1960 Rome C: 17, N: 17, D: 9.6.

		ROUND ELIMINATED	PEN. PTS.	FINAL ROUND
1. Wilfried Dietrich	GER	–	1	2
2. Hamit Kaplan	TUR	–	5	4
3. Savkuds Dzarasov	SOV/RUS	–	2	6
4. Pietro Marascalchi	ITA	5	8	
5. Lyutvi Ahmedov	BUL	4	6	
5. János Reznák	HUN	4	6	
7. Bertil Antonsson	SWE	4	7	
8. William Kerslake	USA	4	8	

Dietrich won Greco-Roman silver medals in 1956 and 1960, but his only gold came in freestyle wrestling, after he held defending champion Hamit Kaplan to a draw in the final match.

1964 Tokyo C: 13, N: 13, D: 10.14.

		ROUND ELIMINATED	PEN. PTS.	FINAL ROUND
1. Oleksander Ivanytsky	SOV/UKR	–	2	2
2. Lyutvi Ahmedov	BUL	–	3	2
3. Hamit Kaplan	TUR	4	7	2
4. Bohumil Kubat	CZE	4	7	2
5. Denis McNamara	GBR	4	7	8
6. Ştefan Ştîngu	ROM	4	8	
7. Wilfried Dietrich	GER	3	6	
7. Lawrence Kristoff	USA	3	6	
7. Masanori Saito	JPN	3	6	

Thirty-one-year-old Hamit Kaplan of Amasya, Anatolia, completed his set of Olympic medals by winning the bronze.

1968 Mexico City C: 15, N: 15, D: 10.20.

		ROUND ELIMINATED	PEN. PTS.	FINAL ROUND
1. Oleksander Medvid	SOV/UKR	–	1	1
2. Osman Duraliev	BUL	–	4	3
3. Wilfried Dietrich	GER	–	5	8

4. Ştefan Ştîngu	ROM	5	6
5. Lawrence Kristoff	USA	4	6
6. Abolfazl Anvari	IRN	4	9
7. Erdeneotchir Elziisaihan	MGL	4	9
8. Raymond Uytterheaghe	FRA	3	9

Dietrich won his fifth Olympic medal (one gold, two silver, two bronze) at the age of 35.

1972 Munich C: 13, N: 13, D: 8.31.

		ROUND ELIMINATED	PEN. PTS.	FINAL ROUND
1. Oleksander Medvid	SOV/UKR	–	2	1
2. Osman Duraliev	BUL	–	4	3
3. Christopher Taylor	USA	5	6	
4. Eskandar Filabi	IRN	5	8.5	
5. Wilfried Dietrich	GER	4	6	
6. Peter Germer	GDR	4	8	
7. Ştefan Ştîngu	ROM	4	8.5	
8. Stanisław Makowiecki	POL	3	7.5	

The biggest confrontation of the 1972 tournament came in the very first round, when two-time Olympic champion Oleksander Medvid met 6-foot 5-inch (1.96 meters), 412-pound (186.88 kilograms) Chris Taylor of Dowagiac, Michigan. Medvid had beaten Taylor three times, but this time they fought to a standoff. The 231-pound (104.78 kilograms) Ukrainian was awarded a controversial decision when the Turkish referee, Umit Demirag, penalized Taylor for passivity. This evident injustice led to Demirag's dismissal as an Olympic referee, although the judgment against Taylor was allowed to stand. Both Medvid and Taylor won the rest of their bouts. Medvid became the only freestyle wrestler to win gold medals at three different Olympics. Taylor died in 1979 at the age of 29.

A nasty incident took place in the third-round match between Giyasettin Yilmaz of Turkey and Bulgarian veteran Osman Duraliev. The two men collided in the third minute, and Yilmaz came away with a bleeding nose. Enraged, he refused to go to his corner and was disqualified. Then he went berserk, shouting at the referee, chasing Duraliev, and tearing apart his own dressing room. Yilmaz was finally subdued by 1968 Light Heavyweight gold medalist Ahmet Ayik.

1976 Montreal C: 15, N: 15, D: 7.31.

		ROUND ELIMINATED	PEN. PTS.	FINAL ROUND
1. Soslan Andiyev	SOV/RUS	–	2	1
2. József Balla	HUN	–	7	5
3. Ladislau Simon	ROM	–	6	6
4. Roland Gehrke	GDR	6	8	
5. Nikola Dinev	BUL	5	6	
6. Yorihide Isogai	JPN	4	7	
7. Eskandar Filabi	IRN	4	8	
8. Mamadou Sakho	SEN	4	8.5	

1980 Moscow C: 12, N: 12, D: 7.31.

		ROUND ELIMINATED	PEN. PTS.	FINAL ROUND
1. Soslan Andiyev	SOV/RUS	–	1	1
2. József Balla	HUN	–	5	5
3. Adam Sandurski	POL	–	0	6
4. Roland Gehrke	GDR	4	7	
5. Andrei Ianko	ROM	4	8	
6. Mamadou Sakho	SEN	4	8.5	
7. Petur Ivanov	BUL	3	7	
8. Arturo Díaz Mora	CUB	3	8	

Seven-foot (2.13 meters), 297-pound (134.72 kilograms) Adam Sandurski demolished his first four opponents in 9:50 but then lost on points, 6–3, to defending champion Soslan Andiyev of Ordzhonikidze, North Ossetia.

1984 Los Angeles-Anaheim C: 8, N: 8, D: 8.10.

		FINAL MATCH
1. Bruce Baumgartner	USA	10–2
2. Robert Molle	CAN	
3. Ayhan Taskin	TUR	Fall 1:44
4. Hassan El Hadad	EGY	
5. Mamadou Sakho	SEN	Injury
6. Vasile Andrei	ROM	
7. Koichi Ishimori	JPN	
8. Panayotis Pikilidis	GRE	

An amiable 264-pounder (119.75 kilograms), Bruce Baumgartner of Haledon, New Jersey, was not seriously challenged in his three matches. Silver medalist Bob Molle barely made it to the Olympics. Ten days before the Opening Ceremony, Molle underwent a two-and-a-half-hour operation for a herniation of the fifth lumbar disc.

In a sport where competitors frequently have to go to great lengths to stay below the weight limit for their division, it is sometimes forgotten that super-heavyweights have to make a minimum weight. Harouna Niang of Mauritania had the unfortunate experience of traveling ten thousand miles to the Olympics and then being disqualified and prevented from competing because he weighed in at only 216 pounds (97.98 kilograms).

1988 Seoul C: 14, N: 14, D: 10.1.

		FINAL MATCH
1. David Gobezhishvili	SOV/GEO	3–1
2. Bruce Baumgartner	USA	
3. Andreas Schröder	GDR	Passivity 4:21
4. László Klauz	HUN	
5. Atanas Atanassov	BUL	8–3
6. Daniel Payne	CAN	
7. Adam Sandurski	POL	7–5
8. Ralf Bremmer	GER	

David Gobezhishvili was world champion in 1985, but the following year Bruce Baumgartner defeated him three times. Stung by these losses, Soviet wrestling officials removed Gobezhishvili from the national team and replaced him with Aslan Khardartsev, who went on to win the 1987 world championship and the 1988 European championship. However, Gobezhishvili was allowed to represent the USSR in the 1988 World Cup, where he defeated Baumgartner. Soviet coach Ivan Yarygin decided to let Gobezhishvili and Khardartsev wrestle without a time limit to determine who would go to the Olympics. Gobezhishvili finally won after almost a half hour. In Seoul, Gobezhishvili, who grew up in the tiny mountain village of Khuruti, in Soviet Georgia, scored his first point against Baumgartner only 17 seconds into the final match. He added two more points in the second period before giving up a single point with 10 seconds left.

1992 Barcelona C: 15, N: 15, D: 8.6.

		FINAL MATCH
1. Bruce Baumgartner	USA	8–0
2. Jeffrey Thue	CAN	
3. David Gobezhishvili	GEO	4–0
4. Mahmut Demir	TUR	
5. Andreas Schröder	GER	Injury
6. Ali Reza Soleimani	IRN	
7. Wang Chunguang	CHN	9–0
8. Park Sung-ha	KOR	

Considered by many to be over the hill after he finished seventh at the 1991 world championships, Bruce Baumgartner came roaring back to regain the Olympic championship. He outscored five of six opponents by a combined total of 35–1 and threw the sixth one in 11 seconds. The critical match was his third-round contest with longtime rival David Gobezhishvili. The two had met 16 times before with Baumgartner leading the series, 10 wins to 6. They were tied 0–0 when, with four seconds left, Baumgartner suddenly dropped Gobezhishvili with what the American described as an "old-fashioned, straight-on, high-level, double-leg takedown."

1996 Atlanta C: 18, N: 18, D: 8.2.

		FINAL MATCH
1. Mahmut Demir	TUR	3-0
2. Aleksei Medvedev	BLR	
3. Bruce Baumgartner	USA	1-1 8:00
4. Andrei Shumilin	RUS	
5. Aleksandr Kovalevsky	KYR	3-1
6. Sven Thiele	GER	
7. Merabi Valiyev	UKR	5-1
8. Petros Bourdoulis	GRE	

Mahmut Demir survived a 1-1 victory over Valiyev in his opening match and a 1-0 win over Shumilin in the semifinals before winning the final. After dropping out of gold-medal contention when he lost 6-1 to Shumilin in the second round, Bruce Baumgartner rebounded to earn his fourth Olympic medal by beating Shumilin 1-1 in the bronze medal match on judges' decision.

2000 Sydney C: 18, N: 18, D: 10.1.

		FINAL MATCH
1. David Musul'bes	RUS	5-2
2. Artur Taymazov	UZB	
3. Alexis Rodríguez Valera	CUB	1-0
4. Abbas Jadidi	IRN	
5. Kerry McKoy	USA	Injury
6. Aleksey Medvedev	BLR	
7. Sven Thiele	GER	
8. Aleksandr Kovalevsky	KYR	

One of the most bizarre protest reviews took place after the quarterfinal match between Artur Taymazov and Kerry McCoy. Taymazov led 8-3 in the first period. McCoy scored four more points, but ran out of time before he could score again. The United States protested the scoring in the first period and paid the $500 appeal fee. However, when the jury of appeal reviewed the videotape of the bout, they discovered that the entire first period was missing. The Americans then turned over their own tape. The judges did add the disputed two points to McCoy's total, but then they also discovered three extra points for Taymazov, so that he won anyway, 11-9. Meanwhile, David Musulbes survived a judges' decision following a 0-0 tie with Peter Pecha of Slovakia and defeated Abbas Jadidi 3-0 in the semifinals, before handling Taymazov 5-2 in the final.

2004 Athens C: 20, N: 20, D: 8.28.
(120 kg—264½ lbs)

		FINAL MATCH
1. Artur Taymazov	UZB	Fall (4:33)
2. Ali Reza Rezaei	IRN	
3. Aydın Polatçı	TUR	3-1 6:12
4. Marid Mutalimov	KAZ	
5. Alexis Rodríguez Varela	CUB	WO
6. Kuramagomed Kuramagomedov	RUS	
7. Kerry McCoy	USA	
8. Bozhidar Boyadzhiev	BUL	

In a surprise move, Russian officials chose Kuramagomed Kuramagomedov of Dagestan to represent Russia instead of defending Olympic champion and two-time world champion David Musulbes. This was good news for Artur Taymazov, who had lost to Musulbes in the Sydney final, as well as in the following two world championships. Taymazov faced Kuramagomedov in the qualifying round and defeated him 7-3. He then beat Aydin Polatçı in overtime in the semifinals and scored four points against Ali Reza Rezaei in the final, before sealing the victory by a fall.

2008 Beijing C: 20, N: 20, D: 8.21.
(120 kg–264½lbs)

		FINAL MATCH
1. Artur Taymazov	UZB	3-0, 1-0
2. Bakhtiyar Akhmedov	RUS	
3. David Musul'bes	SVK	
3. Marid Mutalimov	KAZ	
5. Disney Rodríguez Rodríguez	CUB	
5. Fardin Masoumi	IRN	
7. Steven Mocco	USA	
8. Ottó Aubéli	HUN	

3rd Place: Musulbes—Rodríguez 4-0, 4-2
3rd Place: Mutalimov—Masoumi 8-3, 1-1

Defending Olympic champion and twice world champion Artur Taymazov defeated 2000 Olympic gold medalist David Musul'bes 1-0, 1-0 in the semifinals, and then faced 21-year-old former junior world champion Bakhtiyar Akhmedov in the final. There he didn't give up a single point, winning 3-0, 1-0 to successfully defend his title.

DISCONTINUED EVENTS

LIGHT FLYWEIGHT
(48 kg—106 lbs)

1904 St. Louis C: 4, N: 1, D: 10.15.
(47.6 kg—106 lbs)

		FINAL MATCH
1. Robert Curry	USA	Fall 2:38
2. John Hem	USA	
3. Gustav Thiefenthaler	USA	

Curry, of New York City, threw Thiefenthaler in 4:05 to qualify for the final.

1906–1968 not held

1972 Munich C: 14, N: 14, D: 8.31.

		ROUND ELIMINATED	PEN. PTS.	FINAL ROUND
1. Roman Dmitriev	SOV/RUS	–	2	4
2. Ognyan Nikolov	BUL	–	5	4
3. Ebrahim Javadi	IRN	–	3.5	4
4. Sefer Baygin	TUR	4	6.5	
5. Ion Arapu	ROM	4	7	
6. Masahiko Umeda	JPN	4	8	
7. Sergio Gonzalez	USA	3	6	
7. Jürgen Möbius	GDR	3	6	

Dmitriev grew up herding reindeer in Yakutia.

1976 Montreal C: 18, N: 18, D: 7.31.

		ROUND ELIMINATED	PEN. PTS.	FINAL ROUND
1. Hasan Isayev	BUL	–	4	3
2. Roman Dmitriev	SOV/RUS	–	1	5
3. Akira Kudo	JPN	–	0	8
4. Gombo Khishigbaatar	MGL	5	6	
5. Kim Hwa-kyung	KOR	5	6	
6. Li Yong-nam	PRK	5	8	
7. Kuddusi Ozdemir	TUR	4	7	
8. Willi Heckmann	GER	4	8	

Dmitriev actually defeated two-time world champion Isayev, but lost four points as the result of a double disqualification against Kudo.

1980 Moscow C: 14, N: 14, D: 7.29.

		ROUND ELIMINATED	PEN. PTS.	FINAL ROUND
1. Claudio Pollio	ITA	–	5.5	3
2. Jang Se-hong	PRK	–	5	4
3. Sergei Kornilayev	SOV/RUS	–	1	5
4. Jan Falandys	POL	5	6.5	
5. Mahabir Singh	IND	5	9	
6. László Biró	HUN	4	9	
7. Rumen Yordanov	BUL	3	6	
8. Gheorghe Rasovan	ROM	3	7	

Pollio lost to Kornilayev, but won the gold medal anyway after the Soviet wrestler was thrown in the final match by Jang Se-hong, who had been disqualified in his match against Pollio.

1984 Los Angeles-Anaheim C: 7, N: 7, D: 8.9.

		FINAL MATCH
1. Robert Weaver	USA	Fall 2:58
2. Takashi Irie	JPN	
3. Son Gab-do	KOR	13-7
4. Gao Wenhe	CHN	
5. Reiner Heugabel	GER	Passivity 5:21
6. Kent Andersson	SWE	
7. Sunil Dutt	IND	

Freestyle wrestling was hard hit by the Soviet-bloc boycott. Twenty-three of the 30 medalists at the 1983 world championships were from boycotting nations, including nine of the ten gold medal winners. The light flyweight division was so depleted that there were only seven entrants—the smallest wrestling competition since 1932. Bobby Weaver, who had finished second at the 1979 world championships and fifth in 1983, needed a total of only 8 minutes and 26 seconds to dispose of his three opponents.

1988 Seoul C: 19, N: 19, D: 9.29.

		FINAL MATCH
1. Takashi Kobayashi	JPN	16-4
2. Ivan Tzonov	BUL	
3. Sergei Karamchakov	SOV/RUS	3-1
4. Timothy Vanni	USA	
5. Reiner Heugabel	GER	Passivity 4:27
6. Ilyas Sukruoğlü	TUR	
7. Volker Anger	GDR	Forfeit
8. Naser Zeinalnia	IRN	

Two-time defending world champion Li Jae-sik missed the competition because of North Korea's boycott. Lee

Sang-ho of South Korea had finished second to Li at the 1987 world championships, but at the Olympics Lee suffered a broken arm in the first minute of his opening match against Takashi Kobayashi. Thereafter, Kobayashi dominated the tournament except for a close call against Ilyas Sukruoğlü. Sukruoğlü led 5-3 with 10 seconds remaining when Kobayashi scored on a 3-point move to win 6-5 and advance to the final.

1992 Barcelona C 19, N: 19, D: 8.6.

		FINAL MATCH
1. Kim Il	PRK	4-1
2. Kim Jong-shin	KOR	
3. Vugar Orudzhev	BLR	2-1
4. Romică Raşovan	ROM	
5. Tim Vanni	USA	1-0
6. Reiner Heugabel	GER	
7. Aldo Martínez Echavarría	CUB	Injury
8. Tserenbaatar Khosbayar	MGL	

In the final match of the 1991 world championships, Vugar Orudzhev defeated Kim Il 1-0 in overtime. The two met again in the first round at the Olympics. This time Kim won, 9-5. Kim's closest match was a 7-6 victory over Aldo Martínez.

1996 Atlanta C: 19, N: 19, D: 7.30.

		FINAL MATCH
1. Kim Il	PRK	5-4
2. Armen Mkrchyan	ARM	
3. Alexis Vila Perdomo	CUB	5-2
4. Vugar Orudzhov	RUS	
5. Jung Soon-won	KOR	4-0
6. Vitalii Railean	MOL	
7. Gheorghe Corduneanu	ROM	5-1
8. Robert Eiter	USA	

Because of the extreme isolationism of the North Korean government and the collapse of its economy, Kim Il was unable to travel abroad following his Olympic victory in 1992. He missed the next three world championships and did not reappear at an international competition until April 1996 when he won the Asian Olympic qualifying tournament. Kim had to lose 11 kg in order to make weight in Atlanta. In the semifinals, he faced Kim Jong-shin, the same wrestler he had beaten in the 1992 final. This time he defeated the South Korean 3-1 in overtime. In the final, Kim jumped out to a quick 3-0 lead and then survived two gutwrenches by Mkrchyan in the last thirty seconds to hold on for a 5-4 victory.

FLYWEIGHT

(52 kg—114½ lbs)

1904 St. Louis C: 3, N: 1, D: 10.15.
(52.16 kg—115 lbs)

		FINAL MATCH
1. George Mehnert	USA	Dec. 15:00
2. Gustav Bauer	USA	
3. William Nelson	USA	

1906–1936 not held

1948 London C: 11, N: 11, D: 7.31.

		ROUND ELIMINATED	PEN. PTS.	FINAL ROUND
1. Lennart Viitala	FIN	–	2	2
2. Halit Balamir	TUR	–	4	2
3. Thure Johansson	SWE	–	5	6
4. Rassoul Raiisi	IRN	4	6	
5. Pierre Baudric	FRA	4	7	
6. Khashaba Jadav	IND	3	5	
7. William Jernigan	USA	3	7	

1952 Helsinki C: 16, N: 16, D: 7.23.

		ROUND ELIMINATED	PEN. PTS.	FINAL ROUND
1. Hasan Gemici	TUR	–	4	3
2. Yushu Kitano	JPN	–	4	4
3. Mahmoud Mollaghasemi	IRN	–	3	4
4. Georgy Sayadov	SOV/AZR	5	6	
5. Heinrich Weber	GER	4	6	
6. Louis Baise	SAF	4	7	
7. Giordano Degiorgi	ITA	3	5	
7. Robert Peery	USA	3	5	

1956 Melbourne C: 11, N: 11, D: 12.1.

		ROUND ELIMINATED	PEN. PTS.	FINAL ROUND
1. Mirian Tsalkalamanidze	SOV/GEO	–	5	3
2. Mohammad Ali Khojastépour	IRN	–	3	3
3. Huseyin Akbaş	TUR	–	2	4
4. Tadashi Asai	JPN	4	7	
5. Richard Delgado	USA	3	6	
5. André Zoete	FRA	3	6	
7. Abdul Aziz	PAK	3	7	
7. Baban Daware	IND	3	7	

Tsalkalamanidze gained the gold medal by throwing Khojastépour after four minutes.

1960 Rome C: 17, N: 17, D: 9.6.

		ROUND ELIMINATED	PEN. PTS.	FINAL ROUND
1. Ahmet Bilek	TUR	–	5	2
2. Masayuki Matsubara	JPN	–	4	4
3. M. Ebrahim Seifpour Saadabadi	IRN	–	3	6
4. Paul Neff	GER	6	9	
5. Elliott Gray Simons	USA	5	8	
6. Ali Aliyev	SOV/RUS	5	8	
7. Nikola Dimitrov	BUL	4	7	
8. André Zoete	FRA	4	8	

1964 Tokyo C: 22, N: 22, D: 10.14.

		ROUND ELIMINATED	PEN. PTS.	FINAL ROUND
1. Yoshikatsu Yoshida	JPN	–	2	1
2. Chang Chang-sun	KOR	–	3	3
3. S. Ali Akbar Heidari	IRN	5	6	
4. Ali Aliyev	SOV/RUS	5	7	
4. Cemal Yanilmaz	TUR	5	7	
4. André Zoete	FRA	5	7	
7. Elliott Gray Simons	USA	4	6	
8. Muhammed Niaz	PAK	4	7	

1968 Mexico City C: 23, N: 23, D: 10.20.

		ROUND ELIMINATED	PEN. PTS.	FINAL ROUND
1. Shigeo Nakata	JPN	–	3.5	1
2. Richard Sanders	USA	–	0	4
3. Tjimidbazar Damdiharev	MGL	–	5	7
4. Nazar Albaryan	SOV/ARM	5	6.5	
5. Vincenzo Grassi	ITA	5	6.5	
6. Sudesh Kumar	IND	5	7.5	
7. Mohammad Ghorbani	IRN	5	8	
7. Paul Neff	GER	5	8	

1972 Munich C: 24, N: 24, D: 8.31.

		ROUND ELIMINATED	PEN. PTS.	FINAL ROUND
1. Kiyomi Kato	JPN	–	1.5	2
2. Arsen Alakhverdiyev	SOV/RUS	–	5.5	5
3. Kim Gwong-hyong	PRK	–	5.5	5
4. Sudesh Sudeshkumar	IND	6	7	
5. Petru Ciarnău	ROM	6	7.5	
6. Gordon Bertie	CAN	5	7.5	
7. Henrik Gál	HUN	4	7	
7. John Kinsella	AUS	4	7	

1976 Montreal C: 19, N: 19, D: 7.31.

		ROUND ELIMINATED	PEN. PTS.	FINAL ROUND
1. Yuji Takada	JPN	–	0	0.5
2. Aleksandr Ivanov	SOV/KAZ	–	1.5	3.5
3. Jeon Hae-sup	KOR	–	2	8
4. Henrik Gál	HUN	5	7	
5. Nermedin Selimov	BUL	5	8.5	
6. Wladyslaw Stecyk	POL	5	9	
7. Li Bong-sun	PRK	4	7	
8. Eloy Abreu Morales	CUB	4	9	

Two-time world champion Yuji Takada of Gunma Prefecture overwhelmed the field, pinning six of his seven opponents, five of them in less than two minutes. He also outpointed Ivanov 20–11.

1980 Moscow C: 16, N: 16, D: 7.30.

		ROUND ELIMINATED	PEN. PTS.	FINAL ROUND
1. Anatoly Bilohlazov	SOV/UKR	–	1.5	0
2. Władysław Stecyk	POL	–	4	5
3. Nermedin Selimov	BUL	–	4.5	7
4. Lajos Szabó	HUN	6	9	
5. Jang Dok-ryong	PRK	4	6.5	
6. Nanzadying Burgedaa	MGL	4	7	
7. Koce Efremov	YUG/MAC	4	8	
8. Hartmut Reich	GDR	3	6.5	

After winning his first two matches on decisions, Anatoly Bilohlazov needed only 4:54 to dispose of his last four opponents. Twenty-four hours and 48 minutes after Bilohlazov won the Flyweight gold medal, his twin brother, Serhei, won the Bantamweight tournament.

1984 Los Angeles-Anaheim C: 17, N. 17, D: 8.10.

		FINAL MATCH
1. Šaban Trstena	YUG/MAC	Injury
2. Kim Jong-kyu	KOR	
3. Yuji Takada	JPN	12-0 4:34
4. Ray Takahashi	CAN	
5. Aslan Seyhanli	TUR	14-5
6. Mahabir Singh	IND	
7. Fritz Niebler	GER	
8. Liang Dejin	CHN	

Kim tore a muscle in his left shoulder during his match with Fritz Niebler of West Germany and was unable to take part in the final. The crucial match for 19-year-old Šaban Trstena of Skopje, Macedonia, was an 8-8 decision over 1976 Olympic champion Yuji Takada.

1988 Seoul C: 31, N: 31, D: 9.30.

		FINAL MATCH
1. Mitsuru Sato	JPN	13-2
2. Šaban Trstena	YUG/MAC	
3. Vladimir Toguzov	SOV/RUS	14-1
4. László Bíró	HUN	
5. Aslan Seyhanli	TUR	5-4
6. Kim Jong-ho	KOR	
7. Tserenbatar Enebayar	MGL	Injury
8. Valentin Yordanov	BUL	

Sato threw his first five opponents and then outpointed Kim 15-0 in 4:02 to advance to the final. The favorite had been three-time world champion Valentin Yordanov, who competed under the government-imposed surname Dimitrov. Yordanov won his first three matches, then lost 11-5 to Trstena and 14-1 to Toguzov before withdrawing from the "B" final because of injury.

1992 Barcelona C: 18, N: 18, D: 8.5.

		FINAL MATCH
1. Li Hak-son	PRK	8-1
2. Larry "Zeke" Jones	USA	
3. Valentin Yordanov	BUL	9-3
4. Kim Sun-hah	KOR	
5. Ahmet Orel	TUR	Injury
6. Mitsuru Sato	JPN	
7. Majid Torkan	IRN	2-1
8. Christopher Woodcroft	CAN	

Li, a relative newcomer who was unknown to most of his opponents, overwhelmed everyone he faced with his speed and aggressiveness. His only close match was a 6-4 victory over Yordanov.

1996 Atlanta C: 19, N: 19, D: 8.1.

		FINAL MATCH
1. Valentin Yordanov	BUL	4-3 6:29
2. Namiq Abdullayev	AZR	
3. Maulen Mamyrov	KAZ	3-2
4. Chechen-ool Mongush	RUS	
5. Gholam Reza Mohammadi	IRN	4-2
6. Metin Topaktas	TUR	
7. Adkhamdzhon Akhilov	UZB	11-0 2:34
8. Gregory Woodcroft	CAN	

By the time of the 1996 Olympics, 36-year-old Valentin Yordanov had won seven world championships and seven European championships. But at the Olympics he had only managed an eighth place in 1988 and third place in 1992. His overtime victory over Namiq Abdullayev in the 1996 final was not without controversy. While his coach rushed forward to berate the judges, Abdullayev sat in the middle of the mat in silent protest for at least a minute. When Abdullayev returned to Azerbaijan, President Geidar Aliyev rewarded him with the prize money for a gold medal rather than a silver. Sixth place finisher Chechen-ool Mongush was a member of the Tuva minority group.

2000 Sydney C: 19, N: 19, D: 9.30.
(54 kg—119 lbs)

		FINAL MATCH
1. Namiq Abdullayev	AZR	4-3
2. Samuel Henson	USA	
3. Amiran Kardanov	GRE	5-4
4. German Kontoev	BLR	
5. Oleksandr Zakharuk	UKR	8-1
6. Maulen Mamyrov	KAZ	
7. Vitali Railean	MOL	
8. Adkhamdzhon Akhilov	UZB	

The final was a rematch of the final of the 1998 world championships, in which Sammie Henson defeated Namiq Abdullayev 3-1. This time Abdullayev jumped out to a 3-0 lead after only 45 seconds. Henson fought back point by point, first on a caution and then with a takedown before and after the break. With 1½ minutes to go, Abdullayev scored on a reversal to give him a 4-3 advantage that he held to the end. Henson was so distraught at the collapse of his dream that, after he shook Abdullayev's hand, he ran screaming and moaning out of the arena and into a hallway and fell to the ground, where he lay on his back wailing and flailing until assistant US coach John Smith pulled him to his feet and dragged him to a restricted area. Later Henson wept through the medal ceremony and, away from media coverage, tried to throw away his silver medal.

LIGHT HEAVYWEIGHT

1920 Antwerp C: 13, N: 8, D: 8.27.
(80 kg—186½ lbs)

		FINAL MATCH
1. Anders Larsson	SWE	Forfeit
2. Charles Courant	SWI	
3. Walter Maurer	USA	
4. John Redman	USA	
5. Johan Gallén	FIN	
5. Emil Westerlund	FIN	

Courant injured his ankle in the semifinals. He tried to fight in the final, but had to withdraw.

1924 Paris C: 16, N: 10, D: 7.14.
(87 kg—192 lbs)

1. John Spellman	USA
2. Rudolf Svensson	SWE
3. Charles Courant	SWI
4. Carl Westergren	SWE
5. Walter Wilson	GBR
6. George Rumple	CAN

John Spellman went on to play professional football in the NFL.

1928 Amsterdam C: 7, N: 7, D: 8.1.
(87 kg—192 lbs)

1. Thure Sjöstedt	SWE
2. Arnold Bögli	SWI
3. Henri Lefèbre	FRA
4. Heywood Edwards	USA
5. Jacques van Assche	BEL

1932 Los Angeles C: 4, N: 4, D: 8.3.
(87 kg—192 lbs)

1. Peter Mehringer	USA
2. Thure Sjöstedt	SWE
3. Edward Scarf	AUS
4. Henry Madison	CAN

Pete Mehringer of Kinsley, Kansas, first learned how to wrestle from a correspondence course: the Frank Gotch and Farmer Burns School of Wrestling and Physical Culture Course. After the Olympics, he played professional football for eight years and then worked as a stuntman in Hollywood. His credits included *Knute Rockne, All-American.*

1936 Berlin C: 12, N: 12, D: 8.4.
(87 kg—192 lbs)

		ROUND ELIMINATED	PEN. PTS.	FINAL ROUND
1. Knut Fridell	SWE	–	2	1
2. August Neo	EST	–	5	4
3. Erich Siebert	GER	–	5	6
4. Paul Dätwyler	SWI	4	6	
5. Ray Clemons	USA	4	7	
6. Edward Scarf	AUS	3	5	
7. Hubert Prokop	CZE	3	7	
8. Ede Virág-Ébner	HUN	3	7	

1948 London C: 15, N: 15, D: 7.31.
(87 kg—192 lbs)

		ROUND ELIMINATED	PEN. PTS.	FINAL ROUND
1. Henry Wittenberg	USA	–	1	2
2. Fritz Stöckli	SWI	–	1	3
3. Bengt Fahlkvist	SWE	–	2	4
4. Muharrem Candaş	TUR	5	7	
4. Fernand Payette	CAN	5	7	
6. Patrick Morton	SAF	3	5	
7. Spyros Deftreraios	GRE	3	6	
7. John Sullivan	GBR	3	6	
7. Oscar Verona	ITA	3	6	

Henry Wittenberg was a 29-year-old New York City policeman. Shortly before the Games began, his father, Rudolph, fell terminally ill. Wittenberg did not want to leave, but his father insisted, promising to stay alive until he returned. In London, each of the three matches of the final round was an epic struggle and each was decided by a split decision of the judges. Wittenberg returned to New York as quickly as possible and handed over his gold medal to his father. That night, his father died. Wittenberg did not begin wrestling until he entered City College of New York. In high school he had been captain of the chess team.

1952 Helsinki C: 13, N: 13, D: 7.23.
(87 kg—192 lbs)

		ROUND ELIMINATED	PEN. PTS.	FINAL ROUND
1. Wiking Palm	SWE	–	4	2
2. Henry Wittenberg	USA	–	4	3
3. Adil Atan	TUR	–	6	5
4. August Englas	SOV/EST	5	7	
5. Abbas Zandi	IRN	4	5	
6. Jacob Theron	SAF	3	5	
7. Max Leichter	GER	3	7	

1956 Melbourne C: 12, N: 12, D: 12.1.
(87 kg—192 lbs)

		ROUND ELIMINATED	PEN. PTS.	FINAL ROUND
1. Gholam Reza Takhti	IRN	–	0	2
2. Boris Kulayev	SOV/RUS	–	2	4
3. Peter Blair	USA	–	4	6
4. Gerald Martina	IRL	4	6	
5. Adil Atan	TUR	4	7	
5. Kevin Coote	AUS	4	7	
7. Mitsuhiro Ohira	JPN	3	7	
7. Wiking Palm	SWE	3	7	
7. Jacob Theron	SAF	3	7	

Gholamreza Takhti is one of Iran's most revered sports heroes. Competing in four Olympics, he earned one gold medal and two silver. In 1968 he died mysteriously at the age of 37. During his lifetime he was known as J.P. Gholamreza Takhti, the J.P. standing for *Johan Pahlevan* or "world champion." After his death, he gained the honorific *shaid* or "martyr" because he died of unknown cause during the reign of Shah Reza Pahlavi.

1960 Rome C: 19, N: 19, D: 9.6.
(87 kg—192 lbs)

		ROUND ELIMINATED	PEN. PTS.	FINAL ROUND
1. Ismet Atli	TUR	–	5	1
2. Gholam Reza Takhti	IRN	–	0	3
3. Anatoly Albul	SOV/RUS	5	6	
4. Wiking Palm	SWE	5	6	
5. Daniel Brand	USA	5	7	
6. Hermanus van Zyl	SAF	5	9	
7. Singh Saijan	IND	4	8	
8. Kazuo Abe	JPN	4	9	
8. György Gurics	HUN	4	9	

Takhti pinned his first five opponents before losing on points to Atli. Albul was awarded the bronze medal over Palm on the basis of lower bodyweight.

1964 Tokyo C: 16, N: 16, D: 10.14.
(97 kg—214 lbs)

		ROUND ELIMINATED	PEN. PTS.	FINAL ROUND
1. Oleksander Medvid	SOV/UKR	–	3	2
2. Ahmet Ayik	TUR	–	5	4
3. Said Mustafov	BUL	–	5	6
4. Gholam Reza Takhti	IRN	5	6	
5. Peter Jutzeler	SWI	5	9	
6. Gerald Conine	USA	4	6	
7. Heinz Kiehl	GER	4	7	
8. Imre Vigh	HUN	3	6	

Medvid secured the first of his three gold medals by pinning Mustafov in the final bout after only 39 seconds.

1968 Mexico City C: 16, N: 16, D: 10.20.
(97 kg—214 lbs)

		ROUND ELIMINATED	PEN. PTS.	FINAL ROUND
1. Ahmet Ayik	TUR	–	4	2
2. Shota Lomidze	SOV/GEO	–	5	3
3. József Csatári	HUN	–	5	7
4. Said Mustafov	BUL	5	6.5	
5. Khorloo Baianmunkh	MGL	5	8.5	
6. John Thomas "Jess" Lewis	USA	4	7	
7. Ryszard Długosz	POL	4	7	
8. Gerd Bachmann	GDR	3	6	

1972 Munich C: 23, N: 23, D: 8.31.
(90 kg—198½ lbs)

		ROUND ELIMINATED	PEN. PTS.	FINAL ROUND
1. Benjamin Peterson	USA	–	4	2
2. Gennady Strakhov	SOV/RUS	–	4	2
3. Károly Bajkó	HUN	6	6.5	
4. Russi Petrov	BUL	6	8.5	
5. Reza Khorrami	IRN	5	7	
5. Bárbaro Morgan Soroa	CUB	5	7	
7. Günter Spindler	GDR	5	8	
8. Mehmet Güçlü	TUR	4	8	

Ben Peterson, whose brother, John, won a silver medal in the Middleweight division, picked up a surprise gold medal by pinning world champion Russi Petrov after 2:41 of his final bout and placing ahead of Gennady Strakhov on the basis of more total falls.

1976 Montreal C: 21, N: 21, D: 7.31.
(90 kg—198½ lbs)

		ROUND ELIMINATED	PEN. PTS.	FINAL ROUND
1. Levan Tediashvili	SOV/GEO	–	1	2
2. Benjamin Peterson	USA	–	3.5	4
3. Stelica Morcov	ROM	–	7	6
4. Horst Stottmeister	GDR	6	7.5	
5. Terry Paice	CAN	5	7	
6. Paweł Kurczewski	POL	5	8.5	
7. Frank Andersson	SWE	5	8.5	
8. Bárbaro Morgan Soroa	CUB	4	7.5	

One of the greatest amateur wrestlers of all time, Levan "Teddy" Tediashvili had not lost a match since 1971. At the Munich Olympics he had defeated John Peterson to win the Middleweight division. Four years later Tediashvili moved up to Light Heavyweight and outpointed John's brother, Ben, 11-5 for a second gold medal. Tediashvili, a law student and the son of a wine grower, was a brash performer who was known to wink at pretty women in the crowd just before pinning his opponents. In 1988, Tediashvili played the part of bandit folk-hero Gogi Kenkeshvili in the film *Khareba and Gogi.*

1980 Moscow C: 15, N: 15, D: 7.29.
(90 kg—198½ lbs)

		ROUND ELIMINATED	PEN. PTS.	FINAL ROUND
1. Sanasar Oganisyan	SOV/RUS	–	2	1.5
2. Uwe Neupert	GDR	–	4.5	4
3. Aleksander Cichoń	POL	–	0.5	6.5
4. Ivan Ginov	BUL	5	7	
5. Dashdorj Tserentogtokh	MGL	5	8.5	
6. Christophe Andanson	FRA	4	7	
7. Ion Ivanov	ROM	4	7.5	
8. Michael Pikos	AUS	4	8	

1984 Los Angeles-Anaheim C: 16, N: 16, D: 8.9.
(90 kg—198½ lbs)

		FINAL MATCH
1. Edward Banach	USA	15-3 4:02
2. Akira Ota	JPN	
3. Noel Loban	GBR	5-1
4. Clark Davis	CAN	
5. Macauley Appah	NGR	Injury
6. Ismall Temiz	TUR	
7. Majeed Abdul	PAK	
8. Michele Azzola	ITA	

On the way to the final, Ed Banach defeated his first three opponents by a combined score of 37-4, and then threw Majeed Abdul of Pakistan in 48 seconds. Ed was the twin brother of Lou Banach, who won the heavyweight division two nights later.

1988 Seoul C: 28, N: 28, D: 9.29.
(90 kg—198½ lbs)

		FINAL MATCH
1. Makharbek Khadartsev	SOV/RUS	16-0 3:27
2. Akira Ota	JPN	
3. Kim Tae-woo	KOR	1-0
4. Gábor Tóth	HUN	
5. James Scherr	USA	3-1
6. Rumen Alabakov	BUL	
7. Iraklis Deskoulidis	GRE	4-2
8. Zeveg Duvchin	MGL	

Two-time world champion Makharbek Khadartsev pinned four of his seven opponents and outpointed two more in less than 3½ minutes. Only Edwin Lins of Austria lasted the full 6 minutes and even he lost 10-1. Khadartsev, like 68-kilogram champion Arsen Fadzayev, grew up in the North Ossetian region of Russia.

1992 Barcelona C: 17, N: 17, D: 8.7.
(90 kg—198½ lbs)

		FINAL MATCH
1. Makharbek Khadartsev	RUS	1-0
2. Kenan Şimşek	TUR	
3. Christopher Campbell	USA	3-1 7:23
4. Puntsag Sukhbat	MGL	
5. Ayub Bani Nosrat	IRN	3-1 7:42
6. Roberto Limonta Vargas	CUB	
7. Marek Garmulewicz	POL	0-0 8:00
8. Renato Lombardo	ITA	

Between Olympic Games, Khadartsev won three more world championships. He was not seriously challenged on his way to the final, outscoring four opponents 27-3. In the final, he scored midway through the bout and stuck to defense until time ran out. In addition to the gold medal, Khadartsev received a special prize. As soon as the match ended, referee Lassi Toivola, officiating the last match of his career, placed his whistle around the winner's neck.

Khadartsev had qualified to be an attorney, although he had yet to practice law. Coincidentally, bronze medalist Chris Campbell was a corporate attorney for an air-conditioning company. Like Khadartsev, Campbell was also a world champion—but Campbell's championship had come back in 1981. In 1980 Campbell made the United States Olympic team, but the US boycott kept him out of the competition. In 1984 he injured his right knee one week before the United States Olympic trials and was forced to withdraw. Discouraged, Campbell retired, but came back five years later. A strict vegetarian and proponent of tai chi ch'uan, Campbell finally earned his Olympic medal at age 37.

1996 Atlanta C: 21, N: 21, D: 8.2.
(90 kg—198½ lbs)

		FINAL MATCH
1. Rasoul Khadem	IRN	3-0
2. Makharbek Khadartsev	RUS	
3. Eldar Kurtanidze	GEO	5-0
4. Jozef Lohyňa	SLV	
5. Dzambolat Tyedyeyev	UKR	12-0 2:32
6. Victor Kodei	NGR	
7. Melvin Douglas	USA	6-0
8. Kim Ik-hee	KOR	

Rasoul Khadem and his brother Amir Reza both won bronze medals at the 1992 Olympics. They both moved up one weight class for the 1996 Games. Amir earned another bronze, but Rasoul was expected to do better. In the last two world championship finals, he had defeated defending Olympic champion Makharbek Khadartsev. In the Atlanta final, they met again. This time Khadem scored a takedown after four minutes to become Iran's first Olympic champion in 28 years. In 2003, Khadem was elected to the Tehran Council.

WOMEN

FLYWEIGHT
(48 kg—106 lbs)

1896–2000 not held

2004 Athens C: 14, N: 14, D: 8.23.
(48 kg—106 lbs)

		FINAL MATCH
1. Irini Merleni	UKR	2-2 9:00
2. Chiharu Icho	JPN	
3. Patricia Miranda	USA	12-4
4. Angélique Berthenet	FRA	
5. Larisa Oorzhak	RUS	3-1
6. Brigitte Wagner	GER	
7. Lidiya Karamchakova	TJK	
8. Enkhjargal Tsogtbazar	MGL	

Only 1.50 meters (4 feet 11 inches) tall, Irini Merleni entered the Olympics as the three-time defending world champion and as the overwhelming favorite to become women's wrestling's first gold medal winner. In the preliminary round, she easily defeated her three opponents, outscoring them 31-0 in only 4 minutes 36 seconds. In the semifinals, she faced Patricia Miranda, whom she had narrowly beaten, 5-4, in the 2003 world championship final. This time Merleni won easily, 9-0. In the final, Merleni finally met her match: Chiharu Icho, the reigning world champion in a higher weight category. The two struggled through an even contest. Trailing 1-2, Merleni tied the score with 2½ minutes left and then was awarded the victory by judges' decision.

Irini Merleni, 2004
Merleni learns that she has defeated Chiharo Icho by judges' decision to become the first Olympic women's wrestling champion.

Less than a half hour after the final, Icho's younger sister, Kaori, won the gold medal in the middleweight category.

2008 Beijing C: 17, N: 17, D: 8.16.
(48 kg–106 lbs)

		FINAL MATCH
1. Carol Huynh	CAN	4-0, 2-1
2. Chiharu Icho	JPN	
3. Irini Merleni-Mykulchyn	UKR	
3. Mariya Stadnik	AZE	
5. Tatyana Bakatyuk	KAZ	
5. Clarissa Chun	USA	
7. Vanessa Boubryemm	FRA	
8. Kim Hyung-joo	KOR	

3rd Place: Merleni-Mykulchyn—Chun 2-0, 4-1
3rd Place: Stadnik—Bakatyuk 2-1, 8-0

Twenty-seven-year-old Carol Huynh faced two-time reigning world champion and defending Olympic silver medalist Chiharu Icho in the gold medal match. Icho had reached the final after pinning defending Olympic champion Irini Merleni-Mykulchyn in the quarter-finals.

Huynh, whose previous best result at a major international tournament was fifth place at the 2007 world championships, took control of the final, winning the first period 4-0 with a takedown and a point from Icho leaving the ring. She scored twice in the second period on pushouts to clinch the victory.

Huynh was born in British Columbia to ethnic Chinese parents who emigrated from Vietnam to Canada as refugees.

LIGHTWEIGHT

(55 kg—121¼ lbs)

1896–2000 not held

2004 Athens C: 12, N: 12, D: 8.23.
(55 kg—121 lbs)

		FINAL MATCH
1. Saori Yoshida	JPN	6-0
2. Tonya Verbeek	CAN	
3. Anna Gomis	FRA	6-0
4. Ida-Theres Karlsson	SWE	
5. Sun Dongmei	CHN	
6. Tela O'Donnell	USA	
7. Lee Na-lae	KOR	
8. Tetiana Lazareva	UKR	

DISQ (Drugs): Mabel Fonseca (PUR)

The two-time defending world champion, Saori Yoshida outscored three of her four opponents by a combined total of 27-0. Her only real challenge came in the semifinal round, when she narrowly edged out Anna Gomis 7-6. The 21-year-old Yoshida had never lost an international competition.

2008 Beijing C: 16, N: 16, D: 8.16.
(55 kg–121 lbs)

		FINAL MATCH
1. Saori Yoshida	JPN	2-0, Fall (2:43)
2. Xu Li	CHN	
3. Jacqueline Rentería Castillo	COL	
3. Tonya Verbeek	CAN	
5. Ida-Theres Karlsson-Nerell	SWE	
5. Ana-Maria Paval	ROM	
7. Olga Smirnova	KAZ	
8. Nataliya Golts	RUS	

3rd Place: Renteria—Paval fall (1:04)
3rd Place: Verbeek—Karlsson-Nerell 1-0, 1-0

Five-time reigning world champion and defending Olympic champion Saori Yoshida had only lost once in her international career: a 2-0 defeat to American Marcie van Dusen at a World Cup event in January 2008 that broke Yoshida's 119-match winning streak.

In Beijing, Yoshida swept through her first two matches easily and faced Tonya Verbeek, whom she had defeated in the 2004 Olympic final, in the semifinals. This time Yoshida overwhelmed Verbeek, winning the bout 8-0 to reach the gold medal match. Meanwhile, van Dusen lost 12-5 in the quarterfinals to Jacqueline Rentería, who was, in turn, pinned by eighteen-year-old Xu Li in the semifinals.

Yoshida dominated the final from the start, winning the first period 2-0 and pinning Li for a fall after a two-point takedown in the second period.

MIDDLEWEIGHT

(63 kg—139 lbs)

1896–2000 not held

2004 Athens C: 12, N: 12, D: 8.23.
(63 kg—139 lbs)

		FINAL MATCH
1. Kaori Icho	JPN	3-2
2. Sara McMann	USA	
3. Lise Legrand	FRA	Fall (2:04)
4. Stavroula Zygouri	GRE	
5. Viola Yanik	CAN	5-2
6. Volha Khilko	BLR	
7. Stephanie Gross	GER	
8. Alyena Kartashova	RUS	

The Olympic final was a replay of the 2003 world championship final, when Kaori Icho beat Sara McMann by one point in overtime. In Athens, McMann led 2-0 after two takedowns in the first period, before Icho fought back with two one-point takedowns to tie. She then scored a third takedown with 21 seconds remaining.

McMann faced two major tragedies during her career. In 1999 her brother, Jason, was beaten to death after a drug-money-related fight. Five days after the Olympic Closing Ceremony, McMann was driving with her boyfriend in Colorado when she lost control of her Jeep Cherokee at 88mph (142kph) and rolled over. Her boyfriend, wrestler Steve Blackford, who was not wearing a seatbelt, was thrown from the vehicle and killed.

2008 Beijing C: 17, N: 17, D: 8.17.
(63 kg–139 lbs)

		FINAL MATCH
1. Kaori Icho	JPN	1-0, 2-0
2. Alyona Kartashova	RUS	
3. Randi Miller	USA	
3. Yelena Shalygina	KAZ	
5. Martine Dugrenier	CAN	
5. Lise Golliot-Legrand	FRA	
7. Elina Vaseva	BUL	
8. Monika Michalik	POL	

3rd Place: Miller—Dugrenier 1-0, 1-2, 1-1
3rd Place: Shalygina—Golliot-Legrand 5-0, 3-2

Kaori Icho had dominated the 63-kilogram weight class for the past six years, winning five consecutive world championship titles and the 2004 Olympic gold medal.

Icho overwhelmed her first two opponents, beating each by fall, but had a harder time in the semifinals against three-time 67-kilogram world silver medalist Martine Dugrenier. Icho won the first period 1-0, but Dugrenier came back to score the only point in the second period. The two wrestlers finished the third period tied 1-1, but Icho advanced because she scored the last point.

Icho took on reigning European champion Alyona Kartashova in the final, winning the first period 1-0 in overtime. After the second period also ended without a point scored, Icho clinched the gold medal four seconds into overtime, earning two points on a left-knee takedown.

Icho's older sister, Chiharu, had won her second consecutive Olympic silver medal the previous day in the 48-kilogram weight class.

HEAVYWEIGHT
(72 kg—159 lbs)

1896–2000 not held

2004 Athens C: 12, N: 12, D: 8.23.
(72 kg—159 lbs)

		FINAL MATCH
1. Wang Xu	CHN	7-2
2. Guzel Manyurova	RUS	
3. Kyoko Hamaguchi	JPN	4-0
4. Svitlana Saienko	UKR	
5. Christine Nordhagen	CAN	WO
6. Anita Schätzle	GER	
7. Toccara Montgomery	USA	
8. Maria Louiza Vryoni	GRE	

In what would prove to be a controversial semifinal match, five-time world champion Kyoko Hamaguchi faced 18-year-old Wang Xu of Beijing, whom she had beaten in the 2002 world championship final. First there was a dispute about the awarding of two points to Wang after a move that Hamaguchi initiated. Then a scoreboard error caused more turmoil. Looking at the scoreboard, Hamaguchi thought she was trailing 5-4. She scored a one-point takedown with ten seconds to go and thought she had tied the match. But the scoreboard then showed the corrected score of 6-4 for Wang. Hamaguchi's father, former professional wrestler Heigo "The Animal" Hamaguchi, tried to jump out of the stands and had to be restrained by the police. Wang advanced to the final, where she outpointed European champion Guzel Manyurova 7-2.

2008 Beijing C: 16, N: 16, D: 8.17.
(72 kg–159 lbs)

		FINAL MATCH
1. Wang Jiao	CHN	Fall (1:59)
2. Stanka Zlateva	BUL	
3. Kyoko Hamaguchi	JPN	
3. Agnieszka Wieszczek	POL	
5. Ali Bernard	USA	
5. Maider Unda González	SPA	
7. Anita Schätzle	GER	
8. Rosângela Conceição	BRA	

3rd Place: Hamaguchi—Bernard 3-0, 3-1
3rd Place: Wieszczek—Unda 2-1, 1-0

A reserve on the Chinese wrestling team, 20-year-old junior world champion Wang Jiao was only allowed to compete at the Beijing Games because defending Olympic champion Wang Xu injured her shoulder in training three weeks before the event. Wang beat five-time world champion Kyoko Hamaguchi 5-2, 3-0 in the semifinals, earning a place against two-time reigning world and European champion Stanka Zlateva in the final.

Wang dropped Zlateva with about 30 seconds remaining in the first period, and then gradually forced her shoulders to the mat to win by a fall in the final second.

Chapter 33 Greco-Roman Wrestling

MEN

Bantamweight—55 kg	Middleweight—84 kg
Featherweight—60 kg	Heavyweight—96 kg
Lightweight—66 kg	Super Heavyweight—120 kg
Welterweight—74 kg	Discontinued Events

In Greco-Roman wrestling the use of the legs for squeezing, pushing, pressing, or lifting an opponent is prohibited, and no holds may be made below the hips. In Greco-Roman, unlike in freestyle, it is necessary to accompany an opponent to the mat during a takedown. The system of scoring is the same as in freestyle wrestling. Despite its name, Greco-Roman wrestling was actually created in nineteenth-century France. It was called Greco-Roman in honor of the ancient cultures that originated modern sports.

BANTAMWEIGHT
(55 kg—121¼ lbs)

1896–1920 not held

1924 Paris C: 25, N: 15, D: 7.10.
(56 kg—123½ lbs)

1. Eduard Pütsep	EST
2. Anselm Ahlfors	FIN
3. Väinö Ikonen	FIN
4. Sigfrid Hansson	SWE
5. Adolf Herschmann	AUT
6. Ragnvald Olsen	NOR
7. Armand Magyar	HUN
7. Józef Tasnádi	HUN

1928 Amsterdam C: 19, N: 19, D: 8.5.
(56 kg—123½ lbs)

1. Kurt Leucht	GER
2. Jindřich Maudr	CZE
3. Giovanni Gozzi	ITA
4. Oscar Lindelöf	SWE
5. Ödön Zombori	HUN
6. Eduard Pütsep	EST
7. Herman Andersen	DEN
8. Anselm Ahlfors	FIN

1932 Los Angeles C: 7, N: 7, D: 8.7.
(56 kg—123½ lbs)

1. Jakob Brendel	GER
2. Marcello Nizzola	ITA
3. Louis François	FRA
4. Herman Tuvesson	SWE

Jakob Brendel won the final on decision, with the official report noting that Marcello Nizzola "gave up." Evidently Nizzola was dissatisfied with the turn of events, because in the locker room after the match he attacked Brendel with a knife. A policeman intervened and prevented any serious injury. A member of Benito Mussolini's Republican Fascist Party (P.F.R.), Nizzola was assassinated on 22 February 1947, almost two years after the end of World War II. His son, Garibaldo, competed as a freestyle wrestler in four Olympics between 1948 and 1960.

Aleksandr Karelin, 1996
With a gold in Atlanta, Karelin became the first wrestler to win the same weight division three times in a row. He then took silver in 2000.

1936 Berlin C: 18, N: 18, D: 8.9.
(56 kg—123½ lbs)

		ROUND ELIMINATED	PEN. PTS.	FINAL ROUND
1. Márton Lörincz	HUN	—	3	1
2. Egon Svensson	SWE	—	0	3
3. Jakob Brendel	GER	5	5	
4. Väinö Perttunen	FIN	5	5	
5. Iosef Tözer	ROM	5	6	
6. Evald Sikk	EST	4	5	
7. Robert Voigt	DEN	4	7	
8. Dante Bertoli	ITA	4	7	

1948 London C: 13, N: 13, D: 8.6.
(57 kg—125½ lbs)

		ROUND ELIMINATED	PEN. PTS.	FINAL ROUND
1. Kurt Pettersén	SWE	—	4	1
2. Ali Mahmoud Hassan	EGY	—	2	3
3. Halil Kaya	TUR	5	6	
4. Taisto Lempinen	FIN	4	5	
5. Elvidlo Flamini	ARG	4	6	
6. Lajos Bencze	HUN	3	5	
6. Reidar Maerlie	NOR	3	5	
8. Nikolaos Biris	GRE	3	6	

1952 Helsinki C: 17, N: 17, D: 7.27.
(57 kg—125½ lbs)

		ROUND ELIMINATED	PEN. PTS.	FINAL ROUND
1. Imre Hódos	HUN	—	4	4
2. Zakaria Chihab	LEB	—	6	4
3. Artem Teryan	SOV/AZR	—	4	4
4. Hubert Persson	SWE	5	7	
5. Reidar Maerlie	NOR	4	5	
6. Ferdinand Schmitz	GER	4	6	
7. Ion Popescu	ROM	4	7	
8. Pietro Lombardi	ITA	3	5	

1956 Melbourne C: 28, N: 28, D: 8.31.
(57 kg—125½ lbs)

		ROUND ELIMINATED	PEN. PTS.	FINAL ROUND
1. Konsfantin Vyrupayev	SOV/RUS	—	4	4
2. Edvin Westerby	SWE	—	1	4
3. Francisc Horvath	ROM	—	4	4
4. Imre Hódos	HUN	4	5	
5. Alfred Kämmerer	GER	4	5	
6. Dinko Petrov	BUL	3	5	
7. Adolfo Díaz	ARG	3	6	

1960 Rome C: 28, N: 28, D: 8.31.
(57 kg—125½ lbs)

		ROUND ELIMINATED	PEN. PTS.	FINAL ROUND
1. Oleg Karavayev	SOV/BLR	—	2	1
2. Ion Cernea	ROM	—	5	3
3. Dinko Petrov	BUL	5	6	
4. Edvin Westerby	SWE	5	6	
5. Jiří Švec	CZE	5	7	
5. Yaşar Yilmaz	TUR	5	7	
7. Masamitsu Ichiguchi	JPN	5	8	
7. Bernard Knitter	POL	5	8	

1964 Tokyo C: 18, N: 18, D: 10.19.
(57 kg—125½ lbs)

		ROUND ELIMINATED	PEN. PTS.
1. Masamitsu Ichiguchi	JPN	—	4
2. Vladlen Trostyansky	SOV/UKR	5	6
3. Ion Cernea	ROM	5	8
4. Jiří Švec	CZE	5	8
5. Karmal Ali	EGY	4	6
5. Tsviatko Pashkulev	BUL	4	6
5. Fritz Stange	GER	4	6
8. Unver Basergil	TUR	4	7

1968 Mexico City C: 24, N: 24, D: 10.26.
(57 kg—125½ lbs)

		ROUND ELIMINATED	PEN. PTS.	FINAL ROUND
1. János Varga	HUN	—	6	—
2. Ion Baciu	ROM	6	7.5	4
3. Ivan Kochergin	SOV/RUS	6	7.5	6.5
4. Othon Moschidis	GRE	6	7.5	6.5
5. Koji Sakurama	JPN	5	6.5	
6. Elsayad Ibrahim	EGY	5	9	
6. Kaya Öczan	TUR	5	9	
8. Risto Björlin	FIN	4	6	

1972 Munich C: 30, N: 30, D: 9.10.
(57 kg—125½ lbs)

		ROUND ELIMINATED	PEN. PTS.	FINAL ROUND
1. Rustem Kazakov	SOV/UZB	—	5	0
2. Hans-Jürgen Veil	GER	—	4	4
3. Risto Björlin	FIN	7	8	
4. János Varga	HUN	7	9	
5. Hristo Traikov	BUL	6	6	
6. Ion Baciu	ROM	5	6	
7. Ikuei Yamamoto	JPN	5	8.5	
8. Józef Lipień	POL	4	8	

World champion Rustem Kazakov pinned local favorite Hans-Jürgen Veil in 2:58 to win the gold medal.

1976 Montreal C: 17, N: 17, D: 7.24.
(57 kg—125½ lbs)

		ROUND ELIMINATED	PEN. PTS.	FINAL ROUND
1. Pertti Ukkola	FIN	—	4.5	2
2. Ivan Frgić	YUG/SER	—	6	3
3. Farhat Mustafin	SOV/RUS	—	4.5	7
4. Yoshima Suga	JPN	5	8	
5. Mihai Botila	ROM	5	8	
6. Krasimir Stefanov	BUL	4	6	
7. József Doncsecz	HUN	4	7.5	
8. Josef Krysta	CZE	4	8	

Ukkola earned his upset victory by barely outpointing Mustafin and Frgić with scores of 6-5 and 5-4.

1980 Moscow C: 13, N: 13, D: 7.24.
(57 kg—125½ lbs)

		ROUND ELIMINATED	PEN. PTS.	FINAL ROUND
1. Shamil Serikov	SOV/KAZ	—	1	1
2. Józef Lipień	POL	—	6	7

3. Benni Ljungbeck	SWE	—	5	8
4. Mihai Botila	ROM	5	11.5	
5. Antonino Caltabiano	ITA	4	7	
6. Josef Krysta	CZE	4	7	
7. Gyula Molnár	HUN	4	7	
8. Georgi Donev	BUL	3	7	

Serikov outpointed Lipień 11-4 in the final match.

1984 Los Angeles-Anaheim C: 16, N: 16, 0: 8.3.
(57 kg—125½ lbs)

		FINAL MATCH
1. Pasquale Passarelli	GER	8-5 6:00
2. Masaki Eto	JPN	
3. Haralambos Holidis	GRE	2-1 6:00
4. Nicolae Zamfir	ROM	
5. Frank Famiano	USA	Injury
6. Benni Ljungbeck	SWE	
7. Mehmets Erhat Karadag	TUR	
8. Park Byung-hyo	KOR	

Passarelli, a 27-year-old insurance agent, spent the last 96 seconds of his final match with world champion Eto in a back body arch to avoid being pinned. One year after his Olympic triumph, Passarelli was arrested (and subsequently convicted) for smuggling stolen money to France and Paraguay.

1988 Seoul C: 21, N: 21, D: 9.22.
(57 kg—125½ lbs)

		FINAL MATCH	
1. András Sike	HUN	Injury	3:38
2. Stoyan Balov	BUL		
3. Haralambos Holidis	GRE	6-1	
4. Yang Changling	CHN		
5. Huh Byung-ho	KOR	Fall	1:44
6. Ghazi Salah	IRQ		
7. Aleksandr Chestakov	SOV/BLR	Forfeit	
8. Rifat Yildiz	GER		

Sike was leading 9-0 in the final when Balov retired.

1992 Barcelona C: 19, N: 19, D: 7.30.
(57 kg—125½ lbs)

		FINAL MATCH
1. An Han-bong	KOR	6-5 5:36
2. Rifat Yildiz	GER	
3. Sheng Zetian	CHN	5-4
4. Aleksandr Ignatenko	RUS	
5. William Lara Díaz	CUB	8-1
6. Marian Sandu	ROM	
7. Keijo Pehkonen	FIN	6-4
8. Dennis Hall	USA	

Unheralded An Han-bong blasted his first five opponents 41-1. In the final, two-time world champion Rifat Yildiz took a 5-2 lead but ran out of steam as An continued to attack relentlessly.

1996 Atlanta C: 20, N: 20, D: 7.20.
(57 kg—125½ lbs)

		FINAL MATCH
1. Yury Melnichenko	KAZ	4-1
2. Dennis Hall	USA	
3. Sheng Zetian	CHN	4-0 6:49
4. Ruslan Khakymov	UKR	
5. Rifat Yildiz	GER	0-0 0:32
6. Luis Sarmiento Hernández	CUB	
7. Sarkis Elgkian	GRE	5-4
8. Kenkichi Nishimi	JPN	

In 1991, when Yuri Melnichenko was 19 years old, he visited the "Wailing Wall" in Jerusalem and slipped a piece of paper into a crevice expressing his with to become a world and Olympic champion. An ethnic Ukrainian born in the mountains of Kyrgystan, Melnichenko moved to Kazakhstan to train with double Olympic medalist Daulet Turlykhanov. In 1994, Melnichenko fulfilled half of his wish by winning the world championship. When he attempted to defend his title the following year, he was defeated by Dennis Hall on decision after a 2-2 tie. In Atlanta, Melnichenko outscored his first four opponents 26-1. One minute 38 seconds into the final, he surprised Hall with a lift and toss that earned him four points. Melnichenko was the first Olympic champion to represent independent Kazakhstan.

2000 Sydney C: 20, N: 20, D: 9.27.
(58 kg—128 lbs)

		FINAL MATCH
1. Armen Nazaryan	BUL	Fall 2:34
2. Kim In-sub	KOR	
3. Sheng Zetian	CHN	2-0
4. Rifat Yildiz	GER	
5. Ali Ashkani Aghbolagh	IRN	3-2
6. James Gruenwald	USA	
7. Valery Nikonorov	RUS	
8. Makoto Sasamoto	JPN	

After winning the gold medal in the flyweight class at the 1996 Olympics, Armen Nazaryan decided to leave Armenia and compete for another country that could support him financially. His first choice was France, but the French wrestling federation did not have a large enough budget, so he turned to Bulgaria, the home of his girlfriend (and later wife). In Sydney, he outscored his first four opponents 38-3 to earn a place in the final against two-time defending world champion Kim In-sub. Nazaryan was leading Kim 10-3 when he pinned him after 2 minutes 47 seconds.

2004 Athens C: 22, N: 22, D: 8.25.
(55 kg—121 lbs)

		FINAL MATCH
1. István Majoros	HUN	3-1 6:08
2. Geydar Mamedalyev	RUS	
3. Artiom Kiourengian	GRE	6-1
4. Oleksiy Vakulenko	UKR	
5. Lázaro Rivas Scull	CUB	Fall 1:32
6. Irakli Chochua	GEO	
7. Im Dae-won	KOR	
8. Haakan Nyblom	DEN	

István Majoros was an unlikely winner, having finished only 18th at the 2000 Olympics and 12th and 13th at the 2002 and 2003 world championships. In his opening match in Athens, he defeated Masatoshi Toyota of Japan after 86 seconds of overtime. In the qualification round he upset defending silver medalist Lázaro Rivas 6-1, and in the final he beat 2002 world champion Geydar Mamedalyev, again in overtime. Majoros later became a professional wrestler in Japan.

2008 Beijing C: 19, N: 19, D: 8.12.
(55 kg-121 lbs)

		FINAL MATCH
1. Nazyr Mankiev	RUS	4-3, 2-2
2. Rövshan Bayramov	AZE	
3. Roman Amoyan	ARM	
3. Park Eun-chul	KOR	
5. Yagnier Hernández	CUB	
5. Hamid Soryan Reihanpour	IRN	
7. Kristijan Fris	SER	
8. Spenser Mango	USA	

3rd Place: Amoyan—Hernández 3-0, 5-0
3rd Place: Park—Soryan 1-1, 2-2

Hamid Soryan had won the last three world championships, winning 32 of 33 periods. However, in the Olympic quarterfinals he was upset by Nazyr Mankiev, whose previous best result had been a bronze medal at the 2007 world championships. Each of the three periods ended in a tie, but Mankiev won the third-period tie-breaker. Mankiev then beat reigning world silver medalist Park Eun-chu 1-1, 6-0, 2-1 in the semifinals.

Twenty-one-year-old two-time European champion Rövshan Bayramov took the early lead in the final, lifting Mankiev to earn three points. However, Mankiev rallied to score the next four points and win the period. Bayramov scored first in the second period too, but Mankiev again came back, this time tying the period score 2-2, and earning the gold medal by scoring the final point.

FEATHERWEIGHT
(60 kg—132 lbs)

1896–1906 not held

1912 Stockholm C: 38, N: 13, D: 7.15.

1. Kaarlo Koskelo	FIN
2. Georg Gerstäcker	GER
3. Otto Lasanen	FIN
4. Kaarlo Leivonen	FIN
4. Erik Öberg	SWE
6. Lauri Haapanen	FIN
6. Arvo Kangas	FIN
6. H. Vilhelm Lehmusvirta	FIN

In 1918, Koskelo emigrated to the United States and settled in Astoria, Oregon, where he established a Finnish sauna for tired workers and their families.

1920 Antwerp C. 21, N: 12, D: 8.19.

1. Oskar Friman	FIN
2. Heikki Kähkönen	FIN
3. Fritiof Svensson	SWE
4. Aage Torgensen	DEN
5. Alexandre Boumans	BEL
6. Eduard Pütsep	EST

Friman pinned each of his four opponents within eight minutes.

1924 Paris C: 27, N: 15, D: 7.10.
(62 kg—136½ lbs)

1. Kaarlo "Kalle" Anttila	FIN
2. Aleksanteri Toivola	FIN
3. Erik Malmberg	SWE
4. Arthur Nord	NOR
5. Fritiof Svensson	SWE
6. Maurice Capron	FRA
6. Ödön Radvány	HUN

Anttila was 36 years old when he won his second Olympic gold medal. In Antwerp in 1920 he had finished first in the freestyle Lightweight division.

1928 Amsterdam C: 20, N: 20, D: 8.5.

1. Voldemar Väli	EST
2. Erik Malmberg	SWE
3. Giacomo Quaglia	ITA
4. Károly Kárpáti	HUN
5. Ernst Steinig	GER

6. Aage Meier (DEN), Arakan Saim (TUR), Aleksanteri Toivola (FIN)

1932 Los Angeles C: 8, N: 8, D: 8.7.
(61 kg—134½ lbs)

1. Giovanni Gozzi	ITA
2. Wolfgang Ehrl	GER
3. Lauri Koskela	FIN
4. Jindřich Maudr	CZE
5. Kiyoshi Kase	JPN

The bad luck award for 1932 went to Wolfgang Ehrl. He won all of his fights, but was denied the gold medal because Giovanni Gozzi amassed the most points, which, according to the rules, was the determining factor. Four years later, Ehrl made it to the final of the lightweight division of freestyle wrestling, but lost to Károly Kárpáti and ended up with another silver medal.

1936 Berlin C: 19, N: 19, D: 8.9.
(61 kg—134½ lbs)

		ROUND ELIMINATED	PEN. PTS.
1. Yaşar Erkan	TUR	—	4
2. Aarne Reini	FIN	7	5
3. Einar Karlsson	SWE	7	5
4. Sebastian Hering	GER	5	5
5. Kristjanis Kundziņš	LAT	5	6
6. Valentino Borgia	ITA	4	5
7. Henryk Ślązak	POL	4	6
8. Gyula Móri	HUN	4	6

1948 London C: 17, N: 17, D: 8.6.
(61 kg—134½ lbs)

		ROUND ELIMINATED	PEN. PTS.	FINAL ROUND
1. Mehmet Oktav	TUR	—	3	0
2. Olle Anderberg	SWE	—	3	3
3. Ferenc Tóth	HUN	6	6	
4. Georg Weidner	AUT	5	5	
5. Luigi Campanella	ITA	5	6	
6. Sayed Kandil	EGY	4	7	
6. Egil Solsvik	NOR	4	7	
6. Safi Taha	LEB	4	7	
6. Erkki Talosela	FIN	4	7	

The decisive match took place in the third round, when Oktav threw Anderberg in 2:48.

1952 Helsinki C: 17, N: 17, D: 7.27.
(61 kg—134½ lbs)

		ROUND ELIMINATED	PEN. PTS.	FINAL ROUND
1. Yakiv Punkin	SOV/UKR	—	2	0
2. Imre Polyák	HUN	—	3	4
3. Abdel Rashed	EGY	—	5	6
4. Umberto Trippa	ITA	4	5	
5. Bartholomäus Brötzner	AUT	4	6	
6. Hasan Bozbey	TUR	4	7	
7. Safi Taha	LEB	3	3	
8. Ernest Gondzik	POL	3	5	
8. Erkki Talosela	FIN	3	5	

Punkin finished strongly, pinning Polyák in 1:26 and Rashad in 3:28.

1956 Melbourne C: 10, N: 10, D: 12.6.
(61 kg—134½ lbs)

		ROUND ELIMINATED	PEN. PTS.	FINAL ROUND
1. Rauno Mäkinen	FIN	—	4	4
2. Imre Polyák	HUN	—	3	4
3. Roman Dzneladze	SOV/GEO	—	4	4
4. Müzahir Sille	TUR	4	6	
5. Gunnar Håkansson	SWE	3	5	
6. Umberto Trippa	ITA	3	7	
7. Ion Popescu	ROM	3	7	

1960 Rome C: 25, N: 25, D: 8.31.
(61 kg—134½ lbs)

		ROUND ELIMINATED	PEN. PTS.	FINAL ROUND
1. Müzahir Sille	TUR	—	5	1
2. Imre Polyák	HUN	—	3	3
3. Konstantin Vyrupayev	SOV/RUS	6	6	
4. Umberto Trippa	ITA	6	6	
5. Mihai Schultz	ROM	6	8	
6. Saiid Ebrahimian	IRN	5	7	
6. Vojtech Toth	CZE	5	7	
8. Lee Allen	USA	4	7	

1964 Tokyo C: 27, N: 27, D: 10.19
(63 kg—139 lbs)

		ROUND ELIMINATED	PEN. PTS.	FINAL ROUND
1. Imre Polyák	HUN	—	1	2
2. Roman Rurua	SOV/GEO	—	4	2
3. Branislav Martinović	YUG/SER	5	4	
4. Ronald Finley	USA	5	6	
4. Mostafa Mansour	EGY	5	6	
6. Joseph Mewis	BEL	4	6	
6. Rassoul Mirmalek	IRN	4	6	
6. Koji Sakurama	JPN	4	6	

After finishing second three straight times, Polyák finally won an Olympic gold medal.

1968 Mexico City C: 23, N: 23, D: 10.26.
(63 kg—139 lbs)

		ROUND ELIMINATED	PEN. PTS.	FINAL ROUND
1. Roman Rurua	SOV/GEO	—	2	2
2. Hideo Fujimoto	JPN	—	5	2
3. Simeon Popescu	ROM	6	6.5	
4. Dimitar Galinchev	BUL	6	8	
5. Hizir Alakoc	TUR	5	6	
6. Martti Laakso	FIN	4	6	
7. James Hazewinkel	USA	4	8.5	
8. Lothar Schneider	GDR	4	9	

1972 Munich C: 19, N: 19, D: 9.10.
(62 kg—136½ lbs)

		ROUND ELIMINATED	PEN. PTS.	FINAL ROUND
1. Georgi Markov	BUL	—	3	
2. Heinz-Helmut Wehling	GDR	6	6.5	
3. Kazimierz Lipień	POL	6	6.5	
4. Hideo Fujimoto	JPN	6	7.5	
5. Djemal Megrelishvili	SOV/GEO	6	8	
6. Ion Păun	ROM	5	7.5	
7. Martti Laakso	FIN	5	8	
7. Stylianos Mygiakis	GRE	5	8	

1976 Montreal C: 17, N: 17, D: 7.24.
(62 kg—136½ lbs)

		ROUND ELIMINATED	PEN. PTS.	FINAL ROUND
1. Kazimierz Lipień	POL	—	3.5	3.5
2. Nelson Davydyan	SOV/UKR	—	4	4
3. László Réczi	HUN	—	5.5	4.5
4. Teruhiko Miyahara	JPN	7	8	
5. Ion Păun	ROM	6	8	
6. Pekka Hjelt	FIN	4	7	
7. Stylianos Mygiakis	GRE	4	8.5	
8. Stoyan Lazarov	BUL	3	7	

Kazimierz Lipień won the world championship in 1973 and 1974, but in 1975 he lost a controversial decision to Nelson Davydyan. The two met again in the sixth round of the Olympics in Montreal, with Davydyan gaining another controversial victory, 10-6. In that match, Viktor Igumenov, the Soviet coach, was ordered to leave the competition area after he illegally shouted instructions to Davydyan. Igumenov continued to yell orders, but from a greater distance. Lipień salvaged the gold medal anyway by outpointing Róczi 13-4, the nine-point margin reducing Lipień's bad marks for the bout from 1 to 0.5. Lipień's twin brother, Jozef, won a Bantamweight silver medal in 1980. At the 1975 World championships, the Poles were accused of substituting Jozef for Kazimierz in one match. Their accusers should have known better, since Jozef always parted his hair on the left side, while Kazimierz parted his on the right. At the post-tournament press conference in Montreal, Kazimierz, a 27-year-old plumber, advised aspiring wrestlers to abstain from smoking and drinking. "And no women," added bronze medalist László Réczi. But Lipień disagreed. "That is taking sacrifices too far," he said, "women are good to wrestle with, too."

1980 Moscow C: 11, N: 11, D: 7.22.
(62 kg—136½ lbs)

		ROUND ELIMINATED	PEN. PTS.	FINAL ROUND
1. Stylianos Mygiakis	GRE	—	6	2
2. István Tóth	HUN	—	3	4
3. Boris Kramorenko	SOV/TRM	5	7	
4. Ivan Frgić	YUG/SER	5	7	
5. Panayot Kirov	BUL	4	9	
6. Kazimierz Lipień	POL	3	6	
7. Radwan Karout	SYR	3	8	
8. Michal Vejsada	CZE	3	8	

Mygiakis was the first "Greco" ever to win a Greco-Roman gold medal in the Olympics.

1984 Los Angeles-Anaheim C: 20, N: 20, D: 8.1.
(62 kg—136½ lbs)

		FINAL MATCH
1. Kim Weon-kee	KOR	3-3
2. Kent-Olle Johansson	SWE	
3. Hugo Dietsche	SWI	8-4
4. Abdurrahim Kuzu	USA	
5. Douglas Yeats	CAN	15-3 4:41
6. Salem Bekhit	EGY	
7. Bernd Gabriel	GER	
8. Seiichi Osanai	JPN	

1988 Seoul C: 17, N: 17, D: 9.20.
(62 kg—136½ lbs)

		FINAL MATCH
1. Kamandar Madzhidov	SOV/BLR	6-2
2. Zhivko Vangelov	BUL	
3. An Dae-hyun	KOR	Passivity 3:15
4. Jenő Bódi	HUN	
5. Peter Behl	GER	5-1
6. Isaac Anderson	USA	
7. Gilles Jalabert	FRA	Injury
8. Hugo Dietsche	SWI	

Madzhidov, a 26-year-old law student, reversed the defeat he had suffered to Vangelov at the previous world championships.

1992 Barcelona C: 21, N: 21, D: 7.30.
(62 kg—136½ lbs)

		FINAL MATCH
1. M. Akif Pirim	TUR	13-2
2. Sergei Martynov	RUS	
3. Juan Luis Marén Delís	CUB	5-0
4. Włodzimierz Zawadzki	POL	
5. Jenő Bódi	HUN	Injury
6. Anthony "Buddy" Lee	USA	
7. Stanilsav Grigorov	BUL	Forfeit
8. Hugo Dietsche	SWI	

The final was a rematch of the 1991 world championship at which Martynov won a rough and controversial 2-1 victory over Pirim. This time there was no controversy, as Pirim won handily. At the 1993 European championships, Pirim tested positive for the steroid nandrolone and was suspended for two years.

1996 Atlanta C: 19, N: 19, D: 7.22.
(63 kg—139 lbs)

		FINAL MATCH
1. Włodzimierz Zawadzki	POL	3-1
2. Juan Luis Marén Delís	CUB	
3. M. Akif Pirim	TUR	9-0
4. Koba Guliashvili	GEO	
5. Ivan Ivanov	BUL	3-0
6. Hryhoriy Kamyshenko	UKR	
7. Mkhitar Manukyan	ARM	WO
8. Sergei Martynov	RUS	

The critical match leading to the final came in the second round when Sergei Martynov, who had won the last four world championships, was defeated 5-4 by Juan Luis Marén.

2000 Sydney C: 20, N: 20, D: 9.26.
(63 kg—139 lbs)

		FINAL MATCH
1. Varteres Samurgachev	RUS	3-0
2. Juan Luis Marén Delís	CUB	
3. Akaki Chachua	GEO	Fall 1:57
4. Beat Motzer	SWI	
5. Bakhodir Kurbanov	UZB	10-0 4:06
6. Kevin Bracken	USA	
7. Mkhitar Manukyan	KAZ	
8. Hryhoriy Kamyshenko	UKR	

European champion Varteres Samurgachev endured baptism by fire, as his first two matches paired him with world champion runner-up Şeref Eroğlu and defending Olympic champion Włodzimierz Zawadzki. Samurgachev defeated Eroğlu 5-2 and Zawadzki 8-0. In the final, he faced Juan Luis Marén, who had taken out world champion Mkhitar Manukyan 5-3 in his elimination pool. The gold medal match went into overtime, with Samurgachev winning when Manukyan received a caution after 43 seconds.

2004 Athens C: 19, N: 19, D: 8.26.
(60 kg—132 lbs)

		FINAL MATCH
1. Jung Ji-hyun	KOR	3-0 6:08
2. Roberto Monzón González	CUB	
3. Armen Nazaryan	BUL	4-3
4. Aleksei Shevtsov	RUS	
5. Makoto Sasamoto	JPN	4-0
6. Nurlan Koyshaganov	KAZ	
7. Eusebiu Iancu Diaconu	ROM	
8. Şeref Tüfenk	TUR	

Armen Nazaryan arrived in Athens as the overwhelming favorite at 60 kilograms. He had already earned Olympic gold medals in 1996 and 2000 and world championships in 2002 and 2003. He won his first three matches, but in the semifinals he was upset 3-2 by the 21-year-old Asian champion, Jung Ji-hyun. In the final, Jung led 2003 world championship runner-up Roberto Monzón after regulation, but was short of the three points needed for victory. Starting in the defensive position in the overtime period, he scored with a reverse tackle after only eight seconds. Among the rewards Jung earned for his victory was a reduction of his military service from 26 months to four weeks.

2008 Beijing C: 20, N: 20, D: 8.12.
(60 kg-132 lbs)

		FINAL MATCH
1. Islam-Beka Albiev	RUS	2-0, 4-0
2. Vitaliy Rahimov	AZE	
3. Nurbakyt Tengizbayev	KAZ	
3. Ruslan Tyumenbayev	KGZ	
5. Roberto Monzón González	CUB	
5. Sheng Jiang	CHN	
7. Armen Nazaryan	BUL	
8. Eusebiu Diaconu	ROM	

3rd Place: Tengizbayev—Jiang 4-1, 1-2, 3-0
3rd Place: Tyumenbayev—Monzón 8-0, 3-0

Due to the blind draw, nearly all of the favorites were thrown together early in the tournament. Armen Nazaryan, who had earned Olympic gold medals in 1996 and 2000, defeated reigning world champion David Bedinadze of Georgia 1-1, 4-1, 5-0 in the first round, and then took on reigning world silver medalist Makoto Sasamoto of Japan in the second round, winning 0-4, 2-0, 2-0.

The thirty-four-year-old Nazaryan next faced 2005 European champion Vitaliy Rahimov in the quarterfinals, winning the first period 2-0 before Rahimov came back to win the next two periods 3-0 and 7-0. The quarterfinal round also saw defending Olympic champion Jung Ji-hyun lose 1-2, 3-2, 2-0 to Nurbakyt Tengizbayev.

Rahimov reached the final after beating Tengizbayev 1-1, 7-0 in the semifinals. His opponent in the final was 19-year-old Islam-Beka Albiev, who had finished eighth at the 2007 world championships.

Albiyev swept both periods of the final, winning the first 2-0 and the second 4-0. He thus became the youngest Greco-Roman gold medalist in Olympic history, and the second-youngest Olympic wrestling champion ever (being four days older than Šaban Trstena , the 52-kilogram gold medal winner in 1984).

LIGHTWEIGHT
(66 kg—145½ lbs)

1896–1904 not held

1906 Athens C: 12, N: 8, D: 4.26.
(75 kg—165½ lbs)

1. Rudolf Watzl	AUT
2. Karl Karlsen	DEN
3. Ferenc Holubán	HUN
4. René Dobrinovitz	BEL
4. Karel Halik	BOH/CZE
4. Alexander Wendrinsky	AUT

1908 London C: 25, N: 10, D: 7.25.
(66.6 kg—147 lbs)

		FINAL MATCH
1. Enrico Porro	ITA	Dec 30:00: Dec 20:00
2. Nikolai Orlov	RUS	
3. Arvid Lindén	FIN	
4. Gunnar Persson	SWE	

5. Gustaf Malmström (SWE), József Maróthy (HUN), Anders Møller (DEN), Ödön Radvány (HUN)

Porro, a 23-year-old Milanese sailor, was unbeaten in international competition. He was awarded a decision over Orlov after 50 minutes of very little action.

1912 Stockholm C: 48, N: 13, D: 7.15.
(67.5 kg—149 lbs)

1. Emil Väre (Vilén)	FIN
2. Gustaf Malmström	SWE
3. Edvin Matiasson	SWE
4. Carl Eriklund	SWE
4. Ödön Radvány	HUN
6. Jan Balej	BOH/CZE
6. Johan Nilsson	SWE
6. Oscar Kaplur	RUS
6. David "Tatu" Kolehmainen	FIN
6. Volmar Wikström	FIN

Väre pinned all five of his opponents, completing his feat by defeating Malmström after an epic 60-minute struggle.

1920 Antwerp C: 22, N: 12, D: 8.19.
(67.5 kg—149 lbs)

1. Emil Väre (Vilén)	FIN
2. Taavi Tamminen	FIN
3. Frithjof Andersen	NOR
4. Frits Janssens	BEL

1924 Paris C: 28, N: 18, D: 7.10.
(67.5 kg—149 lbs)

1. Oskar Friman	FIN
2. Lajos Keresztes	HUN
3. Kalle Westerlund	FIN
4. Albert Kusnets	EST
5. František Kratochvil	CZE

6. Charles Frisenfeldt (DEN), Arne Gaupseth (NOR), Mihály Matura (HUN)

In 1920 Friman won the Featherweight title. Four years later in Paris, at the age of 31, he gained his second gold medal.

1928 Amsterdam C: 19, N: 19, D: 8.5.
(67.5 kg—149 lbs)

1. Lajos Keresztes	HUN
2. Eduard Sperling	GER
3. Edvard Westerlund	FIN
4. Tayare Yalaz	TUR
5. Vladimir Vávra	CZE
6. Walter Massop	HOL
7. Ryszard Błażyca	POL
7. Frits Janssens	BEL

Keresztes turned to wrestling on the advice of a doctor who prescribed the sport as a cure for "prolonged neurosis".

1932 Los Angeles C: 6, N: 6, D: 8.7.
(66 kg—145½ lbs)

1. Erik Malmberg	SWE
2. Abraham Kurland	DEN
3. Eduard Sperling	GER
4. Aarne Reini	FIN

With this victory the 35-year-old Malmberg completed his set of Olympic medals, having previously earned a Featherweight bronze in 1924 and silver in 1928.

1936 Berlin C: 18, N: 18, D: 8.9.
(66 kg—145½ lbs)

		ROUND ELIMINATED	PEN. PTS.	FINAL ROUND
1. Lauri Koskela	FIN	—	2	2
2. Jozef Herda	CZE/SLV	—	3	3
3. Voldemar Väli	EST	—	2	5
4. Herbert Olofsson	SWE	5	5	
5. Alberto Molfino	ITA	4	6	
6. Arild Dahl	NOR	4	7	
7. Zbigniew Szajewski	POL	4	7	
8. Dragomir Borlovan	ROM	3	5	

1948 London C: 17, N: 17, D: 8.6.
(67 kg—147½ lbs)

		ROUND ELIMINATED	PEN. PTS.	FINAL ROUND
1. Gustav Freij	SWE	—	2	
2. Aage Eriksen	NOR	5	5	
3. Károly Ferencz	HUN	5	6	1
4. Charif Damage	LEB	5	6	2
5. Johannes Munnikes	HOL	4	6	
6. Georgios Petmezas	GRE	4	7	
6. Ahmet Senol	TUR	4	7	
6. Eino Virtanen	FIN	4	7	

1952 Helsinki C: 19, N: 19, D: 7.27.
(67 kg—147½ lbs)

		ROUND ELIMINATED	PEN. PTS.	FINAL ROUND
1. Shazam Saftin	SOV/RUS	—	3	1
2. Gustav Freij	SWE	—	3	3
3. Mikuláš Athanasov	CZE/SLV	—	5	6
4. Gyula Tarr	HUN	5	6	
5. Franco Benedetti	ITA	4	7	
5. Dumitru Cuc	ROM	4	7	
5. Kalle Haapasalmi	FIN	4	7	
8. Kamel Hussein	EGY	3	5	
8. Erich Schmidt	SAA/GER	3	5	

1956 Melbourne C: 10, N: 10, D: 12.6.
(67 kg—147½ lbs)

		ROUND ELIMINATED	PEN. PTS.	FINAL ROUND
1. Kyösti Lehtonen	FIN	—	1	1
2. Riza Dogan	TUR	—	6	3
3. Gyula Tóth	HUN	—	2	6
4. Bartholomäus Brötzner	AUT	4	8	
5. Dimiter Yanchev	BUL	4	9	
6. Dumitru Gheorghe	ROM	3	7	

1960 Rome C: 23, N: 23, D: 8.31.
(67 kg—147½ lbs)

		ROUND ELIMINATED	PEN. PTS.	FINAL ROUND
1. Avtandil Koridze	SOV/GEO	—	5	1
2. Branislav Martinović	YUG/SER	—	4	3
3. Gustav Freij	SWE	5	6	
4. Karel Matoušek	CZE	5	6	
5. Dumitru Gheorghe	ROM	4	7	
5. Ernest Gondzik	POL	4	7	
5. Adil Güngör	TUR	4	7	
5. Mitsuharu Kitamura	JPN	4	7	
5. Kyösti Lehtonen	FIN	4	7	
5. Jacques Pourtau	FRA	4	7	

DISQ: Dimitro Stoyanov (Dimiter Yanchev) (BUL) 5 8

Charges of "fix" were hurled following a fifth round bout between Koridze and Dimiter Yanchev of Bulgaria, then known as Dimitro Stoyanov. Koridze needed to score a fall to force a final showdown with Martinović. Anything less—a draw or even a points victory—would give the gold medal to the Yugoslav. After 11 minutes of inactivity, with only one minute left before the end of the bout, Koridze spoke a few words to Stoyanov and then threw him to the ground and pinned him. The Yugoslavs immediately lodged a protest. Stoyanov, who had originally been awarded fifth place, was disqualified from the tournament, but Koridze was not punished and went on to defeat Martinović and to win the gold medal.

1964 Tokyo C: 19, N: 19, D: 10.19.
(70 kg—154½ lbs)

		ROUND ELIMINATED	PEN. PTS.	FINAL ROUND
1. Kazim Ayvaz	TUR	—	5	
2. Valeriu Bularcă	ROM	5	6	3
3. David Gvantseladze	SOV/GEO	5	6	4
4. Tokuaki Fujita	JPN	5	6	5
5. Stevan Horvat	YUG/SER	5	7	
6. Eero Tapio	FIN	5	8	
7. Bror Jonsson	SWE	4	6	
8. Ivan Ivanov	BUL	4	7	

1968 Mexico City C: 26, N: 26, D: 10.26.
(70 kg—154½ lbs)

		ROUND ELIMINATED	PEN. PTS.	FINAL ROUND
1. Munji Mumemura	JPN	—	5	3.5
2. Stevan Horvat	YUG/SER	—	5	5
3. Petros Galaktopoulos	GRE	—	5	5.5
4. Klaus Rost	GER	6	8	
5. Eero Tapio	FIN	5	7.5	
6. Werner Holzer	USA	5	8	
6. Gennady Sapunov	SOV/RUS	5	8	
8. Antal Steer	HUN	4	6	

1972 Munich C: 23, N: 23, D: 9.10.
(68 kg—149½ lbs)

		ROUND ELIMINATED	PEN. PTS.	FINAL ROUND
1. Shamil Khisamutdinov	SOV/RUS	—	2.5	
2. Stoyan Apostolov	BUL	6	5	
3. Gian-Matteo Ranzi	ITA	6	6	
4. Manfred Schöndorfer	GER	6	7.5	
5. Takashi Tanoue	JPN	5	6	
6. Seyit Hisirli	TUR	4	6	
6. Antal Steer	HUN	4	6	
8. Sreten Damjanović	YUG/SER	4	7.5	

1976 Munich C: 21, N: 21, D: 7.24.
(68 kg—149½ lbs)

		ROUND ELIMINATED	PEN. PTS.	FINAL ROUND
1. Suren Nalbandyan	SOV/ARM	—	3	2
2. Ştefan Rusu	ROM	—	3	3
3. Heinz-Helmut Wehling	GDR	—	8	7
4. Lars-Erik Skiöld	SWE	6	9.5	
5. Andrzej Supron	POL	5	8	
6. Manfred Schöndorfer	GER	5	9	
7. Erol Mutlu	TUR	4	6	
8. Markku Yli-Isotalo	FIN	4	7	

The 20-year-old Nalbandyan gained a crucial 5-3 victory over Rusu in the fourth round and then outpointed Supron 7-4 and Wehling 12-9. In 1984, Nalbandyan was sentenced to three years in a labor camp for selling blackmarket alcohol.

1980 Moscow C 15, N: 15, D: 7.24.
(68 kg—149½ lbs)

		ROUND ELIMINATED	PEN. PTS.	FINAL ROUND
1. Ştefan Rusu	ROM	—	4	2
2. Andrzej Supron	POL	—	1	3
3. Lars-Erik Skiöld	SWE	—	1	7
4. Suren Nalbandyan	SOV/ARM	5	8	
5. Buyandelger Bold	MGL	5	9	
6. Ivan Atanassov	BUL	4	8	
7. Reinhard Hartmann	AUT	4	8	
8. Károly Gaál	HUN	3	7	

The cast of characters was almost the same as it was four years earlier. Nalbandyan was the first of the four favorites to be eliminated when he and Rusu were charged with a double disqualification after 7:09 of their fifth-round match. In the final round-robin Rusu outpointed Supron 3-2 and Skiöld 5-1.

1984 Los Angeles-Anaheim C: 14, N: 14, D: 8.3.
(68 kg—149½ lbs)

		FINAL MATCH
1. Vlado Lisjak	YUG/CRO	Fall 0:57
2. Tapio Sipilä	FIN	
3. James Martinez	USA	Fall 0:25
4. Stefan Negrisan	ROM	
5. Deitmar Streitler	AUT	8-4
6. Mohamed Mutei Alnakdali	SYR	
7. Shaban Ibrahim	EGY	
8. Sümer Koçak	TUR	

In a major upset, the defending world champion, Tapio Sipilä, was quickly thrown by a late substitute to the Yugoslav team, Vlado Lisjak, a 22-year-old truck driver from the village of Petrinja.

1988 Seoul C: 31, N: 31, D: 9.22.
(68 kg—149½ lbs)

		FINAL MATCH
1. Levon Dzhulfalakyan	SOV/ARM	9-3
2. Kim Sung-moon	KOR	
3. Tapio Sipilä	FIN	7-4
4. Petrica Carare	ROM	
5. Jerzy Kopański	POL	Passivity 5:07
6. Yasuhiro Okubo	JPN	
7. Morten Brekke	NOR	6-5 6:42
8. Attila Repka	HUN	

Dzhulfalakyan, a 24-year-old Armenian, faced his stiffest challenge from Carare, who forced him into overtime before succumbing.

1992 Barcelona C: 19, N: 19, D: 7.28.
(68 kg—149½ lbs)

		FINAL MATCH
1. Attila Repka	HUN	1-0 5:38
2. Islam Duguchiyev	RUS	
3. Rodney Smith	USA	6-3
4. Cecilio Rodríguez Pérez	CUB	
5. Ghani Yalouz	FRA	Forfeit
6. Abdollah Chamangoli	IRN	
7. Ryszard Wolny	POL	1-0
8. Douglas Yeats	CAN	

Repka upset Armenian-born Duguchiyev, the two-time defending world champion, by spinning him over from a bodylock position in sudden-death overtime. The match was halted twice so that Repka's badly swollen hand could be tended.

1996 Atlanta C: 22, N: 22, D: 7.20.
(68 kg—149½ lbs)

		FINAL MATCH
1. Ryszard Wolny	POL	7-0
2. Ghani Yalouz	FRA	
3. Aleksandr Tretyakov	RUS	4-0 5:56
4. Kamandar Madzhidov	BLR	
5. Biser Georgiev	BUL	2-1
6. Grigory Pulyayev	UZB	
7. Liubal Colás Oris	CUB	6-1
8. Valeri Nikitin	EST	

Ghani Yalouz outscored his first three opponents 22-1, but was overwhelmed in the final by Ryszard Wolny, whose cumulative score for the tournament was 22-1. Wolny's teammates celebrated his unexpected victory by throwing him in the air six times, a feat which Yalouz no doubt wished he could have done once.

2000 Sydney C: 19, N: 19, D: 9.27.
(69 kg—152 lbs)

		FINAL MATCH
1. Filiberto Azcuy Aguilera	CUB	11-0 1:44
2. Katsuhiko Nagata	JPN	
3. Aleksey Gluchkov	RUS	5-0
4. Valeri Nikitin	EST	
5. Son Sang-pil	KOR	Injury
6. Islam Duguchiyev	AZR	
7. Ryszard Wolny	POL	
8. Rustam Adzhy	UKR	

Filiberto Azcuy won the 1996 Olympic championship in the welterweight division, but at the 1999 world championships, he was unexpectedly eliminated in the round of 16, which meant that Cuba could not have an entry at the 2000 Olympics. Cuba had already qualified in the lightweight division, so Azcuy lost weight and competed there instead. His first match was a difficult 4-3 victory over Ender Memet of Romania. It turned out to be his only serious challenge. He outscored his other four opponents 36-2. In the final, he faced Katsuhiko Nagata, whose medal-earning performance was completely unexpected. Azcuy ended the match by scoring 11 points in 1 minute 44 seconds. In the words of Jeremy Walker, writing for *The Daily Yomiuri* of Tokyo, "The Cuban celebrated with a backward somersault and jumped into the arms of his coaches as Nagata picked himself up and headed for the throng of Japanese media wondering who he was."

2004 Athens C: 21, N: 21, D: 8.25.
(66 kg—145½ lbs)

		FINAL MATCH
1. Farid Mansurov	AZR	4-3
2. Şeref Eroğlu	TUR	
3. Mkhitar Manukyan	KAZ	8-1
4. Jimmy Samuelsson	SWE	
5. Armen Vardanian	UKR	WO
6. Konstantinos Arkoudeas	GRE	
7. Jannis Zamanduridis	GER	
8. Vaghinak Galustyan	ARM	

Farid Mansurov took a 4-0 lead over six-time European champion Şeref Eroğlu in the first half of the final. Eroğlu scored a spectacular three-point throwdown in the second period, but Mansurov held on for the gold.

2008 Beijing C: 20, N: 20, D: 8.13.
(66 kg-145½lbs)

		FINAL MATCH
1. Steeve Guénot	FRA	3-0, 3-1
2. Kanat Begaliyev	KGZ	
3. Armen Vardanian	UKR	
3. Mikhail Semyonov	BLR	
5. Nikolay Gergov	BUL	
5. Darkhan Bayakhmetov	KAZ	
7. Sergei Kovalenko	RUS	
8. Tamás Lőrincz	HUN	

3rd Place: Vardanian—Gergov 4-1, 1-2, 6-1
3rd Place: Semyonov—Bayakmetov 2-0, 1-1, 1-1

Defending Olympic gold medal winner and reigning world champion Farid Mansurov lost his opening bout 3-0, 3-0 to European champion Armen Vardanian, leaving the field wide open. Vardanian then fell to 2006 world silver medalist Kanat Begaliyev after a two-point takedown that nearly took out the referee in the process.

Begaliyev faced world silver medalist Steeve Guénot in the final. Guénot won the first period 3-0, and then took the second period 3-1 after being awarded two points by the judges on a video review

Guénot was the first French Olympic wrestling champion since Henri Deglane in 1924.

A few minutes after Guénot won his gold medal, his older brother Christophe earned a bronze in the 74-kilogram weight class. Both brothers worked for France's national rail system.

WELTERWEIGHT

(74 kg—163 lbs)

1896–1928 not held

1932 Los Angeles C: 8, N: 8, D: 8.7.

(72 kg—159 lbs)

1. Ivar Johansson	SWE
2. Väinö Kajander-Kajukorpi	FIN
3. Ercole Gallegati	ITA
4. Osvald Käpp	EST
5. Börge Jensen	DEN

Ivar Johansson, a 29-year-old policeman from Norrköping, put on a remarkable performance from August 1 through August 7. First he won the freestyle Middleweight division with four bouts in three days. Then he spent the next 24 hours fasting and sweating in a sauna so that he could compete as a welterweight in the Greco-Roman competition. Eleven pounds lighter, he won four more matches and earned a second gold medal.

1936 Berlin C: 14, N: 14, D: 8.9.

(72 kg—159 lbs)

		ROUND ELIMINATED	PEN. PTS.	FINAL ROUND
1. Rudolf Svedberg	SWE	—	2	2
2. Fritz Schäfer	GER	—	1	2
3. Eino Virtanen	FIN	—	4	6
4. Eduard Pütsep	EST	5	6	
5. Nurettin Boytorun	TUR	5	7	
5. Silvio Tozzi	ITA	5	7	
7. Jean De Feu	BEL	4	6	
7. Adolf Rieder	SWI	4	6	

1948 London C: 16, N: 16, D: 8.6.

(73 kg—160 lbs)

		ROUND ELIMINATED	PEN. PTS.	FINAL ROUND
1. Gösta Andersson	SWE	—	3	2
2. Miklós Szilvási	HUN	—	3	3
3. Henrik Hansen	DEN	—	4	6
4. René Chesneau	FRA	4	7	
4. Veikko Männikö	FIN	4	7	
4. Josef Schmidt	DEN	4	7	
7. Bjorn Cook	NOR	3	5	
8. Nicolaos Felgen	LUX	3	6	
8. Luigi Rigamonti	ITA	3	6	

1952 Helsinki C: 18, N: 18, D: 7.27.

(73 kg—160 lbs)

		ROUND ELIMINATED	PEN. PTS.	FINAL ROUND
1. Miklós Szilvási	HUN	—	1	1
2. Gösta Andersson	SWE	—	1	4
3. Khalil Taha	LEB	—	5	6
4. Semen Marushkin	SOV/RUS	4	6	
5. Marin Belushiça	ROM	3	5	
5. René Chesneau	FRA	3	5	
5. Osvaldo Riva	ITA	3	5	
5. Ahmet Şenol	TUR	3	5	

In 1946, while on duty as a policeman, Miklós Szilvási was accidentally shot in the left leg by a machine gun. His left foot was temporarily paralyzed. Through exercise and willpower, Szilvási regained the use of his foot and represented Hungary at the 1948 Olympics. He finished second, losing a decision to Gösta Andersson in the final match. Four years later the two met again for the championship, and this time Szilvási won a split decision.

1956 Melboume C: 11, N: 11, D: 12.6.

(73 kg—160 lbs)

		ROUND ELIMINATED	PEN. PTS.	FINAL ROUND
1. Mithat Bayrak	TUR	—	2	2
2. Vladimir Maneyev	SOV/RUS	—	2	4
3. Per Berlin	SWE	—	0	6
4. Veikko Rantanen	FIN	3	5	
5. James Holt	USA	3	6	
5. Siegfried Schäfer	GDR	3	6	
7. Miklós Szilvási	HUN	3	7	
8. Mitiou Petkov	ROM	3	7	

1960 Rome C: 27, N: 27, D: 8.31.

(73 kg—160 lbs)

		ROUND ELIMINATED	PEN. PTS.	FINAL ROUND
1. Mithat Bayrak	TUR	—	5	1
2. Günter Maritschnigg	GER	—	5	5
3. René Schiermeyer	FRA	—	5	6
4. Stevan Horvat	YUG/SER	6	6	
5. Hrigory Hamarnyk	SOV/UKR	6	7	
6. Matti Laakso	FIN	5	7	
7. Antal Rizmayer	HUN	5	8	
8. Hansjörg Hirschbuhl	SWI	4	7	

1964 Tokyo C: 19, N: 19, D: 10.19.

(78 kg—172 lbs)

		ROUND ELIMINATED	PEN. PTS.	FINAL ROUND
1. Anatoly Kolesov	SOV/KAZ	—	7	5
2. Kiril Petkov	BUL	—	7	6
3. Bertil Nyström	SWE	—	7	6
4. Boleslaw Dubicki	POL	—	7	7
5. Antal Rizmayer	HUN	4	6	
5. Ion Täranu	ROM	4	6	
7. Russell Camilleri	USA	4	7	
7. René Schiermeyer	FRA	4	7	
7. Asghar Zowghian	IRN	4	7	

Five of the last six matches ended in draws, which meant that Kolesov's victory by decision over Dubicki was the tie-breaker.

1968 Mexico City C: 22, N: 22, D: 10.26.
(78 kg—172 lbs)

		ROUND ELIMINATED	PEN. PTS.	FINAL ROUND
1. Rudolf Vesper	GDR	—	4.5	3.5
2. Daniel Robin	FRA	—	5	4
3. Károly Bajkó	HUN	—	5.5	5.5
4. Metodi Zarev	BUL	5	8	
5. Ion Tăranu	ROM	5	9.5	
6. Jan-Ivar Kårström	SWE	4	6	
7. Harald Barlie	NOR	4	7	
7. Franz Berger	AUT	4	7	
7. Milovan Nenadić	YUG/SER	4	7	

1972 Munich C: 21, N: 21, D: 9.10.

		ROUND ELIMINATED	PEN. PTS.	FINAL ROUND
1. Vítězslav Mácha	CZE	—	5.5	1
2. Petros Galaktopoulos	GRE	—	3	3
3. Jan Karlsson	SWE	5	6	
4. Ivan Kolev	BUL	5	6.5	
5. Momir Kecman	YUG/SER	5	7.5	
6. Daniel Robin	FRA	5	8	
7. Klaus-Jürgen Pohl	GDR	5	8	
8. Werner Schröter	GER	4	7.5	

Mácha lost his opening bout to Ivan Kolev, but then won five in a row to secure the gold medal. Married to Miss Bohemia of 1971, Mácha was technically a miner, although he actually spent six to seven hours a day training.

1976 Montreal C: 18, N: 18, D: 7.24.

		ROUND ELIMINATED	PEN. PTS.	FINAL ROUND
1. Anatoly Bykov	SOV/RUS	—	1	1
2. Vítězslav Mácha	CZE	—	1.5	3
3. Karlheinz Helbing	GER	—	6	8
4. Mikko Huhtala	FIN	5	7.5	
5. Klaus-Dieter Göpfert	GDR	5	10	
6. Gheorghe Ciobotaru	ROM	4	7	
7. Jan Karlsson	SWE	4	8	
8. Petros Galaktopoulos	GRE	3	7	

Crucial matches took place in the fourth round when Bykov outpointed Ciobotaru 7-6 and Mácha edged Huhtala 4-3. In the fifth round Bykov was awarded a controversial victory by disqualification over Göpfert, with six seconds left and the score tied 5-5. Bykov's final win over Mácha was by a margin of 7-3.

1980 Moscow C: 14, N: 14, D: 7.23.

		ROUND ELIMINATED	PEN. PTS.	FINAL ROUND
1. Ferenc Kocsis	HUN	—	1	2
2. Anatoly Bykov	SOV/RUS	—	4	5
3. Mikko Huhtala	FIN	—	5	7
4. Yanko Shopov	BUL	5	7	
5. Lennart Lundell	SWE	4	6	
6. Vítězslav Mácha	CZE	4	8	
7. Gheorghe Minea	ROM	4	8	
8. Jacques van Lancker	BEL	3	7	

The final bout between Kocsis and Bykov ended with Bykov disqualified for inactivity after 7:21.

1984 Los Angeles-Anaheim C: 17, N: 17, D: 8.2.

		FINAL MATCH
1. Jouko Salomäki	FIN	5-4
2. Roger Tallroth	SWE	
3. Ştefan Rusu	ROM	6-1
4. Kim Young-nam	KOR	
5. Karolj Kasap	YUG/CRO	6-3
6. Martial Mischler	FRA	
7. Christopher Catalfo	USA	
8. Mohamed Hamad	EGY	

Salomäki took a 5-0 lead and held on for the victory. Ştefan Rusu earned a bronze medal to go with the silver and gold he had won in the lightweight division in 1976 and 1980.

1988 Seoul C: 19, N: 19, D: 9.21.

		FINAL MATCH
1. Kim Young-nam	KOR	2-1
2. Daulet Turlykhanov	SOV/KAZ	
3. Józef Tracz	POL	2-0
4. János Takács	HUN	
5. Martial Mischler	FRA	4-1
6. Borislav Velichkov	BUL	
7. Roger Tallroth	SWE	5-1
8. Hiromichi Ito	JPN	

Defending Olympic and world champion Jouko Salomäki was quickly eliminated when he lost his first two bouts to Tallroth and Mischler. In 1990 Salomäki was arrested by customs officers for smuggling steroid tablets from Estonia into Finland.

The final pitted Turlykhanov, a Soviet of Korean descent, against Kim, the 28-year-old son of poor farmers in Hampyong in Cholla province. When Kim began wrestling, he practiced on the wooden floor of his high school gymnasium, which was sparsely covered with dried rice stalks because the school could not afford mats. Turlykhanov led 1-0 at the break. But 25 seconds into the second round, Kim rolled his opponent onto his back for a 2-point score, then repelled Turlykhanov's advances for the remainder of the match. Kim was South Korea's first gold-medal winner of the Seoul Olympics. His victory brought great joy to the entire nation and earned him an $800 monthly pension for the rest of his life.

1992 Barcelona C: 21, N: 21, D: 7.29.

		FINAL MATCH
1. Mnatsakan Iskandaryan	ARM	6-3
2. Józef Tracz	POL	
3. Torbjörn Kornbakk	SWE	5-1
4. Nestor Almanza Baro	CUB	
5. Yvon Riemer	FRA	12-0
6. Anton Marchl	AUT	
7. Jaroslav Zeman	CZE	
8. Karlo Kasap	CAN	

Dobri Ivanov of Bulgaria qualified for the seventh-place match, but refused to take part and was disqualified.

1996 Atlanta C: 20, N: 20, D: 7.22.

		FINAL MATCH
1. Filiberto Azcuy Aguilera	CUB	3-2
2. Marko Asell	FIN	
3. Józef Tracz	POL	4-2
4. Erik Hahn	GER	
5. Mnatsakan Iskandaryan	RUS	
6. Tamás Berzicza	HUN	
7. Kim Jin-soo	KOR	
8. Takamitsu Katayama	JPN	

In the final, Azcuy took a 3-0 lead and then survived being thrown over Asell's shoulder. The Finns protested that Asell should have been awarded three points for this move instead of one, but their protest was rejected. Artur Dzikasov of the Ukraine and Stoyan Stoyanov of Bulgaria qualified for and refused to take part in the matches for fifth and seventh places respectively and were disqualified.

2000 Sydney C: 20, N: 20, D: 9.26.
(76 kg—167½ lbs)

		FINAL MATCH
1. Murat Kardanov	RUS	3-0
2. Matt Lindland	USA	
3. Marko Yli-Hannuksela	FIN	4-2
4. David Manukian	UKR	
5. Kim Jin-soo	KOR	9-0
6. Ara Abrahamian	SWE	
7. Vyacheslav Makarenko	BLR	
8. Tarieli Melelashvili	GEO	

Matt Lindland lost the final in the US trials 2-1 to Keith Sieracki, but protested that Sieracki had used his legs to trip him. Sieracki countered that Lindland had bitten his ear. In the midst of arbitration, Lindland won a rematch 8-0. The case was appealed all the way to the US Supreme Court and eventually it was Lindland who was allowed to compete in the Olympics. He made it all the way to the finals where he faced Mourat Kardanov, who gave up only one point in the entire tournament. Against Lindland, Kardanov scored three points in the first 80 seconds and successfully defended for the rest of the match.

2004 Athens C: 21, N: 21, D: 8.26.
(74 kg—163 lbs)

		FINAL MATCH
1. Aleksandr Dokturishivili	UZB	4-1
2. Marko Yli-Hannuksela	FIN	
3. Varteres Samurgashev	RUS	10-0 1:07
4. Reto Bucher	SWI	
5. Danil Khalimov	KAZ	WO
6. Filiberto Azcuy Aguilera	CUB	
7. Konstantin Schneider	GER	
8. Tamás Berzicza	HUN	

Aleksandr Dokturishivili eliminated Sydney 63-kilogram gold medalist Varteres Samurgashev 5-2 in the semifinals, and then beat 2000 bronze medalist Marko Yli-Hannuksela for gold. Dokturishivili had competed for his native Georgia until 2001, when he was knocked off the national team. In 2003 he relocated to Uzbekistan.

2008 Beijing C: 20, N: 20, D: 8.13.
(74 kg–163 lbs)

		FINAL MATCH
1. Manuchar Kvirkelia	GEO	6-0, 3-0
2. Chang Yongxiang	CHN	
3. Christophe Guénot	FRA	
3. Yavor Yanakiev	BUL	
5. Péter Bácsi	HUN	
5. Oleg Mikhalovich	BLR	
7. Varteres Samurgashev	RUS	
8. Roman Melyoshin	KAZ	

3rd Place: Guénot—Bácsi 3-1, 0-4, 4-2
3rd Place: Yankiev—Mikhalovic 0-3, 2-0, 2-0

Twenty-three-year-old Chang Yongxiang upset reigning world champion Yavor Yanakiev in the first round 3-2, 1-1. Chang was an unexpected finalist, having finished 36th and 26th at the last two world championships.

His opponent in the final was 30-year-old veteran Manuchar Kvirkelia, who had won the 2003 world championship title and the 2007 European title. Kvirkelia reached the final after pinning reigning European champion Péter Bácsi for a fall in the semifinals.

Kvirkelia dominated the final match, ending the first period with a five-point throw and earning two points on a gut wrench in the second period to take the gold medal 6-0, 3-0.

MIDDLEWEIGHT
(84 kg—185¼ lbs)

1896–1904 not held

1906 Athens C: 16, N: 9, D: 4.27.

		FINAL MATCH
1. Verner Weckman	FIN	
2. Rudolf Lindmayer	AUT	Fall 8:00
3. Robert Behrens	DEN	
4. Wenzel Goldbach	AUT	
5. Václav Hradecký	BOH/CZE	
5. Elia Pampuri	ITA	
5. Saveur	BEL	
5. Franz Solar	AUT	

1908 London C: 21, N: 9, D: 7.25.
(73 kg—161 lbs)

		FINAL MATCH
1. Frithiof Mårtensson	SWE	Dec 20:00; Fall 6:25
2. Mauritz Andersson	SWE	
3. Anders Andersen	DEN	WO
4. Jóhannes Jósefsson	DEN/ICE	

5. Jacob Belmer (HOL), Johannes Eriksen (DEN), Axel Frank (SWE), Axel Larson (DEN)

The final between Mårtensson and Mauritz Andersson was postponed overnight due to a minor injury to Mårtensson. Jósefsson, an Icelandic nationalist forced to compete under the Danish flag, fractured his arm in the semifinals and had to forfeit the match for third place.

1912 Stockholm C: 38, N: 14, D: 7.15.
(75 kg—165½ lbs)

1. Claes Johanson	SWE
2. Martin "Max" Klein	RUS/EST
3. Alfred "Alppo" Asikainen	FIN
4. K. Konrad Åberg	FIN
4. August Jokinen	FIN
6. Johannes Sint	HOL
7. Edvin Fältström	SWE
7. Mikko Holm	FIN
7. Emil Westerlund	FIN

The longest wrestling contest in Olympic history was the semifinal bout between Klein and Asikainen. The two men struggled on for hours under the hot sun, stopping every half hour for a brief refreshment break. Finally, after 11 hours, Klein, an Estonian competing for Czarist Russia, pinned his opponent. However, he was so exhausted by his ordeal that he was unable to take part in the final. Johanson was awarded first place by default.

1920 Antwerp C: 23, N: 12, D: 8.19.
(75 kg—165½ lbs)

1. Carl Westergren	SWE
2. Artur Lindfors	FIN
3. Matti Perttilä	FIN
4. Sjur Johnsen	NOR

The phenomenal Carl Westergren won the first of his three Olympic gold medals, each in a different division. He pinned Lindfors after 31 minutes 25 seconds.

1924 Paris C: 27, N: 19, D: 7.10.
(75 kg—165½ lbs)

1. Edvard Westerlund	FIN
2. Artur Lindfors	FIN
3. Roman Steinberg	EST
4. Giuseppe Gorletti	ITA
5. Viktor Fischer	AUT
5. Nikola Grbić	YUG/SER
7. Robert Christoffersen	DEN
7. Waclaw Okulicz-Kozaryn	POL

1928 Amsterdam C: 17, N: 17, D: 8.5.
(75 kg—165½ lbs)

1. Väinö Kokkinen	FIN
2. László Papp	HUN
3. Albert Kusnets	EST
4. Johannes Jacobsen	DEN
5. Jean Saenen	BEL
6. František Hála	CZE
7. Enrico Bonassin	ITA
7. Nurettin Boyturun	TUR

Kokkinen, a restaurant owner from Helsinki, pinned all five of his opponents.

1932 Los Angeles C: 4, N: 4, D: 8.7.
(79kg—174 lbs)

1. Väinö Kokkinen	FIN
2. Jean Földeak	GER
3. Axel Cadier	SWE

1936 Berlin C: 16, N: 16, D: 8.9.
(79kg—174 lbs)

		ROUND ELIMINATED	PEN. PTS.	FINAL ROUND
1. Ivar Johansson	SWE	—	2	
2. Ludwig Schweikert	GER	—	3	2
3. József Palotás	HUN	—	4	6
4. Väinö Kokkinen	FIN	5	6	
5. Ibrahim Erabi	EGY	4	6	
6. Ercole Gallegati	ITA	4	6	
7. Francisc Cocoş	ROM	4	6	
8. Kalman Kiš	YUG/SER	3	6	
8. Johans Pointner	AUT	3	6	
8. Josef Pribyl	CZE	3	6	

1948 London C: 13, N: 13, D: 8.6.
(79kg—174 lbs)

		ROUND ELIMINATED	PEN. PTS.	FINAL ROUND
1. Axel Grönberg	SWE	—	2	1
2. Muhlis Tayfur	TUR	—	4	3
3. Ercole Gallegati	ITA	5	5	
4. Jean-Baptiste Benoy	BEL	5	6	
5. Kaare Larsen	NOR	5	7	
6. Juho Kinnunen	FIN	4	5	
7. Gyula Németi	HUN	4	5	
8. Anton Vogel	AUT	3	6	

1952 Helsinki C: 11, N: 11, D: 7.27.
(79kg—174 lbs)

		ROUND ELIMINATED	PEN. PTS.	FINAL ROUND
1. Axel Grönberg	SWE	—	4	2
2. Kalervo Rauhala	FIN	—	3	4
3. Nikolai Belov	SOV/RUS	—	3	6
4. Gyula Németi	HUN	4	5	
5. Ali Özdemir	TUR	3	5	
6. Ercole Gallegati	ITA	3	6	
7. Gustav Gocke	GER	3	7	

1956 Melbourne C: 10, N: 10, D: 12.6.
(79kg—174 lbs)

		ROUND ELIMINATED	PEN. PTS.	FINAL ROUND
1. Givy Kartoziya	SOV/GEO	—	3	2
2. Dimiter Dobrev	BUL	—	4	4

3. Karl-Axel Rune Jansson	SWE	—	5	6
4. Johann Sterr	GER	4	6	
5. György Gurics	HUN	3	5	
6. Viljo Punkari	FIN	3	6	
7. James Peckham	USA	3	7	

This tournament saw the fastest pin in Olympic history when Rune Jansson beat Viljo Punkari in 11 seconds.

1960 Rome C: 24, N: 24, D: 8.31.
(79kg—174 lbs)

		ROUND ELIMINATED	PEN. PTS.
1. Dimiter Dobrev	BUL	—	4
2. Lothar Metz	GDR	6	6
3. Ion Tăranu	ROM	6	7
4. Kazim Ayvaz	TUR	6	7
5. Boleslaw Dubicki	POL	5	7
5. Nikolai Chuchalov	SOV/RUS	5	7
7. Yacous Romanos	LEB	4	7
8. Russell Camilleri	USA	4	7

1964 Tokyo C: 20, N: 20, D: 10.19.
(87 kg—192 lbs)

		ROUND ELIMINATED	PEN. PTS.	FINAL ROUND
1. Branislav Simić	YUG/SER	—	4	
2. Jiři Kormanik	CZE	5	6	
3. Lothar Metz	GDR	5	6	3
4. Géza Hollósi	HUN	5	7	
4. Valentin Olenik	SOV/RUS	5	7	
6. Kraliu Bimbalov	BUL	5	8	
7. Richard Wayne Baughman	USA	4	7	
8. Ismail Selekman	TUR	4	7	

Simić, competing in his third Olympics, managed to take first place without having to face either Kormanik or Metz.

1968 Mexico City C: 19, N: 19, D: 10.26.
(87 kg—192 lbs)

		ROUND ELIMINATED	PEN. PTS.
1. Lothar Metz	GDR	—	5
2. Valentin Olenik	SOV/RUS	6	6
3. Branislav Simić	YUG/SER	6	6
4. Nicolae Neguț	ROM	6	8.5
5. Richard Wayne Baughman	USA	5	8
5. Peter Krumov	BUL	5	8
7. Czesław Kwieciński	POL	4	7
8. Häkon Overby	NOR	4	7

1972 Munich C: 20, N: 20, D: 9.10.
(82 kg—181 lbs)

		ROUND ELIMINATED	PEN. PTS.	FINAL ROUND
1. Csaba Hegedüs	HUN	—	3	2
2. Anatoly Nazarenko	SOV/KAZ	—	4	3
3. Milan Nenadić	YUG/CRO	—	4	7
4. Miroslav Janota	CZE	5	7	
5. Ion Gabor	ROM	5	9	
6. Frank Hartmann	GDR	4	6	
7. Ali Yagmur	TUR	4	7	
8. Kiril Dimitrov	BUL	4	7.5	

Nazarenko, the 1970 world champion, and Hegedüs, the 1971 world champion, met in the very first round, with Hegedüs winning a decision. Neither man lost another bout for the rest of the tournament.

1976 Montreal C: 17, N: 17, D: 7.24.
(82 kg—181 lbs)

		ROUND ELIMINATED	PEN. PTS.	FINAL ROUND
1. Momir Petković	YUG/SER	—	4.5	2
2. Vladimir Cheboksarov	SOV/RUS	—	6	4
3. Ivan Kolev	BUL	—	7	6
4. Leif Andersson	SWE	6	8	
5. Miroslav Janota	CZE	5	8	
6. Kazuhiro Takanishi	JPN	5	8.5	
7. Ion Enache	ROM	4	7	
8. Adam Ostrowski	POL	4	7	

The crucial third-round contest between Petković and Cheboksarov ended in a 6-6 tie, but Petković was given the victory after complex tie-breaker rules were invoked.

1980 Moscow C: 12, N: 12, D: 7.24.
(82 kg—181 lbs)

		ROUND ELIMINATED	PEN. PTS.	FINAL ROUND
1. Gennady Korban	SOV/RUS	—	1	2
2. Jan Dolgowicz	POL	—	7	3
3. Pavel Pavlov	BUL	—	1	7
4. Leif Andersson	SWE	4	8	
5. Detlef Kühn	GDR	3	8	
6. Mihály Toma	HUN	3	8	
7. Mohammad Eloulabi	SYR	3	9	
8. Miroslaw Janota	CZE	2	7	

Korban defeated Dolgowicz, 11-4, and Pavlov, 13-7.

1984 Los Angeles-Anaheim C: 15, N: 15, D: 8.3.
(82 kg—181 lbs)

		FINAL MATCH
1. Ion Draica	ROM	4-3
2. Dimitrios Thanopoulos	GRE	
3. Sören Claesson	SWE	5-2
4. Momir Petković	YUG/SER	
5. Jarmo Övermark	FIN	5-3
6. Mohamed El Ashram	EGY	
7. Louis Santerre	CAN	
8. Kim Sang-kyu	KOR	

1988 Seoul C: 21, N: 21, D: 9.22.
(82 kg—181 lbs)

		FINAL MATCH
1. Mikhail Mamiashvili	SOV/RUS	10-1
2. Tibor Komáromi	HUN	
3. Kim Sang-kyu	KOR	6-5
4. Stig Arild Kleven	NOR	
5. Goran Kasum	YUG/SER	Passivity 4:26
6. Magnus Fredriksson	SWE	
7. John Morgan	USA	Forfeit
8. Bogdan Daras	POL	

Mamiashvili had already won three world championships at 74 kilograms when he moved up to challenge

Mikhail Mamiashvili, 1988

Middleweight Greco-Roman wrestler Mikhail Mamiashvili finds himself in a tight squeeze in his 1988 final match against Tibor Komáromi. Mamiashvili emerged victorious.

82-kilogram world champion Komáromi in 1988. He defeated the Hungarian at the European championships in May and then again at the Olympics in Seoul. By the time of the next Olympics, Mamiashvili was the head coach of the Greco-Roman team of the ex-Soviet republics, even though he was only 28 years old.

1992 Barcelona C: 20, N: 20, D: 7.30.
(82 kg—181 lbs)

		FINAL MATCH
1. Péter Farkas	HUN	6-1
2. Piotr Stępień	POL	
3. Daulet Turlykhanov	KAZ	2-0
4. Magnus Fredriksson	SWE	
5. Timo Niemi	FIN	3-1
6. Goran Kasum	YUG/SER	
7. Thomas Zander	GER	3-1
8. Pavel Frinta	CZE	

Péter Farkas became a popular heart-throb singer in Hungary. In 2004 he and his brother Karoly, were arrested after police discovered more than 3,000 marijuana plants growing in their mother's basement in Budapest. Péter and Karoly escaped from police custody in November 2008 shortly before being sentenced to five years in prison. Karoly pretended to be ill and the two left the court room during the break between the announcement of the verdict and sentencing, and did not return. Karoly was captured almost immediately, but Péter was not rearrested until a year later in Andorra. Their sentences were subsequently extended to seven years.

1996 Atlanta C: 19, N: 19, D: 7.20.
(82 kg—181 lbs)

		FINAL MATCH
1. Hamza Yerlikaya	TUR	3-0
2. Thomas Zander	GER	
3. Valery Tsilent	BLR	4-0
4. Daulet Turlykhanov	KAZ	
5. Gotcha Tsitsiashvili	ISR	WO
6. Martin Lidberg	SWE	
7. Levon Geghamyan	ARM	WO
8. Raatbek Sanatbayev	KYR	

Hamza Yerlikaya was only sixteen years old when he won his first world championship in 1993. At the Olympics he earned the gold medal without giving up a single point, while scoring sixteen in four matches. Silver medalist Zander was a full-time policeman in Aalen.

2000 Sydney C: 20, N: 20, D: 9.27
(85 kg—187½ lbs)

		FINAL MATCH
1. Hamza Yerlikaya	TUR	3-3
2. Sándor Bárdosi	HUN	
3. Mukhran Vakhtangadze	GEO	4-0
4. Valery Tsilent	BLR	4-0
5. Luis Enrique Méndez	CUB	
6. Gotcha Tsitsiashvili	ISR	
7. Martin Lidberg	SWE	
8. Mohamed Mohamed	EGY	

The finalists from 1996, Hamza Yerlikaya and Thomas Zander, ended up in the same elimination pool, with Yerlikaya prevailing 5-1. Zander's point was the only one scored against Yerlikaya until he reached the final, where he met Sándor Bárdosi, who had also given up only one point. Bárdosi, who had been added to the Hungarian team only two months before the Olympics, almost pinned the defending champion in the first period, but Yerlikaya successfully resisted. The match went into overtime and then to judges' decision. The judges gave the nod to Yerlikaya. Bárdosi was naturally disappointed, but conceded that the decision was correct. Fritz Aanes of Norway was originally placed fourth, however he failed a doping test.

In 2007 Yerlikaya was elected to a seat in Turkey's Parliament.

2004 Athens C: 22, N: 22, D: 8.25.
(84 kg—185 lbs)

		FINAL MATCH
1. Aleksei Mishin	RUS	1-1 9:00
2. Ara Abrahamian	SWE	
3. Vyacheslav Makarenko	BLR	2-1 9:00
4. Hamza Yerlikaya	TUR	
5. Dimitrios Avramis	GRE	WO
6. Oleksandr Darahan	UKR	
7. Shingo Matsumoto	JPN	
8. Levon Geghamyan	ARM	

The 2003 European champion, Aleksei Mishin was one of 2004's least dominating Olympic champions in wrestling. In his elimination pool, he was beaten 3-1 by Melonin Noumonvi of France. He advanced to the qualification round, where he defeated Dimitrios Avramis 5-2. In the semifinals, Mishin outscored Vyacheslav Makarenko 6-0, while two-time world champion Ara Abrahamian beat two-time defending Olympic champion Hamza Yerlikaya 5-2. Tied 1-1 at the end of regulation and overtime in the final, Mishin was awarded the gold medal by referee decision.

2008 Beijing C: 20, N: 20, D: 8.14.
(84 kg–185 lbs)

		FINAL MATCH
1. Andrea Minguzzi	ITA	1-1, 1-1, 4-0
2. Zoltán Fodor	HUN	
3. Nazmi Avluca	TUR	
—Ara Abrahamian	SWE	
5. Ma Sanyi	CHN	
5. Mélonin Noumonvi	FRA	
7. Denis Forov	ARM	
8. Şalma Qodabadze	AZE	

3rd Place: Avluca—Ma 0-4, 5-0, 6-0
3rd Place: Abrahamian—Noumonvi 4-0, 1-1

Reigning Olympic, world and European champion Aleksei Mishin was upset in the quarterfinals by 26-year-old Italian policeman Andrea Minguzzi, who had finished 45th at the 2007 world championships.

Minguzzi defeated defending Olympic silver medalist Ara Abrahamian, 1-1, 2-1 in the semifinals after Abrahamian had a point deducted after the second period ended for allegedly having placed his hand on the out-of-bounds line. The Swedish team protested the result and asked that a video replay be viewed, but their request to even consider the evidence was denied.

Minguzzi won the gold medal after two cautious periods against Hungary's Zoltán Fodor. Tied 1-1, 1-1, Minguzzi scored on a late throw to win the third period 4-0.

The medal ceremony was disrupted when Abrahamian dropped his bronze medal to the mat and stormed off stage to protest what he thought was biased judging. He was stripped of his medal and disqualified, but no other athletes were moved up in the rankings. The Court of Arbitration for Sport (CAS) later ruled that FILA, the international wrestling federation, had acted improperly in not allowing Abrahamian to appeal.

HEAVYWEIGHT
(100 kg—220 lbs)

1896–1968 not held

1972 Munich C: 15, N: 15, D: 9.10.
(100 kg—220 lbs)

		ROUND ELIMINATED	PEN. PTS.	FINAL ROUND
1. Nicolae Martinescu	ROM	—	5.5	0
2. Nikolai Yakovenko	SOV/RUS	—	1	4
3. Ferenc Kiss	HUN	5	6.5	
4. Hristo Ignatov	BUL	5	9	
5. Fredi Albrecht	GDR	4	7	
6. Tore Hem	NOR	4	8	
7. Andrzej Skrzydlewski	POL	4	8.5	
8. Rudolf Luescher	SWI	2	6	

1976 Montreal C: 13, N: 13, D: 7.24.
(100 kg—220 lbs)

		ROUND ELIMINATED	PEN. PTS.	FINAL ROUND
1. Nikolai Balboshin	SOV/RUS	—	0	0
2. Kamen Goranov	BUL	—	4	5
3. Andrzej Skrzydlewski	POL	—	3	7
4. Brad Rheingans	USA	4	6	
5. Tore Hem	NOR	4	7	
6. Heinz Schäfer	GER	4	8	
7. József Farkas	HUN	3	8	
7. Nicolae Martinescu	ROM	3	8	

Balboshin needed only 16 minutes and 48 seconds to win his five matches.

1980 Moscow C: 9, N: 9, D: 7.23.
(100 kg—220 lbs)

		ROUND ELIMINATED	PEN. PTS.	FINAL ROUND
1. Georgi Raikov	BUL	—	1	2
2. Roman Bierla	POL	—	1	4
3. Vasile Andrei	ROM	4	7	
4. Refik Memišević	YUG/SER	4	7	
5. Georgios Pikilidis	GRE	3	8	
6. Oldřich Dvořák	CZE	3	8	
7. Nikolai Balboshin	SOV/RUS	2	4	
8. Svend Erik Studsgaard	DEN	2	8	

Raikov defeated Bierla by disqualification after 7:52. Defending champion Nikolai Balboshin, injured during the second round, was forced to withdraw.

1984 Los Angeles-Anaheim C: 8, N: 8, D: 8.3.
(100 kg—220 lbs)

		FINAL MATCH
1. Vasile Andrei	ROM	12-0 4:16
2. Greg Gibson	USA	
3. Jožef Tertei	YUG/SER	3-0
4. Georgios Pikilidis	GRE	
5. Franz Pitschmann	AUT	7-5
6. Fritz Gerdsmeier	GER	
7. Yoshiro Fujita	JPN	
7. Karl-Johan Gustafsson	SWE	

Andrei defeated each of his four opponents in less than 4½ minutes.

1988 Seoul C: 18, N: 18, D:9.21.
(100 kg—220 lbs)

		FINAL MATCH
1. Andrzej Wroński	POL	3-1
2. Gerhard Himmel	GER	
3. Dennis Koslowski	USA	6-0
4. Ilia Georgiev	BUL	
5. Jožef Tertei	YUG/SER	Injury
6. Yoo Young-tai	KOR	
7. Guram Gedekhauri	SOV/GEO	Injury
8. Tamás Gáspár	HUN	

Andrzej Wroński was one of the most unexpected winners of the Seoul Olympics. Before 1988 he had never placed in the top eight of a major international competition. His most noteworthy accomplishment was finishing *third* in the 1987 Polish championships. Meanwhile, the Olympic field was filled with winners, most notably the defending Olympic champion, Vasile Andrei; the defending world champion, Guram Gedekhauri; the world championship runner-up, Dennis Koslowski; the 1986 world champion, Tamás Gáspár; the 1986 European champion, Jožef Tertei; and the 1987 European champion, Ilia Georgiev. None of these worthies made it to the final. Gáspár was forced to withdraw after he was injured in his match with Gerhard Himmel, the bronze medalist at the 1988 European championship. The others proceeded to knock each other off. Andrei defeated Gedekhauri, as did Tertei. Tertei beat Andrei. Koslowski beat Tertei. Gedekhauri beat Koslowski. Georgiev lost to both Gáspár and Himmel. Even Wroński lost once when he was pinned by Gedekhauri. In fact, he was the only wrestler at the 1988 Olympics to win a gold medal despite having lost a match. What Wroński did do was to register three upset victories: 1-0 over Tertei, 1-0 over Koslowski, and a passivity win over Andrei. In the final he scored all of his points when he lifted Himmel from a prone position and threw him to the mat.

1992 Barcelona C: 16, N: 16, D: 7.28.
(100 kg—220 lbs)

		FINAL MATCH
1. Hector Milián Pérez	CUB	2-1 5:25
2. Dennis Koslowski	USA	
3. Sergei Demyashkevich	BLR	1-0
4. Andrzej Wroński	POL	
5. Andreas Steinbach	GER	4-2
6. Ion Iremciuc	ROM	
7. Norbert Növényi	HUN	Forfeit
8. Song Sung-il	KOR	

In the final, Milián scored on a gutwrench at 1:08, then Koslowski tied the score with a front headlock takedown at 3:26. Milián attacked quickly in overtime, got behind Koslowski, and scored with a sudden snapdown at the edge of the mat after only 25 seconds.

1996 Atlanta C: 20, N: 20, D: 7.20.
(100 kg—220 lbs)

		FINAL MATCH
1. Andrzej Wroński	POL	0-0
2. Sergei Lishtvan	BLR	
3. Mikael Ljungberg	SWE	3-0 1:50
4. Teymuraz Edisherashvili	RUS	
5. Héctor Milián Pérez	CUB	WO
6. Igor Grabovetski	MOL	
7. Heorhiy Soldadze	UKR	WO
8. Todor Manov	BUL	

Wroński won the gold medal without giving up a point. However, after disposing of Mohamed Naouar of Tunisia in one minute 14 seconds, he was hardly overwhelming. His victories over Igor Grabovetski and Sergei Lishtvan were both referee's decisions following scoreless ties.

2000 Sydney C: 20, N: 20, D: 9.26.
(97 kg—213¾ lbs)

		FINAL MATCH
1. Mikael Ljungberg	SWE	2-1
2. Davyd Saldadze	UKR	
3. Garrett Lowney	USA	3-1
4. Konstantinos Thanos	GRE	
5. Gennady Chkhaidze	GEO	1-1
6. Sergei Matviyenko	KAZ	
7. Urs Bürgler	SWI	
8. Mindaugas Ezerskis	LIT	

This was expected to be an easy victory for three-time defending world champion Gogi Koguashvili. However, in a stunning upset, he was eliminated early when, in overtime, Garrett Lowney picked him up and threw him. Lowney made it to the semifinals, but was no match for Mikael Ljungberg, who defeated him 8-1. Ljungberg, who went on to win the gold medal, placed fourth at the 1992 Olympics, won the 1993 world championship, the 1995 world championship and the bronze medal at the 1996 Olympics.

In 2004, Ljungberg committed suicide while being treated for depression in a hospital near Göteborg.

2004 Athens C: 21, N: 21, D: 8.26.
(96 kg—212 lbs)

		FINAL MATCH
1. Karam Gaber Ibrahim	EGY	12-1 3:22
2. Ramaz Nozadze	GEO	
3. Mehmet Özal	TUR	3-2
4. Ernesto Pena Williams	CUB	4-0
5. Gennady Chkhaidze	KGZ	
6. Gogi Koguashvili	RUS	
7. Georgios Koutsioumpas	GRE	
8. Kaloyan Dinchev	BUL	

DISQ: Masoud Hashemzadeh (IRN)

In the semifinals, two-time world silver medalist Karam Gaber Ibrahim needed only 69 seconds to throw 2002 world champion Mehmet Özal three times, winning 11-0. In the final, the flamboyant Gaber built up a 9-1 advantage over junior world champion Ramaz Nozadze in just 95 seconds before securing the win less than two minutes later. In addition to wrestling, Gaber owned a company that manufactured women's clothing. Karam was the first Egyptian athlete in any sport to earn an Olympic gold medal since 1948.

2008 Beijing C: 20, N: 20, D: 8.14.
(96 kg–212 lbs)

		FINAL MATCH
1. Aslanbek Khushtov	RUS	6-0, 3-0
2. Mirko Englich	GER	
3. Aset Mambetov	KAZ	
3. Adam Wheeler	USA	
5. Marek Švec	CZE	
5. Han Tae-young	KOR	
7. Mindaugas Ežerskis	LIT	
8. Elis Guri	ALB	

3rd Place: Membetov—Švec 1-1, 6-0
3rd Place: Wheeler—Han 2-1, 4-1

The pre-competition favorites, defending Olympic champion Karam Garber and silver medalist Ramaz Nozadze, were both knocked out early in the competition, leaving the gold medal up for grabs.

The final match was a repeat of the 2008 European championship final. European champion Aslanbek Khushtov used a gut wrench to throw Mirko Englich for five points to win the first period 6-0, and then threw him again to win the second period 3-0.

Khushtov finished the tournament with a perfect 30-0 score, including one fall.

SUPER HEAVYWEIGHT
(Heavyweight 1896–1968)

A maximum weight limit—286 lbs. (130 kg)—was imposed for the first time at the 1988 Olympics.

1896 Athens C: 5, N: 4, D: 4.11.

		FINAL MATCH
1. Carl Schuhmann	GER	Fall 55:00e
2. Georgios Tsitas	GRE	
3. Stephanos Christopoulos	GRE	

All the matches were held outdoors in a sand pit. Although this was technically a Greco-Roman event, legholds were allowed. Schuhmann and Tsitas, an Athenian baker, fought for 40 minutes until it became dark. The match was postponed until the following morning, at which time Schuhmann threw Tsitas to the ground after 15 or 20 minutes. Schuhmann, who was 1.59 meters (5 feet 2¾ inches) tall, also won three gold medals in the gymnastics competition and competed in the shot put, long jump and triple jump.

1900–1904 not held

1906 Athens C: 10, N: 6, D: 4.28.

1. Søren Marinus Jensen	DEN
2. Henri Baur	AUT
3. Marcel Dubois	BEL
4. Stephanos Christopoulos	GRE
4. Dimitrios Psaltopoulos	GRE

1908 London C: 7, N: 4, D: 7.24.

		FINAL MATCH
1. Richárd Weisz	HUN	Dec 30:00; Dec 30:00
2. Aleksandr Petrov	RUS	
3 Søren Marius Jensen	DEN	
4. Hugó Payr	HUN	

Weisz was a popular and colorful character who was also the Hungarian national champion in weightlifting.

1912 Stockholm C: 17, N: 9, D: 7.14.

1. Yrjö Saarela	FIN
2. Johan Olin	FIN
3. Søren Marinus Jensen	DEN
4. Jakob Neser	GER
5. Emil Backenius	FIN
5. Kaarlo "Kalle" Viljamaa	FIN
7. Adolf Lindfors	FIN

The final match between Saarela and Jensen ended when the Dane was overcome by the sun and retired after three hours of wrestling.

1920 Antwerp C: 21, N: 13, D: 8.19.

1. Adolf Lindfors	FIN
2. Poul Hansen	DEN
3. Martti Nieminen	FIN
4. Alexander Weyand	USA

Lindfors pinned Anders Ahlgren of Sweden in the final after 47 minutes 38 seconds. Ahlgren was so worn out from the match that he withdrew from the contest to decide second place.

1924 Paris C: 17, N: 10, D: 7.10.

1. Henri Deglane	FRA
2. Edil Rosenqvist	FIN
3. Rajmund Badó	HUN
4. Emil Larsen	DEN

5. Harry Nilsson (SWE), Jánis Polis (LAT), Lucien Pothier (BEL)

One of the many incidents which plagued the judgeable sports at the Paris Olympics occurred in the second round of the Greco-Roman Heavyweight tournament. Local favorite Henri Deglane, age 22, was pitted against 39-year-old Claes Johanson, who had won the Middleweight title in 1912 and the Light Heavyweight title in 1920. After 20 minutes of fighting, Johanson was declared the winner on points. The French team protested the decision, and the Jury of Appeal ordered the two men to wrestle for six more minutes, after which Deglane was declared the victor. Johanson was so disgusted that he withdrew from the competition. Deglane went on to win four more decisions and the gold medal.

1928 Amsterdam C: 15, N: 15, D: 8.5.

1. Rudolf Svensson	SWE
2. Hjalmar Eemil Nyström	FIN
3. Georg Gehring	GER
4. Eugen Wiesberger	AUT
5. Josef Urban	CZE
6. Rajmund Badó	HUN
7. Mehmed Çoban	TUR
7. Aleardo Donati	ITA

1932 Los Angeles C: 5, N: 5, D: 8.7.

1. Carl Westergren	SWE
2. Josef Urban	CZE
3. Nikolaus Hirschi	AUT
4. Georg Gehring	GER
5. Aleardo Donati	ITA

Westergren, a bus driver from Malmö, compiled an outstanding record at the Olympics. Following in the footsteps of Claes Johanson, he won the Middleweight title in 1920 and the Light Heavyweight title in 1924. In 1928, as a light heavyweight, he was pinned in the first round by Onni Pellinen. However he returned to the Olympics in 1932 as a 36-year-old heavyweight and won a third gold medal. Westergren is considered the inventor of the forward takedown and the lateral gut wrench.

1936 Berlin C: 12, N: 12, D: 8.9.

		ROUND ELIMINATED	PEN. PTS.	FINAL ROUND
1. Kristjan Palusalu	EST	—	3	1
2. John Nyman	SWE	—	3	3
3. Kurt Hornfischer	GER	5	5	
4. Mehmet Çoban	TUR	4	6	
5. Hjalmar Eemil Nyström	FIN	4	6	
6. Aleardo Donati	ITA	4	7	
7. Joseph Klapuch	CZE	3	6	
8. Alberts Zvejnieks	LAT	3	6	

1948 London C: 9, N: 9, D: 8.6.

		ROUND ELIMINATED	PEN. PTS.	FINAL ROUND
1. Ahmet Kireççi	TUR	—	1	1
2. Tor Nilsson	SWE	—	3	3
3. Guido Fantoni	ITA	—	1	6
4. Taisto Kangasniemi	FIN	3	5	
5. József Tarányi	HUN	3	6	
6. Moritz Inderbitzin	SWI	3	7	

Kireççi had received a bronze medal in the freestyle middleweight 12 years earlier in Berlin.

Carl Westergren, 1932
Westergren won three Greco-Roman wrestling gold medals in three different weight divisions: Middleweight in 1920, Light Heavyweight in 1924, and Heavyweight in 1932 (at the age of 36).

1952 Helsinki C: 10, N: 10, D: 7.27.

		ROUND ELIMINATED	PEN. PTS.	FINAL ROUND
1. Johannes Kotkas	SOV/EST	—	0	0
2. Josef Růžička	CZE	—	3	3
3. Tauno Kovanen	FIN	—	6	6
4. Willi Waltner	GER	4	7	
5. Alexandru Suli	ROM	3	5	
6. Bengt Fahlkvist	SWE	3	6	
6. Antoine Georgoulis	GRE	3	6	
8. Guido Fantoni	ITA	3	7	

Kotkas, a 37-year-old Estonian from Tartu, pinned his four opponents in an elapsed time of 13 minutes 36 seconds. He had won the European championship in 1938 and was also the Soviet hammer throw champion in 1943.

1956 Melbourne C: 10, N: 10, D: 12.6.

		ROUND ELIMINATED	PEN. PTS.	FINAL ROUND
1. Anatoly Parfenov	SOV/RUS	—	4	2
2. Wilfried Dietrich	GER	—	5	4
3. Adelmo Bulgarelli	ITA	—	4	6
4. Hamit Kaplan	TUR	4	6	
5. Bertíl Antonsson	SWE	4	7	
6. Taisto Kangasniemi	FIN	3	6	
7. Yusein Mehmedov	BUL	3	7	
7. Antoine Georgoulis	GRE	3	7	

Parfenov was one of the least overwhelming Olympic champions ever. He was originally declared the loser in his opening contest with Dietrich. However, a protest by the Soviet team was upheld by the Jury of Appeal. In the second round Parfenov lost to Antonsson. Then he won a forfeit in the third round and received a bye in the fourth round. In the fifth round he gained his only undisputed victory, a decision over Bulgarelli. Fortunately for Parfenov, his two wins were enough to take first place.

1960 Rome C: 12, N: 12, D: 8.31.

		ROUND ELIMINATED	PEN. PTS.	FINAL ROUND
1. Ivan Bohdan	SOV/UKR	—	4	4
2. Wilfried Dietrich	GER	—	5	4
3. Bohumil Kubát	CZE	—	5	4
4. István Kozma	HUN	4	6	
S. Lucjan Sosnowski	POL	4	6	
6. Radoslav Kasabov	BUL	4	8	
7. Adelmo Bulgarelli	ITA	3	6	
8. Sten Ragnar Svensson	SWE	3	9	

Dietrich was awarded the silver medal because his bodyweight was less than that of Bohumil "Weeny" Kubát. In fact, it was 40 kg (88 pounds) less than Kubát's. Dietrich weighed 90 kg (198 pounds), while Kubát weighed 130 kg (286 pounds).

1964 Tokyo C: 11, N: 11, D: 10.19.

		ROUND ELIMINATED	PEN. PTS.	FINAL ROUND
1. István Kozma	HUN	—	1	2
2. Anatoly Roshin	SOV/RUS	—	3	2
3. Wilfried Dietrich	GER	5	7	
4. Petr Kment	CZE	5	8	
S. Sten Ragnar Svensson	SWE	4	6	
6. Robert Pickens	USA	3	7	
7. Radoslav Kasabov	BUL	3	8	
8. Tsuneharu Sugiyama	JPN	3	8	

Kozma weighed in at 140 kg (320 pounds).

1968 Mexico City C: 15, N: 15, D: 10.26.

		ROUND ELIMINATED	PEN. PTS.	FINAL ROUND
1. István Kozma	HUN	—	2.5	2.5
2. Anatoly Roshin	SOV/RUS	—	3.5	2.5
3. Petr Kment	CZE	—	5	8
4. Sten Ragnar Svensson	SWE	5	7	
5. Constantin Buşiu	ROM	4	7	
6. Stefan Petrov	BUL	4	8	
7. Raymond Uytterheaghe	FRA	4	9	
8. Edward Wojda	POL	4	9.5	

As in 1964, Kozma won the gold medal despite being held to a draw by Roshin. This time the huge Hungarian threw his other four opponents, two of them within 40 seconds. Kment was injured and forced to withdraw from his final two matches against Kozma and Roshin.

1972 Munich C: 13, N: 13, D: 9.10.

		ROUND ELIMINATED	PEN. PTS.	FINAL ROUND
1. Anatoly Roshin	SOV/RUS	—	2	1
2. Aleksandr Tomov	BUL	—	3	5
3. Victor Dolîpschi	ROM	—	4	6
4. József Csatári	HUN	4	8	
4. Wilfried Dietrich	GER	4	8	
4. Ištvan Semeredi	YUG/SER	4	8	
7. Petr Kment	CZE	3	7	

Thirty-eight-year-old Wilfried Dietrich, attempting to win a medal in his fifth consecutive Olympics, was disqualified in his third-round match against Victor Dolîpschi. Dietrich was so upset by the decision that he withdrew from the competition even though he only had four negative points. Forty-year-old Anatoly Roshin was the oldest wrestler ever to win an Olympic medal.

1976 Montreal C: 12, N: 12, D: 7.24.

		ROUND ELIMINATED	PEN. PTS.	FINAL ROUND
1. Oleksander Kolchynsky	SOV/UKR	—	0	1
2. Aleksandr Tomov	BUL	—	4	3
3. Roman Codreanu	ROM	—	2	8
4. Henryk Tomanek	POL	4	8	
5. William "Pete" Lee	USA	4	8	
6. Janos Rovnyai	HUN	3	8	
7. Einar Gundersen	NOR	3	8	
7. Richard Wolff	GER	3	8	

Three-time defending world champion Aleksandr Tomov had defeated Kolchynsky six straight times, culminating in the European championships three months before the Olympics. However, in Montreal Tomov was upset in the first round when he was pinned in only 1:14 by 331-pound (150.14 kg) Pete Lee of Muncie, Indiana. Tomov recovered to win his next three matches and qualify for the final round-robin. In the meantime, Kolchynsky used up only six minutes and 38 seconds in finishing off his first four opponents. He followed this by outpointing Tomov 12-6 in his final bout.

1980 Moscow C: 10, N: 10, D: 7.24.

		ROUND ELIMINATED	PEN. PTS.	FINAL ROUND
1. Oleksander Kolchynsky	SOV/UKR	—	0	1
2. Aleksandr Tomov	BUL	—	0	3
3. Hassan Bchara	LEB	—	8	8
4. József Farkas	HUN	4	10	
5. Prvoslav Ilić	YUG/SER	3	8	
6. Roman Codreanu	ROM	3	8	
6. Arturo Díaz Mora	CUB	3	8	
8. Marek Galinski	POL	2	8	

The superiority of Kolchynsky and Tomov was shown by the fact that the other eight wrestlers all reached eight penalty points before the two champions had even received their first bad mark. Kolchynsky, the lightest man in the tournament at 220 pounds, defeated 375-pound Roman Codreanu in 7:50 in his opening bout. Then he disposed of his next four opponents in an elapsed time of 11:27. In the final contest Kolchynsky outpointed Tomov 4-2 to win his second straight gold medal.

1984 Los Angeles-Anaheim C: 8, N: 8, D: 8.2.

		FINAL MATCH
1. Jeffrey Blatnick	USA	2-0
2. Refik Memišević	YUG/SER	Passivity 4:16
3. Victor Dolîpschi	ROM	
4. Panagiotis Pikilidis	GRE	7-3
5. Hassan El Hadad	EGY	
6. Masaya Ando	JPN	
6. Antonio Lapenna	ITA	

DISQ (Drugs): Tomas Johansson (SWE)

In October of 1982, Jeff Blatnick of Niskayuna, New York, seemed a most unlikely candidate to win a gold medal in the Olympics. To begin with, no US athlete in his sport, Greco-Roman wrestling, had ever won an Olympic medal in any division. And, although he had qualified for the 1980 team that was not allowed to go to Moscow, he was no longer considered number one in the nation. And then there was the matter of his health. In May he had noticed small lumps on his neck. In July he was diagnosed as suffering from Hodgkin's disease; a form of cancer. In August his spleen and appendix were removed and in October he began radiation therapy.

But Jeffrey Blatnick was no quitter. Inspired by the memory of his brother David, who had died in a motorcycle accident in 1977, Blatnick resumed training almost immediately, despite warnings from his doctors. At the 1984 US Olympic trials, he won a controversial two-match victory over 390-pound favorite Pete Lee. Lee was disqualified for slapping in the first match and for inactivity in the second.

Blatnick entered the Olympic tournament as an underdog, but in his first bout he upset gold medal favorite Refik Memišević, when the latter was disqualified for passivity. However, in his second match, Blatnick was defeated 4-3 by Panagiotis Pikilidis. It is unusual for a wrestler to qualify for the final after losing a match, particularly when his preliminary pool consists of only four men. But the next day, Memišević beat Pikilidis and Blatnick found himself one victory away from an Olympic championship. His opponent in the final would be Tomas Johansson, who, at 275 pounds, outweighed Blatnick by over 35 pounds.

Just before he went out to wrestle Johansson, Blatnick saw his parents underneath the stands and approached them.

"It's so close, Jeff, so close," said his father, Carl. "The Swede is big, but you've come too far to let anything

Jeff Blatnick, 1984

Blatnick drops to his knees and gives thanks after winning a gold medal in the Super Heavyweight division of the 1984 Greco-Roman wrestling competition. Two years earlier, suffering from cancer, Blatnick had undergone extensive radiation treatment following the removal of his spleen and appendix.

stop you now." Following a family ritual, Carl added, "Get mad, Son!" To which Jeff gave his usual reply: "If you get mad, you get stupid."

Then his mother, Angela, whispered to him, "For David, Jeffrey, for David."

The final match was close and hard-fought. After 4½ minutes neither wrestler had scored a point, but Blatnick had been cautioned twice, Johansson only once. Then, with only 64 seconds left, Blatnick took Johansson to the mat for a score. With the screams of the crowd getting louder and louder, Blatnick scored again 38 seconds later.

The audience counted down the final seconds and when they reached zero, the arena was filled with emotional celebration. Blatnick fell to his knees, crossed himself, joined his hands in prayer and looked up, far beyond the ceiling. Then, for the first time since his older brother had died seven years earlier, Jeffrey Blatnick cried. And cried and cried and cried. And, judging from the mail he would subsequently receive, all over the world millions of people cried with him. But not all dramatic stories have clean, happy endings. In September of 1985, Blatnick's cancer returned. This time he required 28 sessions of chemotherapy to send it into remission.

As for Johansson, he tested positive for the steroid methendone and lost his medal. After serving an 18-month suspension, he won the 1986 world championship, finished third at the 1988 Olympics, and second at the 1992 Olympics.

1988 Seoul C: 16, N: 16, D: 9.22.

		FINAL MATCH
1. Aleksandr Karelin	SOV/RUS	5-3
2. Rangel Gerovski	BUL	
3. Tomas Johansson	SWE	Passivity 5:04
4. Hassan El Hadad	EGY	
5. László Klauz	HUN	Passivity 5:00
6. Kazuya Deguchi	JPN	
7. Roman Wrocławski	POL	Forfeit
8. Duane Koslowski	USA	

Twenty-one-year-old Aleksandr Karelin trailed 3-0 with 30 seconds left in the final, then used a reverse body lift to score a 5-point takedown. Gerovski was the only one of his five opponents to last the full 6 minutes.

1992 Barcelona C: 16, N: 16, D: 7.29.

		FINAL MATCH
1. Aleksandr Karelin	RUS	Fall 1:33
2. Tomas Johansson	SWE	
3. Ioan Grigoraş	ROM	1-0
4. László Klauz	HUN	
5. Andrew Borodow	CAN	12-0
6. Tian Lei	CHN	
7. Juha Ahokas	FIN	1-0 6:27
8. Panagiotis Poikilidis	GRE	

Karelin, undefeated in five years, disposed of his opponents as if they were inanimate objects. Only Ahokas lasted the full five minutes. Karelin needed only 5 minutes 32 seconds to pin the other four. A 6-foot, 3¾-inch (1.92 meters), 286-pound (130 kg) giant from Siberia, Karelin weighed 15 pounds at birth. Despite his intimidating presence, he was a soft-spoken student of literature and rhetoric.

1996 Atlanta C: 19, N: 19, D: 7.22.

		FINAL MATCH
1. Aleksandr Karelin	RUS	1-0
2. Siamak "Matt" Ghaffari	USA	
3. Sergei Mureiko	MOL	1-0
4. Petro Kotok	UKR	
5. Panagiotis Poikilidis	GRE	3-0
6. René Schiekel	GER	
7. Tomas Johansson	SWE	8-0 2:17
8. Kenichi Suzuki	JPN	

Matt Ghaffari was born in Tehran, Iran, and moved to the United States when he was 15 years old. While Ghaffari was still in high school, Iranian militants took over the US embassy in Tehran and held 52 Americans hostage for more than a year. Ghaffari's wrestling coach in Paramus, New Jersey, added an "o" to his name so that he would appear to be Italian instead of Iranian. Ghaffari did not win his first national championship until 1990 when he was 28 years old. He medaled at the 1991 and 1995 world championships but was eliminated early at the Barcelona Olympics. For many years, Ghaffari had been driven by the desire to beat Aleksandr Karelin—just once. By the time of the 1996 Olympics, the 34-year-old Ghaffai had faced Karelin twenty times (including exhibitions) and lost every time. Ghaffari kept a photograph of Karelin in his locker, another in his home and was also known to put a similar photo in his wallet.

To say that Karelin was the favorite would be a gross understatement. He had not lost a match in nine years and had never been beaten by a foreign opponent. Only once had he been pushed to overtime (by Ghaffari). At the 1993 world championships, Ghaffari broke Karelin's rib in a preliminary match. Karelin went on to win the championship anyway. "I didn't want to appear weak," he would say, "and skip a fight because of such a trifle as broken ribs."

However, in 1996 there was a glimmer of hope for Ghaffari and Karelin's other challengers. Only three months before the Olympics, Karelin underwent shoulder surgery in Hungary. In his second match in Atlanta, he was actually forced into overtime by Sergei Moureiko, although he did win 2-0. In fact, Karelin entered the final against Ghaffari by outscoring his four opponents 24-0. When Ghaffari raced onto the mat, the public address system blared the theme from "Rocky." Karelin walked in calmly, apparently unfazed by the wildly pro-Ghaffari crowd. One minute 51 seconds into the bout Karelin secured a body lock that led to a one-point takedown. For six more minutes, Ghaffari attacked, but to no avail. Karelin became the first wrestler to win the same weight division three times. In 1999 he won his twelfth world or Olympic championship, outdistancing the previous record of ten set by freestyle specialist Oleksander Medvid.

In December 1999, Karelin was elected to the State Duma lower house as a representative of Novosibirsk, Siberia.

2000 Sydney C: 20, N: 20, D: 9.27.

		FINAL MATCH
1. Rulon Gardner	USA	1-0
2. Aleksandr Karelin	RUS	
3. Dmitry Debelka	BLR	3-2
4. Yuri Yevseychyc	ISR	
5. Hector Milián Pérez	CUB	5-3
6. Heorhiy Saldadze	UKR	
7. Giuseppe Giunta	ITA	
8. Fatih Bakir	TUR	

By the time of the 2000 Olympics, Aleksandr Karelin was 59-0 in the Olympics and world championships and had not lost a match of any kind since 1987, when Igor Rostorosky beat him 1-0 at the Soviet national championships. Until 1999, Karelin had not given up a single point in six years. Although Karelin, who turned 33 during the Sydney Olympics, was starting to suffer the pain and injuries of age, he was the overwhelming favorite to become only the fourth person in Olympic history in any sport to win the same individual event four times. Any doubts about his fitness were dispelled when he qualified for the final by shutting out all four of his opponents. Karelin's adversary in the final was Rulon Gardner, a 29-year-old Mormon who grew up, the youngest of nine children, on a dairy farm in Afton, Wyoming. The Olympics was only Gardner's second major international tournament. The first had been the 1997 world championships, where he wrestled Karelin for the first time. Karelin hoisted Gardner in the air with his signature reverse body lift and the match was over. Gardner reacted good-naturedly to the experience. "I had never flown before," he would say, "so I thought it was pretty cool." Gardner knew that his only chance to beat Karelin in the Olympic final was to fight a perfect match. He survived the first period 0-0. The second period began with the two wrestlers in a face-to-face clinch with their arms wrapped around each other. Thirty seconds later, the unexpected happened: Karelin's hands slipped apart. The mat referee didn not see it, but the judges stopped the fight, reviewed the video and awarded a point to Gardner for Karelin's penalty. For the rest of regulation time and overtime, 5 minutes in all, Gardner resisted every attempt that Karelin made to pick him up or turn him around and the match ended with Gardner scoring one of the most surprising upsets in Olympic history. About a half hour after the match, Gardner was asked when he realized he could beat Karelin. Gardner replied, "About ten minutes ago."

2004 Athens C: 20, N: 20, D: 8.25.
(120 kg—264½ lbs)

		FINAL MATCH
1. Khasan Baroyev	RUS	4-2
2. Georgy Tsurtsumia	KAZ	
3. Rulon Gardner	USA	3-0 6:39
4. Sajad Barzi	IRN	
5. Mijal López	CUB	WO
6. Yannick Szczepaniak	FRA	
7. Xenofon Koutsioumpas	GRE	
8. Sergei Mureiko	BUL	

Reigning world champion Khasan Baroyev reached the final by outscoring his four opponents 14-0. In the final, Georgy Tsurtsumia held a 2-0 lead with less than one minute left, when Baroyev suddenly threw him on his back to score four points and earn the gold medal.

Bronze medalist Rulon Gardner was unusually accident-prone following his 2000 Olympic triumph. In February 2002, he became lost while snowmobiling in Wyoming, spent seventeen hours in sub-zero temperatures and lost one toe to frostbite. He returned to competition 10 months later, but was involved in a motorcycle crash. Then, barely a month before the 2004 US Olympic Trials, he dislocated his wrist during a pick-up basketball game Gardner retired after his last Athens match, following tradition by leaving his shoes in the middle of the ring.

In February 2007, Gardner had yet another brush with death when he and two friends crashed a single-engine plane into a lake in southeastern Utah. The trio swam more than a mile in 44-degree Fahrenheit (6.67° Celsius) water and spent the night in the wilderness before being found by a fisherman the next day.

2008 Beijing C: 20, N: 20, D: 8.14.
(120 kg–264½ lbs)

		FINAL MATCH
1. Mijaín López Núñez	CUB	5-0, 1-1
2. Khasan Baroyev	RUS	
3. Mindaugas Mizgaitis	LIT	
3. Yury Patrikeyev	ARM	
5. Jalmar Sjöberg	SWE	

5. Yannick Szczepaniak	FRA
7. Dremiel Byers	USA
8. Mihály Deák-Bárdos HUN	

3rd Place: Mizgaitis—Szczepaniak 2-1, 2-1
3rd Place: Patrikeyev—Sjöberg 2-1, 1-1, 3-0

Defending Olympic champion Khasan Baroyev and 2005 world champion Mijaín López had faced each other in each of the past two world championship finals, with Baroyev winning in 2006 and López winning in 2007.

As expected, the two faced off again in the Beijing Olympic final. López threw Baroyev to gain five points in the first period. In the second period, Baroyev scored first, but López evened the score 1-1, earning the victory by scoring the final point.

DISCONTINUED EVENTS

LIGHT FLYWEIGHT
(48 kg—106 lbs)

1972 Munich C: 20, N: 20, D: 9.10.

		ROUND ELIMINATED	PEN. PTS.	FINAL ROUND
1. Gheorghe Berceanu	ROM	—	1	1
2. Rahim Aliabadi	IRN	—	5	3
3. Stefan Angelov	BUL	—	3.5	8
4. Raimo Hirvonen	FIN	5	6	
5. Kazuharu Ishida	JPN	5	7	
6. Lorenzo Calafiore	ITA	5	8	
7. Bernd Drechsel	GDR	4	7	
8. Günter Maas	GER	3	6.5	

1976 Montreal C: 15, N: 15, D: 7.24.

		ROUND ELIMINATED	PEN. PTS.	FINAL ROUND
1. Aleksei Shumakov	SOV/RUS	—	0	2
2. Gheorghe Berceanu	ROM	—	2	4
3. Stefan Angelov	BUL	—	3	6
4. Yoshite Moriwaki	JPN	5	8	
5. Dietmar Hinz	GDR	4	6	
6. Mitchell Kawasaki	CAN	4	7	
7. Salin Bora	TUR	4	7	
8. Michael Farina	USA	3	8	
8. Rashid Mohammadzadé	IRN	3	8	

In the final round Shumakov outpointed Angelov 5-4 and Berceanu 10-6.

1980 Moscow C: 10, N: 10, D: 7.22.

		ROUND ELIMINATED	PEN. PTS.	FINAL ROUND
1. Zaksylik Ushkempirov	SOV/KAZ	—	3.5	1.5
2. Constantin Alexandru	ROM	—	6	4
3. Ferenc Seres	HUN	—	7	6.5
4. Pavel Hristov	BUL	5	7.5	
5. Reijo Haaparanta	FIN	4	9	
6. Alfredo Olvera	MEX	3	7.5	
7. Vincenzo Maenza	ITA	2	6.5	
8. Roman Kierpacz	POL	2	7	

1984 Los Angeles-Anaheim C: 12, N: 12, D: 8.1.

		FINAL MATCH
1. Vincenzo Maenza	ITA	12-0 1:59
2. Markus Scherer	GER	
3. Ikuzo Saito	JPN	7-5
4. Salih Bora	TUR	
5. Kent Andersson	SWE	10-3
6. Jun Dae-je	KOR	
7. Li Haisheng	CHN	
8. Lars Ronningen	NOR	

Twenty-two-year-old Vincenzo Maenza of Faenza outscored his four opponents 31-0.

1988 Seoul C: 15, N: 15, D: 9.20.

		FINAL MATCH	
1. Vincenzo Maenza	ITA	3-0	
2. Andrzej Glab	POL		
3. Bratan Tzenov	BUL	Passivity	7:28
4. Magyatdin Allakhverdyev	SOV/AZR		
5. Khaled Alfaraj	SYR	16-6	
6. Markus Scherer	GER		
7. Yang Zhizong	CHN	Injury	
8. Gooun Duk-yong	KOR		

Maenza proved that his 1984 victory over a boycott-depleted field was no fluke by earning an emotional repeat victory in Seoul. He reached the final by defeating Tzenov 4-3 after 42 seconds of sudden death overtime.

1992 Barcelona C: 19, N: 19, D: 7.29.

		FINAL MATCH
1. Oleg Kucherenko	UKR	3-0
2. Vincenzo Maenza	ITA	
3. Wilber Sánchez Amita	CUB	5-0
4. Fuat Yildiz	GER	
5. Iliuță Dăscălescu	ROM	Forfeit
6. Reza Simkhah Asil	IRN	
7. Lars Rønningen	NOR	Forfeit
8. Pappu Yadav	IND	

Vincenzo Maenza, going for a third straight gold medal, qualified for the final by outpointing his four opponents 54-1. In the final, however, Kucherenko scored three points with a high dive and a gutwrench a mere five seconds after the match began. He spent most of the rest of the bout crawling around the mat while Maenza tried unsuccessfully to turn him.

1996 Atlanta C: 19, N: 19, D: 7.20.

		FINAL MATCH
1. Sim Kwon-ho	KOR	4-0 6:44
2. Aleksandr Pavlov	BLR	
3. Zafar Guliyev	RUS	4-0
4. Kang Yong-gyun	PRK	
5. Wilber Sánchez Amita	CUB	4-0
6. Gela Papashvili	GEO	
7. Hiroshi Kado	JPN	1-0 0:14 (injury)
8. V. Ioannis Agakatzanian	GRE	

Sim defeated Pavlov by scoring two points with a chest-high roll-through with 42 seconds left in regulation and another two points with another roll in overtime.

FLYWEIGHT

(52kg—114½ lbs)

1948 London C: 13, N: 13, D: 8.6.

		ROUND ELIMINATED	PEN. PTS.	FINAL ROUND
1. Pietro Lombardi	ITA	—	3	1
2. Kenan Olcay	TUR	—	3	3
3. Reino Kangasmaki	FIN	5	6	
4. Malte Möller	SWE	5	6	
5. Gyula Szilágyi	HUN	5	5	
6. Fridtjof Clausen	NOR	4	7	
7. Mohamed Abd El Al	EGY	3	6	
7. Manuel Varela	ARG	3	6	

1952 Helsinki C: 17, N: 17, D: 7.27.

		ROUND ELIMINATED	PEN. PTS.	FINAL ROUND
1. Boris Gurevich	SOV/RUS	—	3	2
2. Ignazio Fabra	ITA	—	3	4
3. Leo Honkala	FIN	—	2	6
4. Heinrich Weber	GER	4	5	
5. Mahmoud Omar Fawzy	EGY	4	6	
5. Bengt Johansson	SWE	4	6	
7. Maurice Mewis	BEL	4	7	
7. Borivoje Vukov	YUG/SER	4	7	

1956 Melbourne C: 11, N: 11, D: 12.6.

		ROUND ELIMINATED	PEN. PTS.	FINAL ROUND
1. Nikolai Solovyov	SOV/RUS	—	4	3
2. Ignazio Fabra	ITA	—	4	4
3. Durum Ali Egribaş	TUR	—	4	4
4. Dumitru Pirvulescu	ROM	4	7	
5. István Baranya	HUN	3	5	
5. Borivoje Vukov	YUG/SER	3	5	
7. Maurice Mewis	BEL	3	6	

1960 Rome C: 18, N: 18, D: 8.31.

		ROUND ELIMINATED	PEN. PTS.	FINAL ROUND
1. Dumitru Pirvulescu	ROM	—	5	
2. Osman Sayed	EGY	5	6	
3. Mohammad Paziraii	IRN	5	6	
4. Takashi Hirata	JPN	5	7	
5. Ignazio Fabra	ITA	5	8	
5. Ivan Kochergin	SOV/RUS	5	8	
7. Borivoje Vukov	YUG/SER	4	6	
8. Bengt Frandfors	SWE	4	7	

1964 Tokyo C: 18, N: 18, D: 10.19.

		ROUND ELIMINATED	PEN. PTS.	FINAL ROUND
1. Tsutomu Hanahara	JPN	—	3	
2. Angel Kerezov	BUL	—	4	4
3. Dumitru Pirvulescu	ROM	—	2	7
4. Ignazio Fabra	ITA	4	6	
4. Rolf Lacour	GER	4	6	
4. Maurice Mewis	BEL	4	6	
4. J. Richard Wilson	USA	4	6	
8. Burhan Bozkurt	TUR	3	6	
8. Vasilios Ganotis	GRE	3	6	
8. Shin Sang-shik	KOR	3	6	

1968 Mexico City C: 24, N: 24, D: 10.26.

		ROUND ELIMINATED	PEN. PTS.	FINAL ROUND
1. Peter Kirov	BUL	—	5	
2. Vladimir Bakulin	SOV/KAZ	6	6	
3. Miroslav Zeman	CZE	6	8	
4. Imre Alker	HUN	6	8.5	
5. Rolf Lacour	GER	5	6	
6. Jussi Vesterinen	FIN	5	7.5	
7. Enrique Jiménez	MEX	4	6	
8. Metin Cikmaz	TUR	4	7	
8. Shin Sang-shik	KOR	4	7	

1972 Munich C: 22, N: 22, D: 9.10.

		ROUND ELIMINATED	PEN. PTS.	FINAL ROUND
1. Peter Kirov	BUL	—	2	4
2. Koichiro Hirayama	JPN	—	3	5
3. Giuseppe Bognanni	ITA	—	5	7
4. József Doncsecz	HUN	5	8	
4. Jan Michalik	POL	5	8	
4. Miroslav Zeman	CZE	5	8	
7. Vassilios Ganotis	GRE	4	6	
8. Jamsran Munkhotchir	MGL	4	8	

1976 Montreal C: 17, N: 11, D: 7.24.

		ROUND ELIMINATED	PEN. PTS.	FINAL ROUND
1. Vitaly Konstantinov	SOV/RUS	—	3	4
2. Nicu Ginga	ROM	—	5.5	5
3. Koichiro Hirayama	JPN	—	8	5
4. Rolf Krauss	GER	5	8.5	
5. Lajos Rácz	HUN	4	6	
6. Moradali Shirani	IRN	4	7	
7. Antonio Caltabiano	ITA	4	7.5	
8. Baek Seung-hyun	KOR	4	9	

1980 Moscow C: 10, N: 10, D: 7.23.

		ROUND ELIMINATED	PEN. PTS.	FINAL ROUND
1. Vakhtang Blagidze	SOV/GEO	—	1	1
2. Lajos Rácz	HUN	—	4	5
3. Mladen Mladenov	BUL	—	5	6
4. Nicu Ginga	ROM	4	8	
5. Antonín Jeliňek	CZE	4	8	
6. Stanisław Wróblewski	POL	3	7	
7. Taisto Halonen	FIN	2	7	
8. Abdulnasser Eloulabi	SYR	2	8	

Blagidze defeated Rácz, 19-1, in the final match.

1984 Los Angeles-Anaheim C: 12, N: 12, D: 8.2.

		FINAL MATCH
1. Atsuji Miyahara	JPN	9-4
2. Daniel Aceves	MEX	
3. Bang Dae-du	KOR	13-1 3:46
4. Hu Richa	CHN	
5. Jon Rønningen	NOR	14-0 2:54

6. Taisto Halonen	FIN	
7. Erol Kemah	TUR	
8. Mihai Cismasu	ROM	

1988 Seoul C: 21, N: 21, D: 9.21.

		FINAL MATCH
1. Jon Rønningen	NOR	12-7
2. Atsuji Miyahara	JPN	
3. Lee Jae-suk	KOR	4-3
4. Aleksandr Ignatenko	SOV/RUS	
5. Roman Kierpacz	POL	Passivity 3:29
6. Tibor Jankovics	CZE	
7. Hristo Fliev	BUL	9-3
8. Peter Stjernberg	SWE	

1992 Barcelona C: 17, N: 17, D: 7.28.

		FINAL MATCH
1. Jon Rønningen	NOR	2-1
2. Alfred Ter-Mkrtychyan	RUS	
3. Min Kyung-kap	KOR	Forfeit
4. Shawn Sheldon	USA	
5. Bratan Tzenov	BUL	6-1
6. Valentin Rebegea	ROM	
7. Ismo Kamesaki	FIN	2-1
8. Senad Rizvanović	YUG/SER	

Ter-Mkrtychyan was leading 1-0 when Rønningen scored a two-point takedown just as time ran out. Both wrestlers began celebrating. Ter-Mkrtychyan was lifted into the air by his coach at the same time that Norwegian fans were screaming with joy. One side was about to be severely disappointed. After huddling for several seconds, the officials announced that the takedown had occurred before the buzzer and that Rønningen was the victor. Twice Ter-Mkrtychyan collapsed in anguish on his way to the dressing room, while the Norwegians were still dancing in the streets an hour later. Min gained the bronze medal when Sheldon failed to make weight for the final match.

1996 Atlanta C: 20, N: 20, D: 7.20.

		FINAL MATCH
1. Armen Nazaryan	ARM	5-1
2. Brandon Paulson	USA	
3. Andriy Kalashnikov	UKR	4-1
4. Samvel Danielyan	RUS	
5. Lázaro Rivas Scull	CUB	5-0
6. Yordan Anev	BUL	
7. Ha Tae-yeon	KOR	3-2
8. Dariusz Jabłoński	POL	

In March 1996, Andriy Kalashnikov defeated Armen Nazaryan in the final of the European championships. They met again in the first round of the Olympics three and a half months later. This time Nazaryan overwhelmed Kalashnikov 10-0 in 4 minutes 22 seconds. In the quarterfinals Nazaryan defeated defending world champion Samvel Danielyan 3-0. In the final he faced Brandon Paulson, an upset winner of the US trials. Nazaryan, leading 1-0 after a minute and a half, scored four points with a lift and turn from the top position and the match was effectively over. Nazaryan was the first gold medalist to represent independent Armenia. Coincidentally, three of wrestlers he defeated, Alfred Ter-Mkrtichyan of Germany, Rouslan Vartanov of Lithuania and Samvel Danielyan of Russia, were also Armenians. After the Olympics, Nazaryan moved to Bulgaria and became a Bulgarian citizen.

2000 Sydney C: 20, N: 20, D: 9.26.
(54 kg—119 lbs)

		FINAL MATCH
1. Sim Kwon-ho	KOR	8-0
2. Lázaro Rivas Scull	CUB	
3. Kang Yong-gyun	PRK	7-0
4. Andriy Kalashnikov	UKR	
5. Alfred Ter-Mkrtchyan	GER	6-0
6. Wang Hui	CHN	
7. Natig Eyvazov	AZR	
8. Uran Kalilov	KYR	

Fast-moving world champion Lázaro Rivas blitzed his way to the final, outscoring his four opponents 41-1. But in the final, he was no match for 1996 Light Flyweight Olympic champion Sim Kwon-ho. Sim scored early and often and won 8-0. In the semifinals, Sim, of South Korea, had defeated Kang Yong-gyun of North Korea 10-0. Before the medal matches, Kang told Sim everything he knew about Rivas' fighting style and Sim gave Kang a scouting report on Andriy Kalashnikov. Both Koreans won.

LIGHT HEAVYWEIGHT

1908 London C: 21, N: 9, D: 7.22.
(93 kg—205 lbs)

		FINAL MATCH
1. Verner Weckman	FIN	Lost Fall 4:22; Fall 5:07; Fall 16:10
2. Yrjö Saarela	FIN	
3. Carl Jensen	DEN	Fall 2:04; Fall 1:40
4. Hugó Payr	HUN	

5. Arthur Banbrook (GBR), Marcel Dubois (BEL), Fritz Larsson (SWE), Jacob van Westrop (HOL)

Weckman, who had won the Middleweight gold medal in 1906, was a 25-year-old engineer. At the award ceremony the Finnish flag was not hoisted. In its place was a sign bearing the word "Finland." Rumors spread that the tyrannical Czarist Russian government had forbidden the use of the Finnish national flag. However, the Finnish colors were raised up the flagpole later in the day.

1912 Stockholm C: 29, N: 12, D: 7.15.
(82.5 kg—182 lbs)

1. —	
2. Anders Ahlgren	SWE
2. Ivar Böling	FIN
3. Béla Varga	HUN
4. Fritz Lange	GER
4. A. August Rajala	FIN
6. Harald Christiansen	DEN
6. Johannes Eriksen	DEN
6. Knut Lindberg	FIN
6. Sigurjón Pétursson	ICE

Ahlgren fought his way to the final match by pinning six opponents, each within 35 minutes. But in Böling he met his equal—literally. Ahlgren and Böling struggled hour after hour without either man giving in, until finally, after nine hours, officials called the contest a double loss. The rules of the Olympic competition stated that it was necessary for a first-place winner actually to defeat his adversary, so the officials decided to declare Ahlgren and Böling co-winners of the second prize.

Anders Ahlgren and Ivar Böling, 1912
They wrestled for nine hours in the final of the Light Heavyweight division before a double loss was declared.

1920 Antwerp C: 18, N: 11, D: 8.19.
(82 kg—182 lbs)

1. Claes Johanson	SWE
2. Edil Rosenqvist	FIN
3. Johannes Eriksen	DEN

1924 Paris C: 22, N: 15, D: 7.10.
(82.5 kg—182 lbs)

1. Carl Westergren	SWE
2. Rudolf Svensson	SWE
3. Onni Pellinen	FIN
4. Ibrahim Moustafa	EGY
5. Emil Weckstén	FIN
6. Rudolf Loos (EST), A. Misset (HOL), Béla Varga (HUN)	

Westergren had won the Middleweight title four years earlier in Antwerp.

1928 Amsterdam C: 17, N: 17, D: 8.5.
(82.5 kg—182 lbs)

1. Ibrahim Moustafa	EGY
2. Adolf Rieger	GER
3. Onni Pellinen	FIN
4. Nicolas Appels	BEL
5. Ejnar Hansen	DEN
6. Imre Szalay	HUN

1932 Los Angeles C: 3, N: 3, D: 8.7.
(87 kg—192 lbs)

		PEN. PTS.
1. Rudolf Svensson	SWE	1
2. Onni Pellinen	FIN	3
3. Mario Gruppioni	ITA	6

1936 Berlin C: 13, N: 13, D: 8.9.
(87 kg—192 lbs)

		ROUND ELIMINATED	PEN. PTS.	FINAL ROUND
1. Axel Cardier	SWE	—	2	1
2. Edvins Bietags	LAT	—	1	3
3. August Neo	EST	5	5	
4. Werner Seelenbinder	GER	5	6	
5. Umberto Silvestri	ITA	4	6	
6. Olaf Knutsen	NOR	4	6	
7. Franz Foidl	AUT	4	6	
8. Mustafa Çakmak (Avcioğlu)	TUR	3	5	

A member of the German Communist Party, Werner Seelenbinder was an anti-Nazi hero who was executed in 1944 because of his opposition to Adolf Hitler.

1948 London C: 14, N: 14, D: 8.6.
(87 kg—192 lbs)

		ROUND ELIMINATED	PEN. PTS.	FINAL ROUND
1. Karl-Erik Nilsson	SWE	—	2	1
2. Kaelpo Gröndahl	FIN	—	1	3
3. Ibrahim Orabi	EGY	5	6	
4. Gyula Kovács	HUN	4	5	
5. Kenneth Richmond	GBR	4	6	
6. Erling Lauridsen	DEN	4	7	
7. Peter Enzinger	AUT	3	6	
8. Mustafa Çakmak (Avcioğlu)	TUR	3	7	
8. Charles Istaz	BEL	3	7	

An incident of sorts took place in the fifth round, when Nilsson threw Orabi over his head and the referee ruled it a fall. While the Egyptians protested, Orabi stretched out on the mat and refused to move. After 15 minutes Nilsson was called back from the dressing room and ordered to continue the match. Nilsson then scored another fall and the matter was settled.

1952 Helsinki C: 10, N: 10, D: 7.27.
(87 kg—192 lbs)

		ROUND ELIMINATED	PEN. PTS.	FINAL ROUND
1. Kaelpo Gröndahl	FIN	—	2	2
2. Shalva Chikhladze	SOV/RUS	—	4	3
3. Karl-Erik Nilsson	SWE	—	5	6
4. Gyula Kovács	HUN	4	5	
5. Ismet Atli	TUR	3	6	
6. Umberto Silvestri	ITA	3	7	
6. Michel Skaff	LEB	3	7	

The final bout between Gröndahl and Chikhladze was dull and cautious and was won by Gröndahl on a split decision.

1956 Melbourne C: 10, N: 10, D: 12.6.
(87 kg—192 lbs)

		ROUND ELIMINATED	PEN. PTS.	FINAL ROUND
1. Valentin Nikolayev	SOV/RUS	—	4	
2. Petko Sirakov	BUL	4	5	1
3. Karl-Erik Nilsson	SWE	4	5	3
4. Robert Steckle	CAN	4	7	
5. Dale Thomas	USA	3	6	
5. Eugen Wiesberger	AUT	3	6	
7. Veikko Lahti	FIN	3	7	
8. Adil Atan	TUR	3	7	

1960 Rome C: 17, N: 17, D: 8.31.
(87 kg—192 lbs)

		ROUND ELIMINATED	PEN. PTS.	FINAL ROUND
1. Tevfik Kiş	TUR	—	6	2
2. Kralyu Bimbalov	BUL	—	6	2
3. Givy Kartoziya	SOV/GEO	6	8	
4. Péter Piti	HUN	6	8	
5. Antero Vanhanen	FIN	5	7	
6. José Panizo Rodríguez	SPA	4	7	
7. Gheorghe Popovici	ROM	4	8	
8. Eugen Wiesberger	AUT	4	8	

Kiş was awarded first place because he weighed less than Bimbalov.

1964 Tokyo C: 18, N: 18, D: 10.19.
(97 kg—214 lbs)

		ROUND ELIMINATED	PEN. PTS.	FINAL ROUND
1. Boyan Radev	BUL	—	2	
2. Per Svensson	SWE	5	6	
3. Heinz Kiehl	GER	5	6	
4. Nicolae Martinescu	ROM	5	8	
5. Rostom Abashidze	SOV/GEO	4	6	
5. Ferenc Kiss	HUN	4	6	
5. Peter Jutzeler	SWI	4	6	
8. Eugen Wiesberger	AUT	4	7	

Radev breezed through the tournament, aided by the fact that he faced only one wrestler, Martinescu, who finished in the top eight.

1968 Mexico City C: 16, N: 16, D: 10.26.
(97 kg—214 lbs)

		ROUND ELIMINATED	PEN. PTS.	FINAL ROUND
1. Boyan Radev	BUL	—	0.5	2.5
2. Nikolai Yakovenko	SOV/RUS	—	1	3.5
3. Nicolae Martinescu	ROM	—	4	7
4. Per Svensson	SWE	4	6	
5. Tore Hem	NOR	4	8	
6. Peter Jutzeler	SWI	3	6	
6. Cay Malmberg	FIN	3	6	
6. Wacław Orlowski	POL	3	6	

Radev and Yakovenko tied, but Radev threw Martinescu in 4:58 to win the gold medal.

In 2010 Communist-era secret service files revealed that Radev was working as an intelligence officer for the Bulgarian State Security at the same time that he was competing at the Olympics. After the fall of communism he became a noted art collector.

1972 Munich C: 14, N: 14, D: 9.10.
(90 kg—198½ lbs)

		ROUND ELIMINATED	PEN. PTS.	FINAL ROUND
1. Valery Rezantsev	SOV/KAZ	—	2	2
2. Josip Čorak	YUG/SER	—	3	5
3. Czesław Kwieciński	POL	—	5	5
4. József Percsi	HUN	5	6.5	
5. Håkon Överbye	NOR	5	9	
6. Nicolae Neguţ	ROM	4	8	
7. Kimiichi Tani	JPN	4	9	
8. Günter Kowalewski	GER	3	8	

Rezantsev suffered a first-round draw with Neguţ and then won six straight bouts.

1976 Montreal C: 13, N: 13, D: 7.24.
(90 kg—198½ lbs)

		ROUND ELIMINATED	PEN. PTS.	FINAL ROUND
1. Valery Rezantsev	SOV/KAZ	—	2	2
2. Stoyan Ivanov	BUL	—	5	5
3. Czesław Kwieciński	POL	—	3	7
4. Darko Nišavić	YUG/SER	5	9	
5. Frank Andersson	SWE	4	6	
6. István Séllyei	HUN	4	8	
7. James Johnson	USA	3	8	
7. Sadao Sato	JPN	3	8	

Valery Rezantsev dominated Light Heavyweight Greco-Roman wrestling in the 1970s. He went to Montreal as the defending Olympic champion and the five-time defending world champion. In his final bout he was held to a 6-6 tie by Ivanov, but a tie-breaker gave him the victory anyway.

1980 Moscow C: 15, N: 15, D: 7.22.
(90 kg—198½ lbs)

		ROUND ELIMINATED	PEN. PTS.	FINAL ROUND
1. Norbert Növényi	HUN	—	1	2
2. Igor Kanygin	SOV/BLR	—	6.5	5
3. Petre Dicu	ROM	—	6	7
4. Frank Andersson	SWE	5	7	
5. Thomas Horschel	GDR	4	8	
6. José Poll Martínez	CUB	4	8.5	
7. Christophe Andanson	FRA	3	6.5	
8. Georgios Pozidis	GRE	3	7	

Növényi scattered four opponents and then outpointed Kanygin 7-6 and Dicu 4-1.

1984 Los Angeles-Anaheim C: 13, N: 13, D: 8.1.
(90 kg—198½ lbs)

		FINAL MATCH
1. Steven Fraser	USA	1-1
2. Ilie Matei	ROM	
3. Frank Andersson	SWE	5-0
4. Uwe Sachs	GER	
5. Jean-François Court	FRA	4-2
6. Georgios Pozidis	GRE	
7. Toni Hannula	FIN	
8. Franz Marx	AUT	

Fraser, a deputy sheriff from Ann Arbor, Michigan, became the first US Greco-Roman wrestler ever to win an Olympic medal. With less than 50 seconds remaining in the final, he trailed Matei 1-0. But then Fraser caught the Romanian in a front headlock. The roar of the crowd seemed to give Fraser an extra injection of strength and he scored a takedown to gain the final point of the match and consequently the victory.

1988 Seoul C: 22, N: 22, D: 9.20.
(90 kg—198½ lbs)

		FINAL MATCH
1. Atanas Komchev	BUL	4-0
2. Harri Koskela	FIN	
3. Vladimir Popov	SOV/RUS	Fall 1:36
4. Christer Gullded	SWE	
5. Andreas Steinbach	GER	Passivity 4:43
6. Franz Pitschmann	AUT	
7. Olaf Koschnitzke	GDR	Forfeit
8. Georgios Pikilidis	GRE	

1992 Barcelona C: 19, N: 19, D: 7.30.
(90 kg—198½ lbs)

		FINAL MATCH
1. Maik Bullmann	GER	5-0
2. Hakki Başar	TUR	
3. Gogi Koguashvili	GEO	2-0
4. Mikael Ljungberg	SWE	
5. Hassan Babak	IRN	17-1 3:56
6. Michial Foy	USA	
7. Reynaldo Peña Borroto	CUB	Forfeit
8. Salvatore Campanella	ITA	

Bullmann was the overwhelming favorite, having won the last three world championships. In Barcelona his closest match was a 3-1 victory over Babak. He outscored all five of his opponents by a combined total of 33-1.

1996 Atlanta C: 23, N: 23, D: 7.22.
(90 kg—198½ lbs)

		FINAL MATCH
1. Vyacheslav Oliynyk	UKR	6-0
2. Jacek Fafiński	POL	
3. Maik Bullmann	GER	2-0
4. Aleksandr Sidorenko	BLR	
5. Hakki Başar	TUR	4-1
6. Iordanis Konstantin	GRE	
7. Derrick Waldroup	USA	10-2
8. Marek Švec	CZE	

Before he left for the Olympics, Vyacheslav Oliynyk's wife told him, "You're 30 years old. You're old. Stay home, find a job, be with your child." In the quarter-finals Oliynyk defeated defending Olympic champion Maik Bullmann 3-2. In the semis he beat defending world champion Hakki Başar.

ALL-AROUND

1906 Athens C: 3, N: 3, D: 5.1.

1. Søren Marinus Jensen	DEN
2. Verner Weckman	FIN
3. Rudolf Watzl	AUT

This event brought together the winners of the three weight categories. Jensen defeated Watzl and then Weckman, who was awarded second place without winning a match.

Discontinued Sports

Baseball
Cricket
Croquet
Golf
Jeu De Paume
Lacrosse
Motor Boating
Pelota Basque
Polo
Rackets
Rugby
Softball
Tug of War

BASEBALL

In 2005 the IOC voted to drop baseball and softball from the Olympic program for the 2012 London Games. The decision was made in part to make room for other sports (although no other sports were added to the 2012 program), but primarily because Major League Baseball refused to release its players in the middle of the season to compete at the Olympics. Before its inclusion as an official medal sport, baseball had appeared as a demonstration or exhibition sport in 1912, 1936, 1956, 1964, 1984 and 1988—more often than any sport in Olympic history.

1992 Barcelona-L'Hospitalet T: 8, N: 8, D: 8.5.

	W	L	RF	RA
1. CUB	9	0	95	16
2. TAI	6	3	67	34
3. JPN	6	3	70	23
4. USA	5	4	53	42
5. PUR	2	5	22	48
6. DOM	2	5	23	60
7. ITA	1	6	25	62
8. SPA	1	6	15	85

Final: CUB 11-1 TAI
3rd Place: JPN 8-3 USA

1. CUB—Luis Ulacia Álvarez, Alberto Hernández Pérez, Lázaro Vargas Álvarez, Omar Linares Izquierdo, Germán Mesa Fresneda, Juan Padilla Alfonso, Lourdes Gurriel Delgado, José Estrada González, Osvaldo Fernández Rodríguez, Orlando Hernández Pedroso, Giorge Díaz Loren, Omar Ajete Iglesias, Victor Mesa Martínez, Jorge Valdés Berriel, José Delgado Diez, Rolando Arrojo Ávila, Orestes Kindelán Olivares, Antonio Pacheco Masso, Juan Pérez Rondón, Ermidelio Urrutia Quiroga
2. TAI—Lin Chao-huang, Lin Kun-han, Wang Kuang-shih, Chen Wei-chen, Huang Wen-po, Wu Shih-hsih, Chang Yaw-teing, Liao Ming-hsiung, Lo Kuo-chong, Huang Chung-yi, Lo Chen-jung, Chen Chi-hsin, Chiang Tai-chuan, Pai Kun-hong, Kuo Lee Chien-fu, Ku Kuo-chian, Tsai Ming-hung, Chang Cheng-hsien, Chang Wen-chung, Jong Yeu-jeng
3. JPN—Koichi Oshima, Shigeki Wakabayashi, Masafumi Nishi, Koji Tokunaga, Akihiro Togo, Hirotami Kojima, Hiroki Kokubo, Hiroyuki Sakaguchi, Yasunoni Takami, Yasuhiro Sato, Kento Sugiyama, Katsumi Watanabe, Kazutaka Nishiyama, Masahito Kohiyama, Tomohito Ito, Masonori Sugiura, Takashi Miwa, Shinichi Sato, Hiroshi Nakamoto, Shinichiro Kawabata

Tug of War, 1920
Tough pulling in Antwerp.

4. USA—Anthony Garciaparra, Calvin Murray, Chris Wimmer, Craig Wilson, Jeffrey Hammonds, Michael Tucker, Billy Wallace, Jason Giambi, Phillip Nevin, William Adams, Ronald Villone, Jason Varitek, Christopher Roberts, Richard Greene, Ricky Helling, Robert Alkire, Daron Kirkreit, Darron Dreifort, Chad McConnell, Charles Johnson
5. PUR—Abimael Rosario Marrero, Albert Bracero Chévere, Jorge Aranzamendi Torres, José Lorenzana Oquendo, Efraín Nieves Soto, Gualberto López Camacho, Luis Ramos Torres, Wilfredo Vélez León, Manuel Serrano, Ángel Morales Rodríguez, James Figueroa, Rafael Santiago Rivera, Jesús Feliciano Amadeo, José Mateo Rosario, Roberto López Ocasio, Efraín García Santiago, Orlando López Bobian, Helson Rodríguez Santiago, José Sepúlveda Pinto, Silvio Censale
6. DOM—Féliz Nova, José Veras, Manuel Guzmán, Fabio Aquino, Roberto Casey García, Eugenio Váldez Cuevas, Rafaelito Mercedes Díaz, Félix Tejada, Teófilo Peña Dilone, Alexis Peña, Fausto Peña Pichardo, Teodoro Novas, Cipriano Ventura, Juan Sánchez Fernández, Juan Viñas, Roque Solano, Silvestre Popoteur, Elías Olivo, Benjamín Heredia, José Santana
7. ITA—Massimo Ciaramella, Guglielmo Trinci, Claudio Cecconi, Elio Gambuti, Marco Ubani, Maurizio De Sanctis, Francesco Petruzzelli, Fulvio Valle, Massimiliano Masin, Andrea Succi, Claudio Taglienti, Paolo Ceccaroli, Ruggero Bagialemani, Rolando Cretis, Alberto D'Auria, Roberto Bianchi, Leonardo Schianchi, Luigi Carrozza, Massimo Fochi, Massimo Melassi
8. SPA—Manuel Martínez Carrasco, Jesús Lisarri Tomás, Juan Belza Jaurrieta, Antonio Salazar Calzado, Enrique Cortés Gallego, Miguel Pariente Álvarez, José Arza Laurenz, Javier Díez Serra, Juan Damborenea García, Francisco Aristu Lozano, Luis León Anguiano, Felix Cano Riduejo, Juan Salmerón Agullo, Xavier Camps Qulbus, José Pulido Aranda, Miguel Stella Pérez, Gabriel Valarezo Camps, José Becerra Puente, Xavier Civit Forner

Baseball is the only sport to have been included as an exhibition or demonstration sport seven times before finally achieving official medal status. Exhibition games were staged in Paris in 1900, in Stockholm in 1912, in Berlin in 1936 (before a bewildered crowd of 90,000), and in Melbourne in 1956. Because the 1956 game was played in the main stadium while spectators filed in for a track and field session, it is thought that the late innings were seen by the largest live audience in baseball history—almost 114,000 people. In 1964, a team of United States college all-stars played a Japanese amateur all-star team in Tokyo. In 1984, when the Olympics were held in Los Angeles, a six-team tournament was organized. Cuba qualified, but joined the boycott led by the Soviet Union. Nicaragua, ruled by another Soviet-client regime, also qualified. So great was the excitement in Nicaragua about this achievement that the government resisted Soviet pressure to join the boycott and sent their team anyway. Japan won the tournament, defeating the United States 6-3 in the final. The 1988 tournament, this time including eight teams, was boycotted by Cuba again. The final saw a United States-Japan rematch, with the Americans coming out on top, 5-3.

After such a long buildup, the first official Olympic baseball tournament, held in Barcelona, was a major anticlimax because Olympic rules prohibited the use of professional players. This meant that only Communist Cuba was allowed to use their best players, while the other qualifying nations had to choose their squads from college or amateur ranks. The Cubans had won the previous 12 world championships in which they had participated, going back to 1969, and they were 64 and 1 in international tournaments played between 1986 and 1992. Not surprisingly, the Cubans swept through the Olympics as if they were, well, in another league. In nine games, they outscored their opponents 95-16. The Cuban *team* batting average was .404, their slugging percentage .646, and their team's earned run average 1.27. They trailed only once, when the United States scored five runs in the first inning. Even then, by the fourth inning the Cubans were back on top. So dull was the tournament from a competitive standpoint that of the 32 games played, only two were decided by one run and only one went into extra innings.

1996 Atlanta T: 8, N: 8, D: 8.2.

	W	L	RF	RA
1. CUB	9	0	118	59
2. JPN	5	4	89	60
3. USA	7	2	93	41
4. NIC	4	5	48	48
5. HOL	2	5	32	76
6. ITA	2	5	33	71
7. AUS	2	5	47	86
8. KOR	1	6	40	59

Final: CUB 13-9 JPN
3rd Place: USA 10-3 NIC

1. CUB—Luis Ulacia Álvarez, Alberto Hernández Pérez, Eduardo Paret Pérez, Omar Linares Izquierdo, Rey Isaac Vaillant, Juan Padilla Alfonso, Miguel Caldés Luis, Osmani Romero Turcas, Lázaro Vargas Álvarez, Omar Luis Martínez, José Estrada González, Antonio Scull Hernández, Omar Ajete Iglesias, Pedro Luis Lazo Iglesias, Eliecer Montes de Oca Fleites, Juan Manrique García, Orestes Kindelán Olivares, Antonio Pacheco Massó, José Antonio Contreras Camejo, Jorge Fumero
2. JPN—Kosuke Fukudome, Masahiro Nojima, Nobuhiko Matsunaka, Makoto Imaoka, Takao Kuwamoto, Tadahito Iguchi, Yasuyuki Saigo, Hideaki Okubo, Daishin Nakamura, Koichi Misawa, Masao Morinaka, Jutaro Kimura, Takeo Kawamura, Hitoshi Ono, Masahiko Mori, Masanori Sugiura, Takashi Kurosu, Takayuki Takabayashi, Tomoaki Sato, Yoshitomo Tani
3. USA—Robert "R. A." Dickey, Warren Morris, Octavio "Augie" Ojeda, Mark Kotsay, Jason Williams, J. Chad Allen, Chad Green, Kiplan Harkrider, Braden Looper, Travis Lee, Andrew "A. J." Hinch, Jacque Jones, Brian Loyd, Troy Glaus, Seth Greisinger, Matthew LeCroy, Kristin Benson, Jim Parque, Jeff Weaver, Billy Koch
4. NIC—Bayardo Dávila Montiel, Martín Alemán, Norman Cardoze, Oswaldo Mairena, Nemesio Porras, José Luis Quiroz, Carlos Alberto Berrios, Sandy Moreno, Omar Obando Varela, José Ramon Padilla, Fredy Zamora, Julio Cesar Osejo, Eduardo Bojorge, Asdrudes Flores, Anibal Vega, Erasmo Baca, Luis Daniel Miranda, Fredy Corea, Jorge Luis Avellán, Henry Roa
5. HOL—Eric de Bruin, Andreas van Maris, Eddie Dix, Geoffry Kohl, Marcel Joost, Eelco Jansen, Ruben Ward, Randolph Balentina, Giel ten Bosch, Jeffrey Cranston, Daniel Wout, Tom Nanne, Paul Nanne, Evert-Jan t'Hoen, Marlon Fluonia, Rob Cordemans, Adenis Kemp, Marcel Kruyt, Edsel Martis, Peter Callenbach
6. ITA—Claudio Liverziani, Pier Paolo Illuminati, Roberto De Franceschi, David Rigoli, Marco Urbani, Francesco Casolari, Andrea Evangelisti, Enrico Vecchi, Massimiliano Masin, Paolo Ceccaroli, Ruggero Bagialemani, Paolo Passerini, Massimo Fochi, Alberto D'Auria, Roberto Cabalisti, Dante Carbini, Marco Barboni, Rolando Cretis, Luigi Carrozza, Fabio Betto
7. AUS—Jeffrey Williams, Mark Doubleday, Scott Tunkin, Michael Nakamura, Steven Hinton, Richard Vagg, Andrew Scott, Shane Tonkin, Jason Hewitt, Andrew McNally, Matthew Sheldon-Collins, Peter Vogler, David Hynes, Grant McDonald, Scott Dawes, Stuart Howell, Sten Lindberg, Simon Sheldon-Collins, Stuart Thompson, John Moore
8. KOR—Son Min-han, Kim Soo-kwan, Back Jae-ho, Cho In-sung, Kang Hyuk, Cho Jin-ho, Jin Kab-yong, Cho Kyung-hwam, Lee Dong, Kang Pil-sun, Lim Sun-dong, Lee Byoung-kyu, Oh Chul-min, Jeon Seung-nam, Kim Young-soo, Mun Dong-hwan, Choi Man-ho, An Hee-bong, Kim Sun-woo, Chea Jong-kook

The Olympic baseball tournament continued to be weakened in significance by the fact that only one of the major powers, Cuba, was allowed to use its best players. The average age of the Cubans was 28, while the average US player was 21 years old. The Cubans went through the tournament undefeated, but their dominance was clearly diminished from the days of the 1992 Olympics. Rolando Arroyo, who had pitched nine shutout innings at the Barcelona Games and was expected to perform important duty in Atlanta, defected ten days before the Opening Ceremony. Pitching was the Cuban weak point. In Barcelona the team earned run average had been 1.27; in Atlanta it was 6.31. Fortunately, the Cuban batters were hotter than ever. The team batting average was .402 and the team slugging percentage was a phenomenal .812. In nine games, the Cubans hit 38 home runs, including eight in the gold medal game alone.

In pool play, Cuba trailed Japan 7-6 after 9½ innings, but scored two runs in the bottom of the tenth to win 8-7. Against Nicaragua, they had to come from behind four times before prevailing 8-7 again. In the final, Cuba faced Japan a second time. Cuba led 6-0 after only two innings, but a fifth-inning grand slam by Nobuhiko Matsunaka tied the score. However, in the bottom of the sixth, Cuba scored four runs on three home runs and held on to win 13-9.

During the nine-game tournament, Cuba's designated hitter, Orestes Kindelán, batted .432 and slugged nine home runs while third baseman Omar Linares batted .541 and hit eight home runs.

2000 Sydney T: 8, N: 8, D: 9.27.

	W	L	RF	RA
1. USA	8	1	57	19
2. CUB	7	2	45	18
3. KOR	5	4	45	30
4. JPN	4	5	42	29
5. HOL	3	4	19	29
6. ITA	2	5	33	43
7. AUS	2	5	30	41
8. SAF	1	6	11	73

Final: USA 4-0 CUB
3rd Place: KOR 3-1 JPN

1. USA—Bret Abernathy, Kurt Ainsworth, Pat Borders, Sean Burroughs, John Cotton Travis Dawkins, Adam Everett, Ryan Franklin, Chris George, Shane Heams, Marcus Jensen, Mike Kinkade, Rick Krivida, Doug Mientkiewicz, Mike Neil, Roy Oswalt, Jon Rauch, Anthony Sanders, Bobby Seay, Ben Sheets, Brad Wilkerson, Todd Williams, Ernie Young, Tim Young
2. CUB—Omar Ajete Iglesia, Yovany Aragón Rodríguez, Miguel Caldés Luis, Danel Castro Muñagorri, José Antonio Contreras Camejo, Yobal Dueñas Martínez, Yasser Gómez Soto, José Ibar Medina, Orestes Kindelán Olivares, Pedro Luis Lazo Iglesias, Omar Linares Izquierdo, Oscar Macías Hernández, Juan Manrique García, Javier Méndez González, Rolando Meriño Betancourt, Germán Mesa Fresneda, Antonio Pacheco Massó, Ariel Pestano Valdés, Gabriel Pierre Rojas, Maels Rodríguez Corrales, Antonio Scull Hernández, Luis Ulacia Álvarez, Lázaro Valle Martell, Norge Luis Vera Peralta
3. KOR—Chong Tae-hyon, Chung Min-tae, Hong Sung-heon, Jang Sung-ho, Jin Pil-jung, Jung Soo-keun, Kim Dong-joo, Kim Han-soo, Kim Ki-tai, Kim Soo-kyung, Kim Tae-gyun, Koo Dae-sung, Lee Byung-kyu, Lee Sung-ho, Lee Seung-ho, Lim Chang-yong, Lim Sun-dong, Park Jae-hong, Park Jin-man, Park Jong-ho, Park Kyung-oan, Park Seok-jin, Son Min-han, Song Jin-woo
4. JPN—Shinnosuke Abe, Norihiro Akahoshi, Yoshikazu Doi, Jun Heima, Jun Hirose, Tomohiro Iizuka, Masanori Ishikaawa, Yoshihiko Kajiyama, Masato Kawano, Tomohiro Kuroki, Nobuhiko Matsunaka, Daisuke Marsuzaka, Norihiro Nakamura, Kosuke Noda, Osamu Nogami, Yoshinori Okihara, Toshiya Sugiuchi, Masanori Sugiura, Fumihiro Suzuki, So Taguchi, Yukio Tanaka, Shunsuke Watanabe, Akichika Yamada, Yuji Yoshimi
5. HOL—Evert-Jan t'Hoen, Sharnol Adriana, Johnny Balentina, Patrick Beljaards, Ken Brauckmiller, Rob Cordemans, Jeffrey Cranston, Mike Crouwel, Patrick de Lange, Radhames Dijkhoff, Robert Eenhoom, Rikkert Faneyte, Charion Isenia, Percy Isenia, Eelco Jansen, Ference Jongejan, Reily Legito, Jurriaan Lobbezoo, Remy Maduro, Hensley Muelens, Ralph Milliard, Erik Remmerswaal, Orlando Stewart, Dirk van 't Klooster
6. ITA—Matteo Baldacci, Fabio Betto, Roberto Cabalisti, Luigi Carrozza, Francesco Casolari, Marc Cerbone, Alberto D'Auria, Davide Dallospedale, Roberto De Franceschi, Daniel Di Pace, Andrea Evangelisti, Daniele Frignani, Emiliano Ginanneschi, Seth La Fera, Stefano Landuzzi, Christopher Madonna, Claudio Liverziani, Christian Mura, Daniel Newman, Battista Perri, Diego Ricci, David Sheldon, Jason Simontacchi, Michelle Toriaco
7. AUS—Craig Anderson, Grant Balfour, Tom Becker, Shayne Bennett, Mathew Buckley, Adam Burton, Clayton Byrne, Mark Hutton, Ron Johnson, Grant McDonald, Adrian Meagher, Michael Moyle, Michael Nakamura, David Nilsson, Glenne Reeves, Brette Roneberg, Chris Snelling, Brad Thomas, Rodney van Buizen, David White, Gary White, Glen Williams
8. SAF—Clint Alfino, Francisco Alfino, Paul Bell, Vaughn Berriman, Jason Cook, Errol Davis, Simon de la Rey, Nick Dempsey, Ashley Dove, Darryl Gonsalves, Brian Harrell, Richard Harrell, Tim Harrell, Ian Holness, Kevin Johnson, Bles Kemp, Morne MacKay, Liall Mauritz, Carl Michaels, Alan Phillips, Darryn Smith, Russell van Niekerk

Cuba's 152-game winning streak in international competition was finally ended by Japan in 1997. Cuba's prospects for winning another Olympic title were further threatened by two developments: the continuing defections of leading Cuban players, mostly pitchers, to the United States, and the 1996 decision by the International Baseball Association to allow professionals to take part in the Olympics. Major League Baseball softened this second blow by refusing to release its players. In South Korea, the professional season was suspended for two weeks, allowing the Koreans to field a strong team that lacked only those players who played in the major leagues in North America. In Japan, the Pacific League agreed to have each of its eight teams contribute one player to the Japanese Olympic team, but the Central League would only release reserve players. The United States, which was coached by 73-year-old Tommy Lasorda, was made up of minor league players, twelve of whom had played in the major leagues at one point or another, most notably 37-year-old catcher Pat Borders, who was voted the Most Valuable Player of the 1992 World Series.

In Sydney, the Cubans opened with two easy victories over South Africa and Italy, but then their road turned rocky. They fell behind South Korea 0-4 before rallying to win 6-5. The next day, the Cubans' 21 game Olympic winning streak was stopped, not by one of baseball's traditional powers, but by the Netherlands, as the Dutch stunned the Cubans 4-2. After barely beating Australia 1-0, Cuba regrouped and whipped the United States 6-1 and Japan 6-2. They then defeated the

Japanese again, 3-0, in the semi-finals to qualify for the gold-medal game.

The Americans, meanwhile, had to work hard to make it to the final. They faced Japan in their very first game, which turned out to be the longest in baseball's brief Olympic history. The score was 2-2 when Mike Neill hit a two-run home run with no outs in the bottom of the 13th inning. After victories over South Africa and the Netherlands, the Americans beat South Korea 4-0 on an 8th inning grand slam home run by first-baseman Doug Mientkiewicz. The United States faced the Koreans again in the semifinals. The score was tied 2-2 in the bottom of the eighth when play was suspended by a two-hour rain delay. With one out in the bottom of the ninth, Mientkiewicz hit a solo homer to put the US into the final.

Cuba entered the gold-medal game having scored 53 runs in 8 games. Thus it came as a shock when 22-year-old Ben Sheets dominated the Cuban batters, throwing a three-hit complete game shutout. Only one Cuban batter managed to make it to second base. Meanwhile, Mike Neill hit a first inning home run and the Americans added three more runs in the fifth to win 4-0.

2004 Athens T: 8, N: 8, D: 8.5.

	W	L	RF	RA
1. CUB	8	1	55	24
2. AUS	5	4	52	36
3. JPN	7	2	60	23
4. CAN	5	4	46	36
5. TAI	3	4	24	28
6. HOL	2	5	29	55
7. GRE	1	6	24	49
8. ITA	1	6	19	58

Final: CUB 6-2 AUS
3rd Place: JPN 11-2 CAN

1. CUB—Danny Betancourt Chacón, Luis Borroto Jiménez, Frederich Cepeda Cruz, Yorelvis Charles Martínez, Michel Enríquez Tamayo, Norberto González Miranda, Yulieski Gourriel Castillo, Eriel Sanchez León Sánchez, Pedro Luis Lazo, Roger Machado Morales, Jonder Martínez, Danny Miranda Agramonte, Frank Andy Montieth Herrera, Vicyohandri Odelín Sanamé, Adiel Palma López, Eduardo Paret Pérez, Ariel Pestano, Alexei Ramírez Rodríguez, Antonio Scull Hernández, Carlos Alberto Tabares Padilla, Yoandri Urgellés Cobas, Osmani Urrutia, Manuel Alberto Vega Tamayo, Norge Luis Vera Peralta
2. AUS—Craig Anderson, Thomas Brice, Adrian Burnside, Gavin Fingleson, Paul Gonzalez, Nick Kimpton, Brendan Kingman, Craig Lewis, Graeme Lloyd, David Nilsson, Trent Oeltjen, Wayne Ough, Chris Oxspring, Brett Roneberg, Ryan Rowland Smith, John Stephens, Phil Stockman, Brett Tamburrino, Richard Thompson, Andrew Utting, Rodney van Buizen, Ben Wigmore, Glenn Williams, Jeff Williams
3. JPN—Yuya Ando, Atsushi Fujimoto, Kosuke Fukudome, Hirotoshi Ishii, Hisashi Iwakuma, Hitoki Iwase, Kenji Jojima, Makoto Kaneko, Takuya Kimura, Masahide Kobayashi, Hiroki Kuroda, Daisuke Matsuzaka, Daisuke Miura, Shinya Miyamoto, Arihito Muramatsu, Norihiro Nakamura, Michihiro Ogasawara, Naoyuki Shimizu, Yoshinobu Takahashi, Yoshitomo Tani, Koji Uehara, Kazuhiro Wada, Tsuyoshi Wada, Ryoji Aikawa
4. CAN—Chris Begg, Todd Betts, Richard "Stubby" Clapp, Eric Cyr, Phil Devey, Jason Dickson, Rob Ducey, Jeff Guiel, Shawn Hill, Mike Johnson, Danny Klassen, Mike Kusiewicz, Pierre-Luc "Pete" Laforest, Chris Mears, Aaron Myette, Kevin Nicholson, John Ogiltree, Peter Orr, Simon Pond, Ryan Radmanovich, Paul Spoljaric, Adam Stern, Andy Stewart, Jeremy Ware
5. TAI—Chang Chih-chia, Chang Tai-shan, Chen Chih-yuan, Chen Chin-feng, Chen Wei-yin, Chen Yung-chi, Cheng Chang-ming, Cheng Chao-hang, Hsieh Chia-shian, "Kevin" Huang Chun-chung, Huang Chung-yi, Kao Chih-kang, Keng Po-hsuan, Lin En-yu, Lin Wei-chu, Lin Ying-chieh, Pan Wei-lun, Peng Cheng-min, Tsai Feng-an, Tsao Chin-hui, Tu Chang-wei, Wang Chien-ming, Yang Chien-fu, Yeh Chun-chang
6. HOL—Sharnol Adriana, Wladimir Balentien, Johnny Balentina, Patrick Beljaards, Maikel Benner, Ivanon Coffie, Rob Cordemans, Yurundell de Caster, Sidney de Jong, Patrick de Lange, Dave Draijer, Chairon Isenia, Eelco Jansen, Ferenc Jongejan, Eugene Kingsale, Reily Legito, Calvin Maduro, Diego Markwell, Ralph Milliard, Harvey Monte, Alexander Smit, Evert-Jan 't Hoen, Robin van Doornspeek, Dirk van 't Klooster
7. GRE—Clay Bellinger, Alex Cremidans, Chris Demetral, Larry Heisler, Jim Kavourias, Bobby Kingsbury, George Kottaras, Nick Markakis, Panagiotis "Pete" Sikaras, Nick Theodorou, Clint Zavaras, Dimitrios Douros, Cory Antony Harris, Michael Koutsantonakis, Peter Maestrales, Meleti Ross Melehes, Erik Daniel Pappas, Panagiotis "Peter" Rasmusen, Khristoforos Robinson, Peter Soteropoulos, Vasili Spanos, Sean Spencer, Jared Theodorakos
8. ITA—Luca Bischeri, James Buccheri, Francesco Casolari, Mario Chiarini, Davide Dallospedale, Riccardo de Santis, David Francia, Daniele Frignani, Seth La Fera, Claudio Liverziani, William Lucena, Marcello Malagoli, Michael Marchesano, Anthony Massimino, Giuseppe Mazzanti, Fabio Milano, Peter Nyari, Kasey Olemberger, Giovanni Pantaleoni, Vincent Parisi, Jairo Ramos Gizzi, Carlo Richetti, David Rollandini, Igor Schiavetti

Although they were the defending Olympic champions, the United States still had to qualify for the 2004 Olympics by playing in an Americas qualifying competition in which the top two teams, expected to be the US and Cuba, would go through to Athens. Held in Panama City in November 2003, the tournament began with two pools and then moved on to a single elimination format beginning with quarterfinals. The US team won all three of their pool games, outscored their opponents 21-0. This earned them a quarterfinal matchup with the last place team in the other pool, Mexico, which had lost all three of their games. Mexican pitcher Rigo Beltran held the US team to one run and three hits in seven innings. With the score tied 1-1 in the top of the ninth inning, Mexico's first baseman, Luis Garcia, hit a home run that held up for a 2-1 victory. The Mexicans were then eliminated by Canada.

With the United States out of the competition, Cuba was the overwhelming favorite in Athens. Their national team had won nineteen consecutive world titles, as well as three of four gold medals since baseball had become an Olympic sport. Japan was expected to be Cuba's most serious contender. Drawing two players from each major league team in the country, they were hailed as a Japanese "dream team." In fact, in pool play, Japan handed Cuba their only loss, building a 6-0 lead until the Cubans scored three runs in the bottom of the ninth. In the first semifinal, Japan faced Australia, which had upset them 9-4 in pool play. The rematch was a pitchers' battle with Australia earning a surprise place in the final when Brendan Kingman doubled home Brett Roneberg in the sixth inning for the only run of the game. In the second semi, the Cubans trailed Canada 2-3 after seven innings, but then scored six runs in the bottom of the eighth and won 8-5.

In the final. Cuba opened the scoring in the fourth inning when Frederich Cepeda hit a two-run home run. In the bottom of the fourth, with two men on base, Australia's Thomas Brice hit a deep line drive that Cuban center-fielder Carlos Tabares caught as it hit the fence. Brice was called out, but Australian coach Jon Deeble protested the call and was ejected from the game for widening his eyes while discussing the play with home plate umpire Willie Rodriguez. Subsequent TV replays showed the ball hit Tabares' mitt and bounced against the wall before Tabares was able to control it.

Australian left-fielder Paul Gonzalez narrowed the lead to 2-1 with a fifth inning home run off Cuban starting pitcher Norge Luis Vera, the 33-year-old who, until then, had pitched 13 scoreless innings in three games in Athens. Cuba solidified their lead in the sixth inning, scoring two runs on four straight singles, and two more on a double by Eduardo Parent. Gonzalez singled in another run in the eighth inning, but it wasn't enough to turn the game around.

As host of the 2004 Olympics, Greece was automatically given a berth in the baseball competition. However, there was a problem: at the time, Greece had no baseball federation, no teams, and only two baseball diamonds in the entire country, both of them on a former US military base. Pitcher Clint Zavaras had been retired for eight years when he received a call from the Greek baseball federation, who found his name in a baseball registry. Zavaras was shocked, "I think they went down the list of names and called anyone whose name even sounded Greek." In the end, the Greek team included only two players who had actually been born in Greece. Most of the rest were from the United States and Canada.

If baseball was new to the team, it was also new to the fans. The enthusiastic crowd would cheer even when the Greek pitchers missed the strike zone. When Zavaras missed on his first pitch in the Olympic opener the fans cheered so hard he double-checked the scoreboard to see if the pitch had been ruled a strike. When the first foul ball flew into the stands, the crowd threw it back into play. An announcer soon clarified, "Ladies and Gentlemen, if a fly ball lands near you, please accept it as our gift."

Greece lost their first game of the tournament 11-0 to the Netherlands. Their second game, against Cuba, was surprisingly more even. Cuba took a two run lead in the first two innings, but Greece narrowed the score by earning a run in the top of the fourth. Cuba score three more runs in the sixth and seventh innings, but Greece came back with three runs in the top of the ninth. The Cubans responded by sending out their star relief pitcher, Pedro Luis Lazo, who was competing in his third Olympics. Lazo shut down the Greek hitters and closed the game 5-4. As Greek sportswriter Lazaros Souskas put it, "Our fans had never seen a pitcher like this. Our players, I'm not sure they could even see the ball when he pitched it." The Greek team did manage one victory, defeating Italy 11-7.

2008 Beijing T: 8, N: 8, D: 8.23.

	W	L	RF	RA
1. KOR	9	0	50	26
2. CUB	7	2	64	28
3. USA	6	3	50	36
4. JPN	4	5	36	28
5. TAI	2	5	29	33
6. CAN	2	5	29	20
7. HOL	1	6	9	50
8. CHN	1	6	14	60

Final: KOR 3-2 CUB
3rd Place: USA 8-4 JPN

1. KOR—Bong Jung-keun, Jeong Dae-hyeon, Han Gi-ju, Jang Won-sam, Jeong Geun-u, Jin Gab-yong, Gang Min-ho, Kim Dong-ju, Kim Hyeon-su, Kim Gwang-hyeon, Kim Min-jae, Go Yeong-min, Gwon Hyeok, Lee Dae-ho, Lee Jin-yeong, Lee Jong-uk, Lee Seung-yeop, Lee Taek-geun, Lee Yong-kyu, O Seung-hwan, Park Jin-man, Ryu Hyeon-jin, Song Seung-jun, Yoon Suk-min
2. CUB—Alexei Bell Quintero, Frederich Cepeda Cruz, Alfredo Despaigne Rodríguez, Giorvis Duvergel Rojas, Michel Enríquez Tamayo, Norberto González Miranda, Yulieski Gourriel Castillo, Miguel La Hera Betancourt, Pedro Luis Lazo Iglesias, Alexander Mayeta Kerr, Jonder Martínez Martínez, Rolando Meriño Betancourt, Luis Miguel Navas González, Vicyohandri Odelín Sanamé, Héctor Olivera Amaro, Adiel Palma López, Eduardo Paret Pérez, Yadier Pedroso González, Ariel Pestano Valdez, Luis Miguel Rodríguez Ricardo, Elier Sánchez Quesada, Eriel Sánchez Leon, Yoandri Urgellés Cobas, Norge Luis Vera Peralta
3. USA—Brett Anderson, Jacob Arrieta, Brian Barden, Matthew Brown, Trevor Cahill, Jeremy Cummings, Jason Donald, Brian Duensing, W. Dexter Fowler, John Gall, Michael Hessman, Kevin Jepsen, Brandon Knight, Michael Koplove, Matthew LaPorta, Louis Marson, Blaine Neal, Jayson Nix, Nathan Schierholtz, Jeffrey Stevens, Stephen Strasburg, Taylor Teagarden, Terry Tiffee, Casey Weathers
4. JPN—Shinnosuke Abe, Norichika Aoki, Takahiro Arai, Masahiro Araki, Yu Darvish, Kyuji Fujikawa, Atsunori Inaba, Hitoki Iwase, Kenshin Kawakami, Munenori Kawasaki, Shinya Miyamoto, Masahiko Morino, Shuichi Murata, Hiroyuki Nakajima, Yoshihisa Naruse, Tsuyoshi Nishioka, Takahiko Sato, Tomoya Satozaki, Toshiya Sugiuchi, Masahiro Tanaka, Koji Uehara, Tsuyoshi Wada, Hideaki Wakui, Akihiro Yano

5. TAI—Chang Chien-ming, Chang Chih-chia, Chen Chin-feng, Chen Feng-min, Chen Wei-yin, Kao Chih-kang, Chiang Chih-hsien, Hsu Wen-hsiung, Cheng Kai-wen, Kuo Yen-wen, Lee Chen-chang, Lin Che-hsuan, Lin Chih-sheng, Lo Chia-jen, Lo Kuo-hui, Ni Fu-te, Pan Wei-lun, Pan Wu-hsiung, Peng Cheng-min, Shih Chih-wei, Tsao Chin-hui, Yang Chien-fu, Yeh Chun-chang
6. CAN—James Avery, Christopher Begg, Timothy "T. J." Burton, Richard "Stubby" Clapp, Rhéal Cormier, David Corrente, David Davidson, Emerson Frostad, Emmanuel Garcia, Steve Green, Michael Johnson, Brett Lawrie, Jonathan Lockwood, Brooks McNiven, Ryan Radmanovich, Christopher Reitsma, Christopher Robinson, Matthew Rogelstad, Michael Saunders, Adam Stern, Robert "R.J." Swindle, Scott Thorman, James Van Ostrand, Nicholas Weglarz
7. HOL—Sharnol Adriana, David Bergman, Leon Boyd, Robbie Cordemans, Yurendell de Caster, Sidney de Jong, Dorotheus "Dave" Draijer, Michael Duursma, Bryan Engelhardt, Percy Isenia, Eugene Kingsale, Roel Koolen, Reily Legito, Diego Markwell, Shairon Martis, Martijn Meeuwis, Danny Rombley, Jeroen Sluijter, Tjerk Smeets, Alexander Smit, Juan-Carlos Sulbaran, Michiel van Kampen, Dirk van 't Klooster, Pim Walsma
8. CHN—Bu Tao, Chen Junyi, Chen Kun, Feng Fei, Guo Youhua, Hou Fenglian, Jia Delong, Jia Yubing, Li Chenhao, Li Lei, Li Weiliang, Liu Kai, Lu Jiangang, Sun Guoqiang, Sun Lingfeng, Sun Wei, Wang Chao, Wang Nan, Wang Wei, Xu Zheng, Yang Yang, Zhang Hongbo, Zhang Li, Zhang Yufeng

The Cuban team, three-time Olympic champions, had been sapped by defections and was no longer the overwhelming favorite. After winning the 2005 World Cup they lost to Japan in the final of the inaugural World Baseball Classic in 2006 and were beaten by the US at the 2007 Baseball World Cup, the first time Cuba had lost the Cup since 1984.

Despite the attention lavished on the big three—Cuba, the United States and Japan—the real star of the round-robin stage was the unheralded South Korean squad. The Koreans opened with an 8-7 victory against the US and 1-0 shutouts of China and Canada. Then, facing longtime rival Japan, South Korea came from two runs down in the bottom of the sixth inning to score on a two-run shot by Lee Dae-ho in the seventh inning and went on to win 5-3. The team wrapped up pool play with a 9-8 win over Taiwan, a 7-4 defeat of Cuba, and finally a 10-0 rout of the Netherlands, making it through the round-robin undefeated.

Cuba finished second in the round-robin, having lost only to South Korea. The Cubans beat Japan 4-2 and the US 5-4. After their painful loss to the Koreans, they pulverized China 17-1, with Giorvis Duvergel hitting the first grand slam home run of the tournament.

Japan and the US faced each other in the last game of the round-robin stage. Both already assured of reaching the semifinals, the two teams battled through 10 scoreless innings until the US pulled ahead to win 4-2, thanks to a new Olympic tie-breaker system in which play began with runners on first and second base with no outs starting in the 11th inning.

South Korea faced Japan again in the semifinals. Korean slugger Lee Seung-yeop broke a 2-2 tie in the bottom of the eighth with a two-run home run, and the Koreans added two more runs in the same inning to close out the game 6-2.

The US–Cuba semifinal remained close through the first seven innings. Up 3-2, Cuba blew open the game in the bottom of the eighth with two three-run home runs, one from catcher Ariel Pestano and the other from outfielder Alexei Bell, crushing the US 10-2 to reach the final.

Japan took a 4-1 lead in the bronze medal match, before the US came back to tie 4-4 in the bottom of the third inning. The US took control of the game in the bottom of the fifth, with catcher Tayler Teagarden hitting a two-run double that was followed by a two-run homer from shortstop Jason Donald to give the US an 8-4 victory.

In the final, South Korea opened the scoring in the first inning with a two-out two-run home run by Lee Seung-yeop. Cuba responded with a homer by Michel Enríquez in the bottom of the first. The score stayed 2-1 until the seventh inning, when rightfielder Lee Yong-kyu added an RBI (runs batted in) double to put the Koreans up 3-1. Cuba's Bell cut the lead to 3-2 with a solo homer in the seventh. With two strikes and the bases loaded in the bottom of the ninth, Cuba's Yulieski Gourriel hit a ground ball to shortstop Park Jin-man, who started a 6-4-3 double play to end the inning and clinch the Olympic title.

"A few days ago I had a dream of giving interviews to news reporters naked," South Korean coach Kim Kyung-moon said after the game. " I wasn't sure if it was a good omen or a bad one. Now, I guess I have to credit the dream for bringing me the gold."

CRICKET

1900 Paris T: 2, N: 2, D: 8.20.

1. GBR—C.B.K. Beachcroft, John Symes, Frederick Cuming, Montagu Toller, Alfred Bowerman, Alfred Powlesland, William Donne, Frederick Christian, George Buckley, Francis Burchell, Harry Corner, Arthur Birkett
2. FRA—T.H. Jordan, A.J. Schneidau, R. Horne, Henry Terry, F. Rogues, W. Anderson, D. Robinson, W.T. Attrill, W. Browning, Arthur McEvoy, Philip Tomalin, J. Braid

Final: GBR 117 & 145/5—78 & 26 FRA

Great Britain was represented by the Devon and Somerset Wanderers Cricket Club, France by a team made up of players from the British embassy in Paris. According to a contemporary French magazine, "Cricket is . . . a sport which appears monotonous and without color to the uninitiated." On the other hand, a British report observed that, "We found the French temperament is too excitable to enjoy the game and no Frenchman can be persuaded to play more than once." The French innings of 26 remains the lowest score made by any team in an international match of two innings, equaled only by New Zealand against England in 1955. Toller dismissed seven French batsmen in the second innings, while conceding only nine runs.

CROQUET

1900 Paris

Singles—1 Ball C: 9, N: 2, D: 6.28.

1. Aumoitte	FRA
2. John	FRA
3. Waydelich	FRA
4. Blachère	FRA
5. Desprès	FRA

Final: Aumoitte 21-15 John

Singles—2 Balls C: 6?, N: 1, D: 7.11.

1. Waydelich	FRA
2. Vignerot	FRA
3. Sautereau	FRA

Doubles T: ?, N: ?, D : 6.18?

1. FRA (John, Aumoitte)

The 1900 croquet tournament was noteworthy for the participation of three women: Madame Després, the wife of the tournament's organizer, Madame Filleaul Brohy and Maidemoiselle Marie Ohnier. The Official Report of the Paris Games used their inclusion as part of its defense of croquet as a sport. "This game," it explained, "French in name and origin . . . has hardly any pretensions to athleticism . . . One would be wrong, however, to disdain croquet. It develops a combinative mind—one has only to see it transform young girls into reasoners and from reasoners into reasonable people."

The events were not well-attended. There was apparently one paying spectator: an English gentleman who travelled to Paris from Nice to watch the early rounds.

GOLF

1900 Paris-Compiègne C: 12, N: 3, D: 10.2.

Men

		SHOTS
1. Charles Sands	USA	167
2. Walter Rutherford	GBR	168
3. David Robertson	GBR	175
4. Frederick Taylor	USA	182
5. H.E. Daunt	FRA	184
6. George Thorne	GBR	185
7. William Dove	GBR	186
8. Albert Lambert	USA	189

Charles Sands also took part in the 1900 tennis competition. He returned to the Olympics in 1908 as a participant in the jeu de paume tournament. Albert Lambert, who placed eighth in Paris, was the primary financial supporter of Charles Lindbergh's 1927 trans-Atlantic flight. The international airport in St. Louis is named after Lambert.

1900 Paris-Compiègne C: 10, N: 2, D: 10.3

Women

		SHOTS
1. Margaret Abbott	USA	47
2. Pauline "Polly" Whittier	USA	49
3. Daria Pratt	USA	53
4. Froment-Meurice	FRA	56
5. Ellen Ridgeway	USA	57
6. Fournier-Salovèze	FRA	58
7. Mary Abbott	USA	65
7. Baronne Fain	FRA	65

Margaret Abbott was the first US woman to win an Olympic gold medal. A 5-foot 11-inch, 22-year-old Chicago socialite, she traveled to Paris in 1899 with her mother, literary editor and novelist Mary Ives Abbott, so that she could study art. Ten women took part in the final nine-hole round of the ladies' golf competition. Abbott later told relatives that she won the tournament "because all the French girls apparently misunderstood the nature of the game scheduled for that day and turned up to play in high heels and tight skirts." Two years later Margaret Abbott, by then a resident of New York City, married political satirist Finley Peter Dunne. She died in 1955, unaware that the tournament she had won was a part of the Olympics.

1904 St. Louis C: 75, N: 2, D: 9.24.

Men

1. George Lyon	CAN	3 and 2
2. H. Chandler Egan	USA	
3. Burt McKinnie	USA	
3. Francis Newton	USA	

5. Harry Allen (USA), Albert Lambert (USA), Mason Phelps (USA), Daniel "Ned" Sawyer (USA)

George Lyon was an eccentric athlete who didn't pick up a golf club until he was 38 years old. Before that he had competed successfully in baseball, tennis, and cricket. Once, in 1876, he even set a Canadian record in the pole vault and in 1894 he made 234 runs at cricket before going out. Lyon was 46 when he traveled down from Toronto to take part in the Olympics. He caused

George Lyon, 1904
Lyon, winner of the 1904 golf event, keeping his ball on the eye.

quite a stir when he played in St. Louis because of his unorthodox swing. He wielded the club more like a cricket bat, provoking some newspapers to criticize his "coal-heaver's swing." On the course he was an endless source of cheerful energy, singing, telling jokes and even doing handstands. A 36-hole qualifying round reduced the field from 75 to 32. The survivors then engaged in a match play elimination tournament. In the semifinals Lyon defeated Francis Newton, the Pacific Coast champion, on the last of 36 holes. His final match was a surprise victory over the 23-year-old US champion, Chandler Egan. Lyon was awarded a $1500 sterling silver trophy, which he accepted after walking down the path to the ceremony on his hands. In 1908 George Lyon traveled to England to compete in the London Olympics. However, an internal dispute among British golfers caused them to boycott the games, leaving Lyon as the only entrant. Offered the gold medal by default, he refused it. Lyon was still winning championships twenty years later and shot his age for 18 holes from 64 years old until he was 78 years old. He died the following year.

1904 St. Louis T: 3, N: 1, D: 9.17.
Teams

	SHOTS
1. USA—Western Golf Association: H. Chandler Egan, Daniel "Ned" Sawyer, Robert Hunter, Kenneth Edwards, Clement Smoot, Warren Wood, Mason Phelps, Walter Egan, Edward "Ned" Cummins, Nathaniel Moore	1749
2. USA—Trans Mississippi Golf Association: Francis Newton, Henry Potter, Ralph McKittrick, Albert Lambert, Frederick Semple, Stuart Stickney, William Stickney, Burt McKinnie, John Maxwell, John Cady	1770
3. USA—United States Golf Association: Douglas Cadwalader, Allen Lard, Jesse Carleton, Simeon Price, Harold Weber, John Rahm, Arthur Hussey, Orus Jones, Harold Fraser, George Oliver	1839

JEU DE PAUME

Jeu de Paume, also known as "court tennis" or "real tennis," was the forerunner of modern-day tennis.

1908 London C: 11, N: 2, D: 5.28.

1. Jay Gould	USA	6-5, 6-4, 6-4
2. Eustace Miles	GBR	
3. Neville Lytton	GBR	6-2, 6-4, 6-4
4. Arthur Page	GBR	
5. Evan Noel	GBR	
5. Vane Pennell	GBR	

Although Gould, the son of the famous robber baron, won the final in straight sets, he came from behind in each set.

LACROSSE

1904 St. Louis T: 3, N: 2, D: 7.7.

1. CAN—Shamrock Lacrosse Team, Winnipeg, Manitoba: George Cloutier, George Cattanach, Benjamin Jamieson, Jack Flett, George Bretz, Eli Blanchard, Hilliard Laidlaw, H. Lyle, W. Brennaugh, L.H. Pentland, Sandy Cowan, William Laurie Burns
2. USA—St. Louis Amateur Athletic Association, St. Louis, Missouri: Hunter, Patrick Grogan, George Passmore, William Passmore, J.W. Dowling, A.H. Venn, Sullivan, Murphy, Gibson, Woods, Partridge, Ross
3. CAN—Mohawk Indians, Brantford, Ontario: Black Hawk, Black Eagle, Almighty Voice, Flat Iron, Spotted Tail, Half Moon, Lightfoot, Snake Eater, Red Jacket, Night Hawk, Rain in Face, Man Afraid Soap

Final: Shamrock 6-1 St. Louis; Shamrock 8-2 St. Louis

1906 not held

1908 London T: 2, N: 2, D: 10.24.

1. CAN—Frank Dixon, George "Doc" Campbell, Angus Dillon, Richard Duckett, George Rennie, Clarence McKerrow, Alexander Turnbull, Henry Hoobin, Ernest Hamilton, John Broderick, Thomas Gorman, Patrick "Paddy" Brennan
2. GBR—Charles Scott, G. Mason, H.W. Ramsay, E.O. Dutton, J. Parker-Smith, Wilfrid Johnson, Norman Whitley, George Buckland, S.N. Hayes, Gustav Alexander, R.G.W. Martin, Edward Jones

Final: CAN 14-10 GBR

Good sportsmanship was the order of the day in the lacrosse competition. When Angus Dillon of Canada broke his stick, R.G.W. Martin of Great Britain offered to withdraw from the game until a new one could be found. The contest was tied at 9-9 when the Canadians scored five straight goals to clinch the victory.

MOTOR BOATING

1908 London T: 2, N: 1, D: 8.29.
8-Meter class, 40 Nautical Miles

1. GBR	I. Thomas Thornycroft, Bernard Redwood, John Field-Richards	2:28:26

DNF: GBR (Warwick Wright, Thomas Wynn Weston)

1908 London T: 2, N: 1, D: 8.28.
Under 60-Foot class, 40 Nautical Miles

1. GBR	I. Thomas Thornycroft, Bernard Redwood, John Field-Richards	2:28:58

DNF: GBR (John Gorham, Mrs. John Gorham)

Forty-four years after his victories at the 1908 Olympics, Thornycroft was selected as an alternate for the 1952 British yachting team. He traveled to Helsinki, but did not compete. He was 70 years old at the time.

1908 London T: 3, N: 2, D: 8.29.
Open class, 40 Nautical Miles

1. FRA	Émile Thubron	2:26:53

DNF: GBR (Duke of Westminster, Winchester St. George Clowes, Joseph Laycock, George Atkinson)

PELOTA BASQUE

1900 Paris T: 2, N: 2, D: 6.14.

1. SPA	Villota/Amezola
2. FRA	Maurice Durquetty/Etchegaray

Pelota reappeared as a demonstration sport at the 1968 and 1992 Olympics.

POLO

1900 Paris T: 4, N: 5, D: 6.2.

1. GBR & USA & GBR/IRL—Foxhunters Hurlingham: Alfred Rawlinson, Frank Mackay, Foxhall Keene, Denis Daly, John Beresford
2. GBR & USA & SPA—Rugby: Walter McCreery, Frederick Freake, Walter Buckmaster, José de Madre
3. FRA & GBR—Bagatelle Paris: Maurice Raoul-Duval, Frederick Gill, Robert Fournier-Sarlovèze, Edouard Alphonse de Rothschild
3. MEX—Guillermo Hayden Wright, Eustaquio de Escandón y Barrón, Pablo de Escandón y Barrón, Manuel de Escandón y Barrón

Final: Foxhunters 3-1 Rugby

1904–1906 not held

1908 London T: 3, N: 1, D: 6.21.

1. GBR—Roehampton: Charles Miller, Patteson Nickalls, George Miller, Herbert Wilson
2. GBR—Hurlingham: John Wodehouse, Walter Buckmaster, Frederick Freake, Walter Jones
2. GBR/IRL—Ireland: Percy O'Reilly, John Hardress Lloyd, John McCann, Auston Rotherham

Scores: Roehampton 4-1 Hurlingham
Roehampton 8-1 Ireland

1912 not held

1920 Antwerp-Ostende T: 4, N: 4, D: 7.31.

	W	L	PF	PA
1. GBR & GBR/IRL	2	0	21	14
2. SPA	1	1	24	16
3. USA	1	1	14	16
4. BEL	0	2	6	19

1. GBR & GBR/IRL—Teignmouth "Timothy" Melvill, Frederick Barrett, John Wodehouse, Vivian Lockett
2. SPA—Leopoldo Sáinz de la Maza y Gutiérrez-Solano, Jacobo Fitz-James Stuart y Falcó, Alvaro de Figueroa y Alonso-Martínez, Hernando Fitz-James Stuart y Falcó
3. USA—Arthur Harris, Terry Allen, John Montgomery, Nelson Margetts
4. BEL—Alfred Grisar, Maurice Lysen, Clement van der Straten, Gaston Peers de Nieuwburgh

Final: GBR 13-11 SPA

1924 Paris T: 5, N: 5, D: 7.12.

	W	L	PF	PA
1. ARG	4	0	46	14
2. USA	3	1	43	11
3. GBR	2	2	33	24
4. SPA	1	3	22	42
5. FRA	0	4	6	59

1. ARG—Arturo Kenny, Jack Nelson, Enrique Padilla, Juan Miles, Guillermo Brooke Naylor
2. USA—Elmer Boeseke, Thomas Hitchcock, Frederick Roe, Rodman Wanamaker
3. GBR—Frederick Guest, Frederick Barrett, Dennis Bingham, Percival Wise
4. SPA—Leopoldo Sáinz de la Maza y Gutiérrez-Solano, Justo San Miguel y de la Gandara, Luis de Figueroa y Alonso-Martínez, Rafael Henestrosa, Hernando Fitz-James Stuart y Falcó
5. FRA—Charles de Polignac, Pierre de Jumilhac, Jules Macaire, Hubert de Monbrison, Jean Pastra

The decisive match was the one between Argentina and the United States. Jack Nelson was the hero of the game, scoring a goal in the closing seconds of the seventh and final chukker to give Argentina a surprise 6-5 victory.

1928–1932 not held

1936 Berlin T: 5, N: 5, D: 7.8.

	W	L	T	PF	PA
1. ARG—Luis Duggan, Roberto Cavanagh, Andrés Gazzotti, Manuel Andrada	2	0	0	26	5
2. GBR—Bryan Fowler, William Hinde, David Dawnay, Humphrey Guinness	1	1	0	13	22
3. MEX—Juan García Zazueta, Antonio Nava Castillo, Julio Muller Luján, Aberto Ramos Sesma	1	2	0	32	30
4. HUN—Tivadar Dienes-Ohm, Imre Szentpály, Dezső Kovács, István Bethlen, Kálmán Bartalis	1	1	1	26	30
5. GER—Heinrich Amsinck, Walter Bartram, Miles Reincke, Arthur Köser	0	1	1	14	24

Final: ARG 11-0 GBR **3rd Place:** MEX 16-2 HUN

Hungary and Germany were so outclassed that they weren't even included in the competition for first or second place. Instead, the tournament was arranged so that they played for the right to play for the bronze medal against the loser among the other three teams. Over 45,000 people watched Argentina's final victory over Great Britain.

RACKETS

Rackets was a precursor of the modern sport of squash.

1908 London C: 6, N: 1, D: 5.1.
Men's Singles

1. GBR	Evan Noel
2. GBR	Henry Leaf
3. GBR	John Jacob Astor
3. GBR	Henry Brougham

Final: Noel—Leaf WO

Leaf had to withdraw from the final because he had injured his hand in the doubles competition.

1908 London T: 3, N: 1, D: 5.1.
Men's Doubles

1. GBR	Vane Pennell/John Jacob Astor
2. GBR	Edmund Bury/Cecil Browning
3. GBR	Evan Noel/Henry Leaf

Final: Pennell/Astor—Bury/Browning, 6-15,15-7,16-15, 15-6, 15-7

RUGBY

1900 Paris T: 3, N: 3, D: 10.28.

	W	L	PF	PA
1. FRA	2	0	54	25
2. GBR	0	1	8	27
2. GER	0	1	17	27

1. FRA—Alexandre Pharamond, Frantz Reichel, Jean Collas, Constantin Henriquez de Zubiera, Auguste Giroux, André Rischmann, Leon Binoche, A. Albert, Charles Gondouin, Hubert Lefebvre, Émile Sarrade, Vladimir Aitoff, Joseph Olivier, Jean-Guy Gautier, Victor Larchandat, Jean Hervé, Albert Roosevelt
2. GBR—H.A. Loveitt, Raymond Whittindale, Herbert Nicol, Claude Whittindale, L. Hood, J. Henry Birtles, James Cantion, Clement Deykin, Joseph Wallis, V. Smith, M.L. Logan, F.C. Baylis, M.W. Talbott, Francis Wilson, Arthur Darby
2. GER—Hermann Kreuzer, Arnold Landvoigt, Heinrich Reitz, Jacob Herrmann, Erich Ludwig, Hugo Betting, August Schmierer, Fritz Müller, Adolt Stockhausen, Hans Latscha, Willy Hofmeister, Georg Wenderoth, Eduard Poppe, Richard Ludwig, Albert Amrheim

The match between France and England on October 28 was attended by 6000 spectators, 4389 of them paying. This was the largest crowd at any event of the 1900 Olympics. France, which had beaten Germany 27-17, defeated the British team 27-8. The British were represented by the Moseley Wanderers, who arrived in Paris the morning of the match and left that evening. It would appear that Constantin Henriquez de Zubiera of the French team was the first black athlete to compete at the Olympics. Three months earlier he had taken part in the tug-of-war.

1904–1906 not held

1908 London T: 2, N: 2, D: 10.26.

1. AUS—F. Bede Smith, Phillip Carmichael, Charles Russell, Daniel Carroll, John "Darb" Hickey, Francis Bede-Smith, Christopher McKiviat, Arthur McCabe, Thomas Griffen, John "Towser" Barnett, Patrick McCue, Sydney Middleton, Thomas Richards, Malcolm "Mannie" McArthur, Charles McMurtrie, Robert Craig
2. GBR—Edward Jackett, John "Barney" Solomon, Bertram Solomon, L.F. Dean, J.T. Jose, Thomas Wedge, James "Maffer" Davey, Richard Jackett, E.J. Jones, Arthur Wilson, Nicholas Tregurtha, A. Lawry, C.R. Marshall, A. Wilcocks, John Trevaskis

Final: AUS 32-3 GBR

1912 not held

1920 Antwerp T: 2, N: 2, D: 9.5.

1. USA—Daniel Carroll, Charles Doe, George Fish, James Fitzpatrick, Joseph Hunter, Morris Kirksey, Charles Mehan, John Muldoon, John O'Neil, John Patrick, Cornelius Righter, Rudolph Scholz, Richard "Dink" Templeton, Charles Tilden, Heaton Wrenn,
2. FRA—Andre Chilo, Grenet, François Bordes, René Crabos, Edouard Bader, Raoul Thiercelin, Curtet, Jacques Forestier, Maurice Labeyrie, Alfred Eluère, Robert Levasseur, Adolphe Bousquel, Jean Bruneval, Casteix, Maurice Petiteau

Final: USA 8-0 FRA

The US team included Morris Kirksey, who also won a silver medal in the 100-meter dash and a gold in the 4 × 100-meter relay, and Dink Templeton, who later became a famous track coach. Another American player was Daniel Carroll, who had been a member of the victorious Australian squad 12 years earlier. He is one of only two people in any sport to win gold medals while representing different countries (the other is weightlifter Akakide Kakhiashvili.)

1924 Paris T: 3, N: 3, D: 5.18.

	W	L	PF	PA
1. USA	2	0	54	3
2. FRA	1	1	64	20
3. ROM	0	2	3	98

1. USA—Philip Clark, Norman Cleveland, Hugh Cunningham, Dudley De Groot, Robert Devereaux, George Dixon, Charles Doe, Linn Farrish, Edward Graff, Richard Hyland, Caesar Manelli, John ONeil, John Patrick, William Rogers, Rudolph Scholz, Colby Slater, Norman Slater, Edward Turkington, Alan Valentine, Alan Williams
2. FRA—René Araou, Jean Bayard, Louis Beguet, André Béhotéguy, Alexandre Bioussa, Etienne Bonnes, René Bousquet, Aimé Cassayet, Clément Dupont, Albert Dupouy, Jean Etchberry, Henri Galau, Gilbert Gerintes, Raoul Got, Adolphe Jauréguy, René Lasserre, Marcel Frédéric Lubin-Lebrère, Etienne Piquirai, Jean Vaysse
3. ROM—Dumitru Armăşel, Sorin Mihălhescu, Paul Nedelcovici, Teodor Marian, Mihai Vardala, Sterian Soare, Iosif Nemeş Anastasie Tănălsescu, Dumitru Volvoreanu, Paul Vidraşcu, Mărăscu Nicolae, Mircea Sfetescu, Gheorghe Benția, Teodor Florian, Ion Gîrleşteanu, Eugen Sfetescu

Almost 40,000 French spectators watched in horror as their team was thrashed 17-3 by the upstart Americans. After two French players were injured, the US team was booed and hissed for the remainder of the game. Fighting broke out in the stands, and Gideon Nelson, an art student from De Kalb, Illinois, was knocked unconscious after being hit in the face with a walking stick. At the awards ceremony "The Star-Spangled Banner" was drowned out by the booing of the crowd, and the US team had to be escorted from the field under police protection.

SOFTBALL

1996 Atlanta-Columbus T: 8, N: 8, D: 7.30.

	W	L	RF	RA
1. USA	8	1	41	8
2. CHN	6	4	34	13
3. AUS	6	3	27	15
4. JPN	5	3	24	21
5. CAN	3	4	15	17
6. TAI	2	5	19	19
7. HOL	1	6	4	32
8. PUR	1	6	5	44

Final: USA 3-1 CHN

1. USA—Laura Berg, Gillian Boxx, Sheila Cornell, Lisa Fernandez, Michele Granger, Lori Harrigan, Dionna Harris, Kim Maher, Leah O'Brien, Dorothy "Dot" Richardson, Julie Smith, Michele Smith, Shelly Stokes, Dani Tyler, Christa Williams
2. CHN—An Zhongxin, Chen Hong, He Liping, Lei Li, Liu Xuqing, Liu Yaju, Ma Ying, Ou Jingbai, Tao Hua, Wang Lihong, Wang Ying, Wei Qiang, Xu Jian, Yan Fang, Zhang Chungfang
3. AUS—Joanne Brown, Kim Cooper, Carolyn Crudgington, Kerry Dienelt, Peta Edebone, Tanya Harding, Jennifer Holliday, Jocelyn Lester, Sally McDermid, Francine McRae, Haylea Petrie, Nicole Richardson, Melanie Roche, Natalie Ward, Brooke Wilkins
4. JPN—Misako Ando, Yoshiko Fujimoto, Ikuko Fukita, Noriko Harada, Mayumi Inoue, Kyoko Kobayashi, Chika Kodama, Naomi Matsumoto, Kyoko Mochida, Haruka Saito, Juri Takayama, Emi Tsukada, Masako Watanabe, Tomoko Watanabe, Noriko Yamaji
5. CAN—Sandra Beasley, Juanita Clayton, Karen Doell, Carrie Flemmer, Kelly Kelland, Kara McGaw, Pauline Maurice, Candace Murray, Christine Parris-Washington, Lori Sippel, Karen Snelgrove, Debbie Sonnenberg, Alecia Stephenson, Colleen Thorburn, Carmelina Vairo
6. TAI—Chang Nsiao-ching, Chien Chen-ju, Chien Pei-chi, Chiu Chen-ting, Chung Chiung-yao, Han Hsin-lin, Lee Ming-chieh, Liu Chia-chi, Liu Tzu-hsin, Ou Ching-chieh, Tu Hui-mei, Tu Hui-ping, Wang Ya-fen, Yang Hui-chen, Yen Show-tzu
7. HOL—Jacqueline de Heer, Marjolein de Jong, Penny le Noble, Maria van der Putten, Madelon Beek, Petra Beek, Luciene Geels, Jacqueline Knol, Anita Kossen, Anouk Mels, Sandra Nieuwveen, Corrine Ockhuysen, Sonja Pannen, Gerardina Reijnen, Martine Stiemer
8. PUR—Lourdes Baez, Sheree Corniel, Ivelisse Echevarría, María González, Elba Lebron, Lisa Martínez, Aida Miranda, Lisa Mize, Jacqueline Ortíz, Janice Parks, Penelope Rosario, Sandra Rosario, Myriam Segarra, Eve Soto, Clara Vázquez

Beginning in 1986, the US softball team won 106 straight games in international competition. That streak ended August 4, 1995, in a preliminary game at the Superball Classic in what would soon be the Olympic venue in Columbus, Georgia, when Tao Hua of China hit a solo home run in the top of the ninth inning and relief pitcher Wang Lihong shut down a US threat in the bottom of the ninth. The US beat China in the gold medal match 8-0 and another streak began.

At the Olympics, the US won its first five games and then faced Australia in the penultimate round of the preliminary round-robin. In the fifth inning, Dani Tyler of the United States hit a bases empty home run that should have given the US a 1-0 lead. But in her excitement, she looked up to celebrate with her teammates—and missed touching home plate. The Australians caught the blunder immediately and Tyler was called out. It was a mistake that would ultimately cost the US the game.

Meanwhile, US pitcher Lisa Fernandez was throwing a perfect game. With two outs in the bottom of the tenth, the US was leading 1-0 on an unearned run in the top of the inning. Fernandez had retired 29 batters in a row, 15 on strikeouts. The Australians had yet to hit a ball out of the infield. Fernandez faced her former UCLA teammate Joanne Brown. Fernandez fired two straight strikes and was one pitch away from a perfect game victory. But that pitch turned into a home run by Brown over the center-field fence. If this had been a baseball game, play would have continued with the score tied 1-1. But this was softball, so, according to the rules, Australia began the inning with a player on second base. Final score: 2-1 Australia. Not only had the US been beaten for only the second time in ten years, but Lisa Fernandez had the bizarre experience of losing a game in which one of her teammates hit a home run and she retired all but one batter.

In their last game of the preliminary round, the US beat China 3-2 when Sheila Cornell hit a two-run home run off Wang Lihong. They faced the Chinese again in the semifinals and again Cornell connected with the winning hit against Wang, this time a base-loaded single in the bottom of the tenth inning for a 1-0 victory.

The next day, in sweltering heat, China beat Australia 4-2 to qualify for the final, which started only a half hour later. Because of the bizarre format of the softball tournament, the Chinese found themselves playing three games in 27½ hours and playing the United States for the third time in four days. The critical events of the final took place in the third inning. In the top of the inning, with the score 0-0 and runners on first and third, the Chinese tried a double steal. Zhang Chunfang appeared to be safe at home plate, but Canadian umpire Lucy Carmichael ruled otherwise. Chinese coach Li Minkuan contained his anger at the bad call. In the bottom of the third, with one runner on, Dot Richardson, a 34-year-old orthopedic surgeon, sliced the ball down the right field line and into the stands. It landed foul, but right-field umpire Geralyn Lindberg of Sweden ruled that it passed inside the foul pole before twisting foul. Home run: 2-0 United States. This was too much for coach Li and the Chinese, who protested for ten minutes before play was resumed. The Xinhua News Agency expressed the general Chinese consensus by writing, "a woman umpire with a helmet stole the limelight by ruling fair a clear outside hit." Xinhua also complained that "with no time even to relax from the earlier two-hour competition, the Chinese women were forced to challenge the United States in front of the partisan crowd in the remote venue." Valid as some of the Chinese complaints may have been, television replays clearly showed that Richardson's ball did pass inside the foul line and that Lindberg's home run call was correct. The US went on to win 3-1.

2000 Sydney T: 8, N: 8, D: 9.26.

	W	L	RF	RA
1. USA	7	3	25	7
2. JPN	8	1	20	9
3. AUS	6	3	22	7
4. CHI	5	3	26	7
5. ITA	2	5	3	27
6. NZL	2	5	12	22
7. CUB	1	6	6	30
8. CAN	1	6	13	18

Final: USA 2-1JPN

1. USA—Dorothy "Dot" Richardson, Laura Berg, Lisa Fernandez, Crystl Bustos, Sheila Douty, Jennifer McFalls, Jennifer Brundage, Stacey Nuveman, Leah O'Brien-Amico, Christine Ambrosi, Lori Harrigan, Danielle Henderson, Christa Williams, Michelle Venturella, Michele Smith
2. JPN—Hiroko Tamoto, Yosdhimi Kobayashi, Emi Naito, Misako Ando, Naomi Matsumoto, Yumiko Fujii, Taeko Ishikawa, Juri Takayama, Kazue Ito, Mariko Masubuchi, Shiori Koseki, Noriko Yamaji, Haruka Saito, Miyo Yamada, Reika Utsugi
3. AUS—Melanie Roche, Natalie Ward, Tanya Harding, Sandra Allen, Joanne Brown, Brooke Wilkins, Peta Edebone, Kerry Dienelt, Sally McDermid-McCreedy, Selina Follas, Natallie Titcume, Kelly Hardie, Fiona Hanes, Simmone Morrow, Sue Fairhurst
4. CHI—Xu Jian, Yu Yanjong, Zhang Chunfang, Deng Xiaoling, Zhou Yan, Yan Fang, Wang Ying, Qiu Haitao, An Zhongxin, Mu Xia, Wei Qiang, Wang Lihong, Zhang Yanqing, Qin Xuejing, Tao Hua
5. ITA—Verusca Patemoster, Giovanna Palermi, Jie Hun, Cleilia Ailara, Sabrina Combernato, Marta Gambella, Daniela Castellani, Claudia Petracchi, Susan Bugliarello, Loredana Auletta, Jue-Fen Sun, Francesca Francolini, Alessandra Gorla, Nicole Di Salvio, Marina Cergol
6. NZL—Char Pouaka, Cindy Potae, Fiona Timu, Gina Weber, Helen Townsend, Jackie Smith, Jaye Bailey, Kim Dermott, Kiri Shaw, Lisa Kersten, Melanie Hulme, Melisa Upu, Rhonda Hira, Ruta Lealamanua, Zavana Aranga
7. CUB—Diamela Puente, Estela Milañes, Haydee Hernández, Laritza Espinosa, Luisa Medina, Maria Arceco, María Santana, María Zamora, Niolis Ramos, Olga Ruyol, Vilma Alvarez, Yamila Degrase Yamila Flor, Yarisleidis Peña, Yuneisy Castillo
8. CAN—Cherene Hiestl-Boyer, Colleen Thorbum Smith, Denise Carriere, Erin Woods, Heather Newsham, Jacki Nichol, Jackie Lance, Lesley Attwell, Nathalie Fradette, Sommer West, Vicky Bastarache, Hayley Wickenheiser, Kristy Odamura, Meggan Wilton, Sandy Newsham

The US women arrived at the Olympics with a 110–game winning streak over the past two years. They won their first two games easily, but in their third game against Japan they lost their aura of invulnerability. The game was tied 0-0 after 10 innings. In the top of the 11th, the US committed three errors, including two by Dot Richardson, and the Japanese capitalized by scoring two runs. In the bottom of the inning, the US managed one run, but with a runner on third and one out, the game ended with two called strikeouts. The Americans had left on a base a record-setting 20 runners. The next night, the Americans faced China . . . and lost 2-0 in the 14th inning. It was the first time in 17 years that a USA softball team had lost two games in a row. Stunned, the Americans moved on the next day to play Australia. For the third straight time, the game went into extra innings with the scored tied 0-0. The US scored one run in the top of the 13th inning, but with two outs in the bottom of the inning, Lisa Fernandez, who had struck out 25 batters, gave up a two-run home run to Peta Edebone. Faced with the unexpected reality of a three-game losing streak, the Americans met and decided that what they needed was a five-game winning streak. They defeated New Zealand and Italy and reached the medal round by ending up in fourth place in pool play.

The US began their shot at redemption against China. Once again, the game went into extra innings tied 0-0. In the bottom of the 10th, with one out, Stacey Newman hit a three-run home run to win the game. Next came the Australians. Dot Richardson drove in a run in the fifth inning and Lisa Fernandez pitched a one-hitter to preserve the victory. And so the Americans made it to the final, their third game in 33 hours. Japan opened the scoring with a fourth-inning line drive home run by Reika Utsugi. In the bottom of the fifth, Stacey Newman singled in a run to tie the score. It would turn out to be the Americans' only hit of the game. Late in the game, it began to rain. The Americans picked up two walks in the bottom of the 8th inning. With one out, Laura Berg hit a fly ball to left field. As Shiori Koseki reached up to make the catch, she slipped and fell back and the ball popped out of her glove. Pinch-runner Jennifer McFalls raced home from second base and the United States won the Olympic championship by defeating each of the three teams to whom they had lost.

Hayley Wickenheiser, the Canadian shortstop, had earned a silver medal in ice hockey at the 1998 Winter Olympics and added a gold medal in 2002.

2004 Athens T: 8, N: 8, D: 8.23.

	W	L	T	RF	RA
1. USA	9	0	0	51	1
2. AUS	7	3	0	26	24
3. JPN	5	4	0	18	11
4. CHN	3	5	0	15	21
5. CAN	3	4	0	6	14
6. TAI	2	5	0	3	13
7. GRE	2	5	0	6	24
8. ITA	1	6	0	8	25

Final: USA 5-1 AUS

1. USA—Leah O'Brien-Amico, Laura Berg, Crystl Bustos, Lisa Fernandez, Jennie Finch, Tairia Flowers, Amanda Freed, Lori Harrigan, Lovieanne Jung, Kelly Kretschman, Jessica Mendoza, Stacey Nuveman, Catherine "Cat" Osterman, Jenny Topping, Natasha Watley
2. AUS—Sandra Allen, Marissa Carpadios, Fiona Hanes-Crawford, Amanda Doman, Peta Edebone, Tanya Harding, Natalie Hodgskin, Simmone Morrow, Tracey Mosley, Stacey Porter, Melanie Roche, Natalie Titcume, Natalie Ward, Brooke Wilkins, Kerry Wyborn
3. JPN—Kazue Ito, Yumi Iwabuchi, Masumi Mishina, Emi Naito, Haruka Saito, Hiroko Sakai, Naoko Sakamoto, Rie Sato, Yuki Sato, Juri Takayama, Yukiko Ueno, Reika Utsugi, Eri Yamada, Noriko Yamaji
4. CHN—Deng Xiaoling, Guo Jia, Li Chunxia, Li Qi, Lu Wei, Luo Lin, Mi Renrong, Mu Xia, Tao Hua, Wang Xiaoyan, Wei Qiang, Wu Di, Zhang Ai, Zhang Lixia, Zhou Yi
5. CAN—Lauren Bay, Alison Bradley, Erin Cumpstone, Cindy Eadie, Kaila Holtz, Jackie Lance, Sheena Lawrick, Angela Lichty, Andrea "Ani" Nyhus, Kristy Odamura, Alexandra "Sasha" Olson, Kim Sarrazin, Rachel Schill, Auburn Sigurdson, Erin Woods-White
6. TAI—Wu Chia-yen, Li Chiu-ching, Chen Feng-yin, Wang Hsiao-ping, Yang Hui-chun, Huang Hui-wen, Chang Li-chiu, Chen Miao-yi, Lin Po-jen, Lai Sheng-jung, Yen Show-tzu, Lin Su-hua, Pan Tzu-hui, Wang Ya-fen, Tung Yun-chi
7. GRE—Jessica Bashor, Lindsey Bashor, Ioanna Bouziou, Vanessa Czarnecki, Jamie Farnworth, Sarah Farnworth, Stacey Farnworth, Joanna Gail, Ginny Georgantas, Lindsay James, Chloe Kloezeman, Aikaterini Koutoungou, Katina Kramos, Stephanie Skegas-Maxwell
8. ITA—Natalie Anter, Samanta Bardini, Susan Bugliarello, Daniela Castellani, Natalia Cimin, Sabrina Del Mastio, Nicole Di Salvio, Francesca Francolini, Marta Gambella, Leslie Malerich, Ilaria Pino, Jennifer Spediacci, Eva Trevisan, Annalisa Turci, Stefania Vitaliani

The US team arrived in Athens with a 70-game winning streak and having been ranked number one in the world for the past 18 years. Four years earlier, the Americans had come to the Olympics with an even longer string of victories, only to lose three games in a row before rebounding to win the tournament. This time, however, the US overwhelmed the competition. They swept through the round-robin preliminary round, outscoring their seven opponents 41-0, although the Japanese did extend the Americans to extra innings. In their second game of the tournament, the US team stunned Australia 10-0 in a game that was stopped after 4½ innings because of the mercy rule. The Australians won all six of their other preliminary games.

In the semifinals, Australia managed to last the full seven innings against the US, but the Americans still won 5-0. The next day, the Australians qualified for the final by beating Japan 3-0.

In the gold medal match, the US scored three runs in the first inning, highlighted by a two-run home run by Crystl Bustos. In the third inning, Bustos hit another home run and Stacey Nuveman added one of her own to make the score 5-0. In the sixth inning, Australia gained a pyrrhic victory by scoring a run against the US, when Stacey Porter hit a double to leftfield with Sandra Allen on second, breaking the US Olympic streak of 58 shutout innings going back to 2000. The 5-1 victory gave the US an aggregate score of 51-1 and earned them their third consecutive Olympic championship. US pitcher Lisa Fernandez ended the tournament with four victories. She also batted .545, with 12 hits in 22 at bats, and with a slugging percentage of .818. Another US pitcher, Cat Osterman, gave up only two hits in 14⅔ innings, while striking out 23. Crystl Bustos, with a slugging percentage of .923, hit five home runs.

2008 Beijing T: 8, N: 8, D: 8.21.

	W	L	T	RF	RA
1. JPN	8	2	0	31	21
2. USA	8	1	0	58	5
3. AUS	6	3	0	38	18
4. CAN	3	5	0	20	28
5. TAI	2	5	0	10	23
6. CHN	2	5	0	19	21
7. VEN	2	5	0	15	35
8. HOL	1	6	0	8	48

Final: JPN 3-1 USA

1. JPN—Nano Emoto, Motoko Fujimoto, Megu Hirose, Emi Inui, Sachiko Ito, Ayumi Karino, Satoko Mabuchi, Yukiyo Mine, Masumi Mishina, Rei Nishiyama, Hiroko Sakai, Rie Sato, Mika Someya, Yukiko Ueno, Eri Yamada
2. USA—Monica Abbott, Laura Berg, Crystl Bustos, Andrea Duran, Jennie Finch, Tairia Flowers, Victoria Galindo, Lovieanne Jung, Kelly Kretschman, Lauren Lappin, Caitlin Lowe, Jessica Mendoza, Stacey Nuveman, Catherine Osterman, Natasha Watley
3. AUS—Jodie Bowering, Kylie Cronk, Kelly Hardie, Tanya Harding, Sandra Allen-Lewis, Simmone Morrow, Tracey Mosley, Stacey Porter, Melanie Roche, Justine Smethurst, Danielle Stewart, Natalie Titcume, Natalie Ward, Belinda Wright, Kerry Wyborn
4. CAN—Lauren Bay-Regula, Alison Bradley, Erin Cumpstone, Sheena Lawrick, Danielle Lawrie, Caitlin Lever, Robin Mackin, Noémie Marin, Melanie Matthews, Erin McLean, Dione Meier, Kaleigh Rafter, Jennifer Salling, Megan Timpf, Jennifer Yee
5. TAI—Chen Miao-yi, Chiang Hui-chuan, Chueh Ming-hui, Hsu Hsiu-ling, Huang Hui-wen, Lai Meng-ting, Lai Sheng-jung, Li Chiu-ching, Lin Su-hua, Lo Hsiao-ting, Lu Hsueh-mei, Pan Tzu-hui, Tung Yun-chi, Wen Li-hsiu, Wu Chia-yen
6. CHN—Guo Jia, Lei Donghui, Li Chunxia, Li Qi, Lu Wei, Pan Xia, Sun Li, Tan Ying, Wu Di, Xin Minhong, Yu Huili, Yu Yanhong, Zhang Ai, Zhang Lifang, Zhou Yi
7. VEN—Yuruby Alicart Ramírez, Mariangee Bogado González, Marianella Castellanos Martínez, Zuleyma Cirimele Heredia, Denisse Fuenmayor Arcila, Johana Gómez Sequera, Bheiglys Mujica Duarte,

Yusmary Pérez Medina, Jineth Pimentel Belisaro, Geraldine Puertas Flores, Maribel Riera, Mayles Rodríguez Pérez, Rubilena Rojas Guerena, Yaciey Sojo Pacheco, María Soto Gil
8. HOL—Judith van Kampen, Noémi Boekel, Daisy de Peinder, Kristi de Vries, Marloes Fellinger, Sandra Gouverneur, Kim Kluijskens, Sandra "Saskia" Kosterink, Jolanda Kroesen, Marjan Smit, Rebecca Soumeru, Nathalie Timmermans, Petra van Heijst, Helena Venker, Britt Vonk

After winning their third straight Olympic gold medal in 2004, the US continued to dominate the international softball scene, winning both the 2006 and 2007 World Cups and the 2006 World championships. When rain canceled the final of the 2007 Pan American Games between the US and Venezuela, the organizing committee didn't even bother rescheduling it, simply declaring the US the champion.

As expected, the US swept through pool play, winning all seven of their games easily and finishing with a combined total score of 53-1. Japan finished second in the pool, winning six of their seven games, including a 4-3 opener over defending Olympic silver medalist Australia.

When the US faced Japan in the first semifinal, pitchers Monica Abbot and Yukiko Ueno kept the game scoreless through seven innings of regulation play and the first extra inning. The US finally broke through in the top of the eighth, scoring four runs, including a three-run home run by slugger Crystl Bustos. They closed out the game at 4-1 to advance directly to the gold medal match.

Australia beat Canada in the other semifinal, breaking a 3-3 tie with two runs in the top of the sixth inning to win 5-3. Because of the playoff system, Australia played Japan to determine who would advance to the Grand Final against the US. Tied 2-2 after seven innings, the score remained unchanged until the eleventh inning, when both teams scored single runs. Japan finally clinched the victory in the bottom of the twelfth inning on an RBI (run batted in) by shortstop Rei Nishiyama.

Japan scored first in the final, when rightfielder Ayumi Karino hit an RBI single in the third inning. A home run by centerfielder Eri Yamada put Japan up 2-0 in the top of the fourth, but the US came back with a homer from Bustos to narrow the score. The Americans loaded the bases in the sixth inning, but were unable to score, and Japan added a third run in the top of the seventh. Japanese pitcher Yukiko Ueno closed out the seventh inning, her 28th inning in two days, to complete the upset. "I was able to throw three games in a row because of my strong feeling that we must win the gold, and I didn't want to lose." Ueno said afterwards, "It was more psychologically demanding. At times I thought my head would burst."

It was the first US defeat in 22 Olympic softball matches.

TUG OF WAR

In each contest, the first team to pull the other team six feet was declared the winner. If neither team succeeded in so doing in five minutes, the one which had pulled the furthest was given the victory.

1900 Paris T: 2, N: 3, D: 7.16.

1. SWE & DEN—Gustaf Söderstrbm, Karl Gustaf Staaf, August Nilsson, Eugen Schmidt, Edgar Aabye, Charles Winckler
2. FRA—Raymond Basset, Jean Collas, Charles Gondouin, Joseph Roffo, Emile Sarrade, Constantin Henriquez de Zubiera

The US team was unable to take part because three of its six members were engaged in the final of the hammer throw. After the official competition, the American team took part in a "friendly" tug against the Scandivanians, which broke up when American spectators rushed forward and joined in. Edgar Aaybe of Denmark was a journalist covering the Games for *Politiken*. He was asked to join the tug of war and ended up on the winning team.

1904 St. Louis T: 6, N: 3, D: 9.1.

1. USA—Milwaukee Athletic Club: Oscar Olson, Sidney Johnson, Henry Seiling, Conrad Magnussen, Patrick Flanagan
2. USA—St. Louis Southwest Turnverein #1: Max Braun, William Seiling, Orrin Upshaw, Charles Rose, August Rodenberg
3. USA—St. Louis Southwest Turnverein #2: Charles Haberkorn, Frank Kungler, Charles Thias, Harry Jacobs, Oscar Friede
4. USA—New York Athletic Club: Charles Dieges, Samuel Jones, Lawrence Feuerbach, Charles Chadwick, James Mitchel
5. GRE—Pan-Hellenic Athletic Club: Nicolaos Georgantas, Perikies Kakousis, Dimitrios Dimitracopoulos, Anastasios Georgopoulos, Vasilios Metalos
5. SAF—Boer Team: Christopher Walker, Pieter Hillense, Johannes Schutte, Pieter Lombard, Paulus Visser

1906 Athens T: 4, N: 5, D: 4.30.

1. GER & SWI—Heinrich Schneidereit, Heinrich Rondi, Wilhelm Born, Wilhelm Dörr, Karl Kaltenbach, Wilhelm Ritzenhoff, Josef Kramer, Julius Wagner [SWI]
2. GRE—Spyros Vellas, Panagiotis Trivoulidis, Vasilios Psachos, Georgios Psachos, Konstantinos Lazaros, Spyros Lazaros, Georgios Papachristou, Antonios Tsitas
3. SWE—Carl Svensson, Anton Gustafsson, Axel Norling, Ture Wersäll, Oswald Holmberg, Erik Granfelt, Gustaf Grönberger, Eric Lemming
4. AUT—Josef Steinbach, Rudolf Arnold, Henri Baur, Rudolf Watzl, Rudolf Lindmayer, Leopold Lahner, Franz Solar, Josef Wittmann, Karl Höltl

1908 London T: 5, N: 3, D: 7.18.

1. GBR—City of London Police: William Hirons, Frederick Goodfellow, Edward Barrett, J. James Shephard, Frederick Humphreys, Edwin Mills, Albert Ireton, Frederick Merriman

2. GBR—Liverpool Police: Patrick Philbin, James Clark, Thomas Butler, Alexander Kidd, George Smith, Thomas Swindlehurst, Daniel McLowry, William Greggan
3. GBR—K Division, Metropolitan Police: Walter Tammas, William Slade, Alexander Munro, Ernest Ebbage, Thomas Homewood, Walter Chaffe, James Woodget, Joseph Dowler

Surprising as it may seem, the friendly sport of tug of war touched off one of the biggest controversies of the 1908 Games. In the first round, the Liverpool Police pulled the US team over the line in a matter of seconds. The Americans immediately protested that the Liverpudlians had used special illegal boots with steel cleats, spikes, and heels. The British maintained that they were wearing standard, run-of-the-mill police boots, and the protest was disallowed, whereupon the Americans withdrew from the remainder of the competition. After the tournament, the captain of the victorious London City Police team challenged the Americans to a pull in their stockinged feet, but there is no record of such a contest actually taking place.

1912 Stockholm T: 2, N: 2, D: 7.8.

1. SWE—Adolf Bergman, Arvid Andersson, Johan Edman, Erik Fredriksson, Carl Jonsson, Erik Larsson, August Gustafsson, Herbert Lindström
2. GBR—Alexander Munro, J. James Shepherd, John Sewell, Joseph Dowler, Edwin Mills, Frederick Humphreys, Mathias Hynes, Walter Chaffe

After losing the first pull, the British team was disqualified for continually sitting down.

1920 Antwerp T: 5, N: 5, D: 8.18.

	W	L
1. GBR—George Canning, Frederick Holmes, Edwin Mills, J. James Shepherd, Harold Stiff, John Sewell, Frederick Humphreys, Ernest Thorne	3	0
2. HOL—Wilhelmus Bekkers, Johannes Hengeveld, Sijtse Jansma, Hendrikus Janssen, Antonius van Loon, Willem van Loon, Marinus van Rekum, Willem van Rekum	2	1
3. BEL—Edouard Bourguignon, Alphonse Ducatillon, Rémy Maertens, Christian Piek, Henri Pintens, Charles van den Broeck, François van Hoorenbeek, Gustave Wuyts	2	2
4. USA—Carlton Brosius, Stephen Fields, Sylvester Granrose, Floyd Kelsey, Joseph Kszyczewiski, William Penn, Joseph Rond, Joseph Winston	1	3
5. ITA—Adriano Arnoldo, Silvio Calzolari, Romolo Carpi, Giovanni Forno, Rodolfo Rambozzi, Carlo Schiappapietra, Giuseppe Tonani, Amedeo Zotti	0	2

Final: GBR 2-0 HOL

The British team won their two pulls against the Dutch in 28.2 seconds and 13.4 seconds.

Summer Olympic Records

These records do not include the Intercalated Games of 1906.

Most Medals
18 Larysa Latynina (SOV/UKR, Gymnastics, 1956-1964)

Most Medals, Men
16 Michael Phelps (USA, Swimming, 2004-2008)

Most Gold Medals
14 Michael Phelps (USA, Swimming, 2004-2008)

Most Gold Medals In One Day
4 Vitaly Scherbo (SOV/BLR, Gymnastics, 1992)

Most Silver Medals
6 Mikhail Voronin (SOV/RUS, Gymnastics, 1968-1972)
6 Shirley Babashoff (USA, Swimming, 1972-1976)
6 Aleksandr Dityatin (SOV/RUS, Gymnastics, 1976-1980)
Four of Babashoff's six silver medals were earned behind chemically augmented East German swimmers

Most Bronze Medals
6 Heikki Savolainen (FIN, Gymnastics, 1928-1936, 1952)

Most Bronze Medals, Women
5 Merlene Ottey (JAM, Track and Field, 1980-1984, 1992-1996)

Most Years Between Medals
28 Tore Holm (SWE, Sailing, 1920-1948)
28 Aladár Gerevich (HUN, Fencing, 1932-1960)

Most Years Between Medals, Women
24 Birgit Fischer (GDR, GER, Canoeing, 1980-2004)
24 Dara Torres (USA, Swimming, 1984-2008)
24 Josefa Idem (GER, ITA, Canoeing, 1984-2008)

Most Years Between Gold Medals
28 Aladár Gerevich (HUN, Fencing, 1932-1960)

Most Years Between Gold Medals, Women
24 Birgit Fischer (GDR, GER, Canoeing, 1980-2004)

Most Medals in Individual Events
14 Larysa Latynina (SOV/UKR, Gymnastics, 1956-1964)

Most Medals in Individual Events, Men
12 Nikolai Andrianov (SOV/RUS, Gymnastics, 1972-1980)

Most Gold Medals in Individual Events
9 Michael Phelps (USA, Swimming, 2004-2008)

Most Gold Medals in Individual Events, Women
7 Vera Cáslavská (CZE, Gymnastics, 1964-1968)

Most Consecutive Victories In the Same Event
6 Aladár Gerevich (HUN, Team Sabre Fencing, 1932-1960)

Most Consecutive Victories In the Same Individual Event
4 Paul Elvstrøm (DEN, Finn class Yachting, 1948-1960)
4 Al Oerter (USA, Discus Throw, 1956-1968)
4 Carl Lewis (USA, Long Jump, 1984-1996)

Most Consecutive Victories In the Same Individual Event, Women
3 Larysa Latynina (SOV/UKR, Floor Exercises, 1956-1964)
3 Dawn Fraser (AUS, 100-Meter Freestyle, 1956-1964)
3 Krisztina Egerszegi (HUN, 200-Meter Backstroke, 1988-1996)

Youngest Known Medalist
At the time that he placed third in the 1896 team parallel bars event, Dimitrious Loundrous of Greece was 10 years 218 days old. Of course, it happened that third place in the 1896 team parallel bars event also meant last place. The youngest known medalist who actually finished ahead of someone else was Luigina Giavotta of Italy, who earned a silver medal in Women's team gymnastics in 1928. She was 11 years 302 days old. In addition, please see the discussion on pages 806–7 about the coxswains in the 1900 coxed pairs rowing event.

Youngest Medalist In an Individual Event
12 years 24 days Inge Sørensen (DEN, 200-Meter Breaststroke, 1936)

Youngest Medalist In an Individual Event, Men
14 years 11 days Nils Skoglund (SWE, Plain High Diving, 1920

Youngest Gold Medalist, Women
13 years 268 days Marjorie Gestring (USA, Springboard Diving, 1936)

Youngest Known Gold Medalist, Men
13 years 283 days Klaus Zerta (GER, Pair-Oared shell With Coxswain, 1960)

Youngest Gold Medalist in an Individual Event, Men
14 years 309 days Kuzuo Kitamura (JPN, 1500-Meter Freestyle, 1932)

Oldest Medalist
72 years 279 days Oscar Swahn (SWE, Team Double-Shot Running Deer Shooting, 1920)

Oldest Medalist and Gold Medalist, Women
53 years 277 days Sybil "Oueenie" Newell (GBR, Archery, 1908)

Oldest Medalist in an Individual Event
64 years 256 days Oscar Swahn (SWE, Double-Shot Running Deer Shooting, 1912)

Oldest Medallst and Gold Medalist in an Individual Event, Women
53 years 277 days Sybil "Queenie" Newell (GBR, Archery, 1908)

Oldest Gold Medalist
64 years 257 days Oscar Swahn (SWE, Team Single-Shot Running Deer Shooting, 1912)

Oldest Gold Medalist in an Individual Event
61 years 4 days Joshua Millner (GBR/IRL, Free Rifle Shooting, 1908)

Most Olympics Competed In
9 Hubert Raudaschl (AUT, Sailing, 1964-1996). He earned silver medals in 1968 and 1980.
9 Ian Millar (CAN, Equestrian, 1972-1976, 1984-2008) Millar won his only medal, a silver in team jumping, in 2008.

Longest Olympic Career
44 years Hiroshi Hoketsu (JPN, Equestrian, 1964 and 2008)

Youngest Competitor
See Youngest Medalist.

Youngest Competitor, Women
See Youngest Medalist.

Oldest Competitor
See Oldest Medalist.

Oldest Competitor, Women
70 years 5 days Lorna Johnstone (GBR, Dressage, 1972)

Heaviest Competitor
463 pounds (210 kilograms) Ricardo Blas, Jr. (GUM, Heavyweight Judo, 2008)

Heaviest Competitor, Women
344 ¼ pounds (156.14 kilograms) Olha Korobka (Ukraine, Super Heavyweight Weightlifting, 2004)

Most Competitors in an Individual Event
183 Men's Cycling Road Race, 1996
In a sense this record could also go to the 185 who took part in the 1952 Men's Gymnastics team event because scores in the team event also applied to the Individual All-Around event.

Most Nations Represented in a Single Event
79 Men's Marathon, 1996

Longest National Win Streak in a Single Event
16 United States, Pole Vault, 1896-1968

Longest Streak in an Event with a Different Nation Winning Each Time
10 Men's Small-Bore Rifle, Prone, 1924-1972

Most Consecutive Boycotts
4 Albania, 1976-1988

First Known Winner in Ancient Olympics
Koroibos (Elis, Stadion [sprint], 776 BC)

First Winner In the Ancient Olympics, Women
Kyniska (Sparta, Tethrippon [four-horse chariot race], 396 BC

Most Championships, Ancient Olympics
12 Leonidas (Rhodes, Running, 164 BC–152 BC)

Key to Abbreviations

NATIONS

AFG	Afghanistan
ALG	Algeria
ANG	Angola
ARG	Argentina
ARM	Armenia
ASA	American Samoa
AUS	Australia
AUT	Austria
AZR	Azerbaijan
BAH	Bahamas
BAR	Barbados
BEL	Belgium
BER	Bermuda
BLR	Belarus
BOH	Bohemia
BOT	Botswana
BRA	Brazil
BRD	Burundi
BRN	Bahrein
BSH	Bosnia-Herzegovina
BUL	Bulgaria
BUR	Burma (Myanmar)
BWI	British West Indies (Jamaica and Trinidad)
CAM	Cameroon
CAN	Canada
CHI	Chile
CHN	China
CMR	Cameroon
COL	Colombia
CON	Congo
CRC	Costa Rica
CRO	Croatia
CUB	Cuba
CYP	Cyprus
CZE	Czech Republic (Czechoslovakia, 1920-1992)
DEN	Denmark
DJI	Djibouti
DOM	Dominican Republic
ECU	Ecuador
EGY	Egypt
ENG	England
ERI	Eritrea
ESA	El Salvador
EST	Estonia
ETH	Ethiopia
FIN	Finland
FRA	France
GBR	Great Britain and Northern Ireland
GDR	East Germany (German Democratic Republic, 1956-1988)
GEO	Georgia
GER	Germany; West Germany (Federal Republic of Germany, 1952-1988)
GHA	Ghana
GRE	Greece
GRN	Granada
GUA	Guatemala
GUY	Guyana
HAI	Haiti
HKG	Hong Kong
HOL	Holland (Netherlands)
HUN	Hungary
ICE	Iceland
INA	Indonesia
IND	India
INT	International team
IRL	Ireland (Eire)
IRN	Iran
IRQ	Iraq
ISR	Israel
ITA	Italy
IVC	Ivory Coast
JAM	Jamaica
JOR	Jordan
JPN	Japan
KAZ	Kazakhstan
KEN	Kenya
KGZ	Kyrgyzstan
KOR	South Korea
KOS	Kosovo
KUW	Kuwait
KYR	Kyrgyzstan
LAT	Latvia
LEB	Lebanon
LES	Lesotho
LIE	Liechtenstein
LIT	Lithuania
LUX	Luxembourg
MAC	Macedonia
MAD	Madagascar
MAL	Malaysia
MEX	Mexico
MGL	Mongolia

MLI	Mali
MLT	Malta
MLW	Malawi
MOL	Moldova
MON	Monaco
MOR	Morocco
MOZ	Mozambique
MNE	Montenegro
MRI	Mauritius
NAM	Namibia
NEP	Nepal
NGR	Nigeria
NIC	Nicaragua
NIG	Niger
NLA	Netherland Antilles
NOR	Norway
NRU	Nauru
NZL	New Zealand
OMA	Oman
PAK	Pakistan
PAN	Panama
PAR	Paraguay
PER	Peru
PHI	Philippines
PNG	Papua New Guinea
POL	Poland
POR	Portugal
PRK	North Korea (People's Republic of Korea)
PUR	Puerto Rico
QAT	Qatar
ROM	Romania
RUS	Russia
RWA	Rwanda
SAA	Saar
SAF	South Africa
SAU	Saudi Arabia
SCO	Scotland
SEN	Senegal
SER	Serbia
SEY	Seychelles
SIN	Singapore
SKN	St. Kitts and Nevis
SLE	Sierra Leone
SLO	Slovenia
SLV	Slovakia
SMR	San Marino
SOM	Somalia
SOV	Soviet Union (Unified Team, 1992)
SPA	Spain
SRL	Sri Lanka (Ceylon)
SUD	Sudan
SUR	Suriname
SWE	Sweden
SWI	Switzerland
SYR	Syria
TAI	Taiwan
TAN	Tanzania
THA	Thailand
TJK	Tajikistan
TOG	Togo
TON	Tonga
TRI	Trinidad and Tobago
TRM	Turkmenistan
TUN	Tunisia
TUR	Turkey
UAE	United Arab Emirates
UGA	Uganda
UKR	Ukraine
URU	Uruguay
USA	United States of America
UZB	Uzbekistan
VEN	Venezuela
VIE	Vietnam
VIR	US Virgin Islands
YUG	Yugoslavia
ZAM	Zambia
ZIM	Zimbabwe

Please note that some of the national abbreviations used in this book are different than those used by the International Olympic Committee. These official abbreviations can be found on page 1180.

TERMS

AAA	Amateur Athletic Association
AAU	Amateur Athletic Union
AC	Also competed
AIBA	International Amateur Boxing Association
c	Approximately
C:	Number of competitors entered
D:	Date of final
Dec.	Won by judges' decision
DISC	Discus throw
DISQ	Disqualified
DNC	Did not compete in final
DNF	Did not finish
DNS	Did not start in final
e	Estimated
elim	Eliminated
EOR	Equaled Olympic record
EWR	Equaled world record
FINA	International Amateur Swimming Federation

FITA	International Archery Federation
FT.	Feet
GA	Goals against
GF	Goals for
GRW	Greco-Roman wrestling
H	Hurdles
HAM	Hammer throw
HJ	High jump
IAAF	International Amateur Athletic Federation
IN.	Inches
IOC	International Olympic Committee
JAV	Javelin throw
kg	Kilograms
km	Kilometers
KO	Knockout
L	Lost
lbs	Pounds
LJ	Long jump (broad jump)
M	Meters
m.p.h.	Miles per hour
m.p.s.	Meters per second
N:	Number of nations represented
NCAA	National Collegiate Athletic Association
OR	Olympic record
PA	Points against
Pen.	Penalty
PF	Points for
PTS.	Points
PV	Pole vault
RA	Runs against
Ret	Retired
RF	Runs for
RSC	Referee stopped contest
SLJ	Standing long jump
SP	Shot put
T:	Number of teams entered
T	Tied
TG	Touches given
TR	Touches received
USOC	United States Olympic Committee
W	Won
w	Wind-aided
with	Withdrawn
WB	World best
WADA	World Anti-Doping Agency
WO	Walkover
WR	World record
YDS.	Yards

Official Abbreviations

Some of the national designations used in this book (see page 39) differ from those approved by the International Olympic Committee. Here is a complete list of the 205 nations and political entities that are currently recognized by the IOC.

AFG	Afghanistan
AHO	Netherlands Antilles
ALB	Albania
ALG	Algeria
AND	Andorra
ANG	Angola
ANT	Antigua and Barbuda
ARG	Argentina
ARM	Armenia
ARU	Aruba
ASA	American Samoa
AUS	Australia
AUT	Austria
AZE	Azerbaijan
BAH	Bahamas
BAN	Bangladesh
BAR	Barbados
BDI	Burundi
BEL	Belgium
BEN	Benin
BER	Bermuda
BHU	Bhutan
BIH	Bosnia-Herzegovina
BIZ	Belize
BLR	Belarus
BOL	Bolivia
BOT	Botswana
BRA	Brazil
BRN	Bahrain
BRU	Brunei
BUL	Bulgaria
BUR	Burkina Faso
CAF	Central African Republic
CAM	Cambodia
CAN	Canada
CAY	Cayman Islands
CGO	Congo (Brazzaville)
CHA	Chad
CHI	Chile
CHN	China
CIV	Côte d'Ivoire
CMR	Cameroon
COD	Congo (Kinshasa)
COK	Cook Islands
COL	Colombia
COM	Comoros
CPV	Cape Verde
CRC	Costa Rica
CRO	Croatia
CUB	Cuba
CYP	Cyprus
CZE	Czech Republic
DEN	Denmark
DJI	Djibouti
DMA	Dominica
DOM	Dominican Republic
ECU	Ecuador
EGY	Egypt
ERI	Eritrea
ESA	El Salvador
ESP	Spain
EST	Estonia
ETH	Ethiopia
FIJ	Fiji
FIN	Finland
FRA	France
FSM	Micronesia
GAB	Gabon
GAM	Gambia
GBR	Great Britain and Northern Ireland
GBS	Guinea-Bissau
GEO	Georgia
GEQ	Equatorial Guinea
GER	Germany
GHA	Ghana
GRE	Greece
GRN	Grenada
GUA	Guatemala
GUI	Guinea
GUM	Guam
GUY	Guyana
HAI	Haiti
HKG	Hong Kong
HON	Honduras
HUN	Hungary
INA	Indonesia
IND	India
IRI	Iran
IRL	Ireland
IRQ	Iraq
ISL	Iceland
ISR	Israel
ISV	US Virgin Islands
ITA	Italy
IVB	British Virgin Islands
JAM	Jamaica
JOR	Jordan
JPN	Japan
KAZ	Kazakhstan
KEN	Kenya
KGZ	Kyrgyzstan
KIR	Kiribati
KOR	South Korea
KSA	Saudi Arabia
KUW	Kuwait
LAO	Laos
LAT	Latvia
LBA	Libya
LBR	Liberia
LCA	Saint Lucia
LES	Lesotho
LIB	Lebanon
LIE	Liechtenstein
LTU	Lithuania
LUX	Luxembourg
MAD	Madagascar
MAR	Morocco
MAS	Malaysia
MAW	Malawi
MDA	Moldova
MDV	Maldives
MEX	Mexico
MGL	Mongolia
MHL	Marshall Islands
MKD	Macedonia
MLI	Mali
MLT	Malta
MNE	Montenegro
MON	Monaco
MOZ	Mozambique
MRI	Mauritius
MTN	Mauritania
MYA	Burma (Myanmar)
NAM	Namibia
NCA	Nicaragua

NED	Netherlands
NEP	Nepal
NGR	Nigeria
NIG	Niger
NOR	Norway
NRU	Nauru
NZL	New Zealand
OMA	Oman
PAK	Pakistan
PAN	Panama
PAR	Paraguay
PER	Peru
PHI	Philippines
PLE	Palestine
PLW	Palau
PNG	Papua New Guinea
POL	Poland
POR	Portugal
PRK	North Korea
PUR	Puerto Rico
QAT	Qatar
ROM	Romania
RSA	South Africa
RUS	Russia
RWA	Rwanda
SAM	Samoa
SEN	Senegal
SEY	Seychelles
SIN	Singapore
SKN	Saint Kitts and Nevis
SLE	Sierra Leone
SLO	Slovenia
SMR	San Marino
SOL	Solomon Islands
SOM	Somalia
SRB	Serbia
SRI	Sri Lanka
STP	São Tomé and Príncipe
SUD	Sudan
SUI	Switzerland
SUR	Suriname
SVK	Slovakia
SWE	Sweden
SWZ	Swaziland
SYR	Syria
TAN	Tanzania
TGA	Tonga
THA	Thailand
TJK	Tajikistan
TKM	Turkmenistan
TLS	Timor-Leste
TOG	Togo
TPE	Taiwan (Chinese Taipei)
TRI	Trinidad and Tobago
TUN	Tunisia
TUR	Turkey
TUV	Tuvalu
UAE	United Arab Emirates
UGA	Uganda
UKR	Ukraine
URU	Uruguay
USA	United States of America
UZB	Uzbekistan
VAN	Vanuatu
VEN	Venezuela
VIE	Vietnam
VIN	St Vincent and the Grenadines
YEM	Yemen
ZAM	Zambia
ZIM	Zimbabwe

Photographic Credits

Agence France-Press: 339
All Sport/Simon Bruty/IOC: 832
All Sport/Mike Hewitt/IOC: 113
All Sport/Ross Kinnaird/IOC: 885
AP/Amy Sancetta: 794
AP/Charles Dharapak: 843
AP/Christophe Ena: 548, 585
AP/Elizabeth Dalziel: 609
AP/Michael Lipchitz: 1264
AP/Lynne Sladky: 239
AP/Mark J. Terrill: 337, 1063
AP/Thomas Keinzle: 381
AP/Wide World Photos: 86, 93, 109, 130, 200, 436, 439, 451, 463, 481, 1121, 1296, 1302
Athanassios Trassouleas: 1311
Erik Betting/Pressehusel: 645
Tony Bijkerk: 899
Brown Bros: 49
Canada's Sports Hall of Fame: 366, 958
Paul Chinn/LA Herald Examiner: 342
Christo/Fairfax Photo Library: 888
Rick Clarkson/Sports Illustrated © Time Inc: 406
The Alice Coachman Track and Field Foundation: 367
By Permission of Coward, McCann & Geoghegan, Inc., from *The Miracle Machine* by Doug Gilbert, copyright 1980 by PLT Consultants Ltd.: 1083
Rich Cruse/RC Photo: 586
Curuchet, SIPA via AP Images: 138
J. Fairfax and Sons Ltd: 204
Frederik Fliegner Pub: 400, 1245
Fitzkultura Isdalesvo, Moscow: 1029
Getty Images: 51, 56, 115, 337, 373, 386, 397, 430, 538, 584, 635, 951, 1105, 1143, 1277
The Henning Library/International Swimming Hall of Fame: 592, 1064
Hulton-Deutsch Collection: 1147
Hungarian Olympic Committee: 481, 998
Inter-Sport Publicity: 58
IOC-Olympic Museum: 144, 145, 857
Erich Kamper: 242
Andrew Kent: 343
Eddie Keogh/Today Newspaper: 189
Copyright Kishimoto/Live Action: 595
Kyodo via AP Images: 138
Steve Lange: 809
Lia Manoliu: 389
Long Photography: 804
Bob Mathias: 283
Melbourne Herald and Weekly Times Ltd: 106
Melbourne Pictures: 106
Missouri Historical Society: 142
National Olympic Committee of Yugoslavia: 987
Pelham Books: 178, 213
Popperfoto: 72, 129, 164, 179
Michael Porte: 582
Pressebild-Argentur Schirner: 193, 288
Pressen Bild: 181, 199, 289, 317, 600
Progress Publishers: 1232
Proteus Books Ltd: 784
Reportagebild: 226, 572
Reuters/Archive Photos: 931
Reuters/Kevin Lamarque/Archive Photos: 855
The Sport Collection: 43, 45, 54, 55, 68, 69, 70, 84, 94, 96, 151, 222, 224, 252, 264, 279, 285, 305, 328, 591, 750, 782, 785, 1001, 1019, 1068, 1071, 1075, 1080, 1096, 1101, 1103, 1193
Sportverlag Berlin: 1014
Stu Forster/Allsport/Getty Images: 136
Swiss Timing: 59
Szwarc Photo Sport: 406
Toni Nett: 214
University of Michigan Archives: 232
UPI: 132, 153, 213, 235, 1051
UPI/Bettmann: 1281
USOC: 46, 49, 52, 78, 79, 80, 105, 116, 117, 119, 147, 169, 199, 223, 234, 236, 250, 260, 282, 285, 298, 306, 308, 316, 348, 382, 386, 396, 463, 864, 1002, 1012, 1061, 1206
VMS Publications: 558
David Wallechinsky: 505
David Webster Collection: 1194, 1227
David Wool/Dallas Morning News: 1201
Xinhua Photo: 1200